D1450622

Encyclopedia of

SOCIAL MEASUREMENT

VOLUME 2

F–O

Encyclopedia of SOCIAL MEASUREMENT

Editor-in-Chief

Kimberly Kempf-Leonard

University of Texas at Dallas
Richardson, Texas, USA

VOLUME 2

F–O

ELSEVIER
ACADEMIC
PRESS

Amsterdam Boston Heidelberg London New York Oxford Paris San Diego San Francisco Singapore Sydney Tokyo

5/20/05

Elsevier Ltd., The Boulevard, Langford Lane, Kidlington, Oxford, OX5 1GB, UK

First edition 2005

Library of Congress Control Number: 2004104292

A catalogue record for this book is available from the British Library

ISBN 0-12-443890-3 (set)

This book is printed on acid-free paper
Printed and bound in the United Kingdom

Contents

Volume 1

A

B

Volume 2

F

G

T

U

Contents by Subject Area

Analytical Techniques

Constructs and Variables

Data Collection

Data Sets and Websites

Data Sources and Subjects

Fields and Applications

Historical Events and Figures

Interpretation and Data Limitations

Measurement Models

Research Designs

Sampling Design

Contributors

Alberto Abadie
Harvard University, Cambridge, Massachusetts, USA

Chris Adams
Cranfield School of Management, Bedfordshire, United Kingdom

Scott Akins
Oregon State University, Oregon, USA

Faye Allard
The University of Pennsylvania, Philadelphia, Pennsylvania, USA

Garland E. Allen
Washington University, St. Louis, Missouri, USA

Micah Altman
Harvard University, Cambridge, Massachusetts, USA

R. Michael Alvarez
California Institute of Technology, Pasadena, California, USA

Duane F. Alwin
Pennsylvania State University, University Park, Pennsylvania, USA

Erling B. Andersen
University of Copenhagen, Copenhagen, Denmark

Elijah Anderson
The University of Pennsylvania, Philadelphia, Pennsylvania, USA

Leon Anderson
Ohio University, Athens, Ohio, USA

Margo Anderson
University of Wisconsin, Milwaukee, Wisconsin, USA

David Andrich
Murdoch University, Murdoch, Western Australia

Carol S. Aneshensel
University of California, Los Angeles, California, USA

Phipps Arabie
Rutgers Business School, Newark and New Brunswick, New Jersey, USA

Marc Artzrouni
University of Pau, Pau, France

Peter M. Atkinson
University of Southampton, Southampton, United Kingdom

Paul Auerbach
Kingston University, Surrey, United Kingdom

Mie Augier
Stanford University, Stanford, California, USA

Robert D. Austin
Harvard Business School, Boston, Massachusetts, USA

Kenneth D. Bailey
University of California, Los Angeles, California, USA

Christopher Baird
National Council on Crime and Delinquency, Oakland, California, USA

Robert C. Bannister
Swarthmore College, Swarthmore, Pennsylvania, USA

Kevin G. Barnhurst
University of Illinois at Chicago, Chicago, Illinois, USA

Yvette Bartholomée
University of Groningen, Groningen, The Netherlands

David J. Bartholomew
London School of Economics, London, England, United Kingdom

Jeffrey Bass
University of Missouri-Columbia, Department of Anthropology, Columbia, Missouri, USA

Nathaniel Beck
New York University, New York, New York, USA

James Beebe
Gonzaga University, Spokane, Washington, USA

Bryan Benham
University of Utah, Salt Lake City, Utah, USA

Gail R. Benjamin
University of Pittsburgh, Pittsburgh, Pennsylvania, USA

Nathan Berg
University of Texas, Dallas, Richardson, Texas, USA

Ira H. Bernstein
University of Texas, Arlington, Arlington, Texas, USA

William D. Berry
Florida State University, Tallahassee, Florida, USA

John Carlo Bertot
Florida State University, Tallahassee, Florida, USA

James J. Biles
Western Michigan University, Kalamazoo, Michigan, USA

David C. Black
The University of Toledo, Toledo, Ohio, USA

Mihai C. Bocarnea
Regent University, Virginia Beach, Virginia, USA

R. Darrell Bock
University of Chicago, Chicago, Illinois, USA

Ulf Böckenholt
McGill University, Montreal, Quebec, Canada

Hennie R. Boeije
Utrecht University, Utrecht, The Netherlands

Doug Bond
Harvard University, Cambridge, Massachusetts, USA

Marc H. Bornstein
National Institute of Child Health and Human Development, Bethesda, Maryland, USA

Avram Bornstein
John Jay College of Criminal Justice in the City University of New York, New York, New York, USA

Marcel Boumans
University of Amsterdam, Amsterdam, The Netherlands

Tony Bovaird
University of the West of England, Bristol, United Kingdom

Timothy M. Bray
University of Texas, Dallas, Richardson, Texas, USA

Chester L. Britt
Arizona State University West, Phoenix, Arizona, USA

Michael Bromwich
London School of Economics and Political Science, London, United Kingdom

Rod Buchanan
University of Groningen, Groningen, The Netherlands

C. Victor Bunderson
The EduMetrics Institute, Provo, Utah, USA

John A. Bunge
Cornell University, Ithaca, New York, USA

Annie M. Burrows
Duquesne University, Pittsburgh, Pennsylvania, USA

George W. Burruss
Southern Illinois University at Carbondale, Illinois

Ferry Butar Butar
Sam Houston State University, Huntsville, Texas, USA

Michelle Butler
University of Cambridge, Cambridge, United Kingdom

John Bynner
Institute of Education, London, United Kingdom

David Byrne
University of Durham, Durham, United Kingdom

David E. Campbell
University of Notre Dame, Notre Dame, Indiana, USA

Stephanie Carmichael
University of Florida, Gainesville, Florida, USA

Edward G. Carmines
Indiana University, Bloomington, Indiana, USA

J. Douglas Carroll
Rutgers Business School, Newark and New Brunswick, New Jersey, USA

Shannan Catalano
Bureau of Justice Statistics, Washington DC, USA

Sanjay Chawla
University of Sydney, New South Wales, Australia

Charissa S. L. Cheah
University of Maryland, Baltimore, County, USA

Peter Y. Chen
Colorado State University, Fort Collins, Colorado, USA

Oleksandr S. Chernyshenko
University of Canterbury, Christchurch, New Zealand

Mike W. L. Cheung
The university of Hongkong, Hongkong

Josef Cihlar
Canada Centre for Remote Sensing, Natural Resources Canada, Ottawa, Canada

Constance F. Citro
National Research Council of The National Academies, Washington, DC, USA

D. Jean Clandinin
University of Alberta, Edmonton, Alberta, Canada

William A. V. Clark
University of California, Los Angeles, Los Angeles, California, USA

Terry Nichols Clark
University of Chicago, Chicago, Illinois, USA

Harold D. Clarke
University of Texas, Dallas, Richardson, Texas, USA

Andrew Cliff
University of Cambridge, Cambridge, UK

Ethan Cohen-Cole
University of Wisconsin, Madison, Wisconsin, USA

Flavio Comim
St. Edmund's College, Cambridge, United Kingdom; and Universidade Federal do Rio Grande do Sul, Brazil

Wade D. Cook
Seymour Schulich School of Business, York University, Toronto, Canada

Pierre Crépel
CNRS—Université de Lyon 1, Villeurbanne, France

Kevin M. Curtin
The University of Texas at Dallas, Richardson, Texas, USA

Susan L. Cutter
University of South Carolina, Columbia, South Carolina, USA

Andrew I. Dale
University of KwaZulu-Natal, Durban, South Africa

Eric van Damme
Tilburg University, Tilburg, The Netherlands

Ton de Jong
University of Twente, Enschede, The Netherlands

Victor C. de Munck
State University of New York at New Paltz, New Paltz, New York, USA

Jamie DeCoster
Free University Amsterdam, Amsterdam, The Netherlands

Trudy Dehue
University of Groningen, Groningen, The Netherlands

Alain Desrosières
National Institute for Statistics and Economic Studies, Paris, France

Marinus C. Deurloo
University of Amsterdam, Amsterdam, The Netherlands

Robert F. DeVellis
University of North Carolina, Chapel Hill, North Carolina, USA

Karim Dharamsi
University of Winnipeg, Winnipeg, Manitoba, Canada

Carmen Diego Gonçalves
Minho University, Braga, Portugal

Don A. Dillman
Washington State University, Pullman, Washington, USA

Mustafa Dinc
The World Bank, Washington, D.C., USA

John F. Disterhoft
Northwestern University Feinberg School of Medicine, Chicago, Illinois, USA

Alesha E. Doan
California Polytechnic State University, San Luis Obispo, California, USA

Michael R. Dowd
The University of Toledo, Toledo, Ohio, USA

Laurie A. Drapela
Washington State University, Vancouver, Washington, USA

Fritz Drasgow
University of Illinois, Urbana–Champaign, Illinois, USA

William W. Dressler
University of Alabama, Tuscaloosa, Alabama, USA

Christopher S. Dunn
Bowling Green State University, Bowling Green, Ohio, USA

Peter K. Dunn
University of Southern Queensland, Toowoomba, Queensland, Australia

Steven Durlauf
University of Wisconsin, Madison, Wisconsin, USA

E. Paul Durrenberger
Pennsylvania State University, University Park, Pennsylvania, USA

Daniel R. Eignor
Educational Testing Service, Princeton, New Jersey, USA

Horst A. Eiselt
University of New Brunswick, Fredericton, New Brunswick, Canada

Joseph W. Elder
University of Wisconsin, Madison, Wisconsin, USA

Mark Elliot
University of Manchester, Manchester, United Kingdom

Charles W. Emerson
Western Michigan University, Kalamazoo, Michigan, USA

George Engelhard, Jr.
Emory University, Atlanta, Georgia, USA

Richard L. Engstrom
University of New Orleans, New Orleans, Louisiana, USA

Lee Epstein
Washington University, St. Louis, Missouri, USA

Michael T. Eskey
Troy State University, Troy, Alabama, USA

Wendy Nelson Espeland
Northwestern University, Evanston, Illinois, USA

K.J. Euske
Naval Postgraduate School, Monterey, California, USA

Michael E. Ezell
Vanderbilt University, Nashville, Tennessee, USA

David F. Gillespie
Washington University, St. Louis, Missouri, USA

George Farkas
The Pennsylvania State University, University Park, Pennsylvania, USA

Peter J. Fensham
Monash University, Victoria, Australia

Chandi Fernando
University of Toronto, Toronto, Ontario, Canada

Michel Ferrari
University of Toronto, Toronto, Ontario, Canada

Dail Fields
Regent University, Virginia Beach, Virginia, USA

Stephen E. Fienberg
Carnegie Mellon University, Pittsburgh, Pennsylvania, USA

Jeffrey A. Fine
University of Kentucky, Lexington, Kentucky, USA

Gerhard H. Fischer
University of Vienna, Vienna, Austria

Donald W. Fiske
University of Chicago, Chicago, Illinois, USA

Susan T. Fiske
Princeton University, Princeton, New Jersey, USA

Raymond J. G. M. Florax
Free University Amsterdam, Amsterdam, The Netherlands

Johnny R. J. Fontaine
Ghent University, Ghent, Belgium

John Fox
McMaster University, Hamilton, Ontario, Canada

Karen A. Franck
New Jersey Institute of Technology, Newark, New Jersey, USA

Charles H. Franklin
University of Wisconsin, Madison, Wisconsin, USA

Howard S. Friedman
University of California, Riverside, California, USA

Peter A. Furia
Wake Forest University, Winston–Salem, North Carolina, USA

Emmanuela Gakidou
Center for Basic Research in the Social Sciences, Harvard University, USA

Alison Galloway
Queen Margaret University College, Edinburgh, United Kingdom

Elizabeth Garner
Colorado State University, Fort Collins, Colorado, USA

Gilbert Geis
University of California, Irvine, Irvine, California, USA

Alan S. Gerber
Yale University, New Haven, Connecticut, USA

Arthur Getis
San Diego State University, San Diego, California, USA

Andrew S. Gibbons
Brigham Young University, Provo, Utah, USA

Jeff Gill
University of Florida, Gainesville, Florida, USA

Nicholas W. Gillham
Duke University, Durham, North Carolina, USA

Alberto Giordano
Texas State University, San Marcos, Texas, USA

Eduard Glas
Delft University of Technology, Delft, The Netherlands

Cees A. W. Glas
University of Twente, Enschede, The Netherlands

Garrett Glasgow
University of California, Santa Barbara, California, USA

Jack Glazier
Oberlin College, Oberlin, Ohio, USA

Norval D. Glenn
University of Texas, Austin, Texas, USA

Reginald G. Golledge
University of California, Santa Barbara, California, USA

Michael F. Goodchild
University of California, Santa Barbara, California, USA

Timothy R. Graeff
Middle Tennessee State University, Murfreesboro, Tennessee, USA

Jim Granato
National Science Foundation, Arlington, Virginia, USA

Louis N. Gray
Washington State University, Pullman, Washington, USA

Donald P. Green
Yale University, New Haven, Connecticut, USA

Michael J. Greenwood
University of Colorado, Boulder, Colorado, USA

Scott Greer
University of Prince Edward Island, Charlottetown, Prince Edward Island, Canada

Bhajan S. Grewal
Victoria University, Melbourne, Australia

Daniel A. Griffith
University of Miami, Coral Gables, Florida, USA

Donald A. Gross
University of Kentucky, Lexington, Kentucky, USA

John A. Grummel
West Virginia State University, Institute, West Virginia, USA

Peter Haggett
University of Bristol, Bristol, UK

John R. Hall
University of California, Davis, Davis, California, USA

Nancy S. Hall
University of Delaware, Newark, Delaware, USA and University of Maryland, College Park, Maryland, USA

W. Penn Handwerker
University of Connecticut, Storrs, Connecticut, USA

Dean M. Hanink
University of Connecticut, Storrs, Connecticut, USA

Bruce Hannon
University of Illinois, Champaign-Urbana, Champaign, Illinois, USA

Rachel Harter
National Opinion Research Center (NORC), Chicago, Illinois, USA

Kingsley E. Haynes
George Mason University, Fairfax, Virginia, USA

Linda Heath
Loyola University Chicago, Chicago, Illinois, USA

James J. Heckman
The University of Chicago, Chicago, Illinois, USA

David M. Hedge
University of Florida, Gainesville, Florida, USA

Leslie Hepple
The University of Bristol, Bristol, UK

Frederick M. Hess
American Enterprise Institute, Washington, DC, USA

David R. Hodge
University of Pennsylvania, Philadelphia, Pennsylvania, USA

Margaret Hogan
World Health Organization, Geneva, Switzerland

Herbert Hoijtink
University of Utrecht, Utrecht, The Netherlands

Søren Holm
Cardiff University, Cardiff, United Kingdom

Joop J. Hox
Utrecht University, Utrecht, The Netherlands

Lawrence J. Hubert
University of Illinois at Champaign, Champaign, Illinois, USA

John Hudson
University of Bath, Bath, United Kingdom

Casper D. Hulshof
University of Twente, Enschede, The Netherlands

Louise Irving
University of Manchester, Manchester, United Kingdom

Paul T. Jaeger
Florida State University, Tallahassee, Florida, USA

Donald G. Janelle
University of California, Santa Barbara, Santa Barbara, California, USA

Paul A. Jargowsky
University of Texas, Dallas, Richardson, Texas, USA

Jana L. Jasinski
University of Central Florida, Orlando, Florida, USA

Gayle R. Jennings
Central Queensland University, Rockhampton, Queensland, Australia

Bertram Johnson
Middlebury College, Middlebury, Vermont, USA

Robert L. Johnson
University of South Carolina, Columbia, South Carolina, USA

Renée J. Johnson
University of Florida, Gainesville, Florida, USA

Karen D. Johnson-Webb
Bowling Green State University, Bowling Green, Ohio, USA

Ron Johnston
University of Bristol, Bristol, United Kingdom

Lyle V. Jones
University of North Carolina, Chapel Hill, North Carolina, USA

Dean H. Judson
U.S. Census Bureau, Washington, D.C., USA

George Julnes
Utah State University, Logan, Utah, USA

Giora Kaplan
The Gertner Institute, Israel

Jeffrey D. Karpicke
Washington University, St. Louis, Missouri, USA

James Edwin Kee
George Washington University, Washington, DC, USA

Peter Keenan
University College, Dublin, Ireland

Jeremy T. Kerr
University of Ottawa, Ottawa, Canada

Ann H. Kim
Brown University, Providence, Rhode Island, USA

Ryuichi Kitamura
Kyoto University, Kyoto, Japan

Anastasia Kitsantas
George Mason University, Fairfax, Virginia, USA

Panagiota Kitsantas
East Carolina University, Greenville, North Carolina, USA

Amy L. Klekotka
University of Virginia, Charlottesville, Virginia, USA

Casey A. Klofstad
Harvard University, Cambridge, Massachusetts, USA

David Knoke
University of Minnesota, Minneapolis, Minnesota, USA

Ari Kohen
Duke University, Durham, North Carolina, USA

Dolph Kohnstamm
Emeritus, Leiden University, Leiden, The Netherlands

Michael J. Kolen
University of Iowa, Iowa City, Iowa, USA

John L. Korey
California State Polytechnic University, Pomona, California, USA

Autumn D. Krauss
Colorado State University, Fort Collins, Colorado, USA

Philip Kreager
Somerville College, Oxford University, Oxford, England, United Kingdom

David B. Kronenfeld
University of California, Riverside, Riverside, California, USA

John A. Kupfer
University of Arizona, Tucson, Arizona, USA

Kenneth C. Land
Duke University, Durham, North Carolina, USA

Jan de Lange
Utrecht University, Utrecht, The Netherlands

J. Stephen Lansing
University of Arizona, Tucson, Arizona, USA

Janet L. Lauritsen
University of Missouri, St. Louis, St. Louis, Missouri, USA

Danielle Lavin-Loucks
University of Texas, Dallas, Richardson, Texas, USA

Anthony C. Lea
Environics Analytics Group, Toronto, Ontario, Canada

Murray J. Leaf
University of Texas at Dallas, Richardson, Texas, USA

Raymond M. Lee
Royal Holloway University of London, Egham, Surrey, United Kingdom

Eveline S. van Leeuwen
Free University, Amsterdam, The Netherlands

James G. Lennox
University of Pittsburgh, Pittsburgh, Pennsylvania, USA

Gerty J. L. M. Lensvelt-Mulders
Utrecht University, Utrecht, The Netherlands

Charles W. Leonard
University of Texas, Dallas, Richardson, Texas, USA

Lyle E. Leritz
University of Oklahoma, Norman, Oklahoma, USA

James P. LeSage
University of Toledo, Toledo, Ohio, USA

Baruch Lev
New York University, New York, New York, USA

Mairi Levitt
Lancaster University, Lancaster, England, United Kingdom

Shlomit Levy
The Hebrew University of Jerusalem, Jerusalem, Israel

Allan J. Lichtman
American University, Washington, DC, USA

Wim J. van der Linden
University of Twente, Enschede, The Netherlands

Christy Lleras
Pennsylvania State University, University Park, Pennsylvania, USA

Stephen C. Locke
Florida Atlantic University, Boca Raton, Florida, USA

Paul A. Longley
University College London, London, UK

Sylvia Lorek
Sustainable Europe Research Institute, Cologne, Germany

Will Lowe
Harvard University, Cambridge, Massachusetts, USA

Richard M. Luecht
University of North Carolina at Greensboro, Greensboro, North Carolina, USA

Guanzhong Luo
Murdoch University, Perth, Western Australia and South China Normal University, Guangzhou, China

Scott M. Lynch
Princeton University, Princeton, New Jersey, USA

Peter J. Lynn
University of Essex, Colchester, United Kingdom

Harro Maas
University of Amsterdam, Amsterdam, The Netherlands

Cora J. M. Maas
Utrecht University, Utrecht, The Netherlands

M. Eileen Magnello
University College London/Wellcome Trust Center for the History of Medicine, London, United Kingdom

Bryan F. J. Manly
Universidade de São Paulo, Piracicaba, Brazil

Peter Kirby Manning
Northeastern University, Boston, Massachusetts, USA

Peter V. Marsden
Harvard University, Cambridge, Massachusetts, USA

Stephen W. Marshall
University of North Carolina at Chapel Hill, Chapel Hill, North Carolina, USA

Monty G. Marshall
University of Maryland, College Park, Maryland, USA

Stephen M. Marson
University of North Carolina, Pembroke, North Carolina, USA

Andrew Martin
Washington University, St. Louis, Missouri, USA

Elizabeth Martin
U.S. Census Bureau, Washington, DC, USA

Antonio Marturano
University of Exeter, Exeter, England, United Kingdom

Shadd Maruna
University of Cambridge, Cambridge, United Kingdom

Antonio Massieu
World Tourism Organization, Madrid, Spain

Geoff N. Masters
Australian Council for Educational Research, Camberwell, Australia

Richard E. Mayer
University of California, Santa Barbara, California, USA

Allyssa McCabe
University of Massachusetts, Lowell, Lowell, Massachusetts, USA

Charles R. McClure
Florida State University, Tallahassee, Florida, USA

Rose McDermott
University of California, Santa Barbara, California, USA

Michael P. McDonald
George Mason University, Fairfax, Virginia, USA

Daniel P. McMillen
University of Illinois, Chicago, Illinois, USA

Will Medd
University of Salford, Salford, Greater Manchester, United Kingdom

Scott Menard
University of Colorado, Boulder, Colorado, USA

Joel Michell
University of Sydney, Sydney, Australia

Henry L. Minton
University of Windsor, Windsor, Ontario, Canada

David L. Morgan
Portland State University, Portland, Oregon, USA

Calvin Morrill
University of California, Irvine, California, USA

Clayton Mosher
Washington State University, Vancouver, Washington, USA

Michael D. Mumford
University of Oklahoma, Norman, Oklahoma, USA

Gerardo L. Munck
University of Southern California, Los Angeles, California, USA

Darla K. Munroe
University of North Carolina, Charlotte, North Carolina, USA

David J. Murray
Queen's University, Kingston, Ontario, Canada

Andy Neely
Cranfield School of Management, Bedfordshire, United Kingdom

K. Bruce Newbold
McMaster University, Hamilton, Ontario, Canada

Frank Newport
Editor in Chief of the Gallup Poll, Princeton, New Jersey, USA

John M. Nicholas
University of Western Ontario, London, Ontario, Canada

Peter Nijkamp
Free University Amsterdam, Amsterdam, The Netherlands

Shizuhiko Nishisato
University of Toronto, Ontario, Canada

Anthony Oberschall
University of North Carolina at Chapel Hill, Chapel Hill, North Carolina, USA

Thomas R. O'Connor
North Carolina Wesleyan College, Rocky Mount, North Carolina, USA

Ayo Oyeleye
University of Central England in Birmingham, Birmingham, United Kingdom

Barnett R. Parker
Pfeiffer University, Charlotte, North Carolina, USA

Michael Quinn Patton
Union Institute and University, Minneapolis, Minnesota, USA

Dorothy Pawluch
McMaster University Hamilton, Ontario, Canada

James Penny[†]
CASTLE Worldwide, Inc., Morrisville, North Carolina, USA

Trond Petersen
University of California, Berkeley, Berkeley, California, USA

Anthony Petrosino
Nashuah, New Hampshire, USA

Thomas F. Pettigrew
University of California, Santa Cruz, Santa Cruz, California, USA

Andrew Pickles
University of Manchester, Manchester, UK

Richard J. Pike
U.S. Geological Survey, Menlo Park, California, USA

Steven Piker
Swarthmore College, Swarthmore, Pennsylvania, USA

Alex R. Piquero
University of Florida, Gainesville, Florida, USA

Alan E. Pisarski
Independent Consultant, Falls Church, Virginia, USA

Louis G. Pol
University of Nebraska, Omaha, Nebraska, USA

Carole L. Popoff
U.S. Census Bureau, Washington, D.C., USA

Carole L. Popoff
U.S. Census Bureau, Washington, D.C., USA

Eric A. Posner
University of Chicago, Chicago, Illinois, USA

Mick J. Power
University of Edinburgh, Edinburgh, United Kingdom

Ronda Priest
University of Southern Indiana, Evansville, Indiana, USA

Ram C. Rao
University of Texas, Dallas, Richardson, Texas, USA

C. Radhakrishna Rao
Pennsylvania State University, University Park, Pennsylvania, United States

Kenneth A. Rasinski
NORC, University of Chicago, Chicago, Illinois, USA

Daniel Read
London School of Economics and Political Science, London, United Kingdom

Dwight W. Read
University of California at Los Angeles, Los Angeles, California, USA

Mark D. Reckase
Michigan State University, East Lansing, Michigan, USA

Charles S. Reichardt
University of Denver, Denver, Colorado, USA

Arnold Reisman[†]
Sabanci University, Istanbul, Turkey and Reisman and Associates, Shaker Heights, Ohio, USA

Charles G. Renfro
Journal of Economic and Social Measurement, New York, New York, USA

Wilma C. M. Resing
Leiden University, Leiden, The Netherlands

Charles S. ReVelle
Johns Hopkins University, Baltimore, Maryland, USA

Christine Rider
St. John's University, Queens, New York, USA

Marc Riedel
Southeastern Louisiana University, Hammond, Louisiana, USA

Piet Rietveld
Free University, Amsterdam, The Netherlands

Violina P. Rindova
University of Maryland, College Park, Maryland, USA

Paul Robbins
The Ohio State University, Columbus, Ohio, USA

Henry L. Roediger, III
Washington University in St. Louis, St. Louis, Missouri, USA

Peter A. Rogerson
State University of New York, Buffalo, New York, USA

Robert Rosenthal
University of California, Riverside, Riverside, California, USA

Steven Rubenstein
Ohio University, Athens, Ohio, USA

Gidi Rubinstein
Netanya Academic College, Tel Aviv, Israel

Doris McGartland Rubio
University of Pittsburgh, Pittsburgh, Pennsylvania, USA

Bruce Russett
Yale University, New Haven, Connecticut, USA

Fumiko Samejima
University of Tennessee, Knoxville, Tennessee, USA

Shekhar Saxena
Mental Health: Evidence and Research, World Health Organization, Geneva, Switzerland

Erica Scharrer
University of Massachusetts, Amherst, Massachusetts, USA

Silke Schmidt
University of Hamburg, Hamburg, Germany

Ivo Schneider
University of the German Armed Forces Munich, Munich, Germany

Arthur M. Schneiderman
Independent Consultant, Boxford, Massachusetts, USA

Peter H. Schonemann
Purdue University, West Lafayette, Indiana, USA

Miriam W. Schustack
California State University, San Marcos, California, USA

Christof Schuster
University of Notre Dame, Indiana, USA

Libby Schweber
Harvard University, Boston, Massachusetts, USA

Daniel O. Segall
Defense Manpower Data Center, U.S. Department of Defense, Washington, D.C., USA

Richard J. Shavelson
Stanford University, Stanford, California, USA

Peter J. Sheehan
Victoria University, Melbourne, Australia

Shashi Shekhar
University of Minnesota, Minneapolis, Minnesota, USA

Charles Shimp
University of Utah, Salt Lake City, Utah, USA

Klaas Sijtsma
Tilburg University, Tilburg, The Netherlands

Francisco J. Silva
University of Redlands, Redlands, California, USA

Stephen G. Sireci
University of Massachusetts, Amherst, Massachusetts, USA

Maria Anne Skaates
Aarhus School of Business, Aarhus, Denmark

Garry J. Smith
University of Alberta, Edmonton, Alberta, Canada

Timothy D. Smith
Slippery Rock University, Slippery Rock, Pennsylvania, USA

Tom W. Smith
University of Chicago, Chicago, Illinois, USA

Stephen L. J. Smith
University of Waterloo, Waterloo, Ontario, Canada

J. T. Snead
Florida State University, Tallahassee, Florida, USA

David A. Snow
University of California, Irvine, California, USA

Joachim H. Spangenberg
Sustainable Europe Research Institute, Cologne, Germany

Ian Spence
University of Toronto, Toronto, Ontario, Canada

Stephen Stark
University of South Florida, Tampa, Florida, USA

David G. Steel
University of Wollongong, Wollongong, NSW, Australia

Michael Stein
Lindenwood University, St. Charles, Missouri, USA

Magnus Stenbeck
Centre for Epidemiology, National Board of Health and Welfare, Stockholm, Sweden

Mitchell L. Stevens
New York University, New York, USA

Chirayath M. Suchindran
University of North Carolina, Chapel Hill, North Carolina, USA

Joweria M. Teera
University of Bath, Bath, United Kingdom

Dawn Thilmany
Colorado State University, Fort Collins, Colorado, USA

Wendy L. Thomas
University of Minnesota, Minneapolis, Minnesota, USA

Kim M. Thompson
Florida State University, Tallahassee, Florida, USA

Kenneth W. Thompson
University of Virginia, Charlottesville, Virginia, USA

Barbara Tillmann
Université Claude Bernard Lyon 1, CNRS-UMR 5020, Lyon, France

Barbara Townley
University of Edinburgh, Edinburgh, Scotland, United Kingdom

Paul E. Tracy
University of Texas, Dallas, Richardson, Texas, USA

Lisa Troyer
University of Iowa, Iowa City, Iowa, USA

Nancy Brandon Tuma
Stanford University, Stanford, California, USA

Stephen P. Turner
University of South Florida, Tampa, Florida, USA

J. Rodney Turner
Groupe ESC Lille, Lille, France

Patricia A. Urban
Kenyon College, Gambier, Ohio, USA

Wim J. van der Linden
University of Twente, Enschede, The Netherlands

Mark van Ommeren
Mental Health: Evidence and Research, World Health Organization, Geneva, Switzerland

Carla VanBeselaere
Mount Allison University, Sackville, New Brunswick, Canada

Marina Vasilyeva
University of Chicago, Chicago, Illinois, USA

Liwen Vaughan
University of Western Ontario, London, Ontario, Canada

Marcel V. J. Veenman
Leiden University, Leiden, The Netherlands, and University of Amsterdam, Amsterdam, The Netherlands

Bernard P. Veldkamp
University of Twente, Enschede, The Netherlands

Sandra Vergari
University at Albany, State University of New York, Albany, New York, USA

Jay Verkuilen
University of Illinois, Champaign-Urbana, Champaign, Illinois, USA

D. Stephen Voss
University of Kentucky, Lexington, Kentucky, USA

Johan Wagemans
University of Leuven, Leuven, Belgium

Theodore C. Wagenaar
Miami University, Oxford, Ohio, USA

Howard Wainer
National Board of Medical Examiners, Philadelphia, Pennsylvania, USA

Lee Demetrius Walker
University of Kentucky, Lexington, Kentucky, USA

Herbert W. Ware
George Mason University, Fairfax, Virginia, USA

Noreen M. Webb
University of California, Los Angeles, Los Angeles, California, USA

Murray Webster, Jr.
University of North Carolina, Charlotte, North Carolina, USA

John R. Weeks
San Diego State University, San Diego, California, USA

Marc D. Weiner
Rutgers University, New Brunswick, New Jersey, USA

David Weisburd
Hebrew University, Jerusalem, Israel, and University of Maryland, College Park, Maryland, USA

Craig Weiss
Northwestern University Feinberg School of Medicine, Chicago, Illinois, USA

Susan C. Weller
University of Texas Medical Branch, Galveston, Texas, USA

E. Christian Wells
University of South Florida, Tampa, Florida, USA

James O. Wheeler
University of Georgia, Athens, Georgia, USA

Michael J. White
Brown University, Providence, Rhode Island, USA

Andrew B. Whitford
University of Kansas, Lawrence, Kansas, USA

Mark Wilcox
Cranfield University, Cranfield, England, United Kingdom

Willem Jan Willemse
University of Amsterdam, Amsterdam, The Netherlands

Garrath Williams
Lancaster University, Lancaster, England, United Kingdom

Phoebe D. Williams
University of Kansas School of Nursing, Kansas City, Kansas, USA

Arthur R. Williams
Mayo Clinic, Rochester, Minnesota, USA

Tamar Diana Wilson
University of Missouri, St. Louis, Missouri, USA

Gabriel K. Wolfenstein
University of California, Los Angeles, Los Angeles, California, USA

Henk Wolthuis
University of Amsterdam, Amsterdam, The Netherlands

James W. Wood
Pennsylvania State University, University Park, Pennsylvania, USA

James A. Woods
West Virginia University, Morgantown, West Virginia, USA

Richard Wright
University of Missouri, St. Louis, St. Louis, Missouri, USA

Rebecca Yang
University of Texas, Dallas, Texas, USA

Majid Yar
Lancaster University, Lancaster, United Kingdom

Paul S. F. Yip
The University of Hong Kong, Hong Kong

Yoosik Youm
University of Illinois at Chicago, Chicago, Illinois, USA

Reef Youngreen
University of Iowa, Iowa City, Iowa, USA

Chong Ho Yu
Cisco Systems/Aries Technology, Tempe, Arizona, USA

Ke-Hai Yuan
University of Notre Dame, Indiana, USA

L. A. Zander
Naval Postgraduate School, Monterey, California, USA

Richard A. Zeller
Kent State University, Kent, Ohio, USA

Pusheng Zhang
University of Minnesota, Minneapolis, Minnesota, USA

Editorial Board

Editor Biography

Dr. Kempf-Leonard is Professor of Sociology, Crime and Justice Studies, and Political Economy at the University of Texas at Dallas. Prior to her appointment at UTD in 2000, she was Associate Professor and Graduate Director of Criminology and Criminal Justice at the University of Missouri at St. Louis. She also served for ten years as a gubernatorial appointee to the Missouri Juvenile Justice Advisory Group. She received her Ph.D. at the University of Pennsylvania in 1986; M.A. at the University of Pennsylvania in 1983; M.S. at the Pennsylvania State University in 1982; B.S. at the University of Nebraska in 1980. Her book *Minorities in Juvenile Justice* won the 1997 Gustavus Myers Award for Human Rights in North America. Her publications have appeared in: *Criminology, Justice Quarterly, Journal of Criminal Law & Criminology, Crime & Delinquency, Journal of Quantitative Criminology, Advances in Criminological Theory, Punishment & Society, Corrections Management Quarterly, the Journal of Criminal Justice, Criminal Justice Policy Review, The Justice Professional, Youth and Society, The Corporate Finance Reader*, and *The Modern Gang Reader*.

Foreword

Not long ago, and perhaps still today, many would expect an encyclopedia of social measurement to be about quantitative social science. The *Encyclopedia of Social Measurement* excellently defies this expectation by covering and integrating both qualitative and quantitative approaches to social science and social measurement. The *Encyclopedia of Social Measurement* is the best and strongest sign I have seen in a long time that the barren opposition between quantitative and qualitative research, which has afflicted the social sciences for half a century, is on its way out for good. As if the Science Wars proper—between the social and natural sciences—were not enough, some social scientists found it fitting to invent another war within the social sciences, in effect a civil war, between quantitative and qualitative social science. Often younger faculty and doctoral students would be forced to take sides, and the war would reproduce within disciplines and departments, sometimes with devastating effects. This, no doubt, has set social science back. We cannot thank the editors and contributors to the *Encyclopedia of Social Measurement* enough for showing us there is an effective way out of the malaise.

This volume demonstrates that the sharp separation often seen in the literature between qualitative and quantitative methods of measurement is a spurious one. The separation is an unfortunate artifact of power relations and time constraints in graduate training; it is not a logical consequence of what graduates and scholars need to know to do their studies and do them well. The *Encyclopedia of Social Measurement* shows that good social science is opposed to an either/or and stands for a both/and on the question of qualitative versus quantitative methods. Good social science is problem-driven and not methodology-driven, in the sense that it employs those methods which for a given problematic best help answer the research questions at hand. To use a simple metaphor, asking whether social science is best served by qualitative or quantitative methods is about as intelligent as asking a carpenter whether a hammer or a saw is the better tool.

So far every effort has been unsuccessful in the social sciences at arriving at one canon for how to do science, most conspicuously the attempt at emulating the natural science model. Different explanations exist of this phenomenon, from Anthony Giddens' so-called double hermeneutic to Hubert Dreyfus' tacit skills argument. It is a great strength of the *Encyclopedia of Social Measurement* that it stays clear of the unity of science argument for social science, and of any other attempts at imposing one dominant paradigm on what social science is and how it should be conducted. The editors and most of the contributors have rightly seen that success in social science and social measurement lies with the type of methodological and epistemological pluralism, which is a distinguishing feature of the encyclopedia. Together with its impressive substantive breadth—covering the full range of social measurement from anthropology, sociology, political science, economics, and business administration over urban studies, environment, geography, demography, history, criminology, and law to neuroscience, biomedicine, nursing, psychology, linguistics, and communication—this healthy pluralism will prove the *Encyclopedia of Social Measurement* to be a robust and indispensable companion to all working social scientists for many years to come.

BENT FLYVBJERG
Professor of Planning,
Department of Development and Planning,
Aalborg University, Denmark

Preface

Methodology ... [has] developed as a bent of mind rather than as a system of organized principles and procedures. The methodologist is a scholar who is above all analytical in his approach to his subject matter. He tells other scholars what they have done, or might do, rather than what they should do. He tells them what order of finding has emerged from their research, not what kind of result is or is not preferable. This kind of analytical approach requires self-awareness on the one hand, and tolerance, on the other. The methodologist knows that the same goal can be reached by alternative roads.

(Lazarsfeld and Rosenberg, 1955, p. 4)

In the social sciences we use methodology to try to answer questions about how and why people behave as they do. Some types of behavior are very common or routine, while others happen rarely or only in certain situations. When you realize that every conceivable type of behavior is within the realm of possible subjects for us to study, you can begin to appreciate the scope of social science. Beyond identifying human activities and the boundaries in which they occur, social scientists also want to explain why behaviors happen. In looking for causes, social scientists pursue all dimensions of the social world. We look at personal traits of individuals, characteristics of interactions between people, and contextual features of the communities and cultures in which they live. We study people who lived in the past, try to improve the quality of life today, and anticipate what the future will hold. It is difficult to think of a topic that involves people for which a social scientist could not investigate.

Given all we do, it is good that there are so many of us. You will find social scientists in university departments as professors of sociology, psychology, anthropology, political science, and economics. You will also find professors of geography, history, philosophy, math, management, planning, finance, journalism, architecture, humanities, and art who are social scientists. Even this multidisciplinary list is not exhaustive. There are important and prevalent social science investigations that influence decision-making in the world outside of universities too. Social scientists are world-wide and work in all branches of government, large and small organizations, and many types of businesses. Daily life for most people is influenced by social science research in marketing, insurance, and government. However, not everyone in these positions is a social scientist; the distinction involves scientific inquiry, or the approach used to try to answer questions about behavior. As the definition cited above conveys, good science includes tolerance and appreciation for many methodological paths. This encyclopedia of social science methodology provides 356 entries written by social scientists about what they do.

The entries in this encyclopedia cover many forms of measurement used by social scientists to study behavior. Eleven substantive sections delineate social sciences and the research processes they follow to measure and provide knowledge on a wide range of topics. The encyclopedia has an extensive index too, because many topics include issues that are relevant in more than one section. From many perspectives and strategies, these volumes describe the research questions social scientists ask, the sources and methods they use to collect information, and the techniques they use to analyze these data and provide answers to the important questions.

Each section includes entries that address important components of quantitative and qualitative research methods, which are dissected and illustrated with examples from diverse fields of study. The articles convey research basics in sufficient detail to explain even the most complicated statistical technique, and references for additional information are noted for each topic. Most entries describe actual research experiences to illustrate both the realm of possibilities and the potential challenges that might be encountered. Some entries describe major contributions and the social scientists who made them. The authors are accomplished methodologists in their fields of study. They explain the steps necessary to accomplish the measurement goals, as well as provide their practical advice for ways in which to overcome the likely obstacles.

Collectively, the entries in this encyclopedia also convey that no single approach, type of data, or technique of analysis reigns supreme. Indeed, plenty of disagreements exist among social scientists about what constitutes the "best" measurement strategy. Often distinctions are made between quantitative and qualitative methodologies, or are discipline-specific. Some preferences can be linked to a specific field of study or research topic; others, related to time and location, coincide with how new ideas and advances in technology are shared. Sometimes we don't even agree on what is the appropriate question we should try to answer!

Although our views differ on what is ideal, and even on what are the appropriate standards for assessing measurement quality, social scientists generally *do* agree that the following five issues should be considered:

1. We agree on the need to be clear about the scope and purpose of our pursuits. The benchmarks for evaluating success differ depending on whether our intent is to describe, explain, or predict and whether we focus extensively on a single subject or case (e.g., person, family, organization, or culture) or more generally on patterns among many cases.
2. We agree on the need to make assurances for the ethical treatment of the people we study.
3. We agree on the need to be aware of potential sources of measurement error associated with our study design, data collection, and techniques of analysis.
4. We agree it is important to understand the extent to which our research is a reliable and valid measure of what we contend. Our measures are reliable if they are consistent with what others would have found in the same circumstances. If our measures also are consistent with those from different research circumstances, for example in studies of other behaviors or with alternate measurement strategies, then such replication helps us to be confident about the quality of our efforts. Sometimes we'd like the results of our study to extend beyond the people and behavior we observed. This focus on a wider applicability for our measures involves the issue of generalizability. When we're concerned about an accurate portrayal of reality, we use tools to assess validity. When we don't agree about the adequacy of the tools we use to assess validity, sometimes the source of our disagreements is different views on scientific objectivity.
5. We also agree that objectivity merits consideration, although we don't agree on the role of objectivity or our capabilities to be objective in our research. Some social scientists contend that our inquiries must be objective to have credibility. In a contrasting view of social science, or epistemology, objectivity is not possible and, according to some, not preferable. Given that we study people and are human ourselves, it is important that we recognize that life experiences necessarily shape the lens through which people see reality.

Besides a lack of consensus within the social sciences, other skeptics challenge our measures and methods. In what some recently have labeled "the science wars," external critics contend that social scientists suffer "physics envy" and that human behavior is not amenable to scientific investigation. Social scientists have responded to "anti-science" sentiments from the very beginning, such as Emile Durkhiem's efforts in the 19th century to identify "social facts." As entertaining as some of the debates and mudslinging can be, they are unlikely to be resolved anytime soon, if ever. One reason that Lazarsfeld and Rosenberg contend that tolerance and appreciation for different methodological pathways make for better science is that no individual scientist can have expertise in all the available options. We recognize this now more than ever, as multidisciplinary teams and collaborations between scientists with diverse methodological expertise are commonplace, and even required by some sources of research funding.

Meanwhile, people who can be our research subjects continue to behave in ways that intrigue, new strategies are proffered to reduce social problems and make life better, and the tool kits or arsenals available to social scientists continue to grow. The entries in these volumes provide useful information about how to accomplish social measurement and standards or "rules of thumb." As you learn these standards, keep in mind the following advice from one of my favorite methodologists: "Avoid the fallacy fallacy. When a theorist or methodologist tells you you cannot do something, do it anyway. Breaking rules can be fun!" Hirschi (1973, pp. 171–2). In my view nothing could be more fun than contemporary social science, and I hope this encyclopedia will inspire even more social science inquiry!

In preparing this encyclopedia the goal has been to compile entries that cover the entire spectrum of measurement approaches, methods of data collection, and techniques of analysis used by social scientists in their efforts to understand all sorts of behaviors. The goal of this project was ambitious, and to the extent that the encyclopedia is successful there are many to people to thank. My first thank you goes to the members of the Executive Advisory Board and the Editorial Advisory Board who helped me to identify my own biased views about social science and hopefully to achieve greater tolerance and appreciation. These scientists helped identify the ideal measurement topics, locate the experts and convince them to be authors, review drafts of the articles, and make the difficult recommendations required by time and space considerations as the project came to a close. My second thank you goes to the many authors of these 356 entries. Collectively, these scholars represent well the methodological status of social science today. Third, I thank the many reviewers whose generous recommendations improved the final product. In particular I extend my personal thanks to colleagues at the University of Texas at Dallas, many of whom participated in large and small roles in this project, and all of whom have helped me to broaden my appreciation of social measurement. Finally, I thank Scott Bentley, Kirsten Funk, Kristi Anderson, and their colleagues at Elsevier for the opportunity and their encouragement when the tasks seemed overwhelming. Scott's insights to the possibilities of a project such as this and the administrative prowess of both Kirsten and Kristi helped make this a reality.

Good science is a cumulative process, and we hope this project will be ongoing and always improving. Despite our best efforts to identify topics and authors, sometimes we failed. If you have suggestions, criticisms, or information worth considering, I hope you will let me know.

Hirschi, Travis (1973). Procedural rules and the study of deviant behavior. *Social Problems* **21**(2), 159–173.

Lazarsfeld, Paul and Morris Rosenberg (1955). *The Language of Social Research.* The Free Press, New York.

KIMBERLY KEMPF-LEONARD

Guide to Using the Encyclopedia

The *Encyclopedia of Social Measurement* is a comprehensive and authoritative study covering the data, techniques, theories, designs, histories, and implications of assigning numerical values to social phenomena. It consists of three volumes and includes 356 articles written by leading international authorities. Each article provides a focused description intended to inform a broad spectrum of readers, ranging from research professionals to students and the general public.

In order that you, the reader, will derive the greatest benefit from the *Encyclopedia of Social Measurement*, we have provided this Guide. It explains how the *Encyclopedia* is organized and how to locate information within it.

Organization

All the articles in the *Encyclopedia of Social Measurement* are arranged in a single alphabetical sequence by title. Articles whose titles begin with the letters A to E are in Volume 1, articles with titles from F to O are in Volume 2, and articles from P to Y are in Volume 3.

Volume 3 also includes a complete subject index for the entire work along with an alphabetical list of article reviewers, whose silent contributions were essential to the success of the project.

Article Titles

Article titles generally begin with the key term describing the topic, and if necessary they have an inverted word order so the title begins with this term. For example, "Democracy, Measures of" is the article title rather than "Measures of Democracy," and "Education, Tests and Measures in" is the title, not "Tests and Measures in Education." Thus, all the articles on quantitative analysis applications appear together in the third volume of the *Encyclopedia.*

Because each article was composed for the *Encyclopedia of Social Measurement*, for the sake of simplicity we have omitted the phrase "social measurement" from article titles.

Index

The index appears as the last element of Volume 3. Subjects are listed alphabetically and indicate the volume and page number where relevant information can be found. The *Encyclopedia of Social Measurement* contains approximately 13,000 index entries. This index is the most convenient way to locate a topic, and thus it should be the starting point for any reader.

In addition, articles are also divided into key subject areas, and a contents list by area is provided for reference in each volume. The table of contents by subject area functions as an index because it lists all the topics covered in a given area; e.g., the *Encyclopedia* has 48 articles dealing with constructs and variables.

Article Format

Articles in the *Encyclopedia of Social Measurement* are arranged in this standard format:

- Title and Author
- Glossary
- Defining Statement
- Main Body of the Article
- Cross-References
- Bibliography

Glossary

The Glossary section contains terms that are important to an understanding of the article and that may be unfamiliar to the reader. Each term is defined in the context of the particular article in which it is used. The same term may appear as a glossary entry in different articles, with the details of the definition varying slightly from one article to another. The *Encyclopedia* includes approximately 2,500 glossary entries. For example, the article "Scales and Indexes, Types of" includes this entry (among others):

scale A cluster of items that taps into measurements developed on face validity and/or professional judgment of measuring what one intends to measure. The intent is to measure the relative degree, amount, or differences between variables.

Defining Paragraph

The text of each article begins with a single introductory paragraph. This introduction defines the topic under discussion and summarizes the content of the article. For example, the article "Libraries" begins with the following defining paragraph:

Social measurement in libraries involves the collection of evaluation data through social science methods. The goal is to determine the extent to which resources utilized in the management, planning, and presentation of collected sources of information, programs, and services by libraries meet the specific needs of a broad range of library users.

Cross-References

The entry list for the *Encyclopedia of Social Measurement* has been constructed so that each entry is supported by one or more other entries that provide additional information. Therefore all articles have cross-references to other articles. These appear at the end of the article, following the end of the narrative text, and preceding the further reading section. The *Encyclopedia* contains about 1,500 cross-references. The cross-references indicate related articles that can be consulted for further information on the same topic, or for information on a related topic. For example, the article "Case Study" provides the following cross-references:

- Anthropology, Psychological
- Basic vs. Applied Social Science Research
- Ethnography
- Field Experimentation
- Observational Studies
- Qualitative Analysis, Anthropology
- Quantitative Analysis, Anthropology

Bibliography

The further reading section appears next. It presents recent secondary sources that can aid the reader in locating more detailed or technical information. Review articles and research papers that are important to an understanding of the topic are also included. For example, the article "Autocorrelation" has the following references (among others):

Franses, P. H. (1998). *Time Series Models for Business and Economic Forecasting.* Cambridge University Press, Cambridge, UK.

Ghysels, E., Swanson, N. R., and Watson, M. W. (2001). *Collected Papers of Clive W. J. Granger, Volume II, Causality, Integration and Cointegration, and Long Memory.* Cambridge University Press, Cambridge, UK.

Godfrey, L. G. (1988). *Misspecification Tests in Econometrics.* Cambridge University Press, Cambridge, UK.

The further reading references do not represent a complete list of all the materials consulted by the author in preparing the article. Instead, the titles are the author's recommendations of the best and most appropriate starting points for further research.

Factor Analysis

Christof Schuster
University of Notre Dame, Indiana, USA

Ke-Hai Yuan
University of Notre Dame, Indiana, USA

Glossary

communality Variance of a variable accounted for by the factors.

factor Latent variable that determines to a considerable extent the values of the observed variables.

factor loading Weight indicating the direct influence of a factor on a variable.

factor structure Matrix of covariances between factors and variables. If the variables are standardized, then the factor structure matrix contains correlations rather than covariances.

oblique rotation Factor transformation designed to achieve a simple interpretation of the factors.

orthogonal rotation Factor transformation designed to achieve a simple interpretation of mutually uncorrelated factors.

uniqueness Amount of variable variance unrelated to factors.

Factor analysis is a multivariate statistical technique for finding theoretical concepts that underlie the association between observed variables. To this end, the factor model introduces latent variables, commonly referred to as factors, and posits that the observed variables are determined, except for random error, by these factors. Factor analysis is particularly well-suited to psychology, wherein concepts such as "intelligence" can be observed only indirectly—for instance, by noticing which test problems an individual is able to solve correctly.

Introduction

Spearman noted in 1904 that measures of performance for certain cognitive tasks are often positively correlated. If an individual performs well on, say, an intelligence-related task, he or she also tends to do well on similar tasks. To explain this phenomenon, Spearman introduced a general ability factor, commonly referred to as the g-factor, that he claimed determines performance of intelligence-related tasks to a considerable extent, albeit not completely. Thus, positive correlations between intelligence-related tasks were explained by Spearman in terms of the g-factor's influence on each of these tasks. During the first half of the 20th century, factor analysis developed rapidly from a substantive theory on intelligence into a general statistical procedure. An early comprehensive account of factor analysis was given in 1947 by Thurstone.

The main idea of factor analysis is to "explain" correlations between observed variables in terms of a few unobservable variables, commonly called factors or latent variables. It will be convenient to refer to the observable and unobservable variables simply as variables and factors, respectively. More specifically, the model states that the factors determine the variables in such a way that when holding the factors constant, the residual variation of the variables is uncorrelated. If the number of factors needed to explain the correlations is "small," compared to the number of variables, then the factor model is appealing because the associations between the variables can be explained in a parsimonious manner.

Factor analysis is used if latent variables are assumed to underlie the association among the variables, but the conceptual nature of the factors is unclear before fitting the factor model to data. Because the purpose of factor analysis is to clarify the nature of the factors, one also speaks of exploratory factor analysis as opposed to confirmatory factor analysis, a closely related statistical technique that requires specific *a priori* assumptions about the factors and their relationships to the variables. Although in practice the factor model is almost always fitted to the sample correlation matrix, it is common to discuss the model in terms of the sample covariance matrix. This convention is followed here. Finally, note that factor analysis is different from principal component analysis. Although these two statistical techniques are frequently confused, they address different issues. While factor analysis explains observed correlations in terms of latent factors, principal component analysis is a data reduction technique that yields linear composites of the observed variables referred to as "components."

The Factor Model

Consider p variables, each having zero expectation, that is, $E(x_i) = 0$, $i = 1, \ldots, p$. The factor model states that the conditional expectation of each variables is a linear function of q factors, $\xi_1, \ldots, \xi_q$. In other words, the factor model claims

$$E(x_i \mid \xi_1 \cdots \xi_q) = \lambda_{i1}\xi_1 + \cdots + \lambda_{iq}\xi_q,$$

for $i = 1, \ldots, p$. The factor loadings, λ_{ij}, are regression coefficients that indicate the expected change in the ith variable that is related to a unit change in the jth factor, holding all other factors constant. Thus, the loadings measure the direct influence of a factor on the variables. Expressing the equations of all variables simultaneously in a single equation using matrix notation yields

$$E(\boldsymbol{x} \mid \boldsymbol{\xi}) = \boldsymbol{\Lambda\xi}, \tag{1}$$

where $\boldsymbol{x}$ is a $(p \times 1)$ vector of random variables that have zero mean, $\boldsymbol{\xi}$ is a $(q \times 1)$ vector of random factors, and $\boldsymbol{\Lambda} = (\lambda_{ij})$ is a $(p \times q)$ matrix of factor loadings.

In addition to Eq. (1), the factor model makes two further assumptions. First, as has been mentioned, the variables are assumed to be uncorrelated when controlling for the factors. If the conditional covariance matrix is denoted as $\boldsymbol{\Psi}$, that is, $\boldsymbol{\Psi} = \mathrm{Var}(\boldsymbol{x} \mid \boldsymbol{\xi})$, then this assumption can be expressed as $\boldsymbol{\Psi} = \mathrm{diag}(\psi_{11}, \ldots, \psi_{pp})$. The ψ-parameters are referred to as uniquenesses. Second, the model assumes $E(\xi_j) = 0$ and $\mathrm{Var}(\xi_j) = 1$, for $j = 1, \ldots, q$. This assumption removes the arbitrariness in the scales of the factors and does not restrict the generality of the factor model.

Defining the residual vector as $\boldsymbol{\epsilon} = \boldsymbol{x} - E(\boldsymbol{x} \mid \boldsymbol{\xi})$, it is not difficult to see that $\boldsymbol{\Psi} = \mathrm{Var}(\boldsymbol{\epsilon})$. Both specific factors and measurement error may contribute to the residual term. However, because the factor model does not allow for the separation of these two sources of observed score variability, we do not distinguish between them.

From Eq. (1) and the preceding assumptions, it follows that the covariance matrix of the variables is

$$\boldsymbol{\Sigma} = \boldsymbol{\Lambda\Phi\Lambda}' + \boldsymbol{\Psi}, \tag{2}$$

where $\boldsymbol{\Phi} = (\phi_{ij})$ denotes the correlation matrix of the factors. Equation (2) shows that each variable's variance is the sum of two separate sources. One source encompasses the influences of specific factors and measurement error and is referred to as the variable's uniqueness, ψ_{ii}. The other source, commonly referred to as the variable's communality, h_i^2, is the influence the factors have on determining the variable values. More specifically, the communality is defined as $h_i^2 = \mathrm{Var}(E(x_i \mid \boldsymbol{\xi}))$ and is given in terms of the model parameters by the ith diagonal element of $\boldsymbol{\Lambda\Phi\Lambda}'$.

The covariance between factors and variables,

$$\mathrm{Cov}(\mathbf{x}, \boldsymbol{\xi}) = \boldsymbol{\Lambda\Phi}, \tag{3}$$

is called the factor structure. Specializing this expression to a variable–factor pair yields $\mathrm{Cov}(x_i, \xi_j) = \lambda_{i1}\phi_{1j} + \cdots + \lambda_{iq}\phi_{qj}$. The covariances of the factor structure matrix do not control for other factors. This means that even if a particular variable has a zero loading on, say, the first factor, it still can be correlated with the first factor because of indirect effects. Specifically, if the variable loads on a factor that is also correlated with the first factor, the variable will be correlated with the first factor despite its zero loading on this factor. Also note that for standardized variables, the factor structure matrix gives the correlations rather than the covariances between the factors and the variables.

An important special case occurs if the factors are uncorrelated, that is, $\boldsymbol{\Phi} = \boldsymbol{I}$. In this case, the factors are said to be orthogonal and several of the preceding equations simplify. First, the communality of the ith variable reduces to $h_i^2 = \lambda_{i1}^2 + \cdots + \lambda_{iq}^2$. Second, the factor structure matrix [see Eq. (3)] is equal to the factor loading matrix, that is, $\mathrm{Cov}(\boldsymbol{x}, \boldsymbol{\xi}) = \boldsymbol{\Lambda}$. Thus, if the factors are orthogonal, a zero loading will imply a zero covariance between the corresponding variable–factor pair. Again, note that for standardized variables, the λ parameters represent correlations rather than covariances between variables–factor pairs.

Estimating the Model Parameters

Before discussing approaches to estimating the factor loadings, it should be noted that factor loadings are not uniquely defined. If $\boldsymbol{T}$ is a nonsingular $(q \times q)$ matrix such that $\mathrm{diag}(\boldsymbol{T\Phi T}') = \boldsymbol{I}$, then $\boldsymbol{\xi}^* = \boldsymbol{T\xi}$ will be an equally legitimate set of factors with $\mathbf{\Lambda}^* = \mathbf{\Lambda}\boldsymbol{T}^{-1}$. This follows because the assumptions of the factor model are also fulfilled by the new factors $\boldsymbol{\xi}^*$ and the fact that the conditional expectation of the variables is invariant to this transformation. This is easily seen by noting that $\mathrm{E}(\boldsymbol{x} \mid \boldsymbol{\xi}^*) = \mathbf{\Lambda}^*\boldsymbol{\xi}^* = (\mathbf{\Lambda}\boldsymbol{T}^{-1})(\boldsymbol{T}\boldsymbol{\xi}) = \mathbf{\Lambda}\boldsymbol{\xi} = \mathrm{E}(\boldsymbol{x} \mid \boldsymbol{\xi})$. When the factors are uncorrelated, the set of legitimate transformation matrices $\boldsymbol{T}$ is limited to orthogonal matrices, which fulfill the condition $\boldsymbol{TT}' = \boldsymbol{I}$. In order to obtain a solution for the factor loadings, it is desirable to remove this indeterminacy. This can be achieved if the factors are uncorrelated, that is, $\mathbf{\Phi} = \boldsymbol{I}$, and if the so-called canonical constraint, which requires $\mathbf{\Lambda}'\mathbf{\Psi}^{-1}\mathbf{\Lambda}$ to be diagonal, is satisfied.

Having imposed sufficient model restrictions to define the parameters uniquely, the degrees of freedom (df) can be determined. The degrees of freedom are equal to the difference between the $p(p+1)/2$ freely varying elements in the unconstrained population covariance matrix $\mathbf{\Sigma}$ and the number of unrestricted model parameters. The degrees of freedom characterize the extent to which the factor model offers a simple explanation of the correlations among the variables. A necessary condition for the identification of the model parameters is $\mathrm{df} \geq 0$. Clearly, if the factors are uncorrelated, all model parameters are either loadings or uniquenesses and the total number of model parameters is $pq + p$. Because the canonical constraint introduces $q(q-1)/2$ restrictions on the model parameters, the degrees of freedom are

$$\begin{aligned} \mathrm{df} &= p(p+1)/2 - [pq + p - q(q-1)/2] \\ &= (1/2)\left[(p-q)^2 - (p+q)\right]. \end{aligned} \tag{4}$$

Estimation procedures may yield negative estimates for the ψ parameters that are outside the permissible range. Such inadmissible solutions are commonly referred to as Heywood cases. Heywood cases occur quite frequently in practice. A simple strategy of dealing with negative uniquenesses is to set them equal to zero. However, this strategy implies an unrealistic model characteristic, namely, that the factors perfectly explain the variation of the variables having zero uniquenesses. Finally, note that methods for estimating the factor loadings assume that the number of factors is known.

Maximum-Likelihood Factor Analysis

When estimating the factor loadings by maximum-likelihood, a multivariate normal distribution is assumed to underlie the variables. The maximum-likelihood estimates of loadings and uniquenesses are obtained from minimizing the discrepancy function

$$F(\mathbf{\Lambda}) = \log|\mathbf{\Sigma}| + \mathrm{trace}(\boldsymbol{S}\mathbf{\Sigma}^{-1}), \tag{5}$$

where $\boldsymbol{S}$ denotes the usual sample covariance matrix and $\mathbf{\Sigma} = \mathbf{\Lambda\Lambda}' + \mathbf{\Psi}$. Note that the expression for $\mathbf{\Sigma}$ differs from that in Eq. (2) because of the requirement $\mathbf{\Phi} = \boldsymbol{I}$ discussed previously. Minimization of Eq. (5) with respect to the λ and ψ parameters requires iterative numerical methods.

If the assumptions underlying maximum-likelihood estimation are met, then this parameter estimation method has several desirable properties. First, it provides a likelihood-ratio statistic for testing the hypothesis that a particular number of factors is sufficient to describe the sample covariance matrix adequately. Second, standard errors for the loadings can be derived that allow testing of whether the loadings are different from zero. Third, the solution is scale-free in the sense that the results obtained from analyzing the correlation matrix can be obtained by rescaling the results obtained from analyzing the covariance matrix, and vice versa. A drawback of maximum-likelihood factor analysis is that the sample covariance matrix has to be of full rank.

Principal-Axis Factor Analysis

Principal-axis factoring starts by considering the matrix $\mathbf{S}_r = \boldsymbol{S} - \tilde{\mathbf{\Psi}}$, where $\mathbf{\Psi}$ contains initial estimates of the uniquenesses. One popular method of obtaining these initial estimates is to calculate $\tilde{\psi}_{ii} = s_{ii}(1 - R_i^2)$, where s_{ii} is the ith variable's variance and R_i^2 is the squared multiple correlation coefficient obtained from a regression of x_i on the remaining variables.

Because $\mathbf{S}_r$ is symmetric, it is possible to write $\mathbf{S}_r = \mathbf{\Gamma\Theta\Gamma}'$, where the columns of $\mathbf{\Gamma}$ contain p eigenvectors of $\mathbf{S}_r$ and $\mathbf{\Theta} = \mathrm{diag}(\theta_1, \ldots, \theta_p)$ contains the corresponding eigenvalues $\theta_j, j = 1, \ldots, p$. Without loss of generality, the eigenvalues can be assumed ordered such that $\theta_1 \geq \theta_2 \cdots \geq \theta_p$. Note that some of these eigenvalues may be negative. Let the number of positive eigenvalues be greater or equal to q, then $\mathbf{\Lambda}_q = \mathbf{\Gamma}_q\ \mathrm{diag}(\theta_1^{1/2}, \ldots, \theta_q^{1/2})$ can be defined, where $\mathbf{\Gamma}_q$ contains the first q columns of $\mathbf{\Gamma}$.

If one defines $\tilde{\mathbf{\Sigma}} = \mathbf{\Lambda}_q\mathbf{\Lambda}_q'$, then it can be shown that this matrix minimizes the least-squares discrepancy function

$$F(\mathbf{\Lambda}) = \mathrm{trace}[(\mathbf{S}_r - \tilde{\mathbf{\Sigma}})^2] \tag{6}$$

for fixed q. In other words, $\mathbf{S}_r$ can be optimally approximated in the least-squares sense by $\mathbf{\Lambda}_q\mathbf{\Lambda}_q'$, and therefore $\mathbf{S}$ is closely approximated by $\mathbf{\Lambda}_q\mathbf{\Lambda}_q' + \tilde{\mathbf{\Psi}}$. It is possible to iteratively apply this procedure. Having estimated $\mathbf{\Lambda}_q$ using the procedure just explained, the initial estimate of $\mathbf{\Psi}$ can be updated by calculating $\tilde{\mathbf{\Psi}} = \mathrm{diag}(\boldsymbol{S} - \mathbf{\Lambda}_q\mathbf{\Lambda}_q')$. An updated $\mathbf{S}_r$ matrix can then be calculated that leads to a new estimates of $\mathbf{\Lambda}_q$. The iteration is continued in this manner until the change in the factor loadings across successive iterations becomes negligible. Minimizing Eq. (6) has been recommended as more likely to find real but small factors when compared to the number of factors extracted from minimizing the maximum-likelihood discrepancy function [see Eq. (5)].

Determining the Number of Factors

Approaches to estimating the factor loadings require the number of factors to be known. However, this is hardly ever the case in practice. Therefore, starting with a one-factor model, models are fitted to the data, increasing the number of factors sequentially by one.

If the factor model has been fitted by maximum likelihood and the variables follow a multivariate normal distribution, a likelihood-ratio test can be used to test whether a specific number of factors is sufficient to explain the sample covariances. The null hypothesis states that at most q factors underlie the sample covariances. If H_0 is true, the test statistic follows asymptotically a chi-squared distribution, with degrees of freedom given by Eq. (4). A drawback of the likelihood-ratio test is that the number of significant factors will be overestimated if the factor model is only approximately true, especially when sample size is large. In addition, if several models are estimated by varying the number of factors, the test procedure is open to criticism because of an inflated type-one error rate due to multiple testing. Therefore, it is useful to consider two other commonly used rules of thumb for deciding on the number of factors that do not require specific distributional assumptions. However, both rules apply only if the sample correlation matrix $\boldsymbol{R}$ rather than the sample covariance matrix $\boldsymbol{S}$ is used to fit the factor model.

The first rule is based on the eigenvalues of $\boldsymbol{R}$. Because only a few of these eigenvalues will be larger than 1.0, this rule states that the number of factors should equal the number of eigenvalues greater than 1.0. The second rule for choosing the number of factors is a visual plotting procedure called the scree test, which plots the ordered eigenvalues against their rank. Ideally, the decreasing trend in the eigenvalues exhibited by this plot has a clifflike shape. Such a shape results if only the first few eigenvalues are "large" and the remaining eigenvalues exhibit a linear decreasing trend, representing the "scree." It has been recommended to retain as many factors as there are eigenvalues too large to be considered part of the scree. Although there is no mathematical rationale behind this procedure, the validity of the scree test has become accepted in standard factor analysis books. A drawback of the scree test is that it may be difficult sometimes to determine by visual inspection whether a particular eigenvalue should be considered large or small. To remedy the subjectivity involved in the scree test, there is a statistical test for the hypothesis, that the decrease in a set of eigenvalues follows a linear trend. Finally, note that the criteria discussed in this section may not agree when applied to a particular data set. In these cases, researchers may want to decide on the number of factors by taking substantive knowledge into consideration.

Rotating Factors to Simple Structure

Because the estimated factor loadings are based on arbitrary constraints used to define uniquely the model parameters, the initial solution may not be ideal for interpretation. Recall that any factor transformation $\boldsymbol{\xi}^* = \boldsymbol{T}\boldsymbol{\xi}$ for which $\text{diag}(\boldsymbol{T}\boldsymbol{\Phi}\boldsymbol{T}') = \boldsymbol{I}$ is an equally legitimate solution to Eq. (1). To simplify interpretation, it is desirable to rotate the factor loading matrix to simple structure, which has been defined in terms of five criteria: (1) each row of $\boldsymbol{\Lambda}$ should have at least one zero; (2) each of the q columns of $\boldsymbol{\Lambda}$ should have at least q zeros; (3) for every pair of columns of $\boldsymbol{\Lambda}$, there should be several variables with a zero loading in one column but not in the other; (4) for every pair of columns of $\boldsymbol{\Lambda}$, there should be a considerable proportion of loadings that are zero in both columns if $q \geq 4$; and (5) for every pair of columns of $\boldsymbol{\Lambda}$, only few variables should have nonzero loadings in both columns. Rotation techniques differ according to their emphasis on particular simple structure criteria.

Generally, a distinction is made between orthogonal and oblique rotation techniques, which yield uncorrelated or correlated factors, respectively. If the substantive concepts identified by the factors are related, correlated factors are appealing because they allow for a more realistic representation of the concepts, as compared to orthogonal factors.

One of the most popular orthogonal rotation methods is the varimax approach. This approach aims at finding a loading pattern such that the variables have either large (positive or negative) loadings or loadings that are close to zero. The varimax approach tries to accomplish this loading pattern by maximizing the variance of the squared loadings for each factor. Another popular orthogonal rotation techniques is the quartimax rotation, which maximizes the variance of the squared factor loadings in each row.

One of the most common oblique rotation techniques is the promax approach. This approach improves the loading pattern obtained from an orthogonal rotation in the sense of further increasing large loadings and further decreasing small loadings. Varimax rotation is commonly used as prerotation to promax. The promax approach accomplishes this goal in two steps. First a "target" matrix is obtained from the normalized loading matrix by replacing each factor loading by its kth power. For even powers, the signs of the loading matrix elements carry over to the corresponing target matrix elements. Common values for k are 3 and 4. Second, the orthogonal factors are rotated such that the variable loadings are, in the least-squares sense, as close as possible to the corresponding elements of the target matrix.

Predicting the Factor Scores

Because the factor model assumes that the variables are determined to a considerable extent by a linear combination of the factors $\xi_{i1}, \ldots, \xi_{iq}$, it is often of interest to determine the factor scores for each individual. Two approaches to predicting factor scores from the variable raw scores are discussed here. Both approaches assume variables and factors to be jointly normally distributed.

The so-called regression factor scores are obtained as

$$\hat{\boldsymbol{\xi}} = \boldsymbol{\Phi}\boldsymbol{\Lambda}'\boldsymbol{\Sigma}^{-1}\boldsymbol{x}.$$

It can be shown that this predictor minimizes the average squared prediction error, $\mathrm{E}\{\sum_{j=1}^{q}(\hat{\xi}_j - \xi_j)^2\}$, among all factor score predictors that are linear combinations of the variables.

The Bartlett factor score predictor is given by

$$\tilde{\boldsymbol{\xi}} = (\boldsymbol{\Lambda}'\boldsymbol{\Psi}^{-1}\boldsymbol{\Lambda})^{-1}\boldsymbol{\Lambda}'\boldsymbol{\Psi}^{-1}\boldsymbol{x}.$$

This expression also minimizes the average squared prediction error among all factor score predictors that are linear combinations of the variables. In addition, the Bartlett factor score predictor is conditionally unbiased, that is, $\mathrm{E}(\tilde{\boldsymbol{\xi}} \mid \boldsymbol{\xi}) = \boldsymbol{\xi}$. Notice that when calculating the factor scores, the matrices $\boldsymbol{\Lambda}$ and $\boldsymbol{\Psi}$ are replaced by their estimates. In these cases, the optimum property under which the predictors have been derived may not apply. The formula for the Bartlett factor scores can be expressed equivalently when $\boldsymbol{\Psi}$ is replaced with $\boldsymbol{\Sigma}$. An advantage of this formulation is that the factor scores can be calculated even if $\boldsymbol{\Psi}$ is singular, which may occur if uniquenesses are zero (Heywood case).

The use of factor scores is problematic because the factor loadings and the factor intercorrelations cannot be defined uniquely. The predicted factor scores will depend on the selected rotation procedure; therefore, factor scores resulting from different rotation procedures may rank order individuals differently. In addition, factor scores are problematic to use as independent variables in regression models because their values differ from the true values, which typically leads to bias in the regression coefficients.

Example

Generally, the results from a factor analysis of a correlation matrix and the corresponding covariance matrix are not identical. When analyzing a covariance matrix, variables having large variance will influence the results of the analysis more than will variables having small variance. Because the variances of the variables are intrinsically linked to the measurement units, it is preferable to analyze standardized variables, which is equivalent to fitting the factor model based on the correlation matrix, if the variables have been measured using different units.

Factor analysis can be illustrated using the artificial data set given in Table I. The data set contains standardized performance scores of 10 individuals obtained from an algebra problem, a trigonometry problem, a logic puzzle, a crossword puzzle, a word recognition task, and a word completion task. The correlation matrix of

Table I Standardized Raw Scores of Six Performance Measures[a]

Observation	x_1	x_2	x_3	x_4	x_5	x_6
1	−0.697	−0.700	−1.268	−2.245	−1.973	−1.674
2	−1.787	−1.538	−2.018	0.486	−0.163	−0.065
3	0.206	−0.913	0.079	0.801	0.964	1.043
4	−0.191	−0.430	1.074	0.002	−0.071	−0.159
5	−0.606	−0.225	0.296	−0.602	−0.990	−1.174
6	0.171	−0.417	−0.620	−0.519	0.694	0.648
7	1.460	1.038	0.532	1.261	−0.364	0.848
8	−0.639	0.888	0.306	−0.372	−0.305	1.101
9	0.779	1.595	0.775	0.499	1.215	−1.055
10	1.304	0.702	0.844	0.688	0.992	0.488

[a] The performance measures (x_1–x_6) are scores obtained on six tests: an algebra problem, a trigonometry problem, a logic puzzle, a crossword puzzle, a word recognition task, and a word completion task.

the six performance measures calculated from the raw data of Table I is

$$
\boldsymbol{R} = \begin{pmatrix} 1.0 & 0.7 & 0.7 & 0.5 & 0.5 & 0.3 \\ 0.7 & 1.0 & 0.7 & 0.3 & 0.3 & 0.1 \\ 0.7 & 0.7 & 1.0 & 0.4 & 0.4 & 0.2 \\ 0.5 & 0.3 & 0.4 & 1.0 & 0.7 & 0.6 \\ 0.5 & 0.3 & 0.4 & 0.7 & 1.0 & 0.5 \\ 0.3 & 0.1 & 0.2 & 0.6 & 0.5 & 1.0 \end{pmatrix}.
$$

It is hoped that subjecting this matrix to factor analysis will explain the correlations between the performance scores in terms of a small number of factors having easily interpretable relations to the tasks. First, the number of factors has to be determined. The eigenvalues of the sample correlation matrix are 3.34, 1.35, 0.47, 0.30, 0.28, and 0.26. Clearly, if the criterion to retain as many factors as there are eigenvalues greater than 1.0 is employed, two factors are retained. The scree plot in Fig. 1 confirms this conclusion. Clearly, the "small" eigenvalues appear to decrease linearly.

Finally, because the factor model has been fitted by maximum likelihood, the likelihood-ratio test can be used to evaluate the hypothesis that two factors are sufficient to explain the sample correlations. The test statistic yields a value of 0.0334 that can be compared against a suitable quantile of the chi-square distribution based on $\text{df} = 4$. If the nominal type-one error rate is set to 0.05, this test does not provide evidence against the null hypothesis. As a result, for this artificial data set, all three criteria for determining the number of factors agree.

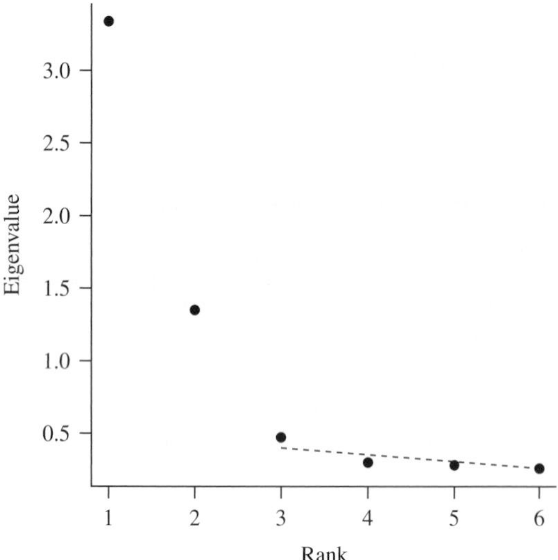

Figure 1 Scree plot depicting the ordered eigenvalues plotted against their rank. "Small" eigenvalues follow a linear decreasing trend.

Table II Maximum-Likelihood Estimates of Factor Loadings before Rotation and after Varimax and Promax Rotation

	Rotation method					
	Unrotated		*Varimax*		*Promax*	
Variable	ξ_1	ξ_2	ξ_1	ξ_2	ξ_1	ξ_2
x_1	0.828	−0.226	0.781	0.356	0.758	0.184
x_2	0.711	−0.489	0.860	0.079	0.920	−0.141
x_3	0.754	−0.335	0.794	0.225	0.807	0.037
x_4	0.746	0.486	0.263	0.851	0.055	0.864
x_5	0.693	0.373	0.294	0.730	0.123	0.722
x_6	0.482	0.485	0.061	0.681	−0.120	0.731

Next the focus is on the interpretation of the factors. Table II contains the factor loadings for the unrotated factors, the factor loadings after varimax rotation, and the factor loadings after promax rotation (the target matrix is created using $k = 3$ and varimax rotation). Because the maximum-likelihood estimates of the loadings on the unrotated factors satisfy the canonical constraint, the unrotated loadings are typically not of substantive interest. However, note that maximum-likelihood factor analysis together with the constraint $\boldsymbol{\Lambda}'\boldsymbol{\Psi}^{-1}\boldsymbol{\Lambda}$ is equivalent to Rao's canonical factor analysis. Because the orthogonal varimax rotation and the oblique promax rotation attempt to provide loadings that fulfill Thurstone's simple structure criteria, these loadings are more useful for interpretation.

First, consider the factor loadings after varimax rotation. Because varimax is an orthogonal rotation, the loadings can be interpreted as correlations between the variables and the factors. Based on the pattern of these loadings, each of the six variables can be identified with one and only one of the factors. Variables x_1, x_2, and x_3 are considerably influenced by the first factor whereas variables x_4, x_5, and x_6 are mainly determined by the second factor. Because the first three variables involve cognitive processing of formal and abstract material, it may be desirable to label the first factor as "formal ability" or "mathematical ability." Similarly, because the last three variables, which involve cognitive processing of verbal material, load highly on the second factor, it may be convenient to label the second factor "verbal ability."

Based on the loadings from the oblique promax rotation, the conclusions about the direct influence of the factors on the variables are essentially the same as before. Overall, the comparison between the loadings from the orthogonal and the oblique rotation shows that the relationships between the factors and the variables have become clearer by allowing for correlated factors. Based on the promax rotation, the correlation between the factors is estimated to be moderately high—specifically, $\phi_{12} = 0.46$.

It is also interesting to consider the factor structure matrix, which for correlated factors gives the correlations between the variables and the factors. Using the factor

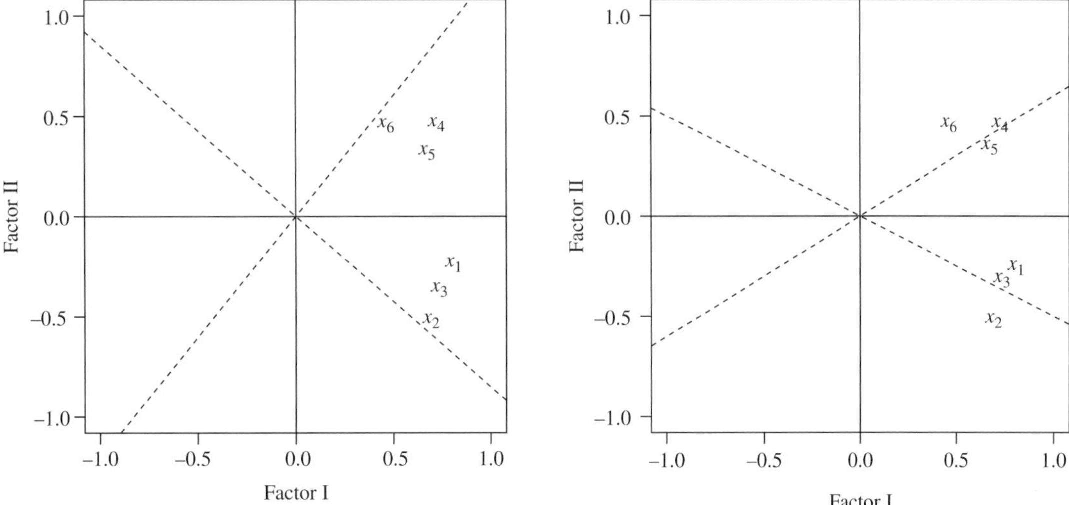

Figure 2 Loadings of variables on unrotated and rotated axes. The left-hand panel depicts the loadings with respect to the unrotated and varimax-rotated factors. The right-hand panel depicts the loadings with the respect to the unrotated and promax-rotated axes.

loadings from the promax rotation, the factor structure matrix is

$$\mathrm{Corr}(\boldsymbol{x}, \boldsymbol{\xi}) = \begin{pmatrix} 0.843 & 0.534 \\ 0.855 & 0.285 \\ 0.824 & 0.411 \\ 0.455 & 0.889 \\ 0.457 & 0.779 \\ 0.218 & 0.676 \end{pmatrix}.$$

This matrix shows that because of the factor intercorrelation, a small factor loading does not necessarily imply a small correlation between the corresponding variable–factor pair. In fact, the correlations in the factor structure matrix that correspond to small factor loadings have a moderately high value.

For the present example, factor rotation can be illustrated graphically. The left-hand panel of Fig. 2 depicts the loadings with respect to both the unrotated factors (solid lines) and the factors after varimax rotation (dashed lines). The right-hand panel of Fig. 2 depicts the loadings with respect to both the unrotated factors (solid lines) and the factors after promax rotation (dashed lines).

Finally, both the regression factor scores and the Bartlett factor scores are given in Table III. These scores are based on the results of the promax rotation. Because the factor scores are centered, positive and negative values can be interpreted as being above and below average, respectively. From Table III, the first individual appears to be considerably below average in terms of both math and verbal abilities. The second individual is considerably below average for math ability but about average for verbal ability. The factor scores of the other individuals may be interpreted similarly. Although there are small discrepancies between the regression factor scores and the Bartlett factor scores, overall they appear to agree well for this data set.

Table III Regression and Bartlett Factor Scores Calculated from the Result of a Maximum-Likelihood Factor Analysis after Promax Rotation

	Factor score			
	Regression		*Bartlett*	
Observation	ξ_1	ξ_2	ξ_1	ξ_2
1	−1.008	−2.122	−0.994	−2.463
2	−1.764	0.093	−2.076	0.300
3	−0.230	0.968	−0.356	1.197
4	0.070	−0.014	0.083	−0.024
5	−0.244	−0.846	−0.211	−0.998
6	−0.296	0.036	−0.351	0.075
7	1.065	0.862	1.173	0.931
8	0.187	−0.199	0.237	−0.261
9	1.214	0.389	1.389	0.342
10	1.007	0.833	1.107	0.902

See Also the Following Articles

Eysenck, Hans Jürgen • Guttman, Louis • Maximum Likelihood Estimation • Thurstone's Scales of Primary Abilities • Thurstone, L.L.

Further Reading

Bartholomew, D. J., and Knott, M. (1999). *Latent Variable Models and Factor Analysis,* 2nd Ed. Arnold, London.

Bartlett, M. S. (1937). The statistical conception of mental factors. *Br. J. Psychol.* **28,** 97–104.

Bentler, P. M., and Yuan, K.-H. (1997). Optimal conditionally unbiased equivariant factor score estimators. In *Latent Variable Modeling and Applications to Causality* (M. Berkane, ed.), pp. 259–281. Springer, New York.

Bentler, P. M., and Yuan, K.-H. (1998). Tests for linear trend in the smallest eigenvalues on the correlation matrix. *Pychometrika* **63**(2), 131–144.

Briggs, N. E., and MacCallum, R. C. (2003). Recovery of weak common factors by maximum likelihood and ordinary least squares estimation. *Multivar. Behav. Res.* **38,** 25–56.

Browne, M. W. (2001). An overview of analytic rotation in exploratory factor analysis. *Multivar. Behav. Res.* **36,** 111–150.

Cattell, R. B. (1978). *The Scientific Use of Factor Analysis in Behavioral and Life Sciences.* Plenum, New York.

Chen, F., Bollen, K. A., Paxton, P., Curran, P. J., and Kirby, J. B. (2001). Improper solutions in structural equation models. *Sociol. Meth. Res.* **29**(4), 468–508.

Cudeck, R., and O'Dell, L. L. (1994). Applications of standard error estimates in unrestricted factor analysis: Significance tests for factor loadings and correlations. *Psychol. Bull.* **115,** 475–487.

Fuller, W. A. (1987). *Measurement Error Models.* Wiley, New York.

Gorsuch, R. L. (1983). *Factor Analysis,* 2nd Ed. Lawrence Erlbaum, Hillsdale, New Jersey.

Harman, H. H. (1976). *Modern Factor Analysis,* 3rd Ed. University of Chicago Press, Chicago.

Hendrickson, A. E., and White, P. O. (1964). Promax: A quick method for rotation to orthogonal oblique structure. *Br. J. Statist. Psychol.* **17,** 65–70.

Kaiser, H. F. (1958). The varimax criterion for analytic rotation in factor analysis. *Psychometrika* **23,** 187–200.

Lawley, D. N., and Maxwell, A. E. (1971). *Factor Analysis as a Statistical Method,* 2nd Ed. Butterworths, London.

Rao, C. R. (1955). Estimation and tests of significance in factor analysis. *Psychometrika* **20,** 93–111.

Spearman, C. (1904). General intelligence, objectively determined and measured. *Am. J. Psychol.* **15,** 201–293.

Thurstone, L. L. (1947). *Multiple Factor Analysis.* University of Chicago Press, Chicago.

Yuan, K.-H., Marshall, L. L., and Bentler, P. M. (2002). A unified approach to exploratory factor analysis with missing data, nonnormal data, and in the presence of outliers. *Psychometrika* **67**(1), 95–122.

Falsification in Social Science Method and Theory

Bryan Benham
University of Utah, Salt Lake City, Utah, USA

Charles Shimp
University of Utah, Salt Lake City, Utah, USA

Glossary

Bayesian inference A use of Bayes' theorem relating conditional and unconditional probabilities, by which it has sometimes been hoped to interrelate objective and subjective probabilities.

falsification Any method by which scientific claims are evaluated by empirical disconfirmation.

induction Any method for confirming general scientific laws or theories by appealing to the accumulation of specific experimental observations.

methodological pluralism The position according to which diverse methods, perhaps having different ontological implications, may nevertheless be legitimate means of discovering scientific truths.

positivism A philosophy of science according to which scientific observation is independent of theoretical commitments and science does and should rest on a secure empirical foundation.

Quine–Duhem thesis The position according to which the meaning or truth of statements cannot be determined individually, but only holistically.

scientific method Any means by which scientific truths are reliably obtained and scientific claims are evaluated.

underdetermination The condition in which two or more mutually inconsistent theories can equally account for the same data and for which evidence alone does not determine theory selection.

Falsification originated in the problem of determining scientific truth. Answers based on induction and on the confirmation of hypotheses were discovered to have theoretical and practical problems. Falsification was proposed as an alternative answer, in terms of which science can rest on a secure foundation, provided that its hypotheses and theories are required to be subject to possible empirical falsification. Contemporary views of falsification vary greatly. In the philosophy of science, it is seen chiefly in logical and historical terms. In introductory social science texts on methodology, it is often seen as a way to reduce scientists' self-imposed biases that reflect theoretical preferences. Accordingly, in texts on rigorous, quantitative methodology, falsification tends to be praised either explicitly or implicitly as an essential part of the scientific method. Alternatively, in texts on qualitative research methods, it is sometimes described as a largely unhelpful or even counterproductive method. In social science practice, there is often an appeal to informal falsification, along with parsimony, as key evaluative criteria by which theories and empirical claims about truth can be evaluated. In theories of choice, decision making, and rational judgment, humans are seen as hypothesis-testing organisms who, in some contexts, may use an intuitive form of falsification. In mathematical statistics, many alternatives have been developed in response to the somewhat counterintuitive, negative logic of falsification. Similarly, the philosophical context from which falsification is viewed has broadened, so that to some scholars, positivism, within which falsification developed, is often seen as only a historical phase in the development of the philosophy of science. To other scholars, the scientific method is seen as successfully applying to the physical sciences but not to the social sciences. Most radically, some scholars see the scientific method within which falsification is defined as an unworkable method and in any case as a political tool. This constructionist and historicist view is compatible with the increasing use of narratives and other qualitative methods in sociological, anthropological, and psychological research methods. How the tension between this approach and the traditional scientific method will be resolved remains to be seen.

Introduction and Overview

Falsification is often viewed as central to the scientific method, essential for correct experimental design, and thus required for scientific progress. It is a view strongly associated with Karl Popper's argument that a genuine scientific claim must be subject to a critical empirical test. According to this view, science ideally proceeds by formulating hypotheses that are subject to empirical testing in such a way that the results could, in principle, show the hypotheses to be false. The critical empirical test should have two conceivable outcomes, one that is compatible with the hypothesis, and one that disconfirms it. Hypotheses that are not falsifiable in principle may be seen, according to this view, as having some potential heuristic value, but having no factual scientific status. Such unfalsifiable hypotheses belong merely to prescientific or pseudoscientific endeavors. From this perspective, falsification is designed as a tool to ensure that scientific claims are grounded in empirical observation, rather than in entrenched theoretical or ideological commitments. Falsification is an attempt to overcome various methodological problems in earlier views of science that were based in induction. These problems include worries about the effectiveness of induction, deriving from the underdetermination of theory by confirming evidence. Falsification, however, faces its own set of problems. Among these is that falsification does not accurately describe the historical practice of scientific discovery or justification. Neither can it account for how evidence can, in practice, falsify any hypothesis at all, given that any hypothesis can always be saved by ad hoc hypotheses, or even by the outright rejection of seemingly falsifying evidence. Perhaps a more sophisticated version of falsification can avoid some or all of these problems; on purely logical grounds, however, falsification seems no better than induction as a means for promoting scientific progress.

In the social sciences, falsification has both defenders and detractors. Proponents accept falsification as an essential part of the scientific method. This is sometimes explicitly stated in introductory social science texts, and it is often implicit in experimental design and in the context of hypothesis testing in inferential statistics, where "negative logic" may be used to test a null hypothesis according to which a variable is hypothesized to have no effect. Opponents, on the other hand, point to the methodological and conceptual problems mentioned previously. These problems with falsification have motivated the development of many alternative methodologies, some of them explicitly designed to preserve some of the logic of induction. In addition, some detractors argue that applying falsification to the social sciences is fundamentally illegitimate because it relies more on the quantitative methods and logic of the physical sciences, whereas its requirements are not met by the social sciences that do or should rely on qualitative and interpretive methods. Despite these criticisms, falsification retains a substantial presence in social science method and theory. This persistence of falsification in the social sciences raises a number of questions regarding the sociology of science as well as the possibility of a legitimate methodological pluralism in the social sciences.

Origins of Falsification

Induction and Scientific Method

Falsification originated in part as a response to various problems raised by earlier views of scientific methods based on induction. Induction has the intuitively desirable property that data that agree with a scientific hypothesis support or confirm that hypothesis. Few claims about scientific method seem more natural to a beginning science student. For example, suppose it is predicted that it will rain if the temperature falls below the dew point. To many students, it seems reasonable that there is confirmation of the prediction when the temperature falls below the dew point and it indeed starts to rain. From the perspective of induction, science progresses by the formulation of a hypothesis and the collection of sufficient empirical data that agree with the hypothesis. When accumulated evidence consistent with the hypothesis is sufficient, the hypothesis is confirmed. Although this account is oversimplified, insofar as induction exists in sophisticated forms, the goal of induction may be simply stated as the confirmation of scientific claims by the accumulation of data that agree with those claims.

Problems with Induction

Both theoretical and practical problems have been identified with induction. Consider the problem that arises if scientific method were based on induction: A universal empirical claim such as "All crows are black," or "Rate of information processing is a linear function of uncertainty," could never be conclusively verified, because it is unclear what finite amount of evidence could ever confirm its truth. Similarly, a probabilistic empirical claim faces the same problem. No finite amount of evidence could conclusively confirm the objective accuracy of a claim such as, "Most crows are black," or "Rate of information processing varies randomly but is on the average a linear function of uncertainty." In social science practice, of course, statements such as these are made in the context of additional assumptions that specify experimental and observational requirements. Nevertheless, the problem remains the same. But more damaging is that induction in general requires inferences from a sample of evidence. As Hume observed in 1739, the only reason to accept an inductive generalization as reliable is based on accepting a principle of reasoning—the future will be like the past, similar causes have similar effects, etc.—which is inherently either not subject to empirical confirmation or employs an inductive method to justify itself. The justification for induction therefore is subject to vicious circularity. Thus, if science rests on induction, it would appear that science involves a fundamental irrationality. Even if this skepticism about induction could somehow be satisfactorily overcome, there would remain the problem of underdetermination. Evidence underdetermines hypotheses in the sense that hypotheses or theories established by an accumulated amount of inductive support, aside from not being conclusively verified, are not uniquely confirmed. For any finite set of data, there is no unique hypothesis that is consistent with that data. It is always possible that two or more theories or hypotheses, each logically inconsistent with the others, will be equally consistent with the supporting data. That is to say, inductive support by data, by itself, never logically suffices to permit a scientist to choose between competing theories that are equally consistent with the data. Other criteria, including parsimony, explanatory power, esthetic qualities, perceived heuristic power, perceived social utility, and political and social values, are needed to supplement an inductive method of choosing between theories. But these additional evaluative criteria are obviously based on exactly the kinds of arbitrary, personal, subjective, potentially irrational human values science conventionally hopes to avoid.

Falsification as a Solution to the Problems of Induction

Falsification aims to overcome these problems with induction. According to falsification, the hallmark of scientific methodology is not that it uses observation or empirical evidence to verify or confirm its hypotheses. After all, many "nonscientific" practices, e.g., astrology, also employ this strategy. Rather, according to falsificationists, what makes science unique is that its claims are open to empirical falsification. What makes a generalization such as "All crows are black" genuinely scientific is not that there is a huge amount of observational evidence in its support, but that we know what type of evidence would count decisively against it; namely, the observation of only one nonblack crow would falsify it. Although such universal claims may never be conclusively verified, they can, in principle, be conclusively falsified. According to this view then, empirical evidence should be used to test scientific hypotheses, not to confirm them. More importantly, falsification is possible without the use of induction, thus avoiding the skeptical problems just described, and to some extent the problems associated with the underdetermination of theory by evidence. In this way, falsification is seen as an improvement over induction. Accordingly, falsification has become a widely accepted feature of accepted scientific method.

Problems with Falsification

Falsification, however, has its own serious logical and methodological problems. First, falsification as described by Popper does not appear to describe accurately historical scientific practice, either of scientific discovery or theory justification. The history of science reveals cases when observational data seemingly incompatible with a hypothesis did not lead to the abandonment of that hypothesis, and for good reason. Copernican theory, for example, initially failed to predict the trajectories of falling terrestrial bodies or why objects do not fly off the surface of the spinning Earth. (Early critics argued, for example, that if Earth spins, as Copernican theory claims, then objects dropped from a tower should fall some distance from the tower base, but this is not what is observed.) Such potentially falsifying observations did not, however, lead to the rejection of Copernican theory. Contemporary social science reveals many other such examples (see later). Second, it is not obvious either in principle or in practice how to determine what counts as a falsifying observation for a specified hypothesis. In the philosophy of science, this problem is described by the Quine–Duhem thesis, according to which hypotheses are not tested in isolation from background theory. That is to say, hypotheses are always tested in clusters consisting of the explicitly tested hypothesis and a complex background theory, which in turn consists of definitions, concepts, conventional methods, instrumentation, and so on. The result of this type of holistic view of hypothesis testing is that an instance of falsifying evidence does not necessarily falsify the hypothesis explicitly being tested. Falsifying evidence, or evidence seemingly incompatible with the tested hypothesis, can only demonstrate that the cluster of claims (the hypothesis plus background theory, etc.) used in the experiment is, at worst, inconsistent. The evidence does not indicate which particular claim to discard. Thus, it is relatively easy to save a hypothesis by rejecting another claim in a background theory, or to propose auxiliary hypotheses not in the original set that would explain the inconsistency. Thus, deciding when to abandon a hypothesis, or when to choose one theory over another, is not merely a matter of seeing falsifying evidence.

Instead, other criteria are needed. Some candidates include considerations of parsimony (e.g., Occam's razor), consistency with already accepted theory, productivity, and predictive power, each of which has its own methodological problems. More insidious problems arise for theory selection if scientific method is viewed from a historicist or sociological view, according to which science involves metatheoretical, arbitrary, possibly irrational, and ideological or political features. From this view, falsification does not provide a methodology from which to escape these idiosyncratic features of scientific research methodology.

Falsification in Contemporary Social Science Research

The Persistence of Falsification

Despite the problems with falsification, it retains a prominent position in social science. One reason why falsification, in one form or another, continues to be used may be that it so effectively captures a widespread view of science: Virtually everyone seems to agree that, in some sense, empirical scientific claims should be subject to refutation by empirical observation. In theory evaluation, in research methods, and especially in statistical methods, falsification is often held up as an essential component of scientific method. Falsification remains prominent even in cases in which it is the object of criticism, in part for reasons already described and in part because some assert that it does not apply constructively to qualitative and interpretive methods that are increasingly employed in the social sciences. The proper place for falsification in social science research is therefore still a matter of some debate.

Diverse Forms of Usage

There are many ways in which falsification is currently used, among which are the following five. First, to gain some small empirical perspective on the extent to which social science texts agree that falsification has a useful role, the present authors informally reviewed various introductory texts on scientific method in psychology and sociology (including statistical methodology). Falsification appears in several guises. (Excluded from consideration are historically related meanings, such as when one scientist criticizes another for having falsified or misrepresented something.) According to most of the introductory texts reviewed, most prominently in psychology texts, science involves a method that relies on observation, empirical data, and hypothesis testing. Some of these texts refer to a self-correcting process of peer review in which, sooner or later, false claims will be laid to rest. Some texts explicitly state that science does not address basic moral or religious issues because such issues involve claims that are not testable or falsifiable. Sociology texts were found somewhat more often than psychology texts to advocate various qualitative methods not involving rigorous hypothesis testing or falsification. Second, statistical methods often explicitly rely on falsification when, for example, the sampling distribution of a statistic of theoretical interest is derived to permit a null hypothesis to be tested. Such a test is motivated by a commitment to falsification, namely, that empirical data will show the hypothesis is falsified, i.e., is unacceptably improbable. If the null hypothesis is falsified in this sense, it is widely believed that scientific progress has been made. Third, falsification appears in its most basic form when a scientist concludes (perhaps most often in the case involving a theory contrary to the scientist's own theoretical predisposition) that the outcome of a single experiment falsifies an opponent's theoretical position. In accordance with the problems with falsification described previously, the theorist whose theoretical position Nevin ostensibly falsified was moved only to generalize and strengthen it, not to reject it. Fourth, on a grander scale, falsification appears in the idea of a "critical experiment" or "critical test." This idea was central to classic contests in the 1930s and 1940s between behavioral and Gestalt learning theorists. Hull and Tolman conducted numerous experiments, each designed to show that the competing theory was wrong. Again, in accordance with one of the problems with falsification described previously, neither side seemed much fazed by this series of critical tests wherein each side successively claimed their opponent's position had been falsified. More recently, the "cognitive revolution" is often said to have shown a basic inadequacy of behaviorism, and to have led to the death of behaviorism. Although cognitive psychologists appear not to claim explicitly that behaviorism was "falsified," the practical consequences seem similar: Behaviorism is declared dead, presumably on the basis of empirical results. As in the case of Hull and Tolman, many behaviorists continue to live happily, however, with their commitment to behaviorism, and care little that cognitive psychologists believe behaviorism is dead. Fifth, falsification as part of the logic of hypothesis testing appears in theories of human and nonhuman animal naturalistic decision making. That is, humans and animals have been studied as intuitive statisticians, especially in terms of the rationality and optimality of their decisions.

Alternative Methods

Not all social scientists are willing to accept falsification as an essential part of scientific method, for reasons previously described. Others reject falsification and associated views about rigorous hypothesis testing because they believe those views derive from methods appropriate to the physical sciences, but not necessarily to the social sciences. These scientists believe that the subject matter of the physical sciences allows for falsification only because of the quantitative and observational methods available to them. These methods, they argue, are not available to social scientists, because human behavior can be adequately understood only by using hermeneutic methods. They therefore worry that transferring the commitments of falsification to the social sciences may be illegitimate and ultimately damaging to the social sciences. These and other concerns have motivated the development of alternative methods and design criteria that avoid some of the problems raised by falsification. Some of these alternative methods are designed to restore a more confirmatory and inductionist approach to statistical analyses. These methods include techniques such as confidence intervals and other forms of Bayesian inference, and the development and evaluation of mathematical and computer simulation theories, some of which have been developed without appeal to falsification. In addition, case studies, narratives, and other qualitative methods are often not committed to falsification or hypothesis testing. Falsificationists tend to worry that some of these alternative methods merely raise again the problems falsification was designed to avoid.

The Broader Impact of Falsification

Philosophy and Sociology of Science

Falsification is often seen as coming out of a positivist view of science, according to which progress is real and cumulative, and which employs methods that are empirical and objective, and which has a self-correcting process in the form of peer review. The critique of falsificationism in the philosophy of science has focused much-needed attention on metatheoretical issues in the practice of science, rather than on idealized logical reconstructions of scientific method. The end result is a richer appreciation for the historical and sociological features of scientific theorizing. Although falsificationism is rejected by philosophers of science as an adequate account of scientific method, it motivates important questions in the sociology and rationality of science.

Falsification from the Perspective of Evolutionary Theory

Falsification has also raised questions about the extent to which hypothesis testing is a natural or default form of decision making. If it is not, then it is possible that humans, including scientists, may find it difficult to behave in accordance with the rational logic of scientific hypothesis testing. For example, Tversky and Kahneman have argued, especially in terms of base-rate neglect, that human categorical judgment displays large-scale irrationality. In another series of experiments to determine whether humans are naturally Popperian falsificationists, Wason presented subjects with a selection task aimed at testing an abstract rule. The result was that participants demonstrated a strong bias toward selecting potentially confirming evidence, and not equally available potentially disconfirming evidence. However, others have argued that rationality in these types of experiments must be interpreted in terms of cognitive processes evolution has provided, not in terms of the logic of falsificationist hypothesis testing. Thus, Tooby and Cosmides showed that participants in the Wason selection task actually did use something like falsificationist logic when the rule to be tested was placed in a more naturalistic setting, involving detecting cheaters in a social setting, not as a form of abstract rule testing. These types of experiments are provocative in what they can tell us about the standards of scientific methodology and research design.

Methodological Pluralism

The acceptance of falsification has been so pervasive in some circles that it has caused concern among researchers, who have felt its weaknesses have been underestimated and that domination by a single method is unhealthy. Alternative methods less committed to falsification and more in line with the tradition of induction seem to be finding growing acceptance in some parts of social science. The increasing use of narrative and other qualitative methods in sociological, anthropological, and psychological research raises controversial questions about the feasibility and appropriateness of methodological pluralism. Legitimate scientific method may not be a unified system relying heavily on falsification in the context of hypothesis testing, but may involve a great diversity of methods that may or may not be consistent with one another. How the tension between these competing approaches and the traditional view of scientific method will be resolved remains to be seen.

Acknowledgment

The authors thank Dr. Frank Drews for helpful references to naturalistic decision making as hypothesis testing.

See Also the Following Articles

Bayesian Statistics • Deduction and Induction

Further Reading

Cosmides, L., and Tooby, J. (1992). Cognitive adaptations for social exchange. *The Adapted Mind: Evolutionary Psychology and the Generation of Culture* (J. H. Barkow, *et al.*, eds.), pp. 163–228. Oxford University Press, Oxford, England.

Duhem, P. (1906/1954). *The Aim and Structure of Physical Theory* (translated by P. P. Wiener). Princeton University Press, Princeton, New Jersey.

Feyerabend, P. K. (1987). *Farewell to Reason.* Verso, London.

Gigerenzer, G. (1996). The psychology of good judgment: Frequency formats and simple algorithms. *Med. Decis. Making* **16,** 273–280.

Hanson, N. R. (1969). *Perception and Discovery.* Freeman, Cooper, San Francisco.

Hume, D. (1739–1740/2000). *Treatise on Human Nature.* Dent, London.

Kuhn, T. S. (2000). *The Road since Structure.* University of Chicago Press, Chicago.

Leahey, T. H. (1992). *A History of Psychology,* 3rd Ed. Prentice Hall, Englewood Cliffs, New Jersey.

Nevin, J. A. (1969). Interval reinforcement of choice behavior in discrete trials. *J. Exp. Anal. Behav.* **12,** 875–885.

Pickering, A. (1995). *The Mangle of Practice.* University of Chicago Press, Chicago.

Popper, K. (1935/1959). *The Logic of Scientific Discovery.* Basic Books, New York.

Quine, W. V. (1951). Two dogmas of empiricism. *Philos. Rev.* **60,** 20–43.

Shimp, C. P., and Hightower, F. A. (1990). Intuitive statistical inference: How pigeons categorize binomial samples. *Animal Learn. Behav.* **18,** 401–409.

Stuart, A., Ord, K., and Arnold, S. (eds.) (1999). *Kendall's Advanced Theory of Statistics, Vol. 2A: Classical Inference and the Linear Model,* 6th Ed. Arnold, London.

Taylor, C. (1994). Interpretation and the sciences of man. In *Readings in the Philosophy of Social Science* (M. Martin and L. C. McIntyre, eds.), pp. 181–211. MIT Press, Cambridge, Massachusetts.

Tversky, A., and Kahneman, D. (eds.) (1982). *Judgement under Uncertainty: Heuristics and Biases.* Cambridge University Press, Cambridge.

Zsambok, C. E., and Klein, G. (eds.) (1997). *Naturalistic Decision Making.* Lawrence Erlbaum, Mahwah, New Jersey.

Federalism: Local, State, Federal, and International Data Sources

Bertram Johnson

Middlebury College, Middlebury, Vermont, USA

Glossary

federalism A system of government in which national and local units possess autonomous domains of decision making.

fiscal federalism The division of responsibility for public services, taxation, and debt across multilevel jurisdictions.

general-purpose government A government, such as a state, municipal, county, or township government, that performs a variety of functions; in contrast to school districts or special districts, which perform only one or a few specific roles.

obligation In U.S. budgeting terms, a transaction that may either be paid in the present period or require payment in a future period.

State, federal, and international data sources comprise a variety of data that may be employed to better understand the relationships between autonomous regions and central governments, as well as the diversity among regions, in fiscal, political, and cultural terms.

Introduction

In the *Federalist Papers*, James Madison characterized the U.S. constitution as a mixture of federal and national elements. For Madison, "federal" meant "decentralized," but more recently, students of intergovernmental relations have used the word "federalism" to refer to a system of government in which national and local units divide sovereignty, each level possessing its own decision-making domain. There are many such nations in the world today, including Argentina, Australia, Austria, Brazil, Canada, Germany, India, Malaysia, Mexico, Nigeria, Russia, Spain, Switzerland, and the United States. The European Union and even China have also been analyzed as federal systems.

Divided sovereignty naturally raises a number of important social science research questions. Because federalism is defined in terms of relationships between governments, and because governments tend to keep track of their activities, data on the consequences of federalism for public finance are abundant, both for the United States and for other countries. Records concerning the electoral implications of federal systems are less common. Finally, information on federalism's effect on public opinion and political culture is rare, and scholars have only begun to develop useful resources in this area.

There are innumerable sources of data, many produced at a local level, thus a comprehensive listing of all empirical information available concerning federalism is not possible. For example, numerous U.S. state comptrollers' offices maintain publicly accessible depositories of budgetary data, but the availability of such data varies widely, depending on the jurisdiction. Nevertheless, several major U.S. and international data sources concerning fiscal federalism are reviewed here, with the focus being on the electoral implications of federalism and regional variations in individual behavior.

U.S. Fiscal Federalism Data

Much of what has been written on federalism in the United States concerns so-called fiscal federalism, i.e., the division of responsibilities for public service provision, taxation, and debt across multilevel jurisdictions. Data available for the study of fiscal federalism may be divided into two components: data on national funds distributed to local levels and data concerning state and local public finance.

Data on U.S. Federal Funds Distributed Locally

"All politics is local," former House Speaker Tip O'Neill famously pronounced, and indeed, in the United States, voters may judge their representatives and senators by how much national money they can deliver to their districts. Data on federal program funds distributed to localities are organized according to protocols developed by the Catalog of Federal Domestic Assistance (CFDA). Once a year (in June), the General Services Administration (GSA) issues the CFDA paper, but the online version is updated in December as well. It was first published in 1965 by the Office of Economic Opportunity; it was moved to the Bureau of the Budget (later the Office of Management and Budget) in 1971 and was transferred to the GSA in 1984.

The CFDA is comprehensive, describing federal domestic assistance programs available to: state and local governments (including the District of Columbia and federally recognized Indian tribal governments); territories (and possessions) of the United States; domestic public, quasi-public, and private profit and nonprofit organizations and institutions; specialized groups; and individuals. For each program, the CFDA provides the authorization history, eligibility requirements, and application guidelines. Each program is also assigned a five-digit program identification number.

Federal Assistance Awards Data System

The Federal Assistance Awards Data System (FAADS) is a quarterly report, organized and published by the U.S. Bureau of the Census, describing financial assistance awards of federal agencies to local individuals and local governments, either representing direct payments, guaranteed loans, direct loans, or insurance program expenditures. The FAADS has existed since 1982; records dating back to 1996 are available online (via www.census.gov). These data are listed by CFDA program number, and are disaggregated down to the county level. Scholars should be aware that the data represent federal agency obligations—that is, transactions that either may be paid or will require payment in a future period, rather than actual expenditures. For this reason, the Census Bureau advises caution when interpreting such data.

Federal Aid to the States

The Census Bureau's annual Federal Aid to the States publication reports actual expenditures made by federal agencies to state and local government entities only during a given fiscal year. These data are presented at a higher level of aggregation compared to the FAADS data, but are useful for those who are interested in annual federal grant aid to governments, rather than to individuals or private organizations.

Consolidated Federal Funds Report

The Consolidated Federal Funds Report (CFFR) is published annually by the U.S. Census Bureau and includes data (based on CFDA classifications, with records from 1993 to present available online) on distribution of federal funds to local areas at least down to the county level (sometimes down to the city level). This publication combines data from the FAADS, the Federal Aid to the States report, and several other (relatively minor) sources. An online query system at the Census Bureau web site allows users to search for data by geographic area and by agency (and subagency if applicable). This search produces summary tables with program names, program codes, and annual dollar figures. Consolidated data files are also available for download in comma-delimited format.

Data on State and Local Government Finances and Employment

The major source on state and local government finances and employment is the U.S. Census of Governments, which is undertaken in full every 5 years, most recently in 2002. All Census of Governments data are available from the U.S. Census Bureau (www.census.gov), along with extensive explanatory documentation.

Each year, the Census Bureau conducts annual finance and employment surveys of between 10,000 and 14,000 local governments. In Census of Governments years, this survey expands to data collection on all 87,525 state and local governments in the United States. The result of this undertaking is as exhaustive picture of state and local governance in the United States, organized in three data files (government organization, public employment, and government finances), with corresponding summary reports.

Government Organization

This section of the census describes the number of state and local governments, classifies each of them according to type, and indicates the services they provide. Important here is the distinction between general-purpose local governments, such as counties, municipalities, and township governments, which provide a variety of services to residents, and school districts or special districts, which may overlap general-purpose governments and typically perform only one or a few functions.

Public Employment
Here the census includes statistics on employment and payrolls at several different levels of aggregation: nationally by function, by states, and by county area. It also contains detailed data on "major local governments," which includes all counties, general-purpose governments of greater than 25,000 population, and school districts of over 7500 students.

Government Finances
Of most interest for those studying intergovernmental public finance, this section of the census details all revenue, expenditure, debt, and financial assets of governments for the fiscal year. Within these broad categories, data are further broken down into very specific classifications. A scholar interested in transportation expenditures, for example, encounters spending data for highways, air transportation, parking facilities, sea and inland port facilities, and transit subsidies.

U.S. Electoral Data

Data on state and local elections and/or the relationships between national elections and intergovernmental aid are less substantial, compared to public finance data. Nevertheless, in recent years, a number of excellent data collection efforts have expanded the list of available data in this area considerably.

Data on State Elections

Several major data sets exist for the study of U.S. state-level elections. First, the Inter-University Consortium for Political and Social Research and scholar Christian Collet have collected state legislative race data at the district, county, candidate, and constituency level from 1968 to 1989, and in the 1993/1994 cycle. Second, Gary King and colleagues have collected and organized precinct-level data on election returns for races from state legislative to presidential from 1984 to 1990. This unusually low level of aggregation, coupled with included demographic and socioeconomic information, make this data set particularly useful for studies examining the microconsequences of macropolitical phenomena. Finally, the Federal Elections Project, directed by David Lublin of American University and D. Stephen Voss of the University of Kentucky, aims to link electoral data at the precinct level with 2000 Census demographic data. Although this data set is primarily concerned with federal elections, it also contains data on the 11 governors' races that were held in 2000.

Data on Elections and Intergovernmental Processes

Kenneth Bickers and Robert Stein have developed a useful tool for analyzing how elections to the U.S. Congress affect the distribution of federal grant aid to local areas. They aggregate FAADS data on intergovernmental grant awards to the congressional district level. At present, they have created data sets for each year from 1983 to 1997. In their own work, Bickers and Stein use these data to test theories of distributive policymaking. The records of the National Election Studies' Senate Election Study, conducted each election year from 1988 to 1992, contain state data samples that researchers may use to examine state electoral phenomena. This data set has been most productive in comparing gubernatorial elections to senate elections.

U.S. Public Opinion, Culture, and Policy

At least since the publication of Daniel Elazar's influential book, *Federalism: A View from the States*, students of federalism have been concerned with the diversity of culture and public opinion that federalism may play a role in preserving. The recent major work in this area has been Erikson, Wright, and McIver's ongoing state public opinion and policy project, which evaluates the relationship between local preferences and government policy decisions. At this writing, they have updated their publicly available state-level ideology estimates, based on aggregated CBS News/*New York Times* polls, to cover the years 1977 to 1999.

In 2000, Harvard University's Saguaro Seminar and affiliated organizations conducted the Social Capital Benchmark Survey nationally, as well as in 41 distinct U.S. communities. Survey questions included queries about individual levels of participation in group activities, attitudes toward politics, and community involvement. The investigators, led by Harvard's Robert Putnam, hope to use the survey as a baseline measure, for future comparison, of civic engagement in the communities studied.

Finally, the number of American state-level policy data sources, which are often used to measure the links between public opinion and public policy, continues to grow. Many of these data sets are available at the Florida State University (FSU) State Politics and Policy Data Archives, maintained by FSU's Charles Barrilleaux.

International Data Sources

International sources of data on federalism are more widely scattered than are data on the United States, so it is difficult to evaluate all of them here. As in the United States, in general, data on fiscal federalism is easier to come by than are data on electoral behavior or public opinion.

Fiscal Federalism

Studies of fiscal federalism in individual nations may rely on data from national finance or statistics agencies, or on data collected or analyzed by several private research organizations, such as Argentina's Fundación de Investigaciones Económicas Latinoamericanas (www.fiel.org), or the Center for Monitoring Indian Economy (www.cmie.com). Many single-nation and multinational analyses of fiscal federalism must rely on World Bank and International Monetary Fund figures, however. The World Bank has published studies of fiscal federalism in individual countries, in addition to managing a significant educational and research program on fiscal decentralization. The International Monetary Fund (IMF) maintains its comprehensive *Government Finance Statistics Yearbook*, which includes annual figures on region and local government taxes and spending; in 1997, IMF published *Fiscal Federalism in Theory and Practice*, which contains information on intergovernmental grants and borrowing.

Politics and Elections

Basic data on politics and elections in federal states are available from state agencies, or from a comprehensive reference such as the *Europa World Yearbook*. A newer arrival, the Forum of Federations, a nongovernmental organization founded in 1998 and based in Ottawa, Canada, shows promise of being an excellent resource on the political aspects of federalism (www.forumoffederations.org). In addition to serving as a depository for scholarly articles, opinion pieces, and other materials on federal states, the fund's web site includes links to affiliates in a number of countries.

Public Opinion and Culture

Only in the past several decades have public opinion surveys been widely used in many federal countries, and, as in the United States, when these surveys have been conducted, they are rarely designed to enable studies of within-country regional variation. There are several notable exceptions, however, which suggest that the amount of data in this area will steadily improve. The unprecedented international World Values Survey, which measures basic values and belief systems, completed a fourth wave of research in 2001. Components of this study allow local comparisons, such as the separate surveys from four regions in Spain and from the Moscow region in Russia, in addition to the standard national surveys for those countries.

See Also the Following Articles

County and City Data • International Economics • State Data for the United States

Further Reading

Collet, C. (1997). *State Legislative Election Candidate and Constituency Data, 1993–1994.* ICPSR 2019. Inter-University Consortium for Political and Social Research, Ann Arbor, Michigan.

Erikson, R. S., Wright, G. C., and McIver, J. P. (1993). *Statehouse Democracy: Public Opinion and Policy in the American States.* Cambridge University Press, New York.

Inglehart, R., *et al.* (2000). *World Values Surveys and European Values Surveys 1981–1984, 1990–1993, 1995–1997.* ICPSR 2790. (electronic file). Inter-University Consortium for Political and Social Research, Ann Arbor, Michigan.

Inter-University Consortium for Political and Social Research (1992). *State Legislative Election Returns in the United States, 1968–1989.* ICPSR 8907. Inter-University Consortium for Political and Social Research, Ann Arbor, Michigan.

King, G., Palmquist, B., Adams, G., Altman, M., Benoit, K., Gay, C., Lewis, J. B., Mayer, R., and Reinhardt, E. (1998). *Record of American Democracy, 1984–1990.* ICPSR 2162. Inter-University Consortium for Political and Social Research, Ann Arbor, Michigan.

Rodden, J. (2002). The dilemma of fiscal federalism: Grants and fiscal performance around the world. *Am. J. Pol. Sci.* **46**(3), 670–687.

Roper Center for Public Opinion Research. (2001). *Social Capital Benchmark Survey, 2000.* (electronic file).

Saguaro Seminar at the John F. Kennedy School of Government, Harvard University. Available on the Internet at www.ropercenter.uconn.edu

Saez, L. (1999). India's economic liberalization, interjurisdictional competition and development. *Contemp. S. Asia* **8**(3), 323–345.

Saiegh, S. M., and Tommasi, M. (1999). Why is Argentina's fiscal federalism so inefficient? Entering the labyrinth. *J. Appl. Econ.* **2**(1), 169–209.

Stein, R. M., and Bickers, K. N. (1995). *Perpetuating the Pork Barrel: Policy Subsystems and American Democracy.* Cambridge University Press, New York.

Ter-Minassian, T. (ed.) (1997). *Fiscal Federalism in Theory and Practice*. International Monetary Fund, Washington, D.C.

U.S. Bureau of the Census. (2000). *1997 Census of Governments, Volume 3-2, Compendium of Public Employment.* U.S. Government Printing Office, Washington, D.C.

U.S. Bureau of the Census. (2000). *1997 Census of Governments: Volume 4-5, Compendium of Government Finances.* U.S. Government Printing Office, Washington, D.C.

U.S. Bureau of the Census. (2002). *Federal Aid to the States for Fiscal Year: 2001.* U.S. Government Printing Office, Washington, D.C.

Wright, G. C., McIver, J. P., and Erickson, R. S. (2003). *Pooled CBS/NYT Party ID and Ideology Estimates, 1977–1999,* (electronic file). Available on the Internet at http://sobek.colorado.edu

Field Experimentation

Donald P. Green
Yale University, New Haven, Connecticut, USA

Alan S. Gerber
Yale University, New Haven, Connecticut, USA

Glossary

dependent variable The outcome variable to be explained.

external validity The extent to which the results from a given study inform the understanding of cause and effect in other settings or populations.

independent variable The explanatory or treatment variable.

instrumental variables regression A statistical technique designed to correct for the contamination or mismeasurement of an independent variable. The technique involves predicting this independent variable with one or more variables that are uncorrelated with unmodeled causes of the dependent variable.

random assignment A method of distributing experimental subjects to treatment and control groups such that every observation has an equal probability of receiving the treatment.

spurious correlation A correlation between two variables that occurs, not because one variable causes the other but rather because both variables are correlated with a third variable.

Field experiments are randomized interventions that take place in naturalistic settings. Well-executed field experiments combine the strengths of randomized designs with the external validity of field studies. When ethically and practically feasible, field experimentation represents the strongest basis for sound causal inference.

Introduction

Field experiments, as distinct from laboratory experiments, are studies conducted in natural social settings, such as schools, voting wards, or police precincts. In contrast to ethnographic or descriptive research, field experiments are principally designed to establish causal relationships. When well executed, this type of inquiry represents the conjunction of four methodological precepts: intervention, controlled comparison, randomization, and verisimilitude.

Intervention

Unlike passive observation, which tracks putative causes and effects as they unfold over time or turn up in different places, intervention-based research seeks to identify causal patterns by disrupting the normal flow of social activity, for example, through the introduction of a new policy, dissemination of information, or creation of new social arrangements.

Controlled Comparison

Intervention research has a long intellectual history, but the scientific value of intervention research depends on the procedures used to determine when and where to intervene. Although massive interventions such as the creation of the Soviet Union are sometimes dubbed experiments in the colloquial sense, a basic requirement of any experiment is the use of a control group against which changes in the treatment group are to be gauged. Control groups may be formed in a number of ways. We may compare different sets of observations to one another, track a single set of observations over time, or follow multiple groups over time. But to draw meaningful comparisons between treatment and control groups, they must be formed in ways that make them equally likely to respond to a particular intervention and they must be exposed to similar influences other than the intervention.

Randomization

The comparability of treatment and control groups is ensured by random assignment. The assignment of observations is said to be random when each observation has the same *ex ante* probability of winding up in the treatment or control groups. The integrity of randomization is best ensured through a set of assignment procedures, whether it be flipping coins or consulting a sequence of random numbers. Note that randomization procedures may be under the control of the experimenter or some other agency or institution in charge of a lottery (e.g., the random assignment of judges to court cases).

Other approaches, such as assigning observations to treatment groups on an alternating basis, might be termed near-randomization, because we cannot be certain that the treatment and control groups differ by chance alone. Still less secure are attempts to simulate random assignment after the fact by matching treatment and control observations as closely as possible in terms of other observable characteristics. This approach, the logic of which undergirds the overwhelming majority of social science research, is known as quasi-experimentation.

The advantage of randomization is that it guarantees that treatment and control groups differ solely by chance prior to an intervention. Moreover, randomization guarantees that chance differences will disappear as the number of observations increases, so that remaining differences reflect the intervention's influence on the treatment group. No such guarantees govern near-random or quasi-experimental research. The first to recognize the full significance of this point was R. A. Fisher, who in 1926 argued vigorously on the advantages of assigning the units of observation at random to treatment and control conditions, as reported by Box:

> *As Fisher put it in correspondence, the experimenter games with the devil; he must be prepared by his layout to accommodate whatever pattern of soil fertilities the devil may have chosen in advance. A systematic arrangement is prepared to deal only with a certain sort of devilish plan. But the devil may have chosen any plan, even the one for which the systematic arrangement is appropriate. To play this game with the greatest chance of success, the experimenter cannot afford to exclude the possibility of* any *possible arrangement of soil fertilities, and his best strategy is to equalize the chance that any treatment shall fall on any plot by determining it by chance himself.*

Verisimilitude

Finally, field experimentation reflects the notion that research best occurs in settings that most closely approximate the domain in which knowledge is to be applied. The term field harkens to the agricultural origins of modern experimentation. Near-experiments in agriculture date back to the eighteenth century and grew increasingly sophisticated by the late nineteenth century. The pathbreaking work of R. A. Fisher in the 1920s, which laid the foundation for randomized experimentation, grew out of and was first applied to agricultural research. That research program had the down-to-earth objective of raising crop yields and lowering production costs on English farms. In a similar vein, many field experiments in social science are conceived as an attempt to evaluate specific programs or pilot projects. Often, however, they inform larger theoretical debates about behavioral responses to incentives, coercion, information, and moral suasion.

Recent Examples of Field Experiments in Social Science

Since their introduction into social science in the 1940s, randomized field experiments have been conducted in a variety of disciplines, particularly those that take a special interest in the behavior of institutionalized populations, students, prisoners, soldiers, recipients of public assistance, and the like. The basic features of field experiments are illustrated by the following selected examples.

1. The Moving to Opportunity experiment conducted by the U.S. Department of Housing and Urban Development randomly assigned 638 applicant families living in high-poverty neighborhoods to a control group or to one of two housing subsidy programs designed to facilitate residential relocation to neighborhoods with lower poverty rates. In 2001, Ludwig, Duncan, and Hirschfeld examined the arrest rates of teenage children in the three experimental groups over a 4-year posttreatment period.
2. Dartmouth College freshmen are randomly assigned dorms and roommates. This procedure sets the stage for an investigation on the effects of interpersonal influence. In 2001, Sacerdote examined the extent to which a student's grade point average, choice of major, and decision to join a fraternity was influenced by roommate characteristics.
3. The Tennessee Student/Teacher Achievement Ratio experiment randomly assigned 11,600 students in 80 schools to large or small classrooms from kindergarten through third grade. Students were given a battery of standardized tests at the end of each year, enabling researchers to gauge the short- and long-term effects of class size on academic performance. Krueger, in a 1999 report,

provides a careful analysis of the data that takes into account the practical problems that arose during the course of the study.

Advantages of Field Experimentation

Field experimentation may be viewed as a response to the limitations of both laboratory experimentation and observational research. In this section, we briefly summarize these limitations and the advantages of field experimentation.

Advantages over Laboratory Experiments

Inferences drawn from social science laboratory experiments confront somewhat different problems of inference. Such experiments create artificial environments designed to simulate the effects of market regulation, legislative voting rules, television consumption, and many other social institutions and processes. Randomization enables the researcher to draw secure inferences about cause and effect, but the question is whether laboratory results say anything about the operation of cause and effect outside the lab. The issue of external validity, or generalizing beyond the confines of a given study, surrounds all research, but it has special force in the case of laboratory studies. The social environment of the laboratory is often unusual, at very least because the participants typically realize that they are under observation in a university setting. The experimental manipulations are often contrived, and the participants tend to be college undergraduates. Whether these features of laboratory experiments threaten the external validity of their results is always unclear. Even under the best conditions, in which sampling and obtrusive measurement are not an issue, the simulated environment of the lab raises questions about generalizability to natural settings.

These concerns are especially pronounced when the aim is to evaluate the effects of a particular policy or program. A reading-enrichment program, for example, may work well in a laboratory setting; but if the aim is to gauge whether it will work in school settings, the experiment must take into account the manner in which schools are likely to administer the program. In contrast, a field experiment in one school will not settle the question of how the program fares on average across the population of schools, but the interpretation of the data requires a smaller inferential leap.

Another practical advantage of field experiments concerns the tracking of behavioral outcomes over time. For example, studies of how exposure to televised political advertisements affects voter preference go to great lengths to have subjects view television in a relaxed environment akin to their own homes, yet the evaluation of these exposure effects consists of a survey administered shortly afterward. It is difficult to know how to translate these survey responses into the terms that matter politically, namely, votes on election day. The advantage of randomizing media markets in which political advertisements are aired is that we can link the treatment to election results. Similar arguments could be made about laboratory versus field studies of whether policing deters crime or pre-school programs augment high school graduation rates.

Advantages over Nonexperimental Research

In nonexperimental research, causal inference is fraught with uncertainty. Lacking a procedure such as random assignment to ensure comparability of treatment and control groups, the researcher is forced to fall back on theoretical stipulations. For example, researchers who argue that active participation in civic organizations encourages the belief that most other people are trustworthy stipulate that beliefs follow from actions when interpreting the correlation between the two in survey data. This correlation, however, is also consistent with the hypothesis that trust encourages participation or that trust and participation bear no causal relationship to one another but happen to share similar causes. Unless the researchers manipulate political participation through some randomized mechanism, they cannot rule out the possibility that the putative relationship between participation and trust is spurious.

A variety of statistical analyses can be used to buttress causal claims based on observational data. Each technique aims to simulate the conditions of an experiment and does so by introducing certain theoretical assumptions. One approach involves the use of multivariate analysis in order to eliminate pretreatment differences between treatment and control groups. Multivariate regression, for example, eliminates the covariance between the treatment variable and other observable factors that are thought to influence the dependent variable. This approach works as long as no unobserved or imperfectly measured factors remain correlated with both the treatment and the outcome variable. Unfortunately, this assumption cannot be tested directly except by means of an experiment.

Another approach involves the use of instrumental variables regression. Here the researcher posits an instrumental variable that predicts the treatment, yet is uncorrelated with unmodeled causes of the outcome variable. Note that the randomization procedures used in experimentation are designed to generate just such an instrumental variable—a sequence of random numbers that predict nothing other than who gets the treatment. In nonexperimental work, the selection of an appropriate instrumental variable is a matter of speculation. Sometimes the proposed instruments are quite compelling. Whether a child's birthday falls immediately before or after the cut-off date for acceptance into kindergarten predicts educational attainment but seems unlikely to affect wage rates, and whether municipal government faces an election year predicts how much money is budgeted for police but seems unlikely to affect crime rates. More often, however, instrumental variables regression languishes for lack of plausible instruments.

The advantages of field experimentation go beyond random assignment. Because the experimenter is often in direct control of how a treatment is administered, there is less measurement uncertainty than is often the case with nonexperimental research, much of which relies on surveys. Asking a sample of survey respondents to report whether they have participated in a job-training program, read the newspaper, or attended the meeting of a civic organization often invites misreports and fails to garner detailed information about the specific content of these stimuli.

Finally, field experimentation can be used to create circumstances that are rare yet informative. Consider the case in which a researcher seeks to study the effects of marginal tax rates on a region's labor supply but tax rates historically vary little around a long-term average. With limited variance in the independent variable, the researcher cannot estimate the effects of tax rates with precision (putting aside the usual uncertainties associated with drawing causal inferences from nonexperimental correlations). An income tax field experiment has the advantage of creating new observations so that widely varying tax rates may be compared, permitting more precise estimates of the effects of tax rates. This experimental approach has the further advantage of enabling researchers to examine whether their modeling assumptions, hold outside the confines of historical data.

Field Experimentation in Practice

To appreciate the relative merits of experimental and nonexperimental research in practice, it is instructive to examine a research literature that features both types of investigation. One such literature concerns voter mobilization. This line of research dates back to Harold Gosnell's efforts in the mid-1920s to register voters and impel them to vote by mailing them leaflets. The handful of experiments following Gosnell have been overshadowed by a plethora of nonexperimental studies that use survey data to gauge whether citizens recall having been contacted by political campaigns. In a typical statistical analysis, reported campaign contact predicts voter turnout, controlling for background variables such as partisanship, interest in politics, and demographic characteristics.

This approach has certain inherent drawbacks. First, the researcher must take the respondent's word that reported contacts actually occurred. In addition, the vague way in which campaign contacts are defined and measured raises further concerns. Little attempt is made to distinguish between personal and phone contacts or between single and multiple contacts. Serious though these measurement concerns may be, they are in some sense eclipsed by even more serious doubts about spuriousness. If parties direct their appeals disproportionately to committed partisans and frequent voters, those most likely to vote will be the ones most likely to receive political contact, and the apparent link between contact and turnout may be spurious.

In principle, these problems may be corrected statistically. For example, we may use instrumental variables regression to offset biases associated with endogeneity and misreporting. None of the aforementioned studies uses instrumental variables regression. This gap in the literature is not hard to understand. Valid instrumental variables are difficult to think of, let alone find in existing surveys. In this case, we must find a variable that predicts campaign contact but remains uncorrelated with unmodeled determinants of voting. We might look for natural experiments in which exogenous events, such as unexpected policy changes or technological innovations, altered campaign contact. Even then, the validity of the instrumental variable would remain a matter of speculation. Only randomization provides a procedure for generating valid instrumental variables.

A more common but nonetheless problematic strategy for avoiding bias is to formulate an exhaustive model of voting, hoping that the control variables in the model eliminate any correlation between campaign contacts and the disturbance term. Unlike the instrumental variable approach, this methodological tack fails to address biases arising from mismeasurement. Given the seriousness of the measurement problem in most survey-based studies, this defect may altogether invalidate the results. Holding measurement concerns in abeyance, this statistical approach nonetheless requires a leap of faith. How can we tell whether a given set of control variables performs its appointed task?

In the case of voter mobilization, it would be very difficult to predict *ex ante* whether experimental and nonexperimental results will coincide. Random errors in survey measures of campaign contacts might lead to an underestimate of their effects; on the other hand, if voters are more likely than nonvoters to report campaign contact when none occurred, regression analysis might overestimate the effects of mobilization. If parties and candidates target likely voters, the effects will also be overestimated. Under these conditions, the sign and magnitude of the biases in nonexperimental research are knotty functions of variances and covariances of observed and unobserved determinants of the vote. Even if by some accident of fate the positive biases were to offset the negative, our ability to compare experimental and nonexperimental findings is hampered by the fact that most surveys fail to gauge the precise nature and frequency of campaign contact.

As it turns out, experimental studies have found that the effectiveness of mobilization varies markedly depending on whether voters are contacted by phone, mail, or face-to-face. In 2000, Gerber and Green conducted a randomized field experiment using a population of 30,000 registered voters in New Haven. Their results indicated that personal canvassing boosts turnout by approximately 9 percentage points, whereas phone calls have no discernible effect. Both experimental and nonexperimental studies find statistically significant effects of campaign activities on voter turnout. Experimental studies, however, speak to the issue of causality with far greater clarity and nuance because the researchers have control over the content of the campaign stimulus and can rule out threats to valid inference.

Drawbacks

Performing randomized experiments in real-world settings presents a number of practical challenges, the magnitude of which in part explains the relative paucity of this form of research in social science.

Limited Access to Manipulations

Social scientists seldom have the opportunity to assign resources, institutions, or experiences at random. Despite Campbell's 1969 plea for an "experimenting society" in which innovations are routinely attempted and subjected to rigorous scientific evaluation, the fact remains that such randomized interventions are rare. A failure to appreciate the special advantages of randomization combines with a reluctance on the part of administrators to be seen to act randomly, preventing experimentation from becoming one of the ordinary data-gathering tasks used in evaluation.

Resource Limitations

Field experiments are often expensive. Even relatively inexpensive field experiments that require a change in administrative behavior (e.g., mandatory arrests in domestic violence cases) rather than the allocation of additional resources still require more funding and effort than the typical observational study.

Implementation Failure

Assigning subjects at random to treatment and control groups is no guarantee that subjects will actually receive the treatment on a purely random basis. Sometimes those who administer or participate in experiments subvert randomization in various ways. A classic instance of implementation failure may be found in the Lanarkshire milk study, one of the first randomized experiments ever conducted. Thousands of children in Lanarkshire schools were randomly assigned during the 1920s to dietary supplements of pasteurized milk, raw milk, or nothing. Their physical development was tracked over several years. Out of concern for the well-being of their students, teachers reassigned some of the smallest and most needy children from the control group into one of the milk-drinking conditions, thereby undermining the randomness of the treatment. Similar problems arise in social experiments in which administrators steer certain subjects into the treatment group or when subjects themselves insist on being reassigned.

Sampling

The central aim of field experimentation is to estimate the average treatment effect in a given population. For example, a study may seek to estimate the average extent to which preparatory classes improve performance on college entrance examinations. Although it is conceivable that all students react in the same way to such classes, it may be that certain types of students benefit more than others. If effects vary, and the aim is to estimate the average treatment effect, we must either draw a representative sample of students or narrow our focus (and conclusions) to students of a particular type.

The issue of sampling and generalizability arises in several ways. First, the challenges of orchestrating field experiments means that they tend to occur in a small number of sites that are chosen for reasons of logistics rather than representativeness. Second, within a given experiment, the numbers of observations may be attenuated by subjects' refusal to participate or decision to drop out of the study. Noncompliance and attrition are remediable problems as long as the decision to participate is unrelated to the strength of the treatment effect. The statistical correction is to perform an instrumental variables regression in which the independent variable is whether a subject was actually treated and the instrumental variable is whether a subject was originally assigned to the treatment group.

The situation becomes more complex if participation and responsiveness to the experimental treatment interact. In this case, the study's conclusions apply only to the types of people who actually participate in an experiment. The way to address this concern empirically is to replicate the experiment under conditions that lead to varying participation rates in order to see whether the results vary. In general, replication is the appropriate response to concerns about drawing conclusions based on studies of particular times, places, and people.

Conclusion

The results from large-scale field experiments command unusual attention in both academic circles and the public at large. Although every experiment has its limitations, field experiments are widely regarded as exceptionally authoritative. By combining the power of randomization with the external validity of field research, these studies have the potential to eclipse or significantly bolster findings derived from laboratory experiments or nonexperimental research.

Further contributing to the strength of field experimentation is the transparent manner in which the data are analyzed. In contrast to nonexperimental data analysis, in which the results often vary markedly depending on the model the researcher imposes on the data and in which researchers often fit a great many models in an effort to find the right one, experimental data analysis tends to be quite robust. Simple comparisons between control and treatment groups often suffice to give an unbiased account of the treatment effect, and additional analysis merely estimates the causal parameters with greater precision. This is not to say that experimental research is free from data mining, but the transformation of raw data into statistical results involves less discretion and therefore fewer moral hazards.

See Also the Following Articles

Laboratory Experiments in Social Science • Randomization

Further Reading

Angrist, J. D., Imbens, G. W., and Rubin, D. B. (1996). Identification of casual effects using instrumental variables. *J. Am. Statist. Assoc.* **91**(June), 444–455.

Box, J. F. (1980). R. A. Fisher and the design of experiments, 1922–1926. *Am. Statist.* **34**(February), 1–7.

Campbell, D. T. (1969). Reforms as experiments. *Am. Psychol.* **24,** 409–429.

Campbell, D. T., and Stanley, J. C. (1963). *Experimental and Quasi-Experimental Designs for Research.* Houghton Mifflin, Boston.

Fisher, R. (1935). *Design of Experiments.* Hafner Publishing, New York.

Gerber, A. S., and Green, D. P. (2000). The effects of canvassing, direct mail, and telephone contact on voter turnout: A field experiment. *Am. Polit. Sci. Rev.* **94,** 653–663.

Gosnell, H. F. (1927). *Getting-Out-The-Vote: An Experiment in the Stimulation of Voting.* University of Chicago Press, Chicago, IL.

Heckman, J. J., and Smith, J. A. (1995). Assessing the case for social experiments. *J. Econ. Perspect.* **9**(spring), 85–110.

Heinsman, D. T., and Shadish, W. R. (1996). Assignment methods in experimentation: When do nonrandomized experiments approximate the answers from randomized experiments? *Psychol. Methods* **1,** 154–169.

Krueger, A. B. (1999). Experimental estimates of education production functions. *Q. J. Econ.* **114**(May), 457–532.

Ludwig, J., Duncan, G. J., and Hirschfeld, P. (2001). Urban poverty and juvenile crime: Evidence from a randomized housing experiment. *Q. J. Econ.* **116**(May), 655–679.

Rosenzweig, M. R., and Wolpin, K. I. (2000). Natural "natural experiments" in economics. *J. Econ. Lit.* **38**(December), 827–874.

Sherman, L. W., and Berk, R. A. (1984). The specific deterrent effects of arrest for domestic assault. *Am. Sociol. Rev.* **49,** 261–272.

Sacerdote, B. (2001). Peer effects with random assignment: Results for Dartmouth roommates. *Q. J. Econ.* **116**(May), 681–704.

Student. (1931). The Lanarkshire milk experiment. *Biometrika* **23,** 398–406.

Word, E. J., Johnston, J., Bain, H., *et al.* (1990). *The State of Tennessee's Student/Teacher Achievement Ratio (STAR) Project: Technical Report 1985–90.* Tennessee State Department of Education, Nashville, TN.

Yinger, J. (1995). *Closed Doors, Opportunities Lost: The Continuing Costs of Housing Discrimination.* Russell Sage, New York.

Field Relations

David A. Snow
University of California, Irvine, California, USA

Calvin Morrill
University of California, Irvine, California, USA

Glossary

derived dimension of roles The highly variable, situationally specific behaviors and orientations associated with the role, and through which actual relations are negotiated and maintained.

fieldwork relations The set of researcher/informant relationships established between the fieldworkers and those members of the scene or setting who function as hosts and objects of the research.

fieldwork roles The various negotiated positions or vantage points that situate the fieldworker in relation to the phenomenon of interest, or in relation to some set of members of the group or setting studied.

rapport/trust A property of a relationship, referring to the point in the development of fieldwork relationships at which the informant feels reasonably comfortable in functioning as a behavioral and orientational guide to the setting/group/social world being studied, thus divulging what s/he knows and does not know, and the corresponding confidence the fieldworker has in his/her informants and the information elicited from them.

structural dimension of roles The generic, skeletal boundaries of a role (such as the role of a fieldworker), but without explicitly defining the various behaviors and orientations associated with the actual performance of the role.

Field relations encompass the set of relationships established, in the scene or setting being studied, between the researcher and those informants who function as the hosts and objects of the research. Because of the importance of field relations to successful field research, such relationships have received considerable attention among field researchers, particularly ethnographers, in their research reports and texts. Examination of the literature detailing these experiences suggests five sets of factors that can affect the development and maintenance of field relations: fieldwork roles, setting or group attributes and characteristics, researcher attributes and characteristics, strategies to facilitate trust or rapport, and strategies to modify relational involvement.

Introduction

Of the various issues that qualitative field researchers must consider and negotiate during the course of their fieldwork, few are as fundamental to the success of a project as the kinds of field relations established with members of a research setting. Indeed, it is arguable that nothing is more determinative of what a field researcher sees and hears, and thus learns about aspects of a social context, than the numbers and types of field relationships developed with informants. This is so for two reasons: first, intimate, up-close access to the happenings, events, and routines that constitute any particular social setting is contingent on establishing relationships in that setting with one or more members who function as "guides" to the organization and perspectives associated with those happenings, events, and routines. Second, different kinds of relationships with different individuals variously situated within the setting are likely to yield different perspectives and understandings. Ethnographic knowledge of any particular family, for example, is likely to vary somewhat, depending on whether the family is accessed and explored from the perspective or vantage point of the mother, or the father, or each of the children, or perhaps even the neighbors.

This intimate connection between field relations and what is seen or heard, and thus learned, has long been acknowledged, both directly and indirectly, by practitioners and observers of ethnographic fieldwork, although not always in the same terminology. For example, using the language of roles, which are relational entities, McCall and Simmons argue that the role the field researcher claims or is assigned "is perhaps the single most important determinant of what he (or she) will be able to learn." Rosaldo makes a similar point with the terminology of "position" and "angles of vision," noting that what the fieldworker sees and what is made of it depends in large measure on how he or she is positioned in relation to those being studied. And Emerson and Pollner emphasize "embodied presence in the daily lives of those who host the research" as "the sin qua non of ethnography," thus accenting the importance of field relations by emphasizing that "the ethnographer constructs the field not simply through gaze and representation but also, and more fundamentally, by negotiating interactional presence to local events and scenes that can then be made subject to disciplinary gaze and textual representation." In each instance, the implication is that what is seen and heard in the context of fieldwork, and thus what ultimately constitutes the basis for the data log or field notes, is contingent on the kinds of field relationships negotiated between field researchers and those who are both their research hosts and objects of study.

Fieldwork Roles and Field Relations

Traditionally, the concept of fieldwork roles has been the primary conceptual vehicle through which field relations have been discussed and analyzed. The logic or cornerstone rationale for approaching field relations via the concept of roles resides in the fact that roles are relational entities, the essence of which derives from the set of other roles with which they are intertwined, and thus they function as avenues or barriers to other roles and their information bases and standpoints. Accordingly, the claim that the fieldwork role is the primary determinant of what the researcher will learn rests on the presumption that the role determines where, what, and with whom the fieldworker can go, do, and interact, what the fieldworker can ask and observe, and what the fieldworker will be told.

Not all field researchers find the concept of fieldwork roles particularly useful, because of the overly structural, rational, deterministic, and impersonal baggage often associated with the idea of roles. However, these troublesome accouterments can be bypassed if roles are understood more flexibly as having two components: the structural dimension, which delimits the skeletal or generic boundaries of roles, and the derived dimension, which denotes the more situationally specific, negotiated, and thus emergent aspects of roles. Although not always framed in terms of these two dimensions of roles, much of the discussion of fieldwork roles can be usefully understood in terms of these components. For example, Raymond Gold's now classic distinction concerning the observational roles of the complete observer, the observer-as-participant; the participant-as-observer, and the complete participant, Herbert Gans' similar distinction concerning the total participant, the researcher-participant, and the total researcher; and John and Lyn Lofland's even more parsimonious distinction between known (overt) and unknown (covert) investigators all identify two or more ideal-typical fieldwork roles, with each implying different kinds of field relations and informational yield.

Although these typologies of fieldwork roles are useful insofar as they sensitize researchers to possible variations in the degree of participation/membership and openness with respect to research identity and interests, and the advantages and disadvantages associated with such variations, such typologies are not very helpful with respect to actually negotiating and maintaining field relationships. Moreover, they gloss over the multitude of ways in which it is possible to be a participant-observer within a setting, or a member of a group, whether known or unknown. For example, Adler and Adler's examination of a large number of ethnographic field studies in which the researcher was a member of the setting or group revealed that membership roles can vary considerably, ranging from peripheral through active to complete membership roles, with each entailing different kinds of relationships with members and commitments to the group or setting. In the case of peripheral membership roles, for example, the researcher participates in some of the activities associated with the group or setting being studied, but refrains from engaging in its central activities, as illustrated in Ruth Horowitz's study of Chicano youth gangs in Chicago. Though she hung out with members in some places and at some times, she avoided participation in their more dangerous and sexual activities, thus foregoing the kinds of knowledge that derive from relationships and experiences forged in certain group-specific contexts. In the active membership role, by contrast, the researcher participates in the group's core activities, but without fully embracing the group's values and goals, as illustrated by Burke Rochford's study of the Hare Krishna movement in the United States in the 1980s. And exhibiting both thoroughgoing engagement in a group's activities and embracing its goals and values is the complete membership role, as reflected in Barrie Thorne's study of the draft resistance movement of the 1960s.

Each of the varieties of membership roles points to the interactionally negotiated and derived character of fieldwork roles and their associated field relations, and show that the broad, generic fieldwork roles of participant-observer, known investigator, or member are at best skeletal shells that have to be filled in and modified throughout the research process. Thus, the concept of fieldwork roles constitutes a useful conceptual tool for getting a handle on field relations, but only insofar as fieldwork roles are understood as relational entities that position researchers in relation to some set of members and activities within the research setting, and as interactionally negotiated rather than merely structurally given.

Setting or Group Attributes/ Characteristics and Field Relations

One of the reasons why field-role relationships are negotiated relates to the kinds of relationships that evolve during the course of fieldwork—they are not simply a matter of the researcher's own choosing. Whatever the objectives and interests of the field researcher, they have to be melded with various characteristics of the group or setting, which constitutes constraints on the kinds of role relationships that can be developed. Settings that are public or private, or groups that conduct their business in one context rather than another, call for somewhat different kinds of fieldwork roles and relations. In public settings, such as parks and malls, researchers typically have greater latitude with respect to access and movement, whereas in quasi-private and private places, such as offices and homes, access and movement are contingent on negotiating an invitation and a more concrete role relationship. Because of such differences, the issue of whether to be overt or covert, or open or closed about research identity and interests, is less complicated interactionally and ethically in public contexts than it is in private ones. To study lifestyle of the street homeless, for example, it is not necessary to knock on doors and negotiate with formal gatekeepers, as might be required in order to study corporate elites.

Similarly, whether a group is inclusive or exclusive in terms of membership criteria affects the kinds of relationships that need to be and can be developed. Studying exclusive religious movements that require the researcher to drop out and join one of its communes mandates nothing less than an active membership role, whereas research on inclusive religious groups that do not require such encompassing commitment allows for greater flexibility in terms of the kind of research role that might be negotiated. Whether the activities associated with the setting or group studied are legal or illegal has significant implications for the kind of role relationships that should be negotiated as well.

Researcher Attributes/ Characteristics and Field Relations

Also significantly affecting the kinds of fieldwork roles and relations that can be negotiated are the researcher's social attributes (gender, age, race, and ethnicity) and personal characteristics and experiences, including biography, personality, and perspectives. Such personal and social characteristics can be relevant to all social research, but they are especially significant in the case of fieldwork, and particularly ethnographic fieldwork, because it is the most embodied of all social research in the sense that the fieldworker is the primary research instrument. Because of this characteristic of fieldwork, the social attributes of the researcher are likely to be especially relevant to those studied, not only closing or opening doors, but also influencing the character of the relationships that evolve.

Given that we live in a gendered social world, with gender figuring in the organization of relationships in most social settings and scenes, the gender of the researcher is likely to be an especially significant factor in accessing and negotiating relationships in most settings and groups. Not surprisingly, the settings and activities that are most gendered, in the sense of being associated primarily with women or men, tend to get studied primarily by the matched gender, or used accordingly as research sites. Public restrooms, for example, can be particularly good sites for developing fleeting relationships that yield information about activities and interests that extend beyond the restroom, but both experience and research show that access and the possibility of developing such fleeting relationships is highly gendered. In other words, women fieldworkers traditionally have been more likely to study topics and issues stereotypically associated with women, such as child care, emotion work, and veiling, whereas male fieldworkers have been more are likely to focus on topics and issues more stereotypically associated with men, such as hunting, police work, and drinking. But just as gender barriers and logics have changed, so have there been changes in the link between gender and research; women, in particular, have negotiated sexually ambiguous roles and relationships. Prominent examples of this loosening of the connection between gender and research foci include Arlene Kaplan Daniels' study of military psychiatrists and Jennifer Hunt's field research among police patrol officers. In both cases, however, the derived research roles were impacted by gender considerations, i.e., Daniels was regarded as an "amusing and ornamental mascot, treated with friendly affection but little respect," and Hunt was treated as an "honorary male."

Age is another factor that can influence access to and the development of functional field relations. Certainly this makes sense, especially in fieldwork with children, but it is often difficult to distinguish the effects of age from those of other social attributes. As well, the research experiences of various fieldworkers suggest that variation in the ages of those studied and in the age of the researcher can often facilitate relational access and informational flow, as when the dependent elderly are interviewed by younger fieldworkers.

The attributes of race and ethnicity can also affect the prospect of developing viable fieldwork relationships. As with any attribute, however, their salience in negotiating functional research relationships varies with what is being studied and the context in which it is studied. If the object of research is an exclusionary group in which membership is based on race or ethnicity, then the prospect of negotiating a viable research relationship is contingent on sharing the same race or ethnicity. But if the research is conducted in more public or quasi-public contexts, such as street corners, sidewalks, parks, and neighborhood bars or eating establishments, a number of prominent studies indicate that viable research relationships between fieldworkers and the objects of their research can evolve independently of racial or ethnic homogeneity. Examples include William F. Whyte's field research among Italian cornerboys, Elliot Liebow's field study of Blacks hanging around Tally's corner, and Mitchell Duneier's research among Black book peddlers in New York's Greenwich Village.

Though the researcher's various social attributes can affect the kind of fieldwork roles and relationships that can develop, attribute heterogeneity or dissimilarity does not preclude the possibility of negotiating viable field researcher relationships. In other words, it is not always a necessary condition for researchers to be "insiders" in the sense of sharing the same attributes (gender, age, race, and ethnicity) and orientations or perspectives of the objects of study. Obviously, there are both advantages and disadvantages to being an "insider" and "outsider"; for example, initial access is easier for the insider but subsequent access to certain kinds of information may be less complicated for the outsider to negotiate. The point, then, is that though researcher attributes are indeed important, attribute heterogeneity can be successfully negotiated and managed in many contexts with heightened sensitivity to its limitations and advantages.

Strategies to Facilitate Relational Access and the Development of Rapport/Trust

Although the character of fieldwork roles and the development of corresponding field relations are constrained by both group and researcher attributes and characteristics, they are rarely determinative of the kinds of fieldwork roles and relations that evolve. If they were, then there would be little substance to the repeated claim that both fieldwork roles and relations are interactionally derived or negotiated. Part of what gets negotiated are these very constraints, because the fieldworker attempts to find a role or vantage point within the group or setting, or in relation to some set of members, that optimizes what is likely to be learned per the objectives of the study. Thus, for most field studies, the fieldworker is likely to have some elbowroom or latitude for negotiating functionally viable fieldwork roles and relationships. Primary field research monographs and secondary works synthesizing these original works are filled with accounts of an array of strategies that have been used to facilitate relational access and informant rapport or trust.

Perhaps the most basic and frequently mentioned strategy involves framing the research in terms of an exchange relationship, such that both parties are beneficiaries of the research project. Simply put, the fieldworker provides context-, group-, or member-appropriate favors or assistance in exchange for relational access and information. Often key to the development of such an exchange relationship is the negotiation of a role relationship that lends itself to exchange. The "buddy researcher" is an example of such a role. Based on a blending of the roles of researcher and friend, it has been used repeatedly to develop rapport and facilitate information flow in studies of street corner men, hoboes and tramps, and contemporary homeless individuals.

A related strategy is the negotiated creation of auxiliary derived roles. Formulations include the derivation of the role of the "controlled skeptic," in which the researcher engages in group-specific behaviors and rituals but does not publicly avow allegiance to the group's beliefs and values (an example being a study of recruitment and conversion to an eastern religious movement); the "ardent activist," who embraces behaviorally and verbally the group ideology, goals, and rhetoric (used to study the peace movement groups); and the "credentialed expert," which involves the use of professional credentials and an institutional base as the grounds for justifying and legitimating research (e.g., for studying social service agencies and for securing access to their clients records). These are only a few of the strategies used by field researchers to facilitate relational access and rapport, but they are sufficient to underscore both the importance and negotiated character of fieldwork relations and thus access and rapport. As well, they subtly suggest what Maurice Punch has called the "muddy" realities of creating trust with informants in the field. Indeed, creating socially intimate ties with informants along the lines just suggested often entails numerous moral dilemmas, including the ultimate aims and boundaries of relationships, the veracities of researcher identities, and even various forms of interactional deceit. Although it is beyond the purview of this essay to elaborate fully the implications of these dilemmas, suffice to say that ethnographers should be conscious of these issues in the everyday conduct of field relations. Formal regulatory approaches to these challenges may be inappropriate, given the unpredictability and negotiated nature of field research. Competent management of these dilemmas thus begins with what Punch called the researchers' "individual responsibility and professional accountability," but this must be attuned to the particular exigencies faced in the field.

Strategies to Control Relational Intimacy/Closeness

An ongoing challenge in field research is to secure and maintain a research role and its associated relationships that enables successful negotiation of the centrifugal forces that distance researchers from the events and information sources necessary for understanding the setting under study. An equally important challenge is to counter the centripetal tendencies that sometimes pull the researcher in too closely, clouding analytic capacities, draining emotions, and creating unnecessary ethical or political complications. In order to neutralize these centripetal tendencies and thereby successfully negotiate the occasional pull toward deeper involvement and even surrender, various strategies and tactics have been employed, sometimes with considerable foresight and sometimes on the spot. Such countercentripetal strategies include "preempting" at the outset of a project, by articulating certain limitations and constraints on what will be done; "finessing" through the utterance of evasions and ambiguities in relation to member overtures and entreaties; "declining" directly and unambiguously member appeals; and "withdrawal" from activities. Such responses to centripetal overtures and appeals further underscore the negotiated character of the development and maintenance of viable fieldwork relationships and of the fieldwork process more generally.

See Also the Following Articles

Field Experimentation • Field Studies

Further Reading

Adler, P. A., and Adler, P. (1987). *Membership Roles in Field Research.* Sage, Newbury Park, CA.

Emerson, R. M. (2001). *Contemporary Field Research: Perspectives and Formulations,* 2nd Ed. Waveland Press, Prospect Heights, IL.

Fine, G. A., and Sandstrom, K. L. (1988). *Knowing Children: Participant Observation with Minors.* Sage, Newbury Park, CA.

Johnson, J. M. (1975). *Doing Field Research.* The Free Press, New York.

Lofland, J., and Lofland, L. (1995). *Analyzing Social Settings,* 3rd Ed. Wadsworth, Belmont, CA.

McCall, G. J., and Simmons, J. L. (eds.) (1969). *Issues in Participant Observation: A Text and Reader.* Addison-Wesley, Reading, MA.

Punch, M. (1986). *The Politics and Ethics of Fieldwork.* Sage, Newbury Park, CA.

Rosaldo, R. (1989). *Culture & Truth: The Remaking of Social Analysis.* Beacon Press, Boston, MA.

Snow, D. A., Benford, R. D., and Anderson, L. (1986). Fieldwork Roles and Informational Yield: A Comparison of Alternative Settings and Roles. *Urban Life* **14,** 377–408.

Warren, C. A. B., and Hackney, J. K. (2000). *Gender Issues in Ethnography,* 2nd Ed. Sage, Thousand Oaks, CA.

Wax, R. H. (1971). *Doing Fieldwork: Warnings and Advice.* University of Chicago Press, Chicago, IL.

Field Studies

Leon Anderson
Ohio University, Athens, Ohio, USA

Steven Rubenstein
Ohio University, Athens, Ohio, USA

Glossary

analytic induction Theory building in field studies through the collection of new cases that require the revision of extant theoretical understandings of the phenomenon.

emic The description and analysis of culturally significant categories of meaning used by the people in a social setting or culture under study.

etic The description of universal categories of human behavior for purposes of cross-cultural comparison irrespective of cultural significance.

grounded theory An inductive approach for generating and confirming theory that emerges from recursive field research.

informant The individual studied by field researchers.

member validation The sharing of research ideas and reports with informants in order to correct mistakes or to provide alternative interpretations of reported events.

purposeful sampling The selection of information-rich cases in order to deepen understanding of specific aspects of the topic of study.

triangulation The application of multiple research methods to provide complementary kinds of data in order to develop a multidimensional analysis.

Field study represents one of the earliest forms of social science research. The definitive characteristic of this type of research is that it includes *in situ* observation of naturally occurring social life. Field studies range from case studies of communities or social groups (e.g., classrooms) to comparative studies of generic social phenomena (e.g., crowd assembly and dispersal). Whatever the focus of investigation, all such research shares a commitment to observation in close proximity to the social groups and phenomena under study. Unlike more narrowly circumscribed methods and techniques, field studies employ a wide range of information-gathering strategies and analytic approaches. Field researchers often triangulate with multiple methods (e.g., interviews, participant observation, unobtrusive measures) to provide various types of data and angles of vision from which to develop holistic analyses of their topics of investigation.

Historical Roots of Field Studies

Different research traditions and theoretical orientations tend to favor different methods. Interpretive traditions of social science inquiry emphasize cultural and contextual understanding of social action, and thus share more of an affinity with field research than is typically the case for more macrostructural and positivistic traditions of inquiry. Field studies facilitate rich understanding of social groups and settings, and are open to unexpected findings that redirect or modify analytic focus during the research process. Ethnography, a term often used synonymously with field study, entails not only an omnibus of data collection strategies, but also frequently includes reflexive self-observation in which the researcher's own experiences and relationships in the field are critical data for analysis. Though field studies can contribute to hypothetico-deductive research, they are particularly valuable when the research goal is to ascertain interpretive meanings and constructions of social action.

Modern field studies grow out of the two similar yet distinct social science disciplines of anthropology and sociology. The roots of sociological field research can be traced to 19th-century proto-social scientists, such as British journalist Henry Mayhew, who conducted a massive observational study of poverty in mid-19th-century London. In the 1920s and 1930s, the University of Chicago's Department of Sociology developed a highly influential tradition of sociological field research under the guidance of Robert Park. Associated with the pragmatist philosophy of John Dewey and George Herbert Mead, and the closely aligned sociological perspective of "symbolic interactionism," "Chicago school" sociology produced major exemplars of field research, and largely defined this type of sociological inquiry in the United States. There were few explicit guidelines for sociological field research, however, until the 1960s, when sociologists began to focus attention on clarifying the skills and techniques most useful in this style of research.

Ethnographic field study has been the defining feature of sociocultural anthropology since the 1920s. Many people have contributed to this method, and to its centrality in anthropology, but the two people most responsible were Columbia University's Franz Boas, and Bronislaw Malinowski at the London School of Economics. Boas and Malinowski practiced and advocated for field observation by anthropologists, as opposed to the earlier practice of anthropologists' reliance on other observers, such as travelers, missionaries, and colonial officials. Boas and Malinowski independently developed similar programs that built on earlier methods. They instructed their students to take a census of the community under study and to map out the different social roles and groups and the relationships among them. Nevertheless, the approach they advocated, known today as participant observation, may be better understood as an antimethod. It was perhaps best characterized by Boas' student Ruth Benedict, as a form of "surrender," in which the researcher allows conditions of the field or interests of the informants to dictate foci and methods of investigation. These anthropologists, however, did not see the role of the anthropologist as a naive reporter of how other people live; they were struck by an often profound gap between what people do and how people account for what they do. They conceived of "culture" as some underlying or unconscious pattern, in the context of which beliefs and behaviors had sense and meaning that were often far from obvious. Above any particular method for discovering this "culture," they counseled time, patience, sympathy, and improvisation. Most of all, Boas and Malinowski established as the crucial elements of successful fieldwork two features that remain the *sine qua non* for ethnographic fieldwork: knowledge of the language and prolonged residence among the people. Consistent with sociological field researchers, Malinowski, Boas, and those who followed them argued that research questions and methods should emerge in the process of field research.

Anthropology has, of course, entertained theories that call for more specific and rigorous methods, but there have been relatively few field manuals written by or for anthropologists, and those that are in print are seldom cited in ethnographic monographs. Far more influential than discussions of specific field techniques have been individual accounts of particular fieldwork experiences. Any concrete advice these books offer—from wearing canvas sneakers and maintaining good health, to being patient, sympathetic, and good humored—would likely seem banal to anyone who has not actually done participant-observation fieldwork. But the main task of these books is to provide inspirational examples of how a researcher might innovate and improvise in the field, and cautionary tales of the psychological and emotional challenges of fieldwork. All of these works suggest that, in participant observation fieldwork, the ethnographer's own body and persona are the primary tools of research—that objective facts about a culture are learned only through the most subjective and personal relationships with other people.

Field studies have been a consistent feature of interpretive sociology and cultural anthropology. Though field research has long been used by some notable researchers in various fields (e.g., education, business, and medicine), this methodological approach exploded in popularity during the 1990s as researchers across a wide range of disciplines sought to achieve more contextualized understanding of social life. Today, ethnographic field studies are a common and accepted (if sometimes controversial) research strategy in the human sciences.

Field Study Design

Given the wide range of variation in field studies, it is not appropriate to define the method's techniques and strategies narrowly. It is fitting, however, to explore the basic generic tasks that are fundamental to most field research. Specifically, all field researchers face the tasks of accessing observational sites, collecting observations, and analyzing data. Important issues must be addressed in accomplishing these tasks.

Accessing Observational Sites

The accessing of observational sites by field researchers typically includes at least four basic tasks: locating appropriate research sites, establishing viable fieldwork roles, gaining Institutional Review Board approval of informed consent procedures, and getting informed consent. As with all aspects of field research, the accessing of observational sites is an emergent process of discovery and creativity. Researchers begin this process with varying degrees of focus on their topic of study, whether it is a social group (e.g., a religious denomination) or a category of activity (e.g., social protest). The initial phase of field research involves exploring prospective sites and evaluating their potential for yielding data for analysis. At this stage, the researcher should cast a wide net and pay attention to the potential availability of various kinds of data—prominently including participation in and observation of ongoing social action, but also including opportunities for interviews, the availability of artifacts related to the topic of study, and unobtrusive forms of data (e.g., documents such as group newsletters). So, for instance, an educational field researcher interested in the classroom performance of elementary school students would want to explore (among other things) the opportunities for classroom observation, willingness and availability of key individuals (e.g., teachers and students) to be interviewed, and accessibility of pertinent documents (e.g., student projects and grade reports). In the course of early, exploratory research, some settings are likely to be found to be more easily accessible and to have richer potential for data collection and triangulation. These locations then are likely to become key initial sites for field observation, but it is important to maintain openness to new potential sites and valuable kinds of data.

Access to social settings and social actors requires gatekeeper approval and the creation or appropriation of fieldwork roles. Observational field research entails the researcher becoming the "research instrument"—that is, the medium through which data are collected via observation and are rendered into field notes. Social scientists have extensively debated the ethics of covert observation, in which the researchers' goals are not revealed or disguised. The American Anthropological Association's code of ethics expressly prohibits covert research, and Institutional Review Board procedures and the code of ethics of the American Sociological Association severely limit covert studies. Overt researchers (by far the majority of fieldworkers today) must create or assume fieldwork roles that maximize access to data. In some cases, a role will exist in the field that can be appropriated for this purpose—such as an educational researcher taking on the role of teacher's aide. In other settings, roles need to be created or improvised, as in improvisation of the "buddy-researcher" role in fieldwork with the homeless. The main goal is to facilitate effective data collection, which may require different fieldwork roles in different settings. Team field research offers advantages in the range of fieldwork roles (including multiple roles within the same setting) and access to various kinds of data.

The ability to access research sites and "subjects" (typically referred to as "individuals," "informants," or "participants") is also frequently conditional on gaining university-based Institutional Review Board approval for the research. Though Institutional Review Board (IRB) procedures were originally developed to protect human participants in federally funded medical research, in recent years IRBs have taken an increasingly active role in evaluating and sanctioning research in the social sciences. The requirements for IRB approval vary dramatically across universities. At some universities, only funded research requires IRB approval, and at many universities, certain kinds of data, such as observation in public settings, are exempt from IRB approval requirements. Given that approval protocols and criteria of evaluation are somewhat institutionally idiosyncratic, researchers must become familiar with their specific university's requirements.

Field studies pose several significant problems in relation to Institutional Review Board procedures. First, because the research design and foci of investigation in field studies tend to emerge during the research process rather than being tidily formulated prior to beginning data collection, field researchers' proposals cannot be as neatly specified as, say, those of experimental researchers. Field researchers must be careful to provide sufficient detail in their IRB proposals to satisfy review board members, while maintaining flexibility in pursuing new research leads along the way. This may require, among other things, the submission of revisions to IRB proposals at later stages in the research. Second, informed consent requirements have been formulated primarily for medical research in the United States and are ill suited for many fieldwork situations. By "informed consent," institutional review boards generally mean that the researcher must provide prospective informants with a clear account of the potential costs, or risks, and benefits of participation in the research. IRBs typically conceive of consent as an individual act. Notions of "risk," "benefit," and "consent," however, are culture bound, and academic IRBs are largely unable to guide fieldworkers in the negotiation of consent across a cultural boundary. Fieldworkers, moreover, often work within communities that have collective representation and require collective consent. In addition, research in foreign countries usually requires the authorization of the local government. In many field sites, gender, class, and ethnic divisions may complicate the consent process, because individuals, community organizations, and governments may be in conflict. In such situations, conventional informed consent formulas may be inadequate, and true informed consent may require careful negotiation across several local group boundaries.

In actuality, as the foregoing comments suggest, field researchers have a long tradition of endeavoring to protect their research informants, often extending far beyond the protocols of Institutional Review Boards. However, fieldworkers face a significant problem in relation to the protection of human participants, because social science researchers do not have legal authority to protect those whom they study. Unlike attorneys and medical professionals, social scientists may be subpoenaed to release their research data, if the data are believed to be relevant to the potential prosecution of their research participants. Researchers who study illegal behavior, or who may acquire knowledge of illegal behavior inadvertently as a result of their research, may thus be placed in a difficult position in which research ethics are in conflict with legal demands. There is no standard protocol for handling these conflicts. Lacking legal protection, several scholars in recent years have served jail time rather than turn over their research data to legal authorities. As long as field researchers feel a responsibility not to harm those whom they research, while having none of the legal authority accorded to medical and legal professionals, fieldworkers must be prepared to face legal challenges and ethical dilemmas in the protection of the foci of their research. Fortunately, the overwhelming majority of field studies do not generate such dilemmas.

Gathering Data

Field Notes

Field notes describing the researcher's experiences and observations in the field are the fundamental data of field research, representing the most crucial data log from which analysis is developed. The most widely recommended technique for writing field notes is for the researcher to make jotted notes inconspicuously in the field and to expand on them later. Conscientious—indeed compulsive—field note writing is critical to high-quality research and analysis, and it is important to write field notes promptly after observations in order to ensure maximum recall. Field notes should be concrete and richly descriptive accounts of events, people, things heard and overheard, conversations among people, and conversations with people. The purpose of field notes is to provide a fertile informational base from which to create rich, descriptive, and analytic accounts. Because fieldworkers often alternate between outsider's and insider's perspectives, they frequently distinguish between two different kinds of accounts. An etic account provides a description of observed actors, actions, and objects in a language that the fieldworker considers "objective" or "universal" (in other words, employing distinctions and categories that can apply to many different cultures; such a description would prove the basis of a "cross-cultural analysis"). An emic account provides a description of observed actors, actions, and objects in terms of distinctions meaningful (either consciously or unconsciously) for the informants (in other words, the description of actors, actions, and objects is a means to elicit a description of locally used categories).

In addition to descriptive accounts of field observations and experiences, field notes should also include researchers' protoanalytic musings as they emerge during the course of research. Such musings are an essential part of the field research process. They can be highly useful in guiding the direction of emergent field research (e.g., sensitizing the researcher to the need to explore new settings) and in creating analytic foci for their studies. As mentioned earlier, field studies rely on a range of data beyond the researcher's field notes. Indeed, field research has two advantages over more predesigned research strategies. First, it is more open to the emergence of the research design through attention and surrender to the leads of accumulated data; second, researchers are situated in social settings where new kinds of data, from cultural artifacts to agency records, may be found. Researchers should be consistently alert to the possibilities of both revising their foci on the basis of emerging analyses, and of pursuing serendipitously emerging data.

Sampling

Though sampling issues are important in field studies, just as in other forms of social science research, sampling strategies in field studies vary according to the goals of the research and field practicalities. If the goal is to generalize individual characteristics or behaviors to a population, then random probability sampling is the most appropriate technique. However, most field researchers seek instead to develop holistic understandings of social groups, cultural settings, and/or generic social processes. In these cases, random sampling is less useful. Insofar as sampling strategies are consciously pursued in field studies (and this varies widely), assorted types of "purposeful" sampling tend to be invoked. In contrast to probability sampling, purposeful sampling is designed in the course of inquiry to pursue emergent analytic leads or to facilitate the development of analytic insights. A range of purposeful sampling techniques has been developed, including the relatively widespread techniques of maximum variation sampling and negative case sampling. Maximum variation sampling involves searching for the range of variation in a particular phenomenon (e.g., kinds of behavior exhibited in a specific social settings or situation). Utilizing this method involves observing and documenting unique cases until saturation is achieved. Negative case sampling—often used in conjunction with analytic induction (discussed later)—entails seeking out manifestations of the phenomenon of interest that do not fit existing theoretical understandings.

Whatever the sampling strategies pursued by field researchers, the cases sampled (whether they are individuals, groups, or social settings) must be informationally rich so as to provide ample contextual data for understanding and illustrative or anecdotal information for writing field reports. The point of sampling in field studies is to maximize richness of observations so as to enable detailed holistic analysis and recursive development of theoretical formulations regarding the topic of study.

Relationality, Reflexivity, and Recursivity

All field research involves relationships with local people. These relationships may be more or less detached. More positivist studies rely on a high degree of detachment, in which the researcher is studying the people in question, and the people may be identified as "subjects" or "respondents." Researchers working within such a paradigm may consider relationships with local people to be a means to the ends of research; in such cases, emotional, conceptual, economic and political differences between researchers and locals are obstacles that intrepid fieldworkers must overcome.

In more humanistic or interpretive paradigms, researchers conceive of field relationship as analytically significant in and of themselves, or as significant proxies for the political or economic relationship between the researcher's society and the informants' society. In these cases, emotional, conceptual, economic, and political differences between researchers and locals may be objects of study and sources of insight. Thus, humanistic or interpretive studies rely more on attachment, in which the researcher is learning about some aspect of the local people's world or lives, and the people are identified as "informants" or "collaborators."

The heart of the participant observation method of fieldwork is to rely on personal relationships as a way of learning about another culture. Indeed, newly arrived fieldworkers are commonly childlike in their naiveté, and rely on their hosts for all sorts of practical knowledge and assistance. The acceptance of dependency and of a "student" role in relation to field informants facilitates the fieldworkers' rapport with those they study, acknowledges the informants' status and power, and eases access to local meanings and practices that are the focus of ethnographic research. Thus, although a successful grant proposal suggests a certain mastery on the part of the researcher, fieldwork effects a massive reversal.

It is seldom possible to achieve a consistent or stable balance between attachment and detachment in relationships. Most fieldworkers alternate between one extreme and the other. Researchers often experience a tension between these two extremes (leading some to identify themselves oxymoronically as "stranger and friend" or "marginal native"). Nevertheless, the tension between these two extremes can be highly productive, yielding analytic insights through the processes of reflexivity and recursivity. Reflexivity involves a reversal in perspective in which the research becomes the object of study—to achieve what Paul Ricoeur called knowledge of one's self by means of a detour through the other. Some degree of self-reflection is practically inevitable during fieldwork because informants often question and comment on the researcher. Moreover, fieldwork typically reveals psychological and cultural biases on the part of the fieldworker. Those who pursue objective research are wise to attend to these revelations in any attempt to reduce observer bias. In addition to research-driven field notes, fieldworkers should therefore keep a diary or journal in which they record their own feelings and personal judgments. Such reflection is also important because it helps fieldworkers to monitor their own mental and physical health, which is essential because, in field research, the person is an instrument of research. In the 1950s and 1960s, some anthropologists published memoirs or autobiographical novels in which they reflected on these personal thoughts and feelings; such works were meant both to inspire and to caution future fieldworkers. In recent years, reflections on fieldwork have become more popular and influential, in part because they reveal not only personal biases on the part of fieldworkers, but shared biases that reveal fieldwork to be not so much a form of scientific study as a cross-cultural encounter. Consequently, fieldwork sometimes reveals as much about the culture of the researcher as it does about the culture being studied.

Recursivity refers to the effect that experiences in the field have on the direction of research. This process often occurs in the course of research in the field: regardless of the theoretical orientation of the researcher, or the questions or methods established before entering the field, field research inevitably reveals unanticipated phenomena and questions. Unexpected political, economic, or physical barriers to research, or the demands of local informants, may also lead to revision of the project. In some cases, the researcher must immediately revise his or her foci, questions, and methods. In other cases, it is precisely the successful conclusion of a well-planned research project that raises new questions. Recursivity may also occur in the course of writing after returning from the field. For many anthropologists, recursivity is made possible by the detachment that comes from distance in time, space, and mind (achieved through the process of academic writing). Thus, much recent ethnography is dedicated to discovering the questions raised by field research, in order to suggest new research.

Data Analysis

Field researchers utilize various data analysis strategies that range along a continuum of procedural rigor and explicit specification. More explicit and codified strategies, such as Anselm Strauss and Juliet Corbin's version of grounded theory, James Spradley's elaboration of Ward Goodenough's componential analysis, and Christina Gladwin's work, presented in her book *Ethnographic Decision Tree Modeling*, involve standardized techniques for manipulating data. Similarly, computer-assisted qualitative data analysis software (CAQDAS) packages, such as ETHNOGRAPH and NVIVO, provide techniques and frameworks for logging and categorizing data in ways that facilitate specific kinds of analysis. However, many field researchers feel that standardized techniques and CAQDAS programs are overly mechanistic and that they insert their own logic into the research process, prematurely obstructing the emergence of analysis. Such divergences notwithstanding, most field researchers engage in some form of field note coding, sorting their data into different themes and issues. The initial coding of field notes should occur during the research process, as field notes are being written. Though researchers vary widely in their coding practices, the coding should enable easy access to materials relevant to a particular issue or theme, as well as access to all materials relevant to specific informants. Subsequent waves of data coding, or refinement of coding categories, may be useful as analysis proceeds.

Whatever the coded categories and analytic agenda, the hallmark of high-quality field research is the development of theoretically relevant and informed analysis that is based in detailed and nuanced "thick descriptions" of social phenomena. Therefore, field researchers must strive to ensure that their descriptions accurately represent the beliefs and experiences of their informants. Extended field observation enhances the likelihood of attaining deep familiarity with the social world under investigation, as does frequent checking of observations with informants while in the field. Further, field researchers often share their written reports with their informants—a process sometimes referred to as member validation—asking them for feedback, to correct mistakes or to provide alternative interpretations of reported events. Such feedback may be used to revise the analysis or, in some cases, may influence the researcher to reformulate the entire study, as in Mitchell Duneier's research with Greenwich Village sidewalk magazine vendors in the 1990s.

Writing Field Study Reports

Field study reports (e.g., articles, books, and official reports) vary depending on the researchers' goals, their audiences, and the social science traditions within which the studies are situated. Two important interrelated issues in this regard are idiographic versus nomothetic levels of analysis, and realist versus subjective or evocative narrative styles. The analytic agenda of field reports may range along a continuum from idiographic to nomothetic in focus. Idiographic reports focus solely on understanding individual cases in their full particularity, whereas nomothetic reports compare the individual case or cases studied with other cases and seek to establish generalizable theoretical propositions. Both idiographic and nomothetic reports should include substantial descriptive material, such as field note and interview excerpts, but the heightened emphasis on generalization in nomothetic reports typically means that more of the text will be written at an abstract theoretical level than is the case for idiographic reports.

Similarly, narrative styles in field reports range along a continuum from realist "objective" accounts to subjective confessional accounts. The presentation of data and the acceptable evidentiary claims of these different narrative styles vary. Authors who provide realist objective accounts tend to utilize more standardized types of data collection analysis. These authors typically devote a section of their reports to explicit discussion traditional methodological issues such as sampling strategies and analytic protocols. Their reports focus primarily on others in the research settings, with relatively little of the analysis proceeding from self-reflexive observations on the part of the researcher. In contrast, in confessional or subjective field study reports, the researcher's experiences and personal reflections assume a far more prominent role. Indeed, some confessional subjective accounts—often referred to as "evocative autoethnography"—tend to focus almost exclusively on the researcher's personal experience. The goal of such confessional narratives is primarily to evoke in the reader an understanding of the researcher's emotional experience.

Whatever the level of analysis and narrative style, field study reports are characterized by a faithful and richly descriptive rendering of situated action and cultural understandings in the setting or area of study. This is in keeping with the two fundamental criteria of field research: (1) *in situ* observation of naturally occurring social life and (2) an emergent research design that allows observations in the field to influence the direction and foci of analyses. These principles of field research, which served as guiding lights for the early sociological and anthropological researchers who developed them, remain the most important legacy of field study methods.

See Also the Following Articles

Field Experimentation • Field Relations

Further Reading

Adler, P. A., and Adler, P. (1987). *Membership Roles in Field Research.* Sage, Newbury Park, CA.

Atkinson, P., Coffey, A., Delamont, S., Lofland, J., and Lofland, L. (2001). *Handbook of Ethnography.* Sage, Thousand Oaks, CA.

Bernard, H. R. (1995). *Research Methods in Anthropology,* 2nd Ed. Altamira Press, Walnut Creek, CA.

Davies, C. (1999). *Reflexive Ethnography.* Routledge, New York.

Denzin, N., and Lincoln, Y. (eds.) (2000). *Handbook of Qualitative Research*, 2nd Ed. Sage, Thousand Oaks, CA.

Emerson, R. (2001). *Contemporary Field Research,* 2nd Ed. Waveland Press, Prospect Heights, IL.

Emerson, R., Fretz, R., and Shaw, L. (1995). *Writing Ethnographic Fieldnotes.* University of Chicago Press, Chicago, IL.

Lincoln, Y., and Guba, E. (1985). *Naturalistic Inquiry.* Sage, Thousand Oaks, CA.

Lofland, J., and Lofland, L. (1995). *Analyzing Social Settings,* 3rd Ed. Wadsworth, Belmont, CA.

Patton, M. Q. (2002). *Qualitative Research and Evaluation Methods,* 3rd Ed. Sage, Thousand Oaks, CA.

Sanjek, R. (1990). *Fieldnotes: The Makings of Anthropology.* Cornell University Press, Ithaca, New York.

Seale, C. (1999). *The Quality of Qualitative Research.* Sage, Thousand Oaks, CA.

VanMaanen, J. (1988). *Tales of the Field.* University of Chicago Press, Chicago, IL.

Wolcott, H. F. (1995). *The Art of Fieldwork.* AltaMira Press, Walnut Creek, CA.

Fisher, Sir Ronald

Nancy S. Hall
University of Delaware, Newark, Delaware, USA and
University of Maryland, College Park, Maryland, USA

Glossary

eugenics The concept of improving a breed by the careful selection of parents, especially in regard to the human race.

Fundamental Theorem of Natural Selection The rate of increase in fitness of any organism at any time is equal to its genetic variance in fitness at that time.

genetics The science of heredity, concerning the similarities and differences that appear among related organisms.

natural selection Sometimes called "survival of the fittest"; Charles Darwin's theory that those organisms that can best adapt to their environment are the most likely to survive.

statistics The science of the collection, analysis, and interpretation of numerical data.

Sir Ronald Fisher made major contributions in the fields of both statistics and genetics. He provided a rigorous theoretical foundation for modern statistics, revolutionized the methodology of experimentation on variable material, helped to reconcile the theories of Mendel and Darwin, suggested a numerical basis for natural selection, and made many discoveries about how the mechanisms of heredity actually operate.

Introduction

Sir Ronald Fisher (1890–1962) was one of the most prolific scientists of the 20th century. Statisticians consider him to be one of the founders of modern statistics, both for his contributions to theory and for his many developments of applied techniques. In population genetics, Ronald Fisher is one of the first names mentioned. Along with J. B. S. Haldane and Sewall Wright, Fisher contributed to the neo-Darwinian synthesis, the integration of Darwin's theory of natural selection with Mendel's theory of heredity. Fisher was active in statistics and genetics for all of his professional life, doing his own research and publishing prodigiously.

Biography and Honors

Ronald Aylmer Fisher was born on February 17, 1890, in London, England. He was the youngest son of George and Katie Heath Fisher. Young Fisher was educated at Harrow School and then at Gonville and Caius College, Cambridge University, where he excelled at mathematics but maintained a strong interest in biology. After graduating in 1912, he spent an extra year at Cambridge, studying statistical mechanics under Sir James Jeans and the theory of errors under F. J. M. Stratton.

As a child he was precocious, but it was apparent that his vision was poor. He wore thick glasses all of his life. Because of his poor vision, Fisher was ineligible for military service during World War I and spent the war years as a teacher at several boys' schools. In 1919, he accepted a 6 months' position at Rothamsted Experimental Station at Harpenden, north of London; there nearly 80 years of agricultural research data had not been rigorously analyzed. Six months, however, became 14 years. In 1917, he married Ruth Eileen Guinness and began raising a family; eventually they had eight children.

At Rothamsted, between 1919 and 1933, Fisher published articles and books on statistics, genetics, and eugenics. He received his Sc.D. degree from Cambridge University, in 1926 and was elected a Fellow in the Royal Society in 1929. In 1933, he became Galton Professor of Eugenics at University College, London, and continued to publish prodigiously. In 1943, he accepted the post of Arthur Balfour Professor of Genetics at

Cambridge, where he stayed until his retirement in 1957. He was knighted in 1952, becoming Sir Ronald Fisher.

Fisher moved to Adelaide, Australia, in 1959 and died there in 1962, of complications following cancer surgery. During his lifetime, he published seven books, 594 articles, and several hundred book reviews. He was knighted, received nine honorary degrees, was awarded the Royal Society's Darwin and Copley Medals, received numerous other honors, and was elected to membership of five foreign academies of science.

Fisher as Statistician

Fisher is regarded by many as one of the founders of modern statistics. Any beginning student of statistics will find in his text a detailed description of the analysis of variance, without any mention that the technique was developed in the 1920s by Sir Ronald Fisher. Similarly, the student will learn to use the *F*-ratio without being informed that it is so named as a tribute to Fisher. But Fisher's importance in the field of statistics ranges far beyond elementary applications. Fisher's work in statistics can be largely grouped in three areas, all of equal prominence: the theoretical foundations of statistics, practical applications and methods, and experimental design.

In 1922, Fisher published "On the Mathematical Foundations of Theoretical Statistics." In earlier papers he had begun considering the accuracy of estimates based on samples drawn from large populations. The 1922 paper clarified the method of maximum likelihood, defined several terms important to the field, and made clear the necessity of considering the sample and the larger population separately. According to Fisher, the population has "parameters" that one does not know; from the sample one calculates one or more "statistics," such as the mean or the standard deviation, in order to estimate the unknown parameters. Ideally, a statistic should be "sufficient"; the statistic computed from the sample should contain all possible information about the unknown parameter. That is, for example, the sample standard deviation s should contain all of the information about the population standard deviation σ that can be obtained from the sample. Additionally, a statistic should be "efficient"; that is, information that the sample contains should not be lost in the process of computing the statistic from the data. Finally, a statistic should be always be "consistent"; the larger the sample size, the closer the statistic should come to the actual parameter.

The 1922 paper, published in the *Philosophical Transactions of the Royal Society*, was a landmark achievement. Fisher followed it with many other papers on statistical theory and applications. (Many of these, in complete text, are available on-line.) Fisher did not always provide adequate mathematical proofs in his papers; there was considerable controversy over some of his statistical proposals. The method of maximum likelihood was later seen to have less generality than Fisher had hoped. However, he was both a visionary and a very competent mathematician. In one memorable paper, proving the general case of a specific theorem put forth by "Student" (William Sealy Gosset, 1876–1937), Fisher offered that something could be seen "instantly" if a geometrical view was considered; what followed were 2 pages of geometry and then 12 pages of calculus. Fisher himself pictured statistical theory in multidimensional spaces. He once suggested at the beginning of a paper that the 10 items of data should be considered as the 10 coordinates of a single point in Euclidean 10-space; needless to say, few people could comfortably follow his reasoning.

Fisher's quick mind and his lack of tolerance for any logical or scientific view with which he disagreed led to lively exchanges and sometimes to disagreements that lasted for years. He had an ongoing disagreement with Karl Pearson and later a similar one with Pearson's son Egon Pearson and with Jerzy Neyman. Their technical disagreements led to personal animosity.

The technique known as analysis of variance, which Fisher regarded as simply a way of arranging arithmetic, is a widely used method of determining whether there really is a mean difference between three or more groups. The statistician would say that there is a significant difference at the 0.05 level, meaning that the probability is less than 5% that the apparent differences happened by pure chance. Suppose that one has three groups of eight people each; each group has been on a different diet plan. One wants to find out which of the three diet plans results in the greatest weight loss—to determine whether one plan really is better than the others. The weight loss of each individual is recorded. The mean is the average of the weight loss within the group. The variance of each group (a term originated by Fisher; actually the square of the standard deviation) is the sum of the squared differences from the mean, divided by 1 less than the group size (here, divided by 7). Fisher's analysis of variance compares the group variances to the variance of the entire set of participants and then uses tables of probabilities to determine whether there is a significant difference between the diet plans.

Closely related to analysis of variance is the more complex analysis of covariance, also developed by Fisher, to remove the influence of an uncontrolled variable on other random variables and thus increase the precision of the experiment. Fisher provided the mathematical techniques to make feasible factorial experiments. For example, a crop can be fertilized with three kinds of fertilizer, singly and in combination, and the effect of each fertilizer as well as interactive effects can be studied.

The development of the analysis of variance reflected Fisher's continuing interests in statistics, genetics, and eugenics. Fisher used an early form of analysis of variance in his 1918 paper, "The Correlation between Relatives on the Supposition of Mendelian Inheritance," in which he demonstrated that the principles of Mendelian genetics could account for similarities and differences among relatives and that, in fact, these observed variations were just what should be expected. (Recall that until Mendel's principles became known, in the early 1900s, there was no understanding of why, for example, a young man might have the hair color of his mother's uncle rather than that of either of his parents, or of why two parents having brown eyes might have a child with blue eyes.)

Fisher then used versions of analysis of variance in his early papers discussing accumulated data at Rothamsted; the 67 years of data from the wheat grown continuously on the Broadbalk fields led to the first of a series of papers entitled "Studies in Crop Variation." That series also included reports of very recent agricultural research at Rothamsted; Fisher himself remarked that he began to develop analysis of variance in the 1918 paper and put it in final form in the second "Studies" paper in 1923, on the fertilizing of potatoes.

In 1925, Fisher's *Statistical Methods for Research Workers* was published and the transformation of research methods was under way. The book was poorly received by statisticians, with several neutral or unfavorable reviews, but was quickly adopted by researchers, first in agriculture, then in biology, then in psychology, and then, within 10 years, by almost everyone whose research involved variable material and relatively small group, or sample, sizes. Between 1925 and 1970, *Statistical Methods* went through 14 editions and was published in seven languages. Part of the statisticians' objection, and the researchers' relief, was that Fisher had deliberately omitted proofs. *Statistical Methods* was a handbook of directions on how to set up experiments and how to evaluate the resulting data. *Statistical Methods*, examined today, looks like any other basic statistics book, but it was the first of its kind.

In 1931, Fisher made the first of several lengthy visits to George Snedecor at Iowa State Agricultural College (now Iowa State University) at Ames, Iowa. At that time, Snedecor's group was virtually the only agricultural statistical research facility in the United States. Through Snedecor and his students, Fisher was influential in the establishment of several more centers combining agricultural research and statistical methods at a number of state universities.

One of Fisher's major innovations in statistics and in research methodology was the concept of randomization. Until the 1925 publication of *Statistical Methods for Research Workers* and Fisher's subsequent activities that promoted the use of randomization, it was customary for the researcher to deliberately arrange the experimental plots, or subjects, and the experimental treatments as she chose, in an effort to eliminate variations extraneous to the experiment. Ideally, all of the subjects should be exactly alike, but this is usually impossible. Fisher was concerned about eliminating extraneous differences, but he was also concerned about the elimination of bias, some covert correlation among the experimental subjects that might influence the data being collected. This bias might be inherent in the experimental material, as, perhaps, a drainage flow from north to south across some of the field plots, or a bias introduced, perhaps accidentally, by the researcher in her groupings: perhaps the subjects in one group were predominantly tall or predominantly of Scottish descent.

Fisher's solution to the elimination of bias was randomization, in concert with ample replication. There should be as many subjects (or experimental plots) as possible and the assignment to treatment should be, not by the whim or plan of the researcher, but by some actual randomizing device, such as a deck of cards, dice, or a random-number table.

A second benefit of randomization, according to Fisher, was that randomization makes possible a valid test of significance—a measure of how dependable the conclusions drawn from the experiment are. Suppose an experiment is carried out, data are collected, and mathematical analysis of those data produces one or more statistics, descriptions of some property of the experimental population. The researcher needs to know whether the results were simply due to chance or whether the indicated differences really do exist. A test of significance is expressed as a probability. If an experimental difference is significant at the 0.05 level, mentioned previously, then there is only 1 chance in 20 that the perceived difference was due to chance. Fisher's concern was that if the experimental material and treatments were arranged systematically rather than through randomization, then more than one test of significance was possible and so none of these was dependable.

Another Fisherian innovation, one that permits very unlike subjects to be used in the same experiment, was an experimental design called randomized block. The essence of a randomized block design is that the material *within* the blocks should be as similar as possible. There can be wide differences, if need be, *between* the blocks. Observed variations within blocks can then be used to allow for the differences between the separate blocks, which may be under very different conditions. As an example, one can consider a case in which there are five types of fertilizer to be tested (on the same crop) with three fields available. However, one field is level and dry, one is on a hillside, and one is marshy. One way to do this is to lay out five plots in each of the three locales, or blocks. Thus, a block consists of five plots in a homogenous locale. Within each block, the assignment of fertilizer types to plots should be made by some randomizing device (a deck of cards, for example, or a random number table). Later, after harvest and measure of the yields, the comparative performances of fertilizer A in the three blocks (and also that of fertilizers B, C, D, and E) could be used to eliminate the "block effects" from the calculations in comparing the five fertilizers.

The last nine pages of the 1925 *Statistical Methods for Research Workers* discussed experimental design. Those pages expanded into an entire book in 1935, *The Design of Experiments*, which went through eight editions and was eventually published in three other languages. In this book, both persuasive and educational about randomization, Fisher presented the classic randomization story: the lady tasting tea. The story was apparently based on an actual event at Rothamsted in the 1920s; at an afternoon tea, a woman declared that she could tell by taste whether the tea or the milk had been placed in the cup first. Fisher and the other men in the group did not believe it, and, partly for its entertainment value, Fisher set about to design an experiment. They assembled eight identical cups, put milk first in four and tea first in four, and presented all eight cups, properly randomized, to the woman for her inspection. Fisher used this tale to introduce the concept of randomization and went on to develop it in later chapters. (Legend has it that the woman got all eight cups right.)

Fisher sometimes used wit to drive home his point. Part of his perspective on experimental methodology was the now customary expectation that the statistical analysis of an experiment will be included in the planning of the research. In 1938 in a speech to the Indian Statistical Institute, he remarked that to call in the statistician after the completion of the experiment may be like calling in the mortician; he can perhaps say what the experiment died of. Fisher's point, of course, was that a plan for analysis of the data is as important as the plan for collecting the data.

Fisher as Geneticist

Among Fisher's major accomplishments in genetics were his genetic theory of natural selection, his work on dominance and the evolution of dominance, and his discovery of the genetic basis for the very complex Rhesus factor in human blood groups. Fisher had a lifelong interest in genetics and always had breeding experiments of some sort under way. Throughout his entire adult life, he kept a breeding population of mice or chickens or, for a time, snails, wherever he was living. In addition to his many papers on genetics, in 1949 Fisher published a book, *The Theory of Inbreeding*.

One problem in genetics early in the 20th century was that Mendel's principles seemed to apply in many plants and animals, but that Mendelism was based on a concept of discrete factors. (Recall that Mendel's experiments with peas involved smooth seed versus wrinkled seed, short plant versus tall plant, etc.) It was difficult to see how discrete factors could be responsible for the continuous variation that was obvious in human heredity. One argument was that human hereditary attributes were dependent not on a single factor, or single gene, but on the additive effects of several genes; that is, any particular human feature was influenced by many genes. Fisher's 1918 paper, discussed above, "The Correlation between Relatives on the Supposition of Mendelian Inheritance," showed mathematically that if one used the rules of Mendelism and a many-gene assumption, then the observed continuous variation was exactly what should be expected.

Fisher's 1930 *Genetical Theory of Natural Selection* began not with his own theory but with a brief review of Darwin. Charles Darwin had introduced the theory of evolution by means of natural selection in his 1859 *On the Origin of Species*. Darwin had assumed that the usual mechanism of inheritance was blending. (There is no evidence that Darwin knew of Mendel's work.) In blending inheritance, the theory was that mating a white flower and a red variant would produce a pink bloom. That pink then mated with a white would produce a lighter pink; within several generations the red variation would be "swamped" out of existence. Since under this theory so much variation disappeared in each generation, Darwin had to assume a very high rate of spontaneous variation in nature, in order to have sufficient variation for natural selection to proceed. In the first chapter of *Genetical Theory*, Fisher pointed out that Mendelism, in effect, solved Darwin's problem, because in Mendelian inheritance variation was conserved, rather than being usually lost, and could reappear in later generations.

Fisher stated his Fundamental Theorem of Natural Selection as "The rate of increase in fitness of any organism at any time is equal to its genetic variance in fitness at that time." One result of this is that large populations, likely to have more variance, are more likely to adapt to changing conditions and thus more plentiful species are more likely to survive than less numerous ones. Also, the larger populations have a greater opportunity for favorable variation to occur, because more variations will be present in the population. By treating Darwinian natural selection from a mathematical viewpoint, Fisher helped to develop the theoretical foundations of what came to be called the Neo-Darwinian Synthesis (of Mendelian genetics and Darwinian natural selection), as did J. B. S. Haldane and Sewall Wright. Fisher and Wright had an ongoing difference of opinion, sometimes referred to as the Fisher–Wright debate, about whether species change was more likely to happen within a large population (Fisher) or within a small isolated population (Wright).

Fisher as Eugenicist

In the later chapters of *Genetical Theory of Natural Selection*, Fisher expressed his concerns for the future of human civilization. A staunch believer in eugenics, he believed that since the lower classes, whom he regarded as less fit, were reproducing at a faster rate than the upper classes, this was working to the detriment of society. As an undergraduate at Cambridge, Fisher was a founder and first president of the Cambridge University Eugenics Society. This brought him into contact with Major Leonard Darwin, a son of Charles Darwin and president of the Eugenics Education Society of London. Leonard Darwin became a close friend and advisor of Fisher's.

A survey of Fisher's publications will show that in addition to his many papers on statistics and genetics, interspersed are papers dealing solely with eugenics and the state of mankind. When Fisher became Galton Professor of Eugenics at University College London in 1933, along with the position came the editorship of the *Annals of Eugenics*. Fisher edited the *Annals* for many years. In addition to his many papers on eugenics in a variety of journals, Fisher contributed several hundred book reviews to the *Eugenics Review*.

See Also the Following Articles

Eugenics • Human and Population Genetics • Randomization • Research Designs • Sample Design • Survey Design

Further Reading

Archive of papers and correspondence of R. A. Fisher. Barr Smith Library, University of Adelaide, Adelaide, Australia. Available at http://www.library.adelaide.edu.au/digitised/fisher/index.html

Bennett, J. H. (ed.) (1971–1974). *Collected Papers of R. A. Fisher*, Vol. 1–5. University of Adelaide, Adelaide, Australia.

Box, J. F. (1978). *R. A. Fisher: The Life of a Scientist.* Wiley, New York.

Yates, F., and Mather, K. (1963). Ronald Aylmer Fisher. *Biogr. Mem. Fellows R. Soc.* **9,** 91–129.

Fixed-Effects Models

George Farkas
The Pennsylvania State University, University Park, Pennsylvania, USA

Glossary

analysis of variance Statistical methods for comparing means by dividing the overall variance into parts.

fixed-effects models Statistical methods for estimating causal effects, in which each individual serves as his or her own control.

panel data Information on each survey unit for multiple time points.

pooled time-series cross-section data A single data set formed from pooled panel data, containing information on multiple survey units for multiple time points.

random-effects models Statistical methods in which the data describe a hierarchy of different populations, with differences constrained by the hierarchy.

Fixed-effects models are a statistical technique (a form of regression analysis) for analyzing nonexperimental data. In the presence of unmeasured, unchanging variables that are correlated with the independent variable of interest and also exert their own effect on the dependent variable, fixed-effects models come closer than does ordinary regression analysis to achieving unbiased estimates of causal effect.

Introduction

Problems of Causal Inference with Nonexperimental Data

Random-assignment experiments provide the best means for testing causal effects. When trying to learn the effect of a treatment (for example, a medical treatment) on humans, there is no better evidence than the results of a randomized experiment. In this situation, a target population is identified, a sample is drawn, and individuals are randomly assigned, some to receive the treatment, others not. After a period of time, outcomes for the two groups are compared. Because of randomization, in the average sample, the two groups will be identical prior to treatment (although there will be some deviations from sample to sample). This similarity between the groups prior to treatment extends to all possible characteristics, including those that may be difficult or impossible to measure. As a consequence, in the absence of other forces acting differentially on the two groups during and after the treatment period, any later (posttreatment) average differences between the two groups must be attributed to the effect of the treatment. No better evidence can be brought forward for the effect of one variable on another.

But experiments are difficult and costly to undertake. And resources aside, there are legal and moral restrictions to undertaking random assignment to "treatment" involving most variables that are the usual subjects of social scientific inquiry. Examples include parental and family characteristics, education, marriage, childbearing, employment, union membership, and so on. Thus, for most variables involving effects that social scientists would like to understand, no experimental random assignment to values of the variable ever has been, or likely ever will be, undertaken.

Without random assignment, individuals who score higher on a variable (for example, those who spend many years in a certain type of job) also differ systematically on other characteristics, compared to those who score lower on this variable. As a consequence, any differences in outcomes between the two groups (say, earnings during or postemployment) may be due not to the variable of interest (in this case, the particular job type), but to some other variable with which it happens to correlate. This uncertainty as to whether differences in outcomes among individuals who differ on an independent variable of interest are really caused by this variable, or are merely caused by some other variable correlated with it, is the chief problem of causal inference with nonexperimental data. The usual solution attempted for this problem is to estimate a multivariate statistical model, in which the independent variable of interest, and other variables correlated with it, act together to determine the outcome. Such models (usually regression analysis models) enable estimation of the effect of interest, "controlling for" other variables that may be correlated with it. That is, if Y is the outcome, X is the independent variable of interest, and $Z_1, \ldots, Z_k$ are the variables correlated with X, the effects of which it is desired to control, regression analysis allows adjusting Y for the effects of the Z values and estimating the "pure" or "net" effect of X on Y, thus controlling for the effects of the Z values on Y.

Because of the importance of this issue, some version of this regression approach has for some time been the most common data analysis technique in social scientific research. However, it has a flaw. It can only control (adjust for) Z variables for which there are measures available on the data. And investigators have come to realize that many potentially important Z variables may not be measured on commonly available data sets. For example, individuals who attain more years of schooling (X) may also be more intelligent or ambitious (unmeasured Z). Or, workers employed in typically "female" jobs (X) may be less motivated by money and more motivated to help people (unmeasured Z). Thus, even after a standard regression analysis, the danger still exists that unmeasured Z variables, correlated with X, and exerting their own effect on Y, may cause incorrect (biased) judgments of the effect of X on Y. This is the problem for which the method of fixed effects is a partial solution.

Fixed-Effects Models as a Partial Solution

How, in the absence of randomization, is it possible to control (adjust for) correlated variables that are not even measured on a data set? The answer is to utilize, for each variable and unit of analysis under study, multiple measures of the variable. Suppose, for example, that it is desired to estimate the effect on an individual's earnings of being employed in job that is predominantly performed by female workers. And suppose that there are work histories for a sample of workers, and that these histories include information on the percentage of females employed in each of the different jobs a worker has held over her or his lifetime. Then, for each of the multiple measures of the variables to be included in the analysis, subtract the average score (across the multiple measures) for the unit of analysis. (For example, take each of the percent female scores for every job an individual has held, and subtract the individual's average of these from each score. Also take the amount of money the worker earned in each of these jobs, and subtract the worker's average of these from each score. Do the same for all variables that are under study and change across jobs (for example, the years of work experience the worker had at the time she or he took each job).) Then pool the multiple observations for each individual (in this case, each job held by each individual) into one data set. Finally, regress the dependent variable, with its within-person mean subtracted (in this case, the worker's earnings in each job minus the average of the worker's earnings across all jobs) against the set of independent variables, also with their within-person mean subtracted. (Thus, the set of independent variables includes the percentage of females in each job held by each individual minus the within-person mean of these across jobs, the work experience of each individual at the time they took each job minus the within-person mean of these across jobs, and so on.) The resulting coefficient for the effect of the percentage of females on earnings is called the fixed-effects estimator.

How does this estimator control for unmeasured Z variables, such as the ambition to earn a lot of money? It is likely that workers scoring high on this ambition remain this way throughout their careers. A high level of ambition may have helped them to earn more, compared to many otherwise identical workers, and may have caused them to seek employment in jobs with a lower percentage of females, compared to many otherwise identical workers. In this case, the fixed-effects estimator uses the individual as "his or her own control," and, as a consequence, the effect of the ambition Z variable has been differenced away.

In an ordinary regression analysis, the result of failing to control this variable would be a biased coefficient for the effect of the percentage of females. But with the fixed-effects estimator, these effects of ambition have been removed from the analysis by the differencing procedure. This is because, for each job the individual held, their earnings were computed as a difference from their average earnings, and their "percent female" factor was computed as a difference from their average "percent female." Thus, whatever the effects of the person's monetary ambitions on each of these variables, it is captured in the person's average for the dependent and independent variables, and subtracted from these variables. As a result, the fixed-effects regression coefficient measures the extent to which, for this individual, the jobs they held that were above their own average "percent female" produced earnings above their own average earnings. That is, by centering the observed variables on the person's average over time, what is being measured is the extent to which, when this person holds a job that is, say, 1% more "female" than is usual for them, their earnings fall below the level that is usual for them. The effects of the unmeasured Z variables are not permitted to bias the calculation because they determine the person's average, and these effects have been eliminated by the construction of variables that are differences around this average.

Two caveats are in order. First, to succeed in removing the effects of variables such as Z in the preceding example, the variables should be unchanging across the multiple observations for each individual. Thus, the method works best for variables Z that can be assumed to be unchanging, or at most, are very slowly changing, across the multiple observations for each individual. Second, the method requires multiple observations for each individual, and that X, the independent variable of interest, vary across these observations. (Thus, for example, this method cannot be used to measure the effects of X variables such as race or gender, which do not change as an individual ages.) When these conditions are met, the fixed-effects method can be quite flexible and powerful. It applies when the same individual or other unit of observation (for example, a state or nation) is observed over time. It also applies to situations in which, for example, multiple siblings from the same family are observed, and the aim is to estimate the effect of family size (number of siblings) on outcomes for each sibling, and to do so while avoiding bias from the effects of unmeasured, unchanging family characteristics (such as genetic endowments and child-raising procedures).

Formal Aspects of the Models

Pooled Time-Series Cross-Section Data

The earliest and still most common use of fixed-effects models is to analyze pooled time-series cross-section data. These are data collected for a sample of cross-sectional units (for example, people, businesses, or nations) so that, for each unit, observations are made on the same variables at different points in time. (That is, a time series of observations is obtained for each cross-sectional unit.) These are then pooled together to make a data set that, for each variable, consists of multiple over-time observations for each cross-sectional unit.

If Y_{it} is the dependent variable for individual i at time t, and $X_{1it}, \ldots, X_{kit}$ are the independent variables $X_1, \ldots, X_k$ for individual i at time t, then the fixed-effects model for pooled time-series cross-section data can be written as follows:

$$Y_{it} = b_1X_{1it} + \cdots + b_kX_{kit} + D_1 + \cdots + D_n + e_{it}, \quad (1)$$

where $D_1, \ldots, D_n$ are dummy variables, each of which is coded 1 for all observations on one of the n cross-sectional units and 0 for observations on all other units, and e_{it} is an error term possessing the usual properties for error terms in ordinary least-squares regression analysis. Thus, a fixed-effects model for pooled time-series cross-section data has essentially the same form as an "ordinary" regression analysis, but (1) with multiple observations over time for each unit of analysis (for example, persons) pooled into one data set and (2) with dummy variables for each of these units of analysis included among the independent variables. This implements the description of deviating each variable from its group mean, because the dummy control variables estimate the group means and net them out from the calculation. The dummy variables, $D_1, \ldots, D_n$, measure the effects of individual otherwise unmeasured variables (such as ambition or ability) that are assumed to be relatively unchanging over time.

Families and Other Groupings

The fixed-effects method has another important social science application. This is when the multiple observations to be pooled for each unit, rather than occurring over time, occur for different members of a group. In research applications, this has most often been a group of siblings. In this case, Eq. (1) once again applies, whereby i indexes particular families, t indexes a particular brother or sister within each family, and the $D_1, \ldots, D_n$ estimate family averages for the outcome variable. As before, these dummy variable fixed-effects estimate and remove the effects of unchanging, unmeasured variables that may be correlated with the X variable of interest. For example, suppose that Y is child cognitive outcomes, X is family size, and there is an unmeasured, unchanging parental variable, "family intellectual climate," which is negatively correlated with family size. In this case, the failure to measure and control family intellectual climate may lead to a biased estimate of the effect of family size on child cognitive outcomes. However, the fixed-effect estimate would be relatively free of such bias.

This example can be extended to other situations in which the data consist of multiple individual units of observation that are sorted into groups, whereby the individual units within each group may be subject to a causal force that is group specific and unmeasured. Examples include students in classrooms, workers in workplaces, patients in hospitals, cities within states or countries, work units within firms, and so on.

Dichotomous and Categorical Outcomes

In general, the preceding models are designed for, and have been most widely applied to, the prediction of dependent variables that are measured on a continuous scale. However, techniques do exist, and are beginning to be more widely used, for extending these methods to the analysis of dichotomous and categorical variables.

Competing Models

A large literature exists for estimating models similar to those in Eq. (1), but instead of using dummy variables and "fixed effects," these models assume "random effects." That is, rather than assuming that these effects are fixed constants present in a particular observed sample, this method assumes that they are random variables from a distribution of values. (This "fixed" rather than "random" distinction is the source of the name, "fixed effects.") The result is a more parsimonious specification, but one that, for estimation, must assume that the random effects are uncorrelated with the *X* variables in the model. This is a disadvantage, because it makes it impossible to net out correlated unmeasured variables that are the chief source of bias in nonexperimental studies.

Data Demands

Multiple Observations per Unit

As already noted, the fixed-effects methodology requires multiple observations per unit, with the dependent variable measured in the same metric at each time point. For pooled time-series cross-section, this means having over-time data for each unit. When individuals are involved, this is usually referred to as panel (compared to cross-sectional) data. Any individual who has data only for a single time point must be dropped from the analysis. Similarly, for families and other groupings, there must be multiple observations for each family or group members. Thus, any family or group having only one sibling (member) in the data must also be dropped from the analysis. When families are involved, this could lead to the nonrandom loss of a large percentage of cases from the analysis, and could potentially be a significant cause of bias in the study.

Other Issues

The fixed-effects methodology makes additional demands on the data to be analyzed. Perhaps most significantly, it removes only the effects of unchanging unmeasured variables. Also, it estimates effects only for those *X* variables that change their values at least somewhat across the multiple observations for each unit. For example, if individuals are being observed over time, it is possible to estimate effects only for those variables that show change over time. Examples include age, work experience, job characteristics (to the extent that at least some workers do change their jobs over the period covered by our data), family characteristics such as married or not, and number of children (if these change for at least some individuals over time), and so on. Variables that do not change (gender, race/ethnicity, year of birth, innate personal characteristics) cannot have their effects estimated [although these effects are removed from the analysis by the dummy variable (fixed-effect) coefficients]. Variables that change only a little bit, and only for a relatively small percentage of individuals (for example, years of schooling completed, when observed for adults who are in the middle of their employment careers), can have their effects estimated, but these estimates will be based only on those individuals whose variables do change, and only on those years during which they are observed. Thus, if fixed-effects estimation is thought of as taking the place of an actual experiment, then, in this case, the experiment involves increasing the schooling of some workers who have begun their employment career, rather than of younger students who have been continuously in school. Similarly, in the case of families and other groupings, families with only one sibling must be dropped from the analysis, and effects are estimated only for those variables that vary across siblings.

Incidentally, the time-series cross-section model has another strength. In addition to dummy variables (fixed effects) for individual units of observation, dummy variables can be included for each of the years the data are observed. This controls the effects of year-specific variables that might otherwise go unmeasured, and thus not accounted for in the analysis.

Estimation and Testing

The Dummy Variable and Difference Estimators

Equation (1) can be estimated using ordinary least-squares (OLS) regression, by simply using one dummy variable for each of the underlying units of observation (for example, each person, for which data for multiple observations per person have been pooled, or each family, for which data for multiple siblings per family have been pooled). As usual, when dummy variables represent a set of categories, if a constant term is included in the regression, one dummy variable must be omitted to avoid perfect multicollinearity. However, it is often quite cumbersome to code a dummy variable for each individual unit of analysis. Indeed, many panel data sets have thousands of individuals in the study, each of which is observed for as many as 10 or more time periods. Utilizing many thousands of dummy variables may go beyond what is possible with some statistical software, as well as leading to computational difficulties.

The solution is to construct each variable as a deviation (difference) from the group mean, and to perform a regression calculation with these deviated variables.

To understand how this works, consider the simple case of Eq. (1), in which there are only two time points, $t = 1$ or 2. Write this equation for each of these time points:

$$Y_{i2} = b_1 X_{1i2} + \cdots + b_k X_{ki2} + D_1 + \cdots + D_n + e_{i2}, \quad (2)$$

$$Y_{i1} = b_1 X_{1i1} + \cdots + b_k X_{ki1} + D_1 + \cdots + D_n + e_{i1}. \quad (3)$$

Now, subtract Eq. (3) from Eq. (2). The result is

$$(Y_{i2} - Y_{i1}) = b_1(X_{1i2} - X_{1i1}) + \cdots + b_k(X_{ki2} - X_{ki1}) + (e_{i2} - e_{i1}). \quad (4)$$

As a result of subtraction, the individual-specific dummy variables have disappeared from the equation, leaving an ordinary regression of the change in Y on the change in X variables. This "first difference" model is the simplest form of fixed effects. When there are more than two time points, this differencing method can be extended by calculating the over-time average score of Y and the X variables for each individual, and subtracting this average from each time-specific score for the individual. Once again, the dummy variable (individual) fixed effects are differenced away, leaving each person/time-specific Y score minus the mean of these for the person regressed against similarly computed X variables. In this case, the OLS regression will give unbiased estimates, but the standard errors will have to be corrected. An identical development occurs when multiple siblings are grouped according to families. In this case, each variable for each sibling is deviated from the family mean, and the computation proceeds as described.

The fixed-effects estimator can also be understood as a "within-group estimator." In an analysis-of-variance framework, there is also a "between-group estimator" that uses only the group-specific means. It can be shown that the ordinary least-squares estimator without fixed effects is actually a weighted average of the within- and between-group estimators.

Data Layout and Computation

In fixed-effects estimation, it is useful to sort the data so that the multiple observations for each unit of analysis (a person over time or siblings from the same family) are next to one another on the data. Typically, there is a variable, the values of which are the same for each of the multiple observations that are to be grouped together. Suppose this variable is called ID. Using the application SAS, a statistical analysis computer program created by the SAS Institute, the fixed-effects estimates are obtained using the PROC GLM procedure. This has a command called ABSORB, which will use the ID variable to group the data, create the deviations from group means, and perform the statistical analysis required. This also gives the correct standard errors for the effect estimates. Other computer programs provide even more elaborate procedures for conducting these calculations. Particularly noteworthy is STATA, created by StataCorp, which has subprograms for cross-section time-series data that begin with "xt."

Testing Goodness of Fit

As previously noted, the model usually competing with fixed effects is the random-effects model. This has the disadvantage that it assumes that the individual random effects are uncorrelated with the regressors X. It is just the possibility of such correlation that requires use of the fixed-effects model. The issue then becomes, is it possible to test the goodness of fit to the data of the fixed- versus random-effects model? The answer is yes. The Hausman test can reveal whether the fixed- or random-effects model fits the data better, and thus which one to use.

Substantive Uses of the Models

Effects of Occupations, Unions, and Other Memberships

One principal use of fixed-effects models has been to estimate the effects of membership in work-related organizations (occupations, unions, and so on) on earnings, net of variables that may be correlated with such membership, including unchanging variables (such as skill, energy, or motivation) that may be unmeasured. This technique has been used to demonstrate that employment in a highly female-worker-dominated occupation lowers wages, net of other characteristics, for both women and men. Labor economists have used the model to show that union membership raises earnings, with worker characteristics constant. Similar analyses of pooled time-series cross-section data are increasingly being used to measure the effects of marriage, childbearing, and divorce on outcomes such as mental health and earnings, controlling for unmeasured, unchanging characteristics of the individuals concerned.

Effects of Families and Other Groupings

A second use of these techniques has been to estimate the effects of changing group membership variables on child outcomes, net of unchanging, unmeasured group membership variables. In one study, twins were used to control for genetic factors when measuring the effect of schooling on earnings. Families with multiple siblings were used in another study to test the effect of the number of children in the household on the intellectual attainment of these children, net of unmeasured, unchanging characteristics, such as family intellectual climate. In contrast to prior studies that did not use fixed effects, the latter study found that the number of siblings has no causal effect on children's intellectual attainment, once unmeasured, unchanging family variables are controlled via fixed-effects estimation.

Program Evaluation

A particularly attractive use of fixed effects occurs for evaluating social programs and interventions using quasi-experimental data collected over time. For example, suppose U.S. states are observed over a time period in which some program or policy (for example, welfare eligibility regulations, or capital punishment as a deterrent to homicide) is "turned on and off" by legislation. The data can then be pooled for each state over time, allowing estimation of a fixed-effects model with dummy variables for states, in which the key independent variable indicates, for each state in each time period, whether the policy is on or off. Here the state dummy variables control a host of state-specific factors, such as local culture, institutions, and social structure, that might otherwise bias the estimate of program effects. Fixed effects have also been used in program evaluations based on individual-level data and labor markets.

Other Areas

Increasingly, social scientists are coming to realize that fixed-effects estimation is potentially useful across a very broad range of circumstances in which pooled cross-section time-series or otherwise grouped data are analyzed, including economic and political science scenarios.

Strengths and Limitations

Strengths of the Model

As previously noted, the great strength of fixed-effects estimation is that it controls for the effects of correlated unmeasured, unchanging variables that may otherwise bias estimates of causal effect.

Limitations of the Model

Fixed-effects estimation uses only data on individuals having multiple observations, and estimates effects only for those variables that change across these observations. It assumes that the effects of unchanging unmeasured variables can be captured by time-invariant individual-specific dummy variables. Bias from measurement error is usually increased in fixed-effects estimators, which may be why fixed-effects estimates are usually smaller than those from cross-sectional data. Also, problems can arise when fixed-effects estimation is used with models containing a lagged dependent variable, although methods exist to deal with these problems.

The Decision to Use Fixed Effects

In assessing panel or other grouped data, fixed-effects regression models are an attractive option to reduce possible bias due to unmeasured, unchanging variables that may be correlated with the variable of interest. The competing model is random effects, but this requires the assumption that the individual-level effects are uncorrelated with the regressors. Best practice is to test for this, using the test developed by Hausman.

See Also the Following Articles

Longitudinal Studies, Panel • Randomization • Time-Series–Cross-Section Data

Further Reading

Allison, P. D. (1996). Fixed-Effects Partial Likelihood for Repeated Events. *Sociol. Meth. Res.* **25,** 207–222.

Allison, P. D. (2004). *Fixed Effects Regression Methods Using the SAS System.* The SAS Institute, Cary, NC.

Angrist, J. D., and Krueger, A. B. (1999). Empirical strategies in labor economics. In *Handbook of Labor Economics,* (O. Ashenfelter and D. Card, eds.), Vol. 3, Chap. 23. Elsevier, Amsterdam.

Ashenfelter, O., and Krueger, A. B. (1994). Estimating the returns to schooling using a new sample of twins. *Am. Econ. Rev.* **84,** 1157–1173.

Beck, N., and Katz, J. N. (1995). What to do (and not to do) with time-series cross-section data. *Am. Pol. Sci. Rev.* **89,** 634–647.

England, P., Farkas, G., Kilbourne, B. S., and Dou, T. (1988). Explaining occupational sex segregation and wages: findings from a model with fixed effects. *Am. Sociol. Rev.* **53,** 544–558.

Greene, W. H. (2000). *Econometric Analysis,* 4th Ed. Prentice Hall, Upper Saddle River, New Jersey.

Griliches, Z., and Hausman, J. (1986). Errors in variables in panel data. *J. Econometr.* **31,** 93–118.

Guo, G., and VanWey, L. K. (1999). Sibship size and intellectual development: Is the relationship causal? *Am. Sociol. Rev.* **64,** 169–187.

Heckman, J. J., and Hotz, J. (1989). Choosing among alternative nonexperimental methods for estimating the impact of social programs: The case of manpower training. *J. Am. Statist. Assoc.* **84,** 862–874.

Matyas, L., and Sevestre, P. (1996). *The Econometrics of Panel Data.* Kluwer Academic Publ., Dordrecht.

Mundlak, Y. (1978). On the pooling of time series and cross sectional data. *Econometrica* **56,** 69–86.

StataCorp. (1999). *Stata Statistical Software: Release 6.0.* Stata Corporation, College Station, TX.

Focus Groups

David L. Morgan
Portland State University, Portland, Oregon, USA

Glossary

degree of structure The extent to which the focus group interview is either directed by the research team ("more structured") or left in the hands of the group participants ("less structured").

funnel approach An interviewing technique that begins with broad, open questions in a less structured format, and then proceeds to more narrowly defined questions in a more structured format.

homogeneity The extent to which all of the participants in the focus group share a similar orientation to, or perspective on, the discussion topic.

question wording The actual content of the items in survey questionnaires and related measurement instruments.

saturation In qualitative research, the extent to which there is less new information in each additional round of data collection.

segmentation A strategy for creating homogeneous subsets of focus groups within a larger project, by assigning participants to groups according to prespecified characteristics, e.g., gender or previous experiences.

The use of focus groups is a technique for collecting qualitative data. Focus groups typically bring together six to eight participants who engage in an open-ended discussion about topics that are supplied by the researchers. Focus groups are thus a form of interviewing whereby the researcher provides the focus, which the group uses as the basis for their discussion. For measurement purposes, focus groups are most often used as a preliminary method that provides input to the development of survey instruments, questionnaires, and other measurement instruments in the social sciences. With that emphasis in mind, the first portion of this article describes the advantages of using focus groups as a preliminary step in creating questionnaires; this is followed by a summary of the most important concerns in designing and using focus groups.

Introduction

Focus groups serve a general-purpose method for collecting data, and as such, they can serve a wide range of purposes. In particular, qualitative researchers frequently use focus groups in a self-contained fashion, in that the groups are the sole source of data for a study. From a measurement perspective, however, focus groups are most frequently used as a preliminary method that generates insights into what should be measured and how those measures should be constructed.

Various forms of group interviewing have played a role in the development of social science measures from very early in the 20th century. The basic format for what are now known as focus groups arose subsequently, in the 1990s, from the work of Paul Lazarsfeld and Robert Merton, although their approach applied to both individual and group interviews. From the 1950s through the 1970s, focus groups were far more common in marketing research than in the social sciences. This changed as group interviewing began to play a more prominent role in creating survey instruments, from the 1980s onward. This strategy relies on a sequential approach that begins by using focus groups as an input to the creation of quantitative research instruments. This amounts to collecting focus group data to enhance the effectiveness of measures that will be used in survey or experimental research, especially in areas in which researchers want to take a fresh approach to well-studied topics and for new topics for which researchers lack basic information. As the following discussions show, however, the knowledge gained through such preliminary focus groups can also serve a variety of other related purposes.

Advantages of Focus Groups in Creating Measures

It might initially seem more logical to use individual rather than group interviews in the development of questionnaire items, because it is almost always individuals who respond to these instruments. In reality, however, the choice of a preliminary method needs to be driven by developmental work. Focus groups have a distinct advantage for this task, because they can reveal a wide range of responses to topic in question. This is notably useful in designing measurement items that apply equally well to the full range of people who will respond to a questionnaire.

Researchers have offered three specific justifications for using focus groups (and other qualitative methods) as inputs to the development of quantitative measures. In discovery-oriented uses, the focus groups are largely exploratory, and the goal is to uncover topics that should be measured. In development-oriented uses, the focus groups examine a prespecified set of issues, and the goal is to locate ways to measure these substantive topics. Finally, in definition-oriented uses, the focus groups supply detailed information, in order to specify the final question wording for specific research topics. This distinction between discovery, development, and definition as three different uses for preliminary focus groups is most useful for heuristic purposes. Actual research projects often include more than one of these purposes. Even so, distinguishing among these three uses has important implications for how the focus groups are conducted. In particular, the research designs that are most effective for discovering new ideas are likely to be quite different from the designs that are best for defining well-developed concepts.

The use of focus groups as inputs to measurement goals that emphasize either discovery, development, or definition is examined in the next three sections. The emphasis is on applications in the area of survey research, along with a brief, concluding discussion on related uses for focus groups in the development of experiments and interventions.

Discovery-Oriented Uses of Focus Groups

The primary reason for beginning a survey project with discovery-oriented focus groups is to gather basic information about a poorly understood topic or population of respondents. This approach emphasizes the strengths that qualitative methods offer in exploratory research. Too often, preliminary focus groups in survey research are stereotyped as dealing solely with issues of question wording, but in an explicitly exploratory study, the essential goal is to learn what should be asked, prior to worrying about how to phrase the actual questions. Early social science research on autoimmune disease syndrome/human immunodeficiency virus (AIDS/HIV) is a classic example of using preliminary focus groups when entering a new field of study. Although the need for epidemiological data led these projects to rely on large-scale surveys, the researchers recognized that they knew very little about the lives of the people who were at highest risk. Hence several of these projects began with focus groups and other open-ended interviewing techniques as a way to learn more about the range of issues that the survey should cover.

One of the key advantages of discovery-oriented designs is to improve the specification of the models that the quantitative research will test. When relatively little is known about either the topic being studied or the people being surveyed, there is a serious danger that a crucial topic will get omitted. This failure to include important variables is not just a matter of missed opportunities, it is actually a source of potentially serious statistical bias in the form of "specification error." For example, leaving an important variable out of a multiple regression will affect the values of all of the coefficients that are estimated. There is no statistical solution for specification error, so, if there are doubts about whether a survey includes a wide enough range of relevant variables, then a set of preliminary, discovery-oriented, focus groups studies can help clarify the factors that matter to the respondents. In general, discovery-oriented focus groups are most useful when a researcher is uncertain about what to measure with regard to a topic or population of interest.

Development-Oriented Uses of Focus Groups

In projects that rely on preliminary focus groups for development, the goal is to learn how a set of key issues operates in the lives of the people being studied. Often this amounts to locating questions that will operationalize a theoretical concept. This approach emphasizes the strengths of qualitative methods for learning about others' perspectives on the things that interest the researcher.

Development-oriented versions of focus groups typically search for a set of questions that can adequately cover a predetermined topic. The discussions in focus groups let researchers hear the respondents' perspectives on that topic. Using preliminary focus groups to develop operationalizations for the key concepts in a survey reveals the behaviors and opinions that the respondents associate with the research topics. This can be especially helpful when creating sets of questions that apply equally well to several categories of respondents, such as men and women, different ethnic groups or age groups, and so on. For this purpose, comparing focus groups from each of the major categories of respondents can increase the likelihood of developing questions that are equally meaningful to all the respondents. In general, development-oriented groups are most useful when a researcher has clear ideas about the topics to measure, but is uncertain about the proper items to capture these domains.

Definition-Oriented Uses of Focus Groups

When definition is the purpose that drives the use of preliminary focus groups in a project, the goal is to determine the final content of the survey instrument. This approach emphasizes the strengths of qualitative methods for studying social life both in detail and in context. The primary reason for beginning a survey research project with a definition-oriented qualitative study is to assist in creating the actual item wording for the questionnaire. Because the quality of the data in a survey depends directly on the questions that are asked, it is not enough just to ask about the right topics (discovery), or to locate question topics that cover the researchers' interests (development); beyond those essential goals, it is also necessary to write the questions in language that the respondents cannot only understand easily, but in language that also means essentially the same thing to both the respondents and the researchers (definition).

Regardless of the theoretical or practical concerns that motivate an interest in a particular research topic, asking effective survey questions requires an understanding of how the survey respondents talk about these topics. Put simply, researchers cannot create meaningful questions unless they understand the language that the respondents use. Once again, a useful example comes from research on AIDS with gay and bisexual men; focus groups helped researchers to locate appropriate wordings for asking about a range of sexual behaviors. In general, definition-oriented groups are most useful when a researcher knows the content areas for the measurement instrument, but is uncertain about the best ways to state the final wording.

Preliminary Focus Groups in Experimental Interventions

One obvious parallel between survey research and experimental inventions is that both methods frequently rely on similar kinds of measurement instruments, such as self-completed questionnaires or in-person surveys. The measurement instruments in experimental interventions can thus benefit from preliminary focus groups in the same ways that survey research can.

A different purpose for preliminary focus groups in intervention studies is to create and deliver programs that are well suited to the people who will participate in them. The same set of three basic advantages also applies to these practical purposes, because it is useful to (1) discover the program participants' needs and constraints, (2) develop programs that will effectively meet these needs, and (3) define program procedures that will work in practice and not just in theory. This similarity follows directly from the shared goal of generating preliminary input, in order to develop materials that will match the thoughts, feelings, and experiences of those who will participate in the subsequent portion of the project.

Additional Advantages of Preliminary Focus Groups

Two different sets of advantages can arise from using preliminary focus groups to develop measures. The first set involves the classic criteria of reliability and validity. The second set is less directly related to the properties of the measures, but may be just as important for the overall success of the research project.

Increased validity is the most obvious attraction of locating questions that are meaningful to the people who will respond to measurement instruments, including the essential goal of ensuring that the questions mean the same thing to both the researchers and the respondents. In the extreme case, preliminary focus groups may show that a set of theoretically generated constructs of interest to the researchers actually has very little relevance to the respondents. For example, research group was asked to use focus groups in developing survey questions that would operationalize a particular theory of how couples handled household finances; instead, the researchers found that almost no one described their lives in terms that fit the prespecified theoretical categories. Without this qualitative research, it still would have been possible to write questions that captured this particular theory, even though those items might not measure anything that was meaningful to the respondents.

The reliability of the survey instrument can also benefit from preliminary focus groups. This is especially true for checklists and attitude scales, which require parallel measures, i.e., multiple items, each targeting the same underlying phenomenon in a similar way. Thus, preliminary focus groups can improve both the reliability and validity of survey measures by generating a sufficient number of survey items that effectively capture what a topic means to the survey respondents.

The uses for preliminary focus groups can also go beyond improvements to reliability and validity. Often, quantitative researchers start with relatively limited purposes for focus groups, such as defining the wording for survey questions or program materials, but come away from this preliminary qualitative work with a whole new set of ideas. In particular, preliminary focus groups can also contribute to surveys and experiments by generating hypotheses and by building relationships between the research team and the research participants.

Quantitative researchers seldom undertake focus groups solely for the purpose of generating hypotheses, because they almost always have a set of research questions already in place. This does not, however, preclude the possibility of pursuing additional hypotheses. Further, there is no requirement that hypotheses must be deduced strictly from theory. In many situations, it makes just as much sense to generate hypotheses inductively through qualitative research, which provides direct contact with the people whose behavior the researchers are trying to understand.

Another common benefit in preliminary focus groups comes from building relationships with the people who will actually be participating in the research project. The value of these relationships is particularly obvious in projects that work with a specific community or target population. In those cases, access to the people who provide the data may require both an understanding of and a connection to the local community. Even with random sampling, this kind of prior contact can provide practical insights that increase the efficiency and effectiveness of the actual fieldwork.

Generating hypotheses and building relationships are further demonstrations of the benefits that can result from using focus groups to create careful connections between those who design research projects and those who participate in them. In each case, the advantages of this approach arise from learning more about the research participants' perspectives and understanding more about the context in which the larger research project will operate.

Designing Focus Groups for Measurement Purposes

Given that focus groups can be used in a number of different ways for a number of different purposes, what are the essential considerations in designing preliminary focus groups as an input to creating measures?

Group Composition

Focus groups work best when the participants are as interested in the topic as the researchers are. Because the conversation among the participants produces the data in focus groups, it is important to bring together a set of people who can easily talk to each other about the topic of interest. The selection of participants for a focus group must thus consider not only the information that individuals have to share with the researchers, but also the ability of the participants to carry on a comfortable group discussion.

The classic approach to facilitating comfortable group discussions is to emphasize homogeneity in the composition of focus groups by bringing together people who share a similar perspective on the topic in question. One obvious advantage of this similarity is the tendency to minimize conflict. In addition, an initial degree of homogeneity can be used to stimulate a process of "sharing and comparing," whereby the participants explore the ways that they are both similar and different with regard to the topic. Conversations that contain such comparisons can be especially useful for developing measures, because they provide insight into the range of issues that need to be considered in constructing measures.

The idea of segmentation is an important extension of relying on homogeneity in the composition of focus groups. With this approach, the total set of participants is divided into a set of homogeneous segments, and different focus groups are conducted with the members of each segment. For example, if a series of questions need to be equally effective in measuring the responses of Americans of European and African descent, then the focus groups would be segmented into separate groups by race. Dividing a set of focus groups into separate, homogeneous segments has two basic advantages. In addition to using the similarity within each group to facilitate conversations among the participants, concentrating the differences between groups also simplifies analytic comparisons across the segments. This approach is well suited to creating measures for use in diverse populations because it allows the researcher to compare the sets of separate groups to determine the ways that the various segments are either similar or different.

Another aspect of group composition that needs to be considered is the number of people in each group, and this also depends on how the participants relate to the topic. If the topic is important to the participants, then each of them will have a fair amount to say, and a smaller group will allow everyone an opportunity to be heard. When the participants are less involved with the topic, however, a larger group is more likely to produce enough ideas to generate a discussion through the participants' reactions to those ideas.

Interview Structure

In addition to planning who will participate in the groups, it is also important to decide how the group discussions will be conducted. This aspect of focus groups is usually summarized in terms of interview structure, with some research projects using a more structured approach than others.

Interview structure consists of two interrelated aspects of focus groups: the interview questions and the moderating strategy. These two elements are connected because an interview that contains a relatively small number of broad questions requires a different moderator style than does an interview that asks about a larger number of more specific topics. Thus, a less structured interview will usually combine a smaller number of very open-ended questions with a moderating style that emphasizes hearing from the participants. In contrast, a more structured interview will combine a larger number of more specific questions with a moderating style that emphasizes the needs and interests of the research team.

For measurement purposes, less structured focus groups are typically associated with discovery-oriented purposes, whereas more structured approaches are well matched to definition-oriented purposes. When the research goals emphasize discovery, the researchers are trying to learn the participants' perspectives on the topic, so a less structured discussion gives the participants the opportunity to pursue a broad set of topics in whatever ways they see fit. Alternatively, when the research goals emphasize definition, the researchers already have a well-specified agenda, so a more structured approach ensures that participants concentrate on the predefined needs of the research team.

In the intermediate case of development-oriented research, a "funnel approach" is frequently useful because it combines elements of both more and less structured interviews. A funnel approach begins the interview with one or two broad, open questions, which lead into a series of more specific questions. The interview thus starts with a less structured approach that emphasizes the participants' point of view, and proceeds to a more structured approach that concentrates on the researchers' agenda. This funnel approach is also useful in projects that combine a range of goals in terms of discovery, development, and definition.

Number of Groups

There are no hard and fast rules that determine the number of focus groups to conduct. Ultimately, the number of groups depends on the familiar constraint imposed by the underlying variability of the population. When there is relatively little variability in the population, then the researcher will begin to hear the same things during the second or third group. This sense that additional data gathering is not producing new information is known as saturation in qualitative research. If, however, there is a wide range of opinions or experiences in the larger population, then it will take a larger number of focus groups before nothing new is being said in each additional group.

Because the level of variability in the population is difficult to specify when working with new topics or new categories of participants, it is especially dangerous to limit preliminary research to only one focus group. Conducting only one group does not provide any information about the variability of the population, so it is impossible to know whether a second group would be nearly identical or completely different. In projects that use multiple segments, the same concern applies to running only one group per segment. It is thus advisable to conduct a minimum of at least two groups per segment.

Analysis Procedures

The analysis strategy for these focus groups should be determined by the larger goal of generating inputs for measurement construction. Because this goal is simpler than the interpretive work that accompanies many full-scale qualitative studies, the analysis procedures can also be simpler. In particular, it would seldom be necessary to use either qualitative analysis software or a detailed coding system to analyze data that serve primarily as an input to creating questionnaires.

The standard procedure for capturing data in focus groups is to audiotape the discussions. Transcribing these tapes can be a time-consuming and difficult task, which is most useful either when there are a great many tapes to be compared or when the content of each discussion needs to be examined in careful detail. One common alternative to transcribing is to have more than one member of the research team present during the group discussion, so they can meet and debrief after the discussion. This approach is most effective when the observers have a prior protocol that directs their attention to the aspects of the discussion that are most likely to be useful for the purpose at hand.

Practical Concerns in Using Preliminary Focus Groups

The most serious limitation in the use of focus groups arises from the fact that they almost always rely on small nonrandom samples. Hence, the data that they produce must be used with caution, even when the goal is simply to provide preliminary inputs. In particular, both the nonrandom samples and the subjective group discussions undermine the value of producing numerical data as part of the focus group process. There may, however, be other purposes for quantitative techniques within a research project that uses focus groups. For example, a brief preliminary questionnaire can provide useful background data about the participants. In addition, interview questions that use a show of hands or other forms of counting can help stimulate the group discussion. The danger arises from going beyond such simple, descriptive purposes to a more dubious attempt to drawing meaningful, numerical conclusions from such data.

A different limitation arises from the fact that focus groups only produce verbal statements about attitudes and preferences, which may not translate into actual behaviors. This potential gap between attitudes and behaviors is a problem in all forms of self-reported data. Still, there is a vividness to hearing people state and defend their beliefs in focus groups, and this can mislead researchers into placing an unjustifiable amount of faith in these attitudes.

Donald Dillman provides a useful counterexample from a project that he and his co-workers conducted at the U.S. census, when their extensive experience with a topic led them to question what they heard in focus groups. In that case, the participants examined a number of different envelopes that could be used to mail census materials, and reported a strong negative response to an official-looking format. Because of their past success with official-looking envelopes, these researchers did a test and found that such a mailing actually produced a significantly higher response rate, compared to the format that the focus group participants preferred. The moral of this story is that focus groups are more useful for learning about experiences, feelings, and opinions, rather than for predicting behavior.

This tendency to rely too heavily on the data from focus groups is also present in the mistaken assumption that preliminary qualitative research reduces the need for thorough pretesting. It is thus essential to remember that preliminary focus groups provide only inputs to the development of measures; they do not provide any guarantee that those measures will perform as desired. As always, the only way to determine the actual effectiveness of a measure is to test it.

Future Directions

The relationship between focus groups and pretesting, as just discussed, is part of a broader series of issues involving different techniques for improving the quality of questionnaire measurements. In particular, even though focus groups are frequently grouped together with cognitive interviewing as "developmental tools" in survey research, these methods typically serve distinct purposes. Currently, very little is known about optimum strategies for combining focus groups with cognitive interviewing and other developmental strategies.

One simple hypothesis is that items and instruments developed via focus groups would need less refinement through cognitive interviewing, based on the assumption that such items were already "closer" to the respondents' perspective. This is, however, an empirical question. What is needed is research that investigates the potential overlap in the preliminary contributions of focus groups, cognitive interviewing, and other developmental strategies. An increase in our understanding of what each of these techniques can contribute would not only increase efficiency but would also allow researchers with limited resources to select the tools that were most likely to address their particular problems.

This lack of data about the relationships between various developmental tools is, however, only one part of a larger gap in knowledge about the value of focus groups as a preliminary input to measurement construction. In fact, there is no clear-cut evidence that preliminary focus groups actually improve the quality of measurement instruments in the social sciences. Instead, it simply seems to be an article of faith that researchers who listen to their future respondents will produce instruments that are superior to what they would have written in the absence of this additional input. This oversight is especially surprising in light of the considerable research literature that investigates the effectiveness of a wide range of practices in survey research.

Questioning the extent to which focus groups truly do contribute to measurement points to a paradoxical situation. On the one hand, the past two decades have produced a tremendous increase in the use of focus groups as a preliminary tool in the development of surveys and questionnaires. On the other hand, there is little systematic evidence that addresses the value of these procedures. At this point, it is necessary to produce clear demonstrations of the increased quality in measures that is due to focus groups—and making use of that evidence will provide the best way to improve futures uses of focus groups for this purpose.

The widespread use of focus groups in the development of measures supports the value of hearing from research participants prior to presenting them with questionnaires. Despite the lack of research on how developmental focus groups affect the quality of measures, there is little doubt about the value of improving our understanding of the people who will provide the data. This is where focus groups make the biggest difference, by helping us do the best possible job of asking people meaningful questions about the things that matter most to them.

See Also the Following Articles

Experimenter Effects • Interviews

Further Reading

Barbour, R. S., and Kitzinger, J. (1999). *Developing Focus Group Research*. Sage, Thousand Oaks, California.

Berry, W. D., and Feldman, S. (1985). *Multiple Regression in Practice.* Sage, Thousand Oaks, California.

Dillman, D. A., Singer, E., Clark, J. R., and Treat, J. B. (1996). Effects of benefits appeals, mandatory appeals, and variations in statements of confidentiality on completion rates for census questionnaires. *Public Opin. Q.* **60,** 376–389.

Edmunds, H. (1999). *The Focus Group Research Handbook.* NTC Business Books (in association with the American Marketing Association), Chicago.

Fern, E. F. (2001). *Advanced Focus Group Research.* Sage, Thousand Oaks, California.

Greenbaum, T. L. (1998). *The Handbook for Focus Group Research,* 2nd Ed. Sage, Thousand Oaks, California.

Joseph, J. G., Emmons, C.-A., Kessler, R. C., Wortman, C. B., O'Brien, K. J., Hocker, W. T., and Schaefer, C. (1984). Coping with the threat of AIDS: An approach to psychosocial assessment. *Am. Psychol.* **39,** 1297–1302.

Krueger, Richard A. (1998). *Analyzing and Reporting Focus Group Results.* Sage, Thousand Oaks, California.

Krueger, R. A., and Casey, M. A. (2004). *Focus Groups: A Practical Guide for Applied Research,* 3rd Ed. Sage, Thousand Oaks, California.

Laurie, H., and Sullivan, O. (1991). Combining qualitative and quantitative data in the longitudinal study of household allocations. *Sociol. Rev.* **39,** 113–130.

Merton, R. K., Fiske, M., and Kendall, P. L. (1990). *The Focused Interview,* 2nd Ed. Free Press, New York.

Morgan, D. L. (1993). *Successful Focus Groups.* Sage, Thousand Oaks, California.

Morgan, D. L. (1997). *Focus Groups as Qualitative Research,* 2nd Ed. (Vol. 16 in the Sage Publications series on qualitative research methods). Sage, Thousand Oaks, California.

Morgan, D. L. (1998). Practical strategies for combining qualitative and quantitative methods: applications to health research. *Qualitat. Health Res.* **8,** 362–376.

Morgan, D. L., and Krueger, R. A. (1998). *The Focus Group Kit* (6 vols). Sage, Thousand Oaks, California.

Tanur, J. M. (1992). *Questions about Questions: Inquiries into the Cognitive Bases of Surveys.* Russell Sage Foundation, New York.

Thurstone, L. L., and Chave, E. J. (1929). *The Measurement of Attitude.* University of Chicago Press, Chicago.

Frameworks of Probabilistic Models for Unfolding Responses

Guanzhong Luo
Murdoch University, Perth, Western Australia and South China Normal University, Guangzhou, China

Glossary

cumulative response process A response process in which the ideal direction principle applies.

ideal direction principle The probability that a person gives a positive response to an item depends on the difference between the locations of the person and the item. This person–item difference may be positive or negative. The probability is 1 when the person–item difference is positive infinity.

ideal point principle The probability that a person gives a positive response to an item depends on the distance (absolute value of the difference) between the locations of the person and the item. This person–item distance is always non-negative. The probability is maximized when the person–item distance is 0.

unfolding process A response process in which the ideal point principle applies.

This article provides a summary of the frameworks of models for unfolding responses. The origin of the term "unfolding" is first explained in the context of constructing a deterministic unfolding model, which is a prototype of modern probabilistic unfolding models. Among the three different response formats for the unfolding process, the single-stimulus format is fundamental. Second, a general form of probabilistic unfolding models for dichotomous responses in the single-stimulus format is described, with the focus on the significance of the item unit parameter for the structure of the model. This general form highlights the role of a single peaked function in the unfolding process. Then a general form of probabilistic unfolding models for responses in pairwise format is derived. Consequently, a general form of probabilistic unfolding models for polytomous responses is then established using the rating formulation approach. As direct results of the frameworks of unfolding models, some basic techniques of confirming the desirable response process are presented.

Structure of the Unfolding Response Process

Psychological measurement in social sciences, which concerns the attitudes, beliefs, preferences, or other constructs (topics) of individuals, is often carried out by means of questionnaires. A questionnaire consists of statements (items) expressing certain affective evaluation of the construct concerned. A primary task of the measurement is to locate respondents and statements on an affective continuum (unidimensional) or space (multidimensional) according to the responses given by the respondents. Responses can be invoked in various formats, including single-stimulus (direct-response), pairwise-preference, and ranking formats. A questionnaire in a single-stimulus format asks respondents to give each of the statements in the questionnaire a direct preference level. This preference level may range from highly negative to highly positive (e.g., from "strongly disagree" to "strongly agree") or may be expressed as a frequency scale (e.g., from "never" to "always"). A questionnaire in a pairwise-preference format gives a pair of items at a time and asks respondents to choose the more preferable one against the other. A questionnaire in a ranking format asks respondents to rank the items according to their preference, from the most preferable to the least preferable. Among these three response formats, the single-stimulus format, also known as the direct-response format, is fundamental, because a response within this format is governed directly by a single person–item distance. A response with pairwise-preference and ranking formats is governed by the comparison of the distances between the person and the items involved. The focus of this article is on a framework of probabilistic models for responses with a single-stimulus format, though a framework for the pairwise-preference format will also be derived from the framework for the single-stimulus format. The rest of this article is restricted on unidimensional situations.

Louis Thurstone pioneered studies on attitude measurement in the 1920s, using both the ideal direction and the ideal point principle. Clyde H. Coombs, a student of Thurstone's, carried on the research within the ideal point framework with a more systematic approach. Coombs introduced the term "unfolding" when he analyzed ranking data (collected with a questionnaire in ranking format) in the early 1950s. Based on this concept, he established his unfolding theory, which covered various types of data in different response formats. In particular, his milestone work in dealing with single-stimulus data (collected with a questionnaire in single-stimulus format) provided a prototype of the modern probabilistic unfolding models. In the unidimensional case, the affective continuum on which the person and the item are located is termed the "latent trait" continuum. In single-stimulus data, the manifest response that a person n gives to item i is denoted as x_{ni}, which can be dichotomous or polytomous. In the case of dichotomous responses, a legitimate response is either "agree/yes" (positive, $x_{ni}=1$) or "disagree/no" (negative, $x_{ni}=0$). The principle for the unfolding process is that the response x_{ni} is determined by the person–item distance $|\beta_n - \delta_i|$, where β_n is the location of person n and δ_i is the location of item i. Coombs explicitly defined x_{ni} as a step function of the person–item distance:

$$x_{ni} = \begin{cases} 1, & \text{when} \quad |\beta_n - \delta_i| \leq \rho, \\ 0, & \text{when} \quad |\beta_n - \delta_i| > \rho. \end{cases} \tag{1}$$

Here, β_n is also known as the ideal point for the person. The value of ρ in Eq. (1) determines the two thresholds between the response interval for a positive response "yes" ($x_{ni}=1$) and two disjoint segments for a negative response "no" ($x_{ni}=0$), as shown in Fig. 1.

Although two very different segments on the latent trait give rise to a negative response, according to Coombs, a negative manifest response is certain if the absolute value of the person–item difference is greater than the given value of ρ, regardless of in which segment the person is located. In this sense, the responses are folded, as shown by the heavy line in Fig. 1. The task of the data analysis is to unfold these responses to recover the underlying latent trait continuum with the locations of the persons and items involved. In addition, the value of ρ is to be recovered or estimated. The distance

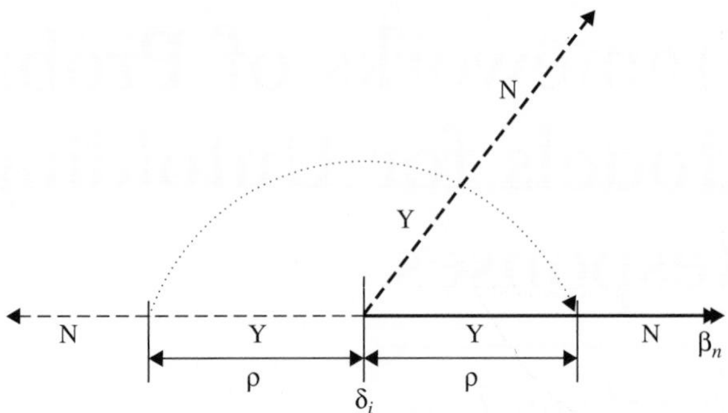

Figure 1 Coombs' deterministic unfolding model, showing the "yes" interval (Y) and "no" segments (N).

between the two thresholds (2ρ) is termed the "latitude of acceptance," an important concept in attitude theory. Originally, ρ was defined as a person parameter. In the frameworks described later in this article, however, ρ is considered as an item parameter in order to avoid the problem of overparameterization.

It can be seen that Coombs' original unfolding model for direct responses in Fig. 1 is deterministic in the sense that the probability for a positive response, $\Pr\{x_{ni}=1\}$, is 1 when the absolute value of the person–item distance is less than ρ, and 0 otherwise. The concept of probabilistic unfolding models naturally arises when a single peaked function is used in the place of the rectangle function. Figure 2 shows that Coombs' deterministic unfolding model for direct responses defines $\{x_{ni}=1\}$ as a certain outcome in the interval $[\delta i - \rho,\ \delta i + \rho]$, whereas a probabilistic unfolding model allows the probability $\Pr\{x_{ni}=1\}$ to be any number between 0 and 1.

Using the concept of probabilistic unfolding models for single-stimulus format, it is straightforward to obtain the probabilities for responses with a pairwise-preference format. For an item pair (i, j), the pairwise responses are coded as $x_{nij}=1$ when person n chooses item i against item j. A pairwise-preference format requires respondents to choose the one that is comparatively more preferable of the pair. It implies that the underlying responses with a single-stimulus format on these two items are either (0, 1) or (1, 0), that is, one and only one item in this pair must be given a positive response. Then the probability that item i is chosen against item j can be expressed in terms of the probability for a positive response on item i and the probability for a negative response on item j, given the condition that only one item in this pair is given a positive response:

$$\Pr\{x_{nij}=1\} = \frac{\Pr\{x_{ni}=1\}\Pr\{x_{nj}=0\}}{\Pr\{x_{ni}=1\}\Pr\{x_{nj}=0\}+\Pr\{x_{ni}=0\}\Pr\{x_{nj}=1\}}. \tag{2}$$

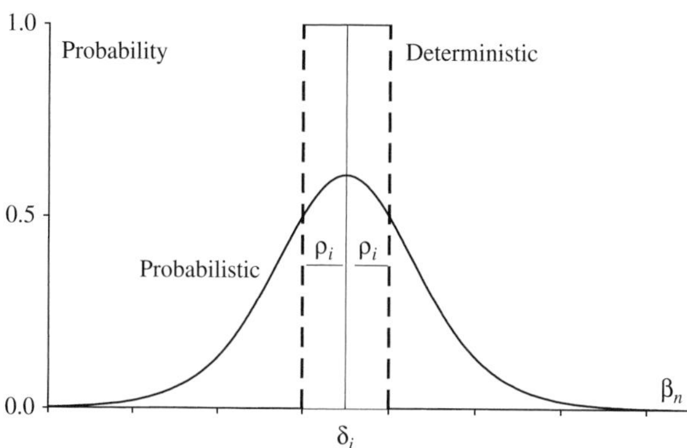

Figure 2 Probabilities of unfolding models: deterministic vs. probabilistic.

From Eq. (2), the probability of any item rank can also be expressed in terms of the probabilities for all item pairs. Therefore, it is widely accepted in the literature that the family of unfolding models includes all the models for all three response formats mentioned earlier, the underlying response function of which is single peaked. Consequently, the response process governed by these models is generally termed the "unfolding" process. Because of the shape of the response functions in Fig. 2, they are also known as single-peaked response processes.

A Framework of Dichotomous Probabilistic Models for the Unfolding Response

During the 30 years since Coombs developed his unfolding theory, particularly in the late 1980s and 1990s, various other specific probabilistic unfolding models for dichotomous responses have been proposed. Suppose that N persons give responses to a questionnaire consisting of I items. For any person n with location β_n and any item i with location δ_i, the response variable is denoted as X_{ni}:$x_{ni} \in \{0, 1\}$. By specifying different probabilistic functions that conform to the unfolding principle, various probabilistic unfolding models have been proposed. In particular, the followings models are frequently referenced in the literature and are used in real applications.

1. The simple square logistic model (SSLM):

$$\Pr\{X_{ni} = 1 \mid \beta_n, \delta_i\} = \frac{1}{1 + \exp[(\beta_n - \delta_i)^2]}. \tag{3}$$

2. The PARELLA (parallelogram analysis) model:

$$\Pr\{X_{ni} = 1 \mid \beta_n, \delta_i, \gamma\} = \frac{1}{1 + [(\beta_n - \delta_i)^2]^\gamma}, \tag{4}$$

where γ (>0) is a structural parameter of the model.

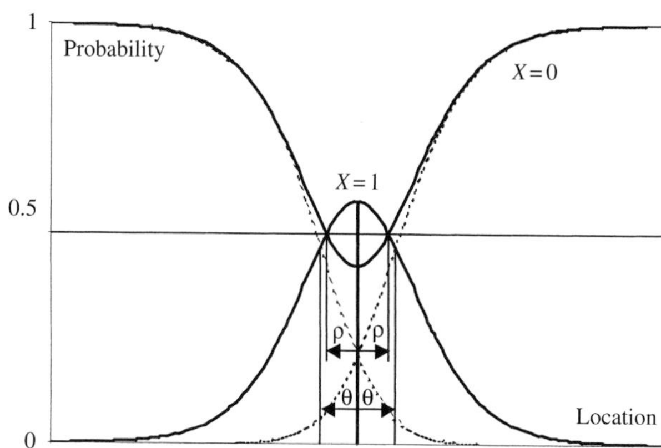

Figure 3 Construction of the hyperbolic cosine model from the Rasch model for polytomous responses.

3. The hyperbolic cosine model (HCM):

$$\Pr\{X_{ni} = 1 \mid \beta_n, \delta_i, \theta_i\} = \frac{\exp(\theta_i)}{\exp(\theta_i) + 2\cosh(\beta_n - \delta_i)}. \tag{5}$$

The probability for a negative response $\Pr\{X_{ni}=0\}$ for the individual models is implied as $\Pr\{X_{ni}=0\} + \Pr\{X_{ni}=1\} = 1$. Among these models, the HCM is distinguished in that it is derived from the Rasch model rather than being specified descriptively. This in fact reveals the relationship between the cumulative process and the unfolding process. In constructing the HCM, the "disagree" response is resolved into two latent components, "disagree below," which reflects that the person may be located below the statement, and "disagree above," which reflects that the person may be located above the statement. Then the Rasch model for three ordered response categories was applied to these two components of the "disagree" response together with the single "agree" response. The final form of the HCM was obtained by summing the probabilities of the two latent components of the "disagree" response to reflect the single manifest "disagree" response. After summing up the probabilities of the two latent components of the "disagree" response, the HCM gives the probabilities for both positive and negative responses as in Eq. (5). Figure 3 shows the probabilistic functions of the HCM (solid lines) and the corresponding Rasch model for three categories (dashed lines).

Another significance of the HCM of Eq. (5) is in involving a second item parameter, θ_i, in addition to the item location, δ_i. However, an obvious limitation of Eq. (5) is that it involves two types of functions. The statistical meaning of θ_i in this form is also unclear because $\delta_i \pm \theta_i$ are not exactly the crossing points of the probabilistic curves for positive and negative responses of the HCM. Let

$$e^{\theta_i} = 2\cosh(\rho_i), \tag{6}$$

then Eq. (5) can be re-expressed into the following form, which involves only the hyperbolic cosine function:

$$\Pr\{X_{ni}=1\,|\,\beta_n,\delta_i,\rho_i\} = \frac{\cosh(\rho_i)}{\cosh(\rho_i)+\cosh(\beta_n-\delta_i)},$$
$$\Pr\{X_{ni}=0\,|\,\beta_n,\delta_i,\rho_i\} = \frac{\cosh(\beta_n-\delta)}{\cosh(\rho_i)+\cosh(\beta_n-\delta_i)}. \tag{7}$$

The parameter ρ_i (≥ 0) in Eq. (7) defines the two thresholds $\delta_i \pm \rho_i$ in the following sense. When $|\beta_n - \delta_i| < \rho_i$, a positive response ($X_{ni}=1$) is more likely: $\Pr\{X_{ni}=1\} > \Pr\{X_{ni}=0\}$. When $|\beta_n-\delta_i| > \rho_i$, a negative response ($X_{ni}=0$) is more likely: $\Pr\{X_{ni}=0\} > \Pr\{X_{ni}=1\}$. When $|\beta_n-\delta_i|=\rho_i$, $\Pr\{X_{ni}=0\}=\Pr\{X_{ni}=1\}=0.5$. As shown in Fig. 3, ($\delta_i \pm \rho_i$) are the two points of intersection of the positive and negative response curves. That is, when $|\beta_n-\delta_i|=\rho_i$, $\Pr\{X_{ni}=0\}= \Pr\{X_{ni}=1\}=0.5$. Based on this fact, ρ_i is termed the unit parameter of item *i*. It is noted that when $\theta_i < \ln 2$, Eq. (6) cannot be solved. Therefore, Eq. (6) is valid only when $\theta_i > \ln 2$. In fact, when $\theta_i > \ln 2$, the probability for a positive response in Eq. (5) is always less than that for a negative response, regardless of the locations of the person and the item.

As shown in the preceding discussion, the hyperbolic cosine function and the item unit parameter ρ_i in Eq. (6) are structural rather than *ad hoc*. It is noted that the hyperbolic cosine is a non-negative monotonic and even function. These properties are considered essential for the HCM. By replacing the hyperbolic cosine function in the equation while retaining its essential properties, a general form of the probabilistic unfolding models for dichotomous responses can be proposed as follows:

$$\Pr\{X_{ni}=1\,|\,\beta_n,\delta_i,\rho_i\} = \frac{\Psi(\rho_i)}{\Psi(\rho_i)+\Psi(\beta_n-\delta_i)},$$
$$\Pr\{X_{ni}=0\,|\,\beta_n,\delta_i,\rho_i\} = \frac{\Psi(\beta_n-\delta_i)}{\Psi(\rho_i)+\Psi(\beta_n-\delta_i)}, \tag{8}$$

where β_n, δ_i, and ρ_i are as defined earlier, and the function Ψ (the operational function) has the following properties:

- (P1) Non-negative: $\Psi(t) \geq 0$ for any real t.
- (P2) Monotonic in the positive domain: $\Psi(t_1) > \Psi(t_2)$ for any $t_1 > t_2 > 0$.
- (P3) Ψ is an even function (symmetric about the origin): $\Psi(t)=\Psi(-t)$ for any real t.

As mentioned before, the hyperbolic cosine function holds these properties. In general, the property P1 ensures that the probability of Eq. (8) is non-negative. Properties P2 and P3 ensure that for any item location δ_i and unit ρ_i, the probability is a single peaked function of person location parameter β_n. Figure 4 shows the probabilistic curves for a positive response when the values of item unit increase. It is observed that for β_n, δ_i fixed at any value, $\Pr\{X_{ni}=1\}$ is a monotonic function of ρ_i.

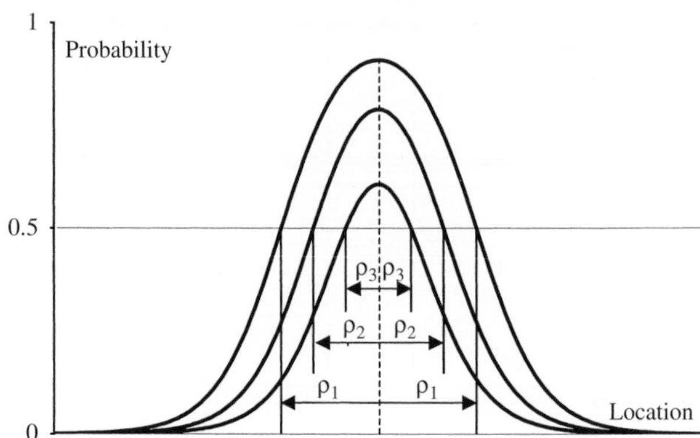

Figure 4 Probabilistic curves of the general unfolding model for dichotomous responses, with different values of the item unit.

It is trivial to confirm that after some simple re-expression, the models in Eqs. (3) and (4) are special cases of Eq. (7). In particular, the implied value for the item unit parameter in the SSLM of Eq. (3) and the PARELLA of Eq. (4) are 0 and 1, respectively. These two models can be extended by allowing a variable item unit. Furthermore, some more new models can also be specified with various operational functions that hold the properties P1–P3. In this sense, Eq. (8) provides a framework of probabilistic unfolding models for dichotomous responses. With this framework, the general properties of probabilistic dichotomous unfolding models are more transparent. For example, it is proved that the item unit ρ_i is not a scale parameter except in the case of the PARELLA model, with which the operational function is specified as $\Psi(t)=[t^2]^\gamma$. In this special situation,

$$\frac{[\rho^2]^\gamma}{[\rho^2]^\gamma+[(\beta_n-\delta_i)^2]^\gamma} = \frac{1}{1+[((\beta_n-\delta_i)/\rho)^2]^\gamma}. \tag{9}$$

Using Eq. (8) with Eq. (2), a general form for pairwise-preference responses can be obtained as

$$\Pr\{X_{nij}=1\} = \frac{\Psi(\rho_i)\Psi(\beta_n-\delta_j)}{\Psi(\rho_i)\Psi(\beta_n-\delta_j)+\Psi(\rho_j)\Psi(\beta_n-\delta_i)}. \tag{10}$$

When $\rho_i=\rho_j$, the general form of Eq. (10) can be further simplified:

$$\Pr\{X_{nij}=1\} = \frac{\Psi(\beta_n-\delta_j)}{\Psi(\beta_n-\delta_j)+\Psi(\beta_n-\delta_i)}. \tag{11}$$

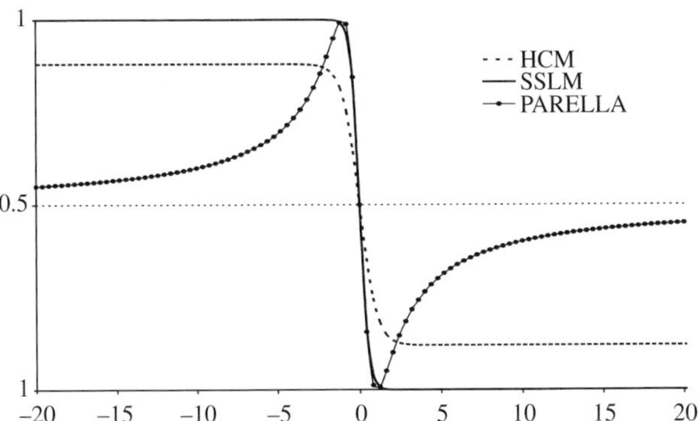

Figure 5 Probabilistic curves of unfolding models with pairwise-preference formats ($\delta_i = -1$, $\delta_j = 1$). HCM, Hyperbolic cosine model; SSLM, simple square logistic model.

Figure 5 shows the probabilities function in Eq. (11) when the underlying models are the HCM, SSLM, and PARELLA, respectively. It is noted that the asymptotic probabilities are different for different underlying models. For example, when $\delta_i < \delta_j$,

$$\lim_{\beta_n \to -\infty} \Pr\{X_{nij}=1\} = \begin{cases} 1, & \text{with the SSLM;} \\ \dfrac{\exp(\delta_j - \delta_i)}{1+\exp(\delta_j - \delta_i)}, & \text{with the HCM;} \\ 0.5, & \text{with PARELLA;} \end{cases}$$

$$\lim_{\beta_n \to +\infty} \Pr\{X_{nij}=1\} = \begin{cases} 0, & \text{with the SSLM;} \\ \dfrac{1}{1+\exp(\delta_j - \delta_i)}, & \text{with the HCM;} \\ 0.5, & \text{with PARELLA.} \end{cases} \tag{12}$$

When $\delta_i > \delta_j$, a similar result [exchange $+\infty$ with $-\infty$ in Eq. (12)] can also be observed. These asymptotic probabilities reveal the difference of the three specific models. Asymptotically, with the SSLM, the preference on item i against item j becomes certain, regardless of the locations of the items involved. With the PARELLA, however, the preference on item i against item j becomes totally random, though also regardless of the locations of the items involved. With the HCM, the asymptotic probability is a logistic function of the location difference of the items, which is the Rasch-type probability for pair comparison. This fact again points to the relationship between the HCM and the Rasch model. In summary, the difference in the asymptotic probabilities reflects the difference in the assumptions on the measurements to be carried out, and it provides a guideline in selecting the right model, i.e., one that conforms to the requirement of a particular measurement task within the unfolding framework.

A Framework of Polytomous Probabilistic Models for Unfolding Responses

It is generally suggested that polytomous responses provide more information, compared to dichotomous responses, when the same set of statements is used. The Likert scale is a pervasive example of using polytomous response. However, the development of probabilistic unfolding models for polytomous responses lagged behind the demand that arises from real applications. In past few years, some probabilistic unfolding models for polytomous responses have been individually developed, either as the extension of the HCM or using the rationale similar to what was used in developing the HCM. The general form of polytomous unfolding models described in this section helps to understand the fundamental structure and properties of the unfolding process in the polytomous response format. The general form is constructed by means of the rating formulation with which the threshold form of the Rasch model for polytomous responses is constructed. The rating formulation for general cumulative and single-peaked processes is summarized in the following discussion, but readers may skip it and jump to the paragraph after Eq. (18).

Rating Formulation

In a general context, a polytomous response variable X with possible value $\{0, 1, \ldots, m\}$ can be mapped into an observation of a random dichotomous vector $Z = (Z_1, Z_2, \ldots, Z_m)$ as

$$(Z = (\underbrace{1, 1, \ldots, 1}_{k}, \underbrace{0, 0, \ldots, 0}_{m-k})) \iff (X = k), \quad k = 0, 1, \ldots, m. \tag{13}$$

The collection of possible mapping observations of X to Z is

$$\Omega' = \{(\underbrace{1, 1, \ldots, 1}_{k}, \underbrace{0, 0, \ldots, 0}_{m-k}), \quad k = 0, \ldots, m\}. \tag{14}$$

Let $\Delta = \{0, 1\}$; all the possible outcomes of $Z = (Z_1, Z_2, \ldots, Z_m)$ are

$$\Omega = \underbrace{\Delta \times \Delta \times \cdots \times \Delta}_{m}.$$

It is evident that $\Omega' \subset \Omega$. Let the marginal probabilities of Z_k on Ω be

$$\begin{aligned} p_k &\equiv \Pr\{Z_k = 1\}, \\ q_k &\equiv 1 - p_k = \Pr\{Z_k = 0\}, \quad k = 1, \ldots, m. \end{aligned} \tag{15}$$

Then according to Eq. (13) and the definition of the conditional probability on $\Omega' \subset \Omega$,

$$\Pr\{X=k\} = \Pr\{Z=(\underbrace{1,1,\ldots,1}_{k},\underbrace{0,0,\ldots,0}_{m-k})\,|\,\Omega'\}$$

$$= \frac{\Pr\{Z=(\underbrace{1,1,\ldots,1}_{k},\underbrace{0,0,\ldots,0}_{m-k})\,|\,\Omega\}}{\Pr\{\Omega'\,|\,\Omega\}}$$

$$= \frac{\left(\prod_{l=1}^{k} p_l\right)\left(\prod_{l=k+1}^{m} q_l\right)}{\gamma}, \quad k=0,\ldots,m; \tag{16}$$

where

$$\gamma = \sum_{j=0}^{m}\left(\prod_{l=1}^{j} p_l\right)\left(\prod_{l=j+1}^{m} q_l\right) \tag{17}$$

(when $j=0$, $\prod_{l=1}^{j} p_l$ is defined as 1; when $j=m$, $\prod_{l=j+1}^{m} q_l$ is also defined as 1). Conversely, $\{p_k, k=1,\ldots, m\}$ can be expressed in terms of $\{\Pr\{X=k\}, k=0, 1, \ldots, m\}$. That is, an equivalent expression of Eq. (16) is

$$p_k = \frac{\Pr\{X=k\}}{\Pr\{X=k-1\}+\Pr\{X=k\}}, \quad k=1,\ldots,m;$$
$$\sum_{k=0}^{m}\Pr\{X=k\}=1. \tag{18}$$

In the context of the cumulative process, the rating formulation was first introduced to construct a class of Rasch models for polytomous responses in terms of a set of latent dichotomous Rasch variables. In the context of unfolding modeling, it was applied to construct the general form of probabilistic unfolding model for polytomous responses. If a set of latent dichotomous unfolding variables have the probabilistic functions as specified in the general form for dichotomous unfolding models,

$$p_k = \frac{\Psi(\rho_{ik})}{\Psi(\rho_{ik})+\Psi(\beta_n-\delta_i)},$$
$$q_k = 1-p_k = \frac{\Psi(\beta_n-\delta_i)}{\Psi(\rho_{ik})+\Psi(\beta_n-\delta_i)}. \tag{19}$$

Then according to Eq. (16), a general form for polytomous unfolding responses is expressed as

$$\Pr\{X_{ni}=k\,|\,\beta_n,\delta_i,(\rho_{il})\} = \frac{\left(\prod_{l=1}^{k}\Psi_l(\rho_{il})\right)\left(\prod_{l=k+1}^{m}\Psi_l(\beta_n-\delta_i)\right)}{\lambda_{ni}}, \quad k=0,\ldots,m; \tag{20}$$

where δ_i and β_n are the location parameters for item i and person n, respectively; $\{\rho_{ik}\}$ are the thresholds for item i; and

$$\lambda_{ni} \equiv \gamma_{ni}\prod_{l=1}^{m}[\Psi_l(\rho_{il})+\Psi_l(\beta_n-\delta_i)]$$
$$= \sum_{k=0}^{m}\left(\prod_{l=1}^{k}\Psi_l(\rho_{il})\right)\left(\prod_{l=k+1}^{m}\Psi_l(\beta_n-\delta_i)\right). \tag{21}$$

The essential properties of the general form of probabilistic unfolding models for polytomous responses include that (1) its expectation is a single peaked function of the person location parameter and (2) for each latent dichotomous variable Z_k, if and only if $|\beta_n-\delta_i|=\rho_k$,

$$p_{nik}=\Pr\{Z_k=1\}=\Pr\{Z_k=0\}=q_{nik}=1/2. \tag{22}$$

These two properties confirm that Eq. (20) follows the unfolding process. In particular, when the thresholds are properly ordered,

$$\rho_{i1}>\rho_{i2}>\cdots>\rho_{ik}>\cdots>\rho_{im}, \tag{23}$$

then within each interval formed by adjacent thresholds, the corresponding category has the greatest probability. Figure 6 shows the probabilistic curves for Eq. (20) (in solid lines), together with the curves for the latent dichotomous variables (in dashed lines) (the operational function is the hyperbolic cosine function).

Specified Probabilistic Models for Unfolding Responses

The Simple Square Logistic Model for Polytomous Responses

Let

$$\Psi(t)=\exp(t^2). \tag{24}$$

Then according to Eq. (20),

$$\Pr\{X_{ni}=k\} = \frac{\exp\{\sum_{l=1}^{k}\rho_{il}^2\}\exp\{(m-k)(\beta_n-\delta_i)^2\}}{\lambda_{ni}},$$
$$k=0,1,\ldots,m-1; \tag{25}$$

where

$$\lambda_{ni}=\sum_{k=0}^{m}\exp\left\{\sum_{l=1}^{k}\rho_{il}^2\right\}\exp\{(m-k)(\beta_n-\delta_i)^2\}. \tag{26}$$

The PARELLA Model for Polytomous Responses

Let

$$\Psi(t)=t^2. \tag{27}$$

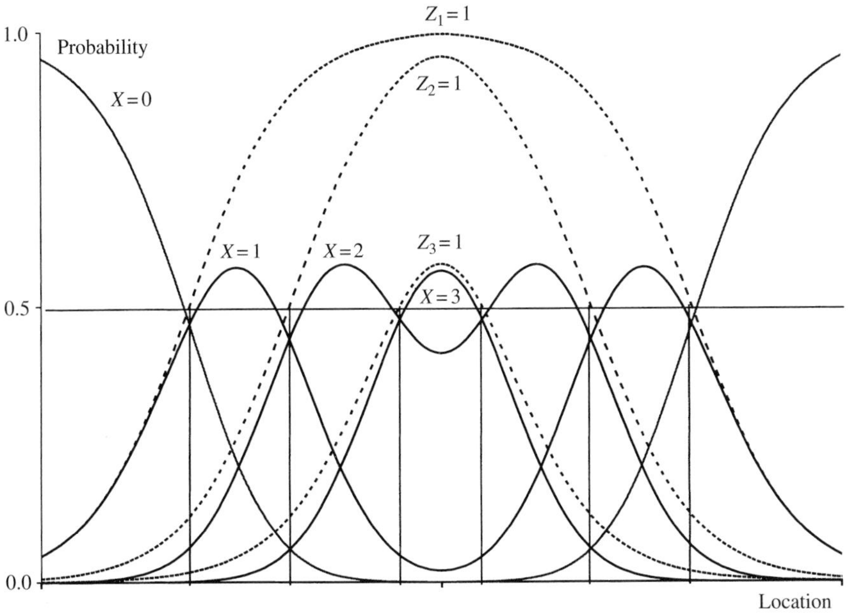

Figure 6 Probabilistic curves of the general unfolding model for polytomous responses.

Then according to Eq. (20),

$$\Pr\{X_{ni}=k\}=(\beta_n-\delta)^{2(m-k)}\prod_{l=1}^{k}\rho_{ik}^2\,/\,\lambda_{ni},\quad k=0,1,\ldots,m-1; \tag{28}$$

where

$$\lambda_{ni}=\sum_{k=0}^{m}(\beta_n-\delta)^{2(m-k)}\prod_{l=1}^{k}\rho_{ik}^2. \tag{29}$$

[For notational convenience, $\beta_n-\delta^{2(m-k)}=1$ when $k=m$, regardless of the value of $(\beta_n-\delta)$.]

The Hyperbolic Cosine Model for Polytomous Responses

Let

$$\Psi(t)=\cosh(t). \tag{30}$$

Then according to Eq. (20),

$$\Pr\{X_{ni}=k\}=[\cosh(\beta_n-\delta)]^{m-k}\prod_{l=1}^{k}\cosh(\rho_{il})/\lambda_{ni},\quad k=0,1,\ldots,m-1; \tag{31}$$

where

$$\lambda_{ni}=\sum_{k=0}^{m}[\cosh(\beta_n-\delta)]^{m-k}\prod_{l=1}^{k}\cosh(\rho_{il}). \tag{32}$$

In addition, it is also known that the general hyperbolic cosine model (GHCM) for polytomous unfolding response and graded unfolding model (GUM), both derived from the Rasch model for polytomous responses, are special cases of Eq. (20). Therefore, all properties held by Eq. (20) apply to these models.

When an Unfolding Model Should Be Used

Compared to the Likert scale, which is still popular in the field of attitude measurement due to its simplicity, the probabilistic models for unfolding responses have advantages: (1) attitudes are identified with latent trait instead of manifest scores, (2) statements and persons are located simultaneously on the attitude continuum, (3) use is made of the development of advanced probability and statistics, in particular as related to parameter estimation and test of fit, and (4) they are operational with modern computing technologies. In attitude measurement or other measures that concern affective perceptions, because the single-peaked or unfolding process is generally implied, use of an unfolding model should be first considered.

However, the cumulative process is also relevant in situations in which the attitudes to be measured indicate degrees of positive affect. For example, it is known in advance that almost all teachers and students in a school think that information technology (IT) is somehow useful. If the purpose is to investigate to what extent teachers and students are positive toward IT use in the school, the use of the cumulative model is appropriate. Items such as “Computers are necessary in the library,” “Computers are necessary in each classroom,” and “Each student in the class should be equipped with a computer”

Table I Comparison of Response Patterns for Cumulative and Unfolding Processes

	Scalogram item						*Parallelogram item*					
Person	*1*	*2*	*3*	*4*	*5*	*6*	*1*	*2*	*3*	*4*	*5*	*6*
1	0	0	0	0	0	0	1	1	0	0	0	0
2	1	0	0	0	0	0	1	1	1	0	0	0
3	1	1	0	0	0	0	0	1	1	1	0	0
4	1	1	1	0	0	0	0	1	1	1	1	0
5	1	1	1	1	0	0	0	0	0	1	1	1
6	1	1	1	1	1	0	0	0	0	0	1	1
7	1	1	1	1	1	1	0	0	0	0	0	1

Table II Structure of the Correlation Coefficient Matrix Confirming the Unfolding Processes

	Item					
Item	*1*	*2*	*3*	*4*	*5*	*6*
1	1.0	+	+	–	–	–
2	+	1.0	+	+	–	–
3	+	+	1.0	+	+	–
4	–	+	+	1.0	+	+
5	–	–	+	+	1.0	+
6	–	–	–	+	+	1.0

are all positive toward the use of IT, but clearly to different degrees. If the cumulative process is applied, the ideal deterministic structure will have a typical pattern, as shown in the first scalogram block in Table I. That is, all items present positive attitudes toward the topic, but to different degrees. A person agrees only to statements with locations lower than that of the person. However, where the attitudes are expected to range from highly negative, through neutral, to highly positive affect, the use of the unfolding process is justified. For example, the use of capital punishment creates a big debate among the general population. Statements reflecting a positive attitude (e.g., "Capital punishment gives the criminal what he deserves") as well as those presenting negative attitude ('Capital punishment is one of the most hideous practices of our time") are needed to cover the whole range of attitude intensity toward capital punishment. If the unfolding process is applied, the ideal deterministic structure will have the typical parallelogram pattern shown in Table I. That is, different items provoke different attitudes (from extremely negative to extremely positive). A person agrees only to statements with locations close to that of the person. Table I shows both patterns when the responses are dichotomous (0 = disagree, 1 = agree) with persons and items are sorted according to their locations (from lowest to highest).

It can be demonstrated that if a general framework of unfolding models [Eq. (8) for dichotomous responses or Eq. (20) for polytomous responses] is applied, the data collected should be essentially in the structure of parallelogram with random variations. This fact can be used after data collection to check if the unfolding process is actually in place. However, it involves ordering items and persons by their locations, which is hardly feasible before the analysis of the data. Nevertheless, the correlation coefficients between the responses on pairs of statements can be used to examine whether the selected process is operating. If the cumulative process is applied, the correlation coefficients should all be positive. If the structure of the data follows the frameworks of unfolding models described in this article, the structure of the correlation coefficient matrix should be as in Table II. The construction of Table II only involves ordering of items by their locations. It is often possible to roughly map out the relative locations of the statements involved according to the conceptual understanding of the statements. Therefore, looking into the correlation coefficient matrix is often used for the purpose of confirming the response process.

It is stressed here that the difference in the structures of the correlation coefficient matrices for the two different response processes is meaningful only in situations when the latent trait continuum involved is unidimensional—that is, the location of an item or a person is described by a real number. In these unidimensional situations, the factor analysis or principal component analysis on these two types of correlation coefficient matrices will produce different results. When the cumulative process is applied, because the correlation coefficients between pairs of items are positive, only one major principal component (factor) will be found and the loadings of all items to this component are positive. When the structure of the data follows an unfolding process, however, two major factors will be found, with the first factor pointing to the items' directions (positive or negative) and the second pointing to the degrees to which the item location is close to the origin (neutral point of the continuum). Therefore, factor analysis could be used for the purpose of detecting the violation of the desirable response process.

See Also the Following Articles

Likert Scale Analysis • Thurstone, L.L.

Further Reading

Andrich, D. (1988). The application of an unfolding model of the PIRT type to the measurement of attitude. *Appl. Psychol. Measure.* **12,** 33–51.

Andrich, D., and Luo, G. (1993). A hyperbolic cosine latent trait model for unfolding dichotomous single-stimulus responses. *Appl. Psychol. Measure.* **17,** 253–276.

Coombs, C. H. (1964). *A Theory of Data.* Wiley, New York.

Hoijtink, H. (1990). A latent trait model for dichotomous choice data. *Psychometrika* **55,** 641–656.

Luo, G. (1998). A general formulation of unidimensional unfolding and pairwise preference models: Making explicit the latitude of acceptance. *J. Math. Psychol.* **42,** 400–417.

Luo, G. (2001). A class of probabilistic unfolding models for polytomous responses. *J. Math. Psychol.* **45,** 224–248.

Michell, J. (1994). Measuring dimensions of belief by unidimensional unfolding. *J. Math. Psychol.* **38,** 244–273.

Roberts, J. S., and Laughlin, J. E. (1996). A unidimensional item response model for unfolding responses from graded disagree–agree response scale. *Appl. Psychol. Measure.* **20,** 231–255.

van Schuur, W. H., and Kiers, H. A. L. (1994). Why factor analysis often is the incorrect model for analyzing bipolar concepts, and what model to use instead. *Appl. Psychol. Measure.* **18**(2), 97–110.

Verhelst, H. D., and Verstralen, H. H. F. M. (1993). A stochastic unfolding model derived from partial credit model. *Kwant. Methoden.* **42,** 93–108.

Galton, Sir Francis

Nicholas W. Gillham
Duke University, Durham, North Carolina, USA

Glossary

correlation The statistical technique that measures and describes the relationship between two variables. The method was invented by Francis Galton, who stated that correlation "was a very wide subject indeed. It exists wherever the variations of two objects are in part due to common causes."

eugenics Defined by Francis Galton as dealing with "questions bearing on what is termed in Greek, *eugenes*, namely, good in stock, hereditarily endowed with noble qualities."

ogive Used by Galton in 1875 to describe the shape of the curve obtained when graphing the inverse normal cumulative distribution function, which has a sinuous shape similar to that of an ogee molding.

regression Used to characterize the manner in which one set of variables (for example, on the *Y* axis of a graph) changes as the other set of variables (for example, on the *X* axis of that graph) changes. For Francis Galton, who invented regression analysis, regression was more a biological problem than a statistical one. Regression to the mean, which he observed in sweet peas and in anthropometric measurements, meant that the underlying hereditary processes were always driving metric characters such as height or weight back toward the mean and would effectively counterbalance natural selection.

Sir Francis Galton (1822–1911) is undoubtedly best remembered as the father and chief cheerleader of the eugenics movement. Because of the great breadth of his interests, Galton has sometimes been called a dilettante. However, his research and published work actually are grouped around two central themes. During the first part of his career, Galton focused on African exploration, geography, and travel writing. He also became interested in meteorology, a natural extension of his interests in exploration and geography, and he constructed retrospective weather maps that led to his discovery of the anticyclone. The second part of Galton's career opened when he read *On the Origin of Species* by his cousin Charles Darwin. He concluded that it might be possible to improve the quality of the human race by selective breeding. He recognized that if what he called "talent and character" were heritable, this should be apparent from pedigree analysis. Hence, he attempted to assess the inheritance of these qualities in the pedigrees of famous men and by comparing qualitative similarities and differences between identical and nonidentical twins. He also made composite photographs of men with similar occupations, whether in crime or in military service, to see whether they shared common facial characteristics. Anyone interested in fingerprinting will soon come across Galton's name, for he was responsible for establishing proper criteria for their identification and also for making a famous calculation suggesting that the probability that two fingerprints from different individuals will match is very low. He also collected great quantities of anthropometric data, probably hoping that this information might relate to "talent and character." Last, he is remembered in psychology for his pioneering studies of mental imagery.

Counting and Measuring

A defining characteristic of all of the work of Sir Francis Galton (1822–1911) was his use of quantitative methods, whether they related to planning for the correct amounts of supplies for his African expedition, the number of fidgets members of an audience made during a scientific presentation, or anthropometry. To analyze these data, Galton made use of existing statistical tools, rudimentary at best, and developed important new ones such as regression and correlation analysis. Galton was passionate about quantitative data and development of new statistical methods for data analysis; he played a central role in founding of the field of biometry.

Establishing the exact point at which Francis Galton became interested in quantitative methods is not possible, but his enthusiasm for mathematics clearly blossomed in 1840 while he was a medical student at King's College in London. His cousin, Charles Darwin, was living nearby. Darwin had also begun his career as a medical student, but at Edinburgh rather than King's College. Darwin hated medicine and eventually wound up at Cambridge. There he was befriended by John Stevens Henslow, a professor of botany, and the *Beagle* voyage followed. Darwin, 13 years older than Galton, newly married, and a recently elected Fellow of the Royal Society, had recently published his *Beagle Journal.* He appears to have been instrumental in stimulating Galton to transfer to Cambridge. Darwin also helped Galton to argue successfully with his father in favor of this move. At Trinity College, Cambridge, Galton's plan was to study for honors in mathematics. In order to improve his chances of succeeding in the mathematics Tripos, Galton took advantage of private tutors or coaches. These were often exceptionally gifted men who did not wish to lead the monastic (and celibate) life of a don. One such coach was William Hopkins, the greatest of the early Victorian mathematics tutors. However, Galton suffered something akin to a nervous breakdown. It also became clear to Hopkins that Galton did not have sufficient talent to succeed as an honors graduate in mathematics, so Galton took an ordinary degree from Cambridge. Nevertheless, for the rest of his life, he was in awe of talented mathematicians and of Cambridge.

After Cambridge, Galton planned to return to his medical studies at King's College, but his father died and Galton, lacking a compass to direct him, spent the next few years in travel and sport. Little is known about this period of Galton's life, with the exception of his journey up the Nile with friends, which was followed by an excursion to the Middle East. Suddenly, in 1849, Galton decided to mount an expedition in South Africa to Lake Ngami, recently discovered by David Livingstone. This expedition did not reach Lake Ngami, but represented the first European exploration of northern Namibia; the details are of concern here primarily as they relate to Galton's passion for quantification. This was evident in the exceptionally careful way in which Galton determined the quantities of supplies that he needed to take with him and in the careful measurements he made of latitudes, longitudes, and temperatures. The leadership of the Royal Geographical Society, which had sponsored Galton's expedition, was so impressed that it awarded him one of the two gold medals the organization presented annually; a year before David Livingstone was so honored. The reason was that Galton, unlike Livingstone, had provided quantitative data to accompany the report of his expedition.

Galton next wrote articles and two books on travel. One of these, a classic called *Art of Travel*, reprinted as recently as 2001, is filled with practical tips for surviving in the bush. In the book, Galton's penchant for numbers also bubbles up time and again. For instance, he discusses the loads different pack animals should be able to carry over long distances, how the outstretched hand and arm can be used as a substitute for a sextant, and the calculations that should be made on becoming "lost." Subsequently, Galton served for many years on the Council of the Royal Geographical Society, where he consistently badgered different explorers for quantitative data. Livingstone got so mad at one point that he complained to Roderick Murchison, the society president, "Put Arrowsmith [the cartographer, John Arrowsmith] and Galton in a hogshead and ask them to take bearings out of the bunghole. I came for discovery and not for survey and if I don't give a clear account of the countries traversed, I shall return the money." Galton's passion for analyzing quantitative data made him instantly receptive to the possibilities provided by the normal distribution and led to his discovery of the important statistical concepts of regression and correlation.

The Normal Distribution

At the time Galton was introduced to the normal distribution by his old friend William Spottiswoode: the distribution, which came from astronomy, was known as the error curve, and was referred to as such during Galton's lifetime. Spottiswoode combined an interest in geography and mathematics with the business of running an important family printing firm. In 1861, Spottiswoode published a paper in which he attempted to fit the normal curve to the distribution of direction of orientation of 11 mountain ranges, to see if they possessed a common pattern. Although the fit was somewhat questionable, Spottiswoode was enthusiastic about the results. Galton must have been familiar with the paper and, when Spottiswoode reviewed the properties of the normal distribution with his friend, Galton was delighted by "the far-reaching applications of that extraordinarily beautiful law which I fully apprehended." Galton was by then interested in human heredity and had written a two-part article entitled "Hereditary Talent and Character," which he published in *Macmillan's Magazine* in 1865. The publication of *On the Origin of Species* by Darwin in 1859 had sparked his interest in this subject and he soon became convinced that human ability was probably a hereditary attribute. But how was he to show this? His starting point was to examine the male relatives of famous men using a kind of partial pedigree analysis. He predicted that if "talent and character" were heritable, the closest male relatives (i.e., fathers and sons) were more likely to be talented than were more distant relatives. He recognized that environment might play a role too, but argued that environmental contributions were negligible in contrast to the role heredity played.

Soon after Galton and Spottiswoode had discussed the properties of the normal distribution, Galton began to study the work of the Belgian astronomer, Adolph Quetelet, who was also an able statistician and population biologist. Quetelet's first attempt in this regard was to compare the actual and theoretical distributions of chest measurements for 5738 Scottish soldiers. The agreement was good and Galton was impressed. The papers published in *Macmillan's* served as precursors for Galton's 1869 book *Hereditary Genius: An Inquiry into Its Laws and Consequences*, in which he presented much more extensive pedigree analysis for large groups of men having different talents (e.g., judges, statesmen, and soldiers). It is reasonable to ask why women were excluded from Galton's pedigrees of the famous: in fact, he does list some notable women in the tables he used to summarize pedigrees of the prominent. However, the nature of Victorian society was such that most occupations and professions were closed to women, so Galton had no way of assessing their abilities in a systematic fashion.

In *Hereditary Genius*, Galton also made use of the normal distribution for the first time. As he did not actually have quantitative data for height, he constructed a theoretical normal distribution for this parameter, which he showed in the book. He cited Quetelet's data on the chest measurements of Scottish soldiers and the heights of French conscripts as evidence that observation fit expectation. But how was Galton to measure mental ability? He decided to see whether examination marks for admission to the Royal Military College at Sandhurst fit a normal distribution. He used only the statistics for 1868, and the data revealed a clear normal distribution at the upper tail and the center, but there were no low scores to fill out the distribution, because the numbers had either been eliminated or those likely to have low scores had eschewed competition. In *Hereditary Genius*, Galton also published a table (Fig. 1) in which he attempted assess the distribution of "ability" in the British male population, which he estimated to be 15 million. He then employed a numerical value he had earlier obtained for men of reputation (~1 in 4000) to establish his highest and lowest (idiots and imbeciles) grades of natural ability; Galton used a Gaussian distribution to calculate the expected number of individuals in each of 12 classes intermediate between the high and low ends.

Galton later invented a new statistical tool. He wished to design a metric that would permit him to arrange any set of measurements on a single statistical scale. He found that if he graphed his data in a series of ranks according to the exponential function that describes the normal

CLASSIFICATION OF MEN ACCORDING TO THEIR NATURAL GIFTS.

Grades of natural ability, separated by equal intervals.		Numbers of men comprised in the several grades of natural ability, whether in respect to their general powers, or to special aptitudes.							
		Proportionate, viz. one in.	In each million of the same age.	In total male population of the United Kingdom, viz. 15 millions, of the under mentioned ages:-					
Below average.	Above average.			20–30	30–40	40–50	50–60	60–70	70–80
a	A	4	256,791	651,000	495,000	391,000	268,000	171,000	77,000
b	B	6	162,279	409,000	312,000	246,000	168,000	107,000	48,000
c	C	16	63,563	161,000	123,000	97,000	66,000	42,000	19,000
d	D	64	15,696	39,800	30,300	23,900	16,400	10,400	4,700
e	E	413	2,423	6,100	4,700	3,700	2,520	1,600	729
f	F	4,300	233	590	450	355	243	155	70
g	G	79,000	14	35	27	21	15	9	4
x all grades below g	X all grades above G	1,000,000	1	3	2	2	2	–	–
On either side of average			500,000	1,268,000	964,000	761,000	521,000	332,000	149,000
Total, both sides			1,000,000	2,536,000	1,928,000	1,522,000	1,042,000	664,000	298,020

Figure 1 The table published in 1869, in Galton's *Hereditary Genius: An Inquiry into Its Laws and Consequences*, showing Galton's attempt to assess the distribution of "ability" in the British male population. Below the table in the original publication, it was explained that "the proportions of men living at different ages are calculated from the proportions that are true for England and Wales." The data were credited to the 1861 census. Redrawn from Galton (1869).

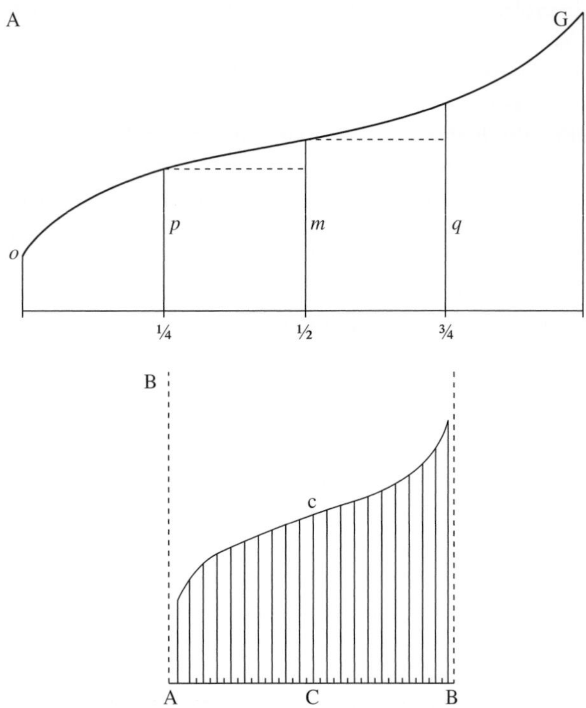

Figure 2 Redrawings of two of Galton's original renditions of the ogive. (A) The earlier drawing, from 1875, shows the median and the quartiles. (B) The later drawing, from 1883, shows spikes with heights representing 21 equally spaced ideal data values. Redrawn from Stigler (1986).

distribution, he obtained a graceful, sinuous curve that was convex at the top and concave at the bottom (Fig. 2). He christened this curve the "ogive," appropriating an architectural term with several meanings, one of which is a molding (an ogee) with the same shape of his curve. The distribution could be divided into quartiles; the middlemost would have a value of 0 (representing the average) whereas an individual in the upper quartile would have a value of 1 (representing one probable error above the mean), etc. Galton's ogive, now known as the inverse normal cumulative distribution function, is one of the most used and abused methods of scaling psychological tests. The terms "quartile" and "median" are also Galton's.

Regression

Not only was Galton interested in applying the normal distribution to continuously varying traits such as height, but he also wanted to study the heritability of such traits. Although he was particularly interested in examining anthropometric data, initially he lacked appropriate data, so, on the advice of Darwin and the botanist Joseph Hooker, Galton turned to a model system, sweet peas. He cited three reasons. Sweet peas had little tendency to cross-fertilize, they were hardy and prolific, and seed weight was not affected by humidity. Galton planted his first experimental crop at Kew in 1874, but the crop failed. In order to avoid this outcome the following year, he dispensed seed packets widely to friends throughout Great Britain. The packets were labeled K, L, M, N, O, P, and Q, with K containing the heaviest seeds, L, the next heaviest, and so forth down to packet Q. Galton obtained fairly complete results from the progeny of 490 carefully weighed seeds. His discovery was that "the processes concerned in simple descent are those of Family Variability and Reversion." By simple descent, Galton meant self-fertilization. Family variability referred to the degree of variation around the mean observed among progeny seeds irrespective of whether they were large, small, or average in size. Although the means of the distributions shifted to some extent between different sets of progeny, the degree of variation around the mean was similar for all. By reversion Galton meant "the tendency of that ideal mean type to depart from the parental type, 'reverting' towards" the mean of the parental population from which the parental seeds were selected. He then drew a diagram that plotted the seed diameter of progeny seeds on the y axis and parental seeds on the x axis, thereby constructing the first regression line (Fig. 3).

At first, Galton referred to the slope of the line as the coefficient of reversion, but then changed this to regression. Later, with aid of partial pedigree data he obtained from his anthropometric laboratory, established in connection with the International Health Exhibition held in London in 1884, Galton was able to show that regression to the mean applied to human stature as well (Table I). This was to have a profound effect on Galton's view of the evolutionary process because Galton believed that regression to the mean would thwart the action of natural selection and that this would create a major problem for Darwin's theory of the origin of species. Hence, Galton supposed that evolution must proceed in discontinuous steps that could not be reversed by regression to the mean. The utility of regression analysis and the regression coefficient as statistical techniques was later recognized by Galton and others, but initially this was of strictly secondary importance to Galton, for whom the evolutionary and, hence, hereditary implications of regression to the mean were of primary significance.

Correlation

There are two accounts of how Galton came upon the idea of correlation. Sadly, the more romantic of these, which envisions Galton as having the notion while seeking refuge from a shower in a reddish recess in a rock near the side of a pathway on the grounds of Naworth Castle, is probably wrong. The plausible, and more believable, account is that Galton was working one day, using his anthropometric

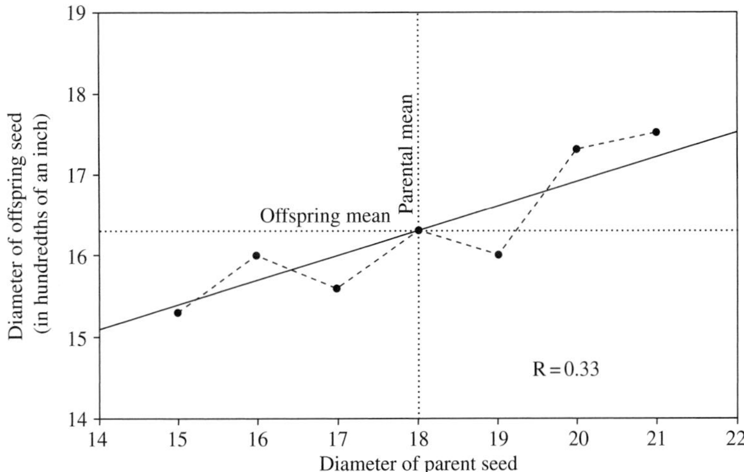

Figure 3 A redrawing of the first regression line for inheritance of size in sweet pea seeds that was presented by Francis Galton at a Royal Institution lecture in 1877. From Pearson (1930).

Table I Number of Adult Children of Various Statures Born of 205 Mid-parents of Various Statures[a]

Height of mid-parents (inches)	*Height of adult children (inches)*														*Total number of*		
	Below	*62.2*	*63.2*	*64.2*	*65.2*	*66.2*	*67.2*	*68.2*	*69.2*	*70.2*	*71.2*	*72.2*	*73.2*	*Above*	*Adult children*	*Mid-parents*	*Median*
Above	—	—	—	—	—	—	—	—	—	—	—	1	3	—	4	5	—
72.5	—	—	—	—	—	—	—	1	2	1	2	7	2	4	19	6	72.2
71.5	—	—	—	—	1	3	4	3	5	10	4	9	2	2	43	11	69.9
70.5	1	—	1	—	1	1	3	12	18	14	7	4	3	3	68	22	69.5
69.5	—	—	1	16	4	17	27	20	33	25	20	11	4	5	183	41	68.9
68.5	1	—	7	11	16	25	31	34	48	21	18	4	3	—	219	49	68.2
67.5	—	3	5	14	15	36	38	28	38	10	11	4	—	—	211	33	67.6
66.5	—	3	3	5	2	17	17	14	13	4	—	—	—	—	78	20	67.2
65.5	1	—	9	5	7	11	11	7	7	5	2	1	—	—	66	12	66.7
64.5	1	1	4	4	1	5	5	—	2	—	—	—	—	—	23	5	65.8
Below	1	—	2	4	1	2	2	1	1	—	—	—	—	—	14	1	—
Totals	5	7	32	59	48	117	138	120	167	99	64	41	17	14	928	205	—
Medians	—	—	66.3	67.8	67.9	67.7	67.9	68.3	68.5	69.0	69.0	70.0	—	—	—	—	—

[a] All female heights have been multiplied by 1.08. In calculating the medians, the entries have been taken as referring to the middle of the squares in which they stand. The reason why the headings run 62.2, 63.2, etc., instead of 62.5, 63.5 etc., is that the observations are unequally distributed between 62 and 63, 63 and 64, etc., there being a strong bias in favor of integral inches. This inequality was not apparent in the case of the mid-parents. From Galton (1886).

data to plot forearm length against height, when he noticed that the problem was essentially the same as that of kinship. He summarized these data in 1888 in a table in one of his most important papers "Co-relations and Their Measurements, Chiefly from Anthropometric Data." Galton extended his correlation data to head breadth versus head length, head breadth versus head height, etc. He also calculated the first set of correlation coefficients, using the familiar symbol r. Most of his values for r were quite high, between 0.7 and 0.9.

Natural Inheritance and the Birth of Biometrics

Galton's paper on correlation, coupled with what is probably his most important book, *Natural Inheritance*, published in 1889, led to the foundation of the field of biometrics. *Natural Inheritance* synthesized much of the work that Galton had done on heredity, anthropometrics, and statistics. From the viewpoint of this article, its chapters on statistics and their application are of most importance. Galton showed his readers how to apply statistical tools to their data by using illustrations from the anthropometric data he had collected. Regression was also discussed, but not correlation; Galton seems to have discovered this statistic after *Natural Inheritance* went to press. He then applied his statistical techniques to human traits such as stature and eye color, and, more fancifully, to artistic ability and disease.

During his long career, Galton had not attracted disciples, but his paper on correlation and *Natural Inheritance* changed that. It is true that prior to the publication of these works, one important British statistician, Francis Ysidro Edgeworth, had been influenced by Galton, but Galton's most important disciples, at least from the viewpoint of statistics and quantitative analysis of biometrical data, were Raphael Weldon, a zoologist, and Karl Pearson, who was able to add to statistical analysis a mathematical rigor that was beyond Galton's reach. Pearson, a mathematics graduate of King's College, Cambridge, had been appointed the Goldsmid Professor of Applied Mathematics and Mechanics at University College, London in 1884. Weldon, originally trained in zoology and morphology at St. John's College, Cambridge, was appointed university lecturer in morphology at St. John's in 1884. Weldon's interest in invertebrate morphology rapidly diminished in favor of quantitative analyses of parameters such as carapace length in samples of the common shrimp, *Crangon vulgaris*. He was quick to recognize the significance of the statistical treatments laid out in *Natural Inheritance* and Galton's correlation paper, and was soon in touch with Galton, who helped him with the statistical analysis of his data, especially as it applied to calculating correlation coefficients. Before long, Weldon and Pearson got to know each other and became fast friends. In 1891, Weldon was appointed a professor at University College, London, where he collaborated with Pearson not only on biometric research, but also on matters relating to university politics. In 1901, largely in a reaction against the nonquantitative geneticist, William Bateson, whom Pearson felt had prevented publication of an important paper submitted to the Royal Society, Pearson and Weldon founded the journal *Biometrika*, with Galton as an advisor. Thus, the science of biometrics was born. Toward the end of his life, Galton endowed a professorship in eugenics at University College. In 1911, the year of Galton's death, Pearson was appointed the first Galton Professor of Eugenics, a position he would hold until 1933, when he was replaced by another great biometrician, R. A. Fisher. The Galton professorship and its predecessor, the Galton Laboratory for the Study of National Eugenics, have long since shed their association with eugenics, and instead have built a reputation for distinction in human genetics.

See Also the Following Articles

Correlations • Eugenics

Further Reading

Bulmer, M. (1999). The development of Francis Galton's ideas on the mechanism of heredity. *J. Hist. Biol.* **32,** 263–292.

Burbridge, D. (2001). Francis Galton on twins, heredity and social class. *Br. J. Hist. Sci.* **34,** 323–340.

Cowan, R. S. (1972). Francis Galton's statistical ideas: The influence of eugenics. *Isis* **63,** 509–598.

Crow, J. F. (1993). Francis Galton: Count and measure, measure and count. *Genetics* **135,** 1–4.

Darwin, C. R. (1859). *On the Origin of Species by Means of Natural Selection, or the Preservation of Favored Races in the Struggle for Life.* Murray, London.

Forrest, D. W. (1974). *Francis Galton: The Life and Work of a Victorian Genius.* Taplinger, New York.

Galton, F. (1865). Hereditary talent and character. *Macmillan's Mag.* **12,** 157–166, 318–327.

Galton, F. (1869). *Hereditary Genius: An Inquiry into its Laws and Consequences.* Macmillan, London.

Galton, F. (1875). Statistics by intercomparison, with remarks on the law of frequency of error. *Philosoph. Mag.* [4th series] **49,** 33–46.

Galton, F. (1883). *Inquiries into Human Faculty and Its Development.* Macmillan, London.

Galton, F. (1886). Regression towards mediocrity in hereditary stature. *J. Anthropol. Inst.* **15,** 246–263.

Galton, F. (1888). Co-relations and their measurements, chiefly from anthropometric data. *Proc. R. Soc. London, Ser. B* **182,** 1–23.

Galton, F. (1889). Presidential address. *J. Anthropol. Inst.* **18,** 401–419 [see p. 403].

Galton, F. (1889). *Natural Inheritance.* Macmillan, London.

Galton, F. (2001). *The Art of Travel; or Shifts and Contrivances Available in Wild Countries,* 5th Ed. [reprint]. London, Phoenix Press.

Gillham, N. W. (2001). *A Life of Sir Francis Galton: From African Exploration to the Birth of Eugenics.* Oxford University Press, New York.

Gillham, N. W. (2001). Sir Francis Galton and the birth of eugenics. *Annu. Rev. Genet.* **35,** 83–101.

Gillham, N. W. (2001). Evolution by jumps: Francis Galton and William Bateson and the mechanism of evolutionary change. *Genetics* **159,** 1383–1392.

Pearson, K. (1914). *The Life, Letters, and Labours of Francis Galton.* Vol. I. Cambridge University Press, Cambridge,

Pearson, K. (1924). *The Life, Letters, and Labours of Francis Galton.* Vol. II. Cambridge University Press, Cambridge,

Pearson, K. (1930). *The Life, Letters, and Labours of Francis Galton.* Vol. III. Cambridge University Press, Cambridge,

Porter, T. (1986). *The Rise of Statistical Thinking.* Princeton University Press, Princeton, NJ.

Stigler, S. M. (1986). *The History of Statistics: The Measurement of Uncertainty before 1900.* Belknap/Harvard University Press, Cambridge, MA.

Stigler, S. M. (1995). Galton and identification by fingerprints. *Genetics* **140,** 857–860.

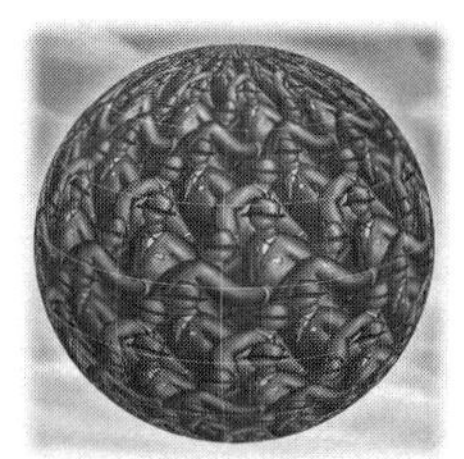

Gambling Studies

Garry J. Smith
University of Alberta, Edmonton, Alberta, Canada

Glossary

chasing An attempt to recoup gambling losses by playing longer, playing more frequently, and/or increasing bet size.

continuous gambling format Any wagering event for which there is a short time interval between placing the bet, playing the game, and learning the outcome.

gambling The act of risking money, property, or something of value on an event for which the outcome is uncertain.

pathological gambling A mental disorder that includes the following essential features: (1) a continuous or periodic loss of control over gambling, (2) a progression in gambling frequency and in the amounts wagered, in the preoccupation with gambling, and in the acquisition of monies with which to gamble, and (3) a continuation of gambling involvement despite adverse consequences.

problem gambling Behavior related to gambling that creates negative consequences for the gambler, for others in his/her social network, or for the community.

A number of prominent social science methodologies are used in the field of gambling studies. Among researchers and scholars, there are debates over the proper terminology to describe problem gambling and over the best practices for determining accurate problem-gambling prevalence rates in general population surveys. Approaches to social measurement of gambling behavior include qualitative, longitudinal, public policy, and sociohistorical analyses.

Introduction

What Are Gambling Studies?

Gambling is a basic human activity dating back to ancient times and found in nearly all cultures through the ages. Although the gambling urge is nearly universal, the public mind-set toward gambling varies considerably among societies, and changes over time within societies. Humankind's experience with gambling shows that the activity has been variously regarded as a sin, a vice, an unfortunate but tolerable weakness of human nature, an evolutionarily appropriate behavior, an adult form of play, a buffer to existential anxieties caused by chance events, and a teacher and mirror of cultural values. Congruent with the global proliferation of legalized gambling over the past few decades, gambling studies have emerged as a multidisciplinary research thrust, focusing on enhancing our understanding of the role that gambling plays in society. Gambling studies encompass diverse academic disciplines such as medicine, psychology, economics, law, business, political science, mathematics, sociology, history, and the humanities, and are fundamentally concerned with explaining the ubiquity and persistence of gambling activity, the behavior patterns of gambling participants, and the personal, social, economic, and cultural consequences of widespread gambling.

Gambling studies research is published in mainstream academic journals; however, the preponderance of academic literature in this field is found in specialized journals, including *International Gambling Studies*, *Journal of Gambling Studies*, *Gaming Law Review*, and *Electronic Journal of Gambling Issues*, and in published conference proceedings and government and research institute reports.

Overview

Gambling-related social science has concentrated more on perceived deviant aspects of the activity than on its normative dimensions and has featured methodologies that include survey, sociohistorical, ethnographic, public policy analysis, and longitudinal perspectives. This article highlights the prominent measures and methods used by social scientists to study the phenomenon of gambling. Included in the analysis are rationales for and descriptions and limitations of the representative methods and measures used.

Problem-Gambling Prevalence Research

Rationale for Gambling Studies

Legislative blessing for gambling is based on the premise that the social good of the activity outweighs any negative outcomes. A problem with this presumption is that most of the benefits of gambling are tangible and easily quantifiable in economic terms, whereas the costs to society are often hidden, indirect, not immediately noticeable, and are impossible to measure precisely. The costs alluded to are burdens that problem gamblers impose on other citizens who gamble responsibly or who do not partake in gambling at all. In order to justify offering legal gambling, governments must allay citizens' concerns that the social costs of the activity are not overly onerous. One way this is done is through problem-gambling prevalence surveys. Such surveys have been completed in nearly one-half of the American states, in 9 of the 10 Canadian provinces, and in several overseas jurisdictions. The object of problem-gambling prevalence surveys is to identify accurately the percentages of individuals in a population with and without the disorder. Generally, the higher the percentage of problem and at-risk gamblers in a population, the higher the social costs of gambling and the greater the need for public policy to ameliorate the situation. For example, in making decisions about funding prevention and treatment services for problem gamblers, legislators need sound estimates of the numbers in the general population who require help for their out-of-control gambling, their demographic profiles, and the likelihood that they will use these services if they are made available.

Semantic Differences

A variety of terms have been applied to individuals whose out-of-control gambling has an adverse effect on their lives and creates harms for those around them (e.g., family, friends, and co-workers) and for society in general. The term often employed by lay audiences and Gamblers Anonymous (GA) members is "compulsive"; however, researchers and problem-gambling treatment specialists avoid this term on the grounds that the label implies that the individual is participating in an unenjoyable activity. Because gambling can be a pleasing activity, even for those who later develop problems, terminology inferring compulsiveness is considered a misnomer.

"Problem gambling" is used by both lay and professional audiences to specify all of the patterns of gambling behavior that compromise, disrupt, or damage personal, family, or vocational pursuits, and covers a continuum from moderate-risk to seriously out-of-control gamblers. Psychiatrists and mental health therapists prefer the term "pathological," which incorporates several assumptions basic to the medical perspective of aberrant gambling, including the notion that pathological gambling is a chronic and progressive disorder and a conviction that there is a clear distinction between a pathological and a social gambler.

Based on the imprecise terminology used to describe out-of-control gambling and the methodological chaos this creates, use of the label "disordered gambling" has been recommended for the following reasons: (1) disordered gambling embraces all of the previously used terms, and (2) a disorder suggests a wide range of gradually shifting behavior. Semantic differences pertaining to uncontrolled gambling continue to confound gambling studies scholars, because no clear-cut choice has emerged; however, "problem gambling" and "disordered gambling" are the terms with the most academic currency at the moment.

Measuring Problem Gambling

The Diagnostic and Statistical Manual of Mental Disorders

After several years of advocacy by problem-gambling treatment specialist Dr. Robert Custer, the 1980 (third) edition of *Diagnostic and Statistical Manual of Mental Disorders* (DSM-III) provided the first official diagnostic criteria for pathological gambling. Classified as an "impulse control disorder," the inclusion of pathological gambling in the American Psychiatric Association publication dramatically altered social attitudes toward out-of-control gambling. Although not officially considered an addiction, pathological gambling was often treated as such by researchers and therapists. With two exceptions ("chasing" and "bailout"), the DSM-III pathological gambling criteria were similar to those used for diagnosing substance and drug dependence. The association between pathological gambling and addiction was further highlighted when "tolerance" and "withdrawal" were included as pathological gambling criteria in the 1994 revised DSM-IV. The fact that pathological gambling was considered a disease or a medical condition challenged the prevailing legal perception of pathological gambling as a vice, and has impacted the justice system in terms of proving culpability, assigning responsibility, and determining type and length of sentencing, when problem gambling is used as a mitigating factor to explain criminal behavior.

The South Oaks Gambling Screen

Several years after publication of the DSM-III pathological gambling criteria, an instrument based on these diagnostic criteria, the South Oaks Gambling Screen (SOGS), quickly became the lead assessment tool for diagnosing and identifying out-of-control gamblers. Although designed and tested for clinical use, the SOGS also became the instrument of choice for estimating problem-gambling prevalence rates in the general population. The SOGS is a 20-item, dichotomous (yes/no) response scale that asks respondents about gambling patterns, behaviors, and impacts that gambling has on their lives. A SOGS score can range from 0 to 20, and cutoff points are used to distinguish between three gambler subtypes: nonproblem (SOGS score of 0, 1, or 2), problem (SOGS score of 3 or 4), and probable pathological (SOGS score of 5 or higher). One advantage of the SOGS is its comparability both across and within jurisdictions; however, challenges have been made regarding its efficacy in nonclinical settings, including the charges that (1) SOGS is an accurate measure in a clinical situation, where the prevalence of the disorder is high, but is less sensitive in population studies, where base rates of problem gambling are much lower; (2) the imprecision of SOGS in population studies leads to classification errors (either false positives or false negatives) that compromise the validity of the scale; (3) SOGS has not been validated for use with special populations (e.g., adolescents and various ethnic groupings); and (4) because of the wider dispersion of legal gambling, prevalence surveys in the early 1990s showed the demographic profile of problem gamblers was changing to include more females and middle income individuals. Consequently, some SOGS items have been considered less than appropriate. For example, SOGS items relating to borrowing from loan sharks or liquidating stocks or securities might pertain to middle-aged, middle-income males, but less so to young males and middle-aged females experiencing problems in controlling their gambling behavior.

The 1994 DSM-IV Problem-Gambling Criteria

As a result of empirical research findings and rigorous statistical testing, new pathological gambling criteria were adopted for the 1994 DSM-IV (Table I). Pathological gambling was then considered to be persistent and recurrent maladaptive gambling behavior as indicated by a positive response to ≥ 5 of the 10 criteria shown in Table I.

The DSM-IV criteria were readily accepted by researchers and treatment specialists as the standard for diagnosing pathological gambling; however, the criteria had not been adapted for population research. As part of the American National Gambling Impact Study Commission in 1998, a new instrument [the National Opinion Research Center DMS Screen (NODS)] was devised to assess the prevalence of problem and pathological gambling in the general population. The NODS uses the 10 DSM-IV pathological gambling criteria, but in some instances asks more than one question per category. The end product is a 17-item scale requiring "yes" or "no" answers from the perspective of two time frames—lifetime and current (within the past year). A maximum NODS score is 10 (even though respondents can answer affirmatively to all 17 questions, only one positive response per category is counted) and the scores are

Table I DSM-IV Criteria for Pathological Gambling

Criterion	*Definition*
Preoccupation	Is preoccupied with gambling (e.g., preoccupied with reliving past gambling experiences, handicapping or planning the next venture, or thinking of ways to get money with which to gamble)
Tolerance	Needs to gamble with increasing amounts of money in order to achieve the desired excitement
Withdrawal	Is restless or irritable when attempting to cut down or stop gambling
Escape	Gambles as a way of escaping from problems or relieving dysphoric mood (e.g., feelings of helplessness, guilt, anxiety, or depression)
Chasing	After losing money gambling, often returns another day in order to get even ("chasing" one's losses)
Lying	Lies to family members, therapists, or others to conceal the extent of involvement with gambling
Loss of control	Has made repeated unsuccessful efforts to control, cut back, or stop gambling
Illegal acts	Has committed illegal acts (e.g., forgery, fraud, theft, or embezzlement) in order to finance gambling
Risked significant relationship	Has jeopardized or lost a significant relationship, job, or educational or career opportunity because of gambling
Bailout	Has relied on others to provide money to relieve a desperate financial situation caused by gambling

used to distinguish four gambler subtypes: (1) low risk—no reported DSM-IV criteria, (2) at risk—one or two DSM-IV criteria, (3) problem gambler—three or four DSM-IV criteria, and (4) pathological gambler—five or more DSM-IV criteria. A unique feature of the NODS is the use of filter questions to determine respondent eligibility for continuing the interview. One filter question asks whether the person had ever lost $100 or more in a single day of gambling; if they had not, respondents are then asked if they had ever lost $100 or more over an entire year of gambling. A yes answer to either question continues the interview. The rationale for the filter questions is based on research showing a strong correlation between problem-gambling behavior and having experienced significant monetary losses. The NODS was tested for validity and reliability with clinical and general populations as well as gambling venue patron samples. NODS was found to have strong internal consistency and retest reliability and to be a superior instrument for estimating problem-gambling prevalence rates and for investigating correlates.

The Canadian Problem Gambling Index

As noted earlier, growing concern with the SOGS prompted Canadian researchers to develop improved ways of measuring problem-gambling prevalence in general population surveys. One of these new instruments, the Canadian Problem Gambling Index (CPGI), has gained currency in Canada, Australia, and New Zealand. The CPGI grew out of an interest in addressing problem gambling from a community public health perspective, as opposed to viewing problem gambling as a disease requiring health care intervention. A three-person team designed the instrument after reviewing the problem-gambling literature, investigating theories and models purporting to explain problem gambling and analyzing various measures (including the SOGS) used to distinguish problem from nonproblem gamblers. Preliminary testing of the CPGI included an evaluation by an international panel of gambling research experts, pilot studies with three groups (i.e., a general population random sample, regular gamblers who responded to newspaper ads, and problem gamblers in treatment), and a national randomly sampled survey of 3120 adult Canadians. CPGI reliability was evaluated by readministering the instrument to a subsample of 417 respondents from the initial national survey and was validated through clinical interviews conducted by problem-gambling treatment specialists with 143 national survey respondents. As a result of this preparation, the CPGI was the first problem-gambling behavior measurement tool to have been rigorously tested prior to its use in general population surveys. Furthermore, it was the first problem-gambling measure to have established and published psychometric properties before its use in problem-gambling prevalence surveys.

Emerging from this process, the CPGI is a 31-item instrument containing an embedded 9-item scale labeled the Problem Gambling Severity Index (PGSI); the PGSI is the measure used to separate respondents into one of four gambler categories (nonproblem, low risk, moderate risk, and problem). As opposed to the SOGS and NODS yes/no response categories, the four possible answers to the PGSI questions include "never," "sometimes," "most of the time," and "almost always." A score of 1 is given for a response of "sometimes"; 2, for "most of the time"; and 3, for "almost always"; thus, there is a range of possible scores from 0 to 27. PGSI cutoff points used to discriminate the four gambler subtypes are nonproblem (PGSI score = 0), low risk (PGSI score = 1 or 2), moderate risk (PGSI score = 3–7), and problem gambler (PGSI score = 8 or more). The CPGI does not use the term "pathological" to categorize a gambler subtype, because in the developers' view, the term is too closely associated with addiction and a medicalized view of gambling disorders, in contrast to the public health orientation of the CPGI.

Comparison of the NODS and CPGI

As a result of updated DSM-IV problem-gambling criteria and an intensification of empirical research, significant progress has been made in developing and refining instruments to measure problem gambling among the general population. The result is fewer misclassifications and increased confidence in problem-gambling prevalence estimates. Still unresolved are questions concerning the cutoff points used to differentiate gambler subtypes, which tend to be arbitrary, and the fact that scale items are not weighted to distinguish between severe and less severe problem-gambling indicators; for example, feeling guilty about gambling behavior, facing criticism of gambling behavior, and lying about gambling activity are scored the same as committing illegal acts to support a gambling habit or family breakups caused by excessive gambling. Moreover, neither of these instruments has been validated for use in adolescent populations.

The NODS is based directly on the DSM-IV pathological gambling criteria, whereas the PGSI (the CPGI subscale used to differentiate gambler subtypes) makes selective use of DSM-IV criteria (e.g., it uses tolerance, chasing, and bailout but omits criteria such as preoccupation, withdrawal, and illegal acts). The NODS items are more amenable to empirical measurement in that questions are asked about specific behaviors (have the respondents ever engaged in them, and if so, how often), whereas the PGSI is concerned more with respondents' perceptions about how gambling impacts their lives. Both measures separate respondents into four gambling subtypes based on problem-gambling severity; the NODS provides both lifetime and current problem-gambling prevalence rates, versus the PGSI, which refers only to the previous 12 months; however, the PGSI offers four response choices versus just two for the NODS, which allows for finer distinctions in assessing gambling behaviors.

Methodological Issues

The academic debate over the best way to measure problem gambling continues. The lack of consensus on methodological issues has practical implications for gambling regulators and treatment specialists who are calling for pertinent, evidence-based data revealing how serious and widespread problem gambling is in their jurisdiction and what they should do about it. Partly because of these snags in problem-gambling measurement, changing the research focus from prevalence to incidence studies has been recommended. In general terms, jurisdictional problem-gambling prevalence rates vary according to the menu of gambling formats offered, the prize structure of the games, and the length of time the games have been operating. In other words, the more legal gambling formats available (especially continuous formats such as electronic gambling machines and casino games) and the longer these formats have been offered, the higher the problem-gambling prevalence rate. Gambling formats differ in terms of their impacts on a citizenry. For example, lotteries and raffle play are relatively benign compared with continuous games such as video lottery terminals (VLTs) and slot machines, which have a more pronounced addictive potency.

Other Problem-Gambling Prevalence Survey Measurement Issues

In addition to scholarly disputes over the most appropriate tool for measuring problem gambling in a population, differences of opinion exist about the value of telephone surveys and the validity of certain survey questionnaire items. Most problem-gambling prevalence studies have been telephone surveys, which have the primary advantage of capacity to reach large numbers of respondents in a short period of time, and in a cost-effective manner. Despite their popularity, telephone surveys generally, and problem-gambling prevalence surveys particularly, contain flaws that can skew response rates (generally in the direction of underestimating the problem):

- Response rates have declined in the past decade partly because of telephone survey and telephone solicitation fatigue; a response rate of 60% is now considered "good."
- Households in upper and lower income categories and in which English is not the primary language spoken tend to be underrepresented.
- Most telephone surveys exclude institutions such as college or university residences, penal institutions, and mental health facilities. Gambling problems have been found at higher rates in all of these populations.
- Respondents being interviewed in the presence of other family members may modify their answers.
- Respondents with a severe gambling problem may refuse to participate in a telephone survey investigating their gambling behavior or, if they do participate, may be reluctant to divulge the truth to a stranger on the telephone. Also, problem gamblers are often not home because they are out gambling, or if at home, do not answer the phone for fear it is a bill collector or loan shark.

To some extent these problems can be reduced by using weighting to adjust sampling imbalances after the data collection is completed, using more complete sampling frames and improving response rates by having more callbacks and better trained interviewers; however, these improvements invariably add time and cost to a project.

The validity of some problem-gambling prevalence survey data has been challenged because of questionnaire item ambiguities; a case in point being questions pertaining to gambling expenditures. Respondents are asked "How much do you spend on gambling?" The reference point is a particular time frame (e.g., a typical session, per week or per month) or a specific gambling format over a specific time period (e.g., horse racing, lotteries, casinos). Gambling expenditure data have been criticized on the grounds that the questioners make no attempt to confirm the uniformity of responses by clarifying how respondents derive their answers. Confusion about gambling expenditures stems from respondents' differing interpretations of how to calculate losses (to wit: is it the net amount lost, the total amount initially staked, or the total amount wagered in a session?). Each can be a reasonable way of interpreting the question; however, accepting responses at face value and averaging those to arrive at community or subsample gambling expenditure rates can lead to data distortion. It is suggested that net expenditure is the most relevant measure because this represents the actual amount lost and is the true cost to the gambler. Consequently, it is recommended that future studies provide clear instructions on how to calculate net gambling expenditures and point out that wins reinvested during a session are not part of the calculation.

Meta-analysis

Meta-analytic research has been conducted on 120 problem-gambling prevalence studies that had taken place in North America over the previous decade. The studies reviewed represent both adults and adolescents in the general population, university students, adults and youth in clinical and prison populations, and a variety of "special" populations, including women, specific ethnic groups, and gambling industry employees. The meta-analysis empirically integrated the findings from these diverse studies for the purpose of establishing more accurate estimations of problem-gambling prevalence rates and identifying factors that affect these rates.

The main findings of the meta-analysis included the following measurement and methodology factors:

- Disordered gambling is a robust phenomenon that research can identify reliably across a wide range of investigative procedures that vary in quality of method.
- Disordered-gambling prevalence rates were assessed by 25 different instruments; the SOGS or a SOGS derivative was used in more than half the studies.
- A substantial degree of collinearity among the studies made it difficult to interpret the meaningfulness and significance of the various prevalence estimates.
- The validity of all the prevalence studies reviewed was questionable to the extent that none of the studies was evaluated by an independent means of assessment (for example, having a sampling of survey respondents undergo a diagnostic interview with a gambling treatment specialist to determine whether they had been properly categorized).
- The meta-analysis also recommended that confidence intervals be routinely reported and that specific problem-gambling prevalence rates be listed (e.g., male rates versus female rates) instead of aggregate rates for an entire population.

Longitudinal Research in Gambling Studies

Prominent gambling studies researchers have stressed the need for longitudinal designs to determine the natural history of both disordered and responsible gambling. As gambling studies research evolves, it is evident that certain questions about gambling and problem gambling cannot be answered definitively by one-time surveys or clinical research. Longitudinal research (or cohort research, as it is sometimes referred to) is required to measure changes in gambling behavior over time, to correlate gambling patterns and behaviors with the availability of various legalized gambling formats, and to determine the social and economic impacts of gambling and problem gambling on communities and society at large. Although in its infancy in gambling studies, longitudinal research is becoming an increasingly popular study design because of its presumed superiority over "snapshot" or "cross-sectional" studies. Longitudinal research includes the following advantages:

- Following a group of respondents over time allows researchers to better understand the onset, development, and maintenance of both normative and problem gambling behavior.
- Longitudinal data allow respondents to be compared with themselves at different times as well as to other respondents in the same cohort.
- Because of the time dimension, longitudinal data help identify factors that moderate and exacerbate an individual's gambling participation and thus allow the researcher to infer causality.
- Sorely needed research on the social and economic impacts of legalized gambling on individuals, families, and communities can be done most precisely and expeditiously using a longitudinal design.
- Longitudinal studies produce broad and deep databases that can be used by researchers across many academic disciplines; they may prove more cost-efficient in the long run, as compared to creating many smaller data pools with each new project.

Despite the obvious benefits of longitudinal studies, practical and logistical barriers make them difficult to mount; for example, there is the massive funding required for a multiyear commitment; there are problems with maintaining research team continuity over a lengthy time period and with sample attrition; there is the danger that repeated testing of individuals may influence gambling behavior and/or behavioral reports; and there is the knowledge that longitudinal data confound aging and period effects (e.g., is a person's sudden gambling interest due to being 18 and at the age of majority, or because a casino opened in the area?). Although not yet abundant, longitudinal research in gambling studies is becoming more commonplace, sophisticated, and theory based.

Qualitative Research Methodology in Gambling Studies

The focus of qualitative research in gambling studies has been on particular gambling settings, whereby researchers use firsthand observations to describe ongoing gambling scenes; identify social roles, rewards, and what constitutes deviant behavior; and illustrate how gambling participation is integrated into players' lifestyles. Examples of gambling scenes investigated in this manner include poker clubs, horse race betting (both on and off track), bridge, pool, and golf. Studies of this nature have also investigated the processes and impacts of gambling addiction; for example, in one study working with Gamblers Anonymous members, the research identified the phenomenon of "chasing" after lost money in an attempt to remain in action. In another study, addicted female electronic gambling-machine players were observed and interviewed, with the aim of explaining gender differences in gambling behavior.

Classic studies in this genre have used a form of participant observation known as autoethnography, which is a cultural study conducted among one's own people. Autoethnographers share the perspective of a participant and present the view of an insider; the advantages of this approach include ease of entrée into the gambling scene, familiarity with the gambling scene, knowledge of the jargon, and a longitudinal outlook (because of a lengthy immersion in the scene). The primary drawbacks of this method are potential researcher bias and loss of objectivity (insiders may take basic assumptions for granted and may be incapable of viewing the scene impartially). To overcome this inclination, the researcher must constantly analyze his/her motivation and deal with the question of bias straightforwardly via a transparent disclosure of the data-gathering methods used.

Typically, these studies are classified as "exploratory" or "preliminary," because they are not always guided by a preconceived model; indeed, they are often informed by the grounded theory perspective. This approach features interdependence and reflexivity in the collection, coding, and analysis of data; this should cause data to blend and merge throughout the investigation. Data gathering often includes "purposive sampling," which is the practice of identifying and interviewing respondents known to be familiar with the subject in question. The "snowball" method is frequently used in combination with purposive sampling to expand the base of potential key informants; this technique allows identified authorities on the topic to recommend others whom they know to be conversant with the gambling scene. The researcher typically proceeds from raw data (observations and interviews), to classification (which involves the "constant comparative" method to ensure that conceptual categories accurately represent reality), to hypothesis generation, and, ultimately, to formal theory.

The grounded theory approach is used to develop substantive and formal theory through a process whereby the researcher continually redesigns and integrates theoretical concepts as new material is received. The researcher may not know in advance where the data will lead and the resultant hypotheses are always subject to revision. In other words, the emerging theory directs the efforts of future research. Using this approach to study the Nevada race book scene in the 1980s, John Rosecrance began by identifying participant demographic characteristics, attributes, social groupings, and degree of integration into society at large. Next, Rosecrance depicted the social world of the race book by describing the routine activities of the participants (e.g., horse selection, betting behavior, rationalizing race results) and outlining the roles, norms, sanctions, and social hierarchy that regulate group behavior. From this general milieu perspective, Rosecrance moved to an analysis of individual gambling careers, describing how an interest in race horse betting started and evolved, the coping mechanisms used to stay in the activity, and how respondents rationalized their involvement in this social world. Finally, Rosecrance used his empirical data to generate substantive hypotheses relating to the costs and rewards of participation in the gambling scene, thus explaining how individuals were able to sustain their involvement. These hypotheses were then integrated into a theory that depicted participant behavior in the race book social world and produced insights that could be extrapolated into similar social worlds.

Another approach to gambling-related ethnographic research is the work of Natasha Dow Schull on the links between gender, the lived experience of addiction, and the increasingly technological circumstances of life in modern society. Focusing on self-declared, video poker-addicted Las Vegas mothers, Dow Schull conducted fieldwork at casinos, supermarkets, gaming industry trade shows, and technology laboratories; she also attended Gamblers Anonymous meetings and group therapy sessions for problem gamblers and interned at a hospital where a pharmaceutical drug trial for video poker addicts was based. Besides observing in these settings, Dow Schull interviewed medical doctors, problem-gambling counselors, gaming engineers, and casino managers, as well as the mothers hooked on video poker. Using this eclectic data-gathering approach, Dow Schull presented findings that challenge gender stereotypes of female video poker players. On the one hand, Dow Schull's study concurred with previous research showing that escape from daily routines is the main motivation for addicted female video poker players; however, Dow Schull claimed that this desire to escape is triggered by the stress experienced in meeting the demands and responsibilities in performing the societal role of "good mother." Paradoxically, by escaping into machine gambling play, these women become "antimothers"—uncaring, unemotional, self-absorbed individuals whose behavior jeopardizes their children's welfare. Complicit in fostering this role transformation, according to Dow Schull, is the gaming industry, which develops technologies that capitalize on some women's propensity to seek an altered state of reality.

Cultural Studies

Several noteworthy gambling-related works have emerged from the "cultural studies" tradition, which is a blend of social history and sociology. The premise of this approach is that past events cannot be understood without reference to prevailing social structures, and that universal categories such as class, race, and gender must be applied to the analysis. Central to the cultural studies schema is the concept of hegemony or social control—the process whereby dominant ideas, ideologies, meanings, and values are transmitted through various cultural practices so as to maintain patterns of power and privilege in society. Ostensibly, the moral and philosophical legitimacy of this elite worldview is tacitly accepted and taken for granted by the general populace, with the effect being that alternative structures and meanings are downplayed or ignored.

Gambling studies within the cultural studies framework typically track community sentiments, competing discourses, strategic partnerships, and legislative activity to show how gambling laws and public policies have been shaped and framed. Temporally, these studies cover eras in which gambling went through stages of being considered a sin, a vice, and ultimately, a harmless amusement. For example, there have been cultural studies of Canada's gambling landscape from 1919 to 1969, of lower class gambling practices in England from 1845 to 1960, and of Western culture gambling practices from the earliest time to the present. These studies rely on archival data from diverse sources, including government, police, newspaper, church, and reformist group records; social and legal histories; and, depending on the time period under review, interviews with key informants. Pitfalls are encountered in reconstructing history from these sources: urban, upper class, and male voices tend to dominate over rural, lower class, and female voices, and more historical data are available from groups opposed to gambling than from adherents of the activity. In addition, there is always the possibility that researchers' opinions, prejudices, and other biases may affect data processing and interpretation.

The analytical hook used by researcher Suzanne Morton in studying Canadian gambling is the social values pertaining to gambling—in particular, their derivation, negotiation, and maintenance. Morton found that (1) antigambling views had been softened by the general secularization of a pluralistic society as reflected in more permissive attitudes toward activities such as marijuana use, extramarital sex, and Sunday observance; (2) vested interest groups, hoping to benefit from looser gambling laws, have euphemized the vocabulary of gambling by using "gaming" and "gaming revenue" as opposed to "gambling" and 'gambling losses' to subtly change public discourse on the activity; and (3) by tying gambling-generated funds to charitable causes and keeping taxes down, governments effectively neutered morality arguments and helped launch gambling as a powerful social, economic, and political force in Western society.

Public Policy Analyses

Policy analysis, as defined by Leslie Pal, is "the disciplined application of intellect to public problems." Discipline implies that the analysis is systematic, rational, and empirical—more than perfunctory musings. As a recognized academic subdiscipline, public policy analysis explores public policies, the elements that comprise them, the processes that produce them, and the impacts they have on society. For the majority of participants, gambling may be the harmless amusement it was intended to be; however, because of the potential for cheating, exploitation, and overindulgence, the law has historically taken an iron-fisted approach toward gambling. At the same time, history has shown that the activity cannot be completely suppressed and that there is no good reason to outlaw all forms of gambling because it is a long-standing, naturally occurring, mainstream, cultural practice. Given this reality, policymakers strive to create a balance between regulation and outright prohibition by enacting legislation that stipulates where, when, in what form, and under what conditions gambling is permissible. Because of the state and provincial autonomy that exists throughout North America, the gambling terrain is characterized by a patchwork of conflicting jurisdictional policies. Indeed, Dr. Margaret Beare argues that the expansion of legal gambling formats in North America has created a sense of ambiguity that has "resulted in inconsistent policy, limited research and evaluation, inadequate funding for gaming regulation and enforcement, and little concern for the potential social consequences of gambling."

Academic analyses and critiques of gambling policy have highlighted inadequate gambling policies and the adverse impacts they create, with an outlook toward fostering sound gambling policy and responsible gambling industry practices. Examples of works in this genre include Clotfelter and Cook's *Selling Hope: State Lotteries in America* and Goodman's *The Luck Business*. These studies use interview data from industry leaders, government officials, and academic experts and publicly available information such as gambling revenues, unemployment rates, crime data, advertising expenses, economic impacts, and so forth to ascertain the efficacy of government gambling policies. Clotfelter and Cook showed that American state lotteries function as a significant source of state revenue; they are an attraction for individuals from low-income, low-education and minority backgrounds and are deceptively marketed to attract new players. To remedy this situation, the Clotfelter and Cook recommend a new lottery model that is consumer oriented rather than profit driven. This would mean greater transparency in advertising sales pitches, informing consumers about the odds of winning, higher payouts for winners, and more innovative product lines.

In *The Luck Business*, Goodman questioned the economic justifications used by policymakers to expand legal gambling offerings in the 1980s and 1990s—in particular, the promise of an economic renaissance. In Goodman's view, pre-expansion economic impact studies were distorted because many of these reports were commissioned by casino companies and governments failed to recognize the degree to which expanded gambling formats would cannibalize existing businesses. Governmental underestimation of the financial and social burdens created by addicted gamblers may end up outweighing any societal benefits accrued from the activity. To redress the economic imbalance of existing gambling policies, Goodman made the following recommendations:

1. Rethinking the ways that state and local governments use gambling as a public policy tool and greater involvement in the process by federal governments.
2. Limiting the ways that states and private industry can advertise and encourage gambling.
3. A national moratorium on gambling expansion until the social and economic impacts of widespread legal gambling have been assessed.
4. Based on the preceding assessment, deciding a new which gambling formats should be allowed, how much gambling is appropriate in a jurisdiction, where gambling outlets should be located, and how gambling revenues should be dispersed.

Final Thoughts

Until 20 years ago, gambling in North America was a low-profile public issue in terms of its variety and availability; immoderate gambling was rarely framed as being problematic, governmental concern about gambling was minimal, and scholars were indifferent to the activity. However, social science research has significantly broadened and deepened our understanding of gambling to the point where there is general concurrence on the following points:

- Gambling is a mainstream cultural activity that is practiced in a socially responsible manner by the majority of those who partake in the activity.
- There is such a phenomenon as problem gambling and it is exacerbated by intermittent reinforcement schedules and fast-paced gambling formats.
- Elevated problem-gambling prevalence rates and higher per capita annual wagering rates in a jurisdiction are associated with the widespread availability of gambling outlets, particularly electronic gambling devices.
- Pressure to expand gambling comes not from the public, but from vested interest groups (e.g., governments, the gambling industry, aboriginal groups, and charities) that stand to benefit from the expansion; as a consequence, commercial considerations generally take priority over social ones.
- Governments that sanction gambling are faced with the conundrum of maintaining gambling revenues, while at the same time suppressing its harmful impacts. Costly treatment programs for problem gambling are seen to be less effective than is public policy that emphasizes preventative measures that immunize those susceptible to gambling addiction, or at least minimize the trauma for those who already have a gambling problem.

As legalized gambling offerings proliferate, social science research will continue being a critical means of assessing the societal impacts of this expansion and, it is hoped, will provide the basis for enlightened public policy in this domain.

See Also the Following Articles

Meta-Analysis • Survey Design

Further Reading

American Psychiatric Association. (1980). *Diagnostic and Statistical Manual of Mental Disorders,* 3rd Ed. American Psychiatric Association, Washington, DC.

American Psychiatric Association. (1994). *Diagnostic and Statistical Manual of Mental Disorders,* 4th Ed. American Psychiatric Association, Washington, DC.

Beare, M. (1989). Current law enforcement issues in Canadian gambling. In *Gambling in Canada: Golden Goose or Trojan Horse?* (C. Campbell and J. Lowman, eds.), pp. 177–194. School of Criminology–Simon Fraser University, Burnaby, British Columbia.

Blaszczynski, A., Dumlao, V., and Lange, M. (1997). "How much do you spend gambling?" Ambiguities in survey questionnaire items. *J. Gambling Stud.* **13**(3), 237–252.

Castellani, B. (2000). *Pathological Gambling.* State University of New York Press, Albany.

Clotfelter, C., and Cook, P. (1989). *Selling Hope: State Lotteries in America.* Harvard University Press, Cambridge, Massachusetts.

Dixon, D. (1991). *From Prohibition to Regulation: Anti-gambling and the Law.* Claredon, Oxford, United Kingdom.

Dow Schull, N. (2002). *Escape Mechanism: Women, Caretaking, and Compulsive Machine Gambling.* Working Paper No. 41. Center for Working Families. University of California, Berkeley.

Ferris, J., and Wynne, H. (2001). *The Canadian Problem Gambling Index: Final Report.* Canadian Centre on Substance Abuse, Ottawa, Ontario.

Ferris, J., Wynne, H., and Single, E. (1999). *Measuring Problem Gambling in Canada.* Phase 1 Final Report to the Canadian Inter-Provincial Task Force on Problem Gambling.

Glaser, B., and Strauss, A. (1967). *The Discovery of Grounded Theory.* Aldine, New York.

Goodman, R. (1995). *The Luck Business.* Free Press, New York.

Hayano, D. (1982). *Poker Faces.* University of California Press, Berkeley.

Herman, R. (1974). Gambling as work: A sociological study of the racetrack. In *Sociology for Pleasure* (M. Truzzi, ed.), pp. 298–314. Prentice-Hall, Englewood Cliffs, New Jersey.

Lesieur, H. (1977). *The Chase: Career of the Compulsive Gambler.* Anchor Books, Garden City, New York.

Lesieur, H., and Blume, S. (1987). The South Oaks Gambling Screen (SOGS): A new instrument for the identification of pathological gamblers. *Am. J. Psychiatr.* **144,** 1184–1188.

Morton, S. (2003). *At Odds: Gambling and Canadians, 1919–1969.* University of Toronto Press, Toronto, Ontario.

National Gambling Impact Study Commission. (1999). *Final Report.* U.S. Government Printing Office, Washington, DC.

Pal, L. (1997). *Beyond Policy Analysis.* International Thompson Publ., Scarborough, Ontario.

Polsky, N. (1969). *Hustlers, Beats, and Others.* Anchor Books, Garden City, New York.

Reith, G. (1999). *The Age of Chance: Gambling in Western Culture.* Routledge, London, United Kingdom.

Rose, I. N. (1988). Compulsive gambling and the law: From sin to vice to disease. *J. Gambling Behav.* **4**(4), 240–260.

Rosecrance, J. (1985). *The Degenerates of Lake Tahoe.* Peter Lang, New York.

Scott, M. (1968). *The Racing Game.* Aldine, Chicago.

Shaffer, H., Hall, M., and Vander Bilt, J. (1997). *Estimating the Prevalence of Disordered Gambling Behavior in the United States and Canada: A Meta-analysis.* Harvard Medical School Division on Addictions, Boston.

Smith, G., and Paley, R. (2001). Par for the course: A study of gambling on the links and a commentary on physical skill-based gambling formats. *Int. Gambling Stud.* **1**(1), 103–134.

Smith, G., and Wynne, H. (2002). *Measuring Gambling and Problem Gambling in Alberta Using the Canadian Problem Gambling Index.* Report prepared for the Alberta Gaming Research Institute, Edmonton, Alberta.

Volberg, R. (1996). Prevalence studies of problem gambling in the United States. *J. Gambling Stud.* **12**(2), 111–128.

Volberg, R. (2001). *When the Chips are Down: Problem Gambling in America.* The Century Foundation, New York.

Volberg, R., Moore, W., Christiansen, E., Cummings, W., and Banks, S. (1998). Unaffordable losses: Estimating the proportion of gambling revenues derived from problem gamblers. *Gaming Law Rev.* **2**(4), 349–360.

Walker, M. (1992). *The Psychology of Gambling.* Butterworth, Oxford, United Kingdom.

Game Theory, Overview

Ram C. Rao

University of Texas, Dallas, Richardson, Texas, USA

Glossary

asymmetric information The type of data acquired when a move by Nature occurs before any player acts, and some, but not all, players are ignorant of what Nature chose.

best response A player's optimal choice of action in response to a particular choice of others.

common knowledge Something that all players know, with the shared understanding among all players that they all know the same thing.

contractible Some element that can be written into a contract so that the disposition of the contract is based on the exact outcome of the element, and a third party, other than the players, can help in verifying the outcome.

cooperative game An activity in which players can make binding agreements as to their actions.

equilibrium and Nash equilibrium A set of actions chosen by all players such that, given the choices of others, no player wants to change his choice unilaterally.

folk theorem A result, especially in repeated games, that many hold to be true, but which is proved formally much later.

incomplete information The type of data acquired when a move by Nature occurs before any player acts, and some players do not know what Nature chose.

informed player A game participant who has observed Nature's move in a game of asymmetric information.

mixed strategy A player's choice of action that attaches a probability to more than one available action.

Nature An entity that makes a probabilistic move with respect to one of the elements of the game.

noncooperative game A type of game in which players cannot make binding agreements as to their actions.

payoff Profits or utility to players after all players have chosen their action.

perfect information The type of data acquired when players know all that has occurred before their move.

players Participants in a game.

pure strategy A player's choice of a single action with probability 1, from among all available actions.

strategy Specifies action for a player at each information set in which he must move.

subgame perfect Nash equilibrium A Nash equilibrium to a game that is also a Nash equilibrium in every subgame.

Game theory may be used as a modeling device. The rudiments of noncooperative game theory include analyses of games of incomplete information, emphasizing the concepts of Nash equilibrium, subgame perfection, and perfect Bayesian equilibrium. Both illustrative examples and applications in economics and management are used here to provide the reader with a grasp of the scope and usefulness of the game theoretic model. Also presented are the challenges facing modelers who want to use game theory, and how some of those are being met by continuing research.

Game Theory as a Model

Why Game Theory?

Game theory can be viewed in terms of its mathematics or as a tool to model the interaction between decision makers. The word "game" is an apt one to describe this because, just as in common parlor games such as Chess or Hex, much of game theory is concerned with how individual entities (persons, or organizations) choose actions, taking into account how other participants do the same. These entities are called players, even though the decisions that they make are in the context of situations with real-world consequences, quite different from the entertainment that parlor games yield. Players are assumed to choose actions to maximize their expected utility, following the accepted model of single-person decision making. In this sense, game theory may be viewed as a generalization of single-person decision theory to multiperson decision making. But there are many differences between the two. The utility resulting from a player's action cannot be determined without also taking into account the actions chosen by other players. Thus, game theory cannot prescribe an optimal action for an individual player without also offering a way for each player to anticipate what other players would choose. In other words, game theory is concerned with specifying actions for all players, ensuring that for each player, his/her chosen actions are optimal, given the actions of other players, implying that optimality is relative. As a result, it is generally difficult to define the best outcome from the view of all players. The value of game theory, then, lies in its ability to model the interaction between players. Such a model can help to explain observations involving multiperson decision-making situations, and can also rule out certain outcomes that might not otherwise be contemplated. There is another potential use of game theory. If one of the players can "go" (act) first and choose an action that he can commit to, then it is possible to come up with choices that will ensure outcomes favorable to the first player. For example, the tax code can be viewed as a choice of lawmakers. Based on that, citizens and corporations choose actions, given the tax code. Thus, the lawmakers and citizens can be viewed as playing a game. An analysis of such a game can help determine the best code from the lawmakers' viewpoint. And, what is more important, it would help to disabuse wishful lawmakers of predictions of outcomes that are deemed unreasonable in light of the analysis.

Questions

What should a person know about game theory to be able to apply it to problems in social science? This question can be answered using applications and illustrative examples, mainly in economics and management, that do not require advanced training. The deeper problems in economics and management that game theory has been used to analyze can be accessed in a large body of literature. The hard problems in game theory are not discussed here, yet the reader can get a feel for how the game theoretic model has been successfully used based on minimal domain knowledge beyond everyday experience. Issues that some would regard as drawbacks in using game theory are presented here, although others, including the author, view them as challenges.

Definitions

A game, denoted by G, can be defined as consisting of three elements: players, indexed by i ($i = 1, 2, \ldots, N$); an action or strategy a_i, possibly a vector, chosen by player i, from a set $A_i = \{a_i\}$; and a payoff to player i, $\pi_i(a_i, a_{-i})$, where a_{-i} denotes the actions of all players other than i. The payoff π_i is to be thought of as the utility to player i when he chooses a_i and the other players choose a_{-i}. A game defined in this way is represented in strategic form. An alternative representation of a game, called extensive form, is illustrated by considering a game such as chess. In chess, each player has a turn to make a move by choosing an action a_i, followed by other players, each in turn. The sequence of decisions forms a decision tree, or more correctly a game tree. Each turn to move by any player can be thought of as a stage in a multistage game. A multistage game is to game theory what dynamic programming is to single-person decision theory. In a multistage game, when it is a player's turn to move, he/she may or may not know what some or all of others' choices are. Depending on what the player knows, he/she is at a particular information set at each turn to move. Viewed this way, player i's strategy, s_i, is defined as a specification of an action, a_i, at each information set, satisfying $s_i \in S_i$. Payoffs can be denoted in this case by $\pi_i(s_i, s_{-i})$, $s_i \in S_i$. In chess and other games, there could be a chance element, similar to the toss of a coin, that determines who moves first. Any such chance event is ascribed to what is denoted "Nature." Finally, assume that each player knows the payoffs and the structure of the game, and further that each player knows that the other players know the same information, and also knows that other players know that the other players know, and so on, *ad infinitum*. This type of knowledge of the game by all of the players is known as common knowledge.

Classification of Games

There are many ways to classify games. First, a game can be a cooperative or noncooperative game. In a cooperative game, the players can make binding commitments with respect to their strategies. Thus, members of the Organization of Petroleum Exporting Countries (OPEC), for example, play a cooperative game when they agree to what level of oil production each is to maintain. In contrast, supermarkets, say, choose pricing strategies noncooperatively. Here the concern is only with noncooperative games.

A very important basis for classifying games is the information that players have at the time of making a move. A game is said to be one of perfect information if, at his/her turn to move, each player knows all that has occurred up to that point in the game. Chess is an example of this type of game. In contrast, consider two firms submitting sealed bids on a contract. This can be conceptualized as similar to a game of chess, with one firm moving first and submitting a bid, followed by the other. Naturally, the first player does not know what the other will do. But what is more important is that the second player does not know what the first bid is.

The second player's information set consists of all possible bids that the first player could have made. Stated differently, the second player's information set contains many elements, each element corresponding to a possible bid by the first player. A game is said to be one of perfect information if, at each player's turn to move, his/her information set is a singleton. With this definition, it is easy to see that bidding for the contract is not a game of perfect information. When players move simultaneously, as in this case, the game is always one of imperfect information. An even more important distinction arises if Nature moves first, and the move is not revealed to at least one player. For example, suppose a human plays chess against a computer but does not know whether the computer is playing at the beginner or advanced level. When the human sees a particular move by the computer, he/she must recognize that the move could have resulted from either the beginner or the advanced level of playing. The player's information set is therefore not a singleton, even though he/she observed the move. In fact, it can be said that the human does not know which game he/she is playing; chess against beginner level or chess against advanced level. This is called a game of incomplete information. More generally, in games of incomplete information, one or more players do not know the game structure. Naturally, all games of incomplete information are also games of imperfect information. A special case of a game of incomplete information is one of asymmetric information. In a game of asymmetric information, the move by Nature is observed by some players but not by others. Consider the interaction between a car salesperson and a potential buyer. The buyer knows his/her budget but the salesperson does not. Thus, in the game of haggling, the salesperson's information is different from that of the buyer, and so there is a game of asymmetric information. As far as the salesperson is concerned, the buyer is a random draw, attributable to a move by Nature. And so, it is a game of incomplete information.

Equilibrium

Nash Equilibrium

In single-person decision theory, the main task is to characterize the optimal solution. In game theory, the task is to characterize the equilibrium. The equilibrium is understandable if the concept of best response is first understood. Consider player i's choice in response to actions by the other players. Denote $b_i(s_{-i})$ to be i's best response to s_{-i}. It is then defined as

$$b_i(s_{-i}) = \arg\max_{a_i \in A_i} \pi_i(s_i, s_{-i}). \quad (1)$$

An equilibrium s^* to a game is defined as the strategies of all players such that its components (s_i^*, s_{-i}^*) satisfy the following relationship:

$$s_i^* = b_i(s_{-1}^*) \quad \forall i \quad (2)$$

In other words, at equilibrium, each player's choice is a best response to the choices of the remaining players. In this sense, each player's choice is the solution to an appropriately defined optimization problem. Because each player is at his best response, each player is content with his/her choice. For this reason, this is called an equilibrium. Another equivalent way to define the equilibrium choices s^* is to impose the following inequalities at the equilibrium:

$$\pi_i(s_i^*, s_{-i}^*) \geq \pi_i(s_i, s_{-i}^*)\, s_i \in S_i \quad \forall i \quad (3)$$

An equilibrium s^* is usually called a Nash equilibrium, named after John Nash. The essential property of Nash equilibrium is that once players arrive at such an equilibrium, no player can profit by deviating unilaterally from it.

Pure and Mixed Strategies

Thus far, strategies have been viewed as actions, or rules for action, at each information set of a player. The definition of strategies can be broadened by specifying a strategy as a probability function over the actions $a_i \in A_i$ corresponding to each information set of the player. A nondegenerate probability distribution would imply that the player's strategy tells him/her to mix among his/her actions, rather than have a unique action for a choice. For this reason, strategies defined in this way are called mixed strategies. A simple example will help illustrate the idea of mixed strategies. Consider a baseball pitcher pitching to a new batter. Suppose the pitcher is restricted to pitch a strike (meaning that the ball goes over the plate at the right height for the batter to be in a position to hit) or a ball (meaning that the ball goes far away from the batter, making it difficult to hit). So the pitcher has two possible actions from which to choose. Now, suppose the batter also has two options: to take a swing or to "see" the ball, meaning not to take a swing. If the batter swings at a strike or sees a ball, the batter wins, whereas the pitcher wins if he/she throws a strike and the batter sees, or he/she throws a ball at which the batter swings. If the pitcher decides to throw a strike for certain, the batter would swing and win. Likewise, if the pitcher decides to throw a ball for certain, the batter would see and win. The pitcher may then consider mixing pitches so that there is uncertainty as to whether he/she throws a strike or a ball. In other words, the pitcher may choose to employ a mixed strategy. In contrast, if the pitcher chooses to assign a probability of 1 to either of his/her actions, he/she would be employing a pure strategy. Thus, a pure strategy is a special case of mixed strategies in which all actions but one have a zero probability of being chosen.

One advantage with broadening the definition of strategies in this way is that it assures us of the existence of a Nash equilibrium, possibly in mixed strategies, for any game G with a finite number of players, each of whose action sets contain a finite number of elements. John Nash first established this existence result in 1950.

Equilibrium in Pure and Mixed Strategies

Examination of a few game structures will help illustrate Nash equilibrium in pure and mixed strategies. Three of these structures are celebrated, both for their ability to illuminate key concepts and because they represent generic models of competition. All three games have two players, and each player has two possible courses of action.

Product Introduction (Prisoners' Dilemma)

This game contemplates two firms who may each introduce (I) or shelve (S) a new product (P). Table I shows the payoffs to each firm under the four possible combinations of actions. In the table, the rows represent the possible actions of firm 1, and the columns represent the possible actions of firm 2. The entries in each cell are the payoffs to the two firms. Thus, if both choose S, both are at status quo with a utility of 0; if both choose I, they incur costs, but no gains, with utility of −2. Consider first the best responses of firm 1. It is obvious that $b_1(S) = I$ and $b_1(I) = I$. In other words, regardless of what firm 2 chooses, the best response of firm 1 is to choose I. For firm 1, the strategy S is strictly dominated because it is inferior in both scenarios (with firm 2 choosing S or I). The dominated strategy S for firm 1 can therefore be eliminated or deleted. By symmetry, S for firm 2 can also be deleted. This leaves a unique outcome arising from the dominant strategy of I for each firm. The Nash equilibrium for this game then is (I, I), as indicated by (−2, −2) in Table I. It can be seen that the Nash equilibrium is in pure strategies. Note also that the Nash equilibrium is unique. Finally, it yields lower utility to both firms than what they could achieve by cooperating and choosing S. Of course, then they would not be at a best response. Though the best response ensures optimality in an appropriately defined maximization problem, the maximization problem may be undesirable if it is compared to what is possible under cooperative behavior, a feature that is a property of many noncooperative games. This game is often referred to as the prisoners' dilemma, replacing firms by prisoners, actions S and I by "deny" and "confess" (to a crime), and leaving the ordering of the utilities the same. In that game, "confess" is a dominant strategy for both, but if they could cooperate to choose "deny," they would be better off. This will be discussed further later.

Table I Product Introduction[a]

Firm 2 (P2) / *Firm 1 (P1)*	*S*	*I*
S	(0, −0)	(−5, 10)
I	(10, −5)	(−2, −2)

[a] Product P is either introduced (I) or shelved (S).

Battle of the Sexes

The next illustrative game is called the battle of the sexes. In this game, the two players are a man and a woman. Each can choose to go to the ballet or to the baseball game. The payoffs to the two players are shown in Table II. In the table, when both the man and the woman choose baseball, the man gets a utility of 2 and the woman gets a utility of 1, and so on. It is easy to see that the man's best responses are given by b_M(baseball) = baseball and b_M(ballet) = ballet. Likewise, the woman's best responses are b_W(baseball) = baseball and b_W(ballet) = ballet. Thus, there are two Nash equilibria in pure strategies in this case. The first one has both players choosing baseball, and the second one has both choosing ballet. An important point to note here is that the Nash equilibrium is not necessarily unique. Moreover, whereas the man would prefer the first equilibrium—he obtains a utility of 2 as opposed to 1 in the second—the woman would prefer the second equilibrium. Thus, it is not possible, in general, to rank order Nash equilibria in terms of desirability. Finally, it is not clear how the two players can agree on one of the two equilibria if they cannot communicate in some way. Perhaps even talk that is nonbinding can help the two to get to one of the pure strategy Nash equilibria. Such talk that is nonbinding is termed "cheap talk."

Table II Battle of the Sexes

Woman / *Man*	*Baseball*	*Ballet*
Baseball	2, 1	0, 0
Ballet	0, 0	1, 2

Monitoring a Franchisee (Inspection Problem)

The final example will help illustrate the Nash equilibrium in mixed strategies. In this example, a franchisor may choose to monitor the performance of a franchisee or may choose "don't monitor." The franchisee can choose shirk or "don't shirk." The payoffs are shown in Table III.

Table III Monitoring a Franchisee

Franchisor \ *Franchisee*	*Shirk*	*Don't Shirk*
Monitor	−1, −1	−3, 0
Don't monitor	−4, 1	0, 0

This game is also referred to as the "inspection problem," for obvious reasons. Once again, the best responses of the franchisor can be seen to be $b_{\mathrm{FR}}(\text{shirk}) = \text{monitor}$ and $b_{\mathrm{FR}}(\text{don't shirk}) = \text{don't monitor}$. And the best responses of the franchisee are $b_{\mathrm{FE}}(\text{monitor}) = \text{don't shirk}$ and b_{FE} (don't monitor) = shirk. It is obvious that there is no pure strategy Nash equilibrium by an examination of the best responses. For example, taking the outcome (monitor, shirk), though the franchisor is at a best response, the franchisee is not. Similarly, all four possible outcomes can be ruled out. Although there is no Nash equilibrium in pure strategies in this case, there exists a Nash equilibrium in mixed strategies. Let p denote the probability that the franchisor chooses monitor and let q denote the probability that the franchisee chooses shirk. Suppose $q = 0.5$. Then, the franchisor's expected profits are $0.5 \times (-1) + 0.5 \times (-3) = -2$, if he/she chooses monitor, and $0.5 \times (-4) + 0.5 \times (0) = -2$, if he/she chooses don't monitor. In other words, the franchisor is indifferent between his/her two actions if the franchisee follows the mixed strategy of $q = 0.5$. Because the franchisor is indifferent between the two actions, he/she can randomize across them. Suppose the franchisor chooses the mixed strategy $p = 0.5$. Then, it can be verified that the franchisee is indifferent between his/her two actions. The franchisee could, therefore, choose to randomize across his/her actions, and indeed choose $q = 0.5$. Thus, it is obvious that the pair ($p = 0.5$, $q = 0.5$) is a best response for each player and so constitutes a Nash equilibrium in mixed strategies. The key point to note here is that in mixed-strategy equilibrium, a player is indifferent across actions chosen with nonzero probability. Indeed, each of these actions is a best response to the other players' equilibrium mixed strategy. Moreover, if an action is not a best response at equilibrium, it is chosen with zero probability. Finally, the mixing probabilities of the other players make each player indifferent across actions chosen with nonzero probability. In fact, the battle-of-the-sexes game also a mixed-strategy equilibrium in addition to the two pure-strategy equilibria.

Informational Issues

Perfect Equilibrium

One of the central ideas in dynamic programming is Bellman's principle of optimality. This has force in multistage games in the following sense: a player's strategy should be such that it is a best response at each information set. To see how this might affect Nash equilibrium, consider the following variation of the battle of the sexes.

Subgame Perfection

Suppose in the game of battle of the sexes, the man moves first in stage 1 and makes a choice, followed by the woman, in stage 2, and the man gets to have the final say in stage 3. This multistage game can be represented in extensive form by the game tree in Fig. 1, similar to a decision tree in single-person decision situations. At the end of each terminal branch in the game tree are the payoffs to both of the players. Read Fig. 1 as follows: If in stage 1, at node 1, the man chooses baseball (BS), this leads to node 2 in stage 2 of the tree. If, on the other

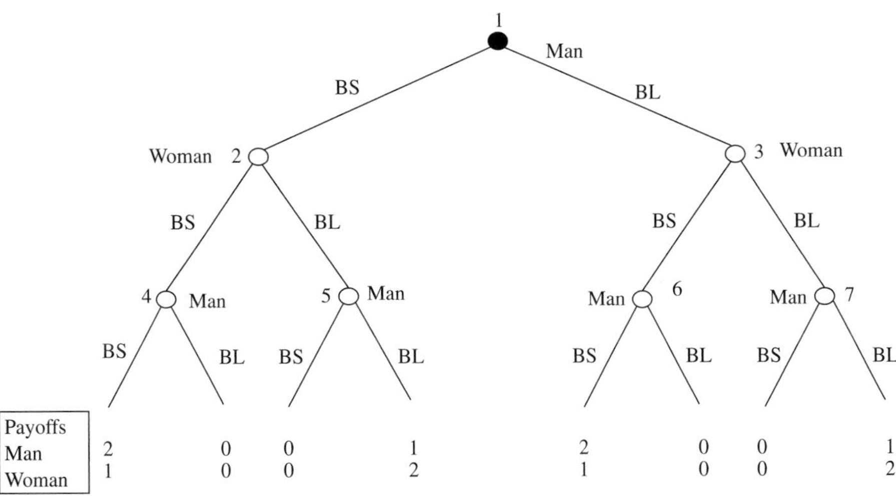

Figure 1 A three-stage battle-of-the-sexes game in extensive form. BS, baseball; BL, ballet.

hand, the man chooses ballet (BL), this leads to node 3 in stage 2. At node 2, if the woman chooses ballet, this leads to node 5 in stage 3, and the man would choose again. At node 5, the best that the man could do is to choose ballet and get a payoff of 1, as opposed to a payoff of 0 by choosing baseball. Note that node 5 would give a payoff of 2 to the woman, and, using the same logic, node 4 would give her 1. Knowing this, at node 2, she would choose ballet. And similarly, at node 3, she would choose ballet. Given this, at node 1, the man could choose either ballet or baseball. The Nash equilibrium outcome to the three-stage battle of the sexes is unique: both the man and the woman go to the ballet. The equilibrium is specified as follows:

Man: Stage 1—at node 1, choose either ballet or baseball; stage 3—at nodes 4 and 6, choose baseball and at nodes 5 and 7 choose ballet.

Woman: Stage 2—at nodes 2 and 3, choose ballet.

One of the interesting things about specifying the equilibrium in this way is that even though, in equilibrium, nodes 4 and 6 would never be reached, what the man should do if the game ever got there is specified; i.e., the man's strategies are specified on off-equilibrium paths. Also, note that in solving for the equilibrium to the game starting at node 1, the games are first solved for starting at nodes 4–7 in stage 3, then these strategies are used from stage 3 to solve for games starting from nodes 2 and 3 in stage 2, resorting to backward induction to solve for the game. In doing so, the equilibrium is solved for all subgames, starting from every node. Thus, the equilibrium specified is a Nash equilibrium, not only to the game starting from node 1, but to every subgame. For this reason, the equilibrium is known as a subgame perfect Nash equilibrium. It is important to note that if sub-game perfection was not required, other Nash equilibria would be admitted, including, for example, the man choosing baseball at nodes 1 and 4–7, and the woman choosing baseball at nodes 2 and 3. Finally, note that if the three-stage game had only two stages, containing nodes 1–3, with the man choosing in stage 1, at node 1, and the woman choosing in stage 2, at nodes 2 and 3, the subgame perfect equilibrium would be for both to choose baseball. In this way, it is seen that the concept of subgame perfect equilibrium has real force. It has been used to study many problems in economics, especially related to entry of firms, including sequential and preemptive entry. Essentially, the idea is that once a firm has entered, an incumbent would take that as given, and the subsequent behavior would be an equilibrium to the new subgame postentry, and it is this that must govern a firm's entry decision.

Incomplete and Asymmetric Information

Recall that if there is a move by Nature—a chance move—at the beginning of a multistage game, then the game is one of incomplete information. Consider the following example. A seller of an appliance, say, a refrigerator, knows that there is a probability p that the refrigerator has a defect that cannot be observed. Suppose the buyer also knows this. In other words, the defect rate is common knowledge. The buyer would pay $1000 for a "good" refrigerator and $900 for a "bad" one. Should the seller set a price, P, of $1000 or $900? (for the sake of exposition, ignore other possible prices). And, what would be the equilibrium action for the buyer: buy, B, or not buy, N? This is a game of incomplete information, which can be depicted as in Fig. 2. Note that the seller's information set consists of the two nodes {1, 2} because he/she does not know whether Nature chose a good

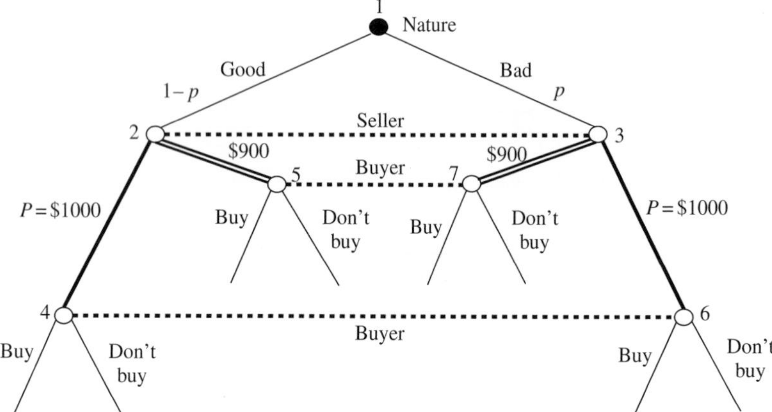

Figure 2 Game of incomplete, symmetric information. The dashed lines indicate the same information set.

refrigerator or a bad one. If the seller chooses a price of \$1000, the buyer is at the information set consisting of the two nodes {4, 6}, and if the seller chooses a price of \$900, the buyer is at {5, 7}. This game might be solved by invoking, for example, the expected value criterion. What is important to note here, though, is that in evaluating the best response based on expected value at an information set with multiple nodes, a decision maker must know the payoffs for any combination of node and action and must know the probability of being at a certain node conditioned on being at the information set. Figure 2 represents a game in which information is incomplete and symmetric, because neither seller nor buyer knows what Nature chose.

Now consider games of asymmetric information, which provide useful models for many interesting situations. Returning to the refrigerator example, suppose it can be one of two types with a defect rate of $p_i, i = 1, 2$, and $p_1 < p_2$. So, product 1 is good and product 2 is bad. Moreover, assume that buyers value a working refrigerator at \$1000 and a defective one at zero. Further, buyers are risk neutral, so they would pay $\$1000(1-p)$ for a refrigerator with a known defect rate p. The cost to the seller of a type i refrigerator is assumed to be C_i. Thus, the profits from selling type i refrigerator, if buyers were informed of the type, is $1000(1-p_i) - C_i$. Finally, assume that the probability that the seller has a good refrigerator is θ, and bad is $1-\theta$. If consumers had no information on the type that the seller has, they would be willing to pay $1000[(1-p_1)\theta + (1-p_2)(1-\theta)]$. Let P denote the price that the seller sets. Then, the buyer–seller interaction is depicted as a game of asymmetric information in Fig. 3. Here, as in Fig. 2, Nature picks the type of refrigerator at node 1, the seller picks a price at nodes 2 and 3, and the buyer makes a decision to buy or not at an information set consisting of nodes 4 and 5. The key point to note here is that the seller knows the node at which he/she is located but the buyer does not, resulting in asymmetric information. The more interesting question is what the seller can do about it. There are two possibilities. One is for the seller to condition his/her equilibrium strategy on the node where he/she is located. This, in turn, would reveal information to the buyer, and so the buyer should revise his/her probability of a good refrigerator θ (being at 4 or 5) suitably, using Bayes' rule. The buyer's equilibrium strategy at the information set containing nodes 4 and 5 should then be arrived at using these revised probabilities. The second possibility is that the seller's equilibrium strategy is independent of the information he/she has, and so of the node where he/she is located. In this case, the buyer needs to make sense of an off-equilibrium outcome in stage 1. In particular, how should the buyer revise his/her probability of a good refrigerator? As will be seen, this has force in perfect Bayesian Nash equilibrium (PBNE), which extends the concept of subgame perfect Nash equilibrium to the case of asymmetric information.

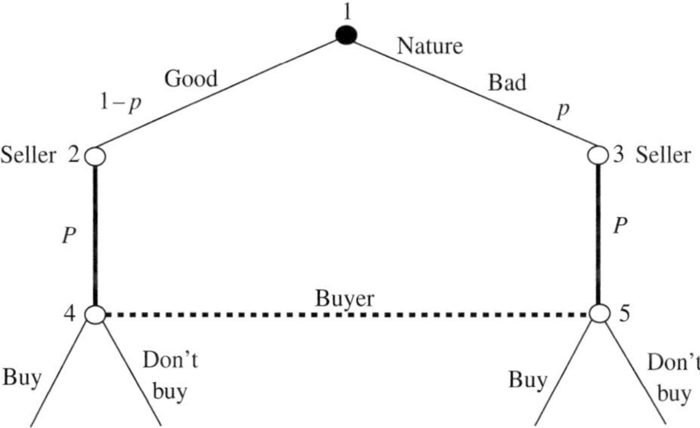

Figure 3 Game of incomplete, asymmetric information. The dashed lines indicate the same information set.

Perfect Bayesian Nash Equilibrium

Perfect Bayesian Nash equilibrium is now illustrated to show how it applies in a simple signaling model. Revisit the refrigerator example with specific numerical values: $p_1 = 0.1, p_2 = 0.2, \theta = 0.5, C_1 = 845$, and $C_2 = 750$. Then, consider the following candidate PBNE:

Seller: $P = 1000[(1-p_1)\theta + (1-p_2)(1-\theta)] = 850$.
Buyer: Buy.
Beliefs (off-equilibrium): $\Pr(\text{Good} \mid P > \neq 850) = \theta$.

Given the strategies of the other, both the buyer and the seller are at their best response. However, for a subgame perfect equilibrium to this two-stage game, it should be specified what the buyer would do in stage 2 if the seller were to deviate from the equilibrium price of \$850 in stage 1. In a game of asymmetric information, it is specified how the buyer would revise his/her prior probability of a good refrigerator, θ, in this case as $\Pr(\text{Good} \mid P \neq 850) = \theta$. These are known as beliefs. The subject of what beliefs are appropriate has preoccupied game theorists considerably. In this case, what are known as passive conjectures have been proposed, so that on seeing an out-of-equilibrium outcome, the posterior is the same as the prior. Given this, it is easy to verify that this is indeed a PBNE. In this equilibrium, both types of sellers take the same equilibrium action, and so cannot be separated based on their actions. For this reason, the equilibrium is called a pooling equilibrium. Note that in this equilibrium, a bad product makes a large profit, $(850 - 750 = \$100)$, and a good one makes a small profit $(850 - 845 = \$5)$.

It might be conjectured that there are other equilibria in this case, because consumers would be willing to pay \$900 for a good refrigerator if there were no asymmetric information. In particular, is there an equilibrium in which the seller charges a high price in node 2 for a good refrigerator and a low price in node 3 for a bad refrigerator? An equilibrium of this type that identifies the type of seller by the seller's actions is known as a separating equilibrium. It turns out that a separating equilibrium does not exist in this case. To see why, suppose it did. Then, on seeing a high price, the buyer would have to conclude that the refrigerator is good, and so be willing to pay a higher price. But then, why would a seller with a bad refrigerator not mimic the good type? Indeed, in this case, the seller would. Thus, for a separating equilibrium to exist, it must be that no type wants to mimic the other.

Next consider how the seller can profitably enforce a separating equilibrium by designing a contract before setting the price. This will make it not profitable for the bad type to mimic the good type. Specifically, suppose the seller can offer a money-back guarantee that costs \$25 to administer. Consider the following PBNE:

> Seller: At node 2, offer a money-back guarantee, but not at node 3.
> Seller: $P = 1000$ at node 2, \$800 at node 3.
> Buyer: Buy.

Now, given the money-back guarantee, the buyer would pay \$1000 regardless of the defect rate. The buyer would certainly pay \$800 even for the bad product. So the buyer's strategy is a best response. For the seller, at nodes 2 and 3, profits are, respectively, $1000(0.9) - 25(0.1) - 845 = \$52.5$, or $800 - 750 = \$50$. It is obvious that the good seller would not want to mimic the bad, but how about the other way around? If, at node 3, the seller were to offer the same terms as at node 2, his/her profits would be $1000(0.8) - 25(0.2) - 750 = \$45$. It is clear that the seller would not want to mimic the action at 2. Thus, a way has been devised for the informed player, the seller, to communicate his/her private information to the buyer, the uninformed player. This was done by a signal of quality in this case. Interestingly, the signal alone did not affect quality. The signaling model as a way to offset asymmetric information is used in many contexts, including job market signaling, if worker's abilities are not known to employers; advertising, if product quality is known to seller but not buyer; and dividend payments, to convey information on a company's future prospects.

The Revelation Principle

A large class of problems in which there are two players, one informed and the other uninformed, has come to be known as principal–agent problems. A principal is one who designs a contract that an agent can accept or reject. From a game theoretic perspective, the key question is whether the informed or the uninformed player moves first. In the signaling model, the informed player moves first. In the particular example of the preceding section, the principal was informed. Signaling can also occur in situations in which the agent is informed. Employers (principals) are uninformed of workers' (agents') abilities, but workers are informed. In this case, the employer designs the contract conditioned on a signal from the worker. Workers accept or reject the contract depending on their abilities.

Consider now situations in which the uninformed player must move first. In particular, assume that the principal is uninformed and must design a contract. There are many examples of this kind of situation. For example, insurance contracts are designed without knowing the driving characteristics of the insured. For illustrative purposes, consider a sales manager as the principal who must design a compensation plan (contract) for his/her salespersons, who are the agents. Assume that the agent in this model is informed. To what information might a salesperson, but not the manager, have access? It could be the salesperson's ability. In this case, the salesperson would be informed before accepting the contract. Another kind of information would be whether a customer the salesperson approached turned out to be easy or hard to sell to, because it would be difficult for the manager to observe this sales response. In this case, the salesperson becomes informed after accepting the contract but before putting in the effort to sell to the customer. Thus, the effort level of the agent depends on information that he/she, but not the principal, has. Finally, the manager would be uninformed about the effort put in by a salesperson. This would occur if sales have a random component to them, because knowing sales is not sufficient to infer the effort. More relevant, a manager, even if he/she could observe the salesperson, cannot write a contract that is conditioned on a salesperson's ability, the random customer response, or effort. Thus the type (of salesperson), the state of the world chosen by Nature, and effort are all not contractible, meaning that there would be no way for a third party, such as a court, to verify the claims of ability, customer response, and salesperson effort. And yet all of these factors would affect the sales generated by the salesperson. What the manager can do is to write an "optimal" contract conditional on sales. What are some properties that such optimal contracts must satisfy?

A contract based on sales (verifiable outcome) must satisfy three conditions to be practical. First, it must be acceptable to the salesperson. Usually, it must afford the agent expected utility that is not less than what the agent would obtain if he/she were to reject the contract. This is known as the individual rationality (IR) constraint. Second, it must take into account that the salesperson would take the contract as given and then choose effort to maximize his/her expected utility. In other words, the incentive structure in the contract would determine the effort level. This is known as the incentive compatibility (IC) constraint. Third, a contract that is optimal for the manager would maximize his/her expected utility subject to the IR and IC constraints. This problem can be formulated as a constrained maximization problem.

The problem can also be viewed as a multistage game in which the principal first designs a mechanism, M, that specifies the terms of the contract. In particular, it says what the salesperson would have to sell, and what he/she would earn, both depending on what message he/she sends. After the mechanism has been designed, the salesperson accepts or rejects the contract. Suppose the salesperson accepts. Then, the information he/she has and the terms of the contract he/she chooses simultaneously send a costless message to the manager that will determine the salesperson's payoff. Thus, the principal chooses the mechanism and the agent chooses the message (and the effort), and the equilibrium in this game solves for the optimal contract. An important result in the theory of contracts is that the message can be restricted to be the information the agent has, and an optimal contract has the property that the agent would not have an incentive to report his/her information falsely. This is known as the revelation principle, because the optimal contract uncovers the information that the principal does not have. To see the intuition behind the revelation principle, suppose in the salesperson compensation problem that there are two salespersons with differing abilities, high (H) and low (L). Consider the (optimal) mechanism that offers $m(H)$ and $m(L)$, $m(H) \neq m(L)$, if salespersons report H and L, respectively. Suppose, contrary to the revelation principle, the mechanism induces H to lie, and to report L instead. Then, because the mechanism is optimal, the manager would have lost nothing by making $m(H) = m(L)$. This sort of reasoning can be established more rigorously. This is useful because it can restrict our attention to a subset of all possible contracts. In light of the revelation principle, the problem of optimal contracting can now be thought of as maximizing expected utility of the principal subject to three constraints: IR, IC, and truth telling.

Using the Game Theoretic Model

There are far too many interesting applications of game theory to cover here, but three examples with managerial implications will give the reader a feel for how the concepts developed in the preceding discussions can be used in modeling.

Auctions

Auctions play a major role in many spheres of economic activity, including e-commerce, government sale of communication frequencies, sale of state-owned assets to private firms, and, of course, art. Sellers are interested in maximizing their revenue and so analysis of equilibrium under different auction rules for particular situations would be helpful. From a larger perspective, it would be desirable that the auctioned object goes to the person who values it most. Again, how this is affected by specific auction rules can be studied using game theory. At its core, an auction involves competitive bidding, with bidders taking turns. Bidders in an auction differ in their valuation for an object and their knowledge of the true value, so auctions can be viewed as games of asymmetric information. Here the Nash equilibrium strategies are characterized in the simple English and Dutch auctions. Consider a single object being auctioned to N potential bidders, indexed by i. Bidder i knows his/her valuation v_i, of the object. Assume that $0 \leq v_i \leq V < \infty$, so that all bidders have a nonzero valuation and none has an infinite valuation. This type of auction is called a private value auction because each bidder knows with certainty his/her value, but not others' values. [In contrast, an auction in which all bidders have the same (common) value for the object, but each has an error-prone estimate of the common value, is usually called a common value auction. In this case, knowing others' estimates can help refine an individual bidder's estimate. The following discussion relates only to private value auctions.]

In a Dutch auction, the auctioneer starts off at a high price and decreases the price in small steps until a bidder steps in. The bidder wins at that price, but no information is generated about the valuations of the other potential bidders, except that they are lower than the winning bid. Because the bidder pays the highest price, and nothing is learned during the auction, a Dutch auction is equivalent to a first-price sealed-bid auction. In an English auction, the auctioneer cries out bids in incremental steps, and bidders stay in or opt out. When a single bidder remains, he/she wins the auction, and must pay the last bid at which the second highest bidder stayed in. During the course of the auction, information on the valuation of the other bidders becomes available from the price at which each dropped out, which could be useful, especially in common value auctions. In a private value auction, because nothing is learned during the auction, an English auction is equivalent to a second-price sealed-bid auction. Seminal work by William Vickrey in 1961 showed that both first-price and second-price auctions in a private value auctions yield the same expected revenue to the seller.

Second-Price Auction

In a second-price sealed-bid auction, the highest bidder wins but pays the second highest bid. Let B_i denote i's bid. The payoff to bidder i is then

$$\pi_i(B_i, B_{-i}) = \begin{cases} v_i - \max(B_{-i}) & \text{if } B_i > \max(B_{-i}), \\ 0 & \text{else.} \end{cases} \tag{4}$$

The possibility of bids being tied is ignored. It is easy to see that a Nash equilibrium to this game is for each bidder to bid $B_i = v_i$. In the event that the bidder loses, this strategy is not dominated. In the event that the bidder wins, given other bidders' strategies, this is a best response. Thus, this strategy of bidding true valuation is a weakly dominant strategy, resulting in a Nash equilibrium because all players are at their best response.

The seller is interested in the equilibrium revenue to the seller, not the bids alone, and so would like to know what the revenues are when using a second-price rule. Revenue would depend on the distribution of values over bidders. Let $F(v)$ denote the cumulative distribution function of the v_i values. In other words, each bidder's value is a draw from this distribution. Assume that the draws are independent, and assume that F is differentiable and the values are in a closed interval. Given the Nash equilibrium strategies, a bidder with valuation v_i wins if all others have a valuation less than v_i, and this occurs, say, with probability $P(v_i)$. Of course, P depends on F. Knowing F, it is also possible to calculate the expected value of the second highest bid as the maximum of $(N-1)$ independent draws from F conditioned on the maximum being less than v_i. Denote this by $M(v_i)$. Then, clearly the revenue to the seller conditioned on v_i is $P(v_i)M(v_i)$. The expected revenue can be obtained by unconditioning on v_i. In other words, expected revenue to the seller is simply $\int P(v)M(v)\, dF(v)$.

First-Price Auction

In a first-price auction, the Nash equilibrium strategies are slightly more complicated. Assume that bidders maximize their expected payoff. Suppose all bidders follow a strategy $s(v_i)$, with s monotonically increasing in v_i. Then, $s : v_i \rightarrow B_i$. It can be shown that a Nash equilibrium in this case is $s(v_i) = M(v_i) < v_i$. Thus, in a first-price auction, all bidders bid less than their true value. But, the revenue to the seller, computed, as before, by first conditioning on v_i and then taking expectations, is identical to that in the second-price auction. This is Vickrey's result. Thus, from the seller's point of view, the two types of auctions produce the same outcome. In both cases, the object goes to the person who values it most. The equivalence outcome under different auction rules does not always obtain. Indeed, many features of auctions, such as the use of reserve prices, auctions of multiple objects, common value auctions, and so on, would be part of a model, depending on the situation. Since the time of Vickrey's work, many game theoretic models have been developed to incorporate these features.

Government Procurement

How might the government design a contract for defense purchases? This is game of asymmetric information because the (supplying) firm is likely to know more about its cost of supplying to the government than the knows about prices. Suppose the firm is one of two types, H and L, with abilities a_H and a_L, $a_H > a_L$, where cost of supplying the defense item is

$$c_i = c_0 - a_i - e_i, \quad i = H, L, \tag{5}$$

where e_i is the effort expended by firm i to control costs. The cost of the effort for the firm is $V(e)$, V', $V'' > 0$. Of course, the government cannot observe the effort level of a firm, but can observe the final cost. The government offers a contract that pays $t(c)$ if the firm's reported cost is c. The firm's objective is to maximize

$$\pi_i = t(c_i) - V(e_i). \tag{6}$$

The government cares about the cost, the social benefit B of the defense item, and the firm's profits. So it wants to maximize

$$\pi_G = B_{-c} - V(e_i) - \lambda[c + t(c_i)]. \tag{7}$$

The last term represents the social cost of taxes that must be used to pay the firm. Although the government does not know which type the firm is, it is assumed to know the probability that the firm is type H or L, and it is common knowledge. This problem can be seen as one of mechanism design, with the government specifying a payment $s(H)$ and $s(L)$, and associated costs $s(H)$ and $s(L)$, corresponding to messages H and L. For realizations of other costs, the payment would be zero.

The solution to this problem yields a surprisingly simple incentive contract. The contract reimburses a high-cost firm for its effort e, but this effort is lower than what would be optimal if there were no information asymmetry and the government knew that it was dealing with a high-cost firm. On the other hand, with a low-cost firm, the government reimburses the cost of effort plus an additional amount that elicits truth telling by the low-cost firm. The effort level chosen by the low-cost firm is exactly what it would have been with no asymmetric information. When there are many types of firms, rather than two, and cost observation is noisy, this result generalizes to a contract in which a firm receives a fixed payment and a variable payment that reimburses a fraction of the observed cost. The fixed payment is higher for a lower cost firm whereas a higher fraction of the cost is reimbursed for a high-cost firm.

Retail Advertising and Pricing Practice

Supermarkets carry many products, and must decide which products they should price relatively low to induce customers to shop at their store, and also whether they should advertise the price of such products. A game theoretic model can help answer such questions. Consider two retailers, indexed by j, A and B located at the ends of a straight line. Suppose that each carries two goods 1 and 2, indexed by i, and the price of good i at store j is P_{ij}. Consumers are willing to pay up to $\$R$ for either good. They are located on the line AB, are uniformly distributed, and are assumed to incur a cost to visit a store proportional to the distance of their location from the store. How might the competing stores price the products?

Peter Diamond has argued that, once at a store, a consumer would find it cheaper to buy at that store, even if the other store had a slightly higher price, because of the transportation cost. This would allow each store to price a little above the other, eventually to the monopoly price, in this case, R. This counterintuitive result of monopoly prices under competition has come to be known as the Diamond paradox. The question is how this would be affected if firms carrying multiple products could advertise prices of only a subset of products? This sort of question is relevant to supermarkets that carry many products but can advertise only a few. This can be modeled as a two-stage game in which firms advertise the price of one item (1 or 2) in the first stage, and then, after knowing the advertising strategies, set the price of the other item in the second stage. Of course, consumers would know the prices of advertised goods, but not the unadvertised ones. A Nash equilibrium to this game takes the following form:

Stage 1: Each firm advertises either item with probability 0.5, and chooses a price $P_a^* < R$ for it.

Stage 2: If both stores advertised the same item (1 or 2) in stage 1, they set the price of the unadvertised good at R. If they advertised different items, they set the price of the unadvertised good at $P_a^* + c < R$, where c is the incremental cost for a consumer located at the midpoint of route AB to visit an additional store.

In this equilibrium, consumers find it optimal to buy both items at the nearest store, even when the stores advertise different items, because, once they are at this store, it would not pay them to take advantage of a lower price on one of the items at the other store. When both stores advertise the same item, it is clearly optimal for consumers to shop at the nearest store.

The mixed-strategy equilibrium is consistent with casual observation of stores advertising both the same and different products on occasion, stores offering unadvertised price specials, and consumers content to make store choices without knowing all prices. It also shows that at least one item would always be below monopoly price R, while the expected price of the other item is also below R. The first effect is a consequence of permitting advertising, the second is a consequence of rational expectations on the part of consumers. Thus, a game theoretic model can provide insights into pricing practice.

Adapting the Game Theoretic Model

Repeated Games

An issue that has received a great deal of attention is the effect of players repeatedly playing a game such as the prisoners' dilemma. If played only once, the equilibrium is for both players to play their dominant strategy and to get a lower utility than what they would get with cooperation, but it can be conjectured that they could seek, and even obtain, some sort of cooperation if they encountered each other repeatedly, in turn leading to an outcome that is not a Nash equilibrium in a single play of the game. This line of thinking goes at least as far back as 1957, to the work of R. Duncan Luce and Howard Raiffa, who argued that "we feel that in most cases [of repetitions of Prisoners' Dilemma] an unarticulated collusion between the players will develop... this arises from the knowledge that... reprisals are possible." However, for some games, including the prisoners' dilemma, it can be shown that finite repetitions do not change the outcome, leading to what has come to be known as the chain-store paradox. Infinite repetitions are another matter, however. In this case, it is possible, under certain conditions, to support many payoff outcomes as a subgame perfect equilibrium, even if the outcome would not be a Nash equilibrium in a one-shot play of the game. Define, for each player, his/her security level or minmax value, m_{is}, as follows:

$$m_{is} = \min_{a_{-i}}[\max_{a_i} \pi_i(a_i, a_{-i})]. \tag{8}$$

An individually rational payoff for player i is a payoff that is not less than m_{is}. Let players discount future payoffs by a factor δ, $0 < \delta < 1$. Let $G(\delta)$ denote an infinite repetition of a game G, with discount factor δ. Then, the result, called a folk theorem, holds for infinitely repeated games.

Folk Theorem

Any vector of individually rational payoffs in a game G can be supported as a subgame perfect Nash equilibrium in an infinitely repeated version of G for a sufficiently large δ. The folk theorem actually requires an additional technical condition that the set of payoffs that strictly pareto-dominate the individually rational payoffs be of dimension N. It is best to think of a desired level of payoffs to support in equilibrium as a desired outcome. When a player deviates from the desired outcome, the other players would punish him/her. Now, the intuitive condition that players should not discount the future too much allows players to inflict sufficient punishment to any deviant behavior by a player. This is the reprisal contemplated by Luce and Raiffa. The technical condition allows players to punish a deviant player without punishing themselves. No punishment can lead to a player receiving a payoff lower than his/her minmax value. One of the consequences of the folk theorem is that sub-game perfect Nash equilibrium admits too many possible outcomes, calling into question the usefulness of the equilibrium concept as a modeling device. The challenge then is to model a situation carefully about what players can observe and how they can implement punishments. The main contribution of results such as the folk theorem is the reasonable way it offers to capture tacit understanding among players who interact repeatedly.

Experiments and Games

There has been a good bit of effort to see how good a model of human behavior game theory really is. Most of this work has consisted of laboratory experiments using human participants and creating environments that would correspond to typical game theoretic models of competitive interaction, whether it be auctions or price determination. In one study, it was reported that some predictions of game theory describe behavior well. In particular, games with unique Nash equilibrium are replicated well in the lab. On the other hand, in the presence of multiple equilibria, theoretical procedures to refine them do not find support in the lab. One of the concepts emphasized here is the subgame perfect equilibrium. However, participants in an experiment may have difficulty in implementing such a complicated computational procedure. In contrast, the concept of fairness seems to affect experimental outcomes, as do institutional structures (for example, the number of players).

An issue in real-world competition is how players learn. In game theoretic models, the usual way to model learning is to use some sort of Bayesian updating. This does not always accord well with experimental evidence. The capacity of individuals to learn in the course of auctions appears to be limited. Similar findings have been found in a large number of experiments. These considerations have led researchers to find ways of modeling learning, resulting in the growing area of evolutionary game theory. The goal of these efforts is to find a good way to incorporate learning in a game theoretic model. Some scholars who have explored this and related issues say there is little doubt that game theory has much to offer as a model, and alternatives are not nearly as attractive. Even so, one question remains: what is the best way to use and adapt game theory as a model of rational players?

Acknowledgments

I thank Professors Nanda Kumar, Uday Rajan, and Miguel Vilas-Boas for their suggestions on early drafts of this article.

See Also the Following Articles

Gambling Studies • Quantitative Analysis, Economics

Further Reading

Abreu, D. (19880). Towards a theory of discounted repeated games. *Econometrica* **56,** 383–396.

Ackerlof, G. (1970). The market for lemons: Quality Uncertainty and the market mechanism. *Q. J. Econ.* **84,** 488–500.

Aumann, R., and Hart, S. (1992). *Handbook of Game Theory with Economic Applications.* North Holland, New York.

Benoit, J.-P., and Krishna, V. (1985). Finitely repeated games. *Econometrica* **17,** 317–320.

Binmore, K. (1990). *Essays on the Foundations of Game Theory.* Basil Blackwell Ltd., Oxford.

Davis, D. D., and Holt, C. A. (1993). *Experimental Economics.* Princeton University Press, Princeton, NJ.

Diamond, P. A. (1971). A model of price adjustment. *J. Econ. Theory* **3,** 156–168.

Fudenberg, D., and Levine, D. K. (1998). *The Theory of Learning in Games.* MIT Press, Cambridge, MA.

Fudenberg, D., and Maskin, E. (1986). The folk theorem in repeated games with discounting or with incomplete information. *Econometrica* **54,** 533–554.

Fudenberg, D., and Tirole, J. (1991). *Game Theory.* MIT Press, Cambridge, MA.

Harsanyi, J., and Selten, R. (1988). *A General Theory of Equilibrium Selection in Games.* MIT Press, Cambridge, MA.

Kagel, J. H., and Roth, A. E. (1995). *The Handbook of Experimental Economics.* Princeton University Press, Princeton, NJ.

Krishna, V. (2002). *Auction Theory.* Academic Press, San Diego, CA.

Lal, R., and Matutes, C. (1994). Retail pricing and advertising strategies. *J. Bus.* **67**(3), 345–370.

Luce, R. D., and Raiffa, H. (1957). *Games and Decisions: Introduction and Critical Survey.* Wiley, New York.

McAfee, R. P., and McMillan, J. (1987). Auctions and bidding. *J. Econ. Lit.* **25,** 699–754.

Milgrom, P., and Roberts, J. (1986). Price and advertising signals of product quality. *J. Pol. Econ.* **94,** 796–821.

Milgrom, P., and Weber, R. (1982). A theory of auctions and competitive bidding. *Econometrica* **50,** 1089–1122.

Nash, J. (1950). Equilibrium points in n-person games. *Proc. Natl. Acad. Sci. U.S.A.* **36,** 48–49.

Rao, R. C., and Syam, N. (2000). Equilibrium price communication and unadvertised specials by competing supermarkets. *Market. Sci.* **20**(1), 66–81.

Ross, S. (1977). The determination of financial structure: The incentive-signalling approach. *Bell J. Econ.* **8,** 23–40.

Selten, R. (1965). Spieltheoretische Behandlung eines Oligopolmodells mit Nachfragetragheit. *Z. Ges. Staatswiss.* **121,** 301–324, 667–689.

Selten, R. (1978). The chain-store paradox. *Theory Decis.* **9,** 127–159.

Smith, V. L. (1989). Theory, experiment and economics. *J. Econ. Perspect.* **3**(1), 151–169.

Spence, A. M. (1974). *Market Signalling: Informational Transfer in Hiring and Related Processes.* Harvard University Press, Cambridge.

Stahl, D. O. (1989). Oligopolistic pricing with sequential consumer search. *Am. Econ. Sci. Rev.* **14**(4), 700–712.

Vickrey, W. (1961). Counterspeculation, auctions, and competitive sealed tenders. *J. Finance* **16,** 8–37.

Wilson, R. (1993). Strategic analysis of auctions. *Handbook of Game Theory* (R. Aumann and S. Hart, eds.). Amsterdam, North Holland.

Generalizability Theory

Richard J. Shavelson
Stanford University, Stanford, California, USA

Noreen M. Webb
University of California, Los Angeles, Los Angeles, California, USA

Glossary

condition The levels of a facet (e.g., task 1, task 2, ..., task k).

decision (D) study A study that uses information from a G study to design a measurement procedure that minimizes error for a particular purpose.

facet A characteristic of a measurement procedure such as a task, occasion, or observer that is defined as a potential source of measurement error.

generalizability (G) study A study specifically designed to provide estimates of the variability of as many possible facets of measurement as economically and logistically feasible considering the various uses a test might be put to.

universe of admissible observations All possible observations that a test user would considerable acceptable substitutes for the observation in hand.

universe of generalization The conditions of a facet to which a decision maker wants to generalize.

universe score The expected value of a person's observed scores over all observations in the universe of generalization (analogous to a person's true score in classical test theory); denoted μ_p.

variance component The variance of an effect in a G study.

Generalizability (G) theory, a statistical theory for evaluating the dependability (reliability) of behavioral measurements, grew from the recognition that the undifferentiated error in classical test theory provided too gross a characterization of the multiple sources of measurement error. Whereas in classical test theory, measurement error is random variation and the multiple error sources are undifferentiated, G theory considers both systematic and unsystematic sources of error variation and disentangles them simultaneously. Moreover, in contrast to the classical parallel-test assumptions of equal means, variances, and covariances, G theory assumes only randomly parallel tests sampled from the same universe. These developments expanded the conceptions of error variability and reliability that can be applied to different kinds of decisions using behavioral measurements. In G theory a behavioral measurement (e.g., achievement test score) is conceived of as a sample from a universe of admissible observations, which consists of all possible observations that decision makers consider to be acceptable substitutes for the observation in hand. Each characteristic of the measurement situation (e.g., test form, item, or occasion) is called a facet and a universe of admissible observations is defined by all possible combinations of the levels of the facets. To estimate different sources of measurement error, G theory extends earlier analysis-of-variance approaches to reliability and focuses heavily on variance component estimation and interpretation to isolate different sources of variation in measurements and to describe the accuracy of generalizations made from the observed to the universe scores of individuals. In contrast to experimental studies, analysis of variance is not used to formally test hypotheses.

Generalizability Studies

In order to evaluate the dependability of behavioral measurements, a generalizability (G) study is designed to isolate particular sources of measurement error. The facets that the decision maker might want to generalize over (e.g., items or occasions) must be included.

Universe of Generalization

The universe of generalization is defined as the set of conditions to which a decision maker wants to generalize. A person's universe score (denoted μ_p) is defined as the expected value of his or her observed scores over all observations in the universe of generalization (analogous to a person's true score in classical test theory).

Decomposition of Observed Score

With data collected in a G study, an observed measurement can be decomposed into a component or effect for the universe score and one or more error components. Consider a random-effects two-facet crossed $p \times i \times o$ (person by item by occasion) design. The object of measurement, here people, is not a source of error and, therefore, is not a facet. In the $p \times i \times o$ design with generalization over all admissible test items and occasions taken from an indefinitely large universe, the observed score for a particular person (p) on a particular item (i) and occasion (o) is:

$$\begin{aligned}
X_{pio} = {} & \mu && \text{grand mean} \\
& + \mu_p - \mu && \text{person effect} \\
& + \mu_i - \mu && \text{item effect} \\
& + \mu_o - \mu && \text{occasion effect} \\
& + \mu_{pi} - \mu_p - \mu_i + \mu && \text{person} \times \text{item effect} \\
& + \mu_{po} - \mu_p - \mu_o + \mu && \text{person} \times \text{occasion effect} \\
& + \mu_{io} - \mu_i - \mu_o + \mu && \text{item} \times \text{occasion effect} \\
& + X_{pio} - \mu_p - \mu_i - \mu_o \\
& \quad + \mu_{pi} + \mu_{po} + \mu_{io} - \mu && \text{residual} \qquad (1)
\end{aligned}$$

where $\mu = E_o E_i E_p X_{pio}$ and $\mu_p = E_o E_i X_{pio}$, and E means expectation. The other terms in (1) are defined analogously. Assuming a random-effects model, the distribution of each effect, except for the grand mean, has a mean of zero and a variance σ^2 (called the variance component). The variance of the person effect, $\sigma_p^2 = E_p(\mu_p - \mu)^2$, called universe-score variance, is analogous to the true-score variance of classical test theory. The variance components for the other effects are defined similarly. The residual variance component, $\sigma^2_{pio,e}$, indicates that the person × item × occasion interaction is confounded with residual error because there is one observation per cell. The collection of observed scores, X_{pio}, has a variance, $\sigma^2(X_{pio}) = E_o E_i E_p \times (X_{pio} - \mu)^2$, which equals the sum of the variance components:

$$\sigma^2(X_{pio}) = \sigma_p^2 + \sigma_i^2 + \sigma_o^2 + \sigma_{pi}^2 + \sigma_{po}^2 + \sigma_{io}^2 + \sigma_{pio,e}^2 \qquad (2)$$

An estimate of each variance component can be obtained from a traditional analysis of variance (or other methods such as maximum likelihood). The relative magnitudes of the estimated variance components provide information about potential sources of error influencing a behavioral measurement. Statistical tests are not used in G theory; instead, standard errors for variance component estimates provide information about sampling variability of estimated variance components.

Decision Studies

G theory distinguishes a decision (D) study from a G study. The G study is associated with the development of a measurement procedure and the D study uses information from a G study to design a measurement that minimizes error for a particular purpose. In planning a D study, the decision maker defines the universe that he or wishes to generalize to, called the universe of generalization, which may contain some or all of the facets and conditions in the universe of admissible observations. In the D study, decisions usually are based on the mean over multiple observations rather than on a single observation. The mean score over a sample of n'_i items and n'_o occasions, for example, is denoted as X_{pIO}, in contrast to a score on a single item and occasion, X_{pio}. A two-facet, crossed D-study design in which decisions are to be made on the basis of X_{pIO} is, then, denoted as $p \times I \times O$.

Types of Decisions and Measurement Error

G theory recognizes that the decision maker might want to make two types of decisions based on a behavioral measurement: relative and absolute.

Measurement Error for Relative Decisions

A relative decision concerns the rank ordering of individuals (e.g., norm-referenced interpretations of test scores). For relative decisions, the error in a random-effects $p \times I \times O$ design is defined as:

$$\delta_{pIO} = (X_{pIO} - \mu_{IO}) - (\mu_p - \mu) \qquad (3)$$

where $\mu_p = E_O E_I X_{pIO}$ and $\mu_{IO} = E_p X_{pIO}$. The variance of the errors for relative decisions is:

$$\sigma_\delta^2 = E_p E_I E_O \delta_{pIO}^2 = \sigma_{pI}^2 + \sigma_{pO}^2 + \sigma_{pIO,e}^2 = \frac{\sigma_{pi}^2}{n'_i} + \frac{\sigma_{po}^2}{n'_o} + \frac{\sigma_{pio,e}^2}{n'_i n'_o} \qquad (4)$$

In order to reduce σ_δ^2, n'_i and n'_o may be increased (analogous to the Spearman-Brown prophecy formula in classical test theory and the standard error of the mean in sampling theory).

Measurement Error for Absolute Decisions

An absolute decision focuses on the absolute level of an individual's performance independent of others' performance (cf. domain-referenced interpretations). For absolute decisions, the error in a random-effects $p \times I \times O$ design is defined as:

$$\Delta_{pIO} = X_{pIO} - \mu_p \quad (5)$$

and the variance of the errors is:

$$\begin{aligned}\sigma^2_\Delta &= E_p E_I E_O \Delta^2_{pIO} \\ &= \sigma^2_I + \sigma^2_O + \sigma^2_{pI} + \sigma^2_{pO} + \sigma^2_{IO} + \sigma^2_{pIO,e} \\ &= \frac{\sigma^2_i}{n'_i} + \frac{\sigma^2_o}{n'_o} + \frac{\sigma^2_{pi}}{n'_i} + \frac{\sigma^2_{po}}{n'_o} + \frac{\sigma^2_{io}}{n'_i n'_o} + \frac{\sigma^2_{pio,e}}{n'_i n'_o}\end{aligned} \quad (6)$$

Coefficients

Although G theory stresses the importance of variance components and measurement error, it provides summary coefficients that are analogous to the reliability coefficient in classical test theory (i.e., true-score variance divided by observed-score variance; an intraclass correlation). The theory distinguishes between a generalizability coefficient for relative decisions and an index of dependability for absolute decisions.

Generalizability Coefficient

The generalizability coefficient is analogous to classical test theory's reliability coefficient (the ratio of the universe-score variance to the expected observed-score variance; an intraclass correlation). For relative decisions and a $p \times I \times O$ random-effects design, the generalizability coefficient is:

$$E\rho^2(X_{pIO}, \mu_p) = E\rho^2 = \frac{E_p(\mu_p - \mu)^2}{E_O E_I E_p (X_{pIO} - \mu_{IO})^2} = \frac{\sigma^2_p}{\sigma^2_p + \sigma^2_\delta} \quad (7)$$

Dependability Index

For absolute decisions with a $p \times I \times O$ random-effects design, the index of dependability is:

$$\Phi = \frac{\sigma^2_p}{\sigma^2_p + \sigma^2_\Delta} \quad (8)$$

The right-hand side of Eqs. (7) and (8) are generic expressions that apply to any design and universe. For domain-referenced decisions involving a fixed cutting score λ (often called criterion-referenced measurements), and assuming that λ is a constant that is specified *a priori*, the error of measurement is:

$$\Delta_{pIO} = (X_{pIO} - \lambda) - (\mu_p - \lambda) = X_{pIO} - \mu_p \quad (9)$$

and the index of dependability is:

$$\Phi(\lambda) = \frac{E_p(\mu_p - \lambda)^2}{E_O E_I E_P (X_{pIO} - \lambda)^2} = \frac{\sigma^2_p + (\mu - \lambda)^2}{\sigma^2_p + (\mu - \lambda)^2 + \sigma^2_\Delta} \quad (10)$$

An unbiased estimator of $(\mu - \lambda)^2$ is $(\bar{X} - \lambda)^2 - \sigma^2(\bar{X})$, where $\bar{X}$ is the observed grand mean over sampled objects of measurement and sampled conditions of measurement in a D-study design.

Generalizability- and Decision-Study Designs

G theory allows the decision maker to use different designs in the G and D studies. Although G studies should use crossed designs whenever possible to avoid confounding of effects, D studies may use nested designs for convenience or for increasing sample size, which typically reduces estimated error variance and, hence, increases estimated generalizability. For example, compare σ^2_δ in a crossed $p \times I \times O$ design and a partially nested $p \times (I{:}O)$ design, where facet i is nested in facet o, and n' denotes the number of conditions of a facet under a decision maker's control:

$$\begin{aligned}\sigma^2_\delta \text{ in a } p \times I \times O \text{ design} &= pI + \sigma^2_{pO} + \sigma^2_{pIO} \\ &= \frac{\sigma^2_{pi}}{n'_i} + \frac{\sigma^2_{po}}{n'_o} + \frac{\sigma^2_{pio,e}}{n'_i n'_o}\end{aligned} \quad (11)$$

$$\begin{aligned}\sigma^2_\delta \text{ in a } p \times (I:O) \text{ design} &= \sigma^2_{pO} + \sigma^2_{pI:O} \\ &= \frac{\sigma^2_{po}}{n'_o} + \frac{\sigma^2_{pi,pio,e}}{n'_i n'_o}\end{aligned} \quad (12)$$

In Eqs. (11) and (12), σ^2_{pi}, σ^2_{po}, and $\sigma^2_{pio,e}$ are directly available from a G study with design $p \times xi \times o$ and $\sigma^2_{pi,pio,e}$ is the sum of σ^2_{pi} and $\sigma^2_{pio,e}$. Moreover, given cost, logistics, and other considerations, n' can be manipulated to minimize error variance, trading off, in this example, items and occasions. Due to the difference in the designs, σ^2_δ is smaller in Eq. (12) than in (11).

Random and Fixed Facets

Generalizability theory is essentially a random effects theory. Typically a random facet is created by randomly sampling conditions of a measurement procedure (e.g., tasks from a job in observations of job performance). When the conditions of a facet have not been sampled randomly from the universe of admissible observations but the intended universe of generalization is infinitely large, the concept of exchangeability may be invoked to consider the facet as random.

A fixed facet (cf. fixed factor in analysis of variance) arises when (1) the decision maker purposely selects certain conditions and is not interested in generalizing beyond them, (2) it is unreasonable to generalize beyond conditions, or (3) the entire universe of conditions is small and all conditions are included in the measurement design. G theory typically treats fixed facets by averaging over the conditions of the fixed facet and examining the generalizability of the average over the random facets. When it does not make conceptual sense to average over the conditions of a fixed facet, a separate G study may be conducted within each condition of the fixed facet or a full multivariate analysis may be performed.

G theory recognizes that the universe of admissible observations encompassed by a G study may be broader than the universe to which a decision maker wishes to generalize in a D study, the universe of generalization. The decision maker may reduce the levels of a facet (creating a fixed facet), select (and thereby control) one level of a facet, or ignore a facet. A facet is fixed in a D study when $n' = N'$, where n' is the number of conditions for a facet in the D study and N' is the total number of conditions for a facet in the universe of generalization. From a random-effects G study with design $p \times i \times o$ in which the universe of admissible observations is defined by facets i and o of infinite size, fixing facet i in the D study and averaging over the n_i conditions of facet i in the G study ($n_i = n'_i$) yields the following estimated universe-score variance:

$$\sigma^2_\tau = \sigma^2_p + \sigma^2_{pI} = \sigma^2_p + \frac{\sigma^2_{pi}}{n'_i} \qquad (13)$$

where σ^2_τ denotes estimated universe-score variance in generic terms. σ^2_τ in Eq. (13) is an unbiased estimator of universe-score variance for the mixed model only when the same levels of facet i are used in the G and D studies. Estimates of relative and absolute error variance, respectively, are:

$$\sigma^2_\delta = \sigma^2_{pO} + \sigma^2_{pIO} = \frac{\sigma^2_{po}}{n'_o} + \frac{\sigma^2_{pio,e}}{n'_i n'_o} \qquad (14)$$

$$\sigma^2_\Delta = \sigma^2_O + \sigma^2_{pO} + \sigma^2_{IO} + \sigma^2_{pIO} = \frac{\sigma^2_o}{n'_o} + \frac{\sigma^2_{po}}{n'_o} + \frac{\sigma^2_{io}}{n'_i n'_o} + \frac{\sigma^2_{pio,e}}{n'_i n'_o} \qquad (15)$$

Numerical Example

As an example, consider the following 1998 G study, by Webb, Nemer, Chizhik, and Sugrue, of science achievement test scores. In this study, 33 eighth-grade students completed a six-item test on knowledge of concepts in electricity on two occasions, 3 weeks apart. The test required students to assemble electric circuits so that the bulb in one circuit was brighter than the bulb in another circuit and to answer questions about the circuits. Students' scores on each item ranged from 0 to 1, based on the accuracy of their judgment and the quality of their explanation about which circuit, for example, had higher voltage. The design was considered fully random.

Table I gives the estimated variance components from the G study. σ^2_p (0.03862) is fairly large compared to the other components (27% of the total variation). This shows that, averaging over items and occasions, students in the sample differed in their science knowledge. Because people constitute the object of measurement, not error, this variability represents systematic individual differences in achievement. The other large estimated variance components concern the item facet more than the occasion facet.

Table I Generalizability Study and Alternative Decision Studies for the Measurement of Science Achievement

		G study	*Alternative D studies*					
		$n'_i = 1$	$n'_i =$	6	6	8	12	12
Source of variation	σ^2	$n'_o = 1$	$n'_i =$	1	2	3	1	2
Person	σ^2_p	0.03862	σ^2_p	0.03862	0.03862	0.03862	0.03862	0.03862
Item	σ^2_i	0.00689	σ^2_I	0.00115	0.00115	0.00086	0.00057	0.00057
Occasion	σ^2_o	0.00136	σ^2_O	0.00136	0.00068	0.00045	0.00136	0.00068
pi	σ^2_{pi}	0.03257	σ^2_{pI}	0.00543	0.00543	0.00407	0.00271	0.00271
po	σ^2_{po}	0.00924	σ^2_{pO}	0.00924	0.00462	0.00308	0.00924	0.00462
io	σ^2_{io}	0[a]	σ^2_{IO}	0	0	0	0	0
pio,e	$\sigma^2_{pio,e}$	0.05657	$\sigma^2_{pIO,e}$	0.00943	0.00471	0.00236	0.00471	0.00236
	σ^2_δ	0.09838		0.02410	0.01476	0.00951	0.01667	0.00969
	σ^2_Δ	0.10663		0.02661	0.01659	0.01082	0.01860	0.01095
	ρ^2	0.28		0.62	0.72	0.80	0.70	0.80
	Φ	0.27		0.59	0.70	0.78	0.67	0.78

[a] Negative estimated variance component (−0.00093) set to zero.

The nonnegligible σ_i^2 (5% of the total variation) shows that items varied somewhat in difficulty level. The large σ_{pi}^2 (22%) reflects different relative standings of people across items. The small σ_o^2 (1% of the total variation) indicates that performance was stable across occasions, averaging over students and items. The nonnegligible σ_{po}^2 (6%) shows that the relative standing of students differed somewhat across occasions. The zero σ_{io}^2 indicates that the rank ordering of item difficulty was the same across occasions. Finally, the large $\sigma_{pio,e}^2$ (39%) reflects the varying relative standing of people across occasions and items and/or other sources of error not systematically incorporated into the G study.

Table I also presents the estimated variance components, error variances, and generalizability coefficients for several decision studies varying in the number of items and occasions. Because more of the variability in achievement scores came from items than from occasions, changing the number of items has a larger effect on the estimated variance components and coefficients than does changing the number of occasions. The optimal number of items and occasions is not clear; for a fixed number of observations per student, different combinations of numbers of items and occasions give rise to similar levels of estimated generalizability. Choosing the optimal number of conditions of each facet in the D study involves logistical and cost considerations as well as issues of generalizability (reliability). Because administering more items on fewer occasions is usually less expensive than administering fewer items on more occasions, a decision maker will probably choose a 12-item test administered twice over an eight-item test administered three times. No feasible test length will produce a comparable level of generalizability for a single administration, however—even administering 50 items on one occasion yields an estimated generalizability coefficient of less than 0.80.

The optimal D study design need not be fully crossed. In this example, administering different items on each occasion (*i:o*) yields slightly higher estimated generalizability than does the fully crossed design; for example, for 12 items and two occasions, $\rho^2 = 0.82$ and $\phi = 0.80$. The larger values of ρ^2 and ϕ for the partially nested design than for the fully crossed design are solely attributable to the difference between Eqs. (11) and (12).

Multivariate Generalizability

For behavioral measurements involving multiple scores describing individuals' aptitudes or skills, multivariate generalizability can be used to (1) estimate the reliability of difference scores, observable correlations, or universe-score and error correlations for various D study designs and sample sizes; (2) estimate the reliability of a profile of scores using multiple regression of universe scores on the observed scores in the profile; or (3) produce a composite of scores with maximum generalizability. For all these purposes, multivariate G theory decomposes both variances and covariances into components. In a two-facet, crossed $p \times i \times o$ design with two dependent variables, the observed scores for the two variables for person p observed under conditions i and o can be denoted as ${}_1X_{pio}$ and ${}_2X_{pio}$, respectively. The variances of observed scores, $\sigma^2({}_1X_{pio})$ and $\sigma^2({}_2X_{pio})$, are decomposed as in Eq. (2).

The covariance, $\sigma({}_1X_{pio}, {}_2X_{pio})$, is decomposed in analogous fashion:

$$\begin{aligned}\sigma({}_1X_{pio}, {}_2X_{pio}) = {} & \sigma({}_1p, {}_2p) + \sigma({}_1i, {}_2i) + \sigma({}_1o, {}_2o) \\ & + \sigma({}_1pi, {}_2pi) + \sigma({}_1po, {}_2po) \\ & + \sigma({}_1io, {}_2io) + \sigma({}_1pio,e, {}_2pio,e)\end{aligned} \tag{16}$$

In Eq. (16) the term $\sigma({}_1p, {}_2p)$ is the covariance between universe scores on variables 1 and 2, say, ratings on two aspects of writing: organization and coherence. The remaining terms in Eq. (16) are error covariance components. The term $\sigma({}_1i, {}_2i)$, for example, is the covariance between scores on the two variables due to the conditions of observation for facet i.

An important aspect of the development of multivariate G theory is the distinction between linked and unlinked conditions. The expected values of error covariance components are zero when conditions for observing different variables are unlinked, that is, selected independently (e.g., the items used to obtain scores on one variable in a profile, writing organization, are selected independently of the items used to obtain scores on another variable, writing coherence). The expected values of error covariance components are nonzero when conditions are linked or jointly sampled (e.g., scores on two variables in a profile, organization and coherence, come from the same items).

In 1976, Joe and Woodward presented a G coefficient for a multivariate composite that maximizes the ratio of universe-score variation to the universe score plus error variation. Alternatives to using canonical weights that maximize the reliability of a composite are to determine variable weights on the basis of expert judgment or to use weights derived from a confirmatory factor analysis.

Issues in the Estimation of Variance Components

Given the emphasis on estimated variance components in G theory, any fallibility of their estimates is a concern. One issue is the sampling variability of estimated variance components; a second is how to estimate variance components, especially in unbalanced designs.

Sampling Variability of Variance Component Estimates

Assuming that mean squares are independent and score effects have a multivariate normal distribution, the sampling variance of an estimated variance component (σ^2) is:

$$\sigma^2(\sigma^2) = \frac{2}{c^2}\sum_q \frac{E(MS_q)^2}{\mathrm{df}_q} \tag{17}$$

where c is the constant associated with the estimated variance component; $E(MS_q)$ is the expected value of the mean square, MS_q; and df_q is the degrees of freedom associated with the MS_q. In the $p \times i \times o$ design, for example, σ_p^2 is estimated by $(MS_p - MS_{pi} - MS_{po} + MS_{pio,e})/(n_i * n_o)$. Using Eq. (17) to estimate the variance of $\sigma_p{}^2$, c refers to $n_i * n_o$, and MS_q refers to MS_p, MS_{pi}, MS_{po}, and $MS_{pio,e}$. The more mean squares that are involved in estimating variance components, the larger the estimated variances are likely to be (e.g., compare standard errors $\sigma(\sigma_p^2) = 0.01360$ and $\sigma(\sigma_{pio,e}^2) = 0.00632$ for the results in Table I). Furthermore, the variances of estimated variance components will be larger with smaller numbers of observations per person (reflected in smaller df_q). Although exact confidence intervals for variance components are generally unavailable (due to the inability to derive exact distributions for variance component estimates), approximate confidence intervals are available, as are resampling techniques such as bootstrapping.

Estimates of Variance Components

Although analysis-of-variance methods for estimating variance components is straightforward when applied to balanced data and has the advantages of requiring few distributional assumptions and producing unbiased estimators, problems arise with unbalanced data. They include many different decompositions of the total sums of squares without an obvious basis for choosing among them (which leads to a variety of ways in which mean squares can be adjusted for other effects in the model), biased estimation in mixed models (not a problem in G theory because G theory averages over fixed facets in a mixed model and estimates only variances of random effects, or mixed models can be handled via multivariate G theory), and algebraically and computationally complex rules for deriving expected values of mean squares.

In 1987, Searle reviewed several alternative methods of estimating variance components that do not have the drawbacks of analysis-of-variance methods. Maximum likelihood (ML) and restricted maximum likelihood (REML) methods of estimation produce estimators that are normally distributed and have known sampling variances at least under large-sample conditions. Minimum norm quadratic unbiased estimation (MINQUE) and minimum variance quadratic unbiased estimation (MIVQUE), unlike ML and REML, do not assume normality and do not involve iterative estimation, thus reducing computational complexity. However, MINQUE and MIVQUE can produce different estimators from the same data set, and estimates may be negative and are usually biased. In 2001, Brennan described two resampling techniques, bootstrap and jackknife, that can be used to estimate variance components and standard errors. Drawing on Wiley's 2001 dissertation, bootstrap now appears to be potentially applicable to estimating variance components and their standard errors and confidence intervals when the assumption of normality is suspect.

Another concern with variance component estimation is when a negative estimate arises because of sampling errors or because of model misspecification. Possible solutions when negative estimates are small in relative magnitude are to (1) substitute zero for the negative estimate and carry through the zero in other expected mean square equations from the analysis of variance, which produces biased estimates; (2) set negative estimates to zero but use the negative estimates in expected mean square equations for other components; (3) use a Bayesian approach that sets a lower bound of zero on the estimated variance component; and (4) use ML or REML methods, which preclude negative estimates.

See Also the Following Articles

Measurement Error, Issues and Solutions • Reliability Assessment

Further Reading

Brennan, R. L. (2001). *Generalizability Theory.* Springer-Verlag, New York.

Cronbach, L. J., Gleser, G. C., Nanda, H., and Rajaratnam, N. (1972). *The Dependability of Behavioral Measurements.* John Wiley, New York.

Feldt, L. S., and Brennan, R. L. (1989). Reliability. In *Educational Measurement* (R. L. Linn, ed.), 3rd Ed., pp. 105–146. American Council on Education/Macmillan, Washington, D.C.

Marcoulides, G. A. (1994). Selecting weighting schemes in multivariate generalizability studies. *Educ. Psychol. Meas.* **54,** 3–7.

Searle, S. R. (1987). *Linear Models for Unbalanced Data.* John Wiley, New York.

Shavelson, R. J., and Webb, N. M. (1981). Generalizability theory: 1973–1980. *Br. J. Math. Statist. Psychol.* **34,** 133–166.

Shavelson, R. J., and Webb, N. M. (1991). *Generalizability Theory: A Primer.* Sage, Newbury Park, CA.

Webb, N. M., Nemer, K., Chizhik, A., and Sugrue, B. (1998). Equity issues in collaborative group assessment: Group composition and performance. *Am. Educ. Res. J.* **35,** 607–651.

Webb, N. M., Shavelson, R. J., and Maddahian, E. (1983). Multivariate generalizability theory. In *Generalizability Theory: Inferences and Practical Applications* (L. J. Fyans, ed.), pp. 67–81. Jossey-Bass, San Francisco, CA.

Wiley, E. (2000). *Bootstrap Strategies for Variance Component Estimation: Theoretical and Empirical Results.* Unpublished doctoral diss., Stanford University, Stanford, CA.

Geographic Information Systems

Michael F. Goodchild
University of California, Santa Barbara, California, USA

Glossary

datum Basis for measurement of position on the Earth's surface.

discrete object view Conceptualization of geographic phenomena as analogous to a tabletop littered with countable, possibly movable objects.

ecological fallacy The fallacy of making inferences about individuals from aggregated data.

field view Conceptualization of geographic phenomena as a set of functions over geographic space.

geocoding Conversion of addresses, place names, or other geographic references to coordinates, such as latitude and longitude.

modifiable areal unit problem The dependence of analysis of aggregate data on the precise reporting zones used for aggregation.

polyline Representation of a line as a sequence of points connected by straight segments.

spatial analysis A method of analysis whose results depend on the locations of the objects being analyzed.

street centerline data set Representation of a street network as a collection of lines approximately centered along each street.

A geographic information system is designed to capture, store, display, communicate, transform, analyze, and archive georeferenced information, that is, information tied to specific locations on the Earth's surface. Geographic information systems enhance and to some extent replace the traditional role played by maps, but are also capable of handling information in the form of satellite images of the Earth's surface, as well as information from surveys and administrative records that have been georeferenced. They are increasingly used in the social sciences to support research based on cross-sectional data or studies for which geographic location and context are important and useful.

Introduction

The origins of geographic information systems (GISs) can be traced to the mid-1960s. Early computers were designed primarily for numerical processing, following the lead of Babbage and others. But by 1965, other applications had begun to appear, supported in part by the development of specialized peripherals, notably pen plotters and map digitizers. About this time, the Canada Land Inventory faced a massive problem of map data processing: how to take the very large number of maps created to document Canada's underutilized land resource and to produce tables of the amounts of land available for various types of development and use. Measurement of area from maps had always been time-consuming, tedious, and inaccurate when performed by hand. But if the maps could be converted to digital form, simple algorithms would allow areas to be measured and tabulated electronically. The Canada Geographic Information System (CGIS) was thus a response to a well-defined need.

By the 1980s, commercial GISs had begun to appear, offering a wide range of functions that in various ways were too complex, tedious, inaccurate, or expensive for humans to perform by hand. These included simple measurement of area and length, transformations needed to alter data formats, simple statistical analyses such as the calculation of means and standard deviations, and a host of more complex and sophisticated methods generally termed spatial analysis. In addition, GISs were provided with advanced capabilities for data display, including mapping and various forms of data visualization (see Fig. 1). The scientific community was quick to recognize the potential of GIS, and through the 1980s and 1990s GIS emerged as an indispensable tool for research in any discipline dealing with the surface of the Earth or the near-surface. In the social sciences, some of the first applications were in archaeology, but political scientists, criminologists,

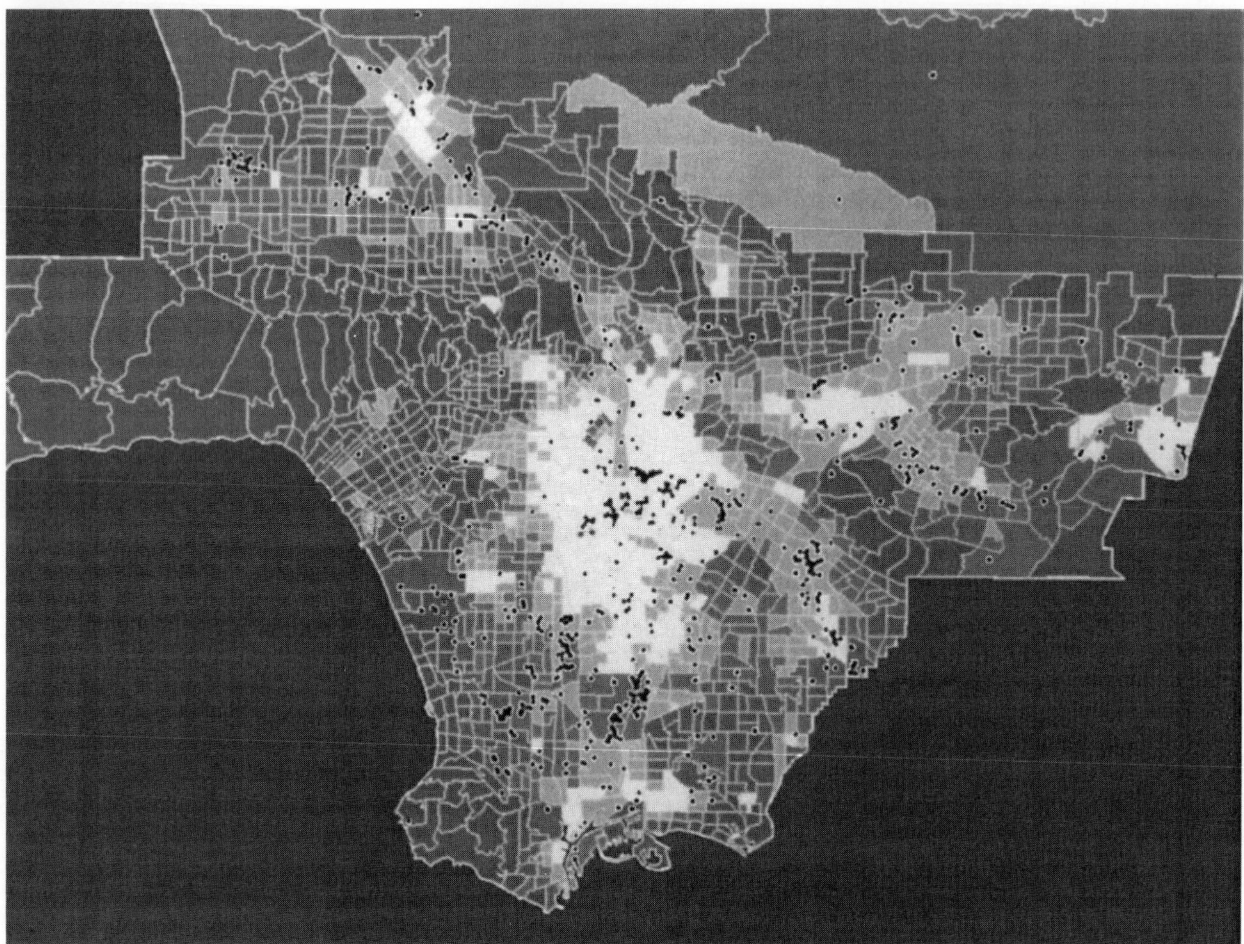

Figure 1 A GIS-generated map showing the locations of polluting industrial plants (black dots, from the Environmental Protection Agency's Toxic Release Inventory) and average income by census tract (white denotes lowest average income) for Los Angeles County. The map shows a clear association between pollution and low income. Reprinted from Burke (1993), with permission.

demographers, and epidemiologists were also prominent early adopters. For extensive bibliographies covering applications of GIS and spatial analysis in the social sciences, as well as information on sources of tools, data, and other resources, see the Web site of the Center for Spatially Integrated Social Science (http://www.csiss.org).

GIS has undergone significant transformation, as applications have emerged that go well beyond the early notion of a digital assistant performing tasks that humans find difficult. The advent of the Internet and the World Wide Web had by 1995 induced a sharp change of perspective, in which GIS was viewed as a means for sharing information between people, in addition to its more traditional role. Many Web sites were created, offering to supply visitors with geographic data sets, or to create maps on demand, or to perform simple GIS services to user specifications, using data provided by the user or by the site. Maps are compelling ways of presenting information and spatial analysis has been reinterpreted as a set of methods by which one person adds value to information, by making visible what might otherwise be invisible to another person, thus strengthening the message.

Advances in technology have brought the promise of GIS that is no longer confined to the office, but carried into the field in the form of portable and wearable devices. Wireless communication is available to download and upload data to and from Internet sites and sufficient power is available in portable devices to support virtually any GIS operation. The advent of field GIS offers to revolutionize the nature and practice of field work, in social surveys and other field-based social science.

Representation

At the heart of a GIS is a system of representation, by which features in the real world are coded in the binary alphabet of the digital computer. GIS representations typically include three aspects of real-world features: their locations on the Earth's surface, using a convenient coordinate system such as latitude and longitude; their attributes, or the things that are known about them; and any relationships of importance between them. Examples of relationships include adjacency, such as the adjacency that might exist between two neighborhoods, and connectivity, such as the connections that might exist between parts of a street network.

Attributes provide much of the richness of a GIS representation, especially in the social sciences. Reporting zones such as census tracts might carry large numbers of descriptive attributes, created from the summary tables provided by the census, such as average income or percentage unemployed. Points representing the locations of individuals in a sample survey might carry as attributes the information collected in the survey from each individual.

Underlying the representation of geographic variation are two distinct conceptualizations. In the first, the features on the Earth's surface are discrete objects, much as a tabletop might be littered by books, pens, or coffee mugs. Discrete objects can overlap and empty space can exist between them. This discrete object view is particularly appropriate in the representation of moving or persistent objects, such as individual people or vehicles. Objects can be represented as points, lines, or areas depending on their size in relation to the geographic extent of the representation. Areas are represented as sequences of points connected by straight lines (polygons) and lines are similarly represented (polylines).

The second is the field view. In this conceptualization, geographic variation is characterized by the continuous variation of a number of variables, each a function of position. Elevation is of this nature, since it can be determined at every point on the surface of the planet, and so is population density. Note that a field of population density is a generalization of a discrete object view, in which each person is a point, surrounded by empty space. This process of generalization is termed density estimation and is an important function of a GIS.

Somewhat confusingly, representations of fields must also be built from points, polylines, and polygons, using one of six recognized methods (see Fig. 2). A field can be represented by values at sample points, distributed either irregularly, or regularly on a grid. It may be represented by a set of nonoverlapping polygons that collectively exhaust the space, each having the mean value or the integral of the field over the area as an attribute (e.g., mean population density or total population). Polylines can also be used, if the isolines (contours) of the field variable are digitized. Finally, a field can be represented as a mesh of nonoverlapping triangles, with values of the field associated with each triangle vertex, and linear variation within each triangle, in the model known as the triangulated irregular network.

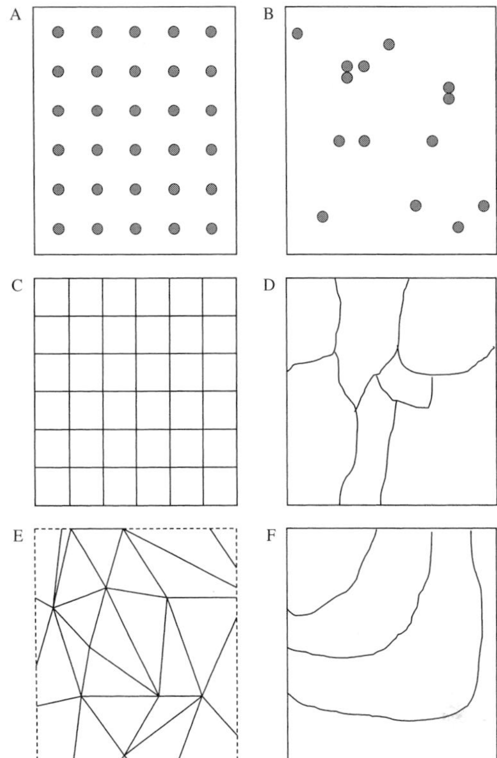

Figure 2 The six alternative representations of a field used in GIS. (A) Regularly spaced sample points. (B) Irregularly spaced sample points. (C) Rectangular cells. (D) Irregularly shaped polygons. (E) Irregular network of triangles, with linear variation over each triangle (the triangulated irregular network or TIN model; the bounding box is shown dashed in this case because the unshown portions of complete triangles extend outside it). (F) Polylines representing contours.

Social scientists are likely to use both discrete object and field conceptualizations. Individual crimes, archaeological artifacts, or deaths from a disease are viewed as discrete objects. But aggregate variables, such as those available in census summary statistics, are more likely to be viewed in terms of fields that have been averaged within reporting zones, which must behave according to the rules of a polygon-based field representation: polygons may not overlap and must collectively exhaust the space. Other phenomena likely to be conceptualized as fields include crowding, ambient noise, or topographic slope.

Georeferencing

Measuring Location

A system for accurately identifying location on the surface of the Earth is an essential component of any GIS representation. The Meridian Conference of 1884 established latitude and longitude as the universal standard for georeferencing, based on measurements from the Greenwich

Meridian and the Equator. Unfortunately, the Earth is not a perfect sphere and has been approximated by a variety of mathematical functions over time and in different parts of the world, each of which potentially leads to a slightly different latitude and longitude. The system or datum of choice in North America is the North American Datums of 1983 (NAD83), but other data may be encountered, such as the earlier NAD27, and the data used in other countries. All of this means that it is impossible to determine location exactly and variations of as much as 200 m on the ground may exist between determinations of latitude and longitude using different data. Modern GIS software makes it possible to convert easily from one datum to another, but nevertheless social scientists will occasionally encounter datum differences.

In addition to latitude and longitude, georeferencing often makes use of methods for projecting the Earth's curved surface onto a plane and associated planar coordinate systems. These include the universal transverse mercator (UTM) system, the NATO standard widely used by national mapping agencies. UTM consists of 60 distinct map projections and coordinate systems, each designed to provide accuracy within a 6° zone of longitude (for example, Zone 11 runs from 120° West to 114° West). U.S. users of GIS may also encounter the State Plane Coordinate systems, adopted by each state for high-accuracy survey; U.K. users may be familiar with the National Grid and many other countries also have national grids.

The use of map projections and the practice of flattening the Earth were essential in the era of paper maps, but are somewhat paradoxical in a technology based on digital representation, since nothing in a digital computer requires flattening. But paper maps are still a very important product of GIS, as well as an important source of input. Moreover, most social science research is conducted over small areas, where the distortions introduced by flattening the Earth are small and where the benefits of being able to work in a simple rectangular coordinate system are compelling. Distance and area are comparatively difficult to compute from latitude and longitude and much easier from planar coordinates expressed in meters.

Street Addresses and Place Names

Although latitude and longitude and planar coordinate systems are convenient, they are essentially inaccessible to the average person, who is more likely to remember and report location in more familiar ways, such as through the use of place names or street addresses. GIS techniques have been developed for easy recognition and conversion, in effect providing an interface between the vague world of human discourse and the precise world of georeferencing. These processes are known by a variety of terms, including geocoding and address matching.

Consider, for example, a survey conducted with a sample of households, in which each household is identified by street address. In order to map the results of the survey, it is necessary to identify the coordinates corresponding to each address. This can be accomplished by making use of one of a number of available street centerline data sets, which represent streets as polylines and include the ranges of addresses on each side of each street segment (the stretch of a street between two adjacent intersections). The first street centerline data sets for the United States were developed in conjunction with the census and distributed free to interested users. The TIGER (Topologically Integrated Geographic Encoding and Referencing) data set, which was first developed for the 1980 census, stimulated a substantial industry concerned with adding value and exploiting the applications of TIGER.

Unfortunately, geocoding is not as simple as it sounds. Specific addresses must be interpolated between the addresses of the end-points of each segment (e.g., 951 would be placed just over halfway between 901 and 999 in the 900 block), which is a dubious assumption in rural areas, where street addresses may not even exist, and in condominium complexes and townhouse developments. In Japan, houses are often numbered by date of construction rather than order along a street. Spelling variations, the lack of a standard syntax, and other problems typically result in success rates of less than 80% for automated geocoding and require expensive human intervention, even in urban areas of the United States.

Place names also provide the basis for a second method of geocoding, although at much coarser scale. An index providing the basis for translation between place names and coordinates is known as a gazetteer and there has been much interest in these data sets, in conjunction with information retrieval. Suppose, for example, that one wants to conduct a study of a particular city and to collect and assess any data that may be available. Many large archives of GIS data, such as the Geography Network (www.geographynetwork.com), developed and maintained by Environmental Systems Research Institute (a major vendor of GIS software), or the Alexandria Digital Library (www.alexandria.ucsb.edu), an online map and imagery library developed by the University of California, Santa Barbara, allow users to search for data within the archive by starting with a place name and using the services of a gazetteer to translate it into a latitude and longitude reference. This reference is then used, along with other user-supplied criteria, to search the archive for suitable data, which can then be retrieved, examined, and downloaded. Other services based on gazetteers have also emerged; geoparsing, for example, allows large masses of text to be searched for place names, which are then used to establish geographic context.

Visualization

GIS is an inherently visual technology, inviting its users to take advantage of the power and effectiveness of data when rendered visually. Maps are the traditional way of visualizing geographic information and GIS owes much to the legacy of cartography, the science and art of mapmaking, and to successful efforts by cartographers to systematize the discipline. Summary or aggregate data associated with polygons are often displayed in the form of choropleth maps, using shading and other forms of polygon fill to distinguish values of the variable of interest. Point data are typically displayed as symbols, again with color or symbol size used to distinguish attribute values. Commercial GIS software supports a vast array of possible mapping techniques, including contour or isopleth maps of fields, and cosmetic features such as legends, north arrows, annotation, and scale bars.

It is important, however, to recognize the fundamental differences between GIS displays and paper maps and the advantages that the digital technology provides over traditional methods. First, GIS has changed mapmaking from an expensive and slow process carried out by a few highly trained cartographers to a fast and cheap process available to all. Anyone armed with a computer, data, and simple software can produce compelling maps (and also misleading maps).

Second, GIS displays are inherently dynamic and interactive, whereas paper maps are essentially immutable once created. GIS displays can portray changes through time or allow users to zoom and pan to expose new areas or greater detail. More than one display can be created simultaneously on a single screen. Maps can also be displayed beside other forms of presentation, such as tables, and tables and maps can be linked in interesting ways (e.g., clicking on a polygon in a map display can highlight the corresponding row in a table). The term "exploratory spatial data analysis" has been coined to describe the interactive exploration of GIS data through maps and other forms of presentation.

Spatial Analysis

Although the display of geographic information in the form of maps can be powerful, the true power of GIS lies in its ability to analyze, either inductively in searching for patterns and anomalies or deductively in attempts to confirm or deny hypotheses based on theory. The techniques of analysis available in GIS are collectively described as spatial analysis, reflecting the importance of location. More precisely, spatial analysis can be defined as a set of techniques whose results depend on the locations of the objects of analysis. This test of locational dependence clearly distinguishes techniques of spatial analysis from more familiar statistical techniques, such as regression, that are invariant under relocation of the objects of analysis. Thus, GIS can be understood as a technology facilitating methods of spatial analysis, just as the familiar statistical packages facilitate methods of statistical analysis or word processors facilitate the process of writing.

Since about the 1950s, a vast array of methods of spatial analysis have been devised for the detection of patterns and anomalies and the testing of hypotheses. Many texts, such as that by Bailey and Gatrell, organize spatial analysis according to the types of data for which they are designed: techniques for the analysis of point patterns, or polygon data, for example. In 2001, Longley *et al.* used a somewhat different approach based on the objectives of analysis and that approach is followed here in a brief review. Interested readers are referred to the more detailed discussion in that source.

Query

Interactive displays allow users to determine answers to simple queries, such as "What are the attributes of this object?" or "Where are the objects with this attribute value?" Some queries are best answered by interacting with a map view, by pointing to objects of interest. Other queries are better answered by interacting with a table view, by searching the table for objects whose attributes satisfy particular requirements. A histogram view is useful for finding objects whose attribute values lie within ranges of interest and a scatterplot view allows objects to be selected based on comparisons of pairs of attributes. Finally, a catalog view allows the user to explore the contents of the many data sets that might constitute a complete GIS project.

Measurement

Earlier discussion of the origins of GIS emphasized the importance of area measurement in the development of CGIS. Many other simple measurements are supported by GIS, including distance, length, terrain slope and aspect, and polygon shape. Measurements are typically returned as additional attributes of objects and can then be summarized or used as input to more complex forms of analysis.

Transformation

Many techniques of spatial analysis exist for the purpose of transforming objects, creating new objects with new attributes or relationships. The buffer operation creates new polygons containing areas lying within a specified distance of existing objects and is used in the analysis of spatial proximity. The point in polygon operation determines which of a set of polygons contains each of a set of points and is used to summarize point data by area, in the analysis of crime or disease (e.g., Fig. 1). Polygon overlay determines the areas of overlap between polygons and is often used by social scientists to estimate summary statistics for new areas that do not coincide with reporting zones (e.g., to estimate populations of communities whose boundaries do not respect census zone boundaries). Density estimation also falls into this category, since it transforms point data sets into representations of continuous fields.

Summary Statistics

Search for pattern is often conducted by computing statistics that summarize various interesting properties of GIS data sets. The center of a point data set is a useful two-dimensional equivalent to the mean and dispersion is a useful equivalent to the standard deviation. Measures of spatial dependence are used to determine the degree of order in the spatial arrangement of high and low values of an attribute. For example, rates of unemployment by census tract might be highly clustered, with adjacent tracts tending to have similarly high or similarly low values, or they might be arranged essentially independently, or adjacent tracts might be found to have values that are more different than expected in a random arrangement.

Optimization

A large number of methods have been devised to search for solutions that optimize specific objectives. These include methods for finding point locations for services such as libraries or retail stores, for finding optimum routes through street networks that minimize time or cost, for locating power lines or highways across terrain, or for planning optimal arrangements of land use. These methods are often embedded in spatial-decision support systems and underpinned by GIS software.

Hypothesis Testing

The sixth class consists of methods that apply the concepts of statistical inference, in reasoning from a sample to the characteristics of some larger population. Inference is well established in science and it is common to subject numerical results to significance tests, in order to determine whether differences or effects could have arisen by chance because of limited sample size or are truly indicative of effects in the population as a whole.

It is tempting to adopt statistical inference in dealing with geographic information, but several problems stand in the way. First, geographic data sets are often formed from *all* of the information available in an area of interest and it is therefore difficult to believe that the data are representative of some larger universe and that results can be generalized. Instead, one tends to believe in spatial heterogeneity or the variation of conditions from place to place; in this context, it is difficult to regard a study area as representative of any larger area. Second, geographic data sets typically exhibit spatial dependence, which means that one object's attributes are unlikely to be truly independent of the attributes of its neighboring objects. The endemic presence of spatial dependence in geographic data has been called the First Law of Geography and is often attributed to Waldo Tobler.

There are several possible solutions to this dilemma. First, objects might be chosen sufficiently far apart, allowing the assumption of independence to be acceptable, but this results in discarding data. Second, one might limit analysis to a description of the data and area of study and avoid any suggestion of inference about larger areas or other data sets, but this flies in the face of scientific tradition and the norms of peer review. Third, one might assume that the universe consists of all possible spatial arrangements of the data, in a form of randomization, particularly if the actual spatial arrangement of the data is the issue of interest. But this approach, though attractive, does not support inference in areas not covered by the data.

Issues

As will be obvious from the previous section, the use of GIS raises numerous issues concerning the nature of geographic information and inference from cross-sectional data. It is generally accepted that cross-sectional data cannot be used to confirm hypotheses about process, but they can certainly be used to reject certain false hypotheses and to explore data in the interests of hypothesis generation. Although GIS has evolved from the static view inherent in paper maps, there is much interest in adding dynamics and in developing methods of spatiotemporal analysis.

Uncertainty is a pervasive issue in GIS. It is impossible to measure location on the Earth's surface exactly and other forms of uncertainty are common also. For example, summary statistics for reporting zones are means or totals and clearly cannot be assumed to apply uniformly within zones, despite efforts to ensure that census tracts are approximately homogenous in socioeconomic characteristics. Results of analysis of aggregated data are dependent on the boundaries used to aggregate (the modifiable areal unit problem) and inferences from aggregated data regarding individuals are subject to the ecological fallacy.

Nevertheless, the outcomes of the widespread adoption of GIS in the social sciences since the 1980s are impressive. It is clear that GIS has brought new power to the analysis of cross-sectional data and the integration of diverse data sets. It has also shifted the ground of social science to some degree, by increasing the emphasis on local data, geographic variation, and highly disaggregated analysis, in contrast to the pervasive nomethetic approach of earlier decades.

See Also the Following Articles

Computer-Based Mapping • Ecological Fallacy • Geolibraries • Land Use Mapping • Remote Sensing • Spatial Databases • Spatial Pattern Analysis

Further Reading

Allen, K. M. S., Green, S. W., and Zubrow, E. B. W. (eds.) (1990). *Interpreting Space: GIS and Archaeology*. Taylor and Francis, New York.

Bailey, T. C., and Gatrell, A. C. (1995). *Interactive Spatial Data Analysis.* Longman, Harlow, UK.

Burke, L. M. (1993). *Environmental Equity in Los Angeles*. Unpublished M.A. thesis, University of California, Santa Barbara.

Goodchild, M. F. (2000). Communicating geographic information in a digital age. *Ann. Assoc. Am. Geogr.* **90,** 344–355.

King, G. (1997). *A Solution to the Ecological Inference Problem: Reconstructing Individual Behavior from Aggregate Data.* Princeton University Press, Princeton, NJ.

Longley, P. A., Goodchild, M. F., Maguire, D. J., and Rhind, D. W. (2001). *Geographic Information Systems and Science.* Wiley, New York.

Monmonier, M. S. (1991). *How to Lie with Maps.* University of Chicago Press, Chicago, IL.

Openshaw, S. (1984). *The Modifiable Areal Unit Problem.* GeoBooks, Norwich, UK.

Robinson, A. H., Morrison, J. L., Muehrcke, P. C., Kimerling, A. J., and Guptill, S. C. (1995). *Elements of Cartography,* 6th Ed. Wiley, New York.

Silverman, B. W. (1986). *Density Estimation for Statistics and Data Analysis.* Chapman and Hall, New York.

Tobler, W. R. (1970). A computer movie: Simulation of population growth in the Detroit region. *Econ. Geogr.* **46,** 234–240.

Tufte, E. R. (1990). *Envisioning Information.* Graphics Press, Cheshire, CT.

Geography

James O. Wheeler
University of Georgia, Athens, Georgia, USA

We cannot talk any better than our ancestors ... cannot figure any better than the best mathematicians of old, but we have not only thousands of tricks that have been gathered through the years, but machinery which enables a rather simple-minded person to get calculations done accurately and quickly.

Benjamin C. Gruenberg,
Biology and Human Life, 1925

Glossary

gravity model A model that compares the volume of flow, or spatial interaction, between two or more places based on the mass (population) of these places and the distance between the places.

index of dissimilarity A measure that compares the proportions of different occupational types within the study area.

index of segregation A measure that provides a single statistic summarizing the spatial distribution between a subcategory and the category as a whole.

information gain statistic A statistic indicating the overall spatial relationship. It is also used as a goodness-of-fit statistic comparing two spatial distributions, P_i and Q_i; the smaller the fit between the two distributions, the lower the value of I.

location quotient A ratio of ratios used to measure and map relative distributions or relative concentrations of a subarea to the area as a whole.

principal components analysis A data transformation technique that measures the degree to which n variables in a data set are intercorrelated. The technique uses unities in the $m \times n$ correlation matrix, where m refers to places or areas, and transforms the n variable into a smaller number of independent components, with each component accounting for a decreasing proportion of the total variance.

social area analysis The application of factor analysis to socioeconomic and demographic data for a number of places (often census tracts) to identify the major dimensions (characteristics) of residential areas of a city.

Human geography is a social science that focuses on the location, spatial distribution, and spatial interaction of human beings and their social, economic, cultural, and political activities. The interest is in places and geographic spaces. The term spatial interaction entails the volume or intensity of linkages between and among two or more places, such as the number of work trips originating in a particular neighborhood and terminating in various office complexes or industrial districts within a metropolitan area. This essay provides a general overview of the quantitative methods used in contemporary geography. Particular attention is given to locational or spatial statistics, the gravity model, and factor and principal components analysis.

Introduction and Background

Although some examples of the use of quantitative methods—primarily statistics—appeared in geographic research prior to the mid- to late 1950s, the full introduction of quantitative modeling and statistical analysis did not occur until the early 1960s, building strength throughout that decade. The quantitative approach to human geography has continued powerfully into twenty-first century, although many other competitive nonquantitative advances have also been made, beginning in the early 1970s. Currently, quantitative statistical approaches represent only one of several different competing ways of conducting research in human geography. Some of these competing research styles, such as postmodernism, are frankly antagonistic to numerical analysis.

Whereas social sciences such as psychology and economics embraced quantitative statistical analysis long before geography adopted these methods, other fields such as anthropology, and especially history, were much slower to accept the value of enumerative procedures in research. Human geography's acknowledgment of the advantages of statistical analysis and mathematical modeling fell somewhere near the middle of the acceptance trajectory within the social sciences and was a major factor in placing human geography squarely within the social sciences.

The Origin and Expansion of Quantitative Methodology in American Geography

In the mid- to late 1950s, a number of exceptionally bright and highly motivated graduate students joined the Department of Geography at the University of Washington in Seattle, then and now one of the leading geography programs in the United States and Canada. Many of these students chose to study at University of Washington in order to work with Professor Edward L. Ullman, one of the most prominent geographers in North America, who in 1951 had moved from Harvard University to the University of Washington. As Doug Eyre wrote in 1978:

> *by a stroke of fortune, there was assembled not only a fine group of able young faculty but also a group of outstanding graduate students, a truly vintage assemblage whose members were to play a leading role in the profession. Chief among these was Brian Berry, who with young Dr. William Garrison pioneered the path that led to the "quantitative revolution" in geography across the county after the mid-1950s. It was a period of unusual intellectual ferment that moved the Seattle department to a position of national leadership. The ferment was not always positive or reasoned—there were unavoidable, sometimes acrimonious, clashes in the department between the traditionalist and the Young Turks who were intent upon sweeping reforms. Ed was an early supporter of the latter's emphasis upon theory-building and quantitation, but he became gradually disenchanted with their extreme positions and dogmatic excesses. In turn, they reciprocated by ignoring or undervaluing his scholarly output.*

Those who were attracted to Seattle by Ullman—including Brian Berry, with his undergraduate degree from University College, University of London—instead chose William Garrison as their mentor. Garrison had just returned from a year's leave of absence in the newly formed Regional Science program at the University of Pennsylvania, headed by Walter Isard, where Garrison had immersed himself in statistics, mathematical modeling, and theory development and hypotheses testing procedures. Many graduate students were attracted to Garrison and his new geography, emphasizing the use of statistical methods, theory development, and hypothesis testing. These students included, in addition to Berry, William Bunge, Michael Dacey, Art Getis, David Huff, Duane Marble, Richard Morrill, John Nystuen, and Waldo Tobler. As Berry wrote in 1993, "Within five years of beginning of their graduate studies, the initial cohort had positions in leading centers of geographic education."

In a 1967 study, LaValle, McConnell, and Brown mapped the spread of quantitative methods courses offered in Ph.D.-granting programs. The first to offer such a course was Bill Garrison at the University of Washington, then Edwin N. Thomas at the University of Iowa (under the leadership of Harold H. McCarty), Brian J. L. Berry at the University of Chicago, Edward J. Taaffe at Northwestern University, and James Barnes at the University of Georgia—a total of only five departments as of 1958 (Fig. 1A). By 1965, 24 of the 32 Ph.D.-granting geography departments in the United States offered a quantitative geography course (Fig. 1B). The then-new approach, sometimes dubbed the quantitative revolution, was quickly and widely adopted in geography. Programs in the Midwest and, somewhat later, on the East Coast were especially responsive, swiftly and vigorously embracing the quantitative approach to geographic research.

Locational Indices in Geography

Because human geography is primarily interested in the location of people and their activities, it follows that certain basic descriptive quantitative measures are commonly used in data analysis. Those indices discussed here are the location quotient, the index of dissimilarity, the index of segregation, and the information gain statistic.

Location Quotient

The location quotient, a ratio of ratios, is a widely used geographic index. It is used to measure and map relative distributions or relative concentrations of a subarea to the area as a whole. An example of its use might be to measure the residential distribution of scientists within a metropolitan area compared to total workers. The formula is:

$$LQ = \frac{X_i/\sum X_i}{N_i/\sum N_i} \cdot 100$$

where LQ is the location quotient, X_i is the value of a variable (scientists) in area i, $\sum X_i$ is the value of the variable (scientists) in all the subareas combined (metropolitan area), N_i is the total of workers in each subarea of the metropolitan area, and $\sum N_i$ is the total number of workers in the metropolitan area (Tables I and II). Thus, the location quotient varies in our example with the proportion of scientists in a given subarea to the total number of

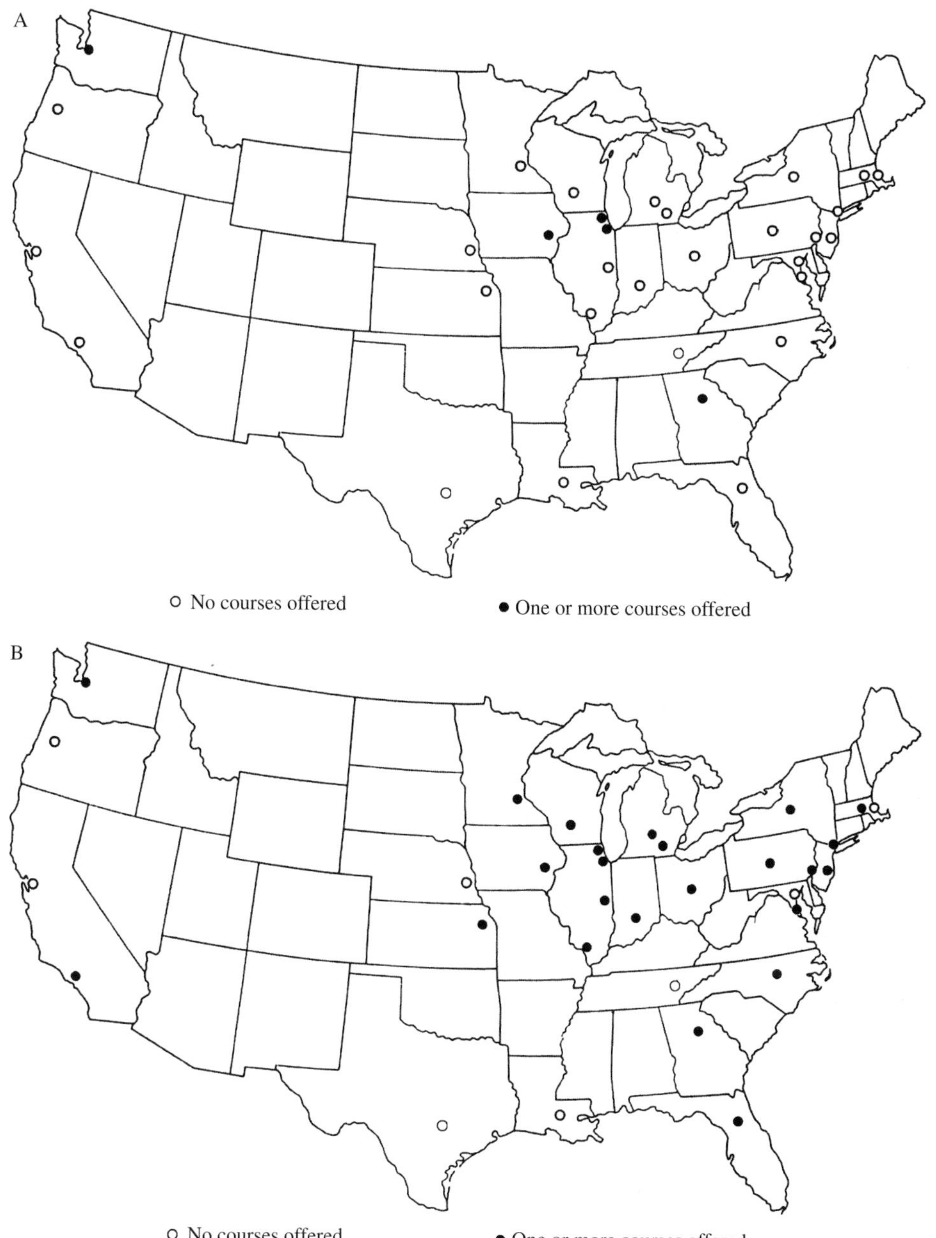

Figure 1 Ph.D.-granting geography departments offering quantitative methods courses, (A) 1958 and (B) 1965. After LaValle, McConnell, and Brown (1967) with permission.

Table I Sample Data for Computing Locational Quotient

Subarea	*Scientists, X_i*	*Total workers, N_i*
1	5	100
2	10	50
3	20	50
4	20	200
5	50	600
Total	100	1000

Table II Computing the Locational Quotient

Subarea	$X_i/\sum X_i$	$N_i/\sum X_i$	*LQ*
1	0.05	0.10	50
2	0.10	0.05	200
3	0.20	0.05	400
4	0.20	0.20	100
5	0.50	0.60	83

Table III Location Quotient for Help-Supply Service Workers in the U.S. South by Metropolitan-Area Population Size Categories, 1999

Metropolitan hierarchy	*Location quotient*
2.5 million and above	1.14
1 million to 2,499,999	1.22
250,000 to 999,999	1.04
100,000 to 249,999	0.73
Less than 100,000	0.58

Source: Hongmian Gong (2002, 54).

Table IV Residential Dissimilarity between Chinese Americans and Selected Racial and Ethnic Groups in Four Counties in the Atlanta Metropolitan Area, 1990

	Index of dissimilarity			
County	*Whites*	*Blacks*	*Hispanic*	*Asian Indians*
Cobb	53	62	51	62
DeKalb	38	74	46	46
Fulton	51	89	52	62
Gwinnett	44	44	35	41
Average	47	67	46	53

Source: Zhang (1998, 132).

workers in that subarea. A value of 100 indicates that there is the same proportion of scientists as total workers. In areas 1 and 5 in Table II, the values less than 100 shows that there are fewer scientists than "expected" compared to the total number of workers. In contrast, values greater than 100 indicate that there is a higher proportion of scientists than "expected" living in the subareas 2 and 3 compared to the total number of workers.

The 2002 study by Gong provides an illustration. Her interest is in measuring the relative metropolitan concentration of employees in help-supply services in the U.S. South. Help-supply services provide temporary workers to other businesses on a fee basis. Here the focus is on how the number of help-supply service employees vary among metropolitan areas of different sizes compared to the total number of workers. Table III shows a clear hierarchical distribution; the larger the metropolitan area, the higher the location quotient (except for metropolitan areas with more than 2.5 million in population). Gong's results indicate that larger metropolitan areas tend to have a greater need for temporary workers compared to total workers.

Index of Dissimilarity

The index of dissimilarity compares the proportional distribution of two subcategories, in contrast to the location quotient, which compares the relative distribution of a subcategory within a larger category. If, for example, we wish to compare the number of help-supply service workers with the number of manufacturing workers, the index of dissimilarity is the appropriate measure.

$$\mathrm{ID} = \sum_{i=1}^{N} \frac{|(X_i/\sum X_i) - (Y_i/\sum Y_i)|}{2} \cdot 100$$

where ID is the index of dissimilarity, X_i is the value of one subcategory (help-supply service workers) and Y_i is the value of another subcategory (manufacturing workers), and i represents observations or areas such as census tracts or counties. For every area i, the absolute value of the difference of the two subcategory proportions $|(X_i/\sum x_i - Y_i/\sum y_i)|$ is taken. These absolute differences are summed for all areas i and divided by two to avoid double counting. The index is multiplied by 100 in order to express the index in whole numbers. Its value ranges from 0 to 100, where 0 reflects identical proportional distributions between the two subcategories and 100 indicates a totally opposite spatial distribution.

The 1998 study by Zhang provides a useful example of the application of the index of dissimilarity. His study was of the residential locations of racial and ethnic groups in four counties of the Atlanta metropolitan area (Table IV). His findings show that Chinese Americans in Atlanta had residential patterns that were most similar to Hispanics and Whites, least similar to Blacks, and in an intermediate position with respect to Asian Indians. The index of dissimilarity here is interpreted as the percentage of Chinese Americans that would have to change census tracts within a county in order for their residential locations to be identical with another racial or ethnic group. Thus, 89% of Chinese Americans would have to shift census tracts in Fulton County to achieve an even spatial distribution with Blacks, representing the highest level of dissimilarity in Table IV.

Index of Segregation

The index of segregation is related to the index of dissimilarity. The difference is that the index of segregation provides a single statistic that summarizes the proportional spatial distribution between a subgroup and the group as a whole:

$$\mathrm{IS} = \sum_{i=1}^{N} \frac{|(X_i/\sum X_i) - (N_i/\sum N_i)|}{2} \cdot 100$$

Its value ranges from 0 to 100, with the same interpretation as the index of dissimilarity.

Boelhouwer, in his 2002 study, used the index of segregation to represent the levels of residential segregation in the four largest cities in the Netherlands (Table V).

He found that the percentage of minorities (Turks, Moroccans, southern Europeans, Surinamese, and Antilleans) was approximately 30% in 1995 for Amsterdam, Rotterdam, and The Hague, but only 21% for Utrecht. Boelhouwer confirmed that, despite a significant growth in minority populations in these four largest cities, the index of segregation has stayed more or less the same and, in fact, dropped somewhat in Rotterdam and The Hague.

The Information Gain Statistic

The information gain statistic has been used by geographers in a variety of ways. It is a goodness-of-fit model that has the advantage over correlation-regression analysis in that it does not assume that the data are normally distributed. The information gain statistic allows the comparison of two variables at a time, such as actual population scores versus predicted population numbers for, say, counties in North Georgia. Conceptually, information is gained from a set of N messages that transform a set of N *a priori* probabilities (Q_i) into a set of N *a posteriori* probabilities (P_i). Thus, there is an initial message (Q_i) and a subsequent message (P_i). At issue is whether the subsequent message improves the information beyond the initial message.

The information gain statistic (I_i) is calculated as follows:

$$I_i = P_i \ln\left(\frac{P_i}{Q_i}\right) \tag{1}$$

Table V Index of Segregation of Minorities in the Four Largest Cities in the Netherlands, 1980–1995

City	*1980*[a]	*1987*[a]	*1995*[a]
Amsterdam	30	32	31
Rotterdam	47	43	43
The Hague	56	53	51
Utrecht	37	33	33

Source: Boelhouwer (2002, 568).
[a] Turks, Moroccans, southern Europeans, Surinamese, and Antilleans.

Note that the natural logarithm (ln), not the common logarithm, is used. Thus, if, for example, $Q_i = 0.25$ and $P_i = 0.25$, no additional information is gained and $I_i = 0$. If $P_i > Q_i$, I_i is positive, reflecting a gain in information. If, however, $Q_i > P_i$, I_i is negative, indicating a loss of information. For example:

$$I_i = P_i \ln\left(\frac{P_i}{Q_i}\right) = 0.36 \ln\left(\frac{0.36}{0.20}\right) = 0.2116$$

We can compute not only the *a priori* and *a posteriori* probabilities for each observation (where i = counties, for example), but we can also sum over all observations to obtain a single summary statistic for the entire data set:

$$I_1 = \sum_{i=1}^{N} P_i \ln\left(\frac{P_i}{Q_i}\right) \tag{2}$$

The poorer the fit between the two sets of probabilities, the larger the value of I_1, the summary statistic.

Table VI shows a hypothetical computational example of the use of the information gain statistic. The first step is to take the absolute data (corporate assets and population totals) and convert them into probabilities, Q_i and P_i, respectively. Carrying out the operations of Eq. (1) provides the individual city probabilities that allow the determination of I_i. When these city values of I_i are summed, following Eq. (2), we find $I_1 = 0.08$ in this example has a positive value.

The information gain statistic can be used to compare actual population totals with projected population, where the latter is the *a posteriori* probability, or to compare two distributions within a region, for example, manufacturing employment and service employment. It can be used, in fact, to compare any two spatial distributions or more than two distributions. In the latter case, the *a priori* probability acts as a kind of dependent variable, with which a set of *a posteriori* probabilities, acting as independent variables, is compared. Here, the summary statistic (I_1) is of prime interest.

Table VI Hypothetical Computational Example of the Information Gain Statistic

Metropolitan area	*Corporate assets*	Q_i	*Population size*	P_i	I_i[a]
Houston	103.4	0.3427	2905	0.2306	−0.0914
Dallas	84.7	0.2805	2975	0.2362	−0.0406
Washington	69.4	0.2299	3061	0.2430	0.0135
Atlanta	26.4	0.0875	2030	0.1612	0.0985
Miami	17.9	0.0594	1626	0.1290	0.1000
Total	301.8	1.0	12,597	1.0	

[a] $I_1 = 0.08$.

Spatial Interaction Modeling

Geographers not only are interested in describing and interpreting the characteristics of places but are also intent on understanding how places are linked or connected with one another. In fact, to comprehend the nature of a place we need to know the linkage structure of that place with other places. Linkages among places may be measured on a binary scale, link or no link. A binary measure leads to measures of accessibility. More commonly, however, linkages among places are calibrated on an interval scale to measure the volume of interaction among places. Because this interaction takes place over space, the term spatial interaction is normally used by geographers. Spatial interaction models have been used, for example, to understand human migration among cities and regions, commuting within metropolitan areas, customer and expenditure flows from residential areas to stores and shopping destinations, and commodity flows among cities and regions.

The Gravity Model

The gravity model is the most common example of spatial interaction modeling. The gravity model uses two variables to predict or estimate the volume of spatial interaction between or among places, be they cities, counties, or regions. These are (1) population totals of the places and (2) the distance separating these places or the time or cost of overcoming distance. The expectation is that there will be a positive association between flow volume and population size; that is, when two places have large populations we expect the volume of migrants or commuters to be large, but when places are separated by a great distance we expect that the effect of distance, as mediated by distance, cost, or travel time, will reduce the level of interaction. Thus, whereas population size leads to a positive relationship, distance leads to an inverse correlation (the volume of spatial interaction decreases as distance separation increases). The gravity model is written as follows:

$$I_{ij} = k\left(\frac{P_i \cdot P_j}{D_{ij}^b}\right)$$

where I_{ij} is the estimate of the volume of spatial interaction between place of origin i and place of destination j, k is a constant, D_{ij} is the distance between i and j, b is the exponent of distance, and P_i and P_j represent the population sizes of the places of origin and destination. The values of k and b vary depending on the specific data set.

Applications of the Gravity Model

We provide two examples of the application of the gravity model. The first is from a 1999 study by Wheeler and measures the extent to which small metropolitan areas are linked to the regional and national metropolitan economies. The specific case study used the numbers of overnight letters, packages, and boxes sent via FedEx from Athens, Georgia (population in 2000 of approximately 150,000) to 42 large U.S. metropolitan areas. The gravity model took the following form:

$$\log \text{FedEx} = \log k(\log P_j - \log D_{ij})$$

where the model is calibrated in log form, P_j is the population of metropolitan area j, and D_{ij} is the distance between Athens (i) and destination j. P_i need not enter the equation because it is the population of Athens. The model is solved by using ordinary least squares regression.

The results are of interest. First, the R^2 for the equation is 0.65, reflecting a moderately strong relationship between FedEx flow volume and the population size of the 42 metropolitan destinations and the airline distance separating them from Athens, Georgia. The standardized parameter estimates for population and distance were, respectively, 0.83 and 0.37. Thus, the population size of the 48 metropolitan areas to which FedEx letters, packages, and boxes were sent from Athens was a very strong indicator of the volume of packages sent. In contrast, the distance separating Athens from the high-volume destinations was only a weak measure of the FedEx flow magnitude—a −0.37 parameter shows only a modest decline in volume with increasing distance. In fact, the five leading metropolitan destinations for FedEx shipments from Athens were Atlanta, New York, Chicago, Dallas-Fort Worth, and Los Angeles, in that order. From this listing it is obvious that population size was of paramount importance, not distance. For FedEx shipments, which take on something of a perishable nature or may be said to be information-based, how far they are sent is less important than where they are sent.

The second gravity model application, from a 1990 study by Wheeler, examines the links between major corporate headquarters in New York City and the U.S. location of subsidiaries under their control. We know that New York is the preeminent location for major corporate headquarters in the United States. The question is in which metropolitan areas do these New York-based corporations locate their subsidiaries. Again, what is the role of metropolitan population size and of distance separation? In the study, the approximately 550 New York parent companies had nearly 2000 subsidiaries in the United States, 93% of which were in 129 metropolitan areas. The eight leading metropolitan locations of the subsidiaries were Chicago, Los Angeles, Newark, Boston, Houston, Philadelphia, St. Louis, and Hartford.

The model is:

$$\log \mathrm{OL} = \log a_1 + a_2 \log(P_j) - a_3 \log(D_{ij})$$

where OL is the number of ownership links, P_j the population of the 129 U.S. metropolitan areas having at least one subsidiary with its headquarters in New York City, D_{ij} is the airline distance from New York to the subsidiary metropolitan area, and a_1 is a constant and a_2 and a_3 are parameter estimates. As before, the model is solved using ordinary least squares. Table VII reports the results of the gravity model application. A modestly strong R^2 is found (0.66). The population size of the metropolitan areas is a strong predictor of where the subsidiaries are located; New York parent firms prefer to locate their subsidiaries in large metropolitan areas. All states except Montana and North Dakota have subsidiaries of the New York parent companies. Distance shows an extremely weak inverse relationship, although the parameter estimate (−0.24) is negative as expected. Thus, distance is negatively associated with subsidiary location, with slightly more subsidiaries near New York City.

Geographic Application of Factor and Principal Components Analysis

In his classic book *Applied Factor Analysis*, R. J. Rummel considered factor analysis to be "A Calculus of Social Science." Most applications of factor analysis by human geographers have followed the typical social science methodological applications and procedures. The unique contribution by geographers, however, has been that the observation inputs to factor analysis have involved areal units or locational points. As do other social scientists, geographers have typically used factor analysis as a data reduction technique whereby N attributes measured over M areal units (observations) result in a number of factors or components considerably smaller than N. Geographers are not only interested in the composition of the factors but also the geographic pattern of the factor scores. In fact, the factor scores for each observation (areal units) can be displayed on maps, providing a rich basis for geographic interpretation. Factor analysis and principal components analysis are both types of factorial analysis. Factor and component scores are often used as independent variables in regression analysis and cluster analysis. Because the scores are independent of one another, they are ideal inputs for these multivarient techniques.

Table VII Model of Subsidiary Linkages with New York Parent Firms

Variables	*Standardized parameters*
Population	0.79
Distance	−0.24
$N = 129$	
$R^2 = 0.66$	

Source: Wheeler (1990) with permission of the American Geographical Society; Dun and Bradstreet data.

Social Area Analysis

One of the most common examples of the use factor analysis in geography is known as social area analysis (also known as factorial ecology). In these applications to various U.S. cities, a considerable number of variables (sometimes up to 50) are inputed for an even larger number of census tracts, defined by the U.S. Census Bureau. The purpose of this use of factor analysis is to measure and map the social space in the city and to break the large number of variables down into a small number of social factors.

Analyses of several U.S. cities have yielded remarkably similar results. Whether the number of variables used is 20 or 50, three basic factors have emerged in virtually all of these studies. (To be considered a factor, the potential factor must have an eigenvalue greater than unity.) Table VIII lists the generalized variables typically employed to measure social areas in the city and the three factors that commonly result from social area analysis.

The socioeconomic status factor is usually the strongest indicator of the various social areas in the city. Census tracts fall into high, medium, and low on the factor scores, and, as indicated earlier, these can be mapped. The socioeconomic factor, as indicated by factor scores for the census tracts, take on sectoral patterns, radiating away from the center of the city and expanding into the

Table VIII Typical Factors and Variables Used in Social Area Analysis

Factors	*Variables*
Socioeconomic status	Income
	Occupation
	Education
	Housing value
Family status	Marital status
	Fertility
	Family size
	Age of adults
Ethnic status	Black population
	Hispanic population
	Asian population
	Linguistic groups

suburban areas. Thus, high-income sectors or wedges extend from the inner city into suburban space and medium-income sectors and low-income sectors have their own corresponding social spaces. Although factor analysis provides a quantitative index to the differentiated socioeconomic characteristics of neighborhoods, even a casual observer driving through the various neighborhoods in a city can see and experience the different socioeconomic levels. Such observations are usually based merely on housing indicators, such as the size and age of the house, lot size, and landscaping quality.

The second factor identified in social area analysis is family status, sometimes termed the life-cycle stage or urbanization index. This factor largely measures the demographic characteristics of census tracts. From mapping factor scores, the family status factor displays a pattern of concentric circles.

The third factor measures minority or ethnic status and is sometimes referred to as the segregation index. Here the social areas of the city are clumped into different racial, language, and accent groups and often on the basis of level of poverty and unemployment.

Because these three identified factors are derived by the use of factor analysis, the three factors are independent of one another. It is the composite of these three factors that gives rise to the social structure of the city.

Principal Components Analysis and Origin-Destination Matrixes

Another distinctive geographic application of a data reduction technique is the use of principal components analysis to understand complex origin-destination (O-D) matrixes. Principal components analysis uses unities on the diagonal rather than communalities, where communalities reflect the extent to which a particular variable enters into the factors. In O-D matrixes, the rows represent the origins and the columns are the destinations. The O-D matrix may measure work trips among census tracts or planning areas within a city, migration flows among the 50 U.S. states, or the movement of container freight from one U.S. port to a state or metropolitan destination. The basic questions being asked is how do the origins differ from one another in their spatial pattern of destinations? The same questions may be asked of destinations with respect to origins. Do inner-city areas differ notably from suburban areas? Again, factor scores may be mapped.

Table IX shows a hypothetical set of factor loadings for three factors, based on Varimax rotations of destinations (columns). Each destination is correlated (zero-order correlation coefficients) with one another to show common patterns of origins. The correlation matrix is then subjected to principal components analysis and then rotated. Factor I accounts for just more than 30% of the variance in the matrix, and the three factors combined show a cumulative sum of more than 67%. The highest loadings for the three factors show that they are largely concentrated among contiguous traffic zones.

Table IX Varimax Rotation of Destinations, Highest Factor Loadings

	Factors		
Traffic zones	*I*	*II*	*III*
1			
2	0.90		
3	0.59		
4			
5			
6			
7			
8			
9			
10	0.76		
11	0.73		
12	0.57		
13			
14			
15			
16	0.85		
17	0.83		
18	0.75		
19	0.80		
20			
21		0.58	
22			0.64
23			0.86
24			0.85
25			
26		0.79	
27		0.76	
28		0.74	
29			0.56
30			
Percentage of variance	30.1	21.4	15.6
Cumulative percentage	30.1	51.5	67.1

Summary Comments

Because simple and multiple linear correlation and regression are commonly used throughout the social sciences, including geography, no attempt has been made here to introduce these techniques. Suffice it to say, that geographers typically use places or areas as the observational units. Geographers, as do other social scientists,

Table X Other Common Statistical Techniques Used by Geographers

Geographic sampling
Measures of central tendency
Measures of spatial dispersion
Chi-square
Point pattern and neighbor analysis
Rank correlation
Spatial autocorrelation
Trend surface models
Graph theoretic techniques
Multidimensional scaling
Analysis of variance
Analysis of covariance
Correlation-regression analysis
Cluster analysis
Discriminant analysis
Cononical correlation

select a dependent variable as the primary feature to be understood and correlate it with one or more independent variables, with all variables representing points, places, or areas. Table X lists other statistical techniques commonly used by geographers. The treatment of these techniques lies beyond the scope of this article.

One final issue is worth noting. Over the past 15–20 years, there has been a decline in the use of quantitative techniques in geography and a gradual rise in the application of qualitative methods. There has also been a notable rise in the narrative approach in journal articles in the field, in which no numerical data are introduced at all. This narrative approach to presenting geography has also led to a reduced reliance on the use of maps by geographers. Moreover, there is a small minority of geographers who embrace postmodernism and are antiscientific and antiquantitative. Geography became a recognized social science primarily during the 1960s, when the discipline began using many of the basic quantitative methods common throughout the social sciences, adapting them to spatial analysis and developing various additional locational techniques. Whereas, in the 1960s, graduate programs in geography required at least one quantitative methods course, today almost no graduate department in geography requires such a course, though quantitative courses continue to be taught. Commonly, however, courses in qualitative techniques and GIS (geographic information science) are offered and eagerly sought out by graduate students.

See Also the Following Articles

Factor Analysis • Geographic Information Systems • Location Analysis • Locational Decision Making • Spatial Autocorrelation • Spatial Databases • Spatial Pattern Analysis • Spatial Scale, Problems of

Further Reading

Berry, B. J. L. (1993). Geography's quantitative revolution: Initial conditions, 1954–1960. A personal memoir. *Urban Geogr.* **14,** 434–441.

Boelhouwer, P. J. (2002). Segregation and problem accumulation in the Netherlands: The case of The Hague. *Urban Geog.* **23,** 560–580.

Clark, W. A. V., and Hoskins, P. (1986). *Statistical Methods for Geographers.* John Wiley & Sons, New York.

Eyre, J. D. (1978). A man for all regions: The contributions of Edward L. Ullman to geography. *Stud. Geogr.* (University of North Carolina, Chapel Hill) No. 11, pp. 1–15.

Fatheringham, A. S., Brunsdon, C., and Charlton, M. (2000). *Quantitative Geography: Perspectives on Spatial Data Analysis.* Sage, Thousand Oaks, CA.

Gong, H. (2002). Location and expansion of help supply services in the U.S. South. *Southeastern Geogr.* **42,** 49–64.

Griffeth, D. A., and Amrhein, C. G. (1991). *Statistical Analysis for Geographers.* Prentice Hall, Englewood Cliffs, NJ.

Gruenberg, B. C. (1925). *Biology and Human Life.* Ginn and Company, New York.

LaValle, P., McConnell, H., and Brown, R. G. (1967). Certain aspects of the expansion of quantitative methodology in American geography. *Ann. Assoc. Am. Geogr.* **57,** 423–436.

McCrew, J. C. and Monroe, C. B. (2000). *An Introduction to Statistical Problem Solving in Geography*, 2nd Ed. McGraw Hill, New York.

Rogerson, P. A. (2001). *Statistical Methods for Geography.* Sage, Thousand Oaks, CA.

Rummel, R. J. (1970). *Applied Factor Analysis.* Northwestern University Press, Evanston, IL.

Wheeler, J. O. (1990). Corporate role of New York City in metropolitan hierarchy. *Geogr. Rev.* **80,** 370–381.

Wheeler, J. O. (1999). Local information links to the national metropolitan hierarchy: The southeastern United States. *Environ. Plann. A* **31,** 841–854.

Wringley, N. (2002). *Categorical Data Analysis for Geographers and Environmental Scientists.* Blackburn Press, Caldwell, NJ.

Zhang, Q. (1998). Residential segregation of Asian Americans in the Atlanta metropolitan area, 1990. *Southeastern Geogr.* **38,** 125–141.

Geolibraries

Peter Keenan
University College, Dublin, Ireland

Glossary

digital library An integrated and cataloged collection of data stored in electronic format.

gazetteer A list of named places together with a geographic reference for identifying locations.

Geographic Information System (GIS) A computer system for storing, manipulating, and displaying geographically referenced information.

geolibrary A digital library that stores information in a format searchable by geographic location in addition to traditional search methods.

georeferenced information Data indexed by location with a distinct geographic footprint.

metadata Information about data, used to facilitate the building of large data sets of diverse information.

spatial data Information about the location and shape of, and relationships between, geographic features.

The digital indexing of library content has greatly facilitated social research, making the searching and cross-referencing of research material much easier than with paper formats. The digital format allows the easy search of a variety of data types in addition to traditional text content. Geographic (or spatial) data are becoming increasingly available in digital form, which allows searching the data by geographic location. Digital search techniques, applied in geolibraries, may be of considerable value to researchers as an extension of traditional paper libraries or nonspatial digital libraries. Digital geolibraries provide a comprehensive collection of all forms of data related to place, suitably indexed and cataloged to allow easy access by researchers. Use of geolibraries is optimized by understanding their potential advantages and some of the problems that exist in building comprehensive geolibraries.

Introduction to Geolibraries

Digital Data Sources

Social researchers are accustomed to using libraries and other sources of secondary information. These sources have traditionally been indexed in paper format by author, date of publication, title, or keyword. Traditional research approaches exploited paper-based indexes and catalogs to locate material in paper-based libraries. Information technology has enhanced research in two major ways via enhancement of library operations: digital techniques can be used for indexing library content and for storage of that content. In particular, the use of database techniques for library catalogs allows easier searching and cross-referencing of material (though the material need not necessarily be digital in nature). The digital Social Science Citation Index, for example, is much more powerful and convenient to use than its traditional paper-based equivalent. Though the digital indexing of offline resources is useful, additional cross-referencing becomes possible when the source material is stored in digital form, and in recent years large databases of computerized text and numerical data have been compiled. In addition to the advantages resulting from easier searching, the use of digital data representation eliminates or reduces traditional problems of bulky physical storage, restricted accessibility, limited portability, and concurrent use.

These advantages mean that digital libraries have much to offer for traditional library content, and researchers are already accustomed to using digital data in this form. However, conventional text-based material represents only a small part of the total data that may be of interest to researchers. The contribution of other formats, such as spatial, audio, or pictorial material, may be overlooked if they are not properly associated with related text-based content. Consequently, the full potential of the new digital technologies can be realized only if a greater range of information sources can be searched and if new relationships can be identified in data.

Geolibraries

A geolibrary is a digital library that, in addition to being searchable by traditional methods, stores information in a format searchable by geographic location; such data are thus georeferenced. In principle, a geolibrary need not use online techniques for indexing or storage of content, and paper-based map collections with appropriate catalogs have existed in libraries for many years. However, geographic location-based indexing is very difficult to implement using paper-based approaches, and comprehensive indexes of this form are not common in traditional libraries. Computerized techniques have now made comprehensive spatial indexing feasible and this will lead to spatial referencing becoming increasingly important in the future. Just as database management techniques made possible the development of digital library catalogs for traditional content, the development of the Geographic Information Systems (GIS) facilitated digital indexing of geographically referenced information. These techniques are especially valuable for the indexing of inherently spatial data that might be used for further processing by a GIS, but geographical referencing also has a major contribution to make for other forms of content across a wide range of social science disciplines.

A traditional index might identify resources associated with a particular author or date of publication; potentially this could also include multimedia formats, such as a piece of music by a particular composer. A georeferenced catalog will store material connected with a particular place. For instance, a geolibrary might store pictures of an urban street or sound recordings of traffic noise at that location. Another example is the combination of geographic data with pictorial records to produce three-dimensional representations of urban environments. Though these multimedia formats have great potential, the seamless integration of these diverse data poses difficulties in all digital libraries and the coherent georeferencing of multimedia content poses a distinct challenge in a geolibrary.

The concept of a geolibrary originated in the 1990s, and the Alexandria Digital Library at the University of California in Santa Barbara is generally regarded as the first major prototype geolibrary. The geolibrary model was further defined within the GIS community by the Workshop on Distributed Geolibraries: Spatial Information Resources, convened by the Mapping Science Committee of the U.S. National Research Council in June 1998. The idea of a geolibrary is therefore a relatively new one, and the data-intensive nature of geographic information has meant that geolibraries have inevitably lagged behind the construction of digital resources for simpler forms of data, such as text or statistics. The concept of a geolibrary is likely to evolve further as potential users become aware of the contribution of geolibraries and as sophisticated real systems become available.

Comprehensive georeferencing of digital library content requires the availability of digital spatial data for the geographic areas concerned. By the end of the 20th century, large amounts of digital spatial data had already been collected in most developed countries, and this may form the basis for the georeferencing of library content. One obstacle to building geolibraries arises because spatial data resources are somewhat fragmented and thus difficult to assemble for applications that require the synthesis of data originating in different organizations. Improved spatial processing techniques and comprehensive geographic databases mean that spatial data relationships are potentially of interest to a much wider audience than those in the traditional geographic disciplines, for whom the data were initially collected. Existing spatial data collections are often designed for the particular needs of specific user communities and it is difficult to integrate these together. Currently, the wider potential user community lacks the training and experience to make full use of the latent potential provided by the spatial association of information. The introduction of properly organized and cataloged geolibraries can make a major contribution to extending the use of spatial information and techniques to a broader community.

In many respects, geolibraries have both the problems and advantages of other types of databases. Data are collected for particular purposes by organizations that have a good understanding of the nature and immediate applications of the specific data. Nevertheless, once data have been collected and organized, their use can be justified for further downstream applications. The increasing availability of conventional digital libraries has already allowed social researchers exploit these resources for research purposes, using data in ways that were not envisaged by the original users and collectors. Such an integrated database of georeferenced data, properly indexed and cataloged in the form of a geolibrary, will also allow researchers investigate new geographic relationships that may have been difficult to research using traditional libraries.

Geolibrary Applications

Geolibrary Software

For any digital data, accessibility is largely determined by the availability of appropriate tools. A geolibrary will comprise both georeferenced data and the tools to access the data. Michael Goodchild, the most prominent researcher in geolibraries, has identified a number of key components of a geolibrary; these include a geolibrary browser, a basemap, a gazetteer, and search facilities. The geolibrary browser is a specialized software application running on the user's computer and providing access to the geolibrary via a computer network. In a sense, the many existing Internet-based mapping applications with zoom functionality offer an immature example of how such a system might operate (for example, the link to maps at http://www.mapquest.com).

The basemap provides an image of Earth, allowing the user to identify the area of interest and to display the results of a geolibrary search. Goodchild has also identified the need to search across geolibraries containing distributed information. In principle, a single geolibrary should exist for the whole planet Earth, but in practice, geolibraries will combine resources located in different databases. The large volume of data in geolibraries means that transmission of the data requires high-capacity network links. The locations containing the component parts of the geolibrary can be connected by high-speed connections, but the absence of universal high-speed network connections poses problems for user access to large volumes of geographic data. One suggestion is to distribute common geographic data (basemaps) by compact disk with read-only memory (CD-ROM) or digital videodisk (DVD), allowing the browser software to concentrate on the downloading of specialized data sets from the geolibrary. If the user had the basic geographic data in place on their machine, additional layers or attribute data could be obtained as required from the geolibrary.

A gazetteer is a list of named places together with geographic coordinates identifying locations. Gazetteers were traditionally found in printed atlases; the Times Atlas of the World, for instance, contains over 200,000 items in its gazetteer. The Geographic Names Information Service of the U.S. Geological survey (http://mapping.usgs.gov) is one digital equivalent of the atlas gazetteer. Traditional gazetteers have a number of problems from a geolibrary perspective. First, official gazetteers tend to concentrate on place names with some legal use or definition, and other widely used informal place names may not be included. There may be no clear definition of commonly used terms such as the "Midwest" of the United States or "Western Europe." Second, traditional gazetteers tended to give only a point location for a place name, but many place names refer to regions or districts rather than single points. Because point locations lack an extent, data could not be used to establish the geographic footprint associated with the name. A gazetteer could define the extent of a geographic region by indicating its component parts; for example, Iberia could be defined as Spain and Portugal together. A geographic region may also be defined by delineating its boundaries. The latter approach is data intensive and is infrequently used by traditional gazetteers, but is required for an effective geolibrary.

Limitations of Traditional Techniques

Traditional library content is organized into a few discrete objects for indexing purposes; common examples include books, sections in books, journals, and articles in journals. In contrast, georeferenced data relate to part of a continuum of space, with a geographic footprint that characterizes each piece of data. Such footprints can be precise, for example, when a unique identifier refers to a legally defined area. Other footprints are fuzzy in nature, when the limits of the area are unclear. Imprecise footprints can arise with physical objects; the boundaries of a valley or a mountain may be vaguely defined. More often, fuzzy footprints arise when there is no clear definition of commonly used terms. Though what these expressions mean in context is generally understandable, they lack the type of clear definition required for straightforward computer processing.

Traditional digital databases make it possible to search for an attribute value. This could include data with a geographic element; for example, the search could be for all people whose address is in a certain town or who share the same postal code. However, though this approach is widely used, it has several limitations. First, the same name may refer to differently defined spatial regions. For example, a variety of organizations may have an administrative center based in a town; the exact region served by these offices may differ from one body to another. A city may have an urban administration covering only part of the greater urban area; for research purposes, this limited definition of the urban area may not be of interest. In many cases, a county or state may share the same name as a town or city. Furthermore, the same place name may occur in different locations; for instance, Washington State may be confused with Washington, D.C. A web search engine search for "Dublin" may return information on Ireland's capital city or on Dublin, Ohio in the United States. A third problem is that place names may be used to label nonspatial information. A search for "Dublin" may also return information on data standards developed in Dublin, California. This is an instance of a geographic location being used as a label for something not in itself of a spatial nature (other examples include the Treaty of Rome and foodstuffs such as Brussels sprouts, Parma ham, or Peking duck). Consequently, the frequent confusion of different entities with a similar name is a major obstacle to the use of conventional text-based approaches for searching for establishing spatial associations.

Geolibrary Operations

A geolibrary should allow the user to overcome these problems by providing tools and data to answer questions related to geographic entities of interest, in addition to the standard units used by standard digital databases. For instance, demographic data is collected in small districts, which are combined into larger regions for reporting purposes. This can present a problem if these larger regions are not identical to the region of interest to the researcher. A geolibrary with detailed data would allow the combination of that data into any larger unit, to allow definition of a footprint to correspond exactly with the focus of the research (Fig. 1). Other types of analysis may not be based on administrative districts, but may be concerned with the regions served by shopping facilities or regions where commuting takes place to a large urban center.

Digital data processing is most powerful when it allows different sources of data to be synthesized together. Consequently, geolibraries provide a spatial indexing structure that facilitates the combination of different spatial data sets; for example, a digital library catalog allows searching for both keyword and author. In a similar way, a geolibrary search can identify whether spatial features overlap with the footprints of other spatial objects. For example, a search might identify the administrative districts that lie along a river, allowing the discovery of content relating to these regions. Another use of these techniques would be to identify the regions close to a political boundary, i.e., suburbs of a city or other fringe

Figure 1 Use of a bounding box for aggregation of data from subdistricts into a new area of interest.

areas. In addition to using overlay operations to identify where footprints overlap, spatial operations can be used to identify which lines or points lie within specific areas. For instance, it would be possible to identify the modern towns lying within the boundary of a historic political entity, such as a province of the Roman Empire. Other spatial processing techniques include network analysis, which can be used to calculate travel times on road networks. These techniques are probably less important in a geolibrary context, but could be used to identify information associated with travel to work regions and other spatial patterns not reflected in administrative boundaries.

Geolibrary Example

A number of geolibrary prototype systems exist, although these presently fall some way short of the ultimate potential of a geolibrary, they are constantly evolving to include more information. Examples of current systems available over the World Wide Web include the Alexandria Digital Library web client (http://webclient.alexandria.ucsb.edu/) located at the University of California in Santa Barbara and the Geography Network (http://www.geographynetwork.com) hosted by ESRI Corporation. Because of the limitations of the software commonly used on the web, these provide a relatively unsophisticated geolibrary browser access to georeferenced material and a gazetteer.

Using the Alexandria web client as an example, the user is initially presented with a screen with an interactive map in one window and the ability to enter text commands. User interaction through the map browser or text dialogue boxes can change the bounding box that determines the footprint being examined. The interface allows different shapes of bounding box to be selected and the user can zoom in to the level of detail required (Fig. 2). The object of a search is to identify information in the database with a geographic footprint that overlaps in some way with the footprint of the region of interest to the user. The user can request information with a georeferenced footprint that lies entirely inside the selected region, footprints that overlap with it, or indeed footprints that are entirely outside the region. The library will return the results of such a search as database entries with the required footprint. These might include gazetteer entries for towns in the area selected, details of relevant offline information such as books, and links to online information such as digital maps and aerial photographs of the region.

In their present immature state, geolibrary services inevitably lack much potentially useful information that will be added in such resources in the future. The limitations of web technology mean that the interfaces are not as easy to use as they might be, and dedicated geographic browser software may be needed to address this

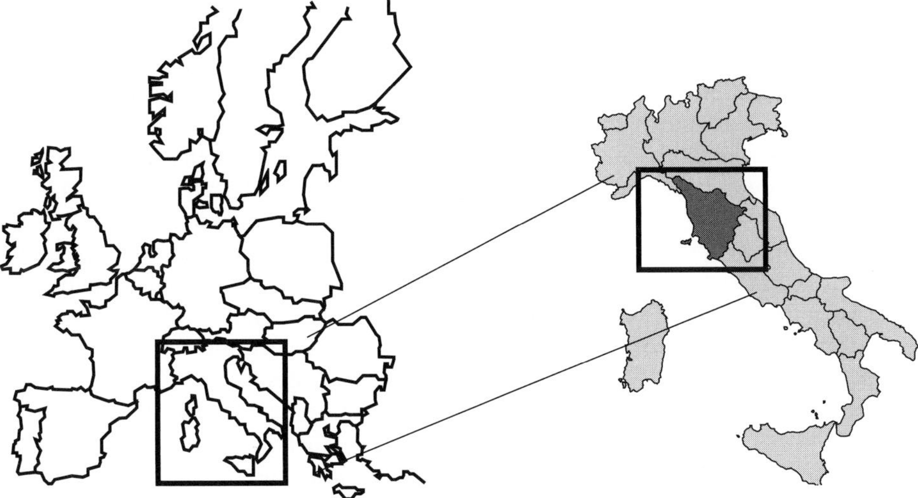

Figure 2 Defining a more detailed bounding box.

problem. Nevertheless, these prototypes demonstrate the potential power of the geolibrary model and can advance to provide a fuller implementation of the concept.

Issues in Geolibraries

Difficulties in Using Spatial Techniques

Social science researchers have become accustomed to using digital tools such as database queries and statistics. Though these tools are widely used, not every user makes full use of their potential, in part because of a lack of understanding of the techniques involved. Modern statistical analysis packages provide a range of powerful statistical techniques, but the limitations of these may not be fully comprehended by a user whose primary domain is not statistics. Spatial techniques are even more complex and the development of appropriate interfaces to make these approaches accessible to the nonspecialist user is an important challenge for geolibrary designers. Geographic interfaces often assume user familiarity with specialist geographic terminology; this assumption is unlikely to hold true for a broader user community. Training can offer one solution to this lack of experience with spatial techniques, but it is always likely to be the case that the desire of social researchers to use geolibraries exceeds their willingness to undergo long training courses. There is a danger that inexperienced users may fail to use a geolibrary to its full potential, owing to ignorance of many of its capabilities. The geolibrary tools need to make access as convenient as possible, while preventing inexperienced users from using the system inappropriately.

Geolibrary interfaces need to address a number of issues: the formulation of the problem, the identification of relevant data, the correct spatial association of the data, the performance of any spatial operations required on the data, and the presentation of the results in a format comprehensible to a nonspecialist user. Problem formulation is made more difficult by differences of terminology and nomenclature between different disciplines. One strategy for resolving this difficulty is to provide a direct manipulation interface that provides a visual interactive description of the operation required. Using this approach, the user might specify the region to be processed by drawing a boundary on an onscreen map. Successful geolibrary initiatives are likely to offer more sophisticated interfaces, including this type of functionality, exploiting artificial intelligence and visual interactive modeling techniques to interpret user requirements and facilitate presentation of output in customized formats.

Metadata

Identification of the relevant data for a specific problem requires that the contents of the geolibrary be comprehensively spatially indexed. As the volume of spatially referenced data continues to grow, indexing of these data resources plays a vital role in facilitating the wider use of spatial techniques. The correct spatial association between spatial entities is complicated by the use of different spatial units for the aggregation. This is a problem faced by other forms of digital data storage, and techniques such as data dictionaries are used to facilitate the organization of digital databases. The spatial equivalent of these approaches is needed to facilitate the use of geolibraries. A variety of spatial directories exist; for example, in the All Fields Postcode Directory in the United Kingdom, these relate spatial units such as postal codes to other spatial representations. However, to document spatial relations comprehensively, metadata, or data (information) about data, are needed. As the building of geolibraries requires the synthesis of different spatial data sets, metadata have a major role to play in clarifying any ambiguities in the definition of spatial data. The objective of metadata is to facilitate the discovery of data, their suitability and their availability, and to identify any technical parameters required for their use.

To fulfill these requirements, metadata must be quite complex, and consequently are not likely to be understood by potential geolibrary users. Raw metadata are likely to be used mainly by librarians and other professionals rather than end users. Less experienced users will use the geolibrary through its interaction tools; this software will use the metadata to structure user access to data. Much of the data imported into a geolibrary will be geographically referenced in the form of traditional database fields. For example, attribute data will be associated in a database table with "east region" or "Smallville urban area." A metadata description is needed to identify exactly what is meant by these terms, because other data sets in the geolibrary may deal with other regions known as "east" and other regions based on the "Smallville area." The definitions of these regions may change over time; for instance, the regions used in one census may differ from those used in subsequent censuses. A metadata definition of a data set will clarify any ambiguities in these definitions.

Traditional library metadata approaches have concentrated on documents and these need to be extended to take account of spatial databases. Various national and regional initiatives exist; one example is the U.S. initiative on the Content Standard for Digital Geospatial Metadata (CSDGM). More than 30 countries are coordinating their standards to be compatible with an international standard, IS 19115. This provides a schema for describing digital geographic data sets using a comprehensive set of mandatory and conditional metadata elements. The challenge is for geolibrary builders to integrate the various metadata approaches successfully, in a way that is largely seamless to the user.

Economics of Geolibraries

A geolibrary is a combination of various data sources, collected by different organizations, often at considerable cost. If spatially related data are to become freely available for inclusion in geolibraries, then the question of the funding of these libraries arises. One approach is for geolibraries to be regarded as a public benefit that should be funded by the government. Many spatial data are of public interest, and a large volume of spatial data originates with government agencies such as traditional cartographic agencies (e.g., the Ordnance Survey in the United Kingdom, or the Bundesamt für Kartographie und Geodäsie in Germany) and local government bodies. However, differing approaches are taken internationally to the distribution of these data. In the United States, government policy is to make basic geographic data collected with taxpayers' money freely available to citizens; this has led to initiatives such as the National Spatial Data Infrastructure (NSDI) and the funding in 1994 of the Alexandria Digital Library by the U.S. National Science Foundation. There have also been geolibrary-type initiatives at the state and local level in the United States (for instance, the Idaho Geospatial Data Center). In contrast, in most European countries, government policy is to seek to recover some or all of the cost of spatial data collection from those who use it, thus posing a major challenge to the builders of geolibraries. Then again, the comprehensive nature of a geolibrary raises the question of a charging model even in the more favorable public sector environment found in the United States. First, when a geolibrary integrates data from private and public sector sources, the economic rationale for these data providers is different. Second, digital data may be readily copied, so the traditional library model of a loan for a restricted period may not be relevant.

This problem of building digital databases from multiple private sector sources is one faced by other sectors; for example, the music industry has experienced great difficulty in establishing a working model for the download of copyright music. In electronic commerce generally, copyright issues remain problematic and proposed solutions such as micropayment mechanisms have had only limited success. A geolibrary might operate by allowing access to the database only through tools provided by the library, thereby enforcing economic restrictions on user access to the data. However, these types of restrictions inhibit access to the data, compromising the objective of the geolibrary. The design of an appropriate charging structure for geolibraries is likely to prove as big an obstacle to their widespread use as any technical problems with data storage or transmission.

Conclusion

Digital indexing and storage of data allow many extended possibilities for social research. These partly arise from the convenience of the digital format, but also because new types of data and data relationships can be exploited. One such opportunity exists for exploiting spatial relationships; this requires the georeferencing of data, which has been greatly facilitated by digital processing. For this form of data to be easily used, the traditional library needs to be extended in the form of a geolibrary. This would provide a comprehensive collection of all forms of data related to any one place, indexed and cataloged to allow spatial operations on different combinations of data in the geolibrary.

Though the potential of geolibraries is clear, their development poses many problems. Social researchers are typically not familiar with either the power or the limitations of spatial techniques. The geolibrary must make these accessible to researchers in all domains; this requirement poses a strong challenge for the designers of geolibraries and their interfaces. Geolibraries will be at their most successful if they contain a wide range of georeferenced data. However, georeferencing requires the availability of digital spatial data, which are usually expensive to collect and which typically originate from different sources. Consequently, it is difficult to devise an appropriate economic model for geolibraries that provides an appropriate return to the data providers. This problem is likely to prove even more difficult than the purely technical obstacles to geolibrary development. Despite these difficulties, the research potential for the use of spatial data is so great that geolibraries will play an important and growing role in research work in the social sciences in the future.

See Also the Following Articles

Computer-Based Mapping • Geographic Information Systems • Spatial Autocorrelation • Spatial Databases

Further Reading

Boxall, J. (2002). Geolibraries, the Global Spatial Data Infrastructure and Digital Earth. *Int. J. Special Librar.* **36**(1), 1–21.

Goodchild, M. F. (1998). The geolibrary. In *Innovations in GIS* (V. S. Carver, ed.), pp. 59–68. Taylor and Francis, London.

Jankowska, M. A., and Jankowska, P. (2000). Is this a geolibrary? A case of the Idaho Geospatial Data Center. *Inf. Technol. Librar.* **19**(1), 4–10.

Larson, R. R. (1996). Geographic information retrieval and spatial browsing. In *GIS and Libraries: Patrons, Maps and Spatial Information* (L. Smith and M. Gluck, eds.), pp. 81–124. University of Illinois, Urbana.

Mapping Science Committee. (1999). *Distributed Geolibraries: Spatial Information Resources*. National Academy Press, Washington, D.C. Available on the Internet at http://www.nap.edu

Giddings, Franklin Henry

Stephen P. Turner
University of South Florida, Tampa, Florida, USA

Glossary

ballistic relations Causal associations that are probabilistic in the sense of being better depicted as a joint statistical distribution than as a deterministic law.

concerted volition The sum of the distinctive responses made by individuals subjected to common stimuli and interstimulation that produced similar behavior, such as cooperation or competition.

consciousness of kind Sympathy, especially through the recognition of similarity or common membership in a category, usually with social consequences, for example, group identity.

index numbers Numbers derived typically by adding heterogeneous items that are assigned predetermined numerical values.

profit-sharing A method by which workers are rewarded a fraction of the net profit of an enterprise.

Franklin H. Giddings was the founder of sociology at Columbia University, and, with Lester F. Ward, William Graham Sumner, and Albion Small, one of the four founders of American sociology. Through his writings and his students, he played a pivotal role in establishing mainstream quantitative sociology in the United States. Among his prominent students were William Fielding Ogburn, Howard W. Odum, and F. Stuart Chapin. In *Inductive Sociology* (1901) and *The Scientific Study of Human Society* (1924) he outlined an account of the relation of social theory and quantification in a way that broke with the nineteenth-century tradition of sociological commentary on tabular material and provided an alternative model more closely resembling the model of statistical hypothesis testing characteristic of twentieth-century social science. Giddings was also a theorist, who developed the idea of "consciousness of kind" and applied models from early population genetics to the question of the development of social types.

Background and Career

Giddings, born in Sherman, Connecticut, was the son of a Congregational minister and came from a distinguished Massachusetts family that had arrived on the Mayflower and provided generals in the Revolutionary War. Rebelling against his father's Calvinism, he entered Union College in 1873 to study civil engineering, but was forced to drop out after 2 years as a result of his father's death. He took up a career in journalism, working for the *Springfield Republican* and other newspapers during a period of intense debate over labor and monetary issues. He also became involved with the Connecticut Valley Economic Association and the cooperative movement and played a role in the early history of the American Economic Association (AEA), editing its book series. His interest in the social sciences appears in his early journalistic work, which included an effort at the quantification of inflation using a price index. Giddings's earliest writing included an empirical, although not statistical, study of cooperative labor and profit-sharing published in 1886 by the Massachusetts Bureau of Labor Statistics under the name of its director, Carroll Wright. Giddings received a B. A. from Union College in 1888 as a member of the class of 1877.

Although cooperativist ideas were central to his thought, they took various forms throughout his career. At the time, state offices concerned with the solution of the labor problem collected labor statistics and routinely printed studies analyzing cases of profit-sharing and cooperation. Giddings had a strong interest in the theoretical implications of cooperation and founded an organization called the American Sociologic Association, about which little is known other than its statement of principles, which prefigured his later analysis of concerted volition and his support for the League of Nations. Eventually, however, his empirical work undermined his commitment to cooperativism as a solution to the labor question; he found participants in successful cooperative adventures typically aspired to having their own business and used the experiences of cooperative labor as a means of learning the business.

Academic Career

Giddings's academic career began when he was appointed to Bryn Mawr in 1888, taking over the position that Woodrow Wilson vacated for Princeton. He continued to write essays, notably an 1898 essay "Imperialism" (collected in *Democracy and Empire*, 1900) that responded to William Graham Sumner's attack on the emergence of American imperialism in the wake of the Spanish-American War, in which he argued that empires could be social aggregations founded on positive common ideals. At Bryn Mawr, he taught economics, history, and politics and introduced sociology. At the beginning of his career, he was active in the AEA, holding several positions in the association. He published various articles on economics, two of which were included in *The Modern Distributive Process*, which he produced with his mentor, the economist John Bates Clark, in 1888. His first-published discussion of sociology appeared in 1890, but he had presented a paper on "The Sociological Character of Political Economy" to the AEA in 1887. In 1891, he published an article on "Sociology as a University Subject" and engaged in a series of exchanges on the general theme of the relation between sociology and economics and the other social sciences. He also began in 1892 to travel to New York to lecture at the rapidly developing faculty of social and political science at Columbia University. Statistics in this Columbia faculty was then taught by the economic and social statistician Richmond Mayo-Smith, who represented the tabular tradition in statistics and directed the first American social science dissertation on a recognizably sociological topic, Walter Willcox's 1891 study of divorce. Giddings was appointed Professor of Sociology at Columbia in 1894 (the first sociology professorship in an American college, established through the efforts of active social reformer Seth Low). In 1906, Giddings held both the chair in Sociology and the newly established chair in the History of Civilization as the Carpentier Professor of Sociology and the History of Civilization, a position he held until 1928. He was awarded a D.L.D. by Columbia in 1929.

Giddings published his key theoretical work, *The Principles of Sociology*, in 1896, and it was promptly and widely translated; his key early methodological work, *Inductive Sociology*, was published in 1901. His subsequent work mostly consisted of essays, which were either published as short books or collected as books. His most important later books were *Studies in the Theory of Human Society* (1922) and his final methodological book *The Scientific Study of Human Society* (1924), based on a series of articles published in *Social Forces*. During the war years Giddings wrote *The Responsible State: A Re-examination of the Fundamental Political Doctrines in the Light of World War and the Menace of Anarchism*, published in 1918, but the war prevented him from carrying out some major planned projects, including one on the history of civilization and an extensive empirical study of working men's time and leisure.

Public Intellectual

Giddings was a public intellectual and served as a member of the school board; various commissions; the Committee of One Hundred, which was organized to chose a non-partisan candidate for Mayor of New York City; and on the board of the Charity Organization Society. He continued to produce for the press throughout his career, notably for Hamilton Holt's *Independent*, to which for many years he contributed an editorial a week, as well as writing regularly for *Van Nordens* and the *New York Times Magazine*. Never one to shy from controversy, he spoke regularly at the Rand School, a center for radical and socialist lectures, often antagonizing his audience. He was, in general, a defender of the middle class and a skeptic about social amelioration, considering many of the ills to which reform was addressed to be better understood as costs of progress. He was an early supporter of the American entry into World War I and was one of the principal speakers at Carnegie Hall at the Lusitania dinner. He later toured the country for the national Security League in support of the war and was an officer of the League to Enforce Peace. His outspoken position embroiled him in controversy at Columbia, which was the site of conflict over the war (and of a famous academic freedom issue involving James McKeen Catell, which divided the faculty from the administration), and at the end of his career he was seen by the administration and funding agencies to be an obstacle to the development of sociology at Columbia.

Giddings's Influence

Although his early years at Columbia were occupied with the problems of training social workers and meeting the demand for lectures on social reform topics, he quickly established general sociology, particularly theory and method, as his primary concern, publishing his *Principles of Sociology* in 1896 and in it staking a claim to the scientific approach to the field. Columbia at the time required training in several fields for its social science graduates, so Giddings was presented with the peculiar situation of having to define the field not only for students of sociology but also for the students of other social science fields. Many of the students he taught sociology to, such as Robert Merriam, became influential figures in their own disciplines. His own students were themselves trained in economics as well as sociology and statistics, and several of them, including, William Fielding Ogburn and F. Stuart Chapin, were in the early years of their careers identified as economists as well as sociologists in their writings and took up such topics as municipal socialism.

The *Principles* was concerned with a problem that appears in various forms in the thinking of each of the early sociologists, but which is nowadays rarely mentioned, although it appears today in evolutionary approaches to social life. The issue was social causation, which was a concern to identify the basic forces that contributed to the making of social life and produced its various forms. Giddings's central concept of consciousness of kind, although it was later applied to a variety of topics, arose in connection with this concern for identifying the basic motivating forces relevant to social life. In a later book, *A Theory of Socialization* (1897), his concern was with the processes by which individuals were made social by being brought into contact with others. He continued to reformulate his position on these issues throughout his career, but never made a major statement of his theoretical position. However, it evolved from its original emphasis on the physical conditions of social life that produced different social forms to an emphasis on the idea that the effects even of physical conditions of life operate through a social medium that is itself produced by past conditions. Thus, he recognized the significance of tradition. Like several of his contemporaries, however, Giddings was careful not to treat society as a teleological object but was concerned with what he called the analysis and correlation of moral and social forces, which included the problem of social reaction on individual character and the reverse problem of the social effect of individual will; this concern for processes informs his methodological thought.

His first major work in the area of methodology, *Inductive Sociology*, was little read, but nevertheless was a pivotal text in the history of American sociology. In this book, Giddings listed dozens of concepts and provided numerical measures for them or in many cases merely definitions that allowed for counting. This was very primitive as measurement, but the radical significance of this project was apparent. Giddings did not simply take over the categories of official statistics but attempted to construct a systematic scheme of concepts that was susceptible of precise definition or measurement. Although Giddings was aware of currents in contemporary French sociology, particularly the work of Gabriel Tarde, which may have provided some distant inspiration for this project, there is no contemporary example of a comparable large-scale effort to find quantifiable versions of social concepts.

Giddings conveyed this conception to his students, encouraging them to make the steps toward verification that he himself did not take. In this school-building effort he was extremely successful. With the help of Mayo-Smith, the first Columbia economist; the celebrated anthropologist Franz Boas; who developed and applied them to physical anthropology; and Henry L. Moore, a proto-econometrician—each of whom taught statistics—and later two other young social statisticians, Robert Chaddock and Frank A. Ross, sometime members of Giddings's department, Giddings created at Columbia an intellectual setting dominated by questions of statistical method. He personally reinforced the association by holding a kind of salon called the (Franklin H. Giddings) Club, which one of his students, F. S. Chapin, recalled as "a small group of graduate students and past students of Professor Giddings who met regularly at his house and enjoyed his hospitality and the rare stimulus of intimate association with him," during which, as another student, Charles Gehlke, reminisced, "we discussed the universe very thoroughly" before the evening "wound up with beer or gingerale and pretzels and cakes." Index numbers continued to interest Giddings throughout his career and the interest continued in his students, such as Chapin, whose famous living-room scale of social class was an index number.

In the first decade of the twentieth century, Giddings attempted, with the help of his students, to revise and update *Inductive Sociology*. Although no revision ever appeared, the group of students that worked with Giddings during this period, including Ogburn, Howard W. Odum, and Chapin, continued to further work out the implications of Giddings's own basic ideas. They went on to become not only leading figures in American social science in statistics, the most important practitioners of statistical empirical sociology in the interwar period, but also dominated the discipline—one-third of the presidents of the American Sociological Association from 1920 to 1940 were his students. By the late 1920s, their methodological ideas, which had been acquired during their time with Giddings, became the basis of textbook methodology in sociology. Giddings himself was the author of the first widely used methodology textbook, *The Scientific Study of Human Society*.

A central theme in Giddings's theoretical work was biological and social evolution from diversity into stable types, an issue identified by British biometrician Karl Pearson. Giddings's student William Ogburn, for example, studied the creation of culture by a process of selection in which environmental forces, including social pressure, eliminated deviations. This was an application of Giddings's idea of "concerted volition" as a product of a process of interstimulation. In his doctoral thesis, Ogburn had examined the transformation of diverse state labor laws into standard form. In *Social Change* (1922), the book for which he was best known, Ogburn coined the term cultural lag to describe how, in response to selective forces, material conditions change before a culture does and different parts of cultures themselves change at different rates. These processes Giddings termed "ballistic," that is, probabilistic rather than machinelike.

The Problem of Social Science Theory and Statistical Verification

Giddings learned his methodology from Mill and Jevons, and later from Mach and Pearson, and among the founding figures of American sociology was the only one who concerned himself in any detail with methodological questions and with the questions of whether the theories of sociology could be made into science and whether the empirical material was available to the sociologist to test them. Giddings can be credited with inventing the account of this problem, which became dominant in American sociology. He was eager to apply the methodological lessons being retailed by contemporary scientists to the question of what empirical inquiry can warrant in the way of theory. From Mach, Giddings took the idea that mechanics is nothing more than description and concluded that "no other branch of knowledge can claim to be more." This prepared him for Pearson's similar but even more extreme message that not only was developed science no more than description but that the laws of physics themselves were not, properly speaking, descriptions but rather idealization of relationships that involved variation. In *The Grammar of Science* (1892) Pearson included a figure of a scattergram of data points that showed the data points arranged in a typical pattern of random error variation around a curve to which a line could be fitted. Inserted into this scattergram was a blown-up section of the pattern, which of course appeared as a high level of variation. Pearson's point was that physics was based on correlations no less than other areas of knowledge and that variation was built into nature itself. Like Comte before him, Pearson regarded the idea of cause as intellectually retrograde, a step backward toward animism; Giddings followed Pearson and Comte in this respect, regarding causation as a metaphysical notion and explanation itself as a suspect concept.

Giddings's embrace of these Pearsonian and Machian doctrines created obvious difficulties for him as a theorist. But he resolved these by placing sociological theory within what he called the three normal stages of the scientific method: guesswork, deduction, and verification. The three stages are a modification of Pearson's stages of ideological, observational, and metrical, which Giddings quoted in his lectures and which themselves were a modification of Comte's three stages. In 1920, Giddings gave the following formulation:

> *Science cannot, as a distinguished scientific thinker said the other day, even get on without guessing, and one of its most useful functions is to displace bad and fruitless guessing by the good guessing that ultimately leads to the demonstration of new truth. Strictly speaking, all true induction* is *guessing; it is a swift intuitive glance at a mass of facts to see if they* mean *anything, while exact scientific demonstration is a complex process of* deducing *conclusions by the observations of more facts.*

His own work, he hoped, would enable his readers "to see that much sociology is as yet nothing more than careful and suggestive guesswork; that some of it is deductive; and that a little of it, enough to encourage us to continue our researches, is verified knowledge." The solution to the puzzle of the relation between statistical sociology and sociological theory this suggests is that speculative social theory is a source from which the sociologist may take basic concepts to see if statistical data "mean anything," then deduce conclusions from strict formulations of these guesses, and test them on more facts, thus gradually adding to the stock of verified knowledge that thus consists of the accumulation of statistical results that serve, if not to answer theoretical questions, to replace theoretical answers with metrical descriptions of relations.

Measurement

Statistics and Sociology (1895) by Giddings's Columbia colleague Richmond Mayo-Smith remained squarely in the nineteenth-century tradition of moral statistics. In it, Mayo-Smith commented, with a sociological purpose, on material of the sort collected by state bureaus, such as tables of vital statistics. In his *Inductive Sociology* and his articles, such as "The Measurement of Social Pressure" (1908), Giddings attempted something quite different—the measurement of magnitudes that derive either from sociological theories or from social concepts such as labor unrest. The data he proposed to use were not very different from the sort discussed by Mayo-Smith, but they were conceived in a distinctly new fashion.

The key difference was how the problem arose. Giddings was concerned with a theoretical question, with the constraints on political evolution (especially the achievement of democracy) that result from conflicts with primordial ties such as kinship and from the inadequate psychological and characterological evolution of personalities. His approach to this problem is indicative of his approach to sociology. We might investigate this kind of problem impressionistically by deciding if some group has some characteristic, such as "forcefulness" (one of Giddings's four basic psychological types), that is pertinent to the theoretical question of their capacity for sustaining particular forms of political association. But only systematic quantitative evidence in the form of magnitudes can enable the precise determination of correlations. So in *Inductive Sociology* he constructs a magnitude:

> *Suppose that we desire to know whether the men of Montana represent a type of character that might be described as forceful, but that we find no testimony, no record of personal observations, directly bearing on our inquiry. We know, however, that by the general consent of mankind, men who follow adventurous and daring occupations are described as forceful. Turning, then, to the census, we learn that a majority of men in Montana follow adventurous and daring occupations.*
>
> *Accordingly, by substitution, we affirm that a majority of the men of Montana are of the forceful type of character.*

The explicit idea of measurement "by substitution" warranted by "the general consent of mankind" (or "face validity" in later parlance) represented a genuine innovation that allowed him to extend the concept of magnitude to other social concepts.

The primary inspiration for Giddings's innovation here was the problem of race, one of the defining issues for Columbia at the time. Giddings's student, Frank H. Hankins, makes the point in *Introduction to the Study of Society* (1929) that "all the customary indices of racial difference, viz., stature, cephalic index, hair color, eye color, skin color, nasal index, hair form, alveolar index, etc. in fact extensively overlap one another."

> *Norwegians are obviously taller on an average than Japanese, but some Japanese are taller than many Norwegians. White and Negro cannot be distinguished by stature; nor by cephalic index; even as regards skin color and hair form the border areas of distribution overlap. It is this overlapping that makes it necessary to think of a race as a* group set apart by a complex of traits inherited together within a limited range of variability. *Since tall stature shades into short, long head into round, and dark complexion into light, it must be shown that with tall stature are found also a certain head form, eye color, shape of hair, etc.*

The underlying idea here that a race is not definable by a single criterion but by correlated statistical distributions of several properties, and this justifies the practice of using a wide variety of measures, each of which can be plausibly used as a surrogate for the variable of interest.

If we consider only Giddings's early attempts at using distributions, for example, of the number of people in daring occupations as imperfect indicators of the preponderance of psychological types, such as "forceful," his achievement may appear to be rather trivial, even preposterous. Certainly it is questionable whether these "traits" are traits and whether this sort of substitution is properly regarded as a form of measurement. But it was very difficult to pass from the abstract ideal of metricizing social theory to the actual creation of metrical substitutes for theoretical concepts. Before Giddings, there were some abstract discussions of measuring happiness (the felicific calculus), and, at the other extreme, a body of data collected for a wide variety of official purposes such as vital statistics, suicide statistics, and crime statistics. There were also some rudimentary data on opinions and attitudes. Opinion data collected by the Bureaus of Labor Statistics took the form of queries to officials or people presumed to be knowledgeable regarding the causes of a phenomenon of interest, which could be classified by these causes. This was very far from Giddings's goal, to be algebraic, or concerned with magnitude, rather than arithmetic, or concerned only with counting items in the social world.

In this effort, he was a genuine pioneer in creating a quantitative sociology organized around the measurement of variables and the determinations of the correlations between them. The existing theoretical discussions of measuring belief and desire were far removed from data collection, and the concepts used by theorists were not readily measured. Giddings closed this gap. He reconceptualized commonly used concepts, such as "the unsocial," "the degraded," and "the immoral," which he specified in terms of what moral statisticians had termed drunkenness, begging, and the like. He also defined measures of various social phenomena, such as "domestic peace and order," which he specified in terms of "the number of insurrections and riots experienced," and devised measures of equity in the distribution of wealth. This huge enterprise of identifying measures had a limited direct impact on research, but prepared students for a revolution in research practice.

Yet, in *Inductive Sociology*, Giddings did produce some influential models of analysis, including what may be the first example of statistical hypothesis testing in sociology. The speculative concept "consciousness of kind" suggested the following deduction: "Concerted volition" of forms of political association depend on sympathy or consciousness of kind. Hence, there should be a relationship (which he spelled out at length, discursively, on the theoretical level) between the degree of social sympathy and what we might call political culture. He tested this hypothesis by constructing an index number corresponding to a weighted formula based on the addition of these fractions: the proportion of the numbers of native born of native parents; the proportion of native born of native parents and native born of foreign parents to foreign born; and this proportion to the proportion of colored. The number was understood to correspond to the degree of homogeneity in the population. After calculating this number for each state of the union, he constructed three categories based on the scores. The relationship was verified by examining the lists of states falling into each category. In the highest index number category, he said, "it will be observed that the states which are distinguished for a rather pronounced 'Americanism' in politics and legislation are chiefly found, as might be expected." In those states where the population was "neither perfectly homogeneous nor excessively heterogeneous," signifying the existence of more intellectual ties as distinct from primordial group feelings, are to be found the highest degree of "progress and social leadership."

The statistical association between the metricized concept of heterogeneity and the nonmetricized concept of progressiveness provides a kind of paradigmatic example of the kind of social research that became conventional in sociology by 1935. It was motivated by some theoretical ideas about the political effects of heterogeneity. Heterogeneity was an abstract variable measured indirectly. The association was imperfect, but it confirmed and metricized a theoretical idea. In time, Giddings's suggestions about measurement became far more clever. In his 1924 textbook, he gave an example that might be used today—to measure "discriminative reaction to nationalities," he gave 70 people a list of 2 dozen nationalities and asked each of them to distribute places for 100 hypothetical immigrants among them. He used a similar method to measure interest in causes, asking his respondents to distribute $100 among up to 20 possible causes, such as scientific research, the suppression of vice, and so forth.

Causation

Giddings and his students also struggled with the relationship between correlation and cause. In the 1911 edition of *The Grammar of Science*, Pearson treated the difference between cause and correlation as merely a matter of degree; the difference between the laws of physics and the relations between parental and adult children's stature, for example, is the quantitative fact of degree of variation, and even observations in physics do not perfectly match up with the idealized laws of physics. Accordingly, he urged the abandonment of the distinction between laws and correlations. Almost everything is correlated with everything else, Pearson insisted. Analogously, as Giddings explained, "every manifestation of energy is associated with other manifestations, every condition with other conditions, every known mode of behavior with other modes." Giddings and his students attempted, as did their biometric colleagues, to find a proper middle ground between collapsing cause into correlation and adhering to the traditional notions of cause and law while searching for an adequate formulation of the compromise.

Giddings made several striking contributions to what was to be the ultimate resolution of the problem in sociology. In *Inductive Sociology*, he corrected the deficiencies of Mill's purism by redefining the task of social science. Although "it is not always possible perfectly to isolate our phenomena [f]or example, in Mill's familiar example of the effect of a protective tariff, we may nevertheless be certain that we have found the only one commensurate with results." The paradigmatic means of establishing this result is "systematic observations of the resemblances and differences of occurrence in a series, and of magnitude," meaning correlational analysis. The terminology of resemblances is Mill's and John Venn's (in his *Logic of Chance*, 1876); the idea of the mathematical expression of a comparison between "classes or series of figures," or the notion that a correlation coefficient is "always equivalent to a generalization or law" is taken from Pearson, but is also exemplified by Edward Tylor's much simpler diagrammatic method in an 1889 study of the relation between matrilineality and matrifocal residence patterns.

Yet Giddings's comment on Mill in *Inductive Sociology* posed a dilemma. To the extent that we retain the possibility of isolating sufficient antecedents or major causes, it is not sufficient to point to correlations, however high. As Giddings explained in his methodology textbook of 1924, "If, in a large number of cases, we find a high correlation of the occurrence of frequencies of our experimental factor with the occurrence frequencies of the result attributed to it, the presumption of causal nexus is strong." Giddings conceded that there was no rule that distinguished causal associations from merely statistical associations, but he identified a key indicator—a high correlation "points to the major causal nexus" when it persists, "while other factors and correlations come and go." He thought of these relations as similar to those captured by the notion of constants in physical science and suggested that social science also pursued constants but that these could never be as precisely determined. The intuition that a correlation can be presumed not to be a mere arithmetical accident when the hypothesis of a common cause can be excluded and where there are no highly correlated causes that may be confounded with the putative cause pointed to issues that were to concern statistical sociology for much of the century.

See Also the Following Articles

Causal Inference • Sociology

Further Reading

Bannister, R. C. (1987). *Sociology and Scientism: The American Quest for Objectivity, 1880–1940*. University of North Carolina Press, Chapel Hill, NC.

Camic, C. (1994). The statistical turn in American social science: Columbia University, 1890 to 1915. *Am. Sociol. Rev.* **59,** 773–805.

Turner, S. P. (1991). The world of academic quantifiers: The Columbia University family and its connections. In *The Social Survey in Historical Perspective: 1880–1940* (M. Bulmer, K. Bales, and K. Sklar, eds.), pp. 269–290. University of Chicago Press, Chicago, IL.

Wallace, R. (1989). *The Institutionalization of a New Discipline: The Case of Sociology at Columbia University, 1891–1931.* Ph.D. diss. Columbia University, New York.

Goal-Based vs. Goal-Free Evaluation

Michael Quinn Patton
Union Institute University, Minneapolis, Minnesota, USA

Glossary

external evaluation Inquiries aimed at judging the merit, worth, quality, and effectiveness of an intervention conducted by independent evaluators.

goal-based evaluation Program evaluation that assesses the degree and nature of goal attainment.

goal-free evaluation Program evaluation that assesses the extent to which and ways in which the real needs of participants are met by the program without regard to the program's stated goals.

internal evaluation Evaluative inquiries undertaken by staff within a program or organization.

needs assessment Determining those things that are essential and requisite for a particular population that are lacking, the degree to which they are lacking, and the barriers to their being provided or met.

program evaluation The systematic collection of information about the activities, characteristics, and outcomes of programs to make judgments about the program, improve program effectiveness, and/or inform decisions about future programming.

program goals The desired and targeted outcomes or results of program activities.

Goal-based versus goal-free evaluation involves a debate among evaluators about the degree to which measuring goal attainment ought to be the central focus of program evaluations. The alternative to the traditional and still-predominant goal-based approach is goal-free evaluation, which proposes to replace measuring goal attainment with assessing the extent to which and ways in which *the real needs* of participants are met by the program without regard to the program's stated goals.

The Centrality of Goals in Evaluation

Traditionally, evaluation has been synonymous with measuring goal attainment. Evaluation textbooks have typically taken the position that a program must have clearly stated goals in order to be evaluated and that the primary purpose of evaluation is to assess goal attainment. Conversely, a program that does not have clearly specified goals cannot be evaluated. This perspective took on the status of being a truism. For example, evaluators have long been fond of citing the Cheshire Cat's witty reply to Alice in Wonderland that if you don't know where you're going, any road will get you there. A widely disseminated evaluation cartoon shows an archer shooting an arrow into a wall and then drawing a circle around wherever the arrow lodged and proclaiming, "I hit the target dead center," a way of poking fun at the seemingly absurd notion that one could take credit for hitting a target (attaining a goal) without having a bull's-eye to aim at in advance (stating a targeted goal in advance). In short, early definitions of evaluation viewed the purpose of evaluation as assessing a program's goal attainment.

Clear, Specific, and Measurable Goals

The trinity of goal-based evaluation is clarity, specificity, and measurability. Thus, an evaluable goal is one that is clear, specific, and measurable. However, evaluators have frequently found that, on starting to conduct an evaluation, they must begin by refining the program's goal statements because the goals are fuzzy, vague, and immeasurable. The process of refining goals can be difficult and conflict-laden.

The Goals Clarification Challenge

Fuzzy and Vague Goals

When evaluators work with program staff to clarify goals and attain clarity, specificity, and measurability, the program's goals may not just get clarified, they may also get changed. In some cases, changing the goals is helpful and appropriate. In other cases, however, program staff may feel forced to adopt goals they do not believe in and are not committed to in order to come up with goal statements that have the virtues of clarity, specificity, and measurability. If staff and evaluators do not know how to measure goal attainment, they may adopt goals that are unsuitable and inappropriate to meet the evaluation criteria of a "good" goal.

Multiple Goals

Another challenge in conducting goal-based evaluations involves prioritizing goals. Few programs have only one primary goal. For example, the Headstart program aims to prepare preschool children for success in school, but it also includes health assessment goals, nutrition goals, parenting goals, and sometimes even employment or community organizing goals. Evaluation priorities must be set to determine which goals get evaluated and how scarce resources should be allocated to evaluating different goals.

Conflicts over Goals

Another barrier to goals clarification and goal-based evaluation is conflict over priorities. Conflict among different stakeholder groups over program goals is common. For example, in criminal justice programs, battles are waged over whether the purpose of a program is punitive (punish criminal offenders for wrongdoing), custodial (keep criminal offenders off the streets), or rehabilitative (return offenders to society after treatment). In education and training programs, conflicts often emerge over whether the priority goal is attitude change or behavior change. In welfare agencies, disagreements can be found over whether the primary purpose is to get clients off welfare or out of poverty and whether the focus should be long-term change or short-term crisis intervention. In health settings, staff dissension may emerge over the relative emphasis to be placed on preventive versus curative medical practice. Chemical dependency programs are often enmeshed in controversy over whether the desired outcome is sobriety or responsible use. Even police and fire departments can get caught in controversy about the purposes and actual effects of sirens, with critics arguing that there are more a nuisance than a help. Virtually any time that a group of people assemble to determine program goals, conflict can emerge resulting in a lengthy, frustrating, and inconclusive meeting.

Evaluation of school busing programs to achieve racial balance offers an example rich with conflict. By what criteria ought busing programs be evaluated? Changed racial attitudes? Changed interracial behaviors? Improved student achievement? Degree of parent involvement? Access to educational resources? All are candidates for the honor of primary program goal. Is school busing supposed to achieve desegregation (representative proportions of minority students in all schools) or integration (positive interracial attitudes, cooperation, and interaction)? Many communities, school boards, and school staffs are in open warfare over these issues. Central to the battles fought are basic disagreements about what evaluation criteria to apply and how to assess results.

Goal-Free Evaluation

Philosopher and evaluator Michael Scriven has been a strong critic of goal-based evaluation and, as an alternative, an advocate of what he has called "goal-free evaluation." Goal-free evaluation involves gathering data on a broad array of *actual effects* and evaluating the importance of these effects in meeting demonstrated needs. The evaluator makes a deliberate attempt to avoid all rhetoric related to program goals. No discussion about goals is held with staff and no program brochures or proposals are read; only the program's actual outcomes and measurable effects are studied and these are judged on the extent to which they meet *demonstrated participant needs*.

Reasons for Shifting to Goal-Free Evaluation

Scriven has offered four reasons for doing goal-free/needs-based evaluations:

(1) to avoid the risk of narrowly studying stated program objectives and thereby missing important unanticipated outcomes;
(2) to remove the negative connotations attached to the discovery of unanticipated effects, side effects, or secondary effects;
(3) to eliminate the perceptual biases introduced into an evaluation by knowledge of goals; and
(4) to maintain evaluator objectivity and independence through goal-free conditions.

Avoiding the Tunnel Vision of Goals

Scriven has argued that focusing on goals in evaluation is unnecessary. To the contrary, too much attention to goals can distort an evaluation and lead to tunnel-vision. The less an external evaluator hears about the goals of the project, the less tunnel-vision will develop and the more attention will be paid to *looking for actual effects* (rather than checking on *alleged* effects), including attention to side effects and unanticipated consequences of program activities.

Avoiding Grandiosity and Unrealistic Goals

By reducing the emphasis on goals, goal-free evaluation strives to reduce the tendency in programs to overpromise what they can achieve in order to obtain funding. Unrealistic goals contribute to negative evaluation findings. Even if a program is achieving significant results, that finding may be disguised and lead to negative judgments when goals were unrealistic from the outset.

Avoiding the Problem of Real Goals versus Alleged Goals

Organizational theorists, such as Argyris and Schon, have long distinguished between rhetorical goals (what a program says it aims to accomplish) and real goals (what staff actually care about and work toward). The problem of distinguishing real from alleged goals is avoided in goal-free evaluation.

Goal Clarification Becomes Unnecessary

Goal-free evaluation also removes the evaluator from playing the role of facilitating a staff exercise in goals clarification in a search for clear, specific, and measurable goals. In this way, the evaluator avoids becoming caught in goals conflicts among competing stakeholder groups. The problems of multiple goals and changing goals (shifting goals in the middle of a project) are also avoided.

The Focus of Goal-Free Evaluation

Needs Fulfillment versus Goal Attainment

Goal-free evaluation is *needs-based instead of goal-based*; that is, it focuses on assessing the extent to which the real needs of the program's clients or recipients are being met by the program. Thus, the evaluation does not focus on measuring the goals of the people in the program and goal-free evaluators never need to know the stated goals and should not even look at them. The outcome of a goal-free evaluation is an assessment of the merit of the program, not goal attainment.

Determining Priority Needs of Participants

Scriven has argued that determining priority needs is typically as obvious as the difference between soap and cancer. People need a cure for cancer more than they need soap. Hungry people need food more than they need books or self-esteem enhancement. Conducting a careful and rigorous needs assessment provides the baseline for goal-free evaluation.

Internal and External Evaluation Combinations

Scriven's ideal goal-free proposal assumes both internal and external evaluators. Under this ideal, the external evaluators can ignore program staff and local project goals because the internal evaluator takes care of measuring goal attainment and providing feedback to managers and staff. Scriven has acknowledged that planning and production require goals and formulating them in testable terms is necessary for the manager as well as the internal evaluator who keeps the manager informed. This frees external evaluators to assess whether priority needs are being met rather than repeating the internal work of measuring goal attainment.

Criticisms of Goal-Free Evaluation

Goal-free evaluation was derived from a critique of goal-based evaluation, especially the problem of possibly missing side effects when measuring goal attainment and the entanglement of evaluators in stakeholder politics when trying to clarify vague, general, and immeasurable goals. But goal-based evaluators have countered with what they perceive as weaknesses in goal-free evaluation.

Who Determines Goals (and Needs)?

Critics argue that the issue is whose goals will be evaluated. The goal-free model keeps program staff from determining and controlling the focus of an evaluation (stated goals), but in so doing it directs data away from the stated concerns of the people who run the program, thereby reducing the evaluation's usefulness to those closest to the program participants and in the best position to use evaluation findings. Goal-free evaluation typically addresses the concerns of an external audience, such as legislative or philanthropic funders. But, in as much as these audiences are often ill-defined and lack organization, the standards an evaluator applies in determining real needs in a goal-free evaluation may turn out to be none other than the evaluator's very own preferences about what program effects are appropriate and of priority interest. Goal-free evaluation carries the danger of substituting the evaluator's preferred program goals for those of the program staff.

Accuracy of the Name "Goal-Free"

Evaluation theorist Marv Alkin has argued that the term "goal-free evaluation" is not to be taken literally. Goal-free evaluation *does* recognize goals, but they are wider context, socially inferred goals rather than the specific stated objectives of the program. This, Alkin argues, means that goal-free evaluation is not really goal-free at all but rather is an approach that frees the evaluator to focus on the goals of different and usually more distant decision makers and audiences. The question is whether such distant decision audiences ought to be given the highest priority.

The Problem of Defining Needs

Goal-free evaluation recommends focusing on assessing real program effects and judging those effects in relation to real needs. The third area of criticism concerns this focus on needs in goal-free evaluation. This critique has both conceptual and methodological dimensions. What is a "need" and how is it measured? In addition to the challenge of distinguishing needs from wants, there is the challenge of making explicit the values and assumptions that undergird needs assessments. Does a battered woman need motivational counseling, therapy to deal with childhood abuse, shelter to escape the abuser, higher self-esteem, financial support to escape the abuser, community support, religion, or some other form of assistance?

Status of Goal-Based and Goal-Free Evaluation

Goal-Based Evaluation Remains Dominant in Evaluation

Most evaluation designs focus on assessing goal attainment and goals clarification remains a major task undertaken by evaluators early in the evaluation design process. Goal-free evaluation has not resonated much either with evaluators or with those who commission and use evaluations. Relatively few goal-free evaluations have been reported in the literature. A few comprehensive evaluations include hybrid designs in which a goal-free evaluator works parallel to a goal-based evaluator, but such efforts are expensive and, accordingly, rare.

Beyond the Rhetoric of Goal-Free Evaluation

Scriven's original goal-free proposal provoked considerable controversy and stimulated professionals in the field of evaluation to examine more closely both theory and practice with regard to goals. In particular, goal-free evaluation has directed more attention to the need for measuring a program's real effects, side effects, and unanticipated consequences in addition to measuring goal attainment. Emphasizing and calling attention to the importance of looking beyond narrow goal attainment measures has been the real and lasting contribution of goal-free evaluation, but the term itself—goal-free evaluation—has proven to be no more than a rhetorical thrust that provoked controversy, as intended. The notion that an evaluation can and ought to be goal-free has not been taken seriously by many as a viable primary approach to actually conducting evaluations.

Diverse Options Now Available for Conducting Evaluations

The idea of performing goal-free evaluation also helped bring attention to other ways of focusing evaluations besides measuring goal attainment, including designing evaluations to improve programs, illuminate important issues, answer the questions of primary decision makers, and support dialogue about future programming directions. Evaluation has become a field rich with options for focusing designs, only two of which are goal-based and goal-free evaluations.

See Also the Following Article

Risk and Needs Assessments

Further Reading

Alkin, M. C. (1972). Wider context goals and goals-based evaluators. *Eval. Comment J. Educ. Eval.* **3,** 10–11.

Argyris, C., and Schon, D. (1978). *Organizational Effectiveness.* Addison-Wesley, Reading, MA.

Montefiore, A., and Noble, D. (eds.) (1989). *Goals, No-Goals and Own Goals: A Debate on Goal-Directed and Intentional Behaviour.* Routledge, New York.

Morris, L., and Fitz-Gibbon, C. (1978). *How to Deal with Goals and Objectives.* Sage Publications, Beverly Hills, CA.

Patton, M. Q. (1997). *Utilization-Focused Evaluation: The New Century Text,* 3rd Ed. Sage Publications, Thousand Oaks, CA.

Scriven, M. (1972). Prose and cons about goal-free evaluation. *Eval. Comment J. Educ. Eval.* **3,** 1–7.

Scriven, M. (1991). *Evaluation Thesaurus,* 4th Ed. Sage Publications, Newbury Park, CA.

Scriven, M. (1993). *Hard-Won Lessons in Program Evaluation,* New Directions For Program Evaluation, Vol. 58, Jossey-Bass, San Francisco, CA.

Graded Response Model

Fumiko Samejima
University of Tennessee, Knoxville, Tennessee, USA

Glossary

continuous response model The analysis of continuous responses, for example, marking a range between "Totally disagree" and "Totally agree."

dichotomous response model The analysis of dichotomous responses, for example, a choice between "True" and "False."

graded response model The analysis of graded responses, for example, a choice among five responses, "Strongly disagree," "Disagree," "Neutral," "Agree," "Strongly agree."

For several decades item response theory dealt with solely dichotomous responses, such as correct/incorrect, true/false, and so on. In 1969, the general graded response model was proposed. This model represents a family of mathematical models that deal with ordered polytomous responses in general. This entry introduces graded response models and considers their relationships with dichotomous and continuous response models. Although the example here are simple, graded response models have many innovative applications, and for future research it has a big potential.

Introduction

Psychometrics, or mathematical psychology, distinguishes itself from the general statistics in two ways: (1) Psychology has its own goal of understanding the behavior of individuals rather than dealing with them as mass products and (2) psychometrics includes measurement of hypothetical constructs, such as ability, attitude, etc. Item response theory (IRT) started as modern mental test theory in psychological measurement and as latent structure analysis in social attitude measurement. In its early days, IRT was called latent trait theory, a term that is still used in latent trait models, which represent mathematical models in IRT.

For several decades IRT dealt with solely dichotomous responses such as correct/incorrect, true/false, and so on. In 1969, the general graded response model was proposed by Samejima. This model represents a family of mathematical models that deal with ordered polytomous responses in general. To understand the need for the graded response model, the following example may be useful. Suppose that included in a questionnaire measuring social attitudes toward the war is the statement: "A war is necessary to protect our own country." Figure 1 presents examples of three possible types of answer formats. Figure 1A shows a dichotomous response that allows the subject choose one of the two categories: "Disagree" and "Agree." Figure 1B shows a graded response that allows the subject to select one of the five response categories: "Strongly

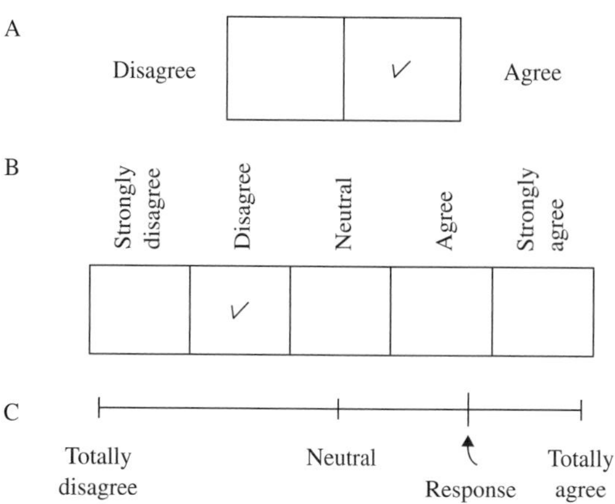

Figure 1 The three response formats. (A) Dichotomous response format. (B) Graded response format. (C) Continuous response format.

disagree," "Disagree," "Neutral," "Agree," and "Strongly agree." Figure 1C shows a continuous response that allows the subject choose any position on the line segment ranging from "Totally disagree" to "Totally agree." The general graded response model uses the second format, the graded response, which makes use of more abundant information from the subject's reaction than the general dichotomous response model. Note that the number of response categories can be any positive integer and that the number of categories can be different for each item (statements, questions, X-ray films, etc.). The example in Figure 1 is one of the simplest, most straightforward applications of the graded response model. However, the graded response model has many innovative applications, and for future research it has a big potential.

The expansion of dichotomous response models to graded response models resulted in a substantial enhancement of the applicability of IRT for various areas of social and natural science measurements. The graded response model is applicable whenever we measure a hypothetical construct based on the subject's graded responses to items or whenever each item response is evaluated and a graded score is given. Examples of the use of the graded response model are the Likert-type attitude measurement and the skeletal maturity scale in medical science. In the latter example, expert medical scientists evaluate and grade the maturity level of a knee joint (graded responses) on X-ray films (items) taken from various angles and, on the basis of the sequence of graded responses (response pattern), the patient's skeletal maturity level is estimated following a specified graded response model. The skeletal maturity scale is especially useful for young patients because there is no one-to-one correspondence between a patient's chronological age and skeletal maturity and the optimal time for a specific surgery will depend on his or her skeletal maturity, not chronological age.

General Graded Response Model

Let θ be the unidimensional latent trait that represents the target hypothetical construct to measure and that is assumed to take on any real number. Let g denote an item, which is the smallest unit of manifest entity in observable data (e.g., "[3/11] − [12/5] = " in an arithmetic test); X_g $(=0, 1, \ldots, m_g)$ denote a graded item score to item g; and x_g be its realization. Note that, unlike dichotomous responses, the values of m_g can be different for separate items, the feature that makes the graded response model more widely applicable to different types of data. The dichotomous response model is included in the graded response model as a special case where $m_g = 1$.

The operating characteristic, $P_{x_g}(\theta)$, of the graded item score x_g is defined by:

$$P_{x_g}(\theta) \equiv \text{prob.}\left[X_g = x_g \mid \theta\right]. \tag{1}$$

The general graded response model is represented by:

$$P_{x_g}(\theta) = \left[\prod_{u \le x_g} M_u(\theta)\right]\left[1 - M_{(x_g+1)}(\theta)\right] \tag{2}$$

where $M_{x_g}(\theta)$ is called the processing function, which is strictly increasing in θ except:

$$M_{x_g}(\theta) = \begin{cases} 1 & \text{for} \quad x_g = 0 \\ 0 & \text{for} \quad x_g = m_g + 1 \end{cases}. \tag{3}$$

Let $P^*_{x_g}(\theta)$ be the cumulative operating characteristic of the graded item score, $X_g = x_g$, defined by:

$$P^*_{x_g}(\theta) = \prod_{u \le x_g} M_u(\theta). \tag{4}$$

From Eqs. (2) and (4), the operating characteristic $P_{x_g}(\theta)$ can be written as:

$$P_{x_g}(\theta) = P^*_{x_g}(\theta) - P^*_{(x_g+1)}(\theta) \tag{5}$$

for $x_g = 0, 1, 2, \ldots, m_g$. The operating characteristic $P_{x_g}(\theta)$ is the sole basis of the graded response model, and all other functions such as various types of information functions, the basic function for each of $m_g + 1$ grades, and the bias function of the maximum likelihood estimate of θ (MLE bias function) of a test are derived from $P_{x_g}(\theta)$. Note from Eqs. (2), (3), (4), and (5), however, that any specific mathematical model can be represented by either $M_{x_g}(\theta)$ or $P^*_{x_g}(\theta)$ also.

Homogeneous and Heterogeneous Cases

Let U_g $(=0, 1)$ denote a binary score for dichotomous responses. The item characteristic function (ICF) is defined by:

$$P_g(\theta) \equiv \text{prob.}\left[U_g = 1 \mid \theta\right]. \tag{6}$$

This is a special case of Eq. (1), which is obtainable by replacing the graded item score X_g by the dichotomous item score U_g, and by replacing its realization x_g by a specific value, 1. It is noted that, when $m_g > 1$, the $m_g + 1$ graded response categories can be redichotomized by choosing one of the m_g borderlines between any pair of adjacent graded response categories and creating two binary categories, as is done when the letter grades A, B, and C are categorized into "Pass" and D and F into "Fail." When the borderline was set between the categories $(x_g - 1)$ and x_g, the cumulative operating characteristic $P^*_{x_g}(\theta)$, defined by the right-hand-side of

Eq. (4), equals the ICF given by Eq. (6). If these m_g ICFs are identical except for the positions alongside the θ dimension, the model is said to be homogeneous; otherwise it is heterogeneous.

A homogeneous model can be represented by:

$$P^*_{x_g}(\theta) = \int_{-\infty}^{a_g(\theta - b_{x_g})} \psi(t)\, dt \tag{7}$$

where $\psi(\cdot)$ denotes a four times differentiable density function with $\lim_{t \to -\infty} \psi(t) = 0$ (which is required for obtaining other functions from the operating characteristics $P_{x_g}(\theta)$, including the MLE bias function), and the item response parameter b_{x_g} satisfies:

$$-\infty = b_0 < b_1 < b_2 \cdots < b_{m_g} < b_{m_g+1} = \infty. \tag{8}$$

Models that are homogeneous imply that each and every graded response boundary has the same discrimination power, a principle that may fit categorical judgment data. If in Eq. (7) $\psi(t)$ is replaced by the standard normal density function,

$$\frac{1}{\sqrt{2\pi}} \exp\left[-\frac{t^2}{2}\right]$$

for example, it will provide the cumulative operating characteristic in the normal ogive model for graded responses. Another widely used homogeneous model is the logistic model, expanded from the model for dichotomous responses proposed by Birnbaum in 1968.

Examples of heterogeneous models are those derived from Bock's 1972 nominal response model, Samejima's 1995 acceleration model, and Samejima's 2003 logistic positive exponent model; the last is a graded response model expanded from Samejima's 2000 logistic positive exponent family (LPEF) of models for dichotomous responses in which the item parameter $\xi_g > 0$ controls the principle incorporated in ordering the MLE of θ. To be more precise, when $0 < \xi_g < 1$ the principle is to penalize the failure to answer an easy item correctly, and when $\xi_g > 1$ it is to give credit to the success in answering a difficult question correctly, with the logistic model ($\xi_g = 1$) as their transition, which is not affected by either of the two principles. Let $\Psi_g(\theta)$ be such that:

$$\Psi_g(\theta) = \frac{1}{1 + \exp[-Da_g(\theta - b_g)]} \tag{9}$$

which equals the logistic ICF for dichotomous responses with a_g (>0) and b_g as the discrimination and difficulty parameters, respectively. The cumulative operating characteristic in this model is given by:

$$P^*_{x_g}(\theta) = [\Psi_g(\theta)]^{\xi_{x_g}} \tag{10}$$

where the acceleration parameter ξ_{x_g} satisfies:

$$0 = \xi_0 < \xi_1 < \cdots < \xi_{m_g} < \xi_{m_g+1} = \infty. \tag{11}$$

The operating characteristic in this model is obtained by substituting the right-hand-side of Eq. (10) into Eq. (5) for the graded scores x_g and $(x_g + 1)$. The processing function in this model can be written as:

$$M_{x_g}(\theta) = [\Psi_g(\theta)]^{\xi_{x_g} - \xi_{x_g - 1}} \quad \text{for} \quad x_g = 1, 2, \ldots, m_g. \tag{12}$$

The 1995 acceleration model was proposed by Samejima for cognitive diagnosis such as problem solving. Let $\Psi_g(\theta)$ in Eq. (9) be replaced by $\Psi_{x_g}(\theta)$, with the item parameters a_g and b_g changed to the item response parameters a_{x_g} and b_{x_g}, respectively, and $\Psi_g(\theta)$ in Eq. (10) be replaced by $\Psi_{x_g}(\theta)$. Setting the step acceleration parameter $\xi^*_{x_g} = \xi_{x_g} - \xi_{x_g - 1}$, if this parameter is used in Eq. (12) and $\Psi_g(\theta)$ is replaced by $\Psi_{x_g}(\theta)$, the formula will become the processing function of the acceleration model, although in this model $\Psi_{x_g}(\theta)$ is not restricted to the logistic function. Figure 2 presents a set of seven $P_{x_g}(\theta)$ of a graded response item following the acceleration model, with $m_g = 6$ and the item response parameters: $a_{x_g} = 1.0$ for all x_g; $b_{x_g} = -1.0$ for $x_g = 1, 2, 3$; and $b_{x_g} = 1.0$ for $x_g = 4, 5, 6$; with $\xi^*_{x_g} = 0.5$ for $x_g = 1, 4$; $\xi^*_{x_g} = 1.0$ for $x_g = 2, 5$; and $\xi^*_{x_g} = 1.5$ for $x_g = 3, 6$.

In general, $P_{x_g}(\theta)$ for $x_g = 1, 2, \ldots, m_g - 1$ are not symmetric in a model that is heterogeneous, as illustrated in Figure 2. They are symmetric and unimodal in homogeneous cases, however, if the model provides point-symmetric $P^*_{x_g}(\theta)$, as is the case with the normal ogive and logistic models. The modal points of $P_{x_g}(\theta)$ are ordered in accordance with the graded item score x_g in the logistic positive exponent model and in models derived from Bock's nominal model, as well as in the normal ogive and logistic models. In the acceleration model, however, this is not rigorously true, although it does hold in most practical situations, as in Figure 2.

Relationship with Continuous Response Models

We can categorize the family of general graded response model into (1) models that can be naturally expanded to continuous response models and (2) those that are discrete in nature. Most models in category 1 also have additivity in the sense that:

1. If two or more adjacent graded response categories (e.g., grades A, B, and C) are combined into one new category (e.g., "Pass"), the operating characteristic of the resulting new category, which is the sum total of the original separate operating characteristics, also belongs to the original model.
2. If we divide a graded response category (e.g., "Agree") into two or more graded categories (e.g.,

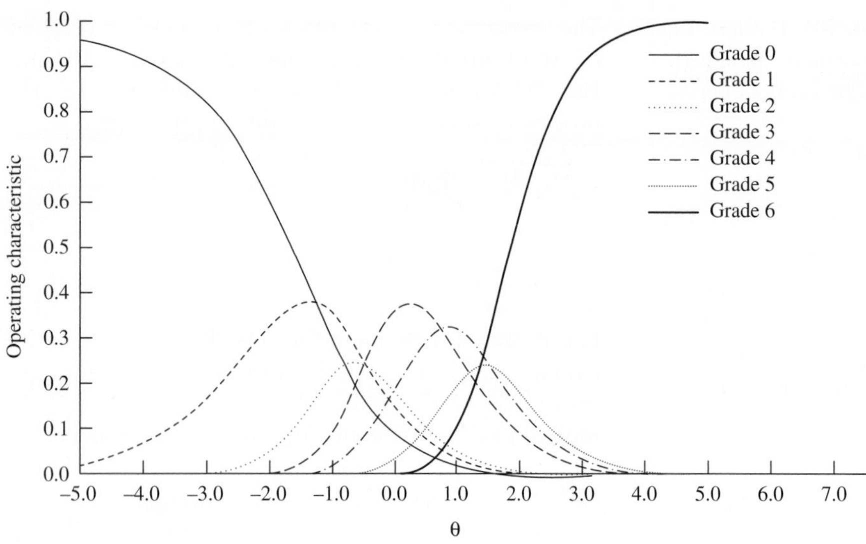

Figure 2 Example of a set of operating characteristics of graded responses. Acceleration model with seven graded scores, 0 through 6.

"Strongly agree" and "Moderately agree"), the operating characteristics of these new categories can be found in the original mathematical model.

In the acceleration model, however, the first kind of additivity does not rigorously hold, although it does hold in most practical situations. It can be said that models in category 1 are less restrictive and have a broader range of applicability because of their additivity.

Models That Can Be Naturally Expanded to Continuous Response Models

Let Z_g be a continuous item score that assumes any real number between 0 and 1 and z_g denote its realization. An example of a response format in social psychological measurement for which a continuous response model is used is given in Figure 1C. In this example, $Z_g = 0$ is assigned to the end point labeled "Totally disagree," and $Z_g = 1$ to the other end point labeled "Totally agree." To every other point on the line segment, the value between zero and unity that is proportional to the length from the left end point (i.e., where $Z_g = 0$) is assigned as z_g, when the statement is phrased positively. (If it is phrased negatively, the positions of $Z_g = 0$ and $Z_g = 1$ are reversed.)

When a specific graded response model is expandable to a continuous response model, the operating density characteristic, denoted by $H_{z_g}(\theta)$, is defined by:

$$H_{z_g}(\theta) = \lim_{\Delta z_g \to 0} \frac{P^*_{z_g}(\theta) - P^*_{(z_g+\Delta z_g)}(\theta)}{\Delta z_g} = -\frac{\partial}{\partial z_g} P^*_{z_g}(\theta) \tag{13}$$

where $P^*_{z_g}(\theta)$ is analogous to $P^*_{x_g}(\theta)$ in Eq. (7) for the graded response $X_g = x_g$. In homogeneous cases, the operating density characteristic for a continuous response is given by, from Eqs. (7) and (13):

$$H_{z_g}(\theta) = a_g \psi_g \{a_g(\theta - b_{z_g})\} \left[\frac{\partial}{\partial z_g} b_{z_g}\right] \tag{14}$$

provided that b_{z_g} is a strictly increasing and differentiable function of z_g. Samejima proposed in 1973 and 1974 the normal ogive and logistic models for continuous responses expanded from those for graded responses; they are specific cases of the general outcome given by Eq. (14). Additivity holds in these models in the homogeneous case, as can be seen in Eqs. (5), (7), and (8).

Whereas generally graded response models that are homogeneous can be naturally expanded to continuous response models, models that are heterogeneous are more diverse, namely some belonging to category 1 and others to category 2—that is, they are discrete in nature. The logistic positive exponent model for graded responses is a good example of a graded response model that can be naturally expanded to a continuous response model. The operating density characteristic of the resulting continuous response model is obtained from Eqs. (10) and (13):

$$H_{z_g}(\theta) = -\left[\Psi_g(\theta)\right]^{\xi_{z_g}} \log \Psi_g(\theta) \left[\frac{\partial}{\partial z_g} \xi_{z_g}\right] \tag{15}$$

provided that ξ_{z_g} is a nonnegative, strictly increasing, and differentiable function of z_g. It is also obvious from Eqs. (5), (10), and (11) that additivity holds for the logistic positive exponent model.

Models that are Discrete in Nature

A typical example of models that are discrete and cannot be naturally expanded to continuous response models is a model that is derived from Bock's 1972 nominal response model, which is represented by:

$$P_{k_g}(\theta) = \frac{\exp\left[\alpha_{k_g}\theta + \beta_{k_g}\right]}{\sum_{u \in K_g} \exp[\alpha_u \theta + \beta_u]} \tag{16}$$

where K_g denotes a nominal response to item g, and k_g is its realization, and $\alpha_{k_g}(>0)$ and β_{k_g} are item response parameters. Samejima (1972) pointed out that Bock's nominal model can be considered as a heterogeneous graded response model with the replacement of K_g in Eq. (16) by X_g and k_g by x_g and with the ordering:

$$\alpha_0 \leq \alpha_1 \leq \alpha_2 \leq \cdots \leq \alpha_{m_g} \tag{17}$$

where a strict inequality should hold at least at one place. When two or more adjacent parameters, say, α_{x_g} and $\alpha_{x_g}+1$, are equal, the operating characteristics of these adjacent graded responses share the same modal point, and this enables the model to deal with multiple correct answers and multiple incorrect answers. Thissen and Steinberg called this family of models, which includes Masters's 1982 partial credit model and Muraki's 1992 generalized partial credit model, the divided-by-total model. The processing function $M_{x_g}(\theta)$ in this model can be written:

$$M_{x_g}(\theta) = \frac{\sum_{u=x_g}^{m_g} \exp[\alpha_u \theta + \beta_u]}{\sum_{u=x_{g-1}}^{m_g} \exp[\alpha_u \theta + \beta_u]} \quad \text{for} \quad x_g = 1, 2, \ldots, m_g \tag{18}$$

in addition to Eq. (3) for $x_g = 0$ and $x_g = m_g + 1$.

It can be seen in Eq. (16) that the conditional ratio, given θ, of the operating characteristics of any two responses, k_g and h_g, equals the ratio of the numerators of the respective operating characteristics, each of which consists solely of its own item response parameters and θ. This means that the ratio is unchanged regardless of the other elements of the set K_g; a similar assumption is used by Luce's 1959 individual choice behavior. This principle makes the model discrete and provides an excellent model for nominal responses. As models for graded responses, however, this principle of the invariance of the conditional ratio, given θ, between the operating characteristics of any pair of discrete item responses to the same item g is rather restrictive. For example, for the category obtained by combining the responses k_g and h_g, the operating characteristic becomes:

$$P_{k_g}(\theta) + P_{h_g}(\theta) = \frac{\exp[\alpha_{k_g}\theta + \beta_{k_g}] + \exp[\alpha_{h_g}\theta + \beta_{h_g}]}{\sum_{u \in K_g} \exp[\alpha_u \theta + \beta_u]} \tag{19}$$

which does not belong to the model represented by Eq. (16); that is, first type of additivity does not hold.

Estimation of the Operating Characteristics

Methods for estimating the operating characteristics of graded item responses can be categorized as (1) nonparametric methods and (2) parametric methods. Nonparametric approaches are characterized by the discovery of the true shapes of the operating characteristics directly from the data, without assuming any mathematical form for $P_{x_g}(\theta)$. In contrast, parametric approaches assume a specific mathematical form for the operating characteristic, and the estimation of $P_{x_g}(\theta)$ is replaced by that of item parameters incorporated in the specific mathematical model.

For any scientific research, it is advisable to first use a nonparametric method to discover the shapes of the operating characteristics and then parameterize them by selecting a model that suits the nature of the data and that also fits the shapes of the $P_{x_g}(\theta)$ uncovered by the nonparametric estimation method. Note that a good fit of the ICF provided by a specific model to the uncovered curve is not sufficient because many mathematical models with completely different rationale can produce almost identical sets of $P_{x_g}(\theta)$ values.

Well-developed nonparametric estimation methods include the Levine's 1984 multilinear formula score theory, Ramsay's 1991 kernel smoothing approaches, and Samejim's 1998 conditional probability density function (pdf) approach. Computer software for parametric estimation methods has been developed mainly for Samejima's logistic model for graded responses and models based on Bock's nominal response model, using the marginal likelihood method and expectation-maximization (EM) algorithm. In particular, Thissen's Multilog (1991) and Muraki and Bock's Parscale (1993) have been used by many researchers.

Operating Characteristic of a Response Pattern

Let V denote the response pattern, which represents the individual's performance for n graded response items by a sequence of graded item score X_g for n items, and let v be its realization. Thus,

$$v = \{x_g\}' \quad \text{for} \quad g = 1, 2, \ldots, n. \tag{20}$$

It is assumed the local independence, or conditional independence, of item scores holds, so that the conditional distributions of n item scores are independent of one another, given θ. Thus, the likelihood function for $V = v$ is given as the operating characteristic of the response patterns, $P_v(\theta)$:

$$L(v \mid \theta) = P_v(\theta) \equiv \text{prob.}[V = v \mid \theta] = \prod_{x_g \in v} P_{x_g}(\theta). \tag{21}$$

Information Functions

Samejima proposed the item response information function for a general discrete item response. For a graded response x_g, it is denoted by $I_{x_g}(\theta)$ and defined by:

$$\begin{aligned} I_{x_g}(\theta) &\equiv -\frac{\partial^2}{\partial\theta^2}\log P_{x_g}(\theta) \\ &= \left[\frac{(\partial/\partial\theta)P_{x_g}(\theta)}{P_{x_g}(\theta)}\right]^2 - \frac{(\partial^2/\partial\theta^2)P_{x_g}(\theta)}{P_{x_g}(\theta)} \end{aligned} \tag{22}$$

She also defined the item information function for general discrete responses as the conditional expectation of the item response information function, given θ. For a graded response x_g, this function can be written:

$$\begin{aligned} I_g(\theta) &\equiv E[I_{x_g}(\theta) \mid \theta] = \sum_{x_g} I_{x_g}(\theta)P_{x_g}(\theta) \\ &= \sum_{x_g}\left[\frac{(\partial/\partial\theta)P_{x_g}(\theta)}{P_{x_g}(\theta)}\right]^2. \end{aligned} \tag{23}$$

Note that Eq. (23) includes Birnbaum's 1968 item information function for the dichotomous item, which is based on a somewhat different rationale, as a special case.

Samejima also proposed the response pattern information function, $I_v(\theta)$. For graded responses, it is given by:

$$I_v(\theta) \equiv -\frac{\partial^2}{\partial\theta^2}\log P_v(\theta) = \sum_{x_g \in v} I_{x_g}(\theta) \tag{24}$$

and the test information fuction, $I(\theta)$, as the conditional expectation of $I_v(\theta)$, given θ, which, from Eqs. (22), (23), and (24), can be written as

$$\begin{aligned} I(\theta) &\equiv E[I_v(\theta) \mid \theta] = \sum_{v} I_v(\theta)P_v(\theta) \\ &= -\sum_{v}\left[\frac{\partial^2}{\partial\theta^2}\log P_v(\theta)\right]P_v(\theta) = \sum_{g=1}^{n} I_g(\theta). \end{aligned} \tag{25}$$

The outcome of Eq. (25) also includes Birnbaum's 1968 test information function for dichotomous responses as a special case.

In general, the amount of test information is larger for graded response items than for dichotomous response items, and more importantly, it is substantially larger for a wider range of θ. In computerized adaptive testing (CAT), we construct a set of several hundred or more appropriate questions (items), called an item pool. These items have already been calibrated, and we let the computer select an optimal subset of items to a given examinee based on his or her performance on the previously presented question(s), so that an individual's ability level (individual parameter) can be estimated accurately without presenting too many questions to each examinee.

CAT is now widely used for the administration of the Graduate Record Examinations (GRE) and other large-scale tests, and dichotomous response items are used in the item pool in most cases because of the ease of writing items (questions). However, if we include several items that can be graded polytomously, presenting them to the examinee in the initial stage of CAT and analyzing the examinee's performance using a graded response model, CAT becomes more efficient because these graded response items direct the examinee closer to his or her true position on the latent trait scale with higher probabilities.

Figure 3 illustrates the shift of $\hat{\theta}_v$, the MLE of the individual parameter θ, in CAT after the presentation of each selected item, using simulated data for each of two hypothetical examinees who have the same (true) ability level, $\theta = 54.8$. The hypothetical item pool consists of dichotomous response items following the normal ogive model whose ICF, defined by Eq. (6), is identical with the cumulative operating characteristic, $P^*_{x_g}(\theta)$, in the normal ogive model for graded responses provided by Eq. (7), with the replacement of the item response difficulty parameter b_{x_g} by the item difficulty parameter b_g and of the density function ψ by the standard normal density function. For the first examinee (hollow circles), six to nine items were needed before $\hat{\theta}_v$ converged to the true θ, whereas for the second examinee (black square) as many as thirteen or more items were needed before $\hat{\theta}_v$ reached this stage. Note that with dichotomous items, after the examinee has answered the first question in CAT the current $\hat{\theta}_v$ is either negative infinity or positive infinity, depending on whether the answer is incorrect or correct. Although for the first examinee in Figure 3 this happened solely after the first item presentation, for the second examinee

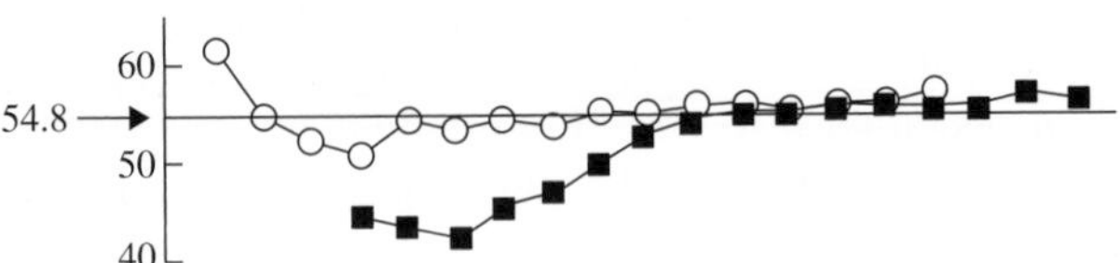

Figure 3 Shifts of the maximum likelihood estimate of ability after each dichotomous response item has been presented and responded to, for two hypothetical examinees with equal ability levels, 54.8.

the item score continued to be zero up to the fourth item, and thus the corresponding $\hat{\theta}_v$ were uniformly negative infinity, which cannot be plotted in the figure. It is expected that, if graded response items are presented on the initial stage of CAT instead of dichotomous response items, the convergence of $\hat{\theta}_v$ to the true θ will be facilitated and that the slow convergence with substantial discrepancies between the current $\hat{\theta}_v$ and the true θ illustrated by the second examinee in Figure (3) will be substantially less likely to happen.

Very few researchers have paid attention to the fact that the amount of test information can be reduced unless the estimation of θ is done directly from the response pattern. Let T be any aggregate (union) of response patterns, and t denote its realization. Because the response patterns are disjoint, the operating characteristic of $T = t$ becomes:

$$P_t(\theta) = \sum_{v \in t} P_v(\theta). \tag{26}$$

Let $I^*(\theta)$ denote the test information function based on such an aggregate t instead of each response pattern v. This is obtained by replacing $P_v(\theta)$ in the fourth expression of Eq. (25) by $P_t(\theta)$, given by Eq. (26). For these two test information functions, there exists the relationship:

$$I(\theta) \geq I^*(\theta). \tag{27}$$

Eq. (27) has an important implication because the reduction in the amount of test information leads to the inaccuracy of the estimation of θ. A good example of the aggregate T is the test score, which is the sum total of the $n x_g$ values in $V = v$. Because the reciprocal of the square root of the test information function can be used as an approximate local standard error of estimation, it is obvious from Eq. (27) that the accuracy of the estimation of the latent trait θ will be reduced if the test score is used as the intervening variable. Thus, it is essential that θ be estimated directly from the response pattern, not from the test score.

It should also be noted that the item response information function $I_{x_g}(\theta)$ and the response pattern information function $I_v(\theta)$, which are defined by Eqs. (22) and (24), respectively, have important roles in the estimation of the latent trait θ based on the subject's response pattern v. For example, even if $I_{x_g}(\theta)$ of one or more x_g that belong to the response pattern v assumes negative values for some interval(s) of θ, the item information function $I_g(\theta)$ that is defined by Eq. (23) will still assume nonnegative values for the same interval(s), as is obvious from the far right-hand-side expression in the equation. The consideration of this fact is especially necessary in programming CAT to select an item to present to an individual subject when the three-parameter logistic model is adopted for multiple-choice test items in the item pool.

These information functions and observations can be considered extensions of Fisher information functions. In most of the statistics literature, however, the discussion and theorizing concern a restricted situation in which all observations are based on a random sample from a *single* distribution. In the context of IRT, however, such a situation will not happen unless all items are equivalent, which can be stated on the graded response level as: (1) all the n items have the same values of m_g, and, moreover, (2) the sets of $(m_g + 1)$ operating characteristics for the n separate items are all identical. In most research based on IRT, we need a variety of different sets of operating characteristics, and thus the assumption of equivalence of the n items is not acceptable.

To make the information functions useful in the context of IRT, therefore, the theorems based on a random sample will have to be expanded to apply to cases in which separate observations come from separate distributions, combined with the principle of local independence, which states that the conditional distributions of item scores, given θ, are independent of one another.

With some research data, the assumption of local or conditional independence can also go beyond the level of tolerance. There are ways of ameliorating the situation in pilot studies, however, by modifying or even replacing one or more items, without affecting the contents of the latent trait. Items are human-made, and they are only tools for measuring the individual's latent trait, so such modifications are perfectly justifiable.

In addition, in the statistics literature very little attention is paid to the information provided by individual responses. In IRT, however, the item response information function, $I_{x_g}(\theta)$, is very important because the item responses are the elements of a specific response pattern $V = v$, on which the individual parameter θ is estimated. Credit should be given, however, to the few exceptions to this (such as Lindgen's 1976 study), in which such information is presented and discussed in the context of a random sample from a single distribution.

Unique Maximum Condition for the Likelihood Function

The beauty of IRT lies in that, unlike classical test theory, θ can be estimated straightforwardly from the response pattern, without the intervention of the test score. Let $A_{x_g}(\theta)$ be:

$$\begin{aligned} A_{x_g}(\theta) &\equiv \frac{\partial}{\partial\theta}\log\, P_{x_g}(\theta) \\ &= \sum_{u \leq x_g} \frac{\partial}{\partial\theta}\log\, M_u(\theta) + \frac{\partial}{\partial\theta}\log[1 - M_{(x_g+1)}(\theta)]. \end{aligned} \tag{28}$$

Because, from Eqs. (21) and (28), the likelihood equation can be written:

$$\begin{aligned}\frac{\partial}{\partial\theta}\log L(x\,|\,\theta) &= \frac{\partial}{\partial\theta}\log P_v(\theta)\\ &= \sum_{x_g\in v}\frac{\partial}{\partial\theta}\log P_{x_g}(\theta)\\ &= \sum_{x_g\in v}A_{x_g}(\theta)\ \equiv\ 0 \qquad (29)\end{aligned}$$

a straightforward computer program can be written for any model in such a way that $A_{x_g}(\theta)$ is selected and computed for each $x_g \in v$ for $g = 1, 2, \ldots, n$ and added, and the values of θ that makes the sum total of these n functions equal to zero are located as the MLE of θ for the individual whose performance is represented by v. Samejima called $A_{x_g}(\theta)$ the basic function, because this function provides the basis for computer programming for estimating θ from the response pattern v.

From Eqs. (28) and (29), it is obvious that a sufficient condition for the likelihood function to have a unique modal point for *any* response pattern is that the basic function $A_{x_g}(\theta)$ be strictly decreasing in θ, with a nonnegative upper asymptote and a nonpositive lower asymptote. It can be seen from Eqs. (22) and (28) that this unique maximum condition will be satisfied if the item response information function $I_{x_g}(\theta)$ is positive for all θ, except at a finite or enumerably infinite number of points.

The normal ogive model, the logistic model, the logistic positive exponent model, the acceleration model, and models derived from Bock's nominal response model all satisfy the unique maximum condition. Notably, however, the three-parameter logistic model for dichotomous responses, which has been widely used for multiple-choice test data, does not satisfy the unique maximum condition, and multiple MLEs of θ may exist for some response patterns.

Discussion

A strength of the graded response model in IRT is that it can be used in many different types of research, and there is still room for innovation. In doing so, model selection for specific research data should be made substantively, considering the nature of the data and the characteristics of the models.

Acknowledgments

The author is obliged to Wim J. Van der Linden and Philip S. Livingston for their thorough reviewing and comments.

See Also the Following Articles

Item Response Theory • Maximum Likelihood Estimation

Further Reading

Birnbaum, A. (1968). Some latent trait models and their use in inferring an examinee's ability. In *Statistical Theories of Mental Test Scores* (F. M. Lord and M. R. Novick, eds.) Chaps. 17–20. Addison Wesley, Reading, MA.

Bock, R. D. (1972). Estimating item parameters and latent ability when responses are scored in two or more nominal categories. *Psychometrika* **37,** 29–51.

Dodd, B. G., Koch, W. R., and De Ayala, R. J. (1989). Operational characteristics of adaptive testing procedures using the graded response model. *Appl. Psychol. Meas.* **13,** 129–143.

Koch, W. R. (1983). Likert scaling using the graded response latent trait model. *Appl. Psychol. Meas.* **7,** 15–32.

Levine, M. (1984). *An Introduction to Multilinear Formula Scoring Theory.* Office of Naval Research Report 84-4, N00014-83-K-0397. University of Illinois, Champaign, IL.

Lindgen, B. W. (1976). *Statistical Theory.* John Wiley, New York.

Lord, F. M., and Novick, M. R. (1968). *Statistical Theories of Mental Test Scores.* Addison Wesley, Reading, MA.

Luce, R. D. (1959). *Individual Choice Behavior.* John Wiley, New York.

Masters, G. N. (1982). A Rasch model for partial credit scoring. *Psychometrika* **47,** 149–174.

Muraki, E. (1992). A generalized partial credit model: Application of an EM algorithm. *Appl. Psychol. Meas.* **16,** 159–176.

Muraki, E., and Bock, R. D. (1993). Parscale, 11. Scientific Software.

Ramsay, J. O. (1991). Kernel smoothing approaches to nonparametric item characteristic estimation. *Psychometrika* **56,** 611–630.

Roche, A. F., Wainer, H., and Thissen, D. (1975). *Skeletal Maturity: The Knee Joint as a Biological Indicator.* Plenum Medical, New York.

Samejima, F. (1969). A general model for free responce data. *Psychometrika* Monograph No. 17.

Samejima, F. (1972). Estimation of ability using a response pattern of graded scores. *Psychometrika* Monograph No. 18.

Samejima, F. (1973a). A comment on Birnbaum's three-parameter logistic model in the latent trait theory. *Psychometrika* **38,** 221–233.

Samejima, F. (1973b). Homogeneous case of the continuous response model. *Psychometrika* **38,** 203–219.

Samejima, F. (1974). Normal ogive model on the continuous response level in the multi-dimensional latent space. *Psychometrika* **39,** 111–121.

Samejima, F. (1977). A use of the information function in tailored testing. *Appl. Psychol. Meas.* **1,** 233–247.

Samejima, F. (1980). Latent trait theory and its applications. In *Multivariate Analysis,* (P. R. Krishnaiah, ed.), Vol. 5 North Holland.

Samejima, F. (1993). An approximation for the bias function of the maximum likelihood of a latent variable for the general case where the item responses are discrete. *Psychometrika* **58,** 119–138.

Samejima, F. (1994). Roles of Fisher type information in latent trait models. In *Proceedings of the First US/Japan Conference Modeling: An Informational Approach* (H. Bozdogan, ed.), pp. 347–387.

Samejima, F. (1995). Acceleration model in the heterogeneous case of the general graded response model. *Psychometrika* **60,** 549–572.

Samejima, F. (1996). Evaluation of mathematical models for ordered polychotomous responses. *Behaviometrika* **23**, 17–35.

Samejima, F. (1997). Graded response model. *Handbook of Modern Item Response Theory* (W. J. Van der Linden and R. K. Hambleton, eds.) Springer-Verlag, New York.

Samejima, F. (1998). Efficient nonparametric approaches for estimating the operating characteristics of discrete item responses. *Psychometrika* **63,** 111–130.

Samejima, F. (2000). Logistic positive exponent family of models: Virtue of asymmetric item characteristic curves. *Psychometrika* **65,** 319–335.

Samejima, F. (2003). Logistic positive exponent model for graded responses (in preparation).

Thissen, D. (1991). *Multilog User's Guide—Version 6.* Scientific Software, Chicago, IL.

Thissen, D., and Steinberg, L. (1986). A taxonomy of item response models. *Psychometrika* **51,** 567–577.

Van der Linden, W. J., and Hambleton, R. K. (eds.) (1997). *Handbook of Modern Item Response Theory*. Springer-Verlag, New York.

Graph Theory

Stephen C. Locke
Florida Atlantic University, Boca Raton, Florida, USA

Glossary

algorithm A procedure for solving a problem.

bipartite graph A graph that has two classes of vertices; for example, vertices may represent men and women, with the additional property that no edge joins two members of the same class.

connected A graph is connected if for each pair of vertices, there is a path from one to the other.

cycle A route, using at least one edge, that returns to its starting point, but does not repeat any vertex except for the first and the last.

directed graph A generalization of a graph, in which some edges may have directions; similar to one-way streets in a city.

edge A connection between a pair of vertices, denoting that the two vertices are related in some way.

heuristic A procedure for obtaining an approximate solution to a problem.

matching A pairing of some vertices, so that the vertices in each pair are joined by an edge.

NP-complete A set of problems currently assumed to be computationally difficult; a subset of nondeterministic polynomial (NP)-time.

path A route that can be followed from one vertex to another by means of edges between successive vertices of the path.

simple Without loops or multiple edges.

tree A connected graph with no cycles.

vertex A basic element of the graph, possibly representing physical objects or places.

A graph can be thought of as a representation of a relationship on a given set. For example, the set might be the set of people in some town, and the relationship between two people might be that they share a grandparent. Graph theory is the study of properties of graphs. In particular, if a graph is known to have one property, what other properties must it possess? Can certain features of the graph be found in a reasonable amount of time? In this article, a few of the more common properties of graphs and some theorems relating these properties are mentioned, with reference to some methods for finding structures within a graph.

History

The river Pregel flows through the city of Königsberg (Kaliningrad). In the middle of the river is an island, the Kneiphof, after which the river branches. There are seven bridges over various parts of the river. The citizens of the town enjoy strolling through the city and are curious whether there is a route that crosses each bridge exactly once. This problem, a popular mathematical game known as the "Königsberg Bridge Problem," was solved by Leonhard Euler in 1736, and, in doing so, Euler stated the first theorem in the field of graph theory.

Another popular amusement is the "Knight's Tour Problem": can a knight travel around a standard chessboard, landing on each square exactly once, and returning to its initial square? This problem was treated by Alexandre-Theophile Vandermonde in 1771. A similar problem using the vertices and edges of a dodecahedron was marketed as the "Icosian Game" by Sir William Rowan Hamilton in 1857. The game was a flop, but over 1600 research papers on Hamilton cycles (cycles through all of the vertices) have since been published, and thousands more papers have explored related topics.

The word "graph" is derived from "graphical notation," introduced by Alexander Crum Brown in a paper on isomers in 1864. Crum Brown was a contemporary of Arthur Cayley and James Joseph Sylvester, who used related graphs to study chemical properties. One of the most notorious problems in graph theory originated in 1852, when Frederick Guthrie asked his professor, Augustus De Morgan, whether four colors were always sufficient to color the regions of a map drawn on a sphere. A mere 124 years later, Wolfgang Haken and Kenneth Appel finished the proof with extensive assistance from a computer program. There is, of course, an ongoing debate among mathematicians whether a computer-assisted proof should be accepted if the resulting proof is so lengthy that most mathematicians would not have time to read the entire proof. In other areas of mathematics, there are theorems with long, human-constructed proofs. Andrew Wiles wrote a 200-page proof of a 400-year-old number theoretic conjecture by Fermat. The record length for a proof done entirely by humans is 15,000 pages (for the classification of simple groups). It is expected that this proof can be condensed to 3000 pages.

In 1890, Percy John Heawood extended the idea of map-coloring problems to consider colorings on surfaces other than the sphere. For example, seven colors suffice for coloring regions on a torus (a doughnut). It is perhaps counterintuitive that the torus is easier to handle than the sphere. Heawood provided the upper bound for all of the orientable (two-sided, like a sphere or torus) surfaces and a few years later Heinrich Tietze provided the upper bound for the nonorientable (one-sided, like a Möbius strip) surfaces.

Notation

Figure 1 is a labeled graph depicting the relationships between various pairs of people. In the figure, vertices representing people have been drawn as small open circles, and an edge (connection) between two vertices indicates that the two people have spoken to each other. Thus, for example, Brad has spoken with Janet, and both have spoken with Frank. It would be easy to modify the picture to record that the interchanges had been in one direction. An arrow on the edge from Brad to Janet, pointing in the direction of the communication, would show that Brad has spoken to Janet, but Janet did not respond. To show that Brad spoke to himself, an edge (loop) could be drawn from Brad back to Brad. Five edges (a multiple edge) could also be drawn from Brad to Janet if they have spoken on five occasions. In the following discussions, unless otherwise specified, only simple graphs—those that are undirected, loopless, and lacking multiple edges—are considered.

Graph theory notation is not completely standardized and the reader should be aware that vertices may sometimes be called "nodes" or "points," and edges may be called "lines" or "links." Graphs can be used to model social relationships, transportation networks, hierarchies, chemical or physical structures, or flow of control in an algorithm. Perhaps one of the largest examples of a (directed) graph that many people use every day is the World Wide Web. The files are the vertices. A link from one file to another is a directed edge (or arc).

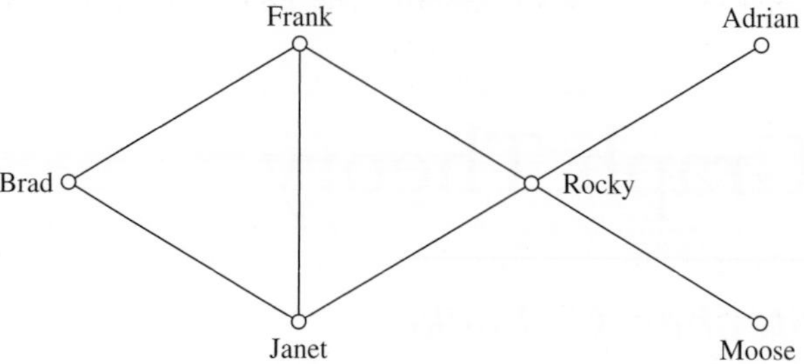

Figure 1 A graph depicting the relationships between pairs of people. Vertices representing people have been drawn as small open circles; an edge (connection) between two vertices indicates that two people have spoken to each other.

Several properties of graphs can be studied. In Fig. 1, Frank and Janet would be called neighbors of Brad. If Brad wished to get a message to Moose, he could tell Janet, who would pass the message along to Rocky, and then Rocky would give the message to Moose. This describes a path from Brad to Moose. In this figure, there is a path connecting any two of the vertices and the graph is connected, or the graph has one component. The number of edges in the path is its length. The length of a shortest path between any two vertices is the distance between those vertices. The diameter of a graph is the maximum number that occurs as a distance. Figure 1 has diameter 3, because there is no path from Brad to Moose using fewer than three edges, but for every pair of vertices the path length is at most three. There are Internet web sites that will compute the driving distance between any two points in the United States. A famous metaconjecture (and movie title, "Six Degrees of Separation") proposes building a graph similar to the example in Fig. 1, but with each person in the United States as a vertex, and edges between two people if they normally communicate with each other; that graph should have diameter 6 at most. This is a metaconjecture because it would take a great deal of trouble to prove it—the graph would be constantly changing and it would never be quite correct.

In Fig. 1, if Rocky were to move away from the social circle, Brad, Janet, and Frank could still communicate with each other, but Moose and Adrian would have no route for their communications, nor could they talk to the other group. Rocky would thus be defined as a cut vertex, i.e., a vertex that increases the number of components when deleted (in this case, disconnecting the graph). If both Frank and Janet were to leave, instead of Rocky, there would again be no way for Brad to communicate with Moose. Thus {Janet, Frank} is a cut set of vertices. Now, consider removing edges instead of vertices. Suppose that Rocky and Adrian have an argument and are unwilling to speak to each other. Then, there would be no way for, say,

Janet and Adrian to interact. The edge from Rocky to Adrian is a cut edge, i.e., an edge that increases the number of components when deleted. The two edges from Rocky to Janet and Frank constitute a cut set of edges.

Next consider Fig. 1 as representing members of a committee, with an edge between those pairs who are willing to work together. Perhaps some of the members of the committee need to pair off for some important tasks. For example, Brad (B) and Janet (J) could work together and Rocky (R) and Adrian (A) could work together. The juxtaposition of two letters will refer to the edge between the two vertices labeled by the letters of the committee members' names. The set {BJ, RA} is a matching or independent set of edges. A perfect matching, or 1-factor, is a matching that includes all of the vertices. Figure 1 does not have a perfect matching, but if an edge between Adrian and Moose is included, a perfect matching could then be found.

A complete graph is a graph in which every vertex is a neighbor of every other vertex. A subgraph of a graph consists of a subset of the edge set and a subset of the vertex set, with the proviso that both ends of every edge must be included. In Fig. 1, one of the subgraphs would be obtained by taking the edges {BJ, JF, BF} and the vertex set {B, J, F}. This subgraph is complete. Because it is not contained in any larger complete subgraph, it is sometimes called a "clique." The reader is encouraged to identify the four cliques in Fig. 1.

A set of vertices, no two of which are joined by an edge, is called an independent set of vertices or a stable set of vertices. There are 17 nonempty stable sets in Fig. 1; 6 of these have one vertex each, 8 have two vertices, and 3 have three vertices. The complement of a simple graph is the graph with same set of vertices, but with an edge between two vertices if and only if there was no edge in the original graph. The complement of the graph of Fig. 1 would have eight edges: AM, AJ, MJ, AB, MB, AF, MF, and BR. Maximal stable sets in any graph correspond to cliques in its complement.

A graph is bipartite if its vertex set can be partitioned into two sets **X** and **Y**, such that no edge has both ends in **X** or both ends in **Y**. The pair (**X**, **Y**) is called a bipartition of **G**. Suppose the vertices in **X** represent people and those in **Y** represent jobs and that an edge from person P to job J means that person P is capable of completing job J. We might wish to assign people to jobs so that nobody gets more than one job, and no two people get the same job. That is, we ask for a matching in this bipartite graph. If the edges are assigned weights representing the value to the company of that person doing that job, we might ask for a maximum weight matching. For a set **S**, we write **S** for the cardinality (number of elements of) of **S**.

A **k**-edge-coloring of a graph **G** is an assignment of a color (number) from {**1**, **2**, ..., **k**} to the edges of **G** so that each edge receives exactly one color. It is not necessary to use all **k** colors. A proper **k**-edge coloring is one for which no two edges of the same color meet at any vertex; **G** is **k**-edge colorable if **G** has a proper **k**-edge coloring. A **k**-coloring of a graph **G** is an assignment of a color (number) from {**1**, **2**, ..., **k**} to the vertices of **G** so that each vertex receives exactly one color. Again, it is not necessary to use all **k** colors. A proper **k**-coloring is one for which no two vertices of the same color are adjacent; **G** is **k**-colorable if **G** has a proper **k**-coloring. If **G** is a bipartite graph with bipartition (**X**, **Y**), and if the vertices of **X** are colored red and those in **Y** are colored blue, the graph would have been properly 2-colored, because no edge would have both ends of the same color.

Suppose the vertices in the graph **G** represent courses at a university, with an edge joining two courses if some student is enrolled in both courses. At exam time, it is necessary to schedule the exams in **k** time slots, so that no student has two exams at the same time. If it is possible to schedule the exams with no conflicts, the assignment of time slots from {**1**, **2**, ..., **k**} to the courses is a proper **k**-coloring of **G**. The vertices of a bipartite graph could also be used to represent the instructors at a high school and the classes they have to teach. The colors of a proper edge-coloring could designate the time slots in the school day.

Colorings have also been used to speed up testing for short-circuits on circuit boards. Two points within a certain specified distance might short, but two at greater distance are unlikely to short. In the graph representing the circuit board, an edge between two vertices that could short would be drawn. If the points are properly colored, with points that are adjacent designated by different colors, it is possible to test if there is any current flow between all the points of one color and all of the points of another. (Imagine a device designed to touch all of the red vertices simultaneously, and another designed to touch all of the blue.) Current flow between the set of red vertices and set of blue vertices would indicate that there is a short on the board. No flow for any pair of colors could reasonably ascertain that there is no short-circuit. Among the other uses for colorings are optimization of assignment of variables to registers by computer language compilers.

Consider an ant starting at a vertex of a graph **G** and crawling along the edges of **G** from one vertex to another. A cycle of **G** is the route traversed by the ant if that route uses at least one edge, repeats no edges or internal vertices (vertices of the cycle, which are neither the first nor the last vertex of the cycle), and returns to where it started. An alternative definition of a cycle is that it is a graph with an equal number of vertices and edges, and the vertices can be placed around a circle so that two vertices are adjacent if and only if they appear consecutively along the circle. A tree is a connected graph with no cycles. A forest is a graph with no cycles (a collection of trees). A Hamilton cycle of a graph is a cycle that passes through every vertex. A graph that has a Hamilton cycle is called hamiltonian. The "Traveling Salesman Problem" seeks to find the minimum-weight Hamilton cycle in a graph that has edges with weights. Although this may seem a bit artificial, there is an application: in some manufacturing processes, it is necessary for a robotic arm to visit 100,000 sites on each article manufactured, and it is essential to have the trip take as little time as possible.

Algorithms

Having a list of problems that can be addressed with the language of graph theory is a useful end in itself. Even better, once a problem has been identified, problems of a similar nature can be sought. Often, these problems have been solved, and there will be an algorithm available. An algorithm is a finite, terminating set of instructions to solve a given problem. An algorithm is of order $\mathbf{T(n)}$, or $\mathbf{O(T(n))}$, if there is a constant $\mathbf{c}$, such that for any input of size $\mathbf{n}$, the algorithm takes no more than $\mathbf{cT(n)}$ steps to complete its task, as long as $\mathbf{n}$ is large enough. If $\mathbf{T(n)}$ is a polynomial in $\mathbf{n}$, the algorithm is polynomial-time, or good. There is a special, very well-studied class of yes/no problems for which there are no known good algorithms, but the existence of a good algorithm for any one problem in the class would give a good algorithm for all problems in the class. This is the class of NP-complete problems (the technical definition of which is complicated and beyond the scope here). If a mathematician is having difficulty solving a problem from this class, the excuse that nobody else knows how to do it efficiently either is a good excuse!

Consider now some of the standard problems from graph theory, starting with some NP-complete problems. Assume in each case there is a graph $\mathbf{G}$, and in some cases, there is an integer $\mathbf{k}$:

1. Does $\mathbf{G}$ have a Hamilton cycle?
2. Does $\mathbf{G}$ have an independent set of $\mathbf{k}$ vertices?
3. Does $\mathbf{G}$ have a complete subgraph on $\mathbf{k}$ vertices?
4. Can the vertices of $\mathbf{G}$ be properly colored with $\mathbf{k}$-colors, where $\mathbf{k} \geq 3$?

These questions (problems) all have yes/no answers. If, for example, we wanted to see a Hamilton cycle, an independent set or complete graph of the specified size, or a proper $\mathbf{k}$-coloring, this is at least as difficult. Such problems are called NP-hard. For these problems, we must settle for approximation algorithms, heuristics, or brute force.

Some Elegant Theorems

There are polynomial-time algorithms to address the problems discussed next. For simplicity, the algorithms are not displayed, and the fastest algorithm to solve each problem is not necessarily presented.

1. Given a maze (labyrinth), consider the intersections as vertices and the passages between intersections as edges. If the entire maze is visible, a way out of the maze can be found, or it can be shown that no way out exists, by using Dijskstra's algorithm. Dijkstra's algorithm states that, given a graph $\mathbf{G}$ and a vertex $\mathbf{v}$ in $\mathbf{G}$, the distances from $\mathbf{v}$ to all other vertices in $\mathbf{G}$ in $\mathbf{O(n^2)}$ time can be found. A bipartite graph can be characterized as one that has no cycles with an odd number of edges. A minor variant of Dijkstra's algorithm can be used to either find an odd cycle in a given graph or to find a bipartition of that graph.

2. Ford–Fulkerson algorithm. Given a graph $\mathbf{G}$, the distances between every pair of vertices in $\mathbf{G}$ in $\mathbf{O(n^3)}$ time can be found.

3. The southeastern coast of Florida has more than occasional heavy rain. Covered walkways between buildings are very useful. If the cost of connecting each pair of buildings by a walkway is known, the cheapest way to connect the buildings using walkways between pairs of buildings can be calculated so that it is always possible to walk from one building to another by some sequence of walkways. To minimize the cost, there would be no cycles. Thus, a minimum weight spanning (reaches all buildings) tree is sought. If it is allowed to choose some extra locations and build walkways to those locations as well as using direct connections, the problem becomes much harder. This Steiner tree problem is NP-hard.

Kruskal's algorithm. Given a graph $\mathbf{G}$, with weighted edges, a minimum weight spanning tree in $\mathbf{G}$ in $\mathbf{O(n^2)}$ time can be found.

4. A set $\mathbf{S}$ isolates a vertex $\mathbf{w}$ if all of the neighbors of $\mathbf{w}$ are members of $\mathbf{S}$. A set of vertices $\mathbf{C}$ is a cover if every edge has at least one end in $\mathbf{C}$.

Consider operating a dating service; it has already been determined which pairs of people are suitable as a couple. Presuming interest only in the pairings of males with females, the data could be represented as a bipartite graph. Assume also that no person will be matched with more than one other person. This case is a matching in a bipartite graph. Hall's theorem and König's theorem give conditions on a maximum matching. These theorems yield algorithms that quickly find maximum matchings. The reader will notice that conditions have been introduced that may not exist in the original problem (male–female matching, no multiple partners). Adapting a known algorithm to fit the particular problem may be necessary. If weights are placed on the edges, perhaps to show a compatibility index between the people using the dating service, maximum weight matching could be attained, with the hope that the solution provided provides the best satisfaction level overall. Again, presuming the graph is bipartite, this is the same problem as given in the problem of assigning jobs, mentioned previously.

Hall's matching theorem. If **G** is a bipartite graph, with bipartition (**X**, **Y**), then **G** has a matching that meets every vertex of **X** if and only if no subset **S** of **Y** isolates more than |**S**| vertices of **X**. An easy consequence of Hall's theorem is that if a bipartite graph has maximum degree **Δ**, then it is **Δ**-edge-colorable. Obviously, any color class of a proper **k**-edge-coloring of a graph **G** is a matching. This edge-coloring can be thought of as having the following meaning: In time slot one, the edges of the first color give us a matching; in time slot two, the edges of the second color give us a matching; etc. This could be useful for scheduling examinations or for designing an experiment.

König–Egervary matching theorem. If **G** is a bipartite graph, then the cardinality of a maximum matching equals the cardinality of a minimum cover. There is a polynomial-time algorithm to find a maximum matching **M** in a bipartite graph and a corresponding cover **C**. This is exceptionally elegant and useful;—it not only provides a method of finding the primary object (**M**), but also receives a certificate (**C**) to prove that **M** is optimum. If **M** and **C** are passed to another person, that person does not have to understand how the algorithm works. The only requirement is to check that **M** is a matching, **C** is a cover, and that $|\mathbf{M}| = |\mathbf{C}|$. The Kuhn–Menkres algorithm produces similar solutions for weighted bipartite graphs in $\mathbf{O(n^4)}$ time. These results and other minimax theorems using network flows can be considered as special cases of the fundamental theorem of linear programming.

5. Consider the job of setting up a round-robin chess tournament. People can be paired in round one, possibly with some people not playing that round. Then, pairing is done a different way for round two, etc. In effect, this is asking for a coloring of the edges of a complete graph. In a more general case, a way to color the edges of an arbitrary simple graph might be sought. It is obvious that at least as many colors as the edges meeting any vertex are needed. Surprisingly, many more are not needed.

Vizing's theorem. If a simple graph has maximum degree **Δ**, then it is $(\mathbf{\Delta + 1})$-edge-colorable. Suppose that a zoo is being built and putting certain animals together, if one is likely to eat the other, must be avoided. The animals could be represented as vertices in a graph and two animals would be connected if they are not compatible. The number of habitats needed is the number of colors needed to color the vertices of the graph.

6. Brooks' theorem. If a simple graph **G** has maximum degree **Δ**, then it is **Δ**-colorable, unless **G** is an odd cycle or a complete graph. In this latter case, $\mathbf{\Delta + 1}$ colors are necessary and sufficient.

7. Having mentioned matchings in bipartite graphs, consider nonbipartite graphs, for which Tutte's theorem applies. To actually find a maximum matching, Edmonds algorithm can be used. Tutte's matching theorem states that if **G** is a graph, then **G** has a matching that meets every vertex of **G** if and only if for every subset of **S** of **V(G)** the number of odd components of $\mathbf{G - S}$ is at most |**S**|.

8. Ramsey's theorem. Any sufficiently large graph has a complete subgraph on **k** vertices, or an independent set of **k** vertices.

9. Dirac's theorem. If every vertex of the simple graph **G** has degree at least **k**, and if **G** has at most **2k** vertices, then **G** is a hamiltonian.

Unsolved Problems

In many areas of mathematics, it takes years of study to reach the point where it is possible to understand the interesting unsolved problems. In graph theory, a few hours of study already leads one to unsolved problems. The four-color problem, mentioned previously was unsolved for 140 years, yet it takes little to understand the statement of the problem. Bondy and Murty made up a list of 50 unsolved problems in 1976, and most of those problems are still open today. The two following problems interest many researchers.

1. The "cycle double cover problem": If a graph has no edge whose deletion disconnects the graph, is there a collection of cycles that together contain every edge exactly twice? If a graph can be drawn in the plane, and if that graph has no edge whose deletion disconnects the graph, then the faces of the graph are cycles that together contain every edge exactly twice.

2. The "reconstruction problem": Given the deck of a graph on at least three vertices, can we determine uniquely what the original graph was? Given a graph **G**, with vertices $v_1, \ldots, v_n$, let $\mathbf{G_k}$ denote the subgraph of **G** obtained by deleting the vertex $\mathbf{v_k}$. Now, draw these vertex-deleted subgraphs, $\mathbf{G_1}, \ldots, \mathrm{G_k}$, as unlabeled graphs, each on a separate index card. This is called the deck of **G**.

See Also the Following Articles

Heuristics • Network Analysis

Further Reading

The books by Chartrand (1985) and Trudeau (1976) are accessible to high school students. For an undergraduate or beginning graduate presentation, Bondy and Murty (1976) or West (2001) would be useful. For further information on algorithms, see Even (1979). At the graduate level, there are texts on algebraic graph theory, algorithmic graph theory, cycles in graphs, graphical enumeration, matroid theory, random graphs, topological graph theory, as well as texts on specific unsolved problems.

Biggs, N. L., Lloyd, E. K., and Wilson, R. J. (1976). *Graph Theory 1736–1936.* Clarendon Press, Oxford.

Bondy, J. A., and Murty, U. S. R. (1976). *Graph Theory with Applications.* Elsevier North-Holland, Amsterdam.

Chartrand, G. (1985). *Introductory Graph Theory.* Dover, New York.

Edmonds, J. (1965). Paths, trees and flowers. *Canad. J. Math.* **17,** 449–467.

Even, S. (1979). *Graph Algorithms.* Computer Science Press, Rockville Maryland.

Locke, S. C. (2004). *Graph Theory Definitions.* Available on the Internet at www.math.fau.edu

Trudeau, R. J. (1976). *Dots and Lines.* Kent State University Press, Kent, Ohio.

West, D. B. (2001). *Introduction to Graph Theory.* Prentice Hall, New Jersey.

Graunt, John

Philip Kreager
Somerville College, Oxford University, Oxford, England, United Kingdom

Glossary

life expectation The average number of additional years a person would live, when the rate of mortality indicated by a given life table holds.

life table A detailed descriptive model of the mortality of a population, giving the probability of dying at each age; 17th- and 18th-century tables were based on the assumption that populations are stationary, i.e., their total number and age distribution are constant.

natural history The scientific study of animals and plants based on observation rather than on experiment.

scholasticism Teaching based on the medieval university framework of the trivium (grammar, logic, and rhetoric) and quadrivium (mathematical arts of arithmetic, geometry, astronomy, and music); although developed originally in the context of theology and philosophy, Scholastic models continued to shape school curricula into the 17th century.

John Graunt's *Natural and Political Observations upon the London Bills of Mortality*, published in 1662, marks the inception of scientific social measurement. Immediate acclaim at the time of publication of the work led the Royal Society to make Graunt a charter member, and a long line of analysts from Farr and Pearson to Glass and Kendall have not hesitated to declare him the founder of statistics and demography. Graunt's book defined the direction of early modern numerical description and analysis of society, in which the state was seen as a population possessed of inherent quantitative regularities, natural in kind, but susceptible to political, medical, and economic management. Many of the quantitative measures Graunt invented, and his critical scrutiny of available numerical sources, make his population arithmetic appear modern. His work quickly became central to developments in the nascent calculus of probability. In the process, one of his inventions (a hypothetical table of mortality by age) was elaborated to become demography's fundamental population model (the life table). Yet the concepts of method Graunt employed and the idea of population he developed differ profoundly from demography and statistics as they emerged much later, in the 19th and 20th centuries. The enduring importance of his work rests not only on its seeming anticipation of many aspects of later methodology, but on the originality and distinctiveness of his conception and what it can tell us about the nature of quantitative social inquiry.

The Historical Context of the *Observations*

John Graunt (1620–1674) wrote at a time when scientific uses of mathematics, confined largely to chemistry, astronomy, and physics, were commonly bound up with religious questions, alchemy, and astrology. The idea of a science of social and economic life was unformulated, and specialized disciplines such as demography and statistics were inconceivable. That man should develop mathematics in order to intervene into patterns of life and death was morally and theologically dubious to the great majority of Graunt's contemporaries. Graunt was, in any case, expressly not proficient in the new natural sciences, nor in higher mathematics. Yet he was able to compose a method of measuring populations that excited Huygens, Leibnitz, Halley, and other distinguished mathematicians and natural scientists of the time. The sensation Graunt's work created was not confined to the elite. Despite its unprecedented and questionable subject matter, and a text composed largely of computations and sustained quantitative reasoning, the *Observations* immediately attracted a wide readership, going through three reprintings by 1665, and subsequent editions, translations, excerpts, and summaries over the course of the next century. Graunt's own life and the stated purposes of his work direct us to the contemporary issues that gave population arithmetic its immediate importance.

Biographical Note

The fragmentary but coherent record of Graunt's life owes largely to the careful research of David Glass. The story is at once brilliant and tragic. Graunt's formal education was limited to common schooling, based at the time on the Scholastic curriculum of logic and rhetoric. His mathematics was confined to bookkeeping arithmetic, learned presumably when apprenticed at age 16 to his father's London haberdashery business. From these modest beginnings, Graunt rose to be a respected London figure, holding a number of senior offices in the city council and the merchant community, and gaining a reputation as a shrewd and fair arbitrator of trade disputes. Graunt's success coincided with the period of the English Commonwealth, the period of religious and civil conflict that divided the country following the execution of Charles I. Graunt was a junior officer in Cromwell's forces, and knowledgeable in the dissenting faith of Socinianism, which denied claims to divine authority made by monarchists and the church, in favor of more egalitarian ideals. Contemporaries record Graunt as an assiduous scholar, competent in Latin and French, and articulate and witty across a range of philosophical, artistic, and economic topics. His independent learning and reputation in the city brought Graunt into contact with Royal Society members (who likewise had combined interests in science and trade), notably William Petty, for whom Graunt was able to use influence to secure a professorship in the 1650s.

English society by the early 1660s, however, had arrived at an important point of transition. The restoration of the monarchy in 1660 put an end to the Commonwealth. Religious and political differences, over which many lives had been lost, remained critical in science as well as in government, but there could be much tolerance for privately held views. The method of the *Observations*, as will be discussed later, reflects the ambivalence of Graunt's position at this time. It is noteworthy that his membership in the Royal Society, almost unique for merchants at the time, was favored expressly by Charles II. The new king's support would have certainly helped to alleviate any questions concerning Graunt's past. Yet, in the early 1670s, Graunt's life took an abrupt turn. Converting publicly to Catholicism, he rejected religious moderation and science, and alienated himself from most friends and contemporaries. Suffering financial ruin, Graunt died shortly thereafter in poverty.

Avowed Aims of Graunt's Text

The reasons underlying the reversal of Graunt's fortunes will probably never be known for certain. The tensions experienced by an acute and original mind, however, in an era in which the need to accommodate science, politics, and religion was an overriding concern, are evident in his text. The *Observations* is prefaced by two dedicatory letters that, despite their adroit use of literary conventions, do not quite conceal the conflicting orientations of the work. The first, addressed to a Minister of the Crown, concerns the usefulness of Graunt's many specific findings for government, particularly as they relate to defense, trade, disease, and the person of the King. Graunt here adopted the customary terminology of the body politic, which recurs in his text. By this long-established convention, the King is likened to the head and soul of the state; the strength of the body politic depends on the relative size and balanced proportion of its members, or population. Graunt's conventions were well chosen. The idea that a well-balanced polity implies a justly governed one had wide currency at the time, cutting across all political persuasions from critics of monarchy to believers in the divine right of kings. Good government, by general agreement, was government in conformity with natural law and God's will.

What was new was that Graunt's arithmetic opened up for the first time the possibility of taking these traditional images seriously, and showing precisely what proportions actually exist. The text of the *Observations* demonstrates repeatedly and in considerable detail the presence of enduring natural balances (for example, in sex ratios, reproductive levels, and causes of death). Where his ratios might be interpreted to imply imbalance (e.g., in certain causes of death, or the excessive growth of London relative to the kingdom as a whole), Graunt carefully stressed the regularity of numerical series over the long term. Evidence of natural order and national strength thus appeared to give consistent support to existing sovereign rule. The sensitivity of the subject is nonetheless acknowledged in the concluding sentence of the *Observations*, in which Graunt leaves the King and his ministers to decide whether such evidence should be confined to themselves.

Graunt addressed his second dedication to the President of the Royal Society. Here he acknowledges the methodological inspiration of his work in Baconian natural history. Francis Bacon, whose work directly inspired the Society, emphasized the importance of direct observation, of numerical representation, and of open methods of exposition that allow any experienced observer to test other researchers' evidence. Like Bacon, Graunt did not always succeed in adhering to these precepts, but his step-by-step presentation of numerical evidence and analysis follows Bacon's respected methodology closely. Bacon wrote a natural history concerned with the vital forces that enable some people to live longer than others do, and Graunt's text, in proposing a natural arithmetic of life and death, followed logically from this. Graunt, moreover, encouraged readers to use his numerical evidence and methods to develop observations of their own. Knowledge of the population of a state is at base a scientific matter that his method opens to anyone prepared to follow it. This line of reasoning led Graunt to conclusions more consistent with his Socinianism than with his first dedication. The second dedication ends with a comparison of observation to political representation. Graunt likens the Royal Society to a "Parliament of Nature," saying that even though an observer like himself may be a mere commoner, he and his observations are entitled to be represented by the Society. The role of such a "parliament," by implication, is to serve as a forum in which proportional balances in the body politic may be discussed openly, so that scientific knowledge of natural forces can be brought to bear on whether governments actually pursue just policies that conform with nature.

The Method of the *Observations*

For more than a century before Graunt, the humanist writings that initiated the modern theory of the state had sought to define a legitimate basis for human government, a problem that well after Graunt continued to be concerned chiefly with defining proper relations between rulers and subjects. By Graunt's time, the need to control population distribution, size, and growth for political and economic purposes was generally recognized as a central difficulty in such relations, but the problem of means to reliable knowledge of population had not been broached. Graunt, writing in a context in which issues of legitimacy were unquestionably alive, broke new ground in European thought by restating the issue primarily in quantitative and scientific terms. More than this, Graunt's contribution was to see the specific problems that population raised as a question of method: such problems could be resolved at least in part by regular, replicable procedures applied from the level of the state down to particular subpopulations sharing specific vital, economic, or other characteristics.

Almost two centuries passed before national censuses and registration systems enabled Graunt's conception of a state, defined and evaluated by quantitative parameters, to become common practice, and before "statistics" became synonymous with quantitative data and its analysis. It is easy to forget that in the world in which Graunt wrote he needed to improvise terms if his new way of thinking was to be intelligible. In the absence of general terms of quantitative reference (e.g., wherein nouns such as "data," "population," and "statistics" would now be used), Graunt adopted customary bookkeeping phraseology ("accompts"), or stuck to popular usage ("inhabitants," "people," "city," "the whole pile"). Conventional formulas such as "the body politic" had to suffice for discussion of structural relationships in society. Standards of argument drawn from established rhetorical procedures enabled Graunt to develop his "observations," based on methods of natural history, as persuasive "positions," and to demonstrate, for example, why the sex ratio is the "true *ratio formalis* of the evil of adulteries and fornications." Unacquainted with the advanced mathematics that contemporary probabilists such as Pascal were developing, Graunt dealt with differing chances of death using the arithmetic that merchants employed to assess the "hazard," "odds," or "even lay" of risky business ventures.

Histories of statistics and demography have ignored, until recently, the imaginative process Graunt needed to create and present the first method of quantitative social inquiry. The focus instead has been on picking out those features that anticipate modern practice, and then assessing their limitations in light of current techniques. Three enduring accomplishments have been noted. Glass called attention to the "characteristically statistical" critical apparatus Graunt developed to evaluate and adjust 17th-century enumerations. For Sutherland, the *Observations* constituted "a methodology of descriptive statistical analysis" that included many later demographic measures and concepts. And Pearson, noting that Graunt's analysis "depends on the stability of statistical ratios," saw his method as grounded implicitly in mathematical statistics. Graunt's ability to reason along statistical lines almost two centuries before the emergence of demography and mathematical statistics testifies to the power of his vision. Yet the question of how he devised his method, and what it was, cannot be answered by projecting later developments back onto his work. How he arrived at his insights becomes understandable once they are considered in light of the three ideas of method, current in the 17th century, which shaped his text.

Baconian Natural History and Graunt's Critical Apparatus

The Bills of Mortality kept by London parish clerks provided Graunt with a substantial record of burials and baptisms from 1603 to 1660, distributed by locality and including causes of death from 1629. He supplemented this record with registers from a rural parish in Hampshire and added other sources in later editions. The difficult problems of how to present such bulky materials and to assess their reliability he solved by following Bacon's twofold account of natural observation. First, it must be confirmed that evidence is based on direct sense impression, that those doing the observing are reliable, and that the record of observation allows independent confirmation.

The first issues addressed in the *Observations*, therefore, are to assess the acuity of the "searchers" who reported vital events to the clerks, and to provide the reader with a comprehensive summary of the Bills using a tabular form such as Bacon had recommended. Second, observation presupposes classification, the grouping together of related phenomena. The observer's objective should be to isolate the simplest elements of which nature is composed, and this requires that he build up a body of experience so that regular patterns can be expressed as general rules or standards that convey concisely the implications of nature for society. Observation, in other words, entails judgment. Graunt's second concern was to assess the overlapping classifications and numerical irregularities in the Bills, and reduce them to a reliable order, regrouping them as necessary into a set of primary topics. Conscious of Bacon's insistence on open methods of exposition, Graunt informs the reader at each step of adjustments he has made to the figures and draws attention to their implications as balances in the body politic.

It is not difficult to see why this method so impressed Graunt's contemporaries. His first set of observations includes proportions contrasting the combined impact of several causes of infant and child death to the mortality of plagues. The marked difference was plain to see: over a 20-year period, infant and child mortality accounted for one-third of all deaths, several times greater than the most feared of epidemics. Turning to Bacon's interest in patterns of longevity, Graunt provided an elaborate but concise answer, showing the need to separate "acute" (i.e., epidemic) causes from "chronical" (i.e., endemic), and giving examples of how to calculate the odds of dying of particular diseases. The "absolute standard" of longevity is given by the proportion over age 70 to the total number of deaths in a given locality. Graunt provides the reader with direct and practical means of calculating which localities are most healthy and which causes of death are most dangerous in them.

The modernity that Sutherland and many others have noted in Graunt's descriptive methodology arises not only from the critical and empirical attitude he took to his numerical sources, but from the topics that Bacon's method led him to observe. These topics remained central when texts in medical statistics and demography began to appear in the 19th century. Following his discussion of endemic and epidemic causes of death, their relations, and causes relating to particular age groups, Graunt treats in turn the seasonality of births and deaths; natural increase (including rural and urban differentials); sex ratios; ratios showing the growth of London over time, and the differing contributions of localities within it; estimates of the population size of London and England; and the use of age structures to determine numbers of women of reproductive age and manpower.

Graunt's Concept of a Population

Graunt's application of arithmetic to natural history was not confined entirely to Bacon's precepts, because the latter gave no quantitative guidance beyond stating the need for careful enumeration and classification. Graunt's second dedication remarks the second methodological practice on which he relied, which he calls "the mathematics of my shop-arithmetic." The Bills, like a merchant's account books, provided a continuous record of additions and subtractions in a constantly changing numerical whole. Graunt, in effect, treated the idea that nature has an inherent quantitative order as analogous to the balance of debt and credit in merchant bookkeeping. His seeming prescience in assuming the "stability of statistical ratios" arises from this analogy. Graunt referred to each cause of death in the Bills as a separate "accompt"; the series of deaths from 1603 onward showed the changing debt or credit in this accompt as a proportion of one of the wider populations of burials or christenings he was analyzing. Abrupt changes in a given series led Graunt, as natural bookkeeper, to question his accompts, just as a merchant would, for instance, check whether a striking disproportion might be due to misclassification (e.g., confusion with entries in some other accompt), to some error of calculation, or to unusual events. In each case, the disproportion might be corrected by applying a proportion as a multiplier to the series; the irregularity was, in effect, smoothed. Merchants also applied multipliers where they lacked information, for example, to compare potential profits and losses in ongoing accompts; Graunt used this technique to estimate national population totals and to distribute the population into age groups. The *Observations* employs many of the standard devices of double-entry bookkeeping in use in the mid-17th century.

Graunt's accompts are not populations as demographers now understand them, and it is of note that Graunt nowhere uses the term. Vital rates in demographic analysis are computed with reference to a single base population, but Graunt, following contemporary accounting practice, used different denominators and applied proportions derived from one accompt as multipliers in the analysis of unrelated accompts when relevant information was lacking. Observation for Graunt, as for Bacon, cannot be separated from experience and judgment. The actual number of inhabitants, like a merchant's total worth, involved many debts and credits that were changing all the time; experience showed that such figures were mere abstractions, and much less important than assessing the state of profit or loss in a particular accompt. Graunt's assumption of the inhering proportional regularity in human accompts for the first time enabled merchants, king's ministers, and natural historians to estimate relative orders of magnitude, providing an informed basis for opinion.

Contemporary Rhetorical Method and the Calculus of Probability

The *Observations* addressed a recognized need for reliable knowledge of life and death, whether for the individual, in managing his own affairs, or the state, in which the distribution and size of population were considered a material factor in the success of policies of war and trade. As Graunt made clear, no matter how candid or experienced an observer might be, the observer's results depended on judgments and were subject to the judgments of others. Graunt's guarded attitude to whether the natural balances he calculated really demonstrate the legitimacy of kingly rule is a reminder of just how loaded apparently simple arithmetical measures can be. Not surprisingly, Graunt's work was taken up immediately by other thinkers who saw in quantitative methods a means of systematizing judgment. Probability, or the calculus of chance, emerged at this time in the attempt to construct a mathematics of degrees of belief. Huygens, DeWitt, Hudde, Leibnitz, and Bernoulli found in Graunt's observations the only materials other than hypothetical gaming problems in which this mathematics could be explored. Within a decade of the publication of the *Observations*, Graunt's proportional accompt of age structure was redeveloped by the first three of these analysts to make the first calculation of life expectation, which they applied to data on the mortality of Dutch annuitants.

The additions that Graunt made to later printings of his work show no awareness of these developments, and there is no indication in the records of the Royal Society that he contributed to advanced mathematical discussion. As noted, Graunt was able to conceive his "statistical" ideas on the basis of established bookkeeping practice, employing an arithmetic of risk familiar in the merchant community. His handling of longevity was confined to the questions Bacon had raised, and he never applied his accompt of age structure to calculating life chances. Mathematical probability was, in any case, known only to a tiny elite of specialist mathematicians. Graunt adopted instead the approach to matters of opinion that prevailed in his time, and in which he proved to be very skilled.

Schooling based on logic and rhetoric taught that matters of opinion are decided largely by systematic and artful presentation. Although Bacon argued that rhetorical methods had no place in natural history, neither he nor Graunt were able to keep them out. The *Observations* shows Graunt to be a master of rhetorical technique, using it to structure his numerical evidence, to organize the sequence of primary topics, and to argue impressively from them to the lessons of population arithmetic for managing the body politic. There is some irony, of course, that the first scientific social measurement should begin in the methodology of the Scholastic curriculum. This dependence was, however, characteristic of many important 17th-century scientific developments, and belongs to a wider Humanist rethinking of the role of rhetoric in science and government. Graunt's awareness of these developments is, moreover, no secondary matter in the lasting importance of his work. First, it enabled contemporaries, who were reared in the same intellectual traditions, to appreciate his work readily, despite its questionable subject matter and unprecedented numerical approach. Second, it enabled Graunt to present his method as visibly supportive of the existing political order, despite its pronounced republican undercurrent. Third, the positive and general reception of Graunt's work established a place for population arithmetic, even though the need for basic vital data as a basis of informed government was not accepted by most European states for another two centuries. That Graunt succeeded in persuading his audience of the potential of his method is shown by the diversity of his readership over that intervening period, which extended far beyond scientific circles to include the full range of religious persuasions (Catholic, Anglican, Dissenting, Atheist), royalists, and republicans, and a diverse professional audience of physicians, public officials, surveyors, estate managers, economists, and schoolteachers, as well as his fellow merchants.

Graunt's Influence

The sensitivity of population arithmetic as a matter of state remained a dominant factor into the later 18th century. Before the revolutions in France and America, only powerful monarchies such as those in Prussia, Sweden, and France dared to establish systems of data collection, but were careful to restrict public access to information. The *Observations*, however, opened the door to quantitative inquiries by individuals, and the intellectual and technical development of population arithmetic owes to their initiative. Four main developments followed from Graunt's work. Each entailed a significant narrowing of his vision, but together they laid the foundation for the generalization of population arithmetic in the statistical reforms of the 19th century.

First, Huygens' reinterpretation of Graunt's accompt of age structure initiated the first formal population model, the life table, subsequently developed by a distinguished line of mathematicians including Halley, De Moivre, Euler, and Price. By the early 19th century, this tradition had given rise to the first large-scale corporate structures based on mathematical models (life insurance), and was able to exercise a major influence on data requirements of the new national census and registration systems then being erected in Europe. Many simple proportional measures pioneered by Graunt were reintroduced at this time as key parameters of medical and social evaluation.

The numerical regularity of mortality, together with the consistency of sex ratios that Graunt also first demonstrated, became important in a second, "physico-theological" interpretation of population arithmetic, which attained wide influence in European thought through the writings of Süssmilch. Here the political conservatism of Graunt's first dedication prevailed entirely. The potential of population arithmetic to demonstrate deficiencies of government was ignored, and its use was confined to demonstrating the apparently seamless unity of divine, natural, and monarchical order—an approach that certainly helped to make social measurement acceptable in the *ancien régime*.

The ambiguities and deficiencies of population arithmetic became apparent with the rise of a third successor to Graunt's method, known as "political arithmetic." This phrase was introduced by Petty in the 1670s to refer jointly to Graunt's work and his own. Graunt's discredit at that time appears to have encouraged a few later authors, especially Petty's heirs, to attribute the *Observations* to Petty, but later scholarship has found no substance in these claims. The choice of "political arithmetic" as a rubric in itself indicates the major divide that separates Petty's thinking from Graunt's. With Petty, the practice of natural history, with its critical emphasis on the quality and open presentation of numerical evidence, ceased to be a primary concern. Nor was the careful use of arts of persuasion continued in order to secure support for quantitative approaches. Dispensing with the overall methodological framework Graunt had provided, Petty extended and popularized the use of multipliers in arguments that supported particular landed, royal, and merchant interests. The relative simplicity of multipliers, the frankness of party interests, and the lax attitude to numerical sources all made political arithmetic topical, as well as much easier to practice. A wide range of medical, religious, and economic writers responded, drawing on an *ad hoc* selection of Graunt's ratios and applying them to parish, hospital, and other records. Stimulating but inconclusive debates followed, and by the mid-18th century, a more critical attitude began to be reasserted, particularly in France. Much greater care was again taken by some writers to ensure the accuracy of figures. Declining population was linked to the condition of the poor and attributed to defects of monarchical rule.

Finally, the need for reliable numerical records was a theme often repeated by Graunt's successors, but the scrutiny and openness he advocated was pursued by few. Probabilists developing life tables for use in welfare and insurance, such as Price, and public officials who sought to show their governments that accurate censuses were realizable, such as Vauban and Michodiere, are cases in point. Graunt's most direct legacy in this respect was to Gregory King, whose scrutiny and analysis of population and tax records in the 1690s initiated the study of national income. The sensitivity of King's subject, however, delayed its publication until the 19th century.

In conclusion, the sources, method, and subsequent development of Graunt's observations show that social measurement owes its beginning to a specific conjunction of historical, cultural, and scientific circumstances. Population arithmetic was premised in an idea of inhering quantitative order that raised difficult questions about the legitimacy of differing forms of government and religious belief. Graunt's method was an attempt to clarify, and potentially to resolve, such difficulties via an original synthesis of three methodological traditions: observation, as practiced in natural history; the accounting model of merchant bookkeeping; and Scholastic and Humanist methods of rhetorical presentation.

See Also the Following Articles

Attrition, Mortality, and Exposure Time • Demography • Insurance Industry, Mortality Tables in • Population vs. Sample • World Health Organization Instruments for Quality of Life Measurement in Health Settings

Further Reading

Glass, D. V. (1963). John Graunt and his *Natural and Political Observations*. *Proc. Royal Soc., Ser. B* **159,** 2–37.

Graunt, J. (1662). *Natural and Political Observations upon the Bills of Mortality*. John Martyn, London.

Hacking, I. (1975). *The Emergence of Probability*. Cambridge University Press, Cambridge.

Kreager, P. (1988). New light on Graunt. *Pop. Stud.* **42,** 129–140.

Kreager, P. (1993). Histories of demography. *Pop. Stud.* **47,** 519–539.

Kreager, P. (2002). Death and method: The rhetorical space of 17th-century vital measurement. In *The Road to Medical Statistics* (E. Magnello and A. Hardy, eds.), pp. 1–35. Rodopi, Amsterdam.

Laslett, P. (ed.) (1973). *The Earliest Classics: Pioneers of Demography*. Gregg Int., Farnborough, Hants.

Pearson, K. (1978). . *The History of Statistics in the 17th and 18th Centuries* (E. S. Pearson, ed.). Charles Griffin and Co., London.

Rusnock, A. (1995). Quantification, precision and accuracy: Determinations of population in the Ancien Régime. In *The Values of Precision* (M. N. Wise, ed.), pp. 17–38. Princeton University Press, Princeton.

Sutherland, I. (1963). John Graunt: A tercentenary tribute. *J. Royal Statist. Soc., Ser. A* **126,** 537–556.

Guttman Scaling

George Engelhard, Jr.
Emory University, Atlanta, Georgia, USA

Glossary

coefficient of reproducibility Indicator of fit between data and requirements of a Guttman scale; defined as 1 minus the ratio of the number of errors predicted by a Guttman scale divided by the total number of responses; this coefficient ranges from zero to 1.

item characteristic curve Representation of the probabilistic relationship between a response to an item and person locations on a latent variable.

items Any set of stimuli intended to provide a structural framework for observing person responses; synonymous with tasks, exercises, questions.

latent variable The construct that is being measured or represented by the scale; also called an attribute.

perfect scale Another name for a Guttman scale.

persons The object of measurement; synonymous with subjects, participants, examinees, respondents, and individuals; groups or institutions can also be objects of measurement.

population of objects Target group of persons that a scale is designed to measure.

scalogram analysis Another name for Guttman scaling.

universe of attributes Target set of items that a scale is designed to represent; universe of content.

Guttman scaling (also called scalogram analysis) is a technique for examining whether or not a set of items administered to a group of persons is unidimensional. A data matrix (persons by items or persons by categories within items) meets the requirements of Guttman scaling when person scores reproduce the exact item responses in the data matrix. A set of items that meets this condition is defined as a Guttman scale.

Introduction

In the 1940s, Louis Guttman laid the groundwork for a new technique designed to explore the unidimensionality of a set of test items. Guttman considered the quest for unidimensionality to be one of the fundamental problems in scaling. Guttman scaling stresses the idea that the items or questions included in a scale should have the same meaning for all persons responding to the items. If the meaning of the items is invariant across persons, then persons can be ranked on the same dimension. Items that do not provide the same stimulus to different persons cannot be used as a basis for developing a unidimensional Guttman scale. Guttman proposed a set of requirements that can be used to test the hypothesis of unidimensionality. Guttman scaling, or scalogram analysis, is the specific technique that he recommended for determining whether or not a set of items and group of persons met the requirements of a Guttman scale.

Guttman scales are also called perfect scales. Guttman determined the requirements of these perfect scales based on an ideal model of a scale. Methodologically, this is related to the concept of ideal types proposed by the German sociologist Max Weber. This methodological approach involves comparisons between theory-based ideal types and observed cases in order to test specific hypotheses about events and to identify deviant cases. Guttman used this style of comparative analysis by first identifying the requirements of an ideal or perfect scale and contrasting these perfect scale patterns derived from theory with observed response patterns. Guttman focused not only on the item patterns that met the requirements of a perfect scale, but also stressed the importance of case studies of persons with deviant response patterns. Guttman suggested that imperfect item-response patterns may yield important new understandings of both items and persons. The study of deviants and apparently anomalous results can play an important role in scientific progress.

Defining a Guttman Scale

Guttman scales can be defined in several ways. These definitions apply to data matrices composed of either dichotomous or polytomous responses, but the presentation here will be limited to the dichotomous case (two response categories: right/wrong, correct/incorrect, agree/disagree, etc.). A data matrix (persons by items) meets the requirements of Guttman scaling when person scores reproduce the exact item responses in the data matrix. Guttman sought a method of scaling that would yield numerical values for each item and person that could be used to reproduce the observations or responses of each person on each item. Guttman's ideal scale meets these requirements and he proposed a variety of graphical and numerical methods for determining whether or not a scale deviates from the ideal scale patterns.

One popular graphical method is called a scalogram. When persons and items are ordered and displayed in a table, then the data matrix forms a distinctive triangular pattern for an ideal or a perfect scale. This pattern is shown in the left-hand panel of Table I. The person scores are listed in descending order (4 to 0) and the items are ordered from easy to hard (A is easy, D is hard). It should be noted that person scores assigned to each response pattern exactly identify the specific items that the person answered correctly or incorrectly. No information is lost by replacing item-response patterns with person scores. For example, a person with a score of 3 and a perfect response pattern is expected to respond correctly to the three easiest items (A, B, and C) and incorrectly to the hardest item (D). A four-item test composed of dichotomous items has 16 possible response patterns ($2^4 = 16$). There are 5 perfect response patterns and 11 imperfect patterns. The 11 imperfect patterns are shown in the right-hand panel of Table I.

Another way to illustrate a Guttman scale is to use item-response theory. A scale can be represented as a line with items ordered from easy to hard and persons ordered from low to high. This line reflects the attribute or latent variable that defines the construct being measured. Item characteristic curves can be used to show the relationship between the latent variable or attribute being measured and the probability of correctly answering an item. A Guttman scale is considered a deterministic model because Guttman items yield the distinctive pattern that is shown in Fig. 1. The x axis in Fig. 1 represents the attribute or latent variable with Items A to D ordered from easy to hard. The items are rank-ordered and there is no requirement that the x axis have equal intervals. The y axis represents the probability of responding with a correct

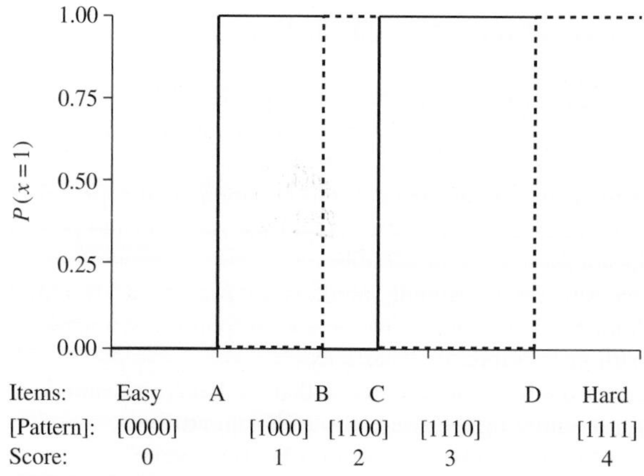

Figure 1 Illustrative item characteristic curves for Guttman items (deterministic model).

Table I Possible Response Patterns for Four Dichotomous Items

	Items (Perfect patterns)					*Items (Imperfect patterns)*			
Person scores	*A*	*B*	*C*	*D*	*Person scores*	*A*	*B*	*C*	*D*
4	1	1	1	1	4	None	None	None	None
3	1	1	1	0	3	1	1	0	1
2	1	1	0	0	3	1	0	1	1
1	1	0	0	0	3	0	1	1	1
0	0	0	0	0	2	1	0	1	0
					2	0	1	1	0
					2	1	0	0	1
					2	0	1	0	1
					2	0	0	1	1
					1	0	1	0	0
					1	0	0	1	0
					1	0	0	0	1
					0	None	None	None	None

Note: Four dichotomous items yield 16 ($2^4 = 2 \times 2 \times 2 \times 2$) response patterns. Items are ordered from easy (Item A) to hard (Item D). There are 5 perfect Guttman patterns and 11 imperfect Guttman patterns.

answer to each item. For example, a person located on the x axis between Items B and C is expected to answer Items A and B correctly (probability is 1.00) and Items C and D incorrectly (probability is 0.00); this yields a score of 2 and a perfect response pattern [1100]. These distinctive step functions also serve to define a Guttman scale. It will be shown later that the Rasch measurement model is a probabilistic form of a Guttman scale.

Algebraically, Guttman scales yield perfect conjoint transitivity based on the requirement that a person who endorses a more extreme statement or item should endorse all of the less extreme statements. This property is represented by the ordering of the items (typically by an estimate of item difficulty) that reflects the following relationships:

$$\text{If Item A} < \text{Item B} \quad \text{and} \quad \text{Item B} < \text{Item C},$$
$$\text{then} \quad \text{Item A} < \text{Item C}.$$

In a perfect Guttman scale, the property of transitive inequality is invariant over persons. If this requirement of perfect conjoint transitivity is met and the items define a common content, then this data matrix can be summarized as a Guttman scale.

Guttman recognized that obtaining perfect conjoint transitivity was necessary, but not sufficient for creating a useful scale. Two other concepts play a key role in Guttman's theoretical perspective on scaling. These concepts are the universe of attributes and population of objects. Guttman defined the universe of attributes as all of the possible items from a common content area that could be used to define the construct. The universe of attributes has also been called the universe of content. Guttman makes clear that items must have common content if they are to be used to define a unidimensional scale and that these items should be viewed as being sampled in some sense from a larger universe of potential items that could be used to define the construct or latent variable. Based on person responses to a sample of items, researchers can draw inferences about the universe of content. If the requirements of a Guttman scale are achieved, then invariant scaling of persons is possible regardless of the particular sample of items used to rank-order the persons.

The population of objects defines the objects of measurement. Guttman stressed the importance of defining and describing the population of persons that define the target group for the scale. In some ways, the concept of a population of objects corresponds to the standard statistical problems of sampling persons from a population with the object of measurement and person population defined differently depending on the purpose of the scale. In other ways, Guttman put his own unique twist on the issue by considering that the scalability of a set of items may not be invariant over different groups of persons. This becomes a very important issue because if the items are not invariant over groups, then it is not possible to compare them. This concern with item invariance across groups appears within modern measurement in the form of differential item functioning.

Evaluating a Guttman Scale

There is a variety of methods that have been proposed for determining whether or not the requirements of a Guttman scale have been achieved. The methods that are briefly described here are Guttman's reproducibility coefficient, Loevinger's coefficient of homogeneity, and Rasch's simple logistic model. These indices were chosen because of their didactic value and strong connections to current work in measurement theory.

The methods proposed for evaluating Guttman scales involve a comparison between observed and expected or perfect response patterns. The differences between methods depend on how errors are defined and summarized. Guttman recognized that perfect scales are not to be expected in practice and suggested that deviations from a perfect scale be measured by a coefficient of reproducibility. Guttman's coefficient of reproducibility was defined by summing the number of errors predicted by perfect response patterns, dividing by total number of responses, and subtracting this fraction from 1. Although Guttman proposed different acceptable values for his coefficient of reproducibility, 90% reproducibility or higher is generally considered necessary for an acceptable Guttman scale. This coefficient of reproducibility is defined as

$$Rep_{\mathrm{GG}} = \frac{1 - \text{total number of errors}}{\text{total number of responses}} = 1 - \left[\frac{E_{\mathrm{GG}}}{nk}\right],$$

where E represents an error count, n is the number of persons, and k is the number of items. This definition of reproducibility follows a similar definition by Goodenough and is called the Guttman-Goodenough coefficient of reproducibility.

Another coefficient of reproducibility was described by Suchman. Suchman derived a method that attempts to minimize the number of errors obtained when observed item-response patterns are assigned to score groups based on perfect Guttman patterns. This coefficient is called the Guttman-Suchman coefficient of reproducibility by Mokken. This coefficient of reproducibility is defined as

$$Rep_{\mathrm{GS}} = \frac{1 - \text{total number of errors}}{\text{total number of responses}} = 1 - \left[\frac{E_{\mathrm{GS}}}{nk}\right],$$

where E_{GS} is defined based on Suchman's definition of errors.

Another way to count errors in Guttman scales is to create a cross-tabulation of ordered item pairs. If items form a perfect scale, then there is a distinctive pattern in these tables. This distinctive pattern is based on the fact that with a perfect scale, no one who succeeds on a harder item fails on an easier item. This yields a zero cell that must always occur with the cross-tabulation of two dichotomous items that meet the requirements of a Guttman scale. Any persons in this cell constitute errors. Loevinger developed her coefficient of homogeneity independently of Guttman's work, but it has been used frequently to evaluate Guttman scales. Mokken has shown how Loevinger's coefficient of homogeneity (H coefficient) can be estimated using item pairs and counts of error cells. For a scale composed of k items, there are $k(k-1)/2$ unique cross-tabulations of item pairs. Loevinger's coefficient of homogeneity can be defined as

$$H_{\text{tot}} = 1 - \left(\frac{\sum F}{\sum E}\right),$$

where F is the count of the persons in the observed error cell (easier item wrong, harder item right) in the 2×2 cross-tabulation of item pairs, E is the expected number of persons in the error cell assuming statistical independence, and the summation is understood to be over the $k(k-1)/2$ ordered item pairs. As will be shown later in the empirical example, these values can also be summed for an individual item to create a scalability coefficient for each item. Loevinger's coefficient of homogeneity is of particular importance because it was incorporated and extended by Mokken and others into nonparametric item-response theory.

The Rasch model can also be used to compare observed and expected response patterns with error counts. Andrich has made a compelling case for viewing the Rasch model as a probabilistic realization of a Guttman scale. Rasch's simple logistic model (SLM) can be used to model the probability of dichotomous item responses as a logistic function of item difficulty and person location on the latent variable. The SLM can be written as

$$\Pr(x_{ni} = 1 \mid \theta_n, \delta_i) = \frac{\exp(\theta_n - \delta_i)}{[1 + \exp(\theta_n - \delta_i)]}$$

and

$$\Pr(x_{ni} = 0 \mid \theta_n, \delta_i) = \frac{1}{[1 + \exp(\theta_n - \delta_i)]},$$

where x_{ni} is the observed response from person n on item i (0 = wrong, 1 = right), θ_n is the location of person n on the latent variable, and δ_i is the difficulty of item i on the same scale. Once estimates of θ_n and δ_i are available, then the probability of each item response and item-response pattern can be calculated based on the SLM. Model–data fit can then be based on the comparison between the observed and expected response patterns that is conceptually equivalent to othe methods of evaluating a Guttman scale. If the Guttman's model is written within this framework, then Guttman items can be represented as follows:

$$\Pr(x_{ni} = 1 \mid \theta_n, \delta_i) = 1, \quad \text{if} \quad \theta_n \geq \delta_i$$

and

$$\Pr(x_{ni} = 0 \mid \theta_n, \delta_i) = 0, \quad \text{if} \quad \theta_n < \delta_i.$$

This reflects the deterministic nature of Guttman items that was illustrated in Fig. 1.

One of the challenges in evaluating a Guttman scale is that there are different ways to define errors. Mokken has pointed out that there may even be errors in the perfect response patterns. Probabilistic models provide a more flexible framework for comparing observed to expected item-response patterns and a less rigid perspective on errors. Guttman's requirement of perfect transitivity appears within the Rasch measurement model as perfect transitivity in the probabilities of ordered item responses.

Empirical Example

Table II presents data from Stouffer and Toby that are used to illustrate the indices for evaluating a Guttman scale presented in the previous section. Table I provides the response patterns for 261 persons responding to four items (A, B, C, and D) designed to measure whether or not persons tend toward universalistic values or particularistic values when confronted by four different situations of role conflict. Persons with higher scores provide more particularistic responses (reactions to role conflicts are based on friendship). It should be noted that earlier reanalyses coded positive (+) and negative (−) responses differently. Table I reflects the original Stouffer-Toby scoring with positive responses (+) coded 1 and negative responses (−) coded 0; the items are reordered from easy to hard to endorse (e.g., Stouffer-Toby Item 4 is Item A here) for Form A (Ego faces dilemma).

The four items in the Stouffer-Toby data have the following difficulties (Item A to Item D): 0.21, 0.49, 0.50, and 0.69. Item A is the hardest to endorse, whereas Item D is the easiest to endorse for these persons. Based on this difficulty in ordering, the expected patterns for a perfect scale are shown in column 2 of Table II. Column 3 presents the observed patterns and their assignment to a particular expected item pattern based on the sum of the items. For example, the observed pattern [1110] sums to person score 3 and it is assigned to the expected item pattern of [1110]; there were 38 persons with this observed pattern and there are no errors. In contrast, the

Table II Response Patterns for Empirical Example

		Guttman-Goodenough				*Guttman-Suchman*			
Person scores	*Expected item pattern*	*Item pattern (ABCD)*	*Frequency*	*Errors*	*Error frequency*	*Item pattern (ABCD)*	*Frequency*	*Errors*	*Error frequency*
4	1111	1111	20	0	0	1111	20	0	0
						1101	9	1	9
						1011	6	1	6
						0111	2	1	2
						0101	2	2	4
						0011	1	2	2
3	1110	1110	38	0	0	1110	38	0	0
		1101	9	2	18	0110	7	1	7
		1011	6	2	12				
		0111	2	2	4				
2	1100	1100	24	0	0	1100	24	0	0
		1010	25	2	50	0100	6	1	6
		0110	7	2	14				
		1001	4	2	8				
		0101	2	2	4				
		0011	1	4	4				
1	1000	1000	23	0	0	1000	23	0	0
		0100	6	2	12	1010	25	1	25
		0010	6	2	12	1001	4	1	4
		0001	1	2	2				
0	0000	0000	42	0	0	0000	42	0	0
						0010	6	1	6
						0001	1	1	1
		$k=4$	$n=216$	24	140	$k=4$	$n=216$	13	72

Note: Higher person scores indicate a more particularistic response, whereas lower person scores indicate a more universalistic response. Items are ordered from easy (Item A) to hard (Item D). Guttman-Goodenough reproducibility coefficient: $1-[140/(216\times 4)]=0.84$. Guttman-Suchman reproducibility coefficient: $1-[72/(216\times 4)]=0.92$.

observed pattern [1101] also sums to person score 3, but when the expected and observed response patterns are compared, there are two errors. The Guttman-Goodenough reproducibility coefficient for these data is 0.84: $1-[140/(216\times 4)]$. This value is lower than the value of 0.90 recommended by Guttman for an acceptable scale. The last four columns of Table II illustrate another approach for classifying observed item-response patterns to expected item patterns. Using the Guttman-Suchman approach for classifying observed to expected patterns, there are significantly fewer errors. The Guttman-Goodenough reproducibility coefficient is 0.92: $1-[72/(216\times 4)]$. Under the Guttman-Suchman error counting system, the number of errors has dropped from 140 to 72. This approach was used by Stouffer and Toby. This higher value indicates an acceptable Guttman scale. Unfortunately, the Guttman-Suchman approach seems to be somewhat arbitrary and destroys the simple relationship between the expected and observed item-response patterns based on ordered items and person scores. The Guttman-Suchman approach changes the goal of scaling from the comparison of observed and theory-based definitions of expected item patterns to the minimization of errors that is highly dependent on the vagaries of the particular sample of persons that responded to the scale.

Table III provides the cross-tabulation of Items A and B that form the basis for calculating Loevinger's homogeneity coefficient based on Mokken. Item A is easier than Item B and, thus, based on the requirements of Guttman scaling, there should not be any persons in the error cell. For the Stouffer-Toby data, there are 17 persons who failed Item A (easier item) and succeeded on Item B (harder item). Based on the assumption of statistical independence, the expected number of errors is 33.5: $(108\times 67)/216$. Table IV summarizes the results of the Loevinger's analyses based on Mokken scaling. The estimated H_{tot} for this set of items is 0.41 with individual item results ranging from 0.35 to 0.51. Mokken

Table III Cross-Tabulation of Items A and B (Observed and Expected counts), Stouffer-Toby Data

	Item B (harder)		
Item A (easier)	*0*	*1*	*Total*
0		*(Error cell)*	
Observed	50	17	67
Expected	33.5	33.5	67.0
1			
Observed	58	91	149
Expected	74.5	74.5	149.0
Total			
Observed	111	108	216
Expected	111.0	108.0	216.0

Note: Error cell includes persons who fail (0) the easier item (item A) and succeed on the harder item (item B).

Table IV Loevinger's Coefficient of Homogeneity for Stouffer-Toby Data

Item cross-tabulations	*Observed error cell*	*Expected error cell*	*H coefficient*
A × B	17	33.5	
A × C	16	32.6	
A × D	6	14	
B × C	38	52.5	
B × D	12	22.5	
C × D	16	23.1	
Total	105	178.2	0.41
Items			
A	39	80.1	0.51
B	67	108.5	0.38
C	70	108.2	0.35
D	34	59.6	0.43

Note: H coefficient for the total scale is $1 - [105/178.2] = 0.41$. H coefficients for items are based on the sum over pairwise tables that include the target item. For example, the H coefficient for Item is A is $1 - [39/80.1] = 0.51$.

recommends the following interpretive scheme for the H coefficient:

$$0.50 \leq H \quad : \text{ strong scale;}$$
$$0.40 \leq H < 0.50 : \text{ medium scale;}$$
$$0.30 \leq H < 0.40 : \text{ weak scale.}$$

Based on these guidelines, the Stouffer-Toby data would be considered a medium scale.

Table V presents the results of using Rasch's SLM to analyze the Stouffer-Toby data. The estimated Rasch item difficulties are −1.89, −0.20, −0.10, and 2.20 logits for Items A to D, respectively, and the estimated person locations on the latent variable are 1.52, −0.06, and −1.54 logits. Estimates of person locations under the Rasch model are not provided for perfect scores of 0 and 4, although estimates can be obtained for these scores if additional assumptions are made about the data. The item characteristic curves for these four items are shown in Fig. 2. It is important to note how close Items B and C are in terms of difficulty. Column 4 gives the probability of observing a perfect item-response pattern for each person score. For example, a person with a score of 3 ($\theta = 1.51$) has an expected response pattern in the probability metric of 0.97, 0.85, 0.84, and 0.34 for Items A to D, respectively. It is clear that persons with scores of 3 are expected to have more than a 50/50 chance of succeeding on Items A, B, and C, whereas they have less than a 50/50 chance of succeeding on Item D. This ordering reflects a probabilistic transitivity for these items that mirrors the deterministic transitivity of the perfect item pattern [1110] for a person with a score of 3. Column 5 gives the conditional probability within each person score group of obtaining the various item-response patterns. These values were obtained by estimating the likelihood of each pattern conditional on θ and standardizing these values so that the likelihoods sum to 1 within each score group. As pointed out by Andrich, the conditional probability of observing a Guttman pattern within a score group is more likely than the other patterns. For example, the probability of a person with a θ of 1.52 (score of 3) having an observed response pattern of [1110] is 0.830, whereas the probability of this person having an observed response pattern of [0111] is only 0.013. In order to follow the theme of error counting, Rasch measurement theory provides an index of person fit that quantifies the difference between the observed and expected response probabilities. The person fit statistics (standardized residuals) are reported in the last column of Table V. It is clear that the most unusual patterns have the highest standardized residuals, with values greater than 2.00 reported for patterns [0111], [0101], [0011], and [0001].

Conceptual Contributions to Measurement

Guttman made quite a few significant conceptual contributions regarding scaling and measurement theory. One index of his influence is reflected in the strong and opposing views generated by his work. Cliff viewed Guttman scales as one of the good ideas in all of measurement, whereas Nunnally cautioned that the intuitive attractiveness of Guttman scaling does not overcome its fundamental impracticality.

Table V Probabilities of Item-Response Patterns Based on the Rasch Model

Person scores	*Item patterns ABCD*	*Frequency*	*Expected response pattern*	*Conditional probability of response pattern*	*Person fit (standardized residual)*
4	1111	20		1.000	0.00
3 ($\theta_3 = 1.52$)	1110	38	0.97, 0.85, 0.84, 0.34	0.830	−0.78
	1101	9		0.082	0.44
	1011	6		0.075	0.50
	0111	2		0.013	2.03
2 ($\theta_2 = -0.06$)	1100	24	0.86, 0.54, 0.51, 0.09	0.461	−0.63
	1010	25		0.408	−0.55
	0110	7		0.078	0.93
	1001	4		0.039	1.51
	0101	2		0.007	2.22
	0011	1		0.007	2.24
1 ($\theta_1 = -1.54$)	1000	23	0.59, 0.21, 0.19, 0.02	0.734	−0.58
	0100	6		0.136	0.20
	0010	6		0.120	0.25
	0001	1		0.010	2.20
0	0000	42		1.000	0.00
	$k = 4$	$n = 216$			

Note: Rasch item difficulties are −1.89, −0.20, −0.10, and 2.20 logits for Items A to D respectively. Higher person scores indicate a more particularistic response, whereas lower person scores indicate a more universalistic response.

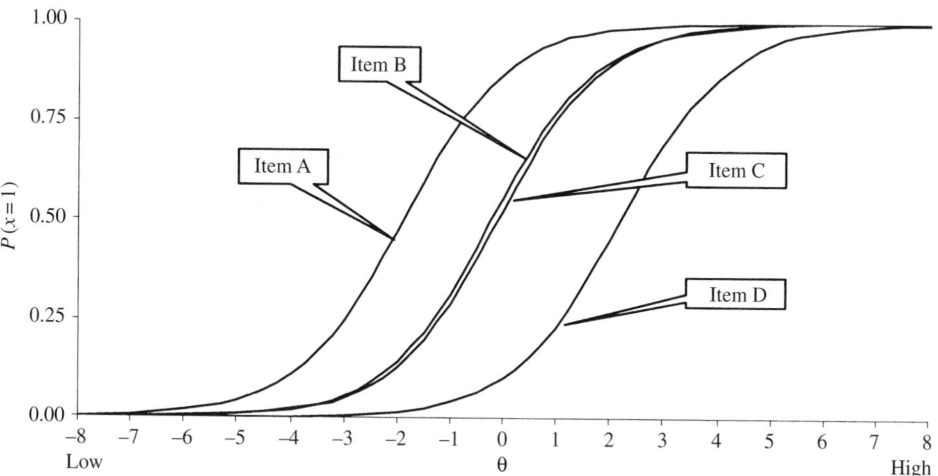

Figure 2 Item characteristic curves for Rasch model (probabilistic model) using Stouffer-Toby data.

Guttman scaling is important because it lays out in a very obvious way many of the issues and requirements that are necessary for the development of a scale. Guttman preferred to limit his approach to scaling to ranks and ordinal-level person measures that reflect a deterministic and nonparametric approach to scaling. Even though his requirements for a perfect scale are imbedded within a deterministic framework, Andrich has shown how a probabilistic model based on Rasch measurement theory can achieve these theory-based requirements. Andrich has pointed out the close connections between Guttman's deterministic model and Rasch's probabilistic model. Andrich stresses that these connections are not a coincidence and that both Guttman scaling and Rasch scaling embody the same essential requirements of invariance of item and person locations on the latent variable. In addition to the strong relationship between Guttman scaling and Rasch measurement theory, the origins of nonparametric item-response theory can be found in Guttman's early work. Mokken scaling has its origins in Guttman scaling.

In many introductory textbooks, a Guttman scale is simply defined for the dichotomous case and the other conceptual contributions of Guttman scaling are not discussed. The concepts of a perfect scale, universe of attributes, and population of objects have been very influential in areas as diverse as generalizability theory, item-response theory, and nonparametric item-response theory. In summary, Guttman made several fundamental contributions to measurement and scaling theory that are well worth revisiting. Even though much of the work on Guttman scaling was performed more than 50 years ago, a careful reading of Guttman's original texts still forms a sound introduction to most of the major scaling issues that researchers continue to face.

See Also the Following Articles

Guttman, Louis • Rasch, Georg • Scales and Indexes, Types of

Further Reading

Andrich, D. A. (1985). An elaboration of Guttman scaling with Rasch models for measurement. In *Sociological Methodology* (N. B. Tuma, ed.), pp. 33–80. Jossey-Bass, San Francisco, CA.

Cliff, N. (1983). Evaluating Guttman scales: Some old and new thoughts. In *Principles of Modern Psychological Measurement: A Festschrift for Frederic M. Lord* (H. Wainer and S. Messick, eds.), pp. 283–301. Erlbaum, Hillsdale, NJ.

Goodenough, W. H. (1944). A technique for scale analysis. *Educ. Psychol. Measure.* **4,** 179–190.

Guttman, L. (1944). A basis for scaling qualitative data. *Am. Sociol. Rev.* **9,** 139–150.

Guttman, L. (1950). The basis for scalogram analysis. In *Measurement and Prediction* (S. A. Stouffer, L. Guttman, E. A. Suchman, P. F. Lazarsfeld, S. A. Star, and J. A. Clausen, eds.), pp. 60–90. Princeton University Press, Princeton, NJ.

Loevinger, J. (1948). The technic of homogeneous test compared with some aspects of "scale analysis" and factor analysis. *Psychol. Bull.* **45,** 507–530.

Mokken, R. J. (1971). *A Theory and Procedure of Scale Analysis.* De Gruyter, The Hague, The Netherlands and Berlin, Germany.

Mokken, R. J. (1997). Nonparametric models for dichotomous responses. In *Handbook of Modern Item Response Theory* (W. J. van der Linden and R. K. Hambleton, eds.), pp. 351–367. Springer-Verlag, New York.

Nunnally, J. C. (1967). *Psychometric Theory.* McGraw-Hill, New York.

Rasch (1960/1980) *Probabilistic Models for Some Intelligence and Attainment Tests.* Danish Institute for Educational Research, Copenhagen, Denmark. [Expanded edition (1980) University of Chicago Press, Chicago, IL.]

Stouffer, S. A., Guttman, L., Suchman, E. A., Lazarsfeld, P. F., Star, S. A., and Clausen, J. A. (1950). *Measurement and Prediction.* Vol. IV. Princeton University Press, Princeton, NJ.

Stouffer, S. A., and Toby, J. (1951). Role conflict and personality. *Am. J. Sociol.* **56,** 395–406.

Suchman, E. A. (1950). The scalogram board technique. In *Measurement and Prediction* (S. A. Stouffer *et al.*, ed.), pp. 91–121. Princeton University Press, Princeton, NJ.

Wright, B. D. (1997). A history of social science measurement. *Educ. Measure. Issues Pract.* **52,** 33–45.

Wright, B. D., and Masters, G. (1982). *Rating Scale Analysis: Rasch Measurement.* MESA Press, Chicago, IL.

Guttman, Louis

Shlomit Levy

The Hebrew University of Jerusalem, Jerusalem, Israel

Glossary

categorical mapping A mapping having one set for its domain (population) and a Cartesian set for its range (items are the facets of the range).

facet One way of classifying variables according to some rule; a set that plays the role of a component set of a Cartesian set.

Guttman scale A perfect scale; a unidimensional scale.

mapping A rule by which elements from one set are assigned to elements from another set.

monotone regression A relationship in which the replies on variable $-x$ increase in a particular direction as the replies on variable $-y$ increase without assuming that the increase is exactly according to a straight line. The trend is always in one direction (upward or downward) with the possibility that variable y can occasionally stand still.

perfect scale A set of profiles in which there is a one-to-one correspondence between the profiles and the scale ranks; a Guttman scale.

stem facet A content facet that directly modifies the name of the range of a structioned mapping sentence, but does not modify any other facet.

structioned mapping sentence A mapping having two major varieties of facets for its domain (population and content) and one facet (or few) for the range.

structuple A profile.

Louis Guttman (1916–1987) contributed to the social sciences in a large variety of areas. His first developments on scaling theory were made while he was a student at the University of Minnesota. He later continued this work in two stages: as an expert consultant to the U.S. Secretary of War during World War II and, after his immigration to Israel in 1947, when he established the Israel Institute of Applied Social Research. His pioneering work on scaling theory is cited in 1971 in *Science*, one of 62 "major advances" in the social sciences from 1900 to 1965. In the 1960s, Guttman started another wave of new developments in intrinsic data analysis and facet theory. These topics constituted his major teaching and research activities at the Hebrew University in Jerusalem and at the Israel Institute of Applied Social Research. In particular, he developed new substantive theories concerning structural lawfulness for social attitudes, intelligence tests, and other aspects of human behavior.

Biographical Highlights

Louis Guttman was born in Brooklyn, New York, on February 10, 1916, to Russian immigrant parents. When he was 3 years old the family moved to Minneapolis where he completed his formal education. His father was a self-taught amateur mathematician who published several papers in the *American Mathematical Monthly*.

Although skilled in mathematics he decided to major in sociology. His studies also included courses in psychology equivalent to a major in the field. Upon realizing the importance of statistics to social research, he returned to his study of mathematics, of which he had a solid knowledge. This led him to formalize—while still a graduate student—techniques for data analysis, some of which were published in 1941 and constitute the foundations of his later work on scale theory, factor analysis, and other topics (his first publication was in 1938 in *Regression Analysis*). Guttman attained his B.A. (1936), M.A. (1939), and Ph.D. (1942) degrees in sociology from the University of Minnesota. Guttman's doctoral dissertation constituted original formulations to the algebra of matrices in general and to the algebra of factor analysis in particular.

For 1 year he studied at the University of Chicago (a predoctoral fellowship), which was at that time the only place in the United States where factor analysis was taught. His ties with Samuel Stouffer began at that time. His theorems concerning communalities that he developed while a graduate student are still part and parcel of the basics of factor analysis theory. The issues associated with factor analysis and reliability theory were addressed by Guttman in a series of articles that appeared between 1941 and 1961. Some 15 years later, in the mid-1970s, the factor indeterminacy problem led to controversial publications that Guttman called "the Watergate of Factor Analysis." His two then-unpublished papers concerning this issue can be found in Levy's 1994 compilation of his work.

In the 1970s, he also summarized his insights regarding statistics in a paper entitled "What Is Not What in Statistics" (1977). In this paper, he unmasks maltreatments of statistics and conceptualization in the social sciences by use of aphoristic and challenging headings such as "Partial Correlation Does Not Partial Anything," "Proportion (or Percentage) of Variance Is Never 'Explained'," and "Nominal, Interval and Ratio Scales Are Not Scales." With these, he not only exposed the naive lack of understanding of researchers, but indicated that most data analysis techniques, in particular statistical inference, do not provide answers to substantive problems and are irrelevant to replication, which is the "heart of cumulative science."

Of special importance are the monotonicity coefficients developed by Guttman. Of these, the weak monotonicity coefficient, denoted by μ_2 can be compared directly to Pearson's product-moment correlation coefficient. μ_2 expresses the extent to which replies on one variable increase in a particular direction as the replies to the other variable increase, without assuming that the increase is exactly according to a straight line (as in Fig. 1 below). It varies between -1 and $+1$. $\mu_2 = +1$ implies a perfect monotone trend in a positive direction; $\mu_2 = -1$ implies a perfect monotone trend in a negative or descending direction. By *weak* monotonicity is meant that ties in one variable may be untied in the order without penalty. Unlike Pearson's product-moment coefficient, μ_2 can equal $+1$ or -1, even though the marginal distributions of the two variables differ from one another. Therefore, it is especially appropriate in conditions, as in the social sciences, in which marginal distributions differ from item to item.

The formula for weak μ_2 is as follows:

$$\mu_2 = \frac{\sum_{h=1}^{n}\sum_{i=1}^{n}(x_h - x_i)(y_h - y_i)}{\sum_{h=1}^{n}\sum_{i=1}^{n}|x_h - x_i||y_h - y_i|}$$

When Pearson's coefficient equals $+1.00$, 0, or -1.00, the weak monotonicity coefficient μ_2 for the same data will have the same values. In all other cases, the absolute value of μ_2 will be higher than that of Pearson's coefficient, including the phi coefficient for dichotomies—in which case μ_2 equals Yule's Q. Most similarity coefficients are special cases of Guttman's coefficient of monotonicity.

As for the problem of the misuse of statistical inference, Guttman developed a new kind of efficacy coefficient for comparing arithmetical means, based on the monotone concept. The coefficient is called a discrimination coefficient (DISCO). It is distribution-free, avoiding both unrealistic assumptions about the normality of population distributions and equality of variances within the populations. DISCO equals 1 if there is no overlap between the distributions, no matter how large the within variance. It equals 0 if there are no differences among the means.

He regarded none of the methods that he developed as sociology or psychology. It may come as a surprise to the uninitiated that theory, not method, was Guttman's primary interest. In fact, he saw the two as inseparable, arguing in 1982 that "A theory that is not stated in terms of the data analysis to be used cannot be tested. . . . the form of data analysis is part of the hypothesis." Hence, his main interest lay in developing structural theories, which led to empirical lawfulness as evidenced in his definition of theory.

Guttman did not believe in mathematical psychology or mathematical sociology, and he rejected formalized axiomatic theories. The mathematics he used was not for the substantive theory but rather for technical features of data analysis. He stated that

> *Those who firmly believe that rigorous science must consist largely of mathematics and statistics have something to unlearn. Such a belief implies emasculating science of its basic substantive nature. Mathematics is contentless, and hence—by itself—not empirical science. . . . rather rigorous treatment of content or subject matter is needed before some mathematics can be thought of as a possibly useful (but limited) partner for empirical science.*
>
> (Guttman 1991, p. 42)

During Guttman's service as expert consultant to the Secretary of War with the Research Branch of the Education Division of the U.S. Army in World War II, he developed scale analysis (1944) and techniques that were used for attitude research in many aspects of army life. These developments were documented and published in 1950 in the volume edited by Stouffer and colleagues, *Measurement and Prediction* (Vol. 4 of the *American Soldier: Studies in Social Psychology*).

Guttman's academic base during that period (beginning in 1941) was Cornell University, where he was associate professor of Sociology. There he met Ruth Halpern, a student at the upper campus, whom he married in 1943. In 1947 he received a postdoctoral fellowship from the Social Science Research Council (SSRC) of the United States, and they left for Palestine. They lived in Jerusalem, where their three children were born. Years later, his connections with Cornell University were renewed, and he served as a professor-at-large from 1972 to 1978.

The social science know-how accumulated during World War II at the Research Branch was useful in setting up a similar unit for the Hagana (the Jewish underground army in Palestine) while the British Mandate was expiring (1948). His collaboration with Uriel Foa began in this framework. The underground research group of volunteers developed into the Psychological Research Unit of the Israel Defence Forces, headed by Guttman. This unit provided the basis for the Behavioral Science Unit of the Israel Defence Forces. The Public Opinion Section of the army's Psychological Research Unit developed into the Israel Institute of Applied Social Research in 1955, of which Guttman was the scientific director. The history of the Institute, its unique continuing survey, and its scientific activities can be found in Gratch (1973). In 1955, he became professor of Social and Psychological Assessment at the Hebrew University of Jerusalem. Louis Guttman passed away on October 25, 1987.

Guttman's work on factor analysis and other multivariate problems led him to nonmetric structural ideas such as the simplex, circumplex, and radex and to the idea of facets for definitional frameworks and structural theories. Guttman introduced the term circumplex in 1954 to indicate a particular kind of correlational pattern, having a circular arrangement. Since then, the circumplex model has been applied by many researchers to personal traits and interpersonal behaviors as an alternative to explanatory factor analysis.

The breakthrough for facet theory occurred in the mid-1960s when structural lawfulness in the area of intelligence tests was established, both with the advent of the electronic computer and with his collaboration with Lingoes, who was the first to program Guttman's nonmetric techniques. Only then did Guttman finally feel that he was "'doing' sociology and psychology," as a flourishing facet theory helped to establish substantive structural laws of human behavior in a variety of areas such as well-being, adjustive behavior, values, intelligence tests, and involvement. Thus, he pioneered the road to a cumulative social science.

Even a brief inspection of his proposed tentative outline for his planned book on facet theory reflects the great variety of issues with which he was involved. A selection of a wide variety of Guttman's works, including the first two chapters from his unfinished book on facet theory, together with a full comprehensive and detailed bibliography (approximately 250 publications), is to be found in Levy's 1994 compilation.

Scientific Societies

Guttman participated in a diversity of professional organizations. He was a member of the Israel Academy of Sciences and was appointed chairman of the Israel Psychological Association, the Israel Association for Research and Labor Relations, the Israel Sociological Association, and the Israel Statistical Association. He was the first nonresident president of the Psychometric Society (of the United States), and was elected a foreign member of the American Academy of Arts and Sciences.

Awards

Awards and honors bestowed on Guttman during his career include fellow at the Center for Advanced Study in the Behavioral Sciences (1955–1956), the Rothschild Prize for Social Science (1963), Outstanding Achievement Award from the University of Minnesota (1974), the Israel Prize in the Social Sciences (1978), the Educational Testing Service Award for Distinguished Service to Measurement (1984), and the Helen Dinermann Award from the World Association of Public Opinion Research (1988, posthumously).

Scale Theory

Introduction

The overall concept that underlies Guttman's work is structural theory, with the universe of content to be studied as the starting point. Very early, he realized that focusing on concepts and classifying content must precede data analysis; that is, content alone defines the universe and not data analysis. It is the empirical structure of the universe of content that is at issue.

For qualitative data, the first complete example of structural theory was that of a perfect scale of a class of attitudes (or attributes), developed in the U.S. Army during World War II.

The Definition of a Scale

Guttman defined a scale in 1944:

> *For a given population of objects, the multivariable frequency distribution of a universe of attributes (attitudes) will be called a "scale," if it is possible to derive from the distribution a quantitative variable with which to characterize the objects such that each attribute is a simple function of that quantitative variable. Such a quantitative variable is called a scale variable.*

A variable y with m distinct ordered values is said to be a simple function of a variable x, with n distinct ordered values, if for each value of x there is one and only one value of y. The converse need not hold; for the same value of y, there may be two or more values of x. This relationship is illustrated in the regression curve in

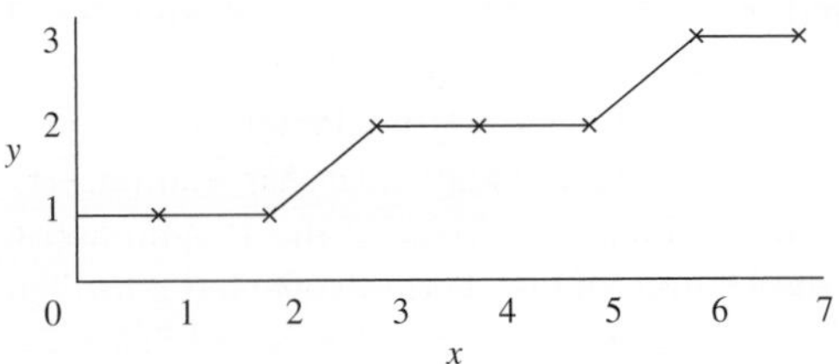

Figure 1 A simple function of variable y on variable x: the monotone trend.

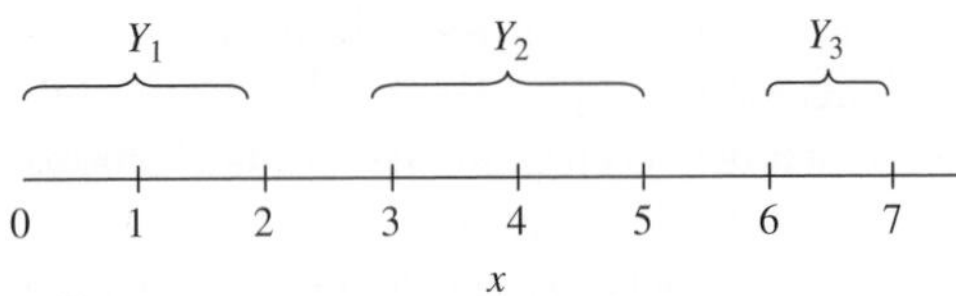

Figure 2 A graphical presentation of a perfect scale.

Fig. 1. Obviously, if y is to be a single-valued function of x, then its distinct values cannot be higher than the distinct values of x $(m \leq n)$. The regression in Fig. 1 is of a monotone trend. Indeed, monotonicity is the underlying feature in all of Guttman's intrinsic multidimensional methods—similarity structure analysis, SSA; multidimensional structuple analysis, MSA; and partial-order structuple (scalogram) analysis with base coordinates, POSAC—that serve as partners to the definitional framework (by facets) of the universe of content.

The simple function of y on x can also be presented graphically as a perfect scale by plotting the x values on a straight line and cutting it into numerical intervals (scale scores), according to which the objects are ordered (Fig. 2). Figure 2 is a perfect scale because it has the property of perfect interval consistency, the intervals along the straight line being the one-dimensional regions of the scale. Because there is a one-to-one correspondence between the profiles over the observed two-item categories and the scale ranks, predictability from the ranks is exactly the same as from the profile.

Thus, the basic concepts that underlie Guttman's later developments in intrinsic data analysis and facet theory—universe or content, monotonicity, and regionality—can be traced to his early scale theory.

Departure from a Perfect Scale: Image Analysis

Perfect scales are very rare. According to Guttman "perfect scales are not to be expected in practice." The first measure he developed (in 1944) for deviation from perfection was the coefficient of reproducibility. Later (in 1953), he developed a general theory of deviations, namely, image theory. Image theory provides general techniques for discovering the common structure in the observed data by first defining and eliminating the deviations. This is done by predicting, in turn, each item in the given observed set from all the rest of the items. The predicted values are called images. Because image techniques allow us to deal systematically with deviations, the concept of reproducibility is no longer of central importance in measuring deviations from a perfect scale. Image analysis for the departure from unidimensionality is used, *inter alia*, for job evaluation, defined by Guttman in terms of the level of restriction in performing a job. This issue has been found repeatedly to be essentially unidimensional. In later years, the perfect scale constituted a special case of MSA and POSA.

Principal Components of Scalable Attitudes

In 1954, scale theory expanded in the direction of developing substantive psychological and sociological theories for principal components of scalable attitudes. The first principal component is a monotone function of the scale ranks. The second, third, and fourth components are expected to have certain polytone regressions on the ranking of the population on the attitude: The second (intensity) is a U-shaped function, the third component (closure) is an N-shaped function with two bending points, and the fourth component (involvement) is an M- or W-shaped function with three bending points. Guttman hypothesized that certain types of personal norms for involvement may often serve as direction finders for predicting when to expect a W- or an M-shaped function.

The principal components have proven indispensable for properly interpreting survey results and for making predictions, especially by marking the proper zero point of the scale. They also illuminate the problem of attitude change.

Facet Theory: Structural Lawfulness—Spaces of Variables

Introduction

The problem that pertains to scale analysis (as well as to any structural analysis) is that of defining the universe of content. The facet theory approach was developed by Guttman to answer this problem. Scale theory, its insights already achieved in the 1940s, constitutes the basis of facet theory, which was introduced and elaborated by Guttman later on. As Guttman put it in 1960, "Facet Theory is proving to be a vast topic in which scale analysis occupies but one small—though important—corner."

Definition of Theory

The point of departure of facet theory is Guttman's definition of the concept of theory itself: "A theory is an hypothesis of a correspondence between a definitional system for a universe of observations and an aspect of the empirical structure of those observations, together with a rationale for such an hypothesis." This definition implies that we as researchers have to worry about two distinct things: (1) the design of the observations and (2) the empirical structure of those observations. The theoretical leap requires thinking about these two things in partnership. The mapping sentence device is intended to promote this partnership. The concept of rationale is added because it enables us to proceed cumulatively on the basis of already established hypotheses.

Guttman proposed four theoretical constructs for theory development: (1) definition, (2) specification, (3) rationale, and (4) hypothesis. These constructs constitute a basic facet in his 1972 "Mapping Sentence for Strategies of Theory Development."

The Concept of a Mapping Sentence

The mapping sentence generalizes R. A. Fisher's design of experiments to the design of any observations. It coordinates formal concepts (facets) and informal verbal connectives. Each facet is one way of classifying variables according to some rule, and the elements of the facet conform to the rule. Guttman's more formal (1972) definition of facet is "a set playing the role of a component set of a Cartesian set." A properly defined set of m facets, namely the mapping sentence, "provides an m-way simultaneous classification of variables."

A mapping sentence includes three varieties of facets. The first, usually symbolized by X, designates the population of respondents being researched. The second variety of facets classifies the content of the variables. These two varieties of facets together define the domain of the mapping sentence. The third kind of facet is the range, namely the set of response categories specified for the universe of items under study.

The mapping can be expressed abstractly in the following nonverbal form:

$$\underbrace{\underbrace{X}_{\text{Population}}\quad\underbrace{ABC\ldots N}_{\text{Content facets}}}_{\text{Domain}} \longrightarrow \underset{\text{Range}}{R}$$

The left member, or domain of the mapping is the Cartesian set $XABC\ldots N$, giving all possible combinations of the form $xab\ldots n$, that is, of each member of the population x with each of the content facets of the Cartesian set $ABC\ldots N$. The arrow indicates the mapping of the domain onto the set R of possible responses; namely, facet R (the range facet) is the image of the domain. An actual observation is made by choosing one and only one element from the range facet for each sentence generated by the domain facets. Hence, each respondent (x) has one and only one response in R for each question (or test, or any other stimulus) classified by the elements of the content facets $ABC\ldots N$. This classification of elements is known as structuple, the components of which make up a structuple that is known as struct.

The Structioned Mapping Sentence: A Definitional Framework for Variables

In order to give an abstract mapping empirical meaning, Guttman proposed to add verbal connectives and further literary additions to make the mapping readable in ordinary language. Such a substantive elaboration of the mapping is called a mapping sentence. For example, here is a mapping sentence for the Revised Wechsler Intelligence Tests for Children (WISC-R):

$$\textit{The } \textbf{correctness} \textit{ of the response of testee } (x) \textit{ to rule } \textbf{task} \overset{\textbf{A}}{\left\{\begin{matrix} \textit{1. inference} \\ \textit{2. application} \\ \textit{3. learning} \end{matrix}\right\}}$$

$$\textit{through} \overset{\textbf{\textit{B}}}{\left\{\begin{matrix} \textit{1. oral} \\ \textit{2. manual manipulation} \\ \textit{3. paper and pencil} \end{matrix}\right\}} \textbf{\textit{expression}} \textit{ on an item presented}$$

$$\textit{orally by the tester in} \overset{\textbf{\textit{C}}}{\left\{\begin{matrix} \textit{1. verbal} \\ \textit{2. numerical} \\ \textit{3. geometrical} \end{matrix}\right\}} \textbf{\textit{format}} \rightarrow \overset{\textbf{\textit{R}}}{\left\{\begin{matrix} \textit{high} \\ \textit{to} \\ \textit{low} \end{matrix}\right\}} \textbf{\textit{Correctness.}}$$

(Guttman and Levy 1991).

This mapping sentence defines the varied substance of the WISC-R in terms of three distinct content facets. The sentence is very clear with respect to the rule of each facet, with the elements of each facet being mutually exclusive. Each facet appears in the mapping sentence as a set of elements listed in bracketed columnar form. The name (rule) of each facet appears (in boldface) right before or after its list of elements, depending on the verbal structure of the sentence. Verbal connectives are added to make the mapping sentence readable in ordinary language. The common range for intelligence-test items is expressed in the mapping sentence by the level of correctness of the responses (facet R) after the arrow. Note that the meaning of the range is also indicated in the domain—the left member of the mapping. (The content facets are detailed and discussed later, in the context of regional hypotheses.) Such a mapping sentence is termed a structioned mapping sentence. A structioned mapping sentence should make sense in ordinary speech, regardless of the number of the facets involved. Otherwise there may be conceptual flaws in the proposed facets. ("Making sense" is no guarantee of theoretical or practical fruitfulness; it is only a necessary condition, not a sufficient one.)

It should be noted that even the facets of a given design are generally only a sample from a much larger set of possible facets. Hence, "developing a fruitful facet design for content is an evolutionary process—in a sense never-ending as is all science."

Sampling of Items

The number of ordinary sentences derivable from the mapping sentence presented in the previous section is 27 $(3 \times 3 \times 3 = 27)$. These serve as guides for actual item construction, specifying both the similarities and differences among the designed items. Each test is defined by the mapping sentence in a manner independent of its specific formulation. Consider, for example, the faceted definition $a_2b_1c_1$: The task imposed on the testee is application (a_2) of a rule expressed orally (b_1) in a verbal format (c_1). A possible test item constructed according to this structuple is: "Who is the president of the United States?" Similarly, a possible test item constructed according to the structuple $a_3b_1c_2$ can read as follows: "I will now cite loudly some numbers. Listen carefully, and immediately after I finish, repeat the numbers." Namely, the task imposed on the testee is learning (a_3) expressed orally (b_1) in a numerical (c_2) format. Many other items can be constructed for each of these two structuples. The same holds for all the structuples derivable from the faceted definition. The Wechsler Manual specifies only 12 subtests, and yet these allow for structural lawfulness because each element of each facet is represented in at least one of the subtests.

The number of derivable sentences from a structioned mapping may be very large, depending on the number of facets and the number of elements within each facet. Although generally "there is no probability distribution for a facet design of content," in each case a small sample of items that will nevertheless suffice to yield the essential information about the facets can be systematically constructed. The actual item construction has to conform to the research topic, which may result in placing different emphases on certain facets and, within facets, on certain elements. A structioned mapping sentence can also be used as a culling rule for a universe of content that already exists, telling us how to choose items from among existing ones.

Are Scientific Definitions "Correct"?

Scientific definitions can never be "correct" (or "incorrect"); rather, they can be reliable or clear (or unreliable). Hypotheses are classified as correct or incorrect. Scientific definitions are not fruitful by themselves, but only in partnership with other concepts. The issue is whether they fit into some partnership that leads to some form of empirical lawfulness. The definitional framework provided by the structioned mapping sentence helps ensure clarity and reliability, and it also facilitates the formulation of empirical lawfulness. Furthermore, it helps ensure continuities in research: "through knowing what facets are common to different studies, one can begin to learn about lawfulness in several studies."

Strategies of Modification

Formal definitions are necessary for scientific progress. Though striving for formality by its formal facets, the structioned mapping sentence enables the use of fruitful strategies for systematic theory development because it lends itself easily to correction, deletion, submission, extension (adding elements to a facet), and intension (adding content facets), based on cumulative research.

The Common Range: Laws of Positive Monotonicity (First Laws)

A central feature of the design of observations is the range facet. In the previous mapping sentence, all the Wechsler intelligence subtests are assigned a common range of extent of "correctness," namely a right-to-wrong range with respect to an objective rule.

There are two conditions for a universe of items to have a common range: (1) The range of each item in the universe must be ordered, and (2) the ranges must have a uniform meaning of their orders, regardless of their actual phrasing. The problem of meaning is semantic (substantive) and is related to the general framework of the research, whereas phrasing is a technical problem.

The observation that the right-to-wrong range is most common to almost all traditional mental testing (the Wechsler tests among them) led Guttman to propose in 1973 the following faceted definition of the universe of intelligence items, specifying both range and domain for the items:

"An item belongs to the universe of intelligence items if and only if its

$$\text{domain asks about a} \left\{ \begin{array}{l} \text{logical} \\ \text{scientific (factual)} \\ \text{semantic} \end{array} \right\} \text{objective rule, and its range}$$

$$\text{is ordered from} \left\{ \begin{array}{c} \text{very right} \\ \text{to} \\ \text{very wrong} \end{array} \right\} \text{with respect to that rule."}$$

(Guttman in Gratch 1973; Guttman and Levy 1991).

This definition encompasses all approaches to intelligence, known in this field. It was published simultaneously with the First Law of intelligence testing. (A short time before his death, Guttman suggested the term "The Law of Positive Monotonicity" to replace the term "First Law.") The law reads, "If any two items are selected from the universe of intelligence test items, and if the population observed is not selected artificially, then the population regressions between these two items will be monotone and with positive or zero sign."

The regression curve is obtained by plotting the range of one variable against the range of the other. Thus, the definitional communality of range provides part of the rationale for the positiveness of regression slope. The law has been known implicitly since mental testing began some 100 years ago. For ordinary populations (child or adult), only positive correlations have been observed between mental test items. Now, there is a rationale for the phenomenon of positive correlations, namely the common range. However, this phenomenon cannot be termed a law without the formal definition just cited. This law, like any scientific law, states the conditions under which positive or zero correlations (based on monotone regressions) are to be expected. In the case of intelligence items, two conditions are stated: (1) The items must be intelligence items according to the definition and (2) the population is not specially selected with respect to the test items.

Many replications supporting the Positive Monotonicity Law of Intelligence Tests can be found in the literature. Similarly, Guttman's mapping definition of attitude facilitated the formation of the Positive Monotonicity Law of Attitude. These were published together with the First Law of Intelligence in 1973. According to Guttman (in 1982):

> *I would not have thought that the First Law of Attitude was a law had I not been aware of the phenomenon of intelligence, well established in research .... Actually, I thought about the two laws simultaneously. It is doubtful that I would have had the courage to state either law separately .... The sheer idea of seeing similarity in two different areas of human behavior of this sort lent support to the idea that laws are possible, and the similar rationale of the laws gave further support – and courage.*

Guttman's mapping definition of the universe of attitude items followed by the First Law of Attitude (Positive Monotonicity Law) is as follows:

"An item belongs to the universe of attitude items if and only if its

domain asks about behavior in a $\left\{\begin{array}{l}\textit{cognitive}\\ \textit{affective}\\ \textit{instrumental}\end{array}\right\}$ *modality toward an*

object, and its range is ordered from $\left\{\begin{array}{c}\textit{very positive}\\ \textit{to}\\ \textit{very negative}\end{array}\right\}$ *towards that object"*

(Guttman, in Gratch 1973, 1982; Levy 1985).

The Positive Monotonicity Law of Attitude stating the conditions under which positive or zero correlations are to be expected among attitudinal items reads as follows: "If any two items are selected from the universe of attitude items towards a given object, and if the population observed is not selected artificially, then the population regressions between these two items will be monotone and with positive or zero sign."

Like intelligence and attitude, most of the concepts of social science are multivariate, and the technique of a mapping definition is helpful in defining them. Indeed, further concepts were defined through mapping sentences, some of them being special cases of attitudes. Examples are:

Attitudinal: well-being, worry, coping (stress reaction), value, protest.
Nonattitudinal: modernization, involvement, social problem indicators.

The First Law of Attitude has been reconfirmed cross-culturally in a large array of research areas. A First Law, like the other laws to be discussed, refers to the overall trend within the population as a whole, but not to individuals. Any correlation that is not precisely equal to $+1$ implies that there are individuals who are "contradictory" in their behavior.

Positive monotonicity laws are concerned with the shape (monotone) and fixed sign of the regression and are derived from a consideration of the range (or ranges) of the mapping definition. These laws make redundant most of the work merely aimed at establishing the existence of positive correlations among various classes of behavior. Progress has been made in developing hypotheses about lawfulness concerning the sizes (i.e., relative sizes) of the correlations, using further facets to define the items under study (such as the mapping sentence for defining the WISC-R).

Roles of Facets in Establishing Structural Lawfulness

The General Hypothesis of Facet Theory

The general hypothesis of facet theory is that the specification of formal roles for the facets in a mapping sentence provides a rationale for structural theories concerning a correspondence between the definitional framework (the mapping sentence) and an aspect of the empirical data, thereby facilitating the formation of scientific lawfulness in a cumulative fashion.

Theories in social science concern qualitative observations for the most part. In the quest for lawful relations between the content design and the observed data, Guttman's problem was how to present the data "in some numerical form without losing the qualitative features of the data." This led Guttman to develop his intrinsic data analysis methods, especially similarity structure analysis (SSA; previously called smallest space analysis). In this technique, as well as in the other techniques developed by Guttman, the data are treated intrinsically in terms of inequalities, needing no explicit prespecified model.

Similarity Structure Analysis

SSA is a technique for viewing a similarity (correlation) coefficient matrix. It is an intrinsic data analysis technique with an emphasis on looking at regions in the space of variables rather than on coordinate systems.

The Symmetric Case The symmetric case (SSA-I) is the first of the Guttman-Lingoes series designed for analyzing symmetric matrices. SSA treats each variable as a point in a Euclidean space in such a way that the higher the correlation between two variables, the closer they are in the space. The space used is of the smallest dimensionality that allows such an inverse relationship between all the pairs of observed correlations and the geometric distances. Reference axes are *not* in the general definition of SSA. (The empirical data to be analyzed are not limited to coefficients of similarity. They can also be dissimilarity coefficients, such as geographical distances. In such a case the monotonicity condition becomes as follows: the smaller the dissimilarity coefficients between two variables, the closer their points are in the space.) Only the relative sizes of coefficients and the relative distances are of concern. The goodness of fit between the observed coefficients and the geometrical distances is assessed by the coefficient of alienation, which varies between 0 and 1, where 0 designates a perfect fit. The goodness of fit is also expressed graphically by plotting the input coefficients versus the computed distances. This scattergram is called shepard diagram, and it actually portrays the metric nature of the implied monotone function. The less the spread around the negative monotone regression, the better the fit. To put it in another way, the shepard diagram is a graphical representation of the coefficient of alienation. Any such coefficient is blind to content considerations and, hence, alone is inadequate for cumulative science. There is always a need for a partnership with some content theory in determining the shape of the space. Lawfulness regarding sizes of correlations has been established largely in terms of regions of content of the SSA space.

The Asymmetric Case The Guttman-Lingoes SSA series also treats asymmetric matrices (SSA-II). In this program, each item is presented as a point in a Euclidean space, in such a manner that, for any three variables, the two most dissimilar will be farthest apart. Namely, distances are produced within rows or within columns, but not between rows and columns.

Asymmetric Matrix as a Submatrix of a Symmetric Matrix: Weighted Similarity Structure Analysis Producing distances only within rows or within columns, as is done in SSA-II, raises both theoretical and algorithmic questions. To solve these questions Guttman introduced in the mid-1980s the WSSA technique for symmetric matrices, with the inclusion of missing submatrices. WSSA, like SSA-I, requires symmetric matrices, but, unlike SSA-I, it enables us to treat missing data by assigning them zero weight. By doing this, the asymmetric matrix can be regarded as a submatrix of a larger symmetric matrix. Thus it is possible to treat the original asymmetric matrix via the WSSA technique, having the distances produced simultaneously for rows and columns in the same space.

Among other uses, this has facilitated the development of a new theoretical approach to sociometric issues involving square-asymmetric matrices. The same holds for rectangular matrices. Guttman considered this to be the only SSA program with no mathematical problems.

The Concept of Regionality

The regional laws with which the SSA acts as a partner support the general hypothesis of facet theory. Regional hypotheses relate to the roles that the content facets of the variables play in partitioning the SSA space. Three major roles emanate from considerations of order among elements in the facets: the polar, modular, and axial:

> Polar Role: *Unordered facet (or alternatively, a facet whose elements have a circular order). Each element of the facet corresponds to a different direction in the SSA space, emanating from a common origin.*
> Modular Role: *Simply (or partly) ordered facet, with an "absolute" origin, this origin being common to that of a polar facet.*
> Axial Role: *Simply ordered facet, where the notion of order is* unrelated *to that of other facets.*
> (Guttman 1977, in Levy 1994, Ch. 10)

Each content facet corresponds to a certain partitioning of the SSA space into as many regions as there are elements to the facet. Having several content facets, each with its own role, leads to intersecting partitions that generate various geometrical structures such as radex, cylindrex, duplex, and multiplex.

The regionality concept is coordinate-free; regions are to be defined by content considerations. Regions are indicated by—and usually share—boundary points; they are usually not clusters that are discernible by empty space around them. Regional hypotheses are for a space that in principle has points everywhere. This means that some variables in one region may correlate less with other variables of the same region than they do with variables from other regions. Such variables are substantively dissimilar, yet statistically closer to one another than to similar variables (from the same region). This is a relatively new principle initiated by facet theory, and it enables the detection of lawfulness in data that has hitherto been unobserved or misinterpreted. Attaining more and more refined regions leads to more and more refined restrictions on sizes of correlations.

Stem versus Modifying Content Facets

A rational for partitioning correspondences can come not only from considerations of order among elements in the facets, but also from the roles that the content facets play within the framework of the mapping sentence.

A differentiation is made between two varieties of content facets: stem and modifying facets. (The term "stem" was suggested by Guttman a short time before his death; earlier this facet was known by different names.) A stem facet directly modifies the name of the range, but does not modify the other facets. An inspection of the mapping sentence for defining the WISC-R, presented previously, suggests that the task imposed on the testee (facet *A*) is a stem facet. The range of the mapping sentence refers back directly to facet *A* because what is being assessed from "correct" to "incorrect" is the task ("inference," "application," or "learning" a rule) imposed on the testee.

According to Guttman, "stem facets should partition the space orthogonally to each other. A modifying facet sub-partitions into stem facets." Guttman's hypothesis was actually confirmed in the 1970s for the area of well-being and was reconfirmed and extended in 1990.

The conceptual independence between the stem and the modifying facets may provide a rationale for their orthogonality. Furthermore, because a stem facet modifies only the range of the mapping sentence, it is by definition an ordered facet; this is because the range (or ranges) of a structioned mapping is ordered (according to a common meaning) and hence may play an axial or modular role in partitioning the space.

Number of Facets and Dimensionality of Similarity Structure Analysis

The hypothesized dimensionality of the SSA space is not necessarily connected to the number of content facets in the structioned mapping sentence. In general, the dimensionality of SSA can be equal to, greater than, or less than the number of content facets.

Regional Lawfulness in Practice: The Cylindrical Structure for Intelligence Tests

The following is an illustration of the regional theory for the WISC-R, which are defined by the mapping sentence presented previously. This mapping sentence includes three distinct content facets. Facet *A* distinguishes among the tasks imposed on the testee according to three elements: rule inferring, rule applying, and rule learning. The elements of facet *B* are the modalities of expression of the testee, and facet *C* lists three formats of communication: verbal, numerical, and geometrical. The data come from a 1991 study by Guttman and Levy of two populations; U.S. and Israeli children ages 6–16.

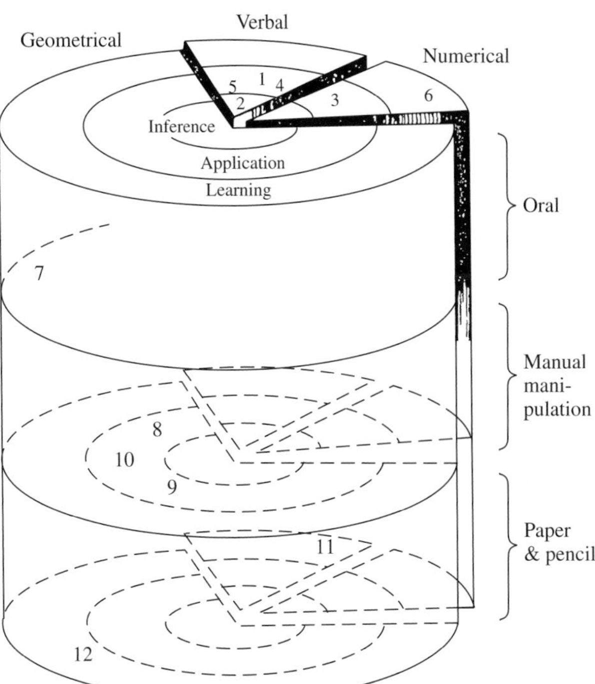

Figure 3 Schematic representation of the cylindrical structure of the Revised Wechsler Intelligence Tests for Children. Reprinted from *Intelligence*, Vol. 15, L. Guttman and S. Levy, "Two Structural Laws of Intelligence Tests," pp. 79–103, Copyright 1991, with permission from Elsevier Science.

The correlation coefficients for each of the observed matrices yield a three-dimensional structure that can be described schematically by a cylinder (Fig. 3). The placement of points of the subtests of the WISC-R are presented schematically in the cylinder of Fig. 3, which also shows the three intersecting partitions of the space corresponding to facets *A*, *B*, and *C*. The circle (radex) and the axis orthogonal to it provide the cylindrical framework.

The Circular Base (Radex) of the Cylinder The elements of the format facet (*C*) have the rationale for a polarizing facet because there is no notion of order among the formats of communication (verbal, numerical, and geometrical). Emanating from a common origin, each of the formats corresponds to a different direction in the SSA space, resulting in a partitioning of the space into three wedgelike regions.

A further partitioning of the circular base is by the distance of the subtests from the origin, conforming to the order of the elements of facet *A*, the task imposed on the testee. Thus, the task facet plays a modulating role corresponding to the notion of order that results both from being a stem facet and from substantive considerations of the meaning of the order among the elements. Tests in the inner circle around the origin have the element of rule inference, whereas those in the outer bands have the elements of rule application and rule learning. Thus, the task facet modulates the order from the origin from inference to application and to learning (instant memory) an objective rule.

The radex lawfulness of the cylinder base means that subtests requiring rule inference tend to be highly correlated among themselves, even though they may be presented in different formats that correspond to different directions of the space. In contrast, correlations among rule-application tests may even approach zero, depending on differences in their format. This radex lawfulness has repeatedly been verified for paper-and-pencil intelligence tests; their regionality prowess was first published by Guttman in 1965.

The Axis of the Cylinder Because the WISC-R are not limited to expression by paper and pencil, an additional dimension is needed to allow the portrayal of the axial role of the additional mode-of-expression facet (facet *B*). The elements of this axial facet are ordered from oral to written expression, with manual manipulation in between.

Cross-Cultural Replication The same cylindrical lawfulness has been replicated separately for each age group in the United States and in Israel, even though the apparent averages are different.

The Road to Cumulative Social Science

Our example demonstrates the efficacy of the mapping sentence in establishing scientific lawfulness. The mapping sentence provides both the definitional framework for the observations and the rationale for regional hypotheses by assigning formal roles to the content facets that correspond to regional partitioning of the empirical space of the observations.

When a few facets are used, they generally partition the space into relatively large regions. The finer the partitioning into regions, the sharper the delimitation of the sizes of the correlation. The road to finer partitioning is through increasing the number of content facets (intension of the mapping sentence). Most research until now has been limited to a relatively few facets, but these have sufficed to establish basic lawfulness.

The effectiveness of the facet approach in establishing lawfulness for the structure of similarity (correlation) coefficients matrices in the social sciences in fields such as intelligence, attitudes, social indicators, well-being, values, ethnic identities, involvement, multitrait multimethod matrices, and so forth has been documented by a collection of cross-cultural and long-term replications. They continue to be replicated and extended. The facet approach has also been successfully applied in other scientific disciplines such as engineering, medicine, architecture, and zoology. The many published examples that use the facet approach and arrive at structural lawfulness provide growing evidence that supports the general hypothesis of facet theory. As in all science, attention should be paid to "deviants" from an anticipated structural lawfulness because these may be springboards to further growth.

Facet Theory: Typologies and Spaces of Subjects

Introduction

The formation of scientific structural laws hitherto discussed has concerned typologies and spaces of variables. Here we discuss the branch of theory construction that typologizes subjects (of any population), namely the scalogram, defined as any tabular way of printing out a listing of structuples (profiles). The roots of scalogram analysis are in the unidimensional scale developed by Guttman in the early 1940s. The rarity of the perfect scale raised the need for higher-dimensionality methods to enable a systematic representation of complex multivariate distributions. Multidimensional structuple analysis (MSA) addresses the problem of defining dimensionality for structuples of subjects, with no restrictions whatsoever on the nature of the variables categories. MSA provides a geometrical portrayal of the multivariate distribution in as few dimensions as possible using a principle called contiguity. Partial-order structuple analysis (POSA) deals with the dimensionality of structuples of subjects with ordered categories.

Partly Ordered Typologies

Classification of Subjects: The Categorical Mapping Sentence

A frequent variety of typology is one that results when a given population is classified simultaneously by several criteria (variables), the categories of each criterion being ordered in a sense common to all criteria. Each member of the population has an observed structuple (profile) composed of *n* structs (categories), one from each criterion, the categories of each criterion being empirically exclusive and exhaustive. In other words, the population is mapped onto a Cartesian set of a common range. This mapping is termed a categorical mapping sentence and can be expressed abstractly in the following form:

$$x \longrightarrow \mathrm{V}_1\ \mathrm{V}_2\ \mathrm{V}_3\ \mathrm{V}_4 \ldots \mathrm{V}_n$$

Thus, in the categorical mapping, there is one set for the domain, namely population, and a Cartesian set for the range, the items or criteria. Hence, the items are the facets of the range, and their categories are the elements of the range facets.

The Concept of Partial-Order

Although the subjects are simply ordered on each item separately, they are only partly ordered by their structuples from all the items simultaneously because there may be several structuples for each rank. Hence, the overall partial order is an automatic consequence of the simple orders on each item separately. The empirical problem is to ascertain the dimensionality and the substantive meaning of the partly ordered system.

Consider the following set (scalogram) of seven structuples (profiles) observed from a certain population. The four items (facets) *A*, *B*, *C*, and *D* all have a commonly ordered range, where within each item $1 < 2$. The structuples are listed in Table I according to their structuple "sum" or rank. Clearly, this set is not a perfect scale because there is not a one-to-one correspondence between the structuples and the ranks. But it can be easily portrayed as a two-dimensional POSA (Fig. 4). Four symbols for comparability are used: $>$, $<$, $=$, and #. By definition, a structuple is "higher" than another structuple (IV > II) if and only if it is higher on at least one item and not lower on any other item; therefore for structuples II (2111) and IV (2121); IV is higher than II. A similar definition holds for a "lower" relationship: I (1111) < II (2111). Two structuples are "equal" if they are equal in all items. Two structuples are comparable whenever one of these three relationships ("higher," "lower," or "equal") holds. In Fig. 4, comparable structuples are connected by a line. Two structuples are noncomparable (#) if and only if one structuple is the higher on at least one struct while the other structuple is higher on at least one other struct; for example, structuples II (2111) # III (1112). In Fig. 4, all structuples in the same row are noncomparable, indicating similarity in rank but difference in content. In other words, two structuples with the same score are noncomparable. A scalogram containing noncomparable structuples requires two or more dimensions for its portrayal. A Guttman scale presented earlier, is the case in which all structuples are comparable. The one-to-one correspondence between the structuples and the ranks of a Guttman scale, implies that all the monotonicity coefficients between the scale items equal 1. This means that, in SSA terms, a perfect scale constitutes only one point (zero-dimensional space). However, in the case in which the scale items are only a subset of the items included in an SSA space, the scale items may be presented by more than one point because their monotonicity coefficients with the remaining items may differ and the monotonicity condition of SSA breaks ties.

Table I List of Structuples

	A	*B*	*C*	*D*
I	1	1	1	1
II	2	1	1	1
III	1	1	1	2
IV	2	1	2	1
V	2	1	1	2
VI	1	2	1	2
VII	2	2	2	2

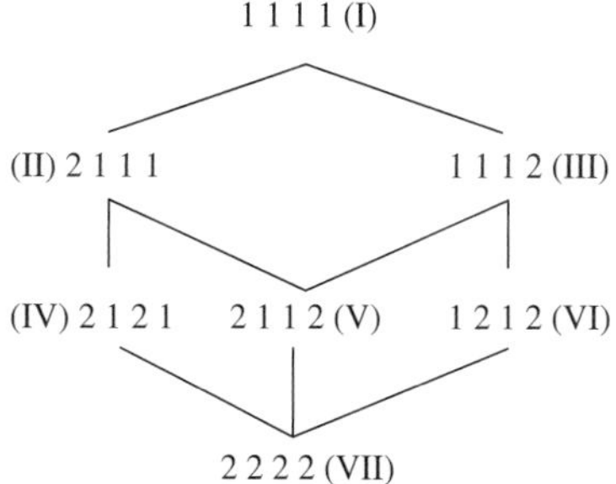

Figure 4 A two-dimensional partial-order.

The stratification of subjects among themselves is automatically a part of the stratification of the entire population that they are a part of. Because the partial order of a subset does not depend on the partial order of the total set, the internal ordering holds regardless of the subjects not in the sample.

The Partial-Order Structuple (Scalogram) Analysis with Base Coordinates (POSAC) Technique for Portraying a Partial Order

The systematic, yet detailed, study of the similarities and differences among the structuples is facilitated by viewing them in the space of the smallest dimensionality that can preserve the partial order. To determine the (smallest) dimensionality of the partial order, the POSAC technique was introduced by Guttman.

POSAC calculates a mathematically optimal pair of base axes (x and y) for the empirical partial order. Each structuple appears as a point in the two-dimensional space. Any two comparable structuples will have their two points on a line with a positive slope, namely the joint direction $(x+y)$. Hence, in the case of a perfect (unidimensional) scale, all the structuples have their points on a line with positive slope. In contrast, two noncomparable profiles have their points on a line with a negative slope, that is in the lateral direction $(x-y)$. "All four kinds of directions in the 2-space (x, y, *joint* and *lateral*) have a role in interpreting the results." These directions are presented schematically in Fig. 5.

The program provides a coefficient for the goodness of fit for the representation of the partial order, named CORREP. It specifies the proportion of structuple pairs correctly represented by POSAC. Three CORREP coefficients are specified, for the entire partial order for the comparable structuples and for the noncomparable structuples.

As already stated, such coefficients alone are not sufficient for determining the shape of the space. A detailed analysis of the systematic differences among the items is made in terms of n POSAC diagrams, one for each item. These are called item diagrams.

The concept of regionality plays a basic role also in the spaces of structuples. The role of the items (which are the facets of the categorical mapping) is to partition the space of the subjects into exclusive and exhaustive regions ordered according to their categories in one or more of the directions of the POSAC space (Fig. 6). The cell (or point) of a structuple as a whole, is the intersection of all the regions of its structs. Although there need not always be items that correspond to one or more of the POSAC main directions, we may assume that in any universe of items that partly orders a population there will be at least one item corresponding to a main direction, while the others will correspond to directions that are a combination of the main directions.

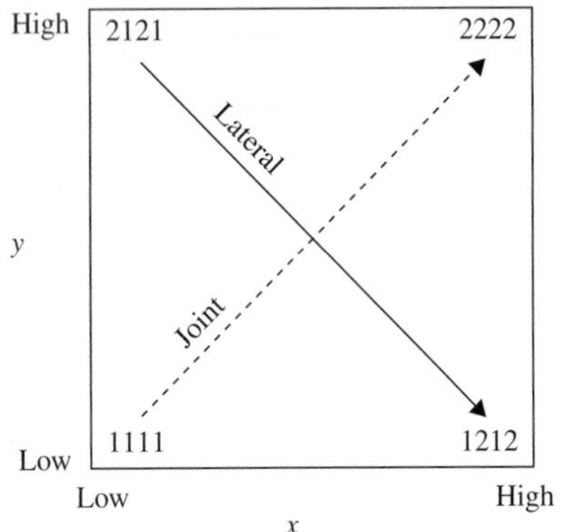

Figure 5 Schematic presentation of the directions of the POSAC space (base coordinates, joint direction, and lateral direction).

In case there are variables that correspond to the base coordinates, the partly ordered space is essentially spanned by these two variables. For example, in a 1985 study Levy and Guttman present a partly ordered typology of thyroid cancer patients, according to eight prognostic variables. Two of the prognostic variables were found to correspond to the respective base axes (x and y), meaning that the partly ordered space is essentially spanned by these two prognostic variables. The base axes were then assigned a substantive meaning and the items were termed basic items. Thus, the POSAC revealed systematic differences according to the *kind* of prognostic variables and not just according to the *level* of severity of symptoms. These differences may have implications for treatment procedures as well as for progress toward a richer theory.

Partial-Order Structuple (Scalogram) Analysis with Base Coordinates and Discriminant Analysis for External Criteria

POSAC has an optional routine for predicting an external criteria. The external criteria to be predicted are transcribed onto the partial order. Such a superimposition helps reveal the relationship (if any) between the partial order and the criteria to be predicted. In the 1985 thyroid cancer study, almost a perfect discriminant function was provided by the joint direction for prognosis of survival. This example demonstrates the power of POSAC in bringing out the substantive lawfulness in terms of internal discrimination of symptoms and in establishing the optimal discriminant function for prognostic purposes. "POSAC, with its space diagrams and item diagrams, milks the multivariable distribution to the maximum, and hence provides the best possible

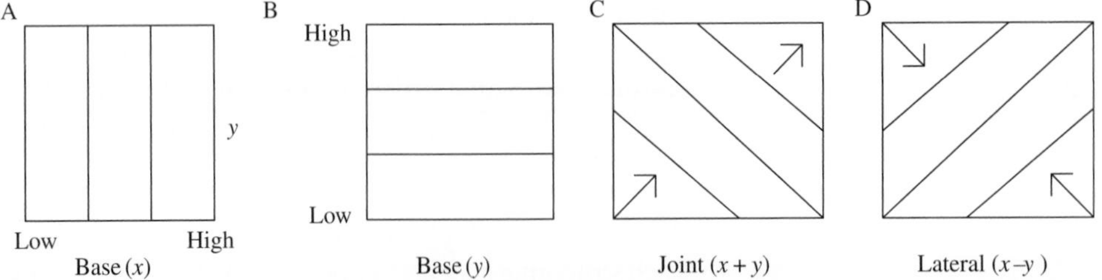

Figure 6 Schematic presentation of item diagrams partitioning the POSAC space into regions by item categories, corresponding to the directions of the POSAC.

basis for discriminant analysis, without preconceived assumptions."

Toward a Richer Theory: Transforming from a categorial to a structioned Mapping

The structuples of partial order result from a categorical mapping. This raises the question of constructing a richer theory.

In a structioned mapping sentence, there is a Cartesian set for the domain (population and content facets) and one facet (or a few) for the range; however, in a categorical mapping there is a Cartesian set for the range (the items are facets) and one set for the domain (population). Unlike the categorical mapping, the structioned mapping sentence leads to theory construction because it enables a simultaneous definition of the universe of observations to be analyzed in accordance with the definitional system. Hence, the main issue for theory construction is the transition from categorical mapping to structioned mapping. The first step in doing this is, of course, to consider the uniform substantive meaning of the common range facet. Next we may consider the substantive meaning of the items in the space of the subjects' structuples, such as meaningful base items, as representing elements of content facet(s).

I conclude with the words of Clyde Coombs regarding facet theory. When discussing the complex problem of defining domain boundaries in the social sciences in 1982, he stated that he believed that Guttman's facet theory is "the only substantial attempt to provide a general theory for characterizing domains; in this sense it is a metatheory. As behavioral science advances, so will the need for such theory."

See Also the Following Articles

Categorical Modeling/Automatic Interaction Detection • Factor Analysis • Guttman Scaling

Further Reading

Borg, I., and Lingoes, J. (1987). *Multidimensional Similarity Structure Analysis.* Springer Verlag, New York.

Borg, I., and Shye, S. (1995). *Facet Theory Format and Content.* Sage, Thousand Oaks, CA.

Canter, D. (ed.) (1985). *Facet Theory: Approaches to Social Research*. Springer Verlag, New York.

Elizur, D. (1987). *Systematic Job Evaluation and Comparable Worth.* Gower, Aldershot, UK.

Gratch, H. (ed.) (1973). *Twenty-Five Years of Social Research in Israel.* Jerusalem Academic Press, Jerusalem.

Guttman, L. (1941). The quantification of a class of attributes—A theory and method of scale construction. In *The Prediction of Personal Adjustment* (P. Horst, ed.), pp. 319–348. Social Science Research Council, New York.

Guttman, L. (1944). A basis for scaling qualitative data. *Am. Sociol. Rev.* **91,** 139–150.

Guttman, L. (1953). Image theory for the structure of quantitative variates. *Psychometrika* **18,** 277–296.

Guttman, L. (1954). A new approach to factor analysis: The radex. In *Mathematical Thinking in the Social Sciences* (P. F. Lazarsfeld, ed.), pp. 258–348. Free Press, Glencoe, IL.

Guttman, L. (1954). An outline of some new methodology for social research. *Public Opinion Q.* **18,** 395–404.

Guttman, L. (1954). The principal components of scalable attitudes. In *Mathematical Thinking in the Social Sciences* (P. F. Lazarsfeld, ed.), pp. 216–257. Free Press, Glencoe, IL.

Guttman, L. (1968). A general nonmetric technique for finding the smallest coordinate space for a configuration of points. *Psychometrika* **33,** 469–506.

Guttman, L. (1972). The Facet Approach to Theory Development (mimeo).

Guttman, L. (1977). What is not what in statistics. *The Statistician* **26**(2), 81–107.

Guttman, L. (1980). Integration of Test Design and Analysis: Status in 1979. In *New Directions for Testing and Measurement,* (W. B. Schrader, ed.), vol. 5, pp. 93–98. Jossey-Bass, San Francisco, CA.

Guttman, L. (1982). What is not what in theory construction. In *Social Structure and Behavior* (R. M. Hauser, D. Mechanic, and A. Haller, eds.), pp. 331–348. Academic Press, New York.

Guttman, L. (1985). Multidimensional Structuple Analysis (MSA-1) for the Classification of Cetacea: Whales, Porpoises and Dolphins. In *Data Analysis in Real Life Environment: Ins and Outs of Solving Problems* (J. F. Marcotorchina, J. M. Proth, and J. Janssen, eds.), pp. 45–53. Elsevier Science, North Holland.

Guttman, L. (1986). Coefficients of polytonicity and monotonicity. In *Encyclopedia of Statistical Sciences,* Vol. 7, pp. 80–87. John Wiley and Sons, New York.

Guttman, L. (1988). Eta, DISCO, ODISCO, and F. *Psychometrika* **53**(3), 393–405.

Guttman, L. (1991). The language of science. In *In Memoriam: Chapters from an Unfinished Textbook on Facet Theory,* Chap. 1. Israel Academy of Sciences and Humanities, and The Hebrew University of Jerusalem, Jerusalem.

Guttman, L., and Levy, S. (1987). Similarity Structure Analysis of European Elections. In *Data Analysis* (J. Janssen, F. Marcotorchino, and J. M. Proth, eds.), pp. 192–204. Plenum Press, New York.

Guttman, L., and Levy, S. (1991). Two Structural Laws for Intelligence Tests. *Intelligence* **15,** 79–103.

Levy, S. (1985). Lawful roles of facets in social theories. In *Facet Theory: Approaches to Social Research* (D. Canter, ed.), pp. 59–96. Springer Verlag, New York.

Levy, S. (1990). The Mapping Sentence in Cumulative Theory Construction: Well-Being as an Example. In *Operationalization and Research Strategy* (J. J. Hox and J. de Yong-Gierveld, eds.), pp. 155–177. Swetz & Zeitlinger, Amsterdam.

Levy, S. (ed.) (1994). *Louis Guttman on Theory and Methodology: Selected Writings*. Dartmouth, Aldershot, UK.

Levy, S., and Amar, L. (2002). Processing square-asymmetric matrices via the intrinsic data analysis technique WSSA: A new outlook on sociometric issues [CD-ROM]. *Social Science Methodology in the New Millennium* (J. Blasius, J. Hox, E. de Leeuw, and P. Schmidt, eds.). Leske and Budrich, Opladen, Germany.

Levy, S., and Guttman, L. (1975). On the multivariate structure of well-being. *Soc. Indicators Res.* **2,** 361–388.

Levy, S., and Guttman, L. (1985). The partial order of severity of thyroid cancer with the prognosis of survival. In *Data Analysis in Real Life Environment: Ins and outs of Solving Problems* (J. F. Marcotorchino, J. M. Proth, and J. Janssen, eds.), pp. 111–119. Elsevier Science, North Holland.

Levy, S., and Guttman, L. (1989). The conical structure of adjustive behavior. *Soc. Indicators Res.* **21,** 455–479.

Lingoes, J. C. (1968). The multivariate analysis of qualitative data. *Multivariate Behav. Res.* **3,** 61–94.

Raveh, A. (1989). A nonmetric approach to linear discriminant analysis. *J. Am. Statist. Assoc.* **84,** 176–183.

Shye, S. (ed.) (1978). *Theory Construction and Data Analysis in the Behavioral Sciences*. Jossey-Bass, San Francisco, CA.

Shye, S., and Amar, R. (1985). Partial-order scalogram analysis by base coordinates and lattice mapping of the items by their scalogram poles. In *Facet Theory: Approach to Social Research* (D. Canter, ed.), pp. 277–298. Springer Verlag, New York.

Waks, S. (1995). *Curriculum Design: from an Art towards a Science.* Tempus Publications, Hamburg, Germany.

Zvulun, E. (1978). Multidimensional scalogram analysis: The method and its application. In *Theory Construction and Data Analysis in the Behavioral Sciences* (S. Shye, ed.), pp. 237–264. Jossey-Bass, San Francisco, CA.

Half-Life Method

Arthur M. Schneiderman
Independent Consultant, Boxford, Massachusetts, USA

Glossary

balanced scorecard (BSC) A deployment approach for linking strategy to action.

experience curve A normative model of cost reduction based on the learning curve.

half-life method A normative model for predicting rates of incremental improvement for processes of different complexity.

incremental improvement Continuous process improvement achieved by breaking a big problem into many easily solvable little pieces.

organizational complexity The degree to which activities or decisions within a process confront conflicting demands or considerations caused by the way that the participants are organized.

outsourcing Moving an internal process or process step to an independent external source.

PDCA (Plan-Do-Check-Act) cycle The Shewhart/Deming cycle used in improvement activities.

quality circle A supervisor and his or her direct reports who meet regularly to improve the process that they execute.

redesign To fundamentally change the technology employed by or the reporting relationships of the participants in a process.

systematic problem-solving method A documented step-by-step improvement process based on scientific methodology, for example the 7-step method.

SDCA (Standard-Do-Check-Act) cycle The cycle that a worker follows in doing his or her daily job.

technical complexity The degree to which employed technology is understood and mastered by its users.

total quality management (TQM) An evolving set of tools and methods used as part of a companywide focus on continuous improvement.

Don't burden me with more ideas about how to farm better.... I'm not doing what I know how now.
Anonymous Iowa Farmer

The half-life method is a normative model for predicting the rate of incremental improvement of nonfinancial performance measures. It can be used both as a diagnostic tool and to set goals. Because it identifies the fastest rate at which a measure can be improved using current incremental improvement tools and methods, it is particularly valuable in testing the achievability of strategically significant balanced-scorecard (BSC) goals without major process redesign (reengineering) or outsourcing.

Introduction

Consider the following situation. You have identified the vital few things that you need to do in order to achieve your strategic objectives, developed actionable metrics, and determined appropriate time-based goals for each of them. Now the question is: Can you achieve those goals in a timely way and thereby feel confident that you have done everything that you possible can in order to assure your strategic success?

Today many organizations have implemented some form of a balanced scorecard (BSC) that promises to help them translate their strategy into action. But from my experience, only a very small fraction of them have thoughtfully addressed the question of meaningful goals for each of their scorecard measures—goals whose achievement will really make a strategic difference. An even smaller percentage of them have addressed the issue of which methodology or approach they will use in order to achieve these goals. That exercise is generally left to those who will be held responsible for their achievement. There do not appear to be any rigorous impartial studies that provide evidence in conflict with my observations.

What is clear is that simply extrapolating historical performance improvement trends on each of the selected scorecard measures will not get them to their strategic objectives. Or as the saying goes, "Doing what you did, will (at best) get you what you got," and in most cases that is just not good enough.

It is now widely recognized that improvement of performance measures requires a process focus—the identification and improvement of those underlying processes within an organization that are the leveraged drivers for closing those strategically identified stakeholder-requirement gaps that must be rapidly eliminated if the strategy is to succeed. Once these have been identified, there appear to be three options open to the organization for closing these gaps:

1. Incrementally improve the process.
2. Redesign (reengineer) the process.
3. Outsource the process.

Deciding which is the best choice requires a thorough understanding, for each of them, of the amount of improvement that can be achieved, how long it will take, and how much it will cost. The outsourcing option is further restricted to noncore processes; those that simply support core competencies that differentiate the organization from its competition. These usually are not the processes that can really make a strategic difference. In other words, organizations cannot outsource those crown-jewel processes that give them their distinct competitive advantage.

The cost of achieving the goal, must be addressed on a case-by-case basis. But as a general rule of thumb, outsourcing is the least costly in terms of required cash outlay and redesigning is the most costly. Fortunately, the other two criteria—the greatest possible improvement and the time it will take to achieve it—can be viewed from a normative perspective. That is the principal subject of this entry.

The Half-Life Method

Let us start by considering Fig. 1, which frames the issue by looking at a typical performance measure as a function of future time. The figure shows the measure's current state. Assume that the measure is defined so that its decrease represents improvement. For incremental improvement, experience shows that improvement follows a typical path. At first, it as rapid as the "low-hanging fruit" is plucked; but it gradually slows as root-cause and solution identification become more elusive. This is sometimes called the law of diminishing returns. Eventually improvement stalls as fundamental limits on the process's inherent capability are encountered; the results just cannot get any better because of basic technological or human limitations.

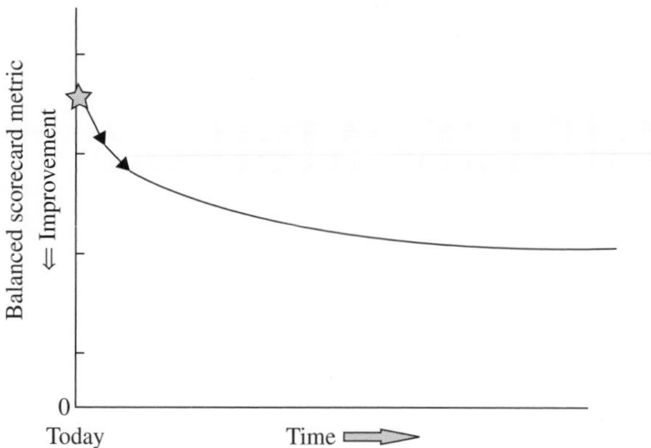

Figure 1 Typical improvement curve. Time history of improvement.

There are many causes of technological limitations, including fundamental machine variability, finite cycle times, and cues caused by clumps in demand. In the manufacture of semiconductors, the density of airborne dust particles above a certain size in the clean room determines the maximum possible yield that a given facility can achieve. Humans are subject to inevitable and predictable errors, particularly when carrying out highly repetitive tasks such as inspection. So every process has fundamental limits that can only be overcome with new technology (including automation) or by structural reorganization. This almost always involves significant financial cost. Once we acknowledge that zero-defects are economically impossible for any real-world situation and that physics dictates what any process can ultimately achieve, we must recognize that, without significant capital investment, there exists a fundamental limiting performance level for any given process.

It is worth noting here that process reengineering, which is often referred to as discontinuous or stepwise improvement, is not often so in reality. The fundamental effect of process reengineering is a significant improvement in the process's inherent capability—its theoretical performance limit. Usually this involves replacing people or older machines with automated systems that produce the desired output better, faster, and cheaper. As a rule of thumb, this improvement must be approximately 10-fold to justify it economically in the first place.

And when the new process is activated, at first performance often gets worse, not better! It takes time to iron out the initial wrinkles in the reengineered process and to establish new standard operating procedures to be followed by both operators and the machines themselves (called software). Once startup is complete, the new process, like the old one, must then be incrementally improved in order to approach, over time, its new and improved limits. In fact, actual performance-improvement histories after process reengineering have a strikingly similar appearance to Fig. 1, but hopefully with a lower asymptote.

To make the economically rational decision whether to improve, reengineer, or outsource, we need some way to predict the expected performance improvement over time.

Serendipity

In 1984, on a flight returning from a study mission to Japan, I made a remarkable discovery. Like many such discoveries, this one was also serendipitous. I was reviewing materials from a presentation given by Kenzo Sasaoka, then president of Yokagowa Hewlett-Packard (YHP). YHP had recently won the coveted Deming Prize. One display (see Fig. 2) showed the multiyear efforts of a quality circle working on the reduction of soldering defects in the manufacture of printed circuit boards.

Starting at a defect level of 0.4%, which corresponded on average to two defects on each board produced, the team systematically reduced the defect level to near zero—or so it appeared. Each of the pointing fingers in the figure represented the implementation of a major corrective action resulting from one cycle of their improvement process. Recognizing that their near perfection was a graphical illusion, the team generated the second graph, which measured the defect level in the smaller units of parts per million (ppm; 1 ppm = 0.0001% and is equivalent to 6.3σ). With this magnified view, the incremental improvement trend was seen to continue. Over a period of 5 years, the team reduced the defect level by a factor of more than 10,000. Now, instead of having to rework every board on average, only one in 600 required this costly and non-value-adding step.

This is interesting data, but how did it help reduce the boredom of a 15-hour flight? Well, I am an engineer; so faced with those two graphs, I recognized that they could be combined into a single graph if a logarithmic scale was used for the defect level. But I am also a manager and no longer travel with semilog graph paper in my briefcase—and, remember, that was before the now-ubiquitous laptop computer. Therein lay my first challenge. The next few hours were spent creating semilog paper using my calculator and a ruler and regraphing the YHP data. Figure 3 is the result.

Looking at that result, I recognized that radioactive decay has the same general behavior. It is characterized by the constant amount of time it takes for the radiation level to drop by 50%, which is called the half-life. Using that analogy, I calculated the "half-life" for the printed-circuit-board defect rate; it was 3.6 months! In other words, starting at a defect level of 0.4%, after 3.6 months it was down to 0.2%, in another 3.6 months down to 0.1%, in another 3.6 months down to 0.05%, and on and on. In fact, the team went through more than seven halvings of the defect level before something happened and the rate of improvement slowed dramatically to a new and again constant half-life of approximately 8 months. I return to why that happened later.

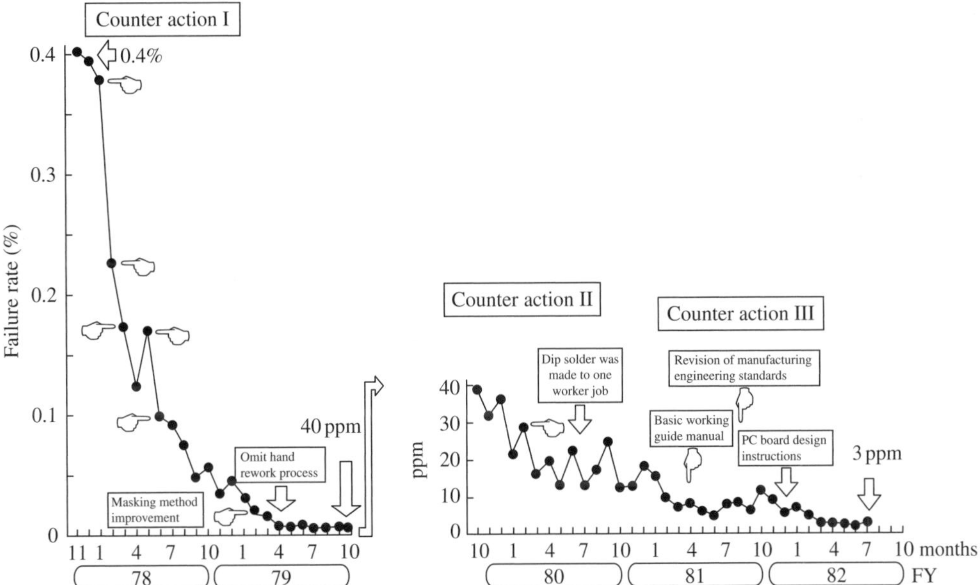

Figure 2 Process quality improvement. Reduction of soldering defects in a dip soldering process.

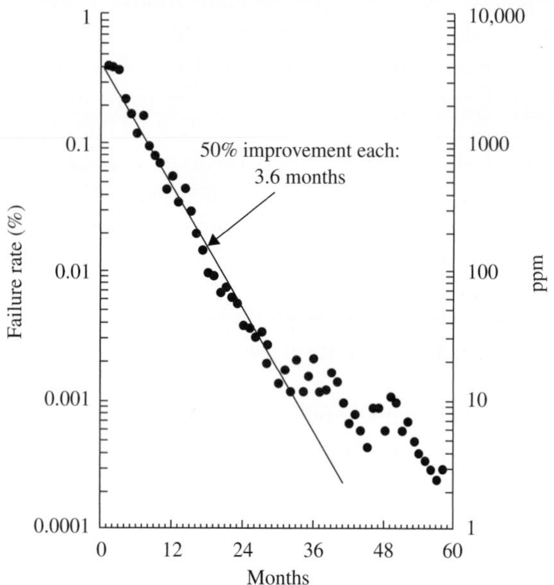

Figure 3 Yokogowa Hewlett-Packard dip soldering defects graph.

By the way, John Young, at that time CEO of HP, in describing these same accomplishments commented that:

> *It's worth noting that the machinery used by YHP was considered obsolete by another HP division in 1973. The insertion defect rate, at 100 ppm, is more than 50 times better than we've achieved at Cupertino.*

On my last visit to YHP, that same team was measuring their defect levels in parts per billion (ppb). So the incrementally improvement versus reengineering decision is not always as obvious as it may seem.

Half-Life Math

A mathematically inclined reader will immediately recognize that the path of improvement shown in Figs. 1–3 follows an exponential curve described by the formula:

$$m - m_{\min} = (m_0 - m_{\min})e^{-a(t-t_0)/t_{1/2}}$$

where:

m = current value of the scorecard metric

$m_{\min}$ = minimum possible value of m

m_0 = initial value of m at t_0

t = current time

t_0 = initial time

$t_{1/2}$ = half-life constant

$a = \ln 2 \approx 0.7$

The half-life is measured in units of time, typically months, and represents the amount of time it takes to achieve a 50% improvement in the metric. One of the remarkable features of exponential improvement is that the half-life does not depend on the initial point; in other words, it is a constant over the large range of improvement. Let us say, for example, that our scorecard metric is on-time delivery. If the current performance is 75% and the best possible performance given the processes fundamental limitations is 95%, then there is a performance gap of 20%. If we assume a 6-month half-life, then we should achieve 85% performance after 6 months, leaving a 10% gap remaining. In the 6 months after this, we should be able to reduce the gap by 50% (which is 5%), so our resulting performance after a total of 1 year should be 90%. This pattern continues with each successive 6-month period chewing up half of the remaining gap.

In calculating the half-life from historic data, it is only necessary to get an approximate value. If the data are provided using a linear axis, start by drawing a smooth curve through the data shaped roughly like the curve in Fig. 1. Then simply choose a convenient initial point on that your curve and estimate the time it took for half that value to be reached. Repeat this at several points on the curve and simply average the results. If the data are plotted using a semilog scale, then fit a straight line through the data and repeat the described procedure. It is straightforward to determine the half-life more rigorously using software packages such as Excel or Lotus 123. Using them provides the additional benefit of providing a measure of statistical significance of how well the model fits the data.

What Determines the Improvement Half-Life?

The obvious question that arises is "What determines the improvement half-life?" I discovered the answer to this question nearly 15 years ago and published my findings in two articles that appeared in *Quality Progress*, a publication of the then American Society for Quality Control, now called the American Society for Quality. The answer is that the improvement methodology employed, as well as the complexity of the process that the metric represents, determines the half-life.

Over the millennia, various means have been employed to change the current state to a more desirable one. Figure 4 is my attempt to capture many of these approaches. The ones of interest here are on the branch containing the various systematic methodologies that rely on real-world data and are based on the scientific methodology embodied in the Shewhart-Deming or PDCA (Plan-Do-Check-Act) cycle.

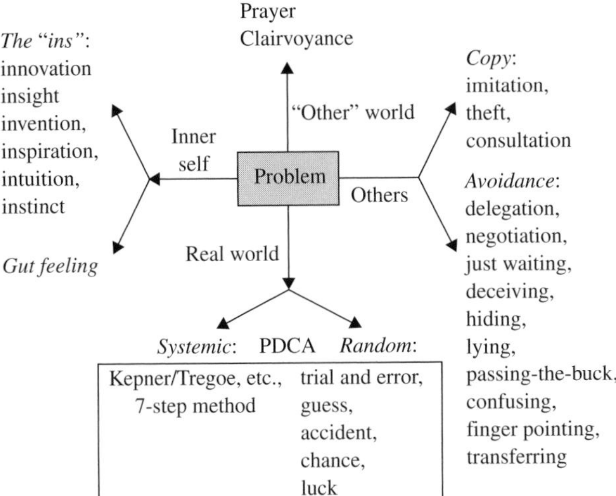

Figure 4 Options for problem solving.

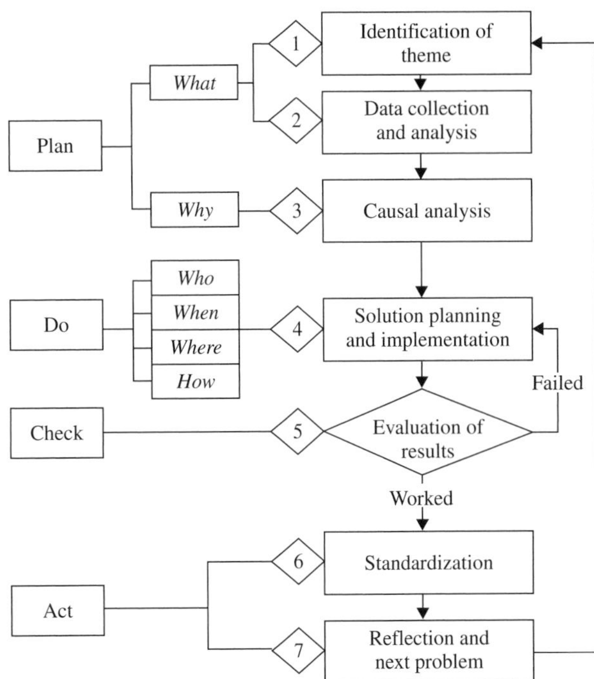

Figure 5 Incremental improvement, the PDCA cycle and the 7-step method.

Science versus Chance

Although scientific methodology has been around for thousands of years, its application has been restricted to a very small set of individuals who have been trained in its use. By using a scientific approach, the rate of improvement is increased 10-fold over trial and error, evolution's apparent approach to improvement. The Industrial Revolution prompted a desire to broaden its user base. In the early part of the twentieth century, leaders such as Frederick W. Taylor and Walter Shewhart were teaching simplified versions of the scientific method of discovery to nontechnically trained individuals out on the shop floor. In the late 1930s, Kepner and Tregoe even made a franchised consulting business of it. By the 1950s, at the prompting of Ed Deming, the Japanese Union of Scientists and Engineers (JUSE) institutionalized it in their Quality Circle movement. Figure 5 is an example of its current state of refinement, known as the 7-step method.

The 7-step method shown in Fig. 5 distinguishes itself from trial and error in a number of critical ways. It uses root-cause analysis to mitigate the waste inherent in the trial-and-error approach (steps 2 and 3). It validates candidate solutions to assure that they have the desired effect (step 5). It retains improvements in the process's memory by incorporating them in written standards (step 6). And, perhaps most important, it embodies double-loop learning by encouraging its users to consider ways to improve their problem-solving methods and skills and to prepare for their next cycle of improvement (step 7). Compare this 7-step method to its more commonly used cousin that consists only of steps 1 and 4.

Motivated by what I discovered at YHP, I studied nearly 100 separate exemplary process-improvement efforts, each of which employed what was essentially this 7-step method. On average, these projects achieved a sevenfold improvement in their metric over a 3-year period by maintaining an 11-month half-life. I discovered in all cases that the rate of improvement, captured by the half-life metric, was essentially constant (average $r^2 = 0.77$) within each effort, but varied from project to project ranging from less than 1 month to more than 4 years.

The Role of Process Complexity

The stratification of the resulting observed half-lives demonstrated that this variation was the result of differences in the organizational and technical complexity of the process being improved. The half-life matrix shown in Fig. 6 summarizes my findings.

Organizational complexity spans the range from unifunctional to cross-functional to cross-business processes. Technical complexity captures the maturity of the embodied technology from simple and well established to new and not yet fully developed. For processes of average organizational and technical complexity, the use of a systematic improvement methodology such as the 7-step method will usually yield a half-life of 9 months; that is, the gap between current and potential performance will close at the rate of 50% every 9 months.

For the most complex processes, the half-life increases to nearly 2 years, whereas for the least complex ones a half-life of 1 month is more typical. An inspection of

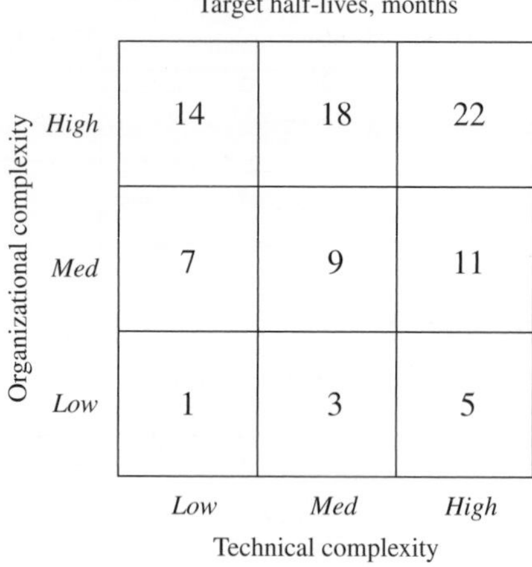

Figure 6 Half-life matrix.

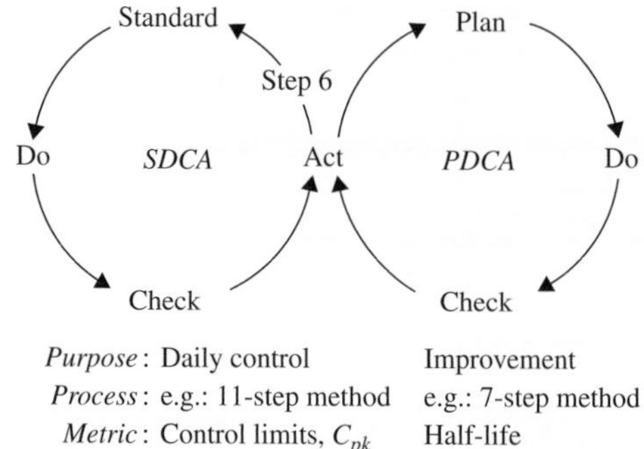

Figure 7 The dual function of work, SDCA and PDCA cycles.

Fig. 6 shows that increasing organizational complexity has about three times the slowing effect of increased technological complexity. This clearly supports the current notion that organizations should be structured around processes rather than functions in order to increase their potential rates of improvement.

Returning to the YHP example, what caused the observed half-life to suddenly change from 3.6 to 8 months? At a subsequent visit to YHP, I shared Fig. 3 with Mr. Sasaoka and his vice president of manufacturing. After much discussion, we discovered that around the time that the improvement rate slowed, the team discovered that most of the root causes of the remaining defects lay not with manufacturing but with the design of the boards themselves. The team needed to be expanded to include the design function, not just manufacturing, thus increasing the organizational complexity of the process.

Why the Half-Life Method Works

The half-life method is an empirically based normative model for process improvement. Yet there is a simple explanation of why it works. First, consider the notion of the dual function of work depicted in Fig. 7. In this contemporary view of the purpose of work, all members of an organization have two distinct responsibilities. The first is to do their daily job of contributing to the organization's ongoing value-creating activities. They do this by executing their current process using its associated standard operating procedure. But, unlike Charlie Chaplin's character in the classic movie *Modern Times*, they are also empowered to spend a portion of their time improving the way that they do that job. These two activities are referred to as the SDCA (Standard-Do-Check-Act) and PDCA (Plan-Do-Check-Act) cycles.

The portion of time spent and the tool set employed in PDCA activities vary by organizational level. Typically, production workers spend 5–10% of their time in improvement activities, whereas people in top management spend approximately one-half of their time improving or managing the improvement of the organization's critical processes. Because, in general, process complexity increases as the organizational level of its executors increases, the tools change from simple statistical analysis to more complex language-based and modeling methods.

Like any normative model, it is difficult to mathematically prove why the half-life method works. But by studying how continuous process improvement is done in practice, we can understand its underlying "physics." First, we need to look at the typical findings of steps 2 and 3 in the 7-step method. A common format for presenting these findings is the Pareto diagram, a rank-ordered bar chart showing the identified causes of the performance gap. It should come as no surprise that all possible causes are not created equal; some are more important than others. So in nearly all cases, the 80-20 rule applies, with 20% of the likely causes being responsible for 80% of the gap. In fact, Pareto charts almost always show an exponential decline in the significance of each successive rank-ordered cause. Typically, the most significant one, called the root cause, is responsible for 30–50% of the total gap. Once this root cause has been mitigated, the Pareto chart for the remaining gap looks very similar in shape to the original one. The new root cause (usually the second bar on the earlier chart) now represents 30–50% of the new and smaller gap.

The nature of the continuous improvement process is such that the team that is executing it continuously cycles through the 7-step method, gnawing away at the remaining ever-decreasing gap. How long does it take for each cycle? The answer depends on the complexity of the process that is being improved, but in general it ranges from 3 to 6 months. Both worker and manager impatience and the need to see short-term results conspire so that the total gap be broken down into small enough pieces to assure visible progress can be made in that time frame.

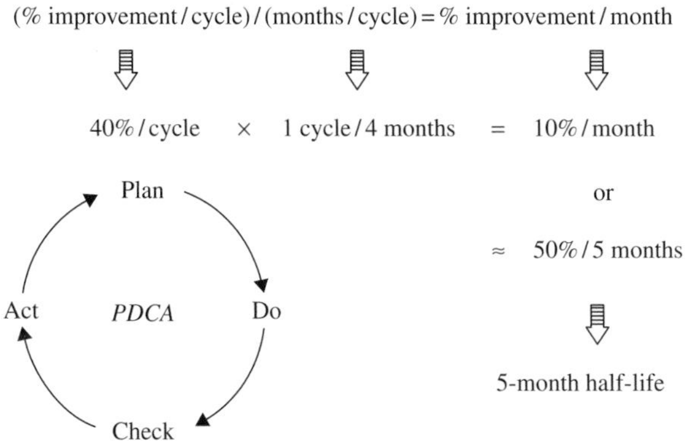

(% improvement / cycle) / (months / cycle) = % improvement / month

40% / cycle × 1 cycle / 4 months = 10% / month

or

≈ 50% / 5 months

5-month half-life

Plan

Do

Check

Act

PDCA

Figure 8 Why the half-life method works.

Knowing the percentage improvement per cycle and the number of months it takes per cycle allows us to determine the improvement per month (by simple division). Figure 8 depicts this calculation, showing how a 40% improvement every 4 months corresponds to a 5-month half-life.

Process complexity affects both the improvement per cycle and the months per cycle. Complex processes have more potential causes, and each causes tends to have a smaller individual effect; in other words they have flatter Pareto diagrams. Also, it takes longer to complete each cycle because cross-functional issues and technological complexities inevitably slow progress. So the half-life method works because the causes of the remaining gap nearly always obey the 80-20 rule and because the time required to execute each PDCA cycle remains roughly constant for a given level of organizational and technological complexity.

Half-Life Method versus Experience Curve

I am often asked how the half-life method differs from the experience curve popularized in the 1960s by Bruce Henderson, founder of the Boston Consulting Group. Henderson promoted, under a new name, the learning curve that was discovered by T. P. Wright and published by him in 1936. The learning curve, developed in the aircraft industry, was based on the observation that unit direct-labor use, expressed in total worker-months, declined with increasing experience. Henderson noted that the same was also true for unit cost. Based on this observation, he went on to develop a strategy model that had the experience curve at its cornerstone.

The experience curve, like the half-life, is also an empirical observation. It states that for each doubling of cumulative experience (total units produced from the very beginning, not just this year), real unit cost drops by a constant percentage, for example 20%. If your first million units have an average cost of $10 each, then your next million units should average $8 each, your next 2 million units, $6.40, your next 4 million units, $5.12, and so on. Given that cost is driven by cumulative units produced (1 million + 1 million + 2 million + 4 million in our example), the rate of decline of the cost tends to drop over time unless unit volume grows at a sufficiently high offsetting rate.

The half-life method, on the other hand, predicts that the rate of decline of the defect level is constant over time. Why the difference? We cannot say for sure because the experience curve is purely an empirical observation and is not based on any underlying theory. We can list the things that probably affect the slope of the experience curve, but we cannot write an equation in which they are the independent variables. On the other hand, as already described, there is a theoretical basis for the half-life method.

Also, keep in mind that the half-life deals with defects, not cost or labor hours. Of course, defects, defined as any gap between current and potential performance, are often a principal driver of unit costs, so the two are clearly related. Twenty years ago, the unexplainable leapfrogging done by Japanese industry baffled experience-curve practitioners. How could they possibly achieve experience-curve slopes two or more times steeper than their Western counterparts? The initial reaction was that they were using predatory pricing, selling below cost in order to buy market share. The furor even made its way to the U.S. Congress. But careful study of the situation, the object of my first visit to Japan, showed that their hyperfast cost reduction was real and the result of their new approach to process improvement: Total Quality Management (TQM).

The experience curve became the very basis of competitive strategy for several decades after its discovery, leading to a focus on the positive feedback loop between market share, cumulative experience, and unit cost. The half-life method can be used to form the basis of a similar competitive dynamic.

Using the Half-Life Method

There are two basic uses for the half-life method: improvement process diagnosis and goal setting. If we benchmark similarly complex processes and find that the best-practice half-life is significantly shorter than what we are experiencing, then we can infer that the best-practice organization's improvement process itself is capable of faster rates of improvement than the one that we are using. This should trigger careful study of what they are doing that we are not, thus providing a valuable source for organizational learning.

The second use, goal setting, is in a critical step (step 9) in the creation of a type 7 balanced scorecard, an approach for linking strategy and action. It is also used in step 5 of my seven steps of process management. Earlier in this entry, I described a key strategic decision that must be explicitly made if an organization is to have any chance of achieving its strategic objectives—whether to incrementally improve, redesign, or outsource. Those objectives have been translated into a few vital set of metrics and associated time-based goals that must be achieved for strategic success. The half-life method provides a tool for assessing the likelihood that the goal can be achieved through best-practice incremental improvement. By placing the driving process in the appropriate cell of Fig. 6, a target half-life can be determined. Using this half-life value and estimating the gap between current and potential performance, that performance can be projected to the date associated with the achievement of the scorecard goal. If the result is better than the goal, then in principle it can be realized using state-of-the-art incremental improvement. If it fails to meet the goal, then no amount of wishing or cajoling will produce success. You just cannot get there from here by merely improving the existing process.

In making this calculation, it is important to consider the underlying assumptions that form the basis for the half-life method:

1. The people who execute the process will do the improving.
2. They only spend a small portion of their time on it.
3. They will use a systematic problem-solving methodology equivalent to the 7-step method.

Modify any of these assumptions and you must reflect that change in the half-life value that you assume. For example, assigning expert resources such as a trained process engineer or statistician to assist the team will usually lead to faster improvement. The same holds if you increase the amount of time spent on improvement versus daily job activities.

If incremental improvement still cannot get you there, then process redesign or outsourcing are your only alternatives. If neither of those are feasible, then the only remaining recourse is to change your strategy or accept the fact that the strategy you are pursuing is just not achievable.

Talk (of Action) Is Cheap

Reading the current popular literature on new management practices is often very frustrating. Many of the "new" ideas promoted by today's leaders are merely the repackaging of old ones with at best a slightly new twist. I believe that this phenomenon arises from the difficulty organizations often have in truly institutionalizing new ideas. A case in point is the inculcation of TQM into an organization's culture. Ask nearly any major organization if they do TQM and their answer will more than likely be, "Oh yes, why we did that 10 years ago." But seek evidence that it has become a real part of their way of doing business, and you will begin to doubt their assertion.

In particular, look at the rates of improvement that they have achieved on their BSC metrics. You will most likely find them significantly slower than the half-life method would predict. In fact, they probably will differ little from the pre-TQM rates of approximately ~5% per year; and most of that will have come from technology, not process improvement. In other words, as that anonymous Iowa farmer said, "We're not doing what we know how now."

The half-life method gained much visibility in the business world as the result of a still-popular Harvard Business School case study by Kaplan, first published in 1989. The Board of Directors of one Fortune 100 aerospace company, a well-known TQM advocate, even adopted it as its official nonfinancial metric for judging business unit performance. However, after a few years of embarrassingly long half-life results, it was relegated to the back burner as a management tool. Why? Was the concept incorrect, or was this just another case of shooting the messenger?

I believe that the half-life method is a measure of process learning and that the reduction of a half-life over time is an indicator of organizational learning. As such, it is only useful to organizations that are committed to continuous applied learning. For others, it will probably be of questionable value as a performance metric.

See Also the Following Articles

Accounting Measures • Critical Views of Performance Measurement • History of Business Performance Measurement

Further Reading

Kaplan, R. S. (1991). Analog devices: The half-life system. (Harvard Business School case number 9-190-061, 3/16/90; revised 7/12/91.). In *The Design of Cost Management Systems* (R. Cooper and R. S. Kaplan, eds.), pp. 226–239. Prentice Hall, Englewood Cliffs, NJ.

Schneiderman, A. M. (1986). Optimum quality costs and zero defects: Are they contradictory concepts? *Quality Prog.* (November), 28.

Schneiderman, A. M. (1988). Setting quality goals. *Quality Prog.* (April), 51.

Schneiderman, A. M. (1998). Are there limits to TQM? *Strategy Business* (11), 35.

Schneiderman, A. M. (2001). How to build a balanced scorecard. In *Handbook of Performance Measurement* (Mike Bourne, ed.) Gee Publishing, London.

Schneiderman, A. M. http://www.schneiderman.com

Hazards Measurement

Susan L. Cutter
University of South Carolina, Columbia, South Carolina, USA

Glossary

disaster A singular hazard event that results in widespread human losses or has profound impacts on local environments.

discharge The quantity of water flowing past a point on a stream or river per some unit time.

exposure models Statistical or analytical models that delineate the probability of risk, its source, the type of risk, and the geographic extent of danger.

hazard The potential threat to humans (risk) as well as the impact of an event on society and the environment.

intensity The measure of event severity based on subjective human experience of it.

magnitude The strength or force of a hazard event.

recurrence intervals The time between events of a given magnitude or the magnitude range for a specific location.

risk The likelihood or probability of occurrence of a hazard event.

temporal spacing The sequencing and seasonality of hazard events.

vulnerability The potential for loss or the capacity to suffer harm from a hazard event.

Hazards measurement entails a suite of models, methods, and tools used to assess what makes people and places vulnerable to environmental threats, including the source and physical characteristics of environmental threats, and an evaluation of their impacts on society over time and across space.

The Origin of Environmental Hazards

Environmental hazards are threats to people and the things we value. They have many different origins, yet we normally think of hazards as occurring as a consequence of the interaction between natural systems, technological systems, and human systems. As such, we often classify hazards according to their causal agents—natural events that are infrequent (earthquakes and hurricanes) and relatively common (blizzards and coastal erosion), technological events (extreme and common events such as nuclear power plant accidents or chemical spills), social disruptions (terrorism, riots, and warfare), biological agents or biohazards (epidemics, infestations, and bioterrorism), and chronic and global significant hazards (climate change, pollution, and environmental degradation) (Table I).

Hazard Identification

The identification of hazards poses real challenges because we discover new sources of threats on a daily basis. For example, the rediscovery of anthrax as a biological hazard came to light only after the terrorist attacks of September 11, 2001, despite its longevity as a known hazard to the agricultural community. Likewise, a recent federal survey of streams found trace amounts of antibiotics, steroidal compounds, nonprescription drugs, and disinfectants, all of which are found in consumer products. This prompted the Food and Drug Administration (which approves these products for human and animal use) to begin thinking about the adverse environmental impact of these substances after they have been excreted from the body (human and animal), thus identifying yet another hazard in the environment.

Two methods are primarily used to identify risks and hazards: quantitative risk assessment, a procedure used to identify human health risks from involuntary exposures to hazardous substances; and environmental indicators, which monitor ecosystem diversity and

Table I Origins of Environmental Hazards

Causal agent	*Example*
Natural hazards	
Hydrologic	Drought, floods, flash floods
Atmospheric	Hurricanes (cyclones), tropical storms, tornadoes, severe storms, temperature extremes, lightning
Seismic	Earthquakes, volcanic eruptions, tsunamis
Geomorphic	Landslides, mass movements, avalanches, soil subsidence, rockfalls
Other	Wildfires
Biological agents	
Epidemics	Influenza, cholera, AIDS
Infestations	Locusts, termites, bees, grasshoppers
Other	Bioengineered substances, bioterrorism
Social disruptions	
Civil disorders	Ethnic violence, urban riots
Terrorism	Bombings, chemical/biological weapons, hijackings
Warfare	Conventional war, weapons of mass destruction
Technological	
Extreme Failures	Nuclear accidents, dam failures, industrial explosions
Common Occurrences	Hazardous materials spills, chemical accidents, oil spills
Chronic/globally catastrophic hazards	Pollution, environmental degradation, famine, nuclear war, global environmental change, natural resources depletion

Source: J. T. Mitchell and S. L. Cutter, 1997. Global Change and Environmental Hazards: Is the World Becoming More Disastrous?, in *Hands On! An Active Learning Module on the Human Dimensions of Global Change*. Washington D.C.: Association of American Geographers.

health. Traditionally, human health risks have been identified through disease clusters (a large number of outbreaks of illnesses in one location that exceed the random probability of such events), such as the cancer clusters found in Love Canal, NY, or Woburn, MA; epidemiological surveys that involve detailed field surveys to determine the linkage between an environmental contaminant and human disease, such as John Snow's nineteenth-century classic study of cholera in London; and bioassay data, the foundation of toxicological research, in which chemical exposures in laboratory animals determine dose-response relationships that are then extrapolated to human populations.

For environmental hazards, the most often used methods for hazard identification are surveillance and monitoring. Documenting variability in spatial and temporal patterns of environmental indicators is a first step in identifying environmental hazards. The real-time detection of seismic events anywhere in the world is now possible through the global seismic network. The development of WSR-88D Doppler radar has improved our ability to forecast and track the path of tornadoes, for example, whereas light airborne detection and ranging (LIDAR) systems are able to predict the potential extent of flooding based on digital terrain models or establish the height of the debris pile from the collapse of New York City's World Trade Center. Improvements in sensor technology and the satellites have resulted in better spatial resolution (1×1 meter) than in the past, thereby improving the remote monitoring of floods, wildfires, volcanic eruptions, snow cover, hurricanes and tropical storms, chemical releases, and nuclear accidents, among others. These systems have been instrumental in developing better forecasting information, resulting in fewer injuries and loss of life from environmental hazards.

Hazard Characteristics and Risk Characterization

Because the origins of environmental hazards are so diverse, it is difficult to compare them over time and space. However, we can use a common set of characteristics that enable us to measure the relative strength or impact of a particular hazard event and in this way compare them. Unfortunately, not all types of hazards have sufficient quantifiable measures of each of these characteristics. As a consequence, for some hazard events these characteristics are described in qualitative terminology such as large or small, strong or weak, fast or slow, whereas others have quantifiable scales. The parameters used to characterize hazards and risks are described next.

Magnitude

The sheer strength or force of an event is one characteristic that can be used to compare hazards. For earthquakes, the Richter scale, developed in 1935, provides a measure of the seismic energy released (in ergs) from an earthquake, using a logarithmic scale. The magnitude of an earthquake increases 10-fold from one Richter number to the next, so that an earthquake measured as 7.2 on the Richter scale produces 10 times more ground motion than a magnitude 6.2 earthquake, but it releases nearly 32 times more energy. The energy release best indicates the destructive power of an earthquake. The Saffir-Simpson hurricane scale (ranging from category 1 to 5) is a measure of hurricane strength based on maximum sustained winds. In the case of floods, the magnitude is simply quantified as the maximum height of floodwaters above some base elevation (mean sea level, flood stage, or above ground). Snow avalanches also have a magnitude scale ranging from 1 to 5, based on avalanche size relative to the avalanche path size. Finally, the volcanic explosivity index (VEI) provides a relative measure of the explosiveness on a 0–8 scale based on the volume of materials (tephra) released, eruption cloud heights, explosive energy, and the distance traveled by the ejecta. For example, the 1980 eruption of Mt. St. Helens is rated 5 on the VEI, whereas the 1815 Tambora, Indonesia, eruption that killed more than 92,000 people is rated 7 on the VEI.

Intensity

In addition to magnitude based solely on physical characteristics, intensity offers a metric to gauge the severity of an event based on the subjective human experience of it. The modified Mercalli scale (class I to XII) is a measure of the effects at a particular location. On the modified Mercalli scale, the intensity of earthquakes is based on magnitude, distance from the epicenter, building construction, and local geology, all of which contribute to the damage of structures and human experiences (e.g., whether they are felt by people or not). The Saffir-Simpson hurricane scale also has an intensity element within it, offering qualitative descriptions of probable property damage and potential flood levels based on anticipated storm surges. The Fujita scale of tornado intensity is another index used to measure hazard severity. Based on postevent structural-damage assessments, tornadoes are classified (with approximate wind speeds) as F0 (minimal tornado) to F5 (catastrophic and totally devastating). In the case of drought, there are quite a few drought intensity indices. The most well known in the United States is the Palmer drought severity index based on precipitation, temperature, and local availability of water in the soil (water balance) and is used to delineate abnormally wet or dry conditions. Last, the international nuclear event scale (developed in 1990 in the aftermath of the Chernobyl nuclear power plant accident) is used to distinguish accidents based on the type of release (off site vs. on site), the amount of radioactivity released, reactor damage, and potential human health and environmental impacts. The scale ranges from 0 (nonsignificant) to 7 (major accident with acute health effect and long term environmental consequences).

Frequency

This characteristic details how often an event of a given magnitude or intensity occurs. More often than not, the frequency of events is based on qualitative judgments of rare or frequent. More quantitative assessments are available in the form of recurrence intervals or frequency of occurrence (the number of events per number of years in the period of record) metrics. Flood frequency curves are generated based on the available history of discharge for a river or river stretch. For regulatory purposes involving floodplain management, a commonly used indicator for flood events is the 100-year flood. This does not mean an expectation of one large flood every 100 years (a common misperception) but rather signifies a 1% chance of a flood with this specific discharge occurring in any given year. Snow avalanche return intervals are common as well, but these are normally based on the age of trees on the avalanche path rather than some arbitrary time frame such as 100 years.

Duration

Another temporal dimension of environmental hazards describes how long the event lasts. Some hazard events have a very short duration measured in seconds to minutes (earthquakes), whereas others are prolonged events that can last years to decades (droughts). There are no specific scales or indices that depict duration.

Speed of Onset

The speed of onset provides a measure of the length of time between the first appearance of an event and its peak. Hazards are often described as rapid-onset hazards (earthquakes and tornadoes) when they offer little or no opportunity for warnings to get people out of harm's way once the impending signals are received or slow-onset hazards (soil erosion and drought), which take a year to decades to fully develop from their initial appearance. Of course, there is the occasional extreme drought year such as the 1976–1977 drought in California, the Great Plains, and Upper Midwest, which caused more than $10 billion in direct losses.

Temporal Spacing

Some hazards events are quite random in their timing, whereas others have a distinct seasonality (hurricanes and blizzards) to them. The designation of "hazard seasons" (June 1–November 30 for Atlantic basin hurricanes, April–November for tornadoes, winter for blizzards, and summer for heat) assists in the emergency preparedness, planning, and management of these hazards.

Areal Extent

This is a measure of how much of the geographic area was affected by the hazard event and is usually described as large or small. It should not be confused with hazard zones, which are clearly demarcated areas that are high risk such as floodplains or barrier islands. Disasters normally have large areal extents, whereas a small tornado or hazardous material spill has a more localized impact (one house or one segment of a road). There are no consistent scales that empirically define the areal extent of impacts from hazards.

Spatial Dispersion

Hazards are also described and compared based on their spatial distribution. For example, at a national scale we can see some cluster of tornado touchdowns in particular regions (such as the so-called "Tornado Alley"), yet when we examine the distributions within this region, they appear to be more random. Tornadoes at smaller spatial scales may relate more to the nuances of physiography, whereas at larger scales atmospheric circulation and air masses are more likely to dictate the spatial dispersion of tornadoes. Spatial concepts (dispersion, contiguity, density, and concentration) and geographic-scale differences are useful in examining hazard events because they provide additional information on the distribution of those types of events in a given area.

Nature of Exposure

The final characteristic of hazards is less indicative of the physical characteristics of the hazard, but more oriented toward how individuals and society respond to them. Primarily using the criterion voluntary or involuntary, this dimension differentiates hazards in which there is some degree of human intervention in the level of exposure, either through locational choices (residing in a known floodplain or on a coastal barrier island), voluntary participation in certain risky activities (sky diving, smoking, and scuba diving), or consumer preferences for products (herbal supplements, organic produce, child restraints in cars, or bicycle helmets). Oftentimes, these hazards and risks are perceived as more acceptable and less frequent in their occurrence. On the other hand, risks and hazards that we are involuntarily exposed to, such as nuclear fallout, climate change, and radioactive waste disposal, produce greater societal concern to reduce their adverse impacts.

Assessment Tools and Techniques

Risk Estimation Models and Indices

The majority of risk estimation models are hazard specific, such as hurricane strike predictions or the pathway of a toxic plume. They are designed to assist in the issuance of hazard warnings to the public and in the development of protective actions to guard against potential harm. In some instances, they can be used to determine the population that is potentially exposed to the risk. As mentioned previously, the hazards field is so diverse that it is virtually impossible to identify, let alone describe, all the risk estimation models. The discussion here highlights some of the most important ones currently in use.

Dispersion Models for Hazardous Air Pollutants

Dispersion models are crude mathematical representations of the airborne transport of contaminants and the downwind concentrations. Many can accommodate multiple sources, multiple receptors, and varied timing and duration of releases. The most commonly used are the U.S. Environmental Protection Agency's (USEPA's) Industrial Source Complex (ISC) suite of models, such as the short-term version called ISCST3. For emergency managers, USEPA's Areal Locations of Hazardous Atmospheres/Computer-Aided Management of Emergency Operations (ALOHA/CAMEO) model is the most widely used air dispersion model.

Coastal Storm Surge Inundation

Areas subject to flooding in hurricanes are measured by the Sea, Lake, and Overland Surges (SLOSH) model developed by the U.S. National Weather Service. This dynamic model was initially developed to forecast real-time hurricane surges, but has proven so successful that it is now widely used for preimpact hurricane planning, including the delineation of evacuation zones.

Hurricane Strike and Wind Field Intensity

The National Hurricane Center provides forecast information on storm track, intensity, and surface winds for both tropical storms and hurricanes. Using dynamic and statistical models such as Navy Operational Global

Atmospheric Prediction System (NOGAPS) and Geophysical Fluid Dynamics Laboratory (GFDL), improvements in storm path designations have been made. At the same time, enhancements of some of the cyclone intensity models have resulted in better estimations of the wind field strengths in advance of the storm.

Tornado Risk

Tornado risks were first identified visually by people who happened to see a funnel cloud and called the local weather station or by designated tornado spotters whose job was to go out and watch the sky. With the development of Doppler radar, detection improved with the ability to identify rotation and air velocity in parent storms (mesocyclone signatures) that spawn tornadoes as well as the distinct hook-shaped feature on the radar. These improvements have increased our warning times from less than 5 minutes 20 years ago to more than 10 minutes today.

Flood Events

Flood risk models require precipitation inputs and runoff estimates. Working in tandem, both the U.S. Geological Survey (USGS) and the U.S. Weather Service provide the relevant exposure data for flood events. There are a variety of runoff-rainfall models that are used for flood hazards such as the USGS's Distributed Routing Rainfall-Runoff model (DR3M). The most widely used flood damage model is the U.S. Army Corps of Engineers's Hydrologic Engineering Center's Flood Damage Assessment model (HEC-FDA). Finally, the National Weather Service has a couple of models that examine the potentially affected downstream areas from floods caused by dam failures (DAMBRK and BREACH).

Nonpoint Source Pollution

Developed by the U.S. Department of Agriculture, the Agricultural Nonpoint Source (AGNPS) pollution suite of models is a widely used tool to predict soil erosion and nutrient loadings from agricultural watersheds. This model captures runoff, sediment, and nutrient transport (especially nitrogen and phosphorus) inputs in trying to assess surface water quality.

Seismic Risk

Seismic risks are determined either through mapping of known surface and/or subsurface faults and by estimates of ground motion. Both approaches employ historical analogs. Probability approaches that include some indicator of the likelihood of an event or the exceedence of some ground-shaking threshold are the mostly commonly used. The Federal Emergency Management Agency (FEMA) uses effective peak acceleration and effective peak velocity measures to delineate seismic risks.

Extremes of Heat and Cold

The heat index (based on temperature and humidity) provides a measure of the "felt" temperature and sends warning information to residents to reduce physical activity so as to not induce heat stroke. Its corollary, the wind chill index, is used to monitor the effect of wind on "felt" temperatures to forecast conditions that are conducive to hypothermia.

Social Consequences and Loss Estimation

There is very little consistent data on what environmental hazards cost the United States on an annual basis. This is a direct function of measurement issues. For example, there is no consistent agreement on what is meant by loss, yet the prevailing wisdom is to equate losses with costs, expenditures, and lost benefits. These can be direct or indirect, tangible or intangible. Direct losses relate to actual building damage, injury, or loss of life as a consequence of a hazard event. Some of these losses are privately insured or are reimbursed to individuals and communities by the government. Indirect losses are more difficult to measure and monitor because they are often hidden and appear much later after the initiating event. An example of indirect costs are losses incurred relating to the lack of revenue from tourism on a barrier island beach in the aftermath of a hurricane. An additional complicating factor in measuring losses is how to quantify some of the intangible losses such as loss of life or debilitating injuries caused by an environmental hazard. There are no uniform standards or criteria for these, so loss estimations from environmental hazards events often are more an art than a science.

A number of models are currently in use to assess direct losses from natural hazards. These tools are specific to the type of loss (direct economic or environmental) and scale (individual structure, county, or region). Private-sector approaches examine direct losses through financial risk assessments based on probabilistic models of event frequency and magnitude and potential property exposure. Reinsurance companies use financial risk assessment models as well, but these are usually based on worst-case scenarios, which are then used to set the premiums charged to insurance companies.

Hazards US

FEMA has developed a tool, called Hazards US (HAZUS), that forecasts damage estimates and economic impacts from earthquakes at the local level. Using a scenario earthquake, HAZUS incorporates the physical characteristics of the event coupled with building inventory, infrastructure, and population data. This tool is quite effective in providing loss estimates at a variety of geographic units for earthquake-induced damages throughout the country. Recently, a wind module and a flood module were added so that the top three natural hazards (earthquakes, floods, and hurricanes) are now part of the multi-hazard assessment tool.

Ecological Risk Assessments

Ecological risk assessments provide a quantitative estimate of ecosystems or species damage due to toxic chemical contamination. Similar to human health risk assessments, ecological risk assessments normally focus on a single contaminant at a time and on a single species. However, the use of multiple stressors (contaminants), end points (type of damage), and scales (species to ecosystem) is beginning to take hold.

Geographical Information Systems

Geographical information systems (GIS) is a computer-based tool that enables the integration of disparate data (topography, infrastructure, hazard zones, population, and surveillance data) in order to analyze, model, and map information. In this regard, GIS offers the capability to manage, store, and analyze large volumes of data within a specific geographic setting. These data can contribute to loss-estimation modeling, help determine the potential population at risk, or be used in preimpact planning and mitigation efforts. GIS is widely used throughout the U.S. federal agencies involved in hazards measurement and monitoring.

Data Caveats

There are many federal, state, and local agencies as well as the private-sector organizations that collect and disseminate data on hazard events and losses. The methods used vary widely, as do the definitions of losses. The temporal and geographic coverage is equally variable, rendering much of these data incompatible with one another. For example, FEMA compiles statistics on presidential disaster declarations, but does not archive hazard event or economic loss data that do not qualify for that designation. Similarly, flood event and loss data are compiled by three different federal agencies (USGS, National Weather Service, and the U.S. Army Corps of Engineers) for very different purposes, yet are rarely shared or reconciled. Natural hazards are cataloged differently than technological hazards. Private insurance companies compile insured loss data, but what about uninsured losses? Access to data is limited (especially in the private sector) and is increasingly becoming more so. Along with issues of accuracy, precision, incompatibility, and dissemination come concern about data maintenance and archiving. It is often not in the purview of a mission agency to warehouse historical data on hazard events. The result is fragmented and incomplete data on hazard events, their characteristics, and the losses incurred from them. Thus, the measurement of hazards poses significant challenges for the future and until such time as there is a national clearinghouse for such data, the United States will continue to underestimate the true extent of the annual costs of hazards to this country.

See Also the Following Articles

Geographic Information Systems • Remote Sensing • Risk and Needs Assessments

Further Reading

Cutter, S. L. (1993). *Living with Risk.* Edward Arnold, London.

Cutter, S. L. (ed.) (2001). *American Hazardscapes: The Regionalization of Hazards and Disasters.* Joseph Henry Press, Washington, DC.

Federal Emergency Management Agency (FEMA). (1997). *Multi Hazard Identification and Risk Assessment.* Government Printing Office, Washington, DC.

Heinz Center for Science, Economic, and the Environment. (2000). *The Hidden Costs of Coastal Hazards: Implications for Risk Assessment and Mitigation.* Island Press, Covello, CA.

Jensen, J. R. (2000). *Remote Sensing of the Environment: An Earth Resource Perspective.* Prentice-Hall, Upper Saddle River, NJ.

Kunreuther, H., and Roth, R. J., Sr. (eds.) (1998). *Paying the Price: The Status and Role of Insurance against Natural Disasters in the United States.* Joseph Henry Press, Washington, DC.

Monmonier, M. (1997). *Cartographies of Danger: Mapping Hazards in America.* University of Chicago Press, Chicago, IL.

Mitchell, J. T., and Cutter, S. L. (1997). Global change and environmental hazards: Is the world becoming more disastrous? *Hands On! An Active Learning Module on the Human Dimensions of Global Change* (ed.) Association of American Geographers, Washington, DC.

National Research Council. (1999). *Reducing Disaster Losses through Better Information.* National Academy Press, Washington, DC.

National Research Council. (1999). *The Impacts of Natural Disasters: Framework for Loss Estimation.* National Academy Press, Washington, DC.

National Research Council. (2000). *Ecological Indicators for the Nation.* National Academy Press, Washington, DC.

National Research Council. (2000). *Risk Analysis and Uncertainty in Flood Damage Reduction Studies.* National Academy Press, Washington, DC.

Platt, R. H. (1999). *Disasters and Democracy. The Politics of Extreme Natural Events.* Island Press, Washington, DC.

White, G. F. (1994). A perspective on reducing losses from natural hazards. *Bull. Am. Meteorol. Soc.* **75,** 1237–1240.

Heuristics

Michael D. Mumford
University of Oklahoma, Norman, Oklahoma, USA

Lyle E. Leritz
University of Oklahoma, Norman, Oklahoma, USA

Glossary

correlation A measure of the strength of the relationship between two measures.

divergent thinking tests Open-ended problem-solving tasks in which people are asked to generate multiple solutions.

domain An area of work or task performance involving a shared body of knowledge and skills.

heuristics Strategies for executing the processing of operations involved in complex problem solving.

ill-defined problems Situations in which the goals are unclear and multiple paths to problem solutions are available.

problem construction The cognitive process involved in structuring, or defining, the problem to be solved.

processes Major cognitive operations that must be executed during problem solving.

scenario A written description of a problem and its setting.

think aloud A procedure for analyzing problem solving based on verbalizations during task performance.

The strategies people use to solve complex problems are commonly referred to as heuristics. The particular heuristics people apply in problem-solving, and the effectiveness with which they execute these heuristics, represent critical influences on performance in a variety of settings. In the present article, the procedures used to identify the heuristics involved in performance and the procedures used to measure the effectiveness of heuristic application are examined.

Introduction

History

The term "heuristics" was first applied in the social sciences some 50 years ago. Initially, this term was used to refer to the strategies people employed to reduce the cognitive demand associated with certain decision-making tasks. These strategies involved, for example, "satisficing," which refers to peoples' tendency to use readily available representations as a basis for framing decision tasks. "Means-end analysis" was the term coined to describe a strategy whereby people work backward from a given goal using trial and error to identify the operations needed for problem solving.

As interest grew in problem-solving, planning, and decision-making on the complex, ill-defined cognitive tasks encountered in the real-world (such as planning the Olympic games, creating a new aircraft, or selecting an investment portfolio), it became apparent that multiple solution paths exist that might lead to successful performance. Alternative solution paths, often paths in which simplification proves useful, allow for multiple alternative strategies that might contribute to performance. Accordingly, the concept of heuristics was expanded, and the term is now commonly used to describe both effective and ineffective strategies people apply in executing complex cognitive processing operations, although some scholars prefer to limit use of this term to strategies that simplify complex cognitive operations.

Illustrations and Applications

The shift in conceptualization of cognitive processing has led to a new wave of research intended to identify the various heuristics linked to good and poor performance on different kinds of complex cognitive tasks. In one study along these lines, there was an attempt to identify the heuristics related to performance when people are gathering information for use in creative problem-solving. It was found that better performance was observed on creative problem-solving tasks when people searched for key facts and anomalies rather than for a wide array of information. In another study along these lines, the researchers sought to identify the heuristics contributing to performance on managerial planning tasks. They found that performance improved when plans were structured around a limited number of key causes—specifically, key causes under ready managerial control. These illustrations of recent research are noteworthy in part because they illustrate one reason why social scientists are interested in heuristics. By identifying the heuristics associated with good and poor performance, it becomes possible to identify the kind of interventions that might be used to improve performance. In fact, studies of heuristics have provided a basis for job redesign efforts, software development, reconfiguration of control systems, and the design of new educational curriculum. Moreover, studies of heuristics have provided a new way for looking at, and assessing, complex cognitive skills.

Although few would dispute the importance of these practical applications, studies of heuristics have proved even more important for theoretical work. Studies of heuristics have not only allowed validation of models of complex processing operations, they have allowed social scientists to specify how various processes are executed in certain performance domains. Indeed, many advances in theories of problem-solving, decision-making, and planning can be traced to identification of heuristics associated with more or less effective execution of certain key cognitive processes.

Objective

Despite the theoretical importance of heuristics, the practical implications of studies of heuristics beg a question: How is it possible to go about identifying relevant heuristics and measuring their application? The intent here is to examine the relative strengths and weaknesses of the various approaches that have been used to identify, and measure, the heuristics people apply to tasks calling for complex cognitive processing activities. More specifically, three general approaches that have been applied are examined: observational, experimental, and psychometric. In examining the methods applied in each of these three approaches, there is no attempt to provide a comprehensive review of all pertinent studies. Instead, the general approach is described and illustrated through select example studies.

Observational Methods

Naturalistic Observations

Although they are not commonly used to assess differential effectiveness, naturalistic observations are used to identify the heuristics people apply as they work on real-world problems, primarily complex problems in which performance unfolds over a long period of time. Investigator observations represent one of the more frequently used observational techniques. In one example of how this technique has been applied in studies of heuristics, research meetings in six microbiology laboratories varying in productivity were recorded. The video and audio recordings, along with relevant documents and notes, were then analyzed for content indicative of select cognitive operations identified in prior research. This content analysis, focusing on problem-solving behaviors, led to the identification of a number of heuristics that appeared to contribute to scientific problem-solving, such as a focus on explanation of inconsistent results and the application of local, or near, analogies in formulating problem solutions.

Observations require ongoing access to people working on a problem. When ongoing access cannot be obtained, naturalistic investigators commonly turn to an alternative technique for identifying heuristics, the interview. In interviews intended to identify heuristics, questions are developed that focus on the actions taken in producing a piece of work. Interviewees' recall of their activities is used to draw inferences about the heuristics being applied. For example, in one study, the interest was in the heuristics used by artists as they developed, over a period of months, pieces of work for exhibition or commission. Sixteen artists were interviewed for 1 or 2 hours on three occasions: (1) as they began work on the project, (2) midway through the project, and (3) after the project was completed. A structured interview format was applied such that these artists were asked to describe the specific actions they took during each phase of work on the project. A content analysis of the resulting interview data indicated that, during idea development, artists were not concerned simply with expression. Instead, they structured ideas, expanded initial ideas, and restructured these ideas before they began work on the piece.

In contrast to direct observations, studies seeking to identify the heuristics applied to complex real-world tasks have, from time to time, used an indirect observational approach based on analysis of historic records. Use of record-based approaches has been most common in studies of scientists, engineers, musicians, and writers, who work in fields in which a substantial body of written material (e.g., articles, drafts, notes) is typically produced. Content analysis of this material, especially analysis of changes in peoples' strategies over time as they move toward completion of a project, is used to draw inferences about the heuristics involved in the work. One illustration of this approach involved an historic analysis of the heuristics used by Bell and Edison in their attempts to develop the first working telephone. Although the need for a sizable body of records tracking progress on a project has limited application of this technique to select fields, the widespread use of computers may, in the future, permit application of historic techniques in a wider range of domains.

Structured Observations

All unstructured observational techniques suffer, to some extent, from the problem of selective information presentation in the presence, or assumed presence, of observers. However, a more critical problem lies in the fact that these techniques do not capture data about heuristics that remain unarticulated. To address this problem, many researchers have come to rely on "think-aloud" protocols. In this technique, people are asked to verbalize, or think aloud, as they work on a cognitive task. Transcripts, or recordings, of these verbalizations are obtained. Heuristics are identified through a content analysis focusing on verbalizations about strategy selection, justifications for the actions being taken, and the sequences of actions described. This approach has been used to identify the heuristics used by anesthesiologists planning medical operations and to identify the heuristics used by students working on creative problem-solving tasks.

The widespread use of think-aloud procedures in heuristic identification may be traced to three advantageous characteristics of this technique. First, protocols can be obtained for people who presumably are more or less skilled with respect to the application of relevant heuristics—experts versus novices, successful versus unsuccessful problem solvers, and gifted versus nongifted students. Comparison of these groups, of course, allows relatively unambiguous identification of the heuristics associated with good and poor performance. Moreover, vis-à-vis careful structuring of the conditions of task performance, situational factors moderating heuristic application can be identified. Second, because all groups are exposed to a common task, or set of tasks, controlled inferences about heuristic application are possible. Third, content coding schemes can be tailored to specific actions on a known set of problems, thereby enhancing the reliability and validity of assessments.

Although these observations recommend the application of think-aloud procedures in identifying heuristics, this technique does have limitations. Due to the nature of verbalization techniques, it is difficult to apply this approach to highly complex real-world tasks, especially tasks for which performance unfolds over substantial periods of time. Moreover, unless multiple, carefully selected, stimulus tasks are applied, the generality of the conclusions flowing from application of this technique are open to question. Along related lines, it is difficult to collect protocol information for a large number of people, a characteristic of the technique that limits power and population inferences. Finally, due to the complexity of the material obtained, it is difficult to apply this technique in appraising differences among people in the effectiveness of heuristic application.

Scenario-based measures represent an alternative technique used to examine the effectiveness of heuristic application. Scenario assessments present people with written descriptions of a complex real-world cognitive task. Subsequently, people are asked to respond, in writing, to a series of questions about the kinds of actions they would take to address the problem broached in a scenario. The questions asked following a scenario are intended to elicit the exhibition of certain heuristics. Judges' evaluations of either the nature, or effectiveness, of heuristic application provide a basis for assessment.

One illustration of the scenario technique may be found in a study in which 1818 army officers were presented with a set of military planning scenarios calling for creative problem-solving. Subsequently, these officers were asked to provide short answers, in writing, to a series of questions intended to elicit heuristic application. Questions asked, for example, what information should be gathered in planning an invasion, or what would be key problems once the invasion began. Judges' evaluations of responses to these questions with respect to the effective application of the relevant heuristics produced interrater agreement coefficients near 0.70. More centrally, these measures of heuristic application were found to yield multiple correlations in the 0.40s when used to predict various measures of on-the-job performance.

Experimental Methods

Experimental techniques are used in both the identification of heuristics and the assessments of heuristic application. Experimental techniques base identification and assessment of heuristics on observable performances on a particular task or set of tasks. Four general kinds of tasks are commonly applied in studies of heuristics based on the experimental approach: optimization tasks, choice tasks, skill acquisition tasks, and simulation/gaming tasks.

Optimization Tasks

The basic principle underlying optimization tasks is that departures from an optimal standard can be used to appraise the heuristics associated with sub par performance. Some studies apply a variation on this approach whereby departures from a theoretical minimum are used to identify the heuristics that contribute to performance. Accordingly, application of this approach, an approach commonly applied in studies of decision-making heuristics, is contingent on the feasibility of determining theoretical minimums and maximums.

One illustration of this approach may be found in a study that used computational modeling to define best and worst possible performance on a medical diagnosis task. The maximum possible performance was specified using statistical decision theory. The worst possible performance was defined based on a randomization model. Six heuristics involved in medial diagnosis were examined. It was found that performance approached the statistical optimum when a schema, or principle-based search, was applied in information acquisition, and multiple hypotheses were generated concerning the cause of the illness.

Of course, when optimization techniques are applied, the kind of heuristics identified will depend on the standards, either minimum or maximum, being used as benchmarks. Heuristics associated with suboptimal performance, biases, or errors will be identified when maximum standards are applied. Heuristics contributing to enhanced performance will be identified when minimum standards are applied. Though the referencing of heuristics against *a priori* theoretical standards is an attractive feature of this approach, the conclusions drawn in optimization studies will depend on the validity of the minimums and/or maximums applied. As a result, when strong *a priori* theory cannot be used to define applicable standards, it will prove difficult to apply this approach.

Choice Tasks

Choice tasks, in contrast to optimization tasks, apply relative, rather than absolute, standards to measure heuristics. More specifically, choice tasks measure heuristics by examining preferences for applying one heuristic over another as people work on certain cognitive tasks. Assessment is based on the assumption that people will use preferred heuristics in performing both the task at hand and in performing other tasks lying in the same domain. As a result, use of this approach typically requires prior identification of relevant heuristics. It is applied when the concern at hand is identifying more or less useful heuristics. When these conditions are met, however, the ability to link heuristic preferences to performance on a variety of tasks makes this approach an attractive vehicle for assessing heuristic application.

This approach has been used to assess the heuristics involved in problem construction, a processing operation commonly held to play a key role in creative problem-solving. In one study, people were presented with a short written description of four scenarios in which the problem at hand could be defined in a number of different ways. People were to review 16 alternative problem definitions and were asked to select the best four definitions under conditions in which these alternatives were structured to reflect the tendency to define problems in terms of (a) goals, (b) procedures, (c) restrictions, and (d) key information. It was found that most people tended to define problems in terms of key information. However, performance on two complex creative problem-solving tasks was related to a preference for defining problems in terms of procedures and restrictions. Thus, people apparently preferred to use a heuristic that was not one of those contributing to subsequent performance.

Skill Acquisition Tasks

When prior research has provided strong theory concerning the heuristics underlying performance, an alternative to choice tasks may be found in skill acquisition tasks. The assumption underlying the skill acquisition approach is that differences among people in heuristic application can be induced through training. Thus, this approach is applied when heuristics can be developed, typically through relatively short-term interventions. Subsequent comparison of trained and untrained groups with respect to performance on one or more transfer tasks provides the basis for identifying the heuristics contributing to performance.

This approach was used to examine three heuristics held to be involved in creative problem-solving: (1) a hierarchical heuristic whereby ideas are generated by looking for communalities among concepts, (2) a brainstorming heuristic whereby performance is held to depend on generation of many ideas, and (3) a changing perspectives heuristic whereby ideas are generated by considering the views of others. Undergraduates were trained in the application of one of these heuristics, and their ability to generate novel solutions to a roommate interaction problem was assessed. It was found that the hierarchical heuristic resulted in significantly better solutions on this creative problem-solving task as compared to the brainstorming and changing-perspectives heuristics.

Not only can skill acquisition tasks be used to identify the heuristics contributing to performance, variations of this approach can be used to assess the effectiveness of heuristic application. For example, in one study, people were trained in the application of various heuristics involved in the processing activities required for creative problem-solving. The rate of heuristic application and the knowledge about relevant heuristics were assessed. It was found that these measures evidenced adequate validity in performance prediction, suggesting that learning may at times provide a basis for assessing heuristic application.

Simulations/Gaming Tasks

The fourth, and final, experimental procedure used in the identification and assessment of heuristics is simulation or gaming. In simulation and gaming exercises, heuristics are identified and measured through the choices people make as they work on the exercise. In one study, a record was kept of operating decisions and requests for information as managers worked on a simulation exercise intended to model the operations of a small manufacturing company. It was found that the level of profits, a criterion measured through quarterly profits, was associated with a smaller number of decisions and a tendency to focus decision-making on a limited number of key issues linked to efficiency considerations.

Though simulations and gaming exercises provide an appealing tool for identifying and measuring heuristics, three points should be borne in mind when applying this approach. First, simulation and gaming exercises will prove useful only if decision and action metrics are formulated in such a way that they capture relevant heuristics. Second, the validity of the resulting assessments will depend on these metrics as much as the apparent realism of the exercise. Third, when these exercises are applied, some attempt should be made to control for gaming heuristics, i.e., heuristics specific to the exercise that are not relevant to the general form of task performance.

Psychometric Methods

In the psychometric approach, heuristics are identified and assessed with respect to people, and the performance differences observed among people, rather than with respect to the particular actions observed for a given set of tasks. This point is of some importance because the psychometric approach tends to emphasize heuristics associated with performance differences, discounting heuristics that are applied in a similar fashion by all individuals. To elicit these individual differences, psychometric studies rely on one of two basic techniques: self-report and tests.

Self-Report

One version of the self-report approach assumes that people are aware of, and understand the implications of, the strategies they apply as they execute tasks lying in different domains. Of course, given this assumption, it is possible to identify heuristics simply by asking people about the heuristics they apply in different endeavors. In accordance with this proposition, in one study, undergraduates were asked to indicate whether they applied heuristics such as visualization, step-by-step analysis, and analogies when working on interpersonal, academic, or daily life tasks. It was found that people could describe where, and how frequently, they applied these general heuristics. This direct reporting approach, however, has proved less effective when specific heuristics, particularly heuristics applied nearly automatically, are under consideration.

When it is open to question whether people can say when, and how, they apply heuristics, an alternative strategy is often used. In an approach referred to as the critical-incidents technique, people are not asked to report on strategies applied. Instead, they are asked to indicate the behaviors they exhibited when performing certain tasks. Specifically, they are asked to describe the setting, the event prompting performance, the actions taken in response to the event, and the outcomes of these actions. Content analysis comparing good and poor performers, or good and poor performances, is used to identify more or less effective performance strategies and the behaviors associated with application of these strategies. Assessment occurs by having people indicate either the frequency or extent to which they manifest behaviors associated with an identified heuristic.

Testing

In testing, people are not asked to describe heuristics or the behaviors associated with these heuristics. Instead, the capability for applying heuristics is inferred based on peoples' responses to a series of test items. In one variation on this approach, the objective scoring approach, test items are developed such that the problems presented call for certain processing activities. Response options are structured to capture the application of heuristics linked to effective process application. In one study, test items were developed to measure selective encoding, selective comparison, and selective combination. It was found that gifted students differed from nongifted students in that they were better able to identify relevant information (selective encoding).

In the subjective scoring approach, problems (typically open-ended problems) are developed in a way that a variety of responses might be used to address the problem. Judges are then asked to review peoples' responses and assess the extent to which they reflect the application of certain heuristics. This approach is applied in scoring the divergent thinking tests commonly used to measure creativity by having judges evaluate responses with respect to three creative strategies: generating a number of ideas (fluency), generating unusual ideas (originality), and generating ideas through the use of multiple concepts (flexibility). In another illustration of this approach, army officers were asked to list the changes in peoples' lives that might happen if certain events occurred (e.g., What would happen if the sea level rose?). Judges scored these responses for heuristics such as use of a longer time frame, application of principles, and a focus on positive versus negative consequences. Use of longer time frames and application of principles were found to be related to both performance on managerial problem-solving tasks and indices of real-world leader performance, yielding multiple correlations in the 0.40s.

Conclusions

Clearly, a variety of procedures have been developed for identification and assessment of the heuristics people use in working on complex, ill-defined problems. Moreover, these procedures have proved useful in identifying heuristics, and measuring heuristic application, across a number of performance domains calling for complex cognition. What should be recognized, however, is that all of these approaches evidence certain strengths and weaknesses. The observational approach has typically proved most useful in heuristic identification. Experimental and psychometric methods are more commonly used to identify the impact of heuristics on performance and measure individual differences in heuristic application. Along similar lines, certain techniques subsumed under these three basic methods appear, by virtue of their assumptions, more appropriate than are others for addressing some questions, and measuring some heuristics. These observations are of some importance because they suggest that a comprehensive understanding of the heuristics involved in a certain type of performance will require a multimethod, multitechnique approach.

Although the kind of multimethod, multitechnique studies called for are not a simple undertaking, the evidence indicates that work along these lines will be worth the time and effort. Not only has identification of the heuristics involved in high-level cognitive performance proved critical in theory development, the information provided by these studies has provided new tools for developing and assessing peoples' performance capacities. Given the foundation of human performance in complex cognitive activities such as planning, decision making, and creative problem-solving, it can be expected that heuristic measurement will become an increasingly important aspect of social measurement over the course of the 21st century.

See Also the Following Articles

Intelligence Testing • Problem-Solving Methodologies • Psychological Testing, Overview

Further Reading

Antonietti, A., Ignazi, S., and Perego, P. (2000). Metacognitive knowledge about problem-solving methods. *Br. J. Educat. Psychol.* **70,** 1–16.

Badke-Schaub, P., and Strohschneider, S. (1998). Complex problem solving in the cultural context. *Travail Humain* **61,** 1–28.

Butler, D. L., and Kline, M. A. (1998). Good versus creative solutions: A comparison of brainstorming, hierarchical, and perspective-changing heuristics. *Creativ. Res. J.* **11,** 325–331.

Carlson, W. B., and Gorman, M. E. (1992). A cognitive framework to understand technological creativity: Bell, Edison, and the telephone. In *Inventive Minds: Creativity in Technology* (R. J. Sternberg and D. N. Perkins, eds.), pp. 48–79. Oxford University Press, New York.

Davidson, J. E., and Sternberg, R. J. (1984). The role of insight in intellectual giftedness. *Gifted Child Q.* **28,** 58–64.

Dunbar, K. (1985). How scientists really reason: Scientific reasoning in real-world laboratories. In *The Nature of Insight* (R. J. Sternberg and J. E. Davidson, eds.), pp. 365–396. MIT Press, Cambridge, Massachusetts.

Ericsson, K. A., and Simon, H. A. (1984). *Protocol Analysis: Verbal Reports as Data.* MIT Press, Cambridge, Massachusetts.

Hogarth, R. M., and Makridakis, S. (1981). Forecasting and planning: An evaluation. *Mgmt. Sci.* **27,** 115–138.

Jausovec, N. (1991). Flexible strategy use: A characteristic of creative problem-solving. *Creativ. Res. J.* **4,** 349–366.

Kleimuntz, D. N. (1985). Cognitive heuristics and feedback in a dynamic decision environment. *Mgmt. Sci.* **31,** 680–702.

Mace, M. A., and Ward, T. (2002). Modeling the creative process: A grounded theory analysis of creativity in the domain of art making. *Creativ. Res. J.* **14,** 179–192.

Morse, L. W., and Morse, D. T. (1995). The influence of problem-solving strategies and previous training on performance of convergent and divergent thinking. *J. Instruct. Psychol.* **22,** 341–348.

Mumford, M. D., Baugman, W. A., and Sager, C. E. (2003). Picking the right material: Cognitive processing skills and their role in creative thought. In *Critical Creative Thinking* (M. A. Runco, ed.), pp. 19–68. Hampton, Cresskill, New Jersey.

Mumford, M. D., Baughman, W. A., Supinski, E. P., and Maher, M. A. (1996). Process-based measures of creative problem-solving skills: II. Information encoding. *Creativ. Res. J.* **9,** 77–88.

Mumford, M. D., Baughman, W. A., Threfall, K. V., Supinski, E. P., and Costanza, D. P. (1996). Process-based measures of creative problem-solving skills: I. Problem construction. *Creativ. Res. J.* **9,** 63–76.

Mumford, M. D., Marks, M. A., Connelly, M. S., Zaccaro, S. J., and Johnson, J. F. (1998). Domain based scoring of divergent thinking tests: Validation evidence in an occupational sample. *Creativ. Res. J.* **11,** 151–164.

Thomas, J. B., and McDaniel, R. R. (1990). Interpreting strategic issues: Effects of strategy and the information processing structure of top management. *Acad. Mgmt. J.* **33,** 286–306.

Xiao, Y., Milgram, P., and Doyle, D. J. (1997). Planning behavior and its functional role in interactions with complex systems. *IEEE Trans. Syst. Man Cybernet.* **27,** 313–325.

Zaccaro, S. J., Mumford, M. D., Connelly, M. S., Marks, M. A., and Gilbert, J. A. (2000). Leader skill assessment: Measures and methods. *Leadership Q.* **11,** 37–64.

Hierarchical Linear Models

Jeff Gill
University of Florida, Gainesville, Florida, USA

Glossary

analysis of covariance model (ANCOVA) A varying intercept hierarchical linear model with the second-level effect fixed across groups.

between-unit model The component of a hierarchical linear model that describes the variability across the groups.

context-level variables Variables defined at the second or higher level of the hierarchical linear model.

empirical Bayes Using the observed data to estimate terminal-level hierarchical model parameters.

exchangeability The property of a hierarchical linear model that the joint probability distribution is not changed by re-ordering the data values.

expectation-maximization (EM) algorithm An iterative procedure for computing modal quantities when the data are incomplete.

fixed effects coefficients Model coefficients that are assumed to pertain to the entire population and therefore do not need to be distinguished by subgroups.

hierarchy The structure of data that identifies units and subunits in the form of nesting.

interaction term A model specification term that applies to some mathematical composite of explanatory variables, usually a product.

random coefficients regression model A hierarchical linear model in which the only specified effect from the second level is seen through error terms.

random effects coefficients Model coefficients that are specified to differ by subgroups and are treated probabilistically at the next highest level of the model.

two-level model A hierarchical linear model that specifies a group level and a single contextual level.

varying intercept model A hierarchical linear model with only one (noninteractive) effect from the second level of the model.

within-unit model The component of a hierarchical linear model that describes variability confined to individual groups.

Hierarchical linear models (HLMs) are statistical specifications that explicitly recognize multiple levels in data. Because explanatory variables can be measured at different points of aggregation, it is often important to structure inferences that specifically identify multilevel relationships. In the classic example, student achievement can be measured at multiple levels: individually, by class, by school, by district, by state, or nationally. This is not just an issue of clarity and organization. If there exist differing effects by level, then the substantive interpretation of the coefficients will be wrong if levels are ignored. HLMs take the standard linear model specification and remove the restriction that the estimated coefficients be constant across individual cases by specifying levels of additional effects to be estimated. This approach is also called random effects modeling because the regression coefficients are now presumed to be random quantities according to additionally specified distributions.

Essential Description of Hierarchical Linear Models

The development hierarchical linear model (HLM) starts with a simple bivariate linear regression specification for individual i:

$$Y_i = \beta_0 + \beta_1 X_i + \varepsilon_i \tag{1}$$

which relates the outcome variable to the systematic component and the error term. The standard conditions for this model include the Gauss-Markov assumptions (linear functional form, independent errors with mean zero and constant variance, and no relationship between regressor and errors), and normality of the errors (provided reasonable sample size): $\varepsilon_i \sim \mathcal{N}(0, \sigma^2)$.

Suppose, for example, that we are interested in measuring university student evaluations of faculty teaching through the standard end-of-semester survey. Then the outcome variable, Y_i, is considered the mean score for instructor i for a given class, recorded along with the explanatory variable, X_i, indicating years of teaching experience. In this example setup, the intercept, β_0, is the expected score for a new instructor. Now, consider that this analysis is temporarily taking place only in department j. This means that Eq. (1) becomes:

$$Y_{ij} = \beta_{j0} + \beta_{j1}X_{ij} + \varepsilon_{ij} \tag{2}$$

There is no substantive change here; for the moment, the j coefficient is just a placeholder to remind us that we are studying only the jth department so far.

Now consider broadening the analysis to evaluate student evaluations of teaching across the entire university by looking at multiple departments. Although we expect some differences, it would be rare to find that there was no underlying commonality among the instructors. A more realistic idea is that, although each instructor has idiosyncratic characteristics, because he or she is teaching at the same university at the same point in time and being evaluated by the same student body there is a common distribution from which β_0 and β_1 are drawn. Actually, it would be unfair and inaccurate to calculate these means across all undergraduate majors at the university. It is well known, for instance, that sociology departments enjoy higher mean student evaluations than chemistry departments. So, now add a second level to the model that explicitly nests instructors within departments and index these departments by $j = 1$ to J:

$$\begin{aligned} \beta_{j0} &= \gamma_{00} + \gamma_{10}Z_{j0} + u_{j0} \\ \beta_{j1} &= \gamma_{01} + \gamma_{11}Z_{j1} + u_{j1} \end{aligned} \tag{3}$$

where all individual level variation is assigned to departments producing department-level residuals: u_{j0} and u_{j1}. The variables at this level are called context-level variables, and contextual specificity is the existence of legitimately comparable groups. Here, the example explanatory variables Z_{j0} and Z_{j1} are the average class size for department j and the average annual research output per faculty member in department j, respectively. Note that if we were interested in performing two nonhierarchical department-level analyses, this would be straightforward using these two equations, provided that the data exist. Of course, our interest here is not in developing separate single-level models; the two-level model is produced by inserting the department-level specifications, Eq. (3), into the original expression for instructor evaluations, Eq. (2). Performing this substitution and rearranging produces:

$$\begin{aligned} Y_{ij} &= (\gamma_{00} + \gamma_{10}Z_{j0} + u_{j0}) + (\gamma_{01} + \gamma_{11}Z_{j1} + u_{j1})X_{ij} + \varepsilon_{ij} \\ &= \gamma_{00} + \gamma_{01}X_{ij} + \gamma_{10}Z_{j0} + \gamma_{11}X_{ij}Z_{j1} + u_{j1}X_{ij} + u_{j0} + \varepsilon_{ij} \end{aligned} \tag{4}$$

This equation also shows that the composite error structure, $u_{j1}X_{ij} + u_{j0} + \varepsilon_{ij}$, is now clearly heteroscedastic because it is conditioned on levels of the explanatory variable. Unless the corresponding variance-covariance matrix is known, and therefore incorporated as weights in the general linear model, it must also be estimated. Ignoring this effect and calculating with ordinary least squares (OLS) produces consistent estimators but incorrect standard errors because it is equivalent to assuming zero intraclass correlation.

Often the first-level expression describing the performance of instructor i in a given department, as specified by Eq. (2), is labeled the within-unit model because its effects are confined to the single department; the second-level expressions describing the performance of department j as a whole, as specified by Eq. (3), are labeled the between-unit model because they describe the variability across the departments. Looking closely at Eq. (4) reveals that there are three distinct implications of the effects of the coefficients for the explanatory variables:

γ_{01} gives the slope coefficient for a one-unit effect of teacher experience in department j. This slope varies by department.

γ_{10} gives the slope coefficient for a one-unit change in department class size in department j, completely independent of individual teacher effects in that department.

γ_{11} gives the slope coefficient for the product of individual teacher experience by department and mean annual research output by department.

Because this set of variables contains both fixed and random effects, Eq. (4) is called a mixed model.

The fundamental characteristic of the multilevel data discussed here is that some variables are measured at an individual level and others are measured at differing levels of aggregation. This drives the need for a model such as Eq. (4) that classify variables and coefficients by the level of hierarchy they affect. Interestingly, a large proportion of HLMs in published work come from education policy studies. This is due to natural nesting of education data through the bureaucratic structure of these institutions. Other applications include studies of voting, bureaucracy, medical trials, and crime rates.

Special Cases of the Hierarchical Linear Model

There are several interesting ramifications that come from fixing various quantities in the basic HLM. The most basic is produced by setting the full β_{j1} component and the γ_{10} term in Eq. (4) equal to zero. The result is the standard ANOVA model with random effects:

$$Y_{ij} = \gamma_{00} + u_{j0} + \varepsilon_{ij} \tag{5}$$

In another basic case, if the second-level model defines a fixed-effect rather than random-effect model, (u_{j1}, $u_{j0} = \mathbf{0}$), then the resulting specification is just simple linear regression model with an interaction term between the instructor level explanatory variable and the department level explanatory variable:

$$Y_{ij} = \gamma_{00} + \gamma_{01}X_{ij} + \gamma_{10}Z_{j0} + \gamma_{11}X_{ij}Z_{j1} + \varepsilon_{ij} \tag{6}$$

This is one of the most studied enhancements of the basic linear form in the social sciences.

Another very basic model comes from assuming that the second-level model introduces no new error terms and there is also no interaction effect. Specifically, this means that we can treat the intercept term as a composite of a constant across the sample and a constant across only the j groupings:

$$Y_{ij} = (\gamma_{00} + \gamma_{10}Z_{j0}) + \gamma_{01}X_{ij} + \varepsilon_{ij} \tag{7}$$

This is routinely called a varying intercept model because the parenthetical expression is now a group-specific intercept term. If we add the second assumption that there is no articulated structure within the first term, that is, $(\gamma_{00} + \gamma_{10}Z_{j0})$ is equal to a single context-specific α_j, this is now the analysis of covariance model (ANCOVA).

Sometimes it is possible to take some specific parameter in the model and fix it at a known level. Thus, if substantive information at hand indicates that there is no variability to one of the γ terms, it is appropriate to fix it in the model. It is also possible to design a combination strategy such as to fix the slope coefficient ($\beta_{j1} = \gamma_{10} + \gamma_{11}Z_{j1}$) and let the intercept coefficient remain a random effect, or to fix the intercept coefficient ($\beta_{j0} = \gamma_{00} + \gamma_{10}Z_{j0}$) and let the slope remain a random effect.

Another common variation is to assume that $Z_{j0} = 0$ and $Z_{j1} = 0$, but retain the u_{j0} error term:

$$Y_{ij} = \gamma_{00} + \gamma_{01}X_{ij} + u_{j1}X_{ij} + u_{j0} + \varepsilon_{ij} \tag{8}$$

This model asserts that the j categorization is not important for determining the expected effect on Y_{ij}, but that there is an additional source of error from the categories. Hence, specifying the model with only one source of error is to miss a heteroscedastic effect. A specification of this type is typically called a random coefficients regression model.

Another related variation is to assume that the effect of the within-unit explanatory variable (years of teaching in our example) is uniform across departments. This is equivalent to setting $\gamma_{11}X_{ij}Z_{j1} = 0$, producing:

$$Y_{ij} = \gamma_{00} + \gamma_{01}X_{ij} + \gamma_{10}Z_{j0} + u_{j1}X_{ij} + u_{j0} + \varepsilon_{ij} \tag{9}$$

where sometimes $u_{j1}X_{ij}$ is also set to zero. The common name for this specification is the additive variance components model.

The General Structure of the Hierarchical Linear Model

The previously developed model is actually a substantial simplification in that typical models in social science research contain many more explanatory variables at both the within-unit level and the between-unit levels. It is therefore necessary to generalize HLM to incorporate more specification flexibility. First we recast Eq. (4) in matrix terms, such that the dimensional assumptions will be generalized to accommodate more useful specifications. We define a new $\boldsymbol{\beta}_j$ vector according to:

$$\boldsymbol{\beta}_j = \begin{bmatrix} \beta_{j0} \\ \beta_{j1} \end{bmatrix} = \begin{bmatrix} 1 & Z_{j0} & 0 & 0 \\ 0 & 0 & 1 & Z_{j1} \end{bmatrix} \begin{bmatrix} \gamma_{00} \\ \gamma_{10} \\ \gamma_{01} \\ \gamma_{11} \end{bmatrix} + \begin{bmatrix} u_{j0} \\ u_{j1} \end{bmatrix} \tag{10}$$

which is just the vectorized version of Eq. (3). Therefore, it is possible to express Eq. (4) in the very concise form:

$$Y_{ij} = \boldsymbol{\beta}_j'[1 \quad X_{ij}]' + \varepsilon_{ij} \tag{11}$$

This extra formalism is really not worth the effort for a model of this size; its real utility is demonstrated when there are more explanatory variables at the contextual level. Define k_0 and k_1 to be the number of explanatory variables defined at the second level for β_{j0} and β_{j1}, respectively. Thus far we have had the restrictions: $k_0 = 2$ and $k_1 = 2$; but we can now generalize this dimension:

$$\boldsymbol{\beta}_j = \begin{bmatrix} \beta_{j0} \\ \beta_{j1} \end{bmatrix} = \begin{bmatrix} 1 & Z_{j01} & Z_{j02} & \cdots & Z_{j0(k_0-1)} & 0 & 0 & 0 & \cdots & 0 \\ 0 & 0 & 0 & \cdots & 0 & 1 & Z_{j11} & Z_{j12} & \cdots & Z_{j1(k_1-1)} \end{bmatrix} \begin{bmatrix} \gamma_{00} \\ \gamma_{10} \\ \vdots \\ \gamma_{(k_0-1)0} \\ \gamma_{01} \\ \gamma_{11} \\ \vdots \\ \gamma_{(k_1-1)1} \end{bmatrix} + \begin{bmatrix} u_{j0} \\ u_{j1} \end{bmatrix} \quad (12)$$

The dimension of the matrix of Z variables is now $(2 \times k_0 + k_1)$ and the length of the $\boldsymbol{\gamma}$ vector is $k_0 + k_1$, for any specified values of k_i that are allowed to differ. It is common, and computationally convenient, to assume that the error vector, u_j, is multivariate normally distributed around zero with a given or estimated variance-covariance matrix. Note that the row specifications in the **Z** matrix always begin with a 1 for the constant, which specifies a level-one constant in the first row and a level-one restricted explanatory variable in the second row.

It is important to observe that because the constant in this model is part of the specification, the indices run to $k_0 - 1$ and $k_1 - 1$ to obtain the dimensions k_0 and k_1. Also, when there was only one Z variable specified in the second level of the model, it was sufficient to index simply by the subscripts j and either 0 or 1, as in the first and second equations of (3). However, now that there are arbitrary numbers for each second-level equation they must be further indexed by the third value—here, 1 to $k_0 - 1$ or 1 to $k_1 - 1$. Note that each group is no longer required to contain the same mix of second-level explanatory variables. This turns out to be useful in specifying many varying model specifications.

It is possible that there are also more first-level variables in the model (it is likely, in fact). To accommodate this, we must further generalize the defined matrix structures. Define the $\mathbf{Z}_\ell$ vector as

$$\mathbf{Z}_\ell = \begin{bmatrix} 1 & Z_{j\ell 1} & Z_{j\ell 2} & \cdots & Z_{j\ell(k_\ell-1)} \end{bmatrix} \quad (13)$$

for $\ell = 1$ to L coefficients in the first-level model, including the constant. Therefore the **Z** matrix is now a $(L \times L)$ diagonal matrix according to:

$$\mathbf{Z} = \begin{bmatrix} \mathbf{Z}_1 & 0 & 0 & \ldots & 0 \\ 0 & \mathbf{Z}_2 & 0 & \ldots & 0 \\ 0 & 0 & \mathbf{Z}_3 & \ldots & 0 \\ \vdots & \vdots & \vdots & \ddots & \vdots \\ 0 & 0 & 0 & \ldots & \mathbf{Z}_L \end{bmatrix} \quad (14)$$

where each diagonal value is a $\mathbf{Z}_\ell$ vector. This can also be fully written out as an irregular ℓ-diagonalized matrix, but it would be more cumbersome than the given form. Given the new for of the **Z** matrix, it is necessary to respecify the g vector as follows:

$$\boldsymbol{\gamma} = \begin{bmatrix} \boldsymbol{\gamma}_0 \\ \boldsymbol{\gamma}_1 \\ \vdots \\ \boldsymbol{\gamma}_L \end{bmatrix} \quad (15)$$

where each $\boldsymbol{\gamma}_\ell$ is a column vector whose length is determined by the k_ℓ dimension specification. Putting these new structures together gives:

$$\boldsymbol{\beta}_j = \mathbf{Z}\boldsymbol{\gamma} + \mathbf{u} \quad (16)$$

and:

$$Y_{ij} = \boldsymbol{\beta}_j' \begin{bmatrix} 1 & X_{ij1} & X_{ij2} & \ldots & X_{ijL} \end{bmatrix}' + \varepsilon_{ij} \quad (17)$$

Thus, the HLM in this form allows any number of first- and second-level explanatory variables, as well as differing combinations across contextual levels. Note also that there is no restriction that number of individual units, n_j, be equal across the contexts (although this can make the estimation process more involved).

The final basic way that the HLM can be made more general is to add further levels of hierarchy with respect to levels. That is, it is possible to specify a third level in exactly the way that the second level was added by parameterizing the $\boldsymbol{\gamma}$ terms according to:

$$\gamma_{pq} = \delta_{0q} + \delta_{1q} W_{pq} + v_{pq}$$

where the p subscript indicates a second level of contexts $(p = 1, \ldots, P)$, and the q subscript indexes the number of equations $(q = 1, \ldots, Q)$ specified at this level (analogous to k at the lower level). In this specification, W_{pq} is a third-level measured explanatory variable and v_{pq} is the level-associated error term.

Obviously, the specifications can be made very complex at this level.

The other principle approach to modeling a third level is to specify a Bayesian prior distribution for the $\boldsymbol{\gamma}$ coefficients. These priors are typically assigned normal distributions, but this is not a restriction and many others have been used. As a consequence of linearity, the normal property then ripples down the hierarchy, making estimation relatively easy. This model, then, specifies hierarchies of linear hyperpriors, each of which has its own prior plus an associated matrix of explanatory variables, and only nodes at the highest level of the hierarchy have fixed hyperprior values.

Estimation of the Hierarchical Linear Model

No matter how complex the right-hand side of the HLM equation becomes, the left-hand side always consists of Y_{ij}, which is assumed to be normal, with mean equal to the systematic component of the model and variance from the collected error terms. If it were known that the error structure in the model was uncorrelated to explanatory variables, then it would easy to estimate the coefficients with standard maximum likelihood or least squares approaches. Actually we know that, in general, the form of the errors *is* conditional on the levels of the explanatory variables because in Eq. (4) there is the term, $u_{j1}X_{ij}$. In addition, there are increasing numbers of dependencies as the model becomes progressively more complex and realistic.

If we knew for certain the form of the relationship between the regressors and errors, then it could be expressed through a weighting matrix and general least squares would provide consistent estimates of the coefficients and their standard errors. Unfortunately, this information is rarely available. The classic alternative is to specify a likelihood function and employ a maximum likelihood estimation of the full set of unknown parameters, including variances using Fisher scoring. This is often a cumbersome process, so many software implementations work with the profile likelihood—first estimating the higher order variance terms and only then fixing them in the likelihood function equation for the lower-level parameters. This tends to underestimate the magnitude of the higher-order variance terms because uncertainty is ignored in the first step, leading to overconfident model results. An improved process is to employ restricted maximum likelihood (REML) by integrating out the fixed-effects terms in the calculation of the profile likelihood and, after obtaining the lower-level parameter estimates, recalculating the higher-order variance terms conditional on these. However, the best method is the quasi-Bayesian procedure, empirical Bayes/maximum likelihood (EB/ML). A fundamental principle of Bayesianism is that unknown parameters are treated as random variables possessing their own distributions which can be estimated as a consequence of applying Bayes's law. By analogy, we can consider the unknown HLM estimates as having their own distributions, conditioned on unknown quantities from the higher level of the model. Rather than stipulating explicit priors for the parameters, as a Bayesian would do, it is possible to use a prior suggested by the data, called empirical Bayes.

The expectation-maximization (EM) algorithm is essential to this estimation process and therefore warrants some description. EM is a flexible and often-used method for incomplete data problems; it is used to fill in missing information, given a specified model. The notion of what is "missing" is general here; it can be unknown parameters, missing data, or both. There are two basic steps. First, we assign temporary data that represent a reasonable guess to the missing data (expectation). Second, we proceed with maximum likelihood estimation of the parameters as if there now existed a complete-data problem (maximization). The algorithm is iterative in the sense that it is now possible to use these parameter estimates to update the assignment of the temporary data values with better guesses, and repeat the process. It can be shown that the EM algorithm gives a series of parameter estimates that are monotonically increasing on the likelihood metric and are guaranteed to converge to a unique maximum point under very general and nonrestrictive regularity conditions. The utility here is that the HLM with linear specifications and normal assumptions is a particularly well-behaved application of EM.

Detailed summaries of the EB/ML computational procedure for obtaining coefficient estimates and measures of reliability can be found elsewhere. The basic strategy is to obtain estimates of the variance terms using the EM algorithm and the joint likelihood function for the coefficients and the variances, plug these estimates into the top hierarchy of the model, perform maximum likelihood calculations as if these were the correct weightings, and update the estimate of the coefficients by using the mean of the subsequent posterior. This is a very general description of the procedure; there are many nuances that depend on the particular form of the model and configuration of the data.

Critical Advantages of the Hierarchical Linear Model

HLMs are a compromise between two opposite approaches to clustering. On one side, it is possible to simply pool all the observations and calculate an estimate of the coefficients of interest as if the between-group effects did not matter. Conversely, it is also possible to aggregate the data by the groups and calculate the coefficient estimates on these aggregations as if they were the primary object of interest. The first approach ignores between-group variation and the second approach ignores within-group variation. It is possible that either of these approaches is entirely appropriate and reliable inferences can be obtained. Of course, if there actually are important differences by groupings, then neither will be correct. HLMs provide a method for producing models that explicitly recognize this distinction by incorporating the nesting of the data into the model specification.

HLMs also have several specific methodological advantages over standard linear models:

- Hierarchical models are ideal tools for identifying and measuring structural relationships that fall at different levels of the data generating procedure.
- Hierarchical models have virtually no limit to the dimension of their hierarchy.
- Hierarchical models directly express the exchangeability of units.
- Nonhierarchical models applied to multilevel data typically underestimate the variance.
- Hierarchical models facilitate the testing of hypotheses across different levels of analysis.
- Nonhierarchical models can be nested within hierarchical models, allowing a likelihood or Bayes factor test of the validity of the proposed hierarchical structure.

Although these reasons are compelling, it is only relatively recently that hierarchical models have been actively pursued in the social sciences. This is parallel (and related) to the attachment social scientists have for the linear model in general. What precipitated the change was the dramatic improvement in statistical computing that provided solutions to previously intractable problems. These stochastic simulation tools include the EM algorithm; Markov chain Monte Carlo techniques (MCMC), such as the Metropolis-Hastings algorithm; and the Gibbs sampler, whereby an iterative chain of consecutive computationally generated values is set up carefully enough and run long enough to produce *empirical* estimates of integral quantities of interest from later chain values. Although these approaches are typically associated with Bayesian modeling, such iteration techniques are not *limited* to Bayesian or even hierarchical applications. They do, however, greatly help naturally occurring computational problems in these settings.

See Also the Following Articles

Bayesian Statistics • Maximum Likelihood Estimation • Ordinary Least Squares (OLS)

Further Reading

Goldstein, H. (1995). *Multilevel Statistical Models.* Edward Arnold, New York.

Heck, R. H., and Thomas, S. L. (2000). *Introduction to Multilevel Modeling Techniques.* Lawrence Erlbaum Associates, Mahwah, NJ.

Kreft, I., and de Leeuw, J. (1998). *Introducing Multilevel Modeling.* Sage Publications, Newbury Park, CA.

Leyland, A. H., and Goldstein, H. (2001). *Multilevel Modelling of Health Statistics.* John Wiley & Sons, New York.

Lindley, D. V., and Smith, A. F. M. (1972). Bayes estimates for the linear model. *J. Royal Statist. Soc. B* **34,** 1–41.

Neider, J. A. (1977). A reformulation of linear models (with discussion). *J. Royal Statist. Soc. A* **140,** 48–76.

Raudenbush, S., and Bryk, A. S. (1986). A hierarchical model for studying school effects. *Sociol. Educ.* **59,** 1–17.

Raudenbush, S., and Bryk, A. S. (2002). *Hierarchical Linear Models,* 2nd Ed. Sage Publications, Newbury Park, CA.

Reise, S. P., and Duan, N. (2001). *Multilevel Models: A Special Issue of Multivariate Behavioral Research.* Lawrence Erlbaum Associates, Mahwah, NJ.

Smith, A. F. M. (1973). A general Bayesian linear model. *J. Royal Statist. Soc. B* **35,** 61–75.

Wong, G. Y., and Mason, W. M. (1991). Contextually specific effects and other generalizations of the hierarchical linear model for comparative analysis. *J. Am. Statist. Assoc.* **86,** 487–503.

Highway Statistics

Alan E. Pisarski
Independent Consultant, Falls Church, Virginia, USA

Glossary

fatality rate The measure almost universally used in the United States is fatalities per 100 million miles of travel.

functional classification An engineering classification of roads based on their function (as opposed to their design characteristics).

international roughness index (IRI) A calculation of inches of deflection from the surface per mile of road; e.g., a rating of 150 = 150 inches of ruts measured over a mile.

lane-miles The number of miles of route multiplied by the number of lanes in the road. A four-lane 10-mile road contains 40 lane-miles.

miles of route The actual length of a system; sometimes called centerline miles.

pavement serviceability rating (PSR) A subjective professional measure of road quality on a scale of 1 to 5.

person-miles of travel The travel of an individual rather than a vehicle; two people in a vehicle going 10 miles equals 20 person-miles of travel.

ton-miles of travel The number of miles traveled by trucks multiplied by the cargo weight carried. One truck carrying 10 tons traveling 10 miles = 100 ton-miles.

travel time index (TTI) One of several measures of congestion, but perhaps the most typically used, measuring the ratio of peak-hour travel to off-peak travel. A TTI of 150 indicates that a 10-minute off-peak trip takes 15 minutes in the peak time.

vehicle-miles of travel (VMT) The total travel in miles summed for all vehicles; one vehicle going 10 miles equals 10 VMT.

Highways in the United States are many things—physical engineering artifacts of our culture; economic and social tools that serve our personal and business activities, needs, and preferences; and social products that have complex consequences, both positive and negative. All of these are measurable, and it is through their measurement and description that society recognizes the roles played by the road system, appreciates the significance of the road system in daily life, and forms judgments on future transport needs and expectations. The road–vehicle dyad provides unparalleled mobility and accessibility to the American population.

Introduction

The highway is many things. Clearly, it is a physical object of considerable scope and dimension. Even if no vehicle ever traversed a highway, the description of the attributes and physical characteristics of the entire highway system, just in terms of its dimensions and design, would be a significant task. But an extraordinary variety of vehicles do use the system, and their performance, or the performance of the road serving them, is the object of a broad array of statistical mechanisms. The highway is an economic and social tool that carries prodigious quantities of people and goods to fulfill many economic and social needs; the highway is also a political tool, used to guide economic development to selected areas, to support military logistics, and to create social and economic interactions among regions to bind nations together.

As a societal artifact that interacts with the rest of the world both positively and negatively, in terms of the space it occupies, the highway is associated with deaths and accidents and has other social impacts as well. The vehicle fleet associated with the highway constitutes a world in itself, a world requiring statistical description and understanding—something akin to a demography of the automobile.

Dimensions of the System

The United States has a limited road system, if the system is calculated on the basis of road miles per square mile; on the other hand, the United States probably has the largest road system in the world. At the turn of the new millennium, the United States had almost 4 million miles of road. Although 4 million miles of road seems to be very large, it works out to slightly more than 1 mile of road per square mile of territory (0.69 km of road per square km of area), which, relative to many other countries, is quite limited. France, Germany, and the United Kingdom all have more than double that. This all goes to say that the United States is a very big country and large numbers are typical of almost any effort to describe or characterize its attributes.

The national mileage has actually grown little in the past century. In 1900, the earliest date for which statistics are recorded, the nation had just over 2.3 million miles of road. Less than 20 years later, by 1918, coverage had reached 3 million miles, and it has taken another 80 years to add another million miles of road. The physical nature of the road system has changed also. In 1945, about 80% of the road miles throughout the nation was unpaved roadway, consisting only of gravel or compacted dirt. It was not until 1977 that more than half of the nation's road system was considered paved. Today, the system is still more than one-third unpaved.

Of course, the capacity of the roadways has grown substantially, with the 4 million miles of road now having 8.25 million lane-miles, or slightly more than two travel lanes per mile of road on average. A lane-mile consists of one travel lane over 1 mile. A country road would likely be two lane-miles per mile of road, one in each direction. A major freeway can be 10 lane-miles per mile (five travel lanes in each direction). Statistics in this area have not been collected for long, but the data indicate that growth is not dramatic; in 1993, there were 8.15 million national lane-miles, with an increase of 100,000 miles from that year to the year 2000, or about 1% growth. Most of the lane-mile growth occurs in metropolitan areas, with rural areas often showing declines in lane-miles. The urban lane-mile growth is in large part a product of urban area expansion, in which existing roads are reclassified from rural to urban, as well as a product of increased road capacity as lanes are added to existing streets and streets are built within new housing and commercial developments. Despite the typically wider roads in metropolitan areas, the vast majority of lane-miles, roughly two-thirds, is in rural areas.

System Ownership

According to the U.S. Bureau of the Census, roads in America are owned by approximately 36,000 units of government, utilizing almost every imaginable system of government organization for the management of the roads in the care of different units. Surprisingly, the national government owns few roads; typically these are only minor roads internal to federal lands. Table I, showing ownership of miles of road in 2001 for urban and rural areas, indicates the main entities that own roads in the United States. Although only approximately 20% of roads are under state control, these are often the major roads of the road system in terms of design characteristics and volume of use. The greatest portion of roads is under local control, including county, town, township, or municipal ownership and also including Indian tribes and public authorities especially created to operate roads. Over 3000 counties in America own more than 1.7 million miles of road, almost 45% of the total system in the country. Only about 3% of the road system is under federal control. The mileage of federal roads has tended to decline as roads on public lands are declassified or reclassified. It is also important to note that the road system is predominantly rural in location, with almost 80% of roads in rural areas.

Measures of Physical Condition

Road Condition

Pavement condition has historically been measured by a system called present serviceability rating (PSR), which ranked pavements from 1 (very deteriorated) to 5 (new or nearly new pavements). This rating was a subjective system based on engineering judgments, which, although sound, were capable of inconsistency

Table I Ownership of Roads[a]

	Rural		*Urban*		*Total*	
Jurisdiction	*Mileage*	*Percent*	*Mileage*	*Percent*	*Mileage*	*Percent*
State	665,093	21.7	109,136	12.4	774,229	19.6
Local	2,286,969	74.5	765,633	87.3	3,052,602	77.3
Federal	119,270	3.9	2234	0.3	121,504	3.1
Total	3,071,332	100.0	877,003	100.0	3,948,335	100.0

[a] Data from *Highway Statistics*, Federal Highway Administration (2001).

from place to place. More recently, the PSR has been replaced by a mechanical rating system called the international roughness index (IRI), developed by the World Bank; the IRI uses machinery to calculate the number of inches of cracks or other imperfections in a road surface. In this case, higher measures are worse. The ranges of comparative values between the two scoring systems are shown in Table II.

In addition to describing pavements in terms of the percentage good or very good, a recent extension is to calculate the volumes of traffic on those facilities so that the measure of percentage of traffic on poor pavements can be calculated. There are, of course, other measures of highway characteristics and condition. Those most used in national evaluations are lane width, which can range from 9 to more than 12 feet, and horizontal and vertical alignment. These are effectively measures of safety and measure the adherence to design standards. Alignments are graded on a code of 1 to 4, where 4 indicates frequent grades that impair visibility or curves that are unsafe for the prevailing speed limits.

Bridges

A system as large as the highway system of the United States inevitably would have a large number of bridges. Because of safety concerns, the number, characteristics, and condition of bridges are carefully monitored under federal law. The length threshold for bridges that are monitored is 20 feet. In 2000, there were somewhat more than 587,000 bridges in the National Bridge Inventory distributed functionally as shown in Table III. Like the road system, the number of bridges grows slowly, with about a 1% increase since 1996.

Bridge Condition

The bridges in Table III are grouped by functional class and area. The National Bridge Inventory reviews each bridge at least every 3 years and exhaustively identifies and describes its characteristics. A recently introduced term in this evaluation methodology is "bridge deck area," which weights bridges by their size (length × width); this evaluation is far more effective in terms of recognizing investment needs, compared to simply taking a count of bridges.

The two main distinctions made in bridge condition relate to bridges that are structurally deficient and those that are functionally deficient. A structurally deficient bridge is not necessarily one that is in danger of collapse, but it generally needs significant maintenance or rehabilitation. It may need replacement or it may have special speed limits or load maximums that inhibit use, forcing larger vehicles, such as school buses, to take more circuitous routes. Functional deficiency has more to do with a bridge that is inconsistent in its characteristics with the road that it serves, either in height, width, curvature, or other aspects. The best example would be a four-lane bridge on a six-lane roadway.

Because most bridges are on the local road systems, those systems are most likely to have the deficient bridges; however, the state bridges that tend to be larger and carry more traffic also carry the major portions of traffic that move over deficient bridges. Recent trends have shown significant improvement in structurally deficient bridges as a result of higher levels of funding and greater focus on the problem; deficiencies dropped from 120,000 bridges to 80,000 over the past 10-year period. Functional deficiencies have remained steady at roughly 80,000 bridges.

Table II Pavement Rating Systems[a]

Rating	*PSR*[b]	*IRI*[c]
Very good	≥4.0	<60
Good	3.5–3.9	60–94
Fair	2.6–3.4	95–170
Mediocre	2.1–2.5	171–220
Poor	<2.0	>220

[a] The ranges shown are for roads in general; interstate roads have a more stringent standard, with anything worse than an IRI of 170 deemed poor (an IRI of 170 = 170 inches in depth of cracks per mile). Data from *Condition and Performance Report*, Federal Highway Administration (2002).
[b] PSR, Pavement serviceability rating.
[c] IRI, International roughness index.

The Highway as a Service System

The System as Network

The great strength of the U.S. highway system is its interconnectedness, within the system and with other modal elements. Few places in the nation are located where desired trip destinations cannot be linked with origins with only minor levels of circuity. It is difficult to describe or even measure the degree or character of this connectedness. There are a number of ways in which

Table III Number of Bridges by Location on Functional System[a]

Functional system	*Rural bridges*	*Urban bridges*
Interstate	27,797	27,882
Other arterial	74,796	63,177
Collector	143,357	15,038
Local	209,415	25,684
Total	455,365	131,781

[a] Data from *Condition and Performance Report*, Federal Highway Administration (2002).

to represent the pervasiveness of the network; a composite of many of the measures is probably needed to understand the complete picture. The system interconnectedness can be expressed in terms of the areas covered, the populations, or other activities to be served (in a sense providing a weighting function for a pure area measurement), or it can also be expressed topographically in terms of measures of coverage and connectivity. The following list suggests ways in which to describe the network connectivity of the system.

1. Area: Miles of road per square mile.
2. Population: Miles of road per thousand population.
3. Vehicles: Miles of road per thousand vehicles.

These approaches actually provide measures of coverage density and might not adequately represent the network's true connectivity. A more effective measure of connectivity would consist of ways in which to describe the enforced circuity imposed on travelers by a network. The rectangle shown in Fig. 1 can be seen to consist of a square with four sides meeting at four points. In a network representation, the sides would be called links and the points at which they meet would be called nodes. The nodes can be thought of as four towns connected by four roads, with an average ratio of links to nodes of one. If two new links (the diagonals) are added, the ratio of links to nodes goes to 1.5 and the average distance between nodes drops sharply. If a new node is seen to exist at the center of the square, then the two diagonal links can be considered as four links, resulting in a total of eight links serving five nodes, or a ratio of 1.6. Higher ratios indicate improved connectivity.

Circuity can be measured as the distance that must be traversed on the network from an origin to a desired destination divided by the crow-flies distance between the two points. Sometimes the circuity involved is imposed by land features such as lakes or mountains; in other cases, it might be simply the lack of roads that causes significant detouring from direct travel. Clearly, the diagonals in Fig. 1 reduce the circuity between the nodes to be served in at least some of the cases. If in fact, the nodes are of different "sizes," as measured in terms of population, industrial output, attractiveness, etc., then the average circuity weighted by that measure would be quite different than an average that was derived assuming that all nodes were equal. Early transportation modeling used a formula related to a gravitation equation that weighted travel by the "size" of areas and the distances between them.

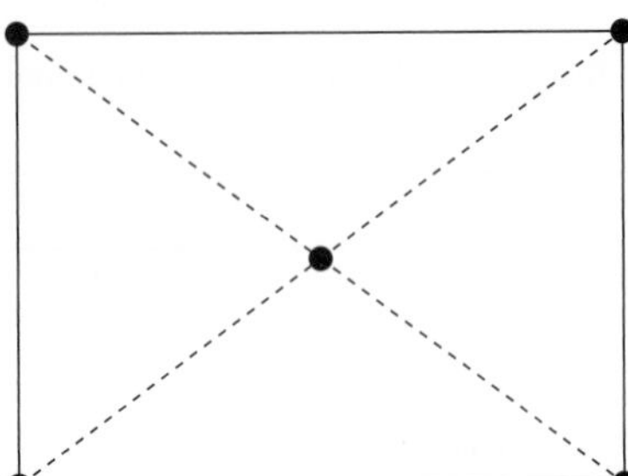

Figure 1 A network representation. The sides (links) connect at nodes. The ratio of links to nodes is 8:5, or 1:6. Higher ratios indicate improved connectivity.

Another way in which to measure the robustness of the system would be to conduct hypothetical exercises in which a link is deleted; for instance, a bridge failure can be simulated and the effects on the circuity of travel measured. This measures the redundancy incorporated in the system and may be an important measure of network effectiveness, in a military or emergency situation, for example.

Function

To understand the true nature and use of the road network as a system, it must be described based on function. A functional classification system has evolved over the years to provide a description of roads according to the function they perform in the overall highway system. There are three major groupings: (1) arterials, which are designed to serve longer distance travel, (2) collectors, which provide an intermediate function between local streets and long distance arterials, and (3) local roads, which primarily serve adjacent properties. As can be seen from Table IV, local roads that serve houses, factories, businesses, and farms constitute the largest share (more than two-thirds) of roads. All arterials constitute only about 11% of the road system, with the collectors making up the remainder. In urban and rural areas, there are subcategorizations within the three main functional groupings to permit more detailed description of specialized functions. The 46,000-mile-long interstate system constitutes the highest level of the functional system; although it accounts for only slightly more than 1% of

Table IV Distribution of Roads by Function[a]

Functional system	*Rural*	*Urban*	*Total*
Interstate	0.8%	0.3%	1.2%
Other freeways/expressways	NA[b]	0.2%	0.2%
Other principal arterials	2.5%	1.4%	3.9%
Minor arterials	3.5%	2.3%	5.8%
Major collector	11.0%	NA[b]	11.0%
Minor collector	7.0%	NA[b]	7.0%
Collector	NA[b]	2.3%	2.3%
Local	53.5%	15.1%	68.6%
All	78.4%	21.6%	100.0%

[a] Data from *Highway Statistics*, Federal Highway Administration (2002).
[b] NA, Not applicable.

roads, it plays a great role in terms of function. There is a considerable degree of linkage between ownership and functional class. Almost all of the interstate roads and roads designated "other principal arterials" are owned by state agencies. Even minor arterials are predominantly owned by states, especially in rural areas. As expected, local roads are owned by local governments, particularly counties in rural areas and municipalities in urban areas. Collectors are more varied in terms of ownership.

The National Highway System

Historically, all roads other than those designated "local" in both rural and local areas, or "minor collectors" in rural areas, were identified as federal-aid highways, indicating that they were eligible for federal financial aid. In 1991, the U.S. Congress established the National Highway System (NHS), a system of nationally significant highways, replacing the previous federal-aid highways concept. The NHS consists of the 46,000-mile interstate system, created in 1944 (the Eisenhower National System of Interstate and Defense Highways), and another 113,759 miles of existing roadway consisting almost exclusively of principal arterials, for a total system of 160,093 miles at present, about 4% of the nation's roads, but almost 44% of vehicle miles of travel. As expected, most of the system, about three-fourths, is in rural areas, and almost 95% of it is state owned. It should be noted that the NHS consists of the redesignation of previous facilities and is not a system of new roads. Only about 3500 miles of additional road will eventually be created, to constitute the full system of 163,611 miles. Table V summarizes the road mileage and travel activity associated with the NHS. Although the NHS constitutes only slightly more than 4% of the road system, it in fact accounts for about 6% of national lane-miles. Almost all of the interstate portion of the NHS is four lanes or more with full access control, with only about 1000 miles with four lanes without access control and another 1000 miles, mostly in Alaska and Puerto Rico, with less than four lanes. Almost two-thirds of the other noninterstate NHS mileage is three lanes or fewer.

Intermodal Connectors

An important aspect of the NHS is that the U.S. Congress recognized in its designation process the two separate roles of national-level highways. The first role is the through-travel, long-distance function, in which highways may be the sole form of transport or may compete with other modes of transport; the second is the service function provided by highways, as the access mode to most other modal alternatives. Although the mileages involved in serving these connection points (terminals, ports, etc.) are very limited, they are a critical part of the nation's transportation system. It is estimated that about 1200 miles of road serve the nation's freight terminal facilities. In total, more than 1400 passenger and freight terminal points are served by the NHS.

The Strategic Highway Corridor Network

The strategic highway corridor network (STRAHNET) is designed to serve military needs, including access to bases and connection to major ports for mobilization purposes. This entire system consists of 61,000 miles of road, 45,376 of which is interstate highway and another 15,668 miles is noninterstate.

Volume of Use of the System

At some time in the next 6 years, reauthorization by Congress of the surface transportation program the nation's highway system will pass a dramatic milestone. The level of highway use will reach 3 trillion vehicle-miles of travel (VMT). (A vehicle-mile equals one vehicle traveling a distance of 1 mile; the sum of vehicle-miles is referred to as the VMT.) As the 20th century began, the (motorized) annual vehicle-miles of travel in the United States was about 100 million miles of travel. It took until 1968 to reach the level of 1 trillion miles of VMT in a year, in a nation in which the population was approaching 200 million. At that time, the share of travel between rural and urban areas had arrived at about a 50/50 split. It took only another 20 years for the road system to reach 2 trillion VMT per year, and the regional shares of travel had reversed from 1962, with 40% rural and 60% urban shares. By 2000, the level of travel was at 2.75 trillion VMT, and is expected to reach 3 trillion in the period 2004–2007; this equals a period of roughly 17–18 years for the increase to the third trillion. The long-term trend is summarized in Table VI.

Table V National Highway System Mileage and Travel, 1998

	Mileage			*Travel miles* ($\times 10^6$)			*Percentage of total travel*		
System[a]	*Rural*	*Urban*	*Total*	*Rural*	*Urban*	*Total*	*Rural*	*Urban*	*Total*
Interstate	32,910	13,424	46,334	252,317	377,840	630,157	9.6	14.3	23.9
Other NHS	85,616	28,143	113,759	214,824	315,243	530,067	8.1	11.9	20.1
Total NHS	118,526	41,567	160,093	467,141	693,083	1,160,224	17.7	26.2	43.9

[a] NHS, National Highway System.

The rates of growth of VMT per decade have declined in each decade following the extraordinary levels of the 1950s, when travel grew by approximately 57%. In the 1960s, the rate of growth dropped to 48%, and then to 38% in both the 1970s and 1980s, and down to roughly 28% during the last decade of the century. However, the actual miles traveled has continued to increase dramatically in each decade, from an increase of about 0.16 trillion VMT in the 1950s to 0.6 trillion new VMT in the last decade of the century. Although such growth seems prodigious, against a background of increase in population of approximately 25 million per decade and a similar number of new vehicles, it appears more comprehensible.

VMT Fleet Mix

The predominant level of growth in travel is attributable to the personal vehicle, responsible for over 92% of travel. This varies significantly by area, comprising only 88% of rural travel and 95% of urban travel. Single-unit and combination trucks comprise almost 3% and 5%, respectively, of overall vehicle travel. Truck travel is greatest in rural areas, comprising more than 11% of travel and almost 21% of rural travel on the interstate system. In fact, combination vehicles alone, consisting of tractors and trailers or semitrailers, account for more than 17% of travel on rural interstate highways. Moreover, the truck share will continue to grow. Growth rates by vehicle on the rural interstate show 3.2% annual growth for personal vehicles from 1987 to 1997 and 4.2% and 4.4% growth for single units and combination unit trucks, respectively. Urban interstate travel showed almost identical annual growth rates of about 3.9% for all vehicle types in the same period.

Functional Classification Mix

The growth in travel has not been distributed evenly across the highway system in either rural or urban areas. Although growth has been substantial almost everywhere over the past 10 years, it is most predominant for the interstate and other high-level arterial travel. Total percentage growth rates in the different elements of the system are shown in Table VII. The 10-year travel growth rate was 30% for the total system, with growth for urban

Table VI VMT Milestones[a]

Year	*VMT*	*Event*
1900	100 million	First year of recorded VMT
1905	1.24 billion	First year of recorded billion VMT
1924	105 billion	First year of recorded 100 billion VMT
1936	0.25 trillion	First year at quarter-trillion VMT
1952	0.50 trillion	First year at half-trillion VMT
1962	0.76 trillion	VMT split, rural 60%/urban 40%
1967	0.96 trillion	Rural/urban VMT split reaches 50/50
1968	1.0 trillion	First year at 1 trillion VMT
1988	2.0 trillion	First year at 2 trillion VMT
1988	2.0 trillion	VMT split, rural 40% urban 60%
2000	2.75 trillion	100-year mark
2005 (est.)	3.0 trillion	Expected third-trillion VMT year

[a] VMT, Vehicle-miles of travel; based on calculations by the author.

Table VII Travel Growth Rates (1988–1998) by Functional System

	Travel growth		
Functional system	*Rural*	*Urban*	*All*
Interstate	39%	46%	43%
Other freeways/expressways	—	43%	43%
Other principal arterials	49%	22%	31%
Minor arterial	10%	34%	24%
Major collector	12%	—	12%
Minor collector	17%	—	17%
Collectors	—	33%	33%
Local	29%	24%	26%
Total	27%	33%	30%

[a] Based on calculations by the author.

and rural systems at 3 percentage points above and below the national average, respectively. In both rural and urban areas, travel on collectors and local roads was below or just at the national overall level, whereas interstate travel growth was more than 10 percentage points above the average. Other freeways and expressways and other principal arterials in rural areas also saw similar levels of growth in travel, often in the 40% and higher range. Only urban principal arterials deviated from the pattern.

As a result of these growth trends, the shares of travel showed even further redistribution toward the high end of the system in both rural and urban areas. From 1980 to 1998, rural interstate travel grew from 20% of rural travel to 24%; in combination with other principal arterials, their overall share grew from 40% to over 47%, with all other functional classes declining in share. In urban areas, interstate travel grew from less than a 19% share to almost 23% of urban travel, and in combination with other freeways and expressways rose from 28% to 35% of the volume from 1980 to 1998. When taken with other principal arterials, this is close to 60% of all travel. The growth trends discussed previously emphasize the importance of the national highway system. As noted earlier, the NHS constitutes about 4% of the road system and now accounts for over 43% of all travel, with about 24% on the interstate and 20% on the other NHS components.

Expected Future Trends

The national annual VMT growth rate over the 20-year period from 1980 to 2000 was 2.99%. Given the slowing of many of the factors of travel growth, an annual growth rate for the 20-year period from 2000 to 2020 of about 2.1% per year is forecast. This varies by area with a rural growth rate of 2.26% and an urban rate of 1.96%. The determinants of travel growth, such as population increase, new households, new driver's licenses, etc., may be decreasing, and part of the forecasts are based on the hope that increasing congestion will cause shifts in transit use or other alternatives and will lessen demand for overall highway travel.

Measures of Condition and Performance

In recent years, as the levels of perceived congestion on the road system have grown, the sophistication of the processes of measuring system performance has grown as well. Although there is still no single adequate definition or measure of congestion, the ability to describe the system's performance has improved, primarily as a result of the work of the Federal Highway Administration (FHWA) and the Texas Transportation Institute. An important facet of understanding has been recognition of the need to identify the depth, extent, and duration of congested travel. Depth measures the severity of congestion; extent measures the range of coverage of the congestion, measured by the number or percentage of roads or riders affected; and duration measures the temporal distribution of the congestion.

Early measures included a volume/capacity (V/C) ratio figure; in a simple sense, the V/C measured how "full" a road segment or road system was. A level of service (LOS) measure accompanied the V/C ratio, defining how certain ratios affected the driving experience. The LOS measure was a letter grade ranging from A (the best) down to F (for failing), graded at traffic standstill levels. In recent times, traffic engineers have felt the need for lower grades or subcategories of grades within F. The characteristics of the letter grades are summarized in Table VIII (note that there are no quantitative boundary measures between the grades). Often the grades were accompanied by photographs, giving the viewer a sense of what the grade looked like on the road. A more recent restructuring of terms has led to the use of a volume/service flow (V/SF) ratio, which is the ratio of the traffic actually using a facility during the peak hour and the theoretical capacity of that

Table VIII Grading System for Traffic Congestion[a]

Grade	*Description*
A	Describes primarily free-flow operations; vehicles are almost completely unimpeded in their ability to maneuver within the traffic stream and the effects of incidents are easily absorbed
B	Also represents reasonable free-flow in which speeds are generally maintained; ability to maneuver is only slightly restricted
C	Flow still at or near free-flow speeds; ability to maneuver restricted and tension increases; incidents cause local deterioration of service
D	Speeds begin to decline with increasing volumes; freedom noticeably restricted; minor incidents cause queuing
E	Operations at or near capacity; operations volatile, with any disruption causing waves of reaction; both physical and psychological comfort is extremely poor
F	Breakdown in flow; queues formed and lower volumes of flow produced

[a] Data abstracted by the author from the *Highway Capacity Manual* 2000, Transportation Research Board (2000).

facility to accommodate the traffic. For example, a V/SF ratio of 0.8 corresponds to a LOS of grade D (Table VIII).

Recent observations of actual experience in highway traffic have actually raised the level of theoretical capacity by 10–15%, from 2000 vehicles/hour to as high as 2400 vehicles/hour. While recognizing actual behavior, this change, at a minimum, creates a discontinuity in measurement and, in fact, may be ratifying an increasingly unsafe set of conditions. Historical measures of traffic congestion have focused on the so-called peak hour in which the highest levels of traffic movement occurred. As most people know, the peak hour is now more of a peak "period" in which congestion is likely to occur. This has confounded measurement in that as traffic conditions have worsened, traffic has spread out, with people and goods traveling both earlier and later. Thus, it might be found that the share of total travel in the peak hour has declined, or just held steady, as congestion has worsened. As a result, peak-period-based measures have diminished in utility. For example, the percentage of peak hour traffic exceeding the V/SF threshold at which congestion begins (V/SF = 0.8) actually shows a decline for urban interstates from 1995 to 2000.

Perhaps the most fundamental measure of congestion is the total volume of travel per lane-mile of road, described as daily VMT (DVMT) per lane-mile. DVMT on urban interstates has grown from 11,300 vehicles per day to 15,300 from 1993 to 2000. By this measure, things are certainly deteriorating. Because this measure tells us nothing about the distribution throughout the day; two roads with the same values of DVMT per lane-mile, but differing temporal distributions of traffic, could conceivably have very different congestion patterns. The broad measures of highway travel growth are shown in Fig. 2.

Among the new measures developed to address the changing nature of travel congestion are those shown in Table IX. Note that these measures are all measures of the facility and its flow. This is different than measuring the effective service provided to individual trips of individual travelers. It is conceivable that measures of system flow could show decline while individual travel was improving as a result of shifts in locations, modes,

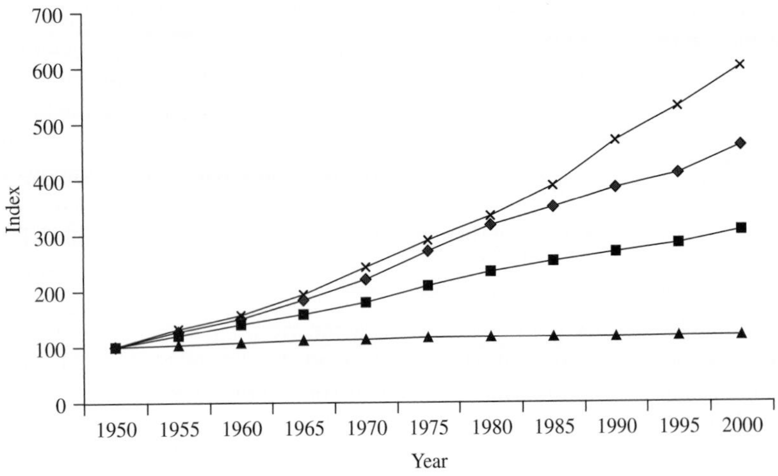

Year	Vehicles	Drivers	Miles of road	VMT
1950	100	100	100	100
1955	127.4	120.1	103.2	132.169
1960	150.2	140.4	107.0	156.853
1965	183.7	158.4	111.4	193.758
1970	220.3	179.3	112.6	242.187
1975	270.3	208.7	115.8	289.764
1980	316.7	233.6	116.5	333.326
1985	349.0	252.3	116.6	387.342
1990	383.7	268.5	116.7	467.983
1995	409.6	283.9	118.1	528.765
2000	458.9	307.1	118.8	600.131

Figure 2 Main trends in highway activity. ♦, Vehicles; ■, drivers; ▲, miles of road; x, vehicle-miles traveled (VMT). Data for selected years from *Highway Statistics*, published by the Federal Highway Administration.

routes, etc.; the most direct user measure is, for instance, average travel time. This information is collected by the Bureau of the Census for work trips and by the National Household Travel Survey (NHTS) of the FHWA for all trips. These averages can improve while the facility-based measures decline. The census measured an increase in work trip travel times of only 40 seconds from 1980 to 1990 but observed a $\geq$2-minute increase from 1990 to 2000.

There are many other measures of congestion that express various aspects of congestion's attributes. The studies of the Texas Transportation Institute (TTI) have been notable in this area; TTI has published a series of annual urban mobility reports since 1982. Their very practical measures have increased as their research has progressed. Much more work needs to be done to arrive at exhaustive measures that are readily understood and applied uniformly. Rolf R. Schmitt of the FHWA has sought to develop theoretically comprehensive measures of congestion attacking all aspects of the topic; his early structure for congestion measures is shown in Table X.

Table IX Selected Highway Performance Measures in Use[a]

Measure	*Approach*	*Purpose*
Average speed	Direct measure of speeds on a facility	Most direct measure of changes in facility service
Travel time index or percentage additional travel time	Ratio of congested travel time to typical off-peak times	Depth measure; measure of loss of time in the peak (140 = 40% more travel time)
Annual hours of delay	Total annual hours delayed in traffic per driver, or per adult, or per capita	Depth × extent measure; accumulated loss of time for the year; provides cost value
Percentage of system congested	Percentage of roadway lane miles operating at less than free-flow speed	Extent measure; percentages of road system affected by congestion
Percentage of travel congested	Percentage of urban daily traffic on principal arterials moving at less than free-flow speed; same as preceding measure weighted by volume	Extent measure; e.g., 40% of total travel was under congested conditions!
Buffer or reliability index	Measure of amount of extra time needed to assure on-time arrival	A measure of variation in speeds and travel times

[a] Data from *Condition and Performance Report, Federal Highway Administration* (2002), *and Urban Mobility Report*, 2003, *Texas Transportation Institute* (2003).

Table X Theoretical Structure for Highway Performance Measures[a]

Measure	*Concept*
Geographic accessibility	Are the origins and destinations linked by the transportation system?
Architectural accessibility	Do the origins and destinations have physical barriers for part of the population?
User cost	Do the origins and destinations have economic barriers for part of the population?
Temporal availability	Is the transportation system available when people want to travel?
Best travel time	How long does it take to get to the desired destination under the best conditions?
Expected travel time	What is the usual expected time to get to the destination?
Buffer time	How much time do people add for a trip or shipment in anticipation of variability in expected travel-time to reach the destination when they need to be there?
Nonoptimal time	How much longer than the best travel time does the usual or scheduled trip take because of routing, speed restrictions, expected delay, etc.?
Tardiness	How late are people and goods when buffer time is exceeded?
On-time performance	How often do trips and shipments reach their destinations by the usual expected time?
Capacity	How many travelers and shipments can be moved over the transportation system under optimum conditions?
Congestion	When and where are the number of trips and shipments that are actually accommodated less than the maximum possible because capacity has been exceeded by the volume of traffic?

[a] Data from R. R. Schmitt, presentation to the North American Statistical Interchange, April 2002.

Highways as an Element in Society

There is an extraordinary number of ways in which highways interact with society, and each has significant ramifications. The impacts include both positive and negative attributes and can be arrayed into three broad categories, economic, social, and safety/energy/environmental. Although the impacts of roads on the land began well before the United States was a nation, the most important impacts of highways ultimately derive from the inception of the great role of the internal combustion engine.

Vehicles

A key measure of the relationship between vehicles, highways, and society is the number of vehicles/household or vehicles/1000 population. In 1910, at the start of the auto age, there were 200 people/vehicle in the United States; 5 years later, this was already down to 40 people/vehicle. By the 1930s, the entire population could be seated in the front and back seats of all of the existing vehicles, and by the 1950s, the entire population could be accommodated in the front seats alone. In 2001, the total motor vehicle fleet exceeded 230 million vehicles; with a population on the order of 285 million, this was a comfortable 1.24 people/vehicle. The vehicle fleet now not only exceeds the number of drivers in the population, it exceeds the number of the total adult population. In many of the recent past decades, vehicle production exceeded population increase.

Other measures of the vehicle/population relationship include the percentage of persons over 16 years of age with drivers licenses, the average number of vehicles per household, the distribution of households by vehicles owned or available for use, and the number of households with no vehicles. Among adults, the United States is near saturation regarding licenses; the same can be said for households, for total number of vehicles. However, these levels are significantly lower among minority groups, which will be a significant source of future growth in vehicle acquisition and travel miles. A key statistical measure of mobility is the number and percentage of households without vehicles in a society highly oriented to mobility. Surprisingly, the number of households without a vehicle has remained at about 10 million for 40 years, and the number of households with one vehicle has remained at about 30 million, but, of course, both are a significantly declining percentage of all households. All growth has occurred in the two- and three-vehicle households. Figure 3 depicts this trend over the past 40 years.

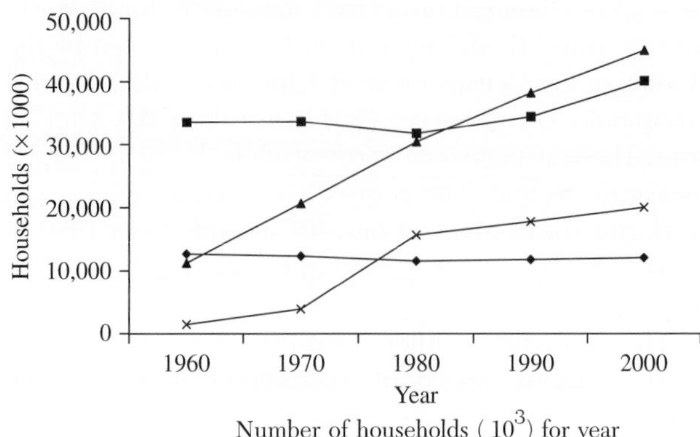

Number of vehicles	Number of households (10^3) for year				
	1960	1970	1980	1990	2000
0	11,400	11,110	10,400	10,600	10,861
1	30,190	30,300	28,600	31,000	36,124
2	10,100	18,600	27,400	34,400	40,462
3+	1300	3500	14,100	16,000	18,033
Total	52,999	63,500	80,500	92,000	105,480

Figure 3 Number of households by number of vehicles owned. ♦, No vehicles; ■, one vehicle; ▲, two vehicles; x, three or more vehicles. Data from the decennial censuses of the U.S. Bureau of the Census.

Household Highway Expenditures

Transportation is of great value to American households, as amply demonstrated by spending behavior. A key measure to monitor is the share of total household spending going to transportation. On average, American households spend about 19% of their total expenditures on transportation, or about \$7600 per year in 2001, with both the amount and the percentage of spending rising with increasing incomes. Of this amount, more than 96%, all but about \$300 of total spending, is oriented to vehicles and road travel. The percentage of expenditures going to transportation has risen slightly over the decades.

Human Purposes

In considering local road travel, particularly when associated with congestion, the tendency is to think of work travel. In fact, work travel is a small ($\approx 20\%$) and declining share of all travel. The share of personal travel accommodated by the road system is prodigious. For work trips, the personal auto accounts for over 92% of trips, with transit and "other" accounting for less than 4% each. Even then, most of the trips via buses and walking or biking are also on roads. For a number of trips for other purposes, such as social/recreational travel or school/church or family/personal business, rail-related usage is far less, as compared to work travel, but walking trips increase.

Long-distance travel (trips over 100 miles) is similarly oriented to the personal vehicle. The personal vehicle accounts for more than 80% of long-distance travel; with intercity bus travel added, the highway share rises to 83%. Even for business travel, the auto predominates for all trips under 1000 miles round trip.

Freight Flows

Americans tend to neglect the role of freight transport in their lives. More than 11 billion tons of freight, valued at $7 trillion, moved in 1997. Measured in ton-miles (moving 1 ton of freight 1 mile), total freight movement was on the order of 2.66 trillion ton-miles. The predominant share of each of the three measures (value, tons, and ton-miles) of freight movement is by highways: 82% of value, 70% of tons, and 42% of ton-miles.

Travel Activity Categories

Categories that are used to structure uses of highways are given in Table XI.

Consumption

Highways are great consumers of resources, including land, steel, concrete, and petroleum, but perhaps the most important element of consumption is time. It has been argued that human beings have tended to spend about 1 hour or so per day in travel since the beginning of civilization. Today, the averages exceed an hour and most of the time spent in travel is spent in autos or trucks. The National Household Travel Survey (NHTS) indicates that the average time spent driving is 66 minutes on weekdays and 54 minutes on weekends, and the time spent in a vehicle driving or as a passenger is closer to 70 minutes per day.

Table XI Travel Activity Categories

Category	*Description*
Commuting	
Other resident travel	School, work-connected business, personal business, shopping, visit friends and relatives, social/recreational, medical/dental, other
Visitor travel	Overnight visitors, same-day visitors, business travel
Services	Telephone, gas, electric, cable TV
Public vehicles	Government/military, police, fire, ambulance/emergency, refuse, road construction/maintenance
Urban goods movement	Couriers, store delivery, home delivery, office delivery, factory delivery, services/repair, construction
Through-passenger travel	Business, social/recreational, visit friends/relatives
Through-freight travel	Agriculture, construction/manufacturing, wholesale/retail, import/export

Safety

Preliminary estimates indicate that the 2002 road-related fatality count rose to 42,850 from 42,116 in 2001. This was a sharp setback; fatalities had been declining as a function of reduced rates of fatalities from crashes and the rate of crashes. Total nonfatal crashes declined as did the number of persons injured in 2002. The highest levels of fatalities occurred in 1969 and in the early 1970s, when for several years fatalities exceeded 55,000; this number dropped sharply over the years to a nadir of 39,000 in 1992, the last time the number was below 40,000. It has been rising sporadically since then.

Measurement of safety is a complex procedure. The tendency is to focus on the absolute numbers of fatalities and of persons injured, but the analytical focus is often on the rates of crashes and fatalities. Among the key measures are the fatalities per million population, fatalities per 100,000 vehicles or per 100,000 drivers licenses, and fatalities per 100 million miles of travel. All of these measures have shown marked improvement over the past 30 or so years. For example, the fatality rate per 100 million miles of travel is less than half of what it was in 1980. Current annual fatalities at 1980 rates would exceed 90,000. The key monitoring question is whether in any given year the rate of improvement in fatalities is sufficient to compensate for the rate of growth in travel. These measures will vary sharply from country to country and can be very misleading, given levels of motorization and levels of management of traffic.

Environmental Concerns

Although road water runoff affecting water quality, noise pollution affecting nearby populations, and habitat impacts are concerns stemming from road use and development, the key environmental concerns related to road use have been those related to air quality. Air quality has been measured over time by focus on four pollutant categories; these are volatile organic compounds (VOCs), oxides of nitrogen (NO_x), carbon monoxide (CO), and particulate matter under 10 μm in diameter (PM10). Lead emissions, a major national concern in the 1960s and 1970s, were totally eliminated because of changes in gasoline formulation by the mid-1980s.

The focus on air quality is in five key areas: share of pollutants generated by transportation, total tons of pollutants emitted, percentage change in emissions, exceedances (of air quality standards) per monitor, and index measures of trends. By almost all of these measures, air quality has been improving dramatically and will continue to do so. Measured against 1970, on-road vehicle emissions are down by the following percentages: VOCs, almost 60%; carbon monoxide, 43%; and PM10, almost

20%; only NO_x is up by 16% as a result of sharp increases in the diesel truck fleet. Carbon monoxide exceedances per monitor are down from 25 per monitor in 1975 to 0.1 in 2000. In all cases, transportation is doing better at improvement compared to the other sources of pollution. In many cases, off-road gasoline engines used for lawn mowing, boating, skimobiling, etc. have shown dramatic increases in emissions.

See Also the Following Articles

Transportation Research • Urban Economics • Urban Studies

Further Reading

Bureau of Transportation Statistics (BTS) (2004). *National Transportation Statistics.* BTS, U.S. Department of Transportation, Washington, D.C.

Bureau of Transportation Statistics (BTS) (2004). *Transportation Statistics Annual Report.* BTS, U.S. Department of Transportation, Washington, D.C.

Federal Highway Administration (FHWA) (2001). *Highway Statistics.* FHWA, U.S. Department of Transportation, Washington, D.C.

Federal Highway Administration (FHWA) (2001). *Summary of Travel Trends; 2001.* FHWA, U.S. Department of Transportation, Washington, D.C.

Federal Highway Administration (FHWA) (2004). *Our Nation's Highways.* FHWA, U.S. Department of Transportation, Washington, D.C.

Federal Highway Administration (FHWA) (2002). *Status and Condition of the Nation's Highways, Bridges and Transit—Condition and Performance Report.* FHWA, Federal Transit Administration, U.S. Department of Transportation, Washington, D.C.

Federal Highway Administration (FHWA) (2004). *Transportation Air Quality—Selected Facts and Figures.* FHWA, U.S. Department of Transportation, Washington, D.C.

Texas Transportation Institute (TTI) (2003). *Urban Mobility Report, 2003.* TTI, College Station, Texas.

Transportation Research Board (TRB) (2000). *Highway Capacity Manual 2000.* National Academy of Sciences, Washington, D.C., ISBN 0-309-06746-4.

U.S. Department of Transportation (2002). *The Changing Face of Transportation; 2002.* U.S. Department of Transportation, Washington, D.C.

History of Business Performance Measurement

K. J. Euske
Naval Postgraduate School, Monterey, California, USA

L. A. Zander
Naval Postgraduate School, Monterey, California, USA

Glossary

cash flow Cash receipts minus cash disbursements.

economies of scale The reduction in the cost of producing goods and services because of increasing size of the producing organization.

effectiveness A measure of the relationship of outputs to goals or objectives.

efficiency A measure of the relationship of inputs to outputs.

performance Behavior that leads to a measured value outcome in the future. It is context specific.

therbligs A set of actions defined by Frank and Lillian Gilbreth for use in time and motion studies.

This history of performance measurement focuses on the development of performance measurement in commercial organizations over the past 500 years. As would be expected, performance measurement over the centuries has been directed at providing stakeholders with a picture of their organization. As the model of business and technology shifted, so did the need for the information to understand the performance of the organization. Models that are viewed as having significant defects today, such as return on investment, did provide useful information for the organizations for which they were designed. There is a continuing challenge to develop a measurement system that effectively and efficiently captures organizational performance in a timely fashion. The highlights of the evolution of performance measurement covered here exemplify changes to performance measurement that have occurred over the centuries. Other examples could have been used. The examples chosen, in the authors' view, capture the spirit of the times and the evolution of performance measurement.

Early Measurement Systems

Luca Pacioli is probably best known for his contributions to accounting. The ideas and processes described in his *Summa de Arithmetica, Geometrica, Proportioni, et Proportionalita* from 1494 are still applied by many in the accounting profession today. However, he can also be characterized as a pioneer in the area of performance measurement. The *Summa* also includes discussions of the topic of performance measurement as well as internal controls, such as numbering and dating ledgers, journals, and memorandums. In addition to describing the double-entry accounting system, Pacioli led businessmen through the necessary steps to account for all of their transactions. He identifies three things that are required to operate a successful business. First, there must be some sort of market need or justification for the endeavor. Second, the businessman must be a good accountant and mathematician. Third, the affairs of the businessman must be arranged systematically so that he may understand the business at a glance. Fundamentally, this means that the businessman must have an orderly record of the performance of the business. For the merchants of the time, this meant understanding the gain or loss for any particular venture. Pacioli described the specific entries required to recognize a profit or loss. Basic financial measures provided a means to evaluate the performance of the individual enterprise.

From the period of Pacioli into the 18th century, businesses tended to be family-run organizations; their primary focus in the area of performance measurement centered on the calculation of profit and loss for projects undertaken. The owners were staking their assets on specific endeavors. The fundamental question was whether the investment (i.e., running the family business) generated sufficient cash flow to continue the venture.

As transportation and technology improved, the focus on the management and measurement of performance evolved. In the 18th century, Josiah Wedgwood, faced with the competition in the pottery industry, realized that the old methods of manufacturing and employee management would no longer suffice. He sought alternative approaches to managing his operations. Wedgwood, through his systematization of production, division of labor, and disciplining of labor, is one of the pioneers of English factory organization. Wedgwood appointed foremen and managers and established what would now be defined as workgroups, or individual workers specializing in each area of manufacturing, from making the pottery through painting. As the organization continued to grow, Wedgwood created the *Potters' Instruction of 1780* to define rules and regulations for manufacturing along with guidance for the foreman regarding rewarding employees and reprimanding employees who were not performing according to expected standards. Additionally, Wedgwood paid piece rates and had bonus schemes to stimulate productivity. His innovations provided a basis for measuring performance at the operational level.

About 40 years after *Potter's Instruction* was printed, one of the first uses of the term "accountability" appeared in a report published for the Springfield Armory. The 1819 report addressed innovations in two specific areas: (1) processes used for manufacturing and inspecting production work and (2) the use of double-entry bookkeeping for every transaction by the employee, related to the manufacturing of items within the armory. The specific transactions recorded information about the physical amounts and value of material used as well as the amount and value of scrap and good inventory received at the end of the workday. In 1834, the Ordnance Department of the Springfield Armory published its own official document, *Ordnance Regulations*. Included in this publication were two objectives related to accountability and management structure: (1) the careful delineation of lines of authority and communication (2) setting standards of uniformity for accounting and manufacturing practices. Daniel Taylor, a West Point graduate who wrote the document, introduced into the manufacturing process within the Armory a new standard for performance measurement and discipline. Taylor's innovations at the Springfield Armory have been traced to studies conducted at West Point under the guidance of Sylvanus Thayer to establish a merit system for student evaluation. Taylor, a student at West Point just prior to the arrival of Thayer, was a part of the transition to a system of grading students and holding them accountable for their performance. It has been proposed that Taylor adapted the accountability and performance measurement ideas from West Point to the armory.

Late 19th–Early 20th Century

As the 19th century came to a close, the U.S. Congress identified a need to eliminate the restraints on trade and competition in the United States. To address the issue, Congress passed the Sherman Anti-Trust Act of 1890. The act was established to protect trade and commerce against unlawful trusts and monopolies. The act also influenced performance measurement. As Thurman Arnold noted in *The Bottlenecks of Business*, when the act was first passed, many interpreted it to be an attack on big business, purely based on their size, perhaps even prohibiting organizations from taking advantage of mass production or distribution. However, there were those who saw the Sherman Anti-Trust Act not as simply a tool to use against any large organization, but rather as a tool to address abuses that might result from the economic power of large organizations. Thurman W. Arnold, who held the office of the head of the Anti-Trust Division of the U.S. Justice Department, took the position that it was not size in and of itself that needed to be controlled, but rather the use of market power to unreasonably restrain trade.

From a production point of view, if organizations could not use their power to restrain trade, competition was more likely to flourish. Given the potential for competition, the leaders of large organizations faced the need to be more competitive. One way to do so was to find more efficient ways to produce their goods and services. Economies of scale became increasingly important. The measurement of performance now more than ever was a necessary part of managing a business. The continuing advances in technology and distribution systems helped transform the manufacturing environment.

With the changes came problems. One was determining performance expectations for individual workers. Frank B. Copley, in his book *Frederick W. Taylor*, explains how Taylor's theory of scientific management resulted from his attempts to address the problem of the appropriate amount of work that any given person ought to complete on any given day with the right tools and materials. Taylor had published a book in 1911, *Scientific Management*, in which he described his methods of gathering and providing to management the knowledge that had traditionally been in the domain of the workers. The process by which he did this included recording and tabulating data and, when appropriate, identifying the relevant rules, laws, and mathematical relationships.

Taylor's work introduced the concept of time standards for processes as well as the need for a standard set of tasks to be completed. A difficulty in using his method of managing the work being performed lies in the ability to collect meaningful data. Getting the workforce to provide information that was surely going to affect their piece-rate system was no easy task. In addition, the machinery might not function properly, or could break down altogether. Taylor applied common sense to decide on which acts to focus to yield the largest return. The focus was on the measurement of performance of the task or tasks that would most likely have an impact on the overall production process, rather than on the measurement of everything.

The standards developed by Taylor were based on a scientific method of gathering data and mathematical formulas, and as such provided a control mechanism to manage the unit. Taylor saw the need for both financial and nonfinancial measures. The blend of information from the time studies, as well as the cost data, provided a set of information that could be used to measure the performance of a given production unit. Taylor's view of cost accounting was that it was not useful unless it was combined with the accurate measurements of the work performed.

In a book written in 1964, *Efficiency and Uplift*, Samuel Haber discussed the establishment in 1911 of the Taylor Society; this group of Taylorites, an informal but exclusive group of individuals, included Frank Gilbreth and Henry Gantt. Both men would soon be cast out of the Taylor Society for their additions and revisions to the "scientific management" way of thinking. Haber describes how Gilbreth concentrated his efforts on the "scientific" aspect of Taylor's work. In 1912, Gilbreth introduced the motion-picture camera as a means of obtaining more exact measurements of work performed by an employee in the manufacturing process. Taylor refuted the process by claiming that it was only an aspect of scientific management, undoubtedly good for investigating the minutiae of motion. Early on, Taylor approved of the experiments, but later he became concerned that the concentration on motion studies was part of a more grandiose scheme and that Gilbreth's focus neglected the broader scope of scientific management.

Gantt's attempt to introduce revisions to the scientific management approach included introducing a focus on social reform and attempting to get at inefficiency in work methods by looking at management, not just the workers. Taylor found these ideas to be unacceptable. Taylor's approach to the work in the factory centered on the problem of setting the tasks of the worker. Gantt, on the other hand, argued that the place to attack inefficiencies was not with the laborer, but with management. Most of Gantt's innovations in the area of management came from his search to set performance standards for management similar to those set for the workers—using a stopwatch. Idleness of man or machine was an indication of management malfeasance. In Gantt's system, costs associated with idleness were not added to product. They were deducted directly from profits. This approach was designed to have a direct effect on those individuals in a management role and to focus performance measurement at a higher level of the organization.

During the same period of time that Taylor was developing his work in scientific management, and continuing after Taylor's death in 1915, Alexander Hamilton Church wrote articles with a focus on areas that included accounting, management, and performance measurement. Richard Vangermeerch, in his authoritative book, *Alexander Hamilton Church* (1988), describes how the foundation of Church's writings centered on the increasing complexity found in the manufacturing environments, focusing on the control of the operation. In the first work that Church published, he concentrated on the increased competition and the necessity for coordination and quick presentation of results. For control to be a reality for Church, inputs and financial results needed to be both forecasted and compared after the fact. Church recognized that scientific management had been around for decades, but also realized that the evolution of this concept was certain to take place as industry continued to go through changes. His view was that scientific management was more a set of principles than a system, and that it provided a means to view the entire production process. Church argued that because scientific management focused only on the human element of management but did not address issues such as capital and labor, it was not a complete system. Vangermeersh traces L. P. Alford's work with Church to develop what they viewed to be the scientific art of management, which focused on more than just one system. In 1912, Alford published an article titled *The Principles of Management*, which presented the foundation for their views. Three basic principles of management were presented:

1. Systematic use of experience.
2. Economic control of effort.
3. Promotion of personal effectiveness.

Each principle was to be measured and analyzed by leadership in conjunction with the workgroups. The resulting information provided a means to capture the performance of the workgroups.

The early 1900s also brought about a systematic identification of critical performance variables; with the publication of a return-on-investment model, Donaldson Brown, working for DuPont at the time, formulated a model to analyze the various components of return on investment. The model provided for a comprehensive series of financial indicators. Brown was later moved to General Motors, a company experiencing a significant upturn in the market in terms of performance. General Motors (GM) was faced with the problem of managing product variation while maintaining production standardization. Ford Motors, on the other hand, lagging behind in the market, sacrificed product differentiation for production volume. While GM measured performance using the model developed at DuPont, Henry Ford had little consideration for the evaluation of financial performance of Ford Motors. Not only did he not develop measures to evaluate such performance, he appeared unconcerned about return rates or other financial measures. His focus was on nonfinancial measures tied directly to the shop floor. This difference in the approach to measuring performance continued for years, not only across organizations but also within organizations. Essentially, Ford was looking at causality from the perspective of a process-based model. GM had what can be described as a results-based model that was more remote from the actual production process. In a 1993 field study of highly successful organizations, Euske and co-workers found that a key midmanagement role was translating or finding a way to tie the top-level financial measures to operational measures of performance.

In the environments in which Brown operated, return on investment was a useful tool. Return on investment, both in nominal and in discounted forms, was a useful form of measurement for organizations that experienced the kind of growth and prosperity that GM saw during the early 1900s. However, return on investment as a measure of performance has a number of weaknesses that are well documented in the literature.

Middle to Late 20th Century

By the mid-1940s, everyone from engineers to social scientists was studying various aspects of control, including performance measurement. Norbert Wiener, a mathematician, coined the term "cybernetics" as a theory of control systems based on communication. It was the work of a number of individuals, including W. Ross Ashby and C. West Churchman, that expanded the idea to complex systems. Their work uses the decision as the unit of analysis. The decision variable then becomes an important element in the system design for performance control (SDPC) model.

The SDPC model, using cybernetics and systems theory as its basis, can be described as a model for guiding the actions of organizational planners using the following seven phases:

1. Identifying the goal: Defining the variables and parameters.
2. Formulating the strategy: Composing the controlled and uncontrolled variables.
3. Organizing the structure: Decomposing the dependent and independent controlled variables.
4. Training the decision makers: Amplifying regulatory capacity over the dependent and independent controlled variables.
5. Coordinating the firm: Recomposing the dependent and independent controlled variables.
6. Monitoring the environment: Synchronizing the controlled and uncontrolled variables.
7. Valuing the performance: Evaluating the variables and parameters.

For the SDPC process to be effective, it must be part of an ongoing planning cycle, continuously applied to the organization. Of particular interest is the last phase of the SDPC process, which addresses the need to evaluate the past performance of the system and the value of that information as it applies to future applications. This phase requires reliable data from various sources. Given a systems theory basis for the SDPC process, the data gathered, once analyzed, can be used as part of an overall evaluation of the entity. First, the data can be used to ensure that the design and decision processes are working properly. Second, the data provide information to stockholders for determining the appropriate resources to allocate to specific processes or systems. Finally, the data can be used to communicate results to the nonstockholders regarding the performance of the organization. Although designed within a systems theory framework, SDPC relies heavily, but not exclusively, on accounting data.

The use of financial data was important during this period not only in models such as SDPC, but also in the return-on-investment model. One variation of the return-on-investment model that had been used for decades was residual income. Although the use of the measure had waned during the latter part of the 20th century, during the 1990s, the use of residual income experienced a resurgence in the form of economic value added (EVA), promoted by Stern Stewart & Co. in publications such as G. Bennett Stewart's *The Quest for Value*.

Return on investment and SDPC proved very useful through the mid-1900s. However, problems began to arise with the use of shorter-term financial measurements. Managers realized that during difficult times, when sales were on the decline and margins were not as acceptable as they had been, profit and return on investment targets could still be met by working a little harder in the finance office. For example, the discretion that existed for the timing of revenue and expense recognition for the current accounting period could affect the outcomes measured by the accounting system.

A different approach addressed the problem of the short-term focus and the ability to manipulate financial measures. In this approach, the focus on performance measures shifted toward nonfinancial measures.

Measures that focused on an organization's strategy and evaluated areas such as research, development, and manufacturing became increasingly important in the 1980s and 1990s. As an example, a company might choose to measure productivity information in order to become more efficient in the manufacturing process, thereby becoming more competitive in the marketplace. Other approaches recognized the need for flexibility in both design and manufacturing and the need to develop ways to measure product design implications as part of the overall research and development process.

The introduction of both financial and nonfinancial measures had the potential to impose on an organization the overwhelming task of trying to manage too many different measurements. Nevertheless, the approach offered the opportunity to capture multiple aspects of performance. However, at any one point in time, it is likely that only a few of the measures would be significant to an organization. The need for a mix or balance of measures was not a new idea. The *Tableau de Bord* used by the French at least since the early 1900s is just such a mix of measures.

The 1990s saw a continuation of the discussion of the relevance of both financial and nonfinancial measurements, but with an emphasis on the employee's role in improving the organization, based on data gathered in the measurement process. In *Relevance Regained* (1992), Johnson, focusing on the global marketplace, argued that if an organization is to be successful, it is essential to capitalize on the potential of the employees and to eliminate any performance measures or other management information that do not support behavior congruent with the imperatives of global competitiveness. Johnson stated that the imperatives for a globally competitive organization create an environment that allows employees to use their skills and talents to the fullest. The globally competitive organization creates an environment such that employees can then begin to understand how the entire organization impacts the way that customers view performance, and to understand their individual responsibilities to meet those customer needs.

The different models that appeared during the 1990s incorporated both financial and nonfinancial measures. For example, in 1991, Lynch and Cross introduced the performance pyramid. The pyramid contained four levels of objectives and measures to link strategy and operations by translating strategic objectives from the top down and measures from the bottom up. The top level of the pyramid is the vision for the organization as stated by the senior management of the company. The second level contains objectives for each business unit in terms of markets and financial data. The third level represents the core processes supporting the organizational strategy, with tangible objectives and priorities as they relate to areas such as customer satisfaction and productivity. Finally, the base of the pyramid represents the conversion of the objectives into specific criteria, such as quality and cycle time for each department or organizational component. The Lynch and Cross model enables the members of the organization to communicate to employees those measures that are important and also provides for an understanding of how those measures relate to the objectives of the organization.

In 1992, Kaplan and Norton popularized a tool developed at Advanced Micro Devices (AMD). The tool was designed to provide managers with the information they deem necessary to be successful in today's business environment. Kaplan and Norton, on the opening pages of their book, *The Balanced Scorecard*, argued that "the Balanced Scorecard translates an organization's mission and strategy into a comprehensive set of performance measures that provides the framework for a strategic measurement and management system. The scorecard measures organizational performance across four balanced perspectives: financial, customers, internal business processes, and learning and growth." The approach to develop a performance pyramid and balanced scorecard are slightly different. Although both models provide for input from employees at all levels of the organization, the balanced scorecard has more of a top-down approach, compared to the pyramid.

As business and technology continue to shift, the need for information to understand the performance of organizations will continue to change. The evolution of performance measurement is a continuing effort to model performance in a fashion that helps the stakeholders understand the organization.

See Also the Following Articles

Critical Views of Performance Measurement • Intangible Assets: Concepts and Measurements

Further Reading

Brown, D. (1924). Pricing policy in relation to financial control: Tuning up General Motors—Article two. *Mgmt. Administr.* **7**(2), 195–198.

Brown, D. (1924). Pricing policy in relation to financial control: Tuning up General Motors—Article three. *Mgmt. Administr.* **7**(3), 283–286.

Brown, D. (1924). Pricing policy in relation to financial control: Tuning up IV—General Motors. *Mgmt. Administr.* **7**(4), 417–422.

Church, A. H. (1900). The meaning of commercial organization. *Engineer. Mag.* 391–398.

Church, A. H. (1911). The meaning of scientific management. *Engineer. Mag.* 97–101.

Epstein, M. J., and Manzoni, J.-F. (1997). Translating strategy into action: The balanced scorecard and the Tableau de Bord. *Strateg. Finance* **79**(2), 28–36.

Euske, K. J., Lebas, M. J., and McNair, C. J. (1993). Performance management in an international setting. *Mgmt. Account. Res.* **4,** 275–299.

Hoskin, K. W., and Macve, R. H. (1988). The genesis of accountability: The West Point connections. *Account. Organiz. Soc.* **13**(1), 37–73.

Johnson, H. T., and Kaplan, R. S. (1987). *Relevance Lost: The Rise and Fall of Management Accounting.* Harvard Business School Press, Boston, Massachusetts.

Kaplan, R. S., and Norton, D. P. (1992). The balanced scorecard—Measures that drive performance. *Harv. Bus. Rev.* **70**(1), 71–79.

Kuhn, A. J. (1986). *GM Passes Ford, 1918–1938.* Pennsylvania State University Press, University Park and London.

Kuhn, A. J. (1986). *Organizational Cybernetics and Business Policy.* Pennsylvania State University Press, University Park and London.

Lynch, R. L., and Cross, K. F. (1991). *Measure Up!* Blackwell Publ., Cambridge, Massachusetts.

McKendrick, N. (1961). Josiah Wedgwood and factory discipline. *Histor. J.* **4**(1), 30–55.

Vatter, W. J. (1959). Does the rate of return measure business efficiency? *NAA Bull.*, January, 33–48.

History, Social Science Methods Used in

Allan J. Lichtman
American University, Washington, DC, USA

Glossary

cliometrics The marriage of metrics with Clio, the muse of history, usually applied to the use of theory and quantitative methods in economic history.

content analysis The application of formal, replicable methods to studying manifest and latent patterns found within texts, including written documents and artifacts such as paintings, coins, films, and buildings.

counterfactual history An answer to a "What If?" question that uses theory and mathematical analysis to assess what might have happened absent particular events, trends, or innovations.

ecological regression The use of regression methods to draw inferences about the behavior of groups from aggregate units in which group members are included.

event history analysis Methods for analyzing life-cycle data such as birth, death, marriage, and divorce that involve few events over extended time periods and for which individuals are traced only for part of their life course.

exploratory data analysis The search for unsuspected regularities and relationships in historical data without testing hypotheses derived from predetermined theory.

game theory Models for analyzing a strategic response to situations in which the outcomes of an individual's or group's decisions are affected by the strategic calculations and choices of others with different and conflicting goals.

Geographic Information Systems (GIS) A computerized system for integrating, analyzing, and displaying digitized maps and other spatial-based data.

postmodernism A view of history that questions whether truth about the past is attainable, no matter how rigorous the methodology used. It suggests that rather than an objective record of the past, historians have only texts or discourses subject to limitless interpretation.

record linkage Computerized methods for recreating life histories by identifying and connecting individuals found in such multiple records as census reports, parish registers, and tax rolls.

time series analysis Methods for analyzing time-dependent data, in which the value of a variable at a particular time, such as spending by governments, is dependent on values at past times.

In the 1960s, historians began to draw extensively on social science methods to recapture the daily experiences of ordinary people, reinterpret history from the bottom up, and reconsider major interpretative questions through the use of quantitative data and verifiable methods of analysis. Since that time, historians have deployed increasingly sophisticated techniques adapted to the special challenges of historical study. Although historians using social science methods have not produced grand new theories of human behavior or come to dominate studies of the past, their work makes an indispensable contribution to every field of history.

History and Social Science

Historians draw on the precise quantitative methods of social science to fill gaps in the historical record, answer causal and interpretive questions about the past, and test theories of human behavior. Methods used by historians range from the simple counting and sorting of data to inferential statistical methods such as multiple regression analysis and quantitative analytic tools such as game theory. The use of social science methods has been influential in shifting the focus of much historical study from the deeds of great men and women to the lives of ordinary people and the challenges they confront in daily life. Through such interdisciplinary procedures historians have studied the masses as well as the elite and day-to-day events and the dramatic episodes of the past. The use of social science methods has opened up the once-hidden history of women, minorities, and poor people who left little or no documentary record of their own. It has cast new light on historical controversies and subjected theories derived from the disciplines of social science to the test of historical experience. However, critics have charged that social science methodology robs history of its human drama, replaces great deeds with the humdrum routine of daily life, condemns historians to arcane specializations, and forces an inherently contingent past into a Procrustean bed of preformed theory.

Origins of Social Science History

Quantitative social science history gained momentum in the 1960s and early 1970s as part of a New History movement that sought to reinterpret history from the bottom up, not the top down; to replace impressionistic, intuitive approaches with formal, verifiable methods of analysis; and to supplant historical narratives with the development and testing of hypotheses. New historians looked to supplement traditional historical sources (letters, diaries, and government documents, for example) with quantifiable sources of information (such as birth and death certificates, census records, business ledgers, ship manifests, and election returns) and to apply rigorous methods of content analysis to wrest hidden meanings from texts. They sought to achieve temporal and cross-cultural comparisons of experience across time and place and to look beneath the headline events of an era to discover the history that is latent rather than manifest in people's experience, such as changes in family size and structure. Their work also had the political objective of giving voice and agency to peoples whose experience was hidden in documentary records, but recoverable through scrutiny of quantitative data from the past.

The new history also reflected changes in social science, which was becoming more self-consciously methodological, abstract, and quantitative. "And still they come," wrote the poet W. H. Auden of the 20th century, "new from those nations to which the study of that which can be weighed and measured is a consuming love." Some new historians, in the words of one pioneering practitioner, Lee Benson, even anticipated that historians guided by quantitative social scientific methods would escape time-bound experience and "participate in the overall scholarly enterprise of discovering and developing general laws of human behavior."

Pragmatically, the development of high-speed computing and machine-readable databases accelerated the pace of work in quantitative social science history in the 1960s. Even the costly and unwieldy mainframe computers available at the time, with hours of turnaround time for a single job, let historians process far more data and apply more sophisticated statistical techniques than in earlier years. By the 1970s, historians were increasingly adept in using programming languages such as FORTRAN, COBOL, and BASIC, as well statistical software applications such as the Statistical Analysis System (SAS) and the Statistical Package for Social Sciences (SPSS), both of which remain in widespread use. Quantitative social science history, because it often requires the compilation and analysis of large bodies of data, led to the rise of government-supported machine-readable data archives—the quantifier's equivalent of manuscript repositories. In the 1960s, aided by funding from the National Science Foundation, the Inter-University Consortium of Political and Social Research (ICPSR) at the University of Michigan began compiling an extensive computerized base of quantitative political and social data that included election returns, survey results, legislative roll calls, and census compilations. By the 1990s, historians had available many hundreds of digital databases covering broad time periods and diverse geographic regions, and they also had desktop computers more powerful than the unwieldy mainframe computers of earlier years. Historians and social scientists also joined together in major collaborative projects that once were unusual in a solitary profession such as history. These included, for example, the Philadelphia Social History Project in the United States and the Cambridge Group for the Study of Population and Social Structure in Britain.

New journals dedicated to publishing work in quantitative social science history helped establish the legitimacy of such interdisciplinary work during the 1960s and 1970s. These included the *Journal of Social History* (1967), *Historical Methods Newsletter* (1967), the *Journal of Interdisciplinary History* (1970), and *Social Science History* (1976). In 1975, a small group of American scholars from history and social science disciplines formed the Social Science History Association (SSHA), dedicated to "encouraging the selective use and adaptation in historical research of relevant theories and methods from related disciplines, particularly the social sciences." The ICPSR and the Newberry Library in Chicago began offering instruction on quantitative applications in history and by the 1980s, an International Commission for the Application of Quantitative Methods in History was holding workshops and sponsoring programs at the meetings of the International Congress of Historical Sciences. Historians outside the United States formed organizations similar to the SSHA and founded several European-based journals dedicated to new historical methods, including *Historical Social Research* (Germany), *Histoire et Mesure* (France), and *History and Computing* (Great Britain). By the 1970s, mainstream historical journals were also publishing considerable historical research based on social science methods. According to a study by John Reynolds, from 1975 to 1981 work in social science history equaled approximately 28% of the research articles published in five major national historical journals in the United States.

Social science history gained prominence and luster through path-breaking work by early practitioners that commanded respect and attention in the profession. Economic history was first among the historical research fields to embrace quantitative social science methods. Perhaps the most notable among the early new economic historians was Robert Fogel. In 1964, with his work *Railroads and American Economic Growth*, Fogel challenged the widely held belief that railroads had been essential to the economic growth of the United States in the 19th century. To test this thesis, Fogel contrived a counterfactual model of a U.S. economy based not on railroads but on an extensive system of canals. Using available documentary data and assumptions drawn from neoclassical economic theory, Fogel estimated the rate of growth under the canal system and concluded that the canals in his hypothesized model would have proven almost as efficient as railroads and that economic growth would not have substantially slowed in the absence of railroads. Fogel's approach to economic history—the development of specific hypotheses about past economies, the testing of hypotheses through counterfactual modeling, and the reliance on quantitative methods and economic theory—became hallmarks of a new economic history that participants termed cliometrics. Much of the work in cliometrics is informed by variants of rational choice theory, which posits that markets and other human institutions arise from purposive, goal-seeking behavior by rationally calculating individuals. Some economic historians, however, including Douglas North (who shared the Nobel Prize with Fogel in 1993), stress the importance of economic and social institutions, bringing economic analysis more closely in line with historical experience, although at the expense of elegant formal models applicable in principle to diverse historical circumstance.

A decade after publication of Fogel's study of railroads, he and co-author Stanley Engerman stunned the world with *Time on the Cross* (1974), which used the techniques of cliometrics to argue that slavery was an efficient, profitable, and relatively humane system of labor. Slaves, the authors found, were well housed, clothed, and fed and were rarely beaten, sexually exploited, or forced to abandon their families. Moreover, they contended that slavery was profitable to slave owners, farms using slaves were more efficient than farms using free labor and the slave was "harder-working and more efficient than his white counterpart." These remarkable conclusions flowed from the application of computer-assisted inferential analysis to numerical data culled from probate records, plantation documents, slave-market registers, and census figures. The authors, for example, used techniques borrowed from demography and population genetics to approximate (from census tallies of mulatto slaves and the current genetic composition of American blacks), the proportion of slave children sired by white fathers. Their work posited that the destruction of the profitable system of slavery after the Civil War accounted for declining economic standards in the South, and that postbellum racism, not slavery, explained the present-day problems of African Americans in the United States. Prior to the publication of *Time on the Cross*, the social scientific revolution in history had largely taken place below the threshold of public awareness. Now a historical study using sophisticated mathematical analysis and social science models influenced policy debates and penetrated popular culture, setting off arguments pro and con in the press, innumerable reviews, and conferences devoted to debating the authors' methods and conclusions.

Economic history—often practiced by scholars such as Fogel with training in economic theory—remains the subdiscipline within history with the most extensive and sophisticated use of social science methods. The work of the cliometricians (most located in economics rather than history departments) came to dominate the field of economic history. The percentage of pages in the *Journal of Economic History* devoted to cliometric articles rose from approximately 6% in the 1950s, to more than 30% in the 1960s, to nearly 80% in the 1970s, and to slightly more than 80% in the 1980s. In 1993, Fogel and fellow cliometrician Douglas North won the Nobel Memorial Prize in economic studies "for having renewed research in economic history by applying economic theory and quantitative methods in order to explain economic and institutional change."

In social history, scholars associated with the *Annales School* of French historiography (founded several decades earlier) gained acclaim during the 1960s through painstaking efforts to achieve the total history of communities by reconstructing quantitatively their economic and demographic structure, material culture, and even mentalities or characteristic perceptions of the world. Much of this work relied not on advanced statistical techniques but on the simple compilation of data from previously unexploited sources such as church registers, court records, and tax rolls. The era's most prominent *Annales School* historian, Ferdinand Braudel, initiated a new kind of history in which clashes among rulers, struggles for economic advantage, and strife on the battlefield faded before more fundamental forces of longer duration: the physical environment, prevailing economic and social structures, and entrenched cultural practices and beliefs. "The history of events," Braudel wrote in the preface to *The Mediterranean and the Mediterranean World in the Age of Philip II*, which gained international attention when published in revised form in 1966, was the history of "surface disturbances, crests of foam that the tides of history carry on their strong backs."

In England, quantitative research on family structure shattered the long-cherished presumption that people lived in extended multigenerational families rather than nuclear families until the upheavals of the Industrial Revolution. Work by Peter Laslett and his associates on reconstructing family structure from local records showed that the nuclear family predominated in England long before the onset of industrialization. His findings indicated that for several centuries before industrialization married couples were expected to establish independent households, separate from elderly relatives. Studies conducted by John Hajnal at about the same time found different family patterns in eastern Europe, with a younger average age of marriage than in the West and a high incidence of complex extended and multifamily households. Later scholarship has modified but not overturned Laslett's conclusions, showing that his data failed to identify the common presence within households of lodgers, boarders, and servants, some of whom may have been family members.

In the United States, social historians led by Stephan Thernstrom examined the validity of the Horatio Alger myth of social mobility in 19th century America. Thernstrom's 1964 work, *Poverty and Progress*, a case study of the town of Newburyport, Massachusetts, between 1850 and 1880, examined the extent to which upward social mobility—defined not only through occupational advance but also the acquisition of savings accounts, land, and homes—was a reality for ordinary workers. Thernstrom drew on the data reported in the enumerator's schedules for four decennial federal censuses, city directories, and tax records to trace changes in the lives of laborers, finding that over a span of 30 years only a small minority of his sample succeeded in moving into nonmanual occupations and less than 25% amassed at least $1000 in property. Stories of rags to riches in the United States, his work and subsequent research suggest, were more myth than reality.

Lee Benson, with his 1961 book on politics and voting patterns in New York state during the era of Andrew Jackson in the United States, expanded the use of interdisciplinary methods into political history, a field once dedicated to the study of statesmen, laws, and institutions. His findings challenged the popular belief that President Jackson led an egalitarian Democratic party, drawing its support largely from the working class, in contrast to the rival Whig party with its base among more affluent voters. Through studying popular voting in relatively homogeneous communities, he found that rich communities did not vote differently from poor communities and that voting alignments often remained stable over relatively long periods of time. Differences in popular voting among communities, he found, were based not on economic class but on ethnic origin and religious affiliation. Benson explained his results by drawing on interest group theory, suggesting that different ethnocultural groups in early-19th century America regarded one another as negative reference groups and responded accordingly in their political allegiances. Benson's work had a profound influence on other political historians, including Ronald Formisano, Robert Kelley, Richard Jensen, and Paul Kleppner, who developed a broad ethnocultural interpretation of 19th century American political history. The ethnocultural thesis focuses on the quantitative study of popular voting, arguing that at least until the 1890s voters divided their political allegiance according to their commitment to "pietistic" religious and cultural values that sought to use government for moral reform or to "ritualistic" values that rejected coerced morality and stressed commitment to church rituals and beliefs.

Beyond popular voting, the new political historians also transformed our understanding of legislative politics through the quantitative analysis of roll-call votes. W. O. Aydolette in a 1963 article used Guttman scaling techniques to examine patterns in voting by members of the British Parliament in the 1840s on such weighty matters as repeal of the Corn Laws, the Chartist petition for voting rights, adoption of income taxes, and the imposition of duties on imported livestock. He found that two scales largely explained the voting patterns of many hundreds of Parliamentarians on numerous, seemingly diverse issues. His findings refuted prevailing class-based interpretations of political conflict and showed instead the importance of ideological and party divisions in the 1840s. By the 1970s, Aydelotte's pioneering work had led to similar studies of legislative voting in the United States, Denmark, France, and Mexico. Especially influential was Joel Silbey's 1967 work on congressional voting in the United States in the 1840s and early 1850s. He found that even as the controversy over slavery escalated, it was largely party loyalty not sectional origin that shaped and organized congressional behavior. Voting in Congress, moreover, closely correlated with the positions taken by parties in newspaper editorials, campaign speeches, and partisan texts.

Development of the Field

During the past 25 years, historians have deployed increasingly sophisticated techniques designed to deal with special challenges of historical study. Political and social historians have sought means for circumventing the ecological fallacy—the false presumption that relationships that prevail among aggregate units such as nations, states, provinces, counties, wards, and precincts correctly describe relationships among the groups contained within the units. For example, a correlation between wealthy counties in 1920s America and counties that voted predominantly Republican does not prove that affluent individuals necessarily tended to vote Republican. Likewise, higher suicide rates in heavily Protestant compared to heavily Catholic countries in 19th century Europe do not necessarily mean that Protestants were more likely than Catholics to commit suicide. To overcome this vexing problem, historians, who often lack data on individuals, turned to the technique of ecological regression, initially developed by sociologist Leo Goodman in the 1950s. This technique uses least-squares regression derived from aggregate-level data to model the underlying behavior of groups contained within the aggregate. In the 1970s, Allan J. Lichtman and J. Morgan Kousser were among the first historians to use ecological regression methods. Lichtman's study of the American presidential election of 1928 documented a powerful pro- and anti-Catholic response to Catholic Democratic candidate Al Smith and showed that, contrary to prior assumptions, voting in 1928 did not foreshadow the later New Deal coalition. Kousser's work documented the processes by which white redemptionists in the American South disenfranchised African Americans. Lichtman and Kousser's historical research also had practical implications because they were called on to testify as expert witnesses on voting behavior, political fairness, and minority political opportunities in scores of redistricting and voting-rights cases litigated in federal and state courts.

Lichtman, Kousser, and others also used multiple regression analyses to disentangle the impact on voting of such variables as race, religion, class, ethnicity, and urban-rural residence. Historians have since routinely used such analyses to study the variables that influence such phenomena as the birth weights of babies in early 20th century Europe, school attendance rates in 19th century Canada, the productivity of 17th century English agriculture, and rates of migration in modern developing nations. Historians have also turned to techniques such as probit, logit, and log-linear analysis to study data that fail to meet the statistical requirements of standard regression methods. They have, for example, used log-linear models to reexamine earlier work on social and economic mobility in the United States and Europe and to estimate change and stability in rates of intermarriage among racial and ethnic groups in Latin America.

Beyond the analysis of cross-sectional historical data such as voting in a particular election, historians have drawn on the special methodology of time series analysis to analyze chronologically organized data, where the value of a variable at a given time is dependent on values at earlier times—for example, spending by governments, deaths from certain kinds of disease, and rates of incarceration. These methods enable historians to discover trends, periodicity, and breakpoints within data independent of seasonal and other fluctuations. Historians have used methods of time series analysis to estimate the periodicity of smallpox epidemics in Europe, the frequency of industrial disputes in Great Britain and the United States, and age and gender patterns in the trans-Atlantic slave trade.

Through time series analyses, researchers have also explored interpretations of events called turning points in history. Researchers using interrupted time series analysis, for example, found that Franklin Roosevelt's New Deal of the 1930s failed to alter political and economic trends begun during the previous decade and that the Industrial Revolution produced less discontinuity in European economic life than previously suspected. In contrast, economic historian Claudia Goldin used both time series analysis and cross-sectional statistical analysis of data from American states to demonstrate that use of the birth control pill had a major impact on the educational, career, and marriage decisions of young women in the United States. New procedures for analyzing time series data, in addition, allow historians to explore how changes over time in historical circumstance affected relationships between variables—for instance, differences in the effects of social movements on policy-making during various stages in the life cycle of a regime.

Historians have used event-history methods to analyze data on people's life cycles, such as birth, death, marriage, and divorce, that are not amenable to standard methods because they involve few events over extended time periods and include individuals who cannot be traced for their full life course because they have moved, they have been inexplicably dropped from the records, or record-keeping ceases prior to their death. Event-history methods code data not according to the occurrence or nonoccurrence of events but to survival time prior to the event, and the methods measure not the number of individuals experiencing an event (e.g., marriage or the birth of a child) but the number of person-years prior to the occurrence of the event. Maximum likelihood methods can be applied to life tables to disentangle the effects of explanatory variables on such duration-dependent events. The analysis may include time-fixed variables such as age differences between married couples or time-changing variables such as the birth or death of a child. In a 1990 study of early modern Japan, Laurel L. Cornell used event-history methods to establish that divorce rates for peasant women were higher than once believed and that age differences at marriage, the lack of children, and the presence of a woman's mother-in-law all increased the likelihood of a marriage ending in divorce. Political historians of 19th century Britain have used event-history analysis to trace the voting history of individuals from poll books that recorded people's names and votes, demonstrating, for example, that the predictability of future from past voting (an indicator of party loyalty) increased significantly after the Reform Act of 1832. The methods of event-history analysis can also be applied to events that occur at the level of groups, organizations, or even nations, such as strikes, racial rioting, policy decisions, and technological innovation.

Historians, working individually and in team projects, have recreated life histories through the computerized linking of records such as census reports, parish records, tax rolls, and land registers. Such work, once laboriously done by hand, can now be conducted through algorithms and programs that probabilistically identify and connect the same individual cited in multiple records. These procedures are designed to overcome such problems as transcription errors, multiple spellings of names, name changes, commonly used names, compound names, abbreviations, and obscure handwritten entries. The prodigious labor required by even computer-assisted record linkage has promoted collaborative work. For decades, the Philadelphia Social History Project has worked on integrating databases to reconstruct ordinary life in Philadelphia for much of the 19th century. The Connecticut Valley Historical Demography Project has studied life cycles in Massachusetts towns from 1850 to 1910 by linking census reports on individuals with municipal death records. Teams of researchers have long been working on linking the rich sources of historical information on individuals available in the records of Scandinavian nations.

Through exploratory data analysis historians discover unsuspected regularities and relationships in historical data without testing hypotheses derived from predetermined theories. Exploratory methods, as demonstrated by the path-breaking work of John Tukey in 1977, are appropriate for historical data that do not satisfy the requirements of interval or ordinal scaling; are not linear in form; do not derive from independent, random sampling methods; suffer from selection bias; cannot be replicated; and contain gaps, dips, and extreme values or outliers. They also give quantitative specificity to historians' impressionistic notions about past trends and events without requiring the assumption that fixed relationships prevail among variables in different times and places. Tukey's innovative procedures rely on the graphical presentation of information to disclose the central tendency of data, reveal anomalies, and classify phenomena according to various attributes. Other methods derive from pattern-recognition techniques used, for example, in geophysics and medical diagnosis.

The use of Geographic Information Systems (GIS) for exploratory data analyses has led to the sophisticated spatial analysis of historical issues. These systems integrate, analyze, and display digitized maps and other spatial-based data on matters such as birth, marriage, and death; race; popular voting; protest demonstrations; economic activity; occupational patterns; home ownership; and transportation networks. Studies based on GIS reveal aspects of the past concealed in nonspatial forms of analysis and help resolve one of the central dilemmas of quantitative historical inquiry—changes in the geographic base for which statistics are collected. Major collaborative GIS projects include the Great Britain Historical GIS Project, China in Time, the United States County Boundary Files, and the worldwide Electronic Cultural Atlas Initiative. Historians have used GIS to study topics such as local migration patterns, geographic distributions of books and other sources of information, transportation networks, language use, political allegiance, local economic development, and demographic histories.

Historians have modeled past behavior using insights from game theory, which analyzes strategic responses to situations in which the outcome of any individual's decisions are affected by the actions of others with different and conflicting goals. Given this situation of strategic interdependence, decision makers cannot predict the consequences of their actions without considering the actions of others. Games can be cooperative or noncooperative, zero-sum (e.g., winner take all) or amenable to differential payoffs for all players involved. They may involve limited or unlimited numbers of actors and varying degrees of uncertainty. The rules of the game specify the resources and strategic options available to players. Critical to game theory are its notions of strategy (each player's plan of action for maximizing payoffs) and of equilibrium (an outcome in which no player can unilaterally improve his payoff provided that other players stick to their chosen strategies as well). Peter Z. Grossman, for example, applied game theory to studying acts of political terror by the state, using the classic one-shot, *n*-person prisoner's dilemma game to analyze decisions made by detainees during Josef Stalin's bloody political purges in the 1930s. Under this scenario, the optimal individual strategy for prisoners is to cooperate with interrogators in implicating other suspects in order to avoid the worst possible outcome—death for noncooperating prisoners implicated by any one of an indefinite number of other known and unknown detainees. However, Grossman demonstrated that prisoners could alter this strategic equilibrium by changing the terms of the game through efforts to implicate their interrogators. Now, a prisoner is no longer playing only against other prisoners but also against the state and its agents, who have no consistent optimal response. He concluded that this rule-changing strategy raised the costs of the purge to authorities and ultimately limited its scope and impact.

Historians have applied game theory to other situations, including the allocation of resources by political campaigners and decisions made by legislators, kings, and religious leaders. A 1998 compendium of game-theoretical studies of history, *Analytic Narratives*, applies game theory to major historical issues in an effort to prove the truth of noted mathematics scholar James R. Newman's claim that "Games are among the most interesting creations of the human mind, and the analysis of their structure is full of adventure and surprises." The work included in this volume explores the rise and fall of the International Coffee Organization in the 20th century, the sources of sectional balance in American politics prior to the Civil War, the development of political institutions under the French and British monarchies and in the commune of Genoa during the late medieval period, and the policies for conscripting men for war in 19th century Britain and the United States. These analyses demonstrate that game theory can illuminate issues central to understanding national and international histories.

In the 1990s, political scientists Keith Poole and Howard Rosenthal achieved a revolutionary breakthrough in studying the history of legislative roll-call voting, including the difficult question of how to compare voting patterns across time periods with changing issues, party systems, and constituencies. Using multidimensional scaling methods to analyze more than 16 million roll calls in the American Congress since 1789, they found that political conflict can be modeled according to the ideological positions of legislators on just one or two dimensions. The first and most important dimension corresponds roughly to liberal-conservative differences on government intervention in and regulation of the economy. The second dimension roughly measures positions on race and civil liberties. Poole and Rosenthal have generously made their data available on the Web, including ideological scores for each member of Congress that are comparable over time. Their results indicate that ideology is more important than constituent influences in shaping congressional voting, that realignments in congressional voting result from the replacement rather than the conversion of legislators, and that congressional voting became both more ideologically polarized in the late 20th century than in earlier years and largely one-dimensional because positions on economic and social issues fell into line for both parties (e.g., legislators who voted for generous welfare programs also voted for civil rights laws and against restrictions on abortion). Their scales can be used to study the polarization between parties and regions, the effects of elections on congressional voting patterns, and correlations between liberal-conservative ideologies and voting on particular issues. Scholars have extended Poole and Rosenthal's methodology to study the history of roll-call voting in legislative bodies outside the United States.

Although interdisciplinary historians have not achieved Lee Benson's dream of formulating new laws of human behavior, their work has challenged the universalistic assumptions of social science theories. Historians, for example, have questioned the application of rational choice theory to contexts in which nonmarket values and institutions predominate and people act according to tradition, altruism, ideology, religious belief, or prejudice and subordinate their own interests to common group goals. Scholars of literacy have challenged linear theories of the relationship between literacy and modernization and called attention to forms of literacy other than alphabetic discernment: oral and numerical abilities, spatial awareness, visual acuity, and aesthetic sensibility. Political historians have contested the regularities of critical election theory, a construct of political science that posits that electoral systems respond to unmet public needs through periodic critical or realigning elections that alter the balance of partisan power, reshuffle coalitions of voters, and introduce policy and institutional change. Historians have also cast doubt on the thesis that modernization marked a sharp transition from societies with high fertility and unregulated birth rates to societies with low fertility and controlled reproduction. Historical demographers have found that patterns of fertility were more variable than previously assumed, that preindustrial societies effectively used traditional methods for regulating birth, and that in many cases fertility rates rose, not fell, during the early stages of industrialization. Historians have in addition discovered that there is no single path to industrialization but, rather, that economic development can follow multiple paths ranging from abrupt economic take-offs to a gradual diffusion of technologies and market systems.

Historians have deployed social science methods to address issues once amenable only to informal interpretation. Methods of social network analysis map and measure networks of individuals, groups, and organizations, discerning often hidden patterns in the dissemination of information and influence and uncovering the causes of stability or collapse. Event structure analysis provides computerized models for drawing on a historian's expertise to derive explicit, replicable models of narrative explanations. It forces the historian to distinguish between what is central and what is incidental to an explanation, and it provides a basis for more abstract formulations applicable to other concrete situations. Economic historian David Galenson achieved new insights into artistic creativity by applying cliometric methods to the analysis of prices at art auctions and reproductions of artistic works in textbooks. He found that artistic productivity follows two distinctive patterns, represented by the archetypes of Picasso who achieved a quick, conceptual breakthrough early in life and of Cezanne who refined and developed his art gradually over time through trial and error and achieved his most valued work late in his career.

Most prolifically, historians have used refined methods for the content analysis of texts, including written documents, and material creations such as paintings, coins, churches, and homes. Content analysis is a global term describing a body of formal, replicable methods of data coding and numerical analysis that supplants or supplements the impressionistic reading of texts. Historians have used methods of content analysis to study the appearance of words and phrases in documents or the spatial display of objects in paintings. For example, social historians have studied the arrangement of subjects in family portraits to document changing representations of age, hierarchy, and gender. More complex applications include the discovery of hidden structures of meaning implied by the relationship among concepts in a text and the cognitive mapping of mental structures reflected in a text. For example, scholars have used methods of content analysis to map the concepts and relations that structured the responses of American opinion leaders to the Cold War and its aftermath. Content analysis may illuminate particular issues such as the response of business publications to New Deal reforms or the grievances expressed by Frenchmen petitioning the regime on the eve of the French Revolution. It may also be applied to broad societal trends. A study of front-page stories in major American newspapers throughout the 20th century, for example, disclosed an increasing depersonalization as generalizations and statistical findings replaced a focus on individuals, anecdotes, and inferences from examples. Historians and social scientists worldwide have used content analysis of sources such as newspaper articles and police reports to document across space and time the occurrence, duration, size, and grievances of protest events (e.g., riots, revolutions, and demonstrations) and the various societal responses (e.g., cooptation, repression, and infiltration).

Reaction and Response

The rise of quantitative, social science history in the 1960s generated debates between equally passionate opponents and champions of this new approach. American colonial historian Carl Bridenbaugh in his 1963 presidential address to the American Historical Association entitled "The Great Mutation," warned, "The finest historians will not be those who succumb to the dehumanizing methods of social sciences, whatever their uses and values, which I hasten to acknowledge. Nor will the historian worship at the shrine of that Bitch-goddess, QUANTIFICATION." Bridenbaugh and other traditionalists worried that arcane statistics about people in the mass would supplant the imaginative reconstruction of individual experience and that writing about the past would take on the hypothesis-testing form of scientific papers, sacrificing the explanatory and expressive power of the historical narrative. They feared that history would assume the barren abstractness of science and lose its capacity for conveying to a broad audience the hopes and dreams, agonies and accomplishments of individuals in times and places different from their own. And history reduced to science, in their view, would no longer cast light on such human preoccupations as freedom and social order, democracy and authority, tradition and innovation, faith and reason, and pluralism and unity.

The most zealous of the early practitioners of quantitative social science history gave little credence to such cautionary tales. Instead, they expected their new methodologies to sweep the field, rendering obsolete the old-fashioned, impressionistic approach to historical evidence and analysis. They believed that more precise and theoretically informed history would revitalize the profession, establish a reliable base of knowledge and theory, suggest intriguing new lines of inquiry, and recover the hidden history of invisible and suppressed peoples. Emmanuel Le Roy Ladurie of the *Annales School* declared in 1967 that the "historian of the year 2000 would be a programmer or would not exist." Although work based on quantitative social science methodology became part of mainstream history during the 1970s and 1980s, it never achieved the dominance predicted by Le Roy Ladurie and other early practitioners. Reynolds's study of major American journals showed that the publication of such work peaked at approximately 30% during the 1980s and fell to about 25% during the first half of the 1990s.

This decline reflects the failure of the historical profession to incorporate expertise in social science methods into the teaching of professional historians and the indifference, if not outright hostility, of younger cohorts of historians following the "cultural turn" aimed at recreating the cultural meaning of past events from the perspective of participants and through approaches not amenable to formal methods of analysis. Recent trends in historical scholarship have also revitalized explanation through narratives rather than hypothesis and an understanding of past time through what is sometimes termed the thick description of events. Also influential are postmodern ideas, which question whether truth about the past is attainable, no matter how rigorous the methodology used. In this view, instead of having an objective record of the past, historians have only texts or discourses that are subject to interpretation and reinterpretation without any objective means for adjudicating among them. Historical work is itself a discourse that may or may not be persuasive, exciting, or compelling, but does not correspond to any concrete verifiable reality. Historians cannot transcend their subjectivity and their own time to produce an objective account of the past. Rather, historians produce a plurality of histories or discourses, shaped not just by historical texts, but by ever-shifting present-day values, conventions of language, intuitions, and prevailing theories of human behavior. There is no finality to historical study—the triumph of one historical discourse over another is always unstable, contingent, and subject to change based on unpredictable, nonobjective criteria. Although postmodern history seems the polar opposite of quantitative social science history, both approaches reflect the common political objective of giving recognition to previously marginalized individuals such as women, poor people, and nondominant racial groups. By equalizing interpretations of texts, postmodernists sought to free subordinated people from the power exerted by mainstream culture and recover for posterity their values and ways of life.

Paradoxically, postmodernist critiques cooled the fires of conflict between traditional practitioners and interdisciplinary historians. Postmodernism questions not just the application of social science methods to history, but also any logically governed, evidentially based study of the past. Traditionalists and social scientific historians both agree that despite wide latitude for interpretation, historical work remains constrained by logical and empirical methods that have stood the test of critical review by generations of scholars. Both camps have also come to recognize that the application of quantitative methodology and theoretical models supplements, not supplants, traditional forms of historical study.

If work in quantitative, social scientific history has not come to stand like a Colossus over the field, it has nonetheless made and continues to make indispensable contributions to studying the human condition in past times. Historians cannot today address such diverse issues as economic development, labor relations, family life, migration, social mobility, crime and policing, health and mortality, state-building, legislative and electoral politics, literacy, protest movements, and warfare without taking into account the questions, findings, and inferences of work in quantitative social science history. Social science historians, in turn, have come to acknowledge the limitations of their methodology as applied to a field in which humans are both the subject and object of study, replicable experimentation is precluded, data are limited and time-bound, and important questions are not amenable to scientifically verifiable answers.

Most practitioners of quantitative social science history have resisted the impulse to reduce their discipline to another social science, remaining aware that history, like the god Janus, faces toward both social science and the humanities. Rather than abstracting universal propositions from past events they follow Thoreau's precept that "He is not a true man of science who does not bring some sympathy to his studies, and expect to learn something by behavior as well as by application." The practitioners of quantitative social science methods are participating with other historians in studying human experience as bounded by time and place, stretching our imagination to grasp conditions and challenges different from our own. Students of interdisciplinary history appreciate the continuing importance of recreating individual experience, interpreting the meaning of past ages, and crafting narratives accessible to nontechnical readers. The best of what is still called the new history combines social scientific and traditional methods of inquiry and communicates its findings in clear and vivid prose that brings home to broad audiences an understanding of their heritage and experience, something that the finest historical scholarship has always done.

See Also the Following Articles

Computerized Record Linkage and Statistical Matching • Content Analysis • Event History Analysis • Game Theory, Overview • Geographic Information Systems • Time Series Analysis in Political Science

Further Reading

Adyelotte, W., Bogue, A., and Fogel, R. (eds.) (1972). *The Dimensions of Quantitative Research in History.* Princeton University Press, Princeton, NJ.

Bates Robert, H., *et al.* (1998). *Analytic Narratives.* Princeton University Press, Princeton, NJ.

Benson, L. (1972). *Toward the Scientific Study of History.* J. B. Lippincott Company, Philadelphia.

Bonnell, V. E., and Hunt, L. (eds.) (1991). *Beyond the Cultural Turn: New Directions in the Study of History and Society.* University of California Press, Berkeley, CA.

Burke, P. (1992). *History and Social Theory.* Policy Press, Cambridge, MA.

Clubb, J., Austin, E., and Kirk, G. (1989). *The Process of Historical Inquiry: Everyday Lives of Working Americans.* Columbia University Press, New York.

Fogel, R., and Elton, G. R. (1983). *Which Road to the Past: Two Views of History.* Yale University Press, New Haven, CT.

Galenson, David W. (2001). *Painting Outside the Lines: Patterns of Creativity in Modern Art.* Harvard University Press, Cambridge, MA.

Griffin, L. J. and van der Linden, M. (eds.) (1998) New methods for social history. *Int. Rev. Soc. Hist.* **43**, 3–8.

Jarausch, K., and Hardy, K. (1991). *Quantitative Methods for Historians: A Guide to Research, Data, and Statistics.* University of North Carolina Press, Chapel Hill, NC.

Kousser, J. M. (1989). The state of social science history in the late 1980s. *Hist. Methods* **22,** 13–22.

Laslett, Peter. (1971). *The World We Have Lost.* Scribners, New York.

Lichtman, A. J. (1974). Correlation, regression, and the ecological fallacy. *J. Interdisciplinary Hist.* **4,** 417–433.

Reynolds, J. F. (1998). Do historians count anymore? *Hist. Methods* **31,** 141–148.

Tilly, C. (1984). *Big Structures, Large Processes, Huge Comparisons.* Russell Sage Foundation, New York.

Tukey, J. W. (1977). *Exploratory Data Analysis.* Addison Wesley, Reading, MA.

Household Behavior and Family Economics

Yoosik Youm

University of Illinois at Chicago, Chicago, Illinois, USA

Glossary

bargaining model An economic model that treats the division of household labor as the result of bargaining between spouses who have different and even conflicting interests.

comparative advantage in market sector A spouse has a comparative advantage in market sector if and only if his/her marginal product ratio of market sector (vs. housework sector) is greater than that of the other spouse.

density-of-friendship circle The proportion of the actual number of friendship ties among a spouse's friends out of the maximum possible number of friendship ties.

doing gender A process of creating and maintaining gender identity by rendering oneself accountably masculine or feminine through everyday activities.

gender theory A model under which the division of household labor is not the result of rational behaviors but instead derives from the process of creating and maintaining gender identity in everyday life.

neoclassical model This economic model assumes that the division of household labor is the result of a couple's harmonized behavior that aims to maximize shared unitary utility: people do housework voluntarily in order to maximize the aggregate consumption of the household.

network approach A sociological approach that pays special attention to how a couple's personal network ties affect the division of household labor. The division of household labor is the result not only of spouses' individual attributes, but also derives from the patterns of their social ties.

power-dependency theory This sociological theory assumes that the division of household labor is the result of a couple's power relationship, which is determined by resource discrepancy.

threat point Minimum welfare level if no agreement can be reached in bargaining. The spouse with the higher threat point has a bargaining advantage when a couple makes decisions about the division of household labor. A threat point is typically measured by options (or resources) outside the relationship.

Recent theoretical debates in the social sciences have dealt with how to obtain the proper measures of household behaviors, especially the division of household labor. In the field of economics, the neoclassical and the bargaining paradigms, in particular, have emerged. Until the early 1990s, most economists treated a household as one economic unit based on common preference assumptions. Although this approach gained popularity, especially because of convenient data acquisition at the household level (instead of the individual level), bargaining models have now been developed that treat the family as a collection of individuals with different utilities. In the field of sociology, instead of focusing only on individual attributes of family members, gender theory and the network approach emphasize that household behaviors are the products of interactions between individual family members. Based on these theoretical developments, the focus here is on examining various measurement issues, such as proper levels (for individuals and couples), data collection methods (survey, observation, and emotion sampling methods), and measurement indices (comparative advantage, options outside, and network properties).

Introduction

The following discussions examine diverse theoretical debates and measurement issues concerning one of the most well-studied examples of household behavior, the division of household labor. Diverse approaches have been developed to explain a persistent empirical puzzle: whether employed or not, women do most of the housework. Numerous studies have found that employed married women in the United States do about twice as much housework as employed married men do. The division of household labor has attracted theoretical interest because it provides an excellent empirical test of theories on intrahousehold resource/power distribution. Discussion of measurement issues herein is in line with theoretical developments in social sciences: special attention is paid to providing a brief summary of measurement concerns that are most relevant to evaluating and developing theoretical issues, without trying to provide an extensive list of measurement issues. In the following two sections, theoretical debates in social sciences are briefly introduced.

Economic Approaches: Neoclassical vs. Bargaining

In economics, two competing paradigms have been established to explain how the division of household labor is determined. Neoclassical economic theory, especially as exemplified by Gary Becker's work, argues that the partner with comparative advantage in the market (for example, the higher wage rate) will specialize in paid work and the other partner will specialize in housework, in order to maximize shared unitary utility. In sharp contrast to the assumption of unitary utility of the family members, a group of economic models has adopted the bargaining approach; developed by John F. Nash, this model states that the division of household labor is the result of bargaining between spouses who have separate and even conflicting interests. According to bargaining models, the person who has a bargaining advantage (normally the one who has more resources outside the marriage/cohabitation) will specialize less in housework.

Until the early 1990s, most economists treated the household as one economic unit in which family members behave as if they share one common utility, or at least as if they agree on every economic activity. This "common preference" (or unitary utility of the couple) is guaranteed by consensus or altruism. Different terms are used to describe this approach: neoclassical model, common preference model, unitary model, or consensus model. The approach has gained popularity based on typical economic consumption data that are usually reported at the household level. It has also allowed economists to analyze household data with relative ease by putting aside the theoretical task of showing how individual preferences are aggregated at the collective household level (the so-called preference aggregation problem). Becker provided the seminal theoretical basis for this approach: as a possible mechanism to ensure the unitary utility of the household, he paid attention to "care." In his well-known "rotten-kid" theorem, he proved that even if only one of the members is taking care of meeting the needs of the others, so that his/her preference depends on the others' utility function, every family member (including a rotten kid) would try to maximize the joint family utility. Now, under the assumption that couples try to maximize their shared consumption in the household, Becker proved that no more than one family member would specialize in both market work and household work if all family members have different comparative advantages. Please note that the theorem is valid no matter what family members' income levels are. Even if both spouses have high income from paid work, there will be still positive gains from specialization as long as it is based on comparative advantage and their goal is to maximize their unitary utility. In conclusion, under the neoclassical approach, the person with a comparative advantage in the market will allocate time mainly to the market sector and the other will spend time mainly on housework, thus maximizing their shared utility (or aggregate consumption).

Although Becker avoids the preference aggregation problem by assuming "caring" (or altruism), the issue over who has the last word (or ultimate power) in the household is not solved. A caring person (or a parent) must have the ultimate power in the household in order that the rotten kid theorem is valid. It disregards the fact that the family is also often the place for conflict and struggle. In economics, many different approaches have been developed to treat the family as a collection of individuals with different utilities and to show how the aggregated outcome emerges from different and even conflicting utilities. As one major approach, bargaining models assuming a cooperative game between two persons have been proposed for the intrahousehold division of labor and thus the division of household labor is the result of bargaining between two persons with separate utility. As the solution of the basic Nash bargaining model expects, a higher threat point (i.e., the minimum welfare level if no agreement can be reached between the players, divorce or break up being the payoff in this case) always decreases housework and increases paid work. There have been several efforts to elaborate the Nash bargaining model—for example, by replacing an external threat point with an internal one. Such efforts attempt to explain intrahousehold decisions without relying on the assumption of a single household utility function. In sum, according to bargaining models, a person with a higher threat point will specialize in paid work and the other person with a lower threat point will specialize in housework.

Many empirical results have challenged the unitary utility argument, especially by showing that family members do not appear to pool their income. But most empirical results can be interpreted in accord with both camps, and thus cannot be judged as conclusive rejections of the neoclassical approach. However, many now believe that the burden of proof should be shifted onto those who argue for the unitary utility of the family.

Sociological Approaches: Macro vs. Micro

In the search for mechanisms that are responsible for the persistent sexual division of household labor, diverse sociological attempts have been proposed and examined at different levels of analysis. Macro studies successfully turn attention to social systems such as capitalism or patriarchy as a cause for society-level oppression of women that is manifested in the sexual division of labor. In the opposite direction of this Socialist/Marxist feminism, micro research highlights individual-level attributes of spouses, such as resource level (or resource gap between spouses). Power-dependency models in sociology (or exchange theory, or a resource-dependency theory) that correspond to bargaining models in economics have focused on the power of each spouse as determined by their relative resource level, such as income, occupation prestige, or education: more power produces less housework hours. Also, some studies focus on gender-role attitudes of individual spouses.

Although many studies have focused on either macro (society) systems or micro (individual) attributes, some attention has been paid to interactions within families or between a family member and his/her social intimates, such as friends, kin, and neighbors. Gender theory is one of the few approaches that put interactions in the center of the research. In contrast to the old concept of gender role, which is supposed to be learned through socialization and to remain internal to the individual mind as fixed form, gender has been conceived as constituted by a set of behavioral displays or sex-specific ways of appearing, acting, and feeling, all of which serve to establish or reaffirm categorical identity. This notion of gender display has been further elaborated and advanced by developing the concept of "doing gender," which is displaying gender by making use of discrete, well-defined bundles of behavior. This behavior is necessarily insufficient to generate and maintain gender identity in society, because the "bundles" cannot simply be endlessly plugged into the continuum of interactional situations to produce recognizable enactments of masculinity and femininity. To be successful, marking or displaying gender must be finely fitted to ever-changing situations and constantly modified or transformed as the interactional occasion demands. Doing gender includes the ongoing task of rendering oneself accountably masculine or feminine in everyday life, and thus, although it is individuals who do gender, the enterprise is fundamentally interactional and institutional in character, for accountability is a feature of social relationships and its idiom is drawn from the institutional arena in which those relationships are enacted.

The network approach is another sociological approach that focuses on the interactions of family members as an essential mechanism for determining the division of household labor. Whereas gender theory focuses on symbolic interactions based on normative constructs and institutional settings, the network approach examines structural interactions based on quantitative measurements of the social networks that create and maintain gender differences. Elizabeth Bott's ethnographic study based on 20 couples in London is considered to be one of the first major network studies to reveal that the degree of segregation in the role-relationship of husband and wife varied directly with the connectedness of the family's social network. Bott found two ideal typical families based on several network properties of couples. Three major network characteristics of the *first type* of family are the focus of discussion here. In this family, the couple took it for granted that the husband would have some recreation with men away from home and the wife had separate relationships in which her husband did not expect to join; there was little shared free time. Second, the husband had male friends as the main members of his network, whereas the wife had relatives or neighbors; the husband and wife had very few mutual friends. Third, although the total network of both spouses was sharply divided into the husband's network and the wife's network, within each network, there was a high degree of connectedness between members, independent of the couple: this represents a very dense friendship circle. This type of family is strongly associated with a highly segregated conjugal role-relationship: the husband and the wife believe that there should be a clear-cut division of labor between them and they actually carry out their internal domestic tasks in a very separate way. This fits the picture of traditional families: husbands spend time with their buddies while wives do housework, chatting with their relatives or neighbors.

The *second type* of family has an opposite network structure. First, joint entertainment of friends is a major form of recreation for both the husband and the wife; much free time is shared. Second, nearly all of the husband's friends and the wife's friends are joint friends with the husband and wife. Third, it is not usual for a large number of the family's friends to be in intimate contact with one another independently of their contact with the family: this represents a sparse friendship circle. In this type of family, although there is a basic differentiation between husband's role as primary breadwinner and the wife's as mother of young children, the division of labor is flexible and there is considerable sharing and interchange of tasks.

The associations were explained by differential pressures from the couples' different patterns of networks. In the first type of family, each spouse is strongly embedded in his/her own external networks and thus each spouse is very sensitive to his/her respective social ties (rather than to each other). Because each spouse's external ties are strongly separated, spouses will have a very separate role. In sharp contrast to this, in the second type of family, the strongest influence on each spouse is self-derived, rather than being derived from social intimates. These partners are much more flexible in their roles and meet their own specific needs without strong monitoring or pressures from their kin and friends. The network approach has extended its theoretical horizon by either being incorporated into the wider theme of autonomy or being integrated into a non-cooperative game-theoretic model through a cohesion (rather than autonomy) mechanism between spouses.

In the following sections, measurement issues are discussed in two parts: first, how the division of household labor can be measured as dependent variables, and second, how main causal factors assumed by various theoretical standpoints can be measured.

Measuring Issues 1: Division of Household Labor

Measuring Units

One of the most widely studied data sets on the division of household labor, the National Survey of Families and Households (NSFH), has revealed that there are systematic interspouse reporting discrepancies on the reported amount of housework time. The NSFH asked each spouse to estimate their housework hours and their spouse's hours ("How many hours do you and your spouse spend on the following tasks?"). In general, both husbands and wives tended to report more hours for self than they reported for their spouses, and the discrepancies were greater for the husband's self-reported hours. Given this kind of discrepancy, it is desirable to measure housework hours at a couple level instead of an individual level: couple-matched data asks for combined housework hour estimates. This is important especially because many studies reveal that the discrepancy is systematically affected by normative attitudes, relational quality, and demographic characteristics. As long as traditional surveys are used to measure housework hours, however, even couple-matched data can suffer from validity issues—i.e., reported hours can be different from actual hours. This leads the discussion to the next issue, measuring instruments.

Measuring Instruments

Many studies have found that direct questions tend to lead to overestimation of housework hours. Given that observing housework would be prohibitive for large-scale representative data, one of the attractive alternatives might be a time-diary method. In time-use studies employing this method, respondents are asked to complete a diary of hours spent on various activities. Especially when people are involved in multiple housework tasks simultaneously (e.g., doing laundry while taking care of a baby), it is hard for them to later recall precisely the hours they spent on each activity; time-diary entries are more reliable compared to retrospective self-reports. The time-diary can be also effective in studying the emotions or feelings people go through during performance of specific housework tasks. Experimental sampling methodology (ESM) developed in psychology studies attempts to collect random sampling of behavior, thoughts, feelings, and experiences in real-life situations. Respondents are provided with a questionnaire booklet in which they record their behavior, thoughts, or feelings when they are beeped by a randomly activated pager. This instrument is especially useful when the interest is in normative constructs around specific housework; for example, some housework tasks are considered "male-work" and thus husbands can maintain and even strengthen their masculinity by doing those specific types of housework. The time-diary method and ESM will be accurate to the extent that diary time and day are representative of the general pattern of everyday activities.

Measuring Issues 2: Factors Responsible for the Division of Household Labor

Measuring Units

Most economic analyses and many sociological approaches to study the division of household labor use individual-level attributes such as income, wage rate, education, occupational prestige, and gender-role attitudes to measure comparative advantage, threat point, resources that define power, or normative attitudes as units of measurement. In contrast, some sociological approaches, including gender theory and the network approach, have paid attention to the interaction properties of couples, based on the premise that measurement units cannot be reduced to each individual spouse's attributes. Given that each approach (focusing on the individual vs. the couple) has gained empirical support from various studies, to obtain solid conclusions in empirical research, the ideal would be to include both units of measurement.

Measuring Objects

Depending on the theoretical approach of a research project, what to measure will be different. Three primary quantitative measurements for the selected approaches relate to comparative advantage, threat point, and network.

Comparative Advantage

To provide an exact operational meaning of comparative advantage as it is used in neoclassical economic theory, it is necessary to examine the equation of the aggregate assumption of household assumed in Becker's original formula. An aggregate consumption Z of the household of a husband and wife is as follows:

$$Z = Z(x, t_h') = Z\left[\alpha\left(wt_p^m/p_x\right) + wt_p^w/p_x,\ \beta\left(t_h^m\right) + t_h^w\right].$$

This formula of aggregate consumption is composed of market goods (x) and household goods (t_h', represented by the effective amount of housework hours), and both the man and the woman produce both types of products. The amount of goods consumed is the sum of goods earned due to the man (αw is the wage rate, t_p^m is the amount of time spent on paid work by the man, and p_x is the price for goods) and due to the woman $\left(wt_p^w/p_x\right)$. Household goods also derive from the man's housework hours $\left(\beta t_h^m\right)$ and from the woman's housework hours $\left(t_h^w\right)$. The husband has a comparative advantage in the market sector relative to the woman if and only if

$$\frac{\partial Z/\partial t_p^w}{\partial Z/\partial t_h^w} < \frac{\partial Z/\partial t_p^m}{\partial Z/\partial t_h^m},$$

which means that $\alpha > \beta$ in the previous equation. The husband has a comparative advantage in the market sector if and only if the marginal product ratio in the market sector (vs. the housework sector) for the husband is greater than the marginal product ratio in the market sector (vs. the housework sector) for the wife. However, to measure the marginal product ratio for each spouse is not straightforward because a valid, reliable price for housework is not available. Under the assumption that marginal product in the housework is the same for each spouse, wage rate can be used as a proxy for the comparative advantage. However, even obtaining wage rate is complicated because there are people who do not currently work (or even never work). For those people, it is possible to use an estimated wage rate based on factors such as years of schooling, estimated years of job experience, gender, and race.

Threat Point

The concept of the threat point came directly from classical Nash bargaining model. The Nash bargaining outcome is the solution to the maximization problem: Max $(u_1 - d_1)\ (u_2 - d_2)$, under the condition that $u_1 + u_2 = u$, where u_1 and u_2 are the payoffs to the two individuals, respectively, and d_1 and d_2 are threat points, or the minimum welfare level if no agreement can be reached between the players. The solution can be derived as $u_1 = 1/2(d_1 - d_2) + 1/2\,u$ and $u_2 = 1/2(d_2 - d_1) + 1/2\,u$. It can be easily confirmed from this solution that higher threat points always increase payoffs (or paid work instead of housework, in this case) once the other partner's threat point is given. The threat point for the bargaining of the division of household labor can be options outside the relationship (e.g., expected welfare in the case of divorce or break up). It can also be conceptualized as including options inside the relationship (such as lower housework production due to shirking).

To measure the threat point (or options outside the relationship), it is possible to use either subjectively perceived options or objective indices for options outside marriage, such as education level or income level. For example, some studies used the respondents' subjective assessment of whether their lives would worsen or improve were they not married. For example, the following question in the NSFH was used to measure the relative power in the relationship: "Even though it may be very unlikely, think for a moment about how various areas of your life might be different if you separated." Unfortunately, there is not enough empirical data to confirm that this kind of direct question correctly measures the options outside the relationship.

Alternatively, it is possible to use income or education level as a proxy for options outside the relationship. However, this also suffers from one problem: the resource level of an individual spouse (nor even the resource gap between spouses) does not accurately measure options outside marriage. Threat in bargaining comes not directly from the bargainers' resource gap but from the availability of alternative options in the case of dissolution. Even if a woman has significantly less education (or wage potential) than her husband has, if she can find a better husband with a higher wage (compared to the current husband) who will spend more time on household chores, she can demand more housework from the current husband. Simple measures of resource level (either in absolute or relative terms) have limitations in gauging potential welfare in the case of dissolution. Potential welfare depends on critical parameters of the marriage market, such as age, physical attractiveness, earning capacity, and occupational prestige; these will work for each gender in different ways.

Before moving on to a discussion of network measures, it is important to clarify a difference between neoclassical economics and bargaining theory with respect to their treatment of the wage rate. In bargaining models, an increase in wage rate always decreases housework hours, but such an increase would not matter in neoclassical economics as long as it does not change the status of comparative advantage.

Network Measures

Although network approaches do not yet have unified theoretical propositions and thus there is not full agreement on what kind of effect each network property has on the division of household labor, it is possible to identify three major network dimensions that are crucial to the mechanisms responsible for the division of household labor: sharing free time, mutual friends, and density-of-friendship circle. First, the extent to which spouses share free time is easily measured either by direct questioning in a traditional survey format or by experimental sampling methodology. Second, mutual friends can be measured either in absolute sense (total number of mutual friends) or in relative sense (the proportion of mutual friends). The proportion of mutual friends of the couple can be calculated as follows:

$$N_m/(N_h + N_w - N_m),$$

where N_m is the number of mutual friends and N_h and N_w are the number of friends of husband and wife, respectively. The denominator represents number of pooled friends of couples. This measure varies from 0, when spouses have no mutual friends, to 1, when all the friends are mutual friends.

The third measure of importance is the density-of-friendship circle for each spouse. This can be calculated as follows: $n/[N(N-1)]$, where N is the total number of friends (not counting the spouse) and n is the number of friendship ties between friends. The denominator is the possible maximum number of friendship ties between N persons and the numerator is the actual number of friendship ties. This measure varies from 0 (if among the spouse's friends, nobody is a friend to anybody) to 1 (when everybody is a friend to everybody).

See Also the Following Articles

Consumption and Saving • Economic Anthropology • Social Interaction Models

Further Reading

Alba, R., and Kadushin, C. (1976). The intersection of social circles. *Sociol. Methods Res.* **5,** 77–102.

Alderman, H., Chiappori, P.-A., Haddad, L., Hoddinott, J., and Kanbur, R. (1995). Unitary versus collective models of the household: Is it time to shift the burden of proof? *World Bank Res. Observ.* **10,** 1–19.

Becker, G. S. (1991). *A Treatise on the Family: An Enlarged Edition.* Harvard University Press, Cambridge, Massachusetts.

Bott, E. (1971). *Family and Social Network: Roles, Norms and External Relationships in Ordinary Urban Families,* 2nd Ed. Routledge, London.

Burt, R. (1992). *Structural Holes: The Social Structure of Competition.* Harvard University Press, Cambridge, Massachusetts.

Csikszentmihalyi, M., Larson, R., and Prescott, S. (1977). The ecology of adolescent activity and experience. *J. Youth Adolesc.* **6,** 281–294.

Folbre, N., and Hartmann, H. I. (1989). The persistence of patriarchal capitalism. *Rethink. Marxism* **2,** 90–96.

Friedman, J. W. (1986). *Game Theory with Applications to Economics.* Oxford University Press, New York.

Goffman, E. (1977). The arrangement between the sexes. *Theory Society* **4,** 301–331.

Huber, J., and Spitze, G. (1983). *Sex Stratification: Children, Housework, and Jobs.* Academic, New York.

Kamo, Y. (2000). He said, she said: Assessing discrepancies in husbands' and wives' reports on the division of household labor. *Social Sci. Res.* **29,** 459–476.

Lennon, M. C., and Rosenfield, S. (1994). Relative fairness and the division of housework: The importance of options. *Am. J. Sociol.* **100,** 506–531.

Lundberg, S., and Pollak, R. A. (1993). Separate spheres bargaining and the marriage market. *J. Polit. Econ.* **101,** 988–1010.

Manser, M., and Brown, M. (1980). Marriage and household decision making: A bargaining analysis. *Int. Econ. Rev.* **21,** 31–44.

McElroy, M. B., and Horney, M. J. (1981). Nash-bargained household decisions: Toward a generalization of the theory of demand. *Int. Econ. Rev.* **22,** 333–349.

Murphy, K. M., and Welch, F. (1992). The structure of wages. *Q. J. Econ.* **107,** 285–326.

Robinson, J. (1985). The validity and reliability of diaries versus alternative time use measures. In *Time, Goods, and Well-Being* (T. Juster and F. P. Stafford, eds.), pp. 33–62. The University of Michigan Survey Research Center, Institute for Social Research, Ann Arbor, Michigan.

Shelton, B. A., and Agger, B. (1993). Shotgun wedding, unhappy marriage, no-fault divorce? Rethinking the Feminism–Marixism relationship. In *Theory on Gender/Feminism on Theory* (P. England, ed.), pp. 25–41. Aldine De Gruyter, Hawthorne, New York.

West, C., and Zimmerman, D. H. (1987). Doing gender. *Gender Society* **1,** 125–151.

Youm, Y., and Laumann, E. O. (2003). The effect of structural embeddedness on the division of household labor: A game-theoretic model using a network approach. *Rational. Society* **15,** 243–280.

Human and Population Genetics

Gerty J. L. M. Lensvelt-Mulders
Utrecht University, Utrecht, The Netherlands

Glossary

behavior genetics The study of the inheritance of behavioral characteristics.

chromosome A structure that carries the genes and is found in pairs in the cell nucleus of humans.

deoxyribonucleic acid (DNA) A nucleic acid polymer that is the basic hereditary material, located within the chromosomes.

genotype All characteristics that an individual has inherited, whether or not they are manifested.

individual differences The relatively persistent differences in behavior between members of the same population.

nature–nurture debate The never-ending debate about the relative importance of inheritance and the results of upbringing on the mature phenotype.

path analysis A statistical procedure used to divide covariation between variables into separated components or path.

phenotype All displayed characteristics of an individual.

quantitative trait locus linkage (QTL) The search for the loci of specific genes, where each locus is the location of a gene on the DNA string.

This article focuses entirely on human genetics. It contains a short overview of the two most important branches of human genetic studies, molecular and population genetics. A bibliography and relevant Web sites are included for the interested reader who wants to study this topic more thoroughly. The content of the current nature–nurture debate in science and society is discussed and the basics of the analysis of mapping the human genome are explained. This article also includes a brief introduction to population genetics. The future directions of human genetics and the scientific challenges that geneticists will face are discussed. This article concludes with a discussion on the ethical issues that surround research into human genetics.

Genetics in Society and Science

The Nature–Nurture Controversy

One of the oldest debates in the social sciences is whether humans are social or biological creatures. This debate can be visualized as a giant seesaw in time. At one end, there are the biological explanations of human behavior, such as evolutionary theories, the influence of genetic factors, and theories that stem from brain research. On the other end, there are the social explanations of behavior, such as cultural differences, upbringing, and learning processes. In the past, biological and social explanations always seemed mutually exclusive, with one approach overriding the other, depending on the "zeitgeist." For instance, from the 1950s to the 1970s, the seesaw totally skipped to social theories of human behavior. Most social scientists will remember the strong statements in favor of social explanations made by the early behaviorists from their introductory courses. In the 1990s, the seesaw reversed and the scientific and social climate became more in favor of biological explanations of human behavior. These days, the nature–nurture debate flares again, due to increased insights into the heredity of behavior. Researchers, policymakers, and the lay public are starting to worry about the implications that the outcomes of genetic studies will have for society. What will be the social consequences of the genetic diagnosis of traits such as intelligence, criminality, or sexual orientation? These are important questions because genetic research is becoming a major field within different sciences. The debate is now about how this new knowledge can be celebrated and how it can be prevented from being misused.

Strange as it seems, behavior genetics has the qualities necessary to bridge the gap between exclusively biological and exclusively social explanations of human behavior, because behavior genetics are rooted in biology. Biologists have always acknowledged the fact that even the most inherited behavior can exist only in the context of the environment. The results of new research in behavior genetics have convincingly showed that biological mechanisms can no longer be ignored. However, contrary to what many seem to think, behavior geneticists are not exclusively interested in genetic effects on individual differences; they are just as interested in the influence of social effects.

The Genetic Study of Individual Differences

The influence of genes on everyday behavior can be studied at two levels. At the microlevel, geneticists are trying to identify pieces of DNA associated with particular behavior; for instance, the mapping of chromosome 20 has elucidated a great deal about leukemia, diabetes, and childhood eczema. At the population level, behavior geneticists seek to understand both the genetic and environmental contributions to individual variations in behavior. The way that genes cause complex behavior is still quite unknown, but it is known that complex traits almost always involve multiple genes, which makes the mapping of such traits a very difficult exercise. Luckily for behavior geneticists, it is not necessary to unravel all the secrets of the genome before judgment can be passed on the causation of behavior. It is possible to attribute behavior to broad causes such as genetic or environmental effects, without understanding all the details of this causation. As Loehlin stated in 1992: "One can be perfectly able to drive a car without understanding the way the engine works."

Human Genetics

Terms and Definitions

The assumptions of behavior genetics are based on the rules of Mendelian inheritance and the knowledge of DNA as the bearer of genetic information. The nucleus of a human cell nucleus contains 46 chromosomes; 23 are inherited from the father's sperm and 23 from the mother's ovum. Every chromosome consists of two strings of DNA. Genes are small segments on these DNA strings that carry exactly one piece of information. The location of a gene on the DNA molecule is called a locus and the complementary sites on both strings are called alleles. Heterozygotes have different alleles on each string. Genes are thus the unit factors of heredity that are at the basis of behavior. However, genes do not underlie behavior in a direct sense. Genes are considered templates for the synthesis of amino acids—the building blocks of proteins, which exert their influence on behavioral structures and processes via the nervous system and the production of behaviorally relevant hormones and neurotransmitters. The whole inherited set of genes on all chromosomes is called the genotype, as opposed to the phenotype, which is defined as the whole of observable characteristics and traits of a person.

Most complex traits, especially those traits that are of interest for behavioral scientists, are controlled by the combined action of multiple genes. This multiple regulation increases the possibility of individual differences and makes the variety in human genotypes incredibly large. Research in behavior genetics suggests that variation in diverse characteristics such as intelligence, personality traits, obesity, criminal behavior, and health depends to a considerable extend on genetic factors.

Mapping the Human Genome

The study of the location of individual genes on the genome is part of the domain of molecular genetics. This article does not provide a detailed tutorial on the laboratory techniques of molecular genetics, but does give a brief explanation of how genes are traced. Genes are traced with the aid of DNA markers. DNA markers make it possible to localize genes that are related to behavioral traits without the necessity of understanding the gene product. DNA markers are polymorphic sequences of amino acids with a known location. There are two main strategies for identifying and locating genes, linkage and association, where linkage is concerned with the localization of genes and association is concerned with identifying genes. Classical linkage techniques use large pedigrees of related individuals to search for genes that are related to a certain trait. The rationale behind linkage is that carriers of a trait or disorder should share markers that are close to the disease locus and that are not shared with noncarriers. The coinheritance of the trait and DNA markers is used as a sign of linkage between the gene and the trait. A problem with linkage techniques, especially in sib-pair-based techniques for complex traits, is that they often lack the statistical power to detect true linkage, because human pedigrees are small and only some of the individuals are infected.

Association is the other method used to detect linkage. Unrelated individuals from large populations are used to map the gene associated with the trait. The idea behind association is that carriers should share the associated gene with other unrelated carriers. Power is not a problem for association studies, because it is easy to increase the sample size of unrelated individuals. The drawback of association studies is that they can be used to map only candidate genes that are associated with the trait prior to the study.

Mixed designs that include linkage as well as association are also used, in which additional different families are studied in concordance. Mixed designs combine the strengths of both designs into a more powerful gene detection system.

Population Genetics

Explaining Variability in the Population

Behavior Genetic Research

The focus of population genetics is the explanation of differences in behavior between individuals in a certain population. Behavior geneticists try to increase the understanding of the genetic and environmental causes of these differences. To accomplish this, research methodology and statistical methods to analyze genetic informative data were developed. The research field of behavior geneticists is very broad, encompassing the disciplines of medicine, psychology, and biology.

Genetic Factors Affecting Behavior

The phenotype, the whole of the observable traits of an individual, develops under the influence of different genetic and environmental factors. Within behavioral genetic analysis, three genetic effects are distinguished: additive effects, dominance effects, and the effects of epistasis. Genetic effects are additive insofar as they add up; an additive effect is thus the sum of the average effects of individual alleles (father has fair hair, mother has dark hair, offspring's hair will be in between). Dominance is the nonadditive interaction of alleles on a single locus or intralocus interaction. This concept is well known from Mendelian studies on the color of peas. Epistasis is the interaction of an allele with alleles on other loci, called interlocus interaction.

Environmental Factors Affecting Behavior

The environment in its broadest sense covers the total of the external input to the behavioral processes. As such, it is a very broad concept, including biochemical factors such as nutrition, physical factors such as temperature, and family factors such as child-raising practices or the influence of sibling rank order on development.

The environment can affect behavior in two ways. First, it can make individuals who differ genetically become more alike in their behavior. Culture and parental upbringing practices are instances of such influences. Upbringing makes children in a family behave more similarly than could be expected on the basis of their genetic resemblance. The greater the extent to which an environment is shared, the more individuals will become alike. In genetic studies, the environmental effects that make individuals more alike are found under the headers shared, between family or common family environmental effects.

The environment can also have the opposite effect: it can make individuals that share the same genotype more different from one another. For instance, when a member of an identical twin pair is involved in a traumatic accident, this can have a lasting effect, making this person more anxious in everyday life than her or his co-twin. The unique experience of the accident has altered the phenotypic relation between these twins; it has made them more different than could be expected on the basis of their identical genotype. This effect of the environment is called the unique, within-family, or idiosyncratic environment effect. In the remainder of this paper, the expression "common environment" is used for environmental effects that make people more alike and the expression "unique environment" is used for all the environmental effects that make them more unique.

The Behavior Genetic Design

Conducting Twin, Family, and Adoption Research

To analyze the differential impact of genotype and environment on individual differences, data are needed from genetically informative individuals. The comparative study of complex behavior within twins, siblings, and family members affords such an approach. The twin design is the most classic design in behavior genetic research and it is based on the fact that there are two kinds of twins: monozygotic or identical twins (MZ) and dizygotic or fraternal twins (DZ). MZ twins share the same genotype; they are genetically (nearly) identical. Because of this, observed differences between MZ twins are assumed to be environmental in origin. DZ twins share 50% of their genes; they are genetically related as first-degree siblings, but they share the family environment to a greater extent than siblings usually do. Differences between DZ twin pairs can be genetic as well as environmental in origin. By comparing the phenotypic similarity of MZ twins with that of DZ twins, researchers conduct a kind of natural experiment to investigate the effects of heredity and environment on behavior.

Assumptions for Conducting Family Studies

Before examining the analysis of family data, three assumptions must be discussed: the equal environment assumption, the assumption of nonassortative mating, and assumptions about correlations and covariations between genes and environment.

The equal environment assumption (EEA) assumes equality of trait-relevant environmental experiences among MZ and DZ twins. Research shows that MZ twins share their environment to a larger extent than

DZ twins, which seems to violate the EEA. MZ twins more often go to the same school and wear the same clothes and as adults they practice the same sports, share their hobbies, and meet each other on a more regular basis. But does this influence similarity? A study executed to test the EEA for the Big Five personality traits showed that although the EEA was violated this did not influence the phenotypic resemblance between MZ co-twins for trait-relevant behavior. No significant correlations were found between levels of shared environmental experiences and the intraclass correlations of MZ twins. More extensive sharing of the environment did not make the twin pairs significantly more equal on these traits.

The second assumption is that no assortative mating is allowed for the observed variables, because this will lead to a greater genotypic similarity of siblings than can be modeled. Assortative mating is the tendency of like to mate with like. There are theories that assume that people seek partners with the same attributes as well as theories that state that "opposites attract." However, for most behavioral traits, assortative mating tends to be slight, although for a few traits, such as intelligence and social attitudes, it can be substantial. The effects of assortative mating can be included in genetic models and its effects on other parameters can be estimated.

The last assumption is that behavior genetic analysis techniques do not allow for interactions or correlations between genes and the environment. It was Plomin who introduced the concepts of gene–environment interactions and correlations. Gene–environment interactions refer to genetic differences in sensitivity to experiences. For example, neurotic and emotionally stable children may not differ much in general adjustment when they are both reared in a warm supportive environment, but may grew apart on the emotional stability scale when they are reared in a harsh and cold environment. Since twin analysis assumes a linear relation between the observed phenotypes and their underlying genetic and environmental variables, interactions should not occur.

Genotype–environment correlations are defined as the extent to which individuals are exposed to environments as a function of their genetic propensities. There are three genotype–environment correlations: passive, evocative, and active. Passive correlations occur because genes are not randomly distributed over environments. Children share genes as well as environment with their family and can thus passively "inherit" environments that match their genetic structure. Evocative correlation refers to the experiences of a child resulting from reactions of other people to its genetic propensities. For instance, people tend to act more favorably to more beautiful children, giving them more positive experiences, which is thought to enhance self-esteem later in life. Active correlations occur when children (and adults) actively select, modify, and construct their environments. Correlations and interactions between genotype and environment are more often the case than not and therefore the assumptions about the occurrence of interactions and correlations are often violated. But this is not as disrupting as it was in the past, given that appropriate multivariate model estimation techniques allow for interaction and correlation. For instance, including parents of twins in the classical design allows the estimation of cultural transmission and genotype–environment correlation.

Methods for Analyzing Twin Data

The Classic Approach: Comparing Intraclass Correlations

Behavior genetic studies estimate which part of the total variance of a trait can be attributed to genetic effects and which part of the variance can be attributed to environmental causes. The proportion of the variance explained by genetic effects is called the "heritability coefficient."

In the classic twin approach, the difference between the intraclass correlations of the MZ and DZ twin pairs is used to estimate the heritability coefficient. The intraclass correlation is a specific type of correlation that takes into account the fact that twin pairs are not independent of one another; ICC are based on ANOVA analysis. The difference between the intraclass correlations of MZ and DZ twins is doubled to estimate this heritability coefficient

$$h^2 = 2(r_{\mathrm{MZ}} - r_{\mathrm{DZ}}).$$

An h^2 of 0.5 for a certain trait, for instance, "emotional stability," means that 50% of the total variance in this trait in a population can be explained by differences in the genetic makeup of its individuals. It is very important to have a precise understanding of the meaning of h^2. The h^2 applies only to a population studied in its own environment; therefore, it can change as a result of changes in the population. It is also important to understand that the heritability coefficient is a descriptive statistic of a trait in a population and as such does not apply to individuals. And last but not least, for many traits h^2 is not stable over the life span; it changes with age during development. Intelligence, for instance, is more influenced by the genotype when a person becomes older than in childhood. It is important to keep an open mind toward the effects of the environment on differences in behavior. An h^2 of 0.5 also means that 50% of the variance is explained by causes other than differences in the genotype. These causes are environmental in origin. In the scientific literature, both effects on behavior should always be mentioned. It is odd that in the public debate these environmental effects are so often overlooked.

Path Analysis for Twin Research

Behavior genetics uses quantitative genetic analysis as a tool. Quantitative genetic analysis is the theoretical basis for the statistical analysis of variation in populations. The statistical tool is more commonly known under the names "structural equation modeling" or "path analysis." Model estimation has many advantages over the classic approach. The graphical reproduction of structural models is very helpful for making the assumptions of the twin design more explicit (see Fig. 1). Using path models makes it possible to test different models against each other and to opt for the model that best fits the data. The fit of the model can be expressed in goodness-of-fit statistics and the estimates for genetic and environmental effects are given together with their standard errors.

Many different complex and multivariate models are already commonly used, but here quantitative genetic analysis using the most basic univariate model for genetic analysis is illustrated. This model can easily be extended to multivariate and longitudinal designs as well as designs that go beyond the twin design and investigate the more complex genetic and environmental relationships between different relatives.

Figure 1 represents the simplest path model for MZ and DZ twins reared together. The genetic theory as outlined above is reflected in the model. By convention, the observed or dependent variables are drawn as rectangles and the latent, independent variables are shown as circles. Single-headed arrows are used to define causal relations or paths and double-headed arrows are used to define covariances. Also by convention, uppercase letters are used to define the latent variables and lowercase letters are used to represent the paths and double-headed arrows. An example from research on extraversion is used to illustrate the model. Extraversion is one of the Big Five personality traits. It is associated with active, impulsive, and social behavior, where people who exhibit high levels of these behaviors are called extraverts and people who exhibit low levels of these behaviors are called introverts. The variables in the squares are the observed levels of extraversion for twin 1 and co-twin 2. The latent variables (circles) come from behavior genetic theory. E stands for the unique environment and by definition random error is incorporated in E; A stands for the additive genetic effects, D stands for the effects of dominant genes and epistasis, and C stands for the effects of the common environment. The covariation between both genetic effects is defined for MZ as well as for DZ twins; where MZ twins show a correlation of 1, they are of the same genotype and DZ twins show a correlation of 0.5 for additive genetic effects and 0.25 for dominance effects.

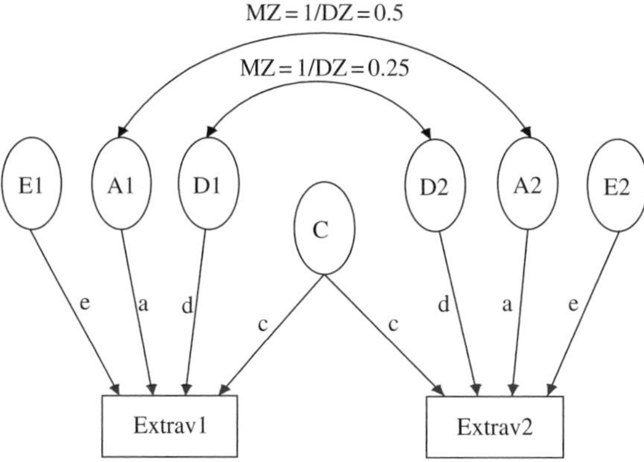

Figure 1 Univariate path model for genetic analysis of twins reared together. Extrav1, level of extraversion for twin 1. Extrav2, level of extraversion for co-twin 2. E, unique environmental effects. A, additive genetic effects. D, effects of dominance and epistatis. C, effect of common environment.

Since quantitative genetic analysis has a strong regression component, the model can be also defined from its underlying regression structures

$$P_1 = eE_1 + aA_1 + dD_1 + cC_1,$$

and

$$P_2 = eE_2 + aA_2 + dD_2 + cC_2,$$

where P_1 and P_2 are the phenotypes of two co-twins. As can be derived from the regression equation, the phenotype is assumed to be a linear function of the underlying genetic and environmental effects. The total variance of the observed measure is composed from the factor loadings as:

$$V_p = a^2 + d^2 + c^2 + e^2.$$

In the classical twin study that uses twins that are reared together, C and D cannot be modeled in one analysis, because then they become confounded and the model cannot be identified. Using this path diagram, different models can be tested. First, the simplest model that takes only the unique environmental and additive genetic effects into account is examined. In the second step, this model can be extended with common environmental or dominance effects, depending on the difference between the intraclass correlations of the MZ and DZ twins in the sample. When the intraclass correlation of the MZ twins is less than twice the intraclass correlation of the DZ twins, a model that allows for common environmental effects is chosen, because the DZ twins resemble each other more than could be expected on the basis of their genotype alone. When the intraclass correlation of the MZ twins is larger than twice the intraclass correlation of the DZ twins, a model that allows for dominance effects is chosen, because the DZ twins differ more than could be expected from theory. Finally, a model that excludes every genetic effect, the CE model that states that all individual differences are attributable to environmental effects, can be chosen.

Using these three models, the way that models are compared and tested is discussed here. In Table I, the

Table I Results of a Univariate Quantitative Genetic Analysis on Extraversion

	Model		
	AE	*ACE*	*CE*
χ^2	3.086	2.405	3.524
df	4	3	4
P	0.544	0.439	0.423
V_A	0.47	0.13	
V_E	0.53	0.56	0.58
V_C		0.31	0.42
NFI	0.98	0.98	0.98
AIC	7.086		7.524

Note: AE, model includes additive genetic and unique environmental effects. ACE, model includes additive genetic and unique and common environmental effects. CE, model includes only environmental effects. V_A, phenotypic variance explained by genetic effects. V_E, phenotypic variance explained by unique environmental effects. V_C, phenotypic variance explained by common environmental effects. NFI, normed fit index for large samples. AIC, Akiaki's information criterion.

path estimates, as well as the goodness-of-fit measure (here, the normed fit index), are given. In the study here examined, the intraclass correlation for MZ twin pairs was 0.5 and for DZ twin pairs it was 0.39, which could be an indication of common environmental effects.

These results show that a model that incorporates only additive genetic and unique environmental effects has a nice fit ($\chi^2/df < 1$; NFI = 0.98). From the data, it can be seen that 47% of the variance in extraversion levels in the population can be attributed to additive genetic effects and 53% of the total variance can be attributed to unique environmental effects. But is this the best-fitting model or has the shared environment also had a significant effect on the development of the trait? To address this question, a model that includes additive genetic effects, unique environmental effects, and common environmental effects needs to be tested. To accomplish this, one degree of freedom must be sacrificed. This model also fits ($\chi^2/df < 1$; NFI = 0.98), but does it fit significantly better compared to the more parsimonious AE model? When models are nested, the likelihood ratio test is used to solve this question. As goodness-of-fit measure, the χ^2 values are obtained. The difference between χ^2 values can be interpreted as a measure for the significance of path C, $\chi^2_{AE} - \chi^2_{ACE} = 0.681$, which is not large enough to compensate for the loss of one degree of freedom. Thus, the model including common environmental effects does not explain the data significantly better than the first model with only additive and unique effects.

The next model tested does not assume any genetic effects on the trait, only environmental effects. This model also seems to fit the data ($\chi^2/df < 1$). Because this model (CE) is not nested in the first model (AE), it is not possible to compare both models using a likelihood ratio test. When models are not nested, the model with the smallest Akaiki's information criterion (AIC) is considered the best model, because AIC is a measure of the parsimoniousness of a model. Therefore, it can be concluded that a model with only additive genetic and unique environmental effects suffices to explain the data.

Future Directions

The Future of Molecular Genetics

Genetic linkage methods with complex inheritance are based on allele sharing between related pairs. As described above, one way to identify the specific loci involved in the development and expression of traits is the use of quantitative trait loci linkage. In the past, the results of QTL have not always been reliable; contradictory outcomes have been seen and there were many problems with the replication of earlier findings. This has led to much criticism of QTL. In turn, this has led to international cooperation and the development of standardized protocols, which will enhance the possibility of finding genetic regions linked to susceptibility of disorders. In the future, the methods for QTL will become more refined and the statistical analysis more powerful in order to detect true linkage and to decrease the number of false-positive outcomes. It will also become possible to determine confidence intervals small enough to become meaningful. To increase the possibility of finding true linkage, related phenotypes can be studied in concordance using selected samples. For instance, in the search for genes linked to diabetes mellitus-related traits glycemia, obesity, blood pressure, and insulin secretion can also be tested.

The Future of Population Genetics

Increasingly more complex and comprehensive models and even more extensive international cooperation will characterize the future of population genetics. Multivariate analysis and the establishment of twin registers have made it possible to start longitudinal studies into different complex traits and diseases. It is expected that these new insights will lead to increased knowledge of the genetic ethiology and environmental contributions to behavioral traits and disorders.

Multivariate analysis also makes it possible to study the genetic relationships between different traits. For instance, the simultaneous analysis of asthma, hay fever, dust allergy, and eczema data showed that there are common environmental and additive genetic influences for all four symptoms of atopy, which means that they have one or more genes in common. The same multivariate models are being used to study the relationship between personality traits and physiological variables, such as the relation between levels of sensation-seeking and cardiovascular reactivity measures.

Genetic analysis and its statistical methods have become so approachable that the twin-only design can be easily extended to other genetically related individuals such as parents and siblings. Adoption studies with twins and siblings reared apart are carried out to obtain greater insight into the combined effects of heredity and environment. Adoption designs will make it possible to identify specific influences of the environment, unconfounded by heredity, and to analyze genotype–environment interactions and correlations. Several types of adoption designs can be used to study the emergence of behavior, such as designs including measures of several different family relationships, e.g., biological parents and their adopted-away offspring, twins separated early in life, spouse correlations, biological and adoptive parent–offspring correlations, and sibling correlations.

And finally, the latest trend is to incorporate specific genetic loci in model-fitting, the so-called biometric model-fitting analysis. The aim of these studies is to gain knowledge about how much of the genetic variance is accounted for by some small set of candidate loci. On the other hand, these models can also provide information about the types of shared environmental effects that influence behavior. For instance, in the study of schizophrenia, specific environmental factors that result in discordance among identical twins are already the subject of extensive investigation.

Ethical Issues

Behavior genetic studies draw a lot of controversy, because the results of such research can have far-reaching political and social implications. Among the topics that are frequently studied are socially sensitive issues such as the genetics of intelligence, homosexuality, and criminal behavior. What does it mean if 75% of the variance in intelligence in a population can be explained by genetic differences between individuals? This type of outcome from international comparative studies evokes a lot of controversy because it seems to collide with the "just world" hypothesis and the thought that all people are born equal. Intelligence may be a fuzzy concept and it is not known exactly what intelligence is, but everyone has some notion that it is an important attribute in society and that those blessed with it appear to be better off. The problem here is that it is not clear enough to the lay public, and to many scientists too, what these outcomes represent. Researchers and the media have not always presented new findings with the necessary care and have not explained carefully enough what these results do and do not mean. One of the tasks of genetic researchers therefore lies in bringing greater clarity to what research on behavior genetics can achieve and what it cannot achieve. The major emphasis on the heritability coefficient has created an idea of genetic determinism at the expense of the environmental outcomes of behavior genetics. Most conditions are determined by multiple causes and therefore also depend on environmental influences. Behavior genetic methods can be used to elucidate such intermediary environmental influences and thus provide a richer explanation of behavioral differences in intelligence.

At the microlevel, genes are studied in DNA studies. The aims of this field of research are to elucidate the mechanisms of gene action and to map the human genome. The mapping of features as diverse as schizophrenia, criminality, and alcohol addiction raises questions about the implications that this knowledge will have for society. What are the social and political implications of the media bulletin that "a gene for violent criminal behavior has been discovered"? Does this mean that violent criminal behavior is inherited and that "violent criminal behavior" is written indelibly in the genes, determining behavior? What should be the consequences of this discovery for society? Is violent behavior suddenly a disease? Should those who commit violent crimes be hospitalized and cured? What should the implications be for the legal system? Should there be genetic screening for violent behavior and ultimately some form of prenatal genetic engineering? These are important issues but they cannot be solved here. In May 2003, a conference was held on these social issues on the occasion of the termination of the Human Genome Project. The topic of the conference was how genetics researchers should engage in a more open dialogue so that the public can become better informed, while those involved in science hear the nature of political and public concerns. Researchers in the field should be aware of the importance of these issues and the responsibilities that come with working in a new and exciting research field. Fortunately, most researchers are.

See Also the Following Articles

Behavioral Psychology • Ethical Issues, Overview • Research Ethics Committees in the Social Sciences

Further Reading

Behavior Genetic Association Web site. Available at http://www.bga.org

Benjamin, J., Ebstein, R. P., and Belmaker, R. H. (2002). *Molecular Genetics and Human Personality.* American Psychiatric Association, Washington, DC.

Boomsma, D., Busjahn, A., and Peltonen, L. (2002). Classical twin studies and beyond: A review. *Nature Rev. Genet.* **3,** 872–882.

Bouchard, T. J., and Propping, P. (1993). *Twins as a Tool of Behavior Genetics.* Wiley, Oxford, UK.

Brown, T. A. (2001). *Genetic Cloning and DNA Analysis: An Introduction.* Blackwell Science, London, UK.

Hall, J. G. (2003). Twinning. *Lancet* **30,** 735–743.

Human Genome Project (regarding ethical and social issues) Web site. Available at http://www.ornl.gov

Institute for Behavioral Genetics at the University of Boulder Colorado Web site. Available at http://www.igwww.colorado.edu

Loehlin, J. C. (1992). *Genes and Environment in Personality Development.* Sage, London.

Neale, M. C., and Cardon, L. R. (1992). *Methodology for Genetic Studies of Twins and Family.* Kluwer Academic, Dordrecht, The Netherlands.

MX Web site: A statistical program for quantitative genetic analysis: Available at http://www.vcu.edu/mx/

Plomin, R., DeFries, J. C., Craig, I., Mcguffin, P., and Kagan, J. (2002). *Behavioral Genetics in the Postgenomic Era.* American Psychological Association, Washington, DC.

Plomin, R., and Rutter, M. (1998). Child development, molecular genetics, and what to do with genes once they are found. *Child Dev.* **69,** 1223–1242.

Virginia State Institute for Psychiatric and Behavior Genetics Web site. Available at http://www.vipbg.vcu.edu

Human Growth and Development

Michel Ferrari
University of Toronto, Toronto, Ontario, Canada

Chandi Fernando
University of Toronto, Toronto, Ontario, Canada

Glossary

change Any physical, psychological, or institutional alteration, without concern for direction or value.

development A process of growth that includes increasing complexity and dynamic directionality over time; typically, but not always, used to refer to a positive change.

electroencephalogram (EEG) A measurement the electrical activity of the brain.

evolution A process of biological growth that includes increasing complexity and dynamic directionality over time; typically, but not always, used to refer to a positive change.

gross domestic product (GDP) The value of the total final output of all goods and services produced in a single year within a country's boundaries.

gross national product (GNP) GDP plus incomes received by residents from abroad minus incomes claimed by nonresidents.

growth An increase in size of the physical body, of knowledge, or of an institution.

individual differences Variation among individuals on all dimensions, as measured by psychometric tests. The study of such differences has been a major focus in the psychology of intelligence and personality and in behavior genetics.

magnetoencephalography (MEG) The measurement of the magnetic activity of the brain, usually conducted externally.

The relations between growth and development are complex, especially because these two words have several, partially overlapping meanings. For our purposes, growth refers to an increase in size of the physical body, of knowledge, or of institutions, whereas development refers to a process of growth that includes increasing complexity and dynamic directionality of growth over time. Growth and development need not imply progress; a cancer tumor is a growth and one can develop a physical or mental illness.

Physical Growth and Development

Physical growth refers to changes in the body (such as height, weight, or hormonal changes) that are the result of maturation, environmental experiences, or some interaction between these two factors. It also involves neurological and sensory development, such as increased visual acuity and mastery of motor skills.

Developmental Milestones (Psychometric Measurement)

The oldest quantitative measures of human growth and development, emerged in the mid-nineteenth century through the work of Quételet. He measured the physical growth of members in a population and calculated statistical norms for the "average man" of different groups (racial types) of people, characterized by measurements of moral and physical qualities. These then came to be considered not just averages, but real ideal or abstract features of these populations. Similar work continues in studies of milestones of "normal" human growth and development that track, for example, the average age at which a person is expected to begin sitting, standing, walking, smiling, grasping, sensory acuity, or later physical changes that accompany puberty, as well as those that occur across the life span into old age. This approach implies a maturational view of physical development. The Bailey Motor Scale, for example, measures quality of movement, sensory integration, motor planning, and perceptual motor integration in infancy. Likewise, tests of bone density measure potential bone loss in old age. Similar kinds of measurement are implicated in assessments of obesity in the population and other measures of health.

Brain Development

Early attempts to understand the development of human brain structure relied on the effects of accident or illness conducted postmortem. However, more recent neuroimaging technologies allow growth generally, and brain activity specifically, to be examined dynamically in living subjects as early as infancy and even during embryogenesis. These include technologies that are less invasive, such as positron emission tomography (PET) scans, magnetic resonance imaging (MRI), and techniques such as magnetoencephalography (MEG) and electroencephalogram (EEG). Studies have examined both large-scale structures such as the spine and internal organs and small-scale structures such as neuronal growth and cell assemblies. Different areas of the brain develop at different times during embryogenesis and ontogenesis. The frontal lobes, for example, develop late compared to more primitive structures such as the brain stem, cerebellum, and limbic system.

Brain growth is influenced both by environmental variables such as nutrition and by learning experiences. Malnutrition negatively affects brain growth, as it does all other aspects of physical development. On a more positive note, learning can increase brain development. For example, a study of London cab drivers found that they have a bigger hippocampus (an area of the brain implicated in memory) than do other Londoners, presumably reflecting their need to remember the many streets of London. And, in general, studies show that learning increases the areas of the brain devoted to particular tasks, often by recruiting neurons from other areas of the brain through new connections and not through the growth of new neurons.

Cognitive Growth and Development

Cognitive growth and development refers to the growth and development of knowledge through experience. Such growth and development can involve information processing needed in planning, attention, or memory, as well as development of expertise in particular knowledge domains. Theorists disagree over whether cognitive development occurs gradually or in stages.

Psychometric Measures of Mental Development

Galton continued the psychometric line of work of Quételet (anthropometry) by extending it to consider individual differences in psychological characteristics, such as those that characterize genius or mental deviance. Galton took these variations to be biological variations that reflected an evolutionary trend toward the greater improvement of the human race, which was hereditary in families. Measures of this hereditary genius included measures of fame, basic skills, and reaction times. Recent work in this vein has been done by Simonton, who shows, using similar statistical methods, that career age and early productivity are the best indicators of exceptional performance within a profession.

The most popular psychometric measurement of cognitive growth is the IQ test, the most famous developed by Binet and Simon at the beginning of the twentieth century. Spearman used a similar logic to measure what he called g, or the basic capacity of individuals to learn. Such tests are the basis for assessments of learning disabilities and giftedness in many content domains.

Galton also held the view, common then, that the different races and different genders differed in their intellectual capacity. The less-evolved races were thought to have less higher-order ability or capacity for abstraction. It is an idea that continues today in books such as *The Bell Curve*, which Gould has effectively challenged in his own book *The Mismeasure of Man*. Although no longer considering evolution to imply progress, evolutionary psychologists are also working in the same spirit as Galton.

Learning and Expertise

Dissatisfied with psychometric norms, which document but do not explain cognitive growth, researchers have measured changes in information-processing capacity (e.g., attentional or memory capacity). Some researchers adopt a maturationist explanation for the observed increases in information processing. Others, such as Ericsson and Sternberg, believe that such changes reflect a growth in expertise. The measurement of growth in expertise is made by comparing the differences in representations and strategies exhibited by experts versus novices, and by comparing the differences in self-regulation and practice habits (deliberate practice of elements and self-explanation) of the greatest experts and most gifted students versus regular experts and students. Assessments by Chi have shown that deep misconceptions can persist even after extensive training if novices do not experience a radical conceptual change and adopt the expert theory in that knowledge domain. The assessment of conceptual change and level of expertise consists of inferring the implicit or explicit representations required to explain patterns of individual problem solving. A unifying position that explains cognitive growth in a way that combines biological variability in basic abilities and the level of expertise proposes that observed skill results from a synthesis of individual differences in capacity and sustained personal efforts to master cultural material that exercise those capacities. Assessments of ability are made through tests of fluid (culture-free) and crystallized (culturally learned) intelligence. Measures are also made of successful life-span adjustments as individuals compensate for their weaknesses and optimize their strengths; for example, elderly individuals rely on documents or others to help recall a forgotten name as their fluid memory ability declines in old age.

Human Evolution

The facts that some individuals learn particular kinds of information better than others and that people can suffer specific cognitive deficits, such as aphasia, have undermined support for Spearman's *g* and suggest instead that the human mind is modular, that is, that people of all ages exhibit a profile of abilities. These profiles can be established by psychomentric tests and also from performance criteria.

Evolutionary psychologists such as Pinker argue that human growth is best understood in terms of the evolution of the human species. This evolution produced a certain biological body that has a basic human nature characterized by modules. This view relies on cross-cultural comparisons of social organization and neurological studies of the effects of brain damage. Evolutionary psychologists mainly rely on an adaptation or design theory regarding the fit between human development and the environments in which we evolved. Support for modules are also provided by infant studies in which innate understandings (e.g., that physical objects are solid) are found to be present from birth and are assumed to be necessary for acquiring later knowledge and skills in the world.

In related work, behavior geneticists such as Plomin have tried to isolate specific genes associated with particular adaptive and maladaptive behaviors (e.g., aggression) or cognitive capacity (e.g., intelligence). These ways of measuring human development presume that human nature is largely set for the species, with individual variations. Individual growth and development, in this view, are analogous to playing the hand one is dealt in poker. Some people are dealt the genetic equivalent of a royal flush and are almost assured to be geniuses, whereas others are given a hand that has no face cards and are mentally deficient; however, most of us have a few good cards and need to play well to win. In other words, our choices may matter, but it is the biology that we inherit that specifies what our smart choices will entail if we want to make the most of our potential abilities.

Stages

Historically, the measurement of children's increasing expertise or ability, especially their ability to understand mathematical and logical relations, has been shown to exhibit structural reorganization characterized by stage-like shifts. This position is usually associated with Piaget, who used a clinical method to observe and interview children about their explanations of events in studies designed to highlight a certain feature of the world (e.g., children's understanding of the conservation of weight or volume). Typically, four main stages are proposed: sensorimotor, preoperational, concrete operational, and abstract propositional (these stages have been given different names by different theorists). The measurement of children's problem-solving behavior and their justifications for particular solutions show an advance through these four stages of understanding in a fixed sequence. Whether this sequence is unique to Western culture or is universal has been disputed but, according to Piaget, the sequence must remain the same—even if not everyone will achieve the most abstract levels of understanding in a given domain.

Neo-Piagetians such as Case, Fischer, and Demetriou have continued in this theoretical tradition. Case shows that children need to master certain core ideas in a domain such as mathematics (which he calls central conceptual structures) before their understanding can advance in that area. Fischer (using, e.g., Gutman scaling) documents that cognitive development can progress along alternative pathways; thus, in learning to read, people can arrive at a comparable level of skill by different routes. Socially supported learning generates an optimal level of functioning and leads to the quickest progression through these stages compared to typical independent performance. Measurements of ability under conditions of increasing social support, called dynamic testing, are increasingly advocated; such assessments reflect what Vygotsky called the zone of proximal development (ZPD). Demetriou has also used statistical techniques to measure the contributions of basic abilities to the development of different levels of knowledge in particular areas of skill (e.g., verbal and spatial areas).

Recent microgenetic assessments of people learning a new task have shown that individuals recapitulate the same levels of understanding, whether they are children or adults developing knowledge over their life span. Surprisingly, this recapitulation can occur many times as individuals construct their understanding of the new task or knowledge domain. Characteristic of microgenetic measurements are multiple measures of performance over a short period of time during the learning of something new. Growth modeling statistics and other methods can be used to assess microgenetic and life-span knowledge development.

In this view, our knowledge is constructed through our biology and our cultural experience jointly, and it greatly depends on our own actions and efforts to master particular kinds of tasks.

Social and Emotional Growth and Development

Another main area of human growth and development is social and emotional development. Social and emotional development refers to the development of personality and the concept of self. It includes at least implicit reference to the ideal ends of development that orient the kind of knowledge people strive to master, including spiritual development and the development of wisdom. Another important topic is how children develop in their social interactions to others. These topics have been measured in a variety of ways, from psychometric assessments to narrative methods.

Personality Development

Personality

In the Galtonian psychometric tradition, personality structure has been measured through factor analytic techniques. These have uncovered what is commonly called the big five-factor structure (openness to experience, conscientiousness, extroversion, agreeableness, and neuroticism). Observational measures also identify differences in temperament that are clearly visible in infants and continue through childhood and adulthood. Other measures examine the extent to which personality embodies multiple, and possibly conflicting, social scripts (e.g., mother and office worker) that individuals fulfill to different degrees. Personality, when considered through narrative methods, becomes synonymous with studies of the self.

Self

Many measurement approaches have been used to study self-concept (e.g., questionnaires, analyzing statistical differences between groups of different ages, and clinical interviews looking for structural reorganization of knowledge). Clinical interview measures of self show that infants first see themselves in terms of their physical features and behaviors. Children later see themselves through isolated concrete events that have occurred in their lives leading to ideas about unique psychological abilities or group affiliations. Only in adolescence do people understand themselves through abstract assessments of the type of person they are or through an integrated in a life story. In this respect, these findings echo those found for cognitive development generally in the work of Piaget and others.

Recent work inspired by that of Bruner has begun to examine self as a narrative. Narrative measures suggest that conceptions of self-growth and development involve considering the self as an actor striving toward goals, using resources (including friends and allies) to overcome some sort of trouble or obstacle. Heroic narrative involves overcoming the obstacles to right a wrong or to achieve an even better state of affairs; tragic narrative involves a failure to do so. As such, narrative approaches necessarily imply cultural conceptions of a good life.

Spirituality

Moral Development

Related to self and development, many attempts have been made to measure moral development. These approaches often use a logic similar to that of Piaget, advancing in stages. The most famous of these is Kohlberg's six stages of moral development: preconventional (stage 1, obedience and punishment orientation; stage 2, individualism and exchange), conventional (stage 3, good interpersonal relationships; stage 4, maintaining the social order), and postconventional (stage 5, social contract and individual rights; stage 6, universal principles). These stages were inspired by Piaget's early work in this area. Research in this area often uses scenarios such as the Hans dilemma (in which Hans must decide whether to steal a drug he cannot afford to save his dying wife) to determine level of moral development. Similar to the work of Piaget, Kohlberg's model relies on the different patterns of response and justifications for particular answers that are considered more developed. These stages have been challenged by Gilligan who proposes an ethics of care rather than one of duty. Recent work on moral development has measured the increasing differentiation of domains of moral knowledge (as assessed through both statistical measures and narrative accounts of personal meaning). In this view, the three main domains of social reasoning are moral reasoning about justice, rights, and welfare; conventional reasoning about rules by authority or traditions; and personal-choice reasoning about duties and responsibilities. Some have also assessed the moral self, that is, the characteristics and narratives through which individuals come to understand themselves as moral beings who must take strong social and political action.

In a different vein, Baltes and Sternberg have measured wisdom, defined either as expertise in the fundamental pragmatics of life (Baltes) or a tacit knowledge of how best to achieve equity or balance among competing interests (Sternberg). Wisdom is measured by analyzing people's answers to scenarios about difficult life situations, especially those involving some sort of negotiation. An alternative view sees wisdom as caring about community and about personal legacy in the face of death. This approach has been inspired by Erikson and is often documented through narrative analysis of people at the end of their lives. McAdams, following Erikson, emphasizes the importance of generativity within life narratives and has shown how measures of generativity correlate to those of general well-being throughout the life span. Buddhist psychologists such as Varela adopt a more radical form of this view in which wisdom involves abandoning fixed habitual responses in favor of a creative response afforded by the specific life situation that an individual is engaged in.

Spiritual Development

Moral development in psychology is assessed in a manner that implies that such development is secular; however, similar approaches have identified spiritual development—the way that people understand their relation to God or to mystical experiences—as underpinning their deepest moral aspirations. For example, Fowler's stages of faith, also modeled on Piaget's stages, document this sort of development. Assessments have been made of mystical experiences and near-death experiences, which rely on narrative methods to assess what is most meaningful and enduring in transformative experiences. These approaches use techniques and analytic strategies often associated with literary studies, such as narrative analysis and character studies. However, statistical methods such as questionnaires have also documented the prevalence of different kinds of spiritual experiences at different ages. For example, children as young as 6 years old have had the experience of a divine presence; mystical experiences of a union with all things is rarer and does not seem to occur before adolescence.

Linked Lives

Human growth and development is not merely a characteristic of isolated individual but of individuals in communities and in families. Cultural differences are not divorced from physical and cognitive aspects of growth and development; rather, they both express and contribute to them in turn. Cohort studies by Elder of the effects of broad cultural events (such as the Great Depression and World War II) show that lives are linked, especially within families, where the actions of parents can have a profound impact on the later lives of children (e.g., a parental decision to abandon their farm to move to the city will transform the lives of their children).

Bronfenbrenner and, more recently, Rogoff have emphasized this point in cultural and ecological models of human development. According to Bronfenbrenner, individuals are embedded in micro, meso, exo, and macro contexts. Rogoff conceptualizes each of these in terms of different planes of analysis, all of which contribute to growth and development. Rogoff documents how participation in social groups changes as individuals grow and develop, going from the periphery (for novices) to the center (for experts).

Culture

Cultural development involves both differences in how cultures conceptualize growth and development and the development of knowledge and artifacts across generations within cultures. Measurements of cultural development include statistical indications of the quality of life and of economic prosperity.

Self-Ways

Work by Bourdieu and Markus shows that individuals interact in groups in ways that conform to an implicit structure unique to specific cultures (e.g., patterns of gift giving), the existence of which participants may deny. These differences are critical to personal assessments of self-worth and a good life, as well as to evaluations of wisdom or maturity. Such cultural expectations are not fixed but are communicated from generation to generation through the institutional practices and narratives within which human life unfolds—whether or not those practices are made explicit. For example, Nelson and her colleagues have shown that the way parents coconstruct the meaning of autobiographical events with children is critical to how children in different (sub)cultures construct their own autobiography. Cultural differences between American and Asian families, for example, have been shown through differences in conversations about self and events, with Asian families include more social actors as integral to their autobiographical narratives.

Knowledge Building

Not only do individuals grow up and develop within social groups and establish their identity within them, cultures and institutions develop technologies (artifacts and practices) that become integral to their ways of life and that are essential to understanding human growth and development. An obvious example is the advance in neonatal care that saves thousands of lives in developed countries. A more problematic issue is the possibility that parents can abort a fetus identified as having a disability or, in the near future, perhaps to alter it through genetic engineering. Along similar lines, eyeglasses and pacemakers have been a boon to quality of life, even extending life, but the possibility of enhancing memory or altering mood through drugs such as Prozac or lithium—and the pharmaceutical industry's stake in developing and promoting such drugs—has profound and problematic implications for human growth and development. Science fiction writers already conceive of developing and improving human nature through marrying the human form and artifacts. In the real world, companies such as Bell Canada have begun to assess whether, for example, wearable computers can improve the work capacity of their technicians.

More abstractly, knowledge itself can be said to develop within a particular culture, the clearest example being the development of mathematical knowledge from Babylonian to modern times. Many argue that knowledge building is precisely the capacity that we foster in education and that such activity is essentially creative. Knowledge building can be supported by artifacts such as Knowledge Forum, a networked collaborative learning environment for schools developed by Bereiter and Scardamalia. Computer simulations and computer modeling are other powerful tools for knowledge development.

Economic Development

In addition to knowledge, there are also indicators of economic growth and development that are taken to indicate the prosperity of nations. Economic development is measured by indicators such as the gross domestic product (GDP) and gross national product (GNP), whereas other measures (e.g., indicators of levels of pollution) target the sustainability of that development or quality of life (e.g., social satisfaction, the amount of disposable income, and level of unemployment).

Seligman, Diener, and Keating all suggest we need indicators of happiness and well-being for citizens as well as of economic prosperity. Diener has measured happiness within various cultural populations using standardized questionnaires. Likewise, Keating has done international comparisons to show that health (and especially, disparities in health among the rich and poor) is an indicator of the overall economic success in different countries.

Particular forms of government are often measured, and we can say that a country is developing into a democracy or a dictatorship by the state of the political institutions, or the level of freedom of the press, within that society. These measures cannot be divorced from ideologies about development and related views about Utopia, or where development ideally should be heading. For Keating, we also need to consider how political, economic, and social conditions interact dynamically with neurobiological differences among children to create the particular habits of mind that characterize them as individuals and, by extension, the forms of life that constitute the culture. Such development may be typical, but it can also be atypical, and to this we turn next.

Atypical Development

Our discussion of growth and development has so far focused on typical development, but we close with a few words on atypical growth and development. It almost goes without saying that all the measures mentioned previously can also be used to document atypical cases. For example, brain imaging technologies are also used to measure human growth in the sense of growth of tumors and other abnormalities in children and adults or the deterioration of the brain in Alzheimer's and Parkinson's disease.

Medical Biography

Medical biographies are an interesting way of measuring physical growth and development. For example, a recent study of the course of illness of U.S. president Franklin Delano Roosevelt questions a long-held view that he had polio. His specific symptoms and the sequence and timing of them in his life (e.g., that he fell ill at the age of 39) make it more likely that he was a victim of Guillain-Barré Syndrome, an autoimmune disorder (although, in any case, the cure for either was not developed until decades later). Similarly, the trajectory of the prognosis of particular diseases can be measured through clinical epidemiology, with important implications for social policy; for example, the trajectory of illness is very different in cases of cancer and cases of organ failure, such as chronic obstructive pulmonary disease (COPD).

Cognitive Differences

Cognitive development can also deviate from the norm. It can be accelerated, or it can be delayed. This logic is what still underpins labels learning disabled and gifted, commonly considered to represent two standard deviations above or below the norm. This approach also highlights alternatives to the norm, for example, attention-deficit hyperactive disorder (ADHD) or autism. Recent work uses different assessments of learning disability and giftedness that are not based on psychometric testing but rather on performance (e.g., Gardner's proposed multiple intelligences); nevertheless, the implicit logic of all of these studies is that extraordinary individuals produce work that is outside the normal range expected within the population. Measurement has also considered alternative pathways to development in atypical cases, for example the work of Karmiloff-Smith on Williams syndrome and its near genetic variants, which highlights the importance of individual development within specific environments even in genetically atypical cases.

Developmental Psychopathology

The importance of individual development is emphasized within developmental psychopathology, in marked contrast to clinical and empirical measurement models of disability. Within the clinical model, the utility of classification measurement models such as the DSM-IV is limited by their insensitivity to age and gender differences, the possibility of diagnostic overinclusion, or the possibility of missing subthreshold cases. Often family factors are only marginally considered and typically accounted for in an unsystematic or noninclusive manner. The empirical approach also tends to group large age spans together; to obscure differences in behavior because of the use of limited behavior descriptions and point scales; and to be insufficiently sensitive to emotional security, relationship quality, and adaptation to environmental functioning.

Because research methodology in developmental psychopathology posits examining the child from multiple domains and perspectives, assessments should include information from a variety of sources. These sources can include tools used in traditional assessments, such as questionnaires, interviews, observations (naturalistic or analog, structured or unstructured), standardized and normed test measures assessing aspects of cognitive functioning, academic achievement, personality, and social competence, along with physiological and biological measures. Although these tools when used in isolation have shortcomings, their use as a multimethod technique allows for a more informative assessment of the child and the processes that influence development to be obtained, including the delineation of the relative risk and protective factors at play. Development is thus conceptualized as an ongoing interaction between an active, changing person and an active, changing context.

Developmental psychopathology research by Cicchetti and others is concerned with positive and negative influences on development, including adaptation (resilience) and maladaptation (psychopathology) when faced with adversity. It also examines positive factors (protective factors) and positive outcomes (i.e., competence despite risk) that are seen as emerging from the transactions between children and their environment. Developmental psychopathology is concerned with mapping development over time, including the form, direction, and shape of pathways. To that end, methodology within developmental psychopathology uses repeated measures over time and assesses functioning through a multimethod approach. Research also draws from multiple domains of functioning (i.e., emotional, cognitive, and social), higher levels of functioning (i.e., patterns of attachment), specific levels of responding in specific situations (i.e., reaction to separation), and information from other disciplines, (i.e., biology) for a more comprehensive understanding of development.

Conclusion

Human growth and development have been conceptualized and measured in a variety of ways. We have chosen to focus on physical, cognitive, social-emotional, and cultural growth in typical populations. We have also briefly considered attempts to assess and measure atypical growth and development. Each of these aspects of growth and development is measured in several ways, including norm-referenced tests, observations, narrative, and longitudinal methods. Despite the wide range of methods reviewed, it is worth remembering that often the most innovative thinkers in an area invent their own theories and methods about what characterizes human development and how to measure it.

See Also the Following Articles

Clinical Psychology • Cognitive Neuroscience • Cognitive Psychology • Galton, Sir Francis • Learning and Memory • Psychometrics of Intelligence • Quetelet, Adolphe • Religious Affiliation and Commitment, Measurement of

Further Reading

Amsterdam, A. G., and Bruner, J. (2000). *Minding the Law: Culture, Cognition, and the Court.* Harvard University Press, New York.

Baltes, Paul, B., and Staudinger, U. M. (2000). Wisdom: A metaheuristic (pragmatic) to orchestrate mind and virtue toward excellence. *Am. Psychol.* **55,** 122–136.

Berieter, C. (2002). *Education and Mind for the Knowledge Age.* Lawrence Erlbaum Associates, Mahwah, NJ.

Damon, W. (ed.). *Handbook of Child Psychology,"* 5th Ed. John Wiley, New York.

Hacking, I. (1990). *The Taming of Chance.* Cambridge University Press, New York.

Keating, D. P., and Hertzman, C. (eds.) (1999). *Developmental Health and the Wealth of Nations: Social, Biological, and Educational Dynamics.* Guilford Press, New York.

Pinker, S. (2002). *The Blank Slate.* Viking Press, New York.

Rogoff, B. (2003). *The Cultural Nature of Human Development.* Oxford University Press, New York.

Rutter, M. (2002). Nature, nurture, and development: From evangelism through science toward policy and practice. *Child Dev.* **73**(1), 1–21.

Spilka, B., Hood, R. W., Hunsberger, B., and Gorsuch, R. (2003). *The Psychology of Religion,* 3rd Ed. Guilford, New York.

Varela, F. (1999). *Ethical Know-How: Action, Wisdom, and Cognition.* Stanford University Press, Stanford, CA. (Originally published in 1992.)

Hypothesis Tests and Proofs

Lee Demetrius Walker

University of Kentucky, Lexington, Kentucky, USA

Glossary

alternative hypothesis The belief the investigator holds about a specified population if the null hypothesis is false.

degrees of freedom Generally, the number of observations minus the number of parameters to be estimated. In some estimation procedures, the degrees of freedom simply represent the parameters to be estimated.

efficient estimator A point estimate that has the lowest possible standard error.

maximum likelihood estimate The value of the parameter that is most consistent with the observed data.

null hypothesis The hypothesis to be tested and the nullification of which by statistical means is taken as evidence in support of the specified alternative hypothesis.

point estimate A simple statistic that predicts the value of the parameter of interest.

***p*-value** The probability of obtaining a test statistic value as large as the one obtained, conditioned on the null hypothesis being true.

test statistic A statistic calculated from the sample data to test the null hypothesis.

type I error The error that occurs from rejecting the null hypothesis when the null hypothesis is true.

unbiased estimator A point estimate with a sampling distribution that is centered around the parameter.

Hypothesis tests and proofs are major aspects of social science research and are the means by which proposed relationships are tested. Hypotheses are developed from theoretical questions that drive research and relate to characteristics of a population. A significance test is a procedure through which a hypothesis is statistically tested by comparing the data to values predicted by the hypothesis. In this article, elements of the significance test and application of the dominant formulation of the test are discussed. This is followed by a discussion of alternatives and enhancements to the hypothesis testing process in the social sciences.

Introduction

A hypothesis about an underlying population is a statement that may be true or false. Relationships in social science are generally probabilistic rather than deterministic, and this fact has major implications in the design of attempts to prove the existence of proposed relationships. Moreover, these relationships are usually asymmetric, with one variable having an influence on another, but not inversely. The testing of hypotheses can take several forms. For example, parametric tests require the population to follow a particular distribution (often the normal); nonparametric tests relax the normality assumption but require that the populations that are to be compared have similar distributional shapes. The dominant method for testing social science hypotheses is the null hypothesis significance test (NHST). This test allows the investigator to test the probability of a null or restricted hypothesis (usually specifying no relationship between the variables of a particular phenomenon) against a research or alternative hypothesis (generally the researcher's belief concerning the relationship of the variables of the phenomenon).

Elements of the Null Hypothesis Significance Test

Like all significance tests, the NHST has five elements: assumptions, hypotheses, test statistics, p-value, and conclusion.

Assumptions

Significance tests require certain assumptions for test validity. These include type and scale of data, the form of the population distribution, method of sampling, and sample size. Data may take quantitative or qualitative form and may spring from different research sources—reactive sources such as attitude surveys and focus group responses, or nonreactive sources such as governmental documents, historical records, newspaper files, voting statistics, or other stored data. Typical distributional forms include the normal, Student's t, gamma, binomial, and chi-squared. Additionally, assumptions must be made concerning the type of sampling that is required for the conclusions drawn from the sample to be applicable to the specified population. Many significance tests require a minimum sample size, and the validity of most tests improves as the sample size increases.

Hypotheses

The NHST examines two hypotheses about the value of a parameter: the null hypothesis and the alternative hypothesis. The null hypothesis (H_0) is the hypothesis to be tested and is usually a statement of a parameter value, say θ, that corresponds to a parameter value of no effect, say θ^*. In many social research applications, θ^* is zero. The alternative hypothesis, represented by H_a or H_1 and also referred to as the research hypothesis, may take the form $H_a\!: \theta \neq \theta^*$. The alternative hypothesis $\theta \neq \theta^*$ constitutes a two-sided test in the sense that the possibility that θ may be either larger or smaller than θ^* is considered. Though the two-sided test is employed most commonly, the investigator may choose to state the direction of the effect in the alternative hypothesis. This one-sided test would take one of the following forms: $H_a\!: \theta < \theta^*$; $H_a\!: \theta > \theta^*$. The investigator designs the research to determine the amount of evidence that exists to support the alternative hypothesis.

Test Statistics

Test statistics generally follow the normal, Student's t, F, or chi-squared distributions. The formation of the test statistic usually involves a point estimate of the parameter to which the hypotheses refer. Maximum likelihood estimators (MLEs) are favored in social research because they are generally unbiased, efficient, and have approximately normal sampling distributions. Commonly used test statistics are the z-score, the t-statistic, the F-statistic, the chi-squared statistic, the likelihood ratio test statistic, and the Wald statistic, defined as follows:

1. The z-score for large sample means ($\bar{Y}$) and proportions ($\hat{\pi}$) is $z = (\bar{Y} - \mu_0)/\hat{\sigma}_{\bar{Y}}$, where $\bar{Y}$ is the sample mean, μ_0 is the population mean, and $\hat{\sigma}_{\bar{Y}}$ is the sample standard deviation, or $z = (\hat{\pi} - \pi_0)/\sigma_{\hat{\pi}}$, where $\hat{\pi}$ is the sample proportion, π_0 is the null hypothesis value of the proportion, and $\sigma_{\hat{\pi}}$ is the standard deviation of the sample.
2. The t-statistic for small-sample means and proportions and individual coefficients in linear regression models is $t = (\bar{Y} - \mu_0)/\hat{\sigma}_{\bar{Y}}$, where $\bar{Y}$ is the sample mean, μ_0 is the population mean, and $\hat{\sigma}_{\bar{Y}}$ is the sample standard deviation, or $t = b_i/\hat{\sigma}_{b_i}$, where b_i is the coefficient of the ith explanatory variable of a regression model and $\hat{\sigma}_{b_i}$ is the coefficient's standard error.
3. The F-statistic to test the significance of multiple regression models is $F =$ model mean square/mean square error, or

$$\frac{R^2/k}{(1 - R^2)/[n - (k+1)]},$$

where R^2 (the coefficient of multiple determination) $= \sum(Y - \bar{Y})^2 - (Y - \star)^2 / \sum(Y - \bar{Y})^2$ ($\bar{Y}$ is the sample mean and $\star$ is the predicted values), k is the number of explanatory variables, and n is the number of observations. The F-statistic can also be used to compare a complete model with k parameters to a reduced model with g parameters (nested models); i.e., $F = [(\text{sum of squared error}_{\text{reduced}} - \text{sum of squared error}_{\text{complete}})/(k - g)]/\text{sum of squared error}_{\text{complete}}/[n - (k+1)]$.
4. The chi-squared statistic (χ^2) to test independence of variables and goodness of fit for generalized linear models (GLMs) is $\chi^2 = \sum(f_o - f_e)^2/f_e$, where f_o is the observed frequency and f_e is the expected frequency of independence.
5. The likelihood ratio test statistic ($-2 \text{ Log } L$) to test nested GLM models is

$$-2 \log(l_0/l_1) = -2[\log(l_0) - \log(l_1)] = -2(L_0 - L_1),$$

where l_0 is the maximized value of the likelihood function for the simpler model and l_1 is the maximized likelihood function for the full model, and L_0 and L_1 represent the maximized log-likelihood functions and are the transformations of l_0 and l_1. This transformation yields a chi-squared statistic with degrees of freedom (df) equal to the number of parameters in the null hypothesis.
6. The Wald statistic (z^2) to test the significance of parameters in GLM models is $z^2 = (\beta/ASE)^2$, where β

is the estimated coefficient and *ASE* is the asymptotic standard error estimate. The statistic is compared to the chi-squared distribution with degree of freedom = 1.

The generalized linear models generalize ordinary regression models by allowing the random component to have a distribution other than the normal and modeling some function of the mean. GLMs have three components: the random component identifies the response variable (Y) and assumes a probability distribution; the systematic component specifies the explanatory variables used as predictors; the link function is a function of the expected value of Y that is linearly predicted by the explanatory variables.

p-Value

The p-value provides a means to interpret the evidence provided by the test statistic on a probability scale. The p-value is the probability of obtaining a test statistic value as large as the one obtained, conditioned on the null hypothesis being true. The smaller the p-value the more strongly the data contradict the null hypothesis. Conversely, a moderate to large p-value indicates that the data are consistent with the null hypothesis. The p-value is the summary of the evidence in the data about the null hypothesis.

Conclusion

The NHST test is designed to minimize a Type I error, which is the error of rejecting the null hypothesis when the null hypothesis is true. To establish the minimization of a Type I error, the investigator sets the predetermined and small α level at which H_0 is rejected. The α level of 0.05 has become the conventional level of statistical significance in social research. The 0.05 level provides that only 5 times out of 100 the null hypothesis will be rejected when the null is true.

The investigator is interested in the range of values of the test statistic for which the null hypothesis will be rejected. Based on the predetermined α level, the distributional form, and the hypothesis to be tested (one sided or two sided), the critical region and corresponding critical value, $T*$, are formed. The task is to determine what values of the test statistic, T, correspond to the cutoffs of the critical region. Figure 1 illustrates this process for the α level of 0.05 with a normal distribution and a two-sided hypothesis. Note that α is divided by 2, so that half of the 0.05 probability is in the left tail of the distribution and half of the probability is in the right tail of the distribution.

The decision to reject H_0 is made if $T < T_1$ or if $T > T_2$. Table I shows the possible conclusions, given the preceding conditions. Note that the investigator does not accept H_0, but rather lacks the necessary evidence to reject H_0.

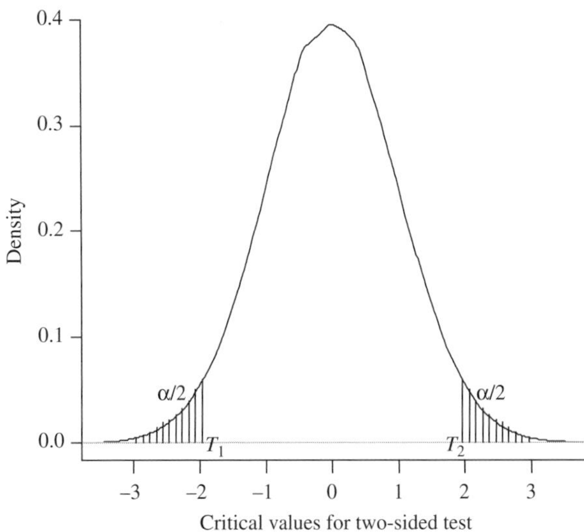

Figure 1 Null hypothesis significance test. Critical values for a two-sided test: $T_1 = -1.96$, $T_2 = 1.96$, $\alpha = 0.05$.

Table I Possible Conclusions of the NHST with an α Level of 0.05[a]

	Conclusion	
p-Value	H_0	H_a
$p \leq 0.05$	Reject	Accept
$p > 0.05$	Do not reject	Do not accept

[a] NHST, Null hypothesis significance test.

A Multiple Regression Application of the NHST

The *F*-Test

To illustrate the NHST, we test whether a linear regression model consisting of income, education, and the interaction between income and education has a statistically significant effect on occupational prestige, and fit the model; $Y = \alpha + \beta_1 x_1 + \beta_2 x_2 + \beta_3 x_3 + e$, where Y is the mean prestige; α is the Y intercept; β_1, β_2, and β_3 are the coefficients for explanatory variables x_1 (income), x_2 (education), and x_3 (the effect created by the interaction between income and education); and e is the $(n \times k)$ error matrix.

The null hypothesis takes the following form: H_0: $\beta_1 = \beta_2 = \beta_3 = 0$. This null hypothesis posits that neither income, nor education, nor the interaction between the two has an effect on prestige. The α level is set at 0.05. Alternatively, we argue that at least one of the explanatory components of the model does have an effect: At least one $\beta_i \neq 0$.

To test the null hypothesis, we investigate Duncan's Occupational Prestige Data, which contains 45 occupational types as observations. Though the sample size is rather small to estimate four parameters, it is useful for illustrative purposes. The F-statistic is selected as the statistic to test the null hypothesis. Recall that $F = (R^2/k)/\{(1-R^2)/[n-(k+1)]\}$. We calculate the F-statistic using the regression results reported in Table II: $F = (0.8287/3)/\{(1-0.8287)/[45-(3+1)]\} = 66.13$. The F of 66.13 is compared to the predetermined critical value extracted from the F distribution, which can only assume nonnegative values and is somewhat skewed to the right. The shape of the F distribution is determined by two separate degrees of freedom measures. In the case of our example, $df_1 = 3$ and $df_2 = 41$. Figure 2 shows the distribution of the F-statistic given the two degrees of freedom, and an F^* that yields $\alpha = 0.05$.

Our test statistic value of 66.13 far exceeds an F^* of 2.935. Given this result, we reject the null hypothesis of no effect and accept the alternative that at least one β_i does not equal zero. This result also indicates that the prediction equation of income, education, and the interaction term produces a significantly better prediction of Y than does the mean of Y.

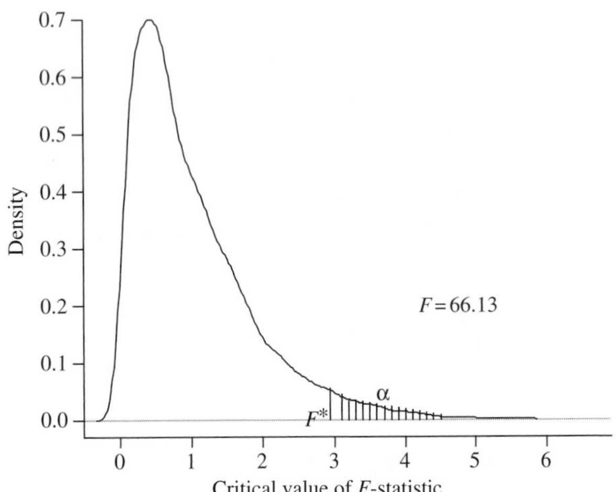

Figure 2 The F-test for the null hypothesis. Critical value of the F-statistic, $F^* = 2.935$; $\alpha = 0.05$, $df_1 = 3$, $df_2 = 41$.

The t-Test

An interaction term is included in the prediction equation, which posits the interaction between income and education as having an effect on prestige that is distinctive from income and education separately. To test the partial effect of the interaction term, the following null and alternative hypotheses are offered: for H_0, $\beta_3 = 0$; for H_a, $\beta_3 \neq 0$, where β_3 is the coefficient of the interaction term x_3 (income $\times$ education). The test statistic is $t = b_3/\hat{\sigma}_{b_3}$. From Table II, $t = -0.001237/0.003386 = -0.365$.

This value is compared to the t distribution and has $df = n - (k+1)$, or 41. Like the standard normal distribution, the t distribution is bell-shaped and symmetric about zero. The spread of the t distribution depends on the degrees of freedom, and the probability of falling in the tails of the distribution is higher than that of the standard normal distribution. However, the larger the degrees of freedom, the more the t distribution resembles the standard normal distribution. For a t-statistic with $df = 41$, the results are practically equivalent to the standard normal distribution. For a two-sided test, the critical value of t^* for $\alpha/2 = 0.025$ is approximately -1.96 (see Fig. 1). Given that the value of the test statistic (-0.365) is less than the value of t^*, we fail to reject H_0, that the coefficient of the interaction term is equal to zero. We can now employ the simpler model. The results of this type of test are generally referenced in footnotes or in a method appendix, because investigators are interested in presenting the most efficient model in the body of the paper.

Table II is illustrative of the manner in which many investigators report the results of the test of the partial effects of each component of the model. The asterisk (*) notation that accompanies the t-values for income and education is an indicator that the coefficients for income and education are significantly different from zero so as to exceed the predetermined α level to the point that they would exceed a predetermined α level of even 0.01. An alternative approach to the use of this notation to indicate significance is to report the

Table II Linear Regression of the Prestige Model[a]

Model term	*Coefficient*	*Estimated standard error*	*t-Value*
Intercept	−8.250934	7.378546	−1.118
Income	0.655621	0.197148	3.326**
Education	0.606030	0.192363	3.150**
Income × education	−0.001237	0.003386	−0.365

Multiple R-squared, 0.8287; F-statistic, 66.13 on 3 and 41 df; p-value, 9.286e−16; significant codes, 0 '***' 0.001 '**' 0.01 '**' 0.05 '.' 0.1 ' ' 1.

[a] Data from Duncan (1961). The Duncan data were extracted from the Companion to Applied Regression (CAR) Library in an **R** statistical-computing environment.

p-values (some advantages of this approach are specified in Section V, B).

The finding that results from the use of the t-test to test the significance of a single coefficient estimate is equivalent to the finding that would result from the use of the F-test to test complete versus reduced models with a single parameter difference. For example, comparing the complete model $Y = \alpha + \beta_1 x_1 + \beta_2 x_2 + \beta_3 x_3 + e$ to the reduced model $Y = \alpha + \beta_1 x_1 + \beta_2 x_2 + e$ would result in the same p-value that the preceding t-test produced.

Controlling for Potentially Spurious Factors

Though parsimony (presenting the model with the fewest parameters) is an important consideration in the presentation of test results, it is equally important that the investigator addresses the possibility of competing explanations. The investigator may accomplish this by including the alternative proposed explanatory variables in the explanatory model. For example, another investigator has shown that father's educational level is a significant factor in an occupation's level of prestige. This result has been widely reported and has begun to gain support in the literature. To demonstrate that the relationship between father's educational level and occupational prestige is spurious, the investigator includes this variable in the full model. A spurious relationship is a relationship between two variables that disappears when it is controlled by a third variable. In this case, the third variable is education. Both the investigator's explanation and the competing explanation are now nested in the full model, and the F- or t-test can be employed to examine the competing explanations. In the case of binary or ordinal outcome variables, the likelihood ratio, chi-squared, or Wald test may be used for the same purpose.

Enhancements and Alternatives to the NHST

Though the NHST has attained a high level of acceptance in social research, it is, nevertheless, controversial because of misunderstandings concerning the application and interpretation of the test by many investigators. Several alternatives have been proposed to enhance the hypothesis testing process.

Report the p-Value

Reporting the p-value is a more objective process that allows the reader to draw conclusions concerning the significance of the relationship, allows for the aggregation of evidence through meta-analyses, and is relatively consistent with conclusions drawn by using the α criterion.

Employ and Interpret Confidence Intervals around Point Estimates

Confidence intervals are attractive because they provide both an estimate for the effect size and an indication of the uncertainty concerning the accuracy of the estimate. Generally, the greater the level of confidence desired, the wider the confidence interval. That is to say, given the same model and data, achieving 99% confidence would require a wider interval than would achieving 95% confidence. A 95% confidence interval for the coefficient b_i is $b_i \pm (t_{0.025} \times \hat{\sigma}_{b_i})$, where b_i is the ith coefficient in a multiple linear regression model, t is taken from the t distribution tail probabilities, and, in this example, the subscript of 0.025 (0.05/2) yields a t-value of 1.96, and $\hat{\sigma}_{b_i}$ is the standard error for b_i.

Table III shows the 95 and 99% confidence intervals for the coefficient estimates of the preceding model. The fact that the confidence intervals for coefficients for income and education are bound above zero indicates that there is strong evidence that the coefficients for both of these explanatory variables are not equal to zero and are positively associated with prestige.

Use Bayesian Analysis

In Bayesian analysis, inferences about unknown parameters are summarized in probability statements of the posterior distribution, which is a product of the likelihood function and some prior belief about the distribution. Contra the frequentist approach to statistical inference, the Bayesian approach allows the investigator to determine the probability of the null hypothesis, or a range of

Table III Linear Regression of the Prestige Model with 95 and 99% CIs

Model term	*Coefficients*	*Estimated standard error*	*t-Value*	*95% confidence interval*	*99% confidence interval*
Intercept	−8.250934	7.3785	−1.118	[−22.713, 6.211]	[−27.288, 10.786]
Income	0.655621	0.1971	3.326	[0.269, 1.042]	[0.147, 1.164]
Education	0.606030	0.1924	3.150	[0.229, 0.983]	[0.110, 1.102]
Income × Education	−0.001237	0.0034	−0.365	[−0.008, 0.005]	[−0.010, 0.007]

values within which the true value lies, with a predetermined level of probability. Using a 95% Bayesian probability interval, the investigator can declare that there is a 95% probability that the interval contains the unknown true value.

See Also the Following Articles

Bayesian Statistics • Confidence Intervals • Maximum Likelihood Estimation • Measurement Error, Issues and Solutions • Type I and Type II Error

Further Reading

Agresti, A., and Finlay, B. (1997). *Statistical Methods for the Social Sciences.* 3rd Ed. Prentice Hall, Upper Saddle River, New Jersey.

Berger, J., and Selke, T. (1987). Testing a point null hypothesis: The irreconcilability of *P*-values and evidence. *J. Am. Statist. Assoc.* **82,** 112–122.

Casella, G., and Berger, R. (1987). Reconciling Bayesian and frequentist evidence in one-sided testing problem. *J. Am. Statist. Assoc.* **82,** 106–111.

Duncan, O. (1961). A socioeconomic index for all occupations. In *Occupations and Social Status* (A. Reiss, Jr., ed.), pp. 109–138. Free Press, New York.

Fisher, R. A. (1970). *Statistical Methods for Research Workers,* 14th Ed. Hafner, New York.

Giles, J., and Giles, D. (1995). Pre-test estimation and testing in econometrics: Recent developments. In *Surveys in Econometrics* (L. Oxley, D. George, C. Roberts, and S. Sayer, eds.), pp. 42–90. Basil Blackwell, Oxford, United Kingdom.

Gill, J. (1999). The insignificance of null hypothesis significance testing. *Pol. Res. Q.* **52,** 647–674.

Hanushek, E., and Jackson, J. (1977). *Statistical Methods for Social Science.* Academic Press, New York.

Isaak, A. (1985). *Scope and Methods of Political Science: An Introduction to the Methodology of Political Inquiry.* Brooks/Cole Publ., Pacific Grove, California.

King, G. (1998). *Unifying Political Methodology: The Likelihood Theory of Statistical Inference.* University of Michigan Press, Ann Arbor.

Liao, T. (1994). *Interpreting Probability Models: Logit, Probit, and Other Generalized Linear Models.* Sage Publ., Thousand Oaks, California.

Nickerson, R. (2000). Null hypothesis testing: A review of an old and continuing controversy. *Psychol. Meth.* **5,** 241–301.

Poole, C. (2001). Lower P-values or narrow confidence intervals: Which are more durable? *Epidemiology* **12,** 291–294.

Raftery, A. (1995). Bayesian model selection in social research. *Sociol. Methodol.* **25,** 111–163.

Sprent, P. (1993). *Applied Nonparametric Statistical Methods,* 2nd Ed. Chapman & Hall, London.

Impact/Outcome Evaluation

Frederick M. Hess
American Enterprise Institute, Washington, DC, USA

Amy L. Klekotka
University of Virginia, Charlottesville, Virginia, USA

Glossary

adaptive behaviors Behaviors that are required by different major life activity areas such as home and community living, school or work, and health and wellness.

benefit-costs The extent to which the program's benefits outweigh the costs.

effectiveness The extent to which a program meets its slated goals and objectives.

habilitation The acquisition of abilities not possessed previously.

impact The extent to which the program makes a difference compared to either having no program or having an alternative program.

objective Observable and measurable data.

outcome/impact evaluation A type of program evaluation that uses valued and objective person-referenced outcomes to analyze a program's effectiveness, impact, or benefit-costs. For instance, an impact evaluation studies whether a counseling program has in fact reduced such factors as recommitment, recidivism, and the crime rate.

outcomes Changes in adaptive behaviors and role status that are logical consequences of the services.

person-referenced outcomes Outcomes related to an individual's adaptive behaviors and role status.

process evaluation A type of program evaluation that analyzes simply whether a program has carried out a stated goal or objective. For instance, a process evaluation studies whether a program has provided counseling to the intended number of clients.

program evaluation A process that leads to judgments about the effectiveness, impact, or benefit-costs of a program.

programs A set of operations, actions, or activities designed to produce certain desired outcomes.

rehabilitation The reacquisition of lost abilities.

role status A set of valued activities that are considered normative for a specific age group. Examples include school, independent living, employment, and recreation/leisure pursuits.

An impact or outcome-based evaluation addresses the essential question of whether education and social programs are delivering the desired results in terms of person-referenced outcomes. Outcome (impact) evaluation is a type of program evaluation that uses valued and objective person-referenced outcomes to analyze a program's effectiveness, impact, or benefit-costs; this is different from process evaluation, which emphasizes simply whether a program has carried out a stated goal or objective. This discussion focuses on effectiveness and impact in impact evaluations.

The Difference between Outcomes and Impacts

It is common to use the words outcome and impact interchangeably, and therefore the terms outcome evaluation and impact evaluation are often considered to be interchangeable. Technically, there is a difference between outcomes and impacts; however, in common parlance, evaluators typically treat them as meaning roughly the same. Strictly speaking, impacts occur on program staff and funders, and possibly some other stakeholders, all of whom are upstream of the outcomes. In this entry, outcome is used to refer to any results or consequences of an intervention, the evaluation model is referred to as outcome evaluation, and impact analysis is considered to be a component of that model.

Impact analysis should be done only after a program has attained a level of stability—we cannot look at the effects of a program before we are certain that the program has been implemented as intended. Attempting to assess the impact of a program that has yet to be put into place is fruitless. In practice, an impact analysis should be preceded by an implementation evaluation designed to determine that the intended program elements are in place. In addition, demonstrating that changes in behavior occur as a result of a program is not always easy because behaviors are likely to naturally change over time. Also, determining which changes occur as a result of natural forces such as experience or maturation and which occur as a result of the interventions provided by a program is difficult.

Uses of Outcome Evaluations

Program evaluations with an outcome or impact focus are especially important for nonprofits, educational institutions, and social programs. These organizations typically design intervention programs that have a particular population with particular needs in mind. Therefore, these organizations have a vested interest in seeing whether or not the programs are meeting the needs of the population. Funding groups are also typically interested in outcome evaluations. These groups hold a vested interest ensuring that their financial and human resources are being allocated to a program that solves social and/or educational problems. An outcome-based evaluation focuses on the notion of efficient allocation of resources—whether an organization's or program's activities are bringing about the desired outcomes. Outcome-based evaluations can be thought of as an accountability measure in that these evaluations seek to prove that programs are not to simply engaging in activities that seem reasonable at the time. Service has traditionally been measured in terms of what is provided (counseling, therapy, guidance, and the like), and "good" service has been viewed as that which is provided by a qualified person. However, service needs to be viewed not only in terms of process, but also in terms of outcomes. Outcomes can be considered as benefits to clients gained through participation in the program. These are usually described in terms of enhanced learning (knowledge, attitudes, or skills) or conditions (increased literacy, self-reliance, or reduced negative behaviors). Outcomes are sometimes confused with program outputs or units of service, which include the number of clients that went through a program. Outcomes are the effects that programs have on clients, whereas outputs are simply the number of services provided to clients.

Outcome-based evaluation is especially important in light of trends currently sweeping educational and social programs. These trends include a quality revolution, consumer empowerment, increased focus on accountability, the emerging paradigm of practical evaluation, and an emphasis on enhanced functioning. The quality revolution focuses on such issues as quality enhancement, teacher quality, school quality, quality-of-life issues, and quality assurance. These emphasize that quality is essential to both the processes of service delivery and the outcomes resulting from those services. The consumer movement is also gaining in power and popularity. Educational and social programs are considering the needs of consumers as a critical concern. For example, this phenomenon can be seen in the issue of school choice. Proponents of school choice emphasize that parents and children are consumers of education and thus design programs and schools tailored to the needs of those consumers. Outcome-based evaluation can become a critical part of the decision-making processes for consumers in terms of where they live or work, what school they send their children to, or what services they use. Accountability data is in demand by the government, funders, program managers, policy makers, and consumers. Accountability is currently defined in terms of outcomes and organizational effectiveness and efficiency. Most states employ an accountability system that requires public reports of school effectiveness. Outcome-based evaluation is consistent with the increasing need for accountability because it provides a value-added system of outcome data.

The field of program evaluation is also changing toward a more practical approach to evaluation. The classic experimental paradigm was very popular in the program evaluations of the 1960s and 1970s because of federal requirements to assess the efficacy of federally funded educational and social service organizations. This model is less practical when it is applied to social or education programs. Educators, social workers, and other providers of social services can rarely meet the required experimental conditions and assumptions. In addition, it is politically undesirable to withhold a potentially beneficial education or social program from human subjects.

The purposes of outcome assessments are to give direction to policy makers, accountability to constituents, and feedback for improving the program and the services provided. The questions to be addressed by an outcome evaluation should originate from the stakeholders: the governing committees, the policy makers, the staff of the program, and the constituents. The reason for this is so that the focus of the evaluation is meaningful to those who have the greatest interest in seeing it be successful. The stakeholders should also have a high level of commitment to use the results of the assessments for the development of policy, accountability, program evaluation, and program improvement. An evaluation whose results are not used in a productive manner or as a means of improvement is a waste of time and money.

Outcomes Are Connected Logically to the Program

Connecting outcomes to the program seems like a simple criterion for outcome evaluations, but it is often overlooked. This criterion requires that the analyzed outcomes logically be the product of the services received through the program and not an unintended effect of externalities. The outcomes should first be identified as being sensitive to change and intervention; otherwise an intervention provided by a program would have no effect. The outcomes should then be attributed to the intervention in such a way that it is obvious that a link exists between the services provided and the outcomes observed.

Outcome-Based Evaluation Model

A common model for outcome-based evaluations has four components. The first stipulates that the mission statement and goals of the agency or program provider should shape the program's efforts. The second is that the interventions or services provided should mirror the goals and mission of the agency or program provider. The third is that outcomes should be value- and person-referenced (related to behaviors and role status or knowledge that can be changed as a result of interventions). The fourth component is that the stakeholders in the program should have a strong voice in the design and management of the program. This can be done through providing formative rather than summative feedback to the stakeholders. Formative feedback allows for the systematic evaluation and improvement of services, as well as identifying focus points for program change.

Recognizing Outcomes and Linkages

The linkage between processes and outcomes is a fundamental issue in many program evaluations. The purpose of an outcome evaluation should be to help define program processes, program outcomes, and the linkages between the two. Identifying and conceptualizing program outcomes and impacts are both inductive and logical processes. Inductively, the evaluator looks for changes in participants, expressions of change, program ideology about outcomes, and ways that service providers make distinctions between those who are receiving the desired outcome and those who are not. In programs that are designed for individual progress or change, statements regarding change from program participants and staff may be global in nature. Such participant outcomes as personal growth, increased awareness, and insight into self are difficult to standardize and quantify, resulting in a situation in which qualitative analysis may be more beneficial and appropriate. The evaluator's job then becomes to describe what exactly happens to those in the program and what they have to say about what happens to them. Once data on both the processes of the program and the outcomes of the participants are available, it must be organized logically so that the processes and outcomes can be linked. A way to do this is to first classify outcomes (i.e., changes in knowledge, attitudes, feelings, behaviors, and skills). It is then possible to organize the data in a way that describes the content and focuses of the program. This enables both stakeholders and those outside the program to know which kinds of changes (outcomes) are occurring. The changes can then, through participant data, be related to specific program processes.

Using a process/outcomes matrix is helpful in organizing these data. In such a matrix, major program processes or implementation components are listed along the left-hand side and types or levels of outcomes are listed across the top. The combination of any process (identified by the mission of the program) with any outcome (identified through participant data from interviews or observations) produces a cell in the matrix. The process/outcome matrix becomes a way to organize, consider, and present the qualitative connections between the dimensions of the program and the outcomes of the program.

Evaluation Designs

The focus of the outcome evaluation is on determining whether the intervention has made a difference for the target groups or individuals. There are several ways to do this and these approaches constitute the evaluation designs. The designs may vary, but the essential question is the extent to which they produce results that allow us to connect the implementation of program elements to the outcomes. This effort to illuminate the causal link between the two is key to outcome evaluations. The most commonly used models are the pretest-posttest design, control/comparison group design, and regression design. Each model must establish a standard against which program results are compared.

Pretest-Posttest Design

The pretest-posttest design is the most common method of assessment that looks at only one group. A group of participants is given the intervention, which can also be considered the treatment, thus creating a treatment group. Data are collected from the group both before and after the treatment. In this model, the expectation is that without the treatment, no changes would occur. Data are collected before treatment to establish a baseline for the individuals in terms of the behavior or skill being intervened on; data are collected after the treatment to look for differences, whether they be positive or negative. The differences that are observed are attributed to the intervention. This design, which uses only one group, is relatively easy and inexpensive to administer; a drawback is that it may not be possible to definitively attribute changes in outcomes to the treatment because extraneous variables are not accounted for.

Control/Comparison Group Design

The expectation in this design is that without the intervention, characteristics of the participants would be very similar to a group of people not in the program. The first step in this design is to identify and select an equivalent or similar setting or group of people. This group does not receive the treatment and thus forms a control group that the treatment group is compared against. The knowledge, behavior, or attitudes of the control group are measured over the same interval of time as those of the participants, or treatment group.

One of the best ways to ensure that the participant and comparison groups are comparable is to employ random assignment. This procedure ensures that each member of each group has an equal chance of being assigned to either of the groups. Random assignment addresses the possibility that the treatment group is different from the comparison group in a manner that affects program outcomes.

Control group designs determine the effects of a treatment in a more rigorous manner than do pretest-posttest designs and are commonly used in experimental design and pharmaceutical studies. However, control group designs are difficult to employ in educational settings because denying a potentially more effective treatment to one group is frowned upon. Moreover, treatment and comparison students may interact, thereby contaminating the groups by potentially sharing aspects of the treatment. The process can be adjusted so that classes or school buildings are randomly assigned to treatment or control status; this would solve the contamination problem because the entire population of the room or school would be in the same group, thus eliminating interaction effects.

An evaluator might also compare the observed results to those that would be anticipated in a hypothetical comparison group formed on the basis of his or her prior knowledge. Such knowledge might be rooted in average outcomes from other closely related programs, preenrollment status, archival data, and current data that can be used as benchmarks for comparison. By relying on a general knowledge of preenrollment status, the evaluator may estimate what would have happened to participants had they not participated in the program. This design obviously presents some inexact estimation, and thus it is much less precision in terms of certainty, comparability, and generalizability.

Regression Model

This model uses statistical analysis to predict what things would have been like without the program. Unlike other designs, a regression design takes into account relevant factors both inside and outside the program. Regression analysis provides advantages over the simple comparison of mean values. In the two previous designs, data are produced at two points—either the same group twice or two groups once each. In order to observe change, the averages (means) from the groups are compared against one another. Regression analyses allow for more powerful tests of the program's potential effects because they statistically control for other extraneous variables. In addition, regression analyses include these variables in the model, allowing for the direct observation of the individual net effects on the outcome variable.

Basic Evaluation Procedures

Regardless of the design of a particular evaluation, some fundamental procedures should generally be followed:

1. Identify the major outcomes to study or examine. This may require reviewing the mission of the program and asking what the intended impacts are for program participants. It is important to look at the activities of the program and the rationale for doing each activity; the rationale for each activity results in an outcome. It is important to avoid the justification of ineffective activities and to focus on examining how well the activities are working. In addition, it is necessary to carefully state the hypothesized effects. In the project/program-planning stage, the developers should carefully state the expectations of the program when it has been implemented correctly. In some programs, the effects may be expected to over an extended period of time. The foci of social and educational programs often target complex problems that are not conducive to short-term solutions. The effects of social and educational programs may also be expected to happen in stages—one stated effect is expected to create another.

2. Prioritize the outcomes. This is especially important if time is an issue because stakeholders may then want to target selected outcomes for the evaluation to concentrate on rather than trying to evaluate a multitude of outcomes. Also, be sure to identify possible unintended effects. Most

programs have possible associated risks that must also be identified in the planning stage. The evaluation can then assess whether the unintended effects occurred.

3. Define the measurement criteria. For each outcome, specify what observable measures or indicators will suggest that the outcome is being achieved with the clients. This is often the most challenging and confusing step of evaluations. The researcher must transfer his or her thinking from rather intangible concepts to specific activities. In this step, it is often useful to have a secondary evaluator to serve as a devil's advocate. The secondary evaluator questions the assumption that an outcome has been reached simply because certain associated indicators are present. Although it may be difficult to define the indicators in social and/or educational programs, they must be clear enough so that evaluators can obtain consistent and reliable data. Terms should be clarified so that evaluators understand exactly what is to be measured and how it is to be measured.

4. Determine the appropriate time periods. Information about the results is important to stakeholders, the people with investments in the program. The stakeholders may need or want information immediately, and this may not always fit with the necessary timelines for data collection. Thus, in order to most effectively work with the stakeholders, evaluators must often compromise the ideal time periods. This step addresses issues such as how far back in time baseline data should be collected and how long the program should operate to give it a fair opportunity to show results.

5. Monitor program implementation. Program monitoring should occur in a systematic way so as to aid program personnel in correcting and overcoming problems, to effect management improvements that may reduce future implementation failures, and to interpret program results correctly. Some evaluators consider this step to be the most important in ensuring that the program is implemented as it was originally planned. As noted earlier, implementation evaluations may also be conducted as separate evaluations, but in the event that separate evaluations are not possible, implementation monitoring is helpful.

6. Decide how data can be efficiently and realistically gathered. Consider program documentation, observations of program personnel, clients in the program, questionnaires and interviews about clients' perceived benefits from the program, documentation of the program failures and successes. If an evaluation is to include reporting on personal information about clients participating in the program, the clients' consent to do so must be gained beforehand. Clients have the right to refuse to participate. Collect data systematically. The data collected on program implementation, hypothesized effects, and unintended effects must be as accurate as possible. If more than one evaluator collects data, each must follow the same rules and use the same definitions. If data are collected over a long period, the same rules and definitions must be used throughout to ensure consistency.

7. Analyze the data. Data analysis should produce a description of the program as it was implemented.

Common Statistical Analyses for Outcome Evaluations

In program evaluations, it is often more useful in practical terms to describe events accurately than it is to test specific hypotheses. First, hypothesis testing is often not practical in social and educational program evaluations due to the constraints on experimental design. Second, stakeholders often do not have the prior knowledge necessary to understand the level of data that will emerge from such studies—thereby making descriptive information more appropriate. Along these lines, an evaluator may simply want to describe the characteristics of the people served by the program, to summarize the services or interventions provided by the program, or to summarize the status of program participants on a range of outcome variables. The two best methods for looking at this type of data are matrices and descriptive statistics. The data can easily be put into a matrix so that it is readily described and exhibited, and these matrices coordinate well with descriptive statistics, especially such calculations as the mean or percentages.

Descriptive statistics can provide clear insight into important characteristics of the program's clientele, the interventions needed by the clientele, the interventions being provided, and the effects of the interventions. Such data allow aspects of the program to be quantified, and questions that will be answered by later stages of the evaluation to be refined. Describing the data at intervals of the evaluation allows the program to be monitored, the evaluation foci to be refined, and any further necessary interventions to be revealed.

Reality Check: Obstacles to Reporting Evaluation Results

Two major problems frequently emerge when evaluators seek to report results from outcome-based evaluation: (1) the equivocal nature of the results and (2) a skeptical audience. Findings are generally equivocal for a number of reasons. First, it is frequently not known how specific interventions produce specific outcomes. Numerous internal and external factors, often called side effects, can have significant influence on the results of a program. Each of these factors must be controlled for experimentally in order to be able to attribute the outcomes to the interventions with certainty. An evaluator is often left uncertain about the degree to which a particular program can be held to have caused observed changes. Second, the results may not be clear or consistent. They may even contradict one another—some results may point in direction, some in quite another. This presents a challenge to the evaluator to explain this contradiction. Third, the data collection method may be inconsistent with the type of analysis performed. For example, if an evaluator collects data that deals with a program's effectiveness, these data should not be used for making cost-benefit statements.

An evaluator may also encounter a skeptical audience. Evaluators must present evidence to an audience that may be resistant to change or criticism. People generally know what they want to believe and are hard to convince that this is incorrect. People also find change difficult and, if the evaluation points to change(s) being needed, this may be met with resistance. The program's stakeholders may often hold differing views as to what the central purpose of the program is and therefore often do not agree about what the purpose of the evaluation should be. Thus, reporting the results of an outcome evaluation may not be easy. Given the need to negotiate these sensitive issues, it is vital that evaluators communicate their results well.

Establishing Credibility

In seeking to establish credibility, evaluators ought to strive to demonstrate competence and to report results in a straightforward fashion. This is more readily accomplished when an evaluator understands the program and its context, works with the stakeholders of the program, and is competent and honest. Before any evaluation is done, the evaluator must become familiar with the program by spending time in the program itself. The evaluator should also familiarize him- or herself with the history of the program, the program's organization, the culture of the program, the services provided by the program, and the community context of the program. The basis of the evaluation—the approach, the questions, and the activities—comes from knowing the context of the program. Because program stakeholders are likely to have varied opinions regarding the goals they hold for the program, working with them is key. In order to be competent, the evaluators must understand the basic requirements of an outcome evaluation. They must be able to analyze the data correctly, meeting the requirements of any statistical analyses performed. Evaluators must also be able to explain to lay people the differences between statistical and practical significance with regard to any statistics found or run. Stakeholders may not understand the concept of statistical significance and how it applies to the results presented to them. Evaluators must be honest in terms of what the evaluation can deliver. It is important not to over-promise. Evaluators should be thorough in their descriptions of the questions asked, the measurement of the outcomes, and the legitimate uses of the data.

See Also the Following Article

Cost–Benefit Analysis

Further Reading

Baker, J. L. (2000). *Evaluating the Impact of Development Projects on Poverty: A Handbook for Practitioners.* World Bank, New York.

Hale, J. (2002). *Performance Based Evaluation: Tools and Techniques to Measure the Impact of Training.* Jossey-Bass, San Francisco, CA.

Joint Committee on Standards for Educational Evaluation, American Association of School Administrators, Joint Committee on Standards for Educational Evaluation Standards., and Sanders, J. (1994). *The Program Evaluation Standards: How to Assess Evaluations of Educational Programs.* Sage, Thousand Oaks, CA.

Merwin, S. (1999). *Evaluation: 10 Significant Ways for Measuring & Improving Training Impact.* Jossey-Bass, San Francisco, CA.

Mohr, L. B. (1996). *Impact Analysis for Program Evaluation.* Sage, Thousand Oaks, CA.

Rossi, P. H., Freeman, H. E., and Lipsey, M. W. (1999). *Evaluation: A Systematic Approach.* Sage, Thousand Oaks, CA.

Weiss, C. (1997). *Evaluation,* 2nd Ed. Prentice-Hall, New York.

Information Management

Paul T. Jaeger
Florida State University, Tallahassee, Florida, USA

Kim M. Thompson
Florida State University, Tallahassee, Florida, USA

Charles R. McClure
Florida State University, Tallahassee, Florida, USA

Glossary

database An electronic means for storing, sorting, cataloging, retrieving, and accessing information.

electronic commerce (e-commerce) The exchange of goods or services at cost to the user via electronic means. Typically, it involves the use of the World Wide Web and related technologies.

electronic government (e-government) The provision of information and services by a government to other government agencies, businesses, and citizens via the Internet. It can span local, state or provincial, national, and supranational levels.

information Anything that informs or produces a difference in knowledge or understanding. Information can be found in many forms and is an essential part of virtually every contemporary activity, event, and interaction.

information access The ability to obtain the information being sought.

information behavior A range of acts that includes seeking, avoiding, sharing, censoring, using, or suppressing available information.

information management The entire range of technical, operational, and social functions of a system handling information, affecting the creation, organization, storage, and disposition of information; the access to that information; the behaviors of users of the information; and the information policy environment in which it exists.

information policy Rules and guidelines, such as laws and regulations, created by government agencies and institutions to steer the creation, management, access, and use of information.

measurement A process by which a value is attached to an observable phenomenon or relationship.

The social measurement of information management is the procedure of employing research strategies to attach a value to an observable phenomenon or relationship involving the management of information in an individual, organizational, or social setting. It encompasses a range of strategies and methods that can be used to describe and assess the social impacts related to the management of information. Studies of information management most often focus on the way information is accessed, the behaviors of individuals as they interact with information, and policy influences on information management. Measurement approaches in these areas of information management are in a process of evolution and refinement.

Introduction

Social measures currently used in information management primarily originate in or are derived from other academic disciplines, because information management is an area of study that is still evolving and expanding. As quickly as information technology changes, so does the way information is relayed, stored, and processed to adjust to incorporate newer, more effective, and more efficient management techniques. For example, governments around the globe are adapting government agency structures to incorporate database and computer technologies in their daily information transfers. Moreover, there is considerable discussion as to the appropriateness of quantitative, qualitative, mixed methods, action research, and other approaches to social science measurement in general. There are several valid ways to examine these issues. As such, the definitions and measurements used herein have been selected as prime examples of the multidisciplinary and evolving nature of this field of inquiry.

The issues related to the social measurement of information management can be examined as they are used in the study of information behavior, information access, and information policy. These three broad areas of research account for many of the areas in which information management can be studied and provide for the discussion of a wide range of different social measurements. To understand how social measures can be applied in the management of information, the meanings of information are first examined. Concepts of information management are then reviewed.

What Is Information?

Information is anything that informs or produces a difference in knowledge or understanding. In its many forms, information is omnipresent in modern society, having a wide array of uses and meanings, with a breadth of purposes and manifestations. The term "information" can indicate a process (such as a message passing from sender to receiver), an item of knowledge (such as a piece of news), or a thing (such as a document). Information can also be the content of a message, anything that is communicated, or data that have a specific purpose. Information can be found in data, text, objects, and events, in both physical and electronic forms. As a result of the multiplicity of its meanings and roles, information is an essential part of virtually every contemporary activity, event, and interaction.

As a result of significant advances in information technologies in the past two decades, information has become a part of practically every interaction in society. This means that the various roles that information plays can be examined using social measures. One of the most important contexts in which information can be measured is the management of information.

What Is Information Management?

Information management is the entire range of technical, operational, and social functions of a system that is used to handle information. Individuals, social networks of individuals, organizations, businesses, and governments all engage in some form of information management. They organize the information they use to communicate, to record history, and to share, store, and create meaning from information. Information management affects the organization of information, the access to information, and the ways in which users can interact with the information. Information management further includes policies that affect the availability and uses of information.

Information management is usually influenced by a strategy or framework that guides the planning, application, and uses of that information. A university, for example, needs a framework for their information systems to accommodate instantaneous changes in student enrollment, across-the-board changes in tuition fees and balances, occasional changes in faculty data, and so forth. Information management strategies influence the relationships between information, technology, and the larger social or organizational information, and have an impact on the functions of information and information systems. Some agencies and businesses do nothing but manage information.

The social measurement of information management is becoming extremely important in this information age, because all organizations employ information in some manner, using and providing some amount of information as a central function of the operation of the organization at some level. Many businesses have embraced electronic commerce (e-commerce) and many governments around the world are providing information and services through electronic government (e-government) web sites. Within these business and government organizations, information has technical, operational, and social roles. Most organizations use information technologies and information systems to provide or deliver information to service populations, such as patrons, customers, or citizens. The increasing usage of information by a diverse range of organizations heightens the importance of measuring information management, as the way in which an organization manages its information affects the organization and the organization's service population.

Social Measurement and the Information Management Process

The general process of the management of information provides numerous opportunities for study. Generally, social measures are intended to translate observable relationships, organizations, characteristics, and events into classifications or data that can be employed to discuss, analyze, and represent the nature of the observed phenomena. Social measurements of information management can be applied inductively or deductively in the research process. They can be used in a range of ways in research, from exploring new aspects of phenomena to evaluating a complex information system. These measures, ideally, allow for describing phenomena and relationships that would otherwise remain hidden.

The process of information management can generally be envisioned as offering several distinct ways to apply social measures:

1. The information can be analyzed for the types of information involved, the purposes of the information, the intended audiences for the information, and the presentation of the information. For example, a department store may perform customer focus groups to elicit feedback on the store's marketing effectiveness. By ranking or even assigning numerical values to the participant responses to focused questioning, the store can determine where and how the information they are presenting is reaching its intended audience and how the information appears to the intended customer group.
2. The life cycle of the information can be researched. Information can be created, collated, processed, disseminated, deleted, and archived. Each of these and many other steps in the information life cycle present opportunities to apply social measurements. For example, a bank will have policies as to how customer information is processed, who can access that information, where it is sent, and how long it will be kept. These policies could then be measured in terms of security and privacy.
3. The decisions made regarding information can be studied. From the original idea to create or collect information to the use of the information by an individual, each decision made to create, retrieve, access, use, and apply the information can be examined with social measurements. For example, the decision-making process can be studied as an individual searches for information on a certain web site. Information seeking-behaviors can be assessed using information search process (ISP) measurement, and these findings can be used to determine how to improve information management on the web site.
4. The impacts of the information on society can also be examined. Issues that can be studied with social measures include how the information is used, who has access to it, how it affects particular populations, and how it shapes social behaviors. The library community, for example, can survey library users and nonusers about their information needs in order to determine how the library affects the community it serves. This data can be combined with other community statistics to create a fuller picture of how the information available at the library influences users in that community.

Though there are likely other opportunities to apply social measurements to the process of information management in specific circumstances, the preceding criteria introduce the breadth of possible applications of social measurements.

Approaches to the Social Measurement of Information Management

Diverse sets of measures have been employed in the study of information management. Many of these measures have been used more as abstract methodologies than as applied measurements. Information management research is influenced by theories and methodologies developed in other social and human sciences, including information studies, communications, sociology, psychology, information technology, management of information systems, business and administration, and education research. Researchers in these diverse fields often employ a range of social measures for various types of research about issues of information management. As a result, many different social measurements are used in the study of information management; a comprehensive review of the social measures that are applied to the management of information would be extensive and is well beyond the scope of the discussion here.

The social measurement of information management can be done with quantitative, qualitative, or action research, or even mixed methods, using many different types of data collection instruments to describe information measurement in individual, organizational, or social settings. A selection of the most common methods, measures, theories, and techniques that can be used in the social measurement of information management is included in Table I.

Given the range of possibilities that could be discussed in terms of the social measurement of information management, the focus here is only on a selection of relevant

Table I Social Measurement Instruments for the Study of Information Management

Analysis of administrative records	Media richness theory
Behavioral intention toward technology usage	Models of question negotiation
Bibliometrics	Narrative research
Case studies	Perceived usefulness
Cognitive authority	Personality tests
Conjoint analysis	Phenomenology
Demand simulation	Policy analysis
Diffusion of innovation	Question answering
Ethnographies	Social network theory
Focus groups	Speech act theory
Genre theory	Surveys
Grounded theory research	Task–system fit
Information search process	Technology acceptance model
Measurement of user information satisfaction	Unobtrusive observation
	Usability assessment
	User modeling

studies and measures. These have been chosen to represent well-respected methodologies in information behavior, information access, and information policy. Of the three, information behavior has been the most heavily studied and has created more generalizable approaches to social measurement. The other two areas are just as valuable as areas of research, but there simply has been less scholarship to date.

Information Behavior

Information behavior is an individual's action (or inaction) when faced with an information need. The range of information behaviors includes deciding that information is needed, searching for information when desired information is not present, sharing or suppressing information once discovered, avoiding information, storing information, and myriad other possible behaviors. Information behaviors affect, and ultimately shape, how individuals manage information. As a result, studying and measuring information behaviors help provide an understanding of how information can be managed to facilitate its use.

Some examples of the use of social measurement to study information behavior include studies that use social network theory (SNT), ethnographic, sense-making, and ISP methodologies to analyze observed behavioral phenomena. SNT is a way to account for the social connections that an individual employs to reach valued information. Researchers study social positioning by studying the relationship between the strength of social connections and the quality and quantity of information that an individual receives. Ethnographic methods used by some researchers measure information behavior to examine how individuals behave in a natural setting with everyday information. Sense-making research focuses on how individuals approach the world with underlying assumptions that affect how they use information to make sense of the world. Sense-making methodologies provide a detailed examination of an information-seeking event in order to determine whether the information need has been met. The information search process methodology is another prominent social measurement in information management behavior. The ISP is a six-stage model for studying how meaning is sought in the information-seeking process from the point of view of the user.

Information Access

Information access is the ability to obtain the information that an individual is seeking. The social measurement of information access can reveal ways in which information can be managed so as to provide greater awareness of available information, to improve access to the information, and to assure that the information can be understood by and be of benefit to those who seek it. Information access can be affected by awareness of the existence of information, the availability of the technology necessary to reach that information, the knowledge to use any necessary technology properly, the ability to locate the desired information, and many other factors. The technical, social, and economic factors that inhibit information access are commonly identified as "barriers," indicating a gap in the abilities of certain groups of individuals to access information in both a print and a digital environment. Specific populations are particularly prone to barriers to information access, and each of these populations and barriers can be examined using social measurements.

Research using social measurement to examine information access often has been related to access to the Internet. These studies have used a range of survey approaches, focus groups, and web site analyses to evaluate levels of information access, for a range of populations, to electronic information and services such as e-commerce and e-government. Examples of research using these approaches include surveys of access to e-government by demographic populations, research by the U.S. Department of Commerce into levels of Internet access in relation to economic factors, and studies of student access to the Internet.

Information Policy

Information policy is the set of guidelines, regulations, and laws that determines how information can be stored, provided, and used. Policy research is, by its nature, complex, multidimensional, and can be examined using a range of theoretical frameworks. Governments, primarily at the national and state levels, pass laws and issue regulations that govern the dissemination and use of information by individuals, private entities, and government organizations. Information policies affect access, use, dissemination, transfer, sharing, storage, transmission, privacy, security, and display of information. These laws and regulations legislate many of the roles of information in a society, but they are also shaped by the social roles of information. For example, in the United States, the First Amendment guarantee of freedom of speech has created a social expectation that information will usually be available, which influences how the government can regulate or direct the flow of information.

Differences in philosophy regarding information policy have led to considerable discrepancies in the ways in which separate nations handle the management of information. The social measurement of information policy can demonstrate how policies impact organizations that manage information and individuals seeking access to the information. Information policy is studied through several types of social measurements, including social interventions, surveys, policy analysis, and case studies.

Specific examples of social measurements of information policy include descriptive modeling of the policy environment, side-by-side analysis, review and analysis of legal and policy instruments, and evaluation of outcomes measures. Examples of these measurement techniques can be found in the literature; some authors have described how such techniques can be used in association with a range of frameworks for studying the policy process, including the "stages heuristic," "institutional rational choice," and a number of other approaches.

This area of information management has been the subject of limited study to date. Some work has been done to bridge issues of information policy with issues of information access and information behavior, such as examination of information poverty in the electronic environment from the interconnected perspectives of information policy, access, and behavior. Further work that investigates policy in relation to access and behavior may help to expand the use of social measurements in information policy.

The Future of Social Measurement in Information Management

As previously noted, social measurement of information management is still evolving and draws on techniques and frameworks from a host of social and behavioral science fields. There is limited agreement on key definitions of terms as fundamental as "information" and "information management," resulting in some disagreements as to how measurement does or should take place. Currently, the measurement approaches are disparate and lack a cohesive or organized relationship. A number of key measurement issues related to information management have yet to be adequately addressed:

- What specific variables best describe the information management process? How are these variables operationalized?
- Does information management, as a process, vary from a print to a digital environment? From an individual to organizational context? If yes, how?
- What social activities or impacts related to information management are most important for measurement?
- How can different epistemological paradigms (e.g., positivism, constructivism, and ethnographic approaches) be best used in social measurement of information management?

These issues only begin to suggest the complexity of work that needs to be addressed in this area. The social measurement approaches identified and proposed in the literature thus far offer only a preliminary understanding of the validity and reliability of these measures and of the situations or contexts in which one versus another measure might be more or less appropriate. Social measurements also need to be studied and applied much more extensively in relation to information access and information policy. Further, there is still limited understanding of how social measurement of information management can "improve" information management in different individual and organizational contexts. In short, there remains much work and research to be done in the development of social measurement of information management.

Conclusion

Social measurement concepts relative to information behavior, information access, and information policy provide a foundation for further research in information management. The array of social measurements discussed herein offer quantitative, qualitative, action research, and mixed-method approaches to the study of information management. The far-reaching nature of information management allows for the use of such a diversity of social measurements. As information technology continues to evolve, the research in this field will parallel these developments, continuing to refine the social measurement of information management.

See Also the Following Articles

Ethnography • Focus Groups • Network Analysis • Phenomenology

Further Reading

Bartholomew, D. J. (1996). *The Statistical Approach to Social Measurement.* Academic Press, San Diego.

Buckland, M. K. (1991). Information as thing. *J. Am. Soc. Inf. Sci.* **42**(5), 351–360.

Campbell, D. T., and Russo, M. J. (2001). *Social Measurement.* Academic Press, San Diego.

Chatman, E. A. (1992). *The Information World of Retired Women.* Greenwood Press, Westport, Connecticut.

Dervin, B., and Nilan, M. (1986). Information needs and uses. *Annu. Rev. Inf. Sci. Technol. (ARIST)* **21,** 3–33.

Earl, M. J. (1989). *Management Strategies for Information Technology.* Prentice Hall, Englewood Cliffs, New Jersey.

Haythornthwaite, C. (1996). Social network analysis: An approach and technique for the study of information exchange. *Library Inf. Sci. Res.* **18,** 323–342.

Jaeger, P. T., and Thompson, K. M. (2004). Social information behavior and the democratic process: Information poverty, normative behavior, and electronic government in the United States. *Library Inf. Sci. Res.* **26**(1), 94–107.

Kuhlthau, C. (1993). *Seeking Meaning: A Process Approach to Library and Information Services.* Ablex, Norwood, New Jersey.

Levin, D., and Arafeh, S. (2002). *The Digital Disconnect: The Widening Gap between Internet-Savvy Students and Their Schools*. Pew Internet and American Life Project. Available on the Internet at www.pewinternet.org

McClure, C. R., Moen, W. E., and Bertot, J. C. (1998). Descriptive assessment of information policy initiatives: The government information locator service (GILS) as an example. *J. Am. Soc. Inf. Sci.* **50**(4), 314–330.

Miller, D. C., and Salkind, N. J. (2003). *Handbook of Research Design and Social Measurement,* 6th Ed. Sage, Thousand Oaks, California.

Sabatier, P. A. (ed.) (1999). *Theories of the Policy Process.* Westview Press, Boulder, Colorado.

Sprehe, T., McClure, C., and Zellner, P. (2001). *Report on Current Recordkeeping Practices within the Federal Government.* SRA International (for the National Archives and Records Administration), Arlington, Virginia.

Stowers, G. N. L. (2002). *The State of Federal Web Sites: The Pursuit of Excellence*. Available on the Internet at www.endowment.pwcglobal.com

Svenonius, E. A. (2000). *The Intellectual Foundation of Information Organization.* The MIT Press, Cambridge, Massachusetts.

U. S. Department of Commerce. (2002). *A Nation Online: How Americans Are Expanding Their Use of the Internet*. Available on the Internet at www.ntia.doc.gov

Innovative Computerized Test Items

Fritz Drasgow
University of Illinois, Urbana–Champaign, Illinois, USA

Glossary

computer adaptive test A computer-administered test in which items are selected from a large item pool so that they are appropriate for each examinee; specifically, a more difficult item is selected following a correct response and an easier item is selected following an incorrect response.

conventional test A test format in which all examinees are administered the same items in the same order.

disattenuated correlation The correlation between two variables that would be obtained if the two variables could be measured without error; classical test theory provides a simple formula for computing this quantity.

dimensions of innovation The fundamental ways in which assessment can vary; specifically, alternatives to paper-and-pencil conventional tests using multiple-choice formats with number-right scoring.

item response theory A measurement theory that relates the probability of a correct or positive response to the underlying trait assessed by a test.

latent trait The underlying skill or ability assessed by a test.

Innovative computerized test items refer to item types that creatively use the computer's capabilities to improve measurement and assessment. For example, multimedia stimuli may be presented, dynamic branching may be used so that the test responds to the examinee, and examinees may construct responses using tools such as spreadsheets or computer-assisted design tools.

Introduction

The traditional multiple-choice test, administered via paper and pencil, provides a highly constrained assessment environment. All examinees receive the same items, they select the best answer from a short list of options written by the test developer, and their scores are usually based on the number of items they answer correctly. Although it is possible to include color pictures, sound clips presented by tape recorder, or video clips from tape or videodisc, the inclusion of such rich stimuli is rare. Consequently, traditional tests seem most suitable for assessing the breadth and depth of an individual's accumulation of information and facts that can be expressed via written communication.

Many skills and proficiencies are not easily assessed by paper-and-pencil multiple-choice items. Consider, for example, musical aptitude, the diagnostic skills of a physician, or the design ability of an architect. Musical aptitude cannot be assessed without the inclusion of sound; the assessment of medical diagnostic skills requires a dynamic environment in which tests can be ordered, some conditions can be ruled out on the basis of the initial results, and then further tests and treatments can be prescribed; and evaluating architectural ability requires an open-ended response format in which individuals can create their own unique designs.

Innovative computerized item formats have been introduced over the past two decades to improve the assessment of skills and abilities not easily measured by paper-and-pencil multiple-choice tests. Computerization allows dynamic interactions between the test and the examinee; multimedia capabilities includes high-resolution color displays, digital sound, and full-motion video; and sophisticated algorithms can be used to score open-ended responses recorded by the computer. This increased flexibility in assessment methodology has led to much innovation and genuine improvement in evaluating critical skills and abilities.

Some History

Test developers and psychometricians recognized the potential benefits of computerized test administration long ago, in an era when computers were quite primitive. Bartram and Bayliss, for example, provided a review of efforts dating to the late 1960s that utilized teletype terminals connected to mainframe computers. This work, largely in the area of clinical psychology, was devoted to automating test delivery by simply using the computer to deliver conventional tests and assessments. Memory on mainframe computers was limited to a few hundred kilobytes, the mouse had not yet been invented, and widespread use of graphical user interfaces lay well in the future.

In the late 1970s, the United States military testing program began a program of research designed to develop and then implement computer adaptive tests (CATs). Such tests not only administer test items via computer, but also use the computer's computational capabilities to determine which item in a large item pool is most informative about an examinee's ability given his or her pattern of responses to already administered items. The first item administered is of intermediate difficulty; if an examinee answers correctly, the computer branches to a more difficult item, whereas the computer branches to an easier item following an incorrect answer. Item response theory (IRT) is used as the basis for ability estimation and branching algorithms. Although computer systems had improved from those in the 1960s, McBride, and Wolfe and co-workers, recounted difficulties encountered due to the limitations of computers in the late 1970s and early 1980s.

It was not until the mid-1990s that personal computers had finally become adequate for innovative item types to proliferate. Graphical user interfaces had finally become pervasive, sound cards and speakers were standard, memory had become relatively inexpensive, video adaptor cards could display full-motion video, and computation power was adequate to implement complex algorithms. Thus, the hardware and operating systems had at last evolved to a point where test developers could innovate without extraordinary efforts.

Dimensions of Innovation

Parshall and co-workers described five dimensions of innovation that can be used to characterize many novel computerized item types. The first two are closely related: item format and the examinee's response action. Item format refers to the distinction between selected response items, with multiple-choice items as a prominent example, and various alternatives. For example, constructed response items, such as essays or architectural designs, require examinees to create a response. Other response formats blur the distinction between selected and constructed responses; for example, examinees may rearrange or organize components via the computer's drag-and-drop functionality to reflect a logical ordering or relationship. Response action describes how examinees make their response. The response action for a traditional multiple-choice test consists of using a No. 2 lead pencil to fill in a bubble on an optical scan sheet. Analogous response actions for computer-administered multiple-choice items include clicking on a bubble with a mouse or speaking aloud to a computer with speech recognition capabilities. Other response actions include drag-and-drop operations, entering text or constructing equations, and using a joystick to track a moving object.

Parshall *et al.*'s third dimension is media inclusion, which refers to the use of nontext material. Examples include Ackerman *et al.*'s high-resolution color images on a test of dermatological skin disorders, Vispoel's sound clips on a computerized test of musical aptitude, and Olson-Buchanan *et al.*'s full-motion video to assess workplace conflict-resolution skills. Note that the capability to include such diverse materials greatly increases the range of knowledge and skills that can be assessed.

Degree of interactivity is Parshall *et al.*'s fourth dimension of innovation. The computer can be used as an electronic page turner to administer a fixed set of multiple-choice items to each examinee in the same order; here the degree of interactivity would be nil. CATs, on the other hand, select items from a large item pool so that their difficulty level matches the ability of each individual examinee, thus illustrating the dynamic capability of computer-administered tests. In addition to this dynamic branching capability (based on the computer "interacting" with the examinee's responses), computerized assessments also allow interactivity between the examinee and the item. Such assessments can have the flexibility seen in video games and allow a wide variety of examinee interactions with the stimulus materials.

The fifth dimension of innovation is the scoring method, which is closely tied to item format and response action. There is relatively little opportunity for innovation with selected response items where examinees click a bubble to indicate their choice; answers are typically scored as correct or incorrect. In contrast, perhaps the greatest challenge for test developers utilizing constructed response items is computerized scoring (note that it is always possible to use human graders, but this is slow, inefficient, and expensive). Scoring algorithms for essays, architectural designs, and mathematical formulas entered by examinees represent some of the most interesting and sophisticated work by psychometricians in the area of innovative item types.

Desiderata

There is little value in innovation for the sake of innovation. Instead, it is important to ask "What is the value added by the innovation?" To address this question, in 1999 Bennett *et al.* examined whether their innovative item type broadened the construct measured by traditional items. Specifically, they constructed tests consisting of 20 items of the new type, estimated reliability, and then computed the disattenuated correlations of the test forms consisting of new items with the old test. Their disattenuated correlations were in the 0.70s, indicating a moderate but not complete overlap of the latent trait measured by the new items with the latent trait assessed by the old test. Thus, adding the new item type to the test has the potential to increase the substantive richness of the assessment by broadening the set of skills that are assessed.

A second consideration is authenticity: to what extent does the test assess the skills required of the candidates? For example, the purpose of licensing exams is to protect the public by ensuring that only individuals who can work competently in their profession receive passing scores. Unfortunately, there is often a substantial gap between proficiency in answering multiple-choice questions about some content area and skill in the practice of the corresponding profession. Consider the difference between answering multiple-choice questions about the physiology of the heart and cardiac system versus performing open-heart surgery. Although this example is obviously an exaggeration, the gap between the knowledge and skills assessed by multiple-choice items and the knowledge and skills essential for competent practice in a profession provides strong motivation for innovative computerized item types. Of course, adding innovation item types to a multiple-choice licensing exam broadens the skills assessed and improves the substantive richness of the exam.

Thus, a goal of computerization is high-fidelity emulation of critical real-world skills and practice. By using graphics, sound, and full-motion video, many real-world activities can be realistically simulated by the computer to provide highly authentic assessments. Performance on a realistic emulation of a real-world activity is then assumed to provide a valid indication of an individual's level of performance on the activity itself and related tasks. Beyond obvious face validity and apparent content validity, empirical demonstrations that such assessments add value beyond traditional multiple-choice tests is very important. Collecting evidence of improved construct validity for these assessments constitutes an important area for future research concerning innovative item types.

Innovation to Improve Existing Tests

It is possible to view innovations as falling into three categories. First, new item types that improve the assessment of some ability or skill can be created. Here the assessment of some well-known construct is enriched by broadening the set of skills that are evaluated; Bennett *et al.*'s research provides a good example. The second category includes assessments designed to improve the authenticity of the assessment. Licensing exams that use computers to create high-fidelity simulations of professional activities, such as the medical and the architectural licensing exams discussed below, fall into this category. Assessments of constructs not easily measured by conventional tests constitute the third category. Examples include tests of musical aptitude and interpersonal skills.

To improve assessment of familiar constructs, a wide variety of innovative item types have been developed. Zenisky and Sireci provide an extensive summary of such item types. They give examples that illustrate drag-and-drop, drag-and-connect, moving objects to create a tree structure, inserting text, editing text, highlighting text, and several other response actions. In this section, a few examples will be given to illustrate how such alternative response actions can be used to improve measurement.

In 2000, Bennett and co-workers noted that traditional mathematical reasoning items are "tightly structured and contain all the information needed to reach a single best answer," which is given as one of the multiple-choice options. To broaden the mathematical reasoning construct, they proposed using an item type that they called mathematical expression. Here a mathematical question is posed and the examinee's task is to write an equation that gives the answer. For example, an item might ask "Suppose a raft drifts M miles down a river in K hours. How far would it drift in 2 hours?" Examinees use a simple equation editor to enter their answers. The challenge for this item type is scoring: many mathematically equivalent expressions can be entered (e.g., $2 \times M/K$, $1/K \times 2 \times M$, and $2M/K$). Bennett *et al.* used symbolic computation principles to reduce answers to a single canonical form that could be compared to the correct answer. In an evaluation of the scoring algorithm, they compared the computer grading to human grading and found an accuracy rate of 99.62% (and most of the discrepancies were actually errors in the examinees' use of subscripts that human graders scored leniently but the computer algorithm scored as incorrect).

Another example concerns the assessment of writing skills. The most direct approach is to have examinees write essays, but human grading is time-consuming and expensive (computerized grading is an area of active research).

Davey *et al.* note that two multiple-choice approaches to assessing writing skills are common. The cloze item type presents examinees with a short piece of text that includes a blank; examinees then select the missing textual element from the multiple-choice options provided. The second item type also presents a short piece of text, but here some part is underlined. Examinees are instructed to select the multiple-choice option that provides the best replacement for the underlined text. Note that both of these approaches highlight the selected response nature of the test in that the item focuses examinees' attention on a specific portion of a sentence.

In contrast, Davey *et al.* present longer essays with no blanks or underlined portions; some portions consist of exemplary prose and others contain errors. Examinees move the cursor to a part of a sentence they wish to edit and press the enter key. Multiple-choice options are then presented for revising that portion of the sentence (one option is to not change the text). Thus, examinees can change grammatical prose to ungrammatical, ungrammatical prose to an alternative ungrammatical form, and ungrammatical text to grammatical. This assessment format appears to constitute an improvement over the two multiple-choice alternatives in that examinees must decide what portions of the essay need revision rather than having the item format focus their attention on what is to be edited.

Of course, having examinees write one or more essays is the most direct means of assessing writing skills. Unfortunately, essay grading is plagued by low interrater agreement and high cost. Computerized grading has been an area of active research and newly developed scoring algorithms show considerable promise.

Improving Authenticity

In this section, three licensing exams that use innovative computer formats to improve authenticity are described. In each case, it would have been much easier for the test developer to construct an exam consisting entirely of multiple-choice items. Instead, these assessments required test developers to reconceptualize the assessment process, to decide what should be measured, and to invent a new approach to testing. The difficulties and challenges of this process were described for a variety of testing programs in a book edited by Drasgow and Olson-Buchanan.

The experiences of the American Institute of Certified Public Accountants (AICPA) provide a good illustration of why licensing exams are moving away from exclusive use of multiple-choice questions. Senior partners in accounting firms expressed concerns to the AICPA that newly hired accountants who had passed the Uniform Certified Public Accountant Examination lacked skills required to perform their jobs. For example, when clients meet with accountants, they do not ask multiple-choice questions, but rather describe complicated dilemmas. The accountant, in turn, may need to conduct research, evaluate several options via spreadsheet analyses, and finally make a recommendation and provide supporting evidence. Multiple-choice questions are poorly suited to assess the higher order skills needed by practicing public accountants.

Uniform Certified Public Accountant Exam

In April 2004, the Uniform Certified Public Accountant exam began to incorporate computer-administered simulations in addition to multiple-choice questions. Each simulation describes a problem that might be encountered by an entry-level CPA. The simulation has a series of tabs across the top of the screen. Clicking the Directions tab causes the directions for the simulation to be displayed, the Situation tab contains details about the simulation, and additional tabs pose questions and guide the examinee through the simulation. Examinees will be assessed on the workaday tasks performed by entry-level accountants: entering values correctly into spreadsheets, determining gains and losses, evaluating risk, and justifying conclusions.

The Research tab is particularly interesting; clicking it produces resources such as a financial calculator, a spreadsheet, and a searchable version of a document containing authoritative accounting standards issued by the appropriate professional association. Examinees can be asked to copy and paste accounting standards that justify their decisions in the simulation; this is an activity commonly performed by practicing accountants.

The AICPA simulations have the "look and feel" of actual client encounters and therefore have considerable face validity. However, do they assess skills beyond those already tested via multiple-choice questions? An important area for future research will be an examination of the extent to which the simulations improve the assessment of candidates' readiness for jobs as CPAs.

Architect Registration Exam

Architectural site-design proficiency is a skill that appears poorly suited to assessment via selected response items: it is easy to recognize Frank Lloyd Wright's Fallingwater as an inspired design, but its creation required genius. Consequently, the Architect Registration Exam (ARE) has long incorporated constructed response items as part of the paper-and-pencil examination. The solutions were subsequently scored holistically by human graders.

A research team from the Educational Testing Service and the Chauncey Group International worked with the

National Council of Architectural Registration Boards to convert the constructed response portions of the ARE to a computerized format scored via algorithm. Part of this effort required the development of tutorial materials and a user interface that enabled all examinees—both computer-naive individuals and computer-sophisticates—to easily create their designs. Bejar and Braun summarize evidence showing that examinees are able to construct all design elements (i.e., the user interface does not impose restrictions on examinees' imaginations) within the exam's time limits.

Interestingly, the research team did not attempt to develop scoring algorithms to emulate human graders. Bennett and Bejar argue that human graders should not be viewed as the ultimate criterion for evaluating computerized scoring because humans are unreliable and may be insensitive to important features of responses. Instead, Bejar and Braun note that the ARE computerized scoring algorithms were developed to be reproducible (not only should the same answer receive the same score when rescored, but the same scoring criteria should be consistently applied across answers), granular (the features of an answer are examined in a detailed way, rather than holistically), and hence more objective. Interestingly, these requirements had important implications for the development of design tasks: they had to be constructed in a way that allowed the scoring algorithm to be consistently applied. Consequently, it was necessary to construct design tasks according to a detailed set of specifications, which imposed a rigor and discipline on item writing.

Rigor in item development was implemented by careful specification of a few basic design tasks, called vignette types by the ARE research team. For each vignette type, many "isomorphs" (i.e., instantiations of the item type) that can be scored according to one algorithm were created. Moreover, these isomorphs are treated as psychometrically equivalent; examinees' scores are not adjusted for differences in difficulty across isomorphs of a given vignette type. Bejar and Braun describe a careful program of research studying characteristics of vignette types that may cause isomorphs to differ in difficulty and the learning process that enabled the development of isomorphs that are virtually identical in their psychometric properties.

National Board of Medical Examiners Case Simulations

In 1999, the National Board of Medical Examiners (NBME) began using computerized case simulations as part of the medical licensing exam. Each simulation begins with the computer providing a description of the patient's presenting symptoms. The user interface then displays an order sheet familiar to physicians. The candidate physician can use it to request the patient's history, order a physical exam, order one or more tests, provide a treatment, or request a consultation; the case simulation software is able to accept orders for thousands of tests and treatments. The information given to the candidate physician following a request for a physical exam, test, or treatment is based on the simulated patient's condition.

In real life, each activity of a physician takes time to complete. The case simulation emulates this process by providing a clock on the computer screen. If the candidate physician orders a test that takes 90 min to complete, the information provided by the test is given when the candidate physician moves the clock ahead by 90 min. Simultaneously, the patient's condition progresses as if 90 min had passed.

Clyman *et al.* note that the NBME case simulation is designed to assess a candidate physician's patient care strategy in a realistic context. Multiple-choice questions artificially segregate components of patient care strategy. In contrast, a case simulation does not provide cues, but instead unfolds over time as does the actual care of a patient. Clyman *et al.* (1999, p. 31) note: "The complex interplay of clinical information about the patient with time and physician action cannot be accurately and comprehensively represented and evaluated by the separation of patient care into many individual parts." Indeed, Clyman *et al.* report that the disattenuated correlation between scores on the case simulations and scores on the multiple-choice portion of the NBME exam is approximately 0.5.

Assessing Constructs not Easily Measured by Conventional Tests

This section reviews assessments of two constructs that are difficult to assess via traditional paper-and-pencil methods. The computer's multimedia capabilities, in addition to its dynamic capabilities, suggest that innovative assessments of many other important human attributes will be developed in the years to come.

Musical Aptitude

Conventional assessments of musical aptitude have the test administrator use a tape recorder to play short audio clips. There are many problems with this approach, including poor-quality sound from old audio tapes, unfair disadvantage caused by sitting far from the tape recorder or another examinee coughing or sneezing as a sound clip is played, and pacing of the exam set by the test administrator rather than the examinee. Computerization solves these problems: audio clips recorded digitally do not degrade over time, each examinee wears headphones so that seating is irrelevant and the effects of coughing and other distracting sounds are minimized, and the computer can proceed to the next item when the examinee is ready.

In programmatic research, Walter Vispoel has pioneered the development of computerized adaptive assessments of musical aptitude. Vispoel reviews earlier approaches to the assessment of musical aptitude and then summarizes his work. Interestingly, he notes that earlier researchers had disputed whether items should be nonmusical (so that they would be culture fair) or musical (so that they would resemble previously encountered melodies). Vispoel constructed test forms with both types of items, which he administered to a sample of college students. In a confirmatory factor analysis, a single overall musical aptitude factor fit the data well, with additional factors not improving fit. Thus, any dispute between musical and nonmusical items is pointless because both item types assess the same underlying musical ability.

Other versions of Vispoel's musical aptitude test have tested tonal memory. The computer plays a melody consisting of four to nine notes. The computer then plays the same melody with perhaps a single note changed. The computer display shows a digit for each note, as well as "0 = no change"; the examinee's task is to click on the digit corresponding to the note that was altered or click on "no change" if there was no change. Using the three-parameter logistic IRT model as the basis for the CAT, Vispoel has found that adaptive measurement provides precise assessment of musical aptitude with many fewer items than conventional tests.

Assessing Interpersonal Skills

Psychologists have been interested in assessing social and interpersonal skills since E. L. Thorndike's 1920 article. However, reviews of attempts to assess interpersonal abilities have concluded that such measures either are unreliable or measure traditional cognitive ability or personality. Attempts to assess interpersonal skills via textual material may be doomed to failure because such a format elicits intellectual processing. Chan and Schmitt, for example, found that a paper-and-pencil test of work habits and interpersonal skills had a correlation of 0.45 with reading comprehension, but a parallel assessment based on video clips had a correlation of only 0.05.

Olson-Buchanan *et al.* developed a computer-administered test of conflict resolution skills in the workplace. The assessment presents video clips depicting common workplace problems such as an employee informing her supervisor that another employee is taking credit for her work, an employee complaining to his supervisor that a co-worker is absent so often that their work group's productivity is affected, an employee telling her supervisor that she has been sexually harassed, and so forth. For each scene, a first video clip depicts the conflict progressing to a critical juncture. Then, the video ends and a multiple-choice question asks the examinee what he or she would do if he or she were the supervisor. After the examinee selects a response, a second video clip presents a follow-up scene showing a likely outcome of the examinee's choice. Again, the video progresses to a critical point, the video ends and a multiple-choice question is presented. After this question is answered, the computer presents an entirely new scene.

In a sample of 347 examinees from six organizations, scores on the conflict resolution assessment showed a correlation of 0.26 with on-the-job performance ratings of the examinees by their supervisors. Correlations of the assessment with verbal and quantitative abilities were near zero. Other research has found relatively small correlations with measures of personality. In sum, this video assessment demonstrates criterion-related validity but is apparently not redundant with cognitive ability or personality.

Future Directions

For more than a third of a century, researchers have sought to improve assessment by computerization. However, for most of this time the researchers' ideas exceeded the capabilities of existing computers. It was not until the mid to late 1990s that graphical user interfaces on powerful personal computers with multimedia functionality became commonplace. Extraordinary efforts are no longer necessary to develop innovative computerized assessments; instead, off-the-shelf hardware and software provide the capabilities to devise a wide variety of assessments.

It is important to recognize that traditional psychometric concerns about reliability and validity pertain to these new assessments. Test developers should examine the psychometric properties of the new item types: item-total correlations, reliability, dimensionality, convergent and discriminant validity, and so forth. Bennett *et al.*'s research examining the value added by their new item type provides a good example of the research that is needed.

In addition to psychometric research, a better understanding of a content domain may be needed for the development of assessments using innovative item types. For example, the Educational Testing Service (ETS) introduced the computer-based Test of English as a Foreign Language (TOEFL) in 1998. Similar to Vispoel's work on musical aptitude, computer-administered audio clips can obviously improve the assessment of English language comprehension. But ETS was dissatisfied with simply utilizing audio clips as a new item type; the TOEFL 2000 project was initiated to develop a conceptual framework for communicative competence, develop test specifications based on the new conceptual framework, and conduct research to test the framework and validate the new item types. Thus, a broad research and development program will be conducted to support this computer-based innovation in assessment.

Some major trends in computerized assessment are obvious. Licensing and credential exams, for example, are evolving in ways that make their assessments more similar to on-the-job practices. It is unlikely that traditional multiple-choice questions will be eliminated, but they will be supplemented by innovative item types that provide high-fidelity emulations of important professional skills. More generally, assessment media are changing to better match the skills and abilities assessed. Audio clips are used for musical aptitude assessment, video clips depicting interpersonal interactions are used to assess social skills, and computer-assisted design tools are used to assess architectural design skills. Matching the assessment media to the relevant skill clearly improves face validity and content validity; evaluations of criterion-related validity and construct validity are needed.

It is likely that the use of innovative assessment will continue to grow. Exams will emphasize the assessment of skills—such as a physician's patient management skills—in addition to measuring the breadth and depth of knowledge. The assessment's administrative medium will be selected to be most appropriate for the trait assessed, rather than the "one-size-fits-all" approach of traditional paper-and-pencil testing. The use of constructed response formats will increase, albeit slowly, because the development of valid scoring algorithms for such items is hard work. Finally, dynamic assessment methods, in which the computer responds to the examinee's actions as in the NBME case simulation, seem likely to proliferate.

See Also the Following Articles

Computer-Based Testing • Computerized Adaptive Testing

Further Reading

Ackerman, T. A., Evans, J., Park, K.-S., Tamassia, C., and Turner, R. (1999). Computer assessment using visual stimuli: A test of dermatological skin disorders. In *Innovations in Computerized Assessment* (F. Drasgow and J. B. Olson-Buchanan, eds.), pp. 137–150. Erlbaum, Mahwah, NJ.

Bartram, D., and Bayliss, R. (1984). Automated testing: Past, present and future. *J. Occup. Psychol.* **57,** 221–237.

Bejar, I. I., and Braun, H. I. (1999). Architectural simulations: From research to implementation. (Research Memorandum 99-2). Educational Testing Service, Princeton, NJ.

Bennett, R. E., and Bejar, I. I. (1998). Validity and automated scoring: It's not only the scoring. *Educ. Measur. Issues Pract.* **17,** 9–17.

Bennett, R. E., Morley, M., and Quardt, D. (2000). Three response types for broadening the conception of mathematical problem solving in computerized tests. *Appl. Psychol. Measur.* **24,** 294–309.

Bennett, R. E., Morley, M., Quardt, D., Rock, D. A., Singley, M. K., Katz, I. R., and Nhouyvanisvong, A. (1999). Psychometric and cognitive functioning of an under-determined computer-based response type for quantitative reasoning. *J. Educ. Measur.* **36,** 233–252.

Chan, D., and Schmitt, N. (1997). Video-based versus paper-and-pencil method of assessment in situational judgment tests: Subgroup differences in test performance and face validity perceptions. *J. Appl. Psychol.* **82,** 143–159.

Clyman, S. G., Melnick, D. E., and Clauser, B. E. (1999). Computer-based case simulations from medicine: Assessing skills in patient management. In *Innovative Simulations for Assessing Professional Competence* (A. Tekian, C. H. McGuire, and W. C. McGahie, eds.), pp. 29–41. University of Illinois, Chicago, IL.

Davey, T., Godwin, J., and Mittelholtz, D. (1997). Developing and scoring an innovative computerized writing assessment. *J. Educ. Measur.* **34,** 21–41.

Drasgow, F., and Olson-Buchanan, J. B. (eds.) (1999). *Innovations in Computerized Assessment.* Erlbaum, Mahwah, NJ.

Davies, M., Stankov, L., and Roberts, R. D. (1998). Emotional intelligence: In search of an elusive construct. *J. Person. and Soc. Psychol.* **75,** 989–1015.

Jamieson, J., Jones, S., Kirsch, I., Mosenthal, P., and Taylor, C. (2000). TOEFL 2000 framework: A working paper. (TOEFL Monograph Series Report Number 16). Educational Testing Service, Princeton, NJ.

McBride, J. R. (1997). The Marine Corps Exploratory Development Project: 1977–1982. In *Computer Adaptive Testing: From Inquiry to Operation* (W. A. Sands, B. K. Waters, and J. R. McBride, eds.), pp. 59–67. American Psychological Association, Washington, DC.

Olson-Buchanan, J. B., Drasgow, F., Moberg, P. J., Mead, A. D., Keenan, P. A., and Donovan, M. A. (1998). Interactive Video Assessment of Conflict Resolution Skills. *Personn. Psychol.* **51,** 1–24.

Parshall, C. G., Spray, J. A., Kalohn, J. C., and Davey, T. (2002). *Practical Considerations in Computer-based Testing.* Springer-Verlag, New York.

Powers, D. E., Burstein, J. C., Chodorow, M., Fowles, M. E., and Kukich, K. (2002). Stumping e-rater: Challenging the validity of automated essay scoring. *Comput. Hum. Behav.* **18,** 103–134.

Thorndike, E. L. (1920). Intelligence and its use. *Harper's Magazine* **140,** 227–235.

Thorndike, R. L., and Stein, S. (1937). An evaluation of the attempts to measure social intelligence. *Psychol. Bull.* **34,** 275–285.

Vispoel, W. P. (1999). Creating computerized adaptive tests of music aptitude: Problems, solutions, and future directions.

In *Innovations in Computerized Assessment* (W. A. Sands, B. K. Waters, and J. R. McBride, eds.), pp. 151–176. Erlbaum, Mahwah, NJ.

Wolfe, J. H., McBride, J. R., and Sympson, J. B. (1997). Development of the experimental CAT-ASVAB system. In *Computer Adaptive Testing: From Inquiry to Operation* (W. A. Sands, B. K. Waters, and J. R. McBride, eds.), pp. 97–101. American Psychological Association, Washington, DC.

Zenisky, A. L., and Sireci, S. G. (2002). Technological innovations in large-scale assessment. *Appl. Measur. Educ.* **15,** 337–362.

Insurance Industry, Mortality Tables in

Henk Wolthuis
University of Amsterdam, Amsterdam, The Netherlands

Willem Jan Willemse
University of Amsterdam, Amsterdam, The Netherlands

Glossary

actuarial valuation A valuation based on a combination of discounting and probabilities.

actuary An insurance mathematician.

antiselection A situation in which individuals with greater than average risk are able to purchase a policy at a standard average premium rate.

discounted value A valuation solely based on discounting cash flows.

equivalence, actuarial Payments having the same actuarial value.

equivalence, interest Payments having the same discounted value.

insurance policy A contract that offers protection (against economic losses) with respect to the time of death of the insured.

insured An individual covered by an insurance policy.

insurer A company offering insurance protection.

mortality table A table showing the rate of death at each age in terms of numbers of death or number of survivors; the basic instrument to determine death and survival probabilities for individuals belonging to a certain group of insured.

net premium The rate that an insured is charged (net of expenses).

premium reserve The amount retained to meet the difference between the actuarial value of future benefits and the actuarial value of future premiums.

risk classification The formulation of different premiums for the same insurance coverage, based on group characteristics.

underwriting The determination of the insurability of the applicant for an insurance policy.

This article gives some insight into the use and significance of mortality tables in the life insurance industry. Actuarial notation is explained and an example of a general mortality table is provided. Rates of mortality q, and how they are estimated, are discussed; an introduction to compound interest and discount calculations is followed by explanations of premiums, premium reserves, standard actuarial methods, risk classification, and some related subjects. In addressing the subject of mortality tables, the question is considered as to which mortality table has to be used for several types of insurance policies. Some aspects of the rich history of insurance are considered in combination with the development of actuarial science.

Introduction

Why Are Mortality Tables Needed in the Insurance Industry?

Mortality tables, also called life tables, are used by the insurance industry to calculate premiums and reserves for insurances and annuities. The tables are used to determine the death and survival probabilities of the insured. Other elements in the premium and reserve calculation are interest and expenses. A primary aspect of life insurance and annuities is the often rather long duration of the issued policies. An actuary (insurance mathematician) uses mortality tables and interest (and expense) assumptions to calculate actuarial values of payments that are contingent on death or survival of the insured. Actuarial values are based on a combination of discounting and probabilities.

Why Are There So Many Different Mortality Tables in Use in the Insurance Industry?

Mortality tables differ per country, per insurance company, and within insurance companies. For different insurance products, different tables are used; tables are differentiated per subclass of risk, based on classification factors involving sex, smoking habits, etc. Also, tables are periodically updated as new data become available.

What Are the Major Problems of an Insurance Company?

Insurance companies must address major problems concerning the mortality tables:

- How to get suitable basic data?
- Should raw data be used, or should analytical mortality functions be used to construct mortality tables?
- How to take account of the long duration of the life insurance policies in premium and reserve calculations with regard to future mortality trends?
- Which actuarial (mathematical) method should be used to calculate premiums and reserves?
- How to assign probabilities to an individual policy, given one or different sets of mortality tables (this also has to do with medical selection and restriction by law)?
- Is there antiselection of the insured in case of life insurance, and if this is the case, how does the insurer have to deal with this problem?

Another important problem of insurance companies, though outside the scope of this article, concerns investments (the reserves of an insurance company have to be balanced by suitable assets). A connected problem is how to value the reserves and the assets; this is the problem of the valuation of the expected cash flows (and connected financial risks) of the insurance portfolio and the investment portfolio. Other problems have to do with expenses of the insurance company and how those expenses have to be related to the policies. This is a complex issue, thus in the following discussions, only net premiums are considered.

Definition of Actuarial and Probabilistic Symbols

The notation used by the International Association of Actuaries is presented in Table I; additional symbols are given in Table II. Each actuarial symbol consists of a core symbol—in general, a single letter for an interest or discount function, a probability function, an insurance or annuity function, etc. The core, or principal, symbol is often combined with auxiliary symbols, mainly subscripts (lower left or lower right) or superscripts (upper left or upper right). The definitions of symbols used here are given in Tables I and II; a complete list of actuarial functions can be found in a 1949 publication of the Comité Permanente. For easy reading and interpretation herein, the actuarial formulas for premiums and reserves, are written using the notation of standard probability theory.

Table I International Actuarial Notation

Symbol	*Definition*
i	Effective annual rate of interest
v	Present value of the amount 1, due at the end of the year
$\ddot{a}_{\overline{n}\vert}$	Present value of an annuity of 1/year
$\ddot{a}_{x:\overline{n}\vert}$	Actuarial present value of a life annuity of 1/year
A_x	Actuarial present value of a term assurance
$A_{x:\overline{n}\vert}$	Actuarial present value of an endowment assurance
l	Expected number, or number of survivors at a given age
d	Expected number, or number of persons dying in a given time period
ω	Limiting age of a mortality table
p	Probability of surviving for a given time period
q	Probability of dying within a given time period
$\hat{q}$	Estimated value of q
P	Net level premium
V	Premium reserve

Table II Other Actuarial Symbols

Symbol	*Definition*
D	Actual number of deaths
E	Number of entries
$K(x)$	Random variable for the future lifetime of an insured aged x; it can only take integer values
L	Actual size of group of insured
O	Number of transitions other than death from group L
$\Pr[K(x)=k]$	Probability that an insured aged x dies between age $x+k$ and age $x+k+1$
$q_x(y)$	Mortality rate at age x depending on (future) calendar year y
r_x	Reduction factor
y	Calendar year

Mortality Tables

A mortality table, also called life table, is a table showing the 1-year rates of death at each age and the number of survivors. Certain tables also show the number of deaths occurring between two ages, and the average remaining lifetime. There are cohort-based tables and period-based tables. The cohort-based table describes the mortality experience from birth to death of a specific cohort (group) of persons, all of whom were born about the same time. This cohort has to be followed until every member dies; so it takes a rather long time to complete such a table. Besides, an insurance company needs more recent mortality experience; this can be acquired from a period-based table based on recent period. For a period-based table, age-specific mortality rates of a population for a given period of time are used to construct a life table from a hypothetical cohort of lives at age 0 (see Table III, which contains the data for a Dutch life table for the period 1995–2000).

For a certain mortality table, d_x denotes the number of deaths between age x and age $x+1$. The number of survivors for the same table is denoted by the symbol l_x, hence for each x,

$$d_x = l_x - l_{x+1}. \qquad (1)$$

For human lives, there is a certain limiting age ω such that $l_x > 0$ for $x > \omega$ and $l_x = 0$ for $x \geq \omega$; ω is, for instance, 115 for a table for females. The number of lives at age 0 has a value that can be arbitrarily chosen (say, $l_0 = 10{,}000{,}000$); l_0 is called the radix of the table. Assume for the moment that the 1-year death rates q_x are known for $x = 0, 1, \ldots, \omega-1, q_{\omega-1} = 1$; then

$$l_{x+1} = (1-q_x)l_x, \qquad x = 0, 1, \ldots, \omega - 1. \qquad (2)$$

An abridged table of numbers of survivors l_x and death rates q_x can be found in Table III. The k-year probability to live for a person of age x, using the notation ${}_kp_x$, is

$${}_kp_x = l_{x+k}/l_x. \qquad (3)$$

Table III Dutch Life Table for 1995–2000

x	l_x	q_x	x	l_x	q_x
0	10,000,000	0.0058395	50	9,498,570	0.0039600
1	9,941,605	0.0004996	55	9,268,954	0.0065635
2	9,936,638	0.0003804	60	8,897,261	0.0111826
3	9,932,858	0.0002480	65	8,276,947	0.0199477
4	9,930,395	0.0002111	70	7,299,388	0.0333654
5	9,928,299	0.0001898	75	5,904,065	0.0559742
10	9,920,504	0.0001347	80	4,131,376	0.0919937
15	9,911,844	0.0003079	85	2,285,035	0.1447875
20	9,888,451	0.0006636	90	881,226	0.2204651
25	9,854,693	0.0006914	95	203,800	0.3128630
30	9,820,644	0.0007232	100	22,068	0.4159440
35	9,781,460	0.0009453	105	1230	0.4756726
40	9,727,241	0.0014687	110	37	0.5439559
45	9,640,014	0.0024149	115	0	—

Using the data from Table III, ${}_1p_{30} = 0.9992768$ and ${}_{35}p_{30} = 0.8428110$.

The probability that an insured of age x dies between age $x+k$ and age $x+k+1$, $k = 0, 1\ldots$, is

$$\Pr[K(x) = k] = {}_kp_xq_{x+k} = (l_{x+k} - l_{x+k+1})/l_x. \qquad (4)$$

In Eq. (4), $K(x)$ is the random variable for the (curtate) future lifetime of x; of course, for each x,

$$\sum_{k=0}^{\omega-x} \Pr[K(x) = k] = \sum_{k=0}^{\omega-x} {}_kp_xq_{x+k} = (l_x - l_\omega)/l_x = 1, \quad (5)$$

and for $n = 0, 1, \ldots,$

$$\Pr[K(x) \geq n] = {}_np_x. \qquad (6)$$

Using the data from Table III, ${}_{35}p_{30}q_{65} = 0.01681214$.

In the random variable model, l_{x+k} is the expected number of survivors at age $x+k$ (in the deterministic model, l_{x+k} denotes the number of survivors at that age). In the following discussions, the only notation needed is $\Pr[K(x) \geq k]$, the probability that an insured x dies between age $x+k$ and age $x+k+1$, and the notation $\Pr[K(x) \geq n] = {}_np_x$, the probability that x is still alive at time n.

Estimation of Rates of Death

In the previous section, Eq. (2) showed how the expected number of survivors l_{x+k} can be determined recursively on the basis of given rates q. The rates q have to be estimated on the basis of actual mortality data of (part of) a country or a portfolio of an insurance company. For a closed group, the actuarial estimator $\hat{q}_x$ is defined for each integer x by

$$\hat{q}_x = \frac{D_x}{L_x}, \qquad (7)$$

where L_x is the number of persons alive at integer age x, and D_x is the number of deceased from the group L_x between age x and $x+1$. For an open group,

$$\hat{q}_x = \frac{D_x}{L_x - 1/2(O_x - E_x)}, \qquad (8)$$

where O_x denotes the number of transitions from group L_x other than by death; E_x is the number of entries into group L_x. In Eq. (8), it is assumed that the number of entries (E_x) and the number of exits (L_x) are approximately uniformly distributed over $[x, x+1)$.

The $\hat{q}_x$ values as defined in Eqs. (7) and (8), or in other formulas, are by definition based on historical data for each separate risk group (e.g., "male smoker," "female nonsmoker"). Normally, the $\hat{q}$ values are rather crude data that are graduated by analytical formulas and the least-squares method. More advanced methods combine a measure of goodness of fit of the graduation and a measure of smoothness (Whittaker–Henderson graduation). It is also possible, and in some countries becoming more popular, to estimate the force of mortality $\mu_x = \ln(1 - q_x)$. If the $\hat{q}$ values are known for a large number of observation periods and if certain trends are observed, they can be used for extrapolation purposes to obtain q values that are suitable for forecasting purposes. This is especially important for life annuities if the $\hat{q}$ values are decreasing for all or most values of x over the last observation periods. The extrapolated death rates are used to determine a mortality table that is suitable for life annuities. The dramatic effect of mortality downward trends on the technical equilibrium of life annuity portfolios and pension plans requires more emphasis on the problem of extrapolating mortality rates. The notation $q_x(y)$ is used to stress that the mortality rate at age x depends on the future calendar year y. An example is the exponential formula, which is widely used in actuarial practice in some countries to forecast mortality rates via extrapolation of observed rates:

$$q_x(y) = q_x(y')[\lambda_x + (1 - \lambda_x)(r_x)^{y-y'}], \tag{8a}$$

where y' denotes the current year and $r_x < 1$ is the reduction factor at age x. A formula like this can be found in the Continuous Mortality Investigation Reports of the Institute and Faculty of Actuaries. For insurance policies with a positive death risk, such as term insurance, the use of an older table does not lead to financial problems for the insurer (see the section on Which Mortality Table to use in Actuarial Practice?).

Accumulation and Discounting

The calculation of actuarial values requires not only a mortality table, but also some theory of compound interest and discounting. A capital 1 at time 0 is accumulated by the effective annual interest i; this means that its value at time 1 is equal to

$$1 + i \tag{9}$$

and at integer time k, because the interest is compounded,

$$(1 + i)^k. \tag{10}$$

The 1-year discount factor v is defined by

$$v = \frac{1}{(1 + i)}. \tag{11}$$

This means that the k-year discount factor of an amount 1 is

$$v^k = \frac{1}{(1 + i)^k}. \tag{12}$$

This means that a single payment of 1 at time k has a value v^k at time 0.

A so-called annuity due with a payment 1 at time k, for $k = 0, 1, \ldots, n - 1$, valued at time 0 and denoted by $\ddot{a}_{\overline{n}|}$, is defined by

$$\ddot{a}_{\overline{n}|} = \sum_{k=0}^{n-1} v^k. \tag{13}$$

This is equivalent under compound interest with a payment of its accumulated value $\ddot{a}_{\overline{n}|}(1 + i)^n$ at time n.

Calculation of Actuarial Premiums and Reserves

The mathematical formulas that are used in actuarial theory and in actuarial practice to calculate individual premiums and reserves are based on the so-called individual equivalence principle. This equivalence principle is in fact an expected value principle based on the assumption that the expected value of the future premiums to be received equals the expected value of the future benefits to be paid out. Although the insurers adopt the equivalence principle in premium calculations, a (positive) expected profit arises from appropriate assumptions concerning both the interest and the mortality table, which must be on the "safe side" with respect to a realistic scenario interest rate and mortality. Expenses are not incorporated into the model for premiums and reserves here. Instead, in this section, we depart from the probability functions that were introduced in the section on Mortality Tables and the discount functions that were introduced in the section on Accumulation and Discounting. As before, a discrete time model is used.

For a whole-life insurance policy, the single premium issued on a life x with insured amount 1, payable at the end of the year of death, by the equivalence principle notation A_x, is

$$A_x = \sum_{k=0}^{\omega-x} v^{k+1} \Pr(K(x) = k). \tag{14}$$

On the right-hand side of Eq. (14), each probability of dying in a certain year is multiplied by the corresponding discount factor. Single premiums are also called actuarial values.

The next policy to consider is an endowment policy; this policy pays the insured amount following the death of the insured or on survival of the insured to the end of the term of the policy. For an endowment policy with duration n and sum assured 1, and payments at the end of the year of death, the single premium is

$$A_{x:\overline{n}|} = \sum_{k=0}^{n-1} v^{k+1} \Pr(K(x) = k) + v^n \Pr(K(x) \geq n). \tag{15}$$

The policy in Eq. (15) is the sum of an n-year term insurance and a pure endowment that pays amount 1 at time n if the insured is still alive at time n.

As a final example of a single premium, consider a life annuity that pays an annual benefit while the insured survives. The annuity of 1 is due at the beginning of each year, issued on a life x, with duration n and notation $\ddot{a}_{x:\overline{n}|}$:

$$\ddot{a}_{x:\overline{n}|} = \sum_{k=0}^{n-1} \ddot{a}_{\overline{k+1}|} \Pr(K(x) = k) = \sum_{k=0}^{n-1} v^k \Pr(K(x) \geq k). \tag{16}$$

In Eq. (16), two alternative definitions are given for the actuarial value of the annuity. In the first expression, an amount $\ddot{a}_{\overline{k+1}|}$ is paid if the insured dies in year $k + 1$; this is a payment valued at time 0, and is equivalent to a payment of $(1 + i)^{k+1}\ddot{a}_{\overline{k+1}|}$ at time $k + 1$. The second summation pays an amount of 1 if the insured is alive at time k. The proof of the equality of both summations follows easily using the definition given by Eq. (13).

The net level periodical premium P for the endowment policy described earlier can be found using the actuarial equivalence principle

$$P\ddot{a}_{x:\overline{n}|} = A_{x:\overline{n}|}, \tag{17}$$

or

$$P = \frac{A_{x:\overline{n}|}}{\ddot{a}_{x:\overline{n}|}}. \tag{18}$$

zThe net level premium is also equal to the ratio of two single premiums for more general single life cases because premiums are based on the equivalence principle.

Implicitly, it is assumed in the equivalence principle that large numbers of similar or identical polices are issued, to reduce the probability of ruin of the insurance company. In fact, the large group has to be homogeneous, and the policies stochastically independent and identical. This is a necessary requirement of the mathematical law of large numbers. A practical law of large numbers has to imitate the mathematical law as far as possible. A first practical requirement is that heterogeneity of the groups of life insurance policies is reduced as much as possible.

An insurer needs reserves to meet its future obligations. Consider two such reserves formulas (net premium reserves) at integer time m, using notation ${}_mV$. For the whole-life policy of Eq. (14),

$${}_mV = A_{x+m}, \tag{19}$$

and for the endowment policy [Eq. (15)] bought by periodical premium P of Eq. (18),

$${}_mV = A_{x+m:\overline{n-m}|} - P\ddot{a}_{x+m:\overline{n-m}|}. \tag{20}$$

In Eq. (20), the term $A_{x+m:\overline{n-m}|}$ is the actuarial value at time m of the future payments of the insurer, whereas $P\ddot{a}_{x+m:\overline{n-m}|}$ is the actuarial value of the net premiums to be received from time m by the insurer.

In the discussions here, the premiums and reserves are based on the same mortality table and the same discount function, which is of course not necessary. By external developments, insurers probably will be obliged to value within a few years, in external reports, the insurance obligations (and the assets) and, as much as possible, actual values (market values). The drawback of such valuation methods is that the annual financial results of insurance companies will vary much more. There also may be differences in the approach made by American and European companies.

Risk Classification, Underwriting

The mortality table defined in the section on Mortality Tables and the estimated rates $\hat{q}$ in the section on Estimation of Rates of Death say little about the probability that a specific insured person will die at a given age. The rates q in the mortality table and the estimated rates $\hat{q}$ are in fact "average" rates for groups that have some previously determined risk characteristics in common.

Life insurances and annuities are traditionally classified according to sex, age, and health. More recently, smoking habits have also been introduced in some countries as a risk factor. Risk classification can be seen as a process by which different premiums are charged by the insurer for the same insurance coverage for insureds belonging to different risk groups. In each risk classification system, it is assumed that the policies can be easily divided into homogeneous risk classes at the time of policy issue. The probabilities of the insured to die will in general depend on many factors, including biological, genetic, life style, social, and geographical factors. Risk classification systems can become more refined if more data are available. The classification system should be as good as the insurance market allows. If competitors do not use smoking as a risk factor, the insurance company can charge a premium based on an "average" mortality table, not taking smoking explicitly into account. An important instrument for an insurance company to obtain (to a certain extent), homogeneity, is in actual practice obtained by classifying the insured in certain risk groups. Risk classification is based on actual risk factors such as age and sex, (rates of dying and survival, etc., and in this special case the mortality table is directly coupled to the risk classification.

The fact, however, remains that each risk group in life insurance will in practice be heterogeneous to some extent, and premiums, according to the equivalence principle, are in fact calculated with reference to some heterogeneous group. As seen in the probabilistic model in the section on Mortality Tables and the premium rating and reserving formulas of the previous section, there is no explicit heterogeneity in the model. This means that homogeneity is a basic assumption in the individual rating system of life insurance mathematics, and the equivalence principle of the previous section. The entire underwriting procedure, which also uses application forms and medical exams, functions to determine if an applicant is insurable at standard rates, substandard rates, etc. The insurer also has to be aware in the underwriting procedure of adverse selection by the applicant, meaning that an applicant tries to select against the risk classification system used by the insurer. For example, a smoker may want to buy insurance from an insurance company that uses only age and sex as risk factors and charges a premium based on these two factors alone.

Which Mortality Table to Use in Actuarial Practice?

The estimated death rates defined in the section on Estimation of the Rates of Death are based on past observations; this means that a mortality table based on such death rates reflects only a certain past period. Future death experience will of course differ from the past due to sociological and medical developments. This means that the insurer, in some way, has to take into account expectations of the future death experience, and higher premiums or higher premium reserves may be necessary. For life insurances, the insurer may use a recent or even older table if mortality is expected to be lower in the future (and competition allows this). Use of an older table leads to higher and thus more conservative premiums. For life annuities, which require taking into account the possibility that the insured live longer than expected, other adjustments are necessary to obtain higher premiums and reserves. A frequently used method in practice is based on extrapolation of probabilities into the future of a series of observed $\hat{q}_x$ values for each x. Extrapolation of probabilities leads to smaller death rates, hence higher survival probabilities. If there is only a limited number of observations or if it can be assumed that the observations do not represent expected future probabilities, then the actuary will usually choose a safe mortality table, which will results in more or less conservative premiums.

Historical Aspects of Insurance, Actuarial Science, and Probability Theory

Nowadays, the determination of insurance premiums and reserves has a sound theoretical basis in actuarial science. However, at the end of the 17th century and the beginning of the 18th century, when the first insurance companies were formed, the relationships between probabilities, statistical data, and life insurance as described by the preceding sections were by no means clear. There was not even a clear distinction between insurance and gambling in terms of taking risks. Insurance was seen as a gamble and the idea of a mathematical approach seemed a strange one. The main reason for the development and growth of the first insurance companies in the 17th century was not the development of a scientific basis of insurance, but the combination of profitable insurance practice and the legal notion of risk as a genuine uncertainty, as opposed to quantifiable uncertainty. The application of probability theory and statistics for problems in insurance and annuities was neglected in the early days of the life industry.

Two important developments provided the possibility of sound theoretical basis. With the growing influence of a middle class, the purpose of life insurance changed from risk taking to aversion of risk, hence a type of insurance had to be created that benefited the family of the deceased. Next there was the emphasis for this new type of insurance based on predictability and not on the contingency of mortality. In fact, a new value system was created, which led to the application of probability theory and statistical data to insurance problems. This theoretical basis resulted in the separation of insurance and gambling, and in the second decade of the 19th century, this separation was almost complete. From that time, faith in statistical regularities and trust in insurance companies were symbiotic. The existence of statistical regularities was proved by the financial success of insurance companies, and the companies saw every new-found regularity as a new foundation of their practice.

In 1762, the Equitable insurance company, based on these new thoughts, was established. The Equitable used an interest rate of 3% (the market rate was at that time 6%) and a mortality table with high death rates (London Table), and only healthy persons were insured. These prudent assumptions and rates led to a very profitable Equitable in the years to come. In 1775, calculations of the Equitable showed that 60% of the assets could be considered as surplus. Recently, the Equitable faced major financial problems because the tariff guarantees of some of their policies were not financially covered by appropriate insurances. This made actuaries more aware of the financial risks involving insurance contracts.

See Also the Following Articles

Attrition, Mortality, and Exposure Time • Risk and Needs Assessments

Further Reading

Bowers, N. L., Gerber, H. U., Hickman, J. C., Jones, D. A., and Nesbitt, C. J. (1997). *Actuarial Mathematics,* 2nd Ed. The Society of Actuaries, Itasca, Illinois.

Comité Permanente. (1949). *Bull. Comité Perm. Congr. Int. d'Actuaires* **46,** June 30.

Continuous Mortality Investigation Bureau of the Institute of Actuaries. (1999). *Contin. Mortal. Invest. Rep.* **17**.

Cummins, J. D., Smith, B. D., Vance, R. N., and VanDerhei, J. L. (1983). *Risk Classification in Life Insurance.* Kluwer Nijhoff, Boston, The Hague, London.

Daston, L. J. (1990). The domestication of risk: mathematical probability and insurance 1650–1830. In *The Probabilistic Revolution, Volume 1: Ideas in History* (L. Krüger, L. J. Daston, and M. Heidelberg, eds.), pp. 237–260. The MIT Press, London.

Dutch Actuarial Association. (2002). *Dutch Life Tables. AG-tafels 1995–2000.* Dutch Actuarial Association, Woerden (U.S. life tables, published by the National Center for Health Statistics, are available on the Internet at http://www.cdc.gov).

Henderson, R. (1924). A new method of graduation. *Trans. Actuar. Soc. Am.* **25,** 29–40.

Intangible Assets: Concepts and Measurements

Baruch Lev
New York University, New York, New York, USA

Glossary

comprehensive valuation of intangibles A methodology for estimating the total value of enterprise intangibles, based on their contribution to profitability.

intangible assets Sources of future benefits that lack a physical embodiment.

intellectual property Intangible assets legally protected by patents, trademarks, or copyrights.

organizational capital Business designs, processes, and employee incentive-compensation systems that create economic value.

partial excludability The inability of owners of intangibles to capture fully the benefits of these assets.

resource allocation The division of national or corporate funds among investments, tangible and intangible.

Intangible assets capture center stage among national and corporate productive investments. The measurement and valuation of these assets—derived from their costs and benefits—are challenging yet crucial to resource allocation decisions made by corporate executives, capital market investors, and public policymakers.

Introduction

The annual investment of the U.S. corporate sector in intangible assets during 2000 amounted to 1 trillion dollars—so estimated Leonard Nakamura, a senior economist with the Philadelphia Federal Reserve. To put this staggering amount in perspective, the same-year investment of the U.S. manufacturing sector in physical assets (primarily property, plant, and equipment) was about \$1.1 trillion. Thus, corporate investment in intangibles almost matched the investment in tangible assets, and given the substantially higher rate of growth of the former, relative to the latter, the rate of investment in intangibles will soon surpass that of physical investments.

Viewed from another perspective, in October 2003, the market value (stock prices times number of shares outstanding) of U.S. publicly traded companies was five times larger than their balance sheet value, which reflects primarily the net worth of physical and financial (stocks, bonds) assets. Thus, about three-quarters of the value of public companies, as perceived by investors, reflects nonphysical and nonfinancial assets. Much of this huge value constitutes intangible assets, which are absent from corporate balance sheets. Even if capital markets will slide, it would take a monumental collapse to erase a 5 : 1 gap between market and balance sheet equity values.

What are those intangible assets, sometimes called intellectual capital or knowledge assets, whose size surpasses the traditional physical assets of business enterprises? This question is addressed in the next two sections, and the reasons for the ascendance of intangibles to the top of corporate investments are presented in the following section. The widespread concerns of corporate managers, investors, and policy makers about the management, valuation, and reporting of intangibles are discussed in the next section, and the measurement and valuation methodologies aimed at alleviating these concerns are articulated in the final section. The aim here is to familiarize the reader with one of the major economic developments of the late 20th and early 21st centuries: intangible assets.

What Are Intangible Assets?

An intangible asset, like any other asset (a machine or a rental property), is a source of future benefits, but in contrast with tangible assets, intangibles lack a physical embodiment. Pfizer's patents on the best-selling drug Celebrex (relief for arthritis) and the Coca Cola' brand name are examples of highly valuable intangible assets that enable their owners to generate substantial revenues and profits over extended periods. (Financial assets, such as stocks and bonds, also lack a physical embodiment, but they are not intangible assets, because they essentially represent claims on corporate assets, both tangible and intangible.) The wide scope of intangibles can be grasped by their categorization as products/services, customer relations, human resources, and organizational capital.

Products/Services

A large and constantly growing share of the gross national product of developed economies is in intangible form; this includes software products, financial and health services, and leisure and entertainment, to name a few intangible products. Furthermore, for many tangible products, such as drugs, computers, or machine tools, the physical component is overshadowed by the intangible ingredient—knowledge—embedded in them. Intangible and intangible-intensive products and services generally emanate from the discovery (research and development) and learning processes of companies. In many cases, the property rights of owners over these assets are secured by patents and trademarks, conferring on owners of such intellectual property a temporary monopoly. This patent-driven monopoly is strongly challenged these days by developing countries and many nongovernmental organizations, claiming, for example, that it puts essential drugs (e.g., for AIDS and malaria) out of reach of poor patients and hinders the technological progress of developing nations (which cannot afford to pay for expensive technology). Nevertheless, the mainstream view, supported by economic theory, is that strictly enforced patent and copyright laws are essential to provide incentives for the heavy investment in research and development, required for sustained innovation and consequent economic growth. Indeed, practically all developed countries and an increasing number of developing ones have and enforce intellectual property laws.

Customer Relations

When the loyalty of customers to a product (e.g., Bayer aspirin) or a company enables a business enterprise to charge higher prices than its competitors charge or to secure a large market share (e.g., the investment bank Goldman Sachs), customer-related intangibles are present. Such intangibles are generally known as brand names, and are secured and enhanced by unique and continuously improved products/services (Microsoft operating systems), coupled with extensive promotion, advertising campaigns, and cultivation of customers (McDonald's, or Disney). The world's 10 most valuable brands according to a *Business Week* ranking (August 5, 2002) are as follows: Coca-Cola (brand value of $70 billion), Microsoft, IBM, General Electric, Intel, Nokia, Disney, McDonald's, Marlboro (cigarettes), and Mercedes ($21 billion).

Human Resources

Unique human resource policies and practices, such as employee incentive and compensation systems, or on-the-job training programs, which consistently enhance labor productivity and reduce employee turnover, create intangible assets. An example of a human resource practice generating substantial benefits is provided by Edward Lazear, a Stanford economist, who has studied the consequences of the transition from a flat hourly rate to a piece-rate compensation of employees in the Safelite Glass Corp., the nation's largest installer of automobile glass. The findings were surprising: a 41% employee productivity jump, enabled in part by a 61% drop in paid sick hours. Such profit-generating human resource practices are, in fact, intangible assets.

Organizational Capital

Intangible assets increasingly come in the form of unique corporate organizational designs and business processes that allow companies to outperform competitors in generating revenues or by economizing on production costs. Dell's built-to-order computers (customers design the configuration of the products they order), Wal-Mart's supply chains (essentially shifting their inventory management to suppliers), and Citibank's online (Internet-based) banking activities are examples of organizationally related intangibles that have created sustained and considerable value for their owners. Unique information processes, such as those of the Italian apparel manufacturer Benetton, relaying real-time information about product colors from stores to production facilities, provide another example of the intangible—organizational capital.

What Is Unique about Intangibles?

Intangibles differ from physical and financial (stocks, bonds) assets in two important aspects that have considerable implications for the management, valuation, and the financial reporting of intangibles.

Partial Excludability

Although the owner of a commercial building or a bond can enjoy to the fullest the benefits of these assets (is able to exclude fully nonowners from sharing in the benefits), the owners of patents, brands, or unique business processes, and the employers of trained personnel, can at best secure some of the benefits of these intangibles for a limited duration (partial excludability). Patents expire after 20 years, but in many cases are infringed upon by competitors long before expiration; there are thousands of patent and trademark infringement lawsuits filed every year. Brand values are fickle, given severe competition in most economic sectors and frequent changes in customers' tastes, as demonstrated by erstwhile leading brands, such as Xerox, Polaroid, or the airlines Pan Am and TWA, which are now financially struggling or bankrupt. Trained employees often shift employers, taking with them the investment in human capital made by employers. In short, the property rights over intangibles are not as tightly defined and secured as are those over physical and financial assets, challenging owners of intangibles to capture large and sustained shares of the benefits.

The difficulties of fully capturing the value of intangibles increase the riskiness of owning these assets (value dissipation) and complicate their valuation by investors, because valuation generally requires a reliable estimate of future cash flows to owners. As for corporate financial reporting to investors, accountants often claim that the absence of complete control over the benefits of intangibles disqualifies these assets from recognition as such in corporate balance sheets.

Nonmarketability

Although many physical and most financial assets are traded in competitive markets (stock exchanges, used car dealerships), intangibles are by and large not traded in active and transparent markets (i.e., those in which prices and volumes of trade are observable). To be sure, there are frequent transactions in some intangibles, particularly the licensing and sale of patents and occasionally of trademarks, but these transactions are not transparent—details of the deals are generally not publicly disclosed. The major reasons for the "nontradability" of intangibles are the incomplete property rights, mentioned previously, and serious information asymmetries, i.e., differences in knowledge about intangible assets between buyer and seller. Thus, for example, developers of drugs or software know about these intangibles and their profit potential much more than do outsiders, and it is difficult to convey to the fullest such information in a credible way. Trade in assets when owners possess a significant information advantage over potential buyers is often limited or nonexistent.

The nontradability of intangibles causes serious valuation problems for investors and managers, because valuation techniques are often based on "comparables," which are observed values (prices) of similar assets traded in transparent markets. Nontradability also increases the risk of owning intangibles, given the difficulties or impossibility of selling them before or after completion of development (no exit strategy). For many accountants, the absence of markets disqualifies intangibles from being considered as assets in corporate balance sheets. Intangibles thus differ inherently from physical and financial assets, and the management, valuation, and financial reporting of intangible assets are challenging. Of particular concern in the early 21st century is the vulnerability of intangibles, as expressed by Federal Reserve chairman Alan Greenspan, in testimony (February 27, 2002) to the House of Representatives: "As the recent events surrounding Enron have highlighted, a firm is inherently fragile if its value added emanates more from conceptual [intangible] as distinct from physical assets. A physical asset, whether an office building or an automotive assembly plant, has the capability of producing goods even if the reputation of the managers of such facilities falls under a cloud. The rapidity of Enron's decline is an effective illustration of the vulnerability of a firm whose market value largely rests on capitalized reputation."

Whence the Ascendance of Intangibles?

If intangibles are so risky, their benefits so difficult to secure, and their liquidity (tradability) low, how did they ascend in the last quarter of the 20th century to become the most valuable corporate assets? What is the upside (benefit) of intangibles? The answer lies in the confluence of two major international economic developments: the ever-increasing intensity of business competition and the commoditization of physical assets. Regarding competition, the globalization of trade and the far-reaching deregulation of vital economic sectors, such as transportation, financial services, and telecommunications, have intensified significantly the competitive environment in which business enterprises operate throughout the world. This severe competitive environment makes innovation—the continuous introduction of new products/services, and of cost efficiency mechanisms—literally a matter of life or death for business enterprises. Computer and semiconductor companies, drug manufacturers, health care providers, and television networks that fail to generate new products continuously and to cut costs soon fall hopelessly behind competitors. Chemical and oil companies that do not constantly economize on costs will fall by the wayside, and retailers that do not improve on inventory management and delivery channels to customers will end up in Chapter 11 (bankruptcy).

How is the necessary level of innovation achieved? Primarily by intangible investments: research and development aimed at generating new products and cutting costs, collaboration with other companies and universities to share technology and minimize risk, training employees to better serve customers, enhancing brand and trademark values to secure competitive positions, and developing unique business processes to streamline operations. Thus, as the competitive pressures intensify, companies respond with enhanced innovation, brought about primarily by intangible investments.

The second economic development to escalate the importance of intangibles is the commoditization (equal access to competitors) of physical assets. These assets, such as machine tools, car-producing robots, or computer-aided design systems, initially conferred significant competitive advantages to their early owners. Nowadays, however, most physical assets are commodities, available to all competitors. For example, all pharmaceutical companies, from the giants Merck and Pfizer to the smaller biotech companies, use state-of-the-art laboratory equipment and computer systems in drug development; General Motors, Ford, and Toyota avail themselves of the most advanced car design and manufacturing systems; and Citibank, Bank of America, and even smaller banks can afford the most advanced computer systems. When competitors have equal access to physical assets, such assets obviously cannot generate abnormally high profits and create sustained values.

In contrast, permanent profits and shareholder value are created by intangible assets, which by their nature are unique to the enterprise: patents, brands, in-house employee-training systems, or cost-cutting business processes. This unique ability of intangibles to enable companies to withstand competitive pressures and prevail is responsible for their remarkable ascendance to the role of premier corporate and national assets. In a sense, intangibles are high-risk/high-reward assets.

So, What Is the Problem?

Having noted that intangibles are fast growing and crucial to the survivorship and growth of business enterprises and national economies, why should there be concern about them? What is the problem with intangibles? In a word—measurement. The adage stating that "what's not measured is not managed" is true for individuals (personal investments are carefully managed by most people, whereas their human capital, which is difficult to measure, rarely is), for business enterprises, and at the national level (national debt, easy to measure, is effectively managed, whereas the hard-to-measure environmental impact of public policies is often ignored). The specific attributes of intangibles—partial excludability, high risk, and nontradability—render the measurement and valuation of intangibles a daunting task. Consider the value of a newly registered patent: like that of any other asset, the value depends on the future cash flows to be generated by it. But given the generally high technological uncertainty prevailing in most industries (competitors developing similar products), cash flows from patents are hard to predict, and consequently patent valuations are often of questionable reliability. For example, studies have shown that about 90% of registered patents turn out to be worthless, namely, their benefits do not cover costs. Even more challenging, how can a value be placed on an employee-training program, given the usually high labor turnover? And, how to value a brand that is constantly threatened by competitors' products? In general, the softer the intangible, such as social capital (value of relationships) or environmentally-friendly policies, the harder its valuation. The absence of transparent markets for intangibles, in which similar transactions and prices can be observed, deprives managers and investors of value gauges for intangibles.

The measurement and valuation challenges raised by intangible assets are of major concern to corporate executives, capital market investors, and public policymakers. The fundamental decision of executives is how best to allocate corporate resources (funds): How much should be invested in new production facilities, international market penetration, technology acquisition, research and development, and labor force development? Such "resource allocation" decisions are generally based on a comparison of investment costs with prospective benefits, i.e., a return on investment computation. But the benefits of intangibles (e.g., cash flows from a drug under development, or future benefits from an employee-training program) are difficult to assess, complicating the decision of how much to invest in intangibles. Investors, too, encounter serious measurement problems in assessing the value of intangible-intensive enterprises. How, for example, can the value of a biotech company with a large investment in early-stage research and development that has uncertain prospects be ascertained? Indeed, empirical evidence indicates that investors systematically misprice the securities of research-and-development-intensive companies.

Accountants, the prime providers of measures and values, essentially have given up on intangibles. Practically all investments in intangibles such as research and development, brand enhancement, employee training, and systems development are expensed in corporate financial reports; such investments are not considered assets that promise future benefits. Physical and financial investments, in contrast, are considered enterprise assets. The large gap—5 : 1 in late 2003—between market values of public companies and their balance sheet values is a reflection of the absence of intangibles from corporate balance sheets, due to the accounting treatment of intangibles as expenses. A ray of hope exists: accounting regulatory bodies, such as the U.S. Financial Accounting Standards Board, are currently considering ways of communicating some information on intangibles to capital markets. Difficulties in measuring intangible investments also beset policymakers in charge of fiscal policies and the measurement of national accounts (e.g., gross national product). Education and research and development, for example, are subsidized by governments throughout developed countries, but how can policymakers assess the adequacies of such intangible investments (too much, too little?) without reliable measures of their benefits (national resource allocation)? These intangibles-related measurement and valuation challenges, which surely cause misallocation of private and public resources, lead to the need to discuss measurement and valuation approaches.

The Measurement and Valuation of Intangibles

It is important to distinguish at the outset between input (cost) and output (benefits) measures of intangibles. Given an effective accounting system, there are no special problems related to the measurement of the costs of most intangible investments. The investments in research and development and software development programs are routinely tracked by business enterprises, as are the expenditures on brand maintenance (advertising, product promotion) and the design of business processes, such as Internet-based supply chains and distribution channels. More challenging is the determination of the cost of employee training. A large part of this activity involves on-the-job training, such as the mentoring of junior employees by veterans, which is not systematically accounted for by most corporations. By and large, though, input measures of intangibles are available, or they could be obtained by corporate executives. However, although available to managers, these investments, with the exception of research and development, are not disclosed to outsiders (investors, policymakers) in corporate financial reports.

The measurement and valuation of the benefits of intangibles' is more challenging. Consider, for example, the valuation of Microsoft's respected brand name. The consistently high profits and large market share of Microsoft are jointly determined by a superior technology (research and development), highly trained employees, and an effective sales and promotion effort. But how can Microsoft's total output (revenues, profits) be allocated among the various intangibles (research and development, human capital, brands) responsible for it, to determine, for example, the brand value and to decide whether to invest more or less in brand enhancement? Stated differently, how can Microsoft's brand be valued and managed independently (stand-alone basis) of its research and development and physical assets? This joint nature of most intangibles is a major challenge to the valuation of individual assets. In fact, most intangibles are not stand-alone assets with unique benefit streams, like a commercial real estate property; rather, they generate benefits collectively with other assets. Pfizer's top-rated scientists, along with its effective sales force and reputation for reliable drugs, are jointly responsible for the success of this company. Given such "jointness," the allocation of Pfizer's revenues to the contributing resources—research and development, sales force, and reputation (brand)—which is required for the valuation of these intangibles and for resource allocation decisions, is a daunting task. Three approaches (benefit allocation, stand-alone valuation, and comprehensive valuation of enterprise intangibles), circumventing some of the difficulties, are often used to measure and assess the desirability of investment in intangibles.

Benefit Allocation

Under certain circumstances, reasonable assumptions can be made that allow the allocation of benefits to individual intangibles, and thereby facilitate their valuation. For example, consider the estimated productivity (return on investment) of research and development and brands for a major chemical company. Return-on-investment measurement requires an evaluation of benefits against costs. The chemical company's annual costs of research and development and expenditures on brand enhancement (advertising, promotion) are routinely recorded by the accounting system. But how could the combined benefits of research and development, brands, and physical facilities—represented by the company's revenues and cash flows—be attributed to the individual intangibles to assess their productivity and value to the organization? Based on consultation with experts, the company's revenues and consequent cash flows (after first deducting a reasonable return on physical assets) can be allocated between research and development and brands according to the following criterion: a brand is manifested by an ability to charge a premium price to customers, namely, a price consistently higher than that of a close competitor. Accordingly, the portion of the company's revenues resulting from the price differential with competitors can be attributed to brands, with the remaining revenues assigned to research and development. This revenue allocation allows estimating the productivity (return on a dollar investment) of research and development and brands individually, based on their costs and benefits. Similar allocation procedures may be used to value other intangibles in different circumstances, for the purpose of resource allocation or valuations in licensing and mergers and acquisitions cases.

Stand-Alone Valuation

Some intangible assets, particularly those with legally protected ownership (intellectual property), generate unique streams of benefits. Such intangibles can be valued on a stand-alone basis by computing the present value of the expected benefit stream. For example, the patent and technology portfolio of IBM is reported to have generated $500 million in licensing revenues in 2001 (*The Wall Street Journal*, February 19, 2002, page A3). It is relatively straightforward to estimate the present value of the forecasted stream of licensing revenues, which yields an estimated value of IBM's licensed intellectual property. A similar approach can be used to assess values of patents, trademarks, and copyrights, as long as reliable forecasts of cash flows from these assets can be made.

A Comprehensive Valuation of Enterprise Intangibles

The problem of jointness of intangibles is mitigated when the objective is to place a combined value on all of the company's intangibles, rather than on individual assets. In many real-world situations, such a comprehensive valuation of intangibles is all that is needed. Investors, for example, are primarily interested in the total value of a company's intangibles, which is missing from its balance sheet. Similarly, in cases of mergers and acquisitions, a comprehensive valuation of the acquired company's intangibles is needed to consummate deals. There is a methodology for such a comprehensive valuation of intangibles. The basic premise (elaborated in Gu and Lev, 2002) is that of an economic production function, whereby the earnings of an enterprise are related to the assets that generate those earnings. Three clusters of corporate or divisional assets are formed: physical, financial (stocks, bonds), and intangible. The initial valuation stage involves an estimate of "normalized earnings," that is, typical annual earnings that can be expected from the enterprise, accounting for both historical and future earnings, and abstracting from nonrecurring, abnormal items (e.g., a loss from a strike, or a gain from selling a subsidiary). The three classes of assets generate these normalized earnings. Accordingly, to isolate the earnings generated by intangibles, the contribution of physical and financial assets is subtracted from normalized earnings, leaving as a residual the "intangibles-driven earnings." An asset's contribution to earnings is based on its value and the return on the asset. The values of physical and financial assets can be obtained, with some adjustments, from published balance sheets; the estimated returns on physical assets (contribution to earnings) are assessed from industry-wide data. The subtraction from normalized earnings of the contributions of physical and financial assets leaves as a residual the earnings contributed by the intangibles: these are the intangibles-driven earnings. The final stage of the comprehensive valuation of intangibles involves computation of the discounted (present) value of the expected stream of intangibles-driven earnings.

Table I demonstrates the outcome of this valuation methodology. It presents the estimated intangibles-driven earnings for the year 2000, along with the estimated total value of intangibles (intangible capital) for the 25 companies with the largest intangible capital in the widely watched Fortune 500 ranking. General Electric, with an estimated $254 billion value of intangible assets captures top rank, followed closely by Pfizer and Microsoft. Walt Disney closes the list with $47 billion of value from intangibles. It is important to note that high values of intangibles are not restricted to high-technology

Table I Comprehensive Value of Intangibles of the Top 25 Companies[a]

Rank	*Company*	*Intangible capital*[b]	*Intangibles-driven earnings*[b]
1	General Electric	254,381	12,435
2	Pfizer	219,202	7686
3	Microsoft	204,515	8735
4	Philip Morris	188,538	10,226
5	Exxon Mobil	176,409	10,050
6	Intel	173,964	7339
7	SBC Communications	155,402	7897
8	IBM	148,679	7534
9	Verizon Communications	141,471	7494
10	Merck	139,494	7497
11	Wal-Mart Stores	99,973	5018
12	Johnson & Johnson	94,769	4976
13	Bristol Myers Squibb	85,837	4709
14	Coca-Cola	73,976	3906
15	Dell Computer	72,985	2499
16	Bellsouth	71,269	4004
17	Procter & Gamble	66,609	3931
18	Ford Motor	59,311	4310
19	Honeywell International	52,798	2533
20	Boeing	51,179	2427
21	PepsiCo	50,614	2607
22	United Parcel Service	48,508	2470
23	Home Depot	48,389	1952
24	Hewlett-Packard	48,226	2500
25	Walt Disney	46,960	2307

[a] Data taken from *Fortune Magazine*, April 18, 2001; values relate to the year 2000.

[b] In millions of U.S. dollars.

or science-based companies. In fact, as made clear by the table, approximately half of the top 25 companies are "old economy": Philip Morris, Exxon Mobil, Wal-Mart, Coca-Cola, Procter & Gamble, Ford, etc. The conclusion is that valuable, productive intangibles are the unique characteristic of innovative, well-run, and successful enterprises, rather than of companies operating in specific industries.

Summary

Intangible assets reached prominence in the business world in the late 20th century and will surely persist to capture center stage in the future. Intangibles are inherently different from physical and financial assets. These differences are responsible for the unique potential of intangibles to generate vast economic value and growth, at both the corporate and national levels, as well as for the serious difficulties in managing, measuring, and reporting the values of intangibles. Various methods are available to overcome the valuations challenges, but efforts to improve the measurement and reporting of intangibles should continue.

See Also the Following Articles

Business, Social Science Methods Used in • Critical Views of Performance Measurement • History of Business Performance Measurement • Knowledge Work

Further Reading

Gu, F., and Lev, B. (2002). *Intangible Assets: Measurement, Drivers, Usefulness.* Working Paper. Stern School of Business. New York University, New York.

Hand, J., and Lev, B. (2003). *Intangible Assets: Values, Measures, and Risks.* Oxford University Press, London.

Lazear, E. (1995). *Performance Pay and Productivity.* Hoover Institution and Stanford Graduate School of Business, Stanford.

Lerner, J. (2000). *150 Years of Patent Protection.* Working Paper 7478. National Bureau of Economic Research, Cambridge, Massachusetts.

Lev, B. (2001). *Intangibles: Management, Measurement, and Reporting.* The Brookings Institution Press, Washington, D.C.

Lev, B., Nissim, D., and Thomas, J. (2002). *On the Informational Usefulness of R&D Capitalization and Amortization.* Working Paper. Columbia Univ., School of Business. Columbia University, New York.

Nakamura, L. (2003). A trillion dollars a year in intangible investment and the new economy. In *Intangible Assets: Values, Measures, and Risks* (J. Hand and B. Lev, eds.), pp. 19–47. Oxford University Press, London.

Rivette, K., and Kline, D. (2000). *Rembrandts in the Attic: Unlocking the Hidden Value of Patents.* Harvard Business School Press, Cambridge, Massachusetts.

Scherer, F., Harhoff, D., and Kukies, J. (1998). Uncertainty and the size distribution of rewards from technological innovation. *J. Evolution. Econ.* **10,** 175–200.

Stewart, T. (2001). *The Wealth of Knowledge: Intellectual Capital and the Twenty-First Century Organization.* Currency Books (Doubleday), New York.

Intelligence Testing

Wilma C. M. Resing
Leiden University, Leiden, The Netherlands

Glossary

academic intelligence The intellectual thinking and problem-solving processes with which academic tasks or academic problems that have a fixed and closed structure are concerned.

culture-fair test Tests with a content related to the knowledge and experience of a wide variety of cultures, avoiding specific cultural-linguistic contexts.

deviation IQ The deviation of an individual's test score from the mean test score achieved by a representative peer group.

Flynn effect The generational raising of IQ scores within populations.

intelligence quotient (ratio IQ) Mental age divided by chronological age multiplied by 100.

mental age The level of correctly solved intelligence test items belonging to a certain age group.

test A systematic measuring procedure, consisting of tasks that are presented in a standardized manner so that the answers can be processed objectively and so that the outcome enables the tester to estimate the (measured) capacity of the examinee or to predict performances in the future.

Interest in intelligence and intelligence testing dates from the start of the twentieth century, but even today a large number of different definitions and theories exist on this subject. In this entry, intelligence is restricted to academic intelligence and, therefore, the emphasis lies on thinking processes and on solving (new) problems. It is important to notice that human intelligence is not static but has a dynamic, developing character. After first sketching the history of the field, the question of whether intelligence has one general dimension or a larger number of independent dimensions is addressed briefly. Modern intelligence theories propose models with a hierarchical structure. Examples of group and individual intelligence tests are described, including the modern way of calculating IQ, deviation IQ. The entry ends by emphasizing several important topics in intelligence testing: whether culturefree tests exist, whether intellectual performance increased or decreased during life span, and whether mean IQ scores rise over generations. Finally, a sketch is given of the characteristics and the applicability of good intelligence tests.

Defining Intelligence

Ever since the start of the twentieth century, we have witnessed a huge increase in intelligence research and intelligence testing. This enduring interest in the subject of intelligence is based on the desire to measure and describe all kinds of human abilities and led to the first test diagnostics being developed.

Academic Intelligence

The concept of intelligence goes back to the Latin verb *intellegere*, meaning the acquirement, processing and storage of information. From this point of view, intelligence is restricted to the cognitive, mental abilities of the human being. Two thousand years later it still seems wise to reserve the term intelligence for what in the scientific literature is frequently called academic intelligence. This is defined as intellectual performance, within a closed system, on academic tasks or on academic problems that have fixed goals, a fixed structure, and known elements, and is distinguished from social, everyday, successful, or practical intelligence. We use the term intelligence here to mean academic intelligence.

Intelligence A, B, and C

If we want to understand and comprehend discussions about intelligence and intelligence testing, it is good to keep in mind the three-way split in intelligence—A, B, and C—made by Vernon in 1967. Intelligence A is the genetically determined disposition or potential to act intelligently that cannot be influenced by culture, environmental stimulation, education, or learning experiences. It is a postulate; it cannot be observed nor measured. Intelligence B is the result of the interaction between this genetic disposition (A), environmental influences, and learning experience. It is culturally bound and can be observed and estimated. It is the visible intelligence, the cognitive abilities that a person has at a particular moment in time that are the result of earlier learning experiences. It changes during an individual's life span. Intelligence C is what intelligence tests—created to estimate intelligence B as well as possible—measure. Intelligence C is the measured intelligence of a person, in terms of the intelligence quotient (IQ); it is restricted to the specific test that is used.

Demarcating Intelligence

Based on the literature, academic intelligence can best be seen as a conglomerate of mental abilities, processes, and aptitudes, such as abstract, logical, and consistent reasoning; detecting relations; (complex) problem solving; detecting rules in seemingly unordered materials; solving new tasks by using existing knowledge; adapting to new situations flexibly; and being able to learn without direct and complete instruction. From this perspective, the accent in intelligence definition(s) lies on thinking processes and on solving (new) problems.

According to Sternberg's 1997 definition, "Intelligence comprises the mental abilities necessary for adaptation to, as well as shaping and selection of any environmental context. According to this definition, intelligence is not just reactive to the environment but also active in forming it. It offers people an opportunity to respond flexibly to challenging situations. Because the landscape of an environmental context changes over time, adequate adaptation, shaping, and selection involve a process of lifelong learning, one that starts in infancy and continues throughout the life span." It is important to notice that intelligence is not static; it has a dynamic character: Humans are always developing themselves, expanding their intellectual expertise.

Intelligence: A Historical Perspective

For almost 100 years, there have been two different research perspectives within the field of intelligence: the psychometric perspective and the experimental cognitive perspective. Within the psychometric tradition, research focuses on the nature and causes of individual differences in intelligent human behavior, particularly in cognitive problem-solving tasks, and on the structure of intelligence. Within the experimental tradition, research focuses more on regularities in both general and specific cognitive processes in problem-solving behavior and in how people perform cognitive tasks in general, how they deal with task demands, and how they use different forms of knowledge and memory. In short, the focus is on shared mechanisms and processes that are the core parts of intelligence.

Pioneers within the Experimental Tradition and Pioneers in Test Development

Experimental studies on intelligence started in France around 1850 with Broca's famous studies on craniometry, relating cranial volume with intelligence. However, after several years of study this relationship was found to be nonexistent. Around the same time, Sir Francis Galton performed the same type of experiments in England. He became strongly influenced by Darwin's theory of evolution and developed a model of the relationship between heredity and intelligence. Galton was the first to try to measure this kind of psychological and physiological relations in the laboratory. He developed experimental tests, such as reaction-time measurement and other sensory tasks, by which, according to him, researchers could differentiate between highly gifted and less gifted individuals. In addition, he collected physiological measures, for instance heart rate and skin conductance. He considered all these variables to be good measures of mental speed, his equivalent of intelligence.

The first pioneers in test development were medical scientists. Esquirol, a Frenchman, was one of the first. In 1838, he developed a test for measuring language disorders in patients with severe mental disorders. Sequin, a second French medical doctor, tested and trained his mentally retarded patients in mental institutions in both France and the United States. These training periods were intended to raise human intelligence. Both scientists practiced early forms of psychodiagnostics with very simple tests. These tests were mainly used as selection instruments for groups of individuals with and without intellectual disorders.

Alfred Binet (1857–1911): Father of the Intelligence Quotient Test

In 1905, Binet and Simon developed the first true intelligence test. According to Binet, mental tests had to include a complex compilation of corresponding mental facets such as attention, comprehension, memory, and verbal and abstract reasoning, which could not be considered separate parts and could not be measured separately. He therefore decided to measure intelligence as one complex conglomeration of interwoven mental facets. Binet examined, for each half-year age cohort, which cognitive tasks had strong correlations with school performance. Based on these data, he then composed a series of test items for each age group, such as naming objects, memory of number series, searching for rhyming words, logical reasoning, and concept defining. All these test components had to be tested in a fixed sequence, making it possible to estimate the mental level of a child. Using this first mental scale, researchers and psychologists in the field were, for the first time, able to compare the mental level of a child with that of its peer group.

The intelligence scale became very popular in the United States thanks to a translation by Goddard in 1908 and further adaptations. He considered intelligence to be a hereditary trait of the human being that could be operationalized in terms of mental age, the age of the group of children whose mean test performance equaled that of the examinee, and later as IQ, which was defined as the child's mental age (MA) divided by the child's chronological age (CA), multiplied by 100.

$$IQ = (MA/CA) \times 100$$

When the scores of a 6-year-old child on an intelligence test equal those of an average 8-year-old child, the mental age (MA) of the child is 8 years and its chronological age (CA) is 6 years. Therefore, this child's $IQ = 8/6 \times 100 = 133$.

The First Group Intelligence Tests

Individually administered tests have an important function in clinical psychodiagnostics, when learning disabilities or social-emotional problems are involved. However, for routine use in school and personnel selection or in industrial and military selection, group tests for measuring intelligence often are more practical and time saving. Group tests were first developed during World War I, when it became necessary to screen and classify recruits for the army on the basis of their general intelligence level as quickly as possible. The groups of recruits were very heterogeneous; some of them could not speak English and could not read at all. Therefore, it was important both to test the general intelligence level of large groups of people at the same time effectively and to bear in mind the large individual ethnic, cultural, and linguistic differences. Two tests were constructed: the Army Alpha, a group test for people who could read and comprehend English and who were able to write down their answers to the test items on paper; and the Army Beta, a nonverbally instructed multiple-choice test in which the examinee had to cross out the right pictures and symbols.

Intelligence Structure

One or More Intelligence Dimensions

The development of psychometric theories on the structure of intelligence ran parallel with the construction of the first instruments. From 1920 onward, answers were sought indirectly to the question "What is intelligence?" by examining whether intelligence has a complex undivided general nature or takes the form of a combined series of separate unique factors, such as abstract reasoning, memory, and vocabulary. Around 1930, Spearman interpreted his test results with newly developed psychometric techniques such as correlational and factor analysis. According to him, a wide variance in intellectual performance on different tasks could be accounted for by one general underlying factor called *g* (for general intelligence). This factor was supplemented by specific, different *s* (for specific intelligence) factors. It soon became evident that Spearman's view was too simple. Several intelligence models added extra factors, mostly intermediary group factors, and some theorists stated that there were several primary factors instead of one general factor. Toward the end of the 1930s, Thurstone reported seven primary intelligence factors; in 1959, Guilford described 120 different intelligence factors in his famous structure-of-intellect model.

However, it became clear that the different cognitive components representing different aspects of intelligence had predominantly positive intercorrelations. To make this conclusion visible, several hierarchical intelligence models were developed in which, in addition to a general intelligence factor as opposed to specific intelligence factors, one or more intermediate levels with group intelligence factors could be discerned. In 1960, Vernon developed a model with a general factor at the first level, intermediate group factors (verbal-educational vs. practical-mechanical-spatial) at the second level, a number of smaller group factors at the third level, and very specific factors at the fourth level. At the same time, Cattell postulated two kinds of intelligence in his model: fluid and crystallized intelligence. In 1993, Carroll confirmed a hierarchical theory of higher-order abilities and combined this with Cattel's fluid-crystallized dimension. In addition to a general intelligence factor, he described at a lower level of analysis fluid intelligence, crystallized intelligence, and a general memory ability. At the same level in this model, he added broad visual and auditory perception, broad retrieval abilities, and broad cognitive speediness. It is this hierarchical intelligence structure and the interconnectedness between most cognitive components that legitimizes the use of one single intelligence score in combination with individually based intelligence profiles.

Information-Processing Theories

More recently, research on the cognitive processes or components of intellectual functioning has been performed from an information-processing perspective. Examples are Sternberg's triarchic theory of intelligence and the PASS (planning, attention, simultaneous and successive processing) model of Das, Naglieri, and Kirby, both developed in the mid-1980s. The PASS model of intelligence is based on Luria's neuropsychological theory of the functioning of the human brain, in which three parts of the brain are described: the brain stem and the limbic system, responsible for attention and arousal processes; the visual, auditory, and general sensory parts of the cerebellum, responsible for simultaneous and successive reasoning processes; and the prefrontal parts of the brain, responsible for the planning and regulation of cognitive processes and activities. In 1985, Sternberg, in his triarchic intelligence model, described various components necessary in intellectual problem solving: performance components, meta components, and knowledge-acquisition components. Later he added the importance of intellectual styles and mental self-government to his model of intelligence.

Current Measures of Intelligence

What is a test? An intelligence test can be defined as a systematic measuring procedure, consisting of a number of carefully selected tasks that are presented in a standardized manner to the examinee in such a way that the answers or solutions can be processed objectively. The last part of this definition allows the psychodiagnostician to interpret and to describe the measured capability of the examined individual, for instance to describe his or her intelligence or to make predictions about his or her school success.

The Intelligence Quotient

When intelligence test development first started, the intelligence of an individual mostly was described in terms of the mental age or the IQ. The use of this measure allows both the delay and the advantage in mental development to be estimated. The ratio IQ seemed to be a good measure for estimating the intellectual level of young children. For older children and adults, this measure of intelligence appeared less suitable. First, the idea behind Binet's test was that mental development is directly related to age and that progression in mental development automatically leads to better test scores. Of course, mental development is related to age, but the progress in mental development will not be the same each year we become older. Apparently, there is no linear progression in development. Second, a 2-year difference between mental age and chronological age at the age of 5 years is not comparable with a 2-year difference at the age of 9 years. This incongruity is even greater after the chronological age of 15–17 years. At this adolescent age level, we hardly see differences in the mean raw scores of the various age groups.

Therefore, the ratio IQ coefficient appears to be a poor measure of intelligence. For this reason, modern tests all have deviation IQs. By using deviation-IQ scores, it is possible to calculate how much an individual's test score deviates from the mean test score achieved by a representative peer group of this individual. The calculation of the deviation IQ goes as follows: (1) large representative norm groups of people of various ages are tested, (2) the mean raw test scores and standard deviations are calculated, and (3) it is assumed that intelligence test scores for each age group have normal distributions. For the calculation of deviation IQs per age group, the raw test scores are transformed into norm scores. Almost all intelligence test constructors follow the rule that the mean raw test scores for each age group are transformed into the deviation IQ of 100, with a standard deviation of 15. Therefore, 68.3% of all IQ scores lie within the 85–115 IQ score range and more than 95% of all IQ scores lie within the 70–130 IQ score range, as Fig. 1 shows.

By using the deviation IQ, the test scores of each examinee can be compared with those of his or her peer group. Instead of the original comparison of the mental age with the chronological age, with deviation IQs the scores of each individual can be related to the norm tables of his or her age group. Scores on different tests easily can be compared with one another because almost all the different instruments have norm scores with equal means and standard deviations.

Intelligence Tests: Some Examples

Although all general intelligence tests aim to measure one and the same concept, their formats are not the same. The commonest way of classifying intelligence tests is in terms of individual and group tests. Individual intelligence tests are to be administered to only one person at a time, whereas group intelligence tests can be administered to whole groups of individuals at the same time. In general, an examiner uses an individual test from a different perspective or for a different goal than a group test. Individual IQ tests can, for example, be used to test more clinical hypotheses, whereas group tests can be used for selection for university or for the prediction of school or job

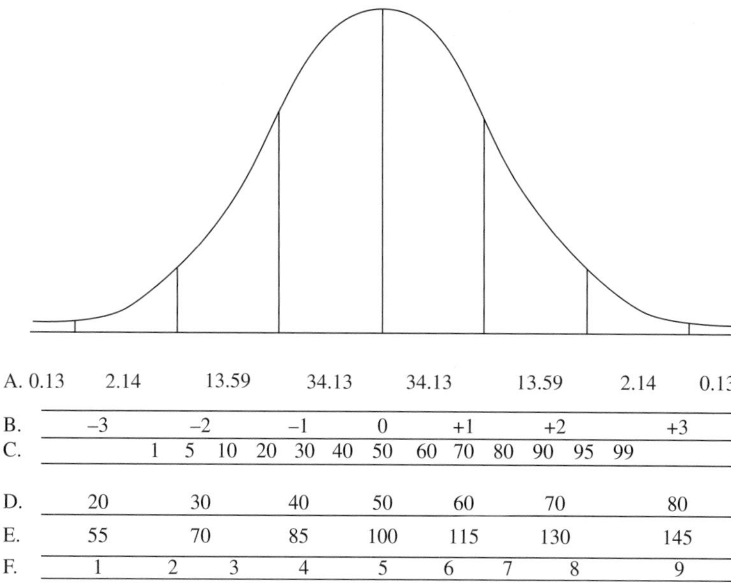

Figure 1 The normal curve with the deviation-IQ scores. (A) Percentages within segments of the normal curve. (B) Standard deviations. (C) Percentile scores. (D) T-scores. (E) Deviation-IQ scores (m = 100, SD = 15). (F) Stanines.

success. Group intelligence tests are more often used for screening, followed by an individual test that can be used to confirm a particular low or high score level.

Individually Administered Tests

Stanford-Binet Intelligence Scales The first individually administered test in the United States was the Standard-Binet Intelligence Scale for children and adolescents. This Stanford-Binet Scale is constructed as an age scale; the items of the scale are grouped into age levels. Items, such as "compares 2 lines" (age 4), "repeats a sentence of 10 syllables" (age 5), and "compares 2 objects from memory" (age 8), are included in the tests when the percentages of correct answers are lower for each successive age level.

Terman tried to include a broad sample of intellectual tasks that were less dependent on specific school learning than the original Binet Scales. He turned the original idea of mental age into the ratio IQ concept: IQ was defined as MA/CA × 100.

In 1937, 1960, and 1972, the Stanford Binet Scale was revised twice, with new floor and ceiling items. In 1960, the deviation IQ was introduced. The fourth edition of the Stanford-Binet Intelligence Scale (SB-IV; 1986, Riverside Publishing Company) was based for the first time on a theoretical and more complex, hierarchical three-level factorial intelligence model, with general intelligence (g level) at the highest level, three broad factors (crystallized intelligence, fluid-analytic intelligence, and short-term memory) at the intermediate level, and three factors (verbal reasoning, quantitative reasoning and abstract/visual abilities) at the lowest level. Carroll's intelligence theory clearly underlies this model. Various empirical studies with SB-IV data, however, have not supported a clear distinction between fluid and crystallized intelligence. The SB-IV is intended to measure intelligence in a broad age range, from 2 years old to adulthood. The test has been constructed using modern test theory (including Rasch scaling). Item-bias analysis for ethnic groups has been performed, making the test as bias-free as possible. This edition no longer focuses only on the general intelligence of children and on detecting mental retardation or giftedness, but also on diagnosing learning disabilities. The reliability of the composite scores is good.

Wechsler's Intelligence Scales In 1939, Wechsler argued that a new instrument with separate subtests—unlike the complex age scales of the Binet scales—could be used to reveal specific disorders in adults by analyzing the individual test profile of the client. Although Wechsler thought that intelligence could only be measured by a complex combination of cognitive tasks, he constructed a test with which both the global intelligence (IQ) of a person could be estimated and a more diagnostic profile analysis could be performed. He published his first Wechsler scale, the Wechsler-Bellevue Scale Form I for adults, in 1939, followed by a revised Form II in 1947. Wechsler noted that the intelligence tests available at that time had been constructed primarily for younger children and that adult examinees found the adapted versions too childish.

Various revisions of the instrument led in 1997 to the Wechsler Adult Intelligence Scale III (WAIS-III;

Psychological Corporation). Like the earlier versions, the WAIS-III has two broad intelligence factors, with subtests loading on a verbal and a performance scale. Verbal subtests are, for example, the detection of Similarities, answering Information questions, and Vocabulary. Performance subtests are, for example, Object Assembly and Block Design tasks. The previously developed WAIS-R had 11 subtests; three new ones are included in the WAIS-III. Therefore, it is possible to provide good estimates for not only the traditional full-scale IQ and the verbal and performance IQs but also for four smaller intelligence factors, described as verbal comprehension, working memory, perceptual organization, and processing speed. The test has been developed for the adult age range from 16 to 90 years. Various clinical groups were tested in addition to a stratified norm group. Reliability coefficients for the full-scale IQ, verbal and performance scales, and the smaller intelligence factors are high.

In 1949, Wechsler published a child and adolescent version of the test, the Wechsler Intelligence Scale for Children (WISC). Revisions were published in 1974 (WISC-R) and 1991 (WISC-III). The WISC-III, constructed for children from 6 to 17 years, has the same format as the adult Wechsler tests with the content adapted to the younger age group. A verbal, performance, and full-scale IQ and four smaller factors scores can be administered: verbal comprehension, freedom from distractibility, perceptual organization, and processing speed. Reliability coefficients for the performance and verbal IQ, the full-scale IQ, and the smaller factors are good. The four factors have been identified in several empirical studies. The WISC-III has been adapted and translated for use in more than 22 different countries. The four smaller factors cannot be identified in the data sets of all countries.

In 1967, Wechsler published a test for young children ages 4–6$\frac{1}{2}$ years, the Wechsler Preschool and Primary Scale of Intelligence (WPPSI), followed in 1989 by the WPPSI-R, the revised version for a broader group of children, ages 3–7 years. The reliability coefficients of the scales are high. Strong evidence for a two-factor structure can be found in the manual. The main criticisms of the WPSSI-R are that the test is too difficult for young intellectually at-risk children.

Kaufman's Intelligence Batteries In 1983, the Kaufman Assessment Battery for Children (K-ABC; American Guidance Service), an intelligence tests for children ages 2.5–12.5 years, was constructed from a theoretical perspective in which Cattell's distinction between fluid and crystallized intelligence was combined with the Luria's neuropsychological ideas about the importance of simultaneous versus sequential mental processing. Test scores on four intellectual domains can be administered: sequential processing, simultaneous processing, mental processing (which is the first two domains combined), and achievement. The scales have high reliability coefficients. Separate percentile norms have been presented for different ethnic and socioeconomic groups.

Kaufman constructed two other intelligence tests: the Kaufman Adolescent and Adult Intelligence Test (KAIT; 1993) and the Kaufman Brief Intelligence Test (K-BIT; 1990). The KAIT was designed for the age range 11–85 years. The test has a good reliability. Validity coefficients with WISC-R and WAIS-R can be interpreted as high. The K-BIT was designed as a screening instrument to get a quick estimation of the intelligence level of an examinee. The structure of the test differs from KAIT or K-ABC, consisting of only two subtests: a vocabulary test and a nonverbal subtest for inductive reasoning (matrices). The K-BIT is designed for the age range 4–90 years and takes only 15–20 minutes.

Das-Naglieri Cognitive Assessment System A new instrument for measuring IQ is the Das-Naglieri Cognitive Assessment System (CAS; 1997, Riverside Publishing). Like, for example, the Woodcock-Johnson tests of cognitive ability (Riverside Publishing), the CAS is based on a cognitive theory linked with parts of Luria's neuropsychological theory, the PASS theory (planning, attention, simultaneous, and successive). Reliabilities and standardization can be interpreted as good.

Group Intelligence Tests

The first group intelligence tests, the Army Alpha and the Army Beta, were constructed for a quick screening of large groups of potentially interesting recruits for the army. At first, the tests were not available to other psychologists. But the idea of mass testing became more and more popular for aims other than military selection. Group tests often differ from individual tests in their content and format. Today, most group tests have multiple-choice formats. They also often have time limits. Examinees have to start and stop at a certain time and have to wait for an order to turn the page; and instruction for each test part takes place for the whole group at once. By using group tests, large numbers of examinees can be tested simultaneously. Personal circumstances that may influence the test scores will not be easily noticed under these conditions. Therefore, the scores on group tests should be considered with extra caution; very low scores should be given extra attention, and these examinees should be given some parallel form of the same test on another day. Multilevel batteries, adaptive testing, and computer-based testing and/or administration could be useful in overcoming the negative aspects of group testing.

Cognitive Abilities Test The Cognitive Abilities Test (CogAT; Riverside Publishing) is a multilevel test assessing children's reasoning and problem solving using both verbal and nonverbal subtests. With multilevel batteries, the examinee does not have to solve a restricted range of test items that are probably good for his age and ability level but can be tested at a level that is the most suitable for him or her. The test is constructed so that most examinees are tested with items with intermediate difficulty levels. Successive batteries overlap one another and the scores on one of the batteries can be compared with various types of norms. The CogAT has levels 1 and 2 for grades K–3 and levels A–H for grades 3–12. At each level, the scores on three subbatteries (verbal, nonverbal, and quantitative) can be administered and converted to various types of norms.

SAT and Otis Many group intelligence tests have been developed to measure aptitude for scholastic work or are intended to measure a combination of intellectual ability and scholastic aptitude. The Otis-Lennon School Ability Test (OSALT; Harcourt Brace, 7th edition) has been constructed to measure verbal comprehension and verbal, figural, quantitative, and pictorial reasoning in children and adolescents in the school-age range K–12.

The Scholastic Assessment Test (SAT) consists of two parts: a reasoning part (verbal and mathematical reasoning) and a subject part (English, history, social studies, mathematics, science, and languages). The test was constructed for college-admission purposes. The reasoning part of the test has good predictive qualities, not only for performance in the first few months of college but also for later performances and examinations.

Nonverbal and Culture-Free Tests

Individual tests (and some group tests as well) that are constructed from the perspective that intelligence must be measured as a conglomerate of scores on a number of different cognitive tasks generally consist of a combination of tasks that depend heavily on language. But word use, relations between words, and verbal instructions are not very suitable for groups of people who do not speak the language very well. Therefore, some tests have been constructed that do not, or hardly, use verbal language or symbols. Most of these tests measure reasoning processes with pictures, geometrical forms, numbers, or symbols instead of verbal materials. The examiner shows how to solve the examples by gestures and pointing. Perhaps the most widely used nonverbal test, often described as culture-free, is the Progressive Matrices test (PM) constructed by Raven in 1958. The PM was designed primarily as an estimator of general intelligence, more specifically of inductive reasoning. The items are presented as matrices, arranged into three rows and three columns, resulting in nine pictures of symbols changing from left to right and from top to bottom. However, the ninth picture is missing and has to be found from several alternatives by reasoning. The test can be administered in groups or individually. The instructions are very simple (e.g., pointing to the right alternative and then to the blank space on the page of the instruction items).

Tests such as Raven's PM were constructed for their potential applicability across cultures. Many studies have been performed trying to establish the hypothesis that nonverbal tests such as the PM are culture-free, meaning that samples of people from different cultures or immigrant groups will perform equally on these tests. However, it has become evident that culture-free tests do not exist.

Studies with intelligence tests so far have shown that culture, as well as other aspects of the environment, influence the test scores to some extent. Consequently, culture-fair tests rather than culture-free tests are being constructed. In designing such tests, the researcher chooses only those items related to the knowledge and experience of a wide variety of cultures. Specific cultural-linguistic contexts are avoided. Items should not be biased toward one or more specific groups of individuals (defined by sex, cultural group, etc.). An example of a culture-fair intelligence test is the Naglieri Nonverbal Ability Test (NNAT; Psychological Corporation), a nonverbal reasoning test with several reasoning components, such as serial reasoning, matrices, and visual spatialization. The test is appropriate for children and adolescents K–12. Item-bias techniques to ensure that tests are unbiased against certain groups are quite normal these days when the construction of new tests and test versions takes place.

The Nature–Nurture Issue

Is intellectual ability innate, having hereditary components only (nature), or can it be influenced by environmental factors, such as nutrition and education (nurture)? For a long time in research on intelligence, proponents of heredity and proponents of environment have debated this question; this battle is known as the nature-nurture controversy. Although most researchers in the field of human intelligence now believe that both factors—innate ability and environmental influences—play important roles in intellectual development, the discussion on the interaction between both aspects still has a central place in testing. The conclusion seems justified that the hereditary component accounts for approximately 50–60% of the variance in intelligence test scores. Given the human genetic foundation, clear restraints are imposed on the maximum level of intelligence of an individual. At the same time, however, intellectual differences among individuals cannot be explained entirely by nature. The 40–50% of the variance in intelligence test scores not attributable to heredity must be attributed to environment, both group environmental influences (e.g., those shared by the family: family characteristics, socioeconomic conditions, parenting styles) and individual, unique environmental influences. Note also that the high percentage of genetic influence does not imply that intelligence test scores have a fixed level for an individual. Changes in the environment, for instance level of schooling, diseases, or nutritional deficiency, certainly will influence the level of the IQ.

Therefore, both environmental influences and the interaction between genetic predisposition and the environment play an important role in IQ. Hence, it is necessary to keep at the back of our mind the distinction between intelligence as a predisposition (i.e., intellectual potential) and actual intelligence (i.e., level of intelligence). Although nature restricts the maximum level of intellectual potential, it is unlikely that anybody will make optimal use of this potential. Goal-directed training programs can therefore make it possible (through nurture) to bring the intelligence scores of individuals closer to their intellectual potential.

Stability and Change over Time

Throughout an individual's lifetime, performance on measures of intelligence increases and decreases. A rapid increase in mastery is seen on cognitive tasks in infants and young children and a less rapid increase is seen in older children, with the slope of the increase in mastery becoming less steep during adolescence. Longitudinal studies with normal samples show that intelligence scores measured before 3 years of age have only limited predictive value for later measured intelligence. Between the ages of 3 and 7, the predictive value becomes much better, and from the age of 8 years on it reaches stability. For each age group, intelligence tests have more difficult items and more complex problems to solve, but large individual differences among children of the same age remain. From the age of approximately 18 years, it is no longer necessary to use more difficult items; cognitive development has been stabilized. Important research questions are: Does the intellectual level remain stabilized after adolescence? And if not, when do cognitive abilities start to decrease? Based on cross-sectional research, Wechsler reported a rapid increase in ability, followed by a very gradual decrease from the age of 20. More recently, in 1996, Schaie presented the results of his Seattle Longitudinal Study. He found no uniform patterns of change in intelligence when looking at the whole spectrum of intellectual abilities. Reasoning ability remains at a very high level as people get older. The vocabulary decreases somewhat after the age of 60 and word fluency decreases after the age of 50. After the age of 80, there is some decrease in perceptual speed and numerical abilities. Schaie stressed individual differences.

Another important question raised in relation to the stability of intelligence over time is whether there are generational differences in intelligence. That is, is the mean intelligence level of a population raising in time? Indeed, mean scores on intelligence tests do increase over time. This effect is called the Flynn effect, after James Flynn who reported it in several studies since the mid-1990s. He collected intelligence test data sets in more than 20 countries and detected a general effect: The mean IQ scores of the populations rose approximately 10 points over a period of 30 years (i.e., one generation). The full reason for this improvement remains unclear. Factors such as better and longer education, better economic circumstances, better information technology, a more complex environment that permits the use of a larger part of the cognitive potential, and better food conditions are all only partial explanations of the reported increase in IQ scores.

What Is a Good Intelligence Test?

How can good tests be characterized? First, good tests are standardized. In a good test, an estimation of a person's intellectual level is always based on a comparison with the standardized norm tables of comparison groups, mostly peers. If a test is good, score fluctuations cannot be attributed to differences in the instructions, in the behavior of the examiner, or in the situation. Every examinee has to have an equal and optimal opportunity to perform as well as possible on the test. Test standardization therefore means that the test material, the test instruction, and the test manual unequivocally prescribe what the examinee has to do to receive and to interpret the test results. Second, the administration of a good test should result in an objective description of the examinee. Two different examiners should arrive at the same results and interpretation. The test scores must be as independent as possible of observations or subjective interpretations. Computerized testing and a good standardized test manual both diminish possible subjective influences. Third, a test should be reliable, meaning that test scores must be influenced as little as possible by the situation or incidental circumstances. Of course, this reliability is partly related to the conditions of standardization and objectivity. But a test score can be influenced by other things as well, for example, illness or emotional upset, the examinee's motivation and work attitude, boring test items, or a boring test room. By using a reliable test, an examiner can be more confident that the test scores estimate the true IQ scores of the examinee. Fourth, a good test is valid. The test should indeed measure the theoretical concept on which it is based. In addition to validity, a test should predict future test scores, for instance school success or job performance in the future. And finally, a good test has good standardized norms and is standardized on large, stratified norm groups. Current intelligence tests should have deviation IQs; it must be possible to compare the test scores of each examinee with the mean test scores of his or her peer group.

Applications of Intelligence Tests

One reason for using intelligence tests lies in the predictive qualities of these tests. The test scores are closely linked with the prediction of future success in school and with future job performance. A second reason is that, in principle, these tests provide an opportunity to describe the cognitive (dys)functioning of the examinee. These tests could thus be used to go one step beyond merely predicting school success by detecting weak cognitive areas. They could thus offer direct advice to teachers and encourage the rearrangement of educational settings. However, the standard intelligence test is not the most suitable instrument for this purpose. For this reason, new test forms such as learning potential tests and other dynamic and adaptive forms of testing, including computerized testing, have been developed. In addition to the static test situation of the traditional intelligence test, with a learning potential test the examinee is tested more than once and is given help or individualized hints. This means that the examiner can look more specifically into the problem-solving process of the examinee and can describe in more detail what is happening during testing, which can add valuable diagnostic information for the interpretation of the test scores itself and can add more information about the examinee's ability to learn and ongoing developing intellectual expertise. Thus, the predictive validity of both static intelligence tests and dynamic learning potential tests guarantee the value of intelligence testing in modern society.

See Also the Following Articles

Binet, Alfred • Psychometrics of Intelligence

Further Reading

Aiken, L. W. (2003). *Psychological Testing and Assessment.* 11th Ed. Allyn & Bacon, Boston.

Annastasi, A., and Urbina, S. (1997). *Psychological Testing*, 7th Ed. Prentice Hall, Upper Saddle River, NJ.

Flynn, J. R. (1987). Massive IQ gains in 14 nations: What IQ tests really measure. *Psychol. Bull.* **101,** 171–191.

Kaufman, A. S. (2000). Tests of intelligence. In *Handbook of Intelligence* (R. J. Sternberg, ed.), pp. 445–476. Cambridge University Press, New York.

Neisser, U., Boodoo, G., Bouchard, T. J., Jr., Boykin, A. W., Brody, N., Ceci, S. J., Halpern, D. F., Loehlin, J. C., Perloff, R., Sternberg, R. J., and Urbina, S. (1996). Intelligence: Knowns and unknowns. *Am. Psychol.* **51,** 77–101.

Schaie, K. W. (1996). *Intellectual Development in Adulthood. The Seattle Longitudinal Study.* Cambridge University Press, New York.

Sternberg, R. J. (1997). The Concept of Intelligence and Its Role in Lifelong Learning and Success. *Am. Psychol.* **52,** 1030–1037.

Sternberg, R. J. (ed.) (2000). *Handbook of Intelligence.* Cambridge University Press, New York.

Sternberg, R. J., and Grigorenko, E. L. (2002). *Dynamic Testing: the Nature and Measurement of Learning Potential.* Cambridge University Press, New York.

Inter-Rater Reliability

Robert F. DeVellis

University of North Carolina, Chapel Hill, North Carolina, USA

Glossary

alpha coefficient A statistic representing internal consistency among items in a set.

intra-class correlation coefficient A class of statistics representing the proportion of true score variance to total variance, expressed as a ratio of variances ascribable to specific sources.

kappa coefficient A statistic representing the chance-corrected extent of agreement between observers.

product-moment correlation coefficient A widely used statistic (often simply called the correlation coefficient) representing the amount of association between continuous variables.

reliability The proportion of variance in a measure that can be ascribed to a true score.

true score The hypothetical error-free component of an obtained score, reflecting the actual state of the variable measured.

Inter-rater reliability is the extent to which assessments of a phenomenon by two or more observers are influenced by some aspect of the phenomenon being observed rather than by some aspect of the observers. Typically, it concerns the degree of consistency or agreement that exists across multiple observers or raters of some phenomenon. Larger discrepancies across observers are interpreted as representing more error in the observers' collective ratings. Several alternative computational approaches have been developed for quantifying inter-rater reliability.

Classical Test Theory and Reliability

According to classical test theory, a score obtained in the process of measurement is influenced by two things: (1) the true score of the object, person, event, or other phenomenon being measured and (2) error (i.e., everything other than the true score of the phenomenon of interest). Reliability, in general, is a proportion corresponding to a ratio between two quantities. The first quantity (denominator) represents the sum total of all influences on the obtained score. The other quantity (numerator) represents the subportion of that total that can be ascribed to the phenomenon of interest, often called the true score. The reliability coefficient is the ratio of variability ascribable to the true score relative to the total variability of the obtained score. Inter-rater reliability is merely a special case of this more general definition. The distinguishing assumption is that the primary source of error is due to the observers, or raters as they are often called.

Multiple Raters

If two or more raters are accurately observing the exact same thing, their reports of what they see should be identical. To the extent that they differ, it is assumed that characteristics of the raters (i.e., biases) are responsible. Such characteristics, of course, are sources of error and consequently the resultant ratings are inaccurate to some degree. It follows from this reasoning that the degree of discrepancy among raters represents the extent of unreliability that the set of observations possesses or, conversely, that the lack of variation from rater to rater represents the extent of reliability. Quantifying discrepancies among raters thus becomes an important part of assessing inter-rater reliability.

A hypothetical example may help to clarify these concepts. Assume that a researcher is content analyzing transcripts collected in the course of a research project. The researcher's aim is to categorize free-form narrative from the transcripts into quantifiable data that can be analyzed using standard inferential statistical procedures. The process may begin by defining units of information, that is, chunks of text corresponding to the unit of analysis chosen on conceptual grounds. Having chosen a unit of analysis, the investigator typically will want to evaluate some quantitative aspect of the units. Therefore, a classification system must be developed that defines the criteria to be used to classify units of speech.

Both the unitization and classification processes require a degree of judgment. For example, if the investigator is interested in coding "affective responses," he or she must determine what text segments (i.e., units) to evaluate for affective content and when a given text segment is an expression of emotion. The judgments involved in both unitization and classification create opportunities for systematic bias.

Still another way of viewing this situation is with respect to sources of variation in the data. Presumably, the investigator wants the data to manifest variation attributable to some aspect of (1) the individuals studied, (2) the situations to which they were exposed, or (3) some combination of these. If, however, in the process of transforming the data from raw to quantifiable form, a personal bias or point of view is superimposed, then characteristics of the coder are an additional source of variation in the data.

One means of addressing the impact that data rating has is to use multiple raters. To the extent that multiple raters are able to produce comparable data (i.e., similar characterizations of affective vs. nonaffective verbalizations within identical transcripts), the likelihood that the ratings are substantially influenced by idiosyncratic perceptions has been attenuated. Consequently, it is customary for research of the type described to employ multiple raters. The idea is that, if independent raters can reach the same conclusions from the same data source, then those conclusions must reflect some aspect of the data examined (which are identical) rather than something about the raters (who are different).

Assessing Inter-Rater Agreement

Consider a simple, if not very realistic, example. Assume that an investigator has a theory that action-oriented people will be more aggressive practitioners of health-promotion behaviors. That is, the theory speculates that action-oriented people will exercise more, seek appropriate professional care, regulate their diets, and generally choose health-benefiting as opposed to health-compromising activities. To test this theory, the investigator reasons that the number of verbs used in individuals' speech should serve as an index of how action-oriented they are. This imaginary theory specifies that people whose speech is more heavily laced with verbs will enjoy an improved health status. So, the task of the investigator is to determine which individuals use more verbs in their speech and, subsequently, to compare verb frequency to various health-status measures. Because certain words can have a verb and a nonverb form (for example, "score" can be either a noun or verb), the investigator feels that there is possibly room for error in the coding of the data and decides to have two independent raters determine how many verbs exist in each transcript. That is, the investigator will determine how reliably a verb score can be assigned to each subject's transcript by comparing the scores given by two raters for each transcript.

Table I Cross-Tabulation of Classifications of Transcript Words

Rater #2 \ *Rater #1*	*Verbs*	*Nouns*	*Adjectives*	*Total*
Verbs	10	2	9	21
Nouns	6	43	0	49
Adjectives	5	5	20	30
Total	21	50	29	100

Let us assume that the two raters evaluate the same transcript and that their results are cross tabulated as shown in Table I. Having tabulated the data for agreement between two raters, we now must determine to what extent the conclusions of the two are comparable.

Percentage Agreement

One of the simplest ways of judging reliability is percentage agreement (i.e., the percentage of cases that raters classify similarly). There are at least two ways to do this, and the difference between them is important. The simplest method is to take a simple count of the number of instances of a category that each rater reports. Assume, as in Table I, that each of two raters found 21 instances of verbs among 100 possibilities. Because they agree on the number of instances, 21 in 100, it might appear that they completely agree on the verb score and that the inter-rater reliability is 1.0. This conclusion may be unwarranted, however, because it does not determine whether the 21 events rater #1 judged to be verbs were the same events that rater #2 assigned to that category. The raters have agreed on the rate of occurrence (i.e., 21%) of the category, "verbs" but not necessarily on specific examples of its occurrence. Rater #1 might have rated the first 21 of 100 words of a transcript as verbs, whereas rater #2 might have described the last 21 words as verbs. In such a case, the raters would not have agreed on the categorization of any of the specific words on the transcript. Rather than simply tallying the number of words each rater assigned to a category, the researcher could determine how the raters evaluated the *same* words. The cross-tabulation shown in Table I accomplishes this by indicating how many words rater #1 classified as verbs, for example, and how many of those same words rater #2 classified similarly. The number of word-by-word agreements for the several categories appear along the main diagonal of the table. This is a more specific indicator of percentage agreement as a measure of inter-rater reliability. In this case, the overall percentage agreement is 73% and, for verbs, it is 10/21 = 47.6%.

Chi-Square

Another method for describing the pattern of ratings is to perform a chi-square test on the data in the 3 × 3 table. The null hypothesis for such a test is that the patterns of ratings for the two raters are random. That is, if the ratings are unreliable (i.e., not influenced by the nature of the words, but only by the proclivities of the raters) the number of verbs identified for a given subject by rater #1 should be independent of the number of verbs seen by rater #2. The chi-square test can be applied to the obtained data to determine whether the pattern of ratings fits the null hypothesis or whether there is some degree of association such that the raters agree with one another more than chance would predict.

The computation of chi-square requires that we compute expected rates of agreement, as shown in Table II. Chi-square (χ^2) can be computed from this table by summing across the cells the squared difference between expected and observed frequencies divided by the expected frequency:

$$\begin{aligned}\chi^2 = \sum\left[(O-E)^2/E\right] &= (10-4.41)^2/4.41 \\ &+ (2-10.50)^2/10.50 + (9-6.09)^2/6.09 \\ &+ (6-10.29)^2/10.29 + (43-24.50)^2/24.50 \\ &+ (0-14.21)^2/14.21 + (5-6.30)^2/6.30 \\ &+ (5-15.00)^2/15.00 + (20-8.70)^2/8.70 \\ &= 66.94\end{aligned}$$

The degrees of freedom (df) for this table is $(3-1) \times (3-1) = 4$, and thus the chi-square statistic is significant beyond $p < 0.000000000000001$. This analysis indicates that the distribution of verbs versus nouns versus adjectives is not independent across raters. Even with a highly significant chi-square, however, we cannot be certain that the rates agree on the number of verbs. All we know is that the overall pattern is nonrandom.

A more appropriate test might collapse categories into "verbs" versus "nonverbs" (i.e., adjectives and nouns combined). This is shown in Table III. Note that the overall percentage agreement has now climbed to 78% because instances in which one rater judged a word to be a noun and the other judged it to be an adjective are now counted as agreements (i.e., "nonverb" matched with "nonverb"). For this table, $\chi^2 = 11.35$ with 1 df. This is significant with $p < 0.001$. Therefore, we can conclude that the pattern of rating words as verbs or nonverbs is not independent across the two raters.

Based on the value of χ^2 alone (or its associated probability), however, we *cannot* conclude that an adequate level of agreement exists between the two raters. Chi-square is a measure of association (i.e., nonrandomness), not agreement. An association might exist that is *not* a reflection of agreement. For example, two sets of ratings may be negatively associated; that is, the assignment of an event to one category by rater #1 may tend to co-occur with the rater #2's assigning the same event to the other category, or one type of disagreement may occur far more often than expected while another type occurs less often. Even though the ratings in such a case would not agree very well, the pattern is indicative of an association and the chi-square would probably be high.

Chi-square looks for departures from zero relationship. It does not care about the direction of association. In addition, it does not care if the amount of agreement is actually quite small as long as it is statistically improbable. A chi-square corresponding to a low degree of agreement might be significantly different from a totally random pattern and, thus, the chi-square statistic would be significant. It does not follow, however, that the level of agreement is substantial. Chi-square can thus be misleading when the extent of agreement is the concern.

Kappa

Cohen's kappa (κ) statistic is a chance-corrected method for assessing agreement (rather than association) among

Table II Cross-Tabulation of Classifications of Transcript Words with Expected Frequencies[a]

Rater #2 \ Rater #1	*Verbs*	*Nouns*	*Adjectives*	*Total*
Verbs	10 (4.41)	2 (10.50)	9 (6.09)	21
Nouns	6 (10.29)	43 (24.50)	0 (14.21)	49
Adjectives	5 (6.30)	5 (15.00)	20 (8.70)	30
Total	21	50	29	100

[a] Expected frequencies are in parentheses.

Table III Cross-Tabulation of Classifications of Transcript Words, Collapsing Nonverb Categories[a]

Rater #2 \ Rater #1	*Verbs*	*Nonverbs*	*Total*
Verbs	10 (4.41)	11 (16.59)	21
Nonverbs	11 (16.59)	68 (62.41)	79
Total	21	79	100

[a] Expected frequencies are in parentheses.

raters. Kappa is defined as follows:

$$\kappa = (f_O - f_E)/(N - f_E)$$

where f_O is the number of observed agreements between raters, f_E is the number of agreements expected by chance, and N is the total number of observations. In essence, kappa answers the following question: What proportion of values not expected to be agreements (by chance) actually *are* agreements?

We can examine the data from Table III using kappa (recall that $N = 100$):

$$f_O = 10 + 68 = 78$$
$$f_E = 4.41 + 62.41 = 66.82$$
$$\kappa = (78 - 66.82)/(100 - 66.82) = 0.34$$

This ratio can be considered conceptually. The numerator is the amount of observed agreement minus the amount expected by chance. The denominator is the total number of observations minus the number of agreements expected by chance—in a sense, this denominator is the number of cases in which the rate of occurrence for the two response classes (verb vs. nonverb) does not guarantee agreement, i.e., the number not determinable merely from the marginal probabilities of the two response classes. It also is equal to the sum of the expected frequencies of the two nonagreement cells (i.e., 16.59 + 16.59). Thus, kappa is equal to the proportion of "observations free to vary" that yields an agreement between raters. Stated in terms of Table III, it is the number of agreements, beyond chance, relative to the number of expected misses. Thus:

$$\kappa = \frac{\text{Actual agreements beyond chance}}{\text{Potential agreements beyond chance}}$$

A $\kappa = 0.34$ is regarded as modest agreement.

As another example of how chi-square and kappa compare, consider the distribution of agreements shown in Table IV. Here $\chi^2 = 6.25$ ($p < 0.02$), whereas $\kappa = 0.20$. Thus, although chi-square is significant, the value of kappa suggests little agreement.

Although kappa is probably the most frequently used measure of agreement, it has come under criticism. One of these criticisms is that kappa is a measure of *exact* agreement and treats approximate agreements in the same way as extreme disagreements. But with some types of data, a "near miss" may be better than a "far miss." Although this is usually not the case when the categories being rated are truly nominal (as in our example of verbs vs. nonverbs), for ordinal categories the idea of a "near miss" makes more sense. Note also that, for a given number of observations, the more categories there are, the smaller kappa is likely to be. Even with our simple percentage agreement, we have seen that collapsing adjectives and nouns into a single category increases the "hit rate." *Weighted kappas* are one way around the "near miss" problem. Essentially, the weighting system can differentiate between relatively proximal and relatively distal ordinal categories. Disagreements that entail different raters choosing nonidentical but proximal categories contribute more positively to the measure of agreement than due disagreements involving highly dissimilar classifications by the raters.

Table IV Hypothetical Data Illustrating Modest but Statistically Significant Association

Rater #2 \ *Rater #1*	A	B	*Total*
A	45 (40)	5 (10)	50
B	35 (40)	15 (10)	50
Total	80	20	100

Product-Moment and Other Correlation Coefficients

In some cases involving ratings of continuous variables, it may be appropriate to evaluate inter-rater agreement by means of the everyday Pearson product-moment correlation coefficient. This is the case when the investigator is interested in to what extent raters agreed in their placement of specific stimuli within their total distributions of all the stimuli being rated. In other words, this method applies when the investigator want to know whether raters agreed on the percentile scores given to the stimuli being rated, but the actual ratings are given in some absolute rather than relative metric. Imagine, for example, that two raters agreed that a certain phrase represented an average degree of emotionality compared to all the phrases in a transcript. If rater #1 considered the whole transcript to be somewhat more emotionally laden than rater #2 did, rater #1 might consistently assign higher scores than rater #2. So, a phrase that both raters considered to be precisely at the midpoint of all phrases with respect to emotionality would receive different numerical scores. Agreement in the literal sense would be zero. But the score discrepancy would result not from a fundamental difference in perceptions but merely in calibration. In such a case, a correlation coefficient, which is blind to units of measurement and is based on similarities of location along a continuum, might actually be preferred as an indicator of inter-rater reliability over a method such as kappa.

The product-moment correlation assumes that the variables (ratings in this case) are measured on a continuous scale. Often, although we may think of the phenomenon being evaluated as inherently continuous, its measurement is not. Rating, in fact, implies assignment to discrete categories. In such circumstances, the tetrachoric (binary case) or polychoric (multiple ordered category case) correlation coefficient can be used as an indicator of inter-rater reliability in a manner analogous to the use of the product-moment correlation with continuous data. Tetrachoric and polychoric correlations are means of estimating what the correlation would have been had the variables been measured continuously. As with the product-moment correlation, the tetrachoric or polychoric correlation between the raters provides a window into the relationship of ratings to true scores and, thus, can serve as an indicator of reliability. A full examination of these methods is beyond the scope of this entry.

Coefficient Alpha

Cronbach's coefficient alpha is used primarily as a means of describing the reliability of multiitem scales. Alpha can also be applied to raters in a manner analogous to its use with items. Using alpha in this way allows us to determine inter-rater agreement when the ratings entail noncategorical data (for example, the degree of emotionality, on a scale of 1 to 10, in various units of text). Scale items and raters both are, in essence, indicators of information about a phenomenon of interest. The information that the items or raters provide is divisible into a portion that is about the phenomenon common to all the indicators and another portion that is due to the idiosyncratic features of each specific data source, be it item or rater. The final score on an item assessing emotionality, for example, will be an amalgam of a respondent's true level of emotionality plus error arising from unintended characteristics of the item, such as confusing language. Similarly, a rater's judgment of the emotionality of a text passage is an amalgam of the actual emotional content of the text plus rater characteristics that affect judgments.

For multiitem scales, alpha can be computed from the correlations among the items. Inter-rater reliability can be computed in like fashion from correlations among the raters. Moreover, just as the alpha for items is driven by the magnitude of inter-item correlations and the number of items, the alpha for inter-rater reliability is determined by the inter-rater correlations and the number of raters. In both the item and rater cases of alpha, the Spearman-Brown equation can be used both to compute alpha and to determine the effect on reliability of adding items or raters. In general, the more numerous and more strongly associated the items or raters are, the higher coefficient alpha will be.

Intra-Class Correlation Coefficient

An analysis of variance (ANOVA) approach can be used to partition variance into discrete sources that can be compared to one another in meaningful ways. Certain ratios of variances can be constructed that correspond to the common definition of reliability, and the proportion expressed by such a ratio is called an intra-class correlation coefficient. That same approach can be, and frequently is, used to assess inter-rater agreement. The suitability of the intra-class correlation coefficient for such purposes underscores the fact that inter-rater reliability is merely a special case of reliability more generally. As it happens, both kappa (weighted or unweighted) and coefficient alpha are special cases of the intra-class correlation coefficient. The latter is not one coefficient but a family of coefficients that varies depending on the nature of the data, research question, and other factors.

Whenever we obtain results from an ANOVA that allows for variance to be partitioned into effect (such as the true score of an observed event) and error (such as differences among raters), it is possible to construct one or more intra-class correlation coefficients. The intra-class correlation coefficient is a general representation of the ratio of effect variance relative to effect-plus-error variance. By constructing the ANOVA appropriately (often treating different indicators as repeated measures of a phenomenon) and then computing the ratio of the appropriate variance terms (i.e., those that correspond to true variation for the numerator and true-plus-error variation for the denominator), a variety of issues related to reliability can be addressed.

In a now-classic 1979 paper, Shrout and Fleiss laid out a series of guidelines for using the intra-class correlation coefficient to assess inter-rater reliability. They noted three issues that help to determine which of several possible analytic strategies should be used: (1) whether different raters observe the same or different events, (2) whether the investigator is interested in assessing the reliability of one rater relative to the others or of all raters as a group, and (3) whether the investigator wishes to generalize to the specific raters used only (as alpha does with items or raters) or to a broader population of raters represented by those sampled in the study. Depending on how the investigator views these three issues, the intra-class correlation coefficient takes on a different form. The advantage of the intra-class correlation coefficient and alpha over kappa is that they can make the most use of the information available (e.g., distinguish between near and far misses in the case of nonnominal data), whereas unweighted kappa cannot.

An extension of this general approach to identifying specific sources of error is generalizability theory. A good introduction to this highly versatile methodology is the 1991 text by Shavelson and Webb.

Conclusion

Assessing inter-rater reliability should be an integral part of all research that involves the use of raters or judges to quantify phenomena. Using a single rater precludes the assessment of inter-rater reliability and thus should be avoided; inter-rater reliability is a special case of reliability more generally. The specific method chosen for assessing inter-rater reliability should be determined by the research questions and the nature of the data to be rated.

See Also the Following Articles

Alpha Reliability • Correlations • Reliability Assessment • Reliability

Further Reading

Lindquist, E. F. (1953). *Design and Analysis of Experiments in Psychology and Education.* Houghton-Mifflin, Boston.

Nunnally, J. C., and Bernstein, I. H. (1994). *Psychometric Theory,* 3rd Ed. McGraw-Hill, New York.

Shavelson, R. J., and Webb, N. M. (1991). *Generalizability Theory: A Primer.* Sage, Thousand Oaks, CA.

Shrout, P. E., and Fleiss, J. L. (1979). Intraclass correlations: Uses in assessing rater reliability. *Psychol. Bull.* **86,** 420–428.

Traub, R. E. (1994). *Reliability for the Social Sciences.* Sage, Thousand Oaks, CA.

Inter-University Consortium of Political and Social Research (ICPSR) Data Sets

Christopher S. Dunn
Bowling Green State University, Bowling Green, Ohio, USA

Glossary

data archive A repository for computerized data files and data documentation.

data documentation Codebooks, record layouts, data collection instruments, descriptions of study procedures, and other materials that describe the contents and organization of computerized data files.

ICPSR study The computerized data files and data documentation from an empirical research study by the Inter-University Consortium of Political and Social Research.

Internet The vast collection of interconnected computer networks that all use TCP/IP protocols.

microdata Data about individual subjects or events; unaggregated data.

World Wide Web (WWW) Internet client-server hypertext distributed information retrieval system, which originated from the CERN High-Energy Physics laboratories in Geneva, Switzerland.

The Inter-University Consortium for Political and Social Research (ICPSR) is the largest social science data archive in the world. ICPSR provides faculty, students, and other researchers at over 550 member institutions with access to 5358 social science data collections (having separate titles). Collectively, these data collections comprise 94,082 available files and add up to nearly 1 terabyte of data—the exact number is 1,051,968,879,000 bytes. ICPSR also provides worldwide public access to some of those data collections through its externally sponsored topical archives. In 2002, ICPSR distributed 334,064 data sets to 1733 member and nonmember institutions, totaling over 8.8 million megabytes (almost 8.5 terabytes) of data. The amount of data distributed to all institutions is the equivalent of nearly 13,650 completely filled CD-ROMs of data. ICPSR also provides educational programs through its well-known Summer Program, enrolling over 650 students from 200 institutions. The students select from among 45 statistics and social science methods courses taught by 40 guest faculty from 30 institutions. ICPSR's core activities of providing access to data and training in its analysis were important elements of its creation and continue to be central to its present mission.

ICPSR's Formation and Growth

The Inter-University Consortium of Political and Social Research (ICPSR) was established in 1962 by a founding set of 21 universities which created a formal organization to institutionalize informal collaborations that had developed during the 1950s for access to survey data about American national elections and participation in advanced quantitative analytical training. ICPSR was originally established as the Inter-University Consortium for Political Research (ICPR) because the impetus for sharing data and providing quantitative analysis training was concentrated among a small number of social scientists who focused on study of political values, attitudes, and voting behavior. Within the University of Michigan's Institute for Social Research, the Political Behavior Program had become a separate research program in 1956 under the leadership of Warren Miller. Throughout the 1950s and early 1960s, Miller's work, and that of Philip Converse and Angus Campbell, introduced methodological innovations into the field of political science through national surveys of the electorate. These included the successful use of the panel survey design to study a mobile population, the integration of individual-level and aggregate data from multiple sources, and the use of social psychological theory and variables to study political attitudes and voting behavior.

Even then, the challenge of continued funding support for the elections studies was an issue for Miller. In part, he conceived of ICPR as an organization that could generate funds from dues-paying member institutions to maintain the 2-year sequence of national election surveys. He also thought that member institutions would provide important voices in support of the continuation of the election studies. Political scientists from other institutions were also convinced by another of Miller's concepts for the consortium. They and their students would have access to national survey data too expensive to develop at individual institutions and they would be able to obtain analytical and methodological training to enable them to stay abreast of the rapid innovations in quantitative research and analysis.

Warren Miller was the first director of ICPR and held that position until 1970 when the Political Behavior Program in the Institute for Social Research (ISR) became the Center for Political Studies and Miller became its first director. By that time, ICPR had grown into an organization with 134 member institutions, a staff of 60, and state-of-the-art computer facilities for cataloging acquired data and preserving it, processing it for use on multiple mainframe-computer-system platforms, and distributing it to member institutions on magnetic reel tape.

During the 1970s, major changes took place at ICPR. A new director, Richard Hofferbert, from Cornell University succeeded Warren Miller. Hofferbert directed ICPR during a time of tightening of federal research budgets in the latter years of the Nixon administration. That research belt-tightening was directly responsible for the withdrawal of some ICPR members and failures to pay dues by others. Reductions in National Science Foundation budgets also affected the ability of ICPR to pay stipends for participants in the Summer Training Program. ICPR responded by broadening the scope of the data in the archive to attract new member institutions and new sources of funding support. A massive historical data collection of county-level election returns from 1789 onward and roll-call records for the U.S. Congress was computerized. Extensive international relations data, including U.N. plenary session and committee voting records; social, political, and economic attributes of nations; and records of international conflicts, were added to the archive. ICPR also began to develop materials (data extracts and syntax setup files) that could be used for undergraduate instruction.

In 1975, ICPR's name was changed to the now familiar (and so easily pronounced) Inter-University Consortium for Political and Social Research (ICPSR) to reflect the broadening of the scope of the data being archived. Also in 1975, Jerome Clubb, director of the Historical Archive, was named to succeed Hofferbert as the director. During Clubb's 16 years as director (1975–1991), ICPSR expanded its membership, its data collections, and its sources of external funding. By the end of Clubb's term as director, there were nearly 350 member institutions and two publicly funded topical archives: the National Archive of Computerized Data on Aging (NACDA) and the National Archive of Criminal Justice Data (NACJD). The basic organization of ICPSR data into 17 thematic categories had also been developed (see Table I). The data distribution system in which official representatives (ORs) at member institutions or their designees transmitted data requests to ICPSR and received requested data collections on reel tapes had been in operation for nearly 30 years. ICPSR became a national resource for the social sciences during the Clubb years.

With Clubb's retirement in 1991 and the appointment of Richard Rockwell from the Social Science Research Council, ICPSR entered a period of significant change. Three additional topical archives were added through externally sponsored projects. The Health and Medical Care Archive (HMCA), supported by the Robert Wood Johnson Foundation, was initiated in 1995. The Substance Abuse and Mental Health Archive (SAMHDA), supported by the Substance Abuse and Mental Health Services Administration of the Department of Health and Human Services (DHHS), was initiated in 1995. The International Archive of Education Data (IAED),

Table I Thematic Categories for ICPSR Data Collections[a]

1. Census Enumerations
2. Community and Urban Studies
3. Conflict, Aggression, Violence, Wars
4. Economic Behavior and Attitudes
5. Education
6. Elites and Leadership
7. Geography and Environment
8. Government Structures, Policies, and Capabilities
9. Health Care and Facilities
10. Instructional Packages
11. International Systems
12. Legal Systems
13. Legislative and Deliberative Bodies
14. Mass Political Behavior and Attitudes
15. Organizational Behavior
16. Social Indicators
17. Social Institutions and Behavior

[a] From ICPSR Web site at http://www.icpsr.umich.edu/access/subject.html

supported by the National Center for Education Statistics, was initiated in 1996. Also in 1996, the NACJD made all its data collections freely available to the public over ICPSR's first-generation World Wide Web (WWW) site. By 1998, almost all the data distribution at ICPSR data was being done over the WWW. With the shift to using the WWW as the primary tool for ORs to access data for their campus users, ICPSR was confronted with the need to provide data documentation in electronic format. This led to the documentation conversion project, which at its conclusion in 2003 had transformed over 500,000 pages of paper codebooks and data collection instruments into electronic files.

The dramatic changes in computing during the Rockwell years (1991–2000) also presented challenges to the original organizational structure and functions of ICPSR. A number of issues emerged concerning the value of membership, the function of the official representative system, the speed of data delivery, individual access to data, and the preservation of data. Essentially, the computing world had changed from a centralized mainframe environment to a decentralized individual environment. Research groups that previously needed a central warehouse for archiving data could by 2000 make their own project data available for downloading on their own WWW sites. Data users could download data from data producers directly to their own computers using only a few mouse clicks on the WWW. ICPSR itself had encouraged the rapid transfer of data directly to individual users by making some of its publicly funded topical archive data available directly to individual users who did not have to be affiliated with a member institution. By mid-2002, 28% of the ICPSR data collection titles were freely available from the ICPSR Web site.

These were the issues that confronted Myron Gutmann when he succeeded Rockwell as director of ICPSR in 2001. Almost immediately, Gutmann responded to these challenges by ordering the rapid implementation of ICPSR Direct, a system of individual access to ICPSR data by users affiliated with member institutions. ICPSR Direct had been in the planning and testing stages during the recruitment of a new director, but it required a leadership decision to fully commit to a data delivery system that bypassed the nearly 40-year tradition of data requests from and delivery to campus ORs. A majority of the 550-plus member institutions now provide direct access to ICPSR data at their campuses. Experience with ICPSR Direct suggests that ORs are still a hugely important link in the data availability chain. With ICPSR Direct, ORs now have administrative, certification, and tutorial responsibilities in the data delivery process rather than hands-on downloading of data and its transfer to users. With ICPSR Direct, the amount of data actually downloaded and used has increased.

Contents of the ICPSR Data Archive

Data collections in the ICPSR archive are organized according to the 17 thematic categories shown in Table I. Each of these thematic categories is the main category for a much more detailed outline and categorization of data collections. These detailed categorizations are used as search terms on the ICPSR Web site to search a database of metadata about the studies. The search returns a list of study titles in the specific category. For example, Table II shows the more detailed outline of subcategories for the first major thematic category, Census Enumerations.

Another way that ICPSR data can be categorized is according to the program units within ICPSR that are responsible for processing the data. This categorization scheme allows the description of collections brought into the archive and made available under the auspices of ICPSR's topical archives, according to data in the "general" archive and the topical archives, providing a more coherent program-related overview of data in the topical archives. In the next section, data are described in terms of the 17 themes, excluding data contained in ICPSR's topical archives. In the section thereafter, data from the ICPSR topical archives are described.

Census Enumerations: Historical and Contemporary Population Characteristics

There are 585 data collection titles in this ICPSR thematic data category. Over 260 of these titles are for data from decennial censuses of population and housing. The other

Table II Subcategories of Data Collections in the Census Enumeration Thematic Category[a]

Census Enumerations: Historical and Contemporary Population Characteristics

A. United States
  1. Decennial censuses
    a. 1790–1960 Censuses
    b. 1970 Census
    c. 1980 Census
    d. 1990 Census
    e. 2000 Census
  2. American Housing Survey Series
  3. Current Population Survey Series
  4. Other Census, Including County and City Data Books
B. Nations Other than the United States

[a] From ICPSR Web site at http://www.icpsr.umich.edu/access/subject.html#I

data collections are almost wholly from three U.S. Census Bureau surveys.

Census data prior to 1970 include a variety of collections. There are data about (1) rural households from northern states in 1860; (2) southern agricultural households in 1880; (3) southern cities from 1870 and 1880; (4) population census data from 1860, 1880, 1900, and 1910; (5) census tract data from 1940, 1950, and 1960; (6) public use microdata sample (PUMS) data from 1940, 1950, and 1960; (7) county-level demographic characteristics of the population from 1930, 1940, and 1950; and (8) one of ICPSR's first data collections, historical, demographic, economic, and social data in the United States from 1790 to 1970. Almost all the collections in the various groups contain multiple data files. Many of these historical census data were keypunched into electronic records from printed census materials and tables.

For the 1970 Census of Population and Housing, the public dissemination of census data on magnetic computer tapes took place for the first time, although electronic machines (keypunches and counter-sorters) had been used for a number of decennial censuses. Major 1970 census data in the ICPSR collection include (1) census tract data on population and housing characteristics and (2) public use microdata samples (PUMS).

The 1980 Census of Population and Housing was the first to have extensive computer files covering a broad range of geographic levels (from states to block-groups) produced by the Census Bureau. These files were released in four different groups, referred to by the Census Bureau as Summary Tape Files (STF) 1, 2, 3, and 4. STF 1 and STF 2 contain data presented at a number of geographic levels from the complete count (100%) of population and housing items. STF 3 and STF 4 contain unweighted and weighted sample data and complete count data on population and housing variables. For each STF group (1, 2, 3, and 4), separate data files were released for each state's data at all the geographic levels. So each STF group contains more than 50 data files. A variety of special-purpose 1980 census files and extract files are also part of the ICPSR collection.

The 1990 Census continued the Census Bureau's provision of data on computerized media. The summary tape file organization of data for the 1980 Census was maintained for the 1990 Census data. A large number of PUMS files are also available, as well as extracts on specific topics.

The 2000 Census represents the most detailed and extensive release of public data in history. When the release of the 2000 Census data is complete, ICPSR expects that there will be over 50,000 data files made available. Data for the 2000 Census are the first to be organized to facilitate their use with personal computers, which accounts for the large number of files. In order to cope with this complexity, ICPSR has developed a topical archive Web site specifically devoted to Census 2000. The topical archive provides for general information about Census 2000 and an overview of the different kinds of data files available, user access to downloading Census 2000 data, and an extensive array of help pages. Figure 1 shows the Census 2000 topical archive Web home page and Table III lists the different types of data available for Census 2000. Three other major Census Bureau data collections are also listed within this general ICPSR thematic section: the American Housing Survey (AHS), the Current Population Survey (CPS), and the Survey of Income and Program Participation (SIPP).

The AHS (formerly the Annual Housing Surveys) is a sample survey conducted by the Census Bureau for the U.S. Department of Housing and Urban Development (HUD). Data collected about the nation's single-family homes, apartments, mobile homes, and vacant housing units include information about household characteristics, household income, housing costs, housing and neighborhood quality, and household moves. An interesting feature of the AHS is that it has used the same sample of housing units since 1985, which facilitates the analysis of the flow of households through housing units (that is, movers and stayers). National sample data are collected every other year and data from 47 specific metropolitan areas are collected once every 4–6 years. Additional information about the AHS can be found at the Web sites for the U.S. Census Bureau, HUD, and ICPSR.

The CPS is a sample survey conducted monthly by the Census Bureau in cooperation with the U.S. Bureau of Labor Statistics (BLS). The Census Bureau describes the CPS as "the primary source of information on the labor force characteristics of the U.S. population. . . . Estimates obtained from the CPS include employment, unemployment, earnings, hours of work, and other indicators. They are available by a variety of demographic characteristics, including age, sex, race, marital status, and educational attainment. They are also available by occupation, industry, and class of worker. Supplemental questions to produce estimates on a variety of topics including school enrollment, income, previous work experience, health, employee benefits, and work schedules are also often added to the regular CPS questionnaire."

The SIPP is a continuous national panel survey conducted by the Census Bureau to collect information about the source and amount of personal income, labor force participation, program participation and eligibility, and demographic characteristics. In addition to these core topics, other questions are added in special topic modules. A comparison of SIPP with other national surveys about income and labor force, for example, the CPS and the Panel Study of Income Dynamics, is available on the SIPP Web site.

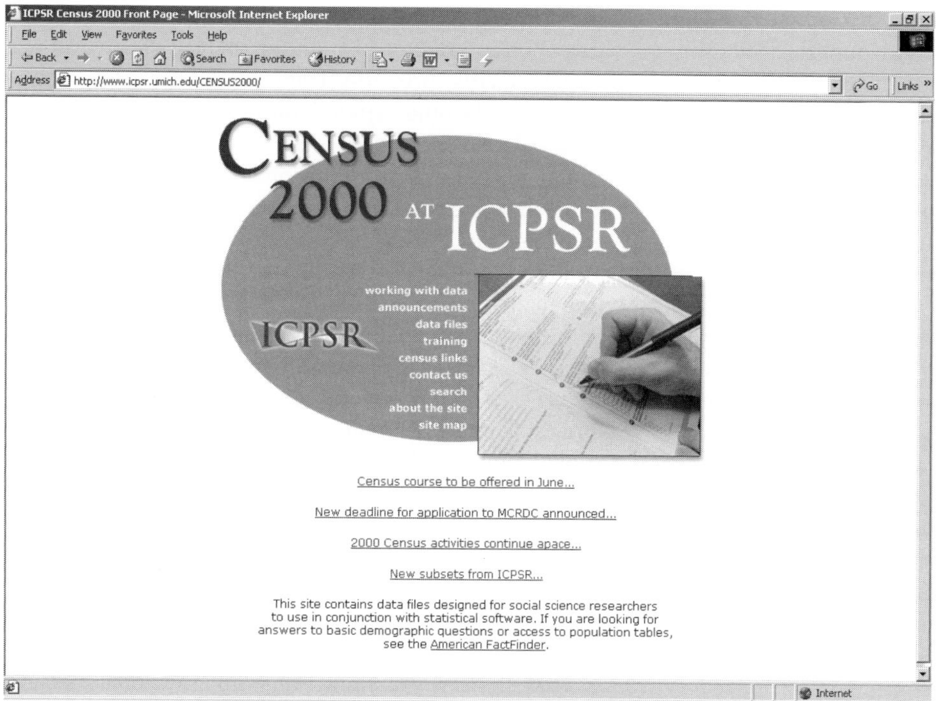

Figure 1 The ICPSR Census 2000 Web site. *Source:* ICPSR Web site at http://www.icpsr.umich.edu/CENSUS2000, with permission.

Table III Census 2000 Data Available from ICPSR[a]

Original Data from the U.S. Census Bureau
Summary File 1
Summary File 2
Summary File 3
Summary File 4
Island Area Summary Files
Redistricting (Public Law 94-171)
Public Use Microdata Sample
Census Tract Relationship Files
1998 Dress Rehearsal, P.L. 94-171 Redistricting Data
Profiles of General Demographic Characteristics
Other Census 2000 Data
Selected Subsets from Summary File 1
Selected Subsets from Summary File 3
Bridged Race and Population Estimates

[a] From ICPSR Web site at http://www.icpsr.umich.edu/CENSUS2000/datafiles.html

Economic Behavior and Attitudes

There are over 505 data collection titles in the ICPSR thematic category for data on economic behavior and attitudes. Surveys of consumers account for the largest subgroup of these economic behavior and attitude data collections. The three major data collections in this subgroup are the BLS Consumer Expenditure Survey, the University of Michigan's Survey of Consumer Attitudes and Behavior, and the Federal Reserve Board's Survey of Consumer Finances. Data from the first two of these surveys are used in the construction and calculation of three of the best-known economic indicators in the United States: the Consumer Price Index, the Index of Consumer Expectations, and the Index of Consumer Sentiment.

The Consumer Expenditure Survey provides information on the purchasing practices of American consumers in regard to a variety of monthly and weekly expenditures on different categories of goods and services. The study involves two independent samples of approximately 7500 each, one which is interviewed quarterly about monthly expenditures and the other which maintains a diary of weekly expenditures. More information about the Consumer Expenditure Survey can be found at its BLS Web site and at the ICPSR Web site.

The University of Michigan's Survey of Consumer Attitudes and Behavior, now known as Surveys of Consumers, was one of the first surveys begun by the fledgling Institute for Social Research in 1946. The survey focuses on 50 core questions that measure aspects of consumer attitudes and expectations in three general areas: personal finances, business conditions, and buying conditions. Two important indexes developed from the survey are used nationally as leading economic indicators. The Index of Consumer Expectations was created using the survey data and is included in the Leading Indicator Composite Index published by the U.S. Department of Commerce. The University of Michigan created and publishes monthly another well-known index, the Index of Consumer Sentiment. More information about these surveys and indexes can be found at the Survey of Consumer Attitudes and Behavior Web site.

The Survey of Consumer Finances was begun at the University of Michigan's Institute for Social Research in 1947 and was later transferred to the auspices of the Federal Reserve Board of Governors. The survey was conducted annually from 1947 to 1971, was also conducted in 1977, and beginning in 1983 has been conducted every 3 years. During the 1980s, the survey was transferred to the Federal Reserve System. Data are now collected for the Federal Reserve System by the National Opinion Research Center (NORC). The survey currently collects information on the income, pensions, balance sheet, and demographic characteristics of U.S. families, as well as their use of financial institutions. Additional information about the current Survey of Consumer Finances is available from the Federal Reserve System and NORC Web sites.

The last major data collection series appearing in the economic data section is the County Business Patterns Series. These data sets contain information about business establishments compiled from the U.S. Bureau of the Census Standard Statistical Establishment List. Data are available by county, state, and national summary levels about the total number of business establishments with one or more employees, the number of employees in mid-March of each year, payroll information, and type of business. Data are provided for the following types of businesses: agricultural services, mining, construction, manufacturing, transportation, public utilities, wholesale trade, retail trade, finance, insurance, real estate, and services. Data is not provided for agriculture production, railroad, government, or household employment.

Data on Political Participation, Politics, and Government

In its beginning (as reflected by its original name), ICPSR data collections came from the research of political scientists. The current ICPSR thematic categories representing those data include: 6. Elites and Leadership; 8. Government Structures, Policies, and Capabilities; 13. Legislative and Deliberative Bodies; and 14. Mass Political Behavior and Attitudes.

The section on Elites and Leadership contains 39 studies about political convention delegates, political party elites, presidential appointees, and foreign policy elites. The section on Government Structures, Policies, and Capabilities contains 32 studies on government employees and 77 studies on government organizations and operations. The section on Legislative and Deliberative Bodies contains 11 studies on legislative roll-call voting records, primarily from the United States Congress, and 24 other studies on a variety of legislatures or legislative processes. The final category of this group, Mass Political Behavior and Attitudes, contains some of ICPSR's most familiar collections, including the American National Election Studies (ANES); other studies about election issues such as campaign finance; and many public opinion polls about political issues, values, and participation. There are 1355 studies in this category, 897 of which are U.S. public opinion polls. Another 72 are ANES data collections, 126 are election studies from other countries, and 116 are European public opinion polls from the Eurobarometer series.

The ANES were begun by Warren E. Miller, ICPSR's founder and first director, in 1948. The ANES studies collect data on Americans' social backgrounds, political preferences, social and political values, perceptions and evaluations of groups and candidates, opinions about public policy, and participation in political life. Most presidential election years and some congressional election years have preelection and postelection surveys. There is a cumulative data file for common questions from 1948 through 2000.

The Eurobarometers collection of public opinion surveys from the European Community (EC) countries began in 1970. The Eurobarometers collect data on public awareness of, and attitudes toward, the Common Market and other EC institutions, the priorities of an individual's own country, perceived quality of life, support for European integration, and a number of special topics. Information can be found on the ICPSR Web site.

Other General Archive Thematic Categories

Six other thematic categories contain most of the other ICPSR data collections not included in ICPSR topical archives: 2. Community and Urban Studies; 3. Conflict, Aggression, Violence, Wars; 7. Geography and Environment; 11. International Systems; 15. Organizational Behavior; and 16. Social Indicators. There are 73 study titles in the Community and Urban Studies thematic category, 44 of which are Detroit Area Studies. The Detroit Area Studies are a student learning project of the University of Michigan's Institute for Social Research (ISR) and the social science departments. Under the direction of ISR scientists and faculty, graduate students design and conduct these annual surveys about the quality of life in the Detroit, Michigan, metropolitan area. The surveys have been conducted since 1953.

There are 58 studies in the thematic category on Conflict, Aggression, Violence, and War. These studies examine various dimensions of conflict and stability within nations and conflict between nations. Topics include civil strife and civil wars, assassinations, coups d'état, minority group conflicts, political violence, correlates of war, Middle East political events, and attributes of terrorist events.

The Geography and Environment thematic category contains only 14 studies, most of which are dated. With the recent attention to PC-based computerized mapping of social phenomena, this is certainly one category in which to expect growth. Some of the topical archives have geocoded data that might otherwise have been included in this section.

The thematic category on International Systems has 54 studies. These studies include data on dyadic or triadic relationships among nations, characteristics of international organizations, arms trade data, and military alliance and expenditure data.

The thematic category of Organizational Behavior has only 29 studies. The category has no large series collections on this topic. The few data sets in the category seem unrelated and are rarely used.

The thematic category of Social Indicators data has a total of 237 data collections, 86 about social indicators in the United States. The topics of these studies range from social problems such as alcohol use, gambling, and drug abuse to use-of-time and quality-of-life indicators. This category also contains the General Social Survey collections available from ICPSR. The major collection in that regard is ICPSR study number 3728, General Social Surveys, 1972–2002. From a comparative research perspective, the U.S. General Social Survey is complemented by its British equivalent, ICPSR study number 3095, the British Social Attitudes Survey, 1983–1991; its German equivalent, ICPSR study number 6523, the German Social Survey (ALLBUS) 1980–1992; and its Polish equivalent, ICPSR study number 3487, the Polish General Social Survey, 1992–1999. Another study that receives a good deal of attention is the World Values Survey, ICPSR study number 2790.

Data from ICPSR Topical Archives

ICPSR began segmenting collections into separate topical archives having both a topical identity and an organizational identity during the 1970s. The NACDA was formed in 1975 and has been continuously supported by the National Institute on Aging. The NACJD was formed in 1978 and has been continuously supported by the Bureau of Justice Statistics since 1978 and by the National Institute of Justice since 1992. Other topical archives were created during the 1990s. The HMCA archive was founded in 1995 and is supported by the Robert Wood Johnson Foundation. The SAMHDA was founded in 1996 and is supported by the Substance Abuse and Mental Health Services Administration of the DHHS. The IAED was founded in 1998 and is supported by the U.S. Department of Education.

National Archive of Computerized Data on Aging

The NACDA seeks to advance research on aging by helping researchers use a broad range of data sets with information about older people, aging processes, or the gerontological sciences. Data identified by NACDA with this potential fall into six categories: (1) demographic characteristics of older adults; (2) social characteristics of older adults; (3) economic characteristics of older adults; (4) psychological characteristics, mental health, and well-being of older adults; (5) physical health and functioning of older adults; and (6) health care needs, use, and financing for older adults. A number of specific data sets with information about older adults have already been described. Data collections from NACDA's data series list are shown in Table IV. NACDA also processes data collections for use in ICPSR's online statistical analysis system. NACDA data collections available to analyze on-line are listed in Table V and can be accessed at the ICPSR NACDA Web site. NACDA also hosts a resident scientist at ICPSR.

National Archive of Criminal Justice Data

The NACJD preserves and distributes computerized crime and justice data from federal agencies, state agencies, and investigator initiated research projects to users for secondary statistical analysis. Staff are available to assist those using NACJD data collections by (1) identification of appropriate criminal justice data collections on specific topics, (2) instruction in extracting customized subsets of selected data files through the ICPSR online data analysis system, and (3) assistance with the retrieval and use of files obtained from the archive.

NACJD has over 1000 criminal justice study titles. Criminal justice data are available in 12 topical areas: (1) attitude surveys; (2) community studies; (3) corrections; (4) court case processing; (5) courts; (6) criminal justice system; (7) crime and delinquency; (8) official statistics; (9) police; (10) victimization; (11) drugs, alcohol, and crime; and (12) computer programs and instructional packages. NACJD has created online Resource Guides to highlight popular criminal justice research topics and provide important information about complex data collections. Table VI shows the complex data collections for which online Resource Guides are available and their Web sites.

Table IV Data Series in the National Archive of Computerized Data on Aging (NACDA)[a]

ABC News/Washington Post Poll Series
American Housing Survey Series
Americans' Use of Time Series
Annual Survey of Governments Series
Census of Population and Housing, 1960 [United States] Series
Census of Population and Housing, 1970 [United States] Series
Census of Population and Housing, 1980 [United States] Series
Census of Population and Housing, 1990 [United States] Series
Census of Population and Housing, 2000 [United States] Series
Center for Research on Social Reality [Spain] Survey Series
Civil War Veterans Series
Community Tracking Study Series
Consumer Expenditure Survey Series
Cost of Living Survey Series
Current Population Survey Series
Detroit Area Studies Series
The Dynamics of Population Aging in ECE Countries
Economics of American Negro Slavery Series
Eurobarometer Survey Series
General Social Survey Series
German Social Survey (ALLBUS) Series
High School and Beyond (HS&B) Series
Immigrants Admitted to the United States Series
Intergenerational Study of Parents and Children, 1962–1985: [Detroit] Series
Knowledge, Attitudes, and Practice of Contraception in Taiwan (KAP) Series
Marital Instability Over the Life Course Series
Medicare Current Beneficiary Survey Series
Mortality Detail Files Series
Multiple Cause of Death Series
National Ambulatory Medical Care Survey Series
National Education Longitudinal Study of 1988 (NELS) Series
National Health and Nutrition Examination Survey (NHANES) and Followup Series
National Health Examination Surveys, Cycles I–III Series
National Health Interview Survey Series
National Home and Hospice Care Survey Series
National Hospital Ambulatory Medical Care Survey Series
National Hospital Discharge Survey Series
National Longitudinal Study of the Class of 1972 Series
National Longitudinal Surveys of Labor Market Experience Series
National Medical Expenditure Survey Series
National Mortality Followback Survey Series
National Nursing Home Survey Series
National Postsecondary Student Aid Study (NPSAS) Series
National Survey of Black Americans Series
National Survey of Families and Households Series
Nationwide Personal Transportation Survey Series
Panel Study of Income Dynamics (PSID) Series
RAND Aging Studies in the Developing World Series
Retirement History Longitudinal Survey Series
State and Metropolitan Area Data Book [United States] Series
Status of Older Persons in Economic Commission for Europe (ECE) Countries, Census Microdata Samples Series
Survey of Consumer Attitudes and Behavior Series
Survey of Consumer Finances Series
Survey of Income and Program Participation (SIPP) Series
Vital Statistics: Marriage Detail [United States] Series
Youth Studies Series

[a] From NACDA Web site at http://www.icpsr.umich.edu/NACDA/archive.html#05

Table V NACDA Data Collections Available for Online Statistical Analysis[a]

Longitudinal Study of Aging, 70 Years and Over, 1984–1990
Multiple Cause of Death, 1999
National Survey Of Self-Care And Aging: Follow-Up, 1994
National Health and Nutrition Examination Survey II: Mortality Study, 1992
National Hospital Discharge Surveys, 1994–1997, 1999–2001
National Health Interview Survey, 1994, Second Supplement On Aging

[a] From NACDA Web site at: http://www.icpsr.umich.edu/NACDA/das.html

NACJD also has ICPSR's most extensive collection of geocoded data, and tools and other resources for computerized mapping and spatial analysis. NACJD has an online tutorial for using data with geographic information system (GIS) software and the CrimeMapTutorial, a program (available for downloading) that enables students to learn crime mapping from their desktop or laptop computers at home or at work and that is designed for self-paced instruction. NACJD also provides access to CrimeStat, a spatial statistics program for the analysis of crime incident locations. NACJD crime mapping resources can be accessed at the ICPSR NACJD Web site.

Health and Medical Care Archive

The HMCA preserves and disseminates data collected by research projects funded by The Robert Wood Johnson (RWJ) Foundation, the largest philanthropy

Table VI Resource Guides for Complex NACJD Data Collections[a]

Collections	*Web site*
Capital Punishment in the United States	http://www.icpsr.umich.edu/NACJD/CP/index.html
Chicago Women's Health Risk Study	http://www.icpsr.umich.edu/NACJD/HELP/faq3002.html
Expenditure and Employment Data for the Criminal Justice System	http://www.icpsr.umich.edu/NACJD/EECJS/index.html
Law Enforcement Management and Administrative Statistics	http://www.icpsr.umich.edu/NACJD/LEMAS/index.html
National Corrections Reporting Program Data	http://www.icpsr.umich.edu/NACJD/NCRP/index.html
National Crime Victimization Survey Data	http://www.icpsr.umich.edu/NACJD/NCVS/index.html
National Incident-Based Reporting System Data	http://www.icpsr.umich.edu/NACJD/NIBRS/index.html
Survey of Inmates in State and Federal Correctional Facilities	http://www.icpsr.umich.edu/NACJD/SISFCF/index.html
Uniform Crime Reporting Program	http://www.icpsr.umich.edu/NACJD/ucr.html

[a] From NACJD Website at http://www.icpsr.umich.edu/NACJD/archive.html#resguide

devoted exclusively to health and health care in the United States.

The RWJ Foundation designates projects that it funds to submit their data to HMCA when it believes that secondary analysis would further its major prevention and health improvement goals. The four topical areas of data in the HMCA are (1) data about health care providers, (2) data about cost and access to health care, (3) data about substance abuse and health, and (4) data about chronic health conditions. (See the ICPSR HMCA Web site.)

Substance Abuse and Mental Health Data Archive

The SAMHDA promotes the use of substance abuse and mental health research data to understand and assess substance abuse and mental health problems and the impact of related treatment systems. SAMHDA data collections include large surveys and administrative record data about substance abuse and mental health. A list of the SAMHDA collections is shown in Table VII; a large number of these studies are available for online data analysis (marked with an asterisk in Table VII). (See the ICPSR SAMHDA Web site.)

Table VII Major Data Collections in the Substance Abuse and Mental Health Data Archive (SAMHDA) at ICPSR[a]

Substance Abuse Collections
Alcohol and Drug Services Study (ADSS)
Cooperative Agreement for AIDS Community-Based Outreach/Intervention Research Program
(Washington) DC Metropolitan Area Drug Study (DC*MADS)*
Drug Abuse Treatment Outcomes Study (DATOS)*
Drug Abuse Warning Network (DAWN)*
Drug Services Research Survey (DSRS)
Health Behavior in School-aged Children (HBSC)*
Monitoring the Future (MTF)*
National Household Survey on Drug Abuse (NHSDA)*
National Pregnancy and Health Survey (NPHS)*
National Survey of Substance Abuse Treatment Services (N-SSATS)*
National Treatment Improvement Evaluation Study (NTIES)*
Services Research Outcomes Study (SROS)
Substance Abuse Treatment Cost Allocation and Analysis Template (SATCAAT)*
Treatment Episode Data Set (TEDS)*
Mental Health Collections
Gambling Impact and Behavior Study*
National Comorbidity Survey*
National Youth Survey (NYS)
Policy Research on Aging and Mental Health Services (PRAMHS)

[a] From SAMHDA Web site at http://www.icpsr.umich.edu/SAMHDA/archive.html#04. Studies marked with an * are available for on-line statistical analysis.

International Archive of Education Data

The IAED archives and disseminates data about education inputs (funding, personnel, teaching resources, facilities, and teacher and student preparation), teaching and learning processes, and education outputs (graduation and matriculation rates, drop-out rates, test scores, job placements, life histories, and life assessments). The IAED is supported by the National Center for Education Statistics of the U.S. Department of Education. Data collections in the IAED are grouped into 10 categories of studies: (1) elementary/secondary surveys, (2) postsecondary surveys, (3) longitudinal surveys, (4) educational assessment, (5) libraries, (6) crime in schools, (7) census in education, (8) vocational education, (9) international education studies, and (10) museum studies. The ICPSR IAED Web site provides listings of specific studies in these categories and also provides information about education research data found at a number of other locations, including the National Center for Educational Statistics.

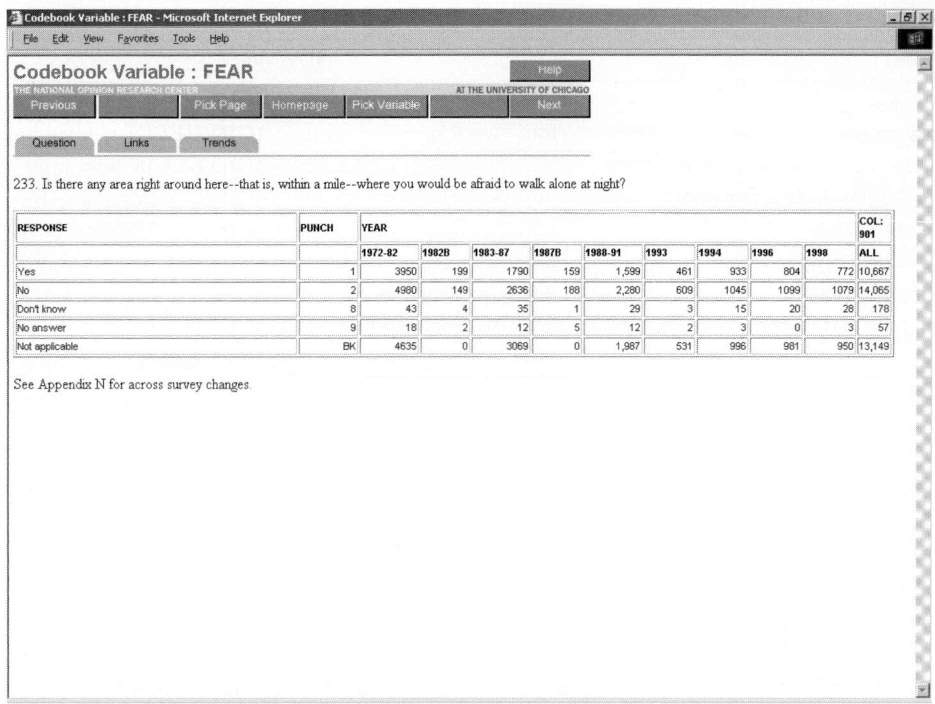

RESPONSE	PUNCH	YEAR									COL: 901
		1972-82	1982B	1983-87	1987B	1988-91	1993	1994	1996	1998	ALL
Yes	1	3950	199	1790	159	1,599	461	933	804	772	10,667
No	2	4980	149	2636	188	2,280	609	1045	1099	1079	14,065
Don't know	8	43	4	35	1	29	3	15	20	28	178
No answer	9	18	2	12	5	12	2	3	0	3	57
Not applicable	BK	4635	0	3069	0	1,987	531	996	981	950	13,149

Figure 2 Example variable-level search and frequency distribution from the ICPSR GSS Web site. *Source:* ICPSR Web site at http://www.icpsr.umich.edu:8080/GSS/homepage.htm, with permission.

Other ICPSR Topical Sites

Although not identified as specific topical archives, ICPSR maintains some other specific Web site collections of data, related documentation, and user tools about (1) Census 2000, (2) Election 2000, and (3) the General Social Survey (GSS).

The Census 2000 Web site has already been mentioned. It functions in much the same way as a topical archive by providing information about Census 2000 data, access to the data files, and other information about using the data or training opportunities related to the data.

Election 2000 is very similar to the Census 2000 Web site. It provides information about data in the ICPSR archive pertaining to the 2000 national and state elections and related public opinion polls. (See the ICPSR Election 2000 Web site.)

The GSS Web site is one of the most detailed topical sites at ICPSR. With National Science Foundation and ICPSR support, NORC, the GSS producer, and ICPSR have collaborated to create an online resource for learning about and doing data analysis and other research with the GSS. One of the most innovative features of the site is that users can do variable-level searches of questions asked in the GSS. This is especially useful because over the 34-year history of the survey, 3260 different questions have been asked across the varying time periods. Once the user locates a particular variable, the user can obtain the question text for that variable and frequency distributions of responses to that question for the years it was asked.

For example, Fig. 2 shows the results for searching for a fear-of-crime variable named FEAR. The specific question text is given along with the distribution of responses over the different periods the question was asked.

New Developments and New Tools at ICPSR

Since Myron Gutmann became director of ICPSR in 2001, a number of new capabilities and tools have been developed and implemented at ICPSR. The first of these, ICPSR Direct, has already been mentioned. ICPSR Direct allows individual users at ICPSR member institutions to access and download data collections on their own. Users at member institutions that have enrolled in ICPSR Direct no longer need to obtain data collections by having the ICPSR OR for the institution download and transfer a data collection.

ICPSR has become more actively involved with providing data collections that have been developed specifically for instructional use. In the past, ICPSR has supported the development of a few teaching-oriented data sets from the National Election Studies. More recently, however, ICPSR has given a renewed focus to data for instruction by creating the Site for

Instructional Materials and Information (SIMI). SIMI is an effort by ICPSR to expand the number and quality of data collections designed specifically for instructional use in substantive or methodological undergraduate and graduate courses. Many of ICPSR's data collections require intensive file management and variable transformations once the data files, syntax files, and documentation have been downloaded to a user's computer. These tasks deter inexperienced student data analysts from conducting empirical research for college classes. They also deter faculty from including empirical exercises as part of a course. Under the general leadership of an ICPSR subcommittee and a group of interested faculty, SIMI has become an ICPSR topical Web site where faculty can submit data sets they have developed for instructional purposes, along with accompanying documentation and course materials. ICPSR uses member institution faculty to review these submissions to ensure that the data are clearly documented and their use in assignments or exercises is clearly explained. Once this review has been done, instructional modules are loaded onto the ICPSR SIMI Web site. There were over 45 instructional modules available as of January 2004.

ICPSR is also interested in developing new topical collections of data. One that is beginning to come to fruition is the Child Care Research Collaboration and Archive (CCRCA). This new topical archive will preserve and disseminate child-care data with the support of the DHHS. It is part of a larger collaborative project with Columbia University's National Center for Children in Poverty. Another area that has been identified in preliminary discussions is a topical archive on population and demographic data.

New developments at ICPSR have also occurred in regard to tools that assist users in their research. In conjunction with work to revise and improve its Web site, ICPSR created a controlled vocabulary system. At the heart of this system are three databases that are used by the ICPSR staff and users: a social science subject thesaurus, a geographic names thesaurus, and a personal names authority list. Of most interest to the user community is the social science subject thesaurus, an alphabetical listing of social science subject terms from the disciplines represented in the ICPSR data collections. It is available for online searching for data collections, as well as for downloading to use in other applications.

Another related tool that ICPSR has developed with National Science Foundation support is a Social Science Variables Database (SSVD). The variables database allows searching at the variable level across studies. The variables database contains over 33,000 discrete variables and can be accessed at the ICPSR SSVD Web site. To search the variables database, a user types in a search term (see Fig. 3), which then returns a list of studies in which the search term links to a variable name (see Fig. 4). From that list, a user can see information

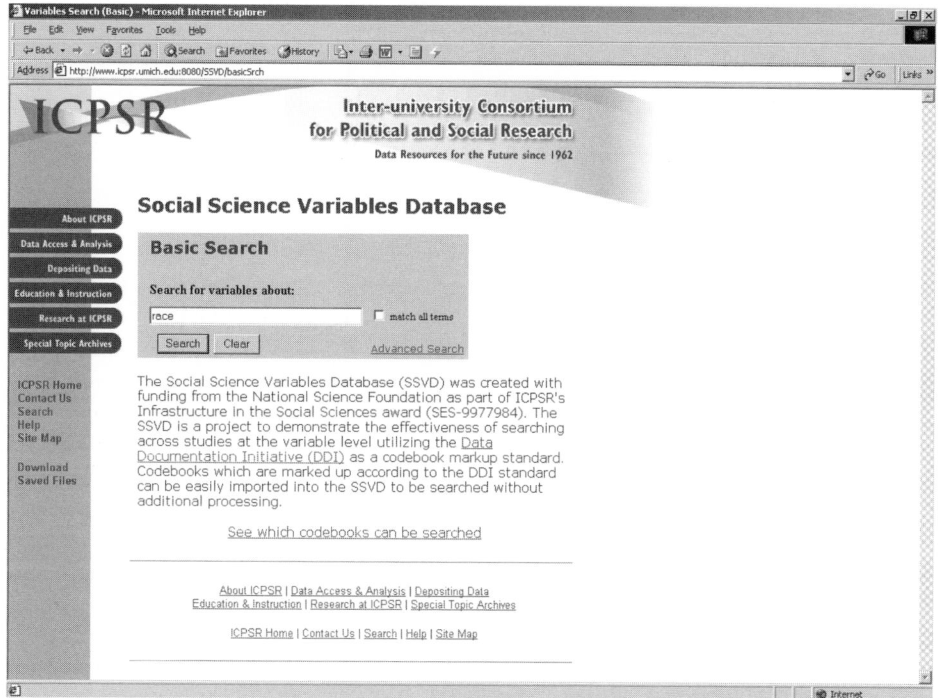

Figure 3 Social science variables database search entry window. *Source:* ICPSR SSVD Web site at http://www.icpsr.umich.edu:8080/SSVD/basicSrch, with permission.

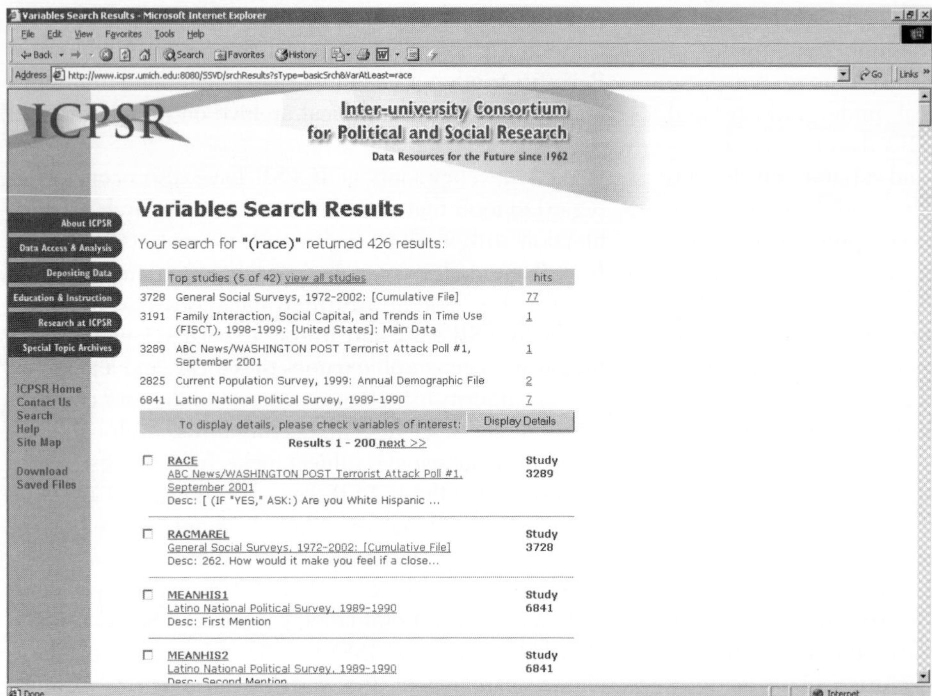

Figure 4 Variable level search results for "race." *Source:* ICPSR SSVD Web site at http://www.icpsr.umich.edu:8080/SSVD/srchResults?sType=basicSrch&VarAtLeast=race, with permission.

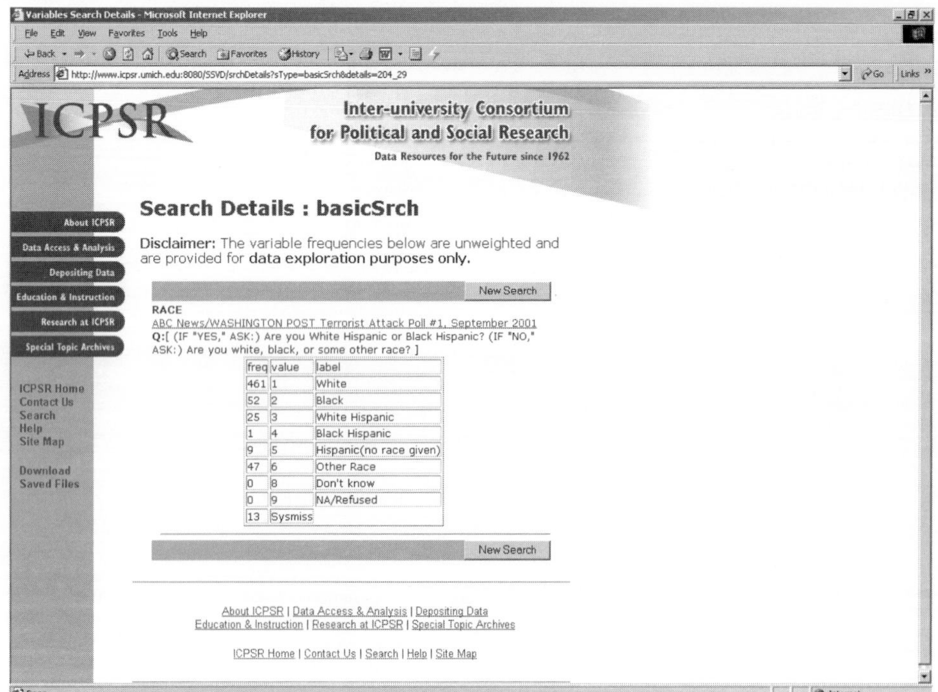

freq	value	label
461	1	White
52	2	Black
25	3	White Hispanic
1	4	Black Hispanic
9	5	Hispanic(no race given)
47	6	Other Race
0	8	Don't know
0	9	NA/Refused
13	Sysmiss	

Figure 5 Variable level search detail results for race, first study listed. *Source:* ICPSR SSVD Web site at http://www.icpsr.umich.edu: 8080/SSVD/srchDetails?sType=basicSrch&details=204_29, with permission.

about the question text for that variable and its frequency distribution (see Fig. 5). The variables database should greatly facilitate research on measurement comparisons and item construction.

Conclusion

ICPSR recently celebrated its fortieth anniversary in October 2003 with a public colloquium on the future of the census given by former Census Bureau director, Kenneth Prewitt, during ICPSR's biennial meeting of ORs. At that gathering, many people gave testimonials about the value and many contributions that ICPSR has made to the social sciences. Past performance notwithstanding, information technology and applications grow exponentially and provide many new capabilities annually. Many people have an erroneous view that ICPSR is just a warehouse for data. Nothing could be further from the truth. During the past 10 years, ICPSR has embraced the capabilities of the Internet and WWW, growing from a tape-copying operation to a sophisticated Web-based organization linking individual users dynamically to data sets, smart documentation, online statistical analysis, data and table extraction tools, and automated computer programs for analyzing complex data sets. In the past 2 years, ICPSR has completed the conversion of half a million pages of paper data set documentation to electronic format and developed the capability to search that documentation at the variable level across studies. ICPSR is collaborating with researchers on new difficult issues involved in protecting the confidentiality of microdata about human subjects in a contradictory environment in which there is public and political demand for enhanced protection of privacy juxtaposed with information technology and data producers capable of creating linked data sets with massive amounts of personal information from multiple sources and agencies. All in all, the state of social science data at ICPSR is excellent. Never before have social scientists had such easy and rapid access to so much data from so many different sources with so many tools to facilitate learning about and using the data accurately and correctly.

See Also the Following Articles

Census, Varieties and Uses of Data • Computerized Record Linkage and Statistical Matching • Web-Based Survey

Further Reading

American Political Science Association. (1982). *Setups: American Politics*. Study #7368 [computer file]. Available from ICPSR, Ann Arbor, MI.

Azar, E. E. (1993). Conflict And Peace Data Bank (COPDAB), 1948–1978. Study #7767 [computer file]. 3rd rel. University of Maryland, Center for International Development and Conflict Management, College Park, MD. Available from ICPSR, Ann Arbor, MI.

Blalock, H., Allan, G. B., Holt, R. T., Rowe, J. S., and Sprague, J. (1989). *Report of the ICPSR Review Committee*. ICPSR, Ann Arbor, MI.

Federal Reserve System. Survey of Consumer Finances. http://www.federalreserve.gov/pubs/oss/oss2/scfindex.html

Frantilla, A. (1998). *Social Science in the Public Interest: A Fiftieth-Year History of the Institute for Social Research*. Bulletin No. 45. Bentley Historical Library, University of Michigan, Ann Arbor, MI.

Inter-University Consortium of Political and Social Research (ICPSR). Census 2000. http://www.icpsr.umich.edu/CENSUS2000/

Inter-University Consortium for Political and Social Research. Election 2000. http://www.icpsr.umich.edu/ELECTION/2000/index.html

Inter-University Consortium for Political and Social Research. General Social Survey. http://www.icpsr.umich.edu:8080/GSS/homepage.htm

Inter-University Consortium for Political and Social Research. Health and Medical Care Archive. http://www.icpsr.umich.edu/HMCA/archive.html

Inter-University Consortium for Political and Social Research. International Archive of Education Data. http://www.icpsr.umich.edu/IAED/welcome.html

Inter-University Consortium for Political and Social Research. National Archive of Computerized Data on Aging. http://www.icpsr.umich.edu/NACDA/das.html

Inter-University Consortium for Political and Social Research. National Archive of Criminal Justice Data crime mapping resources. http://www.icpsr.umich.edu/NACJD/GIS/resources.html

Inter-University Consortium for Political and Social Research. Site for Instructional Materials and Information. http://www.icpsr.umich.edu/SIMI/index.html

Inter-University Consortium for Political and Social Research. Social Science Variables Database. http://www.icpsr.umich.edu:8080/SSVD/basicSrch

Inter-University Consortium for Political and Social Research. Substance Abuse and Mental Health Data Archive. http://www.icpsr.umich.edu/SAMHDA/welcome.html

Inter-University Consortium for Political and Social Research. (1982). *Guide to Resources and Services 1982–1983*. ICPSR, Ann Arbor, MI.

Inter-University Consortium for Political and Social Research. (1982). *United Nations Roll Call Data, 1946–1985*. Study #5512 [computer file]. ICPSR, Ann Arbor, MI.

Inter-University Consortium for Political and Social Research. (1999). *United States Historical Election Returns, 1824–1968*. Study #1 [computer file]. 2nd Ed. ICPSR, Ann Arbor, MI.

Inter-University Consortium for Political and Social Research. (2001). *United States Congressional Roll Call Voting Records, 1789–1990*. Study #4, Pts. 1–202 [computer file]. ICPSR, Ann Arbor, MI.

Inter-University Consortium for Political and Social Research. (2002). *2001–2002 Annual Report.* ICPSR, Ann Arbor, MI.

Inter-University Consortium for Political and Social Research. (2002). *2001–2002 Annual Report Appendices.* ICPSR, Ann Arbor, MI.

National Opinion Research Center. Survey of Consumer Finances. http://www.norc.uchicago.edu/issues/ecopop4.asp

Survey of Consumer Attitudes and Behavior. http://www.sca.isr.umich.edu/

Taylor, C. L., and Amm, J. (1990). *National Capability Data: Annual Series, 1950–1988.* Study #9904 [computer file]. Blacksburg, VA: Charles Lewis Taylor and Joachim Amm, Virginia Polytechnic Institute and State University, Blacksburg VA. Available from ICPSR, Ann Arbor, MI.

U.S. Census Bureau. http://www.census.gov/hhes/www/ahs.html

U.S. Census Bureau. Survey of Income and Program Participation. http://www.sipp.census.gov/sipp/vs.html

U.S. Bureau of Labor Statistics. Current Population Survey. http://www.bls.census.gov/cps/overmain.htm

U.S. Bureau of Labor Statistics. Consumer Expenditure Survey. http://www.bls.gov/cex/home.htm

U.S. Department of Housing and Urban Development. http://www.huduser.org/datasets/ahs.html

International Economics

Bhajan S. Grewal
Victoria University, Melbourne, Australia

Peter J. Sheehan
Victoria University, Melbourne, Australia

Glossary

Atlas conversion factor Used by the World Bank to reduce the impact of exchange rate fluctuations in cross-country comparisons of national income. For any given year, the Atlas conversion factor is the average of a country's exchange rate for that year and its exchange rates for the two preceding years, adjusted for the difference between the rate of inflation in that country and in the G5 countries (France, Germany, Japan, the United Kingdom, and the United States).

Basel II The New Basel Capital Accord issued in April 2003 by the Basel Committee on Banking Supervision. In 1988, the Committee introduced a capital measurement system that became commonly known as the Basel Capital Accord. The Basel II framework aims to introduce more effective supervisory standards for banking institutions.

knowledge-based economy An economy in which research and development, innovation, and the application of knowledge are widespread in all sectors.

purchasing power parity A comparison between any two or more currencies, on the basis of the real purchasing power of the currencies over a common basket of goods and services, rather than on the basis of market exchange rates.

Social measurement involves quantification of different aspects of social phenomena. Increasingly, the search for greater precision, rigor, and accuracy has driven social scientists toward substituting, when possible, the subjective with the objective and the qualitative with the quantitative. The ascendancy of multinational firms and the process of globalization have resulted, in recent years, in a sharp rise in internationalization of production of goods and services (business) and international flows of capital (finance) and of goods and services (trade). These trends have been accompanied by rapidly increasing applications of social measurement techniques in international business, finance, and trade.

Aims of Social Measurement

The principal aim of social measurement is to provide quantitative values of the numerous variables that influence economic and social phenomena. Analysts, policymakers, and other users of such information need to assess these variables with greater precision to gain better understanding of the nature of the underlying concepts and of the changes in the social indicators over time and across regions and nations. Because the concepts and the variables do not always lend themselves to easy quantification, the challenges in social measurement are not only to devise appropriate measures, but also to continue to improve the existing measures.

Role of Social Measurement in International Economics

International economics deals with issues arising from economic interaction among sovereign nations; fields such as international trade, international financial flows, international aid and technical assistance for developing countries, international migration, and exchange rate regimes present international economic challenges. In each of these areas, there are numerous examples of the application of quantitative measurements to analyze the issues and evaluate the solutions. The use of social measurement is particularly important in specific fields of international economics—namely, international business, finance, and trade. These three specific examples have been selected with a view to demonstrating the relevance and the significance of social measurement in relation to purchasing power parity of national currencies, assessments of sovereign credit risk, and the impact of the knowledge economy.

Examples of Social Measurement

International Business: Purchasing Power Parity and International Comparisons

What is Purchasing Power Parity?

Purchasing power parity (PPP) is a form of exchange rate that takes into account the cost of a common basket of goods and services in the two countries compared. PPPs are often expressed in U.S. dollars. Therefore, the PPP between the U.S. dollar and another currency is the exchange rate that would be required to purchase the same quantity of goods and services locally that cost $1 in the United States. Thus, the PPP between any two currencies is the measure of the actual purchasing power of those currencies at a given point in time for buying a given basket of goods and services. As the World Bank explained in its 2002 report *The International Comparison Programme and Purchasing Power Parities*, the PPP for, say, the Indonesian rupiah against the U.S. dollar is defined as the number of rupiahs needed to buy, in Indonesia, the same amount of goods and services as $1 (U.S.) would buy in the United States.

Major Users of PPPs

The Organization of Economic Cooperation and Development (OECD)–Eurostat PPP program was first established at the OECD in 1980 with the aim of providing statistical measures for enabling price and volume comparisons of gross domestic product (GDP) and its components for the OECD member countries. Successive rounds in 1985, 1990, 1993, 1996, and 1999 have resulted in extended coverage from 18 to 43 countries. Procedures for collection of data have also been refined in the process.

The OECD multilateral benchmark studies incorporate price and expenditure data from all the countries included in the comparisons. In addition to the goods and services on the markets being compared, PPPs take into account the economic structure and the market composition in each country. Complexities arise from the different markets for consumers and investments and from the variety of goods and services consumed in different countries. Parallel work is also proceeding through the World Bank and the Statistical Commission of the United Nations, under the auspices of the International Comparison Program (ICP), to extend the coverage of PPP countries not currently covered by the OECD–Eurostat PPP program. Originally launched in 1968 to cover only a small group of countries, the ICP now covers 160 countries in all regions of the world.

Over the past 20 years, the use of PPP-based conversions has grown rapidly, and many users, such as universities, research institutes, international banks, multinational companies and international organizations, have started to use PPPs in making international comparisons.

Significance of PPPs in International Economics

International comparisons of economic performance, standard of living, and productivity of labor force are made every day, for a variety of reasons, by international organizations (such as the United Nations, the World Bank, or the OECD), international banks, multinational companies, tourists and travelers, and researchers. The World Bank also publishes comparisons of national output, not only for individual countries but also for "low-income" or "high-income" groupings of countries. Aggregations and comparisons of this nature require that output be converted into a common currency, i.e., a common unit of value. Often, the U.S. dollar or the Euro is used as the common currency for this purpose. Conversion of national outputs of individual countries to the U.S. dollar basis, for example, is conventionally done by using market exchange rates, which are the rates at which national currencies are officially converted to the U.S. dollar at the relevant time. Because market exchange rates change all the time, generally an average of the exchange rates for a year may be used for representing annual figures. The World Bank irons out fluctuations in exchange rates by using a moving average of 3 years in its Atlas method of reporting.

In recent years, international organizations have also started to calculate and use purchasing power parities for converting variables such as national output or consumption to U.S. dollars. Thus, the World Bank now publishes figures for all countries based on both the exchange rate conversion and the PPPs in its annual *World Development Report*. For most countries, but particularly for the low-income countries, the amounts yielded by the two approaches are very different. Figures for a selected group of countries published in the *World Development Report 2003* are presented in Table I for illustration. It should be noted from Table I that, when converted into PPP gross national income, figures for all countries except Japan, Singapore, and the United States increase

Table I Gross National Income 2001: Two Methods of Measurement[a]

	Gross national income		*PPP gross national income*[b]	
Country	*Billion U.S.$*	*% (of world)*	*Billion U.S.$*	*% (of world)*
Argentina	261.0	0.83	438	0.94
Australia	383.3	1.22	500	1.08
Bangladesh	49.9	0.16	224	0.48
China	1131.0	3.59	5415	11.67
Germany	1948.0	6.18	2098	4.52
India	474.3	1.51	2530	5.45
Japan	4574.2	14.52	3487	7.51
Singapore	99.4	0.32	100	0.22
United Kingdom	1451.4	4.61	1466	3.16
United States	9900.7	31.43	9902	21.34
Low income	1069.1	3.39	5134	11.06
Middle income	4922	15.63	15,235	32.83
High income	25,506.4	80.97	26,431	56.96
World	31,500	100.00	46,403	100.00

[a] Data from *World Development Report 2003* (World Bank, 2003).
[b] PPP, purchasing power parity.

in comparison to the exchange rate-based figures. Significantly, the PPP measures also have the consequence of narrowing the divergence between the low-income countries and the high-income countries. Instead of accounting for only 3.4% of the world economy, the low-income countries now account for 11% of the world economy.

In view of the deficiencies of international comparisons based on exchange rates, PPP is increasingly recognized as a more reliable measure for international comparisons of output, standard of living, and quality of life. Measurements of output based on exchange rates are now increasingly considered to be inappropriate and potentially misleading for making international comparisons. This is because exchange rates are determined by a multitude of factors and generally are not reliable measures of output. At any given time, many countries are known to have exchange rates that are either undervalued or overvalued, but are maintained by their governments for other considerations, such as export promotion or import substitution. The use of such exchange rates for international comparisons is likely to introduce distortions. As the World Bank acknowledges in the *World Bank Development Report 2003*, nominal exchange rates do not always reflect international differences in relative prices.

PPPs and Climate Change

The proper measurement of national output is not an end in itself. As the following example illustrates, proper measurement of output assists the users in making more meaningful judgments about a wide range of economic and social phenomena in which the level of national output is directly or indirectly important—for example, climate change during the course of the 21st century. In 2001, the International Panel on Climate Change (IPCC) released its Special Report on Emission Scenarios (SRES). The purpose of this report was to assess the extent to which emissions of greenhouse gases may lead to a rise in global temperatures on Earth. Because emissions of greenhouse gases in a country are a function of its economic growth, the IPCC made separate projections of economic growth in developing and developed countries over the period 1990–2100, and reported that, based on these projections of growth in national output, global temperatures were projected to increase between 1.4° and 5.8°C over the period 1990–2100. These projections subsequently became what *The Economist* (February 15, 2003) described as the most frequently cited numbers in the field of environmental policy, and quite possibly the most widely cited numbers in any field of public policy. Significantly, the main reason for the controversy that surrounded these numbers was related to the use (or the absence of the use, in this case) of PPPs in estimating national output.

Critics of the IPCC projections argued that the SRES had calculated the rates of growth in the world GDP using market exchange rates. They further argued that, similar to the effect noted in Table I, the use of market exchange rates had the effect of understating the share of the economies of the developing countries in the world economy in 1990, and correspondingly overestimating the rates of GDP growth that the developing countries would achieve in catching up with the developed countries during the 21st century. Because higher rates of growth are associated with higher levels of emissions of greenhouse gases, overestimation of rates of growth by IPCC resulted in a corresponding overestimation of levels of emissions and mean temperatures. The authors of the SRES responded sharply to this critique, arguing that SRES did indeed use both PPPs and market exchange rates, and that market exchange rates are appropriate for certain relevant purposes.

Calculation of PPPs

Calculation of PPPs involves sophisticated and rigorous procedures for selecting the products to be compared, collecting prices of these products, deriving average prices for the whole of a country and a particular year, and determining weights in compiling price indices for groups of products that constitute appropriate headings (such as gross private consumption, gross agricultural or industrial output, and so on). The World Bank and the OECD now coordinate the compilation of PPPs under the International Comparison Program (ICP). The *ICP Handbook 2004*, published by the World Bank in 2003, provides more detail on the procedure for calculating PPPs.

Limitations of PPPs

Notwithstanding increasing acceptance and popularity, PPPs are not without limitations, and are not going to replace exchange rate-based comparisons of international data. PPP rates are based on a limited set of observations and are not free from sampling errors. The World Bank acknowledges that although efforts are made to correct for quality differences, the ICP faces the problem of matching "like with like," which, in some areas, such as services, may be difficult. One problem is that in some cases, price surveys do not cover the entire country or the entire year. As a result, the prices used in PPP calculation may not reflect fully the average national price prevailing in the country under investigation. For nonbenchmark countries, PPP data are basically desk estimates based on regression equations. Consequently, more caution should be exercised when interpreting PPPs for services.

Sovereign Credit Risk Ratings and International Finance

Introduction

Sovereign credit risk ratings, which play a major role in modern international finance, are another example of social measurement in the field of international economics. International movement of capital has been a key feature of globalization, as banks, superannuation funds, managed investment funds, and hedge funds all invest huge amounts in bonds and securities issued by borrowers from all parts of the world.

Both governments and firms borrow funds domestically and internationally to finance their investment projects. The governments of all those countries that borrow funds in the international capital market are obliged to obtain credit risk ratings for their bonds because investors generally prefer to invest in rated rather that unrated securities. Indeed, financial regulators in most developed countries allow their banks to invest only in investment-grade securities. Accordingly, demand for credit ratings comes not only from both borrowers and lenders, but also from financial regulators, such as the Securities and Exchange Commission (SEC) in the United States. Because the key function of sovereign credit ratings is to provide credible information about the risk involved in investment in underlying securities, the independence and the technical competence of the rating organizations are of paramount importance. The number of rating agencies in the business of assessing sovereign credit risk varies from time to time, but the business is dominated by three or four large international rating agencies, including Moody's Investor Services, Standard and Poor's Rating Services, Fitch International Services, and International Bank Credit Analysis.

Although each rating agency follows its own distinctive methodology and procedures, in general, the process of credit rating involves reviewing a broad range of economic, financial, social, and political information on the sovereign and the country, with a view to assessing the ability of the sovereign to meet its debt obligations in a timely manner, according to the contractual conditions of the transaction. Typically, an international rating agency has branch offices around the world and its staff will interview government officials, business leaders, and others for assessing all factors that could affect the capacity of the sovereign in this regard. When the rating agency has formed a preliminary view about the rating to be assigned in a particular case, typically the sovereign is invited to respond confidentially to the assessment, including by making presentations to the rating agency personnel. Before the credit rating is finalized for publication, a final opportunity is provided to the sovereign for contesting the assessment, if necessary, by providing additional information or analysis. Once published, credit ratings are kept under regular review and are updated as warranted by any change in the underlying assumptions and conditions.

Sovereign Risk

Lenders always take into account the risk of default or interruptions in repayments by borrowers. A government's potential inability to service its debt obligations is the main risk underlying sovereign risk. If a government suddenly stops repayments, a loss of income would occur for the bondholders. Sovereign defaults were more frequent in the 1920s and 1930s than they have been after World War II. Generally, outright repudiation of foreign debt is quite rare now and the most common form of default is a temporary disruption in repayments, which requires a rescheduling of debt. Thus, the real risk loss of income and/or capital that may occur is due to such rescheduling of debt.

Rating of Sovereign Risk

A sovereign credit risk rating is an assessment of creditworthiness of a national government and it reflects the degree of confidence that creditors can place on the ability of that government to honor its international debt obligations as they fall due. Thus, for example, a triple-A rating assigned to a government indicates to the lenders that its creditworthiness is excellent and that securities issued by that government are investment grade (see Table II). This assessment would in turn be reflected in the high yield that the lenders would expect from their investment in the bonds issued by such a sovereign.

Many of the factors taken into account by the rating agencies are not quantifiable. Even for those factors that are quantifiable, it is not always clear how relative weights to such factors ought to be assigned and what their influence on final ratings ought to be. In their desire to isolate the most crucial factors, some economists have attempted to second-guess the rating agencies by seeking to replicate the ratings of the rating agencies. For example, one study showed that it was possible to match closely the September 1995 sovereign ratings by Moody's and Standard and Poor's for a sample of countries. The study showed that high credit ratings were positively correlated with per capita income, GDP growth, price stability, and the absence of debt defaults. Although economic development (measured by the level of industrialization of a country) and external debt were also positively correlated, fiscal balance and external balance were not.

Table II Typical Sovereign Credit Risk Ratings of Long-Term Debt[a]

Moody's	*Standard and Poor's*	*Basel II risk-weights*	*Interpretation*
Aaa	AAA	0%	Highest quality
Aa1	AA+	0%	High quality
Aa2	AA	0%	
Aa3	AA−	0%	
A1	A+	20%	Strong payment capacity
A2	A	20%	
A3	A−	20%	
Baa1	BBB+	50%	Adequate payment capacity
Baa2	BBB	50%	
Baa3	BBB−	50%	
Ba1	BB+	100%	Speculative grade
Ba2	BB	100%	
Ba3	BB−	100%	
B1	B+	100%	High-risk obligations
B2	B	100%	
B3	B−	100%	

[a] Data from Cantor and Packer (1996) and Claessens and Embrechts (2002).

Note: To date, agencies have not assigned sovereign ratings below B3 or B−.

The Principle of Sovereign Ceiling

Sovereign ceiling refers to a practice, followed with rare exceptions by international credit rating agencies, according to which any public or private organization from a country is not rated higher than the rating assigned to its sovereign. For example, if the sovereign of a nation has been rated at AA by Standard and Poor's or Aa2 by Moody's, none of the other entities from that country can be rated higher than that rating. The underlying logic of the sovereign ceiling principle is that a financially distressed sovereign government would be likely to impose exchange controls or otherwise interfere with the ability of domestic firms to service their external debt. An exception to this principle occurs, however, when an internationally oriented corporate borrower structures an offshore collateral arrangement under which borrowed funds would never enter the country in which the corporation is domiciled. According to the Basel Committee on Banking Supervision, Standard and Poor's and Fitch are also willing to make exceptions to the sovereign ceiling principle for a high-quality corporate issue domiciled in a low-rated country with a "dollarized" economy, such as Argentina.

Significance of Sovereign Credit Risk Ratings

In addition to their impact on bond yield spreads, sovereign ratings also have an impact on stock prices in the countries for which the ratings are assessed. Indeed, researchers have found that the impact of a ratings downgrade for a particular country may go well beyond the stock markets of that country, impacting those of the neighboring countries as well. During the Asian financial crisis of 1997–1998, a contagion effect of this nature was seen to be the source of spreading the crisis from one country to another.

Sovereign ratings are also considered to be important indicators of fiscal discipline and of the ability of a government to manage the economy. Thus, government ministers, officials, and media generally attach considerable importance to the level of and variations in an international credit rating. Indeed, in Australia, employment contracts of some of the senior government officials have been known to include performance indicators involving the upgrading of the credit rating to the next higher level, the achievement of which would be rewarded by a predetermined bonus.

Because credit ratings are always used by lenders in conjunction with many other considerations, including their own internal credit assessments, and because credit ratings always leave room for subjective considerations, such as the ability of a government to defy trade union pressure for higher wages, the impact of sovereign credit ratings cannot be determined with any degree of precision. It is difficult to say, for example, that a variation in credit ratings of a country was responsible for a particular event. Consistent with this caveat, results of research on the causality from risk ratings to level of bond yields remain inconclusive. Before the Asian financial crisis of 1997, it had been claimed that credit ratings appear to have some independent influence on yields over and above the other publicly available information. One study showed that although rating announcements had a significant impact on spreads of speculative-grade sovereign bonds, no such influence was found on yields of investment-grade sovereign bonds. The international credit rating agencies were widely criticized in the wake of the Asian financial crisis for failing to anticipate the crisis and forewarn investors.

Critics argue that most often credit ratings are grounded in the past and are inappropriate indicators of future events. Indeed, it has been suggested that credit ratings are likely to exacerbate macroeconomic fluctuations, because they tend to be higher in the boom conditions and lower when economic conditions are bad. This procyclical nature of credit ratings has been cited as a possible source of accentuations of business cycles. For example, in one study, rating agencies were criticized for focusing on the "wrong" set of fundamentals, such as debt-to-export ratios, when it came to anticipating financial crises. Similarly, others have observed that instead of leading the market, agencies lag the market and are rather slow to adjust their ratings.

Knowledge Economy, Knowledge Intensity, and International Trade

The Concept of the Knowledge Economy

In times of rapid economic and social change, many new concepts emerge as attempts are made to describe and analyze the process of change. In recent years, the term "knowledge economy" has been the focus of a great deal of comment and has been described variously as the global knowledge economy, knowledge-based economy, information economy, and new economy. The concept of the knowledge economy describes fundamental aspects of the present period of economic change. Quite new activities, structures, and arrangements are emerging on a global basis, characterized above all by rising knowledge intensity in, and increasing globalization of, processes for the creation, production, and distribution of goods and services. This is described as the emergence of the knowledge economy.

The unique role of knowledge as a driving force in economic growth has been extensively discussed and is now widely accepted. The extensive literature on the knowledge economy is concerned with many aspects of the subject, but two main strands deal with (1) the conceptual issues of what is meant by knowledge economy and the other associated terms; and (2) the policy implications for nations flowing from the concepts. Defining the knowledge economy is important for several reasons. First of all, by putting a circle around the factors or features constituting it, a clear definition helps to crystallize the scope of the knowledge economy. Second, a clear definition would permit comparisons to be made between countries in terms of their standing and performance with respect to the knowledge economy. Comparisons would also be possible in the future within a country, tracking its performance over time. Third, and perhaps most importantly, a clear definition of the knowledge economy would sharpen the focus on the enabling reforms and policies and would help in prioritizing those reforms. "A definition offers no shortcut strategy for reforms," noted the APEC Economic Committee in its 2000 report, "but it is the correct starting point for deeper analysis of what the New Economy is and upon what it depends."

Different people have defined the knowledge economy differently, conveying often a partial rather than complete picture of the underlying concept. According to some scholars, the knowledge economy refers to the new overall structure that is emerging, together with its associated institutions, activities, and arrangements. Attention is often given to individual aspects of the emerging economy, such as the new economy or the online economy, the network economy, the learning economy, and the information economy. But these are specific aspects rather than the overall reality. The Internet plays an important part in the knowledge economy, and networks of many different types are also vital. Learning is clearly central to a knowledge economy, as is the rapid exchange of information and other forms of knowledge. Innovation, being the process of applying ideas new to the firm in many different areas, is clearly at the heart of a vibrant knowledge economy, Each of these concepts views the overall reality of the knowledge economy through a different lens, thereby illuminating an important part of the picture.

According to the APEC Economic Committee, the four dimensions that characterize the knowledge-based economy (KBE) are (1) pervasive innovation and technological change, (2) pervasive human resource development, (3) efficient infrastructure, particularly in information and communications technology (ICT), and (4) a business environment supportive of enterprise and innovation. In its attempt to capture the essence of the KBE, the World Bank has developed a more inclusive "knowledge assessment scorecard" consisting of 20 variables, each of which has been normalized on a scale of 0 to 10, so that the lowest value for a variable is at 0 and the highest is at 10. The normalized values of these variables are depicted in a star diagram for comparison among a large group of developed and developing economies with respect to their preparedness for KBE.

Knowledge Intensity, Industry Structure, and Trade

Application of knowledge to economic activities of all types lies at the heart of the knowledge economy. The process of creating and applying economically relevant knowledge is called innovation, and it consists not only of the big discoveries and the high-technology industries, but of "a million little things" that improve the operations of the firms and other economic institutions, to use Paul Romer's characterization in "Two Strategies for Economic Development: Using Ideas and Producing Ideas," published in the World Bank's *Annual World Bank Conference on Development Economics 1992*. It is widely accepted that the process of research and development is only a part of technological innovation. The international standard for the measurement of innovation is the *Oslo Manual*, published by the OECD in 1992, which designates the following activities as components of technological innovation: design; research and development; acquisition of technology; tooling, start-up, and pre-production; training; and marketing new products. In many OECD countries, research and development expenditure accounts for 30–50% of spending on innovation, and expenditures on product design and production start-up also constitute substantial proportions.

The OECD ranks manufacturing industries based on their relative research and development intensity, which is measured in terms of the share of research and development spending in value added in each industry. The high-technology and medium-high-technology industries have played a major role in international trade in the 1990s. Before the Asian economic crisis, between 1990 and 1996, exports of products of these industries by OECD countries increased at the annual average rate of 7%, as compared with 5% for other types of exports. The fastest rates of growth in high-technology exports occurred in Mexico, Iceland, Ireland, New Zealand, and Turkey, which are countries where foreign enterprises had played a major role in developing these industries. Outside OECD, economies of the East Asian countries in general, and of Indonesia, Thailand, China, Malaysia, and Taiwan in particular, benefited enormously from rapid growth in international trade in knowledge-intensive industries. Worldwide high-technology exports accounted for 21% of total exports in 1999. For the countries in the East Asia and Pacific regions, however, the corresponding figure was 31%. These countries also suffered severe setbacks to their economies following the Asian economic crisis of 1997, however, when foreign capital outflows led to a sharp downturn in industrial production and exports.

See Also the Following Articles

Aggregative Macro Models, Micro-Based Macro Models, and Growth Models • Knowledge Creation

Further Reading

Purchasing Power Parity

Castles, I., and Henderson, D. (2002). The IPCC emission scenarios: An economic-statistical critique. *Energy Environ.* **14**(2–3).

Nakicenovic, N., *et al.* (2002). IPCC SRES revisited: A response. *Energy Environ.* **14**(2–3).

United Nations and Commission of the European Communities (1987). *World Comparisons of Purchasing Power and Real Product for 1980: Phase IV of the International Comparison Project: Part One: Summary Results for 60 Countries*. United Nations, New York.

World Bank (2003). *World Development Report 2003*. World Bank, Washington, D.C.

World Bank (2003). *ICP Handbook 2004*. World Bank, Washington, D.C. Available on the Internet at www.worldbank.org

Sovereign Risk

Bank for International Settlements (BIS) (2001). *The New Basel Capital Accord*. Basel Committee on Bank Supervision, Basel. Available on the Internet at www.bis.org

Block, S., and Vaaler, P. (2001). *The Price of Democracy: Sovereign Risk Ratings, Bond Spreads and Political Business Cycles in Developing Countries*. CID Working Paper No. 82. Centre for International Development, Harvard University.

Cantor, R., and Packer, F. (1996). Determinants and impact of sovereign credit ratings. *Econ. Policy Rev.* **2,** 37–53.

Claessens, S., and Embrechts, G. (2002). *Basel II, Sovereign Ratings and Transfer Risk External versus Internal Ratings*. Paper presented at the conference *Basel II: An Economic Assessment, 17–18 May*. Bank for International Settlements, Basel.

Kaminsky, G., and Schmukler, S. (2001). Emerging markets instability: Do sovereign ratings affect country risks and stock returns? *World Bank Econ. Rev.* **16,** 171–195.

Reinhart, C. M. (2001). *Sovereign Credit Ratings before and after Financial Crises*. Paper prepared for the New York University–University of Maryland Project *The Role of Credit Rating Agencies in the International Economy*. University of Maryland, College Park.

Knowledge Economy

Asia–Pacific Economic Cooperation (APEC) (2000). *Towards Knowledge-based Economies in APEC*. APEC Economic Committee, Singapore.

Organization for Economic Cooperation and Development (OECD) (1996). *Employment and Growth in the Knowledge-Based Economy.* OECD, Paris.

World Bank and OECD (2000). *Korea and the Knowledge Based Economy: Making the Transition.* International Bank for Reconstruction and Development, World Bank, Washington DC.

Xue, L., and Sheehan, P. (2002). Foundations of the knowledge economy. *China's Future in the Knowledge Economy: Engaging the New World* (B. Grewal, L. Xue, F. Sun, and P. Sheehan, eds.). Centre for Strategic Economic Studies, Victoria University of Technology and Tsinghua University Press, Melbourne.

International Relations

Bruce Russett
Yale University, New Haven, Connecticut, USA

Glossary

dyad A pair of units, typically countries; may be balanced (same value for both units) or unbalanced.
hierarchy A system that can be ordered from most powerful to least powerful units.
international system A set of interacting countries.
level of analysis The degree of aggregation, from individual decision makers to international system.
polarity The number of major power centers in a system.
political stability The longevity of a political system's or a leader's rule, or the degree to which that rule is challenged.
power The ability to change another's behavior; also the resources that may be used to produce change.

Measurement in international relations scholarship is directed to the development of comparable and valid measures of theoretically important concepts according to international standards of reliability and validity, to developing procedures for their analysis, and to making the data available to a wide range of social scientists.

Introduction

The founding of the scientific study of international relations is properly credited to two scholars, Lewis Frye Richardson and Quincy Wright, both working just before the middle of the 20th century. Both were major theorists, but both also devoted great energy and ingenuity to devising techniques for measuring many aspects of international relations. In the 1960s, the U.S. National Science Foundation made substantial financial support available, and a critical mass of researchers in Europe and North America emerged to improve, extend, and utilize this information. Vast improvements in the quality and quantity of information have combined with comparable improvements in theory and statistical analysis to permit the emergence of international relations as a scientific endeavor. Moreover, the widespread availability of electronic databases for sophisticated analysis is producing greater scholarly convergence on measurement techniques—a necessary though not sufficient condition for scientific success.

Variables and Units of Measurement

What is to be measured of course depends on theory, and theories of international relations operate at several levels of analysis, commonly identified in increasing aggregation as individual decision makers, political unit (i.e., the nation-state, or country), dyads (pairs of countries), and the entire international system. This article concentrates on measurements that can be compiled, with acceptable comparability across countries and years, for most or all countries that are members of the system of international relations.

Individual Decision Makers

Policy-relevant individuals may in principle range from individual voters to heads of state and other key persons responsible for making foreign policy choices. Public opinion surveys measure the direction and intensity of voters' preferences and special-sample surveys can measure the preferences of citizens more directly involved in shaping opinions and policies. Such surveys are possible only in reasonably democratic countries. Even in democracies, the influence of citizens' preferences on actual decisions is a topic of intense inquiry and debate.

The public writings and pronouncements of heads of state can be studied through systematic content analysis, not only for their preferences but for their affective content (friendship or hostility), perception of threat, and complexity of cognition. Formerly a very labor-intensive task, such analysis is now usually carried out on electronic databases compiled from government sources and news organizations. Consequently, the information base has become much richer, and although computational routines rarely match the subtlety of human coders, the gains in quantity and reliability of coding are substantial.

Country

The primary focus of international relations theory has been on the behavior of countries, rather than of individuals or nonstate actors such as international organizations. Often this requires an assumption that the country, or state, behaves as a unitary rational actor. Although this assumption is often sharply challenged, heads of state typically speak in the name of their countries, so information about their pronouncements and actions may be treated as information about the country itself. Country-level information, however, includes much more, notably about the economic, political, and social characteristics and institutions of the country.

Any analysis of international relations must be concerned with power, as the ability to persuade or coerce another actor to do something. The actual ability to affect decisions in this relational sense is difficult to measure, due to the conceptual problems in determining what the other would have done in the absence of coercion or persuasion. At one extreme, if the leader of country A makes a threat so as to deter country B from attacking country C, the mere fact that B subsequently does not attack C does not necessarily indicate that A exerted power over B. Possibly, B's leader had no intention of attacking C anyway. Such problems can be addressed with sophisticated models of strategic actors, with analysis of counterfactuals, and if possible, with detailed *post hoc* documentary information on leaders' deliberations.

More subject to systematic analysis, however, is information on the power bases of nation-states. Much of this involves reasonably straightforward use of preexisting information, often from national censuses or sample surveys. These include levels and growth rates of demographic data (total population, population in the labor force or of military age, literacy and education, health conditions) and economic data (total national income or income per capita, production of various commodities, value and composition of exports and imports, internal and foreign investment, size and composition of government expenditure), and distributional equality within the population of income and wealth. All these data are produced by public agencies in most countries and are subjected to scrutiny and revision by international organizations, economists, demographers, and other scholars. Analysts of international relations also evaluate the cross-national comparability of this information, but are not primarily responsible for their compilation. Similarly, information on military capabilities (quality and quantity of troops under arms, military expenditures, number and types of weapons) is produced by governments—concerning their own countries and their allies and rivals—and critiqued by scholars.

Much analysis, however, requires measuring capabilities and actions within conceptual frameworks arising from theories of international relations. Such measures may be derived from standard measures compiled by other disciplines and agents, but do not exist in any off-the-shelf condition. They may need to be aggregated, disaggregated, or recombined with other existing information or information compiled for the purpose. For example, it is not obvious what the most useful measure of national power is. For nuclear deterrence, of course one counts and evaluates nuclear weapons delivery systems. But for a general-purpose measure of a country's power, one needs a composite indicator of military, economic, and demographic power bases. Moreover, if one wishes to compare all types of countries, and over long time periods, one must take account of the availability and comparability of the measures that make up the composite. Numbers of nuclear weapons are irrelevant before 1945; despite massive research by economists, national income data for many countries in the 19th century are unreliable; demographic data are also of uneven quality depending on national information-gathering capability.

Beyond these data is information on data not so obviously part of standard demographic and economic statistics. One example concerns distribution of services and goods that may affect national power or political stability: relative equality of access to health care, equality of distribution of land and wealth. Some theories of international conflict concern how ethnically homogenous the country is in terms of linguistic/racial/religious characteristics; heterogeneous countries may be less politically stable, especially if major ethnic minorities overlap across national borders with neighbors. These measures must be compiled painstakingly by scholars and evaluated for their reliability and validity.

More directly political measures concern types of political systems, such as relative size of the government in the economy or its degree of democracy or authoritarianism. The latter requires some degree of judgment, but great advances have been made in compiling reasonably objective and internationally accepted codings of types of political systems that cover all countries over a time-scale approaching two centuries. Originally compiled by scholars of comparative politics, they have proved to be very important in testing theories about whether democratic countries are less likely to become involved in international conflict. Still other theories assert that politically unstable countries may be more (or less) likely to engage in international conflict than are stable ones, for example, that unstable governments may attempt to divert their populace toward foreign adversaries and away from problems internal to the country. Depending on the conceptualization, stability may be measured either in terms of the longevity of a particular ruler, party, or constitution, or by the degree of internal conflict manifested in violent protest, rebellion, or civil war. Measures of involvement in international conflict include merely diplomatic disputes in the context of peaceful relations as well as the use of military instruments of violence. The latter may range from relatively low-level military threats up through border skirmishes to full-scale war (conventionally defined in the scholarly literature as involving at least 1000 combat deaths). Hardly any of this kind of information is reported on a comparable basis by national governments. Rather, to be made comparable across countries and time periods, it requires detailed compilation from news media, scattered documentation, and historical documents by teams of scholars. The temporal unit of analysis may be a day or aggregated into monthly or annual slices. Many scholars scrutinize these compilations of political data for accuracy and completeness.

On the whole, country-unit analyses of international behavior have not proved very productive. One exception is the convincing evidence that great powers, with wide-ranging political and economic interests combined with the military power to exert force far from the home country, are many times more likely to become involved in violent conflict than are small or weak states. Other than this, however, strong generalizations about the risk factors for violence by particular kinds of states have proved elusive. There is some evidence that democracies are less likely to engage in violent conflict than are autocracies, but that evidence is contested, the relationship is fairly weak, and the class of autocracies is too varied (communist and fascist regimes, military dictatorships, traditional monarchies) for easy generalization. Many individual state behaviors, of course, are better understood as part of patterns of strategic interaction with at least one other state, in a dyad.

Dyad

A major conceptual breakthrough, focusing on the characteristics of pairs of states, has, however, contributed to greater success in identifying, both theoretically and empirically, the risk factors of international conflict. It drew on the insight that it was less the characteristics of individual countries than their relationships with other countries that mattered. Most countries are neither especially peaceful nor very war-prone in general; their readiness to engage in violent conflict varies over time and with regard to particular other countries. One such hypothesis is that countries will be reluctant to fight other countries of comparable power (with whom the outcome of a war might be unpredictable) but readier to fight weaker countries with which they could be much more confident of victory. This perspective, however, leads to a competing hypothesis for war frequency: the rulers of weak countries, knowing that they would likely lose a war, might make great concessions to powerful ones, making war between very weak and very strong countries unnecessary and rare. Thus, the risk of war might be greatest between two countries of comparable power, leading to great uncertainty as to which would win the war and thus using war as an empirical test of relative capability. Of the two competing hypotheses, the logic beyond the latter (power equality leads to wars, power differential discourages war) seems stronger, but there can be no substitute for empirical investigation over many dyads and years. Such empirical analyses have become possible, since an international system of, for example, 100 countries, has 4850 *pairs* of states $(N \times N - 1)/2$, each of which can be compared over many time intervals. Thus, taking 1-year data slices over a period of a century would give a potential for 485,000 observations—enough observations to make possible the statistical testing of competing hypotheses. In turn, the hypotheses could be refined by careful strategic analysis, including the application of game theory to questions of how states would behave under conditions of uncertainty about each other's intentions or capability.

Thus, dyadic information—typically compiled initially on a country-year (one observation for each year a country is a member of the system) basis and then converted into dyad-year format—permits testing hypotheses about a variety of conditions thought to affect the risk of violent conflict, with enough cases to make statistical generalizations about relative risks. In effect, violence and war can be considered as cases in an epidemic and social scientists can investigate competing hypotheses about what factors promote the onset of violence.

Relevant variables for dyadic analyses include traditional concerns for power and its projection: relative military and economic strength, geographic proximity (contiguous borders, or distance between countries, often transformed into logarithms to represent the rate of decline of power capability over space), and the presence or absence of formal alliance agreements between members of the dyad. Others concern the similarity or difference between political systems (as by subtracting the score for the less democratic country on the democracy–autocracy scale from that of the more democratic one), or the similarity of their behavior internationally (do they ally with more or less the same other countries?), or vote similarly in international organizations (such as the United Nations General Assembly). Still others concern a wider range of economic and institutional ties between countries: trade in goods and services or investment flows, preferential trade agreements, the number and types of international organizations in which they share membership. All of these have been found to be related—sometimes just correlationally, often with plausible grounds for inferring causation—to the degree to which the members of the dyad engage in a wide range of cooperative or conflictful activities. Cooperation and conflict in turn are measured as merely diplomatic cooperation/conflict or as militarized disputes up to and including war. With large databases, it has become possible to assess the relative risk of conflict associated with each variable and to begin to untangle the web of causation. The evidence is that both traditional measures of power and measures of political similarity and political–economic linkage make an impact. A theoretically integrative move has been to combine several measures, such as power, distance, and alliance patterns, under the concept of expected utility; that is, the value or utility of an act weighted by the probability of achieving it.

It is not just the static levels of power or economic relationships that matter. Some analysts have addressed changes, such as if the risk of conflict is greater when one member of the dyad is becoming more democratic from an autocratic base, or if the trend in mutual trade in the dyad is downward. Thus far, these empirical analyses are inconclusive. More productive may be a focus on changes in relative power between potentially antagonistic countries, on the grounds that a narrowing power gap creates larger uncertainty about which country might win a military contest and hence raises the risk of such a contest. It is especially useful to concentrate the analysis on particular kinds of dyads, namely, those with long-standing territorial disputes that periodically erupt into military confrontations, and on the associated political, economic, and military changes in their relationship.

International System

Other efforts have been directed to understanding risk factors according to different kinds of international systems, including both the global international system and regional subsystems. An international system is identified as a group of interacting countries, in which strategic actors make interdependent decisions. For much of history, a truly global international system did not exist, as the level of technology to permit a high level of interaction among distant countries was too low. A system of warring state-like units existed in China at least 3500 years ago, however, and even earlier in Mesopotamia. A regional interstate system existed among Mayan city-states in Central America from approximately 800 B.C. to 800 A.D., with some revival up to the Spanish conquest. But until the conquest, none of them had had any interaction with or even knowledge of a European system, nor European states of them. Not until the 19th century did a sufficiently high level of interaction develop for the concept of a global system to be very useful.

A global system, like a regional system, can be characterized by its degree of hierarchy, or by its polarity. If it were dominated by one great power, a hegemon, it would be unipolar. By contrast, a system dominated by two great powers would be bipolar and a system of three or more great powers would be multipolar. Different theories led to expectations that some kinds of systems were more prone to large-scale international violence than were others, for example, that bipolar systems were likely to experience more small wars than were multipolar systems, but fewer large wars directly between the two great states. The Cold War era between the United States and the Soviet Union was such a system. The evidence available for generalization, however, was so mixed as to prevent any consensus on relative risks. One problem was the small number of different international systems from which to attempt to make any reliable generalizations. For example, most international systems in the "modern" era (even as dated from the Treaty of Westphalia in 1648) have been multipolar, with the less than 50-year Cold War era the major exception. Another was imprecision or lack of consensus on theory. In measuring polarity, some analysts would focus attention more on the structure of alliance systems than on the number of great powers; for example, in 1914 there were perhaps as many as eight great powers in the international system, but only two competing alliance configurations of great powers (Great Britain, France, and Russia versus Germany, Austria-Hungary, and Italy). Consequently, no near-consensus has emerged from the empirical analyses comparing bipolarity with multipolarity.

There is somewhat more agreement that major wars may be less likely to occur under conditions of unipolarity or hegemony, but the empirical base for that generalization is very limited, perhaps only to the years since the end of the Cold War. Moreover, conceptual agreement as to the relevant measures of unipolarity (population, military power, economic strength, even cultural dominance) is elusive. More promising may be attention to changes in the relative power of the leading country or alliance system in the system and that of its putative challenger, as on the dyadic level of analysis.

Another and possibly more productive way to conduct analyses at the system level is to ask whether certain political or economic characteristics become more or less common in the system. Just as systemic measures of power concentration are built up from country-level data on the components of national power, other systemic measures can similarly be constructed. For example, are a larger proportion of countries democratic in one period or another, is the level of economic and financial interdependence higher or lower, and are the number and strength of international organizations greater? Such systemic characteristics do vary over time. The proportion of democratic countries in the system has been higher since the 1990s than at any previous time in world history and by many (but not all) measures the level of economic interdependence has also been at an all-time high. This coincides with the increasing interest in the effects of "globalization" on the world political economy and specifically on constraints that may reduce the incentives to violent conflict. It suggests that system-level changes in, for instance, the proportion of democracies might have an effect in addition to the effects at the national or dyadic levels. That is, a need to obtain commercial ties and foreign investment might constrain even those governments that were not yet closely tied into the global economy. Or the growth of international norms and institutions for peacefully settling disputes, deriving from democratic practice, might constrain even governments that were not themselves democratic. It would thus be useful to analyze the international system as a set of feedback relationships among political, economic, and institutional elements and operating at different levels of analysis.

Analytical Issues

Data Problems

As noted, great progress has been made in creating worldwide information on structural and behavioral phenomena that were not previously well measured and the process of international scholarly scrutiny of these measures has narrowed the range of subjectivity and cultural bias that may infect such measures. Yet data problems go beyond the matter of crude or imperfect measures of the relevant phenomena to situations where data are simply missing for a substantial number of units needed for the analysis. Typically the pattern of missing data is not random, but correlated with and caused by economic underdevelopment or political systems that are closed to external scrutiny. Limiting the analysis to countries where data are reported or can be directly compiled risks introducing serious bias into any "sample" that is subjected to analysis. An analysis confined largely to democratic countries because of missing data for most autocracies, for example, might find that the small variation in their degree of democracy made little difference in their international behavior, whereas analyzing the full number and range of political types might show great behavioral differences.

Fortunately, the existence of large databases on many variables, and the creation of new statistical routines for analysis, often can mitigate these problems. If one knows from previous analyses, for example, that country-level data on income per capita, literacy, life expectancy, and educational achievement are highly correlated with one another, one can estimate the level of any one variable that is missing for a particular country from its levels on the other three measures. Sophisticated computational routines can impute such missing data from a large body of information and even supply a range for the probable error in estimation. Unlike many substantive analyses that require theories about causation, knowledge of correlational patterns is sufficient for this purpose.

Some kinds of selection biases are more insidious. If, for example, one looks at military crises in which a government must decide whether to come to the defense of an attacked ally, one finds many instances where the alliance is not honored. Does this mean alliances do not deter conflict? To reach that conclusion, one would have to look at the many situations where the ally is never attacked. A strong, credible military alliance could deter even the threat of an attack, whereas the alliances that are perceived as weak may attract attack. For repeated interactions, as in a process from normal peace to diplomatic dispute, through military challenge to war or settlement, one must control for selection bias at every step.

Conceptual Problems

The data may be well measured, but if not matched to appropriate concepts they may be useless at best and misleading at worst. In principle, interval measures are preferable to binary ones, if the equal-interval assumption of monotonicity is reasonable or can be made so by some transformation. In the dyadic context, some measures are inherently balanced; e.g., the distance from A to B is the same as that from B to A. Other dyadic measures, however, are inherently unbalanced. To measure the importance of trade to a country's economy and political system, the trade total should be divided by the country's gross national product (GNP). But the same total trade (exports plus imports) between the countries will produce a highly asymmetric measure if the two countries' GNP totals are very disparate. Presumably, the political importance of that trade will be much greater for the smaller country. Behavior is often best measured as that of a directed dyad. Rather than measure the mere existence of a militarized dispute between A and B, one should try to identify the initiator of the dispute. From theory, one should expect a small country to initiate a dispute with a large country far less often than vice versa. Directed measures are especially appropriate for studying sequential patterns of strategic behavior. Behavior may be measured as scales of cooperation or of conflict between countries. Some efforts combine the concepts of cooperation and conflict into a single scale, but this is very problematic. Countries that are politically or economically salient to each other often experience rather high levels of both conflict and cooperation; putting the two concepts on one dimension obscures this reality.

Rare Events

Many aspects of international relations represent common behaviors, especially many acts of cooperation. Trade volumes between countries may vary greatly over time, but the individual commercial transactions are numerous. Other events, such as conflict behavior, are quite rare events. Militarized disputes, for example, arise infrequently. In most years, only approximately 3% of dyads in the international system will experience any such disputes and only one-tenth of those are at war. Popular statistical procedures, such as logistic regression, can sharply underestimate the probability of rare events.

Cross-Sectional versus Cross-Temporal Analysis

Most measures in international relations are utilized both cross-sectionally (comparison across countries at the same point in time) and cross-temporally. Measurement error may be serious in either kind of comparison. Many analyses are performed with pooled time-series, e.g., panels of the same countries or dyads measured at regularly repeated time intervals. Such analyses often raise difficult problems of independence of observations across space and time that are increasingly being addressed in this discipline. The behavior of France, for example, is in part dependent on that of its allies as well as that of its adversaries. War, and even changes in political systems, such as the spread of democracy, may be contagious across space. Trade patterns are relatively constant over time. And, of course, if France had a militarized dispute with Germany in the past year it is much more likely to have one this year than with a country with which it was previously at peace. Most statistical packages contain routines to correct for non-independence of observations, but the choice of correction depends on good theory as well as on statistical options. For instance, controlling current disputes by a term for disputes in the preceding year may obscure the effect of theoretically important variables that raise the risk of a dispute in both years.

In summary, issues of measurement in international relations are inseparable from theoretical issues. The rise of large-scale data sets of quantitative indicators has forced the refinement and formalization of theories that were initially expressed verbally; in turn, mathematical theories have demanded far greater rigor of measurement.

See Also the Following Articles

Rare Events Research • Time-Series–Cross-Section Data

Further Reading

Bueno de Mesquita, B., and Lalman, D. (1992). *War and Reason.* Yale University Press, New Haven, CT.

Diehl, P., and Goertz, G. (2000). *War and Peace in International Rivalry.* University of Michigan Press, Ann Arbor, MI.

Goldstein, J. S. (1992). A conflict–cooperation scale for international events data. *J. Conflict Resol.* **36,** 369–385.

Huth, P., and Allee, T. (2002). *The Democratic Peace and Territorial Conflict in the Twentieth Century.* Cambridge University Press, New York.

Jaggers, D., and Gurr, T. R. (1995). Tracking democracy's third wave with the Polity III data. *J. Peace Res.* **32,** 469–482.

Jones, D. M., Bremer, S. A., and Singer, J. D. (1996). Militarized interstate disputes, 1816–1992: Rationale, coding rules, and empirical patterns. *Conflict Manage. Peace Sci.* **15,** 163–213.

King, G., Honaker, J., Joseph, A., and Scheve, K. (2001). Analyzing incomplete political science data: An alternative algorithm for multiple imputation. *Am. Polit. Sci. Rev.* **95,** 49–70.

King, G., and Zeng, L. (2001). Explaining rare events in international relations. *Int. Organiz.* **55,** 693–715.

Russett, B., and Oneal, J. R. (2001). *Triangulating Peace: Democracy, Interdependence, and International Organizations.* W. W. Norton, New York.

Internet Measurement

Antonio Marturano
University of Exeter, Exeter, England, United Kingdom

Glossary

computer-mediated communications (CMCs) Text-based, interactive communication processes involving computer usage. Examples are chat rooms, Instant Messenger, and ICQ ("I seek you"), programs that allow communication and reveal when other program users are on-line.

epistemic (cognitive) access The possibility of rationally accessing an object, event, or a person's mental state in order to reach a complete understanding.

Internet protocol/transmission control protocol (IP/TCP) Computer software technology that converts messages into streams of packets at the source, then reassembles them back into messages at the destination. IP handles the addressing, seeing to it that packets are routed across multiple nodes and even across multiple networks with multiple standards (not only the early Advanced Research Projects Agency Network's pioneering standard, but also other standards, including Ethernet, Fiber-Distributed Data Interface, and X.25).

virtual community A community of people sharing common interests, ideas, and feelings over the Internet or other collaborative networks. Internet virtual communities are social aggregations that emerge when enough people carry on public discussions long enough and with sufficient human feeling to form webs of personal relationships in cyberspace.

virtual identity In the physical world, there is an inherent unity to the self, for the body provides a compelling and convenient definition of identity. The virtual world is different; it is composed of information rather than matter: a person can have, some claim, as many electronic personas as there is time and energy to create.

The Internet is one of the most important social phenomena today. The Internet is going to be a huge basin for data collection, and Internet measurement is likely to be one of the most valuable means to explore how the human society is evolving. The main feature when considering the social side of the Internet, namely, computer-mediated communications, is the fact that the social boundaries of the physical world are meaningless. On-line communications, indeed, are marked out by the disappearance of the dichotomy of concepts such as private/public and true/false. Because of the very nature of computer-mediated communications (CMCs), qualitative measurement, and in particular observational techniques, turn out as a more fruitful means of inquiry in "opaque" environments. Ethnographics or narrative explanations of on-line behaviors are more powerful than are the classical quantitative analyses. A quantitative explanation of phenomena, or prescriptive analysis, is based on clear causal propositions, which presuppose a wider transparency by the explanandum, but such a transparency is rather problematic in the case of on-line participants. Nonetheless, quantitative measurements are quite useful when used for the application of classical market research to electronic business (e-commerce). Finally, the application of quantitative as well as qualitative measurement to on-line activities raises several ethical concerns, in particular about access and the informed consent.

What Is the Internet?

Internet Protocol/Transmission Control Protocol

The Internet is meant to be a series of computer- and network-assisted activities using the so-called Internet protocol (IP), or transmission control protocol (TCP). These activities, actually, are purely semiotics, namely, they involve only exchange or manipulation of data (for example, credit card number), signs (such as e-mail), and icons (such as photos).

How the Internet Works

The Internet is a development of the Advanced Research Projects Agency (ARPA) system, designed by the Rand Corporation for the United States Department of Defense as a military communications network able to work in the case of nuclear war. The system was designed without a central control in order to keep working if some of its parts were eliminated. The principles were simple. The network would be assumed to be unreliable at all times. All the nodes in the network would be equal in status to all other nodes, each node with its own authority to originate, pass, and receive messages. The messages would be divided into packets, each packet separately addressed. Each packet would begin at some specified source node, and end at some other specified destination node. Each packet would wind its way through the network on an individual basis. The particular route that the packet took would be unimportant. Only final results would count. Basically, the packet would be tossed like a "hot potato" from node to node to node, more or less in the direction of its destination, until it ended up in the proper place. If big pieces of the network had been destroyed, that simply would not matter; the packets would still stay routed, literally wildly across the field by whatever nodes happened to survive. From this design started the legend of an "anarchical" Internet, i.e., the very idea that control of the whole system was impossible. In the autumn of 1969, the first node was installed at the University of California in Los Angeles. By December 1969, there were four nodes on the infant network, which was named ARPANET, after its Pentagon sponsor.

ARPANET remained fairly tightly controlled, at least until 1983, when its military segment broke off and became MILNET. But TCP/IP linked them all. And ARPANET, though it was growing, became a smaller and smaller neighborhood amid the vastly growing galaxy of other linked machines. As the 1970s and 1980s advanced, many very different social groups obtained and used powerful computers. It was fairly easy to link these computers to the growing network of networks. As the use of TCP/IP became more common, other entire networks fell into the digital embrace of the Internet, and messily adhered. Because the TCP/IP software was public domain, and the basic technology was decentralized and rather anarchic by its very nature, it was difficult to stop people from barging in and linking up somewhere within the networks. In point of fact, nobody wanted to stop them from joining this branching complex of networks, which came to be known as the "Internet."

How to Use the Internet

But what is done with the Internet, technically? Four things, basically: e-mail and newsgroup communications, group discussions (computer-mediated communications), long-distance computing (personal web pages), and file transfers. Every kind of Internet usage starts from these original four types of activities. The main focus in the following discussions is on two uses of the Internet: as a tool for e-commerce, namely, as a measurement tool for improving the quality of the on-line selling of products; and as a computer-mediated communication tool.

Measurement and the Internet

The Concept of Measurement

The concept of measurement is widely used to study the Internet. In particular, the "technical" idea of measurement (used by computer scientists and practitioners) is applied to assess data packages flowing in and out of a server, a computer, or a web page. In other words, there are ways of measuring, analyzing, and reporting the services provided to a user's network via the Internet. Engineers, computer scientists, and practitioners use such a notion to measure the data flow. The interest here, however, is in the "social," rather than the technical, measurement of the Internet, although the technical concept could have an interesting role within the quantitative approach.

Internet Research

Another useful distinction to be drawn here is between the Internet as a source of data and the Internet as a social field of study. Internet research is concerned not only with the study of on-line behavior (what people do in virtual and mediated environments), but is also concerned with using computer-based tools and computer-accessible populations to study human behavior in general. On the one hand, then, Internet researchers can access if not potentially infinite data, at least a larger amount of data than is possible in the physical world. The Internet indeed allows researchers to interview participants in different continents and across a complex matrix of university colleges and faculties. It also facilitates participation, which might otherwise have been inhibited due to disability, financial constraints, difficult cultural contexts (socially marginalized communities, such as gay fathers), and/or language and communication differences. But it has been pointed out that those people who assume that the social world of cyberspace is readily accessible once there is technological mastery, once they have more experience, begin to realize that the on-line world has also its hidden areas. On the other hand, the exponential growth of virtual communities makes the Internet one of the most important modern social phenomena: loves, friendships, and contacts are rising and falling daily over the web in a very peculiar way. That makes the web a new and rather sophisticated terrain for research about new forms of human behavior.

Some techniques already used for conventional market research (such as data crossing) are used in e-commerce. An example is the Amazon web site (http://www.amazon.com). Amazon, one of the most widely known Internet business-to-business companies, sells a huge variety of goods. Amazon is quite popular in the academic community as one of the most comprehensive web sites for book purchases. Before approaching the problems encountered in Internet research, the terms "quantitative" and "qualitative" are briefly defined as they relate to measurement.

Quantitative and Qualitative Measurement

There is no agreement about the very notion of quantitative and qualitative research. Some scholars view the two measures as mutually exclusive methodologies for social inquiries, and as such they are essentially divergent clusters of epistemological assumptions—that is, of what should pass as warrantable knowledge about the social world. Others claim that quantitative and qualitative methodologies are just denotations of separate ways of conducting social investigations, which can be integrated in the research design if this strategy addresses the research questions; in this case, they are just simply different approaches to data collection, so that preferences for the first or the latter or some hybrid approach are based on technical issues. Finally, there are claims that much of the discussion in the literature about these two research traditions has created a somewhat exaggerated picture of their differences.

In any case, "quantitative research" here will mean, roughly, a particular kind of research, indeed very similar to the natural science approach, which takes the form of causal propositions. The quantitative approach as used to study causes of delinquency, for example, reflects a concern to follow methods and procedures of positivistic epistemology. In particular, the social survey is the main research tool used with the quantitative approach. Indeed, the survey has a capacity for generating quantifiable data on large numbers of people who are known to be representative of a wider population; this allows testing the validity of pre-existent theories and/or hypotheses, and has been viewed by several scholars as a means of capturing the essence of a science.

"Qualitative measurement" is used here to mean, instead, a kind of approach based on the interpretation or narration of a social phenomenon, starting from a "destructured" understanding of the social reality. The milestone study in this field was the work by Adler on upper-level drug dealers. Adler used a somewhat unstandardized approach, relying on observations, conversations, and some informal interviewing. Adler's approach, indeed, seemed to intentionally avoid the positivistic paradigm, preferring instead to ground the investigations in people's own understanding of their social reality, as phenomenological perspectives are taken to imply. Importantly, it is doubtful whether a group such as Adler's drug dealers would have been accessible to methods that even remotely resembled those used in the previously mentioned quantitative delinquency study, because of the undercover nature of the drug dealers' operations and their considerable secretiveness. This suggests that quantitative and qualitative research are different approaches to carrying out research; the choice between them looks then to be a technical matter about their appropriateness in answering of particular research questions. In the following discussions, it can be seen that the choice between the application of qualitative and quantitative methods, because of their very epistemological nature, will also depend, and in particular regarding the Internet, on the opacity of the studied field.

Applying Qualitative Measurement

The qualitative approach, because of its real nature, seems to be more fruitful for measuring phenomena such as computer-mediated communications (namely, chat rooms, ICQ, or Instant Messenger). Indeed, in such social practices, the boundaries between truth and falsehood, private and public are meaningless. What is the real meaning of sociodemographic data obtained through a structured on-line questionnaire? Importantly, what is really happening when a regular participant in an Internet Relay Chat (IRC) channel, one of the hypothetical cases for a survey sample, says that her name is Mary, she is 30 years old, and she works as secretary? Such information, even if true, provides not the actual data about Mary's real life, but rather provides answers about her on-line symbolic universe, her on-line self-representation. Therefore, accordingly, it is never correct to accept these data without keeping in mind that obtaining information about someone's real physical life through on-line communications, although seemingly easy and convenient, is always a hazardous and uncertain procedure.

A full understanding of Internet usage requires examination of other factors, such as economic and social class issues of access to the technology: Such factors, added to the opacity of data (namely, an ambiguous epistemic access to the real intention by the interviewed), make Internet measurement a very problematic one from a quantitative point of view. Moreover many of the virtual communities are exclusive, and intrusion by an academic researcher could easily be rejected. It is very important to be "a native" when conducting an on-line measurement in a CMC.

A study that tried to set up a game experiment (a typical tool used for quantitative researching) among regular users of Bulletin Board Systems (BBSs) was found to be ineffective in discovering the basic process by which such on-line communication strategies evolve. The artificial and predetermined nature of experiments does not permit participants to manipulate the context creatively, thus it is not surprising that the social-related aspects of CMCs have hardly been explored in laboratories. Issues of anonymity and authenticity remain the core methodological stumbling block for researchers using on-line methods. In structured interviews, the researcher attempts to control the interview by standardizing questions and constraining responses. It is in nonstandardized interviews that the focus moves from the preformulated ideas of the researcher to the meanings and interpretations that individuals attribute to events and relationships.

In the very nature of CMCs lies the difficulty of applying the quantitative approach to the study of virtual communities. The ethnographic approach therefore seems more fruitful when researching with virtual communities. The ethnographic approach, which goes back to Malinowsky's works, entails the sustained immersion of the researcher among those who are being studied, with a view to generating a rounded, in-depth account of the group or organization. The ethnographic approach, however, does not explain phenomena in the classical and impersonal sense of scientific explanation (in the deductive sense, or according to the Hempel–Popper model), whereby explaining a phenomenon means the deduction of a proposition that describes it, using as deductive premises one or more universal laws together with some singular propositions, i.e., the starting conditions. The ethnographic approach means explanation as an "interpretation" of particular phenomena; the ethnographic methodology views human behavior as a product of how people interpret their world. The task for qualitative methodologists is then to capture this process of interpretation in order to grasp the meaning of a person's behavior—that is, to attempt to see things from that person's point of view.

In the ethnographic approach, the main research tools are observational techniques such as participant observation. Such techniques allow the researcher to participate in the activities of the group they are observing. They may be viewed as members of the group, but minimize their participation; they may assume the role of observer without being part of the group, or their presence may be concealed entirely from the people they are observing. Thus, ethnographic methods focus on ordinary, mundane, naturally occurring talk to reveal the way in which meaning is accomplished by everyone involved. Qualitative researchers with an interest in these approaches can, so to speak, observe the natural conversation in various kinds of newsgroups or synchronous conferencing (real-time chat-rooms). By lurking unseen, researchers are able to watch the interaction without intervening in any way.

Some scholars have noted that one of the main problems in applying such techniques to CMCs is the lack of some of the ingredients of face-to-face communications, including nonverbal behavior (such as body language), spatial behavior (such as issues of physical closeness and distance), linguistic behavior (such as parasegmental tracts), and extralinguistic behavior (such as rate of speaking or loudness). A compensatory tool for this lack of physical contact has evolved in the form of "emoticons," typed symbols representing nonverbal and extralinguistic behavior. Although researchers and participants are not in visual or vocal contact, researchers may observe emoticons such as ☺, for smiling; paralinguistic and nonlinguistic cues have also evolved into electronic paralanguage, such as "eheheh" for laughing, or "lol" for "lots of laughs," and the use of capital letters for emphasis.

Applying Quantitative Measurement

The Internet is not only virtual communities, but is also a worldwide supermarket, where shopping can be done at any time. For on-line Internet shopping practices, a quantitative study is more fitting. Classical market research tools can be applied. Such research is based on an underlying design called "correlational" or "cross-sectional," in which data are collected on a cross-section of people at a single point in time in order to discover the ways and degrees to which variables relate to each other. An example of how such a research approach is used on the Internet is the "recommendation for you" section in the Amazon.com website. Based on data pertaining to searching Amazon's website for a particular book title or author, and on purchasing data, Amazon, using a cross-sectional method, is able to recommend and display titles that are likely also to be of interest to the customer (see Figs. 1 and 2). The Amazon example represents well a way in which quantitative research (based on the data-flow analysis, similar to that used in the technical sense of measurement and statistical

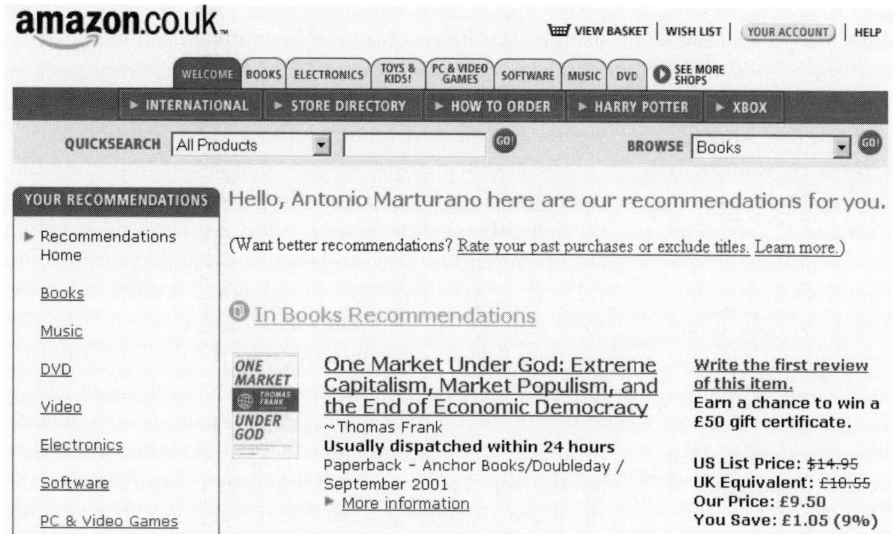

Figure 1 Example of an actual Amazon.com web page from an Internet search for a book (source: http://www.amazon.co.uk; access date, March 3, 2002). © 2004 Amazon.com, Inc. All Rights Reserved.

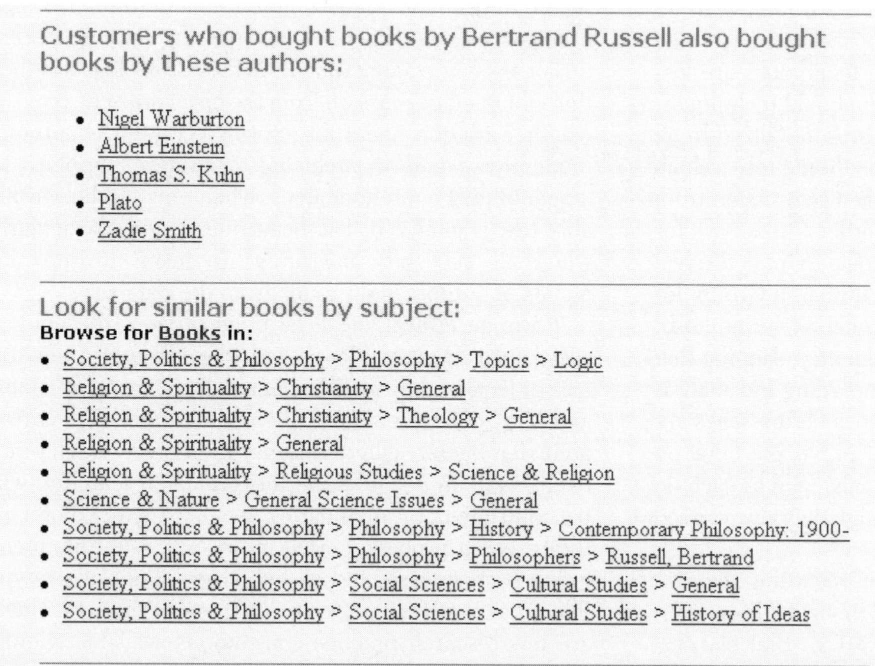

Figure 2 Example of the "recommendation for you" cross-sectional data that Amazon.com provides to customers when they search Amazon for a specific product (source: http://www.amazon.co.uk; access date, March 3, 2002). © 2004 Amazon.com, Inc. All Rights Reserved.

comparison between customers) can be helpful in understanding some social phenomena. (Amazon.co.uk was kindly asked to provide the author some material illustrating how their system works, but said, "due to the extensive number of inquiries that we receive and the competitive nature of our business, our policy is not to give out information to people doing research on the subject.")

Conclusions

Although Internet technology is changing fast, the focus of computer-mediated communications has been primarily on text-based virtual realities, because a majority of studies reflect the fact that only text-based technology is available on-line. Such a technological limitation, rather than being a communication handicap, is an imagination-enhancing challenge. It seems reasonable to suppose that in certain situations, people will prefer textual interactions, even when more advanced technology becomes widely available in the future. Writers such as Neruda, Fo, Hemingway, or Gao Xingjian show us how text alone, without pictures or sounds, is enough to express emotions, experience, and complex ideas. Excellent writing evokes internalized, personal interpretations of sounds or pictures. Nonetheless, on-line technologies are moving toward multimedia systems. Voice and video ("cam") conferencing are becoming affordable and thus very popular among virtual communities, and researchers of virtual communities cannot ignore these new environments. The argument can be made that these technologies have the potential to take the task of the researchers extraordinarily close to that of the traditional field of anthropology.

Internet measurement does raise some ethical issues. A pressing problem in Internet research is privacy; researching as an unobtrusive observer and collecting data, for example, inevitably poses a major ethical problem. Neither can this problem be avoided ad hoc, by using laboratory experiments, because those involve a small number of consenting people. Such techniques are less fruitful compared to "natural" observational techniques, because laboratory findings cannot be generalized to all domains of electronic communication. Some researchers solve this problem by asking for explicit permission from the observed Internet participants; others do not ask for permission and use some obscuring data to mask the real source of their data. The Project H Research Group, focusing on quantitative rather than qualitative methods, after a long debate, issued an ethical policy claiming that they would not seek permission for recording and analysis of publicly posted messages, because such messages are public acts deliberately intended for public consultation (as opposed to private letters or e-mails), and as such do not require specific protection, although they always need to be treated with ordinary care.

A different approach can be taken regarding the protection of privacy for data collected in virtual communities. As stated previously, in CMCs, the classical boundaries between public and private disappear; the interviewer is given data that are not about the participants' physical world, but rather about their on-line self-representation. What happens to the notion of privacy, which is very linked to the very notion of the (physical) private sphere? Indeed, those data, collected using responses from virtual citizens , are likely not expressions of sensitive characteristics. In virtual environments, it could be said, finally, that the notion of privacy plays a less central, if not a marginal, role than it does in the physical world. On the contrary, in on-line shopping, the notion of privacy seems fundamental, because correlated data methods make it possible to obtain very personal profiles of individual consumers. The same databases used by the Internet researcher can be used to construct extremely accurate personal profiles concerning everything from finances to what a person eats, drinks, and wears, as well as revealing intimate personal details.

The notion of informed consent plays an important role in both qualitative and quantitative measurement: giving participants comprehensive and correct information about a research study, and ensuring that they understand fully what participation would entail before securing their consent to take part, should be a key issue to be addressed when creating a framework for ethical Internet research practice. This does raise some problems when applying the ethnographic method to study virtual communities. For example, how will people know when they are the objects of a study? If the researcher "discloses" the intention of studying a particular web-based community, will the result of the research be altered? Is ethnographic electronic research the equivalent to hanging out on street corners (where researchers would never think of wearing large signs identifying themselves as "researchers")? Again, in this field of social measurement, there is a lack of consensus; it is therefore not surprising that researchers do not always declare explicitly in their study logs whether they obtained permission from the observed. The issue of whether a requirement for informed consent of authors, moderators, and/or archiving institutions applies to a quantitative content analysis, when only publicly available text is analyzed, has been questioned, particularly when all necessary measures are taken to separate names of authors and groups from the database.

From an ethical and legal point of view, the field of social measurement shares with the Internet a general lack of legal certainty. Ethical guidelines are insufficient, and very little agreement about how to proceed in a virtual arena has been reached. Because Internet research practice is still in its infancy, the critical researcher will be confronted by quandaries at almost every point in the research process. e-Mail interviews, real time focus group participation, and on-line observations all present dilemmas that Internet researchers must face, yet there are few research practice conventions available. Confidentiality is also quite a problematic issue, because data collected on-line are subject to multiple privacy risks, and there are no easy solutions, although disguising identities still remains the best solution.

To sum up, the Internet does not appear, generally, to be a new or discipline-challenging research ground for social measurement, although virtual communities do represent an exciting exception.

See Also the Following Articles

Computerized Record Linkage and Statistical Matching • Web Hyperlink Analysis • Wundt, Wilhelm

Further Reading

Adler, P. A. (1985). *Wheeling and Dealing: An Ethnography of an Upper-Level Drug Dealing and Smuggling Society.* Columbia University Press, New York.

Bogdan, R., and Taylor, S. J. (1975). *Introduction to Qualitative Research Methods: A Phenomenological Approach to the Social Sciences.* Wiley, New York.

Bryman, A. (1988). *Quantity and Quality in Social Research.* Routledge, London.

Frankfort-Nachmias, C., and Nachmias, D. (1996). *Research Methods in the Social Sciences.* St. Martin's Press, London.

Guba, E. G., and Lincoln, Y. S. (1982). Epistemological and methodological bases of naturalistic enquiry. *Educat. Commun. Technol. J.* **30**(4), 233–252.

Hirschi, T. (1969). *Causes of Delinquency.* University of California Press, Berkeley.

Mann, C., and Stewart, F. (2000). *Internet Communication and Qualitative Research: a Handbook for Researching Online*. Sage, London.

May, T. (1993). *Social Research: Issues, Methods and Processes.* Open University Press, Buckingham.

Myers, D. (1987). Anonymity is part of the magic: Individual manipulation of computer-mediated communications. *Qual. Sociol.* **10,** 251–266.

Paccagnella, L. (1997). Getting the seats of your pants dirty: Strategies for ethnographic research on virtual communities. *J. Computer-Mediated Commun.* **3**(1), June (available on-line at http://www.ascusc.org).

Packard, V. (1957). *The Hidden Persuaders.* McKay & Co., New York.

Popper, K. (1959). *The Logic of Scientific Discovery.* Hutchinson & Co., London.

Shields, R. (ed.) (1996). *Cultures of the Internet: Virtual Spaces, Real Histories, Living Bodies*. Sage London.

Sterling, B. (1993). Internet. *Mag. Fantasy Sci. Fiction* **84**(2), February (available on-line at http://www.lysator.liu.se).

Stone, R. (1991). Will the real body please stand up?: Boundary stories about virtual cultures. In *Cyberspace: First Steps* (M. Benedikt, ed.), pp. 81–118. MIT Press, Cambridge.

Sudweeks, F., and Rafaeli, S. (1996). How do you get a hundred strangers to agree: Computer mediated communication and collaboration. In *Computer Networking and Scholarship in the 21st Century University* (T. M. Harrison and T. D. Stephen, eds.), pp. 115–136. SUNY Press, Albany, New York (available on-line at http://www.it.murdoch.edu).

Walther, J. (1999). *Researching Internet Behavior: Methods, Issues and Concerns*. National Communication Association Summer Conf., Communication and Technology, Washington, D.C.

Interviews

Casey A. Klofstad
Harvard University, Cambridge, Massachusetts, USA

Glossary

close-ended question A question in an interview to which the respondent chooses his or her answer from a set list of choices.

error Any instance in which the data collected through an interview are not an accurate representation of what the researcher thinks he or she is measuring or any instance in which data are not completely representative of the population under study.

focus group A group interview; a moderator leads a group of similar people in discussion on a topic of interest to the researcher. The moderator encourages participants to share their opinions with one another in order to collect data on the topic under study.

incentive A way of increasing the benefits of participating in an interview, relative to the costs, in order to increase participation. Incentives can be solidary or material.

open-ended question A question in an interview to which the respondent must create his or her own answer because a set list of choices is not provided.

personal interview A one-on-one conversation between an interviewer and a respondent; akin to the work of journalists.

questionnaire A predetermined list of interview questions that is either filled out by the interviewee or the researcher. Synonyms include interview schedule and instrument.

respondent A participant in an interview. In some fields, the word subject can be an analogous term.

response rate The number of completed interviews as a percentage of the entire sample size.

response scale The set of answers a respondent chooses from in answering a close-ended question.

sample The subset of a population that is selected to participate in the interview.

An interview is a method of directly collecting data on the attitudes and behaviors of individuals through questions posed by the researcher and answers provided by a respondent.

Introduction

What is an Interview?

An interview is a method of collecting data on the attitudes and behaviors of individuals through some form of conversation between the researcher and a respondent. Unlike research methods that rely on less direct sources of information about social phenomena (for example, indirect observation, archival research, and formal theoretical approaches), interviews are unique because data are collected directly from the individuals who are creating and experiencing the social phenomenon under study.

Direct measurement of social phenomena has its advantages. The data collected are timely. Information can be collected on topics for which archival or other preexisting data sources do not exist, are unreliable, or are incomplete. The social measures derived from interviews, in theory, directly reflect the attitudes and behaviors of individuals in society. And, unlike an archive or a set of economic indicators, the researcher can interact with the subject under study in order to gain a richer understanding of social phenomena. However, interviews can be time-consuming and costly to implement correctly and often require hiring the services of trained professionals. Interview subjects may be less likely to reveal certain types of sensitive or detailed information to a researcher. Interviews also can create a tendency to focus too much on the individual and not enough on his or her social context. Also, as discussed later in this article, direct measurement of social phenomena through interviews can also invite biases and errors in social measurement.

Types of Interviews

Personal Interviews

Personal interviews, akin to the work of journalists, involve one-on-one conversations with a set of respondents. An example here would be a researcher who is interested in the role of lobbyists in policymaking interviewing a number of lobbyists and members of Congress. This type of interview has a tendency to be less structured than the other types discussed in this article because the process can be more spontaneous and open-ended. The interview schedule may be defined in some manner by the interviewer before the interview takes place, but the conversation may deviate from this preset format as the researcher discovers new information. Because of the relatively large amount of work involved in comprehensively studying each respondent, this type of interview often forces the researcher to focus on interviewing a smaller number of respondents. However, this procedure also allows the researcher to obtain rich narrative information from those few individuals.

Focus Groups

A focus group is conducted by engaging a group of respondents who are of interest to the researcher in a group conversation. The individuals are often similar to one another in some way that is germane to the research question (for example, a group of teachers could be gathered to conduct a focus group on the resource needs of educators). During the discussion, participants are encouraged by the moderator to share their opinions, "without pressuring participants to vote or reach consensus" (Krueger and Casey, 2000: p. 4). The moderator strives to create a nonjudgmental environment in order to make the participants more willing to express their opinions openly. It is standard practice for the researcher to conduct many focus group sessions in order to discover potentially meaningful trends across the groups. Like the personal interview, this type of interview can be structured *a priori*. However, because focus group respondents are engaged in free discussion, the researcher does not have complete control over the path of the conversation. In addition, because of the cost and effort involved in gathering and running focus groups, the method often allows the researcher to interview a relatively small number of individuals. Therefore, focus groups are not commonly used when the researcher needs to generate data that are statistically representative of a large population. However, the more open mode of a focus group discussion allows the researcher to find out what matters are of greater interest to respondents. Such data can also be used to develop more formally structured questionnaires (see below). The ability to dig deeper into issues through focus groups can also allow the researcher to untangle complicated topics.

Questionnaires

A questionnaire is a predetermined list of interview questions that is filled out by either the respondent or the researcher. This form of interview is highly structured because the path of the conversation is determined before it begins and is not deviated from. As questionnaires came into wider use, these types of interviews were likely to be conducted in person, usually in the respondent's home. However, with the spread of telecommunications technology during the 1970s, along with decreasing success and increasing costs associated with administering questionnaires face-to-face, these types of interviews began to be increasingly conducted through the mail and over the telephone. Self-administered questionnaires have also been conducted over the Internet. However, because the number of individuals in the general public that have access to the Internet is relatively small, this method is controversial in certain applications. A key benefit of questionnaires is that they can be administered to many people. This allows the researcher to make more reliable inferences about the entire population under study. However, the tradeoff involved is that the researcher is usually not able to obtain as much rich narrative information as with other methods, because respondents are often reluctant or unable to provide detailed or in-depth information on a predefined questionnaire. Either respondents can be unwilling to supply such information or the format of a questionnaire can be too constrictive to allow for the collection of such detailed information.

What Type of Interview is the Best?

In the end, choosing what type of interview method to use comes down to determining what the particular needs of the research project are and how those needs are best met within budgetary constraints. There are, therefore, many different issues that can be taken into consideration when deciding what type of interview procedure to use. However, one very important way to determine what type of interview technique to utilize is to determine what type of data is needed and how generalizable the data need to be. Research designs that allow the researcher to interview many people (questionnaire-based studies) can have the benefit of allowing the researcher, if enough interviews are completed, to make reliable statistical inferences about the population under study. However, questionaire-based interviews can be less effective if the researcher does not know what specific types of questions to ask or if the researcher needs to obtain a sizable amount of deep narrative information about specific types of respondents. Interview designs that commonly yield fewer interviews (focus groups and personal interviews) typically have the benefit of allowing the researcher to gather a large amount of rich narrative data from a smaller subset of the population. The method also allows the researcher to learn about topics that he or she might not have much knowledge on yet. However, this method is likely to be less useful if the researcher is looking to make more generalizable statistical inferences about a large population.

It is important to note that there are cases where a mixed-mode approach may be useful. For example, a researcher may want to learn about how many individuals feel about a certain issue, but he or she may also be unsure what specific issues are important to cover in the interviews. In this case, it may be useful to begin with a series of focus groups in order to learn what questions to ask in questionnaire-based interviews conducted on a larger sample. In these and other cases, results from one style of interview can serve to augment and inform the results of another. However, it is important to consider that different interview modes can produce incompatible findings. For example, the type of person that is more likely to complete a telephone interview might be different from the type of person that is more likely to respond to a mail survey.

Issues in Interview Design and Execution

Types of Interview Questions: Closed- and Open-Ended

There are two ways to structure the responses that respondents offer: open- and close-ended questions. Open-ended questions are "fill-in-the-blank" items, where the respondent offers his or her own answer. Close-ended questions are those that give the respondent a finite set of specified responses from which to choose. In general, close-ended questions are more appropriate when the respondent has a specific answer to give (for example, gender), when the researcher has a predefined set of answers in mind to a question, when detailed narrative information is not needed, or when there is a finite number of ways to answer a question (for example, gender). Open-ended items are more useful when the respondent is able to provide a ready-made answer of his or her own, when the researcher is not certain what answers to provide or wants to conduct more exploratory research, when the researcher wants to obtain narrative data, or when the number of potential responses to a question is known but large and difficult to specify *a priori* for the respondent (for example, occupation). Both types of questions can be used in the same interview because the different types allow researchers to accomplish different goals.

Use of Response Scales in Close-Ended Questions

A key issue to consider in using close-ended questions is how to structure response scales. The type of scale chosen should reflect what the question is trying to measure. Ordered scales ask the respondent to place himself or herself on an opinion continuum. For example, Likert-type scales are 4- or 5-point scales that probe for feelings on issues in reference to agreement or disagreement with a statement (for example, "agree," "somewhat agree," "somewhat disagree," "disagree"). The Likert-type scale can also be modified to measure other types of opinions and behaviors (for example, a scale that runs from "Poor" to "Excellent" to measure how individuals rate a governmental program or from "All of the Time" to "Never" to see how often individuals engage in a certain behavior). Feeling thermometers allow the respondent to choose a number from 0 to 100 in order to rate how "warm" or "cold" he or she feels toward a certain concept, policy, person, or the like. Polar point scales ask the respondent to place himself or herself on a numbered scale, where the ends signify opposite opinions. Unlike the scales just discussed, unordered or nominal scales offer different classes or categories to choose from (for example, types of sports that the respondent plays, or, of the options listed, which public policy should be funded).

Question Ordering

It is important to consider how to order questions in an interview. Research on "context effects" in interviews has shown that the content of a question can affect responses to the questions that follow it. This occurs because respondents create their answers to interview questions, in part, based on what material they have been thinking about beforehand. As one example of such context effects, in thinking about how a respondent might answer a question about Bill Clinton's integrity, Moore shows that if a "... question about Clinton's integrity is preceded by a similar question about Al Gore's integrity... it is likely that some people, to varying degrees, will include their assessment of Gore as a part of the comparative standard by which they judge Clinton" (2002, p. 82). In short, the order of questions matters because individuals make use of the context that they are in when they form responses.

Potential Sources of Error

Measurement Error

Measurement error, a case in which the respondent has somehow provided inaccurate or uninterpretable information, has many potential sources.

Question Wording In thinking about the errors that question wording can produce, it is helpful to consider the following two questions:

1993 Roper Poll Question: "Does it seem possible or does it seem impossible to you that the Nazi extermination of the Jews never happened?"

1993 Gallup Poll Question: "Does it seem possible to you that the Nazi extermination of the Jews never happened or do you feel certain that it happened?"

These questions, although seemingly similar, produced strikingly different results. The Roper poll showed that over one-third of Americans were either unsure or thought that the Holocaust was a hoax. In sharp contrast, the Gallup poll question showed that only 10% of the population were Holocaust doubters.

What this example highlights is how question wording can significantly impact the data collected. As Dillman aptly points out, "The goal of writing a survey question . . . is to develop a query that every potential respondent will interpret in the same way, be able to respond to accurately, and be willing to answer" (2000, p. 32). In other words, in order to reduce measurement error, researchers need to construct questions that are understandable and that give the same "stimulus" to each respondent. To achieve this, Dillman suggests that numerous questions need to be considered when wording questions: Will the respondent be able to understand the question? Does the respondent have the knowledge to answer the question? Does the question wording somehow "frame" the question in a certain manner? Does the wording bias, *a priori*, how the respondent is likely to answer? Will the respondent be willing to answer the question or is the question too personal or sensitive in nature? Are all of the questions worded in a fairly consistent manner?

Issues with Respondents Measurement can also be in error in terms of how the respondent understands and responds to the question. Respondents may not understand a question, may not know how to use the scales provided, may become fatigued or disinterested in the interview, or may feel that the researcher wants them to answer in a certain "socially desirable" way. Any and all of these factors can lead to inaccurate measurement.

Issues with Interviewers Measurement error can also occur because of the traits or behaviors of the interviewer. These errors can occur because of the intentional actions of the interviewer, e.g., if questions are not read accurately or if respondents are encouraged to answer questions in a specific way by the interviewer. Research has also shown that there are various unintentional sources of measurement error caused by interviewers. For example, a 1993 study by Kane and Macaulay shows that in some cases, respondents provide more "pro-woman" responses when interviewed by a female. A 1991 study by Finkel *et al.* finds similar results due to race. Numerous other examples exist.

Sampling and Coverage Error

Interview data can also be imprecise because of errors in sampling and coverage. Sampling error is the product of collecting data from only some, and not all, of the individuals in a population. If one were to interview every individual in a population, the social measures constructed from those data would be a statistically accurate representation of the population with 100% confidence. One would know how everyone in the population responded to the question and hence there would be no error in one's assessment of how the population responded to the question. However, if every member of a population is not interviewed, statistically random error creeps into the measures calculated from interview data because one cannot know with 100% confidence how the population as a whole would have responded to the interview questions. Sampling error accordingly reduces confidence in the precision of measurement. Because of this, the size or margin of this random sampling error must be presented whenever presenting interview results.

Similarly, coverage errors occur when each individual in the population does not have an equal chance of being included in the sample. For example, consider a study of political participation that has generated a sample from voter registration records. This sample would clearly be biased because it failed to cover individuals who are not politically active, in this case nonvoters.

Nonresponse Error

Nonresponse errors result when the individuals who complete the interview are somehow systematically different than those who were unable to be contacted and those who chose not to participate. For example, consider an interview project that is being conducted on political participation. Based on its content, individuals who are more politically active may be more interested in participating in the interview, leaving the attitudes and behaviors of those who are less politically active out of the analysis. Thus, in order to reduce such errors, it is essential to conduct interviews with as many individuals in the sample as possible. It is also helpful to examine interview data carefully to see whether the individuals who are choosing to respond are somehow different than the population at large in a way that is germane to the topic under study.

Getting People to Respond: The Key to Any Interview Project

Maximizing response rate is vital to the success of any interviewer project. As alluded to in the section above on sampling and coverage error, higher response rates translate into more precise and representative measures of the population under study.

Scores of ideas about how to increase respondent participation exist, but these various techniques can be easily summarized through the concepts of costs and benefits. Social relationships are defined by a system of social exchange; individuals engage with others socially if the benefits that others provide exceed the costs of social interaction. Thus, in order to encourage a potential respondent to participate in an interview, the costs of participation need to be reduced and the benefits need to be increased. Numerous techniques are utilized to reduce costs, including trying to gain the trust of the respondent, wording questions in a way that makes them easy to understand and respond to, and laying out self-administered questionnaires in a way that makes them easy to follow. Benefits are increased through offering the respondent material benefits (for example, money, a souvenir) or solidary benefits (for example, communicating how participation will aid the researcher in resolving an important public policy issue of interest to the respondent).

Although reducing costs and increasing benefits is effective, the greatest challenge facing those who use interview techniques will be to adapt and apply this theory of social exchange to new technologies and a changing society. It usually takes a great amount of effort and skill on the part of many professionals in order to finish an interview project with a high response rate. However, it is becoming harder to maintain high response rates. Three related reasons likely account for falling response rates. The first is technology: from caller ID to answering machines and Internet spam filters, households are becoming more equipped to block out messages from strangers. Second, direct marketing through the mail, telephone, and Internet has left the public "fatigued" and less willing to converse with or respond to strangers. Finally, researchers have also documented that the American public has become more withdrawn and less socially engaged since the mid-1900s.

Acknowledgments

Thanks are extended to Robert Lee (University of California–Berkeley Survey Research Center), Jordan Petchenik (State of Wisconsin Department of Natural Resources), John Stevenson (University of Wisconsin–Madison Survey Center), and an anonymous reviewer for comments.

See Also the Following Articles

Focus Groups • Surveys

Further Reading

American Association for Public Opinion Research Web Site. Refer to numerous documents on how to design and conduct interviews. http://www.aapor.com

Crabb, P. B. (1999). The use of answering machines and caller ID to regulate home privacy. *Environ. Behav.* **31,** 657–670.

Dillman, D. (1978). *Mail and Telephone Surveys: The Total Design Method.* Wiley, New York.

Dillman, D. (2000). *Mail and Internet Surveys: The Tailored Design Method.* Wiley, New York.

Finkel, S. E., Guterbock, T. M., and Borg, M. J. (1991). Race-of-interviewer effects in a preelection poll: Virginia 1989. *Public Opin. Q.* **55,** 313–330.

Fox, R. J., Crask, M. R., and Kim, J. (1988). Mail survey response rate: A meta-analysis of selected techniques for inducing response. *Public Opin. Q.* **52,** 467–491.

Kane, E. W., and Macaulay, L. J. (1993). Interviewer gender and gender attitudes. *Public Opin. Q.* **57,** 1–28.

Krueger, R. A., and Casey, M. A. (2000). *Focus Groups: A Practical Guide for Applied Research.* Sage, Thousand Oaks, CA.

Mertinko, E., Novotney, L. C., Baker, T. K., and Lange, J. (2000). *Evaluating Your Program: A Beginner's Self-Evaluation Workbook for Mentoring Programs.* Information Technology International, Inc., Potomac, MD. Available at http://www.itiincorporated.com/publications.htm

Moore, D. W. (2002). Measuring new types of question-order effects. *Public Opin. Q.* **66,** 80–91.

Putnam, R. (2000). *Bowling Alone: The Collapse and Revival of American Community.* Simon & Schuster, New York.

Sharp, L. M., and Frankel, J. (1983). Respondent burden: A test of some common assumptions. *Public Opin. Q.* **47,** 36–53.

Snyder, M. L. (1990). Self-monitoring of expressive behavior. In *Social Psychology Readings* (A. G. Halberstadt and S. L. Ellyson, eds.), pp. 67–79. McGraw-Hill, New York.

Yammarino, F. J., Skinner, S. J., and Childers, T. L. (1991). Understanding mail survey response behavior: A meta-analysis. *Public Opin. Q.* **55,** 613–639.

Item and Test Bias

Howard Wainer
National Board of Medical Examiners, Philadelphia, Pennsylvania, USA

Stephen G. Sireci
University of Massachusetts, Amherst, Massachusetts, USA

Glossary

construct The unobservable attribute purportedly measured by a test.

differential item functioning A statistically significant difference in performance on a test item across two or more groups of examinees, after the examinees have been matched on the construct of interest.

differential predictive validity A statistically significant difference across two or more groups of examinees, in the degree to which test scores predict a relevant criterion.

item bias A statistically significant difference across two or more groups of examinees due to characteristics of the item unrelated to the construct being measured.

test bias A systematic increase or reduction in test scores for one or more groups of examinees due to factors unrelated to the construct measured by the test.

validity The credibility and the relevance of the evidence provided by the measuring instrument for the inferences that the users of the test want to draw.

A test is an instrument that provides evidence from which inferences can be drawn. A test score is a summary of this evidence. The degree to which test evidence is credible and relevant is characterized by the psychometric term "validity." Valid decisions based on test scores for a particular purpose must be supported by theory and empirical evidence. Biases in test scores diminish validity, and so great effort is expended in ameliorating them. In this article, some of the relevant issues related to this topic are discussed, as well as some of the statistical methodologies that are commonly used to detect both bias and differential item functioning.

Introduction: Validity and Invalidity

Understanding Validity Nomenclature

Bias in measurement instruments is a concern for all scientists, which is why scales for measuring weight and other physical properties are regularly recalibrated. However, in the social sciences, the more intangible, psychological attributes measured are much more susceptible to error. For this reason, evaluation of the measurement instrument is intertwined with measurement of the construct of interest. In 1955, Cronbach and Meehl introduced the term "construct" to acknowledge the fact that the "thing" being measured by educational and psychological tests is often an unobservable, postulated attribute "constructed" by theorists and test developers.

Sources of bias in testing are typically attributed to either construct-irrelevant variance or construct under representation. Construct-irrelevant variance refers to one or more systematic sources of variation in test scores irrelevant to the construct the test is trying to measure. Examples of such bias in test scores include contextual effects and response biases. A context effect may occur, for example, when a mathematics test includes a preponderance of word problems that are related to baseball. In such a case, baseball knowledge may interfere with measurement of mathematics proficiency. Response biases would include "yea-saying" and other types of social desirability on surveys and personality inventories, or test-taking strategies on educational exams. In such cases, test scores are influenced by a construct different from the one the test is designed to measure.

Construct underrepresentation occurs when the test measures the construct too narrowly and some important aspects of it are left out. Some obvious examples might be a general science test that includes optics and thermodynamics but not genetics, a licensing test for physicians that includes scientific but not clinical knowledge, or tests of physical ability, such as those used for selecting fire fighters, that focus on physical strength to the exclusion of flexibility and dexterity. It is easy to imagine how the difference in the distribution of scores of men and women could be manipulated by arbitrarily varying the composition of the test.

Quality assessments strive for adequate construct representation and try to eliminate or minimize construct-irrelevant factors that may influence test performance. If such factors affect test scores, bias is present and the interpretations based on test scores may be invalid.

Bias and Impact

To understand test and item bias requires, first, understanding the difference between impact and bias. Impact refers to significant group differences in performance on a test or on a test item. The observation that women, as a group, score noticeably lower in height than men is an example of impact. Such observed differences do not necessarily signify that the ruler is biased, because the difference in heights could very well reflect a true difference between the groups. The potential causes of such a difference are a separate issue beyond the scope here, but the important point is that between-group differences in test scores could reflect true group differences, and so impact does not necessarily signify bias. A determination of bias requires additional evidence indicating that systematic and construct-irrelevant material does differentially affect scores.

A large number of methods have been developed to investigate item and test bias. Four methods that have been suggested for investigating item bias, and one for investigating test bias, are described in the following sections. One method, the delta plot, is included for historical reasons. Two others, the Mantel–Haenszel procedure and the item response theory (IRT)-based maximum likelihood method, are included because they are representative of the two broad classes of methods (observed score and model based) that are widely used. Moreover, each of these procedures is statistically optimal under plausible conditions. Other, similar methods are sometimes used, but do not enjoy either the same breadth of usage or the same level of statistical efficiency. This latter characteristic is very important, because organizations that produce tests would like to look for differential item functioning (DIF) and not find any. Thus it is a moral imperative that any attempts to find DIF must use the largest samples and the most powerful statistical procedures possible. It is only in this way that it can credibly be claimed that the test has been examined for fairness and no flaws were discovered.

Item Bias and Differential Item Functioning

Item bias refers to the situation wherein a statistically significant difference in performance on an item is observed across two or more groups of examinees, and the reason for the difference can be traced to a source other than the construct measured by the test. When there is a quantitative criterion that the test is predicting (e.g., using a college admissions test to predict freshman grade point average), the conclusion that an item is biased can be based on purely empirical evidence. But in those circumstances when the criterion is not so easily characterized quantitatively (e.g., a medical licensing exam in which the criterion is whether the person will become a good doctor), the decision about bias requires both statistical and judgmental information. In either instance, it must first be concluded that the item "functions" differentially across groups. When there is a quantitative criterion, "functions differently" means the test underpredicts one group relative to the other. When such a criterion does not exist, subject-matter experts and other experts familiar with the groups of examinees must be able to identify a source of bias that explains the differential performance.

The assessment of differential performance can be done on all tests using information contained in the scores, without reference to an external criterion. Such assessments are called differential item functioning. DIF analyses evaluate whether examinees from different groups (e.g., females and males) who are of comparable ability on the entire test have equal probabilities of success on an item. In DIF analyses, conditioning procedures are used systematically to match examinees of similar proficiency across groups, to distinguish between overall group differences on an item (item impact) and potential item bias. That is, DIF procedures focus on differences in item performance across groups after the groups are matched on the construct measured by the test. In DIF analyses, test-takers from different groups are matched on the psychological attribute measured, and the probability of differential responses across matched test-takers is evaluated. Items are considered to be functioning differentially across groups if the probability of a particular response differs significantly across test-takers who are equivalent (i.e., matched) on proficiency. The most common conditioning variable used in DIF analyses is the total test score. If the conditioning variable is the criterion score, what is uncovered is bias and not merely DIF.

Adverse Impact and Test Bias

Score differences between two or more groups of examinees are common in educational and psychological testing. Such differences are called "impact," and in some cases when a minority group exhibits lower average performance, it is called "adverse impact" or "disparate impact." Disparate impact has received significant attention in the courts because Title VII of the Civil Rights Act of 1964 (Title VII, 1999) forbids employers from refusing to hire individuals on the basis of race, color, religion, sex, or national origin, and so when disparate impact appears on employment tests, minorities get hired at lower rates, as compared to nonminorities. A common definition of disparate impact is when the "passing" (or selection) rate for members of a particular protected group is less than 80% of the passing rate for the group with the highest rate of selection. However, impact does not signify bias, and so the courts require testing agencies to establish that there is a sound scientific basis for use of the test and that the test is not biased against the protected group. Test bias occurs when the test scores for one or more groups are systematically increased or reduced due to factors unrelated to the construct measured by the test. If a test is biased against one or more groups, the differences observed between groups are misleading and the test scores cannot be assumed to have the same meaning across groups.

As for item bias, several statistical methods for investigating test bias exist. One way test developers reduce the likelihood of test bias and disparate impact is to pretest items and screen them for DIF before assembling the final test form. Thus, before describing methods for evaluating test bias, methods for evaluating DIF must first be described.

Evaluating Item Bias

There are many statistical methods for evaluating DIF. The four methods most commonly used in high-stakes testing environments are the delta plot, standardization, Mantel–Haenszel, and a method based on item response theory. All DIF procedures have, as their goal an estimate of the difference between groups, after controlling for the construct measured on the test. Typically, DIF detection methods evaluate item functioning across two groups. The group about which there is concern is denoted the focal group. The other group is called the reference group.

The Delta Plot Method

The delta plot method provides a visual comparison of item difficulty statistics to allow the identification of items that function differentially across groups. This relatively early procedure was designed for identifying potentially biased educational test items that were scored correct or incorrect. The procedure involves first calculating the proportions of examinees in the reference and focal groups who answer an item correctly (p-values). Next, the normal transform of these p-values is calculated and scaled to any convenient metric (historically, they were scaled so that the mean over both groups is 13 and the standard deviation is 4). These transformed p-values were originally called "group-specific item difficulties" and denoted as "item deltas," the eponymic source of the method's name. These calculations yield group-specific deltas for each item. They are then plotted against one another, with the reference group on the horizontal axis and the focal group on the vertical one. If the relative difficulties of the items are consistent across groups, they will fall on a 45° line. If the difficulty of any item is different in the two groups, that item will deviate from this line.

The overall difference in ability between groups in a delta plot is characterized by the intercept of the regression line running through the scatter plot. If the intercept is at 0, the two groups have the same ability distributions. If the intercept on the focal group's axis is, say, 1, it means that the mean of the focal group's ability distribution is 1 delta (a fourth of a standard deviation) lower than the mean of the reference group. Items that fall within a narrow ellipse around the 45° line have approximately equal difficulty in both groups and thus can be considered as equivalent or unbiased. Items that deviate significantly from this line are said to have demonstrated DIF. The delta plot makes clear that DIF is a concept of interaction. The main effects represent overall item difficulty and group mean ability. When an item deviates from the simple combination of these two main effects and shows a significant interaction, it is singled out for closer study. The delta plot example in Fig. 1 presents the delta values computed from fictitious examinees. The fact that the 45° line does not emanate from the origin reflects the overall difference in proficiency between the two groups, which is 1.0 (in favor of group 1) in this case. A confidence band is drawn around this line, and the four items that fall far enough outside this band are flagged for DIF.

The delta plot method is relatively easy to do and interpret. However, it has been shown to miss items that function differently across groups if the discriminating power of the item is low, and to flag items for DIF erroneously if the discriminating power of the item is high. For these reasons, although it is of historical interest, the delta plot is rarely used today.

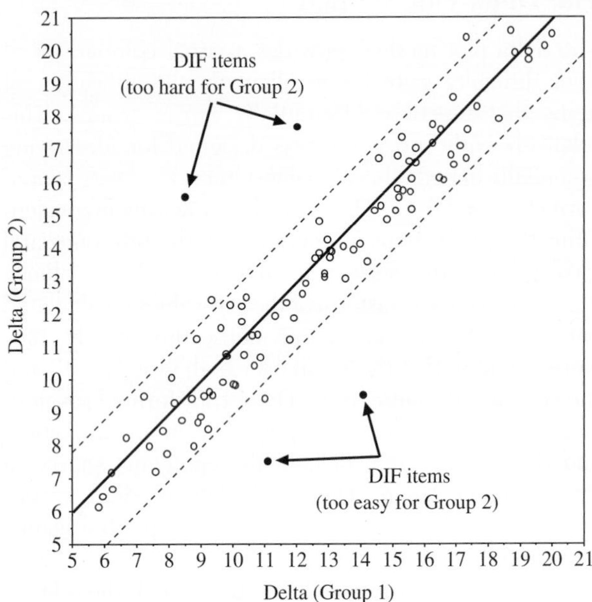

Figure 1 An example of the graphical method (delta plot) of differential item functioning (DIF) detection, now of primarily historical interest.

The Standardization Index

In 1986, Dorans and Kulick suggested using traditional standardization methods to construct an index for detecting DIF. This method is a "conditional p-value" procedure, whereby separate p-values are computed for each item conditional on total test score for each group. The difference between these estimates is then calculated between the reference and the focal groups. A summary statistic is then calculated by summing up these differences weighted by score distribution of the reference group. In practice, test score intervals are computed to match examinees (i.e., thick matching) so that the sample sizes per test score interval are not too small. The standardized proportion (STD-P) index that Dorans and Kulick proposed is computed as follows:

$$\text{STD-P} = \frac{\sum_m w_m (E_{\text{fm}} - E_{\text{rm}})}{\sum_m w_m}, \tag{1}$$

where w_m is the relative frequency of the reference group at score level m, and E_{fm} and E_{rm} are the proportion of examinees at score level m who answered the item correctly in the focal and reference groups, respectively. The standardization index ranges from −1 to 1. (Although Dorans and Kulick did not propose a statistical test for this statistic, one can easily be computed using the jackknife technique introduced by Rupert Miller.) The STD-P has an easy and direct interpretation. For example, if STD-P is 0.10, it means that, on average, examinees in the reference group who are matched to examinees in the focal group have a 10% greater chance of answering the item correctly.

The Mantel–Haenszel Method

In 1959, Mantel and Haenszel developed a summary statistic for examining the efficacy of a cancer treatment. Patients were stratified by the severity of their illness, and at each level of severity, a 2-by-2 frequency table was constructed. One factor of this table was "treatment" or "control" and the other factor was "survived" or "didn't." Computing a measure of the independence of the two factors at each level was well established. Mantel and Haenszel's contribution was the derivation of a clever weighting scheme to combine the results of all of these 2-by-2 tables across the severity strata in a statistically optimal fashion. The resulting summary statistic has become known as the Mantel–Haenszel statistic, in their honor.

It is clear that if we substitute performance on the test for severity, "reference" and "focal" for "treatment" and "control," and "correct" and "incorrect" for "survive" or "didn't," the Mantel–Haenszel statistic can be directly applied to the problem of estimating DIF. The recognition that Mantel–Haenszel (MH) was well suited for this problem took almost 30 years; it was not until 1988 that Holland and Thayer suggested it. MH is similar to the standardization index in that examinees from two different groups are matched on the proficiency of interest, and the likelihood of success on the item is compared across groups. It is different, however, in that it looks at the odds ratio of success on each item rather than the difference in the probabilities. More importantly, it was a well-researched summary statistic with optimality characteristics that fit well with the moral imperative described earlier. Moreover, it is cheap and easy to compute and so is currently the most commonly used DIF method.

To compute the MH statistic, the following frequencies are calculated at each level of the conditioning variable: the total numbers of examinees in each group, and the numbers of examinees in each group who answered the item correctly and who answered the item incorrectly. An example of the necessary data at just one level of the conditioning variable is presented in Table I.

The null hypothesis tested is that the ratios of the proportions (correct to incorrect) for each group are the same. Using the notation in Table I, the common-odds ratio α_{MH} is estimated by

$$\hat{\alpha}_{\text{MH}} = \frac{\sum_j A_j D_j / T_j}{\sum_j B_j C_j / T_j}. \tag{2}$$

When $\alpha_{\text{MH}} = 1$, the likelihood of responding correctly to the item is the same for both the focal and reference group, across j score levels. The significance of the

Table I Frequencies Needed to Compute the MH Statistic at Each Level of Conditioning Variable

Group	*Answer*[a] *Correct*	*Incorrect*	*Total*
Reference	A_j	B_j	N_{rj}
Focal	C_j	D_j	N_{fj}
Total	M_{1j}	M_{0j}	T_j

[a] M denotes one level of conditioning variable.

deviation of the MH statistic is easily determined through a one-degree of freedom chi-square statistic:

$$\text{MH-}\chi^2 = \frac{\left[\left|\sum_j A_j - \sum_j E(A_j)\right| - 0.5\right]^2}{\sum_j \text{Var}(A_j)}, \tag{3}$$

where

$$\text{Var}(A_j) = \frac{N_{rj}N_{fj}M_{1j}M_{0j}}{T_j^2(T_j - 1)}. \tag{4}$$

In addition to providing a test for statistical significance, an effect size can also be computed, and rules of thumb exist for classifying these effect sizes into small, medium, and large DIF (Dorans & Holland, 1993).

The MH method has been shown to be particularly powerful in detecting DIF. For this reason, it is often used as the standard for comparison in studies that compare DIF detection methods. The MH statistic achieves its power by focusing all evidence on the detection of a single parameter (hence the single degree of freedom), which is the extent to which the log-odds ratio is consistently different than one across all strata. It is trying to detect what has come to be called uniform DIF. The cost of this single-mindedness is that it cannot detect other sorts of deviations; specifically, it cannot detect deviations that vary systematically across strata ("nonuniform" DIF). Many studies have shown that both types of DIF can occur on educational tests. Other methods do not have these limitations, and the most powerful of these are discussed next.

Methods Based on Item Response Theory

The three methods for DIF detection described previously were all observed score methods in that they do not posit a strong model for item responses. Because of its optimality characteristics, the MH does about as well as is possible with observed score methods. Thus the most logical way to try to achieve greater flexibility and power is to lean on a stronger test response model. This path has been followed and there are several methods for detecting DIF based on item response theory, which is the most common test scoring methodology in current use. All these methods test whether a common set of item parameters can be used to describe the functioning of an item in each group. If different parameters are needed to describe the functioning of the item in each group, then the item is flagged for DIF.

Fitting an IRT model to an entire test in which all items are assumed to behave the same in both groups, and then fitting a slightly more general model in which the studied item is allowed to have different parameters in the two groups, immediately suggests a likelihood ratio procedure to determine if the fit is improved with the more general model. If the fit is improved, there is DIF; if it is not, there is no DIF. Such a procedure has both flexibility and power. It is flexible in that it can assess differences in item behavior in any way that can be characterized by the model. It is powerful in that it has all of the optimality of maximum likelihood. Thissen, Steinberg, and Wainer developed this procedure, in two papers in 1988 and 1993, following a suggestion by Lord in 1980.

This procedure requires rather heavy computing; for each item, multiple IRT models must be fit to the data. When the assessment comprises a large number of items, and the no-DIF model is rejected, isolating the specific DIF items can be an arduous process. Modern computing has eased this task considerably. In 2001, Thissen prepared a computer program that does the analyses for long sequences of items automatically, and so the computing is a long way from the back-of-the-envelope calculations required for the observed score methods; it is no longer as daunting a task as it was when first proposed. Even for operational-length tests, a full IRT DIF analysis can be done on a standard desktop computer in the time it takes to get a cup of coffee.

Evaluating Test Bias

The evaluation of test bias focuses on test scores rather than on test items. In most cases, evaluation of bias operates within a predictive validity framework. Predictive validity is the degree to which test scores accurately predict scores on a criterion measure. A conspicuous example is the degree to which college admissions test scores predict college grade point average (GPA). Given this predictive context, it should not be surprising that regression models are used to evaluate predictive validity. The analysis of test bias typically investigates whether the relationship between test and criterion scores is consistent across examinees from different groups. Such studies of test bias are often referred to as studies of differential predictive validity.

There are two common methods for evaluating test bias using regression procedures. The first involves fitting separate regression lines to the predictor (test score) and criterion data for each group and then testing for differences in regression coefficients and intercepts. When sufficient data for separate equations are not available, a different method must be used. This method involves fitting only one regression equation. In one variation of this method, the coefficients in the equation are estimated using only the data from the majority group. The analysis of test bias then focuses on predicting the criterion data for examinees in the minority group and examining the errors of prediction (residuals). In another variation of this method, the data from all examinees (i.e., majority and minority examinees) are used to compute the regression equation. The residuals are then compared across groups.

The simplest form of a regression model used in test bias research is $y = b_1X_1 + a + e$, where y is the predicted criterion value, b_1 is a coefficient describing the utility of variable 1 for predicting the criterion, a is the intercept of the regression line (i.e., the predicted value of the criterion when the value of the predictor is zero), and e represents error (i.e., variation in the criterion not explained by the predictors). If the criterion variable were freshman-year GPA and the predictor variable were Scholastic Aptitude Test (SAT) score, b_1 would represent the utility of the SAT for predicting freshman GPA. To estimate the parameters in this equation, data on the predictor and criterion are needed. The residuals (e in the equation) represent the difference between the criterion value predicted by the equation and the actual criterion variable. Every examinee in a predictive validity study has a test score and criterion score. The residual is simply the criterion score minus the score predicted by the test.

Analysis of the residuals in a test bias study focuses on overprediction and underprediction. Overprediction errors occur, for example, when the predicted GPA for a student is higher than her/his actual GPA. Underprediction errors would occur when the predicted GPA for a student is lower than her/his actual GPA. By examining the patterns of over- and underprediction across the examinees from different groups, evidence of differential predictive accuracy is obtained. For example, if the errors of prediction tended to be primarily underprediction errors for females, it could be concluded that the test is biased against females.

This method is flawed, because it can indicate test bias when there is none if the group means are different. Such a result, illustrated in Fig. 2, is merely a regression effect and the use of this methodology when group means are different on both the test and the criterion leads to incorrect inferences. The confusion of impact with bias in the popular media has long added confusion to discussions of this delicate issue. The use of regression methods for detection is not an unmixed blessing.

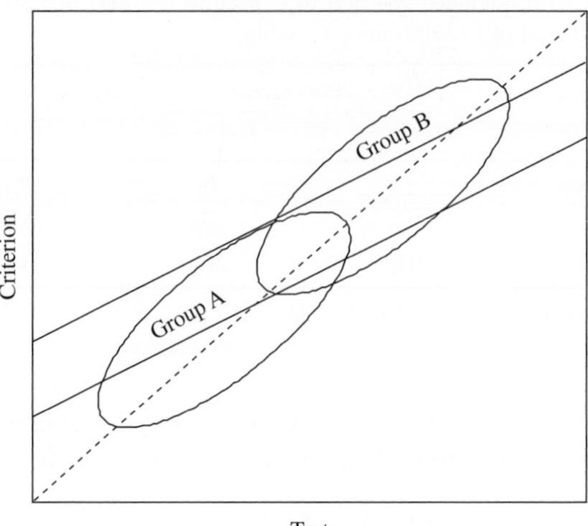

Figure 2 A graphical counterexample to provide a warning for those who would use regression methods to detect test bias when the groups being investigated show substantial differences in level. The two ellipses represent the bivariate distributions of scores on the prediction and the criterion for two different groups (group A and group B). The principal axes of both ellipses lie on the 45° line, but the regression lines are tilted, yielding differential predictions based on group membership. This is not bias, but rather an example of a regression effect.

Bias and Fairness for the Future

Tests have assumed an important role in all meritocratic societies in which the positions within those societies are based principally on the promise of what a person can do, rather than on the ancient criteria of family connections and wealth. Any society that has limited resources must make triage decisions concerning who shall be granted admission to an elite school or who is to be chosen for a particular job opening, for example. Meritocracies use empirical evidence related to the openings to make those decisions. Tests are a special form of evidence. In a real sense, a test score is the result of an experiment. As such, it can be studied, flaws can be detected, and it can be improved. Contrast this with other kinds of evidence, such as interviews and letters of recommendation. These are very much the result of an observational study. A biased letter writer is hard to detect and almost surely cannot be corrected. The methods discussed here are a sampling of a powerful set of statistical procedures designed to examine and improve test scores. Recent trends in education suggest the future holds an ever-increasing role of tests in policy decisions. Because of statistical methods such as these, there is the hope that tests can be made fair enough to satisfy that need properly.

See Also the Following Articles

Classical Test Theory • Item Response Theory • Optimal Test Construction • Test Equating • Validity Assessment

Further Reading

Angoff, W. H. (1972). Use of difficulty and discrimination indices for detecting item bias. In *Handbook of Methods for Detecting Test Bias* (R. A. Berk, ed.), pp. 96–116. Johns Hopkins University Press, Baltimore.

Cronbach, L. J., and Meehl, P. E. (1955). Construct validity in psychological tests. *Psychol. Bull.* **52,** 281–302.

Dorans, N. J., and Holland, P. W. (1993). DIF detection and description: Mantel–Haenszel and standardization. In *Differential Item Functioning* (P. W. Holland and H. Wainer, eds.), pp. 35–66. Lawrence Erlbaum, Hillsdale, New Jersey.

Dorans, N. J., and Kulick, E. (1986). Demonstrating the utility of the standardization approach to assessing unexpected differential item performance on the scholastic aptitude test. *J. Educat. Measure.* **23,** 355–368.

Holland, P. W., and Thayer, D. T. (1988). Differential item functioning and the Mantel–Haenszel procedure. In *Test Validity* (H. Wainer and H. I. Braun, eds.), pp. 129–145. Lawrence Erlbaum, Hillsdale, New Jersey.

Holland, P. W., and Wainer, H. (eds.) (1993). *Differential Item Functioning*. Lawrence Erlbaum, Hillsdale, New Jersey.

Lord, F. M. (1980). *Applications of Item Response Theory to Practical Testing Problems*. Lawrence Erlbaum, Hillsdale, New Jersey.

Miller, R. G., Jr. (1964). A trustworthy jackknife. *Ann. Math. Stat.* **35,** 1594–1605.

Raju, N. S. (1988). The area between two item characteristic curves. *Psychometrika* **53,** 495–502.

Swaminathan, H., and Rogers, H. J. (1990). Detecting differential item functioning using logistic regression procedures. *J. Edu. Measure.* **27,** 361–370.

Thissen, D. (2001). IRTLRDIF v.2.0b: Software for the Computation of the Statistics Involved in Item Response Theory Likelihood-Ratio Tests for Differential Item Functioning. Unpublished manuscript.

Thissen, D., Steinberg, L., and Wainer, H. (1988). Use of item response theory in the study of group differences in trace lines. In *Test Validity* (H. Wainer and H. I. Braun, eds.), pp. 147–169. Lawrence Erlbaum, Hillsdale, New Jersey.

Thissen, D., Steinberg, L., and Wainer, H. (1993). Detection of differential item functioning using the parameters of item response models. In *Differential Item Functioning* (P. W. Holland and H. Wainer, eds.), pp. 67–114. Lawrence Erlbaum, Hillsdale, New Jersey.

Yerushalmy, J. (1947). Statistical problems in assessing methods of medical diagnosis, with special reference to X-ray techniques. *Public Health Rep.* **62,** 1432–1449.

Item Response Models for Nonmonotone Items

Herbert Hoijtink

University of Utrecht, Utrecht, The Netherlands

Glossary

dominance relation The relationship that, the higher the location of a person is on the latent trait, the larger the probability is that the person will respond positively to an item.

item characteristic curve The probability of an item response as a function of the location of a person on the latent trait.

item response models Models in which the probability of an item response is related to the location of both the person and the item on a latent trait.

latent trait A characteristic of either a person or an item that is not directly observable.

measurement instrument A joint one-dimensional representation of individuals and items.

monotone items Items for which the item characteristic curve is a monotonically increasing function of the latent trait.

nonmonotone items Items for which the item characteristic curve is a single-peaked function of the latent trait.

proximity relation The relationship that the closer the locations of a person and an item are on the latent trait, the larger the probability is that the person will respond positively to the item.

Item response models can be used to infer the locations of individuals on a latent trait from the responses of the individuals to a set of items indicative of the latent trait. Item response models for nonmonotone items are developed for the situation in which the trait of interest is an attitude or a preference. A distinguishing feature of these models is the use of proximity relations—the closer the locations of a person and an item on the latent trait, the larger the probability is that the person will respond positively to the item. Goodness-of-fit tests can be used to evaluate the appropriateness of the model and the quality of the resulting measurement instrument (a joint one-dimensional representation of individuals and items) for the data at hand.

The Models of Guttman and Coombs

Guttman's Scalogram Model

In the mid-1950s Guttman developed the first item response model—the scalogram model. The scalogram model assumes that there is a joint one-dimensional representation of person $i = 1, \ldots, I$ with location θ_i and items $j = 1, \ldots, J$ with location δ_j such that the item response x_{ij} equals 1 if $\theta_i > \delta_j$ and 0 otherwise. The scalogram model assumes that the item responses result from dominance relations among individuals and items; that is, it is especially suited for the measurement of traits that are abilities. Table I presents a data matrix for $I = 5$ and $J = 4$ that is typical for the scalogram model. The table shows that person 1 is not very able (none of the items are dominated), and person 3 is more able (two of the items are dominated). Based on Table I, it can be concluded that $\theta_1 < \theta_2 < \cdots < \theta_5$ (i.e., person 1 is least and person 5 is most able) and also that $\delta_1 < \cdots < \delta_4$ (i.e., item 1 is the easiest and item 4 the most difficult). A drawback of

Table I Data Matrix Typical for the Scalogram Model

i	x_{i1}	x_{i2}	x_{i3}	x_{i4}
1	0	0	0	0
2	1	0	0	0
3	1	1	0	0
4	1	1	1	0
5	1	1	1	1

the scalogram model is its deterministic nature, that is, $P_{ij} = P(x_{ij} = 1 \mid \theta_i, \delta_j)$ is either 1 or 0. This is illustrated in Fig. 1, in which the item characteristic curve of item j (P_{ij} as a function of θ_i) is displayed. Guttman's scalogram model has been the point of departure for the development of probabilistic dominance relation-based item response models such as the Rasch model, the two-parameter logistic model, and the Mokken model, which do not have this drawback.

Coombs's Parallelogram Model

In the mid-1960s, Coombs developed the model on which all the models discussed in this entry are based—the parallelogram model. Where the scalogram model assumes dominance relations among individuals and items, the parallelogram model assumes proximity relations; that is, the item response x_{ij} equals 1 if $|\theta_i - \delta_j| \leq \tau$ and 0 otherwise. The parameter τ is a threshold; that is, it is the largest distance between a person and item still leading to a response of 1. The parallelogram model is especially suited for the measurement of traits that are attitudes or preferences. Table II presents a data matrix for $I = 5$ and $J = 4$ that is typical for the parallelogram model. According to this data matrix, individuals and items can be ordered along the latent trait using i and j, respectively, to indicate the rank number in the ordering. As can be seen the item responses are positive if the person and item are located close to one another. The parallelogram model has the same drawback as the scalogram model—it is deterministic. In Fig. 2, the item characteristic curve of item j is displayed. As can be seen, P_{ij} can attain only the values 0 and 1. Coombs's parallelogram model has been the point of departure for the development of probabilistic proximity relation-based item response models such as the Parella model and the hyperbolic cosine model. The hyperbolic cosine model has a counterpart that can accommodate both dichotomous and polytomous item responses, called the generalized graded unfolding model.

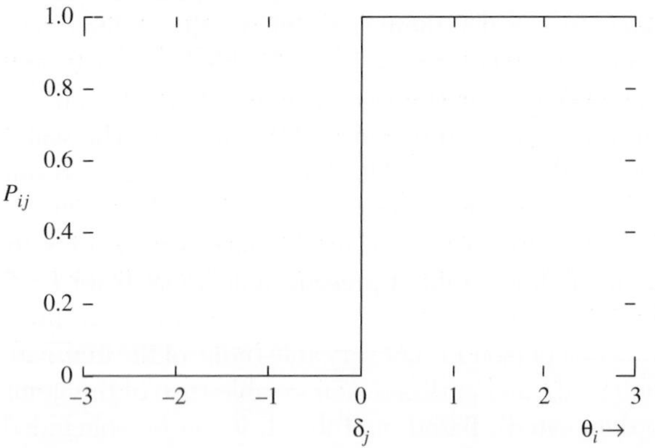

Figure 1 Item characteristic curve for Guttman's scalogram model.

Table II Data Matrix Typical for the Parallelogram Model

i	x_{i1}	x_{i2}	x_{i3}	x_{i4}
1	1	0	0	0
2	1	1	0	0
3	0	1	1	0
4	0	0	1	1
5	0	0	0	1

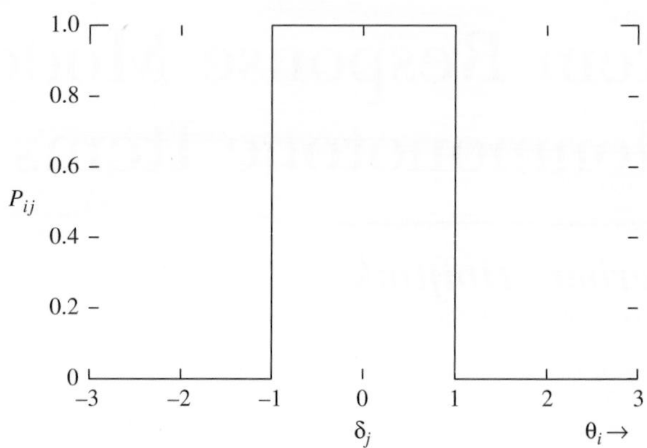

Figure 2 Item characteristic curve for Coombs's parallelogram model.

Probabilistic Models for Dichotomous Item Responses

The Parella Model

In the early 1990s the Parella model, a probabilistic counterpart of the deterministic parallelogram model, was developed. In this model:

$$P_{ij} = P(x_{ij} = 1 \mid \theta_i, \delta_j, \gamma) = \frac{1}{1 + |\theta_i - \delta_j|^{2\gamma}} \tag{1}$$

As indicated in Fig. 3, γ is a parameter that governs the degree with which the model deviates from the deterministic parallelogram model. If $\gamma = \infty$ the Parella model equals Coombs's model with $\tau = 1$; that is, a person will respond positively to all items within a distance of 1 of his or her location. As can be seen in Fig. 3, if γ decreases, both the probabilities of responding negatively to items located within a distance of 1 and responding positively to items located outside a distance of 1 are increasing. This is an important feature of the model because data as perfect as the data in Table II are rarely (if ever) observed.

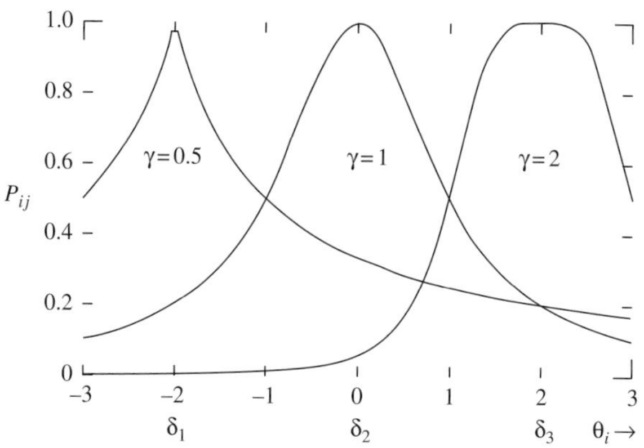

Figure 3 Item characteristic curves for the Parella model.

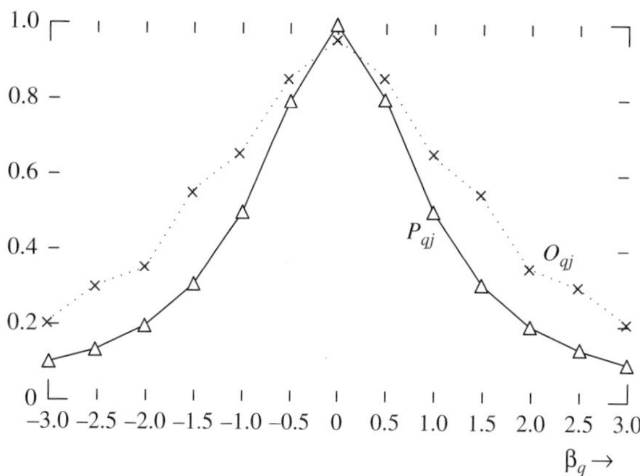

Figure 4 Comparison of observed and expected item characteristic curves for a hypothetical item.

The Parella model is not just defined by Eq. (1); an additional assumption is that θ_i is a random effect. The distribution of θ_i is a step-function with nodes β_q and weights π_q, where $q = 1, \ldots, Q$. The step-function is preferred over the more traditional normal distribution for random effects because, especially when attitudes and preferences are measured, bimodal distributions of θ_i are rather common. The (nonrandom) parameters of the Parella model are estimated using marginal maximum likelihood (MML). Because the addition of a constant to both the person and the item locations does not change the likelihood, identification problems are avoided using the restriction $\sum_j \delta_j = 0$. An additional restriction (used to reduce the complexity of the estimation procedure) is the use of equidistant nodes. The (random) person locations are estimated using an expected *a posteriori* estimator.

Two goodness-of-fit procedures have been developed for the Parella model: a diagnostic with which the adequacy of the item characteristic curve can be investigated and a test for differential item functioning. According to Eq. (1), the expected proportion of individuals located at node q responding positively to item j is:

$$P_{qj} = \frac{1}{1 + |\beta_q - \delta_j|^{2\gamma}} \tag{2}$$

The "observed" proportion of individuals located at node q responding positively to item j is:

$$O_{qj} = \sum_i \frac{x_{ij} P(\mathbf{x}_i \mid \beta_q)\pi_q}{\sum_q P(\mathbf{x}_i \mid \beta_q)\pi_q} \bigg/ (\pi_q N) \tag{3}$$

where observed is placed between quotation marks because both data and parameters are used to compute O_{qj}, and $P(\mathbf{x}_i \mid \beta_q) = \Pi_j P_{qj}^{x_{ij}}(1 - P_{qj}^{1-x_{ij}})$. In Fig. 4, for a hypothetical item, the P_{qj} and O_{qj} are displayed for $q = 1, \ldots, Q$. As can be seen in the figure, the "observed" threshold of this item is larger than the threshold predicted by the Parella model.

Also according to Eq. (1), the response probabilities depend only on θ_i and not on other *person* characteristics. In item response models this characteristic is usually referred to as the absence of item bias or the absence of differential item functioning. Consider, for example, a latent trait that ranges from "progressive" to "conservative." Consider also one of the items used to operationalize this trait: "When the baby is born, I will happily quit working in order to be able to take care of the baby." If a man responds "yes" or "agree" to this item, it is usually considered to be an indication of a progressive attitude. Stated otherwise, for men this item is located at the progressive side of the latent trait. If a woman responds "yes" or "agree" to this item, it usually considered to be an indication of a conservative attitude. For women this item is located at the conservative side of the latent trait. Because the item location depends on gender, Eq. (1) is not sufficient to model the item responses. However, the Parella model has been generalized so that it can be tested for one or more items about whether their locations depend on some person characteristic such as gender, and for one or more items the locations can be estimated for each of a number of subgroups of individuals. Furthermore, it can be tested whether or not γ is subgroup dependent, and γ can be estimated for each subgroup separately.

The Hyperbolic Cosine Model

In 1993 the hyperbolic cosine model was introduced. This model is a derivative of the partial credit model for polytomous dominance data. The principles involved in this derivation are presented in the next section. In the hyperbolic cosine model:

$$\begin{aligned} P_{ij} &= P(x_{ij} = 1 \mid \theta_i, \delta_j, \lambda_j) \\ &= \frac{\exp(\theta_i - \delta_j + \lambda_j)}{1 + \exp(\theta_i - \delta_j + \lambda_j) + \exp(2(\theta_i - \delta_j))} \end{aligned} \tag{4}$$

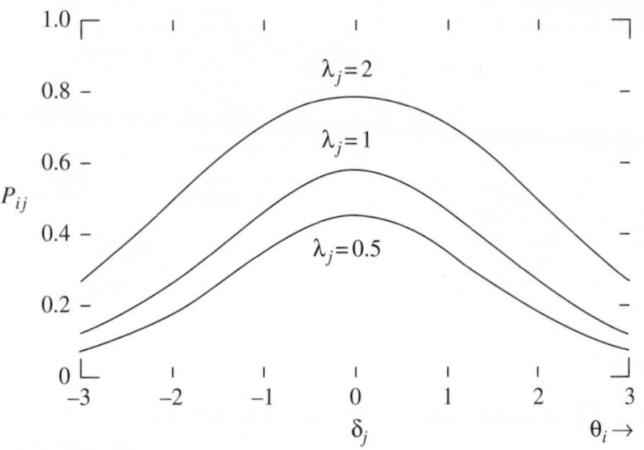

Figure 5 Item characteristic curves for the hyperbolic cosine model.

where λ_j denotes unit parameter of item j. As indicated in Fig. 5, the unit parameter influences both the threshold and the maximum of the item characteristic curve—the larger λj, the larger the threshold and the maximum. Because the addition of a constant to both the person and the item location does not change P_{ij}, like the Parella model the hyperbolic cosine model is not identified. Here too problems are avoided using the restriction that $\sum_j \delta_j = 0$.

Both MML (treating the θ_i as random parameters, as described for the Parella model) and joint maximum likelihood (JML; treating the θ_i as fixed parameters) have been used to estimate the parameters of the hyperbolic cosine model. From a theoretical perspective, MML has to be preferred over JML. JML estimates are known to be inconsistent. Furthermore, it is not very natural to assume that a renewed data collection involves the same individuals. The latter is a direct consequence of treating the θ_i as fixed parameters. Whereas MML assumes that both the individuals and the item responses are sampled, JML assumes that only the item responses are sampled. However, as shown by a number of simulation studies, in practice JML appears to perform quite well. All authors agree that parameter estimation using the restriction $\lambda_j = \cdots = \lambda$ for $j = 1, \ldots, J$ is unproblematic. Without this restriction a large correlation between λ_j and δ_j may lead to inflated parameter estimates, especially if an item is located at either end of the latent trait of interest. A pragmatic solution for this problem is to estimate λ and, subsequently, to estimate the λ_j using the restriction $\sum_j \lambda_j = \lambda$.

As far as the hyperbolic cosine model is concerned, goodness-of-fit tests have not yet received a lot of attention. The only model-based test reported in the literature is a likelihood ratio test for differential item functioning for the model where the unit parameters are restricted to be equal. The null hypothesis being tested was equality of item locations and unit parameter across two subsamples of individuals.

Probabilistic Models for Polytomous Item Responses

Towards the end of the 1990s models for dichotomous item responses were generalized so that polytomous or graded responses could be handled. The most general model, the generalized graded unfolding model (GGUM), was derived from the generalized partial credit model (GPCM). The GPCM can be used to analyze graded dominance data. Let $y_{ij} \in \{0, \ldots, k, \ldots, K\}$ denote the response of person i to item j. Then, according to the GPCM:

$$P_{ikj} = P(y_{ij} = k \mid \theta_i, \delta_j, \alpha_j, \lambda_{j1}, \ldots, \lambda_{jK}) = \frac{\exp(\alpha_j[k(\theta_i - \delta_j) - \sum_{v=1}^{k} \lambda_{jv}])}{\sum_{z=0}^{K} \exp(\alpha_j[z(\theta_i - \delta_j) - \sum_{v=1}^{z} \lambda_{jv}])} \quad (5)$$

For a hypothetical item and $k = 0, \ldots, 5$, the item category characteristic curves (P_{ikj} as a function of θ_i) are displayed in Fig. 6. Note that λ_{jk} marks the intersection of the response curves for categories k and $k-1$. Because this entry deals with models that can handle proximity data, a straightforward interpretation of the parameters of the GPCM is not given here. However, if K is an odd number, using the restrictions $\lambda_{j,(K+1)/2} = 0$ and $\lambda_{j,k} = -\lambda_{j,K+1-k}$ (which applies to Fig. 6) the GPCM can be interpreted as a proximity relation-based model for the analysis of polytomous or graded responses.

Let $x_{ij} \in \{0, \ldots, c, \ldots, (K-1)/2\}$ denote the responses to an item used to operationalize a preference or an attitude. With $K = 5$ these responses could, for example, be labeled 0 = Disagree, 1 = Undecided, and 2 = Agree or 0 = No, 1 = Don't know, and 2 = Yes. In proximity relation-based models, it is assumed that the distance between individuals and items is the main determinant of the item responses. In the example at hand, a response

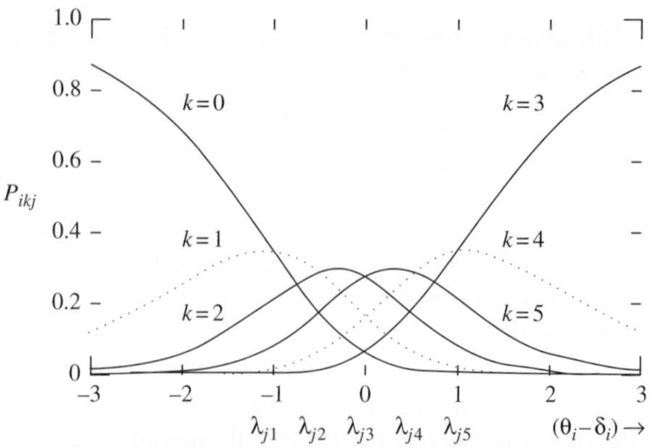

Figure 6 Item characteristic curves for the generalized partial credit model.

of 2 indicates that a person is located closely to the left or right of the item, a response of 1 indicates that a person is located some distance from (either to the left or to the right of) the item, and a response of 0 indicates that a person is located relatively far to the left or right of the item. Based on the GPCM, the probability that person i responds in category c of item j can consequently be modeled as:

$$\begin{aligned} P_{icj} &= P(x_{ij} = c \mid \theta_i, \delta_j, \alpha_j, \lambda_{j1}, \ldots, \lambda_{jK}) \\ &= P(y_{ij} = c \mid \theta_i, \delta_j, \alpha_j, \lambda_{j1}, \ldots, \lambda_{jK}) \\ &\quad + P(y_{ij} = K - c \mid \theta_i, \delta_j, \alpha_j, \lambda_{j1}, \ldots, \lambda_{jK}) \end{aligned} \tag{6}$$

The resulting item category characteristic curves are displayed in Fig. 7 ($\alpha_i = 1$). As shown in the figure, the probability of responding 2 decreases with increasing distance between person and item. The probability of responding 0 increases with increasing distance. On a relatively moderate distance of the item, response 1 is the most likely. These curves show nicely that the response probabilities depend mainly on the distance between person and item. The effect of the unit parameters λ_{jk} on the shape of the curves is similar to the effect of the unit parameter in the hyperbolic cosine model—the larger the values, the larger the thresholds and maximum of the associated curves. As is illustrated in Fig. 8 ($\alpha_i = 8$), increasing values of the discrimination parameter α_i lead to larger maxima and smaller thresholds. Stated in another way, the larger the α_i, the more the item responses are determined by the distance between person and item.

The GGUM model is not defined only by Eq. (5); an additional assumption is that θ_i is a random effect having a standard normal distribution. Consequently, the (nonrandom) parameters of the GGUM are estimated using MML. The (random) person locations are estimated using expected *a posteriori* estimates. Two goodness-of-fit procedures have been developed for the GGUM. First,

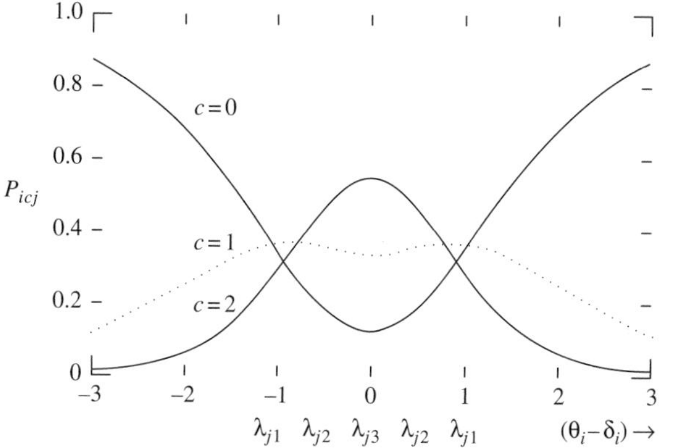

Figure 7 Item characteristic curves for the generalized graded unfolding model ($\alpha_i = 1$).

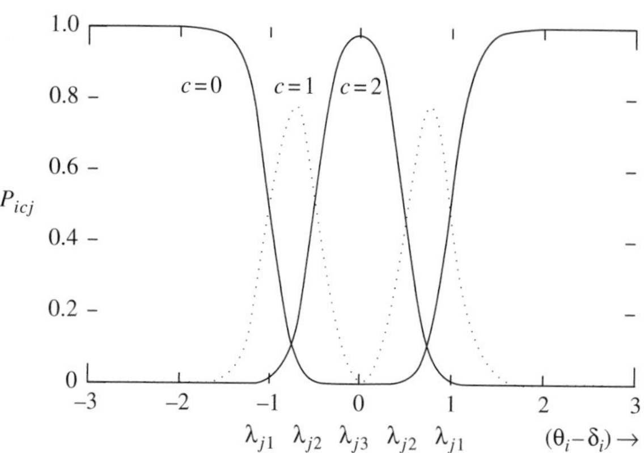

Figure 8 Item characteristic curves for the generalized graded unfolding model ($\alpha_i = 8$).

there is a likelihood ratio test for the comparison of GGUMs of increasing complexity. The simplest GGUM is the model for which $\alpha_1 = \cdots = \alpha_J$ and $\lambda_{1c} = \cdots = \lambda_{Jc}$ for $c = 0, \ldots, (K-1)/2$. In the most complex GGUM, none of the parameters are restricted. Second, a diagnostic has been proposed to roughly investigate the adequacy of Eq. (5). If individuals are grouped using the expected *a posteriori* estimates of their locations, then, for each item, the observed and expected item responses can be compared for each group.

Nonparametric and Monotone-Nonmonotone Models

The focus of this entry is on parametric models for nonmonotone items. The interested reader is referred to the work of van Schuur and Post to learn about nonparametric models for nonmonotone items. These models use nonparametric assumptions about the response process to order items (and individuals) along the latent trait. The most important assumption is that the item characteristic curves are single-peaked.

Baarsen, van Duijn, Klinkenberg, and Post have evaluated the performance of item response models for nonmonotone items in practical applications. They concluded that it is not always clear whether models assuming nonmonotone items or models assuming monotonically increasing and decreasing items were most appropriate for the data at hand. Note that the latter can be translated into dominance relation-based item response models via a reversion of the responses to the items with monotonically decreasing item characteristic curves. The interested reader is referred to Gunther Maris's 1991 dissertation, in which the first model able to handle both nonmonotone and monotonically increasing and decreasing items is proposed.

See Also the Following Articles

Guttman, Louis • Item Response Theory • Nonparametric Item Response Theory Models

Further Reading

Andrich, D. (1996). A hyperbolic cosine latent trait model for unfolding polytomous responses: Reconciling Thurstone and Likert methodologies. *Br. J. Math. Statist. Psychol.* **49,** 347–365.

Andrich, D., and Luo, G. (1993). A hyperbolic cosine latent trait model for unfolding dichotomous single stimulus responses. *Appl. Psychol. Meas.* **17,** 253–276.

Hoijtink, H. (1990). A latent trait model for dichotomous choice data. *Psychometrika* **55,** 641–656.

Hoijtink, H. (1991). The measurement of latent traits by proximity items. *Appl. Psychol. Meas.* **15,** 153–170.

Hoijtink, H., and Molenaar, I. W. (1992). Testing for DIF in a model with single peaked item characteristic curves: The PARELLA model. *Psychometrika* **57,** 383–397.

Klinkenberg, E. L. (2001). A logistic IRT model for decreasing and increasing item characteristic curves. In *Essays on Item Response Theory* (A. Boomsma, M. A. J. van Duijn, and T. A. B. Snijders, eds.), pp. 173–192. Springer Verlag, New York.

Luo, G. (1998). A general formulation for unidimensional unfolding and pairwise preference models: Making explicit the latitude of acceptance. *J. Math. Psychol.* **42,** 400–417.

Luo, G. (2000). A joint maximum likelihood estimation procedure for the hyperbolic cosine model for single stimulus responses. *Appl. Psychol. Meas.* **24,** 33–49.

Luo, G. (2001). A class of probabilistic unfolding models for polytomous responses. *J. Math. Psychol.* **45,** 224–248.

Maris, G. (1991). *Statistical Contributions to Psychological Modelling.* Ph.D. diss., University of Nijmegen, The Netherlands.

Post, W. J. (1992). *Nonparametric Unfolding Models: A Latent Structure Approach.* DSWO Press, Leiden.

Post, W. J., van Duijn, M. A. J., and van Baarsen, B. (2001). Single peaked or monotone tracelines? On the choice of an IRT model for scaling data. In *Essays on Item Response Theory* (A. Boomsma, M. A. J van Duijn, and T. A. B. Snijders, eds.), pp. 173–192. Springer Verlag, New York.

Roberts, J. S. (2002). Item response theory models for unfolding. Available at: http://www.education.umd.edu/Depts/EDMS/tutorials/

Roberts, J. S., Donoghue, J. R., and Laughlin, J. E. (2000). A general item response theory model for unfolding unidimensional polytomous responses. *Appl. Psychol. Meas.* **24**, 3–32.

van Schuur, W. H. (1993). Nonparametric unidimensional unfolding for multicategory data. *Polit. Analysis* **4,** 41–74.

Verhelst, N. D., and Verstralen, H. H. F. M. (1993). A stochastic unfolding model derived from the partial credit model. *Kwantitatieve Methoden* **42,** 73–92.

Item Response Theory

Wim J. van der Linden
University of Twente, Enschede, The Netherlands

Glossary

ability parameter Generic name for the parameter in a response model that represents the person's ability, skill, personality trait, or any other human property measured by the item.

computerized adaptive testing A mode of testing based on sequential item selection in which the person's ability estimate is updated after each item and the next item is selected to be optimal at the last update.

dichotomous response models Response models for items with dichotomously scored responses, such as correct-incorrect, true-false, and agree-disagree items.

information function Fisher's measure for the information on an ability parameter in an item or test score.

item parameters The parameters in a response model that represent such properties of the item as its difficulty, discriminating power, and probability of a correct response when guessing randomly.

monotone items Dichotomously scored items with a monotonically increasing response function for the correct response.

multidimensional response models Response models with a vector-valued ability parameter.

nonmonotone items Dichotomously scored items with a singly peaked response function for the agree response.

optimal test assembly The use of techniques from mathematical programming to assemble a test from a calibrated pool that is optimal with respect to an objective function and meets a potentially large set of constraints representing the content specifications of the test.

polytomous response models Response models for items with polytomously scored responses, such as nominal response, graded response, rating, and partial credit items.

response function The probability of a response as a function of the ability parameter.

Item response theory (IRT) consists of probabilistic models for responses of individuals to test items, procedures for the statistical treatment of the models, and principles that can be used in their application. The models are probabilistic in that they specify a probability distribution over the set of possible responses. The mathematical function used for describing a response probability as a function of the parameter for the person's property measured by the test, such as an ability, skill, attitude, or personality trait, is known as a response function. If the responses are scored as correct-incorrect, we usually present the model as a response function for the correct response. In addition to the person's property, IRT models have parameters for such item properties as its difficulty, discriminating power, and the probability of a correct response when the person guesses randomly. In more complex models, we can also have parameters representing the different conditions under which the individuals respond to the items, properties of possible raters who evaluate the responses, more specific mental operations needed to solve the item, or the speed at which a person responds. As a rule, any factor with a systematic impact on the probability of a response should be represented by a parameter in the model.

History

Although item response theory (IRT) has its roots in a few papers published in the 1940s, the original idea of a response model can be traced back to the method of absolute scaling developed by Thurstone in the mid 1920s. Thurstone's method is based on the assumption of a latent scale underlying the responses on which both the items and individuals can be mapped. No doubt his idea of a scale was inspired by earlier developments in psychophysics, in which probabilities of psychological responses to physical stimuli are modeled as a function of the strength of the stimulus. An example of a psychophysical response function is one that represents the probability of detecting a tone of a certain frequency as a function of its loudness. The unique twist by Thurstone was that, although these psychophysical functions were defined on a measurable physical variable, the response functions in his model were defined on a hypothetical, unmeasured variable. For this reason, Thurstone's model can be considered as one of the first models of a kind now generally known as latent variable models.

The idea of a response function was picked up again by authors such as Ferguson, Lawley, and Mosier in the 1940s. Their papers were somewhat confusing for two reasons. First, some of them struggled with the latent nature of the person parameter and modeled the response function as a regression function of the item score on the observed test scores instead of this parameter. Second, Thurstone's method of absolute scaling did not distinguish clearly between a normal-ogive response function defined over replicated item administrations and a normal distribution function for the sampling of a person from a population. As a result, it took later authors some time to entangle these two notions.

The first to present a coherent treatment of a response model for dichotomous items that did not suffer from these problems was Lord in 1950. His model had a normal-ogive response function. Birnbaum replaced Lord's model by a logistic model in the late 1960s. Statistical procedures for his model were introduced in the 1970s to 1980s, and the model obtained its current position as the main instrument in the test specialists' tool kit in the 1990s.

IRT has been developed in interaction with two other statistical areas of response modeling. The first is the area of bioassay with its models for data on the biological responses of organisms exposed to varying doses of a chemical substance. Although IRT and bioassay models have the same structure of a regression function for a response on a variable, the critical difference between them is the latent nature of the variable in the former and a known experimental dose in the latter. The second area is latent-structure analysis, developed by Lazarsfeld. Although the major portion of latent-structure analysis has been devoted to models with individuals classified in a finite number of latent classes, this area has also produced models with continuous responses functions. The most important contributions of latent-structure analysis to IRT have been conceptual, however. It introduced the essential distinction between manifest (=observed) qualitative data and latent (=unobservable) quantitative parameters or variables, and convinced test theorists that the two quantities can only be related by a probabilistic model.

Review of Response Models

It is hard to give a comprehensive review of the current types of response models. In all, some 30–40 models are available in the literature for which sound statistical procedures have been developed. The models reviewed in this section are examples of the more popular models for items with dichotomous and polytomous response formats, multidimensional abilities, and nonmonotone items. In addition, we review nonparametric approaches to response probabilities on items with a dichotomous and polytomous format. We thus skip cognitive-component models, which specify success probabilities at the level of the individual cognitive operations needed to solve an item and use probability calculus to model the entire solution process. Also omitted are models for response times on items. These models typically have separate parameters for the time required by the item and the speed at which the individual works, and they have become increasingly important due to computerization of testing. Other models not reviewed are models for items with continuous response formats, models with multilevel parameter structures to deal with sampling of individuals from subpopulations defined by differences on background variables or with sampling of items from families sharing important structural characteristics, as well as several models developed to deal with more specific applications.

Dichotomous Models

Lord's model for dichotomous items was based on the choice of the normal distribution function as response function. Let U_i denote the response to item i, where $U_i = 1$ if the response is correct and $U_i = 0$ if it is incorrect. The response function for the correct response is:

$$p_i(\theta) = \Pr\{U_i = 1\} = \int_{-\infty}^{a_i(\theta - b_i)} \frac{1}{\sqrt{2\pi}} \exp^{-z^2/2} dz \quad (1)$$

where $\theta \in (-\infty, \infty)$ is the ability parameter, $b_i \in (-\infty, \infty)$ the item-difficulty parameter, and $a_i \in [0, \infty)$ the item-discrimination parameter.

The model soon became unpopular for the following two reasons. First, it did not allow for guessing on multiple-choice items and could therefore not be used for high-stakes testing programs in which testees always guess if they do not know the answer. Second, the use of the normal distribution function in Eq. (1) led to computationally intensive procedures for parameter estimation, and the computer power needed to estimate the model parameters on a routine basis simply was not yet available at the time. (In an ironic twist of history, the normal distribution function has recently regained its popularity, just for computational reasons.)

An important impetus to the popularity of IRT was Birnbaum's suggestion in 1968 to replace the two-parameter normal ogive (2PNO) model in Eq. (1) by a logistic model with an additional guessing parameters.

Birnbaum's three-parameter logistic (3PL) model has the following response function:

$$p_i(\theta) = c_i + (1 - c_i)\Psi(\theta;\, a_i, b_i) \tag{2}$$

where

$$\Psi(\theta;\, a_i, b_i) = \frac{\exp(a_i(\theta - b_i))}{1 + \exp(a_i(\theta - b_i))} \tag{3}$$

is the logistic distribution function.

Parameter $c_i \in [0,1]$ represents a lower asymptote for the probability of a correct response, which is approached for $\theta \to -\infty$. It is easy to show that the structure of this model is the result of a knowledge-or-random-guessing assumption; the structure in Eq. (2) reflects the assumption that the person knows the correct answer with a probability given by the logistic part of the model equation in (3) or does not know it and guesses with a probability equal to c_i. Parameter b_i can be interpreted as the difficulty parameter of item i because it represents the location of the distribution function in Eq. (3) on the θ scale; more difficult items are located more to the right and require a higher level of ability for the same probability of success. Parameter a_i is proportional to the slope of the logistic function in Eq. (3) at $\theta = b_i$ and can be interpreted as the discrimination parameter of item i. A larger value for this parameter means a steeper slope for the response function and, hence, an item that discriminates better between the success probabilities for individuals with ability levels just to the left and right of $\theta = b_i$.

Because of its parameter structure, the 3PL model is flexible and has been shown to fit large pools of items written for the same content domain in educational and psychological testing. In fact, it has become the standard of the testing industry for tests with dichotomous items that are neither multidimensional nor nonmonotone.

The models in Eqs. (1) and (2)–(3) are not yet identified. We can easily change the unit or origin of the scale of the parameters θ, a_i, or b_i and compensate for this by a change in the scales of the other parameters. In practice, we remove this indeterminacy by fixing the scale of θ to a convenient unit and origin. All later models discussed in this entry need a comparable kind of fixing to become identifiable.

Polytomous Models

Responses to an item with a polytomous format can be denoted by a response variable U_i with possible variables $h = 1, \ldots, m_i > 2$. The dependency of m_i on i indicates that different items in the test may have different numbers of possible responses. To choose an appropriate polytomous model, the structure of the responses should be charted more precisely. In particular, we should distinguish between a format with responses that can only be classified and one with an *a priori* order of the responses. The former is known as a nominal response format, the latter as a graded response format.

Nominal Response Model

The nominal response model specifies the response function for $U_i = h$ as:

$$p_{ih}(\theta) = \Pr\{U_i = h\} = \frac{\exp(a_{ih}(\theta - b_{ih}))}{\sum_{h=1}^{m_i} \exp(a_{ih}(\theta - b_{ih}))} \tag{4}$$

The function for response $U_i = h$ has parameters a_{ih} and b_{ih}. These parameters keep their interpretation as discrimination and difficulty parameters. The difficulty parameter represents the location of the response function on the θ scale (i.e., the point at which it shows its largest change in curvature), whereas the discrimination parameter a_{ih} is proportional to this change.

Although the responses are not ordered *a priori*, the estimates of the parameter b_{ih} do show an empirical order. That is, the response data always indicate that some responses are more typical of lower ability values and others of higher values. Graphically, the model can be displayed as a set of response functions with a function for the "lowest" response that is monotonically decreasing with θ, a function for the "highest" response that is monotonically increasing with θ, and functions for the remaining responses that have a single peak.

The model in Eq. (4) does not allow explicitly for guessing. If guessing occurs, the response functions should be taken to represent a mixture of the probabilities of "knowing the response" and "not knowing any response but guessing the current one." A version of the nominal response model with explicit mixing parameters is available, however.

Graded Response Model

If the responses are ordered *a priori*, a different type of modeling becomes necessary. Suppose the values of index h reflect the order of the responses. We consider the probabilities of the compound events $U_i \geq h$ as a function of the ability parameter, θ, and define:

$$P_{ih}(\theta) = \begin{cases} \Pr\{U_i \geq h \mid \theta\} & \text{for } h = 1, \ldots, m \\ 0 & \text{for } h > m \end{cases} \tag{5}$$

Observe that $P_{ih}(\theta) = 1$ for $h = 1$. Obviously, for $h = 2, \ldots, m$ these functions increase monotonically with θ; for any of these values, the probability of responding with h or a higher response goes to 1 if $\theta \to \infty$.

It follows that the response function for response h can be written as:

$$p_{ih}(\theta) = P_{ih}(\theta) - P_{i(h+1)}(\theta) \tag{6}$$

A convenient choice for the functions $P_{ih}(\theta)$ in Eq. (6) is the logistic function in Eq. (3) for $h = 2, \ldots, m$. More stringent versions of the logistic function are obtained if we set $a_i = 1$ for all i. This case is known as the homogenous case of the graded response model in Eq. (6).

Partial Credit Models

Polytomous model for ordered responses that have gained considerable popularity because of their statistical tractability are the partial credit models. These model are appropriate for the case in which increasing credit is given to the responses $h = 1, \ldots, m_i$. The first version of the partial credit model was based on the assumption that the probability of response h relative to adjacent response $h - 1$ can be represented by the version of the logistic function in Eq. (3) with $a_i = 1$. After some probability calculus, this assumption can be shown to lead to the following response functions:

$$p_{ih}(\theta) = \frac{\exp\left(\sum_{k=1}^{h}(\theta - b_{ik})\right)}{\sum_{h=1}^{m_i}\exp\left(\sum_{k=1}^{h}(\theta - b_{ik})\right)} \quad (7)$$

A generalized version of the model exists in which the parameter structure in Eq. (7) is extended with discrimination parameters a_{ik}.

Alternatively, suppose that the number of possible responses for each item is a common constant, m. If we constrain the parameters b_{ih} for the responses in this model to $b_{ih} = b_h$ for all i, with $\{b_1, \ldots, b_m\}$ being a set of equidistant numbers, the model becomes appropriate for analyzing responses to a set of rating scales of the Likert type. The equidistant numbers $b_1, \ldots, b_m$ are the parameters for the fixed number of categories that the person can check on such scales.

Multidimensional Models

The need for a multidimensional response model arises if the items appear to be sensitive to more than one ability. For some areas of testing, this happens out of necessity. For example, if we test a nonverbal ability (e.g., a mathematical ability), it may nonetheless be necessary to use items with a considerable verbal component. If so, the items may become sensitive to a verbal ability too. But testing for multidimensional abilities can also be intentional. Now that the statistical methods for dealing with such items have matured, it becomes more efficient to measure multiple abilities by a single multidimensional test instead of multiple unidimensional tests.

If the items are multidimensional, we need to adjust the unidimensional model that otherwise would have been appropriate for their response format and by including more than one ability parameter. If our choice is the 3PL model in Eq. (2), an obvious generalization of this model to the case of two ability parameters, θ_1 and θ_2, is:

$$p_i(\theta_1, \theta_2) = c_i + (1 - c_i)\frac{e^{a_{i1}\theta_1 + a_{i2}\theta_2 - b_i}}{1 + e^{a_{i1}\theta_1 + a_{i2}\theta_2 - b_i}} \quad (8)$$

This model defines the probability of a correct response as function of (θ_1, θ_2). It is customary to refer to a multidimensional response function as a response surface. The model in Eq. (8) has two discrimination parameters, a_{i1} and a_{i2}, which control the slope of the response surface along θ_1 and θ_2, respectively. But it has only one generalized difficulty parameter b_i; a parameter structure with two parameters $b_{i1} - b_{i2}$ would have lead to a nonidentifiable version of the model. If θ_1, $\theta_2 \to \infty$, the probability of a correct response goes to c_i.

The generalization of the model to an ability space with more than two dimensions is straightforward. But in practice, for a professionally constructed test, unless it consists of different sections with items written to entirely different specifications, we seldom need more than two or three ability parameters to obtain a fitting model.

Models for Nonmonotone Items

An item is called monotone if the response function for its correct response is monotonically increasing with the ability measured by the items. Monotone items are usually found in "power tests," such as achievement tests.

Items in an attitude scale cannot be expected to be monotone. Such items typically consist of statements that the person is asked to endorse or not to endorse. It is not uncommon to meet statements with a low probability of endorsement by individuals with an opposite attitude. For such nonmonotone items, a response function with a single peak is more appropriate.

Instead of an algorithmic approach to scoring tests with nonmonotone items, using what is known as an unfolding algorithm, an approach based on probabilistic modeling and parameter estimation, can be followed. An example of a model appropriate for nonmonotone items is the hyperbolic cosine model.

Let $U_i = 1$ denote an agree response to the item and $U_i = 0$ denote a disagree response. The model can be represented by the following function for the agree response:

$$p_i(\theta) = \frac{\exp(\lambda_i)}{\exp(\lambda_i) + 2\cosh(\theta - b_i)}, \quad (9)$$

where $\cosh(\cdot)$ is the hyperbolic cosine function, parameter b_i represents the location of the agree response for item i, and λ_i is the common distance from b_i to the locations of the two disagree responses at the opposite ends of the scale.

The model seems to differ from all previous models in that it has an expression with a hyperbolic cosine function that is not exponential. But this conclusion is wrong—this part of the model is the result of an assumption of an underlying structure with two opposite latent disagree responses that do have an exponential type of response function.

Nonparametric Approaches

Nonparametric approaches in IRT avoid the parametric families of response functions assumed in the preceding sections. Instead, they depart from ordinal assumptions on the response functions.

As an alternative to the dichotomous models, a nonparametric approach assumes probabilities p_{ij} for a correct response by a person $j = 1, \ldots, J$ to an item $i = 1, \ldots, n$ that are constrained by monotonicity conditions. Weaker and stronger assumptions of monotonicity are possible.

The assumption of monotonic homogeneity stipulates that the individuals $j = 1, \ldots, J$ be ordered by each item; that is, for every possible $j, j' = 1, \ldots, J$, it holds that

$$p_{ij} < p_{ij'} \quad \text{if} \quad j \prec_i j'. \tag{10}$$

A stronger assumption requires the individuals to be ordered similarly by the probabilities for each item; that is, for every j it holds that

$$\begin{aligned} &\text{if} \quad p_{ij} < p_{ij'} \quad \text{for any } i = 1, \ldots, n, \\ &\text{then} \quad p_{ij} < p_{ij'} \quad \text{for all } i \end{aligned} \tag{11}$$

The assumption in (10) is necessary for each item to be monotone according to our definition. The assumption in (11) is necessary for a unidimensional representation of the probabilities, that is, for the constraint $p_{ij} = p_i(\theta_j)$ to hold for the same scalar θ for all person-item combinations.

The set of assumptions becomes stronger still if we also require all items to be ordered similarly by the probabilities for each person. This assumption, which is known both as the assumption of double monotonicity and monotonic homogeneity, stipulates that for every pair items i, $i' = 1, \ldots, n$ it hold that

$$\begin{aligned} &\text{if} \quad p_{ij} < p_{i'j} \quad \text{for any } j = 1, \ldots, J, \\ &\text{then} \quad p_{ij} < p_{i'j} \quad \text{for all } j \end{aligned} \tag{12}$$

This assumption is necessary for a representation of the probabilities by response functions that do not intersect.

A nonparametric approach to items with a polytomous format also exists. This approach is based on the reduction of the polytomous format to sets of dichotomous variables:

$$U_{ijh} = \begin{cases} 1 & \text{if } U_{ij} \geq h \\ 0 & \text{otherwise} \end{cases} \tag{13}$$

for the responses $h = 1, \ldots, m$ to item i by person j. The sum of these variables over all responses for an item is the person's actual score h on it.

Let

$$p_{ijh} = \Pr\{U_{ijh} = 1\} \tag{14}$$

For these probabilities, the same monotonicity assumptions can be made as in Eq. (10)–(12) for the dichotomous case. These assumptions hold trivially for the probabilities for the same item, but do constrain the relations between the probabilities for different items.

Statistical procedures for checking these monotonicity assumptions have been developed. These allow us to see if an entire tests admits a unidimensional representation. If it does not, these procedures help us to identify the items and individuals that do not fit the assumptions. Nonparametric IRT is less appropriate for dealing with problems that involve missing data, however. We discuss test-item banking, optimal test assembly, and adaptive testing as examples of such problems in a later section.

Discussion

Several generalizations of the models in the preceding sections exist. Some of these models, for example, the partial credit model in Eq. (7), specify a family of response distributions that belong to the exponential family in statistics. The recognition of this relation helps us to profit from the body of statistical procedures valid for this family.

The graded response model is based on the definition of the probabilities for the compound events in Eq. (5). It is interesting to note that the nonparametric polytomous approach in the preceding section is based on the same type of probabilities in Eq. (14). Models of this type are more generally known as cumulative models in ordinal categorical data analysis. On the other hand, the partial credit model in Eq. (7) is based on the assumption of a logistic model for the pairs of dichotomous events $\{U_{ij} = h,\ U_{ij} = h - 1\}$. Models of this type are known as adjacent category models. It is also possible to model the events $\{U_{ij} = h \mid U_{ij} \leq h - 1\}$. Models of this type are know as continuation ratio or sequential response models.

Statistical Treatment of Models

The statistical treatment of IRT models usually consists of two stages: item calibration and measurement. During the stage of item calibration, the item parameters are estimated from response data and the validity of the model for the data is checked. If the model is used as a measurement model, the item parameters are treated as known and the value of the ability parameter for a person is estimated from his or her vector of responses to the items in the test. In this section, we briefly outline these activities for the case of the 3PL model in Eqs. (2)–(3).

Parameter Estimation

If a test of n items is administered to individuals $j=1,\ldots,J$, we can collect the responses for each person in a vector $\mathbf{u}_j=(u_{j1},\ldots,u_{jn})$. Let $\mathbf{a}=(a_1,\ldots,a_n)$, $\mathbf{b}=(b_1,\ldots,b_n)$, and $\mathbf{c}=(c_1,\ldots,c_n)$ be vectors with the item parameters, and $\boldsymbol{\theta}=(\theta_1,\ldots,\theta_J)$ the vector with the ability parameters for the individuals. The likelihood function for all parameters associated with the response vectors $(\mathbf{u}_1,\ldots,\mathbf{u}_J)$ is:

$$L(\boldsymbol{\theta},\mathbf{a},\mathbf{b},\mathbf{c};\,\mathbf{u}_1,\ldots,\mathbf{u}_J)=\prod_{j=1}^{J}\prod_{i=1}^{n}p_i(1;\theta_j,a_i,b_i,c_i)^{u_{ij}}\times p_i(0;\theta_j,a_i,b_i,c_i)^{1-u_{ij}} \quad (15)$$

Suppose we have a prior distribution with density function $f(\boldsymbol{\theta},\mathbf{a},\mathbf{b},\mathbf{c})$ for these parameters. All parameters in this distribution can be taken to be independent, with the exception of the parameters for the same item. The posterior distribution of all parameters is given by:

$$f(\boldsymbol{\theta},\mathbf{a},\mathbf{b},\mathbf{c}\mid\mathbf{u}_1,\ldots,\mathbf{u}_J)\propto L(\boldsymbol{\theta},\mathbf{a},\mathbf{b},\mathbf{c};\mathbf{u}_1,\ldots,\mathbf{u}_J)\times f(\boldsymbol{\theta},\mathbf{a},\mathbf{b},\mathbf{c}) \quad (16)$$

To obtain maximum likelihood (ML) estimates for the parameters, we have to find values for them at which the likelihood function reaches its maximum. In Bayesian estimation, we estimate the parameters by their joint posterior distribution or by a measure of its central tendency, such as the mode. If the prior distribution is uniform, ML and Bayes modal estimates are equal.

The estimation based on the joint likelihood in Eq. (15) is known as joint maximum likelihood (JML) estimation. Unfortunately, in item calibration the interest is in the item parameters, whereas the ability parameters behave as incidental parameters. Under this condition, the estimators of the item parameters are inconsistent. A standard way of getting rid of incidental ability parameters in item calibration is to assume that their values have been drawn from a common ability distribution, integrate the parameters out of the joint likelihood, and estimate their values from the remaining marginal likelihood function. This method, which results in the following likelihood function,

$$L(\mathbf{a},\mathbf{b},\mathbf{c};\mathbf{u}_1,\ldots,\mathbf{u}_J)=\prod_{j=1}^{J}\int\prod_{i=1}^{n}p_i(1;\theta_j,a_i,b_i,c_i)^{u_{ij}}\times p_i(0;\theta_j,a_i,b_i,c_i)^{1-u_{ij}}\,d\varphi(\theta_j) \quad (17)$$

with $\varphi(\theta)$ the density function for the ability distribution in the population, is known as the method of marginal likelihood (MML) estimation.

In a Bayesian approach, we would integrate the ability parameters out of the joint posterior distribution in Eq. (16) and use the marginal posterior distribution:

$$f(\mathbf{a},\mathbf{b},\mathbf{c}\mid\mathbf{u}_1,\ldots,\mathbf{u}_J)\propto\int L(\boldsymbol{\theta},\mathbf{a},\mathbf{b},\mathbf{c};\,\mathbf{u}_1,\ldots,\mathbf{u}_J)\times f(\boldsymbol{\theta},\mathbf{a},\mathbf{b},\mathbf{c})\,d\boldsymbol{\theta} \quad (18)$$

MML estimates of the item parameters as well as the mode of the marginal posterior distribution in Eq. (18) can be found using the well-known expectation-maximization (EM) algorithm.

For models with response distributions that belong to the exponential family, sufficient statistics for the ability parameters exist. We can get rid of the ability parameters in these models by conditioning the likelihood on these statistics. This method of conditional maximum likelihood (CML) has been popular for the Rasch model—that is, the logistic model in Eq. (3) with $a_i=1$ for all items, as well as for the partial credit model in Eq. (7).

If the items have been calibrated and the model is used as a measurement model, it is customary to treat the estimates of the item parameters as their true values. We then estimate θ for person j from the likelihood function of this parameter for a vector of responses $\mathbf{u}_j=(u_{1j},\ldots,u_{nj})$ on the test. The likelihood function is

$$L(\theta_j\mid u_{1j},\ldots,u_{nj})=\prod_{i=1}^{n}p_i(1;\theta_j)^{u_{ij}}p_i(0;\theta_j)]^{1-u_{ij}} \quad (19)$$

Alternatively, in a Bayesian approach, we can estimate θ_j by the (mode or mean of) its posterior distribution, which is calculated as:

$$f(\theta_j\mid u_{1j},\ldots,u_{nj})\propto L(\theta_j\mid u_{1j},\ldots,u_{nj})f(\theta_j) \quad (20)$$

where $f(\theta_j)$ is the density function of the prior distribution for θ_j.

Model Validation

When the validity of a model for the response data is checked, we assess the fit of the model to the items and the individuals. If misfitting items or individuals are detected, we try to find an explanation and improve the fit. For example, it may be necessary to reformulate some of the items, move to a multidimensional model, break up the set of items into subsets with different abilities, or change the instructions of the test. But if the items have been well written, in most cases we have to remove no more than an occasional item to get a satisfactory fit of the model.

IRT has had a relatively long tradition of evaluating the fit of the 3PL model using informative but rather informal statistical procedures. One of these procedures was to group the individuals in the sample into ranges of ability estimates and calculate Pearson's chi-square statistic on the differences between the proportions of correct responses and the average response probabilities for these groups predicted by the model. Another informal procedure was to inspect visually the residual responses after fitting the response probabilities to a response vector for a person or an item.

More recently, statistically correct goodness-of-fit tests for the 3PL model have become available. These tests are more diagnostic in that they are sensitive to specific assumptions underlying the model, such as on the unidimensionality of θ, monotonicity of the response functions, or local independence between responses. The recent arrival in IRT of Bayesian procedure for model checking has further enlarged our repertory of procedures for diagnosing item and person fit.

Applications

IRT can be used for solving any problem for which classical test theory offers a solution. In addition, IRT has special advantages when solving problems that involve scaling or have missing data. The following sections illustrate the IRT approach to some of these problems.

Variable Construction

A traditional social science approach to establishing a new variable is to define a theoretical construct, write a set of items for measuring it, and define a total score on the item responses. However, deeper insight is gained if we fit an IRT model and study the location of the items on the scale.

A graphical technique for doing so is item mapping. In this technique, we identify a sample of items critical of the definition of the variable, calibrate them, and mark their location on the scale by labels with a brief content description. It is possible to use the value of the difficulty parameter for locating an item on the scale, but a fixed probability of a correct response indicating a higher level of mastery of item content (0.80, say) may be more meaningful. Item maps help us to illustrate how the empirical content of a variable develops with an increase in its numerical values.

We can also place individuals on the scale using their ability score, or parameters of certain distributions, such as average abilities for subpopulations of individuals after a certain program or with a certain symptom. The same can be done, for example, with minimal levels of ability required to be admitted to a program.

The idea of item mapping originated with Thurstone, who applied the technique to his method of absolute scaling in the mid-1920s to give a behavioral interpretation to the scale of an intelligence test in use at the time.

Item Banking

Traditionally, test construction went through a cycle in which a set of items was written that represented the variable best. The set was typically somewhat larger than needed to allow for some items to fail an empirical pretest. The set was then pretested and the item statistics were analyzed. The final step was to put the test together using the item statistics. If a new test was needed, the same cycle of item writing, pretesting, and item analysis was repeated.

In item banking, items are written, pretested, and calibrated on a continuous basis. Items that pass the quality criteria are added to a pool of items from which new tests are assembled when needed. The advantage of item banking is not only a more efficient use of the resources, but also tests of higher quality assembled from a larger stock of pretested items, less vulnerability to the consequences of possible item security breaches, and stable scales defined by larger pools of items.

In item banking, problems of item calibration and person scoring are always subject to large numbers of missing data, due to the fact that no person responds to all items in the pool. IRT deals with these problems in a natural way. If new items are calibrated, a few existing items from the pool are added to the tests and their known item parameter values are used to link the new items to the scale already established for the pool. Likewise, if a person is tested, any set of items from the pool can be used as a test. When estimating the person's score, the estimation equation has known values for the item parameters and automatically accounts for the properties of the items. Consequently, in more statistical terms, differences in item selection do not create any (asymptotic) bias in the ability estimates.

Optimal Test Assembly

Although item selection does not create any bias in the ability estimates, it does have an impact on their accuracy. For example, if a test is too difficult, it is hardly possible to discriminate between the ability levels of less able individuals.

An obvious measure of the inaccuracy of an estimator of θ is the variance of its sampling distribution, $\text{Var}(\hat{\theta} \mid \theta)$. But instead of this variance, we often use Fisher's information measure, which for a dichotomous item is equal to

$$I_i(\theta) = \frac{(p_i'(\theta))^2}{p_i(\theta)[1 - p_i(\theta)]} \tag{21}$$

where $p_i'(\theta)$ being the first derivative of $p_i(\theta)$ with respect to θ. In IRT, this measure is treated as a function of θ; it is therefore known as the item information function. If $p_i(\theta)$ is the response function of the 3PL model in Eqs. (2)–(3), the item information function can be written as

$$I_i(\theta) = \frac{a_i^2[1 - p_i(\theta)]}{p_i(\theta)} \left(\frac{p_i(\theta) - c_i}{1 - c_i} \right)^2 \tag{22}$$

A fortunate property of information functions is their additivity due to conditional independence between item responses. Hence, for the test information function, $I(\theta)$, it holds that:

$$I(\theta) = \sum_{i=1}^{n} I_i(\theta) \tag{23}$$

Another well-known property of the test information function is that if $\hat{\theta}$ is an ML estimator, it holds (asymptotically) that:

$$I(\theta) = \frac{1}{\text{Var}(\hat{\theta} \mid \theta)} \tag{24}$$

The two properties explain why we generally prefer using $I(\theta)$ over $\text{Var}(\hat{\theta} \mid \theta)$—both are a measure of the accuracy of the ability estimator, but $I(\theta)$ is additive in the items.

Optimal test assembly in IRT is based on the idea of a target for the test information function chosen to represent the goal of the test, for example, a uniform target over a certain ability range if the test has to be diagnostic or a peaked function at the cut-off score in a decision problem. Because of the additivity in Eq. (23), the optimization problem involved in matching a target for the test information function is linear in the items.

Let $i = 1, \ldots, I$ be the items in the pool. We use 0-1 decision variables x_i to indicate whether $(x_i = 1)$ or not $(x_i = 0)$ item i is selected in the test. If $T(\theta_k)$ is the value of the target function at a set of well-chosen points θ_k, $k = 1, \ldots, K$, the optimization problem for selecting a test of n item can be formulated as

$$\text{minimize} \sum_{k=1}^{K} \sum_{i=1}^{I} I_i(\theta_k) x_i \tag{25}$$

subject to

$$\sum_{i=1}^{I} I_i(\theta_k) x_i \geq T(\theta_k) \quad \text{for } k = 1, \ldots, K \tag{26}$$

$$\sum_{i=1}^{n} x_i = n \tag{27}$$

$$x_i \in \{0, 1\} \quad \text{for } i = 1, \ldots, I \tag{28}$$

The objective function in Eq. (25) minimizes the sum of the test information function values at the points θ_k, whereas Eq. (26) requires these values to be larger than the target values $T(\theta_k)$. The constraint in Eq. (27) sets the length of the test equal to n.

The problem in (25)–(28) is an example of a linear integer programming problem and can easily be solved using standard commercial software for such problems. It is an example of a problem from an area known as optimal test assembly, which addresses test assembly problems with various objective functions and sets of constraint that model the specifications for the test.

Computerized Adaptive Testing

In computerized adaptive testing (CAT), the items in the test are selected sequentially from a pool of calibrated items while the person takes the test. After the response to an item in the test, the person's ability estimate, $\hat{\theta}$, is updated. The next item is selected to be optimal at the last estimate. During the test $\hat{\theta}$ converges to θ, and consequently the composition of the test moves to the ideal of items with maximum information at θ.

The most popular criterion of item selection in CAT is the maximum-information criterion. This criterion selects the item with the maximum value for its information function at the last estimate, that is, for which $I_i(\hat{\theta})$ is maximal. Bayesian item selection criteria have also been developed. One of the best-known Bayesian criteria is based on the principle of posterior prediction. This criterion selects as the next item the one with the largest predicted reduction of the posterior variance of θ in the pool.

The idea of adaptive testing was already well developed during the early days of IRT. But we had to wait for the first applications until computers became powerful enough for real-time ability estimation and item selection. The first large-scale testing programs introduced the adaptive format for their tests in the 1990s, and many programs have followed since then.

Current Developments

IRT is still being extended with new types of models and procedures. Particularly fruitful areas of expansion are those leading toward the integration of IRT with multilevel modeling, covariance structure analysis, and cognitive modeling.

This expansion results in models that are far more complex than our current models and, in principle, more difficult to treat statistically. However, these new models appear to lend themselves naturally to the application of Bayesian parameter estimation and model validation using Monte Carlo Markov chain (MCMC) sampling from the posterior distributions of their parameters. Unlike the early history of IRT, the introduction of these new models can be therefore immediately followed by empirical applications that highlight their features.

See Also the Following Articles

Computerized Adaptive Testing • Graded Response Model • Item Response Models for Nonmonotone Items • Multidimensional Item Response Models • Nonparametric Item Response Theory Models • Structural Item Response Models

References

Bartholomew, D. J. (1987). *Latent Variable Models and Factor Analysis.* Griffin, London.

Birnbaum, A. (1968). Some latent trait models and their use in inferring an examinee's ability. In *Statistical Theories of Mental Test Scores* (F. M. Lord and M. R. Novick, eds.), pp. 397–479. Addison-Wesley, Reading, MA.

Glas, C. A. W., and Meijer, R. R. (2003). A Bayesian approach to person-fit analysis in item response theory models. *Appl. Psychol. Meas.* **27,** 217–233.

Glas, C. A. W., and Suarez Falcon, J. C. (2003). A comparison of item-fit statistics for the three-parameter logistic model. *Appl. Psychol. Meas.* **27,** 87–106.

Hambleton, R. K., and Swaminathan, H. (1985). *Item Response Theory: Principles and Applications.* Kluwer, Boston.

Lazarsfeld, P. F., and Henry, N. W. (1968). *Latent-Structure Analysis.* Houghton Mifflin, Boston.

Lord, F. M. (1950). *A Theory of Test Scores.* Psychometric Monograph No.7.

Lord, F. M. (1980). *Applications of Item Response Theory to Practical Testing Problems.* Erlbaum, Hillsdale, NJ.

Mellenbergh, G. J. (1994). Generalized linear item response theory. *Psychol. Bull.* **115,** 300–307.

van der Linden, W. J. (2005). *Linear Models for Optimal Test Design.* Springer-Verlag, New York.

van der Linden, W. J., and Glas, C. A. W. (eds.) (2000). *Computerized Adaptive Testing: Theory and Practice.* Kluwer Academic, Boston.

van der Linden, W. J., and Hambleton, R. K. (1997). *Handbook of Modern Test Theory.* Springer-Verlag, New York.

Jevons, William Stanley

Harro Maas
University of Amsterdam, Amsterdam, The Netherlands

Glossary

***a priori* method** A combination of inductive and deductive inquiry proposed and defended by John Stuart Mill. Mill considered the method of special relevance for political economy. The method basically combined introspection with the deduction of tendency laws.

aliis exterendum Literally: to be threshed out by others. Motto of the Statistical Society of London, which expressed its research restriction to data-gathering only, preferably in tabular form. It meant to exclude politics and opinion from its research, in favor of "objective" numerical information.

analogical reasoning Using analogies with known phenomena on the basis of alleged similarities in properties or relationships to explain the unknown.

complexity An event is complex if it is the result of multiple causes. Jevons assumed that by taking averages, erratic causes cancel out, leaving a simple causal relationship.

distinction of mind and matter A widely held distinction in Victorian England, which legitimated different modes of inquiry for the natural and mental (moral) sciences.

disturbing causes Causes that interfere with tendency laws.

index number A (weighted) ratio comparing the values of one or a basket of items to a base value of these items.

introspection A mode of inquiry reserved for the mental sciences in which the truth of the first principles is established by a reasoned inquiry of one's own mind.

inverse deductive method Making inferences from data to simple general laws by framing hypotheses.

method of graphs In the course of the 19th century, graphs came be seen as important aids in uncovering (causal) explanations in functional form. The use of graphs with this purpose is referred to as the graphical method or the method of graphs.

method of means A mode of correcting for errors in measurement by averaging.

tendency laws The notion of tendency laws was widely held among 19th century political economists. It signified laws that were true irrespective of disturbing causes that obfuscated their observation in practice.

The Victorian polymath William Stanley Jevons (1835–1882) revolutionized measurement practices in political economy and statistics. Rather than treating political economy and statistics as separate disciplines, Jevons integrated both. Using his training in and knowledge of the natural sciences, especially chemistry and meteorology, Jevons made functional form relevant to economic theory and numbers relevant to empirical evidence. The general statement of his scientific method is found in *The Principles of Science* (1874), the structure of which is heavily dependent on his formal logical system. From Jevons' time onward, it became increasingly acceptable to think of economics as a natural science in all ways.

Introduction

William Stanley Jevons (1835–1882) is widely acknowledged as one of the Victorian political economists who greatly contributed to the transformation of political economy on a theoretical and empirical plane. This article concentrates on Jevons' innovative measurement strategies in economics, although it will be seen that these cannot be separated from his approach to theory. Jevons' measurement strategies stemmed to a large extent from then-current research strategies in the natural sciences (most notably astronomy and meteorology). They transgressed the then-prevailing distinction between the deductive approach of political economists and the inductive approach of what then went for statistics. Jevons revolutionized measurement in economics on the assumption that the universe, the natural and the social, was governed by mechanical laws; mechanical analogies were of major importance in Jevons' work. Jevons summarized his strategies of measurement in *The Principles of Science* (1874), as he had practiced them in his major statistical studies in the 1860s.

After a short introduction to Jevons' life and work, this article lays out Jevons' general views on measurement in the (social) sciences in relation to the prevailing and institutionalized opinions on economic methodology. It also examines how Jevons put his views into practice in his empirical studies in economics.

Jevons' Life and Work

William Stanley Jevons was born into a well-to-do middle-class family of iron traders in Liverpool in 1835. His father, Thomas Jevons, was a man of some ability with Utilitarian sympathies, who is said to have invented the first floating iron ship. Jevons' mother, Mary-Ann Roscoe, was the daughter of William Roscoe, an important Liverpool banker and art connoisseur, who rediscovered and ardently collected neglected Italian and Flemish masters.

The Jevons and Roscoe families were Unitarians. Closely related to the Huttons and the Martineaus, among others, they constituted part of the intellectual Unitarian circles in Lancashire who were important in promoting the natural sciences. Middle-class Unitarians greatly contributed to the establishment of Mechanics' Institutes designed for the education of the higher working class in the principles of the natural sciences and in the formation of the various literary, philosophical, and statistical societies. The advancement of society was the goal, the progress of science the means.

It was therefore not surprising that education, especially in the natural sciences, was considered of utmost importance by Jevons' parents, though he also became well acquainted with various aspects of culture, especially music, via his mother. When Jevons was 11 years old, he attended Liverpool Mechanics' Institute High School and then, after an interlude of 2 years at a grammar school, he was sent first to University College London School, to enter the College 1 year later, in 1851. For Unitarians and other dissenters from the Anglican Church, University College, London, was one of the few possibilities for receiving a higher education.

Jevons progressed well at the college, especially in chemistry and experimental philosophy, in which he won gold medals. However, he derived most enjoyment from the teachings of one of the permanent influences of his later life, the first Professor of Mathematics at University College, Augustus De Morgan.

Jevons received his education despite the enormous distress suffered by the family, first by the death of his mother when Jevons was only 10, and then, shortly after, by the bankruptcy of his father's iron-trading business in 1848 in the aftermath of the great railway crisis of 1847. This forced the family to move to Manchester. The family's financial difficulties were instrumental in Stanley sailing off to Australia in 1854 before having finished his college education, to take up a position as a gold assayer at the newly established mint in Sydney.

His work in Sydney left Jevons with ample spare time to pursue his scientific interests. In this period, Jevons at first turned to meteorological issues. The best overview of Jevons' studies in meteorology is provided by Nicholls. Jevons was the first to systematically collect data on the Australian weather. He also made some ingenious experiments on the formation of clouds that were taken up in later years by Lord Rayleigh in quite a different context—in the study of heat diffusion. Jevons published on these subjects in Australian and English journals for natural philosophy, most notably the *London, Dublin, and Edinburgh Philosophical Journal*. Jevons actively participated in the scientific societies of Sydney as well. When he returned to England in 1859, the editors of the *Sydney Magazine of Science and Art* remarked in its columns that "Australia is about to lose this laborious and unassuming yet most promising natural philosopher."

It is generally held that Jevons' decision to return to England was prompted by a sharp shift in interest to political economy. The railway controversy in New South Wales (on which Jevons commented in the newspapers), his reading of Dionysius Lardner's *Railway Economy* (1850), and a growing interest in Bentham's *felicific calculus* gathered from lectures and secondary sources are all mentioned as more or less important influences on this shift in Jevons' scientific orientation. By 1858, Jevons undisputedly considered the study of the social sciences, most notably political economy, the most "cogent business." Jevons returned to London in 1859 to take up his studies in political economy.

Having returned to University College, London, Jevons worked in a frenzy in a variety of fields. He not only studied the standard Mill–Ricardian theories of political economy, but he embarked on ambitious statistical studies and studies in the emerging field of formal logic as well. His approach to formal logic was in line with that of George Boole rather than Augustus De Morgan. Clearly inspired by Babbage's calculating engines project, Jevons became interested in the construction of a logical machine, showing mechanically the virtues of the new systems of logic. Jevons' studies in formal logic are less known today, though some of them were highly successful in his own days. His *Primer of Logic* (1876) even went through 40 (!) reprints.

Jevons felt a growing uneasiness with the deductive Mill–Ricardian approach to political economy, but his new ideas found a skeptical hearing. His first airing of his new approach to the field, the *Notice of a General Mathematical Theory of Political Economy*, read in his absence in October at Section F of the British Association for the Advancement of Science (BAAS) in 1862, was "received without a word of interest or belief." Even worse, the *Philosophical Journal*, which until then had received his studies quite favorably, refused the manuscript for publication. Initially, Jevons also failed to get the statisticians of his day, like William Newmarch, interested in his equally innovative use of diagrams to display economic data. These diagrams were inspired by William Playfair's *Commercial and Political Atlas* and part of an equally ambitious *Statistical Atlas* project that Jevons never completed.

His study on the influence of the gold discoveries in Australia and California on the value of gold, introducing index numbers in economics, was received much more favorably. One year later, in 1864, Jevons was elected as a member of the Statistical Society of London and could write that he was generally considered a "competent statistician." His definitive breakthrough as a statistician was *The Coal Question* (1865), examining the consequences of the expected decline of commercially extractable coal on British prosperity. In 1865, Jevons had a part-time professorship in logic, moral philosophy, and political economy at Queens College, Liverpool, which he combined with a tutorship at Owens College, Manchester. *The Coal Question* was certainly instrumental in bringing him the Cobden Chair in logic and political economy at Owens College, a post he exchanged in 1876 for a professorship in political economy at University College, London. He resigned in 1881 in order to devote his time to reading and study, especially to his planned large work on economics.

In 1871, Jevons published his seminal work *The Theory of Political Economy*. Jevons was prompted to a rapid publication because of the publication of Fleeming Jenkin's graphical representation of supply and demand in 1870. Jevons' book introduced the calculus in economics and was one of the starting points of so-called neoclassical economic theory. Value came to be based on utility rather than labor. Economic agents, workers, manufacturers, consumers, and landowners were all considered to base their decisions on the same form of deliberation at the margin, in Jevons' words: on the "final degree of utility." The generalized notion of maximizing a goal function (utility or profits) under given constraints has come to be widely applied in sociology, political science, and ethics as well. Jevons' *magnum opus* is *The Principles of Science* (1874), synthesizing much of the Victorian literature on scientific method and showing a thorough knowledge of scientific practice as well. This book has been of considerable influence on early logical positivism, especially on Otto Neurath, and was republished in the 1950s by Ernest Nagel. It was also an important source of inspiration for the statistician Karl Pearson.

The publications dating after the *Theory* and the *Principles* are generally considered to be of minor importance. His sunspot studies of the 1870s, which attempted to establish a causal nexus between solar activity and commercial crises, though not as absurd as they are sometimes described, are usually thought of as a failure and as having contributed to the bad name associated with the analytical use of statistics at the turn of the 19th century. Jevons worked on an encompassing *Principles of Economics*, the manuscript of which was published by Henry Higgs in 1905. From what can be judged from this unfinished material, the end result would not have been too promising. In the second half of the 1870s, Jevons wrote four vehement articles against John Stuart Mill, which did not have the effect he must have hoped for. Quite to the contrary, they isolated him from political economists such as John Elliot Cairnes, Henry Sidgwick, and Alfred Marshall, who were, in method or content, devoted to Mill's work. Jevons also worked on a second edition of the *Theory*, containing the first bibliography of all the mathematical precursors in economics whom Jevons had been able to trace. In *The State in Relation to Labour* (1882) and the posthumous collection of essays on social reform (1883), Jevons turned more explicitly to the social and political issues of the day, issues that were never far from his mind. These essays undeniably lack the sharpness and innovative force of his early statistical studies and of his *Theory*. In all its bluntness, there is something to be said for Keynes' horrifying remark that when Jevons so untimely drowned in 1882, leaving his wife and three young children, "his work was done." An extensive bibliography of Jevons' work can be found in the 1992 article by White and Inoue, which is reprinted in Inoue's 2002 collection of reviews and obituaries of Jevons' work.

Relation of Political Economy to Statistics

To understand how Jevons' measurement strategies changed the outlook of political economy, it is helpful to sketch the background of the division of labor between political economy and statistics that is characteristic of the largest part of the 19th century in England. Within the scope of this article, it is impossible to do full justice to the variety of positions that are to be found. Jevons steered through a deductive and an inductive approach to economics. These approaches may be affiliated with the names of John Stuart Mill and William Whewell.

Mill's Defense of Ricardian Deductivism

The dominant view on economic method for 19th century England had been formulated by John Stuart Mill in two key publications that served as a vindication of Ricardian deductive economics. The first is *On the Definition of Political Economy; and on the Method of*

Investigation Proper to It (1836, 1844); the second is his monumental *Logic* (1843). It was generally considered one of the great advantages of the *Logic* that it contained an explicit treatment of the methods of the "moral or mental sciences," including political economy. John Stuart Mill staked out political economy from the other moral sciences in that it was capable of attaining the same certainty as obtained in "the most demonstrative parts of physics" ([1836] 1967). This he did by limiting the scope of political economy to the study of just three motives of action (the desire for wealth, the striving for luxury, and the aversion of labor) confronted with Malthus' law of population growth and Ricardo's law of diminishing marginal returns on land. The certainty of this so-called *a priori* method of the political economists was secured by reliance on introspection. Introspection guaranteed the general and universal truth of the first principles of political economy and by consequence of all deductions derived from them. The many disturbing causes operating in practice were responsible for the fact that the laws or tendencies of political economy could seldom be observed. By distinguishing between the *science* and the *art* of economics, Mill relegated to the practical politician the task to draw policy inferences from the tendency laws of political economy in a complex social reality.

Mill's position was not inconsistent with the need felt among political economists for statistical facts (as had been emphasized by McCulloch and, of course, Thomas Tooke). The common strategy was, however, to explain the individual fact, rather than show how these facts bear on the theory itself. This "curious separation between abstract theory and empirical work" found general support among political economists, even though debate has been opened up as to what extent Mill subscribed to his own methodological views in his practical economic writing. In correspondence with Adolphe Quetelet, Nassau Senior even went so far as to claim that he did "not consider the truths of political economy" to depend on "statistical facts." This separation of theory and data is largely responsible for the division of labor between political economists and statisticians, or "statists" as they were called in the early 19th century.

Whewell's Inductivist Criticism of Ricardian Economics

The sharp split between political economy and statistics was anathema to a group of scientists in which William Whewell is considered to be of central importance. This group included, among others, the political economist Richard Jones and the polymath Charles Babbage. Thomas Malthus was also sympathetic to their cause. Even granting the somewhat different status of political economy, and the moral sciences in general, Whewell emphasized that political economy could not evade the tedious path followed by the natural sciences to become genuinely scientific. Whewell was aware that institutional support was of utmost importance in promoting an inductive approach to political economy.

Section F of the BAAS and the Statistical Society of London

In 1833, the group around Whewell managed to persuade the BAAS to allow the establishment of a new section, the so-called Section F, devoted to political economy and statistics. This new section should explicitly restrict its research to facts that could be expressed in numbers and that promised to indicate general laws. This was to exclude the intrusion of opinion into the domain of science, something that was especially feared by the members of the powerful Section A (mathematics and physics). As the offspring of the establishment of Section F, the Statistical Society of London was founded in 1834, involving the same group of inductivists.

The logo of the Statistical Society (selected by Charles Babbage)—a loosely bound wheatsheaf with the words *Aliis Exterendum* (to be threshed out by others)—precisely expressed the aim of restricting research to objective information only, that is, to quantitative data, preferably stated in tabular form and excluding all references to opinions. In practice, this limitation of statistical research to naive Baconian data-gathering proved impossible. Many of the members of statistical societies were practical businessmen with hardly any knowledge, or interest, in science. Indeed, not only for the Statistical Society of London, but for other statistical societies as well (such as its main competitor, the Manchester Statistical Society), political goals determined heavily how use was made of the data gathered. The intrusion of politics into statistical research made Whewell, at the end of the 1850s, so unhappy with the turn and the tone of statistical research in Great Britain that he attempted to abolish the Section F that he had helped to found.

The insecure status of statistical research in the early 19th century served to enforce the alleged superiority of deductive Ricardian political economy. John Elliot Cairnes' eloquently written 1857 lectures on the "character and logical method of political economy" summarized the prevailing opinion that "for the ultimate truths of economic science we are independent of this inductive process, having the direct proof afforded by our own senses and consciousness."

Jevons Cutting through the Distinction of Political Economy and Statistics

Jevons made it his lifelong task to combat this division of labor between political economy and statistics, which in his view had detrimental consequences on both sides. Much in line with Whewell's inductivist methodology, he made it his aim to install political economy on a "truly scientific" basis, using statistics for this purpose. In his aforementioned lectures, Cairnes claimed that many of the principles of political economy "from their nature" did not "admit of being weighed and measured like the elements and forces of the natural world" and of consequence were "not susceptible of arithmetical or mathematical expression." Considering Jevons' empirical and theoretical work in economics, one obtains the impression that it is planned as a word-for-word refutation of the "uninquiring and unhoping spirit" embodied in Cairnes' words.

Even some of the topics of Jevons' inquiries seem to have been given from the examples Cairnes chose: the relationship of man's physiology to the phenomena of the mind, the so-called King-Davenant price quantity table of corn, and the influence of the Australian and Californian gold discoveries on the value of gold. For all these cases, Cairnes argued that because political economy was not an exact, quantitative science, it was "impracticable" to strive for the "precision which is attainable in physical science." Cairnes added that if political economy were treated similarly to physics, it would become a "wholly different study" from that known so far. But this was just what Jevons aimed at. Before examining these three examples in turn, a more general account of Jevons' views on scientific method will be given.

Jevons' Views on Scientific Method

The Uniformity of Scientific Method

Jevons laid out his views on scientific method in *The Principles of Science* (1874), that is, after his major empirical and theoretical work in economics had seen the light. Jevons did not devote separate attention to the method of the social sciences, including political economy, as his great predecessor John Stuart Mill had done. From the foregoing, it should not come as a surprise that Jevons did not do so. Jevons did not accept the categorical distinction between the sciences of mind and nature as defended by Mill and Cairnes and its implications for scientific method. In the introduction to the *Principles*, Jevons stated, by contrast, that "the application of Scientific Method cannot be restricted to the sphere of lifeless objects. We must sooner or later have strict sciences of those mental and social phenomena, which, if comparison be possible, are of more interest to us than purely material phenomena."

Complexity of the Social Sciences

The only apparent difference between the natural and the mental or moral sciences seemed to consist in the complexity of mental and social phenomena. But complexity was, for Jevons, as much a problem for the natural sciences as for the social sciences. Like astronomers infer their mathematical laws from observations, so do political economists from their statistics. Neither of them was an experimental science, but this did not entail, for Jevons, that complexity prohibited the use of mathematics in the study of society any more than it did in astronomy. Jevons referred to Airy's *Theory of the Tides* as an instance where it had been shown to be possible to obtain numerical exactness in a branch of science that formerly had been considered intractable because of its complexity. Jevons considered mastering complexity to be the genuine problem of induction and this problem was no different for natural and social scientists.

Induction: The Inverse Process of Deduction

In the *Principles of Science* (1874), Jevons used his logical machine to elucidate and circumvent the problem of induction. Not incidentally, an image of the machine was printed opposite to the title page of the book. Jevons explained how deductively an avalanche of conclusions could be drawn on the basis of only a limited set of premises. The scientist was depicted as having only nature's conclusions, but not its premises—its laws—at hand. The problem for the scientist was how to infer back to the simple premises producing the observed complexity of nature. Jevons' solution was to equate induction with what he called the "inverse deductive method." This was a reasoned process of searching for the simplest premises from which the observed conclusions could be derived. The logical machine embodied essentially the same process of striking out contradictory conclusions that Jevons used in this reasoning process. The conclusions of the machine, which was referred to as the "logical piano" and which was of only limited capacity, could be read from the display at the front (see Fig. 1).

Jevons' description of the inverse deductive method suggested to Peirce the notion of "abduction" as a mode of drawing inferences, as becomes clear from the small exchange of letters between the young Peirce and Jevons. In the empirical sciences (all of which Jevons considered as quantitative sciences), this reasoned process could proceed only on the basis of a limited set of observations. The inverse deductive method—induction—thus became "imperfect." The premises were hypotheses about the laws of nature: mathematical, not logical, formulae. The problem of induction was how such reasoned guesses were to be made. Analogical reasoning, the method of

Figure 1 Jevons' logical machine. Courtesy of the Museum of the History of Science, Oxford, UK, Inventory No. 18,230 with permission.

means, and graphical methods were all methods that could be used to tackle this problem. In highlighting the importance of these methods for the quantitative sciences, Jevons followed William Whewell's *Philosophy of the Inductive Sciences*. The goal of these methods was to find "rational laws," that is, mathematical functions explaining the relationship between cause and effect over the whole range of possible observations, not only for the range of observations made.

Reasoning by Analogies

Reasoning by analogies was widely practiced by 19th century natural scientists. Faraday, Lord Kelvin, and Maxwell are perhaps the most prominent and it formed a natural part of Jevons' educational background as well. In the *Principles*, Jevons highlights Faraday's use of analogical reasoning as an example to be followed. Jevons' favorite analogies stemmed from mechanics. The great advantage of mechanical analogies is that they carry their mathematics with them or at least suggest that mathematical formulae may be formulated, if not now, then in the future.

In his experiments on cloud formation, Jevons constructed an elaborate analogy between the formation of clouds and the formation of precipitates in liquids. If it can be shown, so Jevons' argument goes, that precipitates are formed by principles of hydrodynamics only, then by analogy the same holds for the formation of clouds.

Jevons constructed his analogies on the strong conviction that nature is ultimately ruled by mechanistic and deterministic laws. The aforementioned experiments on cloud formation are a case in point. His studies on the cyclical behavior of trade cycles, which are discussed in more detail below, is an even more dramatic example.

The Role of Probability

The hypothetical character of the formulae arrived at made science essentially probabilistic. This did not mean that nature itself is probabilistic—quite the contrary. Jevons' framing of the problem of induction in terms of his logical machine made sense only on the assumption that the universe is governed by deterministic laws, like the conclusions of the logical machine follow mechanically from the underlying set of premises. Referring to Laplace as his authority, Jevons considered it due to one's ignorance, to the principled impossibility of predicting the outcome when all causes are not known, that one needs to reason probabilistically: "*Probability belongs wholly to the mind.*" Limited knowledge and limited data made probability arguments unavoidable in arguing for the existence of laws and regularities in nature. Jevons presented many such arguments in a rather offhanded way to illustrate how regularity in observations gives reason to assume the existence of a causal mechanism, even though the possibility of "fortuitous coincidences" could never be excluded.

Apart from the general acknowledgment that all knowledge is uncertain and hypothetical, it remained unclear how exactly to apply probabilistic reasoning to empirical events in a rigorous way, as is also clear from the scarce examples of probabilistic reasoning in Jevons' statistical studies. In England, this was reserved for the mathematically more talented Edgeworth, Yule, Galton, and Pearson.

Averages and Means

As in the natural sciences, the exactness of political economy depended on the quality of the data, the quality of the measuring instruments, and the abilities of the scientists to search for regularities in a sea of numbers. Two related strategies were of special help. The first was the reliance on averages, rather than raw data. By taking averages, errors in measurement could be corrected for. Jevons' confidence in averaging practices can partly be traced to his great acquaintance with the balance, which he considered one of the most perfect measuring instruments.

Averaging practices were also useful in attempting to circumvent the problem of multiple causation. On the assumption that disturbing causes cancel out one another on average, Jevons considered obtaining data that were "more true" than the individual data themselves. With regard to political economy, Jevons even went so far as to say that the only way of turning it into a science was by averaging out the "whims of the individual." In his emphasis on averages and means, Jevons was clearly influenced by Adolphe Quetelet, whom he considered the "true founder of the social sciences."

The Method of Graphs

The second method of correction for errors was the graphical method. Like Whewell, Jevons considered the use of graphs an important aid in the discovery of a causal relationship between two variables. Indeed, Whewell's description of the method of graphs fits perfectly with Jevons. Whewell referred to Sir John Herschel's use of the method of curves in his *Investigation of the Orbits of Double Stars* (1833), drawn "with a bold but careful hand," as a fine example of how to "discover the laws of change and succession." Reliance on such methods enabled the scientist to "obtain data which are *more true than the* individual *facts themselves*." Jevons' predilection for the graphical method in threshing out causal relations can be gathered from the use he made of it, in his published as well as in his unpublished work, and in the repeated discussions he devoted to their use. Visually, graphs are certainly the most spectacular innovation Jevons brought to economics.

Jevons' Measurement Strategies in Economics

To see how Jevons put his general views into practice, three examples of Jevons' work will be examined in some detail. It will be attempted to bring out how Jevons combined economic theory and statistics to genuinely turn political economy into a science. The distinction between Jevons' deductive, theoretical work and his statistical studies in this regard has been historically overemphasized and, perhaps, biased by the great influence that John Stuart Mill has had on discussions on economic method.

Jevons' Experiments on Work and Fatigue

Developments within physiology, in part related to the emerging theory of thermodynamics, seriously undermined the existing classification of the sciences in those of mind and matter. There is a burgeoning literature on these topics.

Jevons, like many other natural scientists, was clearly influenced by these developments, which he considered to bear on the fundamentals of economic theory, most notably his theory of labor. Jevons was most impressed by the book of a lawyer, Richard Jennings, *Natural Elements of Political Economy* (1855), which in a highly contrived and confused style founded the principles of political economy in man's physiology. In his *Theory of Political Economy*, Jevons praised Jennings' suggestion to "exhibit the results of the principles of human nature . . . by the different methods of Algebra and Fluxions" as "a clear statement of the views which I have also adopted."

In a short 1870 article in *Nature*, Jevons attempted to integrate physiological research with political economy. Referring to Coulomb and Babbage, Jevons conducted three experiments that aimed to give insight into the "chemical and physiological conditions" of work and might be of help in "defining the mathematical relations upon which the science of economics is grounded." It is highly probable that Jevons got the idea for these particular experiments from Richard Jennings' 1855 *Natural Elements of Political Economy*.

Jevons conducted these experiments on himself. Notwithstanding this questionable set-up, the experiments shed light on how Jevons adopted methods from the natural sciences in political economy. Repeating the experiments several times (so that, in all, 456 experiments were performed), Jevons computed mean values for the outcomes. From the results, Jevons was able to derive a numerical formula for only one type of experiment, a formula that he distrusted on the grounds that it fitted the experimental outcomes "embarrassingly close." Jevons added that he would have been comforted if he had been able to explain the result "on mechanical principles." In subsequent issues of *Nature*, the physicist Samuel Houghton came to Jevons' aid. Houghton argued that by proper comparison of the work done by the human arm with a "compound pendulum," it was possible to derive formulae fitting the experimental outcomes quite closely.

Jevons was extremely pleased with Houghton's results and referred to them on two important occasions: in the *Theory of Political Economy* (1871) and in the *Principles of Science* (1874). In the first instance, Jevons emphasized that experiments like those he had conducted might be of help in empirically substantiating his theory of labor, in which the disutility of labor was traded off against the utility of the wage received. In the *Principles*, Jevons referred to Houghton's finding as a happy instance where an empirical mathematical relation had been explained on mechanical grounds, thus extending the range of its validity.

Jevons' study in work and fatigue aimed to link the experimental method with theory formation in economics. It also shows how mechanical analogies were of help in transforming experimental results into Jevons' ultimate standard of scientificity; rational laws in functional form.

The King Davenant Price Quantity "Law"

Another importance instance linking economic data with theory is Jevons' discussion of the so-called King Davenant table of prices and quantities of wheat. Jevons used this table in the *Theory of Political Economy* to demonstrate how a mathematical function might be inferred from statistical data as positive evidence for his theory of the final (marginal) degree of utility—"the all-important element in Economics."

Jevons' choice of this table was not incidental. It was discussed in Whewell (1830), Tooke (1838), and Cairnes (1857), among others, and played an important role in arguments at the time for and against the possibility of mathematizing economics. In contrast with Cairnes and Tooke, Jevons argued that the table could be rendered mathematically and gave numerical support for his theory of utility. Jevons was fully aware of the many obstacles, but did not consider them prohibitive (see Table I).

Jevons first made a conjecture about the functional form of the relation and solved for the parameter values. The formula Jevons considered was

$$p = \frac{a}{(x-b)^2}.$$

Stephen Stigler uncovered the method of computation of a and b that Jevons most likely followed. First, Jevons computed the extreme values to pin down the slope of the line. He then used the value of b thus obtained to compute a by taking the simple arithmetic mean. This mode of computing was common practice in astronomy, dating back to the 17th century. Otherwise than has been assumed, Jevons used neither least-squares nor any other probability-based method.

If it had been Jevons' sole aim to arrive at the best fit, his choice for the general form of the equation is far from logical. Whewell had already found that the data could be exactly fitted by a cubic. The exact fit is $p = 25 - 62\frac{1}{3}x + 55x^2 - 16\frac{2}{3}x^3$. "An astute numerical scientist" like Jevons would certainly have stumbled on this equation. It was, however, not Jevons' purpose to find the best fit. In line with his exposition of the graphical method, Jevons argued that a function or curve was not meant to intersect all individual observations. A polynomial to fit the data could always be found. Jevons was aware, however, that data are loaded with errors in measurement. Even though a polynomial may give an indication of the "rational function," theoretical considerations must be brought into play to decide on the form of the function. In the case at hand, the function loosely embodies considerations stemming from Jevons' theory of utility, thus providing an explanation of the data, not just a rendering in mathematical form.

Table I Jevons' Rendering of the King Davenant Price Quantity Table of Corn

Changes in Quantity of	
Corn	*Price*
1.0	1.0
0.9	1.3
0.8	1.8
0.7	2.6
0.6	3.8
0.5	5.5

Jevons' Gold Study (1863)

The foregoing two examples show how Jevons attempted to introduce methods from the natural sciences in political economy, such as the use of experiments, the graphical method, and the reliance on mean values rather than individual data. Exemplary for Jevons' major innovations in statistics is his study of the fall of the value of gold.

At the start of the 1860s, the influence of the gold discoveries in California and Australia on the value of gold was a subject of heated debate. The common explanatory strategy was to attribute the changes in observations on prices to the gold discoveries, achieved by eliminating all other possible causes successively. This explanatory strategy has recently been happily compared by Hoover and Dowell with Mill's so-called method of residues. As might be expected, there was thus no conclusive way to decide on the influence of gold on prices. Jevons broke with this explanatory strategy and in doing so introduced a wealth of new tools for research in economics: index numbers, graphs, and ratio charts.

Instead of focusing on individual prices, Jevons simplified the problem dramatically by considering it as a balancing problem. Since all goods were traded against gold, Jevons compared the change in the market conditions of gold (the gold influx) against the change in the market conditions of all other goods. Jevons went on to argue that if a change in this balance was observed, it was far more likely that the cause of the change was on the side of gold than on the side of goods, all other changes on the side of goods most probably canceling one another out. Thus, shifting from an analogy with a mechanical balance to probabilistic reasoning, Jevons argued for a causal claim as well as a measurement strategy.

Instead of considering all price changes in isolation, all prices should be lumped together. If an average rise in prices could then be observed against a base year or period, the percentage change gave an indication of the fall in the value of gold *as well as* a confirmation of the probable cause: the gold discoveries. This setup made index numbers relevant for economic research. Index numbers had been known since at least the turn of the 18th century and had even been used by a prominent statistician, William Newmarch, in the early 1850s. Most statisticians had refused their use, however, because they considered index numbers to provide delusory information. A major obstacle to their use was the problem of weighting.

Jevons made notice of the problem, but he left its solution "amid the obscurities of economic science in general." Jevons similarly mentioned and then passed over the obvious problem that his way of framing the inquiry ignored the interdependencies of price changes of goods. In a different context, Jevons remarked that "all the measurements with which we perform our measurements are faulty." This remark equally applies here. Even though the computation of an index number was surrounded by difficulties, it could be seen as a first approximation to solving these difficulties. Indeed, had scientists waited until their instruments and data had been perfect, Jevons argued, "we should have still been in the age of science which terminated at the time of Galileo."

Jevons chose the unweighted geometric mean as the price index. The argument for the choice was that in the case of ratio changes, the geometric mean is the natural choice. He computed the geometric mean for a set of 39 commodities and subsequently checked the outcome against a considerably enlarged set of 118 commodities. From these computations, Jevons safely concluded an increase of the geometric mean *"by about* $9\frac{1}{3}$ *percent."* Jevons drew two ratio charts, one picturing the general course of the price level throughout time and the other spectacularly plotting the ratios of the prices of the individual goods in 1862 against the base period (see Fig. 2).

Jevons' accomplishment was stunning, especially considering the standards of statistical inquiry of his days. Jevons convincingly transgressed the self-chosen limitations set to statistical inquiry to data-gathering only,

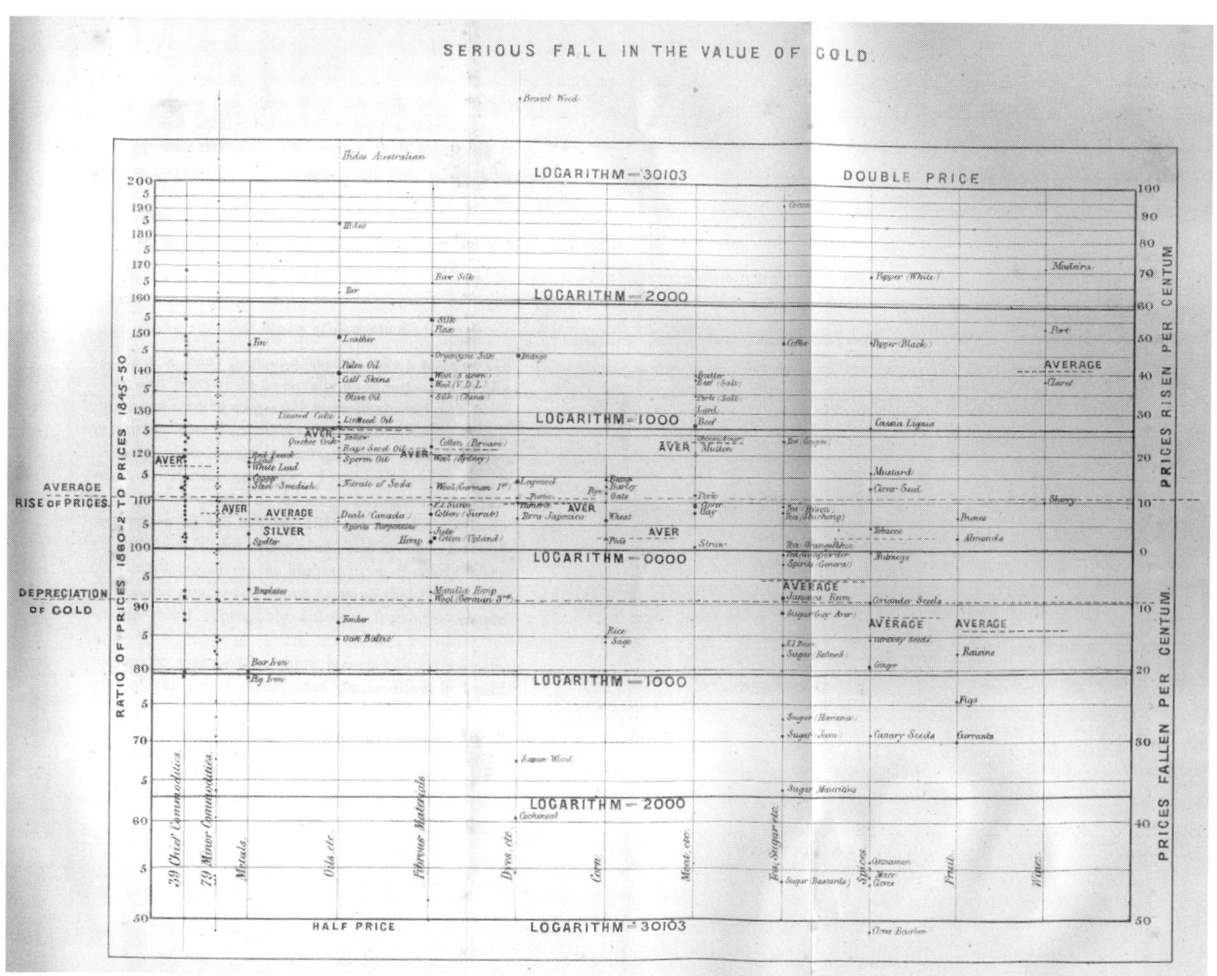

Figure 2 Ratio chart displaying the average individual prices of Jevons' extended sample of commodities from 1860 to 1862 against their average values in the base period (from 1845 to 1850).

preferably in tabular form and leaving it to the political economists to thresh out conclusions. Here, the data were put to work to obtain quantitative causal inferences and instruments were designed and used to make this possible; index numbers, graphs, and ratio charts.

John Elliot Cairnes immediately acknowledged Jevons' accomplishment and referred most favorably to Jevons' study in a letter to the *Times*. The more so, since Cairnes essentially argued for the same position: that the gold influx had led to a fall in the value of gold. The correspondence between Jevons and Cairnes on the subject is revealing, however. In it, both Jevons and Cairnes show their awareness that they came to their results via "entirely distinct methods of inquiry."

Other Statistical Work

Jevons' other statistical studies concerned mainly cyclical fluctuations in the economy, the currency system, and the issue of women working in factories. It is generally held that most of his statistical work was the offspring of his abandoned *Statistical Atlas* project of the early 1860s. Some of this work, like his study in the seasonal variations of the money supply, was as thorough and innovative as

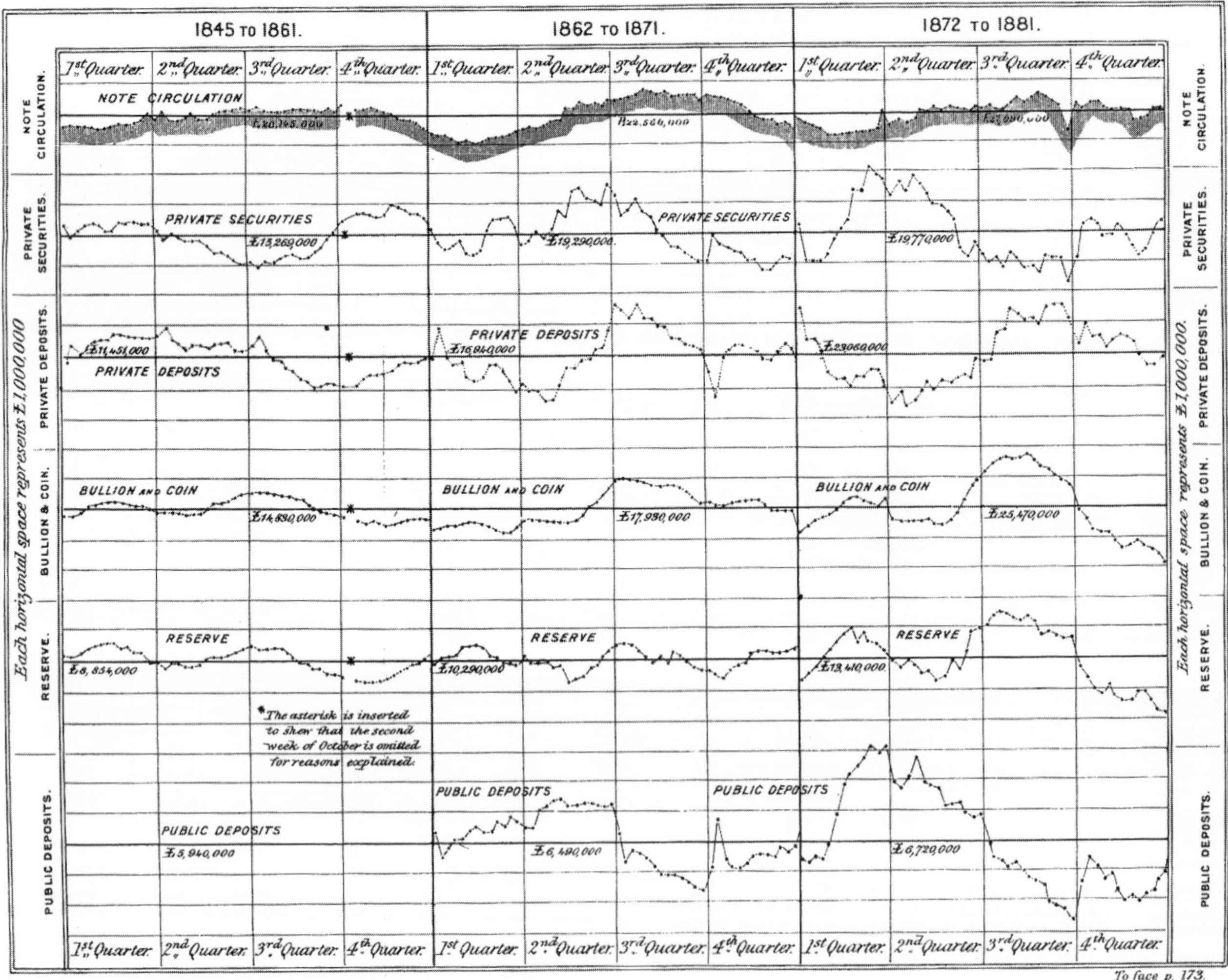

Figure 3 Jevons' diagram (reduced) showing the divergence of the accounts of the Bank of England from their average values after elimination of quarterly variations. Reading from the top, the diagram shows notes in circulation, private securities, private deposits, bullion and coin, reserves, and public deposits respectively. From *On the Frequent Autumnal Pressure in the Money Market, and the Action of the Bank of England*, reprinted in *Investigations in Currency and Finance* (1884), London: Macmillan, between pp. 192–193. Courtesy Palgrave/Macmillan Press.

his gold study. Jevons skillfully used simple averaging over weekly, quarterly, and yearly periods, to average out for different periodic variations. One of his diagrams, after elimination of quarterly variations in a number of economic variables, is given here (see Fig. 3).

Jevons was less successful in his attempt to explain commercial fluctuations from cyclical failures of the harvest. Jevons conjectured that failures in harvests might be caused by the cyclical activity of the sun, a cycle for which sunspots gave an indication. Jevons based this idea on the "well-known principle of mechanics that the effects of a periodically varying cause are themselves periodic." Jevons was never able to substantiate this conjecture appropriately. One of the difficulties was the establishment of the appropriate coincidence in periodicity between the activity of the sun (measured by sunspot activity) and commercial cycles. Once Jevons had managed to more or less synchronize both cycles, the causal chain of events linking both involved massive reactions of British trade on failures in the Indian harvests from at least 1700 onward, a causal link that was considered inconceivable by contemporary commentators. A fine example of Jevons' attempt to synchronize the periodicity of sunspot activity and commercial cycles is given in Fig. 4.

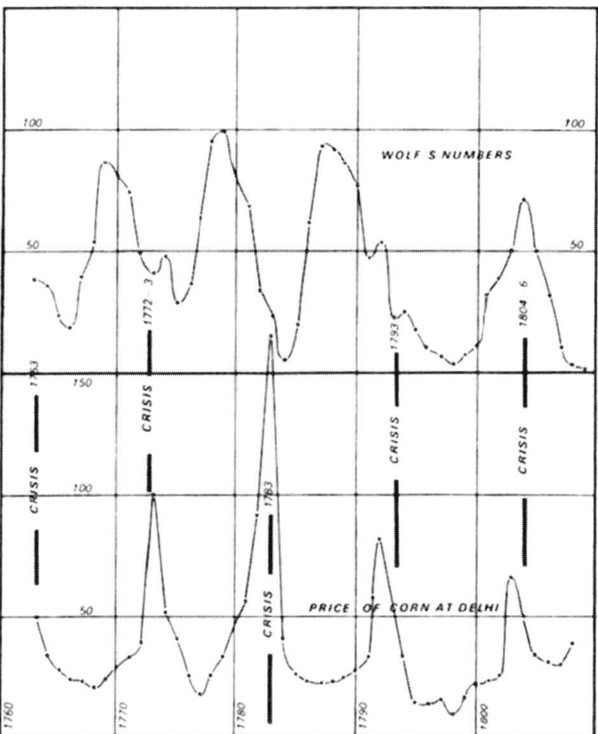

Figure 4 Jevons' diagram showing fluctuations in sunspot activity (represented by Wolf's numbers) and fluctuations in commercial activity (represented by the prices of corn at Delhi). Time is depicted on the horizontal axis. Jevons did not provide a description of what exactly is stated on the vertical axis. From "The Solar–Commercial Cycle" (1882) and reprinted from Black (1972–1981), **7**, 112, with permission.

His involvement in the issue of women working in factories turned out to be equally unsatisfying. When put to task on the subject, Jevons generously admitted that his plea for the abolishment of women's work in case there were children was not backed by his statistics. He remained convinced, however, of his conclusions.

Jevons: Humboldtian Scientist

In a brilliant essay, Susan Faye Cannon argued that "if you find a 19th century scientist mapping or graphing his data, chances are good you have found a Humboldtian." The Humboldtian scientist combines the use of these techniques with a vivid interest in scientific instruments and he does not restrict all these methods and tools to the laboratory, but applies them to the complex variety of real phenomena, whether they belong to the physical, biological, or human world. Without insisting on the label Humboldtian scientist, it is of use in pinpointing a type of scientist highly interested in precise and accurate measurements, not for their own sake, but to derive general laws from them, preferably in mathematical form. Such a scientist does not fit with the image of naive Baconianism. Rather, hypotheses are formed in a loose way from the data, making use of the tools and instruments indicated, with the aim of arriving at general explanations.

Jevons fits this image. And it may well be argued that perhaps the founder of the application of statistics to the social sciences, Adolphe Quetelet, fits the image as well. There was no walk in the country on which Jevons did not take his barometer and thermometer with him to determine the height of mountains and to make meteorological observations. Even when remembering an elder brother, Roscoe Jevons, who turned insane at the age of 18, Jevons thinks first of the wooden balance with which they were able to make fairly precise measurements.

Jevons clearly was not scared off by nature's complexity. He ingeniously made use of an inverted world map to compare the climate of Australia with that of North Africa. He consciously used averaging techniques to bring out the general course of the Australian climate from the data collected. His experiments on clouds not only tried to reproduce the existing classification of forms of clouds, but searched for a unifying mechanism explaining their formation as well. His experiments on work and fatigue, aiming to shed light on the "physical groundwork" of political economy, and his introduction of index numbers to thresh out a causal relation between the influx of gold and price changes are other cases in point.

In retrospect, all this may be considered more or less successful, as many of the scientific endeavors of the 19th century are now considered to be stupefyingly off the mark. But they show the opposite of the "uninquiring and unhoping spirit" that Jevons so much criticized in his later battles with political economists and statisticians. Quoting Herschel, he considered all sciences in the end capable of quantification and—depending on the quality of the data gathered and the measuring instruments used—capable of finding the laws governing the universe, the natural and the social. Slightly exaggerating, one might say that Jevons opened up the "age of measurement" in economics, as the period from Jevons onward has been called.

See Also the Following Articles

Complexity Science and the Social World • Deduction and Induction • Graph Theory

Further Reading

Aldrich, J. (1987). Jevons as statistician: The role of probability. *The Manchester School* **55,** 233–256.

Black, R. D. C., and Könekamp, R. (1972–1981). *Jevons, William Stanley. Papers and Correspondence, Vols I–VII.* Macmillan, London.

Goldmann, L. (1983). The origins of British 'social science': Political economy, natural science and statistics, 1830–1835. *Hist. J.* **26,** 587–616.

Henderson, J. P. (1996). *Early Mathematical Economics: William Whewell and the British Case.* Rowman & Littlefield, Lanham.

Kim, J. (1995). Jevons versus Cairnes on exact economic laws. In *Numeracy in Economics* (I. H. Rima, ed.), pp. 140–156. Routledge, London.

Klein, J. L. (1995). The method of diagrams and the black art of inductive economics. In *Numeracy in Economics* (I. H. Rima, ed.), pp. 98–139. Routledge, London.

Maas, H. (2005) *William Stanley Jevons and the Making of Modern Economics.* Cambridge University Press, Cambridge.

Maas, H., and Morgan, M. S. (2002). Timing history: The introduction of graphical analysis in 19th century British economics. *Rev. Hist. Sci. Hum.* **7,** 97–127.

Morgan, M. S., and Klein, J. (eds.) (2001). *The Age of Economic Measurement: 1850–1950.* Duke University Press, Durham, NC.

Nicholls, N. (1998). William Stanley Jevons and the climate of Australia. *Austr. Meteorol. Mag.* **47,** 285–293.

Peart, S. J. (1996). *The Economics of William Stanley Jevons.* Routledge, London.

Peart, S. J. (1995). 'Disturbing Causes,' 'Noxious Errors,' and the Theory–Practice Distinction in the Economics of J. S. Mill and W. S. Jevons. *Canadian Journal of Economics* **28.4b,** 1194–1211.

Porter, T. (1986). *The Rise of Statistical Thinking: 1820–1900.* Princeton University Press, Princeton, NJ.

Schabas, M. (1990). *A World Ruled by Numbers: William Stanley Jevons and the Rise of Mathematical Economics.* Princeton University Press, Princeton, NJ.

Schabas, M. (1996). Victorian economics and the science of the mind. In *Victorian Science in Context* (B. Lightman, ed.), pp. 72–93. Chicago University Press, Chicago, IL.

Schmitt, R. W. (1995). The Salt Finger experiments of Jevons (1857) and Rayleigh (1880). *J. Phys. Oceanogr.* **25,** 8–17.

Stigler, S. M. (1982). Jevons as Statistician. *The Manchester School.* **50,** 354–365.

White, M. V. (1994). The moment of Richard Jennings: The production of Jevons's marginalist economic agent. In *Natural Images in Economic Thought: Markets Read in Tooth and Claw* (P. Mirowski, ed.), pp. 197–230. Cambridge University Press, Cambridge, UK.

White, M. V. (1995). *Perpetual Motion and Change: Statics and Dynamics in the Political Economy of W. S. Jevons.* Mimeo, Monash University.

White, M. V., and Inoue, T. (1993). Bibliography of published works by W. S. Jevons. *J. Hist. Econ. Thought* **15,** 122–147.

Wise, N., and Smith, C. (1989,1990) Work and waste: Political economy and natural philosophy in nineteenth century Britain. *Hist. Sci.* **27,** 263–301, 391–449; *Hist. Sci.* **28,** 89–123.

Wood, J. C. (ed.) (1988). *William Stanley Jevons: Critical Assessments.* Routledge, London.

Judgment and Choice

Daniel Read
London School of Economics and Political Science, London, United Kingdom

Glossary

bootstrapping The use of a model derived from a judgment, in place of the judge.

choice Generally, the act of selecting among options. In research, however, the term is often differentiated from the act of putting a specific value on options, as in pricing or matching.

judgment The process of evaluating evidence, modifying beliefs based on the evidence, and stating or otherwise acting on those beliefs. The measurement of judgment involves observing these statements or acts.

matching A method for assessing value using a "fill-in" form in which one or more variables of options are left blank, and the respondent fills in the blanks so that the options are equal in value.

subjective probability The degree of belief that a proposition or set of propositions is true.

utility This term is used in two senses. First, it is often used to describe the benefit yielded by an action or course of action (someone who chooses A over B is therefore presumed to believe they will get more benefit from A than B). Second, it is a measure that reflects or summarizes choice. The outcome of utility measurement is often assumed to say something about the first kind of utility.

Central to the social sciences is some version of belief–desire psychology: We perform act X because we want Y, and believe that by doing X we will obtain Y. Ideally, acts can be divided into two sorts—judgments (or acts that reflect beliefs) and choices (or acts that reflect preferences). Beliefs and preferences can be distinguished in the following way: beliefs can be compared against a standard of accuracy, whereas preferences cannot. In reality, no act is a pure judgment or choice, but the goal of measurement is to distill these beliefs and preferences in as pure a form as possible. This article focuses on four key aspects of measurement in judgment and choice. These have been chosen both because they are among the most important and because they provide a broad picture of the range of measurement methods used by decision scientists, and the problems that arise in their use.

The Lens Model

The lens model is a general framework for measuring judgment and assessing its validity. It was first described by Egon Brunswik in the context of perception and was later extended to clinical judgment by Kenneth Hammond and colleagues. In principle, the lens model can accommodate all relationships between judgments, outcomes, and the data on which those judgments are based. In many, and perhaps even most, practical cases, some of the information necessary for such a complete analysis is missing, but the lens model summarizes ideal conditions of analysis that can inform research under less ideal ones.

Imagine a doctor assessing a patient's health. The doctor observes some attributes, such as blood pressure, heart rate, and temperature, and from them makes a judgment about the patient's health. The patient, moreover, has a true health status that may differ from the doctor's judgment. We can formally conceptualize problems like this using the framework depicted in Fig. 1, which shows why this is called the "lens" model. A judgment is made based on observable predictor variables ($\mathbf{x} = \{x_1, x_2, \ldots, x_n\}$). For each specific set of predictors a judgment y_s is made, and there is a corresponding objective outcome y_o. That is, the doctor estimates the health of the patient and the patient actually has a specific health status. From knowledge of the judgments, the outcomes, and the predictors, we can construct a statistical model of the judge

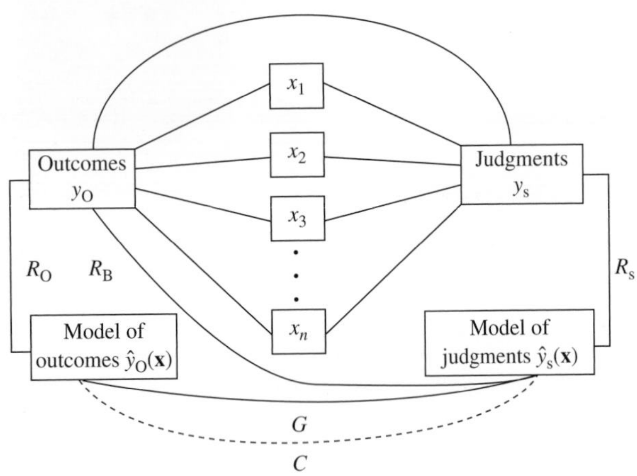

Figure 1 Relationships between components of the lens model.

and of the environment. These models are typically (but need not be) constructed using multiple linear regression. Figure 1 shows the important measurements that can be made, given many sets of judgments, outcomes, and predictors. These are summarized as follows:

- r_A: The accuracy or achievement of the judge, or the correlation between outcomes and judgments.
- $\hat{y}_J(\mathbf{x})$ and $\hat{y}_O(\mathbf{x})$: The predictions from a model mapping predictor variables onto predicted values.
- R_J and R_O: The correlation between judgments and outcomes and the predictions of their respective models ($R_J = R_{y_J\hat{y}_J}$, $R_O = R_{y_O\hat{y}_O}$) R_J is sometimes labeled "cognitive control," because it reflects how consistently judges use the available information.
- G: The correlation between the predictions from the two models, or $R_{\hat{y}_J\hat{y}_O}$. This can be called modeled knowledge.
- C: The correlation between the residuals from the two models. This can be called unmodeled knowledge, because it means that the judgments contain useful information that is not incorporated in the model.
- R_B: The relationship between the outcomes and the predictions of the judgment model (the subscript B is for bootstrapping; see later).

The lens model equation decomposes accuracy into components attributable to how information is used by the judge, how useful the information is, and the predictability of the environment:

$$r_A = GR_OR_J + C\sqrt{(1 - R_O)(1 - R_J)}.$$

The second term in the right-hand side is the unmodeled component of judgment. The modeled component is thus the product of modeled knowledge × task predictability × cognitive control. Several methodological issues must be addressed when applying the lens model. First, r_A must be assessed using a representative research design, meaning that the predictors and outcomes used to assess the judges are a representative sample of the environment in question. Second, because predictors are partially redundant (i.e., they are intercorrelated), there can be many equally reliable models relating judgments and outcomes to the predictor variables. Third, models of the judge and of the environment should always be cross-validated on a holdout sample, or at least subjected to statistical tests of shrinkage.

A number of generalizations about human judgment have come from studies conducted within the lens theory framework. First, the linear regression model usually provides an excellent fit to judgment, even when there are significant nonlinearities in the environment. Second, the best-fitting model also contains a lot of unsystematic error, meaning that people are inconsistent. Third, people draw on relatively few cues, usually no more than three and often less. Finally, what people say their judgment policies are often differs from what statistical models show. The latter finding is important for those wishing to study judgment—we cannot simply ask people what they are doing, we must actually observe them doing it.

The term "bootstrapping" is used to describe the use of a statistical model of a judge to stand in for the judge. These models virtually always outperform real judges. It appears that people are pretty good (but not great) at working out a tacit model of how data should be combined, but their judgments contain a lot of error that can mask this relationship. Moreover, judges are almost never as good as the best-fitting linear model; indeed, it has been a matter of great concern to researchers why actuarial models that outperform "clinical" (or unaided) judgment do not play a greater role in real-world diagnosis.

Probability Judgment

From the perspective of decision making, the most important judgment is of the likelihood of events, or their subjective probability. The nature of probability remains controversial, and this controversy has seeped into research on probability assessment. However, it is generally assumed that a subjective probability is a degree of belief (DOB) in a statement or set of statements.

Statements of DOB can be elicited in the form of verbal reports, meaning the use of everyday language such as "very likely" and "probable." People like giving probabilities in this form, but the subjective meanings of the terms they use vary so much that they provide a poor guide to action. Likelihood ratings are a more formalized version of verbal reports. Here a standard set of terms having a clear ordering in terms of probability is used to form response categories. An example is the 4-point scale "very likely," "likely," "unlikely," and "very unlikely." Such a scale is useful when all that matters is the rank of likelihood judgments. But there is no correct level of accuracy associated with each rating. Moreover, even for the same person, the terms will not have the same meaning in different contexts; the term "very likely" will denote a very different numerical probability when it refers to rain tomorrow, compared to a supernova of the sun within the next decade.

Most research into DOB assessment is based on numerical assessments. This is done using two classes of methods. When estimating quantities, such as "next year's sales projection," an interval-probability method is used. The typical method is the elicitation of a confidence interval in which the respondent provides an interval that he/she believes has an *X*% chance of containing the true value, as in "there is a 95% chance that next year's sales will be between £3 and £4 million." A related method is the fractile method, whereby the respondent reports fractile values for the quantity. For instance, they might be asked to specify three values such that there is a 5, 50, and 95% chance that the true value is no more than the corresponding value.

When assessing the likelihood of propositions (i.e., "Shakespeare wrote *Doctor Faustus*"), probability judgments are used; these are responses that can be directly transformed into a number on the 0–1 scale, where 0 means there is no chance of a statement being true, 1 means it is certain to be true, and intermediate values reflect proportionate degrees of uncertainty. The methods used are manifold, with the most common being statements of percentage likelihood or probability, and other methods being the use of a probability wheel (whereby the area on the wheel is adjusted to correspond to the probability of being correct), relative frequency estimates (e.g., "for 100 cases about which I was this sure, I would expect about 60 to be correct"), and odds judgments (e.g., "I would assign it odds of 3 to 1," meaning it has a chance of being correct three out of four times).

The important measurement issues in subjective probability judgment concern accuracy. This is usually indexed by calibration and discrimination (see Table I for more details). Calibration refers to the difference between the proportion of correct statements given a specific numerical judgment and the value of that judgment. For instance, do we find that of those patients given a 95% chance of surviving an operation that 95% do indeed survive? Discrimination refers to the ability to distinguish between cases. For instance, is the probability different (whether higher or lower) for a group given a 95% chance of survival and a group given a 5% chance of survival? Perfect calibration is found when the judged probability equals the observed probability, and perfect discrimination is found when judgment categories all have either 0 or 100% true statements. Signal detection theory uses the analogous terms bias (c) and sensitivity (d') to denote, respectively, calibration and discrimination.

Most research into DOB has focused on calibration. Fig. 2, which plots subjective probabilities (p) against objective probabilities or the proportion correct ($\bar{x}$), summarizes the stylized outcomes of dozens, if not hundreds, of experiments. First, people are generally overconfident, meaning their probability judgments are too high. Second, overconfidence declines as the task becomes easier. Some, although not all, overconfidence is caused by researchers often (inadvertently) choosing trick questions that are likely to be answered incorrectly (e.g., "Who invented the telescope, Galileo or Leeuwenhook?").

As with any judgment task, participants can be motivated to give responses differing from their true beliefs for strategic reasons. They might, for instance, give lots of high-confidence responses because they want to be seen as confident, or may give lots of 50% responses because they do not want to commit. One way to ensure that respondents give their true probability judgments is by paying them according to a strictly proper scoring rule, which assigns payoffs to subjective probabilities such that the maximum reward comes from reporting one's best probability estimate. The most widely used approach is based on the quadratic score (often called the Brier score):

$$s = \frac{1}{n}\sum_{i=1}^{n}(p_i - x_i)^2,$$

where p_i is the stated probability that the event will occur; $x_i = 1$ if the event occurs and 0 otherwise. If we let ψ_i be the subject's true belief about the probability of an outcome, the expected value of this score is

$$E(s) = \psi_i(1-p)^2 + (1-\psi_i)p^2.$$

This is minimized when $\psi_i = p_i$, so a good incentive scheme is one that pays or punishes by an amount equal to $a - bs$, where b is a positive amount of reward and s is the quadratic score. This payoff function is maximized when $\psi_i = p_i$.

Valuation

Central to the study of preference and choice is the measurement of the value of things. There are two straightforward and widely used methods of finding out how much something is worth to somebody: we can ask them to put a price on it, or we can ask them to choose between it and something else.

Four pricing methods are illustrated in Fig. 3. If you already own an object, you can state how much you would require to give it up (willingness to accept; WTA) or you can state how much you would pay to prevent having to give it up (equivalent loss; EL); if you do not own an object, you can state how much you would pay to obtain

Table I Components of Judgment Skill: Decomposition of the Quadratic Score

The quadratic score can be decomposed into three components, each of which reflects a different aspect of the decision maker's skill:

$$s = \bar{x}(1-\bar{x}) + \frac{1}{n}\sum_{j=1}^{t} n_j(p_j - \bar{x}_j)^2 - \frac{1}{n}\sum_{j=1}^{t} n_j(\bar{x}_j - \bar{x})^2,$$

where $\bar{x}$ is the proportion correct, p_j is a specific probability judgment (e.g., $p = 0.55$), n_j is the number of times this judgment is used, and $\bar{x}_j$ is the proportion of items assigned this probability that are correct. The first term on the right-hand side, the variance of the observed outcomes, is called "knowledge" when used for tasks in which a respondent states their belief and then assigns a probability to it. The second component, "calibration," indicates the squared deviation of the average confidence judgment from the average proportion correct. Calibration ranges from 0 to 1. It does not discriminate between over- and underconfidence.

Perfect calibration could be achieved by giving the average proportion correct for each probability judgment ($p = \bar{x}$), but this would make the individual judgments all but useless. The third component in the decomposition, called "resolution" or "discrimination", indicates whether the judge gives different probability judgments for tasks differing in their average outcome (analogous to r_A in the lens model). Resolution does not depend on what the judgments are, but only on the fact that the different values of $\bar{x}_j$ differ. A judge who gave probabilities of 1 whenever they were incorrect, and 0.5 when they were correct would have perfect resolution. The maximum value of resolution is the knowledge score, so many scholars suggest that a normalized discrimination index (NDI) be used, where NDI = resolution/knowledge.

it (willingness to pay; WTP) or you can state how much you would be willing to accept in place of obtaining the object (equivalent gain; EG). These methods are all widely used in valuation studies. In studies of intertemporal choice, EL and EG are almost the norm (e.g., "how much in 6 months would be the same to you as receiving £100 now" is an example of EG); in studies of consumer choice, WTP is natural ("how much would you pay for this toaster?"); in contingent valuation, WTP and WTA are widely used ("how much would you need to be paid to permit this river to be polluted?" or "how much would you pay to prevent it from happening?").

Economic theory states that, under most circumstances, all methods of pricing should yield the same price, but this is far from true. One of the most celebrated findings in choice research is what Daniel Kahneman, Jack Knetsch, and Richard Thaler called the "endowment effect," which means that WTA is typically far greater than WTP. This is true for commonplace consumer goods such as pens and coffee mugs, and for more momentous goods as well. To illustrate, one study found that if the risk of injury from a household cleaner is increased from 10 to 15 injuries per 10,000, most consumers will not buy the good at any price; but they would only pay, on average, \$0.65 more to decrease the risk from 15 to 10 injuries per 10,000. The major reason for the WTA/WTP discrepancy appears to be that people are systematically loss averse, meaning they treat a gain of x as being not as good as a loss of x is bad. When stating their WTP, therefore, they are trading off a loss of money against a gain of some good, and so loss aversion leads them to put more weight on the money. For WTA, the situation is reversed, and the loss of a good is traded against the gain of money. Other pricing methods fall in between, and Bateman and associates provide strong evidence that the pattern is WTP < EL ≤ EG < WTA.

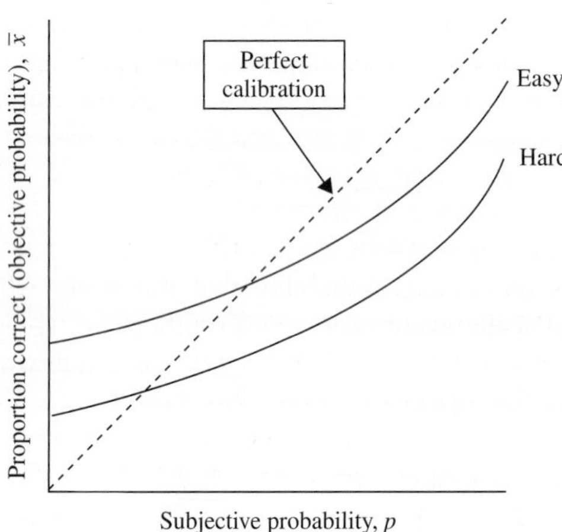

Figure 2 Calibration plot showing overconfidence and the hard–easy effect.

		Good: Gain	Good: Lose
Money	Gain	Equivalent gain (**EG**); you own neither, but you can receive one or the other	Willingness to accept (**WTA**); you are the owner, but you will give up ownership in exchange for a gain
	Lose	Willingness to pay (**WTP**); you are not the owner; but you will acquire ownership in exchange for a loss	Equivalent loss (**EL**); you own both, but you must give up one or the other

Figure 3 Four ways of eliciting a price.

Pricing is a specific example of a general method of preference measurement called matching. In general, one option is fully specified and another has some missing information. For example, respondents are asked what value of x would make the following options equivalent:

(A): A 3-week trip to Australia at a cost to you of \$2000, or
(B): A x-week trip to Australia at a cost to you of \$3000.

Another method is choice, whereby respondents are presented with two or more options and they choose the one they prefer. The experimenter would fill in a value for x, and ask "which would you prefer, A or B?" The comparison between choice and matching is most important from the perspective of preference measurement, because it has yielded evidence of widespread preference reversals, meaning that under one measurement technique people prefer A to B, but under another they prefer B to A. Preference reversals were first shown by Paul Slovic and Sarah Lichtenstein in the domain of gambles. When people choose between gambles, when one choice offers a high probability of winning a small amount (P-bet; e.g., a 0.8 chance of \$10) and the other offers a low probability of winning a high amount (\$-bet; e.g., a 0.1 chance of \$80), they tend to prefer the P-bet. On the other hand, they will put a higher price on the \$-bet. This appears to be one expression of a general phenomenon called the "compatibility effect": when stating one's preferences (or making judgments in general), dimensions that are more compatible with the response mode get more decision weight. For the gamble example, when pricing a gamble, the money dimension gets more weight because it is compatible with (i.e., easy to translate into) price.

Utility Measurement

Central to the study of choice is the concept of utility, which is, very roughly speaking, an index or measure of the benefit provided by an option. Utility is an inherently subjective concept, although it has been shown that given a small number of consistency or coherence conditions (the axioms of John von Neumann and Oskar Morgenstern), a cardinal utility function can be derived from gambles. Most utility measurement methods are based on the assumption that people are expected utility maximizers, where the expected utility of a prospect is given by the sum of the products of the probability of outcomes multiplied by their utilities $[EU = \sum p_i u(x_i)]$, meaning that they will always choose the prospect having the highest expected utility. Of the many utility measurement methods available, the following discussion focuses primarily on three that are solidly rooted in the axioms of utility theory. These are the certainty equivalent (CE), probability equivalent (PE), and gamble-trade-off methods.

The CE and PE methods are used to fit a utility function between a minimum utility level and a maximum utility level, which are given arbitrary values, usually 0 and 1. Imagine a set of possible outcomes, $\{s, x_1, x_2, \ldots, x_n, l\}$, where s and l are, respectively, the smallest and largest outcome, and all x_i take on intermediate values. The CE and PE methods work by offering the decision maker a choice between x_i for sure, and a gamble between s and l:

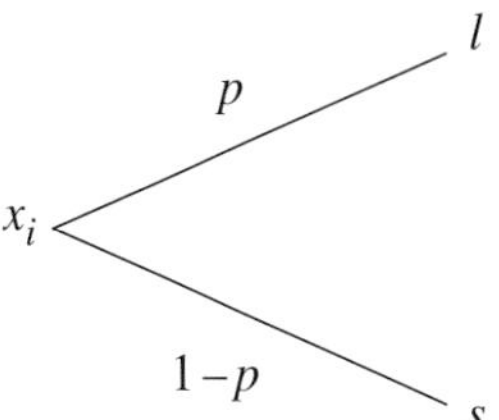

We start by assigning utility values to s and l. Because utility is measured on an interval scale (unique up to a linear transformation), these values are arbitrary as long as $u(l) > u(s)$, and for computational reasons it is best to choose $u(s) = 0$ and $u(l) = 1$. In the PE method, the value of p is varied until the decision maker is indifferent between the gamble and the sure thing, meaning that $u(x_i) = (1 - p)u(s) + pu(l) = p$. For different values of x_i, the same process is repeated until all possible values of x_i have been assigned their utility value. The CE method proceeds similarly, except now the value of p is fixed and the value of x_i is varied until indifference is reached. The interpretation of the numbers is the same as before. With the PE method, x_i is specified and $u(x_i)$ is derived; with the CE method, $u(x_i)$ is specified and x_i is derived. Both methods have shortcomings. A major one is the assumption that people maximize expectations, meaning that the decision weight they put on probabilities is equal to the probabilities. It is well known that this is not true, and that the true probability weighting function is more like the one illustrated in Fig. 4, first proposed by Kahneman and Tversky, which plots psychological weights $\pi(p)$ against probabilities. The function gives too much weight to small probabilities, and too little weight to intermediate ones; moreover, there is a rapid increase (even a discontinuity) when going from $p = 0$ to $p > 0$ and from $p < 1$ to $p = 1$. To account for such problems, utility assessment procedures that "cancel out" the effects of probability weighting have been developed. Most notable of these is the gamble-trade-off method proposed by Peter Wakker.

In the gamble-trade-off model, participants begin by equating a pair of gambles, as illustrated in Fig. 5. One gamble offers a p chance of l' and a $(1 - p)$ chance of

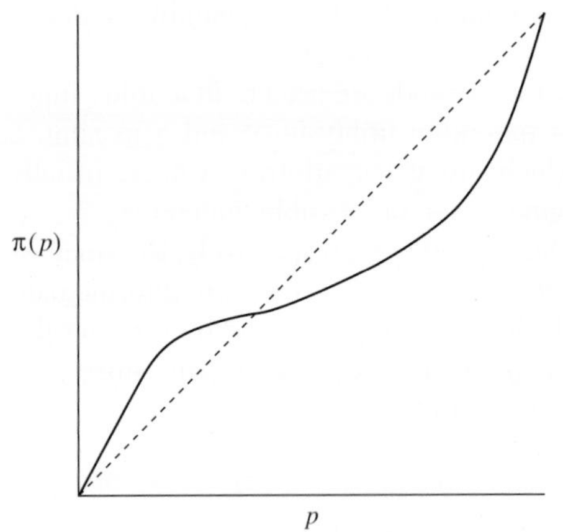

Figure 4 Psychological decision weights associated with different probability values.

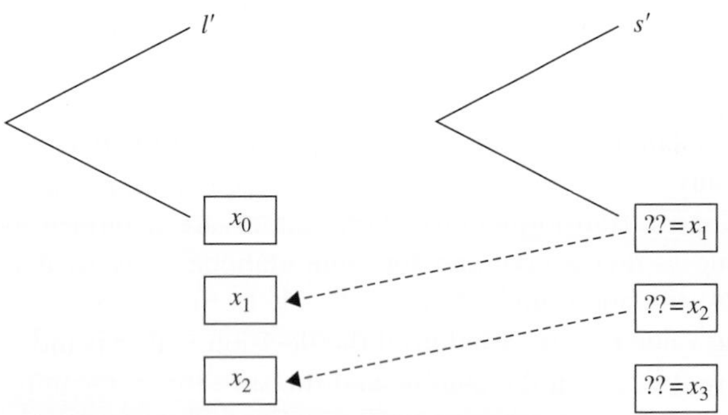

Figure 5 The gamble-trade-off method for utility measurement.

x_0 (less than l'); the other offers a p chance of s' ($<l'$; note that s' and l' probably will not be the largest and smallest possible values) and a $(1-p)$ chance of an unspecified x_1. Once x_1 is specified, it replaces x_0 in the next gamble and x_2 is obtained in the same way. The process continues until the range of values x_0 to x_n covers the range over which a utility function is needed. The logic is that the difference in utility between all consecutive values of x is equal, regardless of how the decision maker weights probabilities. That is, for all x_i and x_{i-1},

$$\pi(p)u(l') + \pi(1 - p)u(x_{i-1}) = \pi(p)u(s') + \pi(1 - p)u(x_i),$$

$$\therefore \quad u(x_i) - u(x_{i-1}) = [\pi(p)/\pi(1-p)] \times [u(l') - u(s')],$$

where the right-hand side in the second expression is a constant. In this way, a number of values of x can be produced that are equally spaced in utility, and a utility function can be derived as shown in Fig. 6. The shape of the utility function reflects risk attitude: concave (downward) functions mean risk aversion, and convex functions mean risk seeking. That is, a concave function,

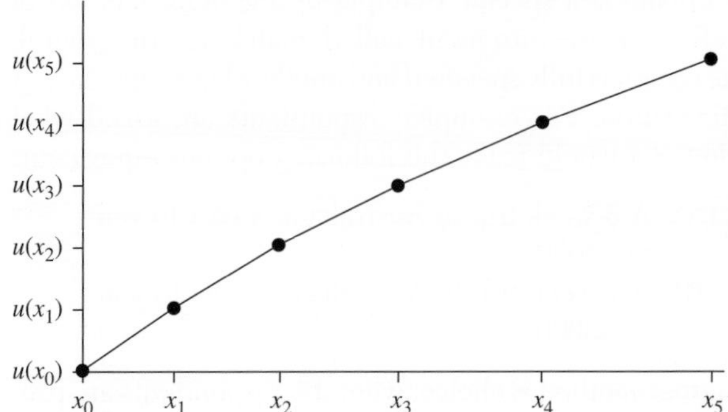

Figure 6 Utility function derived from the gamble-trade-off method. Note that the illustrated function is concave, but the utility function can take any shape.

such as the one in Fig. 6, means someone will turn down a fair gamble (i.e., with expected value of 0) in favor of a sure thing; a convex function means they will accept it. There is controversy over how utility functions derived in this way can be interpreted. The usual economic interpretation is that there is a global function defined over states of wealth, and the measured utility function constitutes only a small slice of it. Yet the concavity usually observed in this slice is, as Matthew Rabin has demonstrated, incompatible with any reasonable global utility function. More realistic is a utility function, as first proposed by Harry Markowitz and developed by Kahneman and Tversky, having a "kink" at one's current state of wealth, with convexity for losses and concavity for gains. The methods just described, therefore, are best interpreted as telling us about the local utility function, just above or below this kink.

Another issue concerns how utilities can be combined. Suppose, for instance, you find that £100 is worth 0.6 on a scale, and a diamond ring is worth 0.2. It is not possible to conclude that £100 and a diamond ring have a utility of 0.8; the utility analysis permits us to conclude no more than we knew without it: the ring-plus-£100 is worth no less than the ring or the £100 alone. There are two reasons for this. First, utility is measured only up to a linear transformation. Second, because of complementarity and substitution effects, the utility of each part of a bundle cannot be combined in a linear fashion. To find the utility of the money and the ring requires subjecting the entire bundle to a utility analysis.

The Problem of Response Variance

Measures of judgment and choice should conform to "description invariance" and "procedure invariance": different representations of the same problem, and different ways of measuring responses, should yield compatible judgments and choices. In fact, as already mentioned, this precondition is far from being met. The judgments and choices people make are highly dependent on irrelevant task features, and so researchers must always ask whether the results they obtain represent the decision maker's beliefs or preferences. The problem is so acute that many researchers have suggested that measured judgments and preferences are often "constructed" in response to the task, rather than "reported." Consequently, a word of caution is offered to researchers and consumers of research: always ask how much judgments and choices reflect true beliefs or preferences, and how much they reflect how the task was described and the responses elicited.

See Also the Following Article

Utility

Further Reading

Bateman, I., Munro, A., Rhodes, B., Starmer, C., and Sugden, R. (1997). A test of reference dependent preferences. *Q. J. Econ.* 479–505.

Hammond, K. R., and Stewart, T. R. (2001). *The Essential Brunswik: Beginnings, Applications and Extensions.* Oxford University Press, Oxford.

Kahneman, D., and Tversky, A. (1979). Prospect theory: An analysis of decision under risk. *Econometrica* **47,** 263–291.

Keeney, R. L., and Raiffa, H. (1976). *Decisions with multiple objectives: Preferences and value tradeoffs.* Cambridge University Press, Cambridge.

Luce, R. D. (2000). *Utility of Gains and Losses: Measurement Theoretic and Experimental Approaches.* Erlbaum, Mahwah, New Jersey.

Payne, J. W., Bettman, J. R., and Schkade, D. (1999). Measuring constructed preferences: Towards a building code. *J. Risk Uncertainty* **19,** 243–271.

Rabin, M. (2000). Diminishing marginal utility of wealth cannot explain risk aversion. In *Choices, Values and Frames* (D. Kahneman and A. Tversky, eds.). Cambridge University Press, Cambridge.

Wakker, P. P., and Deneffe, D. (1996). Eliciting von Neumann–Morgenstern utilities when probabilities are distorted or unknown. *Mgmt. Sci.* **42,** 1131–1150.

Yates, J. F. (1990). *Judgement and Decision Making.* Prentice-Hall, Englewood Cliffs, New Jersey.

Knowledge Creation

Gidi Rubinstein
Netanya Academic College, Tel Aviv, Israel

Glossary

empiricism The view that all knowledge is based on or derived from sensory experience.

factor analysis A mathematical technique used to determine the minimum number of factors required to explain an observed pattern of correlations.

induction The method by which a general statement, suggesting a regular association between two or more variables, is derived from a series of empirical observations.

interpretivism A perspective or method that emphasizes understanding of intentional human conduct.

ontology A branch of philosophy dealing with the nature of existence or reality.

paradigm A number of theories that depend partly on the shared metaphysical beliefs of the scientific community (Kuhn).

positivism A strict empiricism that recognizes as valid only knowledge claims based on experience.

realism The assertion that the objects in the world have an existence independent of our conception of them.

refutation An approach opposed to verification, claiming that the scientific process begins when observations clash with existing theories (Popper).

relativism A doctrine that claims that the conceptions of good and evil are relative rather than absolute.

This article describes attempts to create knowledge through the process of social measurement. The main approaches in the philosophy of science are presented and the processes through which quantitative measurement instruments are developed to test hypotheses, and how they generate new questions and create new knowledge, are reviewed. Qualitative attempts to study phenomena, the investigation of which cannot be carried out by standardized quantitative measures, are described. Intelligence quotient (IQ) tests, emotional intelligence tests (developed in response to the inadequacy of the IQ tests to predict success in real-life situations), the F scale (based on the authoritarian personality theory), and the Big Five (a measure to map the various dimensions of personality, which started by attempts to find words that refer to characteristics of behavior) exemplify the contribution of quantitative measures to knowledge creation; Frieilich's anthropological study about the Mohawk men who worked as building molders in New York of the 1960s, as well as various explorative attempts to study the life of gay couples, are described to exemplify qualitative ways of knowledge creation, when quantitative measures are inappropriate.

Introduction: Knowledge and Science

The word "science" has its origins in the Latin verb *scire*, meaning "to know." We can "know" through tenacity, authority, faith, intuition, or science. The major purpose of science is to develop laws and theories to explain, predict, understand, and control phenomena. The scientific method is distinct in its notion of intersubjective certification, but all observation is potentially contaminated, whether by theories or by worldview or by past experiences. Scientific knowledge is tentative and subject to revision on the basis of new evidence. Science cannot provide certainty, but it is the most objective mode of pursuing knowledge. It is generally believed that the goal of the pursuit of knowledge is the discovery of truth, which may either take shape in the mind of the observer or is to be approached only through the evidence of the senses. Two additional views of science are the consensual, according to which the goal of science is a consensus of rational opinion over the widest possible field, and the dissension, according to which scientific research is much more controversy laden.

An enormous amount of knowledge resides in the ability to notice and interpret phenomena. Knowledge can be stable or flexible, shared by all or residing in special individuals, taking the form of general rules learned by rote or treating new situations in an imaginative way. What a person sees depends both on what is observed and on what previous visual/conceptual experience has taught a person to see. Every description of observable events has what might be called "objective" and "subjective" sides, i.e., "fits" are recognized in a particular situation, but the process of fitting to a situation modifies it.

From Logical Positivism to Scientific Realism

The concepts discussed so far are related to the evolution of scientific thought from logical positivism to postpositivism and scientific realism. For many years, "positivism," a strict empiricism that recognizes as valid only knowledge claims based on experience, has dominated discussions of scientific method. During the 1920s, positivism emerged as a full-fledged philosophy of science in the form of logical positivism. Developed by the Vienna Circle, a group of scientists and philosophers, logical positivism accepted as its central doctrine Wittgenstein's verification theory of meaning, which holds that statements are meaningful only if they can be empirically verified, and inductive inference can never be justified on purely logical grounds. A more moderate version of positivism is known as logical empiricism, which became the "received view" in the philosophy of science. The concept of verification was replaced with the idea of gradually increasing confirmation. Verification is considered a complete and definitive establishment of truth. Universal statements can never be verified, but may be confirmed by the accumulation of successful empirical tests. Logical empiricists believe that all knowledge begins with observations, which lead to generalizations. Science and knowledge are believed to occur inductively from data to theory. A finite number of observations are believed to lead to the logical conclusion that a universal statement is "probably true," tentative, and in need of permanent proof. Observations are always subject to measurement error, and theory depends on observation.

Unlike the positivists, Karl Popper (1902–1994) accepted the fact that observation always presupposes the existence of expectations; hence, the scientific process should begin when observations clash with existing theories, which are subjected to rigorous empirical refutation tests. Contrary to Popper's refutation rule, Thomas Kuhn's (1922–1996) model emphasizes the conceptual frameworks that guide research activities. Kuhn's paradigm includes a number of theories that depend partly on the shared metaphysical beliefs of the scientific community. Given its advocacy of relativism, Kuhn's *Structure of Scientific Revolutions* became one of the most carefully analyzed works in the philosophy of sciences. Larry Laudan (1952–), on the other hand, sees science operating within a conceptual framework that he calls research tradition, which consists of a number of specific theories, along with a set of metaphysical and conceptual assumptions that are shared by those scientists who adhere to the tradition. The "truth" or "falsity" of a theory is therefore irrelevant as an appraisal criterion.

Critical relativism is a multifaceted philosophy of science, arguing that knowledge production in the social sciences is impacted by the broader cultural milieu and there is no "scientific method," but disciplinary knowledge claims are viewed as contingent on the particular beliefs of its practitioners. It rejects the basic premise of the positivistic approaches that there is a single knowable reality and accepts different ways of exploring natural phenomena, each with its own advantages and liabilities.

Classical realism believes that the world exists independently of its being perceived and that the role of science is to use its method to improve our perceptual measurement processes, separate illusion from reality, and thereby generate the most accurate possible description and understanding of the world. The claim that a scientific proposition seems true does not mean that it is certain, but rather that the world is as the proposition says it is.

Objectivity, Standardization, and Behavior Sampling

In the positivist approach, as a whole, measurements are developed to test hypotheses. However, often the existence of a measurement instrument is an impetus to the generation of new questions, and the creation of new knowledge. Anastasi (1908–), one of the best known psychologists in the field of testing, tells us that psychological tests are tools that can be instruments of good or harm, depending on how they are used. She defines a test as an "objective" and "standardized" measure of a sample of behavior. This definition focuses our attention on three elements: (1) objectivity, which tells us that most aspects of a test are based on objective criteria, such as how the test is scored and how the score is interpreted, and are not a function of the subjective decision of a particular examiner; (2) standardization, so that no matter who administers, scores, and interprets the test, there is uniformity of procedure; and (3) a sample of (a person's) behavior, desirably a representative sample, from which we can draw inferences and hypotheses. A test is not a psychological X ray, nor does it necessarily reveal hidden conflicts and forbidden wishes.

Measurement Instruments as an Impetus of New Questions

As far as knowledge creation is concerned, the effect of measurement on the objects being observed is of major importance. Even in the hard sciences, wherein knowledge is usually considered an objective, reproducible truth derived through the scientific method, measurement affects results in the most physical sense. To gain any knowledge of a system requires interaction with it. When something is seen, it is because quanta of light hit the object and are reflected to the eyes (or to an instrument). This is not an issue as long as the objects are macroscopic, because then the interaction is vanishingly small relative to the object. However, when the objects are on atomic scale, the interaction energy is on the order of the object energy. This is the physical reason for the famous Heisenberg Uncertainty Principle, which fundamentally affects quantum mechanics, the basis of physics. Observation and measurement always involve interaction with the observed object. Because of quantization, this interaction cannot be made infinitely small. Therefore, for atomic-scale objects, the interaction is similar in size to measured quantities, leading to inability to measure everything with infinite precision.

The Case of Intelligence Quotient Tests

When Alfred Binet (1859–1911) began research on the measurement of intelligence, he did not realize the Pandora's box that he was going to open. With the creation of the Binet scale (later modified by W. Stern and renamed the intelligence quotient), human beings were given a quantitative, objective method of gauging "intelligence." Originally, Binet intended his test to be a rough guide for identifying mildly retarded and learning-disabled children, with the hope of administering these children special training to improve their mental capacity. Scientists such as Goddard, Terman, Yerkes, and countless others saw this new test as a means of identifying inferior individuals who needed to be regulated and, most importantly, prevented from reproducing. Many of these scientists used their data to create a hereditarian theory of IQ that relied primarily on within- and between-group heredity. In other words, they would identify an estimate of heritability within a single population and then say that this similarity within the group also explains the common differences between groups. It was these assumptions that created a major problem: human beings now had quantitative scientific data to support racism and discrimination. The demons were out of the box.

The Case of Emotional Quotient Tests

Another question raised with respect to IQ tests relates to their inadequacy to measure success in real-life situations; assessing this has contributed to the creation of new knowledge. When psychologists began to write and think about intelligence, they focused on cognitive aspects, such as memory and problem solving. However, there were researchers who recognized early on that the noncognitive aspects were also important. As early as 1943, Wechsler (1896–1981) was proposing that the nonintellective abilities are essential for predicting a person's ability to succeed in life. Robert Thorndike (1943–), to take another example, was writing about "social intelligence" in the late 1930s. The work of these early pioneers was largely forgotten or overlooked until 1983, when Howard Gardner began to write about "multiple intelligence." Gardner proposed that "intrapersonal" and "interpersonal" intelligences are as important as the type of intelligence typically measured by IQ and related tests. In 1990, Peter Salovey and John Mayer coined the term "emotional intelligence," defining it as "a form of social intelligence that involves the ability to monitor one's own and others' feelings and emotions, to discriminate among them, and to use this information to guide one's thinking and action." Salovey and Mayer also initiated a research program intended to develop valid measures of emotional intelligence and to explore its significance. In 1995, Daniel Goleman became aware of Salovey and Mayer's work, and this eventually led to his book, *Emotional Intelligence*. To be a scientist, probably an IQ of 120 or so is needed simply to get a doctorate and a job. But it is more important to be able to persist in the face of difficulty and to get along well with colleagues and subordinates than it is to have an extra 10 or 15 points of IQ. The same is true in many other occupations. In doing the research for his first book, Goleman became familiar with a wealth of research pointing to the importance of social and emotional abilities for personal success. Some of this research came from personality and social psychology, and some came from the burgeoning field of neuropsychology. Research now emerging suggests that emotional intelligence, and particularly the new measures that have been developed to assess it, is in fact a distinct entity.

The Case of the F Scale

The problems resulting from Anastasi's demand for objectivity may be exemplified by the authoritarian personality theory and the various scales to measure authoritarianism and related variables. The study of authoritarianism, an example of an inductive empirical personality research, has grown out of the deductive psychoanalytic theory. It began with an attempt to find the personality variables related to anti-Semitism, continued with defining anti-Semitism as a part of ethnocentricity (prejudices against ethnic minorities in general), and ended up with considering ethnocentricity as a general fascistic tendency, the origin of which is a personality structure called the "authoritarian personality." Authoritarian individuals were perceived as having a strong primitive id, a weak ego, and a rigid superego, which is based on a fear of punishment rather than on a true internalization of morality. This personality structure is behaviorally expressed by authoritarian aggression, obedience, projectivity, and other traits, according to which the F(ascism) scale was developed. As was the case with the IQ tests, the F scale was politically, methodologically, and theoretically criticized. It was argued that it represents an ideological bias of politically leftist researchers, hence focusing only on authoritarianism of the political right, associated with fascism, and ignoring the existence of left-wing authoritarianism, associated with communism. An immediate attempt to develop a measure unrelated to political attitudes resulted in the development of the Dogmatism scale. Here it can be seen how the effects of believed flaws in a measurement instrument result in an attempt to correct it and create new knowledge. Methodologically, it was argued that the F scale is not valid, because all its items are phrased in the same direction; hence it cannot be known whether an agreement with a certain statement is a valid evidence of authoritarianism or rather expresses a general tendency to agree with every statement in general (a response-set bias). Intensive research efforts were invested in the attempts to test this claim and in the development of an alternative biased scale. Theoretically, it was argued that the whole research method of authoritarianism is wrong. First, a relation between authoritarian attitudes and behavior does not necessarily exist, and second, each one of the different personality characteristics has to be measured separately to prove the alleged relations among them, rather than starting with a scale that presupposes that such relations do exist. The effect of this alleged flaw of the F scale resulted in the development of separate measures of the different variables that are supposedly characteristic of the authoritarian personality, thus promoting the creation of new knowledge. A series of studies investigating authoritarianism in court, authoritarianism and repression, and authoritarianism and obedience to instructions enlightened the issue of validity, which becomes complicated given the complexity of the concept of authoritarianism. The sources of authoritarianism among children, as well as the interaction between authoritarianism and various situations and its effect on intragroup preferences, are two additional fields that exemplify how developing the F scale and its related variables contributed to the creation of new knowledge. Finally, it is important not to ignore the possibility that the study of authoritarianism has been influenced by different sociopolitical climates; from the 1930s till nowadays, both researchers and the groups they study have been affected by sociopolitical realities.

The Case of the Big Five

Personality can be defined as the distinctive and characteristic patterns of thought, emotion, and behavior that define an individual's personal style of interaction with the physical and social environment. When people are asked in daily life to describe a personality, the response is likely framed in terms of personality traits, e.g., adjectives such as "intelligent," "extroverted," "conscientious," and so forth. One way to begin the task of deriving a comprehensive but manageable number of traits is to consult a dictionary. The assumption is that through linguistic evolution, the language will encode most, if not all, of the important distinctions among individuals that make a difference in everyday life. Allport and Odbert actually undertook this task by going through the unabridged dictionary. They found approximately 18,000 words that refer to characteristics of behavior—nearly 5% of the English lexicon. Next, the list was reduced to about 4500 terms by eliminating obscure words and synonyms, and this shortened list was then organized into psychologically meaningful subsets. Subsequent researchers have used such trait terms to obtain personality ratings of an individual. Peers who know the individual well are asked to rate him/her on a scale of each trait. For example, a rater might be asked to rate the person on the trait of friendliness using a 7-point scale that ranges from "not at all friendly" to "very friendly." Individuals can also be asked to rate themselves on the scales. For example, Raymond Cattell (1905–) first condensed the Allport–Odbert list to less than 200 terms and then obtained both peer and self-ratings. He then used the method of factor analysis to determine how many underlying personality factors could account for the pattern of correlations among the trait ratings. His analysis yielded 16 factors. A similar procedure was used by the British psychologist Hans Eysenck (1916–1997) to arrive at two personality factors, introversion/extroversion, a dimension first identified by the psychoanalyst Carl Jung (1875–1961) that refers to the degree to which a person's basic orientation is turned inward toward the self or outward toward the external world, and emotional instability/stability, which Eysenck calls neuroticism, defined as a dimension of emotionality, with moody/anxious, temperamental, and maladjusted individuals at the neurotic or unstable end and calm, well-adjusted individuals at the other. Nowadays many trait researchers agree that five trait dimensions (the "Big Five") may provide the best compromise. There is still disagreement about how best to name and interpret the factors, but one reasonable way to summarize them is with the acronym OCEAN: openness to experience, conscientiousness, extroversion, agreeableness, and neuroticism. Many personality psychologists consider the discovery and validation of the Big Five to be one of the major breakthroughs of contemporary personality psychology. Thus, the 18,000 words found by Allport and Odbert in 1936 were reduced to five major factors that express a personality. Moreover, the introversion/extroversion dimension, suggested by Jung on purely deductive theoretical basis, is one of the current Big Five factors, which are the result of thorough inductive empirical testing, as was the case with the authoritarian personality theory and the F scale. Have the Big Five created new knowledge? Interestingly enough, the same two researchers who validated the Big Five have just recently edited and published an almost 500-page volume of research, connecting the Big Five to personality disorders, which are the most frequently recognized psychopathologies today. Thus, the Big Five seems to be not merely a valid instrument to characterize personality, but has a diagnostic value in the realm of psychopathology. And, if it is possible to characterize individuals who suffer from different personality disorders by the Big Five, how does this relate to the other diagnostics? Is it possible to predict that authoritarian individuals, to take only one example, would have low scores on the openness-to-experience factor? How would authoritarians, whose superego is supposed to be weak, score on the conscientiousness factor? How about the emotional intelligence of authoritarians, who are supposed to be rigid and dogmatic? Does it seem reasonable to predict that emotionally intelligent individuals would have high scores on the extroversion and openness-to-experience factors? Finally, how would psychologists score on these and other measures? Only future research will tell.

Alternatives to Quantitative Research

A perennial debate in the philosophy of social sciences is whether they should strive to emulate natural science methods, or whether understanding social phenomena is something essentially different from explanation in the natural sciences. The naturalists say that the social sciences should be like the natural sciences, whereas the interpretivists assert the contrary. Interpretivism can be roughly divided into two conceptual parts: a positive program for how to do social science and a set of arguments for why any attempt to implement natural science methods in the social sciences is doomed to failure.

Some have argued that the social sciences cannot explain events by causes because they cannot capture all the complex contributing factors, because there is no material constitution to social facts (such as marriage or money), or because human reason is necessarily involved. But if science has the goal of providing the means for explanation, prediction, and intervention, then social science must also be able to do this in order to be considered science. Causal relations are the basis of this type of reasoning. When the function of an artifact or practice is identified (the function of the Hindu taboo on eating cattle is to provide traction animals for farming; the function of Potlatch is to redistribute food, etc.), what is explained? Carl Gustav Hempel (1905–1997) argued that functions cannot explain why the functional item is present (why the Hindu's have the taboo, or why the Kwakiutl have the Potlatch). But identifying functions is ubiquitous in social science (as is the case in biology), and functions seem to be playing an explanatory role. Philosophers have taken up the challenge to analyze how and what function ascription explains. The role of laws as essential to explanation has been defended by Hempel and formalized in his deductive–nomological model of explanation, arguing that, if they are necessary in physical science, then they must be necessary also in social science. The problem then arises that there appear to be no laws in social science, hence these explanations are impossible.

Another relevant issue in the context of qualitative methods is the Individualism–Holism debate, which is often dated back to Emil Durkheim's formulation of the holistic position and Weber's definition of the individualist position. Today the discussion of the two positions is typically divided into three different issues:

1. The ontological issue: Are there any irreducible social phenomena?
2. The explanatory issue: Are there any explanations that are irreducible to the individual level?
3. The semantic issue: Are there social concepts that cannot be defined by reference to individuals only?

Schön's approach about reflection-in-action and reflection-on-action is a process that reshapes what we are working on, while we are working on it. If something is not working correctly, then we "reflect" (a conscious activity) in the action-present. A critical aspect is the questioning of the assumptional nature of knowing-in-action, which is often left unexplained or unmentioned when we describe what we do, but is revealed in skillful performance. Reflecting-in-action is generally called forth when a surprise appears in the process of accomplishing the task. That surprise causes us to question how the surprise occurred, given our usual thinking process. As we work on a project, many of the "surprises" we will encounter will appear because the knowing-in-action, on which we draw, is largely skills that we perhaps developed in other fields. Thus, the surprises occur because our old model does not work without modification for the new task. We reflect-in-action and find out what is different and how we can change our thinking to address this new task. We reflect-on-action, thinking back on what we have done in order to discover how our knowing-in-action may have contributed to an unexpected outcome. How do we reflect-on-action? First, we choose a critical incident, which could be something that we believe we finally did correctly after much ado, or something that even in the end we believe we did not do very well. Then, we think about the components of that incident from two different time frames. For example, if it is something with which we struggled and were proud of the accomplishment in the end, we will try to find that "light bulb" that helped us make sense of it and try to find out what was it like before that time and what was it like after that time. Next, we discuss the thinking process that either existed, or needed to exist, between the two time frames. What was not right in the knowing-in-action? We see if we can find specific examples to link in this discussion and draw on our resources (book, articles, etc.) that help explain the incident. Finally, we wrap it all up: What have we learned so next time our knowing-in-action (or at least our reflection-in-action) will be different and will reflect our new understanding?

In addition to these issues, we should also be aware of certain social phenomena for which either the quantitative methods or random sampling are inapplicable.

Mohawk Heroes in Structural Steel

During the 1950s, New York residents could occasionally read in the newspapers about a unique phenomenon, the Indians from the Mohawk tribe who worked as structural steel molders on high-rise buildings. The members of the Mohawk were described as "brave" and "physically stable." Why were so many Indians of the Mohawk tribe molders? It was argued that, for some reason, the Mohawk Indians do not suffer from acrophobia. Morris Frieilich tried to understand the reasons for this lack of acrophobia among the Mohawks by investigating the Caughnawaga reserve, which was considered the home of the Mohawk Indians. During the participant observations, Frieilich carried a small notebook and a pencil, trying not to be obtrusive, and recorded the names of the people with whom he was talking, the topics of the conversations, the time, unusual events, and statistical data that he might have otherwise forgotten, such as salary, age, frequency of travels to the reserve, and the like. He revealed that the life of the Mohawk Indian is focused in the role of the fearless hero who uses every opportunity to demonstrate disdain for the security, laws, authorities, and social conventions of other groups. According to the Mohawk culture, being a man equals being a warrior. In the original Mohawk society, Mohawk Indians were involved in battles of small groups, and the social role of the warrior was prestigious and socially rewarded. "The game of the warrior" during the 1950s equated to the danger of being a high-rise molder, expressing the continuity of the ancient Mohawk social structure. The warrior-molder formula was developed because of the similarity between the two modes of life and because being a "real" warrior was no longer possible; the modern parallel was the molder, who carried out dangerous tasks in a group of young men with an older leader (the supervisor).

In terms of social measurement, Frieilich's research methods, compared to quantitative methods, are much more prone to subjectivity, personal interpretation, and bias as a result of his contacts with the study participants. His participant observations have not met Anastasi's requirements of objectivity, standardization, and the representativeness of the behaviors being sampled. However, applying quantitative systematic methods not only was impossible, but would have never yielded the findings discovered by Frieilich. Unlike the quantitative approach, adopted by social scientists from life and hard sciences, qualitative researchers do not have any hypotheses to be tested in their studies. The question whether Frieilich "measured" the phenomena at hand remains open. There is no doubt, though, that he created knowledge.

Knowledge Creation without Measurement: Gay and Lesbian Couples

Gays and lesbians are a minority in the population in every society. One of the arguments used by mental health professionals who consider homosexuality a mental disorder is that homosexual individuals are usually incapable of establishing solid, lasting relationships. Yet little is known about gay and lesbian relationships. How many gays and lesbians live as couples? What is the average duration of a relationship? How many open vs. monogamous relationships are there among gay and lesbian couples? Research into gay couples is relatively new, and gay people remain a largely invisible segment of the population. Problems in obtaining study participants who reflect the diversity of this group continue to plague studies of homosexual relationships; some of the published research on same-sex couples is based on small samples, and many studies are only anecdotal. Statistics about the percentages of singles, married, and divorced men and women in different age groups is well-documented among heterosexuals, but a similar database has not been established for the gay community. What can be asked, however, putting aside aspirations to generalize the results, is how (rather than how many) gay and lesbian couples live.

Americans live in a society where strong feelings against homosexuals are expressed openly and in almost every context. Legal, religious, and social institutions are constructed with a significant bias toward heterosexual marriage and, implicitly or explicitly, against homosexual partnerships. David McWhirter and Andrew Mattison have noted many of the ways that internalized social fears and prejudices toward homosexuals can create havoc within gay partnerships, and several other authors have discussed the role these social attitudes play in the relationships of gay couples. McWhirter and Mattison undertook an extensive investigation of 156 gay couples in order to ascertain patterns of change as the couples aged. They were dissatisfied with attempts to impose heterosexual models of the family life cycle on gay couples. Their interpretation of the data led to a developmental theory of male couples composed of six stages: blending, nesting, maintaining, building, releasing, and renewing. Loosely based on the age of the relationship, the model has been broadly used to describe the development of gay male couples.

Douglas Carl cautioned that gay men who come out of the closet as adults may become sexually involved with several men or may rapidly move in with someone they are dating, only to break up within a year. Carl equated this phenomenon to adolescents going steady, only without the restraints typical of the younger age. For most gay men, this period of unbridled sexuality subsides with time. Carl also noted that many gay couples join across racial, cultural, or socioeconomic lines. He speculated that this occurs because a smaller pool exists from which to choose partners in the gay community. Nonetheless, these couples will face many of the same strains that cross-cultural marriages experience. McWhirter and Mattison stated that limerence (intense sexual attraction that usually accompanies the early stages of intimate relationships) usually begins to decline after the first year or two of the relationship, and at the same time there is greater interest in "nesting" urges. This developmental change in the relationship is sometimes misinterpreted as loss of love or as ambivalence about remaining committed.

In conclusion, male couples have been shown to face unique challenges. However, many men feel that their love for one another is worth every sacrifice. Because the recognition of gay-couple relationships is relatively new in society and gays are a sometimes invisible segment of the population, hypotheses have not been developed on the basis of previous knowledge nor has a quantitative approach been applied; even so, knowledge of these groups of people has been created.

Conclusion

The question as to whether social sciences are "scientific," as life sciences or hard sciences are, continues to bother some social scientists (particularly those who deal with the philosophy of science). Those who doubt the "scientificness" of social sciences claim that social researchers, those individuals who study human behavior, cannot be objective enough because of the lack of the necessary distance or detachment between the researcher and those being investigated. There are social scientists and philosophers of science who think that human behavior should be measured like any natural phenomenon, and that what exists is only what can be observed and quantitatively measured. According to this view, the social scientist is supposed to be objective, and although the issue investigated could be subjectively selected, its scientific measurement should be value free. Measures that exemplify this positivist approach provide examples that demonstrate how the development of measurement instruments results in the generation of new questions and knowledge. Flaws in measurement instruments, and their correction, have an effect on the creation of knowledge (e.g., the development of emotional intelligence measures as a result of the inadequacy of IQ tests to predict success in real-life situations).

An opposite view argues that human behavior should be investigated only qualitatively, and that the efforts to measure it quantitatively leave important elements out of the picture. Moreover, there are phenomena that cannot be quantitatively measured because of various reasons. Attempts to investigate such phenomena qualitatively contribute to the creation of new knowledge. In some instances, as in anthropology, this contribution remains qualitative; in other cases, qualitative measurements can be a basis for formulating hypotheses that can be tested by quantitative measures.

See Also the Following Articles

Binet, Alfred • Factor Analysis • Information Management • Psychometrics of Intelligence

Further Reading

Anastasi, A. (1988). *Psychological Testing*. 6th Ed. Macmillan, New York.

Chalmers, A. (1990). *Science and Its Fabrication*. Minnesota Press, Minnesota.

Hempel, C. G. (1966). *Philosophy of Natural Science*. Prentice-Hall, New Jersey.

Hunt, S. D. (1991). *Modern Marketing Theory: Conceptual Foundations of Research in Marketing*. Southwestern Publ., Mason, Ohio.

Kuhn, T. (1996). *The Structure of Scientific Revolutions.* 3rd Ed. University of Chicago Press, Chicago.

Laudan, L. (1984). *Science and Values.* University of California Press, Berkeley.

Popper, K. (2002). *The Logic of Scientific Discovery.* 15th Ed. Routledge, New York.

Schön, D. A. (1987). Teaching artistry through reflection-in-action. *Educating the Reflective Practitioner*, pp. 22–40. Jossey-Bass Publ., San Francisco.

Yogesh, M. (1994). *Role of Science in Knowledge Creation: A Philosophy of Science Perspective*. Available on the Internet at http://www.brint.com

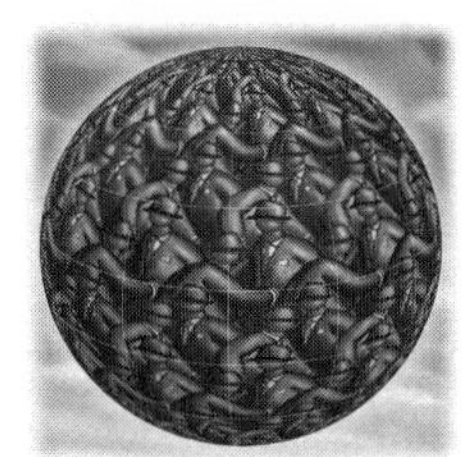

Knowledge Work

Robert D. Austin

Harvard Business School, Boston, Massachusetts, USA

Glossary

agency theory A theory that addresses the dynamics of an agency relationship, with particular emphasis on the alignment (or lack thereof) of incentives between principal and agent, and on the use of measurement coupled with payments to adjust incentives.

agent Someone who does work on behalf of another, a principal, in exchange for payment.

attributability The degree to which a measurement can be attributed to some causal object—an individual, a group, or a process.

evaluability The degree to which the normative adequacy of a measurement can be judged.

measurability The degree to which important aspects of the observed work yield to cognitively simple and relatively compact quantification.

observability The degree to which activities involved in work are easy to see, understand, and evaluate.

precision The degree to which a change in a measure indicates change in the underlying quantity of interest rather than random disturbance.

principal Someone who pays another, an agent, to do work.

reliability The degree to which a measurement indicator retains, over time, its integrity as a representation of an underlying quantity of interest.

sensitivity The degree to which a change in an underlying quantity of interest tends to change a measurement indicator.

separability The degree to which the outcomes or effects of the work of one individual or group can be differentiated from the outcomes or effects of the work of another individual or group.

Knowledge work is work in which important value-creating transformations occur in the realm of ideas or in which substantial amounts of productive activity is intellectual rather than physical; as Drucker put it in 1959, "work that is based on the mind rather than on the hand." It is now widely accepted that organizations' abilities to create, communicate, retain, and use knowledge are critical to their success. In high-technology sectors of industrialized economies, rapid growth has underscored the economic importance of knowledge work and created entirely new occupational categories—network manager, software engineer, and biotech researcher, to name but a few. These knowledge workers produce economic value primarily by manipulating thoughts, ideas, and symbols. Their work has distinctive characteristics that affect our ability to measure it. Specifically, knowledge work is difficult to observe because its materials and products are intangible and complex. Its processes are highly interdependent, which leads to difficulties in attributing outcomes to specific people or causal factors. Because the work is often highly specialized, it is difficult to evaluate; often managers (and other observers) of knowledge workers cannot do what they do and are not qualified to judge the work outcomes, especially interim work products. In addition, innovation—by definition, doing or making something different—is *the* key to value creation in much knowledge work; this fact presents challenges in that previously established forms of measurement may not adequately capture what is novel and important in such work.

Categories of Difficulty in Measuring Knowledge Work

There are three categories of difficulty in measuring knowledge work. First, knowledge work is less observable than physical work. The activities involved in loading coal into a rail car are easier to see, understand, and evaluate than the activities involved in progressing toward a successful database design. Although the problem of observability has long been known and studied, it takes on new depth when the activity being measured is intangible thought-stuff.

Second, the motivation of knowledge workers is more reliably intrinsic than it is for many physical workers. Knowledge work is often idiosyncratic and oriented toward creative activities and problem solving; hence, it is interesting for workers. Physical work is more often repetitive and oriented toward compliance and, hence, less interesting. The possibility that strong intrinsic motivation can be relied on to direct workers' activities requires rethinking research based on less optimistic assumptions about human motivation (such as economic agency theory) and suggests additional dimensions of measurement relevant to work outcomes.

Third, it is the nature of knowledge work that a high degree of individual capability in the worker is often the critical factor in achieving successful outcomes rather than, as with much physical work, his or her consistent compliance with a plan or efficient participation in an externally programmed system. An excellent technical support person is excellent not because of his or her performance on well-known and well-understood tasks but rather because he or she is good at the exploration, knowledge creation, and analysis needed to perform excellently in solving unprecedented problems or in other vaguely defined tasks. In knowledge work, talent, skill, and knowledge (TASK) differentials matter a great deal; performance is often more about what a worker can do than about the level of effort he or she exerts. Levels of talent and skill interact strongly with performance and therefore must also be measured.

Although problems in the second and third categories are important, the focus here is on the first category, problems of observability. This is because problems of motivation and TASK differentials often manifest themselves in terms of observability.

How Economists Approach Work Observation Difficulties

Problems of discerning performance in social phenomena have been much studied. Economic agency theories, recent and direct attempts to address issues of observability, are notable for their growing prominence in research and practical contexts; they are, for example, employed in debates about how business executives should be paid. The foundational agency model was introduced in 1973 by Ross and refined in 1979 by Holmstrom; all subsequent models have been variations on this Ross-Holmstrom (R-H) model. Although such models ultimately fail to capture the full complexities of the problem of measuring knowledge work, they are a useful starting point in considering this subject because they distill observability problems into their simplest, most fundamental elements.

The R-H model depicts an organization in highly simplified form: two individuals and the contractual relationship between them. A principal has control over resources and hires an agent to transform resources into output with money value. The principal tries to maximize profit—the difference between the value of the agent's output and the payment required to induce effort from the agent. The agent's motivations are also self-interested and simple—he or she wants to maximize his or her income while minimizing effort and avoiding risk. The interests of the two are therefore opposed. The principal wants to extract as much effort as possible from the agent while paying him or her as little as possible. The agent wants to do as little work and bear as little risk as possible while being paid as much as possible.

The principal cannot directly observe the agent's work. This assumption is justified by noting that (1) often it is not feasible for a manager to watch an employee at every moment, and doing so would in any case obviate the efficiencies sought in hiring the agent; and (2) often workers are hired for specialized abilities that the principal does not possess and has only limited ability to understand and evaluate. Because the principal cannot observe how much effort the agent is exerting, the principal cannot compensate the agent on the basis of how hard he or she works (his or her level of effort). The principal does have available, however, a signal of the agent's effort level, although that is complicated by a random component (representing factors that are beyond the agent's control; e.g., rainstorms that depress a salesperson's performance in a given week). The signal's random component has distributional properties such that unfavorable signal outcomes become less likely when the agent's effort level increases. Hence, the signal is statistically, although not directly, indicative of the agent's effort level and can serve as a measure of performance. There is also an assumption, often implicit, that higher levels of effort by the agent will make more valuable work outputs more likely.

An optimal compensation schedule based on the signal of agent effort can be derived from this theoretical setup. The schedule maximizes expected profits for the principal and expected utility for the agent, subject to a constraint that ensures that the agent expects enough reward to remove him or her from the labor market. The consideration of the properties of this schedule produces the following conclusions.

1. The agent demands additional compensation for bearing the risk associated with the probabilistic signal

of his or her performance; thus, measuring and rewarding performance is more costly for the principal than if effort could be observed directly because of the agent's risk aversion.

2. The outcome is Pareto inferior to the outcome that would result if direct observation of effort were possible; that is, the principal and agent would be collectively better off, and neither would be worse off, if effort were directly observable; hence, there is economic value lost due to observation difficulties.

3. The optimal compensation contract includes a variable component that increases with the signal (the measure of performance).

This last conclusion is offered both as an explanation and an endorsement of increasing-in-output payment schedules (such as sales commission systems).

Banker and Datar have broadened this discussion of observability to include problems of precision and sensitivity of the performance measure, which may complicate the discernment of the agent's underlying effort levels and prevent the creation of effective compensation schemes. Precision, roughly defined, is the degree to which movement in the signal indicates movement in the underlying quantity of interest (e.g., effort) rather than random disturbance. A very low precision signal is not useful because too many of its changes are due to random noise. Sensitivity, roughly defined, is the degree to which a change in an underlying quantity of interest (e.g., effort) tends to change a measurement indicator. A measure that is very low in sensitivity is not useful because even large movements in the underlying quantity of interest result in small, difficult-to-discern movements in the signal. The fields of statistical process and quality control address related issues involved in separating signal from noise in repetitive and stable industrial processes.

How Behavioral Scientists Approach Work Observation Difficulties

In contrast with the rigorous theorizing of agency economics, behavioral science has tended to study observability via detailed, often field-based, empirical examinations. Early work focused on pathological phenomena. In 1963, Blau conducted research on government bureaucracies and found that well-intentioned measurement programs were consistently dysfunctional. In one study, agents at an employment office reacted to a system that measured job-applicant interviews by shifting most of their efforts to interviewing, away from locating new job opportunities; fewer job placements resulted, even though that was the organization's *raison d'etre*. Office managers then enhanced the system to include eight measures, some of them ratios, such as "percentage of interviews that resulted in job referrals." At first the enhancements seemed to work, but Blau's replication of the study revealed that earlier dysfunctional behaviors had been replaced by more sophisticated dysfunction. Agents "engaged in outright falsification . . . by destroying at the end of the day those interview slips that indicated that no referrals to jobs had taken place." Further attempts to fix this system by adding many more measures were also ineffective; employees always adapted and dysfunction resulted.

As described by Blau, the pattern of dysfunction that resulted from observability problems had three unfortunate characteristics. First, dysfunction seemed inherent in the attempt to measure these administrative organizational activities; regardless of the incentive effect designers of a measurement system intended—regardless even of whether they meant to create any incentive effect at all—unintended incentive effects appeared. Second, dysfunction was persistent; it resisted efforts to eradicate it by adjusting the measurement technology. Finally, dysfunction was hidden from the designers and users of the measurement system, often until some catastrophic failure occurred; the question "how do you know your system is not dysfunctional?" could not readily be answered. In 1956, Ridgway summarized the findings of several studies that reported similar dysfunctional patterns by concluding, "quantitative performance measurements—whether single, multiple, or composite . . . have undesirable consequences for overall organizational performance."

This persistent dysfunctional pattern has often been explained as resulting from incompleteness in measures. A measurement system suffers from incompleteness when measures do not capture all critical dimensions of productive work. (A dimension of activity is critical when no value can be produced without devoting effort to it.)

The R-H model offers no explanation for the pattern of dysfunction that results from incompleteness in measures because it assumes implicitly that measures are complete. In fact, the increasing-in-measured-output payment schedules that seem implicated in the pattern of dysfunction identified by Blau (and others) seem to be specifically recommended by the R-H model. The two streams of research were at odds on this point.

Economists have since modified their models to address the problem of incompleteness and consequent dysfunction. In 1991, Holmstrom and Milgrom modeled a situation in which the agent allocates effort across tasks, some of which are measurable and some of which are not. They show that if one of the unmeasurable tasks is critical to value creation and rewards increase with measurements on measurable tasks, then dysfunction will result. If the agent is willing to do valuable work without measurement-linked rewards, then letting him work for a flat fee is the best you can do with incomplete measures. Milgrom and Roberts concede that this result "imposes a serious constraint on the incentive compensation formulas that can be used in practice." Holmstrom and Milgrom have argued that the measurability of specific effort dimensions may be a determining factor in work efficiency, organization, and organizational structure.

Knowledge Work and Observability

As Holmstrom and Milgrom have shown, if the problem of completeness remains unsolved, then solutions to the problem of unobservable effort that tie variable payments to signal outcomes (e.g., output measures) are dysfunctional. Furthermore, because knowledge work tends to be oriented toward innovation and problem solving, it may benefit from efforts on dimensions that were unanticipated. Knowledge work is multidimensional, and the criticalness of dimensions often evolves dynamically. To put this another, less formal way: in work that is about smartness, how smart someone works (i.e., how cleverly one allocates effort across tasks) is necessarily of great importance. For these reasons (and others), the problem of completeness is especially prominent when the work being performed is knowledge work.

Prescriptive works on the subject of organizational measurement often include recommendations that measures be as complete as possible. One popular treatment, for example, urges that organizational scorecards be balanced by including nonfinancial as well as financial measures, in categories that more exhaustively cover what really matters to a business. Although balance might not be precisely the same thing as completeness, the evoked intuition is often the same. Although recommendations of balance or completeness may be a step in the direction of improved practice, it remains important to understand when completeness can be achieved and in which work settings.

Observability issues that arise in physical settings have typically been framed in terms of asymmetry in information about workers' hidden acts (usually effort allocations). Knowledge work generates more pronounced asymmetries, based not only on information asymmetries but also on talent, skill, or knowledge asymmetries between a manager and those he or she manages. A manager who has the same information as a worker can still lack the expertise needed to understand, attribute, evaluate, and act on what he or she observes. Hence, observability problems that afflict knowledge work may be particularly severe and persistent.

Knowledge asymmetries and resulting observability problems cannot necessarily be designed away. Prescriptive treatments of organizational measurement often focus almost exclusively on the measurement technology—on "choosing the right measures"—as if observability were entirely dependent on the shrewdness of measurement system designers. In fact, observability problems derive ultimately from the characteristics of the specific organizational setting that are the site of a productive act—not just from the design of the measurement technology.

Persistent observability problems common in knowledge-work settings can be decomposed into three categories. Difficulties in any of these categories can suffice to undermine performance measurement objectives.

1. Measurability is the degree to which important aspects of the observed work yield to cognitively simple and relatively compact quantification. If we cannot measure what we care about in a way that is meaningful, with acceptable confidence in the validity of the measure, then measurement becomes more difficult. In such situations, less direct proxy measures are often sought, which creates potential for problems in the other two categories. For example, the quality of work during software development is notoriously difficult to measure. Counts of defects in the final product, a common measure, are at best only suggestive of quality as a customer defines it, which is in terms of suitability for the customer's evolving intended purpose.
2. Attributability is the degree to which a measurement can be attributed to some causal object—an individual, a group, or a process. Measuring something without knowing (or at least confidently hypothesizing) its relationship to a causal action or object is not very useful. Moreover, the ability to measure a thing does not assure that the thing can be easily or usefully attributed to an actionable underlying cause. Often, there are important interdependencies in knowledge work; it is rarely easy, even after the fact, to say who contributed what to the value in the final product.
3. Evaluability is the degree to which the normative adequacy of a measurement can be judged. Measuring and attributing without knowing whether the measurement reflects favorably on the object of attribution is not very useful. Standards and benchmarks assist with evaluability issues. But the ability to measure and attribute a thing does not assure that the thing can be easily or usefully evaluated. Much knowledge work results in products that are distinctive and, in general, the greater the distinctiveness, the lower the evaluability.

Prescriptive treatments and economic models have often assumed away these problems, especially the second and third. The R-H model, for example, deals in a limited way with measurability in that the agent's effort expenditure cannot be directly observed. Because there is only one agent, however, there are no issues of attributability.

Evaluability is assumed, in that signal and work outputs are usefully related and effort allocation occurs along a single dimension. More effort is good; less effort is bad.

The situation is usually considerably less simple or convenient in knowledge-work settings. Because much of the work is intangible and conceptually complex, measurability problems are common. Proxy measures are not obvious, and usually there are questions about the attributability of a chosen proxy measure. The collaborative and interdependent nature of much knowledge work makes it difficult to draw lines of causality, especially when progress is evolutionary and proceeds at an uneven pace. Determining who or what was responsible for a favorable or unfavorable outcome can be difficult if not impossible for an idiosyncratic, evolving, or poorly understood work process. These same difficulties complicate evaluability. Activities and outputs may be unprecedented. No obvious standard of evaluation may exist. Comparison with what was done last time may not be meaningful because of changes in process and the work environment since then.

Measurability issues necessitate the use of proxy measures in place of true measures—measures of what the organization truly values. Once proxy measures are introduced, questions about their relationship to true measures arise. Attributability concerns complicate attempts to establish persistent relationships between proxy and true measures, leaving workers latitude to engage in dysfunctional behaviors. Problems of evaluability hinder the detection of dysfunctional behaviors as the pattern unfolds.

Several characteristics of organizational situations that have often been observed to complicate work measurement create particularly difficult problems for knowledge-work measurement. Measures of knowledge work are more likely to be incomplete due to these factors.

- Context insensitivity. Because measurement designers may lack vital knowledge about the work, contextual variables that have independent effects on proxy measures may remain unknown. Even if they are known, they may be ignored because of the conceptual complexity involved in measuring them. Ways of affecting proxy measures that are known to workers but not to measurers create potential for incompleteness and dysfunction.
- Separability. Because of knowledge asymmetries and the collaborative nature of some knowledge work, measurement users may have difficulty separating the work of one individual or group from that of another because the work is (or seems) so interdependent. Consequently, workers may have the ability to move proxy measures in what seems like a favorable direction by shifting work difficulties onto other workers. Needless to say, a system that rewards such behavior does not foster cooperation among workers and may result in undesired outcomes from the overall collaborative activity.
- Reliability. For knowledge work that is rapidly changing, attribution and evaluation may become difficult because comparisons of a process from repetition to repetition are not obviously valid. The degree to which measures succumb to problems of context insensitivity and inseparability may change from repetition to repetition. Empirically discovered correlations between measured quantities and underlying phenomena may not persist. If the measurement process is a statistical one, the problem manifests itself as a fundamental incoherence in the population definition.
- *Ex post* causal ambiguity. Knowledge asymmetries provide latitude for variation in *ex post* interpretation of events. If a complex computer error shuts down a production facility, for example, there may be only two or three people who truly understand what has happened. The parties involved may take advantage of this fact by lobbying for specific interpretations of measurements and events. This practice has a destabilizing effect on efforts to establish underlying causal attributions.

In established or more physical measurement settings there is often a consensus on the causal models that underlie measurement. In many knowledge-work settings, no such consensus exists. Moreover, the extent to which such a consensus is realizable may be limited by the rapidly changing nature of knowledge work.

Measuring Knowledge Work in Research

Many of the difficulties that afflict managers as they attempt to measure the performance of knowledge workers also carry over to researchers as they attempt to understand the same work. Researchers have attempted to overcome the observability difficulties inherent in knowledge work in a number of ways.

Simon and others conducted comprehensive investigations in 1979 into the nature of human problem solving by using talk-aloud protocols, in which research subjects verbalized their thoughts while attempting to solve a problem. Although these experiments have led to insights into human cognition, they provide limited assistance in quantifying important aspects of knowledge work; most such studies were not conducted in real work settings, and observations often did not yield compact quantification. Also, human problem solving, although a significant component of knowledge work, by no means exhausts value-producing activities. For example, many creative activities involved in knowledge work may not be usefully conceptualizable as problem-solving activities.

In 2002, Amabile *et al.* pioneered empirical methods for examining creative activities by engineers through several means that vary in their obtrusiveness, including close examination of their daily work products, coding of subjective records kept by workers (such as diaries), and direct observation of work processes. In the tradition of Blau, ethnographers have continued to apply their methods to achieving an understanding that takes into account the rich contexts and deep expertise levels that exist in knowledge-work settings. Austin and Devin have suggested in 2003 a formalized approach to analyzing differences in subsequent versions of knowledge-work outputs (e.g., software) as a means to gaining insight into work processes. Ways of gaining empirical insights into the nature and essential characteristics of knowledge work are evolving; this is likely to continue in the near future.

See Also the Following Articles

Business, Social Science Methods Used in • Critical Views of Performance Measurement • History of Business Performance Measurement • Intangible Assets: Concepts and Measurements • Knowledge Creation

Further Reading

Austin, R. D., and Devin, L. (2003). *Artful Making: What Managers Need to Know about How Artists Work.* Prentice Hall, Upper Saddle River, NJ.

Austin, R. D. (1996). *Measuring and Managing Performance in Organizations.* Dorset House, New York.

Blau, P. M. (1963). *The Dynamics of Bureaucracy: A Study of Interpersonal Relations in Two Government Agencies.* University of Chicago Press, Chicago, IL.

Drucker, P. (1992). *The Age of Discontinuity.* Transaction Publications, New York. (Originally published 1969.)

Lawler, E. E., III. and Rhode, J. G. (1976). *Information and Control in Organizations.* Goodyear, Santa Monica, CA.

Leonard-Barton, D. A. (1995). *Wellsprings of Knowledge: Building and Sustaining the Sources of Innovation.* Harvard Business School Press, Boston, MA.

Mason, R. O., and Swanson, E. B. (1981). *Measurement for Management Decision.* Addison-Wesley, Reading, MA.

Milgrom, P., and Roberts, J. (1992). *Economics, Organization and Management.* Prentice-Hall, Englewood Cliffs, NJ.

Nonaka, I., and Takeuchi, H. (1995). *The Knowledge Creating Company: How Japanese Companies Create the Dynamics of Innovation.* Oxford University Press, Oxford.

Ridgeway, V. F. (1956). Dysfunctional consequences of performance measurement. *Adm. Sci. Q.* **1**(2), 240–247.

Laboratory Experiments in Social Science

Murray Webster, Jr.
University of North Carolina, Charlotte, North Carolina, USA

Glossary

condition (Theoretical) Abstract and historical fact or given, e.g., "task-focused group," "motivated actors," "full knowledge of payoffs." (Experimental) State of a theoretical condition under examination, e.g., "Condition 1, higher status for self than other."

design Abstract features of a situation intended for an experiment. E.g., "The design included four conditions, differing by status position of the focal actor, in which all actors were task-focused." Cf. operation.

operation Specific structural fact and action during an experiment. "Design" refers to abstract criteria; "operations" refers to observable facts. E.g., "The operational measure of satisfaction was marking above the midpoint on the questionnaire item."

phase Temporal part of an experiment, often tied to independent and dependent variables. E.g., "Independent variables regarding the task and each subject's status position were introduced in phase 1; dependent measures of behavior were recorded in phase 2."

variable Structural fact and action taking different values during an experiment. Independent variables are controlled by an experimenter to create the experimental design; dependent variables are uncontrolled and are measured to test predictions.

Experiments entail creating and manipulating independent variables, and, following those operations, measuring the dependent variables. The temporal ordering distinguishes experiments from other methods. For instance, in surveys, responses (dependent variables) are analyzed by statistically controlling the independent variable(s) *after* data collection. Laboratories are physical locations for data collection. In most cases, a laboratory's design allows optimal conditions for accurately measuring changes in dependent variables, often including arrangements to improve visibility and technology to present information and record behavior and other responses.

Role of Experiments in Social Sciences

Contemporary social science methods are diverse, including unstructured, structured, and participant observation; surveys of attitudes or behavior; content analysis of written or photographic material; analyses of archived data; and different kinds of experiments. Experimental types include those conducted in the field (e.g., large-scale drug trials), in contained natural settings (e.g., new classroom techniques, employee incentive programs), and in a laboratory. Data collection thus uses observational, survey, or experimental methods and data from each type can be subjected to various analytic methods. Surveys and experiments lend themselves to inferential statistics, whereas observational methods lend themselves to qualitative analytic techniques. However, qualitative analyses of some experimental data, such as postsession interviews, may be important and inferential statistics are appropriate for some kinds of observational data, such as records of repeated events.

An experiment is a simplified constructed reality in which an investigator controls the level of an independent variable(s) before measuring a dependent variable(s). Attempting to reduce or eliminate extraneous factors, deliberately creating different levels of independent variables, and then measuring effects permits strong inferences, though not proof, of causal relationships. Laboratory experiments developed first in the natural sciences (see Table I), becoming the standard research method whenever they can be used (astronomy and meteorology, for instance, also use other methods). Social

Table I Some Historical Uses of Experiments in Social Sciences

Psychology has the oldest tradition of experimental methods in the social sciences. Around 1900 in Russia, Ivan Petrovich Pavlov, trained as a physiologist specializing in the digestive system, naturally turned to an experimental laboratory for his famous studies of the relationship between time of bell ringing and saliva production. U.S. psychologists Edward L. Thorndike at Harvard University and J. B. Watson at Johns Hopkins University developed laboratory methods for their studies, and experimental methods have become standard in many areas of psychology.

In social psychology Solomon Asch studied conformity and Muzafer Sherif studied norm formation and transmission in laboratories. Soon afterward, Leon Festinger and his many colleagues and students investigated social comparison and cognitive dissonance. Both editions of *The Handbook of Social Psychology* contain didactic chapters on experimental methods.

In economics, Chamberlin introduced laboratory studies of markets in the 1940s, Siegel and Fouraker analyzed games, and von Neumann and Morgenstern pioneered the study of rational choices. Davis and Holt, and Kagel and Roth, provide comprehensive overviews of experimental economics.

In political science, many experimental studies were stimulated by Thomas Schelling's theory of negotiation strategies. Axelrod studied cooperation experimentally using rational choice and other approaches.

In sociology, Robert Freed Bales studied discussion groups in his Harvard University laboratory beginning in the 1940s, and Joseph Berger, a research assistant for Bales, helped to found a continuing tradition of experimental research at Stanford University.

References

Psychology and Social Psychology

Aronson, E., and Carlsmith, J. M. (1968). Experimentation in social psychology. In *The Handbook of Social Psychology* (G. Lindzey and E. Aronson, eds.), 2nd Ed., Vol. 2, pp. 1–79. Addison-Wesley, Reading, MA.

Asch, S. (1951). Effects of group pressure upon the modification and distortion of judgement. In *Groups, Leadership, and Men* (H. Guetzkow, ed.), pp. 177–190. Carnegie Press, Pittsburgh, PA.

Edwards, A. L. (1954). Experiments: Their planning and execution. In *The Handbook of Social Psychology* (G. Lindzey, ed.), 1st Ed., Vol. 1, Chap. 7, pp. 259–288. Addison-Wesley, Cambridge, MA.

Festinger, L., and Carlsmith, J. M. (1959). Cognitive consequences of forced compliance. *J. Abnormal Soc. Psychol.* **58,** 203–210.

Sherif, M. (1948). *An Outline of Social Psychology*. Harper & Brothers, New York.

Thorndike, E. L. (1905). *The Elements of Psychology*. Seiler, New York.

Watson, J. B. (1913). Psychology as the behaviorist view it. *Psychol. Rev.* **20,** 158–177.

Watson, R. I. (1968). *The Great Psychologists: From Aristotle to Freud*, 2nd Ed. Lippincott, New York.

Economics

Chamberlin, E. H. (1948). An experimental imperfect market. *J. Polit. Econ.* **56,** 95–108.

Davis, D. D., and Holt, C. A. (1993). *Experimental Economics*. Princeton University Press, Princeton, NJ.

Kagel, J. H., and Roth, A. E. (1995). *The Handbook of Experimental Economics*. Princeton University Press, Princeton, NJ.

Siegel, S., and Fouraker, L. E. (1960). *Bargaining and Group Decision Making*. McGraw-Hill, New York.

Von Neumann, J., and Morgenstern, O. (1944). *Theory of Games and Economic Behavior*. Princeton University Press, Princeton, NJ.

Political Science

Axelrod, R. M. (1984). *The Evolution of Cooperation*. Basic Books, New York.

Schelling, T. C. (1960). *The Strategy of Conflict*. Harvard University Press, Cambridge, MA.

Sociology

Bales, R. F. (1999). *Social Interaction Systems: Theory and Measurement*. Transaction Publishers, New Brunswick, NJ.

Berger, J., and Zelditch, M., Jr. (1997). *Status, Power, and Legitimacy*. Stanford University Press, Stanford, CA.

science borrowed and adapted laboratory methods and there has been dramatic growth in the use of this method, although other methods, primarily surveys, are still more common.

Sometimes people wonder whether results would differ if an experiment were repeated with a different subject population. Results would differ, though that fact may well be irrelevant to the researcher's real interest. For instance, Swedish, Japanese, and Argentine citizens might well exhibit different rates of overall influence in a laboratory conformity experiment, but so what? It does not matter whether Argentines or Swedes accept influence in contrived situations. One might want to know how they act in everyday settings, but the laboratory is hardly an everyday setting. Laboratory resources are too valuable to waste on whimsical explorations of "What would happen if . . . ?"

However, demographic characteristics of a population, such as gender, nationality, or skin color, may operationalize theoretical factors, in which case laboratory results are informative. For instance, one might use gender as an instance of the theoretical construct "status characteristic," or one might want to know the extent to which fairness norms are important in experimental participants' social systems. In 1980, Foschi distinguished experimental limitations of culture from theory-testing uses of cultural facts and discussed some theoretical uses of cross-cultural comparisons.

A well-designed experiment tests hypotheses contrasting two or more possible outcomes, derived from a theoretical base. Those may include a theoretically derived hypothesis and a null hypothesis, or contrasting outcomes that would support contrasting theories. The theory is the abstract template for the experimental design. Experimental design means creating an alternate social reality—a theoretically guided virtual reality—that creates independent variables and facilitates measurement of dependent variables. Experiments are somewhat similar to theatrical performances and an experimenter is in some ways similar to a director. In complexity and difficulty, the parallels are obvious. In other ways, however, laboratories are unlike theaters. Participants in an experiment must truly believe that the created situation is real; they must interact, rather than adopting the largely passive role of theatrical patrons. Nuance, individuality, and variable performance are desirable in the theater because they make characters seem more "human" and "interesting." In an experiment, uniformity and standardization become crucial; variability and measurement variance (within conditions) are unwanted. Subtlety, complexity, and ambiguity often are prized in the theater; in experiments, everything must be obvious and clear. Experiments are often less exciting to watch or act in than theater. Yet "boring" would be irrelevant. The excitement of experiments comes from puzzle-solving and from the challenges of producing the design and assessing theoretical ideas in it.

Designing an effective experiment is difficult and time-consuming. Survey and observational research is heavy on the back end: it may take years before a data set has been fully analyzed and interpreted. Experimental research is heavy on the front end. It may require months, even years, to construct a setting and operations. However, experimental data usually are simple and readily interpretable. The main "work" of laboratory experiments takes place before the data come in. What experimental data show—their theoretical meaning—is often clear as soon as they appear.

Uses of Experiments in Social Science

Appropriately used, laboratory experiments are the best method to develop and test many kinds of theories. However, not every research question is appropriate for experimentation. For instance:

- Experiments are not useful when a theory's constructs cannot readily be created. For instance, theories of the cultural antecedents of modern attitudes or of the relation of family structure to educational attainment are not easily translated into operations permitting experimental assessment.
- Experiments are not useful for analyzing existing data and secondary analyses of experimental data seldom are as useful as those for which an experiment was designed. Meta-analyses of comparable experiments, however, can be very useful.
- Experiments are not useful for characterizing populations. Social science experiments, like chemistry experiments, are highly unusual situations, unlikely ever to appear in natural settings. Except for what experimental data show regarding a theory, the data themselves are uninteresting.
- Experiments usually are not useful absent a testable theory. Without an explicit theoretical question, there are no guides as to which features of the experiment, or which outcomes, are significant. Any analysis is open to infinite alternate interpretations, with no way to choose among them. In other words, one might "see what happens," but one will have no idea why, under what conditions that effect appears, or whether it ever will recur. Without a guiding theory, too many experiments are needed to make any real progress. Thomas Edison, it is said, tried out 997 materials to find a suitable filament for light bulbs, but his efforts were unusually well funded. Theoretically driven experiments might have achieved the result more quickly.

However, when appropriate—which means when used to test derivations from a theory—experiments can be enormously useful.

- Experiments generally offer the most convincing evidence in favor of theoretical explanations. No other kind of data matches that from experiments for being directly relevant to the ideas under test and no other data suggest causality as conclusively as experiments do.
- Experiments, being deliberately constructed observational settings, can offer unobstructed measurements. For example, Bales-type discussion groups typically work in laboratories with one-way mirrors, videotapes and sound tapes, computerized voice analyses, and a variety of paper and pencil recording mechanisms that offer optimal data collection. Comparable groups in natural settings—juries, committees, sports teams, etc.—entail many observational difficulties and compromises. Furthermore, such natural groups always include

unmeasured amounts of personal history, biases, other agendas, and the like that a researcher is unaware of. The best control for unknown factors is random assignment to experimental conditions, which is virtually impossible in naturally occurring groups.

- Related to the above point, experiments permit a high degree of isolation of processes that may be confounded with other processes in a natural setting. For instance, in a laboratory it is possible to study, say, influence caused by gender differences independent of many other factors that are—for this purpose—irrelevant, such as liking, romantic attraction, or appearance.
- Experiments permit studying unusual or rare situations that, nevertheless, may be highly informative for some theory. For instance, many experimental studies of status processes induce almost continuous disagreements among work partners, something that seldom if ever occurs among real work groups, because influence is a proven useful laboratory measure of status effects.

Experiments are artificial and that is the great strength of this kind of research. Well-designed experiments include *all* and *only* those features of a situation that are most informative for the ideas under test. Experiments readily permit random assignment of individuals to experimental conditions. They permit optimal measurement, often using unusual technology and other techniques. Experiments do not *directly* tell about the natural world, where several social processes tend to occur together and where measurement may be difficult or impossible. Experiments are ideal for showing how specified elements of social structure and social process affect one another and isolating conditions under which the effects appear.

At one time, social science experiments sometimes were criticized for being artificial. That criticism never arises in developed sciences where experiments are the dominant empirical method. What happens in a chemistry laboratory bears little resemblance to chemical reactions in nature—the laboratory situation is simpler, it may involve elements and compounds that do not exist in nature, and it simplifies the complexity of a natural environment. Chemistry experiments are artificial. They are valuable for what they tell about theoretical questions under investigation. The theories, after laboratory confirmation, may be applied outside a laboratory, but application is different from theory development and theory testing.

Elements of Experimental Design

Effective experimental design begins with a list of a new experiment's essential abstract features. As noted above, a theory is the template for experimental design. Experimental design begins with the theory's scope conditions—telling classes of situations to which the theory claims to apply—and antecedent and initial conditions describing specific instances for testing the theory's predictions. Fully stated hypotheses have the form "Given SC_1 and SC_2 and AC_1, if X_1 and X_2, then Y." Here, scope and antecedent conditions are given as SC's and AC's whose values are constant across experimental conditions, "X's" are independent variables whose values are controlled to test hypotheses, and "Y's" are dependent variables that will be measured as data.

Individuals will be assigned to experimental conditions at random, to control for the variety of unwanted sources of variance: history, prior experiences, etc. Next, an experimenter turns to devising operational measures of predicted outcomes. For instance, bargaining experiments may be developed to test a rational choice theory of behavior that claims as a scope condition to apply to all individuals who want to maximize winnings. An experiment testing derivations from such a theory would need a provision to motivate participants, such as highly desirable winnings; money would be appropriate here, whereas game points might not be. Whether behavior conformed to predictions might be measured as each participant's winnings or some other appropriate instance of the predicted outcomes.

Sometimes investigators are surprised to realize that information that they thought was obvious in a design got overlooked by a number of participants. For instance, if it is crucial for participants to know the gender of a real or simulated interactant, that information must be presented clearly and emphatically. Gender, like all other conditions, must be created fully rather than minimally. If one's partner is to be a male, a picture creates the condition more powerfully than a verbal description. A male wearing obviously gender-typed clothing and saying he has gender-typed hobbies produces a more uniform effect than leaving the gender characteristic partly undefined. A good rule of thumb for experimental instructions is to repeat every significant fact *three* times. For some, the repetition is excessive, but spurious variance is reduced to the extent that everyone shares the same information within an experimental condition. Pretesting is essential (see below) to ensure that none of the instructions are reactive, for instance, that the repetition is not unduly annoying and therefore excessive.

Once an experimental design incorporates scope, antecedent, and initial conditions, attention turns to dependent variables and their measurement. The first question is what consequences the investigator has predicted from combinations of circumstances; that is, what would constitute predictive success in this situation? Often a theory predicts several different sorts of consequences and an investigator will select one or a few of them as most informative or most practical to measure. Selecting among alternatives is partly a matter of taste and partly governed by ease, cost, measurement, and other practical considerations. In selecting dependent measures, it is wise to keep these concerns in mind:

- Is a measure unambiguous and clearly related to the predictions? For instance, in bargaining experiments, the value of winnings makes a better measure than participants' subjective satisfaction because measuring winnings is straightforward, whereas measuring subjective states requires inferential leaps.
- Is an experimental situation clear and simple? Complex situations may be harder for participants to understand, thus increasing unwanted variance in the data. Even worse, complex situations may trigger other processes, not of interest at the moment, that affect the dependent variables. For instance, participants might, in addition to winnings, be concerned with self-presentation ("Do I seem like a nice person?"), equity ("Am I treating the other person unfairly?"), or hostility ("I'm going to show that guy I don't like him, even if it costs me a few points!"). Competing processes may obscure the effects of theoretical processes under test.

Example: An Experimental Investigation of Gender and Performance Scores

A laboratory experiment by Martha Foschi and her students illustrates many features of good design. Researchers investigated consequences of status (instantiated by gender) and performance assessment (whether a particular score was "good," "average," etc.) in task groups.

The theoretical foundation for this work is the family of theories of status generalization. Those theories take as scope conditions that individuals are task-focused and collectively oriented, and within those conditions, they seek to explain behavioral inequality, such as influence from the structure of status relations in the group and evaluative information provided to interactants. The main outcome is performance expectation states, a theoretical construct operationally measured by resistance to influence in cases of disagreement.

Foschi *et al.* took the following questions (among others) for research:

(1) In status-homogenous (e.g., same sex, age, skin color) dyads, do individuals form expectations consistent with evaluative feedback during interaction?

(2) Do women and men form different levels of self-expectations, given the same structure of status relations and evaluative feedback?

(3) How do self-expectations affect the standards that individuals develop to assign someone high or low ability?

Participants were 156 Canadian college student volunteers who served in same-gender dyads, with 39 dyads of each gender. To create the scope conditions, the researchers told participants that they were working on a team task, judging pairs of abstract patterns to tell which of each pair contained more white area. They also told them that the team with the best score at the end of the project would receive a cash bonus.

The experiment had two phases, corresponding to inducing independent variables (phase 1) and measuring dependent variables (phase 2). It had six conditions. Because within a dyad, members were equated on age, gender, and educational level, they began as status equals. In two conditions, individuals received no evaluative information as they worked on the task. In other conditions, participants were told that they received either high scores (15 correct out of 20) or low scores (9 out of 20), and in some conditions, high or low scores were also announced for their partners. Thus, phase 1 instantiates scope conditions (task focus, collective orientation) and antecedent and initial conditions (status equality, evaluative information).

Phase 2 measured performance expectations behaviorally and ability standards subjectively. For a behavioral measure of expectations, participants work on a set of two-stage problems, exchanging "initial choices" and making private "final decisions." Experimenters control feedback from partners such that the partner's initial choices appear to disagree with the participant's. The proportion of times a person resolves disagreements in favor of self measures her or his relative performance expectations. For standards, Foschi *et al.* distributed questionnaires asking how many trials participants would require for a convincing assessment of ability level and the percentage of correct answers required to infer either high or low ability for a person. Responses give subjective assessments of standards used by people in different conditions of the experiment.

Foschi *et al.*, of course, were crucially interested in results of this experiment, but this article does not focus on the hypotheses, which were confirmed. Instead, it emphasizes the translation processes that take investigators from abstract considerations, such as task focus and evaluative feedback, to concrete manifestations in the experiment and then back again from proportion of influence rejection and marks on questionnaires to interpretations in terms of expectation states and ability standards. Theories and interpretations of results use abstractions; experiment use substantive, concrete instances of them.

The task of instantiating abstract ideas requires imagination and role-taking. Participants do not know the abstract theoretical ideas under test; they understand their situation as a concrete instance. Creating independent variables experimentally entails finding ways to instantiate them in concrete features of a situation. Here, creating self-expectations (as required for the third research question above) meant administering a plausible test of ability and returning believable "scores" to the participants. Similarly, dependent variables must be created operationally. In this case, rejection of influence has proven a good way to assess relative performance expectations and questionnaires are widely accepted as means to understand respondents' subjective experiences. Both measures have been widely used in other experimental settings, increasing confidence in their adequacy.

Foschi and associates employed two other crucial kinds of assessments of the design: manipulation checks and postsession interviews. Various checks are employed to assess whether participants understood the situation as the experimenter intended. For instance, researchers asked participants how many correct answers they and their partners received in phase 1. Those given high or low scores (15 or 9) all recalled exactly those scores. Furthermore, the researchers asked them to rate those performances on scales from Poor (1) to Excellent (6) and found the mean scale points ordered as they should be: 4.73 for those told 15/20, 3.45 for those given no feedback, and 2.34 for those told 9/20. Postsession interviews provide additional information about beliefs and motivations. They also allow an experimenter to inquire about any surprising behavior or other occurrences during an experimental session and allow participants to ask about any aspects of interest to them. Foschi *et al.*'s participants all recalled perfectly that they and their partners were of the same gender, age, and education. The postsession interview provides another opportunity to ask about task focus and undesirable possibilities, such as suspicion that the disagreements did not truly originate with a participant's partner. Investigators fully debriefed the participants, explaining all aspects of the study to them and answering any questions they might have.

Assessing Experimental Design and Operations

Effective design is not subtle, and effective instructions are deliberately repetitious. Working from a list of things that participants need to know, investigators design an experiment to make those points emphatically, to make them salient and memorable. Clarity and uniformity are essential.

Effective experimental design requires great attention to detail and creative imagination, but it never is possible to anticipate the effects of every design detail. Therefore, assessment is essential; experimenters must use available measures of success or create new measures to tell whether they have created all intended features of the situation. Pretests, checks, and postsession interviews are the main ways to monitor success.

Pretesting "tries out" a design to assess whether it functions as required. At the pretest stage, it is important to gather as much information as possible about possible problems and to be open to possible unanticipated interpretations by participants. Pretesting may involve extensive questionnaires, interviewing, and other means to obtain information on aspects of experimental operations. Once pretesting shows a design to be satisfactory, the experiment may be stripped of those assessment measures to save time and to focus on theory testing.

Checks assess at each experimental session how successfully various conditions were created. It is important not to take for granted that some feature that seems obvious to the investigator also will be apparent to every experimental participant. For instance, if it is crucial for a participant to know a real or simulated interactant's age or gender, not only should the design stress those points, but the design should allow for assessing whether participants notice, understand, believe, and remember crucial facts.

Postsession interviews generally have three goals: (1) additional manipulation checks and follow-up on any idiosyncratic behavior or other occurrences relevant to the independent or dependent variables or scope conditions; (2) explaining any deception in the experiment, as well as the reasons for it; and (3) inviting participants to inquire further about any aspects of their experience that they wish to explore. As with other aspects of experimental design, the postsession interview requires considerable thought and pretesting so that it yields the information an investigator needs, as well as protecting and enhancing the welfare of participants.

Some Contemporary Issues in Laboratory Experimentation

New Technology: Television and Computers in the Laboratory

Networked personal computers are ideal for many operations of laboratory experimentation. They carry communication, either actual or controlled, among experimenters and participants; they can present all manner of information, such as independent variables; they also can administer questionnaires and tests; and they collect and store data. When integrated with closed-circuit live and taped video, they improve both the ease with which experiments are conducted and the quality of presentation. Among the advantages from technology are the following:

- Ease of presentation, reducing fatigue among experimenters and interviewers.
- Uniformity of stimuli, reducing variability of administration that can show up as random variance in data.
- Error-free data, better than human experimenters could record. This advantage is particularly significant because errors in data recording are particularly difficult, sometimes impossible, to identify afterward.

Technology also brings new challenges, among them:

- It may be less involving than live administration, if participants treat videotaped presentations as "entertainment" and do not give them their full attention.
- Clear, fully explained, unambiguous instructions and procedures become crucial because participants cannot ask questions during an automated experiment and experimenters generally cannot intervene if they seem puzzled or act inappropriately on some experimental task.
- For programmatic research, it is valuable to ascertain how data from experiments using new technology compare to data from older designs. This can be especially important when an investigator wants to compare results of conditions from different experiments or when performing meta-analyses.

Data Inclusion: Whether to Retain a Participant in the Sample for Analysis

In a perfect world, every experiment would perfectly instantiate the scope conditions and independent variables, and the dependent variables would perfectly reflect all and only the theoretical concepts of interest. In the real world, that happy state is not likely. Some participants will not pay attention, or will misunderstand, information related to crucial antecedent conditions. Some will disbelieve some things they are told. Others will respond to internal factors (unshakeable prior beliefs, extreme tiredness, recreational or prescription drugs) rather than to social factors in behavior affecting the dependent variable. If scope or antecedent conditions have not been created for a particular participant, then her or his behavior is irrelevant for the theory under test. Success at creating experimental conditions must be assessed for every participant so that the investigator can decide whether that person's data should be included in the sample for analysis. There is no point in analyzing data ("Y") from someone whose experience does not instantiate ("If X") in an hypothesis of the form "If X, then Y." Assessing, through manipulation checks and interview, whether someone's experience did place her or him in the kind of situation required is always a matter of judgment and in most cases the decision is not clear-cut. A participant may say she paid attention most of the time, for instance, and the interviewer must then decide whether, on balance, she was "in" the desired situation often enough to retain her data. Practice, attention, and empathy help, but even with the best efforts some errors will take place. That is why good design requires $n > 1$ for conditions!

Every investigator will from time to time develop a feeling that "Something just is not right, but I can't put my finger on what that is." This cannot be a reason to exclude. Someone whose behavior "is not right" might well be someone whose behavior does not conform to the investigator's theory. This is theoretical disconfirmation; it is not failure of experimental design. When, then, should data be excluded?

Three useful rules of thumb on exclusion of data are as follows:

(1) If it appears that, say, more than ~20% of participants' data should be excluded, probably the experimental design should still be considered at the pretest stage. Most social science experiments are not so complicated that more than 20% will need to be excluded, once design flaws have been corrected.

(2) An investigator *never* uses the dependent variable measures to decide exclusions. This could easily shade into excluding disconfirming data but retaining confirming data—a practice better suited to psychics than to scientists.

(3) Exclusion is properly done by reference to predetermined rules and standards. In other words, if someone's data are to be excluded, it requires justification by a rule established before that person entered the laboratory. Such rules include successful creation of all scope, antecedent, and initial conditions, though it will be important to give operational indicators of just what "success" means for those. Overall, unless an investigator can cite a specific reason to exclude, the data must be included.

Ethics: Stress, Deception, Informed Consent and Care of Participants

Whereas an investigator properly focuses attention on theoretical and methodological issues, it is important not to forget the larger picture. Laboratory experimentation in the social sciences is partly a humanistic endeavor. It relies on humans who volunteer their time and efforts (either freely or for pay or course credit) and its ultimate purpose is to inform and to benefit other humans. Because of some particularly egregious examples of unethical procedures (in medical, not in social research), U.S. and some other governmental funding agencies have developed standards for protecting human subjects. For most research, federal agencies rely on Institutional Review Boards (IRBs) delegated to examine each proposal and certify that it does not unduly threaten the welfare of those to be studied. Regulations evolve, and a wise experimenter checks with the local IRB or a federal Web site at the proposal-writing stage.

The main concerns are (1) psychological stress, discomfort, or embarrassment during the session and (2) privacy and security of information afterward.

An experimental laboratory in most cases is an unfamiliar setting and it usually contains several potentially frightening elements: microphones and video cameras directed toward participants, experimenters dressed in lab coats, questionnaires that resemble coursework examinations, etc. Interaction processes in behavioral experiments are other potential stressors, possibly triggering concerns with self-presentation, test anxiety, behaving appropriately, and the like. Finally, many—though not all—social science experiments include deceptive elements, such as the near-continuous disagreements in the Foschi *et al.* experiment outlined above. Two points are crucial here. First, experimenters must think carefully about potential sources of stress, avoiding or minimizing them where possible through design changes and, always, through observing participants during every session to watch for evidence of discomfort. Second, experimenters have a moral obligation to explain fully every deceptive element of a design and reasons for it immediately at the end of the session. It is unacceptable to allow anyone to leave a laboratory with induced misunderstandings or false ideas—including "test scores" and simulated behaviors of others—that may have been created during the group.

Even something as simple as word choice can make a surprising difference. It has been found that substituting "participant" for "subject" and "study" for "experiment," to cite just two examples, reduces anxiety considerably. Generally, it is helpful to go over all details of every experiment with an eye to reducing unnecessary anxiety-provoking elements.

Unfortunately, informed consent is better suited to medical research than it is to social research. The reason is that most people simply do not know what they will find "too stressful to bear." Many college sophomores think they could, for instance, shrug off an experiment in which they were told they gave heavy electric shocks to a nice man, even though in an actual experiment where they did that, some participants had nightmares for weeks afterward. Participants do not understand their resilience, and lack thereof, as well as an experimenter and an IRB must. Responsibility clearly is with them, not with participants, to make the experience harmless and beneficial to those who undertake it.

Thorough planning, full explanation, giving all participants chances to express their feelings and reactions to a study, and freely discussing all significant elements of design (including anything that a participant thinks is significant even if the experimenter does not think it is crucial) are obligations that laboratory experiments entail. With those elements in place, most participants report that they find the experience interesting and beneficial, for they learn about research and, sometimes, about themselves in the process.

In fact, ethical considerations are, in some ways, easier to achieve in laboratory experiments than in other research settings. In experiments, one has the advantage of postsession interviews to detect potential lingering adverse effects and concerns. The research is also explained face to face, allowing greater sensitivity to potential distress and offering participants the chance to ask questions and receive full explanations. Observational settings, in contrast, usually do not readily achieve informed consent and surveys usually are not well explained to participants. That is not to say that those methods are ethically deficient, only to note that experimental methods offer the potential to be conducted in a highly ethical, sensitive, and beneficial manner.

Artificiality, Realism, and Generalization from Results

Laboratory experiments are, by design, artificial settings, in the dictionary sense of being socially constructed. They create unusual situations and ask people to participate as others observe and record what they do. Participants may work on contrived tasks, interacting with fictitious people having unusual characteristics, under conditions that would be impossible to sustain in any natural setting.

Some ask, using the term introduced by Campbell and Stanley in 1966, "What about external validity?" Yet concern with the external validity of experiments often is misguided, because although processes of theoretical interest should occur both in the laboratory and in the natural world, they do not occur in the same way. The laboratory, by design, should be "artificial"; otherwise why go to the trouble to create an experimental setting? "Valid" might incorrectly suggest that without direct generalization from the laboratory to a natural setting, findings are not valid. Laboratory results are valid if they inform about theoretical ideas, not if they accurately reproduce concrete features of some natural setting. A laboratory is as real as any other situation in which participants might find themselves and it certainly is involving for them. Laboratories are different from natural settings and they are simpler than natural settings, but they are certainly valid and real.

As noted earlier, an experiment itself does not *directly* tell about the natural world. Experimental results illuminate a theory. Applying that theory later to a natural setting makes a better world, perhaps, but by that stage the experimental laboratory work that developed the theory is finished. In 1998, Jonathan Turner explored the benefits to basic science from applying theories for useful purposes. Among them, application forces theorists to confront explicitly what their theories claim will happen and conditions under which those effects should appear.

Reliability, Multiple Measurements, and Programmatic Research

No important information should come from a single observation, for every observation contains (often unknown) amounts of error. This caution applies to dependent variables in an experiment and also to measurements designed to assess success at creating the scope and antecedent conditions of an experimental condition. An experiment in which a dependent variable is measured only once is a much weaker design than one in which multiple measures are collected. For instance, suppose an investigator wanted to study responses to violations of fair distributions of rewards. A design that creates either fair or unfair allocations of rewards among individuals, and then allows a subject to reallocate rewards once, is much weaker than a design permitting multiple reallocations. With repeated opportunities to reallocate, transient sources of error decline in importance. With multiple measures, one might measure reaction to unfairness by the mean amount reallocated. Even better, a design that permits multiple measures of different types will reduce unwanted effects of error variance even further. If one measures several different reactions to unfairness, such as self-reported anger, physiological changes, and attempts to leave the situation in addition to the amount reallocated, data would be less affected by random error than they are with a single type of measurement.

Although most experimenters understand the importance of multiple measures of dependent variables, many experimental designs still depend on single measures. For instance, for an experimental study of bargaining, participants might be asked on a questionnaire how much they cared about winning points in the game: "Winning was my only concern," "I very much wanted to win," "I wanted to win," "So-so," "I somewhat wanted to win," "Winning was not very important," and "Winning was unimportant to me." Then, the experimenter might exclude data from any participant who answered "so-so" or below. That would mean making inclusion decisions on a single data point. A better design would use multiple measures of the scope and antecedent conditions, as Foschi *et al.* did above. Their design employed five bipolar scales to assess task focus and belief that the experimental task was unrelated to other skills that an individual might believe she possessed.

A 2000 paper by Thye provides several ways to assess the impact of error variance in experimental research. Among other useful analyses in that paper, the author points out that even random measurement error can result in either type 1 (falsely concluding that experimental conditions do differ) or type 2 (missing a true difference between conditions) errors. Although problems of systematic measurement error and of type 2 errors from random measurement error are perhaps well recognized, it is useful to remember also that measurement error that is differentially associated with experimental conditions can create differences in data unrelated to the theoretical variables of interest.

Results of any single entire experiment too are subject to unknown amounts of measurement error. Thus, a single study is much less reliable than a replicated study. Furthermore, the more unlike the first study a replication is in terms of concrete details of design, subject pool, cultural background, and measurement operations, the more impressive it is when it obtains similar results. Cohen (1989, p. 262) observed that, "The hypotheses, procedures and measures of an experiment represent only one set of instantiations of the concepts contained in [theoretical] explanations . . . ." Reliable assessment of theories requires programmatic research, sets of sequential experiments, in order to develop cumulative knowledge about the adequacy of theories. Replications, though probably considerably more common than *published* replications, still are not undertaken as often as would be desirable from a measurement or a knowledge-developing perspective. Although there are undoubtedly many reasons for this, including cost, love of novelty, a preference for new or disconfirming evidence, and the enormous variety of theoretical perspectives in many social sciences, the quality of knowledge can be improved markedly by more frequent replication of all research, including that emanating from the laboratory.

The best way to reduce the uncertainty and effort needed to conduct laboratory experiments is to make use of existing designs and measurement techniques wherever possible. There is still an unfortunate reluctance among social scientists to adopt and adapt proven experimental designs, perhaps reflecting a love of novelty or a misplaced view that one is going to revolutionize the field by a single, brilliant experiment. This is a waste of effort. Some designs have proven themselves excellent for studying certain social processes—the Asch conformity experiment and the basic status experiment that Foschi *et al.* adapted are examples. More seriously, refusing to adapt standard techniques makes the results of different experiments difficult to compare and the knowledge produced is not cumulative. A great deal of wasted effort could be avoided if social science experimenters copied their sisters and brothers in the natural sciences and sought to build on existing experimental designs to develop and assess new theoretical ideas.

The most useful single piece of advice for a beginning experimenter is to look around and see how someone else has studied the phenomenon you are interested in and then adopt and adapt as much of that design as possible. That way you can focus your efforts on the new ideas that you are investigating and you have the best chance of contributing to knowledge in your discipline.

Conclusions

Laboratory experiments in social science require creating artificial settings and asking participants to engage in specific kinds of behaviors that are recorded. In a well-designed experiment, all operations are concrete manifestations of abstract factors in a theory. Experimental research should be readily interpretable by moving from concrete measures produced in a laboratory to abstract theoretical dependent variables and that information should be used to assess the derivations and assist in developing theories.

In addition to thoughtful design, it is important to include provision for monitoring the quality of an experiment. Useful techniques include pretesting and measures during the conduct of an experiment and in a postsession interview. The more aspects of a design that can be assessed in these ways, the stronger the confidence an investigator may place in conclusions drawn from this type of research.

In addition to scientifically adequate design, social science experiments must incorporate ethical concerns for the welfare of participants, during the experiment itself and afterward. Responsibility for ethical concerns properly rests with the investigators; relying on participants to know their limits and to understand the dangers through varieties of informed consent generally abdicates that responsibility and places it on people lacking the experience they would need to protect themselves.

Single measures and single experiments can mislead because of measurement error. Multiple measures should always be used for important variables and replication is essential for important theoretical questions. Programmatic experiments generally result in more reliable information than one-shot studies. They always partially replicate past work (in operations and measures, most typically), and through differences in setting and populations studied, they permit assessing different aspects of the design.

Laboratory experiments are complicated, and effective design presents many challenges. In return for the effort involved, they often return reliable data permitting strong inferences that are useful for theory building.

Acknowledgments

Martha Foschi, Michael Lovaglia, Lisa Rashotte, Lisa Troyer, and David Wagner read drafts of this article and offered suggestions and comments that greatly strengthened it. The author thanks them, while retaining responsibility for any remaining errors. National Science Foundation Grant 9911135 supported preparation of this work.

See Also the Following Articles

Experiments, Overview • Experiments, Psychology • Explore, Explain, Design • Research Designs

Further Reading

Berger, J. (1992). Expectations, theory, and group processes. *Soc. Psychol. Q.* **55,** 3–11.

Campbell, D., and Stanley, J. (1966). *Experimental and Quasi-Experimental Designs for Research.* Rand McNally, New York.

Cohen, B. P. (1989). *Developing Sociological Knowledge: Theory and Method,* 2nd Ed. Nelson-Hall, Chicago, IL.

Dobbins, G. H., Lane, I. M., and Steiner, D. D. (1988). A note on the role of laboratory methodologies in applied behavioral research: Don't throw out the baby with the bath water. *J. Organiz. Behav.* **9,** 281–286.

Foschi, M. (1980). Theory, experimentation, and cross-cultural comparisons in social psychology. *Can. J. Sociol.* **5,** 91–102.

Foschi, M. (1997). On scope conditions. *Small Group Res.* **28,** 535–555.

Foschi, M., Enns, S., and Lapointe, V. (2001). Processing performance evaluations in homogeneous task groups: Feedback and gender effects. In *Advances in Group Processes* (S. R. Thye, E. J. Lawler, M. W. Macy, and H. A. Walker, eds.), Vol. 18, pp. 185–216. JAI Press, New York.

Markovsky, B., Lovaglia, M., and Thye, S. (1997). Computer-aided research at the Iowa Center for the Study of Group Processes. *Soc. Sci. Comput. Rev.* **15,** 48–64.

Mook, D. (1983). In defense of external invalidity. *Am. Psychol.* **38,** 379–387.

Rashotte, L., Webster, M., Jr., and Whitmeyer, J. M. (2002). *Some Effects of Appearance and Presentation Style in Experimental Research.* Paper presented at the Annual Meeting of Group Processes, Chicago, IL.

Thye, S. R. (2000). Reliability in experimental sociology. *Soc. Forces* **78,** 1277–1309.

Troyer, L. (2001). Effects of protocol differences on the study of status and social influence. *Curr. Res. Soc. Psychol.* **6,** 13. Available at http://www.uiowa.edu/~grpproc/crisp/crisp.6.13.htm

Turner, J. (1998). Must sociological theory and sociological practice be so far apart? A polemical answer. *Sociological Perspectives* **41,** 243–258.

Walker, H. A., and Cohen, B. P. (1985). Scope statements: Imperatives for evaluating theory. *Am. Sociol. Rev.* **50,** 288–301.

Webster, M., Jr. (1994). Experimental methods. In *Group Processes* (M. Foschi and E. J. Lawler, eds.), pp. 43–69. Nelson-Hall, Chicago, IL.

Whitmeyer, J. (2003). Using theory to guide empirical research. In *The Growth of Social Knowledge: Theory, Simulation, and Empirical Research in Group Processes* (J. Szmatka, M. J. Lovaglia, and K. Wysienska, eds.), pp. 149–164. Praeger, New York.

Willer, D., Rutstrom, L., Karr, L. B., Corra, M., and Girard, D. (1999). A web-lab to enhance social science infrastructure: Experiments, simulations, and archiving. *J. Knowledge Manage.* **3,** 276–287.

Laboratory Studies

Donald W. Fiske
University of Chicago, Chicago, Illinois, USA

Susan T. Fiske
Princeton University, Princeton, New Jersey, USA

Glossary

confounding Varying an unintended variable along with the variable of interest, particularly as applied to experimental manipulations of independent variables.

correlational research Studies concerned with the relationships among a set of measured variables; the variables are not directly under the control of the experimenter.

demand characteristics The features of the situation that constrain the participants' behavior by communicating the hypothesis to them.

dependent variable In an experiment, the measured variable presumed to be influenced by the experimental manipulation of the independent variable.

expectancy effects The impact on participants of experimenters communicating their prior beliefs concerning the participants' likely responses.

experiment A study of the effects of randomly assigned independent variables, which are manipulated by the experimenter, on dependent ones, which are measured by the experimenter.

external validity The extent to which an investigator can generalize beyond the immediate data and findings.

independent variable In an experiment, the manipulated variable, levels of which the experimenter randomly assigns to participants; the experiment tests the causal effects of this variable.

internal validity The extent to which an investigator's conclusions hold for the particular participants, measuring procedures, and conditions studied.

method specificity The extent to which a set of data is determined by a particular procedure used to collect it. The term "method" may be applied to a range of procedures.

response rates The percentage of the sampled population that, when contacted, will agree to participate in the research, or the percentage of participants who complete the researcher's measures.

unobtrusive measures Assessments taken without the participant's awareness.

A laboratory study is an investigation that occurs in a place dedicated to research, its conditions being designed to eliminate, or at least minimize, effects from unwanted influences. Laboratory studies often are experiments, but sometimes are correlational studies, including those that investigate individual or group differences. Laboratory studies have advantages with regard to design, setting, researcher, participants, and measurement; the advantages primarily relate to precision, control, and internal validity. Laboratory studies also have disadvantages with regard to each of these factors, method specificity and external validity being primary among these.

Background: Correlational and Experimental Research

The laboratory has been the site of research investigations for centuries. Researchers can control many conditions in the laboratory and can keep specialized equipment there. Psychology was one of the most recent disciplines to enter the laboratory, only about a century ago; other social sciences, such as economics, are only now expanding their use of the laboratory. This article concerns the quality of laboratory research on behavior, focusing on what affects the behavior that can be observed in the laboratory or, more precisely, what affects the measurements that can be taken for later statistical analysis. Although many of these factors have similar effects outside of the laboratory, they come into particular focus in the laboratory, where so much can be precisely controlled. This article addresses both the laboratory's advantages and its disadvantages, classifying them by issues of design, setting, researcher, participants, and measurement.

Two primary kinds of research occur in the laboratory: correlational and experimental. (A third kind, descriptive research, estimating the population's levels on variables, as in opinion surveys or the census, rarely occurs in the laboratory.) Correlational research has the goal of assessing the relationships among two or more measured variables; these can include nominal (categorical) variables, such as gender; ordinal (sequential but not ratio-scaled) variables, such as birth order; and continuous variables (either scaled or not), such as age, response time, measured amount of a particular personality trait, or number of correct answers. Correlational research cannot draw strong causal inferences. Experimental research aims to allow valid causal inferences. It requires (1) an independent variable that experimenters can manipulate, assigning participants to different levels of the variable, such as experimental and control groups; (2) the ability to assign participants randomly to the different levels; and (3) the ability to control extraneous variables that might either covary with the independent variable (creating a confound) or create unwanted random variance (error).

Advantages

Whether correlational or experimental, well-conducted laboratory studies excel at internal validity, which is potential precision, control, and confidence that the conceptual variables have been operationalized as intended.

Design

Laboratory studies allow precise design. Because the researcher determines the variables, the series of manipulations and measures can be specified precisely, then administered in the desired sequence, with high response rates and relative attention. Researchers can identify relevant variables and operationalize them deliberately. Because of time and space constraints, laboratory researchers typically are forced to focus on a few critical variables in their designs, whether correlational or experimental. This focus disciplines the questions that researchers ask, often making hypotheses more precise.

Setting

The laboratory setting by definition is isolated from ordinary life; as a place that the researcher can control to a great extent, the laboratory can block or minimize certain stimuli that might interfere with observing the effects of the variables of interest. For example, consider weather conditions as intruders (open windows might create unacceptable variation in noise, wind currents, temperatures, and humidity). In a more general sense, researchers can minimize most forms of stimulation except the experimental variables or critical measures. That is, the laboratory setting can isolate the variables of interest. Participants' reactions can be gauged with a minimum of distraction or input from extraneous variables. Spotlighting manipulations and measures allows them to have maximum potential impact and perhaps the most pure assessment.

The setting is a psychological phenomenon. Its nature depends largely on the particular participant construing it. The point here is that it is not the objective setting that determines the behavior of the participant, but the setting as interpreted by the participant. In order to ascertain how most participants construe the setting, researchers can pilot test their setting, procedures, and variables.

Researcher

The laboratory researcher can easily control characteristics of the researcher who comes in contact with participants. For example, a researcher's appearance, manner, script, and demographic categories can be held constant, varied systematically, or counterbalanced. Of equal importance, the laboratory can control the participating researchers' knowledge of the hypotheses, as well as individual participants' conditions or status on critical measures, any of which could affect the outcome via expectancy effects. The degree and type of interactions between the researcher running the study and the study participants also can be controlled, monitored, and assessed.

Participants

Laboratory research participants frequently are selected for convenience and availability. In studies of adult humans, college students, usually psychology majors, often serve as participants, in order to fulfill a departmental requirement. In studies of children, those whose parents have the time, contacts, interest, and ability are overrepresented. In studies of animals, those bred for the purpose often serve. In all cases, no attempt is made to sample randomly a study population from a larger population of interest. This limits the external validity or generalizability from the laboratory sample to participants in the field.

The compensating factor with laboratory samples is their relative convenience and low cost. Researchers do not have to go out to find the participants in their natural habitat, but instead participants come to them. This may allow research to occur more efficiently.

Measurement

At its best, the laboratory affords precision of measurement. Laboratory researchers can specify the conditions and methods of measurement in fine-grained ways. For example, the laboratory can minimize the problem of bias, error, or disagreement in observer reports by using direct observation (for behaviors amenable to being observed in the laboratory). The laboratory can collect extremely fine-grained physiological measures at the level of single neurons, responses of extremely short duration at the level of milliseconds, and actions in small well-defined units (a blink or a nod).

The psychometric properties of laboratory measures can be well specified. For each of the major variables in a researcher's plan, two attributes of each measuring procedure need to be considered: reliability and validity. Reliability is essentially replicability: the question concerns how well the researchers can reproduce this array of measurements if they change the particular operationalization to which the participants are responding, or if they ask them to respond again at a different time. Validity asks how well researchers are measuring whatever it is that they want to measure. But first, researchers must specify exactly what they want to measure. To measure intelligence, is it just verbal intelligence, or is it active vocabulary, or is it the number of words for which the participant can give good definitions? For the sake of research processes and for ease in communicating with fellow researchers, each major variable should be described precisely. As a research program progresses, key terms should become increasingly clear and better specified.

Disadvantages

The great deficit of laboratory studies is external validity—that is, whether the results observed in that context generalize to other contexts in other laboratories or outside of the laboratory. Much of the problem in external validity can be understood as method specificity: some results may be a product of the method, not the construct the researcher hopes to assess.

Design

Laboratory studies typically are limited in time and space. Thus, on average, they are less likely to be longitudinal and extended over long periods, either within a single session or across repeated visits to the laboratory. Except for captive laboratory animals, the setting limits the time researchers can interact with their participants. Limits of time and space also constrain the number of variables, whether manipulated variables or measured variables, that can be assessed in a laboratory setting.

Setting

For behavior that occurs in the laboratory, the questions to ask concern what it represents and what it means. Participants may react to the fact of being measured. Reactivity to the setting may cause anxiety, self-consciousness, impression management, or a whole host of unknowable effects. Researchers can deduce the effects of the laboratory setting by replicating the study in a field setting or even in other laboratory settings that systematically vary the potentially contaminating variables, to discover their effect.

Nevertheless, one major disadvantage of the laboratory is verisimilitude. Because the laboratory is an artificial setting controlled by researchers, set aside and isolated for the purposes of research, it may seem removed from everyday life. Researchers distinguish between mundane realism of the setting (how much does it resemble life outside the laboratory) and experimental realism (to what extent are participants involved and spontaneous). Using experimental realism, researchers can demonstrate the possibility of particular patterns of behavior by showing that they can occur, at least in some settings. Sometimes, capability for particular behaviors is all that is needed to meet the goals of the research. It may be important to know, even if in a laboratory setting, that people or animals are capable of particular behaviors. For example, demonstrating that young infants can distinguish groups of objects by number (i.e., they can distinguish twos from threes, and both from fours), regardless of the specific objects, is important, no matter where it is shown to occur.

As noted, one advantage of the laboratory setting is a researcher's ability to isolate the variables (stimuli) of interest, in order to maximize their impact. This control can go too far, in the sense of creating what are called demand characteristics. That is, the setting can be constructed in such a constrained way that other researchers judge that cooperative participants had no choice except to respond in the predicted manner. A subtle criticism, it reflects a judgment that the setting required only one kind of response, in ways beyond the presentation of the stimulus. As Martin Orne observed, participants play a certain role and place themselves under the control of the experimenter, cheerfully performing push-ups for no apparent reason or adding numbers for 5 hours and tearing up the results. Participants think the "good-subject" role is to help validate the experimenter's hypothesis, so the participant looks for cues in the environment that will convey the hypothesis, in order to behave accordingly. The set of cues to the experiment's hypothesis constitutes its demand characteristics. If participants do not behave spontaneously but instead try to confirm the hypothesis, this artifact clearly threatens internal validity.

Researcher

Closely linked to demand characteristics of the setting are the expectancies and authority of the experimenter. Just as the laboratory researcher exquisitely controls the setting, so too does the researcher, if not monitored, control the participant. Stanley Milgram's famous social psychology study showed that laboratory participants would shock another participant (seemingly to dangerous levels), merely because the researcher in authority told them to do so. Experimenter effects, effects generated unwittingly by experimenters, have been a source of much thought and research for several decades, ever since Robert Rosenthal introduced the concept and a line of research on the topic.

A typical demonstration of the experimenter effect uses a number of participants as experimenters. Half of these are led subtly to believe that the participants will perform a certain way and the other half are given a different expectation. Almost invariably, the participants as a group respond in conformity with the expectation given by their "experimenters." The actual experimenters were puzzled about how to explain this dependable and replicable finding. The central question concerned how an experimenter's expectation was transferred to the participants. Two groups of "experimenters" read to their participants exactly the same instructions, except, of course, for the word or words that made the instructions different for the two groups of participants. No one heard any difference in the readings. Finally, a colleague detected a slight difference in the emphasis given a key word. In a carefully designed and executed study by Duncan and Rosenthal, some student instructors were led to expect that the participants they would be working with would tend to make ratings toward the success end of a scale while other student instructors were led to believe that their participants would tend to make ratings toward the failure end of that scale. And that is the way the two groups of participants tipped their judgments. The researchers concluded that the way in which the experimenter reads instructions to participants, even when instructions are read accurately, can significantly determine the participants' responses to an experimental procedure.

Researchers can influence participants in many subtle ways. As demonstrated by Rosenthal's program of research, when experimenters know their hypotheses (which will be the case for all except hired staff), and they know the experimental condition or assessed selection score of the participants, they may inadvertently behave in ways that confirm their own hypotheses.

Participants

External validity constitutes the obvious limit in laboratory studies, and one of the laboratory's clearest restrictions is generalizability beyond the sample. Volunteer participants are not a random sample even of the departmental subject pool. They certainly are not a representative random sample of their age cohort or of people more generally. Specific biases arise from using volunteers, as Rosenthal and Rosnow have documented, and from using college students, as David Sears has documented.

Measurement

Many of the main problems concerning reactivity and response set result from people constraining their own responses to fit their view of the most socially desirable response. People do not want to look deviant, foolish, or bad, even when their individual responses are confidential and anonymous. People do not even like to make other people look bad, and their ratings often have a clear positivity bias.

Reactivity to the fact of being measured in a laboratory may be handled by the use of unobtrusive measures that participants do not perceive. Or the critical manipulations and measures may be disguised by being embedded among innocuous filler stimuli and items. Participants may not be told the full purpose of the study until afterward, to minimize their reacting to the hypotheses, in a misguided effort to help, hurt, or present themselves in the best possible light. Disguising the fact of measurement, its purpose, its method, and its timing all can minimize problems of reactivity. However, the ethical issues involved must be resolved thoughtfully, in consultation with Institutional Review Boards.

Every method makes a unique kind of contribution to the observation of behavior. The term "method specificity" captures this problem, which is that the measurement method adds unwanted variance to the observation. Campbell and Fiske identified this issue with regard to multiple methods to assess multiple personality traits, demonstrating method effects, independent of trait effects. One solution is to use multiple methods and to estimate method effects. Response sets form a particular class of method effects; they are most relevant to a participant's responses on a paper and pencil test with multiple response alternatives to each item, and are most often seen in responses to personality measures

Table I Response Sets or Systematic Reactions to Measuring Procedures

Kind of procedure	*Response set or systematic reaction*	*Manifestation*
Self-report	Social desirability	Marking the response alternative perceived to give the most favorable impression
Self-report	Acquiescence	Giving "yes" responses, agreeing with the attitude statement
Rating behavior	Halo	Allowing a general impression of the person rated to affect their ratings on specific characteristics
Rating behavior	Leniency	Tendency to rate everyone as above average
Rating behavior	Position set	Tendency to mark an item, especially on a multistep scale, in the same position as the preceding item

of self or others and in responses to attitude measures. A response set contributes unwanted variance to data.

Table I presents a sample of response sets. At the top is the most common and best studied one, social desirability. At the bottom of this list is a fairly uncommon set, position set, which consists of repeating the response just made to the preceding item. Especially when the participant is working toward the end of a test, the repetition of the same response may occur out of frustration, fatigue, or boredom, when the participant does not want to take the trouble to figure out the best response.

When researchers suspect that a response set is contributing unwanted variance to the data, they can record the response alternatives for each item on the measure that would indicate a participant showing that response set, and simply score the measure for the sum of those alternatives. The researchers could statistically control for that response set. And they could then see if the response set score from this test had an appreciable correlation with that from some other test, perhaps a fairly similar test that might be expected to show it. Any response set that appears in the test-taking world can be construed as a psychological trait. The best known instance of this is social desirability, which has been identified in social discourse and elsewhere. Other response sets may be consistencies in respondents' ways of handling items that they find difficult to answer. Rewriting or removing items may be the best way to reduce the influence of response sets.

Conclusion

The laboratory study excels at internal validity and precision, but it is not designed to foster external validity (generalizability beyond specific methods, participants, settings, and designs). Multiplism, in the form of multiple measures and multiple replications, can ameliorate these problems, but they remain an intrinsic challenge to laboratory research. Research programs do well with methodological pluralism, combining laboratory and field studies.

See Also the Following Articles

Content Validity • Laboratory Experiments in Social Science • Validity, Data Sources

Further Reading

Aronson, E., Wilson, T. D., and Brewer, M. B. (1998). Experimentation in social psychology. *Handbook of Social Psychology* (D. T. Gilbert, S. T. Fiske, and G. Lindzey, eds.), 4th Ed., Vol. 1, pp. 99–142. McGraw-Hill, New York.

Fiske, D. W., and Shweder, R. A. (eds.) (1986). *Metatheory in Social Science: Pluralisms and Subjectivities*. University of Chicago Press, Chicago.

Pelham, B. W. (1999). *Conducting Research in Psychology: Measuring the Weight of Smoke.* Brooks/Cole, New York.

Reis, H. T., and Judd, C. M. (eds.) (2000). *Handbook of Research Methods in Social and Personality Psychology*. Cambridge University Press, New York.

Rosenthal, R., and Rosnow, R. L. (1999). *Beginning Behavioral Research: A Conceptual Primer,* 3rd Ed. Prentice-Hall, Upper Saddle River, New Jersey.

Sansone, C., Morf, C. C., and Panter, A. T. (eds.) (2004). *Handbook of Methods in Social Psychology*. Sage, Thousand Oaks, California.

Zechmeister, J. S., Zechmeister, E. B., and Shaughnessy, J. J. (2001). *Essentials of Research Methods in Psychology*. McGraw-Hill, New York.

Land Use Mapping

Jeremy T. Kerr
University of Ottawa, Ottawa, Canada

Josef Cihlar
Canada Centre for Remote Sensing, Natural Resources Canada, Ottawa, Canada

Glossary

classification The ordering or arrangement of a group of objects into categories based on their physical characteristics, with the objective of producing a thematic representation of those objects (e.g., a map).

hierarchical classification system The ordering or arrangement of classes of objects such that the more detailed classes comprise subsets of the more general classes.

land cover The physical characteristics of the terrestrial surface, most generally described by the dominant, observable vegetation or structures.

land use Human exploitation of biospheric resources in terrestrial ecosystems, either above or below the surface and potentially including groundwater reserves and wildlife.

land use change Temporal shifts in the type or intensity of human exploitation of biospheric resources in terrestrial ecosystems.

land use management The process by which human land use is controlled to attain a specific goal, such as the maximization of resource extraction, minimization of environmental impact, or some combination of both.

legend The classes (e.g., of land use or land cover) drawn from the classification scheme that appear in an accompanying map or data set.

mapping The process by which the actual geographical arrangement of entities of interest (e.g., different land uses) is determined and depicted in a digital or paper product.

minimum mapping unit The size of the smallest feature on a map.

resolution The ability of a sensor (e.g., satellite-borne) to distinguish two closely spaced objects or lines as two, rather than one, object or line; alternately, the smallest object or narrowest detectable line.

Land use mapping encompasses a range of procedures and data sources that are used to determine the spatial arrangement of human activities in terrestrial ecosystems and their change over time. Land use mapping techniques are employed to monitor and help predict the environmental and human health impacts of different land uses.

Introduction

People live on land and thereby make use of the resources land provides. The capabilities and limitations of land from the "use" perspective are therefore fundamental factors modifying the "way of life" locally, regionally, and globally. A particular land use is a result of decisions based on environmental, socioeconomic, and cultural factors. Because these vary over time, land use also changes. Ultimately, individuals make land use decisions regarding specific patches of land. Individual decisions are difficult to predict, yet affect land use patterns and trends over large areas.

Knowledge of current land use is critical for many environmental monitoring activities. At the local level, environmental planning and management are necessarily founded on current land use. Regionally to globally, land use has been recognized as a critical factor mediating between socioeconomic, political, and cultural behaviors and global environmental change, including changes in atmospheric chemistry and climate. Because of the difficulty in predicting land use decisions, a method is needed for acquiring such information. Land use mapping is a tool to meet this need.

What Is Land Use?

In simple terms, land use refers to human activities that are directly related to the land. More specifically, land use encompasses the human exploitation of biospheric resources immediately above or below the surface; bodies of water (shallow lakes, rivers, marshes, and swamps), the near-surface sedimentary layers and associated groundwater reserve, the plant and animal populations, the human settlement pattern, and the physical results of past and present human activity (terracing, water storage or drainage structures, roads, buildings, etc.) are included in assessing resource exploitation. Land use, therefore, is a broadly inclusive term reflecting the terrestrial consequences of the human–land interaction.

Land use may be considered from various perspectives, two of which are discussed here. An "urban" perspective focuses on the use of land in urban areas where most people live, the modification of land through creation of infrastructure, and the capture of detailed information about human actions and their consequences in these settings. A "resource" perspective would place a more balanced emphasis on various land surface components, regardless of human population density or degree of landscape modification. There are valid reasons for each perspective, depending on the intended use of the information. The urban perspective is most useful for urban planning and development purposes. This need is typically met through specially designed mapping or information gathering at the local level. On the other hand, the resource viewpoint refers to the use of all land, and because most landmass is not urbanized, issues relating to agriculture, forested areas, or other ecosystems tend to dominate. From the viewpoint of climate change or of sustainable development of natural resources, the resource perspective is of primary interest.

Present land use indicates that the human "footprint" is undeniably large and continues to expand, with perhaps 40% of terrestrial net productivity and half of the available freshwater resource diverted for human use. High-quality land use mapping data are an important descriptor of the distribution and intensity of human environmental impacts and are required for many other applications as well. These may include models and measurements of carbon cycles or assessments of the extinction risk among endangered species. Land use mapping from this resource perspective forms the basis for the remaining discussion.

Historical and Contemporary Examples of Land Use Mapping

The importance of land use mapping has been recognized since at least the Middle Ages. The medieval Domesday Book, based on survey data and completed in 1086, summarizes for most of England an array of land use characteristics that remain foci of present-day land use mapping activities, such as extent of agriculture and natural areas that might be used to increase agricultural production. Detailed maps of land use in England were developed in the 18th century using similar survey techniques and questionnaires. The methods employed for these ancient land use inquiries are still in use but have been refined by the addition of new data sources from remote sensing, a technology that reduces the cost, effort, and subjectivity of purely survey-based mapping enterprises. Remote sensing and geographic modeling increase the ability of the surveyor to measure temporal changes in land use. Measurement and mapping of land use across broad and often sparsely populated geographical regions are usually impractical without remote sensing data, even though remote sensing and modeling approaches are most appropriately used to infer land use, not to measure it directly.

Various approaches to determining land use or land use change using geographic information and remote sensing techniques have been developed over broad, often agricultural, areas; the characteristics of such major efforts are summarized in Table I. Coarse-resolution (e.g., 0.0833 degree cells) land use change models synthesize a wide variety of national statistical data sources and interpolate predicted global patterns of conversion of natural habitats to agriculture from the beginning of the Industrial Revolution. Agricultural land use maps that exist for China depict the extent of major agricultural practices that correlate very well with census-based estimates of the extent of individual agricultural land use practices. In Canada, a national-scale land use map was produced by fusing Census of Agriculture statistics with moderate-resolution imagery in a procedure called "Land Use and Cover with Intensity of Agriculture" (LUCIA). The secondary result of the LUCIA land use mapping initiative has been the production of agricultural pollution data that can be related to aspects of environmental degradation, such as species endangerment. Similar national data now exist for the United States, and the European Union has developed high-resolution land use/land cover data for member countries under the auspices of its Coordination of Information on the Environment (CORINE) program. Remote sensing and ancillary data sources were combined to demonstrate that as much as 83% of global land area is significantly modified by human land use activities. One of the hallmarks of many of the large land use mapping projects has been data availability: the new maps are often available freely in digital format through various Internet access systems, a quantum leap forward from historical land use documentation through laborious censuses and limited distribution.

Table I Examples of Leading Land Use or Land Use Change Data for Various Regions

Data source	*Description of data*	*Resolution*	*Location/extent*
Ramankutty and Foley (1999)	Global land use change data describing land use conversions to and from agriculture	5 minutes	Global agricultural regions
Frolking *et al.* (1999)	Agricultural land use derived from the Advanced Very High Resolution Radiometer	1 km	China
Kerr and Cihlar (2003)	All types of land use/land cover, but especially detailed within agricultural regions, derived from the vegetation sensor aboard SPOT4 using the LUCIA process	1 km	Canada
Hurtt *et al.* (2001)	All types of land use/land cover but at a very low level of thematic detail (small number of land use/cover classes)	30 minutes	United States
Coordination of Information on the Environment (a European union program; separate sources for each European country)	Hierarchical classification and land use/land cover mapping initiative based on satellite data interpretation (minimum mapping unit is generally 25 hectares)	Variable (about 100 m, but with a minimum mapping unit of 25 ha)	Europe
Sanderson *et al.* (2002)	Estimates of the extent of human modifications of natural ecosystems	1 km (source data often of coarser resolution)	Global

Land Use/Land Cover Relationship

"Use" and "cover" are two terms commonly associated with land, and they are often considered synonymous. However, this is not the case, and a conceptual difference exists between the two terms. Interestingly, the confusion seems to have emerged as a result of the need for mapping. In this section, the land use/land cover relationship is reviewed and implications for mapping are discussed.

Strictly speaking, land cover refers to the physical characteristics of Earth's surface. The Earth may be observed directly (on the ground) or indirectly (through remote sensing). Land cover typically includes vegetation, bare ground, water, human constructs such as buildings or roads, and mixtures of these. On the other hand, land use is characterized by the arrangements, activities, and inputs people undertake with respect to a certain land cover to produce, change, or maintain it. Because possible uses are to a large degree determined by physical land characteristics, land cover is an important factor in determining or indicating land use; in fact, this relationship is the basis for land use mapping. However, the strength of the relationship between land cover and land use varies.

Land use implies the application of a management strategy or input for the purpose of deriving a product or benefit from an area. The socioeconomic forces shaping land use are also part of its study, but these cannot be easily mapped. Land use is determined by many factors—natural as well as economic, institutional, cultural, and legal. In general, possible types of land use are limited by biophysical constraints: climate, topography, soils and the geological substrate, availability of water, and the type of vegetation. Frequently, these factors also find consistent expression in land cover. For example, the presence, type, and characteristics of vegetation cover are effective indicators of the biophysical conditions.

Although environmental conditions provide strong constraints on possible land uses, they are not necessarily decisive; some types of land use are, at most, weakly constrained by local biophysical parameters. This is especially true for those land uses that result in new land cover (transportation infrastructure, buildings), in which the biophysical constraints are mitigated by the investment of energy and materials. Furthermore, land cover provides only an approximate guidance as to land use. A forested area may have an agricultural land use if it is also used for grazing. The same area could also be used for recreation, wildlife protection, or resource extraction if the forest is intended for harvest. A single patch of forested land may thus have a combination of different uses. Conversely, different land cover types may have identical land use, such as if both a grassland and a forest are used for recreation. Land use is also influenced by cultural factors. For example, agricultural practices differ from one region to another depending on the history, local traditions, and the way of life, entirely separately from biophysical constraints.

Land cover can be a cause of, or a constraint on, land use. In the latter case, the relationship between cover and use tends to be strong because the land use in question is implied by the land cover's physical characteristics. When the modification of land cover is less profound (i.e., if the change is not large enough to cause a shift from one cover type to another), the type of land use may be more difficult to infer, and the reliability of the inference tends to be lower. The distinctions will vary with the type of use, geographic region, and time. For example, cropland is relatively easily mapped from remotely sensed data in most cases, provided that the sensor's spatial resolution is adequate. The type and intensity of management are much less evident, although they may be inferred, given knowledge of local practices. Similarly, multiple or mixed land uses, such as agroforestry, are also difficult to distinguish solely from land cover data. Because land use practices change with time, so may the relationship of land use to land cover.

Given the multifaceted nature of land use and the variety of causal factors affecting it, precise mapping of land use over large areas becomes a challenge. Remote sensing methods developed during the past ~60 years permit the mapping of land cover types and their properties, which may be discerned from electromagnetic radiation that is detected by sensors aboard satellites or aircraft. There are no equivalent direct sensing methodologies for land use, and the land cover/land use link is therefore the only conceptual approach to mapping land use over large areas. However, the success of "translating" land cover information into land use depends on several main factors: classification scheme and legend, environmental setting, and both the types and characteristics of remotely sensed data (particularly spectral and spatial). These factors are discussed in subsequent sections.

Land Use Classification and Legends

Classification is an abstract representation of the field conditions, using a particular set of diagnostic criteria; more simply, it is the ordering or arrangement of objects into groups or sets on the basis of their relationships. Classification thus necessarily involves the definition of class boundaries, which should be clear, precise, possibly quantitative, and based on objective criteria. Ideally, a classification should be scale independent (the classes should be applicable at any scale) and source independent (the scheme does not depend on a particular data source). For some purposes, it is desirable to establish a hierarchical classification scheme that permits the identification of progressively more specific land uses given additional mapping resources and/or data sources. For example, a hierarchical classification of a particular region with three "tiers" might proceed as follows: agricultural land → cropland and pasture → permanent pasture lands.

A legend is the application of a particular classification in a specific geographic area using a defined mapping scale and a specific data set. Thus, a legend may contain only a subset of the possible classes, and its content depends on the mapping scale as well as on the data source and the mapping methodology. The transition from an abstract classification to a particular legend requires assessment of the minimum mapping unit (MMU).

In the past, two approaches have been employed for mapping land use over large areas. Both are founded on the relationship between land use and land cover, and they differ primarily in the definition or selection of an appropriate land use classification and of the associated legend. In 1976, Anderson and colleagues described a land use classification scheme that combines aspects of land cover and land use and that is designed for use with remotely sensed data. A more recent proposal by Cihlar and Jansen involves a stepwise approach in which the land use classification and associated legend are defined separately from those for land cover. The 1976 scheme, which has also formed the template for land cover classifications, has been used extensively in the United States and to a lesser degree elsewhere. The conceptual advantage of the second approach is its flexibility and the transparency in the definition and application of land use categories. The two approaches are referred to in the following discussions as "parallel" and "sequential," respectively.

Parallel Strategy

The United States Geological Survey sponsored an early, and particularly influential, land use mapping program. The classification system developed for this project was hierarchical, with relatively coarse land use classes being progressively subdivided into more detailed uses. For example, a first-tier land use is "agriculture," which can be subdivided into a number of second-tier uses, such as "cropland and pasture" and "confined feeding operations." These uses may then be further subdivided to include progressively more detailed classification items. The overall classification system was designed to represent those parts of the United States that are of highest relevance for natural resource use (i.e., a resource perspective). The initial classification contained little thematic detail for urban areas, but was designed to permit detailed descriptions of land use even in these areas.

In the 1976 approach, land use is determined based on land cover as the principal surrogate. However, it assumes that other information is also available and would be used, e.g., the image interpreter's customary references to pattern, geographic location, or knowledge of local practices. The classification is formulated in land use terms when possible, but the mapping is conducted by considering primarily land cover features recorded by the remotely sensed data. The first two tiers of the hierarchical system were fully defined as follows:

1 Urban and built-up land
- 11 Residential
- 12 Commercial and services
- 13 Industrial
- 14 Transportation, communications, utilities
- 15 Industrial and commercial complexes
- 16 Mixed urban or built-up land
- 17 Other urban or built-up land

2 Agricultural land
- 21 Cropland and pasture
- 22 Orchards, groves, vineyards, nurseries, and ornamental horticultural areas
- 23 Confined feeding operations
- 24 Other agricultural land

3 Rangeland
- 31 Herbaceous rangeland
- 32 Shrub and brush rangeland
- 33 Mixed rangeland

4 Forest land
- 41 Deciduous forest land
- 42 Evergreen forest land
- 43 Mixed forest land

5 Water
- 51 Streams and canals
- 52 Lakes
- 53 Reservoirs
- 54 Bays and estuaries

6 Wetlands
- 61 Forested wetland
- 62 Nonforested wetland

7 Barren land
- 71 Dry salt flats
- 72 Beaches
- 73 Sandy areas other than beaches
- 74 Bare exposed rock
- 75 Strip mines, quarries, and gravel pits
- 76 Transitional areas
- 77 Mixed barren land

8 Tundra
- 81 Shrub and brush tundra
- 82 Herbaceous tundra
- 83 Bare ground tundra
- 84 Wet tundra
- 85 Mixed tundra

9 Perennial snow or ice
- 91 Perennial snowfields
- 92 Glaciers

The conclusion from the 1976 approach was that level I land use data (categories 1 through 9) could be gathered from the Landsat Multi-Spectral Scanner (resolution, 80 m) or more detailed sources; Anderson's group indicated that level II classification required high-altitude photos. The Landsat Thematic Mapper (resolution, 30 m; these data were not available when Anderson's group designed their land use classification system) or other, more detailed satellite remote sensing data sources may now be used to replace or supplement aerial photography. In principle, the result of this approach is a land use map that extracts all discernible information from the available data sources.

Sequential Strategy

This is a new approach that divides land use and land cover mapping into separate, distinct steps. The rationale is threefold: land use and land cover are fundamentally different, i.e., land cover maps are easier to prepare and exist in many cases with a land cover-specific legend, and land cover is an important determinant of land use. The sequential approach accommodates any land cover classification scheme and mapping legend, but it does assume that such a legend has been chosen. For the geographic domain of interest, it then analyzes the relationships between this legend and the envisioned land use classification. Four relationships may exist between the polygon boundaries outlining individual mapping units for land cover and land use categories: (1) one-to-one, in which the boundaries of land cover polygons and land use polygons coincide, (2) many-to-one, (3) one-to many, but constant across the mapping domain, and (4) one-to-many, varying across the domain. For a particular area, the existence of these relationships needs to be established from field observations or another source (e.g., expert knowledge). For the first two situations (one-to-one and many-to-one), land use maps may be derived from land cover alone. For the one-to-many cases, three increasingly costly options exist: modify land use legend (and, if feasible, land cover legend), provide additional data or information (e.g., elevation), and collect more field observations. It is possible that all three solutions need to be employed, but these can then be restricted to the specific land cover types, thus keeping the mapping costs down.

The advantages of the sequential strategy are that the land cover and land use are conceptually separated, the potential confusions between the two are known, and that it may be applied to existing land cover maps. When applied to a new area for which no land cover map exists and with appropriate source data, the sequential approach could result in a map very similar to that of Anderson's group (depending on the amount of supplementary data); it may thus be viewed as a generalization of the earlier methodology. This strategy has not yet been extensively tested but provides a sound theoretical basis for land use mapping.

Land Use from Remote Sensing and Ancillary Data

Remotely sensed data from satellites or aircraft are the main data source used for land use mapping. Remote sensing techniques are able to provide synoptic, spatially, and spectrally consistent, frequently updated measurements of land surface characteristics. Passive optical measurements (using the sun as the source of electromagnetic radiation) in the visible (0.4 to 0.7 μm) and the infrared (0.7 to ~2.5 μm) parts of the electromagnetic spectrum provide the most information and are therefore used most frequently. Physically, these measurements capture the solar radiation reflected in the individual spectral bands that are delimited by spectral filters. The bands and filters are carefully selected to maximize the contrasts between various surface targets while being affected as little as possible by atmospheric conditions.

The radiation reflected by the surface is captured by sensors carried aboard aircraft or satellites. Until the 1980s, the aerial photographic camera was the leading sensor type. Following technological developments during and after the World War II, this technique provided much flexibility in the type of film and mapping scales used, from black and white panchromatic to color infrared films and mapping scales ranging from 1 : 1000 to >1 : 100,000 (the mapping scale can be precisely controlled by choosing the camera lens focal length and the aircraft flying height). The data are analog in format, thus requiring analysis by experienced photointerpreters, but aerial photographs are usually maintained in regional and national archives. The art of photointerpretation also developed during and after World War II. Compared to digital methods (see later), an important advantage of visual interpretation methods is the ability to use effectively various clues in the image in addition to tone; these include pattern, shadows, size and shape (in two or three dimensions), and context. Land use change may also be measured effectively because of the relatively long data record: aerial photographs for some regions are available as far back as the 1930s or even earlier.

Publicly available satellite data suitable for land cover and land use mapping have been archived since 1972. Following the launch of Landsat and its Multi-Spectral Scanner (MSS), with a resolution of 80 m, optical satellite data have been acquired continuously; spatial resolution has increased to the current range of between ~5 and 30 m. Although the data have not been systematically and completely retained around the world, extensive archives are nevertheless available, and are sufficient for repeated land cover/land use mapping of large areas. Major archives are maintained by the space agencies that launched the respective satellites, and by individual countries that operate satellite receiving stations through agreements. For example, Canada has comprehensive coverage of its territory provided by satellite programs of the United States (the Landsat MSS and Thematic Mapper since 1972, and the National Oceanic and Atmospheric Administration since 1989) and France (Système Probatoire pour l'Observation de la Terre since 1986). Compared to aerial photography, satellite data have the advantages of radiometric calibration (thus permitting analysis by computers), generally much more frequent coverage, spatial consistency, and retrospective availability (mapping of previous conditions is feasible even if not planned at the time), among others. Aerial photographs, on the other hand, compared to satellite imagery, are generally available from earlier time periods.

Regardless of the sensor and data type, land use mapping requires that raw data be converted into information, a process termed information extraction. Strictly speaking, the information that can be directly extracted refers to land cover type or other target characteristics (e.g., percent vegetation cover). This is because the reflected electromagnetic radiation carries an imprint of physical or chemical properties of the target. The science and art of mapping land cover from remote sensing data have been well established for aerial photography and studied extensively for satellite data. To extract land use information, the additional step of establishing the relationship between land cover and land use is required (see the preceding discussion of parallel and sequential strategies).

From the viewpoint of land use information, a major difference between analog aerial photography and digital satellite images is in the ability to use context at the information extraction stage. This includes not only the direct clues embedded in the image, such as spatial patterns, but also—and especially—the expert knowledge and understanding of land use practices, local conditions, the peculiarities of land use/land cover relationships, and the ease with which additional information from other sources can be brought to bear on the preparation of the land use map. Although, in principle, many of these inputs could also be included in digital analysis, such a process is more complex and difficult. On the other hand, intermediate solutions employing both digital analysis and external knowledge are feasible, but their effectiveness will depend on the degree to which systematic relationships exist between land use and land cover. This aspect becomes less important as the mapping scale becomes less detailed.

Issues in Land Use Mapping

As evident from the discussions so far, there is no simple formula for land use mapping that will apply to all situations. As with most mapping methodologies, the success will depend on the type and level of detail in the desired information, the available data that may be used to extract that information, and the compromises in the mapping process, for which both the map producer and the user must be prepared. There are three areas where flexibility exists: scale influences, supplementary data use, and accuracy assessment.

Scale Influences on Land Use Mapping

Land use mapping requires consideration of different aspects of scale and resolution. First, the minimum mapping unit, defined as the smallest area a mapped feature can occupy on the land use map, should be determined. In general, as the MMU becomes smaller, the spatial resolution of the input data must increase, concomitant with the increasing likelihood of errors. The needs of the users of a land use map affect the MMU substantially. For example, a land use map might be developed to identify the spatial distribution of meadow habitats for wildlife conservation purposes. If the users are interested primarily in large animal conservation, meadows that are less than 0.5 hectares may not need to be mapped. Therefore, there will be significant interplay between the MMU and the spatial resolution of the data used for the mapping task. Landsat Thematic Mapper (TM) data, a commonly employed source, consists of pixels that are 30×30 m, or 900 m^2 (0.09 hectares) in size. Consequently, the smallest possible MMU of a land use map that draws primarily on Landsat TM data is a single pixel of 0.09 hectares, but a more practical MMU (one that was less error prone) would be several pixels. Supplementary data should be sought wherever practicable because they may improve, or at least maintain, the accuracy of the land use map while simultaneously allowing for a reduction in the MMU. Commonly used land use mapping ancillary data sources include agricultural or population statistics, but other sources, such as high-resolution imagery, may also be helpful. Specific supplementary data needs, as with the MMU, will be influenced strongly by the needs of land use map users and by the map legend.

The extent over which land use is to be mapped exerts considerable influence on mapping methodologies. Many local land use mapping efforts may be performed entirely through direct survey of the land. These do not require a great deal of conceptual refinement beyond the need to design a suitable sampling strategy for cases where the survey is not exhaustive. Across broad regions, thematically detailed land use characteristics may be mapped at coarse, and usually variable, resolution using census questionnaires, but this technique is most useful for populated areas. Land that has no permanent, or easily contacted, human population is still often subject to human-based land uses, such as resource extraction or wildlife conservation.

Supplementary Data

Several modern land use mapping efforts have used supplemental data from censuses and surveys to derive land use classes at the final stage of standard image classification procedures. Supplemental data (e.g., those derived from questionnaires or field samples) used in this way "train" the classification procedure to discern the effect of prevailing land use in the spectral signal of the land surface. Combinations of remotely sensed and census data have been used to create land use maps in many places, including Europe, United States, Canada, and China. The spatial resolution of such land use maps can be as high as the satellite sensor resolution (most commonly 1 km across such large regions) or, depending on the specific methods used and quality of census data, can be a compromise between the spatial resolutions of the remotely sensed and census data. The accuracy of the resulting maps depends on the tightness of the land cover/land use relationships (refer to the previous discussion of sequential strategy).

Accuracy Assessment of Land Use Maps

Validation of land use and land cover maps can be difficult because supplemental data are frequently needed to help distinguish land use from land cover (which can be derived from remote sensing data alone). The supplemental data, such as from an agricultural census or survey, may be the only source of information over large areas that can be employed to characterize land use. In the absence of independent information on land uses within an area, as well as their spatial distribution (e.g., from field surveys), the approach to validation is likely to be restricted to measurements of consistency between the completed land use map and the supplemental or ancillary data sets that permitted the land use map to be derived from remote sensing data. For example, the extent of a particular land use can be compared between the completed land use map and summary statistics provided at a county level by an ancillary data source, such as a census of agriculture. It is worth noting that, given the 1976 criterion of the Anderson group, that land uses should be represented by a particular cover type whenever possible, it may be possible to derive use from cover without extensive reliance on ancillary data sources. In that case, alternative estimates of land use, perhaps derived from supplemental data sources, could provide truly independent estimates of land use that could be used for validation purposes.

When spatially explicit land use data that are independent of the land use map are available, standard

Table II Construction of an Error or Confusion Matrix[a]

Mapped land use pixels	*Ground truth land use pixels*[b]			
	I	*II*	*III*	*Total*
I	25	5	9	39
II	7	21	5	33
III	8	2	30	40
Number of ground truth pixels	40	28	44	112

[a] In this example, matrix construction enables the land use map producer to estimate rates of commission and omission errors for each land use class; there are three land use classes, labeled I–III.

[b] From ancillary data sources.

classification accuracy assessment is possible. This method requires the production of a confusion (or error) matrix. Confusion matrices allow the analyst to compare the results of the mapping procedure to ancillary data describing known characteristics of the area under consideration, often referred to as ground truth, and to identify magnitudes and types of mapping error (Table II). There are two error categories. First, errors of omission (which can be assessed to estimate so-called user's accuracy) occur when pixels that are identified by the ground truth data set are misclassified. Second, errors of commission (also known as "user's accuracy") occur when a particular mapped class belongs to a different class, as identified by the ground truth data.

In Table II, the producer's accuracy for land use type I is $25/(25+7+8)=62.5\%$, so the error of omission is 37.5% for this land use class (i.e., 15 pixels that are actually of land use class I were mapped as different land uses). However, of greater interest is the user's accuracy, which is $25/(25+5+9)=64.1\%$, so the error of commission is 35.9% (i.e., of the 39 pixels in the map that should have been labeled as land use class I, 25 were correctly labeled). Overall, in this example, the land use map is 64.1% accurate with respect to land use class I, but only 60% of the ground truth pixels with class I have been correctly mapped. The user's accuracy (which is the complement to the rate at which errors of commission occur) is the more important of the two statistics because it directly measures the accuracy of the final land use map with respect to the classes that are included.

Two questions need to be addressed regarding the accuracy of a particular land use map. First, what is the required accuracy? There is no agreed-upon accuracy value, but Anderson's group suggested in 1976 that land use and land cover maps at high spatial resolutions should have a classification accuracy of at least 85% and should have equivalent classification accuracies between individual legend items. Second, what level of confidence in the final accuracy value does the user need? Obviously, this will depend on the users' needs and the degree to which the accuracy may be traded against the resources required. In reality, both questions translate into mapping costs. Costs in the preparation of the map are inevitable (although they may be modulated by trade-offs regarding the legend and the input data type), but the accuracy assessment costs are, in principle, optional, and, furthermore, are highly variable ,depending on the approach chosen to establish the map accuracy. In practice, accuracy assessment of derived land cover or land use maps often suffers due to the significant resources required to obtain reliable accuracy estimates. This is significant because once a map is produced, it tends to be used regardless of its accuracy (if the latter remains unknown), particularly if such a map is the only map and the information is needed urgently.

Conclusion

Land use, which is the product of human interactions with the land, is crucial for environmental monitoring purposes. The importance of land use stems in part from its tendency to "feed back" on the human enterprise by modifying human health, agricultural productivity, or the capacity for resource extraction from an area. Beyond such straightforward measures of the importance of land use as a characteristic of the environment, human/land interaction affects the natural environment's capacity to provide ecosystem goods and services; the goods and services, in turn, enable the conventional economy to exist and to support functioning natural ecosystems. There is virtually no major aspect of human activity that can be considered to be truly independent of the human/land interaction. The task of managing land use to minimize negative economic, health, and environmental feedbacks is a rapidly evolving process that relies on accurate information concerning the variety and spatial distribution of particular land uses. Land use mapping is a key technique for meeting these requirements.

See Also the Following Articles

Digital Terrain Modeling • Geographic Information Systems • Remote Sensing • Spatial Scale, Problems of

Further Reading

Anderson, J. R., Hardy, E. E., Roach, J. T., and Witmer, R. E. (1976). A land-use and land cover classification system for use with remote sensor data. Geological Survey Professional Paper No. 964. U.S. Government Printing Office, Washington, D.C.

Cihlar, J. (2000). Land cover mapping of large areas from satellites: status and research priorities. *Int. J. Remote Sensing* **21,** 1093–1114.

Cihlar, J., and Jansen, L. J. M. (2001). From land cover to land use: A methodology for efficient land use mapping over large areas. *Profess. Geogr.* **53,** 275–289.

Clawson, M., and Stewart, C. L. (1965). *Land Use Information. A Critical Survey of U.S. Statistics Including Possibilities for Greater Uniformity.* Johns Hopkins Press for Resources for the Future, Baltimore, Maryland.

Colwell, R. N. (ed.) (1960). *Manual for photographic interpretation.* American Society of Photogrammetry, Washington, D.C.

Di Gregorio, A., and Jansen, L. J. M. (2000). Land Cover Classification System (LCCS): classification concepts and user manual. Environment and Natural Resources Service, GCP/RAF/287/ITA Africover-East Africa Project and Soil Resources, Management and Conservation Service. FAO, Rome.

Frolking, S., Xiao, X., Zhuang, Y., Salas, W., and Li, C. (1999). Agricultural land-use in China: A comparison of area estimates from ground-based census and satellite-borne remote sensing. *Global Ecol. Biogeogr.* **8,** 407–416.

Hurtt, G. C., Rosentrater, L., Frolking, S., and Moore, B. (2001). Linking remote-sensing estimates of land cover and census statistics on land use of the conterminous United States. *Global Biogeochem. Cycles* **15,** 673–685.

Kerr, J. T., and Cihlar, J. (2003). Land use and cover with intensity assessment for Canada from satellite and census data. *Global Ecol. Biogeogr.*

McConnell, W. J., and Moran, E. F. (eds.) (2000). Meeting in the middle: The challenge of meso-level integration: LUCC Report Series No. 5. LUCC International Project Office, Belgium.

Ramankutty, N., and Foley, J. (1999). Estimating historical changes in land cover: North American croplands from 1850 to 1992. *Global Ecol. Biogeogr.* **8,** 381–396.

Sanderson, E., Jaiteh, M., Levy, M., Redford, K., Wannebo, A., and Woolmer, G. (2002). The human footprint and the last of the wild. *BioScience* **52,** 891–904.

Sokal, R. (1974). Classification: purposes, principles, progress, prospects. *Science* **185,** 1115–1123.

Stehman, S. V., and Czaplewski, R. L. (1998). Design and analysis for thematic map accuracy assessment: fundamental principles. *Remote Sensing Environ.* **64,** 331–344.

Language Acquisition

Allyssa McCabe

University of Massachusetts, Lowell, Lowell, Massachusetts, USA

Glossary

competence The internalized knowledge of language, especially rules and structures. Competence contrasts with performance and is assumed to surpass it.

elicitation The prompting or stimulation of children's production of language.

mean length of utterance (MLU) A measure used to assess early syntactic development; the average length of a child's utterances calculated in morphemes.

morpheme The minimal unit of meaning; the word "cats" consists of two morphemes, "cat" and the plural morpheme "s."

morphology The rules that govern use of morphemes in language.

narrative A story, usually given in past tense and usually consisting of a sequence of events, either factual or fictional.

performance The production of speech, which contrasts with competence.

phonology The study of the sound system of a language, especially rules for combining sounds into words.

pragmatics The study of the rules for the social, often conversational, use of language.

rule Knowledge of a linguistic pattern, which may range widely from very implicit knowledge expressed by means of regular patterning of speech sounds to the ability to articulate grammatical laws.

specific language impairment (SLI) A condition in which children struggle with acquisition of many aspects of language even though they are largely of normal nonverbal intelligence.

syntax The rules for ordering words into sentences such as declaratives, interrogatives, and negatives.

Language is a cultural, social, emotional, and cognitive phenomenon, and its acquisition reflects and affects every aspect of an individual's life. Research has demonstrated that children who excel in language acquisition (1) connect better with parents, peers, and teachers, among others; (2) are substantially less aggressive and more socially competent in a variety of ways; and (3) achieve higher scores on most intelligence tests. Technically, language acquisition is the process by which children develop the ability to produce and understand oral and written language. This process begins before birth with the onset of hearing *in utero* 4 months after conception and, ideally, continues throughout life, although the vast majority of research looks at language acquisition between birth and 12 years of age. Measuring children's language acquisition requires attention to both the comprehension and production of language. Both naturalistic observation and structured elicitation of language production are essential methods for fully understanding this complex process. Language acquisition is a complicated French braid of different strands or levels of language, so researchers must consider a child's progress in mastering phonology, vocabulary, syntax and morphology, discourse, reading, and writing. Parents, clinicians, and educators want to know whether a child's pronunciation, vocabulary, use of plurals and past tense, and narration are normal. Some children acquire more than one language and their progress in all these dimensions must be considered for each language separately, although the acquisition of one language facilitates the acquisition of others. A few children struggle with acquisition of many aspects of language even though they are largely of normal nonverbal intelligence; specific language impairment (SLI) is the technical name for this condition, and early identification of SLI aids in obtaining optimal intervention to minimize the negative consequences of atypical language development. Measuring language acquisition is critical for many reasons.

Introduction

Why Measure Language Acquisition?

The acquisition of language is of considerable importance for many reasons. First of all, language enables children to negotiate social relationships, allowing them, for example, to communicate what is bothering them or what they want and to assert themselves without resorting to physical aggression. Language also becomes increasingly necessary for cognitive development. In fact, most tests of intelligence involve an extensive assessment of verbal ability. In recent years, researchers have become increasingly aware that early language ability predicts subsequent literacy achievement. Many learning disabilities involve language-based reading disabilities that could potentially have been mitigated or even prevented by the diagnosis of language delay in the preschool years. Some children suffer from specific language impairment (SLI), and early identification of SLI allows for more effective intervention. Thus, measuring language acquisition is essential to ensure children's optimal social, cognitive, linguistic, and literate functioning.

When researchers began to assess language acquisition, they were primarily interested in the phenomenon in and of itself, as well as what the close observation of that phenomenon implied about how language is acquired. Those early endeavors have now permitted us to assess individual children, predicting cases in which delay is noticeable in the preschool years. Language is a very complex process, and the disruption of one of its components can compromise others. The measurement of this complex process requires numerous measures, both to understand the process in general and to chart the progress of any child in particular.

Measures of Language Acquisition

There are thousands of measures of language acquisition. Some of these attempt to assess children's linguistic competence, namely, their ability to understand the rules of a language. Others try to assess children's simpler competence at understanding language. Still others depict aspects of children's performance, their use of language. All these aspects are important. Children are unlikely to mark distinctions of which they have no comprehension, but they often comprehend language they cannot yet perform. For example, a girl may understand very well that her name is pronounced "Cassy," yet because she has a lisp she may respond "Cathy" when asked to tell someone her name. We cover here measures of both competence and performance.

Assessment of Acquisition of Bilingualism (or Trilingualism)

Many children all over the world acquire more than one language, either at the same time or staggered. The assessment of language acquisition in such cases is quite complicated and ideally would involve a comparable assessment of all languages the child is acquiring. Children are often more competent and/or productive in one of their languages, usually the first one spoken to them at home by their parents. Knowledge of this dominant language will transfer to the acquisition of other languages. The notion that bilingualism interferes with language acquisition has been countered by numerous studies and is now viewed as the unfortunate remnant of long-outdated and methodologically unsound research (i.e., experimenters tested children in their new language and/or used tests that had not been standardized for their native language).

Article Overview

There are thousands of tests of language acquisition, so we are not able to review them exhaustively here. We first address issues to be faced in assessing language acquisition, focusing on concerns that must be taken into consideration and trade-offs anyone faces in selecting among the many available measures. Rarely is it the case that any researcher or clinician can rely on only one measure to answer their questions. Next, we introduce some representative measures of the various levels of language acquisition. The final section discusses computer-assisted measurement in this area.

Issues in Assessing Language Acquisition

Age Concerns

The first important consideration in measuring language acquisition is the age of the child. Virtually all measures are devised to address the language acquisition of individuals in a specified age range. Related to this concern is the mental age or stage of language acquisition of the child. For example, although the mean length of utterance (MLU) in morphemes is appropriate until that measure reaches 3.5 morphemes, a point usually reached by children when they are 3 years old, the measure may continue to be of use with older, delayed children. That is, MLU is no longer appropriate to use for children who routinely produce longer sentences (e.g., "I jump/ed out of the car" or "He did/n't cry too much today," both consist of seven morphemes).

Control versus Generalizability of Results

Psychologists have long stressed the importance of standardizing the procedure of a study, or arranging for as many circumstances to be the same for all participants as possible. Through the exercise of such scientific control, experimenters believe that they can attribute outcomes to the independent variable of interest to them rather than some other, extraneous variable. The difficulty is that such control comes at the inevitable expense of generalizability (the extent to which findings can be applied to other situations outside the laboratory). For example, an experimenter might adopt the method Ebbinghaus used in the 1880s to study the acquisition of words. Ebbinghaus used consonant-vowel-consonant trigrams—nonsense syllables—in an effort to avoid contaminating the experimental procedure by the intrusion of meaning on the laboratory experience. He then measured precisely how many repetitions of "JUM" or "PID" were required for subjects to memorize those nonsense syllables. Researchers eventually discovered that such procedures told them very little about how people learn words in the real world; in other words, generalizability had all but completely been sacrificed for the sake of control. Moreover, unbeknownst to researchers, subjects often turned nonsense syllables into meaningful ones (e.g., "JUM" became "JUMP" or "CHUM") to ease memorization.

On the other hand, simply observing language in the real world, which maximizes generalizability, would not tell us much about which of the many aspects of some particular situation were responsible for triggering the language observed. Once again, multiple methods of assessment are required.

Naturalistic Observation versus Elicitation

Related to the trade-off between experimental control and generalizability is that between naturalistic observation and elicitation. One of the earliest means used to study language acquisition was a diary of a child's progress, kept by parents who were also often linguists. Such an approach can yield ample, rich data that are true of real situations because they were derived from such situations. However, observation of what a child does, even day in and day out, does not necessarily tell us about a child's capability. Elicitation procedures are best suited to informing us of children's capacity, and by far the best-known such procedure is the wug test developed by Berko Gleason in 1958. Berko Gleason showed children a picture of a strange creature and said, "This is a wug." She then showed children a picture of two of the strange creatures, saying, "Now there is another one. There are two of them. There are two ____." Using this procedure, Berko Gleason was able to demonstrate that children were capable of producing grammatical morphemes (e.g., saying, "wugs") in response to nonsense words they had never heard of before. Children had apparently implicitly acquired certain rules (e.g., for forming plurals) rather than simply mindlessly imitating their parents' productions.

Longitudinal versus Cross-Sectional Assessment

The assessment of language acquisition can be accomplished by testing groups of individuals of different ages at approximately the same time, called the cross-sectional approach. Alternatively, the same individuals can be tested repeatedly over a number of years, called the longitudinal approach. The cross-sectional approach is more economical of a researcher's time, because wide age spans can be assessed in a relatively short period of time. However, that method gives no information about the particular path or paths of development of individual children, nor does it provide any hints about the possible causes of such development. The longitudinal method, in contrast, provides information both about individuals and potential causes, although it is expensive in terms of time and money and liable to problems if participants drop out. Furthermore, the results of longitudinal studies may not be generalizable to other groups or other generations.

Production versus Comprehension

At first glance the distinction between children's production of language and their comprehension of language may seem identical to the distinction between performance and competence already noted. However, whereas production and performance may be used interchangeably, comprehension and competence cannot. Specifically, comprehension refers to children's understanding of language directed to them (e.g., can the child perform a sequence of orders directed to him or her?), whereas their competence refers to their internalized knowledge of linguistic rules, a more esoteric ability often tapped by asking people to judge the grammatical acceptability of a sentence. For most children, the comprehension of language precedes and exceeds production. Some estimate that children comprehend five times as many words as they produce, for example. Thus, the discrepancy between comprehension and production must be kept keenly in mind by those assessing children.

Research versus Clinical Assessment

Any type of language assessment can in theory be used either to address research issues about the language development of children in general or for clinical purposes to assess the relative progress of a particular child in acquiring language relative to his or her peers. In fact, research on children in general is essential for the clinical assessment of specific children. Whereas some measures are used interchangeably, many tend to be used primarily in one setting or another.

Levels of Language Acquisition to be Assessed

Thousands of measures of language acquisition differ along all the aforementioned dimensions. Such measures also differ in the aspects or levels of language they assess. A comprehensive survey is thus impossible here. Table I lists examples of measures that assess the comprehension and/or production of language at various levels; such measures differ as to the ages for which they are appropriate, the amount of control versus generalizability they display, whether they are primarily observation or elicitation, and whether they are used most often for research or for clinical assessment. Despite such variety and ingenuity of methodology, the most important method of assessing language acquisition has been and remains the audio tape recorder, along with typed transcriptions of language recorded.

Phonology

At birth, a child's cries consist of speech sounds that can be audio-tape-recorded and measured by researchers listening carefully or by spectrographic analysis, which gives a visual display of audio signals. These methods of assessing production are useful for individuals of any age. Infants' perceptions of speech sounds have been assessed by means of what is called high-amplitude sucking, in which an infant sucks a pacifier connected to a sound-generating system. Infants quickly learn that sucking causes a sound to be produced, and at first they suck frequently in order to hear that sound. After a while, however, infants lose interest, or habituate to the sound, and slow down or stop sucking altogether. At this point, experimenters introduce another sound. If infants begin to suck again eagerly, we can infer that they perceive the new sound to be different from the old one. Using such a method, experimenters have discovered that young infants perceive the difference between speech sounds even of languages they have never heard. By the end of the first year, infants have lost the ability to perceive speech sounds not meaningfully distinguished in the languages to which they have been exposed.

Table I Examples of Measures of Comprehension versus Production of Language Acquisition by Level

	Comprehension	*Production*
Phonology	Habituation in high-amplitude sucking	Tape-recording child's productions
Vocabulary	Peabody Picture Vocabulary Test-III	MacArthur Communicative Development Inventories
Syntax/morphology	Preferential looking paradigm	Wug test
Discourse/narrative	Story retelling	Personal narratives Wordless picture book story
Literacy	Reading comprehension section of California Achievement Tests	TROLL (preschool)

Vocabulary

A child's earliest words emerge toward the end of the first year of life in the context of interaction usually with parents and are the result of parents imitating children's babbling and connecting those sounds to objects of interest to the child (e.g., "dada" with the child's father). Thus, parents are in a good position to report the words their children produce, especially when systematically prompted to do so, which is the approach taken by the MacArthur Communicative Development Inventories. That instrument also asks mothers to report which words their children comprehend. However, a more objective means of assessing a child's receptive vocabulary is the Peabody Picture Vocabulary Test (3rd edition), which can be used beginning when the child is two and one-half years old and has been normed for individuals throughout the life span.

Morphology and Syntax

When infants are only 12 months old, their comprehension of syntax and morphology can be assessed using the preferential looking paradigm. Infants are seated on their mothers' laps equidistant from two video monitors, each of which presents a different image. A message that matches one image is presented from a central location. A hidden experimenter measures how long a child watches each of the two videos. Even children who at 17 months can still produce only single words have been discovered to prefer looking at the video congruent with the message. For example, when "Cookie Monster is tickling Big Bird" is presented, children reveal their understanding of word order by looking at the image of Cookie Monster tickling Big Bird rather than of Big Bird tickling Cookie Monster. Older children's understanding of syntax and morphology is often studied by asking them to repeat complex sentences because they can repeat grammatical structures only slightly beyond their productive grasp. Alternatively, children's understanding can be assessed by asking them to act out what the sentence says.

Children's own production of morphology in spontaneous speech was one of the first aspects of language development studied using the tape recorder. However, Berko Gleason developed the wug test, already described, to reveal children's competence in this area by eliciting responses to novel nouns and verbs. Children performed as if they had acquired a rule for the grammatical procedure, albeit implicitly.

Pragmatics and Narrative/Discourse

Language is a social phenomenon, and a key aspect of its acquisition is its use in various social settings, settings in which speakers often string sentences together into some type of discourse. One frequently studied type of discourse is narrative. When children are approximately 27 months old, they begin to talk about past events. As always, production can be studied by audio-recording children's productions and subsequently transcribing and analyzing them using one of a number of available analyses. Personal narratives have been recorded in many different natural settings, particularly meal times.

A procedure has been developed to elicit personal narratives in a structured but naturalistic conversation by having researchers tell personal stories of their own to prompt children. For example, after making sure a child is comfortable and talks readily with an adult, the adult might say, "See this bandage? Yesterday I was peeling a potato, and I cut my finger. Has anything like that ever happened to you?" This procedure has worked well with children from many different cultural backgrounds.

Fictional narratives are also frequently elicited by using pictures or story prompts (e.g., "Once there was a rabbit who was very, very hungry. ...") and having children make up the rest of the story. One method that has been widely used in different languages consists of having individuals of many ages peruse a wordless picture book and then retell the story told in the pictures.

The comprehension of stories has been more difficult to study, and most often this is assessed by asking individuals questions about (usually fictional) stories they have heard or read or by requesting that the individuals retell the stories. The assessment of story comprehension by retelling is complicated when the individuals being assessed are from a culture other than the one that gave rise to the story in question because individuals of all ages tend to recall stories from cultures not their own in ways that distort those stories to conform to their own expectations of what makes a good story.

Literacy

The last strand or level of language to begin to be acquired is literacy, the ability to read and write. There are numerous measures of individuals' literacy skills, including some that are appropriate when the child is as young as three years (e.g., the TROLL test). Numerous school assignments and many standardized tests such as the Reading Comprehension Section of the California Achievement Tests (CTB) are geared to assessing the literacy skills of school-age children.

Computer-Assisted Assessment of Developing Language

The transcription of tape-recorded language is the most often used means of assessing oral language acquisition at any level. Such transcription is time-consuming and yields data that can take many years and numerous researchers to be adequately analyzed. In order to facilitate this process, MacWhinney and Snow and their colleagues developed in 1990 the Child Language Data Exchange System (CHILDES; this is available to scholars at the Web site). It includes a consistent and fully documented system for transcribing tape-recorded data, automatic processes for data analysis (e.g., calculation of MLU), and a database of transcripts available to researchers. This program facilitates the use of multiple methods of assessment of children's language, which researchers and clinicians alike agree is essential for the measurement of language acquisition.

See Also the Following Articles

Conversation Analysis • Linguistics

Further Reading

Berko, J. (1958). The child's learning of English morphology. *Word* **14,** 150–177.

Berko Gleason, J. (2001). *The Development of Language,* 5th ed. Allyn & Bacon, Boston.

Berman, R. A., and Slobin, D. I. (1994). *Relating Events in Narrative: A Crosslinguistic Developmental Study.* Erlbaum, Hillsdale, NJ.

Child Language Data Exchange System (CHILDES). Available at: http://childes.psy.cmu.edu/

Cole, K. N., Dale, P. S., and Thal, D. J. (1996). *Assessment of Communication and Language.* Brookes, Baltimore, MD.

CTB Macmillan/McGraw-Hill (1992). *California Achievement Tests,* 5th ed. Macmillan/McGraw-Hill, Monterey, CA.

Dickinson, D. K., McCabe, A., and Sprague, K. (2003). Teacher rating of oral language and literacy (TROLL): A research-based tool. *Reading Teacher* **56,** 1–11.

Dunn, L., and Dunn, L. (1997). *The Peabody Picture Vocabulary Test,* 3rd ed. American Guidance Service, Circle Pines, MN.

Eimas, P. D., Siqueland, E. R., Jusczyk, P., and Vigorito, J. (1971). Speech perception in infants. *Science* **171,** 303–306.

Fenson, L., Dale, P. S., Reznick, J. S., Thal, D., Bates, E., Hartung, J., Pethick, S., and Reilly, J. (1993). *The MacArthur Communicative Development Inventories: User's Guide and Technical Manual.* Singular Publishing Group, San Diego, CA.

Hirsh-Pasek, K., and Golinkoff, R. M. (1996). *The Origins of Grammar: Evidence from Early Language Comprehension.* MIT Press, Cambridge, MA.

MacWhinney, B., and Snow, C. (1990). The child language data exchange system: An update. *J. Child Lang.* **17,** 457–472.

McCabe, A. (1996). *Chameleon Readers: Teaching Children to Appreciate All Kinds of Good Stories.* McGraw-Hill, New York.

Menn, L., and Ratner, N. B. (2000). *Methods for Studying Language Production.* Erlbaum, Mahwah, NJ.

Peterson, C., and McCabe, A. (1983). *Developmental Psycholinguistics.* Plenum, New York.

Snow, C. E., Burns, M. S., and Griffin, P. (eds.) (1998). *Preventing Reading Difficulties in Young Children.* National Academy Press, Washington, DC.

Laplace, Pierre-Simon

Eduard Glas
Delft University of Technology, Delft, The Netherlands

Glossary

Bayesian probability A measure of the confidence that should be conferred on a statement in view of the available evidence. Degrees of belief should, in any case, be comparable (greater or smaller), but they need not be absolutely quantifiable. Also called subjective probability.

determinism The view that nothing happens without a cause; everything depends on fixed causal laws that with perfect certainty determine what happens. The appearance of chance is due only to the fact that in many cases the causal situation is too complex for us to comprehend.

frequentist probability The relevant frequency of the occurrence of an event in a class of equally possible events. When events occur in large numbers, their probability is often considered (for instance, by Laplace) to converge on a limit in proportion to the number of events. Also called object probability.

naturalism The position that philosophical statements should not be defended by appeals to anything that transcends nature or goes beyond the empirical. Many enlightenment intellectuals held that just moral and legal principles should be founded on empirical knowledge of man and nature (e.g., natural laws and natural rights).

probabilism The view that there is an essential uncertainty at the quantum level of phenomena, for instance, the Copenhagen interpretation of quantum mechanics.

Although living at a time and place of great scientific and political upheaval, Laplace was not a revolutionary, either in his political or in his scientific outlook. In his physics and astronomy, he was a vindicator of the Newtonian science of the epoch rather than an innovator. Apart from his technical contributions to mathematics and science, Laplace was important for the philosophical views that he developed in the presentation of his work and for the development of quantitative methods in areas in which mathematical treatment had previously been unknown.

Introduction

From the outset, Laplace's research centered on the analytical approach to astronomy and the theory of probability, which in his work were intimately connected. He remained faithful to this pattern throughout his life. The final results were incorporated in his two major treatises: *Traité de mécanique céleste* (1799–1825) and *Théorie analytique des probabilités* (1812). Both were accompanied by verbal paraphrases addressed to an informed but nonmathematical public. The *Essai philosophique sur les probabilités*, first printed in 1814, had a longer life and probably a wider audience than any of his other writings, including its counterpart in celestial mechanics, the *Exposition du système du monde* (published in 1796). The reason for its continuing impact has been, of course, the importance that probability, statistics, and stochastic analysis have increasingly assumed in the natural and social sciences and in the philosophy of science.

Laplace broadened the subject from the mathematics of games of chance into a basis for statistical inference, philosophy of causality, theory of errors, and measurement of the credibility of evidence. He built from old and often hackneyed problems into areas to which quantification and mathematical treatment had never before been applied. As, in his own words, just "good sense reduced to calculation," he applied his probability calculus to various political and social sciences and practices such as demography, the procedures of judicial panels and electoral bodies, the credibility of testimony, and the determination of insurance risk and annuities.

Laplace was a firm believer in the determinism of nature. The concept of chance in his view does not pertain to reality: it merely expresses our ignorance of the ways in which various aspects of phenomena are interconnected. Imperceptibly small variations in the initial conditions of a mechanism may entail enormous differences in the outcomes after a sufficiently long time, but that mechanism itself must behave in a perfectly determined fashion. The central tenet of Laplace's work was to show how in the final analysis there is a regularity underlying the very things that seem to us to pertain entirely to chance and to unveil the hidden but constant causes on which that regularity depends.

Life and Times

Laplace was born on March 23, 1749, in Beaumont-en-Auge (Normandy). His father was probably in the cider business and certainly well off. There is no record of particular intellectual distinction in the family. Originally destined to enter the Church, the young Laplace enrolled as a theology student at the University of Caen. After 2 years—at the age of 19—he discovered his mathematical inclinations and talents, aborted his studies, and went to Paris (1768). He gained the patronage of d'Alembert, who found him a teaching position at the Ecole Militaire. He held this post till 1776. At that time, it was almost impossible to earn a living in mathematics outside the sphere of the military.

Once settled in Paris, Laplace began reading papers at the Académie des Sciences, but it was only after 3 years and 13 remarkable papers that he finally was elected an adjoint to this venerable institution (1773). In the 1780s, Laplace achieved the depth of results that placed him on a par with Lagrange as an uncontested leader of mathematical analysis. He acquired a senior position in the Académie in 1785 and came to participate in various of its influential committees, among them the committee of weights and measures. The establishment of a metric system was the sole revolutionary endeavor that consistently engaged his warm interest.

His post as examiner at the Corps Royal d'Artillerie (which began in 1784) brought him into contact with ministers and others in positions of power and introduced him to the practice of recruiting an elite by competitive examination. This practice was later greatly expanded in scale and intensified in mathematical content in the procedures for selecting students to enter the Ecole Polytechnique (founded, together with the Ecole Normale, in 1794). Although he never actually taught at the Ecole Polytechnique, Laplace was closely involved in the organization of its educational program and later, especially under Bonaparte, came to dominate it completely. Having kept himself at a safe distance from Paris during the Reign of Terror (which suppressed the Académie and other learned societies of the Ancien Régime), he was recalled to the capital after its fall (in July 1794) to participate in the reorganization of science at the two newly founded Ecoles. He became a professor at the Ecole Normale.

It was part of this school's mission to carry through a thorough rectification of the language of mathematics, in order to make it more accessible to ordinary people as an essential tool for their various practices rather than remaining the prerogative of leisured gentleman-scholars. At that time, language was taken as constitutive of thought, and the *langue des calculs* as its highest manifestation. By implication, all thought processes were conceived to be in the last analysis forms of calculation. This view had been developed especially by the philosopher Condillac. It represented the received view of the time, as is underlined by the fact that the Ecole Normale in 1794 purchased hundreds of copies of Condillac's *Logique*. Laplace certainly shared the view that calculation was the basis of all human intelligent action.

The revolutionaries had not thought highly of Laplace, but the Emperor Napoleon showed himself sensitive to his great prestige among distinguished mathematicians in France and abroad. He was given a leading role in the militarization of the Ecole Polytechnique, whose enduring egalitarian and republican spirit had to be curbed. The educational program came to turn on mathematical analysis, whereas previously descriptive geometry (a creation of the revolutionary Monge) had played the role of the universal mathematical basis for all the arts of engineering. Later, Laplace was also commissioned by the restored Bourbon monarchy to oversee a further reorganization (1816).

Around 1805, Laplace, with the chemist Berthollet, began to organize scientific meetings at their neighboring homes in Arcueil (just outside Paris), out of which grew the informal Société d'Arcueil, headed by Laplace. Its members, among them the mathematicians Biot and Poisson, strongly advocated a mathematical approach to natural and social sciences and practices. The group had a strong influence on the Institut (successor of the suppressed Académie) and on the program of courses of the Ecole Polytechnique.

During the Arcueil period, Laplace worked mainly on a physical program of research, which for a time was highly influential. The Laplacian School of Physics, as it has come to be called, was founded on the belief that phenomena such as refraction, capillary action, cohesion, crystallization, and even chemical reactions were the result of an attractive molecular force, which was identified with gravity. Laplace hoped in this way to raise the physics of terrestrial bodies to the state of perfection to which celestial physics had been brought by the discovery of universal gravitation. By 1812, however, members of the Société began to favor theories that were in contradiction with Laplace's views. They, for instance, criticized Newton's corpuscular theory of light and Lavoisier's caloric theory of heat, which had been further elaborated by Laplace and to which he would stick tenaciously for the rest of his days.

Napoleon made him chancellor of the Senate and, subsequently, count of the Empire (1806). In 1814, Laplace sided with the monarchists and voted against Napoleon in the Senate. In 1817, the king honored him for his services with the title of marquis. Laplace died on March 5, 1827 in Paris.

Determinism of Nature

The idea of changing the cherished Newtonian system of the world seems never to have entered Laplace's mind. Rather, he sought to perfect it by the means proper to his generation and milieu, that is, by mathematical analysis. The overwhelming success of Newtonian mechanics induced the belief in the universal validity of mechanistic philosophy, whose core is the explanation of phenomena in terms of a mechanism in which the whole succession of motions is determined by the state of the moving system at any particular time. In contrast to religious belief, the belief in a fully determined universe was a faith that supported naturalism. Well known is Laplace's remark to Napoleon that there is no need for the hypothesis of God's intervention in the system of the world. On the other hand, because natural phenomena can be described by differential equations, the determinism of nature was supposed to guarantee under specified initial conditions the existence of unique solutions to differential equations—unless they are altogether "unnatural."

Laplace shared the optimistic enlightenment views of the universal applicability of analytical procedures: "What one observes in Analysis happens similarly in Nature, whose phenomena are indeed just the mathematical consequences of a small number of invariant laws." He defined his program as "reducing the whole of mechanics to pure analysis," followed by its application to celestial mechanics, the paradigm case of purely analytical calculation of "the changes that the course of time has effected, and still effects, in this system." Commenting on Clairaut's corrected prediction of Halley's comet, Laplace concluded, "the regularity which astronomy shows us in the movements of the comets doubtless exists also in all (other) phenomena. The curve described by a simple molecule of air or vapor is regulated in a manner just as certain as the planetary orbits." Consistent with this view, in his Arcueil period he set out to solve the problems of capillary action, the speed of sound, and the refraction of light and to develop a general theory of heat and gases through the analysis of a microastronomical model of central forces of attraction acting on point masses. Using the same deterministic model, he also tackled psychology, which he conceived as a continuation of empirical physiology. Roughly speaking, he modeled the seat of our thoughts after a system of resonators coupled to the environment, whose vibrations are subjected to the laws of dynamics.

Laplace saw himself as a strict follower of Newton, who was believed to have been a pure inductivist abhorring hypothetical reasoning. He went so far as to claim that Newton's successes derived from the circumstance that in his time just enough empirical knowledge of mechanical phenomena had been assembled for him to infer the general principles and laws of mechanics from these facts. Newton's works, Laplace asserted in 1796, have supplied

> *the best models ... for gathering data and subjecting them to the calculus.. One must select or produce the phenomena that are best suited to this purpose, multiply them under varying circumstances, and find out what they have in common. In this way one ascends successively to more and more extensive relationships, to reach finally the general laws, which then have to be verified .... This analytical relation of particular facts with a general fact is what constitutes a theory.*

Although Newton himself had had serious qualms about the possibility of action at a distance, Laplace used it as a necessary basis of all mathematical physics, claiming that natural phenomena are in the last analysis reducible to intermolecular attraction on the model of Newton's theory of gravitation. As we have already seen, he also stubbornly stuck to the corpuscular theory of light, even after the experiments of Fresnel had tipped the balance so much in favor of the wave theory.

He set himself the task of proving that Newton's theory of gravitation suffices to solve all problems in its domain and therefore constituted "the true System of the World." The best statement of Laplacian determinism undoubtedly is that given by Laplace, himself:

> *We ought then to regard the present state of the universe as the effect of its anterior state and as the cause of the one that is to follow. Given for one instant an intelligence which could comprehend all the forces by which nature is animated and the respective situations of the bodies of which it is composed—an intelligence sufficiently vast to submit these data to analysis—it would embrace in the same formula the movements of the biggest bodies of the universe as well as those of the lightest atom; for this intelligence nothing would be uncertain and the future as well as the past would be present to its eyes. The human mind offers, in the perfection which it has been able to give to astronomy, a feeble idea of this intelligence. Its discoveries in mechanics and mathematics, added to that of universal gravity, have enabled it to comprehend in the same analytical expressions the past and future states of the system of the world. Applying the same method to some other objects of knowledge, it has succeeded in*

referring observed phenomena to general laws, and in foreseeing phenomena which given circumstances ought to produce.

Probability and Human Affairs

It is only because of our lack of knowledge and our limited mental capacity that we have to appeal to the theory of probability, which is, as it were, an instrument for repairing defects in our knowledge. Chance has no reality in itself; it is nothing but a term for expressing our ignorance of the way in which the various aspects of a phenomenon are interconnected. Because nature knows nothing of chance, the notion of a statistical law (of nature) was a contradiction in terms for Laplace. The object of probability theory is precisely to show that the very things that seem to pertain entirely to chance in the final analysis exhibit a certain regularity and to unveil the hidden but constant causes on which that regularity depends. Thus, he, for instance, established that the planets' seeming aberrations from Newtonian law were periodic and hence part of the determined order of Nature—they were due to the gravitational influence of the other planets and of comets.

It was from mathematics, especially his investigations of difference equations, that Laplace came to the theory of probability. In articles written around 1773, he applied the analytical methods that he had developed to the theory of chance, and they at the same time complemented his new departure into the determination of cause. These were the writings in which, according to Gillispie, Laplace "began broadening probability from the mathematics of actual games and hypothetical urns into the basis for statistical inference, philosophic causality, estimation of scientific error, and estimation of the credibility of evidence, to use terms not then coined."

The theory of probability owes more to Laplace than to any other individual. He considered the theory from all aspects and at all levels, and his *Théorie analytique des probabilités* is replete with new analytical methods still in use today. We find there for instance the theory of generating functions, which Laplace had already developed in the 1770s as a means of estimating the ratio of the number of favorable cases to the total number of all possible cases. The book contains also the method of least squares for the combination of numerous observations. This method had been suggested by Legendre on practical grounds, without any principled basis in probability theory, but Gauss and then Laplace gave it a variety of formal proofs, on which the entire theory of errors has since been based. It is with reference to least squares that Laplace conceived the ideas that now serve as the foundations of statistical theory: the idea that every statistical procedure is a game of chance played with nature, the idea of a loss function and of risk, and the idea that risk may be used for defining the optimality of the statistical method concerned. Further important new mathematical tools were the method of recurrent sequences and of characteristic functions, also called Laplace transforms, which are widely used today for tackling differential equations.

The second edition (1814) contained, apart from several new supplements, an introduction that subsequently was published separately as *Essai philosophique sur les probabilités*. Laplace introduced it as an extended version of lessons that he gave at the Ecole Normale in 1795: "I present here without the aid of analysis the principles and general results of this theory, applying them to the most important questions of life, which are indeed for the most part only problems of probability." This explains the avoidance of formulas and technical mathematics; actually large tracts of the *Essai* are transpositions into common language of what in the *Théorie analytique* had been developed mathematically.

"Strictly speaking," Laplace went on, "it may even be said that nearly all our knowledge is problematical; and in the small number of things which we are able to know with certainty, even in the mathematical sciences themselves, the principal means for ascertaining truth—induction and analogy—are based on probabilities; so that the entire system of human knowledge is connected with the theory set forth in this essay."

The leading idea of the book is that each particular phenomenon in reality, including social and political phenomena, is governed by causes of two distinct kinds, the permanent and the accidental causes. In each particular phenomenon, the effect of accidental causes may appear stronger than that of the permanent causes, with the result that such phenomena become the subject for probabilistic investigations. On the other hand, in a long series of similar occurrences, the accidental causes average out and the permanent causes prevail. This is called the weak version of the theorem of large numbers formulated by Bernoulli, who is given due credit by Laplace. Considerations such as these are, of course, quite usual with reference to lotteries, games of chance, insurance risk, and so on, but Laplace built them into areas in which quantification and calculation had previously been nonexistent, especially various political and social sciences and practices (e.g., demography, procedures of judicial panels and electoral bodies, and credibility of testimony).

It follows again from this theorem that in a series of events indefinitely prolonged the action of regular and constant causes ought to prevail in the long run over that of irregular causes. It is this which renders the gains of lotteries just as certain as the products of agriculture; the chances which they reserve assure them a benefit in the totality of a great number of throws. Thus favorable and numerous chances being constantly attached to the observation of the eternal principles of reason, of justice, and of humanity which establish and maintain societies, there is a great advantage in conforming to these principles and of grave inconvenience in departing from them. If one consults histories and his own experience, one will see all the facts come to the aid of this result of calculus. Consider the happy effects of institutions founded upon reason and the natural rights of man among the peoples who have known how to establish and to preserve them.

Laplace defined the probability of an event as the ratio of the number of cases favorable to that event to the number of all the possible cases. This suggests a frequentist interpretation of probability, which is often contrasted with the subjective notion (attributed to Bayes, who is mentioned once in the *Théorie analytique*) of "degree of belief." At that time, however, this distinction was not made. The *Essai philosophique* became the fountainhead of the frequentist interpretation, because the decisive role is given to frequencies, but in many places Laplace also handles probability as a (Bayesian) measure of confidence or diffidence, independent of any frequency connotations.

Laplace arrived at results very similar to those of Bayes, tacitly relying on the assumption that possible causes are equally likely if there is no reason to believe that one of them is more probable than any other. As the inverse square law was the final touchstone of mathematical astronomy, so the principle of equal prior probabilities was the touchstone of his mathematical theory of probability.

The intensity of rational expectations appears here as the decisive moment in assigning probabilities. On the other hand, a considerable part of the *Essai* is devoted to illusions that give rise to mistakes in assigning probabilities to events, and here probability appears as something independent of the subjective state of mind of individuals.

So it seems that Laplace used an objective notion of probability in the cases for which we have sufficient information and a subjective notion in the cases for which insufficient information is available. On the one hand, his calculations depend on the consideration that the probability of events that occur in large numbers converges on a limit in proportion to the number of events; on the other hand, he held that probability is relative to our state of knowledge or ignorance and not to nature. The more frequently a certain correlation between events is observed, the greater is its probability and the stronger our belief; hence, the objective probabilities of experience and the subjective probabilities of belief were, in his mind, mirror images of one another.

The mathematical theory of probability was, in Laplace's words, just "good sense reduced to a calculus." The apparent mishmash of applications to gambling, insurance, astronomy, medicine, reliability of testimony, accuracy of tribunal judgments, economic theory of value, and reasoning from known effects to unknown causes had as a common background that all were posed in terms of reasonable belief and action based on that belief. The calculus of probabilities shared with the social sciences and practices of the Enlightenment a common ground in that they all had as their object of study the psychology of the rational individual. But when Laplace discussed the relationship between psychology and probability, this was primarily to expose the psychological roots of probabilistic illusions, which included beliefs in astrology and divination. The "good sense" that in Laplace's theory was reduced to a calculus was the good sense of the *homme de lumières*, combating ignorance, error, prejudice, and superstition.

See Also the Following Articles

Bayesian Statistics • Bernoulli, Jakob

Further Reading

Crosland, M. (1967). *The Society of Arcueil.* Heineman, London.

Dale, A. I. (1991). *A History of Inverse Probability.* Springer-Verlag, New York.

Daston, L. (1988). *Classical Probability in the Enlightenment.* Princeton University Press, Princeton, NJ.

Dhombres, J. (1980). L'enseignement des mathématiques par la méthode révolutionnaire: les leçons de Laplace à l'Ecole Normale de l'an III. *Revue de l'Histoire des Sciences* **33,** 315–348.

Dhombres, N., and Dhombres, J. (1989). *Naissance d'un Nouveau Pouvoir: Sciences et Savants en France, 1793–1824.* Payot, Paris.

Fox, R. (1974). The rise and fall of Laplacian physics. *Historic. Stud. Phys. Sci.* **4,** 89–136.

Fox, R. (1997). The Laplacian school. In *Pierre-Simon Laplace* (C. C. Gillispie, ed.), Chap. 24. Princeton University Press, Princeton, NJ.

Frängsmyr, T., Heilbron, J. L., and Rider, R. E. (eds.) (1990). *The Quantifying Spirit in the Eighteenth Century.* University of California Press, Berkeley, CA.

Gillispie, C. C. (1997). *Pierre-Simon Laplace.* Princeton University Press, Princeton, NJ.

Hahn, R. (1967). *Laplace as a Newtonian Scientist.* University of California, Los Angeles, CA.

Krüger, L., Daston, L. J., and Heidelberger, M. (eds.) (1990). *The Probabilistic Revolution, Vol. 1. Ideas in History.* MIT Press, Cambridge, MA.

Laplace, P. S. de (1796). Exposition du système du monde. In *Oeuvres Complètes,* Vol. 6. Gauthiers-Villars, Paris. 1884.

Laplace, P. S. de (1951). *A Philosophical Essay on Probabilities.* F. W. Truscott and F. L. Emory, trans. Dover Publications, New York.

Sheynin, O. B. (1976). P. S. Laplace's work on probability. *Arch. Hist. Exact Sci.* **16,** 137–187.

Sheynin, O. B. (1977). Laplace's theory of errors. *Arch. Hist. Exact Sci.* **17,** 1–61.

Stigler, S. M. (1986). *The History of Statistics: The Measurement of Uncertainty before 1900.* Harvard University Press, Cambridge, MA.

Law

Eric A. Posner
University of Chicago, Chicago, Illinois, USA

Glossary

civil law A system of law in France, Germany, and many other countries that is based mainly on statute (the civil code), rather than on judge-made law.

Coase theorem If transaction costs are zero, then the allocation of legal entitlements does not determine their use; instead, the entitlements will be traded to their most efficient use.

common law A system of law originating in England, and characteristic of the United States and other countries, that is based on judge-made law.

exemption law A law that protects the assets of defaulting debtors against seizure and liquidation by creditors.

expectation damages The standard remedy for breach of contract; the victim of the breach is entitled to the amount of money that would put him in the financial position that he would have been in if the contract had been performed.

formalism A characteristic of legal systems, or areas of law within them, formalistic laws are those that are clear rules rather than vague standards.

liability rule A type of legal remedy that grants a person who has been wronged the right to monetary damages.

property rule A type of legal remedy that permits the person who has been wronged to obtain an injunction against the wrongful act.

specific performance A remedy for breach of contract that gives the victim of breach the right to have the contract performed.

transaction cost The cost of negotiating, writing, monitoring performance with, and enforcing a contract.

Examples of social science methods used in law come mainly from efforts to apply economics, psychology, and sociology to legal questions. The methods from these disciplines permit one to evaluate the influence of laws or legal institutions (such as courts) on social behavior such as crime, to explain how legal institutions function, and to explain why existing laws and legal institutions came into existence.

Introduction

Traditional legal scholarship, sometimes called doctrinal scholarship, is an interpretive enterprise. Using legal materials such as statutes and judicial opinions, scholars attempt to identify what the law is, that is, whether some particular act X is permitted or regulated by the law, and in the latter case, what the sanction will be if the law is violated. Although doctrinal scholarship continues to be conducted, it was attacked in the early 20th century for its preoccupation with the "law on the books" to the exclusion of "law in action." A statute might prohibit X, but have no influence on social behavior because the statute is ignored by prosecutors, judges, juries, potential litigants, and others, or because the people to whom the law is directed can accomplish their original goals without violating the statute. The critique of doctrinal scholarship provoked a turn toward social science; legal scholars hoped that social science methods would enable them to understand how the law works, how it influences behavior in society, and how people and governments achieve their goals through law rather than through other means.

The earliest social science work in legal scholarship occurred during the 1920s and 1930s under the influence of a movement known as legal realism. It is generally regarded as a failure: it counted things rather than proposing and testing theories. Many decades passed before social scientific methods in legal scholarship became influential. In the 1960s, a movement known as "law and society" applied empirical sociological techniques to legal problems. Law and society scholars used surveys and other data sources to investigate how people thought about law, whether they understood or paid attention to it, and how the law affected behavior.

Beginning in the late 1960s and early 1970s, a movement known as "law and economics" applied rational choice theory to legal problems. Law and economics, which has become the dominant social science methodology in legal scholarship, typically asks, What effect will some law Y, as opposed to some other possible law Z, have on people's behavior, assuming that people are rational in the sense defined by economics? There is also a growing empirical literature that uses statistical and qualitative methods to evaluate the theoretical predictions.

A third important methodology is psychology. The law and psychology literature typically looks at how psychological theories predict behavior in legal settings and tests these predictions usually under experimental conditions. A large literature of jury studies investigates how jurors make decisions. Additional work applies insights from cognitive psychology to a wide range of laws and legal institutions.

This article discusses a few examples of social science-inspired theory and testing in legal scholarship. Comprehensiveness is impossible; the examples will illustrate the main trends.

Law and Economics

Criminal Law

The application of economics to criminal law has its roots in Beccaria and Bentham, but the first modern piece of scholarship is an influential 1968 article by Gary Becker. Becker's methodological innovation was to treat the criminal sanction as the "price" of engaging in socially disapproved behavior, such as murder and robbery. Individuals rationally choose to engage in crime when the benefits, which include monetary returns as well as intrinsic pleasure, exceed the expected cost, which is the criminal sanction discounted by the probability of arrest and conviction. An increase in a criminal sanction should have the same effect as the increase in the price of ordinary goods: individuals will engage in less of the sanctioned behavior. (Many criminologists reject Becker's views.)

Lawyers and policy analysts typically want to know more than this. If the sanction for robbery is increased, will potential robbers switch to a lawful occupation or to burglary instead? If the punishment for robbery is too severe, and thus too close to the punishment for murder, will robbers be more likely to murder their victims because the extra sanction is now so low? Should repeat offenders receive higher sentences? These, and similar questions, can be addressed using Becker's framework.

The focus of the empirical literature has been the relationship between the criminal sanction and the crime rate. Authors test the hypothesis that an increase in punishment reduces crime through the deterrence effect, as opposed to some other process, such as the incapacitation of people who would commit crimes if they were not in prison. It is also possible that criminals are not deterrable: they might discount future payoffs or sanctions too much, miscalculate the probability of being caught or convicted, and so forth.

One representative empirical study attempts to distinguish the effects of deterrence and incapacitation. In a 1999 paper, Kessler and Levitt studied California's Proposition 8, one of the most famous "three-strikes laws," which increased the punishment for certain repeat offenders. If imprisonment has a deterrent effect, then a three-strikes law should immediately deter people from committing the crimes to which it applies. If imprisonment has no deterrent effect, but only incapacitates, then the effect of these laws will be felt only after a delay. The reason is that the new incapacitation effect created by the laws will be felt only after criminals serve as much time in prison as they would have if the laws had not been enacted.

Kessler and Levitt tested the deterrence and incapacitation effects of Proposition 8 by comparing two sets of data. They distinguished the crimes eligible for the sentencing enhancement under Proposition 8 (generally, serious felonies) and those that were not. The rates for eligible crimes and ineligible crimes declined immediately after Proposition 8 came into effect, but the rate for eligible crimes declined more rapidly, suggesting that the law, rather than an omitted variable, caused some of the reduction in crime. In addition, they compared the difference between the eligible and ineligible crime rates in California and the difference between two similar sets of crime rates nationwide. The difference in California increased more than the difference nationwide, indicating that the law, rather than an omitted variable, caused the increase in the difference between the eligible and ineligible crime rates. In these ways controlling for trends within California as well as national trends, Kessler and Levitt found an immediate 3.9% drop in the eligible crime rate. After 3 years, the decline was 7.9%. By this time, the incapacitation effect could have kicked in, but the study suggests the initial 3.9% drop was due entirely to the deterrence effect.

Kessler and Levitt relied on a simple comparison of changes in the crime rate, rather than regression analysis, because California was the only state in which three-strikes laws were both created and vigorously enforced. Many other empirical studies of criminal law exploit interstate variation in criminal law and punishment and therefore can rely on cross-sectional and, sometimes, panel data.

Debtor–Creditor Law

Many people have trouble paying their debts and default on their loans. Numerous federal and state laws regulate the means by which creditors may obtain compensation for their losses. Under federal bankruptcy law, debtors may periodically file for bankruptcy, which usually results in the discharge of their debts. But even if debtors do not file for bankruptcy, state garnishment laws prevent creditors from obtaining more than a fraction of future income, and state exemption laws limit the assets that can be seized and liquidated.

State exemption laws hold particular interest for scholars. One reason for this is that the federal bankruptcy system incorporates the state exemption laws and, in addition, creates a generous system of federal exemptions that serve as a floor for the state exemptions unless states take the trouble of opting out of the federal system. The state and federal exemption laws typically allow individuals to protect their principal residence, or some fraction of the equity (in some states, an unlimited amount of equity), and furniture and other goods up to designated values, sometimes tens of thousands of dollars. However, many states are less generous, and the extreme cross-state variation in the generosity of exemption laws makes them an attractive subject for empirical study.

Although the modern system of American bankruptcy law originated in 1899, and many state exemptions are even older, current law was heavily influenced by a reform act passed in 1978. This law greatly expanded bankruptcy protections; one of its provisions was the creation of the parallel federal system of exemptions described above. Supporters of the 1978 reform act argued that these expanded protections were justified by sharp credit practices that took advantage of unsophisticated debtors, who often filed for bankruptcy because of unanticipated events such as divorce or illness. Although opposition to the reform was muted, shortly after the reform became law the bankruptcy filing rate skyrocketed. Creditors complained to Congress, which cut back some of the protections a few years later, but these protections remained more generous than they had been prior to 1978.

Economists and legal scholars have studied the effect of bankruptcy protection on the credit market. Economic models of the credit market posit that individuals borrow money in order to smooth consumption over time. If income increases with age, while the marginal value of a dollar remains constant, the individual would want to move dollars from the future to the present. Creditors will supply these dollars as long as debtors pay back the loans plus interest to compensate for the time value of money, inflation, the risk of default, and similar factors. In a competitive market, the interest rate will be just enough to cover these costs; everyone willing to pay the interest will be given credit.

Debtor protection law, including bankruptcy and exemption law, has two opposing effects on the unregulated equilibrium. On the one hand, debtor protection makes credit more attractive because it limits the adverse consequences of default; this should increase the demand for credit. On the other hand, debtor protection increases the losses of creditors; this should reduce supply. Many economists would assume that debtor protection law in the aggregate restricts credit—reduces the supply, increases the cost, or both—because debtors and creditors could individually negotiate insurance contracts if debtors wanted to be protected from default. They do not, for the most part, suggesting (unless there is a market failure of some sort) that debtors are simply not willing to pay for insurance. But this is only theory; the actual effect of debtor protection laws can be determined only by empirical tests.

Gropp *et al.* conducted one such test in 1997. Because exemption laws vary by state, one can gauge the effect of these laws through cross-sectional comparison. The main independent variable is the effective exemption level (divided into quartiles): in each state, this is the higher of the federal floor and the state exemption (except in the states that have exercised the right to opt out of the federal system, in which case residents must use the state exemption). The hypothesis is that credit will be tighter in states with higher exemptions.

Gropp *et al.* conducted a number of tests. Their first regression shows that individuals in the highest exemption states are significantly more likely to be turned down for credit than individuals in the lowest exemption states. A second regression shows that the amount of debt carried by individuals is higher in low-exemption states than in high-exemption states. A third regression shows that interest rates are higher in states with generous exemptions, although not for debtors with significant assets, who probably pose less of a risk for creditors, who would be able to obtain a greater proportion of the debtor's wealth even in bankruptcy. The three regressions are consistent with the hypothesis that generous debt protection reduces the supply of credit. Because creditors expect that they will not recover the full value of their debt when debtors default, they charge a higher interest rate or refuse to issue loans in the first place.

There are many other studies on the regulation of the credit market. These studies tend to find that the regulations restrict credit without providing any offsetting benefits, though some studies find no effect.

Comparative Law

La Porta and his coauthors have written a series of papers examining cross-country differences in the law; they seek to explain why laws differ across countries, and what effect these legal differences have on economic performance and institutional structure. Because legal traditions are so different, these studies face significant empirical difficulties.

In 1998, La Porta *et al.* investigated investor protection laws in 49 countries. These laws are designed to prevent managers of corporations from violating the rights of equity-holders and debt-holders. Generally speaking, equity-holders have the right to a share of the corporation's profits and to vote on certain decisions made by the firm, including appointment of directors. Debt-holders have the right to principal and interest and to seize a portion of the corporation's assets if it defaults on the debt. These rights have value only if legal institutions enforce them; if they do not, managers can pocket the money that would otherwise be due to the holders of securities. The law is designed to prevent managers from taking assets that belong to corporations, both directly and through subterfuge, when these assets should be used to generate revenues for distribution to debt-holders and equity-holders. This is true in all countries, though the details differ significantly, as does the quality of legal enforcement.

One of the problems with studies such as La Porta *et al.*'s is that legal rights in different countries vary along many dimensions. Some countries have a one-share–one-vote rule, which prohibits corporations from issuing shares with different voting rights. Other rules, which can be found in some countries but not others, regulate the use of proxies for voting, cumulative voting procedures, and the treatment of minority shareholders by the majority, mandate dividends, and so forth. In order to enable cross-country comparisons, La Porta *et al.* constructed various indices. The main index is a score from 0 to 6, which is derived by giving each country 1 point for each of six major shareholder rights that are protected in its legal system. A simple regression shows that countries with an English common law origin offer significantly greater shareholder protections than countries with French, German, or Scandinavian civil law origins.

Countries also afford a diverse array of legal protections to creditors. Rules govern whether creditors can immediately repossess assets when the debtor enters bankruptcy or must wait, subordinate creditors' claims to those of other interests, give management more or less control in bankruptcy, and so forth. La Porta *et al.* constructed an index of creditor rights and again found a great deal of variation across countries, with common law countries offering the greatest protections.

Thus far, this article has discussed formal investor protection laws, but there is the equally important question of whether these laws are enforced. La Porta *et al.* examined a variety of measurements of law enforcement, including scores for the efficiency of the judicial system, the rule of law, corruption, risk of expropriation, risk of contract repudiation, and accounting standards. Gross National Product (GNP) per capita is strongly correlated with quality of legal enforcement; when this is controlled for, English common law origin countries score better than French civil law origin countries but worse than German civil law origin countries.

The final question investigated by La Porta *et al.* is whether these differences in investor protection law have any effect on the economy. They focused on ownership concentration: the extent to which ownership of a corporation is concentrated in the hands of a few people rather than dispersed across thousands of shareholders. One hypothesis is that if investor protection laws are weak, then ownership will be concentrated. The reason is that minority shareholders will fear that they will be exploited by majority shareholders and managers unless they have legal protection. A regression with various controls lends support to this hypothesis. French civil law origin countries, for example, have the weakest investor protection laws and the most concentrated ownership. Note that including the legal origin of countries addresses concerns about direction of causality; e.g., governments in countries with highly concentrated ownership are lobbied by businesses to legislate weak protections. The legal origins date back centuries and are likely to be exogenous.

The study reveals a great deal about variation of investor protection laws across countries and the effect of these protections on ownership concentration. Its larger significance is its illustration of the methodological solutions to problems arising from cross-country comparisons of legal systems.

Law and Psychology

Property Rights and the Endowment Effect

One of the most famous ideas in law and economics is that, in the absence of transaction costs, resources will be transferred to their most efficient use. To understand this idea, suppose that two people, A and B, own neighboring parcels of land. A's factory generates noise and pollution, which interferes with B's hotel. Under the law of nuisance, B might have a right to enjoin A from producing noise and pollution; whether B does have such a right depends on numerous legal variables. But Coase argued that it does not matter whether A has the entitlement to make noise and pollution, or B has the entitlement to be free from noise and pollution, because the entitlement will end up in the hands of whoever values it more. If the law grants B the entitlement to be free from noise and pollution, but A's factory makes enough money to fully compensate B for the loss of that entitlement, then B will sell the entitlement to A. If the law does not grant B that entitlement, then there will be no such transaction. Thus, if A values the entitlement more than B does, A will end up with it, and similar logic applies if B values the entitlement more than A does. The initial allocation of entitlements does not affect the final allocation.

This argument has been extended to the topic of legal remedies. Suppose that B is granted the entitlement; there is a further question of whether B should be protected with an injunction or with damages. In the first case, B can sue to enjoin, that is, prohibit, A from producing noise and pollution. In the second case, B cannot stop A from producing noise and pollution but is entitled to monetary compensation equal to B's loss. The Coase idea has been interpreted to suggest that it does not matter for the allocation of the entitlement whether the law gives B damages, an injunction, or indeed no remedy at all. Regardless of the remedy or lack of remedy, A will stop polluting if and only if B's valuation is higher than A's: the only difference is who pays whom, and how much.

One criticism of the Coase idea is that it assumes that a person's valuation of a piece of property is independent of whether he owns it. The psychology literature suggests that there is an "endowment effect," according to which a person values something more if he owns it than if he does not own it. A well-known experiment found that subjects who were given coffee mugs would sell them only for a higher price than similarly situated subjects would buy them for. This is a puzzle for economics, which assumes that people value goods the same regardless of whether they own them. If the endowment effect is significant enough—and there is some doubt about this—then Coase's idea would be wrong. If B is given the entitlement, then B will value quiet and clean air a lot; if B is not given the entitlement, he will value quiet and clean air a little. Although trades will sometimes still be possible, the initial allocation will partly determine the final allocation.

If this is true, then the conclusion about legal remedies might be wrong as well. But here there is a further question: what ownership characteristics are necessary for the endowment effect to function? Most property rights are protected by a mix of injunctive and damages remedies, but is it possible that people might regard these remedies differently and value property that is protected by stricter remedies more? In 1998, Rachlinski and Jourden tested this hypothesis in an experimental setting, in which students were given a story about a nuisance dispute and asked a series of questions about whether they would trade entitlements. Students were told that they owned a piece of property whose value was reduced by the activities of a neighboring landowner. In one scenario, the students were told that their entitlement was protected by damages; in another scenario, the students were told that their entitlement was protected by injunction. Rachlinski and Jourden found that the students valued their entitlement more, and were less willing to sell it to the landowner, if it was protected by an injunction rather than damages. This suggests that the endowment effect is stronger when legal remedies are stricter and implies that the allocation of property rights is not independent of the type of legal remedy.

The study is notable because it relies on an experiment rather than on data collected from the field. Experiments have been heavily criticized: typically, they rely on students, who may not be representative, and subjects are often paid nothing or a small amount, so that their motivation is not the same as that of people in the real world. Nonetheless, experiments are useful for isolating certain phenomena that are not easily observed outside the laboratory and they have become increasingly popular in law, as they have in economics.

Juries and the Psychology of Deliberation

Legal scholars have long been interested in understanding how juries deliberate and make decisions. A literature going back several decades has analyzed jury decision-making using either reports of actual jury deliberations or laboratory experiments in which subjects are asked to play the role of juror.

In 1984, Cowan *et al.*, for example, investigated whether jurors who are unwilling to impose the death penalty are less likely to convict defendants than jurors who are willing to impose the death penalty. This question is important because under traditional rules, a person can serve as a juror for a capital murder trial only if he is not philosophically opposed to the death penalty and is willing to impose it under the appropriate legal conditions. Jurors are required to apply the law and the exclusion rules are designed to ensure that they will. The problem is that people willing to impose the death penalty may not be representative of the population. If people willing to impose the death penalty are more likely to convict, then defendants accused of capital murder are likely to receive a jury biased in favor of conviction.

To test their hypothesis that "excludable" jurors are less likely to convict than "death-qualified jurors," Cowan and her coauthors had their subjects watch a reenactment of a capital murder trial and then deliberate in mock juries. Consistent with the hypothesis, the excludable jurors were significantly less likely to vote for conviction than the death-qualified jurors were, and this was true both prior to deliberations and after the deliberations. Some evidence also suggested that juries with a mixture of excludable and death-qualified jurors performed better than juries composed entirely of death-qualified jurors. These results were consistent with the findings of other studies and have had influence on the development of death penalty doctrine in the courts.

Research on jury decision-making has been influenced by the cognitive psychology literature. A 1998 article by Sunstein *et al.* and a 2000 article by Schkade *et al.* exemplify this research. Both studies were based on large-scale controlled experiments, in which several hundred individuals were given a fictional legal dispute and asked to resolve it as a mock juror. The first study investigated whether the judgments of individual jurors were predictable, in the sense that the judgment of one juror was a good prediction of the judgment of another juror. They found that jurors ranked cases by the severity of the legal wrongdoing in a consistent fashion, but that jurors' judgments about appropriate money damages varied wildly. This result was consistent with psychological studies that indicated that individuals evaluated outcomes more consistently when given a closed scale than when given an open scale. In the study, jurors were asked to rank their outrage and their intent to punish on a scale from 0 to 6 and then to award damages on an unbounded scale (as is usually the case in legal proceedings when damages are intended to punish rather than to compensate). The rankings were consistent because the scale was closed; the damages were inconsistent because the scale was open.

Critics of the first study pointed out that real jurors deliberate in groups before deciding on a monetary award; it is possible that deliberation eliminates extreme outcomes and results in more consistent awards. By contrast, in Sunstein *et al.* the monetary awards were statistically created from randomly matched aggregates. Schkade *et al.* therefore instructed the experimental subjects to deliberate in groups of six. Surprisingly, although the postdeliberation rankings of outrage and intent to punish were similar to the statistical rankings in the prior study, the postdeliberation awards exhibited even greater variance than the statistical awards (they were also more severe). The authors discuss a number of possible explanations for these results; one of the most interesting is group polarization—a phenomenon whereby, in a group, people tend to herd toward one extreme or the other, rather than the median of their original positions.

Law and Society

The "law and society" movement is older than the literatures on law and psychology, and law and economics, but has had less influence in the mainstream legal journals. The reason for this may be that law and society scholarship draws on many different academic traditions and thus lacks a unified theoretical core.

Contractual Relationships

Macaulay's 1963 study of business relations among firms that do business in Wisconsin is a landmark in law and society scholarship. Macaulay interviewed 68 businessmen and lawyers and asked them to describe how they use contracts to structure their business relations. He found that businessmen, to a surprising extent, avoided using detailed contracts and refrained from litigation if a dispute arose. Businessmen believed that too much emphasis on legal rights and lawyers, and too much planning in advance of possible disputes, can undermine the establishment of trust.

The main significance of Macaulay's study was its demonstration that the law on the books and the law in action can be very different. Although legal scholars had suspected as much, there had been no persuasive empirical support for this view and Macaulay's study showed that even sophisticated people who had access to legal advice frequently did not pay attention to their legal rights. Macaulay's work stimulated empirical scholarship of the legal system and especially the use of the survey to measure the law's effect on behavior. His influence has also been felt in law and economics, including the work of Ellickson (1991) and Bernstein (1992), who have followed Macaulay's lead in arguing that people frequently ignore, or are ignorant of, their legal rights and rely on social norms and informal groups to regulate their behavior.

The Distributive Impact of Litigation

In 1974, Galanter launched a long line of studies by arguing that wealthier individuals and business are more likely to win lawsuits than poorer individuals are. Studies of trial and appellate litigation, in the United States and other countries, have confirmed that the win rate is positively correlated with wealth and that businesses and governments win more frequently than individuals do. These studies have relied mainly on records of judicial decisions, which are widely available.

Many explanations have been proposed for this pattern. One theory is that the law is biased in favor of the wealthy. But there is no baseline for determining whether the law is biased or unbiased, and in any event when the law is changed in favor of the poor, the win rates do not change. Another theory is that wealthier people hire better lawyers. But better lawyers settle (or should settle) in order to save their clients unnecessary litigation expenses and they should take on harder cases. Thus, it is not clear whether wealthier people should win more often or instead should settle more often and litigate more difficult cases. A third theory is that wealthier individuals, and especially businesses and the government, are repeat players and are willing to fight harder in order to discourage others from bringing new suits against them and to establish favorable precedents.

Citation Studies

Legal materials have been available on computer databases for many years. Judicial opinions, statutes, scholarly articles, and similar sources can therefore be easily collected, converted into data, and analyzed with statistical methods. A new focus has been the use of citations to measure, and to determine the causes of, the influence of judges and scholars.

Judges play an important but poorly understood role in the legal system. The legal system is divided into federal and state law; the federal government and the state governments all have their own judiciaries. The federal system is divided into trial (district) courts, appellate (circuit) courts, and a court of last resort (the Supreme Court). There are hundreds of federal judges and thousands of state judges.

In 1998, Landes *et al.* focused on the federal circuit judges. Judges hear cases in panels of three (usually), and the senior judge on the panel chooses one of the judges to write an opinion for each case that they hear. The opinion is usually signed by the judge who writes it and is published. The opinion is binding precedent in the circuit and can be a nonbinding but persuasive authority for judges outside the circuit. If well-reasoned opinions are influential, then one would expect this influence to show up particularly in citations to the opinions by judges outside the circuit in which the opinions were issued. These judges do not have to cite a relevant extracircuit opinion because it is not binding; if they do so, the reason is likely to be that the opinion is persuasive.

Landes *et al.*'s database consisted of opinions written by most of the judges sitting on the courts of appeal in 1992. The question that interested Landes and his co-authors is what determines the level of "influence" of a judge, where influence is assumed here to be the frequency of citation. Citations, they argue, are a function of the judge's "capital"—his stock of opinions—and other judges' demand for that capital. Capital is a function of the judge's years of experience, whether he has retired, and so forth. Demand is a function of the judicial workload at any given time, the size of the circuit in which the judge operates (because each circuit has its own interpretations of the law, within-circuit citations are higher than inter-circuit citations), whether the judge has the power to assign opinions to himself (the chief judge of the circuit), and similar variables. The capital variable in the equation reflects the assumption that judges who work for a long time build up a reputation for writing good or bad opinions, and demand reflects the assumption that some opinions are more useful than others. The two variables are multiplied together in the regression equation.

Regressions confirm that citations increase with tenure but at a decreasing rate. Each new opinion builds up the capital stock but the earlier opinions depreciate at a rate faster than replacement. Retired judges and judges on senior status (a twilight before retirement) are cited less often than other judges. Chief judgeships do not increase citations. The regressions enable the authors to rank judges by comparing their residuals, that is, the fraction of citations that cannot be attributed to years of experience and the other independent variables. Circuits are also ranked for influence.

Next, the authors tried to determine the factors that explain influence, that is, the citation ranking. They collected demographic and other variables that might be relevant. Their findings are as follows: (1) Judges who cite their own opinions a lot are also frequently cited by other judges; perhaps this is because self-citers take more of an interest in writing opinions (many judges do not write their opinions but delegate to law clerks). (2) Judges in specialized circuits (for example, the Federal Circuit, which specializes in patent disputes) have less influence on judges outside their circuits, no doubt because their opinions have less relevance to the average case. (3) Judges with law degrees from Harvard University and Yale University have more influence than other judges; this may be because they are more intelligent, received better training when in law school, or benefit from networks. (4) The race and sex of a judge do not have an impact on his or her influence. (5) Academic achievement (honors) has little or no impact. (6) Prior judicial experience has little or no impact. (7) Conservative judges are no more influential outside their circuit than liberal judges, but are more influential within circuits. (8) American Bar Association ratings of judicial nominees were not predictive of influence, except that those judges who received the lowest rating were less influential.

Citation analysis has been heavily criticized. Citations are a crude proxy for influence and other variables that one might care about, and citation studies often seem to be driven by data rather than theory. Nonetheless, law enforcement depends to a great extent on judges, prosecutors, and other legal actors caring about their reputations, and the citation is, thus far, the most objective measure of this important variable.

See Also the Following Article

Expert Witness Testimony

Further Reading

Bernstein, L. (1992). Opting out of the legal system: Extralegal contractual relations in the diamond industry. *J. Legal Stud.* **21,** 115–157.

Cowan, C. L., Thompson, W. C., and Ellsworth, P. C. (1984). The effects of death qualification on jurors' predisposition to convict and on the quality of deliberation. *Law Hum. Behav.* **8,** 53–79.

Ellickson, R. C. (1991). *Order Without Law: How Neighbors Settle Disputes.* Harvard University Press, Cambridge, MA.

Gropp, R., Scholz, J. K., and White, M. J. (1997). Personal bankruptcy and credit supply and demand. *Q. J. Econ.* **112,** 217–251.

Kahneman, D., Knetsch, J. L., and Thaler, R. H. (1990). Experimental tests of the endowment effect and the Coase theorem. *J. Polit. Econ.* **98,** 1325–1348.

Kessler, D., and Levitt, S. D. (1999). Using sentence enhancements to distinguish between deterrence and incapacitation. *J. Law Econ.* **42,** 343–361.

Landes, W. M., Lessig, L., and Solimine, M. (1998). Judicial influence: A citation analysis of federal courts of appeals judges. *J. Legal Stud.* **27,** 271–332.

La Porta, R., Lopez-de-Silanes, F., Shleifer, A., and Vishny, R. (1998). Law and finance. *J. Polit. Econ.* **106,** 1113–1155.

Posner, R. A. (1998). *Economic Analysis of Law.* Aspen Law, and Business, New York.

Rachlinski, J. J., and Jourden, F. (1998). Remedies and the psychology of ownership. *Vanderbilt Law Rev.* **51,** 1541–1582.

Schkade, D., Sunstein, C. R., and Kahneman, D. (2000). Deliberating about dollars: The severity shift. *Columbia Law Rev.* **100,** 1139–1175.

Songer, D. R., Sheehan, R. S., and Haire, S. B. (1999). Do the "haves" come out ahead over time? *Law Soc. Rev.* **33,** 811–832.

Sunstein, C. R. (ed.) (2000). *Behavioral Law and Economics.* Cambridge University Press, Cambridge, UK.

Sunstein, C. R., Kahneman, D., and Schkade, D. (1998). Assessing punitive damages (with notes on cognition and valuation in law). *Yale Law J.* **107,** 2071–2152.

Lazarsfeld, Paul

Terry Nichols Clark
University of Chicago, Chicago, Illinois, USA

Glossary

contextual analysis Comparing patterns of individuals across different contexts (such as big and small cities) to measure distinct individual and contextual effects.

fourfold table/cross-tabulation Simple tabular presentations to quantify processes that have otherwise been handled casually.

panel study Repeated surveys of the same persons over time, to help specify causal paths.

postindustrial society A label signifying the paradigmatic revolution that Lazarsfeld and associates helped generate.

Paul Lazarsfeld and his many associates made multiple specific contributions to social science by cumulatively encouraging two paradigmatic transformations: the first was the joining of European theory with systematic empirical research, and the second was the shifting of focus from production and work to consumption and leisure, to understand postindustrial society. Lazarsfeld changed the social sciences. He might have worked on mathematically sophisticated issues with a coterie of like-minded associates, but instead collaborated with dozens of talented persons, some strongly nonquantitative. This makes his unique contribution harder to specify. Born in Vienna in 1901, he studied mathematics and social science at the University of Vienna. In America after 1933, he worked on survey research in New York and was professor of sociology at Columbia University until his death in 1976.

Research Overview

Major Contributions

Paul Lazarsfeld helped launch several new fields of social measurement and approaches to study them. Before Lazarsfeld, market research was anecdotal and casual. His techniques for large empirical surveys of consumers today define market research. He developed surveys to measure the policy views of individual voters, to assess personal friendships, and to chart other processes previously handled more intuitively. His books *The People's Choice* (1944) and *Voting* (1954) are the foundations of contemporary political behavior studies. Lazarsfeld refined survey methods for mass communications. Before him, many believed that radio and newspapers manipulated individuals and had huge impacts. These "mass society" arguments held sway with most intellectuals and commercial firms. He showed instead how media effects were generally more limited and operated differently.

In politics, product marketing, and mass communication, Lazarsfeld showed that direct messages from elites were seldom accepted by individual citizens, as many had suggested; rather, key impacts were indirect, often via "opinion leaders" who would talk with their friends, thus selectively accepting, rejecting, or adapting news, advertisements, and political messages. Such processes constituted a "two-step flow of communication"—first through the media, second through the personal contact—which Lazarsfeld documented with detailed analyses of neighbors discussing politics and women choosing groceries and clothes. He considerably strengthened social science methodology, by developing new techniques and writing about how to refine or transform older methods by more self-conscious analysis.

Although his Ph.D. was in mathematics, most of his methodological work was written in very clear, simple language, and aimed to change how social scientists and policymakers thought and worked. His success was impressive. His impact came often from finding a new, creative solution to a "hot" problem that others had addressed more casually. Many of his solutions were so elegantly clear that others could and did immediately adopt them, and extend them further. The mathematics and statistics used were the simplest possible for the task. For instance, to sort out distinct effects of media content, personal discussions, and other factors, Lazarsfeld developed the "panel study," reinterviewing the same persons over time to monitor change, such as during a political or advertising campaign. He reported differences in cross-tabulations, and analyzed turnover across cells.

In a paper on "The Art of Asking Why?," Lazarsfeld showed that simply asking "why" often gets a simplified response, but that a richer picture of processes often emerges if the process is studied and an accounting scheme of likely answers is developed and is used to structure probes. To analyze effects of several variables, Lazarsfeld showed how multicausal analysis was necessary. But he continually sought to transcend the simple, linear models (as in ordinary least-squares regression) by showing how to measure interaction effects (such as a third variable Z shifting the effect of X on Y) or contextual effects (such as Marx's suggestion that low salaries generate more worker discontent in large, as compared to small, factories). The methodological treatise by Lazarsfeld, *The Language of Social Research*, became popular in America as a guide for practitioners and students. With a former student, Raymond Boudon, the treatise was transformed into a theoretical–philosophical work in the French adaptation, *Le Vocabulaire des Sciences Sociales*. Lazarsfeld encouraged mathematical work in social science and developed "latent structure analysis," but such approaches went beyond most of his collaborators. His creative thrust was to claim large, new terrains and analyze them in a more self-conscious and methodologically explicit manner than did his predecessors. He showed how past simplifications brought misleading results. Unhappy that most history of social science considered only theories, he helped develop the history of empirical social research as a subfield. Most contributions by Paul F. Lazarsfeld were by-products of collaborative work with Robert K. Merton and many talented students and colleagues, first in Vienna, then at Columbia University.

Father of Postindustrial Society?

"In Russia the Revolution succeeded, so they need engineers; in America, the revolution failed, so we need Sociology." Here is classic Lazarsfeld: self-deprecating humor, the whiff of a secret agenda, an ideological program, and an immigrant's revolutionary commitment to build a new society. Consider one specific reading of Lazarsfeld's slogan: that sociologists, especially at Columbia, helped chart and explain the workings of postindustrial society—even if "postindustrial society" was not conceptualized until years after their major contributions. This is a broader formulation than Lazarsfeld proposed, but it clarifies his impact. The major counterinterpretation is that Columbia sociology was a handmaiden to capitalism. Lazarsfeld's neosocialist slogan directly contradicts the simple view that Lazarsfeld and Columbia "sold out" to American capitalism—as argued in various ways by critics, from C. Wright Mills to Alvin Gouldner to the Frankfurt sociologists.

In contrast to some critics, it can be posited that Marxism was incorporated into the Columbia amalgam of sociology from its very origins in the 1930s, and continued in ways often overlooked. For instance, *Marienthal* was Lazarsfeld's 1932 study of the unemployed in a depression-devastated community, detailing how persons out of work suffered psychological damage. Merton's 1937 *Science, Technology and Society* showed how modern science was driven ahead by the twin forces of technology (in a broadly Marxist manner) and the Protestant religion (broadly Weberian). Merton and Lazarsfeld's personal involvements with left political movements in their formative years were deep and intense, as others have detailed. Columbia sociologists, led by Lazarsfeld and Merton, helped create modern sociology through a continuous dialogue, albeit often latent, with Marxist themes and concepts. This holds in many areas, on examination of their shifts from past topics chosen for study (dress shoppers in Decatur, Illinois, rather than unemployed workers), or of their shift from a top-down focus in organizations to bottom-up cooptation. Core concepts were invented or redefined (e.g., from the proletariat to student activist, from politics as part of production to part of consumption).

Lazarsfeld's contribution may be framed with the concept of postindustrial society, first by identifying sources for the concept in subfields of Columbia sociologists after the 1930s. The gradually resulting framework generated a paradigm shift away from Marxist-inspired thinking, but this shift was largely "unannounced," in that elements of Marx continued in many Columbia studies. The big bang built on smaller "revolutions" in subparadigms, such as organization theory and mass media; together, they generated a deeper overall change. This is all the more intriguing because the label and conceptualization of "postindustrial" from Bell only came later, following much of the innovative Columbia work. Alternatives are charted in Table I, showing the specific concepts and their main competitors, Marxism and Individualism.

More generally, Lazarsfeld and the Columbia armory of ideas have an elective affinity with postindustrial society in ways that were not recognized or scarcely mentioned in earlier years. This is in good part because the concept of the postindustrial society crystallized only after the most vibrant years of Lazarsfeld and Merton. Similarly, Hegel's owl of Minerva took flight only as dawn neared. The label "postindustrial society" came

Table I A Core List of Elements Contrasting Columbia Sociology with Neo-Marxist and Individualistic Concepts[a]

Columbia/postindustrial society concept	*Neo-Marxist concept*	*Individualistic concept*[b]
Consumption	Production	Utility, preferences (more abstract)
Leisure	Jobs	Work and amenities
Consumers	Workers	Subsets of utilities, clusters of attitudes
Home	Workplace	Individual
Women and their families	Men and their work	Less attention to context
Personal influence, social interaction	Social structural characteristics (class, etc.)	Interaction
Citizen focused	System focused, e.g., capitalism, aristocracy	Individual/preferences/personality focused
Buying consumer products	Investing capital	Maximizing utility
Talking with friends to form opinions	Organizing class consciousness	—
Informal organization; unanticipated consequences	Class conflict	—
Organizational/management structure	Ownership of the means of production	—
Goal displacement; cooptation; subcultures	*Classe an sich* to *classe fuer sich*	—
Issue politics, issue specificity	Coherent party program	Cognitive consistency
More social liberalism, e.g., new women's roles	Fiscal/economic policy positions	Attitude structure
Voluntary associations	Vanguard party focus	—
Cross-pressures, role conflict	False consciousness	Cognitive dissonance
Pluralism	Power elites	—
Autonomous mass media	Class-controlled propaganda	—
Autonomous scientific community	Science subordinated to hierarchy	—
Students as political vanguard	Proletariat moving toward revolution	—
New class	Fordism/regulation theory	—
Knowledge research and development/ high technology	Manufacturing products	—
Rising professional autonomy of workers	Rising global monopolies, regulated by states	—
Weak unions and parties, strong individualism	Strong unions and class-based parties	—
Consumer-based indvidual aesthetics	Historical materialism	—
Democratic processes	Class responsiveness	—
Intellectuals/cultural creation	Class domination, surplus value	—

[a] Source: A decidedly flawed memory of a former Columbia student (T. N. Clark).
[b] Individualistic theories tend not to address some more social structural items, hence the column is sometimes left blank.

from two books by Daniel Bell, published in 1973 and 1978. Overlapping ideas were elaborated by Seymour Martin Lipset, Ronald Inglehart, and the present author's writings in *The New Political Culture* (Table II charts the main themes). Deeper than labels and specific studies are the prototheory, implicit hunches, and a prescient sensitivity as to how society worked—or what Weber called choosing the research topic. Lazarsfeld often operated with brilliant intuition. Later, Merton clarified the operation of identifying "strategic research sites." Choosing the precise topic and angle is often the single most critical aspect of a brilliant study, as the following examples suggest.

The Columbia synthesis built on elements of American society that distinctly differed from European society, with its peasantry, class, work, and party-defined patriarchal, authoritarian social structure. Instead, the new structure was driven by consumption, not production; by the household, not the job; by leisure, not work. Thus voting was not seen as "explained" exclusively by men and fathers working on an assembly line, but also by women and mothers, chatting with their neighbors about whom to vote for while listening to soap operas. These new participants in the system made decisions for political candidates following rules like those for buying Campbell's soup and, later, Mary Kay cosmetics. The core elements charted in Table I were refined in works such as those cited in Table II. These works comprise an exploration of only a few of the themes that illustrate the transformations wrought by Lazarsfeld and his collaborators.

Table II Contrasting Emphases in Alternative Versions of Postindustrial Theories[a]

	Bell				
Columbia/postindustrial society concept	*TCPIS*	*CCC*	*Inglehart*	*Lipset*	*Clark, NPC*
Consumption		×	×		×
Leisure		×	×		×
Consumers		×	×		×
Home		×			×
Women and their families		×			×
Personal influence, social interaction					
Citizen focused			×		×
Buying consumer products		×			
Talking with friends to form opinions					
Informal organization, unanticipated consequences					
Organizational/management structure					
Goal displacement, cooptation, subcultures					
Issue politics, issue specificity			×		×
More social liberalism, e.g., new women's roles		×	×		×
Voluntary associations			×		×
Cross-pressures, role conflict				×	
Pluralism			×	×	×
Autonomous mass media					
Autonomous scientific community	×				
Students as political vanguard		×		×	
New class	×	×		×	
Knowledge/research and development / high technology	×		×	×	×
Rising professional autonomy of workers	×		×		×
Weak unions and parties, strong individualism				×	×
Consumer-based indvidual aesthetics		×			×
Democratic processes				×	×
Intellectuals/cultural creation	×	×		×	

[a] The point of this table is merely to highlight, quite roughly, major differences in emphasis among alternative formulations of postindustrial society. The main references are Bell's *The Coming of Post-Industrial Society* (TCPIS) and *The Cultural Contradictions of Capitalism* (CCC), various works by Lipset, especially *Political Man* and *American Exceptionalism*, and by Inglehart (*Modernism and Post-Modernism*), and *The New Political Culture* (NPC) by Clark *et al.*

Discussion of Selected Core Concepts

Consumption vs. Production, Leisure vs. Jobs, Consumers vs. Workers, Home vs. Workplace, Autonomous Mass Media vs. Class-Controlled Propaganda

With support and encouragement from Frank Stanton, chief researcher and then president of the new Columbia Broadcasting Company, Lazarsfeld charted the rise of the media and how it related to average citizens. Many studies were published in *Radio Research,* which Lazarsfeld and Stanton edited. What they found in these first-ever serious media studies did not support the Adorno/Horkheimer/Marcuse Frankfurt Marxist view that the media organizations were capitalist tools to dominate and manipulate citizens. Lazarsfeld and Stanton instead suggested a limited, information-purveying role; citizen-shoppers used the media, but core views were seldom transformed by the media.

This "limited effects" interpretation of the media is considered a main finding of Lazarsfeld-inspired research. Yet it is often overdrawn. The media could have impact, in some situations. Indeed, in 1948, prefiguring a much-repeated theme, Lazarsfeld and Merton elaborated contextual characteristics that should enhance or suppress media impacts (monopoly of information, consistency with values, and personal contacts).

Columbia sociology and preeminently Lazarsfeld have been criticized for being opportunistic, responding to market demands, following the money, and consequently defending capitalism. This is too simple and deterministic. It ignores the fact that much if not most money for social science in the depths of the depression came not from corporate sources, but from the federal government—as judged by prefaces of major books by W. Lloyd Warner, Stuart Chapin, and others. Lazarsfeld did work on government propaganda studies during World War II.

The New York foundations had a long and strong tradition of supporting work on poverty, such as Lazarsfeld's *Marienthal*. The media supported polls, and *Life* magazine even underwrote *The People's Choice*. Why did Lazarsfeld not pursue such more established funding sources and research questions? The view that he "simply" followed the money illustrates precisely the sort of one-factor thinking that Lazarsfeld critiqued in his famous "The Art of Asking Why?," the main point of which is analogous to Marx's criticism of simple self-interest, income-maximizing interpretations, which he dismissed by labeling them *Benthamismus*.

Clearly, Lazarsfeld's fund-raising had a colorful and opportunistic flair—which he loved to flaunt in the right company. The simple critics were taken in by (or interpreted too literally) his *double entendres* and teasingly exaggerated bravado. Yet other smart persons at the time made other choices, perhaps equally opportunistic or rewarding—as the contrasts in Table I indicate. Lazarsfeld's uncanny instinct for capturing what was new and distinctive about American society, and its driving changes (radio, advertising, marketing research, citizen-oriented voting studies, etc.), led him both to propose new and innovative research on these topics and to work with foundation and corporate officials attracted by the cutting-edge quality of these concerns (including Frank Stanton at CBS, Bernard Berelson at the Ford Foundation, and Jeremiah Kaplan at the Free Press.)

Merton and Lazarsfeld did not analyze Hitler's or Roosevelt's speeches, but did examine Kate Smith's talk shows, her war bond sales appeals to average folks, and similar messages. This resulted in elevating Smith, a 1940s Oprah Winfrey, in a way elitist Europeans found repulsive. The media do not plead, they command, was the Frankfurt counterinterpretation. As a methodological by-product, the F(ascism) scale was generated, to capture the deep structure of authoritarianism that lay behind fascist dominance, yet that remains hidden perhaps in all of us. By contrast, Merton and Lazarsfeld developed and refined methods for recording emotion as people watched a documentary or short film, urging them, for instance, to use less meat in their cooking; a follow-up focus interview probed as to how and why people made their actual choices. Merton and Lazarsfeld sought to build a disciplined way of making researchers listen to and converse with their "subjects," and genuinely learn from them, not to use them simply to test or to illustrate theories.

A persistent subtheme of Lazarsfeld's media work was a critique of simple individualism, as a simplifying aspect of American ideology and misleading "explanation." For instance, Lazarsfeld wrote that "radio has so far been a conservative force in American life.... [In many radio stories or soap operas] all problems are of an individualistic nature. It is not social forces but the virtue and vices of the central characters that move the events along. People lose their jobs not for economic reasons but because their fellow men lie or are envious." This general skepticism about individual explanations persists in most Columbia sociology. Lazarsfeld was criticized by some as promoting atomistic views of society by using surveys of individuals. But he and others consistently distinguished their interpretations from the more classically individualistic perspective common among many psychologists, economists, and some political scientists then and later.

Organizational/Management Structure vs. Ownership of the Means of Production; Goal Displacement; Cooptation; Subcultures vs. Classe An Sich *to* Classe Fuer Sich

Weber studied the Prussian bureaucracy, elevating it as the ideal type of modern society. The specter that it would dominate led him to the "iron cage" metaphor. When he wrote *Politics as a Vocation*, he spoke of parties and their leaders—minimally of citizens or civic groups. Similarly, his student Robert Michels formulated the "iron law of oligarchy" in studying the leadership of the German Social Democratic Party. Lazarsfeld grew up in the heady air of Socialist Party political leadership and elite personal intrigue in Vienna. He not only knew the issues intimately; they drove much of his professional agenda in his early adult years. He did surveys of socialist youth groups, and sought to codify how to attract recruits and mobilize them effectively.

In America, Lazarsfeld turned to the extreme non-elite—in Elmira, New York or Decatur, Illinois—to study how housewives chose to buy red shoes and vote for Franklin Delano Roosevelt. Charting the cognitive maps and social contexts of average Americans to understand their decisions led to some revolutionary findings, contrasting with those of his Columbia colleague Robert Lynd (known for his best-sellers *Middletown* and *Middletown in Transition*). Lynd's second book relied heavily on neo-Marxist concepts and had much in common with Lazarsfeld's *Marienthal*. But in the first large-scale survey studies of voting and political behavior ever conducted, *The People's Choice* and *Voting*, Lazarsfeld and his associates contradicted the Lynds, the Marxist organizers, and the League of Women Voters in suggesting that citizen "apathy" (nonvoting and low participation in civic groups and parties) could make democracies more flexible. Unlike Weber's focus on Prussian bureaucrats and party leaders, Columbia researchers studied organizations less from the top than from the middle (where bureaucrats redefined goals and rationality) and the outside (in how organizations interfaced with their environments), leading to concepts such as Selznick's cooptation.

Organizational Subcultures and Their Autonomy vs. Ownership of the Means of Production

The work of Lazarsfeld and colleagues led to a new paradigm for organizational theorizing. By including corporations, governments, and universities, and looking for common themes, they transcended the "capitalist–worker" or "public–private" divides. Rather, they reported multiple sources of change and conflicts. The Columbia synthesis moved the social psychological theorizing about organizations from Harvard and Michigan into more structural coherence, by blending it with the European institutional traditions, and added a new subtlety and complexity. Merton stressed organizational subcultures and contextual variability, whereby the subcultures and tensions inside organizations led to and explained slacking soldiers or alienated government staff, such as postal workers.

The most dramatic American manifestation of the authoritarian leader in the 1950s was Senator Joseph McCarthy, whose House Un-American Activities Committee pursued labor union leaders, academics, and others suspected of "anti-Americanism." Many lost their jobs, especially in Hollywood. This Cold War virulent anti-Communism was seen as a clear product of capitalism by observers such as the Frankfort sociologists. But Lazarsfeld, always the skeptic, proposed a major national study to assess the impacts of McCarthy and other political constraints on academic freedom in universities and colleges. Did McCarthy really lead people to be more cautious in what they said and wrote and taught? He showed that universities resembled other organizations studied by Columbia researchers. The American academic community was not a simple top-down structure, not a factory-like hierarchy in which a board of trustees or even Senator McCarthy could cajole students to embrace capitalist theories and consume capitalist products. Rather, in *The Academic Mind*, Lazarsfeld, Felix, and Thielens sought to probe empirically what Parsons and later Habermas did theoretically: contrast the authoritarian, controlling specter of a McCarthy (or Hitler) with the egalitarian/collegial/decentralized ethos of the professional. This was a model for a new sort of workplace, one that deeply conflicts again with the Prussian/Weberian imagery. Lazarsfeld engaged David Riesman, a nationally renowned academic, skilled ethnographic observer, and openly leftist and anti-McCarthy figure, to review *The Academic Mind* and to reinterview some of the same academics across the country. Riesman did, and endorsed the main findings of the book: most academics were not scared of McCarthy and carried on their activities without fear. This added another piece to the picture of a paradigm change.

Contextual Analysis

The opposite extreme from the Prussian bureaucracy was the atomized individual of Michigan voting studies or neo-classical economist consumers. These theories have an elective affinity with the ideological individualism of the broad Protestant majority in political science and American politics. But Lazarsfeld and the Columbia group differed in locating the individual in a strong social context. They strategically chose research sites and methodology to highlight such contextual effects. They did not use national surveys of individuals like Campbell and Converse did at Michigan, or an ecological neighborhood voting method like Gosnell did in the Chicago tradition, which submerged the individual voter into the neighborhood mass. Rather, the genius of *Voting* and *Personal Influence* was showing how networks of friendship would bring filiation and encouragement toward voting for FDR or buying dresses. These constraints and subtle influences may have had more visibility to an immigrant Jewish observer who was self-consciously marginal.

Transforming Social Science

Lazarsfeld's largest contribution is the hardest to specify: he transformed social science. Sociology, economics, and political science in the 1930s had theoretical traditions and empirical traditions, but they seldom joined. The grand theories of social science were European. Public opinion, basic values, political support, confidence in government, and even the Gross National Product were unmeasured concepts in 1930. In America, Pitirim Sorokin and Talcott Parsons continued this European tradition at Harvard. Distinctly American work was problem-oriented and empirical. The center of social science was The University of Chicago in the 1920s and 30s. Its leaders in sociology, Robert Park and Ernest Burgess, did not seriously join their empirical work with European theories. Sociology changed at Columbia in the 1940s and 1950s, when Lazarsfeld, Merton, and talented students set a new tone in their many publications. They seriously joined the European theories with empirical work to create a new amalgam: "middle-range theories" were codified and tested using fourfold contingency tables. Previously disparate activities were merged, generating far more powerful results. Students from Columbia became professors at other leading universities, and in the 1960s the social sciences changed irrevocably. The persons and organizations mentioned here all helped. Although these are large claims, they are supported by at least one slim bit of evidence. The following excerpt is from a major theoretical work of two non-Columbia centers, Harvard and Chicago (*Theories of Society*, 1961, by Edward Shils, edited by Talcott Parsons, Edward Shils, and two Parsons students, pp. 1407–1408):

> *In the 1930s, American sociology underwent a marked expansion . . . It was helped by the Great Depression, by*

the influx of German and Austrian refugees . . . Research became more sophisticated through the development of a new statistical discipline, and through the improvement in interviewing techniques under the influence of psychoanalysis and the public opinion polling industry . . . Sociology—which was once an earnest, uncouth subject, a subject of the American Middle West, a dreary scholastic classificatory scheme of the German universities—has invaded the parlors of the most refined intellectuals of the United States and Europe.

Admiring the Columbia team, Parsons sought to recruit a "Lazarsfeld" (Sam Stouffer) and join his theory to empirical work. Chicago hired a series of Columbia graduates. In economics, econometric work increasingly joined abstract theory, encouraged by the National Bureau of Economic Research, which brought many academics to its New York headquarters. Political science was analogously revolutionized, by Robert Dahl and Gabriel Almond at Yale, V. O. Key at Harvard, Philip Converse at Michigan, and others. Lazarsfeld was a leading consultant to the Ford Foundation, which substantially funded such developments in the 1950s and 1960s in the United States and internationally. Lazarsfeld and Merton proposed to Ford a new center, which became the Center for the Advanced Study of the Behavioral Sciences in Palo Alto, California, fostering these approaches. In Europe, the European Consortium for Political Research (ECPR) was launched by Stein Rokkan, who collaborated with Columbia-trained Seymour Martin Lipset. The ECPR included just a few young turks in the 1960s; by the 1980s, it was the European establishment. International professional groups such as the International Sociological Association and its research committees, the International Political Science Association, and others brought social scientists the world over into contact with analogous developments. The tone and focus of the social sciences obviously shifted. Did Lazarsfeld and Columbia play a role in this? Why and how? Paul Lazarsfeld was charming and engaging when captivated by a new idea, as well as dynamic, manipulative, original, and stimulating. He sought to have global impact, and engaged many to join the effort.

The Intellectual Machine: Research Institutes and More

Columbia sociology sometimes looked more like the French model of the national clientelist university than the normal American model of departmental domination. How did Clark and Merton build such a vast intellectual empire, converting Columbia sociology into a global standard? Lazarsfeld said many times that to advance an intellectual agenda required a machine. His major examples were the research institutes that joined the methods of survey research, the money of government and commerce, and the intellectual ferment of the university. He delighted in recounting incidents illustrating his manipulative prowess; he would grin and laugh and tease as he cajoled others to join in. He evoked images of a political candidate, a mafia boss, a Wall Street banker, and Don Juan. He fascinated and entertained while deliberately shocking. He was a European prince who created his own court and intrigues.

What precisely did he mean by a machine? And how did it influence so powerfully? Though he often discussed research institutes as examples, he surely did not intend the impersonal, bureaucratic, efficient sort of organization that thrives on many American state university campuses. His archetype was rather the Bureau of Applied Social Research (BASR), and later Chicago's National Opinion Research Center (NORC) of the Pete Rossi era (1960s). How were they distinct? The term "machine" suggests an informal organization that permits exchange of resources in ways sometimes interstitial, if not illegitimate, for official organizations, such as governments or universities. Merton's famous essay on manifest and latent functions stressed the opportunity structure that political machines provide to ambitious persons who might not succeed by following normal rules.

Clientelism is a more general concept than machine, but overlaps in meaning. Clientelism refers to allocation of private goods, such as jobs or grants, by a patron to his clients, with an expected return of favors that reinforces patron leadership. In an officially universalistic context, the clientelist resource exchanges are thus quasilegitimate or illegitimate insofar as they shift decisions and reward patterns. The BASR's clientelism was clear. Like the Sorbonne patron, Lazarsfeld would allocate jobs, grants, and favors to his subordinates in princely manner, expecting total loyalty. His classic strategy was to win large grants from corporations or foundations, then siphon off funds to aid poorer projects, illustrating what his students labeled "Robin Hooding" (they would be paid to work on one project, but advance a second or third or fourth as well). At the Paris conference, others noted similar patterns. Merton termed the BASR a "commune, a family, a *Gemeinschaft*, a youth group." According to David Sills, Lazarsfeld said that "nepotism is my key to administration. Who can you trust more than your family to carry things out?" This dramatically self-deprecating language was more than chance. Merton noted that Lazarsfeld would say that he "overcharged clients," regularly "used nepotism," and "schemed and plotted" about future plans.

But a clientelist model is too simple to explain Lazarsfeld and the BASR. It was interpenetrated by the more universalistic norms of science, stressing new ideas, creativity, original publication, and corresponding international, market-driven rewards. Lazarsfeld sometimes leaned over to build in checks against personal bias, to counter the particularistic tendencies. He engaged students to help refocus and rewrite even work by stars such as Nicholas Rachevsky, if it could be improved. Lazarsfeld applied the same stringent criticism to himself, even if it meant that he missed the deadlines of foundations and book publishers. More than once he said that "when the book is published, will they ask did it meet the deadline? No! People will ask, is it a good book?" He distrusted mere reputation; he sought independent readings, again and again, by the young, by outsiders, to cross-validate and stimulate repeatedly. These various examples illustrate his powerful commitment to scientific universalism, the Mertonian norms. Even so, they do not suffice to explain his machine.

The early to mid-1960s were years of great affluence for social science research; it was much less necessary to engage in Robin Hooding. However, this also meant a shift toward more universalistic criteria for awarding grants, and put the BASR in more open, direct competition with institutes at other universities. Perhaps Lazarsfeld's shift of interest toward Paris and Europe in the 1960s was related to this shift in the U.S. rules of the game toward universalism. In his last years, he wrote about adding his own tradition to the history of social science. His place is now secure.

See Also the Following Articles

Playfair, William • Survey Design • Typology Construction, Methods and Issues

Further Reading

Barton, A. H. (1979). Paul Lazarsfeld and the invention of the university applied social research institute. *Organizing for Social Research* (B. Holzner and J. Nehnevajsa, eds.). Schenkman, Cambridge.

Bell, D. (1973/1999). *The Coming of Post-Industrial Society.* Basic Books, New York. (The 1999 edition includes a new foreword.)

Bell, D. (1978/1996). *The Cultural Contradictions of Capitalism.* Perseus/Basic Books, New York.

Boudon, R. (1993). *Paul F. Lazarsfeld: On Social Research and Its Language.* The University of Chicago Press, Heritage of Sociology Series, Chicago.

Clark, T. N. (1998). Paul Lazarsfeld and the Columbia sociology machine. In *Paul Lazarsfeld (1901–1976) La Sociologie de Vienne a New York* (J. Lautman and B.-P. Lecuyer, eds.), pp. 289–360. Editions L'Harmattan, Paris.

Clark, T. N. (2001). *The Construction of Post-Industrial Society: An Unannounced Paradigm Shift.* Prepared for presentation to the Paul Lazarsfeld Centennial Celebration and Conference, Columbia University, September 29.

Clark, T. N., and Hoffmann-Martinot, V. (eds.) (1998). *The New Political Culture.* Westview, Boulder.

Lautman, J., and Lecuyer, B.-P. (eds.) (1998). *Paul Lazarsfeld (1901–1976). La Sociologie de Vienne à New York.* Editions L'Harmattan, Paris.

Lazarsfeld, P. F. (1962). The sociology of empirical social research. *Am. Sociol. Rev.* **27**(6), 757–767.

Lazarsfeld, P. F., Jahoda, M., and Ziesel, H. (1932). *Die Arbeitslosen von Marienthal.* Herzel, Leipzig.

Lazarsfeld, P. F., and Spivak, S. S. (1961). Observations on the organization of empirical social research in the United States. *Inf. Bull. Int. Social Sci. Counc.* **19,** 1–35.

Lipset, S. M. (1981). *Political Man: The Social Bases of Politics.* Johns Hopkins University Press, Baltimore.

Merton, R. K. (1968). *Social Theory and Social Structure.* Free Press, New York.

Merton, R. K., *The Sociology of Science* (N. W. Storer eds.), University of Chicago Press, Chicago.

Merton, R. K. (1995). Opportunity structure: The emergence, diffusion, and differentiation of a sociological concept, 1930s–1950s. In *The Legacy of Anomie Theory, Advances in Criminological Theory* (F. Adler and W. S. Laufer, eds.), Vol. 6, pp. 3–78. Transaction Publ., New Brunswick, New Jersey.

Platt, J. (1986). Stouffer and Lazarsfeld: Patterns of influence. *Knowl. Society* **6,** 99–117.

Pollak, M. (1984). Projet scientifique, carriere professionelle et strategie politique. *Act. Recher. Sci. Social.* **55,** 54–62.

Shils, E. (1961). The calling of sociology. In *Theories of Society* (T. Parsons, E. Shils, K. D. Naegele, and J. R. Pitts, eds.), Vol. 2, pp. 1405–1451. Free Press, New York.

Simonson, P., and Weimann, G. (2002). Critical research at Columbia. *Canonic Texts in Media Studies* (E. Katz, J. D. Peters, and T. Liebes, eds.). Polity, London.

Learning and Memory

Henry L. Roediger III
Washington University in St. Louis, St. Louis, Missouri, USA

Jeffrey D. Karpicke
Washington University, St. Louis, Missouri, USA

Glossary

conceptual tests Measures of priming using retrieval cues that are conceptually related to studied items; these tests are considered to be conceptually driven because performance on them is affected by manipulating conceptual (meaning-based) processing.

cued recall A technique in which participants are provided with retrieval cues and are asked to recall studied items related to the cues.

explicit memory tests Measures of conscious, intentional recollection of specific learning events.

free recall A test in which participants recall as many studied items as they can, in any order they choose.

implicit memory tests Indirect measures of retention.

perceptual tests Measures in which participants are asked to identify or complete degraded stimuli; these tests are considered to be perceptually driven because performance on them is affected by manipulating perceptual processing.

priming Improvement in performance on a test that assesses retention indirectly; the measure of primary interest in implicit memory tests.

recognition tests Measures in which test participants are asked to decide whether they recognize test items from the study list, amid distracters or lures(a yes/no recognition test), or are asked to pick out the correct test item from a set containing distracter items (a forced-choice recognition test).

word fragment completion Test in which participants are presented with word fragments and are asked to complete them; priming is measured as the improved ability to complete fragments with words that had been previously presented.

Learning and memory can be measured in a variety of ways. Some of the prominent methods of measuring retention are based on several popular paradigms used in cognitive psychology. These are surveyed in this article; coverage is selective and other techniques exist for more specialized purposes. Different measures of memory, even for the same experiences, may not always agree in their assessment, and such dissociations among memory tests provide important insights into the proper understanding of human memory.

Origins of Memory Measurement

Achievements of Hermann Ebbinghaus

The measurement of learning and memory dates back to the seminal work of Hermann Ebbinghaus, who developed the first reliable measures of memory and published his original results in 1885 in his great monograph, *Memory: A Contribution to Experimental Psychology*. Ebbinghaus created lists of nonsense syllables (e.g., JUK-WAF-KOB, etc.) that varied in terms of their length. He measured the number of trials (or the amount of time) it took to learn each series of syllables, to accomplish one perfect recitation of the entire list, a measure he called original learning. After a retention interval that could last several minutes, hours, days, or even weeks, Ebbinghaus measured the number of trials (or the time) it took to relearn the list of syllables. The difference between measures of original learning (OL) and later relearning (RL) is known as the savings in relearning. For example, if it took 20 trials to learn a series of syllables perfectly during original learning and, later, it took 10 trials to relearn the series, the savings in relearning would be 10 trials. Ebbinghaus expressed retention performance as a savings score, defined as [(OL − RL) ÷ OL] × 100 (or 50% savings, in this example).

One beauty of the savings method, and one reason Ebbinghaus preferred it, was that retention could be measured independently from whether the person being tested could consciously recall anything from the original learning experience. Even if a person does not have any recollection of the original list, retention of the experience can be detected by the method of calculating savings in relearning. Thus, a decade before Freud proposed his ideas about unconscious memories, which led several generations of psychologists to wonder how unconscious memories could be studied empirically, Ebbinghaus had already supplied one promising solution to the problem: the method of savings in relearning.

Strength Theory and Measurement

One beguiling idea about human memory is that memories vary in terms of a unidimensional quantity, often referred to as "memory strength." Memories that can be easily recalled are thought to have greater strength, whereas those that can be recalled only with difficulty are thought to be weaker. Although (without further elaboration) strength theory simply redescribes the phenomenon to be explained, nonetheless, the notion of memory strength has been reified in several conceptions of memory and still holds currency in various forms even today. Strength theory also makes a strong prediction regarding the measurement of memory: if memory strength is the critical quality determining performance on any memory test, then different measures of memory should be correlated (even though they may vary in their ability to detect memories of different strengths). That is, although some measures may be more sensitive than others, all memory tests ultimately assess the same underlying quality of memory strength.

Consider the following simple example. A typical laboratory method of assessing retention involves the initial presentation of a list of words and the measurement of performance on one or more memory tests given at a later time. Consider five words (items A, B, C, D, and E) presented within a longer list of words. After studying the list, one group of individuals is given a sheet of paper and simply asked to recall as many of the words as they can remember, in any order they choose. Assume that B and D are recalled on this free recall test. A second group of individuals is given a memory test in which words that are associated with the studied words are presented as cues. For example, if "chair" had been a word presented on the study list, "table" might be given as a cue. The study participants might now recall more items on this cued recall test than they could on the free recall test. Finally, a third group of individuals is given a memory test in which items that had actually been presented on the study list (such as chair) are mixed in with other plausible candidate items that had not been presented (such as stool). In this recognition memory test, study participants are asked to identify the items that had been presented on the original study list.

The ideas behind strength theory are illustrated in Fig. 1. The different items presented on the study list (A through E) vary in terms of their strength, with items B and D being the strongest. According to strength theory, free recall is an insensitive measure of memory, because only memories with the greatest level of strength are recalled. Free recall tests require a great amount of strength to cross the conversion threshold for recall, indicated by the top dashed line in Fig. 1. Cued recall tests are more sensitive measures and are able to detect weaker memories, such as item C in Fig. 1. Finally, recognition memory tests are the most sensitive measures of memory strength; they are able to detect all items recalled in free and cued recall tests and one additional item (E) that was too weak to be detected by the other methods. In short, the principal assumptions of strength theory are that particular memories vary in terms of their strength and that methods of assessing retention differ only in terms of their sensitivity to memory strength.

This story is tidy but wrong. In fact, different measures of memory assessed across items, people, or other independent variables are not always positively correlated, as predicted by strength theory. In fact, measures of memory may be completely uncorrelated or even negatively correlated with each other. For example, consider the effects of word frequency (i.e., the frequency with which a word occurs in a language) on memory performance measured on two different memory tests. In free recall tests, high-frequency words tend to be better recalled

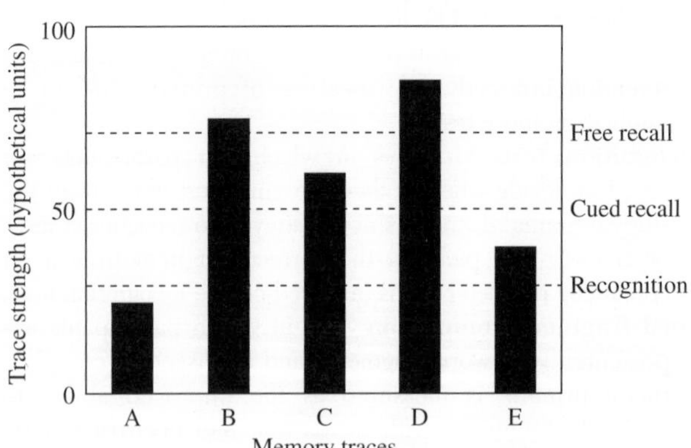

Figure 1 Strength theory. Different memory traces (A through E) vary in terms of their strength, and different measures of memory differ in their sensitivity to memory strength.

than low-frequency words are. Thus, it is reasonable to conclude that high-frequency words are stronger compared to low-frequency words. However, in recognition memory tests, low-frequency words better recognized than high-frequency words, leading to the odd conclusion that low-frequency words must have greater memory strength than high frequency words. Neither conclusion is correct. Instead, interactions between independent variables and performance on different memory tests indicate that strength theory is simply the wrong way to conceptualize human memory. Different measures of memory do not assess a single quality that varies along a single dimension.

Encoding/Retrieval Interactions and Their Implications

Processes of learning and memory are typically conceptualized as involving three stages: encoding, storage, and retrieval. Encoding is the initial registration and acquisition of information, storage is the maintenance of information over time in the nervous system (represented as a memory trace), and retrieval is the process whereby stored information is brought back into conscious awareness or otherwise affects ongoing behavior. Strength theory essentially proposes that encoding conditions will produce main effects on performance measured on different memory tests and will never interact with retrieval conditions, because different memory tests simply vary in terms of their sensitivity to memory strength. However, the literature on human memory is replete with examples in which encoding and retrieval conditions interact. The example mentioned previously, that high-frequency words are better recalled than low-frequency words are, whereas low-frequency words are better recognized than high-frequency words are, is one example of an encoding/retrieval interaction.

Larry Jacoby has designed compelling experiments demonstrating that two different measures of memory with great surface similarity can be uncorrelated or even negatively correlated. Participants in Jacoby's experiments were presented with lists of words under various study conditions and were given one of two different memory tests. One group of individuals was given a standard yes/no recognition memory test, in which they were presented with a long list of test words and were asked to determine which words had been previously studied. The other group of individuals was given a test that involved identifying words presented at very fast rates (around 30 msec per word). The proportion of words correctly identified was the dependent measure. Some of the words flashed during the test had been presented on the study list but other test words had not been previously studied. In this speeded word identification test, the improved ability to name the briefly flashed words that had been presented during the study phase is known as priming.

In one of Jacoby's experiments, the independent variable was the level of processing of words during the study phase. Students were presented with one of three questions that oriented them toward either the surface features of the target word (e.g., "Is the word in all capitals?"), the sound of the word (e.g., "Does the word rhyme with chair?"), or the meaning of the word (e.g., "Is the word a type of animal?") before the presentation of each target word (e.g., BEAR). These three different orienting questions manipulated the level of processing that individuals performed on each word. The effects of levels of processing on performance in the two different memory tests are depicted in Fig. 2. In the recognition memory test, the typical levels of processing effect was observed: individuals were best at recognizing words they had processed at a meaningful level and worst at recognizing words they had processed at only a surface level, whereas processing the sounds of the words produced intermediate recognition performance. In contrast, consider performance on the speeded word identification test, shown in the right panel of Fig. 2. In this test, priming was measured as the difference in performance between naming studied and nonstudied words. Although all of the priming scores were positive, indicating retention of the studied words, all three encoding conditions produced equivalent levels of priming! Levels of processing, which had such a profound effect on recognition memory, had no effect on priming. Although both tests were measuring retention of the same list of items, the two measures were completely uncorrelated in this experiment.

In another experiment, Jacoby demonstrated that measures of recognition memory and speeded word identification could even be negatively correlated. In this experiment, individuals studied a list of words under one of three different encoding conditions: they were either asked to read the target words in a neutral context (XXXX-cold), to read each word paired with its opposite (hot-cold), or to generate each target word given its opposite (hot-????). Thus, in all three conditions, participants said out loud the same list of target words, but the means of having participants produce the words differed dramatically. The effects of these encoding manipulations on performance in the two different memory tests are shown in Fig. 3. Although generating the target words produced the best performance on the recognition test and reading the words in a neutral context produced the worst performance (a finding known as the "generation effect"), the opposite pattern of results was observed in the speeded word identification test: reading the words produced better identification performance than did generating the words! The results of Jacoby's experiment demonstrate that two

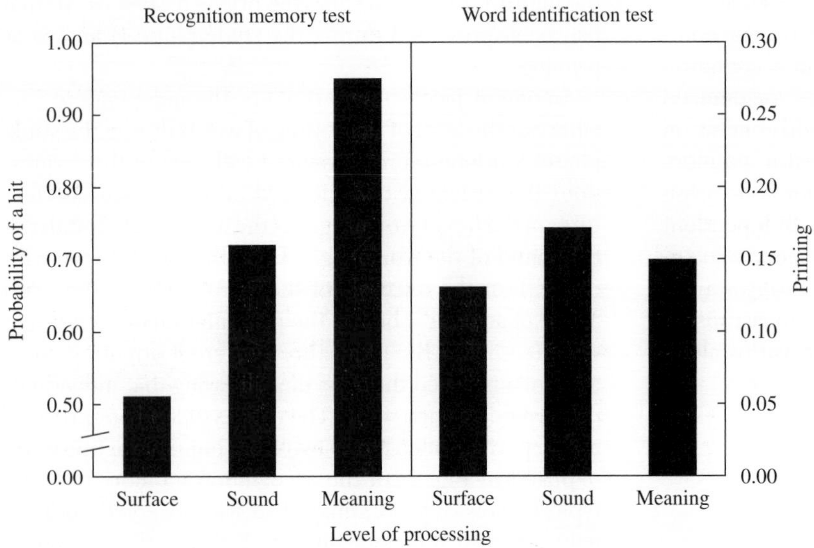

Figure 2 Levels of processing during encoding have a profound effect on recognition memory performance, but no effect on speeded word identification. The two memory tests are not correlated. Based on data from Jacoby and Dallas (1981).

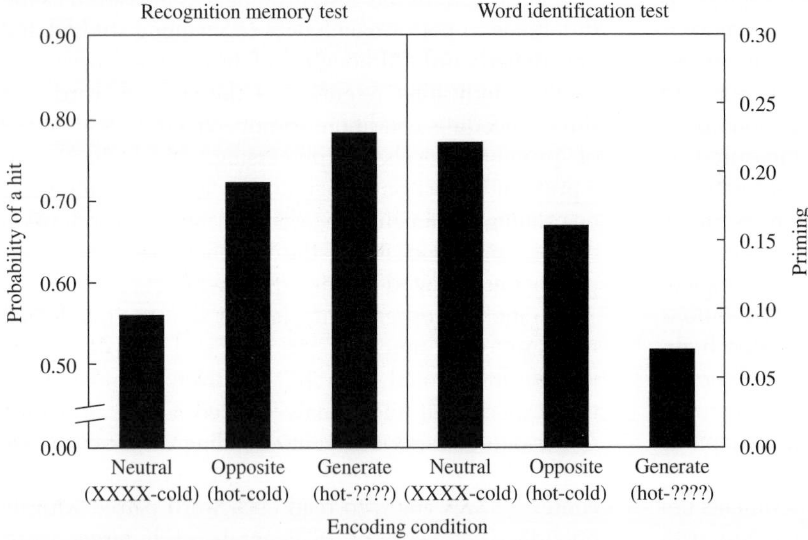

Figure 3 Generating words during encoding produced better recognition, compared to simply reading words (the generation effect). In contrast, reading words produced better performance on the word identification test, compared to generating words. The two memory tests are negatively correlated. Based on data from Jacoby (1983).

measures of memory that appear to be very similar on the surface may be negatively correlated with each other under some circumstances.

Interactions between encoding and retrieval conditions demonstrate that measures of retention can reveal positive, zero, or negative correlations with one another. These encoding/retrieval interactions have an important implication for understanding human memory: although the concept of memory is labeled with a single word, it is hardly a single entity. Many different types of memory exist, and there are several different valid measures of memory. Some of the most prominent ways to measure memory are considered in the following discussions.

Explicit Measures of Retention

One important distinction in the field of human memory is that between explicit and implicit measures of memory. Briefly, explicit memory tests involve conscious, intentional recollection. If you are asked to describe what you had for dinner two nights ago, you must mentally travel back in time and retrieve information about that specific event. Explicit retrieval involves conscious awareness of this mental time travel. Endel Tulving has referred to explicit retrieval as involving the use of episodic memory, a memory system that enables people to remember their personally experienced past. There are several differences between explicit and implicit measures of retention; in the next section, several different explicit tests commonly used in research on human memory are described.

Free Recall

In most explicit tests of memory, participants are exposed to a set of material on which they will be tested at a later point in time. The material can consist of words, pictures, sentences, stories, videotapes, and other types of data. In a free recall test, participants are asked to recall as many of the studied items as they can, in any order they choose. Because no overt retrieval cues are provided, they must rely on their own strategies in order to retrieve the items. Free recall is perhaps the most effortful explicit memory test.

Cued Recall

In a cued recall test, participants are provided with retrieval cues and are asked to recall the studied items related to the cues. Retrieval cues can have a high or low associative strength (a measure of their degree of association with the target words). For example, "table" might be a strong cue to retrieve the word "chair," whereas "glue" would be a weak cue in this case. A retrieval cue can also be a graphemic cue, in which a portion of the word is provided at test (e.g., "ta___ or ___le" or "t_b__"). Yet another type of retrieval cue is a phonemic or rhyming cue: participants may be told to recall studied words that rhyme with the cue words. For example, "bear" might be provided as a cue to recall "chair." Although these are the most common types of retrieval cues, others can also be developed.

Recognition Tests

Recognition memory tests are perhaps the most popular measures of explicit memory used in cognitive psychology. There are two basic types of recognition memory tests. In a free choice or yes/no recognition memory test, participants are presented with a long list of test words and are asked to say "yes" if they recognize a word from the study list (thus, they are free to say "yes" or "no" to each item). For example, if participants studied 100 words, they might be presented with 200 words during the test (the 100 studied words mixed in with 100 distracter words) and asked to make a yes/no response for each item. Two basic measures of recognition performance are obtained in this test: the hit rate (the probability of saying "yes" to words that were actually studied) and the false alarm rate (the probability of saying "yes" to words that were not studied). The false alarm rate can be interpreted as a measure of false recognition and can also be used to correct performance for guessing (by subtracting the false alarm rate from the hit rate). Although a yes/no recognition memory test can be thought of as a 2-point scale for judging recognition, the scale can also be expanded by asking participants to provide confidence ratings. For example, participants might be asked to judge each item according to a 6-point scale, ranging from 1 (sure the item was not studied) to 6 (sure the item was studied). Such fine-grained scales provide the researcher with more information regarding participants' decisions during the recognition memory test.

The other primary type of recognition memory test is the forced choice recognition memory test. In a forced choice test, participants are presented with several alternatives on the test (one previously studied item embedded among several distracter or lure items) and are required to choose the item that they think was presented in the study list. For example, participants might be presented with "chair table dresser lamp" and asked to choose the item that they studied. If all of the response alternatives are equally likely to have been studied, the guessing level can be determined depending on the number of alternatives. For example, in a two-alternative test, 50% reflects chance-level performance, whereas in a three-alternative test, 33% reflects chance-level performance.

Although recognition and recall tests are both explicit measures of memory, they do not always produce the same results. As mentioned previously, although people are better at recalling high-frequency words than low-frequency words, they are better at recognizing low-frequency words than high-frequency words. As another example, when adults of different ages are compared in their performance on a free recall test, older adults typically recall less than younger adults do. However, on recognition memory tests, older adults often perform just as well as younger adults do. These dissociations illustrate that recall and recognition memory tests measure different aspects of retention and cannot be considered equivalent.

Paired Associate Learning

Another popular method of studying memory is paired associate learning. In a paired associate learning test, participants are presented with pairs of items, such as knight–heaven, elephant–house, flower–camera, and so on. Later, they are given the left-hand member of the pair (e.g., knight) and are asked to recall the right-hand member of the pair (heaven). This type of paired associate learning test measures the forward association between the pairs of words that is formed during learning. Researchers can also investigate backward associations by providing the right-hand member (heaven) and asking participants to recall the left-hand member (knight). In general, recall of forward associations is better than recall of backward associations. Because forming associations among experiences is thought to be a basic mechanism of learning, paired associate learning has been investigated since the beginning of memory research, notably by Mary Calkins, in 1894. Note that the paired associate learning procedure can be considered a type of cued recall.

Serial Recall

Although paired associate learning has been used for over 100 years, serial recall is actually the oldest memory paradigm, first used by Francis Nipher in 1878 and by Ebbinghaus in 1885. In a serial recall test, participants are presented with a series of items (such as digits, letters, words, or pictures) and are asked to recall the items in the order in which they were presented, working from the beginning to the end of the series. Recalling a telephone number is an everyday example of a serial recall task: the digits in a telephone number must be remembered in correct sequential order. Thus, memory both for the items and for the order in which they occurred is critical. A more difficult variation on this task is backward serial recall, in which a person is presented with a sequence, such as 7923948, and is asked to recall the sequence in backward order (8493297). Backward recall is often used in memory assessment batteries, because people with brain damage, for example, show greatly impaired performance on this type of task.

Implicit Measures of Retention

In addition to the explicit measures of memory, there is an entire other class of tests, implicit memory tests; these are superficially similar to explicit tests, but measure retention indirectly. For example, consider an experiment in which some participants are presented with a list of pictures (with one being of an elephant) and other participants are presented with a list of words (the names of the pictures, so the word "elephant" is presented). Following this initial presentation phase, participants are told that they will now perform a different, unrelated task, and nothing is said about testing their memory for the list of items. In one such test, participants are presented with word fragments ("e_e_h_n_") and are asked to complete them (as in the game Wheel of Fortune). Some of the correct answers, such as "elephant," were presented on the study list, whereas others are not. The difference in the ability to complete studied versus nonstudied fragments is a measure of priming, the measure of primary interest in studies of implicit memory.

In the rest of this section, two main types of implicit memory tests, perceptual tests and conceptual tests, are described.

Perceptual Implicit Memory Tests

Perceptual tests present a puzzle or challenge to the perceptual system. Participants are typically asked to identify or complete a degraded stimulus, such as identifying a briefly flashed item or completing an object presented in a fragmented format. These implicit memory tests are considered to be perceptually driven because performance on them is affected greatly by manipulations of perceptual processing and less (if at all) by manipulations of meaning-based processing. Several examples are considered in the following discussions.

Word Fragment Completion

In a word fragment completion test, individuals are presented with word fragments and are asked to complete them, which is difficult if the correct answer has not been recently primed and much easier if it has been primed. In a typical word fragment completion experiment, the probability of completing a fragment that was not primed is about 0.30, and the probability of completing fragments after studying a list of words is about 0.60 (a 30% priming effect). However, after studying a series of pictures (such as a picture of an elephant), negligible priming effects are observed (0–5%), which indicates that even though the concept (elephant) may be primed, performance on a word fragment completion test depends on priming specific perceptual representations. In contrast, on explicit memory tests such as recall or recognition, pictures are remembered better than words are, a finding known as the "picture superiority effect." Changes in presentation modality (i.e., auditory or visual) also affect priming in word fragment completion. Visual presentation of words produces the greatest amount of priming, whereas auditory presentation produces reduced levels of priming. The effects of presentation modality on word fragment completion provide additional evidence that it is a perceptually driven test.

Word Stem Completion

In a word stem completion test, individuals are presented with the first three letters of a word ("ele______") and are asked to complete the stem with the first word that comes to mind. This test differs from word fragment completion because participants could potentially produce several different words from the same stem ("element, elegant, elevate, eleven," etc.). Priming in a word stem completion test is measured as the difference between the ability to complete primed word stems versus those that were not primed. Like word fragment completion tests, performance on word stem completion tests is also affected by perceptual manipulations.

Word Identification

Priming can also be measured in a word identification test. In a typical word identification test, participants are asked to identify briefly presented words, and priming is measured as the difference between identifying previously studied versus nonstudied words. Priming in word identification tests can also be measured under auditory presentation conditions, in which participants might be asked to identify words presented against a background of noise.

Other Perceptual Tests

There are several other implicit memory tests that are perceptual in nature. For example, participants might be presented with picture fragments and, following the same logic presented previously, asked to guess the identity of the picture. Likewise, there are several auditory implicit memory tests, in which test words are presented in noise or with portions of the words deleted. Because these tests are also affected greatly by manipulations of perceptual processing during encoding, they are classified as perceptual implicit memory tests.

Conceptual Implicit Tests

In conceptual implicit memory tests, participants are provided with cues that are conceptually related to primed items. Whereas perceptual tests are affected by manipulations of perceptual processing, conceptual tests are not affected by perceptual manipulations but, instead, are affected by manipulating conceptual (meaning-based) processing. Three examples are category association, word association, and general knowledge tests.

Category Association

In category association tests, participants are presented with lists of items (such as "elephant") during an initial phase and are later asked to generate as many instances from a category (such as "animals") as they can during a brief testing period (lasting 30–60 seconds). Priming is measured as the greater probability of producing words that had been presented earlier than words that were not presented. In category association and other conceptually driven tests, priming is increased when the words are initially encoded in a way that emphasizes their meaning rather than other aspects of the words (such as the surface features or sound of the words).

Word Association

Word association tests are very similar to category association tests. However, the retrieval cue in a word association test is an associate of the target word (such as "tusk"), rather than the name of a category. Priming in word association tests is also affected by manipulations of conceptual processing during encoding.

General Knowledge Tests

As the name implies, general knowledge tests require participants to answer general knowledge questions. For example, they might be asked, "What animal aided the general Hannibal in his attack on Rome?" Participants who had previously been presented with the word "elephant" will be more likely to produce the correct answer to this question, compared to participants who had not been primed with the correct answer. Once again, priming on this test is not affected by manipulating perceptual processing of the studied words (e.g., modality of presentation) but is affected by manipulating conceptual processing.

Other Measures of Memory

In addition to the measures of learning and memory already discussed, there are many more ways to test memory. Several tests have been designed to measure working memory capacity, which is the ability to hold information in mind and resist interfering information. One popular measure of working memory capacity is the operation span task, in which test participants are presented with a series of math problems followed by target words (for example, "$12 \times 8 = 96$, WINE"). Participants must read the problem out loud, say whether it is true or false, and then read the target word. After a series of 2 to 10 operations such as these, participants are asked to recall all of the target words in the order in which they were presented. The average length of the lists that are recalled in correct serial order is the participant's operation span. Measures of working memory capacity such as the operation span task are correlated with measures of general fluid intelligence and also predict performance on a wide variety of other cognitive tasks.

Other memory tests have been designed to measure autobiographical memory, which is a person's memory for their own life history. One popular technique for measuring autobiographical memory is the Galton–Crovitz cue word method, in which participants are presented with a word or phrase naming a common object or activity and are asked to recollect an experience from their lives related to this cue. For example, a person who is presented with the cue "nurse" may recall an event from when they were 5 years old in which they went to the hospital and were frightened by a scary nurse. One finding from research using this technique is that people in later life (50 years and older) most frequently retrieve memories from the period of their life lasting from late adolescence to young adulthood (roughly ages 16 to 25). Experiences from these formative years seem especially likely to come to mind.

There are also several standardized measures of memory used in educational testing and neuropsychological testing (for example, to assess whether a person with brain damage has memory impairments). The Wechsler Memory Scale and the California Verbal Learning Test are two widely used standardized memory tests. Tests such as the Scholastic Assessment Test (SAT) or even different measures of intelligence can also be considered as tests that, in part, measure recall of information learned during a lifetime (similar to the general knowledge tests).

Concluding Remarks

Although measuring human learning and memory may seem to be a straightforward enterprise at first blush, there is no single correct method of measuring retention. Instead, several diverse measures are used for different purposes to assess various aspects of a person's memory. Most importantly, different methods of testing memory for the same experiences can be completely uncorrelated or even negatively correlated with each other. These findings have important implications for our conceptualization of memory. Memory does not refer to a single, unitary property of the mind, and dissociations among measures of retention indicate that several different memory processes and systems work together to produce the complexity of human memory.

See Also the Following Articles

Behavioral Psychology • Cognitive Maps • Cognitive Psychology • Music Cognition • Spatial Cognition and Perception

Further Reading

Balota, D. A., Dolan, P. O., and Duchek, J. M. (2000). Memory changes in healthy older adults. In *The Oxford Handbook of Memory* (E. Tulving and F. I. M. Craik, eds.), pp. 395–410. Oxford University Press, Oxford.

Blaxton, T. A. (1989). Investigating dissociations among memory measures: Support for a transfer-appropriate processing framework. *J. Exp. Psychol. Learn. Mem. Cognit.* **15,** 657–668.

Calkins, M. W. (1894). Association: I. *Psychol. Rev.* **1,** 476–483.

Conway, M. A. (1996). Autobiographical memory. In *Memory* (E. L. Bjork and R. A. Bjork, eds.), pp. 165–194. Academic Press, San Diego.

Craik, F. I. M., and Tulving, E. (1975). Depth of processing and the retention of words in episodic memory. *J. Exp. Psychol. Gen.* **104,** 268–294.

Ebbinghaus, H. (1964). *Memory: A Contribution to Experimental Psychology* (H. A. Ruger and C. E. Bussenius, trans.). Dover, New York. (Original work published in 1885.)

Engle, R. W. (2002). Working memory capacity as executive attention. *Curr. Dir. Psychol. Sci.* **11,** 19–23.

Freud, S., and Breuer, J. (1960). *Studies on Hysteria* (J. Strachey, trans.). Avon Books, New York. (Original work published in 1895.)

Gregg, V. (1976). Word frequency, recognition and recall. In *Recall and Recognition* (J. Brown, ed.), pp. 183–216. Wiley, New York.

Jacoby, L. L., and Dallas, M. (1981). On the relationship between autobiographical memory and perceptual learning. *J. Exp. Psychol. Gen.* **110,** 306–340.

Jacoby, L. L. (1983). Remembering the data: Analyzing interactive processes in reading. *J. Verbal Learn. Verbal Behav.* **22,** 485–508.

Nipher, F. E. (1878). On the distribution of errors in numbers written from memory. *Trans. Acad. Sci. St. Louis* **3,** ccx–ccxi.

Roediger, H. L., Marsh, E. J., and Lee, S. C. (2002). Varieties of memory. In *Stevens' Handbook of Experimental Psychology, Third Edition, Volume 2: Memory and Cognitive Processes* (D. L. Medin and H. Pashler, eds.), pp. 1–41. Wiley, New York.

Tulving, E. (1983). *Elements of Episodic Memory.* Clarendon, Oxford.

Weldon, M. S., and Roediger, H. L. (1987). Altering retrieval demands reverses the picture superiority effect. *Mem. Cognit.* **15,** 269–280.

Libraries

John Carlo Bertot
Florida State University, Tallahassee, Florida, USA

J. T. Snead
Florida State University, Tallahassee, Florida, USA

Glossary

activities The library services/resources (e.g., licensed resources availability, story hours, training sessions) actually generated by inputs.

evaluation The process of determining or setting a value or amount.

evaluation approach The framework or methodology used for evaluative purposes.

indicators Also known as performance indicators or performance measures; used to measure the effectiveness and efficiency of library resources and services.

inputs The resources that libraries invest (e.g., money, staff, workstations, and on-line commercial databases).

outcomes The benefits from and/or changes in knowledge, skills, or behavior that library users gain after involvement with library resources, services, or programs.

outputs The number of services/resources generated from library investments (e.g., number of public-access workstations, number of databases licensed, and print material purchased).

service quality The evaluation of how well a library provides a service or program.

Social measurement in libraries involves the collection of evaluation data through social science methods. The goal is to determine the extent to which resources utilized in the management, planning, and presentation of collected sources of information, programs, and services by libraries meet the specific needs of a broad range of library users.

Introduction

Libraries in the 21st century exist within a complex and rapidly changing environment. Library services and resources are shifting increasingly from the traditional brick-and-mortar setting to one that includes network-based services, creating a hybrid library operating environment. This new environment includes services such as material lending, interlibrary loan, reference, and instruction. It also includes programs delivered and available via the Web and other Internet-based technologies; the creation of digital collections; access to on-line databases, books, and other content; and services such as digital reference.

With the growing use of technology in the development of library services and resources, patrons use libraries in what has been coined as an "anytime, anywhere" atmosphere. Access to and availability of library resources and services has changed from the limiting hours of operation within a traditional setting to anytime of the day and from anywhere a patron has access to a library's on-line presence. The trend within libraries today is a steady increase in the volume of resources available electronically from within the library and from geographically dispersed locations. At the same time, however, libraries continue to provide building-based services and resources. This dual operation mode creates an evaluation environment in which libraries need to assess both their traditional and their networked resources and services from multiple perspectives. Indeed, though libraries have a long tradition of planning and evaluation initiatives that employ multiple techniques and strategies, the networked environment requires librarians to learn new ways to apply traditional evaluative strategies and to develop new, specific approaches to assess network-based resources and services.

A key issue facing researchers, library managers, and others in this context is the determination of the extent to which library services, resources, or programs meet the information needs of a wide range of library users, including on-site and remote users. Libraries have a history of evaluating library activities through a number of research methods (surveys, focus groups, interviews, and systems-based data collection involving circulation records). In using such methods, librarians and researchers adopt a number of evaluation frameworks to assess whether library services/resources meet user information needs and expectations. In the following discussions, the ways in which libraries evaluate library services, resources, and programs are explored.

Social Change in Libraries

Historically, the primary role of the library has been to function as an information collection center for dissemination and use purposes. Materials have been typically collected and services developed for use by patrons and for archival or historical purposes. Essentially, librarians (1) determined what materials to collect and archive within these collections and how to do so; (2) were responsible for providing the expertise and guidance for use of these collections by patrons; (3) were instrumental in developing structures for the presentation and ordering of the materials; and (4) developed services for the delivery of materials, for training, and for managing the collections. During the past three decades, however, many changes have occurred within the library environment. The following changes have affected how librarians function in this collection and development process for the presentation of materials and services:

- Development of user-centered evaluative strategies within the research community.
- Development of professional librarian degree programs that focus on delivering user-based library services and resources.
- Evolution of information-seeking behavior of users to reflect a diversity of information resources and services from a number of access points.
- Increased availability and use of technology, development of a networked environment, and increased impact of the Internet, which has affected the information-seeking behavior of users.

Additionally, each of these areas is interrelated, creating a cumulative impact on libraries, their resources and services, and the communities that they serve.

Changing Role of Libraries

During the 1970s, evaluation within libraries underwent a shift in perspective. Understanding libraries from the library point of view shifted to understanding libraries from the user perspective. In 1973, Douglas Zweizig conducted a study that focused on the role of libraries in the lives of adult users. This study evaluated how library resources and services affected the users of the resources and services—the patrons. The results of this study and others like it led to the recognition by a growing number of researchers of the need for the development of user-centered evaluation strategies of library collections and services from a user perspective, as well as from the library's perspective.

Prior to 1980, most of the complex research conducted within a library setting was conducted by librarians and a select few professional researchers. Library staff members acted as intermediaries for library users and directed and instructed these users in the use of the library's resources and services. Patrons were generally dependent on libraries and their staff for the fulfillment of more complex research needs, particularly for access to exclusive and expensive databases. During the 1980s and continuing into the 1990s, however, the introduction of personal computers and the digitization of resources changed the way patrons could access information within the library setting. Patrons learned to use digitized resources to conduct research, and their dependency on library staff decreased over time as users developed personal skills in the use of technology to access information directly. The evolution of the Internet throughout the 1990s expanded access to information for library patrons by providing access from a growing number of access mechanisms and locations. Patrons no longer needed to go to a library or to consult as often with a librarian to access many of the library's resources. This change in access to resources also signaled a change in the information-seeking behavior of patrons.

Technology and the Development of Resources

With the development of the Internet, library web sites began to include remote resources developed and located outside the library's primary collections, along with links to other sources of information available via the Internet. Libraries made the following changes:

- Formed consortiums with other libraries to share databases and other resources in an effort to control costs of maintaining and developing collections.
- Subscribed to databases maintained outside the library's collections and maintained by vendors.
- Expanded Internet access for their patrons by increasing the number of workstations.

• Expanded the scope and use of their web sites as portals to other sources of information, such as federal, state, and local government web sites.

• Expanded access to a variety of information resources and services available via the Internet for many library patrons.

Technology and the development of the Internet have served to enhance information dissemination by creating a medium that effectively and efficiently delivers resources to library patrons located within libraries and from remote locations.

Challenges Faced by Libraries due to Changing Roles and Technology

Operating in a dual environment in which many of the traditional physical services and resources are offered alongside Web-based services and resources, 21st century librarians find themselves in need of reevaluating their role as a central repository for information services, resources, and programs. As the roles of libraries change, new challenges arise for librarians. These challenges include the presentation of traditional and Web-based collections, services, and programs by means of a web page; the need for software that integrates multiple databases and applications; the need to balance expenditures between physical resources and services and digital resources and services; the development of various policies, such as privacy and security, created by the on-line environment; and changes in the behavior of patrons due to the development of a dual environment—the traditional and the networked. Librarians recognize these challenges and attempt to meet many of them through the use of planning and evaluation efforts.

Planning, managing, and implementing collections, services, and programs may also be affected by other factors as well, such as meeting the needs of multiple stakeholders; weighing quality of resources and services against quantity; addressing issues of accountability to staff, library volunteers, patrons, boards of directors, and in some instances organizations offering funding; and developing evaluative measures and approaches to understand the effects of planning, managing, and implementing collections, services, and programs. Together, these challenges form the basis for library evaluation activities through a number of methods and approaches.

Evaluative Strategies in Libraries

Libraries use a variety of approaches for the collection of data and statistics, and various data standards have been created and agreed on for the collection of a number of the usage-based statistics. For example, the National Information Standards Organization (NISO) has the NISO Z39.7 *Library Statistics* standard that provides data elements and definitions for U.S. libraries. The International Standards Organization (ISO) has the ISO *Standard on Library Statistics* (ISO 2789) and the *Standard on Library Performance Indicators* (ISO 11620). Also, individual library organizations such as the Association of Research Libraries (ARL), or state or national library agencies, agree to a number of library use statistics to collect and report on an annual basis. Use of these approaches alone, however, is not sufficient to offer all the needed answers regarding library services and resources in general, and the management of such resources and services in particular. Michael Buckland suggests that library administrators must identify problems or decisions that need solutions and prioritize them; determine what areas within a library are affected; determine if research is the answer to the problem or decision; determine what research needs to be done to provide potential solutions to the problems and the potential effectiveness of the research; and link what they want to know with specific evaluative approaches.

Today's libraries are often faced with decisions that require timely results; issues of accountability in the use of diminishing funding are ever present, and simply conducting more research is not always the answer. Managing and planning evaluation have become imperative in a rapidly changing technological environment, and identifying areas that need evaluation has become the real challenge. The traditional approach of turning to research when problems arise or when there is a need to make decisions is still a viable approach. The addition of planning and developing an overall evaluative scheme, however, enhances the evaluative process. Identifying the focus from specific perspectives in this process recognizes the need to understand a complex environment. Approaching evaluation as an overall process is not new either. An evaluative process that encompasses many areas of a library's functions describes the evaluative evolution that has already occurred within libraries over the past three decades. Incorporating a management plan into the evaluative approaches enhances evaluation efforts.

Evaluation

The primary purpose of conducting research using evaluative approaches in a library setting is twofold: (1) to understand user interaction with library resources and services and (2) to capture data that inform the planning, management, and implementation of library resources and services. Integrated research, evaluation, and planning efforts, through various measurement approaches and methods, can assist libraries in efficiently and effectively developing, implementing, and changing resources and services that meet user information needs over time.

They can also provide an understanding of the broader social context of libraries from a user perspective.

Evaluative Approaches

Evaluative approaches are difficult to define or even to standardize. Each evaluative approach typically offers potential information, based on collected data, particular to a specific area of focus within a library. The area of focus may be broad in scope or defined narrowly for a specific task within a specific setting. Also, evaluative approaches tend to be tailored to particular needs of an organization; to be linked to available time and funding; to be limited by scope and breadth of application due to funding, planning, etc.; and to be determined by direction that ranges from what libraries collect historically to immediate learning needs regarding library services, resources, and programs. Data and statistics captured due to the evaluative effort of an approach may be qualitative or quantitative, descriptive, anecdotal or definitive, collected using traditional manual methods, or tabulated electronically. Whatever approach is used, the guiding principle for researchers is to answer questions such as "what do libraries need or want to know?" through an evaluation planning process within a library setting.

Library evaluation activities can be complex and include a number of factors throughout the process. In general, however, library evaluation centers on three key components (see Fig. 1):

1. Inputs. These are the resources that libraries invest (e.g., money, staff, workstations, on-line commercial databases).
2. Activities. These are the library services/resources that the inputs actually generate (e.g., licensed resources availability, story hours, training sessions).
3. Outputs. These are the number of services/resources generated from library investments (e.g., number of workstations, number of databases licensed, print material purchased, number of training sessions).

These three components form the basis for essentially all library evaluation strategies, because they provide vital baseline data regarding costs, investments, services, and resources.

Types of Evaluative Approaches

There are many approaches used to evaluate library resources and services from multiple perspectives, and the approaches may be library-centered or user-centered. Each approach is part of an evaluative process that includes planning, data collection, and evaluation as components of the evaluation. For purposes of this discussion, evaluative approaches are briefly presented within four broad areas based on the inputs, activities, and outputs: outputs assessment, performance measures, service quality, and outcomes assessment (see Table I). Each of these areas represents multiple approaches. The application of an approach may be broad in coverage or limited and specific. The approaches are malleable. Researchers modify each to fit specific needs and to answer questions based on decision-making needs, in the presentation of resources or services, and on particular perspectives. Library-centered approaches evaluate the presentation of resources and services with an emphasis on efficiency and effectiveness. User-centered approaches evaluate the quality of the presentation of resources and services and the inclusion of the needs of users (or patrons) in accessing resources and services, and may include the library community in general within the approach or may target specific stakeholder groups.

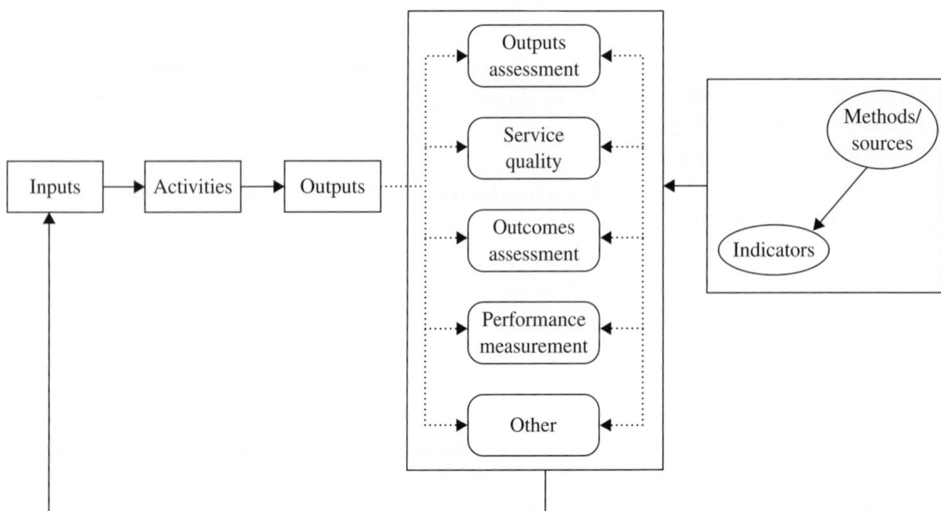

Figure 1 Library services and assessment frameworks.

Table I Overview of Four Broad Areas of Evaluative Approaches

Evaluation approach	*Description*	*Examples of evaluative practices*	*Applications*
Outputs assessment	Collection of counts from use of resources, services, or programming	1. Collection of traditional counts, e.g., reference, circulation, etc. 2. Focus groups 3. Interviews	1. Evaluation of resources, services, and programs 2. Planning
Performance measures	Developed for evaluating the presentation and/or delivery of specific library resources, services, or programs	1. Availability studies 2. Usability studies 3. Web page analysis 4. Content analysis 5. Functionality analysis	1. Usability of resources, services, or programs 2. Availability of resources 3. Determine efficiency or effectiveness of presentation of resources, services, or programs, etc.
Service quality	Developed to determine the overall quality of both traditional and network-based resources and services	1. ServQual 2. LibQual+ 3. Balanced scorecard 4. Best practices 5. Benchmarking	1. User satisfaction with library services 2. Library staff/management appraisal and/or desired level of service provision
Outcomes assessment	Developed to assess the effects of programming on patrons in terms of benefits to patrons	1. Outcomes as a product of programming 2. Outcomes as the effect of programming	1. As a product, initial measurable affect of programs on patrons 2. As an effect, initial to long-term evaluation of measurable benefits for patrons based on specific programming

Outputs Evaluation

Outputs assessments typically involve the identification of the number of library activities in which patrons engage (e.g., number of database sessions, number of database items examined, and number of training sessions conducted). They may also, however, include data that are qualitative in nature, such as the results of focus groups and interviews. Outputs are collected to determine the usage of library resources and services and as part of a library's planning process. Table II includes examples of outputs evaluation techniques.

Traditionally, libraries have collected output data in many forms from reference and circulation departments, facility usage, etc. With the advent of networked resources and services, however, outputs today include usage statistics of the networked environment that include data and usage statistics from digital reference services, database article downloads, remote visits to library web sites, and others. Typically, these on-line data and usage statistics are collected using electronic means. Electronic means of collection include data from log files that track and document the information-seeking behavior of users; network traffic statistics that offer data on where users originate, the browsers used, the files accessed, and other data; and use of databases that can be tracked from statistics gathered directly from library-developed databases and from statistics supplied by vendors of databases. As technology continues to evolve, the development of electronic means to collect outputs will evolve as well.

Performance Measures

Performance measures (also known as performance indicators) have a long history within the tradition of library research. They are used to measure the effectiveness and efficiency of library resources and services from both the library and the user perspectives. These forms of measures are versatile and changeable, determine efficiency and effectiveness, offer measures of satisfaction, and are used to determine needs of users (see Table III). Performance measures include availability and usability studies and studies utilizing focus groups and interviews; with the evolution of electronic presentations, they also include content analysis, web page analysis, and functionality testing. Performance measures developed for measuring impacts of physical resources and services are often adaptable to the networked environment and may be inclusive of outputs evaluation counts and approaches. Examples of performance measures include cost per item circulated,

Table II Overview of Outputs Evaluative Approaches

Evaluation approaches	*Description*	*Examples of types of data collected*	*Applications*
Tradition counts	Counts collected by physical means	1. Reference statistics 2. Circulation statistics 3. Library patron counts	Used to determine usage of library resources and services
Focus groups and interviews	Typically consists of 1–10 individuals and used to collect information in the form of opinions, perceptions, concerns, and experiences	1. Qualitative data 2. Anecdotal data 3. Quantitative data	1. Planning 2. Exploration 3. Evaluation 4. Assessment 5. Description
Network statistics	Counts collected electronically	1. Web log file statistics 2. Network traffic statistics 3. Database use statistics 4. Vendor statistics	Used to determine usage of library electronic resources and services

Table III Overview of Performance Measures

Evaluation approach	*Description*	*Examples of types of data collected*	*Applications*
Performance measures	Developed for evaluating the presentation and/or delivery of specific library resources, services, or programs	1. User-centered 2. Library-centered statistics 3. Technology related statistics	1. Usability of resources, services, or programs 2. Availability of resources 3. Determine efficiency or effectiveness of presentation of resources, services, or programs, etc. 4. Identify needs, strengths, and weaknesses of resources and services

items downloaded per registered borrower, and correct answer fill rate.

Service Quality

In general, service quality is an evaluation of how well a library provides a service, resource, or program. Service quality approaches include evaluation from the library and user perspectives, of libraries as a field, and of the library as an institution (see Table IV). Approaches used to determine service quality saw rapid growth during the 1980s with the shift to user-centered research and with the development of electronic resources and services. Approaches developed in the business environment such as best practices, benchmarking, customer satisfaction assessment tools (e.g., ServQual), and others were adapted for use in a library environment in the measuring of service quality. ServQual was developed specifically to measure quality of business services based on perceptions, desires, and a minimal level of expectation of consumers. LibQual+ was developed specifically to measure satisfaction in the quality of library services based on perceptions, desires, and a minimal level of expectation of users.

More recently, libraries have applied the balanced-scorecard approach to evaluating library services. The balanced-scorecard method determines overall organizational performance along four dimensions—financial, customer, internal, and innovation/learning dimensions. This approach provides libraries with an overall assessment technique that involves the multiple evaluation frameworks of outputs, service quality, and outcomes.

Outcomes Assessment

Outcomes assessment is relatively new to library evaluation. This evaluation approach seeks to determine the impact of library resources and services on the users of library resources and services. In particular, outcomes assessment seeks to determine the benefits or changes in knowledge or skill level, behavior, attitudes, or any change that may be seen as a benefit for the participants. As a product, outcomes are immediate measurable benefits for users with potential long-term effects. As an evaluative approach, a large body of work is available from the

Table IV Overview of Service Quality Evaluative Approaches

Evaluation approaches	*Description*	*Examples of types of data collected*	*Applications*
Service quality (ServQual)	Library-centered approach developed to determine library service quality or effectiveness in the presentation and/or delivery of specific library resources, services, or programs	Quantitative data of library performance based on patrons' perceptions, desires, and minimum expectations of five ServQual dimensions: 1. Tangibles 2. Reliability 3. Responsiveness 4. Assurance 5. Empathy	1. Strategic analysis 2. Gap Analysis 3. Input analysis 4. Production capability 5. Determine efficiency of resources, services, and programs
Library quality (LibQual+)	User-centered approach developed to determine library service quality or effectiveness in the development, presentation, and/or delivery of specific library resources, services, or programs based on the wants and needs of users	Quantitative data of user-centered wants and needs of library performance based on patrons' perceptions, desires, and minimum expectations	1. Output analysis 2. Outcomes analysis (where outcomes are measurable results) 3. Results targeted for benchmarking 4. Long-range planning
Balanced scorecard	Developed to balance past measures of success with future measures of success based on four dimensions—financial, customer, internal, and innovation/learning dimensions	Qualitative and quantitative data collected by means of performance measures and outputs	1. Planning for future services or programs 2. Financial, customer, internal, and innovation/learning dimensions 3. Strategic planning at an organizational level
Best practice and benchmarking	The process of initiating industry best practices in developing standards or benchmarks to gauge future developments or practices	Qualitative and quantitative data collected from products, processes, programs, etc.	1. Improve efficiency and effectiveness of services and programs 2. Future strategic planning 3. Identify user-centered quality programs and services

fields of education and sociology in which outcomes are typically measurable results of interventions or programs. Table V presents selected examples of outcomes assessment strategies. When viewed as an effect, the measurable change is part of the assessment process in determining the initial to long-term impact of specifically developed programs on participants of the programs. Developed programs are designed in terms of institution goals or standards to create benefits for participants, and performance measures are used within the programs to measure the differences produced by the programs.

Summary of Evaluative Approaches

Evaluative approaches are developed to answer the questions of what libraries need or want to know regarding their resources and services (see Fig. 2). A library's need/desire to know may be influenced by a number of factors, including internal and external stakeholders such as library management, governing boards, or other community-based stakeholders. To meet these data needs, evaluation activities within libraries often use multiple assessment strategies and approaches, because no single approach is likely to

Table V Overview of Outcomes Assessment

Evaluation approaches	*Description*	*Examples of types of data collected*	*Applications*
Outcomes assessment	Developed to assess the initial to long-term effects of programming on patrons in terms of benefits to patrons such as changes in skills, knowledge, or behavior	1. Outcomes as a measurable qualitative product of programs 2. Outcomes as the qualitative effects of programming	1. As a product, initial measurable affect of programs on patrons 2. As an effect, initial to long-term evaluation of measurable benefits for patrons based on specific programming

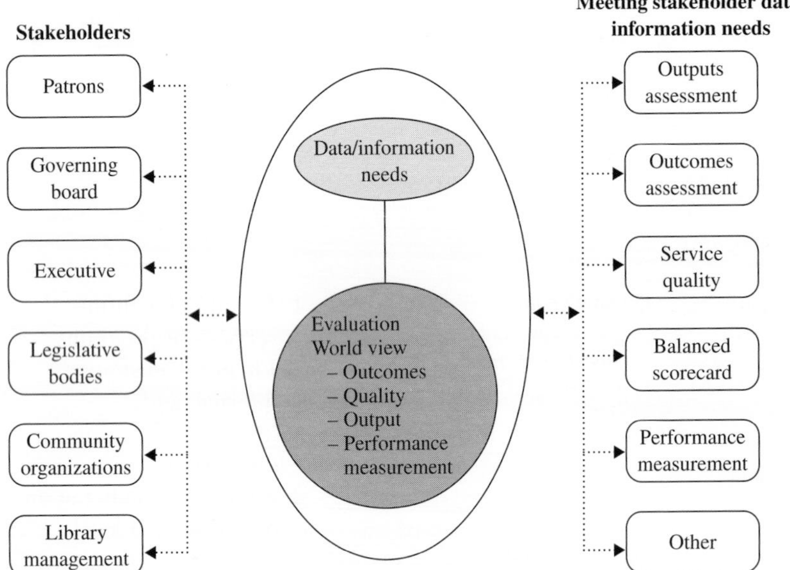

Figure 2 Needs-driven evaluation strategies.

provide all the answers for library management and decision-making purposes. The approaches are versatile and, as presented here within four broad categories, often overlap and may serve multiple purposes. Performance measures may use aspects of outputs approaches within the evaluative scheme and the results may serve as indicators of service quality. Approaches developed for physical settings are adapted and utilized in the networked environments.

As researchers of library environments continue to develop evaluative schemes, more complex approaches to evaluation are beginning to appear. For example, evaluative schemes can include the collection of traditional and networked data and statistics, combined with the use of performance measures in understanding service quality or outcomes. Researchers and practitioners in library settings are aware of the need to develop evaluative strategies that include multiple approaches, methods, and evaluation frameworks to gain a better understanding of a complex library environment and are working to develop approaches to address this need.

Challenges of a Networked Environment

Although the fundamentals of evaluation efforts and the measurement frameworks and paradigms in which evaluation activities reside remain essentially constant, the networked environment continues to usher in a whole host of new library resource and service use measures. At present, these measures occur in essentially two areas: (1) resource/service availability, related to the number of items available (e.g., full-text titles, e-books, digitized images), instruction tools, and digital references, and

(2) user actions, related to the items examined and/or downloaded, the number of searches conducted, the number of digital reference questions submitted, etc. As of this writing, libraries are only in the early stages of considering service quality and outcomes assessment for networked services. Moreover, the "what," "how much," and "how often" questions in the networked environment will be in a continual development cycle as new technologies and capabilities enable a variety of networked library resources and services.

Future of Evaluation in Libraries

Libraries will continue to evaluate their resources and services and how users interact with and engage in those resources and services. The core of these evaluation strategies—inputs, activities, and outputs—will likely remain the same. Differing internal and external factors and library situational factors, however, will influence the assessment strategies that libraries employ and methodologies that enable useful data collection for decision-making and research purposes. For example, an external program evaluation paradigm, such as institutional accreditation in higher education for academic libraries or results-oriented government in public libraries, can drive the assessment activities within a library. Indeed, this serves as the impetus for outcomes assessment in academic and public libraries. Also, user behavior and expectations for library services continue to evolve. Thus, user expectations, the library's situational context, and program reporting requirements combine to influence library evaluation activities of the present and future.

See Also the Following Articles

Computerized Record Linkage and Statistical Matching • Information Management

Further Reading

Bertot, J. C. (2001). Measuring service quality in the networked environment: Approaches and considerations. *Library Trends* **49**(4), 758–775.

Bertot, J. C., and McClure, C. R. (2003). Outcomes assessment in the networked environment: Research questions, issues, considerations, and moving forward. *Library Trends* **51**(4), 590–613.

Bertot, J. C., McClure, C. R., and Ryan, J. (2000). *Statistics and Performance Measures for Public Library Networked Services.* American Library Association, Chicago.

Buckland, M. (2003). Five grand challenges for library research. *Library Trends* **51**(4), 675–686.

Cook, C., and Thompson, B. (2000). Reliability and validity of SERVQUAL scores used to evaluate perceptions of library service quality. *J. Academ. Librarian.* **26**(4), 248–258.

Cook, C., Heath, F., and Thompson, B. (2000). LIBQUAL+: One instrument in the new measures toolbox. *Am. Res. Libraries* **212**(4-7), O.

Hernon, P., and Dugan, R. E. (2002). *An Action Plan for Outcomes Assessment in Your Library.* American Library Association, Chicago.

Kaplan, R., and Norton, D. (1996). *Translating Strategy into Action: The Balanced Scorecard.* Harvard Business School Press, Boston.

McClure, C. R., and Bertot, J. C. (2001). *Evaluating Networked Information Services.* Information Today, Medford, New Jersey.

McKie, S. (2001). *E-Business Best Practices: Leveraging Technology for Business Advantage.* John Wiley & Sons, New York.

National Information Standards Organization. (2003). *Z39.50—Library Statistics.* National Information Standards Organization, Bethesda, Maryland. Retrieved on the Internet, November 1, 2003, at www.niso.org

Parasuraman, A., Berry, L. L., and Zeithaml, V. A. (1988). ServQual: A multiple-item scale for measuring customer perceptions of service quality. *J. Retail.* **64,** 12–40.

Phipps, S. (2001). Beyond measuring service quality: Learning from the voices of the customers, the staff, the processes, and the organization. *Library Trends* **49**(4), 635–661.

Reider, R. (2000). *Benchmarking Strategies: A Tool for Profit Improvement.* John Wiley & Sons, New York.

Tenopir, C. (2003). Reflections on two decades. *Library J.* **128**(2), 36F1.

United Way of America. (1996). *Measuring Program Outcomes: A Practical Approach.* United Way of America, Alexandria, Virginia.

Zweizig, D. (1973). *Predicting Amount of Library Use: An Empirical Study of the Role of the Public Library in the Life of the Adult Public.* Syracuse University, Syracuse, New York.

Likert Scale Analysis

Ira H. Bernstein
University of Texas, Arlington, Arlington, Texas, USA

Glossary

bipolar domain Dimensions that have meaningful and opposite extremes, such as good vs. bad.

congeneric (test) model Tests that have the following properties: (1) their true components are linearly related and (2) their error components are unrelated across respondents.

error component The latent (unobservable) part of an observed score that is independent of the actual trait of interest.

Likert scales of agreement Scales that allow the respondent to express degrees of agreement (like) vs. disagreement (dislike), for example, "Strongly agree," "Agree," "Agree somewhat," "Disagree somewhat," "Disagree," and "Strongly disagree."

Likert scaling An approach to scaling that treats ordinal (ordered) alternatives as if they are equally spaced. For example, "Strongly agree," "Agree," "Agree somewhat," "Disagree somewhat," "Disagree," and "Strongly disagree" would be coded 1–6. This scaling principal is not limited to Likert scales of agreement.

observed score The score a person is assigned on a test or test item.

parallel (test) model Two congeneric tests that have the following properties: (1) their true components are identical and (2) their true and error components are the same across respondents.

systematic (true) component The latent (unobservable) part of an observed score that measures the actual trait of interest.

Likert scales are named after Rensis Likert (1903–1981) and are also known as summated rating scales because the scale score is a simple sum of responses over items. They are perhaps best known from items that allow respondents to express degrees of agreement, such as "Strongly agree," "Agree," "Agree somewhat," "Disagree somewhat," "Disagree,"and "Strongly disagree" rather than a simple choice between agreement and disagreement. However, Likert scales contain a second element that Likert actually stressed more in his original article. This involves using equally spaced integral scale values, most simply, 1, 2, 3, . . . , to scale items with ordinal response categories instead of a more formal algorithm. Consequently, the logic he used in his classic 1932 paper applies to any ordinal multicategory rating scale, which includes estimates of frequency, anchored scales, and confidence ratings. This entry is concerned with the issues that surround their analysis. The terms Likert scales of agreement and Likert scaling thus describe Likert items in their familiar application and the use of equally spaced scale values, respectively, noting that the former is a special case of the latter.

Likert's Basic Idea

Thurstone proposed a method of scaling responses to ordered multicategory items that was designed to transform the categories to points on an equal-interval scale. This sigma method assumed that the latent scale values could be inferred from the response proportions in the various categories. Likert presents an example using proportions of 0.13, 0.43, 0.21, 0.13, and 0.10 in five categories. Thurstone's method generates cited values of −1.63, −0.43, +0.43, +0.99, and +1.76, using a simplified algorithm described in Thurstone's original article. A close approximation to these values may be obtained by (1) adding the proportion of observations below a given interval and one-half the proportion within the given interval and (2) converting this sum of proportions to a z score. In the case of the second interval, the result is the z score corresponding to $0.13 + 0.5 \times 0.43$ or 0.345, which is -0.40.

Likert's scaling method was simpler—give unit scores to the categories. As anyone who has ever used a Likert scale of agreement knows, this simply means assigning weights such as 1, 2, 3, 4, and 5 (or -2, -1, 0, $+1$, and $+2$) with a five-category scale. This simplification was extremely useful before computers became widely available, but it ran counter to the apparent precision of Thurstone's method. However, Likert showed that the reliabilities and validities of scales scored with his method were at least as high, and often were higher, than those scored with Thurstone's method, even with fewer items. Unlike Thurstone's many other contributions, which are still used, his method of constructing equal intervals from multicategory scales is now rarely employed.

Many, however, still question the interval assumptions underlying Likert's scaling method, as seen by the frequency of related questions in various Internet discussion groups. Of course, perhaps the majority of critics have not read his original justification. Likert's scaling method employs *a priori* weights, so it avoids the tendency of Thurstone's category estimates to contain a lot of sampling error.

Allen Edwards was among the first to support Likert's approach, although he was concerned about the issue of a middle category failing to differentiate true neutrality or lack of concern with ambivalence. This point emerges periodically; indeed I was once briefly involved in the topic. Of interest is the fact that at that time Edwards and others were exploring a variety of scale-construction procedures such as Guttman scales. Guttman scales are now rarely used, but were an important precursor of item response theory.

There is a direct link between Likert's scaling logic and what Kaiser and, later, Wainer referred to as the "It don't make no nevermind principle," which notes that simplified weightings in multivariate applications such as factor analysis and multiple regression are often more robust than "exact" values. Wainer later modified his conclusions somewhat, but the gist of the story is that little, if anything, is gained by using complex weighting schemes with multicategory items in classical multivariate applications.

Likert's scaling model may be pursued more formally. One way to do so is to assume that the categorized overt responses to individual items are a product of implicit responses that are available internally along a continuum (there are also decision threshold models that assume that even the implicit response is categorical, but these are not considered here). The present theory consists of two models: (1) the implicit model, which generates the latent responses and (2) the categorization model, which can be used to categorize these latent responses into overt responses.

The Implicit Model

One way to state Likert's scaling model is as follows, following classical psychometric theory. Assume that asking any question, such as attitudes toward a commercial product, evokes a latent response, λ_{ij}, where i denotes the subject (out of n subjects) and j denotes the response (out of k items defining the scale). Next, assume that λ_{ij} is a weighted combination of a systematic (true) component (τ_{ij}) and an error component (ε_{ij}), as defined by the following general model:

$$\lambda_{ij} = \beta_i \tau_{ij} + \gamma_i \varepsilon_{ij} \quad (1)$$

where both the true and error components are standard normal random variables, β_i is the weight allocated to that true score, and γ_i is the weight allocated the error term for that item. As a result, all that is assumed at this point is that the true and error scores are independent (uncorrelated) and that they combine linearly. Further, assume that the error scores for different items are also uncorrelated. The scalings of the two weights can reflect the assumption that they are also definable as standard normal variables. Because even nonlinear relations are often approximated by linear ones and the very meanings of the terms "true score" and "error" imply independence, only one point is controversial. That is the view that the absolute magnitude of the response is the critical variable. This is generally regarded as a good assumption in such areas as intellectual functioning (the smarter you are, the better you perform). However, in many attitudinal areas, an unfolding model using distances from an ideal point may be more relevant; for example, a candidate may be either too liberal or too conservative to be preferred optimally by a given voter.

In addition, even this model is far too general. One common assumption is that the implicit responses are normally distributed, which we assume here for its illustrative value; however, Micceri has made a well-stated objection to this Gaussian model. More critically, an important class of restrictions is often made that lead to the congeneric (i.e., measuring the same thing) test model:

1. True score components across items are linearly related to one another for a given respondent.
2. Errors are independent over items and respondents.

The parallel test model is even more restrictive. It further assumes that:

1. True score components for a given respondent across items are the same.
2. Their weighting is the same across items.

This leads to:

$$\lambda_i = \beta\tau_i + (1-\beta^2)^{0.5}\varepsilon_{ij} \quad (2)$$

Because of the first parallelism assumption, the item subscript can be dropped for a given respondent, and because of the second parallelism assumption, the item subscript can be dropped from the item weighting. The second congeneric assumption allows the same weight to be applied to each error observation. It can be shown that letting the γ_i of Eq. (1) equal $(1-\beta^2)^{0.5}$ simply standardizes the values of λ_i. Given this standardization, it makes sense to define β as the item reliability. Finally, if we simply keep in mind that respondents inherently vary, their subscript can be eliminated, giving rise to:

$$\lambda = \beta\tau + (1-\beta^2)^{0.5}\varepsilon_j \quad (3)$$

As strong as this model is, it probably fits quite well when items are sampled from a homogeneous pool (domain sampling). That is the case, for example, in an abilities test that requires respondents to add randomly selected pairs of three-digit numbers, in which the pool (domain) consists of the numbers 000, 001, . . . , 999. The concept of domain sampling may not apply to an unselected set of attitudinal items, but may at least be approximately true of a scale following item analysis in which the items have similar item/total correlations. The demonstrations that follow assume parallelism for simplicity.

The Categorization Model

Assume that a latent response is classified into one of m response categories using a series of $m-1$ cut-offs. This follows the standard logic of signal detection theory, which also traces back to Thurstone. In other words, let c_j ($j = 1, 2, \ldots, k-1$) and the response to a given item be assigned to overt category C_i if $\lambda > c_i - 1$ and $\lambda \leq c_i$. In other words, if standardized data are dichotomized symmetrically ($c_1 = 0$), then $C_i = 1$ if $\lambda < 0$ and $C_i = 2$ if $\lambda \geq 0$. Of course, these can be transformed linearly to -1 and $+1$ or any other pair of distinct values.

Note that there are at least two potential ways to justify Likert's assumption of equality. The first is to assume that the cut-offs partition responses into equal proportions of observations over respondents. For example, cut-offs of -0.675, 0, and $+0.675$ will divide normally distributed observations into equal quartiles. The alternative is to assume that the intervals themselves are equal. This is meaningless if we assume the continuum extends from $-\infty$ to $+\infty$; but if, say, we assume it only extends from -3 to $+3$, the cut-offs can be -1.5, 0, and $+1.5$. However, neither seems exceptionally plausible in general because response distributions are usually demonstrably unequal, and there is little to justify a rectangular distribution of observations.

Likert Scaling and Cohen's Dictum

Jacob Cohen noted that we pay an extremely high price in loss of power when we dichotomize, which is referred to here as Cohen's dictum. This is not limited to the present situation; it also occurs when we discard, say, continuous information contained in age as a variable and replaces it with "Young" vs. "Old." Specifically, he estimated that a value of r^2 obtained with two continuous, normally distributed variables would shrink by a factor of 0.65 when one variable is dichotomized and by a factor of 0.41 when both are dichotomized. This implies losses in power of 38% and 60%—the equivalent of discarding the respective numbers of cases. Often this dichotomization is done because investigators are familiar with the analysis of variance but not with more general forms of regression. Of course, there are techniques such as biserial r and tetrachoric r that are designed to offset the reduction in r^2 produced by categorization, but these statistics have much greater sampling errors than ordinary Pearson r, can lead to anomalous results in procedures such as factor analysis, and make little sense when the original continuous variables are available in the first place. Cohen's dictum applies to Type II errors for dichotomized data in null hypothesis testing (which, as an incidental point, he was actually opposed to), as well as such things as confidence intervals (which he supported). Cohen's general focus on statistical inference contrasts somewhat with this entry's emphasis on description, particularly with regard to internal consistency. However, we would normally expect increases in reliability to reduce Type II errors.

Several have looked at Type I and Type II error rates as a function of the number of categories that data are placed into. In 1987, Gregoire and Driver performed an extensive series of computer simulations and concluded that the results for Type I error even with five-point scales were unsatisfactory. In 1989, Rasmussen argued that their conclusion reflected an erroneous assumption about the mean used to test the various confidence intervals. When they corrected this assumption, Type I error rates were in accord with expectation. In 1977, Jenkins and Taber also showed that problems that arise with a dichotomization do not arise when a five-point scale is used. This is consistent with Likert's scaling assumption.

Multicategory Scales and Coefficient α

Consider how using multiple categories affects coefficient α reliability for a set of k parallel test items. This is done here in terms of the simple latent variable model for parallel items already discussed.

The cut-offs were chosen to yield equal population item frequencies at three levels of categorization, 2, 4, and 8. As result, the cut-offs were (1) 0, (2) −0.675, 0, and +0.675, and (3) −1.15, −0.675, −0.32, 0, +0.32, +0.675, and +1.15. These were combined with three values of β (0.4, 0.6, and 0.8) and three test lengths (5, 10, and 20 items) on 10,000 replications/simulation. Figures 1–3 contain the coefficients α for 5, 10, and 20 items, respectively, across number of categories (including the latent data), with β as the parameter.

The three figures collectively illustrate how coefficient α is a joint function of scale length, item intercorrelation, and number of categories, but also they indicate that these effects are clearly not linear. It is perhaps useful to examine these differences in the light of the commonly suggested (but arbitrary) standards of 0.8 and 0.9 for tests used to measure group differences and tests used for individual classification, respectively. The five-item data in Fig. 1 indicate that an item reliability of 0.8 is required to meet the standard for group discrimination using dichotomized data, but this level of item reliability produces a value of coefficient α that nearly meets the individual standards with eight-category data. The 10-item data in Fig. 2 indicate that the individual-level criterion is reached at an item reliability of 0.6 and four or eight categories or at an item reliability of 0.8 regardless of the number of categories. Indeed, the latter scale almost meets the individual-level criterion. Finally, the 20-item data in Fig. 3 indicate that dichotomized data and an item reliability of at least 0.6 are satisfactory for group-level discrimination and dichotomized data and an item reliability of 0.8 are satisfactory for individual-level discrimination, regardless of the number of categories. Note that the lowest level of item discrimination does not lead to a satisfactory group-level discrimination, let alone an individual-level scale, with the parameters studied. Further analysis, not detailed here, suggests that dichotomized data with an item reliability of 0.4 requires at least 40 items for group-level discrimination and at least 70 items for individual-level discrimination, which may not be practical. This was improved only slightly to roughly 30 and 60 items using four categories, which differed but marginally from the eight-category results. In other words, although using as few as four categories can make a substantial difference for scales of at least moderate (β = 0.6 in the present case) item reliability, nothing can save a scale made up of low (β = 0.4) item reliability items. At the same time, the group-level criterion is met

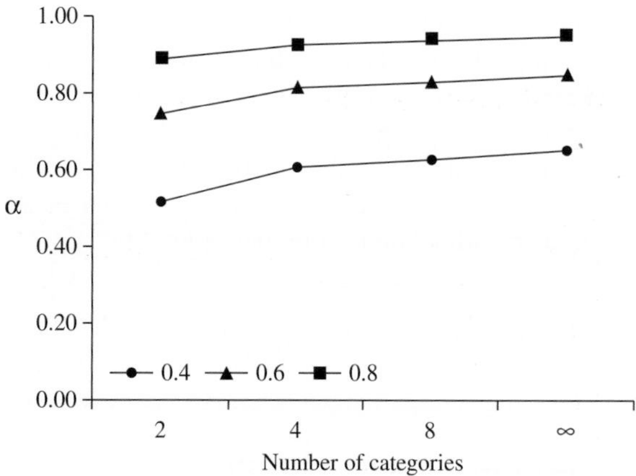

Figure 2 Values of coefficient α as a function of the number of categories into which latent observations are categorized for a hypothetical parallel 10-item scale; the parameter is the item reliability, β (simulated data).

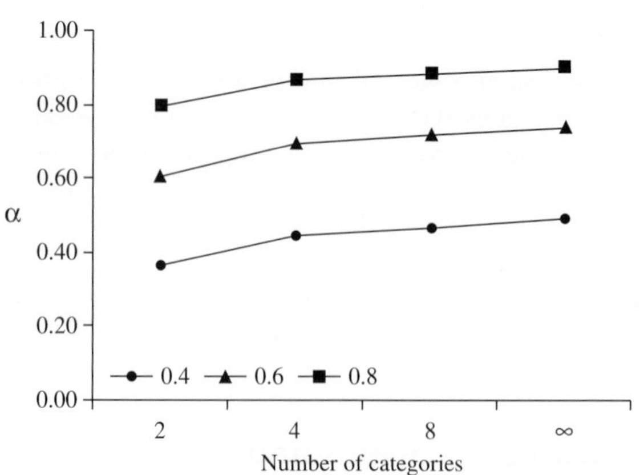

Figure 1 Values of coefficient α as a function of the number of categories into which latent observations are categorized for a hypothetical parallel five-item scale; the parameter is the item reliability, β (simulated data).

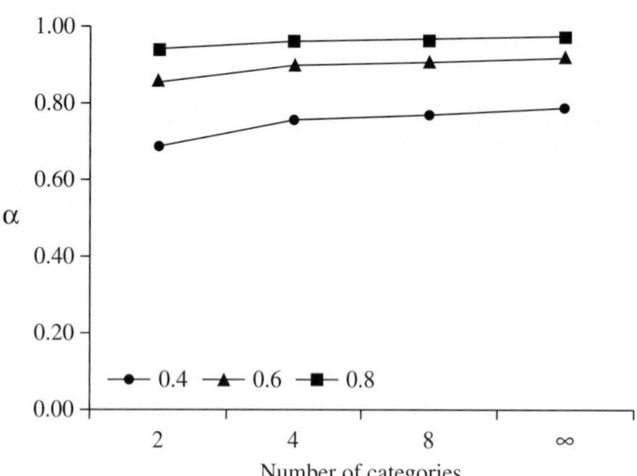

Figure 3 Values of coefficient α as a function of the number of categories into which latent observations are categorized for a hypothetical parallel 20-item scale; the parameter is the item reliability, β (simulated data).

with four-category data and an item reliability of 0.6 with only 10 items and the individual-level criterion is met with 20 items. Thus, the ability of multiple categories to save a scale requires at least moderate item reliability. In general, the effect of going from four to eight categories was marginal. These results are in accord with Jenkins and Taber's more extensive simulations.

The choice of items with the same distribution may be a bit extreme because it is often desirable to obtain a spread of item difficulties so that further simulations along these lines may be of interest. However, the choice of cut-offs that make the response frequencies equal provides a best-case scenario over the effects of categorization. The more extreme the difference in response frequencies for the various categories (as in scales that assess rare symptoms), the less dramatic the advantage of any multicategory format becomes.

Effects of Item Reliability on Inter-Item Correlations

Table I contain the correlation between items 1 and 2 (r_{12}) as a joint function of the number of categories, the number of items, and the item reliability ($\beta = 0.4$, 0.6, and 0.8). Holding the number of categories and item reliabilities constant, the r_{12} is identical across scale lengths because the first five items employed identical data (likewise, the first 10 item responses were identical in the 10- and 20-item data, again holding number of categories and item reliabilities constant). As we expect from the coefficients α data, the effects of increasing the number of categories are minimal with an item reliability of 0.4, but increase as the item reliability increases; with $\beta = 0.8$, there is considerable attenuation in r_{12} with dichotomized data compared to the latent data, but relatively little with eight-category data.

Effects of Item Reliability on the Factor Structure

Bernstein and Teng noted that the effects of using multicategory scales are as we might expect with older exploratory methods, but can lead to some surprising outcomes with inferences derived from newer maximum likelihood–based methods.

Table I also contains the first and second eigenvalues (λ_1 and λ_2) obtained from analyzing the 20-item data for $\beta = 0.4$, 0.6, and 0.8, respectively. Recognizing the limitations of the Kaiser-Guttman criterion (the number of components whose eigenvalues are less than 1) for the number of factors, these results are consistent with a single-factor solution. Moreover, all other common criteria for the number of factors (parallel analysis and minimum average partial) lead to the same conclusion. Specifically, parallel analysis (factoring null matrices based on 10,000 observations and 20 variables) generated mean values λ_1 and λ_2 values of 1.08 and 1.06 with 20 variables. The obtained λ_1 is clearly larger and the obtained λ_2, is clearly smaller than these values with all degrees of categorization. However, also note that λ_1 becomes larger and, accordingly, λ_2 becomes smaller as the number of categories increases from 2 to ∞. The same held true with the shorter scales, although with a smaller magnitude of difference.

Table I Values of the Correlation between Items 1 and 2 (r_{12}) and the First Two Eigenvalues, λ_1 and λ_2[a]

Number of categories	*Number of items*	$\beta = 0.4$			$\beta = 0.6$			$\beta = 0.8$		
		r_{12}	λ_1	λ_2	r_{12}	λ_1	λ_2	r_{12}	λ_1	λ_2
2	5	0.11	1.41	0.92	0.24	1.94	0.79	0.44	2.77	0.57
4	5	0.13	1.55	0.88	0.31	2.25	0.70	0.56	3.26	0.45
8	5	0.15	1.59	0.87	0.34	2.34	0.68	0.60	3.41	0.41
∞	5	0.15	1.64	0.86	0.35	2.43	0.66	0.63	3.55	0.37
2	10	0.11	1.87	0.94	0.24	3.05	0.81	0.44	4.90	0.60
4	10	0.13	2.19	0.90	0.31	3.74	0.73	0.56	6.04	0.46
8	10	0.15	2.28	0.89	0.34	3.95	0.70	0.60	6.39	0.42
∞	10	0.15	2.39	0.88	0.35	4.18	0.68	0.63	6.71	0.38
2	20	0.11	2.89	0.98	0.24	5.37	0.84	0.44	9.30	0.61
4	20	0.13	3.56	0.94	0.31	6.85	0.76	0.56	11.69	0.48
8	20	0.15	3.76	0.92	0.34	7.29	0.73	0.60	12.44	0.44
∞	20	0.15	4.00	0.91	0.35	7.77	0.69	0.63	13.10	0.39

[a] Eigenvalues obtained from factoring scales varying in number of categories (2, 4, 8, and ∞), number of items (5, 10, and 20) and item reliability (β).

Exploratory maximum likelihood solutions for 5, 10, and 20 items were based on 10, 45, and 190 df in testing the null hypothesis that at least one factor was present and on 5, 35, and 170 df in testing the null hypothesis that the residual from a single-factor solution was nonsignificant. There was never any issue of a single factor being present nor, in my experience, is this ever the case with any reasonable number of variables. However, the value of the χ^2 statistic used to test for the presence of a single factor does increase with the number of categories with the difference between two and four categories being much larger than that between four and eight, which, in turn, is larger than that between eight and ∞.

More interesting and complex results are found in looking at the test for residual variance, which are consistent with Bernstein and Teng's results. Table II contains the values of χ^2 as a joint function of number of categories, number of items, and item reliabilities.

The key point to note is that the minimum value of χ^2 for a test of the residual is *not* necessarily reached with the latent (∞) data, in general, because these values were actually lower with the four- and, especially, eight-category Likert scales when the item reliability was low. Even worse is the problem that longer scales made up of more reliable items lead to significant residuals and that this tendency increases rather than decreases with number of categories (the latent data conformed to theoretical expectations throughout). What happens is that the more reliable Likert data make the effects of categorization more (rather than less) apparent. In other words, using Likert scales may increase (rather than decrease) the probability of falsely concluding a unidimensional scale is multidimensional when inferential criteria are used, at least those based on maximum likelihood tests!

Table II Values of χ^2 Associated with the Null Hypothesis[a]

Number of categories	*Number of items*	β 0.4	β 0.6	β 0.8
2	5	6.15	8.54	0.66
4	5	1.25	2.42	3.98
8	5	0.79	2.38	1.83
∞	5	2.04	2.05	2.06
2	10	29.60	43.33	31.01
4	10	22.73	31.04	33.35
8	10	24.65	30.03	34.43
∞	10	29.56	29.56	29.57
2	20	181.17	214.44*	220.28**
4	20	200.10	226.71**	231.68**
8	20	201.22	217.04**	234.84**
∞	20	178.08	178.20	178.27

[a] H_0: One factor is sufficient to explain the data as a function of number of categories (2, 4, 8, and ∞), number of items (5, 10, and 20), and item reliability (β) = 0.4, 0.6, or 0.8).

* $p < 0.05$.

** $p < 0.01$.

Effects on Item Response Theory Parameters

An alternative way to look at the data is in terms of item response theory. In particular, the data for the $\beta = 0.6$ for 10-item dichotomous data and $\beta = 0.6$ for10-item eight-category data were fit to rating scale models (in the case of the dichotomous data, this led to the same outcome as a one-parameter model). The results of greatest interest are the test information functions. The higher the value of this function, the more precise the statement about small differences in the estimation of the latent attribute, θ, in this region in the scale. Figure 4 contains these results.

As can be seen, both functions peak at $\theta = 0$, which results from the symmetric manner in which the various distributions were constructed and the fact that the items are parallel (have the same true and error components). Note, however, that the Likert scale falls above the dichotomized data, meaning that it is more informative about the latent attribute, and that it is nearly flat from $\theta = -2$ to $\theta = +2$, whereas the function for the dichotomized data is approximately normal because it falls off fairly rapidly. This will not be the case if items vary in their means, unlike the present simulations.

Bipolar Domains

Likert scales of agreement (but not Likert scaling in general) imply an underlying bipolar continuum. For

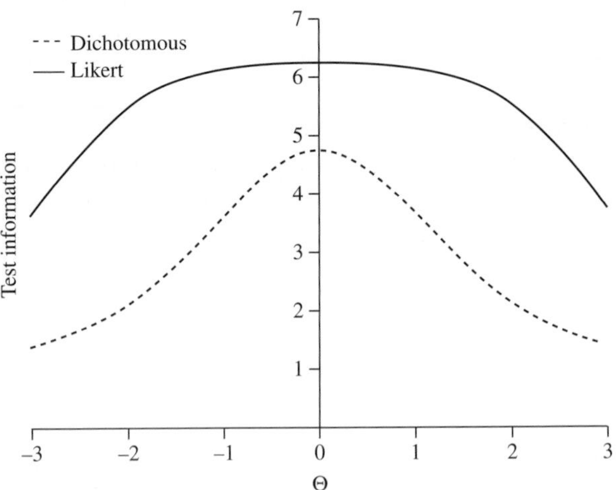

Figure 4 Test information function for eight-category Likert and dichotomized data, assuming 10 parallel items with item reliabilities of 0.6.

example, agreement with an item such as "parents should receive vouchers from their state government to pay for private school education of their children" implies support for a conservative position and disagreement implies support for a liberal position, where conservative and liberal are poles of a single dimension.

In 1965, Green and Goldfried challenged the view that common scales such as "Good/Bad," "Large/Small," and "Active/Passive" are, in fact, bipolar. These bipolar dimensions are presumed to underlie the semantic differential, a once highly popular type of rating scale. Instead of having respondents employ a single bipolar dimension, they had the respondents respond to the two poles separately, for example, using separate "Good" and "Bad" scales. Whereas the bipolar view suggests that the "Good" scale ratings of a series of stimuli should have a strong negative correlation with the "Bad" scale ratings, this often did not happen. However, Bentler pointed out that these minimal correlations may have been influenced by the tendency to acquiesce (agree). When this trait was partialled out, the expected strong negative correlations between the putatively bipolar scales were in fact obtained, supporting the bipolarity assumed by Likert scales of agreement.

A related problem arises when certain items are phrased so that agreement denotes the presence of a trait and other items are phrased so that agreement denotes either the absence of the trait or its polar opposite. In other words, suppose one self-descriptive item asks, "I am presently in a good frame of mind," and another asks, "I am presently unhappy," (it does not matter here whether the items use Likert scales of agreement or are simply binary). Assuming we wish positive scores to reflect happiness, we would simply subtract the rating on the second question from seven (the number of categories plus 1). Conversely, if we wish positive scores to reflect unhappiness, we would apply the same transformation to the first item. Note that either of these is straightforward and neither is a matter for disagreement among experts and that your choice of measuring happiness or unhappiness leads to equivalent outcomes.

Be prepared for two items phrased positively to correlate more highly and for two items phrased negatively to correlate more highly than a positively worded item with a negatively worded item. However, this typically reflects the method rather than content variance. The history of this distinction traces back to a classical 1959 paper by Campbell and Fiske.

How Many Categories to Use?

Another common question is how many categories to employ. Part of this question involves whether to employ a neutral category. Many investigators (such as this author) prefer to try to force a decision out of the respondent, which leads to avoiding a neutral category by incorporating an even number of categories. However, this makes no difference in some methods, such as signal detection rating scale analysis.

As for choosing the number of categories, the first point to keep in mind is that we can always condense a scale containing a larger number of categories to a smaller number. The second point is that we need to determine whether there is an optimal number of categories to use. The simulations so far suggest that there is little need for more than eight categories, but these simulations have only touched the surface of a vast literature. Indeed, rather strong assumptions were made in the simulations. Note that the limitation to "seven plus or minus two" categories, so artfully summarized by George Miller, does not really apply because this limitation applies to judgments of unidimensional stimuli such as height and weight and not the complex attributes usually scaled. However, it is good to keep in mind that respondents may not be fully able to use, say, a 100-point scale and that items with 10 or fewer categories fit nicely within many mark-sense forms.

At the same time, there are several studies that indicate that subjects can use a relatively large number of categories profitably. Bendig found that the amount of information transmitted, a type of nonmetric correlation, increased up to at least nine categories. Green and Rao, using simulated data and a multidimensional-scaling-fit criterion, found support for more rather than fewer categories. On the other hand, Komorita and Mattell and Jacoby used respondent's ratings and found that the reliability of a scale was independent of the number of categories; Mattell and Jacoby also found that the scale's validity was likewise unaffected by the number of categories. Moreover, Lissitz and Green, using simulated data, argued that seven categories are optimal, noting a leveling off of coefficient α and a decrease in standard deviations as the number of categories increases, holding the covariance structure constant. In 1973, Ramsay developed a maximum likelihood algorithm. Using the precision of estimation (reciprocal standard errors) as a criterion, his model predicts a leveling off at approximately seven categories. Perhaps as interesting is the finding that estimating the category boundaries from the data degraded the model's performance considerably compared to treating them as fixed.

Note that the conclusions often differ because different investigators used different criteria (e.g., information transmitted vs. coefficient α). Although not recent, Cox provides a useful summary of the considerations relevant to this complex issue (indeed, the complexity of the issue has become so widely recognized that recent textbooks tend not to even suggest an optimal number). Perhaps it is best to conclude this section by suggesting that each investigator consider which criteria will be used to evaluate the scale's performance and act accordingly.

Mixing Items with Different Numbers of Scale Points

Suppose we wish to combine some items scored on, say, a five-point scale with others scaled on an eight-point scale. The simplest possibility is simply to mix the two types of items without making adjustments for the difference in the numbers of categories and, therefore, item variance. A more complex procedure is to spread the five categories over an eight-point range by assigning values of 1, 2.75, 4.5, 6.25, and 8 to the five categories. In general, if we want the first category have a value of A_0, have a total of C intervals, and have $V_{\max}$ be the values of the highest numbered category, we let the value of category C_i be $A_0 + (V_{\max} - 1) \times (C_i - 1)/(C - 1)$. Thus, in the present example, the scale value of the second category is $1 + (8 - 1) \times (2 - 1)/(5 - 1) = 1 + 7/4 = 11/4 = 2.75$.

It is instructive to compare this with simply mixing in the two types of items with their original scalings, that is, spreading the five-category items over a five-point range and the eight-category items over an eight-point range. Consistent with Likert's scaling thesis (and those of many others who advocate scaling in the simplest manner), we will probably find the two scores correlate nearly perfectly.

The Use of Anchors

It is always a good idea to make the descriptors of the various response categories (anchors) as clear as possible. Ideally, we should also choose categories that are chosen by respondents a reasonable percentage of the time, say at least 0.5%. A third consideration is not to bias responses, for example, by asking respondents about how much they like something and providing only positive options. Of course, the desire to achieve reasonable proportions of choice may conflict with the need to balance categories to avoid bias. It is suggested that this last consideration take precedence.

See Also the Following Articles

Item Response Theory • Reliability Assessment • Thurstone's Scales of Primary Abilities

Further Reading

Cheung, K. C., and Mooi, L. C. (1994). A comparison between the rating scale model and dual scaling for Likert scales. *Appl. Psychol. Meas.* **18,** 1–13.

Ferrando, P. J. (1999). Likert scaling using continuous, censored, and graded response models: Effects on criterion-rated validity. *Appl. Psychol. Meas.* **23,** 161–175.

Gardner, D. G., Cummings, L. L., Dunham, R. B., and Pierce, J. L. (1998). Single-item versus multiple-item measurement scales: An empirical comparison. *Educ. Psychol. Meas.* **58,** 898–915.

Igou, E. R., Bless, H., and Schwarz, N. (2002). Making sense of standardized survey questions: The influence of reference periods and their repetition. *Commun. Monogr.* **69,** 179–187.

Sudman, S., Bradburn, N. M., and Schwarz, N. (1996). *Thinking About Answers: The Application of Cognitive Processes to Survey Methodology.* Jossey-Bass, San Francisco, CA.

Van Schuur, W. H., and Kiers, H. A. (1994). Why factor analysis often is the incorrect model for analyzing bipolar concepts, and what model to use instead. *Appl. Psychol. Meas.* **18,** 97–110.

Linear Logistic Test Models

Gerhard H. Fischer

University of Vienna, Vienna, Austria

Glossary

basic parameters Parameters that are the source of differences in item difficulty; examples are parameters measuring the complexity of cognitive operations or subtasks and the effects of test conditions or treatments.

Bradley-Terry-Luce (BTL) model A probabilistic model for paired comparisons of objects or of players in a tournament.

item generation The production (typically of large numbers) of items on the basis of a formalized theory of their cognitive complexity, yielding sets of items of predefined difficulty levels.

linear Bradley-Terry-Luce (LBTL) model A BTL model in which the object parameters are linear combinations of certain basic parameters.

linear logistic test model (LLTM) A logistic test model in which the difficulty of each item is a linear combination of certain basic parameters.

linear partial credit model (LPCM) A partial credit model in which the parameters of items × categories are linear combinations of certain basic parameters.

linear rating scale model (LRSM) A rating scale model in which the item parameters are linear combinations of certain basic parameters.

partial credit model (PCM) A model for polytomous test items in which the numbers of ordered response categories and their attractiveness parameters can vary between items.

Rasch model (RM) A model for dichotomous test items in which the probability of a right response is a logistic function of the difference between a person's ability and the item difficulty.

rating scale model (RSM) A model for polytomous test items in which both the numbers of ordered response categories and their attractiveness parameters are the same for all items.

virtual item An item that is characterized by an item parameter in a model but does not necessarily exist in reality; for example, if a real item is given under two testing conditions influencing the response probabilities, the item is represented in the model by two virtual items with different item parameters.

This entry introduces the linear logistic test model (LLTM), which aims at explaining the difficulty of test items or tasks in terms of underlying factors such as rules, cognitive operations, treatments or training, and trend effects (e.g., development). The estimation of the model and properties of the estimators, testing of fit, hypothesis testing, relationship of the LLTM to the linear Bradley-Terry-Luce (LBTL) model, typical fields of application (analysis of the cognitive complexity of tasks, cross-cultural research, and group- and individual-centered analysis of change), a multivariate reinterpretation of the LLTM, its estimation and properties of the estimators, and hypothesis testing in multivariate LLTMs are outlined. Polytomous extensions and specialized software products are briefly mentioned.

Definition of the Linear Logistic Test Model

The linear logistic test model (LLTM) is an extension of the Rasch model (RM) assuming that the item difficulty parameters β_i, $i = 1, \ldots, k$, of the RM can be linearly decomposed into a weighted sum of basic parameters α_l, $l = 1, \ldots, p$, with $p \leq k - 1$. (For a list of the mathematical symbols used here, see Table I; for abbreviations, see Table II.) The motivation for this extension is the notion that, in some classes of tests, the differences between the difficulties of any two items, I_i and I_j, can be accounted for by the sum of the difficulties of the cognitive operations that are needed for item I_i but not for item I_j minus the sum of the difficulties of those cognitive operations that

Table I Mathematical Symbols

k	Number of items in a test or in an item sample
p	Number of basic parameters
β_i	Item (difficulty) parameter of item I_i
$\boldsymbol{\beta}$	Column vector of item parameters β_i, $i=1,\ldots,k$
β_i^*	Item (difficulty) parameter of virtual item I_i^*
α_l	Basic parameter no. l
$\boldsymbol{\alpha}$	Column vector of basic parameters α_l, $l=1,\ldots,p$
$\mathbf{1}_k$	A k-dimensional column vector of ones
w_{il}	Weight of basic parameter α_l in item I_i
$\mathbf{W}=((w_{il}))$	Matrix of weights
$\mathbf{W}^+=(\mathbf{W},\ \mathbf{1}_k)$	Matrix of weights extended by a column of ones
$\mathbf{V}$	Asymptotic covariance matrix of basic parameter estimators
θ_v	Position of testee S_v on trait Θ (unidimensional case)
θ_{vi}	Position of testee S_v on trait Θ_i (multidimensional case)
Θ	Latent trait dimension
x_{vi}	Item score of testee S_v on item I_i
$x_{.i}=\sum_v x_{vi}$	Item marginal sum (item score)
$x_{..}=\sum_v\sum_i x_{vi}$	Total sum of item scores
$\mathbf{X}=((x_{vi}))$	Item score matrix
$\boldsymbol{y}$	An arbitrary vector of responses to k items, with raw score r
c	Normalization constant
L_c	Conditional likelihood fuction
$\gamma_r(\boldsymbol{\beta})$	Elementary symmetric function of order r of parameters $\exp(-\beta_i)$
$\gamma_{r-1}^{(i)}(\boldsymbol{\beta})$	Elementary symmetric function of order $r-1$ of parameters $\exp(-\beta_1),\ldots,\exp(-\beta_{i-1}),\exp(-\beta_{i+1}),\ldots,\exp(-\beta_k)$
$s_l=\sum_i x_{.i}w_{il}$	Realization of sufficient statistic for α_l
$r=\sum_i x_{vi}$	Raw score of testee S_v
n_r	Number of testees with raw score r
$n=\sum_r n_r$	Testee sample size
$\boldsymbol{r}$	Column vector of raw scores of all S_v, $v=1,\ldots,n$
$\boldsymbol{D}=((d_{ij}))$	Adjacency matrix of digraph D
q_{gjt}	Dosage of treatment B_j given to all $S_v\in G_g$ up to time point T_t
η_j	Effect of one dosage unit of treatment B_j
$\boldsymbol{\eta}$	Column vector of treatment effects η_j, $j=1,\ldots,p$
τ	Trend effect
ρ_{jl}	Treatment interaction effect $B_j\times B_l$
δ_v	Amount of change in testee S_v
$\boldsymbol{M}$	$p\times p'$-dimensional matrix expressing a H_0 about $\boldsymbol{\eta}$

are required for I_j but not for I_i; or that changes of item difficulties over time can be explained as the sum of effects of treatments, training, or information given between testing occasions. The LLTM therefore assumes, for all pairs of items, that:

$$\beta_i-\beta_j=\sum_{l=1}^{p}(w_{il}-w_{jl})\alpha_l \tag{1}$$

where w_{il} denotes the weight of the basic (or effect) parameter α_l for item I_i. When the difficulty of items is analyzed in terms of their cognitive structure, w_{il} is usually defined either as the number of times cognitive operation O_l is needed to solve I_i or more simply as $w_{il}=1$ if O_l is needed for I_i, and $w_{il}=0$ otherwise. The difficulties of operations needed equally for both items or not needed for either item (implying $w_{il}-w_{jl}=0$ for $l=1,\ldots,p$) obviously do not influence the difference $\beta_i-\beta_j$ in Eq. (1). In treatment effect studies, typically the weights w_{ij} are the cumulative dosages of the treatments given prior to the testing occasions.

Formally, the LLTM is constituted by the following two equations. First, the RM is defined by:

$$P(X_{vi}=1\mid\theta_v,\beta_i)=\frac{\exp(\theta_v-\beta_i)}{1+\exp(\theta_v-\beta_i)} \tag{2}$$

Table II Abbreviations

ACER ConQuest	Software for generalized IRT models with embedded linear structures
B_j	Treatment number j
BTL	Bradley-Terry-Luce model
CML	Conditional maximum likelihood
CLR	Conditional likelihood ratio
D	Directed graph (digraph) associated with item score matrix $\mathbf{X}$
df	Degrees of freedom
FACETS	Software for multi-facet Rasch models
F & M (1998)	Fischer & Molenaar (1998)
G_g	Treatment group number g
H_0	Null hypothesis
H_1	Alternative hypothesis
iff	If and only if
I_i	Real item number i
I_i^*	Virtual item number i
IRT	Item response theory
n.s.	Necessary and sufficient
LBTL	Linear Bradley-Terry-Luce model
LLTM	Linear logistic test model
LPCM	Linear partial credit model
LPCM Win	Software for PCMs with embedded linear structures
LRSM	Linear rating scale model
ML	Maximum likelihood
MML	Marginal maximum likelihood
O_l	Cognitive operation number l
RM	Rasch model
S_v	Testee (person) number v
T_t	Time point number t
$\mathcal{T}_1$	Pretest
$\mathcal{T}_2$	Posttest

for k items I_i, where X_{vi} is the response variable with realizations $x_{vi}=1$ if testee S_v gives the response "+" to I_i and $x_{vi}=0$ if S_v gives the response "−" to I_i; θ_v is the latent ability of S_v; and β_i the difficulty of item I_i. All item responses are assumed to be locally independent. Parameters θ_v and β_i are defined only up to a common additive normalization constant c.

Second, the following linear constraints are imposed on the β_i:

$$\beta_i = \sum_{i=1}^{p} w_{il}\alpha_l + c \tag{3}$$

for $i=1,\ldots,k$, with weights w_{il}, basic parameters α_l, and normalization constant c. The weights are considered to be given constants (unless explicitly stated otherwise). Inserting the item parameters according to Eq. (3) into the difference $\beta_i - \beta_j$ obviously leads to cancellation of c and thus yields Eq. (1).

Estimation of the Basic Parameters

Conditional Maximum Likelihood Estimation

The most satisfactory method for the estimation of the basic parameters α_l is the conditional maximum likelihood (CML) method. It maximizes the likelihood of the item response matrix $\mathbf{X}=((x_{vi}))$, conditional on the testees' raw scores r_v, $v=1,\ldots,n$. This likelihood function is:

$$L_C(\boldsymbol{\beta} \mid r) = \Big(\prod_r \gamma_r(\boldsymbol{\beta})^{n_r}\Big)^{-1} \prod_i \exp(-x_{.i}\beta_i) \tag{4}$$

where $\boldsymbol{\beta}$ denotes the (column) vector of item parameters β_i, $\boldsymbol{r}$ the vector of testees raw scores, n_r the number of testees with raw score r, $x_{.i}$ the sum of the ith column of $\mathbf{X}$, that is, $x_{.i}=\Sigma_v x_{vi}$; and γ_r the elementary symmetric function of order r of the transformed item parameters $\exp(-\beta_i)$, $i=1,\ldots,k$. These well-known functions, which are of fundamental importance (e.g., in algebra), are defined as:

$$\gamma_r(\boldsymbol{\beta}) = \sum_{\boldsymbol{y}|r} \prod_i \exp(-y_i \beta_i) \tag{5}$$

where the summation is taken over all possible response vectors $\boldsymbol{y}$ that are compatible with raw score r, implying $\sum_i y_i = r$.

Inserting constraints (3) into Eq. (4) and rearranging terms:

$$L_C(\boldsymbol{\beta}\,|\,\boldsymbol{r}) = \left(\prod_r \gamma_r(\boldsymbol{\beta})^{n_r}\right)^{-1} \exp(-x_{..}c)\exp\left(-\sum_l s_l \alpha_l\right) \tag{6}$$

with $x_{..} = \sum_i x_{.i} = \sum_r r n_r$ and $s_l = \sum_i x_{.i} w_{il}$. The likelihood in Eq. (6) thus depends on the data only via the s_l (and the n_r, which, however, are considered fixed constants), from which it can be concluded that the s_l are realizations of jointly sufficient statistics for the parameters α_l. Note that L_C actually is independent of the normalization constant c because, by Eq. (5), it holds that $\gamma_r(\boldsymbol{\beta} - c\mathbf{1}_k) = \gamma_r(\boldsymbol{\beta})\exp(cr)$, where $\mathbf{1}_k$ denotes a column vector of dimension k with all elements equal to 1.

Therefore, $\prod_r \gamma_r(\boldsymbol{\beta})^{n_r} = \exp(-x_{..}c)\prod_r \gamma_r(\boldsymbol{\beta} - c\mathbf{1}_k)$, so that the expression $\exp(-x_{..}c)$ cancels out of Eq. (6), yielding $L_C(\boldsymbol{\beta} - c\mathbf{1}_k\,|\,\boldsymbol{r}) = (\prod_r \gamma_r(\boldsymbol{\beta} - c\mathbf{1}_k)^{n_r})^{-1} \times \exp(-\sum_l s_l \alpha_l)$.

Taking partial derivatives of ln L_C in Eq. (6) with respect to the $\alpha_l, l = 1, \ldots, p$, and setting these derivatives to zero yields the CML estimation equations:

$$\sum_i w_{il}\left[x_{.i} - \sum_r n_r \frac{\gamma_{r-1}^{(i)}(\boldsymbol{\beta})\exp(-\beta_i)}{\gamma_r(\boldsymbol{\beta})}\right] = 0 \tag{7}$$

for $l = 1, \ldots, p$. The functions $\gamma_{r-1}^{(i)}(\beta)$, for $r = 1, \ldots, k$, denote elementary symmetric functions of order $r-1$ of transformed item parameters $\exp(-\beta_j)$ where, however, the ith parameter $\exp(-\beta_i)$ is omitted; therefore, the arguments of these functions are $\exp(-\beta_1), \ldots, \exp(-\beta_{i-1}), \exp(-\beta_{i+1}), \ldots, \exp(-\beta_k)$.

A software product specifically designed for CML estimation and hypothesis testing in the LLTM and some of its extensions in LPCM-Win by Fischer and Ponocny-Seliger. It uses recursions for computing the functions γ and, as a fast iterative method for solving the CML equations, the so-called Broyden–Fletcher–Goldfarb–Shanno algorithm.

Some Properties of the Conditional Maximum Likelihood Estimators

It is noteworthy that the CML Eqs. (7) do not involve the person parameters any more; by conditioning on the observed raw scores r_v, which in any RM are realizations of sufficient statistics for the θ_v, the likelihood in Eq. (6) becomes independent of the θ_v, and hence the same holds for Eqs. (7). This property, typical for all RMs, has the consequence that the distribution of the θ_v in the given sample (or in the reference population) is irrelevant. This is only true, however, as long as the raw score distribution in the sample (i.e., the n_r) is considered fixed. There remains the problem, however, that this distribution in samples of size n *does* depend on the Θ distribution of the population from which the testees have been sampled, which influences the information in the sample with respect to the item parameters β_i (and the basic parameters α_l in the case of an LLTM).

A more exact and unequivocal formulation of these important properties of the RM and the LLTM can be based on two results: (1) the uniqueness of the CML estimator in finite samples and (2) its consistency for $n \to \infty$.

The Uniqueness of the CML Estimator in Finite Samples

For a condensed description of a fundamental property of the item score matrix $\mathbf{X}$ of an RM, the following directed graph (or digraph) D is most serviceable. Assign one-to-one nodes (or vertices) to the k items and define the adjacency matrix $\boldsymbol{D} = ((d_{ij}))$ by putting $d_{ij} = 1$ if some testee S_v has given the response "+" to item I_i and the response "−" to item I_j and by putting $d_{ij} = 0$ otherwise. Each element $d_{ij} = 1$ is then represented by a directed line from node i to node j, for all $i, j = 1, \ldots, k$. The crucial property of $\mathbf{X}$ is whether D is strongly connected. (Efficient algorithms to determine strong connectedness of a digraph are standard instruments of graph theory and thus are not discussed here.)

A sufficient condition for uniqueness of the CML estimator $\hat{\boldsymbol{\alpha}}$ is the following. If D is strongly connected, then a unique (finite) CML estimate (i.e., a unique solution of the CML equations) $\hat{\boldsymbol{\alpha}}$ exists iff the rank of matrix $\mathbf{W}^+$ is $p+1$, where $\mathbf{W}^+$ is the matrix $\boldsymbol{W}$ extended by a $(p+1)$st column of 1s, $\mathbf{W}^+ = (\mathbf{W}, \mathbf{1}_k)$. If D fails to be strongly connected (i.e., has more than one strong component), the CML estimator $\hat{\boldsymbol{\alpha}}$ still may be unique because a weaker necessary and sufficient (n.s.) condition holds for uniqueness. This n.s. condition, however, is more complicated, involving a set of linear inequalities based on a partial order of the strong components of D. Further details can be found in the book *Rasch Models* by Fischer and Molenaar, Chapter 8.

In complete designs in which each person responds to each item, the probability of obtaining a strongly connected digraph D tends to 1 very fast as n increases, so in practice the uniqueness of the CML estimator depends only on the rank of the extended weight matrix $\mathbf{W}^+$. LLTMs in which $\mathbf{W}^+$ has full column rank are therefore denoted identifiable. It should be noted, however, that in some cases of incomplete designs digraph D may necessarily have more than one strong component, so that the uniqueness question regarding the CML estimator $\hat{\boldsymbol{\alpha}}$ can be decided only by means of the more complicated n.s. condition previously mentioned.

The CML Estimator's Consistency

An important asymptotic result about the CML estimator in the RM is given by Pfanzagl: it states that the normalized estimator $\hat{\boldsymbol{\beta}}$ is consistent iff for $n \to \infty$,

$$\sum_{v=1}^{n} \exp(-|\theta_v|) \to \infty \qquad (8)$$

Therefore, the CML estimator $\hat{\boldsymbol{\alpha}}$ in the LLTM is also consistent iff Eq. (8) holds true and $\mathbf{W}^+$ has rank $p+1$. Condition (8) rules out degenerate Θ distributions where almost all $|\theta_v|$ are infinitely large, which, by the way, would entail also the violation of the condition of strong connectedness of digraph D. Whenever Eq. (8) is satisfied, however, the particular form of the Θ distribution becomes irrelevant to the question of consistency of $\hat{\boldsymbol{\alpha}}$. Then asymptotic normality of $\hat{\boldsymbol{\alpha}}$ around $\boldsymbol{\alpha}$, with asymptotic covariance matrix $\mathbf{V}$, taken at $\boldsymbol{\alpha} = \hat{\boldsymbol{\alpha}}$,

$$\mathbf{V} = -\left(\frac{\partial^2 \ln L_C}{\partial\boldsymbol{\alpha}\partial\boldsymbol{\alpha}'}\right)^{-1} = -\left(\mathbf{W}'\frac{\partial^2 \ln L_C}{\partial\boldsymbol{\beta}\partial\boldsymbol{\beta}'}\mathbf{W}\right)^{-1} \qquad (9)$$

can be proved.

These results hold only, however, if the weight matrix $\mathbf{W}$, which represents the researcher's hypothesis about the factors causing differences of difficulties between items, is fixed and given. Bechger, Verstralen, and Verhelst point out in 2002 that LLTMs with different weight matrices and different basic parameters may be equivalent (i.e., may yield the same likelihood for any data matrix $\mathbf{X}$ and thus be empirically indistinguishable). They prove a result that is equivalent to the following: Two identifiable LLTMs with weight matrices $\mathbf{W}_1$ and $\mathbf{W}_2$ are equivalent iff the columns of either of the matrices $\mathbf{W}_1^+$ and $\mathbf{W}_2^+$ lie within the column space of the other, which is equivalent to saying that matrix $(\mathbf{W}_1^+, \mathbf{W}_2^+)$ has rank $p+1$.

Other Estimation Methods

Two other popular methods of estimation in item response theory (IRT) can also be employed for the LLTM. The first is the joint maximum likelihood (JML) method that maximizes the likelihood of the data as a function of both the basic and the person parameters. A program employing this method for a family of many-facet RMs (including the LLTM) is FACETS by Linacre. An advantage of this approach is its relative simplicity; its disadvantage is the lack of consistency, which, moreover, implies that nothing is known about the asymptotic properties of the estimators. The second method is the parametric marginal maximum likelihood (MML) method, which extends the IRT model by assuming a parametric population distribution of Θ. These parameters are then integrated out of the likelihood, which becomes a function of the item and distribution parameters. The software program ACER ConQest by Wu, Adams, and Wilson uses this approach. Its advantage lies in the complexity of the models that can be handled; its disadvantage lies in the bias occurring when the unknown Θ distribution has not been specified correctly.

Testing of Fit

Testing the fit of an LLTM comprises two steps. First, it is necessary to ascertain that the RM fits the item score matrix $\mathbf{X}$. (A state-of-the-art account of methods for testing of fit in the RM is given by Glas and Verhelst.) If the RM does not fit at least approximately, there is no point in attempting to decompose $\boldsymbol{\beta}$ because then $\boldsymbol{\alpha}$ (and its estimator) would lack an empirical meaning.

Second, if the RM has been found to fit, we may check whether the decomposition in Eq. (3) is empirically valid. In that case, the $\hat{\beta}_i^{(RM)}$ that result from fitting the RM and the $\hat{\beta}_i^{(LLTM)}$ reproduced from the LLTM via Eq. (3) should be the same except for random deviations (assuming in both cases the same normalization). A Pearson correlation can be used as a rough indicator of agreement; however, it has often been seen that such correlations can be quite high (>0.90), even in the presence of significant model violations. Therefore, a more rigorous test of significance for the null hypothesis represented by Eq. (3) is indicated.

A global test of Eq. (3) under the assumption of the validity of the RM is easily made using (once more) the conditional likelihood function L_C, both under the LLTM (as H_0) and under the RM (as H_1). Denote the respective likelihoods as $L_C(H_0) = L_C(\hat{\boldsymbol{\alpha}} \mid \boldsymbol{r}, \mathbf{W}, \mathbf{X})$ and $L_C(H_1) = L_C(\hat{\boldsymbol{\beta}} \mid \boldsymbol{r}, \mathbf{X})$; then under H_0 the statistic:

$$\chi^2 = -2\ln\left(\frac{L_C(H_0)}{L_C(H_1)}\right) \quad \text{with df} = k-1-p \qquad (10)$$

follows a central chi-square distribution and thus can be used for a conditional likelihood ratio (CLR) test of H_0. Moreover, there exists a Lagrange multiplier test of the LLTM by Glas and Verhelst.

This CLR test of the LLTM against the RM is quite powerful for detecting departures from the restrictions in Eq. (3). Lack of fit can be caused, for instance, by neglect of some relevant factors (e.g., p too small) or by wrong entries in matrix $\mathbf{W}$. Researchers may therefore wish to carry out tests of significance for particular elements of the weight matrix $\mathbf{W}$ and, if the model does not fit sufficiently well, make improvements on these elements. Bechger, Verstralen, and Verhelst develop a test for a single element of $\mathbf{W}$ plus a specific method to estimate it empirically. There is a simpler way, however, to achieve the same goal, completely in line with the methods previously presented.

Suppose that w_{ab} is the element of interest. Under H_0, let $\mathbf{W}_0 = \mathbf{W}$, so that the contribution to the difficulty parameter β_a pertaining to w_{ab}, is $w_{ab}\alpha_b$. Under H_1, w_{ab} becomes a free parameter ω. To bring the H_1 model, however, back to the form of an LLTM, we replace $w\hat{\alpha}_b$ by $w_{ab}\hat{\alpha}_b + \hat{\alpha}_{p+1}$, where the new parameter α_{p+1} is a correction term. For the estimation of α_{p+1} under H_1, the weight matrix is:

$$\mathbf{W}_1 = \begin{pmatrix} w_{11} & \dots & w_{1b} & \dots & w_{1p} & 0 \\ \dots & \dots & \dots & \dots & \dots & \dots \\ w_{a1} & \dots & w_{ab} & \dots & w_{ap} & 1 \\ \dots & \dots & \dots & \dots & \dots & \dots \\ w_{k1} & \dots & w_{kb} & \dots & w_{kp} & 0 \end{pmatrix} \quad (11)$$

This model is identified iff the rank of $\mathbf{W}_1^+$ is $p+2$. The two LLTMs with weight matrices $\mathbf{W}_0$ and $\mathbf{W}_1$ may be compared by means of a conditional likelihood ratio test as previously described. If the test is significant, the H_1 model is accepted and the unknown element ω is estimated by means of the estimator $\hat{\omega} = w_{ab} + \hat{\boldsymbol{\alpha}}_{p+1}/\hat{\boldsymbol{\alpha}}_b$. (This requires $\alpha_b \neq 0$, of course; but if $\alpha_b = 0$, the element ω becomes arbitrary and thus cannot be estimated.)

An obvious advantage of this approach is that it applies also to the estimation and testing of two or more independent unknown elements in different rows of $\mathbf{W}$. A warning to researchers, however, seems to be indicated: such methods entail a considerable danger of overfitting the model.

Relationship to the Bradley-Terry-Luce Model

It is well known that the RM can be regarded as a Bradley-Terry-Luce (BTL) model for the pairwise comparison of testees with items. This BTL model is incomplete by design because no direct comparisons are made between testees and none between items. The LLTM therefore is also an incomplete BTL, however, with a linear structure embedded in the object parameters; hence, it is denoted linear Bradley-Terry-Luce (LBTL) model. The correspondence between LLTM and LBTL is twofold. First, the unconditional likelihood of any LLTM is the likelihood function of an incomplete LBTL. Second, it can be shown that the likelihood function of any LBTL is the conditional likelihood function of a particular incomplete LLTM, where each testee responds to only $k_v = 2$ items. This equivalence implies several useful results both for the LLTM and the LBTL. Among these are n.s. uniqueness conditions both for the maximum likelihood (ML) estimation in the LBTL and for unconditional (or joint) ML estimation in the LLTM. These n.s. conditions again involve systems of linear inequalities based on the partial order of the strong components of certain digraphs and are, for instance, weaker than the sufficient condition for the LBTL given by Bradley and El-Helbawy.

It is obvious that the LBTL can have many interesting applications both in experimental and applied (e.g., marketing and consumer) psychology. Unfortunately, the potential of this model has so far not been fully recognized in psychometrics.

Fields of Application

Analysis of the Cognitive Complexity of Tasks and Item Generation

The focus of early applications of the LLTM was on the explanation of the difficulty of test items (e.g., in matrix completion tests), of syllogisms, or of tasks from subject matters such as physics, mathematics, and statistics (in school and university education) in terms of their cognitive complexity—the kinds and numbers of cognitive operations or rules that have to be applied to solve a given task. Many references to the first decade of research using the LLTM can be found, for instance, in articles by Fischer and Formann or Spada and May. The rapid development of computer-based testing technologies, especially of adaptive testing strategies, in the last two decades has created an increasing demand for large item banks and has triggered research on item generation principles and techniques. An up-to-date description of these methods is given by Irvine and Kyllonen. Some of this research has built on the LLTM or related IRT models; however, often simpler regression techniques, which do not enjoy the advantageous statistical properties of the LLTM, have been employed.

A frequent problem in applications of the LLTM was that the model failed to fit the data; the likelihood ratio tests specified in Eq. (10) often came out significant, especially when the LLTM was applied to existing test materials rather than to items that had been constructed strictly on the basis of an appropriate cognitive model. Nevertheless, item difficulty could often be explained at least approximately.

An exemplary early study employing matrix completion items is due to Nährer. First, the basic parameters α_l of the factors underlying item difficulty were estimated using the data of one item sample and one testee sample. Second, a new item sample was constructed and the parameters of the items were predicted based on their cognitive structures, using the estimates $\hat{\alpha}_j$ obtained from the first sample. (Let the predicted item parameters be denoted $\hat{\beta}_i^{(\mathrm{LLTM})}$.) Third, these new items were presented to a new testee sample, from which item parameter estimates $\hat{\beta}_i^{(\mathrm{RM})}$ were derived using the RM. Fourth, a comparison of both sets of estimates, $\hat{\boldsymbol{\beta}}^{(\mathrm{LLTM})}$ and $\hat{\boldsymbol{\beta}}^{(\mathrm{RM})}$, was made, indicating a considerable degree of correspondence. These results can be viewed as an example of a genuine prediction of the difficulty of new items in a new testee sample.

There remains, however, the unsolved question: What is a sufficient approximation of predicted item difficulty? The answer should depend in a complex way on the purpose of the particular LLTM application.

Cross-Cultural Research and Item Bias

A major strength of the LLTM lies in the consistency of the estimator $\hat{\boldsymbol{\alpha}}$ irrespective of the form of the distribution of the person parameters θ_v. This implies that the researcher can carry out a rigorous comparison of the difficulty of cognitive operations or of the application of rules between different populations, such as age groups, gender groups, and cultural groups. In other words, the LLTM is very suitable for testing the generalizability of results over different person populations. Under H_0, the basic parameters are equal in two (or more) populations of interest, $\boldsymbol{\alpha}_1 = \boldsymbol{\alpha}_2 = \boldsymbol{\alpha}$; under H_1, they are independent parameter vectors. Therefore, the conditional likelihood under H_0 is $L_C(H_0) = L_C(\hat{\boldsymbol{\alpha}} \mid \boldsymbol{r}, \mathbf{W}, \mathbf{X})$, whereas under H_1 it is $L_C(H_1) = L_C^{(1)}(\hat{\boldsymbol{\alpha}}_1 \mid \boldsymbol{r}_1, \mathbf{W}_1, \mathbf{X}_1) L_C^{(2)}(\hat{\boldsymbol{\alpha}}_2 \mid \boldsymbol{r}_2, \mathbf{W}_2, \mathbf{X}_2)$ (where the indexes 1 and 2 refer to the two populations). H_0 can be tested against H_1 by means of a CLR test statistic analogous to Eq. (10), $\chi^2 = -2\ln(L_C(H_0)/L_C(H_1))$ with $\mathrm{df} = 2p - p = p$.

A study of this kind was carried out by Formann and Piswanger already in 1979, described later in English language in an article by Fischer and Formann. A set of matrix completion items was constructed, systematically grounded on a set of rules, and was used for a comparison of the test performance of Austrian and African high school students. The application of the LLTM revealed an unexpected influence of Arabic versus Latin writing habits on the difficulty of these nonverbal (purely graphical) items, due to their item format. This conclusion was possible irrespective of the fact that the distributions of ability Θ differed significantly between the two populations. A more recent cross-cultural study was done by Tanzer, Gittler, and Ellis.

Obviously, item bias (or differential item functioning) studies are just special cases of cross-cultural studies, as already sketched.

Group-Oriented Analysis of Change

The LLTM has been found to be very useful for the description of change within individuals and to attribute the change to causes such as treatments and training. An illustrative example is a study by Gittler and Glück on the effect of learning mechanical geometry in high school on the development of spatial abilities in male versus female students. An LLTM-based unidimensional model of change assumes that the RM defined in Eq. (2) holds, with virtual item parameters:

$$\beta_{git}^* = \beta_i + \sum_j q_{gjt}\eta_j + \tau \tag{12}$$

where

- β_i is the difficulty parameter of item I_i;
- q_{gjt} is the cumulative dosage of treatment B_j given to individuals S_v of treatment group G_g up to the time point of testing, T_t;
- η_j is the effect of one unit of treatment B_j (with respect to the latent dimension Θ);
- τ is the trend effect, an effect occurring in all individuals (e.g., the effect of aging or maturation); formally, the trend can be conceived as a treatment given to all individuals with same dosage 1;
- β_{git}^* is the 'virtual' difficulty parameter of item I_i for testees $S_v \in G_g$ at time T_t, which is a result of initial item difficulty β_i plus the cumulative treatment effects up to the time of the testing.

This LLTM-based model of change requires that testees be observed or tested at least twice because otherwise the item difficulty parameters β_i would not be separable from the effect parameters η_j and trend τ. This approach to analyzing change has been seen to be a flexible and powerful tool in the analysis of repeated measurement data.

Individual Change

Suppose the researcher focuses on a single individual S (the index v is omitted for simplicity), and assume that an item pool is available for which a previous calibration study has established the fit of the RM. If S is tested at some time T_1 with an item sample (test) $\mathcal{T}_1$ taken from that pool, the appropriate model for the item responses is the RM in Eq. (2), for all items $I_i \in \mathcal{T}_1$. If, subsequently, S's trait parameter θ undergoes some change (due to treatments given or to development), the appropriate model for S's responses given to another sample of items from the pool, denoted $\mathcal{T}_2$, presented at time T_2, is still the RM with the item parameters β_i, for $I_i \in \mathcal{T}_2$, however, with person parameter $\theta + \eta$, where η denotes the amount of change in S. The latter RM can be written as:

$$P(X_i = 1 \mid \theta, \eta, \beta_i; T_2) = \frac{\exp(\theta + \eta - \beta_i)}{1 + \exp(\theta + \eta - \beta_i)} = \frac{\exp(\theta - \beta_i^*)}{1 + \exp(\theta - \beta_i^*)} \tag{13}$$

with $\beta_i^* = \beta_i - \eta$, for all $I_i \in \mathcal{T}_2$. The reparameterization in the right-hand formula of Eq. (13) has the advantage that, in spite of the change of S's position on trait Θ, person parameter θ_v in the model is kept constant while change is projected into the virtual item parameters β_i^*. Therefore, both RMs for time points T_1 and T_2 can jointly be considered one RM with item parameters β_i for $I_i \in \mathcal{T}_1$ and $\beta_i^* = \beta_i + \eta$ for $I_i \in \mathcal{T}_2$, with a fixed person parameters θ_v. Clearly, this is a special LLTM.

Assuming that the item parameters β_i have previously been estimated based on a calibration sample of sufficient size, they can now be treated as known constants, so that the model involves only one unknown parameter η (in addition to θ). The person parameter θ can again be conditioned out and η estimated via the CML method, one- or two-sided uniformly most accurate confidence intervals can be computed, and uniformly most powerful unbiased statistical tests can be made (e.g., of the H_0: $\eta = 0$ of no change). Moreover, if pretest $\mathcal{T}_1$ and posttest $\mathcal{T}_2$ are presented to many testees, it makes sense to tabulate significance probabilities for all possible score combinations (r_1, r_2) and to use that table without further computations in each individual case. Such tables have been published, for example, in the manual for the Progressive Matrices test by Raven, Raven, and Court.

Reinterpretation as a Multidimensional Model

A Multidimensional Linear Logistic Test Model of Change

A multidimensional reinterpretation of the unidimensional LLTM of change is possible by setting, in Eq. (2), $\theta_v - \beta_i = \theta_{vi}$ and treating these θ_{vi} as multidimensional trait parameters, so that θ_{vi} can be understood as S_v's position on latent trait Θ_i, $i = 1, \ldots, k$. No assumptions are made about whether the k dimensions Θ_i are functionally related, correlated, or independent. Owing to this weakness of assumptions about the underlying dimensions, the model has been denoted "linear logistic model with relaxed assumptions" (LLRA). Avoiding to specify the true dimensionality is possible because, by virtue of conditional inference methods, estimation and hypothesis testing become independent of the true values of the person parameters θ_{vi}. Under the assumption that the same set of items, $I_1, \ldots, I_k$, is presented to the testees at two time points, T_1 and T_2, the model can be defined by:

$$P(X_{vi1} = 1 \mid S_v, I_i, T_1) = \frac{\exp(\theta_{vi})}{1 + \exp(\theta_{vi})} \quad \text{for } T_1 \tag{14}$$

$$P(X_{vi1} = 1 \mid S_v, I_i, T_2) = \frac{\exp(\theta_{vi} + \delta_v)}{1 + \exp(\theta_{vi} + \delta_v)} \quad \text{for } T_2 \tag{15}$$

$$\delta_v = \sum_{j=1}^{p} q_{vj}\eta_j + \tau + \sum_{j<l} q_{vj}q_{vl}\rho_{jl} \tag{16}$$

where

δ_v denotes the amount of change of S_v under the treatment(s) given,
η_j denotes the effect of one dosage unit of treatment B_j,
q_{vj} denotes the dosage of B_j given to S_v,
τ denotes a trend effect that is independent of the treatment(s),
ρ_{jl} denotes a treatment interaction effect $B_j \times B_l$.

Eq. (16) can be rewritten without loss of generality as:

$$\delta_v = \sum_{j=1}^{p^*} q_{vj}\eta_j \tag{17}$$

This is possible because the right-hand side of Eq. (16) is a linear function of the effect parameters η_j, τ, and ρ_{jl}: all these $p^* = p + 1 + \binom{p}{2}$ parameters can be denoted by $\eta_j, j = 1, \ldots, p^*$, with accordingly redefined weights q_{vj}, so that Eq. (17) results immediately. The latter is notationally more convenient.

The conditional likelihood function of the two response matrices $\mathbf{X}_1$ and $\mathbf{X}_2$ can be shown to be:

$$\ln L_C = \sum_v \sum_i (x_{vi1} - x_{vi2})^2 \times \left[x_{vi2} \sum_j q_{vj}\eta_j - \ln\left(1 + \exp\left(\sum_j q_{vj}\eta_j\right)\right) \right] \tag{18}$$

Differentiating this with respect to η_a, $a = 1, \ldots, p^*$, and setting the derivatives to zero yields the CML equations:

$$\sum_v q_{va} \sum_i (x_{vi1} - x_{vi2})^2 \left[x_{vi2} - \frac{\exp(\sum_j q_{vj}\eta_j)}{1 + \exp(\sum_j q_{vj}\eta_j)} \right] = 0 \tag{19}$$

for $a = 1, \ldots, p^*$. Similarly, the second-order partial derivatives are:

$$\frac{\partial^2 \ln L_C}{\partial \eta_a \partial \eta_b} = -\sum_v q_{va} q_{vb} \sum_i (x_{vi1} - x_{vi2})^2 \times \frac{\exp\left(\sum_j q_{vj}\eta_j\right)}{\left(1 + \exp\left(\sum_j q_{vj}\eta_j\right)\right)^2} \quad (20)$$

which are needed, for instance, to solve Eq. (19) by means of the Newton-Raphson algorithm or to compute the asymptotic information matrix. Both the likelihood function and the estimation equations can be seen to be special cases of those for the LLTM.

Some Properties of the Multidimensional Model of Change

In spite of the multidimensionality of the latent traits Θ_i and, consequently, the large number of person parameters, the CML approach allows us to eliminate all the nk parameters θ_{vi} and thus enables a statistically stable and consistent estimation of the (treatment) effect parameters η_j. Consider, for instance, a clinical depression scale comprising 15 items (psychopathological symptoms) that cannot be meaningfully modeled by means of a unidimensional IRT approach. Suppose further a study design with three treatments and three treatment groups plus a control group. Such a design obviously does not permit us to estimate treatment interactions, so only three treatment effect parameters $\eta_j, j = 1, 2, 3$, and one trend parameter τ are estimable. If the treatment groups as well as the control group consist of 30 patients each, the model comprises $n \times k = 120 \times 15 = 1800$ person parameters plus four effect parameters. It would be hopeless to try to estimate these 1804 parameters jointly, whereas it is a statistically meaningful and feasible enterprise to estimate, by means of the CML method, the four effect parameters alone and to test hypotheses on them.

The price to be paid for this, however, is that, by conditioning on all $r_{vi} = x_{vi1} + x_{vi2}$, all response combinations with $x_{vi1} + x_{vi2} = 2$ or 0 become uninformative (because the respective conditional probability of such pairs of responses is trivially equal to 1) and cancel out the likelihood function. Technically, this is achieved by means of the term $(x_{vi1} - x_{vi2})^2$ in Eqs. (18) and (19), which filters out the uninformative score combinations. Their elimination implies a considerable loss of statistical information, but at the same time drastically reduces the number of parameters to be estimated and on which hypotheses are to be tested.

Conditioning the θ_{vi} out yields also another equally important advantage: for a multidimensional model (e.g., with 15 latent dimensions), it is practically impossible to ascertain whether a sample of testees (or patients) is representative of a specified population. The present conditional method, however, is not sensitive to the nonrepresentativeness of the sample because the estimator $\hat{\boldsymbol{\eta}}$ is consistent independently of the distribution of the θ_{vi} parameters (again except for certain degenerate distributions). This more than compensates for the disadvantage of the loss of part of the information.

Hypothesis Tests

The main goal in applications of the LLRA is the testing of hypotheses on change or on treatment effects. A general tool for the construction of such tests is the CLR statistic that compares the conditional likelihoods under H_0 and H_1, assuming that H_1 is true. Consider null hypotheses of the form:

$$\boldsymbol{\eta} = \boldsymbol{M}\boldsymbol{\alpha} \quad (21)$$

where $\boldsymbol{\eta} = (\eta_1, \ldots, \eta_p)'$ is the column vector of effect parameters under H_1; $\boldsymbol{\alpha} = (\alpha_1, \ldots, \alpha_{p'})'$, with $p' < p$, is a column vector of effect parameters under H_0; and $\boldsymbol{M}$ is a $p \times p'$ matrix of full column rank. Then asymptotically:

$$\chi^2 = -2 \ln\left(\frac{L_C(H_0)}{L_C(H_1)}\right), \quad \text{with df} = p - p' \quad (22)$$

is a centrally chi-square distributed statistic for testing H_0 against H_1.

Typical null hypotheses are that (1) a particular treatment effect parameter (or trend) is zero, (2) two or more effect parameters are equal, (3) some or all effect parameters generalize over all items or over certain subgroups of items, and (4) some or all effect parameters generalize over certain subgroups of persons. A software program specifically designed for the analysis of treatment effects using the powerful conditional likelihood approach is LPCM-Win by Fischer and Ponocny-Seliger.

Polytomous Extensions

The models discussed here have been generalized also to polytomous items with ordered response categories. Two cases must be distinguished: (1) if all items have the same categories, then the basic model is a rating scale model (RSM) with a linear structure imposed on the item parameters and (b) if different items may have different response categories, then the basic model is a partial credit model (PCM) with a linear structure embedded in the item × category parameters. A description of these "linear rating scale models" (LRSMs) and "linear partial credit models" (LPCMs) is given in the book *Rasch Models* by Fischer and Molenaar, Chapter 19, and in more detailed form in the LPCM-Win manual by Fischer and Ponocny-Seliger. Related models have been suggested by Wilson and Adams as well as by Meiser. Further programs capable of estimating multidimensional LRSMs and LPCMs are FACETS by Linacre and Acer ConQest by Adams, Wu, and Wilson.

See Also the Following Articles

Item and Test Bias • Maximum Likelihood Estimation • Partial Credit Model • Rating Scale Model

Further Reading

Andersen, E. B. (1980). *Discrete Statistical Models with Social Science Applications.* North-Holland, Amsterdam.

Bechger, T. M., Verstralen, H. H. F. M., and Verhelst, N. D. (2002). Equivalent linear logistic test models. *Psychometrika* **67,** 123–136.

Bradley, R. A., and El-Helbawy, A. T. (1976). Treatment contrasts in paired comparisons: Basic procedures with applications to factorials. *Biometrika* **63,** 255–262.

Fischer, G. H. (2003). The precision of gain scores under an item response theory perspective: A comparison of asymptotic and exact conditional inference about change. *Appl. Psychol. Measmt.* **27,** 3–26.

Fischer, G. H., and Formann, A. K. (1982). Some applications of logistic latent trait models with linear constraints on the parameters. *Appl. Psychol. Measmt.* **4,** 397–416.

Fischer, G. H., and Molenaar, I. W. (eds.) (1995). *Rasch Models: Foundations, Recent Developments, and Applications*. Springer-Verlag, New York.

Fischer, G. H., and Ponocny-Seliger, E. (1998). *Structural Rasch Modeling: Handbook of the Usage of LPCM-WIN 1.0.* ProGAMMA, Groningen, The Netherlands (see www.scienceplus.nl).

Gittler, G., and Glück, J. (1998). Differential transfer of learning: Effects of instruction in descriptive geometry on spatial test performance. *J. Geometry and Graphics* **2,** 71–84.

Glas, C. A. W., and Verhelst, N. D. (1995). Testing the Rasch model. In *Rasch Models: Foundations, Recent Developments, and Applications* (G. H. Fischer and I. W. Molenaar, eds.), pp. 69–95. Springer-Verlag, New York.

Irvine, S. H., and Kyllonen, P. C. (eds.) (2002). *Item Generation for Test Development*. Lawrence Erlbaum, Mahwah, NJ.

Linacre, J. M. (1996). *A User's Guide to FACETS.* MESA Press, Chicago, IL.

Linacre, J. M. (1994). *Many-Facet Rasch Measurement.* MESA Press, Chicago, IL.

Meiser, T. (1996). Loglinear Rasch models for the analysis of stability and change. *Psychometrika* **61,** 629–645.

Nährer, W. (1980). Zur Analyse von Matrizenaufgaben mit dem linearen logistischen Testmodell [On the analysis of matrices items by means of the linear logistic test model]. *Zeitschrift für Experimentelle und Angewandte Psychologie* **27,** 553–564.

Pfanzagl, J. (1993). On the consistency of conditional maximum likelihood estimators. *Ann. Inst. Statist. Math.* **45,** 703–719.

Rasch, G. (1980). Probabilistic models for some intelligence and attainment tests. Expanded ed. University of Chicago Press, Chicago, IL. (Originally published 1960, Pædagogiske Institut, Copenhagen.)

Raven, J., Raven, J. C., and Court, J. H. (2000). Standard progressive matrices. In *Raven Manual,* Sec. 3, App. 3. Oxford Psychologists Press, Oxford.

Spada, H., and May, R. (1982). The linear logistic test model and its application in educational research. In *The Improvement of Measurement in Education and Psychology* (D. Spearritt, ed.), pp. 67–84. Australian Council for Educational Research, Hawthorn, Victoria, Australia.

Tanzer, N. K., Gittler, G., and Ellis, B. B. (1995). Cross-cultural validation of item complexity in an LLTM-calibrated spatial ability test. *Eur. J. Psychol. Assess.* **11,** 170–183.

Wilson, M. R., and Adams, R. J. (1995). Rasch models for item bundles. *Psychometrika* **60,** 181–198.

Wu, M. L., Adams, R. J., and Wilson, M. R. (1998). *ACER ConQest.* Australian Council for Educational Research, Melbourne, Australia.

Linear Models, Problems

John Fox
McMaster University, Hamilton, Ontario, Canada

Glossary

added-variable plot A diagnostic graph for showing leverage and influence of observations on a regression coefficient.

Breusch–Pagan test A score test for nonconstant error variance (heteroscedasticity).

collinearity (multicollinearity) Strong linear relationships among the columns of the model matrix in a linear model, reducing the precision of coefficient estimates.

component-plus-residual plot A diagnostic graph for nonlinearity, plotting partial residuals against an explanatory variable.

Durbin–Watson statistics Test statistics for serial correlation of the errors in a time-series regression.

heteroscedastic-consistent covariance matrix An estimate of the covariance matrix of the least-squares regression coefficients that is consistent even when the error variance is not constant.

high-leverage observation An observation that can exert substantial influence on the least-squares estimates by virtue of its unusual combination of values of the explanatory variables; hat-values are measures of leverage.

influential observation An observation that, when removed, substantially changes the regression coefficients; dfbeta, dfbetas, and Cook's distances are measures of influence.

outlier In a linear model, a value of the response variable that is conditionally unusual, given the values of the explanatory variables; studentized residuals may be used to locate outliers.

variance-inflation factor (VIF) A measure of the impact of collinearity on the precision of estimation of a coefficient.

Despite its broad direct applicability, the normal linear model makes strong assumptions about the structure of the data. If these assumptions are not satisfied, data analysis based on the linear model may be suboptimal or even wholly misleading. The use of linear models in data analysis should therefore be accompanied by diagnostic techniques meant to reveal inadequacies in the model or weaknesses in the data. In favorable instances, diagnostics that reveal such problems also point toward their solution. Problems that can afflict linear models and least-squares estimation include unusual data, non-normal errors, nonconstant error variance, nonindependent errors, nonlinear relationships, collinearity, and measurement error in the explanatory variables.

The Normal Linear Model: Structure and Assumptions

Most of applied statistics is based, directly or indirectly, on the normal linear model fit by least squares: linear models for simple and multiple regression, analysis of variance, and analysis of covariance (dummy regression) have broad direct application. Various extensions and generalizations of the linear model—for example, generalized linear models (logistic regression, Poisson regression, etc.), robust regression, additive regression, Cox regression for survival data, linear structural-equation models, linear models fit by generalized least squares—retain central features of the normal linear model. Finally, many kinds of statistical models are fit by adaptations of linear least squares, such as the method of iteratively reweighted least squares (IRLS) commonly employed to fit generalized linear models. In this article, the terms "linear model" and "regression" are used more or less interchangeably.

The normal linear model may be written in matrix form as

$$\begin{aligned} \mathbf{y} &= \mathbf{X}\beta + \varepsilon, \\ \varepsilon &\sim \mathbf{N}_n(\mathbf{0}, \sigma^2\mathbf{I}_n). \end{aligned} \tag{1}$$

The variables in Eq. (1) have the following meanings:

- $\mathbf{y} = (y_1, y_2, \ldots, y_n)^T$ is a column vector of observations on the response variable.
- $\mathbf{X} = \{x_{ij}\}$ is an $n \times p$ model (or design) matrix of regressors. The regressors comprising the columns of **X** may be quantitative explanatory variables, transformations of quantitative explanatory variables, polynomial terms, dummy regressors or other contrasts representing categorical explanatory variables, interaction regressors, and so on.
- $\beta = (\beta_1, \beta_2, \ldots, \beta_p)^T$ is a column vector of regression coefficients. Usually, β_1 is a constant or intercept term, in which case $x_{i1} = 1$.
- $\varepsilon = (\varepsilon_1, \varepsilon_2, \ldots, \varepsilon_n)^T$ is a column vector of errors. The errors are assumed to be normally and independently distributed, with zero expectations and common variance σ^2.
- $\mathbf{N}_n$ is the n-variable multivariate-normal distribution.
- $\mathbf{0}$ is a column vector of n zeroes.
- $\mathbf{I}_n$ is the order-n identity matrix.

If the x values are random rather than fixed, then the errors are additionally assumed to be independent of the x values, and the x values are assumed to be measured without error. Fixed values of x occur in experimental research, because the explanatory variables are under the direct control of the researcher; in observational research, the x values are usually construed as random. Assuming that random x values are independent of the errors implies that omitted explanatory variables (which are components of the errors) are independent (or somewhat more weakly, uncorrelated) with the explanatory variables that appear explicitly in the model.

The central task of linear-model analysis is to estimate the parameters of the model—that is, the regression coefficients (the β values) and the error variance (σ^2). Under the model, including the assumption of normality, the least-squares estimate of β, $\mathbf{b} = (\mathbf{X}^T\mathbf{X})^{-1}\mathbf{X}^T\mathbf{y}$, has a variety of desirable and even optimal properties. This solution implies that the model matrix **X** is of full column rank p; otherwise, the least-squares coefficients **b** are not unique. The least-squares residuals are $\mathbf{e} = \mathbf{y} - \mathbf{Xb}$, and an unbiased estimate of the error variance is $s^2 = \mathbf{e}^T\mathbf{e}/(n-p)$.

Diagnostics and Remedies

As mentioned, the normal linear model incorporates strong assumptions about the data, including assumptions of linearity, constant error variance (homoscedasticity), normality, and independence. Linearity follows from the assumption that the average error is zero, for then $E(\mathbf{y}) = \mathbf{X}\beta$. The assumption of linearity is to be broadly construed, because through transformations, polynomial regressors, and so on, the linear model may incorporate what are conventionally thought of as nonlinear partial relationships. That is, the linear model is linear in the parameters but not necessarily in the explanatory variables.

Not all of the assumptions of the model are checkable. For example, when **X** is random, it is assumed that it is independent of the errors ε, but because the least-squares residuals **e** are necessarily uncorrelated with **X**, the assumption is partly reflected in the estimated model. Certain departures from the assumptions can be detected (such as certain forms of nonlinearity, nonconstant error variance, nonnormality, or serial correlation of the errors), but not a correlation between the errors and a particular column of **X**, for example, induced by an omitted (confounding or lurking) explanatory variable. Although there are tests for omitted explanatory variables (such as Ramsey's RESET test), these necessarily make assumptions about the nature of the omission. Likewise, except when there are replicated observations at each unique row of **X**, possible departures from linearity are so diverse as to preclude effective, fully general, methods for detecting them.

The consequences of violating the assumptions of the normal linear model range in seriousness from benign to fatal. For example, depending partly on the configuration of the model matrix, moderate violation of the assumption of constant error variance may have only a minor impact on the efficiency of estimation. In contrast, substantial violation of the assumption of linearity suggests that the wrong mean function is fit to the data, rendering the results of the analysis entirely meaningless. Diagnostic methods, which are the focus here, are designed to discover violations of the assumptions of the model and data conditions that threaten the integrity of the analysis. Two general approaches to linear-model problems are numerical diagnostics, including statistical hypothesis tests, and graphical diagnostics. Tests determine, for example, whether there is evidence in the data to reject one or another assumption of the model, or to determine whether there is evidence that particular observations do not belong with the others. Graphical methods seek to reveal patterns that are indicative of problems with either the model or the data, and often are useful in suggesting ways to improve the data analysis, for example, by transformation of the variables or other respecification of the model. The two approaches, numerical diagnostics and graphs, are often complementary—for example, using a test to check a pattern discerned in a graph, or drawing a graph to display numerical diagnostics. The emphasis here is on graphical displays; more information on tests may be found in the literature.

With a few exceptions, space considerations preclude the presentation of examples in this article. Likewise, the presentation is limited to basic and widely available methods, excluding some newer and more advanced techniques, and the generalization of diagnostics to other kinds of statistical models. Examples, advanced methods, and generalizations are copiously available in the sources cited at the end of this article.

Unusual Data

Least-squares estimates, and other statistics associated with them, such as coefficient standard errors, correlation coefficients, and the regression standard error (standard deviation of the residuals), can be seriously influenced by unusual data. It is useful to distinguish among outliers, high-leverage observations, and influential observations. In the context of a linear model, an outlier is an observation for which the y value is unusual, conditional on the x values. (Thus, a univariate outlier on y or an x need not be a regression outlier.) A high-leverage observation, in contrast, is one that has an unusual combination of x values. Observations that combine outlyingness and leverage influence the values of the least-squares coefficients, in the sense that the removal of such observations changes the coefficients substantially. Other regression quantities, however, can be strongly affected under other circumstances. For example, a high-leverage, in-line observation decreases the standard errors of (some of) the regression coefficients; such an observation may in certain circumstances be regarded as a source of precision in estimation and in other circumstances as providing an illusion of precision. Similarly, an outlying observation at a low-leverage point will not affect the coefficients much, but will decrease the correlation, increase the residual standard error, and increase the standard errors of the coefficients.

Standard numerical diagnostics for outliers, leverage, and influence, along with a graphical method for examining leverage and influence on the coefficients are described in the follow subsections.

Leverage: Hat-Values

The fitted values $\hat{\mathbf{y}}$ in linear least-squares regression are a linear transformation of the observed response variable: $\hat{\mathbf{y}} = \mathbf{Xb} = \mathbf{X}(\mathbf{X}^T\mathbf{X})^{-1}\mathbf{X}^T\mathbf{y} = \mathbf{Hy}$, where $\mathbf{H} = \mathbf{X}(\mathbf{X}^T\mathbf{X})^{-1}\mathbf{X}^T$ is called the hat-matrix (because it transforms $\mathbf{y}$ to $\hat{\mathbf{y}}$). The matrix $\mathbf{H}$ is symmetric ($\mathbf{H} = \mathbf{H}^T$) and idempotent ($\mathbf{H} = \mathbf{H}^2$), and thus its ith diagonal entry, h_{ii}, gives the sum of squared entries in its ith row or column. Because the ith row of $\mathbf{H}$ represents the weight associated with the ith observed response in determining each of the fitted values, $h_i = h_{ii}$, called the hat-value, summarizes the potential contribution of observation i to the fitted values collectively, and is a suitable measure of the leverage of this observation in the least-squares fit.

Because $\mathbf{H}$ is a projection matrix (projecting $\mathbf{y}$ orthogonally onto the subspace spanned by the columns of $\mathbf{X}$), the average hat-value is p/n. By rule of thumb, hat-values are considered noteworthy when they exceed twice (or in small samples, three times) the average value. It is best, however, to examine hat-values graphically—for example, in an index plot (a scatterplot with hat-values on the vertical axis and observation indices on the horizontal axis)—using the numerical cutoffs to aid interpretation of the graph.

Outliers: Studentized Residuals

Although residuals are regarded as estimates of the errors, and although the residuals are the key to outlying observations, it is a sad fact that even when the standard assumptions hold, the least-squares residuals, though normally distributed, are dependent and heteroscedastic: $\mathbf{e} = \mathbf{y} - \hat{\mathbf{y}} = \mathbf{y} - \mathbf{Hy} = (\mathbf{I}_n - \mathbf{H})\mathbf{y}$. In most circumstances, the diagonal entries of $\mathbf{H}$ are unequal and the off-diagonal entries are nonzero. One approach is to standardize the residuals, as $e_i^* = e_i/[s\sqrt{(1-h_i)}]$, but the standardized residuals do not have a simple distribution. The more useful studentized residuals, however, are each t-distributed (under the model) with $n - p - 1$ degrees of freedom: $\text{rstudent}_i = e_i/[s_{(-i)}\sqrt{(1-h_i)}]$, where $s_{(-i)}$ is the estimated standard deviation of the errors computed from a regression with observation i deleted. (There are efficient computational formulas for the studentized residuals that do not require refitting the model, removing each observation in turn.)

Although the studentized residuals are each distributed as t, different studentized residuals are correlated, and there is, moreover, a problem of simultaneous inference when, as is usually the case, attention is drawn to the largest $|\text{rstudent}_i|$. A solution is to employ a Bonferroni adjustment for the outlier test, multiplying the usual two-sided p-value for the biggest absolute studentized residual by the number of observations. It is also helpful in this context to examine plots of the studentized residuals (see Non-Normal Errors, below).

Influence: dfbeta, dfbetas, and Cook's Distances

Although, as noted previously, unusual data can exert influence on all regression outputs, the focus here is on the coefficient estimates. A straightforward approach to the influence of individual observations is to ask how much the coefficients change when an observation is deleted. The change in the regression coefficients attending the deletion of observation i can be computed without literally refitting the model: $\mathbf{dfbeta}_i = (\mathbf{X}^T\mathbf{X})^{-1}\mathbf{x}_i e_i/(1-h_i)$, where $\mathbf{x}_i$ is the ith row of the model matrix (written as a column vector); dfbeta_{ij} gives the influence of observation i on coefficient j. A standardized version of this statistic, called dfbetas_{ij}, simply divides dfbeta_{ij} by the standard error of b_j.

There are $n \times p$ of each of dfbeta_{ij} and dfbetas_{ij}, and so their examination can be tedious, even in graphs such as index plots. Several similar measures have been proposed to examine the influence of individual observations on the vector of coefficient estimates. The most popular such measure is Cook's distance, $D_i = (\mathbf{b} - \mathbf{b}_{(-i)})^T\mathbf{X}^T\mathbf{X}(\mathbf{b} - \mathbf{b}_{(-i)})/ps^2$, where $\mathbf{b}$ is the least-squares coefficient vector computed on the full data set and $\mathbf{b}_{(-i)}$ is the coefficient vector with observation i omitted. As in the case of rstudent and dfbeta, Cook's D can be calculated without refitting the model. Cook's distance is invariant with respect to rescaling of columns of $\mathbf{X}$, and can be conveniently viewed in a graphical display such as an index plot.

Joint Influence: Added-Variable Plots

Single-observation deletion statistics such as dfbeta, dfbetas, and Cook's distances can fail to detect observations that are jointly influential. A good graphical diagnostic that works in such instances, and more generally, is the added-variable plot, also called a partial-regression plot. One such plot is constructed for each coefficient in the model. The collection of p added-variable plots represents projections of the $p-1$ dimensional regression surface onto a series of planes.

For example, for b_2, begin by regressing y on all columns of the model matrix excluding the second, $\mathbf{X}_{(-2)}$, obtaining residuals $\mathbf{y}^*_{(2)} = \mathbf{y} - \mathbf{X}^T_{(-2)}(\mathbf{X}^T_{(-2)}\mathbf{X}_{(-2)})^{-1}\mathbf{X}^T_{(-2)}\mathbf{y}$ Then compute residuals for the regression of the second column, $\mathbf{x}_{(2)}$, on the others: $\mathbf{x}^*_{(2)} = \mathbf{x}_{(2)} - \mathbf{X}^T_{(-2)} \times (\mathbf{X}^T_{(-2)}\mathbf{X}_{(-2)})^{-1}\mathbf{X}^T_{(-2)}\mathbf{x}_{(2)}$ (skipping over the first column of the model matrix, because it is typically a column of ones, representing the regression constant; it is possible to construct an added-variable plot for the constant, but the other coefficients are almost always of greater interest). The added-variable plot graphs $\mathbf{y}^*_{(2)}$, on the vertical axis, against $\mathbf{x}^*_{(2)}$, on the horizontal axis. The least-squares slope corresponding to this scatterplot is the coefficient b_2 from the original least-squares fit, the residuals are the original least-squares residuals e_i, and the standard error of the slope for the simple regression of $\mathbf{y}^*_{(2)}$ on $\mathbf{x}^*_{(2)}$ is (except for degrees of freedom) the standard error of the coefficient b_2 in the original model. The added-variable plot therefore shows the leverage and influence of the observations in determining b_2, along with the precision of the estimate b_2. An example is shown in Fig. 1.

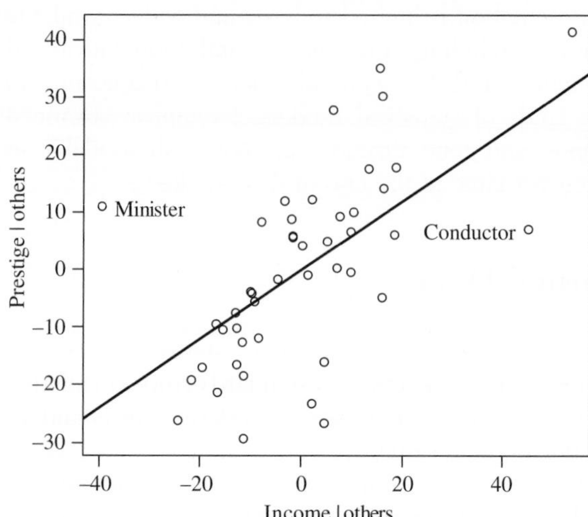

Figure 1 Added-variable plot for income in the regression of occupational prestige on the income and educational levels of occupations. This regression has been employed by Duncan (1961) in the construction of a prestige scale for occupations. The two labeled observations, ministers and railroad conductors, serve to decrease the income slope. The least-squares line on the plot represents the regression plane in the direction of income controlling for education.

Non-Normal Errors

Violations of the assumption of normally distributed errors can threaten the efficiency of estimation (for example, in the case of heavy-tailed error distributions) or can compromise the interpretability of the least-squares fit, which estimates the conditional mean of y as a function of the x values (for example, in the case of skewed errors). As explained in the preceding section, least-squares residuals and the errors have some different properties; nevertheless, examining the distribution of the residuals can be informative about the distribution of the errors. Quantile-comparison plots of studentized residuals help in focusing on the tails of the distribution. Such plots graph ordered residuals (usually on the vertical axis) against approximate expected quantiles of a reference distribution—either the normal distribution or the t distribution with $n - p - 1$ degrees of freedom. If the residuals follow the reference distribution, then the plot will be approximately linear. Systematic nonlinear patterns are indicative, for example, of skewed residuals or heavy-tailed residuals. Enhancing the plot with a bootstrapped confidence envelope, computed assuming the truth of the fitted model, provides a visual guide to the extremity of departures from normality; this is illustrated in Fig. 2.

There are several methods for testing departures from normality. One approach is to embed the normal linear model in a more general model that indexes

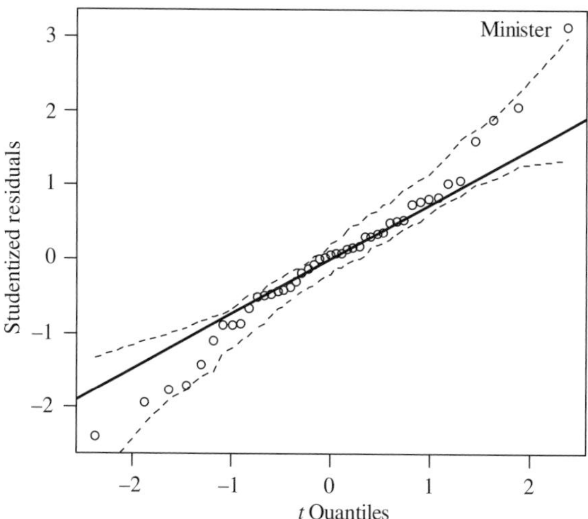

Figure 2 A t quantile-comparison plot for the studentized residuals from Duncan's occupational-prestige regression. The dashed lines represent a pointwise bootstrapped 95% confidence envelope. The residual distribution looks heavy tailed in comparison with the t-distribution, and one observation (minister) is slightly outside the confidence envelope.

non-normality by one or more parameters. Consider, for example, the Box–Cox regression model:

$$y_i^{(\lambda)} = \beta_1 x_{i1} + \beta_2 x_{i2} + \cdots + \beta_p x_{ip} + \varepsilon_i,$$
$$\varepsilon_i \sim \text{NID}(0, \sigma^2),$$

where

$$y_i^{(\lambda)} = \begin{cases} (y_i^\lambda - 1)/\lambda & \text{for } \lambda \neq 0, \\ \log_e y_i & \text{for } \lambda = 0, \end{cases}$$

is a modified power transformation (and the y_i are all positive). This model, with parameters $\beta_1, \beta_2, \ldots, \beta_p, \sigma^2$, and λ, is estimated by the method of maximum likelihood. A value of $\hat{\lambda}$ significantly different from 1 is indicative of non-normal errors (corrected by the Box–Cox transformation).

Nonconstant Error Variance

Nonconstant error variance (or heteroscedasticity) also threatens the efficiency of least-squares estimation as well as the validity of statistical inference. In principle, it is possible to examine the spread of residuals around the fitted regression surface, but because this usually is a high-dimensional surface, it is, except in the simplest cases, impractical to do so. An alternative is to look for common patterns of nonconstant residual variation. One such pattern is a tendency for residual spread to increase with the level of the response, a pattern that may be discernible in a plot of residuals (for example, rstudent_i or $|\text{rstudent}_i|$) against fitted values ($\hat{y}_i$).

A simple score test for the dependence of spread on level (called the Breusch–Pagan test, but independently developed by Cook and Weisberg) is to regress squared standardized residuals, $e_i^2/\hat{\sigma}^2$, on the fitted values, where $\hat{\sigma}^2 = \mathbf{e}^T\mathbf{e}/n$ is the maximum-likelihood estimator of the error variance. Half of the regression sum of squares from this auxiliary regression is distributed as chi square with one degree of freedom under the null hypothesis of constant error variance. The test can be extended to other, more general, models for the error variance.

Once discovered, nonconstant error variance can often be corrected by transformation of the response variable. In other instances, weighted-least-squares (WLS) estimation can be employed to obtain efficient coefficient estimates and accurate standard errors. Finally, it is possible to correct the standard errors of the ordinary least-squares estimates for unmodeled heteroscedasticity. A commonly employed approach estimates the covariance matrix of the least-squares coefficients consistently even in the presence of heteroscedasticity:

$$\tilde{\mathbf{V}}(\mathbf{b}) = (\mathbf{X}'\mathbf{X})^{-1}\mathbf{X}'\tilde{\mathbf{\Sigma}}\mathbf{X}(\mathbf{X}'\mathbf{X})^{-1},$$

where $\tilde{\mathbf{\Sigma}} = \text{diag}(e_i^2)$. The estimator $\tilde{\mathbf{V}}(\mathbf{b})$ is used in place of the usual $\hat{V}(\mathbf{b}) = s^2(\mathbf{X}'\mathbf{X})^{-1}$. Discovering the form of nonconstant error variance and taking it into account is advantageous, however, because doing so improves the efficiency of estimation.

Nonindependence

The potential ill effects of nonindependent errors are similar to those of nonconstant error variance. Departures from independence can occur in a variety of ways. Usually, the assumption of independence must be justified by the method of data collection. Common sources of nonindependence include clustered data (for example, hierarchical data, such as data collected on children within schools), longitudinal data collected on individuals over time, and time-series data.

How nonindependence is ascertained depends on the structure of the data. In time-series regression, for example, it is common to examine the autocorrelations of the residuals, where the autocorrelation at lag t is $r_t = \sum_{i=t+1}^{n} e_i e_{i-t} / \sum_{i=1}^{n} e_i^2$. Tests for serial correlation in the errors may be based on the Durbin–Watson statistics $D_t = \sum_{i=t+1}^{n} (e_i - e_{i-t})^2 / \sum_{i=1}^{n} e_i^2$. The D_t values have a complex sampling distribution that depends on the configuration of the model matrix for the regression, but there are good approximations available for the p-values, which may also be estimated by bootstrapping. Remedies for nonindependence depend on its source. For example, serial correlation of errors in time-series regression may be handled by generalized least-squares estimation. Likewise, linear and nonlinear mixed-effects models provide efficient estimates for clustered and longitudinal data.

Nonlinearity

Nonlinearity is in a sense the most serious violation of the assumptions of the linear model, because it implies that the wrong equation is being fit to the data. As employed here, "nonlinearity" encompasses all departures from the specified functional form of the model; as mentioned, the linear model of Eq. (1) encompasses specifications that are nonlinear in the explanatory variables but linear in the parameters, such as polynomial regression models, models including interactions, models with dummy regressors, and so on. As with the other problems that have been discussed here, however, nonlinearity can vary in degree from trivial to serious. If there are one or two explanatory variables, nonlinearity can be discerned directly, in a smoothed two- or three-dimensional scatterplot of the data, but the higher dimensional problem is much less tractable.

If combinations of values of the explanatory variables are replicated in the data, then lack of fit can be tested for by contrasting the model fit to the data with a model that simply partitions the observations according to the unique rows of the model matrix. This strategy can be adapted as an approximation in other cases by partitioning the space of the explanatory variables into regions. An alternative general approach is to look for nonlinearity of a particular form, such as a nonlinear partial relationship between the response and each explanatory variable. This approach can be implemented both in graphical diagnostics and in tests.

A frequently useful graphical diagnostic is the component-plus-residual (or partial residual) plot. Suppose that the coefficient β_1 in the linear model is a regression constant, and focus on the partial relationship between y and x_2 conditional on the other x values. The partial residual associated with x_2 is $\mathbf{e}_{2|3,\ldots,p} = b_2\mathbf{x}_2 + \mathbf{e}$, where $\mathbf{e}$ is the vector of least-squares residuals and $\mathbf{x}_2$ is the second column of the model matrix. The component-plus-residual plot is a scatterplot of the partial residuals, on the vertical axis, against the values of x_2, on the horizontal axis. Smoothing the plot with a nonparametric-regression line aids interpretation. Once the nature of a nonlinear partial relationship between the response and a particular predictor x_j is discerned, it is possible to determine how to model it—for example, by a transformation of x_j or by a polynomial in x_j. An illustrative component-plus-residual plot appears in Fig. 3.

When there are strong nonlinear relationships among the explanatory variables, component-plus-residuals plots can prove misleading. More sophisticated versions of

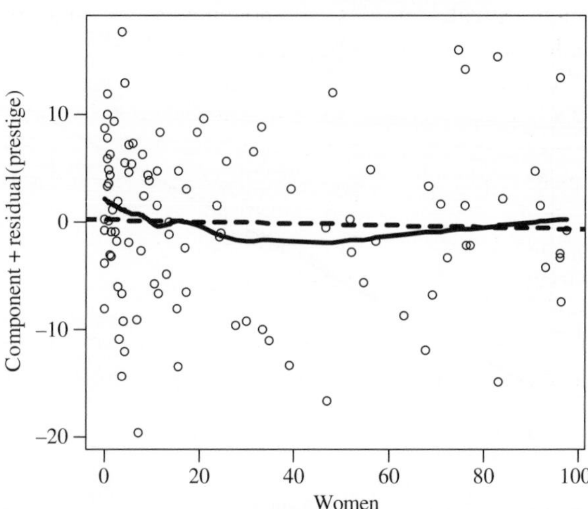

Figure 3 Component-plus-residual plot for the percentage of women in the regression of occupational prestige on the income level, education level, and percentage of women in 102 Canadian occupations. The dashed line in the plot represents the edge of the regression hyperplane, which is nearly horizontal in the direction of percentage of women. The solid line is for a nonparametric-regression smooth, which suggests a weak quadratic partial relationship.

these diagnostics based on polynomial or nonparametric regression are more robust. Nonlinearity can be tested for in a partial relationship by embedding the linear model in a more general model. For example, the Box–Tidwell regression model includes parameters for the power transformation of one or more predictors. In a similar spirit, the linear model can be replaced with a semiparametric additive model in which certain terms are modeled nonparametrically, contrasting the fit of this model with the linear model by an approximate incremental F-test. Likewise, if an explanatory variable is discrete, it can be treated as a set of dummy regressors, contrasting the resulting fit with the original linear model.

Collinearity and Other Sources of Imprecision

Consider fitting a linear model in which β_1 is the regression constant. The sampling variance of the least-squares estimate b_2 of β_2 is

$$V(b_2) = \frac{\sigma^2}{(n-1)s_2^2} \times \frac{1}{1-R_2^2}, \qquad (2)$$

where σ^2 is the error variance (estimated by s^2 in a application), n is the sample size, s_2^2 is the sample variance of x_2, and R_2^2 is the squared multiple correlation from the regression of x_2 on the other x variables. Thus, imprecise estimates are the product of large error variance, small samples, homogeneous explanatory variables, and strong linear relationships among (some of) the explanatory variables, termed collinearity or multicollinearity. The second factor in Eq. (2), $1/(1-R_2^2)$, called the variance-inflation factor (VIF), expresses the harm produced by collinearity. The square root of the VIF is the expansion of the size of the confidence interval for β_2 due to collinearity.

Variance-inflation factors are applicable to one-degree-of-freedom effects, but not, for example, to sets of related dummy regressors or polynomial terms. Write the linear model as follows:

$$\mathbf{y} = \beta_1 \mathbf{1} + \mathbf{X}_2\beta_2 + \mathbf{X}_3\beta_3 + \varepsilon,$$

where $\mathbf{1}$ is a vector of ones, $\mathbf{X}_2$ contains the columns of the model matrix pertaining to a particular multiple-degree-of-freedom effect, and $\mathbf{X}_3$ contains the remaining columns of the model matrix. Then the generalized variance-inflation factor is $\text{GVIF} = \det \mathbf{R}_{22} \det \mathbf{R}_{33} / \det \mathbf{R}$, where $\mathbf{R}_{22}$ is the correlation matrix among the columns of $\mathbf{X}_2$, $\mathbf{R}_{33}$ is the correlation matrix among the columns of $\mathbf{X}_3$, $\mathbf{R}$ is the correlation matrix for $[\mathbf{X}_2, \mathbf{X}_3]$ (i.e., the full model matrix, omitting the constant regressor), and det stands for the determinant. The GVIF gives the inflation in the squared (hyper)volume of the joint confidence region for the coefficients in β_2 due to collinearity between the columns of $\mathbf{X}_2$ and $\mathbf{X}_3$.

There are other diagnostics for collinearity (based, for example, on eigenvalue–eigenvector or singular-value decompositions of the model matrix or of the cross-products or correlations among the columns of the model matrix), but variance-inflation factors are particularly easy to interpret. Once collinear relationships are located, they can be explored by regressing one column (or set of columns) of the model matrix on the others. What to do about collinearity is a thornier issue. Unlike most of the other problems discussed in this article, collinearity is usually best understood as a problem with the data rather than with the model: because of strong correlations among the x variables, the data are uninformative about certain partial relationships between the response and explanatory variables. Common approaches to collinearity, such as variable selection and biased estimation, make the problem *seem* to disappear by (often surreptitiously) altering the questions asked of the data.

Measurement Error in the Explanatory Variables

Consider the following regression model:

$$y_i = \beta_1\xi_i + \beta_2 x_{i2} + \varepsilon_i,$$

where the "latent" explanatory variable ξ is not directly observed (hence the Greek letter); x_2 is directly observed and measured without error; and the regression error ε behaves according to the usual assumptions—in particular, $E(\varepsilon_i) = 0$, and the errors are uncorrelated with each other and with the explanatory variables. To simplify the exposition, but without loss of generality, suppose that all of the variables, y, ξ, and x_2 (along with ε), have means of 0, eliminating the regression constant from the model. Imagine that we have a fallible observable indicator x_1 of ξ,

$$x_{i1} = \xi_i + \delta_i,$$

where δ is the measurement-error component of x_1. Suppose further that the measurement errors are "well behaved": $E(\delta) = 0$; $E(\xi\delta) = 0$ (the measurement errors and "true scores" are uncorrelated); $E(x_2\delta) = 0$ (the measurement errors in x_1 are uncorrelated with the other explanatory variable); and $E(\varepsilon\delta) = 0$ (the measurement and regression errors are uncorrelated).

Under these circumstances, it is not hard to show that

$$\begin{aligned}\beta_1 &= \frac{\sigma_{y1}\sigma_2^2 - \sigma_{12}\sigma_{y2}}{\sigma_1^2\sigma_2^2 - \sigma_{12}^2 - \sigma_\delta^2\sigma_2^2},\\ \beta_2 &= \frac{\sigma_{y2}\sigma_1^2 - \sigma_{12}\sigma_{y1}}{\sigma_1^2\sigma_2^2 - \sigma_{12}^2} - \frac{\beta_1\sigma_{12}\sigma_\delta^2}{\sigma_1^2\sigma_2^2 - \sigma_{12}^2},\end{aligned} \qquad (3)$$

but that the population analogues of the least-squares coefficients (i.e., the quantities that the least-squares coefficients estimate) are

$$\begin{aligned}\beta_1' &= \frac{\sigma_{y1}\sigma_2^2 - \sigma_{12}\sigma_{y2}}{\sigma_1^2\sigma_2^2 - \sigma_{12}^2},\\ \beta_2' &= \frac{\sigma_{y2}\sigma_1^2 - \sigma_{12}\sigma_{y1}}{\sigma_1^2\sigma_2^2 - \sigma_{12}^2}.\end{aligned} \qquad (4)$$

In these equations, the σ values are variances and covariances: for example, σ_{y1} is the covariance of y and x_1, σ_1^2 is the variance of x_1, and σ_δ^2 is the measurement-error variance (which supposedly is nonzero). Comparing Eqs. (3) and (4) reveals that the least-squares coefficients are biased as estimators of β_1 and β_2: because the denominator of β_1 in Eq. (3) must be positive, and $-\sigma_\delta^2\sigma_2^2$ is necessarily negative, the least-squares estimand β_1' is "attenuated" toward zero.

The bias in β_2' has a different (and more interesting) characterization: Write $\beta_2' = \beta_2 + \text{bias}$, where

$$\text{bias} = \frac{\beta_1\sigma_{12}\sigma_\delta^2}{\sigma_1^2\sigma_2^2 - \sigma_{12}^2}.$$

The bias can be in either direction, but as the measurement-error variance σ_δ^2 grows, the least-squares estimand β_2' is driven toward σ_{y2}/σ_2^2, which is the population analogue of the least-squares coefficient for the regression of y on x_2 alone. That is, a large measurement-error component in x_1 makes it a weak statistical control, in effect removing it from the regression equation. Of course, when there are several explanatory variables, all subject to measurement error, the effects are more complex.

What can be done about measurement error in the predictors? Under certain circumstances—for example, when there are multiple indicators of latent explanatory variables—it is possible to derive unbiased estimators that take account of the measurement errors.

See Also the Following Articles

Measurement Error, Issues and Solutions • Multicollinearity

Further Reading

Atkinson, A. C. (1985). *Plots, Transformations and Regression.* Oxford University Press, Oxford.

Atkinson, A. C., and Riani, M. (2000). *Robust Diagnostic Regression Analysis.* Springer, New York.

Belsley, D. A., Kuh, E., and Welsch, R. E. (1980). *Regression Diagnostics.* Wiley, New York.

Bollen, K. A. (1989). *Structural Equations With Latent Variables.* Wiley, New York.

Chatterjee, S., and Hadi, A. S. (1988). *Sensitivity Analysis in Linear Regression.* Wiley, New York.

Cook, R. D. (1998). *Regression Graphics.* Wiley, New York.

Cook, R. D., and Weisberg, S. (1982). *Residuals and Influence in Regression.* Chapman and Hall, New York.

Cook, R. D., and Weisberg, S. (1999). *Applied Regression Including Computing and Graphics.* Wiley, New York.

Duncan, O. D. (1961). A socioeconomic index for all occupations. In *Occupations and Social Status* (A. J. Reiss, Jr., ed.), pp. 109–138. Free Press, New York.

Fox, J. (1991). *Regression Diagnostics.* Sage, Newbury Park, California.

Fox, J. (1997). *Applied Regression, Linear Models, and Related Methods.* Sage, Thousand Oaks, California.

Fox, J., and Suschnigg, C. (1989). A note on gender and the prestige of occupations. *Can. J. Sociol.* **14,** 353–360.

Godfrey, L. G. (1988). *Misspecification Tests in Econometrics: The Lagrange Multiplier Principle and Other Approaches.* Cambridge University Press, Cambridge.

Long, J. S., and Ervin, L. H. (2000). Using heteroscedasticity consistent standard errors in the linear regression model. *Am. Statist.* **54,** 217–224.

White, H. (1980). A heteroskedastic consistent covariance matrix estimator and a direct test of heteroskedasticity. *Econometrica* **48,** 817–838.

Linguistics

Gail R. Benjamin
University of Pittsburgh, Pittsburgh, Pennsylvania, USA

Glossary

dialect A variety of a language, spoken by an identifiable group of speakers or in identifiable circumstances.

ethnography A description of the thought and behavior of a cultural group.

grammar The (finite set of) rules for formulating/describing the (infinite) set of sentences of a given language.

lexicon The set of meaningful units of a language; words, but also smaller and larger units.

phonology The set of sounds and sound categories of a language, and the rules for combining them into words or larger units.

register A variety of language usage patterns, confined to identifiable situations.

Language as observed in action, rather than as patterns divorced from usage, has been of interest as an insight into the nature of language, and also as an insight into social structure, culture, and individual psychology. How language use varies between groups of speakers and in different situations, how it functions in power relationships, and how it changes are studied to gain cultural and psychological perspectives. Social structures can be understood by examining how language is involved in social constructs and how it relates to achieving social coherence.

Individual/Social Nature of Language

Language appears to analysts in two guises: innate knowledge and speech. Language seems to be something that individuals "know" and to suggest an internal, psychological structuring of knowledge that is self-contained in an individual. Ferdinand DeSaussure, in lecture notes from 1906 to 1911 collected by his students, formulated the distinction between language as the object of study of linguistics, and speech, as behavior in social settings, subject to study by sociologists, historians, and anthropologists. Language is the human faculty to use a particular semiological system, "a system of distinct signs corresponding to distinct ideas.... Language exists in the form of a sum of impressions deposited in the brain of each member of a community, almost like a dictionary of which identical copies have been distributed to each individual. Language exists in each individual, yet is common to all." Speech, on the other hand, is behavior, not a faculty. It is characterized by individual will, imperfection, and variation, and is subject to many (linguistically) extraneous social, cultural, physical, and other vagaries.

Many important insights into the structure and nature of languages were gained using this perspective, and the practical work of writing grammars, dictionaries, translations, and teaching materials in numerous languages was made possible by the working assumption that one, or a very few, speakers could provide linguists with a complete sample of the structures of a language, and that all other speakers would be able to understand performance based on the competence-derived grammars of one or a few speakers. This was the traditional approach to the task of gaining knowledge of previously unknown languages, too. One teacher could teach a learner a language.

But the second guise of language is intensely social, and the social nature of language seems to many linguists to pervade all the questions of a linguistics of pure language and languages. Many linguists have found the data of linguistic performance, in all its messiness, to be the only evidence for linguistic competence, the language faculty, and essential to understanding the structure of language and languages, as those abstract entities are used in the world, and in people's minds. The functions of language, in this view, are a necessary focus for understanding the structure of language and languages.

The nonsocial criterion for sharing knowledge of a language is agreement on what strings, or sentences, are grammatical strings of the language. Thus English speakers are expected to share common judgments of the grammaticalness of strings such as *Colorless green ideas sleep furiously* and *Furiously ideas colorless sleep green*. Sharing judgments of grammaticality in this way means that two speakers speak the same language. Many linguists adopt the view that writing a grammar means specifying the rules for isolated grammatical strings. The social criterion for sharing knowledge of a language is mutual intelligibility. In this framework, the ability of speakers mutually to understand strings such as *He didn't give me anything* and *He dint give me nothin'* means that both forms have to be accepted as grammatical strings of the language in question, and the formulation of the rules, or knowledge, of the language must encompass the possibility of both strings, just as the rules must include both *Do you want coffee?* and *Would you like some coffee?* In both cases, social and discourse factors play a role in the formulation of the strings, in their comprehension, and in their acceptability.

Patterned, shared variations in the performance of linguistic features, such as vowel systems, may reduce users' sense of comprehension. Thus American English, in any of its varied forms, may have a vowel system essentially the same as Australian English, but both Australian and American speakers will experience some sense of diminished comprehension when first experiencing the other performance. If language users are able to learn to interpret the different patterns as readily as American and Australian speakers do, then the communities are said to share high levels of mutual intelligibility. A common writing system increases the sense of mutual intelligibility, of the "same language." A number of situations have been observed in which chains of linguistic variation have resulted in intelligibility between near neighbors, but an accumulation of differences prevents intelligibility between far distant communities. Within one geographical community, one social group may claim that another's language is mutually intelligible with theirs, but this claim may be denied by the second group. When they act "as if" they do not understand others, it is difficult to dispute their assertion. In other cases, members of one part of a "monolingual" language community may be able to adjust their linguistic performance so that it is either easily understood by people from a different segment of the community, or so that it is understood with great difficulty, or perhaps not at all.

Beyond the recognition of variables in the feelings of degrees of intelligibility between language communities, or language users, little work has been done trying to quantify intelligibility, or to evaluate the relative impact of different linguistic factors in contributing to intelligibility or the lack thereof. And anecdotally, speakers have sometimes reported high degrees of comprehension in language communication with other people without any basis for linguistic comprehension at all. If language is considered as the major component of a human communication system, then observing its use in social contexts is an essential method of discovering its communicative resources and structures. Questions of interest to linguists and the social science techniques that have been used to approach each follow.

How Does Language Use Vary between Groups of Speakers?

The earliest modern interest in language variation arose in conjunction with the interest in historical linguistics, the attempts to trace "family trees" of languages and their evolutionary origins. Regional differences were salient and noticeable to the linguists doing this work, and the methods used were targeted surveys of usage in different regions. The preferred sources of data were the oldest, least educated, least mobile speakers that could be found, usually males. There was an emotional tension in scholars between the feeling that newer forms were somehow degenerations from purer forms, and the sense that newer, better, more advanced standard forms were inevitable.

It is generally recognized that regional variations in language use can be found in phonology, lexicon, grammar, and semantics, but it is easiest to collect data about phonological and lexical differences. A few minutes of talk will reveal almost all of the phonetic variation in vowel and consonant systems, especially with a few questions calculated to highlight "interesting" questions: in American English, for example, does a speaker use different vowels in pin/pen, caught/cot, merry/Mary/marry? Are the initial consonants of "we'll" and "wheel'" different? Using a word list can quickly elicit words used for common objects. Much more data is needed to establish grammatical and semantic differences. Again, in American English, "anymore" and "whenever" have different meanings in different regions, and the use of multiple modals, "might could," for example, is regionally bounded. These variations could well be absent from short samples of speech.

The notion of dialect has been associated with the social characteristics of the informants providing dialect data: in early research, dialect indicated language use patterns that were nonstandard, provincial, uneducated, and less modern. Both in Europe and the United States, social class and education differences in language use were apparent to everyone, but these were generally treated as either "good" or "bad" French, English, German, etc.

Studies of a wide variety of speakers in a given region, and in a wide variety of social circumstances, have caused a reformulation of the meaning of the term "dialect." No longer is it seen as a question of identifying speakers who speak a dialect. Rather, dialect is seen as a tool of speech performance that speakers can use strategically in interactions, both to establish self-identities in interactions, and to manipulate the nature of interactions. Speaking "casually" is part of what makes a situation casual; a sense of self in interaction is signaled by speech performance variables. Situational or identity-marking variation in speech performance is sometimes referred to as register variation, to differentiate it from regional dialect, some aspects of which may be less malleable and less available for strategic interactional use than a speaker's repertoire of registers.

One of the nonregional factors that correlates with variables in speech performance is gender. Investigations of male and female speech behaviors have endeavored to document differences in the behaviors of males and females, the ages at which they are acquired, the situations in which they are apparent, the implications for the linguistic competence of males and females, and the causes for differences. Do females speak in forms that de-emphasize self-assertion because they are females, or because they usually find themselves in situations in which they have lesser power, and de-emphasis of self is the gender-neutral speech response to such situations? What are the costs and benefits for using male/female speech patterns?

Sociolinguists have focused attention on correlations between ethnicity, class, and linguistic variables; they have been interested in social analysis and the discovery of the role of language behavior in social behavior, as well as implications for understandings of language per se. Linguistic and social constraints on code switching, moving from one language to another, or one marked dialect to another, in the course of the same discourse or the same sentence, have been investigated. When collecting data in more extended formats than word lists, from people who attach social and emotional meanings to speech variations, who are found to vary speech patterns in different interactions and social settings, who are not indifferent to others' speech, or to their own, the observer effect becomes an evident problem. Mechanically recording speech behavior without the knowledge and consent of the recorded is usually unethical and often illegal.

Various techniques for recording "natural" speech have been developed. First, of course, is the practice of being alert to speech patterns of interest, and writing down instances of their use as they occur in the investigator's presence. This is feasible if the investigator is present in the community for a long time. A Pittsburgh resident can collect uses of the "it needs painted" construction over a period of months or years, to determine the scope of the use in grammatical and social terms of this regional variation. Because it is stigmatized in its local environment, recording would usually be done after the interaction.

William Labov, in *Sociolinguistic Patterns*, interested in the distribution of a New York City dialect feature, the omission of "r" in postvocalic positions ("park," "car," "guard"), elicited performances of "fourth floor" from a socially stratified sample of New Yorkers by asking employees of (socially stratified) department stores for the location of something Labov knew to be found on the fourth floor. He asked for a repetition of the answer. After each encounter, he recorded the gender, approximate age, and job of the speaker, along with the responses, which could contain from zero to four occurrences of "r." His report on findings fails to indicate anything about his own speech (New York dialect or not?) or appearance, often taken to indicate class membership. But insofar as the store employees can be assumed in this instance to be speaking with little self-consciousness, the data can be used as "natural" speech.

Another study of New York City speech by Labov was designed to collect large samples of speech from a stratified random sample of New York City speakers, in a wide range of speech styles. Interviews, which were identified as part of an American Language Survey, were conducted at people's homes. As part of the interview, Labov asked informants to read a six-paragraph story highlighting the linguistic variables he had chosen to measure and to provide quantitative data on linguistic variables. He also asked them to recite "jump-rope" rhymes from their childhood, to tell about a time in their life when they felt they might die, and to read a second story containing words that are distinctive in many American dialects but not always in New York City speech (e.g., dark/dock, source/sauce, chalk/chocolate). Then he asked them to read lists of these pairs of words and to discuss whether the words were the same or not, showing by reading the lists again how they sounded in very careful pronunciation. These tasks were expected to provide some speech samples of careful self-conscious speech, and others of less self-conscious speech. Because the interviews were lengthy and conducted in homes, there were usually interruptions, and talk occurred that was not part of the interview. Telephone calls were made and received, neighbors and children came in and out, and interviewers were offered refreshments and accompanying chitchat.

The overall impression of the quality of talk in all these situations was that each speaker exhibited a wide variety of speech patterns, and much of it seemed very spontaneous and vernacular. Quantitative measurements of speech variables confirmed the impressions. These interviews could not provide samples of the full range of the repertoire of speech performances of any individual speaker, but they did show that recording in itself, even when it was announced that the subject of interest was the speaker's speech, does not contaminate behavior beyond usefulness.

How Does Language Use Vary in Different Situations?

Ethnography of communication, associated with Dell Hymes and other anthropologists, emphasizes the competence to communicate and interact, involving much more than the formulation of isolated grammatical sentences. The approach also calls into question a narrow understanding of which features of speech performance fall within the scope of analysis. Linguists working in this tradition have looked at socially defined situations, social actions, and the speech performance patterns associated with them. Examples include greetings, narratives, question/answer sequences, prayers, testimonies, riddles, curing rituals, examinations, medical interviews, lectures, compliments, ritual insult duels, political debates, and trials. A complete list of situations and tasks would amount to a complete ethnography of a group. Nonwritten communication has been emphasized, but the approach is also fully compatible with the analysis of written genres.

Hymes formulated a mnemonic for fieldwork, the **SPEAKING** framework, that emphasizes the difference in the research agenda for this approach and for a grammatical strings approach. Communication and language behavior take place in **S**ettings, the time and physical attributes of which often influence the behaviors involved. The **P**articipants in a communicative event may be present, in different roles (speaker and listener, teacher and student, performer and audience, etc.), or not all co-present (as in the case of the recipient of a letter). Communicative events have **E**nds, both as goals of interactors and as results of interactions. What is communicated has both form and content, and both aspects of these **A**cts should be considered. The overall tone or manner of an interaction is indicated by the term **K**ey, whether the event is mock or serious, perfunctory or full, or humorous or not, and similar variations. **I**nstrumentalities refer to the channels used (face-to-face speaking, writing, telephone talk, silence, code or open signaling, singing, chanting, whispering, etc.) and to the forms selected from the speaker's repertoire of languages, dialects, registers, and varieties. **N**orms of interaction refer to expected ways of carrying out communicative events and are often detected by reactions when the norms are not followed. Finally, **G**enre refers to emically recognized types of communicative events in the speech community being studied.

The primary method for gathering data for an ethnography of communication is participant observation recorded in written field notes, tape recording, and video recording. Video recording seems the most obtrusive, but may still be mostly ignored by participants who are caught up in the interaction being recorded. It also provides more data than can be easily analyzed. Sampling problems also must be faced. How many "events," selected on what bases, are needed to describe in order to talk about events in general? What about the numbers and types of members of a speech community who need to be studied in order to talk about the community in general? These issues tend to be dealt with on *ad hoc* bases, in each study or research project. Usually, extensive event-related observation of participants is carried out before tape or video recording is done, so that the ethnographer has a sense of what is normal for such an event and what might be significantly unique in the recorded interaction.

It should be noted theoretically that, in narrow terms, just as a language can be defined as an infinite set of grammatical strings, generated by a limited set of units and rules for combining them, such that ungrammatical strings can be identified but grammatical ones cannot be predicted or exhaustively listed, so communicative competence will lead to communicative performances that are unique, unpredictable, and "grammatical." Thus, a small sample of speakers/actors/events should be sufficient. (Though ethnographers who take the communication competence approach tend to be very wary of the "one or a few" speakers who suffice for grammatical studies, in the narrow sense.) Often, published descriptions present one representative event (or a few) or a composite representation of a type of event.

What Do Users Accomplish through Language?

Conversational analysis, first widely publicized by Harvey Sacks, Emanuel Schegloff, and Gail Jefferson, building on phenomenological approaches to social analysis by Erving Goffman and others, took conversational interaction as a way to understand social order at the most basic microlevel. They took "conversation" as one of the most common, least specified forms of social interaction available for inspection, and considered how participants accomplish this interaction. Their focus was on speech, or language accompanied with the messiness of performance: hesitations, false starts, interruptions, volume changes, speed variations, overlaps, and mistakes. They regarded these as all potentially useful tools in the "construction" of conversational interaction. They also focused attention on the phonological, grammatical, and semantic relations of utterances to preceding ones in interaction. One feature of their approach which differs from the ethnography of communication orientation is that they see themselves as formulating universal understandings of social interaction, and base their analysis as little as possible on individual (social) identities of the interactors, or cultural variations. They are interested in the competence exhibited by anyone participating in social interaction. This orientation has proved difficult to adhere to; there seem not to be many "anyones" in the social world.

Conversational analysts use two tactics. One is to identify some general (language) interactional activity, such as greetings, ending conversations, asking questions, etc., and to look for the contexts in which these take place, and at what is accomplished, with what language/speech tools. Given the assumption that the competences of interest are very general and very widespread, data is often found in transcribed or recorded interactions originally collected for other purposes. This addresses to some degree the bias that might be introduced by purposive recording of speech interaction. Again, for the competences of interest in this framework, it does not matter who is interacting or being recorded.

The second entrée for conversational analysis is to choose some microphenomenon that recurs in speech, such as the use of proper names or laughter, then to look for its contexts and reasonable explanations of the function, or "work" of the phenomenon. A classic example is Gail Jefferson's article, "A Case of Precision Timing: Overlapped Tag-Positioned Address Terms in Closing Sequences." This article first points out that sometimes names or other address terms ("Joe," "honey," "sir") are added to the ends of sentences in English. This use is always optional; it is never required by rules of English grammar. Second, when these forms of address are used, the speech of the addressee often overlaps them; the addressee starts talking before the speaker is finished. And third, such events often happen during the closings of conversations. Jefferson states these as simple general observations, and they seem plausible enough. She then establishes that such overlaps could be either deliberate, and not just the result of quick-paced talk, or accidental. By looking at transcripts of interruptions in speech, she shows that interruptions are not randomly placed, and at least sometimes take place just after the first syllable at which a listener could be sure of the information being conveyed by a speaker in a turn; precision timing is an available tool for talkers. She then offers the following example, a sequence of six turns at the end of a telephone conversation, containing two instances of names attached to the end of utterances, overlapped by the following speech of the addressee:

Jean: Okay.
Mel: Okeydoke.
Jean: Thank you Mel.
Mel: Thank you Jean.
Jean: Bye bye.
Mel: Bye.

Jefferson's analysis posits that tag-positioned address terms are likely to be overlapped because they are optional and unpredictable, and because the precise timing of a next turn that follows a completed turn, with no empty time, is one way for interactors to show that they are fully attending to an interaction and thus know when to take their own turn. But address terms are important signals of the relationship between interactors in any situation, given that any individual may be accurately addressed with many different terms. If an address term is used in interaction, it is often (usually?) followed by a responding address term, here validating or questioning the term first used. If an addressee does not hear or ignores the use of an address term, here "Mel," the understanding of the ongoing relationship offered by the speaker who used it may have been rejected, leaving the user in some doubt about the appropriateness of its use. Or, because it was overlapped, it may just not have been heard. A use of a responding term in the tag position, hear "Jean," is equally vulnerable to overlapping, as in this case. Jefferson even suggests that not overlapping it, and leaving a potentially silent time, just in case it might be used, would draw undue attention to its (potential) absence. Here, however, Jean's use of the two-syllable "bye bye" in effect signals that she has heard Mel's end tag, "Jean," in spite of its occurring during her own speech, because using two syllables instead of one gives Mel a chance to make his one syllable "bye" match hers, thus achieving the preferred simultaneous ending of conversation. Similarly, Mel's use of "okeydoke" accomplished the task of establishing that the next turn at the beginning of this excerpt should be Jean's, because Mel finished last, even though they began simultaneously. What these two conversationalists have accomplished, in this excerpt, is a mutually attentive simultaneous closing incorporating reciprocal namings—not the namings they employed at the beginning of the conversation—and the tools they have employed, from the range offered by their language competence, include precision timing of speech. Conversations, as well as other consequential interactions—interviews, trials, medical examinations, contracts—in this sociological framework are "work" accomplished by speech interaction, and the study of language in use and the structure of language has both linguistic and sociological import.

Penelope Brown and Steven Levinson (in their 1978 *Language Universals: Politeness Phenomena*) have looked at how language use varies as speakers accomplish face-threatening acts (FTAs). Their analysis is both sociological, in defining FTAs and in providing a framework for interactors' evaluation of FTAs, and linguistic, in looking at the many ways of saying the same thing that natural languages offer. They define "face" as the competing desires of people to be left alone and unimpeded in pursuit of their wants, and to be liked and admired. FTAs occur when one person wants or needs to threaten the "face wants" of another, in making requests or demands, in acknowledging the other or ignoring them, for instance. Nearly any utterance can be construed as an FTA, even simple statements.

Though most things can be FTAs, not all FTAs are equal. They are distinguished, in Brown and Levinson's framework, by the power relationships of the interactors, by the "social distance" relationship, and by the ranking of the imposition. Some method of measuring each of these is assumed to be collected into a score for the composite FTA, and each score is associated with a set of linguistic devices for appropriately accomplishing the FTA. The following approaches are examples of FTAs:

- *What time is it?* (bald, on record, no mitigating actions).
- *Do you have the time?* (conventional indirectness, literal answer not expected, assumes nice addressee).
- *Pardon me, could you tell me what time it is?* (imposition recognized, past tense distances the action, conventional indirectness in question, assumes cooperation).
- *Excuse me, my watch doesn't seem to be working; could you just tell me what time it is?* (imposition recognized, excuse offered, request minimized (*just*), past tense, conventional question form).
- *How come they don't have any clocks in this building?* (off-record request could be denied, blame for imposition placed on impersonal others, assumption of ability and willingness of hearer to identify need and respond).

Finally, people may decide not to attempt the FTA at all.

Though communicative competence may belong to everyone, observation of the distribution of speech variables strongly suggests that variation in performance is a key to establishing "who" is interacting. To the extent that individuals are involved in ongoing and relatively unchanging social relationships with others, their use of appropriate speech variations may come to be part of their identity and self-identity. What is required to establish this phenomenon is observation of many individuals in one role, and one individual in a number of roles. One outstanding example of work in this vein is Leslie Milroy's Belfast work, reported in 1980 in *Language and Social Networks*. After collecting recorded speech samples from casual conversations in natural settings from an undisclosed number of speakers, Milroy chose the speech of 23 men and 23 women, from three communities, and two age groups each, for careful analysis of a correlation of speech variables with social variables. (This is a small sample in sociological practice, but a large sample in sociolinguistic/linguistic practice.) The eight linguistic variables chosen for analysis were each cast in terms that were amenable to quantitative analysis. For variations in vowel quality, a continuum was established between two extremes of variation, and a speaker's performance was placed at a point on the continuum; three to five point scales were used. For features that are more or less dichotomous, percentage scores were used (e.g., to indicate how often lip rounding was used in monosyllables containing the vowel [ʌ], as in *hut*, *mud*). Linguistic variables are commonly quantified in these ways, but care must be taken with specifying the linguistic context.

In Milroy's case, the sociological variables of interest were gender, age, community, and social network. Milroy was able to establish a six-point scale for network multiplexity and density for all of the 46 individuals. (One point was given for each of the following variables: membership of a high-density, territorially based cluster; kinship ties in the neighborhood; working at the same place as at least two others from the same area; working at the same place as at least two others of the same sex from the area; and voluntary association with workmates in leisure hours.) Individual scores covered the full range of the scale. Each speaker's performance could be correlated, for eight variables, with gender, age, community, and network score. The findings of significant associations showed that different variables were associated with different features of social identity, some with gender, some with age, some with community, and some with network scores. In one community, for instance, though men were found overall, compared to women, to use more vernacular forms, they also had higher network scores compared to women overall, but women's use of vernacular forms also correlated with their network scores.

Milroy suggests that the use of these variables (assumed to be under speakers' control, if not in their awareness) by individuals is best understood as tools for signaling different aspects of social identity: women in one community, for instance, may use vernacular forms less often than men do, this difference being a gender marker, but the women still use some forms that differentiate their community from others, exhibiting community loyalty. The particular vernacular forms that are correlated with network scores may vary from community to community. Milroy's work suggests, as does work by other sociologists and linguists, that dense, multiplex networks operate as norm enforcement mechanisms. A speaker's choices from variables exhibits social identity features and enacts social identity roles, an explanation for the persistence of nonstandard stigmatized forms. What speakers accomplish through the use of language can thus be seen to encompass both short-term social interactions, such as conversations and FTAs, and long-term social roles, identities, and relationships.

How Does Language Function in Power Relationships?

Ethnography of communication and conversational analysis tends to exhibit an orientation to language use as individually motivated, and as a cooperative enterprise of those involved in a speech situation, but it is also possible to view the conventions and practices of language usage as much less benign and more coercive. Instead of seeing an interview as a joint elicitation/production of information sharing, it is possible to see the interview as antagonistic efforts to shape or manipulate the information that forms the basis for following action. Thus the interview becomes an occasion and an instance of a power relationship, not a cooperative one. Conversations or narratives or question/answer sequences, or curing rituals or trials or any other speech events, can be similarly construed.

Looking at interactions between people who are clearly unequal in power—questioning of suspects or witnesses in legal disputes, talk between doctors and patients, discussions directed by teachers—shows how the power to accept or reject replies or information offered by the powerless, to shape the flow of information, culminates in events that usually reaffirm the prevailing power relationships and ideology. Because there is no one-to-one relationship between linguistic formulations and the real world, choosing formulations is an attempt to manipulate perceptions of the world and actions, available in principle to all language users and demonstrably used by both the powerful and the powerless (*My jacket got lost*; *The computer crashed*; *I'm in a bad mood*). But the powerful have more power to coerce compliance with their formulations, and their formulations are used to enhance their power. The more powerful speaker often interrupts, cuts off talk by the other, rephrases contributions of the less powerful, proceeds as though the less powerful had accepted the offered interpretation of events or information, or coerces agreement under threat, open or implied. The methodology used here, as in much of linguistic analysis, is to look at events of language usage (or transcriptions more or less rich), and to ask of each element of the event what set of alternatives it was chosen from, then to set forth the effects or results of the particular choices made, validated by comparison with the effects in other instances of use.

How Does Language Structure Enable Users to Achieve Coherence?

Language is used for sharing both intellectual (*There is a herd of deer over the next hill*) and phatic/social (*Dr. White, how are you?*) meaning. There are formidable barriers to communication in both spheres, stemming from the nonexistent one-to-one relationship between world states and talk about the world, and from issues of intentions of speakers and listeners. Linguistic utterances proceed in a one-after-another fashion, and incorporate structures to facilitate all parties attending to the same world states and phatic/social states during a linguistic interaction. Analysis that looks for the phonological, grammatical, and semantic features that play a role in this coordination commonly adopts two strategies.

Sometimes a set of linguistic exchanges is searched to catalog the occurrences, and a rationale is sought for their appearances in those places. Thus in *Discourse Markers*, Deborah Schiffrin's investigation of the word "oh" in American conversation began with proposed identifications of contexts for "oh." One such identification was that "oh" is used when one speaker requests clarification from another of something contained in a previous turn. This is the use in Val's first utterance:

Freda: Sometimes he got a notice for staying out past curfew. Recently. In August, that was.
Val: Oh curfew? What's curfew?
Freda: A certain time that children have to be in.
Val: Oh your children. Oh I see. Oh it's personal. Oh I . . . I thought there might be police or something.

In Val's second utterance she signals with "oh" each element of her understanding of the clarification offered by Freda, and her own new understandings of the situation Freda is talking about. Such enumeration of new understandings enables both parties to continue with relative assurance that mutual comprehension is available as the basis for further talk. Counts of the occurrences of "oh" in the large corpus studied show that it occurred in 11% of environments analogous to Val's first use (so it is not the only device available for this task), that it never occurred in contexts like Freda's response, and that it occurred in 41% of contexts like Val's last utterance. Similar specification of contexts proceeds until there are no more anomalous occurrences of the item under investigation.

The range of variations that can be studied this way is large. Examples are changes in language or register, use of particular grammatical forms (passives or other rhetorical devices), changes in voice quality, use of feedback or echoing devices, repetitions of previous speakers' talk, puns, manipulation of deictic markers, proverbs, and conventional summaries.

Alternatively, an environment is specified, and data are searched to find different devices used. Thus, one speaker's questions may be the environment, and it can then be determined what follows the questions (usually, but not always, an answer, not always in the same forms).

How Do Users Employ Language to Construct Social Structures?

Talk about the real world is subject to many manipulations outside the truth/falsity framework. In talk, the answers to questions concerning whether a reference to the world will be made now, what aspects of the world will be mentioned, what kind of reference will be made, and what recipients will do with it will be made in the context of the current state of interaction, and will in turn influence the subsequent states and talk. That talk then becomes a feature of the interactional world within which speakers act.

William Hanks, in *Referential Practice: Language and Lived Space among the Maya*, has provided a linguistically and anthropologically complex analysis of everyday and ritual speech patterns that reflect and enact sociocultural realities. Deictic features in languages are the ones that establish interactors and referents in time and space, absolutely and with regard to each other. They are pervasive and unobtrusive. Tenses, pronouns, and demonstratives are included in this category. One interaction analyzed by Hanks is given here:

ti? e kàanal k-im-b'èetik a? → ká?a p'eé sùurko kén u-b'i seh →
"In this ditch I'm making two rows it will take,

ump'é té?el a → ump'eé tée bey a? →
one right here (pointing), one like this here (pointing).

ká?a ȼol pak'aál kén in-ȼ'aáeh
Two rows of plants will I put (there)."

This talk was produced by DP when DP, VC, and WH were engaged in digging an irrigation ditch. WH was loosening soil with a pickax, VC was shoveling the dirt out of the way, and DP was sitting on the ground watching them. Nevertheless, it is DP who uses the first-person singular pronoun "I" in "I'm making" and "I will put." He is the father of VC, the leader of the work team and of all economic activity they undertake together, and it is appropriate for him to use this form about an activity being carried out by others. But it would not have been inappropriate for him to use "this ditch you're making" or "this ditch we're making" either. Though the content of the three forms is different, each is an acceptable one (no one objected, or even particularly noticed) only in the context of a set of social understandings that validates DP's ownership of work done by others, and his position as the focal point of the collectivity he heads. In other contexts, he is also treated in this way: an inquiry about "how is DP?" on another occasion produced information about various people in DP's homestead.

The Maya language includes a number of terms that translate into English as "here" and "there." In this talk, DP had available two appropriate forms, "té?el a" and "té?el o," both used in shared perceptual, spatial, and actional frames. But "té?el a" is better used for information that is not shared by all participants, and the information was new to WH, though not to VC. DP thus claims the information as his, and indicates that it is addressed to WH, not VC, though VC is also a full participant in the work and the talk about it. A little later, DP was standing very close to VC, watching him dig a hole for a bush. He pointed to the side of the hole and told VC to enlarge the hole:

tían tée xčik'in o? →
"There's where it is there on the west."

Here DP uses a nonimmediate deictic, "there," even though what he is indicating is closer to him and to VC than the referent of "here" in the previous example. (Note also the cardinal direction used, "on the west" for a point about a meter from the speaker and addressee.) This utterance also includes the particle, "tían," which indicates previous mention of the referent, the hole, though it was not talked about in the immediately preceding exchanges. The utterance thus places the activity in VC's space, nonimmediate to DP, but also acknowledges the shared background knowledge about the activity common to VC and DP. The very ordinariness of these exchanges emphasizes the nature of the real-world situation as a creation of interactors, speakers in ongoing talk. Deictic features are a general feature of all human languages, and nowhere is their use any more straightforward than in these examples.

George Lakoff's work, notably in *Women, Fire and Dangerous Things*, has shown that metaphor is among the most pervasive ways of structuring information in talk (and thought), and the use of cohesive devices in talk strengthens its role. Cohesive devices for demonstrating comprehension of ongoing talk include repetitions and extensions of a metaphor in following talk. These lead to more and more talk adopting the same line of thought, reinforcing the metaphor. An example from English concerns the conceptions of time. Lakoff contends that talk (and thought) in English incorporates two underlying notions of the nature of time. One is that time is a thing—it is formally a noun and can be used with active verbs—that it is in front of us, and that it is moving toward us. English habitually treats things in front of us as having a face, and as facing us, as people most commonly do in conversation. Thus if a person, a ball, and a table are in a row, English speakers will most often say that the ball is in front of the table, not behind the table, as though the table were "facing" the speaker. This is not the habitual formulation of speakers from speech communities who ordinarily do not converse face to face, but commonly talk side by side, looking in the same direction. For them, the ball would be characterized as behind the table, because the table is "facing" the same direction as the speaker.

Because time is facing English speakers, it is moving toward the speaker. It is this pervasive metaphorical framework that makes English speakers accept formulations such as "we look ahead to the next season," "it's behind us now," "in the following weeks," "in the preceding months," and so on. When speakers participate, over and over, in ongoing talk utilizing this metaphorical set, the argument goes, they come to conceptualize time in this way. They may also entertain other frameworks, such as the cyclical one of "thank God it's Friday" or "every summer we go to the beach," or the time travel framework of science fiction, and when these are invoked, speakers also structure subsequent talk and thought. Thus both the social world and the real world in which it exists are structured for speakers by forms of talk about them.

How Do Language Use and Language Change?

Two modern insights have provided linguistics with a way to deal with language changes. First is the notion of rule change emphasized in Chomsky's linguistics. Thus the set of changes exemplified in the correspondences between *pater/father, tres/three, canus/hound*, where in each case, a stop in Latin (p, t, k) corresponds to a fricative in English (f, th, h), can be accounted for if we posit a rule change that says "change a stop (in specified contexts) to a fricative at the same point of articulation." (This rule change must have happened before English began borrowing words from Latin, at some point when the Germanic languages as a whole diverged from Proto Indo-European in a different way than the Latin family developed.) Rule changes are internal to a speaker's language competence, and can account for changes in language behavior in a holistic and plausible way. The alternative is to imagine whole communities somehow "missing the target" of their ideal notion of a large set of words in their performance. Especially because English (Germanic) retained "p" in other contexts, this is not a very convincing picture. The question remains as to why would anyone, or any community, comes up with such a rule change. Language change, in general, imposes costs in communication, between generations and between communities, so there would seem to be strong pressures to minimize change. In terms of linguistic competence, or the language faculty, nothing is gained by language change (except for vocabulary enlargement).

A groundbreaking study by William Labov (in *Sociolinguistic Patterns*) showed how linguistic change could be observed in a time period amenable to observation, and provided a motivation for a rule change. Labov noticed that speakers living on Martha's Vineyard, an island off the coast of Massachusetts, were using a different vowel in certain contexts than had been recorded only 30 to 40 years earlier in a dialect survey. The vowel change involved the diphthongs /ai/ and /au/, as in the words "knife" and "life" and "about" "house." In each case, the first part of the diphthong was centralized, starting at a position closer to /ə/ than to /a/. The change can be specified in linguistic terms as a rule change, operating in certain environments. The costs of the rule change in terms of intelligibility are small; English speakers tolerate wide variations in the realization of vowels, but it is noticeable. It is not evenly distributed over the whole population of Martha's Vineyard speakers. The speakers who showed the sound change were among those who most strongly held as part of their personal identity a sense of themselves as Vineyarders, different from other Massachusetts residents, or other Americans. These others were typically encountered in the form of rich vacationers who summer on the island, and until recently they tended to come from Boston. When dialect data from the 1940s were collected in New England, Boston speakers widely used the rule calling for deletion of the postvocalic "r." Martha's Vineyarders did not use this rule, and were linguistically distinct in this way from other New Englanders. Over the course of 30 years, Bostonians, like other "r" deleters in the United States, were influenced by nonlocal prestige speech patterns to abandon this rule, to become "r"-speakers. This made their speech less different from that of Vineyarders. Labov proposed that the vowel change he observed was adopted to preserve a linguistic distinction by those Vineyarders who did not want to be absorbed into a larger sociolinguistic entity. He also observed that a personal decision to be a Vineyarder entailed a decision to remain poor, to forgo the economic benefits that came from leaving the island community. Thus "prestige," if it is to be invoked as a motivation for linguistic modeling, must be construed in local, nonobvious forms.

Variation is now seen as either a change in progress or as a manifestation of sustained diversity within a speech community. Increasing social complexity is expected to be accompanied by increasing linguistic diversity, and universal movement to "standard" forms of a language is no longer expected. The explanations of language change are both linguistic and sociological in nature.

See Also the Following Articles

Ethnography • Language Acquisition

Further Reading

Briggs, C. L. (1986). *Learning How to Ask.* Cambridge University Press, New York.

Coates, J. (ed.) (1998). *Language and Gender: A Reader.* Blackwell, Oxford.

Hanks, W. F. (1990). *Referential Practice: Language and Lived Space among the Maya.* University of Chicago Press, Chicago.

Johnstone, B. (2000). *Qualitative Methods in Sociolinguistics.* Oxford University Press, New York.

Labov, W. (1972). *Sociolinguistic Patterns.* University of Pennsylvania Press, Philadelphia.

Lakoff, G. (1987). *Women, Fire and Dangerous Things: What Categories Reveal about the Mind.* University of Chicago Press, Chicago.

Milroy, L. (1987). *Language and Social Networks.* Basil Blackwell, New York.

Literacy, Mathematical

Jan de Lange
Utrecht University, Utrecht, The Netherlands

Glossary

assessment (educational) A method for determining how well students are learning; provides feedback to students, educators, parents, policymakers, and the public about the effectiveness of educational services.

competencies (mathematical) Processes that students apply as they (attempt to) solve problems. Aspects of mathematical competencies are organization of knowledge, problem representation, connecting the real world with mathematics (mathematization), metacognition, use of different strategies, and contributions to group problem-solving, but also knowledge of basic facts, mathematical language, and procedures.

context The specific setting, within a situation, of an assessment item. An important aspect in measuring mathematical literacy is inclusion of a variety of situations.

mathematical literacy An individual's capacity to identify and understand the role that mathematics plays in the world, to make well-founded judgments, and to engage in mathematics in ways that meet the needs of that individual's current and future life as a constructive, concerned, and reflective citizen.

mathematics The science of structure, order, patterns, and relations that has evolved from the practices of counting, measuring, and describing the shapes of objects.

Mathematical literacy has evolved as a subject for discussion because of a growing awareness that we are increasingly surrounded by numbers and data, but that we fail to reason and think about these in a sensible way. Fundamental questions about this subject concern identifying the ingredients of mathematical literacy, how the capacity to be literate is related to mathematics, the essential competencies needed to be mathematically literate, the role of literacy in real-world contexts, and how to measure mathematical literacy, especially in large-scale assessments.

Introduction

According to a widely accepted definition, mathematical literacy is an individual's capacity to identify and understand the role that mathematics plays in the world, to make well-founded judgments, and to engage in mathematics in ways that meet the needs of that individual's current and future life as a constructive, concerned, and reflective citizen. This definition is widely accepted, in part because it comes from the Organization for Economic Cooperation and Development/Program for International Student Assessment (OECD/PISA) study in 2003, which was supported by the 29 OECD countries and by a number of other countries, and in part because the definition is quite comprehensive.

Innumeracy, or the inability to handle numbers and data correctly and to evaluate statements regarding problems and situations that invite mental processing and estimating, is a greater problem than our society generally recognizes. "Fixing" this problem, however, requires dealing with several issues: from a mathematical perspective, how do we define literacy? Does literacy relate to mathematics (and to what kind of mathematics)? What kind of competencies are we looking for? And how do we measure mathematical literacy?

Mathematical Literacy

Before trying to understand what knowledge of mathematics is important, it seems wise first to look at a "comfortable" definition of quantitative literacy (QL). Lynn Arthur Steen pointed out that there are small but important differences in the several existing definitions and, although he did not suggest the phrase as a definition, referred to QL as the "capacity to deal effectively with the quantitative aspects of life." Indeed, most existing definitions Steen mentioned give explicit attention to numbers, arithmetic, and quantitative situations, either in a rather narrow way, as in the National Adult Literacy Survey, or more broadly, as in the International Life Skills Survey. The National Adult Literacy Survey, conducted by the National Center for Education Statistics (NCES), narrowly defines QL as "the knowledge and skills required in applying arithmetic operations, either alone or sequentially, using numbers embedded in printed material (e.g., balancing a checkbook, completing an order form)." The International Life Skills Survey (ILSS) broader definition of QL is "an aggregate of skills, knowledge, beliefs, dispositions, habits of mind, communication capabilities, and problem solving skills that people need in order to engage effectively in quantitative situations arising in life and work."

These definitions emphasize quantity. Mathematical literacy is not restricted to the ability to apply quantitative aspects of mathematics, but also involves knowledge of mathematics in the broadest sense. Spatial literacy can also be defined—it deals with aspects such as map reading and interpretation; spatial awareness; "grasping space;" and understanding a range of things, such as great circle routes, plans for a new house, patterns, distances, scale, symmetry, and so on. All kinds of visualization of data belong also to the literacy aspect of mathematics and constitute an absolutely essential component for literacy.

Against this background of varying perspectives, the most recent and widely spread definition of mathematical literacy is broad but also rather "mathematical." As stated in the OECD/PISA 2003 assessment, "Mathematics literacy is an individual's capacity to identify and understand the role that mathematics plays in the world, to make well-founded judgments, and to engage in mathematics in ways that meet the needs of that individual's current and future life as a constructive, concerned and reflective citizen." This definition was developed by the Expert Group for Mathematics of PISA. There is some confusion, as indicated previously, about the boundaries of the definitions. For instance, some equate numeracy with quantitative literacy, whereas others equate quantitative and mathematical literacy. It is thus helpful to discriminate between different aspects of literacy in relation to mathematics, i.e., spatial literacy, numeracy, quantitative literacy, and mathematical literacy:

1. Spatial literacy (SL) is the simplest and most neglected aspect of literacy in relation to mathematics. SL supports our understanding of the (three-dimensional) world in which we live and move. To deal with what surrounds us, we must understand properties of objects, the relative positions of objects, and the effect thereof on our visual perception; this involves the creation of all kinds of two- and three-dimensional paths and routes, navigational practices, shadows—even the art of Escher.
2. The next obvious literacy is numeracy (N), fitting as it does directly into quantity. Most definitions stress the ability to handle numbers and data and to evaluate statements regarding problems and situations that invite mental processing and estimating in real-world contexts.
3. When we look at quantitative literacy, we are actually looking at literacy dealing with a cluster of phenomenological categories: quantity, change and relationships, and uncertainty. These categories stress understanding of, and mathematical abilities concerned with, certainties (quantity), uncertainties (quantity as well as uncertainty), and relations (types of, recognition of, changes in, and reasons for those changes).
4. We think of mathematical literacy (ML) as the overarching literacy comprising all others.

It goes without saying that every definition of mathematical literacy will have it shortcomings and that different scholars put different emphasis on the aspects of mathematical literacy. Some, for instance, stress the fact that an approach to mathematical literacy must never lead logically to the conclusion that only the expert can be mathematical literate: it is an obvious condition of mathematical literacy, and literacy in general, that it be directed toward and attainable by the greater part of society. This seems certainly a valid observation for the aforementioned OECD study.

Discussion

In an interview in *Mathematics and Democracy*, Peter T. Ewell was asked the following question: "*The Case for Quantitative Literacy* argues that quantitative literacy (QL) is not merely a euphemism for mathematics but is something significantly different—less formal and more intuitive, less abstract and more contextual, less symbolic and more concrete. Is this a legitimate and helpful distinction?" Ewell answered that indeed this distinction is meaningful and powerful. The answer to this question, however, depends in large part on the interpretation of what constitutes good mathematics. We can guess that in Ewell's perception, mathematics is formal, abstract, and symbolic—a picture of mathematics still widely held. Ewell continued to say that literacy implies an integrated ability to function seamlessly within a given community of practice. Functionality is surely a key point, both in itself and in relation to a community of practice, which includes the community of mathematicians. Focusing on functionality gives us better opportunity to bridge gaps or identify overlaps. In the same volume, Alan H. Schoenfeld observed that in the past, literacy and what is learned in mathematics classes were largely disjointed. Now, however, they should be thought of as largely overlapping and taught as largely overlapping. In this approach, which takes into consideration the changing perception of what constitutes mathematics, mathematics and mathematical literacy are positively not disjointed.

For Schoenfeld, the distinction most likely lies in the fact that, as a student, he never encountered problem-solving situations, that he studied only "pure" mathematics and, finally, that he never saw or worked with real data. Each of these real-world approaches is absolutely essential for literate citizenship, but none even hints at defining what mathematics is needed for ML, at least not in the traditional school mathematics curricula descriptions of arithmetic, algebra, geometry, and so on. Again, in *Mathematics and Democracy*, Wade Ellis, Jr. observed that many algebra teachers provide instruction that constricts rather than expands student thinking. He discovered that students leaving an elementary algebra course could solve fewer real-world problems after the course than before it: after completing the course, they thought that they had to use symbols to solve problems they had previously solved using only simple reasoning and arithmetic. It may come as no surprise that Ellis promotes a new kind of common sense, i.e., a quantitative common sense based on mathematical concepts, skills, and know-how. Despite their differences, however, Schoenfeld and Ellis seem to share Treffers' observation that innumeracy might be caused by a flaw in the structural design of instruction.

These several observers seem to agree that, in comparison with traditional school mathematics, ML is less formal and more intuitive, less abstract and more contextual, and less symbolic and more concrete. ML also focuses on reasoning, thinking, and interpreting, as well as on other very mathematical competencies. To get a better picture of what is involved in this distinction, it is first necessary to describe the "elements" needed for ML. With a working definition of ML and an understanding of the elements (or "competencies," as they are described in the PISA framework) needed for ML, we might come closer to answering the original question (what mathematics is important?) or formulating a better one.

What Is Mathematics in Relation to Mathematical Literacy?

To provide a clearer picture of literacy in mathematics, it seems wise to reflect for a moment on what constitutes mathematics. There is no intention here to offer a deep philosophical treatment—there are many good publications around—but it is not unlikely that many readers might think of school mathematics as representing mathematics as a science. Several authors in *Mathematics and Democracy* clearly pointed this out quite often, based on their own experiences (Schoenfeld, Schneider, Kennedy, and Ellis, among others). Lynn Steen (observed in *On the Shoulders of Giants: New Approaches to Numeracy*) that traditional school mathematics picks a very few strands (e.g., arithmetic, algebra, and geometry) and arranges them horizontally to form the curriculum: first arithmetic, then simple algebra, then geometry, then more algebra, and, finally, as if it were the epitome of mathematical knowledge, calculus. Each course seems designed primarily to prepare for the next. These courses give a distorted view of mathematics as a science, do not seem to be related to the educational experience of children, and bear no relevance for society. A result of this is that the informal development of intuition along the multiple roots of mathematics, a key characteristic in the development of ML, is effectively prevented. To overcome this misimpression about the nature of mathematics created by such courses, we will try to sketch how we see mathematics and, subsequently, what the consequences can be for mathematics education.

Mathematical concepts, structures, and ideas have been invented as tools to organize phenomena in the natural, social, and mental worlds. In the real world, the phenomena that lend themselves to mathematical treatment do not come organized as they are in school curriculum structures. Rarely do real-life problems arise in ways and contexts that allow their understanding and solutions to be achieved through an application of knowledge from a single content strand. If mathematics is viewed as a science that helps solve real problems, it makes sense to use a phenomenological approach to describe mathematical concepts, structures, and ideas. This approach has been followed by Freudenthal and by others, such as Steen. They state that if mathematics curricula featured multiple parallel strands, each grounded in appropriate childhood experiences, the collective effect would be to develop among children diverse mathematical insight into the many different roots of mathematics. Steen then suggested that we should seek inspiration in the developmental power of five deep mathematical ideas: dimension, quantity, uncertainty, shape, and change. The OECD/PISA mathematics expert group has adapted these, creating four phenomenological categories to describe what constitutes mathematics: (1) quantity/space, (2) shape/change, (3) relationships, and (4) uncertainty. Using these four categories, mathematics content can be organized into a sufficient number of areas to help ensure a spread of items across the curriculum, but also a small enough number to avoid an excessively fine division, which would work against a focus on problems based in real-life situations. Each phenomenological category is an encompassing set of phenomena and concepts that make sense together and may be encountered within and across a multitude of quite different situations. By their very nature, each idea can be perceived as a general notion dealing with a generalized content dimension. This implies that the categories or ideas cannot be sharply delineated vis-à-vis one another. Rather, each represents a certain perspective, or point of view, which can be thought of as possessing a core, a center of gravity, and a somewhat blurred penumbra that allow intersection with other ideas. In principle, any idea can intersect with any other idea.

Competencies Needed for ML

The competencies that form the heart of the ML description in PISA seem, for the most part, well in line with the elements proposed by Steen. The following list of eight competencies rely on the work of Mogens Niss and his Danish colleagues, but similar formulations can be found in the work of many others representing different countries:

1. Mathematical thinking and reasoning. Posing questions characteristic of mathematics, knowing the kinds of answers that mathematics offers and distinguishing among different kinds of statements, and understanding and handling the extent and limits of mathematical concepts.
2. Mathematical argumentation. Knowing what proofs are, knowing how proofs differ from other forms of mathematical reasoning, following and assessing chains of arguments, having a feel for heuristics, and creating and expressing mathematical arguments.
3. Mathematical communication. Expressing oneself in a variety of ways in oral, written, and other visual form and understanding someone else's work.
4. Modeling. Structuring the field to be modeled; translating reality into mathematical structures; interpreting mathematical models in terms of context or reality; working with models; validating models; reflecting, analyzing, and offering critiques of models or solutions; and reflecting on the modeling process.
5. Problem posing and solving. Posing, formulating, defining, and solving problems in a variety of ways.
6. Representation. Decoding, encoding, translating, distinguishing between, and interpreting different forms of representations of mathematical objects and situations as well as understanding the relationship among different representations.
7. Symbols. Using symbolic, formal, and technical language and operations.
8. Tools and technology. Using aids and tools, including technology when appropriate.

To be mathematically literate, individuals need all these competencies to varying degrees, but they also need confidence in their own ability to use mathematics and need to be comfortable with quantitative ideas. An appreciation of mathematics from historical, philosophical, and societal points of view is also desirable. This list of competencies is just one example. Other studies have chosen, instead of emphasizing competencies, to question what it means to be successful in mathematics. Recognizing that no term completely captures all aspects of expertise, competence, knowledge, and facility in mathematics, the study *Adding It Up* has chosen to identify five strands for mathematical proficiency:

1. Understanding. Comprehending mathematical concepts, operations, and relations, i.e., knowing what mathematical symbols, diagrams, and procedures mean.
2. Computing. Carrying out mathematical procedures, such as adding, subtracting, multiplying, and dividing numbers flexibility, accurately, efficiently, and appropriately.
3. Applying. Being able to formulate problems mathematically and to devise strategies for solving them using concepts and procedures appropriately.
4. Reasoning. Using logic to explain and justify a solution to a problem or to extend from something known to something not yet known.
5. Engaging. Seeing mathematics as sensible, useful, and doable (if effort is exerted) and being willing to do the work.

Kilpatrick and Ball, the authors of *Adding It Up*, stress that students are open to mathematics, and all students can and should be mathematically proficient.

Without comparing the competencies and strands of proficiency in detail, it is clear that there are some similarities, albeit that the emphasis is placed somewhat differently. If the five strands are reordered as computing, applying and 'reasoning, and understanding, we come very close to the clustering of competencies as used for the PISA study. This will be discussed next.

Competency Clustering

PISA defines three competency clusters for mathematical literacy. The "reproduction" cluster involves reproduction and recall of practiced knowledge, common problem representations, recognition of equivalents, recall of familiar mathematical objects and properties, routine procedures, and carrying out standard computations. The "connections" cluster addresses competencies needed to plan for solving problems by drawing connections from different mathematical content strands. The competencies include students' abilities to combine and integrate information in order to solve problems. They also include the ability of students to interpret the meaning of a solution and to check the validity and meaning of their work. The "reflection" cluster activities include the ability to reflect on the processes needed to solve a problem. They relate to the students' abilities to plan solution strategies and implement them in more complex problem settings. Items measuring the competencies of this cluster should reflect students' abilities to analyze. In other words, they must be able to interpret, to reflect, to explain, and to present mathematical generalizations, arguments, and proofs.

Context and Situations

An important part of mathematical literacy is using, doing, and recognizing mathematics in a variety of situations. In dealing with issues that lend themselves to a mathematical treatment, the choice of mathematical methods and representations often depends on the situations in which the problems are presented. Teachers of mathematics often complain that students have difficulty applying the mathematics they have learned in different contexts. Students who do not excel in science often dislike contexts involving physics applications in mathematics, because they do not understand the physics. Building from this, it seems necessary to examine the wisdom of confronting nonscience students with mathematics applications that need specific science literacy at a nonbasic level. As has been pointed out before, to transfer their knowledge effectively from one area of application to another, students need experience solving problems in many different situations and contexts. Making competencies a central emphasis facilitates this process: competencies are independent of the area of application. Students should be offered real-world situations that they recognize as relevant. This can be either real-world situations that will help them to function as informed and intelligent citizens, or real-world situations that are relevant to their areas of interest, either professionally or educationally.

The term "situation" is used here in the context of the part of the student's world in which a certain problem is embedded. It is very convenient and relevant to the art of teaching for ML to see situations as having certain distances in relation to the student. The closest distance is the student's personal life; next is school (educational) life, then work (occupational) and leisure, followed by the local community and society as encountered in daily life. Furthest away are scientific situations. It might be desirable to enlarge the distance domain as the age of the students increases, but not in a strict way. Steen itemized an impressive list of expressions of numeracy, most of which can be seen as having a certain "distance" from citizens. "Personal life" includes, depending on age, games, daily scheduling, sports, shopping, saving, interpersonal relations, finances, voting, reading maps, reading tables, health, insurance, and so on. School life relates to understanding the role of mathematics in society and school events (e.g., sports, teams, scheduling) and understanding data, computers, and so on. Work and leisure involve reasoning and understanding data, statistics, finances, taxes, risks, rates, samples, scheduling, geometric patterns, two- and three-dimensional representations, budgets, visualizations, and so on. In the local community, the intelligent citizen makes appropriate judgments and decisions, evaluates conclusions, gathers data and makes inferences, and in general adopts a critical attitude, i.e., sees the reasoning behind decisions.

Last, we come to science situations. To function as an intelligent citizen, individuals need to be literate in many fields, not only in mathematics. The use of scientific situations or contexts in mathematics classes should not be avoided per se, but some care must be taken. If we try to teach students the right competencies but use the wrong context, we are creating a problem, not solving it. A good but rather unscientific example concerns work with middle-school students in the United States. The designed lesson sequence had archeology as a context. Archeologists sometimes use rather straightforward but quite unexpected and rather "subjective" mathematical methods in their research—just the kind of mathematics middle-school students can handle. The question, therefore, was not whether the students could do the mathematics but whether the context was engaging enough in this short-attention-span society. Without giving the specifics, the students were highly engaged because of the unexpectedness of what they were learning and the relevance of the methods used. In this instance, it was learned that connecting to the students' real world can be a complex but highly rewarding journey.

It has become clear in dealing with mathematics in context over the past 25 years that making mathematics relevant by teaching it in context is quite possible and very rewarding, despite the many pitfalls. Much more experience and research are needed, but based on previous experiences it appears that teaching both mathematical literacy and relevant mathematics at almost the same time might very well prove feasible.

Items and Assessment Structure

In general, mathematical literacy will be measured by an assessment system consisting of restricted-time written tests. For literacy, context or a real-world situation is an essential part of any item designed to measure mathematical literacy. This implies that typically an item will consist of some stimulus material or information, an introduction, and the actual question. In addition, for non-multiple-choice items, a detailed coding scheme will be developed to enable trained markers. It goes without saying that there is an inherent tension between the traditional choice of item formats, usually with very restricted time limits (1–2 minutes per item), and the rather ambitious definitions of what constitutes mathematical literacy. It still has to be proved that, in this respect, tests such as PISA (and many others) are valid in the sense that they really measure mathematical literacy. But it is also clear that much progress has been made in the past 40 years on the quality and especially the authenticity of items used in ML studies. Authenticity is especially important when measuring ML, meaning here that tasks represent one of a variety of real-world situations, and that they have a context for which the use of mathematics to solve the problem that is authentic.

Although experts do not completely agree on the subject, careful observations make clear that items requiring competencies that go beyond mere reproduction and basic skills are quite difficult to operationalize with items of the multiple-choice format. Closed-constructed response items and open-constructed response question are often used to operationalize these competencies (see Fig. 1). For items in these formats, guessing is not likely to be a concern, and the provision of distracters (which influence the construct that is being assessed) is not necessary. Open-constructed response items differ from closed-constructed response in that they require a more extended response, and the process of producing the answer requires often higher order cognitive activities.

The assessment structure that is popular when measuring ML is the rotating test design. Items are clustered in a number-cluster of items, with each item-cluster representing a fixed amount of time. The item-clusters will be placed in booklets according to the rotated test design. In order to ensure reliable scoring, detailed guidelines have been developed for the scoring guides, the training materials to recruit scorers, and the workshop materials used for training national scorers. For each test item, the intent of the question is described, and how to code the student's response to each item. This description allows for giving partial credit. Also included is a system of double-digit coding, allowing not only for correctness of the answer but also for identifying strategies or misconceptions. In order to examine the consistency of the marking process, an interscorer reliability study has to be carried out.

In the diagram below, you see the pattern of a certain lighthouse. The light flashes alternate with dark periods. It is a regular pattern. After some time the pattern repeats itself. The time taken by one complete cycle of a pattern, before it starts to repeat, is called the period. When you find the period of a pattern, it is easy to extend the diagram for the next seconds or minutes or even hours.

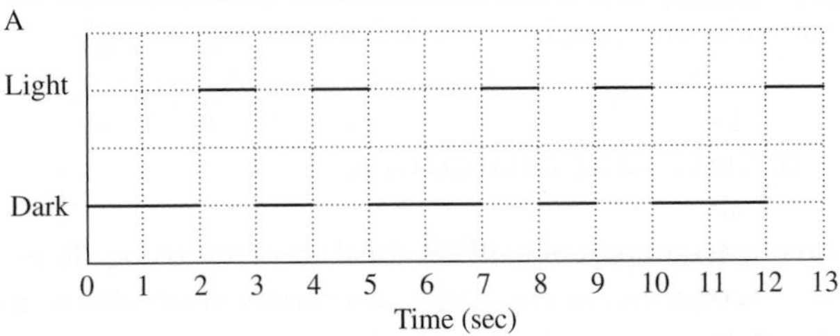

In the diagram below, make a graph of a possible pattern of light flashes of a lighthouse that sends out light flashes for 30 seconds per minute. The period of this pattern must be equal to 6 seconds.

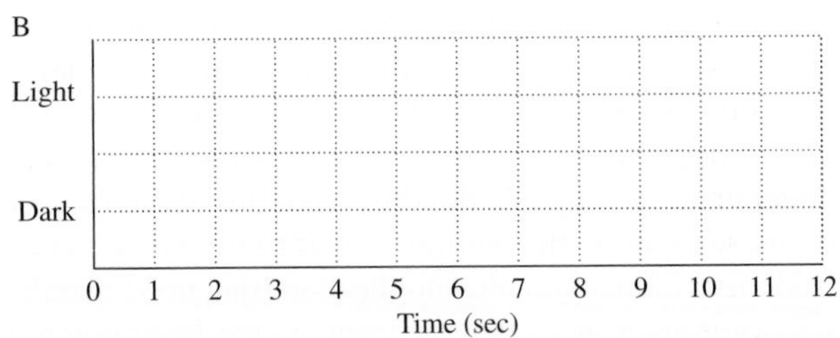

Figure 1 The type of problem that was used in the PISA 2003 Assessment Framework. The wording of the description (A) and of the instruction (B) indicates the openness of the problem (note the use of the word "possible"). The problem presents a challenge to students to construct or design a solution. This challenge to express mathematical competency in an active and underived manner is an important aspect of mathematical literacy. There are two conditions to solving the problem: there must be equal amounts of light and dark in a 1-minute period, and each period must last for a specified time (6 seconds). These conditions require comprehension on a conceptual level, indicating that the students are being confronted with the "reflection" competency cluster. Adapted from Organization for Economic Cooperation and Development (OECD) (2003).

Methodological Aspects

The 2003 PISA is, by any measure, the largest study yet in the area of mathematical literacy (in the 2003 study, mathematics is the main study subject). Some technical aspects of this study are summarized here. PISA developed quality standards, procedures, instruments, and verification mechanisms to ensure that national samples yielded comparable data. The data quality standards required minimum participation rates for educational institutions as well as for students. The minimum participation rate had to be met at a national level, not necessarily for each participating country (details of the quality assurance report are contained in the 2003 OECD publication). PISA used item response theory (IRT) methods to produce scale scores that summarized the achievement results. The model (mixed-coefficients multinomial logit IRT) used to produce the test results is similar to the more familiar two-parameter IRT model. With this method, the performance of a sample of students is a subject area or subarea can be summarized on a single scale or a series of scales, even when different students do different items. IRT scaling provides estimates of item parameters (such as difficulty and discrimination) that define relationships between items and underlying variables measured by the test. Parameters of the IRT model are estimated for each test question, with an overall scale being established as well as scales for each predefined content area.

One of the key problems of a study that deals with a matter as complex as measuring mathematical literacy, on such a large international scale, is the problem of keeping the burden for students as low as possible, and obtaining results that are accurate nevertheless. In the PISA study, because so few items were done by students, it was impossible to produce accurate content-related scale scores for each student. To account for this, the plausible-value theory can be applied. For example, PISA administered few assessment items to each student and generated five possible scale scores for each student. The five scale scores represented selections from the distribution of scale scores of students with similar backgrounds who answered the items in the same way. In this way, PISA used the plausible-values methodology to represent what the true performance of an individual might have been, had it been observed, using a small number of random draws from an empirically derived distribution of score values based on the student's observed responses to assessment items and on background variables. Because of this plausible-values approach, secondary researchers can use the data to carry out a wide range of analysis.

Developments and Studies on Mathematical Literacy

Some of the publications in the field of mathematical literacy have had a proven impact. In 1977, the Education Department of Western Australia published a policy paper on literacy and numeracy, stating that the "term 'numerate' is understood to mean mathematical literacy. A person is considered to be literate and numerate when he has acquired the skills and concepts that enable him to function effectively in his group and community, and when his attainment in reading, writing and mathematics make it possible for him to continue to use these skills to further his own and his community's development." The report stresses a more traditional view by emphasizing mastery of number facts, competence in operations, skills in estimation, skills in interpreting graphs, etc.

A noteworthy publication in the United Kingdom, Cockcroft's *Mathematics Counts*, contained David Stringer's survey *Make It Count*. The survey mentioned that "there are many adults in Britain—not just the unintelligent and uneducated—that are hopeless in arithmetic and they want to do something about it . . . Functional innumeracy is far more widespread than anyone has cared to believe." The entire Cockroft report was an important source of information and especially was motivation to rethink mathematics education in many countries, especially the United States and Australia. One part of this report stated that "it is important to have the feeling for number, which permits sensible estimation and approximation and which enables straightforward mental calculation to be accomplished. Most important of all is the need to have sufficient confidence to make effective use of whatever mathematical skill and understanding is possessed, whether this be little or much."

In 1989, the United States followed the UK report *Make It Count* with the report *Everybody Counts*. In this report, it was stated that "numeracy requires more than just familiarity with numbers. To cope confidently with the demands of today's society, one must be able to grasp the implications of many mathematical concepts—for example, chance, logic, and graphs—that permeate daily news and routine decisions." Almost at the same time, the National Council of Teachers in Mathematics (NCTM) published its *Standards*. In this publication, the authors refer to mathematical literacy and recognize its importance. This was again emphasized in the more recent revised edition of the *Standards*. Literacy is not only a Western world problem. On the contrary, the push for literacy in general started with the work of Paulo Freire. His pleas for literacy for all were reflected at several United Nations Educational, Scientific, and Cultural Organization (UNESCO) conferences. One of the most well-known conferences took place in Yomtien in 1990, when Freire stated that "every person shall be able to benefit from educational opportunities designed to meet their basic learning needs. These needs comprise both essential learning tools (as literacy, oral expression, numeracy, and problem solving)."

Studies have followed the many reports. In 1986, an important start was made with national research into quantitative literacy skills of adults as part of the National Assessment of Educational Progress (NAEP) project in the United States. In a first study, the Young Adult Literacy Skills (YALS), young adults were assessed on tasks related to three literacy scales, one being quantitative literacy. As reported by John Dossey in 1997, the scale measures the ability to apply the knowledge and skills to understand and use the information from texts similar to newspapers and popular magazines; to locate and use information contained in job applications, schedules, maps, tables, and indexes; and to apply arithmetic operations embedded in printed materials, such as recording checks in a check register, computing the amount of a tip, completing an order form, or determining the amount of a loan. According to Dossey, the results "were less than what the nation required in human talent for long-term international competitiveness." A follow-up of YALS was the National Adult Literacy Study (NALS), again with rather disappointing results. Performance on tasks used in the NALS suggests that many everyday or work-related literacy tasks, involving either manipulation of numbers or comprehension of quantitative data, that are embedded in various types of text prove difficult for a large proportion of adults in the United States.

The Organization for Economic Cooperation and Development carried out an international study, the International Adults Literacy Skills Survey (IALS), in the period from 1990 to 1996. In 2000, the first phase of the OECD/PISA study was carried out; the second phase of the OECD/PISA study occurred in 2003, stressing mathematical literacy as its main component. In the same year, the follow-up survey of IALS, the Adult Literacy and Life Skills survey, was fielded. Other, more local studies on mathematical literacy include the National Completion Examinations in mathematics (NCEM) in Israel and the Victoria Common Assessment Tasks in Australia. Although the list of studies and reports mentioned here is far from exhaustive, it is clear that measuring mathematical literacy has taken full flight. The discussion about the consequences of the measurements and the true meaning of the data, however, just has started.

See Also the Following Articles

Education, Tests and Measures in • Literacy, Scientific

Further Reading

Amit, M., and Fried, M. N. (2002). High-stakes assessment as a tool for promoting mathematical literacy and the democratization of mathematics education. *J. Math. Behav.* **21,** 499–514 Elsevier, Amsterdam.

Cockroft, W. H. (1982). *Mathematics Counts*. Report of the Committee of Inquiry into the Teaching of Mathematics in Schools. Her Majesty's Stationery Office, London.

De Lange, J. (2003). Mathematics for literacy. In *Quantitative Literacy. Why Numeracy Matters for Schools and Colleges* (B. L. Madison and L. A. Steen, eds.), pp. 75–89. The National Council on Education and the Disciplines, Princeton, New Jersey.

Dossey, J. A. (1997). National indicators of quantitative literacy. In *Why Numbers Count. Quantitative Literacy for Tomorrow's America* (L. A. Steen, ed.), pp. 45–59. College Entrance Examination Board, New York.

Freudenthal, H. (1973). *Mathematics as an Educational Task.* Reidel, Dordrecht.

Gal, I. (1993). *Issues and Challenges in Adult Numeracy.* Technical Report TR93-15. National Center of Adult Literacy, University of Pennsylvania Philadelphia.

International Life Skills Survey (ILSS). (2000). *Policy Research Initiative. Statistics Canada.* Policy Research Initiative, Ottawa.

Kilpatrick, J., and Swafford, J. (eds.) (2002). *Helping Children Learn Mathematics*. National Academy Press, Washington, D.C.

National Center for Education Statistics (NCES). (1993). *National Adult Literacy Survey.* NCES, Washington, D.C. (Available on the Internet at http://nces.ed.gov.)

National Research Council (NRC). (1989). *Everybody Counts: A Report to the Nation on the Future of Mathematics Education.* National Academy Press, Washington, D.C.

Neubrand, N., *et al.* (2001). Grundlager der Ergänzung des Internationalen PISA-Mathematik-Tests in der Deutschen Zusatzerhebung. *ZDM* **33**(2), 45–59.

Niss, M. (1999). Kompetencer og Uddannelsesbeskrivelse (Competencies and Subject-Description). *Uddanneise* **9,** 21–29.

Organization for Economic Cooperation and Development (OECD). (2000). *PISA 2000 Technical Report*. (Available on the Internet at www.oecd.org)

Organization for Economic Cooperation and Development (OECD) (2003). *The PISA 2003 Assessment Framework—Mathematics, Reading, Science and Problem Solving Knowledge and Skills.* OECD, Paris.

Reeves, H. (1994). *Numeracy, a Background Discussion Paper.* Department of Education and the Arts, Tasmania (Available on the Internet at http://www.cs.tased.edu.au/maths/num.html).

Steen, L. A. (1990). *On the Shoulders of Giants: New Approaches to Numeracy.* National Academy Press, Washington, D.C.

Steen, L. A. (ed.) (2001). *Mathematics and Democracy: The Case for Quantitative Literacy*. National Council on Education and the Disciplines, Princeton, New Jersey.

Willis, S. (ed.) (1990). *Being Numerate: What Counts*. Australian Council for Educational Research (ACER), Melbourne.

Literacy, Scientific

Peter J. Fensham
Monash University, Victoria, Australia

Glossary

need-to-know science The knowledge of science that citizens urgently require in order to cope with real-life situations in which they are involved.

public understanding of science A measure of the knowledge that members of the public have of science and its procedures of inquiry.

school science What is intended to be taught and learned about science in the years of formal schooling.

science for all A belief that meaningful learning of science can be extended to all students and citizens, not just those with interests in science-related careers.

scientific inquiry Processes and ways that scientists acquire knowledge in order to elucidate and explain the natural world.

scientific literacy Competencies and understandings about science that persons can acquire through formal and informal education.

the public The citizens of a society in general, in groups and individually.

The measurement of scientific literacy and of public understanding of science involves assessing what students and the public need to know about science and how scientific knowledge can be surveyed reliably and validly. Scientific literacy acquired in educational systems is now understood to be closely linked to public understanding of science; schools, as the major source of scientific teachings, are the source also of hope for a well-informed citizenry.

Introduction

The Public and Science

The interest of the general public in understanding science has a long history. Mechanics institutes, an early 19th-century innovation, flourished in many towns and villages and served a central purpose of providing citizens with knowledge of science and technology. Early in the 19th century, magazines such as *Popular Science* and *Popular Mechanics* had substantial readerships; the contemporary equivalents, for English readers, are *Scientific American* and *New Scientist*, and similar magazines published in many languages are widely read throughout the world. In 1938, Lancelot Hogben published the first of many reprints and editions of *Science for the Citizen—A Self-Educator Based on the Social Background of Science Discoveries*. Numerous books by leading scientists for interested public readers were published in the 1940s. Since then, many well-known writers, such as Isaac Asimov, Stephen J. Gould, Stephen Hawking, Dava Sobel, and Margaret Wertheim, to name just a few, have been successful purveyors of the fascination of science and of background on how scientists develop scientific knowledge.

Paralleling the print media popularizations of science are the television programs about investigations by scientists in many fields, especially the natural world and the medical sciences. Science fiction, with its mix of reality and fantasy science, is a genre of literature that is read by large numbers of the public, and it is even more popular in the media of film and television. Interactive science museums and science centers are also now commonplace and are increasingly visited by members of the public as well as by school students. The Internet currently is an important means of access for the public to an ever-increasing amount scientific information. Finally, governments are the impetus for the public need for scientific knowledge, given that science-based regulations confront citizens everyday, from use-by dates in supermarkets to the compulsion to wear seat belts in cars. How much of this science does the public at large, or its subgroups of citizens, including students, understand, or need to understand?

School Science and Public Understanding of Science

It is only from the perspective of the 1960s onward that an association between school-taught science and public understanding of science makes any general sense. Prior to the 1960s, only a small minority of students in most countries undertook serious studies of science at school. A great period of science curriculum reform in the 1960s and 1970s initiated the rise of science as a more universal and serious component of academic curricula. This process also began to shift the locus of the public's understanding of science from adult sources to what was being taught and learned by future citizens in grade school through high school. This link between school science and public understanding was given further impetus in the 1980s, when a number of countries (Canada, the United States, and the United Kingdom) and the United Nations Educational, Scientific, and Cultural Organization (UNESCO) committed to the slogan of "Science for All" as a new goal for school science. The science education of all students, who are the general public of the future, was to be put on an equal footing with the original and traditional goal of school science, which was the selection and preparation of future scientists. Implementation of these new educational goals would require all students to study science for some years at school; the intent was to provide a base for the general public's understanding of science, regardless of what other community sources might contribute. By 1990, the original international slogan had evolved to become "Scientific Literacy," thus aligning the goal of school science with the educational imperatives of literacy in language and numbers. Furthermore, because measuring student learning is a standard aspect of schooling, it is not surprising that measuring student scientific literacy, as an indicator of what the future public's understanding of science would be, became, alongside measurement of learning, a national and international activity.

Public Understanding of Science

Nature of Public Interactions

In 1975, Benjamin Shen suggested that the interactions of the public with science involve three types of scientific literacy: practical, cultural, and civic. By practical, Shen meant scientific knowledge that has personal and practical usefulness. Cultural scientific literacy is associated with knowledge of, and interest in, science for personal appreciation, and civic scientific literacy is concerned with the knowledge that is required to follow the essence of the arguments that are presented, say, in the media about disputed socioscientific issues. Shen regarded the last of these as "the cornerstone of informed public policy." These different types of knowing about science might also have led Shen and others to a recognition of different "publics," but such a differentiation of this target population has only more recently been a feature of the issue.

Need-to-Know Science

In the early 1990s, David Layton and his colleagues at the University of Leeds studied small groups of citizens who were in situations in which they had an urgent need to know some aspect of science. These case studies helped identify some specific abilities that are associated with Shen's practical and civic scientific literacies: the ability to access scientific information when required, to differentiate between the worth of different sources, to weigh the value of the information in relation to other social knowledge, and to differentiate between scientific questions and other questions about the pressing problem. These features of understanding science are not about a "conceptual cathedral" of science knowledge to be remembered, but rather about a "quarry to be raided" for information, to be put to use when needed. On the other hand, cultural scientific literacy involves a level of understanding that enables members of the public to share vicariously the investigations of scientists past and present—their questions, their quest for answers, and what they found.

Measuring Public Understanding

Beginnings

The notion that a public understanding of science should or could be measured is a recent idea, and, accordingly, there is still debate about the meaning of what is to be measured and how the measures can and should be obtained. An increase in media and tools for public access to science in the 20th century spurred the development of means to measure the public's interest in science. In 1957, the National Association of Science Writers surveyed American adults about their patterns of access to, and consumption of, writings about science. The issues about access to science have not been pursued in the more recent measurement studies, despite their increased importance in the age of the Internet.

In 1963, Michael Bassey published the results of a modest study under the title of *Science for Tomorrow's Citizens*, reminiscent of Hogben's title. He surveyed university-level humanities students who had studied some science at school, but not as their central interest or future intention. Bassey's view of the science to be understood consisted of some basic content knowledge that students should or could have been taught in science in secondary schooling, and that they would be able to describe the standard scientific method in terms that included the role of hypothesis. The level of the content knowledge can be seen from some of Bassey's questions:

- Are there atoms in air, water, clay, and wood?
- Which of the following are properties of chlorine?
- Which of the following are basic aspects of the modern theory of evolution?

The residual memory among Bassey's respondents of the two fundamental aspects of science knowledge (basics and the scientific method) was not substantial, and the experience of school science that the university students remembered was that it seemed to be a long list of irrelevant facts. Bassey made a prescient link between his sense of citizens' understanding of science and the learning of science in schooling by starting with the question "What effect does learning science in school have on persons not engaged in science after they leave school?"

Political Interest

In the 1970s and 1980s, modern contradictions—how science and technology lead to rising standards of living in the developed countries and how the same combination of knowledge and application degrades the biophysical environment—began to be recognized nationally and internationally. The political awareness that yet more applications of science and technology would be necessary to resolve this dilemma has led to pressure for greater public understanding (and hence measures) of the role of science and technology in relation to decision making about the many socioscientific issues all societies now face. Shen's description of civic scientific literacy relates directly to this political pressure. The Royal Society in London released a report in 1985 entitled *The Public Understanding of Science*. It addressed the need for more education, of both the public and those in school, about science. It forcefully urged that there were a number of benefits, personal and national, to be gained from a public that was more informed about science. The Royal Society has been criticized for overemphasizing the public deficiency in factual knowledge of science, but the report also expressed concern about inadequate knowledge of the methods of science, its potential for achievement, and its limitations.

Scope of Understanding

The limited nature of the science understanding Bassey set out to measure (a few direct knowledge items and an open question about scientific inquiry) invited other aspects of understanding to be included in such measuring. In 1974, Peter Fensham made an attempt with several accessible work groups of adults. They were interviewed about a range of questions:

- What type of scientist would be relevant to plagues of locusts, bridge failures, water quality, etc?
- Where would you look in an encyclopedia for information on colors in soap bubbles, on objects floating in satellites, on egg yolks blackening spoons, etc?
- How could observations such as warmer patches of water in a lake, skin rash in children in a neighborhood, etc. be investigated?

These questions were so hypothetical for the respondents that this direction of measuring a rather wider meaning of understanding science was not pursued.

Systematic Measuring

In 1972, the National Science Board in United States produced the first of a series of biennial reports on a set of science indicators. The initial focus was on the public's attitude to science in general and to some specific science issues, but subsequently this was widened in scope. In 1973 and 1977, the National Assessment of Educational Progress in the United States used a survey methodology to test large, but not generally representative, groups of adults to measure their factual science knowledge and their interest in science. In 1982 Arthur Lucas reported the use of the process of public opinion polling to survey the knowledge British adults had of some topics in biology, using questions that could have been on tests in the mid-years of secondary school biology. The use of the survey methods for polling public opinion thereafter became the main method of measuring public understanding of science. These have the strengths of representativeness and measure reliability that were lacking in the earlier studies of specific groups, but they have the validity limitation of what can be asked about science on such a wide scale, using the methods for data collection of this type of survey research (questionnaires or interviews asked face-to-face or by telephone).

J. D. Miller in the United States and J. Durant in the United Kingdom are two key figures in the measuring process at the public level. Miller, in 1983, suggested that public understanding of science can be thought of in three dimensions. The first dimension is like Shen's civic scientific literacy. It is about having a sufficiently confident knowledge of the vocabulary of science constructs that a media report involving conflicting aspects of science can be read and appreciated. The second dimension is an understanding of the processes of scientific inquiry, and the third is the understanding citizens have of the impact of science on society. The early attempts to measure the third of these dimensions suggested that it varied widely across and within countries, and researchers have not persisted with this measure in the larger national and international comparative studies that have been undertaken since the 1980s. In the 1990s, when major surveys had also been undertaken in Europe, Bauer and Schoon argued that variation in the public's understanding of science (as, for example, in this dimension) should be seen as something interesting to investigate. To measure or record this variation, however, raises serious methodological problems.

In his first testing of the vocabulary dimension in 1983, Miller surveyed more than 1000 adults in the United States; Miller used a range of true/false factual statements such as "It is the father's gene that determines the sex of the child," "all radioactivity is man-made," and "the center of the earth is very hot." He concluded that the great majority on this dimension were scientifically illiterate, a conclusion that was supported when Miller and John Durant collaborated in the late 1980s to produce a set of knowledge items for use as a core set in surveys in Canada, China, Japan, Korea, New Zealand, and Spain, in addition to the United States and the United Kingdom. In 1992, a survey by telephone interview of 12,000 adults in the 12 member states of the European Union produced what was described as the Eurobarometer—measures on a broad set of knowledge and attitude items about science.

Scientific Inquiry

For Miller's second dimension, understanding scientific inquiry, a single open-ended item ("What does it mean to study something scientifically?") was found to produce useful results in both the United States and the United Kingdom. More concrete cases (for example, "Which approach [briefly described] of two scientists wishing to studying the effect of a certain drug on high blood pressure is better, and why?") have also been used with interesting outcomes.

Psychometric Aspects

Miller, in particular, has given attention to several of the psychometric issues associated with measuring public understanding of science. One issue is the durability of the measure: Can a measure be developed that has an enduring relevance to different publics and to these publics over time, so that changes in public understanding of science can be recognized? A second issue is the reliability of the measures: Can reliable scores be obtained from tests that contain a minimum number of common items? A third issue is the type of item to use in the measure? What type of item facilitates data collection and data richness? Finally, there has been the issue of level of understanding: What levels of understanding should be used when reporting cross-national comparisons?

Factor analysis of the results of testings in both the United States and Europe, using items designed to test Miller's first two dimensions, confirmed that two factors were present. one concerned with vocabulary and one concerned with the process of scientific inquiry. The scores on the two dimensions correlated highly, but were considered sufficiently different to be regarded as separate dimensions. Nine vocabulary items were common, although their loadings on the factor differed in the two studies. The use of a combination of factor analysis and the methods of item response theory on the data from their national studies enabled Miller and Durant to identify a core set of knowledge items that were then used in the eight-nation study referred to previously. When multiple groups are involved, as in this study, the methods of item response theory were used to compute item values and test scores that take into account the relative difficulty of items and the different composition of each national test. Reliable results were obtained with a minimum of 10 items. These items required respondents to provide, for example, definitions of DNA and a molecule and to answer true/false to statements such as "light is faster than sound," "all radioactivity is man-made," "earliest humans lived at same time as the dinosaurs," and "antibiotics kill viruses and bacteria." The type of item is very related to the mode of interaction between the researcher and the responding public. Both open-ended and closed items have been tried in studies in the United States and United Kingdom. In general, open-ended questions lead to measures that are likely to be more valid, but they are more difficult to interpret and hence to score compared to closed questions.

If a printed questionnaire is presented, multiple-choice items are feasible, although adults are more likely to be confused by this format than are students at school. When the interview is conducted by telephone, simple open-ended questions, such as asking for definitions, and the closed true/false items are much more appropriate. In either case, having more than one part to an item greatly helps to distinguish guessing from understanding. For example, when the true/false item "Earth rotates around the sun" was followed with a related question ("Does this rotation take a day, a month, or a year?"), a more realistic indication of the level of understanding was achieved. Of those who knew Earth goes around sun, 47% in the United States and 33% in Great Britain knew the period correctly.

The scoring of large-scale surveys that have quantitative comparative measures as their primary purpose requires a convergence of response to the various items—that is a "correct" response. Although this can be achieved when printed questionnaires and closed items are used, telephone interviewing, even with intentionally closed questions, leads to a wider range of responses. Respondents in the Eurobarometer study were asked the open question, "What does it mean to study something scientifically?" Analysis of the responses by Bauer and Schoon found a richness in the respondents' understanding that would not have been possible with closed questions directed at a "correct" response. For reporting purposes, three levels have been established: literate or well informed (≥67% correct), partially literate (33–66%), and not literate (<33%). In the comparative study between the United States, in 1995, and Europe, in 1993, the findings for these levels were United States, 12, 25, and 62%; and Europe, 5, 22, and 73%.

Political Needs

Political Interest

Politicians seem fatally attracted to the survey measures, despite the overall dismal message of the outcomes. On the one hand, there always seems to be one or two items to which politicians can point successfully, emphasizing that their own ministry outscored some other rival ministry. On the other hand, the generally poor scores enable political arguments to be made for more funds for particular ministries. More fundamentally, survey measures may provide politicians with data that are only marginally related to the issues for which they need to produce policy.

Understanding and Support for Science

There is some evidence from repeated studies, and from the breakdown of responses by age, that young adults and those who have continued to study science do have a greater measure of scientific understanding. This trend has been acknowledged, but with the caveat that the presence of correct bits of science knowledge is not the same as being able to respond to science messages, a much more difficult thing to measure. In 1995, Evans and Durant looked at the relationship between the measures of understanding of science and the attitude to science, which has been of such interest to politicians. More understanding was weakly related to positive attitudes, but was more related to coherence in the attitude responses and to more discriminating attitudes about specific cases of the application of science. Miller's studies in the United States also found similarly real, but modest, linkages. When science applications were posed in general terms and in cases involving research that could be classified as useful and basic, understanding and support were directly related. For research that was controversial, such as embryo research or searching for new stars and planets, the most knowledgeable citizens were more strongly opposed. Martin Bauer analyzed the Eurobarometer data in terms of the degree of industrialization of the participating European countries. The most industrialized countries had higher levels of understanding, but they recorded less interest in science. Age, gender, and level of education are also determinants of these attitudes, so the relationship is complex and by no means as clear-cut as some politicians have hoped or tended to assume.

Criticism

Methodological Limitations

The limitation that the opinion poll method of data collection places on the types of questions that can be asked and simply scored has already been mentioned. It is just one aspect of a basic concern about psychometric measures of complex things, such as having an understanding of science. Some aspects of this complexity may be amenable to large-scale measuring, whereas other important aspects of it are not. If measuring the accessible aspects goes ahead, and scores of the public's performance on these aspects are reported, the nonmeasurable aspects recede in importance or may be discounted entirely, even though originally they may have been seen to be of equal or greater importance. The previously mentioned caveat, concerning possessing bits of science as opposed to being able to construe science messages, relates to this problem, as does the absence of measures of the public's ability to access scientific information when it is needed. Cultural scientific literacy as an aspect of public understanding of science has been totally disregarded in the most widely publicized measures, even though the evidence of its importance, provided by best-selling books that popularize science and by the success of science programs on television, is readily available.

Multiple Publics/Multiple Sciences

The polling of random samples of adults about a common set of science knowledge items discounts entirely any sense of the local in citizens' need to know, or of their particular interests among the multitude of science topics. In this regard, in 1997, Edgar Jenkins, a colleague of Layton in the Leeds study, urged that the interest in measurement should recognize that there are a number of distinct, segmented "publics," differentiated by interest and situational need. Furthermore, there is a multiplicity of knowledge and understandings of science, and all of these entities are essentially functional and directed toward specific personal and social purposes. These ideas have generated a quite different approach to exploring the public understanding of science. It begins by identifying the needs for scientific knowledge that adults have, as they function in the variety of societal contexts that make up life in modern society. Rather than discounting the need-to-know aspect (from the Leeds case studies) as idiosyncratic to particular situations, the approach suggests that there are aspects of science in the need-to-know category that large numbers of citizens may indeed share in common in their daily lives and work. The terms "citizen science" and "practical science-knowledge-in-action" have been proposed to replace the general term "scientific literacy." In recent studies in three large cities in China, the perspective of citizens rather than science experts was deliberately sought. This has revealed some interesting examples of science knowledge that the different publics in these studies commonly needed to know.

Unjustified Importance

There has been serious criticism of the very idea of measuring public understanding of science. The argument is that, because scientific knowledge is a socially constructed form of knowledge, to measure its presence among the public at large gives it an unjustified and unhelpful status, relative to other types of socially constructed knowledge, such as the local knowledge of citizens.

Projections from School Measures

The Trends in International Mathematics and Science Study

The link between the science learning by all students in schooling and the public understanding of science in adult life means that a measure of the understanding achieved in schooling will provide some indication of what the public understanding may be in the years ahead. The Trends in International Mathematics and Science Study (TIMSS; formerly called the Third International Mathematics and Science Study) in 1994 was the first attempt to do this cross-nationally. As one of the tests of TIMSS, its creators, the National Center for Education Statistics and various partners in the United States, prepared an instrument referred to as Mathematics and Science Literacy. This test was taken by students in the final year of secondary schooling, whether or not they were still studying science. Despite a very considerable debate about the possible emphases this test's items might be given, it was finally developed as a rather traditional test with isolated items that required an understanding of the vocabulary of science constructs, some of which related to ongoing environmental contexts. Understanding of the nature of scientific inquiry was not included. The findings provided a useful cross-national baseline for future studies of the vocabulary knowledge of the young adult populations of the 21 countries that took part in TIMSS. There were, however, indications from studies associated with TIMSS that this type of knowledge was being forgotten even before the students had left school.

Organization for Economic Cooperation and Development/Program for International Student Assessment

Although both Shen's description of civic scientific literacy and Miller's elaboration of the first dimension of public understanding of science referred to the ability to read mass media science reports that include conflicting or competing science views, the abilities associated with such meaningful reading have not been directly measured at the public level. This is another example of the constraint that opinion poll testing places on the type of item used in the data collection. The captive populations that school contexts provide, however, makes it possible to include the test tasks of reading and critiquing actual media reports of science.

The Program for International Student Assessment (PISA) in Science, launched by the Organization for Economic Cooperation and Development (OECD) in 1998, based its first testing of 15-year-old students in 2000 on just such a set of tasks. It is thus more interesting than TIMSS as an example of projecting from school understanding. The purpose of this PISA survey was to provide measures of the extent to which the students' education in science had prepared them to "play a constructive role as citizens in society." In this way, the PISA Science project took a large step away from the idea that the outcome of school science is, or ought to be, simply an accumulation of scientific knowledge and skills in the form in which they are presented in most science textbooks and classrooms. The project's view of scientific literacy is much more active. For the first limited measurement of science in 2000, the goal was defined as "being able to combine science knowledge with the ability to draw evidence-based conclusions in order to understand and help make decisions about the natural world and the changes made to it through human activity." The measure the project was seeking would place students along a continuum of developing scientific understanding and procedural ability.

Five scientific procedures were selected for the design of the items of this initial measuring instrument:

1. Recognizing scientifically investigable questions.
2. Identifying evidence/data needed in a scientific investigation to test an explanation.
3. Drawing or evaluating conclusions.
4. Communicating valid conclusions.
5. Demonstrating understanding of scientific concepts.

The items were devised to involve these knowledge/process combinations as applied to media reports involving science, as examples of authentic, public socioscientific situations. The science constructs in the items were chosen based on criteria of everyday relevance, enduring relevance, and relevance to the media context. The instruments that resulted contrast markedly with those used in TIMSS and in traditional school science tests, in which the question situations are so often contrived for the purpose, and hence fail to reflect the dynamic nature of either pure or applied science.

The immediate reactions to this proposed testing were that most 15-year-old respondents would not be able to deal with these types of tasks. It was suggested that the students were not mature enough to think in these ways about science issues or that, even if potentially mature enough, their education in science at school had not given them the opportunity or the incentive to develop these skills. The results of the first PISA testing in 32 countries in 2000 were encouraging beyond such expectations. Two-thirds of the students in the OECD countries achieved scores within one standard deviation of the average level, and the highest national averages meant achievement on about 75% of the items. This means that a majority of the students were able to use a number of the required scientific constructs to make predictions or provide explanations, to recognize questions that can be answered by scientific investigation, and/or to identify details of what is involved in a scientific investigation, and that they were able to select relevant information from competing data or chains of reasoning in drawing or evaluating conclusions. There were, of course, differences in the average scores of the students in the various countries, and attention has inevitably tended to focus on these differences and the rankings. This should not, however, obscure the promise that the results of the PISA project suggest for public understanding of science in the future.

See Also the Following Articles

Literacy, Mathematical • Polling Industry • Surveys

Further Reading

Bauer, M., and Schoon, I. (1993). Mapping variety in public understanding of science. *Public Understand. Sci.* **2**(2), 141–155.

Durant, J., Evans, G., and Thomas, G. (1989). The public understanding of science. *Nature (London)* **340,** 11–14.

Evans, G., and Durant, J. (1995). The relation between knowledge and attitude in public understanding of science in Britain. *Public Understand. Sci.* **4**(1), 57–74.

Fensham, P. J., and Harlen, W. (1999). School science and public understanding of science. *Int. J. Sci. Edu.* **21**(7), 755–764.

Institut National de la Recherche Agronomique (INRA)—Europe. (1993). *European Co-ordination Office for the Commission of the European Community DG XII, Eurobarometer 39.1, Biotechnology and Genetic Engineering: What Europeans Think about It.* Commission of the European Community, Brussels.

Irwin, A., and Wynne, B. (eds.) (1996). *Misunderstanding Science*. Cambridge University Press, Cambridge.

Jenkins, E. (1997). Towards a functional public understanding of science. *Science Today: Problem or Crisis? (R.. Levinson and J. Thomas, eds.)*, pp. 137–150. Routledge, London.

Layton, D., Jenkins, E., Macgill, S., and Davey, A. (1993). *Inarticulate Science? Perspectives on the Public Understanding of Science and some Implications for Science Education.* Studies in Science Education, Driffield, United Kingdom.

Miller, J. D. (1983). Scientific literacy: A conceptual and empirical review. *Daedalus* **11**(2), 29–48.

Miller, J. D. (1992). Towards a scientific understanding of science and technology. *Public Understand. Sci.* **1**(1), 23–26.

Miller, J. D. (1998). The measurement of civic scientific literacy. *Public Understand. Sci.* **7,** 203–223.

Organization for Economic Cooperation and Development (OECD). (1999). *Measuring Student Knowledge and Skills: A New Framework for Assessment.* OECD Publ., Paris.

Organization for Economic Cooperation and Development (OECD). (2000). *Measuring Student Knowledge and Skills: The PISA 2000 Assessment of Reading, Mathematical; and Scientific Literacy.* OECD Publ., Paris.

Shen, B. S. P. (1975). Scientific literacy and the public understanding of science. In *Communication of Scientific Information* (S. B. Day, ed.), pp. 44–52. Karger, Basel.

Wynne, A. (1994). Public understanding of science. In *Handbook of Science and Technology Studies* (G. E. Jasanoff S., Markle, J. C. Peterson, and T. Pinch, eds.), pp. 361–388. Sage, London.

Ziman, J. (1991). Public understanding of science. *Sci. Technol. Human Values* **16**(1), 99–105.

Location Analysis

Charles S. ReVelle

Johns Hopkins University, Baltimore, Maryland, USA

Horst A. Eiselt

University of New Brunswick, Fredericton, New Brunswick, Canada

Glossary

competitive location problems Models in which each competitor takes the existing locations and the potential reactions of its competitors to its own actions into account.

dispersion problems Location problems in which the decision maker locates facilities so as to maximize the spatial separation between them.

flow capturing (intercepting) problems Location problems in which customers are assumed to travel on a path between home and work, and decision makers try to capture or intercept as much of the flow of customers as possible.

hierarchical location problems Location problems in which higher-level facilities offer specialized services in addition to the type of service that lower-level facilities offer. Problems of this type typically include some type of referral system.

location set covering problems (LSCPs) Location models in which the decision maker attempts to locate the least number of facilities that guarantee that each customer is no farther than a prespecified distance from a facility.

maximum covering location problems (MCLPs) Location models in which a decision maker sites facilities so that as many customers as possible are located within a certain radius.

***p*-center location** A set of p facility locations that minimizes the longest distance between any customer and the facility closest to it.

***p*-median location** A set of p facility locations on a network that minimizes the sum of weighted distances between the customers and the facility closest to them.

simple plant location problems (SPLPs) Location models that minimize the sum of transportation costs and fixed (establishment) costs of the facilities, so that the number of facilities is endogenous in the model.

undesirable facility location The location of facilities to maximize a function of distances between the facilities and their customers. Typically associated with (ob-)noxious facilities.

Weber problem A set of p facility locations in the plane that minimizes the sum of weighted distances between the customers and the facility closest to them.

Location models are designed to represent the process of siting facilities in some given space. Typical examples of such models deal with supermarkets, fast-food outlets, gas stations, landfills, and power-generating stations. Each application has its own idiosyncrasies, so that a large number of models is needed to model the many different scenarios in practice. With the exception of some fairly basic models, most realistic location problems tend to result in fairly complex nonlinear and/or integer optimization problems. The difficulties are exacerbated by the fact that most location problems require long-term planning, for which exact data are typically not available; have multiple objectives; and may require more than a single decision maker. This makes it even more important than in other optimization problems to treat the results of location models as suggestions rather than exact recommendations.

Introduction

The term location analysis refers to the modeling, formulation, and solution of a class of problems that can best be described as siting facilities in some given space.

The expressions "deployment," "positioning," and "siting" are frequently used as synonyms. We distinguish between location and layout problems. In location analysis, the facilities are small relative to the space in which they are sited and interaction between the facilities may or may not occur. In layout problems, in contrast, the facilities to be located are fairly large relative to the space in which they are positioned, and interaction between facilities is the norm rather than an exception. Four components characterize location problems: (1) customers, who are presumed to be already located; (2) facilities that will be located; (3) a space in which customers and facilities are located; and (4) a metric that indicates distances or times between customers and facilities. Applications of location problems abound, ranging from gas stations and fast food outlets to landfills and power plants.

In some nontraditional location problems such as product positioning, each facility represents a product, which is mapped into a feature space, each of whose dimensions represents a relevant feature of the product. Similarly, each customer (or, typically, group of customers) is mapped into the feature space, and the distance between customers and products will give an indication of which products the customers are going to purchase, thus allowing estimates concerning the sales of the products. In 1992, Eiselt provided a survey of many distinct applications of location models. As opposed to routing problems, location problems tend to be higher on the strategic, or tactical, operational continuum. As a result, location problems are likely to have multiple objectives; they tend to be fuzzy and ill-posed, making them doubly challenging—they must first be modeled before they can be solved.

The Space of Location Decisions

Location scientists often use the space in which facilities are located to distinguish between classes of location problems. We here distinguish between planar location problems and network location problems, each of which can be further subdivided into continuous or discrete location problems. The space in planar location problems is the two-dimensional real space of the plane. Distances in planar problems are most often either the rectilinear (or rectangular, or Manhattan, or ℓ_1) distance metric or the Euclidean (or straight line, or ℓ_2) metric, although other functions are possible and have been suggested. For the estimation of road distances between points based purely on the coordinates of the end points, Love and co-researchers have worked with a number of additional metrics, for example, in their 1988 study. The main reason for calculating distances between points whenever needed rather than storing them is the sharply decreased need for storage space; the coordinates of n given points require $O(n)$ storage space, whereas all point-to-point distances require $O(n^2)$ memory.

In contrast, distances in network location problems are measured on the network itself—typically as the shortest route on the network of arcs connecting the two points. Using the shortest path usually requires a preprocessing phase to find all shortest paths between all relevant pairs of points.

Both planar problems and network problems can be further subdivided into continuous and discrete location problems. In continuous problems, the points to be sited can generally be placed anywhere on the plane or on the network. An example of a continuous location problem in the plane is the placement of a helicopter for trauma pickup; an example of a continuous problem on a network is the location of an ambulance or a tow truck along a stretch of highway. In discrete problems, the points to be positioned, in addition, can conceptually be placed only at a limited number of eligible points on the plane or network. Thus, discrete location models have gone through an additional preprocessing phase that has preselected candidate sites at which the facilities may be sited. An example of a discrete location problem in the plane is the positioning of transmitter stations that are to be placed at some permissible points within a region, such as mountaintops; an example of a discrete network location problem is the location of retail facilities that can only be sited on lots that are zoned for them.

As a result, continuous location problems, which are for the most part planar problems, typically tend to be nonlinear optimization problems, whereas discrete location problems, which are most often network problems, involve 0-1 variables that result in integer programming or combinatorial optimization problems. Clearly, there are countless hybrid models, many of which do not fall into these neat categories. Whereas some researchers concentrate on a space of their choice, many shuttle between classes of models.

Classes of Location Objectives

A variety of factors other than customers, facilities, space, and distance functions play important roles in location modeling. One such factor is the objective that is employed by the decision maker. Traditionally, the facilities that were to be located were assumed to be desirable in the sense that the closer they were to the customers, the better the value of the objective function. As Eiselt and Laporte pointed out in 1995, these are pull objectives. Clearly, there is a large variety of pull objectives, but two of the most prominent objectives within this class are the minisum objective, which minimizes the sum of transport costs or weighted distances, and minimax objectives, which minimize the largest customer-facility distance.

In planar continuous models, the minisum objectives are usually called Weber problems, after the German economist who worked on these problems at the beginning of the twentieth century and summarized his findings in his classical treatise, summarized by Wesolowsky in 1993. In network location models, facility sites that are chosen with a minisum objective are typically referred to as medians, or sometimes as points of production or of distribution. Solutions to problems with a minimax objective are usually referred to as centers.

As discussed by Erkut and Newman in 1989, since the late 1970s, researchers have also considered the location of noxious or obnoxious (or simply undesirable) facilities. In contrast to facilities for which nearness is desirable, customers wish, as one of their objectives, to push undesirable facilities as far from them as possible. By themselves and without any further restrictions, push objectives attempt to locate toward infinity. This is why they are often coupled with other, predominantly pull objectives. An example of a problem with these two conflicting objectives is the location of a (nuclear) power plant, an arguably undesirable facility. Whereas the customers and the population at large would like to push the power plant as far away as possible, the hydro commission, who has to pay for the connection of all customers to the power grid, would prefer to pull the power plant as close as possible. Combining the two objectives requires statements regarding the trade-off between the cost of connecting the customers and the proximity to a part of the population of the power plant. Finally, a third class of objectives is the achievement of equity. Models with such objectives attempt to locate the facilities so that the customer-to-facility distances may be as similar to one another as possible. This equalization gives rise to the term "balancing objectives." Alternatively, the distances from clients to the nearest facility may be bounded by some generally recognized distance standard. This is done so as to provide relatively equal access to the facility or, equivalently in the case of undesirable facilities, to distribute the unpleasantness as equally as possible.

Other features of interest to the modeler include the number of facilities that are to be located. The simplest of the models attempt to locate a single facility, whereas more complex models might locate p facilities, where the parameter p may be fixed by the decision maker or imposed by a budget limitation. Alternatively, the number of facilities may be unknown at the outset and determined endogenously through the elements of the model's objective. The best known in this category of models with free entry is the plant location problem that minimizes the sum of plant-opening costs and distribution costs and that allows the number of facilities to be an output or consequence of the minimum cost solution. Another type of model in this category is the location set covering model, first introduced in 1971 by Toregas *et al.* The idea is to find the least number of facilities so that all demand points are covered within a prespecified distance standard.

Other enhancements of location models include uncertainty or risk with respect to the ability to service demands within desirable distances. Sometimes barriers may exist that cannot be crossed in continuous location models. In addition, there is a category of facilities referred to as extensive facilities that cannot be modeled as points but that have length as well as position characteristics, thus providing a link between location models, layout models, and network models.

An early characterization of model forms and objectives that is still in use, provided in 1970 by ReVelle *et al.*, divides location problems into private-sector problems and public-sector problems. The private-sector problems seek the sites for plants and or warehouses; these sites are those that minimize the sum of the annual costs of distribution and amortized plant costs. Public-sector problems, in contrast, seek sites for facilities that optimize the population's access (measured in the various ways already discussed) to those facilities, the facilities being constrained either in number or by some investment level. Clearly, there are many shades of gray between the extremes of private and public. For instance, if a decision maker in the public sector accepts the measure of the average customer-facility distance as a proxy for accessibility, then the resulting model could be viewed as a special case of a transport-cost minimizing model that is typical for the private sector.

Continuous Location Problems

Minisum planar location problems dominated the location discussion until the mid-1960s. From the first three-customer, one-facility location problem posed by Torricelli in 1648, to Weber's seminal work in 1909 (discussed by Wesolowsky in 1993), to Kuhn and Kuenne's 1962 and Cooper's 1963 contributions, location problems were mostly discussed by geographers or regional scientists whose space of choice was the two-dimensional plane. The first algorithm for the minisum planar problem with one facility and Euclidean distance, however, was offered by Weiszfeld in 1937. His algorithm (written in French and published in a Japanese journal of mathematics) predated the similar algorithms of Cooper and Kuhn and Kuenne, but escaped attention until the 1970s when his early contribution was finally recognized, as described by Wesolowsky in 1993.

Setting up the two-variable objective function (the only variables are the two coordinates of the new facility) leads to Min $z = \sum_{i \in I} d_i w_i$, where d_i denotes the Euclidean distance between a customer at (a_i, b_i) and the facility at (x, y) to be sited; w_i is the known demand (or weight) of customer i; and I is the set of customers. This nonlinear function can be differentiated, resulting in two nonlinear equations that are set equal to zero but for which no closed form solution exists. A clever iterative technique tends to converge quickly. In contrast, when the objective of the minimum weighted squared distances is differentiated with respect to the x and y coordinates of the facility, the resulting equations are separable and a simple closed-form solution exists, providing the well-known center of gravity of the points. (For an excellent exposition of the history of continuous problems on the plane, see Wesolowsky's 1993 review.) Similarly, as shown by Vergin and Rogers in 1967, the single-facility location problem in the plane using the sum of rectilinear distances also has a separable objective function and can be solved easily.

As far as center problems (or minimax distance problems) are concerned, the model with Euclidean distances is typically solved by using either the 1972 approach of Elzinga and Hearn or, more efficiently, the methods from computational geometry involving farthest-point Voronoi diagrams. Elzinga and Hearn have also shown that the 1-center problem in the plane with rectilinear distances has a remarkable closed-form solution that results from the reduction of a large linear programming formulation to just four constraints that can be solved graphically.

The solution of planar location problems with multiple facilities requires not only the siting of facilities but also the allocation of customers to those facilities. Here, we typically distinguish between customer choice (or user-attracting) models and allocation models (or delivery systems). In customer choice models, the customers decide which facility to patronize—a system typically appropriate in the retail sector. On the other hand, allocation models are appropriate when the facility planner is also in charge of deciding which facility supplies a given customer. It is quite natural in allocation models for customers to be allocated to their closest facility (except in capacitated models). However, many customer choice models also allocate customers to their closest facility. Such an assumption makes sense only if (1) customers engage in separate trips to the facility and (2) customers are rational (i.e., utility maximizing) planners with utility functions that include only transportation costs that are assumed to be proportional to customer-facility distances. Presuming these assumptions are satisfied, we can define a set J of facility locations, where the point (x_j, y_j) is the location of the jth facility for all $j \in J$. Defining u_{ij} as the proportion of customer i's demand that is served by the jth facility, the multifacility location problem can then be written as:

$$\text{Min } z = \sum_{i \in I} \sum_{j \in J} w_i d_{ij} u_{ij}$$

$$\text{s.t.} \sum_{j \in J} u_{ij} = 1 \, \forall \, i \in I$$

$$u_{ij} \in \mathbb{R} \forall i \in I, j \in J$$

$$x_j, y_j \in \mathbb{R} \forall j \in J$$

where the variables x_j and $y_j, j \in J$, appear only implicitly in the formulation in the guise of the distances d_{ij}.

Except for the case of rectilinear distances, in which the formulation can be solved by a linear programming problem, the problem is NP-hard for most distance functions. Hence, most exact algorithms can only solve problems of moderate size. One interesting approach that uses set partitioning and a form of column generation is due to Rosing. His method first enumerates all feasible partitions of the customers, solving within each of these subsets of customers a single-facility problem. The outputs of these subproblems supply the parameters of the larger problem that is solved as a set partitioning problem. Because the number of partitions is exponential in the number of customers, the approach is probably best used as a heuristic by simply considering only a subset of potentially promising or spatially reasonable partitions of customers. A well-known heuristic is Cooper's 1963 "alternate" method for location allocation. The algorithm switches back and forth between a siting phase and an allocation phase. Many other heuristics exist, including greedy methods and genetic algorithms. Multifacility minimax problems frequently use extensions of the Elzinga-Hearn procedure previously mentioned.

Network Location Problems

Although a few papers on network-based plant and warehouse location appeared in the operations research literature in the 1950s, serious attention to network-based problems was not paid until the middle 1960s. In 1964, Hakimi in a pair of seminal papers investigated the minimum weighted distance location of p facilities on a network of n demand nodes—a problem class he termed the p-median problem. Although he did not provide a solution method for the p-median problem, he proved the existence of at least one optimal solution in which all p facilities are located solely at the nodes of the network. His contribution is similar to that of Dantzig for linear programming in that it reduced the set of optimal solutions from a potentially infinite set to a finite (albeit astronomically finite) set. This result is commonly referred to as Hakimi's theorem or the node property.

Although Hakimi was actually dealing with a wiring problem in electrical engineering, his contribution may be viewed as the first in the line of research that we have referred to as public-sector location. In public-sector location, people's access to publicly owned facilities is optimized subject to a limit on the number of or investment in facilities. In contrast to the p-median problem, which focuses on aggregate access, the p-center problem on the network seeks the set of facilities that minimizes the maximum distance that separates any demand node from its nearest facility. It is easy to demonstrate that solutions to the p-center problem typically do *not* have at least one solution in which the facilities are all at nodes of the network. That is, centers are usually located somewhere along an edge of the network. As a result, location scientists distinguish between node centers (in which the eligible facility locations may be restricted to vertices of the network) and absolute centers, in which the facility location could be anywhere on the network. It is apparent that the determination of a single node center would require the enumeration of each node as the eligible center. Determining a single absolute center is more involved. In particular, it is the minimum on the upper envelope of piecewise linear concave functions, so that the examination of a finite set of break points is sufficient to determine the optimal solution. The general case of p facility locations is considerably more difficult.

In 1971, Goldman showed that 1-median problems on trees have very simple properties somewhat reminiscent of single-Weber problems with ℓ_1 distances (a result that was independently derived by Hua Lo-Keng *et al.* in 1962). He also showed that 1-median problems on general graphs can be solved by a brute-force search in $O(n^3)$ time. However, no such results are available for the general p-median problem. In fact, Kariv and Hakimi demonstrated in 1979 that the general p-median problem is NP-hard. However, invoking Hakimi's theorem, we know that it is sufficient to search for the optimal solution on the set of nodes. Using this result, ReVelle and Swain were the first, in 1970, to formulate the p-median as a 0-1 programming problem. A variant of their original formulation is:

$$\text{Min } z = \sum_{i \in I} \sum_{j \in J} w_i d_{ij} x_{ij}$$

$$\text{s.t.} \sum_{j \in J} x_{ij} = 1 \forall i \in I$$

$$x_{ij} \leq y_j \quad \forall i \in I, j \in J$$

$$\sum_{j \in J} y_j = p$$

$$x_{ij} = 0 \vee 1 \forall i \in I, j \in J$$

$$y_i = 0 \vee 1 \forall j \in J$$

where the locational variables y_j are 1 if a facility is located at node j and 0 otherwise. Here, the allocation variables x_{ij} denote the proportion of the demand of the customer at node i that is assigned to a facility at node j, and p denotes the number of facilities that are to be located; the remaining parameters are as previously defined. To be sure that the optimal solution is truly found requires that the set of facility nodes include not only demand nodes but also empty nodes (i.e., nodes without demand that are simply network intersection points). These network intersection points are not, however, included in the set of demand nodes I because they do not require assignment.

Among the exact algorithms is a 1993 procedure due to Galvão that employs Lagrangean relaxation and the 1970 linear programming relaxation of ReVelle and Swain. It is also possible to apply iteratively the dual descent techniques developed for the plant location problem in 1977 by Bilde and Krarup as well as Erlenkotter's 1978 dualoc procedure; Daskin, in 1995, provided an insightful description. Among traditional heuristic methods applied to the p-median problem is the 1964 location allocation heuristic of Maranzana, which is actually a co-temporaneous nodal version of Cooper's alternate method. Another of the older, but widely known, heuristics is the more powerful vertex substitution technique of Teitz and Bart, reported in 1968. A speedier adaptation of the exchange heuristic was described by Densham and Rushton in 1992. In 1997, Rosing and ReVelle incorporated the exchange heuristic into a metaheuristic known as heuristic concentration, which has performed well, even against Rosing *et al*'s 1999 tabu search. In 2000, Schilling *et al.* showed that the performance of both exact and heuristic algorithms on p-median problems depends on the extent to which the triangle inequality is satisfied in those problems. Genetic algorithms have also assumed their place in the context of solving p-median problems.

Standing in contrast to the p-median problem, in which the number of facilities is given in advance, is the simple plant location problem (SPLP). In this problem, an unknown number of plants is to be located so as to serve the demand and minimize the sum of transportation and facility costs. In 1965, Balinski provided a formulation that is very similar to the p-median formulation, except for addition cost terms in the objective that represent the costs of opening and potentially operating the facilities. The constraint that requires that p facilities are to be located is absent in the SPLP. Morris, in 1978, and ReVelle and Swain, in 1970, demonstrated through experiments that p-median problems and the SPLPs are integer-friendly, a term used by ReVelle in 1993; that is, their linear programming relaxations tend to have integer or near-integer solutions that require only a few branchings in a subsequent branch-and-bound procedure. Although many have worked on plant location solution methods, (see, for example, Galvão's 1993 report), the methodology that currently reports the best results in SPLPs is that described by Körkel in 1989.

The related capacitated plant location problem is identical to the SPLP, with the addition of capacity constraints on the facilities. Work in this area seems to offer ambiguous results. These additional capacity constraints destroy the property that all demand of a customer is satisfied from a single facility, making the problem much more difficult to solve.

In 1996, ReVelle and Laporte exposed new and challenging problems in plant location. In 2000, Brimberg and ReVelle offered a solution to one of the many problems posed there, the maximum return on investment problem; however, to a large degree many practical plant location problems remain unsolved.

Although the p-median and the plant location problems, with their aggregate access and cost measures, have occupied a great deal of the discussion in the location community, especially for those interested in algorithms, another line of location thought has grown up, related to these two classic problems but aside from them. In some instances, particularly when emergency facilities are to be located, the concept of coverage may apply to siting decisions. A customer or demand node is said to be covered by a facility if the distance or time between a customer and its closest facility is no greater than a prespecified value of S, the distance or time standard. For example, it may be required that no tract of houses in a municipality be farther than 1.5 miles (or 5 min) from the nearest fire station or ambulance.

To illustrate the models, we again define 0-1 variables x_j, which equal 1 if a facility is located at node j and 0 otherwise. We denote d_{ji} as the distance between the jth facility site and the ith customer. We can then define coverage sets $N_i = \{j\colon d_{ji} \leq S\}$. The set N_i includes all potential facility locations that can dispatch to and reach customer i within the time standard S. The location set covering problem (LSCP) as introduced by Toregas *et al.* in 1971 and ReVelle *et al.* in 1976 can then be formulated as:

$$\text{Min } z = \sum_{j \in J} x_j$$

$$\text{s.t.} \sum_{j \in N_i} x_j \geq 1 \forall i \in I$$

$$x_j = 0 \vee 1 \forall j \in J$$

Although the problem is formally NP-hard, large instances of network-based LSCPs have been solved easily by linear programming and the occasional addition of solution-derived cutting plane constraints. The repetitive application of reduction rules that use the principles of row and column dominance and essential columns, discussed by Toregas and ReVelle in 1973, is usually capable of reducing the size of LSCPs dramatically and even of solving problems *ab initio*. A consequence of the ability of the location scientist to solve the LSCP easily is that the p-center or minimax distance problem on a network with a prespecified number of facilities can also be solved efficiently. In particular, Minieka suggested in 1970 a solution of the minimax distance problem for p given facilities by solving a series of LSCPs with successively decreasing distance or time standard S. As the distance standards are tightened (i.e., decreased), the number of required facilities remain the same for a number of values and then suddenly increase. At the smallest distance value before the number of facilities increases from p to $p+1$, the maximum distance from any demand node to its nearest facility is, by definition, a minimum—that is, the p facilities and their positions at this distance value minimize the maximum distance.

The LSCP requires that each customer must be covered, a requirement that is very restrictive. In a problem with many spatially dispersed population nodes, the requirement of complete coverage of all demands may produce solutions with an unrealistic number of facilities. Several possibilities for problem restatement emerge immediately. The first is known as the maximum covering location problem (MCLP), introduced by Church and ReVelle in 1974. Using weights w_i as the number of customers located at node i, the MCLP seeks to locate an economically feasible number of facilities, say p, in such a way that the number of customers covered within the time standard S by the facilities, is the maximum. The reduction rules for the LSCP no longer apply easily, making the MCLP potentially more challenging to solve. Nonetheless, linear programming supplemented by branch-and-bound, greedy, and exchange heuristics have all been applied with success. A thorough review of the application of covering problems from the location as well as other perspectives was offered by Schilling *et al.* in 1993.

Another possibility to get around the complete coverage requirement is to maximize the expected coverage of demand nodes, a problem that Daskin formulated in 1983 and solved. Still a third possibility is to solve the p-center problem given a number of facilities that reflects a realistic budget limitation. That is, in lieu of minimizing the number of facilities needed to cover all the demand nodes within the preset standard S, a realistic number of facilities is examined to determine the value of the smallest distance standard that can be achieved for all demands with p facilities. The problem can also be extended into the probabilistic realm with chance constraints on the reliability of coverage being available within a distance or time standard. Further, multiple types of interrelated facilities may be modeled. A review of location covering problems that apply principally to emergency services was provided in 1995 by Marianov and ReVelle.

Other Location Problems

In this section, we discuss some of the more interesting other location models, focusing on innovative structures, settings, and objectives that have been developed. The concept of undesirable facility locations has already been mentioned. An immediate observation is that, as opposed to minisum and minimax problems, a bounded set is required, in which the location of the facility is to be chosen; otherwise, the optimal location moves to infinity.

The problems with balancing objectives have also been mentioned. There are very few actual (as opposed to potential) applications of location models with balancing objectives. The main reason for this appears to be the problem of measurement. It is not surprising that the definition of equity does, of course, lend itself to socioeconomic and even philosophical interpretations. Typical equity objectives use the variance, the Lorenz curve, or the Gini index as an expression that measures the equity or inequity of a set of sites.

A simple example demonstrates that equity objectives should be used in conjunction with an efficiency objective. Consider three customers, whose locations form a triangle, in which one angle approaches 180°. The point that optimizes the equality of distances is the center of the circle on whose circumference the three points are located. This point can be very distant. In moving the distant facility toward the three customers, each customer gains in that the customer-facility distance decreases. However, this gain is achieved at the expense of making the three distances more unequal. Equity objectives were discussed by Marsh and Schilling in 1994 and by Eiselt and Laporte in 1995.

Hierarchical location problems occur in many health-care contexts. There are different levels of health care: a doctor's office (or maybe just a nursing station) at the lowest level, a small clinic on the next level, and a full-service hospital at the highest level. Each facility on some level may be assumed to provide all the services of a facility on the next-lower level plus other services. The question is then how to cover as many people as well as possible within feasibility (e.g., cost) constraints. This topic was discussed in 1984 by Narula, and in 1993 and 1994 by Serra and ReVelle.

Hub location problems, an area of research introduced by O'Kelly in 1986, arise in contexts in which customers require transport between a large number of origin-destination pairs. Frequently, it is cheaper for the carrier, albeit more tedious for the passenger, to avoid direct routing between all pairs with traffic demand. Instead, hub networks are assembled that require customers to travel from their origin to a central hub, from there either to their destination or to another hub, and, if to a second hub, then to continue on to their final destination. Hub systems are very popular in the airline industry; a special 1996 issue of *Location Science* was devoted to such problems, and Bryan and O'Kelly provided a comprehensive review in 1999.

Competitive location problems may incorporate not only location decisions, but also pricing decisions as variables in the model. In its simplest form, a competitive location problem seeks the positions and prices that maximize market capture (as measured in customers or profit) from previously positioned competitors. The field emerged with the Hotelling's 1929 contribution of duopolists competing in a linear market—Hotelling's famous "main street." The possibility of being undercut results in a large degree of instability, as shown by literature surveys by Eiselt *et al.* in 1993, Serra and ReVelle in 1995, and Plastria in 2001. The contributions in the economics literature typically deal with the existence of equilibria, as derived using the tools of game theory. Another approach described by Serra and ReVelle in 1993 and 1994 is the sequential competitive location, in which a leader in the (location or pricing) game is followed by a follower in the game. The earliest analytical location contribution in this area was in 1983 by Hakimi, who termed the locations of the follower medianoids. Medianoids result from conditional location problems, in the sense that the follower takes the locations of the leader as given. Hakimi referred to the leader's location as centroids; the leader of the game will take the optimized reaction of the follower into consideration and protect against it by using a minimax strategy. The first location science solution methodology applied to the siting of the follower was called the maximum capture problem and was offered in 1986 by ReVelle, who recognized capture as a form of covering and defined coverage/capture sets characterized by distance to nearest competitor.

Location-routing problems incorporate the issues of location and routing. For example, consider the simultaneous location of postal relay boxes and the routing of postal trucks for deliveries and pickups. Clearly, as just almost all known routing problems are NP-hard, the addition of a location component does not make them any easier to solve.

We also need to mention p-dispersion problems, which do not include any customers but which attempt to locate facilities so as to maximize the shortest distance between any facility and its nearest neighbor. Typical applications of this type of problem are found in the location of franchises, in which the head office attempts to locate its branches so that each can exist comfortably without interfering with the markets of the others.

As previously discussed, location-allocation models typically treat demand expressed at points and serve this demand through point-to-point travel. For many types of service, service stations, fast-food outlets, and automatic teller machines, customer demand does not occur at a point (e.g., the residence of the customer) but along a path (e.g., a customer's daily route to work). The idea now is to capture or intercept as much potential demand as possible. For that purpose, Hodgson introduced in 1990 the flow capturing location-allocation model (FCLM), which serves such demands by locating facilities to intercept them *en route*. He indicated that the model has the structure of the MCLP and stressed the need to avoid flow cannibalization, or double counting.

The model has been adapted by Hodgson and Berman in 1977 to the location of billboards, as well as to vehicle inspection stations. These models were reviewed by Berman *et al.* in 1995.

Outlook

As reviewed by ReVelle in 1997, the field of facility location is very active, with many interesting problems still being investigated, both from a problem statement/formulation standpoint and from an algorithm point of view. Although the field is active from a research perspective, when it comes to applications, there appears to be a significant deficit, at least as compared to other similar fields. One reason may be a preference of researchers for the solitary pursuit of ideas without regard to profit. Related to this preference is the fact that few location packages or turn-key software programs seem to exist. At the same time, it seems possible that the deficit of applications is a consequence of the fact that many of the practical location problems faced by executives and public-sector decision makers are strategic problems, having multiple objectives and structures that do not fall into the relatively easy categories outlined here. One possible way to overcome this barrier is to build more comprehensive, integrated models at the expense of an exponentially increasing complexity of the models and required algorithms. Other, possibly more promising, approaches would be to employ fairly simple subproblems with structures that fit our categories within the context of decision-support systems. Coupled with extensive sensitivity analyses, this approach appears to have potential. However, falling back onto a one-size-fits-all general mixed-integer programming problem may be required in the case of more complex scenarios.

Finally, the dearth of applications may be due to an inability of researchers to communicate results effectively. It is not that location scientists cannot explain what they do but that spatial decisions may demand spatial display. Geographic information systems software, coupled with location models and algorithms and bundled in user-friendly packages, may, in fact, provide the keys to unlock the city's gates.

See Also the Following Articles

Spatial Discounting • Spatial Scale, Problems of

Further Reading

Balinski, M. L. (1965). Integer programming: Methods, uses, computation. *Manage. Sci.* **12,** 253–313.

Berman, O., Hodgson, M. J., and Krass, D. (1995). Flow intercepting models. In *Facility Location: A Survey of Applications and Methods* (Z. Drezner, ed.), pp. 427–452. Springer-Verlag, New York.

Bilde, O., and Krarup, J. (1977). Sharp lower bounds and efficient algorithms for the simple plant location problem. *Ann. Discrete Math.* **1,** 79–97.

Brimberg, J., and ReVelle, C. (2000). The maximum return on investment plant location problem. *J. Operational Res. Soc.* **51,** 729–735.

Bryan, D., and O'Kelly, M. (1999). Hub-and-spoke networks in air transportation: An analytical review. *J. Reg. Sci.* **39,** 275–295.

Cooper, L. (1963). Location—Allocation problems. *Operations Res.* **11,** 331–343.

Church, R. L., and ReVelle, C. (1974). The maximal covering location problem. *Pap. Reg. Sci. Assoc.* **32,** 101–118.

Daskin, M. L. (1983). Maximal expected covering location model: Formulation, properties, and heuristic solution. *Transportation Sci.* **17,** 48–70.

Daskin, M. S. (1995). *Network and Discrete Location: Models, Algorithms, and Applications.* John Wiley & Sons, New York.

Densham, P., and Rushton, G. (1992). A more efficient heuristic for solving large p-median problems. *Pap. Reg. Sci.* **71,** 307–329.

Eiselt, H. A. (1992). Location modeling in practice. *Am. J. Math. Manage. Sci.* **12,** 3–18.

Eiselt, H. A., and Laporte, G. (1995). Objectives in location problems. In *Facility Location: A Survey of Applications and Methods* (Z. Drezner, ed.), pp. 151–180. Springer Verlag, New York.

Eiselt, H. A., Laporte, G., and Thisse, J.-F. (1993). Competitive location models: A framework and bibliography. *Transportation Sci.* **27,** 44–54.

Elzinga, J., and Hearn, D. W. (1972). Geometrical solutions for some minimax location problems. *Transportation Sci.* **6,** 379–394.

Erkut, E., and Newman, S. (1989). Analytical models for locating undesirable facilities. *Eur. J. Operational Res.* **40,** 275–279.

Erlenkotter, D. (1978). A dual-based procedure for uncapacitated facility location. *Operations Res.* **26,** 992–1009.

Galvão, R. (1993). The use of Lagrangean relaxation in the solution of uncapacitated facility location problems. *Location Sci.* **1,** 57–79.

Goldman, A. J. (1971). Optimal Center Location in Simple Networks. *Transportation Sci.* **5,** 212–221.

Hakimi, S. L. (1964). Optimal locations of switching centers and the absolute centers and medians of a graph. *Operations Res.* **12,** 450–459.

Hakimi, S. L. (1983). On locating new facilities in a competitive environment. *Eur. J. Operational Res.* **12,** 29–35.

Hodgson, M. J. (1990). A flow-capturing location-allocation model. *Geogr. Analysis* **22,** 270–279.

Hodgson, M. J., and Berman, O. (1997). A billboard location model. *Geogr. Environ. Modelling* **1,** 25–45.

Hotelling, H. (1929). Stability in competition. *Econ. J.* **39,** 41–57.

Hua, Lo-Keng and others (1962). Application of mathematical methods to wheat harvesting. *Chin. Math.* **2,** 77–91.

Kariv, O., and Hakimi, S. L. (1979). An algorithmic approach to network location problems, Part II: The p-median. *SIAM J. Appl. Math.* **37,** 539–560.

Körkel, M. (1989). On the Exact Solution of Large-Scale Simple Plant Location Problems. *Eur. J. Operational Res.* **39,** 157–173.

Kuhn, K., and Kuenne, R. (1962). An efficient algorithm for the numerical solution of the generalized Weber problem in spatial economics. *J. Reg. Sci.* **4,** 21–33.

Love, R. F., Morris, J. G., and Wesolowsky, G. O. (1988). *Facilities Location: Models and Methods.* North Holland, New York.

Maranzana, F. (1964). On the location of supply points to minimize transport costs. *Operations Res. Q.* **15,** 261–270.

Marianov, V., and ReVelle, C. (1995). Siting emergency services. In *Facility Location* (Zvi Drezner, ed.), pp. 203–227. Springer-Verlag, New York.

Marsh, M. T., and Schilling, D. A. (1994). Equity measurement in facility location analysis: A review and framework. *Eur. J. Operational Res.* **74,** 1–17.

Minieka, E. (1970). The m-center problem. *SIAM Rev.* **12,** 138–141.

Morris, J. G. (1978). On the extent to which certain fixed-charge depot location problems can be solved by lp. *J. Operational Res. Soc.* **29,** 71–76.

Narula, S. C. (1984). Hierarchical location—Allocation problems, a classification scheme. *Eur. J. Operational Res.* **15,** 183–189.

O'Kelly, M. (1986). The location of interacting hub facilities. *Transportation Sci.* **20,** 92–106.

Plastria, F. (2001). Static competitive facility location: An overview of optimization approaches. *Eur. J. Operational Res.* **129,** 461–470.

ReVelle, C. (1986). The maximum capture or sphere of influence location problem—Hotelling revisited on a network. *J. Reg. Sci.* **26,** 343–358.

ReVelle, C. (1993). Facility siting and integer friendly programming. *Eur. J. Operational Res.* **65,** 147–158.

ReVelle, C. (1997). A perspective on location science. *Location Sci.* **5,** 3–13.

ReVelle, C., and Laporte, G. (1996). The plant location problem: New models and research prospects. *Operations Res.* **44,** 864–874.

ReVelle, C., Marks, D., and Liebman, J. (1970). Analysis of private and public sector location problems. *Manage. Sci.* **16,** 692–707.

ReVelle, C., and Swain, R. W. (1970). Central facilities location. *Geogr. Analysis* **2,** 30–42.

ReVelle, C., Toregas, C., and Falkson, L. (1976). Applications of the location set covering problem. *Geogr. Analysis* **8,** 67–76.

Rosing, K. E. (1992). An optimal method for solving the (generalized) multi-Weber problem. *Eur. J. Operational Res.* **58,** 414–426.

Rosing, K., and ReVelle, C. (1997). Heuristic concentration: Two stage solution construction. *Eur. J. Operational Res.* **97,** 75–86.

Rosing, K., ReVelle, C., Rolland, E., Schilling, D., and Current, J. (1998). Heuristic concentration and tabu search: A head to head comparison. *Eur. J. Operational Res.* **104,** 93–99.

Rosing, K., ReVelle, C., and Schilling, D. (1999). A gamma heuristic for the p-median problem. *Eur. J. Operational Res.* **117,** 522–532.

Schilling, D., Jayaraman, V., and Barkhi, R. (1993). A review of covering problems in facility location. *Location Sci.* **1,** 22–55.

Schilling, D., Rosing, K., and ReVelle, C. (2000). Network distance characteristics that affect computational effort in the p-median problem. *Eur. J. Operational Res.* **127,** 525–536.

Serra, D., and ReVelle, C. (1993). The pq-median problem—Location and districting of hierarchical facilities, Part I: An exact solution method. *Location Sci.* **1,** 299–312.

Serra, D., and ReVelle, C. (1995). Competitive location in discrete space. In *Facility Location* (Zvi Drezner, ed.), pp. 337–356. Springer-Verlag, New York.

Serra, D., and ReVelle, C. (1994). Market capture by 2 competitors—The preemptive location problem. *J. Reg. Sci.* **34,** 549–561.

Serra, D., and ReVelle, C. (1994). The pq-median problem—Location and districting of hierarchical facilities, Part II: Heuristic solution methods. *Location Sci.* **2,** 63–82.

Teitz, M., and Bart, P. (1968). Heuristic methods for estimating the generalized vertex median of a weighted graph. *Operations Res.* **16,** 955–961.

Toregas, C., and ReVelle, C. (1973). Binary logic solutions to a class of location problems. *Geogr. Analysis* **5,** 145–155.

Toregas, C., Swain, R., ReVelle, C., and Bergman, L. (1971). The location of emergency service facilities. *Operations Res.* **19,** 1363–1373.

Vergin, R. C., and Rogers, J. D. (1967). An algorithm and computational procedure for locating economic facilities. *Manage. Sci.* **13,** B240–B254.

Wesolowsky, G. O. (1993). The Weber problem: History and procedures. *Location Sci.* **1,** 5–23.

Locational Decision Making

Daniel A. Griffith
University of Miami, Coral Gables, Florida, USA

Anthony C. Lea
Environics Analytics Group, Toronto, Ontario, Canada

Glossary

agglomeration economy Centripetal forces that encourage the geographic clustering of economic activities; a type of external economy of scale comprising localization economies (e.g., the clustering of special suppliers or customers) and urbanization economies (e.g., the existence in an urban area of inexpensive services such as high-quality water or special garbage disposal), and the minimization of assembly and distribution transport costs for intermediate goods and services.

decision making The act of making a judgment that results in a choice, often based on the use of selection principles and rules coupled with imperfect/incomplete information, and frequently involving computational tools.

economies of scale The quantity of production output increasing more than proportional to the quantity of inputs, resulting in a decrease in the per unit cost of production, especially because fixed costs are spread across more output units of production.

geographic accessibility A measure of aggregate nearness of a given point to a set of points that are important or desirable to be near in a region, taking into account the locational configuration of these points and their interlinkages.

geographic cluster A disproportionate concentration at a single location, or in a relatively small area, of individual objects exhibiting a commonality in terms of one or more attributes.

geographic information system (GIS) Computer software and associated georeferenced data in which the spatial features and their associated attributes are housed in a structured database management system, and in which the software allows users to manage, integrate, edit, manipulate, analyze, display, and map these data to plan, design, and solve problems.

geographic scale The absolute size of a region, often indexed by the ratio between the size of this region on a map and the size of its corresponding segment of Earth's surface, and frequently accompanied by increasing detail with decreasing size.

least-cost location The location where the sum of assembly and distribution transportation costs plus production costs are at a minimum; usually considered to be the optimal location because assumptions are made that effectively hold revenues constant over different locations.

locational advantage A combination of attributes of a location that differentiates it from other locations and gives it a comparative advantage over other locations when a choice is made among them; important attributes include geographic accessibility, resource endowments, and the nature and degree of existing nearby agglomeration economies.

location–allocation model An optimization model, designed to identify the "best" (e.g., minimum aggregate travel distance) single or multiple centralized locations within a region, while at the same time optimally allocating geographically distributed demand (which is to be efficiently serviced) to these selected centralized locations; more sophisticated versions of these models take into account the fixed costs of establishing facilities at the centralized locations, resulting in the optimum number of facilities becoming an additional solution variable.

location rent The economic rent due to a given location's relative positional advantage, with respect to the locations of buyers/suppliers, over the location of the marginal consumer/supplier.

optimal location A location that is better than all other considered or relevant locations, each having a given value for some criterion defining "best" attached to it, in the sense that the criterion function is either minimized or maximized at that location.

spatial dependence The correlation of attributes for nearby locations that arises because of proximity; attributable sometimes to interactions among these locations, and sometimes to geographic influences or factors they share in common.

spatial externality An external economy—or a (joint and nonexclusive) effect unpriced in the market—in an explicitly geographic context, for which a person, firm, or organization is made better off without paying (the full price) or worse off without being compensated (the full expense); common examples are congestion, pollution, and housing price, each of which tends to have a geographically articulated, distance-decaying influence zone.

transportation costs The total of costs incurred when an item is shipped between locations, or a person (e.g., a customer) travels between locations, including a rate per item per unit of distance separating the origin and destination, and associated overhead costs, such as insurance, consular fees, forwarders' charges, and loading/unloading fixed costs.

Locational decision making is the process of evaluating a set of alternative geographic locations, given a certain quantity and quality of information, in order to answer a "where" question concerning the location of homes, stores, businesses, or any type of facility used by individuals or society.

Introduction

Individually and collectively, people frequently must select geographic locations for purposes such as owning a residence, operating a store, and/or visiting a recreational facility, regularly engaging in economic, and sometimes other types of, locational decision making. Their judgments for selecting among alternative locations involve hard copy, digital, and/or mental maps housing geographic information with various degrees of completeness and uncertainty. Locational decision making has been guided through the ages by selection rules based on locational advantage. Prior to urbanization, locational advantage apparently was defined in terms of safety and defense. The rise of cities added commerce and resource (such as water) accessibility to the criterion list. The development of advanced economies in the 18th century extended this list to more abstract economic considerations.

Locational advantage has a different flavor in different contexts. Most commonly, but not exclusively, this advantage is conceptualized in economic terms. A gas station on the corner of two high-traffic streets has a locational advantage as far as access to traffic is concerned. An oil refinery located beside a large oil well has a locational advantage. A drug store inside of a hospital has a different type of locational advantage. Common to establishing these various forms of locational advantage are specific principles that guide judgments differentiating among geographic locations. These principles exploit prominent geographic patterns and variability, conferring privilege on or disenfranchising particular locations.

The Principle of Optimizing Distance

Geographic distance—the measure of separation between two locations on Earth's surface—may be measured in various ways, including as a great circle distance (i.e., a straight line in relatively small regions), as a minimum path through a network of connections, as the cost (e.g., time, money) incurred to move from one place to another, and as the similarity of attributes. Using this metric, locations can be differentiated with a distance-minimizing, a distance-maximizing, or a min–max criterion.

Distance minimization is often employed when locational decision making involves the selection of new locations from among a set of existing locations, even if these new locations are a subset of the existing ones. Alfred Weber, the German economist/sociologist and younger brother of Max Weber, exploited this principle in 1909 to describe normative (i.e., what works the best, according to some criteria) patterns of manufacturing on a continuous surface. His fundamental idea, extended to general facility location under the heading of the "*P*-median" problem, gave rise to the location–allocation literature, either on a continuous surface or a network. The principal objective function (i.e., a function, associated with patterns, that rigorously defines what is the best) minimizes distance weighted by the quantity of material shipped. Additional selections may require placing constraints on this objective function in order to satisfy criteria such as minimizing the maximum distance of any location from a facility, or minimizing the number of facilities required to serve efficiently some constituency. Maximizing rather than minimizing distance, Walter Christaller (in 1933) and August Lösch (in 1938) exploited this principle to describe the normative number, size, and geographic distribution of urban places. The foundations of their work optimize profits by quantifying sales with a hexagonally truncated concave demand cone in order to determine the spacing of locations.

The seminal work of Johann Heinrich von Thünen in 1826 exploited the distance-optimizing principle to describe normative land use patterns, and as such bridges these minimization and maximization classes of location decision making. The key idea of von Thünen was location rent (LR), or the locational advantage a relatively better positioned producer has over the location of the marginal producer of a commodity. The additional location decision-making input here is the commodity to produce.

von Thünen described the geographic pattern of agricultural production around a market town on an undifferentiated plane. This conceptualization also can be applied to spatially separated markets, yielding the transportation problem, the solution of which renders two types of LR: one is established by the marginal producer and quantifies locational advantage in production; the other is established by the marginal consumer and quantifies locational advantage in terms of the marginal market. Much of what became known as the new urban economics is founded on von Thünen's work, which was extended in the 20th century by the seminal contributions to this literature by William Alonso.

Measures of geographic accessibility—the aggregate nearness of some location to selected other locations—differ from the distance minimizing specifications by using distance as a discounting factor. One simple version of this quantity, called the potential model, derives from the notion of social gravitation and is calculated for each location as a weighted sum of distance-discounted "masses" for all locations. Some versions of this measure then standardize the quantities by dividing by the total of all accessibility measures. This latter specification relates to entropy-maximizing trip distribution models as well as to market-potential models.

Spatial Competition, Agglomeration Economies, and Externalities

The role of spatial competition in locational decision making was first examined analytically by Hotelling in 1929. Hotelling cast the delivered price of a commodity as a function of distance. The increase in price due to transportation costs imposes geographic limits on suppliers, establishing market areas in which one supplier has a clear advantage. A simultaneous mutual attraction between supplier and demander coincides with a mutual dispersal of suppliers, another situation—in which one type of distance is minimized while simultaneously another type is maximized—that links directly to the work of Christaller and Lösch. One outcome is the emergence of spatial monopolies within market areas. Locational decision making involves the selection of strategic locations and results in spatial dependencies, because each locational choice is vitally affected by the positions of competitors.

Agglomeration economies are an important component of locational decision making. Economies of scale (decreasing per unit production cost with increasing quantity of output) are critical to an efficient space-economy. These scale economies can be either internal or external to an organization, with external ones motivating geographic clustering of activities (i.e., agglomeration). Such concentrations bring intermediate producers together as a way of deliberately minimizing transportation costs. These concentrations also set in motion centripetal forces that attract complementary activities, allowing specialization to emerge. The selection of a location when agglomeration economies prevail may well deviate from that suggested by a purely distance-minimizing criterion. External diseconomies of scale have the opposite impact, setting in motion centrifugal forces that repel activities.

Spatial externalities (unintentional and incidental impacts on the production of one activity by normal actions of another) are also a function of proximity. A given activity generates an externality field, where the maximum effect takes place only at its location, with this effect decreasing as distance from its location increases. Locational decision making here results in the selection of places that allow some activities to transfer costs to other activities without compensation. Positive spatial externalities promote clustering; negative spatial externalities promote scattering.

The Role of Geographic Scale, Hierarchy, and Spatial Dependence

Geographic scale is determined by the ratio of the distance between two locations on a map and the corresponding distance on Earth's surface. Geographic scale refers to the order of magnitude of the size of a regional landscape, and may be illustrated by considering the continuum ranging from the microscale of an individual household location to the macroscale of a continent. Moving across this continuum often involves the geographic (dis)aggregation of locations. The extent of aggregation determines geographic resolution, with relatively little aggregation referring to a fine resolution and considerable aggregation referring to a coarse resolution. Uncertainty in locational decision making increases as coarseness of resolution increases, because less is known about the geography within aggregations. Locational decision making is compromised by increasing scale with decreasing resolution, because the combinatorial nature of alternative location comparisons increases exponentially. Often a compromise is struck between scale and resolution in order to ensure feasibility with reasonable accuracy. The massive amounts of data that emerge with increasing scale also lead to sequential rather than simultaneous selection assessments.

In many instances, spatial organization comprises articulated layers of maps. According to some graded ranking, each location is assigned to a layer, with layers nesting to form a hierarchy. The most publicized geographical hierarchy is that associated with urban places. Two classes of spatial dependencies (nearby things tend to be more similar and more prone to interact) are depicted by this resilient conceptualization of geographic space, one functioning within a layer, or hierarchical level, and the other functioning between hierarchical levels. Geographic diffusion characterizes these dependencies in terms of contagious and hierarchical components. Trans-hierarchy-level dependencies result in locational decision making needing to take into account geographic scale, with interscale distance possibly being measured as the number of intervening hierarchical levels.

Conceptual Background

Basic conceptual features of locational decision making essential to understanding it are introduced in the following sections. Definitions of notation used throughout appear in Table I.

Descriptive, Predictive, and Normative Considerations

Theories may be classified as being descriptive, predictive, or normative. Descriptive theory seeks to describe a state of affairs, or how something is done or happens. It is the most basic form of theory and the first task of science. Descriptive theories of location focus on a description of a part of reality in which location is celebrated; they describe how people, firms, agencies, and other organizations select/choose locations. Predictive theory seeks to predict what will happen either in the future or under certain specified conditions. Predictive theories of location are of two broad types: those that predict which locations will be selected and those that predict the impacts on people, firms, institutions, or the environment of a particular location being selected. Normative or prescriptive theory is often viewed as the highest form of theory; it seeks to state what should happen or what would be optimal. Normative location theory seeks to prescribe what the best or optimal location, or set of locations, would be under certain assumptions or conditions.

All three forms of theory (descriptive, predictive, and normative) are valid and have different roles to play. In general, good predictive theory requires or builds on good descriptive theory. Although normative theory can be based on descriptive and predictive theories, it does not require them. Rather, it may simply be a statement postulating that if certain processes are followed and/or conditions are met, then the resulting locations are best or optimal. However, truly useful or applicable normative theory should be based on some principles, norms, or values on which there can be wide agreement. For example, in locating emergency medical facilities, most people would agree that facility locations should be positioned so as to minimize distances or travel times. In recent years, most scholarly interest and research

Table I Symbols Used in Locational Decision Making

Symbol/acronym	*Description*
α	Store attractiveness parameter in the Huff model
A_j	Measure of the attractiveness of store j in the Huff model
β	Market-specific distance decoy parameter in the Huff model
D	Distance
D_{ij}	The distance separating households area i from store location j in the Huff model
GIS	Geographic information system
LA	Location–allocation
LCL	Least-cost location
M	Market
n	Number of existing locations
P	Number of facilities
P-median	The Pth central facility
P_{ij}	Huff model probability of a household from area i patronizing a store at location j
r	The exponent for the Weberian model distance calculation
RM	Raw material
(u_i, v_i)	Cartersian coordinates for demand point i
(U, V)	Cartesian coordinates of the optimal location point
w_i	Weight associated with existing location i
Z	Objective function value being minimized
$\sum$	Summation notation
$\binom{m}{n}$	The combinatorial number of m objects, taken n at a time, which equals $m!/[(n!)(m-n)!]$ using factorial notation

efforts have been in the predictive and normative forms of location theory. Earlier in the 20th century, more effort was devoted to descriptive theories of location. In the case of normative location theory, much of the work that has been done, especially in terms of determining solutions, falls under the disciplinary heading of operations research, wherein considerable emphasis has been given to algorithms that find or compute optimal locations.

The Entities Being Located

Any physical entities can be the subject of location theory and locational decision making. Indeed, the field of locational analysis and decision making is very wide ranging. Location plays a more fundamental role and is of greater intrinsic interest for certain entities that have been of particular interest to geographers, regional scientists, economists, and planners, who are the ones most likely to study locational issues. Although many location principles relate to all or most types of entities, certain types of entities require slightly different versions or theories. One very distinctive entity is the city or town, and a body of principles and theories has been designed for urban areas. There are some important differences between public entities and private entities (in the literature specific to this field, the words "facilities" or "activities" are typically used instead of "entities"; for simplicity, the word "facility" is used here to refer to what is being located). Public facilities or activities are owned and/or operated by some level of the state. Their locations reflect public decision making that incorporates politics, social welfare, equity, fairness, justice, and other similar considerations. Normative theories of public location are interesting because the focus is on locating facilities in the public interest, which can be defined in many ways.

The largest body of literature and theory relating to location relates to the private sector in Western-style economies. One of the most important features here relates to economic sectors: resource extraction, resource conversion, primary manufacturing, secondary manufacturing, utilities, wholesaling, shopping centers, retail stores, professional services and medical offices, business services, and so on. Most empirical research and theory construction focuses on one or a few of these sectors because the issues involved are often quite different.

Trade-offs between Transportation and Other Costs

In locational analysis and decision making, the costs associated with overcoming space or separation are always important (if they were not, locational issues would be unimportant). The costs associated with overcoming distance go by different names. When goods or materials are physically moved, the costs are variously called transportation, shipping, delivery, or forwarding costs. Sometimes the organizing firm or agency (the "shipper") pays these costs, and sometimes the recipient pays them. Who actually pays is an important factor in constructing principles, theory, and decision rules. If shippers pay, and these costs are not incorporated into prices, then buyers or recipients care less about shippers' locations; but shippers care because poorly selected locations with respect to buyers come with a significant cost penalty. For some types of facilities customers, clients or citizens effectively pay for overcoming space by paying for delivery charges directly—as would be the case for furniture—and indirectly—as would be the case for pizza (incorporated into the price) and for garbage collection (incorporated into property taxes). A very common way end-users effectively pay is via travel costs and time. Most retailing functions in this manner.

Because transportation/travel costs are key costs in location studies, they are often pitted against all other costs. For example, the main costs associated with manufacturing are raw materials, including possible transportation costs, labor, energy, water/sewage utilities, communications, shipping output, and the annualized costs of capital (land, plant, and equipment). Minimum transportation costs suggest that there should be many supply or service locations—in the limit, one for each customer or buyer. But this would be an extreme and inefficient solution. Why? Because building many separate small facilities is often very expensive per unit of "output" compared to a single large facility, which could service everyone. It is not only the facility construction or capital costs that support solutions with fewer facilities, but also production costs. Most production processes and many service processes have economies of scale, or increasing returns to scale. This means that both average and marginal costs become smaller as the scale of the facility or plant becomes larger. Larger scales of facilities mean fewer facilities and larger transport-related costs or travel costs. The trade-off discussed here is in terms of the total costs of a service or production facility, including the travel/transport costs. Sometimes different constituencies pay different transportation costs for their output. Manufacturing plants always pay the production costs and sometimes pay the transport costs. If they pay delivery costs directly, then they are concerned about being close to their customers. If buyers pay these transport costs (directly or embedded in the price), then manufacturers do not trade these off against production costs. Rather, these costs are still important to producers because (1) buyers will buy less because the effective price they pay is higher, and (2) competitors could take advantage of space by locating in such a way as to serve these customers less expensively. All organizations that have, or could have, multiple facilities face these trade-offs.

Seeking Optimal Locations

Organizations and firms that have facility systems do tend to seek optimal locations for one facility or for all facilities that are part of the system. Facilities are built infrequently, and hence the selection of locations at which to build them usually is considered a long-run decision. One exception is traveling units, such as bookmobiles and street vendors (e.g., mobile hotdog carts). Another exception is when the activity in the facilities can relocate to other nonspecialized facilities easily and inexpensively (e.g., automatic teller machines). Relocation is always a possibility but often comes at a very large cost, whether this is in terms of renovating or building custom facilities, lost production time, or lost customer business in retailing. To the extent that facilities last a long time or are specialized, that relocating is expensive, or that location is part of the package being sold (as in designer women's wear), location decisions should be well informed and should take all relevant present and future costs and benefits into account.

In almost all systems of facilities, the optimal location for any individual facility is clearly dependent on the locations of the other facilities. For example, the optimal location of a school, a retail chain store, or a national beer company brewing plant is profoundly affected by the location of other facilities. Interdependence is driven by one or both of these issues. If the customer pays the costs of travel to the facility, as is common, then the facility of choice will tend to be the most accessible or cheapest. If locations are added to the network, then facility usage pattern will be altered and some facilities could be underused and others overused. On the other hand, a facility system that delivers generally finds supplying each customer from one facility to be efficient. The supplying facility is the one that is the cheapest overall supplier for that customer, which usually means it is the one with the lowest transport costs. The addition of facilities changes the best pattern of who gets supplied by which facilities, and this can affect the overall costs of the network. Of note is that, for these problems, the "other facilities" that are part of the system effectively are treated as competitors. In most senses they really are! A customer served from one facility tends to be a customer that is not served from another facility in the same system. Because of facility locational interdependence, the optimum location of facilities in a system is a difficult analytical problem; this has been called the "location–allocation problem."

Optimal locations may be defined in various ways: the consideration may be to minimize costs; to maximize revenues or benefits; or to maximize profits, net benefit, or social welfare. Another important consideration is whose costs and benefits or profits are to be optimized. In the private sector, it is clear that this is the firm. In the public sector, it should be society, an objective that can be defined and operationalized in many ways. Sometimes the system owner or controller is not aware that locations are being selected to optimize something. But that is just a case of incomplete conceptualization or information. In general, if locations are not optimized in a competitive environment, firms may go out of business in the long run, and certainly forgo profits in the short and long runs.

The true "optimum" must always relate to profit, net benefit, or social welfare because both costs and benefits must be considered simultaneously. Following a long tradition in location theory, a location or system of locations that minimizes costs or maximizes revenues is often considered to be an "optimal location"—even if it is not formally optimal. A location that minimizes costs could be clearly nonoptimal. For example, a location of a brewery at the North Pole would likely have no demand, and hence no production, and no costs. A location or system that minimizes costs must have some constraint on it (usually relating to revenues or benefits) if it is to be considered a proxy for optimal. Examples of constraints are "supply the demand locations with an average price lower than X," "be within 10 miles of all customers," "revenue from sales must be at least N," or simply "using a fixed number of facilities." Similarly, constraints are also necessary for maximizing revenue to be considered a reasonable proxy for "optimal." Maximizing revenue can always be done with very high costs—as would be the case in which each customer had her/his own supplier facility located next door. Typical constraints here would be that costs of the system must be lower than X, or the number of facilities must be less than or equal to Y.

Choosing a Single Location

Most of the literature, case studies, and theory relating to location decisions pertain to single locations. For example, the location of a single plant, warehouse, retailer, office, or dwelling is at issue. We seek to understand its location if it exists and seek to predict or optimize its location if it does not yet exist. The extension of this is to multiple locations being considered simultaneously or sequentially; this more complex case is treated in the next section.

Key Variables in the Decision-Making Process

The question being addressed here concerns the identity of the important variables that influence, affect, or help determine locations. A variable can be important descriptively, predictively, or prescriptively. If being near a waterfall on a river is important for a town (as was the case in 18th-century New England), or if being close to consumer households is important for a grocery store, then this is an important descriptor, a good predictor of location and a good prescriptive variable. The type of entity for which location is being discussed is critical for assessing the importance of variables. Certain variables are more or less important to selecting a location because they influence one or more of the following parameters: direct costs, direct revenues or benefits, indirect costs or via negative externalities, and indirect benefits or via positive externalities. Of note is that some cost- and benefit-type variables do not vary by location. If a variable does not vary over space, it cannot affect locational decisions in that space. For example, because the cost of basic telephone service is constant within most cities, the selection of a location for a house is not affected by this cost.

One of the entities that has had a very long tradition of location theory—the manufacturing plant—can serve as a helpful illustration here. A summary of locational factors considered when selecting a plant location appears in Table II. Many of the variables reported in Table II also are important when locational decisions are made for cities, exhibitions, warehouses, shopping centers, stores, service facilities, offices, public facilities, dwellings, and so on. The variables that are the most important in any particular case are those that either contribute significantly to the costs of running an enterprise or contribute to the benefits of its output, or are those costs/benefits that vary most appreciably over space. For example, steel plants require a steady supply of iron ore and coal/coke (which are very expensive to ship), a cheap source of power, ready access to lots of water for cooling, and a trained labor source. Being close to buyers is also important because steel is heavy and expensive to ship. The importance of these key variables is strongly affected by production technology. In contrast, the key variables for warehousing seldom are the actual costs of running the facility or skilled labor; rather, they are a combination of shipping costs of goods from manufacturing plants and to stores or final consumers. These principles can be extended to nonmanufacturing locational decisions.

Geographical Scale and the Nesting of Locational Decisions

The selection of "locations" for activities can span geographic scales, ranging from continents, through countries, regions, and cities or markets, to neighborhoods and street addresses or points. The entity and the context of the location decision determine the appropriate scale or scales that must be addressed. International firms or organizations usually start searches for best new locations (or closures) within continents, countries, and regions. They then progress to smaller scales, and eventually particular sites. Sometimes all scales are addressed simultaneously, as when a real estate director has pro forma information on many sites in different countries. For firms that operate

Table II Key Variables Relating to the Location of Manufacturing Plants

Variable class	*Variable*
Direct costs	Access to/price of raw materials to process, or primary suppliers
	Cost of shipping to buyers/customers
	Labor costs
	Power costs
	Water/sewage costs
	General local/regional transport and communication costs
	Taxes (beyond labor and power costs)
	Availability of/cost of supporting services (e.g., doctors, lawyers, accountants, insurers)
	Marketing/advertising costs
Indirect costs	Pollution
	Congestion
	Crime
Direct revenues or benefits	Locating close to buyers whose principal considerations are low delivered prices, short delivery times, good service, or a combination of these factors
	When customers are citizens and the facility is public, the benefit is easy/fast/convenient access to the facility in order to "consume" the good or service being offered there
Indirect revenues or benefits[a]	Urbanization economies—The reduced costs of a wide range of more general services characterizing cities because of their clustering together near the location (a good example is universities)
	Localization economies—The reduced costs of interacting with a set of specialized suppliers or buyers because they already have clustered together near the location (a good example is offices clustering in order to facilitate face-to-face communication)

[a] Indirect benefits are often realizations of low costs for one or more important inputs or services.

in particular countries, regions, or cities, the normal process would be to select locations in only these familiar territories. The decision to expand outside these areas is taken with considerable trepidation. An entrepreneur in a city or region has a very strong incentive to add facilities in local territory because the costs, benefits, and risks are more likely to be known, better understood, and better controlled, and she/he has successful logistics experience there.

The variables that are important in locational decisions vary with the scale being considered. At the international scale, political stability, national government policy, currency value, exchange rates, culture, and language are critical. At intermediate scales, access to markets and the costs of raw materials, transportation, labor, power, taxes, and so on (see Table II) are most important. At local scales, local variables come to the fore. Density of demand, accessibility considerations (e.g., the availability of parking, nearness to public transit stops, and availability of local shopping and restaurants), the security environment, and land costs or rental rates become important. At very small scales (sometimes not considered location problems), other interesting variables become important. The location of a soda cooler inside a store must take into account location of the cash register, the candy displays, the electrical outlets, and available space, for example.

Sometimes the distinctive requirements of a location mean that specific site attributes are more important than country or regional variables are. For very upscale fashion retailers, being located in areas next to other similar retailers is critical. Even if the population and income of a new region appear able to sustain such a retailer—if there is not an agglomeration yet—selecting a location in this situation will be very risky. The location of large new sports stadia in North American cities has been dominated by issues of available unencumbered land, first, and by access or convenience, second. The location of manufacturing is strongly influenced by the availability of highly skilled labor for its industry coupled with a large number of underemployed workers. The selection of large-scale areas commonly affects the types of variables that are important at smaller geographical scales. Selecting rural locations means that access to labor and to adequate supplies of water will be critical. Selecting New York City means that proximity to the subway system and land costs or rent will be critical. In general, the location decision at one scale is strongly affected by the location decision at other spatial scales.

Least-Cost Models and Decision Support Tools

The optimal-location theory literature celebrates the selection of single best locations. As noted previously, there are effectively three approaches to this locational decision making: (1) cost minimization, (2) revenue or benefit maximization, and, (3) profit or net benefit maximization. For either the first or second to be a good proxy for "optimal," assumptions have to be made. For example, meaningful cost minimization requires assuming that revenues or benefits are constant.

The premier seminal theory for the cost minimization criterion was proposed by Alfred Weber in 1909. Weber dealt with the problem of selecting the location of a plant with respect to three points—a market and two raw material suppliers. He described the conditions under which the best location would be at one of these three points, and those situations in which the location would be at an interior location. The generalization of the Weber problem from 3 to n points—either material locations or markets—has been a well-known problem in location theory since the early 1960s (and the $n \geq 3$ reference points are no longer restricted to manufacturing-oriented locations). The point location that minimizes the sum of transportation costs in supplying a fixed amount of materials to each of the reference points is known to be the bivariate median location. Its coordinates in continuous space are not easily found; rather, they must be solved for using nonlinear programming. This n-point Weber problem is a key component of the location–allocation problem in which the goal is to locate a set of facilities so that total transportation or travel costs associated with required flows to/from other points are minimized. The continuous space location–allocation problem has been further generalized to discrete space as the problem of selecting the cost-minimizing location, or locations, from a set of predetermined feasible, or available, point locations in a transportation network setting.

Maximum Revenue and the Hotelling Problem

For retail locational analysis and similar applications, a cost minimization framework is not as suitable as a revenue maximization framework. Customers incur the cost of travel; retailers want to locate stores such that sales are maximized. Two common assumptions underlie this perspective: (1) customers patronize the closest store or (2) customers patronize a number of nearby stores, taking into account the attractiveness of a store and its intervening distance, relative to other competing stores that offer the same goods. In the former case, a retailer seeks to maximize the number of people who are closer to his/her store than to other stores; this would be the reference point with a large Thiessen polygon around it. This approach is also consistent with people buying at the lowest price and reducing the amount consumed as the price increases. The classic reference to demand maximizing location and locational competition is the 1929 work of the famous economist Harold Hotelling, who used the example of two mobile ice cream vendors on a beach with a uniform distribution of bathers. When consumers are pure cost minimizers, each vendor has an incentive to locate immediately beside the other one but on the longer stretch of the beach. Because customers would go to the closest vendor, this locational decision would maximize revenue. But the vendor adjacent to the short stretch of beach has an incentive to relocate on the opposite side of the other vendor in order to secure the longer stretch of beach. Leap frogging would continue until both vendors are located at the center of the beach. And, there they would stay. This is a good example of a situation in which competition would lead to a socially suboptimal result. Customers (society) would be better off if the two sellers locate at the quartiles of the beach length—the average distance traveled would be minimized.

The second, more realistic, assumption also recognizes such factors as people's realistic multiple trip-making behavior (for a wide range of purposes), people's uncertainty about the availability of goods at specific destinations, and uncertainty about traffic. David Huff, writing in 1964, was able to apply the Luce choice axiom (i.e., a rule for calculating the probability that a possible alternative will be chosen) to store and shopping center patronage in a spatial context, using principles of distance and store attractiveness trade-offs—extending the 1929 work of William J. Reilly known as the "law of retail gravitation." The Huff model generates probabilities of a person or household at location i selecting a retail choice at location j from a set of alternative stores. The alternatives include stores in a particular chain, and all competitors. Attractiveness variables associated with destination store j include measures of store size, visibility, parking, modernity of the store interior, price, and service. Based on this model, a retail trade area is not a Thiessen polygon, nor indeed a polygon at all; rather, it is a surface depicted as a set of concentric rings surrounding a store that represent increasingly lower probabilities of patronage. This spatial interaction type of model can be extended to underpin a good estimate of the expected revenue at a store. An estimate of the total demand available in each customer source area (i) is multiplied by these probabilities and then summed over i to estimate the expected sales of a store at j. To find the optimal location for a new store in a system, a retail location analyst would compute the expected revenue using this approach for all available feasible locations. The one with the highest expected revenue would be the recommended site.

Other types of retail site evaluation models have been perfected as decision support tools. The objective of this type of model is to estimate the sales at an existing store in a network or at a hypothetical new store location. These models also can be used to estimate the sales effects of dropping either an existing store or a competitor. Similar models can be developed for certain services, offices, and recreational facilities or areas, too. A common and popular tool here is the multiple regression model, the dependent variable of which may be store sales in the preceding year. Independent variables include demand-related surrogates, represented by trade area socioeconomics and demographics; situation variables such as local traffic volumes and number of nearby stores; site variables such as size, age, and visibility of store, signage quality measures, hours of service, and parking places; and, measures of in-store features such as management quality, number of cashiers, and stock depth. Retail companies either build these types of site evaluation models or contract with service firms/consultants who specialize in constructing them. Collecting, cleaning, and structuring the necessary data usually take longer than the time required to calibrate these models. Some retailers also build optimization models that search for best single sites—with a site evaluation model as the engine. Both types of model recently have been embedded into user-friendly software with mapping (geographic information system) interfaces. Users can query what the sales would be at a proposed new location by clicking on a point on a map, then keying the attributes of this site/store into a pop-up window, and finally automatically running the model.

Choosing Multiple Locations

The exercise of choosing multiple locations can take two forms. The first is selecting single locations many times (for example, in sequence; if mutually independent selections of different locations are made, then no new discussion needs to be added to the Conceptual Background section). The second form is selecting, typically at one time, multiple locations where the resulting network functions as a system of interdependent locations.

Key Variables in the Decision-Making Process

With a few important exceptions, the key variables in the locational decision-making process for multiple-location problems are the same as those that are important in single-location decision contexts. If closeness to raw material sources or markets of particular types is important to a single plant, then these factors still will be important when multiple plants are being located. If parking availability or nearness to upscale shopping is important to one store, then these factors still will be important to multiple stores in a chain.

The new variables that become important in multiple-location problems are the ones that capture the interdependencies of locations. These variables are typically not like the variables concerning availability of cheap power, skilled labor, parking, or hours of service. Rather, they are variables such as distance between facilities, and relative closeness to customers or markets. A second type of variable also becomes more important—one that relates to the optimal number of facilities in a system. The key variable underpinning the optimal number of facilities is the trade-off between the fixed costs of production (driving economies of scale) and transportation costs, as is previously discussed. Typically the fixed costs of production (dominated by the costs of land, physical plant, and equipment) are relatively simple matters to account for in single-location problems. If the economic activity to be undertaken is justified, the costs of setting up at least one facility must be incurred. But the overall size and spatial variation in these costs take on an additional importance when designing a multiple-locational system. If fixed costs are relatively low (as, for example, in dry-cleaning storefronts without processing equipment, or ATM banking), then the number of facilities in the system will be relatively large if finished good transport costs or travel costs are important. With more facilities to locate, more possible locations need to be considered, and hence the data collection process becomes more onerous. If fixed costs are high, then economies of scale become a key issue in a trade-off with the number of (small) facilities, and the optimal solution is fewer larger facilities.

Costs related to relative distances and accessibilities are more difficult to conceptualize. Imagine a problem in which there are already three facilities in a city—plants, warehouses, stores, or offices. Why should a search for additional locations avoid the areas close to these three facilities? Additional facilities that ship products to demand points virtually always reduce the aggregate costs of transportation. But if the new facility is close to one of the existing ones, then only small reductions in costs of shipping to customers would be realized. Thus the best locations for new facilities are in areas where they can service customers at a lower cost, compared to the existing facilities. This trade-off is complicated when the location of a new facility can help secure additional customers because the effective delivered price to them is lower than the price charged by competitors. Serving additional customers requires additional capacity, which in turn could lower per unit production costs at existing facilities if economies of scale exist. Possibly the only way of securing the additional customers is by adding additional facilities.

If people travel to the facilities to buy or be serviced there, the reason for spacing out the facilities is intuitive and compelling. Putting facilities side by side fails to capture many new customers (from competitors or a present state of nonconsumption). A cost-effective strategy is to place additional facilities at locations in which they will capture as many new customers as possible while not cannibalizing existing customers from existing facilities of the store chain. Cannibalization, a critical consideration in multiple-location systems, is not present when locating a single facility—this is the case even if a single new facility is being added to an existing system. In addition, new facilities would greatly benefit by avoiding locations close to strong competitors who would detract from a likely incremental draw. Moreover, in multiple-location systems, distances to other facilities in the system can be as important as distances to suppliers and customers, and to competitors. In systems involving specialized facilities that have to ship to or receive from other facilities, or involving certain service or technical employees who must travel between the facilities, the importance of interfacility distance increases, resulting in a tendency for facilities to be located closer to one another.

Geographical Scale and the Nesting of Locational Decisions

In multiple-location systems, selection of the geographical scale of the system is a very concrete and strategic decision. Because the system is interdependent, its boundaries must be especially clear. If Canada is the appropriate scope for an auto muffler franchise chain, then the whole country must be treated as one system at this scale. If, because of legal or cultural issues, the province of Quebec has to be treated differently, then there should be two systems treated separately. This change in objectives, which is geographically articulated, gives rise to a significant impact on the number of locations and on the specific locations selected. The optimal configuration of facilities in a system clearly depends on the scope of geography being served by the system. Sometimes there are legal, economic, political, or even cultural constraints on the size of the region to be served.

What is the optimum configuration of fire stations to serve a political jurisdiction—for example, a city? If the city in question is one political unit, the locational problem for fire stations is a system-wide problem. If the city contains n political jurisdictions (examples being Minneapolis-St. Paul or the Dallas-Forth Worth areas), then the problem becomes n different unrelated systems problems. In a multiple-jurisdiction situation, many neighborhoods ultimately are served by fire stations that are not the closest facilities to them—because the closest fire station may be in another jurisdiction. The average distance between serving facilities and demand points can be shown mathematically to be larger when there is any division of the overall space into different jurisdictions. The general moral of this story is that anytime a system is divided into smaller autonomous subsystems, the optimal solution for this system becomes suboptimal in global terms, no matter how the optimum is measured. Moreover, an optimal solution to a larger problem cannot be obtained by optimally locating facilities in smaller subareas first. If the constraints that create subregional systems can be removed, then a good case can be made for doing so. However, there may be sound reasons for having smaller regions. In a political context, smaller jurisdictions tend to be more sensitive to the preferences of common subgroups. In an economic context, smaller markets have more in common, and can be better served with similar packages of merchandise, store concepts, and policies. If smaller regions make sense—taking all matters into account—then locational systems designed for these smaller regions should not be referred to as suboptimal. In general, the optimal number of facilities to serve a region or a market depends on the level of service that is desired and for which customers or people (via governments) are willing to pay.

Models and Decision Support Tools

Multiple-location problems have been well studied, classified, and modeled, and have generated a large body of literature about solutions, formulations, and algorithms. Almost all of these problems/models now are called "location–allocation" (LA) problems/models. A common feature of all of these problems is that the locations of multiple facilities—in a system—are being selected. They have to deal with both the locations of facilities and the allocation of demand points to these located facilities. Describing all of these problems, models, and solution approaches is an impossible task; the literature comprises at least 2500 scientific papers. This literature is remarkably diverse in its disciplinary heritage and scope, and can be found in the journals of operations research, management science, industrial engineering, geography, regional science, transportation science, logistics, applied economics, agricultural economics, applied mathematics, combinatorics, integer and nonlinear programming, and computer science.

Before dissecting these problems, their application contexts merit some comments. These models can be applied to any set of facilities that functions as a system, including manufacturing and processing plants of all kinds, refineries, warehouses, storage and distribution facilities of all kinds, transshipment points that are not warehouses, shopping centers, stores, offices, health care facilities, and kiosks. Furthermore, these models can be applied to any set of public facilities that functions as a system, including schools, hospitals, day care facilities, police stations, fire stations, ambulance dispatch centers, airports, parks, playgrounds, recreational facilities (e.g., tennis courts and swimming pools), and solid waste and other dump sites. The following taxonomic principles are helpful in formulating discussions of these problems:

1. Types of geographic space in which facilities can be located.
2. The number of facilities as an additional solution variable.
3. Capacity constraints for facilities.
4. Distinctive types of objective functions.
5. Interactions among the facilities being located (e.g., hierarchies of facilities).
6. Static versus dynamic settings.
7. Deterministic versus probabilistic variables (especially demand).
8. Closest facility assignments or multiple facility allocations.
9. Elasticity of demand.
10. Solution procedures.

Types of Geographic Space in which Facilities are Located

Three types of geographic space are discussed in the literature. The first is continuous space, meaning that facilities can locate anywhere on a plane. The location of a single facility to serve a set of n demand points distributed in continuous space is the generalized Weber problem previously mentioned. Each demand point is to be served by the closest facility, and all of the demand points need to be optimally partitioned into n compact subsets, each with its own optimally located central facility. This is the classic and first formally articulated LA problem initially discussed in the literature in the early 1960s by Leon Cooper. The continuous space feature of this LA problem generally is accompanied by the assumption that travel can take place in every direction at the same cost, which is computed as Euclidian distance. Other metrics also have been used, including the Manhattan metric, or city block distance. Advantages of this conceptualization of space include simplicity, classical geometric underpinnings, and solutions based on commonplace mathematics. Disadvantages include that one or more facilities can be placed at infeasible geographic locations. Although extensions to this problem allow solutions to avoid infeasible subareas (e.g., lakes), this complication can be circumvented by employing another type of space.

The second type of space is a network or graph theoretic structure. Demand is located on an explicit transportation network, usually at the nodes, and the service facilities must be located on this network. In 1965, S. Louis Hakimi proved that an optimal solution to the N-facility location problem (known today as the P-median problem) is such that the facilities are located at nodes of the network. Accordingly, the problem becomes one of selecting a subset of n nodes of a network, or vertices of a graph, so that the total cost of transportation or travel between the demand points and the service facilities is minimized. Demand points in the simple version of this problem are always served by the closest supply points, and transportation or travel distances are computed as shortest paths through the network.

The third type of space is discrete or punctiform in nature. Demand is located at a set of points in a continuous space. The supply points are to be located only at a subset of preidentified points in this space, usually a subset restricted to the demand points. These feasible points may be actually or conceptually the nodes of a network, or points that have been shown to be feasible (e.g., have available real estate) locations. In these conceptualizations (often found in the geography and regional science literatures), distances are typically computed as Euclidian distances (or sometimes Manhattan distances). If network distances are computed, this space is identical to a network space.

The Number of Facilities: An Additional Solution Variable

Whereas the literatures of geography, regional science, applied economics, and mathematics largely deal with the simpler LA problem, the more complex problem in which the number of facilities is also a solution variable is dominantly treated as an operations research, management science, or transportation science problem. The more complex problem has at least a fixed cost associated with establishing a facility; this fixed cost could be uniform or variable across locations. The existence of nonzero fixed costs is sufficient for the number of locations to become a solution variable in the LA problem, primarily because fixed costs are associated with economies of scale. Other forms of cost often are associated with more realistic LA problem formulations, including concave total cost curves characterizing continuous economies of scale. This form of the problem in which the number of facilities is a solution variable is called the "plant or warehouse location problem," a mixed-integer programming problem with zero/one variables associated with the existence of a facility at a location, and continuous variables associated with amounts shipped between the plants and the demand points. In general, the solution to this problem involves solving a series of subproblems, called "transportation problems of linear programming," in which the goal is to ship supplies from known supply points to known demand points at minimal cost. One such computationally onerous transportation problem has to be solved for each of a set of combinatorial alternatives featuring a different number of supply points at different locations. In general, the cheapest facility is the facility to serve a demand point. However, if the facilities are capacitated (see the Choosing a Single Location section), then facilities other than the cheapest often must be selected. The key to solving practical-sized problems of this type, consisting of hundreds of possible supply points, is to be able to "implicitly enumerate" (i.e., not actually do the work to solve or totally enumerate) many solution configurations, and then rule them out because they can be proven to be either infeasible or more expensive than a known solution.

Capacity Constraints for Facilities

Initially, simple LA problems were defined and solved with facilities lacking capacity constraints, the assumption being that these facilities could serve whatever demands were made on them. Indeed, in some contexts the capacity of a facility was planned on the basis of the demands made on it in an LA solution. The existence of modern mixed-integer programming code means that capacitated plant location problems can be solved quite easily by exploiting the framework of the "transportation problem," which has capacities built into it. A natural extension to this formulation is to select among several differently sized facilities with different fixed costs and different capacities—the "multilevel fixed-charge LA problem." Although almost all capacitated problems in the literature today are plant location-type problems, an early problem defined in continuous space was an LA problem with capacity constraints on the amount of demand that could be met by each facility. Today, this problem formulation is used for political redistricting or sales territory planning, whereby the goal is to create a set of compact districts with equal populations or demands. The focus in this problem is on the compactness and rationality of territories (assigned to each facility), rather than on the location of central facilities per se (which are merely incidental entities necessary to achieve compactness).

Distinctive Types of Objective Functions

The type of objective function being optimized has a profound impact on a solution. The most common objective by some margin is minimization of all relevant costs. Although appearing to be different conceptually, this is mathematically identical to maximizing revenue or profit objectives. Minimization of all travel or transportation costs alone frequently is referred to as a distance or transportation cost minimization problems. If fact, objective functions can be defined in many possible ways.

Another type of objective emerges in public facility location problems, one that often is nonstandard or requires the use of a proxy for something that is not easily measured. Consider, for example, locating fire stations, hospitals with emergency departments, or ambulance dispatch centers. A reasonable objective for this problem might be to minimize the maximum distance that has to be overcome in the geographic distribution of demand points—known as the minimax LA problem. In other words, the multiple locational pattern should be such that the distance between the least accessible ("the worst off") neighborhood and its closest facility is to be as small as possible. The objective is designed to maximize equity or fairness in a geographic context. (Indeed, in the past 20 years, the literature on justice and fairness has tended to use minimax concepts.) This minimax location problem also has been called the M-center problem in a continuous space. The optimal solution can be shown to contain a number of neighborhoods that are tied for being the worse off.

The number of facilities also can be treated as a solution variable. The "location set covering problem" requires finding the minimum number of facilities and their locations such that all demand points can be "covered" within a maximum of D distance units from the closest facility to each. To solve this problem, decision makers first must select a distance D beyond which travel distance is considered to be unacceptable. The number of facilities required clearly increases as this coverage distance D becomes smaller. These problems can be solved with relatively simple linear programming formulations, and typically have a number of different facility location configurations as solutions. Differentiating among these configurations has motivated consideration of supplementary objectives, such as to find the solution that covers as much demand as possible at least twice.

When the goal is to minimize "inefficiency" as the sum of distances traveled or shipped subject to an equity maximum distance constraint, the formulation becomes the P-median problem with maximum distance constraints. If P is given (e.g., as a generalized budget constraint) and D, the maximum distance allowed, is very large and nonbinding, then this extended problem reduces to the simple P-median problem. As D becomes smaller and the constraint becomes binding—to the point where further reductions make the problem infeasible—then this formulation approaches the M-center, or minimax location problem. For intermediate binding constraint levels of D, the problem is truly a mixed-breed problem; but it is still tractable.

Changing the objective to one of locating P facilities in such a way that the maximum amount of demand is included in the coverage distance D renders the multiple facility "maximal covering problem." As before, D denotes the maximal service distance that is "acceptable." This formulation differs from the location set-covering problem, in which the objective is to minimize the number of facilities required to achieve a certain coverage. The location set-covering problem frequently is defined in continuous space, whereas discussions of maximal covering problems typically have been defined in discrete or network spaces. The "maximal covering problem" also has been extended to one in which there are additional maximal distance constraints imposed on demand points not covered within the coverage distance D—as a concession to equity. In this version of the problem, a fixed number of facilities may not permit a feasible solution as D decreases.

Finally, the problem could be to locate some set of facilities that most people consider locally noxious, such as toxic waste dumps and sewage treatment plants, or even hostels for the homeless, halfway houses for former inmates, or psychiatric hospitals. One suitable objective here is to select a fixed number of locations such that the minimum distance is maximized—a maximin solution.

Interactions among the Facilities being Located

The type of facility system that is the optimum for delivering certain kinds of services can be quite complex. Some systems require the optimal locations to support interfacility shipping, travel, and/or communication. Such requirements arise because of specialization of facilities and/or employee positions. Entering interfacility distances or travel costs into most simpler LA problems makes them more complex but not intractable, partly because solution procedures already deal with space efficiently and tend to be interactive so that the locations of facilities in the last iteration can be treated as if they were demand points in the current iteration.

An interesting and practical extension to this problem formulation is one in which the facilities to be located are multilevel. A typical example is a system of both plants and warehouses; these need to be located in a way that will minimize total costs in meeting fixed demands at known locations. Plants must be located by taking real estate costs into account and dealing with distances to both raw materials and warehouse locations. Warehouses must be located by taking real estate costs into account and with respect to both plant locations (for their source of shipments) and the location of the demand points or markets. The literature contains examples of solutions to practical multilevel fixed-cost problems like these. A simple formulation involves using "transshipment problem of linear programming" shipment subproblems instead of transportation problem subproblems in the overall LA problem formulation.

The more intellectually and computationally challenging extension is the "hierarchical location–allocation problem," which contains several levels of facilities, such as plants, warehouses, stores, and kiosks. Each level of facility might interact only with facilities at adjacent levels in the hierarchy. Thus, for example, warehouses would get all their supplies from plants, and would ship their stock just to stores. The "central place problem" of locating a system of cities, towns, and villages optimally to service a consuming public is a similar problem. Here the consumers travel to all levels of "facilities" rather than to just one (or two). Thus, people will go to the smaller local facility, say, twice a week for milk and bread; to a larger nearby town, say, once a week for meat and vegetables; and, to the closest but more distant city, say, once a month for clothes and specialty items. These last two complex problems can be formulated as mixed-integer programming problems, and then solved with sufficient computer resources. The multilevel and constrained flows problem is easily accommodated within this problem formulation. The key tractability issue in this case is the number of zero/one variables involved.

Static versus Dynamic Settings

In all of the versions of the location–allocation problem discussed in the preceding sections, the problem is conceptualized as a one-shot static solution—albeit to a long-run problem. Because building a facility system all at once that will be optimal in the long run is extremely expensive, an additional feature of the problem becomes the optimal sequencing of investment over time. If the time horizon is truly long run, a facility system that is optimal for the long run should be determined, followed by solving the optimal sequencing as an independent problem. Sequencing can focus on short-term (i.e., myopic) or long-term (i.e., hyperopic) impacts. In a stagnant situation, the first facility locations optimize the objective function for the current time, having the largest effects across the time horizon. Facilities added in later time periods have smaller effects on the objective function value. This dynamic location–allocation formulation becomes even more compelling if, for instance, demand is projected to grow over time. Although the ultimate configuration of locations is best for the long run, short-run decisions may appear suboptimal when the long-run objective function is being optimized. In contrast, optimization of short-run objective function values could be suboptimal across the time horizon. Although dynamic LA problems were formulated in the early 1970s, only small problems could be solved because they require zero/one variables for each potential facility location for each time period, resulting in a combinatorial explosion in the number of variables as the number of feasible locations or time periods increases. More powerful computers coupled with more efficient mixed-integer programming code allow relatively quick solutions to be obtained today for problems with several hundred feasible locations and up to about 20 time periods.

Deterministic versus Probabilistic Variables

The LA problems described in preceding sections contain no probabilistic components. In reality, many components of these problems should be formulated in probabilistic terms. But probabilistic components are not very interesting if they do not really change a solution. For example, the projections of demand that are (or will be) present at demand points in a system really are expected values based on a selected probability distribution. Accordingly, if mean values are inserted as the effective demands when optimizing an objective function, solutions are not affected. However, if demand projections inserted are random drawings from the probability distribution, the different sequences can be deemed optimal. Repeating these random drawings many times allows confidence bounds to be attached to optimal facility numbers, facility locations, and overall costs. Other components of the problem have been treated as probabilistic, including transportation or travel costs, fixed costs, and production costs.

Closest Facility Assignments or Multiple Facility Allocations

One of the strongest assumptions in conventional LA problem formulations is that all interactions take place only between demand points and their closest or cheapest supply points. Though typically reasonable for systems in which a single undifferentiated product is being shipped by a facility system owner to demand points, this assumption is not reasonable in many situations in which customers travel to facilities that they have selected. Patronizing retail stores is a case in point. The personal decision of selecting facilities to patronize is a multidimensional behavioral problem that is truly complex. Customers are observed to patronize multiple facilities over a period of time, even for the same category or product. One reason for this behavior is that customers have multiple origins, not just home; for example, they go to stores from work, from grocery shopping, or from dental appointments. Further, traffic can change, for which convenience may suggest different choices at different times of the day. In addition, customers may be simply uncertain about the availability of stores or products at particular locations.

The "allocation problem" can be recast as a non-closest-store behavior patronage problem. For example, a Huff-type model can be used to capture realistic store patronage behavior. In the Huff model, the probability of a customer at a demand point patronizing a store is a function of the distance to this store (relative to other stores) and the attractiveness attributes (e.g., size or hours of operation) of the store. Demand areas are assigned probabilities of patronizing each member of a set of reasonably close stores. In these problems, competitor stores along with their attractiveness attributes are entered into the model as possible choices for consumers even if the model does not attempt to locate or relocate these competitors optimally. The problem becomes especially difficult to solve optimally because it is even more nonlinear in structure than a traditional location–allocation model is. Supply–demand interactions are no longer just zero/one variables. These problems are solvable using heuristic approaches that find very good, although not necessarily optimal, solutions. Retail location analysts have begun using these types of models to solve what are called "optimal store" or "bank branch" network problems. This formulation typically is used in the context of the P-median problem in which the analyst decides the value of P, as opposed to the fixed-cost "plant location" type of model, which nevertheless offers a reasonable formulation and tractability.

Elastic Demand

In the preceding discussions, even for the Huff-type extended problem, demands points are assumed to be known and constant. Besides the issue of defining these as random variables, two types of situations require that demand levels should be considered variable—in this case, "elastic." The first situation is one in which the existence of a facility in a neighborhood would cause more money to be spent on the goods sold there than would be the case if people had to travel some distance to buy them. Examples of this include an ice cream specialty store and a donut or coffee shop. Selecting good locations for such stores can cause the total amount spent in a market on specialty ice cream or coffee or donuts to increase. Rigorously specifying the level of total elasticity of demand requires a study to be conducted in one or more markets with significantly varying densities of stores.

The second situation is one in which a system is only partially modeled. For example, the number and locations of existing grocery stores clearly affect revenue expectations when adding new stores to a network. Rather than putting all of the grocery stores in the model as explicit competitors, it is possible to deal with their effects indirectly by building an elastic demand function. In this approach, the amount of demand in a small area that is available for new stores is an inverse function of the accessibility of fixed grocery stores to that demand area. This latter accessibility can be measured using "mathematical potentials" (see the Choosing a Single Location and The Principle of Optimizing sections).

This second type of problem, in which demand is a function of accessibility to fixed facilities, is structurally identical to one with simple fixed demands. It is therefore solvable using conventional LA solution approaches. The first formulation, in which the demand in a small area is a function of distances to the facilities being located, is especially difficult to solve optimally because of the substantial increase in nonlinearities. Nevertheless, fairly robust heuristic solutions (e.g., the vertex substitution approach; see the Least Cost Models and Decision Support Tools section) have been shown to work well in solving these problems.

Solution Procedures

Most location–allocation problems are very difficult to solve optimally—they are combinatorially explosive problems. For example, the number of possible ways of locating 20 facilities in a subset of 100 feasible locations is

$$\binom{100}{20},$$

or approximately 5.3×10^{20}. Furthermore, many of the problem formulations involve nonlinearities in the objective function, the constraints, or, worse, both. In general, the size and difficulty of a problem are most strongly influenced by the number of feasible locations for the facilities being located. Second in importance is the number of facilities to be located. The number of demand points to be served is typically the least important variable affecting problem size and solvability. Finally, problems in which transportation or travel costs are computed as shortest paths through a network are more onerous.

Geographic Cluster Generators

Sometimes locations are selected on the basis of clustering in geographic space, rather than strictly on the basis of some distance optimization process. Geographic clusters usually emerge from nonlinear relationships, agglomeration effects, or dependencies arising from tangible and/or intangible spatial interactions.

Trade-offs between Economies of Scale and Transportation Costs

A multilocational enterprise seeks to minimize distance to both its input sources and output demand points, while maintaining at least a minimum distance between its individual facility site locations in an effort to prevent self-duplication or overlapping of geographic coverage. But the cost of maintaining multiple sites often disproportionately increases as the number of sites increases. A certain overhead is incurred with each site, intersite communication multiplies disproportionately with more sites, and the enterprise tends to acquire more unutilized capacity as it expands its number of sites. Consequently, a trade-off materializes between benefits attributable to fewer larger, more centrally located sites and those attributable to a more intensive network of smaller sites covering a geographic landscape—a site at every location incurs too much overhead, whereas a single site often has inadequate accessibility. For economic activities, this trade-off has three salient components: assembly costs, production costs, and distribution costs. Reducing fixed costs, such as overhead, per unit of production means economies of scale are being tapped. The number, size, and spacing of site locations to be selected are those for which an increase in sizes no longer reduces fixed costs by more than accompanying increased assembly and distribution costs, and a decrease in sizes no longer reduces assembly and distribution costs by more than accompanying increased fixed costs. Final sizes determine spacing, and hence the relative number of facilities, through the supply–demand relationship. Mass production requires clustering in geographic space, and as such becomes a standard for selecting among geographic locations.

Agglomeration Economies and Spatial Externalities

Assembly and distribution costs frequently are impacted by a clustering of enterprises. The maxim "the whole is greater than the sum of its parts" describes this situation. When individual entities congregate in geographic space, many of their common requirements can be more effectively and efficiently furnished. For example, a transportation terminal can be operated to service both passenger travel and regional importing and exporting of industrial goods for all of an area's manufacturers. Agglomerating such transportation needs into a single location results in the terminal being more fully used and prevents the need to duplicate repeatedly a smaller version of the same facility throughout a region. Cost reduction benefits from this type of agglomeration also accrue when specialized infrastructure and ancillary services are needed, encouraging the construction of industrial parks, shopping centers and malls, and housing developments. Increased costs due to increased congestion and an overloading of infrastructure and ancillary services also can exist. The locational decision is whether to gravitate to geographic clusters in a deliberate effort to reduce various types of transport costs that are not offset by other costs.

Activities that are gathered together in space also reap benefits or incur costs from spatial externalities, or spillovers from one site to another that are unable to be internalized by the occupiers of each site. This is a scale economy arising from the size of a geographic cluster, rather than from the size of an individual activity within the cluster—an external economy of scale. One commonly cited example of a positive form of this effect is called "urbanization economies." These include the spatial concentration of labor forces, educational institutions, research establishments, and cultural facilities, coupled with the dampening impact of large numbers of actors on cyclical fluctuations in local supply and demand. A commonly cited example of a negative form is pollution. These spatial externalities also materialize as localization economies, promoting a clustering of, for example, hospitals, in order to share medical specialists and better utilize expensive equipment; shoe stores, in order to disproportionately increase patronage through provision of a wider range of selections and a comparison shopping environment; similar housing stock, in order to preserve house prices; and, office activities, in order to facilitate face-to-face contact. In other words, the decision to locate becomes one involving "urban considerations."

Spatial Dependencies

Spatial externalities are a special case of spatial dependencies, or spatial autocorrelation. Nearby geographic locations tend to have similar attributes associated with them. For example, soil types, geological structures, altitudes, moisture contents, and temperatures for two juxtaposed locations will be similar. Continuity of the geographic distributions of many physical phenomena means common factors generate geographic clustering. Agricultural regions emerge from the clustering of particular farming activities. Spatial interaction is facilitated by nearness, promoting contagious diffusion of everything from ideas to communicable diseases. The existence of a differentiated geographic landscape, in which various chemical elements vary in concentration rather than being ubiquitous and homogeneous, results in hot spots of environmental contamination. And, preferences of households to reside in localities inhabited by other households similar to them create segregated, ethnic neighborhoods. The geographic clustering of similar attributes sometimes furnishes a selection criterion for locational decision making—if a cluster of activities is thriving, then joining the cluster becomes appealing.

The Geographic Information System: A Tool for Locational Decision-Making Support

Locational decision making addresses the problem of finding one or more suitable sites for some activity. Inputs for solving this problem include skilled analysts, georeferenced attribute data, models for evaluating relevant data, and an ability to construct maps displaying the data and enabling identification of potential sites. Many of these tasks can be efficiently and effectively executed with the help of a geographic information system (GIS). This computer software tool supports locational decision making by furnishing an attribute data viewer table, data manipulation facilities, and graphics capabilities for displaying results as layers on a map. A GIS helps guide a decision-making progress—albeit operational, tactical, or strategic— by furnishing timely access to attribute data, speedy data manipulations, and rapid map updates. The focus is on decision support, not replacement of a decision maker. GIS, in its spatial analysis mode, is applicable to this spatial decision-making context.

See Also the Following Articles

Clustering • Geographic Information Systems • Location Analysis • Spatial Scale, Problems of • Transportation Research

Further Reading

Alonso, W. (1960). *Location and Land Use.* Harvard University Press, Cambridge, Massachusetts.

Applebaum, W. (1970). *Shopping Center Strategy.* International Council of Shopping Centers, New York.

Beckmann, M. (1968). *Location Theory.* Random House, New York.

Burns, E. (1997). Nested hexagons: Central place theory. In *10 Geographic Ideas That Changed the World* (S. Hanson, ed.), pp. 163–181. Rutgers University Press, New Brunswick, New Jersey.

Christaller, W. (1966). *Central Places in Southern Germany.* (translated by C. W. Baskin). Prentice-Hall, Englewood Cliffs, New Jersey.

Daskin, M. (1995). *Network and Discrete Location: Models, Algorithms and Applications.* Wiley, New York.

Ghosh, A., and Rushton, G. (eds.) (1987). *Spatial Analysis and Location–Allocation Models.* Van Nostrand Reinhold, New York.

Greenhut, M. (1956). *Plant Location in Theory and in Practice.* University of North Carolina Press, Chapel Hill.

Griffith, D. (1999). Statistical and mathematical sources of regional science theory: Map pattern analysis as an example. *Pap. Regional Sci.* **78,** 21–45.

Hall, P. (ed.) (1966). *Von Thünen's Isolated State.* (translated by C. Wartenberg). Pergamon Press, Oxford.

Hotelling, H. (1929). Stability in competition. *Econ. J.* **39,** 41–57.

Huff, D. (1964). Defining and estimating a trading area. *J. Market.* **28,** 34–38.

Isard, W. (1956). *Location and Space Economy.* MIT Press, Cambridge, Massachusetts.

Krugman, P. (1993). *Development, Geography, and Economic Theory.* MIT Press, Cambridge, Massachusetts.

Lösch, A. (1954). *The Economics of Location.* Yale University Press, New Haven, Connecticut.

Ponsard, C. (1983). *History of Spatial Economic Theory.* Springer-Verlag, Berlin.

Weber, A. (1909). *Theory of the Location of Industries.* University of Chicago Press, Chicago.

Wilson, A. (1970). *Entropy in Urban and Regional Modelling.* Pion, London.

Log File Analysis

Casper D. Hulshof
University of Twente, Enschede, The Netherlands

Glossary

frequency analysis A method for log file analysis that focuses on the frequency with which operations are performed.

interaction As used in this article, the interplay between human behavior and feedback generated by a computer program.

log file A sequence of behavioral data, stored on a permanent medium.

protocol analysis A method for obtaining information on cognitive processing of persons who are carrying out a specific task, by having them think aloud.

sequence analysis A method of log file analysis that focuses on the sequence in which operations are performed.

transition analysis A method for analyzing cognitive processing; can be used to classify persons by focusing on transitions in reasoning.

Log file analysis encompasses those strategies that can be applied in order to analyze behavioral patterns. One of the basic assumptions in contemporary psychology is that (invisible) cognitive processes can, in principle, be inferred from studying and comparing types of overt behavior. Log file analysis can be used when the purpose is to infer the cognitive processes of persons who interact with a computer program. Log files can be obtained by a number of methods, such as by having the computer register a person's operations or by having a person think aloud. Subsequent analysis can then be performed in a number of ways—for example, by examining the frequency with which different operations are carried out or by focusing on the sequence in which operations occur. In social measurement, the best results may be obtained by using an experimental design in which a combination of different methods of analysis is applied.

General Description of Log File Analysis

Log file analysis is the systematic approach to examining and interpreting the content of behavioral data. Its goal is to assist in finding patterns in the behavior of people as they interact with a computer. The behavior that people demonstrate while working with a computer program is influenced both by the program (its interface, or how it responds to user behavior) and by cognitive factors (e.g., the expectations and beliefs the user has in mind at any moment). Log file analysis can be applied to gain insight in the way these factors influence behavior. Keeping track of user behavior is of interest in two contexts, practical and scientific.

In a practical context, knowing the interaction style that people pursue while working with a computer program can be of great value. Because the number of people who use the computer on a daily basis continues to increase, human–computer interaction plays a role in an increasing number of areas. The implication is that there are more and more cases in which there is a need for studying the way users interact with a computer application. As the complexity and scope of software packages increase all the time (e.g., updated versions of Microsoft Word always add new, more complex features), not only people's judgment about the usefulness of a computer program and its interface should be studied, but also the way they use computer programs. This leads to insight about features that are preferred and about sequences of operations that are more typical than others. Based on this, a program's interface can be modified to suit the users' expectations and preferences. For a business, it is of the utmost importance that its product, rather than that of competitors, is experienced by users as better and easier to use.

In a scientific context, the way people interact with a computer program is of great interest to social science.

For example, in education, many studies have examined the (sometimes lack of) effectiveness of learning with computers. Although a computer can add value to the learning experience, many students experience trouble in making sense of the computer programs that are used. As has been pointed out by John Sweller and his colleagues, the interface that is used and the way in which information is presented to a learner influence cognitive load, which in turn influences learning effectivity. A large body of research has been devoted to studying the way these factors affect learning. Research on discovery learning with computer simulations has found sustaining evidence about types of support (assignments, model progression, interactive feedback) that learners need. In these studies, both computer-registered operations and analysis of think-aloud data have been used to examine behavior.

Before a system of keeping track of human–computer interaction is implemented, the purpose of measuring user behavior should be determined. Three purposes can be distinguished: supervising, monitoring, and examining interaction. The purpose of supervising interaction is either to keep a constant check on whether a user does nothing that is deemed "illegal" or to guide users through a program, with rigid restrictions on behavior that is out of bounds. Monitoring interaction means being able to interfere with a user's actions at certain moments, to avoid or minimize the effects of any mistakes. Constant monitoring provides users with a certain level of freedom, but this is limited in order to avoid actions that are considered to be mistakes. Finally, examining interaction means keeping track of the actions without any interference at all. Users experience complete freedom of action while interacting with a computer program. The decision to supervise, monitor, or examine behavior has implications for the method of obtaining log files and storing data on a permanent medium (e.g., the compact disk read-only memory).

Obtaining Log Files

One of the underlying assumptions in research on cognitive processes has always been that these processes are ordered in time, that is, they proceed in a serial fashion (e.g., the modal model of memory). This assumption, which is based on the computer metaphor of thought, links behavioral processes (that overtly proceed in time) with cognitive processes. An implication of this assumption is that cognition can be studied through the behavior that a person exhibits. Behavior that is expressed explicitly—through actions that are performed or through verbal statements that are made during a task—can be measured and subjected to analysis. Interaction can be analyzed either while a person works with the computer (real-time analysis), or afterward (*post-hoc* analysis). In real-time analysis, what is known to the system is someone's behavior up to the point in time that the analysis is carried out. An example is the field of intelligent tutoring systems, a goal of which is the creation of suitable learner models. An intelligent tutoring system (ITS) can develop a model of a learner's knowledge state while he or she works with a computer program. This model consists of all information that can be gathered, and can be put to use to provide appropriate and intelligent feedback.

In a practical sense, it can sometimes be useful to track behavior in real time, without storing it on a permanent medium. This is the case when personal data cannot be stored due to privacy issues, but also when a user's behavior during just one session with a computer program is needed. As an example, consider the "dynamic menu system," a software feature that tracks the computer program options that people prefer to use. This feature can be seen in recent versions of Microsoft Office. Available options of the software that are used infrequently will eventually disappear from sight on the menus. The idea is that menus are kept uncluttered by limiting the number of visible options. What should be visible is induced from frequency of use. In this example, it is necessary to track only one thing: the options that are chosen by a user from the available menus. Other operations, such as the text that is typed or the sequence in which different menu options are selected, are not of interest, and should therefore not be registered. Real-time analysis differs from *post-hoc* analysis in that it tries to capture as much relevant information as possible about the human–computer interaction.

A number of methods can be used to obtain log files. Three methods that are most widely used are eye movement registration, protocol analysis, and computer-registered operations. Although different methods can be combined, usually only one type of measurement is chosen.

Eye Movement Registration

Eye movement registration is discussed in detail in the book by Duchowski, *Eye Tracking Methodology: Theory and Practice*. The method entails recording eye fixations while a person is performing a task. Afterward, fixation points can be combined with the things that happened on a video screen. It is assumed that the direction and duration of eye gazes indicate what part of the visual field people are paying attention to, and hence the type of information they are processing. Eye movement registration results in very detailed log files. When a task has a large visual component, eye movements may provide researchers with more information than other methods of obtaining log files would provide. However, interpreting fixations can be difficult, which may deem the method less suitable for tasks in which high-level cognitive processes are studied. Also, only one subject at a time can be tested using eye movement registration. One implication is that in many practical applications of social measurement (e.g., collaborative problem solving or studying group processes in a classroom), it makes no sense to just measure eye movements.

Protocol Analysis

Protocol analysis (also referred to as the "think-aloud method") is a popular method for obtaining a detailed report of real-time cognitive processing. The method was made into a coherent system by Allen Newell and Herbert Simon in their seminal work on problem solving; a subsequent overview of the method by K. A. Ericsson and Simon was published in 1993. Obtaining a log file of think-aloud data involves three steps: transcribing, segmenting, and encoding. Transcribing refers to the process of typing in the verbal data. Segmenting a protocol means breaking it down into separate meaningful chunks (or "segments"). Encoding means categorizing each segment and developing a descriptive behavioral model based on the sequence of categories. Interpretation and encoding of a protocol influence each other, which means that the whole process occurs in cycles. However, Ericsson and Simon have noted that segments should be encoded in isolation, that is, disregarding the particular sequence in which they occur. Obtaining think-aloud data is a suitable method when there is interest in higher order cognitive processing, although the segmenting and encoding process involves some subjective judgment.

Computer-Registered Operations

Computer-registered operations is a method that involves keeping track of all interaction, where interaction is defined as all user-initiated behavior that leads to a change, visible or invisible, in the computer program for which the interaction pattern is studied. In practice, this means registering all mouse-button presses and keyboard operations that a user undertakes during a task. The resulting log files usually are extensive, but do not explain people's reasoning behind the actions they have performed, which makes interpretation a complex affair. An important advantage of the method is that it can be applied to a group of people simultaneously, which can be very practical. This makes the method most useful when the purpose is to get a global overview of the operations that people perform when they interact with a computer program, or when groups of subjects are expected to vary in the activities they display when they work with different configurations of a computer program. When human reasoning is the focus of research, registered operations may be too ambiguous or shallow to merit a reliable interpretation.

Practical Issues in Registering Interaction

A log file represents a recorded version of the behavior that a person has displayed while working with a computer program. The goal in creating a log file is to store a person's behavioral pattern in such a way that it can be faithfully "played back" afterward. In other words, it should be possible to reconstruct the sequence of relevant operations from the log file data. Whichever method of obtaining log file data is applied, the result is a sequence of actions that can be subjected to analysis. The following discussion explores the type of information that a log file can contain, and the way this information can be systematically stored. To illustrate how guidelines for storing registered interaction in a log file work in practice, an example case is described.

A number of guidelines can be given for storing interaction behavior in a log file. In addition to user-initiated behavior that changes the computer program, a log file should include information on the type of operations, the time operations take to complete, and the object(s) on which an operation is performed. In logging interaction, a distinction can be made between different types of operations. Some operations change only the "mode" of a program. For example, a word processor could allow the active font to be changed by pressing a button on the screen. This action, which in itself does not have a visible effect, will have a visible effect on subsequent operations. Thus, the type of operation that is performed can be included in a log file. Furthermore, a distinction can be made between operations that take place instantly (the mode operation in the previous example) and operations that take some time to be completed. For example, a drawing program may allow objects to be dragged on the screen. The operation of selecting an object and dragging it to a new destination takes a certain amount of time. Thus, the time that operations take to complete should also be included in a log file. Finally, some operations that are carried out in a computer program are performed on one or more objects. Again, an example is dragging an object to a specific spot. A log file should include not only the operation "drag," but also the type of object that the operation affects. The application of these guidelines can be illustrated by an example from research by Casper Hulshof on the computer simulation "Optics." An excerpt from a structured log file is displayed in Fig. 1. Reference source not found," is displayed. It represents a raw log file, i.e., one that is not yet edited or filtered for specific operations. The excerpt shows a short

```
@ (478.0, action(delete_all)).
@ (490.0, mode(one_lightbeam)).
@ (492.0, add(l2 = lamp3(switch(true),
                    angle(80),
                    divergence(5),
                    pos_x(3),
                    pos_y(0.1),
                    instrument_name(one_lightbeam)))).
@ (493.0, mode(rotlamp)).
@ (495.0 – 498.0, rotate(l2,
        [       @ (0.0, drag(–2.00955)),
                @ (1.0, drag(–0.498212)),
                @ (2.0, drag(0.498212)),
                @ (3.0, drag(0))
        ])).
.
.
.
@ (521.0, mode(screen)).
@ (524.0, add(s5 = shield(pos_x(7.65),
                    unit(1),
                    instrument_name(screen)))).
```

Figure 1 Excerpt from a log file (see text for discussion). Adapted from Hulshof (2001).

time sequence in which a number of different operations are carried out with the Optics computer simulation. The program helps students discover properties of geometrical optics. In experiments that were carried out with Optics, students worked individually with the simulation. The method for obtaining log files was computer-registered operations (Fig. 1). As can be seen from close examination of Fig. 1, structure was put into Optics log files by separating different operations. Each operation has a clearly defined beginning and ending; in this case, an easily recognized "@" symbol is at the start of each operation and a dot is at the end. Starting time and (in case of operations that took more than a second to perform) ending time were included with each operation. The mode operation on the second line indicates that a student intended to add a lamp to the simulation, an operation that occurs immediately afterward (at time 492.0). After this operation, the "rotate lightbeam" mode is entered and the direction of the lightbeam is altered. The object on which this rotation operation is performed is included in the log file (the lamp is identified in the log file as 'lamp3'). In the example, some information about dragging of objects with the mouse was also registered (the "drag" operations). This example shows that a mechanism for registering user operations results in an elaborate and informative log file that conforms to all guidelines. What remains is the actual analysis.

Methods for Analyzing Log Files

To analyze the string of operations that a log file consists of, usually some sort of conversion of the log file to a format that can be processed by tools such as Microsoft Excel or SPSS is needed. This can be done by applying clever sorting mechanisms in either of these programs, or through a conversion script. For example, the log files that resulted from the studies with Optics (as shown in the example in Fig. 1) were converted to SPSS-readable format through the use of a program script written in Practical Extraction and Reporting Language (Perl, for short). Not only are there no generally available algorithms for converting log files to files that can be processed, nor are there as yet general guidelines for analyzing log files once they are processed. Studies in which log files were obtained have usually applied their own type of log file analysis method. When a log file is examined, at first operations may appear to follow each other in seemingly random fashion. Analysis means probing for regularities or patterns in the string of operations. Different strategies can be used to discover regularities, which differ in complexity and in the way results are interpreted. Some methods can be applied to a single log file; for others, a number of log files should be available for analysis. In the following overview, four general methods are discussed: transition analysis, frequency analysis, learning indicators, and sequence analysis. An outline for a fifth method, which combines frequency and sequence analysis, is briefly discussed.

Transition Analysis

A simple yet powerful way to draw conclusions from people's behavior is to examine whether some typical transition in behavior is displayed. This mechanism can be applied to classify persons based on only one distinguishing action. An example is a study on the process of discovery. In the study, the distinction between two strategies in rule discovery (experiment or hypothesis based) was grounded in the way subjects came up with the correct rule: either by using an experiment that pointed in the right direction or by just coming up with the idea to change the frame of reference. The defining transition in this case is the frame shift that occurs: either doing an experiment in a new "space of experiments" and reaching the right conclusion (the experimenter approach) or reaching the right conclusion without having done any experiments in the "right" space of experiments (the theorist approach). The discovery study was designed in such a way to allow for a careful distinction in the way a transition occurred. The dimensions of the experimental domain were relatively small, which means that all operations within the domain could be fully described as occurring at a specific location in the experimental space. Other studies make use of domains in which there are many variables with complex relations; it is impossible to describe fully the experimental domain or to describe formally one defining transition that differentiates between subjects. Domains in which it is possible to observe the kind of transition as in the discovery process study appear to make up the most appropriate setting for this type of analysis. Other domains need a more complex type of analysis.

Frequency Analysis

Frequency analysis is a generic method of analysis that is used not only in studies that apply to social measurement but also in studies in many other scientific fields. Because it has always been so widely used, the method is usually not acknowledged when it is used, in contrast to other methods of log file analysis. The reason for its popularity is that it provides a simple way to measure quantitative aspects of behavior. Groups of subjects can easily be compared using a variety of standardized statistical tests. However, frequency analysis can also be used to examine the interaction pattern of a single person. In such a case, the relative frequency with which different operations are performed supplies most information.

Performing a frequency analysis means tallying the frequency with which each operation occurs. In the case of protocol analysis, segmented codes are counted. Different statistics, e.g., averages and standard deviations, can be computed for each operation. These averages can be compared (for example, to examine which operation has the lowest occurrence and which one the highest). Depending on the questions that a researcher has in mind, statistical tests can be performed to compare the frequencies of specific operations.

Although frequency analysis is relatively easy to perform, it has its drawbacks when used as the sole method of log file analysis. This is most evident when a comparison between two or more subject groups is made. When no difference is found in the frequency with which different operations are carried out, it can easily be concluded that the groups generally interacted similarly with a computer program, and experienced working with the program in a similar way. But do they? Frequency analysis tends to "even things out," which means that the interesting variation in the level of activity that people show is filtered out of the equation. Also, although the overall level of activity may be similar, the reasons people have for acting the way they do may be completely different for different groups. Intentional problem-solving behavior in one group may look similar to random guessing in another group, when only frequencies of operations are compared. When a theoretical research question predicts differences in the behavioral pattern of different groups of subjects, it may be sensible to perform more than just frequency analysis.

Learning Indicators

The learning indicator approach can be seen as an offshoot of frequency analysis, and has similar advantages and disadvantages. The method consists of constructing clusters of operations that roughly occur roughly with the same frequency. An example of this approach to studying behavior is the Smithtown study by Shute and Glaser in 1990. Smithtown is a computerized learning environment. Shute and Glaser were able to derive global learner differences on the basis of learner interaction measures. The analysis that was pursued focused on the large-scale extraction of clusters of interaction patterns. The method was to take operations together (these operations were called "learning indicators") to distinguish between global processes that take place during learning. The learning indicators were derived from both log files and protocols, by clustering similar operations. Based on this analysis, three types of broad "rational categories" were distinguished: a general activity level (e.g., total number of experiments), data management skills (e.g., total number of notebook entries), and thinking and planning behaviors (e.g., number of variables changed per experiment). The approach by Shute and Glaser can be summarized as involving (1) counting frequencies of actions, (2) categorizing them into meaningful units, and (3) making comparisons across groups. This approach can be helpful to compare groups of subjects at a global level. However, as in the case of frequency analysis, it can also be a misleading approach, because differences between learners can even everyone out. When students of high and low competence are compared, other factors (e.g., prior knowledge about the domain) may influence interaction with a computer program.

A main disadvantage of both frequency analysis and the learning indicator approach is that they both ignore the way behavior changes or progresses over time. A broad overview of the activity level of subjects does not provide answers with respect to the reason for any differences. For this, analysis of the sequence in which operations occur may be a more appropriate method.

Sequence Analysis

Frequency analysis looks at user-initiated operations as isolated events. When interaction with a computer program is studied, it is not very realistic to assume that each operation that people perform is not connected in any way to the operations that come before it and after it. As Bakeman and Gottman have argued, interaction "reveals itself unfolded in time." This implies that the information that is contained in the sequence of operations may be just as meaningful as the information contained in the overall number of specific operations. (The mathematical and statistical details of sequence analysis cannot be discussed in detail here, but an introduction to the topic of sequence analysis can be found in the work by Bakeman and Gottman.) The purpose of sequence analysis is to examine the connection between operations as they occur over time. Such an analysis is performed by computing, for each possible operation, the probability of that operation following or preceding each of the other operations. An advantage of sequence analysis over other types of analysis is that it takes account of interaction as it occurs over time. Sequences of operations that occur together are recognized as such. This creates the possibility of inferring from a log file, to some extent, a user's intention in performing certain behavior. When looking at different phases of working with a computer program, sequence analysis may also reveal the type of operations a user focuses on in the beginning (when not everything about the computer program is known) and at the end (when knowledge about the program has been acquired). In spite of these advantages, sequence analysis is used only infrequently in social measurement. This has both a practical and a theoretical reason. From a practical point of view, sequence analysis is difficult to perform. Standard statistical software packages usually have only limited functionality for computing sequence probabilities. Also, the level of expertise needed to understand and interpret p-values of sequences may pose a barrier for researchers with basic statistical training. From a theoretical point of view, there is a risk in performing a sequence analysis, because it may lead to a misinterpretation of operations that appear to occur after one another. Because sequence analysis looks at the probabilities of each operation occurring before and after the other operations, there is a high chance that "noise" will lead to a significant probability. Separating relevant from irrelevant patterns of behavior can be a complex affair, for which no standard method exists yet.

A Different Approach: Finding Patterns in Variable Manipulation

Each of the four methods of analyzing log files that have been discussed has its own advantages and disadvantages. In this section, a method of analysis that combines frequency analysis with sequential analysis is outlined. The idea is that by taking advantage of the strong points of these two methods, another type method for analyzing log files can be constructed. The underlying idea is that the relevant operations within a computer program can be seen as consisting of the manipulation of variables. A variable is here defined as anything in a computer program that changes, by manipulation by a user or by manipulation by the computer program. Manipulating variables means that users apply a change to one or more parameters in a computer program, and then observe the effect of these changes. When defined this way, three types of variable manipulation can be distinguished: single, alternating, and sequential. Single manipulation means that a variable A is changed a number of times. Alternating variable manipulation means that, first, variable A is modified, then variable B is modified, then A again, and so on. Sequential manipulation means that available variables are all changed, one after another. In Table I, the three types are shown together with the possible goal that can be inferred from that type of manipulation.

Table I Variable Manipulation and Possible Intended Behavior

Manipulation type	*Possible goal*
Single	Effect of variable A
Alternating	Relation between A and B
Sequential	Exploring available options

When variable manipulation is used as a starting point for analyzing a log file, frequency analysis can be combined with sequence analysis. The idea is to combine the variable manipulations that a computer program allows into meaningful sequences that conform themselves to one of the three types of variable manipulation, as shown in Table I. It is important to note that this construction of meaningful sequences can be done at a stage of research when no log file is yet available. Also, the sequences that are defined are different for each computer program with which interaction is studied, because they depend on the way variable manipulation is implemented in a particular computer program. Once sequences are defined, the frequency with which they occur can be computed by analyzing log files. The frequency of different sequences of variable manipulation gives information on the different goals that people pursue while they work with a computer program. This method of computing frequencies of sequences does not require sophisticated techniques, so that it can be performed within standard statistical software packages. The outlined method combines some of the strengths of the other methods, but it is unlikely that it could completely replace them.

Conclusions

Log file analysis is a powerful tool for gaining insight into the cognitive processes that underlie behavior—specifically, interaction with a computer program. Obtaining a detailed record of interaction can be achieved relatively unobtrusively through a number of different methods, and resulting log files can be structured in such a way that different methods of analysis can be applied. Each method has its own advantages and disadvantages. An analysis method that uses types of variable manipulation as a stepping stone to combining frequency analysis with sequence analysis has been outlined. There is room for the development of new analysis methods or improved schemes for the classification of interaction behavior. It is clear that in log file analysis the problem is not so much one of collecting interesting information on the type of operations that are performed, as it is one of inferring people's intentions in carrying out these operations in the first place. At least protocol analysis allows users to state clearly their intentions while interacting with a computer program. In conclusion, the strongest experimental design may be created when the behavior of a limited number of subjects is measured using protocol analysis, in combination with a large-scale measurement of computer-registered operations. In such a research design, the power and elegance of statistical analysis of registered eye movements or computer-registered operations can be used in conjunction with the depth and thoroughness of protocol analysis.

See Also the Following Articles

Cognitive Neuroscience • Cognitive Psychology • Cognitive Research Methods • Spatial Cognition and Perception

Further Reading

Atkinson, R. C., and Shiffrin, R. M. (1971). The control of short-term memory. *Sci. Am.* **225,** 82–90.

Bakeman, R., and Gottman, J. M. (1986). *Observing Interaction: An Introduction to Sequential Analysis,* 2nd Ed. Cambridge University Press, New York.

Chandler, P., and Sweller, J. (1991). Cognitive load theory and the format of instruction. *Cognit. Instruct.* **8,** 293–332.

de Jong, T., and van Joolingen, W. R. (1998). Scientific discovery learning with computer simulations of conceptual domains. *Rev. Educat. Res.* **68,** 179–201.

Duchowski, A. T. (2003). *Eye Tracking Methodology: Theory and Practice.* Springer-Verlag, New York.

Ericsson, K. A., and Simon, H. A. (1993). *Protocol Analysis: Verbal Reports as Data,* 2nd Ed. MIT Press, Cambridge, MA.

Hulshof, C. D. (2001). *Discovery of Ideas and Ideas about Discovery: The Influence of Prior Knowledge on Scientific Discovery Learning in Computer-Based Simulations.* Ph.D. Thesis, University of Twente, The Netherlands.

Klahr, D., and Dunbar, K. (1988). Dual space search during scientific reasoning. *Cognit. Sci.* **12,** 1–48.

Newell, A., and Simon, H. A. (1972). *Human Problem Solving.* Prentice-Hall, Englewood Cliffs and New Jersey.

Shute, V. J., and Glaser, R. (1990). A large-scale evaluation of an intelligent discovery world: Smithtown. *Interact. Learn. Environ.* **1,** 51–77.

van Someren, M. W., Barnard, Y., and Sandberg, J. (1994). *The Think Aloud Method: A Practical Approach to Modelling Cognitive Processes.* Academic Press, London.

Log-Linear Models

Peter K. Dunn
University of Southern Queensland, Toowoomba, Queensland, Australia

Glossary

contingency table A table in which individuals are cross-classified as belonging to particular levels of various factors.

factor A variable for which the individuals are classified into one of many categories.

level One of the categories of a factor into which an individual can be categorized.

Poisson distribution A statistical distribution used to model counts.

treatment coding A method for converting the levels of a factor into a numerical variable for inclusion in a mathematical model.

A large amount of data collected in the social sciences are counts cross-classified into categories. These counts are nonnegative integers and require special methods of analysis to model appropriately; log-linear models are one sophisticated method. The counts are modeled by the Poisson distribution, and related to the classifying variables through a logarithm. Models can then be built, critically analyzed, evaluated, and compared to develop a suitable statistical model for modeling the count data. Log-linear models are powerful enough to cope with many classifying variables, and permit many model-building ideas similar to those in standard statistical regression.

Introduction and Background

Log-linear models (also written as log linear models or loglinear models) are analysis tools for modeling counts cross-classified into categories. Initially, count data itself is discussed.

Classifying Count Data

Count data can be cross-classified by a number of variables; for example, Gender (with values "male" or "female") and Employment Status (with values "employed," "unemployed," or "not in workforce"). Both of these variables are categorical variables, also called *factors*: the values of the variable refer to the different classifications (in contrast to numerical measurements). Gender has two levels or categories; Employment Status has three. Categories must be both mutually exclusive (no observation can appear in more than one level of each factor) and exhaustive (any individual must belong to one of the given levels for each factor).

Noncategorical variables, such as Age, may be coerced to factors. For example, ages may be classified into the categories "Under 20," "20 to under 35," "35 to under 50," and "50 or over." (Note the categories are mutually exclusive and exhaustive.) Some noncategorical variables have so few possible values they are often considered categorical; for example, the number of political party memberships currently held is a numerical variable. However, this (numerical) variable could be treated as categorical with levels "0," "1," and "2 or more."

Types of Factors

Factors can be identified as either ordinal (or ordered) or nominal. The levels of a nominal factor can be ordered in any convenient way. University faculties can be listed alphabetically, by size, or by some other criteria; there is no natural ordering. An ordinal factor implies the categories have some natural order. Examples include smoking habits ("do not smoke," "light smoker," "heavy smoker") or opinions rated on a Likert scale ("strongly disagree," "disagree," "neutral," "agree," "strongly agree"). Specific models for ordered factors are available but are beyond the scope of this article. In general, ordinal factors can be adequately treated as nominal factors.

Displaying Data

Conveniently, counts can be displayed in a contingency table; see Table I for example. There are four factors: Age (say A) is an ordered factor on three levels, Depression Level (D) is an ordered factor on two levels, Label (L) and Gender (G) are both nominal factors on two levels. The data form a $3 \times 2 \times 2 \times 2$ table, with $3 \times 2 \times 2 \times 2 = 24$ cells.

None of the totals in this table has been fixed beforehand: selected subjects are just classified according to their age, label, gender, and depression level. Tables may, however, have some totals fixed (for example, a fixed number of males and females are interviewed, or a fixed total number of people are interviewed). Fixed totals are not variables, which has implications for the model fitting but is beyond the scope of this article. Briefly, those parameters referring to fixed totals must be included in the model.

Purpose

It is difficult to grasp the connections between levels of each factor, especially for large numbers of factors, when the data are presented in a contingency table. Log-linear models are used to examine associations among levels of categorical variables. As in any modeling exercise, the analyst is searching for the simplest model not contradicted by the data. In some special cases it may be possible to summarize the data by collapsing the table over one of the factors.

Table I The Number of Seriously Emotionally Disturbed (SED) and Learning Disabled (LD) Adolescents Classified by Age (A), Gender (G), and Depression Level (D)

		Depression (D)			
		Males		*Females*	
Age (A)	*Label (L)*	*High*	*Low*	*High*	*Low*
12–14	LD	79	18	34	14
	SED	14	5	5	8
15–16	LD	63	10	26	11
	SED	32	3	15	7
17–18	LD	36	13	16	1
	SED	36	5	12	2

Note: The data are from Maag, J. W., and Behrens, J. T. (1989). Epidemiologic data on seriously emotionally disturbed and learning disabled adolescents: reporting extreme depressive symptomology. *Behav. Disorders* **15**, 21–27.

The Model

The counts in a contingency table are assumed to be possibly related to the factors by which they are cross-classified; the interest is in quantifying this relationship. (A contingency table with one of the factors on two levels may also be modeled using a logistic regression model.) The two most important aspects of the log-linear model considered herein are the underlying assumption of a Poisson distribution for the counts, and the logarithm which relates the factors to the counts.

The Poisson Distribution

In the log-linear model considered here, the response variable is the number of observations, say y_i, in each cell i of a contingency table. The data are non-negative integers; an appropriate distribution for modeling counts is the *Poisson distribution*. For a given cell i with mean μ_i, the Poisson probability function is

$$f_Y(y_i;\mu_i) = \Pr(Y = y_i) = \frac{\exp(-\mu_i)\mu_i^{y_i}}{y_i!} \tag{1}$$

for $y_i = 0, 1, 2, \ldots$ and $\mu_i > 0$. For the Poisson distribution, the mean equals the variance; that is, $\mu_i = \mathrm{E}(Y_i) = \mathrm{var}(Y_i)$.

Coding of Factors

Before fitting a log-linear model, the classifying factors need to be coded numerically; additions and multiplications cannot be performed on a factor level "male." A factor with k levels is coded into $k - 1$ binary variables (variables that take only two values, often 0 and 1), called *dummy variables*.

Many coding systems exist (and are sometimes called *contrasts* under special conditions). One of the simplest is treatment coding, described next.

The factor Gender has two levels and requires one dummy variable. This dummy variable could code 0 for females and 1 for males (or 0 for males and 1 for females). These numbers are merely identifiers. Similarly, coding "female" as 1 and "male" as 2 does not imply males are in some way twice the value of females; the numbers merely identify the levels of the factor.

For the Table I data, the factor Age has three levels; two dummy variables are needed. Define variable A_1 as 1 for subjects 15–16 years of age, and zero otherwise; define variable A_2 as 1 for subjects 17–18 years of age and zero otherwise. The age group "12–14" is called the *reference*, or *baseline* category. Age group "12–14" is assigned the codes $A_1 = A_2 = 0$; age group "15–16" is assigned the codes $A_1 = 1$ and $A_2 = 0$; age group "17–18" is assigned the codes $A_1 = 0$ and $A_2 = 1$. Thus Age

(A) has been unambiguously coded numerically using dummy variables A_1 and A_2 for incorporation into the mathematical model. Similarly, code L_1 as 1 for the SED label, and zero otherwise; G_1 as 1 for males, and zero otherwise; D_1 as 1 for low depression, and zero otherwise.

The Logarithm Link

In log-linear models, the counts in each cell are assumed to follow the Poisson distribution. In addition, the mean of the distribution in each cell is perhaps related to the classifying factors. After appropriate coding, the factors in Table I are then related to the Poisson mean in each cell through

$$\log\mu_i = \beta_0 + \beta_1 A_1 + \beta_2 A_2 + \beta_3 L_1 + \beta_4 G_1 + \beta_5 D_1, \tag{1}$$

where the parameters β_0, β_1, β_2, ... are values to be estimated, and A_1, A_2, L_1, ... are the (dummy) variables. (The log function is the natural log with base $e \approx 2.71828\ldots$.) This equation gives rise to the name "log-linear models," as the model is linear on the logarithmic scale. Technically, the logarithm is called the *link function* in the nomenclature of generalized linear models. Equivalently, but more concisely, the right-hand side of the model can be written as $1 + A + L + G + D$.

Equation (1) can be rewritten as $\mu_i = \exp(\beta_0 + \beta_1 A_1 + \beta_2 A_2 + \ldots)$; thus the logarithm ensures the Poisson means μ_i always remain positive. Using the log implicitly assumes the factors have a multiplicative effect on the response, not an additive effect. (Equivalently, the effect of the factors is additive on the log-scale.)

Fitting the Model

Log-linear models have a firm theoretical foundation and established fitting algorithms as they are a subset of generalized linear models. Iterative algorithms such as iteratively reweighted least squares (IRLS) are used to fit the models; the algorithms are quite robust. Most statistical software has the facility to fit log-linear models.

Interactions

The model that considers only the effect of each factor on the counts is called the *main effects model*; this models the numbers of observations in the totals for each factor level. For example, the model only incorporating the factor Gender would model differences in the number of observations for each level of Gender. This is of limited interest; of more interest are the interactions between the factors.

Commonly, the levels of the factors interact with each other. For example, interaction between Age and Gender in Table I would indicate how the proportions of males and females differ across the age groups. This interaction is written using as $A.G$. Since Age has two dummy variables and Gender has one, the interaction is specified by $2 \times 1 = 2$ dummy variables.

Zero Counts

The presence of zeros, or of many small counts, in a contingency table can adversely affect parameter estimation. Two types of zeros exist. Structural zeros refer to necessarily zero counts, such as the number of males receiving a hysterectomy. These cells should be discarded from the analysis.

Sampling zeros are counts that are not necessarily zero; a larger sample may produce counts for those cells. Because these cells contain legitimate counts, they should not be discarded. Some authors recommend adding 1/2 to each count in a table with zeros and/or small counts. Alternatively, some factor levels may be combined if possible and sensible (for example, combine "strongly agree" and "agree" into one category "agree").

Model Criticism and Comparison

The process of building a suitable log-linear model for given data is an art as much as a science. In a typical contingency table with more than two factors, numerous models are possible. Each must be evaluated and compared to find a best model. Some evaluation criteria are discussed below.

Residual Analysis

The differences between the observed counts y_i, and the expected (modeled) counts μ_i are an indicator of the adequacy of the fitted model. Using the Poisson distribution implies the mean equals the variance, implying large difference are more likely when μ_i is large compared to when μ_i is small. (That is, a predicted count of 3 is unlikely to be in error by as much as 10, but is reasonable for a predicted count of 2000.) Thus, the residuals must be scaled appropriately. The Pearson residuals are therefore defined for the Poisson distribution as

$$r_{P,i} = \frac{y_i - \mu_i}{\sqrt{\mu_i}}.$$

Alternatively, deviance residuals can be used, defined for the Poisson distribution as

$$r_{D,i} = \text{sign}(y_i - \mu_i)\sqrt{2[y_i \log(y_i/\mu_i) - (y_i - \mu_i)]}.$$

(The function sign (x) is 1 if $x>0$, is -1 if $x<0$, and is 0 if $x=0$.) Both types of residuals should have approximately a normal distribution.

Overall Measures of Discrepancy

Residuals indicate how well the model fits for each observed count. It is useful to also have an overall measure of discrepancy for the model. The X^2 statistic for a table of n cells is defined as

$$X^2 = \sum_{i=1}^{n} r_{P,i}^2 = \sum_{i=1}^{n} \frac{(y_i - \mu_i)^2}{\mu_i}.$$

Similarly, the deviance can be defined as

$$D = \sum_{i=1}^{n} r_{D,i}^2 = 2\sum_{i=1}^{n} y_i \log(y_i/\mu_i) + (y_i - \mu_i).$$

This form of the deviance but without the term $(y_i - \mu_i)$ is also known as the G^2 statistic.

The deviance is actually related to the log-likelihood for the Poisson distribution, and is often defined as

$$D = -2\sum_{i=1}^{n} \log f_Y(y_i;\, \mu_i),$$

where $f_Y\,(y_i;\, \mu_i)$ is the probability function for the Poisson distribution defined in Equation (1). For any given data, the two forms of the deviance differ only by a constant. Hereafter, the second form will be used.

Approximately, the change in deviance between nested models has a χ^2 distribution; often this approximation is poor. (Model 1 is nested in Model 2 if Model 2 has all the parameters fitted in Model 1, plus additional parameters.) Hence, significant changes in the deviance are identified by comparing the change in deviance to the appropriate χ^2 distribution.

For both X^2 and D, smaller values indicate a better model. However, a model having both X^2 and D equal to zero, indicating a "perfect" model (see the Example), can be created simply by adding more classifying factors and interactions. Typically, this model, called the *saturated* or the *full* model, is unnecessarily complicated; a simpler model may be just as useful. The Akaike Information Criterion (AIC) addresses this difficulty. It is defined as $AIC = D + 2p$, where p is the number of estimated parameters in the model. The AIC penalizes the deviance by $2p$ to discourage the inclusion of unnecessary parameters. (Other similar criteria also exist with different penalties.) The best model has the smallest AIC.

Model Building

Sometimes, prior information (either theoretical or otherwise) may be used to propose the preferred log-linear model, or at least a set of possible models. However, it is also possible to have no prior expectations of the model. In either case, many possible models may exist for modeling a contingency table with many factors. As stated earlier, models may be compared using the deviance.

Consider Model A with p_A estimated parameters and deviance D_A, and Model B with p_B estimated parameters and deviance D_B. If Model B is nested within Model A, $p_B < p_A$ and $D_B \geq D_A$. Then $(D_B - D_A)/(p_A - p_B)$ has approximately a χ^2 distribution on $p_A - p_B$ degrees of freedom (df).

Important factors (and interactions) may be identified in two ways using the above ideas: by adding terms to a main effects model sequentially, or by removing terms from a saturated model sequentially. The two methods may produce a different set of important factors.

Over- (and Under-) Dispersion

Using the Poisson distribution for the counts implies the mean of the counts equals the variance. Commonly, the (estimated) variance is larger than the (estimated) mean; this is called *over-dispersion*. *Under-dispersion* is less common in practice.

The degree of over- or under-dispersion can be estimated using the Pearson estimator $\tilde{\phi} = X^2/(n-p)$ or the mean-deviance estimator $\hat{\phi} = D/(n-p)$. An estimate greater than 1 indicates over-dispersion, and an estimate less than 1 indicates under-dispersion. Serious over-dispersion results in inflated standard errors, and inferior inference.

In the case of over-dispersion, a negative binomial distribution may be of use. Discussion of this model is beyond the scope of this article.

Model Interpretation

It is often difficult to find an interpretation for a log-linear model, though some useful interpretations exist for two- and three-factor models. A table may be collapsed to aid understanding and interpretation; rather than use, for example, a $3 \times 4 \times 2$ table, there may be no information loss to consider the equivalent 3×2 table. This must be done with great care: in a three-factor case, a collapsed table cannot be formed unless at least the three-factor interaction and one two-factor interaction is unnecessary in the model.

This implies that a contingency table with more than two factors should not by analysed by considering each two-factor table separately.

Example: Fitting a Model

Consider the data in Table I with coding as defined above; numerous models are possible. Initially, however, it is

Table II Predicted Values, Deviance (D), Number of Estimated Parameters (p), and the AIC for Five Log-Linear Models Fitted to the Data in Table I

	Predictions from the models				
Count	*M1*	*M2*	*M3*	*M4*	*M5*
79	77.5	81.1	76.2	77.1	79
18	20.4	16.8	18.8	19.1	18
34	37.3	33.7	31.9	31.2	34
14	9.8	13.4	18.0	17.6	14
14	17.1	17.9	16.8	15.9	14
5	4.5	3.7	4.2	3.9	5
⋮	⋮	⋮	⋮	⋮	⋮
12	14.1	12.8	12.7	13.7	12
2	3.7	5.1	1.4	1.5	2
D	60.24	25.57	10.35	9.66	0.00
p	6	9	15	16	24
AIC	176.91	148.24	145.02	146.33	152.67

Note: Model 1 has only main effects; Model 2 has insufficient terms; Model 3 is a good model; Model 4 includes one unnecessary interaction term; Model 5 includes all interactions. For full details, see the text.

common to include all the main effects in the model. For this example, the main effects model (denoted $1+A+L+G+D$) gives a deviance of $D=60.24$ on 18 df.

There are six second-order interactions ($A.L, A.G, A.D, L.G, L.D$, and $G.D$), four third-order interactions ($A.L.G$, $A.L.D$, $A.G.D$, and $L.G.D$), and one fourth-order interaction ($A.L.G.D$), plus all the additive combinations of these. Commonly, but not universally, higher order interactions may be included only when lower order interactions are already in the model; these models are called *hierarchical* models. For example, the interaction $A.D.G$ is only permitted provided $A, D, G, A.D, A.G$, and $D.G$ are in the model. This reduces the number of possible models, but the number is still large.

One simple model is

$$1+A+L+G+D+A.L+D.G+A.G+A.D+A.D.G;$$

adding more terms does not produce a significant reduction in deviance.

As a demonstration, five models have been fitted here: Model 1 has only main effects; Model 2 adds the interaction $A.L$ and $D.G$ only; Model 3 is the model above; Model 4 adds the interaction $L.G$ unnecessarily to Model 3; and Model 5 is the saturated model. A comparison of the models is given in Table II. Note the deviance decreases as more terms are added, but the AIC begins to increase as unnecessary terms are added to the model.

In this example, Model 3 gives $\hat{\phi}=25.57/(24-9)=1.71$, indicating slight over-dispersion.

See Also the Following Articles

Contingency Tables and Log-Linear Models • Data Distribution and Cataloging

Further Reading

Agresti, A. (1996). *An Introduction to Categorical Data Analysis.* Wiley, New York.

Christensen, R. (1997). *Log-Linear Models and Logistic Regression,* 2nd Ed. Springer, New York.

Dobson, A. (2000). *An Introduction to Generalized Linear Models,* 2nd Ed. CRC/Chapman and Hall, London.

Fienberg, S. E. (2000). Contingency tables and log-linear models: Basic results and new developments. *J. Am. Statist. Assoc.* **95,** 643–647.

Gilbert, G. N. (1981). *Modelling Society: An Introduction to Loglinear Analysis for Social Researchers.* Allen & Unwin, London.

Hutcheson, G. D., and Sofroniou, N. (1999). *The Multivariate Social Scientist.* Sage, London.

Raftery, A. E. (2001). Statistics in sociology, 1950–2000: A selective review. *Soc. Methodol.* **31,** 1–45.

Longitudinal Cohort Designs

John Bynner
Institute of Education, London, United Kingdom

Glossary

age, cohort, and period effects The different extrinsic components of variation in a cohort study data point, as opposed to the intrinsic variation reflecting developmental processes unique to the individual.

attrition Loss of sample members due to death, movement, noncontact, or dropout from the study.

cohort Any subgroup of a population defined by a demographic attribute, such as age or gender, for which the members of the group are followed up individually across time.

event histories The individual record of statuses, such as jobs, partnerships, and housing, and their duration in the intervals between follow-ups.

fading relevance The tendency for theoretical frameworks that informed the early stages of the study and the variables used to operationalize them to lose scientific salience for later users of the data.

net and gross effects Changes in a population over time compared with changes in a population and among the population members over time.

period The historical era or time when data are collected.

prospective and retrospective enquiry The distinction between collecting event data contemporaneously with each sweep or retrospectively through recall.

quasi-experiment Follow-up of a treatment and a control group, when there has been no random allocation of individuals to the two conditions.

sequential and quasi-sequential cohort designs The distinction between designs that follow up different cohorts of the same age and those that follow up cohorts of different ages.

sweeps and waves The follow-up surveys to collect data at each time point as the cohort study progresses.

This article discusses the main features of cohort studies, examining their scientific aims and the main forms that they take within the context of longitudinal research designs and draw on a number of exemplar studies to illustrate their main features. The distinctions between the intrinsic and extrinsic (age, cohort, and period) components of the variation that they embrace are discussed. Methodological challenges are considered, focusing particularly on sample attrition, missing data, reliability, and validity, including the problem of "fading relevance." Ways of enhancing the data through administrative records are then discussed, bringing in the ethical questions that arise in relation to certain types of data linked at the individual level. Finally, it is concluded that despite their weaknesses, cohort studies are one of the most powerful instruments available to social scientists for understanding how the human life-course is shaped under changing conditions. They therefore fully merit the high levels of investment that go into them.

The Cohort Study

Growing interest in long-term life-course processes has led to a burgeoning of longitudinal cohort enquiries in social science—the equivalent of the large-scale facilities such as "atom smashers" in the physical sciences and the Human Genome Project in medicine. The 1994 inventory published by the European Science Foundation (ESF) (1985-1991) Network on Longitudinal Studies concerned with Individual Development lists over 500 studies that met the ESF criteria of follow-up with more than 30 subjects over more than three time points and a minimum of 3 years' duration. Another major inventory of U.S. longitudinal studies published by the Henry Murray Research Center in the Radcliff Institute at Harvard University, lists in 2003, 270 high-quality, fully documented studies available in their archive for secondary analysis.

What is meant by cohort study and what information can it provide that other types of research cannot? Cohorts were subdivisions of Roman legions, originally 10% (600–800) soldiers, but soon becoming any specified subdivision. The idea of a group "marching forward" from a home base to some designated destination carries over, in modern usage, to that of any subdivision of a population followed up through time. Age cohorts are identified with groups of a particular age; birth cohorts are defined as people born at a particular time. There are also sex cohorts and social class cohorts, cohorts defined by social situation, cohorts defined by health condition, and so on. Cohort studies are concerned with charting the development of such groups from a particular time point either prospectively, by following them up subsequently, or retrospectively, by asking them to recall past events in their lives.

In other words, cohort studies are about the life histories, recorded over a designated period, of sections of a population and the individuals who constitute them. They can throw light on the circumstances in early life that are associated with the population's characteristics in later life—what encourages development in particular directions and what appears to impede it? Development can be studied across any stage of life in any life domain: education, employment, housing, family formation, citizenship, and health.

There are, therefore, two immediate payoffs from cohort studies. They help in forecasting the effects of particular early experiences and circumstances on outcomes in later life. Working retrospectively from particular outcomes, they also provide the opportunity to model the life-courses of the people who exhibit the given outcomes. When the same model is applied to different cohorts, there is an opportunity to determine how social (or secular) change is affecting the parameters of the model and consequently the life-course processes involved. Thus, Glen Elder, one of the leading proponents of life-course studies, compared the lives of cohort members in the Oakland Growth study, starting with births in 1920–1921, with those of cohort members in the Berkeley Guidance study starting with births in 1928–1929. He used the comparison to demonstrate the dominance of the Great Depression in the United States as a lasting influence across the whole of the latter cohort's lives.

Cohort studies are therefore a special case of the broader set of longitudinal or panel enquiries defined by any set of measurements or observations taken on the same set of units across time. They contrast with other types of panel study that take whole cross sections of a population and follow them up over time, e.g., household panel studies, audience research panels, and product testing panels.

Interpreting Cohort Data

Cross-sectional data collected on repeated occasions are longitudinal at the macrolevel in the sense that they enable one to monitor the effects of societal (or secular) change on a population's characteristics—"net effects." Cohort data are essential for investigating changes in individuals within the population as well—"gross effects." These incorporate information about changes in the individual members of the cohort as well as the cohort as a whole and are essential for gaining any purchase on possible causal processes. Researchers need to know about sequences of life experiences and events, and which individuals appear to be affected by changes in their external environment, while others remain impervious to them. Thus, poor educational performance can be attributed in part to low parental aspirations, if changes in the former follow changes in the latter. A cross-sectional survey could establish only a correlation between parents' aspirations and children's educational attainment, with no basis on which to infer cause and effect.

Cohort studies come into the category of what are called "quasi-experimental designs." One cannot allocate individuals randomly to different conditions in the way that the "true experiment" demands. Hence, one can never be certain that a variable identified with an hypothesized cause is not confounded with another variable that has not been measured. Is it aspiration or social class that one is really measuring? On the other hand, one can unravel how particular life histories develop, and draw strong quantitative or qualitative inferences through the experience that some individuals rather than others have had, as to what has shaped them. Who moves up through the social structure, who moves downward, and who stays immobile?

Types of Research Design

Figure 1 shows the way that the cohort study relates to other kinds of research design. Each of the large blocks represents a population or (subpopulation) of a country. The vertical axis of each block shows chronological age and the horizontal axis shows the time (or "period") of data collection in chronological years. Each vertical section represents a population survey at a particular time point. Each horizontal section represents repeated surveys of a single age group across time—3 year olds, 10 year olds, and so on. Such "time series" of observations on one or more age groups or the whole population provide a means of monitoring changes in the population, indicating response to policy shifts or where policy development is needed. The Connecticut crackdown on drunk driving, which was accompanied by a fall in deaths from

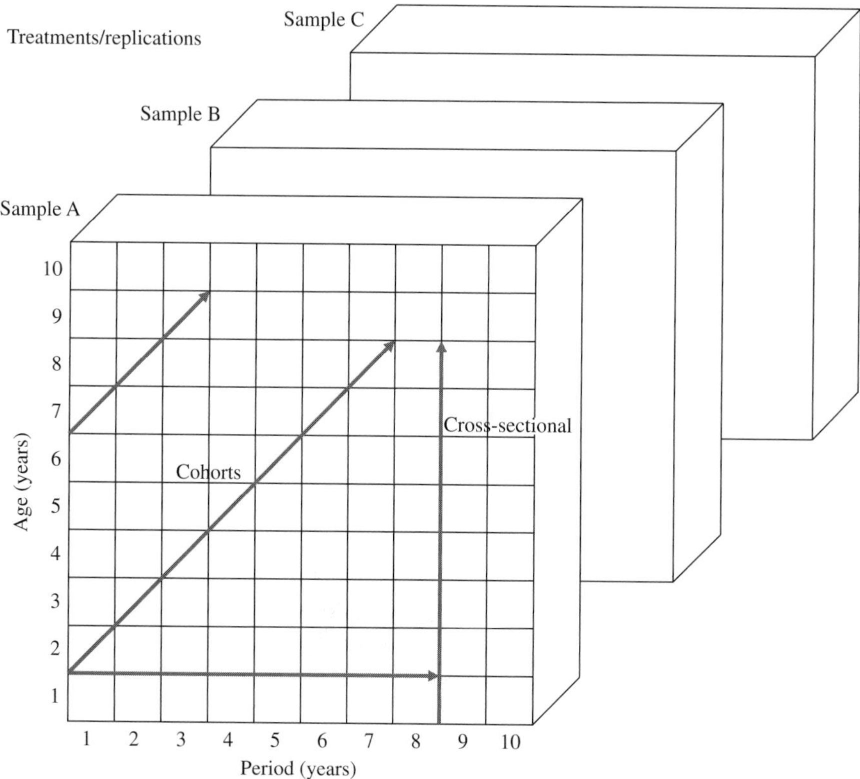

Figure 1 Longitudinal research designs.

driving, was used by Donald Campbell as an example of a quasi-experiment in his classic paper, *Reforms as Experiments*.

Cohort Designs

The cohort study is represented by the diagonal line, which shows the age the cohort has reached at each year in historical time. Thus, a baby born in the year 2002 will be age 8 in the year 2010 and age 43 in the year 2045. The cohort is generally identified here with a particular age group of a population usually described as a birth cohort because all the members must share a common age. These can encompass all births over the given year, as in the British Millennium Cohort Study (see Fig. 2), or all births in a single week, as in the earlier 1946, 1958 and 1970 cohort studies. The U.S. National Children's Study focusing on the effects of environmental factors (biological, chemical, physical, and social) on children's health, and scheduled to begin in 2005, will be based on 100,000 births with follow-up over the next 20 years. Many cohort studies follow a wider range of groups including the birth year conceived either as a single cohort or as a set of birth cohorts. The variable intervals between follow-ups are also shown in Fig. 2, indicating the scope for cross-cohort comparison. Cohort studies in Scandinavian countries, such as Sweden, start at much later ages than birth, e.g., 10 or 13 years of age, relying on the comprehensive administrative data held on state registers to supply information about earlier ages.

The cohort study can extend to multiple populations representing one or more countries, such as the Paths of the Generation Longitudinal Study established by Mik Titma following up high school graduates. In its second version, this extended from Estonia, where it began, to 15 countries and regions of the old Soviet Union—a sample size approaching 50,000 individuals. The study can also be based on the populations of different towns or regions within countries, such as the Dunedin Multi-Disciplinary Study and the Christchurch Child Development Study in New Zealand or the Malmo Longitudinal Study and the Gothenburg Evaluation through Follow-up Studies in Sweden, starting in 1938 and 1961 respectively. Alternatively, the study can involve follow-up of different groups (subpopulations), including those that have been subjected to some form of treatment or policy intervention, while others have not. Under "true" experimental conditions, there would be an allocation of individuals to such groups on a random basis, who then become the cohorts for investigation. In the absence of such allocation, i.e., the cohorts are naturally occurring, one has another form of quasi-experiment. The validity of such a design for experimental purposes depends on the extent to which the groups are matched with respect to all attributes related to the outcome.

The temporal sequencing of the longitudinal data that cohort studies produce offers a powerful means of control in comparison with a cross-sectional survey. One can monitor the circumstances and experiences through which cohort members' life histories unfold to assess how these interact with personal characteristics to produce particular social, economic, psychological, or health outcomes. Contemporary data accumulated over the life cycle—establishing the sequencing of events, circumstances, and characteristics—provide a particularly valuable tool in the search for causal explanations of differential development and its outcomes. Dated event histories can be used to describe and model dynamic processes, rather than the static states observed in cross-sectional "snapshots." Such possibilities have been greatly enhanced by advances in statistical methodology for the analysis of longitudinal data and the development of high-powered computer technology to apply them.

Sequential and Quasi-sequential Cohort Designs

Figure 1 also introduces another distinction in cohort study design: "sequential" or "quasi-sequential" cohorts. Sequential cohorts have a starting point on one of the horizontal lines. A series of birth cohorts is established with births separated by, for example, 2-, 5-, or 10-year intervals. This is the basis of the "youth cohort studies" set up in many countries to monitor the transition from compulsory schooling to the labor market. In contrast, the quasi-sequential design starts on one of the vertical axes in Fig. 1 and follows the cohorts defined by the different ages on it. For example, one might select age groups separated by 4-year intervals—7 year olds, 11 year olds, 15 year olds, 19 year olds—and follow them up over time. Such age groups are of course also a series of birth cohorts. The difference with the sequential cohorts design is that the latter has full information back to the starting age, whereas for the quasi-sequential design, age-based (developmental) data are missing in increasing amounts the older the cohort's starting age.

The advantage of the quasi-sequential cohort design is that the information is obtained much earlier from the study for older age groups than would be the case if they were all followed up from the same starting age. It will not be until the third decade of the new century, for example, that the "Millennium" birth cohorts started in a number of countries will yield data on adult life. A good example of the quasi-sequential cohort design is the U.S. National Longitudinal Study of Youth (NLSY). In the first and continuing NLSY, a set of age cohorts of 10,000 young people ages 14–21 have been followed up annually since 1979. The new NSLY starting in 1997 comprises a cohort of over 9000 young people ages 12–16 who have been followed up annually since 1997. In contrast, the Canadian National Longitudinal Study of Children that began in 1994–1995 embraces a younger set of cohorts extending from age 11 back to birth, comprising 25,000 children.

Case Control Studies

Another variant in design favored in medical enquiry particularly is the "case control study." This might be based on people with identified characteristics in adult life such as the long-term unemployed, those with criminal

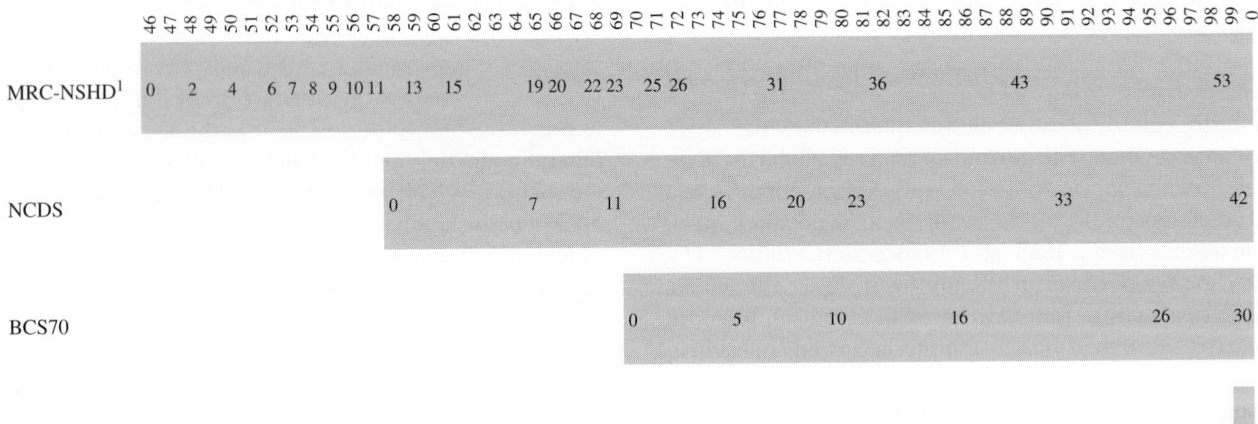

Figure 2 British Birth Cohort Studies Programme. *Note:* 1. Initial survey carried out at ca. 8 weeks. 2. Initial survey carried out at ca. 9 months.

records, or those having a particular medical condition, who are subsequently followed up with a matched control group not showing the specified criterion characteristic. In studies still at the stage of collecting data from children, high-risk and control groups can also be identified and followed up to determine whether hypothesized outcomes later in life are observed.

Intergenerational Studies

A final, though fairly rare, variant of the cohort study design extends data collection to the next generation—that of cohort members' children. This creates unique three-generation data sets involving cohort members, their parents, and their children, with the opportunity to identify intergenerational continuities and discontinuities in development, and the factors associated with these. The data can throw light on such central societal concerns as "cycles of deprivation," i.e., deprivation in families transmitted from one generation to the next. The first U.S. National Longitudinal Study of Youth, for example, collected data from and about female cohort members' children at 2-year intervals from 1986. The British National Child Development Study also collected such data in a substudy of one-third of cohort members and their children, when the cohort members had reached age 33. In such a design, however, the population is still defined by the cohort members because of the built-in logical dependency of the age of the child on the age of the mother. The children therefore must be seen as attributes of their parents and not as a cohort in their own right.

Age, Cohort, and Period Effects

In the 1960s, Schaie, followed by Baltes, pioneered the work on different components of variation in the data yielded by a cohort design. They drew attention to the distinctions between individual variation in the cohort at any particular time that is a function of the experience and biological make up of the cohort members—"intrinsic effects"—as opposed to that which is externally determined—"extrinsic effects." Cohort data confound three extrinsic sources of the individual variation, which need ideally to be accommodated in the research design: age, period, and cohort effects. Data collected at a particular time point in a cohort study may be a product of the age of the individual concerned (age effect), the time when the individual was born (cohort effect), and the period when data were collected (period or secular effect). These effects are logically related through the formula: Period = Age + Cohort and are therefore confounded with one another.

In the interest of unambiguous interpretation of cohort data, it is necessary to determine the significance of these effects and to exercise a degree of control over them through the research design. To assess the cohort effect, controlling for age and/or period (both cannot be controlled simultaneously), one needs to collect data from individuals of the same age but born at different times (cohorts). To assess the age effect, one needs to collect data from individuals of different ages controlling for cohort and/or period. To assess the period effect, one needs to collect data from individuals at different periods controlling for age and/or cohort. Such designs—though an improvement on the single cohort—can never overcome the confounding entirely because of the logical dependencies that remain. To isolate the effect of age, cohort, or period effects, independently of the others, one therefore must assume constancy of one of the effects that are not controlled. Thus, comparing 30 year olds born at 12-year intervals, as in the British birth cohort studies, controls the age effect, leaving cohort and period confounded. If the strong assumption can be made that there is no period effect, which might be reasonable for differences between cohorts in the prevalence of a health condition, for example, then it is justified to attribute variability between cohorts entirely to a cohort effect, i.e., differential exposure of the two cohorts to changing societal circumstances is producing the difference in the health outcome.

The subsidiary requirements of cohort data follow more precisely from the conceptualization of the phenomenon under investigation.

First, to understand long-term processes such as value formation or social exclusion, the developmental data must be collected over a substantial period of people's lives.

Second, to analyze variation within a society between individuals and between socially defined groups, it is necessary to have cohorts comprising large representative samples of the total population. Alternatively, the cohorts can comprise samples of groups with special characteristics with relatively low population prevalence, such as disability, with the facility of a baseline longitudinal study or matched control group for comparison. The most comprehensive cohort study designs combine both features, differentially stratifying the sample to ensure that groups of special scientific interest are adequately represented within a probability sample. Representation of the population as a whole can then be achieved through reweighting.

Third, to embrace societal change itself in the design, one needs ideally more than one birth cohort studied across time (sequential cohorts) or follow-up of broad cross sections embracing multiple age groups (quasi-sequential cohorts).

Fourth, to embrace the historical and cultural context of such change, one needs studies that involve more than one region or more than one country. This third "spatial" feature of cohort study defines with age period and cohort what Alwin, in 1994, referred to as the "space–time coordinates" of longitudinal study.

Finally, the cohort study design needs to incorporate the relevant variables for investigation of the phenomenon of interest. Much cohort study with a medical orientation restricts the data collected to a limited number of variables hypothesized to be implicated in the pathology of a particular medical condition. For studies of developmental processes such as educational achievement, it is necessary to ensure that the data not only embrace experience of the education system, but also the wide range of family circumstances, family and peer relations, and individual functioning and personal attributes that precede or accompany it.

From the above, it can be concluded that large-scale and long-term developmental studies, within what can be described as a broad life-course, or holistic, interdisciplinary perspective, are going to yield the best returns for behavioral and social science. Such developmental studies embrace circumstances and experience across the different domains of life, with a view to revealing connections between them across time.

Methodological Challenges

Attrition and Missing Data

The value of longitudinal study must be judged against the problems of collecting longitudinal data and the implications these have for data quality. Magnusson and Bergman, in 1990, set these out in the third of 10 books resulting from the work of the European Science Foundation's network on longitudinal research referred to earlier. The most serious of these data quality problems is "attrition"—the loss of sample members over time. Subjects may disappear from the study because they have died, moved house, changed their names (through marriage), or are simply no longer interested in taking part; others move in and out of the study depending on their availability at the time a particular survey is to be carried out.

Such changes in the cohort's composition can seriously weaken the research potential of the data. Sample loss reduces the numbers available for data analysis—a particular problem in longitudinal analysis that strictly requires complete records across the time span of the research. Attrition can also bias the data if those who leave the study are not typical of those who started it. On the other hand, unlike the cross-sectional survey, with any longitudinal data set there is full information about the characteristics of the sample when the study began. Accordingly, if reduction in the size of the cohort through attrition occurs differentially across groups, e.g., groups defined by socioeconomic status of parents, then the sample can be reweighted to restore the distributions of such key variables to the form they were earlier. This is only a partial solution, however, as the variables of central interest, on which the missing cohort members differ from those still participating, may not have been measured at the start of the study. The most effective cohort studies, therefore, place a large amount of investment in minimizing attrition by maintaining contact with the cohort in between surveys and tracing the present whereabouts of sample members through administrative records, and even national and local media publicity campaigns, when leading up to a new one.

Missing data are not restricted to loss of cohort members from the study. Nonresponse at the variable level due to respondent failure or refusal to answer a particular question, or accept a particular measurement, can occur across the data set. Much of this nonresponse is unlikely to be occurring at random and thus constitutes another source of potential bias in the data. Again, the problem multiplies across follow-ups, both reducing the numbers available for longitudinal analysis and increasing the bias. The solution must be an analytic one. There have been major developments in the statistical methodology for "imputing" missing data, which are increasingly applied in the analysis of cohort study. But again prevention is better than cure. Comprehensive development work involving much piloting and prepiloting of all survey procedures is an essential prerequisite for any new follow-up. They need to be minimally burdensome and maximally sensitive to the cohort member's situation.

Measurement Quality

Other data quality issues that are common to all social scientific enquiry arise but their effects are likely to be exacerbated in a cohort study. All measurement contains error, which reduces its reliability and can lead to incorrect inferences. This effect will again multiply for repeated measures across time. Questions of validity and usability also arise. Bias due to memory loss may be a serious problem, especially for studies in which events such as unemployment spells are recalled across intervals of several years. As theory shifts about the origins of behavior, i.e., the balance changes between biological, individual, situational, and environmental perspectives, so the variables entered into the design of the longitudinal study will change as well. Often theories in which cohort data are employed specify variables for which data have not been collected and those that have been are no longer of interest: the relevance of the data "fades" with time. The significance of the social and historical context of development, as exemplified in life span developmental psychology, ecological psychology, and life-course study, was not recognized in the more psychogenically oriented approaches to developmental processes that were prominent up to 20 years ago. Moreover, in designing a new follow-up in a cohort study, measurements taken earlier in the study may no longer be considered operationally adequate by those using the data later on, but to change them would rule out repeated measurement on which causal inference strictly depends.

The most effective multipurpose longitudinal studies overcome these measurement difficulties, by using well-developed and trusted measurement procedures, including standardized tests and structured interviews conducted by well-trained interviewers. Analysis can again also play a part through the specification and estimation of more generic and stable latent variables corrected for attenuation, which structural modeling methods such as LISREL offer. The team will also consult as widely as possible in their research communities about the critical variables to include in the attempt to optimize prospective usability before finalizing the data specification. Much effort is invested in documenting the data in considerable detail, and keeping the raw data alongside the computerized data set, so future researchers are able to recode answers in terms of more appropriate variables and new classifications. For example, the classification of occupations usually changes from one census to the next. The International Classification of Diseases is similarly subject to regular review and updating. Only by storing the raw data can researchers be sure that the most up-to-date classification is consistently applied across all data points.

The need to optimize measurement value also demands retention of full information about data sources, so that with cohort members' permission, if necessary, the original sources can be returned to for more information. Medical records have often been used in this way, especially in Scandinavian countries. Of course, it will not always be possible to do such tracking back through the cohort members' lives to enhance the data; often the data sources themselves, e.g., schools, teachers, doctors, and their records, will no longer exist. In such cases, either the past data must be reconstructed from present information, or from what can be recalled by subjects, or treated as "missing".

Retrospective Alternative

These formidable data quality issues in utilizing data collected in a prospective cohort study need to be set against the main alternative: the collection of cohort data entirely retrospectively. All cohort studies contain elements of retrospection to complete the record of events in between follow-ups. Nevertheless, all prospective studies are committed to collection of as much data as possible contemporaneously.

The completely retrospective approach has been effectively used in a program of research under the direction of Karl Ulrich Mayer of the Max Planck Institute for Human Development. Individuals were selected from the German Micro Census in three birth cohorts spanning a period of 50 years to find out to what extent cohort effects had brought about changes in employment and other aspects of life patterns. The Norwegian Life History Project is another example that covers the same period and has been used in comparative research with Germany. The advantage of the method is that the problem of attrition is solved, because there are complete samples of the contemporary population. Also, data collection can be targeted precisely on the variables of interest. The disadvantage of the approach is that problems of long-term memory decay make recall for many life events, such as job change and spells of unemployment, over anything more than a few years, of dubious accuracy. Methodological research involving overlapping recall periods for event histories in the same and different cohort studies (e.g., recall from age 30 to age 16 compared with recall from age 23 to age 16) point to 3 to 4 years as the maximum length of time over which such events as unemployment spells can be recalled accurately.

Even more seriously, although objective information, such as work, family formation, and housing histories, can in principle be collected retrospectively, certain kinds of data involving moods, feelings, states, attitudes, values, knowledge, and skills, can be assessed only at the time that individuals are experiencing them. Such variables are crucial mediators of social relations in transition processes. In studies of the life-course, one might therefore conclude that the best kinds of longitudinal data are those collected prospectively.

Finally, another important feature of cohort studies needs to be mentioned. Large-scale cohort studies can be expensive to carry out and, if they last a long time, require considerable commitment from a dedicated team to keep the study going. Maintaining a continuing flow of funds may be a major challenge, because of the peaks and troughs in activity corresponding to data collection follow-ups and the periods between them. The complexity of the cohort data and the post-fieldwork editing and coding that needs to be carried out before use means that there are also often extended delays before results are reported. More poignantly, those who start the study off are unlikely to be the ones to finish it, and as retirement or other interests beckon, there is always a danger that the study will die. This is why, rather in the nature of a small business, effective cohort studies need a well-funded infrastructure to ensure their continuation. It is where this has happened that the greatest potential for research on a given topic is likely to lie. Despite the huge expansion of longitudinal enquiry, there are still only a limited number of cohort studies that fully meet this requirement.

Data Enhancements and Ethics

The standard prospective cohort enquiry is likely to be relatively self-contained, relying on the research team to collect the required data from cohort members or their parents. There are potential benefits, however, from extending the scope of data collected to other administrative data sources. It is common to link aggregate data, such as local area unemployment and poverty rates, to large-scale cohort study data. More difficult issues arise in relation to linking individual level data.

Individual record linkage is widely employed in Scandinavia and in the United States, where data protection legislation has not inhibited its use as much as it has in some other countries. In its simplest form, record linkage may involve no more than linking administrative data, such as employment or housing records, to a cross-sectional survey of school children via the individual identifiers, when the sample has reached adulthood. In Scandinavian countries, such linkage extends to relying exclusively on state registers to supply the data in the early years of the study. More typically, the method is used in conjunction with longitudinal data collection from the cohort members throughout the study. Thus, Sweden's Project Metropolitan started with a sample of over 15,000 13 year olds in Stockholm in 1964. Childhood data were collected exclusively from education and other records. Further government administrative data were linked to the directly collected data from age 13 onward, including criminal convictions.

However, apart from data protection legislation and other government restrictions on the use of personal data obtained from administrative records for research, there are other problems with record linkage that need to be taken seriously. Administrative records often are inaccurate through clerical error or are incomplete; for example, large numbers of criminal acts go undetected. Thus, within a cohort study to which criminal convictions have been linked, there are likely to be large numbers of "false-negatives," i.e., people who have committed crimes but are not recorded as having committed them.

Another problem arises in relation to research ethics, but may also have practical consequences. Longitudinal data are collected from individuals on the basis of trust within an implicit or, in some cases, explicit contract between them and the researcher. They, or before them their parents, are assured of confidentiality and told that the data will be used only for specified purposes. Other people, such as doctors and teachers, supply data about them on this understanding. During adulthood, permission to use other sources, such as medical records, can be sought directly from the cohort member at the time of a survey. For records of a highly confidential nature, such as those having to do with tax, crime, drug problems, and abortion, the researcher is unlikely to seek permission, and if permission was sought, it is unlikely that it would be given. Using such data sources secretly not only raises the ethical problem of researcher probity, but may also damage the survey directly. If the news that such records have been used gets back to the cohort members, it is likely that many will withdraw from the study. In the case of the Stockholm-based Project Metropolitan, such feedback reached respondents through press reports and the study subsequently collapsed.

The best compromise is the pragmatic one of judging each question of data linkage on its merits. If the data from administrative sources are linked within a framework of what survey practitioners call "informed consent," i.e., it is very unlikely that the respondent, knowing the subject of the study, would object to their use, then it seems legitimate to use them. If there is any doubt about this, their use is best avoided.

Conclusion

This article has revealed the power of cohort studies as an aid to social scientific understanding, while also pointing to some of the problems in undertaking them. They can involve long-term commitment and large-scale funding. There is a risk that the data collected will prove irrelevant to later social scientific purposes. There may be heightened concern about data protection issues ruling out the use of data that may be central to the study's success. There may be growing unwillingness among members of the public and their children to commit themselves to collaboration with a research team involving the supply of information about themselves throughout their lives.

It is perhaps for these reasons that relatively few countries have engaged in large-scale cohort studies based on representative samples. For those that have—such as the United States, Great Britain, Sweden, New Zealand and Canada—there are rich social scientific rewards. A record of the changing lives of a country's citizens in response to social change has been described as a "treasure trove" for learning how the human life-course is shaped under different social conditions. Extending the scope of cohort studies comparatively through cross-national designs, and intergenerationally is the next stage in their development. In a rapidly changing world, there can be few better social scientific investments.

See Also the Following Articles

Age, Period, and Cohort Effects • Explore, Explain, Design • Longitudinal Studies, Panel • Quasi-Experiment

Further Reading

Alwin, D. F. (1994). Aging, personality and social change: The stability of individual differences over the adult life span. In *Life-Span Development and Behaviour* (D. Featherman, R. Lerner, and M. Perlmutter, eds.). Erlbaum, NJ.

Blossfeld, H.-P., and Rohwer, G. (2002). *Techniques of Event History Modelling.* Erlbaum, London.

Brooks-Gunn, J., Phelps, E., and Elder, G. H. (1991). Studying lives through time: Secondary data analyses in developmental psychology. *Dev. Psychol.* **27,** 899–910.

Bynner, J. (1996). *Use of Longitudinal Data in the Study of Social Exclusion*. OECD website, http://www.oecd.org/dataoecd/20/15/1856691.pdf

Chase-Lansdale, P. L., Mott, F. L., Brooks-Gunn, J., and Phillips, D. A. (1991). Children of the National Longitudinal Survey of youth: A unique research opportunity. *Dev. Psychol.* **27,** 918–931.

Davies, R., and Dale, A. (eds.) (1995). *Analysing Social and Political Change.* Sage, London.

Elder, G. H. (1999). *Children of the Great Depression: Social Change in Life Experience,* 25th anniversary Ed. Westview Press, Boulder, CO.

Ferri, E., Bynner, J., and Wadsworth, M. E. (2003). *Changing Britain, Changing Lives.* Institute of Education Press, London.

Giele, J. Z., and Elder, G. H. (1998). *Methods of Life Course Research.* Sage, London.

Janson, C. (1981). Some problems of longitudinal research in the social sciences. In *Longitudinal Research* (F. Schulsinger, *et al.*, eds.). Nijhoff, Dordrecht, The Netherlands.

Magnusson, D., and Bergmann, L. (1990). *Data Quality in Longitudinal Research.* Cambridge University Press, Cambridge, UK.

Mayer, K. H., and Schoeflin, U. (1989). The state and the life course. *Annu. Rev. Sociol.* **15,** 187–209.

Phelps, E., Furstenberg, F. F., and Colby, A. (2003). *Looking at Lives: American Longitudinal Studies of the 20th Century.* Sage, New York.

Robins, L., and Rutter, M. (1990). *Straight and Devious Pathways from Childhood to Adulthood.* Cambridge University Press, Cambridge, UK.

Schaie, K. W. (2000). The impact of longitudinal studies on understanding development from young adulthood to old age. *Int. J. Behav. Dev.* **24,** 257–266.

Shadish, K. W., Cook, T. D., and Campbell, D. (2001). *Experiments and Quasi-Experiments for Generalized Causal Inference.* Houghton-Mifflin, Boston, MA.

Longitudinal Studies, Panel

Scott Menard
University of Colorado, Boulder, Colorado, USA

Glossary

intraindividual change A transition in the attitudes, behaviors, or other characteristics of a specific individual, as opposed to an aggregate of individuals.

measurement interval The time between which measurements are taken; measurements may be taken continuously, but more often are taken at predefined intervals of minutes, hours, days, years, or longer periods, such as the 10-year measurement interval for the U.S. Census.

panel attrition The loss of research participants in the second and subsequent waves of data collection.

panel conditioning Changes in the responses of research participants as a result of their experience as participants in previous waves of the panel.

wave A measurement period, which may be a single moment in time or may span one or more years; the period for which the data are collected; panel studies involve two or more waves of data collection.

Longitudinal panel data have two defining characteristics. First, components (people, cities, nations) of the panel are measured for two or more points or intervals in time (the measurement periods, or waves). The act of measurement may occur only once, at the end of the last wave, or for all of the waves, in a retrospective panel design, or it may occur at the end of each period for which the data are being measured, in a prospective panel design. It is the number of periods for which, not at which, the data are measured that defines the longitudinal panel design. Second, at least one variable is measured for two or more waves. This is the longitudinal aspect of the data, which allows the measurement of qualitative or quantitative change within individuals or cases from one wave to the next. Strictly speaking, a longitudinal panel design is a time series design, insofar as the same participants are measured at two or more waves, but the term "time series" is usually reserved to refer to the repeated measurement of a single case or at most a few cases over many waves. Time series designs allow the measurement of change, but typically not for a panel of respondents representing a total population or a representative sample of that population.

Types of Longitudinal Panel Designs

Longitudinal panel designs in their purest form measure exactly the same participants at every wave, but this ideal is rarely met. In any longitudinal panel design, particularly involving individuals as study participants (although cities and nations change and even cease to exist as well), the study may not be able to follow every individual; some may die, some may relocate, and some may refuse to continue to participate in the research. In some panel designs, participants are added to the study. For example, in the 1992 Panel Study of Income Dynamics, data were collected about families and about all individuals in those families. The panel of individuals may thus not only be reduced by death, failure to locate, or refusal, but may also be increased by birth or marriage. New families have also been added as children have reached adulthood and moved out of the originally sampled household, or as a result of divorce between members of the original households. Allowing for both additions to and losses from a panel, a design that attempts to measure all of the individuals in a population at two or more waves may also be considered one variant of the longitudinal panel design, specifically a total-population design. In another variant of the longitudinal panel design, the revolving panel design, individuals are included in the panel for some number of measurement periods, then are replaced by other individuals. This was the design of the 1989 National Crime Victimization Survey.

The term "longitudinal panel design" is most often used, however, to refer to a design in which the same individuals are measured for every wave, with no additions to the panel and (in principle, but often not in practice) no losses from the panel. The research participants may all be drawn from a single birth cohort (people born in the same year), which results in a single-cohort longitudinal panel design, but more often the participants span several cohorts, which results in a multiple-cohort panel design. Because there are no additions and, ideally, few or no losses, the age structure of the panel changes over time; the oldest age at the last period is older than the oldest age at the first period, and the youngest age at the first period is younger than the youngest age at the last period. The 1989 National Youth Survey is an example of a multiple-cohort panel design; the data were first collected in 1976, when the research participants were 11–17 years old, and the same individuals were followed into adulthood, with the tenth and eleventh waves of data being collected in 2002 and 2003, when the original participants reached their late thirties and early forties. Figure 1 illustrates the structure of the designs for total population, a revolving panel, and a multiple-cohort panel.

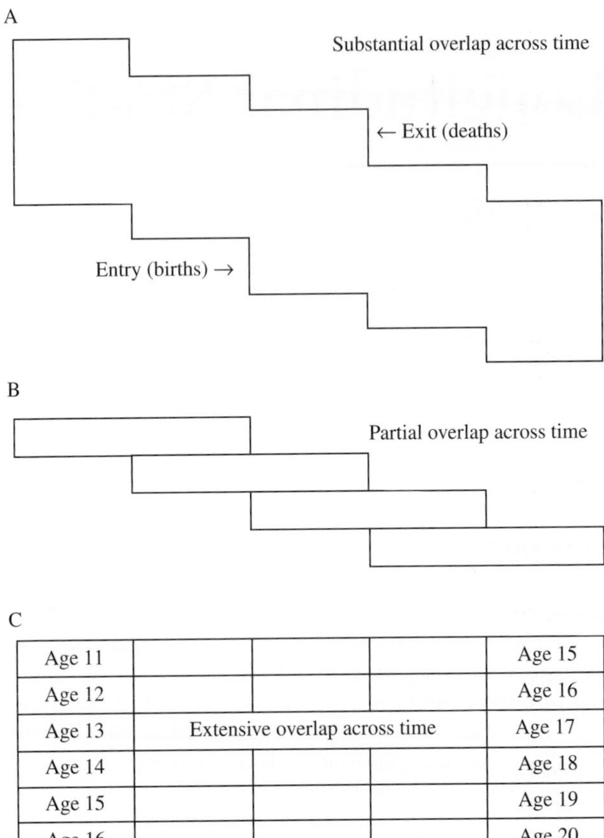

Figure 1 Longitudinal designs for data collection. (A) Total-population design; (B) revolving panel design; (C) multiple-cohort panel design.

Purposes of Longitudinal Panel Studies

Longitudinal research serves two primary purposes: to describe and explain patterns of change and to establish the sign (positive or negative), direction (from X to Y or from Y to X), and magnitude of causal relationships (a relationship of magnitude zero indicates the absence of a causal relationship). Change is typically measured with respect to one of two continua: chronological time or age. Both chronological time and age may be measured in the same units (seconds, minutes, days, or years), but chronological time is measured externally to the research participants, whereas age is an internal measure, in the sense that age is a characteristic of the individual but chronological time is not. Changes associated with age often represent developmental changes, i.e., physiological, psychological, or social contextual changes (for example, puberty, increasing absolute intelligence, and graduation from high school) that occur in conjunction with aging from childhood to adolescence to adulthood to old age. Changes associated with time often represent historical changes; these changes occur as a result of events external to the individual, but may have some common effect on individuals at different ages. It is also possible that historical changes interact with age, with the result that different age groups or cohorts experience different consequences from the same change.

Qualitative and Quantitative Changes

Changes may be qualitative or quantitative. In qualitative change, a particular change either did or did not occur; for example, the individual either got married or remained single. Qualitative changes may vary in specificity; in such cases, an individual did or did not, say, change political parties, or more specifically, changed from Democrat to Republican or from Republican to Democrat, the latter two transitions representing two different and more specific subsets of the more general change in political party. Qualitative change is thus typically measured as a yes-or-no dichotomy. Quantitative change, in contrast, is measured numerically, as the difference between an individual's "scores" or "ranks" on a characteristic at two waves. For ratio variables, but not interval variables, it may also make sense to calculate proportional change (the later score divided by the earlier score) or percentage change (the proportional change multiplied by 100), as long as division by zero is not involved. Changes may also occur in measures of relationships, such as correlation and regression coefficients, and these (because they are measured on a ratio scale) may be represented as differences or percentage changes. These and other measures of change have been described in the literature, but in all cases, the measurement of change at the individual level, whether the focus of the study is a person, a city, or a nation, requires panel data.

Longitudinal Panel Designs and the Study of Change

Longitudinal panel studies may be used to examine changes in individual characteristics within a single individual over time and age (for a single individual, the two cannot be separated), and also to examine changes in relationships among variables. Examples of change in individual characteristics include changes in physical characteristics such as weight, mental characteristics such as cognitive ability, and behavioral characteristics such as frequency of involvement in illegal behavior. Changes in relationships among variables as an individual ages could include the changing influence of diet on weight (a diet that once resulted in weight maintenance now results in weight gain), the changing influence of sleep on cognitive ability (more or less sleep is needed for peak mental performance), and the changing influence of family attachment on involvement in illegal behavior (the influence of the family may first decline from early to late adolescence, then increase in early adulthood). Changes in characteristics and relationships can be historical as well as developmental. For example, at the national level, fertility and mortality rates may decline over time, and the relationship between mortality and fertility rates may be higher or lower in one period than in another.

Single- or multiple-cohort panel designs, in contrast to total-population and revolving panel designs, cannot provide comparable age-specific cross-sectional data from one wave to another (because the age spans are different in different waves), except possibly for a subset of the original sample. For example, in the multiple-cohort panel design diagrammed in Fig. 1, it is possible to compare respondents at ages 15 and 16 at the first and last waves of the panel. The multiple-cohort panel design is, however, well suited to the analysis of developmental changes. The revolving panel design, particularly when it involves a relatively short time span (3 years for the National Crime Victimization Survey), is not as well suited to the measurement of developmental change, because it may cover too small a segment of the life course for the developmental changes of interest to manifest fully. The revolving panel design can, however, provide a reasonably comparable cross-section of individuals at each wave, so it is better than the multiple-cohort panel design for tracing historical changes that occur in aggregates of individuals over time. The total-population design has in principle both the advantage of comparable cross-sections over time plus the ability to follow individuals over a relatively long time span, and can thus be used to study both developmental and historical change.

Longitudinal Panel Designs and the Study of Causal Relationships

In order to establish the existence of a causal relationship between any pair of variables, three criteria are essential: (1) the phenomena or variables in question must covary, as indicated, for example, by differences between experimental and control groups or by a nonzero correlation between the two variables; (2) the relationship must not be attributable to any other variable or set of variables—that is, it must not be spurious, but must remain nonzero even when other variables are controlled experimentally or statistically; and (3) the presumed cause must precede or be simultaneous in time with the presumed effect, as indicated by the change in the cause occurring no later than the associated effect it is supposed to produce. Evidence for covariation may easily be obtained from cross-sectional data. Evidence for nonspuriousness is never really sufficient (there is always something else that could have been controlled), but evidence for spuriousness or its absence in the presence of the controls used in a particular study can also be obtained from cross-sectional data. In some instances, it is also possible to infer temporal (and implicitly causal) order from cross-sectional data. For instance, whether an individual is male or female, along with other genetically determined characteristics, is determined at birth, and necessarily precedes any voluntary behavior on the part of the individual. Thus, although being male is a plausible cause of violent behavior (with respect to covariation, time ordering, and perhaps nonspuriousness), violent behavior is not realistically plausible as a cause of being male.

In the social sciences, however, we are often dealing with time-varying characteristics, and the order of change may not be readily ascertainable at the level of the individual research participant without longitudinal panel data. In the case of qualitative changes, with a short enough measurement interval (the time from one wave to the next), it should be possible to determine which of two changes occurred first (or that they occurred at the same time). That one change preceded another is not sufficient to support the claim that the first change must have caused the second (the "post hoc ergo propter hoc," or "after therefore because of," fallacy), because the criteria of covariation and nonspuriousness must also be satisfied, but it does mean that the second change can probably be ruled out as a cause of the first. For example, in one study, the proposition that substance use (underage alcohol use and illicit drug use) caused other illegal behavior (violent and property crime) was examined; the findings were that the initiation of substance use typically came after, not before, other illegal behavior. Although this evidence does not establish other illegal behavior as a cause of substance use, it seriously weakens the case that initiation of other illegal behavior is a result of substance use, insofar as an effect cannot precede a cause. Besides initiation or onset of a behavior, other possible qualitative changes include escalation of attitudes or behaviors (entry of a higher state on an ordinal scale), de-escalation or reduction (entry of a lower state on an ordinal scale), and suspension (permanent or temporary exit from all states that indicate involvement in a particular kind of behavior or agreement with a particular attitudinal statement).

Issues in Longitudinal Panel Designs

Longitudinal panel designs have the same problems associated with cross-sectional research, and also have additional problems that are not encountered in cross-sectional designs, including problems of (1) changes in measurement over time, and the related problem of distinguishing unreliability in measurement from true change, (2) repeated measurement and panel conditioning, (3) respondent recall, and (4) missing data and panel attrition. In addition to the increased problems, however, longitudinal panel designs offer something that is not readily available in other research designs, i.e., the possibility of detecting and adjusting for these problems, particularly missing data.

Unreliability of Measurement and Measurement Change

In longitudinal panel research, the usual issues of internal and external validity and measurement reliability arise. Measurement reliability may be measured by either test–retest reliability, with a suitably short interval between test and retest, or by internal consistency measures, such as Cronbach's alpha or factor analytic techniques. The issue of longitudinal reliability arises from the possibility that even when identical measurement instruments are used in different waves, and even more when they are not, differences in administration or life course changes may lead to the result that what is measured at one wave is not really comparable to what is measured at another. Four more specific issues within the broader framework of longitudinal reliability illustrate the dilemmas that may arise: consistency of administration, consistency of observation, factorial invariance, and changes in measurement.

Even if the same survey or psychometric tests are administered in each wave of a panel study, how the questions are administered may vary in more obvious or more subtle ways. An example of this is the change from face-to-face to telephone interviews in the National Crime Victimization Survey and the Panel Study of Income Dynamics. More subtle changes may include changes in instructions to interviewers (or in the interviewers' actual behavior, regardless of instructions); one example is whether certain responses elicit probes from the interviewer. The setting of a psychometric test may change, for example, from the researcher's office to the respondent's home or school. These changes in administration all represent inconsistencies in administration, and raise the question of whether any apparent change (or absence of change) in responses from one wave to another represents real changes (or their absence) in characteristics of the research participants, or merely changes in how the participants respond to the administration of the survey or test. Observational inconsistency closely parallels inconsistency in administration. When the observer becomes the measurement instrument, as in ethnographic research, the question arises whether reported changes represent true change in the individuals being observed, or merely changes in the perceptions or perspective of the observer.

When the same sets of items on a scale have the same relationship to the scale (and thus to one another) in each wave of a panel study, the result is called factorial invariance. Strict factorial invariance insists that the numerical relationship be identical across waves; a weaker form of factorial invariance insists only that the same items "belong" to the same scale (as indicated by some numerical criterion, but the numerical relationship need not be exactly the same) at each wave. Factorial invariance is compromised when the relationship of one item to the scale changes. The first question that arises when factorial invariance is absent is whether we are measuring the same variable from one wave to the next, and hence whether it is possible to measure change in that variable, one of the core criteria of longitudinal panel research. If the variable being measured is not the same from one wave to the next, or even if it is the same variable, but measured differently, a second question that arises is whether any change in the relationship of this variable to other variables in the study (or, again, an apparent absence of change) can be attributed to real change (or its absence) or merely to a change in measurement.

In some instances, researchers may deliberately change the measurement instrument (including the observer, in ethnographic studies) from one wave of a panel to another. This may be done to incorporate a "new and improved" measure, because questions that were appropriate at an earlier age or stage of the life course (e.g., how well a student is doing in school at age 14) may no longer be appropriate, or because new questions that would have been inappropriate at an earlier age or stage (e.g., how well an individual is doing at work at age 34) are now appropriate. Of course, it is possible that, for some individuals, work is an important context at age 14 or school is an important context at age 34, but what about ages 9 and 59? In this example, the introduction of new questions without eliminating old ones, or the elimination of old questions without adding new ones, would constitute a change in survey administration, adding to or subtracting from the length of the survey, but the inclusion of the same set of questions at all waves, regardless of their appropriateness to the age or stage of the respondent, could risk unwillingness of the respondent to participate in a survey that seems irrelevant. Unless the same questions are asked in the same order, in the same way, at every wave, the question of comparability of administration arises. Yet at the same time, if the survey covers a substantial span of the life course, the same question at different ages or stages may not have the same meaning for the respondent, either subjectively or in its empirical relationship with other scale items or variables.

Repeated Measurement and Panel Conditioning

Panel conditioning (or in experimental and quasi-experimental research, the effect of testing) refers to the empirical observation that past experience with a psychometric test or a survey questionnaire may lead a respondent to respond differently, compared to how he or she would have responded had the same test been administered at the same time, but without any prior experience on the part of the respondent with the test or survey. For example, different responses to the same question on a survey may lead either to (1) skipping a series of questions or to (2) additional follow-up questions. Respondents may be tempted to answer in a way that avoids the follow-up questions if they regard the follow-ups as burdensome. Alternatively, they may be tempted to give an inappropriate answer that does lead into the follow-up questions if they find the questions particularly interesting! Study participants may also experience real changes as a result of the research, above and beyond the effects that would be expected from their characteristics and environment. For one example, the questions in a survey may provoke a respondent to reflect explicitly and seriously on his/her behavior, and to reassess and attempt, perhaps successfully, to change that behavior. Another possibility is that ethical requirements for the treatment of human participants in mental health research may lead researchers to offer to provide referrals to individuals who show evidence of severe mental health problems, and this in turn may lead to a change in the behavior or psychological condition that would otherwise not have occurred. The problem of panel conditioning appears to be more severe for relatively shorter measurement intervals (for example, 6 months as opposed to a year or more), but it is not clear whether the length of the test or interview has a substantial impact on panel conditioning.

Respondent Recall

Research on short- versus long-term retrospective data typically indicates that (1) memories tend to fade with time; (2) short- and long-term recall data on more salient events or attitudes tend to be more consistent compared to data on less salient events or attitudes; (3) short- and long-term recall data on objective events or characteristics tend to be more consistent compared to data on attitudes or other psychological data; and (4) differences between short- and long-term recall data indicate that the long-term recall data tend to be biased to reflect respondents' current views and attitudes. Regarding this last point, people tend to reconstruct and reinterpret their memories to reflect their current life situations and attitudes, in effect constructing a consistent "life story" for themselves. The potential consequence of this is to generate inconsistencies when prospective (or short-term recall) and retrospective (or long-term recall) data are compared for the same respondents, and the evidence appears to indicate that the prospective data are more valid, both with respect to whether certain events actually occurred, and also with respect to the precise timing of those events. This is not to say that long-term recall data are consistently unreliable or invalid, but it does suggest that they should be used with caution, and that, whenever possible, the shorter term recall data characteristic of prospective longitudinal designs are to be preferred. Attempts have been made to reduce errors associated with long-term recall, but research on the effectiveness of these attempts is generally inconclusive.

Panel Attrition and Missing Data

Missing data can occur in both cross-sectional and longitudinal research, but longitudinal panel research involves more possible types of missing data and more ways in which to address the problem. In longitudinal data, it is possible to have data missing (1) for a single item on a multiple-item scale, (2) for an entire scale, (3) for a particular case at a particular wave but not for all waves (wave nonresponse), (4) for a particular case after the first, second, or subsequent waves [that is, the individual is permanently lost to the study (panel attrition)], or (5) for a particular case for all waves, (for example, as a result of initial nonresponse). Regardless of the type of missing data, there is always a risk that it will lead to biased estimation of predictive or causal models, or inaccurate estimation of descriptive statistics such as means, standard deviations, or trends.

For missing items, if most items in a scale are available, it may be relatively simple to substitute the respondent's scale mean for the missing item, with some confidence that the resulting estimate is likely to be better than just deleting the case with the missing data from the analysis. When a whole scale is missing, there are several choices; none of them is entirely satisfactory, but some at least offer the prospect of improvement over dropping the case entirely. For longitudinal panel data in particular, one possibility is interpolation of data, using data from previous and subsequent waves to estimate the missing data, but this approach, although potentially useful for causal analysis, is problematic for the analysis of change in the variable that has the missing data. For wave nonresponse or initial nonresponse, if there is a clear pattern of "missingness" by a variable that has been measured (e.g., ethnicity or socioeconomic status), weighting cases so that the cases most like the missing cases "count" a little more is a frequently used option; this will reduce potential bias, but it depends on the degree to which the cases that are missing are similar to the nonmissing cases with the same characteristics (again, e.g., ethnicity or socioeconomic status), with respect to other variables and relationships. Alternatively, for wave nonresponse, it is possible to attempt to model the nonresponse, or to interpolate or extrapolate data based on previous or subsequent waves. Insofar as respondents are lost in later waves of data collection, the measurement of change may be confounded because those respondents who are lost may differ from those who are retained in some systematic way (they may have had different average values on variables to begin with, or they may have changed in ways different from the rest of the sample). This is especially serious if losses come disproportionately from those with extreme values on the variables on which the research focuses (for example, the most frequent illicit drug users or the most serious criminals in studies of illegal behavior). It is thus not only the magnitude of attrition, but also the pattern of attrition with respect to critical variables in the study, that may be problematic. It may be possible to use standard statistical tests to see whether, for example, individuals who continued in later waves differed significantly from individuals who were lost in later waves with respect to (1) values on particular variables, (2) strength of relationships (e.g., correlations) among variables, or (3) the structure of relationships (e.g., multiple regression equations or covariance structure) among sets of three or more variables. Still, it remains possible that some source of sample variability that significantly affects the substantive outcome of the analysis may be overlooked. For example, individuals with different behavioral trajectories (e.g., increasing as opposed to decreasing drug use) may be differentially likely to remain in or drop out of the panel, and this may not be readily detectable using the previously suggested methods. This could seriously bias substantive results such as the estimation and explanation of developmental trends in behavior, and may be extremely difficult to detect.

In retrospective panel designs, the problem of attrition takes a different form, one not amenable to assessment by the use of tests of statistical significance. Instead of problems associated with respondents leaving the panel after the first wave of data collection, retrospective studies may have problems of selection. Especially for long-term studies, retrospective studies may miss individuals who, for example, died or moved out of the area from which the sample was drawn, and who did so during the period for which the data were collected. Those individuals may differ systematically from the rest of the population. For example, frequent users of illicit drugs may have higher mortality than the rest of the population. If this is so, then frequent illicit drug users will be undersampled for the period of the study, and this may bias estimates of change in rates of illicit drug use. In effect, this is a problem of attrition, but attrition that takes place before the sample is drawn. It is much more difficult to detect and measure this type of attrition compared to the attrition that arises in conjunction with prospective panel designs.

Analysis of Longitudinal Panel Data

Longitudinal data analysis confronts two major issues: first, the separation of developmental (age) and historical (period) change and their possible interaction, and second, the interdependence among observations of the same variable for the same individual at different times. If we operationalize age as the year of birth, period as calendar year, and cohort as the year of birth, then any one of these three variables is completely determined by the other two; for example, cohort = calendar year − age. Because they are linearly dependent, it is difficult to separate age, period, and cohort effects analytically. Possible solutions to this problem are (1) the use of dummy variable regression models, (2) reconceptualizing the cohort in terms of an event other than birth (for example, entry into the labor force, which may eliminate the linear dependency), or (3) replacing cohort, measured as year of birth, with some characteristic of the cohort (for example, cohort size) in which we are really interested.

Although we are sometimes specifically interested in the effect of being a certain age at a certain time, it is more often the case that it is not the year of birth, but some other characteristic of the cohort in which we are interested, or else that we are only concerned with the cohort effect as a nuisance variable, i.e., something that may confound our analysis of developmental and historical change. An important point is that although age and a period are both measures of time, a cohort is not; it is an aggregation of individuals, a unit of analysis, rather than a continuum along which change can be measured.

Regarding the issue of mutually dependent observations, longitudinal panel data by definition involve two or more observations on the same individuals. Many statistical techniques assume that the observations or measurements of variables are mutually independent, but this is clearly unlikely when the same individual is measured on the same variable more than once, especially for relatively shorter as opposed to longer measurement intervals. Yet additional observations on the same variable for the same individual do provide additional information for causal analysis and especially for the measurement and analysis of intraindividual change, which is based on the expectation that the measure of a variable at one time for an individual is very likely to be related to a later measurement of the same variable for the same individual. One problem that may arise in the analysis of longitudinal panel data is bias in inferential statistics. The interdependence of the observations typically leads to underestimates of the standard errors of estimation, and this in turn increases the risk of Type I error (rejecting the null hypothesis when the null hypothesis is true). A second problem is that apparent intraindividual change (or stability) may be a result of positively (or negatively) correlated within-individual measurement error. This systematic, nonrandom error most typically leads to overestimation of stability and underestimation of the causal impact of other variables in models of change.

A wide range of techniques is available for longitudinal analysis, depending on the number of cases, the number of periods, and the specific research issue (causal analysis of differences; description and analysis of the occurrence and timing of change) for which the analysis is being performed. Specific to longitudinal panel studies, the number of cases is typically large and the number of waves ranges from relatively few (3–10) to relatively many (over 50). For relatively few waves, linear panel analysis and latent growth curve models using structural equation models are often employed, and are especially amenable to the analysis of correlated error structures. When there are many cases and many waves, structural equation models can, in principle, be used, but in practice, because of the technical requirements of structural equation analysis software, they tend to be used for shorter series (fewer waves); with many waves of data, it may become difficult to obtain reliable estimates for complex models. For both relatively few and relatively many waves, event history or survival analysis methods and multilevel growth curve models may be used to model causal relationships and change. For a panel involving few cases and many periods, time series analysis may be appropriate. All of these analytical techniques statistically adjust for the fact that the observations in a longitudinal panel are not independent, but are repeated for individual research participants or cases.

See Also the Following Article

Longitudinal Cohort Designs

Further Reading

Bijleveld, C. C. J. H., van der Kamp, L. J. T., Mooijaart, A., van der Kloot, W. A., van der Leeden, R., and van der Burg, E. (1998). *Longitudinal Data Analysis: Designs, Models, and Methods.* Sage, Thousand Oaks, California.

Blossfeld, J., Hamerle, A., and Mayer, K. U. (1989). *Event History Analysis: Statistical Theory and Application in the Social Sciences.* Lawrence Erlbaum, Hillsdale, New Jersey.

Cantor, D. (1989). Substantive implications of longitudinal design features: The National Crime Survey as a case study. In *Panel Surveys* (D. G. Kasprzyk, G. Duncan, G. Kalton, and M. P. Singh, eds.), pp. 25–51. Wiley, New York.

Elliott, D. S., Huizinga, D., and Menard, S. (1989). *Multiple Problem Youth: Delinquency, Substance Use, and Mental Health Problems.* Springer-Verlag, New York.

Finkel, S. E. (1995). *Causal Analysis With Panel Data.* Sage, Thousand Oaks, California.

Hill, M. S. (1992). *The Panel Study of Income Dynamics: A User's Guide.* Sage, Newbury Park, California.

Kaplan, D. (2000). *Structural Equation Modeling: Foundations and Extensions.* Sage, Thousand Oaks, California.

Kessler, R. C., and Greenberg, D. F. (1981). *Linear Panel Analysis: Models of Quantitative Change.* Wiley, New York.

Menard, S. (2002). *Longitudinal Research,* 2nd Ed. Sage, Thousand Oaks, California.

Raudenbush, S. W., and Bryk, A. S. (2002). *Hierarchical Linear Models: Applications and Data Analysis Methods,* 2nd Ed. Sage, Thousand Oaks, California.

Rutter, M., Maughan, B., Pickles, A., and Simonoff, E. (1998). Retrospective recall recalled. In *Methods and Models for Studying the Individual* (R. B. Cairns, L. R. Bergman, and J. Kagan, eds.), pp. 219–242. Sage, Thousand Oaks, California.

Taris, T. W. (2000). *A Primer in Longitudinal Data Analysis.* Sage, Thousand Oaks, California.

Yaffee, R., and McGee, M. (2000). *An Introduction to Time Series Analysis and Forecasting with Applications of SAS and SPSS.* Academic Press, San Diego.

Zeller, R. A., and Carmines, E. G. (1980). *Measurement in the Social Sciences: The Link Between Theory and Data.* Cambridge University Press, Cambridge, UK.

Mahalanobis, Prasanta Chandra

C. Radhakrishna Rao
Pennsylvania State University, University Park, Pennsylvania, United States

Glossary

Central Statistical Organization (CSO) A government agency at the federal level to oversee data collecting and reporting activities at the national and state levels.

***D*^{2}** The Mahalanobis distance; a measure of dissimilarity between individuals or objects based on multiple measurements.

Indian Statistical Institute (ISI) A research and teaching institution established in 1931.

International Statistical Education Center (ISEC) An organization established in 1950 to train statistical personnel from Asian and other developing countries.

National Sample Survey (NSS) A large-scale sample survey started in India in 1950 to collect socioeconomic data on a continuing basis.

operations research (OR) A technique developed during the Second World War for optimum use of resources.

statistical quality control (SQC) Special statistical techniques developed for use in industry to maintain a specified quality of goods in production and in research and development programs.

The Professor, as Prasanta Chandra Mahalanobis was popularly known, was a physicist by training, a statistician by instinct, and a planner by conviction. He became a professor of physics at Presidency College (Calcutta) in 1922 after completing the Physics Tripos program at Cambridge University (United Kingdom) and taught physics for over 30 years. His statistical interests led him to found the Indian Statistical Institute (ISI) for advanced research and training in statistics and to start a new journal in statistics, *Sankhyā*, both of which enjoy an international reputation. Lack of formal training in economics did not prevent Professor Mahalanobis from undertaking a major responsibility in drafting the Second Five Year Economic Plan for India. He believed in perspective planning and used simple logical ideas in deriving an econometric model for planning in underdeveloped countries. As a member of the Planning Commission, he advocated making large investments in heavy industries, setting aside other sectors of development, a policy that helped the country considerably in achieving rapid industrialization, although agricultural development received a temporary setback. That a physicist-turned-statistician, rather than professional economists, had played a more important role in India's national economic planning could only be true of Mahalanobis, with his sharp intellect and versatile interests.

Early Life

Prasanta Chandra Mahalanobis was born on June 29, 1893 into a family well established in Calcutta; the relatively wealthy family members were enterprising, adventurous, and imbued with liberal traditions. The contacts Mahalanobis had with the great intellectuals and social reformers of Bengal prepared him for the active life he was to lead over the next 79 years.

Mahalanobis received his early education in the Brahmo Boys School in Calcutta, where he passed the entrance (later called matriculation) examination in 1908. He entered Presidency College in Calcutta in the same year and passed the intermediate examination in science in 1910; he earned a Bachelor of Science degree with honors in physics in 1912.

Mahalanobis left for England in the summer of 1913 and joined King's College in Cambridge. He took part I of the Mathematical Tripos program in 1914, and part II of the Physics Tripos program in 1915, which he passed with first-class honors. After finishing the Physics Tripos program, Mahalanobis arranged to work with C. T. R. Wilson at the Cavendish Laboratory in Cambridge and returned to India for a short vacation. But Mahalanobis did not go to Cambridge; during what was to be a brief vacation at home in India, he found a number of problems that so engaged his attention that he did not leave. The story of Mahalanobis would have been different if he had gone back to Cambridge and worked in physics. He might have contributed richly to our understanding of the universe, but the modern development of statistics, which is fundamental to all sciences for information gathering, information processing, and decision making under uncertainty, would have received a great setback. Soon after his return to India, Mahalanobis accepted a teaching position in Presidency College in Calcutta. It was still his intention to return to Cambridge to do research in physics, but he soon gave up the idea because he found so many issues in India that held his interest and absorbed all of his working time.

At the time that Mahalanobis was scheduled to depart form Cambridge to return to India, World War I was on and there was a short delay in his planned journey. Mahalanobis utilized this time browsing in the King's College library. His tutor, Macaulay, found him there one morning and drew his attention to some bound volumes of *Biometrika*, presented by the editor, Karl Pearson, an Honorary Fellow at King's. Macaulay asked Mahalanobis for his opinion of the volumes, and Mahalanobis got so interested that he bought a complete set of *Biometrika* published up to date and brought them to India. He started reading the volumes on the boat during his journey and continued to study and work out exercises on his own during his spare time after arrival in Calcutta. He saw that statistics, a new science connected with measurements and their analysis, had the potential for wide applications. He tried to look for problems where he could apply the new knowledge he was acquiring. Fortunately, he found some extremely interesting problems in educational testing, meteorology, and anthropology, and started working on them. This was the turning point in his scientific career.

It was an accident that brought Mahalanobis into statistics. But it proved to be a lifelong struggle to develop statistics in India the way he had visualized it. Statistics was known in India only in the sense of official data obtained as a by-product of administration. It was not recognized by the universities, research institutes, or academic bodies as a separate discipline, and other scientists did not take kindly to statistics. Government bureaucracy was quite opposed to the introduction of new methods or making changes in existing practices, thus Mahalanobis had to struggle on all fronts—with the scientists and with the government officials—to advance the cause of statistics in India.

Contributions to Statistics

Mahalanobis Distance

The first opportunity to use statistical methods came to Mahalanobis when N. Anandale (then director of the Zoological Survey of India) asked Mahalanobis to analyze anthropometric measurements taken on Anglo-Indians (of mixed British and Indian parentage) in Calcutta. This study led, in 1922, to the first scientific paper published by Mahalanobis, and it was followed by other anthropometric investigations, leading to formulation of the D^2 statistic. The D^2 statistic, known in the statistical literature as the "Mahalanobis distance," is widely used in taxonomic classification.

Suppose each individual of a population is characterized by p measurements. The means (average) of the p measurements can be represented as a point in a p-dimensional space. Corresponding to k given populations, we have a configuration of k points in the p space. If $p = 2$, the points can be represented on a two-dimensional chart, and the affinities between populations, as measured by nearness of mean values, can be graphically examined. We may find that some populations are close to each other in the mean values of the characters studied, thus forming a cluster. The entire configuration of points may then be described in terms of distinct clusters and relations between clusters. We can also determine the groups forming clusters at different levels of mutual distances. Such a description may help in drawing inferences on interrelationships between populations and speculating on their origins.

If p is larger than 2, graphical examination becomes difficult or impossible. How might the difference between the mean vectors of, for example, populations 1 and 2 be sensibly measured? Call these vectors δ_1 and δ_2. A direct approach (one that had been used by anthropologists) works with the squared length of the column vector $\delta_1 - \delta_2$,

$$(\delta_1 - \delta_2)'(\delta_1 - \delta_2),$$

but this approach pays no attention to internal population covariation among the coordinates, nor to heterogeneity of variances. A related disadvantage of this simple sum-of-squares distance is its noninvariance under linear transformations of the coordinate system.

Mahalanobis, perhaps motivated by his studies of mathematical physics, suggested a more useful kind of distance when the dispersion (variance—covariance) matrix of the two populations is the same, say $\wedge$. The Mahalanobis distance, traditionally given in squared form and called D^2, is

$$D^2 = (\delta_1 - \delta_2)'\wedge^{-1}(\delta_1 - \delta_2),$$

so that D^2 is in a sense the standardized squared difference between δ_1 and δ_2, generalizing the univariate version of the standardized difference $(\mu_1 - \mu_2)^2/\sigma^2$, where σ^2 is the common variance and μ_1 and μ_2 are mean values. If Λ is a common dispersion matrix for all k populations, it is then possible to examine the $k(k-1)/2$ different D^2 values and apply on them various statistical analyses, including cluster analysis. One large-scale anthropometric cluster analysis was published by Mahalanobis and colleagues in 1949. Fuller and more precise statements of this exposition appeared in Mahalanobis' later writings.

Mahalanobis argued that inferences based on distances among populations might depend on the particular measurements chosen for study. The configuration may change, and even the order relations between distances may be disturbed, if one set of measurements is replaced by another set. In 1936, Mahalanobis therefore laid down an important axiom for the validity of cluster analysis, the dimensional convergence of D^2.

When a comparison between two real populations is made, ideally all possible (relevant) measurements, typically infinite in number, should be considered. Consequently, cluster analysis of a given set of populations should ideally be based on distances computed on an infinite number of measurements. If D_p^2 and D_∞^2 denote Mahalanobis distances between two populations based on p characters and all possible characters, respectively, then it can be shown under some conditions that

$$D_p^2 \longrightarrow D_\infty^2 \qquad \text{as } p \longrightarrow \infty$$

(naturally, after making that expression precisely). In practice, it is possible to study only a finite number p of characteristics, thus D_p^2 should be a good approximation to D_∞^2 if cluster analysis is to be stable. Mahalanobis showed that stability, in important senses, was possible if and only if D_∞^2 is finite.

Meteorological Research

Sir Gilbert Walker (then director general of observatories in India) referred to Mahalanobis some meteorological problems for statistical study. This resulted in two memoirs and a note on upper air variables in 1923. Correcting meteorological data for errors of observation, Mahalanobis established by purely statistical methods that the region of highest control for changes in weather conditions on the surface of Earth is located about 4 km above sea level (a result rediscovered later by Franz Bauer in Germany, from physical considerations).

Early Examples of Operations Research

In 1922, a disastrous flood occurred in North Bengal. An expert government committee of engineers was about to recommend the construction of expensive retaining basins to hold back the flood water, when the question was referred to Mahalanobis for examination. A statistical study of rainfall and floods extending over a period of 50 years showed that the proposed retaining basins would be of no value in controlling floods in North Bengal. The real need was improvement of rapid drainage, not control of flood water. Specific remedies were recommended, many of which were implemented and proved effective.

A similar question of flood control in Orissa was referred to Mahalanobis, after a severe flood of the Brahmini River in 1926. An expert committee of engineers held the opinion that the bed of the Brahmini had risen, and they recommended increasing the height of river embankments by several feet. A statistical study covering a period of about 60 years showed that no change had occurred in the river bed and that construction of dams for holding excessive flood water in the upper reaches of the river would provide effective flood control. Mahalanobis pointed out that dams could also be used for the generation of electric power, much needed for the economic development of the region. He also gave first calculations for a multipurpose (flood control, irrigation, and power) scheme for the Mahanadi system in Orissa; this formed the basis of the Hirakud hydroelectric project inaugurated about 30 years later in 1957.

Large-Scale Sample Surveys

Large-scale sample survey techniques as practiced today owe much to the pioneering work of Mahalanobis in the 1940s and 1950s. He saw the need for sample surveys in collecting information, especially in developing countries, where official statistical systems are poor and data are treated as an integral part of an administrative system that is regulated by the principle of authority. A sample survey, properly conducted, would provide a wealth of data useful for planning and policy purposes; the survey could be conducted expeditiously, economically, and with a reasonable degree of accuracy, and at the same time would ensure the objectivity of the data.

The methodology of large-scale sample surveys was developed during the period from 1937 to 1944 in connection with the numerous surveys planned and executed by the Indian Statistical Institute. The survey topics included consumer expenditure, tea-drinking habits, public opinion and public preferences, acreage under a crop, crop yields, velocity of circulation of rupee coins, and incidence of plant diseases. The basic results on large-scale sample surveys were published in 1944 and were also presented at a meeting of the Royal Statistical Society. The 1944 *Philosophical Transactions* memoir on sample surveys is a classic in many ways, touching on fundamental questions: What is randomness? What constitutes a random sample? Can different levels of randomness be identified? The memoir gives the basic theory of sample surveys and estimation procedures. Mahalanobis described a variety of designs now in common use, such as simple random sampling with or without replacement, and stratified, systematic, and cluster sampling. He was also familiar with multistage and multiphase sampling and with ratio and regression methods of estimation. He was, in a sense, conscious of selection with probability proportional to size (area); he pointed out that selection of fields on the basis of cumulative totals of the areas of millions of fields was difficult.

Mahalanobis made three notable contributions to sample survey techniques: pilot surveys, concepts of optimum survey design, and interpenetrating networks of samples. A pilot survey provides basic information on operational costs and the variability of characters, which are two important factors in designing an optimum survey. It gives an opportunity to test the suitability of certain schedules or questionnaires to be used in the survey. A pilot survey can also be used to construct a suitable framework for sampling of units.

From the beginning, Mahalanobis was clear about the principles of good sample design. He wrote in 1940 that "from the statistical point of view our aim is to evolve a sampling technique which will give, for any given total expenditure, the highest possible accuracy in the finale estimate and for given precision in the estimates, the minimum possible total expenditure." For this it is necessary to determine three things: (1) the best size of the sample units, (2) the total number of sample units that should be used to obtain the desired degree of accuracy in the final estimates, and (3) the best way of distributing the sampling units among different districts, regions, or zones covered by the survey. Mahalanobis constructed appropriate variance and cost functions in a variety of situations and used them in designing actual surveys.

As a physicist, Mahalanobis was aware of instrumental errors and personal bias in taking measurements, and consequently he stressed the need for repeating measurements with different instruments, different observers, and under different conditions. He maintained that a statistical survey was like a scientific experiment and that the planning of a survey required the same discipline and rigor as do other investigations. He advocated built-in cross-checks to validate survey results. For this purpose, he developed the concept of the interpenetrating network of subsamples (IPNS). A simple design using IPNS is as follows. Suppose that a given area is divided into four strata and that there are four investigators for the fieldwork. The normal practice is to assign one stratum to each investigator to cover all units (randomly) chosen from that particular stratum. With IPNS, however, each investigator works in all of the strata and covers a random quarter of the units. Thus the IPNS design provides four independent (parallel) estimates of the characteristic under study for the region as a whole, corresponding to the four different investigators. The validity of the survey will be in doubt if the four estimates differ widely. In such a case, it may be possible, by further data analysis, to take the differences properly into account when reporting the final estimate. Such a comparison or critical study would not have been possible if the four different strata had been assigned to four different investigators, because stratum and investigator differences would have been confounded.

Fractile Graphical Analysis

Fractile graphical analysis is an important generalization of the method and use of concentration (or Lorenz) curves. A Lorenz curve for wealth in a population tells, for example, that the least wealthy 50% of the population owns 10% of the wealth. (If wealth were equally distributed, the Lorenz curve would be a straight line.) The comparison of Lorenz curves for two or more populations is a graphical way to compare their distributions of wealth, income, numbers of acres owned, frequency of use of library books, and so on.

One of Mahalanobis' contributions in this domain was to stress the extension of the Lorenz curve idea to two variables. Thus, it is possible to consider, for example, both wealth and consumption for families, and to draw a curve from which it may be read that the least wealthy 50% of the families consume 27% of total consumption, or a certain quantity per family on the average. Or, treating the variables in the other direction, it might be found that the 20% least-consuming families account for 15% of the wealth, or a certain value per family. (The numbers in these examples are hypothetical and only for illustration.) Such bivariate generalized Lorenz curves can, of course, also be usefully compared across populations.

Contributions to Economic Planning

Mahalanobis' acquaintance with economics was neither systematic nor complete. The economics he learned was connected with the problems he had to solve, and these came intermingled with problems in other fields. Mahalanobis initiated a number of family budget surveys in rural and urban areas during the 1940s. He also undertook a number of studies on consumer preferences. He even tried his hand at a census of rupees, i.e., estimating the life of a rupee note. A survey of the aftereffects of the great Bengal famine in 1943 made him acutely aware of the poverty of the country.

In 1949, Mahalanobis became the chairman of the Indian National Income Committee; at this time, he began to think about the macroeconomic problems of India. There were gaps in information for computing national income. To fill this, he established the National Sample Survey (NSS) in 1950, and also organized a statistical unit devoted to the study of national income. When Mahalanobis was asked to help in the formulation of 5-year economic plans for India, he took up the study of planning models. He realized that the models suitable for advanced countries might not be applicable for underdeveloped countries. Setting for himself the twin objectives of doubling the national income and reducing unemployment considerably over a period of 20 years, he produced what are known as the Mahalanobis two- and four-sector models for economic development.

In a series of papers, Mahalanobis considered a two-sector model, where the net output of economy is conceived as originating in two sectors, one producing all investment goods and the other producing all consumer goods. Assuming that the total investment every year is split up in the ratio $\lambda_i : \lambda_c (\lambda_i + \lambda_c = 1)$, between the investment and the consumer goods sectors, and introducing income coefficients of investments, β_i, β_c for the respective sectors, Mahalanobis obtained the equation

$$Y_t = Y_0 \left\{ 1 + \alpha_0 \frac{\lambda_i \beta_i + \lambda_c \beta_c}{\lambda_i \beta_i} \left[(1 + \lambda_i \beta_i)^t - 1 \right] \right\},$$

where Y_t is the national income at time t and α_0 is base period investment. Using this equation, Mahalanobis concluded that a value of λ_i of approximately 0.3 would lead to a plausible limiting investment rate of 18%, which was adopted in the Indian Second Five Year Plan. Mahalanobis also considered a four-sector model, distinguishing three types of consumer goods industries, that was used in formulating the Indian Second Five Year Economic Plan.

Mahalanobis' association with the planning commission and his involvement in the formulation of the Second Five Year Plan brought him into contact with problems of wider national and international importance. He wrote extensively on subjects such as (1) the priority of basic industries, (2) the role of scientific research, technical manpower, and education in economic development, (3) world peace and the industrialization of poorer countries, and (4) labor problems, unemployment, and demographic problems. Mahalanobis considered scientific advance as a prerequisite of sustained economic development. He believed that economic progress entailed technological change that could be brought about only by engineers and technologists and that sustained technological research could prosper only in an atmosphere in which science in general flourished. In his writings on scientific research, technical manpower, education, etc., traces of a theory of economic growth are detectable. The role of innovations in economic development has been stressed by Schumpeter and others, but Mahalanobis emphasized the connection between scientific advance and technological innovations and the role of decision making at the appropriate time.

Promotion of Statistics in India and the Asian Region

Mahalanobis will be remembered not only for the outstanding contributions he made to statistical theory and practice, but also for promoting national statistical systems for collection of data that are needed by governments for short-range policy decisions and long-range economic planning, and for promoting statistical quality control (SQC) techniques for use in industry. He was primarily responsible for the establishment of (1) the Central Statistical Organization (CSO) in 1951 to serve as a National Statistical Office at the all-India level, (2) statistical bureaus in each state to collect data at the state level, and (3) an independent National Sample Survey (NSS) organization for collecting socioeconomic data on a continuing basis. Mahalanobis was also responsible for creating consultation services located in different parts of India, for implementing SQC and operations research (OR) techniques in industrial establishments to increase productivity and improve the quality of manufactured goods.

Mahalanobis saw the need for developing statistics in the Asian region for socioeconomic planning. To train the statistical personnel needed in the countries of the Asian region, an International Statistical Educational Center (ISEC) was started at the Indian Statistical Institute in 1950 with the support of the United Nations Educational, Scientific, and Cultural Organization (UNESCO), the government of India, and the International Statistical Institute.

Honors and Awards

Mahalanobis was elected a fellow of the Royal Society of London in 1945, of the Econometric Society (United States) in 1951, and of the Pakistan Statistical Association in 1961; an honorary fellow of the Royal Statistical Society (United Kingdom) in 1954 and of King's College (Cambridge) in 1959; honorary president of the International Statistical Institute in 1957; and a foreign member of the (former) United Soviet Socialist Republics Academy of Science in 1958. He received the Weldon medal from Oxford University in 1944, a gold medal from the Czechoslovak Academy of Sciences in 1963, the Sir Deviprasad Sarvadhikari gold medal in 1957, the Durgaprasad Khaitan gold medal in 1961, and the Srinivasa Ramanujan gold medal in 1968. He received honorary doctorates from Calcutta, Delhi, Stockholm, and Sofia universities and one of the highest civilian awards, Padmavibhushan, from the government of India.

Life With a Mission

The 79 years of Mahalanobis' life were full of activity. His contributions were massive on the academic side as the builder of the Indian Statistical Institute, founder and editor of *Sankhyā*, organizer of the Indian Statistical Systems, pioneer in the applications of statistical techniques to practical problems, promoter of the statistical quality control movement for improvement of industrial products, architect of the Indian Second Five Year Plan, and so on (see Table I).

During his life, he held several distinguished posts, many of them simultaneously. He was the chief executive of the Indian Statistical Institute, serving as secretary and director continuously from the founding of the Institute in 1931; he was honorary statistical advisor to the government of India from 1949; and he was associated with the work of the Planning Commission as a member (1955–1967). He also served as head of the statistics department of Calcutta University (1941–1945) and statistical advisor to the government of Bengal (1945–1948). He was a member of the United Nations Statistical Subcommission on Sampling from the time it was founded in 1946 and served as chairman from 1954 to 1958; he was general secretary of the Indian Science Congress (1945–1948) and, later, its treasurer (1952–1955) and president (1949–1950); and he was president of the Indian National Science Academy (1957–1958) and editor of *Sankhyā: The Indian Journal of Statistics*, from the time of its foundation in 1933.

Statistical science was a virgin field and was practically unknown in India before the 1920s. Developing statistics was like exploring a new territory; it needed a pioneer and adventurer like Mahalanobis, with his indomitable

Table I Chronology of Important Works by Mahalanobis

Year	*Contribution*
1922	Anthropological observations on the Anglo-Indians of Calcutta: Part 1. Analysis of the Male Stature (*Records of the Indian Museum* **23**, 1–96)
1923	Correlation of upper air variables (*Nature* **112**, 323–324)
1927	Report on rainfall and floods in North Bengal, 1870–1922 (submitted to the government of Bengal—volume 1, text; volume 2, 28 maps)
1930	On tests and measures of group divergence: Part 1. Theoretical formulae (*Journal and Proceedings of the Asiatic Society of Bengal, New Series* **26**, 541–588)
1931	Statistical study of the level of the rivers of Orissa and the rainfall in the catchment areas during the period 1868–1928 (report submitted to the government of Bihar and Orissa)
1936	On the generalized distance in statistics (*National Institute of Science, India, Proceedings* **2**, 49–55)
1940	A sample survey of the acreage under jute in Bengal (*Sankhyā* **4**, 511–530); The application of statistical methods in physical anthropometry (*Sankhyā* **4**, 594–598); Rain storms and river floods in Orissa (*Sankhyā* **5**, 1–20)
1944	On large scale sample surveys (*Royal Society of London, Philosophical Transactions, Series B* **231**, 329–451)
1946	Recent experiments in statistical sampling in the Indian Statistical Institute (*Journal of the Royal Statistical Society A* **109**, 325–378)
1949	Anthropometric survey of the United Provinces, 1941: A statistical study (*Sankhyā* **9**, 89–324)
1953	Some observations on the process of growth of national income (*Sankhyā* **12**, 307–312)
1955	Draft plan-frame for the Second Five-Year Plan, 1956/57–1960/61: Recommendations for the formulation of the Second Five-Year Plan (*Sankhyā* **16**, 63–90); The approach of operational research to planning in India (*Sankhyā* **16**, 3–62)
1958	Industrialization of underdeveloped countries: A means to peace (*Bulletin for Atomic Scientists* **15**, 12–17; also in *Sankhyā* **22**, 173–182); A method of fractile graphical analysis with some surmises of results (*Bose Research Institute Transactions* **22**, 223–230)
1960	A method of fractile graphical analysis (*Econometrica* **28**, 325–351; also in *Sankhyā, Series A* **23**, 41–64); A note on problems of scientific personnel (*Science and Culture* **27**, 101–128)
1961	Experiments in statistical sampling in the Indian Statistical Institutes (Calcutta: Asia Publishing House and Statistical Publishing Society; also in *Journal of the Royal Statistical Society, Series A* **109**, 325–378); Statistics for economic development (*Operations Research Society of Japan, Journal* **3**, 97–112)
1965	Statistics as a key technology (*American Statistician* **19**, No. 2, 43–46)

courage and tenacity to fight all opposition, clear all obstacles, and open new paths of knowledge for the advancement of science and society. The Mahalanobis era in statistics, which started in the early 1920s, ended with his death in 1972. It will be remembered as a golden period of statistics, marked by an intensive development of a new (key) technology and its application for the welfare of mankind.

See Also the Following Articles

Operations Research • Sample Design • Sample Size

Further Reading

Ghosh, J. K., Maiti, P., Rao, T. J., and Sinha, B. K. (1999). Evolution of statistics in India. *Int. Statist. Rev.* **67,** 13–34.

Rao, C. R. (1952). *Advanced Statistical Methods in Biometric Research.* Hafner, New York. Reprinted with corrections in 1970 and 1974.

Rao, C. R. (1954). On the use and interpretation of distance functions in statistics. *Int. Statist. Inst. Bull.* **34**(2), 90–97.

Rao, C. R. (1973). Prasanta Chandra Mahalanobis, 1893–1972. *R. Soc. Lond., Biograph. Mem. Fellows* **19,** 455–492.

Rao, C. R. (1973). Mahalanobis era in statistics. *Sankhyā* **35**(suppl.), 12–26.

Mail Surveys

Don A. Dillman
Washington State University, Pullman, Washington, USA

Glossary

response rate The percentage of sample units returning completed questionnaires.

response rate improvement techniques Individual procedures that are applied during the implementation of surveys primarily for the purpose of improving response rates.

tailored design Modifying the procedures used for conducting surveys on the basis of differences in population, purpose, and/or topic, with the goal of improving response rates and response quality.

visual communication Transmission of information through the sense of sight.

visual survey languages The words, symbols, numbers, and graphics used to transmit the meaning of questions that rely on visual communication.

Mail surveys are a means of collecting information from individuals, households, or other units of interest, whereby potential respondents are sent a paper questionnaire by postal mail or other courier. Individuals are asked to complete the questionnaires by self-administration and to return the surveys to the sender. Such surveys have been conducted for hundreds of years; as one of the oldest type of survey methods, the mailed questionnaire remains among the most prevalent procedures for collecting large quantities of information, especially from geographically dispersed respondents.

Introduction

Origins

The origin of mail surveys is unknown. However, in 1577, King Philip II of Spain conducted a census of his New World possessions using 38 written questions sent by official courier. In addition, the first volume of the *Journal of the Royal Statistical Society* published in 1837 included a mail survey of Church of England clergymen. More than a century later, in Volume 124 of the same journal, a lengthy analysis of response rate research became the first of several meta-analyses that attempted to identify the major determinants of response to mail surveys.

Mail surveys are sometimes used for complete censuses. For example, the U.S. Census Bureau used mail surveys as the primary means of collecting population count information in the 2000 decennial census. More than 70 million households responded by mail, with visits from enumerators being used to collect information from nonrespondents. However, the most prevalent use of mail surveys is for scientifically drawn samples of large populations in which attempts are made to produce estimates for the entire population. Mail sample surveys and surveys by telephone or face-to-face methods are subject to the same sources of error—coverage, sampling, measurement, and nonresponse.

Coverage Concerns

In the United States, mail surveys were used extensively in the first half of the 20th century. However, as a method of collecting information from general populations, it was widely criticized. Compared to face-to-face interviews, the standard method for conducting most important surveys from the 1940s through the 1970s, mail surveys suffered from significant coverage problems. Lists did not exist for drawing samples of the general public such that all households (and individuals) would have a known, nonzero chance of being sampled, guaranteeing that scientifically based estimates could be made for that larger population. This shortcoming was demonstrated in an embarrassing way by the infamous *Literary Digest* survey that was conducted by mail in 1936. That survey collected responses from more than 2 million respondents and predicted a landslide victory for Alf Landon (55% to 41%); in the actual election, Franklin Roosevelt beat Landon by an even wider margin (61% to 37%). The coverage problem stemmed from relying on telephone directories and automobile registrations for selecting households to receive their poll, and voters for Roosevelt were less likely than Landon supporters to have either. Coverage remains a major problem that limits the use of mail surveys for conducting surveys of the general public. Surveys of the general public require giving all households a known nonzero chance of being sampled, and it is rare to find lists that would fulfill this goal. In addition, it is important to select randomly the adult household member who responds. It is very costly, if not prohibitive, to achieve fully these requirements for such surveys. However, it is not a problem for more specialized populations, e.g., teachers, organization members, magazine subscribers, union members, and licensed professionals, for which complete address lists can often be obtained.

Response Rate Concerns

A second problem that has limited the use of mail surveys has been their reputation for producing low response rates. However, considerable progress has been made in finding solutions for this concern. In the 1970s, two publications on mail surveys provided research-based advice for improving response rates. The first book, *Professional Mail Surveys*, by Paul Erdos, emphasized the use of mail surveys in marketing research and provided detailed procedures for designing and implementing them. The second book, *Mail and Telephone Surveys: The Total Design Method*, emphasized the use of social exchange theory to design all aspects of the questionnaire and procedures experienced by respondents in ways that reduce perceptions of the social costs of responding (e.g., a sense of subordination) and increase perceptions of social rewards (e.g., a sense of doing something interesting) and trust (e.g., the likelihood that the results would be reported in a useful way). The total design method, or TDM as it is often called, was oriented toward university, government, and private foundation survey sponsors in much the same way that Erdos' procedures were oriented to private-sector organizations. The TDM also emphasized using quite similar procedures for most surveys. Both books established the idea in the 1970s that mail surveys using questionnaires of modest lengths, for most survey situations, could achieve response rates that were close to those normally obtained by other survey methods.

Reasons for Current Use

Mail surveys continued to be used heavily throughout the remainder of the 20th century. A 1981 review of all U.S. government surveys revealed that of the 2137 active government surveys, 69% relied exclusively on self-administered methods (mostly done by mail), compared to 2.2% by telephone and 9.4% by face-to-face interviews; an additional 11% used self-administered questionnaires in combination with other methods.

Several factors have contributed to the heavy use of mail surveys. One of them is lower cost, especially in comparison to face-to-face interviews. Use of mail procedures made it possible to conduct large-scale surveys of thousands or tens of thousands of units; procedures on this scale otherwise would have been prohibitively costly to do. Although the cost of conducting mail surveys has been less than the cost of conducting telephone interviews, that gap narrowed significantly during the late 1980s and 1990s as computer-assisted telephone methods combined interviewing with data entry, thus eliminating a separate activity that is still required for most mail surveys. Another important contributor to the use of mail methods has been the ability of many organizations to use existing personnel and resources to conduct the surveys. Most mail surveys are simple enough to implement, so many organizations conclude that they can do it themselves. Whereas the skills needed for printing questionnaires and making multiple contacts exist in most organizations, the skills and software for conducting structured telephone interviews generally do not. In addition, improvements in list management software and printing capabilities have eased the task of implementing large-scale mail surveys for virtually any user.

In recent years, increased interest has developed for using mail surveys as one of two or more modes for collecting information in a particular survey. Concern over lower response rates, compared to telephone surveys, and coverage problems with the recently developed and less expensive Internet surveys are leading to the use of mail surveys as a way of reaching respondents who cannot be contacted or convinced to respond to the other interview modes.

Factors that Influence Response Rate

Factors that are Often Manipulated

Since the 1940s, hundreds of studies have investigated procedures that affect response rates to mail surveys. Two factors, multiple contacts and token financial incentives sent with the survey, stand out as being particularly effective for improving response rates. Other manipulations found to have a smaller, but significant, positive impact on response rates include respondent-friendly questionnaire design, stamped return envelopes, a request sent by special contact (e.g., courier service or telephone), and personalization of correspondence.

A typical mail protocol might begin with a personalized prenotice letter, followed in a few days with a mail-out package that includes another personalized letter, a respondent-friendly questionnaire, $2 cash incentive, and stamped return envelope. That in turn may be followed in a week by a thank-you/reminder postcard. Then, after waiting 2–3 weeks, a replacement questionnaire with a different explanatory letter and a stamped return envelope is sent. Finally, after a wait of a few more weeks without a response, a final effort might be made using a mailer that has contents similar to the fourth mailing, except for a new letter and being sent by overnight courier delivery. Such procedures consistently produce response rates near 60% or higher for many populations and situations.

Factors Less Subject to Manipulation

Response rates are also influenced by a number of considerations that are not usually subject to design manipulation. For example, it has been shown that salience or interest of respondents in the questionnaire topic has a substantial effect on response rates. The same study showed that questionnaire length, sponsorship by a market research firm, and survey of general populations had negative affects on response rates, whereas government sponsorship and the survey of school and army populations had positive effects. Also, completing mail questionnaires is difficult for people whose reading and writing skills are not well developed. Extensive research on this factor was conducted by the U.S. Bureau of the Census during the 1990s for decennial census test questionnaires. It was shown that response rates in areas of the United States with high proportions of lower income and minority populations (where about 11% of the U.S. population resides) and where education levels are low averaged 16–26 percentage points lower, compared to the remaining areas (where 89% lived). It was also determined that only one factor, i.e., respondent-friendly questionnaire design, of 16 potential response-inducing factors tested across several large-scale experiments, improved response more in the lower responding areas. These data provide evidence that response rates to mail surveys are limited by the characteristics of survey populations.

Tailored Design

Recognition that different survey sponsorship, the survey topic, and the nature of the population being surveyed may discourage the use of some response-inducing techniques and permit others has led to the development of a tailored design approach to improving survey response. Tailored design uses the tenets of social exchange to shape survey implementation features somewhat more precisely for different survey populations and situations. For example, whereas token financial incentives are generally seen as appropriate for many private-sector surveys, they may be seen as quite inappropriate for establishment surveys and certain government-sponsored surveys.

The 2000 decennial census, to which all households are required by law to respond, is an example of tailored design. Extensive experimentation showed that placing a notice on the outside of the envelope, i.e., "U.S. Census Form Enclosed: Your Response is Required by Law," improved response by nearly 10 percentage points. However, such a notice would be inaccurate, as well as inappropriate, on most other surveys. Other contrasts encouraged by a tailored design perspective might include concentrating six to eight contacts within a period of several weeks when asking people to complete a radio or TV diary, but stretching a smaller number of contacts out over many months in a government survey of manufacturers. Tailored strategies have even been used effectively to conduct election surveys, the traditional province of telephone survey methods. For example, for Ohio elections, it has been shown that results from a mail election survey conducted regularly since 1980 have been more accurate than comparable surveys conducted by telephone.

Increasingly, tailored design approaches are being used to ensure that good response is achieved in most mail survey situations. Improvements in response rates do not guarantee that nonresponse error, i.e., differences between respondents and nonrespondents on a variable of interest, will be reduced. However, the higher the response rates, the lower will be the potential biasing effect of even substantial differences in respondents and nonrespondents.

Measurement Considerations

Mail and Telephone Differences

Evidence exists that people answer mail surveys and telephone surveys somewhat differently; these two types of surveys have been most frequently compared, and at least four types of measurement differences have been noted by researchers. One difference is the tendency for mail surveys to be less prone to question-order effects, i.e., the possibility for answers to certain questions to be affected by other items, whether they appear before or after the affected items. Second, a consistent body of research has shown that respondents are less likely to offer socially desirable answers, i.e., answers that reflect attitudes or behaviors approved by the culture, in self-administered surveys than they are in surveys that require respondents to give verbal answers to interviewers. For example, in one of the most recent publications that verifies this tendency, it was found that prostate surgery patients gave more positive answers about their current health by telephone interview than they did by mail.

There is a third type of measurement difference related to mail versus telephone: it has been hypothesized that in mail or self-administered surveys, respondents are more likely to choose from the first answer choices presented. This is called a primacy effect;—in telephone surveys, respondents are more likely to choose the last categories presented, known as a recency effect. Primacy is believed to occur because respondents tend to use their early answers as a base of comparison with others and work down the list only until they have found a satisfactory answer. Recency effects are thought to occur because under conditions of aural communication, the first categories read by an interviewer are less likely to be retained in short-term memory. However, an analysis of 82 experiments involving both mail and telephone surveys found no differences between methods in the occurrence of either primacy or recency effects.

Yet another tendency observed in past research is for mail survey respondents to give less extreme answers compared to those offered over the telephone. For example, on a series of community and neighborhood perception questions deemed to have low, if any, social desirability attributes, telephone respondents were much more likely to choose the extreme positive categories by a substantial margin.

Some Effects of Dependence on Visual Communication

The process of answering mail questionnaires differs in several significant ways from the manner in which telephone surveys are answered. One of these is the complete reliance on visual, rather than aural, communication. Information on self-administered questionnaires is communicated through four languages: words (also used in interviewer-administered questionnaires), numbers (which provide guidance on things such as in which order questions should be read and answered), symbols (e.g., arrows and answer boxes, which communicate navigation and response expectations), and graphics. Variations in graphical language, the conduit through which the other languages are expressed, includes considerations such as variations in size, brightness, color, and location, which communicate how information presented on self-administered questionnaires should be grouped and interpreted by respondents. A theory of how these elements may affect whether information on self-administered gets read and followed has been developed and tested. Results show that answers to mail surveys can be significantly changed by manipulating symbols and the graphical display of information on questionnaire pages. These visual design concepts have also been used in an attempt to reduce certain errors that are much more likely to occur in self-administered questionnaires than in interview surveys—namely, the tendency for respondents to follow branching instructions incorrectly. Branching instructions direct respondents to different questions, depending on which answer choice was selected for a preceding question. It has been shown in a national test of census questionnaires that the effectiveness of branching instructions can be substantially improved through better use of the language constructs (words, numbers, symbols, and graphics) in a way that makes the language constructs more mutually supportive.

Although the use of visual languages plays an obvious role in how respondents interpret and use information in mail questionnaires, much remains to be learned about how differences in answers to specific questions result from differences in graphical composition. It also remains to be determined how important the visual aspects of questionnaire design are in comparison with others for explaining the frequently observed differences in answers to interview questionnaires, such as primacy and extremeness effects.

Effects of Technology

Many of the processes associated with obtaining high response rates to mail surveys, e.g., use of personalized correspondence and repeated mailings, are labor intensive. Development of word processors in the 1970s began to reduce the time and costs required for such efforts, and facilitated keeping track of returns to avoid duplicate mailings. However, most mail questionnaires, even today, require manual data entry, a separate step in processing that is not required for telephone surveys collected through computer-assisted methods.

Since the 1960s, it has been possible to use optical scanning as a means of avoiding manual data entry. However, these early methods relied on a reflective mark technology that required respondents to fill in circles or ovals completely on specially designed questionnaires for which special colors of (drop-out) inks were used to print the questions and the answer spaces. Such questionnaires were often inflexible (answers had to go on certain portions of the pages and be printed in pastel colors) and have been judged not to be respondent friendly. Dramatic changes have occurred in these technologies. Today, instead of being limited to scanning questionnaires under colored lights to read pencil marks in ovals, it is possible to import complete images of questionnaires into computers and to automate further the process of summarizing answers. Software exists for recognizing check marks, numbers, and characters, so they can be read directly during computer processing. The ability to recognize numbers and letters has been improved significantly through the use of visual principles for design. For example, white spaces for answers can be set against colored backgrounds, and segmentation marks can be added to divide internally the answer spaces. As a result, respondents are more likely to print rather than use cursive writing, and to stay within confined spaces, both of which facilitate faster processing. It remains to be seen how these developments will affect the general use of mail surveys.

Future Uses of Mail Surveys

The future use of mail surveys appears somewhat unclear. On the one hand, the high costs of face-to-face interviews and declining response rates to telephone surveys suggest that more surveyors may consider using mail surveys. On the other hand, the ability to conduct self-administered surveys over the Internet, for which costs are substantially less than for mail, especially for large samples, suggests that Web surveys may replace those by mail. The situation is complicated by the fact that for many, if not most, survey populations, access to the Internet is limited. In addition, telephone surveys exhibit an increasing coverage problem, as in some advanced industrial countries the telephone becomes more of a personal device, and some people forgo the traditional household telephone.

It seems likely that surveyors will attempt to deal with these issues through the increased use of mixed-mode surveys, which means that some individuals in a sample will be surveyed by one mode while others respond by alternative modes. This in turn raises the issue of whether mail surveys and surveys using other modes will obtain the same answers to questions, an issue that will no doubt command the attention of researchers for many years to come.

See Also the Following Articles

Communication • Survey Design • Survey Questionnaire Construction • Surveys • Telephone Surveys • Total Survey Error

Further Reading

Bishop, G. H., Hippler, J., Schwarz, N., and Strack, F. (1988). A comparison of response effects in self-administered and telephone surveys. In *Telephone Survey Methodology* (R. M. Groves, P. P. Biemer, L. E. Lyberg, J. T. Massey, W. L. Nicholls, II., and J. Waksberg, eds.), pp. 321–340. Wiley, New York.

Christian, L. M., and Dillman, D. A. (2004). The influence of graphical and symbolic language manipulations on responses to self-administered questions. *Public Opin. Q.* **68,** 57–80.

Church, A. (1993). Estimating the effect of incentives on mail survey response rates: A meta-analysis. *Public Opin. Q.* **57,** 62–79.

Dillman, D. A. (1978). *Mail and Telephone Surveys: The Total Design Method.* John Wiley, New York.

Dillman, D. A. (1991). The Design and Administration of Mail Surveys. *Annu. Rev. Sociol.* **17,** 225–249.

Dillman, D. A. (2000). *Mail and Internet Surveys: The Tailored Design Method.* John Wiley, New York.

Dillman, D. A., Brown, T. L., Carlson, J., Carpenter, E. H., Lorenz, F. O., Mason, R., Saltiel, J., and Sangster, R. L. (1995). Effects of category order on answers to mail and telephone surveys. *Rural Sociol.* **60,** 674–687.

Erdos, P. (1970). *Professional Mail Surveys.* McGraw Hill, New York.

Fowler, F. J., Jr., Roman, A. M., and Di, Z. X. (1998). Mode effects in a survey of Medicare prostate surgery patients. *Public Opin. Q.* **62,** 29–46.

Heberlein, T. A., and Baumgartner, R. (1978). Factors affecting response rates to mailed questionnaires: A quantitative analysis. *Am. Sociol. Rev.* **43,** 447–462.

Jenkins, C. R., and Dillman, D. A. (1997). Towards a theory of self-administered questionnaire design. In *Survey Measurement and Process Quality* (L. Lyberg, P. Biemer, M. Collins, L. Decker, E. de Leeuw, C. Dippo, N. Schwarz, and D. Trewin, eds.), pp. 165–196. Wiley-Interscience, New York.

Krosnick, J., and Alwin, D. F. (1987). An evaluation of a cognitive theory of response-order effects in survey measurement. *Public Opin. Q.* **51,** 201–219.

Literary Digest. (1936). What went wrong with the polls? *Liter. Dig.* **122,** 7–8.

Redline, C. D., and Dillman, D. A. (2002). The influence of alternative visual designs on respondents' performance with branching instructions in self-administered questionnaires. In *Survey Nonresponse* (R. Groves, D. Dillman, J. Eltinge, and R. Little, eds.), pp. 179–193. John, Wiley, New York.

Scott, C. (1961). Research on mail surveys. *J. R. Statist. Soc., Ser. A* **124,** 143–205.

U.S. Office of Management and Budget. (1984). *The Role of Telephone Data Collection in Federal Statistics.* Statistical Policy Working Paper No. 1. U.S. Government Printing Office, Washington, D.C.

Visser, P. S., Krosnick, J. A., Marquette, J., and Curtin, M. (1996). Mail surveys for election forecasting? An Evaluation of the Columbus Dispatch poll. *Public Opin. Q.* **60,** 181–227.

Marketing Industry

Maria Anne Skaates
Aarhus School of Business, Aarhus, Denmark

Glossary

database marketing The creation and use of databases and other information management systems to find potential customers, service them, and monitor their preferences.

interaction marketing Activities concerned with the development of supplier and customer relationships to ensure better creation and delivery of the products or services offered.

marketing The process by which products and services of value to customers and potential customers are created, communicated, and delivered.

marketing industry The collective composed of all firms, organizations, groups, and individuals who collect and analyze information about the needs, preferences, and current and potential future demands of current and potential customers for use in creating, communicating, and delivering goods and services in a way that will ensure sufficient returns.

marketing information system An information management system composed of people, equipment, and methods for collecting and analyzing information about customers and potential customers and delivering the analysis to decision makers.

network marketing The development of relationships to multiple stakeholders, including customers, to enable the optimal offering delivery as well as the optimal coordination of offering-related activities among the stakeholders in the network of relationships.

relationship marketing Activities concerned with creating and optimizing customer relationships. May encompass database, interaction, and/or network marketing practices.

segmentation The subdivision of a market into groups of consumers that have different needs, preferences, or user behavior and thus can be addressed through separate offerings or advertisements.

test market A small, most often geographically defined section of a market with members who are believed to have the same characteristics as are found in the entire market. A test market is used for marketing experiments with, e.g., product design, pricing, or advertising.

transaction marketing A type of marketing that is primarily concerned with optimizing product or service characteristics connected to an individual transaction such as quality, price, promotion, place of sale, etc., in relation to customer preferences.

The marketing industry encompasses firms, organizations, groups, and individuals involved in conducting research about markets and about the needs, preferences, and current and potential future demands of customers. These aspects are examined in this article, first by briefly describing the marketing industry and its areas of focus. Thereafter, research questions and methods pertaining to the market industry are discussed. Finally, future developments in the research done by and methods used by the marketing industry are addressed.

The Marketing Industry and its Areas of Focus

Marketing is a process of activities by which firms, organizations, groups, or individuals create, communicate about, and deliver offerings of value to other firms, organizations, groups, or individuals. The offerings may include any combination of goods, property, services, and other intangibles (e.g., brand name, corporate reputation, supplier and customer relationships, value propositions, experiences, events, individual expertise, or knowledge). In order to create, communicate about, and deliver offerings, marketers must have a profound understanding of the needs, preferences, and current and potential future demands of current and potential customers and of the offerings of competitors. However, in order to make the long-term creation, communication about, and delivery of offerings feasible, sufficient returns need to be obtained on the offerings. Marketers are therefore also necessarily concerned about the economics of the creation, communication, and delivery of current and potential offerings, yet marketers often work with other business researchers, such as those persons responsible for accounting measures or business performance measurement, or technical professionals (logisticians or production engineers), to map the economics of offerings.

The marketing industry encompasses all firms, organizations, groups, and individuals involved in conducting applied social science research by collecting and analyzing information about markets and the needs, preferences, and current and potential future demands of current and potential customers for use in creating, communicating, and delivering offerings that will achieve sufficient returns. From this it follows that the marketing industry includes individuals and groups from private enterprises, governmental institutions, and not-for-profit organizations as well as entire organizational units (e.g., firms specialized in market research or export promotion offices of states, provinces, or countries). However some of these individuals, groups, or organizational units perform marketing only on a part-time basis, in that they also are involved in other organizational tasks such as managing production or service delivery, hiring new staff, or keeping records of income and expenses.

In their marketing research, marketers examine specific issues related to the creation, communication, and delivery of offerings in a way that ensures sufficient returns. In connection with these issues, they pose specific research questions, then gather and analyze data using various methods and research designs. These points are elaborated on further in the following sections of this article.

Marketing Research Questions

Questions Pertaining to the Levels of Business Strategy

In large organizations, business strategy is commonly developed at the levels of the organization as a whole, the business unit, and the operating line. In contrast, in smaller organizations, strategy is often developed at only one level, and the strategy development process may occur either during or after the market-related information is gathered and analyzed. The roles that marketers fulfill in relation to strategy formulation in large organizations have been specified as follows: At the level of the organization as a whole, marketers work with the assessment of market attractiveness and at ensuring that top management understands customer demands. Furthermore, at this level, marketers are involved in the development of a specific global policy concerning the interlinked issues of (1) which types of offerings the organization should develop, (2) which types of customers it should aim to serve, and (3) which types of underlying internal resources and capabilities it should develop. Possible research questions that correspond to these themes are found in Fig. 1, which also lists research questions relevant to the other levels of strategy formulation in large firms.

At the level of the business unit, questions that marketers commonly address include how to target potential customers (including the possible use of market segmentation and relational marketing techniques); how to position the offerings in relation to, e.g., competitors' offerings or the requirements of distributors; and what areas of offering-related development, production, advertisement, and delivery should be outsourced to other firms. At the level of the operating line, marketers are involved in formulating and implementing the quality of specific offerings and the pricing, promotion, and distribution policies; in managing relationships to end customers and distributors; and in problem solving in relation to previous marketing policy mistakes or misjudgments. In relation to the levels of the business unit and the operating line, it is relevant to note that there is some overlap between the types of research questions and research methods used by marketers and those used by practitioners in the field of communication.

Questions Pertaining to Four Types of Marketing Activities

The marketing practices of organizations influence the research questions that their marketers pose. In a study of practices of firms in five countries, Coviello, Brodie, Danaher, and Johnston (2002) took their point of departure in four different types of marketing activities:

1. Transaction marketing: activities concerned with optimizing product characteristics such as quality, price, promotion, place of sale, etc.
2. Database marketing: the creation and use of databases and other information management systems to find potential customers, monitor customers' preferences, and ensure optimal customer service.
3. Interaction marketing: activities concerned with the development of supplier—customer relationships to ensure, e.g., a better creation and delivery of the offering seen from viewpoint of the customers.
4. Network marketing: the development of multiple relationships to enable the optimal offering delivery as

Level of the organization as a whole:

- How much economic benefit would our corporation get out of establishing our own sales subsidiary in Australia?
- Should our fast food chain continue to target business professional eating lunch worldwide?
- Would the largest individual customers of our civil engineering design services also value our company developing facility management services so much that they would ask us to manage the facilities that we have designed for them, if we developed such facilities management capabilities?
- If we divest our own production activities and instead enter production contracts with firms X and Y, will this have a positive or negative effect on our sales to major industrial customers?

Level of the business unit:

- What should characterize our line of specialty drills if we are to differentiate them from those currently sold to do-it-yourselfers in Germany?
- What sorts of salads sell best to our repeat lunchtime customers who use their loyalty program card?
- How should the employees in our shops inform individual customers of the types of fashion trends that this line of clothing seeks to mirror?
- How much of the after-sales service on our product line should we make a specific external provider of such services responsible for?

Level of the operating line:

- If we increase the price of drill X by Y, how will this affect total sales in Germany?
- Does this fat-reduced sandwich appeal to those lunchtime business professionals who are part of our loyalty program?
- To better meet a specific customer's needs, should we arrange for special deliveries and if so, what should we charge this customer for this extra service?
- To what extent do teenagers introduce each other and their parents to the fun of playing this mystery video game by using its "solve the mystery as a group" function?

Figure 1 Examples of marketing research questions at the levels of business strategy.

well as optimal coordination of offering-related activities among the actors of the network of relationships.

In larger organizations, these four types of marketing activities may pertain to all three levels of business strategy formulation mentioned previously, i.e., the levels of the organization as a whole, the business unit, and operating line. Therefore, in Fig. 2, the research questions listed in Fig. 1 have been regrouped to illustrate to which of the four types of marketing activities they pertain. The manner in which the data are presented in Fig. 2 does not represent the only way in which marketing activities may be categorized. For example, looking at an individual offering, i.e., a specific product or service, it would also be possible to categorize the marketing activities according to phases: (1) development of the offering, (2) introduction of the offering to the market, (3) further development or maintenance of the offering on the marketing, and (4) removal of the offering from the market. Nevertheless, the focus on the classifications presented in Fig. 2 is maintained in this article because these classifications deal with the more general, multiple-offering situation. The results of the five-country study indicate that transaction and interaction marketing practices are much more widespread than database and network marketing are. However, this may change in the future, if hardware, software, and methods for database and network marketing develop in coevolution with the increasing levels of knowledge richness and acknowledgment of diversity in advanced societies. Furthermore, the five-country study results showed that firms that sell to consumers focus to a greater extent on transaction and database marketing than do firms that sell to businesses, and that firms that sell goods are generally more transactional than are firms that sell services. However, the results also indicate that there is substantial variation among firms. It is possible to find examples of both transactional and relationship (i.e., database, interaction, or network) marketing practices in all firm types, and around one-third of the firms in the five-country sample combine transactional and relational practices.

The Link between Marketing Research Questions and Views on Measuring Human Behavior

As in other social research, the aims of marketing research questions vary. They may, for example, seek to increase exploration of specific instances of human behavior in relation to a particular offering or to explain trends or patterns in market share or consumer acceptance by documenting relations of causality or teleology. Similarly, the views of marketing researchers and their customers on the possibilities of measuring human behavior vary. Some marketing researchers and marketing research customers

Transaction marketing:

- How much economic benefit would our corporation get out of establishing our own sales subsidiary in Australia?
- What should characterize our line of specialty drills if we are to differentiate them from those currently sold to do-it-yourselfers in Germany?
- If we increase the price of drill X by Y, how will this affect total sales in Germany?

Database marketing:

- Should our fast food chain continue to target business professionals eating lunch worldwide?
- What sorts of salads sell best to our repeat lunchtime customers who use their loyalty program card?
- Does this fat-reduced sandwich appeal to those lunchtime business professionals who are part of our loyalty program?

Interaction marketing:

- Would the largest individual customers of our civil engineering design services also value our company developing facility management services so much that they would ask us to manage the facilities that we have designed for them, if we developed such facilities management capabilities?
- How should the employees in our shops inform individual customers of the types of fashion trends that this line of clothing seeks to mirror?
- To better meet a specific customer's needs, should we arrange for special deliveries and if so, what should we charge this customer for this extra service?

Network marketing:

- If we divest our own production activities and instead enter production contracts with firms X and Y, will this have a positive or negative effect on our sales to major industrial customers?
- How much of the after-sales service on our product line should we make a specific external provider of such services responsible for?
- To what extent do teenagers introduce each other and their parents to the fun of playing this mystery video game by using its "solve the mystery as a group" function?

Figure 2 Examples of marketing research questions by type of marketing activity.

believe strongly in the quest for objectivity and are therefore less open to phenomenological research. Others may be more open to phenomenological marketing research and more critical of efforts to determine cause or correlation through quantitative research; this may be due, for example, to the ongoing discussions about the possibilities of achieving content validity, about the validity of hypotheses tests and proof, and about statistical versus substantive data interpretations.

Marketing Research Methods

Operationalization of Research Questions

Research questions such as the ones presented in Figs. 1 and 2 have to be operationalized, i.e., reformulated to allow for measurement using secondary data and/or primary data (including communication with the persons whose behavior and opinions are to be examined by the marketing researchers via surveys, focus groups, participant observation, or interviews). In connection with this communication, it is paramount that the persons whose behavior and attitudes will be examined understand the questions posed in the same way as the marketing researchers believe they are understood. This can be especially problematic for marketing researchers if cross-cultural data are to be collected and interpreted. Especially if the marketing researchers do not have sufficient knowledge of foreign market and foreign customers, there are risks of ethnocentrism and poor translation equivalence in the formulation of research questions and in the interpretation of responses. Methodologies from anthropology, communications, and linguistics may, however, be used by marketers to minimize ethnocentrism and translation problems in marketing research.

Ethical issues, such as ensuring anonymity and confidentiality of respondents and taking into consideration issues concerning their personal risks, consent, and privacy, are also considered by marketers in connection with the operationalization of research questions as well as with the rest of the marketing research process. In connection with these issues, marketers are subject to substantial national and supranational (e.g., European Union) variations in data protection legislation, and the marketing research industry's own rules, recommendations, and norms also vary from country to country.

Marketing Information Systems

Individuals or organizations that collect and analyze information about the needs, preferences, and current and potential future demands of current and potential customers on a regular basis often make use of previously established marketing information systems. Such systems for marketing information management are composed of individuals, equipment (such as data-mining and data-warehousing software), and methods for collecting and analyzing information about customers and potential customers and then delivering the analysis to relevant decision makers. Thus, with specific regard to the marketing industry, customer listening systems or, in some instances, systematized customer feedback systems can be considered. In contrast, organizations that conduct marketing research only occasionally usually do not develop marketing information systems. Instead, they rely on the more *ad hoc* use of some of the qualitative and quantitative methods discussed in the following sections.

Qualitative Methods of Marketing Research

Marketing research studies using qualitative methods most often explore and describe the nature of offering- or market-related phenomena without using stratified or random samples. This is in contrast to marketing research studies using quantitative methods, which normally seek to measure and explain patterns of predefined offering-related phenomena in an entire population using established sampling methods. Thus, qualitative methods are especially relevant when marketers are concerned with in-depth understanding of phenomena and with "whys" and "hows." Examples of the application of the marketing research questions that were listed in Figs. 1 and 2 to qualitative methods are given in Fig. 3. It is important to note that some of the research questions in Fig. 3 can also be applied to quantitative methods. In fact, there is often the option of doing either qualitative or quantitative research or combining the two research approaches. Qualitative research methodologies used by marketing practitioners include case study-based research, ethnographic and field study research, individual interviews, focus group research, and observational studies.

Case study methodology is especially appropriate for capturing current or recent phenomena in circumstances when the boundaries between the phenomenon and its context cannot be predetermined and when there are multiple sources of empirical data (e.g., interview data and firm-internal documents) available for inspection. Thus, an Irish marketing bureau specializing in helping Irish high-technology firms communicate about their products and services to potential North American customers and capital-providers might undertake case study research of previous Irish high-tech firm internationalizations to North America. Similarly, a South African marketing consulting firm specializing in helping local retailing operations expand nationally might do a case study of the changes in the delivery function during a successful national expansion. Ethnographic and field study research are often used in international marketing research and in research into subcultures in societies. In these cases, one or more researchers also participate actively in the activities of the culture or subcultures, to gain an insider understanding. For example, a market researcher of a new light ale targeted at young adult women on its domestic market might frequent bars and cafés in a foreign country to learn more about the drinking habits and preferences of the young adult women there. This participant observation would enable the researcher to determine reasons why the light ale could/could not be targeted in the same way in the foreign market.

Interviewing of individuals is a major source of information in qualitative research, and as such it is most often

- Would the largest individual customers of our civil engineering design services also value our company developing facility management services so much that they would ask us to manage the facilities that we have designed for them, if we developed such facilities management capabilities?
- If we divest our own production activities and instead enter production contracts with firms X and Y, will this have a positive or negative effect on our sales to major industrial customers?
- What should characterize our line of specialty drills if we are to differentiate them from those currently sold to do-it-yourselfers in Germany?
- What sorts of salads sell best to our repeat lunchtime customers who use their loyalty program card?
- How should the employees in our shops inform individual customers of the types of fashion trends that this line of clothing seeks to mirror?
- How much of the after-sales service on our product line should we make a specific external provider of such services responsible for?
- Does this fat-reduced sandwich appeal to those lunchtime business professionals who are part of our loyalty program?
- To better meet a specific customer's needs, should we arrange for special deliveries and if so, what should we charge this customer for this extra service?
- To what extent do teenagers introduce each other and their parents to the fun of playing this mystery video game by using its "solve the mystery as a group" function?

Figure 3 Examples of marketing research questions suitable for qualitative inquiry.

also used in case studies, ethnographic, and field study research, yet it may also be used alone. For example, a U.S. Chamber of Commerce seeking to increase the demand for its services among its members may conduct market research interviews with selected individuals from member firms. On the other hand, focus group research involves inviting a small group of respondents to a meeting where they will be asked about their attitudes and behavior. In focus group research, group interaction effects may produce data and viewpoints that would not have been accessible through individual interviews. Thus the aforementioned U.S. Chamber of Commerce effort seeking to increase the demand for its services among its members might also have conducted its market research by arranging for a small number of individuals from member firms to participate in focus groups.

Two types of observational studies, participant and passive, are used by the marketing industry. Participant observation, has already been discussed in relationship to ethnographic and field study research. Passive observation is a more unobtrusive method and a method that should guarantee greater neutrality in data collection in that it involves collecting data without interaction with the persons being studied. Passive observation is very much used in consumer research. For example, the marketing department of an Italian company that develops children's toys may conduct passive qualitative observational studies of how children play with various prototype versions of the toys.

Quantitative Methods of Marketing Research

Quantitative methods seek to measure various offering-, consumer-, or market-related phenomena in an entire population and to explain patterns of predefined offering-, consumer-, or market-related phenomena through causal inference or teleological explanation. Such quantitative measurements enable, among other things, segmentation, i.e., the subdivision of a market into groups of consumers that have different needs, preferences, or user behavior and thus can be addressed through separate offerings or advertisements. Those marketing research questions listed in Figs. 1 and 2 that are suitable for quantitative methods of research are shown in Fig. 4. It is important to remember that many of these research questions could have also been studied using qualitative methods. In connection with this point, quantitative methods have the advantage of generating results that can be generalized to larger populations, whereas qualitative methods enable marketing researchers to go into specific instances in great depth.

In quantitative research, the marketing industry most often uses sample research designs; however, occasionally, censuses of entire populations are used. In quantitative international marketing research, marketing researchers must seek to achieve construct equivalence, measurement equivalence (through scale transformation, for example), and sampling equivalence as well as comparability between national research designs. Because markets, consumers, and offerings change over time, the marketing research industry, similar to the polling industry, conducts a substantial portion of both its domestic and international research at intermittent intervals, using either longitudinal panel studies or cross-section data.

Instead of primary data, the marketing research industry very often uses suitable, valid, and reliable secondary data if they are available, because it is usually more expensive to generate primary data. Types of secondary data commonly used by marketers include demographic, psychometric, labor market, polling industry, consumption and saving, household behavior and family economics, and tourism statistics data; census-derived retail trade, wholesale trade, inter- and intraindustry trade, and international trade data; and industry-, nation-, or region-specific data on economic development, technological

- How much economic benefit would our corporation get out of establishing an own sales subsidiary in Australia?
- Should our fast food chain continue to target business professionals eating lunch worldwide?
- What should characterize our line of specialty drills if we are to differentiate them from those currently sold to do-it-yourselfers in Germany?
- What sorts of salads sell best to our repeat lunchtime customers who use their loyalty program card?
- How should the employees in our shops inform individual customers of the types of fashion trends that this line of clothing seeks to mirror?
- How much of the after-sales service on our product line should we make a specific external provider of such services responsible for?
- If we increase the price of drill X by Y, how will this affect total sales in Germany?
- Does this fat-reduced sandwich appeal to those lunchtime business professionals who are part of our loyalty program?
- To what extent do teenagers introduce each other and their parents to the fun of playing this mystery video game by using its "solve the mystery as a group" function?

Figure 4 Examples of marketing research questions suitable for quantitative inquiry.

change, and growth. Such data may be acquired by marketers from governmental organizations at the local, regional, national, or supranational [e.g., European Union (EU), North Atlantic Free Trade Association (NAFTA), Organization for Economic Cooperation and Development (OECD), World Bank, and World Trade Organization (WTO)] levels, from industry or business organizations, or from private firms specializing in publishing market research reports. However, in general, there are fewer available secondary data on markets and consumers from the developing countries.

In cases in which it is necessary for marketers to generate their own primary data, the marketing industry utilizes surveys, quantitative observations, and pre-experimental, quasi-experimental, and true experimental designs. Surveys have traditionally been conducted over the telephone, through personal interviewing, or via mailings to potential respondents. In recent years, the Web-based survey has become increasingly important, especially in countries in which a substantial portion of businesses and most of the general population have access to the Internet. Surveys are appropriate to determine opinions of customers and potential customers about pricing, packaging, promotion, points of sale, and the quality of offerings and the quality of their relationship to the producer or the retailer or to determine general patterns of household behavior and family economics. However, industry experts may also be surveyed for strategic marketing purposes; in this case, these experts are commonly asked about their beliefs concerning future industry or market developments.

Passive observation is used as a quantitative method, too. In quantitative observation, the measurement may concentrate on the number of times something occurs or the amount of time or money spent on something. Human researchers are sometimes involved in quantitative observation, e.g., when a marketing researcher working in a Brazilian shopping center records the number of customers who visit a shop for formal men's attire, the times of day that these customers arrive, and the parts of the shop that they visit. However, quantitative human observation research may also take the form of an audit of stocks. For example, a marketer in a Japanese supply firm that supplies its business-to-business customers according to their materials management policies may take an inventory of the number of the customer's preferred brands, the customer's current quantities of products and packaging, and general size of the customer's storage facilities. A great deal of quantitative observation is also undertaken electronically. Examples of electronic means of recording activity include the use of tracking "cookies" (information stored on a computer user's hard disk, by the server, following a client/server interaction) to monitor consumers' Internet use, the use of "loyalty cards" by retail shops, hotel chains, or airlines to monitor customer purchase patterns, and installation of the A. C. Nielsen audiometer in a consumer's television set to record which channels are accessed.

Pre-experiments do not control for extraneous factors through randomization. For example, through the use of a one-shot case study design, the attitudes of a number of respondents may be measured by marketing researchers immediately after a critical, yet unforeseeable, event such as a company winning a prestigious award or a large-scale product recall. Alternatively, if an event is foreseeable, such as the introduction of new product features, the single group may be exposed to a pretest/posttest design, in which group attitudes are measured before and after the change. Quasi-experiments are characterized by the researcher being able to control when, on whom, or what measurement is to be undertaken, yet not being in total control of the extraneous stimuli that those persons or objects to be measured will experience. Most marketing research field experiments, such as the use of test markets or computer-simulated test markets, are quasi-experiments. A test market is a small, most often geographically defined section of a market with members who are believed to have the same characteristics as are found on the entire market. A test market may be used for marketing experiments with product design, pricing, or advertising. For example, a Pakistani producer of radio commercials wants to test the effectiveness of a commercial jingle by broadcasting it and subsequently surveying two test panels, one located in the area of where the commercial is to be broadcast and the other in a neighboring area. Because the producer cannot be certain of the number of members of the first panel who have heard the jingle or that all the members of the second panel have not heard the jingle, the producer is not in total control of extraneous stimuli.

True experiments are marked by both randomization with regard to the assignment to test units to groups and by a large level of control for extraneous variables. For example, a bank located in a country such as Finland, where consumer Internet banking is very widespread and where the vast majority of I-banking customers use a single bank's I-banking interface, would be able to conduct true experiments concerning variations in its Internet banking interface. For this field experiment to be a true experiment, the Finnish customers involved in the experiment would have to be randomly assigned to the experimental and control groups. Additionally, a high level of control of extraneous variables could be achieved because the Finnish customers would access only the specific I-banking interface and thus would not be subject to uncontrollable communication from competing banks.

Laboratory experiments are sometimes used in marketing research. In these cases, the laboratory may be a restaurant, place of entertainment, shop, or trade fair environment designed exclusively for experimentation purposes. The possibilities for controlling extraneous variables tend to be higher in such laboratories. However, human subjects of research may still respond differently to the stimuli in such laboratories than they would in other situations, especially if they are aware that they are a part of a test and/or are present in a laboratory.

Future Developments in the Marketing Industry

The future of the marketing industry will be influenced by broader societal developments, including the evolution of production and distribution structures, further innovations in the area of information technology, and continued public debate and governmental regulation concerning international trade and the protection of sensitive person-related data. As concerns the evolution of production and distribution structures, in some industries, marketers are faced with increasingly short product development and launch periods. This occurs in industries that are highly influenced by fashion or fads, such as the clothing industry or the entertainment industry. In these cases, the marketing research and its resulting product or service adjustments are often done on a real-time basis, i.e., on the basis of data accumulated in marketing information systems and/or through the use of universal product code (UPC) bar codes, "loyalty cards" in retail shops, or monitoring devices that record the consumer's use of the Internet, the television, or video game equipment. It is expected that this trend toward "real-time" marketing research will continue in the future. In service industries (such as chartered travel, hotels and motels, retailing, airlines, and, in some countries, rail travel), special systems of real-time pricing based on marketing information on achieved sales are being implemented. These systems have revolutionized the marketing industry's possibilities for determining an optimal price at a certain place and time.

The production and distribution structures used by the marketing industry to distribute its market- and customer-related information are also evolving due to new information technology possibilities. Marketers within many multinational companies communicate with each other on a daily basis via either the Internet or an internal network, and they also hold meetings using teleconferencing facilities. Additionally, relationships between client firms and the marketing industry's consulting firms are often reinforced by such telecommunication. These developments are expected to become even more prevalent in the future, as is the trend toward the increased use of Internet (and perhaps even mobile) services in transmitting surveys to and from respondents. Finally, in the future, respondents may also be interviewed individually or in focus groups via teleconferencing, just as Internet discussion groups may also be used for research in many of the same ways that focus groups are currently being used. However, the methodologies for conducting communicative marketing research electronically are not yet as well developed as the corresponding traditional, face-to-face methods are.

Evolutions in information technology have also allowed for more advanced statistical and econometrical analysis than was previously possible, as well as very advanced business information software programs that contain data-mining and data-warehousing features. In many of these business information software programs, the marketing information systems related to customer listening are regarded as just one part of more general management information systems, which also encompass financial planning systems, materials and production management systems, human resource management systems, and systems for monitoring specific competitors' activities. Thus, marketing research and marketing decisions, and here especially the marketing research and decisions at the level of the whole organization, are increasingly also being assessed by business information gatherers who are experts in other fields of business administration. This increases the need for members of the marketing industry as well as all other types of business specialists to have sound generalist knowledge of all of the main areas of decision making in organizations and of the interdependencies between these areas.

The demand for international marketing research is related to the extent of trade liberalization and the harmonization of product requirements in relation to national or international standards, consumer protection issues, and environmental policy. However, due to the progression of trade liberalization talks in the WTO and the General Agreement on Trade in Services (GATS), for example, as well as the creation and further strengthening of trade blocks such as the EU and NAFTA, it can be expected that the marketing industry will be even more involved in international marketing research than it has been. Thus, there will also be a need in the future for marketers who have skills in the methods used to conduct market- and customer-related social measurement in more than one country.

Regarding the protection of person-specific data, it is much more difficult to predict the future, because public opinion and the actions of lawmakers will very likely be influenced by specific events. Such events include possible media disclosure of the illegal use and/or perceived unethical use of such data or, to the contrary, stories in the media of successful product or service improvements that would not have been possible without the generation and combination of such person-specific data. However, it can be said with a high degree of certainty that this is an area that is being watched intensively in many democratic countries by the media as well as by consumer rights organizations and organizations concerned with civil liberties.

See Also the Following Articles

Business, Social Science Methods Used in • Case Study • Economics, Strategies in Social Science • Interviews • Laboratory Experiments in Social Science • Observational Studies

Further Reading

Achrol, R. S. (1991). Evolution of the marketing organization: new forms for turbulent environments. *J. Market.* **55**(4), 77–93.

Backhaus, J. W. (2003). *International Marketing.* Macmillan Press, Hampshire, England.

Carson, D., Gilmore, A., Perry, C., and Gronhaug, K. (2001). *Qualitative Marketing Research.* Sage, London.

Coviello, N. E., Brodie, R. J., Danaher, P. J., and Johnston, W. J. (2002). How firms relate to their markets: an empirical examination of contemporary marketing practices. *J. Market.* **66**(4), 33–46.

Kotler, P. (2003). *Marketing Management,* 11th Ed. Prentice Hall, Upper Saddle River, New Jersey.

Kumar, V. (2000). *International Marketing Research.* Prentice Hall, Upper Saddle River, New Jersey.

Laudon, K., and Laudon, J. (2003). *Management Information Systems,* 8th Ed. Prentice Hall, Upper Saddle River, New Jersey.

Malhotra, N. K., and Birks, D. F. (2003). *Marketing Research: An Applied Approach.* Pearson Education, London.

Tharp, M., and Jeong, J. (2001). Executive insights: The Global Network Communications Agency. *J. Int. Market.* **9**(4), 111–131.

Usunier, J.-C. (2000). *Marketing Across Cultures,* 3rd Ed. Pearson Education, London.

Webster, F. E., Jr. (1992). The changing role of marketing in the corporation. *J. Market.* **56**(4), 1–17.

Wierenga, B., and van Bruggen, G. H. (1997). The integration of marketing problem-solving modes and marketing management support systems. *J. Market.* **61**(3), 21–37.

Mathematical and Statistical Approaches

David J. Bartholomew

London School of Economics, London, England, United Kingdom

Glossary

Bernoulli variable A random variable that takes only two values, usually designated by 0 and 1.

factor analysis A method of statistical analysis designed to show how far a set of correlations between variables can be explained by its dependence on a smaller set of unobserved variables.

factor score The predicted (or "estimated") value of an unobservable variable.

Gini coefficient A scale-free measure of dispersion for a positive random variable.

indicator A directly observable random variable that depends on an unobservable variable and thus "indicates" something about its value.

intelligence quotient (IQ) A widely used measure of cognitive ability.

latent variable A random variable that cannot be directly observed; also known as a hidden variable or a factor.

logit If p lies between 0 and 1, then logit $p = \log_e[p/(1-p)]$.

manifest variable A random variable that is directly observable.

Markov chain A process, developing over time, in which the probability of moving to a new state at any time depends only on the current state.

Social measurement poses particular problems because many of the quantities occurring in social discourse cannot be measured directly. Indirect methods based on mathematical or statistical models provide an important way out of this impasse. This approach enables many measurement problems to be posed as problems of statistical estimation or prediction.

Introduction

Social Measurement

Measurement is the cornerstone of science. Laws of nature typically express the relationship between measured quantities. Ohm's law, for example, states that the voltage divided by the current flowing in a circuit is equal to a constant called the resistance. Physicists have invented instruments for measuring the basic variables of the physical world—length, mass, time, and electric charge. In the social sciences, the position is much more complicated, although social scientists often aspire to the standards of measurement set by their natural science colleagues. In some areas, especially in economics, it is sometimes possible to quantify the concepts in a way that allows them to be measured directly. Time and money, for example, are two variables for which measurement poses relatively few problems. This is "direct" measurement because the quantity of interest is directly expressible in terms of some readily measurable quantity. However, a great many other variables are not so readily captured. For example, cost of living, quality of life, arithmetical ability, or social mobility are all spoken of quantitatively, yet there are no simple measuring instruments to measure them in the direct way that is usual in the natural sciences. What is usually available in such cases is a set of indicators—that is, a collection of directly measurable quantities that are believed to reflect the underlying quantity of real interest to some degree. The problem of measurement is then to distill from this collection of indicators the essence of the variable of interest. Put in another way, the task is to assign numbers to objects in a way that corresponds to the intuitive notion of their "magnitude." Measurement of this kind may be described as *indirect*. It is in indirect measurement that mathematical and statistical methods come in to play.

Examples

Before proceeding, it will help to have a variety of examples in mind. Common examples arise in most of the social sciences and in related areas such as medicine. In economics, quantities such as the cost of living or industrial production need to be measured so that comparisons can be made over time and so that the quantities can be used as inputs to econometric models. Many indicators (for example, of the cost of living) are usually expressed as price relatives (that is, current prices expressed in terms of the prices at some earlier time). Some kind of average (usually weighted) then serves as a measure of the unobserved quantity.

In sociology, a large amount of work (much originating with Karl Schuessler of the University of Indiana) has focused on the measurement of "social life feelings." This covers attitudes such as feeling "down," job satisfaction, and disillusionment with government. One of the main interests of quantitative sociologists has been in social or occupational mobility. Intergenerational mobility is concerned with the movement of family lines between social classes (usually defined by occupation). Sociologists are interested in comparing the mobility of different societies and of the same society at different times. For this they need measures of mobility.

Psychologists have been prominent in the field of social measurement through their interest in human abilities and attributes. First, and most controversial, among these has been the measurement of intelligence, to which we shall return later. The whole field of intelligence assessment has become an area of study in its own right, known as psychometrics.

Finally, but without exhausting the list of examples, there is the issue of quality of life. This is a particularly interesting case because it straddles several disciplines and falls into both of the main categories of measurement that we are about to define. As used in medicine, for example, it usually refers to a characteristic of an individual. It arises in the context of treatment for disabling conditions, when the decision to treat the condition may depend on the quality of life that the patient will expect to enjoy subsequent to treatment. This usually refers to the degree of mobility, the ability to feed and wash oneself, and so on. In other contexts, it refers to the quality of the environment, which is something shared by a whole population. The indicators in this case will include the concentration of atmospheric pollutants, the quality of drinking water, and so on.

Population and Individual Level Measurement

Social measures fall into two broad categories that require different treatment. Some relate to populations and others relate to individuals. Social mobility, for example, is a characteristic of a human population. Such a population is made up of many individuals, or family lines, each pursuing a different path over the generations. However, it is not the individual movements that are of interest, but the collective behavior of the population. Some populations show more movement than others, and that is what a measure of mobility is designed to capture.

A cost-of-living index is, likewise, a population measure, though this time it is the population of commodities purchased. Population measures refer to aggregates and so may be referred to as aggregate measures. Other variables relate to individuals. Abilities or attitudes, for example, are individual characteristics. They may be thought of as if they were real (but unobservable) characteristics of the individual, just like the indicators. To distinguish them from the indicators, they are called "latent" (or hidden) variables.

Mathematical and Statistical Approaches

Formal Statement of the Problem

Many measures in current use have been derived without any overarching theory. In some cases, the way to construct them has seemed so obvious as to make a formal theory unnecessary. For example, the "summated rating scales" widely used in ability scaling simply require the addition of the indicator scores in each row of the data matrix (see later). Teachers have done this kind of thing for generations because it seemed the natural thing to do.

In mobility measurement, there exists, a wide range of similarly *ad hoc* measures that seem to measure mobility in an obvious way. Examples include the proportion of family lines that move to a different class from one generation to the next, or, if the classes are designated by numbers, the correlation between the classes in the first and second generations. Even at this rudimentary level there are indications that intuition may not be enough. There are, in fact, many measures of mobility available, and this fact raises the question of their relative merits. A general theory of measurement should enable making rational choices between existing measures. More importantly, it should enable devising new measures for new situations. As part of this process, it helps to clarify the concept behind the measure.

A convenient way of setting out the unity of the measurement problems is to start with the form of the data from which the problems originate. The differences arise from the differing ways in which the data are supposed to have been generated. Imagine the data for the problem to be set out in a standard data matrix as follows:

	Indicators			
	x_{11}	x_{12}	$\ldots$	x_{1p}
	x_{21}	x_{22}	$\ldots$	x_{2p}
Individuals	$\vdots$	$\vdots$		
	x_{n1}	x_{n2}	$\ldots$	x_{np}

There is one column for each indicator, of which we assume there to be p altogether. The rows are referred to as "individuals." In many applications, these will be persons, but they could be firms, farms, or families. These n individuals will often be sampled randomly from some population, but this need not necessarily be so. There may be missing values, because not all indicators need be observed for all individuals. Posed mathematically, the problem is to find some function of the elements of this table to serve as the measure. The data matrix will be denoted by $\mathbf{X}$.

First look at the matrix from the aggregate measure point of view, taking the simplest possible case when there is only one column. Such an example arises when measuring inequality. Suppose that the income of n families is observed and a measure of inequality is to be constructed. The problem is then to find some function of the elements in the first (and only) column of the table that summarizes what is meant by inequality of income. If the column represents the whole population, this immediately provides the measure. If it is a random sample, an inference must be made from the sample to the population.

The case of social mobility is more complicated, but the same general principles apply. The x values in the first column might represent the class to which each family line belongs in the first generation. The second column would then indicate the class occupied by the next generation, and so on, across the table. In practice, there will often be only two columns to the mobility table. Each row provides information about the mobility pattern of a particular family line. An aggregate measure of mobility must then be obtained by aggregating these patterns in some way.

Next look at the data matrix from the individual measurement point of view. In educational testing, the rows would represent the individuals whose ability is to be measured. In each row are the scores obtained by that individual on a series of p tests. Thus, for example, the x values might be marks out of 100. The individual measurement problem is to use each individual's test scores to arrive at an ability score. In other words, we wish to attach a score, y_i, say, to the ith row that can be regarded as a measure of the ability of individual i. This value, y_i, is a predictor or estimate of the latent variable we seek to measure.

Individual level measurement is thus the problem of extracting a relevant summary of the sample of variables represented by the columns. In this case, it will not be justified, or necessary, to regard them as a random sample. They do need, however, to be representative, in some sense, of the population (or domain) of items that are indicators of the latent variable.

Axiomatic Approaches

The measurement problem can be posed as that of finding a scalar function of the elements of the data matrix, $m(\mathbf{X})$ say, which captures the essence of what it is desired to measure. It may be possible to specify constraints on the function $m(\mathbf{X})$ that restrict the range of functions necessary to consider. Ideally, if there were only one function that met all the requirements, the measurement problem would be solved. This is called the axiomatic approach because it starts with a set of properties (axioms) that any measure must satisfy. More realistically, the method may serve to restrict the search for suitable measures. Used retrospectively, it provides a means of judging the validity of measures arrived at by other means (see section on Validity). The approach has been used in the construction of index numbers and, in an extended form, for social mobility.

In order to illustrate the idea, consider how it might be applied to the construction of a measure of income inequality. In this case, suppose the data matrix has only one column in which the values of income are recorded. Dropping the second subscript, look for a function $m(x_1, x_2, \ldots, x_n)$ that measures the degree on inequality. Inequality is a quantity that is necessarily non-negative. Therefore, limit the class of functions to those for which $m(x_1, x_2, \ldots, x_n) \geq 0$. Second, if all x values were equal, there would be no inequality. Thus, if $x_1 = x_2 = \cdots = x_n = x$, say, then $m(x, x, \ldots, x) = 0$ is required. Third, inequality does not depend on the units in which income is measured. It does not matter whether rupees, dollars, or yen are used. The third axiom then becomes

$$m(ax_1, ax_2, \ldots, ax_n) = m(x_1, x_2, \ldots, x_n) \qquad \text{for any} \quad a > 0.$$

Proceeding further along these lines narrows down the range of options. For example, it might be required that if the distance between any pair of x values increased, the measure of inequality should increase also. However, the procedure has gone far enough to indicate what the approach involves. In practice, it is far less useful than the model-based approach.

Model-Based Approaches

The key idea behind the approach advocated here is that of a statistical model. The model provides the link between the data and the underlying concept. The modeling approach requires specifying the joint probability distribution of the random variables, the observed values of which are given in the data matrix. This specification must include any latent variables. The quantity to be measured is then identified either as a latent variable or as a parameter of this distribution. The measurement problem then resolves itself into the prediction of a random variable or the estimation of a parameter of the distribution. All measurement problems are then reduced to problems of prediction or estimation, which can be tackled by standard statistical methods. In the following sections, it is shown how this simple idea works out in practice.

Modeling Individual Behavior

The basic idea is first introduced by pointing out that it is already implicit in the summated rating scale. Suppose a child is asked to perform a number of tasks, 10, say, as a test of arithmetical ability. What is the rationale behind the idea that a sum of task-performance scores gives a good indication of the child's ability? Because a sum of scores would obviously be much better than any score taken individually, a likely answer would be as follows: the score on any particular task might be affected by many extraneous factors peculiar to the circumstances at the time. The task might, by chance, happen to be one the child had encountered before. Or the child's attention might have been distracted by something happening in the room or by the recollection of some incident that caused daydreaming. Some of these extraneous factors might work in one direction, and some in the other. However, it would not be expected that all factors were present all of the time and for all people. Different factors on different occasions would be likely to produce a haphazard perturbation of the scores. Given enough items, it would confidently be expected that the pluses and the minuses will roughly balance out, thus providing a better idea of the true ability of the child.

This argument may be expressed algebraically as follows. Let there be p items yielding scores $x_1, x_2, \ldots, x_p$. Suppose that the major determinant of x_i is the child's ability, denoted by a. This gives

$$x_i = a + e_i \qquad (i = 1, 2, \ldots, p), \tag{1}$$

where e_i is the effect of all the extraneous factors acting on this occasion. Because each e_i is presumed to be the cumulative effect of many separate factors, it is expected that some are negative and some are positive. Overall, they should approximately "balance out." This idea can be taken further by making assumptions about the frequency distribution of the e_i values, and that, in turn, will indicate whether straight addition is, indeed, the best way of "extracting" a. When extended to include distributional assumptions, Eq. (1) is sometimes referred to as the classical measurement model. Although it is limited in its scope, it incorporates the key elements in any measurement model—namely, (1) a quantitative link between the indicators (the x values and the thing to be measured, a) and (2) a probabilistic statement about the deviations of the indicators from the thing to be measured. In an individual-level measurement problem, it is assumed that each individual (represented by a row of the matrix) is located at a different point on a one-dimensional scale. This means that the rows will all have different distributions. There is, therefore, no way to estimate those distributions directly. Instead, some assumption will have to be made about their form. This is made easier by the fact that the distributions can be broken down into component parts.

The starting point for a model is still the joint probability distribution of the elements in the ith row. (The concern is only with a single row because the focus is only on the value of y linked to that row.) However, this distribution is now conditional on the latent variable, denoted by y. If some way of estimating this distribution can be found, then the roles of y and $\mathbf{x}$ can be inverted by Bayes' theorem to give

$$f(y \mid \mathbf{x}) = \frac{f(y) f(\mathbf{x} \mid y)}{f(\mathbf{x})}, \tag{2}$$

where, for convenience, the subscript i has been omitted from $\mathbf{x}$. To keep things simple, all variables have been treated as continuous, but the idea is perfectly general. All that is known about y, after $\mathbf{x}$ is observed, is contained in $f(y \mid \mathbf{x})$. The value of y is clearly not certain, but its value can be predicted using Eq. (2). There are several ways of doing this, but a natural predictor is $E(y \mid \mathbf{x})$. In principle, this solves the individual measurement problem, but only after selection of $f(\mathbf{x} \mid y)$ and $f(y)$. The relationship between the three distributions appearing on the right-hand side of Eq. (2) is

$$f(\mathbf{x}) = \int_{-\infty}^{+\infty} f(y)\, f(\mathbf{x} \mid y)\, dy. \tag{3}$$

Once $f(y)$ and $f(\mathbf{x} \mid y)$ have been chosen (by whatever means), that they are consistent with the data can be checked using Eq. (3). Here $f(\mathbf{x})$ is the marginal distribution of $\mathbf{x}$ that can be estimated from the data. However, there are infinitely many pairs $\{f(y), f(\mathbf{x} \mid y)\}$ that lead to the same $f(\mathbf{x})$. Once one pair is available, others can be generated simply by making a one-to-one transformation of y. This has no effect on the integral and hence on $f(\mathbf{x})$. Another way of saying this is that $f(y)$, the prior distribution, is arbitrary, and any choice that is made is, therefore, a matter of convention.

This still leaves $f(\mathbf{x} \mid y)$ to be chosen, and here the choice can be narrowed by invoking a variety of considerations. If $\mathbf{x}$ is to tell us anything at all about y, it must be because each individual x_i depends on y. This common dependence on y means that the x values will be correlated among themselves. Conversely, it may be inferred that, if the x values are independent, then, when we condition on y, there are no further latent variables influencing the x values. This means that it is necessary only to choose the form of a univariate distribution rather than a multivariate distribution.

A second criterion for choosing $f(x_i \mid y)$ $(i = 1, 2, \ldots, n)$ is based on the notion of sufficiency. If it turned out that $f(y \mid \mathbf{x})$, given by Eq. (2), depended on $\mathbf{x}$ only through a single statistic t, say, then this would serve as a substitute for y in the sense that, once t is known, the data would provide no more information about y. In other words, any measure of y should be a function of t.

An example is provided by the case when all the x values are binary variables. This is often the case in educational and attitude testing when the responses are YES/NO or RIGHT/WRONG. Each x_i is then a Bernoulli variable defined by the probability of getting a positive response, $\pi_i(y)$, say. The problem is then to choose a suitable functional form for $\pi_i(y)$. As a probability, it must obviously lie between 0 and 1. Further, it should be monotonic in y because the "more y" there is, the greater (or lesser) should be the probability of a positive response. Also, symmetry arguments can be brought into play. Which of the two responses are labeled as 1 and as 0 is quite arbitrary, and the choice of direction to measure y is likewise arbitrary. Any function chosen, therefore, should retain the same form under transformations of this kind. These constraints are not sufficient to determine uniquely $\pi_i(y)$, but they severely limit the range of choices. If it is now asked that the sufficiency condition should also be satisfied, the choice is

$$\text{logit}\ \pi_i(y) = \alpha_{i0} + \alpha_{i1} y \qquad (i = 1, 2, \ldots, n). \tag{4}$$

This is known as the logit model and the function $\pi_i(y)$ is S-shaped, increasing from 0 to 1 as y ranges from $-\infty$ to $+\infty$. The sufficient statistic turns out to be

$$t = \sum_{i=1}^{p} \alpha_{i1} x_i. \tag{5}$$

It is very interesting to note that this approach has led to a weighted sum of x values that is very close to the summated rating scale idea, which owes nothing to the general ideas presented here. The only difference lies in the weights $\{\alpha_{i1}\}$. A large value of α_{i1} means that the corresponding probability changes relatively rapidly with y. In other words, x_i is a good indicator of y and hence it is appropriate that it should receive more weight. The form of the argument here is largely dictated by the fact that x_i was assumed to be a binary variable. Similar reasoning can be used if x_i is polytomous or continuous.

Modeling Collective Behavior

In modeling collective behavior, it is necessary to estimate the joint distribution of the row elements of the data matrix. This is because all rows have the same distribution, because they have been generated by random sampling from some population, the aggregate properties of which are of interest. The previous example of inequality can be used to illustrate how a measure may be derived from this. That is, suppose there is a situation with a single observation on each individual. Suppose, again, that this observation measures the income of the individual and that constructing a measure of income inequality is of interest. That is, it is desired to locate the particular distribution on a scale that can be regarded as measuring inequality. In this case, it is immediately recognized that a measure such as the standard deviation indicates variability, and hence inequality. In passing, note also that the first two axioms are then satisfied but the third is not. Changing the scale of each indicator changes the scales of the standard deviation by the same factor. For example, if income is measured in monetary units such as euros, the standard deviation will be in the same units. The degree of inequality should not depend on such arbitrary units, so the problem might be solved by using instead standard deviation/mean. This would then serve as a measure of inequality. There is thus a way of mapping the possible distributions of income onto a one-dimensional scale extending from zero upward.

Of course, there are other measures of dispersion and other ways of normalizing the incomes so as to make the measure independent of scale. One interesting alternative is to use the Gini coefficient, which ranks the distributions according to their degree of dispersion (inequality) on a scale from 0 to 1 by a measure derived directly from the distribution. Leaving aside the question of how, precisely, to measure scale-free dispersion, this simple example reveals that any measure will be a parameter of the distribution. Most distributions will depend on several parameters, so choosing the right parameter may involve selecting some function of the parameters in terms of which the distribution is specified—as in this case. Constructing a measure thus resolves itself into two stages: (1) determining an appropriate distribution to describe the variation of the data and (2) identifying the relevant (appropriate) parameter of that distribution to serve as a measure.

The case of mobility is much more complicated but the same principles apply. If the classes of the family line are observed over $(p - 1)$ generations, it is possible to estimate the joint distribution $f(\mathbf{x}_i)$, where $\mathbf{x}_i$ represents the ith row of the data matrix. The question now concerns what parameter of that distribution best reflects what is meant by "mobility." To keep things simple, suppose that $p = 2$, so that there is only one generation to consider. The joint distribution $f(\mathbf{x}_i)$, which can be factorized into $f(x_{i2} \mid x_{i1})\, f(x_{i1})$. The set $\{f(x_{i1})\}$ is concerned with how family lines are distributed across classes and it can be plausibly argued that this distribution reveals nothing about mobility that is concerned with transitions between classes. Therefore, only the conditional distributions $\{f(x_{i2} \mid x_{i1})\}$ should be considered. These determine how family lines are distributed across classes at the first step. A simple hypothesis, for which there is empirical evidence, is that the distribution is multinomial with parameters $\pi_{i1}, \pi_{i2}, \ldots, \pi_{ip}$, say $(\sum_{j=1}^{p} \pi_{ij} = 1)\,(i = 1, 2, \ldots, n)$. If that is accepted, mobility is governed by the transition matrix:

$$\mathbf{P} = \begin{bmatrix} \pi_{11} & \pi_{12} & \cdots & \pi_{1p} \\ \pi_{21} & \pi_{22} & \cdots & \pi_{2p} \\ \vdots & & & \\ \pi_{p1} & \pi_{p2} & \cdots & \pi_{pp} \end{bmatrix} \tag{6}$$

The joint distribution obviously has very many parameters; therefore, it has to be decided what single-valued function of those parameters best represents what is meant by mobility. Much work on measuring mobility has centered on finding a suitable one-dimensional summary of this matrix (this question will be further addressed later).

Constructing a joint distribution involves making assumptions and the quality of the resulting measure will depend on the realism of these assumptions. An important part of the measurement process is the validation of the model by testing the assumptions.

Two Examples

Intelligence

The measurement of intelligence has a long and controversial history. There are two distinct strands, both originating independently at the beginning of the 20th century. The first began with Alfred Binet, whose tests were originally devised to identify children who might benefit from remedial education. The basic idea was refined and developed, leading to what became known as the Binet–Simon scale and the Binet–Stanford scale. The latter was largely the work of Lewis Terman. A key figure here was David Wechsler, whose name is still linked with a family of tests in use today. The second strand began with Charles Spearman, whose interest gave birth to factor analysis. Subsequent developments were made on both sides of the Atlantic by Thurstone, Thomson, Cattell, and many others. It is this second strand that falls within the general framework described herein. In the third section, the general approach for the case where the manifest variables are binary was illustrated. Items in intelligence tests are usually treated as continuous variables. In that case, the model becomes a set of regression equations of the x_i values on the latent variables, but the general idea is essentially the same. It is still the case, for example, that information about latent variables is contained in linear combinations of the manifest variables. When scores for test items, such as those in the Wechsler scales, are factor analyzed, it turns out that they cannot be adequately described by a model with only one latent variable. It seems to be necessary to include at least three. This means that the idea of intelligence that lies behind those scales is not a unidimensional quantity, as is commonly supposed. This accounts for much of the confusion and dispute that have surrounded this matter. Spearman, for his part, recognized that the term "intelligence," as used in ordinary discourse, was too imprecise for scientific purposes. He therefore coined the term "*g*" for the major dimension of latent variation. Spearman and his followers regarded this as corresponding to a general dimension of cognitive ability. By identifying those test items that are particularly good indicators of this latent dimension, it is possible to get a more precise idea of what this dimension represents. Items that require abstract problem solving, especially those depending on patterns in numbers and shapes, seem to be close to what this factor measures.

The quantity *g* is, of course, a latent variable and cannot, therefore, be directly observed. Thus, it has to be estimated from the data. These estimates (or factor scores, as they are known) are linear combinations of the item scores. Once again, therefore, the intuitive idea of summing (possibly with weights) turns out to have theoretical support.

Because these *g* scores are linear combinations of indicators, they have the same form as the intelligence quotient (IQ) indices constructed by Wechsler, among others. It may be asked what is the difference between the two. The answer is that IQ reflects the compromise position of the individual on several different dimensions of ability, whereas the *g* score relates to the single dimension identified as general cognitive ability.

The case of intelligence provides another example of the advantages of a model-based approach to measurement. It serves to resolve much of the confusion that has bedeviled the subject for almost a century. Further, it provides a technique for generating a measure with a much clearer meaning.

Social Mobility

Return again to the question of measuring mobility, at the point where the transition matrix **P** had been identified as the set of parameters containing the information about mobility. The next question is how to summarize this information in a single number. If this is possible, it will serve to rank matrices according to the degree of mobility that they represent. A good way to begin is to fix the end points representing the maximum and minimum amount of mobility. The lower limit presents no problems. When $\mathbf{P} = \mathbf{I}$, there is no movement at all and this matrix therefore corresponds to 0 on the mobility scale. The upper limit is not so straightforward. In the case of zero mobility, the son's social class is identical with the father's and so depends on the father's social class to the greatest degree possible. The opposite extreme, when viewed from this angle, is a situation in which the son's class is totally independent of the father's. The condition for this to be so is that the rows of the transition matrix be identical. There are infinitely many matrices having this property, and all should therefore map onto the extreme upper end point of the scale.

A little reflection suggests that the upper limit might be defined in another way. The point may be made by inspecting the following three matrices:

$$\underset{\text{(i)}}{\begin{pmatrix} 1 & 0 \\ 0 & 1 \end{pmatrix}} \quad \underset{\text{(ii)}}{\begin{pmatrix} 2/3 & 1/3 \\ 2/3 & 1/3 \end{pmatrix}} \quad \underset{\text{(iii)}}{\begin{pmatrix} 1/3 & 2/3 \\ 2/3 & 1/3 \end{pmatrix}} \qquad (7)$$

The second matrix is a 2×2 matrix with identical rows. But the third matrix will produce more changes of class than the second will, because 2/3 of the first class move compared with 1/3 in the middle case. This example reveals an ambiguity in the concept of mobility. If it is desired to measure the amount of movement, the upper extreme would occur when

$$\mathbf{P} = \begin{pmatrix} 0 & 1 \\ 1 & 0 \end{pmatrix}$$

because then all family lines move. The intermediate case, whereby the rows are identical, is actually measuring what might be more accurately described as social inheritance—the extent to which the class of the child is dependent on that of the father. For matrices intermediate between matrices (i) and (ii), the concepts of movement and social inheritance are not easy to distinguish. It is only with movement to the upper extreme that the two diverge. This example illustrates how the modeling process may bring to light subtle distinctions that are easily missed in less formal approaches.

The foregoing discussion can be recognized as an example of the axiomatic approach, but this time it is applied to the parameters rather than to the data. This process was carried further by Anthony Shorrocks, to the point where there was no single measure that satisfied all of the axioms that he proposed. This suggested that the concept needed further clarification. Many measures have been suggested. When the primary focus is on social inheritance, there is a whole class of measures based on the distance between the estimated transition matrix and either of the previously identified extremes. Measures of movement typically focus on the number of transitions made. In both cases, account needs to be taken of whether the classes are ordered. If not, all moves to a different class are equivalent so far as the contribution they make to mobility is concerned. If the classes are ordered, a move from class I (the lowest class) to class III can be thought of as two moves—from I to II and from II to III—and so should carry more weight.

All of the measures derived in this way are model dependent. The Markov chain model used here is not the only model capable of describing mobility. It is almost always an oversimplification. In some contexts, another model, known as the vacancy-chain model, is more suitable. This is as it should be, because what is meant by mobility obviously depends on what drives the system. However, bearing in mind that one of the main purposes of measuring mobility is to make comparisons—between societies and within one society at different times—it may be better to settle for a simple model that will allow such comparisons.

Having decided on the appropriate parameter, the final step is to estimate it from the data matrix. This may, or may not, be a simple task but, in principle at least, it is a routine matter.

Validity and Reliability

Validity

Turning all measurement problems into statistical problems of estimation or prediction has also clarified two topics that figure prominently in the measurement literature, namely, validity and reliability. Validity is concerned with whether the measure is measuring the right thing. In a strict sense, it is impossible to answer this question because there is no "gold standard" with which a proposed measure can be compared. If there were, there would be no need of a new measure in the first place! There is no question that a population-based measure provides a measure of the parameter that has been identified as being the thing desired to measure. Equally, statistical theory ensures that the predictor of a latent variable does, indeed, predict the latent variable of interest.

The question of validity, therefore, resolves itself into the question of the appropriateness of the model. In the case of social mobility, for example, there are two aspects to this question. First, does the model adequately describe the movements between classes? Second, does the function of the parameters that were chosen adequately capture the notion of mobility. The first is a statistical question; the second is a matter of semantics. Essentially, it must be asked whether the measure varies in a way that corresponds to the usage of the term in social scientific discourse.

The axiomatic approach often provides a partial way of judging validity, as already noted. Axioms embody the most basic features of the concept we are trying to capture. That a measure of inequality should be non-negative and independent of scale is a very limited but self-evident pair of properties that can be used to weed out totally unsuitable measures. In the case of social mobility, it is easily possible to propose sufficient axioms to identify a single measure. The same is true of index numbers. Roy Allen, for example, has described many desirable properties that, it turns out, cannot be satisfied simultaneously by any single index. Again, this points to lack of precision about what we are trying to measure but, by checking which axioms are satisfied, it is possible to judge how close a proposed measure comes to the ideal and to make a judgment about its validity.

Reliability

Reliability is, essentially, about the closeness of the estimate or predictor to the parameter or latent variable of interest. Appropriate measures of reliability, therefore, arise naturally from general statistical theory. The standard error of an estimator measures reliability. The predictive variance serves the same purpose for predictors. Thus, if we have a factor score $E(y \mid \mathbf{x})$ for y, then the conditional standard deviation $\sigma(y \mid \mathbf{x})$ measures the reliability of the score (as would any other measure of dispersion). In practice, there are a number of other measures in use, all closely related to $\sigma(y \mid \mathbf{x})$. An advantage of the statistical approach recommended here is that it requires nothing new but points directly to the core idea on which any reasonable measure of reliability must depend. For individual-level measurement, there are several reliability coefficients, one of which—Cronbach's alpha—is widely used. Such coefficients are constructed to range over the interval (0, 1), but they are essentially equivalent to measures of variability as defined here. So far as the principles are concerned, therefore, they may be regarded as measures of variability, or unpredictability.

See Also the Following Articles

Bernoulli, Jakob • Contingency Tables and Log-Linear Models • Correlations • Factor Analysis • Population vs. Sample • Psychometrics of Intelligence • Reliability Assessment • Validity Assessment • Validity, Data Sources

Further Reading

Allen, R. G. D. (1975). *Index Numbers in Theory and Practice.* Macmillan, London.

Bartholomew, D. J. (1996). *The Statistical Approach to Social Measurement.* Academic Press, San Diego.

Bartholomew, D. J. (2004). *Measuring Intelligence: Facts and Fallacies.* Cambridge University Press.

Bartholomew, D. J., and Knott, M. (1999). *Latent Variable Models and Factor Analysis.* Arnold, London.

Duncan, O. D. (1984). *Notes on Social Measurement: Historical and Critical.* Russell Sage Foundation, New York.

Hand, D. J. (1996). Statistics and the theory of measurement (with discussion). *J. Roy. Statist. Soc. A* **159,** 445–492.

Krantz, D. H., Luce, R. D., Suppes, P., and Tversky, A. (1971). *Foundations of Measurement, Vol. I. Additional Polynomial Representations.* Academic Press, London.

Luce, R. D., Krantz, D. H., Suppes, P., and Tversky, A. (1990). *Foundations of Measurement, Vol. III. Representation, Axiomatization and Invariance.* Academic Press, San Diego.

Shorrocks, A. F. (1978). The measurement of mobility. *Econometrica* **46,** 1013–1024.

Stevens, S. S. (1946). On the theory of scales of measurement. *Science* **103,** 677–680.

Suppes, P., Krantz, D. H., Luce, R. D., and Tversky, A. (1989). *Foundations of Measurement, Vol. II. Geometric Thresholds and Probabilistic Representation.* Academic Press, San Diego.

Mathematical Demography

Marc Artzrouni
University of Pau, Pau, France

Glossary

carrying capacity The maximum sustainable population, which in the case of the logistic function is the value toward which the population levels off.

cohort A group of individuals sharing a common characteristic (e.g., born the same year).

continuous models Models in which time is any real number.

deterministic models Models in which all quantities are known.

discrete models Models in which time is counted at discrete points in time (0, 1, 2, etc.).

force of mortality at age *x* A measure of the risk of dying during a short time interval after age *x* conditional on surviving to age *x*.

Lexis diagram A schematic representation of the life course of an individual through time.

life expectancy at age *x* Average number of years to be lived beyond age *x*.

life table A table describing statistically the attrition through death (or other causes) of a group of individuals born the same year.

logistic function A function that describes a population that initially grows exponentially and then levels off.

stable population A population with constant age-specific mortality rates and a number of births growing exponentially.

stationary population A population with constant age-specific mortality rates and a number of births that is constant.

stochastic models Models in which all quantities have a certain degree of uncertainly (stochastic is synonymous with random).

strong ergodicity The long-run behavior of a population subjected to constant fertility and mortality rates.

weak ergodicity The long-run behavior of a population subjected to variable fertility and mortality rates.

Mathematical demography uses mathematical and statistical methods to study the size, distribution, composition, and dynamics of human populations. This definition can be broadened to include all biological populations (i.e., cells and animal populations).

Introduction

History up to 1900

It is generally accepted that the modern use of statistical methods for the study of human populations (at least in the Western world) started with the Englishman John Graunt in the 17th century. He produced a fairly detailed statistical description of the populations of London and England. His most important contribution was made in his single published work in which he described for the first time a life table (see Table I). The life table, which is a cornerstone of mathematical demography, describes the attrition through death over time in a cohort of, say,

Table I Graunt's 1662 Life Table

Age	*Survivors*
0	100
6	64
26	40
36	16
46	10
56	6
76	1
80	0

100 individuals born at the same time. Graunt's table makes clear the struggle for life in 17th century England, where only 16% of the population reached their thirty-sixth birthday.

Another cornerstone of mathematical demography is the stable population, first introduced in the 18th century by the Swiss mathematician Leonard Euler. A stable population has a constant age-specific death rate and an annual number of births growing exponentially. A stationary population is a special case of stability with a zero growth rate for births.

Perhaps the first mathematical theory of population growth can be found in the work of the English clergyman Thomas Malthus. Although Malthus's much debated ideas are beyond the scope of this entry, their mathematical expression is laid out simply in his celebrated and controversial 1798 essay. Malthus argues that "Population, when unchecked, increases in a geometric ratio," whereas "Subsistence increases only in an arithmetical ratio." Notwithstanding its naïveté by today's standards, this was the first mathematically formulated attempt at linking population and economic growth.

It was not difficult to realize that a population could not grow indefinitely at an exponential rate. Pierre-François Verhulst was a 19th century Belgian mathematician who first proposed the logistic function, which avoids the pitfall of indefinite growth. This function describes a population that initially grows exponentially, then slows downs, and finally levels off to its carrying capacity (i.e., the maximum population that can be sustained).

20th Century Mathematical Demography

A modern integral equation formulation for a continuous-time deterministic population-growth model was first introduced in 1911. The classical matrix and renewal equation models were developed shortly after World War II. Sophisticated mortality and forecasting models arose during the last third of the 20th century. These models are described in some detail later.

Mathematical demography is a young science that developed only during the second half of the 20th century. This development was made possible because only then were university courses offered in the discipline. Another important factor that contributed to the expansion of the field was the availability of digital computers. Although primitive in the early years following World War II, computers became an increasingly important and indispensable tool for anyone interested in tracking, understanding, and projecting the growth of human and other populations.

Model Types

Important distinctions need to be made between deterministic and stochastic (or random) models and also between continuous and discrete formulations.

Deterministic versus Stochastic

Deterministic models assume that known average rates with no random deviations are applied to large populations. For example if 10,000 individuals each have a 95% chance of surviving 1 year, then we can be reasonably certain that 9500 of them will indeed survive. In stochastic models, in contrast, there are random variations due either to uncertainties on the parameter or to small population sizes for which it may not be reasonable to apply average rates. Consider for example a population of 20 centenarians, each having a probability 0.7 of surviving another year. The average number of survivors will be $20 \times 0.7 = 14$. However, due to the small size of the population, there will be random variations, and a probabilistic description of the population at the end of the year would be preferable. In this case, we would use a binomial model to describe the population. The binomial model provides the probabilities of having zero survivors, one survivor, two survivors, and so on, up to 20 survivors at the end of the year. In other words, a probability distribution is given for the number of survivors, not just an average number.

Continuous versus Discrete

In a continuous model, events can take place at every point in time. For example, the time between birth and death can be any positive decimal number. In a discrete model, events are categorized within time intervals. For example we might count the numbers of deaths between ages 0 and 1, between 1 and 5, between 5 and 10, between 10 and 15, and so on. (This example, which is typical, also shows that the lengths of the intervals need not be the same.) Both deterministic and stochastic models can be either continuous or discrete.

The life table and its applications are first presented. The classical linear and non-linear deterministic models follow. The entry closes with stochastic models, most of which were developed since the 1970s.

The Life Table

Basic Definitions

The Discrete Formulation

Table I is one of the earliest life tables. Table II provides a modern example, an excerpt from the 1989–1991 table for U.S. females. Such tables are typically calculated using census data. The ℓ_x columns gives the number of survivors at exact age x (this corresponds to the "Survivors" column

Table II Life Table for U.S. Females, 1989–1991[a]

Age x	q_x	ℓ_x	d_x	L_x	T_x	e_x
0	0.00828	1,000,000	828	99,341	7,881,156	78.81
1	0.00068	99,172	67	99,139	7,781,815	78.47
2	0.00042	99,105	42	99,084	7,682,676	77.52
3	0.00032	99,063	32	99,047	7,583,592	76.55
4	0.00025	99,031	25	99,019	7,484,545	75.58
⋮	⋮	⋮	⋮	⋮	⋮	⋮
20	0.00052	98,597	51	98,571	5,902,842	59.87
⋮	⋮	⋮	⋮	⋮	⋮	⋮
60	0.00895	89,742	803	89,341	2,055,538	22.90
⋮	⋮	⋮	⋮	⋮	⋮	⋮
99	0.27957	3124	873	2688	8363	2.68
100	0.29635	2251	667	1917	5675	2.52

[a] *Source:* National Center for Health Statistics. Nine years presented.

in Table I). The initial size of the cohort ℓ_0 (the radix) is an arbitrary number that is usually taken for convenience to be equal to a multiple of 100 (here $\ell_0 = 1{,}000{,}000$ female newborns). The other columns are derived from the ℓ_x as explained next.

The d_x column gives the number of deaths between ages x and $x+1$:

$$d_x = \ell_x - \ell_{x+1} \tag{1}$$

The q_x column gives the probability of death during the xth year and is the number of deaths d_x during that year divided by the number ℓ_x of survivors at the beginning of the year:

$$q_x = \frac{d_x}{\ell_x} = \frac{\ell_x - \ell_{x+1}}{\ell_x} \tag{2}$$

The variable L_x is the average number of people alive during the time interval between ages x and $x+1$. If people die uniformly during the interval, then L_x is the average between the numbers alive at the beginning and at the end of the year:

$$L_x = 0.5(\ell_x + \ell_{x+1}). \tag{3}$$

Finally we define the sum:

$$T_x = L_x + L_{x+1} + \cdots + L_\omega \tag{4}$$

where ω is the maximum life span, and T_x is the total future number of years lived by the ℓ_x individuals alive at exact age x. If ω is the maximum life span then $L_\omega = T_\omega = 0$, and we work recursively back from the oldest ages with the formula:

$$T_x = T_{x+1} + L_x \tag{5}$$

Finally, the average future numbers of years lived by those alive at exact age x is:

$$e_x = \frac{T_x}{\ell_x} \tag{6}$$

which is better known as the life expectancy at age x, that is, the average number of years to be lived by those who have reached age x.

Useful information can be obtained from a life table. The value ℓ_{36} (not shown) is 97,497, which means that 97.5% of the female population will survive to be 36—a great improvement compared to the 16% estimated by Graunt. A newborn can expect to live $e_0 = 78.81$ years, but a centenarian will live on average only another $e_{100} = 2.52$ years.

Various probabilities can be calculated from the table. For example the probability that a girl alive at age 4 lives to be 100 is the number of centenarians divided by the number alive at age 4,2251/99,031 = 0.0227.

The Continuous Formulation

The life table provides an intrinsically tabular, discrete, description of mortality over the life span. However, the survivorship function ℓ_x can also be viewed as continuous, that is, as having a value for any real (not only integer) value between 0 and, say, 120. The average number L_x of people alive between x and $x+1$ and the number T_x of people older than x are then:

$$L_x = \int_{t=0}^{t=1} \ell_{x+t}\,dt \qquad T_x = \int_{t=0}^{t=\infty} \ell_{x+t}\,dt \tag{7}$$

The life expectancy at age x is:

$$e_x = \frac{\int_0^\infty \ell_{x+t}\,dt}{\ell_x} \tag{8}$$

If ℓ_x has a derivative, then the continuous equivalent of the number of deaths d_x between exact ages x and $x+1$ is d_x^*, which is the opposite of the instantaneous rate of change in the population (i.e., the derivative):

$$d_x^* = -\frac{d\ell_x}{dx} \tag{9}$$

The continuous equivalent of the probability of death q_x between ages x and $x+1$ is the force of mortality $\mu(x)$, defined as:

$$\mu(x) = -\frac{d_x^*}{\ell_x} = -\frac{d\ell_x}{\ell_x dx} \qquad (10)$$

The probabilistic interpretation of the quantity $\mu(x)$ (which is not necessarily less than 1) is that, for a very small time interval dx, then $\mu(x)dx$ is the infinitesimally small probability that a person alive at age x will die between ages x and $x+dx$. The relation between $\mu(x)$ and ℓ_x is then:

$$\ell_x = \ell_0 \exp\left[-\int_{u=0}^{x} \mu(u)\,du\right] \qquad (11)$$

Oftentimes the force of mortality $\mu(x)$ is known and many useful calculations can be performed with Eq. (11). For example the probability that a person alive at age 40 will still be alive at 60 is:

$$\frac{\ell_{60}}{\ell_{40}} = \exp\left[-\int_{u=0}^{60} \mu(u)\,du\right] \qquad (12)$$

As a numerical illustration, suppose that between 40 and 60 the force of mortality $\mu(x)$ increases approximately as a straight line, say from 0.005 to 0.03. Therefore $\mu(x) = 0.00125x - 0.045$ and

$$\frac{\ell_{60}}{\ell_{40}} = \exp\left[-\int_{u=40}^{60} (0.0125u - 0.045)\,du\right] = 0.705 \qquad (13)$$

This means that a person alive at 40 has a 70.5% chance of being alive at 60.

Life Tables, Stationary/Stable Populations and Lexis Diagrams

The life table describes the attrition within one cohort of individuals born at the same time. There is however a dynamic way of looking at the life table. Suppose that 1,000,000 females are born during each year. Thereafter, they die according to the schedule in Table II. The result is a stationary population, that is, a population characterized by a constant annual arrival of births and an unchanging schedule of mortality. The life table provides information on the corresponding population in a straightforward manner, best explained with a Lexis diagram. (A stable population generalizes this by considering that births increase exponentially, with still unchanging mortality.)

The Lexis diagram has horizontal and vertical axes that represent time and age. The trajectory over time of a particular individual is represented by a line starting at the time of birth and at a 45° angle, because time and age increase in the same manner. The line continues until the time of death. In our example, there are 1,000,000 lines that start off during each 1-year interval.

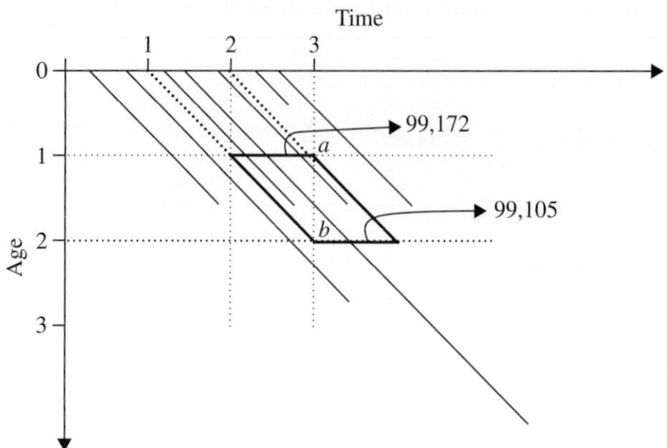

Figure 1 Lexis diagram.

Because $\ell_1 = 99{,}172$ and $\ell_2 = 99{,}105$ there will 99,172 lines crossing a segment of length 1 at age 1 and only 99,105 of those crossing the horizontal line at age 2. (There were 67 deaths, i.e., 67 lines were interrupted between ages 1 and 2.)

The population at age 1 is the number of trajectories crossing any vertical line (e.g., at time 3) for ages between 1 and 2 (i.e., the number of lines crossing the segment from a to b in Fig. 1). Two such lines are depicted in Fig. 1, but in reality there are approximately $0.5(\ell_1 + \ell_2) = (99{,}172 + 99{,}105)/2 = L_1 \approx 99{,}139$ such lines, which is therefore the population at age 1 in the stationary population. More generally then, L_x is the number of individuals at age x in the stationary population; T_x is therefore the population at age x and above.

Applications: Life Insurance and Pension Funds

The life table and the corresponding stationary population have many important applications in actuarial sciences. Two oversimplified but typical examples are given next.

Life Insurance

Suppose a 20-year-old woman has a risk of dying at each age given by Table II. What annual premium can she expect to pay if she wants to buy \$10,000 worth of life insurance? Table II reveals that she can expect to live 59.87 years. A break-even annual premium is simply \$10,000/59.87 = \$167 a year. If the woman lives her average 59.87 years, then at that rate she will have paid out exactly the capital that goes to her estate upon her death. If the insurance company wants to make an annual 5% profit, it must charge 167 × 1.05 = \$175.35 per year. If the woman is 60, she has only 22.9 years, on average, to live, and her break-even premiums are 10,000/22.9 = \$436.68.

This is a highly simplified example that ignores inflation and a person's individual risks. In reality, calculations are more complicated than this and are done with life tables that incorporate the specific risks of a person (e.g., cancer history in the family, smoking, and risks of catastrophic diseases such as AIDS).

Pension Funds

Every year a company hires 100 young women age 20, whose risks or dying are again given in Table II. These women retire at 60 and collect $30,000 a year in pension. Management wants to know how much has to be paid by the pension fund every year. It also wants to know what capital K is needed in order to make these payments entirely from the income earned with a safe return of 5%.

The retired women consist of the population over 60 in the stationary population given by Table II, but with a survivorship function $\ell_0{}^*$ equal to the previous one multiplied by the constant $100/\ell_{20}$ (in order to have $\ell^*{}_{20} = 100$):

$$\ell_x{}^* = \ell_x(100/\ell_{20}) \quad x = 0, 1, \ldots \tag{14}$$

The average population of women 60 and older is then T_{60} multiplied by the same corrective factor $100/\ell_{20}$:

$$T_{60}100/\ell_{20} = 2084.79 \tag{15}$$

The amount paid out every year is therefore:

$$\begin{aligned} 30{,}000 \times T_{60}100/\ell_{20} &= 3 \times 10^6 \times T_{60}/\ell_{20} \\ &= \$62{,}543{,}627 \end{aligned} \tag{16}$$

If this amount is 5% of a capital K, then K must be:

$$K = 3 \times 10^6 \times T_{60}/\ell_{20}/0.05 = \$1{,}250{,}872{,}542 \tag{17}$$

Again, this is an oversimplified example that ignores inflation and many other factors; but it does illustrate the importance of the life table in concrete everyday business applications.

Extensions

The basic life table described so far has many important extensions that make it a fundamental tool of analysis in demography, public health, and sociology. Multiple-decrement life tables recognize the possibility of attrition through different causes. For example, the number of deaths d_x may be decomposed into $d_x = d_x^1 + d_x^2 + d_x^3$, where these three numbers are deaths by cardiovascular disease, cancer, and all other causes. Attrition can be due to causes other than death. For example, we may be interested in the attrition through death and first marriage. Life tables may become even more complicated with possibilities of reentry or movements between different regions or categories. For example, we may wish to track entries into and exits from the labor market or contraceptive use.

Deterministic Models

Aggregate Models

The simplest population dynamics models consider the whole (aggregated) population, without distinguishing between age and sex.

Exponential Model

Let $P(t)$ be the population at time t and $b(t)$, $m(t)$ be the prevailing crude birth and death (mortality) rates at time t. The population at time $t + 1$ is then:

$$P(t + 1) = P(t)(1 + b(t) - m(t)) \tag{18}$$

When birth and death rates are constants b and m, then the growth rate is $r = b - m$ and Eq. (11) becomes:

$$P(t + 1) = P(t)(1 + r) \tag{19}$$

Therefore:

$$P(t) = P(0)(1 + r)^t \tag{20}$$

This is the exponential (or Malthus's "geometric") model—the simplest possible model of population growth. It assumes a constant growth rate r that can be positive, zero, or negative (although not smaller than -1).

The continuous equivalent to Eq. (18) is the differential equation:

$$\frac{dP(t)}{dt} = P(t)r \tag{21}$$

which has the solution:

$$P(t) = P(0)e^{rt} \tag{22}$$

The exponential model is of theoretical interest because it describes the growth of a population under the simplest circumstances, namely with constant birth and death rates.

Perhaps the *raison d'être* of population models is their use for demographic forecasts. However, the exponential model is of limited use for that purpose (beyond the short term) because the resulting population either goes to infinity when $r > 0$ (which is not realistic) or to 0 when $r < 0$ (which is not desirable). When $r = 0$, the population is stationary (constant). An alternative to the exponential model is provided by the logistic function, which always approaches an upper limit over time.

The Logistic Function

Although the logistic function has met with mixed results and has mostly fallen out of favor, it is of interest historically and pedagogically because it has been used extensively as a forecasting tool.

The logistic function is derived from a simple differential equation similar to Eq. (21). Instead of assuming a constant growth rate, the logistic model postulates that the growth rate decreases linearly as the total population increases:

$$\frac{dP(t)}{dt} = P(t)r\left[1 - \frac{P(t)}{A}\right] \tag{23}$$

where $r > 0$ and A is a constant that is larger than the initial value $P(0)$. Equation (23) expresses the saturation of a population whose growth rate decreases as $P(t)$ approaches A. The solution to this differential equation is:

$$P(t) = \frac{A}{1 + (A/P(0) - 1)e^{rt}} \tag{24}$$

This function at first grows exponentially, then levels off and converges to the carrying capacity A (i.e., the maximum sustainable population).

The logistic function can be used for forecasting purposes by first finding the parameters A, $P(0)$, and r for which the modeled population $P(t)$ approximates as closely as possible a population series $P_o(t)$ observed in the past. Then the population is projected by extrapolating the modeled function $P(t)$ beyond the last observed value of $P_o(t)$. The parameters are found by minimizing the squared deviations between fitted and observed values; that is, we seek A, $P(0)$, and r such that:

$$\sum_t \left[\frac{A}{1 + (A/P(0) - 1)e^{rt}} - P_o(t)\right]^2$$

is minimized. As an example, the analysis was performed with decennial U.S. census data from 1790 to 2000. The minimization yields the following estimated parameter values:

$$\begin{aligned} &A = 440.81; \quad P(0) = 7.68; \\ &r = 0.02160 \Longrightarrow A/P(0) - 1 = 56.38 \end{aligned} \tag{25}$$

Therefore the logistic function is:

$$P(t) = \frac{440.81}{1 + 56.38e^{0.02160(t-1790)}} \qquad t = 1790, 1791, \ldots \tag{26}$$

The observed population (census figures) and the modeled logistic population (with an extrapolation up to 2050) are presented in Fig. 2. The logistic function appears to fit the data well. In 2050, the population is projected to be 366 million. According to the model, the U.S. population will converge to the limit value $A = 440.81$ million by the end of the 21st century.

Extreme caution needs to be exercised with such simple extrapolations. If the model is fitted with the census

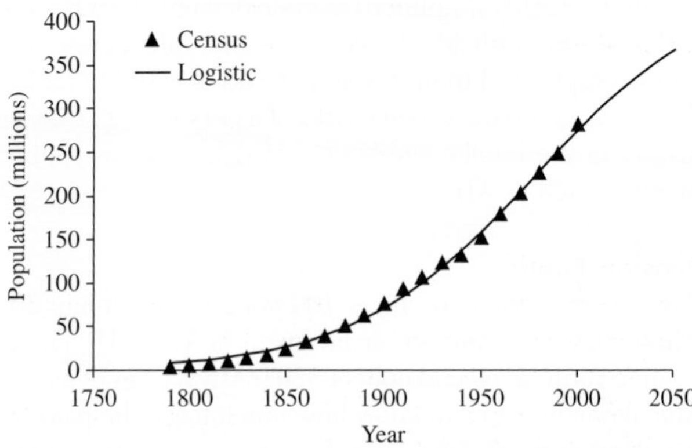

Figure 2 Census data and fitted logistic function for the United States from 1970 to 2000, with forecasts to 2050.

data up to 1960 only, the predicted population in 2000 is 216 million instead of the 281 million actually counted, a figure already larger than the estimated limit population $A = 253$ million we would have obtained in this case. Therefore, a projection made in 1960 using this approach would have severely underestimated the true population at the end of the 20th century.

The logistic function is not a reliable projection tool because the differential Eq. (16) does not express a biological, natural, or social law that a human population is known to follow (unlike, for example, the physical law of gravity, which provides an accurate prediction of the trajectory of an object thrown in the air). The logistic function is merely a convenient mathematical description of a population that levels off.

It should be noted that minimizing a nonlinear function of three variables is not a simple task and, as recently as the 1980s, would have been considerably more cumbersome. Today, however, the whole exercise, including the graphing and minimization of the sum-of-squares needed to estimate the parameters, can be done in a few minutes with an Excel spreadsheet on a PC.

Linear Age-Structured Models

Introduction

Aggregate models are too crude because they do not take into account the fact that mortality and fertility rates depend on age. Age-structured models are defined through the knowledge of $p(t, a)$, a function of two variables that represents the population at time t of age a. In a discrete formulation, t and a will typically be integers that represent years. The total population $P(t)$ at time t is the sum over all ages at time t:

$$P(t) = \sum_{a=0}^{\omega} p(t, a) \tag{27}$$

where ω is the maximum life span. In a continuous formulation, this sum is an integral:

$$P(t) = \int_0^{\omega} P(t,a)\,da \quad (28)$$

Discrete Population Dynamics

The Leslie Matrix Because it is females who give birth, we usually considers that the values $p(t, a)$ represent the female population. (The number of male births is close to that of females and is found by applying a male life table to the radix $p(t, 0)$.)

The number of female births at time $t+1$ is $p(t+1, 0)$ and is obtained by applying age-specific fertility rates $f(a)$ to each age group at time t (i.e., $f(a)$ is the number of girls born to each woman at age a):

$$p(t+1,0) = p(t,0)f(0) + p(t,1)f(1) + \cdots + p(t,\omega)f(\omega) \quad (29)$$

In human populations, the fertility rates $f(a)$ are 0 up to age $a = 15$, then increase rapidly to a maximum around 25, and then decrease to reach 0 around age 50.

The populations in other age groups at $t+1$ are obtained by applying proportions surviving $\sigma(a)$ to each population $p(t, a)$. That is, $\sigma(a)$ is the proportion of those age a who survive to age $a+1$ (the values $\sigma(a)$ are derived from a life table; each $\sigma(a)$ is essentially ℓ_{a+1}/ℓ_a):

$$p(t+1,a+1) = p(t,a)\sigma(a) \quad a = 0,1,2,\ldots,\omega-1 \quad (30)$$

The dynamics of the population are thus entirely defined by Eqs. (29)–(30). These equations can be formulated by considering the population vector $\pi(t)$, whose components are the populations $p(t, a)$ at each age a:

$$\pi(t) = (p(t,0)p(t,1)\cdots p(t,\omega))^T \quad (31)$$

where T denotes the transpose; $\pi(t)$ is a column vector that is the transpose of the row of $p(t, a)$.

We next define the Leslie matrix L having the fertility rates $f(a)$ in its first row and the survival rates $\sigma(a)$ below the main diagonal:

$$L = \begin{bmatrix} f(0) & f(1) & . & . & . & f(\omega) \\ \sigma(0) & 0 & 0 & . & . & 0 \\ 0 & \sigma(1) & 0 & . & . & 0 \\ . & . & . & . & . & . \\ 0 & . & . & \sigma(\omega-2) & 0 & 0 \\ 0 & .. & . & . & \sigma(\omega-1) & 0 \end{bmatrix} \quad (32)$$

Equations (29)–(30) can now compactly be expressed in matrix notations as:

$$\pi(t+1) = L\pi(t) \quad (33)$$

When L remains constant through time, we then have:

$$\pi(t+1) = L\pi(t) = LL\pi(t-1) = \cdots = L^{t+1}\pi(0) \quad (34)$$

which shows that the vector $\pi(t+1)$ can be calculated from the knowledge of the powers L^t. Of particular interest is the long-term behavior of the vector $\pi(t)$ as t becomes very large. From the theory of nonnegative matrices, we know that L will have a positive dominant eigenvalue (spectral radius) ρ, where ρ is the positive root of the characteristic equation:

$$\mathrm{Det}(L - \lambda I) = 0 \quad (35)$$

that dominates all other roots in modulus. (Det denotes the determinant of the matrix $L - \lambda I$, where I is the identity matrix). In the long run, each component $p(t, a)$ of $\pi(t)$ grows as ρ^t. In particular, the first component can be written $p(t, 0) \approx \alpha\rho^t$ for some $\alpha > 0$. If we define the survival rate $s(a)$ from age 0 to a:

$$s(a) = \sigma(0)\sigma(1)\cdots\sigma(a-1) \quad a = 1,2,\ldots,\omega \quad (36)$$

then, in the long run:

$$p(t,a) = p(t-a,0)s(a-1) \approx \alpha\rho^{t-a}s(a-1) \quad a = 1,2,\ldots,\omega \quad (37)$$

Equation (37) shows that after a long time all age groups grow exponentially with the same growth rate $\rho - 1$. Furthermore, the structure of the population is that of the stationary population defined by the survival rates $\sigma(a)$. Depending on whether $\rho > 1$, $\rho = 1$, or $\rho < 1$, the population will grow to infinity, converge, or go to extinction.

The Renewal Equation From Eq. (29) and the first part of Eq. (37) we derive a recurrence relation between births $p(t, 0)$ (with $s(0) = 1$):

$$\begin{aligned} p(t+1,0) = {} & p(t,0)f(0)s(0) + p(t-1,0)f(1)s(1) \\ & + p(t-2,0)f(2)s(2) \\ & + \cdots + p(t-\omega,0)f(\omega)s(\omega) \end{aligned} \quad (38)$$

If we call $B(t)$ the births $p(t,0)$ and define the net maternity rates $m(a) = f(a)s(a)$, then Eq. (38) can be rewritten:

$$\begin{aligned} B(t+1) = {} & B(t)m(0) + B(t-1)m(1) \\ & + B(t-2)m(2) + \cdots + B(t-\omega)m(\omega) \end{aligned} \quad (39)$$

There exists a solution of this renewal equation of the form $B(t) = \alpha\rho^t$ if $\rho > 0$ satisfies the polynomial equation:

$$\begin{aligned} \lambda^{\omega+1} = {} & \lambda^{\omega}m(0) + \lambda^{\omega-1}m(1) + \lambda^{\omega-2}m(2) \\ & + \cdots + \lambda m(\omega-1)m(\omega) \end{aligned} \quad (40)$$

This equation is the same as the characteristic Eq. (35) and its single positive root ρ is therefore equal to the ρ of Eq. (37). The solution $B(t)=\alpha\rho^t$ to the recurrence Eq. (39) is therefore the same as the long-term solution obtained for the Leslie matrix. This is not surprising because those were two different formulations of the same problem.

The Leslie matrix model hinges on the assumption that a proportion $\sigma(a)$ of individuals survives to the next age group. This is a reasonable assumption when populations are large, and probabilities of survival applied to large numbers of people result in numbers surviving that are very close to the average number. If populations are small (say a few dozen), then the proportion $\sigma(a)$ should really be considered a probability and we then have a stochastic version of the Leslie matrix model.

Continuous Population Dynamics

If we consider a density of births $B(t)$, then the continuous equivalent of Eq. (39) is:

$$B(t) = \int_0^{\omega} B(t-x)m(x)\,dx \tag{41}$$

where $m(x)=f(x)s(x)$ as before. In a continuous analog of Eq. (34), a solution $B(t)=\alpha e^{rt}$ of Eq. (41) will exist if r is the unique real root of:

$$1 = \int_0^{\omega} e^{-rs}m(s)\,ds \tag{42}$$

The population density $p(t, a)$ at age a at time t is then the number born $t-a$ years prior multiplied by the proportion $s(a)$ surviving a years:

$$p(t,a) = \alpha e^{r(t-a)}s(a). \tag{43}$$

From Eq (22) the total population $P(t)$ is:

$$P(t) = \int_0^{\omega} p(t,a)\,da = \alpha \exp(rt)\int_0^{\omega} \exp(-rt)s(a)\,da \tag{44}$$

The population is thus stable; that is, mortality rates are constant and the population increases (or decreases) exponentially depending on the value of r relatively to 0; when $r=0$, the population is stationary.

The age distribution $c(a)$ (proportion of population at age a) is constant and equal to:

$$c(a) = \frac{p(t,a)}{P(t)} = be^{-ra}\,s(a) \tag{45}$$

where b is the birth rate:

$$b = \frac{1}{\int_0^{\omega} e^{-ra}s(a)\,da} \tag{46}$$

Coale and Keyfitz have investigated the process by which an arbitrary initial population subjected to the constant survival and fertility rates $s(a)$ and $f(a)$ converges to its stable state, defined by r and the age distribution of Eq. (45). They seek a solution $B(t)$ of the form:

$$B(t) = \sum_{k=0}^{\infty} Q_k \exp(r_k t) \tag{47}$$

where each r_k is a root of Eq. (42) and the values Q_k are chosen so as to satisfy initial conditions determined by the density of births by women alive at time 0, say. The first root r_0 is the only real root r defined here—other roots come in complex conjugate pairs whose real parts are less than r. The influence of these roots on the process of convergence to stability has been studied in detail. The convergence to stability is also known as the strong ergodic theorem of demography.

Applications of Stable Population Theory

Stable population theory has been one of the cornerstones of mathematical demography for two reasons. First the convergence to stability is the outcome of the simplest and most natural assumption we can make when projecting a population, namely that of constant mortality and fertility rates. Indeed, such constant-rates projections provide useful what-if scenarios in the absence of specific information on trends in mortality, fertility, and migration rates. (Stable population theory is easily generalized to incorporate migrations).

Second, stable population theory is of considerable importance when using indirect estimation methods to assess demographic parameters in countries with incomplete vital registration systems. For example, mortality rates or intrinsic growth rates can be estimated in such cases under the assumption that the population has reached stability.

Nonlinear Models

The simple population dynamics models of Eq. (39) or (41) are intrinsically linear. If the number of women of childbearing age doubles, the number of newborns will also double, all other forces remaining unchanged. Whether other forces remain unchanged, however, is precisely what has interested economists who believe that nonlinear feedbacks play an important role in population processes.

The best-known example is provided by the post–World War II baby boom. Easterlin and Condran in 1976 argued that such a boom (and possible echoed busts) could be explained by a feedback of the age structure on fertility rates (a relative scarce young population has better economic opportunities and will have a higher fertility, and *vice versa*).

Mathematical formulations of such feedbacks hinge on nonlinear versions of Eq. (39) or (41), in which the maternity function $m(x)$ is a function of the age x but also of births $B(t-k)$ of women born in the recent past. The discrete equivalent of Eq. (33) with such a feedback might be of the form:

$$B(t+1) = B(t)m_0(\beta(t)) + B(t-1)m_1(\beta(t)) + B(t-2)m_2(\beta(t)) + \cdots + B(t-\omega)m_{t-\omega}(\beta(t)) \quad (48)$$

where the maternity rates $m(a)$ are now functions $m_a(\beta(t))'$ of the vectors $\beta(t) = (B(t-\omega),\ B(t-\omega+1), \ldots, B(t))$ of births during the past $\omega + 1$ periods.

Models along the lines of Eq. (48) have attracted considerable attention in the last 30 years. Even when very simple, such models can exhibit complex behaviors that include bifurcations between stable, cyclic, and chaotic trajectories. These elegant constructions have yet to find their way into the arsenal of mainstream mathematical tools used for population forecasts.

Extensions and Applications

The Weak Ergodic Theorem

In practice, fertility and survival rates always change with time, which means that the matrix L of Eq. (33) is a function $L(t)$ of time. If the strong ergodic theorem provides information on the behavior of a population subjected to constant mortality and fertility rates, the weak ergodic theorem sheds light on the behaviors of two different populations subjected to the same but changing Leslie matrices $L(t)$. Two such populations have age structures that come closer and closer to one another with the passage of time. Cohen and Golubitisky *et al.* made important contributions to the same subject through the use of elegant mathematical tools, particularly the projective distance between vectors that measures how close they are to having the same structure.

Nonstable Extensions

The dynamics of a population subjected to changing vital rates have been formulated and analyzed in various ways. For example, Artzrouni derived approximate closed-form expression for population variables when vital rates change slowly. Kim and Schoen considered the possibility of sinusoidal or quadratically exponential birth trajectories. This latter case means that births $B(t)$ are of the form $B(t) = \exp(h_1 t + h_2 t^2)$.

Multiregional Models

Population geographers have extended the Leslie matrix model to systems that allow migratory flows between regions. Recently much work has dealt with spatial interaction patterns and the spatial structure of population growth. Time series techniques are used to model age-specific and origin-specific migration flows.

Stochastic Models

In recognition of the complexity and elusiveness of population processes, mathematical demographer interested in both mortality models and population forecasts have recently started to move away from deterministic models. Indeed, uncertainty (often arising from heterogeneity within a population) is one of the most important characteristics of population processes.

Stochastic Differential Equations

The simplest example of a stochastic differential equation is a variant of Eq. (21) in which the growth rate r is subjected to infinitesimally small, random fluctuations. The modified equation is then:

$$\frac{dp(t)}{dt} = P(t)[r + sW(t)] \quad (49)$$

where s is a constant and $W(t)$ is the generalized derivative $dB(t)/dt$ of the standard Brownian motion process. There are difficulties with the interpretation of the stochastic differential Eq. (49), which has at least two solutions, depending on whether the Ito or Stratonovich approach is used. With the Ito approach, the expected value $E(P(t))$ of the population at time t is $P(0)\exp(rt)$, which coincides with the solution in the deterministic case. With the Stratonovich approach, the term $s^2t/2$ is added to rt in the exponential.

Frailty Models of Mortality

Recall that $\mu(x)$ denotes the force of mortality at age x; that is, $\mu(x)dx$ is the probability of death between ages x and $x + dx$ for individuals alive at age x. However, much depends on the health, or frailty, of these individuals who have survived to age x. All else being equal, the healthier these individuals are, the smaller $\mu(x)dx$ will be. This simple premise led Vaubel, Yashin, and others to recognize the importance of individual frailty and of selection in any modeling of $\mu(x)$.

A simple mortality model that incorporates individual frailty stipulates that mortality is a function of age but also of a variable Y that captures each individual's indisposition, with $Y(x)$ being an individual's indisposition at age x. A possible construction of $\mu(x)$ is then:

$$\mu(x, Y) = \mu_0(x) + \lambda(x)Y^2(x) \quad (50)$$

where

1. $\mu_o(x)$ is a baseline mortality under optimal conditions.
2. $Y(x)$ is the indisposition that changes randomly from individual to individual.

3. $\lambda(x)$ is an age-dependent vulnerability that determines the extent of the excess mortality due to indisposition.

Each individual is assigned randomly an indisposition at birth $Y(0) = Y_o$; values $Y(x)$ at other ages are obtained through the following differential equation:

$$\frac{dY(x)}{dx} = a_0(x) + a_1(x)Y(x) \tag{51}$$

The overall average observed force of mortality among survivors at age x, denoted $\bar{\mu}(x)$, is then:

$$\bar{\mu}(x) = \mu_0(x) + \lambda(x)(m^2(x) + \gamma(x)) \tag{52}$$

where $m(x)$ and $\gamma(x)$ are the conditional mean and variance of $Y(x)$ among individuals surviving to age x. If Y_o is normally distributed with mean m_o and variance γ_o, then $m(x)$ and $\gamma(x)$ are the solutions of the following system of differential equations:

$$\frac{dm(x)}{dx} = a_0(x) + a_1(x)m(x) - 2\lambda(x)m(x)\gamma(x) \tag{53}$$

$$\frac{d\gamma(x)}{dx} = 2\,a_1(x)\gamma(x) - 2\lambda(x)\gamma^2(x) \tag{54}$$

Numerical solutions to these equations yield the quantities $m(x)$ and $\gamma(x)$ needed to obtain at least the average observed force of mortality $\bar{\mu}(x)$ at age x.

A natural extension has the deterministic $Y(x)$ replaced with a continuous path stochastic process $Y(x)$ obtained as the solution of the stochastic differential equation:

$$\frac{dY(x)}{dx} = b(x)W(x) \tag{55}$$

where $W(x)$ is as in Eq. (49) and $b(x)$ changes over age x.

This simple frailty model has been considerably expanded in the past 20 years and has spawned shared-frailty and correlated frailty models, which have been used extensively with bivariate data.

The Stationary Leslie Matrix

The deterministic Leslie matrix model has a straightforward stochastic version, which we denote as "stationary" to emphasize that probabilities do not change with time. The female population $p(t, a)$, age a at time t, is now a random variable with expected value $e(t, x)$ and variance $C(t, a, a)$. The covariance of $p(t, a)$ and $p(t, b)$ is denoted $C(t, a, b)$. The fertility and survival rates $f(k)$ and $\sigma(k)$ in Eq. (32) are now probabilities of giving birth to one girl and of survival to age k. If $\pi^e(x, t)$ is the vector:

$$\pi^e(x,t) = (e(t,0)\; e(t,1)\cdots e(t,\omega))^T \tag{56}$$

of expected (average) population counts, then as in Eq. (33) the vector $\pi^e(x, t)$ satisfies the matrix equation:

$$\pi^e(x,t+1) = L\pi^e(x,t). \tag{57}$$

There is also a simple linear relationship involving the vector $C(t+1)$ of the covariances $C(t+1, a, b)$ listed in the lexicographic order of the indices a and b:

$$C(t+1) = D\pi^e(x,t) + L \times LC(t) \tag{58}$$

where D is a constant nonnegative matrix (based on A) and $A \times A$ is the Kronecker (or direct) product of A by A. Stochastic equivalents of stable population theory follow fairly simply from Eqs. (57)–(58) (i.e., if ρ is as before the dominant positive eigenvalue of L, then $e(t, 0)/\rho^t$ converges with probability 1).

Stochastic Forecasting

In recent years, arbitrarily defined low, medium, and high variants obtained with deterministic models have come under criticism for not adequately capturing the inherent uncertainties of population forecasts. The stochastic differential equation approach reviewed here is useful only for the total population, as opposed to a population structured by age and sex. The stationary Leslie matrix model is of little use because it does not allow for secular changes in the forces of mortality or fertility, which need to be incorporated in any realistic population forecast. Time series methods have long been used to model and forecast specific demographic variables with statistically sound confidence intervals.

However, what is needed to project human populations is a statistical model that both captures the inherent linear nature of the demographic process (i.e., the Leslie matrix model) and takes into account the uncertainties due to the fluctuating nature of fertility, mortality, and migration rates. In 1986, Cohen proposed the first forecasts based on a nonstationary stochastic version of the Leslie matrix model. However, confidence intervals are provided only for the total population, which limits their usefulness.

In 1994, Lee and Tuljapurkar solved this problem with a method that feeds carefully forecast time series of age-specific mortality and fertility rates into a nonstationary Leslie matrix model that incorporates migrations. Their equation is:

$$\pi(t+1) = L(t+1)\pi(t) + I(t+1) \tag{59}$$

where the population vector $\pi(t+1)$ is now a random variable equal to $\pi(t)$ multiplied on the left by the now random Leslie matrix $L(t+1)$, to which is added the vector $I(t+1)$ of net immigration. Each $L(t)$ is assumed to be a sum $L(t) = M(t) + E(t)$ of a deterministic component $M(t)$ and of a (small) deviation $E(t)$. Complex perturbation methods are used to approximate moments of the random vector $\pi(t+1)$ from which a confidence interval can be found for the predicted population in each age group. For example, the 95% prediction interval for the U.S. population under 20 years old in 2000 is 70.9–85.4 million. The 2000 census yielded 82.2 million for that population, which is in the interval, although on the high side. The interval for the total population in 2050 is 267.6–515.9 million. The predicted value for 2050 is 371.5 million, a figure quite close to the 366 million previously obtained by extrapolating the logistic function.

Confidence intervals reflect the uncertainty within a stochastic model that is assumed to be an accurate reflection of reality. In that respect, stochastic models as well as deterministic ones both depend heavily on the assumptions made concerning vital rates. Indeed, the previous interpretation of the confidence interval is that the actual population in 2050 has a 1 in 20 chance of being outside the (267.6, 515.9) interval, even if the model is correctly specified. However, if the population did fall outside the interval (which is unlikely given the interval's size) it may be the result of an unforeseen drop in fertility or increase in immigration rather than the result of an "unlucky" 1 in 20 realization of an otherwise accurate stochastic process.

Finding stochastic population forecasting models that are as accurate and useful as possible remains one of the major challenges for mathematical demographers of the 21st century.

See Also the Following Articles

Attrition, Mortality, and Exposure Time • Demography • Insurance Industry, Mortality Tables in • Longitudinal Cohort Designs • Population vs. Sample

Further Reading

Artzrouni, M. (1986). On the dynamics of a population subject to slowly changing vital rates. *Math. Biosci.* **80,** 265–290.

Bongaarts, J., and Bulatao, R. (eds.) (2000). *Beyond Six Billion: Forecasting the World Population.* National Research Council. National Academy Press, Washington, DC.

Coale, A. J. (1972). *The Growth and Structure of Human Populations.* Princeton University Press, Princeton, NJ.

Cohen, J. E. (1986). Population forecasts and confidence intervals for Sweden: A comparisons of model-based and empirical approaches. *Demography* **23,** 105–126.

Easterlin, R., and Condran, G. (1976). A note on the recent fertility swing in Australia, Canada, England and Wales, and the United States. In *Population, Factor Movements and Economic Development: Studies Presented to Brinley Thomas* (H. Richards, ed.), pp. 140–151. University of Wales Press, Cardiff, UK.

Graunt, J. (1662). *Natural political observations mentioned in a following index, and made upon the bills of mortality, with reference to the government, religion, trade, growth, ayre, diseases, the several changes of the said city (London).* London: John Martyn. (Republished (1964). *J. Inst. Actuaries* 90(384), 4–61.)

Keyfitz, N. (1968). *Introduction to the Mathematics of Populations with Revisions.* Addison-Wesley, New York.

Kim, Y. J., and Schoen, R. (1996). Populations with quadratic exponential growth. *Math. Popul. Stud.* **6**(1), 19–33.

Lee, R. D. (1974). The formal dynamics of controlled populations and the echo, the boom and the bust. *Demography* **11,** 563–585.

Lee, R. D., and Tuljapurkar, S. (1994). Stochastic population forecasting for the United States: Beyond high, medium, and low. *J. Am. Statist. Assoc.* **89**(428), 1175–1189.

Malthus, T. R. (1798). *An Essay on the Principle of Population.* St. Paul's Churchyard, London.

Pollard, J. (1973). *Mathematical Models for the Growth of Human Populations.* Cambridge University Press, Cambridge, U.K.

Prskawetz, A., Steinmann, G., and Feichtinger, G. (2000). Human capital, technological progress and the demographic transition. *Math. Popul. Stud.* **7**(4), 343–363.

Rogers, A. (1995). *Multiregional Demography: Principles, Methods, and Extensions.* John Wiley, Chichester, U.K.

Vaupel, J., Yashin, A., and Manton, K. (1988). Debilitation's aftermath: Stochastic process models of mortality. *Math. Popul. Stud.* **1**(1), 21–48.

Wachter, K. (1994). The cohort feedback model with symmetric net maternity. *Math. Popul. Stud.* **5**(1), 25–44.

Maximum Likelihood Estimation

Charles H. Franklin
University of Wisconsin, Madison, Wisconsin, USA

Glossary

asymptotic properties The properties of an estimator as the sample size goes to infinity.

consistent estimator An estimator that converges to the population parameter as the sample size goes to infinity.

Cramér-Rao lower bound The minimum variance possible for an estimator in the class of consistent estimators.

data generating process The probability function or density describing the distribution that characterizes the data.

efficient estimator An estimator whose variance-covariance matrix achieves the Cramér-Rao lower bound.

likelihood The joint density of the observed data, treating the parameters as variable and the data as fixed.

maximum likelihood (ML) estimator The value of the parameter(s) at which the likelihood is maximized.

Maximum likelihood (ML) is a method of estimation and inference for parametric models. The ML estimator is the value of the parameter (or parameter vector) that makes the observed data most likely to have occurred given the data generating process assumed to have produced the variable of interest. ML estimates have several desirable asymptotic properties: consistency, efficiency, asymptotic normality, and invariance over continuous transformations. These are asymptotic properties, however, and the small-sample properties of ML estimators are not known in general, although they may be derived for some specific applications. The advantages of ML estimation are that it fully uses all the information about the parameters contained in the data and that it is highly flexible, allowing easy extension to incorporate complex parametric specifications. Most applied ML problems lack closed-form solutions and so rely on numerical maximization of the likelihood function. The advent of fast computers has made this a minor issue in most cases. Hypothesis testing for ML parameter estimates is straightforward due to the asymptotic normal distribution of ML parameter estimates and the Wald likelihood ratio and Lagrange multiplier tests for ML estimates.

Specifying the Data Generating Process

The likelihood approach to statistical estimation and inference begins with the specification of a probability model that represents the process generating the data. The specification of this process rests on scientific knowledge about the phenomena and the observable characteristics of the data, such as whether the variable of interest is discrete or continuous, binary or ordered, and so on. It should be recognized that the choice of model is seldom dictated by theory alone. All models are simplifications of complex reality. Our goal is to make the best model we can consistent with what we know about the phenomena and with the recognition that models must also be tractable to be useful.

Let $\mathbf{y}$ represent the observed variable of interest. The probability model is characterized by a density function (for continuous variables) or probability function (for discrete variables) $f(\mathbf{y} \mid \theta)$, where θ is a vector of one or more parameters that characterize the distribution. For example, if $\mathbf{y}$ is generated by a Poisson process, then

$$f(\mathbf{y} \mid \theta) = \frac{e^{-\lambda}\lambda^{y_i}}{y_i!}$$

with a single parameter, $\theta = \lambda$.

If **y** is normally distributed, then θ contains two parameters, μ and σ^2:

$$f(\mathbf{y} \mid \theta) = \frac{1}{\sqrt{2\pi\sigma^2}} e^{-1/2((y_i - \mu)^2/\sigma^2)}$$

The density, $f(\mathbf{y} \mid \theta)$, is often called the data generating process for the variable **y**. The specification of this process is central to likelihood estimation because without it there can be no likelihood function. Theoretical considerations may help with this specification. For example, processes that generate events over time may suggest a Poisson distribution or one of its relatives. Although social science may lack the strong theories of some physical sciences, there is often more theoretical basis to suggest a particular distribution than a casual first impression might admit.

The nature of the variable **y** may also place some constraints on the data generating process. If **y** is discrete and nonnegative, then this rules out the normal distribution as a potential data generating process because the normal distribution describes variables that are both continuous and unbounded. However, within the class of discrete and nonnegative distributions there may be considerable room for uncertainty as to which data generating process is appropriate. For example, both Poisson and binomial distributions describe discrete and nonnegative variables. In these circumstances, the researcher must be guided in the specification of the data generating process by a combination of substantive theory, observed characteristics of the data, and practicality.

The specification of the data generating process encourages the researcher to be explicit about the assumptions being made and to justify the decision to use one distribution rather than another. This encourages the interaction between the theoretical questions being asked and the statistical specification of the model.

This interaction may be seen in an example. Suppose we wish to model the number of bills approved by a committee of the U.S. House of Representatives during a 2-year-long Congress. The institutional rules of Congress requires that bills be referred to a single committee for consideration. The committee may then modify the bill (or not) and report the bill back to the full House, or it may fail to report the bill, in which case the legislation dies in the committee. We might consider using a binomial distribution:

$$f(\mathbf{y} \mid \theta) = \binom{N}{y} \pi^y (1 - \pi)^{N-y}$$

where $\theta = \pi$ is the probability that a bill is approved by the committee, and N is the number of bills referred to the committee. Because a bill cannot be reported back unless it is first referred to the committee, this model captures an element of the institutional rules of the House. Our knowledge of those rules suggests part of the probability model.

On the other hand, it may make sense to think that members of a committee behave as legislative entrepreneurs who generate legislation rather than passively awaiting bill referrals. In this case, the number of bills referred to a committee has no inherent upper limit. If too few bills are submitted, members will generate new bills. We might prefer to ignore the institutional referral constraint and model the process as a Poisson distribution that places no upper limit on the number of bills a committee might report over a 2-year period. In this case, we adopt a data generating process that captures the entrepreneurship behavior rather than focusing on institutional limits on bills. Which of these distributions, or others, we might prefer is partially a statistical question, but it is also a result of the substantive perspective we bring to the problem. By asking ourselves what the substantive model requires and by asking how different probability models would represent that substance, we benefit from a conversation between the substantive and statistical models. This conversation is very helpful when specifying the data generating process. It informs both the substantive and statistical models.

Definition of the Likelihood

The likelihood of a sample of N observations, **y**, is defined as the joint density of the data, with the parameters, θ, taken as variable and the data as fixed, multiplied by any arbitrary constant or function of the data but not of the parameters:

$$L(\theta \mid \mathbf{y}) = c(\mathbf{y}) f(y_1, y_2, \ldots, y_n \mid \theta)$$

where $f(\cdot)$ is the probability density function (for continuous **y**) or the probability mass function (for discrete **y**). The parameter θ may be a scalar for a single parameter model or a vector for functions of multiple parameters, as is the more common case in practice. The arbitrary constant, $c(\mathbf{y})$ means that the likelihood is proportional to the density of the data given θ:

$$L(\theta \mid \mathbf{y}) \propto f(y_1, y_2, \ldots, y_n \mid \theta)$$

This means that $c(\mathbf{y})$ can be readily ignored when we move on to estimation and inference. This was one of the key insights in Fisher's development of the likelihood notion. The elements of $c(\mathbf{y})$ need not concern us because they do not depend on the parameter, θ. If we compare ratios of likelihoods, the $c(\mathbf{y})$ will cancel in numerator and denominator and so relative likelihoods depend only on the joint density of the data given the parameter.

If the observations are independently distributed, then the likelihood of the sample reduces to the product of the likelihoods for each observation:

$$L(\theta \mid \mathbf{y}) \propto \prod_{i=1}^{N} f(y_i \mid \theta)$$

If the observations are not independent, we can use the general rule for joint probability, $P(ABC) = \text{h}\,P(A) \times P(B \mid A) \times P(C \mid A,B)$, to write the joint likelihood of a sample as:

$$L(\theta \mid \mathbf{y}) \propto f(y_1 \mid \theta) \times f(y_2 \mid \theta, y_1) \times f(y_3 \mid \theta, y_1, y_2) \times \cdots \times f(y_N \mid \theta, y_1, y_2, \ldots, y_{N-1})$$

Although there are practical difficulties with the most general forms of such a likelihood, in many empirical cases it is possible to condition on only a few terms, as, for example, in a time series that is autoregressive for only a small number of lags, say AR(1) or AR(2). Once the data generating process has been specified and the data are observed, our problem is to estimate the parameters of the model based on the likelihood function.

Maximum Likelihood Estimation

The key intuition for estimation in likelihood problems is that the most reasonable estimate is that value of the parameter vector that would make the observed data most likely to occur. More formally we seek a value of θ that maximizes:

$$L(\theta \mid \mathbf{y}) = c(\mathbf{y}) f(y_1, y_2, \ldots, y_n \mid \theta)$$

or, in the case of independent observations, that maximizes:

$$L(\theta \mid \mathbf{y}) = c(y) \prod_{i=1}^{N} f(y_i \mid \theta)$$

Because $c(\mathbf{y})$ does not depend on the parameter θ, it does not change as θ changes. Any value of θ that maximizes $f(y_1, y_2, \ldots, y_n \mid \theta)$ also maximizes $c(\mathbf{y})f(y_1, y_2, \ldots, y_n \mid \theta)$. This means we can ignore $c(\mathbf{y})$ in solving for the maximum likelihood (ML) estimate of the parameters. More formally, $c(\mathbf{y})$ will drop out of the derivative of the likelihood with respect to θ and hence not affect the solution for the ML estimator. For this reason we drop $c(\mathbf{y})$ and the proportionality relation in subsequent discussion.

Maximizing the likelihood can be seen graphically in the following example. Assume that the number of appointments to the U.S. Supreme Court made during each presidential term follows a Poisson distribution (there are various reasons why this may or may not be the case in fact, but we assume it here for the sake of illustration.) The data for the period 1961through 2000 are listed in Table I.

Table I Appointments to the U.S. Supreme Court 1961–2000

Years	*Number appointed*	*Years*	*Number appointed*
1961–1964	2	1981–1984	1
1965–1968	2	1985–1988	3
1969–1972	4	1989–1992	2
1973–1976	1	1993–1996	2
1977–1980	0	1997–2000	0

Assuming independent observations the likelihood for these data is:

$$L(\theta \mid \mathbf{y}) = \prod_{i=1}^{N} \frac{e^{-\lambda}\lambda^{y_i}}{y_i!}$$

For the 10 observations in this data set, we can complete the product, yielding:

$$L(\theta \mid \mathbf{y}) = \frac{e^{-N\lambda}\lambda^{\sum_{i=1}^{N} y_i}}{\prod_{i=1}^{N} y_i!} = \frac{e^{-10\lambda}\lambda^{17}}{2304}$$

This likelihood function is plotted in Fig. 1A for values of λ between 0 and 5. The likelihood peaks between about 1.5 and 2. In Fig. 1B, the likelihood is plotted for a narrower range of values of λ, between 1.5 and 2, to show that the maximum appears to be close to 1.7.

It is usually simpler mathematically to find the maximum of the log of the likelihood rather than the likelihood itself. Because the log is a monotonic transformation, the log-likelihood will be maximized at the same parameter value that maximizes the likelihood. This is illustrated in Fig. 1C–D for the Supreme Court appointments example. Although the shape of the log-likelihood is different from that of the likelihood, it is clear that both are maximized at approximately 1.7.

We may solve analytically for the ML estimator. To maximize any function, we find the value of the parameters that make the first derivatives of the function with respect to the parameters equal to zero. We also check that the second derivatives are negative to ensure that this is a maximum rather than a minimum. To maximize a likelihood function in general we solve the derivative:

$$\frac{\partial L(\theta \mid \mathbf{y})}{\partial \theta} = 0$$

where ∂ denotes partial differentiation of the likelihood with respect to the parameter vector θ.

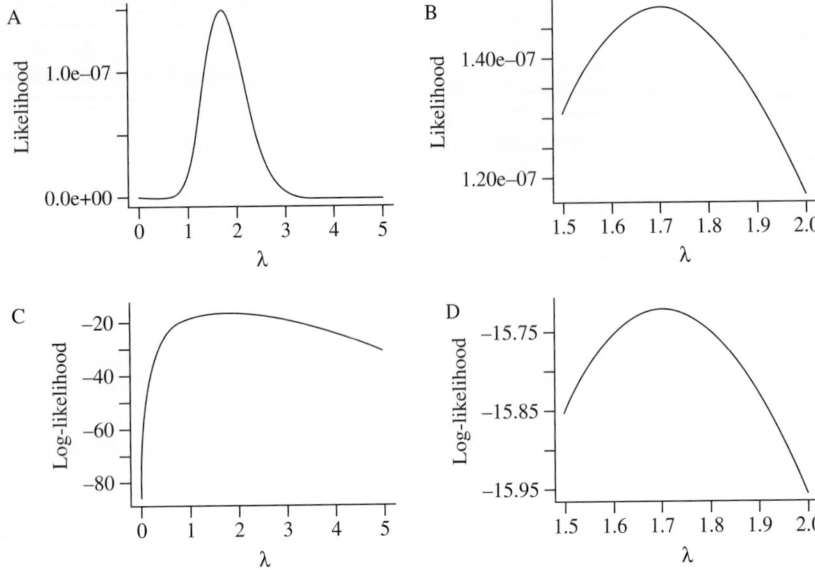

Figure 1 Likelihood and log-likelihood functions for a Poisson model of U.S. Supreme Court appointments, 1961–2000. Both likelihood and log-likelihood functions are maximized at $\lambda = 1.7$.

It is easier to maximize the log-likelihood, written $l(\theta \mid \mathbf{y}) = \log L(\theta \mid \mathbf{y})$. Because the log of a product is the sum of the logs, this simplifies the log-likelihood to a sum:

$$\begin{aligned}\log L(\theta \mid \mathbf{y}) &= \log \prod_{t=1}^{N} f(y_i \mid \theta) \\ &= \sum_{i=1}^{N} \log f(y_i \mid \theta)\end{aligned}$$

Because the derivative of a sum is just the sum of the derivatives, it is easier to differentiate the log-likelihood rather than the likelihood; the latter would involve the more complicated derivative of a product. Because the log transformation is monotonic, any value of the parameter vector that maximizes the log-likelihood will also maximize the likelihood.

For the Poisson example this results in:

$$\begin{aligned}\frac{dl(\lambda \mid \mathbf{y})}{d\lambda} &= \frac{d}{d\lambda}\Big(\sum_{i=1}^{N}\Big(\log \frac{e^{-\lambda}\lambda^{y_i}}{y_i!}\Big)\Big) \\ &= \frac{d}{d\lambda}\Big(\sum_{i=1}^{N}(-\lambda + y_i \log(\lambda) - \log(y_i!))\Big) \\ &= -N + \frac{1}{\lambda}\sum_{i=1}^{N} y_i\end{aligned}$$

Setting the last line equal to zero and solving for λ yields:

$$\lambda = \frac{\sum_{i=1}^{N} y_i}{N}$$

In the Supreme Court appointments data, $N = 10$ and $\sum y_i = 17$, so the ML estimate is $\lambda = 17/10$ or 1.7, which coincides with the apparent maximum in Fig. 1.

To check that this is a maximum, we take the second derivative of the log-likelihood:

$$\begin{aligned}\frac{d^2 l(\lambda \mid \mathbf{y})}{d\lambda^2} &= \frac{d}{d\lambda}\Big(-N + \frac{1}{\lambda}\sum_{i=1} y_i\Big) \\ &= -\lambda^{-2}\sum_{i=1} y_i\end{aligned}$$

which is always negative because λ and $\sum y_i$ must both be positive. Because the second derivative is always negative, this shows that the log-likelihood has a single maximum value.

This illustrates the general process of maximizing any likelihood. We write the likelihood of the data, based on our model specification of the data generating process. We then differentiate the log of the likelihood with respect to the parameters. Setting this derivative equal to zero and solving for the parameters results in an expression for the ML estimator for the model. The second derivative test must be negative to demonstrate that we have found a maximum.

Once we move beyond the simplest models, explicit solutions for the parameters are unlikely to exist. Often the ML estimator is a nonlinear function that does not have an explicit closed-form solution. In this case, we resort to numerical maximization of the likelihood. The widely used logit model for binary dependent variables is an example of this. The derivative of the log-likelihood of the logit model with independent variables $\mathbf{x}$ is:

$$\frac{\partial l(\beta \mid \mathbf{y}, \mathbf{x})}{\partial \beta} = \sum \left(y_i - \frac{e^{\mathbf{x}\beta}}{1 + e^{\mathbf{x}\beta}} \right) \mathbf{x}_i$$

which is nonlinear in β, which precludes an explicit solution for β. There are a number of numerical methods that provide solutions in these cases.

Multiparameter Likelihoods

Aside from classroom examples, there is usually more than a single parameter in the model. In this case, the first derivatives produce a vector of partial derivatives and the second derivatives produce a matrix.

This is easy to see with the normal distribution as an example. In general, we write the parameters as a vector:

$$\theta = \begin{bmatrix} \theta_1 \\ \vdots \\ \theta_k \end{bmatrix}$$

The normal log-likelihood, $l(\sigma^2 \mid \mathbf{y})$, depends on two parameters, μ and σ^2, so this becomes:

$$\theta = \begin{bmatrix} \mu \\ \sigma^2 \end{bmatrix}$$

To simplify the notation we write the log-likelihood function as $l \equiv l(\theta \mid \mathbf{y}) \equiv \log L(\theta \mid \mathbf{y})$. This notation is common in works on likelihood. We also assume that summations are over all cases from $i = 1, \ldots, N$ unless otherwise noted. The likelihood depends on the parameters. The derivative of a likelihood function with respect to a parameter vector, θ, produces a vector of partial derivatives:

$$\frac{\partial l}{\partial \theta} = \begin{bmatrix} \frac{\partial l}{\partial \theta_1} \\ \frac{\partial l}{\partial \theta_2} \\ \vdots \\ \frac{\partial l}{\partial \theta_k} \end{bmatrix}$$

Recall that the likelihood for a normal distribution is:

$$L(\theta \mid \mathbf{y}) = \prod_{i=1}^{N} \frac{1}{\sqrt{2\pi\sigma^2}} e^{-1/2((y_i - \mu)^2/\sigma^2)}$$

so the log-likelihood is:

$$\begin{aligned} l &= \sum \left(-\frac{1}{2}\log(2\pi) - \frac{1}{2}\log\sigma^2 - \frac{1}{2}\frac{(y_i - \mu)^2}{\sigma^2} \right) \\ &= -\frac{N}{2}\log(2\pi) - \frac{N}{2}\log\sigma^2 - \frac{1}{2}\frac{\sum (y_i - \mu)^2}{\sigma^2} \end{aligned}$$

The first derivative of this log-likelihood, where $\theta = (\mu, \sigma^2)'$, is:

$$\begin{aligned} \frac{\partial l}{\partial \theta} &= \begin{bmatrix} \frac{\partial l(\mu, \sigma^2 \mid \mathbf{y})}{\partial \mu} \\ \frac{\partial l(\mu, \sigma^2 \mid \mathbf{y})}{\partial \sigma^2} \end{bmatrix} \\ &= \begin{bmatrix} \frac{1}{\sigma^2}\sum (y_i - \mu) \\ -\frac{N}{2\sigma^2} + \frac{1}{2\sigma^4}\sum (y_i - \mu)^2 \end{bmatrix} \end{aligned}$$

The vector of partials with respect to θ is called the gradient vector, or just the gradient. It tells us how the log-likelihood function is changing as each element of θ changes. We can solve the gradient vector to find the ML estimators for the normal likelihood:

$$\begin{bmatrix} \frac{1}{\sigma^2}\sum (y_i - \mu) \\ -\frac{N}{2\sigma^2} + \frac{1}{2\sigma^4}\sum (y_i - \mu)^2 \end{bmatrix} = \begin{bmatrix} 0 \\ 0 \end{bmatrix}$$

so

$$\mu = \frac{1}{n}\sum y_i$$

$$\sigma^2 = \frac{1}{n}\sum (y_i - \mu)^2$$

Regardless of how many parameters enter into a model, the basic steps of ML estimation remain the same—use the derivatives of the log-likelihood to find the values of the parameters that maximize the likelihood of the sample. This may be done analytically or with numerical methods. These point estimates are of interest, but for statistical inference we must also know how these estimates vary. For this, we turn to the problem of finding the variance-covariance matrix for ML estimators.

Variance-Covariance Matrix of the Maximum Likelihood Estimator

Any estimator will vary across repeated samples. We must be able to calculate this variability in order to express our uncertainty about a parameter value and to conduct statistical inference about the parameters. This variability is measured by the variance-covariance matrix of the parameters or, more briefly, the covariance matrix. This matrix provides the variances for each parameter on the main diagonal while the off-diagonal elements estimate the covariances between all pairs of parameters. In least-squares regression, this covariance matrix is $\sigma^2(X'X)^{-1}$. In ML, the matrix of second derivatives of the log-likelihood is the key.

Fisher showed that the covariance matrix for ML estimators is the inverse of what he called the information matrix:

$$[I(\theta)]^{-1} = \left(-\mathrm{E}\left[\frac{\partial^2 \ln \mathrm{L}(\theta)}{\partial\theta\partial\theta'}\right]\right)^{-1}$$

In words, the covariance matrix of the ML estimator is the inverse of the negative of the expected value of the matrix of second derivatives of the log-likelihood with respect to the parameters.

An intuition into why this makes sense is that the second derivatives measure the rate of change in the first derivatives, which in turn determine the value of the ML estimate. If the first derivatives are changing rapidly near the maximum, then the peak of the likelihood is sharply defined and the maximum is easy to see. In this case, the second derivatives will be large and their inverse small, indicating a small variance of the estimated parameters. If on the other hand the second derivatives are small, then the likelihood function is relatively flat near the maximum and so the parameters are less precisely estimated. The inverse of the second derivatives will produce a large value for the variance of the estimates, indicating low precision of the estimates.

In the case of a typical multiparameter likelihood, we need to find the matrix of second derivatives, then take the expected value of this, and invert to get the covariance matrix. As with single-parameter models, the second partial derivative is the derivative of the first partial derivatives with respect to θ. The first derivatives produce a column vector:

$$\frac{\partial l}{\partial\theta} = \begin{bmatrix} \frac{\partial l}{\partial\theta_1} \\ \frac{\partial l}{\partial\theta_2} \\ \vdots \\ \frac{\partial l}{\partial\theta_k} \end{bmatrix}$$

To get the second derivatives, we differentiate each element of the gradient vector with respect to each element in θ', a row vector. This results in a square matrix of second derivatives:

$$\frac{\partial}{\partial\theta'}\left(\frac{\partial l}{\partial\theta}\right) = \frac{\partial^2 l}{\partial\theta\partial\theta'}$$

or

$$\frac{\partial}{\partial\theta'}\begin{bmatrix} \frac{\partial l}{\partial\theta_1} \\ \frac{\partial l}{\partial\theta_2} \\ \vdots \\ \frac{\partial l}{\partial\theta_k} \end{bmatrix} = \begin{bmatrix} \frac{\partial^2 l}{\partial\theta_1\partial\theta_1} & \frac{\partial^2 l}{\partial\theta_1\partial\theta_2} & \cdots & \frac{\partial^2 l}{\partial\theta_1\partial\theta_k} \\ \frac{\partial^2 l}{\partial\theta_2\partial\theta_1} & \frac{\partial^2 l}{\partial\theta_2\partial\theta_2} & \cdots & \frac{\partial^2 l}{\partial\theta_2\partial\theta_k} \\ \vdots & \vdots & \vdots & \vdots \\ \frac{\partial^2 l}{\partial\theta_k\partial\theta_1} & \frac{\partial^2 l}{\partial\theta_k\partial\theta_2} & \cdots & \frac{\partial^2 l}{\partial\theta_k\partial\theta_k} \end{bmatrix}$$

This matrix of second derivatives is called the Hessian matrix, often abbreviated as H. It is always of dimension $k \times k$, where k is the length of the θ parameter vector. The off-diagonal elements are called the cross-partial derivatives and Young's theorem guarantees that:

$$\frac{\partial^2 l}{\partial\theta_i\theta_j} = \frac{\partial^2 l}{\partial\theta_j\theta_i}$$

which assures us that the Hessian, and hence the covariance matrix, will be symmetric.

In the previous section we found the first derivatives for the two-parameter normal distribution. Here we continue that example to find the covariance matrix for the normal likelihood.

The gradient vector for the normal likelihood is:

$$\frac{\partial l}{\partial\theta} = \begin{bmatrix} \frac{1}{\sigma^2}\sum(y_i - \mu) \\ -\frac{N}{2\sigma^2} + \frac{1}{2\sigma^4}\sum(y_i - \mu)^2 \end{bmatrix}$$

The Hessian is the matrix of second derivatives of this likelihood:

$$\frac{\partial^2 l}{\partial\theta\partial\theta'} = \begin{bmatrix} \frac{\partial^2 l}{\partial\mu\partial\mu} & \frac{\partial^2 l}{\partial\mu\partial\sigma^2} \\ \frac{\partial^2 l}{\partial\sigma^2\partial\mu} & \frac{\partial^2 l}{\partial\sigma^2\partial\sigma^2} \end{bmatrix}$$

Take the appropriate derivatives of the gradient to get:

$$\frac{\partial^2 l}{\partial\mu\partial\mu} = -\frac{N}{\sigma^2}$$

$$\frac{\partial^2 l}{\partial\mu\partial\sigma^2} = -\frac{1}{\sigma^4}\sum(y_i - \mu)$$

$$\frac{\partial^2 l}{\partial\sigma^2\partial\sigma^2} = \frac{N}{2\sigma^4} - \frac{1}{\sigma^6}\sum(y_i - \mu)^2$$

Young's theorem takes care of the other cross-partial derivative. So:

$$H = \begin{bmatrix} -\frac{N}{\sigma^2} & -\frac{1}{\sigma^4}\sum(y_i - \mu) \\ -\frac{1}{\sigma^4}\sum(y_i - \mu) & \frac{N}{2\sigma^4} - \frac{1}{\sigma^6}\sum(y_i - \mu)^2 \end{bmatrix}$$

Because the sum of deviations about the mean is always zero, the off-diagonal terms vanish leaving:

$$H = \begin{bmatrix} -\frac{N}{\sigma^2} & 0 \\ 0 & \frac{N}{2\sigma^4} - \frac{1}{\sigma^6}\sum(y_i - \mu)^2 \end{bmatrix}$$

Taking expected values leaves us with:

$$E(H) = \begin{bmatrix} -\frac{N}{\sigma^2} & 0 \\ 0 & -\frac{N}{2\sigma^4} \end{bmatrix}$$

And the inverse of the negative of this gives us the covariance matrix for the normal likelihood parameter estimates:

$$I(\theta)^{-1} = \begin{bmatrix} -\frac{\sigma^2}{N} & 0 \\ 0 & -\frac{2\sigma^4}{N} \end{bmatrix}$$

The first element in the covariance matrix is the well-known variance of the sample mean. The second element is the less widely discussed variance of the estimated variance parameter, $\hat{\sigma}^2$. The zero covariances in the off-diagonals show that in the case of a simple normal model the estimates of the mean and variance are uncorrelated.

With these results in hand, we know how to find the ML estimator and the variance-covariance matrix for that estimator. It remains to discuss the properties of the ML estimator.

Properties of Maximum Likelihood Estimators

The nearly universal acceptance of ML as a method of estimation and inference rests on the properties of ML estimators. These major properties are:

- Consistency
- Efficiency
- Asymptotic normality
- Invariance under reparameterization

If a ML estimator exists, it is guaranteed to have these properties. This may be ML's greatest strength. The properties need not be proved repeatedly for each application of ML. Amazingly, Fisher discussed all these properties in his 1922 and 1925 papers. ML was born almost full grown (although rigorous proofs did await developments by Cramér, Wald, and Rao during the 1940–1960 period.)

It is important to note that these are asymptotic properties that hold only as the sample size becomes indefinitely large. It is impossible to say in general at what point a sample is large enough for these properties to apply. This, in turn, is a significant limitation of ML. Although some small-sample properties may be derived for specific models, no general results have been discovered. Thus, when applications involve small samples, the use of ML should be carefully evaluated before relying on inferences based on the ML estimates.

Consistency

There are several definitions of consistency, but an intuitive version is that as the sample size gets large the estimator is increasingly likely to fall within a small region around the true value of the parameter. This is called convergence in probability and is defined more formally as follows. A random variable x_n converges in probability to a constant, c, if:

$$\lim_{n \to \infty} \text{Prob}(|\mathbf{x}_n - c| > \epsilon) = 0$$

for any positive ϵ.

For example, if we think of c as the population value of a parameter and x_n as an ML estimator of c based on n cases, then this says that as the sample size increases the probability that we fall outside a small ϵ region around c goes to zero. We are certain to be within ϵ of the true value as long as the sample size is allowed to be large enough.

In 1946, Cramér proved that ML estimators are consistent; Fisher had reached this conclusion less rigorously in the 1920s. From a practical perspective, this means that as long as the likelihood is properly specified we can be confident that the estimates of the parameters will converge to the population parameter values as the sample size becomes sufficiently large.

As an example of consistency, consider the ML estimator for the variance in a normal likelihood. We have already seen that this estimator has a closed form and is:

$$\sigma^2 = \frac{1}{n}\sum(y_i - \mu)^2$$

But it is well know from elementary statistics that this is a biased estimate of the population variance and that:

$$\sigma^2 = \frac{1}{n-1}\sum(y_i - \mu)^2$$

is the unbiased estimator.

This example shows that ML estimators may be biased in finite samples, even though they are consistent in large samples. The convergence of the ML estimator in this case can be seen in Fig. 2. The figure plots the distribution of the ML estimator of σ^2 for four sample sizes when the population variance is set to 10. The small-sample estimates are noticeably biased, but as the sample size increases the distribution of the ML estimator converges toward the true value and the variability of the estimator also decreases.

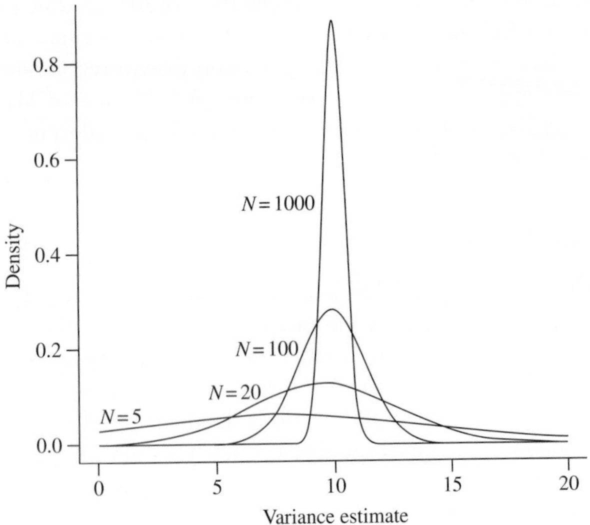

Figure 2 The ML estimator for the variance in a normal likelihood is biased downward in finite samples. As the sample size increases, the estimator converges toward the population value (10 in this example) and the variance of the estimator decreases.

Efficiency

The Cramér-Rao lower-bound theorem shows that (given certain regularity conditions concerning the distribution) the variance of any estimator of a parameter θ must be *at least* as large as:

$$Var\,\hat{\theta} \geq \left(-E\left[\frac{\partial^2 \ln L(\theta)}{\partial\theta\partial\theta'}\right]\right)^{-1}$$

Therefore any estimator that achieves this lower bound is efficient and no "better" (in the sense of smaller variance) estimator is possible.

But this lower bound is exactly the variance-covariance matrix of the ML estimator that we have previously found. Therefore, all ML estimators achieve the Cramér-Rao lower bound. In this sense then, ML estimators are optimal. No other consistent estimator can have a smaller variance. Another way to think of this is that ML estimators incorporate all the available information about the parameters that is contained in the data.

Asymptotic Normality

Combining consistency and the ML covariance result with the Lindberg-Feller central limit theorem produces:

$$\hat{\theta}_{ML} \overset{a}{\sim} N\left[\theta, \{I(\theta)\}^{-1}\right]$$

This says that ML estimators converge in distribution to a normal with mean equal to the population value of the parameter and covariance matrix equal to the inverse of the information matrix. The proof of normality is quite involved and not covered here.

The practical implications of this, however, are quite apparent. This means that regardless of the distribution of the variable of interest the ML estimator of the parameters will have a multivariate normal distribution. Thus, a variable, **y**, may be Poisson distributed, but the ML estimate of the Poisson parameter λ will be normally distributed, and likewise for *any* distribution of **y**. This is particularly valuable for inference and hypothesis testing because it means we can always count on a very simple distribution of the parameter estimates, no matter how complex the underlying likelihood.

Invariance

How does the parameterization of a likelihood affect the resulting inference? ML has the property that any transformation of a parameter can be estimated by the same transformation of the ML estimate of that parameter. This provides substantial flexibility in how we parameterize our models while guaranteeing that we will get the same result if we start with a different parameterization.

The invariance property can be stated formally. If $\gamma = c(\theta)$, where $c(\theta)$ is a one-to-one transformation, then the ML estimator of γ is $c(\hat{\theta}_{ML})$.

To make this more concrete, consider the example of a normal distribution. The usual parameterization is in terms of the mean and variance but an alternative parameterization is in terms of precision, which is the inverse of the variance. If we adopt this parameterization and derive the ML estimator for the precision, how is this related to the ML estimator for the variance?

We reparameterize the normal log-likelihood in terms of precision, $\tau^2 = 1/\sigma^2$:

$$l(\mu, \tau^2 \mid \mathbf{y}) = -(N/2)\ln(2\pi) + (N/2)\ln\tau^2 - \frac{\tau^2}{2}\sum(y_i - \mu)^2$$

The log-likelihood equation for τ^2 is now:

$$\partial l(\mu, \tau^2 \mid \mathbf{y})/\partial\tau^2 = \frac{1}{2}\left[N/\tau^2 - \sum(y_i - \mu)^2\right] = 0$$

which has the solution $\hat{\tau}^2 = N/\sum(y_i - \hat{\mu})^2 = 1/\hat{\sigma}^2$. We see that the invariance property holds. We are free to choose either parameterization, estimate that parameter, and then transform the ML estimate into an alternative parameterization. The results will be consistent with one another regardless of the choice of parameterization. Fisher noted this property in his 1925 paper. In the process he pointed out that Bayesian approaches do not share the invariance property. A Bayesian posterior is sensitive to the parameterization and different parameterizations may lead to different inferences when transformed.

Inference and Hypothesis Tests

Standard hypothesis tests about parameters in ML models are handled quite easily, thanks to the asymptotic normality of the ML estimator. For any single ML parameter estimate, $\hat{\theta}_j \overset{a}{\sim} N[\theta_j, \{I(\theta)\}_{jj}^{-1}]$ and therefore:

$$z = \frac{\hat{\theta}_j - \theta_j}{\{I(\theta)\}_{jj}^{-1}} \overset{a}{\sim} N(0, 1)$$

This is the familiar z score for a standard normal variable developed in all introductory statistics classes. The normality of ML estimates means that our testing of hypotheses about the parameters is as simple as calculating the z score and finding the associated p value from a table or by calling a software function.

In a regression, for example, the hypothesis test that a slope is zero is based on the z score of the slope divided by its standard error. In ordinary least-squares (OLS), this is calculated as a t distribution. However, because the ML properties are all asymptotic we are unable to address the finite sample distribution. Asymptotically, the t distribution converges to the normal as the degrees for freedom grow, so clearly the ML test is the same as that for OLS as long as the number of cases are large enough. However, for small samples the OLS estimator is known to have a t distribution, whereas the small-sample properties for the ML estimator are generally unknown.

In addition to the test of hypotheses about a single parameter, there are three classic tests that encompass hypotheses about sets of parameters as well as one parameter at a time. All are asymptotically equivalent, but they differ in the ease of implementation depending on the particular case: the likelihood ratio (LR), Wald, and Lagrange multiplier (LM) tests.

- The LR test asks, "Did the likelihood change much under the null hypotheses versus the alternative?"
- The Wald test asks, "Are the estimated parameters very far away from what they would be under the null hypothesis?"
- The LM test asks, "If I had a less restrictive likelihood function, would its derivative be close to zero here at the restricted ML estimate?"

The first two are most commonly used. The LM test is particularly useful in specification tests that are beyond the scope of this entry.

The LR test is based on the relative likelihoods between a full and a restricted (or reduced) nested model with fewer parameters. The restricted model must be nested within (i.e., a subset of) the full model. The LR test is actually based on the log of the likelihood ratio, $\ln L_r - \ln L_f$. The test statistic is:

$$-2(\ln L_r - \ln L_f) \sim \chi^2$$

with degrees of freedom equal to the number of parameters in the full model minus the number of parameters in the restricted model. The advantage of the LR test is that it is simple to calculate from the log-likelihoods of the two models. It requires that both models be estimated, however, which may not be entirely trivial. Both full and restricted models must be estimated on exactly the same cases, something that missing data may make less than easy to do in some software packages.

The Wald test provides an alternative to the LR test that requires the estimation of only the full model, not the restricted model. The logic of the Wald test is that if the restrictions are correct then the *unrestricted* parameter estimates should be close to the value hypothesized under the restricted model. For example, a restriction might be that coefficients on three independent variables are all hypothesized to be zero. If this is correct, then the estimated coefficients ought to all be close to zero as well.

The Wald test is based on the distribution of a quadratic form of the weighted sum of squared normal deviates, a form that is known to be distributed as a chi-square distribution. If:

$$x \sim N_J[\mu, \Sigma]$$

then

$$(x - \mu)'\Sigma^{-1}(x - \mu) \sim \chi^2[J]$$

where N_J is a J-dimensional multivariate normal distribution with variance-covariance matrix $\sum$, and $\chi^2[J]$ has J degrees of freedom. If the hypothesis that $E(x) = \mu$ is correct, then the quadratic form is distributed χ^2. If the hypothesis is false, then the quadratic form will on average be larger and we reject the null hypothesis.

For the Wald test, we write the hypothesis as a *constraint* on the parameters:

$$H_0: c(\theta) = q$$

If this is true, then:

$$c(\hat{\theta}) \approx q$$

but, if the constraint is false, then:

$$c(\hat{\theta}) - q$$

should be farther from zero than would be expected.

The test statistic for the Wald test is:

$$W = [c(\hat{\theta}) - q]' \operatorname{Var}(c(\hat{\theta}) - q)^{-1}[c(\hat{\theta}) - q]$$

Under the null hypothesis this has a χ^2 distribution with degrees of freedom equal to the number of restrictions. Further:

$$\mathrm{Var}(c(\hat{\theta}) - q) = \hat{C}\,\mathrm{Var}(\hat{\theta})\hat{C}'$$

and

$$\hat{C} = \left[\frac{\partial c(\hat{\theta})}{\partial \hat{\theta}'}\right]$$

where C is $J \times K$, where K is the number of parameters in the model and J is the number of restrictions.

For the special case of *linear* constraints, this takes on a simple form:

$$c(\theta) - q = R(\theta) - q = 0$$

so

$$\hat{C} = \left[\frac{\partial c(\hat{\theta})}{\partial \hat{\theta}'}\right] = R$$

Hence,

$$\mathrm{Var}(c(\hat{\theta}) - q) = R\ \mathrm{Var}(\hat{\theta})R'$$

and

$$W = [R\hat{\theta} - q]'[R\mathrm{Var}(\hat{\theta})R']^{-1}[R\hat{\theta} - q]$$

with degrees of freedom equal the number of rows in R.

For example, suppose we want to test the hypothesis that $\theta_2 = \theta_3$ when there are five parameters in the model. The restriction implies that $\theta_2 - \theta_3 = 0$. The R matrix is just:

$$R = [0 \quad 1 \quad -1 \quad 0 \quad 0]$$

so that $R\theta = 0$ holds if the restriction $\theta_2 = \theta_3$ is true.

More than one restriction produces more than one row in R— one row for each restriction. If we add the restriction that $\theta_4 = -\theta_5$, then R becomes:

$$R = \begin{bmatrix} 0 & 1 & -1 & 0 & 0 \\ 0 & 0 & 0 & 1 & 1 \end{bmatrix}$$

The p value that results from the Wald test provides a test of the joint hypothesis that all restrictions are simultaneously true.

Three Brief Examples

Here we consider three examples of applications of ML to common social science estimation problems.

Poisson Event Counts

If the data are observed counts of events that occur over time, the Poisson distribution provides a good starting point. The Poisson assumes that events occur independently and at a fixed rate within time periods. If these assumptions are substantively sensible, we might model the number of coups d'etat in the world, the number of wars initiated, the number of troops killed or the number of suicide bombings per year (or month) as Poisson processes.

The Poisson data generating process gives us the log-likelihood for the sample:

$$\begin{aligned} l(\lambda \mid \mathbf{y}) &= \sum_{i=1}^{N}\left(\log\frac{e^{-\lambda}\lambda^{y_i}}{y_i!}\right) \\ &= \sum_{i=1}^{N}(-\lambda + y_i\log(\lambda) - \log(y_i!)) \\ &= -N\lambda + \log(\lambda)\sum y_i - \sum \log(y_i!) \end{aligned}$$

Because the last term does not involve λ, we can drop it from the log-likelihood without affecting the ML estimator.

If we thought that the dependent variable of interest had a constant rate of occurrence in all places and all times, then we could proceed to estimate the parameter as discussed earlier. However, in almost all interesting social science applications we have a variety of variables that we think affect the rate of occurrence. For example, the rate of coups d'état in a year may depend on world economic conditions in that year and might vary by region. The number of combat deaths may depend on the level and type of conflict. If we can measure these independent variables, then we want to incorporate them into the model as explanations of why the rate of events, measured by λ, varies across cases in the data.

To do this, we recognize that there is variation in λ across cases, and so we replace it with λ_i, where i is the unit of analysis. The log-likelihood then becomes:

$$l(\lambda_i \mid y) = -\sum \lambda_i + \sum \log(\lambda_i)y_i$$

ignoring the factorial term. If we leave the model in this form, there are as many parameters λ_i as there are cases. This model is identified only for the trivial case where $\lambda_i = y_i$. This says that each case is different but that we cannot say why it is different and we cannot estimate a variance for λ_i.

However, if we believe that our substantive explanatory variables can account for the variability in λ_i across cases, then we can reparameterize the model in terms of the smaller number of explanatory variables and a small number of parameters. In this case, we might choose the parameterization:

$$\lambda_i = e^{\mathbf{x}_i\beta}$$

We pick this form because λ_i must be nonnegative. This functional form takes values of $\mathbf{x}_i\beta$ between $-\infty$ and $+\infty$ and return estimates of λ_i that respect the nonnegativity required. We assume there are k columns in **x**, so there are also k elements in β. Because it will usually be the case that k is much smaller than n, we have dramatically reduced the number of parameters in the model while also providing a model that explains how the rate of events (λ_i) varies as each **x** varies. The elements of β are the coefficients of this Poisson regression.

After we reparameterize in this way, the log-likelihood becomes

$$l(\beta \mid \mathbf{y}, \mathbf{x}) = -\sum e^{\mathbf{x}_i\beta} + \sum \mathbf{x}_i \beta y_i$$

Because this is nonlinear in β we will not be able to derive a closed-form solution for the parameters. Numerical methods can easily maximize this function, however, and can also return the estimated variance-covariance matrix for the parameters.

To test hypotheses in this model we might focus first on the individual parameters and use the z score for each to calculate a p value against the null hypothesis that the population parameter is zero, that is, that the x variable has no effect on the rate of event counts. Such a test has exactly the same logic as the t test for coefficients in a linear regression.

If we have a more complicated theory, then we might test that some set of variables are all irrelevant to the rate of events. For example, perhaps we want to test the hypothesis that international economic conditions do not affect the rate of coups d'état. We might use several indicators of economic conditions. The null hypothesis in this case is that all the coefficients on the economic variables are zero. We could use either a LR or a Wald test for this. If we fail to reject the null, then the data are not inconsistent with a lack of impact of economic conditions. If we reject the null, then we conclude that at least one of the economic variables affects the rate of coups.

This example illustrates the ability to reparameterize the log-likelihood function in order to incorporate substantive explanations and also to then test hypotheses about these possible explanations. This reparameterization is extremely flexible and can be used to capture a number of alternative specifications and hypotheses.

Heteroskedastic Regression

When a linear regression presents evidence of heteroskedasticity, the usual approach in least-squares is to use a generalized least-squares (GLS) estimator in place of the usual OLS. The virtue of GLS is that we do not need to know anything about *why* the data are heteroskedastic in order to estimate the model by GLS. The GLS estimator will provide consistent estimates of the regression slopes, but will also provide consistent estimates of the standard errors of those slopes, making correct hypothesis tests possible. If the slopes are all we care about, this is a sensible solution.

In many cases, however, we might wish to treat the heteroskedasticity as itself the subject of substantive interest. For example, the content of election campaigns may affect not only how candidates are perceived but also affect the *clarity* of those perceptions. The clarity can be modeled by assuming that the variance parameter, σ^2, varies across individuals depending on both campaign and individual level variables such as the amount of advertising, the number of issues discussed, the individual's level of interest in politics and their amount of television exposure. In this case we wish to reparameterize the variance as $\sigma_i^2 = f(\mathbf{z}_i\gamma)$, where **z** contains the variables that affect clarity of candidate perception and γ is the vector of coefficients measuring these effects. Because σ_i^2 must be nonnegative, we adopt the parameterization $\sigma_i^2 = e^{\mathbf{z}_i\gamma}$.

As with the heteroskedastic regression model, there are also variables that affect the mean of perceptions. For example, liberals may see Democrats as closer to them, whereas conservatives see them as further away. In the normal distribution, this requires another reparameterization. If the mean perception varies across individuals, then the parameterization becomes $\mu_i = \mathbf{x}_i\beta$.

If we assume our dependent variable, candidate perceptions, follows a normal data generating process, then the log-likelihood is:

$$l(\mu_i, \sigma_i^2 \mid \mathbf{y}) = \sum \left(-\frac{1}{2}\log(2\pi) - \frac{1}{2}\log \sigma_i^2 - \frac{1}{2}\frac{(y_i - \mu_i)^2}{\sigma_i^2} \right)$$

Replacing μ_i and σ_i^2 with their reparameterizations gives:

$$l(\beta, \gamma \mid \mathbf{y}, \mathbf{x}, \mathbf{z}) = \sum \left(-\frac{1}{2}\log(2\pi) - \frac{1}{2}\mathbf{z}_i\gamma - \frac{1}{2}\frac{(y_i - \mathbf{x}_i\beta)^2}{\exp(\mathbf{z}_i\gamma)} \right)$$

This parameterization now has, say, k parameters in β and j parameters in γ. This is a significant reduction from the $2N$ parameters we have in μ_i and σ_i^2, which are also underidentified. This provides a parsimonious model of both perceptions and clarity and offers substantive insight, through the γ vector, into why some perceptions are more variable than are others.

Again, there are nonlinear functions of the parameters that preclude a closed-form solution to the log-likelihood equations, so numerical methods are used for estimation. Hypothesis testing is straightforward using z scores for individual parameters or the LR or Wald test for sets of parameters.

Logit Model for Binary Outcomes

Perhaps the single most widely used ML estimator is the logit model for binary outcomes. Many social outcomes are inherently dichotomous: a citizen votes or does not, a person marries or does not, a person is employed or is not. For these models, we start with the simplest data generating process, the Bernoulli distribution:

$$y_i \sim \begin{array}{cc} y & P(y) \\ 1 & \pi \\ 0 & 1-\pi \end{array}$$

where the event occurs with probability π and fails to occur with probability $1-\pi$.

We reparameterize this model to allow the probability of success to vary across observations, so π becomes π_i. The likelihood is therefore:

$$L(\pi_i \mid \mathbf{y}) = \prod \pi_i^{y_i}(1-\pi_i)^{1-y_i}$$

As with the Poisson example, there are N parameters in this form of the model, so some simplification is required.

To construct the logit model, we again reparameterize, this time replacing the probability of success for each case with the cumulative logistic distribution and introducing explanatory variables and parameters to account for the variation in probability. The cumulative standardized logistic distribution is:

$$P(y=1) = \frac{1}{1+e^{-\mathbf{x}\beta}}$$

where $\mathbf{x}$ is the matrix of predictor variables, and β *is* a vector of coefficients. If we reparameterize π_i to equal this function, the log-likelihood becomes:

$$l(\beta \mid \mathbf{y}, \mathbf{x}) = \sum_{i=1}^{N} y_i \log\frac{1}{1+e^{x_i\beta}} + (1-y_i)\log\left(1-\frac{1}{1+e^{-x_i\beta}}\right)$$

Numerical methods are used to maximize this, and hypothesis testing proceeds as before.

We can convert this to the probit model by simply choosing to parameterize in terms of the cumulative normal rather than the cumulative logistic. In that case, the log-likelihood becomes:

$$l(\beta \mid \mathbf{y}, \mathbf{x}) = \sum_{i=1}^{N} y_i \log\Phi(x_i\beta) + (1-y_i)\log(1-\Phi(x_i\beta))$$

where

$$\Phi(x_i\beta) = \int_{-\infty}^{x_i\beta} \frac{1}{\sqrt{2\pi}}\exp\left(-\frac{1}{2}(x_i\beta)^2\right)dx$$

This is the integral of a standard normal variate. It has no closed form and so is usually abbreviated as simply $\Phi(x_i\beta)$.

Here we see that models of binary outcomes rest on a common assumption that the Bernoulli distribution with variable parameter π_i is a reasonable model for binary outcomes. The choice between logit or probit is simply a matter of whether we choose to reparameterize π_i as a cumulative logistic or a cumulative normal. Other binary choice models result from choosing other distributions, such as the complementary log-log or the Cauchy distribution. This also illustrates the flexibility of ML in allowing us to incorporate a variety of alternative parameterizations within a common base likelihood.

Conclusion

ML provides a general and flexible approach to statistical estimation and inference. ML estimators are consistent, efficient, asymptotically normally distributed, and lead to identical inferences when reparameterized. These are powerful reasons for the success of the method. On the negative side of the ledger is the requirement for large samples in order to have confidence in the asymptotic approximations required.

See Also the Following Articles

Contingency Tables and Log-Linear Models • Hypothesis Tests and Proofs • Missing Data, Problems and Solutions • Non-Response Bias • Spatial Econometrics

Further Reading

Azzalini, A. (1996). *Statistical Inference Based on the Likelihood.* Chapman & Hall/CRC, Boca Raton, FL.

Cramér, H. (1946). *Mathematical Methods of Statistics.* Princeton University Press, Princeton, NJ.

Fisher, R. A. (1922). On the mathematical foundation of theoretical statistics. *Philos. Trans. Royal Soc. A* **222,** 308–358.

Fisher, R. A. (1925). Theory of statistical estimation. *Proc. Cambridge Philos. Soc.* **22,** 700–725.

Franklin, C. H. (1991). Eschewing obfuscation? Campaigns and the perception of Senate incumbents. *Am. Polit. Sci. Rev.* **85,** 1193–1214.

Gill, P. E., Murray, W., and Wright, M. H. (1981). *Practical Optimization.* Academic Press, New York.

Godfrey, L. G. (1988). *Misspecification Tests in Econometrics.* Cambridge University Press, Cambridge, U.K.

Greene, W. H. (2000). *Econometric Analysis,* 4th Ed. Prentice Hall, New York.

King, G. (1989). *Unifying Political Methodology: The Likelihood Theory of Statistical Inference.* Cambridge University Press, Cambridge, U.K.

Long, J. S. (1997). *Regression Models for Categorical and Limited Dependent Variables.* Sage, Thousand Oaks, CA.

Norden, R. H. (1972). A survey of maximum likelihood estimation. *Int. Statist. Rev.* **40,** 329–354.

Norden, R. H. (1973). A survey of maximum likelihood estimation, Part 2. *Int. Statist. Rev.* **41,** 39–58.

Rao, C. R. (1945). Information and accuracy attainable in the estimation of statistical parameters. *Bull. Calcutta Math. Soc.* **37,** 81–91.

Wald, A. (1949). A note on the consistency of maximum likelihood estimates. *Ann. Math. Statist.* **20,** 595–601.

Measurement Error, Issues and Solutions

Richard A. Zeller
Kent State University, Kent, Ohio, USA

Glossary

communality The sum of the squared factor loadings for an measure across all factors.

concept A specific idea concerning crucial aspects of a narrow variety of behaviors.

construct A general idea concerning crucial aspects of a wide variety of behaviors.

convergent validity The strong positive correlation among measures of a dimension.

correlation matrix An arrangement of correlation coefficients, each defined by its row and column.

Cronbach's alpha The average of all possible split-half reliabilities projected onto the number of measures in a scale.

dimension The physical specification of the location of a concept in space.

discriminant validity The correlation among measures of each dimension when they are more strongly correlated among themselves than they are with measures of other dimensions.

effect parameter The degree to which a presumed cause affects a presumed effect.

eigenvalue The sum of the squared factor loadings for a factor across all measures.

epistemic correlation The correlation between a concept and an observed variable designed to measure that concept.

epistemic path The strength of the causal effect of a concept on an observed variable designed to measure that concept.

factor analysis A statistical tool designed to reduce a large number of measures to a small number of dimensions.

factor loading The correlation of an measure with a factor.

measurement The link between theory and data.

measurement error The difference between a concept and the observations designed to measure that concept.

operational definition A formulation that specifies a protocol, the quantitative result of which is our attempt to assess the concept.

path coefficient The estimated strength of a causal effect.

random error The haphazard fluctuation of a variable that does not produce the same observation under identical theoretical and observational conditions.

reliability The degree to which an observation designed to measure a concept is free from random error.

scale A dimension created from multiple measures.

systematic error The patterned fluctuation of a variable that produces an observation that differs from the concept it was designed to measure.

validity The degree to which an observation designed to measure a concept is free from both systematic error and random error.

varimax A rotation algorithm that maximizes high and low factor loadings, minimizing mid-value factor loadings.

Measurement is the act of establishing a correspondence between observations and concepts. In a perfect world, we would have perfect measures of our concepts. But in the real world of research, we possess no such perfect measures; we have no "gold standard" against which to evaluate how good our measures are. In order to advance our disciplines, we need pretty good, but not perfect, measures for our concepts. We need measures that are highly, but not perfectly, reliable and valid. We ought not to use woefully inadequate measures. Instead, we should use measures that are, although not perfect, pretty good. This entry establishes how to create and evaluate pretty good measures.

Measurement

Measurement is the link between theory and data. Data are made up of observations of behavior. Theory is made up of constructs. A construct is a general idea concerning crucial aspects of a wide variety of behaviors. Constructs are made up of concepts. A concept is a specific idea concerning crucial aspects of a narrow variety of behaviors. Measurement is the act of establishing a correspondence between observations and concepts. Social science concepts include aggression, pain, co-dependence, self-esteem, alienation, economic output, productivity, satisfaction, conflict, development, safety, communication, political participation, socioeconomic status, deviance, fertility, learning, health, physical fitness, and stress. In a perfect world, we would have perfect measures of our concepts. But in the real world of research, we possess no such perfect measures; we have no "gold standard" against which to evaluate how good our measures are.

Measurement error is the difference between a concept and the observations designed to measure that concept. Measurement error is made up of random error and systematic error. Random error is the haphazard fluctuation of a variable that does not produce the same observation under identical theoretical and observational conditions; systematic error is the patterned fluctuation of a variable that produces an observation that differs from the concept it was designed to measure. Reliability is the degree to which an observation designed to measure a concept is free from random error; validity is the degree to which an observation designed to measure a concept is free from both systematic error and random error.

In order to advance our disciplines, we need pretty good, but not perfect, measures for our concepts. We need measures that are highly, but not perfectly, reliable and valid. We ought not to use woefully inadequate measures; that is, we should not use measures possessing weak reliability and validity. Instead, we should use measures that are, although not perfect, pretty good. Let us illustrate.

Galileo wanted to measure the speed of a falling object. In order to measure speed, he had to measure time and distance. His measure of distance was highly reliable and valid. But what could he use to measure time? For his purposes, the hourglass was inadequate; the pulse was adequate—Galileo did not have (and did not need) a quartz watch! The clever Galileo used the relatively reliable and valid pulse of an assistant as his measure of time. For his purposes, pulse was highly, but not perfectly, reliable and valid.

How could Galileo have evaluated the reliability and validity of a pulse as a measure of the concept time? More generally, how can any scientist evaluate the reliability and validity of any measuring instrument? Answer: Galileo could have had multiple assistants measure a clear interval of time using their respective pulses. That is, he could have had 10 assistants check their pulses during the passage of the same interval of time.

Suppose that Galileo defined a clear interval of time (e.g., from when the object started falling to when it hit the ground). Suppose he asked 10 assistants to measure their pulses during this time interval. Suppose he summed each of the 10 measures for each instrument, creating a pulse scale (a scale is a dimension created from multiple measures). I illustrate in the following the procedures that Galileo could have used to as evaluate the reliability and validity of his pulse (time measurement) scale.

Hauser argued in 1969 that the major challenge in social research is to find and evaluate the reliability and validity of the scales that we use measure our concepts. He notes that "... inadequate measurement, more than inadequate concept or hypothesis, has plagued social researchers and prevented fuller explanations of the variances with which they are confounded."

Given concepts and the hypothesized causal connections among those concepts, sociology researchers are faced with the "reality" test. Does our conceptual structure coincide with what we observe? This is the major challenge of science. In order to evaluate the causal relationships among concepts, we must find an adequate measure for each concept. I now turn to the task of finding adequate measures for concepts. This presentation focuses primarily on exploratory factor analysis. Other studies (e.g., the 1987 Hayduk study) focus primarily on confirmatory factor analysis.

The Criteria for Adequate, but Not Perfect, Measurement

The following are standard protocols of adequate, but not perfect, measurement.

- Multiple measures. There should be multiple measures designed to assess each dimension of the concept.
- Measure clarity. Each measure should be designed to measure one and only one dimension of a concept.
- Convergent and discriminant validity of measures of a concept. There should be a strong positive intercorrelation among measures designed to assess each dimension of the concept. Moreover, these intermeasure correlations should be stronger than the correlations of these measures with measures designed to assess other dimensions.
- Factor analysis. The dimensions in data should be identified.
- Scaling. Once the clarity, convergence, and discriminance of a set of measures have been established, scales should be constructed.

- Equivalence reliability. The equivalence reliability among the measures of each dimension of a concept should be strong.
- Correction for attenuation. Correlations between scales with imperfect reliability will be less than what the correlation would have been if the scales were perfectly reliable, and this underestimate of the correlation should be corrected.

Additional criteria for good measurement, the examination of which goes beyond the present discussion, include:

- Known groups validity. Once scales have been constructed, comparisons of scale scores between groups known to be high and low on the dimensions of the concept should be made.
- Construct validity. Scales should correlate as theoretically specified with measures of other concepts.

Let us discuss each of these target criteria in turn.

Multiple Measures

A dimension is the physical specification of the location of a concept in space. Each dimension is designed to represent its respective concept. A dimension is made up of a set of measures. When a set of concepts represents the general idea of a construct, the space is called multidimensional. For example, in 1966 Nisbet argued that the construct "Alienation" is one of the major unit-ideas of sociology. In 1959, Seeman argued that "Alienation" is an umbrella construct for the concepts "Social isolation," "Powerlessness," "Normlessness," and "Meaninglessness." In 1967, Neil and Rettig constructed multiple measures for each of these concepts. In 1980, Zeller, Neal, and Groat established the reliability and stability of these concepts, as assessed by scales constructed from their respective measures. I now turn to a discussion of the measurement issues raised by the attempt to assess the concepts of "Alienation" and the protocol used by these authors.

Consider only the concepts "Social isolation" and "Powerlessness" under the umbrella construct "Alienation." Zeller, Neal, and Groat conceptually defined "Social isolation" as "... the experience of a social cleavage between oneself and others." They defined "Powerlessness" as "... low subjectively held probabilities for controlling events." Multiple Likert items were developed as measures of these two concepts. For example, as measures of "Social isolation," Zeller, Neal, and Groat used:

S_1, "Real friends are easy to find as ever." (reverse scoring)
S_2, "Sometimes I feel all alone in the world."

As measures of "Powerlessness," they used:

P_1, "People like me can change the course of world events if we make ourselves heard." (reverse scoring)
P_2, "The world is run by the few people in power, and there is not much the little guy can do about it."

Common response categories for Likert items are: 1 = "Strongly disagree"; 2 = "Disagree"; 3 = "Mildly disagree"; 4 = "Neutral"; 5 = "Mildly agree"; 6 = "Agree"; 7 = "Strongly agree." Reverse-scored items assign a 7 (not a 1) to "Strongly disagree"; a 6 (not a 2) to "Disagree"; and so on.

Figure 1 presents a measurement path model of the construct "Alienation." "Alienation" is conceptualized as the umbrella construct that causes the concepts "Social isolation," and "Powerlessness." The model specifies six measures of "Social isolation," labeled s_1, s_2, s_3, s_4, s_5, and s_6, and six measures of "Powerlessness," labeled p_1, p_2, p_3, p_4, p_5, and p_6.

In path models, causal effects are represented by arrows. In path analysis, these causal effects are estimated by path coefficients; a path coefficient is the estimated strength of a causal effect. The theoretical causal effect of

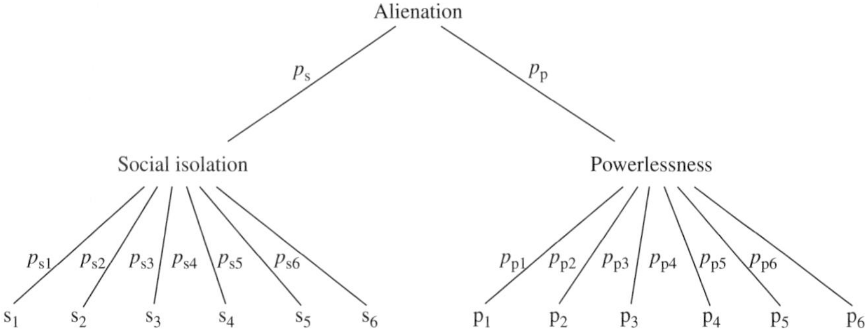

Figure 1 Two-factor measurement path model for "Alienation."

"Alienation" on "Social isolation" is represented by P_s; the theoretical causal effect of "Alienation" on "Powerlessness" is represented by P_p, where P stands for the theoretical path coefficient. Thus, P_s refers to the path from "Alienation" to "Social isolation," and P_p refers to the path from "Alienation" to "Powerlessness."

The epistemic causal effects of "Social isolation" on each of the measures of "Social isolation" (e.g., s_1, s_2, s_3, s_4, s_5, and s_6) are represented by p_{s1}, p_{s2}, p_{s3}, p_{s4}, p_{s5}, and p_{s6}. The epistemic causal effects of "Powerlessness" on each of the measures of "Powerlessness" are represented by p_{p1}, p_{p2}, p_{p3}, p_{p4}, p_{p5}, and p_{p6}, where p stands for the causal, epistemic effect of each concept on its respective measures. The measurement model in Fig. 1 has 12 measures, six for each concept.

The only thing that the researcher observes is the answers provided by the respondent to the items on the questionnaire. The data obtained from the questionnaire are variables; each has a mean and a variance. These variables can be correlated with one another and with other variables relevant to the research questions.

In order to illustrate the principles of factor analysis just described, I present a dimensions of "Alienation" data set. I created this data set using transformations of random numbers. Therefore, the universe that underlies this data set has known parameters. But prior to the research, the researcher does not know what those parameters are. Indeed, if the researcher had foreknowledge of these parameters, there would be no reason to conduct the research. I first show how these parameters are estimated using the standard protocols of factor analysis; I then compare the results of the factor analysis with the parameters.

Table I presents a correlation matrix of the 12 measures of alienation—a correlation matrix is an arrangement of correlation coefficients, each defined by their respective row and column. For example, the correlation between s_1 and s_2 is 0.506 ($r_{s1s2} = 0.506$). This can be seen by looking down column s_1 in Table I and across row s_2. It can also be seen by looking down column s_2 in Table I and across row s_1. Thus, the correlation matrix is a symmetric matrix. That is, $r_{s1s2} = r_{s2s1}$, $r_{s1s3} = r_{s3s1}$, and so on.

The correlation of an item with itself is equal to 1 ($r_{s1s1} = 1.000$). The set of correlations of each item with itself forms a diagonal across the correlation matrix. This diagonal is called the main diagonal. The symmetry of the correlation matrix is that each correlation in the upper right triangle (above and to the right of the main diagonal, as shown in Table I) is identical to its counterpart in the lower left triangle (below and to the left of the main diagonal).

Intercorrelations among measures also form groups. The triangle of correlations among measures of "Social isolation," the triangle of correlations among measures of "Powerlessness," and the rectangle of correlations between the "Social isolation" measures and the "Powerlessness" measures are presented in Table I. A visual inspection of the table shows that the intercorrelations among the measures of "Social isolation" hover around 0.5; the intercorrelations among the measures

Table I Correlation Matrix of 12 Measures of Alienation

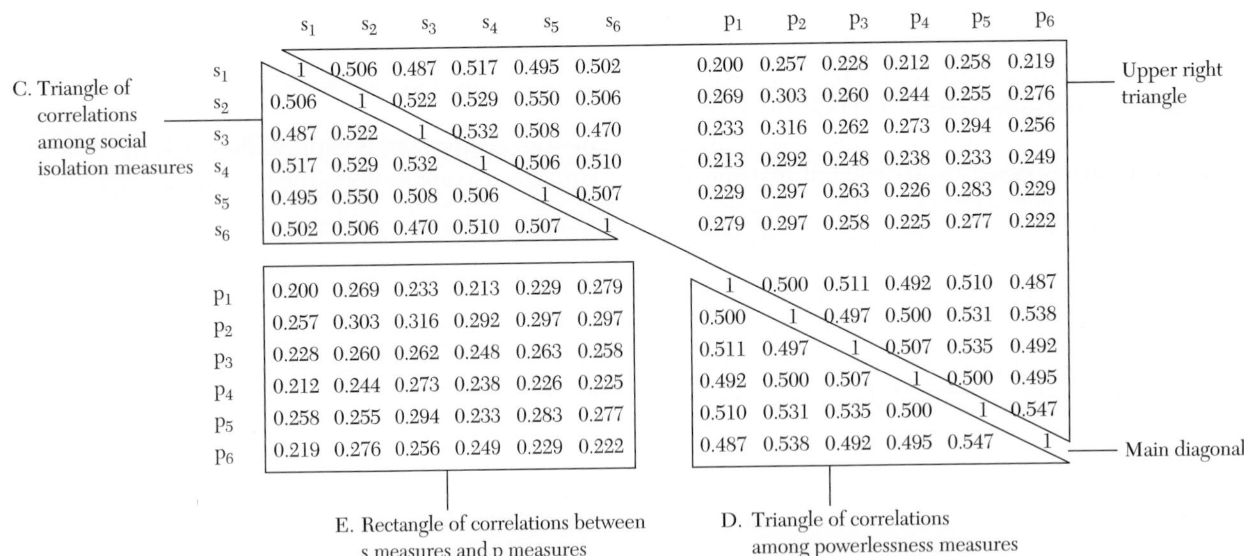

	s_1	s_2	s_3	s_4	s_5	s_6	p_1	p_2	p_3	p_4	p_5	p_6
s_1	1	0.506	0.487	0.517	0.495	0.502	0.200	0.257	0.228	0.212	0.258	0.219
s_2	0.506	1	0.522	0.529	0.550	0.506	0.269	0.303	0.260	0.244	0.255	0.276
s_3	0.487	0.522	1	0.532	0.508	0.470	0.233	0.316	0.262	0.273	0.294	0.256
s_4	0.517	0.529	0.532	1	0.506	0.510	0.213	0.292	0.248	0.238	0.233	0.249
s_5	0.495	0.550	0.508	0.506	1	0.507	0.229	0.297	0.263	0.226	0.283	0.229
s_6	0.502	0.506	0.470	0.510	0.507	1	0.279	0.297	0.258	0.225	0.277	0.222
p_1	0.200	0.269	0.233	0.213	0.229	0.279	1	0.500	0.511	0.492	0.510	0.487
p_2	0.257	0.303	0.316	0.292	0.297	0.297	0.500	1	0.497	0.500	0.531	0.538
p_3	0.228	0.260	0.262	0.248	0.263	0.258	0.511	0.497	1	0.507	0.535	0.492
p_4	0.212	0.244	0.273	0.238	0.226	0.225	0.492	0.500	0.507	1	0.500	0.495
p_5	0.258	0.255	0.294	0.233	0.283	0.277	0.510	0.531	0.535	0.500	1	0.547
p_6	0.219	0.276	0.256	0.249	0.229	0.222	0.487	0.538	0.492	0.495	0.547	1

of "Powerlessness" hover around 0.5; and the correlations between the "Social isolation" measures and the "Powerlessness" measures hover around 0.25.

Table I presents all the information we have. This information is nothing more than marks on a piece of paper. From these marks, we have created variables and a correlation matrix. By no stretch of the imagination does this data collection protocol constitute strong data. Instead, it is subject to all of the foibles known to researchers: social desirability, response set, lying, ignorance, apathy, fatigue. and so on.

Analysis and inference remain to be done. What can we do with the correlations in Table I that will allow us to evaluate the measurement model? In order to answer this question, we must create some principles of analysis and inference.

Let us begin at the beginning. We have a pool of items. We created this pool of items with the specific intent of measuring our concepts. Recall that we created the measurement model presented in Fig. 1 by sheer imagination—we made it up. By no stretch of the imagination does this measurement model constitute strong theory, so we have weak data and weak theory. But, as we shall see, this combination can lead to a rather strong inference about the measurement model. We now turn to the equipment we need to make that inference.

An epistemic correlation is the correlation between a concept and an observed variable designed to measure that concept. The term epistemic path refers to the strength of this causal effect. The epistemic path is the traditional answer to the question: "To what degree is this measure a valid measure of the dimension it is designed to measure?" In Fig. 1, the p_{ij} from either "Social isolation" or "Powerlessness" to their respective measures represent epistemic paths.

The epistemic correlation crosses the line between the theoretical and the observational. The theoretical concept is, in principle, unobservable; nobody has ever seen "Social isolation" or "Powerlessness." We attempt to measure a concept using an operational definition. An operational definition specifies a protocol, the quantitative result of which is our attempt to assess the concept. In our "Alienation" example, each of the 12 items are operational definitions designed to measure their respective concepts. The protocol is that we will ask respondents to provide their opinions on a questionnaire, and we will use their responses on our preestablished quantitative ladder as the relative level of each respondent on each respective concept.

The epistemic correlation is the crux of measurement. It is, in measurement terminology, the validity coefficient. But an epistemic correlation can never be directly observed. We cannot make this observation directly because the concept is unobservable. Therefore, the epistemic correlation requires that the conceptual structure be inferred.

In Fig. 1, the epistemic path from "Social isolation" to measure s_1 is p_{s1}. This path spans the chasm between the theoretical and what is observed; $p_{s1}, \ldots, p_{s6}$ are the six epistemic paths from "Social isolation" to the measures of "Social isolation"; $p_{p1}, \ldots, p_{p6}$ are the six epistemic paths from "Powerlessness" to the measures of "Powerlessness." But how can we evaluate whether the two-dimensional structure in Fig. 1 is the appropriate measurement model? After we have made this inference, how can we assess the strength of the epistemic paths of the inferred model? Finally, how can we assess the pattern of association among the concepts? Clearly, proper inference in measurement presents the scientist with a substantial challenge.

If a measure were perfectly reliable and valid, each epistemic path would be 1.00. When one measure assesses its target concept with perfect reliability and validity, that measure alone is sufficient to measure its respective concept. In this situation, multiple measures are unnecessary and superfluous. Even if the epistemic path from a dimension to a measure were near perfect (i.e., $p_{ij} = 0.95$), the use of more than one measure would add very little to measurement reliability and validity.

As the epistemic path is reduced in strength, the number of measures needed for acceptable measurement reliability increases. Much of the measurement challenge involves evaluating the veracity of the measurement model and finding credible estimates for the epistemic and conceptual paths.

Measure Clarity

Each item should be designed to assess one and only one dimension of a concept. There is no substitute for clear measures. There is no substitute for the depth and breadth of substantive knowledge of a concept and its dimensions. There is no substitute for a researcher's clinical experience with those who exhibit the phenomenon in question. In addition, there is no substitute for diligence, persistence, cleverness, and creativity in the construction of measures. I may have underplayed the importance of item clarity by giving it only one short paragraph. I have seen numerous studies in which item weakness in terms of clarity, substantive knowledge, and construction has led to unsatisfactory measurement results. However, this is a paper on measurement, not on the construction of clear measures.

Convergent and Discriminant Validity of Dimensions within a Concept

When multiple measures are designed to assess a single dimension, the standard of the research industry has long been that these measures should be highly intercorrelated.

Convergent validity is the condition of strong positive correlation among measures of a dimension. The industry also requires that measures of one concept be differentiable from measures of another concept. Discriminant validity is the condition that measures of each dimension are more strongly correlated among themselves then they are with measures of other dimensions. In Fig. 1, correlations among s_i and correlations among p_i (in the triangles of correlations within groups of measures) are convergent correlations; correlations between the s_i and the p_i (in the rectangle of correlations between S measures and P measures) are discriminant correlations. There are two convergent clusters in Fig. 1.

Factor analysis is the major statistical technique designed to describe measure intercorrelations. The purpose of factor analysis is the identification of dimensions in the data. As such, factor analysis enables researchers to (1) describe the dimensions of a set of measures, (2) select those measures that best represent each of the identified dimensions, and (3) estimate the strength of the epistemic path from each dimension to its respective set of measures.

However, when evaluating the degree to which a large set of measures represent a small number of theoretical dimensions, the application of factor analytic techniques is as much an art as it is a science. This is because there are numerous conceptual and empirical ambiguities in the measurement setting. Conceptually, the researcher wants to find out: (1) how many dimensions of the concept are "real" and (2) to what degree each dimension of the concept is related to other dimensions of the same concept and to other concepts. Empirically, the researcher wants to assess the degree to which each measure represents (1) the dimension it is designed to represent, (2) dimensions other than the one it is designed to represent, (3) systematic method artifacts, and (4) random error.

At the same time, the researcher's primary interest is in the substantive association between the dimensions of the concept and other concepts; the measurement effort itself is of secondary importance. Nevertheless, bad measurement most surely will torpedo the best of conceptual schemes and sentence them to the intellectual trash heap, whether they belong there or not. The end result of the factor analysis should be that the researcher has inferred how many dimensions are represented by the measures, which measures define which dimensions, and to what degree.

Factor Analysis

Factor analysis is a statistical tool designed to describe correlations economically. Specifically, factor analysis is designed to reduce a large number of measures to a small number of dimensions. In order to accomplish this objective, a series of mathematical calculations are performed on a correlation matrix. When a researcher has a strong theory and strong data, the appropriate factor analytic tools are confirmatory. However, researchers usually lack such a strong theory and strong data. When a researcher lacks a strong theory and strong data, the appropriate factor analytic tools are exploratory.

Ordinarily, the researcher wants the number of factors to be as small as possible while still maintaining fidelity to the patterns of correlations. Exploratory factor analysis is appropriate in situations in which the researcher is less than highly confident *a priori* about how many factors are necessary and sufficient to describe the data, about which measures define which factors, and about the pattern of association among the factors.

Exploratory factor analysis focuses on the extraction and rotation of factors. Extraction is the process of removing and describing the desired number of factors from a correlation matrix. Rotation is the process of solving for a viewing location of those factors that makes the most theoretical sense. There are a variety of different mathematical approaches to the extraction and rotation of factors. I limit this discussion to principal components extraction and to varimax rotation.

Extraction

Principal components extraction applies a complex mathematical algorithm to a correlation matrix. Components, commonly called factors, are extracted from the correlation matrix sequentially. The first and strongest factor is extracted and then statistically removed from the matrix. Then the second factor is extracted and removed from the matrix. This process continues, extracting weaker and weaker factors, until there are as many factors as there are variables in the correlation matrix. But the analyst only wants to examine the strong systematic factors. Parsimony is achieved when the strong systematic factors are retained in the analysis while the weak random factors are discarded. I examine the criteria for making the decision concerning how many factors are systematic shortly. First, I must define factor loading.

A factor loading is the correlation of an measure with a factor. Like correlation coefficients, factor loadings vary from -1.0 to 1.0. Each measure has a factor loading on each factor. If a measure has a strong positive factor loading (i.e., >0.5) on a factor, that measure is said to define that factor. If a measure has a strong negative factor loading (i.e., <-0.5) on a factor, that measure is said to define the opposite of that factor. As the strength of the factor loading decreases, the capacity of the factor loading to define the factor also decreases.

Two crucial tools in the interpretation of factor analyses are the communality and the eigenvalue. The communality (symbolized h^2) is equal to the sum of the squared factor loadings for a measure across all factors. For any measure, the communality reports the proportion of variance that measure shares with the factor structure.

The higher the communality, the more that measure shares variance with the other measures in the correlation matrix. When the number of factors is equal to the number of measures in the correlation matrix, all principal component communalities will equal 1.00. The sum of the communalities over all measures will equal the number of measures. But the purpose of factor analysis is to reduce a large number of measures to a small number of factors. When this reduction takes place, the communalities reveal how much variance an item shares with the systematic factors retained in the analysis.

The eigenvalue is equal to the sum of the squared factor loadings for a factor across all measures. For any factor, the eigenvalue divided by the number of measures reports the proportion of variance of the correlation matrix on that factor. The sum of the eigenvalues over all factors will equal the number of measures.

But, I reiterate, the analyst only wants to examine the systematic factors. When factors are extracted from a correlation matrix, the systematic factors are extracted first. But the mathematical algorithm does not know when systematic patterns have been exhausted. Instead, the analyst must specify the number of factors to be included in the factor analysis. How does the analyst decide how many factors to include? I now turn to the answer to that question.

How Many Factors? For many measurement questions, good theoretical arguments can be articulated for varying numbers of factors. Ordinarily, none of these arguments constitute strong theory and ordinarily, the researcher does not possess strong data. When faced with either of these liabilities, the factor analyst can provide two rules of thumb designed to assist in the decision about how many factors are sufficiently systematic to be included in subsequent analyses: the 1.0 eigenvalue cut-off and the scree test.

- The 1.0 eigenvalue cut-off rule of thumb is a decision rule for setting the number of factors to be retained in the analysis as equal to the number of factors with eigenvalues ≥ 1.0. Factors with eigenvalues ≥ 1.0 should, according to this rule of thumb, be retained as systematic factors. Factors with eigenvalues < 1.0 should be discarded as random. Table II presents the eigenvalue, the percentage of variance explained, and the cumulative percentage of variance explained for each component. There are 12 factors in this analysis, one for each of the 12 measures. The 12 factors together account for 100% of the variance in the matrix. The eigenvalue for the first component is 5.080; this component accounts for 42.333% of the variance in the matrix (e.g., 5.080/12 = 0.42333). The second factor has an eigenvalue of 2.025 and accounts for 16.875% of the variance in the matrix. Together, factors 1 and 2 account for 59.208% of the variance

Table II Total Variance Explained[a]

Component	*Eigenvalue total*	*Percentage of variance*	*Cumulative (%)*
1	5.080	42.333	42.333
2	2.025[b]	16.875	59.208
3	0.584	4.869	64.078
4	0.537	4.471	68.549
5	0.529	4.410	72.959
6	0.520	4.330	77.290
7	0.493	4.112	81.402
8	0.482	4.015	85.417
9	0.473	3.946	89.363
10	0.452	3.763	93.126
11	0.428	3.570	96.696
12	0.396	3.304	100.000[c]

[a] Extraction method: principal component analysis.
[b] 1.0 eigenvalue cut-off.
[c] Twelve components account for 100% of the variance.

(e.g., 42.333% + 16.875% = 59.208%). Factor 3 has an eigenvalue of only 0.584, and the remaining factors account for successively less variance. The 1.0 eigenvalue cut-off indicates that we should retain two factors in this analysis.

- The scree test rule of thumb is a decision rule for setting the number of factors to be retained by the identification of the point of disjuncture in the pattern of eigenvalues extracted on each subsequent factor. The scree test uses the fact that there are as many factors in a principal components analysis as there are measures. Factors with eigenvalues on the larger side of the disjuncture should be considered systematic; factors with eigenvalues on the smaller side of the disjuncture should be considered random. The scree test is carried out using a scree plot. A scree plot presents the size of the eigenvalue on the vertical axis and the component number on the horizontal axis. A scree plot is read by noting the number of factors for which the eigenvalue is greater than the trajectory of eigenvalues suggests. Figure 2 presents the scree plot for this factor analysis. In Fig. 2, the eigenvalues increase only slightly as we move back from factor 12 to factor 3; then there is a substantial increase in the scree plot line as we move back from 3 to 2. This substantial increase is the disjuncture in the scree plot line that leads the analyst to the inference that there are two systematic factors in the data.

Rotation of Factors

As I have noted, the factors as extracted do not usually present the optimal vantage point from which to examine the results. In addition to the 1.0 eigenvalue cut-off rule and the scree test, analysts can make educated guesses about the number of factors by the number of measures that define each rotated factor. The rotation of factors improves the analysts educated guesses.

Varimax rotation uses a mathematical algorithm that maximizes high- and low-value factor loadings and minimizes mid-value factor loadings. The varimax rotated two-factor matrix is presented in Table III. All factor loadings are positive. The factor loadings on factor 1 are between 0.7 and 0.8 for the s_i, the measures of "Social isolation," and between 0.1 and 0.3 for the p_i, the measures of "Powerlessness." The reverse is true for the factor loadings on factor 2. On this factor, the factor loadings are between 0.1 and 0.3 for the s_i and between 0.7 and 0.8 for the p_i. Given this analysis, we call label factor 1 the social isolation factor and factor 2 the powerlessness factor.

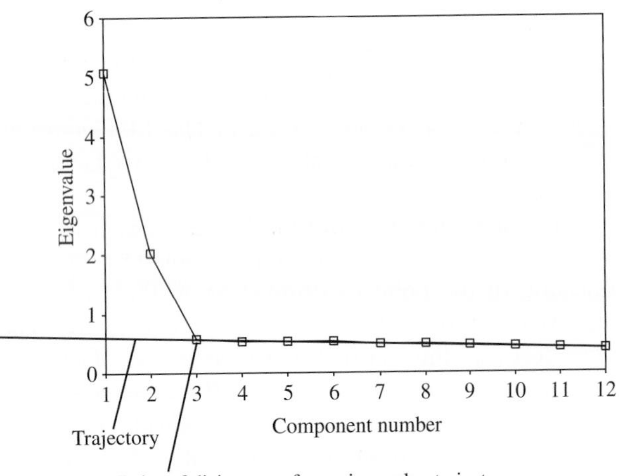

Figure 2 Scree plot of tow-factor structure.

Table III Rotated Two-Factor Matrix[a]

	Factors	
	1 (Social isolation)	*2 (Powerlessness)*
s_1	*0.752*	0.128
s_2	*0.761*	0.186
s_3	*0.733*	0.203
s_4	*0.767*	0.150
s_5	*0.755*	0.168
s_6	*0.732*	0.182
p_1	0.144	*0.746*
p_2	0.236	*0.735*
p_3	0.168	*0.749*
p_4	0.143	*0.744*
p_5	0.184	*0.765*
p_6	0.149	*0.759*

[a] Values in italics indicates high-value factor loadings.

The data warrant the inference that the 12 items measure two dimensions. These dimensions have been named social isolation and powerlessness to coincide with the content of the items created by Neal and Rettig. What would have happened if we had factor analyzed the six "Social isolation" items separately from the six "Powerlessness" items? Figure 3 shows that the scree plots would have indicated that there was a single factor in each of these six-item data sets. Table IV shows that all items designed to measure each of these factors separately have strong factor loadings.

Scaling

Once the number of factors and which measure defines which factors have been established, the researcher needs to create scales. One scale should be created to represent each dimension. If the measures defining each dimension have roughly equal variances,

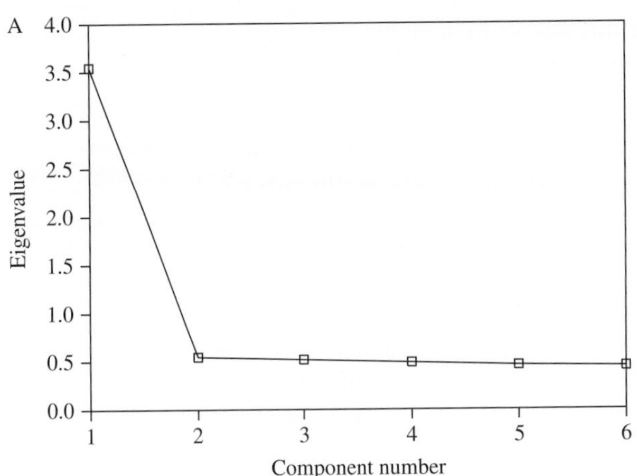

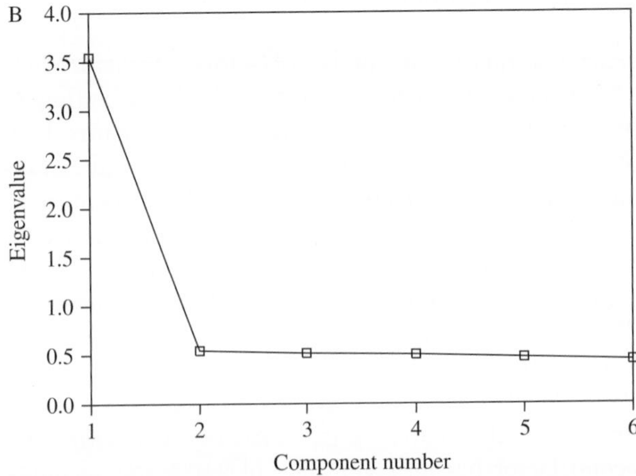

Figure 3 Scree plots of two single-factor structures. (A) "Social isolation" measures. (B) "Powerlessness" measures.

Table IV Rotated Single-Factor Matrices

Social isolation		*Powerlessness*	
s_1	0.759	p_1	0.757
s_2	0.785	p_2	0.774
s_3	0.762	p_3	0.768
s_4	0.780	p_4	0.755
s_5	0.773	p_5	0.788
s_6	0.755	p_6	0.772

the simplest way to create a scale is to sum the measures defining each scale. In practice, researchers can tolerate moderate variation in the measure variances.

The standard deviations of the items in this analysis are roughly comparable, ranging from 1.38 to 1.46. Thus, scales were created by summing the items defining each dimension. Specifically:

$$\text{Social isolation scale} = s_1 + s_2 + s_3 + s_4 + s_5 + s_6$$

$$\text{Powerlessness scale} = p_1 + p_2 + p_3 + p_4 + p_5 + p_6$$

Given that we have scales for each dimension of "Alienation," we can solve for the correlation as follows:

$$r = \frac{e}{\sqrt{a+2b}\,\sqrt{c+2d}} \quad (1)$$

where

a is the number of items in scale 1.
b is the sum of the off-diagonal correlations among the items in scale 1.
c is the number of items in scale 2.
d is the sum of the off-diagonal correlations among the items in scale 2.
e is the sum of the intercorrelations between the items in scale 1 and the items in scale 2.

Let scale 1 be the six-item social isolation scale and scale 2 be the six-item powerlessness scale. From Table I, we get:

$$a = 6$$

$$b = 0.506 + 0.487 + 0.522 + 0.517 + \cdots + 0.510 + 0.507 = 7.647$$

$$c = 6$$

$$d = 0.500 + 0.511 + 0.497 + 0.492 + \cdots + 0.495 + 0.547 = 7.642$$

$$e = 0.200 + 0.257 + 0.228 + 0.212 + \cdots + 0.277 + 0.222 = 9.144$$

Substituting these values into formula 1, we get:

$$r = \frac{e}{\sqrt{a+2b}\,\sqrt{c+2d}} = \frac{9.144}{\sqrt{6+2(7.647)}\,\sqrt{6+2(7.642)}} = \frac{9.144}{21.289} = 0.430$$

Equivalence Reliability

The equivalence reliability of each scale should be assessed. The standard of the research industry is to use Cronbach's alpha for this purpose. Cronbach's alpha is the average of all possible split-half reliabilities projected onto the number of measures in the scale. Standard statistical computer software packages can be used for this purpose. However, care must be taken in using these packages to ensure that all the measures and only the measures that define a specific scale are included in the calculations. As a rule of thumb for adequate measurement, Cronbach's alphas mirror instructional grades:

A—0.9 or higher are considered excellent;
B—0.8 to 0.9 are adequate;
C—0.7 to 0.8 are marginal;
D—0.6 to 0.07 are seriously suspect;
F—less than 0.6 are totally unacceptable.

The formula for Cronbach's alpha using a correlation matrix is:

$$\alpha = \left(\frac{a}{a-1}\right)\left(1 - \frac{a}{a+2b}\right) \quad (2)$$

where a is the number of items, and b is the sum of the off-diagonal correlations.

Substituting the values for the social isolation scale into Eq. (2), we get:

$$\alpha = \left(\frac{a}{a-1}\right)\left(1 - \frac{a}{a+2b}\right) = \left(\frac{6}{6-1}\right)\left(1 - \frac{6}{6+2[7.647]}\right) = 0.862$$

Similarly, for the powerlessness scale, we get:

$$\alpha = \left(\frac{c}{c-1}\right)\left(1 - \frac{c}{(c+2d)}\right) = \left(\frac{6}{6-1}\right)\left(1 - \frac{6}{6+2[7.642]}\right) = 0.862$$

(See Table V.) By our standards, this reliability is adequate but not excellent.

Table V Sample-Size Analysis

	Statistic				*Difference from universe*			
N	r	α_s	α_p	ρ	r	α_s	α_p	ρ
∞(universe)	0.429	0.857	0.857	0.500	—	—	—	—
1000	0.430	0.862	0.862	0.499	0.001	0.005	0.005	−0.001
100	0.421	0.859	0.847	0.494	−0.008	0.002	−0.010	−0.006
50a	0.504	0.883	0.887	0.569	0.075	0.051	0.030	0.069
50b	0.378	0.833	0.865	0.445	−0.051	−0.024	0.008	−0.055
50c	0.395	0.878	0.897	0.445	−0.034	0.021	0.040	−0.055
50d	0.556	0.848	0.831	0.662	0.127	−0.009	−0.026	0.162
30a	0.241	0.887	0.838	0.280	−0.188	0.030	−0.019	−0.220
30b	0.525	0.900	0.864	0.595	0.096	0.043	0.007	0.096
30c	0.555	0.866	0.815	0.661	0.126	0.009	0.042	0.161
30d	0.613	0.903	0.901	0.680	0.184	0.046	0.044	0.180

Correction for Attenuation

The correlation between scales with imperfect reliability is less than what that correlation would have been if the scales were perfectly reliable. Alternatively stated, the correlation between the concepts "Social isolation" and "Powerlessness" is stronger than the correlation between the social isolation scale and the powerlessness scale. This difference, called attenuation, is caused by the less-than-perfect reliability of the scales as measures of their respective concepts. We can use the following formula to correct for attenuation:

$$\rho_{t1t2} = \frac{r_{12}}{\sqrt{(\alpha_1 \alpha_2)}} \qquad (3)$$

where

ρ_{t1t2} is rho, the "true" correlation between concept 1 and concept 2, the correlation that has been corrected for attenuation due to unreliability;
r_{12} is the observed correlation between scale 1 and scale 2;
α_1 is the Cronbach's alpha for scale 1;
α_2 is the Cronbach's alpha for scale 2.

Correcting the observed correlation for attenuation using Eq. (3), we get:

$$\rho_{t1t2} = \frac{r_{12}}{\sqrt{(\alpha_1 \alpha_2)}} = 0.430/\sqrt{(0.862)(0.862)}$$

$$= 0.430/0.862 = 0.499$$

From this analysis, the best estimate of the theoretical correlation between "Social isolation" and "Powerlessness" is 0.499.

An Assessment

Thus, the criteria for adequate, but not perfect, measurement have been achieved:

- Multiple measures. Each concept is represented by multiple items.
- Measure clarity. The items measuring each concept are clear.
- Convergent and discriminant validity of dimensions. There is a strong positive intercorrelation among measures designed to assess each dimension of the concept. Moreover, these intermeasure correlations are stronger than the correlations of these measures with measures designed to assess the other dimension.
- Scaling. Scales have been constructed.
- Equivalence reliability. Cronbach's alphas for each scale are an adequate 0.862.
- Correction for attenuation. Unreliability has been removed from the observed correlation between "Social isolation" and "Powerlessness," providing us with an estimate of the theoretical correlation of 0.499.

Earlier, I said that the data were created "... using transformations of random numbers. The universe that underlies this data set has known parameters." Now I will reveal what those universe parameters were:

$$\alpha_{\text{social isolation}} = \alpha_{\text{powerlessness}} = 0.857$$

$$\rho_{t1t2} = 0.500$$

Wow! The analysis did an incredibly good job of estimating what occurred in the universe! The reliabilities as estimated from the data analysis (0.862) are very close to the universe reliabilities from which the data were generated (0.857). Moreover, the correlation between the concepts as estimated from the data analysis (0.499) was very close to the universe correlation between the concepts (0.500).

Using the presented statistical tools and having a weak theory and weak data, we have emerged with excellent estimates of crucial universe parameters. If the map is isomorphic with the terrain, use the map. These statistical tools are maps. We use them because there is a high degree of isomorphism between the tools and the universe from which the data were generated.

Measurement in the Real Research World

Interpretative clarity rarely is achieved as easily as in our example. Given a research setting in the real world, how should an analyst proceed? I now turn to a brief discussion of the application of these tools in the real research world.

Secrest and Zeller in a 2002 study wanted to develop a brief screening instrument that would reliably and validly measure the dimensions of adjustment by stroke patients following their suffering of a stroke. They created 45 items from the literature, their knowledge of poststroke patients, and their imaginations. They collected data on these 45 items from 55 poststroke patients. They conducted their analysis using the protocols presented in this entry. Specifically, in order to establish the number of factors and to identify which items defined which factors, they used (1) the 1.0 eigenvalue cut-off, (2) the scree test, (3) the minimum communality cut-off, and (4) the pattern of factor loadings criterion. The 1.0 eigenvalue cut-off and the scree test have already been described.

- The minimum communality cut-off. The analyst can also decide to exclude measures that are not useful in the interpretation. Specifically, analysts can make decisions about the inclusion or exclusion of measures based on communalities. Once measures with inadequate communalities have been eliminated from consideration, additional factor analyses are conducted to evaluate the clarity of the results. Communalities of 0.25, 0.275, and 0.30 are common minimum communalities used to eliminate measures in an analysis. Any such minimum communality is arbitrary, but an arbitrary minimum communality for the exclusion of weak measures is better than the default 0 minimum, which includes measures so weak as to be worthless. Secrest and Zeller used a 0.275 communality cut-off to eliminate some of the items.
- The pattern of factor loadings criterion. In general, a well-defined measure has a strong factor loading on its primary factor and relatively weak factor loadings on all other factors. The varimax rotation maximizes this pattern. However, some measures in Secrest and Zeller's study, despite varimax rotation, had strong factor loadings (i.e., >0.5) on more than one factor and/or have roughly equal moderately strong factor loadings (i.e., <0.5 and >0.3) on more than one factor. These difficult-to-interpret patterns of factor loadings reduced the clarity of the definition of the factors. Consequently, for continued inclusion in subsequent principal components analyses, the measures in this rotated component matrix had to have a factor loading on their primary factor of ≥ 0.5 and a difference of ≥ 0.2 between the factor loading on their primary and their secondary factor.

Using a 0.275 communality cut-off and their pattern of factor loadings protocols, Secrest and Zeller reduced the number of items from 45 to 20. These 20 items factored into two clear, theoretically meaningful factors, with 10 items defining each factor. Scales created from these factors had Cronbach's alphas equaling 0.874 and 0.869. They started with vague theory and items of unknown characteristics; they ended with a reliable and valid brief screening instrument measuring the two important dimensions of adjustment by stroke patients following their suffering a stroke. They did this with only 55 observations.

Sample Size: How Many Observations Are Needed?

Did Secrest and Zeller have enough observations (e.g. $N = 55$) to conduct these analyses? Tabachnick and Fidel (in a 1996 study) and Kerlinger (in a 1986 study) answered this question with a resounding "No!" In exploratory factor analytic designs, Tabachnick and Fidel recommended more than 100 respondents and, if possible, 300 subjects per item, and Kerlinger recommended "10 subjects per item."

In my experience, a researcher should have an adequate but not excessive number of respondents to evaluate the factor structure. At some point, additional respondents do not improve the evaluation of the measure and waste precious research resources. Somewhere between too few and too many responses is an optimum sample size. Sample-size deficiency indicates that the number of respondents is less than optimum; sample-size overkill indicates that the number of respondents exceeds the optimum. A body of literature has emerged making this argument. For example, in 1999, MacCallum *et al.* argued:

> *Our theoretical framework and results show clearly that common rules of thumb regarding sample size in factor analysis are not valid or useful.... Good recovery of population factors can be achieved with samples that would traditionally be considered too small for factor analytic studies, even when N is well below 100.... [I]t is better to have more indicators than fewer....*

Just as content validity may be harmed in introducing additional items that are not representative of the domain of interest, so recovery of population factors will be harmed by the addition of new indicators with low communalities.

Sapnas and Zeller, in 2002, argued that for exploratory factor analysis a sample size of 25 observations are inadequate but that 50 or more are adequate. In this tradition, we argue that attention to the optimization of the number of respondents will improve social measurement.

Summary

Measurement is the *sine qua non* of science. Without good measurement, all other scientific activities are futile. Factor analysis is a powerful statistical tool. It serves the goal of the measurement of social constructs best when it is allowed to flow through numerous options and iterations. It operates best on the assumption that the researcher has some insight, but not a strong theory, concerning the topic under investigation. It operates best when used as the statistical midwife assisting the substantive researcher-mother to give birth to the advancement of knowledge. The potential for statistical imagination in the use of exploratory factor analysis in service to the reduction of measurement error provides substantial value-added of substantively driven research efforts.

See Also the Following Articles

Correlations • Equivalence • Factor Analysis • Reliability Assessment • Sample Size • Validity Assessment

Further Reading

Alwin, D. F. (2000). Factor analysis. In *Encyclopedia of Sociology* (E. F. Borgatta and R. J. Montgomery, eds.), 2nd Ed., pp. 905–922. Macmillan, New York.

Asher, H. B. (1976). *Causal Modeling.* Sage, Beverly Hills, CA.

Blalock, H. M. (1969). Multiple indicators and the causal approach to measurement error. *Am. J. Sociol.* **75,** 264–272.

Bohrnstedt, G. W. (1970). Reliability and validity assessment in attitude measurement. In *Attitude Measurement* (G. F. Summers, ed.), pp. XX. Rand McNally, Chicago, IL.

Carmines, E. G., and Zeller, R. A. (1979). *Reliability and Validity Assessment.* Sage, Beverly Hills, CA.

DeVellis, R. (1991). *Scale Development: Theory and Application.* Sage, Newbury Park, CA.

Froman, R. D. (2001). Elements to consider in planning the use of factor analysis. *South. Online J. Nursing Res.* **2**(5).

Gable, R. K., and Wolf, M. B. (1993). *Instrument Development in the Affective Domain,* 2nd Ed. Kluwer, Boston.

Hayduk, L. A. (1987). *Structural Equation Modeling with LISREL.* Johns Hopkins University Press, Baltimore, MD.

Kerlinger, F. (1986). Factor analysis. In *Foundations in Behavioral Research* (F. Kerlinger, ed.), 3rd Ed., pp. 569–593. Holt, Rinehart, and Winston, Fort Worth, TX.

MacCallum, R. C., Widaman, K. F., Zhang, S., and Hong, S. (1999). Sample size in factor analysis. *Psychol. Methods* **4**(1), 84–99.

Neal, A. G., and Rettig, S. (1967). On the multidimensionality of alienation. *Am. Sociol. Rev.* **32,** 54–64.

Nisbet, R. A. (1966). *The Sociological Tradition.* Basic Books, New York.

Sapnas, K. G., and Zeller, R. A. (2002). Minimizing sample size in factor analysis when using items to measure dimensions of constructs. *J. Nursing Meas.* **10,** 135–153.

Secrest, J., and Zeller, R. (2002). A quality of life instrument for stroke survivors. Paper presented at Advanced Nursing Practice Excellence: State of the Science, National Conference of Sigma Theta Tau, Washington, DC.

Seeman, M. (1959). On the meaning of alienation. *Am. Sociol. Rev.* **24,** 772–782.

Tabachnick, B. G., and Fidell, L. S. (2001). *Using Multivariate Statistics,* 4th Ed. Harper Collins, New York.

Zeller, R. A., and Carmines, E. G. (1980). *Measurement in the Social Sciences: The Link between Theory and Data.* Cambridge University Press, New York.

Zeller, R. A., Neal, A. G., and Groat, H. T. (1980). On the reliability and stability of alienation measures: A longitudinal analysis. *Soc. Forces.* **58**(4), 1195–1204.

Measurement Theory

Joel Michell
University of Sydney, Sydney, Australia

Glossary

conjoint measurement The process of simultaneously acquiring evidence that three attributes are quantitative via observing how an increase or decrease on one attribute is affected by trade-offs between magnitudes of the other two.

derived measurement The process of acquiring evidence that an attribute is quantitative via the discovery of system-dependent constants in the relationship between two or more fundamentally measured attributes.

extensive attribute A quantitative attribute, the additive structure of which is directly observable to humans across some range of its magnitudes.

fundamental measurement The process of acquiring evidence that an attribute is quantitative by observing its additive structure directly across some range of its magnitudes employing an operation for concatenating objects.

intensive attribute A quantitative attribute, the additive structure of which is not directly observable to humans across any of its range.

magnitude A specific level of a quantitative attribute, for example, a specific length, such as the length of this page.

measurement The practice of attempting to identify the magnitude of a quantitative attribute by estimating the ratio between that magnitude and an appropriate unit.

quantitative attribute An attribute, the levels of which stand in additive relations to one another.

ratio A relationship between two magnitudes of a quantitative attribute whereby one of them is r times the other, where r is a positive real number.

From the time of Ancient Greece to the present, measurement has been recognized as a scientific method. Since the 17th century, its position has been central. From the 19th century it has been applied to psychological attributes, and from the 20th century, most famously, to cognitive abilities, personality traits, and social attitudes. These applications proved controversial and the ensuing controversies stimulated a revival of interest in measurement theory. Scientists and philosophers had reflected upon measurement prior to this period. Indeed, the earliest work on measurement theory was Book V of Euclid's *Elements*, which has been decisive in guiding subsequent thinking. It was only more recently, however, that measurement theory became a topic treated in its own right, and over the past century, measurement theorists, building upon the contributions of the past, have attempted to advance our understanding of what measurement is and what conditions are necessary for its occurrence.

Central Issues of Measurement Theory

One of the distinguishing features of measurement, as a method of observation, is that it involves numerical terms. For example, a length is observed to be 2.5 meters, a weight, 5.37 grams, and so on. Of course, the involvement of numerical terms is not unique to measurement. Other observational procedures, such as counting, involve them as well. However, measurement is distinguished from counting by the fact that the latter deals with natural, integral, and rational numbers (in the consideration of frequencies, differences between frequencies, and relative frequencies), while measurement also involves real numbers (in the consideration of incommensurable magnitudes). The real numbers include the irrational numbers (such as $\sqrt{2}$, π, and e) and these are neither counted nor arrived at by taking differences or ratios between counts. Irrational numbers seem beyond observation and, yet, they figure within the terms of an observational method, viz., measurement.

As will be shown, this perplexity was resolved early in the history of measurement theory and it focuses attention upon what, for psychologists, is an easily overlooked feature of measurement. If the width of a room measures 2.5 meters, the numerical term, 2.5, is, in fact, a *ratio*. What I mean by this is not the fact that $2.5=25/10$ (because the measure of a quantity does not equal a ratio of natural numbers in every case), but rather that 2.5 is the ratio between two non-numerical terms; that is, in this case, two lengths, viz., the room's width and the meter. As the concept of measurement has been traditionally understood, such ratios are the key to understanding measurement.

Traditionally, measurement is the practice of attempting to identify the magnitude of a quantitative attribute by estimating the ratio between that magnitude and an appropriate unit. Among other things, measurement theory attempts to answer the following questions. (1) What are ratios? (2) What is a quantitative attribute? (3) What is the relationship between ratios and numbers? (4) What kinds of evidence support the conclusion that an attribute is quantitative? This discussion gives some indication of ways in which these questions have been approached.

Ratios

Measure was narrowly defined in antiquity. The measure of something was the number of units it equalled, where *number* meant whole number (or *natural number*, as it is now called). Thus, the measure of a crowd in a stadium might be 1000 persons. Such a concept of measure works well for discrete quantities but not for continuous quantities. The length of the stadium might not equal some whole number of units. For example, it might be $100 \times \sqrt{2}$ meters. In Book V of his *Elements*, Euclid offered a generalization of the concept of measure capable of dealing with continuous quantities.

Like measures, Euclid's ratios are relations between specific levels of a quantitative attribute (call any such level x) and an appropriate unit (call it y). However, while ratios are not natural numbers, Euclid realized that they could be specified by reference to natural numbers. Consider the sequence of natural numbers: 1, 2, 3, ... and so on. Let m and n be any two such numbers. Then for specific x and y, one and only one of the following three propositions will be true:

(i) $mx > ny$
(ii) $mx = ny$
(iii) $mx < ny$.

If (i) is true, then $x/y > m/n$; if (ii) is true, then $x/y = m/n$; and if (iii) is true, then $x/y < m/n$. This means that any ratio of natural numbers (m/n) is exceeded by, equals, or exceeds the ratio of x to y. Letting m and n each range across the set of all natural numbers, it follows that for any specific x and y, the following three exhaustive and disjoint sets of numerical ratios (i.e., ratios of natural numbers) are defined:

1. $R_{(x/y)}$ = the set of all numerical ratios less than x/y (i.e., $\{m/n \mid m/n < x/y\}$);
2. $S_{(x/y)}$ = the set of all numerical ratios equal to x/y (i.e., $\{m/n \mid m/n = x/y\}$); and
3. $T_{(x/y)}$ = the set of all numerical ratios exceeding x/y (i.e., $\{m/n \mid m/n > x/y\}$).

(Of course, (2) may be empty, in which case x is said to be *incommensurable with* y). Euclid implicitly defined the ratio between any x and y by declaring that for any levels of a quantitative attribute, w, x, y, and z,

$$x/y = w/z \text{ if and only if } R_{(x/y)} = R_{(w/z)}, \; S_{(x/y)} = S_{(w/z)} \text{ and } T_{(x/y)} = T_{(w/z)}.$$

This concept of ratio clarifies important issues in measurement theory. First, it specifies precisely what is estimated in measurement: for any x and y, measurement is the attempt to estimate the boundary or "cut" (as Dedekind was to call it later) between $R_{(x/y)}$ and $T_{(x/y)}$. Second, it implies that absolute precision in measurement is generally impossible: for any x and y, the best estimate of x/y will be an interval estimate. Third, the concept makes explicit how numbers get into measurement: both what is estimated and the estimation of it are numerical.

Quantitative Attributes

A measure is always the measure of a quantitative attribute. An attribute is always an attribute of something (i.e., of an object or a system). Furthermore, an attribute is always either a *property* of a thing (such as, for example, the density of a sample of gas) or a relation between things (such as the distance between two objects). Some attributes (for example, length) are quantitative and others (for example, the attribute of biological species) are not. Finding out which an attribute is, requires knowing the character of quantitative attributes.

Given the centrality of the concept of ratio to measurement theory, the concept of a quantitative attribute was defined in a way that ensured any two magnitudes of the same attribute stand in a ratio. Taking the natural numbers as a guide reveals how this can be done: any two natural numbers stand in a ratio because of the additive relation holding between them. For example, the ratios of 40/5 and 80/10 are the same because 40 is eight 5s added together just as 80 is eight 10s. That is, ratios derive from additive structure, so characterizing the structure of quantitative attributes means characterizing additive structure. Measurable attributes (like length) are traditionally thought to differ from natural numbers in being continuous and in possessing no smallest magnitude and, so, characterizations of their structure typically accommodate these features as well.

At the beginning of the 20th century, Hölder characterized quantitative structure, and the following specification for length is based on, but is not identical to, his exposition. In the following characterization, the symbols, a, b, and c refer to specific lengths, that is, specific magnitudes of length independently of any measurements being made. Physical objects have length (i.e., spatial extension) measured or not, and the following conditions characterize all lengths, measured or not. The expression, $a+b=c$, does not refer to any human operations. Most lengths are either too big or two small for human operations and, more importantly, if for any lengths a, b, and c, $a+b=c$, then that is true regardless of human operations. The expression, $a+b=c$, denotes a relation: viz., that length c is entirely composed of discrete parts, a and b. The first four conditions state what it means for lengths to be additive. The remaining three ensure that no lengths are excluded (i.e., there is no greatest nor least length, nor gaps in the length series).

1. For every pair, a and b, one and only one of the following is true:
   (i) $a=b$;
   (ii) there exists a c, such that $a=b+c$;
   (iii) there exists a c, such that $b=a+c$.
2. For any a and b, $a+b>a$.
3. For any a and b, $a+b=b+a$.
4. For any a, b, and c, $a+(b+c)=(a+b)+c$.
5. For any a, there is a b, such that $b<a$.
6. For any a and b there is a c such that $c=a+b$.
7. For every nonempty class of lengths having an upper bound, there is a least upper bound.

Condition 7 may seem obscure. An upper bound of a class is anything not exceeded by any member of the class. A least upper bound is any upper bound not exceeding any other upper bound. The requirement that any class of lengths having an upper bound has a least upper bound ensures that there are no gaps in the sequence of lengths, as follows. Consider, for example, these two classes of lengths: any length, x, is a member of class A if and only if the square of x's measure in meters is less than 2; and any length, y, is a member of B if and only if the square of y's measure in meters exceeds 2. There is no greatest length in class A and, so, A does not contain any length that qualifies as its upper bound. However, any length belonging to class B will be an upper bound of A because no length in A exceeds any length in B. But there is no least member of class B. Thus, if A and B exhausted the class of all lengths, class A would have an upper bound but possess no least upper bound and condition 7 would fail. For condition 7 to be true, there must be a length falling between these two classes (i.e., greater than every length in A and less than every length in B) and that must be the length, z, such that the square of z's measure in meters is 2 (i.e., $z=\sqrt{2}$ meters). Condition 7 ensures that the gap between classes A and B is plugged and, similarly, all such gaps.

Condition 7 is not necessary for an attribute to be measurable. The minimum condition necessary for measurement, in the context of conditions 1–6 above, is the Archimedean condition, 8, below (first described by Euclid and Archimedes in ancient mathematics):

8. For every pair of magnitudes of length, a and b, there exists a natural number, n, such that $na\geq b$ (where $1a=a$ and $na=(n-1)a+a$).

Given the above characterization of length as an unbounded, continuous quantitative attribute, it follows that the class of ratios of lengths is isomorphic to the class of positive real numbers. That is, for every pair of lengths, x and y, there is a positive real number, r, such that $x/y=r$; and given any positive real number, r, there is a pair of lengths, w and z, such that $w/z=r$. Part of what this means is that every length is measurable relative to any other length taken as the unit of measurement. That is, the above characterization guarantees the measurability of lengths.

Length is the quantitative attribute that we are most familiar with and it provides the model for understanding all other quantities. All other quantitative attributes measured in physics are likewise taken to be continuous, quantitative attributes and, so, are taken to satisfy an analogous set of conditions.

Numbers and Representations

For most of the 20th century, the majority view among measurement theorists was some version or other of the representational theory of measurement. According to this view, measurement involves a mapping between the magnitudes of an attribute and numbers in such a way that relations between the numbers represent relations between the magnitudes. Furthermore, according to the representational view, the existence of this mapping is thought to be the key feature upon which measurement depends.

According to the results outlined above, such an isomorphism exists. If there is an isomorphism between ratios of magnitudes of a quantitative attribute and the positive real numbers, then relative to each unit, there is a mapping between magnitudes of the attribute and the real numbers. Furthermore, according to this mapping, not only are all magnitudes of the attribute represented numerically, additive relations between different magnitudes are represented as well.

Two philosophical considerations motivated the representational theory. The first was the view that numbers are abstract entities, rather than constituents of the empirical world. Especially important historically was the fact that the representational view is compatible with logical positivism, a philosophy that dominated the philosophy of science last century. One of the doctrines that the logical positivists were most famous for was that logic (including mathematics) consists only of conventional stipulations about the use of signs and, as a consequence, does not say anything about the world. If this is true, then the overwhelming effectiveness of mathematics in natural science seems, at first sight, quite unreasonable. The representational theory of measurement was used as a way of explaining this apparent unreasonableness away. According to this theory, mathematics is effective, not because it says anything about the world itself, but because it mirrors the form of real-world structures.

The second philosophical consideration motivating the representational view was the desire to understand measurement as far as possible in terms of directly observable operations upon objects. Most early representational measurement theorists, such as N. R. Campbell, Ernest Nagel, and S. S. Stevens, attempted to reformulate the conditions characterizing a quantitative attribute in terms of directly observable conditions applying to empirically identifiable objects. This program encountered considerable difficulty with conditions such as the continuity condition (see condition 7 above). As a result, this condition was abandoned; later, representational theorists replaced it with Archimedean conditions of one form or another, as in the first volume of *Foundations of Measurement.*

Hölder, in his epoch-making 1901 paper, had proved not only that a continuous quantitative attribute must satisfy the Archimedean condition but also that if the Archimedean condition is substituted for the continuity condition, then the resulting structure is isomorphic to a substructure of the positive real numbers. In the literature on the representational theory of measurement, this result is referred to as *Hölder's Theorem* and it was pivotal to the development of representational theory given by Luce, Suppes, Krantz, and Tversky in their *Foundations of Measurement.* However, Archimedean conditions are no more reducible to observational terms than is the continuity condition. Recent versions of the representational theory, such as Volume 3 of *Foundations of Measurement*, have used the continuity condition.

The representational view actually broadens the concept of measurement somewhat because the class of quantitative structures (as characterized by conditions 1–7 above) is a proper subset of the class of empirical structures possessing mappings into the real numbers. In particular, structures that involve no more than equivalence relations; no more than weak order relations; and no more than equivalence or order upon differences; may have mappings into subsystems of the real numbers, yielding what Stevens called *nominal*, *ordinal*, and *interval scales of measurement* in addition to so-called ratio scales (produced by conditions 1–7).

The mappings sustaining these different kinds of scales of measurement have different invariance properties and the validity or meaningfulness of numerical conclusions inferred from measurements are relative to these invariance properties. This fact was first recognized by Stevens and has subsequently been most thoroughly investigated by Louis Narens as part of the theory of meaningfulness.

The alternative to the representational view is the realist theory of measurement. It is based upon the thesis that the real numbers are ratios of magnitudes of continuous quantitative attributes, a view defended early in the 20th century by Frege in *Grundgesetze der Arithmetik* and by Whitehead in the third volume of his and Russell's *Principia Mathematica*, and then, again, toward the end of that century, by a number of realist philosophers, such as David Armstrong. The logic of this view is that if real-world structures (such as quantitative attributes) are isomorphic to mathematical structures, then the world already contains mathematical structure. This is because two systems are isomorphic only if they share the same structure. According to this view, the numbers are not abstract entities but are relations (i.e., ratios) between real things, and mathematics is the study of real (and imagined) structures considered abstractly.

Evidence for Quantity

If there is no logical necessity that attributes studied in any science be quantitative, then the issue of the structure of attributes is always an empirical one. Hence, a part of measurement theory is the investigation of the general forms that evidence for quantitative structure may take.

Historically, the quantitative attributes recognized first were time, weight, and the geometric attributes of length, area, volume, and plane angle. In each case, with such attributes, its additive structure is directly evident to human observers under certain fairly simple conditions. For example, the additive structure of lengths can be seen in extending lengths by concatenating rigid, straight rods. That is, the structure of the attribute (length) is directly reflected in the structure of objects (rods) possessing the attribute. Such attributes are called *extensive*. Ancient philosophers sometimes wrote of other attributes as quantitative (such as temperature, density, and even psychological attributes like pleasure and pain) and, indeed, the Pythagoreans and Platonists thought that the fundamental structure of reality must be quantitative. However, ancient philosophers do not appear to have distinguished the structure of attributes from the structure of the objects manifesting those attributes.

This distinction was explicitly drawn during the Medieval period when a number of philosophers began to analyze intensive quantities. In their work, the hypothesized additive structure of intensive attributes, such as temperature, was modeled upon the structure of extensive attributes, but, at the same time, this modeling went along with the recognition that the additive structure of such attributes was not reflected in the concatenation of relevant objects. Thus, Duns Scotus noted that when volumes of liquid at different temperatures are combined, the volumes add together while the temperatures do not. Nonetheless, he thought that increase or decrease in temperature involved the addition or subtraction of homogeneous parts. However, these were not parts of the objects involved (the liquids), they were parts of temperature. Thinking in these terms involves making a distinction between the structure of the object and the structure of the attribute.

This distinction having been made, the scientists of the 17th century, such as Galileo and Newton, were able to contemplate hitherto unmeasured, intensive attributes, to explore indirect ways of measuring them, and to propose theories relating intensive attributes to extensive attributes. Despite the flowering of quantitative physics, it was not until late in the 19th century that the issue of evidence for quantitative structure was first raised by Helmholtz.

The first to treat this issue in a systematic fashion was the British measurement theorist, N. R. Campbell. Campbell distinguished two forms of evidence: fundamental measurement and derived measurement. Fundamental measurement occurs in the case of extensive attributes, where an operation of concatenation applied to relevant objects directly reflects the additive structure of the attribute. Derived measurement, according to Campbell, depends upon the existence of a system-dependent constant, which occurs as a function of fundamentally measurable attributes. For example, density is a function of mass and volume, the latter two attributes being fundamentally measurable (mass via weight and volume via length) and density is a different constant for each system (or kind of substance). Campbell did not bring out the logic of derived measurement, but it seems sound. If for each different kind of stuff it is observed that the ratio of mass to volume is a constant (for example, one constant for gold, another for silver), then it is sound scientific reasoning to argue that each different kind of stuff possesses a property (its density) that the observed constant reflects. Because the effect (the constant) is quantitative, it is scientifically sound to argue that its cause (the stuff's density) must likewise be quantitative.

The soundness of this reasoning was later confirmed by the development of the theory of conjoint measurement. While the general idea behind conjoint measurement had been variously anticipated, by Hölder among others, it was the series of papers beginning with Luce and Tukey in 1964 and culminating in the three volumes of the *Foundations of Measurement* that thoroughly developed the theory. This work emerged under the auspices of the representational theory of measurement and it was motivated by a desire to identify more or less directly observable, psychological structures that could be given the sort of numerical representation characteristic of measurement (i.e., what Stevens had earlier called interval or ratio scale representations).

The idea behind conjoint measurement is somewhat counterintuitive. Suppose that in some system, under certain conditions, two independent, quantitative attributes combine to produce a third, dependent attribute. Furthermore, suppose that this third attribute is not extensive and that all we are able to observe with respect to it are increases or decreases in order. The theory shows that providing we can identify distinct levels of the two independent attributes (measuring them is not required) and providing the combination of these two attributes to produce the third involves no interactions, then the additive structure of all three attributes is displayed in various order relations between levels of the third attribute. The counterintuitive feature of the theory is that purely ordinal relations are diagnostic of additive structure. This feature means that the theory is potentially useful in sciences like psychology where it is widely believed that attributes are quantitative and, yet, we seem to be restricted to observations of order, not quantity.

For example, it is widely believed by psychometricians that quantitative features of both the task and the person determine a person's performance on an intellectual task. Despite a preference for such quantitative hypotheses, all that can be observed is that one person does better on a task than another. It is in contexts such as this that the theory of conjoint measurement can be applied. If the probability of solving the task correctly is thought to be a noninteractive function of the person's ability and the task's difficulty (increasing with the first and decreasing with the second), then ordinal relations between the probabilities (as estimated via relative frequencies) can be used to assess the evidence for the quantitative hypothesis as opposed to nonquantitative alternatives. A large class of so-called item response models in psychometrics are of this general form.

Item response models are just one class of probabilistic measurement models. During the 20th century, under the influence of positivist philosophy of science, the view became accepted in psychology that scientific theories, including theories of measurement, should account for all relevant observational data. Since data are always fallible and in psychology always include the effects of uncontrolled and, often, unknown factors, characterizations of quantitative structure, such as conditions 1–7 above, do not provide an adequate guide to the form that relevant observational data may take. The preferred alternative is to use probabilistic measurement models, which it is hoped capture the form data takes when evidence for underlying quantitative structures is obscured by the effects of extraneous factors. In recent years, simpler probabilistic models, such as the kind of item response models mentioned above, have been supplemented by more complex models, as represented by, e.g., Regenwetter and Marley.

It should be stressed that fundamental, derived, and conjoint measurement are not the only forms of evidence pertinent to the hypothesis that attributes are quantitative. Other forms are discussed in the three volumes of the *Foundations of Measurement* and, no doubt, others are yet to be recognized. This remains an open-ended area of measurement theory. However, the existence of this area makes it clear that it may well be equally fruitful in psychology and social science to develop nonquantitative theories and methods. Measurement theory undermines Pythagorean pretensions regarding the place of measurement in science. To strive for measurement is appropriate where attributes are quantitative, and inappropriate where they are not; we have no way of knowing which they are other than by considering the evidence.

See Also the Following Articles

Item Response Theory • Literacy, Mathematical • Mathematical and Statistical Approaches

Further Reading

Armstrong, D. M. (1997). *A World of States of Affairs*. Cambridge University Press, Cambridge, UK.

Campbell, N. R. (1920). *Physics, The Elements*. Cambridge University Press, Cambridge, UK.

Frege, G. (1903). *Grundgesetze der Arithmetik*, Vol. 2. Georg Olms, Hildesheim.

Goldstein, H., and Wood, R. (1989). Five decades of item response modelling. *Br. J. Math. Stat. Psych.* **42,** 139–167.

Heath, T. L. (1908). *The Thirteen Books of Euclid's Elements*, Vol. 2. Cambridge University Press, Cambridge, UK.

Helmholtz, H. von (1996). Numbering and measuring from an epistemological viewpoint. In *From Kant to Hilbert: A Sourcebook in the Foundations of Mathematics* (W. Ewald, ed.), Vol. 2, pp. 727–752. Clarendon Press, Oxford.

Hölder, (1901). Die Axiome der Quantität und die Lehre vom Mass. Berichte über die Verhandlungen der Königlich Sächsischen Gesellschaft der Wissenschaften zu Leipzig. *Math. Phys. Klasse* **53,** 1–46. [English translation in Michell, J., and Ernst, C. (1996). The axioms of quantity and the theory of measurement, Part I. *J. Math. Psychol.* **40,** 235–252; Michell, J., and Ernst, C. (1977). The axioms of quantity and the theory of measurement, Part II. *J. Math. Psychol.* **41,** 345–356.]

Krantz, D. H., Luce, R. D., Suppes, P., and Tversky, A. (1971). *Foundations of Measurement*, Vol. 1. Academic Press, New York.

Luce, R. D., and Tukey, A. (1964). Simultaneous conjoint measurement: A new type of fundamental measurement. *J. Math. Psychol.* **1,** 1–27.

Luce, R. D., Krantz, D. H., Suppes, P., and Tversky, A. (1990). *Foundations of Measurement*, Vol. 3. Academic Press, San Diego.

Michell, J. (1999). *Measurement in Psychology: A Critical History of a Methodological Concept.* Cambridge University Press, Cambridge, UK.

Nagel, E. (1931). Measurement. *Erkenntnis* **2,** 313–333.

Narens, L. (2002). *Theories of Meaningfulness.* Erlbaum, Hillsdale, NJ.

Regenwetter, M., and Marley, A. A. J. (2001). Random relations, random utilities, and random functions. *J. Math. Psychol.* **45,** 864–912.

Stevens, S. S. (1951). Mathematics, measurement and psychophysics. In *Handbook of Experimental Psychology* (S. S. Stevens, ed.), pp. 1–49. Wiley, New York.

Suppes, P., Krantz, D. H., Luce, R. D., and Tversky, A. (1989). *Foundations of Measurement*, Vol. 2. Academic Press, San Diego.

Whitehead, A. N., and Russell, B. (1913). *Principia Mathematica*, Vol. 3. Cambridge University Press, Cambridge, UK.

Meta-Analysis

Jamie DeCoster
Free University Amsterdam, Amsterdam, The Netherlands

Glossary

effect A research finding examined in a meta-analysis.

effect size A statistical estimate of the strength of an effect.

heterogeneity The variability observed in a sample of effect sizes.

meta-analytic summary Using meta-analysis to answer a specific research question.

moderator A study characteristic that influences the effect size.

primary research Directly conducted research, in contrast to meta-analytic research, which uses the results of other studies.

quantitative literature review Using meta-analysis to review the behavior of an effect as it is reported in the research literature.

Meta-analysis, also known as quantitative synthesis, refers to a set of statistical procedures that combine the results of multiple studies in a single analysis. Traditionally, when reviewers wanted to make inferences about the results of a set of studies, they had to use vaguely defined, qualitative methods. To introduce the same scientific rigor to the review process that is typically required in primary research, meta-analysis przovides statistically valid rules for aggregating and discriminating the results found within a literature. Its procedures allow researchers to estimate the average strength of a finding observed across several studies, to determine whether the finding is consistent or varies from study to study, and to test whether variability in the finding relates to study characteristics.

Introduction

Since its introduction less than 30 years ago, meta-analysis has strongly influenced research in many areas of the social sciences. It has become the accepted standard for summarizing research in many fields because of its emphasis on objective observation and its openness to critical evaluation. Meta-analysis has also provided the means to investigate new types of research questions, such as how the strength of an effect relates to the setting in which it was investigated. Its growing popularity has even impacted those who perform only primary research, in that the guidelines for writing journal articles in many fields have changed to facilitate meta-analysis. It has therefore become important for all social scientists, even those who never actually plan to perform a meta-analysis, to have at least a basic understanding of these procedures. Knowing the ideas behind meta-analysis is necessary to be able to read and critically evaluate meta-analyses performed by others. It is also important to understand how to best present research so that it can easily be included by meta-analysts in their reviews. Without this knowledge, researchers risk isolation from important sources of information and opportunities for their own ideas to guide future theorizing.

By far the most common use of meta-analysis has been in quantitative literature reviews. These are review articles in which the authors select an effect that has been investigated in primary research under a large number of different circumstances. They then use meta-analysis to describe the overall strength of the effect, as well as the circumstances that affect its magnitude and direction. As knowledge of meta-analytic techniques has become widespread, it is more common to see researchers using simple meta-analytic summaries within primary research papers. In this case, meta-analysis is used to provide support for a specific theoretical statement, usually about the overall strength or consistency of a relationship within the studies being conducted. As might be expected, calculating a meta-analytic summary is typically a much simpler procedure than is performing a quantitative literature review.

Steps to Conduct a Meta-Analysis

There are five basic steps to a meta-analysis. First, the research question that will be addressed by the analysis is defined. Second, a population of primary research studies that can be examined to answer the question is located. Third, an effect size from each study is calculated and its characteristics are coded into "moderating variables." Fourth, the database of effect sizes is statistically analyzed. Finally, the results of the analyses are presented and interpreted. The following discussions provide a basic overview of how to conduct a meta-analysis, focusing on these five steps. Also considered are any differences between the procedures for quantitative literature reviews and those for meta-analytic summaries.

Define the Meta-Analytic Research Question

Forming a clear meta-analytic research question requires three decisions: choosing an effect to examine, defining the population in which to examine the effect, and deciding what information the analysis should provide about the behavior of the effect.

An effect can almost always be thought of as a relationship between a pair of variables, so defining the effect primarily involves choosing appropriate definitions for these variables. An effect size metric must also be chosen to be the basis for the analysis. This is a specific statistic that will be calculated from the results of each study, so that they may all be compared and aggregated. Effect size statistics must provide a measure of the strength of the relationship that is independent of the sample size. Note that the most commonly used statistics (such as t, F, and p-values) are dependent on sample size, and so cannot be used as effect sizes. Descriptions and formulas for a number of acceptable metrics can be found in the literature. Although the choice of effect size metric will not influence the validity or significance of any of the meta-analytic tests, a given effect size is easier to calculate from certain research designs than from others. The effect size metrics most commonly used in the social sciences are the standardized mean difference (g) and the correlation coefficient (r). The standardized mean difference is typically used when most of the studies in the analysis reported t or F statistics, whereas the correlation coefficient is typically used when most of the studies reported correlation or regression coefficients.

To define the population, a decision must be made about the characteristic studies must have to be included in the analysis. The more broadly defined the population of the analysis, the more generally applicable the conclusions drawn from the results. However, it is always important to make sure that the definition is restrictive enough so that the included studies all concern the same phenomenon. For meta-analytic summaries, it is appropriate to limit the consideration to the studies performed in a specific paper or set of papers. Although this limits drawing conclusions to a very small population, this is usually appropriate for the purpose of the analysis. Quantitative literature reviews, on the other hand, require broader definitions that encompass the different ways researchers have examined the effect of interest.

Meta-analysis can provide three levels of information about effect size, with each level requiring somewhat more work to obtain than the last. First, it can provide an estimate of the average strength of an effect. Second, it can reveal whether a set of effect sizes comes from a single distribution, or if there appear to be systematic differences. Third, it can test whether the values of the effect sizes are related to other measured study characteristics. When performing a quantitative literature review, it is generally desirable to examine all of these questions. For a meta-analytic summary, it is best to choose the lowest level of analysis that provides the required information.

Locate the Relevant Literature

Once the boundaries of the meta-analysis have been defined, the next step is to find every study within that area that provides an estimate of the effect of interest. Typically, it is known ahead of time exactly what studies will be included when performing a meta-analytic summary. This is not the case for a quantitative review, which usually requires a comprehensive literature search to locate the relevant articles. Most literature searches start with queries into one or more computerized indices. Indices are available for most topic areas, allowing specific word and phrase searches within the titles and abstracts of relevant articles. One important index that should be examined in almost any search is *Dissertation Abstracts*. This index contains a reference to every doctoral dissertation completed in North America, making it an excellent way to locate research that might not have made it into a published form.

Although computerized indices are fairly easy to use, some care must be taken when selecting search terms to obtain complete results. Theoretical constructs that define the area of analysis should be identified first. Next, to identify each of the constructs, lists should be created of the different words or phrases that have been used in the literatures being searched. If the index being used assigns key words to its entries, the lists must contain any of these words that are related to the relevant constructs. "Wildcards" should be used if they are supported by the index. These are special characters (such as "*" or "?") that can be added to the search terms to indicate that matching entries might have additional characters before or after the specified characters. This helps prevent missing studies that happen to use the desired term in a grammatical form different from what was specified. Once the lists are completed, query the index for studies that include at least one term related to each construct. The best way to do this is to first perform a conjunctive ("or") search for each construct, finding studies related to each list, then perform a disjunctive ("and") search on these results, to locate studies that are related to all of the constructs.

Although computerized indices can quickly provide a large list of studies related to a topic, a thorough literature search does not rely on these alone. After obtaining an initial set of studies, an "ancestor search" can be performed by checking the references within the studies to locate older articles that might be related to the topic. If there is a seminal study that was of theoretical or methodological importance to the field, a "descendent search" can be performed by using the *Social Science Citation Index* or the *Science Citation Index* to locate later articles that list the seminal study in their references. Sometimes external organizations will establish "research registers" for a field that has significant societal impact; these are actively maintained lists of ongoing research projects. If there are any existing reviews of a topic (whether meta-analytic or not), the articles that they have already identified as relevant should be examined. Consider also a hand-search of any journals that commonly publish research on the phenomenon of interest. Finally, contacting active researchers in the field can yield information about recent projects that are not indexed in the usual sources. One good way to locate active researches is through the use of Internet listservers and newsgroups.

Once these different methods have been used to perform a comprehensive search, their results must be combined into a master list lacking redundancies. A review of each study on this list will determine whether it actually fits the area of the meta-analysis. Sometimes it can be determined whether a study fits simply by reading the abstract; at other times the study's method and results will need to be closely examined. This process can be made easier by developing a set of specific criteria that studies must satisfy to be included in the analysis. When deciding to exclude a study from the analysis, the criterion on which this decision is based should be noted. It is not uncommon for researchers to change aspects of the research question as their knowledge of the topic becomes more complete through the course of performing the review. Should the decision be made to redefine the population (and consequently the inclusion criteria), knowing why each study was excluded limits the number of studies that need to be reexamined.

For a quantitative review to draw accurate conclusions, its literature search must be as complete as possible. Researchers wishing to limit the number of studies in their meta-analyses should do so by using more restrictive inclusion criteria instead of by performing a less comprehensive search. This will not be possible when the goal is to review a very general area. In this case, the researcher should first use a comprehensive search to locate the population of studies that examined the effect of interest. From this population, the desired number of studies to analyze can then be randomly sampled.

Calculate Effect Sizes and Code Moderating Variables

Once a set of relevant studies has been obtained, they are used to create a quantitative data set for analysis. The first thing to do is calculate an effect size from each study. Every effect size metric has a computational formula that will allow it to be calculated from raw data. However, meta-analysts will often not have access to this information, especially when conducting a quantitative review. Analysts calculating an effect size from someone else's research must typically rely on whatever statistics are provided in the report (although the authors may sometimes be directly contacted for additional information). It is almost always possible to calculate an estimate of the effect size from a study, although it may be very imprecise for statistically impoverished reports. If there is wide variability in the precision of their estimates, meta-analysts will sometimes perform separate analyses, including only the most precise estimates, to see if the inclusion of imprecise estimates affects the results.

To determine if a study characteristic influences an effect, it must first be coded as a moderating variable. Meta-analysts commonly consider moderators related to the study setting, sample, design, and methodology. For each moderating variable, it is best to write down an explicit coding scheme detailing how to translate study characteristics into values of the moderator. If a moderator has continuous scale, its unit of measurement must be specified. For categorical moderators, the meta-analyst must specify the different groups that compose the variable, as well as what study characteristics are associated with each group. It is typically a good idea to pilot the coding scheme to make sure that it is well understood by the coders, and that it provides reliable data.

The final meta-analytic data set should contain variables for the effect size, the sample size, and any moderators to be examined. For a meta-analysis to produce valid results, it is essential that these values are accurate, so it is standard practice to have at least two different people calculate and code each effect size. This provides an additional check on the accuracy of the calculations and allows the reliability of the moderator codes to be reported.

Analyze the Meta-Analytic Database

As with data from primary research, the basic distribution of effect sizes should always be examined before performing the analyses. It is especially important to determine if the distribution has multiple modes or outliers. A multimodal distribution can indicate that the studies are coming from several different subpopulations. In this case, an attempt should be made to identify a moderating variable that can explain the different groups of effects. If the modes are highly distinct, an analyst might consider analyzing each of the groups separately. Studies that produce outlying effect sizes should be examined closely to make sure that they truly fit within the boundaries of the analysis. Consider excluding any outlier that is particularly extreme, whether its characteristics fit the defined population or not, because it will have an inappropriately large influence on the results.

Descriptive analyses can be used to obtain information about the central tendency and consistency of the effect sizes. The most commonly used estimate of central tendency is the weighted mean effect size, whereby each effect size is weighted by the inverse of its variance. Some other measures that have been used are the mean effect size weighted by the sample size, the unweighted mean effect size, and the median effect size. Estimates of the mean effect size combined with its standard error are often used to calculate confidence intervals around the population effect size.

After estimating the central tendency, how well this single value describes the full pattern of effect sizes can be determined by computing its heterogeneity (Q). The heterogeneity statistic reveals the likelihood of observing the amount of variability present in the sample if the effect sizes were all drawn from a single distribution. A significant amount of heterogeneity indicates that the effect sizes are likely not all from the same distribution. In this case, it is often desirable to explain the variability through moderator analyses. Moderator analyses are used to determine if the effect sizes are related to study characteristics. Before testing any moderators, it is necessary to decide whether to treat the individual studies as fixed or random factors in the statistical models (although this question may be circumvented by using Bayesian analysis). This decision has implications for the formulas used to analyze the data, as well as for the inferences drawn from the results. Fixed-effects models are limited to drawing conclusions about the specific studies and conditions present in the analyses, whereas random-effects models allow drawing conclusions about a wider theoretical population of which the studies in the analysis are considered to be a random sample. Fixed models are used much more often than random models are, although this is more due to the fact that fixed-effects analyses are simpler and typically more powerful, rather than because they are more appropriate.

The method for testing of a moderator depends on how the moderator was coded. A categorical moderator can be examined by using heterogeneity statistics to estimate the between-group and within-group variability. The amount of between-group heterogeneity (Qb) can be used to test whether the moderator can account for a significant amount of the variability in the effect sizes, whereas the amount of within-group heterogeneity (Qw) can be used to test whether there is a significant amount of variability that cannot be accounted for by the moderator. It is possible for both of these statistics to be significant. This would indicate that the moderator has a significant influence on the effect size but that there are other important sources of variability.

A continuous moderator can be tested by using a weighted regression analysis to estimate the strength of the linear relationship between the moderator and the effect size. The weight for a given study is usually set to be the inverse of the effect size variance, although sometimes meta-analysts choose to use the sample size instead. Parameter estimates for the weighted regression can be obtained using any standard statistical program, although the standard errors of the estimates will need to be corrected for the unique characteristics of meta-analytic data.

It is also possible to build more complicated models to predict effect sizes. Models containing multiple predictors, including interaction and higher order polynomial models can be tested using a weighted multiple regression analysis. Categorical predictors may be included in these models, but they must be coded by a set of indicator variables. The parameters from a multiple predictor model can be estimated using a standard statistical program, but it is necessary to correct the standard errors of the estimates as when testing a continuous moderator. When interpreting the results of a multiple predictor model, keep in mind that the precision of the estimates will be reduced if there are correlations among the predictor variables. The significance of the parameters in the model will be determined by the independent ability of each moderator to account for variability in the effect sizes. Moderators that are significant when tested individually may be nonsignificant in the multiple predictor model if they are collinear with other included variables.

Report and Interpret the Results

There are many similarities between performing a meta-analysis and conducting a standard research study. In both cases, the process is to pose a research question, collect data, analyze the results, and draw conclusions about the findings. The presentation of a meta-analysis consequently parallels the presentation of primary research. A quantitative literature review is written using the standard sections found in empirical articles. In the introduction, the theoretical motivation for conducting the analysis is explained and the definitions of the effect and the populations are provided. The method section explains how the studies were selected for inclusion, how the effect sizes were calculated, and how any moderating variables were coded. The reliability of the moderator codes should also be explained in the method section. In the results section, the analyses are described and the findings are reported. Finally, the discussion section should present the theoretical implications of the results and suggest new directions for research.

It is necessary to provide this same information when reporting a meta-analytic summary, though in a compressed format. If the summary includes moderator analyses, these should be presented as a separate study in the paper, using the guidelines for quantitative reviews. If the primary interest is presenting descriptive analyses, however, it will likely be simple to incorporate it directly into the introduction or discussion. In this case, the purpose and method of the meta-analysis should be described in one paragraph, with the results and discussion in a second.

The presentation of the meta-analysis should provide enough detail so that another researcher could replicate the analyses. Even though there are standard guidelines for how to perform a meta-analysis, there are also a number of subjective decisions that are up to the discretion of the analyst. For example, the moderator analyses can be strongly influenced by the author's personal beliefs. Different researchers might have different opinions on what moderators should be examined and how they should be defined. It is therefore important to clearly describe and justify each subjective decision so that others can evaluate the choices.

Although performing a meta-analysis necessarily requires a large number of calculations, it is important not to allow statistics to dominate the presentation. Always embed the analyses in a theoretical framework that provides them with meaning. The report should describe how the theoretical perspectives in the field influenced the way the constructs were defined and how the analysis was conducted. Also be sure to describe any implications that the findings may have for existing models of the phenomenon of interest. Specific effort should go into helping the audience understand the meaning of any effect sizes reported. The easiest way to do this is to compare them to the strengths of other effects that would already be known by the intended audience. Alternatively, other tools to help readers understand the practical significance of your effect sizes can be found in texts on power analysis.

Critically Evaluating a Meta-Analysis

The main purpose of meta-analysis is to provide a scientifically rigorous method for summarizing research, but not every meta-analysis meets this goal. Just as there is variability in the quality of primary research, there can be great differences in the quality of meta-analyses. When judging a meta-analysis, consider whether it uses appropriate methods of data collection and analysis (its internal validity), properly represents the phenomenon of interest (its external validity), and makes a distinct theoretical contribution (its scientific importance).

The first thing to consider when evaluating the internal validity of a meta-analysis is the validity of the studies in its sample. A meta-analysis can be no more valid than the primary research that it aggregates. If there are methodological problems with the studies in the sample, then the validity of the meta-analysis must also be called into question. The meta-analysis should include enough studies so that it has sufficient power to test the proposed research question. If a meta-analysis examines moderating variables, then consider both the reliability of the moderator codes and how the studies are distributed across the levels of each moderator. Unreliable codes and unbalanced designs will reduce the power of moderator analyses. Finally, consider whether confounding variables could provide alternative explanations for any significant moderators.

Possibly the most important factor affecting the external validity of a meta-analysis is the extent that the sample represents the theoretical population of interest. To draw firm conclusions about a given population, the sample should be an unbiased representation of every study that has been conducted within that population. Meta-analytic summaries are typically applied to very specific populations, making external validity less of an issue. The search procedures used for quantitative literature reviews, however, should be closely examined to determine whether any relevant subpopulations were overlooked. For example, some quantitative reviews exclude unpublished or foreign studies because they are difficult to obtain. If there is reason to suspect that these studies might be different than the ones included in the analysis, then valid conclusions cannot be drawn about the literature as a whole. Finally, consider the way the author defined the target population. If it includes highly divergent studies, then the analysis may in fact be combining different phenomena. In this case, the results may have little meaning.

If it is determined that the conclusions drawn from a meta-analysis are valid, the next step is to evaluate the importance of its findings. Sometimes a meta-analysis will simply provide an estimate of an effect size within a set of studies. Although this may be valuable, it does not make as great a scientific contribution as an analysis that additionally uses moderator analyses to determine the conditions under which the effect is stronger, weaker, or even reversed. Finally, consider the extent to which the results of the analysis have theoretical implications. The more implications a meta-analysis has for existing theories, the more likely it will influence future research. The best meta-analyses provide statistically valid information about an internally consistent population, which is then used to provide novel insights about the phenomenon under study.

See Also the Following Articles

Computerized Record Linkage and Statistical Matching • Gambling Studies • Scales and Indexes, Types of

Further Reading

Cohen, J. (1977). *Statistical Power Analysis for the Behavioral Sciences.* 2nd Ed. Academic Press, New York.

DeCoster, J. (2002). *Notes on Meta-Analysis.* Retrieved from the Web June 12, 2002 at http://www.stat-help.com/notes.html

Glass, G. V. (1976). Primary, secondary, and meta-analysis of research. *Educat. Res.* **5,** 3–8.

Hedges, L. V. (1994). Fixed effects models. In *The Handbook of Research Synthesis* (H. Cooper and L. Hedges, eds.), pp. 285–300. Sage, New York.

Hedges, L. V., and Vevea, J. L. (1998). Fixed- and random-effects models in meta-analysis. *Psychol. Methods* **3,** 486–504.

Johnson, B. T., and Eagly, A. H. (2000). Quantitative synthesis in social psychological research. In *Handbook of Research Methods in Social Psychology* (H. T. Reis and C. M. Judd, eds.), pp. 496–528. Cambridge University Press, London.

Lipsey, M. W., and Wilson, D. B. (2000). *Practical Meta-Analysis.* Sage, Thousand Oaks, California.

Louis, T. A., and Zelterman, D. (1994). Bayesian approaches to research synthesis. In *The Handbook of Research Synthesis* (H. Cooper and L. V. Hedges, eds.), pp. 411–422. Sage, New York.

Rosenthal, R. (1991). *Meta-analytic Procedures for Social Research* (rev. ed.). Sage, Beverly Hills, California.

Shadish, W. R., and Haddock, C. K. (1994). Combining estimates of effect size. In *The Handbook of Research Synthesis* (H. Cooper and L. V. Hedges, eds.), pp. 261–281. Sage, New York.

Missing Data, Problems and Solutions

Andrew Pickles

University of Manchester, Manchester, UK

Glossary

censoring and coarsening Forms of imperfect observation of a variable whereby only boundaries can be placed on its value.

imputation Assigning a value to a missing value.

item nonresponse Missing the value of one variable.

missing at random (MAR) Noninformative or ignorable missing data, in reference to a missing-data mechanism in which the probability of missingness depends only on other observed data.

missing completely at random (MCAR) A missing-data mechanism in which the probability of missingness is a constant.

missing not at random (MNAR) Informative or nonignorable (NIGN), in reference to a missing-data mechanism in which the probability of missingness depends on the value of variables that may also be missing.

selection model An equation that relates predictors to the probability of observing some variable.

unit nonresponse The complete absence of data for a sample unit.

Unless proper account is taken, statistical analyses of samples that include units with incomplete data records can result in biased estimates of means, rates, and measures of association (such as regression coefficients) that are intended to represent corresponding values in an entire population. These biases can be avoided, reduced, or at least explored using a number of statistical strategies.

Introduction and Problem

The term missing data is used to refer to circumstances in which the available data on a set of individuals are less than what is intended, planned, or desired for a particular analysis. The last two words are important here, in that how missing data are described and the methods that may be employed to deal with them depend as much on what is desirable to investigate as on the extent and arrangement of missing values in the data file. The problem of missing data is ubiquitous. Though the emphasis here is on the occurrence of this problem within large social surveys, the problem is also common in small experimental studies. A sample unit (a survey participant, for example) may not be located or may refuse to respond (unit nonresponse). Variables may be completely missing (item nonresponse) through an error in questionnaire design or may be missing from just some respondents. In multistage sampling, nonresponse may occur at any of the levels; for example, student record data may be missing if a student's school refuses participation or because a particular student individually refuses. In addition, circumstances arise whereby although some sort of response is obtained, the information content of that response is incomplete. For example, it may be known that an event has occurred in some interval of time, without knowing when (so-called interval censoring), or that the event has not yet occurred (so-called right censoring). Sometimes, the precision of the recorded data is distrusted—for example, when study participants exhibit "digit preference," or rounding their responses to, say, units of 10 years. This loss of information is sometimes referred to as data coarsening.

The problem of missing data does not appear to be solvable by improvements in fieldwork practice alone. As research questions become more complex, so do the necessary data required to answer them, and this increases the burden on respondent participation. Although a good case can be made that one of the responsibilities of social membership is participation in research that is likely to contribute to the common good, participation only by informed consent invariably remains a legitimate individual right, and in attempting to coerce participation and response completion, it is easy to cross the boundary of what is ethically acceptable. It is inevitable that some data will be missing. Rather than making blind attempts to minimize missing data at any cost, there is a good case to be made that this problem should be actively managed. Data that are deliberately allowed to be missing, or data "missing-by-design," present a comparatively tractable analytical problem compared to data that are missing by happenstance. For example, when it is considered that a set of questionnaires or experimental test packs A, B, C, and D are jointly too burdensome, it is appropriate to consider designs in which subjects are randomly assigned to receive packs ABC, ABD, or ACB (pack A being considered a core pack).

Collecting data from a large initial sample with a low participation rate is almost always cheaper than collecting the same amount of data from a small sample, all of whom have been persuaded to participate. Persuading the less willing to provide data is a costly and time-consuming process. Although the presence of missing data implies having less data than intended, it is often not the consequent reduction in available sample size for an analysis that is the critical problem. Instead, the reason to strive for a high participation rate is because those less willing to participate are different from those more willing, and they can be different in all sorts of ways that are unknown. How to be sure that conclusions reached from an analysis of the willing will apply to the less willing? And how is it possible to be sure that results from analyzing the willing subjects describe the whole population and are not biased? There are ways in which the likely bias can be reduced. Sometimes, however, a lack of knowledge about the causes of "missingness" leads to an inability to justify any one adjustment. In such circumstances, a sensitivity analysis exploring the impact of different assumptions should be undertaken.

Types of Missing Data

The choice of how to deal with missing data should be based on how the missing data are generated. A very useful classification is as follows: Let Y_{obs} represent the observed part of the data, Y_{mis} represent the missing values, and R be an indicator for whether an observation is missing. The three principal types of mechanisms using these variables for the missingness are shown in the Fig. 1. If everyone in the population has an equal probability of being missing, then the missing data mechanism is said to be missing completely at random (MCAR). In this case, listwise deletion, or the dropping of any individual with an incomplete set of measures, does not lead to bias and can be understood as being equivalent to simply having a lower sampling fraction and thus smaller sample size. Thus, even when it is applicable (and it often is not),

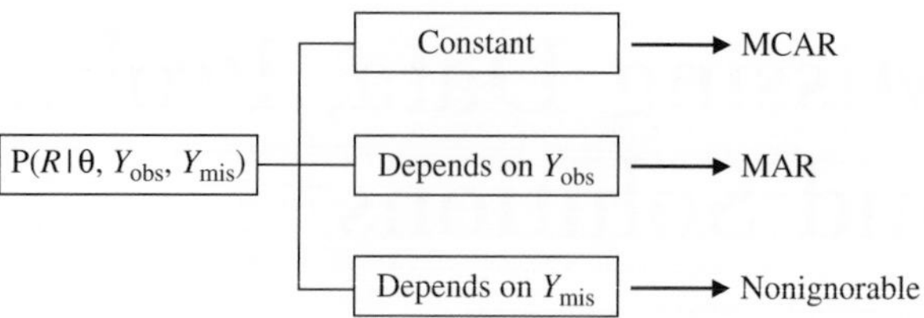

Figure 1 The three principal types of mechanisms using the variables Y_{obs}, Y_{mis}, and R for the missingness.

listwise deletion reduces efficiency, sometimes resulting in a dramatic reduction in sample size. When the probability of missing is not constant, but differences in probability depend solely on data that are not missing, then the missing data are said to be missing at random (MAR). A particularly simple case of MAR is covariate dependent missing data, where the probability of missingness depends only on the value of an explanatory covariate or independent variable. This would include, for example, sex differences in response rate, provided that we knew the sex of all sample members, responders and nonresponders alike. MAR also includes circumstances in which the rate of attrition from a particular wave of a longitudinal study varies with the value of the response from the previous (and thus observed) wave. When the probability of missingness varies in ways that depend on things other than covariates or observed values of the response variable, then the missingness mechanism is described as being informative, or nonignorable. Nonignorable missing data are substantially more difficult to deal with. In the case in which missing data are either MAR or nonignorable, simple listwise deletion is not only inefficient but will lead to bias.

Popular Methods Based on Misconceptions

A number of frequently used methods have some misconceived intuitive logic, lack a proper formal basis, and can be quite misleading.

Single Imputation: Mean Values

In this approach, missing values are replaced by the mean values of those with nonmissing values. This is based on the thinking that no bias is introduced because the estimated mean remains unchanged, or that any bias that might be introduced is conservative because no association between variables is being introduced. Both views are incorrect. Unless the missingness mechanism is MCAR, then it is not justifiable to assume that the mean for the unobserved individuals should be the same as that of the observed individuals. As for measures of association, because variances are systematically reduced by repeated insertion of mean values, correlations can be inflated. In the multiple regression context, covariation of the y variable with the x variable with mean-imputed missing values will be downwardly biased, and as a result the y variable variation that ought to be accounted for by that x variable can be wrongly attributed to other independent variables with which it is correlated. Thus incorrect treatment of missingness in one x variable can result in biased estimates of the effects of all x variables, including those with complete data.

An extension of this approach replaces missing values by mean values but also constructs a dummy variable indicating the records in which this has been done. It is thought that inclusion of this dummy variable as an additional independent variable in subsequent analysis will account for differences between observed and imputed records. In general, it does not.

Single Imputation: Regression Estimates

In this approach, missing values are replaced by the predicted values from a regression (or similar) model. This is based on the thinking that this will mirror the pattern of association in the observed data. This ignores the possibility that the pattern of association among those with missing data may be different from that among the complete-data cases, risking bias. Moreover, because the predicted values include no error variance, the imputed values have less variance than do the observed values. Adding back in simulated "residuals" to reflect the missing error variance can improve this correspondence, but subsequent analyses in which imputed values are treated indistinguishably from properly observed values does not fully take account of the fact that these imputed values are not known, but remain guessed values. Standard errors, confidence intervals, and p-values reported from such analyses thus tend to be smaller than they should be.

In spite of their limitations, almost all studies make some use of these simple methods; for example, they are used to fill in occasional missing items in a many-item rating scale. A range of well-founded methods are now considered.

Covariate Adjustment

Suppose we have covariate dependent missing data, then the probability of missing a response Y or a predictor variable X is dependent on the value of some third variable Z. Except under special circumstances, this missingness will bias naive estimates of the regression relationship between X and Y. However, in the estimation of the regression relationship between X and Y given Z (i.e., where both X and Z are used as predictors of Y), then this missingness, while reducing the precision of the estimate, does not bias the parameters being estimated.

A common response to this is to argue that in the usual circumstance in which it is suspected that missingness might be dependent on a whole set of covariates, all of these variables should then be included as additional covariates in the regression. This can be a perfectly satisfactory approach. However, it can also be entirely misleading. The issue hangs on whether the regression of X on Y, given these additional covariates $Z_1, Z_2, \ldots, Z_n$, is the parameter of interest. For example, suppose the relationship between educational attainment and parental interest is being investigated. It might be decided that the child's truancy rate is a good predictor of nonresponse on the attainment test. Does the regression coefficient for the effect of parental interest on attainment, given the level of truancy, estimate the effect of interest? The answer is "probably not," not if one of the ways in which parental interest exerts its effect is through ensuring school attendance. This regression may seriously underestimate the effect of parental interest. Thus covariate adjustment is only sometimes an effective strategy.

Weighting for Missing Data

An alternative to using variables associated with nonresponse as additional covariates is to use them as covariates in the calculation of nonresponse weights. The clearest example of this approach is for the analysis of studies involving a two-phase design. Under this design, individuals are stratified based on some preliminary measures (e.g., questionnaire report of child abuse), and individuals are selected for a detailed interview with a sampling fraction that depends on their stratum (e.g., oversampling those who experienced child abuse). Clearly those not interviewed will be missing the interview data, but this missingness is by design—the factors related to the probability of missingness are known. The sample is then analyzed using psuedo-likelihood or other design-based or marginal modeling methods that allow for the inclusion of probability weights. The probability weights are the inverse of the stratum-specific sampling fractions. It is important to distinguish probability weights from frequency weights. In probability weighting, whereas one sampled individual is being used to represent, say, 10 other individuals in the population, the variability in their response is nonetheless expected to be that of a single individual. In frequency weighting, the analysis is assuming that there were in fact 10 sampled individuals with identical responses. For many analyses, the estimates of regression-type coefficients are the same whether software is used that properly treats these weights as probability weights or improperly treats them as frequency weights (a risk within programs such as Statistical Packages for the Social Sciences, or SPSS). However, to obtain properly corrected standard errors, confidence intervals, and p-values, software that properly recognizes the weights as probability weights is required. These typically use so-called linearization or sandwich estimators of the parameter covariance matrix, but jackknife or bootstrap methods could be implemented instead.

In order to apply this approach to data missing by happenstance rather than by design, then an exploratory stage is usually required in which predictors of complete response are sought. Once identified, either strata are formed and stratum-specific response rates are calculated (e.g., for men and women), or a binary regression model is estimated (e.g., logit) and the predicted probabilities from this are used as estimated individual specific sampling fractions. In either case, the weight is the inverse of the estimated sampling fraction. Caution is required both to avoid an excessively wide range of estimated sampling fractions and to include the full range of covariates and their possible interactions. As used by survey statisticians, this sometimes seems as much an art as an exact science. The quality of the weighting can be checked by comparing the simple population distribution for variables measured on the whole sample (e.g., all those measured in the phase-1 screen) with that obtained for the same variables but based on the weighted complete-data cases only (the phase-2 sample).

The great advantage of these weighting methods over covariate adjustment is that they leave the user free to estimate all of the effects of interest to them, without the need to involve other covariates that they do not want in their model. Indeed, users of secondary survey data remain largely unaware that weights provided as part of the survey typically adjust for both sampling design and missing data due to unit nonresponse. Their principal disadvantage is that they can be inefficient, though more efficient variations are anticipated. In addition, for those wedded to model-based inference (for example, those wishing to estimate multilevel and latent variable models), available statistical theory to justify their estimation in the presence of probability weights is largely limited to circumstances in which the weights vary only at the highest level. Even in the marginal modeling framework, unless an independence-working model is being assumed, current standard generalized estimating equation (GEE) implementations require the same restriction.

Multiple Imputation

The principal unsolved problem in the use of single imputation of values obtained by some form of regression model was that the proper variability and uncertainty of the imputed records were not being communicated to the analysis stage. This can be achieved by the use of multiple imputation. This is a comparatively new and still developing field. It cannot yet be considered entirely general. However, because the difficult imputation part can be separated from the analysis part, specialist staff and software can be used to generate imputed data sets that can then be analyzed by relatively unsophisticated users equipped with standard software. This can be very effective, particularly for small to moderate levels of missingness, where the missing data mechanism is structured, and for data sets that are to be placed in the public domain.

Successful multiple imputation requires three conditions. First, all associations among variables must be properly reflected in the imputations. Unless the missingness follows a clear pattern of comparatively small sequential blocks of variables, such that primarily it is possible to predict imputed values using variables that are either known or have already been imputed, then the imputation task becomes complex. Second, each imputed value should reflect both the full range of associations with other variables and the full extent of the uncertainty. Technically, the model used for imputation should be at least as "large" (i.e., nonparsimonious) as the model to be used in the analysis. This may require numerous predictors to be included, but Bayesian considerations would suggest that the individual coefficients should be shrunk, requiring the use of specialist methods. Third, to communicate the uncertainty in our imputed values to the analysis stage, several data sets are generated. In each data set, the observed values remain the same but the imputed values may change as a result of using different imputations. These different imputations should reflect the full uncertainty in the estimated models used for imputation (e.g., should draw parameter values from their sampling distribution and not just reuse the same point estimates of the coefficients from the imputation regression) and not just add different "residuals." The foregoing has been described in the context of model-based imputation, but similar considerations apply when the imputation is based on some kind of matching and substitution of incomplete data records by complete data records—so-called hot-deck methods.

Instead of a single file with incomplete records, the end result is several files, but each one is complete. With modest amounts of missing data, five imputation replicates are often sufficient. As the proportion and uncertainty of the missing data increase, so more replicates are required. Each of the, say, m files is then analyzed using naive methods that know nothing about any missing data, and the desired statistic, be that a mean, a difference, or a model coefficient, is estimated as if the data were truly all complete. The results from each of the m analyses are then combined. The average of the estimated statistics is reported as the point estimate. The standard error of this estimate is calculated from combining the simple variance of the point estimates over the m replicates (the between-imputation variance B) and the average of the estimated variances (standard errors squared) as reported by the m naive analyses (the within-variance W), these being combined using what has become known as Rubin's formula, i.e., overall standard error $= \sqrt{\{(1-1/m)B + W\}}$.

Maximum-Likelihood Model-Based Inference

Likelihood inference is based directly on the joint probability density function for the variables and the observation scheme, which, using the notation at the beginning of this article, can be written as $f(y^{(\mathrm{obs})}, y^{(\mathrm{mis})}, r)$. This can be factored into one part describing the probability of the data and the second part describing the probability of observation or missingness:

$$f(y^{(\mathrm{obs})}, y^{(\mathrm{mis})}, r) = f(y^{(\mathrm{obs})}, y^{(\mathrm{mis})})\, f(r \mid y^{(\mathrm{obs})}, y^{(\mathrm{mis})})$$

However, we observe only $f(y^{(\mathrm{obs})}, r)$, and this can be expressed in terms of the above factorization by

$$f(y^{(\mathrm{obs})}, r) = \int f(y^{(\mathrm{obs})}, y^{(\mathrm{mis})})\, f(r \mid y^{(\mathrm{obs})}, y^{(\mathrm{mis})})\, dy^{(\mathrm{mis})}.$$

Integration over $y^{(\mathrm{mis})}$ is a mathematical way of saying that to obtain the probability density for the observed parts of the data, it is necessary to average over all possible values of the missing data, weighting each by their probability of occurrence. That is essentially what is done when multiple imputation is used—this is integration by sampling. However, if the missing data mechanism is random or completely at random, then $f(r \mid y^{(\mathrm{obs})}, y^{(\mathrm{mis})})$ does not depend on $y^{(\mathrm{mis})}$ and, as a consequence,

$$f(y^{(\mathrm{obs})}, r) = f(r \mid y^{(\mathrm{obs})}) \int f(y^{(\mathrm{obs})}, y^{(\mathrm{mis})})\, dy^{(\mathrm{mis})}$$
$$= f(r \mid y^{(\mathrm{obs})})\, f(y^{(\mathrm{obs})}).$$

This gives a log-likelihood of the following form:

$$L = \log f(r \mid y^{(\mathrm{obs})}) + \log f(y^{(\mathrm{obs})}).$$

The first term contains no information about $f(y^{(\mathrm{obs})})$ and so it can be "ignored" within a likelihood-based analysis. Even though the missingness may be highly selective, as long as the probability of missing depends only on observed data and that, conditional on the observed data, it does not depend on the missing data, then it can be ignored if the data are analyzed using full maximum likelihood.

This is an extremely powerful conclusion. It provides one of the major justifications for preferring repeated-measures analyses undertaken in multilevel or random-effects programs, rather than the "same" analysis undertaken in multivariate analysis of variance (MANOVA) procedures, because the standard algorithms for the latter require complete data and use listwise deletion, whereas the former will include those with both complete and incomplete sets of repeated measures. Latent variable and latent class models often lend themselves rather easily to treatments of missing indicator variables under an assumption of missing at random, and the same theory justifies the fitting of a common model across groups identified by different patterns of missing data, an approach that has been used in the structural-equation modeling field. Sometimes, particular implementations of maximum-likelihood methods do not lend themselves easily to MAR analyses. However, these implementations can sometimes be imbedded as the maximization step in an E–M algorithm that iterates between estimating quantities for records with missing data (the E, or expectation, step) and then maximizing the complete data likelihood (the M step).

That maximum likelihood will automatically cater for missing data that are missing at random does not remove from the analyst the onus of checking that the missing data assumptions are met. It also increases the importance of correctly specifying the model. This last arises because results generally become more sensitive to model misspecification biases as the proportion of missing data increases.

Nonignorable Nonresponse and Selection Models

A more direct approach to the problem of missing data is to estimate a joint model of (1) the probability of observing the response of interest and (2) the value of the response if observed. Often associated with the work of James J. Heckman, in economics, model (1) is usually estimated as a probit model and is referred to as the selection equation. With predictors of observing the response, z, with regression-type coefficients γ, the response of subject i is observed only if $z_i\gamma + u_{1i} > 0$ [where $u_1 \sim N(0, 1)$]. If it is observed, then the substantive regression equation for the value of the response (model 2) is a normal linear regression (if the response is continuous or a probit regression if the response is binary/ordinal), i.e., $y_i = x_i\beta + u_{2i}$ [where $u_2 \sim N(0, \sigma)$]. The two error terms, u_1 and u_2, are expected to be correlated if the substantive equation does not contain all the predictors of nonresponse that also predict the substantive response. If the errors are correlated, then the model allows for the possibility that nonresponse depends on unobserved values of the response variable—that is, the missingness is nonignorable. An essentially similar model occurs in the statistical literature in which the probit model is replaced by a logit model.

It is usual to include in the selection equation all the variables in the substantive regression equation, but it is helpful to add other instrumental variables that the analyst assumes are not related to the value of the response. A classic example occurs in the analysis of wages. Wages are missing for those without a job; the number of dependent children can be expected to influence willingness to work, but not the wages offered for a given job. In the absence of such instrumental variables, results from these models can sometimes be unstable, with erratic variation in coefficients and significance for rather modest changes in the set of included covariates and distributional assumptions. It should be noted that covariates are required for all observations, those with and those without the response variable of interest. Elaborations of this basic model for more complex multilevel settings are possible.

Implications for Study Design

A recurring theme has been the value of having at least some data on all subjects, particularly if those data are expected to be related to nonresponse. These data can be used as additional covariates, for calculating weighting strata, for imputing missing values, or as covariates in a selection equation. Thus an important part of any study design is to identify what variables can be collected, even about nonparticipants. Sometimes relevant data can be extracted from other sources; examples include using postal codes to link to small area census data, or calculating weights to match known population proportions. Use of such data allows methods that assume a MAR mechanism (rather than the naive MCAR mechanism) in order to take account of an increasing range of selection effects, and allows postponing or avoiding having to use the much less robust methods that allow for nonignorable missingness. In a similar way, patterns of missingness that have been deliberately created (missing data by design), and are thus amenable to missing-at-random methods, may be preferred over rather more complete data when the reasons for missingness are not known.

See Also the Following Articles

Maximum Likelihood Estimation • Non-Response Bias • Phrase Completion Scales • Randomization

Further Reading

Allison, P. D. (2001). *Missing Data.* Sage, Thousand Oaks, California.

Brick, J. M., and Karlton, G. (1996). Handling missing data in survey research. *Statist. Methods Med. Res.* **5,** 215–238.

Heckman, J. J. (1976). The common structure of statistical models of truncation, sample selection and limited dependent variables, and a simple estimator for such models. *Ann. Econ. Social Measure.* **5,** 475–492.

Jones, M. P. (1996). Indicator and stratification methods for missing explanatory variables in multiple linear regression. *J. Am. Statist. Assoc.* **91,** 222–230.

Little, R. J. A., and Rubin, D. B. (1987). *Statistical Analysis with Missing Data.* Wiley, New York.

Little, R. J. A., and Rubin, D. B. (1989). The analysis of social science data with missing values. *Sociol. Methods Res.* **18,** 292–326.

Rubin, D. B. (1996). Multiple imputation after 18 years. *J. Am. Statist. Assoc.* **91,** 473–489.

Shafer, J. L. (1999). Multiple imputation: A primer. *Statist. Methods Med. Res.* **8,** 3–15.

Winship, C., and Mare, R. D. (1997). Models for sample selection bias. *Annu. Rev. Sociol.* **18,** 327–350.

Misspecification in Linear Spatial Regression Models

Raymond J. G. M. Florax
Free University Amsterdam, Amsterdam, The Netherlands

Peter Nijkamp
Free University Amsterdam, Amsterdam, The Netherlands

Glossary

misspecification test A statistical test, typically used in a regression context, directed toward identifying violations of the standard assumptions of ordinary least squares (heteroscedasticity, autocorrelation, nonnormality) or the functional form and the inclusion of explanatory variables.

spatial autocorrelation Similarity in attribute values, measured either at a nominal, ordinal, or interval scale, over geographical locations; also referred to as spatial dependence or spatial clustering.

spatial effects Catchall term referring to spatial autocorrelation or dependence (spatial clustering), and spatial heterogeneity.

spatial heterogeneity The occurrence of dissimilar attribute values over spatial locations.

spatial process models Spatial regression models, typically with a linear additive specification, in which the relationship among areal units is specified exogenously using a weight matrix that mimics the spatial structure and the spatial interaction pattern.

specification strategy A prespecified series of misspecification tests for regression models aimed at detecting the correct underlying data-generating process.

Abstract

Spatial effects are endemic in models based on spatially referenced data. An increased awareness of the relevance of spatial interactions, spatial externalities, and networking effects among researchers has led to studies in the area of spatial econometrics. Spatial econometrics focuses on the specification and estimation of regression models explicitly incorporating such spatial effects. The multidimensionality of spatial effects calls for misspecification tests and estimators that are notably different from techniques designed for analysis of time series. With that in mind, the focus here centers on spatial effects, referring to both heterogeneity and interdependence of phenomena occurring in two-dimensional space. Spatial autocorrelation or dependence can be detected by means of cross-correlation statistics in univariate and multivariate data settings. There are tools for exploratory spatial data analysis and misspecification tests for spatial effects in linear regression models. Discussions of specification strategies and an overview of available software for spatial regression analysis, including their main functionalities, aim to give practitioners of spatial data analysis a head start.

Spatial Effects

The awareness of and incorporation of space are fundamental to geography. In 1979, the geographer Waldo Tobler formulated the first law of geography, stating "everything is related to everything else, but near things are more related than distant things." The relevance of spatial effects extends, however, beyond geography, and the effects are ubiquitous in many of the social sciences. Relevant to this, a seminal 1991 book by Andrew D. Cliff and J. Keith Ord about models and applications of spatial processes begins with an example from epidemiology. The spatial mortality pattern from cholera in London, from 1848 to 1849, is analyzed and the high incidence of the disease in the London metropolis is attributed to the high organic content of the Chelsea, Southwark, and

Vauxhall waters. Similarly, spatial analysis techniques are used to analyze diffusion–adoption patterns of innovations by farmers, to prescribe spatially differentiated fertilizer doses in precision agriculture, to explain network effects among individuals, and to investigate human–environment interactions in processes of environmental degradation.

Economists have traditionally been more reluctant to consider space as a relevant factor. In 1890, the economist Alfred Marshall acknowledged the role of space, maintaining that the working of the market depends "chiefly on variations in the area of space, and the period of time over which the market in question extends; the influence of time being more fundamental than that of space." It took until the 1950s, however, before Walter Isard opposed this, calling it "Anglo-Saxon bias" that repudiates the factor of space, compresses everything within the economy to a point so that all spatial resistance disappears, and thus confines economic theory to "a wonderland of no spatial dimensions." An ongoing debate has since revolved around whether space is merely a geographical facilitator or medium for movement, or whether space has an intrinsic explanatory function. The monopolistic competition model of Avinash Dixit and Joseph Stiglitz in 1977 inspired a revolution in economic theory that increased awareness of imperfect competition and increasing returns to scale; this model subsequently became apparent in the "new economic geography" of Paul Krugman, Masahisa Fujita, and others. Nowadays, spatial dimensions are taken into account in the study of economic growth, high-tech innovations, urban economics, public sector productivity, fiscal policy interdependence, and international trade.

Spatial Dependence and Spatial Heterogeneity

Spatial effects include spatial heterogeneity and spatial dependence. Spatial heterogeneity refers to structural relations that vary over space, either in a discrete or categorical fashion (for instance, urban vs. rural, or according to an urban hierarchy), or in a continuous manner (such as on a trend surface). Spatial dependence points to systematic spatial variation that results in observable clusters or a systematic spatial pattern. These descriptions already show that in an observational sense, spatial dependence and spatial heterogeneity are not always easily discernible. The clustering of high values in, for instance, urban areas and urban fringes can be interpreted as spatial clustering of high values pertaining to urban areas and to low values to rural areas, but it may as well be viewed as spatial heterogeneity, distinguishing metropolitan areas from their hinterland.

The typical feature of spatial dependence or spatial autocorrelation is that it is two-dimensional and multidirectional. An observation of an attribute at one location can be correlated with the value of the same attribute at a different location, and vice versa, and the causation pattern can occur in different directions. Figure 1 shows two identical (7×10) regular grid systems with distinct spatial distributions of the same values. The absolute location of the nonzero values is the same in both grids, but graph A shows a clustering of relatively low values on the left-hand side and high values to the right. Graph B shows a much more random spatial allocation of values. In terms of spatial effects, note that the distribution in graph A exhibits spatial dependence and spatial heterogeneity, whereas graph B does not.

The occurrence of spatial heterogeneity does not necessarily have severe implications for the information that can be obtained from a spatial data series. Spatial autocorrelation does, however, because an observation is partly predictable from neighboring observations. A series of spatially dependent observations therefore contains less information. This is similar to the situation in time series analysis, wherein a forecast with respect to the future can be partly inferred from what happened in the past. The two-dimensional and multidirectional nature of spatial autocorrelation ensures that the spatial case is more complex.

Spatial Econometrics

The history of analysis of the spatial autocorrelation problem goes back to the work of statisticians such as Thomas Moran, Geary, and Whittle in the late 1940s and early 1950s. The development of the subsequent literature was rather slow until Cliff and Ord published their seminal book about spatial autocorrelation in 1973. Their book focused on the statistical analysis of spatial data series, although not exclusively from a spatial statistical point of view because there was also some attention given to modeling. The modeling context is, however, much more pronounced in the efforts of the Dutch–Belgian economist Jean Paelinck, who coined the term spatial econometrics in the early 1970s. Paelinck and Leo Klaassen jointly wrote the first monograph on spatial econometrics in 1979, stressing the need to model spatial relations explicitly , epitomizing the asymmetry in spatial interrelations and the role of spatial interdependence. The edges of the field in those days were pushed ahead mainly by Dutch regional economists (Bartels, Brandsma, Hordijk, Ketellapper, and Nijkamp). Later, the center of activity shifted to the United States, where both economists and geographers concentrated on introducing new statistical tests (particularly, tests developed in a maximum-likelihood framework) and the specification and estimation of spatial regression models. During the late 1990s, these methodological developments were gradually being picked up in applied spatial research, which, among other things, was facilitated by the availability of spatial econometric software.

The most comprehensive book of modern developments is Luc Anselin's 1988 book on methods and models of spatial econometrics, in which he defined spatial econometrics as "the collection of techniques that deal with the peculiarities caused by space in the statistical analysis of regional science models." The modeling perspective, already pondered by Paelinck, distinguished spatial econometrics from the broader field of spatial statistics, as discussed by Cressie in 1993. Theoretical overviews of spatial econometrics are available in further work by Anselin and Bera in 1998, and Anselin in 2001. The tutorial of the SpaceStat software, available online at http://www.terraseer.com, provides a good introduction to spatial econometrics, and LeSage's contribution to the Web book of regional science, available at http://www.rri.wvu.edu, gives a more applied, hands-on introduction.

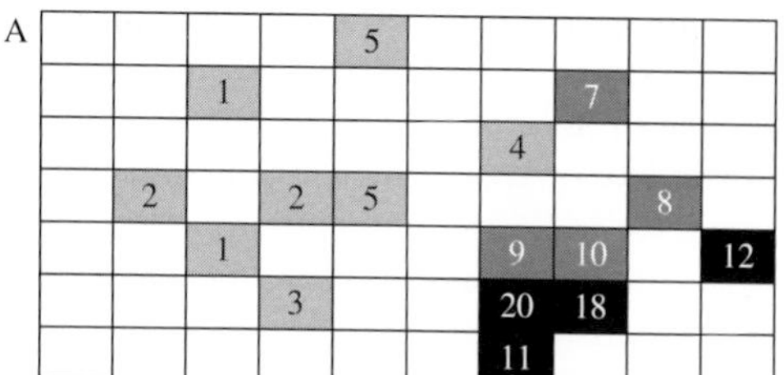

Figure 1 Hypothetical example of a spatial distribution of values on a 7×10 regular grid. Adapted from Upton and Fingleton (1985).

Testing for Spatial Autocorrelation

Definition Spatial Autocorrelation

Two publications of the work of Cliff and Ord, in 1973 and 1981, induced extensive focus on the statistical properties of spatial data, in particular for spatial autocorrelation or dependence. Statistical tests for spatial association or dependence are always based on the null hypothesis of spatial independence. The general notion of independence is easily formalized as follows:

$$\Pr(X_1 < x_1, \ldots, X_n < x_n) = \prod_{i=1}^{n} \Pr(X_i < x_i), \qquad (1)$$

with $i = 1, \ldots, n$. Consequently,

$$\Pr(X_i = a,\ X_j = b) = \Pr(X_i = a) \cdot \Pr(X_j = b). \qquad (2)$$

For independent events, such as tossing an unbiased coin, the probability of the occurrence of a series of events (e.g., throwing 6 and subsequently 5) is determined multiplicatively by the chance of the occurrence of the individual events (i.e., throwing 6 and throwing 5). In the case of dependence, this implication does not hold, because the chance of the second event occurring is somehow conditional on the occurrence of the first event.

The notion of spatial dependence is similar, but is more specific in the sense that the dependence among events is mediated through space—for instance, either through distance or adjacency. Spatial dependence is referred to using informal terms, such as spatial clustering of similar values, an organized pattern, or systematic spatial variation. Strictly speaking, spatial dependence is a characteristic of the joint probability density function. As such, it is verifiable only under simplifying conditions, such as normality. Spatial autocorrelation is simply a moment of that joint distribution. In this article, however, the common practice is followed, and spatial autocorrelation and spatial dependence are used interchangeably.

Spatial autocorrelation is easily observed in Fig. 1. In graph B, observations are randomly distributed over space, so the chances of observing a specific value are independently distributed. Graph A exhibits spatial autocorrelation or dependence, because the probability of a specific value occurring in a specific location depends on the value of neighboring locations.

Statistical Tests for Spatial Autocorrelation

The common element in all tests for spatial autocorrelation is that they relate a vector of attribute values for various locations to all other locations through a matrix representing the structure of the spatial system. Most test statistics are special cases of the general cross-product statistic, developed in various publications by Hubert, Golledge, Costanza, and Gale, given by Eq. (3):

$$\Gamma = \sum_{i=1}^{n} \sum_{j=1}^{n} w_{ij} y_{ij}, \qquad (3)$$

where i and j ($= 1, \ldots, n$) index the locations, w_{ij} are the elements of a matrix of the spatial topology of the system, and y_{ij} are the association between the values of a specific attribute at different locations. It is common to assume no self-association, which is easily incorporated in Eq. (3) by defining $w_{ij} = 0, \forall i = j$. Various metrics can be used to measure the association among attribute values y_{ij}, such as the product of the attribute values $x_i \times x_j$, or the squared difference $(x_i - x_j)^2$. In 1991, Getis provided an overview of spatial association statistics as well as a comparison to spatial interaction models.

Most statistics for spatial association are special cases of the cross-product statistic. For spatial data measured on a nominal level (for example, unity for a location displaying the attribute, and zero otherwise, usually colored black and white on a map), so-called join–count statistics have been developed. They compute the observed frequency of black–black, black–white, and white–white joins. The comparison to what is expected by chance constitutes a formal test for spatial autocorrelation. The test statistics are asymptotically normally distributed and the moments, under free and nonfree sampling, were derived in the 1981 book by Cliff and Ord, in addition to extensions to categorical data organized in multicolored maps.

The most well-known spatial association statistics for ordinal and interval data are Geary's c and Moran's I. These statistics are also special cases of the general cross-product statistic. The univariate Moran's I statistic is given by Eq. (4):

$$I = \left(\frac{n}{S_0}\right) \times \left[\frac{\sum_{i=1}^{n}\sum_{j=1}^{n} w_{ij}(x_i - \bar{x})(x_j - \bar{x})}{\sum_{i=1}^{n}(x_i - \bar{x})^2}\right], \tag{4}$$

or, in matrix terms,

$$I = \left(\frac{n}{S_0}\right) \times \left(\frac{\mathbf{x}'\mathbf{W}\mathbf{x}}{\mathbf{x}'\mathbf{x}}\right), \tag{5}$$

where $\mathbf{x}$ is an $n \times 1$ vector of observations x_i measured in deviations from the mean $\bar{x}$, $\mathbf{W}$ is a spatial weight matrix with $n \times n$ elements w_{ij} representing the topology of the spatial system, and S_0 is the sum of the elements of the spatial weights matrix. The weight matrix is typically exogenously determined and can be defined using contiguity, distance, or more complicated specifications such as those based on the distance and length of the common border, referred to as generalized weights by Cliff and Ord in 1981. As for all autocorrelation statistics, a slight rearrangement of the statistic shows that it is based on a comparison of the covariance of spatially connected observations to the variance of all observations.

Statistical inference can be based on the standardized or z-value of Moran's I, as follows:

$$z_I = [I - \mathrm{E}(I)]/\mathrm{SD}(I), \tag{6}$$

but an assumption about the distribution of the x-variates is needed. The moments of I can be derived analytically assuming that the x follow a normal distribution, or that the distribution is unknown but can be approximated in a nonparametric framework using a randomization approach. Alternatively, an estimated distribution function for Moran's I can be empirically generated following a permutation approach, as shown by Cliff and Ord in 1981.

It is common practice to interpret Moran's I as a correlation coefficient, although its value is, strictly speaking, not restricted to the $[-1, +1]$ interval. High positive values signal the occurrence of similar attribute values over space (either high or low values), and hence spatial clustering. Negative values indicate the joint occurrence of high and low attribute values in nearby locations. A value close to the expected value of Moran's I in the absence of spatial correlation [which equals $-1/(n-1)$ and therefore approaches zero with increasing sample size] can be taken as evidence of a random allocation of attribute values over space.

Concurrent results for Geary's c are developed in a similar fashion. The statistic is based on a different metric, and reads as follows:

$$I = \frac{(n-1)}{2S_0} \times \left[\frac{\sum_{i=1}^{n}\sum_{j=1}^{n} w_{ij}(x_i - x_j)^2}{\sum_{i=1}^{n}(x_i - \bar{x})^2}\right]. \tag{7}$$

In 1981, Cliff and Ord also derived the moments for the Geary statistic, under different assumptions. The expected value of Geary's c is one under the null hypothesis of no spatial autocorrelation, and the variance again depends on the stochastic assumption (normality or randomization). Statistical inference is straightforwardly based on the corresponding z-value of the statistic. Somewhat counterintuitive, a negative (positive) of Geary's c indicates positive (negative) spatial autocorrelation. Cliff and Ord also showed in 1981 that the asymptotic relative efficiency is generally better for the I test than for the c test, and it is therefore common practice to use Moran's I, especially in a regression context. The variance of Geary's c is also more sensitive to the distribution of the sample data. Note that the these statistics and their asymptotic properties refer to "raw data." The moments for regression residuals are different, because residuals are, by definition, correlated, even if the errors are independent. The asymptotic properties of Moran's I for regression residuals have been derived, whereas those for Geary's c are not available.

These autocorrelation statistics have a series of important limitations, which were discussed by Cliff and Ord in 1981 and Anselin in 1988. First, for most straightforward specifications of the weight matrix, the statistics are topologically invariant, implying that changes in the size, shape, and relative strength of the link between the areal units are ignored. Second, in the connection or weights matrix, all links are given equal weight, which does not necessarily conform to an appropriate perception of space. Third, the level of aggregation of the data and the spatial arrangement is usually rather arbitrary, but it affects the magnitude of the statistics. In order to ensure identification, the weights have to be defined *a priori* and exogenously, but this implies that for irregularly spaced areal units, no analytical mathematical properties can be derived. Finally, the specification of the weight matrix is such that out-of-sample observations are simply ignored. This leads to edge effects that are difficult to assess and it is cumbersome, or even impossible, to alleviate their disturbing influence.

Local Statistics and the Moran Scatterplot

During the 1990s, two extensions of the overall or "global" statistics were developed to further intensify exploratory spatial data analysis (ESDA). One extension centers on disaggregating the overall pattern of spatial variation in local spatial patterns, and is caught in so-called local indicators of spatial association (LISA). Exploratory spatial data analysis focuses on identifying spatial dependence patterns and spatial heterogeneity, either as an independent analytical tool or as a tool that assists in identifying the specification of a spatial regression model. The cross-product statistics discussed previously are global in nature in that they identify clusters of spatial association pertaining to the entire spatial system. However, spatial processes may be instable or nonstationary. Within an overall autocorrelated sample, local pockets of randomness may exist. Alternatively, localized clusters of spatial association, sometimes referred to as "hot spots," may be observed within an overall randomly distributed sample of observations. The generalized cross-product statistic and variants such as Moran's I can be disaggregated into local statistics. For instance, for a standardized weights matrix (i.e., the row sums are scaled to unity), the local Moran is given by Eq. (8):

$$I_i = \frac{\left[(x_i - \bar{x})\sum_{i=1}^{n} w_{ij}(x_j - \bar{x})\right]}{\sum_{i=1}^{n}(x_i - \bar{x})^2/n}, \tag{8}$$

which clearly shows that the local Moran is proportional to the global Moran's I up to a scaling constant. Anselin showed in 1995 that the null distribution of the local statistic should not be approximated by the normal, but instead a randomization approach should be used for statistical inference.

The proportionality property distinguishes LISA from other local statistics, notably the Getis–Ord statistics. The latter compare the sum of values in neighboring locations within a certain distance band to the sum over all locations, and have a slightly different interpretation, explained by Getis and Ord in 1992. The LISA and the Getis–Ord statistics can both be used to identify local pockets of nonstationarity or to evaluate the contribution of individual areal units to the global spatial pattern. A second extension of the overall or global statistics builds on the general property that any statistic taking the form of a ratio of a quadratic form and its sum of squares can be interpreted as a bivariate regression coefficient. Equations (4) and (5) show that Moran's I has this form, and it is thus equivalent to the estimated parameter of a regression of $\mathbf{Wx}$ on $\mathbf{x}$. Rearranging gives Eq. (9):

$$I = \mathbf{x}'(\mathbf{x}'\mathbf{x})^{-1}\mathbf{Wx}, \tag{9}$$

omitting the standardization term that is unity for a standardized weights matrix. This result can be visualized in a Moran scatterplot that can be used visually to identify spatial clusters, outliers, and local nonstationarity, shown by Anselin in 1995 and 1996. As reported by Cressie in 1991, the Moran scatterplot is similar to the spatial lag scatterplot in exploratory geostatistics. When the x-variable is standardized (i.e., expressed in deviations from the sample mean, and divided by the standard deviation), and the value of x is plotted on the horizontal axis and the weighted average value of x for the neighbors is plotted on the vertical axis, the scatterplot contains four quadrants(see Fig. 2A, for an example). The quadrants in Fig. 2A possibly show clusters of high–high values (top right quadrant), low–low values (bottom left), and low–high and high–low values (top left and bottom right, respectively). Because the x-variable is standardized, exploratory tools such as the 2σ rule for outliers can be easily assessed. The Moran scatterplot can be used for any variable, including residuals of a regression model.

Illustration of Exploratory Spatial Data Analysis

A simple illustration from neoclassical economic growth theory can also be used for modeling purposes. In their pathbreaking 1992 article in the *Quarterly Journal of Economics*, Gregory Mankiw, David Romer, and David Weil analyzed the economic growth performance of 98 non-oil-producing countries, over the period 1960–1985. The data and the model presented here are identical to those used by the Mankiw–Romer–Weil (MRW) model, except that the spatial effects are considered explicitly here (the data can be found online at http://post.economics.harvard.edu). The weight matrix has been compiled using the centroid function in ArcView (see www.esri.com), and using SpaceStat to compute spherical distances between the countries' centroids.

Figure 3 shows the spatial distribution of per capita income in 1960 and 1985 and the growth rate of per capita gross domestic product (GDP) over the period 1960–1985. The maps reveal that the spatial distribution of the level of GDP per capita is highly persistent over time. The richest countries are clustered in North America and Western Europe, and Australia and New Zealand have high GDP per capita levels as well, both in 1960 and

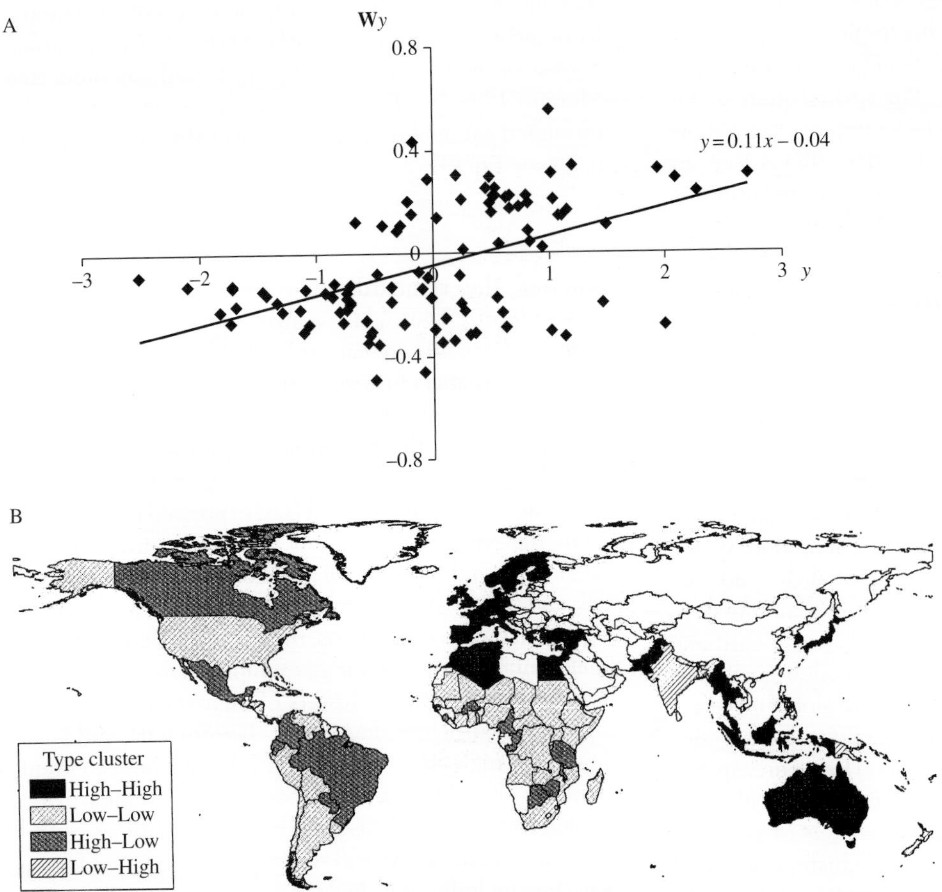

Figure 2 Moran scatterplot of economic growth (A), and a map differentiating between four types of countries based on the quadrants in the Moran scatterplot (B).

in 1985. The spatial distribution of economic growth seems much more random, although, in accordance with the theoretical prediction of neoclassical growth theory, the fast-growing economies are typically located outside the previously mentioned area with high-GDP-level countries. This pattern of spatial clustering is corroborated in the statistical analysis. The elements of the spatial weights matrix are specified as $1/d_{ij}$, where d_{ij} is the spherical distance of the geographical midpoints of the various countries, putting zeros on the diagonal. The weights matrix is standardized, implying that all elements are scaled such that each row sum equals one, in order to avoid scale effects. Table I shows that GDP per capita levels change from approximately $3000 in 1960 to $5300 in 1985 (in 1985 prices, U.S. dollars), and the growth rate of per capita GDP is approximately 2%. The normality test is rejected for the levels, but not for the growth rate, so the normality assumption is used for Moran's *I* in the latter case and the randomization approach is applied for the levels. The Moran *I* tests show that there is significant spatial clustering of similar values for GDP per capita levels. The same is true for GDP per capita growth rates, although at a considerably lower level.

Looking again at the Moran scatterplot of economic growth in Fig. 2, a mapping of the four types of countries identified in the Moran scatterplot is shown in Fig 2B. The scatterplot reveals the equivalence of Moran's *I* to the estimated regression coefficient of the linear trend line. The map shows that low-growth countries tend to cluster together (especially in Africa), but high-growth countries are either surrounded by other high-growth countries (in Europe) or by countries that exhibit considerably lower growth rates (in North and South America, and in Africa). This is a primary visual indication that spatial heterogeneity may be relevant for the regression model, either by varying the coefficients over different types of regions and/or allowing for groupwise heteroskedasticity.

Spatial Regression Models

The specification of spatial dependence in (linear) regression models is usually distinguished according to two types of representation. One is to model the dependence directly, for instance, by means of a distance deterrence function. If a sufficient number of data points are

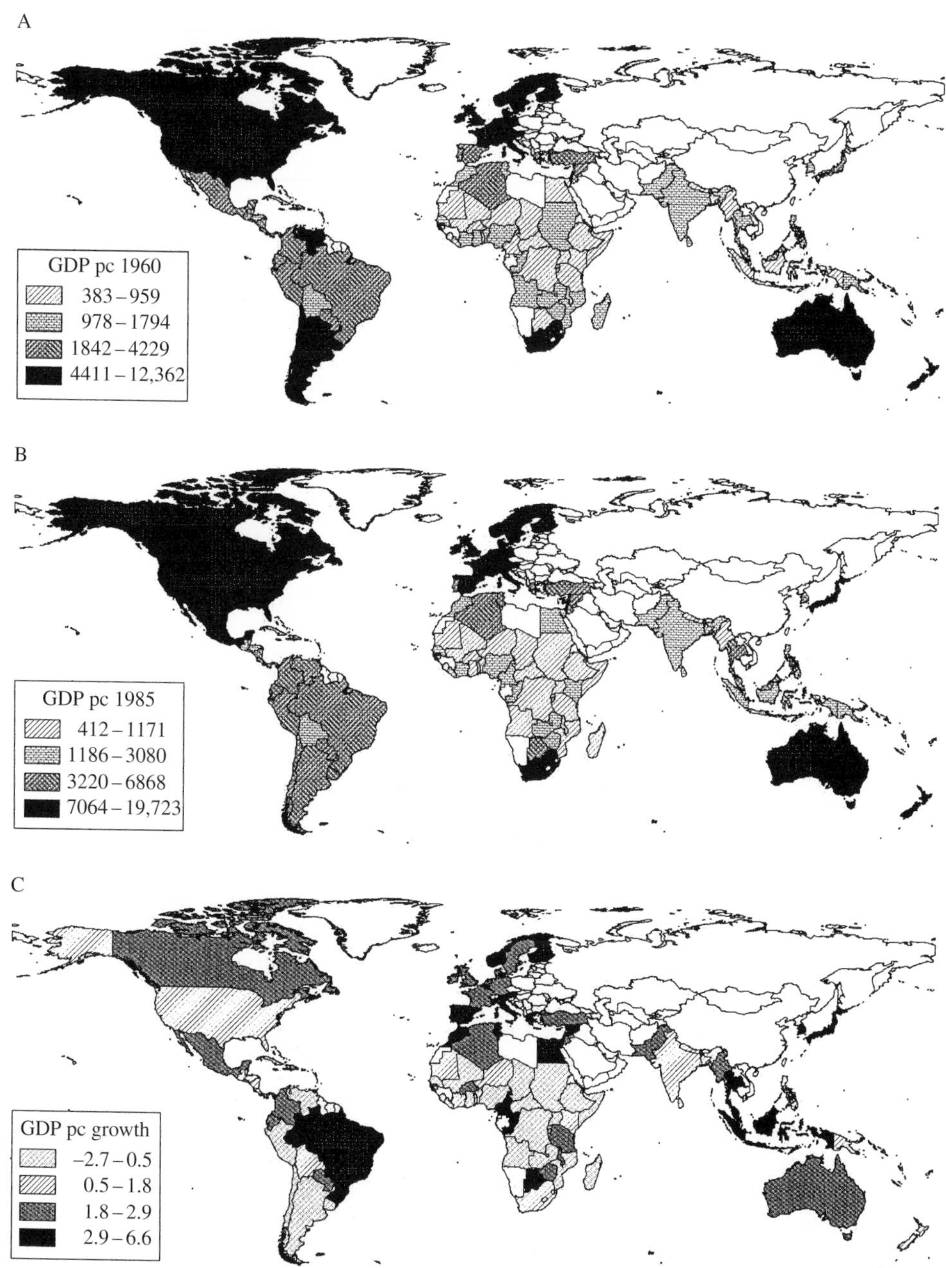

Figure 3 Maps of gross domestic product per capita (GDP pc) for the Mankiw–Romer–Weil sample of 98 non-oil-producing countries in (A) 1960 and (B) 1985. (C) Map of annual GDP growth over the period 1960–1985 for the Mankiw–Romer–Weil sample of 98 non-oil-producing countries.

available, the influence of spatial impediments can be estimated directly. Another approach is to provide exogenous structure by specifying the spatial topology and interaction structure in a spatial weights matrix, in order to avoid the incidental parameter problem that would arise when the influence of neighboring locations is estimated for each region separately. We restrict the discussion to the latter category of so-called spatial process models. There is a third type of model, the so-called conditional autoregressive models, but for these types of models, it is rather cumbersome to attain appropriate estimates.

Spatial Process Models

A general specification for a spatial regression model is the specification combining a spatially autoregressive dependent variable among the set of explanatory variables and spatially autoregressive disturbances. For higher order

Table I Exploratory Statistics for Gross Domestic Product per Capita Levels[a]

Statistic	*Average*	*Wald test for normality*[b]	*Moran's I*[b]
GDP per capita, 1960	2994.90	38.18 (0.00)	0.20[c] (11.44)
GDP per capita, 1985	5309.77	21.79 (0.00)	0.24[c] (13.31)
GDP per capita, annual growth rate	0.02	0.06 (0.97)	0.11[d] (6.69)

[a] In 1985 dollars (U.S.); data are from the Mankiw–Romer–Weil sample comprising 98 non-oil-producing countries from 1960 to 1985.
[b] Probability levels for the Wald test z values for Moran's I are in parentheses.
[c] Using the randomization approach.
[d] Using the normality assumption.

processes, this autoregressive–autoregressive (ARAR) paradigm, the ARAR(i, j) model, is given by Eq. (10):

$$\begin{aligned} \mathbf{y} &= (\rho_1 \mathbf{W}_1 + \cdots + \rho_i \mathbf{W}_i)\mathbf{y} + \mathbf{X}\boldsymbol{\beta} + \boldsymbol{\varepsilon}, \\ \boldsymbol{\varepsilon} &= (\lambda_1 \mathbf{W}_1 + \cdots + \lambda_j \mathbf{W}_j)\boldsymbol{\varepsilon} + \boldsymbol{\mu}. \end{aligned} \tag{10}$$

For a first-order process, this reduces to the ARAR(1, 1) model:

$$\begin{aligned} \mathbf{y} &= \rho \mathbf{W}_1 \mathbf{y} + \mathbf{X}\boldsymbol{\beta} + \boldsymbol{\varepsilon}, \\ \boldsymbol{\varepsilon} &= \lambda \mathbf{W}_1 \boldsymbol{\varepsilon} + \boldsymbol{\mu}, \end{aligned} \tag{11}$$

where $\mathbf{y}$ is the $n \times 1$ vector with observations on the dependent variable, $\mathbf{X}$ is the $n \times k$ design matrix containing the explanatory variables, $\boldsymbol{\beta}$ is the $k \times 1$ vector with parameters, ρ is the scalar spatially autoregressive parameter, is the scalar spatial autoregressive disturbance parameter, and $\boldsymbol{\mu}$ is an $n \times 1$ independently and identically distributed vector of error terms. The spatial interaction pattern can be restricted to first-order neighbors (i.e., neighbors that have a common border) as in Eq. (11), or extended to higher order neighbors (i.e., neighbors of the neighbors, etc.) as in Eq. (10). Alternatively, the weight matrix can be specified using inverse distances, eventually with a cutoff point. In the latter case, an interpretation similar to the higher order interpretation is feasible, using distance bands. The weights matrices for the spatially lagged dependent variable and in the error term do not necessarily have to be identical, but they are assumed to be the same here for reasons of simplicity. Spatial stationarity is assured by constraining the spatial autoregressive parameters to lie in the interval $1/\omega_{min}$ and $1/\omega_{max}$, where ω_{min} and ω_{max} are, respectively, the smallest and the largest eigenvalues (on the real line) of the spatial weights matrix. For a row-standardized spatial weights matrix (i.e., the row sums are scaled to unity), the largest eigenvalue is always +1. The model contains a spatially homogeneous set of coefficients but can trivially be extended to allow for spatially varying coefficients and/or heteroskedasticity. A related model is the autoregressive moving-average (ARMA) variant, ARMA(1, 1), which, for the first-order case, reads as $\mathbf{y} = \rho \mathbf{W}_1 \mathbf{y} + \mathbf{X}\boldsymbol{\beta} + (\mathbf{I} + \lambda \mathbf{W}_1)\boldsymbol{\mu}$.

The most frequently used models are two special cases of the ARAR(1, 1) model, the spatial autoregressive error model, or AR(1) model, obtained for $\rho = 0$, and the spatial lag model when $\lambda = 0$. For ease of notation, one weight matrix is used from here on, and the subscript is omitted. Extensions to higher order cases are trivial. The spatial (autoregressive) error model reads as follows:

$$\mathbf{y} = \mathbf{X}\boldsymbol{\beta} + (\mathbf{I} - \lambda \mathbf{W})^{-1} \boldsymbol{\mu}, \tag{12}$$

The error covariance matrix is given by $\sigma^2[(\mathbf{I} - \lambda\mathbf{W})'(\mathbf{I} - \lambda\mathbf{W})]^{-1}$, showing that heteroscedasticity is present even if the error term is homoscedastic. This applies likewise to the spatial lag model,

$$\mathbf{y} = \rho \mathbf{W} \mathbf{y} + \mathbf{X}\boldsymbol{\beta} + \boldsymbol{\mu}, \tag{13}$$

for which the error covariance is the same as in the AR(1) model, assuming otherwise homoscedastic errors.

As a special case of the spatial ARMA model, the spatial moving average model can be easily derived as $\mathbf{y} = \mathbf{X}\boldsymbol{\beta} + (\mathbf{I} + \lambda\mathbf{W})\boldsymbol{\mu}$, with error covariance matrix $\sigma^2(\mathbf{I} + \lambda\mathbf{W})(\mathbf{I} + \lambda\mathbf{W}')$. Although the AR and MA specifications appear to be similar, the difference in the error covariance shows that the spatial dependence in the MA model is restricted to first- and second-order neighbors, whereas in the AR model the dependence extends throughout the spatial system.

Interpretation of Spatial Effects

The standard spatial process models previously introduced illustrate two quite different interpretations of spatial dependence. As shown by Anselin and Rey in 1991, dependence can be modeled either as a substantive process or as a nuisance. In the spatial lag model, a substantive theoretical interpretation can be given to the spatial interaction. In the spatial error model, spatial dependence is caused either by (erroneously) omitted spatially correlated variables or by boundaries of regions that do not coincide with actual behavioral units. The different specifications of spatial dependence have divergent implications for estimation and statistical inference. The spatial error model is an example of the more general class of models with a nonspherical variance–covariance matrix, although due to the multidirectional nature of spatial dependence, the estimation is more difficult than for time series (in particular, estimated generalized least-squares estimators are inconsistent). The spatial lag model exhibits endogeneity that can be taken into account by instrumental variable or general methods of moments techniques, but should preferably be solved using an appropriate maximum-likelihood estimator; see Anselin's 1988 paper for details. In contrast to the time series case, whereby ordinary least squares (OLS) remains consistent if the errors are not serially correlated and its use is therefore asymptotically warranted, OLS estimators for the spatial lag model are biased and inconsistent, irrespective of the properties of the error term. Nuisance dependence in the error term is less serious because OLS remains unbiased, but it is inefficient.

Rearranging Eq. (12) shows that the spatial error model is equivalent to an extended spatial lag model comprising both the spatially lagged dependent and the spatially lagged exogenous variables:

$$\mathbf{y} = \lambda\mathbf{W}\mathbf{y} + \mathbf{X}\boldsymbol{\beta} - \mathbf{W}\breve{\mathbf{X}}\boldsymbol{\gamma} + \boldsymbol{\mu}, \tag{14}$$

where $\breve{\mathbf{X}}$ is the original design matrix $\mathbf{X}$, except for the constant. The formal equivalence only holds if $k-1$ nonlinear constraints are satisfied, specifically $\lambda\boldsymbol{\beta} = -\boldsymbol{\gamma}$. This model is generally referred to as the "spatial Durbin" or "common factor" model. The similarity between the spatial error and the common factor model, discussed by Anselin in 2001, shows that tests with either the spatial error or the spatial lag model as the alternative hypothesis is likely to have power against the other alternative as well.

Testing for Spatial Effects in Spatial Process Models

Apart from focused tests with an informative alternative hypothesis that points to, for instance, the spatial lag or the spatial error model, various diffuse tests merely reflecting whether the residuals are spatially correlated have been developed. The oldest and best known is Moran's I for regression residuals, given by Eq. (15):

$$I = \left(\frac{n}{S_0}\right) \times \left(\frac{\mathbf{u}'\mathbf{W}\mathbf{u}}{\mathbf{u}'\mathbf{u}}\right), \tag{15}$$

where $\mathbf{u}$ is the $n \times 1$ vector of OLS residuals. As with Moran's I for raw data given in Eq. (5), statistical inference can be based on the assumption of asymptotic normality, but an exact approach depending on the matrix $\mathbf{X}$ is available too, although rather cumbersome to apply. Moran's I for regression residuals is a locally best-invariant test; moments and estimation details were given by Cliff and Ord in 1981 and Anselin in 1988. An alternative large-sample test derived under less restrictive assumptions was derived by Kelejian and Robinson in 1992.

Unidirectional and Multidirectional Tests for Spatial Dependence

Focused tests have a clear alternative hypothesis and are developed in a maximum likelihood framework. They either refer to a unidirectional alternative hypothesis dealing with one specific misspecification or a multidirectional alternative comprising various misspecifications, or they are robust in the sense that the test allows for the potential presence of a second type of misspecification. The Lagrange multiplier tests, LM_λ and LM_ρ, are unidirectional tests with the spatial error and the spatial lag model as their respective alternative hypotheses. The LM error test is identical to a scaled Moran coefficient (for row-standardized weights), and reads as follows:

$$LM_\lambda = \left(\frac{1}{T}\right)\left(\frac{\mathbf{u}'\mathbf{W}\mathbf{u}}{s^2}\right)^2, \tag{16}$$

where s^2 is the maximum likelihood variance $\mathbf{u}'\mathbf{u}/n$; T is a scalar computed as the trace of a quadratic expression in the weight matrix, $T = \mathrm{tr}(\mathbf{W}'\mathbf{W} + \mathbf{W}^2)$; and the test asymptotically follows a χ^2 distribution with one degree of freedom.

The LM lag test has the same asymptotic distribution, and looks similar:

$$LM_\rho = \left(\frac{1}{nJ_{\rho\cdot\beta}}\right)\left(\frac{\mathbf{u}'\mathbf{W}\mathbf{y}}{s^2}\right)^2, \tag{17}$$

where $J_{\rho\beta} = [(\mathbf{W}\mathbf{X}\mathbf{b})'\mathbf{M}(\mathbf{W}\mathbf{X}\mathbf{b}) + Ts^2]/ns^2$ is a part of the estimated information matrix, $\mathbf{b}$ is the OLS estimated parameter vector, and $\mathbf{M}$ is the projection matrix $\mathbf{I} - \mathbf{X}(\mathbf{X}'\mathbf{X})^{-1}\mathbf{X}'$.

Unfortunately, the LM error test cannot be used to distinguish between the spatial autoregressive and the moving-average processes. The same holds for multidirectional tests, such as the test against the ARAR and the ARMA models, a test that is similar but not equal to the sum of the error and the lag tests:

$$\mathrm{LM}_{\rho\lambda} = \frac{(\mathbf{u}'\mathbf{W}\mathbf{y}/s^2 - \mathbf{u}'\mathbf{W}\mathbf{u}/s^2)^2}{RJ_{\rho.\beta} - T} + \frac{(\mathbf{u}'\mathbf{W}\mathbf{u}/s^2)}{T}, \tag{18}$$

and follows a $\chi^2_{(2)}$ distribution.

Finally, a multidirectional test against spatial error dependence and heteroskedasticity does equal the sum of the LM error test and the familiar LM test for heteroskedasticity due to Breusch and Pagan (i.e., the BP test):

$$\mathrm{BP} = \frac{1}{2}\,\mathbf{f}'\mathbf{Z}(\mathbf{Z}'\mathbf{Z})^{-1}\mathbf{Z}'\mathbf{f}, \tag{19}$$

where the elements of **f** are defined as $f_i = (u_i/s)^2 - 1$, and **Z** is an $n \times k$ matrix containing the variables causing the heteroskedasticity. The BP test is asymptotically distributed as χ^2 with k degrees of freedom, and hence this joint test follows a $\chi^2_{(k+1)}$ distribution.

Rather than simple spatial heteroskedasticity, increasingly complex forms of spatial heterogeneity are possible as well. They occur in the case of discrete or continuous spatial variation, and they can be restricted to the means of homogeneous subgroups (spatial analysis of variance or a trend surface) or can extend to all coefficients (spatial regimes, and error component or spatial expansion models). Anselin provided details and appropriate test statistics in 1988.

Robust Tests for Spatial Dependence

The derivation of specification tests with locally misspecified alternatives makes it possible to distinguish more clearly between spatial error and spatial lag dependence. As explained by Anselin *et al.* in 1996, these tests are labeled robust because the test statistics account for the potential presence of a spatial lag or spatially correlated errors when testing for the presence of spatially correlated errors or a spatial lag, respectively. The test for a spatial error process robust to the local presence of a spatial lag is as follows:

$$\mathrm{LM}^*_\kappa = \frac{1}{T - T^2\left(nJ_{\rho\cdot\beta}\right)^{-1}}\left[\frac{\mathbf{u'Wu}}{s^2} - T\left(nJ_{\rho\cdot\beta}\right)^{-1}\frac{\mathbf{u'Wy}}{s^2}\right]^2. \tag{20}$$

This clearly shows the subtraction of a correction factor that accounts for the local misspecification of a spatial lag process. The test for a spatial lag process robust to the local presence of a spatial error is given by Eq. (21):

$$\mathrm{LM}^*_\rho = \frac{1}{nJ_{\rho\cdot\beta} - T}\left(\frac{\mathbf{u'Wy}}{s^2} - \frac{\mathbf{u'Wu}}{s^2}\right)^2. \tag{21}$$

Both tests asymptotically follow a $\chi^2_{(1)}$ distribution.

It would be fruitful if it was also possible to test for a spatial error or a spatial lag model assuming local misspecification in the form of heteroskedasticity. This approach, however, leads to a highly nonlinear problem, discussed in 1988 by Anselin.

Small Samples, Specification Strategies, and Software

In the spatial econometrics literature, the design of misspecification tests has predominantly focused on continuous regression models (although some recent results, e.g., those of Kelejian and Prucha in 2001, are also concerned with categorical models) and on the use of Lagrange multiplier tests. Although LM tests are asymptotically equivalent to Wald and likelihood ratio tests, LM tests are computationally convenient because they are based on parameter estimates under the null hypothesis. Although the increasing availability of large data samples alleviates the problem of the small sample distribution of the tests being markedly different from their asymptotic distribution, substantial efforts have been put into simulating the performance of the tests in small sample situations.

Small Sample Performance and Specification Strategies

The finite sample performance of spatial dependence tests across various "true" models is actually quite well documented; see Florax and De Graaff's 2004 comprehensive overview. For diffuse misspecification tests, it has been shown that the power of Moran's I is greater than the Kelejian–Robinson test. The latter is also more sensitive to departures of the normality of the error distribution, although, on the positive side, it has power against spatial dependence as well as heteroskedasticity. As would be expected, the power of focused LM tests against their correct alternative is very high. In general, the power of the tests in small samples is very satisfactory. Asymptotic results are approached for moderately sized samples of approximately 100 observations.

The power of the Lagrange multiplier spatial error (lag) test against a spatial lag (error) model seriously complicates the work of the practitioner of spatial modeling techniques. If both tests are significant, which underlying model is then correct? This issue is addressed in research on so-called specification strategies. Some researchers (for instance, Haining, Getis, Griffith, and Tiefelsdorf) advocate avoiding the search for the proper model specification altogether. They propose to "prewhiten" or "filter" the variables in such a way that the variables are free of spatial dependence and it is subsequently possible to resort to simple OLS for estimation purposes. As an alternative, it is possible to follow either a "classical" approach (start with simple OLS, perform LM tests, and select the model corresponding to the test with the highest value) or an approach inspired by David F. Hendry's work (start with a very general model including spatial effects, and reduce the model on the basis of significance tests). Florax *et al.* showed, by means of Monte Carlo simulation, that the classical approach outperforms the Hendry approach, but a comparison to the filtering approaches is not yet available. The latter, as well as a specification strategy centering on how to deal with the joint occurrence of heteroskedasticity (or spatial heterogeneity) and spatial dependence, would be extremely relevant for practitioners of spatial econometric modeling.

Apart from further research on the small-sample performance and specification strategies, several other unresolved questions or points deserve further attention. For instance, mainstream econometrics is reluctant to accept the *a priori* imposition of the elements of the weights matrix, which can be avoided by using so-called direct representation models. Moreover, further advances in the treatment of spatial effects in a panel data setting are required (see Baltagi *et al.*'s 2003 discussion), and computational problems when dealing with large data sets need to be further explored.

Software for Spatial Exploratory and Explanatory Analysis

In recent years, there has been an upsurge in the development and availability of software for spatial statistics and spatial econometrics. The two most complete software packages are SpaceStat and James LeSage's extensive spatial econometrics toolkit of routines for the estimation of spatial econometric models developed in MATLAB (see www.spatial-econometrics.com). Anselin's SpaceStat package combines both exploratory tools and an extensive array of classical misspecification tests and estimators for spatial models. The package can be complemented with a free downloadable tool for mapping and exploratory spatial data analysis called GeoDa (see http://sal.agecon.uiuc.edu). This tool also facilitates the building of weighting matrices, and the output can be easily transferred to SpaceStat. LeSage's toolkit is slightly more oriented toward modeling, and contains an array of Bayesian routines in addition to the classical tests and estimators. Several other online software sources are available. In the context of spatial econometric modeling, the following tools are the most relevant:

- Kelly Pace's spatial statistics toolbox (see http://spatial-statistics.com) contains routines for MATLAB and programs to estimate spatial models for large samples.
- Roger Bivand's SPDEP Spatial Analysis Tools website (see http://cran.r-project.org) gives programs for spatial autocorrelation and regression analysis written in R.
- S+ SpatialStats (see http://www.insightful.com) is a complementary tool to the S-Plus statistical package that contains some spatial regression routines.
- Winbugs–Geobugs (see http://www.mrc-bsu.cam.ac.uk) has routines for spatial models based on the Gibbs sampler and Markov chain Monte Carlo (MCMC) estimation.

Two developments are particularly noteworthy and promising. One is the ongoing development of software and the boost to this development that can be expected to result from so-called open-source projects, which are typically Web based and essentially constitute a platform and a common language for anybody who can credibly contribute to the development of software tools. The other development relates to the available information, the integration, and the accessibility of knowledge regarding spatial analysis. The U.S. National Science Foundation has recently funded a large-scale project to establish a Center for Spatially Integrated Social Science (CSISS; see www.csiss.org), which is intended to develop a successful clearinghouse for the tools, case studies, educational opportunities, and other resources needed by a spatially integrated social science approach. On the CSISS website, Luc Anselin has developed a spatial tools search engine that indexes a list of World Wide Web addresses (uniform resource locators, or URLs) and software archives of over 700 individual software titles. A spatial tool listing of links to portals (i.e., collections of links) is available as well.

Illustration of the Spatial Modeling Approach

The workings of the spatial econometric modeling approach can be illustrated by continuing with the economic growth example discussed previously. Table II presents the results for the Mankiw–Romer–Weil analysis in the first column. Economic growth over the period 1960–1985 is regressed on the GDP level in 1960, and three variables (investment share, population growth, and human capital) account for differences across countries. The implication of the estimation findings is that the 98 non-oil-producing countries are converging toward each other (or actually their so-called steady state) at a rate of 1.4% per year. The misspecification tests in column 1(OLS) show that the estimated standard errors are not accurate because of heteroskedasticity, and, more importantly, the estimates are biased because of the erroneously omitted spatially lagged dependent variable. The spatial lag model is therefore estimated, with results being reported in column 2 (Lag). The misspecification tests for this model indicate that there is no remaining spatial error correlation, but the model still suffers from heteroskedasticity. Then the error variance is allowed to differ between slow- and fast-growing economies; these results are presented in column 3 (Lag–Het). Relaxing the homoscedasticity restriction is, however, a rather mechanical solution to the potential relevance of spatial heterogeneity. It does not have a substantive interpretation. Therefore, the possibility of two spatial regimes is introduced, allowing the coefficients and the variances to differ between slow- and fast-growing economies. Columns 4a and 4b (Lag–Reg) show that this is an appropriate model. There is no heteroskedasticity when the regression parameters are allowed to vary between two different "clubs" of countries; the Chow test indicates

Table II Mankiw–Romer–Weil Specification with Diagnostics for Spatial Effects, and Spatial Process Models Allowing for Spatial Dependence and Heterogeneity

Variable				*Lag–Reg*	
	OLS (1)	*Lag (2)*	*Lag–Het (3)*	*Slow (4a)*	*Fast (4b)*
Constant	3.02 (3.65)	3.03 (3.95)	3.81 (5.65)	1.16 (1.17)	3.88 (5.39)
GDP Level, 1960	−0.29 (−4.68)	−0.28 (−4.86)	−0.31 (−5.70)	−0.08 (−1.30)	−0.26 (−3.92)
Investment share	0.52 (6.03)	0.52 (6.44)	0.56 (6.87)	0.21 (2.64)	0.41 (3.62)
Population growth	−0.51 (−1.75)	−0.29 (−1.09)	−0.17 (−0.73)	0.02 (0.07)	0.07 (0.27)
Human capital	0.23 (3.89)	0.19 (3.41)	0.20 (3.73)	0.06 (1.08)	0.17 (2.50)
Spatial lag GDP growth		0.74 (4.73)	0.74 (4.99)	0.60 (3.16)	
Convergence rate[a]	1.4	1.3	1.5	0.3	1.2
R^2 adjusted	0.46	0.50	0.56	0.75	
Maximized log likelihood	−26.95	−23.07	−20.18	9.50	
Breusch–Pagan	10.26**	10.93[b]	5.78[c]	0.83[c]	
Chow–Wald	—	—	—	86.85[d]	
I	3.12	—			
Lagrange multiplier error	2.24	0.06[e]			
Robust Lagrange multiplier error	5.08	—			
Lagrange multiplier lag	10.34	7.76[f]			
Robust Lagrange multiplier lag	13.18	—			

[a] In precents per year. The convergence rate is equal to 100[ln (β + 1)]/−T.

[b] Test on random coefficients. The Breusch–Pagan test for two regimes, groupings of slow- and fast-growing economies, is 1.97 (with probability 0.16) for the spatial lag model.

[c] Likelihood ratio test on groupwise heteroskedasticity (using slow- and fast-growing economies as groups).

[d] For the tests on equality of individual coefficients for the different groups, only the constant and the GDP level are significant (4.09 with probability 0.03, and 4.17 with probability 0.04, respectively).

[e] Lagrange multiplier test on remaining spatial error correlation.

[f] Likelihood ratio test on spatial lag.

that overall the estimated regression parameters for the two types of countries are not identical; and the spatially lagged dependent variable is highly significant and is large in magnitude. From the "reduced" form of the spatial lag model, $\mathbf{y} = (\mathbf{I} - \rho\mathbf{W})^{-1}(\mathbf{X}\boldsymbol{\beta} + \boldsymbol{\varepsilon})$, it is easily seen that the significance of the spatial lag variable can be caused by the omission of spatially correlated exogenous variables, and/or by spatially correlated factors within each country that are not considered in the specification. The modeling results reveal that instead of the 1.4% MRW convergence rate, a differentiation among slow-growing economies converging at a 0.3% rate, and fast-growing economies converging at a 1.2% rate, is more in accordance with reality. The ultimate model specification allows for spatial heterogeneity and accounts for the intrinsic spatial interrelatedness of countries' economies.

Conclusion

The use of appropriate spatial statistical and spatial econometric techniques is imperative. This applies to all analyses in the social sciences that are based, or should be based, on spatially referenced data. Such analyses are not necessarily restricted to cases in which data for a specific spatial area (cities, counties, states, or countries) are employed. For any analysis that is intrinsically spatial, whether it is operationalized using individual data, institutional data (firms, hospitals, and the like), or spatially demarcated data, the use of spatial analysis techniques is a *conditio sine qua non.* The growing availability of easy-to-use software for spatial analysis makes it tempting to simply "try" all kinds of different spatial models and techniques, but it is highly desirable that this blends in with a careful consideration of the inherent subtleties underlying different spatial modeling techniques, and theoretical considerations with respect to the topic at hand.

See Also the Following Articles

Modeling Diffusion Processes • Ordinary Least Squares (OLS) • Spatial Autocorrelation • Spatial Databases • Spatial Econometrics • Spatial Pattern Analysis • Spatial Sampling

Further Reading

Anselin, L. (1988). *Spatial Econometrics: Methods and Models.* Kluwer, Dordrecht.

Anselin, L. (1992). *SpaceStat: A Program for the Analysis of Spatial Data.* National Center for Geographic Information and Analysis, University of California, Santa Barbara.

Anselin, L. (1995). Local indicators of spatial association—LISA. *Geograph. Anal.* **27,** 93–115.

Anselin, L. (1996). The Moran scatterplot as an ESDA tool to assess local instability in spatial association. *Spatial Analytical Perspectives on GIS* (M. Fischer, H. Scholten, and D. Unwin, eds.) Taylor and Francis, London.

Anselin, L. (2001). Spatial econometrics. *Companion to Econometrics* (B. Baltagi, ed.) Basil Blackwell, Oxford.

Anselin, L., and Bera, A. K. (1998). Spatial dependence in linear regression models with an introduction to spatial econometrics. *Handbook of Applied Economic Statistics* (A. Ullah and D. Giles, eds.) Marcel Dekker, New York.

Anselin, L., and Rey, S. (1991). Properties of tests for spatial dependence in linear regression models. *Geograph. Anal.* **23,** 112–131.

Anselin, L., Bera, A. K., Florax, R. J. G. M., and Yoon, M. J. (1996). Simple diagnostic tests for spatial dependence. *Reg. Sci. Urban Econ.* **26,** 77–104.

Baltagi, B. H., Song, S. H., and Koh, W. (2003). Testing panel data regression models with spatial error correlation. *J. Economet.* **117,** 123–150.

Cliff, A. D., and Ord, J. K. (1981). *Spatial Processes: Models and Applications.* 2nd Ed. Pion, London.

Cressie, N. (1993). *Statistics for Spatial Data.* 2nd Ed. Wiley, New York.

Florax, R. J. G. M., and De Graaff, T. (2004). The performance of diagnostics tests for spatial dependence in linear regression models: A meta-analysis of simulation studies. *Advances in Spatial Econometrics: Methodology, Tools and Applications* (L. Anselin, R. J. G. M. Florax, and S. J. Rey, eds.) Springer Verlag, Berlin.

Florax, R. J. G. M., Folmer, H., and Rey, S. (2003). Specification searches in spatial econometrics: The relevance of Hendry's methodology. *Reg. Sci. Urban Econ.* **33,** 557–579.

Getis, A. (1991). Spatial interaction and spatial autocorrelation: A cross-product approach. *Environ. Plan. A* **23,** 1269–1277.

Getis, A., and Ord, K. J. (1992). The analysis of spatial association by means of distance statistics. *Geograph. Anal.* **24,** 189–206.

Kelejian, H. H., and Prucha, I. R. (2001). On the asymptotic distribution of the Moran *I* test statistic with applications. *J. Economet.* **104,** 219–257.

Kelejian, H. H., and Robinson, D. P. (1992). Spatial autocorrelation: A new computationally simple test with an application to per capita county policy expenditures. *Reg. Sci. Urban Econ.* **22,** 317–331.

Paelinck, J. H. P., and Klaassen, L. H. (1979). *Spatial Econometrics.* Saxon House, Farnborough.

Upton, G., and Fingleton, B. (1985). *Spatial Data Analysis by Example.* Wiley, New York.

Modeling Diffusion Processes

Andrew Cliff
University of Cambridge, Cambridge, UK

Peter Haggett
University of Bristol, Bristol, UK

Glossary

adoption curves Rates at which an innovation is adopted by a population through which a diffusion wave is passing. In the Hägerstrand model, the rates show distinctive changes over time.

barrier effects A variant of the Hägerstrand diffusion model developed by Yuill to show the spatial effects on spread of different categories of barrier.

Bartlett model An epidemic model developed by the British statistician M. S. Bartlett to show the relationships between the size of a community measured by population and the spacing of epidemic waves.

Bayesian entropy forecasting An approach to forecasting based on Bayes's theorem, which forecasts future events in a "least prejudiced" manner given any prior information.

contagious diffusion A type of diffusion process in which spatial contact is consistently maintained. It is also called neighborhood diffusion.

diffusion The process of spreading out or scattering over an area of the Earth's surface. It should not be confused with the physicist's use of the term to describe the slow mixing of gases or liquids with one another by molecular interpenetration.

Hägerstrand models A series of spatial diffusion models developed by the Swedish geographer Torsten Hägerstrand based on empirical studies of innovations in farm communities in southern Sweden. The models, first developed in the 1950s, were innovative in their pioneering of simulation using Monte Carlo methods.

hierarchic diffusion A type of diffusion wave that moves through the urban hierarchy in a cascading manner. Unlike contagious diffusion, its geographical pattern of spread may be discontinuous in space.

mean information field (MIF) A weighted matrix used in the Hägerstrand model to provide a probability surface for simulating the spread of a process of interest. Originally used for the spread of information, it has since been widened to include such processes as the spread of disease through a population. Values within the matrix may be symmetric or asymmetric.

Monte Carlo methods Methods for finding solutions to mathematical and statistical problems by simulation. Used when the analytical solution to the problem is either intractable or unacceptably time consuming.

relocation diffusion A type of spatial diffusion in which the center from which the object being spread also changes its location.

serial interval The average time between the observation of symptoms in one case and the observation of symptoms in a second case directly infected from the first.

simulation model The artificial generation of processes (usually by means of pseudo-random numbers on computers) to imitate the behavior of models that reproduce complex, real-world situations. Simulation is a useful heuristic device and can be of considerable help in the development of explanation. Literally, simulation is the art or science of pretending.

In the social sciences, the modeling of diffusion processes involves the study of the mechanisms by which phenomena of interest disperse or are dispersed from a center, to spread widely or disseminate within a region or a population. The areas of disciplinary application are very wide, from economics and sociology to social psychology and history. Here models from the geographical and epidemiological literature are used to illustrate the broad principles involved in model building.

The Nature of Diffusion Processes

Types of Diffusion Process

Expansion and Relocation Diffusion

In the geographical literature, the term diffusion has two distinct usages. Expansion diffusion is the process whereby a phenomenon of interest (this may be information, a material, or a disease) spreads from one place to another. In this expansion process, the item being diffused remains, and often intensifies, in the originating region, but new areas are also occupied by the item in subsequent time periods (Fig. 1A). Relocation diffusion is also a spatial spread process, but the items being diffused leave the areas where they originated as they move to new areas (as in population migration) (Fig. 1B). The two processes of expansion and relocation may be combined (Fig. 1C).

This combination is shown in Figure 1D, which traces the spread of one of the world's great cholera pandemics—the El Tor strain—between 1960 and 1971. In 1961, it began to spread with devastating speed from the Celebes. By 1964, it had reached India, replacing the normal cholera strain that had been endemic in the Ganges delta for centuries, and by the early 1970s, it was pushing south into central Africa and west into Russia and Europe.

Expansion diffusion occurs in two ways. Contagious spread depends on direct contact. It is in this way that many infectious diseases pass through a population, from person to person. This process is strongly influenced by distance, because nearby individuals or regions have a much higher probability of contact than remote individuals or regions. Therefore, contagious spread tends to occur in a centrifugal manner from the source region outward.

Expansion diffusion may, however, occur in a very different fashion, namely, by hierarchical spread. This describes transmission through an ordered sequence of classes or places. The process is typified by the diffusion of innovations from large metropolitan centers to remote villages. Within socially structured populations, innovations may be adopted first on the upper level of the social hierarchy and then trickle down to the lower levels. Cascade diffusion is a term reserved for processes that are always assumed to be downward from larger to smaller centers. When specifying a movement that may be either up or down the hierarchy, the preferred term is hierarchical diffusion.

Types of Diffusion Models

Alternative models of a spatial diffusion process are illustrated schematically in Fig. 2. Given the diffusion process being studied, there are three relevant questions an investigator may wish to ask:

1. From an accurate mapping of a sequence of stages it may be possible to identify the change mechanism and

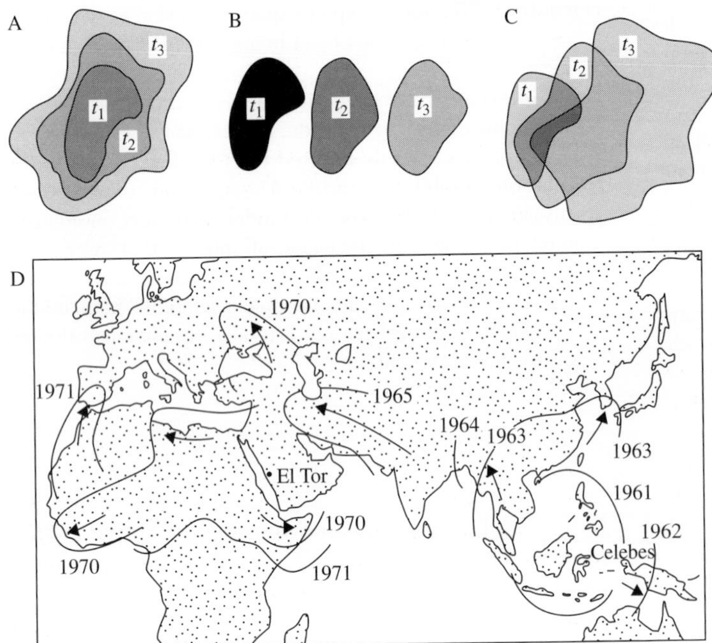

Figure 1 Types of spatial diffusion. (A) Expansion diffusion. (B) Relocation diffusion. (C) Combined expansion and relocation processes. The term t_i denotes the time period. (D) Example of a combined diffusion wave: the spread of the El Tor cholera pandemic, 1960–1971. Reproduced from Haggett (2000, Fig. 1.1, p. 2) by permission of Oxford University Press.

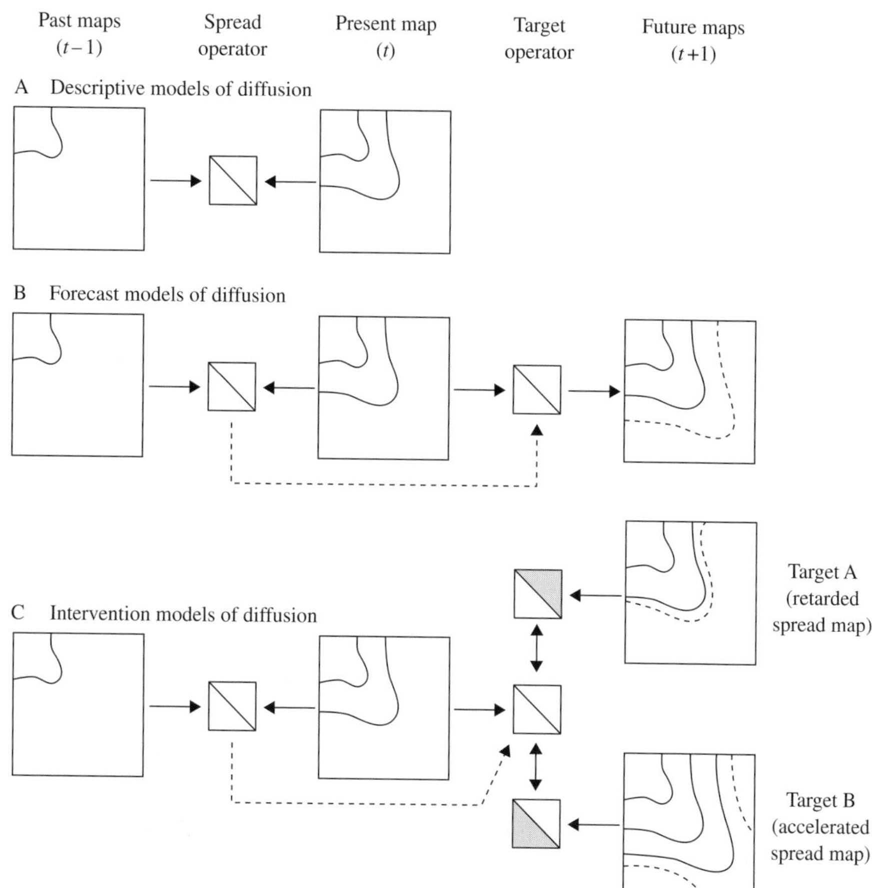

Figure 2 Map sequences as a predictive device. Descriptive, predictive, and interdictive models of a spatial diffusion process. The creation of operators (e.g., mean information fields) from a map sequence allows the forward progression of the map to a future time period. Reproduced from Haggett (2000, Fig. 1.12, p. 30) by permission of Oxford University Press.

summarize the findings in terms of a descriptive model. The key questions here are what is happening, and why?

2. If a model can simulate the sequence of past conditions reasonably accurately, then we may be able to go on to say something about future conditions. This move from the known to the unknown is characteristic of a predictive model: the basic idea is summarized in Fig. 2B. One must search for the target operator that appears—in terms of this model—to convert early maps of the past into later maps of the present and future. If such an operator can be found, and if some continuity can be assumed in this process (the heroic assumption that lies behind so much forecasting), then a future map can be sketched in. The error bands associated with each "contour" will be given by the width of the lines on the map; the further forward in time, the wider those bands are likely to be.

3. But planners and decision makers may want to alter the future, say, to accelerate or stop a diffusion wave. So the third question is what will happen in the future, if there is some specific intervention? Models that try to accommodate this third order of complexity are termed interdictive models. These are shown in Fig. 2C.

Different Disciplinary Approaches to Diffusion Study

Spatial diffusion studies have not been the province of any single discipline. As the surveys by Brown and Rogers showed, approaches have varied with the background and traditions of the researchers involved. In the United States, the Berkeley School of Cultural Geography, led by Carl O. Sauer, played a central role. Sauer and his students were interested in how diffusion processes might help to account for the dispersal of cultural traits from given origins or cultural hearths. Sauer himself considered the cultural diffusion idea at the world scale in his 1952 Bowman lectures, "Agricultural Origins and Dispersals." It was also in the United States that the historian Frederick Jackson Turner developed his great theme of the "frontier" in U.S. history, which has proved to be one of the key ideas of cultural diffusion studies. Turner's work was taken up by Webb in his classic regional study of the central grasslands in the United States, *The Great Plains*.

Purely economic phenomena have similarly been studied within a diffusion framework. An example appears in Fig. 3, taken from work by Lösch on price changes in space. This figure redraws from his data the spread of the business depression of 1929–1931 in the United States through the state of Iowa. Note the steady east-to-west movement of the depression.

Two further lines of approach to diffusion study have come from the fields of sociology and epidemiology. In sociology, the concern has focused on the spread of concepts through a society, the role of leaders in starting innovations, and the problem of resistance to change. Rogers reviewed hundreds of such studies, largely concerned with the innovation of new techniques in farming communities of the United States. Work in this field has concentrated on the factors that influence the propensity to adopt innovations and the speed of take-up. In epidemiology, the analysis of disease transmission as a spatial spread process has been a major interest since the work of Hamer at the turn of the 20th century; it continues to be an important concern.

Diffusion as a Wave Process

Innovation Profiles

Much of the geographical interest in diffusion studies stems from the work of the Swedish geographer Torsten Hägerstrand. His *Innovation Diffusion as a Spatial Process* (1968) was concerned with the acceptance by farmers of several agricultural innovations, such as the control of bovine tuberculosis by vaccination and subsidies for the improvement of grazing, in an area of central Sweden. In one of his early studies, Hägerstrand described a four-stage model for the passage of what he termed innovation waves (innovations *förloppet*), but which are more generally called diffusion waves.

From maps of the diffusion of various innovations in Sweden, ranging from bus routes to agricultural methods,

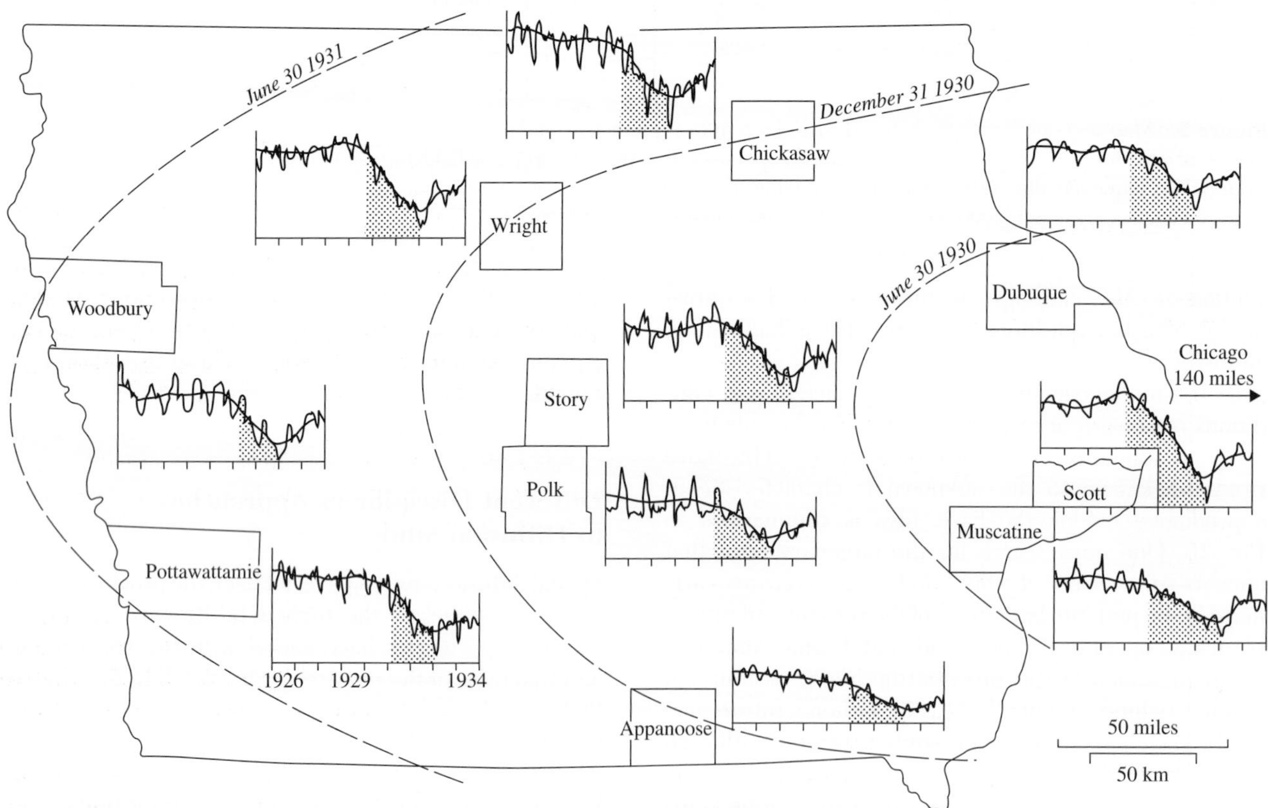

Figure 3 Economic impulses as diffusion waves. Spread of the business depression of 1929–1931 through the state of Iowa in the central United States. Graphs show indices of business activity with their running means for 10 counties. Time contours show time of arrival of the depression "front." Redrawn from Lösch, in Haggett (2000, Fig. 1.2, p. 4) by permission of Oxford University Press.

Hägerstrand drew a series of cross-sections to show the profile of the wave form at different points in time. He suggested that diffusion profiles can be broken into four types, each of which describes a distinct stage in the passage of an innovation through an area. Consider Fig. 4A, which shows the relationship between the proportion of adopters of an innovation against distance from the original center of innovation.

The primary stage marks the beginning of the diffusion process. A center of adoption is established at the origin. There is a strong contrast in the level of adoption between this center and remote areas that is reflected in the steep decline of the level of adoption curve beyond the origin. The diffusion stage signals the start of the actual spread process; there is a powerful centrifugal effect, resulting in the rapid growth of acceptance in areas distant from the origin and by a reduction in the strong regional contrasts typical of the primary stage. This results in a flattening of the slope of the proportion of adopters curve. In the condensing stage, the relative increase in the numbers accepting an item is equal in all locations, regardless of their distance from the original innovation center; the acceptance curve moves in a parallel fashion. The final, saturation stage is marked by a slowing and eventual cessation of the diffusion process, which produces a further flattening of the acceptance curve. In this final stage, the item being diffused has been adopted throughout the country, so that there is very little regional variation.

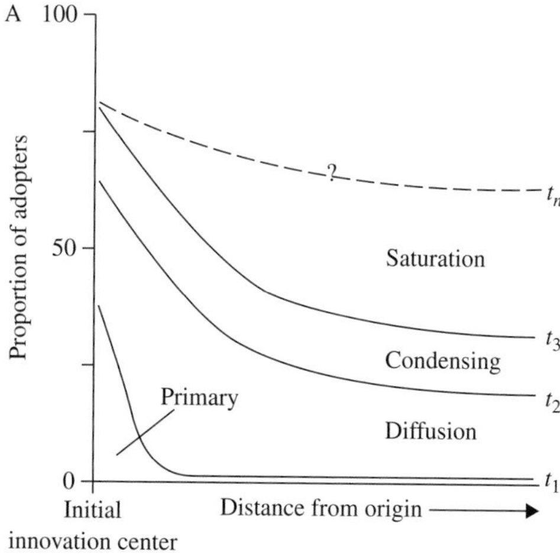

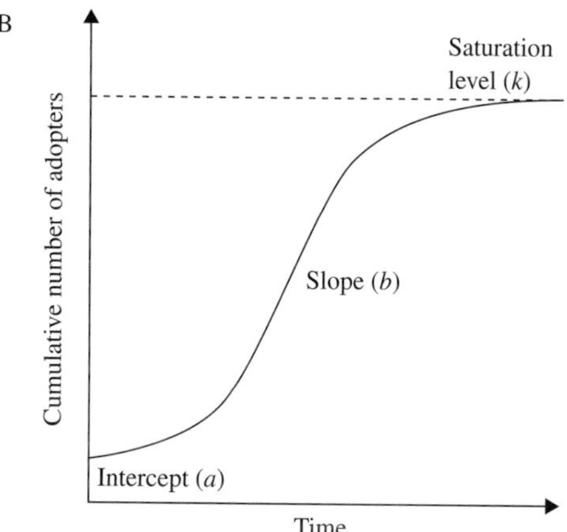

Figure 4 (A) Hägerstrand hypothetical profiles for diffusion waves. (B) Logistic curve. Reproduced from Cliff *et al.* (1981, Figs. 2.9, 2.10, pp. 17–18) with the permission of Cambridge University Press.

Logistic Models

The shape of the profile in time and space has been formally modeled. First the temporal build-up in the number of adopters of an innovation is considered. If the total susceptible population at the start ($t=0$) of the process is known, then the cumulative number of that total who will have become adopters at $t=1, 2, \ldots$ commonly follows an S-shaped curve when plotted against t (see Fig. 4B). y_t is used to denote the cumulative number of adopters in the total population at risk. Acceptance of an innovation is rather slow at first, but is followed by a rapid build-up as the innovation "takes off." Ultimately, there is a leveling off as saturation of the susceptible population is approached. The model most commonly fitted to profiles of the form of Fig. 4B is the logistic model.

The logistic model is given by

$$p_t = (1+e^{a-bt})^{-1} \tag{1}$$

or

$$y_t = k(1+e^{a-bt})^{-1}, \tag{2}$$

where p_t is the proportion of adopters in the population at t, y_t is as defined above, and a, b, and k are parameters. The model is readily fitted by ordinary least squares since both Eqs. (1) and (2) reduce to simple regressions upon taking the appropriate transformation. The parameter k is usually interpreted as the maximum possible number of adopters (saturation level), a is the intercept, and b is the slope coefficient.

The structure of Eq. (2) is made clearer by looking at the first derivative, or the rate of change r_t in p_t with respect to time, where

$$r_t = \frac{dp_t}{dt} = bp_t(1-p_t). \tag{3}$$

Since p_t is the proportion of the susceptible population that has actually adopted by time t, $(1-p_t)$ is the proportion still at risk. The quantity $p_t(1-p_t)$, then, represents the probability that a random meeting between two individuals is between an adopter and a potential adopter, while the parameter b represents the rate at which meetings take place (the rate of mixing). Note that b is the same whatever the distance between the adopter and the potential adopter, that is,

Eq. (1) implies spatially homogenous mixing between adopters and potential adopters. This assumption is in conflict with the contagious diffusion idea discussed earlier. Cliff and Ord in 1975 suggested the following extension of the logistic model that allows homogeneous mixing within n regions ($i = 1, 2, \ldots, n$) but less mixing between regions (compare Rapoport's distance-biased net or island model):

$$r_{it} = (1 - p_{it})\big(b_i p_{it} + \sum_{j \neq i} c_{ij} p_{jt}\big). \tag{4}$$

Here c_{ij} is the rate of mixing between the ith and the jth regions. Extensions of the logistic model to handle inhomogeneous mixing as a function of the distance between adopters and potential adopters may be applied provided that a diffusion pole (that is, the original center from which the diffusion process started) can be specified.

Hägerstrand's Monte Carlo Model

The first major attempt within geography to formulate a model of the process of spatial diffusion was that of Hägerstrand. In developing the model in the context of innovation diffusion, Hägerstrand assumed that the decision of a potential adopter to accept an innovation was based solely upon information received orally at face-to-face meetings between the potential adopter and adopters. He further assumed that the contact probabilities between tellers and receivers conformed to the neighborhood effect.

Rules of the Basic Model

Hägerstrand's model was stochastic and was based upon the following rules:

1. The input numbers and spatial locations of adopters in the model were the actual configurations at the start of the diffusion process. The study area was divided up by a lattice of 5 km × 5 km.
2. A potential adopter was assumed to accept the innovation as soon as he or she was told by an adopter.
3. In each iteration, every adopter was allowed to contact one other person, adopter or non-adopter. The probability, p_i, that a carrier would contact an individual located in the ith cell of the study lattice is shown in Fig. 5. Each cell in this floating grid, which Hägerstrand called a mean information field (MIF), is 5 km × 5 km, and outside the grid, $p_i = 0$. These probabilities were estimated from an analysis of migration and telephone traffic data. The floating grid was placed over each existing adopter in turn, so that the adopter was located in the central cell of the MIF. What Fig. 5 tells us is that an adopter located in the center of the central cell of the MIF has approximately a 44% chance of contacting someone within ~0–2.5 km of him- or herself, and that this contact probability decays over space to less than 1% at a distance of about 14 km (along diagonals) from the adopter and to 0 beyond 14–18 km. Since the probability is taken as 0 beyond 18 km, the MIF is exponentially bounded.

The location of each carrier's contact was determined in two steps. First, a random number r, $0 \leq r \leq 1$, from a rectangular distribution located the cell i according to the rule

$$\sum_{m=1}^{i-1} Q_m < r \sum_{m=1}^{i} \leq Q_m, \tag{5}$$

where Q_m, the probability of a contact in cell m with population n_m, is

$$Q_m = \frac{P_m n_m}{\sum_{m=1}^{25} P_m n_m}. \tag{6}$$

A second random number from a rectangular destruction on $[1, n_m]$ was drawn to locate the receiver in the cell. If the receiver was a potential adopter, he or she immediately became an adopter by rule (2); if the receiver was an existing adopter, the message was lost; if the receiver was identical with the carrier, a new address was sampled.

To take into account the reduction in interpersonal communication likely to be caused by physical features such as rivers and forests, two simplified types of barrier were introduced into the model plane, namely zero- and half-contact barriers. When an address crossed a half-contact barrier, the telling was cancelled with probability 0.5. However, two half-contact barriers in combination were considered equal to one zero-contact barrier. Using this model, Hägerstrand performed a series of computer runs to simulate the spatial pattern of acceptance of a subsidy for the improvement of pasture on small farms in the Asby district of central Sweden (see Fig. 6).

0.0096	0.0140	0.0168	0.0140	0.0096
0.0140	0.0301	0.0547	0.0301	0.0140
0.0168	0.0547	0.4431	0.0547	0.0168
0.0140	0.0301	0.0547	0.0301	0.0140
0.0096	0.0140	0.0168	0.0140	0.0096

Figure 5 Hägerstrand's mean information field (MIF). Each grid cell is 5 km × 5 km. Reproduced from Cliff et al. (1981, Fig. 2.12, p. 21) with the permission of Cambridge University Press.

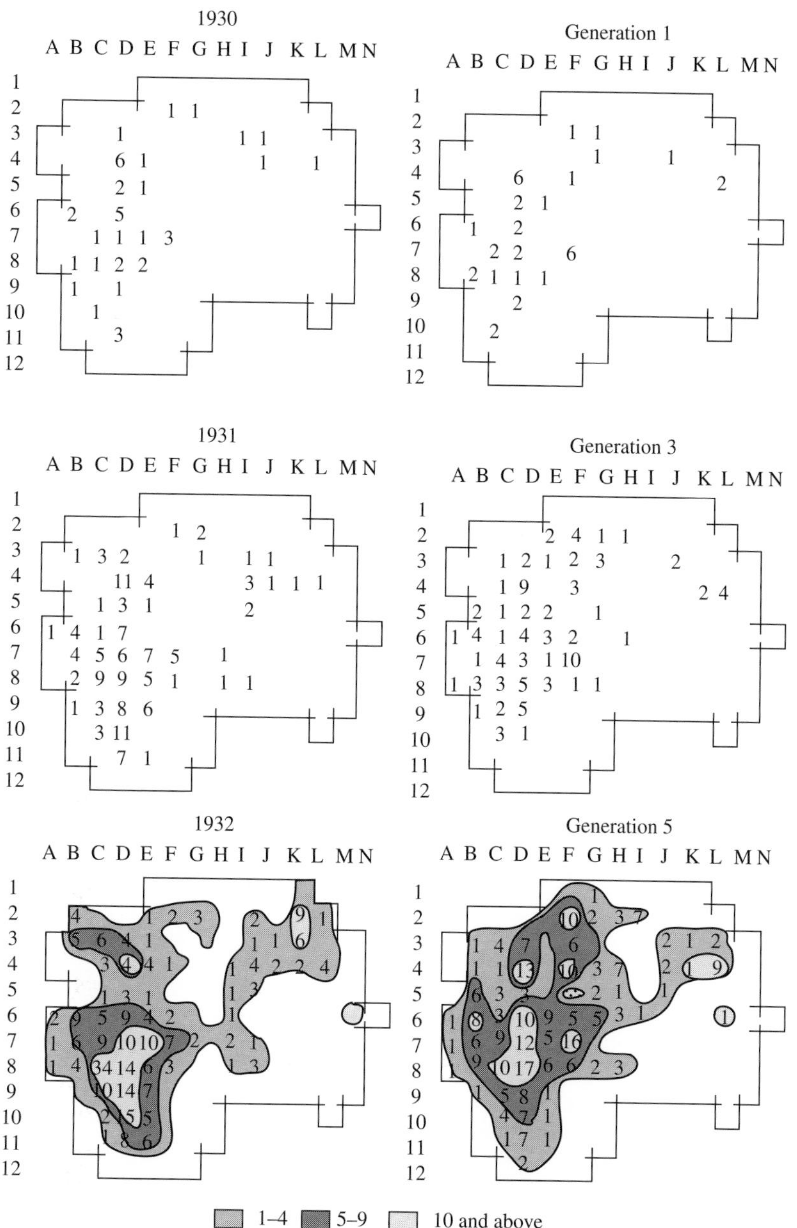

Figure 6 Real and simulated diffusion patterns. Simulation of the spatial pattern of the number of adopters of an improved pasture subsidy in central Sweden. From the initial distribution of adopting farmers in 1929 (generation 0), the next 3 years are shown; the actual distribution on the left (1930, 1931, 1932) and the simulated distribution on the right (generations 1, 3, and 5). Each square cell on the map is 5 km × 5 km on the ground, and numbers give the number of adopters in each cell. Redrawn from Hägerstrand, in Haggett (2000, Fig. 1.3, p. 8) by permission of Oxford University Press.

Modification of the Hägerstrand Model

Barriers

Although in rule (4) of the model, a very simplified system of resistance to communication was proposed by Hägerstrand, barriers to diffusion waves are likely to be much more complex in reality. The effect of barriers has been looked at by Yuill. His study used a 30 × 18 regular lattice of cells, and his MIF used a 3 × 3 grid rather than the 5 × 5 grid used by Hägerstrand. Fig. 7A gives the MIF, and it is assumed that two initial adopters (the solid

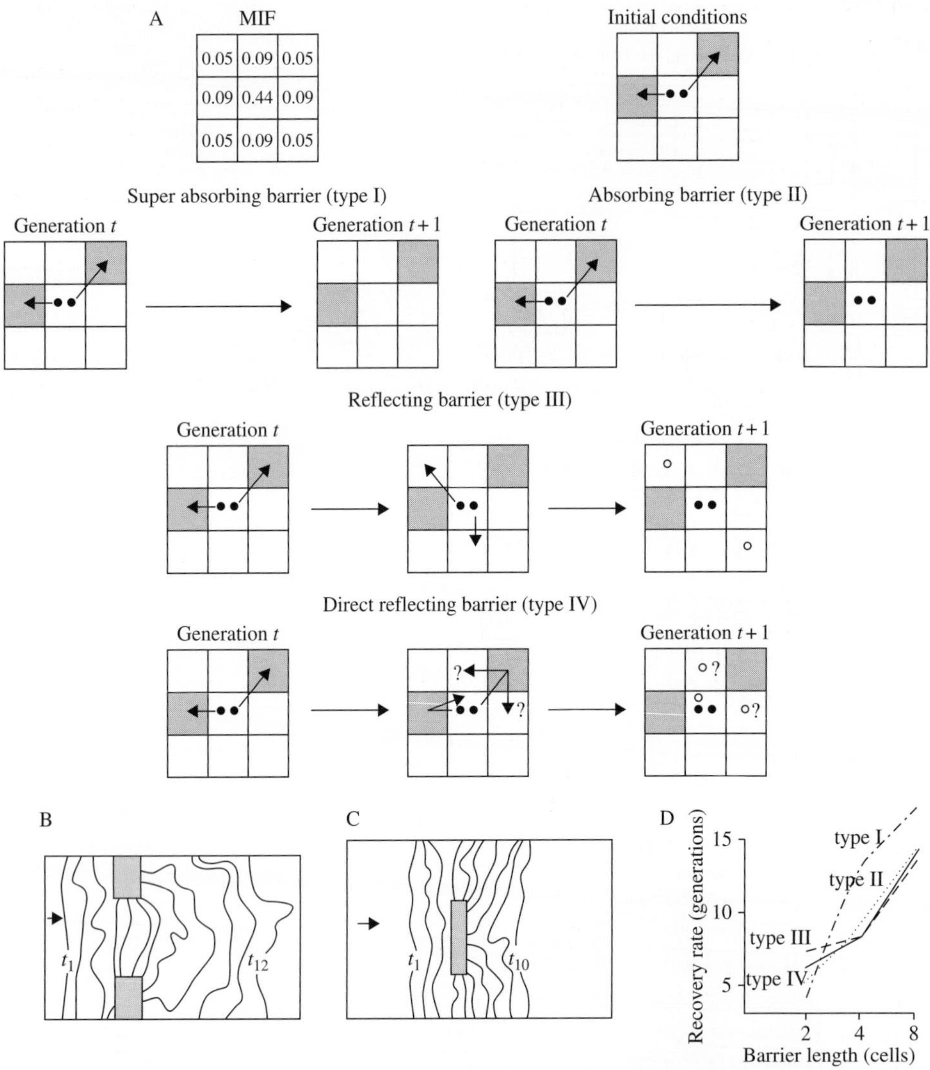

Figure 7 Barrier effects on diffusion waves. (A) Mean information field and the four types of barriers used by Yuill. (B) Diffusion wave passing through opening in an absorbing barrier. (C) Diffusion wave passing around a bar barrier. (D) Recovery rates around bar barriers. Reproduced from Cliff *et al.* (1981, Fig. 2.14, p. 24) with the permission of Cambridge University Press.

circles) have been located in the central cell. Imagine further that centering the grid over those two adopters has caused two cells of the MIF to be occupied by barriers (the stippled cells). The location of each carrier's contact in the next generation of the model (compare Hägerstrand's Monte Carlo experiment) is shown by the arrows.

Yuill envisaged four types of barrier cell in decreasing order of blocking effectiveness: type I, the super-absorbing barrier, which absorbed the new contacts and destroyed the transmitters; type II, the absorbing barrier, which absorbed the new contacts but did not affect the transmitters; type III, the reflecting barrier, which absorbed the new contracts, but the transmitters were allowed to make a new contact in the same generation (the open circles); and type IV, the direct reflecting barrier, which did not absorb the contacts but instead reflected them randomly to the nearest available cell. Each situation was separately programmed and its results plotted. Figure 7B shows the advance of a linear diffusion wave ($t = 1$) through an opening in an absorbing bar barrier. The wave front becomes distorted in its passage through the opening because of the loss of contacts at the barrier edge (a frictional drag effect), but it reforms by about the 12th generation. Yuill referred to the number of generations required for the wave to return to its original form after first encountering the barrier as the recovery rate. An alternative version of the bar barrier is shown in Fig. 7C, where the diffusion wave passes around a bar and reforms after about nine generations. Here the recovery rate is directly related both to the barrier length and to the kind of barrier, with the curve for the type I (super-absorbing) barrier showing strong contrasts to those of the other three types (Fig. 7D).

Corridors

The obverse of a barrier is a corridor of movement, and the identification of such corridors was the theme of a 1973 study by Levison *et al.* They constructed a Monte Carlo model to simulate the pattern of settlement of Polynesia by raft voyagers. The drift tracks of the rafts, from a variety of starting points, were determined by sampling from ancillary probability distributions describing factors such as wind frequency, direction and force, ocean currents, and survival rates. Voyages were terminated by either (1) contact with another island or (2) expiry of the voyage as determined by survival rate probabilities. Mapping the distribution of voyage termination points in Polynesia permitted estimates to be made of the probability of reaching various Polynesian islands from the different starting points.

For certain kinds of innovations, a strong hierarchical effect might be expected in the adoption regime rather than a simple neighborhood effect. Figure 8A shows a

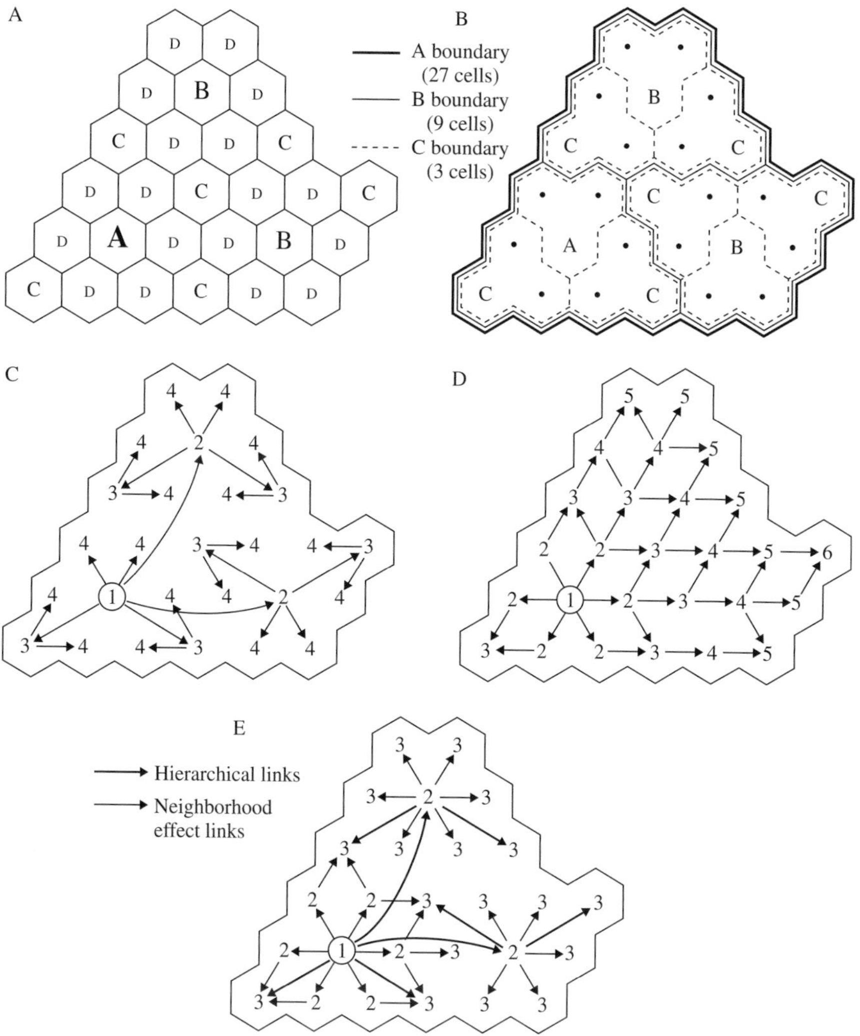

Figure 8 Patterns of diffusion through a system of settlements. (A) Hypothetical landscape with four sizes of settlements ranging from the very large, A (e.g., cities), to very small, D (e.g., villages). (B) Boundaries of spheres of influence of settlements. (C) Purely hierarchical diffusion process from large city A. (D) Purely neighborhood diffusion from city A. (E) Combined hierarchical and neighborhood diffusion processes. Vectors show spread sequence while numbers indicate time period innovation reaches the settlements. Reproduced from Haggett *et al.* (1977, p. 241) with the permission of Hodder Arnold.

hypothetical landscape. Center A is the biggest settlement (e.g., a city) and, for shopping and other social and economic services, influences the largest tract of surrounding countryside. This sphere of influence is demarcated by the solid boundary line in Figure 8. Centers of type D are the smallest settlements (e.g., villages), and influence the smallest amount of surrounding countryside (shown by the broken lines in Fig. 8B). An innovation is introduced in center A and is allowed to diffuse to other places by purely hierarchical spread, purely contagious spread, and by mixed process. The mixed process produces the fastest spread, the purely contagious spread the slowest.

Epidemiological Models

Epidemic Modeling: A Historical Note

Interest in the geographical distribution and spread of diseases around the globe is of some antiquity. Hirsch's *Handbuch der Geographische-Historische Pathologie* was first published nearly a century and a half ago; the history of mathematical modeling of epidemic processes goes back still further. Among the first applications of mathematics to the study of infectious disease was that of Bernoulli in 1760 when he used a mathematical method to evaluate the effectiveness of the techniques of variolation against smallpox. As disease statistics accumulated during the early 19th century, Farr in 1840 was able to fit a normal curve to smoothed quarterly data on deaths from smallpox in England and Wales over the period 1837–1839. This empirical curve-fitting approach was further developed by Brownlee, who considered in detail the geometry of epidemic curves.

The origin of modern mathematical epidemiology owes much to the work of En'ko, Hamer, Ross, Soper, Reed, Frost, Kermack, and McKendrick, who, using different approaches, began to translate specific theories about the transmission of infectious disease into simple, but precise, mathematical statements and to investigate the properties of the resulting models.

The Hamer-Soper Mass Action Model

The simplest form of an epidemic model, the Hamer-Soper model, is shown in Fig. 9A. It was originally developed by Hamer in 1906 to describe the recurring sequences of measles waves affecting large English cities in the late Victorian period. It has been greatly modified over the last half century to incorporate probabilistic, spatial, and public health features.

The basic wave-generating mechanism is a simple one. At any time t, assume that the total population in a region can be divided into three classes: the population at risk or susceptible population of size S_t, the infected population of size I_t, and the removed population of size R_t. The removed population is taken to be composed of people who have had the disease, but who can no longer pass it on to others because of recovery, isolation on the appearance of overt symptoms of the disease, or death. The infected element in a population is augmented by the homogeneous mixing of susceptibles with infectives ($S \times I$) at a rate determined by a diffusion coefficient (β) appropriate to the disease. The infected element is depleted by recovery of individuals after a time period at a rate controlled by the recovery coefficient (γ). As Fig. 9A shows, the addition of further parameters to the model, such as the birth rate, μ, allows more complex models to be generated.

The formal articulation of Fig. 9A into a mathematical model handles three types of transition (Table I):

1. A susceptible being infected by contact with an infective.
2. An infective being removed. It is assumed that infection confers lifelong immunity to further attack after recovery, which is reasonable for many infectious diseases such as measles and whooping cough.
3. A susceptible birth. This can come about through a child growing up into the critical age range (that is, reaching about 6 months of age).

As formulated, this model is aspatial. However, as has already been seen, by their very nature diffusion processes imply geographical spread between areas. Such spread may be result from a variety of social factors

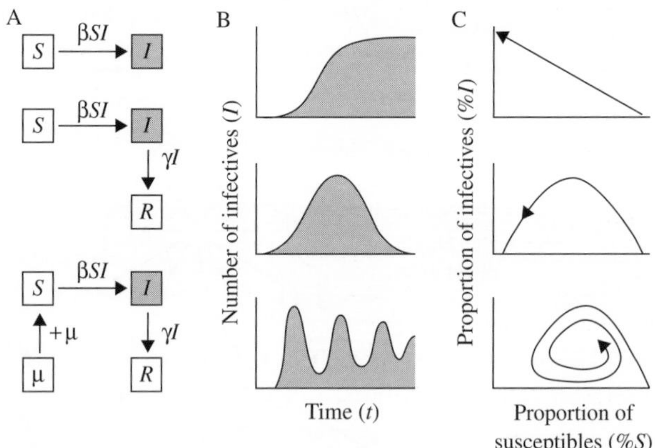

Figure 9 Basic elements in the three simplest mass action models of wave generation. (A) Elements in the model: S, susceptibles; I, infectives; R, recovereds; μ, births; β, infection (diffusion) rate; γ, recovery rate. (B) Typical time profiles for the model with number of infectives stippled. (C) Trajectory of typical waves in infective-susceptible space. Reproduced from Haggett (2000, Fig. 1.7, p. 22) by permission of Oxford University Press.

Table I Mass Action Models: Transition Types and Rates

Transition	*Rate*
1. $S \rightarrow S-1; I \rightarrow I+1; R \rightarrow R$	βIS
2. $S \rightarrow S; I \rightarrow I-1; R \rightarrow R+1$	γI
3. $S \rightarrow S+1; I \rightarrow I; R \rightarrow R$	μ

that cause mixing of people: for example, at the local scale, travel between workplace and home, or shopping and school trips; at the national level, by relocation of homes when seeking new employment; at the international level, by holidays. To allow for the flux of infected and susceptible individuals at all these geographical scales, spatial versions of the basic model are required.

Spatial Versions of the Hamer-Soper Model

Empirical validation of the mass action models described previously was provided by the work of statistician Maurice Bartlett. He investigated the relationship between the periodicity of measles epidemics and population size for a series of urban centers on both sides of the Atlantic. His findings for British cities are summarized in Fig. 10. The largest cities have an endemic pattern with periodic eruptions (type I), while cities below a certain size threshold have an epidemic pattern with fade-outs (type II), or even miss some epidemics altogether (type III cities). For measles, Bartlett found the endemicity size threshold to be approximately a quarter of a million people. Subsequent research has shown that the threshold for any infectious disease is likely to be rather variable, with the level influenced by population densities and vaccination levels, but the threshold principle demonstrated by Bartlett remains intact.

Once the population size of an area falls below the threshold, then, when the disease concerned is eventually extinguished, it can recur only by reintroduction from other reservoir areas. Thus, the generalized persistence of disease implies geographical transmission between regions as shown in Fig. 11. In large cities above the size threshold, like community A, a continuous trickle of cases is reported. These provide the reservoir of infection that sparks a major epidemic when the susceptible population, S, builds up to a critical level. This build-up occurs only as children are born, lose their mother-conferred immunity, and escape vaccination or contact with the disease. Eventually the S population will increase sufficiently for an epidemic to occur. When this happens, the S population is diminished and the stock of infectives, I, increases as individuals are transferred by infection from the S to the I population. This generates the D-shaped

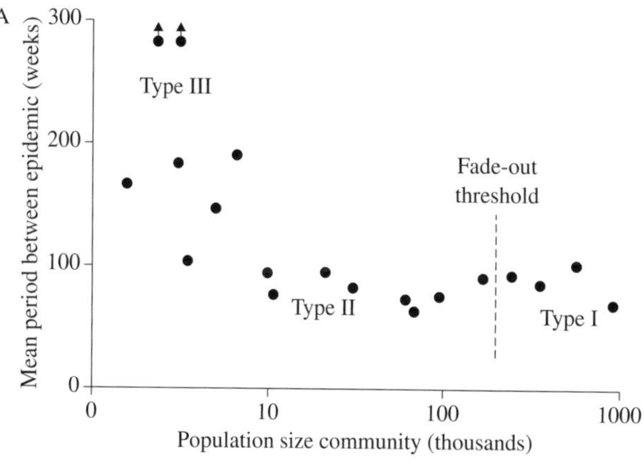

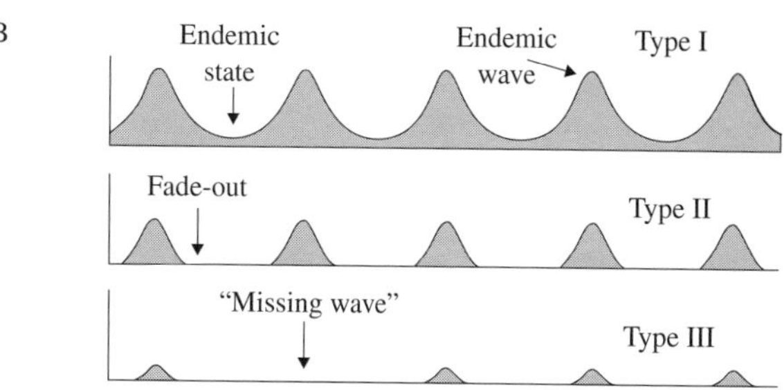

Figure 10 Bartlett's findings on city size and epidemic recurrence. (A) The impact of population size on the spacing of measles epidemics for 19 English towns. (B) Characteristic epidemic profiles for the three types indicated in (A). Reproduced from Haggett (2000, Fig. 1.8, p. 23) by permission of Oxford University Press.

relationship over time between sizes of the S and I populations shown on the end plane of the block diagram.

With measles, if the total population of a community falls below the quarter-million size threshold, as in settlements B and C of Fig. 11, epidemics can, as has been noted above, only arise when the virus is reintroduced by the influx of infected individuals (so-called index cases) from reservoir areas. These movements are shown by the broad arrows in Fig. 11. In such smaller communities, the S population is insufficient to maintain a continuous record of infection. The disease dies out and the S population grows in the absence of infection. Eventually the S population will become large enough to sustain an epidemic when an index case arrives. Given that the total population of the community is insufficient to renew the S population by births as rapidly as it is diminished by infection, the epidemic will eventually die out.

It is the repetition of this basic process that generates the successive epidemic waves witnessed in most communities. Of special significance is the way in which the continuous infection and characteristically regular type I epidemic waves of endemic communities break down as population size diminishes into discrete but regular type II waves in community B and then into discrete

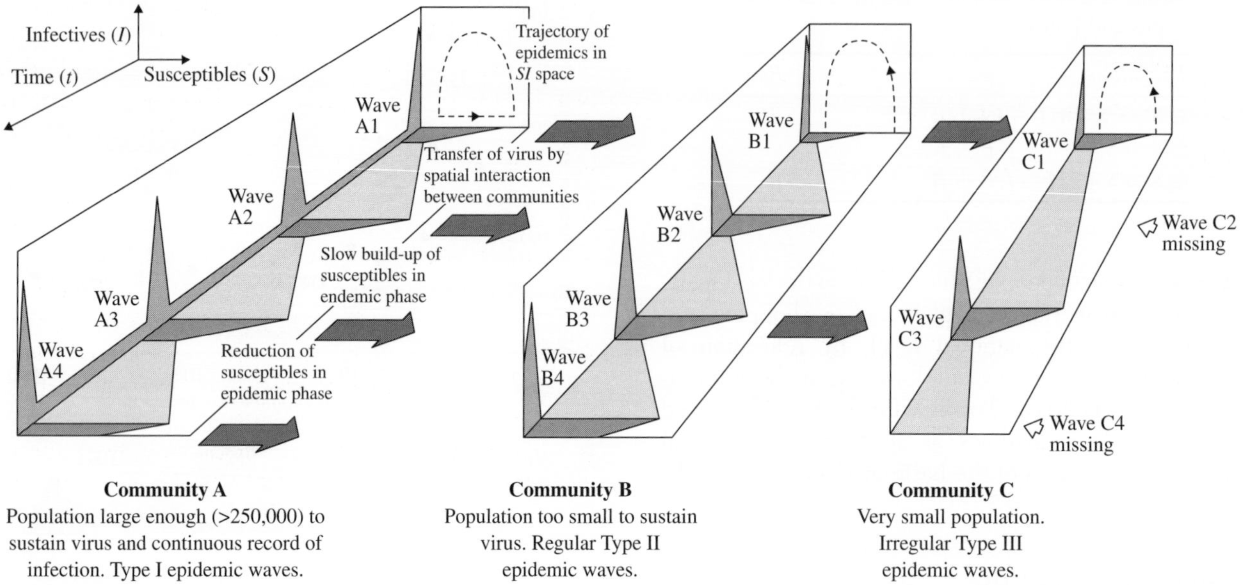

Figure 11 Conceptual view of the spread of a communicable disease (measles) in communities of different population sizes. Stages in spread correspond to the Bartlett model. Reproduced from Haggett (2000, Fig. 1.9, p. 25) by permission of Oxford University Press.

and irregularly spaced type III waves in community C. Thus, disease-free windows will automatically appear in both time and space whenever population totals are small and geographical densities are low.

The Chain Binomial Model

A second set of epidemic models based on chain frequencies has been developed in parallel with the mass action models. A major distinction exists between two types of model in the level of data grouping at which they are designed to operate. The mass action model was constructed for use with aggregated data, and it can be readily adapted to deal with spatial units at the regional, national, and international levels. Conversely, the chain binomial was originally developed for the micro-scale analysis of intra-family chains of transmission of infectious diseases.

Cliff *et al.* adapted the chain binomial to provide forecasts at the aggregated data level used at a regional scale. The basic model for a single district supposes that it is possible to record the state of the system at times $t = 1, 2, \ldots$ Ideally, the time interval between recording points should correspond in length to the serial interval of the disease. This ensures that multiple epidemic cycles in a single time period are not witnessed, provided that each infected individual is isolated after the appearance of symptoms. The total population in a given district at the beginning of time period t, denoted by N_t, will contain S_t susceptibles, I_t infectives, who can transmit the disease to susceptibles, and R_t removals. During the tth time period, N_t may be modified by the addition of A_t arrivals (births and/or immigrants) and the loss of D_t departures (deaths and/or emigrants). Finally, let X_t denote the number of new cases that occur in time period t.

The following accounting identities may then be written down for each medical district:

$$\begin{aligned} N_{t+1} &= N_t + A_t - D_t, \\ N_t &= S_t + I_t + R_t. \end{aligned} \tag{7}$$

If $\alpha_t A_t$ denotes the number of individuals among the new arrivals who are infectives, while $\delta_t D_t$ denotes the number of infectives among the departures, then

$$I_{t+1} = I_t + X_t - [R_{t+1} - R_t] + \alpha_t A_t - \delta_t D_t. \tag{8}$$

The arrivals term in Eq. (8) is vital in cases considering a disease that has to be re-imported into an area after local fade-out; these arrivals are the individuals who trigger a recurrence of the disease when the number of susceptibles is high.

Kendall and Spatial Waves

The relationship between the input and output components in the wave-generating model has been shown by Cambridge statistician David Kendall to be critical. If the magnitude of the input by the diffusion coefficient (β) and the output by the recovery coefficient (γ) is measured, then the ratio of the two, γ/β, defines the threshold (given by the Greek letter rho, ρ) in terms of population size. For example, where γ is 0.5 and β is 0.0001, ρ would be estimated at 5000.

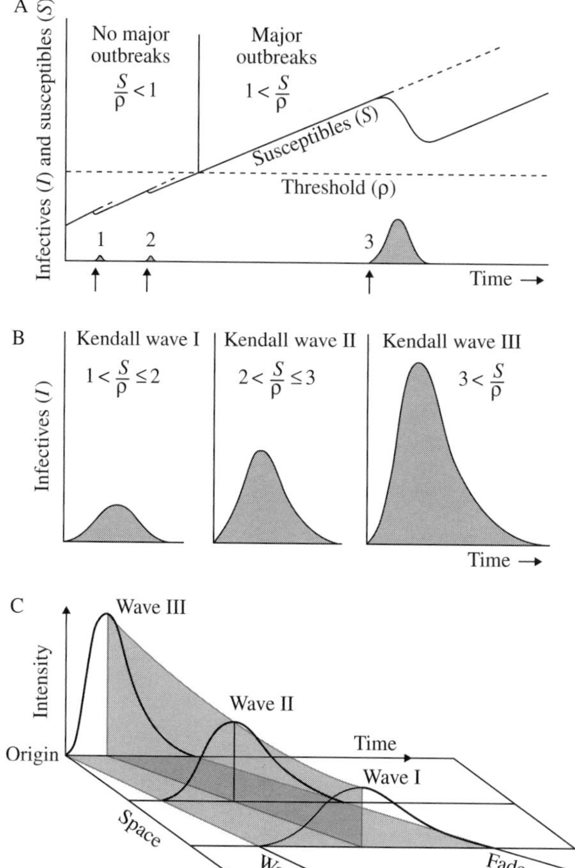

Figure 12 Kendall model of the relationship between the shape of an epidemic wave and the susceptible population/threshold ratio (S/ρ). (A) Growth of a susceptible population over time showing the effect of infections (see arrows). (B) Three typical Kendall waves. (C) Generalized Kendall wave train in time and space. Reproduced from Haggett (2000, Fig. 1.10, p. 27; Fig. 1.11, p. 28) by permission of Oxford University Press.

Figure 12A shows a sequence of outbreaks in a community in which the threshold has a constant value; it is therefore shown as a horizontal dashed line. Given a constant birth rate, the susceptible population increases and appears as the solid diagonal line rising over time. Three examples of virus introductions are illustrated (arrows). In the first two (1, 2), the susceptible population is smaller than the threshold ($S < \rho$), and there are a few secondary cases but no general epidemic. In the third example of virus introduction (3), the susceptible population has grown well beyond the threshold ($S \gg \rho$); the primary case is followed by many secondaries and a substantial outbreak follows. The effect of the outbreak is to reduce the susceptible population as shown by the offset curve in the diagram.

Kendall has investigated the effect of the ratio S/ρ upon the shape of epidemic waves (Fig. 12B). With a ratio of less than one, a major outbreak cannot be generated; above one, both the probability of an outbreak and its shape changes with increasing S/ρ ratio values. In Kendall type I waves, the susceptible population is only slightly above the threshold value. Such waves will have a low case incidence, are symmetric in shape, and have only a modest concentration of cases in the peak period; as Fig. 12B shows, a Kendall wave I approximates a normal curve. In contrast, wave III is generated when the susceptible population is well above the threshold value. The consequent epidemic wave has a higher incidence, is strongly skewed toward the start, and is extremely peaked in shape with many cases concentrated into the peak period. Wave II occupies an intermediate position and is included to emphasize the changing waveforms as examples from a continuum. A generalization of Kendall waves in both time and space is plotted in Fig. 12C.

Time Series Modeling

Autoregressive-Moving Average Methods

The basic philosophy of these methods is that the past behavior of regional systems provides the key to how they will act in the future, and that this can be modeled using autoregressive and moving average components. Figure 13 illustrates such a space-time propagation system for a measles epidemic that affected Iceland in 1958. Measles virus, which is not endemic in Iceland, was introduced into Reykjavíkur, the medical district of the capital city, in August. It then spread to the north coast settlement of Akureyrar in September before diffusing on to Ólafsfjarðar and Grenivíkur by November. Let x_{it} denote the value of a variate in region i at time t—for example, the number of measles cases reported in Akureyrar in October 1958 (see Fig. 13). Time periods earlier than t are indexed by $t-k$, and periods later than t by $t+k$. Let Akureyrar be the reference medical district, i, and let j denote other medical districts. The pattern of dependencies among medical districts outlined above may thus be formulated as shown in Fig. 13.

The dependency of an area's behavior upon what happened in that area in the past is referred to as an autoregressive component, and the dependency upon other areas as space-time covariances. In an extension of the conventional autoregressive notation proposed in Cliff *et al.*, such models may be referred to as space-time autoregressive (STAR) models, and

$$E(X_{it}\,|\,\text{past history}) = b_1 x_{i,t-1} + b_2 \sum_j w_{ij} x_{j,t-1}$$
$$i,j = 1,2,\ldots,n;\ j \neq i \qquad (9)$$

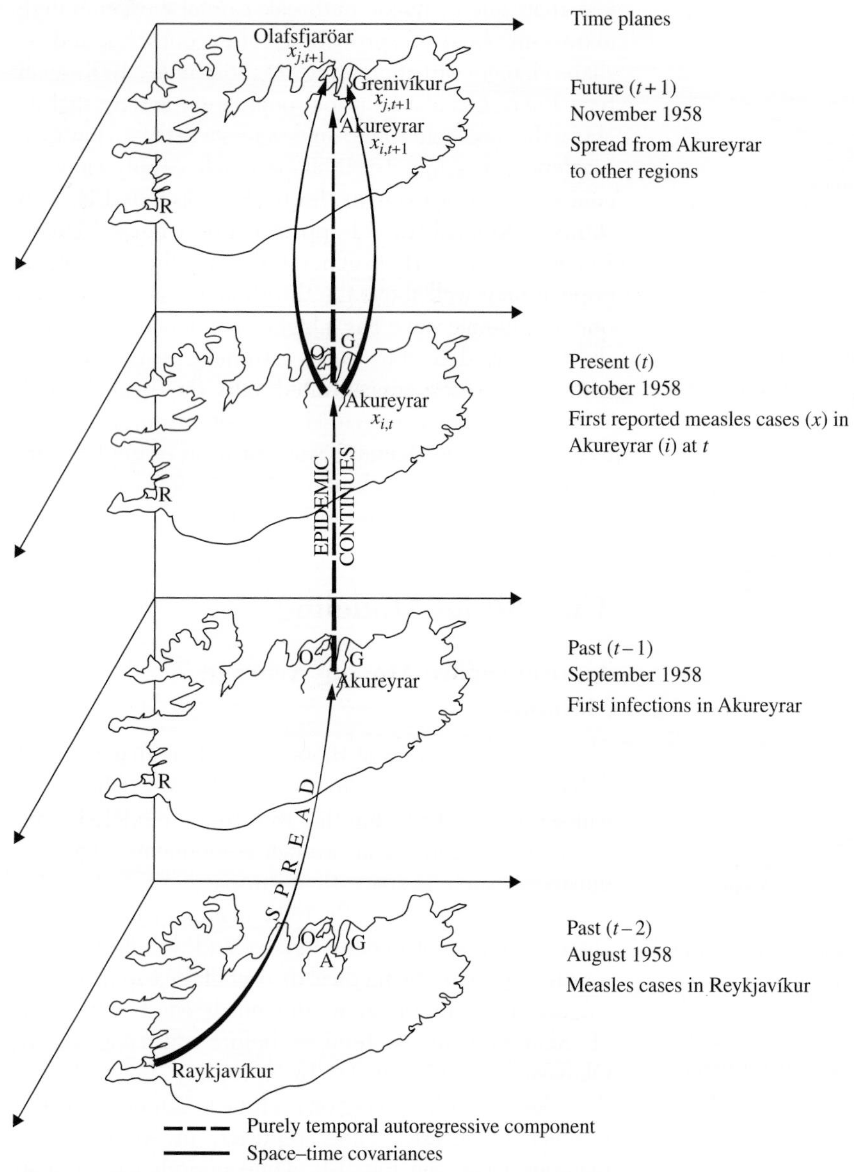

Figure 13 Patterns of dependencies among medical districts for part of the 1958–1959 measles epidemic wave in Iceland. Reproduced from Cliff *et al.* (1981, Fig. 6.1, p. 133) with the permission of Cambridge University Press.

is a typical model. Here, b_1 and b_2 are parameters to be estimated, the w_{ij} are pre-specified, non-negative, structural weights indicating which areas, j, affect i, and the summation is over all areas j for which $w_{ij} \neq 0$. It is assumed that there are n areas of interest in the space-time system. There is no reason why the temporal dependency should be restricted to a single past map, and Eq. (9) could be extended to earlier time periods.

It often happens that change over time cannot be accounted for solely in terms of systematic components such as those in Eq. (9), and random shocks may be envisaged arriving in a region both from other areas and from within itself on past maps. Thus, a space-time random shocks, or moving average, model (STMA) might be postulated as

$$x_{it} = \varepsilon_{it} + b_1\varepsilon_{i,t-1} + b_2 \sum_j w_{ij}\varepsilon_{j,t-1}, \qquad (10)$$

where b_1 and b_2 are parameters, and the epsilons (ε) are random shocks with zero means, constant variances, and zero intercorrelations. As before, the model could be extended to cover more than one time lag and any order of spatial interaction. Additionally, Eqs. (9) and (10) can be combined to define a general STARMA model.

Writing down Eqs. such as (9) and (10) is the easy part of the task. The difficulties arise in three areas: (1) Which model is appropriate for the problem in hand—STAR, STMA, or STARMA? (2) What order of spatial and temporal lags should be included in the model once it is selected? (3) How is the model fitted? Problems (1) and (2) constitute the so-called identification and specification problems, while (3) raises issues of estimation and, in turn, whether the assumptions of the model proposed hold for the data set being analyzed.

Adaptive Time-Series Models

Cliff *et al.* considered a number of alternative time-series models and applied them to Icelandic epidemic data. These are the Kalman models, which formulate a diffusion process that is dynamic in its parameters, that is, whose parameters can be changed and updated as fresh information arrives. Other models are the Bayesian-entropy methods, which handle problems associated with (1) the non-stationarity of the process, in particular, how to handle epidemic/no-epidemic changes to avoid lagged forecasts, and (2) growth/decline in the S population due to changes in birth rates and/or net migration.

Assume that, for a particular study area affected by an epidemic, a Poisson process, I_t is observed for the number of infectives at time t, with mean level φ_t, which depends upon past levels of the process. Suppose that, at any time t, the generating model is a random choice between two models (that is, two states):

$M_t^{(1)}$: Model 1(no epidemic): $\varphi_t = \varphi_c$, where φ_c is a small positive constant (11)

$M_t^{(2)}$: Model 2 (epidemic):
φ_t is a gamma-distributed random variable. (12)

Equation (11) states that when there is no epidemic, the observations come from a Poisson process with a constant, low-valued rate ($\varphi_t = \varphi_c$). This implies the assignment of a high probability to the occurrence of small-valued observations (depending on the selected value for φ_c), and almost zero probability to the occurrence of high-values observations. On the other hand, with $M_t^{(2)}$ in Eq. (12), φ_t is a gamma-distributed random variable, and the model itself corresponds to the single-steady Poisson-gamma Bayesian-entropy forecasting model.

Applications of the models show that the change from epidemic to no-epidemic conditions in medical districts causes difficulties that can be properly tackled only by having separate models for each state, and then switching from one to the other at the appropriate time. Defining a switching mechanism may not be straightforward. One possibility is to have a online surveillance system to pick up early isolated cases heralding the approach of an epidemic, and to use this to trigger a switch between state models. Another is to identify disease lead indicator areas (for example, the capital medical district, Reykjavík, in the case of Iceland) and to allow the presence of infection in this district to give the impulse for an epidemic in other areas. Without this spatial trigger, it is doubtful whether it will be possible to forecast epidemic starts with any reliability, although the mixed-state model allows quick identification of a new epidemic. Nevertheless, early warning of the approach of an epidemic is obviously necessary if control is to be effected through vaccination and isolation programs.

Perspectives on Diffusion Modeling

Over the last century an armada of different models has been developed and applied to spatial diffusion data. From the experience gained in applying such models to epidemiological data, the view of the strengths and weaknesses of such models is as follows:

1. No "Rosetta stone" model that gives reasonable projections of (a) epidemic recurrences and (b) epidemic size has yet been found. Generally, if a model such as the Hamer-Soper model that forecasts well epidemic recurrences is devised, epidemic size is overestimated. This is because to forecast recurrences properly, the model has to be made sensitive to changes signaling the approach of an epidemic, with the result that it can overshoot amplitude when the epidemic is in progress.
2. Models that are based only on the size of the infective population in previous time periods—a common feature of some time-series models—consistently fail to detect the approach of an epidemic. Instead, they provide reasonable estimates of cases reported, but tend to run in arrears.
3. Models with parameters fixed through time have a tendency to smooth through the highs and lows of an epidemic because they are unable to adapt to the changes between build-up and fade-out phases of an epidemic. Time-varying parameter models are better at avoiding this problem.
4. Epidemic recurrences can be reasonably anticipated only by incorporating into the model information on the size of the susceptible population and/or properly identifying the lead-lag structure among medical districts for disease transmission. Incorporation of spatial interaction information markedly improves the ability to forecast recurrences in lagging areas. Information on susceptible population levels also serves to prime a model to the possibility of a recurrence. Models based on susceptible populations, but that are single- rather than multi-region, tend to miss the start of

epidemics but rapidly lock on to the course of an epidemic thereafter. Models that are dominated by spatial transmission information at the expense of information on the level of the susceptible population in the reference region produce estimates of epidemic size that reflect the course of the epidemic in the triggering regions rather than in the reference region.

5. Process models, such as the mass action models described previously, can serve to strengthen the time series models and identify a more reliable scheme for forecasting.

The overall assessment is that spatial diffusion modeling has made significant progress over the last half-century. Part of that progress has come from improved understanding of the epidemic process, part from revolutions in computing, part from changes in the mathematics used, and part from improved incorporation of spatial elements into the models. On the negative side, it should be noted that such progress is broadly asymptotic, with each new improvement step being more difficult to achieve than the earlier ones.

See Also the Following Articles

Epidemiology • Linear Logistic Test Models • Modeling Migration • Spatial Econometrics • Time-Series–Cross-Section Data

Further Reading

Anderson, R. M., and May, R. M. (1991). *Infectious Diseases of Humans: Dynamics and Control.* Oxford University Press, Oxford, UK.

Bailey, N. J. T. (1975). *The Mathematical Theory of Infectious Diseases and Its Application.* Griffin, London, UK.

Bailey, T. C., and Gatrell, A. C. (1995). *Interactive Spatial Data Analysis.* Longman Scientific and Technical, Harlow, UK.

Brown, L. A. (1982). *Innovation Diffusion.* Methuen, London, UK.

Cliff, A. D., and Ord, J. K. (1981). *Spatial Processes: Models and Applications.* Pion, London, UK.

Cliff, A. D., Haggett, P., Ord, J. K., and Versey, G. R. (1981). *Spatial Diffusion: An Historical Geography of Epidemics in an Island Community.* Cambridge University Press, Cambridge, UK.

Cliff, A. D., Haggett, P., and Smallman-Raynor, M. (2000). *Island Epidemics.* Oxford University Press, Oxford.

Gould, P. R. (1969). *Spatial Diffusion.* Association of American Geographers, Commission on College Geography, Resource Paper 4, Washington, D.C.

Hägerstrand, T. (1968). *Innovation Diffusion as a Spatial Process.* (A. Pred, Trans.) Chicago University Press, Chicago, IL.

Haggett, P. (2000). *The Geographical Structure of Epidemics.* Oxford University Press, London, UK.

Haggett, P., Cliff, A. D., and Frey, A. E. (1977). *Locational Analysis in Human Geography,* 2nd Ed. Arnold, London, UK.

Isham, V., and Medley, G. (eds.) (1996). *Models for Infectious Human Diseases: Their Structure and Relation to Data.* Cambridge University Press, Cambridge, UK.

Levison, M., Ward, R. G., and Webb, J. W. (1973). *The Settlement of Polynesia: A Computer Simulation.* University of Minneapolis Press, Minneapolis, MN.

Mollison, D. (ed.) (1995). *Epidemic Models and Their Relation to Data.* Cambridge University Press, Cambridge, UK.

Rogers, E. M. (1995). *Diffusion of Innovations,* 4th Ed. Free Press, New York, NY.

Thomas, R. W. (1992). *Geomedical Systems: Intervention and Control.* Routledge, London, UK.

Modeling Migration

Michael J. Greenwood
University of Colorado, Boulder, Colorado, USA

Glossary

determinants of migration The personal and regional factors that influence migration decisions.

disequilibrium perspective The idea that wage differentials provide opportunities for utility gains.

equilibrium perspective The idea that wage differentials are compensated and therefore do not offer opportunities for utility gains.

gravity model A place-to-place migration model that assumes that interregional migration is directly related to the population of the origin and of the destination regions and inversely related to the distance between them.

human capital model A model that treats migration as an investment with future expected returns and costs and that discounts these to arrive at a best present discounted value of a move.

migration The change of an individual's usual place of residence from one migration defining area to another during a migration interval.

migration interval The period of time over which a migratory move may occur.

migration propensity The probability of making a migratory move.

model The abstract depictions and simplifications of a complex real-world process, which may or may not be expressed mathematically.

modified gravity model A place-to-place migration model that adds to the basic gravity model additional variables relating to origin and destination characteristics.

Modeling migration refers to ascertaining the factors that underlie decisions to migrate (or not migrate). Such models also address the personal as well as the regional consequences of migration. The models are abstract depictions and simplifications of complex real-world processes that may or may not be expressed mathematically. Empirical models attempt to ascertain the relative importance of various determinants of migration and, in the case of models of the consequences of migration, to ascertain migration's role, along with other factors, in various economic and social outcomes at the personal and the regional level (such as personal earnings change and regional employment, unemployment, or wage change).

Introduction

Migration is inherently a spatial phenomenon. It entails a change in an individual's usual place of residence from one migration-defining area to another over a given period of time (called the migration interval), which may be a month, a year, a 5-year period, a life time, or some other interval. Because it is a spatial phenomenon, modeling migration must refer to at least two regions, even if the second region is "somewhere else." Migration phenomena may be modeled theoretically or empirically. The best empirical models have strong theoretical underpinnings. Migration models attempt to explain either the causes of personal, family, or aggregate interregional migration or the consequences of migration. Thus, the distinguishing feature of a migration model is that it is an attempt to explain, which is to say that it constitutes an effort to answer the question: Why does a certain migration phenomenon occur? Like any good model, migration models may also allow the investigation to predict, but migration models have not frequently been used for predictive purposes.

All migration models begin with the basic assumption (most frequently made implicitly) that migration is a voluntary human act. However, much migration is clearly involuntary. Examples of involuntary migration are the movement of prisoners and the relocation of military personnel. The migration of refugees of war, political strife, and religious differences is also regarded as involuntary in the sense that such individuals move to escape persecution and/or death and therefore seek at least initially to get away; the personal consequences of migration for refugees have been studied. Models of voluntary migration seek to explain the presumably utility-maximizing behavior of free individuals.

Migration models address several broad questions: (1) Who migrates? (2) Why do these people migrate? (3) Where do the migrants come from and where do they go? (4) When do they migrate? and (5) What are the consequences of migration for the migrants themselves as well as for others in the origin and destination areas? Theoretical migration models tend to address the "Why?" and the "Where?" questions, and to a lesser extent the "What are the consequences?" question. Very little theoretical work has ever been done on the "Who?" and the "When?" questions, although numerous descriptive accounts of who migrates go back to the nineteenth century. The question "Who migrates?" refers to various characteristics of the migrants, such as age, education, race, income, marital status, and presence of children in the household.

The relationships between age and education, on the one hand, and migration, on the other, are among the most commonly studied migration relationships. Model migration schedules have been developed to shed light on the exact relationship between age and the propensity to migrate for various population subgroups. These schedules indicate that in the United States annual intercounty migration propensities peak at 23–25 years of age (at approximately 7.5%) and decline steadily until approximately 62 years of age (to approximately 1.5%). These propensities differ greatly for various population subgroups. For example, depending on age, migration propensities are between two and four times higher for those with 5 years or more of college compared to those with 8 years or less of elementary school.

Because migration declines sharply with increased distance, propensities to move over longer distances are considerably lower than for shorter distances. Thus, interstate migration propensities, as indicated in Table I, are somewhat lower than the intercounty propensities. The tendency for annual interstate migration propensities to rise with education and fall with age is clearly evident in Table I. For example, 6.18% of those individuals ages 25–29 with only a bachelor's degree made a U.S. interstate move between 1993 and 1994, but 3.67% of those in the same age class with a high school diploma only made a similar move during the same period. And whereas 6.18% of the 25–29 age group with a bachelor's degree made an interstate move, only 2.58% of those in the same education class but ages 45–64 did so.

Theoretical Perspective

Economic models of migration, as well as models that derive from other disciplines, take one of two possible broad theoretical perspectives: (1) the disequilibrium perspective or (2) the equilibrium perspective. The theoretical perspective taken in almost all migration research conducted by economists and others prior to the late 1970s was that of a disequilibrium system. The perspective is called disequilibrium because migration is assumed to be motivated by the existence of a set of nonmarket clearing regional wages. The idea is that spatial differences in wages, earnings, or income reflect opportunities for utility gains that can be realized through migration. In more recent years, this disequilibrium perspective has been challenged by proponents of the equilibrium hypothesis, which assumes that spatial differences in wages are compensating and therefore do not reflect opportunities for utility gains. Thus, a basic assumption underlying models based on one or the other of these perspectives is considerably different.

The disequilibrium approach does not rely on location-specific amenities, and regional wages and regional rents adjust slowly to exogenous disturbances. In the equilibrium approach, migration is conditional on amenities. Moreover, this approach does not rely on long adjustments of wages and rents to disturbances, especially in the United States where institutional and other impediments to factor mobility are relatively low. Systematic long-term forces, such as rising real income in some or all locations, underlie in an important way consumption

Table I U.S. Interstate Migration Propensities by Age and Education Class, 1993–1994[a]

	Age					
Education	*Under 25*	*25–29*	*30–34*	*35–44*	*45–64*	*65 & over*
All 25 & over	2.38	4.72	3.26	2.50	1.68	1.22
Less than ninth grade	1.33	3.69	2.01	2.08	1.03	1.00
High school graduate	1.98	3.67	2.60	2.12	1.53	1.06
Bachelor's degree	3.41	6.18	4.45	2.91	2.58	1.36
Graduate/profession degree	3.14	8.96	5.10	2.79	2.07	2.61

[a] *Source:* Calculated from data provided in Hansen (1995), Table 4.

amenity demand growth and provide the rationale for migration. Thus, both the disequilibrium and equilibrium approaches assume that spatial variations in utility underlie the motive to migrate, but the differences spring from the source and persistence of the variations. The perspective taken by the analyst not only shapes the precise form of the model that is specified and estimated, it also contributes to the interpretation placed on the estimated coefficients of wage and other variables.

Gravity and Modified Gravity Models

Although they are not often credited with the development of the gravity law of spatial interaction, in 1938 economists Makower, Marschak, and Robinson clearly laid out the basic concept: "Quite a close relationship was found between discrepancies in unemployment rates and migration of labour where allowance was made for the size of the insured population and the distance over which migrants had to travel." The key to the gravity model is the relationship between migration and distance, as well as between migration and origin and destination population sizes.

During the 1940s, Princeton astronomer Stewart noted that the distance to his students' home towns seemed to behave like the Newtonian law of gravitation. Thus, Stewart expressed the gravity law of spatial interaction as $F = GP_iP_j/D_{ij}^2$, where F = Gravitational or demographic force, G = Constant, P_i = Population of origin i, P_j = Population of destination j, and D_{ij} = Distance between i and j. This relationship states that demographic force is directly related to the origin and destination population sizes and inversely related to the square of the distance between them. If the square on the distance term is replaced by α and the relationship is placed in the migration context by substituting migration from i to j, M_{ij}, for F, we get $M_{ij} = GP_iP_j/D_{ij}^{\alpha}j$. If this model is expressed in double-log form, it suggests that the population parameters are equal to 1.0, meaning that a 1% increase in origin or in destination population results in a 1% increase in migration from i to j. This assumption is clearly restrictive, and the population elasticities are subject to empirical tests. Thus, the gravity model can be written as:

$$M_{ij} = \frac{GP_i^{\beta 1}P_j^{\beta 2}}{D_{ij}^{\alpha}}.$$

In this form, the values of β_1 and β_2 may be freely estimated, and the hypothesis that they are equal to 1.0 may be tested. This basic form of the gravity model was tested rarely because little additional effort was required to specify and estimate the more appealing modified gravity model. Moreover, when β_1 and β_2 are estimated freely, their values are rarely equal to 1.0.

During the 1960s, the main thrust of migration research took on a decidedly more formal tone that has continued to the present. Most of the research was not formal in a theoretical sense but rather intuitively generated hypotheses were at first tested formally in an econometric sense with aggregate data, typically (but not always) with place-to-place migration data. These aggregate models of migration frequently were specified in the context of modified gravity models. The models are of the gravity type, in that migration is hypothesized to be directly related to the size of relevant origin and destination populations and to be inversely related to distance. The models are modified in the sense that the variables of the basic gravity model are given behavioral content and additional variables that are expected to influence the decision to migrate are included in the estimated relationship.

The modified gravity models that became common in the migration literature beginning in the 1960s add several additional variables to those of the basic gravity model. Thus, we commonly find studies of place-to-place migration that take the following form:

$$\ln M_{ij} = \ln \beta_0 + \beta_1 \ln D_{ij} + \beta_2 \ln P_i + \beta_3 \ln P_j + \beta_4 \ln Y_i + \beta_5 \ln Y_j + \sum_{n=1}^{m} \beta_{in} \ln X_{in} + \sum_{n=1}^{m} \beta_{jn} \ln x_{jn} + e_{ij} \quad (1)$$

where the Y terms refer to income. Other variables that are commonly included (as reflected in terms containing X) are unemployment rates, degree of urbanization, various climatological amenity variables, various measures of public expenditures and/or taxes, and many other factors. For certain variables, some models contain only origin characteristics, such as median age or median number of years of schooling, which are meant as proxies for the characteristics of the population from which the migrants are drawn. Modified gravity models hold an important place in the migration literature because their formulators tried to incorporate behavioral content into the context of the gravity model approach. These efforts subsequently led to formal models of the migration decision process, such as those reflected in many studies that incorporate microdata. Moreover, such models included a mix of disequilibrium and equilibrium notions that anticipated the later, more rigorous development of the equilibrium hypothesis of migration.

The connection between modified gravity models and the migration decision process has not always been tight. The dependent variable in modified gravity models is meant to proxy the probability of moving from i to j. However, the denominator of the dependent variable frequently has been the population measured at the beginning or end of the migration interval. Such a measure falls short of reflecting the population at risk to make a move from i to j. For example, the beginning-of-period population includes people who die during the period over which migration is measured, as well as those who emigrate from the country and who are thus not available to be counted as migrants. The end-of-period measure includes in-migrants who were not at risk of being out-migrants from the area and also introduces simultaneity between migration and the population measure.

Modified gravity models are frequently estimated in double-logarithmic form, presumably because this functional form yields reasonably good fits and the coefficients obtained from it can be directly interpreted as elasticities of migration's response to changes in the various independent variables of the estimated models. However, common use of the double-logarithmic functional form to estimate modified gravity models has led to arguments for the adoption of nonlinear maximum likelihood logit methods over the double-log form of the model. In part, the argument hinges on the geographic size of the regions for which migration is measured. If all regions had the same population and land area, the migration and nonmigration probabilities would reflect the costs and benefits of the various locational choices. However, the regions of any country differ greatly in population and land area. A larger share of all moves will tend to occur within the boundaries of larger regions. Consequently, more nonmigration will appear to exist for such regions. The result is that nonmigration is spuriously correlated with origin population size and land area.

In the polychotomous logistic model, the migration probabilities are expressed as ratios and the probability of not migrating is used in the denominator of the expression to normalize the flows. That is, the dependent variable is $\ln[m_{ij}/(1-m_{ij})]$, which is sometimes called the logarithm of the odds ratio. Here m_{ij} refers to the probability of migration from i to j and is thus measured as M_{ij}, or the actual number of movers from i to j divided by the population at risk to migrate from i. The model can be estimated in one of two ways that make sense in the migration context. First, again assuming the double-log form of the model, the log of the ratio of various destination-to-origin characteristics can be used. This approach, referred to as uniform symmetric, implies that coefficients on variables for corresponding origin and destination characteristics are the same except for sign. Second, a two-step decision process can be assumed in which the decision maker first decides to migrate and then decides where to migrate based on destination characteristics and perhaps other variables (such as distance) that link the areas. In this case, origin and destination characteristics are introduced separately. In an analogous fashion, nested decision trees could be constructed for other levels of the decision process (e.g., whether to move, where to move, and what house to select). Some dissatisfaction has been expressed with the notion that individuals can decide whether to move independently of deciding where to move. Thus, whether to move and where to move are seen as joint decisions and not discrete and independent decisions.

The standard gravity approach is seen as inefficient because it fails to incorporate information on the relative frequency of nonmigration $(1-m_{ij})$. However, as the migration interval grows shorter and shorter, the two specifications approach one another because the population at risk to migrate becomes a better measure of the nonmigrating population when the migration interval is very short. In any case, the logit approach provides a more natural transition from the gravity model to the more behaviorally grounded modified gravity model.

Prior to 1975, virtually all migration research was based on aggregate data. In addition to the problem already noted, modified gravity models were characterized by other problems and shortcomings frequently associated with the use of such data. Aggregate data often were used to proxy the characteristics of the population at risk to move, resulting in empirical estimates that did not reflect accurately the influence of personal characteristics on the decision to migrate. With some notable exceptions, studies of aggregate migration failed to account for different types of moves, such as primary (or new), return, and other repeat migration. Aggregate data also concealed differences in the underlying determinants of migration of various population subgroups, although stratification by age and race was not uncommon. Such data failed to account for the institutional population, of which the military was especially important, and they made the study of family migration decisions difficult. Another problem with modified gravity models was that the variables used to explain migration often were measured at the end of the migration interval and were thus subject to simultaneity bias. During the 1970s, several simultaneous equations models were developed to explain the causes and consequences of migration within the same empirical framework, but for the most part during the last several years these models have not been developed further.

The Human Capital Model

Underlying the disequilibrium perspective, at least implicitly, is the simple income-leisure model of labor economics wherein an optimizing agent maximizes a utility function with two arguments, income and leisure, subject to a full-income constraint. One implication of this model is that the individual will supply labor such that the marginal rate of substitution of consumption for leisure equals the wage rate, which in turn implies that the individual labor supply is a function of the wage rate. If we abstract from mobility costs and accept many other assumptions that underlie this simple yet powerful model, the individual is expected to offer his labor services in the market with the highest wage, which may require migration.

The human capital approach was added to the disequilibrium perspective that was then in vogue. This model provided a paradigm that caught the attention of economists and provided a convenient theoretical framework for their research.

Present Value Comparisons

The potential migrant will select the locality at which the real value of the expected net benefit that accrues to him or her from migration is greatest. The income that the individual expects to earn at each alternative destination enters crucially into his judgment concerning the benefits associated with each location. The relevant income measure for the individual to consider is the present discounted value of his or her expected future stream of net pecuniary returns.

Let the present value of the earnings stream in locality j less that in i be:

$$\sum_{t=1}^{n} \frac{(E_{jt} - E_{it})}{(1+r)^t} \tag{2}$$

where r is the internal rate of discount, which although written as a constant does not have to be constant. Let the present value of net costs associated with residence in this pair of localities be:

$$\sum_{t=1}^{n} \frac{(C_{jt} - C_{it})}{(1+r)^t}. \tag{3}$$

The summation is over the individual's remaining life. Then, the present value of investment in migration from i to j, PV_{ij}, is:

$$PV_{ij} = \sum_{t=1}^{n} \left[\frac{1}{(1+r)^t}\right] [(E_{jt} - C_{jt}) - (E_{it} - C_{it})]. \tag{4}$$

An individual residing in i will presumably select that destination for which PV_{ij} is maximized.

The disequilibrium perspective is clearly evident in this model of migration. In the human capital model, economic opportunity differentials represent potential for household utility gains that can be arbitraged by migration. For all intents and purposes, the human capital model was unrivaled for almost 20 years. Indeed, disequilibrium forces were presumed to be the primary drivers of migration long before the human capital model provided an explanation for migration. Many of the early authors recognized that both disequilibrium and equilibrium forces were at work, but they clearly emphasized the disequilibrium factors.

The human capital model provided an appealing rationale for the presence of income variables in modified gravity models, as well as in other models of migration. Based on the disequilibrium perspective, in modified gravity models the origin wage or income variable is expected to take a negative sign, whereas the destination wage or income variable is expected to take a positive sign because migrants move out of low-income areas and into high-income areas. A number of studies have tested this assertion regarding the importance of wages in explaining migration by examining the factors affecting interregional migration in the United States and in many other countries. Based on aggregate data, the empirical findings associated with income, earnings, and wage variables in modified gravity models have not been uniformly strong, although it is probably fair to conclude that the weight of available evidence favors disequilibrium results, particularly for rural-to-urban migration. Of course, the exact results are sensitive to many factors, such as the precise specification of the model, the country and period studied, the population subgroup under investigation, the type of functional form assumed, and the estimation technique employed. Moreover, income or wage measures have almost never been refined to reflect real consumption wages. This is to say that the role of taxes and public services has not received the attention it deserves.

Spatial Job-Search Models

Another type of migration model that sprang from the human capital approach places migration in the context of a spatial job search. The human capital model suggests that individuals compare their opportunities in alternative localities with their present situation. However, to learn about opportunities in other areas, they must conduct a search that yields a distribution of wage offers in each alternative. Presumably, these individuals have a reservation wage (the lowest wage they would accept in a potentially new region of residence). If the person is unemployed, this reservation wage may fall over time. However, he or she would reject any opportunities that yielded a wage below the reservation wage. The duration of the search extends until the individual receives a wage offer that is at least equal to the reservation wage. The reservation wage itself is dependent on the person's age, education, marital status, family situation, and numerous other personal characteristics, as well as on regional characteristics, such as the unemployment rate.

More on the Equilibrium Perspective

Due in part to the fairly consistent tendency for empirical studies based on aggregate data to fail to confirm the importance of wages or income in migration decisions, the equilibrium approach has been offered as an alternative to the traditional disequilibrium perspective. The equilibrium theorists begin by assuming that households and firms are in proximate equilibrium at any point in time. This assumption means that the marginal household and firm, while maximizing utility and profit, respectively, are spatially arrayed so as to receive zero consumer and producer surplus from their location. Any movement from the general equilibrium configuration cannot improve utility or profit.

According to the equilibrium approach, changes in life-cycle factors or generally rising real incomes continuously change the demand for consumer amenities. Real incomes may rise due, for example, to persistent technical progress. Because amenities are not evenly distributed spatially, migration occurs and quickly re-equilibrates households. Net in-migration to amenity-rich areas tends to drive down wages and drive up the prices of locally produced goods, services, and land, *ceteris paribus*. In amenity-poor areas, opposite patterns of change occur. Wages and local prices diverge across regions until they just compensate households for the differing amenity bundles that the various regions supply.

The equilibrium approach has another important facet. A number of studies use the level of regional wages or rents to measure regional environmental quality, including the quality of the climate. The assumption underlying these studies is that equilibrium prevails so that wage and rent differentials are compensating differentials and thus serve as accurate proxies for differentials in environmental quality. For equilibrium to prevail, regional markets must be efficient so that regional wages and prices quickly realign to clear such markets subsequent to any disequilibrating exogenous disturbances. The equilibrium proponents believe that, at any point in time, it is highly likely that regional wages and prices have adjusted to their equilibrium values.

In the equilibrium approach, regional differentials in wages and prices do not generally reflect utility differences that can be arbitraged through household migration. Only those noncompensating regional differentials that remain after controlling for amenity differentials across regions should represent utility differentials that would induce migration. As previously noted, the implication of this view for migration analysis is that a properly specified migration equation should include both regional amenity and regional wage and rent variables. For this reason, proponents of the equilibrium hypothesis typically include a wide variety of regional amenities in their empirical models. Among the variables frequently included are climatological amenities (e.g., average temperature at some time during the year, average humidity, and degree days) and topological amenities (e.g., the presence or absence of a sea coast, variety of terrain, and national forest lands).

From an economist's perspective, an equilibrium process makes great sense. Without the operation of such forces, economists would be hard pressed to develop a reasonable theory to explain interregional movements and the adjustments that result therefrom. However, for the most part, until recently tests of the equilibrium hypothesis in the context of the migration literature have not been fully convincing.

Modeling Migration with Microdata

As already noted, prior to 1975 virtually all empirical migration models employed aggregate cross-sectional data. However, during the 1970s a number of important advances occurred in the modeling of migration that were contingent on the development of new data sets. Two types of data were critical in the sense that the advances simply could not have occurred without them. The first and certainly the most important involved the development of microdata and micro-based panel data that included a migration component; the second involved the development of aggregate time series migration data.

Aggregate data have a number of limitations for studying migration behavior.

1. Aggregate data, such as census data, have an inherent fixed migration interval, so that, for those who move multiple times, only the first and last location are available for study. Thus, an individual may move from i to j to k, but a move from i to k is recorded for the individual based on original and final places of residence. Moreover, an individual who moves from i to j and back to i during the migration interval appears as a nonmover. Although this objection also applies to certain microdata sets, such as the U.S. Census Public Use Microdata Samples (PUMS), microdata are in many instances better in avoiding this type of problem.
2. Aggregate data conceal the differences in the underlying determinants of migration for various population subgroups that are lumped together. Thus, the motives for migration may differ for the young versus the old, high-income versus low-income people, blacks versus whites, and so on. Some stratification is possible with aggregate data, but it is

generally limited. Thus, in general only variations between groups can be explained with aggregate data, not variations within groups.

3. Aggregate migration studies, with some notable exceptions, fail to account for the different types of moves, namely, new, return, and other repeat migration and long- and short-distance migration. However, in more recent years, with the availability of microdata, these types of distinctions have been more common, and several studies have uncovered significant differences in the magnitudes of the influence of various migration determinants on these different types of moves.
4. Aggregate data frequently fail to account for the movements of institutional populations, for examples, movements of military personnel and college students. Because the motives for such movements may have little or nothing to do with the migration determinants typically studied, these moves obscure the behavioral relationships of interest. Of course, it is often possible to remove institutional populations from the data being studied.
5. Aggregate data, given the heterogeneity that exists within the large regions between which migration is measured, may not represent the average characteristics of many of the moves that actually occur. For example, U.S. migration is frequently measured between states and even between the nine census divisions and between the four census regions. Moreover, many moves over substantial distances are omitted because they occur within the region. To some extent, this type of problem can be avoided by using finely defined regions as the spatial unit, such as counties or metropolitan areas.
6. Aggregate data allow the study of the regionwide consequences of migration, but in no way do they allow the study of the personal consequences of migration. Thus, any assessment of the personal consequences of migration was not possible until the development of microdata sets that included a migration component.

The development and use of several microdata and panel data sets during the 1970s and 1980s led to many important breakthroughs in the social sciences, including the study of migration in economics and sociology. Several data sets particularly stand out. The 1967 Survey of Economic Opportunity was one of the earliest microdata sets used to study migration. The PUMS from various censuses have been invaluable in allowing investigators to introduce personal characteristics into their models. Microdata from the Current Population Surveys have also been used to good advantage. Two panel data sets of particular note are the Panel Study of Income Dynamics (PSID) and the National Longitudinal Surveys (NLS). Canadian microdata, particularly census data, have also been valuable. These are not the only microdata and panel data sets that have allowed major advances in migration modeling, but they are probably the most important.

In general, three types of migration models employ microdata and panel data: (1) those that use a dichotomous or polytomous dependent variable reflecting migration status (e.g., moved, did not move, or moved, changed job; or moved, did not change job; did not move, changed job) or destination choice as a function of various personal, household, and place characteristics; (2) those that use a measure of earnings or wages as a dependent variable and distinguish migrant vs. nonmigrant status and perhaps other characteristics of a move, such as distance—this latter type of study is couched in the human capital framework because it involves the estimation of earnings (or wage) functions; and (3) a small number of studies that use employment status or hours worked as a function of migration status, among other variables. Note that the last two types of studies relate to the personal consequences of migration.

Models of migration based on microdata have had a major impact on four general topics that have received considerable attention from students of migration.

1. They have allowed the development of important insights regarding the relationship between employment status and migration. Models based on aggregate data have frequently found unanticipated signs and/or insignificant coefficients on unemployment rate variables, but the availability of microdata has gone far toward clearing up the earlier puzzles regarding this relationship.
2. They have allowed more proper and more precise estimations of the monetary returns to migration. Studies in this general area have been based on the human capital model and have involved the estimation of earnings functions.
3. They have allowed the study of the relationship between various personal and life-cycle characteristics, on the one hand, and migration, on the other; these relationships are almost impossible to understand in any fundamental way in the absence of microdata and panel data. Although general tendencies are often discernible from aggregate data (e.g., migration propensities decline with age and increase with education), in the absence of microdata investigators are unable to control for many other factors when studying the relationship between any given factor and migration. An associated point is that family migration decisions are difficult to understand in a substantive way without the use of microdata.
4. They have encouraged researchers to examine primary, return, and nonreturn repeat migration more

closely than was possible using aggregate data. Based on microdata, a number of important differences have been uncovered in the responsiveness of different migrant types to the various determinants of migration.

Sample Selection Problems

With the development and use of microdata, a number of new econometric opportunities have become available, but at the same time certain econometric problems have been introduced. One of the most important of these problems in the migration context concerns sample selection.

Sample selection problems arise from situations in which a population subgroup is not representative of the entire population whose behavior is under study. Stated more formally, in the Manski's 1989 formulation, the problem is one "of estimating a regression $E(y \mid x)$ when realizations of (y, x) are sampled randomly but y is observed selectively." Some unobservable variable may distinguish population subgroups. The natural temptation is to analyze only the subgroup for which data are available, but this procedure may result in parameter estimates tainted by selectivity bias.

Sample selection problems in migration studies have many sources; four of the most common are (1) sampling design or population coverage, (2) panel attrition, (3) time-dependent disturbances, and (4) differential behavioral responses. The last of these is the typical cause of sample selection bias.

Sampling Design or Population Coverage

The first possible problem originates in the data used to study migration. Due to sampling design or, if the data are from an administrative source, population coverage, the data may not be representative of the entire population. For example, migration data derived from U.S. Internal Revenue Service files are selective of those with sufficiently high incomes that they are required to file an income tax return, and annual migration data for Canada derived from the Family Allowance System are selective of families with children. Many similar examples are available. This type of data shortcoming does not cause the usual sample selectivity problem, which refers to bias in the estimation of certain parameters. Rather, it leads to an inability to generalize from accurately estimated parameters.

Panel Attrition

Over time, some attrition is almost certain to occur within any panel. Families move and are difficult or impossible to trace. Others do not wish to put up with the effort of being interviewed repeatedly. For others, payments to participants in the panel may become insufficient. Even though the lost panel members may be replaced with seemingly otherwise comparable individuals and families, systematic differences may well exist between those who remain in the panel and those who drop out. This causes bias when the attrition is correlated with the dependent variables in migration studies. Some unobservable differences may distinguish the groups, such as attitudes in general or attitudes toward risk. An advantage of panel data is that fixed-effect estimates may remove this source of bias. Any investigator who uses panel data sets such as the PSID and the NLS should study what is known about panel attrition in the data set and understand how attrition problems might affect the particular study under consideration.

Time-Dependent Selectivity Problems

A third potential source of sample selection problems also arises from the data, but specifically from the time period of the sample. Time-dependent selectivity problems occur when migrants from different periods are compared. The idea is that the model applies over a span of years, but the disturbance term is time-dependent (and perhaps a function of some latent, unobservable variable). Although this type of selectivity problem may occur in many contexts, two are particularly relevant to migration: secular problems and cyclical problems.

Secular Problems The education and training received by individuals during one period may differ from the education and training received during a later period. Thus, estimates of the monetary returns to different cohorts of migrants may be tainted. This type of bias may be especially important in the study of the returns to different cohorts of immigrants, who may differ systematically not only in education, training, and other personal characteristics, but also in the self-selective nature of their decision to migrate.

Cyclical Problems Little or no research has directly addressed the issue of changes in migrant quality over the business cycle, but such changes are expected to occur. Migrants tend to be self-selected in the sense that they are typically of greater innate ability and possess greater motivation for personal achievement than otherwise comparable nonmigrants. The self-selective nature of the migration decision should be more pronounced the greater the costs of migration, including the probability of finding a job and the costs of subsequent adjustment in the new occupational environment. During periods of relatively poor economic conditions, as indicated by slow national growth of job opportunities, the costs associated with migration are higher. These higher costs are due to more intensive job-search activities because access to entry-level jobs, as well as jobs providing specific skill training, is more difficult. In contrast, during periods of more rapid national economic expansion, the probability of gaining access to jobs is increased and, consequently, the costs of migration are lower. Because the costs associated with migration are expected to be lower during a period of economic expansion, a lower degree of self-selection occurs in periods of relatively good economic conditions. In other words, when economic conditions are generally favorable, the average quality of the migrant flow is relatively lower. This lower quality may be manifested in labor force participation patterns or work motivation, as well as by general skill level. Virtually no research has addressed these issues.

Differential Behavioral Responses

The fourth potential source of a selectivity problem is also behavioral and is analogous to the classic selectivity bias. For examples, in 1976 Heckman wrote about the relationship between wage levels and female labor force participation. In the migration context, at least three types of self-selection may occur: favorable opportunities, remigration, and productivity.

Favorable Opportunities Migrants may be selective of those individuals with the most favorable opportunities, as suggested by Marshall in 1948. Rational economic agents select their chosen alternative because they have some basis for believing that it will yield a higher return than their other options. Consequently, those individuals who select a given alternative are not randomly drawn from the population as a whole. The fact that individual A migrates, whereas the otherwise comparable B does not, suggests that an important difference exists between the individuals. These differences may be in the way they view costs or in the way they view future benefits, and therefore could be due to differences in discount rates. Individual A, for example, may be more highly motivated to invest in human capital formation, not only in migration, but in other forms as well. If this is the case, the earnings of the remaining cohort from which the migrant is drawn may not provide an accurate estimate of the earnings the migrant would have received in the absence of migration. The resulting selectivity bias, if not properly taken into account, poses potentially serious problems in econometric attempts to estimate the return to migration. As Lewis pointed out in 1974, due to this type of problem the returns to nonmigrants are also biased.

Remigration Among those who migrate, some stay in the new place, whereas others move back to the original place or move on to a third location. If those who move back or move on are the economically least successful migrants, then the remaining migrants will bias upward any estimate of the returns to migration. The selectivity bias problem as associated with the remigration phenomenon was raised by Yezer and Thurston in 1976: "The departure of unsuccessful migrants from a destination leaves a residual of successful lifetime migrants. Calculation of the returns to migrations based on these individuals alone results in an upward bias." Although remigration selectivity is potentially important in assessing the returns to internal migration, it seems especially relevant in estimating the returns to international migration because the presumably less successful immigrants who later leave are lost completely from any data collection system in the original country of immigration.

Productivity Individuals may sort themselves based on their productivity. In 1951, Roy discussed such self-selection in terms of occupations (hunting and fishing), but the same argument can be made for region of residence as well as for occupation. The sorting could be based on the individual's absolute advantage in a region (and occupation) or on his or her comparative advantage, but the basic idea is that he or she will locate in the region and work in the occupation that yields the highest expected relative earnings.

Controlling for Sample Selection Bias

The effects of sample selection bias are similar to those caused by left-out variables. Controlling for these left-out variables yields consistent estimates. Although a number of econometric procedures are available to accomplish this control, a frequently used approach is to estimate a first-stage (structural) probit in order to form an estimate of the missing expectations in the earnings equation. In the migration context, an example of this probit is to estimate a regression to predict migrant status (i.e., migrant vs. nonmigrant). A practical difficulty is identifying the earnings equation.

See Also the Following Articles

Demography • Dynamic Migration Modeling • Mathematical Demography

Further Reading

Borjas, G. J., Bronars, S. G., and Trejo, S. J. (1992). Self-selection and internal migration in the United States. *J. Urban Econ.* **32,** 159–185.

Charney, A. H. (1993). Migration and the public sector: A survey. *Reg. Stud.* **27,** 313–326.

Greenwood, M. J. (1975). Research on internal migration in the United States: A survey. *J. Econ. Lit.* **13,** 397–433.

Greenwood, M. J. (1985). Human migration: Theory, models, and empirical studies. *J. Reg. Sci.* **25,** 521–544.

Greenwood, M. J. (1997). Internal migration in developed countries. In *Handbook of Population and Family Economics* (M. R. Rosenzweig and O. Stark, eds.), pp. 647–720. Elsevier Science, Amsterdam.

Gronau, R. (1974). Wage comparisons—A selectivity bias. *J. Polit. Econ.* **82,** 1119–1143.

Hansen, K. A. (1995). Geographical mobility: March 1993 to March 1994. In *Current Population Reports* (U.S. Bureau of the Census, ed.), pp. 20–485. U.S. Government Printing Office, Washington, DC.

Hausman, J. McFadden, D. (1984). A specification test for the multinominal logit model. *Econometrica* **52,** 1219–1240.

Hunt, G. L. (1993). Equilibrium and disequilibrium in migration modelling. *Reg. Stud.* **27,** 341–349.

Lewis, H. G. (1963). *Unionism and Relative Wages in the United States.* University of Chicago Press, Chicago, IL.

Lewis, H. G. (1974). Comments on selectivity biases in wage comparisons. *J. Polit. Econ.* **82,** 1145–1155.

Maddala, G. S. (1983). *Limited-Dependent and Qualitative Variables in Econometrics.* Cambridge University Press, Cambridge, U.K.

Manski, D. F. (1989). Anatomy of the selection problem. *J. Hum. Resources* **24,** 343–360.

McFadden, D. (1987). Regression based specification tests for the multinominal logit model. *J. Econometrics* **34,** 63–82.

Mincer, J. (1978). Family migration decisions. *J. Polit. Econ.* **86,** 749–773.

Molho, I. (1986). Theories of migration: A review. *Scott. J. Polit. Econ.* **33,** 396–419.

Ravenstein, E. G. (1885). The laws of migration. *J. Stat. Society* **48,** 167–235.

Roy, A. D. (1951). Some thoughts on the distribution of earnings. *Oxford Econ. Pap.* **3,** 135–146.

Sjaastad, L. A. (1962). The costs and returns of human migration. *J. Polit. Econ.* **70**(Suppl.), 80–89.

Stewart, J. Q. (1941). An inverse distance variation for certain social influences. *Science* **93,** 89–90.

Taylor, J. E., and Martin, P. L. (2001). Human capital: Migration and rural population change. In *Handbook of Agricultural Economics* (B. L. Gardner and G. C. Rausser, eds.). Elsevier Science, New York.

Todaro, M. P. (1976). *Internal Migration is Developing Countries.* International Labour Office, Geneva.

Yezer, A. M. J., and Thurston, L. (1976). Migration patterns and income change: Implications for the human capital approach to migration. *South. Econ. J.* **42,** 693–702.

Models for Paired Comparisons

Ulf Böckenholt
McGill University, Montreal, Quebec, Canada

Glossary

conjoint measurement Facilitates the identification of a quantitative structure of variables without using operations of concatenation or physical addition.

intraclass correlation A measure of the degree of resemblance between microunits that belong to the same macrounit in a multilevel model.

multilevel models Statistical models that contain variables measured at different levels of a hierarchy. Regression coefficients of lower level representations are regressed on higher level explanatory variables to investigate dependencies among the multiple levels.

random utility model Assumes that observed choices are indicators of latent utilities that are specified to be functions of the decision makers and characteristics of the alternatives. The probability that a particular decision maker will choose a particular alternative is given by the probability that the utility of that alternative is greater than the utility of all other available alternatives for that decision maker.

transitivity A relation is transitive relative to a class if and only if, for all x, y, and z in that class, if $R(x, y)$ and $R(y, z)$ then $R(x, z)$.

In the method of paired comparisons, judges are presented with pairs of items and, for each pair, they are asked to choose the preferred item according to some criterion. Paired comparison judgments are collected in a wide range of applications, ranging from sensory testing to investigations of preference and choice behavior. Since L. L. Thurstone's seminal work in 1927 on the measurement of values, attitudes, and preferences, many advances have been made on modeling paired comparison data. These models are useful for investigating the degree to which respondents are consistent in their comparisons and for analyzing the underlying mean and covariance structure of the items that are being compared.

Introduction

The popularity of the paired comparison (PC) method as a data collection tool can be traced back to three reasons. First, by asking for a comparison of two items at a time, the PC method imposes minimal constraints on the response behavior of a judge. Especially when differences between items are small, the PC method is attractive because it is less prone to the influence of context effects that are caused by the presence of other items. Second, internal consistency checks are available; these facilitate the identification of judges who discriminate poorly. Third, paired comparison data provide a rich source of information about the effects of individual differences and perceived similarity relationships among items.

It is important to distinguish two different sampling schemes in the collection of paired comparison data. In the single-judgment case, each judge compares one pair of items only. Typically, this approach is used when substantial carryover effects from one pairwise judgment to the next would interfere with the evaluation of the items. Because a large number of judges are required to determine differences among the items, the second sampling scheme of asking each judge to compare multiple item pairs is used more frequently. An analysis of multiple paired comparisons by each judge must take into account that the data contain variation among judges as well as momentary fluctuations within each person. Disregarding systematic individual differences in the evaluations of the items is a serious model misspecification that can lead to incorrect statistical and substantive conclusions.

An attractive feature of the method of paired comparisons under the multiple-judgment scheme is that in pairwise comparisons of three or more items, the internal consistency of judgments can be investigated by determining the number of "circular triads." For example, when item j is preferred to item k, and item k is preferred to item l, it is expected that item j is also preferred to item l. If a judge selects item l in the last comparison, then this indicates an intransitivity in the judgmental process that may be either systematic or reflective of the stochastic nature of choice behavior.

To account for random violations of the transitivity conditions, a number of probabilistic choice models have been suggested. Perhaps because of its computational convenience and easy interpretation, the family of linear paired comparison models has been used most frequently for the analyses of paired comparison data over the years. Prominent members of this family include the Bradley–Terry–Luce and the Thurstonian models. These models can accommodate single- and multiple-judgment data. In the multiple-judgment case, it is assumed typically that the individual evaluations can be represented by a multivariate normal distribution. The mean vector and covariance matrix of the normal distribution describe the average evaluation of the items and their variability, respectively, in the population of judges. Because multiple-judgment PC models belong to the general class of hierarchical models, they can be fitted with standard multilevel software packages. Instead of requiring every judge to compare all items with each other, incomplete paired comparison designs can be utilized to reduce the judgmental burden of the respondents significantly. Covariates describing the judges and the items to be compared can also be included readily in this statistical framework.

Linear Paired Comparison Models

According to linear paired comparison models, each item j is associated with a parameter μ_{ij} that represents the mean evaluation or utility for this item of person i. Consequently, a comparison between two items reduces to computing the difference between the respective mean evaluations. Fluctuations in the evaluations of the two items j and k are captured by a random variable, ϵ_{ijk}, which is assumed to be identically and independently distributed for all item pairs. Based on these assumptions, the comparative judgment between items j and k can be written as

$$y_{ijk} = \mu_{ij} - \mu_{ik} + \epsilon_{ijk}. \tag{1}$$

Depending on the distributional assumptions that are made about ϵ_{ijk}, different members of the family of linear paired comparison models are obtained. For example, when ϵ_{ijk} is normally distributed, a Thurstonian model is obtained. Specifying a logistic distribution yields the Bradley–Terry–Luce model.

The Within-Judge Level

For multiple comparisons involving r items, the paired comparison judgments can be written conveniently as a linear model. For example, a comparison of the items j, k, l, and m obtains

$$\begin{pmatrix} y_{ijk} \\ y_{ijl} \\ y_{ijm} \\ y_{ikl} \\ y_{ikm} \\ y_{ilm} \end{pmatrix} = \begin{pmatrix} 1 & -1 & 0 & 0 \\ 1 & 0 & -1 & 0 \\ 1 & 0 & 0 & -1 \\ 0 & 1 & -1 & 0 \\ 0 & 1 & 0 & -1 \\ 0 & 0 & 1 & -1 \end{pmatrix} \begin{pmatrix} \mu_{ij} \\ \mu_{ik} \\ \mu_{il} \\ \mu_{im} \end{pmatrix} + \begin{pmatrix} \epsilon_{ijk} \\ \epsilon_{ijl} \\ \epsilon_{ijm} \\ \epsilon_{ikl} \\ \epsilon_{ikm} \\ \epsilon_{ilm} \end{pmatrix} = \mathbf{A}_i \boldsymbol{\mu}_i + \boldsymbol{\epsilon}_i, \tag{2}$$

where $\boldsymbol{\mu}_i$ is an r-dimensional vector containing the item parameters for the mean evaluations by person i, $\boldsymbol{\epsilon}_i$ is an $\binom{r}{2}$-dimensional pair-specific error component, and $\mathbf{A}_i$ is a design matrix describing the difference structure of the paired comparisons for person i. Each column of $\mathbf{A}_i$ corresponds to one of the items, and each row corresponds to one of the $\binom{r}{2}$ paired comparisons. Note that a constant can be added to each of the item values, which cancels out when computing a pairwise difference between the scale values. Thus, only $(r-1)$ item scale values can be estimated and the rth scale value can be set equal to an arbitrary constant without affecting the fit of the paired comparison model. This result has significant implications for the interpretation of individual differences, because they can be assessed only by selecting one of the items as a reference category.

With minor modifications of the design matrix $\mathbf{A}_i$, comparisons between composite stimuli (for example, in the form of risky choice options) can be investigated. Standard examples are gambles of the form (j, p_s, where item j can be won with probability p_s, and nothing otherwise. By using the mean evaluation of the status quo (i.e., "winning nothing") as a reference category, the origin of the individual utility scales can be defined in a natural way. Let μ_{i0} denote the mean evaluation of the status quo outcome. Then, by setting $\mu_{i0} = 0$, the expected utility of lottery (j, p_s) can be written as

$$y_{ij(p_s)} = p_s\mu_{ij} + (1-p_s)\mu_{i0} + \epsilon_{ij(p_s)} = p_s\,\mu_{ij} + \epsilon_{ij(p_s)},$$

and the comparative utility judgment of two lotteries is given by

$$y_{ij(p_s)k(p_u)} = p_s\mu_{ij} - p_u\mu_{ik} + \epsilon_{ij(p_s)k(p_u)}. \qquad (3)$$

To distinguish a risky from a nonrisky choice mode, the winning probabilities are listed in parentheses next to the option label. As an illustration, consider the following scenario in which the items j, k, and l are presented pairwise, first in a nonrisky presentation mode and, next, in the form of gambles:

$$\begin{pmatrix} y_{ijk} \\ y_{ijl} \\ y_{ikl} \\ y_{ij(0.8)k(0.2)} \\ y_{ij(0.8)l(0.2)} \\ y_{ik(0.8)l(0.2)} \\ y_{ij(0.2)k(0.8)} \\ y_{ij(0.2)l(0.8)} \\ y_{ik(0.2)l(0.8)} \end{pmatrix} = \begin{pmatrix} 1 & -1 & 0 \\ 1 & 0 & -1 \\ 0 & 1 & -1 \\ 0.8 & -0.2 & 0 \\ 0.8 & 0 & -0.2 \\ 0 & 0.8 & -0.2 \\ 0.2 & -0.8 & 0 \\ 0.2 & 0 & -0.8 \\ 0 & 0.2 & -0.8 \end{pmatrix} \begin{pmatrix} \mu_{ij} \\ \mu_{ik} \\ \mu_{il} \end{pmatrix} + \begin{pmatrix} \epsilon_{ijk} \\ \epsilon_{ijl} \\ \epsilon_{ikl} \\ \epsilon_{ij(0.8)k(0.2)} \\ \epsilon_{ij(0.8)l(0.2)} \\ \epsilon_{ik(0.8)l(0.2)} \\ \epsilon_{ij(0.2)k(0.8)} \\ \epsilon_{ij(0.2)l(0.8)} \\ \epsilon_{ik(0.2)l(0.8)} \end{pmatrix} = \mathbf{B}_i\boldsymbol{\mu}_i + \boldsymbol{\epsilon}_i.$$

For example, the fourth and last rows of the design matrix $\mathbf{B}_i$ indicate the choices of person i between the lotteries (j, 0.8) and (k, 0.2) and between the lotteries (k, 0.2) and (l, 0.8), respectively. The latter case obtains

$$y_{ik(0.2)l(0.8)} = 0.2\,\mu_{ik} - 0.8\,\mu_{il} + \epsilon_{ik(0.2)l(0.8)}.$$

It is important to note that the design matrix $\mathbf{B}_i$ is of full rank. Thus, although only difference judgments are observed, the mean evaluations and their covariance matrix can be fully identified, provided the expected utility representation of Eq. (3) is in agreement with the data.

Although the latent difference judgment y_{ijk} is specified to be continuous, the response of a judge is typically binary or ordinal. It is assumed that these discrete responses are obtained by mapping the continuous judgments onto a discrete response scale according to a threshold comparison process. For example, in a comparison between items j and k, the response category h is selected when

$$\tau_{h-1} < y_{ijk} < \tau_h, \qquad h = 1, \ldots, H,$$

where $\tau_0 < \tau_1 < \cdots < \tau_H$ are threshold parameters with $\tau_0 = -\infty$ and $\tau_H = \infty$. Under the hypothesis of no order effect in the comparison of two items, $\tau_h = -\tau_{H-h}$, and the sum of the threshold parameters is equal to zero. For binary response categories, $\tau_1 = 0$ is obtained. Another special case of interest includes PC models with an "indifference" category. The three outcomes—that person i selects item j, item k, or is indifferent to both items—are represented by the trinary variable $R_{ijk} = 1$, $R_{ijk} = 2$, and $R_{ijk} = 3$, respectively. The probability that item j is preferred to item k can then be written as

$$\Pr(R_{ijk} = 1) = \Pr(\mu_{ij} - \mu_{ik} \geq \tau_2 + \epsilon_{ijk}), \qquad (4)$$

where τ_2 is a (nonnegative) indifference threshold. By denoting the distribution function of the stochastic choice component by $\Psi(\cdot)$, the probability of observing the three paired comparison judgments is

$$\begin{aligned} \Pr(R_{ijk} = 1) &= \Psi(\mu_{ij} - \mu_{ik} - \tau_2), \\ \Pr(R_{ijk} = 2) &= \Psi(\mu_{ik} - \mu_{ij} - \tau_2), \\ \Pr(R_{ijk} = 3) &= \Psi(\mu_{ij} - \mu_{ik} + \tau_2) - \Psi(\mu_{ij} - \mu_{ik} - \tau_2). \end{aligned}$$

If $\Psi(\cdot)$ is specified to be a logistic distribution function $1/\{1 + \exp[-(\cdot)]\}$, the Rao and Kupper model is obtained. When instead of the logistic distribution function, the standard normal distribution function is selected, the paired comparison model by Glenn and David is obtained. Although both distribution functions are rather similar in form, the logistic distribution seems preferable because it offers computational advantages over the standard normal. The paired comparison probabilities can be expressed in closed form and the interpretation of the model parameters is simplified by an exponential transformation of the model parameters, i.e., $\pi_{il} = \exp(\mu_{il})$ ($l = 1, 2$), which yields

$$\begin{aligned} \Pr(R_{ijk} = 1) &= \pi_{ij}/(\pi_{ij} + \tau_2\pi_{ik}), \\ \Pr(R_{ijk} = 2) &= \pi_{ik}/(\pi_{ik} + \tau_2\pi_{ik}), \\ \Pr(R_{ijk} = 3) &= \pi_{ij}\pi_{ik}(\tau_2^2 - 1)/[(\pi_{ij} + \tau_2\pi_{ik})(\pi_{ik} + \tau_2\pi_{ij})]. \end{aligned}$$

The Between-Judge Level

Individual difference effects can be investigated by decomposing the person-specific utility values into fixed and random components. The fixed model part consists of the overall group mean, μ_j, for each item j. The random component, ν_{ij}, captures the degree to which the evaluation of judge i differs from μ_j. Thus, mean evaluations are written as $\boldsymbol{\mu}_i = \boldsymbol{\mu} + \boldsymbol{\nu}_i$, with $\boldsymbol{\mu} = (\mu_1, \ldots, \mu_r)'$ and $\boldsymbol{\nu}_i = (\nu_{i1}, \ldots, \nu_{ir})'$.

Frequently, in paired comparison studies, information is available about the options to be compared. The effects of the covariates may be either the same for all judges or may vary from judge to judge. In the former case, the mean evaluations can be expressed as $\boldsymbol{\mu} = \mathbf{X}\boldsymbol{\beta}$, where $\mathbf{X}$ contains the values of the design variables and $\boldsymbol{\beta}$ is a regression vector. In the latter case, the covariate information may be incorporated by specifying $\boldsymbol{\nu}_i = \mathbf{X}\boldsymbol{\zeta}_i + \boldsymbol{\delta}_i$, where $\boldsymbol{\zeta}_i$ is a regression vector for person i, and $\boldsymbol{\delta}_i$ is an error term representing the effects that are not accounted for by the covariates. The distributions of the random effects $\boldsymbol{\nu}_i$, or $\boldsymbol{\zeta}_i$, and $\boldsymbol{\delta}_i$, may be either selected *a priori* from some parametric family or estimated from the data.

One special, important case is obtained when specifying the random-effects distributions for the random effects on the within- and between-judge levels to be normal: Let $\boldsymbol{\epsilon}_i$, and $\boldsymbol{\nu}_i$, be normally distributed with $\boldsymbol{\epsilon}_i \sim \mathcal{N}(\mathbf{0}, \sigma^2\mathbf{I}$, $\boldsymbol{\nu}_i \sim \mathcal{N}(\mathbf{0}, \boldsymbol{\Sigma}_\nu)$, and $\boldsymbol{\epsilon}_i$ and $\boldsymbol{\nu}_i$ are independent. Then the joint distribution of $\mathbf{y}_i$, and $\boldsymbol{\nu}_i$, can be written as

$$\begin{bmatrix} \mathbf{y}_i \\ \boldsymbol{\nu}_i \end{bmatrix} \sim \mathcal{N}\left(\begin{bmatrix} \mathbf{A}\boldsymbol{\mu} \\ \mathbf{0} \end{bmatrix}, \begin{bmatrix} \mathbf{V} & \mathbf{A}\boldsymbol{\Sigma}_\nu \\ \boldsymbol{\Sigma}_\nu \mathbf{A}' & \boldsymbol{\Sigma}_\nu \end{bmatrix} \right), \tag{5}$$

where the $\binom{r}{2} \times \binom{r}{2}$ matrix $\mathbf{V} = \mathbf{A}\boldsymbol{\Sigma}_\nu\mathbf{A}' + \sigma^2\mathbf{I}$. Covariates can be taken into account by specifying that $\boldsymbol{\zeta}_i \sim \mathcal{N}(0, \boldsymbol{\Sigma}_\zeta)$, $\boldsymbol{\delta}_i \sim \mathcal{N}(\mathbf{0}, \sigma_\delta^2\mathbf{I})$, and $\boldsymbol{\zeta}_i$ and $\boldsymbol{\delta}_i$ are independent. In this case, $\boldsymbol{\Sigma}_\nu = \mathbf{X}\boldsymbol{\Sigma}_\zeta\mathbf{X}' + \sigma_\delta^2\mathbf{I}$ is obtained.

Identification of Individual Differences

The interpretation of individual differences in the evaluation of the items is complicated in two ways. First, only binary or ordinal judgments of an underlying continuous variable are observed. Second, because paired comparison judgments are conceptualized as difference judgments, the location of the latent judgment $\mathbf{y}$ cannot be identified except when additional assumptions are made about the origin. Thus, in general, only the covariance matrix of $(r - 1)$ scale values can be estimated and the scale value of the rth item needs to be set equal to a constant to fix the origin of the item scale. In this case, the set of covariance matrices $\boldsymbol{\Sigma}_\nu^*$ that are observationally equivalent to $\boldsymbol{\Sigma}_\nu$ is given by $\boldsymbol{\Sigma}_\nu^* = \boldsymbol{\Sigma}_\nu + \mathbf{d}\mathbf{1}' + \mathbf{1}\mathbf{d}'$, where $\mathbf{d}$ is an arbitrary real-valued vector and the variance of $\boldsymbol{\epsilon}_i$ is specified to be a constant. For example, the hypothesis that the utilities of the options are independently distributed with unit variance, i.e., $\boldsymbol{\Sigma}_\nu = \mathbf{I}$, is indistinguishable from the hypothesis that the utilities have variances equal to $1 + e$ and covariances equal to e, i.e., $\boldsymbol{\Sigma}_\nu^* = \boldsymbol{\Sigma}_\nu + e\mathbf{1}\mathbf{1}'$. When covariates are available to describe the choice options with $\boldsymbol{\Sigma}_\nu = \mathbf{X}\boldsymbol{\Sigma}_\zeta\mathbf{X}' + \sigma_\delta^2\mathbf{I}$, both $\boldsymbol{\Sigma}_\zeta$ and σ_δ^2 can be identified, provided there exists no $\mathbf{d}(\neq \mathbf{0})$ such that $\mathrm{R}(\mathbf{d}\mathbf{1}' + \mathbf{1}\mathbf{d}') \subseteq \mathrm{R}(\mathbf{X}')$, where $\mathrm{R}(\mathbf{M})$ denotes the row space of matrix $\mathbf{M}$.

These difficulties in interpreting the covariance matrix of the item utility differences can be alleviated by including composite items in a paired comparison experiment. In this case, it is possible to identify the covariance matrix of the r scale values although only difference judgments are observed.

Consistency Analyses

The paired comparison task belongs to a small group of techniques that provide explicit information about the consistency of individual- and group-level judgments. Individual judgments are rarely deterministically consistent. Only when the perceived differences between items are large can it be expected that a person will arrive at the same response in repeated comparisons. Several probabilistic consistency rules have been proposed in the literature. The most well-known conditions, weak stochastic transitivity (WST), moderate stochastic transitivity (MST), and strong stochastic transitivity (SST), are defined as follows: for all j, k, and l in a given choice set,

$$\begin{aligned}
\text{WST:}\quad & [\Pr(j \to k) \geq 0.50 \ \text{ and } \ \Pr(k \to l)] \geq 0.50 \\
& \Rightarrow \Pr(j \to l) \geq 0.50, \\
\text{MST:}\quad & [\Pr(j \to k) \geq 0.50 \ \text{ and } \ \Pr(k \to l)] \geq 0.50 \\
& \Rightarrow \ \Pr(j \to l) \geq \min[\Pr(j \to k), \Pr(k \to 1)], \\
\text{SST:}\quad & [\Pr(j \to k) \geq 0.50 \ \text{ and } \ \Pr(k \to l)] \geq 0.50 \\
& \Rightarrow \ \Pr(j \to l) \geq \max[\Pr(j \to k), \Pr(k \to 1)].
\end{aligned}$$

For example, under the SST condition, it is expected that if item j is preferred to item k more than 50% of the time, and item k is preferred to item l more than 50% of the time, then item j should be preferred to item l more often than items j and k are preferred in the (j, k) and (k, l) comparisons, respectively.

Although Luce's paired comparison model satisfies SST and hence MST and WST on the individual level, it allows for violations of SST and requires only MST to hold for group-level data. Investigations of stochastic transitivity relationships are valuable only insofar as they provide consistency evaluations of group judgments. They do not allow any inferences about the behavior of the individual judges. Similarly, inconsistencies in group-level judgments cannot be predicted on the basis of individual-level data. Even if judges are perfectly consistent in their paired comparisons, it cannot be concluded that the group-level data exhibit coherence as well.

For multiple-judgment data, individual consistency can be assessed by analyzing the incidence of circular triads. When circular triads are a result of random variability in the judgmental process, intransitive judgments are expected only when the perceived differences between items are small. Similarly, hypotheses about combination rules that are used in assessing composite stimuli can be tested by examining whether the conditions defined for a conjoint measurement structure are satisfied. As an example, consider the double-cancellation condition in risky-choice comparisons. Let $(j, p_t) \succeq (k, p_s)$ denote that gamble (k, p_s) is not preferred to gamble (j, p_t), and let j, k, and l be items from a specified set of items and p_s, p_t, and p_u be any values on the interval (0, 1), then $\succeq$ satisfies double-cancellation if and only if $(k, p_s) \succeq (j, p_t)$ and $(l, p_t) \succeq (k, p_u)$, then $(l, p_s) \succeq (j, p_u)$. When $p_s = p_t = p_u = 1$, double cancellation reduces to the transitivity test in nonrisky choice.

Figure 1 illustrates how the probability of observing violations of the double-cancellation and transitivity conditions depends on mean differences between the items, the size of the winning probabilities, and the intraclass correlation between two latent pairwise judgments. Five different mean specifications are depicted in Fig. 1 ranging from ($\mu_j = 0$, $\mu_k = 0$, $\mu_l = 0$) to ($\mu_j = 1.5$, $\mu_k = 0$, $\mu_l = -1.5$). The within-pair evaluative responses is specified to be normally distributed with a variance of 1 and the between-pair responses are specified to be uncorrelated. The two panels differ in the winning probabilities assigned to p_s, p_t, and p_u, which are listed at the top of each panel in Fig. 1. For example, the second dashed line in the left panel corresponds to the gamble triplet [$(j, 0.5)$, $(k, 0.5)$, $(l, 0.5)$] with means ($\mu_j = -0.5$, $\mu_k = 0$, $\mu_l = -0.5$). The right panel of Fig. 1 contains the likelihood of observing intransitive responses because all winning probabilities are set equal to 1. Figure 1 shows that for zero mean differences, the likelihoods of observing violations of the double cancellation and transitivity conditions reach their maximum of 0.25 when gambles are judged independently of each other (intraclass correlation = 0) and diminish gradually as the intraclass correlation increases to 0.5. Larger mean differences between gambles lead to a smaller percentage of consistency violations.

Because violations of the transitivity and the double-cancellation conditions are by-products of random variability in the repeated evaluation of an item, the two intransitive cycles $j \succeq k \succeq l \succeq j$ and $j \succeq l \succeq k \succeq j$, as well as the two choice patterns that are inconsistent with the double-cancellation condition, have an almost equal probability of occurring. Significant differences in the probabilities of observing the two intransitive cycles can indicate that intransitive choices are systematic and not random. Similarly, violations of the double-cancellation condition may be systematic when the frequencies of the two choice patterns that are inconsistent with the double-cancellation condition differ appreciably from each other. Thus, examining whether inconsistent choice patterns are equally likely can be of diagnostic value in detecting true deviations from transitivity or double cancellation.

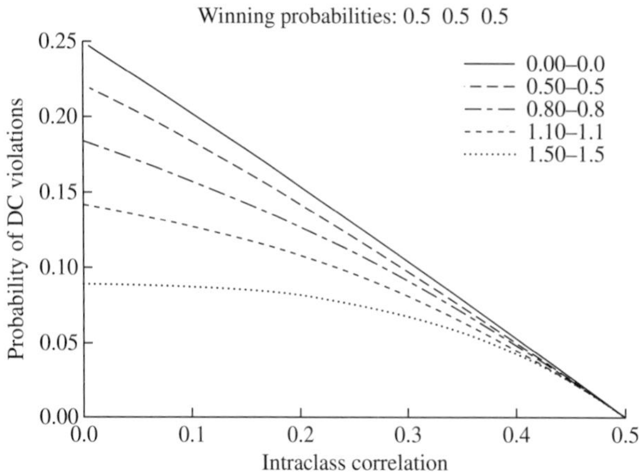

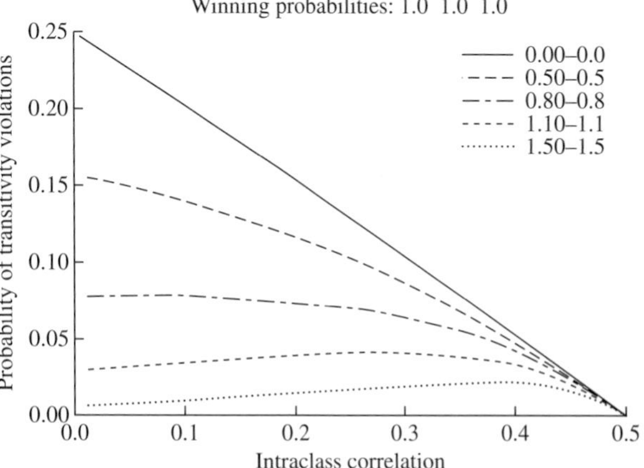

Figure 1 Probability of transitivity and double-cancellation (DC) violations as a function of the intraclass correlation coefficient, winning probabilities, and selected item mean values.

Conclusion

The formulation of linear paired comparison models by postulating latent utilities has a long tradition in biometric, econometric, psychometric, and sociometric disciplines. Applications and technical developments in each of these areas have led to many improvements in the statistical apparatus for estimating and validating paired comparison models. Although the notion that each item can be represented by a person-specific value has proved to be useful in a wide range of applications, its limitations are equally obvious. Important extensions concern the evaluation of cognitive abilities or skills that may vary over time, and the modeling of context-sensitive behavior that takes into account that assessment of an item's utility may depend on pair-specific comparisons drawn between it and another item. Linear paired comparison models are most useful in providing parsimonious descriptions of how judges differ in their evaluations at a particular point in time or over time. However, by emphasizing interindividual differences, this approach can render only limited insights about intraindividual processes influencing a pairwise choice.

See Also the Following Articles

Thurstone's Scales of Primary Abilities • Thurstone, L.L.

Further Reading

Bock, R. D., and Jones, L. V. (1968). *The Measurement and Prediction of Judgment and Choice.* Holden-Day, San Francisco.

Böckenholt, U. (2001). Hierarchical models of paired comparison data. *Psychol. Methods* **6,** 49–66.

Bradley, R. A., and Terry, M. E. (1952). The rank analysis of incomplete block designs. I. The method of paired comparisons. *Biometrika* **39,** 324–345.

David, H. A. (1988). *The Method of Paired Comparisons.* Griffin, London.

Glenn, W. A., and David, H. A. (1960). Ties in paired comparison experiments using a modified Thurstone–Mosteller model. *Biometrics* **16,** 86–109.

Luce, R. D. (1959). *Individual Choice Behavior.* Wiley, New York.

Luce, R. D. (2000). *Utility of Gains and Losses: Measurement—Theoretical and Experimental Approaches.* Lawrence Erlbaum Assoc., Hillsdale.

Maydeu-Olivares, A. (2002). Limited information estimation and testing of Thurstonian models for preference data. *Math. Social Sci.* **43,** 467–483.

Rao, P. V., and Kupper, L. L. (1967). Ties in paired comparison experiments: A generalization of the Bradley–Terry model. *J. Am. Statist. Assoc.* **62,** 194–204.

Snijders, A. B., and Bosker, R. J. (1999). *Multilevel Analyses: An Introduction to Basic and Advanced Multilevel Modelling.* Sage Publ., Thousand Oaks.

Takane, Y. (1987). Analysis of covariance structures and probabilistic binary choice data. *Cogn. Commun.* **20,** 45–62.

Thurstone, L. L. (1927). A law of comparative judgment. *Psychol. Rev.* **34,** 273–286.

Tsai, R.-C., and Böckenholt, U. (2002). Two-level linear paired comparison models: Estimation and identifiability issues. *Math. Social Sci.* **43,** 429–449.

Tversky, A. (1969). Intransitivity of preference. *Psychol. Rev.* **76,** 31–48.

Morgenstern, Oskar

Eric van Damme
Tilburg University, Tilburg, The Netherlands

Glossary

cooperative game A game model that assumes that players can make coalitions and agree on side payments outside of the formal rules.

game theory A mathematical theory to model and analyze conflicts arising from economic, social, and political situations.

Nash equilibrium The solution concept for noncooperative games: a strategy profile is a Nash equilibrium if no player can profit by unilaterally deviating from the solution.

noncooperative game A game model such that the rules of the game fully describe the situation; all possibilities for coalition formation or side payments are explicitly included in the rules.

stable set The solution concept for cooperative games introduced by von Neumann and Morgenstern; a stable set satisfies both internal stability (no element in the set dominates another element in the set) as well as external stability (every element outside is dominated by an element from inside).

von Neumann–Morgenstern utility theory An axiomatic theory of individual decision making under uncertainty; if an individual's choice behavior satisfies certain assumptions, he/she will have a numerical utility function and will evaluate each lottery (random outcome) by its expected utility.

Together with John von Neumann, Oskar Morgenstern wrote *The Theory of Games and Economic Behavior*, one of the great social science books of the 20th century. The book argues strongly that traditional models and methods are unsuited to develop a general theory of rational behavior, and it proposes an alternative based on game theory. Besides expounding the theory of zero-sum two-person games that had earlier been developed by von Neumann, the book contains at least three seminal contributions (the theory of expected utility, the concept of a cooperative game, and the stable set solution concept) and it provides the first applications of game theory to economics and political science. Morgenstern also worked and wrote on economic growth, on predictability of stock prices, on the accuracy of economic observations, and on methodological issues. Morgenstern's work and influence are described here, focusing on his work in game theory.

Early Work: Impossibility of Perfect Foresight

Oskar Morgenstern was born in Görlitz (Germany) on January 24, 1902. When he was 14 years old, the family moved to Vienna, where, in 1925, Oskar received his doctorate for a thesis on marginal productivity; this enabled him to describe himself as a product of the Austrian School of Economics. In the same year, he was awarded a Rockefeller Fellowship, which allowed him to continue studying in London, Paris, and Rome and at Harvard and Columbia. In 1928, he returned to the University of Vienna, where he defended his habilitation thesis *Wirtschaftsprognose* and where he was appointed as Privatdozent in 1929. In this second thesis, a study of the theory and applications of economic forecasting, Morgenstern pointed out two problems in making predictions in the social sciences: that the predictions may influence the predicted events and that an individual makes predictions about the behavior of other individuals, behavior that in turn is guided by their predictions about his own behavior. This raises the issue of whether a (good) prediction is possible at all, and by means of an example, Morgenstern suggested that the answer is no:

> *Sherlock Holmes, pursued by his opponent, Moriarty, leaves for Dover. The train stops at a station on the*

way, and he alights there rather than traveling on to Dover. He has seen Moriarty at the railway station, recognizes that he is very clever, and expects that Moriarty will take a special faster train in order to catch him at Dover. Holmes' anticipation turns out to be correct. But what if Moriarty had been still more clever, had estimated Holmes' mental abilities better and had foreseen his actions accordingly? Then obviously he would have traveled to the intermediate station. Holmes, again, would have had to calculate that, and he himself would have decided to go on to Dover. Whereupon Moriarty would have "reacted" differently. Because of so much thinking they might not have been able to act at all or the intellectually weaker of the two would have surrendered to the other in the Victoria Station, since the whole flight would have become unnecessary. Examples of this kind can be drawn from everywhere. [Morgenstern, 1928, p. 98]

In the same year that Morgenstern published *Wirtschaftsprognose*, John von Neumann published *Zur Theorie der Gesellschaftsspiele*. Morgenstern's example can be viewed as a two-player game in which each of the players, Holmes and Moriarty, has two strategies: to take a slow train that stops at the intermediate station and get out there, or to take a fast train to Dover. Assume that Holmes escapes for sure if they take different types of trains, that he is caught otherwise, and that Holmes (respectively, Moriarty) wants to maximize (respectively, minimize) the probability of escape. Obviously, no player has a *deterministic* optimal strategy and it is not possible to make a determinate prediction of the outcome: if the prediction is that Holmes will take the slow train, Holmes will realize that Moriarty will know this, inducing Holmes to violate the prediction, and similar for every other possibility. In modern game theoretic language, this is a game without pure strategy equilibrium. In his paper, von Neumann, however, showed that equilibrium can be obtained if we allow for randomized decisions: a player that bases his decision on the toss of a coin cannot be outsmarted by his opponent and will be happy with his choice; we can confidently predict that Holmes will escape with probability 1/2. The main result in von Neumann's paper shows that mixed strategies not only solve the prediction problem in this example, but in two-person constant sum games in general.

In 1931, Morgenstern succeeded Friedrich von Hayek as director of the Austrian Institute for Business Cycle Research, but he continued to be bothered by problems of prediction and foresight. He also became editor of the *Zeitschrift für Nationalökonomie*, in which he published his paper *Volkommene Voraussicht und Wirtschaftliches Gleichgewicht*, returning to issues from the 1929 thesis and arguing that the theory of general economic equilibrium crucially depends on this paradoxical assumption of perfect foresight and, hence, is unsatisfactory. After a presentation of this paper in Karl Menger's Vienna Colloquium, the mathematician Eduard Ĉech pointed out to Morgenstern that his work was related to that of von Neumann, and he urged Morgenstern to read the latter's paper. Morgenstern's many duties apparently prevented him from doing so (in addition to being director of the Austrian Institute for Business Cycle Research, he was an advisor to the Austrian National Bank, an advisor to the Ministry of Commerce, and a member of the Committee of Statistical Experts of the League of Nations).

In January 1938, with support of the Carnegie Endowment for International Peace, Morgenstern left for the United States. In March of that year, the Nazis took over in Austria and Morgenstern was dismissed from his Vienna position. Finding himself unable to return to Austria, he accepted a 3-year appointment in political economy at Princeton University, in the hope that he would get to know von Neumann and would be able to work with him.

Collaboration with von Neumann

In Morgenstern's 1976 article in the *Journal of Economic Literature*, the impression is given that, even though von Neumann did most of the work on which Morgenstern and von Neumann had collaborated for the *Theory of Games and Economic Behavior*, and certainly was responsible for the mathematical parts, the writing that they had produced was a truly cooperative effort: "We wrote virtually everything together and in the manuscript there are sometimes long passages written by one or the other and also passages in which the handwriting changes two or three times on the same page." Viewing Morgenstern's diaries, however, it is possible to conclude that this account is somewhat misleading: rather, von Neumann did the bulk of the writing. Morgenstern's direct contributions reside mainly in Chapter 1, in his insistence on the measurement of utility, and in the economic examples, but the indirect contribution should not be underestimated: he succeeded in getting and keeping von Neumann interested in economic problems and inducing him to spend his great intellectual powers on these, thereby advancing social science. As Morgenstern wrote in 1963, "Scientific activity consists largely in asking the right kind of question. There comes a point where economists and mathematicians must get together to do precisely this in order to advance our knowledge." Andrew Schotter wrote in 1976 that "without Oskar Morgenstern we would not have the theory of games as we know it today.... Game theory would probably not have been introduced into the social sciences until many years later.... I can think of no other economists at the time who could have walked into a room with John von Neumann and walked out later with a 600-page book on the theory of games complete with economic examples." By combining their respective comparative advantages—von

Neumann as a creative innovator and Morgenstern as a visionary entrepreneur and arbitrageur between two fields—the two constructed a unique product.

When Morgenstern first met with von Neumann in 1938, the latter had again seriously taken up his interest in game theory. The first intensive discussions between the two took place in October 1939 when Morgenstern was starting to write down the material on "maxims of behavior" that would eventually be published in Chapter 1 of *Theory of Games and Economic Behavior* (*TGEB*); this effort continued till the summer of 1940, when von Neumann gave three lectures on games to the department of mathematics at Washington University in Seattle. After Morgenstern returned to Princeton, von Neumann's cooperation with Morgenstern intensified. He informed Morgenstern about the progress that he had made and wrote two papers, and Morgenstern supplied von Neumann with criticism about established economic thinking and with an agenda of things to do. In the summer of 1941, von Neumann proposed to Morgenstern that they write a paper together and this induced Morgenstern to work on von Neumann's manuscripts, the explicit purpose being to write an introduction to them. The period from June 1941 to Christmas 1942, during which the book was written, probably was the intellectually most stimulating and most productive period of Morgenstern's life. On July 30, 1941, he wrote in his diary, "This is the book I have been dreaming of for years."

Axioms and Measurable Utility

From the outset, the authors of *TGEB* make clear that their work is solidly based on methodological individualism: "In the course of the development of economics, it has been found, and it is now well-nigh universally agreed, that an approach to this vast problem is gained by the analysis of the behavior of the individuals which constitute the economic community." Of course, this approach requires an adequate representation of the motives of the individuals. In 1944, the standard approach in economics was to represent an individual's preferences by a set of indifference curves, which corresponds to an ordinal ranking of alternatives. Even though this standard approach is based on the strong assumption that preferences are complete (the individual is able to compare all possible prospects), it has only limited applicability because it does not allow for uncertainty, and working with it is also somewhat clumsy. von Neumann and Morgenstern argue that the theory should be able to deal with uncertainty, and that willingness to assume completeness of preferences as well as certain other "natural" properties actually obtains a much simpler, numerical representation. Specifically, in the second edition of *TGEB*, von Neumann and Morgenstern propose axioms that imply that utility is measurable, unique up to a positive affine transformation, and linear in the probabilities that represent the uncertainty. *TGEB* provides one of the first applications of the axiomatic method in economics and it shows that this method, which had already been successfully used in mathematics, is equally promising in this domain. In 1963, at the Philadelphia symposium of the American Academy of Political Sciences, Morgenstern provided a brief description of the axiomatic method in general; John F. Nash's work on bargaining and work by Lloyd S. Shapley on value and on measuring political power are excellent examples illustrating how fruitful the approach can be in dealing with economic problems.

It is useful to illustrate the axiomatic approach pioneered by von Neumann and Morgenstern by explicitly deriving their utility function. Assume an individual can choose from a (finite) set of possible outcomes X. The traditional approach assumes that i has a complete preference ordering over X; that is, for each two alternatives x, $y \in X$, he can say whether he (weakly) prefers x to y (written $x \succeq y$) or y to x ($y \succeq x$), and the relation is reflexive ($x \succeq x$ for all x) and transitive (if $x \succeq y$ and $y \succeq z$, then $x \succeq z$). Clearly, associated with $\succeq$, there is a strict preference relation $\succ$ ($x \succ y$ if $x \succeq y$ but not $y \succeq x$) and an indifference relation $\sim$($x \sim y$ if $z \succeq y$ and $y \succeq x$). Because X is finite, it follows that there is a best element b in the set ($b \succeq x$ for all x) as well as a worst element w ($x \succeq w$ for all x).

von Neumann and Morgenstern now assume that the individual can also compare uncertain prospects yielding outcomes in X, as long as these are associated with known, objective probabilities. Formally, if P denotes the set of all lotteries on X, i.e., probability distributions with outcomes in X, we assume that the preference $\succeq$ relation can be extended to a complete, reflexive, transitive relation on P. Now take $x \in X$, assume $b \succ x \succ w$, and write $\langle \lambda;\ w,\ b \rangle = (1-\lambda)w + \lambda b$ for the lottery that yields b with probability λ and w with the complementary probability $1-\lambda$. It is natural to assume that $w \sim \langle 0;\ w,\ b \rangle$, $b \sim \langle 1;\ w,\ b \rangle$ and that the preference relation is continuous, i.e., there exists some $\lambda \in (0, 1)$ such that $x \sim \langle \lambda;\ w,\ b \rangle$. It is equally natural that if $\lambda > \mu$, then $\langle \lambda;\ w,\ b \rangle \succ \langle \mu,\ w,\ b \rangle$, and in this case there exists a unique number, denoted, say, by $u(x)$, such that $x \sim \langle u(x);\ w,\ b \rangle$. Note that $u(w) = 0$ and $u(b) = 1$; we have obtained that the utility of any outcome $x \in X$ is measurable: $u(x)$ is simply the probability needed to put on the good outcome to make the individual indifferent between x and the lottery.

What can be said about the utility of a lottery? Can $u(\cdot)$ be extended from X to P, similarly as we have extended? With an additional assumption, the answer is affirmative. Assume that the individual can also compare compound lotteries, that is, objects of the type $\langle \alpha;\ p,\ q \rangle$, where p, $q \in P$. The final axiom that we need is independence: $p \succeq q$ if and only if $\langle \alpha;\ p,\ r \rangle\ \langle \alpha;\ q,\ r \rangle$ for all $\alpha \in [0, 1]$

and $r \in P$. Again, this appears to be natural: each of the compound lotteries yields r with the same probability, hence, preference should not be guided by that event; in the alternative event, the lottery coincides with p or q, hence, preferences are determined by these lotteries. This assumption implies that the individual is indifferent between a compound lottery and the simple lottery that induces the same distribution on X. Consequently, if $p \in P$ is the lottery that yields outcome x with probability $p(x)$, we have $p \sim \langle u(p); w, b \rangle$, where $u(p) = \sum_{x \in X} p(x) u(x)$. We have derived our main result: if preferences $\succeq$ on P are complete, transitive, continuous, and satisfy the independence axiom, then there exists a function u on X such that $p \succeq q$ if and only if

$$\sum_{x \in X} p(x)\, u(x) \geq \sum_{x \in X} q(x)\, u(x). \qquad (1)$$

Preferences can thus be represented by a numerical utility function, and one lottery is preferred to another if and only if it yields higher expected utility. Furthermore, the utility function $u(\cdot)$ is determined up to a positive affine transformation: because $x \sim \langle u(x); w, b \rangle$, we must have $v(x) = u(x)v(b) + (1 - u(x))v(w)$, or $v(x) = v(w) + u(x)(v(b) - v(w))$ for any alternative utility representation $v(\cdot)$ that satisfies Eq. (1).

This approach has been extended to the case in which the probabilities are subjective. The axiomatic approach makes clear what are the "critical" assumptions underlying expected utility theory; as such, it allows attacking the theory on its weakest points and offers room for alternative development and improvement. Even though these axioms appear natural, actual human behavior violates them in systematic ways. This should not belittle the contribution of von Neumann and Morgenstern; as Morgenstern wrote in 1972, "Each problem solved usually suggests new ones which could not have been stated without a given problem first having been solved."

Games and Solutions

von Neumann and Morgenstern were quick to point out in *TGEB* that a participant in a social-exchange economy faces a much different problem from that just discussed: "He too tries to obtain an optimum result. But in order to achieve this, he must enter into relations of exchange with others. If two or more persons exchange goods with each other, then the result for each one will depend in general not merely upon his own actions but on those of others as well." Obviously, because actions depend on expectations, we are back in the setting of the Holmes–Moriarty example. von Neumann and Morgenstern pointed out that this conceptual problem is neglected in traditional economics and that this kind of problem is nowhere dealt with in classical mathematics. They then proposed an alternative game theoretic solution.

The traditional economic method abstracts away from strategic interaction by focusing on the case in which the number of players is large. Although it may indeed be hoped that the influence of every particular participant is negligible in that case, von Neumann and Morgenstern were right to argue that this had not been formally proved and that such a proof requires explicit consideration of the finite-player case. As they also argued, the traditional approach is all the more unsatisfactory because it makes several assumptions (such as the existence of a price system, the fact that individuals know prices and take them as given, and the absence of coalitions of traders that could wield power) that should preferably should be derived from more primitive ones.

An example may make this clear. Suppose that there is one seller who owns one indivisible unit and who values this at a. Also suppose that there are two potential buyers and that each of these values the unit at b, with $b > a$. As trading generates a surplus, the natural questions are who will trade and how the surplus will be divided. The traditional approach assumes the existence of prices and searches for a price that clears the market. As is clear, the unique price, when supply is equal to demand, is $p = b$, hence, the standard prediction is that the short side of the market appropriates the entire surplus. There is no prediction about who will actually trade, but, because, in equilibrium, each buyer is indifferent between trading or not, this really is irrelevant. However, where do the prices come from? Why focus on a market institution? Why is it justified to assume that the buyers do not form a cartel and negotiate with the seller as a team?

von Neumann and Morgenstern want to address these more basic questions. They clearly state their goal: "We wish to find the mathematically complete principles which define rational 'behavior' for the participants in a social economy, and to derive from them the general characteristics of that behavior." Furthermore, these rules have to deal with all possible situations that may arise: "if the superiority of 'rational behavior' over any other kind is to be established, then its description must include rules of conduct for all conceivable situations—including those where 'the others' behaved irrationally, in the sense of the standards which the theory will set for them."

Noncooperative Games

In defining what should be understood as a solution, it is important, using terminology that was introduced by John Nash, to distinguish between cooperative and noncooperative games. In many parlor games, the rules offer a complete description: it is clear what is allowed and what is not. Such games are said to be noncooperative, i.e., it is not possible to move outside of the game. Note that the game being noncooperative does not mean that coalitions cannot be formed; it simply means that all such possibilities are included in the rules. For such a game, a solution is "a set of rules for each participant which tell him how to behave in every situation which may conceivably arise."

Given Morgenstern's interest in predictability, it is remarkable that Chapter 1 of *TGEB* circumvents the question of what constitutes "rational behavior" in a noncooperative game. For the special zero-sum two-person case, the issue is, however, discussed later in the book. There it is argued that, if a complete and absolutely convincing theory of rational behavior exists, then each player should still be willing to play according to this theory, even if he knows that other players know that he will play that way. von Neumann and Morgenstern use this argument to justify the minmax solution that was originally advocated, and proved to exist in by von Neumann in 1928; that is, they recommend that each player chooses a strategy that guarantees the highest possible payoff under the assumption that his strategy has been found out by the opponent. In later work, John Nash turned around this argument and reasoned that, when a convincing theory exists, each player should not be able to profit from knowing what the others will do: each player's plan should be a best response against the plans of the others. A strategy profile satisfying this condition is known as a Nash equilibrium of the game, hence, the von Neumann and Morgenstern argument seems naturally to lead to the Nash equilibrium concept, by now the most important solution concept for noncooperative games. The Holmes–Moriarty example shows that a Nash equilibrium in pure strategies need not exist, but Nash proved that there is always at least one equilibrium in mixed strategies. He also showed that his concept coincides with that of von Neumann for two-person zero-sum games. Because Nash's concept seems the natural solution to the problem of "perfect foresight" that occupied Morgenstern since the start of his career, it is remarkable that this concept is not discussed in *TGEB*, neither to reject it nor to endorse it. Perhaps von Neumann and Morgenstern rejected this concept because it does not have good "defensive" properties (an equilibrium strategy need not do well when the others do not play according to the solution), but what they thought about this is not known because they did not discuss it, although they mention Nash's work in the preface to the third edition of *TGEB*. In fact, it is quite remarkable that also in his later work Morgenstern never discussed the Nash concept.

Cooperative Games

von Neumann and Morgenstern are, obviously, mainly interested in situations with more than two players, in which coalitions play an important role, thus the bulk of *TGEB* is devoted to cooperative games. What is even more important, and is stressed in *TGEB*, if there are more than two players, they will typically have incentives to agree to coalitions and to make side payments *outside of the formal rules* of the game: it must be expected that a player will be willing to compensate another in order to secure the latter's cooperation. Consequently, even if the rules of the game do not explicitly allow for these possibilities, the formal analysis has to take them into account, and this induced von Neumann and Morgenstern to introduce a different game form, the so-called characteristic function, which describes for each coalition S of players that might form, the total value $v(S)$ that these players can divide among themselves. Note that in moving to this representation, von Neumann and Morgenstern assume that utility is freely transferable between the players. For cooperative games, the question that *TGEB* seeks to answer concerns which coalition S will form and how its members will divide the value $v(S)$?

It should be immediately clear that the theory cannot be expected to give a unique answer to the first question. For example, in the three-person symmetric game in which each two-person coalition has value 1 and all other coalitions have value 0, it may be expected that two players will agree on an equal split (1/2, 1/2), but which players this will be is unknown. As von Neumann and Morgenstern stressed, the competition between coalitions will determine which one will form and how it will divide the surplus. A second example may make this clear. Suppose we have a three-player game with $v(12)=3$, $v(13)=2$, $v(23)=1$, and $v(S)=0$ otherwise. Clearly, the coalition $\{1, 2\}$ is most attractive, but how should it divide the spoils? Each of the players in this coalition will look at what he can get with the outside player, and the outside player (player 3) will clearly investigate what bribe he has to offer to each of the other two in order to induce one of them to form a coalition with him. Consequently, a statement about the division in one coalition can be made only by simultaneously looking at the other coalitions. In this case, if $x=(x_1, x_2, x_3)$ satisfies $x_1+x_2=3, x_1+x_3=2$, and $x_2+x_3=1$, and each coalition $\{i,j\}$ expects $v(ij)$ to be divided according to x, then, in each coalition, each inside player will be satisfied because he cannot get more by switching; hence, x determines a stable division for each possible coalition that might form. Obviously, the unique x that satisfies these conditions is $x=(2,1,0)$. Even if the coalition $\{1,2\}$ is eventually formed, the payoff division (2, 1) associated with this coalition derives its stability only from consideration of the other possible coalitions. The solution consists of a triple $\langle\langle\{1, 2\}, 2, 1\rangle, \langle\{1, 3\}, 2, 0\rangle, \langle\{2, 3\}, 1, 0\rangle\rangle$; it is the system that is stable, not the single imputations from which it is composed.

Accordingly, von Neumann and Morgenstern came to the conclusion that "A solution should be a system of imputations possessing in its entirety some kind of balance and stability the nature of which we shall try to determine." The stability notion that they proposed makes use of the concept of dominance. An imputation x is said to dominate another imputation y ($x \succeq y$) if there exists a coalition S of individuals, each of whom strictly prefers x to y and such that S is able to enforce x. Note that this dominance relation typically will not be transitive: in the one-seller two-buyers example discussed previously, let x_i be the imputation resulting from a trade at price x between S and buyer B_i; then, if $b > x > y > z > a$, we have $y_1 \succeq z_2$ (through the coalition $\{S, B_1\}$) and $x_2 \succeq y_1$, but there is no dominance relation between x_2 and z_2. As a result, a single imputation that dominates all others, in general, need not exist.

When can a set X of imputations be considered stable? A necessary requirement is that X should be free of inner contradictions; no element in X should dominate another element of X. Second, von Neumann and Morgenstern insisted that any alternative imputation (i.e., one that is not in X) can be discredited by referring to some element that is in X: if $y \notin X$, then $x \succeq y$ for some $x \in X$. A set X that satisfies both internal and external stability is called a stable set. von Neumann and Morgenstern argued that such sets correspond to stable standards of behavior for a society: "once they are generally accepted, they overrule anything else and no part of them can be overruled within the limits of the accepted standards. This is clearly how things are in actual social organizations."

The one-seller two-buyers example may be used to illustrate this concept. The characteristic function is given by $v(12) = v(13) = v(123) = 1$ and $v(S) = 0$ otherwise. The competitive solution allocates all surplus to the seller, hence, it produces the imputation (1, 0, 0), and the reader may verify that this imputation is undominated by any other one. However, as a singleton set, this imputation is not stable: for example, it does not dominate the imputation (1/2, 1/4, 1/4) that results if the two buyers decide to collude, bargain with the seller as a team, and insist that the seller gives up half of the pie. Stable sets have to allow for such collusion. It turns out that many stable sets exist. Suppose that the buyers agree that, whatever they get out, they will split this in proportion (α, $1 - \alpha$), and assume, with von Neumann and Morgenstern, that in the bilateral bargaining game between the seller and the team, any distribution of the surplus is possible. Then an outcome in the set $X(\alpha) = \{(1 - x, x\alpha, x(1 - x)): 0 \leq x \leq 1\}$ is predicted and any such set is stable. It is possible to conclude, as Morgenstern had conjectured all along, that other forms of social organization, different from unbridled competition, will be stable.

The fact that a game may have multiple stable sets did not bother von Neumann and Morgenstern: "this has a simple and not unreasonable meaning, namely that given the same physical background different 'established orders of society' or 'accepted standards of behavior' can be built." On the other hand, they write that "there can be, of course, no concessions as regards existence." In 1969, William Lucas constructed an example of a game without a stable set. This counterexample, as well as the others that have been constructed, is, however, contrived and does not correspond to an actual economic, political, or social reality. Given Morgenstern's emphasis on "realistic modeling," it is, hence, unlikely that he would have been bothered by these examples. In "realistic models," stable sets have been found to exist, but stable set theory has nevertheless found only relatively few applications, mainly as a consequence of the fact that the concept is difficult to work with.

Other Contributions

In the preface of *The Selected Economic Writings of Oskar Morgenstern*, Schotter writes:

> *This book contains a selection of writings of one social scientist whose entire scholarly life has been devoted to both building up as well as tearing down the basic traditions of economics. As a builder, he has helped to introduce a radically new way of looking at economic problems, along with hastening the introduction of more powerful mathematical techniques. As a critic, he has constantly attacked economics for refusing to address itself to the empirically given problem, and has asked his profession to confront head-on the enormous complexity of the social world rather than hide behind methodological tools borrowed from other disciplines.*

This characterization is accurate and in line with that of other observers. For example, in his chapter in Weintraub's *Toward a History of Game Theory*, Robert J. Leonard writes that Morgenstern has taken a "position as an arbiter of ideas, an intermediary between theorists in disparate fields, and one ultimately most capable of giving his energy to penetrating criticism rather than alternative theoretical construction." Looking at Morgenstern's later work, it is hard to come to a different conclusion.

Schotter's volume is divided into six sections: game theory and utility theory, linear economic systems, economic theory, economic statistics, methodology, and history of economic theory. Morgenstern's early work on the first topic has already been extensively described; after the death of von Neumann in 1957, new developments in Morgenstern's work in this area are not evident. For sure, there are papers written until the 1970s, but these elaborate on ideas that were already present in earlier work. A similar remark applies to Morgenstern's work on methodology. Morgenstern's main work in economics since the mid-1950s has been on the von Neumann model of the expanding economy. This work successfully relaxed several assumptions in the seminal von Neumann growth model from 1937. In econometrics and statistics, especially noteworthy is Morgenstern's collaboration with Clive Granger, Nobel Prize winner in 2003, on the predictability of stock market prices. This work showed that the short-run movements of prices are well described by a simple random walk, but that for the longer run, the random-walk hypothesis performs less well, and that there is a surprisingly small connection between prices and quantities, thus casting doubt on the standard competitive model of price formation. A lot of work has been done in this area since the collaboration with Nobel Prize Winner Clive Granger.

Morgenstern not only was an arbiter between different fields of science, he also intermediated between science and the community of business and politics. He was a consultant to the Rand Corporation, the Atomic Energy Commission, and the White House and he was active in business as director of the consulting firm Mathematica. This firm was responsible for a large-scale project for the military on games with incomplete information; it gave an important impulse to game theoretic research, and Morgenstern took pride in the fact that Mathematica was a profitable enterprise delivering high-quality work. Morgenstern also employed his entrepreneurial talents elsewhere; he was instrumental, in 1954, in the founding of *Naval Research Logistics Quarterly* and in 1971 he founded the *International Journal of Game Theory,* the first field journal for game theory. In 1963, together with Paul Lazarsfeld, he was one of the founders of the Institute of Advanced Studies in Vienna.

As early as 1957, Morgenstern received an honorary doctorate from the University of Mannheim. He got a second such doctorate, from the University of Basel, in 1960. Later, he also received an honorary doctorate from the University of Vienna. In 1970, Morgenstern left Princeton for New York University. He became an honorary member of the American Economic Association and of the American Academy of Sciences in 1976. Oskar Morgenstern died on July 26, 1977, regretting that he had not received the Bank of Sweden Prize in Economic Sciences in Honor of Alfred Nobel.

See Also the Following Articles

Game Theory, Overview • Utility

Further Reading

Aumann, R. J. (1987). Game theory. In *The New Palgrave Dictionary of Economics* (J. Eatwell, M. Milgate, and P. Newman, eds.), pp. 2, 460–482. MacMillan, London.

Aumann, R. J., and Hart, S. (eds.) (1992–2002). *Handbook of Game Theory with Economic Applications*. Vols. 1 (1992), 2 (1994), and 3 (2002). North Holland Publ., Amsterdam.

Morgenstern, O. (1928). *Wirtschaftsprognose, eine Untersuchung ihrer Voraussetzungen und Möglichkeiten.* Julius Springer Verlag, Vienna.

Morgenstern, O. (1935). Volkommene Voraussicht und wirtschaftliches Gleichgewicht. *Zeitschr. Nationalökon.* **6**(3), 337–357 (English translation by Frank Knight in Schotter, 1976).

Morgenstern, O. (1963). Limits to the uses of mathematics in economics. In *Mathematics and the Social Sciences* (J. Charlesworth, ed.), pp. 12–29. Symposium of the American Academy of Political and Social Sciences, Philadelphia, PA.

Morgenstern, O. (1972). Thirteen critical points in contemporary economic theory: An interpretation. *J. Econ. Lit.* **10**(4), 1163–1189.

Morgenstern, O. (1976). The collaboration between Oskar Morgenstern and John von Neumann on the Theory of Games. *J. Econ. Lit.* **14**(3), 805–816.

Neumann, J. von (1928). Zur theorie der Gesellschaftspiele. *Math. Annal.* **100,** 295–320.

Neumann, J. von, and Morgenstern, O. (1944). *Theory of Games and Economic Behavior.* Princeton University Press, Princeton, NJ.

Nobel Foundation. (2002). *The Bank of Sweden Prize in Economic Sciences in Memory of Alfred Nobel 2002—Advanced Information*. Available on the Internet at www.nobel.se

Nobel Foundation. (2003). *The Bank of Sweden Prize in Economic Sciences in Memory of Alfred Nobel 2003—Advanced Information*. Available on the Internet at www.nobel.se

Schotter, A. (1976). *The Selected Economic Writings of Oskar Morgenstern.* New York University Press, New York.

Weintraub, E. (1992). *Toward a History of Game Theory.* Duke University Press, Durham, NC.

Morgenthau, Hans

Kenneth W. Thompson
University of Virginia, Charlottesville, Virginia, USA

Glossary

diplomacy Seeking to mitigate and minimize conflicts among nations that may lead to war. Through diplomacy, the nation aims to determine its own objectives and power for pursuit of its objectives, the objectives and power of other nations, the extent to which these different objectives are compatible with each other, and the means suited to the reformulation of objectives when they conflict.

elements of national power Comprising some elements that are relatively stable such as geography and others that are subject to constant change such as the relative military power between Germany and France in the interwar period between World Wars I and II. Quality of government and of diplomacy have often changed as one state lost its superior position to another. Such power is relative however, although Britain and America have had advantages for extended periods of time in past centuries.

ethnicity A more primordial force emerging in countries in the Balkans and Eastern Europe where tribal groups and clans have demanded independence and imposed harsh and brutal forms of ethnic cleansing on rival ethnic groups in their struggle for national identity.

force Distinguished from political power by physical violence, which characterizes the abdication of a psychological relationship. The exercise of force is physical while the quest for political power is primarily psychological.

idealism Found in various forms, including a belief in the infinite malleability of human nature, the transforming effects of new international institutions, the good intentions and motivations of particular statesmen, and the belief that for every problem there are resources, financing, and organizations that can solve them. It affirms that no problems are really insoluble, however hopeless they may appear, given well-meaning, well-financed, and up to date scientific approaches.

interest The main sign post that helps political realism find its way through the landscape of international politics. Interest links reason and the facts to be understood and sets politics apart from economics. George Washington wrote: "Small knowledge of human nature will convince us, that, with far the greatest part of mankind, interest is the governing principle." Max Weber wrote: "Interests (material and ideal), not ideas, dominate directly the actions of men."

morality In international politics, morality is significant in political action but takes form in the inevitable tension between the moral command and the requirements of political action. Moral principles must be filtered through the circumstances of time and place and there can be no true political morality without prudence or without consideration of the political consequences of seemingly moral action. Prudence requires the weighing of the consequences of alternate political actions in moral and political terms.

nationalism A social and political force that was the predominant force in the 18th and 19th centuries. Although it proved more powerful than competing forces such as socialism based on common interests of workers in World Wars I and II, it has somewhat weakened after World War II especially in the developed countries such as France and Germany. It has intensified in the less developed countries of Africa and Asia.

power Man's control over the minds and actions of other men and the psychological relation between those who exercise it and those over whom it is exercised. Power derives from three sources: the expectation of benefits, the fear of disadvantages, or the respect for men or institutions. Power is relative, fungible, and subject to change in the ending competition between individuals and groups.

realism The assertion that politics is the result of forces including rivalry and the struggle for power which are inherent in human nature. One must work with these forces as we do internationally through the balance of power and domestically with the separation of powers in the presidency, the Congress, and the courts. It distinguishes between the "is" and "the ought." In such a world, moral principles can never be fully realized but must at best be approximated through the ever temporary balancing of interests and the ever precarious settlement of conflict.

Hans J. Morgenthau is generally considered the father of political realism in the United States. More than a half century after its publication in 1948, his greatest work, *Politics Among Nations: The Struggle for Power and Peace*, remains a leading text for courses in international relations. We have few precedents for a work of this kind to continue as one of the dominant writings for 55 years. As I write, a seventh edition is being planned for publication in 2004 with defenders and critics still in evidence.

In evaluating Morgenthau's contribution to the study of international relations, focusing only on *Politics* would be less than half the story. Indeed, running through Morgenthau's life and work are two underlying commitments, one to philosophy and the other to politics. Two years before *Politics Among Nations*, Morgenthau published *Scientific Man vs. Power Politics*, a treatise that challenged the overall scientific approach to the social sciences. He set forth the idea of a "Philosophy of International Relations," which sought to integrate some of the themes that had marked his earliest writings on legal norms. In 1952, he gave the Walgreen Lectures at Chicago on Marxism and he wrote elsewhere on liberalism and its problems. What emerged was unmistakable evidence of a dual commitment in which his concern with politics was accompanied by a devotion to philosophy, an understanding of which takes us back to his birthplace in Coberg and to Germany during the period 1904–1932.

Youth in Search of Enduring Purpose for His Life

Morgenthau's childhood and youth constituted a quarter of his life, some 19 years of immense promise darkened by overwhelming loneliness. His formative years are remembered more for suffering and unhappiness without as much as a trace of the normal joys of youth; they were spent in the beautiful hills and valley that made up Coburg, which became the capital of the Duchy of Saxony-Coburg in the middle of Germany. His father was a medical doctor and a conservative patriot; he was a Jew who wanted to be a German and who worshipped the Emperor Wilhelm II. The Emperor had abandoned the strategic views of Otto von Bismarck and by his flamboyant policies helped bring on World War I. Yet Hans' father, Dr. Ludwig Morgenthau, wishing to show his patriotism, gave him the middle name of the Emperor youngest son, Prince Joachim. Worse than that, he continuously belittled and criticized Hans often unmercifully until he fell ill with what became a serious respiratory disease. When it came time to choose a college, the father told Hans he could never be admitted to the University of Berlin. His father's ridicule was matched by the scorn fellow students had shown for him and the name calling when they marched in formation. When he received the "First in His Class Award" as the top student of his class preceding the graduating class, he was to climb a high ladder, place a laurel wreath on the statue of the school's founder and give a farewell address to the graduates. Printed leaflets were distributed by townspeople the morning of the ceremony instructing the citizenry to give "Mister Abendnebel" (evening fog) a lesson. It was a pun on Hans' last name—Morgenthau (morning dew). People spit on him and shouted anti-Semitic insults. The former duke appeared at the gymnasium and held his nose at the sight of Morgenthau. From the memory of this harrowing experience, he took refuge in his studies. He wrote a Gymnasium assigned competition on "hopes for the future" inspired by Goethe. In the essay, he addressed two goals he might pursue: (1) to lessen the social apprehension and anti-Semitism from which he suffered and (2) to select one of two types of vocations he would pursue throughout the rest of his life. For each of these, he resolved: (1) to withstand the social ostracism and painful insults from representatives of anti-Semitism, and (2) to choose between two kinds of vocations or goals for his life, one of piling up mountains of wealth accumulating year after year as he became richer and richer or the other of working in the service of some great idea, the fruits of which would outlive him. He chose the latter goal which was to guide him until the end of his life. Such a lesson, discovered at an early age, was to remain with him until the end. As for Coburg, it was to become a battleground between Nazis and the defenders of the Weimar Republic. On October 14 and 15, 1923, Hitler, backed by eight units of 100 men each and his own band of 43 warriors, triumphed.

University Education and Formation

One limiting factor in Morgenthau's education was the harsh evaluation of his father that he was not qualified for admission to the University of Berlin. No doubt this influenced him until the end of his life, perhaps later in life in coveting a permanent appointment at Harvard. His father was determined he study law but from earliest childhood his interest was history. In the beginning it was wars from Cannae to Waterloo, then the Balkan Wars and World War I. Next in his evolving interests was German literature, and from this he was drawn to becoming a writer. Following this, his interest turned to philosophy directed to the ultimate questions of human existence. However, when he chose philosophy in his studies at the University of Frankfurt he became bitterly disappointed. It was a discipline then totally absorbed in epistemological questions that were wholly rational and pseudo-scientific. Moreover, philosophy like literature had little to offer by way of possible financial rewards. A compromise for him was jurisprudence or legal philosophy, and to study this he transferred from Frankfurt University to Munich University. There he was an indifferent student except for courses by two extraordinary professors who offered courses in art history and Max Weber's political thought. He transferred from Munich to the Fredrich Wilhelm University in Berlin where he attended courses in international law, especially with Professor Karl Neumeyer who inspired his interest in the subject.

He passed his first law exam in February, 1927, making this choice partly because of his father's strong urging that he seek academic degrees in law. However, for him a career in law was to have few attractions. He accepted a legal internship appointment with assignments in the Bavarian Ministry of Justice in Munich but then fell ill with tuberculosis and one of his lungs had to be removed. He was allowed to continue his internship in Frankfurt, where he joined the staff of a professor of labor law at the University of Frankfurt who for the rest of his life remained his friend and adviser. Professor Hugo Sinzheimer was a Social Democrat in the National Assembly in Weimar and served on a committee to investigate "the stab in the back theory." According to that theory, Germany with no foreign troops occupying it after World War I, had not been defeated but was a victim of Jews and other groups who conspired against it following the war. Sinzheimer retired from politics as a Deputy in the German Assembly and partially retired from the practice of the law, turning more and more of his duties over to his younger intern. Throughout his association with Senzheimer, Morgenthau met some of the most famous scholars of the day and was drawn into their discussions. Then he returned to his thesis, approaching it less from the canons of international law and more from the sociology of law and the social forces that shaped the law. The thesis was approved and published with the title: *The Judicial Sanction in the International Realm: Its Nature and Limitations*. All the reviews were full of praise. His thesis adviser wrote that the thesis deserved a *summa cum laude* and was equivalent to the second degree for habilitation, the degree above the thesis, which qualified the writer for a tenured position in universities in Germany, Austria, and Switzerland. Professor Paul Guggenheim praised the author for "an astonishing familiarity with the literature." Yet on its completion, Morgenthau found, perhaps because of rising inflation and political uncertainties in Germany, that no academic positions were available. None being available, Morgenthau sought other openings and learned of one at the University of Geneva primarily designed for a professor who would be responsible for German students who came to Geneva to learn French and complete their law training. Morgenthau applied again and again for permission to present himself for the habilitation degree in Geneva. He was accepted provisionally and invited to give a probationary lecture but in French not German. On February 17, 1932, which was his 28th birthday, he crossed the Alps into Geneva expecting to return to Germany with a final degree qualifying him for a professorship.

Education Continues in the Real World

He could not have anticipated the events that followed. His probationary lecture in French was judged to qualify him only for quite limited teaching in Geneva. He appealed to be allowed to give the lecture in German but even here he was only granted permission to teach on a limited basis until he had demonstrated his skills more fully. At first he attributed this ruling to two anti-semitic German professors on the committee. Soon he realized, however, after several appeals to the Dean of the faculty, that the opposition must have come from one or the other of two sources. He decided the one was most likely a result of philosophical differences that were unbridgeable. That left a second referee who turned out to be his so-called friend, Paul Guggenheim. Morgenthau concentrated his response to him. He pointed out that Guggenheim completely misunderstood what his book was all about. Moreover, he noted that his study had been quoted in detail by famous international lawyers such as Hersh Lauterpacht who gave it far more attention than any of Guggenheim's writings. Morgenthau sent copies of his thesis to other professors abroad requesting their evaluation. Finally, he requested that a new commission evaluate his thesis. The commission was appointed and Hans Kelsen was made its chairman. After deliberating, the Kelsen commission approved the thesis and granted habitation. Once approved, however, Morgenthau learned that no positions were available in Germany, the country to which he had planned to return after his habilitation. In fact, German scholars of great repute had already left Germany for positions in the Netherlands, Turkey, and Switzerland. Morgenthau once again turned elsewhere for an appointment.

He found it almost by accident in Spain, where an American international lawyer, Leo Gross whom Morgenthau knew, turned down a little advertised position in Madrid. Morgenthau was recommended by Hans Kelsen and he was appointed. His days in Spain were among the happiest in his life, measured in terms of happiness if not scholarly output. He was appointed to the staff of the *Institute de Estudios Internacionales*

Economaeos in Madrid to give courses in international law, write a research study about international law, and prepare a compilation of international law topics and interests. He went to Madrid where he was married to his longtime friend, Irma Thornvaun. He was appointed for 12 months subject to renewal. He arrived in the spring of 1935 but when civil war broke out he took leave in 1936. He and his wife fled and went to Merano, Italy; Paris; and Switzerland, spending all their resources as they moved across the continent. He turned elsewhere to seek alternatives.

The New World: At Last, the United States

After all that had happened in Spain and Switzerland, Morgenthau decided to make one last effort to find employment in Europe and, if that failed, to obtain a visa to emigrate to the United States. At the end of 1936, Madrid was the scene of the most violent fighting in the Spanish civil war. Returning there was ruled out. Morgenthau tried for a position as foreign editor of the Dutch newspaper *Del Telgraaf* without success. He sought a teaching position in The Hague at the Academy of International Law only to be turned down again. He considered Palestine as a possibility but dropped the idea. He thought seriously about South America if some kind of academic position turned up. Once more he applied to the Rockefeller Foundation to finance a research visit to Argentina but was rejected for the second time. For a time he thought of the United States as the last place worth considering. If he had known the way foundations operate with their own programs and priorities, he might not have been so disappointed. His odyssey in search of opportunities in Amsterdam, the Hague, Merano, Geneva, and Paris were all failures. Then a young Swiss woman tipped him off that the resident American Counsel, who was anti-Semitic, was on vacation. The fact he had lived in Geneva for three years made it appear he had had permanent residence there. His wife received an affidavit from a rich cousin, which impressed the vice consul in Geneva who granted the visa in a few days. A visit to Italy to say goodbye to Morgenthau's parents and to settle financial matters concluded his preparation. They left for the United States with $1200 in their pockets—hardly enough to start over again in the United States. On July 17, 1937, they boarded the steamer Konestein in Antwerp happy that they would finally be catching sight of the Statue of Liberty and to a new life in the United States.

On arriving, Morgethau started his job hunting by immediately traveling to Indiana, Illinois, and Wisconsin. Everywhere the question was the same. Had he experience in teaching in English? If not, no one was ready to take a chance with him. He had known one professor of Semitic languages in Paris who was said to be teaching at Columbia. He climbed the long stairs at the entrance to Low Library and knocked on Professor Richard Gottheil's door only to learn that he had died unexpectedly a few weeks earlier. A German lawyer he met introduced him to Columbia University international law professor Philip Jessup who gave him numerous letters of introduction and names and addresses of scholars who might help. By October 1937, he was still on the street and beginning to apply for nonacademic jobs. He turned down a job as an elevator operator but made it known he would have accepted a job as a proofreader in a publishing house. He left his name and address at various universities and in this way learned that an instructor at Brooklyn College had fallen ill. When the colleague's health did not improve, the temporary job became a regular position for Morgenthau if he wanted it. He taught from eight to eleven o'clock in the evening three times a week, for $3.50 an hour. Even with his wife working as a hat salesperson at Macy's, they earned a combined $180 a month. Long hours, low pay, and a restless, rebellious, and radical student body led him to consider other opportunities. After one year at Brooklyn College, he joined the two faculties of law and the liberal arts college at the University of Kansas City. He remained there from January 1939 until the autumn of 1943, a move that proved to have even more disturbing qualities, mostly revolving around the character of the president. While the Morgenthaus enjoyed midwest friendliness, he soon complained about tight office space, inferior library resources that featured only one book in international law, and a course load that he found required him to give up to a dozen courses in law from administrative to testamentary law. He also ended up teaching European politics in the college. He taught 18 hours a week and colleagues approached that number. The American Association of University Professors surveyed the problem and denounced conditions in its annual report for 1942, recommending the faculty be allowed to assume more responsibility for its courses. In a vote by the faculty for membership in a committee of three to examine the situation, Morgenthau received the highest vote. Once the United States entered World War II, President Decker at the end of 1942–43 fired faculty members including Morgenthau citing lack of qualified students. Decker refused to accept the AAUP action against him and presented his case before the Association of University Professors and the Association of American Law Schools. After hearing the evidence, the two bodies insisted that President Decker withdraw the dismissal of faculty members. By the time this happened, Morgenthau had already left the University. He sought to enlist in the military but was turned down for health reasons, particularly the absence of a lung. In the summer of 1943, he wrote to over one hundred universities from the Ivy League and some third class institutions in Nebraska. None offered him an appointment. Just as he was preparing to give up, Professor Fredrick S. Dunn who was head of the Institute of International Studies at Yale wrote offering him a temporary job in a research project at the Institute. Very shortly after writing to Dunn to accept the offer he received a letter from the University of Chicago asking him if he would be interested in replacing Quincy Wright for six months at a salary of $2600 for the period. With Dunn's approval, he returned the Yale offer and accepted Chicago. He had written earlier in the *Neue Zurcher Zeitung* that the University of Chicago was "one of the greatest, wealthiest, and scientifically most prominent in the country," little imagining he would someday become a member of the faculty.

After all his suffering and disappointments, it would seem that a life rewarded by success and happiness was his due. Yet that was not to be. He joined a department that some have described as "Merriam's Department." Charles Merriam had introduced a brand of political science that was viewed as largely scientific, in the spirit of the age. Not only did it draw inspiration from the age of the enlightenment but he defended his approach as primarily scientific although there was little evidence of this in his writings. It was grounded less in testing and experimentation than in the claims that were made for it. The government department was Merriam's department and he passed judgment on everything that went on in its name. For example, when Morgenthau published *Scientific Man vs. Power Politics*, Merriam promptly advised the newest member of the Department that perhaps he should offer a course in administrative law. The younger faculty whose work attracted Merriam were scholars such as David Easton, Gabriel Almond, and Harold Lasswell, not all of them as yet in the Department. With Merriam's or his allies' strong and energetic support, they became members. The next two chairmen of the Department were Leonard White, who was to write the basic text in public administration, and Herman Pritchett, whose work in administrative law and administrative regulation and the process of change taking place in judicial opinion in the Supreme Court introduced a form of science that Merriam considered appropriate. It was not science as such but it was rather a new methodology that bore the title scientific, using it with supreme confidence as representing the wave of the future. When they thought of additions to the Department, they almost always thought in these terms.

In yet another respect, this approach differed from Morgenthau. He brought to the subject an interest in traditional political theory. He saw his roots in the same kind of political theory that was associated with Aristotle and Plato, not Harold Lasswell or Merriam. The majority of faculty members claimed they were less concerned with the ancients than current political thinkers. None were so extreme as Charles Hyneman of Northwestern University who went on to become president of the American Political Science Association and who once asked "Why study the thought of dead men?" Without using these words, Merriam and others saw the work of present day writers as pointing the way to a new and modern political science. If this suggests that Morgenthau was "on the outside looking in" as a member of the political science department, that was true. It became commonplace that departmental meetings chaired by Leonard White separated difficult and controversial questions, resolved before departmental meetings, from items on the agenda. The sessions that followed dealt largely with housekeeping details such as assignment of office space or of secretaries.

In a word, Morgenthau's brand of political science was not "the wave of the future" as Merriam saw it. Yet as time went on this began to change. Students and GI's returning from military service in World War II had read the literature. They came prepared to study with Merriam, Quincy Wright, or Leonard White. They found they were assigned to these more prestigious figures as assistants for grading student papers or helping with the organization of classes. Yet little by little they came to recognize the teaching and research of the newest and latest addition to the department. At the outset, rumor had it that Morgenthau was a hard grader and a stern taskmaster. Rumor had it that if you were likely to have a thesis or a dissertation questioned and perhaps turned down, Morgenthau was probably your adviser. On the contrary, he graded most student papers himself and was intensely interested in the findings his students reached and the route they followed in reaching them.

My work with Morgenthau began when he sought an assistant to work with him on his major treatise, *Politics Among Nations*. Until then, I mainly assisted Quincy Wright grading term papers, examinations, or helping prepare questions for examinations. Once I began work with Morgenthau, I found him business like and exacting but not someone hell bent to prove I lacked the necessary talents or preparation to be a political scientist. He needed help and I was determined I would assist him according to his kind of schedule. Yet, among some students the image persisted of a gruff and hostile professor with little interest in his assistants or students as distinct and unique personalities. Instead, I found he was always willing to work with and help me in any way he could. It was true that since he worked at virtually every hour of the day and late at night, an assistant had to adjust his schedule to the professor's. Morgenthau had his own work plan which continued well into evening hours. His wife, Irma, had spoken of his bringing sandwiches from home and a container of tea he himself had brewed so that he could continue to work. But I found all this worthwhile for my intellectual growth and development. Hardly a work session passed that I did not gain fresh new insights.

The route to success was fairly obvious for Morgenthau. It differed sharply from Merriam's or Wright's. Charles Merriam's reputation was such that he spent part of most weeks in Washington. He and his colleagues kept an apartment in the Hay Adams Hotel, not far from the White House. This was President Franklin D. Roosevelt's era and his aides were seeking to reorganize and reform the Executive Office. The report of the President's Committee on Administrative Management begins "The President Needs Help." A blue ribbon committee led by Luther Gulick and colleagues sought to map out a plan for reforming the administration of the executive branch of government. Some of the younger faculty in public administration at Chicago "cut their teeth" on this mission. Lurking in the background of the effort was Charles Merriam. He was the *eminence grise* who marked out the course that was to be followed. On the outskirts of the campus of the University of Chicago a substantial center was created called "1313" after its address on 61st Street. It co-opted those who were engaged in the work of the Committee on Administrative Management. When Morgenthau arrived in Chicago, "1313" was the focal point for collaborative work for departmental persons to work with staff at "1313." Some members of the Government Department had joint appointments. There were few other points of contact for the most recent new member of the department faculty.

Notwithstanding, cooperative efforts with Quincy Wright evolved for Morgenthau. One example is the exchange of information by students. Morgenthau asked Quincy Wright for suggestions of a graduate student who might assist him with *Politics Among Nations* and Wright recommended me. I was sorry to leave Professor Wright but working with Morgenthau was an opportunity I could not turn down. When Wright retired from the University of Chicago, he moved to Charlottesville and accepted an appointment as a visiting professor. He continued at the University of Virginia until his death. When Morgenthau participated in a conference at the Miller Center organized by James Sterling Young, Wright had only recently passed away.

The main encouragement Professor Morgenthau received at Chicago came from the University's top leadership, a few junior or lesser colleagues, and most of all from his students. The latter are the easiest to account for because the pattern was so predictable. Most of them came to his classes inclined to make invidious comparisons. They left with moderate to evangelical commitment to his ideas. Idealistic students found they could preserve their ideals at a deeper level while shedding the utopian illusions that earlier moral and political education had given them. Their first weeks in Morgenthau's classes were a time of encounter. His lectures rarely if ever went uninterrupted. As time passed, students saw more clearly that his conception of international politics had coherence because of its grounding in an evolving philosophy of international politics. Students transmitted and exchanged his thinking with others, including Professor Wright, who more and more sensed that questions were being raised with which he had to come to terms. In my time as an assistant to both Wright and Morgenthau, I marveled at their restraint in talking about each other's work. Their days at Chicago were the golden age of international studies. No one doubted to which of the two scholars they were responsible. Both were men of integrity and each had the ability of taking the other's views and subjecting them, as distinct from some outsider's interpretations of them, to searching analysis and criticism. Wright's most deeply held commitment was to the science of international relations, reflected in his *Study of War* and his *Study of International Relations*. Yet throughout a long and varied career, he remained conscious that philosophy had a necessary place in the vast eclectic array of approaches he discussed that comprised international relations.

Multiple Success Stories at Last

Whatever role Morgenthau's friends or foes played in the unfolding of his career, once he emerged as a leading figure in international relations, he alone deserved full responsibility and credit for his ascendancy. From years of intensive study and late nights of laborious drafting of every fragment of his intellectual legacy, he earned his stature. That is not to say that he did not receive help from loyal friends and students or colleagues with whom he had ongoing communication. Students whose devotion to him knew no bounds prepared texts of his lectures. One of his students, Mary Jane Beneditz, made a stenographic transcript of the lectures given in the Winter Quarter of 1946 as well as of the class discussions. Morgenthau paid tribute to her saying "her intelligent and painstaking labor made available the only written record of those lectures; without that record the book could not have been completed in little more than a year." (*Politics Among Nations*, foreword to the first edition, 1988.) Those of us who worked with him were all too familiar with his notes and citations in German shorthand. Through my years of working as an assistant while also enrolled in his classes, I never ceased marveling at the intense concentration he achieved in rapidly reviewing his notes before going into class. It was as though he went into some kind of trance behind the closed doors of his office. We had no doubt that in this interval he would brook no interruptions. Once in class he lectured for the full hour, always without a note or reference. As time went on he lost some of this ability, but to the end he remained free of all notes and texts as he spoke. His reputation spread abroad wherever he went and to whomever he spoke. The world became his classroom as he lectured to groups whose invitations he always treated with respect. From being a professor at a single university, he taught a new generation here and abroad. He traveled and spoke in Asia, Canada, Europe, and South America long before ordinary channels of communications were fully open to distant parts of the globe. He responded especially to invitations in which his students had a hand, occasionally receiving substantial fees but more often then not only what the traffic could bear. It was as if the mission he outlined for himself when a fledgling student "of working in the service of some great idea, the fruits of which outlive him" merited every ounce of his energy in travel and speaking out wherever his goals and purposes carried him. He learned from his travels and questioned oversimplified interpretations, for example, about Asian nationalism. In India and China he looked in vain for the type of revolutionary nationalism often attributed to it by western writers. Instead he argued that for nations there were basic purposes and objective standards by which their foreign policies could be measured. American interests in Asia began in a political and military sense at the turn of the century. Our Open Door policy under Secretary Hay was commercial in the beginning, seeking to keep China open for trade and development by all the major powers. The aim was to keep any one European or Asian power from controlling the great economic and political potential of China. What began as a commercial policy became military and political to prevent any European or Asian power from dominating all Asia. In this way the Open Door policy was transformed into a balance of power policy for Asia. When Russia overcame Japan in 1905, Theodore Roosevelt sought to limit Russian power much as we did after Japan's invasion of Manchuria. In the Summer of 1941 when President Roosevelt and Secretary of State Hull declared we would not countenance any further Japanese expansion, Pearl Harbor became inevitable. After World War II, the United States saw Japan as a check on what was seen as a nearly imperialist power, China. Yet under the postwar policy of the United States, we had convinced the Japanese they should embrace pacifism and rule out regular Japanese military bases. Japan's postwar constitution was inspired and shaped by General Douglas MacArthur. When Morgenthau went to China in 1955 he was convinced that China was being restored, that India and China were not going to be locked in a struggle of competing nationalisms but rather China's goals, especially to its west and southwest, were ones of restraint and not of conquest. China would follow a policy of traditional cultural expansion and not of military conquest. Morgenthau's study of China's history and his 1955 visit led him to an outlook at odds with General MacArthur's. Morgenthau agreed with the policy best defined by Secretary of State Dean Acheson in a speech before the National Press Club in Washington in January 1950.

The New York Story

In 1968, Morgenthau left Chicago and moved to New York. As the years passed, he had discovered that some of his closest friends were no longer in Chicago but in Washington and New York. They included Hannah Arendt, the foremost woman political philosopher, who over the years had encouraged Morgenthau to return to his earlier scholarship in political philosophy, and Robert J. Myers, former publisher of *The New Republic* and *The Washingtonian* and director of the Council on Religion and International Affairs, later the Carnegie Council on Ethics and International Relations. Over the years, his happiest reunions took place in New York and Washington with many of his former students. When he returned from them, he would speak of being renewed and reinvigorated. Of the 26 scholars in international relations who wrote chapters for the Morgenthau festschrift (*Truth and Tragedy: A Tribute to Hans J. Morgenthau*) 17 were in the east, most of them from the Washington to Boston corridor. If the attraction of this group constituted the pull for Morgenthau, the push was the passing or relocation of many of his closest and dearest friends and colleagues and before long his wife in Chicago. Moreover, New York and Washington in particular were the centers of decision making in public policy and that increasingly concerned Morgenthau. He recognized that at some point he would be cutting back on international travel and for this reason these centers became more attractive.

An important factor in his moving to New York was when he received an offer of the Leonard Davis Distinguished Professor of Political Science at City College of the City University of New York. It provided an opportunity to continue teaching, something that he cherished until the end of his life; after leaving City College, he taught at the New School for Social Research. When it appeared that that appointment would be terminated, he asked me to contact President John Everett to correct a possible misunderstanding. I did so and he continued to teach once it was definite that doing so was his wish. He took satisfaction from the fact, despite all his earlier disappointments with foundations, that he was called on repeatedly to serve on advisory committees of the Rockefeller Foundation and others. When someone once asked him why he attended their meetings and served on their committees, he answered "because they asked me." He not only was an officer of an organization that now bears the name of the Carnegie Council on

Ethics in International Relations but on his death they established the Hans J. Morgenthau Lectures.

If he felt disappointment that he was not called upon to the same degree he had been earlier, he came to understand that nothing lasted forever. Sometimes when he was asked to participate, he discovered that his research and writing was more an object for criticism than a subject that earned him praise. He was invited to be a scholar in residence at the Council on Foreign Relations in New York only to discover that the study group that oversaw his work on *A New Foreign Policy for the United States* included a number of his critics. Among members of his committee were Henry Wriston, president of Brown University, Philip Moseley, Columbia professor and director of studies at the Counsil, Frank Altschul who was friendly and sympathetic, and John J. McCloy. A debate between him and members of his committee developed and eventually Morgenthau withdrew and published his book outside the jurisdiction of the Council. Debates were staged in such a way that he was a minority voice but this had been true throughout much of his career. The final verdict was that he was a giant in his field well ahead of his time.

If there were disappointments in New York, there were also rewards. Friends planned receptions in which he was the guest of honor. He had dinners with close friends like Hannah Arendt and she was his companion at anniversaries and lectures of organizations boasting highly distinguished memberships. He enjoyed going to movies with younger friends such as my son Paul and they returned the favor. All in all, he found a rich and stimulating environment even as he contributed to the process.

His trip to China and his critical response to the view that China's military buildup was not for conquest but for cultural expansion was linked with his evolving perspective on Vietnam. For many, his crusade against American policy in Vietnam was a departure from much of his earlier emphasis on power. Many who were his critics saw no connection between his earlier emphasis on power and military strength and his policy for Vietnam. They failed to remember the distinction he always drew between power, which was inevitable in politics, and force, which was a last resort. In effect, he became the number one critic of American policy in the small Asian country. He argued that we had stumbled into the conflict without any plan or well-considered program. First military admirers, next 15,000 troops, and eventually 500,000 troops were sent to Vietnam as one intervention followed another. He could find no basis for our policy either in national interest or compelling international agreement. He took exception to the argument that it was the protocol to the SEATO Agreement that required members to come to the aid of beleaguered fellow members. Because of concern over France's participation in organizations like NATO in Europe, we were taking up the conflict in Asia after France's defeat at Dienbienphu. In Secretary John Foster Dulles' words "we got involved in Vietnam to see what we could salvage." What was unusual about Morgenthau's response to Vietnam was his taking up the unaccustomed role of being the foremost spokesman against a major U.S. policy.

In effect, Morgenthau crisscrossed the country making speeches against our policy in Vietnam. For some he became a leader of the cultural revolution in which the largest number of young people in our history were campaigning against a policy but also against the mainstream culture both in society and the academy. This group turned to him and urged him on at a point in his life when he might have been expected to rest on his laurels. He took part in televised debates on Vietnam with administration spokesmen such as MacGeorge Bundy and Zbigniew Brzezinski, debates about which he complained that his opponents had used heavy handed and dubious arguments and tactics. Vindication came when many in the public took up his cause but by then he was weary and dispirited from what had seemed a losing battle with the more outspoken military and reactionary spokesmen elements in society. Some of his friends asked was this not a role in which he had not been involved earlier? Was he faced to pander to outspoken and radical young people incapable of viewing the subject in the language of international politics? The Vietnam chapter in Morgenthau's life was both courageous and at times unbecoming for a great scholar. Make no mistake however, he might well have used the words of Churchill that he too was not always mistaken. Now that Vietnam is the subject of succession of highly critical monographs and historical studies viewing it as a tragic chapter in U.S. history, it seems clear he had not been engaged in a futile and useless endeavor.

The Crisis and Morgenthau's Legacy

His interpretation was ahead of its time and by the 1970s there was growing discussion of the issue of the decline of the West. Oswald Spengler's book with that title attracted attention in Europe and the United States. The Club of Rome represented an influential group of intellectuals and scholars who saw evidence that the West had suffered significant setbacks both intellectually and morally. There is reference in the preface to *Scientific Man* to the rise and fall of the Roman Empire. The political crisis about which he wrote had grown increasingly obvious in the first four decades of the 20th century. The crisis had roots in a general decay of political thought that for Morgenthau took form in the belief that science could solve all problems, including political problems. The period leading up to World War II was dominated by the rise of Nazism and the failure of many to identify its deeper underlying sources. Critics warned that liberal illusions weakened a more coherent understanding of the threat. What *Scientific Man* offered by contrast was a restatement of fundamental political principles as the basis for political action most of them set forth in classical political philosophy. By juxtaposing the principles of classical political thought and the belief that science could solve all problems, and particularly political problems, Morgenthau sought to demonstrate the superior nature of the former. The idea that both the national and international system as presently constructed made the struggle for power among its units the central phenomenon of political life is discussed as it relates to the quest for political stability. Opposed to this view, the Wilsonian philosophy of liberalism sees an essential harmony of interests underlying the relations among nation states. Morgenthau recognized that political philosophy is an art and not a science, and what is required for its use is not the rationality of the engineer but the wisdom and moral strength of the statesman. He sought to put political philosophy and statesmanship at the center of things political. This was his goal rather than the wholesale reconstruction of political life by new concepts and designs.

Some observers have argued that *Scientific Man* is a call for Western Civilization to rediscover its ultimate purposes and to reconcile traditions with the experiences and exigencies of modern life. The statesman seeks to create an emerging society out of his knowledge of the nature of man. However, neither science nor ethics can resolve the conflict between politics and ethics and bring them into harmony. We have no choice between the pursuit of politics and power and the common good. He wrote: "to act successfully, that is according to the rules of the political art, is political wisdom. To know with despair that the political act is inevitably evil, and to act nevertheless, is moral courage. To choose among several expedient actions the least evil one is moral judgment. In the combination of political wisdom and moral courage and moral judgment, man reconciles his political nature with his moral destiny." (*Scientific Man*, p. 203).

In 1951, Morgenthau published a third book that focused on American foreign policy. The book contained an enlarged version of lectures he gave in the Spring of 1950 at the University of Chicago under the auspices of the Charles A. Walgreen Foundation. For those who attended the lectures and expected a call for a new American foreign policy, they heard a defense of returning to an older American foreign policy. Little did I know when I began working with him on *Politics* that we would soon be engaged in preparing another book, *Principles and Problems of International Politics*, which was published in 1950, a year before *In Defense of the National Interest*. The earlier chapters of the two books overlap, whether or not they coincide. Our book contained selections from opposed viewpoints: Hamilton and Madison, Disraeli and Gladstone. Morgenthau in *In Defense* identifies three periods in American foreign policy: the *realistic*—thinking and acting in terms of power represented by Alexander Hamilton; the *ideological*—thinking in terms of moral principles but acting in terms of power represented by Thomas Jefferson and John Quincy Adams; and the *moralistic*—thinking and acting in terms of moral principles represented by Woodrow Wilson. The three periods in American foreign policy roughly correspond with their definitions, the first covering the opening decades in the history of the United States as an independent nation, the second the 19th century culminating in the Spanish American War and the half century after that war. Morgenthau qualifies his periodization by acknowledging that the three definitions refer only to prevailing tendencies without precluding the appearance of other tendencies in the same period. In *Principles*, Morgenthau and I also tried wherever possible to contrast different points of emphasis, for example, we compared Wilson and W. R. Gladstone as representatives of the idealist view, and then both with Benjamin Disraeli and Lord Salisbury. The book *In Defense* is outmoded in certain respects but in other respects it remains applicable to the present era. In a section on *The Three Revolutions of Our Age*, Morgenthau discusses the Political Revolution, the Technological Revolution, and the Moral Revolution. While the Cold War between the United States and the Soviet Union constitutes the main focus, topics on the rise of political religions and the revolt of Asia are discussed and in this way the rise of Alcaeda and Moslem attitudes toward war and peace are foreshadowed. The use of broad principles and categories advanced in an earlier period opens the door to thinking about developments that have occurred in the last quarter century.

The final volume published in 1960 is *The Purpose of American Politics*, a study of normative and ethical aspects of international relations. One distinguishing feature that stands out in contrast to most normative studies is its consistent use of an historical context. The spotlight is on American history and the extent to which normative concerns, and in particular freedom and equality for the United States, are ordering and defining principles. The study begins with the founding and tracks American history through wars and their resolution, the depression, civil rights and a developing globalization. For our time, it traces the development of U.S. hegemony. The picture is one of advance and retreat. It moves from a strong emphasis on the American purpose to its subordination to partisan and lesser interests and the setting aside of a broader national purpose. As a means to exposing students to the rise and fall, the decline and the rediscovery of moral purposes, the study is a textbook on political morality. I have used it as such for more than a quarter of a century.

While *Scientific Man is Power Politics* came out two years before *Politics*, it was in a certain sense painted on a broader canvas. The opening sentence in *Politics* reads: "This book purports to present a theory of international politics." By contrast, *Scientific Man* was intended as a critique of the social, political, and moral philosophy of contemporary society in the West. If *Politics* received criticism on publication, it came primarily from theorists and historians of international relations more than philosophers of history. In assisting Morgenthau, I remember reading prepublication reviews of *Politics* by Princeton's Harold Sprout and Yale's Arnold Wolfers. Their questions were methodological rather than philosophical. *Scientific Man* was deeply pessimistic in terms of its judgment of history, while *Politics* held out the hope that diplomacy might move the world toward some form of a more unified system of world government. It reflected an attitude of qualified optimism regarding the future, another difference. If *Politics* was primarily a treatise on international peace and order, *Scientific Man* contained the core of principles and prevailing philosophy of political realism in which hope resided for the West. Partly because Morgenthau was less well known when he wrote *Scientific Man*, the critics were more outspoken and more sweeping in defense of science than were the opponents of *Politics* in their evaluations. In turn, at least a select number of those who championed his approach became staunch and outspoken defenders of his political theory and that has continued down to the present day. Whether the issue was relations with the Soviet Union in the Cold War or the War against Terrorism they looked for a reasoned, pragmatic, and sequential approach to the problem at hand rather than a complete and total solution which some would call hard Wilsonianism. Thus, Morgenthau's collection of studies beginning with *Scientific Man*, extended through his systematic and comprehensive study of *Politics* and ending up with *Purpose*, provide a framework for understanding his overall approach to the unfolding crisis in international relations.

See Also the Following Articles

Political Science • Political Violence

Further Reading

Frei, Christoph (2001). *Hans J. Morgenthau: An Intellectual Biography*. Louisiana State University Press, Baton Rouge, LA.

Morgenthau, Hans J. (1958). *Dilemmas of Politics*. University of Chicago Press, Chicago.

Morgenthau, Hans J. (1962). *The Decline of Democratic Politics*, Volume I; Volume II, *The Impasse of American Foreign Policy*; Volume III, *The Restoration of American Politics*. University of Chicago Press, Chicago.

Morgenthau, Hans J. (1974). *Scientific Man vs. Power Politics*, midway reprint. University of Chicago Press, Chicago.

Morgenthau, Hans J., and Hein, David (1983). In *Essays on Lincoln's Faith and Politics* (Kenneth W. Thompson, ed.). University Press of America, New York.

Russell, Greg (1990). *Hans J. Morgenthau and the Ethics of American Statecraft*. Louisiana State University Press, Baton Rouge, LA.

Thompson, Kenneth W. (ed.) (1984). *Moral Dimensions of American Foreign Policy*. Transaction, New Brunswick.

Thompson, Kenneth W., and Myers, Robert J. (1977). *Truth and Tragedy: A Tribute to Hans Morgenthau*. New Republic, Washington, DC.

Thompson, Kenneth W., and Myers, Robert J. (1984). *Truth and Tragedy: A Tribute to Hans Morgenthau*, augmented edition, Council on Religion and International Affairs. New Republic, Washington, DC.

Multicollinearity

D. Stephen Voss
University of Kentucky, Lexington, Kentucky, USA

Glossary

collinearity A special case of multicollinearity in which one variable is a linear function of another. Social scientists often use the two terms synonymously.

full multicollinearity When two or more explanatory variables overlap completely, with one a perfect linear function of the others, such that the method of analysis cannot distinguish them from one another. This condition prevents a multiple regression from estimating coefficients and the equation becomes unsolvable. Also called perfect multicollinearity.

multiplicative model A model that presumes the dependent variable is a multiplicative function of the explanatory variables rather than an additive function. Researchers sometimes induce full collinearity in these models when they attempt to include interaction terms or ratio variables.

partial multicollinearity When two or more explanatory variables overlap, such that they are correlated with one another in a sample but still contain independent variation. This condition limits the extent to which an analysis can distinguish their causal importance, but does not violate any assumptions required for regression.

Multicollinearity (or, as it is sometimes abbreviated, collinearity) describes a condition that may appear when analysts simultaneously consider more than one explanation for a social outcome. It occurs when two or more of the explanatory variables in a sample overlap. Because of the overlap, the methods of analysis cannot fully distinguish the explanatory factors from one another or isolate their independent influence. Social scientists usually apply the term when discussing multiple (linear) regression, in which case it refers to a situation in which one independent variable is fully or partially a linear function of the others; however, many forms of quantitative and qualitative analysis have their own version of the multicollinearity problem. Thus, although this entry explores multicollinearity formally using the notation of linear regression, it outlines the analytical issues more broadly as well.

Introduction

Multicollinearity stands out among the possible pitfalls of empirical analysis for the extent to which it is poorly understood by practitioners. Articles in social science journals often expend an extensive amount of space dismissing the presence of this condition, even though it poses little threat to a properly interpreted analysis.

At its extreme, when explanatory variables overlap completely, multicollinearity violates the assumptions of the classical regression model (CRM). Full (or perfect) multicollinearity is easy to detect, however, because it prevents the estimation of coefficients altogether; an equation becomes unsolvable. This is not the sort of multicollinearity that customarily worries analysts. Full multicollinearity rarely appears in social science data unless the sample is exceedingly small. Otherwise, it generally results from some kind of simple error in the data handling or model specification, one that is easy to diagnose and painless to address. When practitioners speculate about a possible "multicollinearity problem," therefore, they mean some sort of linear relationship among explanatory variables that falls short of complete overlap.

Partial multicollinearity—the use of overlapping variables that still exhibit independent variation—is ubiquitous in multiple regression. Two random variables will almost always correlate at some level in a sample, even if they share no fundamental relationship in the larger population. In other words, multicollinearity is a matter of degree; it is not a problem that either does or does not appear. Furthermore, partial multicollinearity violates absolutely none of the assumptions of linear regression: It does not bias coefficient estimates, does not result in inefficient use of the data available, and does not cause falsely confident conclusions. The sole effect of this data limitation is that it makes conclusions more ambiguous or hesitant than they otherwise might have been. Despite the omnipresence and relative harmlessness of the multicollinearity problem, however, practitioners often write as though it represents an analytical flaw for which everyone must test and that must be solved if it appears. They may select solutions for dealing with multicollinearity that harm an analysis more than they help it. In short, practitioners take partial multicollinearity much more seriously than statistical theory or the methodological literature justifies.

The remainder of this entry proceeds in four sections. First, we treat full multicollinearity in depth, both substantively and statistically. Next, we provide the basic intuition for why collinear variables confound an analysis, using specific examples, and offer various mathematical illustrations of how full multicollinearity prevents the classical regression model from producing coefficient estimates. We then turn to partial multicollinearity, distinguishing the effects of this data condition according to the purposes for which an analyst has included a particular variable. Next we briefly reviews the various symptoms of and tests for multicollinearity customarily used by social scientists. In the last section, we consider the array of methods for dealing with multicollinearity that analysts have available to them.

Full Multicollinearity

Full (or perfect) multicollinearity results when one explanatory variable contains no fluctuation independent of the movement in the others. Because the problem variable is indistinguishable from the remainder of the explanatory variables in such a situation, an empirical analysis cannot parse it out. Conventional techniques break down in the face of such uninformative data, even when the empirical model is not actually a linear one. A maximum likelihood estimation, for example, becomes unsolvable if explanatory variables overlap so completely that they produce a flat likelihood curve and do not allow the method to converge on a set of coefficients. Comparative case analysis, similarly, cannot determine objectively which of the many traits that separate two cases actually account for differences in their outcomes. Additional assumptions or a more detailed analysis become necessary.

Intuitive Discussion

The symptoms of full multicollinearity differ depending on the analytical method, but the overarching problem remains the same: two concepts that cannot be separated from one another within a sample cannot be distinguished from one another empirically in any analysis conducted solely on that sample. In a causal analysis, it becomes impossible to separate out the effects of the problem variable from the effects of the others. In an analysis oriented toward prediction, it becomes impossible to determine how much weight the problem variable should receive, compared to the other variables, when computing forecasts outside of the sample.

The presence of full multicollinearity does not mean that the explanatory concepts are theoretically indistinct in the population or even that the conceptual differences would be indistinguishable in another data set produced using the same sampling method. It does mean that, without incorporating some kind of outside information, the current sample does not allow any way to avoid conflating the overlapping explanatory factors.

Let us start with a simple example. Suppose that a researcher wishes to understand why nations adopt strict censorship laws. One possibility might be to compare the United States, where expressive rights have become relatively permissive, with Canada, where public officials enjoy wide leeway when banning questionable forms of expression. Any number of important traits separate these two nations and therefore could explain the different realities. They achieved independence from Great Britain at a different time and in a different fashion. One elects an independent president, whereas the other selects a prime minister in parliament. One contains two major political parties, whereas the other sustains several. One allows the judiciary more flexibility and authority than the other does. Without incorporating some type of additional information, an analyst cannot say which feature of the two governments caused policy outcomes to deviate, nor would a forecaster know how to predict censorship levels in a third country that shared some traits in common with the United States and others in common with Canada.

This problem becomes even clearer with a statistical analysis. Suppose that an engineering firm faces two simultaneous discrimination lawsuits. An African-American male files the first one, claiming that the company engages in wage discrimination against black employees. A white female files the second one, alleging that the company discriminates against women. An analyst collects a random sample of engineers in the firm, recording each person's race, gender, and salary. However, by chance, the sample ends up containing only two sorts of people: white men and black women. The analyst can compute average salaries for the two sorts of engineers and determine whether they differ more than should be true by chance alone. Indeed, the results might show that black women tend to suffer in their paychecks relative to white men, for one reason or another. This computation would be useless, however, for purposes of deciding which of the lawsuits had merit because the sample conflates the two explanatory factors of race and gender. It is impossible to say how much of the gap reflects racial differences between the two sets of engineers and how much of it represents gender differences. In these data, the two explanations for wage differences are indistinguishable.

These two examples may seem artificial. How likely is it that researchers would try to explain a complicated policy outcome using only two cases, without digging into the underlying policy-making process to parse out the different institutional explanations? How likely is it that a random sample would exclude white women and black men? Of course, neither situation will occur often.

On the other hand, these examples may not be as far-fetched as they seem. Full multicollinearity rarely occurs in quantitative social science research. When it does appear, the problem almost always results from some kind of simple data-handling error created by the analyst. For example, the analyst might accidentally copy from the same column in a data table twice or might accidentally copy one variable over another within a software package. This sort of error would produce two identical variables with different names. An analyst might not realize that a model contains more variables than the sample contains observations, in essence mimicking the United States versus Canada confusion, or might divide up a sample and not realize that within a given subset of data a "variable" actually does not vary. These sorts of theoretically indefensible mistakes, resulting from poor data handling or careless model specification, produce most instances of full multicollinearity that practitioners will encounter. Fixing the mistakes automatically removes the estimation problem.

Formal Presentation

Full multicollinearity appears when one explanatory variable in a regression analysis is a direct linear function of the others. The underlying population relationship among the random variables might or might not be deterministic; the term "multicollinearity" only defines the condition in the sample.

In the classical regression model, full multicollinearity violates the assumptions necessary for successful estimation—a regression model becomes unsolvable. The technique should not even be able to estimate coefficients, although statistical software packages might produce an output if rounding errors create artificial variation sufficient to remove the perfect relationship among variables. More commonly, software packages either will refuse to give results for an unsolvable equation or will drop variables until the model becomes solvable.

There are various ways to illustrate why multivariate linear regression becomes impossible when an explanatory variable is statistically dependent on the others. For example, the notation partly depends on whether we approach the CRM and its assumptions from the vantage of scalar algebra or matrix algebra.

Scalar Notation

The classical regression model selects slope coefficients according to the least-squares criterion. It reports coefficient estimates that minimize the sum-of-squared prediction errors within the sample. For this reason, successful performance requires that some particular set of coefficients meet the least-squares criterion. If two or more sets of coefficients could produce the same minimized sum-of-squared errors, then it becomes impossible to say which one is correct.

Full multicollinearity actually produces a situation in which an infinite number of coefficients would satisfy the least-squares condition. Consider a simple analysis with only two explanatory variables, in which one of them (X_2) is a direct linear function of the other (X_1). We can summarize this relationship as $X_2 = c + dX_1$, where c and d are constants. The usual regression equation poses that the outcome of Interest—the dependent variable (y)—is a linear function of the explanatory variables and a random error term (e). The population model looks like this:

$$y = \beta_0 + \beta_1 X_1 + \beta_2 X_2 + e \tag{1}$$

where β_0 is the intercept, and β_1 and β_2 are the slope coefficients for their respective explanatory variables. If we suppose that X_2 in the sample is a multiple of X_1 (that is, $X_2 = dX_1$), just to keep things simple, then the regression needs to find the coefficient estimates b_1 and b_2 that produced the best predictions **:

$$\begin{aligned} y &= b_0 + b_1X_1 + b_2X_2 \\ &= b_0 + b_1X_1 + b_2(dX_1) \\ &= b_0 + (b_1 + db_2)X_1 \end{aligned} \tag{2}$$

An infinite number of coefficient pairs could produce the same values for **, as long as any change in b_1 from one possible value to another (δb_1) is matched by corresponding change in b_2 to compensate for it ($\delta b_2 = -\delta b_1/d$). Thus, an infinite number of (linearly related) coefficient pairs could produce the minimum sum-of-squared errors, $(y - {**})^2$. Presume, for example, that X_1 is a percentage and X_2 is simply a proportion measure of the same variable, such that $d = 100$. For any possible solution, b_1 and b_2, another pair could produce the same predicted values as long as the increase (or decrease) in b_1 is matched by a decrease (or increase) in b_2 by 1/100 of that amount.

A couple of other common model specification errors can illustrate how full multicollinearity might appear in an analysis and how it foils the estimation. Suppose, for example, that a researcher collects a sample of state-level electoral data for a single year. The dependent variable is the Republican proportion of a state's congressional delegation after a given year's election (Y). The researcher hypothesizes that Republican electoral success is a function of the following explanatory variables:

1. The GOP presidential contender's success in that state in that year, through some sort of coat-tail effect (X_1).
2. The GOP presidential contender's success in that state in the previous election, some sort of signaling effect that influences the quality of candidates fielded by each party (X_2).
3. The state's change in support for the GOP presidential candidate between the two elections, to capture some sort of bandwagon or trend effect ($X_3 = X_1 - X_2$).

Described in this way, these three hypotheses may all sound reasonable. In fact, however, the bandwagon effect is not distinguishable from the other two variables and in any sample it is a perfect linear combination of the other two:

$$\begin{aligned} y &= b_0 + b_1X_1 + b_2X_2 + b_3X_3 \\ &= b_0 + b_1X_1 + b_2X_2 + b_3(X_1 - X_2) \\ &= b_0 + (b_1 + b_3)X_1 + (b_2 - b_3)X_2 \end{aligned} \quad (3)$$

For any estimate of b_3, another will produce the same prediction as long as either b_2 shift in the same direction by the same amount or b_1 shift in the opposite direction by that amount. The equation will permit an infinite number of possible solutions.

Theorists sometimes posit multiplicative rather than additive regression models, such as the Cobb-Douglas function in economics or the gravity model in the study of international trade. Here is an example of a multiplicative model:

$$Y = \beta_0 X_1^{\beta_1} X_2^{\beta_2} \cdots X_K^{\beta_K} e^{\varepsilon} \quad (4)$$

where K represents the number of explanatory variables in a properly specified model and e represents the constant 2.718.... This precise specification is convenient, presuming it is theoretically appropriate, because it means the model is linear with respect to the natural logs (ln) of the variables. Suppose, for example, a three-variable version of the model:

$$\begin{aligned} \ln(Y) &= \ln(\beta_0 X_1^{\beta_1} X_2^{\beta_2} X_3^{\beta_3} e^{\varepsilon}) \\ &= \ln\beta_0 + \beta_1 \ln X_1 + \beta_1 \ln X_2 + \beta_3 \ln X_3 + \varepsilon \end{aligned} \quad (5)$$

What practitioners may overlook is that, when using a multiplicative model of this sort, the way we think about model specification must change. In particular, common practices such as taking a ratio or creating an interaction term can create full multicollinearity. For example, suppose that we wish to predict a nation-state's yearly imports. The three hypothesized explanatory variables might be features of each country's economy:

1. The gross national product, to serve as a measure of the economy's size (X_1).
2. The population, to serve as a measure of consumer needs (X_2).
3. The per capita income, to serve as a measure of wealth ($X_3 = X_1/X_2$).

These three explanations may make superficial sense, but they are not theoretically defensible in such a multiplicative model because $\ln(X_1/X_2) = \ln(X_1) - \ln(X_2)$, which creates a situation directly parallel to Eq. (3). Attempting to create a multiplicative interaction term will create the same problem if the model also includes the two components of the interaction because $\ln(X_1X_2) = \ln(X_1) + \ln(X_2)$.

It is worth considering the effect of full multicollinearity on the measure of uncertainty for multivariate regression coefficients as well. Of course, it may seem silly to investigate standard errors for coefficients that cannot be estimated, but this perspective once again shows how the usual computations fall apart when variables are perfectly collinear. Scalar algebra textbook discussions of multiple regression often present a formula for the standard error (s) of a coefficient (b) for a particular explanatory variable (X_j) along the following lines:

$$S_{b_j} = \sqrt{\frac{\sum_{i=1}^{n}(y_i - \hat{y}_i)^2}{\sum_{i=1}^{n}(x_i - \bar{x}_i)^2(1 - R_j^2)(n-k)}} \quad (6)$$

Most of this notation is standard. The important portion to discuss here is R_j^2, which represents the coefficient of determination that would result if X_j were regressed on the other explanatory variables. In the case of full multicollinearity, $R_j^2 = 1$ because the other explanatory variables account for 100% of the variation in X_j, which means that $(1-R_j^2)=0$, the entire denominator therefore becomes 0, and the ratio becomes undefined. Once again, the regression equations fall apart in the face of full multicollinearity.

Matrix Notation

Matrix-based regression customarily expresses the explanatory variables as a single matrix (X), that might take the following form:

$$X = \begin{bmatrix} 1 & x_{12} & x_{13} & \cdots & x_{1k} \\ 1 & x_{22} & x_{23} & \cdots & x_{2k} \\ 1 & x_{32} & x_{33} & \cdots & x_{3k} \\ \vdots & \vdots & \vdots & \ddots & \vdots \\ 1 & x_{n2} & x_{n3} & \cdots & x_{nk} \end{bmatrix} \quad (7)$$

where n represents the number of observations and k represents the number of independent variables, inclusive of the constant. The first column contains a series of 1s because it corresponds to the intercept, or constant, term in the regression. The dependent variable y, meanwhile, would represent a single column of numbers (a vector) of order n by 1.

The classical regression model's solution for computing its vector of coefficients (b) necessitates the following step:

$$X'Xb = X'y \quad (8)$$

$$b = (X'X)^{-1}X'y \quad (9)$$

where X' is the transpose of X. Going from Eqs. (8) to Eq. (9) requires $X'X$ to be invertible and $(X'X)^{-1}$ actually to exist. In other words, $X'X$ (sometimes written as Q) has to be square and nonsingular. It will always be square because, by definition, the transpose X' will have as many rows as X has columns. When one column of X is a linear combination of the other columns of X, however, the matrix will be singular. One row/column of Q will be a multiple of another row/column, such that the formula $Qb=X'y$ allows an infinite number of solutions for b. The rank of X will be less than k, the determinant of Q will equal zero, and no inverse will exist. In short, the formula cannot produce coefficient estimates in the presence of full multicollinearity. The coefficient standard error equation (σ^2Q^{-1}) also requires $X'X$ to be invertible and therefore produces no results in these cases.

One example of how full multicollinearity often appears becomes easy to illustrate using this notation. Researchers often perform regression on secondary data sets that include categorical variables. For example, a survey of individuals might include a variable to represent each person's religion. If the options include only Protestant, Catholic, Jewish, and Other, the data in X might look like this:

$X =$ (10)

Constant	Faith
1	Protestant
1	Protestant
1	Protestant
1	Catholic
1	Catholic
1	Catholic
1	Jewish
1	Jewish
1	Other

It should be obvious that the Faith variable cannot be included in a regression as is because it is not an ordinal variable, let alone an interval variable. Even if the data processor entered these faiths numerically rather than using text strings, the numbers assigned would be entirely arbitrary. The customary solution is to create a series of binary variables, one for each religion, in which individuals receive a value of 1 if they profess the pertinent faith and a 0 otherwise. One common mistake is for analysts to include all of these dummy variables computed from the categorical variable in a regression. The new data matrix would look like this:

$X =$ (11)

Constant	Protestant	Catholic	Jewish	Other
1	1	0	0	0
1	1	0	0	0
1	1	0	0	0
1	0	1	0	0
1	0	1	0	0
1	0	1	0	0
1	0	0	1	0
1	0	0	1	0
1	0	0	0	1

As long as we assume that no individual professes more than one faith, each row will have a positive value in one and only one of the four religion columns, which means that the constant term is a perfect linear combination of the four dummy variables:

$$\text{Constant} = \text{Protestant} + \text{Catholic} + \text{Jewish} + \text{Other} \quad (12)$$

Including them all with the constant produces full multicollinearity. The analyst must choose between (1) dropping the constant, in which case each of the religion dummies generates an intercept term for people of that faith, and (2) dropping one of the religion dummies, in which case the coefficients for the remainder represent an intercept shift for those who do not appear in the baseline category (that is, the one excluded from the regression).

Is Partial Multicollinearity a Problem?

Whereas full multicollinearity rarely appears in social science data unless sample sizes are tiny or the analyst makes some kind of mistake, partial multicollinearity is rarely absent. One explanatory variable almost always correlates with the other explanatory variables because that happens by chance in a sample most of the time even if the variables have no underlying relationship in the population. Sometimes the theory underlying a model directly mandates some degree of partial collinearity. A parabolic model, for example, includes both an explanatory variable and its square term; these must be correlated. A regression with nested binary variables, in which one singles out a subset of the other, also must exhibit multicollinearity. In short, multicollinearity is a matter of degree rather than one of kind.

Unreliable Coefficient Estimates

Partial multicollinearity violates none of the assumptions required to perform multiple regression, so it undermines none of the desirable features of the classical regression model (such as unbiasedness or efficiency). It also does not prevent accurate measures of uncertainty. Unfortunately, severe cases of multicollinearity can cause that uncertainty to be rather high.

Recall the intuitive example of full multicollinearity previously discussed, in which an analyst attempting to test for wage discrimination against both blacks and women could not distinguish the two cases because the sample only included white men and black women. Suppose that the analyst collected one additional case, a black male. At this point, the two explanatory variables—race and gender—would no longer be perfectly collinear. It would be possible to compute average salaries by race and average salaries by gender without the two gaps necessarily being the same. In particular, when testing for racial discrimination the final engineer would appear among the potentially disadvantaged class, whereas when testing for gender discrimination he would not.

The results of this analysis, however, would not be terribly reliable because they depend entirely on the salary of one randomly selected person. If he happened to collect a salary similar to the other men, the analysis would estimate that the company did not discriminate by race but seriously discriminated by gender; if he happened to collect a salary similar to that of the black women in the sample, by contrast, the analysis would estimate that the company did not discriminate by gender but seriously discriminated by race. If his salary fell at the midpoint between the black women and the white men, the analysis would indicate relatively moderate levels of discrimination against both groups. Adding a single person might have permitted estimates, but it hardly made those estimates trustworthy.

More generally, a high degree of partial multicollinearity adds to the instability of estimates such that the few discordant cases—the limited independent variation across the overlapping explanatory variables—strongly shape the final results. Consider, for example, the results worked out in Eq. (2), but with X_2 only a partial linear function of X_1, $X_2 = c + dX_1 + u$, where c and d are again constants, and u represents the remaining random variation in X_2, centered at 0. Dropping c again for convenience, the ultimate computation becomes:

$$\begin{aligned} y &= b_0 + b_1X_1 + b_2X_2 \\ &= b_0 + b_1X_1 + b_2(dX_1 + u) \\ &= b_0 + (b_1 + db_2)X_1 + b_2u \end{aligned} \tag{13}$$

In this case, multiple regression does allow a solution. If we shift from one possible value of b_2 to another, the sum-of-squared errors change because of alterations in the b_2u term. However, the changes in ** resulting from different possible choices for b_2 will be relatively minor if u contains little variation (that is, if the variables are highly collinear). Adjustments in b_1 could compensate for most of the shift in b_2, allowing a wide range of (b_1, b_2) values to appear roughly equivalent. Furthermore, the estimated balance between b_1 and b_2 would depend heavily on the limited variation in u that happened to appear. If y happened to be particularly high when u crept upward, then the b_2 estimate would be positive and the b_1 estimate would compensate by anchoring predictions downward. If y happened to be notably low when u crept upward, by contrast, b_2 would be selected to drag the predictions down and b_1 would swing in the other direction. In other words, the coefficient estimates will be unstable and negatively correlated with one another.

Regression output will not hide the uncertainty created by a high degree of multicollinearity. Review Eq. (6), which presents the formula for a coefficient standard error in multiple regression. Roughly speaking, errors go down when X and y covary significantly (the numerator) and when the sample size is large relative to the number of explanatory variables (the rightmost term in the denominator). They also go down when the explanatory variable bounces around a lot (the leftmost term in the denominator), but only insofar as this variation is independent of the other explanatory variables, as indicated by the middle term $(1 - R_j^2)$. When partial multicollinearity is high, the middle term $(1 - R_j^2)$ for a variable drops, decreasing the denominator and so ultimately increasing the standard error. In short, the coefficient standard errors from multiple regression correctly indicate the uncertainty, and therefore unreliability, of coefficient estimates produced for variables that offer little to distinguish one from another.

The Implications of Partial Multicollinearity

Explanatory variables subject to partial multicollinearity might appear in an analysis because they interest the researcher as potential causal explanations for the outcome being studied. They might appear in an analysis because the researcher believes they will help forecast outcomes beyond the sample. Or the multicollinear variables might appear simply to hold certain concepts constant—control variables that allow the researcher to isolate the independent effects of one or more other variables that do not exhibit such a high degree of collinearity. The implications of partial multicollinearity differ depending on whether a researcher intends to draw causal inferences and whether the coefficient on the variable in question represents a particular quantity of interest.

Statistical Control

Predictive models often contain a wide variety of explanatory variables, only some of which directly concern the researcher. The remainder, usually called control variables, appear in an analysis simply to increase the accuracy of the theoretically important coefficient estimates. The researcher need not worry whether coefficient estimates for control variables are close to the truth, nor does an analyst necessarily mind if these coefficients are accompanied by high standard errors (that is, whether they achieve statistical significance). What matters is that these rival explanations appeared in the analysis at all, thereby protecting other coefficient estimates from omitted variable bias.

Partial multicollinearity among control variables is almost entirely harmless. It does not undercut their effectiveness in eliminating omitted variable bias. It does not produce any sort of bias. It does not reduce the fit of a regression. Coefficient standard errors properly report the uncertainty attached to each estimate; there should be no opportunity to place more stock in a given coefficient than it deserves. The only risk is if, aside from random noise, the control variables lack independent variation, overlapping so completely that they are redundant. This circumstance would create inefficiency in a regression model, which could be problematic in very small data sets. But such costs appear any time analysts include unnecessary variables in a model; they are not unique to cases of partial multicollinearity. Otherwise, unless the researcher places more confidence in coefficient estimates than is warranted by their level of uncertainty—an indefensible flaw—partial multicollinearity in the control variables does not disrupt an analysis.

Optimizing Prediction and Forecasting

Researchers sometimes care more about the predictive power of a statistical model than they do about identifying causal effects. Forecasting models need not place as much emphasis on why one variable is correlated with another or on the causal ordering among various independent variables, as long as the overall model generates accurate out-of-sample predictions.

Of course, this distinction between forecasting and causal analysis is more conceptual than real. A forecasting model based on causally unrelated, and therefore theoretically inappropriate, independent variables is not likely to perform well outside of the sample on which it is based. A successful causal model that appropriately captures the theoretical process underlying data generation is likely to be successful at forecasting. Nonetheless, to the extent forecasting and causal analysis represent different analytical projects, partial multicollinearity poses little risk to the forecasting side of the enterprise.

Multiple regression takes into account the joint variation in various independent variables when it minimizes the sum-of-squared errors. The technology will not be able to assign responsibility directly to one variable or another, given their covariance, but it does adjust coefficient estimates and predicted values according to the relationship between that shared variance and the dependent variable. Therefore, the regression model milks multicollinear variables of any predictive power that they might bring to the task of forecasting. It uses variables in the sample as efficiently as possible.

Partial multicollinearity does carry some cost in a forecasting situation. Instability in the coefficient estimates for these variables naturally reduces confidence in predictions, increasing standard errors around them. An analyst naturally would like to reduce the imprecision caused by partial multicollinearity, if that is an option. Nevertheless, the problem is only as bad as the standard errors around the predictions. If these errors are already small enough that they produce predictions with an acceptable level of uncertainty, then partial multicollinearity may be ignored.

Determining Causation

Partial multicollinearity really only matters when it interferes with the precision of important coefficient estimates and therefore limits the researcher's ability to identify the causal process leading to a dependent variable. As indicated in Eq. (6), partial multicollinearity drives coefficient standard errors upward. A coefficient that might have passed conventional standards of statistical significance outside the presence of multicollinearity could flunk a hypothesis test because of inflated standard errors. An analyst therefore might fail to reject the null hypothesis only because an explanatory variable of interest overlaps with other variables in the sample.

Partial multicollinearity most resembles a pathology when variables unrelated or only thinly related in the larger population somehow end up highly correlated within our sample because it prevents a precision that otherwise should have been achievable. In essence, this condition means that the analyst possesses poor data with insufficient information about a substantial portion of the larger population, much as is true when the sample simply contains too few observations (which, Goldberger in 1991 termed, tongue in cheek, micronumerosity). Indeed, accidental cases of multicollinearity bear a particularly close relationship to the small-n problem because chance correlations among explanatory variables become increasingly improbable as the sample grows. Leaving aside small samples, therefore, partial multicollinearity usually results when two or more variables actually have some sort of causal relationship among them.

The severity of partial multicollinearity depends on the overall nature of an analysis. For example, as Eq. (6) indicates, a model with impressive predictive power will produce small coefficient standard errors because the numerator in each case will be small. Large data sets also will produce small standard errors, because $(n - k)$ will be large. Even in the presence of heavy multicollinearity, coefficient estimates may be precise enough to satisfy the analyst. Specifically, coefficient standard errors may be small enough for explanatory variables of interest to achieve statistical significance and establish a causal relationship, even if the analyst ignores partial multicollinearity entirely.

Even if some coefficients of interest fail to achieve statistical significance, partial multicollinearity still may pose no barrier to causal analysis, depending on the level of theoretical or causal precision that an analyst requires. For example, it is not uncommon for researchers to include multiple variables intended to capture the same basic theoretical concept: socioeconomic status, trust in government, social anomie, postmaterialist values, and so on. These variables are not multicollinear by chance, through the collection of an unfortunate sample; they covary in the larger population. A package of variables selected to triangulate on a concept naturally will be multicollinear to whatever extent the variables are tapping the same underlying social phenomenon. In fact, the better they perform as proxies for the underlying concept, the more they ought to covary and therefore the greater the multicollinearity—a paradoxical instance in which more multicollinearity is in fact a healthy sign. If the point of model specification is to establish the causal significance of a core concept, not the independent significance of each given proxy, then multicollinearity poses no problem at all. Individually, the variables might fail to pass a significance test, but the package of variables will increase the fit of the model measurably.

At some point the idea of "variable packages" becomes hazy. Two variables may not capture the exact same underlying concept, but researchers nevertheless may be aware that they are causally related to one another in the larger population, so that multicollinearity in the sample is no accident. This sort of multicollinearity, although theoretically meaningful, nonetheless can pose an obstacle to the analyst who wishes to distinguish two or more concepts statistically; it can hinder an analysis based on fine theoretical distinctions. The appearance of such multicollinearity may be helpful because it offers a warning that concepts may not be as theoretically distinct as a modeler initially assumed, but it still risks leaving the analyst with regrettably hesitant causal conclusions. The analyst would only be able to generalize about the overlapping variables as a package, even if a project's needs demand otherwise.

Social science practitioners sometimes express concern when control variables are partially collinear with variables of interest. This worry is symptomatic of the misunderstandings revolving around the "multicollinearity problem." Overlap between control variables and variables of interest in fact serves an important function—it is another instance when the appearance of multicollinearity should be reassuring rather than a cause for concern.

Control variables appear in a model primarily to ward off omitted variable bias. When an analyst omits relevant explanatory variables, the coefficient estimates expected for the remaining variables takes the following form in matrix algebra:

$$E(b_1) = \beta_1 + F\beta_2 \qquad (14)$$

where β_1 is a column vector containing the correct population parameter(s) for the included variables; β_2 is a column vector of population parameters for the omitted variable(s), representing their underlying relationship with the dependent variable; and F is a matrix representing the relationships among the omitted variables and those remaining in the estimated equation. If the term $F\beta_2$ represents a null vector—which it does if either F is a null matrix or β_2 is a null vector—then excluding the variables will not produce omitted variable bias. The expected result of an uncontrolled (that is, restricted) regression will be the correct population parameters, β_1.

What does this mean for multicollinearity? The only time unbiasedness requires the inclusion of a control variable is when we theorize that F is not null—in other words, when that control term *should* be partially collinear with a variable of interest. Including the control variable implicitly acknowledges that variables are expected to be multicollinear. It is therefore odd, if not inexplicable, that practitioners become concerned when the multicollinearity appears as theorized. Omitted variable bias undermines an important statistical property in an analysis—unbiasedness. In contrast, the inflated standard errors that result from multicollinearity are not an analytical flaw but a defense mechanism, an indication of the uncertainty attached to a coefficient of interest once we take into account how much it overlaps with other plausible explanations captured by the statistical controls. Multicollinearity is the solution to a problem, not the problem itself, in these instances.

Special Cases

Some forms of model specification necessarily induce partial multicollinearity and so are worth a separate look: parabolic models, interaction terms, and models with nested binary variables. Parabolic models are one means of rigging linear regression to accommodate nonlinear systematic relationships between dependent and independent variables. If X_1 is the root explanatory variable, for example, the model might include $X_2 = X_1^2$:

$$Y = \beta_0 + \beta_1 X_1 + \beta_2 X_1^2 + e \qquad (15)$$

The inclusion of an explanatory variable in its squared form allows a bend in the systematic component of their relationship. Throwing in the cubed form of the variable allows for a second bend, and so on:

$$Y = \beta_0 + \beta_1 X_1 + \beta_2 X_1^2 + \beta_3 X_1^3 + \cdots + \beta_k X_1^k + e \qquad (16)$$

Because the exponential variables in this sort of model are simply manipulations of the core variable, they naturally covary (although the nature of the collinearity depends on the scale and direction of the source variable).

Does multicollinearity in a parabolic model prevent causal analysis? Not at all. As with using other package variables, applying multiple versions of the source variable does not remove any explanatory power from it. Coefficients will minimize the sum-of-squared errors, taking into account the joint variance among the different manipulated forms of the variable as well as the variance independent to each of them. It is possible that an important variable will fail to achieve statistical significance in any of its exponential forms simply because they overlap so much. But this is an important finding; it means that, even if the variable matters in general, the regression cannot determine with confidence whether the systematic component contains a significant bend. It is a hypothesis test for the functional form rather than for the variable itself. The biggest risk associated with including exponential versions of a variable is that they may be unnecessary, thereby reducing the efficiency of the estimation.

Another form of variable manipulation that necessarily produces multicollinearity is the multiplicative interaction term. For example, the systematic functional form might be:

$$y = \beta_0 + \beta_1 X_1 + \beta_2 X_2 + \beta_3 (X_1 X_2) + e \qquad (17)$$

The purpose of this sort of model is that it allows the coefficient on one variable (say, X_1) to depend linearly on the value of the other variable (in this case X_2). As X_1 increases by one unit, y increases by $\beta_1 + \beta_3 X_2$. The multiplicative term necessarily correlates with its own components. To whatever extent this drives up coefficient standard errors, however, it is not pathological. As always, the joint variation still contributes to coefficient estimates and the model's fit. The inflated standard errors may cause some of the variables to fall short on a hypothesis test, but this is not a test of the overall package; it simply tests the functional form. If the interaction term fails to achieve significance, that means the data do not allow an analyst to conclude that the effect of one variable depends on the value of another.

A final special case that inherently produces multicollinearity is when the researcher uses nested binary variables. For example, suppose that a scholar wishes to gauge the effect of equal protection lawsuits on funding across school districts. The dependent variable might be a measure of inequality in the state's funding system. The explanatory variable of interest might be a representation of the lawsuit. Rather than include only a single variable, however, the analyst might opt for one binary variable representing whether a lawsuit had been filed and another representing whether the complainant won. Because it is necessary to file the lawsuit to win it, the two binary variables will be collinear; a zero on the first variable necessitates a zero on the other.

This collinearity would drive up their standard errors. As with the other special cases, however, this is healthy. The two variables as a package capture the effect of the lawsuit; their independent effects merely probe whether it is the filing or the winning that makes the difference. If the two variables exhibit a high degree of multicollinearity—say, for example, because most legal challenges ultimately prove successful—they may not return significant coefficients. But this is a useful and important result. It means that the act of filing and the act of winning a legal challenge cannot be distinguished theoretically within the bounds of the data.

Symptoms of Partial Multicollinearity

Despite the relative innocuousness of partial multicollinearity, practitioners show a high degree of sensitivity to it. The methodological literature has responded to this concern by outlining a number of ways to detect multicollinearity. The result of this effort is a wide variety of diagnostic tools, more or less rigid in their application. These various diagnostics actually test for a variety of phenomena, no doubt in part because the ill-defined "multicollinearity problem" itself is not a distinct infringement of any statistical principle and does not undermine any important statistical property—it is not entirely clear what we need to test for.

The most informal, and probably the most useful, diagnostic tool is to compare the fit of a model with the uncertainty reported for its various coefficients. When a package of explanatory variables jointly assists in predicting the dependent variable, the variables will markedly improve the model's fit, but they may fail to achieve independent significance if they are highly multicollinear. The partial (or multiple-partial) F test for joint significance formalizes this comparison by determining whether the inclusion of a package of variables—moving from a restricted to an unrestricted model—significantly increases the model's coefficient of determination (R^2):

$$F(k_{\mathrm{U}} - k_{\mathrm{R}}, n - k_{\mathrm{U}}) = \frac{(R_{\mathrm{U}}^2 - R_{\mathrm{R}}^2)/(k_{\mathrm{U}} - k_{\mathrm{R}})}{(1 - R_{\mathrm{U}}^2)/(n - k_{\mathrm{U}})} \tag{18}$$

where n is the total number of observations, k indicates the number of explanatory variables (constant term included), the subscript R indicates the relevant statistic from a model with the package of variables excluded (i.e., their coefficients restricted to be zero), and the subscript U indicates a statistic from a model with the package of variables included (i.e., their coefficients unrestricted and so subject to estimation). A package of variables can achieve statistical significance in a partial F test even if none of them does so individually on the conventional t test.

One common practice in empirical journals is to include a covariance matrix, showing the bivariate relationships among all the difference explanatory variables. As a diagnostic tool, this sort of table serves little purpose. It does not detect complex forms of multicollinearity, when one explanatory variable is a function of several of them. It provides no way to distinguish accidental and population-based forms of multicollinearity and it does not address the substantive question of whether partial multicollinearity undermines the goals of a research project. An alternative but related solution is to present a series of partial regressions, in which each independent variable in turn is regressed on the others. This sort of diagnostic does not address the theoretical difficulties with the bivariate method, but at least it gives a clearer picture of how much independent variation each explanatory variable actually contains.

A number of specific tests for multicollinearity have been proposed. Some people have used the determinant of $(X'X)$ from the matrix regression equation, for example. An even better solution (because it is bounded and unaffected by the dispersion of the explanatory variables) is simply to look at the coefficient of determination, as appears in Eq. (6), for each explanatory variable. Perhaps the most popular test, in recent times, is the variance inflation factor (VIF). It simply represents the inverse of the middle term in Eq. (6):

$$\mathrm{VIF} = \frac{1}{(1 - R_j^2)} \tag{19}$$

The conventional wisdom or rule of thumb seems to be that a VIF of 10 or more signifies trouble, although others use more conservative standards (i.e., higher thresholds). All of these tests share the same basic shortcoming, however—they attempt to systemize what should be a substantive judgment, a matter of analysis and interpretation. Recent scholarship therefore seeks to define the costs of including multicollinear variables in terms of the predictive impact of their presence.

Methods of Dealing with Partial Multicollinearity

Practitioners generally perceive multicollinearity as troublesome. Once in a while partial multicollinearity—especially incidental multicollinearity that obscures causal effects—really does hinder a theoretically appropriate analysis. Analysts concerned about partial multicollinearity face numerous options.

Incorporate Additional Information

Multicollinearity becomes problematic when a sample is not adequately informative about differences among two or more variables, resulting in coefficient estimates that are insufficiently precise and coefficient standard errors that are unacceptably large. Because the cause is at root one of poor data, the most obvious way to remove high degrees of multicollinearity is to get better data.

As Eq. (6) indicates, data improvements can lower coefficient standard errors even if they do not address multicollinearity directly. The analyst could increase the number of observations (n), which would have the additional virtue of making incidental multicollinearity less likely. The analyst also could decrease the number of explanatory variables (k), if some of them are unnecessary, or add other theoretically relevant explanatory variables if they can significantly improve model specification (driving up the numerator). Such changes would compensate for a low $(1 - R_j^2)$.

A researcher also could choose to oversample observations that would increase the independent variation in an explanatory variable, increasing $(1 - R_j^2)$. For example, if a study uses both education and income and these are highly correlated, the researcher could affirmatively select for highly educated poor people or people who are wealthy but uneducated. Selecting on explanatory variables does not induce bias the way that selecting on a dependent variable does. This strategy does entail certain risks, however, because it produces an overall sample that is not representative of the larger population. It may decrease multicollinearity at the expense of inducing bias in other analyses carried out on the data (at least unless those analyses take into account the nonrandom selection through some sort of weighting or similar solution).

These solutions all required pulling new data directly into an ongoing analysis. An alternate way to incorporate additional data is to borrow insights from previous research in the field. The analyst may be able to apportion the joint variance among variables, for example, by assuming a causal order, or otherwise formalize the relationship among multicollinear variables. The analyst may be willing to constrain coefficients for one or more of the partially multicollinear variables, based on previous research. Obviously using prior knowledge is risky; it runs the risk of creating a scholarly literature that is less science and more echo chamber. Nevertheless, researchers trying to exploit imperfect data may decide that their best solution is to take advantage of prior knowledge about the variables being used.

Certain other highly technical solutions also exist. They also incorporate prior information and, therefore, in a sense qualify as Bayesian estimators. Probably the most common example is ridge regression, such as ordinary ridge regression (ORR). This solution relies on the existence of an unmeasured positive constant k that we implicitly can insert into the standard regression equation to derive a new coefficient:

$$** = (X'X + kI)^{-1}X'y \tag{20}$$

where I is the identity matrix, such that k implicitly pumps up the diagonals of Q. This solution depends on the value of k, which is rarely given—the greater that number, the more it reduces variance but the more it biases coefficient estimates toward zero. Because determining k generally requires rather arbitrary deductions from the data, ridge regression is not used frequently.

Remove Additional Information

Adding data is a great idea, but an analyst may not have that luxury. Instead, researchers often react to a poor information source by using the destructive strategy of throwing out even more information. Analysts occasionally toss out partially multicollinear variables, for example. More commonly, analysts combine multicollinear variables into one composite measure. For example, they might perform a factor analysis to isolate the variance that variables share, using the resulting factor score as a new index variable. Such indices are reported on an arbitrary scale and therefore are not interpretable in any direct substantive way. They also strip out any variation unique to the particular variables used to create the index, which may be substantively important. Finally, they might require questionable assumptions, such as the linearity assumption needed for factor analysis. Such indices do have an important virtue, however, which is that the relative weight of each variable in the index is derived statistically using information contained in the data.

Perhaps the most popular sort of index is the additive kind. Unlike indices derived from factor analysis or other statistical methods, the additive index is driven by assumption. Suppose, for example, that a researcher wishes to include "Trust in other people" as an explanatory concept in a causal model. The researcher has two survey questions representing interpersonal trust, one that asks whether people are "selfish" (variable X_1) and one that asks whether people "try to do the right thing" (variable X_2). Presumably these variables will contain some multicollinearity because they are theoretically related, but they also will exhibit some independent variation because they get at the root explanatory concept of interest in different ways. The population model therefore is:

$$y = \beta_0 + \beta_1 X_1 + \beta_2 X_2 + e \tag{21}$$

Recognizing that X_1 and X_2 both represent proxies for the same underlying concept, the analyst may create a new explanatory variable, an additive index $Z = (X_1 + X_2)$. The ostensible purpose of this additive index might be to avoid multicollinearity, or it could be an attempt to simplify the presentation by reducing the overarching concept to a single variable with a single coefficient estimate and a single hypothesis test. The regression equation actually estimated becomes:

$$\begin{aligned} y &= b_0 + b_z Z + e \\ &= b_0 + b_z(X_1 + X_2) + e \\ &= b_0 + b_z X_1 + b_z X_2 + e \end{aligned} \tag{22}$$

Using an additive index therefore produces coefficient estimates under the assumption that, in the population, $\beta_1 = \beta_2$ (a testable proposition that usually goes untested). If this constraint is inappropriate, the fit of the model will decline (imposing inefficiency) and implicit coefficient estimates will be biased because neither $E(b_Z) = \beta_1$ nor $E(b_Z) = \beta_2$.

Practitioners sometimes justify additive indices as reasonable under the assumption that each proxy should receive the same weight (which factor analysis and related methods do not guarantee). Unless X_1 and X_2 are scaled so that they have the same variance, however, forcing two variables to receive the same implicit coefficient actually does not ensure that they receive the same weight. The variance of the additive index is:

$$V(Z) = V(X_1 + X_2) = V(X_1) + V(X_2) + 2\text{Cov}(X_1, X_2) \tag{23}$$

Variation in the new variable therefore depends on which component initially contained more variance. The one with greater variance receives greater weight, both in the additive index before estimation and in the predicted values after estimation. Furthermore, as the rightmost term indicates, movement in the new variable will be overbalanced toward the joint variance between the two questions, washing out the independent variation in each proxy question that presumably justified its separate collection in the first place. In other words, a model constrained by use of an additive index assigns variables unequal influence, imposing a functional form both arbitrarily *and* atheoretically.

In sum, additive indices lack the virtue of statistically derived indices, but they possess all of the drawbacks—a meaningless scale and estimation that neglects the independent information provided by each proxy measure. The only real virtue of this solution to partial multicollinearity is simplicity—they are easy to compute and take up less space when reporting results.

Do Nothing

A final solution to the presence of multicollinearity is to do nothing about it at all. It does no real harm to a regression model aside from making some of the variables less precise, and the standard errors properly report this imprecision. The solution to do nothing may be appropriate when the multicollinearity appears for a theoretically meanginful reason, such as when numerous variables have been computed from the same source. It is also especially tempting in cases when the multicollinearity exists among control variables or within a forecasting model.

However, the option to do nothing is also a viable choice in causal models, as long as the researcher need not parse out the independent effects of the multicollinear variables. The partial F statistic in Eq. (18) allows a test of joint significance for any given package of variables. Although characterizing the effect of a package of variables may be trickier than reporting the effect of only one, it has the virtue of retaining both the scale and the independent variation of the source data.

See Also the Following Article

Economic Forecasts

Further Reading

Anderson, J. E. (1979). A theoretical foundation for the gravity equation. *American Econ. Rev.* **69,** 106–116.

Berry, W. D., and Feldman, S. (1985). *Multiple Regression in Practice.* Sage, Newbury Park, CA.

Fabrycy, M. Z. (1975). Multicollinearity caused by specification errors. *Appl. Statist.* **24**(2), 250–254.

Goldberger, A. S. (1991). *A Course in Econometrics.* Harvard University Press, Cambridge, MA.

Greenberg, E., and Parks, R. P. (1997). A predictive approach to model selection and multicollinearity. *J. Appl. Econometrics* **12,** 67–75.

Harvey, A. C. (1977). Some Comments on Multicollinearity in Regression. *Appl. Statist.* **26**(2), 188–191.

Hoerl, A. E., and Kennard, R. W. (1970). Ridge regression: Biased estimation for non-orthogonal problems. *Technometrics* **12,** 55–67.

King, G., Keohane, R. O., and Verba, S. (1994). *Designing Social Inquiry.* Princeton University Press, Princeton, NJ.

Kmenta, J. (1986). *Elements of Econometrics.* University of Michigan Press, Ann Arbor, MI.

Mansfield, E. R., and Helms, B. P. (1982). Detecting multicollinearity. *Am. Statist.* **36**(3), 158–160.

Multidimensional Item Response Models

Mark D. Reckase

Michigan State University, East Lansing, Michigan, USA

Glossary

computerized adaptive test A computer-administered test that selects test items during the testing process to match the estimated level of performance of the examinee.

dimension A continuum on which individuals vary. The continuum may be directly observable, such as height, or may be a hypothesized continuum, such as verbal ability.

indeterminacy Characteristic of some models that the origin, unit of measurement, or orientation is not determined by the model but has to be arbitrarily set to a value.

item A limited task that is used to assess a person's level on a trait or domain of knowledge.

item response theory (IRT) A theory that hypothesizes a particular mathematical relationship between the levels of a trait and the probability of a response to an item.

latent dimension A dimension that cannot be directly observed but that is hypothesized to exist in at least an abstract sense.

model A mathematical representation of the observed relationships between data.

monotonicity The item response theory assumption that the probability of a response increases as the level on a trait increases.

Multidimensional item response models are probabilistic models for the interaction between persons and measurement tasks, usually called items; these models are based on the assumption that persons vary on numerous latent dimensions and that items are sensitive to differences on multiple dimensions. Item response models can be used to investigate the characteristics of items and to estimate simultaneously a person's location on the dimensions of sensitivity of the items.

Introduction

The Need for Multidimensional Item Response Theory Models

A common approach to measurement in the social sciences is to present persons with a series of tasks (items) and collect their responses to the tasks. For convenience, the responses that a person can give to the task are often limited to a fixed set of choices (such as those given for multiple-choice items), the rating categories for attitude or opinion surveys, or marks on a continuous scale that has been anchored with verbal descriptions to provide meaning to the scale. The observable result from an instrument composed of a set of items is a string of responses for each person that represents the person's interactions with the items. These strings of responses can be aggregated to form a person-by-item matrix of responses for groups of persons. The matrix is usually oriented so that rows correspond to persons and columns correspond to items on the assessment instrument. The goal of much of measurement theory is to determine what can be inferred about persons from their interactions with the items that make up a measurement instrument, when the interactions are summarized as the set of responses included in the person-by-item response matrix.

Much early work in social measurement approached the task of inferring information about the persons from simple models that ordered the persons along a single continuum, often based on a sum of scores given to the responses to the items. For example, achievement items would be scored correct (1) or incorrect (0) and the sum of the item scores would be the number of items answered correctly. This approach implicitly assumes that the major portion of variation in the responses can be accounted for by variation along a single dimension, and that dimension can be approximated by the number-correct score.

However, there is ample evidence in fields of social research that persons have numerous characteristics on which they vary, and the items used in measurement instruments are sensitive to differences in those characteristics. Therefore, to represent the complex information provided in a set of responses to items, multiple characteristics of the respondents need to be taken into account and the complexities of the interactions between the items and the persons need to be modeled. It is the desire to model adequately the complex interactions of persons, using social measurement tasks, that has led to the development of probabilistic models for the person-by-item response matrix; these are collectively called multidimensional item response theory (MIRT) models.

Statistical Rationale for MIRT Models

The need for multidimensional models of the interaction between persons and items can be supported on both statistical and substantive grounds. The statistical support for such models is that it is often the case that the person-by-item response matrix is not well summarized using models based on a single continuum. From a statistical perspective, no further justification beyond lack of fit of a model to data is needed to search for additional parameters to improve the representation of the data.

Substantive Support for MIRT Models

Multidimensional models for the interactions between persons and items can also be supported on substantive grounds. There is a large body of research in most areas of social science that indicates that the number of dimensions needed to describe human behavior is very large, and that even the simplest items are sensitive to differences on multiple dimensions. For example, the variety of cognitive skills found in psychological studies has been catalogued. These results are reinforced by work in cognitive science that shows the wide variety of mental processes that are needed to comprehend and respond to simple tasks. Similar compilations have been done for personality variables and other measures such as attitudes and opinions.

Historical Antecedents to the Current MIRT Models

MIRT models have evolved from two different areas of psychometric theory. The first area is work done throughout the 20th century to relate the performance of persons on items to the location of a person along a continuum. Alfred Binet and Theodore Simon used this concept in 1905 when selecting items for their test of intelligence. The chronological age of students was used as a surrogate for student's location along an ability continuum. Items selected for the test required the level of skill demonstrated by students at increasing age levels. In 1966, the researcher Paul Lazarsfeld (among others) suggested that a straight line could be used to model the increase in the tendency to give a particular response as a person's level on a trait increased. The use of an increasing mathematical function to model the interaction between persons and items became an accepted method for analysis with the work of Frederic Lord in 1980 under the label of item response theory (IRT). Lord had previously suggested that nonlinear relationships using the logistic and normal ogive functions could be used to model the interaction of persons and items. That work was operationalized in a number of computer programs for identifying the probability functions that represent the relationships in the person-by-item response matrix, which have names such as BILOG (for binary logistics) and BIGSTEPS.

The second area that contributed to the development of MIRT was factor analysis, particularly methods for the analysis of items that are scored 0 or 1. Analysis of these types of response data does not meet the assumptions of continuous normally distributed variables used for much of the development of factor analysis. To properly analyze 0/1 data, relationships are hypothesized between a continuous latent variable and the dichotomized observed variable. The form of the relationships is typically very similar to those used in IRT. Numerous researchers have developed factor analysis procedures that are very similar to the current MIRT methods. The major distinction is that factor analysis procedures often standardize the variables being analyzed to have a common mean and variance, whereas MIRT leaves those variables unstandardized so that item characteristics can be studied.

General Assumptions of the Models

The models that fit under the general heading of MIRT are based on a number of assumptions.

Mathematical Form of the Model

A major assumption of MIRT is that a particular mathematical function will provide a reasonable approximation to the relationship between the characteristics of a person, the characteristics of the items, and the probability of the response to the items. Many different mathematical forms are possible, but most assume that the probability of a correct or desirable response increases with an increase in a person's status on a dimension, or any combination of dimensions. This is called the monotonicity assumption. This assumption is not a necessary requirement, but it seems reasonable for many types of measurement instruments, such as achievement or aptitude tests. The cumulative normal or logistic distribution functions have the monotonicity characteristic and are often used as the basis for MIRT. These mathematical forms will be described in detail later.

Local (Conditional) Independence

A second major assumption is that if the model contains a sufficient number of dimensions to well represent the relationships between the persons and the items, then the responses for persons with the same location on the full set of dimensions will be independent of each other. This means, in practice, that the information about a person's level on all of the dimensions totally accounts for the non-random components of the responses. However, responses are expected to be dependent when persons vary in their status on the dimensions. Thus, the independence is "local" to a point in the multidimensional space where persons have the same profile of traits, and, equivalently, the independence is "conditional" on persons having the same profile of traits. The local independence assumption is needed for the estimation procedures used to compute the person and item characteristics.

Models

Introduction

MIRT models are often classified into two types, depending on whether high levels on one dimension can compensate for low levels on another dimension. Compensatory models allow the probability of a correct response to approach 1.0, even when the trait level on one or more dimensions is very low, if the trait levels on the remaining dimensions approach positive infinity. Noncompensatory or, more correctly, partially compensatory models do not allow the probability of a correct response to approach 1.0 when there is a low trait level on one dimension, even when the other traits approach positive infinity.

Compensatory Models

The most commonly used compensatory model is given by the following equation for the probability of a score of 1:

$$\mathrm{P}(x_{ij}=1|\vec{\theta}_j,\vec{a}_i,d_i,c_i)=c_i+(1-c_i)\frac{e^{\vec{a}_i'\vec{\theta}_j+d_i}}{1+e^{\vec{a}_i'\vec{\theta}_j+d_i}}, \tag{1}$$

where x_{ij} is the (0 or 1) response by examinee j to item i, $\vec{a}_i$ is a vector of parameters for item i that indicates how well the item discriminates on each trait dimension, d_i is a parameter that is related to the difficulty of the item or the likelihood of endorsing the item, c_i is the probability of obtaining a score of 1 on the item as the level on all of the traits approaches negative infinity, e is the mathematical constant that is the base of the

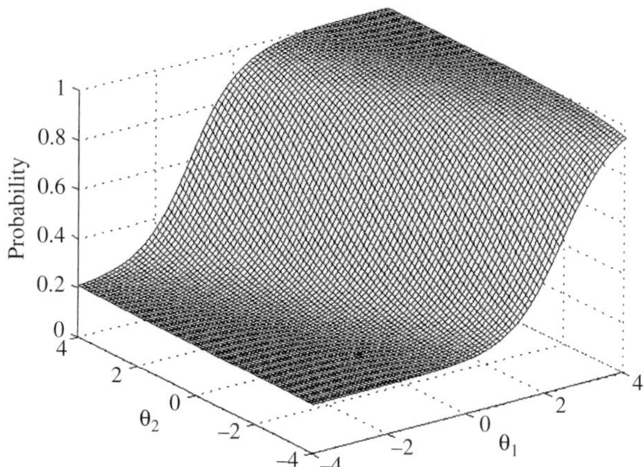

Figure 1 Compensatory multidimensional item response surface; $a_1=1.6$, $a_2=0.7$, $c=0.2$, and $d=-1$.

natural logarithms, and $\vec{\theta}_j$ is a vector of trait levels for examinee j. Note that for a particular vector, $\vec{a}_i$, if one element of $\vec{\theta}_j$ is large, the exponent will be large, resulting in a high probability of correct response even if other elements of $\vec{\theta}_j$ are small. If there are only two trait dimensions in the model, θ_{1j} and θ_{2j}, as elements of $\vec{\theta}_j$, then the model can be represented graphically as a three-dimensional surface. An example of the surface for an item that is better at discriminating on Dimension 1 than Dimension 2 is given in Fig. 1.

The model given in Eq. (1) is a multidimensional extension of the three-parameter logistic model that is widely used for the modeling of test data when a single dominant trait can be assumed. If c_i can be assumed to be zero, then a simplified version of the model is an extension of the two-parameter logistic model. A model that is very similar to the model given in Eq. (1) is based on the cumulative normal distribution rather than the cumulative logistic distribution. Using the same notation as that for Eq. (1), the model is given by

$$\mathrm{P}(x_{ij}=1|\vec{\theta}_j,\vec{a}_i,d_i,c_i)=c_i+(1-c_i)\Psi(\vec{a}_i'\vec{\theta}_j+d_i), \tag{2}$$

where Ψ is the cumulative normal function. In practice, there is little to distinguish the form of the models in Eqs. (1) and (2), but the logistic form in Eq. (2) is somewhat easier to work with mathematically.

Noncompensatory Models

A number of noncompensatory models have been proposed in the literature; the most commonly referenced model assumes that there is a probability of response to the item related to each dimension, and the overall

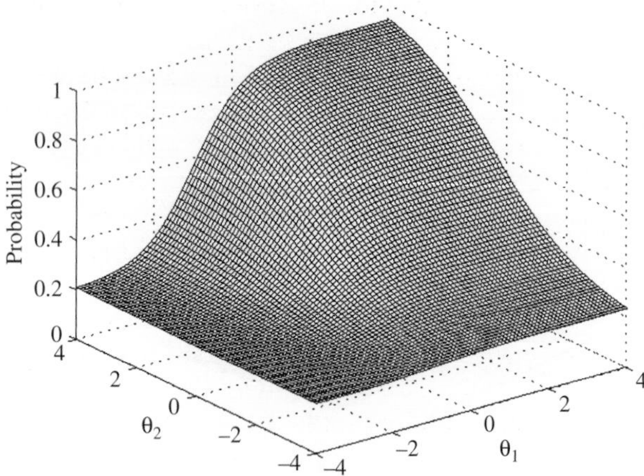

Figure 2 Noncompensatory multidimensional item response surface; $a_1 = 1.6$, $a_2 = 0.7$, $b_1 = -1$, $b_2 = 0.5$, and $c = 0.2$.

probability of correct response is the product of the probabilities from the individual dimensions. The equation for the model is

$$\mathrm{P}(x_{ij} = 1|\vec{\theta}_j, \vec{a}_i, \vec{b}_i, c_i) = c_i + (1 - c_i) \prod_{k=1}^{m} \frac{e^{a_{ik}(\theta_{jk} - b_{ik})}}{1 + e^{a_{ik}(\theta_{jk} - b_{ik})}}, \tag{3}$$

where x_{ij} is the (0 or 1) response by examinee j to item i, $\vec{a}_i$ is a vector of parameters for item i with elements a_{ik} that indicate how well the item discriminates on each trait dimension k, $\vec{b}_i$ is a vector of parameter for item i with elements b_{ik} that indicate the level of difficulty of the item on each trait dimension k or the likelihood of endorsing the item, c_i is the probability of obtaining a score of 1 on the item as the level on all of the traits approaches negative infinity, e is the mathematical constant that is the base of the natural logarithms, and $\vec{\theta}_j$ is a vector of trait levels for examinee j with the individual elements indicated by θ_{jk}, the level of trait on the kth dimension. Note that, for the product term at the right-hand side of the model, the maximum value of the product is controlled by the dimension with the lowest term. When the θ_{jk}-values for the traits go to positive infinity, the corresponding terms go to 1.0. If all but one θ_{jk} goes to positive infinity, the product is equal to the value of the non-infinite term. Some compensation is possible in the model—the probability of correct response increases as each θ_{jk} increases, but the probabilities do not increase to 1.0 unless all θ_{jk} increase to positive infinity. If any one θ_{jk} is less than positive infinity, the value of that term is the limiting factor for the magnitude of the overall probability.

If there are only two trait dimensions in the model, θ_{j1} and θ_{j2}, as elements of $\vec{\theta}_j$, then the model can be represented graphically as a three-dimensional surface. An example of the surface for an item that is better at discriminating on Dimension 1 than Dimension 2 is given in Fig. 2. The values of the discrimination parameters are the same as those used for Fig. 1, but for this model, values are needed for the difficulty parameters b_{ik}.

Estimation of Model Parameters

For the MIRT models to be used in practice, it must be possible to estimate the parameters of the models. The parameters are the item characteristics and the person trait levels. The parameter estimation procedures are quite different for the compensatory and noncompensatory models, so they will be discussed separately in the following two sections.

Compensatory Models

Two computer programs, NOHARM and TESTFACT, are frequently used for the estimation of the item characteristics of the compensatory models. The name "NOHARM" derives from the normal ogive harmonic analysis robust method. This method approximates the MIRT model using a four-term polynomial series; it determines the coefficients of the terms in the series that minimize the squared difference between the observed frequencies of correctly answering items i and j and the predicted frequency of the joint occurrence of the pair of correct responses. This procedure is not very computationally intensive and the input it requires is the collection of all possible two-by-two tables for pairs of item responses. The program will tally the frequencies for the tables from a person-by-item matrix of item responses. If nonzero c-parameters are assumed for the items, those parameters must be estimated by another program and be input to NOHARM. NOHARM does not estimate the lower asymptote for items. In general, the input data are the same that are needed to compute the correlation matrix for dichotomously scored items.

TESTFACT estimates the parameters of the MIRT model using the marginal maximum-likelihood method. That is, the maximum-likelihood estimate is obtained after integrating out an assumed marginal trait distribution. An iterative method based on the expectation maximization (EM) algorithm is used for estimation. As with NOHARM, TESTFACT does not estimate the lower asymptote parameter. It either accepts values as input or uses 1/(number of item choices) as an approximation. TESTFACT is a computationally intensive procedure with limits on the number of dimensions that can be estimated.

Noncompensatory Models

In contrast to the compensatory models, estimation of the parameters for the noncompensatory models is much more challenging. An estimation procedure has been developed for a variation of the model given in Eq. (3), but that estimation procedure requires that data be collected on subtasks within an item as well as performance on the item as a whole. This procedure uses maximum-likelihood estimation. Newer estimation procedures, such as Markov chain Monte Carlo method, are now being applied to this class of models to solve some of the estimation procedures.

Examples of Estimation Results

Estimation software typically provides, at a minimum, estimates of the item parameters for the model. For the compensatory models, the estimates are provided for the a- and d-parameters, often labeled as slope and intercept parameters, respectively. Table I provides the item parameter estimates for the first 10 items from a 40-item tenth-grade mathematics test. The item response data from this test were analyzed using a two-dimensional compensatory model [see Eq. (2)] as implemented in the NOHARM computer program. The a-parameters in the table indicate how well the test items discriminate along the dimension related to that parameter. When the number is large (e.g., $a_1 = 2.37$ for Item 1), it indicates that the item is very discriminating along that dimension. When it is small (e.g., $a_2 = 0.00$ for Item 1), it indicates that the item does not discriminate along the dimension. For this analysis, a_2 was set to 0.0 for Item 1 to remove the rotational indeterminacy of the solution.

When the program estimates the parameters of the items, there are three features of the solution that cannot be determined from the model. They are (1) the location of the 0-point on each of the dimensions (i.e., the origin of the ability space), (2) the units used to measure along each dimension, and (3) the orientation of the axes in the ability space. The 0-point is usually set at the mean level of performance on each dimension for the sample of examinees being analyzed, the unit is usually set as the standard deviation of that group, and the orientation is set by fixing the a-parameters at 0.0 for $m - 1$ items, where m is the number of dimensions in the solution. For this two-dimension solution, the a-parameter needs to be fixed for only one item on one dimension. Setting the a-parameter to 0.0 aligns one of the axes of the solution with the skills assessed by that item with the nonzero loading. The indeterminacy of multivariate solutions has been known for some time, and there are many ways to add constraints to allow solutions to be obtained.

Table I Item Parameter Estimates for the First 10 Test Items[a]

Item number	*Item parameter* a_1	a_2	d
1	2.37	0.00	2.49
2	0.58	0.38	1.00
3	0.63	0.27	0.66
4	0.99	0.47	0.76
5	0.60	0.18	0.26
6	0.78	0.64	−0.01
7	0.75	0.41	0.57
8	1.64	0.15	0.15
9	1.04	0.52	0.61
10	1.26	0.51	0.23

[a] From a tenth-grade mathematics test ($N = 1635$).

Another way of describing the discriminating power of a test item in a multidimensional space is how well the responses to the item divide the space into two parts, i.e., abilities for those who respond correctly to the item and for those who do not. The overall discriminating power of an item, MDISC, is defined by the following equation:

$$\text{MDISC}_i = \sqrt{\sum_{i=1}^{m} a_{ik}^2}. \tag{4}$$

The discrimination of an item is also best in a particular direction in the multidimensional space. The angle with coordinate axis k that gives the direction of best measurement is given by

$$\alpha_{ik} = \arccos\left(\frac{a_{ik}}{\text{MDISC}_i}\right). \tag{5}$$

The conversion of the discrimination parameter estimates to angle measures allows the items to be represented by vectors in the ability space that point in the direction of best measurement.

The distance of the point of best discrimination from the origin [i.e., the (0, 0) point] is given by the following multidimensional difficulty (MDIFF) equation:

$$\text{MDIFF}_i = -\frac{d_i}{\text{MDISC}_i}. \tag{6}$$

The value of MDIFF can be interpreted much like the b-parameter in unidimensional IRT. Positive values indicate difficult items and negative values indicate easy items. The full description of an item in a multidimensional space is given by the direction of best measurement, the discrimination in that direction, and the distance of the point of best discrimination from the origin of the space.

Applications of the Models

Multidimensional item response theory models have been applied in a number of ways: (1) the analysis of the structure of measurement instruments and the processes involved in responding to the instruments, (2) the evaluation of the parallelism of test forms, and (3) multidimensional computerized adaptive testing. Although these have been the dominant applications to date, this is a new methodology and new applications are being developed as this article is being written.

Analysis of Instrument Structure

The data obtained from a measurement instrument is the set of responses to individual items. One of the challenges to the social sciences is to explain the processes behind the generation of the responses. One of the ways of showing that the responses have been explained is to predict the responses using a model such as the MIRT models described here. When the models are applied to data, the item parameter estimates can be used to determine the composite of dimensions that is best measured by an item. If two items have vectors pointing in the same direction, they measure the same composite of abilities. The angle between two item vectors is a measure of the similarity of the construct measured by the items. If the angle is zero, the items measure the same combination of abilities. The information about the similarity of constructs measured by items with cluster analysis methodology has been used to identify the set of constructs measured by achievement tests. Those constructs align closely with the content dimensions built into the test during the test development process. Thus, MIRT procedures are very powerful for investigating the content validity of a measurement instrument.

Multidimensional Parallelism

When measuring instruments purposely have a multidimensional structure, such as when an achievement domain is being assessed, and when multiple forms of the instrument are desired, interchangeable use of those forms requires that the forms measure the same combination of constructs and that those constructs are assessed with equal accuracy. MIRT provides the tools for determining whether multiple forms of a measuring instrument meet these requirements. For example, there have been comparisons of the multidimensional structure and the accuracy of estimation for multiple forms of a mathematics test that covered a wide range of content. Analysis showed that the forms differed in the emphasis given to different content dimensions, even though the forms were constructed to be parallel using classical test theory procedures. The results showed that forms needed to be matched on the bivariate distribution of difficulty and discrimination, rather than matching on each characteristic separately.

Multidimensional Adaptive Testing

The MIRT application that is currently of greatest interest is the use of MIRT models as the basis for computerized adaptive tests. When MIRT models are used for computerized adaptive tests, locations of the examinees on multiple traits are determined simultaneously, rather than estimates of the location on each trait by a separate instrument. Items are acknowledged to require multiple trait dimensions for response and the information from those multiple dimensions is used to estimate the location of persons in the multidimensional space. This means that if items require both reading and mathematical skills for correct solution, that a person can be located on both of those dimensions from a single set of complex items, rather than having individual reading and mathematics tests. One type of MIRT methodology for computerized adaptive testing can increase the efficiency of testing because items contribute information to multiple dimensions. A more complex procedure for MIRT-based adaptive testing includes more constraints on the item development process.

Summary and Conclusions

Great progress has been made in the development of multidimensional item response theory since its initial presentation in the 1970s. Estimation procedures have been developed and several applications of the models are being put in practice. MIRT has also been found useful for explaining observed behavior of test items such as differential item functioning and misfit to unidimensional IRT models. Current work on MIRT is emphasizing the practical application of models to computerized adaptive testing and test equating. It is likely that MIRT methodology will also improve the process for constructing measuring instruments that measure complex composites of traits. More important than the individual applications is the conceptual framework provided by MIRT models; this framework, which allows instrument developers to consider the complex interactions of multiple traits with the subtle characteristics of items, should lead to better understandings about the way that measures of social variables function.

See Also the Following Articles

Computerized Adaptive Testing • Item Response Theory

Further Reading

Ackerman, T. A. (1980). An evaluation of the multidimensional parallelism of the EAAP mathematics test. Paper presented at the meeting of the American Educational Research Association, Boston, MA.

Binet, A., and Simon, T. (1905). New methods for the diagnosis of the intellectual level of subnormals. *L'Annee Psychol.* **11,** 191–244.

Bock, R. D., Gibbons, R., and Muraki, E. (1988). Full information item factor analysis. *Appl. Psychol. Measure.* **12,** 261–280.

Carroll, J. B. (1993). *Human Cognitive Abilities: A Survey of Factor Analytic Studies.* Cambridge University Press, Cambridge, UK.

Dempster, A. P., Laird, N. M., and Rubin, D. B. (1977). Maximum likelihood from incomplete data via the EM algorithm. *J. R. Statist. Soc. Ser. B* **39,** 1–38.

Fraser, C. P., and McDonald, R. P. (2004). *NOHARM.* Available on the Internet at http://www.unt.edu

Harman, H. H. (1976). *Modern Factor Analysis,* 3rd Ed. The University of Chicago Press, Chicago, IL.

Lazarsfeld, P. F. (1966). Latent structure analysis and test theory. In *Readings in Mathematical Social Science* (P. F. Lazarsfeld and N. W. Henry, eds.), pp. 78–88. Science Research Associates, Chicago.

Lord, F. M. (1980). *Applications of Item Response Theory to Practical Testing Problems.* Lawrence Erlbaum Assoc., Hillsdale, NJ.

Lord, F. M., and Novick, M. R. (1968). *Statistical Theories of Mental Test Scores.* Addison-Wesley, Reading, MA.

Lubinski, D. (2000). Scientific and social significance of assessing individual differences: Sinking shafts at a few critical points. In *Annual Review of Psychology* (S. T. Fiske, D. L. Schacter, and C. Zahn-Waxler, eds.), Vol. 51, pp. 405–444. Annual Reviews, Palo Alto, CA.

McDonald, R. P. (1967). Nonlinear factor analysis. *Psychomet. Monogr.* **15,** 1–167.

McDonald, R. P. (1999). *Test Theory: A Unified Approach.* Lawrence Erlbaum Assoc., Mahwah, NJ.

Miller, T. R., and Hirsch, T. M. (1992). Cluster analysis of angular data in applications of multidimensional item-response theory. *Appl. Measure. Edu.* **5,** 193–211.

Mislevy, R. J., and Bock, R. D. (1990). *BILOG 3: Item Analysis and Test Scoring with Binary Logistic Models.* 2nd Ed. Scientific Software, Chicago.

Muthén, B. (1978). Contributions to factor analysis of dichotomous variables. *Psychometrika* **43,** 551–560.

Reckase, M. D., and McKinley, R. L. (1991). The discriminating power of items that measure more than one dimension. *Appl. Psychol. Measure.* **14,** 361–373.

Segall, D. O. (2000). Principles of multidimensional adaptive testing. In *Computerized Adaptive Testing: Theory and Practice* (W. J. C. van der Linden and A. W. Glas, eds.) pp. 53–73. Kluwer Academic Publ., Dordrecht, The Netherlands.

Sympson, J. B. (1978). A model for testing multidimensional items. In *Proceedings of the 1977 Computerized Adaptive Testing Conference* (D. J. Weiss, ed.), pp. 82–98. University of Minnesota, Department of Psychology, Minneapolis, MN.

Tate, R. (2002). Test dimensionality. In *Large-Scale Assessment Programs for All Students: Validity, Technical Adequacy, and Implementation* (G. Tindal and T. M. Haladyna, eds.), pp. 181–211. Lawrence Erlbaum Assoc., Mahwah, NJ.

Veldkamp, B. P., and van der Linden, W. J. (2000). *Multidimensional Adaptive Testing with Constraints on Test Content,* University of Twente, Enschede, The Netherlands (Research Report 00-11).

Wilson, D. T., Wood, R., and Gibbons, R. (1998). *TESTFACT: Test Scoring, Item Statistics, and Item Factor Analysis.* Scientific Software International, Chicago.

Wright, B. D., and Lincare, J. M. (1996). *BIGSTEPS: Rasch-Model Computer Program.* MESA Press, Chicago, IL.

Multidimensional Scaling (MDS)

J. Douglas Carroll
Rutgers University, Newark, New Jersey, USA

Phipps Arabie
Rutgers University, Newark, New Jersey, USA

Lawrence Hubert
University of Illinois, Champaign, Illinois, USA

Glossary

Euclidean distance The distance, given a representation of objects as points in an R-dimensional space with coordinates for the ith object being $x_{i1}, x_{i2}, \ldots, x_{iR}$, between two points i and j, defined as: $d_{ij} = [\sum_{r=1}^{R}(x_{ir} - x_{jr})^2]^{1/2}$.

INDSCAL (individual differences multidimensional scaling) The most widely used method of three-way or individual differences MDS. INDSCAL is, in addition to being the name of this three-way MDS model, also the name of one particular method for metric fitting of this model to three-way proximity data, as well as a class of more general three-way or higher models. In addition, it is the name of the earliest program for implementing this method.

KYST (Kruskal, Young, Shepard and Torgerson MDS) A family of programs for fitting two-way (metric or nonmetric) MDS implemented by Kruskal and others for two-way MDS.

metric multidimensional scaling Multidimensional scaling in which the function relating distances to proximities is assumed to be linear (or in some cases some specific nonlinear function, such as a logarithmic or exponential function). In metric MDS, the scale type of the proximity data is either ratio or interval scale.

multidimensional scaling (MDS) A family of models and methods for representing stimuli or other objects as points in multidimensional space based on proximity (e.g., similarity or dissimilarity) data and relying on the principle that distances (usually, but not necessarily, Euclidean) in that space are related via a simple (usually linear or monotonic) function of the proximities.

nonmetric multidimensional scaling Multidimensional scaling in which the function relating distances to proximities is assumed to be merely monotonic. The scale type of the proximity data in the case of nonmetric MDS is generally ordinal scale. (In some cases, nominal scale or categorical data can also be used in certain forms of nonmetric MDS.)

proximities Measures of similarity(or dissimilarity) or other indices of closeness or proximity of pairs of stimuli or other objects. Proximities are generally assumed to be linearly or monotonically related to distances in an underlying multidimensional space. This function is assumed to have a negative slope (or to be monotonic nonincreasing) if the proximities are similarity-like and to have a positive slope (or to be monotonic nondecreasing) if the proximities are dissimilarity-like.

PROXSCAL (PROXimity multidimensional SCALing) A recently devised program by the Leiden group collaboratively with SPSS, Inc. that allows both metric and nonmetric two-way and three-way MDS, via either the two-way Euclidean model or the three-way INDSCAL model.

three-way multidimensional scaling Three-way MDS is MDS applied to two or more matrices of (usually symmetric) proximity data. Because the overall data array can be represented as a three-way (stimuli by stimuli by subjects or other sources of data) array, as contrasted with a simpler two-way array (or matrix) of stimuli by stimuli proximity data used in ordinary (often called two-way) MDS. Three-way MDS is often referred to as individual differences MDS because the third way of the data very often corresponds to different individual subjects. In three-way MDS, the objective is generally to provide a parsimonious representation of all the proximity data defined by the three-way array of data.

Multidimensional scaling refers to a family of models and methods for representing psychological stimuli of various kinds as points in multidimensional space. These stimuli can range from colors to perceived geometric objects, people, nations, and abstract concepts—in fact, any objects or entities for which judgments of similarity or dissimilarity can be quantified.

Proximity

Proximity is the generic term first introduced by Coombs and later much more fully developed by Shepard. Proximities may result from direct judgments of similarity, dissimilarity, relatedness, friendliness, or other measures of closeness, or proximity, by human subjects or may be derived from other data, such as preferences or rating-scale judgments of the stimuli by human subjects. The goal of multidimensional scaling (MDS) is to produce a representation of the stimuli or other objects as points in a multidimensional space (usually, but not necessarily, Euclidean) in which the distances between distinct pairs of the stimuli or other objects are related by some simple function to the proximity data. For example, if the basic data are similarities, the function relating distances to these similarity data might be, in the metric approaches to MDS, a linear function with a negative slope; in the nonmetric approaches, this function may be a merely monotonic (or order-preserving) function, but a *decreasing* (or, more precisely, a *nonincreasing*) monotonic function (i.e., a weakly monotonic function, in which, as the data values increase in value, the distances either decrease or remain unchanged in value). If the data were dissimilarities (or other proximities expected to be positively related to distances), then the function might be a linear function with a positive slope in the metric case (in which the proximity data are measured on at least an interval scale) or a nondecreasing monotonic function in the nonmetric case (in which the proximity data are measured on a merely ordinal scale). This particular use of the terms "metric" and "nonmetric" to refer to the scale type of the proximity data was first introduced by Coombs and later adopted by Kruskal in his pioneering approach to nonmetric MDS.

Points of View

Tucker and Messick introduced the first computational method for individual differences MDS, which they called the points of view (POV) approach. The POV approach first uses a factor analysis of the extended matrix formed by concatenating all the proximity matrices of all subjects into a single $n \times nm$ matrix (where n is the number of stimuli, and m is the number of subjects), in which the subjects are represented as points, and then looks for clusters of subjects that are assumed to correspond to different points of view. After this initial factor analysis/clustering step, POV analysis then aggregates the data for each point of view and does a two-way, or nonindividual difference, MDS analysis on the aggregate data for each point of view by any one of a number of different metric or nonmetric two-way MDS procedures. Numerous problems have been pointed out concerning this POV approach, including lack of parsimony, a lack of objective criteria for the number or nature of different points of view, and the lack of a strong theoretical justification for this method. These lacunae led eventually to the development of what is now called the INDSCAL (for individual differences multidimensional scaling) model and method for individual differences MDS; this is now, in one form or another, by far the most frequently used approach.

INDSCAL

INDSCAL is the most widely used method of three-way or individual differences MDS. It is based on a model in which different individuals (or other sources of data) use the same (common) set of perceptual dimensions but differ in a profile of dimension weights defining the psychological and/or perceptual salience (or importance) of the various common dimensions (common, that is, to all subjects or other sources of data, who/which are assumed to differ only in the salience or importance weights applied to the different common psychological or perceptual dimensions).

The INDSCAL model assumes a weighted generalization of ordinary Euclidean distances of the form:

$$d_{ijk} = \left[\sum_{r=1}^{R} w_{kr} \left(x_{ir} - x_{jr} \right)^2 \right]^{1/2} \tag{1}$$

where d_{ijk} is the distance between stimuli or objects i and j for subject or other data source k, and w_{kr} is a weight for subject k on the rth common dimension defined for the INDSCAL model. As in two-way MDS, x_{ir} and x_{jr} are the rth coordinates of the ith and jth object points, respectively, in a common or group stimulus space. The total INDSCAL model can be expressed as $F_k(\delta_{ijk}) \cong d_{ijk}$ where δ_{ijk} is the ith, jth, and kth entry in the three-way proximity array, F_k is a function (usually linear or monotonic, depending on whether a metric or nonmetric method is used to fit the model), and d_{ijk} is the weighted Euclidean distance between i and j for k, as defined in Eq. (1). INDSCAL is, in addition to being the name of this three-way MDS model, also the name of one particular method for metric fitting of this model to three-way proximity data, as well as a class of more general three-way or higher-way models. In addition, it is the name of the earliest program for implementing this method.

Among other important properties, the INDSCAL model leads to a unique orientation of the common dimensions. Unlike the representation produced by two-way MDS (with Euclidean distances) the INDSCAL representation can be shown *not* to be subject to an arbitrary orthogonal (or rigid) rotation (even if the subject or source weights are redefined), which leaves ordinary Euclidean distances unchanged or at most multiplies them by a positive constant. The INDSCAL approach assumes basic data that can be viewed as a three-way array. That is, the two-way methods deal with proximity data, defining only a two-way array or matrix of stimuli by stimuli data because either there is only one subject or data source *or*, if there are two or more subjects/sources, these have been averaged or otherwise aggregated to produce a single two-way array or matrix of proximity data. INDSCAL has been shown not only to produce unique (nonrotatable) configurations quite reliably, but also has been demonstrated to result in substantively interpretable dimensions without the need to rotate the stimulus/object configuration to an interpretable set of dimensions (or coordinates)! This need to rotate the stimulus/object configuration often makes two-way MDS methods intractable in practice, especially when the dimensionality of the representation exceeds two or three.

Nonmetric Multidimensional Scaling

A brief history of developments in nonmetric MDS can provide a way to understand the interrelationships among various models and methods as well as guidance in selecting problem-solving methods for social measurement applications.

The earliest description of MDS is the theoretical work published in *Psychometrika* by Gale Young and Alton Householder, which showed how to produce a Euclidean MDS representation with the coordinates' origin placed at any one of the n stimulus points—assuming ratio-scale distance estimates. Marion Richardson followed this with the first paper applying this approach to MDS, a strictly one-dimensional application involving stimuli consisting of various shades of gray (a colorless unidimensional application to the color domain).

The computational intractability of this methodology (no doubt complicated by the onset of World War II) resulted in the field lying fallow until the early 1950s, when, expedited by the emergence of practical digital computer technology, Torgerson and various mentors and collaborators (Gulliksen, Tucker, Abelson, Messick, Bert Green, and probably others) revived and improved this methodology, enabling the use of interval as well as ratio-scale data. They made the method more robust by devising a solution for positioning the origin at the centroid of all these stimuli instead of at some arbitrary particular stimulus point and, probably most importantly, by adapting the method for use on digital computers. This advance led to what is now usually called the classical two-way metric MDS method most typically associated with Warren Torgerson.

Soon after Torgerson's work, Coombs and some of his students developed an approach to what they called nonmetric MDS (now sometimes called completely nonmetric MDS). The Coombs *et al.* approach was not so much a methodology as a set of vaguely expressed ideas and rules of thumb that constituted more a rough outline of a method than a precise algorithm. It did however provide a theoretical basis for the notion that well-defined MDS solutions could, in principle, be derived from even weaker, ordinal-scale (or nonmetric) data on similarities or dissimilarities—that is, proximities.

In 1962, Roger Shepard devised the first successful computer-implemented algorithm, which he called analysis of proximities, for nonmetric MDS in the modern sense. Shepard was (originally, at least) more interested in the theoretical problem of finding the nature and shape of the nonlinear but monotonic distance function, transmuting observed proximities into distances in an underlying Euclidean space, than in the use of nonmetric MDS to infer the underlying dimensions latent within a specific domain of stimuli. It soon became clear, however, that the power of MDS (metric *or* nonmetric) to find such underlying dimensional structures in proximity data was by far the most important potential application of this powerful new methodology. That nonmetric MDS enabled the use of a much wider variety of data types than the metric methods appeared to allow was perhaps the most exciting aspect of Shepard's seminal work.

In 1964, Joseph Kruskal developed the much more mathematically rigorous approach to what he, following Coombs's earlier terminology, explicitly called nonmetric multidimensional scaling by devising an algorithm that uses the method of steepest descent (or gradient method). The Kruskal algorithm optimizes (minimizes) a nonlinear function of many variables, specifically a measure of badness of fit that Kruskal called STRESS, using this gradient-based optimization technique. This technique was essentially unknown to most psychometricians and mathematical psychologists at that time, although now this and more sophisticated optimization techniques are generally well known in these fields, as well as in marketing and other social and behavioral sciences. A different measure of STRESS, called STRESS2, was later introduced, primarily to handle the case of what

Coombs had dubbed off-diagonal conditional proximity data, most often associated with unfolding analysis—which we prefer to call fitting of an ideal point model to individual differences preferential choice data. Kruskal also introduced the idea of fitting MDS models assuming metrics *other* than Euclidean—specifically the Minkowski-p or L_p metrics, the best known and most widely used of which is the well-known L_1, or city block, metric, in which distance is the sum of absolute values of coordinate differences instead of the square root of the sum of squared coordinate differences. The most current and flexible version of Kruskal's algorithm is now implemented in the KYST-2A program.

Two-Way and Three-Way Multidimensional Scaling

In 1969 and 1970, Carroll and Chang introduced the model and method now called the INDSCAL model. It assumes a generalized, weighted, Euclidean metric, with a different profile of weights for each subject (or other source of data), so that a wide variety of different private perceptual spaces can be accommodated within the purview of this model, with a common group stimulus space containing dimensions common to all subjects/sources and only the profile of salience weights for these dimensions differing from subject/source to subject/source. As previously mentioned, the INDSCAL model has the additional important property called dimensional uniqueness, which means that, even though INDSCAL is basically a Euclidean distance model, the dimensions or coordinate axes are uniquely identified and *not* subject to rotational indeterminacy. This feature provides a tremendous advantage in substantively interpreting MDS configurations, which may be almost impossible to interpret in higher than two or three dimensions because of the near intractability of finding the "right" or interpretable rotation of a high-dimensional spatial representation. Experience with the INDSCAL methodology demonstrates that this theoretical property in fact works very well in practice, given that INDSCAL representations are almost always interpretable without rotation!

The most user-friendly implementation of the INDSCAL method is provided by Pruzansky's SINDSCAL program, which is specialized to the case of the kind of three-way symmetric data matrices that most often arise in applications of individual differences MDS. The older INDSCAL program, which is based on use of a general method of multiway data analysis called CANDECOMP (for canonical decomposition of N-way tables), is still useful for more general analyses of three-way or higher data, thus providing, among other things, an approach to three-way or higher factor or components analysis. CANDECOMP is closely related to Harshman and Lundy's PARAFAC approach. The INDSCAL program also allows certain other analyses of more general proximity structures; for example, four-way MDS, in which different subjects, such as consumers, judge the similarity or dissimilarity of pairs of stimuli (products) under different scenarios (e.g., before and after some promotional message has been delivered or after different promotional messages have been delivered).

Other methods of both two-way and three-way (or individual differences) MDS have been devised since then, most notably Takane, Young and de Leeuw's ALSCAL approach, Ramsay's maximum likelihood approach (called MULTISCALE) and Meulman, Heiser, and SPSS, Inc.'s PROXSCAL, a two- and three-way generalization of Heiser and de Leeuw's SMACOF. This recently implemented version of PROXSCAL, now available within the CATEGORIES module for SPSS, includes a three-way nonmetric option (fitting the INDSCAL weighted Euclidean model to ordinal, or nonmetric, data) as well as enabling analysis via two-way metric or nonmetric MDS, with various options for missing data, unfolding analysis, and the like. This program is perhaps the most flexible and dependable for MDS analysis now widely available.

For metric analysis of three-way MDS data, either SINDSCAL or MULTISCALE is the preferred method. For strictly two-way analysis, either the classical two-way MDS method or KYST is probably still the best method for most purposes, although the two-way option in Ramsay's MULTISCALE may be appropriate if a maximum likelihood solution is sought. Various theoretical and methodological problems make ALSCAL less appropriate for most MDS analyses.

Unfolding analysis, which can be implemented by using KYST with appropriate options, appears to be the preferred approach on theoretical grounds for multidimensional analysis of individual differences preference data (using an ideal point model). It is, however, by its very nature, subject to a serious and seemingly intractable degeneracy or quasi-degeneracy problem. In practice, probably the most effective MDS method for the analysis of individual differences preferences is the MDPREF method or some other approach based on the much simpler linear model called the vector model for preferences. Carroll discusses the theoretical basis for this model and the underpinnings of the MDPREF methodology in considerable detail—suffice it to say that the vector model, which MDPREF fits via a straightforward procedure based on the singular value decomposition (SVD), can be viewed as a special (limiting) case of the ideal point model underlying unfolding analysis, with ideal points "infinitely distant" from the stimuli. Apparently, in practice, ideal points for individuals are, if not infinitely distant from the actual stimuli (e.g., products in a marketing application), so far from realistic stimuli (say, products) as to be, for all practical purposes, *effectively* "infinitely distant." For example, if not constrained otherwise, many people would describe their "ideal car" as a spacious, luxurious, comfortable, exceedingly safe sports car that gets as close as possible to an infinite number of miles per gallon and is extremely economical in terms of maintenance and other costs, while having a price equal or very nearly equal to zero! In other words, given no constraints at all, most people would have an "ideal product" that simply does not (and *could* not) exist because such ideal points are necessarily infinitely distant from the actual products (or other stimuli) in various directions. It is for this reason, we believe, that a vector model, which corresponds to the special case of an ideal point model with ideal points at infinity, may be so much more robust and useful in practice than the more theoretically elegant ideal point model of which it is a (*very*) special case!

In addition to these standard approaches to MDS, there have been a number of different proposals to extend the definition of the field to include other (nonspatial) geometric models, such as tree or other network structures, or hybrid models combining spatial structure with such discrete or nonspatial structure as tree, network, and clustering models of various kinds.

See Also the Following Articles

Phrase Completion Scales • Spatial Scale, Problems of

Further Reading

Arabie, P., Carroll, J. D., and DeSarbo, W. S. (1987). *Three-Way Scaling and Clustering.* Sage, Newbury Park, CA.

Carroll, J. D. (1972). Individual differences and multidimensional scaling. In *Multidimensional Scaling: Theory and Applications in the Behavioral Sciences, Vol. 1: Theory* (R. N. Shepard, A. K. Romney, and S. B. Nerlove, eds.), pp. 105–155. Seminar Press, New York.

Carroll, J. D. (1976). Spatial, non-spatial and hybrid models for scaling. *Psychometrika* **41,** 439–463.

Carroll, J. D. (1980). Models and methods for multidimensional analysis of preferential choice (or other dominance) data. In *Similarity and Choice* (E. D. Lantermann and H. Feger, eds.), pp. 234–289. Hans Huber, Bern.

Carroll, J. D. (2002). Psychometrics: Multidimensional scaling in psychology. In *2001 International Encyclopedia of Social and Behavioral Sciences* (N. J. Smelser and P. B. Baltes, eds.), pp. 10189–10193. Pergamon, Oxford.

Carroll, J. D. (2002). Psychometrics: Unfolding and vector models. In *2001 International Encyclopedia of Social and Behavioral Sciences* (N. J. Smelser and P. B. Baltes, eds.), pp. 15962–15968. Pergamon, Oxford.

Carroll, J. D., and Arabie, P. (1980). Multidimensional scaling. In *Annual Review of Psychology* (M. R. Rosenzweig and L. W. Porter, eds.), Vol. 31, pp. 607–649. Annual Reviews, Palo Alto, CA.

Carroll, J. D., and Arabie, P. (1998). Multidimensional scaling. In *Handbook of Perception and Cognition, Vol. 3: Measurement, Judgment and Decision Making* (M. H. Birnbaum, ed.), pp. 179–250. Academic Press, San Diego, CA.

Carroll, J. D., and Chang, J. J. (1970). Analysis of individual differences in multidimensional scaling via an N–way generalization of "Eckart–Young" decomposition. *Psychometrika* **35,** 283–319.

Carroll, J. D., and Chaturvedi, A. (1995). A general approach to clustering and multidimensional scaling of two-way, three-way, or higher-way data. In *Geometric Representations of Perceptual Phenomena* (R. D. Luce, M. D'Zmura, D. D. Hoffman, G. Iverson, and A. K. Romney, eds.), pp. 295–318. Erlbaum, Mahwah, NJ.

Carroll, J. D., and Green, P. E. (1997). Psychometric methods in marketing research, Part II: Multidimensional scaling. *J. Marketing Res.* **34,** 193–204.

Carroll, J. D., and Pruzansky, S. (1980). Discrete and hybrid scaling models. In *Similarity and Choice* (E. D. Lantermann and H. Feger, eds.), pp. 108–139. Hans Huber, Bern.

Carroll, J. D., and Wish, M. (1974). Models and methods for three-way multidimensional scaling. In *Contemporary Developments in Mathematical Psychology* (D. H. Krantz, R. C. Atkinson, R. D. Luce, and P. Suppes, eds.), Vol. 2, pp. 57–105. W. H. Freeman, San Francisco.

Carroll, J. D., and Wish, M. (1974). Multidimensional perceptual models and measurement methods. In *Handbook of Perception* (E. C. Carterette and M. P. Friedman, eds.), Vol. 2, pp. 391–447. Academic Press, New York.

Chang, J. J., and Carroll, J. D. (1969). *How to Use MDPREF, a Computer Program for Multidimensional Analysis of Preference Data.* AT&T Bell Laboratories, Murray Hill, NJ.

Chang, J. J., and Carroll, J. D. (1989). A short–guide to MDPREF: Multidimensional analysis of preference data. In *Multidimensional Scaling: Concepts and Applications* (P. E. Green, F. J. Carmone, and S. M. Smith, eds.), pp. 279–286. Allyn and Bacon, Needham Heights, MA.

Coombs, C. H. (1950). Psychological scaling without a unit of measurement. *Psychol. Rev.* **57,** 148–194.

Coombs, C. H. (1964). *A Theory of Data.* John Wiley, New York.

Davies, P., and Coxon, A. P. M. (eds.) (1984). *Key Texts on Multidimensional Scaling.* Heinemann, Portsmouth, NH.

Green, P. E., Carmone, F. J., and Smith, S. M. (eds.) (1989). *Multidimensional Scaling: Concepts and Applications.* Allyn and Bacon, Newton, MA.

Harshman, R. A., and Lundy, M. E. (1984). The PARAFAC model for three-way factor analysis and multidimensional scaling. In *Research Methods for Multimode Data Analysis* (H. G. Law, C. W. Snyder, J. A. Hattie, and R. P. McDonald, eds.), pp. 372–402. Praeger, New York.

Heiser, W. J., and de Leeuw, J. (1979). *How to Use SMACOF-III.* Research report. Department of Data Theory, Leiden.

Holman, E. W. (1978). Completely nonmetric multidimensional scaling. *J. Math. Psychol.* **18,** 39–51.

Hubert, L., and Arabie, P. (1994). The analysis of proximity matrices through sums of matrices having (anti-)Robinson forms. *Br. J. Math. Statist. Psychol.* **47,** 1–40.

Hubert, L. J., Arabie, P., and Meulman, J. (1997). Linear and circular unidimensional scaling for symmetric proximity matrices. *Br. J. Math. Statist. Psychol.* **50,** 253–284.

Hubert, L. J., Arabie, P., and Meulman, J. (2001). *Combinatorial Data Analysis: Optimization by Dynamic Programming.* Society of Industrial and Applied Mathematics, Philadelphia, PA.

Kruskal, J. B. (1964). Multidimensional scaling by optimizing goodness of fit to a nonmetric hypothesis. *Psychometrika* **29,** 1–27.

Kruskal, J. B. (1964). Nonmetric multidimensional scaling: A numerical method. *Psychometrika* **29,** 115–129.

Kruskal, J. B., and Carroll, J. D. (1969). Geometrical models and badness-of-fit functions. In *Multivariate Analysis II* (P. R. Krishnaiah, ed.), pp. 639–671. Academic Press, New York.

Kruskal, J. B., and Wish, M. (1978). *Multidimensional Scaling.* Sage, Newbury Park, CA.

Kruskal, J. B., Young, F. W., and Seery, J. B. (1973). *How to Use KYST-2A, a Very Flexible Program to Do Multidimensional Scaling and Unfolding.* AT&T Bell Laboratories, Murray Hill, NJ.

MacCallum, R. C. (1977). Effects of conditionality on INDSCAL and ALSCAL weights. *Psychometrika* **42,** 297–305.

Meulman, J., and Heiser, W. J., and SPSS, Inc. (1999). *Categories.* SPSS Inc., Evanston, IL.

Pruzansky, S. (1975). *How to Use SINDSCAL: A Computer Program for Individual Differences in Multidimensional Scaling.* AT&T Bell Laboratories, Murray Hill, NJ.

Ramsay, J. O. (1977). Maximum likelihood estimation in multidimensional scaling. *Psychometrika* **42,** 241–266.

Ramsay, J. O. (1983). MULTISCALE: A multidimensional scaling program. *Am. Statist.* **37,** 326–327.

Richardson, M. (1938). Multidimensional psychophysics [abstract]. *Psychol. Bull.* **35,** 659–660.

Shepard, R. N. (1962). The analysis of proximities: Multidimensional scaling with an unknown distance function, I. *Psychometrika* **27,** 125–140.

Shepard, R. N. (1962). The analysis of proximities: Multidimensional scaling with an unknown distance function, II. *Psychometrika* **27,** 219–246.

Takane, Y., Young, F. W., and de Leeuw, J. (1977). Nonmetric individual differences multidimensional scaling: An alternating least squares method with optimal scaling features. *Psychometrika* **42,** 7–67.

Torgerson, W. S. (1952). Multidimensional scaling, I: Theory and method. *Psychometrika* **17,** 401–419.

Torgerson, W. S. (1958). *Theory and Methods of Scaling.* John Wiley, New York.

Tucker, L. R., and Messick, S. J. (1963). An individual difference model for multidimensional scaling. *Psychometrika* **28,** 333–367.

Weinberg, S. L., and Menil, V. C. (1993). The recovery of structure in linear and ordinal data: INDSCAL versus ALSCAL. *Multivariate Behav. Res.* **28,** 215–233.

Wish, M., and Carroll, J. D. (1974). Applications of individual differences scaling to studies of human perception and judgement. In *Handbook of Perception: Psychophysical Judgement and Measurement* (E. C. Carterette and M. P. Friedman, eds.), Vol. 2, pp. 449–491. Academic Press, New York.

Young, G., and Householder, A. (1938). Discussion of a set of points in terms of their mutual distances. *Psychometrika* **3,** 19–22.

Multilevel Analysis

Joop J. Hox
Utrecht University, Utrecht, The Netherlands

Cora J. M. Maas
Utrecht University, Utrecht, The Netherlands

Glossary

centering Transforming a variable by subtracting the mean. In multilevel data, there are two ways of centering: subtracting the overall mean and subtracting group means. Centering on the overall mean is a straightforward linear transformation, whereas centering on the group mean leads to a radically different model.

cross-level interaction When a regression coefficient of an individual-level variable varies across groups, this variation can be modeled by introducing an interaction term of that variable with one of the group-level variables. Such cross-level interactions are common in multilevel analysis.

cluster sampling A procedure in which data are collected in a two-stage design, starting first with sampling of groups (clusters), followed by sampling of individuals within groups (clusters).

dependence The assumption in cluster sampling and multilevel data that the observations are not sampled independently of one another. The result of this assumption is strongly biased standard errors when standard statistical methods are used.

design effect The amount of bias in the standard errors introduced by having dependent observations.

intraclass correlation The expected correlation between individuals within the same group. When the intraclass correlation is greater than zero, the observations are not independent.

fixed part The part of the model equation that contains the regression coefficients.

generalized linear regression model A regression model that is used when the linearity and distributional assumptions of the linear regression model are not met, for example. when the dependent variable is categorical.

linear regression model A regressions model that describes the relationship between one response variable and one or more explanatory variables by calculating the best-fitting linear line (or plane).

logistic regression A generalized linear regression model for response variables that are dichotomous or proportions.

maximum likelihood (ML) The estimation method most commonly used in multilevel analysis. ML estimation produces estimated parameter values that make the probability of observing the data highest.

multilevel analysis of longitudinal data The analysis of longitudinal data or repeated measurements as multilevel data by viewing these as observations nested within individuals. The advantage is that the analysis deals easily with missing measurement occasions.

multilevel data Data that have a hierarchical or nested structure, usually individuals within groups.

random coefficients The regression coefficients of the lowest-level explanatory variables; these coefficients can vary across groups and part of this variation is assumed to be random (stochastic).

random part The part of the model equation that contains the residual error terms.

variance components The variances (and covariances) of the residual errors. In multilevel analysis, there are variance components at each distinct level.

Social research often concerns the relationship between individuals and the groups to which they belong. This leads to hierarchical or multilevel data structures, with individuals nested within the groups. Examples are educational research with pupils nested within classes nested within schools (a three-level data structure), cross-national studies with individuals nested within national units, and family research with members nested within families. Less obvious applications of multilevel modeling are longitudinal studies with measurement occasions nested within individuals and meta-analysis with subjects nested within studies. More specialized multilevel models have been developed that can incorporate nonnested hierarchical structures and multiple response variables. Multilevel modeling has become popular for the analysis of a variety of problems, going beyond the classical individuals-within-groups applications. This entry gives a brief summary of the reasons for using multilevel models and provides examples why these reasons are indeed valid reasons. Next, the multilevel model is introduced and illustrated with an empirical example. The extension to multilevel logistic regression is briefly discussed.

Introduction

Multilevel modeling is used in the analysis of data that have a hierarchical or clustered structure. Such data arise routinely in various fields, for instance in educational research in which pupils are nested within schools, in family studies in which children are nested within families, in medical research in which patients are nested within physicians or hospitals, and in biomedical research, for instance the analysis of dental anomalies in which teeth are nested within different people's mouths. Clustered data may also arise as a result of the specific research design. For instance, in large-scale survey research the data collection is usually organized in a multistage sampling design that results in clustered or stratified data. Another example is a longitudinal design, in which the data are a series of repeated measurements nested within individual subjects.

A crucial problem in the statistical analysis of hierarchically structured data is the dependence of the observations at the lower levels. Older approaches to the analysis of multilevel data simply ignore this problem and commonly perform the analysis by disaggregating all data to the lowest level and subsequently applying standard analysis methods. The magnitude of the statistical bias introduced by this approach can be illustrated by a simple example from sample surveys. Survey statisticians have long known that the extent to which samples are clustered affects the sampling variance and, hence, causes a bias in statistical significance tests. In his classic 1965 work, Kish defines the design effect (deff) as the ratio of the operating sampling variance to the sampling variance that applies to simple random sampling. Thus, deff is the factor with which the simple random sampling variance must be multiplied to provide the actual operating sampling variance. In simple cluster sampling with equal cluster sizes, deff can be computed by $\text{deff} = [1 + \rho(n_{\text{clus}} - 1)]$, where ρ is the intraclass correlation, and n_{clus} is the common cluster size. (The intraclass correlation ρ indicates the degree of similarity between respondents within the same cluster; the formula is presented in the next section.) It is clear that deff equals 1 only when either the intraclass correlation is zero or the cluster size is 1. In all other situations, deff is larger than 1, which implies that standard statistical formulas will underestimate the sampling variance and therefore lead to biased significance tests with an inflated Type I error rate.

The impact of cluster sampling on the operating α level is often large. For example, assume that we carry out a *t* test at a nominal α level of 0.05. If we have a cluster sample, with a small intraclass correlation of $\rho = 0.05$ and a cluster size of 10, the actual operating α level is 0.11. With larger intraclass correlations and larger cluster sizes, the operating α level increases rapidly. Consider the effect of cluster sampling in educational research, in which data are often collected from classes. Assuming a common class size of 25 pupils, and a typical intraclass correlation for school effects of $\rho = 0.10$, the operating α level is 0.29 for tests performed at a nominal α level of 0.05! Clearly, in such situations *not* adjusting for clustered data produces very misleading significance tests. In addition, for nonlinear models such as logistic regression, not only the standard errors, but also the regression coefficients themselves are biased.

If we have clustered data, the standard statistical tests can be adjusted using deff. However, multilevel modeling is more general. In most multilevel problems, we have not only clustering of individuals within groups, but we also have variables measured at all available levels. Combining variables from different levels in one statistical model is a different problem than estimating and correcting for design effects. Multilevel models are designed to analyze variables from different levels simultaneously, using a statistical model that includes the various dependencies. This leads to research into the direct effects and the interactions between variables that describe the individuals and variables that describe the groups, a kind of research that is now often referred to as multilevel research.

Multilevel research requires multilevel theories, an area that seems underdeveloped compared to the statistical and computational advances. If there are effects of the social context on individuals, these effects must be mediated by intervening processes that depend on characteristics of the social context. Multilevel models in general assume that the grouping criterion is clear and that variables can be assigned unambiguously to their appropriate level. In reality, group boundaries may be somewhat arbitrary and the assignment of variables is not always obvious and simple. In addition, if we have many variables at many levels, there is an enormous number of possible interactions between different levels. Ideally, a multilevel theory should specify which variables belong to which level and which direct effects and cross-level interaction effects can be expected. The common denominator in such theories is that they all postulate processes that mediate between individual variables and group variables, such as communication processes, social comparison processes, and the internal structure of groups.

The Multilevel Regression Model

The multilevel regression model is known in the statistical literature under a variety of names: hierarchical linear model, random coefficient model, variance component model, and mixed (linear) model. Most often it assumes hierarchical data, with one response variable measured at the lowest level and explanatory variables at all existing levels. Conceptually, the model is often viewed as a hierarchical system of regression equations. For example, assume we have data in J groups or contexts and a different number of individuals N_j in each group. On the individual (lowest) level we have the dependent variable Y_{ij} and the explanatory variable X_{ij}, and on the group level we have the explanatory variable Z_j. Thus, we have a separate regression equation in each group:

$$Y_{ij} = \beta_{0j} + \beta_{1j}X_{ij} + e_{ij} \tag{1}$$

In Eq. (1) β_0 is the usual regression intercept, β_1 is the regression slope for the explanatory variable X, and e_{ij} is the residual term. The regression coefficients β carry a subscript j for the groups, which indicates that the regression coefficients may vary across groups. The variation in the regression coefficients β_j is modeled by explanatory variables and random residual terms at the group level:

$$\beta_{0j} = \gamma_{00} + \gamma_{01}Z_j + u_{0j} \tag{2}$$

$$\beta_{1j} = \gamma_{10} + \gamma_{11}Z_j + u_{1j} \tag{3}$$

Substitution of Eqs. (2) and (3) into Eq. (1) produces the single-equation version of the multilevel regression model:

$$Y_{ij} = \gamma_{00} + \gamma_{10}X_{ij} + \gamma_{01}Z_j + \gamma_{11}Z_jX_{ij} + u_{1j}X_{ij} + u_{0j} + e_{ij} \tag{4}$$

In general, there will be more than one explanatory variable at the lowest level and also more than one explanatory variable at the highest level. Assume that we have P explanatory variables X at the lowest level, indicated by the subscript p ($p = 1, \ldots, P$), and Q explanatory variables Z at the highest level, indicated by the subscript q ($q = 1, \ldots, Q$). Then, Eq. (4) becomes the more general equation:

$$Y_{ij} = \gamma_{00} + \sum_p \gamma_{p0}X_{pij} + \sum_q \gamma_{0q}Z_{qj} + \sum_q \sum_p \gamma_{pq}Z_{qj}X_{pij} + \sum_p u_{pj}X_{pij} + u_{oj} + e_{ij} \tag{5}$$

In Eq. (5), the γ are the usual regression coefficients, the u terms are residuals at the group level, and the e term represents the residual at the individual level. The regression coefficients are identified as the fixed part of the model because this part does not change over groups or individuals. The residual error terms are identified as the random or stochastic part of the model.

The assumptions of the most commonly used multilevel regression model are that the residuals at the lowest level e_{ij} have a normal distribution with a mean of zero and a common variance σ^2 in all groups. The second-level residuals u_{0j} and u_{pj} are assumed to be independent of the lowest level errors e_{ij} and to have a multivariate normal distribution with means of zero. Other assumptions, identical to the common assumptions of a multiple regression analysis, are fixed predictors and linear relationships. Most multilevel software assumes by default that the variance of the residual errors e_{ij} is the same in all groups. However, certain forms of heteroscedasticity can be explicitly modeled.

The estimation of parameters (regression coefficients and variance components) in multilevel modeling is generally done using the maximum likelihood (ML) method. The standard errors (SEs) generated by the ML procedure are asymptotic, meaning we need fairly large samples at all levels. These standard errors can be used to establish a p value for the null hypothesis that in the population a specific regression coefficient is zero. Thus, the significance of a regression coefficient can be tested by referring $Z = \beta/SE(\beta)$ to the standard normal distribution. The ML procedure also generates a value for the deviance that is based on the likelihood (the deviance equals -2 times the log-likelihood). In addition to the standard errors, the deviance can also be used to test parameters for significance. When two models are nested, which means that the smaller model can be obtained by removing terms from the larger model, the difference between the deviances of these two models has a chi-square distribution, with degrees of freedom being the difference in numbers of estimated parameters. This is useful for testing the significance of variance terms. The asymptotic Z test previously described is not optimal for testing variances. First, it assumes normality, and variances do not have a normal distribution. Second, testing the null hypothesis that a variance is zero is a test on the boundary of the parameter space (variances cannot be negative), where standard likelihood theory is no longer valid. The significance of a variance component can be tested by comparing the deviance of a model containing this parameter to the deviance of the same model without this one variance parameter. This value can be treated as a chi-square variate with one degree of freedom, and this can be used to test the significance of that variance component. It should be noted that Raudenbush and Bryk present a different chi-square test for variance components, which is not based on the deviance.

Two different likelihood functions are commonly used in multilevel regression analysis. The first is full maximum likelihood (FML). The second is restricted maximum likelihood (RML). The difference is that

RML maximizes a likelihood function that is invariant for the fixed effects. Because RML is more realistic, it should, in theory, lead to better estimates of the variance components, especially when the number of groups is small. Nevertheless, FML has one advantage over RML—because the likelihood is maximized over both the fixed and the random part, the difference between two deviances can be used to test for differences between two nested models that differ only in the fixed part (the regression coefficients). With RML, only differences in the random part (the variance components) can be tested this way.

The proportion of variance in the population explained by the grouping structure is indicated by the intraclass correlation ρ. The model used to estimate ρ is the model that contains no explanatory variables at all, called the intercept-only model:

$$Y_{ij} = \gamma_{00} + u_{0j} + e_{ij} \tag{6}$$

Using this model, the intraclass correlation ρ is estimated by the equation:

$$\rho = \frac{\sigma^2_{u_0}}{\sigma^2_{u_0} + \sigma^2_e} \tag{7}$$

where $\sigma^2_{u_0}$ is the variance of the second-level residuals u_{0j} and σ^2_e is the variance of the lowest level residuals e_{ij}.

Example of Multilevel Regression Analysis

Assume that we have data from school classes. On the pupil level, we have the outcome variable Popularity measured by a self-rating scale that ranges from 0 (very unpopular) to 10 (very popular). We have one explanatory variable Gender (0 = boy, 1 = girl) on the pupil level and one class level explanatory variable Teacher experience (in years). We have data from 2000 pupils from 100 classes, so the average class size is 20 pupils. The data are described and analyzed in more detail in Hox's 2002 handbook.

Table I presents the parameter estimates and standard errors for a series of models. Model M0 is the null model, the intercept-only model. The intercept-only model estimates the intercept as 5.31, which is simply the weighted average popularity across all schools and pupils. The variance of the pupil-level residuals is estimated as 0.64. The variance of the class-level residuals is estimated as 0.87. The intercept estimate is much larger than the corresponding standard error, and the calculation of the Z test shows that it is significant at $p < 0.005$. As previously mentioned, the Z test is not optimal for testing variances. If the second-level variance term is restricted to zero, the deviance of the model goes up to 6489.5. The difference between the deviances is 1376.8, with one more parameter in the intercept-only model. The chi-square of 1376.8 with one degree of freedom is also significant at $p < 0.005$. The intraclass correlation is $\rho = \sigma^2_{u_0}/(\sigma^2_{u_0} + \sigma^2_e) = 0.87/(0.87 + 0.64) = 0.58$. Thus, 58% of the variance of the popularity scores is at the group level, which is very high. Because the intercept-only model contains no explanatory variables, the variances terms represent unexplained residual variance.

Model M1 predicts the outcome variable Popularity by the explanatory variables Gender and Teacher experience, with a random component for the regression coefficient of gender, and model M2 adds the cross-level interaction term between Gender and Teacher experience. We can view these models as built up in the following sequence of steps:

$$\text{Popularity}_{ij} = \beta_{0j} + \beta_{1j}\text{Gender}_{ij} + e_{ij} \tag{8}$$

Table I Multilevel Models for Pupil Popularity

Model	*M0: Intercept-only*	*M1: +Pupil gender and Teacher experience*	*M2: +Cross-level interaction*
Fixed part			
Predictor	Coefficient (SE)	Coefficient (SE)	Coefficient (SE)
Intercept	5.31 (0.10)	3.34 (0.16)	3.31 (0.16)
Pupil gender		0.84 (0.06)	1.33 (0.13)
Teacher experience		0.11 (0.01)	0.11 (0.01)
Pupil gender Teacher exprience			−0.03 (0.01)
Random part			
σ^2_e	0.64 (0.02)	0.39 (0.01)	0.39 (0.01)
$\sigma^2_{u_0}$	0.87 (013)	0.40 (0.06)	0.40 (0.06)
$\sigma^2_{u_1}$		0.27 (0.05)	0.22 (0.04)
$\sigma_{u_{01}}$		0.02 (0.04)	0.02 (0.04)
Deviance	5112.7	4261.2	4245.9

In this regression equation, β_{0j} is the usual intercept, β_{1j} is the usual regression coefficient (regression slope) for the explanatory variable gender, and e_{ij} is the usual residual term. The subscript j is for the classes ($j = 1, \ldots, J$) and the subscript i is for individual pupils ($i = 1, \ldots, N_j$). We assume that the intercepts β_{0j} and the slopes β_{1j} vary across classes.

In our example data, the model corresponding to Eq. (8) results in significant variance components at both levels (as determined by the deviance-difference test). In the next step, we hope to be able to explain at least some of this variation by introducing class-level variables. Generally, we will not be able to explain all the variation of the regression coefficients, and there will be some unexplained residual variation—hence the name random coefficient model, the regression coefficients (intercept and slopes) have some amount of (residual) random variation between groups. Variance component model refers to the statistical problem of estimating the amount of random variation. In our example, the specific value for the intercept and the slope coefficient for the pupil variable Gender are class characteristics. A class with a high intercept is predicted to have more popular pupils than a class with a low value for the intercept. Similarly, differences in the slope coefficient for gender indicate that the relationship between the pupils' gender and their predicted popularity is not the same in all classes. Some classes may have a high value for the slope coefficient of gender; in these classes, the difference between boys and girls is relatively large. Other classes may have a low value for the slope coefficient of gender; in these classes, gender has a small effect on the popularity, which means that the difference between boys and girls is small.

The next step in the hierarchical regression model is to explain the variation of the regression coefficients β_{0j} and β_{1j} by introducing the explanatory variable Teacher experience at the class level. Model M1 models the intercept as follows:

$$\beta_{0j} = \gamma_{00} + \gamma_{01}\ \text{Teacher experience}_j + u_{0j} \tag{9}$$

and model M2 models the slope as follows:

$$\beta_{1j} = \gamma_{10} + \gamma_{11}\ \text{Teacher experience}_j + u_{1j} \tag{10}$$

Equation (9) predicts the average popularity in a class (the intercept β_{0j}) by the teacher's experience. Thus, if γ_{01} is positive, the average popularity is higher in classes with a more experienced teacher. Conversely, if γ_{01} is negative, the average popularity is lower in classes with a more experienced teacher. The interpretation of Eq. (10) is more complicated. Equation (10) states that the *relationship*, as expressed by the slope coefficient β_{1j}, between the popularity and the gender of the pupil, depends on the amount of experience of the teacher. If γ_{11} is positive, the gender effect on popularity is larger with experienced teachers. On the other hand, if γ_{11} is negative, the gender effect on popularity is smaller with experienced teachers. Thus, the amount of experience of the teacher interacts with the relationship between popularity and gender; this relationship varies according to the value of the teacher experience.

The u terms u_{0j} and u_{1j} in Eqs. (9) and (10) are the residual terms at the class level. The variance of the residual u_{0j} is denoted by $\sigma^2_{u_0}$, and the variance of the residual u_{1j} is denoted by $\sigma^2_{u_1}$. The covariance between the residuals u_{0j} and u_{1j} is $\sigma_{u_{01}}$, which is generally *not* assumed to be zero.

Our model with one pupil-level and one class-level explanatory variable including the cross-level interaction can be written as a single complex regression equation by substituting Eqs. (9) and (10) into Eq. (8). This produces:

$$\begin{aligned}\text{Popularity}_{ij} = {} & \gamma_{00} + \gamma_{10}\ \text{Gender}_{ij} \\ & + \gamma_{01}\ \text{Teacher experience}_j \\ & + \gamma_{11}\ \text{Teacher experience}_j \times \text{Gender}_{ij} \\ & + u_{1j}\ \text{Gender}_{ij} + u_{0j} + e_{ij}\end{aligned} \tag{11}$$

Note that the result of modeling the slopes using the class-level variable implies adding an interaction term and second-level residuals u_{1j} that are related to the pupil-level variable Gender. Model M2 is the most complete, including both available explanatory variables and the cross-level interaction term. The interaction term is significant using the Z test. Because we have used FML estimation, we can also test the interaction term by comparing the deviances of models M1 and M2. The deviance-difference is 15.3, which has a chi-square distribution with one degree of freedom and $p < 0.005$. Using a deviance-difference test on the second-level variance components in model M2, by restricting variance terms to zero and then comparing deviances, leads to the conclusion that all variance terms are significant and that the covariance term is not. This means, that not all residual variation in the intercept and slope can be modeled by the explanatory variables.

The interpretation of model M2 is straightforward. The regression coefficients for both explanatory variables are significant. The regression coefficient for pupil gender is 1.33. Because pupil gender is coded 0 = boy and 1 = girl, this means that on average the girls score 1.33 points higher on the popularity measure. The regression coefficient for teacher experience is 0.11, which means that for each year of experience of the teacher, the average popularity score of the class goes up with 0.11 points. Because there is an interaction term in the model, the effect of 1.33 for pupil gender is the expected effect for teachers with zero experience. The regression coefficient for the cross-level interaction is −0.03, which is small but significant. The negative value means that with experienced teachers, the advantage of being a girl is smaller than expected from the direct effects only. Thus, the difference between boys and girls is smaller with more experienced teachers. A comparison of the other results between the two models shows that the variance component for pupil gender goes down from 0.27 in the direct effects model (M1) to 0.22 in the cross-level model (M2). Hence, the cross-level model explains about 19% of the variation of the slopes for pupil gender.

The significant and quite large variance of the regression slopes for pupil gender implies that we should not interpret the estimated value of 1.33 without considering this variation. In an ordinary regression model, without multilevel structure, the value of 1.33 means that girls are expected to differ from boys by 1.33 points, for all pupils in all classes. In our multilevel model, the regression coefficient for pupil gender varies across the classes and the value of 1.33 is just the expected value across all classes (for teachers with zero experience). The variance of the slope is estimated in model M1 as 0.27. Model M2 shows that part of this variation can be explained by variation in teacher experience. The interpretation of the slope variation is easier when we consider their standard deviation, which is the square root of the variance, or 0.52 in our example data. The varying regression coefficients are assumed to follow a normal distribution. Thus, we may expect 95% of the regression slopes to lie between two standard deviations above or below their average. Given the estimated values of 1.33 (in model M2, for inexperienced teachers) or 0.84 (in model M1, average for all teachers) the vast majority of the classes are expected to have positive slopes for the effect of pupil gender. Figure 1 provides a graphical display of the slope variation, which confirms the conclusion that almost all class slopes are expected to be positive.

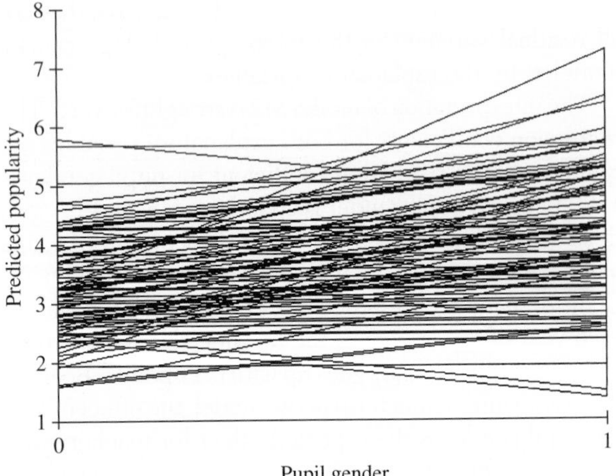

Figure 1 One hundred class slopes for pupil gender.

Analysis of Proportions and Binary Data

The multilevel regression model discussed so far assumes a continuous dependent variable and normal distributions for the residuals. When the response variable is a dichotomous variable or a proportion, both the assumptions of continuous scores and of normality are not met. In addition, the assumption of homoscedastic errors is violated.

The classical approach to the problem of nonnormally distributed variables and heteroscedastic errors is to apply a transformation to achieve normality and reduce heteroskedasticity, followed by a traditional multiple regression analysis. The modern approach to the problem of nonnormally distributed variables is to include the necessary transformation and the choice of the appropriate error distribution (not necessarily a normal distribution) explicitly in the statistical model. This class of statistical models is called generalized linear models. Generalized linear models are defined by three components: (1) a linear regression equation, (2) a specific error distribution, and (3) a link function which is the transformation that links the predicted values for the dependent variable to the observed values. If the link function is the identity function ($f(x) = x$) and the error distribution is normal, the generalized linear model simplifies to the ordinary multiple linear regression model.

Multilevel generalized linear models are described by Raudenbush and Bryk and by Goldstein. Estimating the parameters (regression coefficients and variance components) for such models is more complicated than ordinary multilevel analysis because the likelihood function used in the ML estimation is nonlinear. One approach to estimating such nonlinear models is to linearize the likelihood function. This results in an approximation to the likelihood, and as a result statistical tests based on the likelihood (such as the deviance-difference test) cannot be used. The second approach is to maximize the nonlinear likelihood itself. This is difficult, and therefore it is implemented only in some of the available software and only for a limited set of models. The link functions presently supported in most software are the logistic link function for binary (dichotomous) and binomial data (proportions), the logarithmic function for Poisson data, and the reciprocal link function for γ-distributed data.

The example presented in what follows concerns data from a meta-analysis of studies that compared face-to-face, telephone, and mail surveys on various indicators of data quality. One of these indicators is the response rate—the number of completed interviews divided by the total number of eligible sample units. Overall, the response rates differ among the three data collection methods. In addition, the response rates also differ across studies, which makes it interesting to analyze if study characteristics account for these differences.

These data have a multilevel structure. The lowest level is the condition-level, and the higher level is the study-level. There are three variables at the condition level: the number of completed interviews in that specific condition, the number of eligible respondents in that condition, and an explanatory categorical variable indicating the data collection method used. The categorical data collection variable has three categories: face-to-face, telephone, and mail. It is recoded into two dummy variables: a telephone-dummy and a mail-dummy; this makes the face-to-face condition the reference condition. We use one variable at the study level: the saliency of the questionnaire topic. We have 45 studies in which a total of 99 data collection conditions are compared.

The dependent variable is the response rate. This variable is a proportion—the number of completed interviews divided by the number of eligible respondents. Proportions are analyzed using logistic regression, which is a specific generalized linear model. The link function for binomial data and proportions is the logit function, which is defined as $\text{logit}(x) = \ln[x/(1-x)]$. The corresponding error function is the binomial distribution.

Let P_{ij} be the observed proportion respondents in condition i of study j. Although P_{ij} has a binomial distribution, $\text{logit}(P_{ij})$ has a distribution that is approximately normal, and so we use a linear regression equation at the lowest level. The simplest model, corresponding to the intercept-only model in ordinary multilevel regression analysis, is given by:

$$\text{logit}(P_{ij}) = \beta_{0j} \qquad (12)$$

Note that the usual lowest level error term e_{ij} is not included in Eq. (12). In the binomial distribution, the variance of the observed proportion depends only on the population proportion π. As a consequence, the lowest level variance is determined completely by the predicted value for P_{ij}, and it does not enter the model as a separate term.

The model in Eq. (12) can be extended to include an explanatory variable X_{ij} (e.g., the mail or face-to-face condition) at the condition level:

$$\text{logit}(P_{ij}) = \beta_{0j} + \beta_{1j}X_{ij} \qquad (13)$$

The regression coefficients β are assumed to vary across studies, and this variation is modeled by the study level variable Z_j in the usual second-level regression equations:

$$\beta_{0j} = \gamma_{00} + \gamma_{01}Z_j + u_{0j} \qquad (14)$$

$$\beta_{1j} = \gamma_{10} + \gamma_{11}Z_j + u_{1j} \qquad (15)$$

By substituting Eqs. (15) and (14) into Eq. (13), we get the single-equation version:

$$\text{logit}(P_{ij}) = \gamma_{00} + \gamma_{10}X_{ij} + \gamma_{01}Z_j + \gamma_{11}Z_jX_{ij} + u_{0j} + u_{1j}X_{ij} \qquad (16)$$

It should be kept in mind that the interpretation of the regression parameters is *not* in terms of the response proportions we want to analyze but instead in terms of the underlying variate defined by the logit transformation $\text{logit}(x) = \ln[x/(1-x)]$. The logit link function is nonlinear and transforms the proportions, which are between 0.00 and 1.00 by definition, into values that range from $-\infty$ to $+\infty$. For a quick examination of the analysis results, we can simply inspect the regression parameters. To understand the implications of the regression coefficients for the proportions we are modeling, we must transform the predicted values back to the original scale or transform the regression coefficients to odds ratios. This problem is not specific to multilevel logistic regression.

Table II presents the results for a sequence of three models: the intercept-only model, a model with the two condition dummies, and a model with the two condition dummies and the study-level variable Saliency. In the

Table II Multilevel Logistic Models for Survey Response

Model	*M0: intercept-only*	*M1: +conditions*	*M2: +saliency*
Fixed part			
Predictor	Coefficient (SE)	Coefficient (SE)	Coefficient (SE)
Intercept	1.02 (0.13)	1.29 (0.14)	0.54 (0.22)
Telephone		−0.21 (0.09)	−0.19 (0.10)
Mail		−0.58 (0.16)	−0.56 (0.15)
Saliency			0.68 (0.17)
Random part			
$\sigma^2_{u_0}$	0.84 (0.17)	0.83 (0.19)	0.63 (0.14)
$\sigma^2_{u_1}$		0.26 (0.07)	0.27 (0.08)
σ_{u_2}		0.60 (0.20)	0.56 (0.18)

intercept-only model, the intercept γ_{00} is estimated as 1.02. As noted before, this refers to the underlying distribution established by the logistic link function and *not* to the proportions themselves. To determine the expected proportion, we must use the inverse transformation for the logistic link function, given by:

$$g(x) = \frac{e^x}{1 + e^x}$$

Using this inverse function, the estimated intercept of 1.02 translates back to an expected proportion of 0.73. The study-level variance is considerable and significant by the Z test. Because the estimation method used here is based on the linearization approach, the deviance is approximate and not available for the deviance-difference test. Hence, in this specific case the significance of the variance components is assessed using the Z test.

The next model adds the condition-level variables Telephone-dummy and Mail-dummy, assuming random regression slopes. In this model, the intercept represents the condition in which both explanatory variables are zero, which is the face-to-face condition. Thus, the value for the intercept in model M1 in Table II estimates the expected response in the face-to-face condition, which is 1.29. This corresponds to an expected response proportion of 0.78. The large negative values for the slope coefficients for the Telephone-dummy and Mail-dummy variables indicate that in these conditions the expected response is lower. To find out how much lower, we must use the regression equation to predict the response in the three conditions and transform these values (which refer to the underlying variate) back to proportions. For the telephone condition, which is coded by Telephone = 1 and Mail = 0, the regression equation reads: $Y = 1.29 - 0.21 = 1.08$, which transforms to an expected response proportion of 0.75. For the mail condition, which is coded by Telephone = 0 and Mail = 1, it reads $Y = 1.29 - 0.58 = 0.71$, which transforms to an expected response proportion of 0.67. The variance components for the regression coefficients are significant by the (approximate) Z test.

The final model includes the study-level variable Saliency. Compared to the earlier results, the regression coefficients are about the same, but the value for the intercept is different. This is not informative, because the intercept almost always changes when other variables are added to or deleted from the regression equation. In our case, including the study-level explanatory variable Saliency in the model causes the shift of the intercept value. Saliency is coded as 1 = very salient, 2 = somewhat salient, and 3 = not salient. The coded values for Saliency do not include the value 0. Hence, the estimated value of the intercept has no meaningful interpretation. The regression coefficient for Saliency is positive, indicating that the response rate increases when the study's topic is more salient.

The last logical step is to introduce interaction variables of Saliency with the two condition variables to model the random coefficients. In our example data, it turns out that this interaction variable does not explain any variation of the regression coefficients.

The random coefficient model leads to another interesting conclusion. In general, telephone and mail surveys obtain a lower response rate than face-to-face surveys. For instance, on the underlying scale, the regression coefficient for Telephone is -0.19 in the final model. However, this regression coefficient has a large variance across studies: $\sigma^2_{11} = 0.27$. The corresponding standard deviation is 0.52. Using the standard normal distribution, we can calculate that in 36% of similarly conducted studies this regression coefficient is expected to be larger than zero! It is instructive to see that, even if there is little doubt that *on the average* the telephone interview has a lower response rate than the face-to-face interview, there is still a chance that in a specific study we will find the opposite relation.

Further Topics

Extensions of the Multilevel Regression Model

The multilevel regression model is one attractive approach to analyzing longitudinal data. In this case, the hierarchical structure is viewed as measurement occasions nested within individuals. Extensions of the multilevel regression model are models for data that are not fully nested, such as cross-classified data, and models in which group membership may not be fully known. The nonlinear regression model discussed in the previous section has been extended to models for ordered or unordered categorical response variables and models for the analysis of counts. Finally, multilevel factor analysis and multilevel structural equation models are becoming available.

Software and Internet Resources

Multilevel analysis modules have appeared in most of the large statistical packages, such as SPSS, SAS, Stata, and SPLUS. Although these modules are quite powerful, specialized software for multilevel tends to have more analysis options and more coverage of the model extensions previously mentioned. The best-known specialized multilevel software are HLM and MlwiN. Don Hedeker provides a set of freeware programs for multilevel regression modeling. A 2001 review of some of these packages was given by De Leeuw and Kreft. The multilevel models project in London maintains a large homepage on multilevel modeling, with emphasis on their own product

MlwiN, but also including much general information. Their website also provides links to other multilevel websites, including one to Don Hedeker's freeware packages. There is also an ongoing review of all software that is able to analyze multilevel data. Finally, there is an active Internet multilevel discussion group.

See Also the Following Articles

Clustering • Internet Measurement • Maximum Likelihood Estimation • Misspecification in Linear Spatial Regression Models

Further Reading

Berkhof, J., and Snijders, T. A. B. (2001). Variance component testing in multilevel models. *J. Educ. Behav. Statist.* **26,** 133–152.

De Leeuw, E. D. (1992). *Data Quality in Mail, Telephone, and Face-to-face Surveys.* TT-Publikaties, Amsterdam.

De Leeuw, J., and Kreft, I. (2001). Software for multilevel analysis. In *Multilevel Modelling of Health Statistics* (A. H. Leyland and H. Goldstein, eds.), pp. 187–204. John Wiley, New York.

Iverson, G. R. (1991). *Contextual Analysis.* Sage, Newbury Park, CA.

Goldstein, H. (2003). *Multilevel Statistical Models.* Arnold, London.

Hosmer, D. W., and Lemeshov, S. (1989). *Applied Logistic Regression.* John Wiley, New York.

Hox, J. J. (2002). *Multilevel Analysis. Techniques and Applications.* Erlbaum, Mahwah, NJ.

Hox, J. J., and de Leeuw, E. D. (1994). A comparison of nonresponse in mail, telephone, and face to face surveys. *Quality Quantity* **28,** 329–344.

Kish, L. (1965). *Survey Sampling.* John Wiley, New York.

Maas, C. J. M., and Snijders, T. A. B. (2003). The multilevel approach to repeated measures for complete and incomplete data. *Quality Quantity* **37,** 71–89.

McCullagh, P., and Nelder, J. A. (1989). *Generalized Linear Models.* Chapman & Hall, London.

Multilevel Internet Discussion Group. http://www.jiscmail.ac.uk/lists/multilevel.html

Multilevel Models Project. http://www.multilevel.ioe.ac.uk

Raudenbush, S. W., and Bryk, A. S. (2002). *Hierarchical Linear Models.* Sage, Thousand Oaks, CA.

Searle, S. R., Casella, G., and McCulloch, C. E. (1992). *Variance Components.* Wiley, New York.

Snijders, T. A. B., and Bosker, R. (1999). *Multilevel Analysis.* Sage, Thousand Oaks, CA.

Verbeke, G., and Molenberghs, G. (2000). *Linear Mixed Models for Longitudinal Data.* Springer-Verlag, New York.

Music Cognition

Barbara Tillmann

Université Claude Bernard Lyon 1, CNRS-UMR 5020, Lyon, France

Glossary

cognition Processes linked to perception, learning, memory, attention, and the role of the perceiver's (implicit and explicit) knowledge of these processes.

melodic contour Patterns of ups and downs defined by the tones of a melody with changes in pitch heights.

pitch height, pitch class The pitch height is determined by the fundamental frequency of a tone (e.g., the A tone at 440 Hz). A pitch class is defined by a set of pitches at different pitch heights that are separated by octaves (i.e., an interval defined by multiples of the fundamental frequency of a tone); for example, the A tones at 220, 440, and 880 Hz all belong to the pitch class of A.

tonal acculturation Listeners' familiarization with a musical tonal system resulting from exposure to musical pieces obeying the rules and regularities of the system.

tonal stability A concept linked to the musical function of a tone (or a chord) and its perceptual implication: the more stable a tone is, the stronger the induced feeling of tension implying that the melody should not stop at this point.

Music cognition refers to the cognitive activities involved in the perception, memory, performance, and learning of music. It is one example from the more general domain of auditory cognition. Listeners acquire knowledge about the musical system through mere exposure to musical pieces in everyday life. Research on music cognition aims to understand the nature of listeners' musical knowledge, its acquisition, and the influence of this knowledge on encoding, organizing, remembering, and performing musical patterns.

Introduction

Music is a temporal art combining in a highly structured way events that differ in duration, pitch height, timbre, and dynamics. In order to understand the relations between sounds, listeners have to process the individual events, memorize them, and link them to the preceding events. Listeners who are familiarized with the music of their culture do not perceive a disorganized superposition of sounds, but hear coherent melodic lines and develop expectations and anticipate possible endings of musical pieces. Research in music cognition analyzes how listeners succeed in these processes, and it aims to specify listeners' knowledge about a given musical system and its acquisition, structure, and use in perception and performance.

Interdisciplinary Research on Music

Music cognition represents a growing research domain, bringing together behavioral, neurophysiological, theoretical, and computational perspectives, all adapting an information-processing approach to understand musical knowledge and processing. This article focuses on the cognitive side of music processing and summarizes research that provides evidence for listeners' knowledge of the tonal system and for influence of the tonal system on processing. Other approaches to studies of music perception underline the importance of sensory information, notably psychoacoustical models. Research on music cognition is interdisciplinary and combines music theory with cognitive science (cognitive psychology and neuroscience, neuropsychology, computational modeling, and linguistics). Musicologists describe the different structures and organizational levels in the musical stimulus, and cognitive scientists, beyond this description, are interested in determining which aspects of the structure are relevant for cognition, what is the knowledge acquired by listeners (i.e., acculturation), and how detailed the structural discrimination can be in the perception of this complex, nonverbal material.

Tonal Acculturation

Tonal acculturation is one example of the cognitive capacity to become sensitive to regularities in the environment. Implicit learning processes enable the acquisition of highly complex information, without complete verbalizable knowledge of what has been learned. Music and language are examples of highly structured systems that are learned in an incidental manner: native speakers and nonmusician listeners internalize the regularities underlying linguistic and musical structures with apparent ease merely as a result of exposure. Just by listening to musical pieces in everyday life, listeners become sensitive to regularities of the musical system (e.g., strong regularities on the pitch dimension). Listeners acquire implicit knowledge of the structural patterns used in the musical system, and this knowledge facilitates the processing of music conforming to these patterns. Even nonmusician listeners are "musically expert," as has been shown in numerous behavioral and neurophysiological studies. Tonal acculturation shapes listeners' expectations about the continuity of a musical piece. It allows listeners to detect "wrong" notes in a performance and to judge an unfamiliar musical phrase as incomplete when it stops in the middle. Most contemporary research has used Western tonal music, based on its classical foundations, mainly from the 18th and 19th centuries. Regularities between musical elements also exist in other musical systems (e.g., Indian or Arabic music), and cultural learning and familiarity with these systems lead to auditory experiences different from those of a native Western listener.

Music and Language

The comparison between music and language processing is not only interesting because of acculturation, but also because of parallels in cognitive processes and neural correlates. Music, just like speech, is composed of complex auditory information evolving over time. The auditory stream has to be segmented in smaller units (phrases or words) separated by boundaries between these units. Because of the temporality of the information, there are similar constraints on processing, notably memory limitations (i.e., holding information active in short-term memory). The structures in music and language have similar features; for example, both have periodic and repeating rhythmic patterns (longer and shorter durations), which form meter in both music and poetry. A further example is the conceptual similarity between musical contour and prosody in speech. Based on these structural parallels, the question arises as to what extent cognitive processes and underlying neural correlates for music and language are shared or distinct.

Perception and Memory

Four psychological qualities of sound are important in music: pitch (differentiating high and low sounds), duration, loudness, and timbre. Two of these qualities, pitch and time, serve as form-bearing dimensions in Western tonal music. Other dimensions, such as musical timbre or spatial localization, are helpful in perception. For example, more dissimilar timbres (i.e., instrumental sounds) allow different melodic lines in polyphonic music to be more easily separated. The characteristics of spatial position and timbre become particularly important dimensions in contemporary music, but research on these new musical systems is currently only starting.

Organization Based on the Pitch Dimension

The Western tonal system is based on 12 pitches repeated cyclically over octaves (C–C#–D–D#–E–F–F#–G–G#–A–A#–B–C–C# . . .). Two pitches separated by an octave are functionally equivalent and are perceived as very similar (i.e., voices of men and women singing are often separated by an octave). Strong regularities of co-occurrence and frequencies of occurrence exist among these 12 pitch classes; tones are combined into chords and into keys, forming a three-level organizational system (Fig. 1). Sets of seven tones form scales, which can be either major or minor, depending on the pattern of intervals (i.e., pitch distances) (e.g., C, D, E, F, G, A, B for a C-major scale). Based on the scale, groups of three tones define chords (e.g., C–E–G for a C-major chord). This set of tones and chords defines a tonality, or a key. Inside a key, tones and chords differ in their functional importance. The most referential event (for tones and chords) is the tonic, which gives its name to the key and occurs most frequently in a key context (e.g., it often defines the starting and ending point of simple tonal songs). Keys have more or less close harmonic relations to each other, with keys sharing more tones being more strongly related. A musical piece rarely remains in the same key, but changes key over time. The key changes (i.e., modulations) are often introduced by a pitch that is foreign to the currently instilled key and that primes the new key.

This short description of regularities on the pitch dimension shows that the variety of musical structures is based on a restricted set of events. Consequently, the same musical event fulfills different functions, depending on the key context. The tone C is the most referential tonic tone in a C-major context, but is less stable in a G-major context and out-of-key in an F#-major context (Fig. 2). When the key of the context changes, the functional hierarchies between tones and chords are changing. Understanding this context dependency is crucial for the

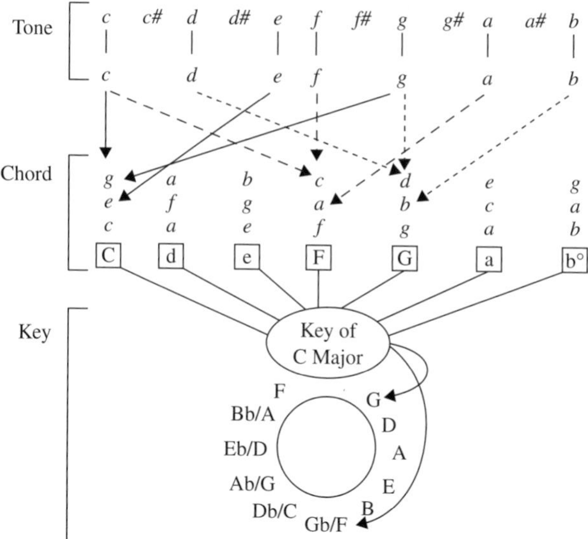

Figure 1 The three organizational levels of the Western tonal system (tones, chords, and keys) illustrated with the example of the C-major key. On the basis of the 12 chromatic tones, a selection of seven tones defines the diatonic scale, which then forms the basis for the construction of seven chords (i.e., associations of three tones, here illustrated with three major chords). At the key level, the C-major key has relationships with other keys, represented here with the "circle of fifths," which shows the harmonic relationships between major keys. Closely related keys are represented next to each other on the circle (e.g., the C- and G-major keys are more closely related to each than are the C- and F#-major keys). (Adapted from Figure 1 is Tillmann *et al.* (2001), "Implicit Learning of Regularities in Western Tonal Music by Self-Organization" (pp. 175–184), Proceedings of the Sixth Neural Computation and Psychology Workshop: Evolution, Learning, and Development (R. M. French and J. P Sougné, Eds) Connectionist Modeling of Learning, Development and Evolution Perspectives in Neural Computing Series © Springer, with permission.)

understanding of musical structures. Context dependency is a characteristic feature of the musical system, and based on listeners' knowledge, the same physical event will be interpreted differently, depending on the tonal context. Acculturated listeners understand these musical structures and changes in an implicit and tacit way.

Tones

The perception of tones is related to absolute pitch, the ability to recognize a specific tone. This ability is quite rare even among musicians; a person with absolute pitch can rapidly identify, without attentional effort, pitches by their note names, even when the tones are presented in isolation. Different explanations of this phenomenon have been proposed, including an early-learning hypothesis postulating a critical period in the fifth or sixth year of life. However, the most important feature for the understanding of music is the perception of relative pitches and of the relative changes in the functional importance of tones, depending on the currently instilled key context. Numerous studies have shown that listeners are sensitive to the functional differences between tones (i.e., tonal hierarchies) and to the functional changes, depending on the key context. The tonal hierarchy described by music theory has a perceptual equivalence for the listeners. Less referential tones are perceived as unstable and instill a feeling of tension, whereas more referential, stable tones bring relaxation. Listeners judge sequences ending on unstable tones as incomplete. The unstable tones demand resolution to stable tones, which work like perceptual anchors or cognitive reference points. In addition to being functionally important, stable tones are also more stable in memory over time, leading to better recognition performance. When listeners are required to judge how well a tone fits into a preceding tonal context, ratings reflect the tonal hierarchy (e.g., with the tonic tone given the

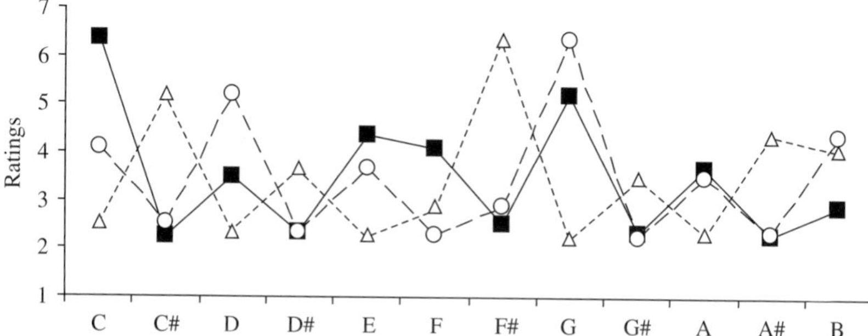

Figure 2 Probe tone ratings for the 12 pitch classes in three key contexts (■, C major; ○, G major; and △, F# major). Tones receiving higher ratings (e.g., C and G in C major) are perceived as more stable and are situated at the top of the tonal hierarchy. The changes in the tone judgments are stronger between two distant keys (i.e., C and F# major) than between two closely related keys (i.e., C and G major). (Values from Table 2.1, *Cognitive Foundations of Musical Pitch*, by C. L. Krumhansl, © 1990 by Oxford University Press Inc. with permission.)

better fit) and the listeners' sensitivity to the functional changes due to the instilled key context (cf. Fig. 2).

Chords

In parallel to the perception of tones, a set of studies has provided evidence that listeners are also sensitive to the functional differences between chords, as described by harmonic hierarchies. Similar paradigms as used for tones have shown that stable chords induce a stronger feeling of completion, are remembered better, or are processed faster than are less stable or unstable chords. Even subtle differences in harmonic functions are perceived by musically untrained listeners.

Keys

Studies on tone and chord perception provide indirect evidence that listeners understand the changes of tonal functions, depending on the key context. They are sensitive to the tonal and harmonic hierarchies in the currently instilled key. This sensitivity to intrakey hierarchy changes is crucial for understanding modulations during a musical piece. When modulations occur, listeners deal with upcoming changes; the perception of tones and chords is reorganized with the new key and adapts to the new hierarchies. The magnitude of perceived changes reflects the harmonic distances between the keys, with small changes for modulations to harmonically closely related keys and larger changes for modulations to more distant keys. Key distances also affect memory for transposed melodies, with better discrimination between melodies separated by distant keys. The changes in keys and functions of events have been compared to travel through a "tonal pitch space," with longer trajectories for more distant key changes. Modulations and associated changes in tone and chord functions have expressive effects for the listener.

Temporal Organization

Besides pitch, temporal regularities (i.e., how events are organized over time) create a second form-bearing dimension in Western tonal music. Temporal regularities include the organization of event-onset intervals through time, leading to a sensation of meter, i.e., a sensation of a regular succession of strong and weak beats superimposed over an isochronous pulse. Temporal regularities include the temporal patterns of onset intervals, creating rhythms that are perceived against the metrical background. For example, when listening to a waltz, the three-beat meter underlying different rhythmical figures is extracted. The metric structure also contains a hierarchy; for example, the first beat in a waltz is more important than the other two beats. Listeners are sensitive to temporal regularities and develop expectations about the temporal occurrence of future events. These expectations influence perception and make it possible to synchronize rhythmic productions with precision. Processing advantages for metrical sequences with a hierarchical structure in comparison to nonmetrical sequences have been observed in perception, production, and memory tasks. Additionally, the processing of rhythms with temporal ratios of 2 : 1 between elements is facilitated in comparison to rhythms with more complex ratios.

Perception of Pitch and Time

In a musical piece, tonal stabilities and temporal organizations (rhythm and meter) are combined in a structural organization. This structure integrates each event and can be described as a structural tree, which is referred to as an event hierarchy (Fig. 3). Currently, research based on behavioral data and on neuropsychological cases has not reached a consensus on the understanding of pitch and time processing: some data suggest that pitch and time dimensions are processed independently and others suggest that they are integrated. Despite this controversy, it has been shown that listeners are sensitive to the underlying organizational structure of musical phrases that are based on both tonal and temporal information.

Musical Structures and Global Organization

A strong characteristic of Western tonal music is its hierarchical nature. The encoding of musical information as a hierarchy of events is attractive for cognitive psychology, because hierarchical structures are economic

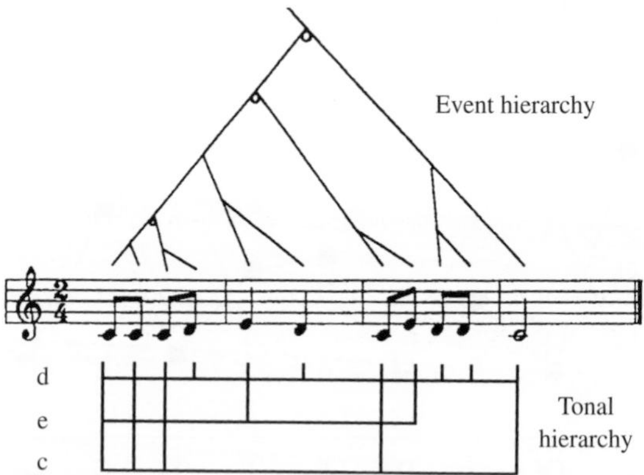

Figure 3 Illustration of tonal hierarchy and event hierarchy concepts. The top of the tonal hierarchy of C major is indicated under the musical score, with C being the tonic tone. Above the score, the event hierarchy of this melody is represented: the structural tree is opened and closed by the tonic tone. (Adapted from Figure 1.4, Percevoir la Musique: une activité cognitive by M. Pineau and B. Tillmann, © 2001, L'Harmattan, Paris, with permission.)

representations with numerous advantages for processing and storage in memory. In music perception, listeners discover the musical events successively within short temporal windows. The perceptual task consists in discovering the structure that underlies the incoming information and that evolves over time. Over short time periods, listeners are sensitive to the underlying musical structures, as shown in perception, memory, and segmentation tasks. For example, listeners indicate more group boundaries at structurally higher level arches of the structural tree (Fig. 3). They also differentiate between melodies that have similar surface characteristics (i.e., similar melodic lines and rhythmic patterns), but differ in the underlying structural trees. Based on tonal knowledge, the perceived hierarchies render melodies more than just a simple succession of tones. Most research has investigated the perception of structural organization with relatively short musical excerpts. It has not been entirely clear how far and in which form this perceptual capacity extends over longer time periods. Some studies have suggested that global organization has less perceptual impact than predicted by music theory and that listeners seem to base their perception mainly on local units of shorter time scale.

Musical Expectations

Expectations guide perceptual processing to important and relevant aspects of incoming patterns and facilitate the processing of expected events (vs. unexpected events). In music perception, it has been shown that processing is faster and more accurate for an expected event occurring at an expected time point (i.e., expected on the basis of musical relations and temporal regularities). Musical expectations can be based on a number of features, some of them reflecting the perceptual organization of the musical sequence (i.e., melodic contour, with its directions and interval sizes), others reflecting the influence of listeners' knowledge about the musical system or about particular musical exemplars. Schematic and episodic musical knowledge facilitates perception, attention, and memory. For example, memory performance is better for tonal than for atonal melodies, and better for tonally stable events than for unstable ones. When two melodies are played at the same time, knowing what melody to listen for enables listeners to focus attention on specific pitch heights and at specific time points, allowing them to pick out the notes necessary to recognize the melody. Tonal expectations based on listeners' schematic knowledge about the musical system have a role not only in the perception and mental organization of music, but are also important for aesthetic experience of music. Meaningful and expressive moments in music arise from the violation of schematic expectations. Listeners use cognitive schemata of prototypical structures to anticipate music (these anticipations are automatic and irrepressible). Aiming to evoke emotions, composers and performers play with these schematic expectations by violating them or by fulfilling them later or differently. These sets of subtle surprises make music interesting, exciting, and emotionally involving. Expectations may thus serve as a concept linking music cognition and emotion. Research on music and emotion is an expanding field of study.

Contributions from Computational Models

Computational models based on music theory or on empirical data have been developed to simulate various aspects of music perception, memory, and performance. A subset of these models uses artificial neural networks (i.e., connectionist models). Neural networks provide modeling frameworks that allow understanding of (1) aspects of cognition as a result of neural pattern associations and (2) the acquisition of these representations through repeated exposure to the material. The networks extract statistical structures from musical material with the help of algorithms that are based on plausible and rather domain-general principles of neuroscience. The learned representations are analyzed and used to simulate human listeners' behavior. This approach has been applied to different aspects of music perception, ranging from basic processes (such as pitch height extraction, octave equivalence, or chord classification), to the learning of either schematic tonal knowledge or specific melodic sequences and even to more complex aspects of music learning and perception (such as categorization and memory of musical style). Computational models contribute to our understanding of music cognition—for example, how listeners build up musical knowledge that allows them to develop expectations, which shapes musical processing and subjective experience.

Developmental Perspectives on Musical Abilities

One of the methods used to investigate music perception skills of infants is the head-turn procedure. Musical stimuli are presented via laterally displaced loudspeakers, and the time it takes infants to look at the loudspeakers is interpreted as "listening time" (i.e., how long the sound captures the infants' attention). In some studies, infants are rewarded with a toy for the detection of changes in sound. Research has provided evidence for strong developmental progress, confirming that music-processing skills become more and more sophisticated with age. Infants do not respond progressively to tonal scale structures; the perception and understanding of tonal scale relationships emerge later. Infants are sensitive to rhythmic groupings of sounds (i.e., perceiving similarity of rhythmic patterns despite tempo changes) and to pitch (i.e., being sensitive to octave equivalence, pitch discrimination, and melodic contour). Melodic contour is a salient feature for infants. For example, melodies with the same melodic contour are processed as the same even when the key is changed. Pitch contour and note duration are important determinants for infants' perception of structural phrases inside musical pieces. Later during childhood, the child's cognitive structure allows having a stable pitch sense while singing. Children at age 5 years are sensitive to stable tonal centers and make the distinction between near- and far-key transpositions. Around the age of 6 years, children distinguish tonal from atonal melodies, allowing them to have better pitch detection performance for tonal melodies than for atonal melodies. With age, the structure of tonal hierarchy becomes more differentiated and pitches are heard more and more in terms of tonal frames of reference: whereas 5-year-old children distinguish only between in-key and out-of-key tones, 7-year-old children additionally distinguish between tones belonging to the triad chord (e.g., CEG) and other in-key tones. Concerning the emotional content of musical excerpts, children are sensitive to the opposition of "happy/sad" at a young age. For example, 3-year-old children attribute smiling faces to positive excerpts in major mode in opposition to negatively connoted excerpts in minor mode. The preference for consonant music over music including dissonant intervals can be observed even for infants.

Musical Performance

Forms of musical abilities include performance of well-learned pieces from memory, sight reading, and improvisation. All of these abilities combine rapid motor skills and elaborated cognitive skills. Analysis of musical performance involves investigating a performer's mental representation of a musical piece, their plan for transforming this representation into sound, and their realization of the movements necessary for this transformation. Studying musical performance is interesting for developing theories on motor behavior and cognition and for understanding the relation between performance and perception. Musical sequences have to be planned and then executed under fine motor control; it is important to control which elements have to be played and the relative timing of these elements. For timing of movements, anticipation and coordination of gestures, and overall motor control, models of internal clocks ("timekeepers") have been proposed. The performer has to coordinate sequences of movements in advance of their execution. Generally, a planned sequence is segmented into smaller units such as phrases. With practice, these units become larger, future events are more strongly anticipated and expressive features of the performance are enhanced. The performer's task is to highlight the structure of the musical piece and also its emotional content. The main expressive parameters that are modified in a performance are timing, loudness, and timbre. Slowing down in tempo at phrase boundaries helps to underline the structural organization of the musical excerpt. A further example taken from piano performances is the melody lead (i.e., onsets of melody precede onsets of other parallel voices by up to 50 msec), which helps to differentiate among simultaneously occurring voices in polyphonic music. Analyzing performance errors provides insight into underlying cognitive processes, such as memory limits (i.e., how far can performers plan ahead) or the influence of the performers' tonal knowledge (i.e., replaced tones are more likely to be in-key tones than out-of-key tones).

Neural Correlates of Music Cognition

The relation between cerebral structures and music perception has been investigated by neuropsychological case studies involving patients with damaged brain regions and by neurophysiological studies using electrophysiological methods and brain imaging. The two approaches provide converging evidence for a hierarchical organization in the brain reflecting stages in music processing: primary auditory areas process spectrotemporal features of the sound, higher order tonal and sequential patterns involve temporo-frontal networks, and the processing of more complex (or real) musical stimuli involve multimodal, widely distributed neuronal networks in both hemispheres.

Neuropsychological Cases

Neurological disorders related to music can take different forms, including musical hallucinations, musicogenic epilepsy (i.e., seizures triggered by music), synesthesia (i.e., hallucinated colors triggered by music), and cases of amusia. Amusia, the most well-studied disorder, represents a disorder of music processing and recognition abilities that can concern specific parameters (i.e., pitch, rhythm, timbre, and emotion) and can be either receptive or expressive, or both. Neurological deficits can be selective to music, with some patients showing amusia without aphasia, or selective to language (i.e., aphasia without amusia). This double dissociation has been taken as an argument that music and language are processed by separate, independent brain structures. Further insight in understanding neural correlates of music processing has been based on patients with right and left temporal damage by comparing their respective performance of tasks varying along different features (i.e., timbre, pitch, rhythm, or memory). For example, in tonal working-memory tasks, performance is decreased in patients with right temporal and frontal lesions. The role of right temporal cortex as well as right frontal cortex in pitch memory has been confirmed by brain imaging studies.

Neurophysiological Approaches

In parallel to the left hemisphere asymmetry observed for language processing, a right hemisphere asymmetry has been suggested for music processing. Recent research allows further qualifying this approach and, more generally, has described bilateral activation networks implied in music processing (i.e., becoming more extended, the more complex the musical materials and tasks are). One of the proposed hypotheses concerns the importance of the auditory cortex in low-level perceptual processing, with the right auditory cortex allowing for fine-grained pitch processing (i.e., pitch height, pitch directions) and the left auditory cortex being involved in the processing of rapid temporal changes. Besides temporal regions, frontal regions (i.e., inferior frontal cortex, dorsolateral frontal areas) become involved in the processing of pitch patterns (e.g., melodies) and for tasks with working-memory aspects (e.g., comparing tones or melodies). For more complex tasks or materials, the parietal cortex also becomes activated, creating a network with frontal, temporal, and parietal components that is similar to neural circuits underlying multiple forms of working memory or attention-demanding activities. Musical imagery occurs when music is internally replayed by imagining it. This musical imagery results in activating auditory regions and other cortical regions involved in the perception of externally presented musical stimuli. This outcome replicates in audition previously observed brain activation patterns for visual imagery. Neurophysiological markers have been detected when listeners are exposed to musical sequences containing deviant musical events that violate expectations. Some of these markers (i.e., the evoked potential P600, a positivity starting 600 msec after the violation onset) have also been observed for language processing: the amplitude of the marker increases with increased difficulty of syntactic integration. In contrast to perception and performance of music, much less is known about cortical networks for emotional processing of music. Preliminary results suggest that there are wide networks, including limbic and sensory areas, with some overlapping networks involved in general emotional processing. Finally, music represents an opportunity to investigate brain plasticity, notably the influence of musical training on brain structures. Extensive practice with an instrument leads to neuroplastic changes in motor cortex. Recent studies have also started to investigate the extent to which increased exposure to particular sounds leads to sensory changes in the auditory cortex.

See Also the Following Articles

Behavioral Psychology • Cognitive Maps • Cognitive Psychology • Learning and Memory

Further Reading

Deutsch, D. (ed.) (1999). *The Psychology of Music*, 2nd Ed. Academic Press, San Diego, CA.

Dowling, W. J., and Harwood, D. L. (1986). *Music Cognition*. Academic Press, Orlando, FL.

Francès, R. (1958). *La Perception de la Musique*. Vrin, Paris. [*The Perception of Music*, W. J. Dowling, trans. (1988). Erlbaum, Hillsdale, NJ.]

Griffith, N., and Todd, P. (eds.) (1999). *Musical Network*. MIT Press, Cambridge.

Juslin, P. N., and Sloboda, J. A. (eds.) (2001). *Music and Emotion: Theory and Research*. Oxford University Press, New York.

Krumhansl, C. L. (1990). *Cognitive Foundations of Musical Pitch*. Oxford University Press, Oxford.

Lerdahl, F. (2001). *Tonal Pitch Space*. Oxford University Press, Oxford.

Lerdahl, F., and Jackendoff, R. (1983). *A Generative Theory of Tonal Music*. MIT Press, Cambridge, MA.

McAdams, S., and Bigand, E. (1993). *Thinking in Sound*. Claredon Press, Oxford.

Meyer, L. B. (1956). *Emotion and Meaning in Music*. University of Chicago Press, Chicago, IL.

Parncutt, R. (1989). *Harmony: A Psychoacoustical Approach*. Springer, Berlin.

Peretz, I., and Zatorre, R. J. (eds.) (2003). *The Cognitive Neuroscience of Music*. Oxford University Press, Oxford.

Pineau, M., and Tillmann, B. (2001). *Percevoir la Musique: Une Activité Cognitive*. L'Harmattan, Paris.

Sloboda, J. A. (1988). *Generative Processes in Music: Psychology of Performance, Improvisation and Composition*. Oxford University Press, London.

Tillmann, B., Bharucha, J. J., and Bigand, E. (2001). Implicit learning of regularities in Western tonal music by self-organization. In *Proceedings of the Sixth Neural Computation and Psychology Workshop: Evolution, Learning, and Development*, pp. 175–184. Springer Verlag, London.

Todd, P., and Loy, G. (eds.) (1991). *Music and Connectionism*. MIT Press, Cambridge, MA.

National Crime Victimization Surveys

Janet L. Lauritsen
University of Missouri, St. Louis, St. Louis, Missouri, USA

Shannan Catalano
Bureau of Justice Statistics, Washington D.C., USA

Glossary

bounding A method for reducing the duplicate reporting of victimizations across repeated interviews. Information from past interviews are used as a reference point or bounding period. If during subsequent interviews a respondent reports a similar victimization experience, the interviewer is able to ascertain whether the current event has been previously reported.

household-based survey A survey in which households are sampled and interviews are conducted with all eligible persons within each household.

nonsampling error The extent to which an estimate of victimization may not represent the true victimization because of errors other than those associated with probability sampling. Examples include question wording, interviewer or coding mistakes, respondent willingness to report crime events, or memory and recall error.

panel rotation A method of implementing the victimization survey to increase efficiency and reliability. The full sample of households consists of six groups, and each group or panel is interviewed once every six months. Interviews are administered to each panel at the beginning of every month. Because interviews are administered continuously on a monthly basis, a panel of newly sampled households is rotated into the full sample each month as an old panel is rotated out of the full sample.

PSU Primary sampling units (PSU) are composed of large metropolitan areas or counties and groups of counties across the United States. PSUs are chosen during the first stage of the sampling process to ensure that selected households are representative of the nation as a whole.

sampling error The extent to which a sample estimate of victimization may not represent the true victimization rate because of error associated with the process of probability sampling.

self-response method A data collection technique in which survey respondents are asked to disclose information regarding their personal victimization experiences.

time in sample bias The error associated with the length of participation in a study. Research has shown that lower victimization rates are associated with increased length of participation (i.e., number of prior interviews).

victimization rate The number of crimes committed against a household or person divided by the total number of households or persons. Household victimization includes crimes of burglary, motor vehicle theft, and other thefts from the household, while personal victimization includes nonlethal violence against persons (i.e., assault, robbery, and rape and sexual assault) and thefts from persons (i.e., purse-snatching and pocket-picking).

"The National Crime Victimization Surveys" describes the methodological features of the nation's only nationally representative, on-going survey designed to measure the extent, nature, and consequences of crime in the United States.

Introduction

Origin and Purpose of the National Crime Victimization Surveys

The National Crime Victimization Survey (NCVS) and its precursor, the National Crime Survey (NCS) began in 1972 as a result of recommendations from the President's Commission on Law Enforcement and the Administration of Justice. The 1967 Commission Report highlighted the importance of having information on crime and its consequences that was independent of police recording practices and available on an on-going basis so that changes in crime rates could be reliably estimated. Prior to the NCS, Uniform Crime Reports (UCR) were the only national source of data on crime and victimization. The NCS was developed to complement the information available in police records by including crimes not reported or recorded by the police. To help inform public policy, greater detail about criminal victimization also was desired, hence the survey contains a wide range of information about crime including weapon use, victim–offender relationships, the extent of injury and property loss, and the reasons for reporting or not reporting crime to the police.

History of the Survey

The Law Enforcement and Administration Association (LEAA) and the Census Bureau developed the methodology for the NCS based on an extensive research program. This research was informed by the Census Bureau's expertise in sampling and survey methodology, a series of reverse record-check studies to test questionnaires and procedures among known crime victims, and supplements to the Quarterly Housing Survey to test procedures among random samples of the population. In July 1972, the National Crime Survey began, consisting of three components: the National Crime Panel, the Commercial Victimization Survey, and an additional 26-city victimization survey. Of these three components, the nationally representative household survey (the NCP) continued and became known as the NCS.

Significant changes to the NCS occurred following an evaluation of the survey by the National Academy of Sciences. The NAS report recommended a series of modifications including better use of screening questions to encourage greater reporting to interviewers as well as additional items to improve understanding of crime and its consequences. The NAS report also advocated a program of on-going methodological research and more timely and user-friendly data and product dissemination.

The evaluations and implementation of these recommendations were performed by a consortium of experts in social science, survey methodology, and statistics and were managed by the Bureau of Social Science Research. Following lengthy review, the consortium proposed that survey modifications be implemented in two phases. In 1986, the first of these changes (known as "near-term" changes) were implemented. Alterations that were unlikely to affect overall crime rates were included at this time so that the continuity of ongoing annual reports could be preserved. The second phase of changes (known as "long-term" changes) were phased into the survey beginning in 1992. This phase-in of the new questionnaire was developed so that changes associated with instrumentation could be assessed independently from temporal changes in crime.

These long-term changes included a more thorough screening section to better stimulate victim recall of events, improved screening to reduce the effects of subjective interpretations of events, and more detailed questions regarding the characteristics and consequences of victimization. Research suggested that victims were less likely to recall victimization incidents or view events as criminal when either the victim knew the offender or when victimization occurred on a regular basis. To better capture events of this type, the redesigned survey incorporated additional prompts to improve the measurement of nonstranger crimes, rape and sexual assault, and domestic violence. In addition, vandalism victimization was added to the survey.

The redesigned interview procedures resulted in significantly higher victimization rates for simple and aggravated assault, rape, household burglary, and theft, but produced no significant changes for robbery, personal theft, or motor vehicle theft. Increased reporting also was somewhat larger for nonstranger crimes, attempted crimes, and crimes not reported to the police. The redesigned interview increased crime reporting for all sociodemographic groups, although the increases were somewhat greater for whites and other racial groups than for blacks, for higher-income households than for lower-income groups, and for middle-aged persons than for younger or older respondents. The National Crime Survey was officially renamed the National Crime Victimization Survey to indicate changes in the interview.

Article Overview

A complete review of the methodological characteristics of the NCVS and the measurement of crime is beyond the scope of this paper. The remainder of this article describes the most important features of the NCVS, including the sample and rotation design, method of administration and interview form, questionnaire content and special supplements, sources of error, and research uses. Emphasis is placed on the characteristics of the current survey.

Sample and Interview Administration

The NCVS is a household-based survey. A random sample of households is generated through a multistage stratified sampling procedure designed to produce a representative sample of all households and individuals 12 years of age and older in the United States. Households are used as the unit of analysis in estimations of household crime (e.g., burglary), and persons are used as the unit of analysis in estimations of personal crimes (e.g., assault). The Census Bureau conducts the sampling procedure and administers the survey for the Bureau of Justice Statistics.

Drawing the Sample

The sample is generated in two stages. During the first stage, primary sampling units (PSUs) are designated to reflect metropolitan areas, counties, and groups of counties. Larger PSUs (reflecting metropolitan areas) are termed self-representing (SR) and are automatically included in the sample. Smaller PSUs (non-self-representing or NSR PSUs) are grouped together in similar strata based on known Census geographic and demographic characteristics. From the NSR PSUs, sample PSUs are selected by probability proportionate to population size.

In the second stage of sampling, the SR PSUs and selected NSR PSUs are divided into sampling frames known as unit, area, permit, and group quarters. Clustered subsamples of approximately four housing units are then selected from each frame. The selection of household addresses differs for each frame, but is derived from Census information for each PSU. Addresses for unit and group quarter frames are generated from the most recent census and sample blocks are used to generate address listings for the area frame. Building permit data are used to generate addresses within the permit frame, ensuring that new housing units not included in the prior census are captured in the sample. This sampling procedure is designed to produce reliable national estimates of criminal victimization and not state or local estimates.

The importance of using a household-based sampling procedure becomes apparent when compared to other sampling procedures such as random digit dialing (RDD). Research has shown that up to 20% of poor households are without telephone service and that poverty rates are correlated with crime rates. By using a household-based sampling strategy, the NCVS is less likely to produce biased victimization rates. In addition, the Census Bureau is renowned for producing very high survey participation rates. The household and person participation rates for the NCVS consistently range from 90% to 95%, while RDD surveys and surveys conducted by other organizations tend to produce substantially lower rates.

Reliable estimates of criminal victimization on an annual basis require very large samples. The NCS sample originally included approximately 60,000 households. However, budget constraints have forced declines in sample size. In 2001, the NCVS sample included about 44,000 households. This decline has implications for statistical estimation, especially for the most rare forms of victimization such as rape. For such crime types, standard errors are larger and thus it is more difficult to detect significant annual changes or subgroup differences.

Interview Procedure

The NCVS uses the self-response method. This means that respondents are asked to disclose information about their victimization experiences. The probability-based sample makes it possible to produce estimates for the population of persons ages 12 and older in the United States. The sample excludes crimes against children younger than age 12, persons without a permanent residence, crew members of merchant vessels, armed forces personnel living in military barracks, institutionalized persons, and businesses or organizations.

Following selection for the sample and notification by mail from the Census Bureau, the NCVS interviewer contacts the household, obtains consent to participate, and conducts the first set of interviews in person. Households selected for the sample are retained for three years, and each person (age 12 and older) in the household is interviewed once every six months about their victimization experiences during the preceding six months. The NAS evaluation suggested a combination of in-person interviews coupled with telephone interviews to balance efficiency, cost and rapport. During early years of the survey, the first, third, fifth, and seventh interview were conducted in person. Currently, only the first interview is conducted in person and the second through seventh interviews are administered by telephone. Exceptions are made if the respondent insists on in-person interviews. The use of Computer-Assisted Telephone Interviewing (CATI) from centralized facilities has increased over time as well.

The NCVS measures experiences with crime in two ways, either as a household or person victimization. One member of the household is surveyed regarding crimes against the household, and all members (age 12 and older) are surveyed regarding personal victimization. The questionnaire uses two components, an initial screening tool administered to all respondents and an incident form designed to collect information and details regarding any events mentioned during the screening portion of the survey. Once household victimization screening is recorded from the head-of-household designate, respondents are screened and interviewed about personal victimization experiences.

Panel Rotation

The NCVS uses a rotating panel design to increase the efficiency of the interviewing process. Sample households are divided into six rotation groups. Each rotation group is interviewed a total of seven times with interviews taking place at the beginning of each month for households in that month's panel. Within each rotation group there are six panels, thus allowing for one-sixth of the rotation group to be interviewed each month. For instance, households in the first panel are interviewed in January and July, those in the second panel are interviewed in February and August, etc. This framework ensures that the sample is balanced, thus minimizing problems in estimating year-to-year changes by reducing "time in sample bias." This procedure also helps to ensure that victimization estimates are not confounded with seasonal differences in crime found to exist in many areas of the country. Once a household panel has completed seven interviews, a new household panel is selected and rotated into the sample to replace the exiting panel. An exception occurs when respondents move out of the household. In this instance, the new residents become part of the sample and complete the remaining number of interviews assigned to the household.

Bounding

An important feature of the NCVS is that bounding is used to limit recall error. Extensive research on survey methodology has shown that respondents often misplace the occurrence of events in time. To reduce this type of error, data from previous household and person interviews are used to "bound" subsequent reports of victimization. For example, if a respondent reports a robbery in the first interview and again in the second interview, the interviewer verifies that these are indeed two separate events. Because unbounded interviews produce estimates of crime that are significantly higher than bounded interviews, the first household interview is excluded from victimization estimates. Bounding however, is tied to the household rotation. Therefore, first-time interviews with new residents in an ongoing household rotation are not bounded and are included in victimization estimates.

Survey Content

Types of Crime Covered

NCVS crime coverage includes both violent and property crimes associated with households and individual victims. Household property crimes include attempted and completed burglary, motor vehicle theft, and household theft (e.g., theft from the yard). Personal crimes (or crimes against individuals) include attempted and completed violent crimes of rape, sexual assault, robbery, aggravated and simple assault, and personal thefts (such as purse snatching). Homicide is excluded due to the victim-based nature of the survey. Arson is excluded as well. Crimes against children under age 12 are not measured because the Census Bureau has determined that the instrument is not valid for younger respondents. The NCVS is able to measure crime more broadly than the UCR because incidents not reported to police are included.

The determination of whether an event is a crime and if so, the type of crime, is not made during the interview. Rather, the characteristics of each reported event are detailed during the interview. Final classification of the crime type occurs during data processing and is based on information provided in the incident report. This is done to minimize definitional variations and to ensure that the use of legal terms such as burglary or robbery matches definitions used by the police and the UCR. Additionally, events are classified according to the most serious aspect of the victimization. For example, if a respondent reports that they were hit (assaulted) and had something taken from them by the use of force (robbed) during the same event, a "hierarchy rule" is applied and the event is classified as a robbery. Specific victimization definitions can be found in Bureau of Justice Statistics (BJS) victimization reports.

Household and Person Characteristics

Characteristics of the household are obtained from the interviewer and from the designated household respondent. Prior to beginning the interview, the interviewer fills out a "control card" that contains demographic information on the household and its members. This information is subsequently transcribed onto the questionnaires. The interviewer records information relevant to the conditions of the interview such as type of living quarters, telephone availability, use of proxy respondents (e.g., for those with difficulty communicating), presence of others during the interview, and reasons for any noninterviews with household members. Information on the control card regarding household characteristics obtained from the household respondent include number of persons in the household, changes in composition since the last interview, income, length of residence, number of times moved in the past five years and presence of a home business. Person characteristics for members of the household include age, sex, race, Hispanic origin, marital status, educational attainment, armed forces membership, employment status and type of job, and relationship to head-of-household.

Incident Characteristics

Details about each incident are gathered after the respondent completes the personal screening questions. For each incident, respondents are asked to provide detail on the time and location of the event and whether the incident was reported to the police by the respondent or some other person. Reasons for reporting or not reporting to police are obtained, as are police actions for events reported. For incidents involving face-to-face contact between the victim and the offender (e.g., most violent crimes), the respondent is asked whether anyone else was present during the incident, the number of offenders involved, actions taken by the offender during the incident, the presence of weapons, the level of injury, whether medical care was received, whether time was lost from work, actions by the victim during the incident and the perceived result of those actions. The respondent also provides the sex, race, and approximate age of the offender, whether the offender appeared to be under the influence of drugs or alcohol, and the victim's relationship to the offender. For property crime incidents (which typically do not involve face-to-face contact), the respondent reports the type and value of property stolen or damaged, whether property was recovered or repaired, and who, if anyone paid for the costs of repair or replacement.

Series Incidents

For some victims, experience with crime is extensive. If the victim is able to describe each incident in sufficient detail, incident characteristics are gathered for each event. However, in cases where the victim reports six or more similar events *and* is unable to distinguish these events, incident data are gathered only for the most recent event. In these cases, the experience is defined as a "series" victimization. Although incident information for the most recent event is gathered, series victimizations are excluded from annual rate estimates because their impact on crime rates is sensitive to counting rule assumptions.

Recent Content Additions

Because of the strength of the NCVS sampling strategy, the survey provides a platform for assessing changing concerns about crime and justice. Various social and political initiatives have resulted in occasional survey supplements as well as additional questions about criminal victimization. Supplements are additional sets of questions that are asked of respondents following completion of the main survey. Recent supplements have addressed school crime experiences among 12- to 18-year-olds, and the nature of public contact with the police outside of crime reporting (e.g., traffic stop information) to persons age 16 and over. Federal crime initiatives have prompted the addition of questions about possible hate crime victimization, personal computer crime victimization, and victimization among the physically and developmentally disabled.

Sources of Error

All sample surveys contain two sources of error—that associated with sampling and that due to other methodological features of the survey, such as nonparticipation, question wording, and the recall tasks that the respondent must accomplish. The former is known as sampling error, while the latter is known as nonsampling error.

Sampling Error

The amount of error associated with random sampling is a function of sample size and the relative rarity of the event under investigation. The amount of this error is estimable and is known as the standard error. In published reports, confidence intervals are included with victimization estimates so that readers can know, for example, whether changes across time or differences across subgroups are statistically significant. The parameters necessary for calculating standard errors can be found in BJS reports.

Nonsampling Error

The error associated with the tasks of the survey is difficult to measure with great precision, but it can be minimized with careful research on the properties of the survey. As noted earlier, the NCS and NCVS items have undergone extensive research to minimize respondent errors, as well as interviewer and data processing errors. When new items or supplements are developed for the survey, they undergo a series of evaluations before they are introduced in the field. These evaluations include cognitive testing and pretesting with specially selected samples and random samples.

Research Uses

Information obtained from the interviews have been used in numerous ways, the most common of which are annual reports on victimization by BJS statisticians that are often cited in the popular press. These reports facilitate and inform public policy debate on a variety of issues such as violence against women, injury and financial costs associated with crime, school crime, and race and contact with the police. The data also have been cited in support of legislation and in various court cases. BJS reports are available at their website (www.ojp.usdoj.gov/bjs). The most commonly produced reports feature estimates of various crime types and the different victimization experiences of selected groups (such as women, teenagers, the elderly). BJS also uses NCVS data to produce reports on special topics such as intimate partner violence, reporting crime to the police, violence at schools, and the costs of crime.

Academic researchers typically use the data to study how victimization risk and reporting to police vary across subgroups and crime types, and how broader changes in society are related to changes in crime. Crime estimates from the NCVS also have been compared to police estimates of crime to understand how police recording practices have changed over time. In addition, the data have been used to study how the outcomes of events (such as the escalation of violence, injury) are related to victim, offender, or third party actions. Public use versions of the NCVS data may be accessed through the National Archive of Criminal Justice Data (NACJD) (www.icpsr.umich.edu/NACJD/index). A link to the NACJD is also accessible through the BJS homepage under the "Dataset and Codebooks" option. As the only source of nationally representative data on victimization, the NCVS data provide an ongoing wealth of information that may be used to inform public policy about crime and its consequences.

See Also the Following Articles

Criminal Justice Records • Criminology • Experiments, Criminology • Survey Design • Surveys • Total Survey Error

Further Reading

Biderman, A., and Lynch, J. (1991). *Understanding Crime Incidence Statistics: Why the UCR Diverges from the NCS.* Springer-Verlag, New York.

Bureau of Justice Statistics (2003). *Criminal Victimization in the United States, Statistical Tables.* U.S. Department of Justice, Washington, DC (www.usdoj.gov/bjs/abstract/cvusst.htm).

Hindelang, M., Gottfredson, M., and Garofalo, J. (1978). *Victims of Personal Crime: An Empirical Foundation for a Theory of Personal Victimization.* Ballinger, Cambridge.

Kindermann, C., Lynch, J., and Cantor, D. (1997). *Effects of the Redesign on Victimization Estimates.* BJS Technical Report NCJ 164381. U.S. Department of Justice, Washington, DC.

Penick, B., and Owens, M. (eds.) (1976). *Surveying Crime. A Report of the Panel for the Evaluation of Crime Surveys.* Washington National Academy of Science, Washington, DC.

President's Commission. (1967). *Task Force Report: Crime and Its Impact: An Assessment.* President's Commission on Law Enforcement and the Administration of Justice. Washington, DC. USGPO.

Skogan, W. (1976). Crime and crime rates. In *Sample Surveys of the Victims of Crime* (W. Skogan, ed.), 1st Ed., pp. 105–119. Ballinger, Cambridge.

Sparks, R. F. (1981). Surveys of victimization: An optimistic assessment. In *Crime and Justice An Annual Review of Research* (M. Tonry and N. Morris, eds.), 1st Ed., pp. 1–60. University of Chicago Press, Chicago.

Tourangeau, R., and McNeely, M. E. (2003). Measuring crime and crime victimization: Methodological issues. In *Measurement Issues in Criminal Justice Research: Workshop Summary* (J. V. Pepper and C. V. Petrie, eds.), pp. 10–42. The National Academies Press, Washington, DC.

National Education Longitudinal Survey of 1988 (NELS:88)

Laurie A. Drapela

Washington State University, Vancouver, Washington, USA

Glossary

base-year ineligible students Students who were excluded from the NELS:88 base-year study participation due to a language barrier or a mental or physical disability.

base-year ineligibles study A study of the base-year ineligible students at the first and second follow-ups of NELS:88 (1990 and 1992).

ceiling effect The effect produced when variation on the NELS:88 cognitive tests is artificially constrained among high-ability examinees due to an insufficient number of difficult questions.

cross-sectional survey A survey design in which data are collected at a single point in time from a cross section of respondents representing a larger population.

Data Analysis System (DAS) A Windows software application providing public access to NCES survey data. Users can generate tables of percentages, means, standard errors, and correlation coefficients for survey items in NELS:88.

design effect (DEFF) A measure of sample efficiency; a design effect is the variance of an estimate divided by the variance of the estimate that would have occurred if a sample of the same size had been selected using simple random sampling.

electronic codebook (ECB) A graphical user interface (GUI) tool listing all the variables, weights, and flags for each unit of analysis at each wave of the data for the particular study period.

flags Dichotomous indicators that isolate respondents based on the questionnaire they completed and/or their participation in a particular wave or waves of NELS:88.

floor effect The effect produced when variation on the NELS:88 cognitive tests is artificially constrained among low-ability examinees, due to an abundance of questions that exceed their abilities.

longitudinal panel sample Survey designs in which the same data are collected from the same respondents across multiple time periods.

National Center for Education Statistics (NCES) The federal sponsoring agency for the longitudinal high school studies, including NELS:88.

sample freshening A sampling technique designed to increase the representativeness of NELS:88 by adding out-of-sequence students to the data file.

survey package Software packages, such as SUDAAN, STATA, and HLM, that take into account complex sampling designs when calculating standard errors for parameter estimates.

waves Points in time at which data were collected for the study; also called follow-ups. Currently, NELS:88 contains five waves of data; a base-year sample (1988) and four follow-up periods (1990, 1992, 1994, and 2000).

weights Factors representing the sampling design that parameter estimates are multiplied by. Typically, sampling weights are used to adjust parameter estimates for the oversampling of certain demographic groups and to adjust items for nonresponse. In NELS:88, Asians, Latinos, and private schools are oversampled.

The National Center for Education Statistics (NCES) is mandated by Congress to conduct longitudinal research on educational outcomes in the United States. The National Education Longitudinal Survey of 1988 (NELS:88, or NELS) is one of three panel studies of students conducted by the NCES to fulfill this mandate. To that end, NELS:88 is designed to measure the determinants of education-related outcomes such as academic achievement, successful transition to secondary and postsecondary institutions, participation in the workforce, and dropping out of high school. The survey also collects data on other types of outcomes for adolescents and young adults. For example, NELS:88 has been used to study the predictors of adolescent deviance (e.g., truancy and teen pregnancy) and delinquency (e.g., fighting, drug use, being arrested, and being detained in a juvenile facility). NELS:88 collects data from students, parents, teachers, and school administrators at several points in time to model these outcomes. This entry describes the structure and analytic populations available in NELS:88 and describes how it has been used to study key constructs in social science research.

Structure of the National Education Longitudinal Survey of 1988

Units of Analysis and Waves of the Data

The National Education Longitudinal Survey of 1988 (NELS:88, or NELS) contains data for four units of analysis: students, parents, teachers, and school administrators (schools). The baseline cohort consisted of 24,599 eighth-graders attending mainstream public and private schools in the United States during 1988. (Bureau of Indian Affairs schools were excluded from the study.) To date, four follow-ups have occurred: 1990, 1992, 1994, and 2000. This set of five waves is typically referred to by NELS:88 users as the base year (BY) and first through fourth follow-ups (F1–F4).

All data collected for teachers, parents, and schools are linked to the students via the students' identification numbers. This enables researchers to model the effects of home, classroom, and/or school environments on the types of student outcomes. These types of analyses typically involve the first three waves of the data (collected in 1988, 1990, and 1992) because most students in the study were attending junior high and high school during this time period. Factors affecting post–secondary school outcomes such as college/university attendance, labor force participation, and marital status typically involve the third and fourth follow-ups of NELS:88 (collected in 1994 and 2000).

The structure of NELS:88 permits both longitudinal and cross-sectional analyses. In terms of its longitudinal capabilities, NELS:88 contains four follow-ups of an initial baseline cohort of 24,599 eighth-graders. These data provide a rich opportunity to model both scholastic and nonscholastic changes among adolescents and young adults over a 12-year period (1988–2000). NELS:88 can also be used to conduct cross-sectional analyses at each wave of the data. In 1990 and 1992, respondents were added to the data file to enhance grade-specific cross-sectional analyses, a process called sample freshening. It increases the representativeness of cross-sectional analyses by adding students to the data file who did not have a chance to be selected into prior rounds of the study. In 1990, the NCES added respondents to NELS:88 who were in the tenth grade in 1990 but not in the eighth grade in the United States in 1988. Similarly, in 1992, the NCES added respondents who were in the twelfth grade but did not attend tenth grade in the United States in 1990 and did not attend eighth grade in the United States in 1988. The addition of freshened students to the first and second follow-ups also permits grade-specific trend comparisons between NELS:88 respondents and the two other NCES longitudinal high school studies: the National Longitudinal High School Class of 1972 (NLS-72) and High School and Beyond (HS&B).

Articulating Analytic Populations for Study in the National Education Longitudinal Survey of 1988: Samples, Scope of Analyses, Flags, and Weights

NELS:88 contains multiple waves of data for multiple units of analysis measured at five points in time (see Table I for a list). Moreover, the time intervals between waves of the data vary from 2 to 6 years, complicating the measurement of longitudinal processes. This section provides a brief description of the types of concepts measured at each wave of the data for each unit of analysis and defines the term analytic population. It further describes the use of questionnaire flags for selecting study participants as well as the use of sampling weights and survey packages to calculate valid parameter estimates.

At the base year, first, and second follow-ups (1988, 1990, and 1992), students were surveyed about their school experiences (e.g., school climate between students and teachers), school activities (extracurricular activities), attitudes concerning pro-conformity and pro-delinquent activities, educational expectations, career aspirations, their family lives, locus-of-control (self-esteem), and language proficiency. There was particular attention devoted to the effect of speaking English as a second language on both the base-year and second follow-up student surveys.

Parent surveys are only available for the base year (1988) and second follow-up (1992) of NELS:88. These questionnaires ask one parent to provide information about his or her relationship to the child, his or her educational expectations for the child, his or her occupation and educational background, the educational tools available in the home for the child, his or her involvement with the school and the child's education (e.g., tutoring), and the family's financial preparation for college.

Teacher surveys are available for the first three waves of the data. Generally speaking, the teacher surveys measure student variables (e.g., whether they have met with the parents of the NELS:88 student in their classes, the quality of the student's work, and the ability grouping of

Table I Available Data in NELS:88[a]

Unit of analysis	Base year, 1988	Follow-up: First follow-up, 1990	Second follow-up, 1992	Third follow-up, 1994	Fourth follow-up, 2000
Student	Survey Cognitive test	Survey Cognitive test	Survey Cognitive test High school transcript	Survey	Survey Post–secondary school transcript
Dropout		Survey	Survey	Survey	Survey
Teacher	Survey	Survey	Survey		
Parent	Survey		Survey		
School administrator	Survey	Survey	Survey		
Other		High school effectiveness study Base year ineligibles study	High school effectiveness study		

[a] *Source:* National Longitudin Education Study of 1988 Base Year to Fourth Follow-Up Data File User's Manual.

the student); classroom variables (e.g., the amount of control they have over selecting texts and structuring the curriculum and the topics taught in their subject area); and the teachers' characteristics (e.g., instructor demographics, training, and credentials). No more than two of the students' teachers completed questionnaires for the base year and first follow-up; only one teacher completed a questionnaire at the second follow-up.

Finally, school administrator surveys are also available at the first three waves of data collection. These surveys contain information about the school characteristics, school services for students (e.g., from computer laboratories to birth control classes), school policies on parental notification for student infractions, faculty qualifications, and graduation requirements.

The analytic populations in NELS:88 are those study populations created by using sample weights and questionnaire flags. Generally speaking, weighting is used to compensate for unequal probabilities of selection into the sample and/or to adjust parameter estimates for nonresponse to survey items. NELS:88 weights are designed to correct for both types of bias. Moreover, the type of weight used determines the scope of an analysis (whether it is cross-sectional or longitudinal). Questionnaire flags isolate those respondents who completed a particular survey (e.g., student, parent, teacher, school administrator, or dropout) at a particular round (or rounds) of the study.

For example, if a researcher wanted to estimate the effects of student reports of school climate on their participation in school-based extracurricular activities (e.g., science club, cheerleading, and sports), such a question could be evaluated with longitudinal and cross-sectional analyses. A cross-sectional investigation of this question at the base year (1988) would require both the use of a questionnaire flag and a questionnaire weight to select the cases for inclusion into the study. In this case, the eighth-grade cross-sectional questionnaire flag would select the appropriate number of cases for the analysis (e.g., BYQFLG (1) = 24,599). This flag, when used in combination with its respective questionnaire weight (BYQWT > 0), produces the appropriate parameter estimates for the analytic populations under study—a nationally representative sample of 1988 eighth graders in the United States.

If we want to investigate the longitudinal effect of tenth-grade assessments of school climate on twelfth-grade participation in school-based extracurricular activities, the first and second follow-ups can be used to conduct the analysis. In this case, the panel flag for the 1990 tenth-graders in 1992 (F2F1PNFL = 2) should be selected to ensure that all 16,749 respondents who completed both questionnaires at both follow-ups are included in the study. The panel weight (F2F1PNWT) should be used to ensure representative analyses for the analytic population—the panel sample of 1990 tenth-graders in 1992. (A table of study populations, flags, and weights can be found in the 1994 study by Ingels, Dowd, Stipe, Baldridge, Bartot, Frankel, and Quinn.)

The mechanical dimensions of using flags and weights to isolate appropriate populations of interest are discussed at length in the NELS:88 user's manuals. However, they take on an additional significance among researchers who use NELS:88 to measure social scientific processes. With four units of analysis over five waves of data, the number of cases selected from NELS:88 for study varies widely, depending on the research question. The number of respondents isolated by the sample flags serves as a benchmark, communicating to other researchers that the appropriate flags and weights are being used to conduct the analysis. If the number of respondents in a researcher's working data file differs from that articulated in the user's manual, researchers are encouraged to explain the relationship between their study's *N* and the sample *N* generated by NELS:88 sample flags.

Muller's 1995 study of base-year maternal labor force participation on first follow-up student mathematics achievement serves an example. After a brief discussion of the NELS:88 study objectives and sampling strategy, the first follow-up panel sample is articulated as the appropriate sample for the study. According to the data documentation, 17,424 students participated in the first follow-up panel sample. Muller articulates additional criteria for selection into her study, noting that students are included in the analyses only if their mothers' employment status was available and the student's natural mother is present in the home. She restricts her analyses to only those respondents who have panel data, and she further notes that "Native Americans were also excluded, making a sample size of 13,381 from the panel sample of 17,424."

NELS:88 users also should take its multistage cluster sampling design into account when generating parameter estimates. Statistical packages assuming simple random sampling can generate biased parameter estimates when used with NELS:88 or other data collected with complex sampling designs. Variances and standard errors of parameter estimates tend to be smaller under simple random sampling than complex sampling designs; thus, researchers are at increased risk of committing a Type I error when interpreting NELS:88 results with software assuming a simple random sample.

If a statistical package must be used, design effects should be employed to ensure the accurate calculation of sample variances. The NCES computed design effects for a subset of variables in the base year and first through third follow-ups of NELS:88. Analysts may calculate design effects for the remaining variables using the Data Analysis System (DAS). The fourth follow-up of NELS:88 (2000) is the only wave of the data for which the NCES calculated design effects for every variable in the analysis.

Users of statistical packages may employ the design effects and weights to calculate a new case weight that better accommodates complex sampling designs. The new weight is a product of the inverse of the design effect and the rescaled case weight: $NEWWGT = (1/DEFF)^* [F2QWT_i/(\sum F2QWT_i/N)]$. This procedure approximates the effect of the sample design, but is not precisely comparable to estimates obtained with survey packages. Nonetheless, it is a more accurate method of using statistical packages with cluster or other less-efficient sampling designs than assuming the data were collected with a simple random sample.

Survey packages such as SUDAAN, STATA, and HLM account for complex sampling designs when calculating sample variances and standard errors. Although these types of packages may be more expensive to obtain and challenging to learn, the researcher gains greater accuracy of parameter estimates, increased validity of study results, and greater flexibility in the selection of variables for analysis.

What Can the National Education Longitudinal Survey of 1988 Measure? A Brief Discussion of Research on Content Areas in the Survey

Because of its broad scope, multiple units of analysis, and multiple waves of data, NELS:88 is ideal for researching scholastic and nonscholastic outcomes among adolescents and young adults. A comprehensive literature review of all studies using NELS:88 is beyond the scope of this entry; this section provides a brief description of some of the more popular content areas in the data set. It also provides examples of studies measuring such concepts.

Academic Achievement

In light of its congressional mandate to track educational progress among American primary and secondary school students, assessing academic achievement is a critical function of NELS:88. Cognitive tests were developed by the Educational Testing Service (ETS) and covered four subject areas: reading comprehension, mathematics, science, and social studies (history, citizenship, and geography). Cognitive tests were administered at the first three waves of data (1988, 1990, and 1992). These multiple measures of achievement allow researchers to measure gains (or losses) in academic achievement among a cohort of students as they made the transition from junior high school to high school.

The ETS designed one form for each of the four base-year cognitive test areas and six forms per subject area for the 1990 and 1992 testing rounds. The difficulty level of the math and reading tests varied on each of the six follow-up test forms. Respondents' scores from the prior wave of testing determined the difficulty level of the reading and math tests at later waves of the study. Thus, if a base-year student scored in the top 10% of students on the 1988 mathematics achievement test, the level of difficulty on his or her 1990 math test would be higher than for a student who had performed at the mean level on the 1988 test. This approach is a more valid measure of the students' cognitive gains over time than a single test per subject at a fixed level of difficulty. Variation in cognitive tests can be constrained if this level of difficulty is too simple for high-ability respondents (i.e., shows a ceiling effect) and/or too challenging for low-ability students (i.e., shows a floor effect).

Students' performances in math and science courses tend to sort them into precollege and noncollege tracks. For this reason, many NELS:88 studies focus on both micro- and macro-level processes that affect mathematics and science achievement. For example, the 1995 micro-level analysis by Muller explored the effect of maternal employment and parental involvement on students' gains in tenth-grade mathematics achievement. Parental involvement is measured using items from both the parent survey (e.g., checking homework, restricting television on weekdays, and parental participation in a parent-teacher organization) and the student surveys (e.g., self-reports of discussions about school activities and subjects, planning of high school program, discussion of college plans, and the amount of time left unsupervised after school). Muller found that although certain types of parental involvement increase math test scores between the eighth and tenth grades (e.g., restricting television and parent-teacher organization participation), students whose mothers were not employed showed significantly fewer gains in mathematics achievement than students whose mothers worked full-time (after unsupervised time after school was controlled).

Other researchers have examined the effects of macro-level processes on mathematics achievement. For example, Ainsworth examined in 2002 the effects of neighborhood-level factors affecting mathematics and science achievement. NELS:88 is ideal for this purpose because a supplemental file allows researchers to match students' zip codes to their census tract identifiers. (Note: Users must obtain a restricted user license in order to link the NELS:88 data to the census tract information.) The neighborhood characteristics under study were the proportion of high-status residents, residential stability, levels of economic deprivation, and levels of racial/ethnic heterogeneity. The proportion of high-status residents is the only one of the four neighborhood-level variables affecting math and reading achievement scores. This positive effect is strongly mediated by the amount of time the student spends on homework and the student's educational expectations.

Social Capital

Social capital is a construct frequently used by sociologists to conceptualize "benefits accruing to individuals or families by virtue of their ties with others." Generally speaking, social capital is conceptualized as the level of obligations, expectations, and trustworthiness of social structures. Put another way, the more interconnected individuals are through social ties at the family, church, and community levels, the greater the level of social capital these individuals possess. The closed nature of the network facilitates both economic and personal interactions among the individuals involved. This is due to the level of trust engendered among the members of a social network, as well as the knowledge that transgressions against any one member of the group has ramifications across critical domains of social life.

NELS:88 can measure several dimensions of social capital because it contains information about the students, their home(s), their school(s), and their neighborhood(s). (Recall from the prior section that respondents' addresses can be linked to their census tracts, allowing for measurements of neighborhood factors such as poverty and the prevalence of female-headed households.) One example is Suet-ling Pong's 1998 analysis of the effect of social capital on the relationship between family structure and academic achievement. The author uses NELS:88 to test the hypothesis that social capital, operationalized as students' reports of their parents' school involvement and social relations with other parents, can mitigate the deleterious effect of high proportions of single-parent families on school academic achievement measures (e.g., tenth-grade math and reading test scores).

These measures of social capital were available on the student surveys, not on the school administrator surveys (school surveys). In order to obtain school-level measures of these indicators of social capital, Pong aggregated them by school and then used them, along with the school administrators' estimates of the proportion of students from single-parent families, to test the mediating and conditioning effects of social capital on family structure and tenth-grade gains in achievement test scores.

She found that school-based social capital (in addition to the school's economic status) mediates the negative effect of moderate proportions of single-parent families on school academic achievement scores. The level of parental acquaintances also conditions the effect of proportions of single-parent families on school achievement test scores. Schools that were one standard deviation below the mean level of parental relations showed a negative effect of high proportions of single-parent families on reading and mathematics achievement. Schools that were one standard deviation above the mean showed that students attending schools with a predominance of students from single-parent families performed as well as or better on achievement tests than schools with a low proportion of students from single-parent homes.

Youth–Early Adult Transitions

The fourth follow-up (2000) is the most recent round of NELS:88. Approximately 12,000 cases of the original 24,599 eighth-grade cohort were retained in this wave of the study; thus, it is a 12-year panel study measuring transitions common to people in early adulthood—namely, college attendance, career development, and family formation.

Because this follow-up of the study was released in August 2002, analysts have just begun to mine its longitudinal capabilities. However, an initial report produced by the NCES assessed the effects of eighth-grade curriculum choices on postsecondary educational attainment and labor market experiences (Ingels *et al.* 2002). Factors such as high eighth-grade mathematics achievement scores, algebra, private schooling, and participation in extracurricular activities increased the likelihood of both enrolling in and completing university degrees 12 years later. Levels of postsecondary educational attainment were positively associated with job satisfaction, professional/managerial occupation, and median income levels.

The report also evaluated the relationship between eighth-grade risk factors for dropping out of high school and life-course transitions such as labor force participation, marriage, and parenthood. Eighth-grade risk factors for dropping out of high school were measured as living in a single-parent household, having neither parent complete high school, having an older sibling drop out, being home alone after school for more than 3 hours per day, having low English proficiency, and being in a low-income family (less than $15,000 total family income per year). Cohort members who had no dropout risk factors were more likely to be childless 12 years later (at age 26) than cohort members with one or more risk factors. Eighth-graders at risk for dropping out who eventually did so were more likely to be working in low-skill jobs (e.g., as laborers or mechanics), be single parents, and receive public assistance 12 years later than their counterparts who graduated from high school.

In their 1998 study, Horn, Chen, and Clifford assessed the effects of student, parent, and peer factors on the odds of 1994 college enrollment. Their study was focused on a subgroup of NELS:88 students identified during the eighth grade as being at risk for dropping out of high school. These students were at risk for dropping out if they exhibited two or more of the following: being in a family in the lowest socioeconomic quartile, living in a single-parent home, earning Cs or lower between the sixth and eighth grades, being held back a grade in school, changing schools two or more times outside of grade-appropriate transitions, and having an older sibling who dropped out. They found that students with peers who had college plans and students with parents who frequently discussed school-related matters with them had greater odds of enrolling in postsecondary education than did students without these factors. Participation in college preparation activities (e.g., financial aid and help with entrance exams) and college outreach programs also increased the odds of a student's enrolling in a university degree program.

High School Dropouts

In NELS:88, dropouts are defined two ways: (1) students who had not been in school for 4 or more consecutive weeks and who had not been absent due to accident or illness and (2) students who had been in school for less than 2 weeks after a period in which he or she had missed school for 4 or more consecutive weeks not due to accident or illness. Dropout status was double-confirmed by both the school and household reports. Dropping out of high school is typically measured along three dimensions: the proportion of students who leave school each year without completing a high school program (event rates); all of the young adults in a specified age range who have dropped out of high school (status rates); and the experiences of students who drop out of high school at various points in time (cohort rates). NELS:88 is one of the NCES data sets used to perform cohort-based analyses of high school dropouts.

Generally speaking, NCES analyses of event and status rates for high school dropout in the United States have found that high school dropout rates are highest among low-income groups, people of color (particularly Latinos and African Americans), and older adolescents (e.g., over two-thirds of event dropouts in 1998 were between the ages of 15 and 18 years old). The proportion of people dropping out of high school has fluctuated between approximately 5 and 6% since 1987.

NELS:88 permits cohort analyses of high school dropouts from the eighth to tenth grades and from the tenth to twelfth grades. Many of these studies focus on factors that significantly affect the likelihood of dropping out of high school. For example, in their 2001 analysis of tenth- to twelfth-grade dropouts, Croninger and Lee found that greater amounts of teacher-centered social capital (operationalized as students' perceptions of teacher-based support of their education and teachers' reports of both school and personal guidance given to students) significantly decreases the probability of a student's leaving high school between the tenth and twelfth grades. This was particularly the case for students with high levels of academic risk (poor school performance) and high levels of social risk (e.g., minority status or single-parent household). High levels of teacher-centered social capital reduced the probability of dropping out of high school by one-half for these students.

Finally, because NELS:88 began data collection with eighth graders, it was able to capture people who dropped out of school before the tenth grade (a population not included in the HS&B data set). One NELS:88 analysis of this group found that although both school and family problems affected dropping out of middle school, students attending lower SES middle schools with fair discipline policies and in non-Catholic religious schools had lower odds of dropout than students in the full sample of schools.

Adolescent Delinquency and Deviance

NELS:88 contains several measures of adolescent delinquency and deviance, most of which are concentrated in the first and second follow-ups (1990 and1992). Base-year measures of law-violating behavior are restricted to one indicator asking the respondent about smoking behavior; the third follow-up (1994) asked the respondents only if they or one of their friends has been arrested in the past year.

First and second follow-up delinquency measures primarily focus on drug use among students and dropouts and school-based misbehavior. For example, students are asked to self-report their use of tobacco, alcohol, marijuana, and cocaine over their lifetime, the previous year, and the previous 30 days. The second follow-up also asks these two groups of adolescents the frequency with which they were under the influence of alcohol, marijuana, or cocaine at while they were at school. There are also measures of fighting, teen pregnancy, cutting classes, being suspended, being transferred for disciplinary reasons, and being arrested. Most of these measures can be found among both student and dropout questionnaires at the 1990 and 1992 waves of NELS:88.

As mentioned earlier, NELS:88 permits contextual analyses of social phenomena because respondents' addresses were linked to their census tract via their zip code. In this case, researchers are able to explore neighborhood-level characteristics affecting delinquency in addition to individual, family, and school characteristics. This is of particular relevance to sociological theories of crime and delinquency, which place a strong emphasis on the role of community characteristics in the etiology of criminal behavior. One example of such a study is John Hoffmann's 2002 contextual analysis of three leading theories of crime and delinquency. This study assesses the effect of delinquent peers, negative emotions (or strain), and social bonds on fighting, school suspension, and being arrested among a sample of 1990 NELS:88 tenth-graders. The study also examines the effects of these variables independently of four tract-level characteristics of each respondent's residence: the level of racial segregation, the percentage of female-headed families, the percentage of jobless males, and the percentage of residents in poverty. Generally speaking, the mediating and conditioning effects of strain and social control theories are strongest for a subset of adolescents living in urban areas (approximately 20% of the study's original sample).

In his 2002 analysis of the contextual effects of family structure on drug use, Hoffmann again uses the NELS:88 data linked to the respondent's census tract. The purpose was to assess whether community-level factors affect the relationship between family structure and juvenile drug use. Drug use is operationalized as a composite measure of the following items: alcohol, marijuana, or cocaine use; having five or more drinks in a row; and attending school while under the influence of the three drugs listed. The only neighborhood-level characteristic significantly affecting drug use was the percentage of unemployed men living in the neighborhood. Adolescents living in neighborhoods with high percentages of male joblessness are at increased risk for drug use, irrespective of their family structure.

The preceding sections merely scratch the surface concerning the breadth of topic areas available in NELS:880. Although it is essential to briefly describe the relevance of NELS:88 to research topics in the fields of education and the sociology of education, a brief introduction to other research areas pertinent to the lives of youth illustrates the possibilities of the data set.

Cautions When Using the National Education Longitudinal Survey of 1988

As can be surmised from the discussion thus far, NELS:88 is a very complex database that permits a diverse array of analyses. Novice users are *strongly* encouraged to read the data file user's manuals as well as any technical reports that pertain to waves of data used in their analyses. The *Quick Guide to Using the NELS:88/200 Data* is a brief introduction that is a must-read for researchers with little to no experience with this data set. This section describes a few features of NELS:88 of which the novice or casual user should be aware.

Subsampling of Cases at the 1990, 1994, and 2000 Waves of the National Education Longitudinal Survey of 1988

Between 1988 and 1990, many eighth-grade students who participated in the base-year study attended high schools with very few or no other base-year study participants. Following up every base-year student proved to be cost-prohibitive. Consequently, the NCES chose to subsample those students participating in the 1990 longitudinal panel study. The subsampling procedure assigned the probability of being included in the first follow-ups to be proportionate to the number of base-year students attending the first follow-up school. Thus, students attending 1990 high schools with 10 or fewer base-year respondents were less likely than students attending high schools with more than 10 base-year participants to be included in the 1990 longitudinal panel sample. These selection criteria resulted in approximately 6000 base-year participants being sampled out of the second wave of the study. Major subsampling also took place at the third (1994) and fourth (2000) follow-ups of NELS:88 (although respondents were randomly selected to be dropped from the analysis at these waves). Users are strongly encouraged to weight their analyses in NELS:88 to adjust for the effects of nonresponse attributed to subsampling. Consult the data file user's manual for the respective wave and respondent type to obtain more information about using specific weights to adjust for item nonresponse.

Abbreviated Questionnaires and Intersurvey Analyses

The NCES used an abbreviated questionnaire to collect data from some respondents at the first follow-up. This shorter version of the questionnaire was disproportionately distributed to dropouts, with approximately 25% of them completing this version of the instrument. Items not included on this abbreviated questionnaire have a nonresponse rate that exceeds acceptable standards by the NCES. A questionnaire weight (F1DPAJWT) was created to adjust for the high nonresponse rate among these items. However, because it was created specifically for dropouts, it cannot be used in analyses combining both student and dropout questionnaire data. Users wishing to combine the adjusted first follow-up dropout weight with other first follow-up weights should consult the NCES for technical assistance.

Users are strongly encouraged to obtain hard copies of survey questionnaires for each type of respondent in their analyses (e.g., student, dropout, and teacher). Although survey questions may be identical across questionnaire types, the differential use of filter questions may produce high rates of item nonresponse between respondent types. For example, at the second follow-up (1992), both students and dropouts are asked the same questions about the quality of their relationships with their parents. However, a filter question precedes this section of the dropout questionnaire, permitting only those dropouts who are currently living with their parents to complete this section of the survey. Many dropouts were not living with their parents; as a result, the nonresponse rate for these indicators is substantially higher among dropouts than students. Thus, combining these indicators between the dropout and student data files could potentially bias results.

Accessing National Education Longitudinal Survey of 1988 Data, Data Documentation, and Information about the Data Set

Two types of NELS:88 data are available on CD-ROM from the NCES: public-use data files and restricted-use data files. In public-use data sets, any information that could potentially identify a respondent has been either encrypted or deleted from the data file. Restricted-use data files do not encrypt this information; thus, the NCES only loan the data set to qualified people who complete a thorough application process. Analysts wishing to obtain a restricted-use NELS:88 data file should refer to the NCES application procedures Web site (http://www.nces.ed.gov/surveys/nels 88).

Each CD-ROM contains data files, the electronic codebook (ECB), and several sets of user's manuals. The ECB is a graphical user interface (GUI) tool listing all the variables, weights, and flags for each unit of analysis at each wave of the data for the particular study period (e.g., 88/92, 88/94, and 88/00). It displays the survey question, frequencies, and percentages of these variables, as well as any other notes or pertinent information about them. The ECB allows users to tag variables of interest for export into SAS, SPSS, or codebook text. This is a very handy feature of NELS:88, allowing the user to create programming code as well as a hardcopy codebook for the variables in an analysis.

In past years, obtaining hard copies of the actual survey instruments used in NELS:88 required contacting the NCES (whose supply could run short, due to demand) or borrowing copies from a colleague. This was also the case for other NELS:88 documentation, from users' manuals to specialty reports. These critical documents were frequently hard to locate and data documentation on the data CD-ROM was often incomplete. Put another way, obtaining the actual NELS:88 data was easy, but obtaining information about using the data was not.

During the past year, the NCES has created digital copies of all surveys used in all waves of NELS:88 and placed it on their Web site. Moreover, most of the data file users' manuals are also available (the first follow-up is the exception), as are many of the technical reports, working papers, and statistical analysis reports. This is a major improvement in accessibility concerning NELS:88. Seasoned users of NELS:88 will happily abandon their quest(s) for various copies of the "big green books" in favor of the Adobe Acrobat files easily downloaded from the Web site.

New users to NELS:88 should take full advantage of two documents available on the Web site. Both are available under the quick guide and example links. The quick guide walks the user through the structure of the database, provides examples of research questions appropriate for NELS:88, gives technical advice on creating working data files, and has a frequently asked questions section. The example link provides step-by-step instructions on how to select variables from the electronic code book, export them to statistical and survey software programs, and use them for basic quantitative analyses.

See Also the Following Articles

Longitudinal Studies, Panel • Survey Questionnaire Construction • Surveys

Further Reading

Ainsworth, J. W. (2002). Why does it take a village? The mediation of neighborhood effects on educational achievement. *Soc. Forces* **81,** 117–152.

Annotated Bibliography of Research with NELS:88. December 2001. Available from: http://www.nces.ed.gov/surveys/nels88/Bibliography.asp

Broene, P., and Rust, K. (2000). *Strengths and Limitations of Using SUDAAN, Stata, and WesVarPC for Computing Variances from NCES Data Sets.* National Center for Education Statistics, Office of Educational Research and Improvement, Washington, DC.

Bursik, R., and Grasmick, H. (1993). *Neighborhoods and Crime: The Dimensions of Effective Community Control.* Lexington Books, New York.

Coleman, J. (1988). Social capital in the creation of human capital. *Am. J. Sociol.* **94,** S95–S120.

Croninger, R. G., and Lee, V. E. (2001). Social capital and dropping out of high school: Benefits to at-risk students of teachers' support and guidance. *Teachers Coll. Rec.* **103,** 548–581.

Curtain, T. R., Ingels, S. J., Wu, S., Heuer, R., and Owings, J. (2002). *National Education Longitudinal Study of 1988: Base-Year to Fourth Follow-Up Data File User's Manual.* National Center for Education Statistics, Washington, DC.

Curtin, T. R., Ingels, S. J., Wu, S., Heuer, R., and Owings, J. (2002). *Quick Guide to Using the NELS:88/2000 Data.* National Center for Education Statistics, Washington, DC.

Data Analysis System. http://www.nces.ed.gov/DAS

Dika, S. L., and Singh, K. (2002). Applications of social capital in educational literature: A critical synthesis. *Rev. Educ. Res.* **72,** 31–60.

Hoffmann, J. P. (2002). The community context of family structure and adolescent drug use. *J. Marriage Fam.* **64,** 314–330.

Hoffmann, J. P. (2004). A contextual analysis of differential association, social control, and strain theories of delinquency. *Soc. Forces* **81,** 753–785.

Horn, L. J., Chen, X., and Adelman, C. (1998). *Toward Resiliency: At-Risk Students Who Make It to College.* Office of Educational Research and Improvement. U.S. Department of Education, Washington, DC.

Ingels, S. J., Curtin, T. R., Kaufman, P., Alt, M. N., and Chen, X. (2002). *Coming of Age in the 1990's: The Eighth-Grade Class of 1988 12 Years Later.* NCES 2002-321. National Center for Education Statistics, Washington DC.

Ingels, S., Dowd, K., Stipe, J., Baldridge, J., Bartot, V., Frankel, M., and Quinn, P. (1994). *National Education Longitudinal Study of 1988: Second Follow-Up Data File User's Manual.* National Center for Education Statistics, Washington, DC.

Jacobson, J., Olsen, C., Rice, J. K., Sweetland, S., and Ralph, J. (2001). *Educational Achievement and Black-White Inequality.* National Center for Education Statistics, Washington, DC.

Johnson, R. A., and Hoffmann, J. P. (2000). Adolescent cigarette smoking in U.S. racial/ethnic subgroups: Findings from the National Education Longitudinal Study. *J. Health Soc. Behav.* **41,** 392–407.

Kaufman, P., Alt, M. N., and Chapman, C. (2001). *Dropout Rates in the United States: 2000.* National Center for Education Statistics, Washington, DC.

Kaufman, P., Kwon, J. Y., Klein, S., and Chapman, C. (1999). *Dropout Rates in the United States: 1998.* NCES #2000-022. National Center for Education Statistics, Washington, DC.

Lee, R. (1994). *NELS:88 First Follow-Up Final Technical Report.* National Center for Education Statistics, Washington, DC.

McNeal, R. B. (1999). Parental involvement as social capital: Differential effectiveness on science achievement, truancy, and dropping out. *Soc. Forces* **78,** 117–144.

Muller, C. (1995). Maternal employment, parent involvement, and mathematics achievement among adolescents. *J. Marriage Fam.* **57,** 85–100.

Muller, C. (1998). Gender differences in parental involvement and adolescents' mathematics achievement. *Sociol. Educ.* **71,** 336–356.

National Center for Education Statistics surveys and documentation. http://www.nces.ed.gov/surveys/nels88/

National Center for Education Statistics application procedures. http://www.nces.ed.gov/statprog/rudman/

Owings, J. (1995). *National Education Longitudinal Study of 1988: Conducting Trend Analyses of NLS-72, HS&B, and NELS:88 Seniors.* National Center for Education Statistics, Washington, DC.

Pong, S. (1998). The school compositional effect of sing parenthood on 10-grade achievement. *Sociol. Educ.* **71,** 24–43.

Quinn, P. (1992). *Language Characteristics and Academic Achievement: A Look At Asian and Hispanic Eighth Graders in NELS:88.* National Center for Education Statistics, Washington, DC.

Ralph, J., and Crouse, J. (1997). *Issue Brief: Reading and Mathematics Achievement: Growth in High School.* NCES 98038. National Center for Education Statistics, Washington, DC.

Rumberger, R. (1995). Dropping out of middle school: A multilevel analysis of students and schools. *Am. Educ. Res. J.* **32,** 583–625.

Spencer, B., Frankel, M., Ingels, S., Rasinski, K., Tourangeau, R., and Owings, J. (1990). *National Education Longitudinal Study of 1988: Base Year Sample Design Report.* National Center for Education Statistics, Washington, DC.

Wilson, W. J. (1987). *The Truly Disadvantaged.* University of Chicago Press, Chicago, IL.

Network Analysis

Peter V. Marsden
Harvard University, Cambridge, Massachusetts, USA

Glossary

blockmodel A summary of the subgroup structure in a network, consisting of an assignment of social units to positions and images of the relationships among those positions.

centrality The prominence or importance of a given unit within a network as reflected in its relationships to other units.

clique A subgroup of mutually related units.

cohesion The strength of the relationship between units; a criterion for assigning units to subgroups.

egocentric network The partial network surrounding a given unit.

mutuality Reciprocity within a relationship from one unit to another.

one-mode design A design focusing on relationships among social units of a single type, for example, friendships among children in a school classroom.

relational property A property of a unit defined by information on its relationships to other units in a collective or group.

structural equivalence A condition in which two units have identical relationships to and from all other units within a collective or group; a criterion for assigning units to subgroups.

structural property A property of a collective or group defined by information on relationships among the units it includes.

transitivity The presence of a relationship from one unit to another when both are related to a third unit, implying closure or clustering within a network.

two-mode design A design focusing on the relationships between social units of two distinct types, for example, the memberships of directors in corporate boards.

whole-network study The study of relationships among units within a bounded social collective or group.

Network analysis identifies regularities in relationships among social units, thereby measuring both relational properties of individual units and structural properties of collectives. Major subjects of network analysis include connectedness, centrality, range, and social differentiation. Mathematical, graphical, and statistical techniques are used to study network data.

Introduction

Network studies measure features of social structure by identifying regularities and patterns in relationships among social units. The properties of interest lie at several distinct levels. They include relational properties of individual social units, such as status, social integration, social support, and social capital, as well as structural properties of entire groups or collectives, including vertical and horizontal differentiation, centralization, and social density.

The social units that compose networks are often individuals, but networks are also made up of other units including families, organizations, or countries, among others. Both formally constituted groups (such as workplaces or schools) and informally defined ones (such as scientific communities or policy domains) can be studied using network analysis. Network studies examine diverse relationships among units including interdependence, communication, membership, solidarity, and affect. Network theories assert that social ties serve as channels for the diffusion of cultural ideas and practices, infectious diseases, and information and as pathways offering access to information, opportunity, and resources. Locations in networks can be sources of power and signals of a unit's social standing. Network analyses are found throughout the social sciences, especially in anthropology, epidemiology, management and organization studies, and sociology.

This entry first covers major network study designs. It then introduces graph-theoretic representations of network data and visual representations. Next, it summarizes network approaches to the measurement of centrality/prominence, network range, and social differentiation. Most of these techniques describe features of the particular networks under study. The entry then introduces some developing statistical approaches to network analysis that seek to draw inferences that extend beyond the available data.

Social Network Data and Research Designs

Beginning in the 1930s, studies of the sociometric measurement of interpersonal affect introduced quantitative methods and tools that were important precursors to network analysis. Ethnographic fieldwork by social anthropologists in the 1950s and 1960s offered a set of concepts, ideas, and methods that informs the study of social networks. Work of both kinds continues, but most contemporary studies use quantitative data. The typical network study uses a nonexperimental design. Common approaches to data collection are surveys, questionnaires, and direct observation. Archival sources also offer rich information on the relationships among certain social units. Designs for network studies are distinguished by whether they assemble data on whole or partial networks and by the number of types (modes) of social units studied.

Whole-network studies examine interrelated units that are analyzed as a bounded social collective; the analytical boundaries of the collective may be based on formal membership criteria, density of interactions, or involvement in a set of events or activities. The most common one-mode whole-network design collects data on relationships linking a set of N social units of a single type. Examples are friendships among students in a school and alliances among businesses in an industry sector. One-mode network data can be represented as a square matrix $\mathbf{X} = \{x_{ij}\}$, where the element x_{ij} represents the strength of the relationship from unit i to unit j; relationships x_{ii} from units to themselves are usually undefined. A data matrix for a binary relationship in a 10-unit network appears in Fig. 1A. A 1 indicates that there is a tie from the row unit to the column unit, and a 0 indicates that there is no such tie. One-mode designs can be extended by observing a relationship at multiple time points, by measuring two or more relationships (e.g., antagonisms as well as friendships) linking the social units, or by obtaining measurements on a single relationship from multiple observers or sources. Each extension leads to a three-way data matrix $\mathbf{X} = \{x_{ijk}\}$, where the subscript k indexes time points, types of relationship, or observers/sources.

In a two-mode whole-network design, basic relationships link two distinct types of units. Data are recorded in a rectangular matrix $\mathbf{Y} = \{y_{ij}\}$, where the element y_{ij} refers to the relationship between the ith unit of the first type and the jth unit of the second type. Studies of interlocking boards of directors exemplify the two-mode design: individuals and corporations are the two types of units, and data elements indicate whether person i is a director of corporation j.

Egocentric network studies collect data on partial networks consisting of a focal social unit i and the other units and relationships clustered in its locality. The social support network surrounding a given person is one example. Egocentric networks are often delimited by including other units that lie within the focal unit's first-order zone, those units directly linked with the focal unit. Unit i's egocentric network, then, consists of those others bearing some criterion relationship to i, and the relationships among them. In Fig. 1B, the egocentric

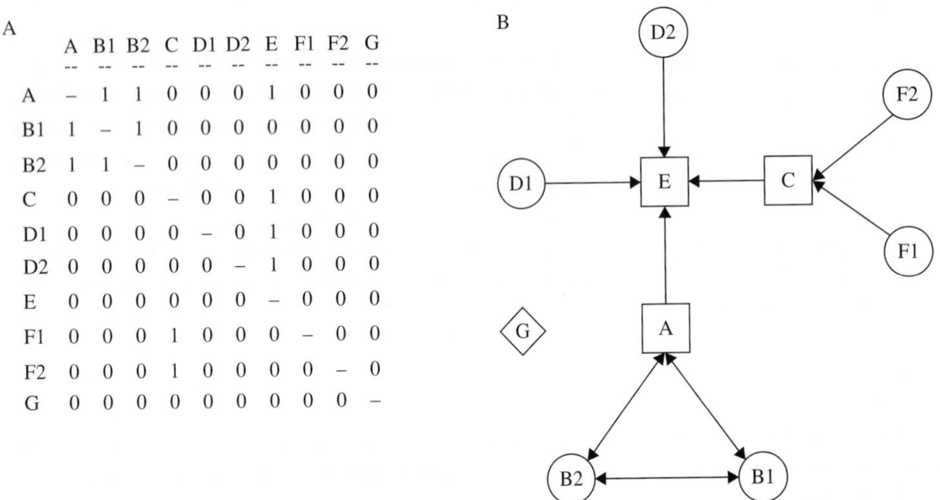

A

	A	B1	B2	C	D1	D2	E	F1	F2	G
A	–	1	1	0	0	0	1	0	0	0
B1	1	–	1	0	0	0	0	0	0	0
B2	1	1	–	0	0	0	0	0	0	0
C	0	0	0	–	0	0	1	0	0	0
D1	0	0	0	0	–	0	1	0	0	0
D2	0	0	0	0	0	–	1	0	0	0
E	0	0	0	0	0	0	–	0	0	0
F1	0	0	0	1	0	0	0	–	0	0
F2	0	0	0	1	0	0	0	0	–	0
G	0	0	0	0	0	0	0	0	0	–

Figure 1 (A) Data matrix and (B) directed graph for a 10-unit, one-mode network.

network for unit A consists of A, B1, B2, and E. Egocentric network data measure relational properties of the social context in which the focal unit is situated. They generally are not well suited to measuring structural properties of collectives.

Most network studies purport to obtain data on a theoretical population of units. Research on network sampling examines the inferences about whole networks that can be drawn using different sampling designs. Node-induced samples observe data on relationships among a sample of social units drawn from a network. Egocentric data are often gathered for a sample of units from a larger population, a design known as sampling of stars.

Graph Theory and Connectedness

Directed graphs (or digraphs) are isomorphic to social networks, providing a fruitful representation for network data. Graph-theoretic concepts provide foundations for many social network measures.

A digraph consists of a set of nodes (corresponding to the units in a network) and a set of (possibly valued) lines linking pairs of nodes. Network analysis makes most use of binary digraphs in which relationships are either present ($x_{ij} = 1$) or absent ($x_{ij} = 0$). The set of such binary relationships $\mathbf{X} = \{x_{ij}\}$ is known as the adjacency matrix of the graph. The matrix in Fig. 1A is an adjacency matrix; the corresponding digraph is shown in Fig. 1B. In the digraph, an arrow denotes the direction of a relationship. There is a one-directional (asymmetric) relationship from unit A to unit E in Fig. 1B, but a mutual relationship linking units B1 and B2. If the relationship under study is not directed, it is represented as a graph rather than a digraph; then $x_{ij} = x_{ji}$ for all pairs of units i and j.

Statistics for the adjacency matrix define elementary structural properties. Probably the most commonly used structural index is network density, the matrix mean:

$$\frac{1}{N(N-1)} \sum_{i=1}^{N} \sum_{\substack{j=1 \\ (j \neq i)}}^{N} x_{ij}$$

For binary data, density gives the number of relationships observed as a proportion of those possible. Sparse, loosely knit networks have low density; closely knit networks have high density. A similar local density index can be defined for the egocentric network surrounding each node; this contrasts interlocking (high-density) and radial (low-density) egocentric networks.

Graph theory defines various forms of connectedness between nodes in a network, of which the most important is indirect connectedness via a path. A path consists of a sequence of distinct nodes, each of which is related to the next. In Fig. 1B, path (B2, B1, A, E) leads from node B2 to node E via intermediary nodes B1 and A. The length of a path is the number of direct relationships included in it; path (B2, B1, A, E) has length 3. If a path exists from one node to another, the second node is reachable from the first. Node E is reachable from B2 in Fig. 1B, but B2 is not reachable from E. A geodesic path is a minimum-length path from one node to another. Path (B2, B1, A, E) is not a geodesic because B2 can also reach E via the length-2 path (B2, A, E). The geodesic (or path) distance d_{ij} from one node to another is the length of the geodesic path between them. The geodesic distance need not be symmetric (i.e., d_{ij} need not equal d_{ji}) and is infinite if one node cannot reach a second.

Two-mode network data can be represented in a bipartite graph including two distinct sets of nodes. All direct relationships in a bipartite graph link nodes in different sets; nodes in one set may be indirectly related to one another via paths involving nodes in the other set. For example, two corporations have an indirect tie of length 2 if their boards include one or more directors in common.

Visualization

Visual images such as the digraph shown in Fig. 1B have long been used to represent and study network data. Such plots capture many intuitions about networks. They depict social distance by placing closely related units near one another while separating weakly related ones. Likewise, they readily identify central and peripheral units.

Network graphics may be enhanced by using symbols of differing shapes or sizes to designate types of units. For example, the different shapes in Fig. 1B could denote differences in rank or social origin. Distinct types of relationships may be illustrated with varying line legends. Solid lines may indicate friendships while dotted lines identify antagonisms, for instance. Variations in the strength of ties can be represented using different line widths. Continuing developments in computer graphics offer many more enhancements, including the use of color and animation.

First termed sociograms, network graphics were long constructed in an *ad hoc* manner dependent on the judgment of the analyst. The emphasis was on presentational clarity, placing units so that few lines crossed one another. More recently, multidimensional scaling and spring embedders have been used to establish locations for units within plots in a standardized fashion and to develop three-dimensional plots. Correspondence analysis and singular value decomposition have proved similarly useful in constructing visual representations of two-mode network data.

Centrality and Centralization

Centrality measures are among the most widely used indices based on network data. They generally reflect a unit's prominence; in different substantive settings, this may be its structural power, status, prestige, or visibility. Studies often use network-based centrality measures in efforts to account for interunit differences in behavior or attitudes.

Distinct centrality measures are sensitive to different aspects of a focal unit's ties to other units. Several important graph-theoretic measures were first defined for binary symmetric graphs. They have since been generalized to include valued and directed ties, but the illustrations in this section assume binary symmetric measurements. A unit's degree centrality $C_{\mathrm{D}}(i)$ reflects its number of relationships:

$$C_{\mathrm{D}}(i) = \sum_{\substack{j=1 \\ (i \neq j)}}^{N} x_{ij}$$

Separate in- and out-degree measures are suitable for nonsymmetric data. In Fig. 1B, for example, unit E has an in-degree centrality 4, but an out-degree centrality 0.

Other common graph-theoretic measures of centrality are based on indirect connectedness measured using geodesic paths. A widely used measure $C_{\mathrm{B}}(i)$ reflects unit i's "betweenness:"

$$C_{\mathrm{B}}(i) = \sum_{\substack{j=1 \\ (j \neq i)}}^{N} \sum_{\substack{k=1 \\ (k \neq i)}}^{j-1} \frac{g_{jk}(i)}{g_{jk}}$$

where g_{jk} is the number of geodesic paths linking units j and k, and $g_{jk}(i)$ is the number of those geodesics on which unit i occupies an intermediary location. Unit C lies between F1 and E in Fig. 1B, for example. Betweenness centrality can reflect a unit's capacity to broker or control social relations involving other units.

A closeness measure conceives of a unit as central to the extent that it is related to other units via short geodesics:

$$C_{\mathrm{C}}(i) = \frac{N-1}{\sum_{j=1}^{N} d_{ij}}$$

Closeness centrality $C_{\mathrm{C}}(i)$ is defined only for sets of units that are mutually related via finite geodesic distances. Units linked to others via short geodesics have comparatively little need for intermediary (broker) units and thus possess relative independence in managing their relationships.

Another useful centrality index defines a unit's power or prominence p_i on the basis of the strength of its relationships to other powerful or prominent units:

$$p_i = \sum_{j=1}^{N} p_j r_{ji}$$

where r_{ji} is a normalized measure of the strength of the relationship from unit j to unit i. This index weights ties to powerful units more heavily than those to less powerful ones. The vector of scores $\mathbf{p} = \{p_i\}$ is an eigenvector of the normalized matrix of relationships $\mathbf{R} = \{r_{ij}\}$, so $\mathbf{p}$ is known as an eigenvector measure of centrality.

The foregoing indices of centrality are relational measures defined for individual social units. Corresponding to each one is a structural measure of centralization defined at the level of the group or collective. Centralization is high if relationships are concentrated on a single unit and low if they are distributed evenly across units. A normalized group-level measure of centralization based on degree centrality is:

$$C_{\mathrm{D}} = \sum_{i=1}^{N} \frac{C_{\mathrm{D}}(\max) - C_{\mathrm{D}}(i)}{(N-1)(N-2)}$$

where $C_{\mathrm{D}}(\max)$ is the maximum degree centrality of any unit within the network under study. Similar centralization measures exist for other unit-level centrality measures.

Range and Composition

Social networks are key constituents of most concepts of social capital. Social actors can gain competitive advantages by making use of resources, information, and opportunities available through their social ties. Such social capital both substitutes for and augments individual capacities or human capital. Social support flowing through networks can improve individual well-being directly and also buffer the impact of stressors on well-being.

The principal network indicators of social capital are indices that measure the range and composition of egocentric networks. Range measures reflect the variety of units with which a focal unit is in direct or indirect contact. The ego units at the center of large, sparse networks are positioned to obtain and synthesize nonredundant information that resides in diverse sectors of a group and thus to be first-movers and early innovators. By virtue of their position as intermediaries bridging structural holes that separate otherwise disconnected alters, such ego units accrue opportunities to profit by exercising entrepreneurial control. In some settings, closely knit, dense egocentric networks also have advantages—they can convey stable social identities and establish well-defined performance expectations.

Basic measures of network range include egocentric network size (degree centrality $C_{\mathrm{D}}(i)$), local density (an inverse indicator of range), and heterogeneity indexes reflecting the level of sociodemographic diversity among those alters tied to a given ego. More refined indicators take simultaneous account of these factors.

Effective network size, for instance, is lower than $C_D(i)$ to the extent that the alter units in unit i's egocentric network are linked to one another and therefore redundant. A unit's structural autonomy is high to the extent that it has many alternative relationships with other units, whereas its transaction partners have comparatively few.

Most network range indicators capture features of the configuration of relationships surrounding a given unit, positing that these features promote access to information and resources. Network composition indicators measure the accessibility of social resources more directly. The status composition of a focal unit's egocentric network, for example, might be measured by the average status of the other units included in it, often weighted by the strength of their relationships to the focal unit.

Social Differentiation: Network Subgroups

Network approaches to studying social differentiation rest on the postulate that social relationships reflect salient social distinctions. Patterns of relationships, then, point to subgroups and statuses within a group or collectivity. Analyses of differentiation seek to assign units to subgroups and develop models of intersubgroup relationships. Two major principles for assigning units to subgroups are extensively used. One defines subgroups as sets of cohesive, densely interconnected units. The other defines them as sets of units occupying common social positions by virtue of their substitutable equivalent profiles of relationships to other units.

Cohesive Subgroups

Cohesive subgroups consist of strongly interconnected units. Such sets of units are thought to be solidary, having a high capacity for collective action. If units in such a subgroup are also isolated from those in other subgroups, an assignment of units to subgroups partitions the network into disjoint clusters of units. For three subgroups, this image of social structure implies the following binary matrix of intersubgroup relationships:

$$\begin{matrix} 1 & 0 & 0 \\ 0 & 1 & 0 \\ 0 & 0 & 1 \end{matrix}$$

where a row and the corresponding column refer to a subgroup and a 1 indicates that units in the row subgroup tend to have relationships with those in the column subgroup.

Formal mathematical models are often used in assigning units to cohesive subgroups. For binary data, an idealized graph-theoretic model is the sociometric clique. Cliques are maximal complete subgraphs, subsets of units in which each unit is tied to all others within the subset. That is, $x_{ij} = 1$ for all distinct units i and j within a clique. In Fig. 1B, units A, B1, and B2 constitute a clique. A given unit may be part of more than one clique. Relaxations of the clique concept consider units to be in a cohesive subgroup if they can reach one another indirectly at a short geodesic distance such as 2 or 3, or if a subgraph is nearly complete—that is, if each unit in the subgroup is directly connected to all but a small number (e.g., one or two) of the others. Strong components of a digraph are disjoint sets of units mutually linked to one another by a path.

Other methods for assigning network elements to subgroups are exploratory. One approach is based on dyadic measures of connectedness such as geodesic distance. Clustering techniques are used to identify subsets of highly interconnected units. A direct approach begins by specifying a criterion function that indicates how closely any given partition of units resembles a target image matrix such as the one just shown. It then uses combinatorial optimization techniques to identify a partition of units that best satisfies the criterion.

Positional Analysis, Structural Equivalence, and Blockmodels

The subgroups identified by cohesion-based analyses have a specific common form—in-group solidarity. Positional analysis takes a much more general approach to studying differentiation in networks. The defining features of some social locations are relationships to others rather than relations to peers, and they do not always include within-group density. Superior positions, for example, are defined by having authority relations to subordinate positions; brokers mediate between buyers and sellers, but are not necessarily connected to other brokers. The distinctions and expectations that define some positions, moreover, may involve multiple, differently patterned types of relationships. A nation in the core of the system of international stratification, for instance, may receive raw materials from countries in peripheral locations, send processed goods to peripheral countries, and have economic and political alliances with other core countries. Cohesion-based approaches to examining differentiation lack the flexibility to examine multiple networks of relationships simultaneously.

Positional analyses map units into subgroups using equivalence criteria. Two units are said to be structurally equivalent if their relationships to and from other units in the group are identical. Units D1 and D2 are structurally equivalent in Fig. 1B because both are unilaterally related to E and unrelated to all other units. Likewise, B1 is structurally equivalent to B2, and F1 is structurally equivalent to F2. Note that structurally equivalent units need not have relationships with one another. Role equivalence is a more general criterion that groups two units together if their profiles of relationships link them to similar, but not necessarily identical, others. The entry-level employees in different bureaucratic organizations are role-equivalent in that they are subject to the authority of first-line supervisors, but they are not structurally equivalent because they are subordinate to different supervisors.

A blockmodel depicts the typical relationships among units grouped into equivalence-based subsets. It consists of an assignment of units to subgroups, together with one or more binary images of intersubgroup ties. The following images for a two-relation, three-subgroup blockmodel might describe a workgroup:

Authority			Friendship		
0	1	1	1	0	1
0	0	0	0	1	0
0	0	0	1	0	0

In the first subgroup (or position) are those who exercise authority over others; they tend to be friendly with one another. The second position includes subordinates who are solidary with one another, whereas the third consists of subordinates who are not friendly with one another, but do maintain friendships with some of the supervisory actors.

The formal mathematical definitions of structural and role equivalence constitute rigorous standards for assigning units to common positions. Empirical studies usually must relax them. Often this begins with a dyadic similarity or dissimilarity measure of the extent to which two relational profiles approach equivalence, such as the Euclidean distance ed_{ij}:

$$\text{ed}_{ij} = \sqrt{\sum_{k=1}^{N} \sum_{m=1}^{M} \left[(x_{ikm} - x_{jkm})^2 + (x_{kim} - x_{kjm})^2 \right]}$$

where M is the number of types of relationship studied. Units i and j are structurally equivalent if $\text{ed}_{ij} = 0$; to the extent that it exceeds 0, they occupy distinct positions or niches in social structure. Once such a measure of relational dissimilarity has been defined, cluster analysis methods are used to identify subsets of units having relatively homogenous profiles. Rather than using an intermediate dissimilarity measure, optimization methods for the empirical construction of blockmodels take a direct approach by seeking a partition of units into blocks that best satisfies a criterion function.

Statistical Network Analyses

By comparison with most other branches of quantitative social science, network analysis has given limited attention to statistical issues. Most techniques and measures examine the structure of specific data sets without addressing sampling variation, measurement error, or other uncertainties. Such issues are complex because of the dependencies inherent in network data, but they are now receiving increased study.

The most widely investigated approach to the statistical analysis of networks stresses the detection of formal regularities in local relational structure. Figure 2 illustrates some of the interrelational dependencies commonly found in analyses of social networks. Many relationships exhibit tendencies toward reciprocity or mutuality, as in Fig. 2A. To the degree that units vary in in-degree centrality, relationships will tend to be directed toward common targets, as in the in-star configuration of Fig. 2B; Fig. 2C illustrates a corresponding out-star pattern in which relationships tend to emanate from common sources. In transitive relationships (Fig. 2D), there is a tendency for direct ties (e.g., from A to C) to accompany indirect ones (e.g., from A to C via B). This redundancy leads to local closure and thus a tendency for the units to separate into subgroups. Another typical structural tendency is known as homophily. It is present, for example, when same-sex friendships are more common than between-sex friendships. This involves an interaction between a property of units and the presence of relationships.

To the extent that a given local configuration is an important basis for structuring a network, the likelihood of observing networks including that configuration increases. The following exponential probability density defines a family of random graph models known as p*:

$$\Pr(\mathbf{X} = \mathbf{X}) = \frac{\exp\{\boldsymbol{\theta}'\mathbf{z}(\mathbf{X})\}}{\kappa(\theta)}$$

where an observed network **X** is a realization of a random variable **X**, **z**(**X**) is a vector of network statistics giving the number of local configurations of particular types found in network **X**, θ is a corresponding vector of parameters

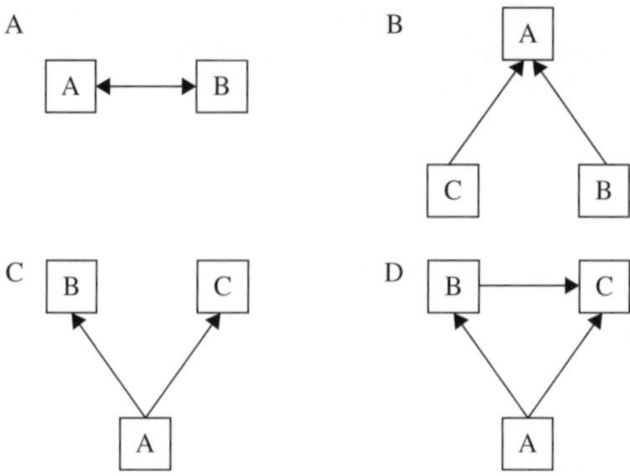

Figure 2 Local configurations commonly found in social networks. (A) Mutuality. (B) Two in-star. (C) Two out-star. (D) Transitivity.

indicating the strength with which different local structural tendencies operate, and $\kappa(\theta)$ is a normalizing constant. The estimation of θ is complicated by the difficulty of evaluating $\kappa(\theta)$; to date most estimates have been obtained via pseudo-likelihood methods.

This modeling framework considers multiple principles underlying social network structure simultaneously and identifies those tendencies that are significant structural patterns. It marks a considerable step beyond previous probability distributions formulated for network data, which included a restrictive specification of dyadic independence. Many extensions and innovations in modeling and estimation methods are underway within this framework.

The p^* density was first formulated by spatial statisticians. Many statistical problems of interest in network analysis have parallels in spatial statistics, although network data are not usually referenced to fixed locations. Network analysts have used spatial regression and spatial autocorrelation techniques when studying processes of influence and diffusion that operate by way of network ties. Other parallels between the analysis of network data and spatial data remain to be explored.

See Also the Following Article

Graph Theory

Further Reading

Borgatti, S. P., and Everett, M. G. (1992). Notions of position in social network analysis. In *Sociological Methodology 1992* (P. V. Marsden, ed.), pp. 1–35. Basil Blackwell, Oxford.

Borgatti, S. P., and Everett, M. G. (1997). Network analysis of 2-mode data. *Soc. Networks* **19,** 243–269.

Breiger, R. L. (1974). The duality of persons and groups. *Soc. Forces* **53,** 181–190.

Burt, R. S. (1992). *Structural Holes: The Social Structure of Competition.* Harvard University Press, Cambridge, MA.

Frank, O. (1981). A survey of statistical methods for graph analysis. In *Sociological Methodology 1981* (S. Leinhardt, ed.), pp. 110–155. Jossey-Bass, San Francisco, CA.

Freeman, L. C. (1979). Centrality in social networks, I: Conceptual clarification. *Soc. Networks* **1,** 215–239.

Freeman, L. C. (2000). Visualizing social networks. *J. So. Struct.* **1**. Available at http://www.heinz.cmu.edu/project/INSNA/joss/.

Harary, F., Norman, R. Z., and Cartwright, D. (1965). *Structural Models: An Introduction to the Theory of Directed Graphs.* John Wiley & Sons, New York.

Lazarsfeld, P. F., and Menzel, H. (1980). On the relation between individual and collective properties. In *A Sociological Reader on Complex Organizations* (A. Etzioni and E. W. Lehman, eds.), 3rd Ed., pp. 508–521. Holt, Rinehart and Winston, New York.

Marsden, P. V. (1990). Network data and measurement. *Ann. Rev. Sociol.* **16,** 435–463.

Mitchell, J. C. (1969). The concept and use of social networks. In *Social Networks in Urban Situations: Analyses of Personal Relationships in Central African Towns* (J. C. Mitchell, ed.), pp. 1–50. Manchester University Press, Manchester, UK.

Scott, J. (2000). *Social Network Analysis: A Handbook.* 2nd edn. Sage, Thousand Oaks, CA.

Wasserman, S., and Faust, K. L. (1994). *Social Network Analysis: Methods and Applications.* Cambridge University Press, New York.

Wasserman, S., and Pattison, P. (1996). Logit models and logistic regressions for social networks: I. An introduction to Markov graphs and p^*. *Psychometrika* **60,** 401–426.

White, H. C., Boorman, S., and Breiger, R. L. (1976). Social structure from multiple networks, I: Blockmodels of roles and positions. *Am. J. Sociol.* **81,** 730–780.

Neutrality in Data Collection

Carmen Diego Gonçalves
Minho University, Braga, Portugal

Glossary

epistemological vigilance The scientific practice of always questioning assumptions, assuring rupture with both externalist and internalist pre-notions about the object of research. As a tool of research, it contributes to scientists' reflexivity, to their being conscious that all empirical research is done within the ambit of a set of theories and accepted technical procedures, within which scientists question what is being observed.

neutrality The scientist's ideological distance from, or non-involvement with, what is being analyzed in social contexts.

objectification The necessary process in empirical research of objectifying all conditions in which the research is done, even research into social processes in which the scientist is developing a role according a *habitus* that has been incorporated into a certain field with theoretical and practical proprieties.

objectivity The scientific position that objective truths are external and independent of the observer's wishes, beliefs, and interests, thus guaranteeing the neutrality of science and scientists.

reflexivity The scientist's capacity to be conscious of the theoretical assumptions and social conditions of research. Therefore, methodological procedures should be explicit, ensuring the objectivity and validity of scientific production.

Neutrality in data collection is always implicit in social science research and is related to two complementary directions of episteme-methodological reflexivity, one orientated toward the assumptions of the scientist and the other toward the object of science, embedded in historical and social contexts.

Introduction

Why Neutrality in Data Collection?

The issue of neutrality in data collection is related to the affirmation of the objective value of scientific truth, which comes from scientific presuppositions about nature joined with a human attempt to produce fixed disciplinary cultures. Therefore, as an important dimension of social science research, neutrality aims to ensure the specific identity of the discipline, in consonance with the independence and impartiality of scientists and the objectivity of their results.

Crucial Debates

In the empirical-positivist tradition, which favors the primacy of observation, science is neutral. By observing the method of neutrality, knowledge will correspond to reality, copying it, and, based on that presupposition, we will have a record of how much of what we are observing is "nature" and how much is "society."

However, there were some writers close to the Vienna Circle who criticized this perspective. Karl Popper, for example, affirmed that observations are impregnated with theory, recognizing, thus, the primacy of theory in opposition to observation. Data that are clearly inconsistent with a hypothesis can show that it is false, as Karl Popper explains in *The Logic of Scientific Discovery*. Lakatos also affirmed that "*all* propositions of science are theoretical," and that "a factual proposition is only a particular type of theoretical proposition."

Admitting that observing necessarily supposes the category of what is being observed (i.e., dividing the world into data processes according to different scientific visions of the world), the aim of the rationalist perspective is the unity and the integration of the research process, in which the epistemological vector, as Bachelard said, is oriented from the rational to the real. Giddens, in turn, considered primordial in the production of scientific knowledge the network of overlapping and intersecting states, whether theoretical or observational, that form changeable connections with empirical objects.

Reflexivity within epistemological vigilance, one of the factors stressed in the thinking of Bourdieu, is much more important because it is certain that, although the object (and objective) of all science is to disclose what is hidden, what is hidden in society and what is hidden in nature are not hidden in the same sense—another difference between the two scientific universes. A more systematic kind of reflexivity claims to take up the ultimate consequences of Bourdieu's concern with the self-objectification of the subject of understanding.

The Problem

Accepting the myth of neutrality in an unquestioning way seems to constitute a dogma of faith, which can contribute to the anti-social applications of science. The problem consists, on the one hand, of knowing whether the science produced is recognized as *representing* social reality, that is, knowing the relationship of scientists and their methods, theories, frames of meaning, and finally idiosyncrasies and contingencies in the production of scientific knowledge, and, on the other hand, of knowing what constitutes the social role of the social scientist, in his or her identity as a scientist and as an actor who intervenes in society.

In fact, knowledge is inseparable from the struggle between different theoretical perspectives through which scientists try to construct and reconstruct society and its scientific interpretations. What exist are technical procedures developed by the scientists with the aim of neutrality. These procedures, as instruments, are only functional departures from previous conventions and decisions about what distinctions must be recorded, and because of this they are always impregnated with theory. There are authors who consider the existence of contextual, cultural, and social conditioning in the production of scientific knowledge. In addition, science is always politically implicated, even if only through its unavoidable relations with politics of science in national or transnational contexts.

In short, the problem is related, on the one hand, to the general demarcation between science and nonscience and, on the other, to the demarcations between the natural and social sciences. The ecology of practices, the demarcation of the objects and subjects of the science(s), and accepted procedures such as instruments for collecting data introduce a form of objectification that can contribute to the illusion of neutrality. All of them, in their turn, contribute to the dualities that sociocultural processes establish between the natural and social, the biological and cultural, the human and nonhuman, and the subject and object. It is clear that the paradigm of modern science is based on an obsession with method, and we can say that never has so much evidence of the illusion of neutrality been seen as in the last decades.

Article Overview

Beginning with questions relating to scientists' and scientific neutrality posed by Max Weber and Robert Merton and the historical contexts that allowed them to reflect on these issues, this entry first presents a (not necessarily chronological) review of authors whose works reflect on neutrality in science, neutrality between science and social contexts, and the distinction between neutrality and objectivity. Whereas as neutrality is shown to be, in fact, an impossible ideal, objectivity may be defended through procedures and the evaluation criteria for these procedures that principally look to make explicit the conditions of knowledge production (cognitive, institutional, cultural, social and political, economic constraints, and the scientists' identifications, including their biographies) in order to permit the identification and criticism of possible bias and other influences on the process of the production of scientific knowledge. From this, we can identify three important essential points. First, science, as a vision of the world based on the values of objectivity and neutrality, imposes itself in opposition to obscurantism and, above all, religion. Second, science has profited from politics, namely in the Second World War, and it is necessary to distance politicians from scientists in terms of ethics and identity. And, finally, in current societies, in which the social implications of the development of science become ethical questions and concerns, what are the conditions under which social scientists must intervene in society. So, considering that ethics seems to be linked to this intervention and the social responsibility of scientists, and if epistemologically it is right, how can scientists guarantee neutrality? The answer seems to lie in the methods and technical tools of research, anchored in the process of the objectification of the presuppositions of the research.

Scientists and Science Neutrality

At the end of the 1930s and the beginning of the 1940s, the belief that science is neutral, objective, and true—the ideology with which science had defined itself as a discipline in opposition to the dogmatic obscurantism of religion in the Middle Ages and that had moved it to the apex of social acceptance in the nineteenth century—received its first significant blows. In Germany, the submission of science to political objectives overthrew the fundamental criteria of scientific validity and the professional competence of scientists.

Max Weber: Axiological Neutrality of Reason

Defending the integrity of scientific activity in the face of political intervention in Germany at the turn of the twentieth century, Max Weber was preoccupied with the demarcation between politicians and scientists. According to Weber, the dimensions that identify the characteristics of politics and of science are, or at least should be, different. Advancing the concept of the "axiological neutrality of Reason," he defined the ethics that must regulate the position of the scientist in opposition to the politician.

This idea presupposed not only the value of neutrality in science and technology, but also the value of the reflexivity of the scientist. In other words, the universal validity of science demands that scientists do not project their value judgements onto the research process or state their preferences in terms of aesthetics or politics. In this sense, Weber thought to overcome a very well-known contradiction that the scientist who is passionate about the object of his or her investigation can never be impartial or objective.

According to Weber, scientists must separate value judgments from their work in the ambit of Reason. The characteristics of science are to be morally and socially free of values. Weber wanted a neutral science, in which professors never use their prestige to impose ideas. But he also wanted a neutral science that would be useful to people of action and politics. The ethics of conviction and responsibility finds itself, in a way, already complementing political vocation. This being so, although society may use science for good or for evil, scientists are no more socially responsible than any other citizens. Science is a double-edged sword. Current authors writing about the social responsibility of scientists affirm that science is limited to the descriptive study of natural laws and is devoid of moral or ethical qualities. This is as true for social science as it is for biological science.

Robert Merton: Scientific Ethos of Science

Robert Merton, beginning in 1942, wanted to guarantee the role of science in a society facing social problems posed by science, namely the negative impact of the development of controversial scientific and technological advances and the engagement of scientists with politics. This is usually identified with his externalist orientation of the development of science. In fact, the lack of confidence in science and scientists' neutrality and the results of the application of science that indicated that continued scientific development might not be unconditionally good created conditions that led to questioning the social functions of science and to imposing fundamental tasks that defined the functional conditions of science that must be practiced.

It is in this historical context that Merton delimited the sociological object of science, which is to study not only the cultural structure itself but also to study the impact on society of the creation of a focus of scientific interest, the selection of research problems, and their development. Merton also enumerated a set of norms, simultaneously moral and technical, that in his understanding constituted the scientific ethos, considered binding by scientists:

- Universalism—not contemplating criteria associated with personal and social attributes, the professional academic position.
- Communalism—openly communicating results as a basic presupposition for the advance of knowledge; because scientific knowledge is a social product, the results of research, as well as the theory that guides it, must be in the public domain.
- Disinterest—maintaining science as independent from other fields and interests, namely economics and politics, that are not related to the normative imperatives of scientific ethos; this is to be understood as an ideal to preserve autonomy.
- Organized skepticism—suspending ideology, controversies, religion, beliefs, and common sense until the facts speak for themselves. This leads us to methodological and institutional questions and to the process of the construction of new scientific knowledge; writers consider that this norm takes form, above all, in institutional appraisals of the validity of scientific knowledge.

Democratic society is the sociopolitical context that permits the maximum realization of these values. Disregarding this set of norms will lead to a situation in which, beyond moral indignation, science begins a process of cumulative dysfunction until it collapses.

Merton, in addition to his analyses of the influence of society on science and of science on society, was concerned with how social factors participate in the construction of scientific facts. He was also dedicated to the analysis of the social relations that constitute scientific institutions, of the processes of scientific production that mediate between theory and analysis in diverse sociocultural contexts, and of the contradictions and conflicts between structures and actors' motivations and perceptions—in other words, to the analysis of the contextualization of scientific production. Nevertheless, from Merton's perspective, the criteria of objectivity, validity, and neutrality and the theoretical conditions and methods are objects of the philosophy of science (or of the theory of science), but never of the sociology of science.

Objectivity, Reflexivity, and Neutrality

Positivism and Objectivity

August Comte: The Syntheses of Scientific Knowledge

August Comte, who is commonly identified as the founder of sociology, verified that the rigorous methods of the natural sciences—linked to positivism, which possesses a universal validity, and based in observation, experimentation, and the establishment of laws—must be widened to include the disciplines we now call the social sciences in the ambit of a reform of collective beliefs, which is a consequence of scientific development. The laws established by scientists are, in Comte's vision, comparable to dogmas; they must be accepted once and for all and not be perpetually questioned. Comte was much more conscious of the necessity of faith than in the legitimacy of doubt as a scientific method, thereby guaranteeing objectivity.

Emile Durkhein: Social Fact Theory

Durkheim's objective was to demonstrate that a sociology can exist that is objective, in agreement with the model of natural sciences, and whose object is social fact. To achieve this, two things are necessary: (1) that the object of this science may be specific, distinguishing itself from the objects of all other sciences and (2) that this object be observed and explained in a manner similar to the facts of other sciences. The rules of Durkheim's sociological method are anchored in the basic ideas that social facts are things and that the characteristic of a social fact is that it exercises coercion on individuals.

Durkheim used a deductive approach (coming from natural science) in which social scientists begin with explanatory hypotheses about a research problem and use logical reasoning to deduce its empirical implications. In this framework, theory building requires that the basic concepts be spelled out before they are used in the formulation of hypotheses. For example, Durkheim's basic concepts (egoism, altruism, anomie, and fatalism) were used as key independent variables in his analysis of suicide rates. The hypotheses were then tested using data in the real world.

The Critics of Positivism—Reflexivity

The positivists were criticized for assuming that society could be described and understood according to an ontology and methodology committed to seeing social behavior as empirically evident and quantifiable and the object of investigation according to a process of validation associated with measurement and quantitative data. Therefore, the deductive model was also criticized for assuming that it was possible, via the use of observer categories and theories, to provide an expert account of the social world superior to the lay accounts of the actors.

The antipositivists discovered or disclosed social reality by being receptive to accepting the actors' own perceptions and interpretations of the world, fashioned through interaction with other actors. Because meaningful human communication depends primarily on language, language is obviously of central interest, according to a validation process based on qualitative data and a comprehension of the way individuals create reality through interactions with others and make sense of it; there is no more to the social world than this. Consequently, they rejected not only the positivist's observational categories, but also any preconceived hypothetical statements about causal relations.

The deductive model was rejected, namely by the critical theorists. They attacked what they called "traditional," or "positivist," theory for suggesting that its deductive arguments could be assessed objectively and for having pure knowledge as a goal. The proponents of critical theory (e.g., Marx Horkheimer) related social phenomena to their notion of historical possibilities that were different from and superior to current reality.

Also, Michael Polanyi, who anticipated some of the ideas of Thomas Kuhn (e.g., conventionism and the importance of scientific community) and of Pierre Bourdieu (e.g., the notion of field), submitted the objectivist and positivist conceptions of the natural sciences to a radical criticism, and the way in which he did this approximated its epistemological status of the one of social sciences. According to him, the knowledge of the natural sciences cannot be distinguished in absolute terms from common sense knowledge; the methods that we use to confirm the facts of daily life logically predate the specific premises of science and must, because of this, be included in a complete description of these premises; also, science is a field of tradition and organized authority, before which only a fiduciary concept of scientific truth seems sustainable. Truth consists of a "scientific consensus" obtained from the scientific community and, because of this, those who speak about science, in the current sense and with the approval of custom, accept that this organized consensus determines what *is* scientific and what is not.

From the moment that the positivism orthodoxy entered this crisis, the concept of reflexivity was extended. The way to attain objectivity was through the subjective reflexivity of scientists, as well as through a profound consideration of the research procedures—the objectivist line of reflexivity, which has less confidence in the self-analysis or introspection of scientists than in the (as far as possible) objective analysis of the scientific theories, methods, and techniques of observation that scientists use—and a consideration of the sociological context in which scientific practice take place: the institutional organization of science; the types of science financing; and the uses of scientific knowledge.

Max Weber: Methodological Individualism

Max Weber, who at the beginning of twentieth century affirmed that "the belief in value of scientific truth does not proceed from nature but is a product of precise cultures," placed himself in the ambit of the important precursors of reflexivity in social sciences. We cannot doubt this when trying to define and legitimize patterns of scientific rationality that are adequate to the irreducible specificity of phenomenon.

Weber's views are related to the idea that objectivity can be applied to social problems only after a distinct value orientation has been established. It follows that political action does not corrupt social scientists' objectivity as long as the scientists' perspectives or values are explicitly acknowledged. So the categories through which social phenomena are conceived are, prior to social scientific analysis, derived from priorities that the researcher brings to the work rather than to universal laws discovered through systematic observation. Once established, these categories also entail ends, and the working objectively toward those ends, which allows social scientists to resolve given social problems scientifically.

Weber contributed powerfully to stimulating a sociological tradition more directly dependent on and contributory to the positivist program of Comte. As did Pareto, Weber, considered sociology to be a science of human behavior, to the extent that it is social. The way was open for the development of a comprehensive social approach and an approach to the technology of empirical research that were very diverse in the way that the positivist paradigm suggested. The recourse to the evidence of social actors on its existence, with a goal to refine the subjectively appraised causes (motives) of action, constitutes a methodology of investigation.

Weber's insistence on referring the motivation and, consequently, the sense of human action, to a set of axiological options defined at the level of the subjective actor, constituted the strategy, which developed into his essential methodological individualism. The self-referential character of reflexivity (subjectivist reflexivity) performs in a way that is very much bound to the personality of the social scientist.

Resisting, however, the extension of the effort of objectification of social processes to the disciplinary internal dynamics of the attribution of the sense that they embody, Weber contributed to the perpetuation of a system of epistemic correspondences (objective-explanation; subjective-comprehension) that today still marks and weakens the scientific analysis of social practices. His own designation of ideology, which Karl Marx substituted, in certain cases for "patterns of conscience," has imposed itself as an obstacle in the analysis.

C. Wright Mills: Explication of Presumptions

In the style of thought that presupposes reflexivity, there are authors who parted from the presupposition that it is not possible to study society with neutrality, and that, instead, because there is always more than one value option, sociologists have to take a position and have to be conscious of the position they take, which implies a conscious reflexivity over their own research practices. If neutrality is always conditioned by internal and external factors of understanding (the ideal type), an objectivity could be found across the methodological procedures that does not dispense with the inherent explication of the conditions of the production of scientific knowledge.

C. Wright Mills, writing in 1959, was the pioneer in the preoccupation with rendering explicit prejudgments, values, and ideological options—in short, the limits by which subjectivity establishes the objectivity of understanding that we produce. In this sense, he can be considered a pioneer of reflexivity in science and in the theoretical and methodological orientation that gained force at the end of the 1960s with the end of the positivist consensus. To Mills, the public explanation of bias is the precondition that makes objectivity possible in the social sciences because these explications can be made by everyone and integrated into scientific debates. The same preoccupation caused Mills to bring to the public domain his "sociological craft." Bravely, at the time, he showed his scientific practice as an intimate practice, personal, empirical, complex, and in constant confrontation with the aridity and simplicity of methodological recipes. Mills presented the task of research and objectification as a task of the artisan, reflexive, which came to constitute the basis of "grounded theory," and identified himself with the use of the inductive perspective.

Scientists using an inductive approach feel that to start an analysis with a clearly defined hypothesis is too rigid and may lead them to ignore important aspects of their subjects. It is far better, they suggest, to get to know a subject and situation well, gradually building up, or inducing, descriptions and explanations of what is really going on. In an inductive approach, the key concepts emerge in the final analysis of the research process. Induction implies an inference from the particular to the general (e.g., Goffman's intensive observations in a mental hospital led him to create the concept "total institution").

The Critics of Positivism—Contextualizing Neutrality

Thomas Kuhn: Frames of Meaning

According to Kuhn, neutrality is not possible in the visions of the world associated with any scientific discipline. We are always socialized into a paradigm or, alternatively, we adhere to a rival paradigm. None of the steps of scientific activity, including the production of information and data, can be neutral.

Kuhn's challenge to logical-positivist philosophy of science was twofold: (1) the development of science is not cumulative and (2) the choice that is made by scientists between alternative paradigms (once the process of rupture has begun in the revolutionary phase) is not founded on scientific theoretical considerations. In such periods of paradigm shift, the question about the direction of transition cannot be based on the requirement of truth precisely because the criteria that legitimize this requirement are, themselves, in question. The fight between paradigms at the moment of transition is more ideological than neutral (Kuhn compared it to a political struggle in which ideologies seek to impose conflicting definitions of the world). Different scientific visions of the world are based on different competing interpretative paradigms and, in this sense, reality offers itself for interpretation like a Picasso painting to the Gestalt dimension.

What is implicit is not a decision about the validity of new discoveries but whether a new perception of reality exists. So, the question will be decided, in the ultimate analysis, by the force of the arguments that the different schools of thought use in defense of their interpretations of the world, which are themselves a consequence of different visions and perceptions of the world.

The process of the imposition of a new paradigm is a process of negotiation among the different groups and among scientists within the groups, defined by relations of authority (scientific and other) and dependence. This leads to psychological and sociological factors of knowledge production. Kuhn stresses that "scientific knowledge as a language is intrinsically the common property of a group or it is nothing. To understand it we must know the special characteristics of the groups that believe and use it."

One of the consequences of Kuhnian epistemology is that rationality and veracity in scientific knowledge can be understandable only inside one paradigm, which provides the frame of meaning for all scientific practice. To explain the reasons for fundamental scientific options, it is necessary to leave the circle of theoretical conditions and internal mechanisms of validation and search for explanations in a vast set of sociological and psychological factors; it is also necessary to study the scientific community in which the different groups are integrated, the process of professional training, the process of socialization into the profession, and the organization of scientific work.

In spite of the fact that his concept of paradigm has a prominent social dimension, Kuhn does not provide evidence of the social causes of scientific knowledge; nor do his works give great importance to events outside the scientific community. Nevertheless, in the sense of reducing the importance of external causes in the revolution initiated by Copernicus, Kuhn used the dichotomy between internal technical factors and external social factors, concepts that were very much in vogue at that time.

Social Conditioning

The sociology of scientific knowledge (SSK) arose in the 1970s and relied on a critical view of the externalist orientation of Merton. Departing from the general idea that knowledge, in its widest sense, is socially conditioned, SSK, independently from the debate about the problem of relativism, had as its object three principal questions: (1) the definition of social conditioning factors, (2) the types of conditioning factors, and (3) the extension of conditioning according to types of knowledge. The treatment of these questions, and above all of the last one, admitted the effect of social conditioning, not only on the theoretical contents of science such as its theoretical and methodological conditions but also on the criteria for validity inherent in the scientific process. This constituted a frontal clash with the positivistic conception of science, in which science is a system of knowledge endowed with internal mechanisms for the validation of the results and the orientation of development, thus guaranteeing objectivity and neutrality.

One of the central streams of SSK was related to what was called the strong program. Within this scope, Bloor and his colleagues wanted to explain how scientific knowledge was caused by social conditions—although not exclusively so. This, in fact, was the first of four canonical principles that he specified for the strong program; the other three were impartiality, symmetry (these two are now usually combined into the postulate or principle of symmetry), and reflexivity (the requirement that the types of explanation given by SSK be to be applied to itself).

To explore this, those practicing the strong program were obliged to look in other directions. Two strategies were explored. The most important of these was to identify the interests of the individuals or small groups under study and use these to explain their choices and judgements. This was inspired, in part, by work on the constituent interests of knowledge by the German philosopher Jürgen Habermas, but the principal focus was specifically orientated toward the influence of social motives in science.

Many debates took place, which eventually led to the fragmentation of SSK at the end of the 1980s. The crucial question in the debate had to do with the characterization of the social range used to explain scientific practice and the nature of the explanations deriving from this. It is important to note that there were questions that were not only derived from Kuhn but that could not be kept apart from questions about the logic of scientific production and patterns of social life. The most important of these was, in fact, the interest in the social causes of scientific beliefs.

Subcultures as Conditioners of the Production of Knowledge

Collins To Collins, the social ties that delimit and maintain the union of subcultures are essential conditions for the production of consensually accepted knowledge (as in Kuhn, the relations of authority are basic to normal science). The majority of scientists, the major part of the time, live their lives in the ambit of a matrix of confidence and support. It is only when that confidence is broken that its social mechanism is exposed to view. Controversies, independently of being frequent or prolonged, acquire primacy because they reveal the relations of authority, credit, and lack of confidence that are hidden in any type of knowledge that has become largely accepted.

The scientific practice was characterized as an undetermined process of opening and shutting up, and scientists were characterized as being compelled by neither logical deductions from existent beliefs nor nonambiguous evidence to develop their ideas in any particular direction. Instead, scientists were presented as making practical judgements that were be related to local subcultures in which their recourses and aptitudes had been invested and in which they pursued their specific objectives. In controversies, the structure of these (normally hidden) compromises is brought to the surface and exposed to view.

Collins also showed that a considerable percentage of tacit knowledge must be drawn upon so that knowledge can be reproduced in another place. In other words, he demonstrated that the universality of scientific knowledge is in fact related to the process of replication, which requires the transference of knowledge from the subculture in which it was originally produced to another subculture. Because they are participants in a subculture, scientists learn to see the objects they observe in a particular way; consequently, the representations of the world, or the (di)visions of the world, that they have are linked as much to the techniques they have acquired as they are to the knowledge shared in the heart of a disciplinary subculture. This is a line of thought that we recognize as coming from Kuhn, Wittgenstein, Hanson, and Fleck.

Ian Hacking Some analysts have defended scientific focus on laboratory work, characterizing scientists as being involved in the creation of an "artificial reality," which is to say, the creation of a configuration of the material world that is *real* but that is not identified with "nature" (which, we suppose, exists *a priori* and independently of human intervention).

The philosopher Ian Hacking spoke of scientific experiences in the laboratory as if they were activities of the creation (representation and construction) of phenomena, treated, stabilized, and reproduced. The phenomena, suggested Hacking, must not be thought of as summer mulberries that have been treated and are available for picking but as identities that have been made via instrumental involvement with the material world. So, laboratories are places where phenomena are reproduced, or constructed—what the French philosopher Gaston Bachelard designated the "phenomena-techniques," phenomena embedded in technical practices. The specific laboratorial resources, human as well as material, make laboratories privileged places for the construction of artificial reality, via its representation.

Ludwick Fleck Both fundamental arguments of ethnography of the laboratory—that scientific work is practical reasoning in a specific place and that human and material recourses construct experimental phenomena—receded before the work of Ludwick Fleck (1896–1961), *Genesis and Development of a Scientific Fact*.

Fleck insisted that the production of knowledge, even of hard experimental facts, consists of social activity and, starting from there, constitutes an appropriate object for sociological analysis. In one of his more emblematic affirmations, which identified his style of thought, he declared, "cognition is the human activity more socially conditioned, and knowledge is the supreme social creation." The social character of knowledge is, in this perspective, revealed by the social circumstances of its production in the heart of an interactive community (a "collective thought") that sustains a distinct mode of reasoning (its "style of thought").

Bruno Latour Bruno Latour was the major defender of the vision that an explanation of scientific practice and the extension of its effects on society required a drastic revision of categories that sociologists of scientific knowledge used. What was required, according to Latour, was the recognition of the status of nonhuman identities as social actors. Many of these points were developed, and largely expressed, in his 1987 work *Science in Action*.

Therefore, it is necessary that the social scientist make a double effort, penetrating the "rituals" that characterize scientific life and achieving a reflexive understanding of details of scientific work, following a hybrid vision of intellectual, technical, and social activities (human and nonhuman) that are mutually dependent and reciprocally influenced. The observer assumes a cautious, but deliberate, position, oscillating between naïve ignorance and the complete acceptance of the pattern as the "natives" see things.

Therefore it is important to incorporate the problem of the consequences or implications (anticipated or probable) of scientific activity that go beyond the circumscribed laboratory space. This is generally associated with and obliges us to rethink, on the one hand, reflexivity and, on the other, the consequences of redividing, reclassifying, or reorganizing the world as a consequence of collecting data.

John Dewey: American Pragmatism Reflection has long been considered by American pragmatists, especially by John Dewey, and is currently being revived today in the context of discussions about risk societies.

John Dewey, as an American pragmatist, used the term "experience" to denote the broad context of the human organism's interrelationship with its environment, not just the domain of human thought alone. In addition, Dewey later substituted "transaction" for his earlier "interaction" to denote the relationship between organism and environment because the former better suggested the dynamic interdependence between the two and, in a new introduction to *Experience and Nature*, he offered the term "culture" as an alternative to "experience." The social dimension and function of belief systems explored by Dewey and other pragmatists have received renewed attention by such writers as Richard Rorty and Jürgen Habermas, particularly Dewey's claims that the human individual is a social being from the start and that individual satisfaction and achievement can be realized only within the context of the social habits and institutions that promote them.

Rejecting fundamentalism, Dewey accepted the view of scientific fallibility that was characteristic of the school of pragmatism—any proposition that is accepted as an item of knowledge has this status only provisionally, contingent on its adequacy in providing a coherent understanding of the world as the basis for human action. According to Dewey, a democratic order, which requires a "socially generous" attitude of mind and "civic efficiency," is neither more nor less than the capacity to share in a give-and-take experience.

Rethinking Objectivity

Forms of Objectivity

We can identify patterns of objectivity:

- Weak objectivity, which suspends references to social, cultural, and identity factors, in short the external factors of scientific work, and reduces objectivity to a question of method, which is understood as being internal to this activity.
- Strong objectivity, which demands the explication of all relevant conditions to the production of scientific knowledge, without a distinction between external or internal conditions. In other words, it is wrong to think that the scientific method requires the elimination of all social values from scientific processes.

Sandra Harding defends the need for a strong objectivity, because, in her perspective, it is necessary to consider the relevance of perspectives other than the dominant one. Thus, democratic values increase objectivity. Harding advocates observer communities (instead of an abstract, individual, or "invisible" observer) in association with the consideration of outside and marginal perspectives to achieve more complete, undistorted accounts in science. She calls attention to the redefinition of political problems as scientific ones; because of this, science can be seen as a contested zone, which means, in her perspective, that we need to reshape objectivity even as we criticize it to prevent dangerous depoliticization in investigating processes, or so-called neutrality.

Disunity of Sciences: Ecology of Practices

According to Galison, the notion of scientific objectivity has changed over time in response to social influences within and outside of specific disciplines. We know much less, however, about the way of constructing alternative visions of the world that are capable of proposing other ways of arranging the world and describing its dynamics, permitting us to face the difficulties that the current dominant "versions of the world" are not capable of resolving.

The reduction of science to a unique epistemological model, such as Newtonian physics, which is based on mathematization as a scientific ideal, gave way to a diversification that created a multiplicity of "ecologies of practices" organized in relation to distinct epistemological models. The principles of legitimating the various practices constituted as sciences began themselves, in this way, to multiply, so that this led not only to different sciences invoking different models of science, but also to tensions between these models of science. Defining the frontiers was a way of autonomizing and legitimizing the distinct ecologies of practices, without their submission to "foreign" epistemological models. Defending the frontiers signified, in many cases, the difference between the consolidation and the fragmentation of new disciplines or scientific dominions.

The demarcation of frontiers comes to mark this period in the history of science. Many more innovative areas of scientific knowledge appear in these territories of "passage" that are the frontiers. We are not speaking about interdisciplinary research but of a collaboration that presupposes a dynamic hybridization, miscegenation, or transgression of boundaries that characterizes modernity as historical process. The work of creating frontiers and the dynamics of transgressing those frontiers will raise the objects and entities that make up the world in which we live today.

The differences between disciplines and the so-called disunity of sciences led to a rethinking of the division between natural and social sciences. Those in the life sciences, cognitive sciences, and environmental sciences, especially, characterized their differences in terms of ecology of practices (as Isabelle Stengers called them) rather than in terms of the classic divisions between the natural and the social sciences. These ecologies of practices permitted the distinction between "naturalist" observation, modeling, simulation, historical research, and experimentation that crosses, transversely, the natural and social sciences.

This means that the problem of collecting data becomes distinct in each of these types of ecology of practice, as referred to by Galison and Stump in *Disunity of Science*. In this sense, the frontiers not only demarcate "science and its others," they determine the diversification or "disunity" inside the sciences.

Social Sciences Specificity

Each science not only describes reality, it also interprets it according to its frames of reference. In sociology, these are essentially related to its social dimension. And, because the preconstructed is everywhere, the breach with common sense (that is, with the representations shared by all) implies a radical doubt according to a reflexive and self-reflexive intention.

The object of social sciences is not "nature"; it is, above all, the systems of historical and social relations that create specific epistemological obstacles (such as the problem of language) and that compel a more accurate epistemological vigilance (to use the terms of Bourdieu, Chamboredon, and Passeron in *Le Métier de Sociologue*). The safeguard of this rationalist construction of social science is, nevertheless, always precarious. The apparent contradiction between the precariousness of this rationalist construction and the "belief," to which Bourdieu subscribes in *Leçon sur la Leçon*, in the transforming character of sociological knowledge, fighting against the "monopoly of legitimate representation of the social world" is resolved in the epistemological plane through reflexivity or perhaps by submitting sociological practice to sociological analysis, using for this the theories and methods that sociology uses to analyze social reality (as pointed out already by the defenders of the strong program).

For Bourdieu, scientific practice that forgets to question itself does not know what it is doing; it may discover something about the object, but it is not truly objectified. It is in this sense that the rupture with both externalist and internalist prenotions is equally important. That is, erudite discourse is not enough; it is also necessary to be aware of the scientific ideology—perhaps better termed "significant representations"—which is inevitably part of the frame of meanings of any scientist. Not taking this into account causes a nonrecognition effect. From there, science reinforces itself while reinforcing scientific criticism, which means that social scientists should take themselves as the object of the instruments that they develop and that the sociology of sociology is an indispensable instrument in the sociological method.

Contrary to what was intended by social physics, it therefore becomes necessary to bear in mind that the object of study does not exist in social life in the direct sense; it is not there, as the positivists thought. Instead, it is a product of our mental exercise; it is constructed by the individual who is going to study it according to the theoretical reference matrix and all the extrinsic and intrinsic constraints of knowledge production, itself the product of the human spirit's capacity of rational elaboration.

This is fundamentally different from a naturalistic descriptive perspective, which assumes that the objects of study already exist and that the scientist only has to describe them. As Bourdieu would say, it is only in accordance with a set of hypotheses derived from a set of theoretical assumptions that any empirical data can work as proof or as evidence. Thus, it becomes necessary to avoid at all costs the basic inclination to think of the social, natural, or physical world in a "realist" instead of a "relational" way, in so far as "real is relational" (as Hegel put it).

In short, we must assume that even in the exact sciences the object of study is not completely independent of (in the sense of being exterior to) the researcher because, even if the perspective is merely descriptive, it becomes necessary to take the analytical instruments used by the researcher into account. This assumption when applied to the social and human sciences leads to an exponential increase in the uncertainties from the outset because the object of study itself interacts with the scientist and can influence the course of the experiment. Therefore, the deterministic characteristics of social and human analyses also decrease exponentially and, in turn, call on the scientists' reflexive capacity to explain the conditions of the research process, with the aim of eliminating what we call the object effect.

Rethinking Neutrality

Once the empiricist innocence had been lost, accessing true knowledge became a sinuous road, full of difficulties. The more neutrality appeared to be an illusion, the more scientific truth became precarious and temporary and the more difficult and risky it became to obtain it.

This consciousness of complexity translated into the idea that if there is no *one* real way to access to the truth, *all* possible ways must be used. The basic idea of Feyerabend, in *Against Method*, is that if there is one methodological rule of absolute value that all other rules are frequently put aside and that this must be if we intend to promote scientific development.

Understanding therefore is a special technique of the social sciences. Social researchers, however, use the same kind of resources as laypeople to give meaning to the conduct that is their object of analysis or explanation, in addition to the fact that the concepts they use are not exterior to the phenomenon observed but are, rather, linked to or dependent on a previous understanding of the concepts used by the laypeople to maintain an intelligible social world. Social scientists, like laypeople in fact, take advantage of the socially available interpretative resources. The difference between scientists and laypeople is that the former take advantage of these resources through the mediation of scientific categories, under the integrated form of a scientific paradigm or frame of meaning; this enables them to have a more developed, but specific, kind of reflexivity, oriented toward scientific presuppositions in order to establish a search for the meaning in itself and whose concepts are dominated as a kind of practical activity that creates specific kinds of description.

As a result of this double relationship between the lay and scientific ways of constructing a universe of meaning, one of the fundamental concepts of Giddens's theory of sociological analysis, called double hermeneutics, is explained, as "the hermeneutic explanation and the mediation of diverging life forms between the descriptive metalanguages of social sciences." This concept should be put into perspective. We start with the assumption that knowledge in itself is part of a production process, which is also the production of facts, data, and actual empirical information. Therefore, we intend to distance ourselves from the perspective of the "unlimited sovereignty" of the subject in an attempt to avoid ending up in an excessive idealism in which it is not very clear where the obstacles of common sense end and where the construction of theoretical prepositions and the perception of the validity of these prepositions by using empirical confirmation starts.

Actually, it defends methodological pluralism, a combination of quantitative and qualitative methods and, consequently, the articulated use of several research techniques. But methodological pluralism should not be confused with methodological anarchy or with methodological eclectism—the first departs from a logic of research that prescribes norms for the selection and use of methods and the second limits the diversity of the methods used and establishes a hierarchy among them. The idea is to leave behind the Weberian tradition of dividing epistemological problems of the production of sociological knowledge between methodology (essentially intensive and qualitative) and philosophical logic and, instead, to carry out a deep exploration of sociological production from the perspective of applied rationalism. Therefore, the meaning of the "epistemological vector" goes from mental elaboration to empirical verification—"from reason to reality"—and in this sense no observation can be made without theoretical assumptions and hypotheses, all data are already results, and no technique can be used except with reference to theoretical options and choices. In addition, theoretical proposals should be informed by appropriate substantive research. The scientific subject is shown to be fragmentary and at the same time equipped with this "technical materialism" (more precisely, the empirical research procedures) of which Bachelard wrote.

Modus Operandus

Assuming a scientific and, presumably, neutral (as conventionally defined) attitude involves choosing to put the acquired theoretical knowledge into action, investing it in new kind of research. This leads to a *modus operandus* that orientates and organizes scientific practice without, however, shaping it solely and definitively into an "ideal" method of a positivist (or other) kind.

This refers to a relational attitude and a reflexive and self-reflexive capacity to *make* science, a fundamental characteristic of the social sciences and of social scientists. This takes time to incorporate; however, it is essential to break with dogmatic elitist attitudes that in the name of orthodox methodologies that cause researchers to end up being unable to notice, see, and question the fundamentals on which the construction of their objects of study, experiments, confirmations, and conclusions are based. Hence, the same reflexivity should be used to create radical diversity between scientific knowledge and common sense.

On this basis, Bourdieu defines *Le Métier de Sociologue* as the capacity to convert abstract problems into practical scientific operations, which is always a relational process between theory and practice in which knowledge is transmitted through modes of transmission, namely between the teacher and the learner. Thus, an operating plan, a scientific *habitus*, is progressively incorporated.

Constructing the object of study, questioning the preconstructed objects, mobilizing all the techniques that, given the definition of the object and practical conditions, always follow a critical and watchful epistemological attitude—these are the assumptions that shape a reflexive methodological proposal that considers research something too serious and too difficult to take the liberty of confusing *rigidity* (which is the opposite of intelligence and invention) with *rigor*. Obviously, the other side of extreme methodological freedom, which seems to be merely good sense, is the use of extreme caution in applying techniques, paying attention to their adequacy to the problem posed and to the conditions of their use.

This methodological position, on the one hand, exceeds the epistemomethodological assumptions of the pioneering masters, but, on the other, it is also rooted in them even though in differentiated substantive-theoretical bases. Thus, just as in the Durkheimian perspective, the break with common sense is important for the construction of the object of study, together with a critical attitude linked not only to the construction of the object but also to the actual research, in the sense of objectification; scientific knowledge is presented to us as constructed knowledge. And just as in the Marxist perspective, the critical vision is extremely important in the research process, in terms of objectification; there is a dialectic relationship between the individual and society that justifies and is justified in social transformation; the positioning in the social structure is an objective condition that interferes with the subjective condition of the individual; social reality is not independent on the mind's construction processes; it is necessary to make the implicit explicit; and historical knowledge is important.

But in addition it is important to stress that this methodological proposal is distinct from those of the classics and that it points out some of their limitations. Although it is clear that the proposal distances itself from the unitary, positivist methodological position, just as the Durkheimian perspective does, it also distances itself in the use of quantitative methods *versus* qualitative methods and in following a course away from mechanical and reductionist materialism. The aim is, in fact, to overcome the radical position between positivism and antipositivism, between the structuralist or phenomenological perspective. An attempt is made, therefore, to pursue a perspective that is articulated and that contributes to the explanation of the construction and comprehension of the social in the action of individuals, they themselves being structured and structuring the actors in social structures, which refers to another fundamental concept of Giddens, the duality of structure. Hence, the individual's position in the structure is important for the explanation of social reality; on the one hand, social reality exists alongside the individual and, on the other, it is the individual who constructs and reconstructs social reality using a dialectic interaction between structures and practices. In addition, social reality must be explained bearing in mind the subjective dimension of the individual him- or herself in so far as he or she contributes to its meaning.

In short, the goal is to account for the subjective dimension of the objective action, objectifying the subjective. Therefore, the construction of the object of study is considered a very important step as is the whole process of choosing research techniques and conducting research, keeping in mind that the attitude that should be adopted is one of epistemological caution so that the research conditions are objectified. Thus, the object of study in social sciences has very specific peculiarities that interact with the researcher, namely with regard to the reflexive-relational capacity of the object, in that at the moment of interaction a situation is generated that is specific in itself and should not be ignored when explaining the actual process of research and the production of results.

Diversity should not be reduced by adopting common dimensions; that is, although it is possible to create an interface among the various scientific perspectives, erasing their diversity, the theoretical-substantive specificities should always be considered in addition to the actual nature of the object of study. Therefore, just as it is completely impossible to accede to intra-individuality, it is completely impossible to reduce to zero the effects on the observed agents of the application of research instruments. The actual discourse of the researcher leads to answers that fall within the range of what is considered desirable or expected as the ideal answer, according to an idealized relationship with the person or entity who analyzes the answers; this in turn unleashes an increase in the reflexive capacity of the observed agents, with more or less observable and lasting effects on the social fabric observed, during the actual research process.

Because it is not possible to research in a vacuum in social sciences, the object is not even there in the direct sense, the objectification of the theoretical priorities and methodological principles becomes important; this not only directs the researcher's way of looking at the object of study, but also controls the actual production of information, in articulation with the researcher's own individualized capacities. Hence, it is understood that different objects of study will be constructed around the same phenomenon in the name of creativity, which is very important to the scientist but which is very specific to each individual. In this way, an attempt is made to explain not only the differences but also the overlap among the various ways of producing scientific knowledge.

It therefore becomes necessary to break with common sense, that is, to be cautious about the preconstructed objects of spontaneous sociology. This, to a certain extent, is rooted in the cardinal rule of the Durkheimian method that social facts should be treated as things and that the main focus should be on dealing with how ("the thing"), on defining a mental attitude, and *not* on conferring an ontological status on the object itself.

The methodological position that is defended here implies not only an epistemological break with preconstructed objects and an attitude of epistemological caution, but also an attitude that systematically questions aspects of reality posed in relation to the questioning to which they are submitted in accordance with theoretical issue. Thus, the whole well-constructed experience results in the intensification of the dialectics between reason and experience and between theory and confirmation, but on the condition that the researcher knows how to think suitably about the results produced, even the negative ones, questioning and specifying the reasons that lead to the results.

Generally speaking, this epistemological and methodological proposal leads to a cautious dialectical position between the theory and the facts observed and between objective and subjective conditions, in a cumulative process marked by breaks and discontinuities through which knowledge is constructed, which is itself in constant change. This position is removed not only from the holistic objectivist perspective of Durkheimian positivism, emptied of the social action meaning, but also removed from the individualist/subjectivist perspective of phenomenology and other forms of antipositivism, which inhibit comparative and causal analyses. Thus, in both a break from and a continuation of the classics, a theoretical-methodological perspective is adopted in the social sciences that overcomes the naïve radical position between positivism and anti-positivism. It gives structure to a tendency to stop the reduction of polarization around alternative paradigms, and orients research on the social toward the agents' self-reflexive capacity in the various fields, leading to the individual's role as structurer through interaction and as reflected in the various structuring dimensions of society.

Therefore, the emerging logic is one of syncretism, following a path of reducing the excesses of the micro/macro dichotomy. That is, neither methodological individualism nor methodological holism leads an open research process along the line of applied rationalism; but methodological situationalism, we believe, does. In short, the art of sociology is objectification, that is, trying to objectify all the research conditions in the actual empirical experience, without forgetting that it, in itself, is a social relationship in which actors (the scientists) finds themselves playing a role in accordance with a specific *habitus*, an incorporated *hexis* that they included in a specific framework of objective properties and that influence and are influenced by the subjective expectations of the researchers in a specific field themselves.

Acknowledgments

The author thanks those colleagues and friends who read and commented on initial drafts of this entry, João Arriscado Nunes and Ruth Chadwick. He also thanks Cecil Williams for his translation of the Portuguese version into English and Kirsten Funk for all her support and for her editing work on the manuscript.

This work is based on the 1994 epistemo-methodologial reflections in C. Diego's *Divulgação Científica um Sistema de Comunicação e Cultura. Entre Reprodução e Diferenciação*, which is awaiting publication by Cosmos Editora, Lisbon.

See Also the Following Articles

Durkheim, Émile • Weber, Max

Further Reading

Bourdieu, P. (1968). *Le Métier de Sociologue.* Mouton, Paris.

Diego, C. (In press) *Divulgação Científica um Sistema de Comunicação e Cultura: Entre Reprodução e Diferenciação.* Cosmos Editora, Lisbon.

Durkheim, E. (1988). *Les Règles de la Méthode Sociologique.* Flammarion, Paris.

Feyerabend, P. K. (1975). *Against Method.* New Left Books, London.

Fleck, L. (1979). *Genesis and Development of a Scientific Fact.* University of Chicago Press, Chicago, IL.

Galison, P., and Stump, D. J. (eds.) (1996). *The Disunity of Science: Boundaries, Contexts and Power.* Sanford University Press, Sanford, CA.

Habermas, J. (1968). Técnica e ciência como "ideologia". *Ed.* **70**

Habermas, J. (1986). *Théorie de l'Agir Communicationnel, Vol 1: Rationalité de L'agir et Rationalization de la Societé.* Fayard.

Hacking, I. (1983). *Representing and Intervening: Introductory Topics in the Philosophy of Natural Science.* Cambridge University Press, Cambridge, UK.

Hacking, I. (1992). The disunified sciences. In *The End of Science?* (R. J. Elvee, ed.). University of America Press, Lanham, MD.

Knorr-Cetina, K. (1981). *The Manufacture of Knowledge: An Essay on the Constructivism and Contextual Nature of Science.* Pergamon Press, Oxford.

Knorr-Cetina, K. (1999). *Epistemic Cultures. How the Sciences Make Knowledge.* Harvard University Press, Cambridge, MA.

Kuhn, T. (1972). *La Structure des Revolutions Scientifiques.* Flammarion, Paris.

Latour, B. (1987). *Science in Action.* Harvard University Press, Cambridge, MA.

Latour, B., and Woolgar, S. (1979). *Laboratory Life: the Social Construction of Scientific Facts.* Sage, Beverly Hills, CA.

Madureira Pinto, J., and Santos Silva, A. (eds.) (1984). *Metodologia das Ciências Sociais.* Afrontamento, Porto.

Merton, R. (1984). *Ciência, Tecnologia y Sociedade en la Inglaterra del Siglo XVII.* Alianza Editorial, Madrid. (First Published in 1970.)

Merton, R. (1985). *La Sociología de la Ciencia, Vol. 1: Investigaciones Teóricas y Empíricas.* Alianza Editorial, Madrid. (First published in 1973.)

Mills, W. (1967). *L'imagination Sociologique.* Maspéro, Paris.

Pickering, A. (ed.) (1992). *Science as Practice and Culture.* University of Chicago Press, Chicago, IL.

Polanyi, M. (1958). *Personal Knowledge: Towards a Post-Critical Philosophy.* Routledge and Kegan Paul, London.

Popper, K. (1983). *La Logique de la Découverte Scientifique.* Payot, Paris.

Verón, E. (1973). Vers une logique naturelle des mondes sociaux. *Communications* **20**.

Weber, M. (1965). *Essais sur la théorie de la science.* Plon, Paris.

Neyman, Jerzy

John M. Nicholas
University of Western Ontario, London, Ontario, Canada

Glossary

confidence interval estimate The determination, with a specified probability, of a random interval that contains an unknown constant parameter value.

test of significance (Fisher) A test of the evidential relation of a sample to a hypothesis, based on the probability, conditional on the hypothesis, that the deviation of the sample or more extreme cases from an expected value will occur. If the probability is small (e.g., 5% or 0.1%), the hypothesis is deemed false or we judge that an improbable event has occurred.

test of significance (Neyman–Pearson) A test of whether a sample warrants a rule of behavior, assuming a given hypothesis as a basis for action, in terms of permissible likely long-term frequencies of Type I and Type II errors in repeated trials.

Type I error The rejection of a hypothesis in favor of an alternative, when the hypothesis is true.

Type II error The acceptance of a hypothesis in favor of an alternative, when the alternative is true.

Jerzy Neyman was one of the magisterial figures of statistical theory and application of the twentieth century. With a taste for foundational studies in mathematics, he brought to statistical theory a demand for clear logical grounding. In a remarkable collaboration with Egon Pearson, he contributed fundamentally to the development of hypothesis testing. He developed influential accounts of confidence interval estimation. He established the core theory of randomized stratified sampling. Throughout his career he was concerned, too, with many applied problems and he made influential contributions in agriculture, meteorology, sidereal astronomy, biomedical research and demography, fastidiously immersing himself in the fundamentals of each field.

Early Years

Neyman was born, Jerzy Splawa-Neyman, on April 16, 1894, in Bendery, Moldavia, then part of Russia. His father, Czeslaw Neyman, was a lawyer. Neyman's family had moved or been removed from what had been Poland, then under Russian, Austrian, and German occupation. After several moves and after the premature death of his father, when Neyman was 12 years old he and his mother settled in Kharkov in the Ukraine. Later, he took up studies at the university there.

Early Career

Neyman was particularly attracted to the foundations of mathematics, including set theory, measure theory, and the theory of integration, possibly stimulated by a deep impression made on him by the work of Lebesgue. He was sufficiently motivated to submit a 500-page essay on Lebesgue integration while at the University of Kharkhov. The essay earned him a Gold Medal.

He was influenced on a number of fronts by the prominent Sorbonne-trained mathematician Sergi Bernstein. Bernstein lectured on probability and statistics and was interested in their application to genetics and agriculture. In addition, he introduced Neyman to the philosophy of science of the British polymath Karl Pearson, arguably the doyen of the nascent field of statistical theory. Neyman later reported that for himself and other students at the time Pearson's uncompromising critiques of a variety of authorities seemed almost unbelievably bold. Pearson became a secular source for a group of young men whose orthodox beliefs had dissipated but whose need for authority had not. It seemed to Neyman's wife, Olga, that he talked of nothing but Karl Pearson. Whether by nature, impressed by this early influence, or both, Neyman was to maintain a philosophical vision of his own work throughout his life, remarkably combining a profound commitment to logical clarity in the conceptual grounding of statistical devices with a prudent sense of the value of applied problems. Concrete problems not only had their intrinsic interest, but also their value as a spur to the development of good theory.

In 1921, Neyman found himself in the newly reconstituted Poland, having been included in an exchange of Polish for Russian prisoners at the conclusion of World War I. But it was not really repatriation for Neyman; it was his first time in the country. He was able to find a position at the National Agricultural Institute in Bydgoszcz; no matter the appeal of measure theory, it was his preparation in statistics that made him employable.

At the end of 1922 he moved to Warsaw and took up employment at the State Meteorological Institute. After that he became an assistant at the University of Warsaw and lectured in mathematics and statistics at the Central College of Agriculture. He also gave lectures at the University of Krakow. He finished his doctorate at Warsaw in 1924. By then Neyman was unique in Poland in his expertise and interests, and, in recognition of this, he was awarded a government fellowship which permitted him to work at the Galton Laboratory at University College London under the direction of Karl Pearson himself.

Neyman and Pearson on Hypothesis Testing

In London, in 1925–1926, Neyman was able to publish several papers in *Biometrika*, employing material that had been published in Poland with little chance of finding an international audience. He was disappointed to find that Pearson's laboratory was not up to date and that Pearson's mathematics was insufficiently modern. Indeed, it seemed to Neyman that Pearson was unwilling to comprehend the difference between independence and absence of correlation, and some strain developed between them, aggravated by Neyman's explanations in impoverished English.

With London now seeming less appealing, he opportunely won a Rockefeller fellowship that permitted him to move to Paris for a year. There, he was able to attend lectures by his revered Borel and Lebesgue and a seminar with Hadamard. Later Neyman remarked that, had it not been for the intervention of Egon Pearson, Karl Pearson's son, he would in all likelihood have returned to work on set theory, measure theory, and the theory of integration.

Researchers in hypothesis testing in the mid-1920s faced a scene that had been remarkably transformed in the previous decade, with new paradigms of statistical appraisal at hand, for the most part introduced by Ronald Fisher between 1915 and 1925 in an almost single-handed revolution. There were new statistical devices and new criteria for their appraisal. Of particular interest were the new results on small-sample distribution theory developed by Student (W. S. Gosset) and Fisher, reflecting a shift in emphasis from the analysis of natural populations to controlled experimentation. Finding a principled basis for choosing between criteria of appraisal in, say, evaluating whether two samples had been drawn from the same population became important because different, equally intuitively plausible criteria yielded different significances from the same data. The stringency of test, in the sense of minimizing the tail-area p value, became a central preoccupation of a number of researchers, including Karl Pearson.

Addressing these issues, Egon Pearson initiated a correspondence with Neyman about the news of Student's suggestive observation that "if there is any alternative hypothesis which will explain the occurrence of the sample with a more reasonable probability . . . you will be very much more inclined to consider that the original hypothesis is not true." This was a not unambiguous proposal, and Neyman did not immediately recognize its import. Although Neyman endorsed Student's insight, he initially read it as implicating Bayesian-style *a priori* probabilities, to which he was at that time still sympathetic. Pearson, however, had a reasonably clear idea that the crucial element was the introduction of an uneliminable role for the alternative hypotheses in tests of significance. This was to be, of course, a central innovation in the Neyman–Pearson accounts of hypothesis testing. It was also an important departure from the model of significance testing that had been advocated by Fisher and, indeed, Fisher would resist the innovation throughout his lengthy career. Pearson did, however, maintain Fisher's central role of the concept of likelihood. Neyman found the viewpoint compelling, although at the same time he was more skeptical than Pearson and looked for a deeper rationalization of the likelihood principle. He was more guarded about embracing its universal applicability in the adjudication of test statistics.

Pearson visited Neyman in Paris in spring 1927, and it is likely that they then set out the plan of their first joint paper, "On the Use and Interpretation of Certain Test Criteria for Purposes of Statistical Inference. Part I," which was accepted by Karl Pearson for *Biometrika*. Already Pearson was opposed to Bayesian inverse probabilities, they flexibly formulated a range of different approaches, direct and inverse, to the problem of determining whether a single sample may plausibly be taken to be drawn randomly from an assumed population. Having introduced a role for an alternative hypothesis to the hypothesis being tested, the authors noted that two sources of error become clearly identifiable: (1) rejecting the test hypothesis when it is true and (2) retaining the test hypothesis when the alternative hypothesis is true. The authors noted the essential role of likelihood to which Fisher had drawn attention in the early 1920s.

In part II of their paper, also published in *Biometrika*, Neyman and Pearson brought the likelihood ratio approach to bear on the grounding of Karl Pearson's χ^2 test, the merits of which had been hotly debated in the early 1920s. The second paper made the distinction between simple and composite hypotheses even more explicit than part I had. Neyman, alone, followed part II with what might have been part III were it not that Pearson felt unable to put his name to it. The paper was published as Neyman's "Contribution to the Theory of Certain Test Criteria" and it offered interesting results, showing convergence in the results of direct and inverse methods. Pearson was not happy about the seemingly sympathetic application of Bayesian methods and possibly found the mathematical character of the paper too extreme. It is likely that his interest in the convergence of results from distinct approaches, and possibly the continued attention of Bayesians such as Harold Jeffreys, motivated Neyman to pursue these parallel approaches.

Despite Pearson's withdrawal from that paper, their collaboration was far from over; in fact, the best was yet to come. The next steps included extending the application of the likelihood principle to the problem of drawing two samples from given normal population, building on the appraisal of several proposed criteria by V. Romanovsky. The result vindicated applications of the t and F tests. The resulting paper, which extended the likelihood principle to the case of an arbitrary number of samples, concluded by commending the principle for its capacity to "deliver the goods" in important problems, validating previously intuitively sound tests and discovering new ones.

Despite his preoccupation at this time with establishing a Biometric Laboratory at the Nencki Institute for Experimental Biology in Warsaw, Neyman was able to start a new initiative—applying the calculus of variations to optimizing the avoidance of error. He intended to find a firm foundation for the likelihood principle. The result was the benchmark joint paper of 1933, "On the Problem of the Most Efficient Tests of Statistical Hypotheses," published in the *Philosophical Transactions of the Royal Society*. Representing the choice of a criterion for testing a hypothesis against an alternative hypothesis as the choice of a critical region in the sample hyperspace, Neyman and Pearson proved the Neyman–Pearson lemma that, for a simple hypothesis and alternative, the "best" critical region, which minimized Type II error at a given risk of Type I error, is picked out by the likelihood ratio principle. Under supplementary constraints, they successfully applied the same strategy to the case of composite hypotheses. In addition, the concepts associated with the uniformly most powerful (UMP) test appeared.

In their *Royal Society* paper, Neyman and Pearson offered a new methodological viewpoint, conceiving of tests as guides to rules governing behavior rather than as inference devices that determine the truth or falsity of hypotheses. Initially, the decisions in question were those of acceptance and rejection, so that a less than prescient reader might take the new viewpoint to be rather innocuous, although serving as a convenient vehicle for linking the costs of acceptance and rejection to the statistician's not being wrong too often. The authors more overtly alluded to Laplace's problem of determining the number of votes of a jury sufficient for conviction, and clear economic and even ethical values are acknowledged to influence the cost of error.

Some of the same ambiguity between epistemological and practical decisions is preserved in their paper "Statistical Hypotheses in Relation to Probabilities A Priori," which applied their strategy to frameworks that appeal to *a priori* probabilities. The paper examined what could be derived from data independently of variation in priors. Notably, they wrote of the different viewpoints possible expressly within the context of scientific inquiry rather than in merely practical and commercial contexts. On the one hand, the researcher may take a hypothesis to be novel and important in scientific terms and not wish to give it up lightly, thus setting the rejection level particularly low. On the other hand, investigating deviations from a standard law, the researcher sets the level high in order to lower the risk of Type II error. However, in "Contributions to the Theory of Testing Statistical Hypotheses," which explored the means for bypassing the difficulty that many problems were not tractable in terms of UMP tests, their exposition of their general approach gave clear priority at the outset to two cases from commercial batch appraisal—one concerning electrical goods, the other pharmacological.

Later, in his *Lectures and Conferences on Mathematical Statistics and Probability* in 1937, Neyman made more explicit his preference for the notion of "inductive behavior" over "inductive reasoning." There he emphasized a more voluntarist notion than hitherto—the crucial phase of deliberation was not reasoning at all but rather an act of will. Problems such as batch acquisition in commercial contexts were easier to solve for definite quantitative costs and benefits than were problems in narrowly scientific work. In such problems, it was often a relatively straightforward matter to adjudicate the particular balance between the permissible risks of Type I and Type II errors. The association of statistical procedures with decision rather than inference and Neyman's denial that belief and conclusion were the appropriate conceptions of the outputs of the procedures received stiff opposition, most notably from Fisher. Although Fisher commended the economically sound methods that might assist the Royal Navy in prudently buying batches of shells for naval guns on the basis of limited sampling of the product, he felt that establishing a reliable scientific body of information, even in as practical a field as agriculture, needed inference, properly speaking. It is no secret that, for him, the disdainful expression "statistics for shopkeepers" was aimed at Neyman's and Pearson's conceptions, together with their generalization to Abraham Wald's statistical decision theory, which had an overtly game-theoretic stance. (There is some evidence that Egon Pearson did not really share Neyman's inductive behaviorist viewpoint.)

Neyman on Confidence Interval Estimation

Neyman had started on the problem of confidence interval estimation in 1930 in Warsaw, spurred by a request from Pytkowski for a measure of the uncertainty of an estimate. At that time he had been aware of neither Fisher's formulation of fiducial probability and fiducial limits nor Hotelling's application of confidence intervals to Student's *t* test. He lectured on his approach for several years in Warsaw and then in London, where Egon Pearson was able to find an appointment for him in the Department of Applied Statistics, which had been split off from the Galton Laboratory when Karl Pearson retired and was replaced by Ronald Fisher.

Neyman applied his approach in his paper "On the Two Different Aspects of the Representative Method." This contribution may be thought to be doubly revolutionary. First, it offered a decisive repudiation of the purposive selection form of sampling and established a theoretical base vindicating random sampling. This work provided a valuable and original platform for much work in sampling theory. In his discussion, Fisher declared Neyman's account to be "luminous." Second, it was the first English-language application of Neyman's method of confidence intervals, giving prominence to its rejection of inverse inference methods. In the face of Neyman's relating his confidence intervals to Fisher's fiducial intervals, Fisher voiced the compliment that it was a "handsome" generalization, although he had reservations about the assumptions that made it possible. Unfortunately, Fisher's goodwill evaporated after Neyman's presentation of arguments that Fisher's *z* test displayed bias in Latin square and randomized block designs in March 1935, results that, according to Fisher, demonstrated that Neyman did not properly appreciate the intent of such tests.

Neyman came to judge that the underlying intuitions of Fisher's fiducial conception defied consistent expression in mathematical terms. Fisher's restriction of the scope of application of fiducial distributions and limits to cases in which there existed sufficient statistics seemed to Neyman to be in itself undesirable and to provide a motivation for finding a more general and explicitly articulated statistical theory. This debate has continued since that time, and there are still widely divergent opinions on the merits of the respective camps, with some authors identifying the Fisher and Neyman approaches, others insisting on the merits and intelligibility of a unique concept of fiducial probability, and yet others identifying the fiducial approach with that of the Bayesian school.

It was only in 1937 that Neyman's systematic treatment of the interval estimation material appeared in "Outline of a Theory of Statistical Estimation Based on the Classical Theory of Probability." Here the method of confidence intervals was scrupulously based on a frequentist interpretation of probability, and Neyman emphasized the crucial point that interval limits were the random variables, not the estimated population parameter, which was in effect an unknown constant. Although Neyman had long given up his early preference for a Bayesian approach, thinking that the Bayesians confused real mathematical probability with a certain psychological feeling, he cheerfully credited the urgings of his student, Churchill Eisenhart as the last straw. It is plain that Neyman was profoundly influenced by the advocacy of the frequentist approach of Richard von Mises.

Neyman in the United States

In July 1935, Neyman was appointed Reader at University College. In time, he became increasingly convinced that his chances of being appointed to a professorial chair were slender. He assumed that Fisher would attempt to obstruct such an appointment—he had voted against Neyman for Reader. Further, he felt that there was little chance of being appointed to a chair in Poland, to which he felt drawn out of gratitude for the support of colleagues and a particular loyalty to his students, to whom he often referred as "my pups." Neyman had been aware of his Russian wife's discomfort at the hostility from some Poles, remembering the Russian occupation. In addition, he was aware that his marshalling of data that indicated the extent of the Polish Catholic Church's holdings of the nation's wealth had earned him the enmity of prominent figures there. He had been informed that there was no chance that he would ever hold a chair in Poland. In addition, the political tensions in Europe were becoming dangerously threatening.

In 1937 he gave some lectures in the United States, having been invited to make presentations at the U.S. Department of Agriculture. His lecture notes were compiled into a celebrated and influential mimeographed edition of *Lectures and Conferences on Mathematical Statistics and Probability*, already mentioned.

A substantially revised edition was published in 1952 and became the canonical statement of the Neyman's statistical theory.

In 1938 he accepted a professorship in the Department of Mathematics at the University of California at Berkeley. There was a lack of statisticians there; the department was a blank slate on which Neyman could write. He moved rapidly to establish a Statistical Laboratory with himself as director.

After the end of the Second World War, Neyman established a symposium on probability and statistics that attracted the participation of preeminent figures in statistical theory, probability theory, and applied statistics. The striking success of the symposium was confirmation of Neyman's stature and of University of California at Berkeley's standing as one of the great centers for the field. A series of Berkeley symposia followed, another five over the next quarter century, and their publication is an invaluable resource for statisticians of all stripes—their influence can scarcely be overstated.

Neyman's revolutionary achievement of the 1920s and 1930s could scarcely be duplicated; inevitably that very achievement required its own elaboration and generalization. Neyman's work did, however, retain its quality, inventiveness, and commitment to grounding in first principles. One widely regarded achievement was the delineation of best asymptotically normal estimators. These have asymptotically normal distributions and, in addition, satisfy other appealing constraints, such as consistency and asymptotic efficiency, while not falling prey to the complexity of computation associated with maximum likelihood estimators. Neyman, with Elizabeth Scott, who became a frequent collaborator, discovered cases of inefficiency and inconsistency of the maximum likelihood estimator.

Lucien LeCam neatly captured Neyman's strategy for addressing problems in applied fields. Neyman's preference was to build and use stochastic models

> *from Astronomy to Zoology following a consistent philosophy throughout: Given a question about a particular phenomenon, Neyman tried to visualize the "mechanism" underlying the phenomenon. He then translated this vision into mathematical assumptions and formulas. After devising the stochastic model to his satisfaction, he would derive the statistical methods appropriate to the case at hand.*

Neyman's outlook was somewhat at odds with his early sympathy with Karl Pearson's philosophy of science, which treated scientific models as mental constructs and which provides little principled basis for the view that, as LeCam put it, "it is better to catch a bit of the mechanism than to use sundry 'interpolation' formulas."

With Scott, Neyman developed a model for epidemics based in part on work he had done in the late 1930s on contagious distributions that had been aimed at evaluating the effects of insecticides on larvae. In the earlier work too, his priority had been to guess "the actual machinery" of movements of larvae rather than simply to model the data. Remarkably, he and Scott discovered that the probability of an epidemic becoming uncontrollable in small community was the same as in the population at large.

Some of the same models were applied by Neyman and Scott, who had migrated from astronomy to statistics, to questions about the clustering of galaxies. Their work on these problems continued for many years and has considerable intrinsic interest, although it has been outflanked by new developments in cosmology. Other areas to which Neyman and his collaborators applied themselves included multistage models of carcinogenesis, natural selection or the struggle for existence, and the interaction of radiation on cells. In 1955, as a result of Neyman's great determination and intense efforts, Berkeley agreed to the establishment of a Department of Statistics distinct from the Mathematics Department.

At his retirement, a move was made to keep Neyman on as director of the Statistical Laboratory, an office he had kept after stepping down as chair of the Statistics Department. It was recognized that it would be an enormous blow to the stature of the admittedly distinguished group to lose his official presence and the administration agreed. Amusingly Neyman began signing his letters as Director of the Laboratory "Recalled to Active Duty."

Conclusion

Neyman lived through times of considerable turmoil. Polish by descent, he was born in Russia. He did live in Poland for a time but did not form, as he put it, "a geographic attachment," although he was deeply committed to his Polish colleagues and students. He was also particularly aware of Poland's intellectual heritage and took great satisfaction in editing *The Heritage of Copernicus: Theories More Pleasing to the Mind.* He was observed reading Copernicus fluently in the Latin he had learned as a youth. He lived in England for some years, but crucial parts of his collaboration with Egon Pearson seem to have taken place as much in brief meetings on the continent as in England. However, he spent half his intellectual life in the United States and seemed genuinely to have felt at home, no longer a stranger in a strange land. As he put it: "In 1921, I finished my studies in Russia, and I was an alien. I came to Poland, and found myself an alien. I went to Britain, and found myself an alien. By 1938, I was feeling, all around, like a professional veteran alien. And then I came to California, and here I stopped being an alien." Jerzy Neyman died in Berkeley on August 5, 1981 at the age of 87.

See Also the Following Articles

Confidence Intervals • Fisher, Sir Ronald • Hypothesis Tests and Proofs • Measurement Error, Issues and Solutions • Pearson, Karl • Type I and Type II Error

Further Reading

LeCam, L. (1994). Neyman and stochastic models. Unpublished paper. Available at: http://stat-www.berkeley.edu/users/rice/LeCam/papers/

Lehmann, E. L. (1994). *Jerzy Neyman*. National Academy of Sciences Biographical Memoirs, Vol. 63. National Academies Press, Washington, DC. Available at: http://books.nap.edu/books/0309049768/html/394.html

Neyman, J. (1937). Outline of a theory of statistical estimation based on the classical theory of probability. *Phil. Trans. Royal Soc. A* **236,** 333–380.

Neyman, J. (1949). *Lectures and Conferences on Mathematical Statistics,* 2nd Ed. U.S. Department of Agriculture Graduate School, Washington, DC.

Neyman, J. (1967). *A Selection of Early Papers of J. Neyman.* Cambridge University Press, Cambridge, UK.

Neyman, J. (1969). Statistical problems in science: The symmetric test of a composite hypothesis. *J. Amer. Statist. Assoc.* **64,** 1154–1171.

Neyman, J. (1974). *The Heritage of Copernicus: Theories 'Pleasing to the Mind.* The Copernican Volume of the National Academy of Sciences. MIT Press, Cambridge, MA.

Neyman, J. (1977). Frequentist probability and frequentist statistics. *Synthese* **36,** 97–131.

Neyman, J., and Pearson, E. S. (1928). On the use and interpretation of certain test criteria for purposes of statistical inference, Part I. *Biometrika* **20A,** 175–240.

Neyman, J., and Pearson, E. S. (1928). On the use and interpretation of certain test criteria for purposes of statistical inference, Part II. *Biometrika* **20A,** 263–294.

Neyman, J., and Pearson, E. S. (1933). On the problem of the most efficient tests of statistical hypotheses. *Phil. Trans. Royal Soc. A* **231,** 289–337.

Neyman, J., and Pearson, E. S. (1933). The testing of statistical hypotheses in relation to probabilities a priori. *Proc. Camb. Phil. Soc.* **24,** 492–495.

Neyman, J., and Scott, E. L. (1948). Consistent estimates based on partially consistent observations. *Econometrica* **16,** 1–32.

Pearson, E. S. (1970). The Neyman-Pearson story: 1926–34: Historical sidelights on an episode in Anglo-Polish collaboration. In *Studies in the History of Statistics and Probability* (E. S. Pearson and M. G. Kendall, eds.), pp. 455–479. Griffin, London.

Reid, C. (1982). *Neyman—from Life.* Springer-Verlag, New York.

Nightingale, Florence

Gabriel K. Wolfenstein

University of California, Los Angeles, Los Angeles, California, USA

Glossary

Adolphe Quetelet Belgian statistician and astronomer (1796–1874), whose application of statistics to social phenomena was central to the practice of statistics in the 19th century.

Crimean War Conflict (1853–1856) between Russia on one side, and Britain, France, and the Ottoman Turks on the other, over control in the region.

miasmatic Theory of disease popular in the 19th century that suggests that poisonous atmosphere emanating from unsanitary conditions causes illness, as opposed to a contagionist theory.

probationers Florence Nightingale's technical term for nurses.

William Farr British statistician (1807–1883), in charge of the statistical section of the General Register Office and a leading authority on vital statistics. He had a significant impact on Nightingale.

zymotic Term created by William Farr to identify infectious and epidemic diseases, specifically caused by a ferment-like process.

The history of modern nursing has become linked with the name of Florence Nightingale (1829–1910), the Lady with the Lamp as she was widely known in the 19th and early 20th centuries. Yet like all historical figures, the history her life reveals is multifaceted. Often portrayed as a sainted hero, she was a shrewd political player who made effective use of her (perhaps psychologically provoked) invalidism to push her reforms. Though her impact has been considerable, her innovations in health care and in the use of statistics must be understood as emerging out of her historical milieu. The story of nursing as a profession does not begin with Nightingale, and we need to be careful not to be directed by her still powerful manipulative skills. But while nursing had a history before Nightingale, she remains central to understanding the changes that took place in both nursing and in health care during her lifetime.

Introduction

Even before her death, Florence Nightingale was known not only as a founder of modern nursing but also as one of the major figures in hospital reform in the 19th century. Though *The London Times* proclaimed her heroism for the saving of British casualties during the Crimean War (she was perhaps the only British hero to emerge from that conflict), it was her work subsequent to the war that secured the historical legacy that we still contend with today. In some ways the popular story of Nightingale as creating the first modern nurses—if not fashioned certainly encouraged by Nightingale and her supporters—has changed little over the course of the century. Though Lytton Strachey exposed the world to a Nightingale different from the admired heroine, demonizing her in his 1918 *Eminent Victorians*, her public persona survives mostly unscathed.

The Metropolitan Life Insurance Company, for example, placed her in their "Health Heroes" series, preserving her image intact, though some influence can be detected from Strachey's work. "In the popular imagination," wrote Grace Hallock and C. E. Turner, "she was the Lady of the Lamp, the Angel of the Crimea, the tender woman whose shadow the soldiers kissed as it fell on their pillows." But, they said, there was another side to her; she was also "an angel with a flaming sword. Her mind was the sword . . . Ruthlessly she bared the easy-going inefficiency which hitherto had made a disgrace of sanitation and nursing, both in military and civil life." She was both nurse and reformer. The recent online edition of the Encyclopedia Britannica defines her primarily as a "nurse and the founder of trained nursing as a profession for women," placing less emphasis on the other important aspects of her life.

However, both Florence Nightingale and the changes in health care which she spearheaded and inspired are far more complex, as recent scholarship has made clear. To this end, the body of this article will proceed in three parts. It will first examine her life to the point when she returned to England from the Crimea. The second section will contextualize her reforms in hospitals and nursing. The third section will discuss her use of statistics, especially as a tool of persuasion.

Florence Nightingale: Early Life and the Crimean War

Florence Nightingale was born May 15, 1820, in Florence, Italy and was named for that city, though she spent much of her childhood in the family house in Derbyshire. Her family was well-to-do. Her father, William Edward Nightingale, was wealthy, and her mother Fanny Nightingale, née Smith, came from a well-known and affluent family. This provided her with political connections, such as a friendship with the future prime minister Lord Palmerston, and the future cabinet minister Sidney Herbert.

She had no formal schooling—as was the norm for women at her time—but was well educated, taught at home at the insistence of, and primarily by, her father. William was a Cambridge-taught man, and perhaps more importantly, a Unitarian. As such, he felt that it was not only young boys who should be educated and cultured, and young Florence benefited from that belief. Her lessons included the standard fare for a young woman: music and drawing taught by the governess. But her father supplemented this with a rigorous, though somewhat superficial, course of study, which included: Latin, Greek, German, French, Italian, philosophy, and history. In addition, she discovered an interest in mathematics and was able to persuade her family to provide her with a tutor for some weeks on the subject. Although it is impossible to know her level of ability, we do know that she had a real fascination with the subject, and sought out a number of the leading mathematicians, statisticians, and men of science of her day. She met Charles Babbage and was a guest of Ada, Countess of Lovelace. She knew Edwin Chadwick, had heard Faraday speak, corresponded with Adolphe Quetelet, and was a close friend of William Farr.

Though she apparently evinced concern about her fellow creatures from a young age—from "her earliest years her strong love of nature and animals manifested itself. Her games, too, were characteristic, for her great delight was to nurse and bandage her dolls"—nursing was initially closed to her. Her parents had forbidden her to take up that mission (she had heard God call her to work in hospitals in 1844), as her father saw nurses as among the most dissolute members of society. William Nightingale would have recognized Sarah Gamp, whose face was "somewhat red and swollen," and whose society "it was difficult to enjoy . . . without becoming conscious of a smell of spirits," as more than just a literary creation of Charles Dickens in *Martin Chuzzlewit*.

This vocation denied to her, she turned to the study of medicine and health care. She was self-motivated, studying by herself many mornings. It was at this time, when the rest of the family was still asleep, that she studied the governmental blue books and other statistical documents relating to the state and health of the nation. She researched in the field as well, examining some London hospitals. Thus before even leaving the confines of her family, she already had some degree of expertise and interest in the subjects of public health and hospital administration.

In 1851 she was finally able to escape her family, and she spent three months working near Düsseldorf at Pastor Theodore Fliedner's Kaiserwerth hospital and orphanage. The stay at Kaiserwerth was particularly important, as it provided her with a model for a dedicated nursing sisterhood. Fliedner had created deaconesses—peasant women whose faith helped shield them from the stigma of poverty—to care for the indigent. Though critical of the conditions at the hospital, Nightingale would later draw from this configuration. After this she served as an apprentice at a hospital near Paris, operated by the Sisters of Mercy. Following this experience of the nursing profession first hand, she was able to obtain a position as a Superintendent of a Harley Street facility in London for the "Sick Gentlewoman in Distressed Circumstances" in 1853. Though unable to formalize any nursing training program, which was her great desire, she was able to put her administrative ideas into practice, and brought the accounts into order. She also began to demonstrate an awareness that reliable statistics were vital in effecting improvements.

Her life was soon to undergo a drastic change. In 1854 the British and French invaded the Crimea, supporting their ally Turkey against Russia. After an early victory, a long siege set in at the naval base at Sevastopol. The death rates among the sick and wounded were high, but this made the military hospitals in the Crimea no different from their counterparts anywhere else at the time. What was different, was the fact that for the first time there were regular newspaper updates, as *The Times* had correspondent William Howard Russell on the scene. When his reports reached London (and the rest of Britain) stating that British soldiers were dying for want of medical attention, and that there were no trained nurses at the

British military hospital at Scutari, there was public outrage and uproar.

Nightingale, though deploring the situation, also saw in it an opportunity to implement her ideas about trained nurses, sober women who could effectively help doctors even in the horrors of the hospital. She wrote to her friend Sidney Herbert, at that time Secretary of State for War, to volunteer her services. She was not to be disappointed. In fact, Herbert had already sent her a letter asking her to gather a group of trained nurses to serve in the Crimea in a manner which agreed with her aims. "If this succeeds," said Herbert, "an enormous amount of good will be done now . . . and a prejudice will be broken through . . . ." When news of her planned service became public, *The Times* raised a significant fund, which she controlled, to aid in her efforts. So less than a year after she had taken her Superintendent position on Harley Street, she left for the Scutari Hospital near Constantinople, where the casualties from the Crimean War were being taken for "treatment."

She soon discovered that the newspaper reports had not exaggerated; the conditions were dreadful. The troops who made it to the hospital—that is, those who had not died from exposure or starvation—had at best a 40% survival rate within its walls. The hospital itself was infested with all sorts of vermin and insects. In addition, it was built on a sewer, which discharged air into the hospital itself. Both surgical and medical equipment were in short supply. Most British soldiers in the Crimea died not from their wounds, but from frostbite, lack of food, or due to postoperative infection with cholera, dysentery, or typhus.

Nightingale's time in London served her well, for the most important changes she was able to effect were administrative. Despite being hindered by the military, who resented her independence from their chain of command and the fact that she was a woman, she was able to make major progress in terms of patient cleanliness and supplies, significantly aided by the funds at her disposal. Thus she was able to cause specific improvements, such as the creation of a laundry, complete with boilers for the heating of water. Most importantly, though, her monetary resources allowed her to supply the entire hospital. This, she initially felt, was the key to higher survival rates which began to appear approximately four months after she arrived. "The men sent down to Scutari in the winter died because they were not sent down till half dead—the men sent down now live and recover because they are sent in time," she told Lord Panmure in August of 1855.

She was not only an administrator. Her nightly rounds comforting the sick and wounded created the legend of the lady with the lamp. She had banned the other nurses from the wards at night, as a way of enforcing good conduct and maintaining order: such were the central tenets of her ideas about nursing. Some nurses had been sent home for "delinquent behaviour," although much of that may have been for disobeying Nightingale as for "dissoluteness." This word covered activities ranging from drinking to fraternization. In the end she felt her time in Scutari had been a great success. It demonstrated the viability of nurses and the care of the soldiers, though the latter probably had to do more with the end of winter and the changes instituted by the Sanitary Commission than with her reforms. Whatever the case, she was credited with the improvements, and when she returned to London from Scutari in 1856 she was a national hero. Though for reasons that remain unclear, she became an invalid from 1857 and remained one (though she regained some mobility after about 10 years) to the end of her life, this did not hinder her impact. Indeed, she became an even more active force for change and reform.

Nightingale and Changes in Nursing and Hospitals

She had already been well known by the time she reached the Crimea, but it was her work, and the reports of it, that made her a household name. This provided her with the political power to push through reforms in health care in the military, as well as to establish nursing training programs that helped to raise the respectability of nursing as a profession. She claimed not to enjoy the publicity, but she used it very effectively to her advantage. Nightingale was able to use her illness in a similar manner. Soon after her return from Scutari she became ill, and would spend the rest of her life often confined to bed. Yet she made excellent use of her confinement, diagnosing her illness to suit correspondents, and making herself more or less available as political situations warranted. "She conscripted her very body to her cause." She was able to parlay her fame, through her authoritative personality and political persuasion, into official support for the sanitary reforms that Scutari had convinced her were necessary.

Upon Nightingale's return, Sidney Herbert set up a committee to raise funds for the training of nurses in a teaching hospital in London. The response was overwhelming, raising nearly 45,000 pounds, and she was able to move forward with her plans. The first issue was one of location. The school was set up at St. Thomas's, though she was less than pleased when it later moved to Lambeth (she wanted a facility in the suburbs). It was not immediately successful, as there was attrition due to ill-health and dismissals for misconduct. Gradually, though, it became more productive, and effective publicity served to support its revolutionary image, and export its ideas.

Nightingale required her nurses, probationers to use the official title, to be "sober, honest, trustworthy, punctual, quiet and orderly, cleanly and neat." There were, of course, specific tasks and certain sets of knowledge required, but the core of her system was one of control and discipline. It was a hierarchical system, with the matron of the hospital having absolute control of all matters related to nursing. Such an arrangement, was not new. The idea that nurses should be clean, presentable, and well behaved predates Nightingale. This should not be surprising, as it was the religious orders that made up an active nursing population whose history goes back to the middle ages. In France, for example, the Sisters of Charity or the Augustinians of the Hôtel-Dieu de Paris were devoted, organized, and professional nurses who would have satisfied Nightingale's regulations for her probationers.

Even in the English case nursing reform has a longer trajectory than the Nightingale legend suggests. Religious sisterhoods, a number of which were founded in the 1830s and 1840s, provided nursing care both in and out of the hospital (Nightingale herself drew upon this resource in her work in the Crimea). It is important to remember that Mrs. Gamp was a Dickensian type—not all nurses behaved like she did. Why does the story retain such power? Part of the reason for the equation of Nightingale with modern nursing is due to Nightingale herself. Nurses in hospitals, she said, "were generally those who were too old, too weak, too drunken, too dirty, too stolid, or too bad to do anything else." Such a story was an effective political device to make a strong case for the necessity of reform among a middle class that had no problem seeing the working class as dissolute. Nightingale's belief, and her tactics, became entrenched in the history of nursing.

This is not to suggest that Nightingale offered nothing new. What was different was the systematization and professionalization of nursing outside a religious framework, which pushed beyond class boundaries. This gave career and status to the women who pursued the occupation. As changes in hospitals over the second half the 19th century led to better hygiene, the Nightingale system was gradually adopted, in whole or in part, as an effective way to encourage that end.

But while some facets of the system still survive, and the popular image of the comforting nurse has not lost its power, nursing as envisaged by Nightingale is very different from the modern form. Nightingale's nurses were not to be educated, technically capable individuals, a central part of a health care unit. Nightingale wanted her nurses to be obedient, to conform to a general pattern as her directives for probationers indicate. The people she envisaged as nurses came from a variety of classes, often with little education, and she sought to instill a type of behavior, rather than an education. Their role was at base a moral one, as her 1860 *Notes on Nursing: What it is, and What it is Not* makes clear. "The everyday management of a large ward, let alone of a hospital ... [does] not come by inspiration to the lady disappointed in love, nor to the poor workhouse drudge hard up for livelihood." For Nightingale, to take up nursing is to take up a vow no less serious than a religious one.

We can see a similar complexity in her hospital reforms. As suggested at the outset, the rise of the modern hospital seems inextricably linked to Florence Nightingale. The popular story suggests that her experience in the Crimea, and her subsequent calls for reforms appear to lead directly to the present-day hospital. Indeed, its three central components—the trained nurse, the hygienic design of the hospital itself, and its orderly administration—all seem to have their origins with her in this narrative.

But, similar to her ideas about nursing, Nightingale's understandings of hospitals and medicine had their basis in far older ideas. Indeed, Charles Rosenberg has convincingly argued that it was the very knowledge of those ideas that made her so successful, that "much of their power lay not in novelty but in their familiarity." Nor were they all the grim places of legend. Nineteenth century voluntary hospitals, for example, had a mortality rate as low as 10% of admissions, though patients with acute conditions would not have been admitted.

Her idea that hospitals should be clean, well-ventilated places was tied directly to the dominant idea of disease causation, a variation of which she learned from Farr; the miasmic theory that ran well through the 19th century. If the atmosphere was the primary spreader of infection, then logic dictated that hospitals should be as well ventilated as possible. The bulk of Nightingale's teachings "were no more than applications of these well-worn speculations—underwritten by the new-style plausibility of statistical analysis." Yet the social and political power she wielded allowed her to make effective use of these well-worn ideas. Her emphasis on the centrality of nurses to the functioning of the hospital, combined with an efficient administration and the physical space itself made her ideas seem original and powerful.

It is, therefore, important to remember that Nightingale was not a convert to the new ideas of disease causation that were emerging in the 1870s. Her ideas "reflected a vision of the world in which volition and disease, environment and regimen, body and mind were woven together so as to create a meaningful structure into which health, healing, and disease could be placed." The ferment model readily explained how atmosphere served as a medium for the transmission of disease, and therefore also fit into Victorian social conceptions. That disease should run rampant in the crowded hospital, no less than in the squalid and cramped tenement house, was no surprise. This also fit into Nightingale's socially reforming mindset. Much as in the hospital, she suggested, if the atmosphere were monitored in the homes and schoolrooms and factories, scarlet fever, and other ills would vanish. "If infection exists," she argued, "it is preventable. If it exists, it is the result of carelessness, or of ignorance." Hospitals, then, were not a place for cure, but were rather a place where the body would be encouraged to heal itself, to regain its natural balance. Her strong belief in the power of fresh air to fight all manner of contagion—physical and moral—is based firmly in this manner of seeing the world.

Just because her ideas were not new should not imply that her reforms were unneeded, that hospitals were bastions of health prior to the reforms inspired by Nightingale, or that the role for women in hospitals was unproblematic; far from it. Though perhaps not always the "sinks of human life in an army" that Benjamin Rush proclaimed them to be, if seriously ill, one undoubtedly had a better chance of survival at home than in the ward. Yet the basis of her reforms are to be found in her time, and we should not mistake similarities in form for similarities in worldview.

Nightingale and the Importance of Statistics

As her modern reputation demonstrates, both in terms of the emergence of the professional nurse, and their role in the functioning of the hospital, Nightingale and the reforms attributed to her were quite successful. Much of that success was based upon her changing ideas about disease after her return from Scutari, and her ability to convince a wider audience that the changes she envisioned were necessary. It was at this point that she turned to statistics, for she saw in them the best way of convincing people of the necessity of her reforms. Though Nightingale certainly had an interest in statistics and hospital administration prior to, and during her, stint in the Crimea, in order to understand her use of statistics it is important to examine her relationship with Dr. William Farr, head of the Statistical section of the General Register Office (GRO), and probably the most famous, if not the leading, British statistician of his day.

Though trained as a doctor, Farr made his name in the collection and publication of statistics, primarily vital statistics, in the over 40 years he spent in the GRO. Farr's statistical work was not primarily mathematical in nature. Rather, he used the information collected by the GRO to produce practical recommendations, based largely upon his "zymotic" theory of diseases, illnesses spread by air or water, rather than direct contact. The tables he produced were primarily data presentation. There was little in the way of mathematics. Nightingale's statistics and medical understandings were of a similar nature. Indeed, it was thanks to her work with Farr in analyzing mortality rates in different areas in the Crimea that she came to believe that bad hygiene, rather than entangled supplies, were responsible for the high death rates at her hospital. This realization perhaps contributed to her invalidism, as it has been suggested that her (self-serving) illnesses were a psychological response to her recent belief regarding her own ineffectiveness at Scutari.

Whatever the case, from the time of her return from the Crimea she and Farr had become close associates. When the commission to study the state of sanitation in the British Army was formed (in response to Nightingale's prodding), Farr presented statistical evidence to the committee and testified before it. He also was appointed to a position that looked into the sanitary state of India thanks in large part to Nightingale's patronage. They worked closely on many of her most statistical publications, including the influential *Notes on Hospitals* (1859) and her *Introductory Notes on Lying-in Institutions* (1871).

She was not a clone of Farr. Though she believed in the value of statistics, especially as a tool for convincing people of the need for change, Nightingale recognized the difficulty even educated people had with the pages and pages of statistics produced by the government. To this end, she was the pioneer in the use of diagrams to convey statistical information.

In 1857 she reported to the politician Sydney Herbert: "I have written to Dr Farr for the diagram which is to affect thro' the Eyes what we may fail to convey to the brains of the public through their word-proof ears." She was referring here to her now famous "coxcombs," which were a type of piechart that showed the mortality rate of the British Army. Prepared under Farr's supervision, they were Nightingale's creation. She knew that only "scientific men" look at the statistics that accompany official reports, but felt that her diagrams would make the statistics more effective and persuasive. She created and utilized polar-area charts, and made effective use of line diagrams as well as pictorial representations to make her statistical arguments more effective.

We should not, however, forget that her belief in statistics was predicated on her social and religious conceptions. For all her practical interest in the use of statistics she also felt that through numbers the laws of society could be discovered. It was here that she diverged from Farr, who felt that statistics should be "the dryest of all reading" and she turned to Adolphe Quetelet. Nightingale met Quetelet in 1860 when the International Statistical Congress was held in London. She was an active participant after a fashion (she was bedridden as always for most of the decade). But a paper of hers, wherein she proposed to create uniform medical statistics for hospitals to aid national and international comparisons, was one of three that were discussed at the Sanitary section of the Congress. There were practical difficulties with her suggestions, as there was no generally accepted theory of communicable disease at the time—there were probably more people who still held the miasmatic or anticontagionist rather than the contagionist theory of disease. Nevertheless, her proposals were generally accepted.

In Quetelet's work she found resonances with her own search for the divine in social laws. "I never read Quetelet's *Physique Sociale* (which I have done over and over again) without being astounded at the force of genius and accurate observation which has produced such a work." It fascinated her on multiple levels. On the one hand, she was quite interested in the practical applications for statistics, as seen in Quetelet's work on mortality rates. In addition, his search for the average man, *l'homme moyen*, gave voice to her own spirituality and belief in improvement, as the average man represented the state of humanity. For her, Quetelet's study of moral statistics were to be understood very much in religious terms. "[H]is was the very highest kind of religion: the seeking in the Laws of the Moral World which he has done so much to discover the action of plan of Supreme Wisdom and Goodness" she told Farr.

Though these interests did not manifest themselves in her use and manipulation of statistics, they lie at the heart of her belief in their truth value, and their utility in her mission of social reform and improvement. She should, thus, be remembered as one of the earliest, and most successful, promoters of the practical application of statistics, rather than a modern statistician. Her ability to bring her own and others' data to the attention, interest, and comprehension of a general public through charts and graphs represented something new in the history of statistics and social measurement. The clear connection she drew between reliable data and policy decisions also should be noted.

Conclusion

The year 1872 marked a change in her life, as she gradually withdrew from political life, "went out of office," as she put it. Though she continued to take an interest in sanitary reform, her activities were much more peripheral for a variety of reasons. One, of course, was her continued ill-health. Another was the fact that a variety of her political friends and allies had begun to leave office or die. Sydney Herbert had died in 1861, and Palmerston in 1865. Farr would die in 1881. Simultaneously, she had begun to pursue friendships of a more philosophical, rather than political, nature, as her relationship with Benjamin Jowett, the Oxford classical scholar, shows. Moreover, she was forced to take a more active role in family affairs, especially caring for her parents.

Florence Nightingale died on August 13, 1910. In 1857 Henry Wadsworth Longfellow had written "Santa Filomena." It read, in part: "Lo! in that house of misery/A lady with a lamp I see/Pass through the glimmering gloom/And flit from room to room." Florence Nightingale's work and exploits during the Crimean War had made her a hero, and poems like Longfellow's combined with her own tactical prowess served to solidify her status and her legend, which survives to this day. Indeed, the history of modern nursing has become virtually synonymous with the name of Florence Nightingale, the Lady with the Lamp. Yet like all historical figures, the history her life reveals is complex and contradictory. She invented neither nursing, nor the changes in health care that she called for. But while nursing had a history before Nightingale, one cannot discuss the changes in both nursing and in health care without discussing her. She was not ahead of her time, rather, she was preeminently of it. In her ideas about medicine and administration, in her use of statistics and her push for sanitation, she reflected the beliefs and advances, and made use of the intellectual tools, of her age. However, it was in implementation that she had the greatest impact. She brought all these advances together in her skillful manipulation of the governmental bureaucracies and utilization of her own renown. In this way, she had a significant influence on her own time and ours.

See Also the Following Articles

Nursing • Quetelet, Adolphe

Further Reading

Ackerknecht, E. (1948). Anticontagionism between 1821 and 1867. *Bull. Hist. Med.* **22,** 562–593.

Baly, M. (1986). *Florence Nightingale and the Nursing Legacy.* Croom Helm, London.

Bullough, V. (ed.) (1990). *Florence Nightingale and Her Era. A Collection of New Scholarship*. Garland, New York.

Cohen, I. B. (1984). Florence Nightingale. *Sci. Amer.* **250,** 128–137.

Diamond, M., and Stone, M. (1981). Nightingale on Quetelet. *J. Roy. Statist. Soc. Ser. A* **144,** 66–79.

Dingwall, R., Rafferty, A., and Webster, C. (1988). *An Introduction to the Social History of Nursing.* Routledge, London.

Rosenberg, C. (1987). *The Care of Strangers. The Rise of America's Hospital System.* Johns Hopkins University Press, Baltimore.

Small, H. (1998). *Florence Nightingale Avenging Angel.* Constable, London.

Smith, F. B. (1982). *Florence Nightingale Reputation and Power.* Croom Helm, London.

Strachey, L. (2002). *Eminent Victorians.* Continuum, London.

Weiner, D. (1972). The French Revolution, Napoleon, and the nursing profession. *Bull. Hist. Med.* **46,** 274–305.

Williamson, L. (ed.) (1999). *Florence Nightingale and the Birth of Professional Nursing*. Thoemmes Press, Bristol.

Woodham-Smith, C. (1983). *Florence Nightingale.* Atheneum, New York.

Nominal Categories Model

R. Darrell Bock
University of Chicago, Chicago, Illinois, USA

Ulf Böckenholt
McGill University, Montreal, Quebec, Canada

Glossary

Fisher information A measure of the precision of maximum-liklihood estimation as a function of the estimate value.

Fisher scoring An interative numerical method for nonlinear maximum-likelihood estimation.

latent dimension A measurement dimension that cannot be observed but can be inferred from the internal consistency of responses to multiple items.

location The origin (zero) of a measurement dimension.

logit A mathematical function for mapping points in the interval zero to one (for example, probabilities) onto a real number continuum of infinite extent.

maximum-likelihood estimation A principle of statistical estimation based on maximizing the probability of a sample observation, the distribution function of which is known, given a putative value of the estimate.

nominal categories Arbitrary categories to which observed responses are assigned, in contrast to ordered categories that represent a coarse grading of quantitative observations.

partial credit model A model based on a logistic response function for responses in ordered categories.

quadrature A numerical method of evaluating integrals that have no explicit solution.

response function A mathematical expression of the probability of an observed qualitative response as a function of a continuous latent or manifest variable.

scale The unit of measurement on a latent or manifest dimension.

unfolding model A mathematical model for rank ordering of objects, whereby order is determined by the distance of each object from the ideal point.

The nominal categories model makes the widely used logit-linear (or log-linear) models for analyzing qualitative frequency data available in the measurement of quantitative attributes. It has been applied mainly to measurement of individual differences among respondents to educational and psychological tests based on multiple-choice items and to measurement of individual attitudes toward public issues or preferences among consumer products. The theory of the nominal model and related estimation methods are reviewed here and illustrated with examples from these fields.

Introduction

The nominal categories model provides a link between the value of an assumed latent variable and the probabilities of a respondent's observed first choice among a number of discrete alternatives. It is one of a larger group of item response models serving the same purpose when the alternatives are dichotomous or form an ordered scale. In the context of modern test theory, several versions of the nominal categories model have appeared in the literature: (1) the initial presentation by R. D. Bock in 1972 applied to the recovery information in responses to wrong alternatives of multiple-choice tests, (2) an extension by F. Samejima in 1972 allowing for possible random choices on the part of the respondents, and (3) a further elaboration by D. Thissen and L. Steinberg in 1984 that included an estimated probability of the respondents' choosing randomly. In connection with his MULTILOG program, Thissen has also shown that the nominal model, when suitably parameterized, specializes to G. N. Masters' partial-credit model for ordinal categories. Takane presented in 1996 a multidimensional model for first choices based on C. H. Coombs' unfolding model for rankings by individual respondents. In the context of modeling individual differences in complete preference rankings, U. Böckenholt introduced in 2001 a multidimensional version of the nominal model that includes Takane's model as a special case.

The nominal model is a particular application of a more general approach to statistical prediction of first choices among competing alternatives. Suppose there are m such alternatives; then the probability that a given respondent will select alternative k as first choice is

$$p_k = \frac{\pi_k}{\pi_1 + \pi_2 + \cdots + \pi_m},$$

where the π values are positive quantities and $\sum_k^m \pi_k = 1$. In this model, the scale of the parameters is obviously indeterminate. To avoid the necessity of estimation under the constraint $\pi > 0$, reparameterize by setting $\pi_h = e^{z_h}$, $h = 1, 2, \ldots, m$. Then

$$p_k = \frac{e^{z_k}}{\sum_h^m e^{z_h}}.$$

In this form of the model, the indeterminacy is one of location and may be fixed by setting $\sum_h^m z_h = 0$ or by reparameterizing the z values in $m - 1$ linearly independent contrasts; for example, $z'_h = z_h - z_1$. In either case, the z values are referred to as multinomial logits, or just logits.

Measurement of Individual Differences

In psychometric applications, where the object is to measure individual differences among respondents with respect to a single latent variable, the logit corresponding to category k of item j may be expressed in terms of the variable, θ, attributed to the respondent, and two parameters, α and γ, attributed to the item category:

$$z_{jk} = \alpha_{jk}\theta + \gamma_{jk}.$$

The unidimensional version of the model may be used in the analysis scoring of standardized tests and psychological scales. In the context of educational achievement testing, the latent variable is typically referred to as "ability" or "proficiency." In psychological testing, the attribute may be any construct descriptive of behavior—"intelligence," "conservatism," "neuroticism," etc. Multiple-choice items may differ in their number of alternatives, m_j. Moreover, the tests or scales do not need to consist of multiple-choice items exclusively: they may be mixed with dichotomous items or with open-ended items, the responses of which are rated in ordered categories.

For purposes of discussing the properties of nominal category items generally, including multiple-choice items, it is useful to define the category response function,

$$P_{jk}(\theta) = \frac{e^{z_{jk}(\theta)}}{\sum_h^{m_j} e^{z_{jh}(\theta)}},$$

which assigns probabilities to the alternatives for any value of θ. The corresponding category information function (Fisher information) is

$$I_{jk}(\theta) = \frac{1}{P_{jk}(\theta)}\left[\frac{\partial P_{jk}(\theta)}{\partial \theta}\right]^2.$$

The following example illustrates the use of these functions in characterizing the operating characteristics of a multiple-choice item.

Example: A Vocabulary Test Item

Figure 1 shows plots of these functions for a multiple-choice item, the word "artifice," appearing in a secondary school vocabulary test. The response alternatives are listed in Table I; number 1 is the correct alternative. The test was administered with the instruction "Do not guess! If you do not know the correct answer, omit the item." This instruction led to an appreciable incidence of omits, which were assigned to a "No response" category in addition to the categories for the alternatives. Two infrequently selected alternatives have been assigned to the same category. The estimated category parameters for this item are shown in Table I. Plots of the corresponding response functions and information curves are shown in Fig. 1.

The information curve for alternative 2 shows that a response to the wrong alternative, "Imitation" is an indication of some vocabulary ability, presumably

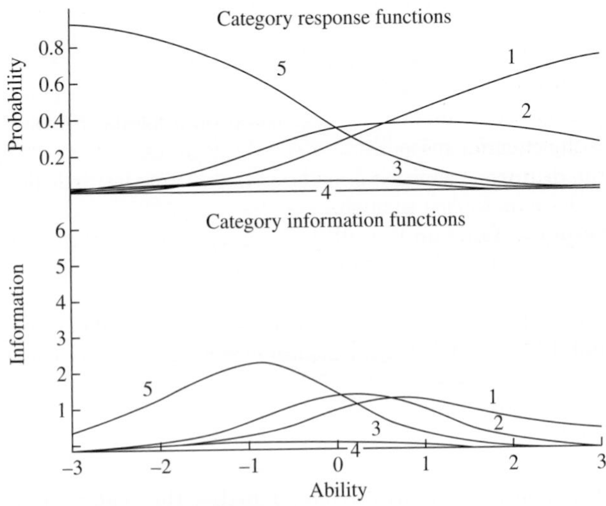

Figure 1 Category response and information functions for the vocabulary test item "artifice."

Table I Category Parameter Estimates for the Vocabulary Word "Artifice"

Alternative	α	γ
1. Clever device	0.565	0.828
2. Imitation	0.865	0.375
3. Careless error	−1.186	−0.357
4. Flavor, accident	−1.199	−0.079
5. No response	0.933	−0.817

because a certain amount of word knowledge is required even to confuse "artifice" and "artificial." Test scoring based on the nominal model would automatically assign full credit to an alternative-1 response and partial credit to an alternative-2 response. It would also make optimal use of the information contained in an omitted response to this item. There is very little information in responses to alternatives 3 and 4.

Item Parameter Estimation and Test Scoring

Data analysis for the nominal model or any of the various item response models is carried out in two steps. In the calibration step, the item parameters are estimated from the responses of a large sample of respondents drawn from the population for which the test is intended. Given these estimates, the attribute values for particular respondents from the population—who are not restricted to the calibration sample—are estimated in a subsequent scoring step. This two-step approach is necessary for maximum-likelihood estimation because the item parameters and respondent attributes cannot be estimated jointly: the number of parameters increases with the sample size and no determinate maximum is obtainable.

The problem of indefinitely many parameters can be avoided by integrating over an assumed or estimated population distribution of θ. This is the so-called method of maximum marginal likelihood. On the assumption that the responses to the n-item test or scale are statistically independent, conditional on θ, the probability of the response pattern $[x_{ijk}]$, $j = 1, 2, \ldots, n$, is, say,

$$L_i(\theta) = \prod_j^n \prod_{h=1}^{m_j} [P_{jh}(\theta)]^{x_{ijhk}},$$

where $P_{jh}(\theta)$ is the response function of category h of item j and $x_{ijhk} = 1$ if the respondent i chooses category k, and zero otherwise.

Assuming that the respondent is drawn from a population with a proper probability density function $g(\theta)$, the marginal probability of the response pattern may be expressed as the definite integral,

$$\bar{P}_i = \int_{-\infty}^{\infty} L_i(\theta) g(\theta)\, d\theta.$$

The marginal likelihood of a general item parameter v_{jk}, given the responses of a sample of N respondents, is then

$$L(v_{jk}) = \prod_i^N \bar{P}_i.$$

The corresponding likelihood equations for m_j-category item response models in general are

$$\sum_i^N \frac{1}{\bar{P}_i} \int_{-\infty}^{\infty} \sum_h^{m_j} \frac{x_{ijhk}}{P_{jh}(\theta)} \cdot \frac{\partial P_{jk}(\theta)}{\partial v_{jk}} L_i(\theta) g(\theta)\, d\theta = 0.$$

Specializing to the nominal model, there are the derivatives

$$\frac{\partial P_{jh}(\theta)}{\partial v_{jk}} = P_{jh}(\theta)[1 - P_{jh}(\theta)] \frac{\partial z_{jh}(\theta)}{\partial v_{jk}}, \qquad h = k;$$

$$\frac{\partial P_{jh}(\theta)}{\partial v_{jk}} = -P_{jh}(\theta) \frac{\partial z_{jh}(\theta)}{\partial v_{jk}}, \qquad h \neq k.$$

The integrals in these equations may be evaluated numerically with sufficient accuracy by Gaussian quadrature formulas—specifically, Gauss–Hermite quadrature when the normal density is assumed for $g(\theta)$. In view of the indeterminacy of location and scale in item response models, the mean and standard deviation of the θ distribution may be set, respectively, to 0 and 1, or other arbitrary values.

Although a direct numerical solution of the likelihood equations is possible in principle, it becomes unwieldy computationally when the number of items, and thus the number of parameters, becomes large in long tests or scales. In that case an expectation–maximization (EM) solution is the best recourse. With quadratures replacing the integrals, the expectations of the E step are the quantities, say,

$$\bar{r}_{jkq} = \sum_i^N \sum_h^{m_j} \frac{x_{ijhk} L_i(X_q)}{\bar{P}_i} A(X_q),$$

and

$$\bar{N}_q = \sum_i^N \frac{L_i(X_q)}{\bar{P}_i} A(X_q),$$

where X_q is a quadrature point, $q = 1, 2, \ldots, Q$, and $A(X_q)$, $\sum_q^Q A(X_q) = 1$, is the corresponding quadrature weight. The quantities $\bar{r}_{jkq}$ and $\bar{N}_q$, $\sum_q^Q \bar{N}_q = N$, comprise the so-called complete data statistics for the M step, which is just the standard procedure for fixed-effects logit-linear analysis of frequency data.

In the present application, procedures can be simplified by provisionally setting the parameters of one of the categories to zero. After all other parameters have been estimated, the locations of the parameters can be moved so that the conventional scaling is recovered. Suppose the parameters of the last category, m_j, are set to zero; then the implicit equations for estimating the parameters of category k and item j are

$$G\begin{bmatrix}\alpha_{jk}\\ \gamma_{jk}\end{bmatrix} = \sum_{q}^{Q}\{\bar{r}_{jkq} - \bar{N}_q P_{jk}(X_q) - [\bar{r}_{jm_jq} - \bar{N}_q P_{jm_jq}(X_q)]\}\cdot\begin{bmatrix}\theta\\ 1\end{bmatrix} = 0.$$

These equations may be solved by the Fisher scoring (Gauss–Newton) method using the corresponding Fisher information function:

$$I\begin{bmatrix}\alpha_{jk}\\ \gamma_{jk}\end{bmatrix} = NP_{jk}(\theta)[1 - P_{jk}(\theta)]\cdot\begin{bmatrix}\theta^2 & \theta\\ \theta & 1\end{bmatrix}.$$

The provisional estimates can then be put in standard form by imposing the constraints $\sum_h^{m_j}\alpha_{jh} = 0$ and $\sum_h^{m_j}\gamma_{jh} = 0$.

Once the estimated item parameters of the test or scale are in hand, maximum-likelihood estimation of θ scores for the respondents is straightforward. The likelihood equation for respondent i,

$$\sum_j^n\sum_h^{m_j} x_{ijhk}[1 - P_{jh}(\hat{\theta})]\alpha_{jh} = 0,$$

may be solved iteratively starting from $\theta = 0$.

The Fisher information with respect to θ contributed by category h of item j is

$$I_{jh}(\theta) = P_{jh}(\theta)[1 - P_{jh}(\theta)]\alpha_{jh}^2,$$

the item information is $I_j(\theta) = \sum_h^{m_j} I_{jh}(\theta)$, and the test information is $I(\theta) = \sum_j^n I_j(\theta)$. The error-variance function is $1/I(\theta)$, and the average error variance in the population is given by, say,

$$\bar{\sigma}_\varepsilon^2 = \int_{-\infty}^{\infty}[1/I(\theta)]g(\theta)\,d\theta.$$

If the population variance is set to 1, the reliability of the test is $1 - \bar{\sigma}_\varepsilon^2$.

The Fisher scoring solution for $\hat{\theta}_i$ converges quickly except in cases where choices of respondent i all fall in the alternative that has the largest algebraic value of α_{jk} or in the alternative with the smallest algebraic value. In those cases $\hat{\theta}_i$, is indefinitely large or indefinitely small, respectively, and cannot be evaluated. Assuming respondent i belongs to a population with proper probability density function, $g(\theta)$, these indeterminate values can be avoided by estimating the Bayes mode, say,

$$\tilde{\theta}_i = \max_{\theta}[L_i(\theta)g(\theta)\,d\theta],$$

with corresponding posterior information function, $I(\theta)g(\theta)$, or the Bayes mean,

$$\bar{\theta}_i = \int_{-\infty}^{\infty}\theta L_i(\theta)g(\theta)\,d\theta,$$

with posterior variance,

$$\sigma_{\bar{\theta}_i}^2 = \int_{-\infty}^{\infty}(\theta - \bar{\theta})^2 L_i(\theta)g(\theta)\,d\theta,$$

when $\int_{-\infty}^{\infty} L_i(\theta)g(\theta)\,d\theta$ is set to 1. Again, the integrals may be evaluated numerically by Gaussian quadrature. If the test is used, for example, to qualify students for advancement or to select the most promising job applicants, the Bayes mean will yield the smallest number of misclassifications in the population in question.

Wainer and co-workers have shown that, if the alternatives of an item are ordered in the sense that a response to an alternative higher in the ordering implies a larger value of θ, then the α parameters must be ordered. The algebraic values of the α parameters may therefore be used to assign an empirical order to the alternatives or to verify a prior ordering. Inspection of the category parameters, category response curves, and category information curves of a multiple-choice item is valuable in any effort to improve the measurement properties of the item by revising some or all of its alternatives.

For any testing program with the necessary computing resources and large sample sizes, these various good properties, including the recovery of information in wrong alternatives and omitted item responses, show nominal-model-based item analysis and test scoring to be superior to any method of right–wrong scoring of multiple-choice items.

Measurement of Group Differences

In research studies in which respondents are identified only by their group membership, the data serve only to describe the distributions of θ within the groups. At minimum, the investigator would like to estimate the group means and standard deviations of θ. If the within-group distributions of θ are assumed normal, the marginal-likelihood equations for μ_u, the mean for group u, and for σ_u^2, the corresponding variance, are

$$\sum_i^{N_u}\int_{-\infty}^{\infty}(\theta - \hat{\mu}_u)L_{ui}(\theta)g_u(\theta)\,d\theta = 0$$

and

$$\sum_i^{N_u}\int_{-\infty}^{\infty}[\hat{\sigma}_u^2 - (\theta - \hat{\mu}_u)^2]L_{ui}(\theta)g_u(\theta)\,d\theta = 0,$$

where N_u is the number of respondents in the sample from group u and

$$g_u(\theta) = \frac{1}{\hat{\sigma}_u\sqrt{2\pi}}\exp\left[\frac{-(\theta-\hat{\mu}_u)^2}{2\hat{\sigma}_u^2}\right].$$

Expressed in terms of the Bayes mean and posterior variance for respondent i in group u, these equations become

$$\hat{\mu}_u = \frac{1}{N_u}\sum_{i}^{N_u}\bar{\theta}_{ui}$$

and

$$\hat{\sigma}_u^2 = \frac{1}{N_u}\sum_{i}^{N_u}\left[(\bar{\theta}_{ui}-\hat{\mu}_u)^2 + \sigma^2_{\bar{\theta}_{ui}}\right].$$

These latter equations are in a form suitable for iterative solution simultaneous with EM estimation of the item parameters. To resolve the indeterminacy of location and scale, the mean and variance of one of the groups may be set arbitrarily.

These results apply to all of the conventional item response models, including the nominal model. They are useful in studies of group differences generally (for example, in educational assessment) when the objective is to measure differences in the effectiveness of school programs.

Analysis of Preference Rankings

Ranking is of particular interest in measurement of preferences for objects of choice, such as political candidates, proposed public policies, occupational choices, or competing consumer goods. When studying preferences, there is an important advantage to asking the respondents to rank rather than rate the objects: ranking avoids undesirable effects of respondents' idiosyncratic interpretations of category labels such as "agree moderately," "agree strongly," etc., found in rating forms. In applying the nominal model to preference studies, the objects take the place of categories. The model can be used to estimate preference functions—that is, the probability that a given object will be first, second, or any lower choice in a preference ranking. The nominal categories model is well suited for this type of analysis because of its computational simplicity and its consistency with other treatments of rankings and ratings, in particular the unfolding representation introduced by Coombs.

In some applications of rankings, the respondents may specify only a certain number of top choices among the objects, as opposed to a complete ranking or ranking of selected subsets of a larger number of objects. The first of these tasks is referred to as incomplete ranking; the second, as partial ranking. In both of these special cases, the additional information provided by making use of all of the rank positions, not just the first choices, can result in gains in efficiency of estimation and improved identifiability of the model parameters.

Using Luce's principle of independence of first choices from irrelevant alternatives, a rank-ordering of objects may be decomposed into a succession of first choices among successively smaller sets of objects. The principle implies that the probabilities of the first choices are independent and that the probability of the ranking as a whole is the continued product of those probabilities. Inasmuch as probabilities of first (or last) choices are given by the nominal model, which is based on an extremal distribution, the conditional probability of a respondent's ranking, given the respondent's location, θ_i, on the latent preference continuum, may be expressed as follows: Let H be a set containing integers $h = 1, 2, \ldots, m$ indexing the objects in the preference study. Let K_i be an ordered subset of elements of H corresponding to the q objects ranked by respondent i, $q = 1, 2, \ldots, m-1$. Let $k_i^{(\ell)}, \ell = 1,2,\ldots,q$, be an element in K_i corresponding to the object in position ℓ in the rank ordering. Then, let $\bar{H}_i^{\ell}$ be the subset of $1+m-\ell$ elements of H excluding elements corresponding to objects above $k_i^{(\ell)}$ in the rank ordering (note that elements of $\bar{H}_i^{\ell}$ not among the elements of K_i need not be ordered). Then the probability of K_i, given θ_i, is

$$P(K_i \mid \theta_i) = \prod_{\ell=1}^{q}\frac{\exp\left[z(k_i^{(\ell)} \mid \theta_i)\right]}{\sum_{h\in\bar{H}_i^{(\ell)}}\exp(z(h \mid \theta_i))}, \tag{1}$$

where

$$z(h \in \bar{H}_i^{(\ell)} \mid \theta_i) = \alpha_h\theta_i + \gamma_h \tag{2}$$

is the logit of the nominal model for the probability of each successive first choice. When $q = 1$, this probability as a function of θ specializes to the category response function, and $\bar{H}_i^{(1)} = H$.

The multistage structure of Eq. (1) imposes constraints on the collection of ranking data. Ideally, rankings should be obtained in the form of successive first choices by requiring respondents to rank the objects from most to least preferred. Deviations from this format that are not consistent with the model's multistage structure may lead to systematic misfits. It is worth noting that Eq. (1) has the same form as the partial likelihood representation of a stratum in a Cox regression, with "surviving" objects corresponding to risk sets and choices corresponding to failures.

Example: A Partial Ranking

Suppose respondent i is presented five objects, A, B, C, D, and E, indexed $h = [1, 2, 3, 4, 5]$. If the respondent reports only the top three ranks, $K_i = \mathrm{DAC}$, the conditional probability of the partial ranking, given θ_i, is

$$P(K_i \mid \theta_i) = \frac{\exp(\alpha_4\theta_i + \gamma_4)}{\sum_{h\in[4,1,3,2,5]} \exp(\alpha_h\theta_i + \gamma_h)} \times \frac{\exp(\alpha_1\theta_i + \gamma_1)}{\sum_{h\in[1,3,2,5]} \exp(\alpha_h\theta_i + \gamma_h)} \times \frac{\exp(\alpha_3\theta_i + \gamma_3)}{\sum_{h\in[3,2,5]} \exp(\alpha_h\theta_i + \gamma_h)}.$$

The role of the logit in an unfolding representation of preference can be shown by reparameterizing Eq. (2) to yield an ideal-point model. In this model, both the object and the respondent have positions on the latent continuum. The unfolding of the preferences follows from setting the origin and unit of scale of θ to 0 and 1, respectively, and writing Eq. (2) as

$$z_h = \kappa_h - (\omega_h - \theta_i)^2, \tag{3}$$

where the θ_i and ω_h represent, respectively, the respondents' so-called ideal point and the object's position on the latent continuum. The equivalence between Eqs. (2) and (3) can be seen by setting $\alpha_h = 2\omega_h$ and $\gamma_h = \kappa_h - \omega_h^2$. The remaining terms may be set to zero because the nominal model is invariant with respect to translation of the logit.

When the postion of an object h, ω_h, coincides with the ideal-point position of person i, the corresponding logit reaches its maximum value of κ_h. The interpretation of Eq. (3) is simplified when these maximum values are equal for all alternatives, leading to the additional constraint that $\kappa_1 = \cdots = \kappa_m = 0$. This constraint yields Takane's model for first choices. The unfolding structure of the nominal model was noted by Samejima, who showed that the category response functions of the nominal model with the smallest and largest γ values are decreasing from 1 (at $\theta = -\infty$) and monotonically increasing to 1 (at $\theta = \infty$), respectively. In contrast, the object preference probabilities with an intermediate value of γ have unique maxima at finite θ values.

When multiple rankings of the same objects are available, it is useful to consider extensions of the unfolding model, including a multidimensional version of the nominal model. Though in educational applications, ability or proficiency measurements are typically based on multiple items with different alternatives, in studies of choice behavior, it is more common to consider rankings of the same objects on either (1) multiple criteria or (2) on the same criterion but at multiple time points. An example of the first ranking is an election study in which respondents are asked to rank political candidates on the criteria integrity, leadership, and expertise; an example of the second ranking is a panel study in which the same respondents are asked to express their preferences for political candidates before and after an election campaign. In these settings, the multiple ratings would be treated as if they were items and an index j, $j = 1, 2, \ldots, n$, would be inserted in the subscript of the logit. This extension is especially important in the multiple-criteria setting, in which the assumption that a one-dimensional latent variable can describe individual taste differences is too restrictive. Although preference functions can be estimated for any rank position, the focus of interest is most often on the first rank. This is the case in the remainder of this discussion including the next example; the subset K_i then contains only one element, k_i^1, and the unnecessary superscript may be omitted.

In the multidimensional case, let the logit of the nominal model be a function of a d latent dimensions indexed by $v = 1, 2, \ldots, d$. Then the d-factor version of the nominal model logit for object k may be expressed as

$$z(k_{ij} \mid \theta_{ij}) = \sum_{v=1}^{d} \alpha_{jkv}\theta_{ijv} + \gamma_{jk}, \tag{4}$$

which describes the individual difference in preference for object k with respect to the jth criterion. The assumption in Eq. (4) of a different θ for each item results in a very heavy parameterization, however, and a more tractable approach is to assume a logistic factor-analysis model in which dependencies among the multiple attributes are attributed to a small number of latent variables that are not specific to each criterion. Equation (4) can then be simplified to

$$z(k_{ij} \mid \theta_i) = \sum_{v=1}^{d} \alpha_{jkv}\theta_{iv} + \gamma_{jk}, \tag{5}$$

where the θ_i vary from person to person according to the multivariate standard normal distribution

$$g(\theta) = \frac{1}{2\pi^{d/2}} \exp\left[\frac{(-\sum_v^d \theta^2)}{2}\right]. \tag{6}$$

In applications involving repeated measurements of a single criterion, Eq. (4) may be simplified to

$$z(k_{it} \mid \theta_{it}) = \alpha_{tk}\theta_{it} + \gamma_{tk}, \tag{7}$$

where subscript j is replaced by t to emphasize the time dimension of the measurements. A parsimonious representation of time-specific effect is obtained by decomposing θ_{it} into a person-specific, time-dependent effect and a random time effect, ν_t,

$$\theta_{it} = \phi_{it} + \nu_t, \tag{8}$$

where ϕ_{it} may vary over time according to an autoregressive process.

Example: Ranking of Political Candidates

In a survey conducted shortly before the 1992 U.S. presidential election, a sample of 81 undergraduate students was asked to order the candidates George H. W. Bush (B), Bill Clinton (C), and Ross Perot (P) according to how well each of them represented their views on education (ED) and economy (EC) issues. The data are reproduced in Table II. For example, 11 respondents ranked the candidates in the order C, B, P on both criteria. Can a common latent trait, reflecting the political orientation of the respondents, account for the observed associations between the rankings? To test this hypothesis the one-dimensional nominal categories model was fitted to the data based on Eqs. (1) and (2) under a normal latent distribution with mean 0 and variance 1. This model yielded a likelihood ratio chi-square of $G^2 = 26.0$ with 27 degrees of freedom (df) and thus provides a superior fit, compared to a multinomial model without a latent trait ($G^2 = 62.2$, $df = 31$). Although a further fit improvement is obtained by a two-dimensional model with $G^2 = 14.9$ ($df = 23$), in view of the small sample size, the one-dimensional nominal categories model seems adequate in capturing the important features of the data set.

The response functions estimated under the one-dimensional model are depicted in Fig. 2. For both ranking criteria, economy (EC) and education (ED), individual differences in the rankings reflect the political orientation of the candidates. Table III shows the estimated item parameters under the ideal-point parameterization. As a consequence of the small number of respondents, the item standard errors are relatively large. With the exception of the κ parameter estimated for Clinton under the education criterion, the remaining κ parameters can be set equal to 0. This result indicates that the respondents favored Clinton's position on this issue regardless of their political views. Yielding a likelihood ratio chi-square of $G^2 = 29.5$ ($df = 30$), this simplified nominal model provides a parsimonious description of the bivariate ranking data.

Table II Bivariate Ranking Data[a]

ED \ EC	BCP	BPC	CBP	CPB	PBC	PCB
BCP	1	1	4	2	0	0
BPC	3	4	4	1	1	2
CBP	1	0	6	2	0	0
CPB	2	0	5	11	0	1
PBC	1	4	1	1	2	1
PCB	1	1	4	12	0	2

[a] Abbreviations: ED, education; EC, economy; B, Bush; C, Clinton; P, Perot (1992 U.S. election).

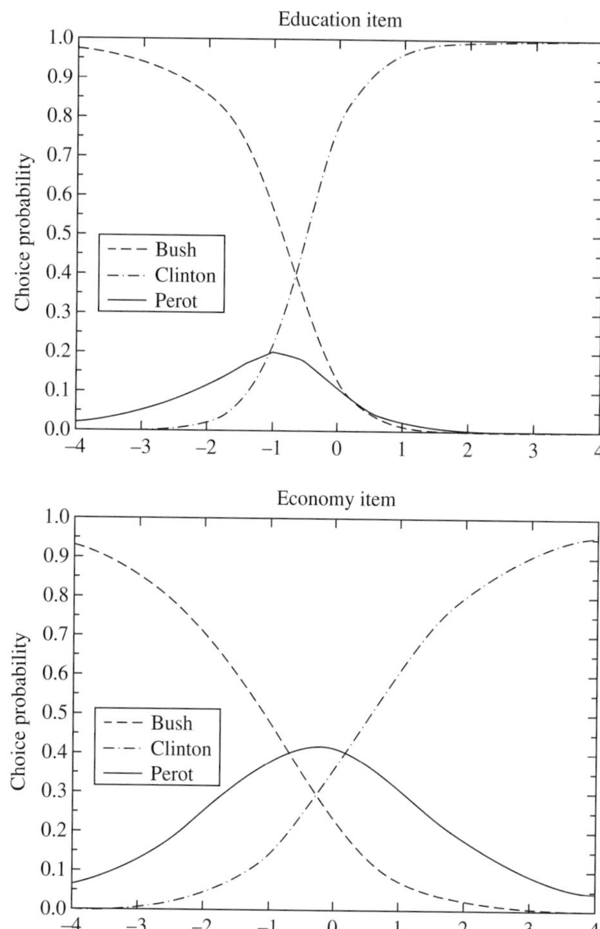

Figure 2 Item response functions of the nominal response model for the education and economy rankings of the three 1992 U.S. presidential candidates.

Table III Estimated Item Parameters of the Bivariate Ranking Data[a]

k	$\kappa_{(ED)k}$	S.E.	$\omega_{(ED)k}$	S.E.	$\kappa_{(EC)k}$	S.E.	$\omega_{(EC)k}$	S.E.
B	0.33	(0.33)	−0.47	(0.21)	−0.44	(0.28)	−0.41	(0.21)
C	2.94	(1.14)	0.97	(0.36)	0.03	(0.29)	0.41	(0.19)

[a] Abbreviations: ED, education; EC, economy, B, Bush, C, Clinton (effects of the Perot category are set equal to 0 to fix the origin of the scale).

See Also the Following Articles

Item Response Theory • Maximum Likelihood Estimation

Further Reading

Bock, R. D. (1985). Multivariate analysis of qualitative data. In *Multivariate Statistical Analysis of Behavioral Research* (R. D. Bock, ed.), Chapter 8. Scientific Software International, Chicago.

Bock, R. D. (1989). Addendum—Measurement of human variation: A two-stage model. In *Multilevel Analysis of Educational Data* (R. D. Bock, ed.), pp. 319–342. Academic Press, New York.

Bock, R. D. (1997). The nominal categories model. In *Handbook of Modern Item Response Theory* (W. J. van der Linden and R. K. Hambleton, eds.), pp. 33–49. Springer-Verlag, New York.

Bock, R. D., and Zimowski, M. F. (1997). Multiple group IRT. In *Handbook of Modern Item Response Theory* (W. J. van der Linden and R. K. Hambleton, eds.), pp. 433–448. Springer-Verlag, New York.

Böckenholt, U. (2001). Mixed-effects analyses of rank-ordered data. *Psychometrika* **66,** 45–62.

Bossuyt, P. (1990). *A Comparison of Probabalistic Unfolding Theories for Paired Comparison Data.* Springer-Verlag, New York.

Coombs, C. H. (1964). *A Theory of Data.* Wiley, New York.

Luce, R. D. (1959). *Individual Choice Behavior: A Theoretical Analysis.* Greenwood Press, Westport, Connecticut.

Marden, J. I. (1995). *Analyzing and Modeling Rank Data.* Chapman & Hall, London.

Masters, G. N. (1982). Rasch model for partial credit scoring. *Psychometrika* **47,** 149–174.

Samejima, F. (1997). Graded response model. In *Handbook of Modern Item Response Theory* (W. J. van der Linden and R. K. Hambleton, eds.), pp. 85–100. Springer-Verlag, New York.

Takane, Y. (1996). An item response model for multidimensional analysis of multiple choice data. *Behaviormetrika* **23,** 153–167.

Takane, Y., and de Leeuw, J. (1987). On the relationship between item response theory and factor analysis of discretized variables. *Psychometrika* **52,** 393–408.

Thissen, D. (1991). *Multilog: Multiple Categorical Item Analysis and Test Scoring Using Item Response Theory.* Scientific Software International, Chicago.

Thissen, D., and Steinberg, L. (1997). A response model for multiple-choice items. In *Handbook of Modern Item Response Theory* (W. J. van der Linden and R. K. Hambleton, eds.), pp. 51–65. Springer-Verlag, New York.

Wainer, H., Sireci, S. G., and Thissen, D. (1991). Differential testlet functioning: Definition and detection. *J. Edu. Measure.* **28,** 197–219.

Non-Probability Sampling

Alison Galloway
Queen Margaret University College, Edinburgh, United Kingdom

Glossary

population The group of people/items/units under investigation, about which the researcher wishes to draw conclusions.

probability sample A sample in which each member of the population has a quantifiable or calculable equal chance of selection.

sampling frame A list of the names and/or addresses of the population under investigation; the data should be comprehensive and up-to-date.

simple random sample A sample in which each element of the population is allocated its own number or identifier, and then random number tables or computer-generated random numbers are used to select a sample; often used as a standard against which other sampling methods are evaluated.

stratified sample A sample whereby the final selection is made to represent the same proportion with which the selected strata (or stratum) occur in the population as a whole.

stratum/strata Group/groups, often demographic, that are identifiable within a sampling frame; may be categorized by age, gender, socioeconomic grouping, income, etc.

systematic sample A form of random sampling whereby, instead of random numbers being selected, the researcher moves through the sampling frame, picking every *n*th entry.

When undertaking any survey, it is essential to obtain data from people who are as representative as possible for the group being studied. Even with the perfect questionnaire (if such a thing exists), survey data will be regarded as useful only if it can be demonstrated that the respondents used are as representative as possible. As with probability methods, non-probability sampling encompasses a range of techniques. The choice of method will depend on the nature of the research problem, the availability (or otherwise) of a good sampling frame, money, time, required level of accuracy in the sample, and data collection methods. Each form has its advantages, each its disadvantages.

Introduction

Definition

In a non-probability sample, some members of the population, compared to other members, have a greater but unknown chance of selection. There are five main types of non-probability sample: convenience, purposive, quota, snowball, and self-selection.

Comparison with Probability Samples

The main feature present in a probability sample, but generally absent in a non-probability sample, is a sampling frame. Probability samples are possible only when there is a complete and up-to-date list of the members (names and/or addresses) of the population under investigation. There are, of course, many situations in which it is not possible to obtain a sampling frame. For example, when researching football supporters, it is not feasible to obtain a list of names or addresses of people who attend games. It should be possible to obtain a list of people who are official members of the team, but this is unlikely to comprise all supporters. Similarly, there is not a sampling frame easily available to researchers of all the elderly in a population. Non-probability techniques therefore have to be used whenever there is no readily available and complete list of the population under investigation.

Advantages and Disadvantages of Non-Probability Sampling

The most obvious advantage in non-probability sampling is clearly the ability to target particular groups of the population. Non-probability methods are often dismissed or criticized because they do not have the statistical foundations of probability methods. However, a survey using, for example, random, systematic, or stratified sampling may adopt methods such as postal delivery, which characteristically has extremely poor response rates. It could certainly be argued that as many valid conclusions can be drawn from a well-constructed study using non-probability methods, compared with a probability survey to which only 10% of the sample responded. Researchers would need to be confident that those 10% were truly representative of the population as a whole.

Non-probability methods also have the advantage in typically being less expensive to conduct. Savings, in terms of both money and time, can be achieved not so much by the sampling method per se, but rather by the forms of delivery that are available for these methods. For example, face-to-face delivery can be cheaper than postal approaches, particularly where oversampling has had to be used to compensate for the typically poor response rates of a mailed survey.

Convenience Sampling

Definition

Convenience sampling involves using respondents who are "convenient" to the researcher. There is no pattern whatsoever in acquiring these respondents—they may be recruited merely asking people who are present in the street, in a public building, or in a workplace, for example. The concept is often confused with "random sampling" because of the notion that people are being stopped "at random" (in other words, haphazardly). However, whereas the correct definition of random sampling (using random numbers to pick potential respondents or participants from a sampling frame) generally results in a statistically balanced selection of the population, a convenience sample has an extremely high degree of bias.

Application

Typically, somebody undertaking a convenience sample will simply ask friends, relatives, colleagues in the workplace, or people in the street to take part in their research. One of the best ways of considering the pitfalls of this form of sampling is to look at this last approach—stopping people in the street. On a typical weekday morning in the shopping area of an average town, the people on the street at that time are likely to result in an overrepresentation of the views of, for example, the unemployed and the elderly retired population. There will be a corresponding underrepresentation of those working in traditional "9-to-5" jobs. This can, of course, be counterbalanced to some extent by careful selection of different times and days of the week to ensure a slightly more balanced sample.

Despite the enormous disadvantage of convenience sampling that stems from an inability to draw statistically significant conclusions from findings obtained, convenience sampling does still have some uses. For example, it can be helpful in obtaining a range of attitudes and opinions and in identifying tentative hypotheses that can be tested more rigorously in further research. Nevertheless, it is perhaps the weakest of all of the non-probability sampling strategies, and it is usually possible to obtain a more effective sample without a dramatic increase in effort by adopting one of the other non-probability methods. The following examples of convenience sampling from published research represent the wide range of applications in the social sciences and in business research:

- A convenience sample of 1117 undergraduate students in American universities explored associations between perceptions of unethical consumer behavior and demographic factors. Instructors on two campuses were contacted to obtain permission to administer the surveys during scheduled classes.
- Questionnaires were distributed using convenience methods in a study of the motives and behaviors of backpackers in Australia. The 475 surveys were delivered in cafes and hostels in areas popular with backpackers.
- Differences in bargaining behavior of 100 American and 100 Chinese respondents were explored using the Fishbein behavioral intention model.

Purposive Sampling

Definition

Purposive sampling is sometimes also referred to as a judgment sample. Whereas convenience sampling involves asking people who happen to be convenient to the researcher (on the street, or using friends and family), those using a purposive sample will endeavor to direct their survey at a range of respondents who are ultimately representative of at least the extremes of variables under consideration. For example, a researcher using purposive methods may strive to ensure that older age groups as well as younger ones are contained within the sample selected. This can be done as a "topping-up" procedure, whereby the researcher can start with what is more or less a convenience sample and may decide that there are insufficient respondents in a particular age category. Some respondents who will fit into the category are then deliberately sought. A number of criteria may be pertinent in accessing a purposive sample. Researchers may, for example, wish to obtain a balanced range of socioeconomic groupings or even incomes, although these are clearly more difficult variables to predict when looking at potential respondents on the street or in another public place.

Application

Purposive samples do not have to be undertaken in public places or even face to face. Potential respondents can be contacted in a variety of ways and it is perfectly feasible to use several of these methods to select a range of characteristics. For example, a researcher wishing to contact a good sample of the elderly to determine any problems they were experiencing with their housing would want to ensure that a range of demographic factors could be encompassed; this can be achieved with a purposive sample. It would clearly be important to include both male and female respondents in such a sample. It could also be considered critical that both the "young old" (the newly retired) and the "old old" (over 80, say) were included. It might also be important to ensure that all housing tenure forms were encompassed when selecting respondents. Accessing such a broad range of variables might require more than one sampling strategy. For example, access may be given to age/sex registers of medical practices, whereby a range of ages of males and females could be located. Renters could be accessed through housing associations or similar organizations, and owners could be located in private housing developments for the elderly. Social clubs for the elderly could also be used as an access point, but this would generally lead to those elderly who might be considered more gregarious.

Another example of the useful application of purposive sampling would be in a study of healthy eating. If the researcher were to resort to convenience sampling, respondents might be of a fairly narrow age band and a limited range of socioeconomic groupings. A purposive sample would ensure that people falling within a good range of ages (e.g., from 18 to 80 years) were contacted and that the group included professionals as well as manual workers. It might even be considered useful to make sure that the sample included people who take plenty of exercise (by delivering some surveys in a health club, for example), as well as those who do not, by contacting social organizations with a more sedentary focus. The following examples of purposive sampling have been reported in research literature:

- A study of nonsmoking parents of adolescents who smoke. A purposive sample of 25 respondents encompassed different ages, levels of education, and genders, and whether the parents had smoked in the past.
- Research into the effectiveness of drama in primary schools in the introduction of sensitive concepts such as child protection and personal safety. Participants who were recruited into focus group research included teachers, actors, and health promotion staff.
- A purposive sample of respondents from different levels of service staff. Persons from senior management, the supervisory level, and front-line operations were used in semistructured interviews with local authority employees to explore the implications and perceived benefits of achieving the "Investors in People" standard (a national quality standard of business practices in the United Kingdom).

Quota Sampling

Definition

There are a number of commonalities between quota and purposive sampling, but a critical difference lies in the fact that the former is invariably undertaken by groups of researchers, whereas the latter can be undertaken by an individual researcher. Quota sampling tries to replicate proportions of demographic factors whereas, in purposive sampling, researchers may be satisfied merely to include a reasonable range of the variables being examined.

Quota sampling is an extremely common technique employed by market research companies, particularly when they are adopting a face-to-face on-street interviewing methodology. It is generally used for large-scale samples of 2000 or more and is a useful alternative to probability samples, such as a random stratified sampling. As with a stratified sample, it is necessary to know certain demographic factors about the sample population (for example, proportions of males/females, age composition, or socioeconomic grouping). This information can be obtained easily through census data. The data are used to calculate quotas for each of the demographic groups that are considered pertinent to the subject of the research being undertaken. Each researcher can then be given a brief that specifies the number of people to interview with these characteristics. Complex quotas can be developed to incorporate all of the critical demographic or other variables.

Application

The main objective in a quota sample is to try to replicate the proportions of particular critical variables in the population as a whole. Imagine, for example, that researchers want to undertake a survey in a town with a population of 64,746 people. They wish to ensure that their sample is representative with respect to three main variables: gender, age, and housing tenure (owner-occupiers, social renters, and private renters). Using census or similar data, they can determine the numbers of people representing these variables in a particular area Tables I and II). Researchers would not necessarily be targeting a particular percentage of the population and could start instead with a total sample number (e.g., 500 or 1000). For the sake of simplicity, though, imagine that a 1% sample is the goal. This would mean that, for their quota sample, the entire group of researchers would have to find the numbers of people shown in Tables III and IV. These figures would be divided up among the team undertaking the fieldwork (perhaps based in different parts of the town). Although gender is usually quite apparent and an approximation of age can be made by the researcher, as the fieldwork progressed and the different quotas were met, the researcher would have to establish housing tenure and confirm age fairly early on in the interview with a short filtering question. The following examples of quota sampling have been reported in research literature:

- Research into the perceived efficacy of sales promotions in UK supermarkets. This research used a quota sample that took account of gender and age. The population profile in the United Kingdom was used to ensure that the study's sample would reflect the general population in these demographic variables.
- The way in which students shop for food. This demographic was explored in a questionnaire-based survey. A quota sample ensured that gender as well as proportional student faculty membership were reflected in the final choice of respondents.

Snowball Sampling

Definition

Just as a snowball gets bigger when rolled in snow, a snowball sample increases in size as a small number of potential respondents suggest the names and/or addresses of other people who fulfill particular criteria. It is a particularly useful technique when looking for respondents with unusual interests/faiths/medical conditions and so on. The researcher begins by contacting two or three people who are thought to fulfill the criteria being sought and asking them if they know of other people with the same interest/condition, etc. If each of three people supplies the names of another three, and those contacts subsequently supply names of potential respondents, a healthy number of participants soon results.

Application

There are countless situations in which a snowball sample can be considered an appropriate strategy, particularly where a criterion for research may be very widely dispersed and difficult to track down using conventional

Table I Quota Sample of Housing Tenure Data for Males[a]

Age (years)	*Owner-occupier*	*Social renter*	*Private renter*
18–25	2149	788	645
26–35	2338	857	701
36–45	4573	1677	1372
46–55	2869	1254	659
56–65	2845	1435	2241
Over 65	1865	1697	1611

[a] Number of people in the sample who represented a particular variable.

Table II Quota Sample of Housing Tenure Data for Females[a]

Age (years)	*Owner-occupier*	*Social renter*	*Private renter*
18–25	2053	920	566
26–35	2247	1007	620
36–45	4217	1890	1163
46–55	2859	1282	789
56–65	4104	1673	1299
Over 65	3759	1884	838

[a] Number of people in the sample who represented a particular variable.

Table III Number of Respondents Required for a 1% Sample of Males[a]

Age (years)	*Owner-occupier*	*Social renter*	*Private renter*
18–25	21	8	6
26–35	23	9	7
36–45	46	17	14
46–55	29	13	7
56–65	28	14	22
Over 65	19	17	16

[a] Relative to quota sample data in Table I.

Table IV Number of Respondents Required for a 1% Sample of Females[a]

Age (years)	*Owner-occupier*	*Social renter*	*Private renter*
18–25	21	9	6
26–35	22	10	6
36–45	42	19	12
46–55	29	13	8
56–65	41	17	13
Over 65	38	19	8

[a] Relative to quota sample data in Table II.

approaches. The following examples are again taken from the literature:

• An exploration of the ethical precepts held by a sample of Chinese professionals. This study used a snowball sample by asking participants in a management development program to complete a questionnaire and to persuade their peers to do the same.

• A study of factors influencing substance use in 16- to 22-year olds. This study used snowballing techniques to include students and even a drug seller as their contact points.

• Two studies of professional women with children (one focusing on lone mothers). This research drew on snowball techniques to acquire sufficient numbers of respondents.

• A cross-cultural study of consumer decision making. This research used a snowball sample because of the difficulty in contacting Indian-Tamil wives located in India. Initial contacts were asked to provide referrals of female married friends and relatives who would be willing to participate.

Self-Selection

Definition

A self-selected sample is simply one in which the respondents put themselves forward for participation in a survey or similar form of research. The possibility of bias in the sample is extremely high, because those most likely to put themselves forward are those who have a particular interest in the subject. Whereas this interest can be a necessary criterion for some research, there may be instances when only those respondents who have extremely positive or extremely negative experiences pertaining to the study subject volunteer for the study, and the "average" viewpoint may thus not emerge.

Application

Self-selection can be implemented in a number of ways. When research is in the form of a survey, questionnaires can simply be left in a variety of appropriate locations (e.g., medical practice waiting rooms and public libraries). This relies to a high extent on altruism, although incentives such as a prize drawing can play an important part in increasing the size of a self-selected sample. Another form of self-selected sampling involves publicizing through posters or flyers. Details of projects can be given with a request for volunteers to contact the researcher by telephone, post, or email. Finally, self-selection can be incorporated into Internet-based surveys. Emails can be sent to appropriate distribution lists or newsgroups, although care has to be taken to avoid doing this in an inappropriate manner ("spamming"). Similarly, Web pages can be used, provided that they are publicized sufficiently to encourage respondents to participate. The following examples of self-selection sampling have been reported in research literature:

• Research into international mobility among business and education professionals. Self-selection sampling was accomplished by the use of institution-wide emails to all academic staff in a sample of higher educational institutions in four different countries.

• Major Internet surveys. These surveys have adopted self-selection as a sampling strategy, the most notable being that done by the Georgia Institute of Technology's Graphics, Visualization, and Usability (GVU), in which Internet usage is monitored on a regular basis.

Conclusions

Although researchers may feel constrained when the lack of an available sampling frame rules out the possibility of a probability sample, there are still a number of options available in the range of non-probability samples. Although non-probability samples do not carry the same weight as probability samples, in statistical terms, they do still provide the opportunity to draw from a representative selection of the population. A true random sample with an extremely low response rate may have no greater chance of being representative than, for example, a carefully constructed quota sample. Not all research requires high degrees of accuracy, and for exploratory research, in particular, a non-probability sample may be a perfectly appropriate strategy.

See Also the Following Articles

Population vs. Sample • Randomization • Sample Size • Snowball Sampling • Stratified Sampling Types

Further Reading

Boys, A., *et al.* (2002). The relative influence of friends and functions: Modelling frequency of substance use in a non-treatment sample of 16–22 year olds. *Health Edu.* **102**(6), 280–288.

Callen, K. S., and Ownbey, S. F. (2003). Associations between demographics and perceptions of unethical consumer behaviour. *Int. J. Consumer Stud.* **27**(2), 99–110.

Douglas, A., *et al.* (1999). The impact of Investors in People on Scottish Local Government services. *J. Workplace Learn.* **11**(5), 164–169.

Ganesh, G. (1997). Spousal influence in consumer decisions: a study of cultural assimilation. *J. Consumer Market* **14**(2), 132–155.

Gilbert, D. C., and Jackaria, N. (2002). The efficacy of sales promotions in UK supermarkets: A consumer view. *Int. J. Retail Distrib. Mgmt.* **30**(6), 315–322.

Gill, S., and Davidson, M. J. (2001). Problems and pressures facing lone mothers in management and professional occupations—A pilot study. *Women Mgmt. Rev.* **16**(8), 383–399.

Gordon, J. R., *et al.* (2002). The midlife transition of professional women with children. *Women Mgmt. Rev.* **17**(7), 328–341.

Lee, D. Y. (2000). Retail bargaining behaviour of American and Chinese customers. *Eur. J. Market* **34**(1), 190–206.

Mohnsin, A., and Ryan, C. (2003). Backpackers in the Northern Territory of Australia—Motives, behaviours and satisfactions. *Int. J. Tourism Res.* **5,** 113–131.

Ness, M., *et al.* (2002). The student food shopper: Segmentation on the basis of attitudes to store features and shopping behaviour. *Br. Food J.* **104**(7), 506–525.

Orme, J., and Salmon, D. (2002). Child protection drama in primary school—An effective educational approach? *Health Edu.* **102**(4), 187–196.

Richardson, J., and McKenna, S. (2002). Leaving and experiencing: Why academics expatriate and how they experience expatriation. *Career Dev. Int.* **7**(2), 67–78.

Small, S. P., *et al.* (2002). Struggling to understand: the experience of non-smoking parents with adolescents who smoke. *Qual. Health Res.* **12**(9), 1202–1219.

Ward, M. R., and Lee, M. J. (2000). Internet shopping, consumer search and product branding. *J. Product Brand Mgmt.* **9**(1), 6–20.

Wright, P. C., *et al.* (2003). Ethical perceptions in China: The reality of business ethics in an international context. *Mgmt. Decis.* **41**(2), 180–189.

Non-Response Bias

Nathan Berg
University of Texas, Dallas, Richardson, Texas, USA

Glossary

bias The expected difference between an estimated characteristic of a population and that population's true characteristic.

item non-response A non-response to a particular survey item accompanied by at least one valid measurement for the same respondent, for example, leaving just one item on a questionnaire blank or responding to some questions by saying, "I don't know," but providing a valid response to other questions.

non-response A survey response that falls outside the range of responses that survey designers consider to be valid.

unit One observation or a single vector of measurements, usually corresponding to a particular individual at a given point in time; many units make up a sample.

unit non-response Refusal or failure to provide any valid responses by someone who survey designers intended to include in the survey.

Non-response bias refers to the mistake researchers expect to make in estimating a population characteristic based on a sample of survey data in which, due to non-response, certain types of survey respondents are under-represented.

Motivation for Analyzing Non-Response Bias

To illustrate and underscore the importance of analyzing non-response bias, consider the following scenario. A researcher working for a marketing firm wishes to estimate the average age of New Yorkers who own telephones. In order to do this, the researcher attempts to conduct a phone survey of 1000 individuals drawn from the population of phone-owning New Yorkers by dialing randomly chosen residential phone numbers. However, after 1000 attempts, the researcher is in possession of only 746 valid responses because 254 individuals never answered the phone and therefore could not be reached. At this point, the researcher averages the ages of the 746 respondents with valid responses and considers whether this average is likely to be too high or too low. Does one expect the 254 non-responders to be roughly the same age as respondents who answered their phones?

After thinking it over, the researcher concludes that the average age of the 746 responders is a biased estimate because the surveys were conducted during business hours when workers (as compared to older retirees) were less likely to be at home. If working age respondents are underrepresented, then the average among the 746 valid age responses is biased upward. In this case, the difference between the biased average and the true but unobserved average age among all telephone owners is precisely non-response bias.

Social scientists often attempt to make inferences about a population by drawing a random sample and studying relationships among the measurements contained in the sample. When individuals from a special subset of the population are systematically omitted from a particular sample, however, the sample cannot be said to be random in the sense that every member of the population is equally likely to be included in the sample. It is important to acknowledge that any patterns uncovered in analyzing a nonrandom sample do not provide valid grounds for generalizing about a population in the same way that patterns present in a random sample do. The mismatch between the average characteristics of respondents in a nonrandom sample and the average characteristics of the population can lead to serious problems in understanding the causes of social phenomena and may lead to misdirected policy action. Therefore, considerable attention has been given to the problem of non-response bias, both at the stages of data collection and data analysis.

Classifying Types of Error and Bias

Sampling Error

Anytime we generalize about a population based on a sample, as opposed to conducting a complete census of the population, there is an unavoidable possibility of mistaken inference. As such, sampling error arises even under the best of circumstances simply because, due to chance, averages of variables in a random sample are not identical to the corresponding averages in the population. Fortunately, sampling error typically disappears as the sample size increases. More important, sampling error does not lead to bias, because population characteristics can be estimated in such a way that the probability-weighted average of possible overestimates and underestimates is precisely zero.

Nonrepresentative Samples

It is important to distinguish from sampling error an entire family of nonsampling errors that arise when a sample is selected from a population in such a way that some members of the population are less likely to be included than others. In such cases, the sample is said to be nonrandom, or nonrepresentative, with respect to the population we intend to study. In contrast to sampling error, a nonrepresentative sample generally leads to biased estimation.

A number of factors may cause a sample to be nonrepresentative. One possibility is that, because of a flawed survey design, the survey simply fails to reach certain segments of the population. In the previous example, a daytime phone survey tended to underrepresent people who work, just as a survey of rural-area dwellers, or of car owners, would underrepresent users of public transportation.

Systematic mistakes by surveyors in coding survey responses can also lead to non-representative samples. The key issue is whether such mistakes are correlated with the characteristics of the individual being surveyed. For instance, a surveyor who, in the course of interviewing survey respondents, sometimes gets carried away discussing sports and forgets to record the respondent's last few responses will end up with a sample in which sports fans are underrepresented among the complete survey responses.

Perhaps the most common reason for nonrepresentative samples, however, is the behavior of survey respondents themselves. Oftentimes, the very fact of being a non-responder correlates with other characteristics of interest. When it does, non-response inevitably leads to nonrandom sampling and creates the potential for biased estimation of the characteristics under study. Researchers working with survey data must always consider the possibility that certain types of individuals are more likely to refuse to respond. This problem is acute when one of the key variables of interest determines, in part, who is more likely to select themselves out of a sample by not answering a survey question.

It is often suspected, for example, that individuals with high incomes are less likely to voluntarily disclose their income, biasing survey-based estimates of income downward. Similarly, those engaged in illicit drug activity, fearing the consequences of divulging potentially incriminating information, are probably less likely to participate in a survey about drug use, leading, again, to the potential for systematic underestimation. A slightly more subtle example is the case of estimating the percentage of a population that supports one of two political candidates. Apathetic voters are often thought to be the least likely to cooperate with political pollsters, even though many of them will in fact vote. Basing election forecasts on a sample of only those who agree to answer the poll can be misleading because the opinions of apathetic voters are underrepresented in pollsters' samples.

Dealing with Nonrepresentativeness before or after Data are Collected: Sample Design and Data Analysis Stages

To deal with nonrepresentative samples, it is helpful to distinguish two broad stages in a social science research project: data collection and data analysis. Some researchers conduct surveys themselves and therefore have direct control over the details of data collection. Others work with data sets originally collected by someone else, in which case the researcher exerts no direct control over the data collection stage.

For those who have a say about how the data are to be collected, it is crucial to try to foresee potential flaws in order to reduce the likelihood of bias. A vast literature exists on the topic of survey design, covering everything from the wording of survey questions to the issue of how many times those who do not answer the phone on a phone survey ought to be called back. Sometimes surveys can be designed in such a way as to provide a means of estimating the non-response bias associated with a particular data collection technique, for example, by comparing the results of face-to-face and phone interviews.

Many researchers in the social sciences, rather than collecting new data themselves, study data that have been collected by others, such as the U.S. Census, the Current Population Survey, and the General Social Survey. As a secondary data analyst, the researcher must decide what to do about survey respondents who failed to answer particular questions, referred to as the missing data problem. An additional issue is what to do about the target respondents who did not participate in the survey at all.

Similarity among Biases with Different Labels

One finds many different labels for biases that are, in fact, instances of one common problem—trying to learn about a population based on a nonrepresentative sample. It is helpful to see the underlying similarity among biases that arise from nonrepresentative samples because a successful approach to dealing with bias in one context often can be applied to new settings. In particular, survey data with missing responses can frequently be analyzed using techniques from the statistical and econometric literature under the heading measurement error. Terms such as "noncompletion bias" or "volunteer bias," referring to the nonrepresentative sample problem that arises when only special kinds of respondents actually complete a survey questionnaire or to situations in which the subpopulation of volunteers is substantively different from the rest of the population, should be viewed as essentially the same problem.

The connection between non-response bias and selection bias warrants special mention. Non-response is special kind of the selection problem of the type analyzed in the work of James Heckman. Thus, selection bias, when referring to the mechanism by which some survey respondents choose not to answer survey questions (thereby selecting themselves out of the sample), overlaps with what is defined here as non-response bias. Heckman interprets the selection problem more generally as a kind of econometric misspecification. As illustration, it is useful to consider a regression model used frequently by labor economists in which the expected wage depends on demographic variables as well as other factors thought to influence workplace productivity. If no account is taken of the mechanism by which only special kinds of individuals choose to become workers and therefore wind up being included in the sample (implying that regressors are correlated with the error term in the regression model), then the econometric model is, in Heckman's words, "misspecified," leading to misspecification bias.

Misreporting versus Non-Response

When those collecting data ask respondents to report on their own behavior in connection with activities such as cheating, personal finance, sex, or alcohol and drug use, some respondents, instead of refusing to answer, will misreport their behavior. When interpreted at face value, a sample in which certain kinds of individuals tend to misreport will not accurately represent the population under study. As with nonrepresentative samples caused by non-response, misreporting usually leads to bias, which can be referred to as misclassification bias, misreporting bias, contaminated data bias, or simply response bias. The task of the researcher is to consider how such misreporting will influence estimates of key population characteristics.

Analysis of Survey Data with Missing Responses

Item versus Unit Non-Response

An important distinction to make regarding non-response is item versus unit non-response, a distinction that turns on whether there is at least one survey item for which a valid response was obtained or whether the entire unit is missing. When entire units are missing from a sample, no test or correction for bias is available without obtaining additional data about the targeted respondents who did not respond to the initial survey. In contrast, samples with item non-response may allow for unbiased estimation because partially completed responses from item non-responders may be used to control for differences across responders and item non-responders. This section discusses techniques for computing unbiased estimates using samples which feature item non-responses.

Little and Rubin's Missing Data Framework

Roderick Little and Donald Rubin, individually and in joint work, have written a number of frequently cited articles on the subject of analyzing data with missing values. Their approach is quite general and applies directly to most situations that applied researchers working with survey data are likely to face.

Imputation

One approach to dealing with missing survey responses is to somehow fill in the missing values, imputing good guesses in place of missing survey entries. Some researchers, for instance, may replace missing measurements with the average value across the complete cases. A more sophisticated approach involves replacing missing values with estimates based on prediction equations that are fitted with the complete cases and subsequently used to predict missing values using the partial responses of item non-responders. After imputing values to fill in the missing data, data analysis proceeds using traditional estimation techniques.

A serious drawback to this technique is that the precision of the estimates computed using the data set with imputed values will be overstated for two reasons. First, imputed values generally are computed by averaging over other observations and, therefore, will be more tightly clustered about the mean than a fresh collection of bona fide observations would be. And second, the use of traditional statistical techniques after imputing values for missing entries in the data matrix will be based on an overstated sample size because a sample of N observations, some of which have been imputed, will contain fewer than N independent pieces of information. This means that standard errors will be too small and that the nominal size of significance tests will be inflated.

Weighting

Another approach to working with incomplete data involves discarding partial observations and assigning a weight to each complete observation so that the weighted sample better represents the average characteristics of the population. For instance, with a sample of 68 men and 32 women in which women appear to be underrepresented, one might consider placing additional weight on female units in the sample, perhaps based on the gender ratio from the U.S. Census, in order to reduce bias. In principle, weighting should correct for bias that arises from estimation based on nonrepresentative samples. A severe complication, however, is knowing how to compute standard errors that accurately account for the imprecision in the weights themselves. Doing so is notoriously difficult. Therefore, many authors, including Little and Rubin, recommend against weighting techniques. Those authors point out that the most common approach to non-response is simply to discard incomplete responses, effectively giving each of the complete sample units the same weight. Except for the unusually lucky case in which the complete-only subsample is a truly random sample of the population, this technique, although simple to use and widely practiced, leads to biased estimates.

The Maximum-Likelihood Approach

The maximum-likelihood approach is, far and away, the preferred approach to correcting for non-response bias, and it is the one advocated by Little and Rubin. The maximum-likelihood approach begins by writing down a probability distribution that defines the likelihood of the observed sample as a function of population and distribution parameters θ. If x_1 and x_2 represent responses to two different survey questions by a single individual, the likelihood associated with a complete response may be expressed as $f(x_1, x_2; \theta)$, where f is the joint probability density function of x_1 and x_2. For individuals who only report x_1, the likelihood associated with x_1 is $\int_{-\infty}^{\infty} f(x_1, x_2; \theta)dx_2$, which can, under the assumption of joint normality, be simplified to a more convenient form. In this way, a likelihood function is specified that includes terms corresponding to each observation, whether completely or only partially observed. The likelihood objective is then maximized with respect to θ, which produces estimates of the desired characteristics, enjoying all the well-known properties of maximum-likelihood estimation.

Most important among those properties, maximum-likelihood estimates converge to the true value of θ under the assumption that the probability distribution is correctly specified. Maximum-likelihood estimates are also asymptotically normal and asymptotically efficient, meaning that, for large samples, the maximum-likelihood estimate of θ is approximately normal and is the best use of the information contained in the sample. In addition to these advantages, the maximum-likelihood approach makes it possible to estimate fairly elaborate multi-equation models in which the probability that an individual fails to respond depends on other observable variables. Within such a framework, it is often possible to construct a quantitative test of the missing-at-random hypothesis, implemented as a straightforward test of an appropriate parameter restriction. The main drawback to maximum-likelihood estimation is that strong assumptions are required about the distribution of the process generating the survey responses. Still, the advantages are usually thought to outweigh the drawbacks, making it the approach of choice for many quantitative researchers.

Missing-at-Random, Missing-Completely-at-Random, Mixture Modeling, and Multiple Imputation

A frequently mentioned distinction in the missing-data literature involves the two terms, missing-at-random and missing-completely-at-random. If the probability of non-response for a variable Y is the same for every unit of observation in the population, then Y is said to be missing-completely-at-random. If, on the other hand, the probability of non-response systematically relates to other variables in the model, but not to the value of Y itself, then Y is said to be missing-at-random. Defining the random variable $R = 0$ if Y is missing, and $R = 1$ otherwise, another important distinction can be expressed as follows. Selection models require the user to observe the conditional distribution $Y \mid R = 1$ and model the conditional probability $R = 1 \mid Y = y$, whereas mixture models require observing $Y \mid R = 1$ and modeling $Y \mid R = 0$.

Other Perspectives on Correcting for Non-Response Bias

Lawrence Marsh and his co-authors have proposed a number of non-response models and developed associated maximum-likelihood estimators that appear to work well in practice. Marsh's work, in addition to providing straightforward maximum-likelihood estimators of non-response bias, compares the performance of maximum-likelihood-based corrections for non-response bias against those associated with alternative techniques of estimation, such as maximum entropy, finding consistent support for the maximum-likelihood approach. These results rest on the existence of auxiliary relations that determine the missing response mechanism. In the absence of auxiliary relations, Lien and Rearden's 1988 article shows that, when the missing observation is the dependent variable in a limited dependent-variable model, nothing is gained by applying maximum-likelihood-based corrections. Thus, special caution is warranted when estimating a model in which the dependent variable is frequently missing.

Measuring Non-Response Bias

Validation

Validation is a general approach to testing for non-response bias that almost always involves comparing two different samples drawn from the same population. The technique of validation permits us to measure non-response bias, to test the hypothesis of no bias, and to identify which variables, if any, are correlated with non-response. This approach is only feasible, however, if we are lucky enough to have two samples drawn from the same population.

Given a pair of samples, it is usually clear, either from the number of missing entries or from descriptive notes attached to the data, which data set has a lower non-response rate. The general philosophy of validation assumes that the sample with the lower non-response rate is, for all practical purposes, the "reliable" one. Accepting this view, significant departures among the observations in the "unreliable" sample relative to the average characteristics in the "reliable" sample can then be attributed to non-response bias, providing a qualitative measure (too high vs. too low) along with a quantitative measure of the severity of the problem.

For instance, it is well accepted that face-to-face interviews typically draw a higher response rate than phone surveys do. Now suppose we draw two samples of measurements on ethnicity, one face-to-face and the other by phone, and discover that the fraction of Asian Americans in the phone data is one-half that of the face-to-face interview data. Taking the estimated racial composition of those who respond to the face-to-face interview as the reliable benchmark, we might plausibly infer that Asian Americans are twice as likely to non-respond in a phone survey compared to other types of Americans. The qualitative finding that phone survey data may underrepresent Asian Americans is valuable in qualifying further estimates of characteristics on which Asian Americans are known to be different from other Americans. Beyond this, the magnitude of the difference, in this case a factor of one-half, can be used to place additional weight on the phone responses of Asian Americans in order to correct for the fact that they tend to be underrepresented in phone surveys.

Sex researchers, who must routinely deal with survey data suffering from very high non-response rates, have applied validation to gain a feel for the ways in which the respondents in their data are different from the U.S. population at large. A straightforward approach is to compare, say, the age distribution among sex survey respondents with the age distribution of the population of Americans as measured by the U.S. Census. Sex survey respondents, in fact, appear to be younger than average Americans are.

Validation is virtually the only way to learn about the characteristics of unit non-responders because, by definition, there is no information on unit non-responders in the rounds of data collection in which non-response occurs. One 1999 study by Heather Turner used validation techniques to uncover some surprising distinctions that need be made among those who are typically categorized together as non-responders. She identified two types of non-responders, differentiating those who refused to participate twice from those who could not be contacted after 17 attempts. Using data from other sources and from follow-up interviews, she discovered that those non-responders who directly refused to participate in the survey tended to be older, attended church more often, and were more skeptical about the confidentiality of interviews.

In an important finding, rich with policy implications, she produced evidence suggesting that, in contrast to the low-risk lifestyles of those who directly refuse to participate, the difficult-to-reach non-responders tended to have significantly more sexual partners and higher frequencies of risk factors for AIDS. This demonstrates how difficult it can be to generalize about non-responders and make reliable guesses as to whether non-response bias skews estimates up or down.

Measuring non-response bias in telephone surveys is a frequent concern for polling organizations and those conducting market research by telephone. A fundamental issue confronting anyone attempting to learn about the entire population of Americans based on a phone survey is the fact that not all American households have telephones. Previous attempts to measure the characteristics of nontelephone households indicate considerable differences with respect to phone-owning households across a number of important characteristics such as the propensity to have health insurance.

In a novel approach to measuring non-response bias published in 1995, Scott Keeter sought to estimate telephone noncoverage bias by conducting a series of phone surveys on the same randomly drawn sample of phone numbers at several points in time. Among those reached at any given time were, of course, some households who had only recently gained access to a telephone. And among those reached in earlier rounds of phone surveying were some households whose number later became disconnected. Labeling those who gained or lost telephone service at least once as "transient" and comparing the number of transients in his sample with government and industry estimates of how many American households are nontelephone households, Keeter determined that transients make up roughly one-half of all nontelephone households. Moreover, the demographic characteristics of nontelephone households recorded in other surveys appeared to match those of the transient group in Keeter's study, bolstering confidence in the ability of existing non-response-corrected phone survey methodologies to produce meaningful insights into the characteristics of American households in general.

Another area of policy research in which non-response bias can play an especially important role is that of valuing natural resources. Developers and government officials often attempt to study the benefits and costs of a proposed building project and must, at some point, put a dollar value on natural resources, including wetlands, endangered animals, and undeveloped green space. Similarly, officials at the Environmental Protection Agency and environmental economists confront the challenge of assessing the value of parks, wildlife, and air quality. Such endeavors must deal with the question of how to reliably elicit valuations that somehow reflect the aggregate preferences of residents. The basic idea is to use samples of citizens to estimate the worth of natural resources in the eyes of an average citizen.

It is fairly obvious that the problem of nonrepresentativeness will have a direct effect on such valuations. Suspecting that those who agree to participate in environmental surveys have higher than average subjective assessments of the value of natural resources, researchers in this area worry that non-response bias may lead to overstated valuations. In a 1993 article, John Whitehead and his colleagues employed a combination mail and phone survey design in an attempt to produce a bias-corrected valuation of a wetlands preservation project. Using the validation principle, these authors attempted to measure differences between non-responders and responders, both in terms of average demographic characteristics and in terms of willingness to pay for environmental amenities. Validation did, in fact, uncover a disparity between those who initially refused to participate and those who participated without hesitation. Although a non-responder with identical observable characteristics was found to be no less willing to pay than a similar responder, the group of eager respondents included more highly educated individuals and more males. After adjusting for non-response bias, the estimated aggregate willingness to pay fell by 33%.

In addition to its application in studying unit non-response, the logic of validation can also be applied to learn about item non-responders. Emil Kupek's 1998 article used a large national sex survey in Britain to study the covariates of item non-response. Kupek partitioned his sample into subsamples based on how reluctant individuals were in answering specific questions about their sexual behavior. Specifying the dependent variable to be a measure of each individual's reluctance to respond, Kupek estimated a model relating other demographic variables to the probability of item non-response. Non-responders in Kupek's sample turned out to be less educated and to include relatively more nonwhites. Perhaps surprisingly, factors such as gender, declared religious affiliation, age, and marital status seemed to have little effect on the probability of non-response. As in this study, simply establishing which variables correlate with non-response can amount to a key step in thinking through the broader consequences of non-response and, in particular, whether our nonrandom sample will actually lead to bias in estimating the population characteristics of interest.

Designing Surveys So That Non-Response Bias Can Be Estimated

An extensive body of research exists analyzing survey methods, seeking to refine their capacity to overcome potential sources of bias. The results, so far, however, are not reassuring. Survey responses are, without question, very sensitive to the way in which they are elicited. This phenomenon underlies disparaging remarks we frequently hear directed at survey findings in general, such as: "By changing the wording, anything can be shown with surveys." Although this statement is undoubtedly an exaggeration, the sensitivity of survey results to the fine detail of survey design has been demonstrated in numerous academic studies.

Hurd *et al.*'s 1998 study uses experimental evidence to analyze survey non-response and presents a thorough discussion of survey-response sensitivity in the context of estimating aspects of consumption and savings behavior. The order of survey questions, the gender of the surveyor, rewordings such as "10% survived" instead of "90% died," and a number of other seemingly innocuous differences in the implementation of surveys can sharply affect the average response. Compared to mail surveys, face-to-face interviews are known to produce higher reported rates of activities with a high degree of social approval such as volunteering, going to church, and engaging in safe rather than unprotected sex. Non-response rates can also vary dramatically depending on whether data are collected using phone, mail, or face-to-face interviews.

Complicating the picture is that these sensitivities to survey design are not always uniform across all segments of the population. For instance, it has been demonstrated that response rates for whites in face-to-face versus mail surveys are about the same, yet they differ significantly for African American respondents. Such findings underscore the delicate nature of survey design while raising important issues of interpretation that demand consideration even at subsequent stages of data analysis.

Randomized Response

The method of randomized response explicitly aims at reducing non-response and misreporting on survey items that concern sensitive topics. The idea behind randomized response is to introduce random questions or random coding procedures into the construction of response data so that it is impossible for the surveyor to infer the respondent's original response by looking at the data recorded for that individual. A survey question on illegal drug use might employ the following survey design. With probability $1 - q$, respondent i is asked, "Have you ever taken an illegal drug," from which the response datum, $y_i = 1$, is recorded if the answer is "Yes," and $y_i = 0$ otherwise. But with probability q, the response datum is coded $y_i = 1$ no matter i's answer (or without ever asking i the sensitive question). The advantage of the randomized design is its capacity to convince respondents that it is safe to truthfully disclose private information. If $y_i = 1$, it may be that i answered "Yes," or it may be that i happened to fall in the $(q \times 100)\%$ of the sample for whom y_i is automatically coded 1.

From randomized response data, an unbiased estimator of the true frequency of drug use is easy to compute, assuming that randomization induces perfect compliance (i.e., full response and no misreporting). Denote the true rate of drug use as λ. Because (equation (1)),

$$Ey_i = (1 - q)\lambda + q, \tag{1}$$

the estimator

$$\hat{\lambda} = \frac{\frac{1}{N}\sum_i^N y_i - q}{1 - q} \tag{2}$$

is unbiased. The price to be paid for introducing randomization, however, is a reduction in the precision of estimation, as can be seen by examining the variance formula for $\hat{\lambda}$.

Multivariate versions of randomization are also possible. Fox and Tracy's 1986 monograph, *Randomized Response: A Method for Sensitive Surveys*, provides further details. The goal of randomization, in all its forms, is to reduce respondents' skepticism about the confidentiality of their responses. Whether randomization accomplishes its goal is open to debate, however, because it is not clear whether respondents understand randomization sufficiently well or trust the survey designers to follow through with an honest implementation.

A Budget Constraint Means a Trade-off between Sampling Error and Bias Reduction

Different survey designs have different price tags and, although more data are always desirable, it is not always obvious how to efficiently allocate spending on data collection given a fixed project budget. In designing surveys with the intention of reducing non-response bias in mind, there is often a nontrivial trade-off to consider when selecting a mix of survey techniques. For a given sum of money, an inexpensive mail survey will probably draw a sample with a higher number of units, thereby reducing sampling error. However, a smaller sample collected using face-to-face interviews will probably enjoy the advantage of a lower unit non-response rate. Thus, we are faced with trading off greater precision (increasing the sample size) against a greater chance that non-response bias will contaminate estimation. In this situation, a sound approach generally involves selecting a mix of sampling techniques that will lead to fairly precise estimates while providing reasonably good controls for non-response bias.

Parsing the Meaning of the "Don't Know" Response

A problem faced by most applied researchers working with survey data is interpreting the meaning of the response "Don't know" to a survey question. Those involved at the survey design stage often contemplate whether one should prompt those who respond "Don't know" to relent and provide a valid answer. Interestingly, there is debate about whether such prompting is a good idea or not. Insofar as prompting induces random guessing, it is not helpful. But when additional prompting succeeds at extracting additional information rather than noise, our estimation should, in principle, improve.

For example, public opinion researchers have demonstrated that opinions about political candidates elicited from respondents who say they know nothing about those candidates are, in fact, meaningful indicators of future voting behavior rather than random noise. But in other settings, the evidence points in the opposite direction. As a general rule, the responses of reluctant responders that we collect by means of a special technique of elicitation should be interpreted cautiously, with full acknowledgement that they probably contain more noise than the responses of other respondents.

In some contexts, it may be useful to try identifying multiple subgroups among item non-responders. The issue at stake is the extent to which we can generalize about non-responders. Qualitative information about non-response bias is particularly helpful in instances in which it can be presumed that non-response bias mitigates against finding a significant difference, referring here to an estimated characteristic such as average income across two groups. In such a case, without doing anything special to correct for bias, discovering a significant difference is especially persuasive, in spite of and, in part, because of the bias. But in other settings, rather than helping to converge to a simple conclusion, gathering additional information about non-responders may complicate the analysis, raising additional questions and revealing the folly of generalizing about non-responders as if they were a homogeneous subset of the population. Oftentimes, they are not.

Panel Data and Attrition

A panel data set contains multiple observations on a fixed group of individuals from whom measurements are collected at several points in time. That is, a random list of individuals is initially chosen, and then those same individuals are surveyed multiple times over the course of months or years. Rather than the snapshot view offered by a cross section in which each observation corresponds to a unique individual, a panel contains a time series for a collection of individuals, which allows researchers to study population characteristics through time.

A frequent problem with panel data is attrition, meaning that some respondents surveyed in the initial period later drop out. Respondents who drop out can be thought of as those who begin as fully cooperative responders but later become non-responders either by choice or circumstance. In this context, non-response bias is sometimes referred to as attrition bias.

Survey panel respondents may be classified as either full-time (those who remain in the sample at all point in time), monotonic attritors, or nonmonotonic attritors. "Nonmonotonic" refers to a respondent who becomes a non-responder at some point in time and then rejoins the survey. When all three types are present in a panel, a three-category logit or probit analysis can demonstrate relationships between the probability of attrition and variables that do not change with time. Simpler still, researchers sometimes run a sequence of regressions and examine the effect on regression coefficients of including or excluding attritors. By creating dummies for full-time, monotonic attritors, and nonmonotonic attritors and interacting those dummies with the regressors of interest, standard t tests on interaction terms can produce evidence that attrition is causing bias. As an example, Burkam and Lee's 1998 article applied these techniques to a panel of U.S. high school students, discovering that gender significantly affects the probability of attrition and also that attrition bias leads to an overstatement of black-white disparity on academic achievement tests.

In another useful example of how to deal with attrition, Fitzgerald *et al.*'s 1998 article estimated a structural model of attrition and studied the severity of attrition bias as it related to a number of standard demographic variables using the Michigan Panel Study on Income Dynamics (PSID). An annual survey panel used frequently by labor economists, the PSID loses roughly 12% of the participants each year. More than 20 years after its inception, fewer than 50% of the original participants remain. Although the observed characteristics of attritors are noticeably different from full-time respondents, coefficient estimates in a variety of models using the PSID, according to Fitzgerald *et al.*, appear to change little when attempts are made to correct for attrition bias. This is good news for researchers attempting to generalize about labor markets in the United States based on the PSID.

Summary

If non-responders are different from responders in ways critical to the main research questions under investigation, the possibility of non-response bias needs to be taken seriously. Whether designing a survey or analyzing previously collected data that have already been collected, a number of useful techniques may be applied to test for and possibly correct for non-response bias. In the data analysis stage, it is usually best, when feasible, to specify a separate equation for the non-response process and estimate all the parameters simultaneously by maximum likelihood. In particular applications, it can be useful to exploit other authors' approaches to dealing with the problem of a nonrepresentative sample, even when the problem is not explicitly referred to as non-response bias. Rather than attempting to solve the problems created by non-response, it is often acceptable simply to be sensitive to the potential problems and state the likely effect of non-response on reported estimates. Careful attention to the problem of non-response is a critical step in conducting high-quality research using survey data.

See Also the Following Articles

Attrition, Mortality, and Exposure Time • Longitudinal Studies, Panel • Maximum Likelihood Estimation • Randomization • Surveys • Weighting

Further Reading

Burkam, D. T., and Lee, V. E. (1998). Effects of monotone and nonmonotone attrition on parameter estimates in regression models with educational data: Demographic effects on achievement, aspirations, and attitudes. *J. Hum. Resources* **33,** 555–575.

Fitzgerald, J., Gottschalk, P., and Moffitt, R. (1998). An analysis of sample attrition in panel data: The Michigan Panel Study of Income Dynamics. *J. Hum. Resources* **33,** 25–74.

Fox, J. A., and Tracy, P. E. (1986). *Randomized Response: A Method for Sensitive Surveys.* Sage, Beverly Hills, CA.

Heckman, J. J. (1979). Sample selection bias as a specification error. *Econometrica* **47,** 153–161.

Hurd, M. D., McFadden, D., Chand, H., Gan, L., Merrill, A., and Roberts, M. (1998). Consumption and savings balances of the elderly: Experimental evidence on survey response bias. In *Frontiers in the Economics of Aging* (J. P. Smith, ed.), pp. 387–391. University of Chicago Press, Chicago, IL.

Keeter, S. (1995). Estimating telephone noncoverage bias with a telephone survey. *Public Opinion Q.* **59,** 196–217.

Kupek, E. (1998). Determinants of item nonresponse in a large national sex survey. *Arch. Sex. Behav.* **27,** 581–589.

Lee, B. J., and Marsh, L. C. (2000). Sample selection bias correction for missing response observations. *Oxford Bull. Econ. Statist.* **62,** 305–322.

Lien, D., and Rearden, D. (1988). Missing measurements in limited dependent variable models. *Econ. Lett.* **26,** 33–36.

Little, R. J. A., and Rubin, D. B. (1990). The analysis of social science data with missing values. In *Modern Methods of Data Analysis* (J. Fox and J. S. Long, eds.), pp. 374–409. Sage, Newbury Park, CA.

Rubin, D. B. (1987). *Multiple Imputation for Nonresponse in Surveys.* John Wiley and Sons, New York.

Turner, H. A. (1999). Participation bias in AIDS-related telephone surveys: Results from the National AIDS Behavioral Survey (NABS) Non-Response Study. *J. Sex Res.* **36,** 52–66.

Whitehead, J. C., Groothuis, P. A., and Blomquist, G. C. (1993). Testing for non-response and sample selection bias in contingent valuation: Analysis of a combination phone/mail survey. *Econ. Lett.* **41,** 215–220.

Nonparametric Item Response Theory Models

Klaas Sijtsma
Tilburg University, Tilburg, The Netherlands

Glossary

invariant item ordering An ordering of items that is the same for each value of the latent trait scale.

monotone homogeneity model A benchmark model within nonparametric item response theory that assumes that all items in a test measure the same latent trait, that the relationship between the item score and the latent trait is monotone, and that the test procedure is free of influences on test performance other than the latent trait.

nonparametric item response theory (NIRT) A version of item response theory that assumes that the relationship between the item score and the latent trait is limited only by order restrictions but is otherwise free.

parametric item response theory (PIRT) A version of item response theory that assumes that the relationship between the item score and the latent trait is defined by a parametric function, such as the logistic or the normal ogive.

stochastic person ordering An ordering of individuals by means of a simple sum score that reflects in a probabilistic way the person ordering on the latent trait scale.

Nonparametric item response theory is a family of item response models for ordinal person and item measurement. The distinctive feature that makes an item response model nonparametric is that in a test either each item response function or the set of all item response functions is restricted by some monotonicity condition, without specifying a parametric family of monotone functions such as the logistic. Instead, item response functions are estimated from the test data and the hypothesized monotonicity condition is evaluated. Several models have been proposed and several methods and software packages are available to evaluate the fit of a model to the data. Nonparametric models are primarily data-oriented in that they study features of the data necessary to obtain ordinal scales for people and sometimes, items as well. Ordinal scales are useful in applications such as selecting the best applicants for a job or identifying the worst-performing students for remedial teaching.

Measurement Using Nonparametric Item Response Theory Models

Tests consist of well-chosen collections of items—exercises, tasks, questions, and statements—that are used to measure different aspects of a hypothetical construct, for example, arithmetic ability, spatial orientation, knowledge of national history, and introversion. A hypothetical construct is a theoretical structure that explains the relationships among a particular set of behaviors. Nonparametric item response theory (NIRT) models are statistical methods that are used to analyze the item response data collected in a sample of individuals to find out whether the items can be considered to be indicators of the same hypothetical construct. If the answer is affirmative, NIRT models provide an ordinal scale for the theoretical construct of interest. This scale is called the latent trait scale. A rank ordering of individuals allows for statements such as "For this expensive follow-up course, we will admit only the 10 students having the highest arithmetic scores" and "For this job, we will hire the candidate with the highest scale score on general knowledge."

In addition to a person scale, a successful NIRT analysis also provides information on the quality of the individual items and the whole test as a measurement instrument for a particular theoretical construct. Information on individual items may reveal two things: (1) Whether the item sharply distinguishes people with relatively low latent trait values from others with relatively high latent trait values, and (2) whether the item measures the same latent trait as the other items in the test. These issues relate to the well-known issues of reliability and validity, respectively. In the phase of test construction, an item that does not distinguish people well or clearly measures a latent trait other than the other items may be removed from the test and replaced by a better one, in order to improve the overall measurement quality of the test.

Assumptions of Nonparametric Item Response Theory Models

Common Assumptions

Methodologically, the latent trait represents an operationalization of the hypothetical construct by means of the collection of items in the test. Semantically, the term latent trait is used to summarize the psychological influences that drive the responses of individuals to each of the items in a test. NIRT assumes that during testing a person's latent trait value is not affected by practice effects, such as those due to learning and development, or flaws in item construction that produce structural dependencies between items. Also, items are related to the latent trait in a way that is specified by the particular NIRT model. This is the common context of most NIRT models. Some models alternatively assume a more complex underlying latent trait structure or formalize practice or training effects during testing that affect test performance. Although potentially interesting and important, these models are not the core of NIRT.

Let X_j be the random variable for the score on item j, and let this score be $x_j = 0, 1, \ldots, m$. The assumption of unidimensionality (UD) means that the relationships between J items in the test can be explained by one common latent trait, that is denoted θ. The assumption of local independence (LI) means that given the latent trait value the probability of a score x_j on item j, $P(X_j = x_j \mid \theta)$, is independent of the scores on the other $J-1$ items in the test. That is, given θ for a vector of J item score random variables, $\mathbf{X}$, and its realization, $\mathbf{x}$, we have:

$$P(\mathbf{X} = \mathbf{x} \mid \theta) = \prod_{j=1}^{J} P(X_j = x_j \mid \theta). \qquad (1)$$

An implication of LI is that for any pair of items, say j and k, their conditional covariance equals 0; that is, $\mathrm{Cov}(X_j, X_k \mid \theta) = 0$.

The third assumption defines the relationship between the item score, X_j, and the latent trait, θ, known as the response function; this is the conditional probability, $P(X_j = x_j \mid \theta)$. NIRT models typically specify order restrictions on this relationship but no other restrictions. For simplicity, we assume that items are scored dichotomously, with $X_j = 0, 1$. These scores may, for example, indicate that the answer was incorrect (score 0) or correct (score 1). Later on, we return to the general case of $m+1$ ordered item scores. The probability $P_j(\theta) = P(X_j = 1 \mid \theta)$ is known as the item response function (IRF). A simple assumption that specifies an order relation on the IRF assumes that it is a monotone nondecreasing function. That is, for item j and two fixed arbitrary values of θ, denoted θ_a and θ_b:

$$P_j(\theta_a) \leq P_j(\theta_b) \quad \text{whenever } \theta_a < \theta_b, \text{and for all } j. \qquad (2)$$

This is the monotonicity (M) assumption. Examples of IRFs that satisfy the assumption M are given in Fig. 1A. The assumptions of UD, LI, and M together define the NIRT model, known as the monotone homogeneity model and introduced in 1971 by Mokken. This model can be seen as a benchmark within NIRT.

Typical of NIRT is the research into relaxations of the assumptions of UD, LI, and, M that seek to restrict the data as little as possible while maintaining important measurement properties such as the ordinal scale for individuals. For example, in 1990 Stout introduced the relaxation of strict unidimensionality to essential unidimensionality, which assumes one dominant latent trait and several nuisance traits whose influence on all statistical properties of the test vanishes for large J (in fact, $J \rightarrow \infty$). Another relaxation is that of LI to essential independence, which allows some conditional interitem covariances to be positive or negative while in the long run ($J \rightarrow \infty$) the mean across all absolute item pair covariances equals 0. A third example is weak monotonicity, which says that the mean of J IRFs is an increasing function in θ. This mean represents the average response to the test and is known as the test response function. Weak monotonicity does not restrict the individual IRFs as long as their mean is increasing; this means that assumption M is dropped at the individual item level. See Fig. 1B for an example of weak monotonicity. Junker showed in 1993 that none of the three assumptions, UD, LI, and M, can be dropped entirely and still leave enough structure in the data for ordering individuals consistently on a dominant latent trait.

Additional Assumptions

Whereas this and other work are aimed at ordinal person measurement under weak (or the weakest possible) assumptions, models that have more restrictions have been defined for studying item properties. For example, it may be assumed that the J IRFs do not intersect; that is, if for some θ_0 we know for items j and k that $P_j(\theta_0) < P_k(\theta)$, then

$$P_j(\theta) \leq P_k(\theta) \quad \text{for all } \theta \quad \text{and} \quad \text{all } j, k; j \neq k. \qquad (3)$$

This is the assumption of invariant item ordering (IIO), which says that the J items have the same ordering by

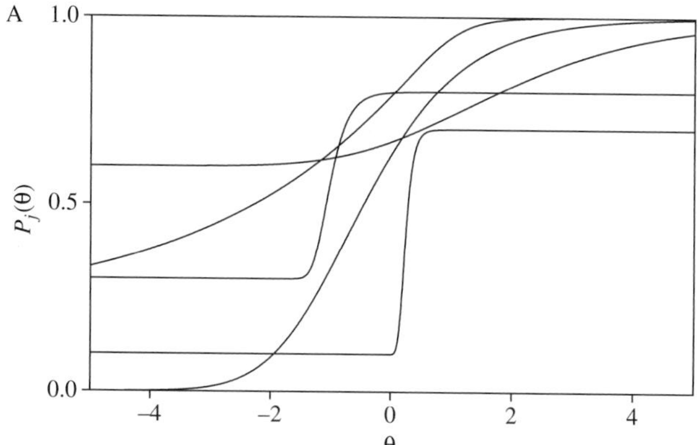

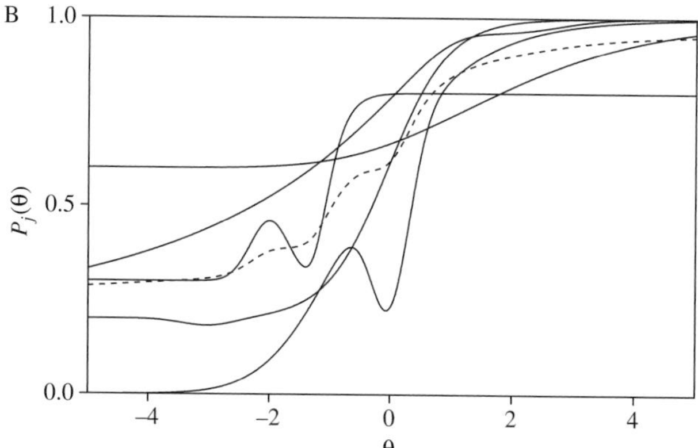

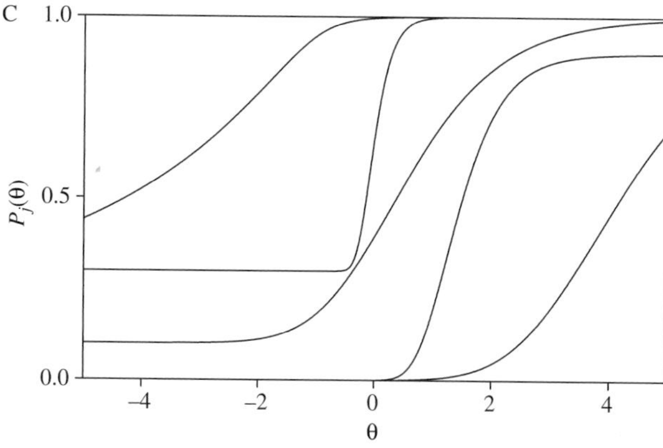

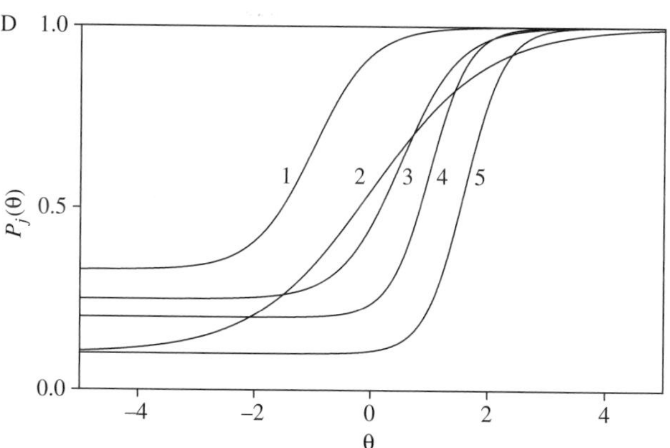

response probability for all θs, with the possible exception of some θs for which ties may exist; see Fig. 1C for examples of nonintersecting IRFs that also satisfy assumption M. An interesting NIRT model that is defined by UD, LI, M, and IIO is the double monotonicity model, which was introduced by Mokken in 1971.

Models that have even more restrictions have been proposed by Sijtsma and Hemker in 1998 for items that have polytomous scoring ($m \geq 2$), and that imply that for J items an ordering,

$$E(X_1 \mid \theta) \leq E(X_2 \mid \theta) \leq \cdots \leq E(X_J \mid \theta) \qquad \text{for all } \theta \quad (4)$$

exists after the appropriate renumbering of the items. For polytomous items, this ordering of expected conditional item scores defines the concept IIO. Because for dichotomous items $E(X_j \mid \theta) = P_j(\theta)$, the item ordering for polytomous items captures IIO for dichotomous items as a special case.

Finally, local homogeneity is an example of an assumption that is needed when it is assumed that an NIRT model holds in each subgroup from the population of interest. Ellis and Van den Wollenberg showed in 1993 that it is necessary to distinguish between latent trait values θ and individuals when it is assumed that the response probability $P_j(\theta)$ is a within-person expectation of a propensity distribution of the item score for that person. Then different individuals with the same θ value must have the same $P_j(\theta)$ and no other person differences can influence this probability. This is important, for example, in differential item functioning research.

Parametric Item Response Theory Models

Parametric item response theory (PIRT) models are different from NIRT models in that they assume a specific parametric IRF, such as a normal ogive or a logistic function. An example is the three-parameter logistic model, defined as:

$$P_j(\theta) = \gamma_j + (1 - \gamma_j)\frac{\exp[\alpha_j(\theta - \delta_j)]}{1 + \exp[\alpha_j(\theta - \delta_j)]}. \qquad (5)$$

Figure 1 (A) Five IRFs satisfying assumption M. (B) Two IRFs (solid curves) that satisfy assumption M, three IRFs that are not monotone increasing, and the test response function that is monotone increasing (dashed curve). (C) Five nonintersecting IRFs that satisfy assumption M. (D) Five IRFs under the three-parameter logistic model (parameter values: $\gamma_1 = 0.33$, $\gamma_2 = 0.10$, $\gamma_3 = 0.25$, $\gamma_4 = 0.20$, $\gamma_5 = 0.10$; $\delta_1 = -0.10$, $\delta_2 = 0.00$, $\delta_3 = 0.50$, $\delta_4 = 1.00$, $\delta_5 = 1.60$; $\alpha_1 = 2.00$, $\alpha_2 = 1.00$, $\alpha_3 = 2.00$, $\alpha_4 = 3.00$, $\alpha_5 = 3.00$).

Here, γ_j is the lower asymptote for $\theta \to -\infty$, α_j is a slope parameter, and δ_j is a location parameter; see Fig. 1D for examples of three-parameter logistic IRFs. For a data matrix produced by N individuals who responded to J items, the likelihood may be solved for each of these item parameters and the latent trait parameter. The resulting estimates give information on the probability (γ_j) that someone with a low scale value correctly solves item j (or gives an affirmative response); the item's location on the scale (δ_j) sometimes called its difficulty; the item's potential to distinguish between people with low and high scale values (α_j, called the discrimination power) to the left and the right of location δ_j; and the individuals' scale values (θ). Because NIRT models impose order restrictions on the IRFs but do not impose a logistic or another parametric restriction, they do not have likelihood functions from which these parameters can be solved. Nevertheless, they also provide information on the latent trait and the item parameters; however, they use other statistics and parameters, to be discussed shortly.

Measurement Properties of Nonparametric Item Response Theory Models

Person Measurement

The monotone homogeneity model is a measurement model for individuals. It implies an ordinal person scale in a stochastic ordering sense. Let test performance be summarized in a total score:

$$X_+ = \sum_{j=1}^{J} X_j \tag{6}$$

and let x_{+a} and x_{+b} be an arbitrarily chosen pair of realizations of X_+ such that $x_{+a} < x_{+b}$. Further, let t be an arbitrary value of θ. Then, the monotone homogeneity model for dichotomous items implies that:

$$P(\theta \geqslant \,|\, X_+ = x_{+a}) \leq P(\theta t \,|\, X_+ = x_{+b}). \tag{7}$$

An implication of this stochastic ordering property is $E(\theta \,|\, X_+ = x_{+a}) \leq E(\theta \,|\, X_+ = x_{+b})$. Thus, the higher the total score X_+, the higher the θ value. In an NIRT context, Grayson showed in 1988 that the observable total score X_+ replaces latent trait θ for ordinally measuring individuals.

For polytomous items, Hemker, Sijtsma, Molenaar, and Junker showed in 1997 that the monotone homogeneity model, defined by UD, LI, and a monotonicity assumption on response function $P(X_j \geq x_j \,|\, \theta)$ for $x_j = 1, \ldots, m$ (for $x_j = 0$, this probability trivially equals 1) does not imply the stochastic ordering property. Van der Ark showed in 2002 that for most realistic tests and distributions of θ an ordering of individuals on X_+ reflects an ordering on θ, but sometimes with reversals for adjacent X_+ values. Reversals of scores this close are unimportant for the practical use of tests because they represent only small differences with respect to the latent trait. For the polytomous NIRT model based on UD, LI, and M, and for NIRT approaches to polytomous items (and dichotomous items as a special case) based on weaker assumptions, X_+ is a consistent estimator of θ. This means that for infinitely many polytomous items the ordering of individuals using X_+ gives the exact ordering on θ, and Junker showed in 1991 that this result is true for several versions of polytomous NIRT models.

Item Measurement

The double monotonicity model is a measurement model for both individuals and items. Because it is a special case of the monotone homogeneity model, it has the same stochastic ordering and consistency properties for person measurement as that model. In addition, it implies an IIO, discussed, for example, by Sijtsma and Molenaar in 2002; see Eq. (4). An IIO implies that for expected item scores in the whole group:

$$E(X_1) \leq E(X_2) \leq \cdots \leq E(X_J). \tag{8}$$

These expectations can be estimated from sample data using the mean item score:

$$\bar{X}_j = J^{-1} \sum_{i=1}^{N} X_{ij}, \qquad j = 1, \ldots, J. \tag{9}$$

If the double monotonicity model fits the data, these sample means are then used to estimate the ordering of the expected conditional item scores, $E(X_j \,|\, \theta)$, $j = 1, \ldots, J$.

The IIO property can be used in several kinds of test applications in which it is important that individuals or subgroups have the same item ordering. For example, person-fit analysis and differential item functioning analysis of real data are better understood if an IIO can be hypothesized for the population, and results that deviate at the level of individuals or subgroups can be interpreted relative to this ordering. Also, in other research an IIO can be the null hypothesis when it is assumed that, for example, the items reflect ascending developmental stages and the equality of this ordering can be tested between age groups. Intelligence tests such as the Wechsler Intelligence Scale for Children use starting and stopping rules that assume an IIO—children of a particular age group start at an item that is easy for them (assuming that the previous items are of trivial difficulty), then are administered items in ascending difficulty ordering, and stop when they fail on several consecutive items (assuming that they would fail also on the next items that are even more difficult).

Fitting Nonparametric Item Response Theory Models to Test Data

If the monotone homogeneity model or a more relaxed version of it fits the test data, an ordinal person scale based on X_+ ordering is implied. If the double monotonicity model fits, not only is an ordinal person scale implied but also an IIO. The question is how to investigate the fit of these models to the test data. NIRT implies two properties of observable variables that are the basis of a variety of methods for investigating model-data fit.

Conditional Association

The first property, introduced by Holland and Rosenbaum in 1986, is conditional association. In principle, if a subgroup of individuals is selected from the population of interest on the basis of their performance on a subset of the items from the test, then within this subgroup the covariance between two sum scores based on another item subset must be nonnegative. The item scores may be dichotomous, polytomous, or continuous. A simple example to start with is that all individuals are selected, thus ignoring a subgroup structure altogether. Then all covariances between two items j and k must be nonnegative $[\mathrm{Cov}(X_j, X_k) \geq 0]$ and negative covariances give evidence of model-data misfit.

A procedure for selecting one or more unidimensional item subsets from a larger item pool uses item scalability coefficients, denoted H_j, based on this nonnegative covariance property. The outcome of this procedure (implemented in the computer program MSP5 introduced in 2000 by Molenaar and Sijtsma) is one or more subsets of items that each measure another latent trait with items that have discrimination power with a lower bound defined by the researcher. Discrimination power is expressed for items by the scalability coefficients H_j and for the total test by the scalability coefficient H.

A more complex example is the following. $J-2$ items, not including items j and k, are used to define a sum score $R_{(-j,-k)} = \sum_{h \neq j,k} X_h$. Then within subgroups of individuals based on values r of $R_{(-j,-k)}$, conditional association means that $\mathrm{Cov}(X_j, X_k \mid R_{(-j,-k)} = r) \geq 0$, for all values r. This is the basis of other procedures (implemented in the computer programs DETECT and HCA/CCPROX, and discussed by Stout *et al.* in 1996) that try to find a subset structure for the whole test that approximates local independence as good as possible. The optimal solution best represents the latent trait structure of the test data.

Manifest Monotonicity

The second property, introduced in 1993 by Junker, is manifest monotonicity. This property can be used to investigate whether an IRF, $P_j(\theta)$, is monotone nondecreasing, as assumption M requires. To estimate the IRF for item j, first a sum score on $J-1$ items excluding item j, $R_{(-j)} = \sum_{k \neq j} X_k$, is used as an estimate of θ and then the conditional probability $P[X_j = 1 \mid R_{(-j)} = r]$ is calculated for all values r of $R_{(-j)}$. Given the monotone homogeneity model, the conditional probability $P[X_j = 1 \mid R_{(-j)}]$ must be nondecreasing in $R_{(-j)}$; this is manifest monotonicity. For real test data, manifest monotonicity is investigated for each item in the test, and violations are tested for significance; see Fig. 2A for an example of a discrete estimate of the IRF that violates assumption M. The program MSP5 can be used for estimating such discrete response functions and testing violations of monotonicity for significance. The program TestGraf98 made available by Ramsay in 2000, estimates continuous response functions using kernel smoothing and provides many graphics. The theory underlying this program was discussed by Ramsay in 1991.

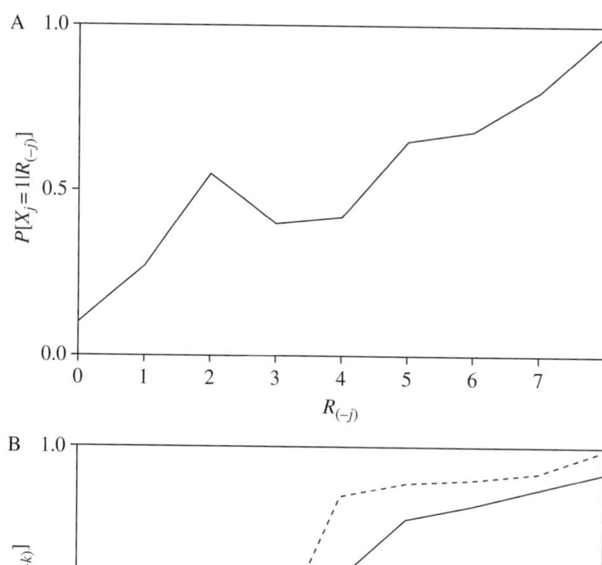

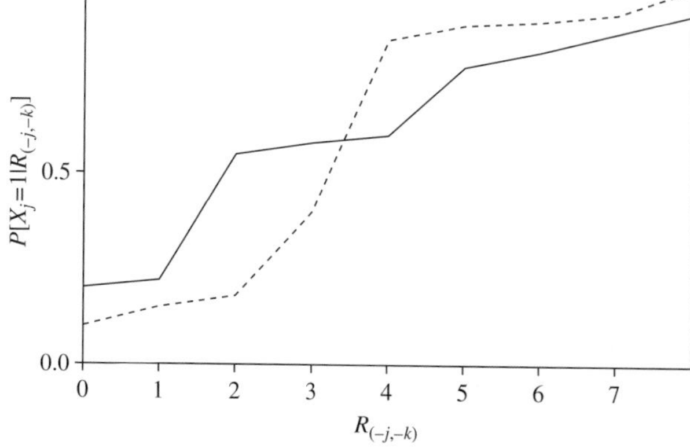

Figure 2 (A) Discrete estimate of an IRF that violates assumption M. (B) Two discrete estimates of IRFs that are intersecting.

Manifest monotonicity is also basic to the investigation whether the IRFs of different items are nonintersecting, as the assumption of IIO requires. To investigate IIO for the items j and k, the sign of the difference of the conditional probabilities $P[X_j = 1 \mid R_{(-j,-k)}]$ and

$P[X_k = 1 | R_{(-j,-k)}]$ can be determined for each value r of the sum score $R_{(-j,-k)}$ and compared with the sign of the difference of the sample item means ($\bar{X}_j$ and $\bar{X}_k$) for the whole group. Opposite signs for some value r of $R_{(-j,-k)}$ indicate intersection of the IRFs and are tested against the null hypothesis that $P[X_j = 1 | R_{(-j,-k)} = r] = P[X_k = 1 | R_{(-j,-k)} = r]$ in the population (which means that these probabilities are the same but that their ordering is not opposite to the overall ordering). See Fig. 2B for an example of two observed IRFs that give evidence of intersecting IRFs in the population. This and other methods for investigating an IIO have been discussed and compared by Sijtsma and Molenaar in 2002. The program MSP5 can be used for investigating IIO.

For evaluating the monotonicity assumption of the response functions of a polytomous item, $P(X_j \geq x_j | \theta)$ for $x_j = 1, \ldots, m$, and the nonintersection of the response functions of different polytomous items, $P(X_j \geq x_j | \theta)$ and $P(X_k \geq x_k | \theta)$, several of these methods are also available in MSP5. Theoretical research to further support the underpinnings of these methods is in progress.

Nonparametric Item Response Theory Models for Nonmonotone Response Functions

For some latent traits and particular item types, a monotone nondecreasing response function cannot adequately describe the probability of an affirmative response. For example, as part of a questionnaire that measures the attitude toward the government's crime-fighting policy people may be asked to indicate whether they think that a 6-month prison term is an adequate sentence for burglary. Both opponents and proponents of long prison sentences may have a low probability of giving an affirmative response to this item, but for opposite reasons, and people having a moderate attitude may have higher probabilities. An NIRT model that successfully describes item scores produced this way thus has to assume that the relationship between the item score and the latent trait first increases and then decreases after a certain latent trait value or interval. In an NIRT context, such a response function could look like the irregular (solid) curve in Fig. 3. The NIRT monotonicity assumption now could be something like: First the IRF increases monotonically, then for some value θ_0 it reaches a maximum value $P_j(\theta_0)$ or a θ range in which it has a constant value, and then it decreases monotonically. Such an order restriction may be compared with a smooth parametric response function (dashed curve in Fig. 3) from a hypothetical parametric model, defined as:

$$P(X_j = 1 | \theta) = \frac{\lambda_j \exp[q(\theta - \delta_j)]}{1 + \exp[q(\theta - \delta_j)]} \qquad (10)$$

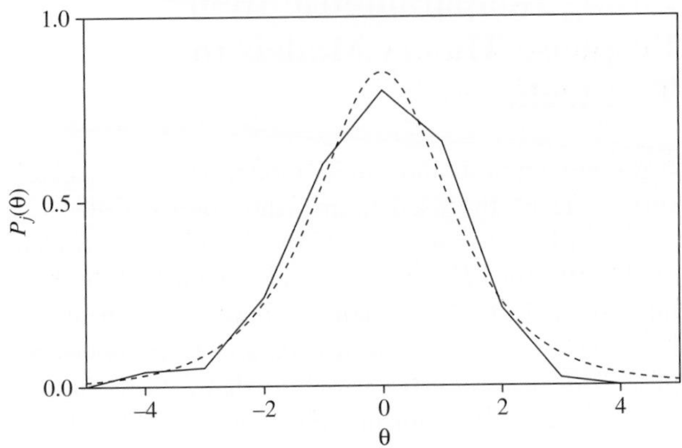

Figure 3 Irregular nonparametric IRF (solid curve) and smooth parametric IRF (dashed curve; $\lambda_j = 1.7$; $\delta_j = 0.0$) for preference data.

with $q = 1$ if $\theta - \delta_j < 0$, and otherwise $q = -1$; and $0 < \lambda_j < 2$. It may be noted that the nonparametric model encompasses the parametric model as a special case.

In 1992, Post studied the theoretical foundation of NIRT models for nonmonotone response functions and also derived methods for investigating model-data fit. Van Schuur proposed in 1984 a scaling procedure for selecting the best fitting items. Due both to their mathematical complexity and to the scarceness of real data that require nonmonotone response functions, NIRT models for nonmonotone response functions have not gained the popularity of the other NIRT models discussed here.

Practical Applications of Nonparametric Item Response Theory Models

NIRT models are particularly useful for the construction of ordinal scales for person and item measurement. They have proven their usefulness in many fields of applied research, such as psychology (nonverbal intelligence, induction reasoning, and tiredness from workload), sociology (attitudes toward abortion and machiavellism), political science (trustworthiness of inhabitants of foreign countries and political efficacy), marketing research (recency, frequency, and monetary value of purchase applied to market segmentation), and health-related quality-of-life research (quality of life for cancer patients and genital sensations and body image after surgery). Each of the scales for these properties allows the ordering of individuals and groups of individuals and, if the double monotonicity model fits, the ordering of items. What are the typical contributions of NIRT to the analysis of test data?

Item Quality

Compare the monotone homogeneity model with the three-parameter logistic model. An item analysis using the monotone homogeneity model investigates the IRFs by means of discrete estimates $P[X_j = 1 \mid R_{(-j)}]$ (in MSP5) or continuous estimates (in TestGraf98), and these estimates provide information on how IRFs may deviate from assumption M. For example, estimated curves may show zero or negative discrimination for parts of the distribution of θ (Fig. 2A) or even suggest that the IRF is bell-shaped (Fig. 3). When the item discriminates weakly for the lower and the middle part of the θ distribution and also has a low $P_j(\theta)$ for those θs, this may suggest that the item would be more appropriate in a test for a higher θ group. Bell-shaped IRFs suggest a nonmonotone NIRT model. An analysis using the three-parameter logistic model fits the S-shaped curve (Fig. 1D) to such items, which has the effect of driving the slope parameter α_j to 0 instead of giving diagnostic information about the misfit. Thus, instead of stretching a grid over the data that bends only in some directions but fails to detect other deviations, as is typical of a PIRT approach, an NIRT approach is more data-oriented in that it catches most of the peculiarities of the IRFs. When assumption M is satisfied, NIRT models use the item mean $E(X_j)$ and the item scalability coefficient H_j to replace location δ_j and slope α_j from PIRT, respectively. Items with empirical IRFs that do not have the typical logistic S-shape but that satisfy assumption M and have item scalability coefficients H_j that are reasonably high may be included in a test because they contribute to reliable person measurement.

Dimensionality

PIRT models usually fit a unidimensional model to the data, and multidimensional PIRT models may be used when the data are suspected to be driven by multiple latent traits. Fitting models yield useful parameter estimates that can be the basis for building item banks, equating scales, and adaptive testing. Within NIRT, algorithms have been produced that explore the data for the optimal dimensionality structure using assumption LI (e.g., program DETECT) or assumption M (program MSP5). Thus, NIRT explores the data more than PIRT, which is typically more oriented toward fitting an *a priori* chosen model. NIRT also imposes restrictions on the data, but compared to PIRT these restrictions are weaker, which renders NIRT more data-oriented and exploratory than PIRT.

NIRT models may be used because often little is known about the hypothetical construct, and a model that forces little structure onto the data, while maintaining ordinal measurement scales, may be a wise choice to start with. Given its exploratory orientation, NIRT could then be used as a precursor to PIRT by exploring the dimensionality structure of the data before a more restrictive hypothesis is tested by means of a PIRT model. Also, when starting with a PIRT model, instead, that does not fit the test data, an NIRT model can then be an alternative to fit to the data. The result of a fitting NIRT model is an ordinal scale for individuals (and items). Depending on the purpose of the test, such a scale is useful for selecting the best applicants for a job, the best students for a follow-up course, or the lowest-scoring pupils for remedial teaching or, in scientific research, for establishing relationships of the test score to other variables of interest.

See Also the Following Articles

Item Response Models for Nonmonotone Items • Item Response Theory

Further Reading

Ellis, J. L., and Van den Wollenberg, A. L. (1993). Local homogeneity in latent trait models: A characterization of the homogeneous monotone IRT model. *Psychometrika* **58,** 417–429.

Grayson, D. A. (1988). Two-group classification in latent trait theory: Scores with monotone likelihood ratio. *Psychometrika* **53,** 383–392.

Hemker, B. T., Sijtsma, K., Molenaar, I. W., and Junker, B. W. (1997). Stochastic ordering using the latent trait and the sum score in polytomous IRT models. *Psychometrika* **62,** 331–347.

Holland, P. W., and Rosenbaum, P. R. (1986). Conditional association and unidimensionality in monotone latent variable models. *Ann. Statist.* **14,** 1523–1543.

Junker, B. W. (1991). Essential independence and likelihood-based ability estimation for polytomous items. *Psychometrika* **56,** 255–278.

Junker, B. W. (1993). Conditional association, essential independence and monotone unidimensional item response models. *Ann. Statist.* **21,** 1359–1378.

Mokken, R. J. (1971). *A Theory and Procedure of Scale Analysis.* De Gruyter, Berlin.

Molenaar, I. W., and Sijtsma, K. (2000). *MSP5 for Windows: User's Manual.* iecProGAMMA, Groningen, The Netherlands.

Post, W. J. (1992). *Nonparametric Unfolding Models: A Latent Structure Approach.* DSWO Press, Leiden, The Netherlands.

Ramsay, J. O. (1991). Kernel smoothing approaches to nonparametric item characteristic curve estimation. *Psychometrika* **56,** 611–630.

Ramsay, J. O. (2000). *A Program for the Graphical Analysis of Multiple Choice Test and Questionnaire Data.* Department of Psychology, McGill University, Montreal.

Sijtsma, K., and Hemker, B. T. (1998). Nonparametric polytomous IRT models for invariant item ordering, with results for parametric models. *Psychometrika* **63,** 183–200.

Sijtsma, K., and Molenaar, I. W. (2002). *Introduction to Nonparametric Item Response Theory.* Sage, Thousand Oaks, CA.

Stout, W. F. (1990). A new item response theory modeling approach with applications to unidimensionality assessment and ability estimation. *Psychometrika* **55,** 293–325.

Stout, W. F., Habing, B., Douglas, J., Kim, H., Roussos, L., and Zhang, J. (1996). Conditional covariance based nonparametric multidimensionality assessment. *Appl. Psychol. Meas.* **20,** 331–354.

Van der Ark, L. A. (2002). Practical consequences of stochastic ordering of the latent trait under various polytomous IRT models. *Psychometrika* (in press).

Van Schuur, W. H. (1984). *Structure in Political Beliefs: A New Model for Stochastic Unfolding with Applications to European Party Activists.* CT Press, Amsterdam.

NORC's 1990 Sampling Design

Rachel Harter
National Opinion Research Center (NORC), Chicago, Illinois, USA

Glossary

cluster sampling Method of sampling in which the ultimate sampling units are naturally grouped in some way, and a sample of the groups (clusters) is selected. If the initial groups are geographical areas, then it is an *area probability design*. If the units within the selected groups are subsampled, then it is a *multistage design*, and the hierarchical clustering and sampling can be repeated for multiple levels. Cluster sampling is often used when a complete list or *frame* of the target population is not available, but a list of the primary sampling units is available. Cluster sampling in this context saves costs by minimizing travel among selected housing units. Because units within a cluster tend to be more alike than units in different clusters, a cluster sample typically provides less information than an unclustered sample of the same size.

design effect A measure of precision of a sample relative to a simple random sample of the same size, defined as the ratio of the variance of a statistic under the design to the variance of the same statistic assuming the sample had been selected by simple random sampling. The lower the design effect, the better. Cluster designs generally have design effects larger than 1, while stratified designs can have design effects less than 1.

half-open interval technique Method of giving housing units not in the national sampling frame a chance of selection, also known as a *missed housing unit procedure*. The half-open interval includes one housing unit on the list as the first closed endpoint, and covers the territory up to but not including the next housing unit on the list as the open endpoint. The interval is well defined because the housing units were originally listed in a prescribed order. A housing unit found within the interval (new construction, for example) has a chance of selection when the first endpoint is selected.

housing unit (HU) A house, apartment, mobile home, trailer, single room, or group of rooms intended for separate living quarters, in which the occupants live and eat separately from others in the building, and having direct access from outside or through a common hall.

Kish table Also called *objective respondent selection table* by Kish, a table of numbers preassigned to the selected housing unit; when combined with a list of eligible persons in the household, the table enables the interviewer to objectively and randomly select one person for interviewing.

national sampling frame Geographically representative sample of geographical areas and the listed housing unit addresses within those geographical areas, used as a sampling frame for national surveys of residential populations. The process of collecting the addresses is called *listing*.

primary sampling unit The units that have an opportunity for selection at the first stage of a multistage design; each selected primary sampling unit is a cluster of subunits (secondary sampling units) for sampling at the second stage. The lowest levels of sampling units are called *ultimate sampling units*.

self-weighting design Design in which each sampling unit has the same chance of selection. For area probability designs of the residential population, often the housing units have an equal chance of selection.

stratification Technique for grouping units into strata according to similarities prior to selection. Stratification differs from cluster designs in that units from every stratum are included in the sample. Selection of units within a stratum is independent of selection of units in other strata. Stratification is usually done to improve the representativeness of the sample.

systematic sampling Probability sampling design in which the units are sorted in an ordered list, a selection interval k is determined to generate the desired sample size, a first unit is selected randomly between 1 and k, and every kth unit thereafter is selected.

Ideally, a sample selected for a survey is drawn from a well-defined list, or frame, of the units being studied. For example, a sample of persons would be selected from a complete list of all eligible persons, or a sample of households would be selected from a complete list of all households. Unfortunately, for studies of the United States population or U.S. households, such lists are not publicly available. Studies of this sort are often accomplished by first selecting a sample of geographical areas, creating lists of all housing units within the selected geographical areas, and then selecting a sample of the listed households. This is known as an area probability design. At least once per decade, generally shortly after the decennial census, the National Opinion Research Center (NORC) goes through the process of selecting geographical areas and collecting lists of housing units within the areas. The resulting list is known as NORC's National Sampling Frame. Many national surveys obtain their samples from this frame. To illustrate the concepts and an area probability design, this chapter describes NORC's National Sampling Frame based on the 1990 census.

Introduction

Studies of households, particularly national studies, have had no national sampling frame of households from which a sample can be selected. Government records typically are not available to social scientists outside the government agency. Frames of potential telephone numbers are impractical when face-to-face interviewing is desired.

Area probability designs were developed to compensate for the lack of a comprehensive national list of households. In area probability designs, the basis is a frame of geographies. The frame units are based on well-defined geographical entities such as states, counties, or metropolitan statistical areas. Geographical areas are selected in a multistage cluster design. Address lists are collected for the smallest geographical units selected, resulting in a frame of housing units for the selected geographies. Housing units can then be selected from this frame. If only certain types of households or persons are eligible for the interview, persons can be selected when the sample households are screened for eligibility.

Area probability designs are clustered, and clustered designs are less efficient, statistically, than simple random sampling or stratified random sampling. Specifically, homogeneity within clusters cause design effects that are larger than 1. But because national lists of housing units have not been publicly available, and the cost of assembling such a list is prohibitive, area probability designs provide a reasonable compromise between statistical efficiency and practicality.

Collecting addresses for a sample of geographical areas is not inexpensive, however. Over the years, very few organizations have been able to develop and maintain area probability frames of addresses for national U.S. samples. The National Opinion Research Center (NORC) at the University of Chicago is one organization that has maintained a national area probability frame. After each decennial census, NORC has redefined and reselected the geographical areas and collected addresses for housing units within the selected addresses. (After the 1980 census, NORC cooperated with the University of Michigan's Institute for Statistical Research in the development of a frame.) The national sampling frames were then used for national studies throughout the decade. The best known of NORC's national area probability studies is the General Social Survey, a repeated cross sectional survey that has been fielded every 1–2 years since 1972.

In this article we describe NORC's national area probability frame as designed following the 1990 decennial census. The design was first described by Tourangeau *et al.* in an NORC internal report, and most of the tables in this article are taken from that report. The design included primary sampling units of counties and metropolitan statistical areas, secondary sampling units of blocks or block groups, subdivisions of blocks under certain circumstances, the selection of housing units, and the selection of persons within housing units. Each stage in the multistage design is described in the following sections.

As of this writing, NORC's 2000 national sampling frame is not yet complete, even though 2000 census data have been available for some time. There are two reasons why the 2000 frame has been deferred. First, national sampling frames are best when they are fresh, before new construction and demolitions alter the landscape. Due to the cyclical nature of many of NORC's area probability studies, the demand for a 2000 frame was not pressing until 2004. NORC opted to develop the new frame as late as possible so that the frame would be as fresh as possible. Second, new informational and technological developments provide opportunities for higher quality and greater efficiency in frame construction. These new developments, which are described at the end of this article, may change the way area probability studies are implemented in the future. By postponing the development of a 2000 national sampling frame, NORC has had additional time to test these new developments and incorporate the best and most up-to-date innovations. Nevertheless, the basic design concepts of a national sampling frame remain the same, and the 1990 national sampling frame illustrates these concepts just as well.

The Multistage Area Probability Design

Primary Sampling Units

The first stage units in the multistage design are called Primary Sampling Units (PSUs). For NORC's 1990 national sampling frame, the PSUs were stratified into two types—metropolitan and non-metropolitan. PSUs in both strata are based on counties or county-like units. All 50 states and the District of Columbia are completely covered by 3141 nonoverlapping counties or county-like units, as of 1990. The metropolitan stratum consisted of all Metropolitan Statistical Areas (MSAs) and New England County Metropolitan Areas (NECMAs), as defined by the Office of Management and Budget. An MSA is a city of at least 50,000 persons with the surrounding county or counties, or an urbanized area of at least 50,000 with a total metropolitan population of at least 100,000, where the U.S. Census Bureau determines urbanized areas. Multiple MSAs with integrated economies and societies are combined into a Consolidated Metropolitan Statistical Area (CMSA) if they have a population of one million or more; each component MSA is called a Primary MSA (PMSA). For example, the Chicago CMSA consists of the Chicago PSMA, the Gary PMSA, and the Kenosha PMSA. Where CMSAs exist, the CMSAs rather than the component PMSAs were the primary sampling units. In New England, MSAs are based on townships rather than counties, which means that MSAs sometimes subdivide a county. NECMAs, on the other hand, are based on whole counties. For consistency with the rest of the frame, NORC used NECMAs rather than MSAs as primary sampling units in New England. Altogether, 259 metropolitan PSUs were defined.

The non-metropolitan PSUs covered 2394 counties that were not part of any metropolitan PSU. Non-metropolitan PSUs were primarily defined by individual counties. If a county had fewer than 2000 housing units (HUs), it was combined with an adjacent county to form a PSU. That is, PSUs had a minimum size of 2000 HUs to support the sampling needs of multiple national studies. Where necessary, smaller counties as identified by census STF-1C files were linked to an adjacent county, where an adjacent county was identified sorting on latitudes and longitudes of county centers. The non-metropolitan stratum consisted of 2197 PSUs. Table I summarizes the number of counties and PSUs defined in the metropolitan and non-metropolitan strata.

Table I PSUs by Stratum

Stratum	*Number of counties*	*Number of PSUs*
Metropolitan PSUs	737	292
CMSAs	87	8
MSAs/NECMAs	660	284
Non-metropolitan PSUs	2394	2197
Total PSUs	3141	2489

Briefly, a sample of PSUs was selected by systematic sampling. The PSUs were first sorted to achieve implicit stratification. The PSUs were selected systematically with probability proportional to size, where the measure of size was the 1990 census count of the number of housing units in the PSUs. Each of these concepts is explained below.

In systematic selection, the units are sorted in an ordered list. A selection interval is determined to generate the desired sample size. For example, for a frame of size N and a desired sample of size n, the interval is $k = N/n$, which is not necessarily an integer. A first unit is selected randomly between 1 and k, and every kth unit thereafter is selected. (When k is not an integer, select the first unit whose position is greater than or equal to the next multiple of k.) In this example, units are selected with equal probability n/N. Systematic sampling is described more fully in Cochran and other sampling texts.

For NORC's national sampling frame, units were selected with probability proportional to the number of housing units in the PSUs. One way of conceptualizing the method is to imagine that N is the number of housing units in the frame, and each PSU is listed multiple times in the frame for the number of HUs in the PSU. For example, a PSU with 10,000 HUs would have 10,000 chances of being selected. The probability of selection is the PSU size divided by the total frame size.

Some PSUs had size greater than the selection interval k, which means that these PSUs were selected with certainty. These PSUs, selected with probability 1, are sometimes referred to as self-representing PSUs. Certainty units were selected through an iterative process. An initial selection interval was calculated based on the desired sample size and the total frame size. Any PSU larger than the selection interval was selected automatically and removed from the list. The frame size and the number of units to select were decreased by the certainty PSUs, and the selection interval was recalculated. Additional PSUs were selected with certainty based on the new selection interval, so they were removed and a newer selection interval was recalculated as before. The process continued until all remaining PSUs had size smaller than the selection interval. The remainder of the sample was selected systematically with probability proportional to size as described above. After iterations, NORC's 1990 frame had 19 metropolitan PSUs selected with certainty. None of the non-metropolitan PSUs was selected with certainty.

Some samplers are uncomfortable calling certainty units PSUs. Because these units were selected with certainty, they were not "sampled" at all. The certainty units can be thought of as comprising a stratum. What would be called secondary sampling units in other PSUs were technically PSUs within these certainty units. Because of the different ways the nomenclature can be used, comparisons of the number of PSUs across designs can be misleading.

Before systematic selection was carried out for the remainder of the sample, the units were sorted to distribute the sample across the spectrum of the sort variables. In this way, the sampled units broadly represented different classes without explicitly stratifying by these classes. The noncertainty PSUs were sorted primarily by level of urbanization, with the metropolitan units listed first followed by the non-metropolitan units. The metropolitan units were sorted geographically by the nine census divisions. If a PSU crossed division boundaries, it was assigned to the single division that contained the majority of its population. Within division the units were sorted by quartiles of the percent minority population (here defined as African-American and Hispanic population), based on 1990 census data. Finally, the metropolitan units were sorted by per capita income, where the income figures were obtained from a private firm. Non-metropolitan units were sorted geographically by census region (Northeast, Midwest, South, and West), state, minority quartile, and per capita income.

To avoid jumps in the sort order for minority quartile and per capita income, NORC used a "serpentine" procedure where variables were alternatively ascending and descending. For example, within one census division the units were sorted by ascending minority quartile, and in the next division they were sorted by descending minority quartile. This serpentine order helped ensure that the sample was representative across all of the sort variables.

Altogether, 100 PSUs were selected, counting the certainty units as sample PSUs. The PSUs covered 51.4% of all housing units in the U.S. The selected PSUs mirrored the distribution of the population of HUs geographically, as well. Table II summarizes the sample of PSUs by geography. Table III compares the distribution of the noncertainty sample of PSUs to the noncertainty population of HUs. For example, 51 of the 81 noncertainty PSUs in the sample (63%) were metropolitan; similarly, 63% of the HUs in the geography covered by the population of noncertainty PSUs were in metropolitan PSUs. For the sake of illustration, Fig. 1 is a map of a hypothetical sample of PSUs.

Secondary Sampling Units

PSUs were still too large to manually obtain complete address lists, so the PSUs were subdivided into Secondary Sampling Units (SSUs). A sample of SSUs was selected for address collection. SSUs were ordered and selected by systematic sampling with probability proportional to size, in much the same fashion as PSUs were selected. Aspects of SSU selection are discussed in this section.

It has been NORC policy to avoid using the same HU more than once during the 10-year life of the frame. Therefore, each SSU should contain enough HUs to support the needs of various area probability samples over the course of a decade. The number of such studies is not known in advance with certainty, so to some extent the decision is a gamble. If the SSUs are too small, all of the HUs are selected eventually, and the SSU must be replaced. If the SSUs are much larger than necessary, the cost of obtaining address lists is wasteful. The size of the SSUs must be balanced with the number of SSUs selected, as both affect costs and design effects.

For the 1990 frame, NORC defined SSUs to be individual blocks or groups of blocks containing at least 50 HUs. For the 1990 census, the entire U.S. was divided into blocks for the first time. Blocks with fewer than 50 HUs were linked to another block in the same census tract. If all the blocks in a tract contained fewer than 50 HUs combined,

Table II Geographical Summary of the Sample of PSUs

	Northeast	*Midwest*	*South*	*West*	*Total*
Certainty PSUs	4	4	6	5	19
Noncertainty Metropolitan PSUs	8	13	21	9	51
Noncertainty Non-metropolitan PSUs	4	9	13	4	30
Total	16	26	40	18	100

Table III Comparison of sample PSUs with population HUs

	Metropolitan		*Non-Metropolitan*	
Noncertainty sample PSUs	63%		37%	
Noncertainty population of HUs	63%		37%	
	Northeast	Midwest	South	West
Noncertainty sample of PSUs	14.8%	27.2%	42.0%	16.0%
Noncertainty population of HUs	14.2%	26.9%	42.9%	16.0%

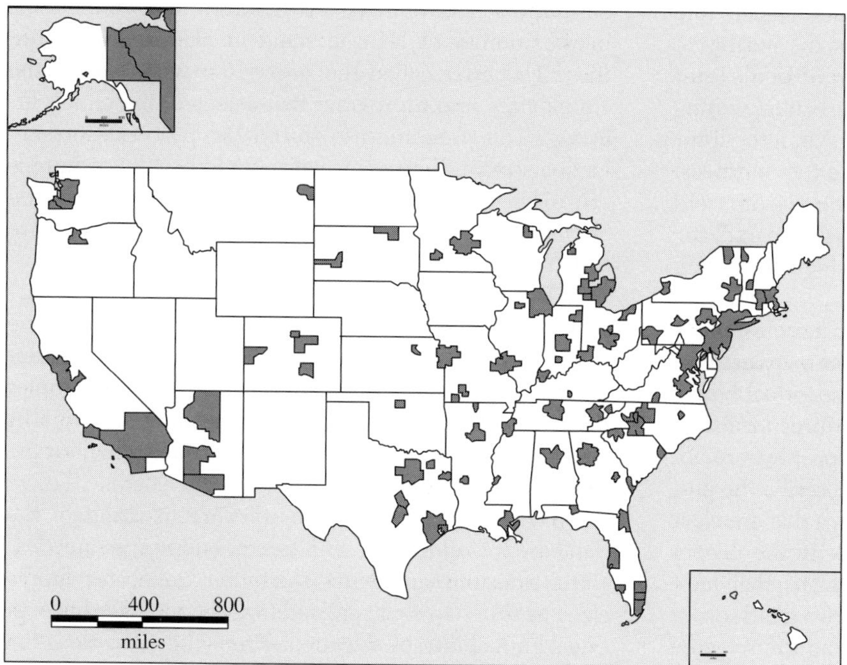

Figure 1 Map of hypothetical sample of PSUs.

then they were linked to the last segment from the previous tract; such multitract SSUs were rare. To link blocks, the blocks were first sorted by census block number within census tract, linking with adjacent blocks in sort order. Usually the linked blocks were geographically adjacent.

Altogether, NORC selected 3046 SSUs. A subsample of 384 SSUs was selected for address collection. The remaining selected SSUs were held in reserve for custom larger studies or for SSU replacement when all HUs in selected SSUs were used up. For all noncertainty PSUs, NORC selected 24 SSUs and subsampled three for address collection. For the certainty PSUs, NORC selected at least 25 SSUs with at least three for address collection; the number selected was proportional to the PSU size. The largest PSU (New York) had 210 selected SSUs, with 26 subsampled for address collection.

The SSUs were selected by systematic sampling with probability proportional to size, where again the measure of size was the number of HUs. The SSUs were sorted prior to selection, imposing an implicit stratification on the sort variables. The purpose of the implicit stratification was to increase precision to the extent that the sort variables were correlated with the survey variables. Within each PSU, SSUs were sorted by (1) central city vs noncentral city, (2) state, (3) county, (4) census place, (5) quartile of tract's percent minority, and (6) census tract. When subsampling for address collection, the sample SSUs were again selected systematically in the order they were first selected from the PSU. Figure 2 illustrates a hypothetical sample of SSUs within a PSU.

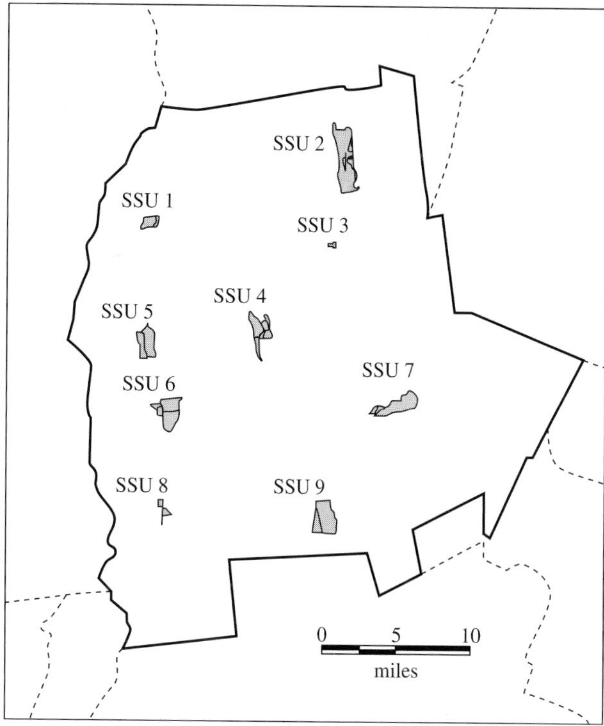

Figure 2 Map of hypothetical sample of SSUs within a PSU.

Housing Units

Before a sample of housing units can be selected from the SSUs, a frame list of HUs in the SSUs is needed. The process of collecting addresses in the SSUs is called listing. The lister, or field person who collects the addresses, travels to the SSU. Starting at the northwest corner of the lowest numbered block in the SSU, the lister travels around the block in a clockwise direction, writing down the address of every HU in order. When the lister returns to the starting place, she moves to the northwest corner of the next lowest numbered block in the SSU and begins listing that block. The process continues until the entire SSU is listed. Figure 3 shows a single SSU with blocks and Hus.

The process of listing is not as simple as it seems. Block boundaries are not always clear, so custom maps are created of the SSU as a whole and of the individual blocks within it. Special rules govern the procedures for listing cul-de-sacs, alleys, and other configurations. Where addresses are not obvious, the lister must describe the permanent characteristics of the HUs in terms that are clear and unambiguous. Additional rules specify the proper order in which to list individual apartments that have the same street address. Having a prescribed order is important to aid interviewers in locating the selected HUs during a study.

In rare instances, an SSU was too large to be practical and cost-effective for listing. Such SSUs consisted of large, urban high-rises, or a broad geographical area requiring extensive travel time. These SSUs were subdivided into smaller areas called chunks, and a single chunk was selected in place of the entire SSU. Technically, chunking was a third stage of sample selection, but it was applied only rarely. The lister first traveled the entire SSU, keeping a quick count of the number of HUs by block, sub-block, or building without writing down individual addresses. If the quick count of HUs exceeded a certain threshold (both 1000 and 500 have been used as thresholds), the lister divided the SSU into chunks; otherwise, the lister collected addresses for the entire SSU. Each chunk was required to have the minimum number of HUs to stand in place of the entire SSU. The lister called the supervisor, who entered the chunk sizes into a program that selected one chunk for listing. The program also stored the probability of selection so that sampling weights could be adjusted properly. The lister then proceeded to list just the selected chunk using the usual procedures for listing an entire SSU.

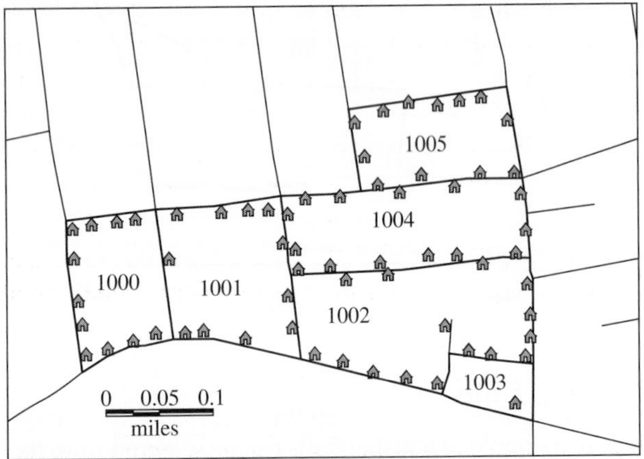

Figure 3 Map of hypothetical SSU (6 blocks) with housing units shown.

When the paper listings were returned to headquarters, the addresses and descriptions were keyed. The keyed listings were compiled into a large database maintained by the sampling statisticians who selected samples of HUs for area probability studies. A number of quality checks were performed before, after, and throughout the transmission processes.

NORC developed custom software to maintain the database of addresses and select samples as needed. Given a desired sample size, the software allocates sample sizes to SSUs so that, unconditionally, all HUs have an equal probability of selection. From the allocation, the software determines a selection interval and selects a sample of HUs systematically in listed order. Selection is independent from one SSU to the next. The software marks the selected HUs so that they are not available for selection in subsequent sample draws. The sample of HUs is provided to the field force for screening and interviewing.

Persons

Sometimes the unit of analysis for a study is the household, in which case no additional sampling is necessary. Any knowledgeable adult in a selected household can respond to the main questionnaire about the household. Other times the person is the unit of analysis. Most studies do not interview all members of a household because of the high correlations in their responses. More commonly, one person per household is selected. Thus, there is one additional stage of sampling.

Often the selection of persons takes place in the field following a short screener interview of the household. Sometimes the household members are rostered, and a person is selected using an objective respondent selection table, commonly known as a Kish table, or a programmed selection routine in the interviewer's computer. Rostering can be a slow process, reducing screener completion rates. An alternative is to use a simple selection routine such as the nearest birthday method, in which the person selected is the one who most recently had a birthday, or some variation of that rule. The method that is used for selecting persons is specific to the study and is not a characteristic of the national area probability frame.

NORC's national sampling frame is designed to give every housing unit in the U.S. an equal probability of selection. (Chunking introduces some deviations, but the effect is assumed to be minor.) Thus, every housing unit has approximately the same sampling weight. Assuming similar response patterns throughout, studies of U.S. households selected from the national sampling frame can be analyzed on an unweighted basis. The design is said to be self-weighting. When persons are the unit of analysis, then the probability of selecting persons within households should be taken into account. Depending on the method used, the person weights may vary according to the size and composition of the households.

Frame Maintenance

The population of housing units is in constant flux. New homes are built, and existing homes are demolished or subdivided. Garages and basements are converted to apartments. Buildings constructed as homes are converted to businesses, and vice-versa. By the time a sample of HUs is selected, the frame is already out of date. The older the frame, the greater the number of HUs that are not on the list. In addition, lister errors and the inaccessibility of some HUs lead to imperfections in the frame from the start. If every HU in the country is to have a chance of selection, then some provision must be made for these situations.

One option is to update the frame periodically through listing updates. For example, listers might periodically return to the SSUs to verify or update the lists. While this approach keeps the frame as fresh as possible, it never entirely eliminates the problem of missed HUs because of inevitable time lags, however small. Listing updates are relatively expensive, as well, because they require on-site visits.

NORC more commonly employs at the interviewing stage a procedure for identifying HUs that are not on the list and giving them a chance of being in the sample. The missed housing unit procedure is based on the concept of half-open intervals. A half-open interval is an interval which includes one endpoint and all points up to but not including the next endpoint. In this context, a half-open interval includes an HU on the list and all territory up to but not including the next HU on the list. Recall that the listing procedure originally specified a process for covering all the area within selected SSUs. Therefore, all geographical points within the SSU would have been searched for HUs in a prescribed order. If a new HU is identified during the interviewing phase of a survey, the interviewer can identify where on the list the new HU would have been if it had been found by the lister. Because the new HU is in the preceding HU's half-open interval, it is added to the sample if and only if the preceding HU on the list is in the sample. In this way, the probability for the new HU is the same as the probability of the HU that precedes it on the list.

If multiple missed HUs are found within the same half-open interval, then all of them have a chance of being included in the sample based on whether or not the preceding listed HU is in the sample. However, if the number of missed HUs in an interval is large, the risk to the interviewing budget and schedule may be unacceptably high. Typically NORC studies restrict the number of missed HUs in a single half-open interval to three; if more than three missed HUs are found in a single selected interval, then three of the missed HUs are selected randomly and weighted accordingly.

New Developments in Area Probability Designs

Design Options

Although NORC's area probability design used HU counts as the primary measure of size, other measures of size are possible. Studies that target minorities might be better served with a design based on the number of minority persons. Studies of youths might be more efficient if the design were based on youth populations. For example, the National Longitudinal Study of Youth 1997 had a custom area probability design that incorporated counts of black and Hispanic youths as a measure of size.

Demographic concepts change over time. The 2000 census was the first to allow persons to classify themselves in multiple race categories. This has implications for the measures of size that can be used, and for the way PSUs and SSUs are sorted for systematic selection.

Geographical area definitions also change over time. Metropolitan areas from the 1980 census were known as Standard Metropolitan Areas. For the 1990 census, the metropolitan areas were redefined and called Metropolitan Statistical Areas. New geographical areas are now defined based on the results of the 2000 census. Not only do geographical areas change in size, which causes different geographies to meet metropolitan criteria, but the criteria themselves may change to define new types of metropolitan areas.

Design changes are not always the result of definitional changes. Sometimes new statistical research and new developments make new ideas practical. One new development is an algorithm for maximizing or minimizing the overlap of new sample units with units selected for another sample from the same frame. The Ernst procedure, for example, can be used to encourage or discourage the selection of the same PSUs and SSUs that were selected last decade. See Further Reading below for more details.

Sometimes design changes are dictated by changes in research interests. The frame may be designed differently depending on whether the analytical needs relate to the residential population, the total population including group quarters and institutions, or specific demographic groups. Alternatively, if customers shift their focus to regional or community studies rather than national studies, the chosen design is likely to be quite different.

Finally, design changes and operational changes, which are related, are sometimes driven by cost concerns. For example, one goal may be to minimize the amount of time between address collection and HU selection; having the interviewers conduct the listing and selection of HUs in the field can reduce or eliminate this time gap.

New Data Sources

The American Community Survey will provide the same information collected in the census long form. The ACS will collect data more often, which may free survey organizations from the once-per-decade frame development cycle. For example, PSUs may be reselected on a rolling basis, spreading the costs over the decade.

Recently, address lists from the U.S. Postal Service have become commercially available through third party vendors. Some survey organizations are researching the use of the address lists in lieu of manually collected addresses. While rural route and post office box addresses will never be an adequate substitute, the use of the USPS list in some geographies is promising.

New Hardware/Software

Traditionally, the listing operation to collect housing unit addresses has been done with pencil and paper. Pencil and paper are inexpensive and highly portable. At some point, however, the listed addresses must be converted into electronic form to consolidate the frame for sample selection. The data entry step, while not difficult, nevertheless adds to the expense, the time, and the chance of errors.

Portable electronic devices are changing rapidly, introducing opportunities for electronic address collection. The variety of devices include laptop computers, tablet computers, palmtop computers, and personal digital assistants. Combined with sophisticated software and easy data transmission, such devices have the potential to allow for electronic updates to maps, built-in edit checks, and rapid assembly of the frame. Barriers to the widespread use of these devices for listing addresses have included high costs, poor battery life, poor visibility of the screen (especially outdoors), poor handwriting recognition capabilities, weight and awkwardness relative to paper, and lack of compatibility with software and systems in the home office. These obstacles are rapidly being overcome.

Another technological development is the accessibility of the Global Positioning System (GPS) and inexpensive devices that record geographical coordinates. In many areas, the precision of the latitudes and longitudes can distinguish individual housing units. The coordinates enable the housing units to be displayed on maps. Combined with on-line travel directions, the availability of coordinates greatly simplifies the interviewer's job of locating a selected housing unit that may have been listed by somebody else. Like names and addresses, geographical coordinates must be strictly protected to avoid the risk of disclosing the identities of respondents.

Mapping software and databases are far more sophisticated than in the past. Most databases are built on the census Topologically Integrated Geographic Encoding and Referencing (TIGER) system, which dramatically improved mapping capabilities when they became publicly available more than a decade ago. Today, commercial vendors enhance the TIGER data with regular updates and additional data sources, making their mapping systems more current and accurate than ever before. Better maps mean less time locating the geographical areas for listing addresses, and less time locating selected housing units. Zoom capabilities and geographical coordinates of individual housing units enhance the usefulness of the maps. Sophisticated mapping software may even be able to optimize travel routes.

Summary

The 1990 National Sampling Frame for area probability studies, as described in this article, was a multistage cluster design with systematic sampling of geographies and housing units. The sampling stages are summarized in Fig. 4. The geographical sampling units in the first two stages were selected with probability proportional to the number of housing units. Lists of addresses were collected for the smallest geographical sampling units. The address listings comprised the frame for nationally representative samples of housing units requiring face-to-face interviewing. When HUs were selected, the sample was allocated to the geographies such that all HUs had an equal probability of selection. The National Sampling Frame was the basis for a number of high profile studies throughout the past decade.

While the basic principles of area probability designs have changed little over the years, technological advancements are making implementation quicker and cheaper. Organizations such as NORC can take advantage of these developments to reduce costs and to increase the statistical efficiency of the basic designs.

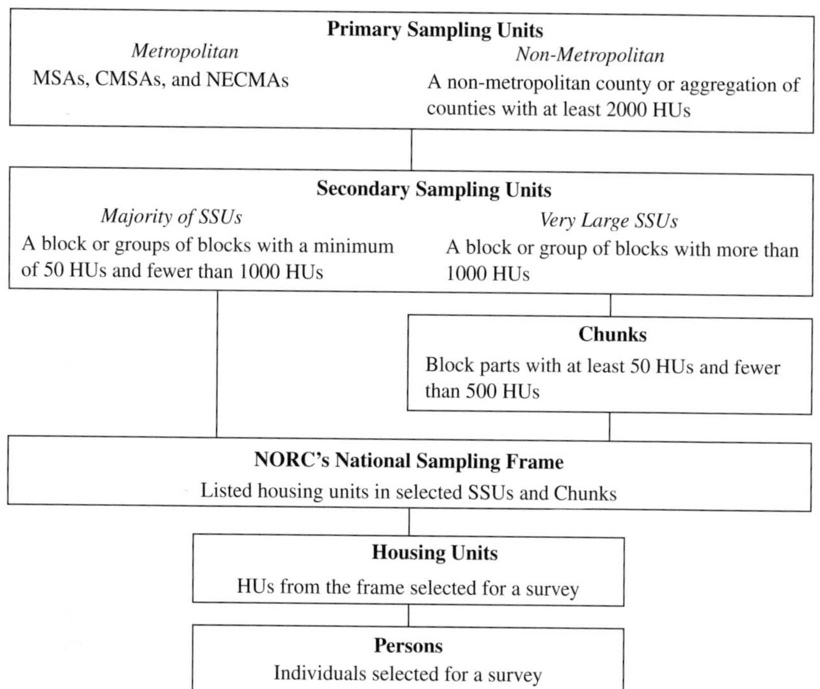

Figure 4 Summary of the multistage sample design in NORC's 1990 National Sampling Frame.

See Also the Following Articles

Clustering • Sample Design • Stratified Sampling Types

Further Reading

For more information on the General Social Survey, see (www.icpsr.umich.edu:8080/GSS/index.html). For the National Longitudinal Study, the *NLS Handbook* is available at (www.bls.gov/nls). Metropolitan Statistical Areas and related concepts are discussed in (www.whitehouse.gov/omb/bulletins/95-04.html). Other terms currently used by the U.S. Census Bureau can be found at the census web site (www.census.gov). In particular, the TIGER geographical system is described at (www.census.gov/geo/wwwtiger/index.html). The technical documentation accompanying census data products are a good source of definitions of census terms.

Binson, D., Canchola, J. A., and Catania, J. A. (2000). Random selection in a national telephone survey: A comparison of the Kish, Next-Birthday, and Last-Birthday methods. *J. Official Statist.* **16,** 53–59.

Cochran, W. G. (1977). *Sampling Techniques,* 2nd Ed. Wiley, New York.

Ernst L. R. (1995). Maximizing and minimizing overlap of ultimate sampling units. In *1995 Proceedings of the Section on Survey Research Methods,* pp. 706–711. American Statistical Association, Alexandria, VA.

Iannacchione, V. G., Staab, J. M., and Redden, D. T (2001). *Evaluating the Use of Residential Mailing Addresses in a Metropolitan Household Survey.* Paper presented at the American Association for Public Opinion Research conference. Montreal, May 2001; Federal Committee on Statistical Methods conference, Arlington, VA, Nov. 2001 (www.fcsm.gov/01papers/Iannacchione.pdf).

Kish, L. (1965). *Survey Sampling.* John Wiley, New York.

Lavrakas, P. J., Bauman, S. L., and Merkle, D. M. (1993). The last-birthday selection method & within-unit coverage problems. In *1993 Proceedings of the Section on Survey Research Methods*, pp. 1107–1112. American Statistical Association Alexandria, VA.

Lohr, S. L. (1999). *Sampling: Design and Analysis.* Duxbury Press, Pacific Grove, CA.

Oldengick, R. W., Bishop, G. F., Sorenson, S. B., and Tuchfarber, A. J. (1988). A comparison of the Kish and Last Birthday Methods of respondent selection in telephone surveys. *J. Official Statist.* **4,** 307–318.

O'Muircheartaigh C., Eckman, S., Weiss, C. (2002). Traditional and enhanced field listing for probability sampling. In *2002 Proceedings of the Section on Survey Research Methods.* American Statistical Association, Alexandria, VA.

Salmon, C. T., and Nichols, J. S. (1983). The next-birthday method of respondent selection. *Public Opin. Quart.* **47,** 270–276.

Technical Documentation, 1990 Census of Population and Housing (1992). Summary tape file 3, CD-Rom. U.S. Department of Commerce, Economic and Statistics Administration, Bureau of the Census, Washington, DC.

Tourangeau, R., Johnson, R. A., Qian, J., and Shin, H.-C. (1993). *Selection of NORC's 1990 National Sample.* Internal report. NORC, Chicago.

Nursing

Phoebe D. Williams

University of Kansas School of Nursing, Kansas City, Kansas, USA

Arthur R. Williams

Mayo Clinic, Rochester, Minnesota, USA

Glossary

generalized estimating equations (GEE) An extension of the generalized linear model developed to deal with clustered and longitudinal data, such as panel models, by first estimating regression parameters then estimating associations among parameters.

latent variable An unmeasured variable that represents an underlying construct (often in the context of structural equation or latent structure modeling).

nonrecursive path model A structural equation model that hypothesizes reciprocal relationships wherein a variable can be both the cause of and an effect of another variable.

principal components Constructions formed from interrelated items that are reduced to a smaller number of well-formed composite measures (components) for further analyses; principal components should not be confused with "factors" that are constructed using a different treatment of the diagonal elements of covariance or correlation matrices.

structural equation modeling (SEM) The development and statistical testing of either an exploratory or explanatory model of hypothesized relationships among variables using simultaneous equations to estimate parameters.

Nursing research involves a systematic search for and validation of knowledge about issues of importance to the nursing profession. Nurses are the largest group of professionals engaged in the provision of health care services in the United States. Like other professionals, nurses are expected to document their "social relevance," including their role in the delivery of services to clients. Nursing research helps to define the unique roles of nurses and their expanding body of professional knowledge. Additionally, nursing research, whether evaluative or basic, contributes to the accountability of the profession for services provided to clients and payers.

Introduction

What Is (and Why) Nursing Research?

Historically, entry into nursing practice has been through a number of paths including diploma programs in hospitals, associates programs at community and technical colleges, and university-based Bachelors of Science in Nursing (BSN) degrees. Increasingly, the emphasis of nursing education has shifted toward the BSN and graduate degrees for advanced practice. Advanced practice programs often require masters theses or research projects, directed by doctorally prepared faculty. This educational upgrading of curricula in nursing is consistent with a currently expanded view of nursing practice. Good nursing practice now is viewed as based on "evidence," continuous measurement, evaluation and review, and practice improvement based on patient outcomes after interventions.

The Context: Outcomes Research and Evidence-Based Nursing Practice

Doctoral programs offering degrees in nursing developed only about three decades ago. As a result, most nurses who obtained research-oriented degrees matriculated in education, the social sciences (particularly psychology and sociology), and a number of other disciplines. Within recent years, research training has expanded in doctoral programs in nursing. Nurses also continue to obtain research degrees in the areas previously mentioned and in physiology, informatics, statistics, and epidemiology. Various academic disciplines emphasize different research methods and strategies; as a consequence, heterogeneity in the advanced education of nurses promotes diversity in methods and research strategies among nurses that may surprise outside observers.

Despite diverse research foci, studies are being done and emphasis given to what is sometimes loosely called "outcomes research"—this concept shall be used as an organizing and limiting construct for this article. Outcomes research emphasizes the use of advanced statistical methods and research designs to determine how interventions used by nurses or other clinicians affect the health trajectories of patients. An outcomes approach to research is now seen by many as useful for building the knowledge base of nursing, providing accountability to clients and society more generally, and, most importantly, promoting improved care. Due to space limitations, research methods now being used by nurses in biomedical bench research, qualitative research, and statistics and epidemiology will not be discussed in this article, although these are important areas of research in nursing.

As health care organizations and governments attempt to promote efficiency, improve effectiveness, and reduce levels of health care expenditures, outcomes research and evidence-based nursing practice have gained attention and support. Outcomes research assesses changes in individuals' (or communities') health status as a result of interventions provided in health care settings. The idea of measuring outcomes or documenting evidence of the value of services is not new in nursing. Barnes (1969), in *Nursing Clinics of North America*, for example, shows that interventions by a pediatric clinical nurse specialist (CNS, a masters prepared nurse) produced valuable patient outcomes. The outcomes identified included the following: An increase in successful oral dilatation without anesthesia. Cost of dilatation decreased. Mastery of the child's care by mother improved. The total hours of CNS care decreased over time. Weight and verbalizations by the child improved. These outcomes are reflected at multiple levels: patient, family, provider, and organizational.

Social science methods were applied in the Barnes study, and they have been applied in the great majority of research done by nurses. Current methods of choice are largely multivariate and correlational, with attempts made to statistically control for covariates that might produce confounding among intervention associated variables.

Although few patient outcomes have been identified that are affected solely by nursing interventions, there are a number of measures of outcomes that are considered "nursing sensitive." Marek gives specific examples with children suffering from sickle cell disease. In the sense noted by Barnes and other nurse researchers, Marek views these nursing outcomes as multilevel. That is, the outcomes of nursing interventions can range from the physiologic (e.g., lower patient complication rate), to family outcomes (e.g., lower parental stress), to "systems" issues (e.g., fewer emergency room visits).

Nursing quality indicators have been developed for acute care settings, and these indicators often capture multilevel outcomes. These quality indicators are often classified into measures of outcome, process, and structure. Patient outcomes and process indicators have included patient injury rate, nosocomial infection rate, maintenance of skin integrity, and patient satisfaction (e.g., with pain management, with educational information, with care). At the nurse provider level, outcomes have included staff satisfaction and intent to stay on the job. Structural or organizational indicators of quality have included the total nursing care hours provided per patient and the "skill mix" of registered nurses (RNs), licensed practical nurses (LPNs), and unlicensed staff caring for patients, and other indicators reflecting the structure of the institutions in which nurses work.

Social Science Measurement Concepts in Nursing Research

Nursing research uses social science measurement methods, concepts, and definitions similar to those in the disciplines of psychology and sociology. Thus, scientific research is defined as the systematic, controlled, empirical, and critical investigation of hypothesized relationships among phenomena. Measurement is defined as the assignment of numbers to objects or events according to rules. Measurement may be nominal, ordinal, interval, or ratio; these measurements determine the type of data analyses (nonparametric, parametric) used. To measure variables in a study, researchers are advised to select instruments or tools that are reliable and valid, also referred to as the tools' psychometric properties. Nurses educated in research-oriented doctoral programs in nursing and other disciplines are thoroughly familiar with such works as those of Kerlinger and others that emphasize assessments of validity and reliability. Research design and statistics is introduced at the undergraduate level in most quality BSN programs and an increasing number of texts present research methods and measurement specifically for nurses (e.g., Polit and Hungler). In general, nursing research has given considerable attention to content validity, criterion-related validity (concurrent, predictive), and construct validity.

Data collection tools used in nursing research include self-report scales, tests that measure various attributes, questionnaires, interview schedules, and observation checklists. Strategies to avoid measurement errors are emphasized. In selecting measurement tools for a study, nurses use various compendia in the social sciences (psychology, sociology) that describe data collection instruments and their psychometric properties. Some nurses are authors of these texts (Waltz *et al.*; Ward and Lindeman). A few of the constructs used in nursing research are outlined below.

Patient/Client

Clinical status as an outcome of care received by individual patients or clients is measured physiologically and behaviorally. Behavioral indicators include measures of *psychosocial status* (such as mood, anxiety, depression, stress, coping, self-esteem), *functional status* (such as activities of daily living); *cognitive status* (such as knowledge of the disease); *attitude* (such as satisfaction with nursing care or care overall or with educational information); and *other aspects* (such as self-care methods for symptom management, quality of life, child development).

Family Members (and the Family System)

Individual family members' behaviors may be studied also using many indicators that measure *psychosocial, functional*, and *cognitive* status, and *attitudes*. In addition, the *role of family members as informal caregivers at home* has been studied in nursing research with concepts such as *motivation to help, preparedness to help*, and *mutuality*, as well as *role strain, burden, and related concepts*. Consistent with systems theory, these variables are recognized as interrelated within the *family system*. For example, our path analysis results in a study of children on apnea monitors and their caregivers (mothers) show that *family cohesion, caregiver self-esteem*, and *social support* are related to positive *family coping strategies*, positive *caregiver-child interactions*, and higher *expressive language development* in the children.

Nurse Providers

Commitment, satisfaction, intent to stay on the job, burn-out, and job stress are some of the individual professional provider variables measured in nursing research. These variables often are correlated with the characteristics of the nurse as well as those of the workplace. For example, Taunton *et al.*, using structural equation modeling based on Leavitt's theory of behavior within an organization, reported that manager leadership characteristics influenced nurse retention through work characteristics, *job stress, job satisfaction, commitment, and nurses' intent to stay on the job*. These findings are consistent with those of many other researchers, including Aiken *et al.*'s cross-cultural study in five countries (United States, Canada, England, Scotland, Germany). These authors report that nurses' negative perceptions of staffing adequacy and workforce management policies are key variables that significantly explained *nurses' job dissatisfaction* and *burn-out*.

Attempts are now being made by a number of nurses to study how provider characteristics and institutional setting directly and indirectly affect patient outcomes. This is a laudable attempt to bring together research at the client and institutional levels to assess how patient care can be immediately improved. Nurses historically and today practice in institutional settings in which they are greatly impacted by organizational structures and processes. These structure and processes are likely to be strongly associated with patient outcomes.

Social Science Research Design Methods and Analyses

Nurse researchers have long been advised that studies need to be planned with careful attention to logical consistency, theory, design, and analysis. Sociological models such as Gibbs' have been cited and discussed in the nursing literature. Using a modified version of the Gibbs substruction model, Dulock and Holzemer describe how a study's conceptual or theoretical model or system are linked with the "operational system" and the empirical indicators that measure the variables studied.

Within nursing research, selection of data analysis technique has been dependent on the study design: descriptive, predictive, experimental, or quasi-experimental. Social science methods of sampling (probability, nonprobability) and sample size determination (power analysis) usually are carefully assessed. Because of its distinct relationship with medical research, nursing research may emphasize power analysis more than some social science disciplines. The use of epidemiologic methods also is growing in nursing. Nurse researchers conduct studies using both experimental and nonexperimental designs, guided by the social science and nursing literature.

Consistent with the outcomes research framework of this article, selected examples of "true experiments" are identified. These are considered to be the strongest designs in that measurement of cause–effect relationships between treatments or interventions and the outcome variables often is less ambiguous than in observational studies. Experimental designs satisfy three criteria: namely, manipulation of the independent variable, presence of a control group, and random assignment of study subjects to the experimental and control groups. The last criterion is not satisfied in "quasi-experiments;" "pre-experiments" meet only the first criterion. Pre-experiments usually are done in nursing as pilot or preliminary studies prior to the implementation of a true experiment. Pre-experimental designs may be combined with nonexperimental approaches including content analysis and other qualitative methods.

Nurses have done nonexperimental and observational research that test patterned or structural relationships among variables (such as structural equation modeling). Outside the discipline of education, nurses were among the earlier adopters of LISREL and structural equation models. Yet, the use of multilevel modeling has grown somewhat slower in nursing than in some other social science disciplines. Due to the inherent multilevel nature of many nursing outcome studies, however, one can anticipate that such modeling is likely to be used increasingly, applying LISREL, HLM, Mplus, or other software.

Due to the fact that many nurse researchers obtained their earlier experiences in educational psychology and that measurement is heavily emphasized in outcomes research, it is not surprising that much attention has been and continues to be given to instrument development and assessment. Current research attention is turning toward how measurement instruments might be more easily adapted to clinical practice settings. Unfortunately, studies of predictive validity in nursing have been few.

New funding sources have enhanced the ability of nurses to engage in outcomes research with strong designs. In 1986, a National Center of Nursing Research was established at the National Institutes of Health; in 1993, the Center became the National Institute of Nursing Research, NINR. Funding through the Institute enables nurse researchers to collaborate with other disciplines, including medicine and the social sciences. Additionally, a number of foundations, particularly those interested in health care, are aggressively supporting well-designed nursing research.

True Experimental Designs in Nursing Intervention and Outcomes Research

Nursing intervention and outcomes research using true experimental designs are mentioned briefly below. In these examples, the measurement of outcomes includes behavioral indicators (in italics) as well as physiologic and organizational ones. Outcomes research done abroad also is mentioned. Outside of clinical settings, true experimental designs have been used to test nursing interventions that have direct implications for clinical practice. As in most clinical disciplines, increasing attention is now being given to the "translation" (or application) of research findings into clinical practice. This "translational research" is a growth area in nursing and medicine.

Brooten *et al.* completed a well-known "true experiment" to test a model of early hospital discharge and transitional care (as compared to a routine care control group) for very low birth weight infants (<1500 Gm). A perinatal clinical nurse specialist or CNS provided instruction, counseling, home visits and daily on-call (telephone) availability for the experimental, E group. Compared to the routine care control group, the E group: (a) was discharged 11 days earlier and 2 weeks younger; (b) was equally as "safe" (that is, there was no difference in *infant growth and development outcomes*, acute care visits, or rehospitalizations; and *maternal health and psychosocial measures*); and (c) had lower cost (hospital charges were 27% less and MD charges were 22% less; hospital cost saving was $18,000 per infant). Brooten *et al.* further tested the "model of transitional care" as provided by a CNS similar to the above in randomized clinical trials on three high risk, high volume, high cost groups of patients, namely those with unplanned Caesarean section births, pregnant women with diabetes, and post-hysterectomy women. They found that compared to the routine care control groups, the E groups showed: higher patient satisfaction, higher infant immunizations, lower rehospitalizations, and health care cost reductions up to 38%. Several of the unique contributions of these studies were their publication in both medical and nursing journals, their strong research design, and the attention paid to the relationship between outcomes and costs.

Naylor *et al.* also tested the "transitional care model" as provided by a CNS to another population: elderly patients with congestive heart failure and their family caregivers, the E group. The CNS care included a comprehensive discharge plan provided while the patient was in the hospital and during the first two weeks after discharge. Findings showed that compared to the routine care group, the E group had fewer total days in hospital, fewer re-admissions, lower re-admission charges, and lower total charges for healthcare services.

Of interest is the review by Brooten and Naylor of nursing studies that used experimental designs. They identified four key questions in nursing research relative to changing patient outcomes. What outcomes should be measured? What "nurse dose" (i.e., what nurse intervention in what amount) is needed to show an effect? What nurse dose is needed in a given health care environment to show a treatment effect? What nurse dose works for which patient group? After a decade, these remain fundamental questions in nursing research. With the varying paths of entry into nursing practice ranging from associate degree, to bachelors degree, to masters or doctorate, the difference in settings in which nurses practice and the varying needs of patients, the measurement of "nursing dose," for example, has been elusive. What combinations of education, credentialing, and setting constitute valid and reliable measures of "dose?"

High quality nursing research has been done outside the United States. These studies are important not only due to their immediate impact on nursing research in the United States, but their distinct differences in organizational and institutional setting provide possible opportunities for assessment of institutional and cross-cultural effects on outcomes. These can impact practice in the United States. Unfortunately, the use of experimental designs in such studies has been limited.

Campbell *et al.* report the results of a randomized trial of nurse-led primary care (the experimental group) in Scotland on the secondary prevention of coronary heart disease, CHD, and a usual care control group. A random sample of 19 general practices in the northeast was used; 1173 participants were under 80 years old, diagnosed with CHD, but not house bound nor with terminal illness or dementia. Eligible patients were stratified by age, gender, and general practice, and randomized (by individual) using a table of random numbers. The components of secondary prevention measured at baseline and one year later included lifestyle measures such as *engagement in physical activity, intake of dietary fat*, and *smoking* as well as other clinical measures such as aspirin use, blood pressure management, and lipid management. One year from baseline, as compared to the control group, significant positive outcomes of the nurse-led primary care were found on all outcome measures, except smoking cessation. Most patients gained at least one effective component of secondary prevention; future cardiovascular events and mortality were reduced by up to one-third.

Research using nonexperimental designs, physiologic, and organizational indicators has demonstrated the value of nursing care, thus increasing the generalizability or external validity of outcomes research findings. For example, conclusions from research on organizational indicators of quality (e.g., total hours of nursing care provided and the RN "skill mix") and patient outcomes have demonstrated that patients have fewer urinary tract infections, falls, pneumonias, and bedsores under a number of conditions. These desired outcomes are more likely to occur when staffing is higher, higher educated nurses are employed, and nurses can devote more time to patients. Aiken *et al.* have shown additionally that mortality rates for such patients can be substantially reduced.

In home health settings, studies have shown immediate and long-term effects on low-income families home visited by nurses that produced *improved pregnancy outcomes* and *lessened child abuse and neglect*. Similar research is being conducted of training families to cope with chronic care at home.

Emerging Nonexperimental Design Approaches

Nonexperimental design approaches to test structural equation relationships among study variables, such as structural equation modeling, also are used in nursing research. An early description of what was then labeled "causal inference" by Blalock has had some impact in nursing. Nursing studies have used path analytic and other modeling approaches. A structural equation modeling example is given below. As noted above, the delivery of nursing care would appear to fit well with techniques now developed for multilevel modeling research. A significant barrier to application is likely to be sample size requirements.

Two areas of immediate need in health services research and policy are studies of costs or expenditure relative to treatment effects and outcomes over time (longitudinal studies). Much work in these areas is likely to remain nonexperimental; however, recent efforts are being made to incorporate cost-effectiveness research into experimental designs including randomized clinical trials (RCT).

Instrument Development Research

To measure constructs and processes of interest to nursing, methods used in education and social sciences have been followed to design instruments with good psychometric properties. Most doctoral programs in nursing contain courses in instrument development, test construction, and item analysis. Nurses have been active in developing instruments and scales to measure patient and provider attitudes, quality of life, patient satisfaction, and other constructs. Work has been directed toward practice settings such as in hospitals in which patients have specific illness conditions such as cancer. Instruments also have been developed for assessment of health promotion services in community settings. Example 3 under the Examples section below includes a brief description of the developmental of a clinical instrument using principal components.

Other Nursing Research

The brief description below is based on two comprehensive summaries of two decades of research reviews (1983–2003) published in the *Annual Review of Nursing Research (ARNR)*. Both summaries use similar categories of content foci or themes; thus, facilitating comparisons of content themes in nursing research over two decades. The content categories used are: life span development, clinical or nursing practice research, research on nursing care delivery, research on professional issues, educational research in nursing, and international nursing research. Life span development has subcategories such as maternal-child health, infants, and young children; school-age children and adolescents; adulthood; older adult issues and problems; and family research. During these two decades, research in life span development was common, with a total of 25 reviews for the first decade and 49 reviews for the second decade.

Nursing Practice Research also has subcategories such as nursing diagnoses and interventions; symptoms and problems; risk behaviors and forms of abuse; physiologic mechanisms and biologic rhythms; care problems of specific diseases; research in nursing specialty areas; crises, grief, loss, and bereavement; and research on special populations such as rural health; health among minorities, migrants, the homeless. The largest number of review chapters published in *ARNR* is in the Nursing Practice Research category, with a total of 42 reviews for the first decade and 61 for the second decade.

Commonly studied were combinations of a nursing practice research problem within a specific age cohort or subcategory of the lifespan. Examples of reviews reflecting these combined categories include: Fatigue During the Childbearing Period, Prenatal and Parenting Programs for Adolescent Mothers; Child Sexual Abuse: Initial Effects; Motivation for Physical Activity Among Children and Adolescents; Children with Epilepsy: Quality of Life and Psychosocial Needs; Family Interventions to Prevent Substance Abuse: Children and Adolescents; Women as Mothers and Grandmothers; Health Promotion for Family Caregivers of Chronically Ill Elders; End-of-Life Care for Older Adults in ICUs; Interventions for Children with Diabetes and their Families; Quality of Life and Caregiving in Technological Home Care; and Sleep Promotion in Adults (*ARNR*, 1994–2002). Also, nursing research in other countries (Scotland, Canada, Philippines, Korea, Israel, Brazil, Taiwan, Italy) has been reviewed (*ARNR*, 1984, 1986, 1988, 1994, 1996, 1997, 1999). Social science methods mentioned above were used in many of the studies reviewed.

Nurse researchers have used several publication guides (e.g., the American Psychological Association). Nursing, medical, social science, and other journals (see Further Reading) are used for research dissemination, as is the *Cumulative Index to Nursing and Allied Health Literature* (*CINAHL*) (www.cinahl.com). Another key bibliographic resource for nursing research is *MEDLINE*, at the U.S. National Library of Medicine (www.nlm.gov).

Examples

Experimental Design: The ISEE Study

(Adapted from Williams *et al.* (2003) with permission of Mosby, Inc.) The Intervention for Siblings: Experience Enhancement (ISEE) was provided to siblings in families of children with a chronic illness or disability. The objective of the study was to determine whether the intervention (designed by nurses and physicians) improved the measured outcomes of *sibling behavior problems, sibling knowledge about the illness of the brother or sister, sibling attitude toward the illness, sibling mood, sibling self-esteem, and sibling feelings of social support*. The six outcomes were identified in a literature review as important to the current and later development of the sibling. Instruments with published psychometric properties were used to measure outcomes.

The ISEE study was designed as a randomized trial. After IRB approval and permissions and assents were obtained, siblings were blocked by age (7–10 versus 11–15 years) and gender. A sibling (closest in age to the ill child) and the mother were then randomized into two experimental and one control group. These groups were as follows: a full experimental group who received the intervention at a five-day residential summer camp; a partial treatment group who did not receive the full intervention but who were provided the usual summer residential experience at one of the regularly scheduled camp sessions; and a waiting list control group who received a residential camp experience after completion of the ISEE study at the same accredited camp.

The siblings in the ISEE study had a brother or sister less than18 years of age who had cystic fibrosis, spina bifida, cancer (more than 18 months survival anticipated by the attending physicians), Type I diabetes, or developmental disabilities such as cerebral palsy, autism, etc. Similar but differentiated intervention materials and educational experiences were designed for siblings in each of these illness or disability groups. Parents in all groups discussed and learned about sibling and family issues as well as general approaches to child behavior management. Appropriately trained advance practice nurses provided the interventions.

Data were collected at baseline, at 5 days, and 4, 9, and 12 months after the delivery of intervention. Two hundred fifty-two parent–child dyads completed the study (13.9% attrition), and were used in data analyses. Technical information concerning randomization, the allocation of subjects, intervention materials, and measurement instruments can be found in Williams *et al.*

Generalized estimating equations (GEE) were used to analyze study outcomes. GEE is sensitive to clustering, repeated measures, conveniently handles covariates, and can lead to improved statistical power. Although these estimating equations have favorable features compared to others commonly used in social and behavioral research such as ANOVA, their use in nursing and health services research is relatively recent.

The results of the above NIH-sponsored study were very favorable to the intervention. The intervention had statistically significant effects on all outcomes over most time periods. The profile of the six outcomes is shown in Table I. These outcomes can be easily displayed graphically to show changes within the three study groups over time, but cannot be done in this chapter due to space constraints. An example of a GEE (sibling knowledge score on independent variables) is shown in Table II. The equation bears some similarity to a multiple regression equation.

The estimates of parameters FULLVIS2 through CONTVIS5 are the ones of central interest, since these exhibit effects from baseline of the knowledge scores in each group over the observation periods, controlling for covariates at baseline. *These covariates are knowledge scores of the siblings in the three study groups at baseline, diagnosis of the ill child, education of the mother, age of the sibling, cohesion within the family, and maternal mood.* Maternal education served as a proxy for socioeconomic status, SES, while cohesion within the family and maternal mood at the beginning of the study (baseline) could otherwise attenuate treatment effects. The other covariates were used to "standardize" the knowledge instruments for sibling age and the differences of items on the instrument related to the specific illness or disability familiar to the sibling.

In terms of nursing and child development research some of the covariates are of interest, but these cannot be further commented upon here. The standard errors in parentheses are semi-robust to account for clustering effects and, as usual for GEE, the Wald chi-square is used in a manner similar to the coefficient of determination in many generalized linear model regressions.

Structural Equation Model: Analysis of ISEE Baseline Measures

(Adapted from Williams *et al.* (2002) with permission of Kluwer Academic/Plenum Publishers.) Alert readers of the above section probably wonder whether some of the outcome variables analyzed as independent in the GEE are in fact interrelated. This, indeed, is the case. These relationships can be assessed using simultaneous equation models. Results reported below examined relationships at baseline. More complex models can be developed to assess changes over time. The model reported below is a nonrecursive path analysis; the only latent variable constructed is SES. AMOS version 4.0 was used to estimate parameters.

Figure 1 shows estimated relationships among the study variables. The numbers on the arrows are path coefficients (beta weights) indicating the effects of each variable on the others. Coefficients of determination are inside the boxes with the abbreviations of the study variables. Covariates related to the "standardization" of the knowledge scores are shown. Additionally, sibling age is used as a covariate with sibling knowledge scores (as mentioned previously), sibling attitude, sibling self-esteem, and sibling behavior scores. These four outcomes were found to be sensitive to age of the sibling in the ISEE

Table I Generalized Estimating Equations (GEE) Results: Summary of Statistically Significant Improvements from Baseline on Six Dependent Variables: Research Hypotheses Supported[a]

Group[a]	*Times of observation*[b]	*Knowledge*	*Social support*	*Self esteem*	*Mood*	*Attitude*	*Behavior*
1	2	***	—	***	—	**	NM
	3	***	*	***	—	**	—
	4	***	**	***	*	***	**
	5	***	*	***	***	***	**
2	2	—	**	**	—	—	NM
	3	—	***	***	—	—	—
	4	***	***	**	—	**	—
	5	—	*	**	—	**	—
3	2	—	—	—	—	***	NM
	3	—	***	**	—	***	—
	4	—	*	—	—	***	—
	5	—	*	—	—	***	***

[a] Summary: (1) Full Treatment Group: 19/23 tests supported improvement on the outcome measures; (2) Partial Treatment Group: 11/23 tests supported improvement on the outcome measures; and (3) Control Group: 9/23 supported improvement on the outcome measures.

[b] Observations (O) 2, 3, 4, 5 were at Day 5 and 4, 9, and 12 months from Baseline, O1.

$*p < 0.05$; $**p < 0.01$; $***p < 0.001$; (—), not significant; NM, not measured.

Note. By permission of Mosby, Inc.

Table II Estimated Relationships from GEE Analysis of Sibling Knowledge about Illness (SKNOW) on Independent Variables ($N = 1260$); Clustering 5 per Study Subject[a]

Variables (Independent)	*Knowledge score*[b]	*Semi-robust standard errors*
FULL (Full Treatment)	−1.3156***	0.5467
PART (Partial Treatment)	−1.9718***	0.6742
DXCYS (Cystic Fibrosis)	−5.2801***	1.2119
DXDIA (Diabetes)	0.2831	0.2979
DXSPI (Spina Bifida)	−5.8056***	1.1962
DXCAN (Cancer)	−5.7134***	0.8490
GRADE (Mother education)	−0.3384	0.1838
AGE (Sibling age)	0.4761***	0.0791
COHES (Family Cohesion)	0.0765***	0.0285
MMOOD (Mother mood)	0.0108	0.0100
FULLVIS2 (Full, Obsn. 2)	3.2532***	0.5274
FULLVIS3 (Full, Obsn. 3)	2.5823***	0.4436
FULLVIS4 (Full, Obsn. 4)	2.4051***	0.4662
FULLVIS5 (Full, Obsn. 5)	2.6329***	0.4577
PARTVIS2 (Part., Obsn. 2)	0.5915	0.5168
PARTVIS3 (Part., Obsn. 3)	0.7042	0.6275
PARTVIS4 (Part., Obsn. 4)	1.6478***	0.6155
PARTVIS5 (Part., Obsn. 5)	0.9718	0.6723
CONTVIS2 (ControlObsn2)	−0.1470	0.2889
CONTVIS3 (ControlObsn3)	0.1667	0.2694
CONTVIS4 (ControlObsn4)	0.1274	0.2822
CONTVIS5 (ControlObsn5)	0.3529	0.2749
(CONSTANT)	16.5877***	2.2545
Wald chi2 p<0.0001	249.81	

[a] Except for Sibling Behavior Problems (by parent report) at Observation 2 (Day 5) because siblings were still at camp.
[b] Sibling Knowledge is one of 6 dependent variables in the study. Similar data were obtained for 5 other variables (sibling social support, self-esteem, mood, attitude, and behavior problems).
$*p < 0.05$; $**p < 0.01$; $***p < 0.001$.
Note: The data in columns 2 and 3 are from Williams *et al.* By permission of Mosby, Inc.

study. All relationships shown in the model are statistically significant at $p < 0.05$ or lower.

Additional material can be reported using tables of total, direct, and indirect effects of each of the variables on the other. For example, the combined effects of the variables account for 45% of the variance in *behavior problems* among study siblings. This is a *combination of direct effects such as sibling knowledge on sibling behavior problems* and *indirect effects of family cohesion*, which has a direct effect of (−0.23) and *several indirect effects, including such complex ones as family cohesion affecting sibling attitude, sibling mood, sibling perceptions of social support, then sibling social support affecting sibling behavior problems*. All such effects can be quantitated, but the use of such complex models depends upon the accumulation of research results that indicate that the model may be reasonable. In this particular instance, components of the model had been tested over almost twenty years by the researchers before the path diagram describing variable interactions was constructed. Additionally, the hypothesized relationships among variables were consistent with our literature review.

The estimation of such a model depends upon having validated and reliable instruments to measure the constructs used in the model. Detailed descriptions of the instruments used in this study appear in the literature by Williams *et al.* (2002). The instruments used in the path analysis and the ISEE study had been developed, tested, and reported in peer-reviewed publications of psychologists, nurses, and others.

A tendency exists to use complex structural equation models with latent variables to incorporate constructs that do not have well known and previously reported measurement properties. Indeed, these models and related computer software were often developed to assist researchers in exploratory studies for model development. Nevertheless, too often these models are used to refit parameters many times until a "good fit" is obtained. Such an approach to data analysis raises a number of troubling issues in both design and measurement and should only

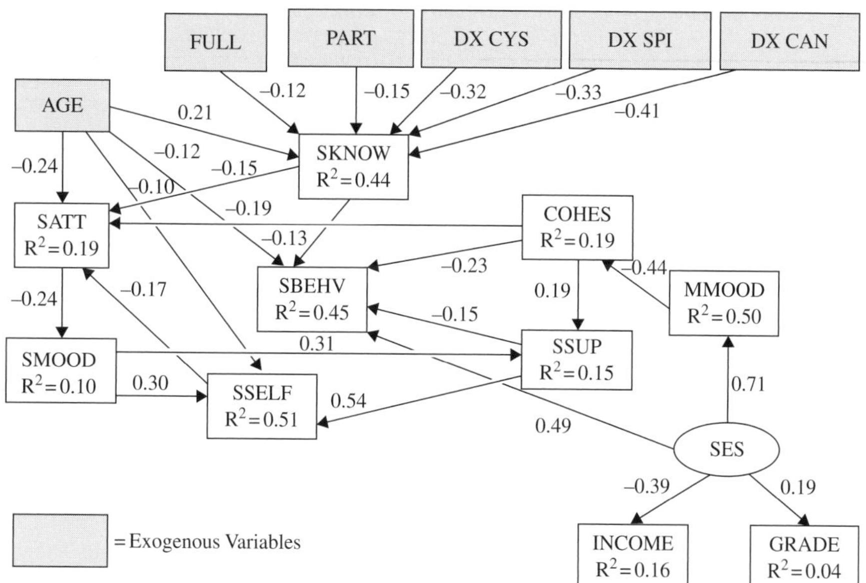

Figure 1 Estimated structural equation model (Baseline). (1) SKNOW, sibling knowledge about illness; (2) SMOOD, sibling mood; (3) SATT, sibling attitude toward illness; (4) SSELF, sibling self esteem; (5) SSUP, sibling social support; (6) SBEHV, sibling behavior problem; (7) MMOOD, mother mood; (8) COHES, family cohesion; (9) AGE, the chronological age of the sibling reported at data collection; (10) FULL, full treatment group; (11) PART, partial treatment group; (12) DX CYS, cystic fibrosis; (13) DX SPI, spina bifida; (14) DX CAN, cancer; (15) SES, socioeconomic status; (16) INCOME, annual family income; (17) GRADE, education of the patient. From Williams *et al.* (2002). *J. Behav. Med.* **25**, 411–424, by permission of Kluwer Academic/Plenum, New York.

be used at the earliest phases of a research program—and even then with great caution.

Instrument Development: The Therapy-Related Symptom Checklist, TRSC

(Adapted from Williams *et al.* (2000, 2001) with permission of the authors and Elsevier Science.) The ISEE study above used a number of valid and reliable instruments to measure treatment outcomes. Such a complex research study could not have been undertaken without measures that had been previously constructed and validated by other researchers. Unfortunately, while the number of measurement instruments available for research is relatively large, the number of instruments available for use by nurses and others in clinic settings is small.

The average clinical consult in the United States is estimated to range between 12 and 15 minutes. Few social measurement instruments, including those designed by providers allegedly for clinic use, can be completed within such a time frame. Perhaps fewer than 36% of instruments designated as "clinical" can be self-administered to patients.

Nurses and others have developed "clinical checklists" that allow patients to subjectively identify their negative or positive responses to items on a list of symptoms, conditions, or signs common to the illness being treated. Usually, these checklists have Likert type scales. The development and use of instruments sensitive to patient subjective concerns is consistent with the recognition that these patient responses can provide essential information to improve treatment regimens. The checklist approach also is consistent with several studies that have shown that unless a systematic listing is used during the clinical consult many treatment symptoms fail to be recorded in the medical record. For example, one study found that medical records contained on average only 1.5 patient symptoms, while patients identified an average of 11 symptoms of concern to them on symptom checklists.

Distinct differences in approach exist between clinical checklist development and commonly used outcome measurement procedures. The development of most instruments designed for outcome measurements tend be more research than clinical oriented. Following the educational, behavioral, and social sciences, a common approach to instrument development in nursing has been the application of data reduction techniques such as factor analysis to produce instruments with the greatest parsimony. The small number of items remaining on such instruments, often as few as 12, is purported to measure a single patient outcome, such as quality of life (QOL). After data reduction and validation, the instrument is frequently assumed to be clinically applicable and interpretable.

Over the past 10 years, a group of nurse researchers have worked to develop an instrument that enables oncology patients to self-report treatment symptoms using a checklist. This instrument also provides researchers with valid and reliable aggregate measures of five therapy-related constructs: fatigue, eating difficulties, oropharynx disturbance, pain, and patient concern with overall treatment symptoms (labeled "symptom concern"). This checklist has been placed in medical records, and is used by clinicians to follow patient symptoms over time. This instrument is shown in Fig. 2. In order to construct an instrument with an optimal number of symptoms (items) for use by clinicians, principal component analysis was used but in a manner different from common factor analysis. These procedures are fully described and justified by Williams *et al.* (2000, 2001).

Initially, 37 symptoms were identified from the literature and clinical experience of the researchers as common to oncology patients undergoing chemotherapy, radiation, or combination therapy. The preliminary

Name: ______________ Hospital# ______________ Date: ______________

PLEASE CHECK THE PROBLEMS YOU HAVE HAD IMMEDIATELY AFTER AND SINCE YOUR LAST TREATMENT.
PLEASE CIRCLE HOW SEVERE THE PROBLEM WAS ACCORDING TO THE FOLLOWING SCALE:

0 = NONE 1 = MILD 2 = MODERATE 3 = SEVERE 4 = VERY SEVERE

EXAMPLE			*Degree of Severity*		
Pain	0	1	2	3	4
Taste Change	0	1	2	3	4
Loss of appetite	0	1	2	3	4
Nausea	0	1	2	3	4
Vomiting	0	1	2	3	4
Weight loss	0	1	2	3	4
Sore mouth	0	1	2	3	4
Cough	0	1	2	3	4
Sore throat	0	1	2	3	4
Difficulty swallowing	0	1	2	3	4
Jaw pain	0	1	2	3	4
Shortness of breath	0	1	2	3	4
Numbness of fingers and/or toes	0	1	2	3	4
Feeling sluggish	0	1	2	3	4
Depression	0	1	2	3	4
Difficulty concentrating	0	1	2	3	4
Fever	0	1	2	3	4
Bruising	0	1	2	3	4
Bleeding	0	1	2	3	4
Hair loss	0	1	2	3	4
Skin changes	0	1	2	3	4
Soreness in vein where chemotherapy was given	0	1	2	3	4
Difficulty sleeping	0	1	2	3	4
Pain	0	1	2	3	4
Decreased interest in sexual activity	0	1	2	3	4
Constipation	0	1	2	3	4
Other problems (please list)	0	1	2	3	4
______	0	1	2	3	4
______	0	1	2	3	4
______	0	1	2	3	4
______	0	1	2	3	4
______	0	1	2	3	4

Figure 2 Therapy-related symptoms checklist (TRSC). From Williams *et al.* (2001). *Int. J. Nursing Stud.* **38**, 359–367, by permission of Elsevier Science.

research checklist developed by these researchers allowed patients to rate the severity of the symptom on a 5-point scale from NONE to VERY SEVERE. The checklist was self-administered to 360 patients who were provided spaces to list other symptoms of concern to them. No additional symptoms were listed.

The data obtained were analyzed using principal component analysis. Measures of sampling adequacy were obtained with items having an adequacy of less than 0.70 excluded from further analysis. This procedure raised the Kaiser–Meyer–Olkin value above 0.80. Unlike most factor analytic approaches, the Jolliffe criterion rather than the Kaiser criterion was used to extract principal components. The former criterion retains components with eigenvalues as small as 0.70 in contrast to the more familiar Kaiser criterion, which retains eigenvalues of only 1.0 or more. Several good statistical reasons exist for choosing the Jolliffe criterion. A most important reason is that a larger amount of variance among patients on symptoms is accounted for in the analysis.

The instrument constructed referred to as the Therapy Related Symptom Checklist (TRSC) retained 25 items with loadings at or exceeding 0.50 on 14 components after varimax rotation. As previously noted, the TRSC has been found to be easily completed, can be retained in medical records (paper or electronic), appears to measure five constructs useful to clinicians and researchers, and has been assessed for discriminant validity, construct validity, and internal consistency.

While the differences between this and factor analytic approaches may appear small, about 20% more variance (79% versus about 59%) was accounted for using this approach, and six additional symptoms or items were retained on the TRSC. Few patients have used the open spaces on the instrument to list additional symptoms. Furthermore, all the items retained on components with eigenvalues between 0.70 and 1.0 correlated significantly with clinician-rated Karnofsky scores of patients. Additionally, these items were statistically significant when a linear discriminant analysis was done to predict the classification of patients into radiation therapy and chemotherapy groups.

Conclusions

Nursing has become a field of professional and advanced (graduate degree) study in the United States that is rapidly developing a distinct body of knowledge through scientific research. The outcomes approach to research is now seen by many as useful for building the knowledge base of nursing, providing accountability to clients and society more generally, and, most importantly, promoting improved care. As in most clinical disciplines, increased attention is now being given to the "translation" (or application) of research findings into clinical practice.

Much nursing research is applied and patient or practice focused. Conspicuously limited in the nursing literature is basic research in areas of methodology. More often, such research is likely to appear in the future as nurses are enrolling in doctoral programs in statistics, epidemiology, psychometrics, and areas specifically emphasizing methods and study design.

Social science research design, sampling, and analytic methods are selectively mentioned in this article. Examples are provided of nursing studies using (a) experimental research design; (b) structural equation modeling; and (c) instrument development. Literature reviews in nursing, a few of which are cited in this article, provide more detailed descriptions of research methods as well as substantive findings.

Acknowledgment

The authors thank Marlené M. Boyd for providing editorial assistance in the preparation of this manuscript.

See Also the Following Articles

Impact/Outcome Evaluation • Structural Equation Models

Further Reading

Aiken, L., Clarke, S., Sloane, D., Sochalski, J., and Silber, J. (2002). Hospital nurse staffing and patient mortality, nurse burnout, and job dissatisfaction. *JAMA* **288,** 1987–1993.

Aiken, L., Clarke, S., Sloane, D., Sochalski, J., Busse, R., Clarke, H., Giovannetti, P., Hunt, J., Rafferty, A., and Shamian, J. (2001). Nurses' reports on hospital care in five countries. *Health Affairs* **20,** 43–53.

American Psychological Association (2001). *Publication Manual of the American Psychological Association.* American Psychological Association, Washington, DC.

Annual Review of Nursing Research (1983–2003). Vols. 1–20. Springer, New York.

Barnes, C. (1969). Support of a mother in the care of a child with esophageal lye burns. *Nursing Clin. N. Am.* **4,** 53–57.

Brooten, D., Kumar, S., Brown, L., Butts, P., Finkler, S., Bakewell-Sachs, S., Gibbons, A., and Delivoria-Papadopoulos, M. (1986). A randomized clinical trial of early hospital discharge and home follow-up of very-low-birth-weight infants. *New Eng. J. Med.* **315,** 934–939.

Brooten, D., and Naylor, M. (1995). Nurses' Effect on Changing Patient Outcomes. *Image J. Nursing Schol.* **27,** 95–99.

Campbell, D., and Stanley, J. (1963). *Experimental and Quasi-Experimental Designs for Research.* Houghton Mifflin, Boston.

Campbell, N., Ritchie, L., Thain, J., Deans, H., Rawles, J., and Squair, J. (1998). Secondary prevention in coronary heart disease: A randomised trial of nurse led clinics in primary care. *Heart* **80,** 447–452.

Dulock, H., and Holzemer, W. (1991). Substruction: Improving the linkage from theory to method. *Nursing Sci. Quart.* **4,** 83–87.

Hardin, J., and Hilbe, J. (2003). *Generalized Estimating Equations.* Chapman & Hall/CRC, Boca Raton, FL.

Hinshaw, A. (1979). Problems in doing research: Planning for logical consistency among three research structures. *West. J. Nursing Res.* **1,** 250–253.

Jolliffe, I. (1986). *Principal Component Analysis.* Springer-Verlag, New York.

Kerlinger, F. (1973). *Foundations of Behavioral Research.* 2nd Ed. Holt, Rinehart, and Winston, New York.

Marek, K. (1997). Measuring the effectiveness of nursing care. *Outcomes Man. Nursing Pract.* **1,** 8–13.

Naylor, M., Brooten, D., Jones, R., Lavizzo-Mourey, R., Mezey, M., and Pauly, M. (1994). Comprehensive discharge planning for the hospitalized elderly: A randomized clinical trial. *Ann. Internal Med.* **120,** 999–1006.

Nunnally, J., and Bernstein, I. (1994). *Psychometric Theory.* 3rd Ed. McGraw-Hill, New York.

Oermann, M., and Huber, D. (1999). Patient outcomes: A measure of nursing's value. *Am. J. Nursing* **99,** 40–48.

Polit, D., and Hungler, B. (1999). *Nursing Research: Principles and Methods.* 6th Ed. Lippincott, Philadelphia.

Smith, C. (1999). Caregiving effectiveness in families managing complex technology at home: Replication of a model. *Nursing Res.* **48,** 120–128.

Taunton, R., Boyle, D., Wood, C., Hansen, H., and Bott, M. (1997). Manager leadership and retention of hospital staff nurses. *West. J. Nursing Res.* **19,** 205–226.

Waltz, C., Strickland, O., and Lenz, E. (1991). *Measurement in Nursing Research.* 2nd Ed. Davis, Philadelphia.

Ward, M., and Lindeman, C. (eds.) (1979). *Instruments for Measuring Nursing Practice and Other Health Care Variables.* DHEW Publication No. HRA 78-53 (Volume 1) and HRA 78-54 (Volume 2), Hyattsville, MD.

Williams, A., Williams, P., Ducey, K., Sears, A., and Tobin, S. (2000). A therapy-related symptom checklist, TRSC, for oncology patients: A self-report instrument. In *Individual, Family and Community: Promoting and Restoring Health and Well-Being* (P. Williams and A. Williams, eds.), pp. 85–100. JMC Press, Quezon City, Philippines.

Williams, P. (1984). The Metro-Manila developmental screening test: A normative study. *Nursing Res.* **33,** 208–212.

Williams, P., and Williams, A. (1997). Transition from hospital to home care by mothers of preterms: Path analytic results over three time periods. *Families Syst. Health* **15,** 429–446.

Williams, P., and Williams, A. (eds.) (2000). *Individual, Family and Community: Promoting and Restoring Health and Well-Being.* JMC Press, Quezon City, Philippines.

Williams, P., Ducey, K., Sears, A., Williams, A., Tobin-Rumelhart, S., and Bunde, P. (2001). Treatment type and symptom severity among oncology patients by self-report. *Int. J. Nursing Stud.* **38,** 359–367.

Williams, P., Williams, A., Graff, J., Hanson, S., Stanton, A., Hafeman, C., Liebergen, A., Leuenberg, K., Setter, R., Ridder, L., Curry, H., Barnard, M., and Sanders, S. (2002). Interrelationships among variables affecting well siblings and mothers in families of children with a chronic illness or disability. *J. Behav. Med.* **25,** 411–424.

Williams, P., Williams, A., Graff, C., Hanson, S., Stanton, A., Hafeman, C., Liebergen, A., Leuenberg, K., Setter, R., Ridder, L., Curry, H., Barnard, M., and Sanders, S. (2003). A community-based intervention for siblings and parents of chronically ill or disabled children. *J. Pediatrics* **143**, 386–393 [*Errata* (2004), **144**, 142].

Objectivity, Quest for

Majid Yar
Lancaster University, Lancaster, United Kingdom

Glossary

deduction The process of logically deriving a conclusion that necessarily follows from a given set of premises; the conclusion must be true if the premises are true.

empiricism The view that all knowledge is based on or derived from sensory experience.

epistemological anarchism The position, associated with Paul Feyerabend, that refuses to acknowledge both the existence of a universal scientific method and the legitimacy of distinguishing between science and nonscientific worldviews on the basis of the former's supposed epistemological superiority.

epistemology A branch of philosophy dealing with the nature of knowledge, what and how it is possible to know.

hypothesis Any proposition that is advanced for testing or appraisal as a generalization about a phenomenon.

incommensurability The radical incompatibility that exists between different paradigms. Different paradigms will have divergent views of fundamental features of reality. Hence, Kuhn claims that adherents of different paradigms are, in some sense, living in different worlds.

induction The method by which a general statement, suggesting a regular association between two or more variables, is derived from a series of empirical observations.

interpretation (*Verstehen*) A perspective or method that emphasizes the understanding of intentional human conduct.

ontology A branch of philosophy dealing with the nature of existence or reality.

paradigm According to Kuhn, a framework "made up of the general theoretical assumptions and laws and the techniques for their application that members of a particular scientific community adopt" that "sets the standards for legitimate work within the science it governs. It co-ordinates and directs the puzzle-solving activity of the scientists that work within it."

positivism The doctrine formulated by Comte that asserts that true knowledge about society is scientific knowledge—it is knowledge that describes and explains the coexistence and succession of observable social phenomena.

realism The ontological assertion that the objects in the world have an existence independent of our conception of them.

This article reviews the attempts to establish social science as an objective form of inquiry and the various challenges with which such objectivism has been met. It begins by outlining the ways in which the natural sciences were established as supposedly objective forms of inquiry, and how 19th century positivist social thinkers borrowed these epistemological and methodological prescriptions so as to place social inquiry on an equally objective footing. It then reviews a number of challenges to this quest for objectivity, including critiques of objectivism emanating from within the philosophy of science and criticisms of social scientific positivism associated variously with interpretive social science, feminism, and postmodernism. The article concludes by outlining the counterresponse to such critiques and the attempts to reassert the possibility of objectivity in some degree, especially in realist contributions to the philosophy of social science.

Introduction

Objectivity is the quality of any account that represents the external world as it is, independent of our subjective conceptions of it. The foundations of social inquiry are bound up with the search for such objective knowledge of the social world. This search is apparent in the philosophical and methodological programs of the social scientific pioneers of the 19th century. By treating the social world as analogous to the natural world and by following (or adapting) the methodology of natural scientific inquiry, these pioneers hoped to place social scientific knowledge on a par with that of other established sciences such as physics and biology. These methodological foundations (usually identified with positivism) continue to exert influence across the social sciences. However, the quest for objectivity has been challenged on a number of fronts from the late 19th century to the 21st. Interpretive social scientists, philosophers and sociologists of natural and social science, feminists, and postmodernists have all assaulted conventional accounts of scientific certitude and its applicability to the social world. More recently, against the supposed relativizing implications of this assault, those favoring a realist philosophy and methodology of social science have sought to reclaim in some form the possibility of objective social scientific knowledge. The dispute between objectivists and anti-objectivists remains unresolved and continues to manifest itself in the wide variety of research paradigms favored by practitioners across the disciplines.

Science and Objectivity

The quest for objectivity in the social sciences is based on the philosophical and methodological warrants given for scientific knowledge as a whole. The groundwork supporting the objectivity of science was developed by natural philosophers such as Francis Bacon. Rejecting rationalist deduction and metaphysical speculation, the modern philosophers of science favored the painstaking collection of empirical data, via observational and experimental methods, and the inductive generalization from these observations and experiments so as to arrive at generally applicable lawlike statements that covered all instances of a similar kind. The possibility of generating objective knowledge in this way was predicated on three basic assumptions:

1. That the universe is ordered and regular, such that the properties of bodies and substances, and the relations of cause and effect that pertain between them, are constant and not subject to random or arbitrary variation.
2. That it is possible neutrally to observe and record the bare facts of experience, such that all normal observers (those in possession of typical human sensory abilities and cognitive faculties) would agree on the phenomenon that has been observed.
3. That by observing the regularities and patterns presented across such observational instances it is possible to generalize to other like instances, including future occurrences. This permits us to formulate general lawlike statements of the kind, "If an acid is added to an alkaline, salt is produced" or "A moving body will continue in a straight line in uniform motion unless it is acted upon by some other force."

In short, objectivity is assured by (1) the regular and ordered character of the natural world, (2) the availability of that world for unbiased and communally available observation, and (3) the reliability of inductive inferences that extrapolate from a finite set of observational instances to anticipate further instances of a like kind.

Social Science and Objectivity: The Positivist Orthodoxy

The pioneering social scientists of the 19th century, such as Comte and Durkheim, drew on the empiricist accounts of science developed by the likes of Bacon, Locke, Hume, and the Enlightenment *philosophes* such as Diderot. August Comte (1798–1857) coined the terms positivist philosophy and social physics (as well as sociology) to postulate a science of society that would be methodologically grounded in the accumulation of empirical evidence alone. Hence, the viability of studying the social world in the manner of the natural scientists was predicated not only on the supposed objectivity of scientific method, but also on the claim that the social world was in principle of the same kind (or logical type) as the natural world. Just as the natural world was seen as regular, ordered, and governed by lawful causal relations and interconnections, so was the social. Human behavior was scientifically explicable by reference to mechanisms of cause and effect of which behavior was the outcome. Detailed observation of the occurrence of social phenomena would permit the formulation of explanatory accounts that identified their causes. Social phenomena were in principle observationally available in the same way as their natural counterparts. Thus Emile Durkheim (1858–1917) claimed that social science ought to concern itself solely with the scientific study of social facts. For Durkheim, society comprised things that existed outside of, and independently from, individuals and their beliefs about the world and thus could be studied objectively by the social scientific observer. Hence, for example, social phenomena such as crime and suicide could be identified and classified by externally manifest signs that distinguished them from other social phenomena. The appearance of these phenomena was explicable by reference to other social facts or phenomena that could be established as their causes.

The extrapolation from the natural to the social world was further supported by analogies drawn from biology and the life sciences. Just as living organisms were seen as coherent systems comprising functionally interdependent elements that acted on one another in a regular way, so the social world was conceived as a unified system in which different functions were assigned to its elements. The influence of evolutionary thinking was also notable, with thinkers from Saint-Simon, Condorcet, and Comte to Spencer and Durkheim arguing that objective evolutionary processes were responsible for social change.

The 19th century positivists' search for objectivity in social inquiry was reiterated and refined in the early 20th century by the philosophers of the Vienna Circle (such as Carnap, Neurath, and Hempel). Their doctrines are generally identified under the label logical positivism. The objectivity of scientific knowledge (natural or social) was to be assured by the application of what they called the verification principle. Only statements that could be verified by sense experience could be considered true. Any statements not of this kind were deemed to be literally meaningless. In this view, social science comprises a set of logically interrelated propositions, each of which is grounded in basic facts derived from sense data alone. The view of the logical positivists (along with revisions such as Popper's falsificationism) contributed to the consolidation of the standard view of social scientific methodology, a view dominant in the middle decades of the 20th century (especially in Anglo-American contexts). The methodological prescription of achieving objective social knowledge was grounded in a logical empiricism that took physics as its ideal model and aspired to reproduce its rigor and reliability.

The positivists' affinity with the natural sciences is evinced in their methods of inquiry. As with the natural sciences, the collection of discrete observational data is emphasized so as to permit generalizations and to establish correlations and causal connections (although the tendency is to eschew the natural scientists' use of experiments, given the near impossibility of artificially recreating social life in a laboratory setting; instead observation and comparison are favored). Equally, a premium is placed on assigning numerical values to social phenomena, permitting quantitative analysis via the use of statistical methods. The apparent association between variables, numerically rendered, thus enables causal hypotheses to be formulated and tested. The use of random sampling permits researchers to make inferential generalizations from that sample to a larger population. In this way, covering laws can be discovered, laws that could account for the appearance of particular social phenomena by relating them to their causal antecedents. In its most systematic application, such an approach yields a mathematical social science, drawing on approaches such as game theory and probabilistic modeling.

The Challenge from Interpretive Social Science

The interpretive challenge to objectivism in social science dates from the 19th century. It emerged primarily in Germany, drawing on the traditions of hermeneutics (the theory and method of textual interpretation, originally concerned with Biblical exegesis) and the *Geisteswissenschaften* ("sciences of spirit"; as opposed to "sciences of nature," *Naturwissenschaften*). The interpretive tradition contests the supposed homology between the natural and social worlds. It claims that the social is distinctive because human action (unlike the behavior of objects in the natural world) issues from motivations, these motivations themselves being constituted in accordance with the meanings or interpretations that conscious human subjects give to the world and their own experiences. Consequently, human conduct cannot be subjected to any explanatory model that sees it as the mechanical effect of causal forces that act on individuals or groups. Nor can humans be treated in behavioral terms like nonhuman animals, attributing human conduct to a stimulus-response mechanism. Humans are instead viewed as agents who attach meanings to the world they encounter and who consequently choose to act in ways that are consonant with those meanings.

The translation of this viewpoint into social scientific methodology is associated primarily with the economic historian and sociologist Max Weber (1864–1920). Weber argued for the methodological centrality of *Verstehen* ("understanding" or "interpretation") in social science. Any valid account of social phenomena (i.e., Why it is that individuals or groups act or behave as they do) has to take into account the meaningful and motivated character of those actions. It is not enough to observe patterns in outward behavior and to link these to other factors, events, or conditions so as to derive a cause-effect type hypothesis. Rather, investigation must give centrality to understanding the meanings that actors themselves attach to their experiences, circumstances and activities. Thus, in his most celebrated study, *The Protestant Ethic and the Spirit of Capitalism*, Weber opposed those accounts that sought to explain the emergence of modern capitalism by sole reference to objective factors, such as the organization of productive forces, the development of new techniques and technologies, demographic changes, the relations of supply and demand, and so on. Instead, he sought to uncover the interpretive frameworks or structures of meaning that disposed certain sociocultural groups to radically reform their economic behavior, thereby setting in motion the process of extensive capital accumulation.

However, beyond a general recognition of the meaningful character of human action, interpretive social scientists have been divided about the extent to which this commitment can be reconciled with the striving for objectivity. Some, following Weber's cue, insist that it is possible for the social scientist to render an objective account of actors' subjective meanings; a systematic method of interpretive inquiry makes this goal achievable, at least in principle. Moreover, actors' motives or reasons can be treated as the causes of their actions, thus permitting the investigator to identify the causal antecedents of particular forms of action. Finally, the supposedly ordered character of human behavior permits the social scientist to make lawlike generalizations (or statements of tendency) from interpretively apprehended data.

However, other interpretive positions have cast greater doubt on the possibility of achieving objective social scientific knowledge. The sociology developed by the symbolic interactionists in the early decades of the 20th century, for example, stressed the symbolically constructed character of actors' worlds, including objects, other people, and individuals' own self-awareness. As such, reality is always and inevitably a variable construct, and this construct is not a fixed formation but continually in the process of production and transformation through interaction and communication with others. Meanings, motivations and actions are thus (1) inextricably intertwined, (2) continually in the process of production, and (3) specific to particular people in particular social-interactional contexts. This carries a number of significant implications. First, social phenomena cannot be conceived as social facts existing independently of subjective conceptions of them; rather, what comes to count as part of a particular class of phenomena (say, crime or deviance) is the contingent outcome of actors' definitions. Second, given the context-specificity of understanding and actions, it is deemed problematic to generalize interpretive accounts across different contexts and interactional engagements. Hence, deriving covering laws (of the kind "When confronted with situation X, individuals will tend to act in manner Y") is likely to lead to inappropriate and distorting explanations. Third, given that symbolic mediation is deemed a universal and fundamental feature of social life, the social scientist him- or herself cannot be exempted from its implications. In other words, the investigator cannot offer a *stricto sensu* objective account of others' subjective understandings, but only a (socially and contextually embedded) interpretation of others' interpretations. Hence, there is no Archimedean point of epistemic neutrality, independent of subjective conceptions, from which the scientist can view the social world. The last point has been captured by Anthony Giddens in terms of the double hermeneutic of social science—just as lay actors produce their world and act on it through their interpretations, so social scientists themselves re-interpret this already interpretively generated domain.

At the most extreme end in the interpretive continuum, the linguistically, culturally, and symbolically constructed character of the social world has been claimed to necessitate a relativist conception of social science. Thus, for example, in 1958 Peter Winch, drawing on Wittgenstein's notion of language games as forms of life, argues that the "truths" pertaining to social phenomena are relative or specific to the order of social practices within which they are embedded. Hence, the aspiration to generalize across local contexts is based on a fundamental misapprehension about the contextual relativity of any given phenomena. Moreover, there is no way of epistemically privileging any one account of reality over any other, including that of the social scientist. The kinds of criteria habitually mobilized by scientists to warrant their claims (evidence, proof, rationality, logical inference, and so on) have no special status, being specific to the practices of inquiry (or form of life) in which they feature.

The Challenge from Philosophy of Science

The possibility of objectivity in the social sciences has also come under challenge as a result of developments in the philosophy of science. The philosophy of science in the 20th century was marked by an increasing skepticism about the picture of epistemically neutral inquiry propounded by objectivist accounts. A number of claims were raised, each of which impacted on the equation of science with objectively valid and universal knowledge. Their effect on the philosophy and methodology of social science has been particularly marked.

First, there was a renewed interest in the skeptical aspects of Humean epistemology, especially in relation to causation. Conventional accounts of scientific method invoked the objective status of relations of cause and effect—these were presented as ontologically prior to and independent of human perceptions. In *An Inquiry Concerning Human Understanding*, Hume claimed that causal relations between events are subjective attributions made by observers. Instead of being real relations between things in the world, causal connections are impositions made by humans in order to organize their sense experiences in a coherent way. Causation, in short, is a way of organizing essentially unconnected sensations, something we learn to do from custom and habit. This being the case, it follows that the relations of different phenomena in causal chains (on which scientific explanation depends) are a contingent outcome of subjective cognitive activities—there is no essential or objective relation between things in the world that necessitates such a connection.

A second philosophical objection posed against objectivism is what is commonly referred to as the problem of induction. Unlike logico-deductive inferences (wherein a conclusion *necessarily* follows from given premises), inductive inferences are logically underwarranted because the validity of the conclusions can only ever be probabilistic in character. That is to say, inductive inference is based on a generalization from a finite set of past observations, extending the observed pattern or relation to other future instances or instances occurring elsewhere. However, there is no *logical* reason why the same pattern or relation should hold in the future or in other places—it can only be a judgment of likelihood based on the fact that this pattern or relation was evident in the instances of a phenomenon already observed. This implies that the transition from a finite set of observations to lawlike generalizations (from "some to all" in Hume's words) cannot be warranted. Thus Karl Popper, for example, claimed that no observationally based generalization about the world can ever be verified as true.

A third, and even more troubling, objection to objectivism concerns the possibility of empirical observations that are free from any prior conceptions about the world on the part of the observer. The objection lodged by philosophers of science often passes under the label the theory-dependence of observation. It is pointed out that even apparently simple and uncontentious observational statements in fact depend on preexisting presuppositions about the world and mobilize already existing cognitive schema that are historically or culturally contingent. Put most simply, what we observe is crucially dependent on the assumptions and knowledge we already have about the world. Moreover, the activity of observation in scientific inquiry necessarily entails a process of selection—only certain phenomena are selected as noteworthy and relevant for the development of an explanatory hypothesis. The criteria for selection can only be derived from presuppositions on the part of the observer vis-à-vis what is likely to be relevant for formulating an explanation, and this notion of relevance is dependent on existing ideas about how the world works.

This point in particular led to the revision of the objectivist account of science. In the work of Thomas Kuhn (1922–1996), scientific practices and criteria of validity are depicted as relative to socially and historically specific paradigms or frameworks of theoretical assumptions. What counts as a legitimate scientific claim will always be determined on the basis of the shared presuppositions that have dominance in a scientific research community in a particular time and place. Because each of these paradigms or frameworks comprises self-contained and interdependent assumptions of a fundamental kind, they are in principle incommensurable with one another. That is to say, they are mutually exclusive standpoints on the world, and there is no standpoint external to such a paradigm from which their competing claims could be assessed or arbitrated.

The work of Paul Feyerabend (1924–1994) presents the most strenuous development of the relativistic implications in Kuhn's work (which Kuhn himself resisted). Feyerabend called his own position one of epistemological anarchism. He claimed that there is no method on the basis of which one paradigmatic structure can be privileged over another. Nor, Feyerabend argued, is it even possible to distinguish some privileged form of knowledge called science from other, supposedly lesser, forms of knowledge; that is, the very privileging of scientific paradigms over other nonscientific worldviews (such as common sense, ideology, magic, and superstition) cannot be sustained. What we call science is, for Feyerabend, just another way of knowing the world, and it has no intrinsic superiority to any other. This being the case, the quest for an objective social science that has a privileged view point on the social world would have to be abandoned.

The Challenges from Feminism and Postmodernism

Quite apart from the impact of philosophy of science, aspirations for social scientific objectivity have also come under pressure from anti-objectivist positions developed within the social sciences themselves. We have already noted the critique developed within the interpretive tradition. More recently, strenuous lines of objection have emerged from feminist and postmodernist perspectives. Each has mobilized both epistemological and normative critiques of objectivist science.

Advocates of feminist epistemology have claimed that objectivist science is profoundly engendered with a masculinist or androcentric bias; dominant masculine experiences, perceptions, ideologies, and values are said to significantly structure the epistemological presuppositions and methodological procedures of mainstream science. Thus, for example, it is claimed that this view of science privileges cognition, rationality, and disinterestedness at the expense of the aesthetic, affective, and somatic dimensions of our experiences. Hence, objectivism mobilizes a distorted and incomplete conception of the knowing subject. Normatively, this view point has been criticized for its imbrication with patterns of male domination in society—the equation of rationality and emotional neutrality with masculinity (and irrationality and emotionality with femininity) amounts to an ideological maneuver that privileges male accounts of the world. This has led some feminist scholars (for example, Evelyn Fox Keller) to advocate the development of a feminist science, one that embodies the neglected epistemological virtues of empathy, holism, and intuitive understanding. In the social sciences, this had led feminists to call for a rejection of objectivist aspirations, disinterested observation, and quantification. Instead, there has emerged an advocacy of qualitative research predicated on interpretation, emotional engagement, and social participation on the part of the researcher. In its most radical form, this appeal to feminist epistemology has lead to the eschewal of formal description and analysis, supplanting it with literary, poetic, and artistic experiments in narrating subjective social experience.

Postmodern thinkers have mobilized epistemological, sociological, and normative critiques to similarly repudiate objectivity, claiming it to be neither possible nor desirable. The philosophies of Kuhn, Winch, and Wittgenstein (among others) have been mobilized so as to press their supposedly relativist implications. Jean-Francois Lyotard viewed the equation of epistemological legitimacy with objectivity as the way in which modern science rhetorically legitimates its authority. By claiming that its criterion of epistemological legitimacy is universally valid, science has set itself up as the sole arbiter of what is to count as knowledge. Yet, Lyotard claimed, the appeal to totalizing, transcendent, and timeless conceptions of legitimacy is now received with incredulity. The loss of faith in such universal criteria exposes the underlying plurality and relativity of language games, each of which has its own internal standards of validity. Behind the rhetoric of objective science, lies the reality of multiple view points that are radically incompatible and cannot be subordinated to some context-independent criteria of legitimacy. The quest for objectivity has also been challenged on political and normative grounds. It is claimed that the search to establish generalizations and laws leads to the violation or suppression of differences and divergences that characterize social life. Zygmunt Bauman identified the objectivist standpoint with the aspiration for legislative prediction and control of society, and as such it stands against human freedom and the cultivation of distinctiveness. In place of the objectivity of science, social inquiry ought to orient itself to interpretive explication of the very plurality of standpoints and experiences that the social world comprises and should eschew the temptation to see its own interpretations as epistemologically superior.

Resistance to the Anti-Objectivist Critique

Despite the many different cases made against the quest for objectivity, much of mainstream social science continues to operate (implicitly or explicitly) under the objectivist influence of the positivist legacy. A number of reasons can be identified for this:

1. The penetration of anti-objectivist critiques has been very uneven, varying in extent across disciplines and subdisciplines and across national and regional research traditions. Thus, for example, although Anglophone sociology has incorporated these positions to a considerable extent, the research paradigms in, say, mainstream economics and psychology retain a strong objectivist orientation.

2. Although the anti-objectivist arguments might be accepted in principle, it has been argued that the practical demands of social inquiry necessitate the retention of some methodological criteria by which to discriminate between more and less sound, partial, or distorted accounts.

3. It has been argued that anti-objectivist accounts of the relativizing kind are logically self-defeating and hence epistemologically vacuous. That is to say, any claim of the kind "all knowledge is relative" inevitably encompasses itself within that claim; hence, the relativist claim can offer no epistemological warrant for its own validity because by logical implication it is itself nonobjective.

4. There have been serious and ongoing philosophical attempts to refute the relativist critique of science. For example, W. V. Quine's (1908–2001) defense of observational language, in a manner conducive to empiricist accounts of science, has been very influential. Others, such as Hilary Putnam (1926–) and Richard Rorty (1931–) have sought to validate a general scientific method on pragmatic grounds (drawing on the philosophical position developed a century or so earlier by C. S. Peirce, William James, and others). For pragmatists, the truth of a belief is distinguished by its leading to a successful action, by the demonstration of its practical efficacy. From this viewpoint, the conventional procedures of scientific inquiry are validated not by some transcendental epistemological warrant but by the fact that they generate robust knowledge that works, that is, that furnishes consistent explanations and predictions about the behavior of the phenomena in question. Hence, for Rorty, it is "better for us to believe" the truths generated by tried-and-tested scientific methods precisely because such truths "are successful in helping us do what we want to do."

Reclaiming Objectivity: The Realist Response

The most significant recent intervention in the debate about objectivity in the social sciences has been that adapted from scientific realism, often passing under the label critical realism. Realists reject the presuppositions of both empiricism (on which the positivist orthodoxy draws) and the relativizing consequences of radical anti-objectivism. Empiricists who follow Hume maintain that any objective characteristics possessed by the external world remain in principle unknowable from the standpoint of a knower, who is limited to his or her subjective sense perceptions of it. Nevertheless, they argue that knowledge generated from the careful attendance to observationally acquired sense data can be judged robust if it is consistent with what we observe of the world and hence enables us to understand it. Antipositivists go much further and insist that not only are the objective properties attributed to things in the world a matter of cognitive construction, but that such constructions are contextually (socially, historically, and politically) specific, and in principle no epistemological discrimination can be made between different constructions of reality.

In contrast, realists such as Roy Bhaskar start from the claim that the external world is characterized by ontological structures, properties, and mechanisms that are objective in character—they are not produced by our subjective conceptions of them. Hence, relations of cause and effect, for example, are mind-independent features of the real world. Things that exist in the world have their own natures and causal powers. To this proposition is added the further claim that in perception we mentally apprehend qualities and objects that are part of that objectively existing world. Hence, the objects of our sense-making activity are not sense perceptions, sense data or phenomena, but real and independently existing features of things themselves. The ontology of the social world is no different from that of the natural world in this respect—real effects occur as the result of real causes. Thus, for example, our reasons for acting can be treated as the causes of our behavior, the latter being an effect of the former. Similarly, social structures are real features of the social world that will have effects quite independently of whether we recognize them or not.

However, critical realists, as the name implies, are not naïve in the sense that our knowledge claims are held to *necessarily* uncover the real structure of social reality. It is quite possible for our particular descriptions of the social world to misapprehend its real features or to be incomplete by having failed to identify all the relevant mechanisms and causes that produce a particular effect or behavior. Nevertheless, because real social structures, objects, and processes are deemed to exist in and of themselves, the production of an adequate account of them becomes possible through scientific investigation that is (1) methodologically refined and (2) open-ended, so as to leave space for the continual correction, revision, and elaboration of our explanatory hypotheses. As Bhaskar put it in 1978, "Things exist and act independently of our descriptions, but we can only know them under particular descriptions. … Science … is the systematic attempt to express in thought the structures and ways of acting of things that exist and act independently of thought."

This position thus attempts to incorporate (1) the view that social reality is an independent order with objective properties and causes and (2) an acknowledgement of the epistemological caution and revisability that scientific attempts to uncover that reality ought to adopt. In such a formulation, the quest for objectivity in social science is reaffirmed, albeit with a modesty that takes cognizance of the objections that have been lodged against a crudely objectivist conception of social inquiry. Nevertheless, practitioners remain profoundly divided over what an objective social scientific view point might entail, whether or not such a stance is in principle possible, and whether or not it is in fact desirable to aspire to such a goal.

See Also the Following Articles

Chapin, Francis Stuart • Deduction and Induction

Further Reading

Bauman, Z. (1992). *Intimations of Postmodernity.* Routledge, London.

Bhaskar, R. (1978). *A Realist Theory of Science.* 2nd Ed. Harverster Press, Sussex, UK.

Chalmers, A. F. (1982). *What Is This Thing Called Science? An Assessment of the Nature and Status of Science and Its Methods.* 2nd Ed. Open University Press, Milton Keynes, UK.

Feyerabend, P. (1975). *Against Method: Outline of an Anarchist Theory of Knowledge.* New Left Books, London.

Hughes, J., and Sharrock, W. (1990). *The Philosophy of Social Research.* 3rd Ed. Longman, Essex, UK.

Keller, E. F. (1985). *Reflections on Gender and Science.* Yale University Press, New Haven, CT.

Kuhn, T. (1996). *The Structure of Scientific Revolutions.* 3rd Ed. University of Chicago Press, Chicago, IL.

Lyotard, J.-F. (1987). *The Postmodern Condition: A Report On Knowledge.* Manchester University, Manchester, UK.

Outhwaite, W. (1987). *New Philosophies of Social Science: Realism, Hermenutics and Critical Theory.* Macmillan, Basingstoke, UK.

Rorty, R. (1980). *Philosophy and the Mirror of Nature.* Blackwell, Oxford.

Sayer, A. (1992). *Method in Social Science: A Realist Approach.* 2nd Ed. Routledge, London.

Winch, P. (1958). *The Idea of a Social Science.* Routledge, London.

Observational Studies

Anastasia Kitsantas
George Mason University, Fairfax, Virginia, USA

Herbert W. Ware
George Mason University, Fairfax, Virginia, USA

Panagiota Kitsantas
East Carolina University, Greenville, North Carolina, USA

Glossary

continuous recording The observer records the sequence of behaviors using predetermined protocols.

duration recording The observer records the time that elapses between the initiation and conclusion of the targeted behavior.

event sampling The observer samples and records the occurrence of a particular form of behavior.

frequency recording The observer tallies the number of times the targeted behaviors occur.

interval recording The observer defines the types of behavior that occur in an interval of specified duration.

lags The observer records the number of events or time units between sequential events.

nonsequential observation The observer records a behavior as a discrete interval or event.

sequential observation The observer records the continuing stem of a behavior.

time sampling The observer samples a particular time period and records the focal behaviors that occur during that time period.

Observational studies are an essential methodological approach for the study of human behavior among many disciplines: sociology, anthropology, education, management, nursing, and psychology. The aim of this entry is to provide the reader with an overview of the scientific methods of using fundamental observational techniques to conduct research. Emphasis is placed on the design, measurement, and data analysis of observational methods. Challenges and practical and ethical issues are also discussed.

Introduction

Observation is an important vehicle of data collection and is used widely in many fields including psychology, sociology, education, anthropology, nursing, and management. It offers the advantage of gathering data of overt behavior directly and systematically. Observation was the most important research tool used by early intellectual forerunners such as Darwin and Freud aiming to study different populations and behaviors in laboratory, clinical, and naturalistic settings. Today, it remains the preferred method for investigating nonverbal behaviors as well as very complex social interactions.

Defining Observational Studies

The meaning of observational studies has two origins: in the context of experimental design it refers to, according to McKinlay, studies "concerned with investigating relationships among characteristics of human populations, after the manner of an experiment, but comparing groups among which the 'treatments' are not randomly assigned." In this context, the observer does not have any control on the subject's exposure status. These characteristics underline the main differences between observational and experimental studies. In the framework of social measurement, observational studies are those in which a researcher seeks to quantify interactive behavior, either human or animal, by systematically assigning codes to behavioral events as they unfold over time. This quantification may occur in either a naturalistic or an experimental setting. Such studies are particularly useful when the interest is in processes (as opposed to outcomes), or in characterization of the stream of behavior through objective quantification by one or more observers. These characterizations are an alternative to those employing tools of survey research that can be biased by the respondents (e.g., self-reporting techniques, interviews). The execution of systematic observational studies requires attention (a) to specifics in design; (b) to the details of measurement procedures and their quality; and (c) to the analysis applied to the data. These topics and some of the challenges associated with implementing observational studies are addressed below.

Design

The design of an observational study is optimally affected by research questions and the related hypotheses. That is, what does the researcher wish to prompt or support? Additionally, the research questions and hypotheses have major implications for what is to be observed and under what conditions; for defining behaviors; for methods of collecting and recording data; and for data analysis. Therefore, theory and prior research determine what behaviors and or interactions are the focus of the observation. For example, is the researcher interested in teacher initiatives or pupil initiatives? In a nursing situation, is the focus the nurses' behavior or the patients' behavior or the interaction between the two? The behaviors or interactions of interest affect (a) the type of setting for the observation; (b) the sampling and recording or coding procedures for the observation; and (c) whether the observation is intrusive or unobtrusive.

Type of Setting and Researcher Control

Data collection associated with observational studies may be gathered either in a naturalistic setting, as with field studies, or in a more controlled, laboratory setting. The investigator may simply observe the stream of interaction without any manipulation of the context or introduce an intervention in which some aspect of the setting is manipulated. In the naturalistic setting, the researcher describes what occurs, including natural changes in the environment of the interaction. In the laboratory or experimental context, the researcher manipulates some aspect of the environment. Thus, a naturalistic context can become an experimental or laboratory setting if the researcher introduces an intervention.

What Is to Be Observed, Sampled, and Recorded

Typically, some form of behavior or interaction is the observational object. It might be the behavior of an individual being considered for social support services, an aspect of teacher–pupil interaction in a classroom, or the interaction of child, mother, and grandmother in a home setting. The form of the observed behavior might be sequential or nonsequential. In the sequential case, the continuing stream of behavior is observed and recorded. In this context, the interest is in the dependencies among successive behaviors. In the non-sequential instance, discrete intervals or events are recorded. This distinction between sequential and non-sequential observation affects both the form of sampling and the methods of recording employed in the observation period.

The more common methods of sampling in observational studies are event sampling and time sampling. In event sampling, the observer looks for the occurrence of a particular form of behavior. For example, in the classroom setting, it might be an open-ended question asked by a teacher. In the child–mother–grandmother context, it might be the mother's or grandmother's support of a child's attention. In these two examples, both behaviors—the questioning and the support—are discrete events. In time sampling, the observer samples a particular time period and records the focal behaviors that occur during that time period. Time sampling involves observation of behaviors in intermittent points in time for periods of predetermined duration.

Once sampling procedures have been identified, defining the behaviors to be observed or developing behavior codes is a critical task in observational studies. Coding of observational data consists of recording events as they occur in time. A behavior code is a written description of the events to be observed and recorded. In addition, a behavior code outlines certain rules regarding how the observation and recording are to be evaluated. The use of existing and appropriate coding systems of known measurement characteristics is recommended over case-specific procedures when possible. However, researchers do develop their own schemes reflecting the variables under study. Overall, attributes of the coding must include a scheme for the coding; specification of coding entries; and extended definitions. Generally, four major recording procedures are reported in the literature: duration recording, frequency recording, interval recording, and continuous recording. In duration recording, the observer records the time that elapses between the initiation and conclusion of the targeted behavior. In frequency recording, the observer tallies the number of times the targeted behaviors occur. In interval recording, the observer specifies the types of behavior that occur in an interval of specified duration. In continuous recording, the observer records the sequence of behaviors using predetermined protocols. Recording methods should facilitate converting observed behavior into quantitative data.

Intrusive vs. Unobtrusive Observation

The settings in which behaviors are recorded differ in terms of whether the observer is actually present during the occurrence of the interaction, in which case the observer intrudes on the setting, or the observer does the recording from a taping—audio or video—of the interaction. In this latter case, the recording may be intrusive but the observer is not the source of the intrusion. Although potentially intrusive, recordings do offer the advantage associated with observer convenience and the use of multiple observers to code the same setting. The latter is useful in training observers and establishing observer agreement or reliability. In addition, some forms of technology used in coding observations are facilitated by the availability of recordings of the observational setting.

Measurement

Measurement is the means by which replication and comparison become possible in observational studies. Measurement here is complex. The complexities relate to obtaining reliable, accurate, and valid observation. Such observation requires care in developing detailed observation manuals, and in selecting, training, and monitoring observers.

The Observation Process: Training and Monitoring Observers

Observing is a human process. The information about behavior that is essential in the social sciences depends heavily on the observing person. Observational studies require the careful selection of observers and their careful training in using observational forms and in recording and evaluating behavior to acceptable levels of agreement and accuracy. Thus, coding schemes must be clearly defined and articulated. Some researchers call for developing an observational manual (see Hartman) that provides explicit definitions and examples assisting the observers in making accurate evaluations and preventing them from drawing unnecessary inferences. Training observers with observations of videotapes accompanied by use of the observational forms and coding schemes is a means of achieving desired levels of rater agreement or reliability. A level of interrater reliability of at least 0.70 has been recommended. Accuracy and reliability are enhanced through monitoring observers during actual data collection.

Agreement, Reliability, and Validity

The criteria for accurate, reliable, and valid observation are of critical importance. Generally, these relate to minimizing error in recording behavior. Traditionally, reliability has been defined as the degree to which data are consistent. However, reliability in observational research is greatly influenced by the continuous interaction between the observer and the recording system. This influence leads to obtaining between and within-observer consistency. In between-observer consistency (or interobserver agreement or interobserver reliability), two or more observers observe the same event. In within-observer consistency (or intraobserver agreement or intraobserver reliability), the same observer observes the behavior of the same subjects under the same conditions. However, there is not universal agreement on the conceptual definitions of these terms.

Methods of computing interobserver agreement include percentages, occurrence agreement (nonoccurrence), and the statistic Kappa. Overall, these indices describe the degree of agreement between observers. A researcher who obtains a high agreement index may conclude that the observers are interchangeable, and that data from any of the observers are free from measurement error. In regard to intraobserver reliability, problems arise from the fact that identical behaviors and conditions cannot be replicated to estimate the consistency of an observer. Pearson's r could be used to compute interobserver reliability, if the classical parallel test assumptions are met between two or more observers. Those assumptions require that two observers produce the same means and standard deviations. Suen argues that this could be possible if the observers are matched (e.g., gender, education, and training). Finally, the intraclass correlation, which does not require the classical parallel assumptions, can be used as an alternative to the intraobserver reliability index and interobserver agreement indices. The approach estimates through analysis of variance the error from different sources.

Validity in observational studies requires that the observation procedure measure the behavior it purports to measure. An important aspect of validity is the accuracy with which the observational protocols measure the behavior of interest. Accuracy refers to the extent to which there is correspondence between an observer's scores and the criterion (e.g., scores from an expert observer). Other kinds of validity in addition to accuracy are required in observational research. Generally, validity in research centers on content, criterion, and construct validity. Content validity refers to behaviors that are to be observed based on the theory that represents a construct. Criterion validity can be established by determining what behaviors relate to the concept under study. The source of those behaviors is the relevant theory of interest to the researcher. Finally, when a set of behaviors are produced deductively from the theory, and postulated to measure a construct, then validation of the construct is necessary.

Improvement in the reliability and validity of an observational study can be accomplished with the aid of technologies. Technologies such as audio recorders, video recorders and computer programs may result in higher reliability and validity by allowing the observer to review (play back) the event many times. This also allows the observer to record several different behaviors that occur closely together and the opportunity of having more than one observer, thereby increasing interobserver reliability.

Data Analysis

Some commonly used descriptive measures and inferential statistics for nonsequential and sequential observations are presented below; aspects of drawing causal inferences in observational studies are discussed.

Descriptive Statistics for Observational Data

In observational studies, the branch of descriptive statistics is composed of a variety of tools whose selection for data representation depends mainly on the manner in which a data set has been recorded. Some simple summary statistics include frequencies and rates. A frequency of an event represents a count, which indicates the number of times that particular event has occurred. Simple event sequences can be represented as frequencies. Frequencies, however, should be converted to rates, which are more informative and appropriate for comparisons across different cases since they take into consideration the element of time in observing a particular behavior.

Probabilities and percentages are also important descriptive statistical tools. Specifically, if a procedure is described as event-based, a percentage or a probability denotes the proportion of events that were coded in a particular way relative to the total number of events coded. Additionally, when onset and offset times are recorded (i.e., the time that elapses between the initiation and conclusion of an activity or behavior) for a behavior, proportions of total time that correspond to different activities can be recorded along with the activity. The selection of a percentage or a probability as means of describing a data set can be justified by the research question posed. Mean event durations can be reported whenever time information is recorded. These measurements are obtained by dividing the amount of time coded for a particular event by the number of times that event was coded. Finally, transitional probabilities constitute a key descriptive measure for sequential observational data. Transitional probabilities are conditional probabilities that indicate the probability of events that occurred at different times. They can be summarized graphically in state transition diagrams, which provide a powerful visual tool for events that are sequenced in time.

Overall, mean durations, percentages, and probabilities provide redundant information. Consequently, researchers choose those that are most informative, given the behavior under investigation. Additional considerations are taken into account when using these summary statistics since the usual parametric assumptions must be satisfied (e.g., a normal distribution of scores).

Nonsequential and Sequential Analyses

In observational studies, statistical analysis and inference are contingent upon numerous elements including the research question, study design, and data coding. Specifically, in a sequential data set where dependencies among behaviors are of interest, the researcher may utilize tools of data analysis that differ from those used in a nonsequential setting. In a nonsequential setting where time is not considered important, the choice of data analytic procedures depends mainly on the research question under investigation. Some commonly utilized data analysis techniques are principal components analysis, orthogonal factor analysis, and discriminant procedures. In principal components analysis, the focus is on transforming the observations into uncorrelated components, while in factor analysis the purpose may be either to produce a set of uncorrelated or correlated factors. In both techniques, the common goal is data reduction. On the other hand, the discriminant function finds the linear combination that best discriminates between two events or behaviors. This procedure is designed for cases where it is difficult to provide an independent check on classifying events.

A traditional approach of sequential data analysis involves tools such as a t-test, ANOVA, or multiple regression methodologies. For instance, these techniques could be used in a two-group design where a researcher may be interested in determining whether a sequential pattern is more characteristic of one group than the other. In other cases, where the purpose is to define a particular sequence by reporting the frequency and probability of its occurrence, a z-score can be utilized to determine the extent to which an observed frequency exceeds its expected value. In general, z-score computations must be based on sufficient data in order to justify significance of

Table I An Example of a 2 × 2 Table with Specified Cell Frequencies

	E	Ê
A	*a*	*b*
Ã	*c*	*d*

results. The *z*-score, however, does not provide information on the magnitude of an effect. If individual or group differences or effects of research factors are of interest, then statistics such as the odds ratio, log odds ratio, Yule's Q and ϕ are utilized. Odds ratio is one of the most common statistics for 2 × 2 tables. The odds ratio varies from 0 to infinity and equals 1 when the odds are the same for two groups. The natural logarithm (ln) of the odds ratio, which is called log odds ratio, is relatively easy to compute and interpret. Yule's Q is a transformation of the odds ratio. It ranges from −1 to +1 with zero indicating no effect. For instance, let us consider a 2 × 2 table (Table I) that consists of events A and E and their complements Ã and Ẽ (where rows represent lag 0 and columns lag 1) with individual cells, which are labeled *a*, *b*, *c*, and *d*, representing cell frequencies. The odds ratio can be estimated as: odds ratio = *ad*/*bc*. The log odds ratio is expressed as ln (*ad*/*bc*), while Yule's Q becomes

$$ab - bc/ad + bc.$$

Another common index for 2 × 2 tables is the ϕ coefficient or the Pearson product–moment correlation coefficient. This statistic also varies from −1 to 1 with zero indicating no association. Although, there are some computational differences between Yule's Q and the ϕ coefficient, Bakeman, McArthur, and Quera concluded that in testing for group differences, the choice of one method versus the other has no impact on inference.

A second approach to sequence detection includes the lag-sequential method. Lags are defined as the number of events or time units between sequential events. Its purpose is to detect commonly occurring sequences by examining codes pairwisely.

Observational data summarized in multiway contingency tables can also be analyzed using log-linear techniques. Log-linear analyses offer an advantageous alternative to lag-sequential analysis. Regardless of overlapping sampling or repetition of consecutive codes, log-linear analysis provides an integrated method for determining whether there are effects at various lags.

Drawing Causal Inferences

In observational studies, statistical associations do not always imply causality. Associations can be classified as spurious, indirect and causal. Spurious associations are the result of selection bias, information bias, and chance. In contrast, indirect associations, which stem from confounding, are real but not causal. Confounding can be controlled by restriction, matching or stratification, while bias can be examined through a variety of techniques. In general, causal inferences in observational studies require a coherent unbiased association between an exposure and outcome. According to Rosenbaum, a coherent association is one that is consistent with the hypothesis under consideration. Criteria for judgment of causal associations include temporal sequence (did exposure precede outcome?), strength and consistency of association, specificity (does exposure lead only to outcome?), coherence with existing knowledge, and analogy (is the association similar to others?). These guidelines for judgment of associations in observational studies can be an asset not only to the researcher but also to the reader in deciding whether a casual link exists.

Challenges

Problems and Ethical Considerations in Observational Studies

Observation of human behavior on interaction is rarely a neutral occasion. How the observer and the observed react to each other and how these reactions affect the contents of the observational record can be problematic. Issues of this kind, as applied to the observers, are generally subsumed under the label of bias and can arise from the gender, race, or cultural perspective of the observer. Additionally, bias can also arise from what the observer views as the intended purpose of the observation. Fatigue, intention, or boredom of the observer may also affect the accuracy, reliability, and validity of the observations. From the perspective of the person being observed, the presence of the observer or the act of being observed has a potential to affect the behavior of the observed. In order to eliminate these problems, observers should record events as unobtrusively as possible.

Other challenges in observational studies are related to recording and coding procedures and enhancing the accuracy, reliability, and validity of those procedures. Laying the groundwork by establishing a training instruction booklet with explicit instructions of what is to be observed and how it is to be recorded and evaluated may positively affect validity and reliability of the study. Reducing the error variance between and within-observers has the potential for increasing the accuracy and reliability of the observations. Additionally, refinement of the observational procedures through the use of generazibility theory can offer promise for addressing these issues. Finally, given that in observational studies replication of a setting is virtually impossible, it is difficult to establish validity using traditional psychometric procedures wherein an instrument is correlated through its use in multiple contexts.

As with any type of research there are ethical considerations that must be taken into account. Research involving observation requires that confidentiality of the participants is protected and that there is no exposure to any physical or psychological harm. Researchers should consider having each coder sign a written statement emphasizing the importance of data confidentiality. Ethical considerations should be outlined clearly in observation manuals.

See Also the Following Articles

Explore, Explain, Design • Research Designs • Stratified Sampling Types

Further Reading

Bakeman, R. (2000). Behavioral observation and coding. In *Handbook of Research Methods in Social and Personality Psychology* (H. T. Reis and C. M. Judd, eds.), pp. 138–159. Cambridge University Press, Cambridge, UK.

Bakeman, R., and Gottman, J. M. (1997). *Observing Interaction: An Introduction to Sequential Analysis,* 2nd Ed. Cambridge University Press, Cambridge, UK.

Bakeman, R., McArthur, D., and Quera, V. (1996). Detecting group differences in sequential association using sampled permutations: Log odds, kappa, and phi compared. *Behav. Res. Methods Instr. and Comput.* **24,** 554–559.

Brennan, R. L. (1991). Statistical models for behavioral observations: A review. *J. Education. Stat.* **16**(3), 253–266.

Brennan, R. L. (1983). *Elements of Generalizability Theory.* American College Testing Program, Iowa City, IA.

Cairns, R. B. (1979). *The Analysis of Social Interactions: Methods, Issues, and Illustrations.* Erlbaum, Hillsdale, NJ.

Gottman, J. M. (1978). Nonsequential data analysis techniques in observational research. In *Observing Behavior* (G. P. Sackett, ed.), Vol. 2, pp. 45–61. University Park Press, Baltimore.

Grimes, D. A., and Schulz, K. F. (2002). Bias and causal associations in observational research. *Lancet* **359,** 248–252.

Hartman, D. P. (1982). Assessing the dependability of observational data. In *Using Observers to Study Behavior: New Directions for Methodology of Social and Behavioral Science* (D. P. Hartmann, ed.), pp. 51–65. Jossey–Bass, San Fransico.

Hennekens, C. H., and Buring, J. E. (1987). *Epidemiology in Medicine.* Little, Brown and Company, Boston.

McKinlay, S. M. (1975). The design and analysis of the observational study—A review. *J. Am. Statist. Assoc.* **70**(351), 503–520.

Parke, R. D. (1979). Interactional designs. In *The Analysis of Social Interactions: Methods, Issues, and Illustrations* (R. B. Cairns, ed.). Erlbaum, Hillsdale, NJ.

Rogosa, D., and Ghandour, G. (1991). Statistical models for behavioral observations. *J. Education. Stat.* **16**(3), 157–252.

Rosenbaum, P. R. (1994). Coherence in observational studies. *Biometrics* **50,** 368–374.

Sackett, G. P. (1978). Measurement in observational research. In *Observing Behavior* (G. P. Sackett, ed.), Vol. 2, pp. 25–43. University Park Press, Baltimore.

Suen, H. K. (1988). Agreement, reliability, accuracy, and validity: Toward a clarification. *Behav. Assess.* **10,** 343–366.

Omitted Variable Bias

Paul A. Jargowsky
University of Texas, Dallas, Richardson, Texas, USA

Glossary

bias The difference between the expected value of an estimator and the parameter being estimated.
coefficient In regression, the estimated effect of an independent variable on the dependent variable, controlling for the other independent variables in the model.
correlation A measure of the linear association between two quantitative variables.
estimator A statistic based on a sample for the purpose of providing information about a population parameter.
expected value The mean of the probability distribution of a random variable.
partial correlation A measure of the linear association between two quantitative variables after controlling for the effect of one or more additional variables.
unbiased The property of an estimator having an expected value equal to the parameter being estimated.

Omitted variable bias, also known as left-out variable bias, is the difference between the expected value of an estimator and the true value of the underlying parameter due to failure to control for a relevant explanatory variable or variables. This entry develops the concept in the context of regression analysis.

The Danger of Omitted Variable Bias

The usual goal of a quantitative social science study is to estimate the direction, magnitude, and statistical significance of the effect of an independent variable on a dependent variable. When one or more variables that ought to be included in a model has been left out, our estimate of the effect of the variables we do include in the model is likely to be in error. Even increasing the sample size or repeating the study multiple times will not help to solve the problem.

Social science phenomena are, by their very nature, multivariate. Yet human reasoning tends to operate in a bivariate manner. When we see two variables correlated in time or space, we tend to leap to the conclusion that one variable must be causing the other. Moreover, data tables and graphics are printed on a two-dimensional page and are most effective at showing bivariate relationships. Unfortunately, except under very favorable circumstances, conclusions based on bivariate reasoning are likely to be incorrect to one degree or another because of omitted variable bias. In fact, even analyses that take dozens of variables into account will still be biased if even one important explanatory variable is overlooked. In all likelihood, omitted variable bias is the most serious and pervasive threat to the validity of social science research.

This entry describes why left-out variable bias occurs, why researchers need to be concerned about it, and how to deal with it. We work here within a linear regression framework, but the concerns are generalizable to many different types of analysis, both more and less sophisticated than linear regression. The entry first describes how an omitted variable biases the coefficient in a bivariate regression, setting forth guidelines for determining the direction of the bias. The analysis is then extended to multiple regression, describing a more refined rule for predicting the direction of the bias, which is less well known than the procedure for the bivariate case. Last, strategies are identified for coping with omitted variable bias.

Omitted Variable Bias in the Bivariate Case

This section addresses omitted variable bias in the context of a bivariate regression.

The Algebra of the Bias

For the purpose of understanding how the influence of an omitted variable can be picked up by other variables in an analysis, we begin with a simple case in which a dependent variable Y is determined by two variables X_2 and X_3, plus a stochastic disturbance term. Thus, the true model is:

$$Y_i = \beta_1 + \beta_2 X_{2i} + \beta_3 X_{3i} + u_i \tag{1}$$

where the βs are the parameters to be estimated, and the disturbance term, u_i, is assumed to be uncorrelated with the X variables.

Let us assume, however, that the researcher lacks data on the variable X_3 and proposes to regress Y on X_2 alone. To clear X_3 from the equation, and thus recast the true model solely as a function of X_2, we first need to express X_3 as a function of X_2:

$$X_{3i} = \gamma_1 + \gamma_2 X_{2i} + \varepsilon_i. \tag{2}$$

We need not concern ourselves with whether Eq. (2) expresses a causal relationship or merely a spurious correlation; the γs are simply the parameters of the ideal line that captures the linear correlation between the two X variables. The ε term is the difference between the actual value of X_3 and the conditional mean of X_3 given X_2. In other words, it is the part of X_3 that is uncorrelated with X_2.

To clear X_3 from the model, we simply substitute Eq. (2) into Eq. (1):

$$\begin{aligned} Y_i &= \beta_1 + \beta_2 X_{2i} + \beta_3(\gamma_1 + \gamma_2 X_{2i} + \varepsilon_i) + u_i \\ &= \beta_1 + \beta_2 X_{2i} + \beta_3\gamma_1 + \beta_3\gamma_2 X_{2i} + \beta_3\varepsilon_i + u_i \\ &= \underbrace{(\beta_1 + \beta_3\gamma_1)}_{\alpha_1} + \underbrace{(\beta_2 + \beta_3\gamma_2)}_{\alpha_2} X_{2i} + \underbrace{(\beta_3\varepsilon_i + u_i)}_{\tilde{u}_i}. \end{aligned} \tag{3}$$

After regrouping, the terms in the first parenthesis are all constants, so for convenience we can label the sum of these constants α_1. The terms in the second parenthesis are slopes—that is, changes in Y associated with changes in X_2. We label the sum of these slopes α_2. The terms in the final parenthesis are a weighted combination of stochastic (random error) terms that are uncorrelated with X_2.

The point is that when we mistakenly estimate the bivariate regression of Y on X_2, omitting X_3 and assuming that the disturbance term is uncorrelated with X_2, we actually obtain an unbiased estimate of α_2 rather than an unbiased estimate of the true causal effect, γ_2. Specifically,

$$E[\hat{\alpha}_2] = \alpha_2 = \beta_2 + \beta_3\gamma_2. \tag{4}$$

The first term (β_2) is the true causal effect, the quantity we wish to estimate. The second term is the omitted variable bias. (The formal derivation of omitted variable bias involves substituting the true model for Y_i into the formula for the ordinary least squares, OLS, slope coefficient and then taking the expectation. See the Appendix at the end of the entry.) Note that the bias has two components. The first (β_3) is the true effect of the omitted variable. The second (γ_2) is the parameter on X_2 in Eq. (2). Because Eq. (2) is in the form of a bivariate regression, we can express this parameter as follows:

$$\gamma_2 = \rho_{23}\left(\frac{\sigma_3}{\sigma_2}\right) \tag{5}$$

in which ρ_{23} is the correlation between X_2 and X_3, and the σs are the standard deviations of the corresponding X variables.

The Direction of the Bias

The two components of the bias make it possible to estimate the direction of the bias. Because standard deviations are always positive, the sign of the bias will be determined by the product of the signs of β_3, the true effect of the omitted variable, and the correlation between the included and the excluded variables. If both are positive, or both are negative, then the bias is positive, meaning that the coefficient estimate in the bivariate estimation is likely to be to high. If one is positive and the other negative, then the bias term is negative, and the coefficient estimate in the bivariate case is likely to be too low. If either of these two terms is zero, then we need not worry about an omitted variable bias.

We do not know these signs for certain; after all, the variable has been omitted from our analysis. But often it is possible to get a good idea about the probable signs of these quantities based on theoretical considerations, prior empirical research, or common sense.

Examples

Suppose we regress wages in dollars on years of education, but omit a variable for experience. We might obtain a result like the following bivariate regression:

$$\text{Wage} = 1.00 + 0.75{*}\text{Educ}.$$

If our model has been correctly specified, we are justified in inferring that an additional year of education leads to an increase of 75 cents in the wage rate. However, we have omitted experience, which is not directly available in most cross-sectional data sets, such as the Current Population Survey.

Even without a variable for experience, we can make an educated guess about the direction of the bias. Based on human capital considerations, we expect the sign of experience to be positive. The correlation between education and experience is likely to be negative, both because people stay out of the labor market to pursue education and because older cohorts of workers generally have obtained less education but have accumulated much work experience. A positive times a negative is negative, so the bias is negative. The bivariate estimate of the effect of education on wage is, therefore, likely to be too low relative to the unbiased estimate that controls for experience.

Although a biased estimate is a bad thing, at least in this case we can say that our estimate of the effect of education on wage is conservative; if we had been able to include experience, the coefficient would probably be even higher. That is, the effect of education on wage is probably greater than 75 cents per year of education.

On the other hand, we have also omitted ability. Ability is likely to have a positive effect on wages and a positive correlation with education. Therefore the bias is positive as well. In this case, the bias is more troubling. Depending on the size of the bias, the true effect of education could be zero or even negative.

As the two examples show, an educated guess about the direction of the bias can be very helpful, particularly if the bias has the opposite sign of the coefficient. A positive coefficient with a negative bias is likely to be an even larger positive number; similarly, a negative coefficient with a positive bias is likely to indicate a larger—that is, more negative—coefficient.

It is worth noting at this point that bias is a property of the expected value of the coefficient, not any specific estimate. In any given sample, the value of a coefficient can be quite different than its expectation, so there is no guarantee that a negatively biased coefficient will be smaller than the true parameter value or vice versa.

Omitted Variable Bias in Multivariate Analyses

The analysis of omitted variable bias in the bivariate case is useful in developing an understanding about the mechanics of the bias. Most of the time, however, we are concerned about the effect of an omitted variable in a multiple regression analysis.

The Algebra of the Bias

Anticipating the direction of the bias is somewhat more complex when we move beyond bivariate regression models. For example, suppose the true causal model is:

$$Y_i = \beta_1 + \beta_2 X_{2i} + \beta_3 X_{3i} + \beta_4 X_{4i} + u_i. \tag{6}$$

Further, suppose that X_4 is related to X_2 and X_3 as follows:

$$X_{4i} = \gamma_1 + \gamma_2 X_{2i} + \gamma_3 X_{3i} + \varepsilon_i. \tag{7}$$

Substituting and rearranging terms:

$$\begin{aligned} Y_i &= \beta_1 + \beta_2 X_{2i} + \beta_3 X_{3i} + \beta_4(\gamma_1 + \gamma_2 X_{2i} + \gamma_3 X_{3i} + \varepsilon_i) + u_i \\ &= \underbrace{(\beta_1 + \beta_4\gamma_1)}_{\alpha_1} + \underbrace{(\beta_2 + \beta_4\gamma_2)}_{\alpha_2} X_{2i} + \underbrace{(\beta_3 + \beta_4\gamma_3)}_{\alpha_3} X_{3i} \\ &\quad + \underbrace{(u_i + \beta_4\varepsilon_i)}_{\tilde{u}_i}. \end{aligned} \tag{8}$$

Thus, when estimating the regression of Y on X_2 and X_3, omitting X_4, the slope parameters for both of the included independent variables are potentially biased. The expected values for the slope parameters are:

$$\begin{aligned} E[\hat{\alpha}_2] &= \beta_2 + \beta_4\gamma_2 \\ E[\hat{\alpha}_3] &= \beta_3 + \beta_4\gamma_3. \end{aligned} \tag{9}$$

As in the bivariate case, there is no bias if β_4 the true effect of the omitted variable, is zero. Unlike the bivariate case, the γs are now multiple regression coefficients. Thus, they cannot be expressed as a function of the simple bivariate correlation coefficients between the omitted variable and the included variables. Instead, γ_2 is the slope coefficient for X_2 that we obtain from a regression of X_4 (the missing variable) on X_2 and X_3. If that coefficient is zero, there is no bias. The sign of the that coefficient is the sign of the *partial* correlation between X_2 and X_4, controlling for X_3. As in the bivariate case, the direction of the bias is determined by the product of the signs of the two terms in the bias equation.

The extension to situations involving more variables is straightforward; Greene (2000) provided a formal derivation of the bias in the multivariate case. If there are two excluded variables, X_4 and X_5, the expected value of the coefficient on X_2 is:

$$E[\hat{\alpha}_2] = \beta_2 + \beta_4\gamma_{42} + \beta_5\gamma_{52} \tag{10}$$

where γ_{42} is the coefficient expressing the partial effect of X_2 on X_4 and γ_{52} is the coefficient expressing the partial effect of X_2 on X_5, with X_3 controlled in both cases.

In general, if X_j are the J variables included in the regression, and Z_k are the K variables omitted from the regression, the expected value of the coefficient any one of the included variables is:

$$E[\hat{\alpha}_j] = \beta_j + \sum_k \beta_k\gamma_{kj}. \tag{11}$$

Thus, each left-out variable potentially contributes to the bias. For a given left-out variable k, there is no bias if the omitted variable has no effect on the dependent variable after controlling for the included variables, that is, $\beta_k = 0$ for that variable. There is also no bias for a given included variable j if the partial correlation

Table I Existence and Direction of Omitted Variable Bias[a]

Partial correlation between omitted variable and the included variable of interest[b]	*Marginal effect of the omitted variable on the dependent variable*[c]		
	Negative	Zero	Positive
Negative	Positive bias	None	Negative bias
Zero	None	None	None
Positive	Negative bias	None	Positive bias

[a] If more than one variable is omitted, each can cause a bias. If the biases are in opposite directions, it is difficult if not impossible to tell the net expected direction of the bias.
[b] Net of the other included variables.
[c] Controlling for all other variables.

between the omitted and the included variables is zero after controlling for the other included variables, that is, $\gamma_{kj} = 0$.

Although it is clearly more difficult in the multivariate case, we can still anticipate the direction of omitted variable bias by making educated guesses about the sign of the effect of the excluded variable and the *partial* correlation of the included variables in questions and the excluded variable. Most of the time, but certainly not always, the sign of the partial correlation and the simple bivariate correlation are the same. Nevertheless, we must guard against uncritically applying the bivariate analysis in the multivariate case, and the distinction is not as well appreciated as it ought to be. Table I summarizes the issues involved in evaluating the existence and direction of the bias. However, if there are several omitted variables and some of the expected biases are positive and some are negative, it may be difficult (if not impossible) to anticipate direction of the net expected bias.

Broader Implications

An often neglected point is that omitting relevant variables affects the standard errors of the included variables as well. There are several potentially offsetting effects, so that the standard errors may be larger or smaller relative to the correctly specified model. However, in view of the bias in the coefficients when relevant variables are left out, the effects on the standard errors seem like a second-order concern because the wrong quantity is being estimated. There is no bias if the omitted variable is not correlated with the included variable, but the standard errors of the coefficients on the included variables will still be affected. On the one hand, including an omitted variable uses up one degree of freedom, potentially increasing the standard error. On the other hand, including an omitted variable reduces the residual variance, which will tend to reduce the standard errors of the coefficients of the included variables. In practice, the latter effect will usually predominate, especially in larger data sets in which degrees of freedom are plentiful.

The foregoing discussion has been framed in the context of OLS regression, but the ideas developed are applicable to a broad array of models that include a linear function of several variables as part of their specification. Omitted variable bias has roughly the same properties in all models in which the dependent variable is modeled as some function of a linear combination of dependent variables and parameters.

For example, a logit model is specified as follows:

$$P_i = \frac{1}{1 + e^{-(\beta_1 + \beta_2 X_{2i} + \cdots + \beta_k X_{kj})}}. \qquad (12)$$

Solving for the linear function of the independent variables, the model can be written as:

$$\ln\left(\frac{P_i}{1 - P_i}\right) = \beta_1 + \beta_2 X_{2i} + \cdots + \beta_k X_{kj}. \qquad (13)$$

Although the relationship between the *Xs* and P_i is clearly nonlinear, the relationship is monotonic; therefore, a positive β implies that the probability increases as X increases, a negative coefficient implies that the probability decreases as X increases, and a larger coefficient implies a larger effect, other things equal. Omitted variable bias is a function of the relationship between the X variables, not the functional form of the relationship with the dependent variable. In other words, we can still make the same generalizations about the *direction* of the bias as previously described when considering logit, probit, tobit, Poisson, and many other models.

On a conceptual level, we can also extend these ideas to tables, graphs, and maps. For example, given the rise of Geographic Information Systems (GIS), it is common for researchers to show maps and note that two variables, say percentage of blacks and the high school dropout rate, are geographically concentrated in the same neighborhoods. This is nothing more than a visual bivariate correlation, without even the benefit of a test of significance. Any conclusion we would wish to draw from such maps is tainted by the omission of other variables, such as the poverty rate, which may well partly or fully determine the outcome variable.

As discussed by Alwyn and Hauser in 1975, omitted variable bias is very closely related to path analysis. In fact, the mathematics of the two are identical; they differ only in the assumptions about the relations among the variables. What has been described as a bias in this entry is called an indirect effect in path analysis. In order for the indirect effect interpretation to be valid, the researcher must be able to correctly specify the causal ordering of the variables in the model.

Coping with Omitted Variable Bias

The definitive solution to omitted variable bias is to conduct a classic experiment, in which individuals are randomly assigned to treatment and control groups. Because both groups are random draws from the same population, they have the same expected value for any variable other than the treatment. Because no other variable, measured or unmeasured, known or unknown, is likely to be correlated with the treatment, there is little reason to be concerned with omitted variable bias in the analysis of experimental data. In many issues studied by social scientists, however, it is not possible to conduct experiments or, in cases in which it might be possible, it is often not ethical. We cannot randomly assign workers to a gender, and we would not randomly assign children to abusive parents. And even when experiments are possible and ethical, they are expensive and difficult to conduct. Thus, nonexperimental research is an unavoidable necessity, despite the possibility and probability of omitted variable bias.

The second best way to correct omitted variable bias is to collect new data that include the variables omitted in previous analyses. We should then include the formerly omitted variables and perform the relevant t or F tests; and, depending on the results of these tests, we should either include or exclude the variable from the final model. However, this is not always practical or possible. For example, some variables are intrinsically hard to measure, such as a person's level of motivation. And in some cases, a researcher may not even be aware of the variable that is being omitted because of a lack of understanding of the phenomenon under study.

For all of these reasons, researchers often have no choice but to conduct analyses on data that may be missing important explanatory variables. This section addresses strategies and techniques for recognizing and addressing omitted variable bias when conducting an experiment or collecting new data is not possible.

Testing for Omitted Variable Bias

Any time the R^2 from a regression is less than 1, some aspect of the process that generates the dependent variable is unknown. Thus, the first diagnostic for omitted variables is a low R^2 statistic. However, R^2 less than 1 is a necessary but not a sufficient condition for omitted variable bias. The unexplained variation could be random noise, or it could be the systematic impact of omitted variables which, taken together, are uncorrelated with any of the included variables.

A number of tests have been developed that can aid the researcher in diagnosing the likelihood of left-out variable bias. The most commonly used is the regression specification error test (RESET) proposed by Ramsey in 1969. The intuition behind the test is that the residuals from a regression with a left-out variable will include a systematic component, reflecting the net influence of the omitted variables. However, by construction, the residuals are orthogonal to both the predicted values and all the included independent variables. Thus, the residuals from the suspect regression are themselves regressed against squares and higher powers of either the predicted values or the independent variables. Under the null hypothesis of no specification error, the sum of the squared residuals from the auxiliary will have an F distribution. Unfortunately, the test is a general misspecification test and cannot distinguish between omitted variables and incorrect functional form.

Correcting Omitted Variable Bias

When the data do not contain one or more variables of interest, there are a number of ways to control for them implicitly. In panel data, fixed effects models may be estimated. The fixed effect model implicitly controls for all variables that are unchanging over the period in question. For example, fixed effects at the individual level can be used to control for innate ability in a wage regression; fixed effects for multiple-sibling families can be used to control for unmeasured characteristics of the parents. Similarly, paired difference tests and difference-in-difference estimators allow individual observations to serve as their own control.

An instrumental variable (IV) approach may be attempted if variables can be found that are related to the included variables but not to the omitted variables. By purging the included variable of its correlation with the omitted variable, consistent estimates of the included variable's influence may be obtained. For example, as Angrist and Krueger explained in 1991, quarter of birth is correlated with schooling because of compulsory education laws, but presumably uncorrelated with ability. Thus, an IV approach based on quarter of birth allows a consistent estimate of the effect of schooling on wage that is not biased by the omission of a measure of ability. Obviously, this technique depends on the availability of suitable instruments.

If there is no way to add the omitted variable or to control for it implicitly, the best we can do is to try to evaluate the likely impact of the bias, as discussed previously.

Conclusion

Social phenomena are the results of complex multivariate processes in which the causal variables are often correlated. Ultimately, the best way to recognize a left-out variable problem is to use theory, prior empirical research, and common sense as guides to what variables ought to be included in the model. Given the near impossibility of measuring all the relevant variables, virtually all social science analyses are plagued by omitted variable bias to some degree. However, understanding the mechanics of omitted variable bias can suggest the probable size and direction of the bias. Perhaps more important, it can help the researcher to decide which left-out variables cause the most serious threat to the validity of research findings and therefore indicate where further time, money, and effort can be most usefully deployed.

Appendix: Expectation of the Bivariate Slope Coefficient with an Omitted Variable

Assume that the true model is:

$$Y_i = \beta_1 + \beta_2 X_{2i} + \beta_3 X_{3i} + u_i \quad u_i \sim N(0, \sigma^2) \tag{14}$$

However, the following model is estimated:

$$Y_i = \alpha_1 + \alpha_2 X_2 + \varepsilon_i \tag{15}$$

For ease of presentation, let lower-case letters represent deviations from the respective means. In other words:

$$\begin{aligned} y_i &= Y_i - \bar{Y} \\ x_{2i} &= X_{2i} - \bar{X}_2 \\ x_{3i} &= X_{3i} - \bar{X}_3. \end{aligned}$$

It is also useful to note the following relation:

$$\sum x_{2i} y_i = \sum x_{2i}(Y_i - \bar{Y}) = \sum x_{2i} Y_i - \bar{Y} \sum x_{2i} = \sum x_{2i} Y_i. \tag{16}$$

The second term disappears because the sum of deviations around a mean is always zero.

The expectation of the slope coefficient from the incorrect bivariate regression is:

$$E[\hat{\alpha}_2] = E\left[\frac{\sum x_{2i} y_i}{\sum x_{2i}^2}\right] = E\left[\frac{\sum x_{2i} Y_i}{\sum x_{2i}^2}\right]. \tag{17}$$

As shown, for example, by Gujarati in 2003, the first step is the standard solution for the bivariate slope coefficient. In the second step, we make use of Eq. (16). Now we substitute the true model, Eq. (14), simplify the expression, and take the expectation:

$$\begin{aligned} E[\hat{\alpha}_2] &= E\left[\frac{\sum x_{2i}(\beta_1 + \beta_2 X_{2i} + \beta_3 X_{3i} + u_i)}{\sum x_{2i}^2}\right] \\ &= E\left[\frac{\beta_1 \sum x_{2i} + \beta_2 \sum x_{2i} X_{2i} + \beta_3 \sum x_{2i} X_{3i} + \sum x_{2i} u_i}{\sum x_{2i}^2}\right] \\ &= E\left[0 + \beta_2 + \beta_3 \left(\frac{\sum x_{2i} x_{3i}}{\sum x_{2i}^2}\right) + \frac{\sum x_{2i} u_i}{\sum x_{2i}^2}\right] \\ &= \beta_2 + \beta_3 \gamma_{32}. \end{aligned} \tag{18}$$

This is the result noted in Eq. (4). The first term goes to zero because the sum of deviations around a mean is always zero, and the final term has an expectation of zero because the model assumes no covariance between the *X*s and the disturbance term. The raw values of X_2 and X_3 are replaced by their deviations (x_2 and x_3) in the third step by making use of the property demonstrated in Eq. (16).

See Also the Following Articles

Correlations • Ecological Fallacy • Path Analysis

Further Reading

Alwin, D. F., and Hauser, R. M. (1975). The decomposition of effects in path analysis. *Am. Sociol. Rev.* **40,** 37–47.

Angrist, J., and Krueger, A. (1991). Does compulsory attendance affect schooling and earnings? *Q. J. Econ.* **106,** 979–1014.

Goldberger, A. S. (1974). Unobservable variables in econometrics. In *Frontiers in Econometrics* (P. Zarembka, ed.) Academic Press, New York.

Greene, W. H. (2000). *Econometric Analysis,* 4th ed. Prentice Hall, Upper Saddle River, NJ.

Griliches, Z. (1957). Specification bias in estimates of production functions. *J. Farm Econ.* **39,** 8–20.

Griliches, Z. (1977). Estimating the returns to schooling: Some econometric problems. *Econometrica* **45,** 1–22.

Gujarati, D. N. (2003). *Basic Econometrics,* 4th ed. McGraw-Hill, New York.

Ramsey, J. B. (1969). Tests for specification errors in classical linear least-squares regression analysis. *J. Royal Statist. Soc. B* **31,** 350–371.

Operations Research

Kevin M. Curtin

The University of Texas at Dallas, Richardson, Texas, USA

Glossary

analytical hierarchy process A method for building a hierarchy of decision elements and comparing and ranking those elements.

branch and bound A search procedure in which relaxations of an integer linear program are organized in a tree structure and solved in order to bound the solution space of the root problem and converge on the optimal solution.

combinatorial complexity The measure of the size of or difficulty in solving a problem based on the number of possible combinations of decision variable values within the problem.

decision variables The elements of an operations research model that represent choices among possible alternative assignments of resources.

Delphi process A structured method for developing consensus among decision makers and experts regarding the significant factors to be included in a model.

enumeration procedure A method for examining all possible alternative solutions in order to identify an optimal solution.

heuristic solution method A "rule-of-thumb" algorithm that will rapidly produce high-quality (though not guaranteed optimal) solutions to a difficult problem.

interior point solution procedure An iterative procedure that identifies a solution within the boundary of the feasible region for a problem and improves on that solution until an optimal solution is found.

linear programming A method for modeling a complex problem as a set of linear functions, including an objective function and a set of constraints.

mathematical modeling The process of structuring complex systems as a set of mathematical functions.

objective function The mathematical expression of the goal of a complex system.

optimization An act, process, or methodology of making something (as a design, system, or decision) as fully perfect, functional, or effective as possible; specifically the mathematical procedures (as finding the maximum of a function) involved in this process.

resource constraint A mathematical representation of a limitation on reaching the objective for an optimization problem.

simplex method An iterative procedure for solving a system of linear equations given in a standardized form, representing constraints on a system.

Operations research is defined as the application of advanced analytical techniques in order to solve complex problems. Its dominant characteristic is the use of mathematical models to analyze problems. With origins in military strategic planning, operations research has found applicability in a wide range of industrial, commercial, and social contexts. Although many of the problems studied are highly combinatorially complex, advanced optimal and heuristic solution procedures have been developed to find alternative solutions for decision-making processes.

Operations Research Defined

The field of operations research (alternately termed operational research or management science) is defined as the application of advanced analytical techniques in order to solve complex problems. Operations research (OR) contains a set of tools used by those who must make organizational decisions. Often these problems involve the allocation of scarce resources in such a way as to achieve a goal maximally (such as profit or level of service) or to minimize some negative consequence of the operation of an organization (such as cost or environmental degradation). In order to solve a complex problem posed by the operation of an organization or system, this problem must be formulated in such a way that it can be efficiently analyzed.

The dominant characteristic of OR is that it constructs and uses mathematical representations, i.e., models, to analyze problems. These models commonly take the form of an objective function that defines the goal of the organization (or one of many goals), and a set of constraints representing the conditions within which the system must operate. Once the general version of problem is formulated, individual instances of that problem may be solved optimally in order to suggest specific allocations of the organization's resources. This solution will be the one that best satisfies the objective that is to be optimized. This distinctive approach is an adaptation of the scientific method used by other sciences.

History of Operations Research

The discipline of OR has its origins in the application of problem-solving techniques in a military context during World War II, when the practice was termed "military OR." In this context, the complex system was designed to wage war, and the components of that system were the enormous resources and requirements of military organizations. Examples of how OR was applied include the determination of the optimal fuse length for depth charges designed to combat submarines, the optimal deployment of radar stations and mining operations, and the optimal arrangement for convoys of ships.

Following the end of the war, two fundamental changes occurred in the practice of OR. First, the methods employed in the conduct of war were quickly adapted to a wide range of industrial applications. Rather than maximizing the efficiency of weapons systems, problems were formulated to increase the efficiency of manufacturing and transportation systems. Second, the development of the simplex method by G. B. Dantzig in 1947 revolutionized the practice of solving mathematical models. The simplex method is a procedure for solving a system of linear equations given in a standardized form, representing the constraints on a system. This iterative method can efficiently evaluate very large numbers of such constraints and associated variables. Due to the computational complexity of such problems and the potential for astronomically large numbers of possible solutions to evaluate, the simplex method effectively unlocked the solutions to a vast number of problems that could not otherwise have been solved.

The two changes in the practice of OR have brought about the steady growth in the development and application of OR techniques for over 50 years. Moreover, these techniques have demonstrated that the efficiencies gained by mathematically modeling a system and solving that model optimally are significant and can in some cases be extraordinary. Recent findings show that major corporations have realized savings in the hundreds of millions of dollars attributable to the implementation of optimization techniques.

An Approach for Conducting Operations Research

Although the mathematical model provides both the message for decision makers and the structure for conveying that message, the model alone is only one part of a process for conducting OR. There are commonly five stages in this process.

Stage 1: Understand and State the Problem

As in any research project, the first step is to state the problem clearly. In the context of OR, such a statement involves an understanding of the system to be modeled and the environment within which the system operates. Understanding the system requires that there is a known goal (or set of goals). Examples of goals are to maximize profit in the context of a commercial enterprise, to minimize cost for a particular manufacturing process, or to minimize distance traveled in the case of transportation applications. Moreover, there may be many factors that influence the extent to which the goal can be met. In terms of commercial gain, there are limits on costs of acquiring goods and constraints imposed by both markets and regulations. In terms of manufacturing processes, there are set requirements for inputs and scheduling considerations. Transportation functions depend on the origin and destination locations, the locations of stops, mode choices, and a host of other factors. All of the pertinent factors must be determined in order to have a reasonable understanding of the problem. These factors can be determined through consultation with the managers of the system and others who are experts in the field, perhaps through a Delphi process. It may be appropriate to determine the importance of different factors through the use of an analytical hierarchy process or some other method of ranking these factors. With an understanding of the factors that influence the system, a clear statement of the problem can be generated.

Stage 2: Formulate the Problem Mathematically

In any research project, models are built in order to find a useful, albeit simplified, representation of a real-world situation. It is no different in OR. A mathematical model is generated from the understanding of the problem gained in stage 1 of the research process. The model often consists of a single objective function that reflects a simplified vision of the goal to be met. The objective function also serves as the quantitative performance measure for the system being modeled. A series of mathematical constraint functions represent simplified versions of the limitations that must be met in the system.

Within these functions many different decisions must be made in order to evaluate the system. Examples of decisions include which roads to travel in order to minimize distance, which locations to choose for warehouses, or how many units of manufactured goods to ship from a particular warehouse to a retail store. These decisions are represented within the functions in the mathematical model with decision variables, and it is the value of these variables that must be determined in such a way as to optimize the system. Decision variables may be binary (e.g., either a road is traveled or it is not), integer (e.g., only whole units of manufactured goods may be shipped), or fractional (e.g., any number of gallons or fractions of gallons of water may be pumped in order to meet the needs of a community). Constants or weights may be associated with particular decision variables if relevant and accurate data exist.

Consider as an example the mathematical formulation for a common OR problem known as the "knapsack" problem. This problem arises when there is limited space to carry or include items (such as in a knapsack) and the objective is to select those items that will be most valuable for inclusion in the limited space. This could pertain to the loading of products for delivery into trucks with limited space or limited weight-carrying capacity. First, the notation used in the formulation is defined as follows: j is the index of item types, N is the number of types of items, c_j is the value of item type j (where $j = 1, 2, \ldots, N$), a_j is the weight of item type j (where $j = 1, 2, \ldots, N$), b is the limit on the total weight of the items that can be included, and x_j is the number of items of type j that are included in the knapsack. The objective or goal is to maximize the value of the items included in the backpack, and thus the objective function can be written as

$$\text{Maximize } Z = c_1x_1 + c_2x_2 + \cdots + c_Nx_N,$$

or alternatively as

$$\text{Maximize } Z = \sum_{j=1}^{N} c_jx_j.$$

This objective function is subject to a constraint on the total amount of weight allowed (room in the knapsack or truck). This constraint can be written mathematically as

$$a_1x_1 + a_2x_2 + \cdots + a_Nx_N \leq b,$$

or alternatively as

$$\sum_{j=1}^{N} a_jx_j \leq b.$$

The x_j variables are the decision variables for this formulation. It must be decided how many of each type of item (if any) ought to be included in the knapsack in order to maximize the objective function, while respecting the constraint. In practice, it is impossible to put negative numbers of items in a knapsack, thus a set of constraints is usually generated to ensure that the decision variables hold only non-negative numbers of items. These can be written as $x_1 \geq 0, x_2 \geq 0, \ldots, x_N \geq 0$, or alternatively as $x_j \geq 0$ for all $j = 1, 2, \ldots, N$. Depending on the nature of the items to be included in the knapsack, these decision variables may be further constrained. For example, if the items to be placed in the knapsack cannot be broken into smaller pieces, they must be constrained to be only integer values. Moreover, if only one item of each type may be included in the knapsack, then the decision variables are binary and $x_j = 1$ if an item of type j is included in the knapsack, and $x_j = 0$ otherwise.

Although the knapsack problem is only one of many different types of problems that are commonly solved in OR, the mathematical formulation is typical of many different problems: there is an objective function, a constraint on the available resources for the system, and a set of constraints on the values of the decision variables. This common type of formulation is called a linear programming formulation, and such formulations are perhaps the chief research area in OR. However, several other research areas command attention, including critical path analysis, dynamic programming, goal programming, nonlinear programming, decision analysis, game theory, Monte Carlo simulation, and queuing theory. Due to the limited space here, the focus remains on using linear programming to model complex systems.

Stage 3: Solve Instances of the Problem

Once an appropriate model formulation has been developed, it must be used to solve real-world instances of the problem. Although there is a fairly large toolbox of solution procedures and variants of such procedures, they can be grouped into five major categories: graphical solution procedures, enumeration methods, simplex-type solution methods, interior point methods, and heuristic solution methods.

Graphical solution methods depend on the fact that all of the parts of a typical mathematical formulation are linear functions. Those functions can therefore be graphed in Cartesian coordinate space in order to determine the optimal solution. Consider a problem instance with two decision variables (x_1 and x_2) and with two resource constraints ($3x_1 + 5x_2 \leq 20$ and $4x_1 + x_2 \leq 15$). The decision variables must be non-negative. The objective function is to Maximize $Z = 2x_1 + x_2$. These functions can be graphed as in Fig. 1. Each axis in the coordinate system represents one of the two decision variables. Each of the constraints can be graphed as linear equalities, whereby one side of the line represents feasible values for the decision variables and the other represents values that would violate the constraint. Taken together, all of the constraints (including the non-negativity constraints) define the feasible region for the problem instance. This area is shaded in Fig. 1. The objective function cuts through the feasible region, and its exact placement depends on the values of the decision variables. With the graphical method, it is easy to see that the objection function value will be greatest when the decision variables have values that allow it to be drawn through the intersection of the two resource constraint lines. Although the graphical method for solving OR problems with linear functions is a very intuitive tool, is usefulness is limited to those cases in which there are only two or three decision variables, since it is difficult to represent four or more dimensions graphically in such a way that they can be easily interpreted. Therefore, other solution procedures must be employed for more complex problem instances.

When there are small numbers of constraints and decision variables in the problem instance, it is conceivable that a complete enumeration procedure could be used to find the optimal solution. That is, each possible combination of decision variable values is tested and the associated objective function value is found. One or more of those combinations will be optimal. It may be more efficient, however, to employ a search method such as "branch and bound" to eliminate some nonoptimal solutions from consideration. The branch and bound method divides the feasible region into partitions in a tree structure and uses the solutions to subproblems to bound the objective function and "prune" branches of the solution tree. In practice, however, many of the problem formulations that must be solved in OR belong to a large family of problems that have been proven to be "NP-complete" (where NP refers to nondeterministic polynomial time). Simply put, this means that there are no algorithmic solutions to such problems, and the size

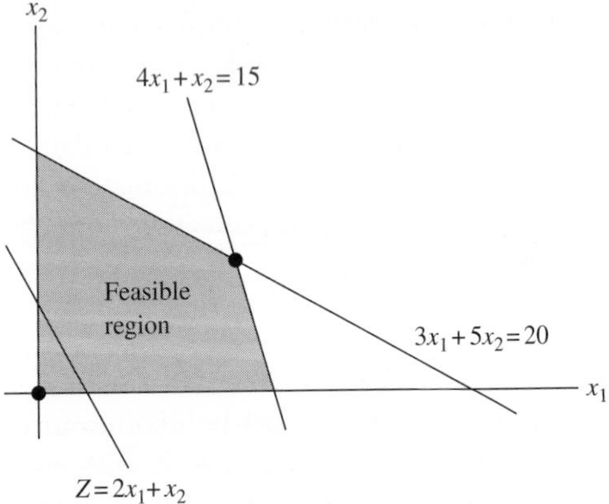

Figure 1 Graphical solution to a two-dimensional problem.

of the problems (as measured by the number of decision variables and constraints) may grow exponentially. Due to the massive resources (in terms of computing time, memory, or storage) that such problems require in order to find a guaranteed optimal solution, it is effectively impossible to solve them through any enumeration procedure. Therefore, an appropriate solution procedure for a problem instance must be chosen based on an understanding of the combinatorial complexity of the problem.

To demonstrate the notion of combinatorial complexity in the context of common OR problems, consider the simple system present in a game of straight pool (billiards). There are 15 billiard balls numbered sequentially, and these must be arranged (in any order) in a rack with 15 places. In the general case, the number of alternatives will be as follows:

$$\text{Number of alternatives} = \binom{n}{p} = \frac{n!}{p!(n-p)!}$$

where n is the number of locations in the rack and p is the number of billiard balls to locate among those potential locations. In the special case of a billiard rack, n is equal to p, so there are 15! (15 factorial) possibilities, or 1,307,674,368,000 possible arrangements of the balls in the rack. In order to determine the optimal solution that describes the best way to arrange the balls through simple enumeration, the objective function must be evaluated for each of the possible arrangements. Depending on the complexity of the objective function chosen for the rack, and on the computing power available, this problem may be unsolvable through inspection. Even a solution protocol that can evaluate the objective function 10,000 times per second would need to run for over 4 years in order to guarantee that the optimal solution had been found. Recall that this problem represents a system with only 15 components! The problems of managing a complex industrial application dwarf this problem by comparison. Given such combinatorial complexity of even small instances of problems in OR, it is clear that enumerative solution procedures are insufficient for many applications.

The development of the simplex method revolutionized OR by providing a standard technique for solving even large optimization problems of the form just described. It is an iterative method that explores the boundary of the feasible region, improving the objective function value with each iteration until the optimal solution has been found. Often the simplex method is used in conjunction with a branch and bound procedure to obtain integer optimal solutions. In other cases, additional constraints (termed "cutting planes") are included in the formulation in order to eliminate parts of the feasible region containing fractional solutions. The "transportation" problem, the "assignment" problem, and the "transshipment" problem are examples of the common problems pertinent to the simplex method. Special versions of the simplex method have been developed to more efficiently solve some problems with particular structural characteristics. The "transportation," "assignment," and "transshipment" problems are among these. These special case solution procedures are sometimes termed "network flow" solution methods.

Interior point solution methods are an alternative to the family of simplex solution procedures. These are iterative methods that find feasible solutions inside the boundary of the feasible region (rather than on the boundary), and at each iteration they find a solution that provides a better objective function value, until the optimal solution is found on the boundary.

When the problem size proves too large for any of the enumeration or iterative methods, heuristic solution methods may be the only practical means of finding a solution. Many heuristics (or rules of thumb) have been developed and tested on problems for which the optimal solutions are known. It is presumed that if a heuristic works well on small problems, it will likely work well on larger instances of the same problem. Some of the most common heuristics include a family of interchange heuristics for which an initial solution is chosen and successive interchanges of the decision variable values are used to search for solutions that improve the objective function value. Interchange heuristics are susceptible to becoming trapped at local optima that may be far from the global optimal solution for the problem, and Tabu (as in "taboo," referring to prohibition) versions of these heuristics have been developed to overcome this limitation. Simulated annealing heuristics use an analogy to the process of heating and cooling metal to harden it, in order to move toward the optimal solution. Lagrangian relaxation heuristics are used to find upper bounds on a problem, ideally narrowing the solution space such that the optimal solution is determined. Although heuristic solution procedures may be the only reasonable method for determining solutions to large problems, and although they may find the optimal solution, there is no guarantee that they will do so.

Stage 4: Validate and Interpret the Results of the Model

Once a general formulation for the model has been formulated and instances of the problem have been solved optimally or heuristically, the researcher must examine the solution and reexamine the model that generated it. Only through the processes of validation and interpretation of the solutions that are generated can the researcher determine whether the model accurately represents the problem environment. The quality of the optimal solution is a function of the suitability of the objective function, the constraints, and the parameters. The nature of mathematical models guarantees that any objective function will be limited in its precision and open to interpretation.

There are several flaws from which models commonly suffer, and which ought to be considered in the validation process: extraneous variables, missing variables, misidentified parameter values, and structural problems. It is possible to use standard statistical analyses such as correlation, regression, and analysis of variance to test for the significance of the variables to the solution. If a variable is not significant to the solution, it may be appropriate to eliminate it and perhaps make the problem easier to solve. Conversely, measures of explained variance might suggest that relevant variables are missing, although they will not help to determine which ones. Sensitivity analysis is useful in determining the amount by which the parameters can be altered before the generated solution will no longer be optimal. The parameters that are varied can include economic and social characteristics such as prices, demands, or population figures, and positional variations in site locations or distance measurements in the case of location optimization problems. If the solution is very sensitive to changes in a particular parameter, then those values must be determined with greater care.

If the model appears to be valid, a critical interpretation of the model should be conducted in the light of the model results. Simply visualizing the solution or presenting it to decision makers can bring to light structural flaws in the model. The optimal solution may expose a missing constraint that would preclude the solution from ever being implemented. The interpretation must be conducted with awareness that the optimality of the solution is always relative to a carefully stated set of constraints, and these constraints are always surrogates for and simplifications of reality. Satisficing solutions that consider qualitative or subjective elements may be close to optimal, but more appropriate in terms of constraints that are well known but not easily expressed as a mathematical function.

Although validation and implementation are discussed here as a fifth step in a research methodology, elements of these processes may be conducted throughout the research program. This highlights the importance in stage 1 of the identification of decision makers and experts for determining objectives, constraints, and significant parameter values.

Stage 5: Implement the Model—Use the model to Explain, Predict, and Decide

The final stage in the OR process is the implementation of the model solutions. Implementation of the solution is the only test of the validity of the results of the research. Because the OR process is concerned largely with optimality, it is tempting to assume that after careful formulation, solution, and validation there could be no possible reason to reject or delay implementation of that optimal solution. In practice, the generation of a valid optimal solution may be less than half the battle. The implementation of a new solution for a complex system may cause massive change in many different but related systems. Resistance to these changes may be substantial and can prevent the implementation of the optimal solution.

In order to ensure implementation of the results of the OR process, those in a position to authorize its implementation must believe that the model is a reasonable simplification of the system and its environment, and they must understand the structural assumptions built into the model. Such understanding can be gained only through clear communication of the model and the ways in which it was generated, and through the involvement of all interested parties. Because OR tries to improve the efficiency of the system under consideration, it implies a tacit criticism of the existing arrangement. Therefore, in order to avoid resentment among those who manage the current system, the results of the research must be considered to be an imaginative exercise in tactful communication and persuasion. Toward this end, decision makers must be presented with a range of alternative solutions, so that they can select the alternative that can be implemented at a reasonable cost. Although they may risk the loss of optimality, they will be able to weigh the cost and time of implementation versus the potential gains.

If the solutions are implemented, it must also be considered that the system is very likely not static, and it will need to be controlled and monitored over its useful life. Changes in the environment may invalidate the assumptions of the model. Additional constraints may be identified, parameter values may change substantially, or objectives may even change. The application of OR requires that all involved are prepared for changes that may have long-lasting implications for the all of the related systems.

Applications of Operations Research

In the few decades since its origin as a tool for military strategy, OR has become involved in an astounding number of applications areas. Due to the interdependence between the military and industrial activities, there was a quick acceptance of this body of methods in manufacturing. OR quickly proved to identify efficiencies in various production systems, including assembly processes, the blending of ingredients, inventory controls, optimal product mixes, trim loss applications, and job shop scheduling. Later, high-technology manufacturing was to use OR to assist in circuit layout design and multiprocessor assignment applications.

Managers of commercial interests other than manufacturing also welcome the cost-effective organizational changes that OR can suggest. Personnel directors can more efficiently schedule a workforce, agricultural decisions under uncertainty can be better evaluated, purchasing decisions can be optimized, and cargo loading can be planned for the greatest efficiency. Those who are concerned with marketing issues can evaluate media mixes to maximize exposure, plan product introductions, arrange portfolios of assets, assess pricing strategies, and propose optimal sales allocations.

A subset of OR applications is concerned with the location of facilities. Examples include the location of warehouses or retail stores, the layout of workstations within a factory, and the placement of public services such as fire or police stations. Location problems will often contain a function of distance, which may be measured in a variety of ways. Some of the most common location problem structures include median problems, center problems, dispersion problems, covering problems, and layout problems. A smaller subset of location applications concerns problems that occur on networks or in systems that can be represented as networks. Such problems take advantage of network topology and the associated graph theoretic concepts of connectivity and adjacency. An enormous number of decisions related to transportation and physical distribution can be constructed and evaluated using these types of models. Other applications on networks involve things such as pipeline construction, highway patrol scheduling, and school bus routing.

Operations Research as a Decision Tool in Social Science

Although OR has proved its worth for practical applications in military, industrial, management, or commercial interests, there are many other applications for which the motivation is to understand social systems. Because many social systems are extraordinarily complex, the model structures and solution procedures designed in OR are capable of providing insights where other methods would be overwhelmed.

Some of the applications of OR in the social sciences are economic in nature, including research into labor costs and market demand under different conditions, capital budgeting and expansion for the public sector, and budget allocation. Other applications concern the distribution of limited common public resources. Others may give insight into the patterns of criminal activity through “hot-spot” analysis. Political campaign strategies and policy platforms can be designed or analyzed using OR methods. Appropriate candidates for committee assignments or the selection of the most diverse set of applicants for acceptance to a graduate program can be modeled with the OR process. Ecological applications exist when the goal is to minimize the risk of natural hazards, optimize forest management, encourage environmental protection, select sites for natural reserves, or implement pollution controls. Still more applications are designed to increase the efficiency of public services, such as minimizing the response time for emergency personnel, or reduce inequities in access to services or workloads among public servants.

Generally speaking, OR offers a structure for modeling the complex relationships among humans or between humans and the environment. Even though these social systems can be highly complex, OR allows simplified versions of these systems to be modeled in such a way that their individual constraints and variables can be examined and used to generate alternative solutions.

Prospects and Opportunities

Although OR has matured quickly over the decades since its inception, its rapid growth and dissemination into a wide variety of applications areas have opened up new areas for fundamental research. Due to the complex nature and computational complexity of the systems being modeled in OR, there is an ongoing search for new methods (or modifications of existing methods) that will allow a greater number of problem instances to be solved optimally. Investigations into "integer-friendly" formulations—that is, formulations that will generate integer solutions without explicit integrality constraints—are one area of interest. New and variant heuristic solution procedures are developed on a regular basis. Of course, the search for an algorithmic solution to NP-complete OR problems or to special cases of such problems is of constant concern. Although the notions of optimality and fuzzy modeling may seem to be at odds with one another, the notion of parameters that are dynamic has produced substantial interest. Perhaps most importantly, each incremental step in OR allows for a greater understanding of complex systems—often social systems—and the models chosen for these systems expose both our understanding of them and the limitations of our ability to capture and study them.

See Also the Following Article

Heuristics

Further Reading

Ackoff, R. L., and Sasieni, M. W. (1968). *Fundamentals of Operations Research.* John Wiley & Sons, New York.

Blumenfeld, D. (2001). *Operations Research Calculations Handbook.* CRC Press, Boca Raton, FL.

Budnick, F. S., Mojena, R., and Vollmann, T. E. (1977). *Principles of Operations Research for Management.* Richard D. Irwin, Homewood, IL.

Dantzig, G. B. (1990). Origins of the simplex method. In *A History of Scientific Computing* (S. G. Nash, ed.), pp. 141–151. ACM Press, New York.

Fisher, M. L. (1981). The Lagrangian relaxation method for solving integer programming problems. *Mgmt. Sci.* **27,** i–18.

French, S., Hartley, R., Thomas, L. C., and White, D. J. (1986). *Operational Research Techniques.* Edward Arnold, Victoria.

Hillier, F. S., and Lieberman, G. J. (1995). *Introduction to Operations Research.* McGraw Hill, New York.

Marsten, R., Saltzman, M., Shanno, D., Pierce, G., and Ballintijn, J. (1989). Implementation of a dual affine interior-point algorithm for linear programming. *ORSA J. Comput.* **1**(4), 287–297.

Nagel, S. S., and Neef, M. (1978). Quantitative applications in social sciences: Operations research methods. *Am. J. Sociol.* **83**(6), 1564–1567.

Singh, J. (1972). *Great Ideas of Operations Research.* Dover Publ., New York.

Optimal Test Construction

Bernard P. Veldkamp
University of Twente, Enschede, The Netherlands

Glossary

0-1 linear programming A method for solving optimal test construction problems.
algorithm A sequence of instructions that solves a computational problem.
constraint The mathematical representation of a test specification.
heuristic An approximation method for finding a near optimal solution.
infeasibility analysis The process of finding contradictions between constraints in the test construction model.
item pool The database of items and their attributes from which the test has to be constructed.
item response theory (IRT) Theory of measurement models with distinct person and item parameters.
linear programming model A model for optimal test construction.
objective function A function that represents the objective for which the test is constructed.
optimal solution A test that performs optimally with respect to the objective function and meets all the test specifications.
shadow test approach A model for constrained computerized adaptive testing.
test information A function that relates the amount of information in the test to the person parameter.
weighted deviation model A model for optimal test construction.

Optimal test construction deals with the selection of items from a pool to construct a test that performs optimally with respect to the objective of the test and simultaneously meets all test specifications. Optimal test construction problems can be formulated as mathematical decision models. Algorithms and heuristics have been developed to solve the models, which can be used to construct tests.

Introduction

In the area of educational and psychological measurement, tests are often used as data collection instruments. The data are used to assess the score of an examinee on an ability. To define the relation between the answers to a test and the ability, a measurement model is formulated. Based on the model and the data, the score of the candidate is estimated.

In the early days of testing, oral tests and interviews were used to assess the abilities. The measurement model was not formulated explicitly, and the score did not depend only on the answers but also on the mood of the rater. In some areas, standardized test forms, such as the Binet-Simon test, were introduced to make scores more comparable. These standardized test forms solved one problem, but introduced another. When items in the test became known, candidates might try to influence their scores by formulating answers in advance and learning them by heart. This is a potential problem especially in educational measurement, and teachers, or test committees, had to formulate new items for every new test administration.

The new items had to be written, pretested, calibrated, edited, and transported to the test location before they could actually be used to collect data. This process was quite expensive, and, because these items were used only once, it meant a waste of efforts and time. To increase efficiency, new items were collected in item pools. In educational measurement, these pools usually contain between a few hundred and a few thousands of items. From these pools, tests can be selected for several purposes. Item selection is based on the test specifications. For a large test construction problem, the number of specifications may easily run to a few hundred. When the number of items to choose from is also large, manual test construction becomes impractical and a computer algorithm is used to construct the tests optimally.

Item Response Theory

The introduction of item response theory (IRT) into large-scale testing provided new opportunities for test assembly. In IRT measurement models, item parameters and person parameters are modeled separately. Apart from sampling variation, the item parameters do not depend on the population or on the other items in the test. For dichotomously scored items the Rasch model, the two-parameter logistic model (2PLM), and the three-parameter logistic model (3PLM) are most often applied. The relation between the item and the person parameters can be formulated by the following logistic expression:

$$P_i(\theta_j) = c_i + (1 - c_i)\frac{e^{a_i(\theta_j - b_i)}}{1 + e^{a_i(\theta_j - b_i)}}, \qquad (1)$$

where $P_i(\theta_j)$ is defined as the probability of obtaining a correct answer to item i for person j. The person parameter θ_j denotes the latent ability and the item parameters a_i, b_i, and c_i denote the discrimination, the difficulty, and the guessing parameters. For the Rasch model and the 2PLM, the guessing parameter is supposed to be zero, and for the Rasch model also all discrimination parameters are supposed to be equal to 1. For polytomously scored items, polytomous IRT models have also been formulated, for example, the graded response model, the graded partial credit model, and the nominal response model.

When IRT models are applied, measurement precision is determined by the amount of information in the test. Test information, which is a function of the person parameter and the parameters of the items in the test, is defined by:

$$I(\theta) = \sum_{i \in \text{test}} I_i(\theta) = \sum_{i \in \text{test}} \frac{[P_i'(\theta)]^2}{P_i(\theta)Q_i(\theta)}, \qquad (2)$$

where $P_i'(\theta)$ is the first derivative of $P_i(\theta)$, and $Q_i(\theta)$ is the probability of obtaining a wrong answer. The focus in optimal test construction is therefore to find a computer algorithm that selects items from the pool that maximize the amount of information in the test but that also meet the test specifications.

Knapsack Problem

To solve optimal test construction problem, all kinds of smart decision rules have been developed. In 1968, Birnbaum presented a rather general approach. His algorithm consists of the following steps.

1. Decide on the shape of the desired test information function.
2. Select items from the pool with information functions to fill areas under the target information function.
3. After each item has been added to the test, calculate the test information function.
4. Continue selecting items until the test information function approximates the desired shape.

However, if more and more test specifications have to be added to the construction problem, the approach becomes hard to adapt. In 1985, Theunissen made the observation that optimal test construction is just another example of a selection problem. Other well-known examples are flight scheduling, work scheduling, human resource planning, inventory management, and the traveling-salesman problem.

In the area of operations research or mathematical programming, algorithms were developed to solve such problems. To find the best algorithm for optimal test construction, algorithms from this area have been adapted and applied. One class of selection problems consists of those called knapsack problems. Before a traveler leaves, he has to fill his knapsack. All possible items he may wish to pack represent a certain value to him, but the volume of the knapsack is limited. The problem is how to maximize the value of all the items in the knapsack while meeting the volume restriction. More formally stated:

$$\max \sum_{i=1}^{n} c_i x_i \qquad (3)$$

subject to:

$$\sum_{i=1}^{n} a_i x_i \leq b \qquad (4)$$

$$x_i \in \{0, 1\} \qquad (5)$$

where c_i denotes the value of item i, a_i denotes the volume of item i, and the volume of the knapsack is denoted by b. The decision variables x_i denote whether an item is selected ($x_i = 1$) or not ($x_i = 0$). In mathematical programming terms, the formula in Eq. (3) is called the objective function, and Eqs. (4) and (5) are called the constraints.

In optimal test construction, a problem can be described as a knapsack problem. The value of a test, that is the information in the test, has to be maximized in order to obtain optimal measurement precision. The volume can be interpreted as all possible tests that meet the constraints defined by the test attributes, and an item has to be either selected ($x_i = 1$) or not ($x_i = 0$) for the test.

Overview

In the remainder of this entry, how to model several kinds of optimal test construction problems is demonstrated using mathematical programming and also some algorithms for solving the problems are described. First, the problem of constructing one linear test form is described. Several objective functions and different kinds of constraints are suggested. This section results in a general formulation of a test construction problem. Then we address models for several major test construction problems. Next, the algorithms and heuristics to solve the problems are described. Finally, we discuss the topic further and gives some recommendations about use.

Constructing a Single Linear Test Form

The traditional format in both educational and psychological testing is the linear test form. A linear test form is a paper-and-pencil (P&P) test that can be used for a population of candidates. To select a linear test form from an item pool, first the objective of the test has to be specified. Then, the test specifications have to be written as a set of constraints.

Objective Functions

How we specify the objective function in a test construction model depends on the goals or objectives of the test. Three examples of objective functions are given next.

A simple objective deals with the security of the item pool and the costs of testing. When more items are exposed to candidates, the item pool becomes known faster and the costs of maintaining the pool are higher. If the objective of the test is to maximize the security of the pool or to minimize costs of testing, a reasonable objective function is to minimize the number of items in a test. In this case, the objective function can be formulated as:

$$\min \sum_{i=1}^{n} x_i. \tag{6}$$

The objective of the test can also be chosen to depend on the decisions that have to be taken based on its scores. In criterion-referenced testing, a cut-off score θ^* is specified in advance. When the estimated ability $\hat{\theta}$ is larger than or equal to θ^*, the candidate passes, otherwise the candidate fails. For candidates who clearly pass or clearly fail, measurement precision need not be optimal. However, for candidates who are close to the cut-off score, measurement precision should be high. To construct a test that serves this purpose, the following objective function can be used:

$$\max \sum_{i=1}^{n} I_i(\theta *)x_i. \tag{7}$$

where $I_i(\theta^*)$ denotes the information item i provides for the cut-off score.

A third example is a broad ability test. The test should measure the abilities of a population of candidates, for example, diagnostic testing in school classes. Before the test is constructed, targets for the information in the test are defined. The objective of the test construction problem is to minimize the distance between the target information function and the test information function. A few points on the θ scale are chosen, and for these points the distance between the target and test function is minimized. This problem leads to the following objective function:

$$\min y \tag{8}$$

subject to:

$$\left| \sum_{i=1}^{n} I_i(\theta_k)x_i - T(\theta_k) \right| \leq y \quad \forall k, \tag{9}$$

where y is the maximum distance between the test information function and the target information function T for the k ability points. If no targets for the test information functions are defined a maximin approach can be applied:

$$\max y \tag{8'}$$

subject to:

$$\sum_{i=1}^{n} I_i(\theta_k)x_i \geq y \quad \forall k, \tag{9'}$$

In this approach the minimum value of the test information function over the k ability points is maximized.

These three objective functions are most commonly used in optimal test construction. The number of objective functions can easily be extended because almost every property of the test can be used to define an objective function. Also, in some optimal test construction problems, multiple objectives are necessary. Later, some other examples of objective functions are given, but first several possible constraints are introduced.

Constraints Based on Test Specifications

Test specifications can be categorized in several ways. Here they are categorized based on the properties of the test construction model. Three kinds of constraints are distinguished.

First, there are categorical constraints. Categorical item attributes partition the pool into a number of subsets.

Examples of categorical item attributes are item content, cognitive level, item format, author, and answer key. In a categorical constraint, the number of items in a category is specified:

$$\sum_{i \in V_c} x_i \leq n_c \quad c = 1, \ldots, C \tag{10}$$

where V_c is the subset of items in category c, n_c is an upper bound to the number of items chosen from category c, and C denotes the number of categories.

Second, there are quantitative constraints. These constraints do not impose direct bounds on the numbers of items but instead on a function of the items. Examples of quantitative attributes are word count, exposure rates, expected response times, and also item parameters. To limit the expected response time for a test, the following constraint can be added:

$$\sum_{i=1}^{n} t_i x_i \leq T \tag{11}$$

The sum of the expected response times t_i, $i = 1, \ldots, n$, is bounded from above by a time limit T. Quantitative constraints are usually indexed with the symbol q.

The third type of constraints deals with inter-item dependencies. They are also called logical constraints. If, for example, one item contains a clue to the solution to another, these items cannot be selected for the same test. Thus we use an exclusion constraint; if one item is chosen, the other one is excluded. An inclusion constraint deals with item sets; if one item in the set is chosen, all items in the set have to be chosen. These kinds of constraints can be formulated as:

$$x_i \leq y_l \quad \forall i \in V_l \tag{12}$$

$$\sum_{i \in V_l} x_i = n_l y_l \tag{13}$$

where V_l denotes a logical set l, and n_l defines the number of items to be chosen from the set. The variable y_l is equal to 1 if an item from the set is chosen. Equation (13) implies that if one item is chosen, all items will be chosen. For an exclusion constraint, $n_l = 1$; for an inclusion constraint, n_l is equal to the number of items to be chosen from the set.

General Model for Construction of Linear Test Forms

Now that the objective functions and constraints have been formulated, a general model for optimal test construction can be given. In this model, generic constraints will be used to denote the different kinds of constraints. For a typical high-stakes achievement test, such as the LSAT, GMAT, or TOEFL, the total number of constraints easily runs into the hundreds. The general model can be formulated as:

$$\min y \tag{14a}$$

subject to:

$$\left| \sum_{i=1}^{n} I_i(\theta_k) x_i - T(\theta_k) \right| \leq y \quad \forall k, \quad \text{(target information)} \tag{14b}$$

$$\sum_{i \in V_c}^{n} x_i \leq n_c \quad c = 1, \ldots, C \quad \text{(categorical constraints)} \tag{14c}$$

$$\sum_{i=1}^{n} f_q(x_i) \leq n_q \quad \text{(quantitative constraints)} \tag{14d}$$

$$\sum_{i \in V_l} x_i \leq n_l \quad \text{(logical constraints)} \tag{14e}$$

$$\sum_{i=1}^{n} x_i = n_t \quad \text{(total test length)} \tag{14f}$$

$$x_i \in \{0, 1\} \quad \text{(decision variables)} \tag{14g}$$

The constraint in Eq. (14g) guarantees that an item is either selected or not. In the remainder this entry, this model is used to formulate optimal test construction problems.

Weighted Deviations Model

In the general model, all test specifications are considered to be constraints that have to be met. For some test construction problems, the test specifications are considered to be desirable properties rather than constraints. As a result, they are allowed to be violated in the test construction process. When properties are considered to be desirable properties, a weighted deviation model can be formulated. In this model, targets are defined for all test attributes. The objective function is a weighted sum of all violations or deviations. This model can be formulated as:

$$\min \sum_{j} w_j d_j \quad \text{(minimize weighted deviation)} \tag{15a}$$

subject to:

$$\sum_{i \in V_c} x_i - n_c \leq d_1 \quad \text{(categorical constraints)} \tag{15b}$$

$$\sum_{i=1}^{n} f_d(x_i) - n_q \leq d_2 \quad \text{(quantitative constraints)} \tag{15c}$$

$$\left| \sum_{i \in V_l} x_i - n_l \right| = d_3 \quad \text{(logical constraints)} \tag{15d}$$

$$x_i \in \{0, 1\} \quad d_j \geq 0 \quad \text{(decision variables)} \tag{15e}$$

where the variables d_j denote the deviations of constraints j, $j = 1, \ldots, J$, with J being the total number of constraints, and w_j denotes the weight of deviation j. In this model, the difference between the target information function and the test information functions is formulated as a quantitative constraint. When some specifications are considered to be of paramount interest, their weights get high values. When other specifications are considered to be less important, the weights get low values. Because the specifications do not have to be met, the model is less restrictive. A less favorable feature of this model is that two different tests constructed by the same model might have different attributes.

Models for Construction of Other Testing Formats

In educational and psychological measurement, a wide variety of testing formats has been developed. Models for the majority of these formats can be formulated by slightly changing the general test construction model defined in the previous section. Next we present a number of testing formats and explain how they differ from the general test construction problem and how the model should be adapted to construct the desired test form.

Parallel Test Forms

In many applications, several linear test forms have to be constructed that meet the same set of specifications. Several versions of the same test might be needed for security reasons or so that the test can be offered to candidates on different occasions. When tests meet the same set of specifications, they are considered to be parallel. Several definitions of parallel tests are given in the literature, but the concept of weakly parallel tests is often applied. This means that the same set of constraints is met by the tests and the test information functions are identical. If a model is developed for constructing parallel tests, a few changes have to be made to the general model stated in Eqs. (14). First, the decision variables have to change. Whereas in the general model variable x_i indicates whether an item is selected for the test, for parallel tests an additional index j is needed to determine for which test the item is selected, where j runs from 1 to the number of parallel tests that have to be constructed. The new decision variables x_{ij} are defined as:

$$\begin{cases} x_{ij} = 1 & \text{item } i \text{ is selected for test } j, \\ x_{ij} = 0 & \text{otherwise.} \end{cases} \tag{16}$$

The same sets of constraints should hold for all parallel tests. However, the objective function has to change slightly. For all parallel tests, the maximum difference between the target information function and the test information function should be minimized. It might also happen that no targets for the information functions have been defined. It that case, the maximum difference between the test information functions of the parallel test can be minimized.

Tests with Item Sets

Some items in the pool may be grouped around a common stimulus. The stimulus can be a text passage, a table, a figure, or a video or music fragment (sometimes called vignettes). Whenever stimulus is selected for the test, all items, or at least a minimum number of items, that belong to the stimulus have to be selected. Several ways of dealing with these inclusion constraints have been presented. One of them has already been discussed in the section on constraints on inter-item dependencies. However, when test specifications at the stimulus level have also been met, this approach does not work.

An alternative approach is to introduce decision variable z_s, where

$$\begin{cases} z_s = 1 & \text{if stimulus } s \text{ is selected,} \\ z_s = 0 & \text{otherwise.} \end{cases} \tag{17}$$

Categorical, quantitative, and logical constraints can be formulated both at the stimulus and item levels. To make sure that the relation of inclusion between the stimulus and the items is also met, the following constraint can be added to the model:

$$\sum_{i \in V_s} x_i = n_s z_s \tag{18}$$

Whenever stimulus s is selected, this constraint guarantees that n_s items from V_s, the set of items that belong to the stimulus, are selected.

Classical Test Construction

Even though classical item parameters depend on the population and the other items in the test, in practice classical test theory is often applied to construct tests. When the assumption can be made that the population for the test does hardly change, test construction may be possible for classical test forms. In general, the objective function for these tests is to optimize reliability of the test. The reliability of the test is hard to estimate, but Cronbach's α defines a lower bound for it. The objective function for maximizing Cronbach's α can be defined for a fixed length test as:

$$\max \frac{n}{(n-1)}\left[1 - \frac{\sum_{i=1}^{n} \sigma_i^2}{\left(\sum_{i=1}^{n} \sigma_i \rho_{iX}\right)^2}\right], \tag{19}$$

where σ_i^2 is the observed score variance, and ρ_{iX} is the item test correlation of item i. These parameters are based on earlier administrations of the items. The expression for Cronbach's α is a nonlinear function of the decision variables. In order to formulate the test construction problem as a linear programming problem the following modification is often made. Instead of maximizing the expression in Eq. (19), the denominator of the last term is maximized and its numerator is bounded from above:

$$\max \sum_{i=1}^{n} \sigma_i \rho_{ix} \tag{20}$$

subject to:

$$\sum_{i=1}^{n} \sigma_i \leq c. \tag{21}$$

Tests Measuring Multiple Abilities

For certain types of items, several abilities are involved in answering the item correctly. When taking a driving test, the candidate has to both master the car and show insight about traffic. In some cases, all abilities are intentional, but in other cases, some of them are considered nuisances. When multiple abilities are involved, optimizing the information in the test is more complicated. Fisher's information measure takes the form of a matrix instead of a function. From optimum design theory, several criteria for optimizing matrices are known, but they all result in nonlinear and complicated objective functions. An alternative approach is to use Kullback-Leibler information instead of Fisher information. Kullback-Leibler information is a linear expression in the decision variables even in the case of multiple abilities. The resulting test constructing model can be written as:

$$\max \sum_{i=1}^{n} \mathrm{KL}_i(\theta) x_i, \tag{22}$$

where $\mathrm{KL}_i(\theta)$ denotes the amount of Kullback-Leibler information of the item, and θ is a vector instead of a scalar.

Tests with Equated Observed-Score Distributions

In many large-scale test programs, observed scores are presented to the candidates. Expensive equating studies have to be carried out to make the observed scores of different test forms comparable. Adding constraints to the optimal test construction model that will guarantee equal observed-score distributions will decrease the costs of testing. It can be proven that the conditional distributions of observed scores given θ for two test forms are identical if:

$$\sum_{i=1}^{n} P_i^r(\theta) = \sum_{j=1}^{n} P_i^r(\theta) \qquad r = 1, \ldots, n \tag{23}$$

where $P_i^r(\theta)$ is the rth power of $P_i(\theta)$. In practice, the impact of high powers of $P_i(\theta)$ vanishes quickly. To construct tests with equated observed scores, the constraints in Eq. (23) should be added for several values of θ.

Computerized Adaptive Testing

Computerized adaptive testing (CAT) can be compared to an oral exam. Instead of a teacher, in CAT a computer algorithm adapts the difficulty of the items to the answers of the candidate. After an item has been administered, the ability level of the candidate is estimated. Based on this estimate, the item that provides most information at the examinee's estimated ability level is selected to be presented next. Compared to P&P tests, CAT reduces the test length by almost 40%. An important dilemma in CAT is that optimal CAT construction requires sequential item selection to maximize the adaptivity of the test but simultaneous test construction to realize all the test specifications. In order to deal with this dilemma, the shadow test approach was developed.

The main idea in this approach is that, to maximize adaptivity, a shadow test is constructed in every iteration. This shadow test contains all previously administered items and meets the test specifications. From the unadministered items in this shadow test, the next item is then selected. Because of this, the complete CAT will also meet the test specifications.

For constructing the shadow test, the objective function is to maximize the information at the current ability estimate. This objective function can be compared with the objective function in Eq. (7). The difference is that the estimated ability is used instead of the cut-off score. The constraints are formulated by the test specifications. However, an additional constraint is needed to guarantee that all the items that are administered are contained in the test. For selecting the kth shadow test, the following constraint is added:

$$\sum_{i \in S_{k-1}} x_i = k - 1 \tag{24}$$

where the set S_{k-1} is the set of items that have been administered in the $k-1$ previous iterations.

Multistage Testing

A multistage test form consists of a network of item sets. The item sets are also called testlets. The path of a candidate through this network of testlets depends on

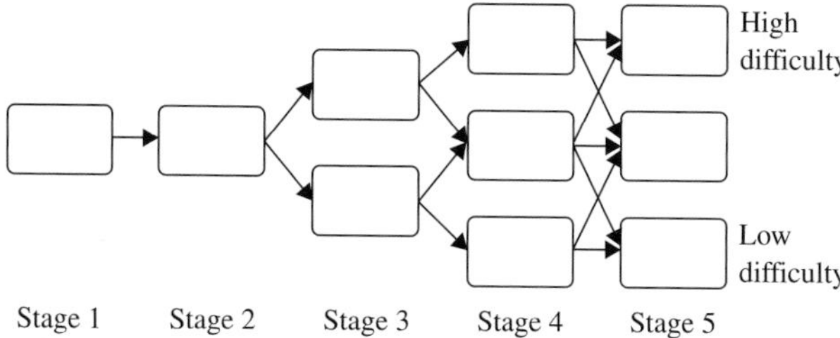

Figure 1 Multistage testing format.

the answers. So, after a testlet is finished, the next testlet is selected adaptively. An example of a network for a multistage test form is shown in Fig. 1. In the first two stages, all candidates answer the same items. At the third stage, the candidates are assigned to either the low-difficulty or high-difficulty testlet. From the fourth to the last stage, based on an estimate of their ability, the candidates are then assigned to the high-, medium-, or low difficulty testlet. The path through the network is chosen to maximize the information in the test as well as to meet the test specifications.

Constructing multistage tests is rather complicated. First, testlets have to be constructed from the item pool, and then they have to be assigned to slots in the network. A testlet can be viewed as a small linear test with its own target information function and a small set of constraints. Constructing one testlet is a straightforward application of the model in Eqs. (14). However, to assemble a multistage test, many testlets have to be constructed. Sequentially solving the model in Eq. (13) would result in high-quality testlets in the beginning and low-quality testlets at the end of the construction process because high-quality items would be selected first. For simultaneous selection, decision variables x_{ij} have to be introduced, which are defined as:

$$\begin{cases} x_{ij} = 1 & \text{item } j \text{ is selected for testlet } j \\ x_{ij} = 0 & \text{otherwise} \end{cases} \tag{25}$$

In addition, Eq. (14b) should be slightly changed because different target information functions are defined for different testlets. The large number of decision variables in this test construction problem makes it very hard to solve.

Algorithms and Heuristics for Solving Optimal Test Construction Problems

In the previous section, models for optimal test construction have been described. An important question is: How do we solve the models? That is, how do we construct optimal tests? Several algorithms and heuristics have been proposed. In this section, 0-1 linear programming techniques, network-flow programming, and a number of heuristics are discussed.

0-1 Linear Programming Techniques

When a problem is formulated in mathematical programming terms, many algorithms are available for solving the model. For example, linear programming, 0-1 linear programming, quadratic programming, and interior point methods can be applied. Which algorithms perform best depends on the kind of decision variables and on the formulation of the constraints. In optimal test construction, the decision variables are 0-1 variables. For the general formulation of a test construction problem in Eqs. (14), all constraints consist of the sums of decision variables. Because the general test construction model only consists of linear constraints, 0-1 linear programming techniques can be applied. 0-1 linear programming problems are known to be non-polynomial (NP)-hard, which means that it is not guaranteed that the optimal solution can be found in polynomial time. However, this is only the worst-case performance.

To find optimal values for the decision variables, standard 0-1 linear programming software such as CPLEX can be used. CPLEX employs an efficient implementation of the branch-and-bound (B&B) algorithm. For most test construction problems, a solution can be found in a reasonable amount of time. Only such problems as multiple-stage testing problems are too time-consuming.

Some models described in the previous section have nonlinear objective functions or constraints. These have to be linearized before the 0-1 linear programming techniques can be applied.

Network-Flow Programming

For some special test construction problems a much faster 0-1 linear programming algorithm is available, the network-flow programming algorithm. In order to apply this algorithm, the model is allowed to have only categorical constraints. When this algorithm is applied, even large test construction problems with thousands of variables can be solved quickly.

Unfortunately, most optimal test construction problems also have to deal with quantitative constraints. To embed these constraints into a network-flow programming algorithm, they are added to the objective function as penalty terms times a Lagrangian multiplier. For example, if a time limit of 30 minutes is to be imposed on a test, the following term is added to the objective function:

$$\lambda\left(30 - \sum_{i=1}^{n} t_i x_i\right) \tag{27}$$

The remaining problem is to find appropriate values for the Lagrangian multipliers λ. These values are usually found iteratively. Even when this iterative process is needed to find the solution of the test construction problem, the algorithm is fast, but the solution might accidentally suffer from a constraint violation.

Logical constraints might also be part of the optimal test construction problem. Some of them can be incorporated in the same way as the quantitative constraints. When it not possible to use Lagrangian multipliers, a heuristic is needed to calculate a solution under these constraints.

Heuristics

For some optimal test construction problems, 0-1 linear programming techniques cannot be applied because of the nonlinearity of the objective function or the constraints or because the techniques may need too much time. In addition, it might not be possible to formulate the problem as a network-flow model. In those cases, heuristical methods can be applied to find a solution. An heuristic is an approximation method that works fast but that tends to result in a good solution rather than in the optimal solution. In optimal test construction, the greedy algorithm, simulated annealing, and genetic algorithms have been applied successfully.

Greedy algorithms work very fast. They select items sequentially. At every iteration, the item is selected that contributes most to the objective function. The normalized weighted absolute deviation heuristic (NWADH) is a well-known application of a greedy heuristic. It has also been applied very successfully in combination with the weighted deviations model in Eqs. (15). However, because these heuristics operate sequentially, the greedy algorithm might run into infeasibility problems at the end of the test, when violations of constraints are not allowed.

Simulated annealing is a much more time-consuming method. First, an initial test is constructed that meets all the specifications. Then, one item is swapped with an item in the pool. If the new test performs better with respect to the objective function, it is accepted; otherwise it is accepted with a probability that decreases during the test assembly process. The method stops when the probability of accepting a worse test is smaller than a lower bound.

When genetic algorithms are applied, several tests are constructed that meet all the specifications. New tests are constructed by selecting one part from one test and another part from a second test. If the new test performs better with respect to the objective function, it is added to the set of candidate tests. At the end, the best candidate in the set is selected.

Infeasibility Analysis

Sometimes, 0-1 linear programming techniques, network-flow programming, and heuristical methods might not be able to construct a test from the item pool that meets all the test specifications. When this occurs, the model is said to be infeasible. The reason might be that there is a logical contradiction between some of the specifications, a writing error may have occurred in the modeling process, or the item pool may be poor. The exact cause of infeasibility is often very hard to detect. A typical test construction model might consist of thousands of variables and hundreds of constraints.

Several methods have been developed to diagnose infeasibility. Because infeasibility is always caused by the specifications in combination with the item pool, the focus of the methods is on the interaction of individual specifications as well as on the interaction of specifications and the item pool. The main idea in most methods is to isolate a small group of specifications that have to be modified in order to construct a test from the pool. A closer investigation of such a group of specifications has to reveal the exact reasons of infeasibility.

Conclusion and Discussion

The main issue in optimal test construction is how to formulate a test assembly model. Models for a number of optimal test construction problems have been introduced. However, all these models are based on the general test construction model in Eqs. (14). They may need a different objective function, some additional constraints, or different definitions of the decision variables, but the structure of the model remains the same. When different optimal test construction problems have to be solved, the question is not how to find a new method but how to define an appropriate objective function and a set of constraints.

The weighted deviations model is an alternative to the linear programming model. All the models presented in the third section could also be written as weighted deviation models. Whether linear programming models or weighted deviation models should be applied depends on the nature of the specifications. When the specifications have to be met, linear programming models are more suitable, but when the specifications are less strict, the weighted deviations model can be used. In practical testing situations, it may even happen that a combination of the two models can be applied if only some of the specifications have to be met. The same algorithms and heuristics can solve both the linear programming models and the weighted deviation models.

Finally, some remarks have to be made about the quality of optimal test construction methods. The models, algorithms, and heuristics presented here are very effective in constructing optimal tests. Additional gains are possible by improving the quality of the item pool. Some efforts have already been made to develop an optimal blueprint for item pool design that would combine test specifications and optimal test construction methods to develop better item pools. This will further increase measurement precision.

See Also the Following Articles

Classical Test Theory • Computerized Adaptive Testing • Heuristics • Item Response Theory

Further Reading

Adema, J. J., and van der Linden, W. J. (1989). Algorithms for computerized test construction using classical item parameters. *J. Educ. Statist.* **14,** 279–290.

Armstrong, R. D., Jones, D. H., and Wang, Z. (1995). Network optimization in constrained standardized test construction. *Applications Manage. Sci.* **8,** 189–212.

Birnbaum, A. (1968). Some latent trait models and their use in inferring an examinee's ability. In *Statistical Theories of Mental Test Scores* (F. M. Lord and M. R. Novick, eds.), pp. 397–479. Addison-Wesley, Reading MA.

Huitzing, H. A. (in press). An interactive method to solve infeasibility in linear programming test assembly models. *J. Educ. Meas.*

Luecht, R. M. (1998). Computer-assisted test assembly using optimization heuristics. *Appl. Psychol. Meas.* **22,** 224–236.

Luecht, R. M., and Nungester, R. J. (1998). Some practical applications of computer adaptive sequential testing. *J. Educ. Meas.* **35,** 229–249.

Papadimitriou, C. H., and Steiglitz, K. (1982). *Combinatorial Optimization.* Prentice Hall, Englewood Cliffs, NJ.

Stocking, M. L., and Swanson, L. (1993). A method for severely constrained item selection in adaptive testing. *Appl. Psychol. Meas.* **17,** 277–292.

Theunissen, T. J. J. M. (1985). Binary programming and test design. *Psychometrika* **50,** 411–420.

van der Linden, W. J. (1998). Optimal assembly of psychological and educational tests. *Appl. Psychol. Meas.* **22,** 195–211.

van der Linden, W. J. (2000). Optimal assembly of tests with item sets. *Appl. Psychol. Meas.* **24,** 225–240.

van der Linden, W. J., and Adema, J. J. (1998). Simultaneous assembly of multiple test forms. *J. Educ. Meas.* **35,** 185–198.

van der Linden, W. J., and Boekkooi-Timminga, E. (1989). A maximin model for test design with practical constraints. *Psychometrika* **54,** 237–247.

van der Linden, W. J., and Glas, C. A. W. (2000). *Computerized Adaptive Testing: Theory and Practice.* Kluwer Academic, Boston.

van der Linden, W. J., and Luecht, R. M. (1998). Observed score equating as a test assembly problem. *Psychometrika* **63,** 401–418.

Veldkamp, B. P. (1999). Multiple objective test assembly problems. *J. Educ. Meas.* **36,** 253–266.

Veldkamp, B. P. (2002). Multidimensional constrained test assembly. *Appl. Psychol, Meas.* **26,** 133–146.

Veldkamp, B. P., and van der Linden, W. J. (2002). Multidimensional adaptive testing with constraints on test content. *Psychometrika* **67,** 575–588.

Wainer, H., Dorans, N. J., Flaugher, R., Green, B. F., Mislevy, R. J., Steinberg, L., and Thissen, D. (1990). *Computerized Adaptive Testing: A Primer.* Lawrence Erlbaum, Hillsdale, NJ.

Ordinary Least Squares (OLS)

Michael E. Ezell
Vanderbilt University, Nashville, Tennessee, USA

Kenneth C. Land
Duke University, Durham, North Carolina, USA

Glossary

assumptions Mathematical conditions used in the derivation of an estimator that are critical for determining the statistical properties of the estimator.

dependent variable The outcome variable on the left-hand side of the equation, which is being explained as a linear function of the independent or explanatory variables.

efficient estimator An unbiased estimator whose sampling distribution has the smallest variance.

error term The population-level difference between an observed value of the dependent variable Y_i and the expected value of the statistical model $E(Y_i)$.

estimator A mathematical method or formula used to calculate a numerical estimate of a population parameter from sample data.

fitting criterion A numerical or scalar index used in the minimization phase of estimation that determines when the residuals of a model are as small as possible.

Gauss–Markov theorem A mathematical theorem that proves that the ordinary least squares (OLS) estimator is the best linear unbiased estimator (BLUE) when the assumptions of the OLS estimator are met.

homoskedasticity The condition whereby the variance of the error terms is constant over the entire range of values of the independent variables. Data with a nonconstant (e.g., increasing or decreasing) variance of the error terms are said to be heteroskedastic.

independent/explanatory variables The variables on the right-hand side of the equation, which are hypothesized to influence or predict the dependent variable.

population parameter A usually unknown characteristic of a population that is estimated using sample data.

residual The sample-based estimate of the true random error term.

serial correlation The amount of correlation between the error terms of any two given observations. Serial correlation is also often referred to as autocorrelation.

unbiased estimator An estimator whose expected value of its sampling distribution equals the true value of the population parameter.

Ordinary least squares (OLS) is a mathematical method often used to numerically estimate a linear relationship between a continuous dependent variable and one or more independent or explanatory variables using sample data. From a statistical point of view, an estimator is a mathematical method or formula used to produce a numerical estimate of an unknown population parameter based on the extractable information contained in a sample of data. The OLS estimator produces the best linear unbiased estimate of the relationship between each independent/explanatory variable (also known as a regressor or predictor) and a continuous dependent variable (also known as the regressand or response variable) while simultaneously eliminating the linear effects of the other included independent variables. The principle of OLS was first published by A. Legendre in 1805, and the theoretical presentation and derivation of its statistical properties was undertaken shortly thereafter by C. Gauss (who claimed to have already been using OLS years prior to Legendre's publication). Even today OLS remains a popular analytical tool in the analysis of social data. Yet, even though the OLS estimator has enjoyed long-standing popularity due to its relative simplicity, ease of computation, and statistical properties, the resulting estimates can be justified only on the basis of whether the assumptions underlying the OLS estimator can be empirically or theoretically satisfied. Herein, we describe the OLS estimator, including its assumptions, its statistical properties, and the consequences of violating the assumptions on which this estimator is based. In an effort to emphasize the substantive principles behind the OLS estimator, we primarily use simple numerical or scalar algebra notation. But, where necessary and relevant, we employ matrix algebra.

Introduction

A common undertaking in the analysis of social science data is to employ the use of a mathematical model to represent a substantive or theoretical social process or issue. This often necessitates formulating a model in which one variable is hypothesized to depend on one or more independent variables. The purpose of this formulation usually is to estimate the effect of each independent variable on the dependent variable while simultaneously adjusting or controlling for the effects of the other relevant independent variables. To quantitatively describe the relationship between a continuous dependent variable, Y, and one or more independent variables, X_k, the population linear regression model is often specified as:

$$Y_i = \beta_0 + \beta_1 X_{i1} + \cdots + \beta_k X_{ik} + \varepsilon_i \tag{1}$$

where β_0 is a constant term (which, geometrically, represents the Y intercept), β_k is the regression parameter characterizing the linear relationship between the kth independent variable and Y, and ε_i is the error or disturbance term for the ith individual ($i = 1, \ldots, n$, where n denotes the sample size). Corresponding to the population linear regression model in Eq. (1) is the sample linear regression model:

$$Y_i = b_0 + b_1 X_{i1} + \cdots + b_k X_{ik} + e_i \tag{2}$$

where b_0 and b_k indicate sample estimates of the unknown population parameters β_0 and β_k, and e_i denotes the error of estimation or residual for the ith observation (corresponding to ε_i). The b_k regression coefficients of this linear function represent the expected change in the continuous dependent variable associated with a one-unit change in the kth independent variable while holding constant the effect of all other independent variables included in the model specification.

From a statistical perspective, the goal is to estimate the population parameter using values that best describe the linear relationship between each of the k regressor variables and the Y regressand variable. This entails generating estimates of the dependent variable, denoted $\hat{Y}$, that best predict the observed values of the dependent variable. Equation (2) can be rewritten as:

$$e_i = Y_i - (b_0 + b_1 X_{i1} + \cdots + b_k X_{ik}) = Y_i - \hat{Y}_i \tag{3}$$

to highlight that the difference between the observed value (Y) and the model's predicted value ($\hat{Y}$) is reflected in the value of the residual term, e_i. Substantively, the residual terms are best thought of as the representation of both the combined effects of all variables not included in the model as specified and any remaining random elements or noise (e.g., measurement error) in the dependent variable. Mathematically, the residuals represent the amount by which an observed value deviates from the predicted conditional mean value (conditional on the values of the regressors). Important for our discussion is that the residuals are estimates of how accurately the model predicts the dependent variable; the smaller the residuals, the better the model fits the observed data, and vice versa. The statistical estimation problem, then, is one of determining how to generate estimates of the population parameters such that the residuals are as small as possible. This is accomplished by using an appropriate fitting criterion that uniquely and objectively determines when such a condition is satisfied.

The linear regression model in Eq. (2) involves fitting a regression surface to the sampled data. In the case of the simple regression model [a regression model involving one regressor or where $k = 1$ in Eq. (1)], we can graphically show the linear dependence of Y on X by fitting a straight line to the scatter plot of the data. Consider Fig. 1, which is a scatter plot of the variables labeled X and Y. Each circle on the graph represents a particular (X_i, Y_i) pair ($n = 8$). The figure also exhibits three lines that have been fitted to these data: a horizontal line equal to the mean of the dependent variable (line A in Fig. 1), a line representing a reasonable eyeball guess at the best-fitting line that was generated by making the line dissect the data points exactly in half (line B), and the OLS regression line itself. The vertical distance between any of the lines and the observed value is each case's residual for that particular line.

As is evident in Fig. 1, a different set of regression coefficients (b_0 and b_1) creates a different estimated line and, therefore, a different set of residuals. Given that each line produces a different set of residuals, there is an important need for a fitting criterion that both selects one particular set of estimates over all other sets of estimates and also can be used when the regression surface is multidimensional. That is, we need a criterion that can be used to determine estimates of the population parameters that best describe the linear relationship between the X_k values and Y for the given sample data. Figure 1 shows that each line fits some observations better than others, which indicates

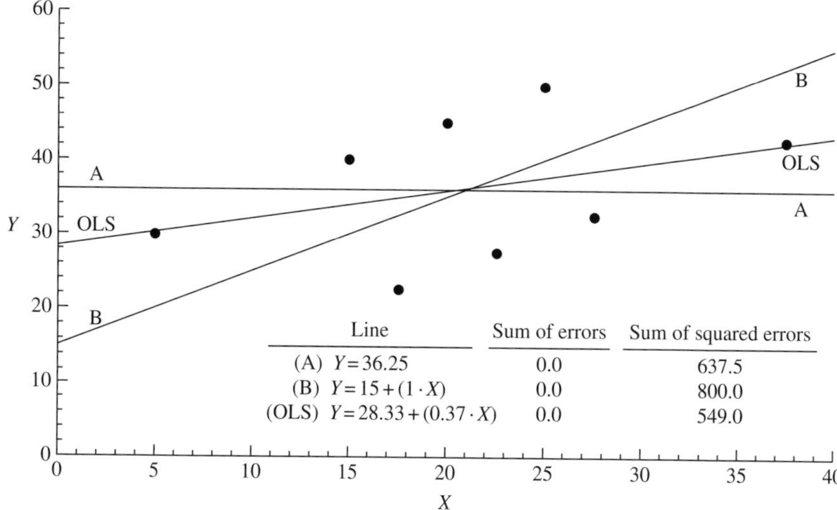

Figure 1 Three lines fitted to eight data points.

that the fitting criterion must simultaneously take into account all the residuals for the sampled data as a whole. In other words, we need to mathematically accumulate the residuals into an overall numerical or scalar index that can be objectively used to generate the best estimates of the population parameters. In the next section we discuss the nature of the fitting criterion used in ordinary least squares (OLS).

Fitting Criterion

In selecting the set of estimates that makes the errors as small as possible, we consider three possible fitting criteria that appear to be useful for this purpose. One possible criterion is the sum of deviations of the observed and predicted Y values, or $\sum_{i=1}^{n}(Y_i - \hat{Y})$. This criterion method, however, is problematic for several reasons. First, there is no unique solution for this fitting criterion. For example, one way to minimize this sum (to 0) is to simply set the b_0 parameter equal to the mean of the dependent variable and set each of the b_k parameters equal to zero. However, any line that passes through both the mean of X and the mean of Y will generate a sum of the residuals that is equal to 0; this is true regardless of the direction of the line. In Fig. 1, all three lines pass through the means of both X and Y and, as a result, the sum of the residuals from all three lines sum to 0. Second, the residual term for any given individual may be quite large (e.g., large positive and negative residuals can cancel one another), and thus the fit of any model satisfying this criterion may be incredibly poor. This fitting criterion clearly is not suitable.

A second fitting criterion that might be advocated is to minimize the sum of the absolute value of the deviations, or $\sum_{i=1}^{n}|Y_i - \hat{Y}|$. Applying the absolute value function avoids the potential problem of large positive and negative residuals canceling one another because all residuals enter this sum as positive values. However, this method does not differentially weight observations on the basis of the size of the residual, and thus large residuals are equal in weight to small residuals. Further, from a computational perspective, this fitting criterion is quite algebraically intractable (due to its nonlinearities) and requires the use of an iterative numerical optimization algorithm.

A final fitting criterion considered here is the sum of squared errors (SSE):

$$\mathrm{SSE} = \sum_{i=1}^{n} e_i^2 = \sum_{i=1}^{n}(Y_i - b_0 - b_1X_{i1} - b_2X_{i2} - \cdots - b_kX_{ik})^2$$
$$= \sum_{i=1}^{n}(Y_i - \hat{Y}_i)^2 \quad (4)$$

By squaring the deviations of $\hat{Y}$ from Y, this fitting criterion simultaneously satisfies both the need for positive values of the residuals and the differential weighting of residuals (i.e., the squaring makes all values positive and weights larger residuals more heavily). Given that it is desirable to avoid larger residuals, this fitting criterion accords more weight to larger residuals than smaller residuals in order to shift the regression surface toward the cases with larger residuals in an effort to reduce the size of their residuals. Computationally, the SSE can be minimized using a simple algebraic equation.

The estimator that minimizes the sum of squared errors in Eq. (4) is the OLS estimator. The statement that the OLS estimator minimizes the SSE implies that no other linear estimator will produce a smaller SSE than the OLS estimator. Consider Fig. 1 again. As shown in the table in the lower part of the figure, all three lines produce prediction errors that sum to 0. The OLS line, however, produces a sum of squared errors that is the lowest of all three lines. For these data, there is no other linear estimator that will produce a SSE value less than 549.0.

The data used in Fig. 1 were specifically generated to emphasize two important points regarding the OLS estimator. First, the fundamental principle behind the OLS estimator is that it uniquely minimizes the sum of the squared residuals. Second, as a consequence of minimizing the sum of squared errors, the OLS regression surface is pulled toward cases farther from the means of the independent and dependent variables. For example, notice that in Fig. 1 the regression line is pulled in the direction of the two cases farthest from the means of both X and Y, and that in fact the OLS regression line nearly passes right through those two data points. Observations that markedly deviate from the typical pattern of the variables are sometimes referred to as extreme cases or outliers. Extreme cases can have a large disproportionate influence on the regression estimates, and thus the results of any OLS estimation should always be checked to ensure that no sample member (or subsets of sample members) exerts significant influence on the values of the parameters.

The Ordinary Least Squares Estimator

Having chosen a fitting criterion, the statistical estimation problem is to find the sample estimates of model parameters that minimize the sum of squared errors. This can be accomplished using differential calculus because Eq. (4) is a quadratic equation and quadratic equations attain a minimum when the first derivative equals 0. Thus, we can find the OLS estimator by taking the partial derivative of the SSE with respect to each of the regression coefficients:

$$\frac{\partial SSE}{\partial b_0} = 2\cdot\sum_{i=1}^{n}(Y_i - b_0 - b_1X_{i1} - b_2X_{i2} - \cdots - b_kX_{ik})\cdot(-1) \tag{5}$$

$$\frac{\partial SSE}{\partial b_1} = 2\cdot\sum_{i=1}^{n}(Y_i - b_0 - b_1X_{i1} - b_2X_{i2} - \cdots - b_kX_{ik})\cdot(-X_{i1}) \tag{6}$$

$$\vdots$$

$$\frac{\partial SSE}{\partial b_k} = 2\cdot\sum_{i=1}^{n}(Y_i - b_0 - b_1X_{i1} - b_2X_{i2} - \cdots - b_kX_{ik})\cdot(-X_{ik}) \tag{7}$$

Setting Eqs. (5)–(7) equal to zero and then multiplying and summing through each of the $k+1$ expressions results in the system of linear equations known as the normal equations:

$$\sum_{i=1}^{n} Y_i = \sum_{i=1}^{n} b_0 + b_1\sum_{i=1}^{n} X_{i1} + \cdots + b_k\sum_{i=1}^{n} X_{ik} \tag{8}$$

$$\sum_{i=1}^{n} Y_iX_{i1} = b_0\sum_{i=1}^{n} X_{i1} + b_1\sum_{i=1}^{n} X_{i1}X_{i1} + \cdots + b_k\sum_{i=1}^{n} X_{ik}X_{i1} \tag{9}$$

$$\vdots$$

$$\sum_{i=1}^{n} Y_iX_{ik} = b_0\sum_{i=1}^{n} X_{ik} + b_1\sum_{i=1}^{n} X_{i1}X_{ik} + \cdots + b_k\sum_{i=1}^{n} X_{ik}X_{ik} \tag{10}$$

Before proceeding, note that these equations can be reexpressed as:

$$\sum_{i=1}^{n} e_i = 0 \tag{11}$$

$$\sum_{i=1}^{n} e_iX_{i1} = 0 \tag{12}$$

$$\vdots$$

$$\sum_{i=1}^{n} e_iX_{ik} = 0 \tag{13}$$

which highlights that the OLS estimator forces *both* the sum of the residuals to equal zero and the covariance between each of the independent variables and the residuals to be zero.

Given that $\sum_{i=1}^{n} b_0 = n\cdot b_0$, solving Eq. (8) yields:

$$b_0 = \bar{Y} - b_1\bar{X}_1 - \cdots - b_k\bar{X}_k \tag{14}$$

The solution in Eq. (14) can then be substituted into the remaining k normal equations, which themselves can then be simultaneously solved. Consider, for example, a regression model that contains two independent variables ($k = 2$). For this model, the normal equations for the independent variables X_1 and X_2, after substituting Eq. (14) for the constant, simplify to:

$$\sum_{i=1}^{n}(Y_i - \bar{Y})\cdot X_{i1} - b_1\sum_{i=1}^{n}(X_{i1} - \bar{X}_1)\cdot X_{i1} - b_2\sum_{i=1}^{n}(X_{i2} - \bar{X}_2)\cdot X_{i1} = 0 \tag{15}$$

$$\sum_{i=1}^{n}(Y_i - \bar{Y}) \cdot X_{i2} - b_1 \sum_{i=1}^{n}(X_{i1} - \bar{X}_1) \cdot X_{i2} - b_2 \times \sum_{i=1}^{n}(X_{i2} - \bar{X}_2) \cdot X_{i2} = 0 \quad (16)$$

Equations (15) and (16) can be rewritten as:

$$\sum_{i=1}^{n} y_i x_{i1} - b_1 \sum_{i=1}^{n} x_{i1}^2 - b_2 \sum_{i=1}^{n} x_{i2} x_{i1} = 0 \quad (17)$$

$$\sum_{i=1}^{n} y_i x_{i2} - b_1 \sum_{i=1}^{n} x_{i1} x_{i2} - b_2 \sum_{i=1}^{n} x_{i2}^2 = 0 \quad (18)$$

where $x_{ik} = (X_{ik} - \bar{X}_k)$ and $y_i = (Y_i - \bar{Y})$. Simultaneously solving Eqs. (17) and (18) yields the solutions for the regression slopes for X_1 and X_2:

$$b_1 = \frac{\sum_{i=1}^{n} x_{i2}^2 \sum_{i=1}^{n} x_{i1} y_i - \sum_{i=1}^{n} x_{i1} x_{i2} \sum_{i=1}^{n} x_{i2} y_i}{\sum_{i=1}^{n} x_{i1}^2 \sum_{i=1}^{n} x_{i2}^2 - \left(\sum_{i=1}^{n} x_{i1} x_{i2}\right)^2} \quad (19)$$

$$b_2 = \frac{\sum_{i=1}^{n} x_{i1}^2 \sum_{i=1}^{n} x_{i2} y_i - \sum_{i=1}^{n} x_{i1} x_{i2} \sum_{i=1}^{n} x_{i1} y_i}{\sum_{i=1}^{n} x_{i1}^2 \sum_{i=1}^{n} x_{i2}^2 - \left(\sum_{i=1}^{n} x_{i1} x_{i2}\right)^2} \quad (20)$$

In the case of the simple regression model ($k = 1$), the regression slope coefficient for each of the independent variables is found by dropping the terms in Eqs. (19) and (20) that involve the other independent variables, or more specifically:

$$b_1 = \frac{\sum_{i=1}^{n} x_{i1} y_i}{\sum_{i=1}^{n} x_{i1}^2} \quad (21)$$

With each additional independent variable, the OLS solutions for the regression coefficients become increasingly more difficult to derive algebraically due to the rapidly increasing number of terms involved. For example, compare Eq. (21) to Eq. (19).

The OLS estimator, however, can be compactly and conveniently described using matrix algebra, and the OLS solution in matrix terms can be applied regardless of the number of independent variables included in the specification. In matrix notation, Eq. (2) can be written as:

$$\mathbf{Y} = \mathbf{X}\mathbf{b} + \mathbf{e} \quad (22)$$

where

$$\underset{n\times 1}{\mathbf{Y}} = \begin{bmatrix} Y_1 \\ Y_2 \\ \vdots \\ Y_n \end{bmatrix}, \quad \underset{n\times p}{\mathbf{X}} = \begin{bmatrix} 1 & X_{11} & \cdots & X_{1k} \\ 1 & X_{21} & \cdots & X_{2k} \\ \vdots & \vdots & & \vdots \\ 1 & X_{n1} & \cdots & X_{nk} \end{bmatrix},$$

$$\underset{p\times 1}{\mathbf{b}} = \begin{bmatrix} b_0 \\ b_1 \\ \vdots \\ b_k \end{bmatrix}, \quad \underset{n\times 1}{\mathbf{e}} = \begin{bmatrix} e_1 \\ e_2 \\ \vdots \\ e_n \end{bmatrix}$$

and $p = k + 1$. The column of 1s in the $\mathbf{X}$ matrix is required for the constant term b_0. In matrix terms, the normal equations are expressed as:

$$(\mathbf{X}'\mathbf{X})\mathbf{b} = \mathbf{X}'\mathbf{Y} \quad (23)$$

Solving Eq. (23) yields the general matrix solution for the OLS estimator:

$$\mathbf{b} = (\mathbf{X}'\mathbf{X})^{-1}\mathbf{X}'\mathbf{Y} \quad (24)$$

where $(\mathbf{X}'\mathbf{X})^{-1}$ denotes the inverse matrix of $\mathbf{X}'\mathbf{X}$.

Assumptions of Ordinary Least Squares

In statistics, precise mathematical conditions are required for the derivation of statistical estimators. These mathematical conditions are referred to as the assumptions of an estimator and are critical for determining the statistical properties of a given estimator. The OLS estimator in Eq. (24) is derived under five assumptions. It should be noted that these assumptions are distinct from the conditions necessary for model identification, which include (1) that there be at least p ($= k + 1$) observations in the sample ($n \geq p$) and (2) that none of the independent variables is an exact linear combination of the other independent variables. These conditions are required for the computation of unique OLS estimates because they ensure the $\mathbf{X}$ matrix is of full rank, a necessary condition for inverting the $\mathbf{X}'\mathbf{X}$ component of Eq. (24).

If the following five mathematical assumptions about the process through which the data were generated can be satisfied, then the OLS estimator will have several desirable statistical properties.

Assumption 1. The model is specified correctly, which implies that Eq. (2),

$$Y_i = b_0 + b_1 X_{i1} + \cdots + b_k X_{ik} + e_i$$

is the correct specification of the regression function such that on average, or by taking the expected value of the estimated regression equation, we obtain the corresponding population or model regression function:

$$\begin{aligned} E(Y_i) &= E(b_0 + b_1X_{i1} + \cdots + b_kX_{ik} + e_i) \\ &= E(b_0 + b_1X_{i1} + \cdots + b_kX_{ik}) + E(e_i) \\ &= \beta_0 + \beta_1X_{i1} + \cdots + \beta_kX_{ik} + 0 \\ &= \beta_0 + \beta_1X_{i1} + \cdots + \beta_kX_{ik} \end{aligned} \tag{25}$$

This assumption implies that there are no relevant independent variables omitted from the specification, that no irrelevant predictors are included, that the relationship between and X_k and Y is linear in the parameters, and that the regression coefficients are additive in nature (e.g., the effects are not multiplicative).

Assumption 2. The conditional expected value of the error term is 0, or:

$$E(\varepsilon_i \mid X_{i1}, \ldots, X_{ik}) = 0 \tag{26}$$

In other words, knowledge of X_k provides no information about the error term.

Assumption 3. The independent variables are uncorrelated with the error term:

$$\operatorname{cov}(\varepsilon_i, X_{ik}) = 0 \tag{27}$$

The importance of this assumption is that if they are correlated, it is impossible to separate the true effect of X_k on Y from the effect of ε on Y. In other words, this assumption is necessary in order to identify the $k+1$ unknowns in the **b** vector.

Assumption 4. The errors have constant variance:

$$\operatorname{var}(\varepsilon_i \mid X_{i1}, \ldots, X_{ik}) = \sigma^2 \tag{28}$$

This assumption is often referred to as the assumption of homoskedasticity and implies that the errors of the predictions or are no more or less variable for some observations than others.

Assumption 5. For any two observations i and j, their corresponding error terms are uncorrelated (i.e., there is no serial correlation among the errors):

$$\operatorname{cov}\left(\varepsilon_i \mid X_{i1}, \ldots, X_{ik}, \varepsilon_j \mid X_{j1}, \ldots, X_{jk}\right) = 0 \tag{29}$$

Assumptions 4 and 5, Eqs. (28) and (29), taken together are often referred to as the assumption of spherical errors or the assumption that the errors are independently and identically distributed (i.i.d.). These two assumptions imply that the variance–covariance matrix of the error terms can be described as:

$$\begin{bmatrix} \sigma^2 & 0 & \cdots & 0 \\ 0 & \sigma^2 & \cdots & 0 \\ & & \vdots & \\ 0 & 0 & \cdots & \sigma^2 \end{bmatrix} = \sigma^2 \begin{bmatrix} 1 & 0 & \cdots & 0 \\ 0 & 1 & \cdots & 0 \\ & & \vdots & \\ 0 & 0 & \cdots & 1 \end{bmatrix} = \sigma^2\mathbf{I} \tag{30}$$

where $\mathbf{I}$ is an $n \times n$ identity matrix with 1s on the diagonal and 0s in the off-diagonals.

The Gauss–Markov Theorem

In statistics, estimators are usually adopted because of their statistical properties, most notably unbiasedness and efficiency. The statistical property of unbiasedness refers to whether the expected value of the sampling distribution of an estimator is equal to the unknown true value of the population parameter. For example, the OLS estimator b_k is unbiased if the mean of the sampling distribution of b_k is equal to β_k. That is, if we repeatedly sampled the population by taking samples of some finite size n, calculated b_k for each sample, and then calculated the mean of the b_k estimates, the mean would be equal to the population parameter i.e., $E(b_k) = \beta_k$.

However, simply knowing that an estimator is unbiased *on average* is not very advantageous if the values of b vary greatly from sample to sample. That is, estimators are adopted not only based on whether they are unbiased, but also based on whether the estimates vary widely from sample to sample. In statistical terminology, an unbiased estimator is maximally efficient when the variance of its sampling distribution is smaller than the variances of the sampling distributions of all other unbiased estimators. For example, consider Fig. 2, which is a graph of the sampling distribution of the two unbiased estimators,

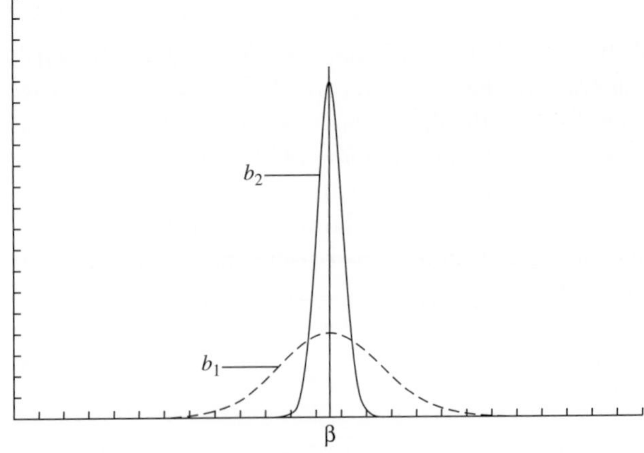

Figure 2 Sampling distributions of two unbiased estimators.

b_1 and b_2 (i.e., the mean of each distribution is equal to the true population parameter β). The variance of the estimator b_1 is much greater than the variance of the estimator b_2. In other words, b_2 is a more efficient estimator than b_1. If either of these distributions were biased, the mean of the distribution would not be equal to the true population parameter value.

The linear estimator with the smallest variance (or highest precision) is said to be the best linear estimator. Under the conditions specified in Eqs. (25)–(29), the OLS estimator is the best linear unbiased estimator (BLUE). This means that among all unbiased linear estimators, the OLS estimator has the smallest variance. This theorem (that the OLS estimator is BLUE) is commonly referred to as the Gauss–Markov theorem after mathematicians C. Gauss and A. Markov. The BLUE property is arguably one of the main reasons why the OLS estimator has been a mainstay of statistical analysis since its derivation, but it is important to emphasize both that the Gauss–Markov theorem applies to the OLS estimator rather than a particular estimate from a given sample and that it is possible that there exists a *biased* estimator that has a sampling distribution with a smaller variance.

By now, some readers are probably wondering why we have not discussed any assumption regarding a particular statistical distribution for the error terms. The reason we have not discussed this issue is that the OLS estimator is BLUE without specifying a particular statistical distribution for the error terms. However, if the error terms can be assumed to be normally distributed, then the OLS estimator becomes the best unbiased estimator. This means that the OLS estimator is the estimator with the smallest variance among *all* unbiased estimators, not just among the linear unbiased estimators. It also can be shown that, under the assumption of normally distributed errors, the OLS estimator is the maximum likelihood estimator (MLE) of β. Thus, minimizing the sum of squared errors is identical to maximizing the likelihood function, or $b_{OLS} = b_{MLE}$. This congruence between the least squares approach and the maximum likelihood approach is another compelling theoretical justification of the OLS estimator. A final crucial item to note about the assumption of normality of the errors is that this assumption also provides the theoretical justification for statistical inference regarding the regression coefficients.

Consequences of Violating the Assumptions of Ordinary Least Squares

We now briefly discuss the consequences of violating the assumptions of the OLS estimator; a complete discussion of these consequences is beyond the scope of this entry. The first three OLS assumptions are fundamentally critical for proving the unbiasedness of the OLS estimator. These assumptions can be violated in a number of ways, including via nonlinearity in the relationship between the independent and dependent variables, via measurement error in the independent variables, via simultaneity or joint dependence between the independent and dependent variables (e.g., Y is a cause of X), or via the model specification's excluding a relevant independent variable that is correlated with both the included independent variables and the dependent variable. If any of these three assumptions is violated, the OLS estimator will be biased. Although violations of either assumptions 4 or 5 will not bias the OLS estimator, the violation of either of these two assumptions will cause the OLS estimator to be inefficient (i.e., no longer the best estimator). Further, violations of assumptions 4 and 5 also will bias the estimator of the variance–covariance matrix of the OLS estimator (which will bias the standard errors of the OLS estimates). Thus, the conventional t tests and F tests used in statistical inference regarding the OLS estimates can no longer be trusted. The important point to remember about the assumptions is that, although OLS estimates can be computed regardless of whether the assumptions can be justified, the statistical properties of the Gauss–Markov theorem *require* that all these assumptions to be met.

The violation of the assumptions of OLS is perhaps best viewed on a continuum from "very mild" to "very severe" rather than as a dichotomy of "yes" or "no." In other words, sample data can rarely be assumed to perfectly satisfy all the assumptions, and thus there will usually be some degree of violation. The critical question of when the violation of an assumption can be considered severe enough to be detrimental to the conclusions has been an ongoing debate among statisticians for decades. This question concerns the robustness of the OLS estimator to violations of its assumptions. The OLS estimator has been argued to be quite robust to moderate violations of some of the assumptions (e.g., heteroskedasticity), and our point here is not to argue for absolute strict adherence to these assumptions in order to use the OLS estimator. Rather we wish to emphasize that the principle of least squares and the Gauss–Markov theorem should not be used as a blanket justification for the application of the OLS estimator without giving due consideration to the assumptions of the model. The user should think critically about the assumptions and be prepared to either empirically or theoretically justify the application of the OLS estimator.

Arguably, the detection of violated assumptions is as much art as science because determining the degree to which the assumptions are satisfied can be a difficult analytical task. For example, as a consequence of the normal equations, the second and third assumptions are guaranteed to be true in the sampled data by the definition of the OLS estimator [see Eqs. (11) and (13)]. Whether these are true in the population from which a sample has been obtained is a much more difficult question that can only be adequately answered with substantive theory about the social issue under consideration. Nonetheless, the user should be aware of the possible consequences of violations of the assumptions on the conclusions of a study, and, if the violation(s) cannot be corrected, the user should make the reading audience keenly aware of the possible consequences.

If the violation of a particular assumption is detected (whether theoretically or empirically), some type of remedial action can usually be taken. Often, violations necessitate the use of a more advanced statistical estimator (e.g., generalized least squares, two-stage least squares), but occasionally a correction can be made to the data (e.g., using a transformation to induce linearity) or the estimator (e.g., applying a heteroskedastic consistent variance-covariance estimator). Recent advances in computing power and the incorporation of advanced statistical estimators in standard statistical software packages have made remedies for data not suitable for the method of OLS much more feasible.

See Also the Following Articles

Hierarchical Linear Models • Linear Models, Problems

Further Reading

Allison, P. (1999). *Multiple Regression: A Primer.* Pine Forge Press, Thousand Oaks, CA.

Berry, W. (1993). *Understanding Regression Assumptions.* Sage, Newbury Park, CA.

Draper, N., and Smith, H. (1998). *Applied Regression Analysis,* 3rd Ed. John Wiley & Sons, New York.

Fox, J. (1991). *Regression Diagnostics.* Sage, Newbury Park, CA.

Greene, W. (2003). *Econometric Analysis,* 5th Ed. Prentice Hall, Upper Saddle River, NJ.

Gujurati, D. (1995). *Basic Econometrics,* 3rd Ed. McGraw-Hill, New York.

Kennedy, P. (1993). *A Guide to Econometrics,* 3rd Ed. MIT Press, Cambridge, MA.

Long, J., and Ervin, L. (2000). Using heteroskedasticity consistent standard errors in the linear regression model. *Am. Statist.* **54,** 217–224.

Wooldridge, J. (2003). *Introductory Econometrics: A Modern Approach,* 2nd Ed. South-Western College Publishing, Mason, Ohio.

Organizational Behavior

Dail Fields
Regent University, Virginia Beach, Virginia, USA

Mihai C. Bocarnea
Regent University, Virginia Beach, Virginia, USA

Glossary

construct validity Empirical evidence that a measure is an acceptable indicator of a particular theoretical concept.

content validity The extent to which the items making up a measure are logical representations of the concepts being measured.

interrater agreement A quantitative indicator of the level of agreement among two or more informants concerning the same measurement.

item A question or a statement that describes a measurable aspect of the concept being measured.

key informant A person with knowledge about the nature of an organization or work group adequate to respond to items describing the collective unit.

latent variable A nonobservable characteristic of people, presumed to underlie observed variables.

multiple-item measure A composite measure, composed of the sum or average of responses to multiple statements or questions about various aspects of the concept being measured.

reliability The extent to which the items of a composite measure of a concept consistently capture various aspects of the concept.

Organizational behavior is the study of humans at work within organizations. It seeks to understand individual workers, work groups, and entire organizations. Measurement in organizational behavior often seeks to assess employee perceptions about work within an organization by quantitatively describing employee attitudes, beliefs, intentions, and behaviors. Organizational behavior is often concerned with which of the variables present within groups and/or organizations positively or negatively affect the attitudes and behaviors of workers. Measurements in organizational behavior may also determine analytical and structural properties of groups or organizations. Global properties of groups or organizations are best detected through measurement of the characteristics of the collective units. However, in some cases, the viewpoints of individuals are aggregated to represent properties of groups and organizations.

Introduction

Organizational behavior research draws on multiple disciplines, including psychology, sociology, and anthropology, but predominantly examines workers within actual organizational settings, rather than in experimental or quasi-experimental settings. Organizational behavior researchers are primarily concerned with measuring the presence of employee motivation, job alienation, organizational commitment, or similar work-related variables in order to understand how these attributes explain employee work behaviors and how they are affected by other variables, such as working conditions, company policies, human resource programs, or pay plans.

Individuals regularly behave in various ways at work, and these behaviors are described in various ways: someone putting forth a great deal of effort might be described as "motivated"; a person who approaches his or her job in a resigned fashion, putting forth only the minimum effort required, might be described as "alienated"; an employee who stays late to help a customer might be described as "committed." In each case, there are alternative possible explanations for the observed behaviors. Plausible alternatives could be that the employee putting forth lots of effort has knowledge about a possible layoff, that the person putting forth the minimum required may be ill or preoccupied with family problems, and that the person staying late may be hoping to secure a job with the customer. Many of the variables of interest in organizational behavior reflect employee perceptions. In fact, many researchers consider the perceptions of organizational members to be the reality within work settings. Perceptions and other similar phenomena on which people may vary are not directly observable as attributes (such as hair color, height, and size), but are nonobservable aspects, or latent variables. Nonobservable variables are latent in that they are assumed to be underlying causes for observable behaviors and actions. Examples of individual latent variables include intelligence, creativity, job satisfaction, and, from the examples previously provided, motivation, job alienation, and organizational commitment. Not all latent variables studied in organizational behavior are individual in nature. Some latent variables apply to groups and organizations. These include variables reflecting aggregate characteristics of the group, such as intragroup communication, group cohesion, and group goal orientation. Furthermore, organizations may be globally described as centralized, flexible, or actively learning, also representing latent variables.

Although some theories in organizational behavior (OB) include manifest variables that are directly observable, such as age, gender, and race of workers or the age and location of a work facility, many OB theories are concerned with relationships among latent variables. For example, job satisfaction is a variable that has been studied extensively over the history of organizational behavior. In particular, researchers (and practitioners) are frequently concerned with which variables are related to higher levels of job satisfaction. Generally, an employee's perceptions of the nature his or her work (interesting, boring, repetitive, difficult, demanding, skill intensive, autonomous) greatly influence job satisfaction. These perceptions are all latent variables. Some researchers have measured these aspects of a worker's job using estimations by trained observers. The agreement between the observer estimations and the worker self-assessments of perceptions is often low, and the observations have a weaker relationship with job satisfaction. Thus, measurement in organizational behavior often deals with how to obtain the specific beliefs, attitudes, and behaviors of individuals that appropriately represent, or operationalize, a latent variable. An example of one way to measure a latent variable, intelligence, is to sum the scores of an individual on tests of verbal, numerical, and spatial abilities. The assumption is that the latent variable, intelligence, underlies a person's ability in these three areas. Thus, if a person has a high score across these three areas, that person is inferred to be intelligent.

A central issue in measurement in organizational behavior is which specific perceptions should be assembled to form adequate measures of latent variables such as job satisfaction and organizational commitment. Because satisfied and committed employees are valued, managers are very interested in what policies, jobs, or pay plans will help promote such states in workers. Researchers, in turn, want to be sure that the things they use to represent satisfaction and commitment are in fact good indicators of the unseen variables. Because latent variables such as satisfaction may be based on different aspects of a job or an organization, it is necessary for an indicator of job satisfaction to include all these aspects—as many as is necessary. The result is that indicators of job satisfaction and other latent variables important in organizational behavior are based on multiple items representing statements or questions addressing measurable aspects of the concept being measured.

Examples of Measures Used in Organizational Behavior

Table I presents examples of multiple item scales capturing various types of employee attitudes, beliefs, intentions, and behaviors that are widely used in measuring employee perceptions concerning organizational commitment, job satisfaction, organizational justice, job stress, and workplace behaviors. These particular measures have been used in multiple research studies that were published in the 1990s in 15 peer-reviewed organizational behavior research journals.

The measures illustrated in Table I describe employee perceptions that are frequently of interest in the field of organizational behavior. For example, organizational commitment has been defined as a strong belief in and acceptance of the organization's goals and values, willingness to exert considerable effort on behalf of the organization, and a strong desire to maintain membership in an organization. Other various definitions reflect three broad themes: (1) commitment reflecting an affective orientation toward the organization, (2) recognition of costs associated with leaving the organization, and (3) the moral obligation to remain with an organization. The concept of job satisfaction is defined as an employee's affective reactions to her or his job based on comparing actual outcomes with desired outcomes. Job satisfaction is generally recognized as a multifaceted construct covering both intrinsic and extrinsic job elements. Organizational justice is measured through a process by which employees judge fairness in the workplace by comparing the equity of their inputs and outcomes to the perceived inputs and outcomes of their co-workers. One aspect of organizational justice is the distributive justice, a summary

Table I Examples of Organizational Behavior Measures

Concept	*Measure*	*Number of items*	*Example items*	*Response scale*
Organizational commitment	Organizational Commitment Questionnaire (OCQ)	15	I am willing to put in a great deal of effort beyond that normally expected in order to help this organization be successful I find that my values and the organization's values are very similar	1, Strongly disagree; 2, moderately disagree; 3, slightly disagree; 4, neither disagree nor agree; 5, slightly agree; 6, moderately agree; 7, strongly agree
Job satisfaction	Minnesota Satisfaction Questionnaire	20 (short form)	The chance to do different things from time to time Being able to do things that don't go against my conscience The feeling of accomplishment I get from the job	1, Very dissatisfied with this aspect of my job; 2, dissatisfied with this aspect of my job; 3, can't decide if I am satisfied or not with this aspect of my job; 4, satisfied with this aspect of my job; 5, very satisfied with this aspect of my job
Organizational justice	Distributive and Procedural Justice	24 (11 for distributive justice and 13 for procedural justice)	I am told promptly when there is a change in policy, rules, or regulations that affect me (procedural) In general, disciplinary actions taken in this organization are fair and justified (procedural) Promotions or unscheduled pay increases here usually depend on how well a person performs on his or her job (distributive) My performance rating presents a fair and accurate picture of my actual job performance (distributive)	Responses are obtained using a five-point scale (1, strongly disagree to 5, strongly agree)
Job stress	Job-Related Tension Index	15	How frequently do you feel bothered by each of these? Feeling that you have too little authority to carry out the responsibilities assigned to you Being unclear on just what the scope and responsibilities of your job are Feeling that you have too heavy a work load, one that you can't possibly finish during an ordinary workday	1, Never; 2, rarely; 3, sometimes; 4, rather often; 5, nearly all the time
Workplace behaviors	Organizational Citizenship Behavior	24	Willingly helps others who have work-related problems Obeys company rules and regulations even when no one is watching Considers the impact of his or her actions on co-workers Attends meetings that are not mandatory, but are considered important	Responses are obtained using a seven-point Likert-type scale (1, strongly disagree to 7, strongly agree); the item wording provided is for supervisor or peer description of a focal employee, and can be modified for self-reporting

judgment about the fairness in distribution of pay, promotions, and other incentives. Another is procedural justice, focused on the process of how reward decisions are made.

Measures of job stress tend to recognize the fact that stress does not reside solely in the environment or solely in the individual, but is established when the interactions between the two are appraised as demanding enough to threaten personal well being. Employee workplace behavior can be generally characterized as either contributing to organizational goals or contributing to the employee's occupational control. A good deal of attention has been devoted to work behavior that is sometimes beyond the reach of traditional definitions of job performance, because these "organizational citizenship behaviors" may contribute to organizational innovation, flexibility, and responsiveness to changing external conditions.

An example of an organization level measure is a three-item measure of the tendency for an organization to be innovative. The items making up the measure were originally designed for a study of hospitals, but are presented here as general statements. The statements are formatted as follows: "(a) This [type of organization] is a little behind in utilizing the most adequate equipment and medicines. (b) This [type of organization] has not introduced any new methods and techniques. (c) This [type of organization] is very behind in the application of new administrative techniques." The responses from organizational members are collected using a five-point scale ranging from 1, strongly agree, to 5, strongly disagree. The use of this type of measure within an organization or group requires identification of an appropriate set of respondents who have been working in the organization long enough to have adequate information about innovative tendencies. These individuals are referred to as "key informants" about the organization. Once collected, the responses from these informants are evaluated in terms of the level of agreement. High levels of agreement and small variations in the responses to the three items would suggest that the measure provides a reliable assessment of the organization's innovativeness. Several different measures can be used to assess agreement among raters. These include the percentage of raters whose responses are the same value (using a Likert-type response with limited choices of responses), the average interitem correlation across raters and the intraclass correlation produced in the analysis of variance (ANOVA) procedure.

The measures described here are designed to be completed as part of a questionnaire or survey, or administered as part of an interview. Measures of this sort can be "closed end," whereby the respondent must choose one of several predefined response options. It is also possible to measure variables in organizational behavior using "open-ended" questions, whereby a respondent can compose an answer using their own words. These types of measures are somewhat difficult to interpret and cannot be evaluated from a reliability point of view because each person's response may be unique.

Response Scales, Reliability, and Validity

The topic of reliability and validity of measures is mentioned here because it is a critical concern in organizational behavior, in part because many of the variables are perceptual in nature. It is important to remember that many organizational behavior measures ask employees to describe aspects of their job or work environment by choosing preselected responses to a series of questions or statements. These measures attempt to capture meaningful aspects of individual perceptions as well as an employee's evaluation of these perceptions. The use of multiple items to attempt to capture employee perceptions and related evaluations is tacit recognition of the difficulty of the task at hand. That is, if a large percentage of workers would all agree on the concept of organizational commitment, much as they would agree about the color red, then a single question or statement could measure commitment in nearly all situations. However, the reality is that organizational commitment is the result of an employee evaluating numerous aspects of the work situation. Attitudes such as commitment to an organization may have affective and cognitive aspects, thus comprehensive measures of commitment must attempt to capture multiple aspects of how employees feel about the organization and how they think about the organization.

Many alternative types of scales can be used to convert human perceptions to numbers based on the statements or questions used in organizational behavior measures. Choice of the type, nature, and anchor values in response scales can be a critical choice in measurements in organizational behavior. For example, to assess the extent to which a sample of students considered a robot to imitate a duck, a list of characteristics such as sound, appearance, walk, flight, and swim could be selected for obtaining assessments from the students. Ratings on each characteristic would be used to compute a score representing how well each student believes that the robot is like a duck. The ratings could be obtained via YES/NO responses, where each YES response is assigned the value 1 and each NO response is assigned the value 0. This approach, however, does not capture much of the variation in the ratings of each characteristic. That is, some students may have voted YES for some characteristics of the robot even if the resemblance to a duck were very limited. In other cases, characteristics may have received a YES vote because they were almost identical to those of a real duck. If the overall score was intended to improve certain aspects of the robot, it would be more informative to know which duck-like characteristics scored high and which scored low. To get such ratings, the students could be asked to rate each characteristic of the robot as "not at all" like a duck, "somewhat" like a duck, "pretty much" like a duck, "a good deal" like a duck, and "very much" like a duck. The values 1 through 7 could then be assigned to these responses and to obtain considerably more information about how the respondents rated the extent to which each of the characteristics were characteristic of a duck.

After getting the responses to the items, a common approach in organizational behavior measurement would be to average the ratings across the characteristics and get a summary score that showed how well the robot approximates a duck overall. The latter approach, using a range of values to collect the ratings, is a commonly used method for obtaining responses from employees in measures of organizational behavior. These Likert-type response scales used in measures of latent variables in organizational behavior often provide respondents with five or seven alternative choices (see Table I for examples of Likert-type response scales frequently used).

Some variation in the extent to which different people see a collection of items as related is expected. However, if the variation is too great, confidence in the stability of the measurement is lessened. The consistency with which a group of statements of questions measure the same concept is referred to as the internal consistency reliability of a measure. There are two commonly used indicators of internal consistency reliability for items for which responses are obtained using a Likert-type scale. These are both readily calculated when using SPSS (Statistical Package for the Social Sciences) or other similar statistical software programs for analyzing organizational behavior data. The most commonly used indicator of internal reliability used for measures in organizational behavior is Chronbach's alpha. An alternative is the Spearman–Brown prophecy. Assessment of the internal consistency reliability is based on a single administration of that measure. Prior to using a measure for research or practice, it is generally wise to consult a reference to determine if the measure's internal consistency reliability has been assessed in multiple samples. It is also relevant to consider whether the responses to the items in a measure are consistent across time periods. This type of reliability, referred to as test–retest reliability, is assessed by examining the correlation of the responses to the items from the same sample of people obtained at two different times. The time between the two measurements should be long enough to limit the likelihood that people will remember their first response, but not so long that there have been substantial changes in jobs or business conditions that could cause legitimately different responses to the items.

The validity of a measure is concerned with the extent to which it actually gauges what it is thought to measure. In other words, validity shows the magnitude of the direct effect of the latent variable on its corresponding observed variables. For example, in the previous example of assessment of the robot duck, the goal was to collect ratings of how well the robot mimics several characteristics of real ducks. The hope is that a measure of the similarity of the robot to a real duck will be obtained. However, it is possible that the measure might actually be of student reactions to a possible robot pet, or an indicator of awe at the technology represented by the robot "quacker." Because many of the concepts measured in organizational behavior are intangible (e.g., motivation, job satisfaction, and organizational justice), the question of a measure's validity is addressed in both direct and indirect ways.

The direct method is called content validity and involves examination of each of the statements or questions used to obtain responses and asking "are these items part of the pool of items that should be used to describe the concept of interest?" Generally, this assessment is made using a panel of judges as a way of approximating the variation that may be found among respondents to the questions or statements. For example, a panel of five judges might have high levels of agreement that five items measure similarity with a duck, but may have low levels of agreement on two other items. The measure with the five items would then have greater content validity than would the measure using all seven.

The indirect approach to validation of organizational behavior measures involves searching for evidence of convergence and discrimination. The idea of convergence is that different versions of measuring the same concept should converge. That is, one measure of a latent variable should produce similar values to other measures of the same latent variable obtained using different techniques. Discrimination in this case means that it should also be possible to show that the measure of a latent variable is distinct from other measures of similar but different latent constructs, and that the measure is not correlated with a set of other latent variables with which it should not be correlated. As an example, the objective might be to validate a measure of the extent to which a person's work interferes with family life. The convergent validity can be examined by comparing a person's reported work/family conflict with independent reports of the frequency that work interferes with a person's planned family activities, as provided by a spouse, children, and co-workers. The discrimination of the measure can be assessed by examining its correlation with pay level, expected to be negative, and the number of pets in the household, expected to be insignificant. Discrimination among measures of similar concepts, e.g., job satisfaction and organizational justice, is often tested empirically using confirmatory factor analysis. This statistical technique evaluates the extent to which the items of the measures of two similar concepts are more strongly related to each of the measures than they are to each other.

Considerations in Organizational Behavior Measurement

There are some issues with which organizational behavior researchers must be particularly concerned in using perceptual measures about work. First, measurement should be made at the appropriate level. For example, the work climate in an organization can affect employee job satisfaction and commitment. However, climate is a property of the organization. It should be measured at the organizational level either by assembling key informants and asking them to provide a consensus response to questions about the organization or aggregating the individual responses of key informants to questions about the organization after assuring there is an acceptable level of interrater agreement. Aggregating responses to statements or questions about an individual's work experience on the job would not provide a valid measure of organizational climate.

Second, self-reports about jobs and related work environments provided by employees do not describe objective job conditions, as might be reported by observers. In general, perceptions of a worker may not agree well with observations by others. In addition, self-reports of behaviors tend to reflect self-serving bias, which is a tendency to describe the self as conforming to some ideal image. Generally, reports by others describing an employee's behaviors do not have high levels of agreement with self-reports. Self-reports can also be contaminated by other forms of bias. For example, it is likely that an employee's descriptions of the autonomy and variety present in his or her job may be influenced by the nature of the employee's relationship with his or her supervisor or by recent events in the work unit, such as promotions or terminations. Self-reports about jobs and work environments provide very meaningful and valuable insights, but do have limitations that are worth keeping in mind. In many cases, the measurement errors introduced by these biases can be controlled in the analysis if data about the biasing condition is collected at the time of the study.

It is also common practice in organizational behavior studies to collect multiple measures within a single questionnaire in order to examine the relationship among concepts. The relationships among variables may be inflated because the measures are all collected within a single instrument. Several alternative statistical methods are available for assessing the degree of impact of method variance. Finally, users of measures in organizational behavior should be aware that the use of English language instruments in other cultures may be fraught with problems. One study used four versions of a measure, each version varying according to the language and the response scale used. There were two reasons for adopting the four versions. First, by comparing the responses of the two language versions, the researchers were able to determine whether respondents were interpreting the Chinese and English questions in a similar way. Second, they could examine the response bias of the Chinese research participants induced by different scales. That is, past studies have found that Chinese respondents may be reluctant to make known their opinion on politically sensitive matters. It is important to examine whether this effect is present when using English language measures in other cultures.

See Also the Following Articles

Content Validity • Organizational Psychology • Reliability Assessment • Validity Assessment

Further Reading

Brief, A. (1998). *Attitudes in and around Organizations.* Sage Publ., Thousand Oaks, CA.

Fields, D. (2002). *Taking the Measure of Work.* Sage Publ., Thousand Oaks, CA.

Jones, A., Johnson, L., Butler, M., and Main, D. (1983). Apples and oranges: An empirical comparison of commonly used indices of inter-rater agreement. *Acad. Mgmt. J.* **26**(3), 507–519.

Kerlinger, F., and Lee, H. (2000). *Foundations of Behavioral Research.* Harcourt College Publ., Fort Worth, TX.

Lazarsfeld, P. F., and Menzel, H. (1961). On the relation between individual and collective properties. *Complex Organizations* (A. Etzioni, ed.). Holt, Rinehart and Winston, New York.

Price, J., and Mueller, C. (1986). *Handbook of Organizational Measurement.* Pitman Publ., Marshfield, MA.

Reis, H., and Judd, C. (eds.) (2000). *Handbook of Research Methods in Social and Personality Psychology.* Cambridge University Press, Cambridge.

Riordan, C., and Vandenburg, R. (1994). A central question in cross-cultural research: Do employees of different cultures interpret work-related measures in an equivalent manner? *J. Mgmt.* **20**(3), 643–671.

Schwab, D. (1999). *Research Methods for Organizational Studies.* Lawrence Erlbaum Assoc., Mahwah, NJ.

Spector, P. (1987). Method variance as an artifact in self-reported affect and perceptions at work: Myth or significant problem. *J. Appl. Psychol.* **72**(3), 438–443.

Spector, P. (1994). Using self-report questionnaires in OB research: A comment on the use of a controversial method. *J. Organiz. Behav.* **15,** 385–392.

Sweeney, P., and McFarlin, D. (1997). Process and outcome: Gender differences in the assessment of organizational justice. *J. Organiz. Behav.* **18**(1), 83–98.

Wong, C., Hui, C., and Law, K. (1998). A longitudinal study of the job perception–job satisfaction relationship: A test of the three alternative specifications. *J. Occupat. Organiz. Psychol.* **71**(2), 127–146.

Organizational Psychology

Oleksandr S. Chernyshenko
University of Canterbury, Christchurch, New Zealand

Stephen Stark
University of South Florida, Tampa, Florida, USA

Glossary

computer adaptive rating scale (CARS) An item response theory-based measure of job performance; the respondent is presented with items consisting of pairs of behavioral statements, representing the same dimension, but different levels of performance.

empirical keying A method of scoring responses to situational judgment tests in which a sample of high-performing employees is assessed and the most frequently endorsed option for each item is keyed as "correct."

faking Intentional distortion of responses to self-report items measuring personality or other noncognitive constructs.

job performance An aggregate of employee behaviors having some expected value to organizations (positive or negative).

personnel selection The process of matching an applicant's qualifications (knowledge, skills, abilities, and other) to job requirements in such a way that job performance is maximized.

Measurement technology is used in the research and practice of organizational psychologists, who specialize in workplace personnel selection and performance management. The focus here is on how measurement technology is used in the workplace and on identifying the main constructs of interest and how they are measured and assessed. Results concerning construct and predictive validity and recent psychometric innovations and avenues for future research are discussed. Measurement equivalence, which is especially important for researchers interested in cross-cultural/national comparisons, is also examined.

Challenges in Measuring Individuals in Contemporary Organizations

The workplace environment has changed dramatically in the past two decades. Development of new technologies, increased globalization, and workforce diversification have transformed "manufacturing style" organizations, characterized by hierarchical structures and well-defined jobs, into "service style" organizations with flat structures, fluid jobs, and the extensive use of teams. The survival of such contemporary organizations is increasingly dependent on their ability to attract, select, and retain workers capable of performing in highly complex, ever-changing, and progressively more social situations. That can be difficult to accomplish without deliberate and continual measurement of workers' abilities, skills, attitudes, and performance. As a result, measurement applications are an important part of organizational efforts to achieve and maintain a competitive advantage.

Measurement in organizations poses numerous challenges for researchers. For example, high test scores usually lead to desirable outcomes, such as job offers, pay raises, and promotions; low test scores, on the other hand, may result in not being selected, being censured, or, possibly, being terminated. Consequently, there are strong incentives for test takers to perform well, if necessary, by manipulating their answers to present themselves in the best light possible. Not surprisingly, this can create difficulties for score use and interpretation, particularly in noncognitive assessment, which often depends on self-report data and subjective performance ratings to select individuals and allocate rewards.

Another challenge for contemporary organizational researchers is to develop measures that assess skills related to the popular concept of "social intelligence." For example, managers usually want to select people with good interpersonal, teamwork, and conflict resolution skills. However, scores on most paper-and-pencil social intelligence measures correlate highly with scores on cognitive ability and personality tests. This raises issues concerning construct and incremental validity (i.e., that which is gained by including social intelligence measures in a selection battery). Hence, the immediate challenge for researchers is to explore alternative methods of assessment and demonstrate discriminant validity.

Measurement Applications for Selection

The use of tests for selection decisions is perhaps the most widely scrutinized and well-researched topic in industrial/organizational psychology. The main purpose of selection is to match an applicant's qualifications, commonly framed as knowledge, skills, abilities, and "other" (KSAOs), to job requirements in such a way that job performance is enhanced. Because the success of selection decisions largely depends on the quality of measures used to assess applicants' KSAOs, organizational psychologists exert a great deal of effort to ensure the reliability and validity of the assessment tools. Overall, the cumulative body of research indicates that measures of cognitive ability, personality, and social skills can be effectively used to predict different aspects of performance, both on the job and in training.

Measurement of Cognitive Ability

Among all the individual difference measures used in organizations, cognitive ability tests (also called intelligence tests) are perhaps the most widely used. Their popularity stems from meta-analytic research indicating that general cognitive ability is the best predictor of performance across thousands of occupations, and the correlations increase as a function of job complexity. For example, the overall meta-analytic estimate of the correlation (corrected for range restriction and unreliability) between general cognitive ability and job performance is 0.51, and the correlation with training performance is 0.53. Years of education, interests, job experience, and biographical data measures provide very little in terms of incremental validity, although the results concerning personality measures, structured interviews, and work samples are more encouraging.

In general, psychometric approaches to measuring cognitive ability in organizational settings are pragmatic, but relatively unexciting. Most organizational researchers are aware of item response theory (IRT) methods of test construction and scoring, but, due to sample size requirements or other practical concerns, they rely on classical test theory methods to develop short tests of general ability; these are scored using "number correct" and are administered via paper-and-pencil or computer programs that act as electronic "page turners." Computerized adaptive testing is far less common in industrial/organizational (I/O) settings than in educational contexts, perhaps because paper-and-pencil measures have traditionally worked well and, possibly, because of competition among organizations. Provided that validity can be demonstrated, organizations are free to develop and purchase tests that best suit their individual needs, in an effort to maximize outcomes with respect to their competitors. A good selection battery is viewed as a competitive advantage or a product that can be licensed for profit, so there is little incentive to cooperate with other companies on research and development or to disclose publicly how scores are obtained. On the other hand, in educational testing, the assessment of college-bound seniors, for example, is relegated to large-scale testing corporations. Rather than developing or purchasing their own tests, universities have agreed to use standardized measures, such as the Scholastic Aptitude Test (SAT), for selection decisions. Development, administration, scoring, and reporting costs are thus absorbed initially by the testing corporation and, ultimately, passed on to applicants, of which there are literally tens of thousands each year. Obviously, there is no analogous situation for job selection; candidates expected to pay for the opportunity to apply would likely seek employment with a different organization. Consequently, organization researchers must be more practical when it comes to evaluating new technology.

There are some recent exceptions, however, involving large organizations. For example, U.S. military psychologists have developed and implemented a computerized adaptive version of the Armed Services Vocational Aptitude Battery (ASVAB), which is used for screening and classifying recruits. In a similar vein, IRT has been recently used to develop parallel forms of several cognitive ability tests for a large telecommunications organization. Both initiatives were motivated by a need for continuous testing and classification of large numbers of applicants, as well as by long-term goals for reducing testing time and costs. In short, given that computer technology is increasing rapidly, which is reducing once prohibitive start-up costs, and there is a growing impetus for workplace globalization, it is likely that IRT-based computer adaptive assessments will become more prevalent in I/O research and practice in the not-too-distant future.

Measurement of Personality

The five-factor structure of personality (extraversion, agreeableness, conscientiousness, neuroticism, and openness to experience) has emerged in the past decade as the predominant framework for describing the basic dimensions of normal personality. Based on this framework, selection researchers have conducted several meta-analyses to examine which "big-five" dimensions are useful for predicting work performance. These studies have shown consistently that conscientiousness is a valid predictor of job performance across all occupations included in the meta-analyses, whereas the other four dimensions predict success in specific occupations, or relate to specific performance criteria. More recently, results of a number of studies have suggested that measures of narrow traits may have higher predictive validity, compared to measures of broad factors. For example, several big-five factor measures, as well as narrow trait measures, were correlated with several performance criteria and it was found that the latter were more effective predictors. Similarly, other studies have shown that narrow facets of a broad factor can have marked but opposite relationships with a performance criterion. Consequently, if measures of the narrow facets are aggregated to assess a broad personality factor, the relationship with an external criterion may fall to zero. In sum, these results suggest that using lower order facets of the big five might increase the validity of personality measures in selection contexts.

There is currently no shortage of personality inventories measuring both broad and narrow big-five traits. Among the most widely used measures for selection are the NEO (neuroticism, extraversion, openness) Personality Inventory (NEO-PI), the Sixteen Personality Factor Questionnaire (16PF), and the California Personality Inventory (CPI). All of these inventories were developed using classical test theory (CTT) methods. They are composed of scales having 10 to 15 self-report items that ask about a respondent's typical behavior. Most measures also contain a lie or social desirability scale to identify respondents who may engage in impression management. Though these scales might work well in research settings, when respondents are motivated to answer honestly, their efficacy in selection contexts is still a matter of concern. Recent research comparing responses to traditional personality items across testing situations has clearly shown that applicants can and will increase their scores, with respect to nonapplicants, when there are incentives to fake "good." In fact, it is not uncommon for applicants to score 1 SD higher compared to respondents in research settings. The main problem, however, is that not all individuals fake, and certainly not to the same extent, so faking affects the rank order of high-scoring individuals and, thus, the quality of hiring decisions. Moreover, because approaches to detect and correct for faking *post hoc*, using social desirability/impression management scores, are generally ineffective, interest may be shifting toward preventing faking by using veiled items, threats of sanctions, or alternative items formats. An example of the latter approach involves the construction of multidimensional forced-choice items that are designed to be fake resistant. By pairing statements on different dimensions that are similar in social desirability and asking a respondent to choose the statement in each pair that is "most like me," items are more difficult to fake. However, important concerns have been raised about the legitimacy of inter-individual comparisons due to ipsativity. In an effort to address that concern, a mathematical model for calibrating statements has been proposed, constructing multidimensional forced-choice tests and scoring respondents. In simulation studies conducted to date, this approach has shown to recover known latent trait scores, representing different personality dimensions, with a reasonable degree of accuracy. But more research is needed to examine the construct and predictive validity of such personality measures in applied settings.

Aside from concerns about faking, there is a basic question that should be examined in the area of personality assessment. Namely, studies are needed to explore the way in which persons respond to personality items. Many measures have been developed and a great deal of research has been conducted, assuming that a dominance process underlies item responding; that is, a person will tend to endorse a positively worded item when his/her standing on the latent dimension is more positive than that of the item. However, some recent studies suggest that an ideal point response process may be better suited for personality items; i.e., respondents tend to agree with items that are located near them on the latent continuum and to disagree with those that are distant in either direction. In IRT terms, this means that some personality items may exhibit nonmonotonic, folded item response functions (IRFs). In the case of neutral items, the IRFs may be bell-shaped when computed based on an ideal point model.

The possibility of using nonmonotone items in personality questionnaires opens new avenues for theoretical and applied research. First, there is a need to determine what features of items can yield nonmonotone response functions and whether some personality dimensions tend to have more such items than others have. Second, the effects on construct and predictive validity due to eliminating or retaining items of neutral standing during personality test construction have not been investigated. If truly nonmonotone items are scored using dominance models (i.e., number right or summated ratings), the rank order of high/low-scoring individuals may be affected by the choice of scoring model; so that the accuracy of hiring decisions could suffer. More research is needed to determine whether these results indeed exert measurable influences on validity and utility in organizations.

Measurement of Social/Emotional Intelligence

Because organizations are sociotechnical systems, successful interaction with others can be a critical competency for any employee. That fact is further recognized by contemporary models of job performance, which now explicitly view helping and cooperating with others as components of performance that contribute to overall organizational effectiveness. Consequently, organizations are increasingly interested in selecting individuals who have good social skills and are able to appraise, express, and regulate emotions in themselves and others. In other words, they want to hire and retain persons having a high degree of social/emotional "intelligence." Many measures of social/emotional intelligence have been designed since the term was first introduced in the 1920s. However most of these measures have been either unreliable or have shown poor discriminant validity. For example, measures that rely on self-reports (e.g., respondents recall typical social behavior) typically correlate highly with personality scales. Others, such as paper-and-pencil situational judgment tests (e.g., respondents are given written scenarios and asked how they would react in that situation) do not correlate with personality measures, but, instead, correlate highly with cognitive ability scores. In sum, though the concept of social/emotional intelligence is intuitively appealing, attempts to measure it have been largely unsuccessful.

Despite the checkered history of social intelligence assessment, considerable progress, in terms of validity, seems to have been made in the past several years. For example, a study using video as a medium of administration for situational judgment tests (SJTs) showed that video-based SJT scores did not correlate with either cognitive ability or personality measures, but the same scenarios were highly correlated with cognitive ability when presented using a paper-and-pencil format. Another study used video-based SJT to assess conflict resolution skills. The measure predicted work performance, and, similar to other SJT findings, this SJT was uncorrelated with cognitive ability and personality. Therefore, the medium of administration seems to play an integral role in SJT validity. At this stage, more research is needed to understand how and why video-based assessment changes the nature of the construct that is assessed. Perhaps the answers here lie in perceptual or cognitive psychology information-processing models.

Scoring video-based SJTs poses a formidable challenge from a psychometric standpoint. Usually, each SJT scenario has several response options (actions) that are derived from interviews with subject matter experts. Because so many reactions to a scenario are possible, those selected and presented as response options in the context of an item often vary widely; i.e., they do not represent a single behavioral dimension. Consequently, unidimensional scoring procedures cannot be applied and alternative approaches must be developed. The most widely used approach to scoring is "empirical keying," wherein a sample of high-performing employees is assessed and most the frequently endorsed option for each item is keyed as "correct." In the end, applicants who earn high scores on empirically keyed SJTs are those that exhibit response patterns similar to high performers. Unfortunately, empirical keying has a number of limitations. First, not all scenarios (items) can be keyed, because high performers sometimes disagree about which response action is better. Second, organization-specific keys are often needed, because there are different preferences and norms for teamwork, leadership, and conflict resolution styles across organizations. A third concern is that empirically derived keys do not cross-validate well, particularly if the sample used for calibration is small; in that case, bootstrap approaches or alternatives to empirically derived keys might be required. And, fourth, empirical keying is not very informative with regard to designing training programs to improve social/emotional skills. In short, despite these limitations, empirical keying of SJTs seems to be more effective than either subject matter/expert-opinion-based scoring methods or rational approaches. More research is needed to explore alternative scoring procedures, medium of administration effects, and incremental validity in job selection.

Performance Measurement

Helping to manage workers' performance is the central task of organizational psychologists. Virtually all organizational interventions target this area. Personnel selection procedures seek to identify applicants who are likely to perform better in the future. Training programs, feedback interventions, and merit pay systems are designed to maintain and improve current performance. Promotion and termination decisions essentially reward (or punish) past performance. None of these interventions is possible without first defining the dimensions of performance and developing valid assessments of the construct.

Dimensions of Job Performance

Job performance is defined as an aggregate of employee behaviors that have some expected value to organizations (positive or negative). These behaviors can be classified into three broad classes: task performance, contextual performance, and counterproductivity. Task performance is composed of behaviors that either (1) directly transform raw materials into products and services or (2) service and maintain the successful transformation of raw materials. Task performance behaviors are role prescribed; that is, they are explicitly written in an employee's job description. In contrast, contextual performance is not role prescribed, but rather includes discretionary behaviors that shape the organizational, social, and psychological context of the workplace. Examples of contextual performance include volunteering to carry out task activities that are not formally part of the job, helping and cooperating with others, and following organizational rules and procedures. In the business literature, these behaviors are also known as organizational citizenship behaviors (OCBs). The third broad dimension of job performance is counterproductivity. It is composed of intentional behaviors that are viewed by the organization as contrary to its interests. Counterproductive behaviors can range from blatantly damaging (i.e., theft, destruction of property) to somewhat less destructive (i.e., poor attendance, misuse of information, intentionally poor work); all of these are detrimental to overall organizational effectiveness.

For many years, task performance was the focus of most applied and research efforts, because it was believed to be the most salient component of job performance. However, recent studies have shown that overall job performance is influenced nearly as much by contextual performance, so there has been an upsurge of research on its antecedents and consequences. Counterproductive behaviors, on the other hand, have been studied primarily in the context of employee attitude surveys, because they tend to correlate highly with job satisfaction. More recently, counterproductivity and contextual performance have been studied together as organizational psychologists attempt to develop more general models of extra-role work behaviors. In summary, research suggests that adequate evaluation of work performance requires assessment of task performance, OCBs, and counterproductive behaviors. Organizations seek to design interventions that discourage counterproductivity, but encourage the task and contextual behaviors.

Psychometric Approaches to Performance Ratings

Assessing job performance is difficult. Often, relatively few "objective," numerical, or easily quantified performance data are available, so organizations must rely on subjective performance ratings obtained from immediate supervisors, co-workers, customers, or even employees. Subjective ratings, however, are often unreliable and prone to a number of rating errors (e.g., halo, leniency, or central tendency). To combat these errors, organizational psychologists have explored many ratings formats over the past 60 years.

The earliest performance ratings were obtained using graphic rating scales (GRSs). These were typically one-item measures, containing a rulerlike response scale. GRSs were quick and easy to administer, but had poor psychometric properties and were susceptible to many rating errors. Manipulations of the GRS format, such as the placement of the scale on the page or the number of response categories on the scale, had little salutary effect on the quality of ratings. In the 1960s, behaviorally anchored rating scales (BARSs) were introduced, wherein behavioral statements representing different levels of job performance are ordered along a scale in terms of effectiveness; the rater's task is to mark the statement that best describes the typical behavior of the ratee. The idea of BARS was to help raters make more objective evaluations by listing prototypical job behaviors, but, like the GRS, the BARS was susceptible to rating errors and exhibited low interrater reliability. Later, other formats, such as behavior observation scales and mixed-standard scales, were developed. These approaches were more complicated, but showed little improvement in terms of rater errors, reliability, and validity. As a result, the quest for improving performance rating formats came to a standstill and organizational psychologists turned, instead, to training raters to more accurately and consistently evaluate employees.

The hope for a better rating format was revived in 2001 using a paired-comparison rating format to measure contextual performance via a computer adaptive ratings scale (CARS). The idea is to present raters with items consisting of pairs of behavioral statements, representing the same dimension, but different levels of performance; the rater's task is to choose the statement in each pair that better describes the performance of the ratee. The novel feature of this approach is the use of a computer adaptive algorithm for composing items and scoring responses, based on an ideal point IRT model. Computer adaptive testing helps raters make more precise estimates of ratees' performance, while simultaneously decreasing the number of items administered per ratee. The results indicate that the CARS format yields more reliable ratings and significantly greater validity and accuracy compared to the GRS or BARS formats. In addition, raters prefer the CARS format to other formats and perceive it to be more accurate. Overall, these findings suggest that improvements in methodology can help raters improve the accuracy of performance assessments. More applications of CARS methodology are likely to appear in the near future.

Emerging Issues in Test Score Use

Measurement Equivalence in Cross-Cultural Research

Industrial/organizational researchers are increasingly interested in comparing test scores across cultural/national groups. The goal of these comparisons can be, for example, to ensure that a test used for selection and promotion decisions is not biased. Alternatively, some researchers may want to identify items and scales that function differently across cultures as a means of generating hypotheses for future experimental research or understanding cultural differences. Others may simply want to know the magnitude of score differences across groups so that appropriate norms can be created. To achieve any of these objectives, measurement equivalence analyses are needed.

Measurement equivalence exists when the relations between observed test scores and a latent attribute measured by a test or scale are identical across groups. Essentially, measurement equivalence refers to the comparability of a scale's internal psychometric properties across subpopulations. It should be distinguished from relational equivalence, which refers to the similarity of a scale's external relationships (i.e., those with other constructs) across subgroups. To date, a majority of measurement equivalence studies have been conducted using either factor analytic or IRT methods. Factor analytic methods, such as confirmatory factor analysis (CFA) and mean and covariance structure (MACS) analysis, involve comparisons of a full model, whereby item parameters are estimated separately for each group, and a series of restricted models, whereby parameters are constrained to be invariant (equal) across groups. Significant change in fit when going from a full to a more constrained model is interpreted as a lack of some form of measurement equivalence (e.g., scalar invariance); the type depends on the specifics of the constrained model.

IRT methods, on the other hand, typically involve comparisons of item/test characteristics curves. For example, Lord's chi-square method compares item parameters estimated for a focal group (e.g., Americans) and a reference group (e.g., Asians), under a particular IRT model, after they have been placed on a common metric. The primary advantage of IRT methods over factor analytic methods is that IRT methods do not confound measurement bias with mean score differences across groups, and they make no assumptions about normality or linearity. Although the number of measurement equivalence studies continue to grow, results from these studies are often difficult to interpret. First, experience shows that CFA and IRT measurement equivalence methods rarely agree when applied to the same data set. That may not be particularly surprising, because the two approaches make somewhat different assumptions about item responding (i.e., linearity or multivariate normality). However, divergent results can obfuscate the interpretation of findings, because it is not apparent which set of results should be trusted. Psychologists therefore need to conduct simulation studies comparing the performance of factor analytic and IRT methods under controlled conditions and examine the relative robustness of these procedures to violations of model assumptions. The second important issue is that a majority of the methods rely on significance testing to detect measurement nonequivalence—i.e., differential item/test functioning (DIF/DTF). However, measurement equivalence analyses typically involve large samples, so small differences in item loadings, item response probabilities, or expected total test scores are often identified as statistically significant, even if they have little practical importance. Furthermore, p-values regarding the tenability of the null hypothesis of no DIF/DTF provide no clue as to what action should be taken when nonequivalence is found. Thus, practical guidelines for interpreting measurement equivalence results are needed.

An effort to improve interpretability of measurement equivalence studies is underway. It involves development of two IRT-based methods to translate findings of test bias into quantities that are easily understood by test users. The first method translates bias into raw score points, so that values can be compared readily to the magnitudes of observed mean differences across groups. If desired, the values can also be transformed to obtain effect size measures similar to those reported in experimental studies. The second method evaluates how bias affects the proportions of reference and focal group members selected using various cut scores, which are commonly used in personnel selection, licensing, and college admissions. More methods, similar to these, should be developed to aid the interpretation of results from measurement equivalence studies.

Summary

There are three areas of burgeoning interest concerning measurement in organizations. As in professional licensing and educational testing, there is a trend in I/O research and practice toward more realistic assessments that can be administered adaptively and delivered, perhaps, over the Internet. Computer simulations and video-based assessments will become more common as technology improves and organizations explore new ways of assessing constructs, such as job performance, personality, and situational judgment. However, the proliferation of new measurement technology from quantitative circles to mainstream research and practice is expected to occur slowly. After all, new technology can only influence mainstream research and practice if results are communicated in a way that is understandable to a general audience, programs are made easier to use, examples and guidelines for interpreting results are provided, and, ultimately, new methods of test construction and evaluation lead to appreciable gains in validity that will offset development and maintenance costs.

See Also the Following Articles

Computerized Adaptive Testing • Organizational Behavior

Further Reading

Barrick, M. R., Mount, M. K., and Judge, T. A. (2001). Personality and performance at the beginning of the new millennium: What do we know and where do we go next? *Int. J. Select. Assess.* **9,** 9–30.

Borman, W. C., Buck, D. E., Hanson, M. A., Motowidlo, S. J., Stark, S., and Drasgow, F. (2001). An examination of the comparative reliability, validity, and accuracy of performance ratings made using computerized adaptive rating scales. *J. Appl. Psychol.* **86,** 965–973.

Chan, D., and Schmitt, N. (1997). Video-based versus paper-and-pencil method of assessment in situational judgment tests: Subgroup differences in test performance and face validity perceptions. *J. Appl. Psychol.* **82,** 143–159.

Chernyshenko, O. S., Stark, S., Chan, K. Y., Drasgow, F., and Williams, B. A. (2001). Examining the fit of IRT models to personality items. *Multivar. Behav. Res.* **36,** 523–562.

Davies, M., Stankov, L., and Roberts, R. D. (1998). Emotional intelligence: In search of an illusive construct. *J. Personal. Soc. Psychol.* **75,** 989–1015.

Motowidlo, S. J. (2003). Job performance. In *Handbook of Psychology: Industrial and Organizational Psychology* (W. C. Borman and D. R. Ilgen, eds.), Vol. 12, pp. 39–53. John Wiley & Sons, New York.

Olson-Buchanan, J. B., Drasgow, F., Moberg, P. J., Mead, A. D., Keenan, P. A., and Donovan, M. A. (1998). Interactive video assessment of conflict resolution skills. *Personn. Psychol.* **51,** 1–24.

Paunonen, S. V. (1998). Hierarchical organization of personality and prediction of behavior. *J. Personal. Soc. Psychol.* **74,** 538–556.

Raju, N. S., Laffitte, L. J., and Byrne, B. M. (2002). Measurement equivalence: A comparison of methods based on confirmatory factor analysis and item response theory. *J. Appl. Psychol.* **87,** 517–529.

Schmidt, F. L., and Hunter, J. E. (1998). The validity and utility of selection methods in personnel psychology: Practical and theoretical implications of 85 years of research findings. *Psychol. Bull.* **124,** 262–274.

Segall, D. O., and Moreno, K. E. (1999). Development of the Computerized Adaptive Testing version of the Armed Services Vocational Aptitude Battery. In *Innovations in Computerized Assessment* (F. Drasgow and J. B. Olson-Buchanan, eds.), pp. 35–65. Lawrence Erlbaum Assoc., Mahwah, NJ.

Stark, S. (2002). A new IRT approach to test construction and scoring designed to reduce the effects of faking in personality assessment: The generalized graded unfolding model for multi-unidimensional paired comparison responses. *Diss. Abstr. Int.: Sect. B: Sci. Engineer.* **63**(2B), 1084.

Stark, S., Chernyshenko, O. S., Chan, K. Y., Lee, W. C., and Drasgow, F. (2001). Effects of the testing situation on item responding: Cause for concern. *J. Appl. Psychol.* **86,** 943–953.

Stark, S., Chernyshenko, O. S., and Drasgow, F. (2004). Examining the effects of differential item/test functioning (DIF/DTF) on selection decisions: When are statistically significant effects practically important? *J. Appl. Psychol.* In press.

Zickar, M. J., and Drasgow, F. (1996). Detecting faking on a personality instrument using appropriateness measurement. *Appl. Psychol. Measure.* **20,** 71–87.